# 48TH EDITION

# KOVELS'
# Antiques &
# Collectibles
# PRICE GUIDE 2016

BLACK DOG
& LEVENTHAL
PUBLISHERS
NEW YORK

RCH
CONT

Front cover photographs, from left to right:
Furniture, rocker, Finn Juhl, beech, Denmark
Toy, Drummer Boy, pushing drum, Marx
Rozenburg, vase, stylized flowers

On the spine:
Silver-English, teapot, curved spout, wood handle, Batemans

Back cover photographs, from top to bottom:
Furniture, chest, bombe style, Dutch
Silver-American, canister, lid, malachite, Henry Petzal
Pairpoint, lamp, puffy, 4 roses, tree trunk base

Authors' photographs © Molly Nook (top) and Alex Montes de Oca (bottom)

Published by
Black Dog & Leventhal Publishers
Hachette Book Group
1290 Avenue of the Americas
New York, NY 10104

www.blackdogandleventhal.com

Printed in the USA

Designed by Sheila Hart Design, Inc.

WW

First Edition: September 2015
10 9 8 7 6 5 4 3 2 1

Black Dog & Leventhal Publishers is an imprint of Hachette Books, a division of Hachette Book Group. The Black Dog & Leventhal Publishers name and logo are trademarks of Hachette Book Group, Inc.

The Hachette Speakers Bureau provides a wide range of authors for speaking events. To find out more, go to www. HachetteSpeakersBureau.com or call (866) 376-6591.

The publisher is not responsible for websites (or their content) that are not owned by the publisher.

Library of Congress Cataloging-in-Publication Data is available on file.

ISBN: 978-1-63191-005-0

# BOOKS BY RALPH AND TERRY KOVEL

*American Country Furniture, 1780–1875*

*A Directory of American Silver, Pewter, and Silver Plate*

*Kovels' Advertising Collectibles Price List*

*Kovels' American Antiques 1750–1900*

*Kovels' American Art Pottery*

*Kovels' American Collectibles 1900–2000*

*Kovels' American Silver Marks, 1650 to the Present*

*Kovels' Antiques & Collectibles Fix-It Source Book*

*Kovels' Antiques & Collectibles Price Guide*

*Kovels' Bid, Buy, and Sell Online*

*Kovels' Book of Antique Labels*

*Kovels' Bottles Price List*

*Kovels' Collector's Guide to American Art Pottery*

*Kovels' Collector's Guide to Limited Editions*

*Kovels' Collectors' Source Book*

*Kovels' Depression Glass & Dinnerware Price List*

*Kovels' Dictionary of Marks— Pottery and Porcelain, 1650 to 1850*

*Kovels' Guide to Selling, Buying, and Fixing Your Antiques and Collectibles*

*Kovels' Guide to Selling Your Antiques & Collectibles*

*Kovels' Illustrated Price Guide to Royal Doulton*

*Kovels' Know Your Antiques*

*Kovels' Know Your Collectibles*

*Kovels' New Dictionary of Marks— Pottery and Porcelain, 1850 to the Present*

*Kovels' Organizer for Collectors*

*Kovels' Price Guide for Collector Plates, Figurines, Paperweights, and Other Limited Edition Items*

*Kovels' Quick Tips: 799 Helpful Hints on How to Care for Your Collectibles*

*Kovels' Yellow Pages: A Resource Guide for Collectors*

*The Label Made Me Buy It: From Aunt Jemima to Zonkers— The Best-Dressed Boxes, Bottles, and Cans from the Past*

# BOOKS BY TERRY KOVEL AND KIM KOVEL

*Kovels' Antiques & Collectibles Price Guide*

# INTRODUCTION

## Changes in Prices, Inflation, and the Economy

This has been another year of the weak "collecting economy" that started in 2008. However, this year, prices are a little better than last, and record prices were set as bidders fought for the best of the best, especially the best of collectibles and art made after 1950. (See page ix for a list of this year's record prices.) There were changes in the way antiques are collected, thanks to the Internet, cell phones, tablets, computers, and other electronic ways to buy and sell. And there are three other major changes in the attitudes of buyers. First, the older collectors (now above 60) wanted collections of as many different toys or plates as possible or a house furnished with only country furniture. A quantity of good to excellent examples was the goal. Now a single perfect piece is the goal. Second, the formal art world now stresses "design." It is a hard term to define since everything is designed by someone. But it seems to refer to great design in any category including, painting, sculpture, jewelry, kitchen tools, cars, packaging, advertising, clothing, and more. That has shifted some buyers' attention in the collector's world to great graphics, unique jewelry, unusual chairs and tables, glass, silver, pottery, and even medical devices. Third is condition. This has altered the pricing for many antiques especially for furniture (refinishing), mechanical banks, and other metal collectibles (amount of original paint and no damage), and bottles, glass, and ceramics (no chips, no cracks, no flaws.) And there is a surprising opposite interest in repaired pieces from years ago, like stapled export porcelain, "do-withs" like broken goblet stems made into candleholders or damaged 18th century porcelain teapots with silver spouts added as replacements. It may be just part of the way being "green" has influenced sales of antiques.

Since 1953, the year we published our first book, the antiques world went from one or two antiques shows in a city per year to one almost every week. But with so many new online ways to buy and sell antiques—and the weak economy—many shows have been discontinued. Auctions of expensive antiques used to be held in New York, Chicago, and a few other large cities. Small towns had "farm auctions" held outside a farmhouse, or a local auctioneer who sold antiques and the tractor and tools in the barn, too. There were no malls, no Internet shops, sales, or auctions. Today New York City auction houses run sales at their galleries with online access that reach buyers in every country. And major auctions are also online from London, Paris, Hong Kong, and sometimes from the home of a special collection. Every day there is an auction you can watch and place bids on from your computer or phone.

Our first book, *Kovels' Dictionary of Marks: Pottery & Porcelain*, was one of just 60 titles about antiques announced that year. In 1969, there were about 200. Now few books about collectibles and antiques are published, but much old and new information is found on the Internet. Much of the information found in old books, company catalogs and advertisements, can be found online. Our years of newspaper columns and questions, newsletters, special reports, books of marks, and other writings are now on our website, Kovels.com. Some can be found with an internet search.

The economic problems that started in 2008 with the stock market crash and housing bust spread to other investments, including antiques and collectibles. There is still a saying that if you buy antiques, they go up in value every year and are a good investment. That is only half true. If you buy the right antiques and sell at the right time, they sell for higher prices than you paid, even when you factor in inflation. Consider this: Our first price book lists a Diamond Dyes cabinet for $50. In the early months of 2008, the same cabinet sold for $1,112 to $2,633. In 2012, two Diamond Dyes cabinets were listed, one at $540, the other $550—very low prices. In 2013, common Diamond Dyes cabinets were $407, $1,320, and $1,540. In 2014, the cabinet featuring Children with Balloons was $896, the Governess was $1,560, and the Washer Woman was $720. Last year Evolution of Women was $360, Maypole was $1,596; Children with Balloons was $2,400, and Blond Fairy was $1,112. And in this book there are six cabinets ranging from $472 to $617 and a rare Washer Woman with a blue background for $1,680. There are twelve original designs used on the tin fronts of these cabinets.

The worldwide recession is still affecting the values of antiques and collectibles. Shows have a little better attendance. There are many more auction bidders because most auctions today are online. But the average auction may end with many unsold lots. Prices for items offered on eBay are still low, and many items don't sell. In 2012, prices had gone up for things with international appeal, like Chinese porcelain and ivory. But in 2013 and 2014, Chinese bidding slowed down for all but top-quality pieces. By 2015, Hummel, Royal Doulton figurines, "country furniture" with peeling paint, and "brown furniture" like period Chippendale desks had gone down in value. However, 1890s oak dining tables that were hard to sell are starting to attract more buyers. Prices for Japanese antiques are down because buyers in Japan are less interested in Satsuma, Nippon, and other Japanese porcelains, but 19th and 20th century woodblock prints have rising prices. A new interest, Western-style Japanese paintings, prints, ceramics, and wood-carvings, are attracting new buyers.

Prices for large advertising signs, enameled metal signs, die-cut cardboard advertising, and even small tins with great graphics as well as rock 'n' roll posters are up. Through it all, shows and shops have seen fewer buyers and lower prices than they could get seven years ago. But collectors and dealers agree that "good stuff sells" and well-run shows, shops, and sales are doing "OK." Usable furniture in good condition and "smalls" are selling for expected prices, and the "best" of every type of antique or collectible is in demand. Some auctions get prices that are close to retail. But easy-to-find antiques are at about one-third of retail because the Internet revealed the large, worldwide supply.

One influence in this market was the demand for Asian antiques—jade, ivory, and cloisonné made in China, Japan, Korea, and other Asian countries. But China's economy is suffering and only top quality brings higher than expected prices. A few items estimated to be worth thousands have sold for millions of dollars. Unfortunately, there is a growing problem with bids from China. Some bidders refuse to honor their bids and instead ask for a large price reduction—or just don't pay for or pick up a piece. Often this "sale" is reported at the time of the auction, but there is rarely a public announcement that the bid was not honored. The highest bids now seem to be from Russian millionaires or a few Middle Eastern and other overseas buyers opening museums.

Laws protecting endangered species are stopping many sales. Laws forbid the sale of parts of elephants (ivory), rhinoceros (horns), eagles (feathers), tigers (skins), and even some types of turtles (shells). Sales of antique Ku Klux Klan items; caricatures of black, Irish, Chinese and Jewish people on postcards; or joke figurines are criticized and result in bad publicity. A group of drawings from the Japanese-American camps during World War II were pulled from an auction because protesters thought it would be too emotional. They wanted to have the drawings put into a special museum exhibit. Legal auctions of historic antique guns caused controversy and unpleasant publicity. There are state laws and EPA (Environmental Protection Agency) laws and it is causing much confusion. Some ivory items including antiques have been seized and even crushed in the hope of saving living elephants.

*Kovels' Antiques and Collectibles Price Guide 2016* has current, reliable information, plus edited content. The book has 2,500 new color photographs and 32,000 prices. You will also find more than two hundred added facts of interest and tips about care and repair. Each photograph is shown with a caption that includes the description, price, and source. The book has color tabs and color-coded paragraphs that make it easy to find listings, and it uses a modern, readable typestyle. More than seven hundred paragraphs introduce price categories that give history and descriptions that help identify an unknown piece. We make some changes in the paragraphs every year to indicate new owners, new distributors, or new information about production dates. This year we made twenty-one updates to paragraphs, many that tell of the sale or closing of a company. All of the antiques and collectibles priced here were offered for sale during the past year, most of them in the United States. Other prices came from sales that accepted bids from all over the world. Almost all auction prices given include the buyer's premium, because that is part of what the buyer paid. Very few include local sales tax and the extra charges involving phone bids, online bids, credit cards, or shipping.

## READ THIS FIRST

This is a book for the buyer and the seller. We check prices, visit shops, shows, and flea markets, read hundreds of publications and catalogs, check Internet sales and other online services, and decide which antiques and collectibles are of most interest to most collectors. We concentrate on the average pieces in any category. Sometimes high-priced items are included so you can see that special rarities are very valuable. Prices of some items were very high because major collections of top-quality pieces were auctioned. Auction houses like to have huge sales of things that belonged to one well-known collector or expert. This year's major sales featured several collections of toys and banks. A few famous bottle collections were auctioned at online only bottle auctions. Single collector auctions of bikes, toy stoves, Victorian glass, Asian art, lamps, and Tiffany of all types including lamps were well advertised and prices were high.

Most listed pieces cost less than $10,000. The highest price in this book is $402,500 for a 15 ½-inch-high stoneware churn with cobalt blue decoration picturing a Civil War soldier. The five-gallon churn with lug handles was made in New York about 1862. The lowest price is $2 for a metal bottle cap with a brown background for "Brownie Chocolate Flavored Drink." The largest antique is a 24 by 14 foot saloon back bar and front bar made of mahogany. It is Princess style, made by Brunswick Balke Collendar Co., and it sold for $79,800. The smallest, only one inch in diameter, is an Orphan Annie pin for the Radio Orphan Annie Secret Service Society. It cost $10.

Many unusual, unique, and weird things are included. This year, we list a quack vibrating medical chair made of wood, leather, and metal. It has a motor. The chair from the Battle Creek, Michigan, sanatorium in the 1900s is 62 inches high by 36 inches wide and cost $4,648. Another strange antique is a model of a guillotine made of bone by a Napoleonic prisoner of war in France about 1810. The $2,446 model is 9 inches high. Ever think of buying a throw made of skunk pelts? A bed-sized 94-inch by 104-inch fur throw lined with brown fabric was bought for $2,100. Many bidders wanted to buy Edison's No. 10110 stock ticker tape machine. It sold for $2,460. But more money was paid for a 17 ½-inch ceremonial cannibal fork from the Fiji Islands. It was made in the 1800s of carved wood and has an iron display stand. A determined bidder paid $3,318. A rare and confusing political miniature flask shaped like Teddy Roosevelt wearing a dress and a banner that says "Suffer-e-'get" sold for $470. It is ridiculing the President for supporting the suffragettes.

Of major interest today, and getting the highest prices, are antique guns and ammunition, the best of modern furniture, and modernist jewelry by artists like Calder or Bertoia. Early comic books in excellent condition are selling at high prices and the editions featuring the first appearances of Batman, Superman, and other superheroes or first issues like Action No. 1 are selling for millions of dollars.

There are still bargains to be had, some that have been emerging as "collectibles" over the last six years. Big is still "big." Group of small figurines or sets of plates are very hard to sell. But large-scale accent pieces with colors and lines that blend in with modern furnishings—pieces like huge crocks, floor vases, centerpieces, bronze sculptures, large posters, and garden statuary—attract decorators as well as the owners of large homes. Blue and white, the colors favored in the 17th and 18th centuries, are back, and black and white are decorator favorites. Anything from clothes and glass to ceramics and furniture in the "newest style" between the 1950s and 2000 is hot. They are all going up in price and attracting new, younger buyers. Iron objects like bookends, doorstops, pots and pans, even snow eagles and carnival shooting targets are getting harder to find. But costume jewelry is the most popular item we see selling at shows. Prices for pieces marked with important makers' names can sell for as much as $1,500. A few very popular collectibles of the past, like Roseville and Rookwood pottery, have come down in price for all but the largest and most important pieces.

The biggest change is silver tableware. The meltdown price of sterling silver the last few years made it profitable to melt many pieces. Hundreds of coin silver items, especially spoons and no-name sterling serving dishes and flatware, disappeared in the meltdown craze. Sterling by well-known companies or designers like Tiffany, Georg Jensen, or Gorham now get top dollar. And very modern unfamiliar shapes make tea services saleable at high prices. Ordinary traditional services are very low priced.

Quality and works of recognized artists sell high—because collectors consider it an "investment" that will increase in value. Newly popular are works by contemporary studio potters that are made in nontraditional shapes. Teapots and vases are not made to be used, but are one-of-a-kind, large, and often colorful sculptures. Tiffany lamps have become so expensive there are now rising prices for all other leaded glass lamps like Handel, Pairpoint, Moe Bridges, and Pittsburgh. Norman Rockwell's oil paintings are selling for thousands of dollars. His prints are selling for hundreds of dollars to those who like the art but have less money. Mixed metal furniture from the 1950's and later by Paul Evans is setting records up to $286,000. Wooden furniture by George Nakashima is popular and expensive. Authentic Western and American Indian items are steadily rising in price. Even some souvenirs made for tourists are wanted. There is more interest and rising prices for TV, radio and computer collectibles. Unique celebrity-related photographs, autographs, clothing or belongings like baseballs or guitars can start bidding wars. Vintage watches like Rolex and Patek Philippe are in demand and prices are getting higher, especially for those made after 1926, when the first waterproof models were made. Many are bought to wear, not just to display. Additions to the auction sales that started less than ten years ago are designer purses by makers like Hermès or Chanel and special edition sneakers made by Nike and other name brands. These are selling for hundreds to thousands of dollars and are not really collected but are bought to use or to resell to make a profit.

The *Kovels' Antiques and Collectibles Price Guide* has gotten younger over the past forty-eight years. Most items in our original book were made before 1860, so they were more than a century old. Today we list pieces made as recently as 2000, and there is great interest in furniture, glass, ceramics, and good design made since 1950.

The book is more than 670 pages long and crammed full of prices and photographs. We try to have a balanced format and not too many items that sell for over $5,000. We list a few very expensive pieces so you can realize that a great paperweight may cost $10,000 but an average one is only $25. Nearly all prices are from the American market for the American market. Only a few European sales are reported. We don't include prices we think result from "auction fever." We do list verified bargains. There are more items under $10 than in any of our earlier price books written in the past fifteen years.

The index is computer-generated. Use it often. It includes categories and much more. For example, there is a category for Celluloid. Most celluloid will be there, but a toy made of celluloid will be listed under Toy and also indexed under Celluloid. There are also cross-references in the listings and in the paragraphs but some searching must be done. For example, Barbie dolls are in the Doll category; there is no Barbie category. And when you look at "doll, Barbie," you find a note that "Barbie" is under "doll, Mattel, Barbie" because Mattel makes Barbie dolls and most dolls are listed by maker.

All photographs and prices are new. Antiques and collectibles pictured are items that were offered for sale or sold for the amount listed in 2014–2015. Auction prices include the buyer's premium. Wherever we had extra space on a page, we filled it with tips about the care of collections and other useful information. Don't discard this book. Old Kovels' price guides can be used for future reference and for tax, estate, and appraisal information.

The prices in this book are reports of the general antiques market. As we said, every price in the book is new. We do not estimate or "update" prices. Prices are either realized prices from auctions, completed sales, or asking prices. We know that a buyer may have negotiated an asking price to a lower selling price, but we report asking prices. We do not pay dealers, collectors, or experts to estimate prices. If the price is from an auction, it includes the buyer's premium if one is charged; but prices do not include sales tax. If a price range is given, at least two identical items were offered for sale at different prices. Price ranges are found only in categories like Pressed Glass, where identical items can be identified. Some prices in *Kovels' Antiques & Collectibles Price Guide* may seem high and some low because of regional variations, but each price is one you could have paid for the object somewhere in the United States. Internet prices from sellers' ads or listings are avoided. Because so many non-collectors sell online but know little about the objects they are describing, there can be inaccuracies in descriptions. Sales from well-known Internet sites, shops, and sales, carefully edited, are included.

If you are selling your collection, do not expect to get retail value unless you are a dealer. Wholesale prices for antiques are 30 to 40 percent of retail prices. The antiques dealer must make a profit or go out of business. Internet auction prices are less predictable—because of an international audience and "auction fever," prices can be higher or lower than retail.

## RECORD PRICES

Record prices for antiques and collectibles make news every year. We report those that relate to the entries in this book. We do not include record prices for works of art that are often seen in museums, like oil paintings, antique sculptures, or very recent work by modern artists unless the artist also worked in decorative arts. Our list is a snapshot of the collectors' market.

### ADVERTISING

**Empire State pocket tin:** $24,000 for a Pete Brothers Tobacco Manufacturers Empire State Granulated Plug vertical pocket tin, 5 in. Morphy Auctions, Denver, Pennsylvania.

**Coca-Cola ephemera, any type:** $210,000 for the 1900 Coca-Cola calendar picturing Hilda Clark, with months pictured below Clark image, enameled colors, embossed, framed, 16 x 20 in. Morphy Auctions, Denver, Pennsylvania.

**1896 Coca-Cola calendar with pad:** $105,000 for the 1896 Coca-Cola calendar with pad beginning in April, framed, 14 ½ x 17 ½ in. Morphy Auctions, Denver, Pennsylvania.

**Syrup dispenser this form:** $84,000 for the 1900 Hires Munimaker salesman's sample dispenser, made of marble, glass, nickel, with zinc liner & coils inside. Morphy Auctions, Denver, Pennsylvania.

**Syrup dispenser this form:** $66,000 for the Grapefruitola ceramic syrup dispenser, in the form of a plump, leaf-embellished grapefruit. Morphy Auctions, Denver, Pennsylvania.

## CLOCK & WATCHES

**Henry Graves Jr. Supercomplication pocket watch:** $23,237,000 for the Patek Philippe Henry Graves Supercomplication pocket watch No. 198.385, case No. 416.769, with 24 complications, seven years to manufacture, started in 1925 and completed in 1932, 74 mm, 1 lb., with original fitted tulipwood box and Patek Philippe Certificate of Origin. Sotheby's, Geneva.

**Chinese clock:** $270,000 for a Chinese triple Fusee and gilt bronze bracket clock with automation, animated acrobats lifting and flipping while rotating on the top, dial surmounted with flowing water and moving ducks in a gilt bronze case, 8 bell musical movement, and engraved rear panel, 30 x 17 in. Clars, Oakland, California.

**Patek Philippe world time pocket watch:** $982,000 for a Patek Philippe Ref. 605, pink gold, open face world time watch with enamel dial, picturing North America, 1951. Sotheby's, New York

## FURNITURE

**Food safe of this form:** $102,500 for a Shenandoah Valley of Virginia food safe, yellow pine & poplar, painted blue, 12 punched tin panels painted white, initials JH, profile portraits of Andrew Jackson, inscriptions "G. Armentrout" (tavern owner) and "Hero! of Orleans, " 1820s. Nicely's Auction, Clifton Forge, Virginia.

**Flying Carpet Daybed:** $162,500 for the 1968 Maria Pergay "Flying Carpet" daybed, curved stainless steel frame around upholstered rectangle, 12 x 117 ½ x 30 in. Los Angeles Modern Auctions, Los Angeles, California.

**Charles Rohlfs:** $262,000 for a drop-front desk on pivoting base by Charles Rohlfs, Buffalo, New York, carved, oak & iron construction, possibly a prototype, c.1898, 56 x 25 x 24 in. Rago, Lambertville, New Jersey.

**Late 18th/early 19th century English console table:** $22,600 for an English mahogany console table, variegated marble top, above a shell carved apron with rosette medallions, single carved in-swept support on a graduated base, c.1900, 29 ½ x 34 x 19 in. Clars, Oakland, California.

## GLASS

**Celery vase:** $37,375 for a Bakewell, Page & Bakewell, Pittsburgh blown and cut celery vase engraved with a seated greyhound, flowers, urn with cascading daisies and initials "S.A.T." in a shield, flared rim, bucket shaped bowl, and pedestal foot, c.1830, 8 5/16 in. Jeffrey S. Evans, Mt. Crawford, Virginia.

## LAMPS

**Tiffany lamp floor model:** $1,066,000 for a Tiffany Studios "Oriental Poppy" floor lamp, patinated bronze, "Chased Pod" floor base, leaded glass shade with pig tail, impressed Tiffany Studios, New York, c.1910, 77 7/8 in., shade diameter 26 in. Sotheby's, New York.

## MISCELLANEOUS

**Apple-1 computer:** $905,000 for an Apple-1 computer, one of only 50 made in Steve Jobs' garage in 1976, with intact motherboard, keyboard and monitor also has a power supply contained in a wooden box and 2 tape decks. Bonhams, New York.

**Ruby or any jewel by Cartier:** $30,335,698 for a ruby & diamond ring by Cartier, "Sunrise Ruby" from Myanmar, in the extremely rare grading of "pigeon's blood" color, weighing 25.59 carats. Sotheby's, Geneva.

## PAINTINGS & PRINTS

**Robert Mapplethorpe, this edition:** $87,500 for Robert Mapplethorpe's gelatin silver print, "Self Portrait," number 3 of 10, signed & dated in black ink, 1985, 15 x 15 in. Los Angeles Modern Auctions, Los Angeles, California.

## PAPER

**Action Comic No. 1:** $3,207,852 for the original 1938 Action Comic No. 1 that introduced Superman, with 10 cent cover price, graded 9 out of 10. EBay.

**Frankenstein movie poster:** $358,500 for a movie poster from the 1931 Universal Studios horror classic Frankenstein, style C, three-sheet, used by the theater as a display for a number of reissues of the film, 41 x 78 ½ in. (the only one of this size known to exist). Heritage Auctions, Dallas, Texas.

## POTTERY & PORCELAIN

**American stoneware:** $402,500 for a stoneware churn decorated with 4 cobalt blue Union Civil War soldiers marching in formation, with tooled shoulder, applied lug handles, Fort Edwards, New York, 1861-65, 5 gal., 15 ½ in. Crocker Farm, Sparks, Maryland.

**Chinese work of art:** $24,723,000 for a Qianlong period imperial vase in a tiered baluster form with gilt bronze ears and 12 lobes, 6 decorated with symbols and 6 decorated with flower and scroll designs in brilliant enamels, 38 ¾ x 10 ¾ in. Skinner, Boston. (pictured)

**Pennsylvania stoneware:** $97,750 for a stoneware jug picturing the profile of a Civil War soldier in cobalt blue by Cowden & Wilcox, Harrisburg, Pennsylvania, c.1865, 2 gal. Crocker Farm, Sparks, Maryland.

**Virginia stoneware:** $92,000 for a stoneware jar stamped Samuel Bell, Winchester, Virginia, with impressed cobalt blue horse and brushed flower decorations, c.1840, 7 gal. Crocker Farm, Sparks, Maryland.

*Qianlong period imperial vase, $24,723,000*

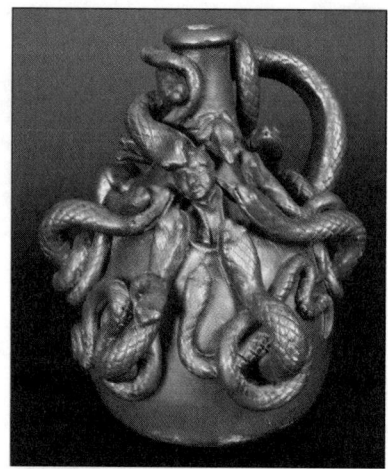

**Anna Pottery:** $87,400 for an Anna Pottery centennial snake temperance jug, applied slithering snakes, brown-red slip glaze rather than the typical salt glaze, incised "By / Kirkpatrick / Anna Union Co Ill / Jan 1st 1876," 10 ¾ in. Crocker Farm, Sparks, Maryland. (pictured )

**Minton majolica cat pitcher:** $20,400 for a Minton majolica figural cat pitcher, tail forms handle, mouse under paw, shape No. 1924, Gustavsburg, c.1890, 9 ½ in. Strawser Auctions, Wolcottville, Indiana.

## SPORTS

**Goudey Babe Ruth baseball card:** $78,870 for a 1933 Goudey Babe Ruth baseball card #149, graded PSA 8. Memory Lane Inc., Tustin, California.

**Paul Hornung rookie card:** $50,323 for a 1957 Topps Paul Hornung rookie card #151, graded PSA 9. Memory Lane Inc., Tustin, California.

**T206 Honus Wagner baseball card in this condition:** $1,320,000 for a T206 Honus Wagner 1909 baseball card, rated 3 out of 10. Robert Edward Auctions, Watchung, New Jersey. (pictured)

## TOYS, DOLLS & BANKS

**Star Wars Boba Fett figure:** $27,000 for the Star Wars action figure bounty hunter Boba Fett, from the 1980 film, *The Empire Strikes Back*, manufactured in Britain by Palitoy, on an unpunched card, 3 ¾ in. Vectis Auctions, Stockton on Tees, England.

**19th century doll:** $285,000 for a Emile Jumeau character doll model 201, bisque socket head, oval face, brown glass paperweight inset eyes, eyeliner, painted curly lashes, brush-stroked and feathered brows, mouth in wide beaming smile showing tongue & teeth, pierced ears, brunette hand-tied human hair wig in long braids, composition and wooden fully-jointed body, marked "201 Depose Tete Jumeau Bte SGDG 11," 24 in. Theriault's, Annapolis, Maryland. (pictured)

*Top to bottom:*
*Anna Pottery centennial snake temperance jug, $87,400;*
*Honus Wagner 1909 baseball card, $1,320,000;*
*Jumeau character doll, model 201, $285,000*

## KOVELS OFFER EVEN MORE
## PRICE INFORMATION SOURCES

### Website: Kovels.com

Join the community of collectors at Kovels.com to keep up on more in the buy-sell world of antiques. Register, but there is no charge for most of the information on the site, years of answers to questions from collectors who read our newspaper column, and over 1,000,000 searchable prices from past years. Other information, including a database of pottery and porcelain marks and makers and another of silver marks and makers, is available for a fee.

### Newsletter: *Kovels on Antiques and Collectibles*

You already know this book is a great overall price guide for antiques and collectibles. Each entry is current, every photograph is new, and all prices are accurate. There is also another Kovel publication designed to keep you up-to-the-minute in the world of collecting. Things change quickly. Important sales produce new record prices. Fakes appear. Rarities are discovered. To keep up with developments, you can read *Kovels on Antiques and Collectibles*, our monthly newsletter. It is now available by subscription in two forms, a print edition that is mailed and an electronic format that is available via an online subscription at Kovels.com. Both provide the identical newsletter, with current information and photos useful to collectors. The electronic edition gives you access to several years of newsletter archives, too. Each newsletter is filled with color photographs, about forty per issue. The newsletter reports prices, trends, auction results, Internet sales, and other news for collectors (see back page to order).

### HOW TO USE THIS BOOK

There are a few rules for using this book. Each listing is arranged in the following manner: CATEGORY (such as silver), OBJECT (such as vase), DESCRIPTION (as much information as possible about size, age, color, and pattern). Some types of glass, pottery, and silver are exceptions to this rule. These are listed CATEGORY, PATTERN, OBJECT, DESCRIPTION. All items are presumed to be in good condition and undamaged, unless otherwise noted. In most sections, if a maker's name is easily recognized, like Gustav Stickley, we include it near the beginning of the entry. If the maker is obscure, the name may be near the end.

- You will find silver flatware in either Silver Flatware Plated or Silver Flatware Sterling. There is also a section for Silver Plate, which includes coffeepots, trays, and other plated hollowware. Most solid or sterling silver is listed by country, so look for Silver-American, Silver-Danish, Silver-English, etc. Silver jewelry is listed under Jewelry. Most pottery and porcelain is listed by factory name, such as Weller; by item, such as Calendar Plate; in sections like Dinnerware or Kitchen; or in a special section, such as Pottery-Art, Pottery-Contemporary, Pottery-Midcentury, etc.

- Sometimes we make arbitrary decisions. Fishing has its own category, but hunting is part of the larger category called Sports. We have omitted most guns except toy guns. These are listed in the Toy category. It is not legal to sell weapons without a special license, so guns are not part of the general antiques market. Air guns, BB guns, rocket guns, and others are listed in the Toy section. Everything is listed according to the computer alphabetizing system.

- We made several editorial decisions. A butter dish is a "butter." A salt dish is called a "salt" to differentiate it from a saltshaker. It is always "sugar and creamer," never "creamer and sugar."

Where one dimension is given, it is the height; or if the object is round, it's the diameter. The height of a picture is listed before width. Glass is clear unless a color is indicated.

- Some antiques terms, such as "Sheffield" or "Pratt," have two meanings. Read the paragraph headings to know the definition being used. All category headings are based on the vocabulary of the average person, and we use terms like "mud figures" even if not technically correct. Some categories are known by several names. Pressed glass is also called pattern glass or EAPG (Early American pattern glass). We use the name pressed glass because much of the information found in old books and articles use that name.

- This book does not include price listings for fine art paintings, antiquities, stamps, coins, or most types of books. Comic books are listed only in special categories like Superman, but original comic art and cels are listed in their own categories.

- Prices for items pictured can be found in the appropriate category. Look for the matching entry with the abbreviation "Illus." The color photograph will be nearby.

- Thanks to computers, the book is produced quickly. The last entries are added in June; the book is available in August. But human help finds prices and checks accuracy. We read everything at least five times, sometimes more. We edit more than 40,000 entries down to the 32,000 entries found here. We correct spelling, remove incorrect data, write category paragraphs, and decide on new categories. We proofread copy and prices many times, but there will always be some misspelled words and other errors. Information in the paragraphs is updated each year and this year more than twenty one updates and additions were made.

- Prices are reported from all parts of the United States, Canada, Europe, and Asia, converted to U.S. dollars at the time of the sale. The average rate of exchange in June 2015 was $1 U.S. to about $1.26 Canadian, €0.90 (euro), and £0.64 (British pound). Prices are from auctions, shops, Internet sales, shows, and even some flea markets. Every price is checked for accuracy, but we are not responsible for errors. We cannot answer your letters asking for price information, but please write if you have any requests for categories to be included or any corrections to the paragraphs or prices. You may find the answers to your other questions at Kovels.com.

- When you see us at shows, auctions, house sales, and flea markets, please stop and say hello. Don't be surprised if we ask for your suggestions. You can write to us at P.O. Box 22192-K, Beachwood, OH 44122, or visit us on our website, Kovels.com.

TERRY KOVEL AND KIM KOVEL
July 2015

# ACKNOWLEDGMENTS

For the past eight years our publisher, Black Dog & Leventhal, and its president, J.P. Leventhal, have helped us continue to rethink, redesign and improve *Kovels Antiques & Collectibles Price Guide.* There are many changes in technology that speeded production, improved the quality of pictures and made it easier to read and use. We changed to color photos, automatic index, easy to read type styles, and added features like marks, tips, sidebars of added information, and even a special section with information to help explain the how and why of buying and selling antiques and collectibles using new technologies. Thanks to J.P. Leventhal; Lisa Tenaglia, our editor; Ankur Ghosh, our production editor; and Kara Thornton for publicity. Mary Flower, Robin Perlow, and Cynthia Schuster Eakin did copyediting and proofreading for the entire book and found the tiniest of errors.

Thanks to Sheila Hart and her assistants, Meredith Bard, Andrea Fowler, Dana Fowler, and Ryker Vulic, who put all the prices, photographs, and paragraphs together and created the look and layout of *Kovels' Antiques & Collectibles Price Guide 2016.* Janet Dodrill and her staff member, Carolyn K. Lewis, outlined each picture to improve its look. Thanks to Lee Markley, who helped proofread the glass categories, including Carnival Glass.

The details and hard work required to record prices, assemble photos and information, check accuracy and spelling, and solve many other problems are all done by our Kovel staff. We thank Mary Ellen Brennan, Katie Karrick, Liz Lillis, Beverly Malone, Renee McRitchie, and Erika Risley. Darlene Craven, our photo editor, chased every photograph, recorded them so we could match the caption to the correct photograph held in a separate file, and had them ready when needed. Extra thanks to Cherrie Smrekar, who made sure every photograph was captioned, tips were edited and entered, record prices were gathered, and other problems were solved. It takes about nine months for the Kovel staff to do the work needed to write the book. And more special thanks to Gay Hunter, our in-house editor-in-chief for the book, who keeps track of all of it. She tracks the sources for prices, watches the descriptions go into files and starts spell checking with the first list of prices. She keeps us on schedule, stores finished work in a safe file, proofreads, corrects paragraphs, handles unexpected problems, and knows all the tricks and shortcuts we have created doing past copies of Kovels. We updated the information about companies and changes in the auctions, shows, shops and publications that control our world of collecting. Special thanks to Kim Kovel, who not only is our expert on the fifties and after, but also makes sure our computers and computing skills are keeping up with the new machines and new ways to write, edit, and store the manuscript. The book is possible only because there are so many of us creating it.

The world of antiques and collectibles is filled with people who have answered our every request for help. Dealers, auction houses, and shops have given advice and opinions, supplied photographs and prices, and made suggestions for changes. Many thanks to all of them:

Photographs were furnished by: Ahlers & Ogletree Auction Gallery, Aleph-Bet Books, Allard Auctions, American Bottle Auctions, Arus Auctions, Bertoia Auctions, Brunk Auctions, Bowers & Merena Auctions, Burchard's Galleries, Clars Auction Gallery, Conestoga Auction Co., Copake Auction, Cottone Auctions, Cowan's Auctions, Dallas Auction Gallery, Dirk Soulis Auctions, DuMouchelles Art Gallery, Early

Auction Co., Eldred's Auctioneers, Fox Auctions, Garth's Auctioneers & Appraisers, Glass Works Auctions, Graceland Auctions, Gray's Auctioneers, Grogan & Co., Hake's Americana & Collectibles, Heritage Auction Galleries, Humler & Nolan, James D. Julia Auctioneers, Jeffrey S. Evans & Associates, Leonard Auction, Los Angeles Modern Auctions (LAMA), Merriman Auction, Morphy Auctions, Mosby & Co. Auctions, Neal Auction Co., New Orleans Auction Galleries, Norman C. Heckler & Co., Old Barn Auction, Palm Beach Modern Auctions, Pook & Pook Auctioneers and Appraisers, Potter & Potter Auctions, Potteries Specialist Auctions, Rachel Davis Fine Arts, Rago Arts and Auction Center, Replacements Ltd., RSL Auction, Santa Margarita Auction Barn, Seeck Auctions, Showtime Auction Services, Skinner Auctioneers & Appraisers, Strawser Auction Group, The Stein Auction Co., Theriault's, Treadway Toomey Galleries, Victorian Casino Antiques, Waterford's Art & Antiques, Willis Henry Auctions, Wm Morford Auctions, Woody Auction, Worthridge Auctions, and Wright.

To the others who knowingly or unknowingly contributed to this book, we say thank you: A.N. Abell Auction Co., Apple Tree Auction Center, Aspire Auctions, Belhorn Auction, Boston Harbor Auctions, Case Antiques, Charlton Hall Auctions, Crescent City Auction Gallery, Doyle New York, Faganarms, Farmer Auctions, Freeman's Auctioneers, Gordon S. Converse & Co., Heisey Collectors of America, Leighton Galleries, Leland Little Auction, Leslie Hindman Auctioneers, Link Auction Galleries, Maine Antique Digest, Manifest Auctions, Morton Kuehnert Auctioneers, Nadeau's Auction Gallery, Noel Barrett Auctions, Northeast Auctions, O'Gallerie Auctioneers, Past Tyme Pleasures, Political Bandwagon, R.G. Munn Auction, Ruby Lane, San Rafael Auction Gallery, Sloans & Kenyon, Stair Galleries, Tradewinds Antiques & Auctions, U.S. Americana Auctions, W. Yoder Auction, Waddington's Auctioneers, Weschler's Auctioneers, and other sites.

**A. WALTER** made pate-de-verre glass under contract at the Daum glassworks from 1908 to 1914. He decorated pottery during his early years in his studio in Sevres, where he also developed his formula for pale, translucent pate-de-verre. He started his own firm in Nancy, France, in 1919. Pieces made before 1914 are signed *Daum, Nancy* with a cross. After 1919 the signature is *A. Walter Nancy.*

| | |
|---|---:|
| **Dish,** Dragonfly, Blue, 6-Sided, 6 Inset Stones, 7 In. | 3444 |
| **Dish,** Fish, 3 x 5 ½ x 4 In. | 1380 |
| **Dish,** Lobster, 5 x 5 ¾ In. | 960 |
| **Figurine,** 2 Brown Mice, Yellow Rocky Base, 2 In. | 1560 |
| **Figurine,** Bird, Fledgling, Amber, Green, 1920s, 4 In. | 500 |
| **Figurine,** Nude Maiden, Lying On Grassy Knoll, Arm Over Head, 5 In. | 2015 |
| **Paperweight,** Beetle, Brown, Black, 2 x 1 ¾ In. | 420 |
| **Paperweight,** Lobster, Yellow, Green, Black, 2 ⅜ x 2 ¾ In. | 420 |
| **Paperweight,** Turkey, 2 ½ In. | 690 |
| **Tray,** Moth Decoration, 1920s, 5 In. .................................*illus* | 1920 |
| **Vase,** Petals, Pink Shaded To Yellow, Shaded Green Leaves, Cream Ground, Flared, 6 In. | 2430 |

**ABC** plates, or children's alphabet plates, were most popular from 1780 to 1860, but are still being made. The letters on the plate were meant as teaching aids for children learning to read. The plates were made of pottery, porcelain, metal, or glass. Mugs and other items were also made with alphabet decorations.

| | |
|---|---:|
| **Dish,** Feeding, Baby In Moon, Green Border, Japan, 1930s, 6 ½ In. | 29 |
| **Mug,** Little Jack Horner, Pearlware, Red, England, c.1880, 2 ¾ In. | 280 |
| **Mug,** Sterling Silver, International Silver Co., c.1910, 2 ¾ In. | 310 |
| **Pitcher,** Milk Glass, Blue, Germany, 3 ⅜ In. | 60 |
| **Plate,** Boy & Girl, Alphabet Border, Buffalo Pottery, c.1935, 7 ½ In. | 38 |
| **Plate,** Famous Places, Transfer, Brown, Brownhills Pottery, c.1880, 8 ¼ In. | 170 |
| **Plate,** Flower, Bud, Transferware, Brown, c.1870, 7 ½ In. | 60 |
| **Plate,** Nations Of The World, Letters On Plate, Greek Couple, Brownhills Pottery, 1800s, 7 In. | 98 |
| **Plate,** Red Riding Hood, Grandmother, Transferware, Brown, Brownhills Pottery, 1880s, 7 In. | 298 |
| **Plate,** Red Riding Hood, Woods, Wolf, England, 1880s, 7 In. | 300 |
| **Plate,** Simple Simon, Transfer, Brownhills Pottery, c.1880, 6 ½ In. | 200 |
| **Plate,** Tin Lithograph, Cats, Sewing Basket, c.1925, 6 In. | 50 |
| **Plate,** Tin, Stamped, Eagle, Numbers, Rolled Edge, 2 ⅜ In. | 95 |
| **Plate,** Tin, Who Killed Cock Robin, Robin On Branch, c.1850, 7 ¾ In. | 120 |
| **Plate,** Wild Animals, Elephant, Brown, England, c.1880, 7 ¼ In. | 255 |
| **Plate,** Woman, Sitting, Child In Bed, 6 ¼ In. | 135 |

**ABINGDON POTTERY** was established in 1908 by Raymond E. Bidwell as the Abingdon Sanitary Manufacturing Company. The company started making art pottery in 1934. The factory ceased production of art pottery in 1950.

| | |
|---|---:|
| **Bookends,** Horse Head, Glossy Black, 6 ½ In. | 52 |
| **Candleholder,** Double, Art Deco, Pink Matte, c.1940, 4 ¼ In. | 16 |
| **Candlestick,** Ruffled Rim, 2-Light, Green, 6 In., Pair | 28 |
| **Centerpiece,** Candleholder, 4-Light, Pink, 14 x 8 In. | 48 |
| **Console,** Pink, Pink Matte Glaze, 14 x 9 x 2 In. | 9 |
| **Cornucopia,** Double, Cameo Pink, 11 x 5 x 4 In. | 26 |
| **Flowerpot,** La Fleur, Poppies, Ribbed, 4 x 4 ¾ In. | 32 |
| **Flowerpot,** Ribbed Panels, Saucer, White, 3 ¼ x 3 ¾ In. | 20 |
| **Planter,** Rectangular, Mustard Yellow, 1960s, 10 x 6 x 2 In. | 18 |
| **Stringholder,** Chinese Face, 5 In. | 250 |
| **Urn,** Curved Handles, Flared Rim, White, 9 x 7 In. | 40 |
| **Vase,** Acanthus Leaf, Handles, Footed, Blue Glossy Glaze, 1940s, 10 In. | 65 |
| **Vase,** Anchor, Pink, 8 In. | 22 |
| **Vase,** Fan Shape, Ribbed Foot, Flower Frog, Pink, 7 x 5 In. | 43 |
| **Vase,** Handles, Footed, Flared, Ivory, 8 In. | 49 |
| **Vase,** Sailing Ships, Green, Oval, c.1940s, 7 In. | 15 |

**ADAMS** china was made by William Adams and Sons of Staffordshire, England. The firm was founded in 1769 and became part of the Wedgwood Group in 1966. The name *Adams* appeared on various items through 1998. All types of tablewares and useful wares were made. Other pieces of Adams may be found listed under Flow Blue and Tea Leaf Ironstone.

| | |
|---|---:|
| **Chamber Pot,** Cream, Scrolled Handle, c.1830, 5 x 9 In. | 100 |
| **Coffeepot,** Paneled Gothic, Jeddo Pattern, 1850s, 8 ¾ In. | 225 |

**A. Walter,** Tray, Moth Decoration, 1920s, 5 In.
$1,920

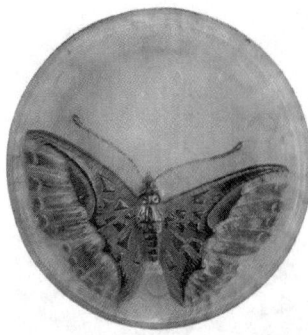

Rago Arts & Auction Center

**Advertising,** Bin, Coffee, Luxury, Pine, Red & Black Letters, Hinged Lid, c.1900, 31 x 21 ½ In.
$531

Garth's Auctioneers & Appraisers

**Advertising,** Bin, Log Cabin, Johnson's Peacemaker Coffee, Tin Lithograph, 28 In.
$1,888

Bertoia Auctions

This is an edited listing of current prices. Visit Kovels.com to check thousands of prices from previous years and sign up for free information on trends, tips, reproductions, marks, and more.

**Advertising,** Box, Frank Siddalls Soap, Wood, Finger Jointed, Philadelphia, 16 x 10½ In.
$60

Morphy Auctions

**Advertising,** Cabinet, DeLaval Cream Separators, Oak, Door, Tin, c.1890, 29 x 18 In.
$1,064

Theriault's

**Advertising,** Cabinet, Diamond Dyes, Washer Woman, Blue Background, Tin, 29½ In.
$1,680

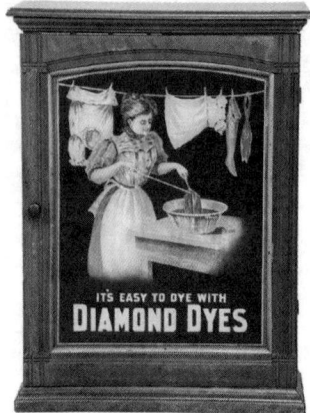

Morphy Auctions

| | |
|---|---:|
| **Cup & Saucer,** Green, White, Farmers Arms | 138 |
| **Eggcup,** Pink Rose Spray, Gold Trim, Double, 1930s, 3¾ In. | 20 |
| **Mug,** Cries Of London, Green & Brown Border, c.1895, 3½ In. | 39 |
| **Pitcher,** Caledonia, Green, Red Transfer, c.1850, 9¾ In. | 345 |
| **Plate,** Mount Vernon, Flow Blue, 10¼ In. | 105 |
| **Plate,** Pastoral Cottage, Lake, Leaf Border, Blue, c.1825, 6¾ In. | 125 |
| **Teapot,** Lid, Rural Scenery, Blue, Footed, c.1820, 8 x 12 In. | 625 |
| **Tureen,** Lid, Flowers, Footed, Titanware, c.1900, 9 x 9 x 5 In. | 120 |

**ADVERTISING** containers and products sold in the old country store are now all collectibles. These stores, with crackers in a barrel and a potbellied stove, are a symbol of an earlier, less hectic time. Listed here are many advertising items. Other similar pieces may be found under the product name, such as Planters Peanuts. We have tried to list items in logical places, so enameled tin dishes will be found under Graniteware, auto-related items in the Auto category, paper items in the Paper category, etc. Store fixtures, cases, signs, and other items that have no advertising as part of the decoration are listed in the Store category. The early Dr Pepper logo included a period after "Dr," but it was dropped in 1950. We list all Dr Pepper items without a period so they alphabetize together. For more prices, go to kovels.com.

| | |
|---|---:|
| **Ashtray,** American Airlines, Airplane Shape, Round Tray, Chrome, 5¾ x 7 In. | 650 |
| **Ashtray,** Champion Spark Plugs, Ceramic, White, 3¼ x 4¼ In. | 184 |
| **Ashtray,** Fisk Co., Tire Shape, Child, Holding Tire, 6½ In. | 264 |
| **Ashtray,** Grand Gas Ranges, Chimney, Cast Iron, Enameled Finish, 5 x 8 x 3 In. | 115 |
| **Ashtray,** Mid-Town Motel, Metal, Green Fleck, Port Allegany, Pa., 1960s, 6 x 4 In. | 14 |
| **Ashtray,** Shell Oil, Compliments Of Petersburg Shell Service Station, Uhl, 2½ In. | 58 |
| **Automaton,** Cush Un Soft Soles, Kitten Bending Shoe | 390 |
| **Banner,** Canvas, House Of Horrors, Bed Of Pain, Blood Alley, Fred Johnson, 96 x 96 In. | 3300 |
| **Banner,** Canvas, Museum Of The Unknown, Devil Man, Frierson Studios, 96 x 96 In. | 480 |
| **Banner,** Gold Dust Washing Powder, Black Twins, Cloth, 30¼ x 22½ In. | 345 |
| **Banner,** Kellogg's Krumbles, Cloth, Frame, 22 x 47 In. | 330 |
| **Banner,** Ladies Home Journal, Multicolor, Cloth, c.1900, 34 x 46 In. | 123 |
| **Bench,** Selz Shoes, Make Your Feet Glad, Oak, 59 x 36 In. | 474 |
| **Bin,** A&P, Wood, Tin Lined, Red, Gold Paint, 18 x 30 In. | 234 |
| **Bin,** Beech-Nut Chewing Tobacco, Tin, Green Ground, Multicolor, 10 x 8¾ In. | 420 |
| **Bin,** Coffee, Luxury, Pine, Red & Black Letters, Hinged Lid, c.1900, 31 x 21½ In. ......*illus* | 531 |
| **Bin,** High Grade Roasted Coffee, Tin, Painted Red, Gold Lettering, Slant Lid, 18 x 18 In. | 354 |
| **Bin,** Honest Scrap Tobacco, Slant Lid, Dog, Cat, Red, Green, Tin, 18 In. | 660 |
| **Bin,** King's Herald Cigar Tobacco, Herald Reading, Cream, F.H. Berning & Sons, 20 In. | 840 |
| **Bin,** Levering's Coffee Baltimore, Tin, Red Paint, 17 x 18 In. | 300 |
| **Bin,** Log Cabin, Johnson's Peacemaker Coffee, Tin Lithograph, 28 In. ......*illus* | 1888 |
| **Bin,** Nic Nac Chewing Tobacco, Dog's Head, Green Ground, 12 In. | 210 |
| **Bin,** Parke's Dry Roast Coffees, Unmatchable, Tin, Paint, Phila., 21 x 20 In. | 265 |
| **Bin,** Polar Bear Scrap Tobacco, Slant Lid, Gold Bear, Letters, Navy Blue, 18 In. | 660 |
| **Bin,** Roundy, Peckham & Dexter Co., Red Cross Choice Coffee, Black, Metal, 20½ In. | 210 |
| **Bin,** Sure Shot Chewing Tobacco, Indian Shooting Arrow, Top Metal Lid, Tin, 15½ In. | 660 |
| **Bin,** Sweet Cuba Tobacco, Angled Lid, Yellow Ground, Tin, 10 In. | 180 |
| **Bin,** Weyman's Cutty Pipe, Green Label, 13 In. | 330 |
| **Books** may be included in the Paper category. | |
| **Bottles** are listed in their own category. | |
| **Bottle Openers** are listed in their own category. | |
| **Bottle Topper,** Orange Crush, Boy, Swimsuit, 1927, 15 In. | 1800 |
| **Box,** see also Box category. | |
| **Box,** Boar's Head Tobacco, Yellow, Blue, Counter, 8½ In. | 780 |
| **Box,** Dr. Miles' Nervine, 2 Heads, Woman's & Anatomic, 2 Doz., Wood, 1906, 14 In. | 392 |
| **Box,** Frank Siddalls Soap, Wood, Finger Jointed, Philadelphia, 16 x 10½ In. ......*illus* | 60 |
| **Box,** Kennedy's Medical Discovery, Cure For Scrofula, Wood, Finger Jointed, 12 In. | 179 |
| **Box,** Larson's Spearmint Gum, Cardboard, 21 Packs, L.P. Larson Jr. Co., 4 x 6 In. | 1208 |
| **Box,** Lily Of Valley Oats, Cardboard, Lithograph, Lauderbach-Griest Co., 7 x 4¼ In. | 81 |
| **Box,** Match, Green Joyce & Co., Fly Shape, Cast Iron, Hinged Wings, 2 x 4¾ In. | 241 |
| **Box,** Soapine The Dirt Killer, Label, c.1900, 24 x 19 In. | 117 |
| **Box,** Spring Valley Chick Hatchery, Pine, Side Latch, Red Paint, c.1915, 14 x 37 In. | 127 |
| **Box,** W.A. Brown Tobacco Co., Slide Top, Oak, Virginia, c.1910, 4 x 13 In. | 115 |
| **Broadside,** New Steamboat Telegraph, Lake Ontario, July 14, 1837, Frame, 20 x 15 In. | 3900 |
| **Bust,** Man, Topper, Black Top Hat, 8 In. | 48 |
| **Cabinet,** Angel Dainty Dyes, Wood | 150 |
| **Cabinet,** Corticelli Thread & Bow, Bowed Glass Front, Drawers, 20½ In. | 510 |

**Advertising,** Cabinet, Dr. A.C. Daniels Dog & Cat Remedies, Woman, Cat & Dog, Tin Litho, 20 x 13 In.
$7,015

Wm Morford Auctions

**Advertising,** Cabinet, Dr. Daniels' Veterinary Medicines, Tin, Embossed, Portrait, Oak, 21 x 29 In.
$2,666

James D. Julia Auctioneers

**Advertising,** Cabinet, Humphrey's Specifics, Oak, Tin, Product & Manual, 22 x 28 In.
$420

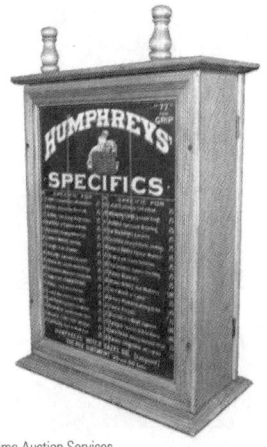

Showtime Auction Services

**Advertising,** Cabinet, Old Judge Cigarettes, Woman, Man, Pillory, Mirror, c.1900, 62 x 25 In.
$780

Garth's Auctioneers & Appraisers

**Advertising,** Cabinet, Spool, J. & P. Coats', Best Six Cord, 4 Drawers, Maple, Refinished, 22 x 16 ½ In.
$593

James D. Julia Auctioneers

**Advertising,** Can, Chippewa Evaporated Milk, Indian Chief, Solder Seal, Paper Label, 4 x 3 In.
$115

Wm Morford Auctions

**Advertising,** Cigarette Box, Chesterfield Cigarettes, Trick Box, Clown Jumps Out
$5

**Advertising,** Clock, Planters Peanuts, Mr. Peanut, Cane, Top Hot, Octagonal, Wall, 18 In.
$960

Morphy Auctions

**Advertising,** Crock, Heinz's Chow Chow, Wire Clamp, Paper Label, 10 In.
$342

Showtime Auction Services

3

**Advertising,** Dispenser, Bromo-Seltzer, Cobalt Blue, Emerson Drug Co., Md., 16 ½ In.
$504

McMurray Antiques & Auctions

**Advertising,** Dispenser, Drink Cherry-Julep, Ball Shape, Ball Pump
$12,000

Morphy Auctions

**Advertising,** Dispenser, Drink Crawford's Cherry-Fizz, 9 Cherries, Ceramic, Pump
$19,200

Morphy Auctions

**Advertising,** Display, Kit, Hershey's, 7 Bottles, Stages Of Cocoa Production, 5 x 9 x 3 ½ In.
$161

Wm Morford Auctions

**Advertising,** Display, Mason's Challenge Blacking, Paper Label, 11 ½ x 8 In.
$86

Showtime Auction Services

**Advertising,** Display, Mazda Lamps, Tin, Arch, Lightbulbs, 27 ½ x 13 In.
$1,920

Showtime Auction Services

**Why Napoleon Lost at Waterloo**
It is reported that Napoleon lost the Battle of Waterloo because he had hemorrhoids. His doctors had given him opiates for pain, and he was woozy the day of the battle. It is said he left the battle to get more medication and delayed deploying the troops, which made him lose the battle.

**Advertising,** Figure, Big Boy, Hamburger On Platter, Red & White Overalls, 54 x 43 In.
$1,920

Morphy Auctions

**Advertising,** Figure, Boy & Dog, Hanes Merrichild Sleepers, Countertop
$210

Morphy Auctions

**Advertising,** Figure, Boy, Squirt Bottle, Just Call Me Squirt, Plaster, 13 In.
$780

Morphy Auctions

| | |
|---|---|
| **Cabinet,** DeLaval Cream Separator, Oak, Door, Tin, c.1890, 29 x 18 In. .............................*illus* | 1064 |
| **Cabinet,** Diamond Dyes, Children Skipping Rope, 24 x 16 In. ...................................................... | 617 |
| **Cabinet,** Diamond Dyes, Children With Balloon, 25 x 15 In. ......................................................... | 472 |
| **Cabinet,** Diamond Dyes, Governess, Children, 22 ½ x 30 In. ......................................................... | 531 |
| **Cabinet,** Diamond Dyes, Maypole, Oak, Children, 22 ½ x 30 In. ................................................... | 531 |
| **Cabinet,** Diamond Dyes, Prism, Color Wheel, Interior Partitions, Hanging, Wood, 29 ½ In. ........ | 660 |
| **Cabinet,** Diamond Dyes, Washer Woman, Blue Background, Tin, 29 ½ In. ........................*illus* | 1680 |
| **Cabinet,** Display, Police Liniment, Universal Rub, Wood, Paint, 6 Shelves, 54 x 18 In. ............... | 472 |
| **Cabinet,** Dr. A.C. Daniels Dog & Cat Remedies, Woman, Cat & Dog, Tin Litho, 20 x 13 In. ..*illus* | 7015 |
| **Cabinet,** Dr. Daniels' Veterinary Medicines, Tin, Embossed, Portrait, Oak, 21 x 29 In. ........*illus* | 2666 |
| **Cabinet,** Dr. King's New Discovery, Wood, Glass, 24 In. ............................................................... | 390 |
| **Cabinet,** Humphrey's Specifics, Oak, Tin, Product & Manual, 22 x 28 In. ......................*illus* | 420 |
| **Cabinet,** Old Judge Cigarettes, Woman, Man, Pillory, Mirror, c.1900, 62 x 25 In. ..............*illus* | 780 |
| **Cabinet,** Open Me & You Will See The Best Accident Eliminator, Door, Wood, 15 x 21 In. ........... | 351 |
| **Cabinet,** Saver's Extract, Gold Leaf Printing, Glass, Hanging, Wood, 21 In. ............................... | 1140 |
| **Cabinet,** Spool, Clark's O.N.T., Oak, Brass Pulls, Beaded Flowers, 6 Drawers, 1800s ..................... | 529 |
| **Cabinet,** Spool, Clark's O.N.T., Oak, Rollfront Door, Glass Windows, c.1890, 22 In. ..................... | 1568 |
| **Cabinet,** Spool, Clark's, Walnut, 6 Drawers, Ruby Glass, c.1910, 29 x 22 In. ............................. | 533 |
| **Cabinet,** Spool, Corticelli, Decals, 22 Drawers, 30 In. .............................................................. | 2160 |
| **Cabinet,** Spool, Goff's Best Braid, Wood Case, 3 Drawers, Gilt Lettering, 17 ½ x 18 In.................. | 127 |
| **Cabinet,** Spool, J. & P. Coats', Best Six Cord, 2 Drawers, Knobs, Embossed, 22 x 17 In. ................. | 236 |
| **Cabinet,** Spool, J. & P. Coats', Best Six Cord, 4 Drawers, Maple, Refinished, 22 x 16 ½ In......*illus* | 593 |
| **Cabinet,** Spool, J. & P. Coats', Oak Case, Paneled Side, 6 Drawers, 22 x 25 ¾ In........................... | 153 |
| **Cabinet,** Spool, J. & P. Coats', Spool Cotton, Stencil Label, c.1900, 24 x 31 In....................... | 553 |
| **Cabinet,** Spool, M. Heminway & Sons, Sublime Quality, Curved Door, 18 In. .............................. | 1560 |
| **Calendars** are listed in their own category. | |
| **Can,** Chippewa Evaporated Milk, Indian Chief, Solder Seal, Paper Label, 4 x 3 In. ..............*illus* | 115 |
| **Can,** Havoline Oil, Indian Refining Company, Gal. ...................................................................... | 316 |
| **Can,** Jack Sprat Coffee, Yellow, 1 Lb. ........................................................................................ | 575 |
| **Can,** Spry Vegetable Shortening, Green, Cream, Bale, Lever Bros., 1940s, 6 Lb. ......................... | 32 |
| **Canisters,** see introductory paragraph to Tins in this category. | |
| **Cards** are listed in the Card category. | |
| **Case,** Cadbury Chocolates, Countertop, Etched Glass, Wood Frame, 31 In. ................................ | 240 |
| **Case,** Curved Glass, Cathedral Tower, Walnut, Nickel, Hoffman, Dahl & Co., 35 x 41 In. ............. | 5130 |
| **Case,** Display, J.P. Priwley, California Fruit & Pepsin Gum, Oak, 19 x 12 In......................... | 840 |
| **Case,** Display, Jacobs & Co., Superior Biscuits, 3 Shelves, 52 x 43 In........................................ | 720 |
| **Case,** Display, Meditation Cigars, Painted Tin, Glass Front, 10 x 10 In........................................ | 59 |
| **Case,** Display, Salisbury's Popcorn, Wood, Glass, 11 In. .............................................................. | 180 |
| **Chair,** Piedmont Cigarette, Folding, 2-Sided Porcelain Back, Wood, c.1920, 30 In. ...................... | 138 |
| **Chalkboard,** Kickapoo Joy Juice, 1965, 30 x 10 ½ In................................................................ | 180 |
| **Change Receiver,** see also Tip Tray in this category. | |
| **Charger,** Cunard Steamship Company, Flags, Crown, 24 In......................................................... | 592 |
| **Cigar Case,** Display, White Owl Cigar, Oak, Iron Claw Feet, 36 x 43 x 26 In............................... | 257 |
| **Cigar Cutter,** Kohler Handmade, Plated, Oak, 2 Blades, c.1890, 10 ½ In. ................................... | 1200 |
| **Cigar Cutter,** Winecke & Doerr Red Box Cigars, Cast Brass, 8 ½ In. ......................................... | 360 |
| **Cigarette Box,** Chesterfield Cigarettes, Trick Box, Clown Jumps Out .........................*illus* | 5 |
| **Clock,** Planters Peanuts, Mr. Peanut, Cane, Top Hot, Octagonal, Wall, 18 In. ................*illus* | 960 |
| **Container,** Franklin Price Foot Powder, Cardboard, 3-Sided, Multicolor Label, 5 x 2 In.............. | 35 |
| **Crock,** Heinz's Chow Chow, Wire Clamp, Paper Label, 10 In. .................................*illus* | 342 |
| **Dispenser,** Birchola, Porcelain, Metal Pump, 15 In..................................................................... | 1440 |
| **Dispenser,** Black Buckeye Root Beer, Black With Gold Letters .................................................. | 1140 |
| **Dispenser,** Bowey's Root Beer, Barrel Shape, Wood Cradle, 13 In.............................................. | 540 |
| **Dispenser,** Bromo-Seltzer, Cobalt Blue, Emerson Drug Co., Md., 16 ½ In. ......................*illus* | 504 |
| **Dispenser,** Buckeye Root Beer Syrup, Acorns, Ceramic, Cleveland Fruit Juice, 16 In. ................. | 2400 |
| **Dispenser,** Buckeye Root Beer Syrup, Cleveland Fruit Juice Co., c.1910, 15 In. .......................... | 2400 |
| **Dispenser,** Cherri Bon Syrup, Red, White, Ball Shape, Ceramic, c.1910, 14 In. ........................... | 31200 |
| **Dispenser,** Cherry Smash Syrup, 5 Cents, White, Red, Round, c.1900, 15 In. ............................. | 3300 |
| **Dispenser,** Dr. Swett's Root Beer Syrup, 75 Years, Boy, Tree Stump, c.1900, 14 In. .................... | 9000 |
| **Dispenser,** Dr. Swett's Root Beer, Bottle Shape, Stoneware, Brown, Tan, 2 Piece ......................... | 1080 |
| **Dispenser,** Dr. Swett's Syrup, Spigot, 2 Parts, Stoneware, Boston, c.1900, 22 In. ......................... | 960 |
| **Dispenser,** Drink Cherry-Julep, Ball Shape, Ball Pump ...........................................*illus* | 12000 |
| **Dispenser,** Drink Crawford's Cherry-Fizz, 9 Cherries, Ceramic, Pump .........................*illus* | 19200 |
| **Dispenser,** Drink Hires It Is Pure, White With Red, 15 In.......................................................... | 420 |
| **Dispenser,** Eberhard Faber Ruby Bands, Rubber Bands, Metal Frame, 15 ½ In............................ | 210 |
| **Dispenser,** Fowler's Cherry Smash Syrup, Ceramic, 3 Cherries, 14 ¾ In..................................... | 2840 |
| **Dispenser,** Fowler's Cherry Smash Syrup, Ceramic, 5 Cent, 14 In.............................................. | 829 |

**Advertising,** Figure, Castle Hall Cigars, Stork, Papier-Mache, Sign In Beak
$380

**Advertising,** Figure, Green Girl, M&M Candy, Plastic, Base, Wheels, 1995, 39 In.
$180

**Advertising,** Figure, Woman, Simplicity Pattern, Composite, Wood, 11 x 33 In.
$308

**Advertising,** Ice Cream Cone Holder, Jack Frost, Embossed Letters, c.1920, 11½ In.
$900

Morphy Auctions

**Advertising,** Jar, Curtis Chicos New Spanish Peanuts, 5 Cent, Glass, Metal, 11 x 9 In.
$390

Morphy Auctions

**Advertising,** Label, Columbia Hair Cream, Columbia Perfume Co., 1¾ x 4 In., 250 Piece
$150

Showtime Auction Services

### The Tiny Heinz Pickle

The tiny Heinz pickle-shaped pin was a giveaway at the 1893 Chicago World's Fair. One million were given away. A Heinz Ketchup bottle pin the same small size was first made in 2000.

| | |
|---|---:|
| **Dispenser,** Getz Blend Root Beer Syrup, Blue, White, Round, Ceramic, c.1920, 15 In. | 4200 |
| **Dispenser,** Heinz Vinegar, Frosted Glass, 15 In. | 180 |
| **Dispenser,** Hires Root Beer, Drink Hires, 5 Cents, Barrel Shape | 450 |
| **Dispenser,** Hires Root Beer, Tan, Red Lettering, Porcelain, Metal, 15 In. | 390 |
| **Dispenser,** Hires Syrup, Ugly Kid, Mettlach Urn, c.1900, 19 In. | 18600 |
| **Dispenser,** Howler's Cherry-Julep Syrup, Ceramic, Red, 15 In. | 2470 |
| **Dispenser,** Ice Tea, KFC, Colonel, White, Blue, Side Handles, 1980s, 20 In. | 480 |
| **Dispenser,** Indian Rock Ginger Ale, Glass, Barrel Shape, Zinc Lid, Gal. | 1568 |
| **Dispenser,** Jersey Creme, Porcelain, Metal, 15½ In. | 1320 |
| **Dispenser,** Josh Slinger, Pointing, Mettlach, c.1900, 19 In. | 10200 |
| **Dispenser,** King's Cherry Drip Syrup, Red, White, 14½ In. | 10800 |
| **Dispenser,** Liberty Root Beer Syrup, Creamy-Kind, Ball Style Pump, 14 In. | 2160 |
| **Dispenser,** Magnus Lime Rickey, Figural, Cast Iron Base, Paper Label, 14 In. | 1800 |
| **Dispenser,** Malted Grape-Nuts, Chrome, Glass, 1920s, 15½ In. | 510 |
| **Dispenser,** Marrowford Syrup, 5 Cents Makes Rich Blood, Christi, c.1915, 15 In. | 8400 |
| **Dispenser,** Mission Orangeade Syrup, Oranges On Top, Metal, Paint, c.1940, 15 In. | 2040 |
| **Dispenser,** Mo-Pep Syrup, Cream, Barrel Shape, c.1920, 14½ In. | 1320 |
| **Dispenser,** Orange Julep, Orange Body, Metal Pump, 16 In. | 1920 |
| **Dispenser,** Orchard Ale Syrup, Taste Tell Milk, Barrel Shape, c.1915, 14½ In. | 1560 |
| **Dispenser,** Schuster's Root Beer Syrup, 5 Cent, Red, White, Barrel, c.1920, 15 In. | 1080 |
| **Dispenser,** Smith's Orangeade Syrup, White, Round, Metal Pump, 12½ In. | 900 |
| **Dispenser,** Taka-Cola Syrup, White, Orange, Round, Footed, c.1900, 14½ In. | 3000 |
| **Dispenser,** Vola Syrup, White, Chicago Concentrating Co., c.1910, 17 In. | 1680 |
| **Dispenser,** Ward's Lemon Crush Syrup, Lemon Shape, Ceramic, c.1920, 14 In. | 3000 |
| **Dispenser,** Zipp's Cherri-O Syrup, Robin Drinking, Barrel Shape, c.1910, 15 In. | 5100 |
| **Display,** Adam's Spearmint Gum, Tin, Lithograph, Adams & Son, Brooklyn, N.Y., 6 x 4 In. | 104 |
| **Display,** Baby Ruth Mint Gum, Lithograph, Reverse Painted Glass, Curtis Candy, 7 x 6 In. | 316 |
| **Display,** Beech-Nut Gum, Holds 4 Boxes, 13¾ In. | 450 |
| **Display,** Bottle, Drink Orange Crush, Oranges, Leaves, Cardboard, 1927, 10 In. | 210 |
| **Display,** Bottle, Howel's, Cardboard, Easel Back, 1940s, 34½ In. | 90 |
| **Display,** Briar Pipe Tobacco, Die Cut, Shop Keeper, Smoking, Crates, 21 In. | 1680 |
| **Display,** Counter, Bethlehem Mocha Coffee, Red, Tin, 20 In. | 180 |
| **Display,** Counter, Monol Pencil, Divided Interior, Tin, 15 In. | 72 |
| **Display,** Curtis Baby Ruth Candy, Glass, Wood, Cylindrical, c.1930, 17 In. | 450 |
| **Display,** Dony's Salve, Sores, Burns, Chilblains, 25 Cents, Cardboard, 6 Tins, 7 x 3 In. | 95 |
| **Display,** Dutch Boy, Paint Can, Papier-Mache, 29½ In. | 270 |
| **Display,** Gainsboro Powder Puffs, Slanted Glass Front Case, Wood Frame, c.1920, 21¾ In. | 450 |
| **Display,** Kit, Hershey's, 7 Bottles, Stages Of Cocoa Production, 5 x 9 x 3½ In. *illus* | 161 |
| **Display,** Mason's Challenge Blacking, Paper Label, 11½ x 8 In. *illus* | 86 |
| **Display,** Mazda Lamps, Tin, Arch, Lightbulbs, 27½ x 13 In. *illus* | 1920 |
| **Display,** Orange Flowers Cigars, 5 Cents, H.B. Granley, Pa., 5¾ In. | 300 |
| **Display,** Pepperidge Farm, Goldfish, Plastic, Product Holder, Wheels, Decals, 40 In. | 201 |
| **Display,** Safety Eczema Ointment, Cures Eczema, Girl On Chair, Cardboard, Die Cut, 9 In. | 84 |
| **Display,** Silver Birch Chewing Gum, Cardboard, R.H. Hickman Co., 5 x 6 x 4 In. | 316 |
| **Display,** Sure Shot Tobacco, Indian, Shooting Arrow, Tin, 15¼ In. | 660 |
| **Display,** Tennyson Cigars, Metal, Glass, c.1915, 15¾ In. | 180 |
| **Display,** West Electric Hair Curler Co., Nets, Ads, Drawer, Metal, 18 x 10 In. | 360 |
| **Display,** Whistle Soda, Iron, Hand Holding Glass Bottle, 1920s, 14 In. | 420 |
| **Display,** Winchester, Medicated Sprucine Chewing Gum, Curved Glass, 17 x 17 In. | 510 |
| **Display,** Wrigley Gum, 3 Rows, Metal, c.1930, 10½ In. | 150 |
| **Display,** Wrigley Gum, 4 Rows, Metal, c.1930, 17½ In. | 210 |
| **Display,** Wrigley Man, Holding 4 Boxes, Tin Lithograph, c.1920, 18½ In. | 1440 |
| **Display,** Zingo Candy, Race Car, Blue, Orange, Tin, 10 x 12 In. | 374 |
| **Dolls** are listed in their own category. | |
| **Door Brace,** Drink Cleo Cola For Goodness Sake, 3-Sided, Green, 1930s, 12 x 6 In. | 150 |
| **Door Pull,** Sunbeam Blue Ribbon Bread, Girl Eating, Adjustable Length, 15 In. | 179 |
| **Door Push,** Mayo's Plug, Crowing Rooster, 13 x 6½ In. | 2280 |
| **Door Push,** National Bohemian, Natty Boh, What A Beer, Tin Lithograph, 6 In. | 78 |
| **Door Push,** Pabst, Your Taste Will Tell You Why, Tin, Century, 8 In. | 112 |
| **Egg Crate,** Lid, IG Cherry Company, Stenciled, Bail Handle, c.1900, 11 x 12 In. | 120 |
| **Fans** are listed in their own category. | |
| **Fashion Plate,** MDS Tailors, Men's Winter Fashions, 1978-79, 24 x 18 In. | 210 |
| **Figure,** Bartender, Pabst Blue Ribbon Beer, Glasses, Bottle, Composition, 12½ In. | 240 |
| **Figure,** Big Boy, French Fries On Base, Wedge Cap, Overalls, Burger, 72 x 92 In. | 7800 |
| **Figure,** Big Boy, Hamburger On Platter, Red & White Overalls, 54 x 43 In. *illus* | 1920 |
| **Figure,** Black Man, Rolling Barrel, The Golden Spirit, Paint, Composition, 10 x 9 In. | 246 |

**Advertising**, Mirror, John C. Roth Packing Co., Hog Spanking A Pig, Metal Frame, Celluloid, 4⅛ In.
$253

**Advertising**, Mirror, Sunset Beach, Lake Ontario, Happy Face, Sad Face, Pocket, c.1910, 2 In.
$115

**Advertising**, Mirror, White Rock, Table Water, Psyche, Goddess, Seminude, Tin, Round, c.1905, 1¹³⁄₁₆ In.
$230

---

**TIP**

*A lithographed can with a picture is of more value than a lithographed can with just names. A paper-labeled can that is dated before 1875 is rare. An ad that pictures an American flag has added value.*

---

**Advertising**, Pail, Dinner Pail Coffee, Tin Lithograph, Bail Handle, 9⅝ x 7 In.
$748

**Advertising**, Pail, Peanut Butter, Jack Sprat, Tin Lithograph, Bail Handle, 3⅝ In.
$374

**Advertising**, Pillow Cover, Holland America Line, Twinscrew Steamers, Linen, Frame, 27 x 23 In.
$143

---

**Advertising**, Plate, Anheuser-Busch, Vienna Art Plate, Woman, Flower In Hair, Tin Litho, 1905, 9 In.
$161

**Advertising**, Ring, Quaker, Gabby Hayes, Cannon, Barrel Shoots Objects, Brass, 1951
$199

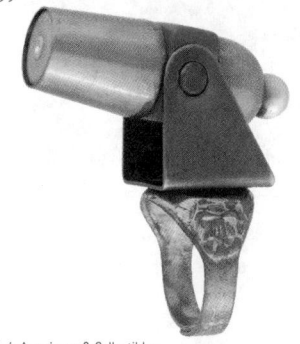

**Advertising**, Sign, Akron Brewing Co., Akron, Ohio, Factory Scene, Wood, 24 x 36 In.
$460

**Advertising,** Sign, American Brewing Company, Bulldog, Doghouse Frame, Tin, 29 ½ x 28 In.
$3,900

Showtime Auction Services

**Advertising,** Sign, Anheuser-Busch, Budweiser Girl, Red Dress, Paper, Frame, 1907, 24 x 39 In.
$855

Showtime Auction Services

**Advertising,** Sign, Anheuser-Busch, Woman, Red Dress, Bird, Letter A, Paper, 1890s, 32 In.
$2,280

Morphy Auctions

| | |
|---|---|
| **Figure,** Boy & Dog, Hanes Merrichild Sleepers, Countertop ...............................*illus* | 210 |
| **Figure,** Boy, Eating Cherry, Red Tame Cherry, Chalkware, c.1900, 26 In.............................. | 480 |
| **Figure,** Boy, Squirt Bottle, Just Call Me Squirt, Plaster, 13 In. ............................*illus* | 780 |
| **Figure,** Bryant Pup, Papier-Mache, Black, White, Old King Cole Mfg., 22 In.................. | 600 |
| **Figure,** Castle Hall Cigars, Stork, Papier-Mache, Sign In Beak ............................*illus* | 380 |
| **Figure,** Donkey, Royal Corona Coffee, Plaster, 10 x 9 x 6 In........................................ | 193 |
| **Figure,** Green Girl, M&M Candy, Plastic, Base, Wheels, 1995, 39 In. .....................*illus* | 180 |
| **Figure,** Green River, Man, Horse, Plaster, 13 In............................................................ | 180 |
| **Figure,** Levis, Jeans, Cowboy, Holding Saddle Royal Navy, Plastic, Wood Base, 29 x 13 In............. | 540 |
| **Figure,** Moxie, Silent Butler, Tuxedo, Wood, 28 In........................................................ | 413 |
| **Figure,** Ronald McDonald, Leather Catcher's Mitt, c.1950 .......................................... | 3300 |
| **Figure,** Ronald McDonald, Plastic, Green Base, Waving Pose, 72 In............................. | 2700 |
| **Figure,** Sleepy Boy, Pajamas, Fisk Tire Co., Time To Re-Tire, Black Base, 60 In............. | 2280 |
| **Figure,** Willie The Penguin, Kool Cigarettes, Mail Carrier, Standee, c.1950, 20 x 30 In........... | 185 |
| **Figure,** Woman, Holding Balloon, Schlitz, Plastic, Light-Up, 1976, 44 In...................... | 300 |
| **Figure,** Woman, Simplicity Pattern, Composite, Wood, 11 x 33 In. ......................*illus* | 308 |
| **Globe,** Beatrice Meadow Gold Ice Cream, Yellow, Red, Black, Round, Metal, 17 In............. | 293 |
| **Ice Cream Cone Holder,** Jack Frost, Embossed Letters, c.1920, 11 ½ In. ...............*illus* | 900 |
| **Jar,** Curtis Chicos New Spanish Peanuts, 5 Cent, Glass, Metal, 11 x 9 In. .............*illus* | 390 |
| **Knife,** Pocket, Anheuser-Busch, Red, Blue, Enameled, Peephole, c.1885, 3 In............. | 570 |
| **Knife,** Pocket, Star Brand Shoes, Shoe Shape, 3 In. ..................................................... | 150 |
| **Label,** Barrel, Queen Shenandoah Brand, Martinsburg Fruit Exchange, Round, 16 In. ....... | 40 |
| **Label,** Columbia Hair Cream, Columbia Perfume Co., 1 ¾ x 4 In., 250 Piece .........*illus* | 150 |
| **Lamps** are listed in the Lamp category. | |
| **Lunch Boxes** are also listed in their own category. | |
| **Match Striker,** Hamlin's Wizard Oil, Elephant, Pack On Back, Cardboard, 5 In........... | 146 |
| **Match Striker,** Wistar's Balsam, Wild Cherry, Cures Asthma, Cardboard, 4 In............ | 90 |
| **Menu Board,** Sealtest Ice Cream, Porcelain, Red, White, 14 x 27 In................................ | 330 |
| **Menu Holder,** Welch's Grape Juice, Bottle, Base, Tin, c.1910, 4 ¾ In............................ | 4800 |

**Advertising mirrors** of all sizes are listed here. Pocket mirrors range in size from 1 ½ to 5 inches in diameter. Most of these mirrors were given away as advertising promotions and include the name of the company in the design.

| | |
|---|---|
| **Mirror,** Cadbury's Chocolate, Etched Lettering, Oak, 22 ¾ x 28 ¾ In. ........................... | 296 |
| **Mirror,** Ceresota Flour, Boy On Stool, Opening Canister, Pocket, 6 ¾ In......................... | 120 |
| **Mirror,** John C. Roth Packing Co., Hog Spanking A Pig, Metal Frame, Celluloid, 4 ⅛ In. ....*illus* | 253 |
| **Mirror,** Sunset Beach, Lake Ontario, Happy Face, Sad Face, Pocket, c.1910, 2 In. .............*illus* | 115 |
| **Mirror,** White Rock, Table Water, Psyche, Goddess, Seminude, Tin, Round, c.1905, 1 ¹³⁄₁₆ In. *illus* | 230 |
| **Nodder,** Colonel Sanders, Cane, Glasses, White Suit, Composition, 1960s, 7 In. ........... | 140 |
| **Pails** are also listed in the Lunch Box category. | |
| **Pail,** Carten's, Lard, Washington Brand, Blue Diamond, Red Square, 6 In.................... | 126 |
| **Pail,** Dinner Pail Coffee, Tin Lithograph, Bail Handle, 9 ⅝ x 7 In. .....................*illus* | 748 |
| **Pail,** Dixie Queen Plug Cut Smoking Tobacco, 6 In. .................................................. | 150 |
| **Pail,** Green Turtle Cigars, Green, Metal, Top, Handle, 7 In........................................ | 120 |
| **Pail,** Green Turtle Cigars, Miners & Puddlers Smoking Tobacco................................. | 900 |
| **Pail,** Old Partner Tobacco, Civil War Soldiers, Yellow Ground, 6 ¼ In........................ | 270 |
| **Pail,** Peanut Butter, Jack Sprat, Tin Lithograph, Bail Handle, 3 ⅝ In. ................*illus* | 374 |
| **Pail,** Pedro Tobacco, Orange, Square, Metal, 7 ¾ In.................................................. | 84 |
| **Pail,** Star Meat Co., Tin, Bail Handle, 4 Lb................................................................ | 236 |
| **Pail,** Tiger, Dark Sweet Chewing Tobacco, Tiger Picture, Handle, 8 ¼ In...................... | 180 |
| **Pail,** Toyland Peanut Butter, Marching Band, Bail Handle, Blue, 2 Lb.......................... | 83 |
| **Pillow Cover,** Holland America Line, Twinscrew Steamers, Linen, Frame, 27 x 23 In. ........*illus* | 143 |
| **Plate,** Anheuser-Busch, Vienna Art Plate, Woman, Flower In Hair, Tin Litho, 1905, 9 In. ....*illus* | 161 |
| **Plate,** Congress Beer, Porcelain, Round, Metal Frame, 12 In........................................ | 2700 |
| **Plate,** 1907 Union Pacific Tea, Girl, Children, Bear Snowball Fight, Tin, 8 In. ............. | 207 |
| **Print,** Hercules Powder Co., Smokeless Shotgun Powder, Woman, Dog, Lithograph, 22 x 32 In. . | 180 |
| **Puzzle,** 24 Hour Corn Cure, N. Stiles, Boston, Cardboard, Foot Shape, Pig Toes, 4 In................ | 106 |
| **Ring,** Jack Armstrong, Whistling, Brass Luster, Egyptian Symbols, Wheaties Premium, 1937....... | 115 |
| **Ring,** Quaker, Gabby Hayes, Cannon, Barrel Shoots Objects, Brass, 1951 ............*illus* | 199 |
| **Ring,** Tom Corbett, Space Cadet, Portrait, Silver Luster, Kellogg's Premium, c.1952.............. | 98 |
| **Rolling Pin,** Compliments Of O.L. Cauble, Ind., Stoneware, Turned Wood Handles, 14 In.......... | 338 |
| **Rolling Pin,** Tulsa Feed Store, Polar Bear Flour, Porcelain, 15 In................................. | 660 |
| **Salt & Pepper Shakers** are listed in their own category. | |
| **Scales** are listed in their own category. | |
| **Scoop,** Peckham's Grocery & Gift Shop, Turquoise, White Lettering, Plastic ..................... | 12 |

**Advertising,** Sign, Auburn Canned Goods, Hemingway Preserving Co., Cardboard, 10 x 13 ½ In.
$184

Wm Morford Auctions

**Advertising,** Sign, Ayer's Cathartic Pills, Cardboard, Easel Back, Dr. & 2 Children, 12 ½ x 7 In.
$265

Wm Morford Auctions

**Advertising,** Sign, Blue Ribbon Bourbon, Colonel's Favorite, Distillery, Plaster, 43 x 34 In.
$1,560

Showtime Auction Services

**Advertising,** Sign, Boericke & Tafel Medicines, Lithograph, Frame, Signed, c.1880, 31 x 25 In.
$1,353

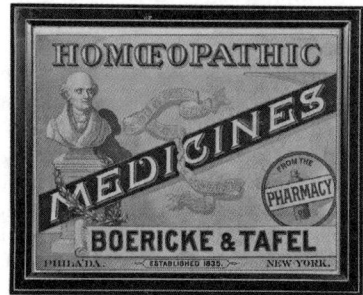

Skinner Auctioneers & Appraisers

**Advertising,** Sign, Cascarets, They Work While You Sleep, Cardboard, Frame, 21 x 11 In.
$1,710

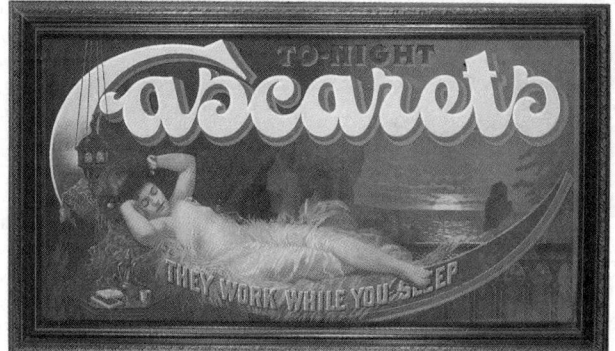

Showtime Auction Services

**Advertising,** Sign, Cascarets, They Work While You Sleep, Mother, Child, 15 x 10 In.
$123

McMurray Antiques & Auctions

**TIP**

*Advertising collectors should check every address, phone number, name, and price information that is on a label, a sticker, or the container. They will help with the research to determine the age of the product.*

**Advertising,** Sign, Centlivre's Nickel Plate Bottled Beer, Paper, Frame, c.1920, 26 x 31 In.
$330

Morphy Auctions

**Advertising,** Sign, Cetacolor, Not A Soap, 10 Cent Package, Linen, 36 x 24 In.
$285

Showtime Auction Services

**Advertising,** Sign, CL Centlivre Brewing Co., Factory Scene, Paper, Fort Wayne, 36 x 24 In.
$59

James D. Julia Auctioneers

**Advertising,** Sign, Columbia Grafonola, Tin, Wood Frame, Hanger, Chain, Jos. K. Fodor, 22 x 28 In.
$360

Morphy Auctions

**Advertising,** Sign, Corn-Fed Hogs, Our Taste Hams, Hall, Luhrs & Co., Metal, c.1905, 19 x 14 In.
$2,688

American Bottle Auctions

**Advertising,** Sign, Cyrus Noble, W.A. Lacy Whiskies, Double O, Crown, 1910, 42 x 27 In.
$1,140

Showtime Auction Services

**Advertising,** Sign, DeLaval Cream Separator, Mother, Child, Tin, Round, Self-Framed, 26 In.
$5,400

Morphy Auctions

| | | |
|---|---|---|
| **Scoop,** Woolson Spice Co., Tin Lithograph, Red, 12 ½ In. | | 248 |
| **Sign,** 136 Steamship Yacht Supplies Marine Hardware, Pumps, Wood, Green Yellow, 42 x 20 In. | | 570 |
| **Sign,** 1940 York Trailers For Sale, Used Trailers, Galvanized Tin, Painted, 17 x 27 In. | | 212 |
| **Sign,** 7 Oaks Dairy, Tree, Porcelain, Round, 30 In. | | 605 |
| **Sign,** A&W Root Beer, Tin, Round, 1950s, 41 In. | | 420 |
| **Sign,** AAA Root Beer, Bottle Shape, Tin, 44 x 12 In. | | 210 |
| **Sign,** Akron Brewing Co., Akron, Ohio, Factory Scene, Wood, 24 x 36 In. | *illus* | 460 |
| **Sign,** Amco Feeds, Tin, Painted, Black Lettering, Feed Bag, Yellow, Red, 24 x 36 In. | | 59 |
| **Sign,** American Brewing Company, Bulldog, Doghouse Frame, Tin, 29 ½ x 28 In. | *illus* | 3900 |
| **Sign,** American Family Soap, Man Writing, Cardboard, Frame, 26 x 34 In. | | 120 |
| **Sign,** American Screw Co. General Office, Black, Gilt Stencil, 24 x 36 In. | | 1020 |
| **Sign,** Anchor, Stoves & Ranges, Burning Anchor, 5-Color Porcelain, c.1900, 21 x 23 In. | | 878 |
| **Sign,** Anheuser-Busch Beer, Reverse Painted Glass, Light-Up, Round, Tin Frame, 18 In. | | 2950 |
| **Sign,** Anheuser-Busch St. Louis Lager, Paper, c.1900, 26 ½ x 41 ½ In. | | 829 |
| **Sign,** Anheuser-Busch, Budweiser Girl, Red Dress, Paper, Frame, 1907, 24 x 39 In. | *illus* | 855 |
| **Sign,** Anheuser-Busch, Woman, Red Dress, Bird, Letter A, Paper, 1890s, 32 In. | *illus* | 2280 |
| **Sign,** Apothecary, Oak, Mortar & Pestle Shape, Hanging, c.1850, 15 x 9 In. | | 431 |
| **Sign,** Ask For Stamina, Self-Supporting Trousers, Man, Boat, Walter Jardine, c.1950, 40 x 30 In. | | 768 |
| **Sign,** Atlantic White Flash, Porcelain, 52 x 35 ½ In. | | 325 |
| **Sign,** Auburn Canned Goods, Hemingway Preserving Co., Cardboard, 10 x 13 ½ In. | *illus* | 184 |
| **Sign,** Australian Apples, Girl, Picking Apples, F. Kenwood Giles, c.1935, 19 x 14 In. | | 438 |
| **Sign,** Ayer's Cathartic Pills, Cardboard, Easel Back, Dr. & 2 Children, 12 ½ x 7 In. | *illus* | 265 |
| **Sign,** B.L. Eaton, Carved, Black, Gold, Paint, 8 x 77 In. | | 1440 |
| **Sign,** Bagdad Smoking Tobacco, Paper, 1908, 33 ½ x 23 ½ In. | | 355 |
| **Sign,** Batteries Recharged & Repaired, Paint, Wood, 25 x 29 In. | | 420 |
| **Sign,** Beauty Shoppe, Wood, Red Paint, 20 ½ x 8 In. | | 176 |
| **Sign,** Beech-Nut Chewing Tobacco, Porcelain, 22 x 10 ½ In. | | 840 |
| **Sign,** Beech-Nut Tobacco, Great Chew, Red, White, Blue, Porcelain, 12 x 9 In. | | 90 |
| **Sign,** Bensdorp Cocoa, Black, White, Porcelain, 23 In. | | 108 |
| **Sign,** Bickmore Shaving Cream, Cardboard, Cutout, 31 In. | | 120 |
| **Sign,** Blue Ribbon Bourbon, Colonel's Favorite, Distillery, Plaster, 43 x 34 In. | *illus* | 1560 |
| **Sign,** Bluff City Beer, Curved Milk Glass, Copper Frame, 22 ½ x 16 In. | | 6792 |
| **Sign,** Boericke & Tafel Medicines, Lithograph, Frame, Signed, c.1880, 31 x 25 In. | *illus* | 1353 |
| **Sign,** Boot Maker, Paint Zinc, c.1920, 28 In. | | 270 |
| **Sign,** Boots, Shoes, Rubbers Repaired C. Edmunds, Boot Shape, Carved, Paint, 60 In. | | 1200 |
| **Sign,** Boxers For Sale, 2-Sided, Painted, 36 x 35 In. | | 390 |
| **Sign,** Brownie Chocolate Soda, Cardboard, M.C.A. Co., 21 x 60 In. | *illus* | 1380 |
| **Sign,** Brylcreem, For Smart Healthy Hair, Porcelain, Red, 18 x 16 In. | | 240 |
| **Sign,** Buck Cigar, King Of The Range, Buck Head, Tin, Die Cut, 12 x 9 In. | | 450 |
| **Sign,** Budweiser Beer Clydesdale Parade, Light-Up, Revolving, Globe, 16 x 24 In. | | 720 |
| **Sign,** Budweiser, Girl, Red Dress, Cardboard, 1907, 16 ½ x 31 In. | | 821 |
| **Sign,** Budweiser, Girl, Standing, Red Dress, Frame, 38 ½ x 23 ¾ In. | | 1440 |
| **Sign,** Buffalo Brewing Co.'s Lager, Iron, Sky & Navy Blue, Corner, 20 x 14 In. | | 4032 |
| **Sign,** Burts Dairy, Diamond Shape, Maple, Green Paint, c.1875, 48 In. | | 723 |
| **Sign,** Bus Stop, Oval, Orange, Black Embossed Lettering, Iron, 10 x 13 In. | | 944 |
| **Sign,** Buscho A Non-Intoxicating Cereal Beverage, 10 x 7 In. | | 150 |
| **Sign,** Call For Philip Morris, 27 x 14 ½ In. | | 300 |
| **Sign,** Campbell's Tomato Soup, Curved Porcelain, 22 ½ x 12 In. | | 3087 |
| **Sign,** Carolina Carriage Co., 35 x 28 In. | | 390 |
| **Sign,** Carr Home Rooms With Running Water, Boarding House, 2-Sided, 26 x 40 In. | | 660 |
| **Sign,** Cascarets, Bowel Troubles, Black Man Eating Watermelon, 43 x 28 In. | | 1680 |
| **Sign,** Cascarets, They Work While You Sleep, Cardboard, Frame, 21 x 11 In. | *illus* | 1710 |
| **Sign,** Cascarets, They Work While You Sleep, Mother, Child, 15 x 10 In. | *illus* | 123 |
| **Sign,** Centlivre's Nickel Plate Bottled Beer, Paper, Frame, c.1920, 26 x 31 In. | *illus* | 330 |
| **Sign,** Cetacolor, Not A Soap, 10 Cent Package, Linen, 36 x 24 In. | *illus* | 285 |
| **Sign,** Chief Paints, 2-Sided, Tin, 28 x 12 In. | | 108 |
| **Sign,** Children's Clothes Miss Homer, 2-Sided, Paint, Wood, Hooks, 26 x 25 In. | | 322 |
| **Sign,** CL Centlivre Brewing Co., Factory Scene, Paper, Fort Wayne, 36 x 24 In. | *illus* | 59 |
| **Sign,** Climax Catarrh & Croup Remedy, Girl With Diploma, Cardboard, Frame, 17 In. | | 179 |
| **Sign,** Cloverland Golden Guernsey Milk, Metal, Cow Head, 15 x 20 In. | | 374 |
| **Sign,** Cognac Monnet, Woman Kissing Glass, Leonetto Cappiello, 1927, 78 x 51 In. | | 2250 |
| **Sign,** Colonial Club Cigars, Woman, Flower Hat, Frame, c.1910, 19 x 25 In. | | 330 |
| **Sign,** Columbia Grafonola, Tin, Wood Frame, Hanger, Chain, Jos. K. Fodor, 22 x 28 In. | *illus* | 360 |
| **Sign,** Corner, American Lady Shoes, Lead The Earth On Simple Worth, c.1915, 20 In. | | 420 |
| **Sign,** Corn-Fed Hogs, Our Taste Hams, Hall, Luhrs & Co., Metal, c.1905, 19 x 14 In. | *illus* | 2688 |
| **Sign,** Cyrus Noble Pure Rye, Purity, Hand Holds Bottle, Metal, Self-Framed, 30 x 24 In. | | 8400 |

**Advertising,** Sign, DeLaval Cream Separator, Red, Tin, Gesso Frame, 30 x 41 In.
$4,500

Showtime Auction Services

**Advertising,** Sign, Dr. D. Jayne's Tonic Vermifuge, Cherub, Reverse Paint, Frame, 12 x 10 In.
$1,659

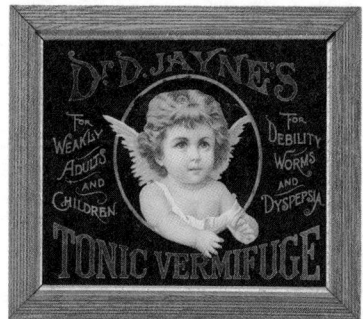

James D. Julia Auctioneers

**Advertising,** Sign, Dr. Daniels Veterinary Medicine, Dogs Playing Cards, Frame, 14 x 18 In.
$196

Wm Morford Auctions

**Advertising,** Sign, Dr. Fuller Private Diseases, Iron, Gilt, 2-Sided, c.1890, 18 x 36 In.
$3,198

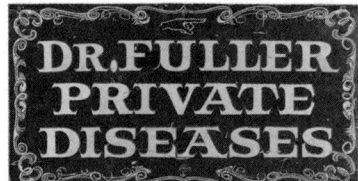

Skinner Auctioneers & Appraisers

**Advertising,** Sign, Dr. Meyer's Foot Soap, Everybody Uses, Foot Troubles, Paper, 25 x 38 In.
$120

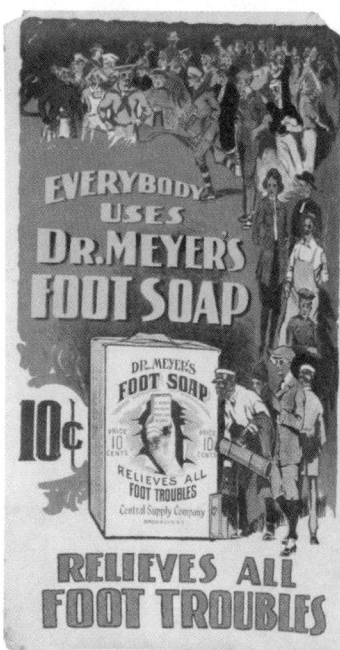

Showtime Auction Services

**Advertising,** Sign, Dr. Swett's, Child, Old Man, Sixty, Cardboard, Frame, c.1915, 16 x 21 In.
$420

Morphy Auctions

**Advertising,** Sign, Dr. Walker's California Vinegar Bitters, Reverse Painted, 21 In.
$1,610

Glass Works Auctions

**Advertising,** Sign, Drink Heart O' Orange, Sold Here, Tin, 1930s, 14¼ In.
$960

Morphy Auctions

**Advertising,** Sign, Drink Hires Rootbeer, Mansfield & Co., Glass, Reverse, Frame, c.1900, 8 x 7 In.
$2,280

Morphy Auctions

**Fast-Food Glasses**
If you collect the decorated glasses from fast-food restaurants, never wash them in the dishwasher. The heat and detergent will change the coloring and lower the value.

**A**

## Beer & Wine Labels

Wine labels are a popular collectible, and now that there are many small local breweries with unusual labels collectors are searching for printed beer bottle labels. Beer collecting magazines have articles, prices, and even some label exchanges.

**Advertising,** Sign, Eberhardt & Ober Brewing Company, Factory, Pa., 52 x 38 In.
$2,280

Morphy Auctions

**Advertising,** Sign, Esslinger Premium Beer, Ask For Little Man, Tin, 1956, 29 x 53 In.
$450

Morphy Auctions

**Advertising,** Sign, Fatima Turkish Cigarettes, Cowgirl, American Tobacco, 21 x 28 In.
$1,938

Showtime Auction Services

**Advertising,** Sign, Figural, Shovel, Treasure Line Stoves & Ranges, Tin Lithograph, 9 3/8 x 4 In.
$210

Wm Morford Auctions

**Advertising,** Sign, Great Atlantic & Pacific Tea, Ten Minutes, Refreshments, Frame, 31 x 21 In.
$210

Showtime Auction Services

**Advertising,** Sign, Hickman-Ebbert, Shade Of Old Apple Tree, Tin, Frame, 1906, 37 x 25 In.
$2,015

James D. Julia Auctioneers

**Advertising,** Sign, Hires, Always Pure, Girl, Yellow, Tin, Embossed, c.1915, 20 x 13 In.
$960

Morphy Auctions

**Advertising,** Sign, Honest Scrap Tobacco, Dog, Cat, Cardboard, Frame, 32 x 22 In.
$1,440

Showtime Auction Services

**Advertising,** Sign, Hawthorn Mellody Ice Cream, Neon, Glass Frame, 36 x 17 In.
$540

Morphy Auctions

| | |
|---|---|
| **Sign,** Cyrus Noble, W.A. Lacy Whiskies, Double O, Crown, 1910, 42 x 27 In. .......................*illus* | 1140 |
| **Sign,** Danger, Thin Ice, Red, White, Black, Metal, 30 x 30 In......................... | 146 |
| **Sign,** Deacons Plug Tobacco, 2 Horse-Drawn Carriages, Frame, c.1880, 26 x 21 In. .................. | 600 |
| **Sign,** Dealer BSA Motorcycles, Tin, 47½ x 27½ In......................... | 948 |
| **Sign,** DeLaval Cream Separator, Mother, Child, Tin, Round, Self-Framed, 26 In. .................*illus* | 5400 |
| **Sign,** DeLaval Cream Separator, Red, Tin, Gesso Frame, 30 x 41 In. .................*illus* | 4500 |
| **Sign,** Dinner, Chicken, Figural, Steel, 2-Sided, Painted, 31 In......................... | 649 |
| **Sign,** Doctor Siegert's Angostura Bitters, c.1880, 12¾ x 29¼ In......................... | 474 |
| **Sign,** Dontophile, Black Man, Showing Off White Teeth, Tin, France, 19 x 8 In......................... | 150 |
| **Sign,** Dr Pepper, 6-Pack, Tin, Embossed, Sidewalk, c.1935, 27 x 19 In......................... | 1680 |
| **Sign,** Dr Pepper, Good For Life, Bottle, Tin Lithograph, Die Cut, 2-Sided, 11 x 23 x 2 In. .............. | 1437 |
| **Sign,** Dr Pepper, Halo Under Logo, Round, Tin, 36 In......................... | 3120 |
| **Sign,** Dr. D. Jayne's Tonic Vermifuge, Cherub, Reverse Paint, Frame, 12 x 10 In. .................*illus* | 1659 |
| **Sign,** Dr. Daniels Veterinary Medicine, Dogs Playing Cards, Frame, 14 x 18 In. .................*illus* | 196 |
| **Sign,** Dr. Fuller Private Diseases, Iron, Gilt, 2-Sided, c.1890, 18 x 36 In. .................*illus* | 3198 |
| **Sign,** Dr. Hobson's Eczema Ointment, Money Back, Porcelain, 2-Sided, 11 x 16½ In......................... | 480 |
| **Sign,** Dr. Lions Bitters National Whiskey, 3 Girls, Cardboard, Die Cut, 15 x 19 In......................... | 24 |
| **Sign,** Dr. Meyer's Foot Soap, Everybody Uses, Foot Troubles, Paper, 25 x 38 In. .................*illus* | 120 |
| **Sign,** Dr. Swett's Root Beer, Woman, Holding Mug, Tin, Curled Edges, 8-Sided, c.1905, 13 In. ..... | 900 |
| **Sign,** Dr. Swett's Root Beer, Woman, Mug, Hanger, Chain, 14 x 14 In......................... | 1006 |
| **Sign,** Dr. Swett's, Child, Old Man, Sixty, Cardboard, Frame, c.1915, 16 x 21 In. .................*illus* | 420 |
| **Sign,** Dr. Walker's California Vinegar Bitters, Reverse Painted, 21 In. .................*illus* | 1610 |
| **Sign,** Dr. Wright, Dentist, Wood, Painted, Gilt, Scrolls, 19th Century, 60 x 48 In......................... | 960 |
| **Sign,** Drink Chero-Cola, There's None So Good, Tin, Embossed, 20 x 9½ In......................... | 390 |
| **Sign,** Drink Dybala's Spring Beverage, White, Orange, Tin, 10 x 27 In......................... | 150 |
| **Sign,** Drink Frostie Root Beer, Red, Yellow, Tin, Embossed, 13 In......................... | 390 |
| **Sign,** Drink Heart O' Orange, Sold Here, Tin, 1930s, 14¼ In. .................*illus* | 960 |
| **Sign,** Drink Hires Rootbeer, Mansfield & Co., Glass, Reverse, Frame, c.1900, 8 x 7 In. ........*illus* | 2280 |
| **Sign,** Drink Hires, 2 Ladies Drinking With Straws, Self-Framed, Tin, c.1915, 19 x 23 In......................... | 510 |
| **Sign,** Drink Moxie, Man, White Coat, Pointing, Paper, 27 x 41 In......................... | 330 |
| **Sign,** Drink Moxie, Red, White, Navy Blue, Tin, Frame, 21 x 30 In......................... | 210 |
| **Sign,** Drink Moxie, Tin Flange, 18 In......................... | 420 |
| **Sign,** Drink Nichol Kola, America's Taste Sensation, Tin, 36 x 12 In......................... | 180 |
| **Sign,** Drink Orange-Julep In Bottles, Orange & White, Tin, Embossed, 13 x 4 In......................... | 180 |
| **Sign,** Drugs, Ralph M. Lord, Mortar, Pestle, Rough-Hewn Wood, 17 x 74 In......................... | 325 |
| **Sign,** Dukes Mixture, Black Men, Riding Horse & Cart, Frame, 22 x 26 In......................... | 330 |
| **Sign,** DuPont Gunpowder, Buffalo Hunt, Dogs, Frame, 14½ x 33 In......................... | 184 |
| **Sign,** Dutch Boy Paint, Tin, Frame, 10 x 28 In......................... | 180 |
| **Sign,** Eat Chicken Dinner Candy, Tin, Paint, 71 x 37½ In......................... | 644 |
| **Sign,** Eat Eskimo Pie, 5 Cents, Enamel, Blue, Red, White Ground, 16 x 2½ In......................... | 270 |
| **Sign,** Eberhardt & Ober Brewing Company, Factory, Pa., 52 x 38 In. .................*illus* | 2280 |
| **Sign,** El Dorado Brewing Co. Valley Brew, Woman, Sitting, Drinking, Rose, Tin, 13 In. Diam....... | 550 |
| **Sign,** Enjoy Hires, Flapper Girl, Tin Over Cardboard, 1920s, 11 In......................... | 480 |
| **Sign,** Enterprise Stoves & Ranges, Black, Yellow, Tin Flange, 18 In......................... | 210 |
| **Sign,** Esslinger Premium Beer, Ask For Little Man, Tin, 1956, 29 x 53 In. .................*illus* | 450 |
| **Sign,** Expert Tattooing Done Here, Woman, Divan, Lithograph, Friedlander, 38 x 24 In.............. | 4720 |
| **Sign,** F.A. Sage Carpet Cleaning, Pine, Arch Shape, Paint, c.1900, 18 x 23 In......................... | 840 |
| **Sign,** Fairy Soap, Cardboard, Die Cut, Easel Back, Countertop, 18 x 12¾ In......................... | 402 |
| **Sign,** Farrier, Horseshoe, Geo. Lutoen, Tin, Painted, Stencil, c.1920, 36 In......................... | 330 |
| **Sign,** Fat Tire, Neon Bicycle, 22½ x 28 In......................... | 325 |
| **Sign,** Fatima Turkish Cigarettes, Cowgirl, American Tobacco, 21 x 28 In. .................*illus* | 1938 |
| **Sign,** Fatsco Ant Poison, Ants Go With Fatsco, Ants, Aluminum, Relief, 22 x 27 In......................... | 325 |
| **Sign,** Figural, Shovel, Treasure Line Stoves & Ranges, Tin Lithograph, 9⅜ x 4 In. .............*illus* | 210 |
| **Sign,** Fish, Tin, Carved, Painted, Wood, Tin, 40 In......................... | 322 |
| **Sign,** Fishmonger, Holding Fish, Wood, Figural, Striped Apron, 46 x 16 In......................... | 325 |
| **Sign,** Fly TWA Superjets, Flemish Woman, Landmarks, David Klein, Litho, c.1960, 25 x 40 In..... | 29 |
| **Sign,** For Sale At Bargain Inquire, J.H. Boothman, Yellow, Red Paint, 32 x 32 In......................... | 600 |
| **Sign,** Frank C. Marston, Wallpapers, Curtains, Stationery, Carved, Blue, 31 x 101 In......................... | 1320 |
| **Sign,** Frank Jones Brewing Co., Portsmouth, N.H., Lithograph, Oak Frame, 35 x 49 In......................... | 6000 |
| **Sign,** Gail & Ax Navy Tobacco, Oak Frame, Paper, 41 x 31½ In......................... | 308 |
| **Sign,** Gerte's Fine Supper & Drinks, Wood, Carved, Painted, 20 x 36½ In......................... | 176 |
| **Sign,** Golden West Coffee, Drink More Coffee, Cardboard, 26 x 38 In......................... | 138 |
| **Sign,** Graduate Optician, Glass, Reverse, Scrolled Silver, Scallop, 6 x 14 In......................... | 264 |
| **Sign,** Grapette, Porcelain, Oval, c.1940, 17 In......................... | 300 |
| **Sign,** Great Atlantic & Pacific Tea, Ten Minutes, Refreshments, Frame, 31 x 21 In. .............*illus* | 210 |
| **Sign,** Guinness, Painted, My Goodness, My Guinness, Toucan, Glass, 11 x 71 In......................... | 1541 |

**Advertising,** Sign, Hy-Quality Coffee, Woman, Swing, Die Cut, String Hanger, 16 x 35 In.
$780

Showtime Auction Services

**Advertising,** Sign, Imported Pilsener, Barmaid, R. Naegeli's Sons, Tin Litho, c.1910, 17 x 21 In.
$500

Hake's Americana & Collectibles

**Advertising,** Sign, Japp's Hair Rejuvenator, Hair Samples, Tin Lithograph, c.1910, 9 x 13 In.
$570

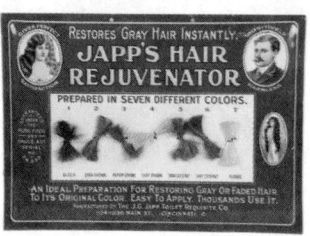

Morphy Auctions

**Advertising,** Sign, La Sena Cigar, 10 Cents, Tin Lithograph, Dogs Drinking, Cigars, Frame, 14 In.
$719

Wm Morford Auctions

**Advertising,** Sign, Last Drop, Stetson, Cowboy, Horse Drinking, Paper, Frame, 18 x 23 In.
$1,680

Showtime Auction Services

**Advertising,** Sign, Lipton's Instant Cocoa, Tin, Cardboard, String Hanger, 9 x 13 In.
$570

Showtime Auction Services

| | |
|---|---:|
| **Sign,** H. Eldridge & Sons Celebrated Portsmouth Ales, Lithograph, Frame, c.1880, 23 x 30 In. | 3300 |
| **Sign,** Hammer Cigars, Hammer, It Keeps A Nocken', 5 Cents, Linen, Colors, 14 x 9 In. | 196 |
| **Sign,** Hamm's Beer, Glass, Metal, 2-Sided, Light-Up, c.1950, 20 x 14 In. | 148 |
| **Sign,** Harrison's Heart O' Lemon, Lemons Drinking, Straws, Tin, 1930s, 14 In. Diam. | 1080 |
| **Sign,** Hartshorn's Dyspeptic, Jaundice Bitters, Key To Health, Cardboard, 11 x 14 In. | 532 |
| **Sign,** Hawthorn Mellody Ice Cream, Neon, Glass Frame, 36 x 17 In. *illus* | 540 |
| **Sign,** Helmar Turkish Cigarettes, Cardboard, Frame, 35¾ x 25½ In. | 247 |
| **Sign,** Henry George, 5 Cent Cigar, Round, Tin, c.1900, 13½ In. | 180 |
| **Sign,** Heurich Brewing Co., Round, Embossed, Tin, c.1905, 17¼ In. | 330 |
| **Sign,** Hickman-Ebbert, Shade Of Old Apple Tree, Tin, Frame, 1906, 37 x 25 In. *illus* | 2015 |
| **Sign,** Hires Cardboard, c.1915, 20 x 12 In. | 360 |
| **Sign,** Hires, Always Pure, Girl, Yellow, Tin, Embossed, c.1915, 20 x 13 In. *illus* | 960 |
| **Sign,** Hires, Bottle, Tin, Embossed, 1950s, 55¾ x 17¾ In. | 330 |
| **Sign,** Hires, Cooling & Refreshing, Golfer, Cardboard, 24¾ x 16 In. | 150 |
| **Sign,** Honest Scrap Tobacco, Dog, Cat, Cardboard, Frame, 32 x 22 In. *illus* | 1440 |
| **Sign,** Honest Scrap Tobacco, Metal, Enameled, 6 Grommets, Trademark Hand, 12 x 9 In. | 1782 |
| **Sign,** Hood's Royal Oak Rubber Boots, Tin, Die Cut, Mayer & Lavenson, 13 x 9 In. | 1500 |
| **Sign,** Hood's Sarsaparilla, Boy, Seated On Box, Cardboard, Cutout, c.1910, 19 In. | 450 |
| **Sign,** Horn & Hardart Strawberry Cream Pie, Plate Of Pie, Frame, 1950s, 31 x 25 In. | 210 |
| **Sign,** Horse Head, Veterinarian Trade, Brown, Flowing Mane, c.1900, 21 In. | 3600 |
| **Sign,** Horsey & Atwell Outfitters, 3 Hanging Fish, Tin Lithograph, Oval, Frame, 19 In. | 920 |
| **Sign,** Horsford's Baking Powder, Cat Holding Can, Chromolitho, Tin, 20 x 16 In. | 266 |
| **Sign,** Horton's Ice Cream, Depots, Addresses, Printed Oilcloth On Board, 27 x 21 In. | 590 |
| **Sign,** Hot French Fried Popcorn, Red, Black, Porcelain, Frame, 22 x 28 In. | 300 |
| **Sign,** Hotel Entrance, Ladies & Escorts, Painted, Plexiglas, 24 x 9 In. | 293 |
| **Sign,** Hotel Lobby, Guest Services, Composite, 10 Sections, Pa., 30 x 66 In. | 9440 |
| **Sign,** Hudson, Red & White, Neon, Light-Up, 22 x 39 In. | 1400 |
| **Sign,** Hy-Quality Coffee, Woman, Swing, Die Cut, String Hanger, 16 x 35 In. *illus* | 780 |
| **Sign,** Imported Pilsener, Barmaid, R. Naegeli's Sons, Tin Litho, c.1910, 17 x 21 In. *illus* | 500 |
| **Sign,** India Tire, Tin, Painted, Molded Wood Frame, 18¼ x 71 In. | 708 |
| **Sign,** Indian Rock Ginger Ale, 2 Bottles, Tin, Embossed, c.1915, 35 x 11 In. | 480 |
| **Sign,** Indianapolis Beer, Blue, White, Liberty, Round, Porcelain, 18 In. | 1697 |
| **Sign,** J.P. Alley's Hambone Cigar, Round, Cardboard, Hanger, 7 In. | 120 |
| **Sign,** Jackson Square Cigar, 2-Sided, Tin Lithograph, Die Cut Hand, 10 x 13 In. | 4600 |
| **Sign,** Japp's Hair Rejuvenator, Hair Samples, Tin Lithograph, c.1910, 9 x 13 In. *illus* | 570 |
| **Sign,** Jersey Cream, Perfect Drink, Buck, Tin, c.1905, 13½ In. Diam. | 780 |
| **Sign,** Job, Woman, Long, Curled Hair, Alphonse Mucha, Champenois, Paris, 1896, 20 x 15 In. | 9375 |
| **Sign,** Johnnie Walker, Golfer, Royal Troon, Artist Proof, Oil, 1900s, 42 x 47 In. | 4148 |
| **Sign,** Johnson Sea Horse, Motor, Seahorse, Boat, Metal, Agent's, 12 x 24 In. | 1200 |
| **Sign,** Kaffee Hag, Man, Mug, Tennis Racket, Ball, Hohlwein, 1913, 35 x 24 In. | 15000 |
| **Sign,** Keens Blue Soap, Cardboard, Frame, 23 x 29 In. | 210 |
| **Sign,** Keil, Key Shape, Red Paint, c.1920, 30 In. | 944 |
| **Sign,** Key For Admission, Brookville Police Hdqts., Tin, Wood, Paint, 14 x 30 In. | 293 |
| **Sign,** Kirk's Flake Soap, Red, White, Porcelain, 40 In. | 660 |
| **Sign,** Kodak Camera, Eastman, Rochester, N.Y., Porcelain, Blue, White, 25 x 19 In. | 1792 |
| **Sign,** La Sena Cigar, 10 Cents, Tin Lithograph, Dogs Drinking, Cigars, Frame, 14 In. *illus* | 719 |
| **Sign,** Ladies Toilet, Blue Paint, Porcelain, 10 x 2½ In. | 47 |
| **Sign,** Last Drop, Stetson, Cowboy, Horse Drinking, Paper, Frame, 18 x 23 In. *illus* | 1680 |
| **Sign,** Lautz Soup, White Man Washing Black Child's Face, c.1880, 32 x 26 In. | 4500 |
| **Sign,** Laverty's Family Liniment, 25 Cents, At Druggists, Tin, Embossed, Frame, 10 In. | 308 |
| **Sign,** Law Offices Of Brinner & Searing, White, Black Paint, 20 x 42 In. | 210 |
| **Sign,** L'Excelsior Sewing Machine, Woman Sewing, Paper, Linen, 33 x 25 In. | 108 |
| **Sign,** License Plate Frame, Famous Pioneer Club, Vegas Vic, Die Cut | 403 |
| **Sign,** Lichtenstein Bros. & Co. Cigar, Manhattan, 27 x 21 In. | 2014 |
| **Sign,** Lion Coffee, Lion, Strength, Purity, Flavor, Zinc, Screen Print, c.1900, 60 x 42 In. | 885 |
| **Sign,** Lipton's Instant Cocoa, Tin, Cardboard, String Hanger, 9 x 13 In. *illus* | 570 |
| **Sign,** Liqueur Maurin Quina, Chromolitho, Green Devil, Black, After Cappiello, c.1910 | 2080 |
| **Sign,** Magnus Root Beer, Tin, Over Cardboard, 1920s, 9 x 6 In. | 210 |
| **Sign,** Marble Head Bakery, Fishermen In Woods, Rutland, Vt., Frame, 16 x 10 In. | 47 |
| **Sign,** McCannes Ice Cream, Baby, Ice Cream Cone, Tin, 28 x 20 In. | 330 |
| **Sign,** Meadow Gold Ice Cream, Neon On Glass Frame, 28 x 13 In. | 510 |
| **Sign,** Medo-Land Ice Cream, Cone Shape, 2-Sided, Tin, Die Cut, 40 x 19 In. | 330 |
| **Sign,** Merchant's Gargling Oil, For Man Or Beast, Tin, Embossed, Diamond Shape, 9 In. | 1344 |
| **Sign,** Miller High Life, Plastic, Light-Up, Metal Box, 22¼ x 12 In. *illus* | 210 |
| **Sign,** Miss H.M. DeForest Modes, Skirt, Tin, Painted, Convex, c.1890, 34 x 26 In. | 1046 |
| **Sign,** Modern Tourist Rooms, Board, Painted Cartouche, Blue, White, 2-Sided, 23 x 36 In. | 767 |

**Advertising,** Sign, Miller High Life, Plastic,
Light-Up, Metal Box, 22¼ x 12 In.
$210

Morphy Auctions

**Advertising,** Sign, Moxie, Girl, Handing Glass,
Tin, Cutout, 2-Sided, 1915, 7 In.
$780

Morphy Auctions

**Advertising,** Sign, Napoleon 10 Cent Cigar,
Framed Under Glass, 29¾ x 9 In.
$120

Showtime Auction Servicesa

**Advertising,** Sign, Pepo Worm Syrup,
25 Cents, Tin, Embossed, Frame, 10 x 7½ In.
$224

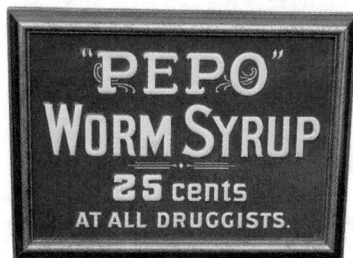

McMurray Antiques & Auctions

**TIP**
*Keeping a list of out-of-state
license plates is a great
travel game for kids.*

**Advertising,** Sign, Plaque, Case Threshing Machine Co., Eagle, Globe, Cast Iron, c.1910, 15 x 18 In.
$1,185

James D. Julia Auctioneers

**Advertising,** Sign, Plumber's Trade, Faucet Shape, Gilded Metal, c.1905, 41 x 58 In.
$2,500

Rago Arts & Auction Center

**Advertising,** Sign, Quick Meal Ranges, Hand, Egg, 2-Sided, Tin Litho, Flange, c.1915, 18 In.
$5,060

Hake's Americana & Collectibles

15

**Advertising,** Sign, Roi-Tan Cigars, Cigarette Girl, Tray, Cardboard, Easel Back, 1940s, 60 In.
$650

Hake's Americana & Collectibles

---

**Advertising,** Sign, Royal Crown Cola, Bottle Shape, Tin, Embossed, Nehi Corp., 1936, 16 x 59 In.
$300

Morphy Auctions

---

**Advertising,** Sign, Scott's Emulsion, Cod Liver Oil, Man Holding Fish, Glass, Frame, 23 x 35 In.
$9,690

Showtime Auction Services

| | | |
|---|---|---:|
| **Sign,** Moose Eye Fruit, Paper, Multicolor, Frame, 48 x 36 In. | | 2280 |
| **Sign,** Mornington Take A Kodak, Bay, Boats, James Northfield, Australia, 1947, 40 x 25 In. | | 1625 |
| **Sign,** Morris Express, Folk Art, Gilt Lettering, Wood, 13½ x 30 In. | | 1006 |
| **Sign,** Morse's Chocolate, Easter Greetings, Die Cut, Cardboard, Rabbit, 7 x 16 In. | | 28 |
| **Sign,** Morton's Salt, It Pours, Black, Gold, 10 x 28 In. | | 180 |
| **Sign,** Mossant, 3 Hats, Yellow Ground, Leonetto Cappiello, c.1925, 63 x 47 In. | | 1080 |
| **Sign,** Moxie, Girl, Handing Glass, Tin, Cutout, 2-Sided, 1915, 7 In. | *illus* | 780 |
| **Sign,** Munsingwear Union Suits, Parade Of Children In Union Suits, Underwear, Metal, 24 In. | | 360 |
| **Sign,** Napoleon 10 Cent Cigar, Framed Under Glass, 29¾ x 9 In. | *illus* | 120 |
| **Sign,** National Hybrids, Corn States, 2-Sided, Flange, Tin, Scioto Sign, Iowa, 17 x 13 In. | | 300 |
| **Sign,** National Joy Smoke Prince Albert, Linen Mount, Brunell Co., 1930s, 61 x 32 In. | | 120 |
| **Sign,** Nectar Tea, Green, White Cup & Saucer Shape, Porcelain, 21 In. | | 330 |
| **Sign,** Nehi, Die Cut, 2-Sided, Flange, Tin, 18 x 13 In. | | 900 |
| **Sign,** Nehi, Tin, Yellow, Red, Woman's Leg, Robertson Steel & Iron, 11¾ x 11½ In. | | 275 |
| **Sign,** New Jersey Seashore, Go By Train, Pennsylvania Railroad, Woman Waving, 41 x 25 In. | | 2750 |
| **Sign,** New York, United Air Lines, Carriage In Rain, Stanley Walter Galli, 39 x 24 In. | | 250 |
| **Sign,** New York's Famous Knickerbocker Beer, Spinner, Neon, 10 In. | | 270 |
| **Sign,** O.F.G. Rye Whiskey, Hunters, Toasting Each Other, Frame, 32 x 22 In. | | 150 |
| **Sign,** Old Crow American Favorite For Seven Generations, Light-Up, 36 x 12 In. | | 390 |
| **Sign,** Orange Crush, 2-Sided, Arrow Shape, Wood, 11½ x 36 In. | | 2530 |
| **Sign,** Orange Crush, Ask For A Crush, Orange, Tin, 3½ x 27 In. | | 210 |
| **Sign,** Orange Crush, Bottle, Tin, Embossed, 54 In. | | 720 |
| **Sign,** Orange Crush, Cardboard, Easel Back, 1940s, 19 x 14 In. | | 210 |
| **Sign,** Orange Crush, Crushy, Paper, 1930s, 18 x 12 In. | | 150 |
| **Sign,** Orange Crush, Girl, At Beach, Bottle, c.1935, 19 x 12 In. | | 240 |
| **Sign,** Orange Crush, Help Yourself, Meet Crushy, Tin, Embossed, 29 x 12 In. | | 660 |
| **Sign,** Orange Crush, Menu, Tin, 39 x 13 In. | | 150 |
| **Sign,** Orange Crush, Pardner, Fred Cole, Cardboard, 21 x 17 In. | | 180 |
| **Sign,** Orange Crush, Tin, Embossed, 1920s, 28 x 20 In. | | 360 to 780 |
| **Sign,** Overholt Pure Rye Whiskey, Yellow Ground, Wood Frame, 42 x 30 In. | | 390 |
| **Sign,** Pabst Blue Ribbon, Bottle, Glass, Food Plate, Frame, 25½ x 22 In. | | 210 |
| **Sign,** Pabst Blue Ribbon, Don't Just Sit There Nag Your Husband, Wood, 1970s, 24 x 11 In. | | 36 |
| **Sign,** Pacific Power & Light Co., Reddy Kilowatt, Green, Yellow, Enamel, 48 x 24 In. | | 540 |
| **Sign,** Panky Oil Truck, Delivery Truck, Red Ground, Tin, 22 In. | | 210 |
| **Sign,** Pennsylvania Railroad, Always Inspiring, New York, Skyscraper, 48 x 30 In. | | 688 |
| **Sign,** Pepo Worm Syrup, 25 Cents, Tin, Embossed, Frame, 10 x 7½ In. | *illus* | 224 |
| **Sign,** Perfection Cigarettes, Woman's Face, Large Red, Green Hat, 30 x 24 In. | | 450 |
| **Sign,** Phillip Morris, Die Cut, 43¾ x 15½ In. | | 494 |
| **Sign,** Plaque, Case Threshing Machine Co., Eagle, Globe, Cast Iron, c.1910, 15 x 18 In. | *illus* | 1185 |
| **Sign,** Plumber's Trade, Faucet Shape, Gilded Metal, c.1905, 41 x 58 In. | *illus* | 2500 |
| **Sign,** Polar Bear Flour, Bear On Iceberg, Tin, 35 In. | | 330 |
| **Sign,** Polly Stamps, Parrot, Plastic, Metal, Light-Up, c.1955, 12 x 25 In. | | 540 |
| **Sign,** Pool Closed, Black, White, Paint, Wood, 25 x 18 In. | | 47 |
| **Sign,** Popper's Ace 10 Cent Cigar, Tin, Enameled, Rolled Edge, Red, 35 x 11 In. | | 300 |
| **Sign,** Popsicle, Art Deco, Cardboard, Yellow, Black, Blue, 25¼ x 17¼ In. | | 489 |
| **Sign,** Pretzel, Strapwork Crown On Top, Metal, Wood, Gilt, 22 x 26 In. | | 1000 |
| **Sign,** Primrose Ice Cream, Woman On Swing, Cardboard, Hanger, 33 x 34 In. | | 374 |
| **Sign,** Prince Albert Tobacco, Chief Joseph, Nez Perce, Reynolds, c.1914, 24 x 20 In. | | 2415 |
| **Sign,** Produits Lavicat Aliments Irradies, Man, Horse, H. Prost, Lyon, France, 35 x 26 In. | | 175 |
| **Sign,** Quality Ice Cream, Melting Snow, Black, White Paint, Cardboard, 48 x 15 In. | | 439 |
| **Sign,** Quick Meal Ranges, Hand, Egg, 2-Sided, Tin Litho, Flange, c.1915, 18 In. | *illus* | 5060 |
| **Sign,** R. Dickson, Paint, Wood, 1830, 29 x 57 In. | | 1560 |
| **Sign,** Railroad, Chicago Normal Training School, Building, Charles Medin, 1927, 82 x 41 In. | | 3250 |
| **Sign,** Railroad, Electricity, Conqueror Of Darkness, Northern Illinois, Hanson, c.1925, 82 x 42 In. | | 2375 |
| **Sign,** Railroad, Shasta Daylight, Southern Pacific, Train, Fred Ludekens, 1952, 23 x 16 In. | | 750 |
| **Sign,** Rainbow Beverages, Tin, Embossed, 24 x 12 In. | | 144 |
| **Sign,** Raleigh, Bicycle, Red, Porcelain, 19 x 29 In. | | 3300 |
| **Sign,** Red Car Oskar Trolley, Porcelain, Red, White, Round, 23 In. | | 360 |
| **Sign,** Red Goose Shoes, Yellow Ground, Tin Flange, 16 In. | | 180 |
| **Sign,** Red Rose Tea, Red, Green, Tin, 29 In. | | 330 |
| **Sign,** Red Wing Shoes, Wing, Neon, Glass Frame, 35½ x 14½ In. | | 150 |
| **Sign,** Redford's Tobacco, Plantation Views, Frame, 27¾ x 21 In. | | 240 |
| **Sign,** Rexall Drugs, Oval, Neon, Porcelain, 2-Sided, 24 x 53 In. | | 1800 |
| **Sign,** Rizla Cigarette Rolling Papers, Woman, Feather Hat, Paper, 45 x 18½ In. | | 1896 |
| **Sign,** Rochester Root Beer, Mug, Girl Looking Thru Glass, Paper, 1920s, 15 In. | | 150 |
| **Sign,** Rock, Rye & Honey, Sure Cure For Coughs, Colds, Cardboard, 14 x 11 In. | | 112 |

| | | |
|---|---|---|
| **Sign,** Roi-Tan Cigars, Cigarette Girl, Tray, Cardboard, Easel Back, 1940s, 60 In. | *illus* | 650 |
| **Sign,** Royal Crown Cola, Bottle Shape, Tin, Embossed, Nehi Corp., 1936, 16 x 59 In. | *illus* | 300 |
| **Sign,** Rutland Shoe Service, Black Shoe, Wood, 2-Sided, 18 x 45 In. | | 266 |
| **Sign,** Schweitzer's, Radio Sales & Service, Wood, Reflective Green, c.1920, 130 x 12 In. | | 540 |
| **Sign,** Scott's Emulsion, Cod Liver Oil, Man Holding Fish, Glass, Frame, 23 x 35 In. | *illus* | 9690 |
| **Sign,** Sherwin-Williams, Cover The Earth, Porcelain, 19 x 35 In. | | 1770 |
| **Sign,** Singer Sewing Machine, Woman, Beautiful Dress, Sepia, Frame, 26 x 35 In. | | 330 |
| **Sign,** Smoke Nickel King Cigars, Gray, Black, Red Paint, Wood, Frame, 18 x 7 In. | | 70 |
| **Sign,** Snow Boy Washing Powder, Sledder, Holding Soap, Plaster, Frame, 33 x 22 In. | | 5700 |
| **Sign,** Sparrow Chocolates, Tin Over Cardboard, Child On Wall, Frame, 17 x 11 In. | | 776 |
| **Sign,** Splendid Stoves, Wood, Painted, 5¾ x 42 In. | | 431 |
| **Sign,** Splendid, Cigar, Box, Matchbook, Color Litho, Neukomm, Frame, 1930, 50 x 36 In. | | 660 |
| **Sign,** Squeeze, Orange Drink, Lithograph Embossed, Red, Yellow, 9½ x 28 In. | | 175 |
| **Sign,** Squirrel Peanuts, Squirrel, Salted Jumbo, 5 Cents, Die Cut, Tin Lithograph 10 x 9 In. | | 747 |
| **Sign,** Squirt, Tin, Embossed, 1941, 17½ x 4 In. | | 240 |
| **Sign,** St. Margaret's Hospital, Infant Asylum & Lying-In, Pointing Hand, Wood, 35 In. | | 767 |
| **Sign,** Stag Brand Glendora Oranges, Ceramic Tile, Wood Frame, 35 x 35 In. | | 720 |
| **Sign,** Stag Trousers, Stag, Glowing Sky, Tin Lithograph, Shaped Circle, 14 In. | | 180 |
| **Sign,** Star Tobacco, Yellow, Black, Red, Frame, 12 x 24 In. | | 450 |
| **Sign,** Stetson's Hats, Tin Lithograph, F. Tuchferber Co., 27½ x 20 In. | | 3555 |
| **Sign,** Stoddard Harness Soap, Black Man, Horse, Frame, 21 x 28 In. | | 480 |
| **Sign,** Street, Drugstore, Pharmacy, Stained & Leaded Glass, c.1900, 35 In. | *illus* | 31200 |
| **Sign,** Strong Quaker Rug, Tin Over Cardboard, Frame, 22 x 16 In. | | 96 |
| **Sign,** Sweetest Maid Chocolates, Girl, Dress, Apron, Tin, Self-Framed, 10 x 22 In. | *illus* | 2280 |
| **Sign,** Sweet-Orr Overalls, Navy, Tug-Of-War, 6 Men, Enamel, Porcelain, 14 x 20 In. | | 3220 |
| **Sign,** Sweet-Orr Overalls, Union Made, Men, Tug-Of-War, Porcelain, Curved, 19 x 14 In. | *illus* | 1440 |
| **Sign,** Tavern, Pineapple, Yellow, Green, Slate Blue Backboard, 48 x 30 In. | | 2400 |
| **Sign,** Tavern, Swan Inn, White Swans, 2-Sided, 39 x 39 In. | | 600 |
| **Sign,** Temperance Hotel, Oval, White, Red, Green, Metal Frame, Scholl, 30 x 36½ In. | | 2040 |
| **Sign,** Texas & Pacific Railway, Native American Maiden, Paper, Frame, 16½ x 21 In. | *illus* | 330 |
| **Sign,** The Rexall Store, Black Enamel, Curved Edges, 38 x 8 In. | | 240 |
| **Sign,** The Station, Wood, Station Man, Giving Directions, Paint, 3 x 44 In. | | 439 |
| **Sign,** This Time It's Hudson, Neon, Light-Up, Blue & White, 1950s, 17 x 35 In. | | 1680 |
| **Sign,** Thomas' Inks & Mucilage, Embossed, Tin, Tuscarora Adv., Frame, 20 x 14 In. | *illus* | 14400 |
| **Sign,** Threshing Machine, Russell & Co, Farm Equipment, Paper, 31½ x 26½ In. | | 3851 |
| **Sign,** Tobias Dale, LTD., Instrument Maker, Carved, Painted, 36 x 25 In. | | 960 |
| **Sign,** Tobias M. Miller's, White Painted Eagle, Wood, Pa., c.1865, 20 x 33 In. | | 1800 |
| **Sign,** Tomahawk Scrap Tobacco, Red Tomahawk, Black Ground, Porcelain, 11 In. | | 390 |
| **Sign,** Tooheys Oatmeal Stout, Beer Mug Overflowing, Walter Jardine, c.1935, 39 x 29 In. | | 704 |
| **Sign,** Tourists Bath, Shower, Mrs. Stone, Wood, 2-Sided, Painted, 21 x 29 In. | | 295 |
| **Sign,** Triple AAA Root Beer Soda, Die Cut, Tin, Bottle Shape, 44 In. | | 480 |
| **Sign,** Tube Rose Snuff Always Mild & Satisfying, Tin, 16 x 23 In. | | 150 |
| **Sign,** Turkish Trophies Cigarettes, Woman, Cityscape, 36¼ x 26¼ In. | | 474 |
| **Sign,** Union Leader Cut Plug, Uncle Sam, Paper, Frame, 36 x 46 In. | *illus* | 3259 |
| **Sign,** Victory Liberty Loan, We'll Finish The Job, Man, Reaching In Pocket, 38 x 26 In. | | 210 |
| **Sign,** W.B. Clarke Apothecary, Established 1868, Brass, 19½ x 34 In. | | 660 |
| **Sign,** Walter Baker & Co., Breakfast Cocoa, Tin Lithograph, Frame, c.1900, 20 x 13 In. | *illus* | 5100 |
| **Sign,** Walter Beer, Curved Milk Glass, Copper Frame, 22½ x 16 In. | | 3087 |
| **Sign,** Ward & Vokes Fun Experts, Vaudeville, 1902, 40 x 26½ In. | | 296 |
| **Sign,** Watch The Wear Overalls & Coats, Red, White, Blue, Porcelain, 24 x 9 In. | | 644 |
| **Sign,** Waterman's Ideal Fountain Pen, Wood, Gilt, Painted, Brass Ring, c.1900, 39 In. | | 923 |
| **Sign,** We Proudly Serve You 7Up, Red Ground, Tin, 1940s, 6 x 9 In. | | 152 |
| **Sign,** We Sell Crisco Shortening, Blue, White, Porcelain, 20 In. | | 450 |
| **Sign,** Week End Cigarettes Man, Top Hat, Sports Equipment, Rene Vincent, 1930s, 12 x 10 In. | | 250 |
| **Sign,** West 'M' Grocery, Drink Nehi Beverages, Tin, Bottle, 52 x 34 In. | | 210 |
| **Sign,** Western Ammo, Cardboard, Die Cut, Easel Back, 12 x 20 In. | | 1495 |
| **Sign,** Western Ammo, Soldier Shooting, Stacked Ammo Boxes, 13 x 10½ In. | | 632 |
| **Sign,** Western Field Shells, Die Cut, Cardboard, Multicolor, Duck, 14 x 6 In. | | 1782 |
| **Sign,** Western Shotgun Shells, Cardboard, Die Cut, Multicolor, 12⅛ x 8 In. | | 1006 |
| **Sign,** Western Union, Light-Up, Porcelain, 2-Sided, 90 x 40 In. | | 1080 |
| **Sign,** Westwood Coal, Enameled Porcelain, Black Lettering, Yellow, 12 x 18 In. | | 266 |
| **Sign,** Whippet, Dollar For Dollar, Tin, Embossed, Willys-Overland, 1920s, 22 x 12 In. | | 360 |
| **Sign,** Whiskey, Pure Rye, Elephant, Reverse Glass, Silver, Copper, Frame, 36 x 32 In. | | 1100 |
| **Sign,** Whistle, Orange, Cardboard, Cutout, 1945, 14 x 10½ In. | | 90 |
| **Sign,** Whistle Soda, Boy Carrying Bottle, Die Cut Cardboard, 13 x 26 In. | | 715 |
| **Sign,** Wiedmann's Fine Beer, Spinner, Round, Eagle Logo, 15¾ In. | | 210 |

**Advertising,** Sign, Street, Drugstore, Pharmacy, Stained & Leaded Glass, c.1900, 35 In.
**$31,200**

Morphy Auctions

**Advertising,** Sign, Sweetest Maid Chocolates, Girl, Dress, Apron, Tin, Self-Framed, 10 x 22 In.
**$2,280**

Showtime Auction Services

**Advertising,** Sign, Sweet-Orr Overalls, Union Made, Men, Tug-Of-War, Porcelain, Curved, 19 x 14 In.
**$1,440**

Morphy Auctions

**Advertising,** Sign, Texas & Pacific Railway, Native American Maiden, Paper, Frame, 16½ x 21 In.
$330

Showtime Auction Services

**Advertising,** Sign, Union Leader Cut Plug, Uncle Sam, Paper, Frame, 36 x 46 In.
$3,259

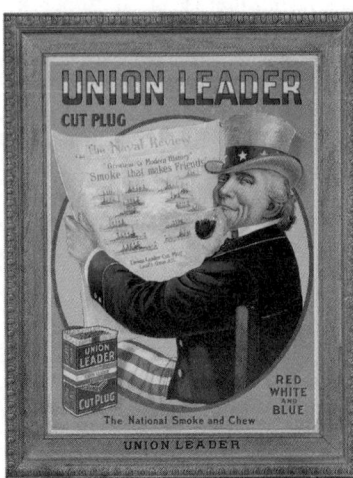

James D. Julia Auctioneers

**Advertising,** Sign, Walter Baker & Co., Breakfast Cocoa, Tin Lithograph, Frame, c.1900, 20 x 13 In.
$5,100

Morphy Auctions

**Advertising,** Sign, Thomas' Inks & Mucilage, Embossed, Tin, Tuscarora Adv., Frame, 20 x 14 In.
$14,400

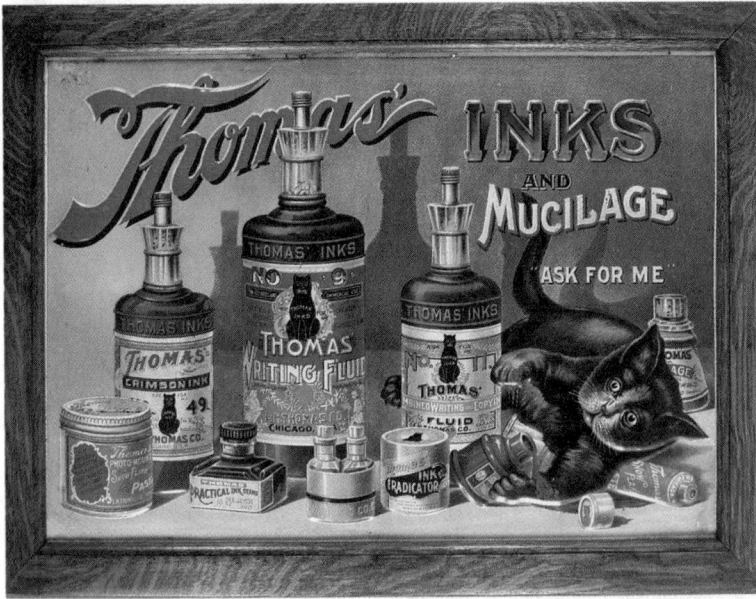

Showtime Auction Services

**Advertising,** Sign, Winchester Repeating Arms Co., Shell Board, Cartridges, 40 x 52½ In.
$19,200

Morphy Auctions

**Advertising,** Sign, Wrigley's Spearmint Gum, Cardboard, After Every Meal, Frame, 15 x 25 In.
$150

Wm Morford Auctions

**Advertising,** Sign, Wrigley's Spearmint, Gum Package, Embossed, 28 x 13½ In.
$805

Showtime Auction Services

---

**TIP**

*Tin signs and cans will fade from the ultraviolet rays coming in a window or from a fluorescent light. Plexiglas UF-1 or UF-3 will cover the window and keep the rays away from your collection. There are also plastic sleeves to cover fluorescent tubes.*

| | |
|---|---|
| **Sign,** Willard Storage Batteries, Porcelain, Red, White Letters, 95¾ x 18 In. | 560 |
| **Sign,** Winchester Repeating Arms Co., Shell Board, Cartridges, 40 x 52½ In. ......*illus* | 19200 |
| **Sign,** Woodward's Peanut Butter Filled Candy, Boy & Girl, Cardboard, 10 x 14 In. | 944 |
| **Sign,** Wrigley's Gum, Smiling Faces, Pack Of Gum, Cardboard, 12 x 22 In. | 150 |
| **Sign,** Wrigley's Spearmint Gum, Cardboard, After Every Meal, Frame, 15 x 25 In. ....*illus* | 150 |
| **Sign,** Wrigley's Spearmint Gum, Women, Boys, Ad On Fence, Cardboard, J. Bliss, 12 x 22 In. | 300 |
| **Sign,** Wrigley's Spearmint, Gum Package, Embossed, 28 x 13½ In. ......*illus* | 805 |
| **Sign,** York Brewing Co., Larger Beer, 27 x 19¾ In. | 5400 |
| **Sign,** Young Ho! Go Chevron!, Cardboard Lithograph Blond Woman Driving, 14 x 49 In. | 390 |
| **Sign,** Yuengling's Beer, Reverse Glass, Convex Oval, 21 x 25 In. | 4400 |
| **Sign,** Zenith Radio, Orange, Red Tin Lithograph, Black Painted Frame, c.1924, 72 x 18 In. | 288 |
| **Stand,** Lady's Legs, Brothel, Prairie Rose, Prescott, Ariz., Clothing, Tokens, 1880s, 42 In. ...*illus* | 3000 |
| **Stein,** Budweiser Bud Man, Pottery, ½ Liter ......*illus* | 36 |
| **Strawholder,** Ask For Welch's Grape Juice, Grape Cluster, Tin, c.1910, 5¾ In. | 7800 |
| **Strawholder,** Hires, Cutout Letters, Iron, Footed, c.1911, 9¾ In. | 1440 |
| **Stringholder,** 7Up, Green, Orange, 16 In. | 120 |
| **Stringholder,** Dutch Boy Anchor Lead Paint, Boy On Swing Painting, 26 In. | 840 |
| **Stringholder,** Dutch Boy Paint, Pail Shape, Bail Handle, 19½ In. | 780 |
| **Stringholder,** Every Table Should Have Daily Ration Of Grape-Nuts, Metal, 12 In. | 210 |
| **Stringholder,** Gold Dust Twins, c.1900, 14 In. | 330 |
| **Stringholder,** Heinz, Pure Foods, Pickle, Chains, 2-Sided, 10½ In. ......*illus* | 6000 |
| **Stringholder,** La Touraine Coffee, 2-Sided, Black, Metal, 17 In. | 1320 |
| **Stringholder,** Moxie, Red Lettering, White, 25½ In. | 300 |
| **Stringholder,** Post Toasties, Bully For Breakfast, Round, 11½ In. | 240 |
| **Stringholder,** Red Goose Shoes, Figural, Tin, 29 In. | 900 |
| **Stringholder,** Yale Coffees, Tin, Red, Green, Yellow, Tin, 16 In. | 390 |

**Thermometers** are listed in their own category.

---

**Advertising tin** cans or canisters were first used commercially in the United States in 1819 and were called tins. Today the word *tin* is used by most collectors to describe many types of containers, including food tins, biscuit boxes, roly poly tobacco containers, gunpowder cans, talcum powder sprinkle-top cans, cigarette flat-fifty tins, and more. Beer Cans are listed in their own category. Things made of undecorated tin are listed under Tinware.

| | |
|---|---|
| **Tin,** 3 Feathers Plug Cut, Vertical, 4 In. | 210 |
| **Tin,** Acme Licorice Pellets, Window, Y & S Pure Calabria Licorice, 5 Lb. ......*illus* | 130 |
| **Tin,** Allen Square Roasted Coffee, Building, Cream Ground, Bail, 5 Lb., 9 In. | 180 |
| **Tin,** Apache Trail Cigar, Indian Brave On Horseback, 6¼ In. ......*illus* | 5400 |
| **Tin,** Apache Trail Tobacco, Indian, Horseback, Blue Ground, 5¾ In. | 3300 |
| **Tin,** Banner Boy, Cloves, Boy, Banner, Black Letters, White Ground, 3 x 2¼ In. | 207 |
| **Tin,** Biscuit, Huntley & Palmers, Green Lizard, Lunch Box Shape, c.1910, 7 In. | 84 |
| **Tin,** Brother Jonathan Tobacco, E.F. Adams Tobacco Co., Man Seated, 10½ In. | 540 |
| **Tin,** Buffalo Bill, Tobacco, Buffalo Bill On Horseback, 4 x 6⅛ In. | 2415 |
| **Tin,** Bunny Spice, Allspice, Color Lithograph, Cardboard, Metal Top, 2½ x 2 In. | 1668 |
| **Tin,** Busy Biddy, Celery Seed, Hen, Red, 3⅛ x 2⅜ In. | 92 |
| **Tin,** Calumet Baking Powder, Indian In Front, Back, 10 Lb., 8½ In. | 72 |
| **Tin,** Cameron & Cameron, Finest Grade Of Smoking Tobacco, Dome Top ......*illus* | 428 |
| **Tin,** Cedar Hill Spice, Ginger, Color Lithograph, Graphic Logo, 3 x 2 x 1 In. | 1323 |
| **Tin,** Checkers, Weisert Brothers Tobacco Co., Vertical, Pocket, 4½ In. | 120 |
| **Tin,** Cigar, Orioles, Birds, On Branches, Lithograph, Multicolor, 50 Ct., 5½ x 5 In. | 719 |
| **Tin,** Continental Cubes Concave, Geo. Washington, Vertical, 4 In. | 180 |
| **Tin,** Continental Cubes Tobacco, 1700s Officer With Message, Curved, Pocket, 3¾ In. | 1200 |
| **Tin,** Cork Town Pipe Tobacco, Tin Lithograph, Hat, Shamrock, Green, 4½ x 3 In. | 345 |
| **Tin,** Desert Gold Tobacco, Horse Reserve, Red Label, 6 In. | 150 |
| **Tin,** Dixie Queen Tobacco, Canister, 7 In. | 240 |
| **Tin,** Electric Mixture, Tobacco, 4 Women, Electric Theme, 3¼ x 4½ In. | 431 |
| **Tin,** English Plug Tobacco, Bull Dog Image, Spalding & Merrik, 4½ In. | 720 |
| **Tin,** Everhead Gold Tobacco, Smiling Woman, Gathering Leaves, Yellow, 7 In. | 150 |
| **Tin,** Extra Long Tom Tobacco Pouch, J. Bagley & Co., Detroit, 1902, 4¾ In. | 1200 |
| **Tin,** Flick & Flock Cigar Tin, 2 Dogs, Brown Ground, 6 In. | 270 |
| **Tin,** Forest & Stream Tobacco, Man Fishing, 5 In. | 84 |
| **Tin,** Forest & Stream Tobacco, Red, Canoe, White Letters, 4¼ x 3 In. | 431 |
| **Tin,** Fountain Fine Cut Tobacco, La Belle Buffington, Round, Handle, Ky., 7 In. | 1020 |
| **Tin,** Greenberg, Whole Cloves, Trademark Iceberg, Yellow, Green, 3 x 2⅜ In. | 115 |
| **Tin,** Hair Tobacco, Orange, Black, Metal Handle, 6½ In. | 540 |
| **Tin,** Hall's Toffee, Boy, Girl, Vintage Attire, Blue Ground, 9 In. | 72 |
| **Tin,** Haywood's Foot Comfort, Cylindrical, Contents, Pfeiffer Chemical, 4 In. | 34 |

**Advertising,** Stand, Lady's Legs, Brothel, Prairie Rose, Prescott, Ariz., Clothing, Tokens, 1880s, 42 In.
**$3,000**

Morphy Auctions

---

**Advertising,** Stein, Budweiser Bud Man, Pottery, ½ Liter
**$36**

Fox Auctions

---

**Advertising,** Stringholder, Heinz, Pure Foods, Pickle, Chains, 2-Sided, 10½ In.
**$6,000**

Morphy Auctions

This is an edited listing of current prices. Visit **Kovels.com** to check thousands of prices from previous years and sign up for free information on trends, tips, reproductions, marks, and more.

**Advertising,** Tin, Acme Licorice Pellets, Window, Y & S Pure Calabria Licorice, 5 Lb.
**$130**

Conestoga Auction Co., Inc.

### Breakfast of Champions
Wheaties, a cold cereal, was introduced by General Mills in 1924. The slogan for the cereal, "Breakfast of Champions," was first used in 1926. The first athlete who had his picture on a box of Wheaties was Lou Gehrig in 1934.

**Advertising,** Tin, Apache Trail Cigar, Indian Brave On Horseback, 6¼ In.
**$5,400**

Morphy Auctions

**Advertising,** Tin, Cameron & Cameron, Finest Grade Of Smoking Tobacco, Dome Top
**$428**

Showtime Auction Services

| | |
|---|---:|
| **Tin,** Hi-Plane, Tobacco, Red, Airplane, White Letters, 4¼ x 3 In. | 489 |
| **Tin,** Hotel Belvedere Spices, Allspice, Brown, Red Building, 3½ x 2⅜ In. | 207 |
| **Tin,** Ideal Brand Spices, Cloves, Girl With Wings, 3⅛ x 2⅜ In. | 207 |
| **Tin,** Indian Rifle Gunpowder, E.J. DuPont De Nemours & Co., Paper Label, 4 In. ...........*illus* | 1200 |
| **Tin,** Kar-A-Van Kiro Coffee, Pry Lid, Tin Lithograph, 1 Lb. | 138 |
| **Tin,** Keen's Mustard, Naval Scenes, Admiral Nelson, 8-Sided, 7½ In. | 72 |
| **Tin,** Life Pipe Tobacco, Red, White, Ryan-Hampton Tobacco Co., 3 x 4 x 1 In. | 120 |
| **Tin,** Lily Of The Valley, Red Pepper, Red Letters, White Ground, 3⅛ x 2¼ In. | 776 |
| **Tin,** Lucky Tiger Dandruff Remedy, c.1915, 10½ In. | 48 |
| **Tin,** Luzianne Coffee, Woman, Bandanna, Holding Tray, Red Label, Bail, 7 In. | 60 |
| **Tin,** Mammoth Salted Nuts, Lithograph, Kelly Co., Ohio, 10 Lb., 11 x 7½ In. ...........*illus* | 518 |
| **Tin,** Mammy's Favorite Brand Coffee, 2-Sided, C.D. Kenny Co., 4 Lb. | 230 |
| **Tin,** Marksman Cigar, Man Shooting Rifle, Paper Label, 5 In. | 300 |
| **Tin,** Mayo's Roly Poly, Mammy Version, 7¼ In. | 420 |
| **Tin,** Merrill's System Tonic, For Blood, Liver & Kidneys, Hinged Lid, 3 x 2 In. | 84 |
| **Tin,** Mohawk Cigar, Indian Profile, Red, Charles Co., 5⅔ In. | 900 |
| **Tin,** Monarch Coffee, White Ground, Lion, Tin Lithograph, 1 Lb. | 92 |
| **Tin,** Monarch Toffees, Lion, Yellow Ground, c.1928, 14½ In. | 210 |
| **Tin,** Newly-Wed Chocolate Bon, 1940s Comic, Blanke-Wenneker, 5 In. ...........*illus* | 510 |
| **Tin,** North Pole Cut Plug, Tobacco, Polar Bears, Walrus, White, 5⅛ x 6 In. | 690 |
| **Tin,** Orange Flower Tobacco, White Blossoms, Orange, Henry Grolley, Pa., 5 In. | 390 |
| **Tin,** Orcico Tobacco, Indian, 3-Feather Headdress, 5½ In. | 450 |
| **Tin,** Pepsikola Tablets, Tonic Digestants, Dr. Davis, Pocket, 3 x 1¾ In. | 67 |
| **Tin,** Pepsin Gum, Edward Beeman Photos, American Chicle Co., 4¾ x 5 In. ...........*illus* | 127 |
| **Tin,** Puritas, Allspice, Trademark Woman, Red, Yellow, 3¼ x 2¼ In. | 115 |
| **Tin,** Queentex Condom, Lipstick Shape, Black, Gold | 240 |
| **Tin,** Roly Poly, Gentleman, Mustache, Pipe, Dixie Queen Tobacco, 8 In. ...........*illus* | 1200 |
| **Tin,** Rose Leaf Chewing Tobacco, Embossed Frog, Inlaid Compass, P. Lorillard & Co., 3½ In. | 180 |
| **Tin,** Scotch Gall Remedy, For Man & Beast, Round, 3½ In. ...........*illus* | 123 |
| **Tin,** Sir Haig Cigar, Military Portrait, Yellow Ground, William Ward & Sons, 5 In. | 36 |
| **Tin,** Sunset Trail Cigar, 2 Riders, Black Ground, 5½ In. | 240 |
| **Tin,** Sweet Cuba Fine Cut Tobacco, Woman's Profile, Green Ground, Lift Lid, 9¾ In. | 90 |
| **Tin,** Sweet Cuba Tobacco, Woman's Profile, Green, Counter, 8 In. | 108 |
| **Tin,** Sweet Loma Fine Cut Tobacco, Woman's Portrait, Orange Ground, 10 In. | 240 |
| **Tin,** Sweet Violet Pocket Tobacco, Violets, Yellow, Vertical, Globe Tobacco Co., 4½ In. | 6600 |
| **Tin,** Target Tobacco, Canister, 5 In. | 24 |
| **Tin,** Thomas Brindley Grain Merchant, Rooster, Farm Scene, Flip Lid, 28 x 19 In. | 406 |
| **Tin,** Tiger Chewing Tobacco, Tiger Head, Blue Ground, 10½ In. | 420 |
| **Tin,** Tiger Chewing Tobacco, Tiger Head, Red, Gray, Cylindrical, 11 In. | 180 |
| **Tin,** Trout Line Pocket Tobacco, Fisherman, Landing Catch, Green, 3¾ In. | 570 |
| **Tin,** Trout Line, Cardboard, Tin Top & Bottom, Vertical, Pocket, c.1910, 3½ In. | 390 |
| **Tin,** Universal Blend Coffee, Uncle Sam, Lithograph, 6½ x 4 In. ...........*illus* | 1495 |
| **Tin,** Wafers, Green Ground, Art Deco Design, Bremner Biscuit Co., c.1924, 12 Oz. | 24 |
| **Tin,** Wagon Wheel Pocket Tobacco, Wheel, Axel, Yellow, Black, American Tin Co., 4½ In. | 360 |
| **Tin,** Wheeling Maid Cigar, Orange Triangle, 5½ In. | 480 |
| **Tin,** White Seal Long Cut Tobacco, White, Black, 1910, 4¾ In. | 120 |
| **Tin,** Wizard Spice, Cloves, Trademark Wizard, 3¼ x 2¼ In. | 1265 |
| **Tin,** Woodfield's Oysters, Lithograph, Sailboat, Lighthouse Scene, Gal., 7¼ In. ...........*illus* | 59 |
| **Tin,** Yankee Boy Vertical Pocket Tobacco, Blond Version, 4 In. | 540 |
| **Tin,** Yellow Kid Ginger Wafers, Round, Brinckerhoff & Co., 1896, 2 x 7½ In. | 240 |

**Advertising tip trays** are usually decorated metal trays less than 5 inches in diameter. They were placed on the table or counter to hold either the bill or the coins that were left as a tip. Change receivers could be made of glass, plastic, or metal. They were kept on the counter near the cash register and held the money passed back and forth by the cashier. Related items may be listed in the Advertising category under Change Receiver.

| | |
|---|---:|
| **Tip Tray,** Adam's Furniture Company, Treasure Stove, Tin Lithograph, Round, 4½ In. | 96 |
| **Tip Tray,** American Ship Line, Steamship, Round, Tin Lithograph, Round, 4½ In. | 84 |
| **Tip Tray,** Bailey's Pure Rye Whiskey, Glasses, Bottle, Tin Lithograph, Round, 4¼ In. | 84 |
| **Tip Tray,** Brilliant Shine Metal Polish, Jar, Tin Lithograph, 4 In. | 48 |
| **Tip Tray,** Budweiser Beer, Columbia, American Flag, Tin Lithograph, Round, 3½ In. | 60 |
| **Tip Tray,** Clarke's Clear Rye Whiskey, Bottle, Tin Lithograph, Round, 4¼ In. | 108 |
| **Tip Tray,** Cleveland & Buffalo Line, Seeandbee Steamer, Tin Lithograph, Oval, 6 In. | 150 |
| **Tip Tray,** Frost Fences, Scallop Edge, Round, 3 White Horses, 4½ In. Diam. | 196 |
| **Tip Tray,** Los Angeles Brewing Co., Brewery, Tin Lithograph, Round, 5 In. | 150 |
| **Tip Tray,** National Beer, Cowboy Holding Beer Bottle, Tin Lithograph, Round, 4½ In. | 240 |

**Advertising,** Tin, Indian Rifle Gunpowder, E.J. DuPont De Nemours & Co., Paper Label, 4 In.
$1,200

Showtime Auction Services

**Advertising,** Tin, Mammoth Salted Nuts, Lithograph, Kelly Co., Ohio, 10 Lb., 11 x 7 ½ In.
$518

Wm Morford Auctions

**Advertising,** Tin, Newly-Wed Chocolate Bon, 1940s Comic, Blanke-Wenneker, 5 In.
$510

Morphy Auctions

**Advertising,** Tin, Pepsin Gum, Edward Beeman Photos, American Chicle Co., 4 ¾ x 5 In.
$127

Wm Morford Auctions

**Advertising,** Tin, Roly Poly, Gentleman, Mustache, Pipe, Dixie Queen Tobacco, 8 In.
$1,200

Morphy Auctions

**Advertising,** Tin, Scotch Gall Remedy, For Man & Beast, Round, 3 ½ In.
$123

McMurray Antiques & Auctions

**Advertising,** Tin, Universal Blend Coffee, Uncle Sam, Lithograph, 6 ½ x 4 In.
$1,495

Wm Morford Auctions

**Advertising,** Tin, Woodfield's Oysters, Lithograph, Sailboat, Lighthouse Scene, Gal., 7 ¼ In.
$59

Conestoga Auction Co., Inc.

**Advertising,** Tip Tray, National Cigar Stands, Woman, Off-The-Shoulder Dress, Tin, 6 ⅛ In.
$316

Wm Morford Auctions

# ADVERTISING

**Advertising,** Tray, Anheuser-Busch, Woman, Flowing Hair, Cherubs, 16½ In.
$660

Morphy Auctions

**Advertising,** Tray, Anheuser-Busch, Young Servant Carrying Tray, Steins, Tin, 18 In.
$5,100

Morphy Auctions

**Advertising,** Tray, Columbia Export, Henry Weinhard City Brewery, Factory, Tin, 16 x 13 In.
$960

Showtime Auction Services

**Advertising,** Tray, Edelweiss Beer, Tin, Alpine Girl, Peter Schoenhofen Brewing, c.1913, 13 In.
$120

Morphy Auctions

**Advertising,** Tray, Hires Root Beer, Just What The Doctor Ordered, Tin, 1914, 13 In.
$1,920

Morphy Auctions

**Advertising,** Tray, You Drink Christo Ginger Ale, Woman, Holding Glass, 1905, 13 In.
$660

Morphy Auctions

| | | |
|---|---|---|
| **Tip Tray,** National Cigar Stands, Woman, Off-The-Shoulder Dress, Tin, 6⅛ In. | *illus* | 316 |
| **Tip Tray,** Old Mt. Vernon Rye Whiskey, Bottle, Tin Lithograph, Round, 3½ In. | | 72 |
| **Tip Tray,** Old Reliable Coffee, Russian Man, Seated, Tin Lithograph, Round, 4 In. | | 84 |
| **Tip Tray,** Pennsy Select Beer, Woman, Bottle, Tin Lithograph, Round, 4¼ In. | | 180 |
| **Tray,** Anheuser-Busch, Woman, Flowing Hair, Cherubs, 16½ In. | *illus* | 660 |
| **Tray,** Anheuser-Busch, Young Servant Carrying Tray, Steins, Tin, 18 In. | *illus* | 5100 |
| **Tray,** Buffalo Brewing Co., Bohemian, Tin, Litho, Round, Oakland Agency, 12 In. | | 570 |
| **Tray,** Columbia Export, Henry Weinhard City Brewery, Factory, Tin, 16 x 13 In. | *illus* | 960 |
| **Tray,** Dr Pepper, Woman, Green Dress, Holding Bottle, Tin Lithograph, 13 In. | | 150 |
| **Tray,** Edelweiss Beer, Tin, Alpine Girl, Peter Schoenhofen Brewing, c.1913, 13 In. | *illus* | 120 |
| **Tray,** Harrington's Ice Cream, Always The Best, Banana Split, Round, Tin, 13 In. | | 240 |
| **Tray,** Hires Root Beer, Just What The Doctor Ordered, Tin, 1914, 13 In. | *illus* | 1920 |
| **Tray,** Hires, 2 Smiling Women, Glasses, Round, Tin, Harry Morse Meyers, c.1920, 23 In. | | 600 |
| **Tray,** Hires, 5 Cents, Josh Slinger, Serving Glass, Tin, 1915, 13¼ In. | | 330 |
| **Tray,** Illinois Brewing Co., Tin, Floral Bouquet, Socorro, New Mexico, 13 x 16 In. | | 510 |
| **Tray,** Leisy's, Beer That Satisfies, The Connoisseur, Man Pouring, Oval, 16 In. | | 112 |
| **Tray,** London Baking Co., Lithograph Rose Girl, American Art Co., 13 In. | | 130 |
| **Tray,** Magnus Beck Brewing Co, Buffalo Brewery, 17 x 12 In. | | 840 |
| **Tray,** NuGrape, Flavor You Can't Forget, Bottle In Hand, 13 x 16 In. | | 60 |
| **Tray,** Old Judge Whiskey, Rothenberg Co., Horses, Field, Metal, Oval, 16½ In. | | 476 |
| **Tray,** Old Pepper Whiskey, Bottle, Colonial Men, Flag Swags, Metal, Oval, 16 In. | | 235 |
| **Tray,** Purity Ice Cream, Girl, Seated, Eating Ice Cream Bowl, Round, 13 In. | | 120 |
| **Tray,** Red Raven Ask The Man, Tin Lithograph, Round, 12 In. | | 360 |
| **Tray,** Red Ribbon Beer, Old Dutch Lager, Tin, Hawaiian Woman, Mathie Brewing Co., 13 In. | | 390 |
| **Tray,** Rustaller Lager & Gilt Edge Steam Beer, Tin, H.D. Beach Co., Factory, 16 x 13 In. | | 513 |
| **Tray,** Serving, Hires, Best Drink On Earth, Josh Slinger, c.1900, 12 In. Diam. | | 1560 |
| **Tray,** Tip, see Tip Trays in this category. | | |
| **Tray,** Webster Cigars, N. Webster Image, Glass, 7½ In. | | 180 |
| **Tray,** Western Air Express, Tin Lithograph, c.1950, 13 In. | | 240 |
| **Tray,** You Drink Christo Ginger Ale, Woman, Holding Glass, 1905, 13 In. | *illus* | 660 |
| **Tray,** Zipp's Cherri-O, Bird, Drinking Out Of Glass, Branch, Tin, 12 In. Diam. | | 1440 |
| **Trolley Sign,** Heinz Mince Meat, Jar, Can, Pie On Plate, Cardboard, 1920s, 11 x 21 In. | *illus* | 115 |
| **Whistle,** Red Goose Shoes For Boys & Girls, Tin, Paint | | 15 |

**AGATA** glass was made by Joseph Locke of the New England Glass Company of Cambridge, Massachusetts, after 1885. A metallic stain was applied to New England Peachblow, which the company called Wild Rose, and the mottled design characteristic of agata appeared. There are a few known items made of opaque green with the mottled finish.

| | | |
|---|---|---|
| **Bowl,** Finger, Amber & Purple Stain, Ruffled Rim, 5¼ In., Pair | | 403 |
| **Bowl,** Finger, Ruffled Rim, Amber, Amethyst Stain, New England, 5 In. | | 201 |
| **Celery Vase,** Pink Mottled, Scalloped Rim, Square, 6¼ In. | | 767 |
| **Celery Vase,** Ruffled Rim, Purple Stain, New England, 4½ In. | | 805 |
| **Pitcher,** Peachblow Shaded To Cream Base, 8½ In. | | 242 |
| **Pitcher,** Water, New England, Bulbous, Amber & Amethyst Stain, 7¼ In. | *illus* | 805 |
| **Punch Cup,** Amber & Purple Staining, Applied Handle, 2½ In. | | 144 |
| **Spooner,** Cylindrical, Square Mouth, Dark Purple Stain, Piecrust Rim, 6¾ In. | *illus* | 1150 |
| **Sugar & Creamer,** Amber, Amethyst Stain, Applied Handles, New England, 4½ In. | | 1495 |
| **Tumbler,** Oil Spot Stain, New England, 3¾ In. | | 173 to 230 |
| **Vase,** Bulbous, Dimpled Body, Smokestack Neck, 13½ In. | | 2875 |
| **Vase,** Lily, Indigo, Amethyst, Amber Stain, New England, 7½ In. | | 690 |
| **Vase,** Lily, Oil Spot, Undulating Rim, New England, 12¼ In. | | 805 |
| **Vase,** Lily, Purple Stain, Footed, Trifold Rim, New England, 7 In. | | 1725 |
| **Vase,** Stick, Dark Amber Stain Over Purple, 6½ In. | | 690 |

**AKRO AGATE** glass was founded in Akron, Ohio, in 1911 and moved to Clarksburg, West Virginia, in 1914. The company made marbles and toys. In the 1930s it began making other products, including vases, lamps, flowerpots, candlesticks, and children's dishes. Most of the glass is marked with a crow flying through the letter *A*. The company was sold to Clarksburg Glass Co. in 1951. Akro Agate marbles are listed in this book in the Marble category.

| | |
|---|---|
| **Ashtray,** Leaf Shape, Blue & White Marbleized, Marked, 1930s, 4 In. | 12 |
| **Dish,** Fish Shape, Jade Green, 5 x 3½ In. | 28 |
| **Planter,** Jonquil, Milk Glass, Blue Marbleized, Embossed, 5 x 3 In. | 17 |
| **Planter,** Orange Glass, Marbleized, Scalloped Edge, Vertical Ribbing, 1940s, 5 x 4 In. | 65 |
| **Pot,** Yellow, Ribbed Rim, 2½ x 2¼ In. | 10 |

**Advertising,** Trolley Sign, Heinz Mince Meat, Jar, Can, Pie On Plate, Cardboard, 1920s, 11 x 21 In.
$115

Hake's Americana & Collectibles

**Agata,** Pitcher, Water, New England, Bulbous, Amber & Amethyst Stain, 7¼ In.
$805

Early Auction Co.

**Agata,** Spooner, Cylindrical, Square Mouth, Dark Purple Stain, Piecrust Rim, 6¾ In.
$1,150

Early Auction Co.

**TIP**

*Bring a price guide book to an auction. It isn't possible to remember everything, but it is possible to look up most items. We think* Kovels' Antiques & Collectibles Price Guide *is the best resource.*

**Aluminum,** Champagne Bucket, Figural, Rhinoceros, Arthur Court, 15 x 31 In. $2,125

Los Angeles Modern Auctions (LAMA)

**Amberina,** Celery Dish, Diamond Optic, Crimped Rim, 6 ½ In. $115

Early Auction Co.

| | |
|---|---|
| **Powder Jar,** Colonial Woman, Opaque Pink, 4 ½ In. | 14 |
| **Powder Jar,** Scottie Dog, Blue, c.1940, 6 x 3 ¾ In. | 24 |
| **Toothpick Holder,** Hand, Orange & White Marbleized, Marked, 3 ¼ In. | 25 |

**ALABASTER** is a very soft form of gypsum, a stone that resembles marble. It was often carved into vases or statues in Victorian times. There are alabaster carvings being made even today.

| | |
|---|---|
| **Bust,** Art Nouveau, Maiden, Hair Tied With Ribbon, 23 In. | 313 |
| **Bust,** Girl, Bonnet, Mourning Dead Bird In Her Basket, Italy, 16 ½ In. | 625 |
| **Bust,** Girl, Smiling, Lace, Bonnet, Emilio Fiaschi, Italy, c.1900, 24 In. | 563 |
| **Bust,** Maiden, Flowers, Ferdinando Vichi, 21 ¼ In. | 185 |
| **Bust,** Verdi, Carved, Green Dyed Base, Incised, Italy, 7 ½ x 3 ¼ In. | 121 |
| **Bust,** Victorian Woman, Wide Brim Hat, Adolpho Cipriani, Italy, c.1915, 29 In. | 2375 |
| **Bust,** Woman, Bangs, Braid, Blouse, Crucifix, Green Pedestal, Italy, 15 ½ x 14 In. | 3936 |
| **Bust,** Woman, Inscribed Ruth, Prof. G. Besji, Italy, c.1850, 40 x 14 In. | 450 |
| **Bust,** Woman, Smiling, Top Knot, Unbuttoned Bodice, 16 ½ x 24 In. | 402 |
| **Bust,** Woman, Wearing Cap, Period Dress, Flowers, Mottled, 16 x 15 In. | 311 |
| **Bust,** Young Beauty, Signed A. Cipriani, 23 ½ In. | 1121 |
| **Bust,** Young Girl, Hair Pulled Back, Ribbon Headband, Lacy Drape, G. Lapini, 1870, 20 In. | 230 |
| **Egg,** Red Highlights, 8 In. | 45 |
| **Figurine,** Art Nouveau, Maiden, Standing, Hand On Balustrade, Urn, Carved, 21 x 10 In. | 604 |
| **Figurine,** Diana, Huntress, Shielding Eyes, Holding Quiver Of Arrows, A. Cipriani, 26 In. | 1230 |
| **Figurine,** Foo Dog, Carved, Male, Female With Pup, Asia, c.1950, 20 In., Pair | 420 |
| **Figurine,** Girl, Bonnet, Holding Grapes, Basket, Italy, 21 In. | 531 |
| **Figurine,** Girl, Butterfly, Raised, Pedestal, Italy, 25 In. | 813 |
| **Figurine,** Laura, Young Woman, Holding Book, Descending Stairs, G. Gennai, 25 In. | 1230 |
| **Figurine,** Woman, Dancing, Italy, 31 In. | 563 |
| **Figurine,** Woman, Standing, Half Draped, Holding Bouquet, 29 In. | 688 |
| **Garniture,** Bronze Mounted, Urn Shape, Scroll Feet, c.1900, 17 ½ x 8 ¼ In., Pair | 3690 |
| **Lamp,** Electric, Carved Eagle On Perch Base, Clear Glass Bead Shade, c.1910, 19 ½ In. | 150 |
| **Lamp,** Electric, Pierced Carved Roses, 20th Century, 45 In., Pair | 540 |
| **Lamp,** Electric, Venus In Shell, Wave Support, Italy, 16 In. | 1125 |
| **Lamp,** Electric, White, Urn Shape, Beaded Borders, Pedestal Base, 16 In., Pair | 420 |
| **Lamp,** Electric, Woman With Jug, Varicolored Stone, Drum Shade, 48 In. | 920 |
| **Lamp,** Figural, Woman, Seminude, Standing, On Pedestal Holding Light Sphere, 99 In. | 6000 |
| **Lamp,** Kerosene, Brass, Diaper Satin Glass Shade, Prisms, Cut Glass, 31 x 10 In. | 122 |
| **Sculpture,** Tiger, Painted Stripes, Marble Base, 1900s, 9 x 19 ½ x 8 In. | 281 |
| **Sculpture,** Woman, Lounging On Chair, Painted, c.1920, 14 x 16 In. | 360 |
| **Urn,** Carved Ribbons, Cornucopias, Flowers, Italy, c.1895, 13 ¼ In., Pair | 875 |
| **Urn,** Carved, Lovebird Finial, Oak Branches, Flowers, Griffin Handles, c.1895, 25 In. | 390 |
| **Vase,** Garniture, Rhyton Shape, Griffin, Leaf & Scroll Carved, Swags, 14 x 12 In. | 922 |
| **Woman,** Playing Pipes, Green Stained, Irregular Shape Panel, 14 ¼ In. | 344 |

**ALUMINUM** was more expensive than gold or silver until the 1850s. Chemists learned how to refine bauxite to get aluminum. Jewelry and other small objects were made of the valuable metal until 1914, when an inexpensive smelting process was invented. The aluminum collected today dates from the 1930s through the 1950s. Hand-hammered pieces are the most popular.

| | |
|---|---|
| **Basket,** Flowers, Reticulated, Ruffled, Handle, 1960s, 7 x 7 In. | 27 |
| **Basket,** Grapevine, Double Round Handle, Square Knot Top, Serrated Edge, 8 In. | 35 |
| **Basket,** Porcelain Center, Roses, Handle, Scroll Trim, 7 x 5 In. | 15 |
| **Bowl,** Flared & Ruffled Edge, Flowers, Blue, 11 x 3 In. | 68 |
| **Bowl,** Flowers, Scrolls, Incised, Krischer, 8 x 13 In. | 19 |
| **Centerpiece,** Stratford, Brushed, Clear Ball Knop, Footed, Kensington, 5 x 14 In. | 58 |
| **Champagne Bucket,** Figural, Rhinoceros, Arthur Court, 15 x 31 In. *illus* | 2125 |
| **Compote,** Hammered, Wild Roses, Continental Silver Co., 4 ½ In. | 28 |
| **Dish,** Hand Forged, Tulips, Rodney Kent, c.1950, 12 x 7 In. | 26 |
| **Dish,** Lid, Whale Form, Red Eyes, Stand With Swimming Whales, A. Court, 1979, 12 In. | 1464 |
| **Grease Container,** Bakelite Lid, Black, c.1965, 4 ¾ In. | 13 |
| **Ice Bucket,** Inverted Top Hat Form, 10 ¾ x 8 x 7 In. | 30 |
| **Lazy Susan,** Embossed, 1960s, 15 In. | 35 |
| **Mailbox,** Flags, Eastern Star, Remington Hardware, c.1930, 13 x 5 In. | 135 |
| **Pitcher,** Water, Hammered, Gailstyn, 1960s, 8 In. | 30 |
| **Plaque,** Virgin Mary, Tombstone Shape, c.1940, 3 x 5 In. | 35 |
| **Pot,** Double Boiler, Mirro, 1 ½ Qt. | 18 |
| **Sculpture,** Conch Shell, Streamlined Style, 20th Century, 13 x 14 x 27 In. | 230 |

| | |
|---|---|
| Silent Butler, Bamboo Design, Hinged Lid, Everlast Metal, 1940s, 10 In. | 40 |
| Silent Butler, Hammered, Applied Rose, Continental, c.1940, 12 x 7 In. | 32 |
| Spurs, Leather, c.1950 | 55 |
| Strainer, Cone Shape, Handle, Wear-Ever, c.1950, 9¾ In. | 13 |
| Teapot, Black Knob, Cornered, Banner Stamping Works, 7 In. | 16 |
| Tray, Embossed, Handles, Everlast Forged, 11 x 11 In. | 38 |
| Tray, Fluted Edge, Leaves, Handles, Cromwell, 17 x 12 In. | 10 |
| Tray, Hammered, Central Well, 24 In. | 55 |
| Tray, Hammered, Fruit, Handles, c.1945, 21 x 12 In. | 85 |
| Tray, Twisted Handles, Crimped Rim, Pomegranate Design, Round, c.1960, 13 In. | 9 |
| Trivet, Hand Forged, Handles, Everlast, 4 x 5 In. | 22 |

**AMBER**, *see Jewelry category.*

**AMBER GLASS** is the name of any glassware with the proper yellow-brown shading. It was a popular color just after the Civil War and many pressed glass pieces were made of amber glass. Depression glass of the 1930s–50s was also made in shades of amber glass. Other pieces may be found in the Depression Glass, Pressed Glass, and other glass categories. All types are being reproduced.

| | |
|---|---|
| Snuff Bottle, Carved Green Jade Leaf Stopper, 3 In. | 767 |
| Snuff Bottle, Garden, Flowers, Bamboo, Butterflies, Birds, Oval, Flat Back, Stopper, 2½ In. | 75 |
| Snuff Bottle, Loops, 2 Relief Dragons, 4 Animal Feet, China, c.1800, 3⅜ In. | 984 |
| Vase, Falconers, Landscape Scene, Enameled, Shouldered, 8½ In. | 125 |

**AMBERINA**, a two-toned glassware, was originally made from 1883 to about 1900. It was patented by Joseph Locke of the New England Glass Company, but was also made by other companies and is still being made. The glass shades from red to amber. Similar pieces of glass may be found in the Baccarat, Libbey, Plated Amberina, and other categories. Glass shaded from blue to amber is called *Blue Amberina* or *Bluerina*.

| | |
|---|---|
| Ashtray, Moon & Stars, Scalloped Edge, L.E. Smith, 1940s, 4½ x 3 In. | 22 |
| Berry Set, Daisy & Button, Squared Shape, Scalloped Edges, 8¾-In. Bowl, 7 Piece | 288 |
| Bowl, Canoe Shape, Reverse Thumbprint, Scalloped Rim, Meriden Silver Plate Frame, 14 In. | 230 |
| Bowl, Daisy & Button, Oval, Scalloped Edge, 10½ In. | 86 |
| Bowl, Quilted, Enamel Flower Interior, Applied Handle, 5¾ x 7½ In. | 148 |
| Celery Dish, Diamond Optic, Crimped Rim, 6½ In. ...................................*illus* | 115 |
| Celery Vase, Diamond Optic, Scalloped Rim, c.1910, 6 x 3 In. | 81 |
| Compote, Coin Spot, Libbey Acid Stamp, 4½ In. | 259 |
| Compote, Diamond Optic, Undulating Rim, 6½ In. | 604 |
| Creamer, Pinch Sided, Coin Spot, 5 In. | 69 |
| Cruet, Diamond-Quilted Body, Applied Amber Handle, Faceted Amber Stopper, 6¼ In. | 86 |
| Cruet, Swirl Pattern, Stopper, Handle, 8½ In. ...................................*illus* | 115 |
| Ice Cream Set, Daisy & Button, Scalloped, Recessed Corners, 14-In. Tray, 7 Piece | 345 |
| Jar, Lid, Diamond Optic, 7 In. ...................................*illus* | 633 |
| Pitcher, Coin Spot, Reeded Handle, Tricorner Mouth, 4¼ In. | 128 |
| Pitcher, Daisy & Button, Tankard Style, Pressed, Hobbs, Brockunier, 5½ In. | 201 |
| Pitcher, Lemonade, Spot Optic, Tapered Tankard, Angled Mouth, c.1880, 9½ In. | 138 |
| Pitcher, Milk, Diamond Optic, Ball Shape, Clear Handle, c.1880, 5½ In. | 69 |
| Pitcher, Water, Hobnail, 7½ In. | 153 |
| Pitcher, Water, Reverse Thumbprint, 8 In. | 115 |
| Punch Set, Optic, Amber To Cranberry, Scalloped Rim, Tapered Bowl, 12 Cups, 7 x 10 In. | 276 |
| Rose Bowl, Coin Spot, Rigaree Collar, 3 In. | 518 |
| Salt Dip, Moon & Stars, Scalloped Edge, Footed, 1½ x 2 In. | 18 |
| Scent Bottle, Cut, Teardrop Shape, Multi-Faceted, Sterling Silver, Twist-Off Cap, 6 In. | 2875 |
| Sugar & Creamer, Coin Spot, Amber Reeded Handles, 4½ In. | 403 |
| Vase, Bottle, Honeycomb Pattern, Star Hexagon Rim, 6½ In. | 633 |
| Vase, Bud, Bulbous, Spreading Petal Shape Rim, 3¼ In. | 173 |
| Vase, Jack-In-The-Pulpit, Amber Stem, Shaded To Cranberry Rim, Green Disc Foot, 5 In. | 748 |
| Vase, Pressed Stock Design, Libbey, 4½ In. | 460 |
| Vase, Reverse Thumbprint, Metal Holder, Spreading Scalloped Rim, 2 Arms, 8¼ In. | 460 |
| Vase, Thumbprint, Swollen Collar, 4-Sided Flared Rim, 5 In. | 58 |
| Vase, Urn Shape, Optic Ribs, Acid Stamped, Libbey, 13 In. | 403 |
| Water Set, Bottle, Pinched Sides, Rigaree Collar, 3 Tumblers, 7 In. | 144 |

**AMERICAN DINNERWARE**, *see Dinnerware.*

**Amberina,** Cruet, Swirl Pattern, Stopper, Handle, 8½ In.
**$115**

Early Auction Co.

**Amberina,** Jar, Lid, Diamond Optic, 7 In.
**$633**

Early Auction Co.

**Animal Trophy,** Antelope, Bushbuck, Shoulder Mount, Africa, 1900s, 32 In.
**$120**

Garth's Auctioneers & Appraisers

**Animal Trophy,** Butterflies, 2 Large, Blue Wings, 2 Small, Blue & Brown Wings, Frame, 15 x 12 In.
$84

DuMouchelles Art Gallery

**Animal Trophy,** Sailfish, Wall Mount, c.1980, 34 x 88 In.
$240

Garth's Auctioneers & Appraisers

**Animal Trophy,** Sea Turtle, Brown, Wall Mounted, Hanger, 5 ¼ x 11 ¼ x 15 In.
$2,706

New Orleans Auction Galleries, Inc.

**Animal Trophy,** Sea Turtle, Wall Mount, 12 ½ x 18 x 6 ¼ In.
$9,532

New Orleans Auction Galleries, Inc.

**AMERICAN ENCAUSTIC TILING COMPANY** was founded in Zanesville, Ohio, in 1875. The company planned to make a variety of tiles to compete with the English tiles that were selling in the United States for use in fireplaces and other architectural designs. The first glazed tiles were made in 1880, embossed tiles in 1881, faience tiles in the 1920s. The firm closed in 1935 and reopened in 1937 as the Shawnee Pottery.

| | |
|---|---:|
| **Bookends,** Child, Dancing With Garland, Black Glaze, c.1925 | 196 |
| **Dish,** Heart Shape, Blue Matte Glaze, c.1920, 3 x 3 In. | 44 |
| **Inkwell,** 2 Wells, Blue Glaze, c.1930, 6 x 5 In. | 95 |
| **Tile,** Man, Hat, Relief, Green Glaze, c.1900, 6 x 6 In. | 77 |
| **Tile,** Man, Profile, Beard, Feather In Hat, Green Glaze, c.1900, 6 ½ x 6 ½ In. | 89 |
| **Tile,** Open Rose, Buds, Leaves, Relief, Burgundy, 6 x 6 In. | 50 |
| **Tile,** Renaissance Man, Green Glaze, c.1900, 6 x 6 In. | 71 |
| **Tile,** Tableau, Shepherdess, Dog, On Hillside, Sheep, 12 x 24 In. | 1725 |
| **Tile,** Torch, Pink Ribbon, Bellflowers, Green Matte Glaze, 9 x 6 In. | 375 |
| **Tray,** Monks, Talking, Scrolled Border, Blue & White Matte Glaze, c.1920, 6 x 5 In. | 52 |

**AMETHYST GLASS** is any of the many glasswares made in the dark purple color of the gemstone amethyst. Included in this category are many pieces made in the nineteenth and twentieth centuries. Very dark pieces are called *black amethyst* and are listed under that heading.

| | |
|---|---:|
| **Box,** Egg Shape, Cut, Gilt Metal Mounts, Hinged Lid, Pineapple Finial, Pedestal Base, 9 In. | 311 |
| **Hurricane Shade,** 12 In., Pair | 120 |

**AMPHORA** *pieces are listed in the Teplitz category.*

**ANDIRONS** *and related fireplace items are included in the Fireplace category.*

**ANIMAL TROPHIES,** such as stuffed animals, rugs made of animal skins, and other similar collectibles made from animal, fish, or bird parts, are listed in this category. Collectors should be aware of the endangered species laws that make it illegal to buy and sell some of these items. Any eagle feathers, many types of pelts or rugs (such as leopard), ivory, and many forms of tortoiseshell can be confiscated by the government. Related trophies may be found in the Fishing category. Ivory items may be found in the Scrimshaw or Ivory categories.

| | |
|---|---:|
| **Antelope,** Bushbuck, Shoulder Mount, Africa, 1900s, 32 In. .........................*illus* | 120 |
| **Baboon,** Wood Tabletop Display Stand, African Continent Inlay, 20th Century, 29 In. | 480 |
| **Birds,** Natural Setting, Branches, Grass, Oval Wood Base, Glass Dome, Victorian, 22 In. | 259 |
| **Bison,** Horn, Shoulder Mount, 38 x 36 In. | 1750 |
| **Blue Wildebeest,** Shoulder Mount, Africa, 20th Century, 27 In. | 240 |
| **Boar,** Shoulder Mount, 20 x 25 In. | 240 |
| **Buck,** Talking Electric Deer Head, Bracket Mount, Gemmy Industries, 36 In. | 345 |
| **Butterflies,** 2 Large, Blue Wings, 2 Small, Blue & Brown Wings, Frame, 15 x 12 In. ..........*illus* | 84 |
| **Caribou,** Shoulder Mount, 54 In. | 1063 |
| **Chihuahua Puppies,** Landscape Setting, Diorama, 19th Century, 10 ¼ x 9 ½ In. | 4159 |
| **Deer Head,** Stag, Whitetail, Wood Plaque, 20 ½ In. | 113 |
| **Deer,** Antler, Shield Plaque, Square Mirror, 19 x 14 In. | 90 |
| **European Mouflon Sheep,** Shoulder Mount, 26 x 25 In. | 120 |
| **Fish,** Large Teeth, Multicolor, Western Hemisphere, 20th Century, 28 In. | 215 |
| **Hereford Bull,** Shoulder Mount, 34 x 36 In. | 875 |
| **Hippopotamus,** Shoulder Mount, Mozambique, 20th Century, 41 x 50 In. | 570 |
| **Kudu Antelope,** Spiral Horns, Wall Mount, Zimbabwe, Africa, 69 In. | 201 |
| **Leopard Hide,** Rue, Felt Backing, Late 19th Century, 48 x 81 In. | 500 |
| **Mountain Goat,** Shoulder Mount, Landscape Scenery, 23 In. | 330 |
| **Mule Deer,** Shoulder Mount, 40 In. | 531 |
| **Mute Swan,** Raised Wings, Mounted To Wood Base, Victorian, 17 x 29 x 19 In. | 604 |
| **Ocelot,** Reclining, Glass Eyes, Victorian, c.1880, 13 ½ x 29 In. | 472 |
| **Ocelot,** With Armadillo, Painted Plaster Base, Victorian, 15 x 39 x 11 In. | 460 |
| **Opossum,** On Branch, New Zealand, 20th Century, 32 In. | 215 |
| **Peacock,** Turned Wood Floor Standing Perch, Victorian, 68 In. | 259 |
| **Peccary,** On Scenic Base, Western Hemisphere, 20th Century, 24 x 33 In. | 270 |
| **Pronghorn Antelope,** Shoulder Mount, 22 In. | 406 |
| **Pronghorn Antelope,** Shoulder Mount, 34 In. | 281 |
| **Quail,** Landscape, Table Mount, 31 ½ In. | 90 |
| **Raccoon,** Mounted On Log, 20th Century, 23 x 8 ½ In. | 183 |
| **Rug,** Black Bear, Full Head, Claws, Felt Pad, Crosby Fur Co., 69 x 72 In. | 322 |

| | |
|---|---|
| **Rug,** Mountain Lion, Full Body, 76 ½ In. | 850 |
| **Rug,** Zebra, 84 x 128 In. | 650 |
| **Rug,** Zebra, Felt Backing, 20th Century, Africa, 70 x 140 In. | 574 |
| **Sailfish,** Wall Mount, c.1980, 34 x 88 In. *illus* | 240 |
| **Sea Turtle,** Brown, Wall Mounted, Hanger, 5 ¼ x 11 ¼ x 15 In. *illus* | 2706 |
| **Sea Turtle,** Wall Mount, 12 ½ x 18 x 6 ¼ In. *illus* | 9532 |
| **Stag,** Wall Mount, Late 20th Century, 29 In. | 180 |
| **Texas Longhorn,** Horns, Leather Strap, 90 In. | 330 |
| **Turkey,** 20th Century, 31 x 28 In. | 90 |
| **Turkey,** Oak Frame Base, Straw, Grass, 20th Century, 39 x 20 In. | 90 |
| **Water Buffalo,** Shoulder Mount, Oak Cabinet Display, Australia, 1900s, 75 In. | 240 |
| **Waterbuck,** Oak Display Stand, Africa, 20th Century, 82 In. | 360 |

**ANIMATION ART** collectibles include cels that are painted drawings on celluloid needed to make animated cartoons shown in movie theaters or on TV. Hundreds of cels were made, then photographed in sequence to make a cartoon showing moving figures. Early examples made by the Walt Disney Studios are popular with collectors today. Original sketches used by the artists are also listed here. Modern animated cartoons are made using computer-generated pictures. Some of these are being produced as cels to be sold to collectors. Other cartoon art is listed in Comic Art and Disneyana.

| | |
|---|---|
| **Cel,** Bambi, Walking In Woods, 1942, 8 x 10 In. | 1375 |
| **Cel,** Dopey, Gouache On Celluloid, Snow White & 7 Dwarfs, 1937, 5 x 4 ½ In. | 1875 |
| **Cel,** Pinocchio & Emperor Of Night, 1987, 26 x 19 In. | 60 |
| **Cel,** Ugly Duckling, Frowning Chicks, Gouache, Frame, 1939, 7 x 9 In. | 1625 |
| **Drawing,** Bashful Dwarf, Snow White & 7 Dwarfs, Graphite Pencil, 1937, 10 x 12 In. | 375 |
| **Drawing,** Donald Duck, Bumblebee, Moose Hunter, Graphite, Paper, 1937, 10 x 12 In. | 250 |
| **Drawing,** Mickey & Minnie Mouse, Bowing, Graphite, Paper, 1932, 9 ½ x 12 In. | 250 |
| **Drawing,** Mickey & Minnie Mouse, Camping Out, Graphite, Paper, 1934, 9 ½ x 12 In. | 375 |
| **Drawing,** Mickey Mouse, Kangaroo, Boxing, Graphite, Pencil, Paper, 1935, 9 ½ x 12 In. | 275 |
| **Drawing,** Peter Pan, Celebrating With Tiger Lily, Gouache, 1953, 7 ½ x 10 In. | 1750 |
| **Film,** Cel Print, Oswald The Rabbit, Poor Papa Cartoon, 1927, 16 mm Kodak Film | 7500 |

**ANNA POTTERY** was started in Anna, Illinois, in 1859 by Cornwall and Wallace *Anna Pottery* Kirkpatrick. They made many types of utilitarian wares, bricks, drain tiles, and giftware. The most collectible pieces made by the pottery are the pig-shaped bottles and jugs with special inscriptions, applied animals, and figures. The pottery closed in 1894.

| | |
|---|---|
| **Flask,** Pig Shape, Incised Eyes, Mouth, Molded, Stoneware, c.1885, 6 ¼ In. | 677 |
| **Flask,** Pig, Cobalt Blue Railroad Map, Albany Slip To Eyes, Stoneware, 1889, 7 ½ In. | 16100 |
| **Flask,** Pig, Incised Railroad, River Guide, Hole At Rear, c.1885, 7 ¾ In. | 4025 |
| **Flask,** Pig, Reclining, Incised Cartoons, Brown Albany Slip Glaze, c.1872, 8 In. | 11500 |
| **Flask,** Pig, Redware, Glazed, Incised Map In A Verse, Fine Old Bourbon, 3 x 7 In. *illus* | 3835 |
| **Flask,** Pig, St. Louis Future Great, Railroad, River Guide, Maps, Anna, Ill., 1890, 4 x 6 In. | 2415 |
| **Jug,** Little Brown Jug, Snake On Neck, Cobalt Blue, Amber Albany Slip, Stoneware, 1885, 5 In. | 50600 |

**APPLE PEELERS** are listed in the Kitchen category under Peeler, Apple.

**ARABIA** began producing ceramics in 1874. The pottery was established in Helsinki, Finland, by Rörstrand, a Swedish pottery that wanted to export porcelain, earthenware, and other pottery from Finland to Russia. Most of the early workers at Arabia were Swedish. Arabia started producing its own models of tiled stoves, vases, and tableware c.1900. Rörstrand sold its interest in Arabia in 1916. By the late 1930s, Arabia was the largest producer of porcelain in Europe. Most of its products were exported. A line of stoneware was introduced in the 1960s. Arabia worked in cooperation with Rörstrand from 1975 to 1977. Arabia was bought by Hackman Group in 1990 and Hackman was bought by Iittala Group in 2004. Arabia is now a brand owned by Iittala Group.

| | |
|---|---|
| **Plaque,** Vase Of Flowers, Blue, 4 x 9 In. | 45 |
| **Vase,** 6-Sided, Green, Flared, Marked | 64 |

**ARCHITECTURAL** antiques include a variety of collectibles, usually very large, that have been removed from buildings. Hardware, backbars, doors, paneling, and even old bathtubs are now wanted by collectors. Pieces of the Victorian, Art Nouveau, and Art Deco styles are in greatest demand.

| | |
|---|---|
| **Bank Counter,** Oak, Paneled, Wrought Iron Frame, Frosted Windows, 132 x 80 In. | 1767 |
| **Bathtub,** Claw Foot, Porcelain, Iron, Victorian, 58 x 30 In. | 82 |
| **Bathtub,** Tin, Round, Flared Sides, Seat Area, Water Trough, Soldered, 1800s, 37 x 41 In. | 83 |

**Anna Pottery,** Flask, Pig, Redware, Glazed, Incised Map In A Verse, Fine Old Bourbon, 3 x 7 In.
$3,835

Conestoga Auction Co., Inc.

**Architectural,** Door & Jamb, Teak, Carved, Sculptured Design, N.M., Federico Armijo, 1970s, 86 x 38 In.
$8,125

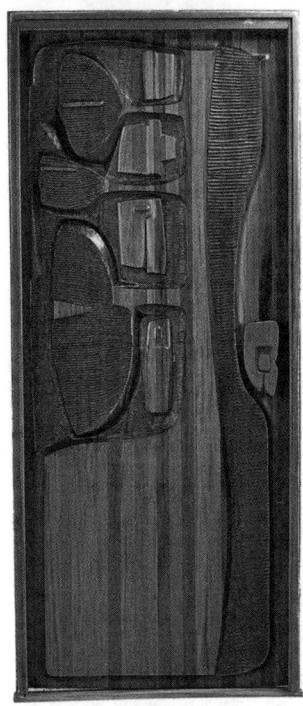

Rago Arts & Auction Center

**Architectural,** Door Handle, Alvar Aalto, 1956-58, 3 ¾ x 9 ¾ In., 4 Piece
$9,375

Los Angeles Modern Auctions (LAMA)

**Architectural,** Door, Wood, Raised Panels, Leaded Glass Panel, Jeweled Abstract, c.1910, 83 x 30 In.
**$1,500**

Rago Arts & Auction Center

**Architectural,** Fireplace Surround, Aesthetic Revival, Walnut, Inlay, Mirror, Tile, c.1880, 105 x 72 In.
**$8,917**

New Orleans Auction Galleries, Inc.

**Architectural,** Gate Finial, Figural, Bust, Woman, Hat, Cast Iron, c.1850, 15½ x 8 In.
**$239**

Neal Auction Co.

| | |
|---|---:|
| **Billet Head,** White Pine, Rosette Terminal, Carved, Yellow, Black, New Eng., 1800s, 21 In. | 2400 |
| **Bracket,** Red, Yellow Roses, Carved, Painted, Italy, 23 x 26 In. | 281 |
| **Cabinet,** Theatre, Painted, Spring Activated Doors, Mirrored, Iron, 1800s, 28 x 20 In. | 123 |
| **Chimney Cap,** Sewer Tile, Figural, Bust, World War I Aviator, E. Thomson, 13½ In. | 492 |
| **Column,** Carved Wood, Elephant Capital, Rectangular Base, Fluted Shaft, 79 x 16 In. | 173 |
| **Column,** Fluted, Carved Acanthus Tops, Bottom, Flat, Partial, 1800s, 55 x 15 In., Pair | 326 |
| **Column,** Neoclassical Style, Wood, White Washed, 104 In., 5 Piece | 500 |
| **Corbel,** Classical Woman Bust, Sandstone, Pa., c.1900 | 6950 |
| **Cornice,** Element, Gothic Revival, Oak, Carved, Pine Brackets, Pierced, c.1850, 18 x 78 In. | 2214 |
| **Crest,** Walnut, Cherubs, Flowers, White, American, 1790-1810, 26½ x 19 In. | 3720 |
| **Doghouse,** French Provincial, Upholstered Sides, Top, Carved Crest, 1800s, 26 x 19 In. | 2337 |
| **Door & Jamb,** Teak, Carved, Sculptured Design, N.M., Federico Armijo, 1970s, 86 x 38 In. *illus* | 8125 |
| **Door Handle,** Alvar Aalto, 1956-58, 3¾ x 9¾ In., 4 Piece *illus* | 9375 |
| **Door Handle,** Fiddler, Sheet Iron, 14½ In. | 351 |
| **Door Handle,** Latch, Heart, 19th Century, 13 In. | 240 |
| **Door Handle,** Metal, Applied Shapes, 1960s, 22½ x 12¾, 4 Piece | 1375 |
| **Door Latch,** Duck Head, Pivoting, c.1900, 8 In. | 542 |
| **Door Latch,** Steel, Engraving, Scrollwork, Key Guard, Middle East, 11 In. | 90 |
| **Door,** Board, Batten, Red, H-Hinges, Latch, New England, 1700s, 70 x 23½ In. | 240 |
| **Door,** F. Armijo, Jamb, Teak, Carved, Sculpted, Abstract, 1970s, 86 x 38 In. | 8125 |
| **Door,** Folding, Elm, Pine Panels, Carved, Pierced, Plants, Chinese, 1800s, 115 x 22 In., Pair | 2337 |
| **Door,** Hardwood, Glass, Scrolled Wrought Iron, Carved, 1800s, 98 x 79 In., Pair | 525 |
| **Door,** Leaded Glass, Stylized Flower, Walnut Frame, c.1920, 80 x 30 In., Pair | 300 |
| **Door,** Mahogany, Divided, Glass Panes, 45 x 75 In. | 59 |
| **Door,** Oak, Swinging, 3 Panels, Beveled Glass, 93½ x 35 In., Pair | 563 |
| **Door,** Wood, Chased White Sheet Metal, Panels, Enameled Flower Baskets, 82 x 42 In. | 720 |
| **Door,** Wood, Raised Panels, Leaded Glass Panel, Jeweled Abstract, c.1910, 83 x 30 In. *illus* | 1500 |
| **Doorknob,** Rosette, Braided Rope Border, Oval, Brass | 135 |
| **Doorknocker,** Brass, Woman's Hand Shape, Lace Sleeve, 5½ In. | 212 |
| **Doorknocker,** Butterfly, Paint, Cast Iron, Waverly Studios, 3½ In. | 120 |
| **Doorknocker,** Cast Iron, Cardinal, Paint, Hubley, Berries, 5 In. | 180 |
| **Doorknocker,** Cast Iron, Dogwood Flower Clapper, 2¾ In. | 780 |
| **Doorknocker,** Cast Iron, Egyptian Head Clapper, Pyramid Shape, Judd Co., 5 In. | 510 |
| **Doorknocker,** Cast Iron, Girl At Door, Hubley, 4 In. | 177 |
| **Doorknocker,** Cast Iron, Masted Ship Shape, 1929, 9½ In. | 163 |
| **Doorknocker,** Cast Iron, Pink Rose, Buds, Painted, Hubley, 5 In. | 360 |
| **Doorknocker,** Cast Iron, Vase, Flowers, Vines, Multicolor, Hubley, 4 x 2¼ In. | 145 |
| **Doorknocker,** Cast Iron, Woodpecker, Push On Tail, Paint, Peckey-Knocker, Tenn., 6¼ In. | 900 |
| **Doorknocker,** Foo Dog, Bronze, Patinated, Round, 6 x 4 In., Pair | 247 |
| **Doorknocker,** Lion's Head, Brass, Loop Knocker, France, c.1900, 9½ x 5 In. | 380 |
| **Doorknocker,** Lion's Head, Ring In Mouth, Cast Iron, 16 In. | 47 |
| **Doorknocker,** Lion's Head, Ring Through Nose, White Paint, Cast Iron, 10 x 16 In. | 263 |
| **Drapery Hook,** Gilt Bronze, Leaves, Scrolling Arm, Leaf Cap, Wall Mount, 9 x 8 In., Pair | 178 |
| **Element,** Hardwood, Carved, Flower Vase, Incense, Dragons, Lei Wen, Chinese, 45 x 27 In. | 474 |
| **Element,** North Wind, Beaded Face, Leaves, Acanthus, Cast Iron, Painted, 9½ In. | 523 |
| **Fan Light,** 10 Rays, Demilune Hub, Black Paint Over White, 1800s, 26 x 83 In. | 800 |
| **Fan Light,** Radiating Baluster, Disc Turned Spindles, Scrolls, White Paint, 21 x 39 In. | 369 |
| **Figure,** Putti, Carved, Painted, 35 In. | 3480 |
| **Finial,** Ball, Wood, White Paint, 38 In. | 480 |
| **Finial,** Baluster, Wood, Twist Carved, Plinth Base, 33 In., Pair | 1063 |
| **Finial,** Carved Festoon, 16 In., Pair | 531 |
| **Finial,** Pineapple, Zinc, Modeled, Hollow, Radiating Diamond Pattern, c.1810, 17 x 8 In. | 1185 |
| **Fireboard,** Wood, Carved Galleon Shape, Painted, c.1900, 42 x 24 In. | 360 |
| **Fireplace Surround,** Aesthetic Revival, Walnut, Inlay, Mirror, Tile, c.1880, 105 x 72 In. *illus* | 8917 |
| **Fireplace Surround,** Applied Scrolls, Rosettes, Scrolls, Birds In Flight, 60 x 72 In. | 6490 |
| **Fireplace Surround,** Cast, Central Sunburst, Torches, Vines, Campfires, Iron, 30 x 30 In. | 344 |
| **Fireplace Surround,** Faux Stone, Mantle, Electric Plug, Shell Medallion, Carved, 48 x 60 In. | 330 |
| **Fireplace Surround,** Federal, Cypress, Charleston, c.1810, 57 x 64 In. | 2006 |
| **Fireplace Surround,** Georgian Style, Pine, Columns, Recessed Panels, Carved, 53 x 59 In. | 250 |
| **Fireplace Surround,** Renaissance Style, Oak, Carved, Dolphin Brass Handles, c.1880, 62 x 67 In. | 295 |
| **Fireplace Surround,** Tile, Cambridge, Center Panel, Dogs Hunting, Cattails, 41 x 56 In. | 563 |
| **Gate Finial,** Figural, Bust, Woman, Hat, Cast Iron, c.1850, 15½ x 8 In. *illus* | 239 |
| **Gate,** Elevator, Brass, 82 x 34 In. | 938 |
| **Gate,** Garden, Carved Star, Compass, Green Paint, Wood, 1800s, 47 x 30 In. | 840 |
| **Gate,** Star & Compass Designs, Crosshatched, Wood, Painted, 47 x 30 In. | 840 |

| | |
|---|---|
| Gate, Wood, Painted White, Vertical Spindles, Horizontal Block, 46 x 81 In., Pair | 1599 |
| Gate, Wrought Iron, Bronze, Bird, Flowers In Circular Scrolls, 78 In., Pair | 7480 |
| Gate, Wrought Iron, Flowers, Vase, Enameled, France, 1940s, 47 x 31 ¾ In., Pair | 4375 |
| Gate, Wrought Iron, Scrolls, Hearts, California, 1930s, 74 x 25 In., Pair | 1024 |
| Grille, Fretwork, Walnut, George Grant Elmslie, c.1923, 9 x 33 In., | 2440 |
| Mailbox, Cast Iron, Molded Horse, Rider Relief, Swing Door, Painted White, 48 In. | 240 |
| Manhole Cover, Iron, City Grid, Round, Le Corbusier, 25 In. | 8540 |
| Mantel, Fireplace, Softwood, Blue Paint, Lancaster County, Pa., c.1790, 60 x 69 In. ...illus | 1062 |
| Mantel, Marble, Neoclassical, Carved, Columns, Draped Relief Maidens, c.1810, 40 x 62 In. | 3936 |
| Mantel, Mixed Woods, Carved, Reeded, Grain Paint, Pennsylvania, c.1810, 61 x 67 In. ...illus | 150 |
| Mantel, Pine, Federal, c.1815, 43 x 61 In. | 90 |
| Mantel, Pine, Federal, Green, Cream Paint, Arched Tympanum, c.1810, 78 x 56 In. | 1680 |
| Mantel, Pine, Federal, Swag Frieze, Carved Capitals, c.1800, 60 ½ x 78 In. | 1560 |
| Mantel, Pine, Federal, White Paint, c.1810, 57 x 79 In. | 246 |
| Mantel, Pine, Fluted Urn Frieze, Carved, c.1800, 51 x 62 In. | 600 |
| Mantel, Pine, Painted, Faux Marble Decorated Surface, c.1810, 54 x 61 In. | 900 |
| Mantel, Walnut, French Provincial, Carved Shells & Scrolls, Marble Top, 48 x 72 In. | 2700 |
| Mantel, Walnut, Renaissance Revival, Shelf, Satyr Mask, Arch Opening, c.1890 ...illus | 1230 |
| Medallion, Wood, Carved, Pierced, Center Phoenix, Scrolls, Paint, 20 In. | 312 |
| Mirror, Parcel Gilt, Louis XVI Style, Garland Swags, Laurel Bands, Painted, c.1920, 63 x 44 In. | 500 |
| Mirror, Trumeau, Walnut, Cast Bronze, Empire, Roman Scene, Columns, c.1820, 60 x 48 In. | 2124 |
| Model, Spiral Staircase, Mahogany, Turned Balusters, Platform, 41 ½ In. ...illus | 2460 |
| Overmantel Mirror, Aesthetic Movement, Apple Blossoms, Painted, Tripart, 49 x 59 In. | 625 |
| Overmantel Mirror, Empire Revival, Giltwood, 3 Sections, Balusters, c.1875, 30 x 72 In. | 1845 |
| Overmantel Mirror, George III Style, Crest, Swags, c.1890, 51 x 60 In. ...illus | 2749 |
| Overmantel Mirror, Giltwood, Egyptian Revival, 3 Sections, Cornice, c.1840, 34 x 80 In. | 2242 |
| Overmantel Mirror, Giltwood, Louis XV Style, Arched, Rocaille Crest, c.1945, 63 x 43 In. | 344 |
| Overmantel Mirror, Giltwood, Louis XVI Style, Pierced Crest, Arched, 80 x 46 In. | 1188 |
| Overmantel Mirror, Giltwood, Napoleon III, Arched Top, c.1890, 68 x 48 In. | 3690 |
| Overmantel Mirror, Giltwood, Neoclassical, Carved, c.1890, 66 x 56 ½ In. | 3750 |
| Overmantel Mirror, Giltwood, Shell, Leaf Crest, Union Shield, 19 Stars, c.1860, 71 x 62 In. | 2500 |
| Overmantel Mirror, Louis XV Style, Carved Garlands, Leaves, Arched Plate, 76 x 52 In. | 1250 |
| Overmantel Mirror, Pendant Acorns, Split Baluster Frame, Rosette Corner Block, 28 x 79 In. | 896 |
| Overmantel Mirror, Wood, Carved, Griffin Figures, Lion Crest, 98 x 77 In. | 1404 |
| Panel, Cast Iron, Colossal Relief, Neptune Head, Crowned Cornice, 34 ½ In. ...illus | 11950 |
| Panel, Engraved, Frosted, Blue, Arched Top, Hanging Basket, c.1900, 43 In., 42 In., Pair | 23 |
| Panel, Gilt Bronze, Art Deco, Chased, Classical Figures, Leaf Borders, c.1910, 74 x 20 In. | 1845 |
| Panel, Parcel Giltwood, Neoclassical Scene, Putto, Playing, Turquoise Ground, 13 x 49 In. | 250 |
| Panel, Patinated Metal, Openwork Scrolls, 48 x 26 In. | 50 |
| Panel, Plaster, Maenad, Satyr, Roman Relief, Spain, c.1860, 29 x 28 In. | 375 |
| Panel, Satinwood, Adam Style, Inlay, Urn & Vine, Frame, 47 x 17 In. | 178 |
| Pedestal, Gothic, Oak, Shelf, Carved Upright, Arches, Oak Leaves, Spires, 96 x 25 In., Pair | 1968 |
| Pedestal, Wood, Painted White, Tiered Cap, Base, Square, 46 In., Pair | 94 |
| Pediment, Baroque, Painted Angel Head, Carved Giltwood Wings, c.1800, 17 x 64 In. | 1353 |
| Plaque, 2 Sisters, Profile Faces, Carved, Painted, 16 In. | 7200 |
| Plaque, Birds, Flower Urn, Cast Iron, Black Paint, c.1870, 12 ½ x 30 ½ In. ...illus | 420 |
| Plaque, Bridge Sign, Cast Iron, Lassig Bridge, Chicago, 1899, 24 x 20 In. | 138 |
| Plaque, Eagle, Zinc, Iron, Spread Wing, Stars, Painted, c.1920, 18 x 31 In. | 540 |
| Plaque, Fan, Wood, White Paint, 1800s, 24 x 74 In., Pair | 300 |
| Plaque, North Wind God Face, Cast Iron, 18 x 24 In. | 70 |
| Plaque, Sun, Triangular Projections, Red, White Paint, c.1900, 69 In. | 805 |
| Plinth, Wood, Painted Red, Applied Diamonds, Gothic Arch Cutouts, 24 In. | 615 |
| Post Office, Window, Boxes, Wood, Metal, Glass, Ledge, 41 x 46 ½ In. ...illus | 480 |
| Roof Spire, Iron, Stylized Flower, Scrolls, Leaves, Black Paint, Wood Base, c.1860, 24 In. | 523 |
| Saloon Backbar, Mahogany, Front Bar, Princess, Brunswick Balke Collendar, 288 x 168 In. | 79800 |
| Screens are also listed in the Fireplace and Furniture categories. | |
| Screen Door, Painted, Blue, White, Red, Stripes, Stars, c.1910, 82 x 39 In. | 356 |
| Sink, Pedestal, Marble, Onyx, Backsplash, Shell Shape Bowl, Gold, Lapis Lazuli, 34 x 36 In. | 2760 |
| Tympanum, Madonna, Child Angels, Instruments, Blue, Demilune, Italy, c.1900, 24 x 47 In. | 1140 |
| Vent, Barn, Sheet Metal, Cylinder Over Taper Over Rectangle, Stamped 1935, 110 In. | 780 |
| Wall Bracket, Baroque Style, Marble Top, Walnut, Carved, Tapered, 23 x 39 In., Pair | 1500 |
| Wall Panel, Oak, Renaissance, Carved, 19th Century, 38 x 11 x 1 In. | 345 |
| Wall Sculpture, 2 Stallions, Enameled Wire, F. Weinberg, Philadelphia, 1950s, 34 x 36 In. | 469 |
| Window Cornice, Giltwood, Neoclassical, Pediment, Masque, Anthemia Surround, 18 x 74 In. | 922 |
| Window Grate, Iron, Oval, Geometric Bars, 1900s, 27 x 18 In. | 322 |

**Architectural,** Mantel, Fireplace, Softwood, Blue Paint, Lancaster County, Pa., c.1790, 60 x 69 In.
$1,062

Conestoga Auction Co., Inc.

**Architectural,** Mantel, Mixed Woods, Carved, Reeded, Grain Paint, Pennsylvania, c.1810, 61 x 67 In.
$150

Garth's Auctioneers & Appraisers

**Architectural,** Mantel, Walnut, Renaissance Revival, Shelf, Satyr Mask, Arch Opening, c.1890
$1,230

Neal Auction Co.

**TIP**
*A stained glass window is probably more stable than it looks. Small cracks in the glass, even a bowed window, are usually not a problem. Cracked solder joints between pieces of glass should be repaired.*

**Architectural,** Model, Spiral Staircase, Mahogany, Turned Balusters, Platform, 41½ In.
$2,460

New Orleans Auction Galleries, Inc.

**Architectural,** Overmantel Mirror, George III Style, Crest, Swags, c.1890, 51 x 60 In.
$2,749

Neal Auction Co.

**Architectural,** Panel, Cast Iron, Colossal Relief, Neptune Head, Crowned Cornice, 34½ In.
$11,950

Neal Auction Co.

**AREQUIPA POTTERY** was produced from 1911 to 1918 by the patients of the Arequipa Sanatorium in Marin County, north of San Francisco. The patients were trained by Frederick Hurten Rhead, who had worked at the Roseville Pottery.

| | |
|---|---:|
| **Vase,** Iris, Purple, Blue, White, Spreading Neck, California, c.1913, 10¾ x 88 In. | 2625 |
| **Vase,** Raised Leaves, Vertical Ribs, Gray Green Matte Glaze, Brown Trim, Shouldered, 6 In. | 580 |
| **Vase,** Scenic Landscape, Blues, Interior Glaze, Impressed Logo, 3½ In. | 690 |
| **Vase,** Stylized Pine Trees, Squeezebag, Frederick Rhead, c.1913, 6 x 3 In. .......*illus* | 32500 |

**ARGY-ROUSSEAU,** *see G. Argy-Rousseau category.*

**ARITA** is a port in Japan. Porcelain was made there from about 1616. Many types of decorations were used, including the popular Imari designs, which are listed under Imari in this book.

| | |
|---|---:|
| **Bowl,** Paneled, Blossoms, 6 In. | 42 |
| **Plate,** Sunrise, Mountain, Sea, Island, Sea Birds, Blue & White, Scalloped Edge, 8 In. | 150 |
| **Tureen,** Money Tree Design, Silkworm Finial, c.1850, 11¾ x 9 x 6 In. | 438 |
| **Vase,** 8-Sided, Flowers, Red, Blue, Green, 8 In. | 140 |

**ART DECO,** or Art Moderne, a style started at the Paris Exposition of 1925, is characterized by linear, geometric designs. All types of furniture and decorative arts, jewelry, book bindings, and even games were designed in this style. Additional items may be found in the Furniture category or in various glass and pottery categories, etc.

| | |
|---|---:|
| **Centerpiece,** Trumpet Vase, Green Glass, Bronze Nude Women Supports, Base, 1920, 19 In. | 923 |
| **Jar,** Lid, Floral Reserves, Gilt Bronze Mounts, Roses, Handles, Louis Dage, c.1925, 4 In. | 800 |
| **Lamp,** Train, Streamliner, 3 Cars, Track, Lighted, Cast Aluminum, Wood, 72 x 2 In. | 5843 |
| **Mirror,** 2 Women, Earthenware, Glazed, Keramos, Austria, 1920s, 16 x 13 In. .......*illus* | 1536 |
| **Mirror,** Patinated Metal, Oval, Edgar Brandt Style, France, 39 x 27½ In. | 2460 |
| **Smoking Stand,** Mico, Lighted Onyx Base, Embossed Tray Supports, Holder, Lighter, 28 In. | 115 |

**ART GLASS,** *see Glass-Art category.*

**ART NOUVEAU** is a style of design that was at its most popular from 1895 to 1905. Famous designers, including Rene Lalique and Emile Galle, produced furniture, glass, silver, metalwork, and buildings in the new style. Ladies with long flowing hair and elongated bodies were among the more easily recognized design elements. Copies of this style are being made today. Many modern pieces of jewelry can be found. Additional Art Nouveau pieces may be found in Furniture or in various glass categories.

| | |
|---|---:|
| **Frame,** Openwork Iris Border, Patinated Metal, Mirror Glass, Hinged Stand, 19 x 10 In. | 615 |
| **Lamp,** Figural, Depicting Loie Fuller, Bronze, Francois-Raoul Larche, c.1900, 18 x 8 In. | 4290 |
| **Vase,** Blue, Green, Porcelain, Gilt Bronze Base, Gold Foundry Disc, Paul Louchet, 9¾ In. | 288 |
| **Vase,** Red, Porcelain, Bronze Mount, Mermaid Leaping In Waves, Paul Louchet, 1898, 15 In. | 2300 |

**ART POTTERY,** *see Pottery-Art category.*

**ARTS & CRAFTS** was a design style popular in American decorative arts from 1894 to 1923. In the 1970s collectors began to rediscover Mission furniture, art pottery, metalwork, linens, and light fixtures from this period. The interest has continued. Today everything from this era is collectible, including jewelry, graphics, and silverware. Additional items may be found in the Furniture category and other categories.

| | |
|---|---:|
| **Cigar Cutter,** Figural, Toucan, Holding Bowl, c.1925, 4¼ x 8½ In. .......*illus* | 210 |
| **Mailbox,** Sheet Iron, Brass, Wood, Gargoyle, Paper Holder, c.1920, 15 x 7 In. | 75 |
| **Vase,** Pierced Copper Overlay, Blue, Green, Amber Glass, Austria, 9¼ x 5 In. | 633 |

**AURENE PIECES** *are listed in the Steuben category.*

**AUSTRIA** *is a collecting term that covers pieces made by a wide variety of factories. They are listed in this book in categories such as Royal Dux or Porcelain.*

**AUTO** parts and accessories are collector's items today. Gas pump globes and license plates are part of this specialty. Prices are determined by age, rarity, and condition. Signs and packaging related to automobiles may also be found in the Advertising category. Lalique hood ornaments will be listed in the Lalique category.

| | |
|---|---:|
| **Can,** Ace High Motor Oil, Race Car, Airplane, Red, Tin Lithograph, Qt. | 488 |
| **Can,** Amalie Motor Oil, The Oiler Oil, Tin, 1967, 33 x 24 In. | 210 |

| | |
|---|---|
| **Can,** Avio Motor Oil, Early Car, Airplane, Red Letters, White Ground, Tin Lithograph, Qt............. | 431 |
| **Can,** Golden Flash Motor Oil, Plane, Cars, Boats, Yellow, Red, Qt. ............................................. | 2400 |
| **Can,** Hi-Plane Motor Oil, Trademark Early Airplane, Red, Tin Lithograph, Soldier Seam, Qt. ...... | 2875 |
| **Can,** Indian Penn Motor Oil, Indian Chief, Yellow Ground, Tin Lithograph, Qt. ......................... | 920 |
| **Can,** Marathon Motor Oil, Green Letters, Cream Ground, Naked Runner, Qt. .............................. | 316 |
| **Can,** Motor Oil, Texaco, 5 Gal. .......................................................................................... | 57 |
| **Can,** Motor Seal Motor Oil, White, Green, Tin Lithograph, Qt................................................... | 150 |
| **Can,** Polarine Motor Oil, Flat, Metal, ½ Gal. ....................................................................... | 150 |
| **Can,** Silent Chief Oil, Cream Separator Oil, Black, Red Letters, Tin Lithograph, Qt. ................. | 1840 |
| **Can,** Sunoco Motor Oil, Yellow, Navy, Tin Lithograph, 5 Gal............................................... | 195 |
| **Can,** Vanderbilt Motor Oil, Cat, Jumping Through V, Yellow, Black, Qt................................... | 1020 |
| **Display,** Mobiloil Gargoyle Oil Can Rack, 2-Sided, Tin, 36 x 20 In....................................... | 660 |
| **Door Push,** Sprig, Marvelous Mixer, Green, Yellow, Porcelain, 12 x 3 ½ In. .......................... | 390 |
| **Flag,** Mobil Pegasus, Blue, White Check Ground, Cloth, Frame, 20 x 26 In. ........................... | 210 |
| **Gas Can,** Century, Outboard Motor, 1940s, 15 In. ................................................................ | 150 |
| **Gas Pump Globe,** Ashland, Flying Octanes, Wide Body, 1930s-40s, 17 ½ In. .............*illus* | 720 |
| **Gas Pump,** Bowser Texaco, Red, Milk Glass Globe, Dial Face .......................................*illus* | 2040 |
| **Gas Pump,** Fry, Mae West, Red & White Crown Shaped Glass Top Globe, Restored, 1920s............ | 5750 |
| **Gas Pump,** Texaco Fire-Chief, Light-Up Globe, Fireman's Hat, Red, White................................ | 2040 |
| **Gas Pump,** Tokheim No. 850, Clock Face, Square ....................................... 1920 to 3600 |
| **Globe Lens,** Unity Oil Co., Oh Boy What A Gas, Glass, Round, 1920s, 15 In., Pair.................... | 4972 |
| **Globe,** Atlantic Hi-Arc Gas, Milk Glass, Gill Lenses ............................................................ | 450 |
| **Globe,** Cyclo Ethyl No-Knock More Power Gas, Green, Red, Milk Glass, 13 ½ In....................... | 1320 |
| **Globe,** Dixie Ethyl, Blue, White, Capco Body, 13 ½ In............................................................ | 360 |
| **Globe,** Hiotane As New As Tomorrow, Rocket Logo, Red, White, Milk Glass, 13 ½ In................ | 780 |
| **Globe,** Lion, Logo Standing On Rock, Red, Black, White, Glass Body, 16 ½ In.......................... | 780 |
| **Globe,** Oil Creek Ethyl Logo, Green, Orange, White, Plastic Body, 15 In.................................. | 3000 |
| **Globe,** Pan-Am Gasoline Motor Oil, Red, Milk Glass, 15 In.................................................. | 570 |
| **Globe,** Service-Plus Premium, Ethyl Logo, Red, White Milk Glass, 13 ½ In. ............................ | 390 |
| **Globe,** Simms Gas, Cone Shape, Milk Glass, 12 In. ............................................................. | 600 |
| **Globe,** Simoniz Wax, Yellow, White, Round, Milk Glass, Etched, 14 In. .................................. | 1080 |
| **Globe,** Sohio Marine Gasoline Lens, Glass, Blue, White, 13 ½ In......................................... | 660 |
| **Globe,** Standard Oil Gold Crown, Milk Glass, 1-Piece Cast, 16 In.......................................... | 510 |
| **Globe,** Standard Oil Of Indiana Red Crown, Milk Glass, 1-Piece Cast, 16 In. .......................... | 330 |
| **Globe,** Sunland, Gasoline Higher Octane Lenses, Orange, White, Round, Metal, 15 In. .............. | 450 |
| **Globe,** That Good Gulf Gasoline, Etched Milk Glass, 16 In. ................................................. | 1320 |
| **Handle,** Gas Pump, Metal, 16 In. .................................................................................... | 234 |
| **Hood Ornament,** Dog, Greyhound, Mid-Sprint, Metal, 1900s, 9 ½ x 3 In. .................*illus* | 156 |
| **Hood Ornament,** Spirit Of Ecstasy, Woman Leaning Forward, Arms Stretched Back, 8 x 4 In..... | 247 |
| **License Plate Topper,** Tydol, Oil Man, White, Black, 6 ¾ x 4 ½ In. .....................*illus* | 94 |
| **License Plate,** Ohio, White, Red Ground, 1966.................................................................. | 8 |
| **License Plate,** Virginia, Green, White Porcelain, Baltimore Enamel & Novelty, 1912, 6 x 11 In. . | 374 |
| **Parking Meter,** Coin-Operated, Martin Red Ball, Pedestal Stand Base ................................. | 300 |
| **Pennant,** Hudson, Black, Yellow, Felt, Frame, 14 x 26 In.................................................... | 60 |
| **Pennant,** Oldsmobile, Red, White, Felt, 15 x 39 In........................................................... | 450 |
| **Plaque,** Chevrolet, America's First Choice In Cars, Trucks, Tin, Wood, 17 x 24 In. ................... | 300 |
| **Plate,** Chevrolet, America's Choice For 18 Yrs., 1930, 10 In.................................................. | 300 |
| **Pump Plate,** Blue Sunoco, Blue, Yellow, Red, Triangle, Porcelain, 22 x 18 In. .......................... | 510 |
| **Pump Plate,** BP, Green Yellow, Porcelain, 6 x 6 In............................................................... | 66 |
| **Pump Plate,** Cities Service Oils, Once Always, Round Black, White, Porcelain, 10 In. ................. | 660 |
| **Pump Plate,** Conoco, Red, White, Triangle Shape, Porcelain, 8 x 8 In.................................... | 150 |
| **Pump Plate,** Dixie 360, White, Red Gray Border, Porcelain, 8 x 13 In.................................... | 360 |
| **Pump Plate,** Douglas Winged Heart, Red, White, Porcelain, 18 x 12 In................................... | 840 |
| **Pump Plate,** Esso Elephant Kerosene, Red, White, Blue, 24 x 12 In........................................ | 420 |
| **Pump Plate,** Fill-Em Fast Gasoline, Red, Yellow, Porcelain, 10 x 16 In................................... | 240 |
| **Pump Plate,** Fire Chief Gasoline, Texaco, White T, Porcelain, Medium, 15 x 10 In. ................... | 270 |
| **Pump Plate,** Indian Gasoline, Art Deco Logo, Porcelain, 1940, 18 x 12 In............................... | 300 |
| **Pump Plate,** Mars, Red, White, Blue, Porcelain, 15 x 14 In.................................................. | 540 |
| **Pump Plate,** Mobilfuel Diesel, Pegasus Logo, Porcelain, 1954, 12 x 12 In. .............................. | 780 |
| **Pump Plate,** Platinum Plus, White, Red, Porcelain, 12 x 12 In............................................... | 390 |
| **Pump Plate,** Power The Gasoline That Has What It Takes, Red, White, Porcelain, 12 In. ............ | 2040 |
| **Pump Plate,** Standard Heating Oils, Red, White, Blue, Porcelain, 13 x 10 In............................ | 570 |
| **Pump Plate,** Texaco Diesel Chief, White T, Red, White, Porcelain, 1945, 18 x 12 In. ................. | 330 |
| **Pump,** Gasboy, Light-Up, Mobilgas Globe, 45 In............................................................... | 880 |
| **Ribbon,** Presentation, Cadillac, 10K Gold, Inlaid Cloisonne, Cloth Ribbon, 6 x 1 ¼ In................ | 604 |
| **Sign,** AAA Emergency Service, Black, White, Red, Oval, 2-Sided, Porcelain, 24 x 36 In............... | 390 |

**Architectural,** Plaque, Birds, Flower
Urn, Cast Iron, Black Paint, c.1870,
12 ½ x 30 ½ In.
$420

Garth's Auctioneers & Appraisers

**Architectural,** Post Office, Window,
Boxes, Wood, Metal, Glass, Ledge,
41 x 46 ½ In.
$480

Morphy Auctions

**Arequipa,** Vase, Stylized Pine Trees,
Squeezebag, Frederick Rhead, c.1913,
6 x 3 In.
$32,500

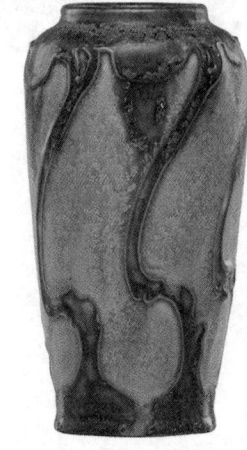

Rago Arts & Auction Center

**Art Deco,** Mirror, 2 Women, Earthenware, Glazed, Keramos, Austria, 1920s, 16 x 13 In.
$1,536

Rago Arts & Auction Center

## Collect License Plates

Why not collect automobile license plates, old, new, and unusual? It's a free hobby. Our local historical society has a display of plates dating back to the early 1900s tacked on a wall. I went to a bottle auction and in the parking lot there were three "bottle," two "ink," one "iclct" (I collect), and one "digger" license plate among the out-of-state cars.

**Arts & Crafts,** Cigar Cutter, Figural, Toucan, Holding Bowl, c.1925, 4¼ x 8½ In.
$210

Garth's Auctioneers & Appraisers

### TIP
*To remove a sticky price tag or instruction label from a newly purchased glass or metal object, try using a hair dryer. The heat should soften the glue and the paper will be easy to peel off.*

**Sign,** AC Spark Plug, Blue, Red, Flange, Tin, 12 x 15 In. ............................................ 330
**Sign,** Alemite Motor Oil, Logo, Die Cut, Green, Yellow, Orange, Porcelain, 6 x 7½ In. ...... 1200
**Sign,** Amalie Pennsylvania Motor Oil Tin Flange, 1950, 15 x 22 In. ............................. 510
**Sign,** Armstrong, Rhino-Flex Tires, Rhino Logo, Red, Cream, Black, Tin, Flange, 17 x 17 In. ...... 2700
**Sign,** Associated Gasoline, Logo, Orange, Green, Round, 2-Sided, Porcelain, 28 In. ............ 1200
**Sign,** Atlantic White Flash, Red, White, Blue, Porcelain, 52 x 36 In. ........................... 300
**Sign,** Atlas Guarantee, Red, Blue, Porcelain, 72 x 17 In. ...................................... 660
**Sign,** Auburn Tires, Red, White, Tin, 18 x 59 In. ........................................ 360 to 450
**Sign,** Auto-Lite Speedometer Service, Black, Yellow, Red, Glass, Light-Up, 10 x 23 In. ........ 900
**Sign,** Beacon Penn Motor Oil, Green, White Stripes, Yellow, 2-Sided, Porcelain, 30 x 30 In. ....... 480
**Sign,** Bear Wheel & Steering Service, Black, Yellow, Die Cut, Tin, 40 x 27 In. ................ 600
**Sign,** Bethlehem Motors, Studebaker, Sales, Service, Phone Number, Wood, 1930s, 77 In. ...... 472
**Sign,** BMW, Blue, White Logo, Black, Rim, Round, Porcelain, 24 In. .......................... 3300
**Sign,** Buick, 3-D, Motorized, 2-Sided, Eagle, Wings Move, Gold, Black, 61 x 31 In. ..........*illus* 1920
**Sign,** Cadillac, Script, Neon, 18 x 48 In. .................................................. 330
**Sign,** Calcoline Marine Products, Convex, Cream, Red, Blue, Tin, 1960, 20 x 28 In. ............ 420
**Sign,** California Route 66, Metal Stand, 25 x 15 In. ......................................*illus* 300
**Sign,** Champions, We Clean & Check Spark Plugs, Tin, Yellow, Black, Tin, 14 x 30 In. ........ 1680
**Sign,** Champlin Motor Oils Gasoline, Frame, 30 x 24 In. ..................................... 300
**Sign,** Chevrolet, Super Service, Porcelain, Blue, Yellow, White, 1930s, 42 In. Diam. ......... 3555
**Sign,** Cities Service Acme Batteries, Embossed, Green, Yellow, Tin, 59 x 16 In. .............. 1140
**Sign,** Cities Service, Black, White, Clover Shape, Porcelain, 15 In. ......................... 390
**Sign,** Cletrac Crawler Tractors, Orange, Blue, Porcelain Flange, 18 x 22 In. ................. 5100
**Sign,** Cliff Brice Quality Gas For Less, Oval, Green, Orange, 2-Sided, Porcelain, 39 x 66 In. ....... 900
**Sign,** Cooper Tires, Knight Logo, Red, Navy, Oval, 2-Sided, Tin, 30 x 48 In. .......... 420 to 480
**Sign,** Curt's Oil Co., Regular Gasoline, Embossed Tin, 16 x 12 In. ........................... 602
**Sign,** Deka Batteries Sold Here, White, Black Orange, Tin, 24 x 60 In. ...................... 120
**Sign,** Delco Batteries, 6 Volt Battery, Red, White, Tin, Wood Back, 1948, 70 x 19 In. ......... 1080
**Sign,** Derby Products, Red, Black, White, Round, 2-Sided, Porcelain, 30 In. .................. 450
**Sign,** Dixel Pioneer Oil Co., Round, Orange, Black, 2-Sided, Porcelain, 42 In. ............... 1320
**Sign,** Durant Motor Cars, Blue, Porcelain, 28 x 42 In. ...................................... 510
**Sign,** Fantasy Oilzum Motorcycle, Porcelain, 14 x 32 In. ................................... 1320
**Sign,** Federal Tires, Good For A Long Safe Ride, Embossed, Self-Framed, 60 x 14 In. ......... 170
**Sign,** Finest Service In Town, Gulflex Lubrication, Woman, Serving Tennis Ball, 42 x 27 In. ... 500
**Sign,** FoMoCo, Ford Parts, Red, White, 2-Sided, Porcelain, 14 x 18 In. ...................... 390
**Sign,** Ford, Oval, 2-Sided, Black, Red, Cream, Oval, Tin, 18 x 30 In. ........................ 1140
**Sign,** Gargoyle Mobil Oil, Red, White, Blue, Porcelain, Flange, 16 x 24 In. .................. 660
**Sign,** General Motors Trucks, Yellow, Black, Round, 2-Sided, Porcelain, 30 In. ............... 2160
**Sign,** Goldol Lion Oil, Lion Logo, Stripes, Stars, Porcelain, 29 x 39 In. ..................... 480
**Sign,** Goodrich Dealer, Silvertown Cord Tires, Blue, White, Tin Flange, 22 x 22 In. .......... 450
**Sign,** Goodrich Guide Post School Sign, Red, White, Round, Porcelain, 20 In. ................ 720
**Sign,** Goodrich Silvertowns, Black, White, 2-Sided, Porcelain Flange, 19 x 23 In. ............ 570
**Sign,** Goodyear Winged Feet, Die Cut, Yellow, Porcelain, 16 x 46 In. ........................ 600
**Sign,** Goodyear, Black, Gray, Yellow, Porcelain Flange, 34 x 2 In. ........................... 720
**Sign,** Gulflube The Highest Mileage Motor Oil, Black, White, Tin, 24 x 48 In. ................ 600
**Sign,** Havoline Motor Oil, Keeps Your Engine Clean, 2-Sided, Tin, 1947, 11 x 22 In. .......... 240
**Sign,** Havoline Motor Oil, Keeps Your Engine Clean, 2-Sided, Tin, 31 x 31 In. ............... 960
**Sign,** Hi-Duty Lubricants, Porcelain, Black, Red, White, 57 x 15 In. ......................... 1140
**Sign,** Highway, California 1, Metal, Shovel Shape, Property State Of California, 24 x 25 In. ...... 510
**Sign,** Highway, Speed Limit 260, Metal, Rectangular, Property Of Texas, 24 x 30 In. .......... 59
**Sign,** Highway, US 101, Metal, Shovel Shape, Property State Of California, 28 x 24 In. ........ 118
**Sign,** Hood Authorized Service, Man, Uniform, Red, White, Die Cut, Porcelain, Life Size ........... 4740
**Sign,** Hood Man, Red, White, Die Cut, Single-Sided Porcelain, 72 In. ....................... 10200
**Sign,** Hood Tires, Logo, Man Saluting, 2-Sided, Porcelain, 32 x 36 In. ...................... 960
**Sign,** Hood Tires, Yellow, Blue, Red, Round, 36 In. ......................................... 690
**Sign,** Hudson Service Essex, Red, White, Blue, 2-Sided, Porcelain, 16 x 30 In. ............... 510
**Sign,** Hudson, This Time It's Hudson, Turquoise Car, Logo, Plaster, Painted, c.1950, 8 x 12 In. ... 295
**Sign,** Interstate California 280, Shield Shape, Metal, Property State Of California, 36 x 36 In. .... 47
**Sign,** Iowa State Route No. 53, Black, Tan, Metal, Restored, 15 In. .......................... 150
**Sign,** Kelly Tires, Navy Blue, Red, Porcelain, 48 x 12 In. ................................... 450
**Sign,** Lacquerwax, Car Graphics, Embossed Tin, Yellow, Red, Green, 13 x 19 In. .............. 540
**Sign,** Linco Gasoline Oils, Round, 2-Sided, White, Red, Blue, Porcelain, 24 In. .............. 390
**Sign,** Linco Gasoline, Ethyl Logo, Round, White, Red, Black, 2-Sided, Porcelain, 30 In. ....... 540
**Sign,** Magolina Gasoline With Ethyl, Logo, Red, White, Round, 2-Sided, Porcelain, 30 In. ..... 780
**Sign,** Marathon Penn Motor Oil, Red Runner, Blue, White, Tin, 24 x 12 In. ................... 420
**Sign,** Mobil, Red, Porcelain, Cookie Cutter, 1952, 72 x 93 In. ............................... 4200

| | |
|---|---|
| **Sign,** Mobilgas, Pledge, Red, White, Porcelain, 8 x 8 In. | 600 |
| **Sign,** Mobiloil D, Motorcycle, Black, White, Porcelain, 9 x 11 In. | 1560 |
| **Sign,** Mobiloil Vacuum Oil Company, Red, White, Blue, Porcelain, Flange, 16 x 24 In. | 450 |
| **Sign,** Mobiloil, Authorized Service, Gargoyle, Red, Black, Porcelain, 1930s, 19 x 24 In. | 1450 |
| **Sign,** Motorcraft, Car, Blue, Red, Light-Up, Plastic, 10 x 23 In. | 270 |
| **Sign,** Nash, Fish Scales, Brown, Orange, White, Round, Light-Up, 32 x 12 In. | 6900 |
| **Sign,** Oak Motor Oil 30 Cents Per Quart, Red, Tin, 12 x 18 In. | 840 |
| **Sign,** Oakland Pontiac Sales, Service, Blue, White, 2-Sided, Porcelain, 24 x 36 In. | 570 |
| **Sign,** Oldsmobile Service, Yellow, Black, Porcelain, Flange, 16 x 22 In. | 900 |
| **Sign,** Parolene Motor Oil, Black, Green, Round, 2-Sided, Porcelain, 24 In. | 2700 |
| **Sign,** Pearl Oil Kerosene, Red, Black, Tin Flange, 18 x 12 In. | 1080 |
| **Sign,** Penn Drake Lubricants, Oil Well, Tan, Black, Tin Flange, 20 x 14 In. | 420 |
| **Sign,** Penn Drake Oil Double Mileage, White, Red, Black, 2-Sided, Die Cut, 27 x 21 In. | 270 |
| **Sign,** Phillips 66, The Gasoline That Won The West, Cowboy, Tin, 16 x 16 In. | 330 to 390 |
| **Sign,** Polarine, Standard Oil For Motor Cars, Porcelain Flange, 12 x 26 In. | 480 |
| **Sign,** Pontiac, Dollar For Dollar You Can't Beat It, Indian, Round, Plastic, Light-Up, 25 In. | 720 |
| **Sign,** Pontiac, Indian Profile, Feather, Round, Red, White, Porcelain, 42 In. | 4200 |
| **Sign,** Quaker State Motor Oil, Convex Green, White, Tin, 24 In. | 420 |
| **Sign,** Quaker State Motor Oil, Tombstone Shape, Porcelain, 26 x 30 In. | 293 |
| **Sign,** Race Car, Speeding, Multicolor, Marked M. Campion, Copyright 1912, 17 x 35 In. | 570 |
| **Sign,** Red Crown Gasoline, Black, Red, White, Round, 2-Sided, Porcelain, 30 In. | 2040 |
| **Sign,** Red Crown Gasoline, Crown, Red, White, Blue, Round, 2-Sided, Porcelain, 30 In. | 556 |
| **Sign,** Red Crown Gasoline, Logo, Red, White, Blue, Round, 2-Sided, Porcelain, 28 In. | 660 |
| **Sign,** Red Owl, Die Cut, Porcelain, 32 In. | 1680 |
| **Sign,** Riley Bros., That's Oil, Yellow, Black, Red, Tin, 6 x 13 In. | 150 |
| **Sign,** Riverside Tires Authorized Dealer, 2-Sided, Porcelain, 30 In. | 2160 |
| **Sign,** Rocolene, Black, Red, White, Round, Tin, 7 ½ x 7 In. | 180 |
| **Sign,** Shell, Gene's Automotive Service, Orange, Yellow, Round, Porcelain, 20 In. | 1920 |
| **Sign,** Shell, Orange, Shell Shape, Porcelain, Embossed, Die Cut, 48 x 48 In. | 1920 |
| **Sign,** Sinclair Gasoline, White, Red, Green Stripes, Round, 2-Sided, Porcelain, 24 In. | 780 |
| **Sign,** Sinclair Pennsylvania Mobiline Motor Oil, Red, White, Porcelain, 60 x 15 In. | 480 to 660 |
| **Sign,** Standard Motor Oil, White, Red, Oval, 2-Sided, Porcelain, 30 In. | 480 |
| **Sign,** Standard Oil Flame, Red, White, Screw Base, 20 In. | 660 |
| **Sign,** Standard Oil Zerolene For Motor Cars, Round, Blue, White, Porcelain, 24 x 25 In. | 660 |
| **Sign,** Standard Products, Cloud Logo, Black, Round, Porcelain, 39 x 66 In. | 1320 |
| **Sign,** Stop, Octagonal, Red & White, Metal, Porcelain, Reflective Buttons, 24 x 24 In. ........*illus* | 180 |
| **Sign,** Studebaker Sold Here, Round, Yellow, Red, Wood Spokes 2-Sided, Tin, c.1916, 14 In. | 4200 |
| **Sign,** Sunoco The Distilled Oil, Blue, Yellow, 2-Sided, Porcelain, 18 x 26 In. | 480 |
| **Sign,** Sunoco, Men's Rest Room, Gold, Blue, White, Porcelain, 3 x 7 In. | 270 |
| **Sign,** Texaco Diesel Chief, Porcelain, 12 x 18 In. | 360 |
| **Sign,** Texaco Diesel Fuel 2, White T, Green Ground, 1954, 18 x 12 In. | 600 |
| **Sign,** Texaco Farm Lubricants Sold Here, White T, Green, Porcelain, 1956, 30 x 42 In. | 510 |
| **Sign,** Texaco Filling Station, Red, Green, White, Round, Porcelain, c.1925, 42 In. | 3600 |
| **Sign,** Texaco Fire Chief, Helmet Logo, White T, Red, Porcelain, 1946, 18 x 12 In. | 240 |
| **Sign,** Texaco Motor Oil, Red, White, Green T, Round, Porcelain, 42 In. | 907 |
| **Sign,** Texaco Sky Chief, Gas Station Pump, Porcelain Plate, 12 x 18 In. | 180 |
| **Sign,** Texaco, Gas Station, Bubble Face, Plastic, Light-Up, Frame, Dimmer Switch, 1970s, 34 In. | 173 |
| **Sign,** Texaco, Light Of The Age Kerosene, Red, White, Porcelain Flange, 9 x 18 In. | 570 |
| **Sign,** Texaco, Red, Black, White, 2-Sided, Porcelain, 84 x 53 In. | 708 |
| **Sign,** Texas Pacific Gasoline, Ethyl Logo, Round, White, Green, 2-Sided, Porcelain, 30 In. | 2280 |
| **Sign,** Tiolene, Motor Oil, Blue, Yellow, Flange, Tin, 18 x 20 In. | 420 |
| **Sign,** TR Triumph, Red, Black, 2-Sided, Porcelain, 36 x 24 In. | 2700 |
| **Sign,** U.S. Tires, Blue, Yellow, Embossed, Tin, 1952, 61 x 16 In. | 570 |
| **Sign,** Use Veedol, World's Most Famous Motor Oil, Red, White, Round, Tin, 42 In. | 780 |
| **Sign,** Valvoline Costs Less, Orange, Green, Embossed, Tin, Donaldson Art Sign Co., 13 x 29 In. | 540 |
| **Sign,** Valvoline Motor Oil, Green, Yellow, Round, 2-Sided, Tin, 30 In. | 780 |
| **Sign,** Veedol 10-30 Motor Oil, Tan, Blue Tin Flange, 19 x 12 In. | 450 |
| **Sign,** Veedol Motor Oil Greases, Black, Orange, 2-Sided, Porcelain, 1930, 28 x 22 In. | 660 |
| **Sign,** Veedol, Motor Oil, Flying A Logo, Yellow, Black, Tombstone, 2-Sided, Tin, 35 x 27 In. | 510 |
| **Sign,** Veedol, Tidewater Logo, White, Red, Black, Round, Porcelain Flange, 20 x 21 In. | 480 |
| **Sign,** Wadhams, Tempered Motor Oil, Lubster Paddle, Round, 2-Sided, Tin, 7 In. | 210 |
| **Sign,** Wakefield Castrol Motor Oil, Yellow, Red, Black, Round, 2-Sided, Porcelain, 24 In. | 480 |
| **Sign,** Welch-Penn Motor Oil, Black, Yellow, Tin, Marked Scioto Sign, Ohio, 9 x 24 In. | 270 to 390 |
| **Sign,** White Star Gasoline, Blue, White, Round, 2-Sided, Porcelain, 41 In. | 1200 |
| **Sign,** William Penn Motor Oil, Lubester Paddle, Green, Red, 2-Sided, Tin, 7 In. | 150 |

**Auto,** Gas Pump Globe, Ashland, Flying Octanes, Wide Body, 1930s-40s, 17 ½ In. $720

Morphy Auctions

**Auto,** Gas Pump, Bowser Texaco, Red, Milk Glass Globe, Dial Face $2,040

Morphy Auctions

**Auto,** Hood Ornament, Dog, Greyhound, Mid-Sprint, Metal, 1900s, 9 ½ x 3 In. $156

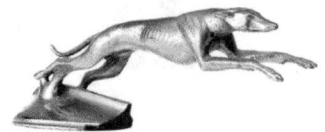

Garth's Auctioneers & Appraisers

**Auto,** License Plate Topper, Tydol, Oil Man, White, Black, 6¾ x 4½ In. $94

Conestoga Auction Co., Inc.

**Auto,** Sign, Buick, 3-D, Motorized, 2-Sided, Eagle, Wings Move, Gold, Black, 61 x 31 In. $1,920

Morphy Auctions

### Road Maps
The first automobile road maps were printed in 1914.

**Auto,** Sign, California Route 66, Metal Stand, 25 x 15 In. $300

Morphy Auctions

| | |
|---|---:|
| **Sign,** Wolf's Head Marine Oils, Red, White, Green, Tin, 1961, 8 x 18 In. | 330 |
| **Sign,** Wolf's Head Motor Oil, Oval, 2-Sided, Tin, 1968, 30 x 23 In. | 240 |
| **Sign,** Wolf's Head Oil, Revelation In Lubrication, Red, White, Green, Embossed, Tin, 14 x 20 In. | 1320 |
| **Sign,** Wyeth Tires, Boy, Driving Attire, Tires, Red, White, Blue, Porcelain, 22 x 16 In. | 19200 |
| **Signal,** Walk, Don't Walk, Signal Co. | 480 |
| **Spinner Steering Wheel Knob,** Bakelite, Marbled Butterscotch, Sinko Mfg., 1940s | 68 |
| **Spinner Steering Wheel Knob,** Wood, Pink, Dome Shape, 1940s | 58 |
| **Steering Wheel,** Nardi BMW, Wood, Aluminum | 420 |
| **Thermometer,** Standard Oil Of Indiana Red Crown, Porcelain, Wood Frame, 72 x 19 In. | 2040 |
| **Tin,** Mohair Top Dressing, Early Car, Yellow, 4 x 3½ In. | 276 |
| **Traffic Light,** Red, Yellow, Green Lights, Yellow Painted Metal, 30 In. | 70 |
| **Winter Engine Front,** Hupmobile, Adjustable Slits, Metal, c.1922, 22 x 19 In. | 21000 |

---

**AUTUMN LEAF** pattern china was made for the Jewel Tea Company beginning in 1933. Hall China Company of East Liverpool, Ohio, Crooksville China Company of Crooksville, Ohio, Harker Potteries of Chester, West Virginia, and Paden City Pottery, Paden City, West Virginia, made dishes with this design. Autumn Leaf has remained popular and was made by Hall China Company until 1978. Some other pieces in the Autumn Leaf pattern are still being made. For more prices, go to kovels.com.

| | |
|---|---:|
| **Baking Dish,** Swirl, 8 In. | 15 |
| **Bowl,** Salad, 9 In. | 14 |
| **Bowl,** Stacking, 1951, 18 Oz., 24 Oz., 34 Oz., 3 Piece | 75 |
| **Bowl,** Vegetable, Oval, 10⅜ In. | 15 to 22 |
| **Cake Plate,** 9½ In. | 28 |
| **Canister Set,** Tea, Coffee, Sugar, Flour, Plastic Lids, 1959 | 130 |
| **Coffeepot,** Drip-O-Lator, Ribbed, 8 Cup | 68 |
| **Cookie Jar,** Handles, Lid, 9 In. | 236 |
| **Creamer,** Fluted, 3½ In. | 45 |
| **Cup & Saucer** | 10 |
| **Custard Cup,** 4 Piece | 32 |
| **Drip Jar,** Lid, 5 In. | 19 |
| **Eggcup,** Double, 3¾ In. | 75 |
| **Gravy Boat** | 47 |
| **Jug,** Ball, 80 Oz. | 38 |
| **Jug,** Utility, 40 Oz. | 22 |
| **Mixing Bowl,** Gilt, Ribbed, Qt., 6 x 3½ In. | 20 |
| **Mixing Bowl,** Gilt, Ribbed, 4 Qt., 8½ x 3¾ In. | 24 |
| **Pitcher,** Milk, Ribbed Sides, Pinched Handle, 5¾ In. | 30 |
| **Pitcher,** Water, Ball | 55 |
| **Plate,** Dinner, 10⅛ In. | 32 |
| **Platter,** 11⅜ In. | 25 |
| **Platter,** 13⅝ In. | 28 |
| **Salt & Pepper,** Handles, 4½ In. | 28 to 29 |
| **Salt & Pepper,** Ruffled Base | 30 |
| **Sugar & Creamer,** Footed, Handles | 47 |
| **Sugar & Creamer,** Ruffled | 74 |
| **Teapot,** Aladdin | 58 |
| **Trivet,** 9½ In. | 25 |

---

**AVON** *bottles are listed in the Bottle category under Avon.*

---

**AZALEA** dinnerware was made for Larkin Company customers from 1918 to 1941. Larkin, the soap company, was in Buffalo, New York. The dishes were made by Noritake China Company of Japan. Each piece of the white china was decorated with pink azaleas.

| | |
|---|---:|
| **Butter Chip** | 59 |
| **Butter Tub,** Insert, 5 x 2½ In. | 45 |
| **Butter,** Cover, Round, Lb. | 70 |
| **Chocolate Pot Set,** Pot, Lid, Cup & Saucer, 6½ In., 10 Piece | 780 |
| **Compote,** 6½ In. | 80 |
| **Cup & Saucer,** Demitasse | 76 |
| **Dish,** Lemon, Handle, 5½ In. | 15 |
| **Gravy Boat,** Underplate, 8¼ In. | 28 |
| **Mustard Jar,** Lid, Spoon, 2 x 2 In. | 35 |
| **Pitcher,** 5½ In. | 89 |
| **Plate,** Bread & Butter, 6 In. | 10 |
| **Plate,** Dinner, 10½ In. | 30 |

| | | |
|---|---|---|
| **Plate,** Salad, 7 x 7 In. | | 50 |
| **Platter,** Oval, 11¾ In. | | 39 |
| **Spoon Holder,** Handles, 8 In. | | 70 |
| **Sugar & Creamer** | | 35 |
| **Sugar Shaker,** Oval, Footed | | 60 |
| **Teapot,** Lid, 5 In. | | 85 |

**BACCARAT** glass was made in France by La Compagnie des Cristalleries de Baccarat, located 150 miles from Paris. The factory was started in 1765. The firm went bankrupt and began operating again about 1822. Cane and millefiori paperweights were made during the 1845 to 1880 period. The firm is still working near Paris making paperweights and glasswares.

| | |
|---|---|
| **Bowl,** Rose Tint, Pillar & Scroll Design, Copper Plate Rim, 5 x 10 In. | 354 |
| **Centerpiece,** Starfish, 15½ In. | 330 |
| **Champagne Coupe,** Narcisse Pattern, Acid Etched Stamp, France, 1900s, 5½ In., 7 Piece | 523 |
| **Cologne Bottle,** Rose Tiente, 5 In. | 52 |
| **Decanter,** Bulbous Base, Prism Stopper, 12 In. | 90 |
| **Decanter,** Lid, Cobalt Blue Geometric Flowers, 17 In. | 563 |
| **Decanter,** Round, Indented Center, Fleur-De-Lis, Spikes, Stopper, 10¾ x 6½ In. | 431 |
| **Figurine,** Angel, Bowed Head, Crossed Arms, 6 In. | 69 |
| **Figurine,** Eagle, Clear, Marked, 10 In. | 200 |
| **Figurine,** Fish, Marked, 5½ x 2½ In. | 149 |
| **Flute,** Champagne, Clear, 8¼ In., 16 Piece | 688 |
| **Goblet,** Red Wine, Lyra, Acid Etched Mark, 7½ In., 16 In. | 1035 |
| **Ice Bucket,** Crystal, Faceted, Tongs, Signed, 1900s, 6 x 5¾ In. | 461 |
| **Ice Bucket,** Faceted Rim, Indented Center Band, Paneled Tapering Sides, 9 x 7½ In. | 184 |
| **Inkwell,** Flaubert, Cut Crystal, Stopper, 6 x 4¼ In. | 431 |
| **Inkwell,** Glass, Clear Swirl, Brass Collar, 5 x 6 In. | 189 |
| **Inkwell,** Hugo, Cut Crystal, Stopper, Signed Baccarat, 6 x 4¼ In. | 800 |
| **Inkwell,** Zola, Cut Crystal, Stopper, Signed Baccarat, 5 x 5½ In. | 431 |
| **Paperweight,** Blue Stars, Grindel Figures, Signed, 1970s, 2⅛ In. | 518 |
| **Paperweight,** Bouquet De Marriage, Stardust Canes, Blue, White, Lattice, 3 In. | 1363 |
| **Paperweight,** Clematis, Amethyst, Leaves, Red & White Cane Garland, 2½ In. | 972 |
| **Paperweight,** Concentric Millefiori, Blue, Brown, No. 13, 1970, 3 In. | 316 |
| **Paperweight,** Interlocking Garland, Blue, White, Salmon, Green Millefiori, 3¼ In. | 1358 |
| **Paperweight,** Millefiori Flowers, Stars, Rooster, Jester, Dog, Horse, 1847, 2 In. | 1375 |
| **Paperweight,** Millefiori Rows, Arrowhead, Stardust, Red, Blue, Green, 2½ In. | 1215 |
| **Paperweight,** Millefiori, Animal Canes, Dog, Monkey, Elephant, Muslin, 3 In. | 2014 |
| **Paperweight,** Millefiori, Arrow, Flower & Star Canes, Multicolor, 1848, 3 In. | 3159 |
| **Paperweight,** Millefiori, Multicolor, 3½ In. | 96 |
| **Paperweight,** Mt. Rushmore, Sulphide, Red, White, Blue, c.1976, 2½ x 4 In. | 58 |
| **Paperweight,** Mushroom, Multicolor, Faceted, 1970, 3 In. | 489 |
| **Paperweight,** Mushroom, Yellow, White Overlay, Faceted, 1970, 3½ In. | 431 |
| **Paperweight,** Pansy, Bud, Starburst Cane Garland, Star Cut Ground, 3 In. | 4148 |
| **Paperweight,** Pansy, Leaves, Purple, Cane Flower, Star Cut Base, 3 In. | 1718 |
| **Paperweight,** Random Millefiori, Latticinio, 1970, 3 In. | 288 |
| **Paperweight,** Yellow Heart, Millefiori Ground, 1970s, 3 In. | 345 |
| **Paperweight,** Yellow Pompom, Leaves, Red Bud, Millefiori Garland Rim, 2¾ In. *illus* | 3555 |
| **Urn,** Campana Shape, Acid Etch Mark, 8 In., Pair | 1179 |
| **Vase,** Angular, 4 Asymmetric Panels, Pinched Neck, Square Rim, 10¾ In. | 207 |
| **Vase,** Edith, 20th Century, 8 In. | 299 |
| **Vase,** Opalescent, Bamboo, Coiled Snake, Insect, Brass Ball Feet, 8¾ In. *illus* | 2963 |
| **Vase,** Repeated Diagonal Cuts, Globular Shape, 10 x 7 In. | 210 |

**BADGES** have been used since before the Civil War. Collectors search for examples of all types, including law enforcement and company identification badges. Well-known prison or law enforcement badges are most desirable. Most are made of nickel or brass. Many recent reproductions have been made.

| | |
|---|---|
| **Assistant Fire Chief,** Montgomery, Ala., Gold Wash, Red Enamel Tooling, c.1890, 1½ In. | 32 |
| **Ford,** Rouge, X1358, Embossed Factory, 1¾ x 1⅛ In. | 125 |
| **Friends Of The Phantom,** Brass, Shield, 1930s, 1 In. | 195 |
| **Indiana Chauffeur License,** Octagonal, 1947, 1¼ In. | 40 |
| **International Livestock Exposition,** Press, Green Enamel, Screw Back, 1 In. | 72 |
| **Masonic,** 14K Yellow Gold, Enamel, Crescent, Pharaoh's Head, Scimitar, Syria, ⅝ x ⅜ In. | 70 |
| **New York Chauffeur License,** Pinback, Oval, 1918, 1¼ x 1 In. | 28 |
| **Ohio Chauffeur,** Silver Tone Metal, Oval, 1950, 1¾ x 1⅜ In. | 35 |

**Auto,** Sign, Stop, Octagonal, Red & White, Metal, Porcelain, Reflective Buttons, 24 x 24 In.
$180

Morphy Auctions

**Baccarat,** Paperweight, Yellow Pompom, Leaves, Red Bud, Millefiori Garland Rim, 2¾ In.
$3,555

James D. Julia Auctioneers

**Baccarat,** Vase, Opalescent, Bamboo, Coiled Snake, Insect, Brass Ball Feet, 8¾ In.
$2,963

James D. Julia Auctioneers

**Bank,** Bank Building, Flat Iron, Kenton, M 1159, c.1915, 8¼ In. $10,200

RSL Auction

**Bank,** Board Of Trade, Bull & Bear, J.M. Harper, Chicago, c.1905, 4¼ In. $39,000

RSL Auction

**TIP**

*Reproduction mechanical banks are usually smaller than the originals because they were made using a real bank as the pattern. But some of the wooden patterns are still available, and banks made from these will be the identical size of an original old bank.*

| | |
|---|---:|
| **Police,** Crow Indian, Coin Silver, 1¾ In. | 308 |
| **Police,** Nevada City, State Of California Seal, 7-Point Star, Leaves, Embossed, 1940s, 3 In. | 135 |
| **Police,** Pittston, Pa., 10, Nickel, Shield, c.1900, 2½ x 2½ In. | 345 |
| **Police,** Sterling, Colorado, Brass, Lapel | 49 |
| **Yellow Cab,** Safe Driver, Enameled, 1930s, 1½ In. | 90 |

**BANKS** of metal have been made since 1868. There are still banks, mechanical banks, and registering banks (those that show the total money deposited on the face of the bank). Many old iron or tin banks have been reproduced since the 1950s in iron or plastic. Some old reproductions marked *Book of Knowledge, John Wright,* or *Capron* may be listed. Pottery, glass, and plastic banks are also listed here. Mickey Mouse and other Disneyana banks are listed in Disneyana. We have added the M numbers based on *The Penny Bank Book: Collecting Still Banks* by Andy and Susan Moore and the R numbers based on *Coin Banks by Banthrico* by James L. Redwine.

| | |
|---|---:|
| **Ambulance,** Red Cross, Gold Paint, Cast Iron, c.1900, 6 In. | 4800 |
| **Andy Gump,** 2 Figures, Pot Metal, Tin, 6 In. | 270 |
| **Andy Gump,** Paint, Cast Iron, Arcade, M 217, 4½ In. | 360 |
| **Bank Building,** Banque, Rooster Finial, Brass, M 1148, 6 In. | 364 |
| **Bank Building,** City Bank, Chimney, Cast Iron, Paint, Multicolor, M 1101, 6½ x 4½ In. | 4740 |
| **Bank Building,** Columbia Savings, Embossed, Cast Iron, Kenton, M 1073, 9 In. | 390 |
| **Bank Building,** Finial Bank, Cast Iron, Gilt Trim, Kyser & Rex, 5½ In. | 711 |
| **Bank Building,** Flat Iron, Cast Iron, Kenton, M 1162, 3¼ In. | 420 |
| **Bank Building,** Flat Iron, Kenton, M 1159, c.1915, 8¼ In. *illus* | 10200 |
| **Bank Building,** Green, Yellow, Orange Paint, Cast Iron, 5½ In. | 330 |
| **Bank Building,** Home Bank, Crown, Cast Iron, J. & E. Stevens, M 1232, 5¼ In. | 784 |
| **Bank Building,** Traders Bank, Yonge St., Cast Iron, Hinged, Cast Iron, c.1891, 8½ In. | 1107 |
| **Baseball Player,** Bat In Hand, Cast Iron, A.C. Williams, 6 In. | 300 |
| **Baseball,** Mobile Oil Premium, Pittsburgh Pirates, Pegasus, Steel Trap, 3 In. | 125 |
| **Battleship,** Oregon, Gray, Yellow, Red, Paint, Cast Iron, 6 In. | 270 |
| **Battleship,** White Paint, Cast Iron, J. & E. Stevens, 10½ In. | 510 |
| **Bear Stealing Pig,** Standing, Gold Paint, Cast Iron, M 593, 6 In. | 450 |
| **Bear With Honey Pot,** Brown, Blue, Yellow Paint, Cast Iron, Hubley, M 717, 7 In. | 150 |
| **Beehive,** Gold Paint, Cast Iron, 8-Footed, John Harper, M 686, 4½ In. | 1920 |
| **Billy Bounce,** Gold Paint, Cast Iron, Hubley, M 15, 4½ In. | 150 |
| **Bird On Stump,** Gold Paint, Cast Iron, A.C. Williams, 5 In. | 360 |
| **Black Man With Umbrella,** Painted, Black, Red Coat, Cane, Cast Iron, 7⅓ In. | 180 |
| **Board Of Trade,** Bull & Bear, J.M. Harper, Chicago, c.1905, 4¼ In. *illus* | 39000 |
| **Boy With Football Over Head,** Paint, Cast Iron, Hubley, M 10, 5⅛ In. | 1180 |
| **Buffalo,** Red Paint, Arcade, 1920-25, M 560, 3 x 4 In. | 78 |
| **Building,** 1882 Church, Cast Iron, Cream, Green Roof, Kyser & Rex, 5¼ x 4 In. | 3258 |
| **Building,** Bungalow, Cast Iron, Tin, Grey Iron Casting, M 999, 3¾ In. | 336 |
| **Building,** Castle With 2 Towers, Cast Iron, John Harper, M 1114, 7 In. | 678 |
| **Building,** Eiffel Tower, Cast Iron, M 1075, 10⅜ In. | 3360 |
| **Building,** Independence Hall, Cast Iron, Enterprise, M 1244, 8⅞ In. | 420 to 1120 |
| **Building,** Independence Tower, Green, Brown Paint, Cast Iron, Enterprise, M 1202, 9½ In. | 240 |
| **Building,** Mosque, Domed, Cast Iron, Yellow, Grey Iron Casting, M 1177, 4¼ In. | 364 |
| **Building,** Multiplying, Gothic Columns, Glass Doorway, Iron, J. & E. Stevens, c.1883, 6½ In. | 1353 |
| **Building,** Palace, Cast Iron, Japanned, Ives, M 1116, c.1885, 7½ x 8 In. *illus* | 2160 |
| **Building,** Palace, Painted, Green, Red Roof, Gold Trim, Ives Blakeslee, 8 x 5 In. *illus* | 18368 |
| **Building,** Palace, Red Finial, Black Paint, Cast Iron, 6 In. | 300 |
| **Building,** Town Hall, Painted Yellow, Cast Iron, Kyser & Rex, M 998, 4½ In. | 4977 |
| **Building,** Westminster Abbey, Cast Iron, 6⅜ In. | 226 |
| **Camel,** Gray Paint, Cast Iron, A.C. Williams, M 767, 7½ In. | 150 |
| **Captain Kidd,** Cast Iron, Ives, M 38, c.1901 | 700 |
| **Car,** Armored, 2 Gens, Red Body, Gold Wheels, A.C. Williams, M 1424, 7 In. | 617 |
| **Cash Register,** Nickels, Dimes, Quarters, Opens Every 10 Dollars, Buddy L. | 20 |
| **Child,** Kneeling, Praying, Green, Blue, Gray Paint, Wood, Composition, 9 In. | 360 |
| **Circuit Rider,** Coin Slot In Mane, Japanned, Gold Trim, M 53, c.1890, 5¾ x 7 In. *illus* | 39600 |
| **Cupola,** Painted, Stenciled Red Roof, J. & E. Stevens, M 1145, 5½ In. | 711 |
| **Dog,** Spaniel, Seated, Facing Left, Chocolate Manganese Glaze, C. Bell, Virginia, 9½ In. | 460 |
| **Dreadnaught,** Cast Iron, Paint, Embossed, Sydenham & McOustra, M 1314, c.1915, 7 In. | 148 |
| **Dutch Girl,** Green Paint, Cast Iron, Grey Iron Casting, M 16, 6½ In. | 150 |
| **Elephant,** Cast Iron, Painted Red, 4 x 3 In. | 59 |
| **Elephant,** White, Red, Blue Paint, Cast Iron, 9½ In. | 210 |
| **Federal Washing Machine,** Figural, Die Cut, Tin Lithograph, 1920s, 2½ x 4¼ In. *illus* | 173 |
| **Football Player,** Cast Iron, A.C. Williams, M 11, 5½ In. | 330 |

B

| | | |
|---|---|---|
| **Frog,** Professor Pug, Green, Yellow Paint, Cast Iron, A.C. Williams, M 311, 3 In. | | 360 |
| **Gas Pump,** Cast Iron, Attached Hose, Paint, Arcade, M 1485, 5¾ x 2¼ In. | | 266 |
| **Globe,** World Bank, As You Save, So You Prosper, Tin, Ohio Art Co., c.1960, 5 In. | | 22 |
| **Golliwog,** Blue, Red, Tan Paint, Cast Iron, England, 6 In. | | 600 |
| **Goodyear Zeppelin,** Hanger, Duralumin, Embossed, Ferrosteel, M 1430, c.1930, 7 In. | | 201 |
| **Grandpa,** Character, Tin Lithograph, Coin Slot In Back, 3¾ x 2¼ In. | *illus* | 316 |
| **Gulf Oil,** Cardboard, 3 Gas Pumps, 3⅞ x 4 x 1 In. | | 23 |
| **House With Bay Window,** Cast Iron, Painted, Multicolor, M 1212, 4 In. | | 2370 |
| **Key Shape,** Cast Iron, 5¾ In. | | 510 |
| **Kneeling Boy,** Yellow Paint, Cast Iron, 7 In. | | 120 |
| **Liberty Bell,** Amber Glass, Original Closure | | 82 |
| **Mammy,** Blue Bandanna, Red, White Dress, M 176, 5½ In. | | 180 |
| **Mammy,** Blue Dress, White Apron, Red Headscarf, Cast Iron, A.C. Williams, c.1905, 6 In. | | 121 |

**Mechanical banks** were first made about 1870. Any bank with moving parts is considered mechanical. The metal banks made before World War I are the most desirable. Copies and new designs of mechanical banks have been made in metal or plastic since the 1920s. The condition of the paint on the old banks is important. Worn paint can lower a price by 90 percent.

| | | |
|---|---|---|
| **Mechanical,** Aeroplane, Spiraling, Paint, Cast Iron, Starkie England, c.1920 | | 5400 |
| **Mechanical,** Artillery Bank, Cast Iron, J.& E. Stevens, c.1920, 8 In. | | 660 |
| **Mechanical,** Bad Accident, Child Frightens Mule, Paint, Cast Iron, J. & E. Stevens, 10 In. | | 780 |
| **Mechanical,** Bank Building, Hall's Excelsior, Paint, Cast Iron, J.& E. Stevens, 6 In. | | 210 |
| **Mechanical,** Bank Building, Hall's Excelsior, Paint, Cast Iron, J. & E. Stevens, c.1870, 5½ In. | | 5100 |
| **Mechanical,** Bank Building, Multicolor Paint, Cast Iron, J. & E. Stevens, 7 In. | | 360 |
| **Mechanical,** Bear, Protruding Tongue, Saalheimer & Strauss, c.1920, 5 In. | | 3600 |
| **Mechanical,** Beehive, Gold Paint, Cast Iron, Embossed Accumulated, 7 In. | | 660 |
| **Mechanical,** Bill E Grin, White, Black, Orange Paint, J. & E. Stevens, 4½ In. | | 540 |
| **Mechanical,** Billy Goat, Paint, Cast Iron, J. & E. Stevens, Pat. 1910 | | 2700 |
| **Mechanical,** Bird In Cage, Nickel Plated Cage, Paint, Iron, G. Zimmerman Co., 1929, 4 In. | | 6000 |
| **Mechanical,** Bird On Roof, Paint, Cast Iron, J. & E. Stevens, c.1880 | | 2400 |
| **Mechanical,** Bonzo Bank, Verse, Tin Lithograph, Saalheimer & Strauss, c.1920, 7 In. | | 1020 |
| **Mechanical,** Bowing Man In Cupola, Building, Paint, Cast Iron, J. & E. Stevens, c.1880 | | 30000 |
| **Mechanical,** Box Only, Funny Clown, Wooden, J. & E. Stevens, 9½ x 6 In. | *illus* | 374 |
| **Mechanical,** Boy On Trapeze, Paint, Cast Iron, J. Barton Smith, c.1888, 9½ In. | | 720 to 6600 |
| **Mechanical,** Boy Robbing Bird's Nest, J. & E. Stevens | *illus* | 3540 |
| **Mechanical,** Boy Scout Camp, Tent, Paint, Cast Iron, J. & E. Stevens, 9 In. | | 2400 |
| **Mechanical,** Boy Stealing Watermelon, Paint, Cast Iron, Kyser & Rex, 6½ In. | | 7800 |
| **Mechanical,** Bread Winners, Hammer Raised, Paint, Cast Iron, J. & E. Stevens, c.1886 | | 20400 |
| **Mechanical,** Buffalo, Head Down, Tail Twists, Brown Paint, Cast Iron, 9 In. | | 540 |
| **Mechanical,** Bulldog, Seated, Red Glass Eyes, Cast Iron, J. & E. Stevens, 8 In. | | 1020 |
| **Mechanical,** Bulldog, Standing, Brown Paint, Cast Iron, Judd Manufacturing, 7 In. | | 300 |
| **Mechanical,** Butting Goat & Tree Stump, Brown Paint, Cast Iron, 4½ In. | | 480 |
| **Mechanical,** Cabin, Cast Iron, Yellow & Red Paint, Figure At Door, J. & E. Stevens, 3¾ In. | | 584 |
| **Mechanical,** Cabin, Green, Black Man, Paint, Cast Iron, J. & E. Stevens, c.1890 | | 2160 |
| **Mechanical,** Cabin, Painted, Cast Iron, J. & E. Stevens, 4¼ In. | | 900 |
| **Mechanical,** Cabin, Yellow Paint, Cast Iron, J. & E. Stevens, 4½ In. | | 240 |
| **Mechanical,** Calamity, Football, Ball Carrier, Paint, Cast Iron, J. & E. Stevens, c.1904, 6 In. | | 27000 |
| **Mechanical,** Called Out, Soldier Leaves Tent, Cast Iron, J. & E. Stevens, c.1917 | | 1200 |
| **Mechanical,** Chief Big Moon, Frog, Indian, J. & E. Stevens, 10 In. | | 4500 |
| **Mechanical,** Chimpanzee, Ledger, Kyser & Rex, Patented 1880 | | 6000 |
| **Mechanical,** Circus, Clown In Cart, Turntable, Crank, Cast Iron, Shepard Hardware, 7 In. | | 3835 |
| **Mechanical,** Clown On Bar, Balancing, Paint, Cast Iron, Tin, C.G. Bush Co., c.1880 | | 120000 |
| **Mechanical,** Clown On Globe, Painted, Windup, Spins, Cast Iron, J. & E. Stevens, 11 In. | | 885 to 1353 |
| **Mechanical,** Cowboy, Tray, Please One Penny!, Tin Lithograph, Klein Co., Germany, 1920s, 6 In. | | 1080 |
| **Mechanical,** Creedmoor, Soldier, Feather Cap, Wood, Cast Iron, J. & E. Stevens, c.1920, 10 In. | | 4200 |
| **Mechanical,** Creedmoor, Soldier, Shooting, Paint, Cast Iron, J. & E. Stevens, c.1880, 10 In. | | 420 |
| **Mechanical,** Darktown Battery, 3 Baseball Players, Paint, Iron, J. & E. Stevens, 9½ In. | | 1020 |
| **Mechanical,** Dinah, Black Woman, Short Sleeves, Cast Iron, England, 7 In. | | 330 |
| **Mechanical,** Dinah, Yellow Dress, Paint, Cast Iron, 6 In. | | 840 |
| **Mechanical,** Dog On Turntable, Brown Paint, Cast Iron, Judd, 5 In. | | 270 |
| **Mechanical,** Dog Tray, Red, Blue Paint, Cast Iron, Kyser & Rex, c.1890, 4 x 4 In. | | 1800 |
| **Mechanical,** Dog, Nodding, Yellow, Saddle, Paint, Tin, c.1910, 5¾ In. | | 1920 |
| **Mechanical,** Eagle & Eaglets, Painted, Glass Eyes, Cast Iron, J. & E. Stevens, 6 In. | | 390 to 690 |
| **Mechanical,** Elephant & 3 Clowns On Tub, Multicolor Paint, Cast Iron, J. & E. Stevens, 6 In. | | 1140 |
| **Mechanical,** Elephant, Howdah, Brown, Green Paint, Cast Iron, 7 In. | | 240 |
| **Mechanical,** Elephant, Trunk Upturned, White, Red Paint, Cast Iron, Hubley, 8 In. | | 120 |

**Bank,** Building, Palace, Cast Iron, Japanned, Ives, M 1116, c.1885, 7½ x 8 In.
$2,160

Bertoia Auctions

**Bank,** Building, Palace, Painted, Green, Red Roof, Gold Trim, Ives Blakeslee, 8 x 5 In.
$18,368

James D. Julia Auctioneers

**Bank,** Circuit Rider, Coin Slot In Mane, Japanned, Gold Trim, M 53, c.1890, 5¾ x 7 In.
$39,600

RSL Auction

**Bank,** Federal Washing Machine, Figural, Die Cut, Tin Lithograph, 1920s, 2½ x 4¼ In.
$173

Hake's Americana & Collectibles

**Bank,** Grandpa, Character, Tin Lithograph, Coin Slot In Back, 3¾ x 2¼ In.
$316

Wm Morford Auctions

**Bank,** Mechanical, Box Only, Funny Clown, Wooden, J. & E. Stevens, 9½ x 6 In.
$374

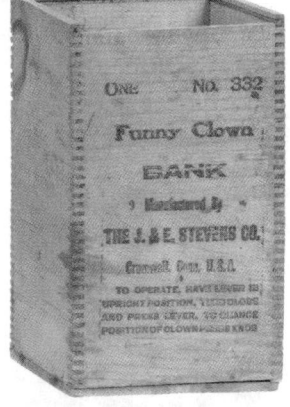

Wm Morford Auctions

**Bank,** Mechanical, Boy Robbing Bird's Nest, J. & E. Stevens
$3,540

Bertoia Auctions

| | |
|---|---|
| **Mechanical,** Feed The Kitty, Cast Iron, Painted, 1925 ...............*illus* | 5400 |
| **Mechanical,** Ferris Wheel, Paint, Cast Iron, Hubley, 1930s............... | 5100 |
| **Mechanical,** Football, Player Kicks Coin Into Net, Cast Iron, Painted, John Harper, 10 In.......... | 1121 |
| **Mechanical,** Fortune Teller Savings, Nickel Plated, Cast Iron, Baumgarten & Co., c.1905, 7 In.. | 4800 |
| **Mechanical,** Frog On Rock, Green, Orange Paint, Cast Iron, Kilgore, c.1920, 3½ In............... | 1020 |
| **Mechanical,** Frog On Round Base, Lattice, Cast Iron, Black, Red, J. & E. Stevens, 4 In............... | 540 |
| **Mechanical,** Frog On Round Base, Lattice, Cast Iron, Green, Red, J. & E. Stevens, 4 In............... | 944 |
| **Mechanical,** Frog On Round Base, Tan Lattice, Paint, Cast Iron, J. & E. Stevens, c.1875, 5 In. .... | 5700 |
| **Mechanical,** Frogs, Two, Cast Iron, J. & E. Stevens, 1882, 8¾ In. | 780 |
| **Mechanical,** Frogs, Two, Cast Iron, Painted, J. & E. Stevens, c.1882, 4¼ In. | 1169 |
| **Mechanical,** Germania Exchange, Goat On Barrel, Cast Iron, J. & E. Stevens, c.1880 ................... | 19200 |
| **Mechanical,** Grenadier, Cast Iron, Painted, John Harper, c.1885, 6¾ In. | 390 to 461 |
| **Mechanical,** Grenadier, Man Pointing Rifle At Tree Stump, Iron, J. & E. Stevens, 10 In. | 300 |
| **Mechanical,** Guessing, Man, Seated, Pays 5 For 1, Cast Iron, c.1880 | 8400 |
| **Mechanical,** Hall's Liliput, Cast Iron, Painted, J. & E. Stevens, 4 In. | 325 |
| **Mechanical,** Hall's Liliput, Man, Tray, Paint, Cast Iron, J.E. Stevens, c.1880, 3 In. | 1560 |
| **Mechanical,** Happy Clown, Tin Lithograph, Germany, 1920s, 3½ In. | 1680 |
| **Mechanical,** Hen & Chick, White, Green Paint, Cast Iron, J. & E. Stevens, 10 In. | 1920 |
| **Mechanical,** Hen On Nest, White Hen, Lever, Paint, Cast Iron, J. & E. Stevens, c.1910 ................ | 1680 |
| **Mechanical,** Hindu, Red Shirt, Paint, Cast Iron, Kyser & Rex, c.1928, 5½ In. | 1800 |
| **Mechanical,** Hold The Fort, Moody & Sanky, Smith & Egge, 5 In. | 5925 |
| **Mechanical,** Horse Race, Cast Iron, J. & E. Stevens, Box, 1871 Patent, 6½ In. | 51000 |
| **Mechanical,** Horse Race, Straight Base, J. & E. Stevens, Patented 1871 | 3540 |
| **Mechanical,** Horse Race, Tin, Paint, Cast Iron, Pull Cord, J. & E. Stevens, c.1875, 6½ In. | 1680 |
| **Mechanical,** Horse, Paws Ground, Black, Red, Paint, Cast Iron, c.1890 | 24000 |
| **Mechanical,** I Always Did 'Spise A Mule, Cast Iron, Painted, J. & E. Stevens, 8 In. | 615 |
| **Mechanical,** I Always Did 'Spise A Mule, Orange, Cast Iron, J. & E. Stevens, Pat. 1897, 10 In. .... | 1440 to 3000 |
| **Mechanical,** Independence Hall Tower, Brown Paint, Cast Iron, Enterprise, 9½ In. ....... | 510 to 2133 |
| **Mechanical,** Indian Shooting Bear, Cast Iron, Brown, Yellow, Red, c.1900, J. & E. Stevens, 10 In. | 1200 |
| **Mechanical,** Initiating, 1st Degree, Black Man, Frog, Goat, Cast Iron, 1886 Patent, 10¼ In. ...... | 9600 |
| **Mechanical,** Jolly Joe Clown, Tin Lithograph, Saalheimer & Strauss, Germany, c.1930, 7 In. ..... | 780 |
| **Mechanical,** Jonah & The Whale, Cast Iron, Shepard Hardware, Pat. 1890, 9½ In. ........ | 600 to 1888 |
| **Mechanical,** King Aqua, Rifle, Red & White Striped Tower, Queen, Iron, Germany, c.1900 .......... | 27000 |
| **Mechanical,** Lehmann London Tower, Blue, Tin Lithograph, Flag, c.1930, 4 In. | 11400 |
| **Mechanical,** Liberty Bell, Centennial, Paint, Cast Iron, Enterprise Mfg., c.1880, 5½ In. ............ | 2400 |
| **Mechanical,** Lighthouse, Red, Green, Black Paint, Cast Iron, 10 In. | 3600 |
| **Mechanical,** Lion & 2 Monkeys, Tree Stump, Cast Iron, Brass, Painted, Kyser & Rex, 9 In. | 649 to 9600 |
| **Mechanical,** Lion Hunter, Paint, Cast Iron, J. & E. Stevens, Pat. 1911 | 9600 |
| **Mechanical,** Little Joe, Paint, Cast Iron, John Harper, c.1920, 5 In. | 1020 |
| **Mechanical,** Magician, Cast Iron, J. & E. Stevens, c.1901, 8 In. | 1353 |
| **Mechanical,** Mammy & Child With Spoon, Paint, Cast Iron, Kyser & Rex, 8 In. | 1080 |
| **Mechanical,** Mammy & Child, With Spoon, Green Dress, Kyser & Rex, 1884 Patent, 7½ In. ........ | 25200 |
| **Mechanical,** Man In Barrel, Paint, Cast Iron, 4 In. | 570 |
| **Mechanical,** Mary Roebling, Trenton Trust, Cast Iron, Painted, Grey Iron Casting ..................... | 420 |
| **Mechanical,** Mason, Bricklayers, Wall, Cast Iron, Shepard Hardware, 7½ In. | 948 |
| **Mechanical,** Milking Cow, J. & E. Stevens, c.1890, 9½ In. | 3600 |
| **Mechanical,** Monkey & Parrot, Tin Lithograph, Saalheimer & Strauss, 1930s, 6 In. | 540 |
| **Mechanical,** Monkey Bank, Green Base, Cast Iron, Hubley, c.1925, 9 In. | 1440 |
| **Mechanical,** Monkey Face, Arched Top, Red, White, Tin Lithograph, England, c.1925, 4⅜ In...... | 3000 |
| **Mechanical,** Monkey With Tray, Tin Lithograph, Maienthau & Wolf, c.1908, 6½ In. | 540 |
| **Mechanical,** Monkey, Man Holding Box, Red, Green, Black Paint, Cast Iron, Hubley, 9 In.......... | 210 |
| **Mechanical,** Mortar Bank, Soldier, Paint, Cast Iron, J. & E. Stevens, c.1892 | 1920 |
| **Mechanical,** Mosque, Dome, Iron, Gorilla, Gilt, Judd Mfg., 8½ x 6 In. | 864 |
| **Mechanical,** Mule Entering Barn, Silver, Orange, Ocher Paint, J. & E. Stevens, 8½ In. | 660 |
| **Mechanical,** New Bank, Soldier In Door, J. & E. Stevens, 6 x 4½ In. | 3318 |
| **Mechanical,** Novelty Bank, Cast Iron, Door Opens, J. & E. Stevens, 6½ In. | 590 to 800 |
| **Mechanical,** Ole Puffer, Bulldog, Hat, Cigar, Cast Iron, Xonex, Reproduction, 8½ In. | 58 |
| **Mechanical,** Organ, Boy & Girl, Cast Iron, Painted, Kyser & Rex, 8 In. | 677 |
| **Mechanical,** Organ, Monkey Tips Cap, Side Crank, Paint, Cast Iron, Judd, 7 In. | 240 |
| **Mechanical,** Owl Turns Head, Blue, Green & Brown Paint, Cast Iron, J. & E. Stevens, 7½ In. ..... | 600 |
| **Mechanical,** Owl Turns Head, Gold, Brown Paint, J. & E. Stevens, 7½ In. | 960 |
| **Mechanical,** Owl Turns Head, Paint, Cast Iron, J. & E. Stevens, Pat. 1880, 7½ In. | 8400 |
| **Mechanical,** Paddy & The Pig, J. & E. Stevens, 7 x 8 In. | 607 |
| **Mechanical,** Panorama, Bank, Paint, Cast Iron, J. & E. Stevens, c.1880, 11 x 18 In. | 14400 |
| **Mechanical,** Peg Leg Beggar, Black Man, Holds Hat, Cast Iron, Judd, 5 In. | 590 |
| **Mechanical,** Pelican With Mammy, Cast Iron, Trenton Hardware, c.1878, 7½ In. | 1280 |

| | | |
|---|---|---|
| Mechanical, Penny Pineapple, Grinning Face, Multicolor, 9 In. | | 210 |
| Mechanical, Pig In High Chair, Paint, Cast Iron, J. & E. Stevens, 6 In. | | 450 to 570 |
| Mechanical, Preacher In The Pulpit, Red, Paint, Cast Iron, J. & E. Stevens, c.1876 | | 252000 |
| Mechanical, Presto, Cast Iron, Kyser & Rex | | 120 |
| Mechanical, Punch & Judy, Cast Iron, Painted, Shepard Hardware, 7 ½ In. | | 330 to 4200 |
| Mechanical, Rabbit Standing, Small, Gold Paint, Cast Iron, Lockwood Mfg., c.1882, 6 x 3 In. | | 1800 |
| Mechanical, Reclining Chinese Man, Holds 4 Aces, Rat, Cast Iron, J. & E. Stevens, 8 In. | | 2242 to 5100 |
| Mechanical, Red Riding Hood By Grandma's Bed, Paint, Cast Iron, c.1880, 8 In. | | 30000 |
| Mechanical, Roller Skating Rink, Skaters, Kyser & Rex, 8¾ x 8½ In. | | 9720 |
| Mechanical, Rooster, Cast Iron, Brown, Red, Green, Kyser & Rex, 6½ In. | | 600 |
| Mechanical, Santa Claus, Chimney, Cast Iron, Shepard Hardware, 6 In. | | 708 |
| Mechanical, Santa Claus, Gray Coat, Shepard Hardware, 1889, 6 In. | | 660 |
| Mechanical, Sentry Bank, Paint, Cast Iron, J. & E. Stevens, c.1872 | | 15600 |
| Mechanical, Sewing Machine, Crank, Needle Moves, Black, Iron, American Bank, 5½ In. | | 27000 |
| Mechanical, Speaking Dog, Girl, Red Dress, Cast Iron, Shepard Hardware, 7½ In. | | 540 to 1020 |
| Mechanical, Stump Speaker, Black Man, Carpet Bag, Cast Iron, Shepard Hardware, 9¾ In. | | 677 to 1440 |
| Mechanical, Tabby, Crouched On Egg, Chick, Black Paint, Cast Iron, Footed, 5 In. | | 420 |
| Mechanical, Tammany, Cast Iron, Painted, J. & E. Stevens, 6 In. | | 246 to 480 |
| Mechanical, Tank & Cannon, Green Paint, Cast Iron, Starkie, 10 In. | | 390 |
| Mechanical, Taxi Cab, Green, Yellow, Tin Lithograph, Fischer, c.1915, 7½ In. | | 8400 |
| Mechanical, Teddy & The Bear, J. & E. Stevens, 1907, 10 In. | | 467 |
| Mechanical, Teddy & The Bear, J. & E. Stevens, c.1910, 10 In. | | 4500 |
| Mechanical, Thrifty Tom's Jigger, Tin Lithograph, Windup, Slot On Base, F. Strauss, c.1915, 10 In. | | 660 |
| Mechanical, Toad On Stump, Brown, Green Paint, Cast Iron, J. & E. Stevens, 3½ In. | | 420 |
| Mechanical, Tommy, Soldier, Rifle, John Harper, England, c.1920 | | 4200 |
| Mechanical, Tower, Dark Brown, Enterprise Manufacturing Co., 9½ In. | | 180 |
| Mechanical, Trick Dog, Multicolor Paint, Cast Iron, Hubley, 8½ In. | | 180 |
| Mechanical, Trick Pony, Cast Iron, Painted, Shepard Hardware, c.1885, 7¾ In. | | 492 |
| Mechanical, Turtle, Black, Green Paint, Cast Iron, Kilgore, c.1926 | | 42000 |
| Mechanical, Uncle Remus, Policeman, Coop, Paint, Iron, Kyser & Rex, Pat. 1891, 4 In. | | 6600 to 18000 |
| Mechanical, Uncle Tom, Green Coat, Cast Iron, Embossed, 5½ In. | | 450 |
| Mechanical, Uncle Tom, Yellow Coat, Paint, Cast Iron, Kyser & Rex, Patent 1882, 5½ In. | | 720 |
| Mechanical, Vending, Automatic Machine, Tin Lithograph, 2 Drawers, Distler, 1920s, 6 In. *illus* | | 1320 |
| Mechanical, Vending, Victoria, Glass, Tin Lithograph, Stollwerk, Germany, 1920s, 10¾ In. | | 660 |
| Mechanical, Volunteer, Man, Rifle, Paint, Cast Iron, John Harper, c.1890s | | 840 |
| Mechanical, Watch Dog, Safe, Cast Iron, Lever, Dog Barks, J. & E. Stevens, 6 In. | | 266 |
| Mechanical, Weedens Plantation Darky Savings Bank, Tin, Dancers, Wood Cabin, 5½ In. | | 1140 |
| Mechanical, Weight Lifter, Tin Lithograph, Bing, Germany, c.1910, 4½ In. | | 7200 |
| Mechanical, William Tell, Cast Iron, Painted, J. & E. Stevens, 6¾ In. | | 483 to 1410 |
| Mechanical, Windmill, Paint, Tin, c.1920, 4½ In. | | 900 |
| Mechanical, Woodpecker, Swiss Musical Movement, Metal, Bing, Germany, c.1890, 6 x 12 In. | | 375 |
| Mechanical, Zoo, Shutters, Monkey, Lion, Bear, Kyser & Rex, c.1894 | | 1416 |
| Merry-Go-Round, Red, Black Paint, Cast Iron, J. & E. Stevens, 5 In. | | 120 |
| Money Bag, 100,000 Number, Cinched Top, Black, Gold Paint, Cast Iron, 3½ In. | | 150 |
| Nipper, RCA Dog, White, Black, Porcelain, 6¼ In. | | 250 |
| Orange Shape, Orange & Green Paint, Metal, M 1283, 2½ In. | | 450 |
| Oriental, Camel, On Rocker, Cast Iron, 5 In. | | 420 |
| Palace, Cast Iron, Ives & Blakeslee, 8 In. | | 1080 |
| Pig, Cast Iron, 7 x 12 In. | | 660 |
| Pig, Pink, Blue, Ears Forward, Cork Nose, Pottery Glossy Glaze, Hull, 1957, 7 x 5 In. | | 132 |
| Polliwog, Blue, Red, Black Paint, Cast Iron, 6½ In. | | 360 |
| Possum, Cast Iron, A.C. Williams & Co., M 561, 2½ x 4½ In. | | 295 to 330 |
| Rabbit, Seated, Black, Green Paint, Cast Iron, 2½ In. | | 1320 |
| Rabbit, Standing, Redware, Signed, Ned Foltz, c.1982, 10 x 10¼ In. | | 112 |
| Rhinoceros, Cast Iron, 5 In. | | 360 |
| Rooster, Kyser & Rex, 1900s | | 800 |
| Safe, Cast Iron, Painted Black, Scrolled Designs, Combination Lock, 1900s, 6 In. | | 59 |
| Safe, Home Savings, Iron, c.1900, 5½ In. | | 96 |
| Safe, Ideal Safe Deposit, Combination, Nickel Plated, 9 x 9 In. | | 250 |
| Safe, Kodak Bank, Cast Iron, J. & E. Stevens Co., 5 In. | | 154 |
| Safe, Meilink's Home Deposit Vault, Black, Red Trim, Metal, 19½ In. | | 300 |
| Safe, Metropolitan, Figure, Key Lock, Iron, J. & E. Stevens, c.1872, M 904, 6 In. *illus* | | 295 |
| Safe, Royal Safe Deposit, Cast Iron, Painted Black, c.1900, 6 In. | | 111 |
| Safe, Young America, Cast Iron, Key, Kyser & Rex, M 881, 4½ In. | | 176 |
| Sailor, Saluting, Tin Lithograph, Lever, Saalheimer & Strauss, 1920s, 6¾ In. | | 1080 |
| Santa At Chimney, Red, White Paint, Cast Iron, Shepard Hardware, 6½ In. | | 960 |

**Bank,** Mechanical, Feed The Kitty, Cast Iron, Painted, 1925
$5,400

Bertoia Auctions

**Bank,** Mechanical, Vending, Automatic Machine, Tin Lithograph, 2 Drawers, Distler, 1920s, 6 In.
$1,320

Bertoia Auctions

**Bank,** Safe, Metropolitan, Figure, Key Lock, Iron, J. & E. Stevens, c.1872, M 904, 6 In.
$295

Bertoia Auctions

**B**

**Bank,** Transvaal Money Box, Cast Iron, Original Pipe, John Harper, M 1, c.1885, 6 In.
**$36,000**

RSL Auction

**Barber,** Chair, Koken, Leather Back & Seat, Gold Plating, 44 x 43 In.
**$1,320**

Morphy Auctions

**Barber,** Chair, Koken, White Porcelain, Leather, Salesman's Sample, 15½ In.
**$31,200**

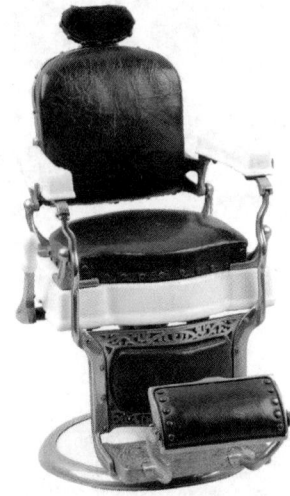

Morphy Auctions

| | |
|---|---:|
| **Santa Claus,** Holding Tree, Red, White Paint, Cast Iron, Hubley, 6 In. | 300 to 780 |
| **Santa Claus,** Wire Tree, Cast Iron, Ives, 7¼ In. | 431 |
| **Shell Out,** Shell, White Paint, Cast Iron, J. & E. Stevens, M 1622, 5½ In. | 330 |
| **Squirrel,** With Nut, Paint, Cast Iron, M 660, 4 In. | 210 |
| **Statue Of Liberty,** Gold Paint, Cast Iron, Kenton, 10 In. | 150 |
| **Stop Sign,** Blue Paint, Cast Iron, 6 In. | 180 |
| **Strongman & Sailor,** Tin Lithograph, Saalheimer & Strauss, c.1920, 6 In. | 27000 |
| **Teddy Roosevelt,** Bust, Rough Rider Uniform, Brass, A.C. Williams, 1919, M 120, 5 In. | 210 |
| **Transvaal Money Box,** Cast Iron, Original Pipe, John Harper, M 1, c.1885, 6 In. ...*illus* | 36000 |
| **Two Faces Black Boy,** A.C. Williams, M 83, c.1901, 4 In. | 250 |
| **Universal Globe,** Tin, Rotating, Wreath, Cribben & Sexton Co., M 787, 4¼ In. | 150 |
| **Yellow Cab,** Orange, Black, Cast Iron, Rubber Tires, Arcade, M 1489, 8 In. | 3540 |
| **Yellow Cab,** Red, Orange Paint, Cast Iron, Arcade, 8 In. | 660 |
| **Zebra Fish,** Black, White, Round Base, Porcelain, Marked Danmark, 4 In. | 58 |

**BARBER** collectibles range from the popular red and white striped pole that used to be found in front of every shop to the small scissors and tools of the trade. Barber chairs are wanted, especially the older models with elaborate iron trim.

| | |
|---|---:|
| **Backbar,** 3 Stations, Emil J. Paidar, Art Deco, Mirrors, Display Cases, 192 x 79 In. | 2040 |
| **Chair,** Booster Seat, Swivel Base, Velvet Upholstery, Wood Base, Koken, Victorian | 1680 |
| **Chair,** Early Koken Congress, Hydraulic, Black, Carved Wood, Cast Iron Footrest | 1200 |
| **Chair,** Early Koken, White Enamel, Red Leather, Child's | 2280 |
| **Chair,** Enameled, Nickel Plated Openwork, Leather Upholstery, Emil Paidar, 47 x 43 In. | 291 |
| **Chair,** Harley Davidson Design, Paidar | 48 |
| **Chair,** Koken, Headrest, Footrest, 24 x 36 In. | 1020 |
| **Chair,** Koken, Leather Back & Seat, Gold Plating, 44 x 43 In. ...*illus* | 1320 |
| **Chair,** Koken, Oak, Cast Iron, Leather | 961 |
| **Chair,** Koken, Round Base, Footrest, Headrest, Child's, 23½ x 47 In. | 1440 |
| **Chair,** Koken, White Porcelain, Leather, Salesman's Sample, 15½ In. ...*illus* | 31200 |
| **Chair,** Koken, Wood, Metal, Leather, Adjustable, c.1900, 48 In. | 351 |
| **Chair,** Red Pedal Car, Whitewall Tires, Faux Rear Spare, Chrome, Child's, 24 x 36 In. | 660 |
| **Chair,** Theo A. Kochs Co., Horse Head, Porcelain Base, Leather Upholstery, Child's ...*illus* | 2400 |
| **Chair,** Wood, Round Back, Tufted Leather, Silver Rivets, Footrest | 5100 |
| **Hat Rack,** Cast Iron, Mirrored Block Top, 2 Tiers Of 6 Hooks, Umbrella Holders, 70 x 18 In. | 1046 |
| **Pole,** Column, Red, White, Blue, Glass Casing, Spins, c.1911, 82 In. | 1260 |
| **Pole,** Iron, Rotating Section, Lighted Globe Top, c.1910, 92 In. | 1625 |
| **Pole,** Koken, Cast Iron, Milk Glass, Red, White, Blue, 81 In. | 1650 |
| **Pole,** Leaded Glass, Red & White, Brass Columns, White Cast Iron Mount | 1560 |
| **Pole,** Medial Ring, Cannonball Ends, Red, White, Blue Paint, c.1880, 18 x 24 In. | 489 |
| **Pole,** Model 405, Light-Up, Red, White, Blue, William Marvy Co., 29¼ x 5¼ In. | 360 |
| **Pole,** Paidar Co., Red, White, Blue, Light-Up, 38 In. | 440 |
| **Pole,** Pine, Fluted Column, Red, Gold Paint, c.1870, 45 In. | 246 |
| **Pole,** Pine, Red & Blue Stripes, White, Gold Ball Finial, Blue Diamonds On Base, 85 In. | 810 |
| **Pole,** Pine, Red, White, Blue Paint, Ball Finial, c.1960, 33 In. | 185 |
| **Pole,** Pine, Round Finial, Red, White, Blue, Stars, Stripes, c.1920, 41 In. | 660 |
| **Pole,** Porcelain, Spinner, Top Globe, Red, White, Blue, 84 In. | 3600 |
| **Pole,** Red & Blue Stripes, White, Red Ball Finial, Wall Mount, c.1900, 40 In. | 1140 |
| **Pole,** Red Stripes, White, Red Ball Finial, Green Square Base, Floor Standing, 44 In. | 1063 |
| **Pole,** Red, White, Blue, Light-Up, Wall Mount, 24 In. | 385 |
| **Pole,** Spinner, Glass, Light-Up, Wall Mount, 26 x 8 In. | 300 |
| **Pole,** Spinner, Light-Up, 75 In. | 2700 |
| **Pole,** Square Base, Turned, Tapered, Gold Ball Finials, Start In Center, 89 In. | 4444 |
| **Pole,** Stained Glass Top Globe, Porcelain, 6-Sided Base, Light-Up, Cast Iron, Copper, 7 In. | 9200 |
| **Pole,** Turned, Red, White, Blue, Ball Finial, Tapered, Gilt, c.1875, 95 In. ...*illus* | 4920 |
| **Pole,** Turned, Red, White, Blue, Painted, Pedestal, c.1890, 98 x 23½ In. ...*illus* | 1534 |
| **Pole,** Wall Mount, Turned, Tapered, Gold Ball Finials, Start In Center, 60 In. | 1976 |
| **Pole,** Wood, Ball Finial, 68 In. | 948 |
| **Pole,** Wood, Carved, Painted, Red, White & Blue, Yellow Ball Finial, c.1910, 73 In. ...*illus* | 1976 |
| **Pole,** Wood, Painted, Red, White & Blue Spiral Stripes, Ball Ends, c.1910, 30 In. | 863 |
| **Pole,** Wood, Red, White, Ball Finials, Wall Mount, c.1920, 7 x 60 In. | 180 |
| **Pole,** Wood, Red, White, Blue, Ball Top, Iron Brackets, c.1900, 10 x 79 In. ...*illus* | 371 |
| **Pole,** Wood, Turned, Ball Finial, 83½ In. | 829 |
| **Pole,** Wood, Twist Carved, Ball Finial, Red, White, Blue Paint, 35 x 3 In. | 176 |
| **Shoeshine Kit,** Brass, Drawers, End Compartments, Photos Under Glass, Turkey, 15 In. | 90 |
| **Sign,** Light-Up, Rotating, Wall Mount, 30 In. | 280 |

Sign, Red, White, Blue Striped Ground, Black Lettering, Frame, c.1910, 12 x 37 In........................ 400
Sign, Shoeshine, Pine Frame, Painted, Barber Stripe, New England, c.1880, 32 x 18 In. .............. 1481

---

**BAROMETERS** are used to forecast the weather. Antique barometers with elaborate wooden cases and brass trim are the most desirable. Mercury column barometers are also popular with collectors. It is difficult to find someone to repair a broken one, so be sure your barometer is in working condition.

Admiral Fitzroy, Walnut, Carved, Gothic Style Case, Pike Optician, c.1890, 49 In......................... 554
Admiral Fitzroy, Walnut, Thermometer, Hygrometer, Pike Optician, N.Y., c.1860, 51 In. ...*illus* 2629
Aneroid, Fox Hunt Theme, Oak Shaped Back Board, Bronze Dog Head, Mesh Bag, 17 x 8 In. ...... 610
Aneroid, Walnut, Pitch Pediment, Columns, Sunburst, 49 In............................................................ 2091
Angle, Mahogany, Molded Edge, Silvered Dials, 35 In...................................................................... 2563
Banjo, Engraved Silvered Main Dial, Convex Mirror, Bond Of Cirencester, Victorian, 43 x 13 In. 104
Barograph, Negretti & Zambra, Lacquered Brass Plate, Recording Drum, 9 In............................ 338
Baroque Style, Giltwood, Cornucopia, Fruit, Flower Swags, Fluted Vase, c.1950, 40 x 20 In........ 1045
Dial, Wood, Flowers, Leaves, Gilt, France, 36 x 20 In..................................................................... 240
Federal, Mahogany, Triangular Crest, England, 1850, 37½ x 6 In. .................................................. 704
Lyre, Flowers, Gesso, Gilt, 8-Sided, Selon Torricelli, 33 In. ..........................................*illus* 1416
Oak, Carved, Scrolling, Porcelain Dial, Thermometer, 9½ x 35½ In. .............................................. 228
Portable, Rectangular, Simmons, 37½ In.......................................................................................... 240
Regency, Veneer, Rosewood, Mother-Of-Pearl, Ivory Adjustor, 1800s, 40 In. ................................ 601
Renaissance Revival Style, Brass Clad, Metal Case, Enameled, France, 20 x 15 In ....................... 522
Scroll Top, Metal Dial, Mahogany, 1800-25, 38 In.......................................................................... 438
Stick, George III, Mahogany, Broken Pediment, Feather Banded Trunk, 39½ x 5¼ In. .................... 984
Stick, George III, Mahogany, Broken Scroll Pediment, Silver Dial, 41 In. ....................................... 498
Stick, Huddleston, Silvered Dial, Thermometer, Cistern, c.1860, 38 In........................................... 492
Stick, Mahogany, Marked Marrett & Short, England, c.1850, 39½ In. ............................................. 250
Stick, Mahogany, Thermometer, Huddleston, Boston, 38 In............................................................ 861
Stick, Oak Case, Thermometer, Mercury, F. Westley, London, c.1820, 36 In.................................... 625
Stick, Regency, Mahogany, Broken Swan Crest, Signed J. Newman, London, c.1810, 40 In........... 1020
Stick, Rosewood, Brass, Bone Panels, Inscribed Bursill & Co., London, c.1800, 38¾ In................. 1080
Stick, Rosewood, Mother-Of-Pearl Inlays, Inscribed E. & G.W. Blunt, N.Y., c.1885, 38 In. ............ 563
Stick, Savage & Son, Arched Hood, Silvered Dial, Glazed Hinged Door, 37 In. .............................. 584
Stick, Thermometer, Spencer, Browning, Rust, England, c.1820.................................................... 1080
Stick, Walnut, Standard Storm King, Spooner, Boston, c.1880, 41 In. ............................................ 492
Sympiesometer, Ship's, Mahogany Gimbaled, W. Desilva, Case, Eng., c.1850, 38 In. .................... 2880
Thermometer, Louis-Philippe, Giltwood, Carved, Lyre Shape Crest, Signed, 38 x 20 In. .............. 1434
Thermometer, Marine, Stick, Rosewood, Brass, Bone, C. Hutchinson, c.1850........................... 960
Thermometer, Storm King, Walnut, Telescope Shape, E.C. Spooner, Boston, c.1850, 42 In. ........ 960
Thermometer, Walnut, Leaf, Scroll Carved Frame, Victorian, 32½ In. ........................................... 123
Wheel, A. Martinell, Mahogany, Swan's Neck Pediment, Alcohol, 38 In. ...................................... 123
Wheel, Hydrometer, Thermometer, Wood Broken Arch Top Case, c.1885, 41 In........................... 189
Wheel, Mahogany, Scroll, Ramsden-Wakefield, 19th Century, 39 In.............................................. 300
Wheel, Mahogany, Veneer, Broken Arch Pediment, Brass Finial, c.1820, 39 In. ............................ 748
Wheel, Regency, Calamander Wood, Thermometer, Hydrometer, Mirror, England, 37 x 10 In. ..... 553
Wheel, Rosewood Case, Carved Floral Pediment, England, 1800s, 36¼ In. ................................... 352
Wheel, Rosewood, Brass, Thermometer, Jackson, England, 39 In. ................................................ 308

---

**BASEBALL** *collectibles are in the Sports category, except for baseball cards, which are listed under Baseball in the Card category.*

---

**BASKETS** of all types are popular with collectors. American Indian, Japanese, African, Nantucket, Shaker, and many other kinds of baskets can be found. Of course, baskets are still being made, so a collector must learn to judge the age and style of a basket to determine its value. Also see Purse.

Applied Leaves, Painted, Blue Ground, Multicolor, Handle, 12½ x 16½ In. ................................... 840
Bamboo, Split, Ikebana, Flared Cylinder, Twisted Handles, Signed Kyohu-Sho, Japan, 12 In....... 732
Bamboo, Woven, Ikebana, Japan, c.1965, 18 x 13 In..................................................................... 938
Berry, Splint, Oak, Signed Aaron Yakim, 2000, 8¾ In. .................................................................. 160
Bowl, Coil, Rye Straw, Oak Splint, Red, White & Blue Paint, Flared, c.1880, 4 x 12 In.................. 978
Buttocks, Market, Splint, White Oak, Round Rim, Ribbed, Bent Wood Handle, 11 x 12 In........... 83
Buttocks, Splint, Oak, Converging Ribs, Wrapped Rim, Arched Handle, 1902, 10 x 11 In. ........... 805
Buttocks, Splint, Oak, Handle, Miniature, 1800s, 3½ In................................................................ 185
Buttocks, Splint, White Oak, Converging Ribs, Arched Handle, Cloth Lining, 5 x 6 In................. 403
Cane, White Oak, Kidney Shape, 32 Converging Ribs, Wrapped Arched Handle, 7 In. ................. 920

B

Barber, Chair, Theo A. Kochs Co., Horse Head, Porcelain Base, Leather Upholstery, Child's
$2,400

Morphy Auctions

---

Barber, Pole, Turned, Red, White, Blue, Ball Finial, Tapered, Gilt, c.1875, 95 In.
$4,920

Skinner Auctioneers & Appraisers

---

Barber, Pole, Turned, Red, White, Blue, Painted, Pedestal, c.1890, 98 x 23½ In.
$1,534

Brunk Auctions

# BASKET

**Barber,** Pole, Wood, Carved, Painted, Red, White & Blue, Yellow Ball Finial, c.1910, 73 In. $1,976

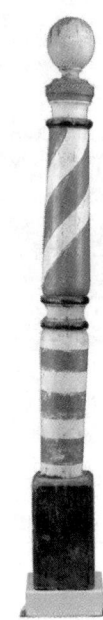

James D. Julia Auctioneers

**Barber,** Pole, Wood, Red, White, Blue, Ball Top, Iron Brackets, c.1900, 10 x 79 In. $371

Showtime Auction Services

**TIP**
*Stains can be removed from woven baskets with a diluted solution of hydrogen peroxide.*

| | |
|---|---:|
| **Cheese,** Splint, White Oak, Hexagonal Open Weave, Square Base, Round, c.1925, 6 x 10 In. | 219 |
| **Cheese,** Split Oak, c.1855, 9 x 17¾ In. | 330 |
| **Egg,** Splint, Oak, Half Kidney Shape, High Arch Handle, Appalachian, c.1910, 8 x 5 In. | 259 |
| **Egg,** Splint, Oak, Handle, Signed Aaron Yakim, 1999, 12 In. | 923 |
| **Egg,** Splint, Oak, Kidney Shape, Double Rim, Arch Handle, Appalachian, c.1905, 4 x 5 In. | 431 |
| **Egg,** Splint, Oak, Rib Type, Low Arch Handle, Va., c.1920, 7 x 8½ In. | 259 |
| **Egg,** Splint, Oak, Ribbed, Kidney Shape, Arch Handle, c.1925, 9¼ x 5¾ In. | 150 |
| **Field,** Splint, Oak, 1800s, 17 x 31 In. | 74 |
| **Gathering,** Oak, Woven, Split, Bentwood Handle, 20 x 23 In. | 177 |
| **Gathering,** Splint, 1800s, 6 x 37 In. | 330 |
| **Gathering,** Splint, Black Painted Handle, Rim, New England, 13 x 19 In. | 300 |
| **Gullah,** Coil, Dyed Bands, Oval Hand Opening, Flared, South Carolina, c.1880, 8 x 18 In. | 115 |
| **Loom,** Splint, 2 Pockets, Arched Brace, Alligatored Mustard Paint, 20 x 12 In. | 360 |
| **Melon,** Splint, Oak, Green Paint, 1800s, 14 x 18 In. | 209 |
| **Nantucket,** Bentwood Swing Handle, c.1890, 4 x 10 In. | 492 |
| **Nantucket,** Hickory, Swing Handle, Ferdinand Sylvaro, Label, 14 x 12 In. .....................*illus* | 1664 |
| **Nantucket,** Lightship, Round, Bushel, Handles, R. Folger, 13 x 18 In. | 5400 |
| **Nantucket,** Lightship, Splint & Cane, Wood Bottom & Swinging Handle, 8 x 7 In. | 978 |
| **Nantucket,** Lightship, Swing Handle, Charles Ray, 19th Century, 8½ x 8½ In. | 240 |
| **Nantucket,** Lightship, Whalebone Clasp & Top Plate Whale, Oval, Handle, 6 x 10 In. | 677 |
| **Nantucket,** Notched Strap Handle, c.1910, 6½ x 9½ In. | 708 |
| **Nantucket,** Oval, Swing Handle, Mitchell Ray, 6 x 7 In. | 840 |
| **Nantucket,** Round, Bentwood Swing Handle, 11 x 11 In. | 360 |
| **Nantucket,** Round, Swing Handle, 8½ x 8½ In. | 540 |
| **Nantucket,** Round, Swing Handle, Brass Ears, F. Chadwick, c.1910, 7¾ x 6 In. .................*illus* | 461 |
| **Nantucket,** Round, Swing Handle, Davis Hall, 10 x 11 In. | 1020 |
| **Nantucket,** Round, Swing Handle, Lightship, Marked Folger, 11 x 7½ In. | 900 |
| **Nantucket,** Round, Swing Handle, Mahogany Bottom, Partial Label, c.1910, 13 x 10½ In. | 861 |
| **Nantucket,** Round, Swing Handle, S.P. Boyer, c.1950, 8 x 6 In. | 1020 |
| **Nantucket,** Swing Handle, c.1950, 4 x 5 In. | 177 |
| **Nantucket,** Swing Handle, Early 20th Century, 3½ In. | 738 |
| **Nantucket,** Swing Handles, Karen Wychock, 1994, 10½ x 12 In. | 431 |
| **Picnic,** Lid, Splint, Metal, Wood, Porcelain Contents, 24 In. | 1320 |
| **Reed,** Kidney Shape, Reinforced Handle, Metal Strap, Virginia, 14 x 23 In. | 90 |
| **Rye Straw,** Round, Pennsylvania, 1800s, 5¼ x 12¼ In. | 74 |
| **Sewing,** Rye Straw, Oval, Open Work, 1800s, 4½ x 13¼ x 8½ In. | 106 |
| **Sewing,** White, Red, Green, Black Paint, Handles, New England, 6 x 16 In. | 120 |
| **Sewing,** Wicker, Green Banding, Lift Lid, Assorted Tools, 6¼ x 4¼ In. | 196 |
| **Splint,** 2 Bentwood Swing Handles, Red & Black Paint, Oval, 5½ x 18 In. | 570 |
| **Splint,** 26 Staves, Oak, Hickory, Pine, Oval, Wood Bottom, X-Wrapped Handle, 7 x 15 In. | 978 |
| **Splint,** Ash, Conical Lid, Handle, Martha Wetherbee, 1988, 12 In. | 123 |
| **Splint,** Ash, Swing Handles, Initialed Martha Wetherbee, 1991, 4½ In. | 185 |
| **Splint,** Basket Weave Panels, Green Paint, Handle, C. Dotter, Scandinavia, 1852, 13 x 12 In. | 450 |
| **Splint,** Lid, Clothespins, American, c.1900, 11 In. | 63 |
| **Splint,** Oak, Gathering, 2 Handles, Stepped, Wrapped Rim, Shenandoah Valley, c.1920, 7 x 31 In. | 575 |
| **Splint,** Oak, Green Paint, Melon Shape, Wrapped Rim, Wedge-Shape Opening, c.1900, 7 x 8 In. | 1265 |
| **Splint,** Oak, Kidney Shape, Navette Rim, Single Bent Loop Handle, 5 x 12 In. | 748 |
| **Splint,** Oak, Kidney Shape, Ribs, Arched Handle, Southern, c.1920, 5 x 6 In. | 196 |
| **Splint,** Oak, Kidney Shape, Ribs, Arched Handle, Va., c.1900, 4 x 3 In. | 184 |
| **Splint,** Oak, Kidney Shape, Ribs, Handle, c.1900, Va., 11½ x 12½ In. | 138 |
| **Splint,** Oak, Mulberry Paint, Black Stain, Square Base, Round Rim, c.1925, 5 x 5 In. | 805 |
| **Splint,** Oak, Oval, Lid, Medial Handles, Shenandoah, c.1960, 25 In. | 115 |
| **Splint,** Oak, Rib, Arched Handle, c.1860, 7 x 8 In. | 184 |
| **Splint,** Oak, Rib, Double Wrapped Rim, Arched Handle, Stained, Southern, c.1945, 7 x 7 In. | 173 |
| **Splint,** Oak, Ribs, Arch Handle, Wrapped Rim, Red, Blue, Green, Pink Paint, c.1900, 9 x 12 In. | 207 |
| **Splint,** Oak, Ribs, Kidney Shape, Arched Handle, Blue Paint, c.1900, 10 x 7 In. | 1380 |
| **Splint,** Oak, Round, Arched Handle, Dark Stain, Shenandoah Valley, c.1890, 7 x 7 In. | 259 |
| **Splint,** Oak, Wood Base, Flared Sides, Arch Handles, Red Paint, c.1930, 12 x 10 In. | 403 |
| **Splint,** Rectangular, Hooded Top, Arched Side Openings, Arched Handle, 8½ In. | 863 |
| **Splint,** Round, Low Handle, c.1900, 10 x 7 In. | 173 |
| **Splint,** Side Loop Handles, New England, c.1840, 5 x 10 In. | 98 |
| **Splint,** Taghkanic Style, Double Lashed Rim, Squared Swing Handle, c.1870, 12 x 10 In. | 210 |
| **Splint,** White Oak, Teal Paint, Melon Shape, Arched Handle, Virginia, 1880s, 7 x 8 In. | 2185 |
| **Splint,** White Oak, Teal Paint, Woven, Kidney Shape, Low-Arched Handle, c.1875, 6 x 9 In. | 1610 |
| **Split,** Oak, Rectangular, c.1860, 11½ x 33 In. | 277 |

| Stave, Mixed Woods, Arched, Rectangular, Canted Sides, Bent Handle, c.1920, 7 x 8 In. | 184 |
| Twig, Red, White, Blue, Paint, c.1890, 14 x 33 In. | 600 |
| Wood, Carved, Red Lacquer, Gilt Relief Bamboo, 1900s, 12 x 7 In. | 40 |

**BATCHELDER** products are made from California clay. Ernest Batchelder established a tile studio in Pasadena, California, in 1909. He went into partnership with Frederick Brown in 1912 and the company became Batchelder and Brown. In 1920 he built a larger factory with a new partner. The Batchelder-Wilson Company made all types of architectural tiles, garden pots, and bookends. The plant closed in 1932. In 1936 Batchelder opened Batchelder Ceramics, also in Pasadena, and made bowls, vases, and earthenware pots. He retired in 1951 and died in 1957. Pieces are marked *Batchelder Pasadena* or *Batchelder Los Angeles*.

BATCHELDER
LOS ANGELES

| Tile, 3 Leaves, Curled Stem, Animals In Corners, Gray Matte Glaze, 5 x 5 In. | 188 |
| Tile, Arts & Crafts, Beige, Blue, Bas Relief, c.1920, 4 x 4 In. | 95 |
| Tile, Dog, Tree, Classic Matte Finish, 1920s, 5 ¾ x 5 ¾ In. | 284 |
| Tile, Flower, Leaves, Vines, c.1920, 5 x 5 In. | 124 |
| Tile, Flowers In Footed Pot, Geometric Border, 6 x 6 In. | 144 |
| Tile, Hunter, Spearing Animal, Bas Relief, c.1920, 3 ¾ x 3 ¾ In. | 65 |
| Tile, Love Birds, Fleur-De-Lis, 6 ⅝ x 5 ⅝ In. | 160 |
| Tile, Man Riding Prancing Horse, Tree Trunk, 3 ¾ x 3 ¾ In. | 96 |
| Tile, Mythical Bird, Gray Matte Glaze, Frame, c.1920, 8 x 8 In. | 292 |
| Tile, Parrot, Diamond Outline, Heart Leaf Corners, 3 ¾ x 3 ¾ In. | 82 |
| Tile, Prancing Deer, 3 Surrounding Circles, 5 ¾ x 5 ¾ In. | 132 |
| Tile, Trees, Farm, House, Fields, 3 ¾ x 3 ¾ In. | 76 |
| Tile, Tulip, Cartouche, Matte Glaze, c.1920, 6 x 6 In. | 196 |

**BATMAN** and Robin are characters from a comic strip by Bob Kane that started in 1939. In 1966, the characters became part of a popular television series. There have been radio and movie serials that featured the pair. The first full-length movie was made in 1989.

| Action Figure, Batgirl, Yvonne Craig, Paint, Resin, Clear Base, T. Reynolds, 1966, 12 In. | 1264 |
| Action Figure, Batman, Adam West, On Batphone, Paint, Resin, T. Reynolds, 1966, 13 In. | 249 |
| Action Figure, Batman, Blue Head, Gray Body, Strunck, Cape, Vinyl, Japan, c.1966, 11 ½ In. | 490 |
| Action Figure, Batman, Blue, Gray, Black, Plastic, DC Comics, Box, 1979, 12 ½ In. | 461 |
| Action Figure, Parachuter, Plastic Bag, Argentina, c.1968, 6 In. | 100 |
| Action Figure, Robin, Burt Ward, Paint, Resin, Clear Base, T. Reynolds, 1966, 12 ¼ In. | 115 |
| Action Figure, Robin, Green Trunks, Shoes, Burbank Toys, Box, 1977, 9 In. | 5693 |
| Bank, Batman, From Waist Up, Bat Symbol On Chest, Blue, Black Hard Plastic, Mego, 8 In. | 139 |
| Belt, Leather, Metal Buckle, Batman, Robin, Package Card, Morris Belt Co., Size 28 | 115 |
| Comic Book, DC Comics, Joker Cover, No. 23, June-July 1944, Dick Sprang Art | 630 |
| Comic Book, DC Comics, Tweedledee, Tweedledum, No. 18, August-September 1943 | 417 |
| Game, Target, 8-In. Tin Dart Gun, 4 Darts, Targets, Batman Scene Box, Tada, Japan, Box | 1123 |
| Glass, Batman Graphics, Standard Oil Premium, Anchor Hocking, Box, 5 In., 18 Piece | 153 |
| Hand Puppet, Batman & Robin, Vinyl Head, Body, Ideal, Box, 11 In., 2 Piece | 886 |
| Inflatable Figure, Vinyl, Ideal, 1970s, 20 In. | 115 |
| Pencil & Paint Set, Batman, Robin, Joker, Coloring Pages, 8 Paints, Box, 12 ½ x 21 In. | 474 |
| Pencil Case, Batman, Yellow, Black Cardboard, Vinyl, Standard Plastic Products, 4 x 10 In. | 156 |
| Ring, 10K Gold, Bat Diamonds Inset, Starburst Corp., Diamond Comic, Box, 1992, Adult | 278 |
| Sign, Holy Detroit The Batmobile Is Here, Robin, 98 Cents, 1966, 9 ½ x 23 In. | 506 |
| Sneakers, Black, Batsignal, Free Batman Ring With Purchase, Red Ring, Box, Size 3 ½ | 759 |
| Suit, Bruce Wayne, On TV, Black Striped Jacket, Pants, 20th Century Fox Tag, 1967, 42 L | 2296 |
| Toy, Bat Bomb, Carded, Cap-Firing, Black, Red, Yellow, 3 ⅓ x 5 In. | 265 |
| Toy, Batcopter, Plastic, Battery, Re El Co., Italy, 1980, 14 ½ In. | 230 |
| Toy, Batman Picture Pistol, Projector Gun, Battery, Box, 8 x 16 In. | 485 |
| Toy, Batmobile, Batman Chest Deep In Car, Blue, Friction, Marx, 1966, 4 In. | 898 |
| Toy, Batmobile, Batman Chest Deep, Red, White, Japanese Text, Japan, 1966, 3 ½ x 9 In. | 1610 |
| Toy, Batmobile, Black, Red Stripes, Batman Driving, Die Cast Metal, 1966, 5 In. | 316 |
| Toy, Batmobile, Blue, Batman, Robin, Vinyl, Crank, Box, Lili Ledy, Mexico, 20 In. | 771 |
| Toy, Batmobile, Slot Car, Red Bat Symbols, Plastic, Metal Chassis, Motor, Box, 1966, 7 In. | 862 |
| Toy, Flying Batman, Inflatable, String, Pulley, Ideal, Box, 1966, 6 x 9 In. | 136 |
| Toy, Glider, Flying Batman, Rubber Band Sling Shot Launch, Plastic, Transogram Co., 12 In. | 216 |
| Toy, Glider, Full-Bodied Batman, Shrink Wrap, 1967, 13 In. | 139 |
| Toy, Model Kit, Unopened Box, Aurora, 13 In. | 360 |
| Toy, Pistol, Sparking, Tin, Plastic Barrel, Bullets, Japanese Batman Name, Nomura, 8 In. | 2657 |
| Toy, Rifle, Sparking, Rubber Barrel, Orange, Running Batman & Robin, 17 ¼ In. | 3858 |
| Toy, Shooting Arcade, Batman, Robin, Spinning Targets, Spring-Loaded BB Gun, 7 In. | 316 |

**Barometer,** Admiral Fitzroy, Walnut, Thermometer, Hygrometer, Pike Optician, N.Y., c.1860, 51 In.
$2,629

Neal Auction Co.

**Barometer,** Lyre, Flowers, Gesso, Gilt, 8-Sided, Selon Torricelli, 33 In.
$1,416

Brunk Auctions

**Basket,** Nantucket, Hickory, Swing Handle, Ferdinand Sylvaro, Label, 14 x 12 In.
$1,664

Rago Arts & Auction Center

**Basket,** Nantucket, Round, Swing Handle, Brass Ears, F. Chadwick, c.1910, 7¾ x 6 In.
**$461**

Skinner Auctioneers & Appraisers

**Beehive,** Bust, Kinderkopf, Boy, Girl, Column Base, Royal Vienna, c.1860, 8¾ In., Pair
**$677**

Neal Auction Co.

**Beehive,** Plate, Portrait Of Ruth, Royal Vienna, Austria, c.1900, 9⅜ In.
**$750**

Rago Arts & Auction Center

> **TIP**
> If you're moving, pack your plates on the sides with pads under and between the plates. The weight of a stack of plates can crack the bottom plates.

| | |
|---|---:|
| **Toy,** Shooting Arcade, Joker, Gotham City, Targets, Spring-Loaded BB Gun, 15 In. | 2087 |
| **Wallpaper,** Batman, Robin, Batmobile, Batcave, Batplane Scenes, Full Roll, 20½ In. | 168 |

**BATTERSEA** enamels, which are enamels painted on copper, were made in the Battersea district of London from about 1750 to 1756. Many similar enamels are mistakenly called Battersea.

| | |
|---|---:|
| **Box,** Cherub, Under Tree, Holding Scythe, Cobalt Blue, Hinged, c.1800, 2 In. | 500 |
| **Box,** Floors Castle, Trees, Oval, Hinged, 2 x 1½ x 1 In. | 129 |
| **Box,** Kneeling Child, Dog, c.1800, 1¾ In. | 495 |
| **Box,** Mother's Day, Your Happiness Is Mine, Flowers, Mushroom Shape, 1976, 1½ In. | 90 |
| **Box,** Woman, Holding Baby, 2 Children By Side, c.1800, 1⅛ In. | 135 |
| **Candlestick,** Flower Sprigs, White Ground, 18th Century, 14 In. | 950 |
| **Etui,** Bilston, Enamel, Gilt Metal, Push Button Latch, Painted, Portrait, 1700s, 4 x 2 In. | 805 |
| **Patch Box,** Esteem The Giver, Scroll, Urn, Garden, Green, c.1780, 1½ x 1½ In. | 495 |
| **Patch Box,** Gingham Green, Flowers, Garland Border, Hinged, Oval, c.1780, 2 x 1 In. | 375 |
| **Patch Box,** Motto, Oval, Hinged, c.1800, 1¼ x 1⅝ In. | 525 |
| **Snuffbox,** Domed, Couple, Garden Scene, Ribbon Band, c.1750, 3 In. | 725 |
| **Snuffbox,** Green, Latticework, Interior Portrait, c.1770, 3½ x 1⅞ x 1⅛ In. | 565 |
| **Trinket Box,** Egg Shape, Flowers, May You Be Happy, 1¼ In. | 50 |
| **Trinket Box,** Lid, Multicolor Flowers, Leaves, Enameled, 1700s, 2½ x 3¾ In. | 118 |

**BAUER** pottery is a California-made ware. J.A. Bauer bought Paducah Pottery in Paducah, Kentucky, in 1885. He moved the pottery to Los Angeles, California, in 1909. The company made art pottery after 1912 and introduced dinnerware marked *Bauer* in 1930. The factory went out of business in 1962 and the molds were destroyed. Since 1998, a new company, Bauer Pottery Company of Los Angeles, has been making Bauer pottery using molds made from original Bauer pieces. The pottery is now made in Highland, California. Most pieces are marked "2000." Original pieces of Bauer pottery are listed here. See also the Russel Wright category.

| | |
|---|---:|
| **Cal-Art,** Planter, Swan, Green, 1930s, 5½ x 10 In. | 98 |
| **Fish Shape,** Salt & Pepper, Blue, Yellow, 2 x 3 In. | 28 |
| **La Linda,** Platter, Green, 10½ In. | 30 |
| **Monterey,** Creamer, Cobalt Blue, Ball Shape, 2¾ x 3½ In. | 101 |
| **Plain,** Chop Plate, Yellow, 13 In. | 125 |
| **Planter,** Swan, White Matte, Ray Murray, 1930s, 13 In. | 47 |
| **Planter,** Swirled, Pink Speckled, 1950s, 7 x 6 In. | 45 |
| **Ring,** Bowl, Measuring, No. 12, Green, 9⅝ In. | 35 |
| **Ring,** Casserole, Chartreuse, Lid, Qt., 7½ In. | 125 |
| **Ring,** Chop Plate, Orange, 12½ In. | 125 |
| **Ring,** Creamer, Blue, 3 x 5 In. | 36 |
| **Ring,** Lid, Green, 7¾ In. | 24 |
| **Ring,** Mixing Bowl, No. 24, 7⅛ In. | 119 |
| **Ring,** Pitcher, Light Blue, 2 Qt., 5½ In. | 125 |
| **Ring,** Pitcher, Green, 5 In. | 86 |
| **Ring,** Pitcher, Green, Marked, 5 x 6¾ In. | 46 |
| **Ring,** Plate, Yellow, 6 In. | 34 |
| **Ring,** Serving Bowl, No. 8 Yellow, 8 In. | 29 |
| **Swirl,** Vase, Globular, Green, 7 x 8 In. | 150 |
| **Turquoise,** Bowl, Flower, 7 x 2¾ In. | 51 |

**BAVARIA** is a region in Europe where many types of porcelain were made. In the nineteenth century, the mark often included the word *Bavaria*. After 1871, the words *Bavaria, Germany*, were used. Listed here are pieces that include the name *Bavaria* in some form, but major porcelain makers, such as Rosenthal, are listed in their own categories.

| | |
|---|---:|
| **Cake Plate,** Pink & Yellow Flowers, Scalloped, Gilt Trim, Handles, c.1900, 11 x 12 In. | 54 |
| **Cup & Saucer,** Jugendstil, White, Cobalt Blue, T. Bayrisch Blau Bavaria, 3 x 4 In., 8 Piece | 35 |
| **Inkwell,** Boy With Dog Finial, Round, 3¼ In. | 155 |
| **Plate,** Service, Bavarian, Raised Gilt, Signed Heinrich & Co., c.1910, 11 In., 12 Piece | 153 |
| **Platter,** Oval, Pale Green Border, Flowers, Leaves, Raised Petals, 14 x 11 In. | 65 |
| **Salt & Pepper,** Oval, Flowers, Multicolor, Gold Trim, 3¼ In. | 22 |
| **Stein,** Old Man Of The Sea, Smoking, 5½ In. | 45 |
| **Wastebasket,** Orange Poppy, Yellow, Brown Ground, Gold Trim, Footed, Marked, 9½ In. | 94 |

**BEADED BAGS** *are included in the Purse category.*

**BEATLES** collectors search for any items picturing the four members of the famous music group or any of their recordings. Because these items are so new, the condition is very important and top prices are paid only for items in mint condition. The Beatles first appeared on American network television in 1964. The group disbanded in 1971. Ringo Starr and Paul McCartney are still performing. John Lennon died in 1980. George Harrison died in 2001.

| | |
|---|---|
| **Album,** The Beatles With Tony Sheridan, Black Label MGM Records, 1964 | 100 |
| **Album,** Yesterday & Today, Butcher Cover, Meat, Headless Dolls, 4 Beatles, 1966 | 3125 |
| **Belt Buckle,** Hologram Logo, 1970s, 3 ½ x 4 ¼ In. | 20 |
| **Binder,** Beatles, Signatures, Vinyl, Yellow, Standard Plastic Products, 1964, 10 x 11 In. | 125 |
| **Bust,** Ringo Starr, Hard Rubber, Gold Finish, Starfans Inc., 1964, 6 ¼ In. | 300 |
| **Button,** Flasher, I Like Beatles, John, Paul, George, Ringo, Vari-Vue, N.Y., 2 ½ In. | 79 |
| **Button,** Ringo For President, On Decca Records, Red On White, 1964, 3 In. | 50 |
| **Doll,** Ringo Starr, Composition, Movable Head, NEMS Ent. Ltd., 1964, 4 ¼ In. | 30 |
| **Doll,** Ringo Starr, Hard Plastic, Rubber Head, Holding Drum, Remco, 1977, 4 In. | 77 |
| **Magazine,** Pageant Magazine, Paul McCartney Cover, Oct. 1976, 5 x 7 In. | 10 |
| **Pennant,** Band Image, Red, White, NEMS Ent. Ltd, 1964, 30 In. | 96 |
| **Pennant,** The Beatles, Liverpool, Black & White, Felt, Song Titles, c.1970, 29 x 11 In. | 140 |
| **Photograph,** Beatles Landing From Austria To Salzburg, Plane, 1965, 7 x 5 In. | 100 |
| **Photograph,** John Lennon, Paul McCartney, Candlestick Park, J. Marshall, 1988, 9 x 6 In. | 475 |
| **Postcard,** Beatles Receiving Award, Variety Club Great Britain, 1963 | 18 |
| **Postcard,** Beatles, Blue Suits, 1960s | 22 |
| **Poster,** Another Day, Butcher Cover, Beatles In Lab Coats, 1973, 24 x 36 In. | 185 |
| **Tie,** Silk, High Heel Shoe, Cactus, Roads, Apple Corps. Ltd., 57 x 4 In. | 24 |
| **Tumbler,** George Harrison Portrait, Black, Red Music Notes, 1964, 4 ¼ In. | 100 |
| **Tumbler,** Ringo Starr Portrait, Black, Red Music Notes, 1964, 4 ¼ In. | 100 |

**BEEHIVE,** Austria, or Beehive, Vienna, are terms used in English-speaking countries to refer to the many types of decorated porcelain bearing a mark that looks like a beehive. The mark is actually a shield, viewed upside down. It was first used in 1744 by the Royal Porcelain Manufactory of Vienna. The firm made what collectors call Royal Vienna porcelains until it closed in 1864. Many other German, Austrian, and Japanese factories have reproduced Royal Vienna wares, complete with the original shield or beehive mark. This listing includes the expensive, original Royal Vienna porcelains and many other types of beehive porcelain. The Royal Vienna pieces include that name in the description.

| | |
|---|---|
| **Bust,** Kinderkopf, Boy, Girl, Column Base, Royal Vienna, c.1860, 8 ¾ In., Pair *illus* | 677 |
| **Charger,** Bacchus & Ariadne In Chariot, 2 Cats Pulling, Pink & Gilt Scrolls, 14 In. | 2750 |
| **Charger,** Painted, Figures, 14 In. | 240 |
| **Charger,** Psyche, Muses, Buildings, Royal Vienna, Frame, 1800s, 18 ¾ In. | 5250 |
| **Cup & Saucer,** Figures, Dancing, Pink, Gold, Cream, Burgundy, 3 ½ In., 2 Piece | 123 |
| **Ewer,** Putti In Spring Landscape, Red Ground, Gilt Vines, Baluster, Footed, 15 x 9 In. | 500 |
| **Group,** Europa & The Bull, Royal Vienna, 22 x 27 In. | 590 |
| **Plate,** Konigen Luise Von Sachsen, Portrait Reserve, Royal Vienna, J. Gold, 9 ¾ In. | 594 |
| **Plate,** Lovers, Whispering, Octagonal, Red, Gold Border, Royal Vienna, c.1890, 9 In. | 1063 |
| **Plate,** Portrait Of Ruth, Royal Vienna, Austria, c.1900, 9 ⅜ In. *illus* | 750 |
| **Plate,** Portrait, Woman, Pink Gown, Curls, Hat, Leaf & Swag Border, 9 ⅝ In., Pair | 1094 |
| **Plate,** Psyche, Seated, Rocks, Lake, Gold, Red Geometric Border, Royal Vienna, c.1890, 9 In. | 1063 |
| **Plate,** Woman, Standing In Field, Geometric Border, Royal Vienna, c.1890, 9 ½ In. | 1188 |
| **Plate,** Woman, Surrounded By Putti, Red, Gold Border, Royal Vienna, c.1890, 8 ⅞ In. | 2750 |
| **Stein,** 3 Graces, Classical Woman, Cherub, Openwork Crown Thumblift, 6 In. | 2185 |
| **Stein,** Crowning Of Leopold The Glorious, Gold Leaves, Magenta Ground, 13 In. | 2415 |
| **Tray,** 3 Classical Maids, Purple Border, Gilt, Oval, Inset Handles, Royal Vienna, 18 In. | 250 |
| **Tray,** Bacchus, Ariadne, Reticulated Border, Rectangle, Royal Vienna, 14 ½ In. | 1750 |
| **Tray,** Painted, Classical Figures, Geometric Border, Royal Vienna, c.1900, 10 ½ x 12 In. | 780 |
| **Tray,** Raised Gilt Carriage Silhouettes, Scrollwork Borders, c.1900, 11 x 13 In. | 461 |
| **Urn,** Lid, Abgeblitz, Amd Ball Auf Der Alm, Scenes, Gilt, Vienna, E.L. Hermann, 44 In. | 11250 |
| **Urn,** Lid, Gilt, Jewels, Nude Panels, Iridescent Puce, Royal Vienna, c.1900, 25 In., Pair | 6875 |
| **Urn,** Painted, Woman Looking In Water, Gilt Serpentine Handles, 1800s, 12 ½ In., Pair | 2560 |
| **Vase,** Cleopatra, Flowers, Gold, Silver, Cobalt Ground, Signed Pilr, 9 ¼ In. | 1380 |
| **Vase,** Flowers, Yellow, Brown, Flower Mold, Gilt, Royal Vienna, 9 In. | 325 |
| **Vase,** Marie Antoinette, Gold, Blue Enamel, Scrolls, Flowers, Wagner, 5 ¾ In. | 1265 |
| **Vase,** Painted Reserve, 2 Children, Confiding, Gold Honeycomb, Royal Vienna, 32 In. | 7500 |
| **Vase,** Ruth, Woman Standing, Maroon Ground, Enamel Trim, Donath, Royal Vienna, 11 In. | 1298 |
| **Vase,** Violets, Yellow, Blue, Lavender, Gold Trim, Double Handles, Royal Vienna, 6 ¾ In. | 354 |
| **Vase,** Woman Seated, Cupid, Bow, Arrow, Gilt Handles, Urn Shape, Royal Vienna, 8 In. | 188 |

**BEER BOTTLES** *are listed in the Bottle category under Beer.*

**Beer Can,** Buffalo Extra Pale, Pride Of Sacramento, Cone Top, 7 ½ In.
$660

Morphy Auctions

**Beer Can,** Krueger Finest, K-Man Carrying Tray, Flat Top, 4 ¾ In.
$150

Morphy Auctions

**Bell,** Bronze, Barrel Shape, Gilt, Chinese Symbols, Dragons, Marked, Chinese, 12 In.
$17,775

James D. Julia Auctioneers

B

**Bell,** Bronze, Inscriptions, Designs, Amedee-Philippe Borrel, France, 1860s, 21 In.
$1,200

Cowan's Auctions

---

**Bell,** Bronze, Servants, Pierrot, Standing, Signed, Peter Tereszczuk, c.1910, 5½ In.
$270

DuMouchelles Art Gallery

---

**Belleek,** Vase, 5 Geishas, Umbrellas, Flowering Wisteria, Lenox, 16 In.
$960

Humler & Nolan

---

**BEER CANS** are a twentieth-century idea. Beer was sold in kegs or returnable bottles until 1934. The first patent for a can was issued to the American Can Company in September of that year, and Gotfried Kruger Brewing Company, Newark, New Jersey, was the first to use the can. The cone-top can was first made in 1935, the aluminum pop-top in 1962. Collectors should look for cans in good condition, with no dents or rust. Serious collectors prefer cans that have been opened from the bottom.

| | |
|---|---:|
| **Alt Heidelberg Guest Beer,** Flat Top, Man Holding Stein, Red, Blue, 5 In. | 660 |
| **Atlantic Beer,** Flat Top, Beer Of The South, 5 In. | 720 |
| **Buffalo Extra Pale,** Pride Of Sacramento, Cone Top, 7½ In. *illus* | 660 |
| **English Lad Beer,** Flat Top, Horse & Rider, Horseshoe, 5 In. | 4200 |
| **Flat Top,** Bull's-Eye, Red, Blue, Silver, 4¾ In. | 1440 |
| **Flat Top,** Grenadier Guards, James Bond, Special Blend, 4¾ In. | 540 to 720 |
| **Flat Top,** Lifeguards, Special Blend, Woman's Face, National Brewing Co., 4¾ In. | 600 |
| **Fort Sutter,** Flat Top, Bert McDonald Company, 5 In. | 480 |
| **Grace Bros. Brewing Extra Pale,** Flat Top, Blue, Orange, 5 In. | 480 |
| **Krueger Finest,** K-Man Carrying Tray, Flat Top, 4¾ In. *illus* | 150 |
| **Mule Wehle Stock Ale,** Flat Top, Mule Head, 4¾ In. | 120 |
| **Pacific Lager,** Flat Top, Blue & White, Sailboat, 5 In. | 2160 |
| **Salute Lager Beer,** Dome Top, Terminal Liquors Limited, 5½ In. | 1560 |
| **Schoenling Old Time Bock Beer,** Flat Top, Ram, 4¾ In. | 2040 |
| **Storz,** All Grain Slow Aged, Man Wearing Hat, Storz Brewing Co. | 3600 |
| **Tacoma Pale Beer,** Cone Top, Blue & White, 6 In. | 570 |
| **Williams Purple Cow,** Flat Top, Lager Beer, Purple, 4¾ In. | 3000 |

**BELL** collectors collect all types of bells. Favorites include glass bells, figural bells, school bells, and cowbells. Bells have been made of porcelain, china, or metal through the centuries.

| | |
|---|---:|
| **Brass,** Dolphin Stand, Cast, Leaf Molded Support, Stepped Base, 19 x 17 In. | 598 |
| **Brass,** Hotel, Bull Dog, Windup, Push Dog's Ears, 3⅜ x 4⅝ In. | 718 |
| **Brass,** Rooster, Green Gemstone Eyes, c.1940, 8 In. | 36 |
| **Brass,** Sleigh, 29 Graduated Bells, Leather Strap, c.1970, 92 In. | 92 |
| **Brass,** Table, Twist Finial, Reticulated, Jugendstil, Germany, c.1900, 3½ x 3⅞ In. | 340 |
| **Brass,** Wall, Engraved, Chain, 1800s, 15 x 7½ In. | 238 |
| **Bronze,** Barrel Shape, Gilt, Chinese Symbols, Dragons, Marked, Chinese, 12 In. *illus* | 17775 |
| **Bronze,** Cast Panels, Inscribed Text, Verdigris Patina, Chinese, 1800s, 10 In. | 120 |
| **Bronze,** Cast, Gothic Tracery Band, Scrolled Yoke, A. Fulton, Pittsburgh, 1800s, 28 In. | 2151 |
| **Bronze,** Crown, Matted Waist, Iron Clapper, Leather, Stamped ER, 20th Century, 38½ In. | 185 |
| **Bronze,** Inscriptions, Designs, Amedee-Philippe Borrel, France, 1860s, 21 In. *illus* | 1200 |
| **Bronze,** Servants, Pierrot, Standing, Signed, Peter Tereszczuk, c.1910, 5½ In. *illus* | 270 |
| **Cast Iron,** Hotel, Turtle, Windup Mechanism, Nickel Plated, 2 x 7 x 3¾ In. | 345 |
| **Cast Iron,** Stamped Fredericktown, Ohio, c.1860, 18½ In. | 90 |
| **Cut Glass,** Colonial, Dorflinger, 5½ In. | 622 |
| **Cut Glass,** Hobstar, Strawberry Diamond, Crosshatch Knob, 5½ In. | 254 |
| **Iron,** Sleigh, Leather Strap, 22 Graduated Strings, 11 & 38 In. | 86 |
| **Temple Gong,** Ebonized, Shaped Frame, Pierced, Chinese, 1900s, 38½ x 23¼ In. | 625 |

**BELLEEK** china was made in Ireland, other European countries, and the United States. The glaze is creamy yellow and appears wet. The first Belleek was made in 1857. All pieces listed here are Irish Belleek. The mark changed through the years. The first mark, black, dates from 1863 to 1890. The second mark, black, dates from 1891 to 1926 and includes the words *Co. Fermanagh, Ireland*. The third mark, black, dates from 1926 to 1946 and has the words *Deanta in Eirinn*. The fourth mark, same as the third mark but green, dates from 1946 to 1955. The fifth mark (second green mark) dates from 1955 to 1965 and has an R in a circle added in the upper right. The sixth mark (third green mark) dates from 1965 to 1981 and the words *Co. Fermanagh* have been omitted. The seventh mark, gold, was used from 1981 to 1992 and omits the words *Deanta in Eirinn*. The eighth mark, used from 1993 to 1996, is similar to the second mark but is printed in blue. The ninth mark, blue, includes the words *Est. 1857* and the words *Co. Fermanagh Ireland* are omitted. The tenth mark, black, is similar to the ninth mark but includes the words *Millennium 2000* and *Ireland*. It was used only in 2000. The eleventh mark, similar to the millennium mark but green, was introduced in 2001. The twelfth mark, black, is similar to the eleventh mark but has a banner above the mark with the words *Celebrating 150 Years*. It was used in 2007. The thirteenth trademark, used from 2008 to 2010, is similar to the twelfth but is brown and has no banner. The fourteenth mark, the Classic Belleek trademark, is similar to the twelfth but includes Belleek's website address. The Belleek Living trademark was introduced in 2010 and is used on items from that giftware line. The word *Belleek* is now used only on the pieces made in Ireland even though earlier pieces from other countries were sometimes marked *Belleek*. These early pieces are listed by manufacturer, such as Ceramic Art Co., Haviland, Lenox, Ott & Brewer, and Willets.

| | | |
|---|---|---|
| **Basket,** Dome Lid, Flower Encrusted, Double Scroll Handles, c.1980, 5 ¼ x 8 ¼ In. | | 469 |
| **Hair Receiver,** Purple Flowers, Leaves, Marked, 4 ¾ x 3 ½ In. | | 135 |
| **Mirror,** Flower Encrusted, Beaded Borders, Oval, c.1910, 17 In. | | 847 |
| **Ring Stand,** Cream, Garland Rim, Footed Basket Shape, Ireland, c.1915, 2 ½ x 4 ¾ In. | | 288 |
| **Tea Set,** Painted Swags, Turquoise Enamel Jewels, Elongated Handles, 10-In. Pot, 3 Piece | | 256 |
| **Vase,** 5 Geishas, Umbrellas, Flowering Wisteria, Lenox, 16 In. | *illus* | 960 |
| **Vase,** Figural, Fish, Entwined, Butterflies, Marked, Ireland, 15 ¾ In. | *illus* | 1250 |
| **Vase,** Impressionist Style Paint, Woodlands, Franz Arthur Bischoff, c.1890, 15 ¾ x 5 In. | | 584 |

**BENNINGTON** ware was the product of two factories working in Bennington, Vermont. Both the Norton Company and Lyman Fenton & Company were out of business by 1896. The wares include brown and yellow mottled pottery, Parian, scroddled ware, stoneware, graniteware, yellowware, and Staffordshire-type vases. The name is also a generic term for mottled brownware of the type made in Bennington.

| | | |
|---|---|---|
| **Bottle,** Coachman, On Barrel, Holding Glass, Bottle, Brown Streaked Glaze, c.1855, 10 ¾ In. | | 780 |
| **Bottle,** Rockingham Glaze, Streaked Brown, Cream, Man, Lyman Fenton & Co., 1855, 10 In. | | 300 |
| **Coffeepot,** Helmet Lid, Lobed, Blue, Yellow Brown Glaze, Lyman Fenton & Co., c.1850, 10 In. | | 360 |
| **Coffeepot,** Lid, Flint Enamel, Cream, Brown, Blue, Scalloped Rib, c.1855, 13 ½ In. | | 210 |
| **Coffeepot,** Ribbed, Brown, Blue, Yellow, Cream Glaze, Lyman Fenton & Co., c.1855, 9 ¾ In. | | 180 |
| **Crock,** Stoneware, Cobalt Blue Spotted Stag, Field, Fence, Lug Handles, J. & E. Norton, 1855, 15 In. | | 11400 |
| **Cuspidor,** Brown, Clubs, Diamonds, Hearts, Spades, Around Bowl | *illus* | 60 |
| **Flask,** Book, Bennington Battle, Blue, Brown, Yellow Streaks, Flint Enamel, c.1855, 7 In., 2 Qt. | | 840 |
| **Flask,** Book, Cream, Scroddled Ware, c.1848, 2 Qt., 6 In. | | 360 |
| **Flask,** Book, Flint Enamel, Blue Accents, Bennington Battle On Spine, 8 In. | | 330 |
| **Flask,** Book, Flint Enamel, Yellow, Brown, Green, Pennington Companion, 2 Qt., 8 In. | | 360 |
| **Flask,** Book, Yellow, Brown, Flint Enamel, c.1855, 2 Qt., 7 ⅝ In. | | 390 |
| **Flask,** Flint Enamel, Molded Seated At Table, Drinking, Cream, Brown, c.1855, 6 In. | | 420 |
| **Footbath,** Flint Enamel, Scalloped Ribs, Cream, Brown, Blue, Orange, c.1850, 20 In. | | 1800 |
| **Footbath,** Green Streaks, Scalloped Ribs, Flint Enamel, Lug Handles, c.1855, 8 In. | | 2400 |
| **Jardiniere,** Rockingham Glaze, Acanthus Leaf Molded, c.1850, 10 In., Pair | | 120 |
| **Jardiniere,** Swirled Alternate Ribs, Flint Enamel, Brown Mottled Glaze, c.1850, 9 In., Pair | | 1020 |
| **Jug,** Bird, Cobalt Blue, Salt Glaze, Julius Norton Co., c.1860, 13 ½ In., 2 Gal. | | 240 |
| **Jug,** Cobalt Blue Bird On Stump, Impressed J. & E. Norton, 1800s, 17 In. | | 450 |
| **Jug,** Cobalt Blue Bird, Slope Shoulder, J. & E. Norton, 13 In. | | 240 |
| **Jug,** Cobalt Blue Flower, Leaves, Gadrooned, J.& E. Norton, c.1855, 3 Gal., 15 ½ In. | | 720 |
| **Jug,** Cobalt Blue Rabbit, Square Spout, Ribbed Handle, Norton & Fenton, c.1845, 2 Gal. | | 2300 |
| **Jug,** Cobalt Blue, Flowering Stem, J. & E. Norton, c.1855, Gal., 10 ¾ In. | | 420 |
| **Jug,** Stoneware, Cobalt Blue Pheasant On Stump, Slip, J. & E. Norton, c.1855, 2 Gal. | | 4313 |
| **Paperweight,** Spaniel, Resting, Rockingham Glaze, c.1850, 4 ½ In. | | 240 |
| **Pitcher,** Basin, Flint Enamel, Diamond Pattern, Cream, Brown, Green, c.1850, 11-In. Pitcher | | 420 |
| **Pitcher,** Basin, Flint Enamel, Scalloped Ribs, Cream, Brown, Blue, Green, c.1855, 13 x 15 In. | | 780 |
| **Pitcher,** Brown Mottled Streaks, Yellow, Green, Diamond Pattern, Flint Enamel, 10 In. | | 390 |
| **Pitcher,** Stoneware, Flowers, Grapes, Albany Slip Glaze, Norton & Fenton, c.1845, 8 ½ In. | | 270 |
| **Snuff Jar,** Lid, Toby, Flint Enamel, Green, Cream, c.1849, 4 In. | | 330 |
| **Tobacco Jar,** Dome Lid, Flint Enamel, Vertical Ribs, c.1850, 9 In. | | 308 |
| **Tobacco Jar,** Flint Enamel, Glaze, Mottled Brown, Ribbed, Lug Handles, Lid, c.1850, 7 In. | *illus* | 288 |
| **Toby Pitcher,** Ben Franklin, Boot Handle, Rockingham Glaze, c.1850, 5 ¾ In. | | 330 |
| **Toby Pitcher,** Brown, Yellow Rockingham Glaze, Grapevine Handle, c.1850, 6 In. | | 480 |
| **Urn,** Coffee, Scalloped Rib, Flint Enamel, Cream, Brown, Orange, Blue, c.1855, 16 In. | | 540 |
| **Vase,** Spill, Flint Enamel, Resting Cow, By Tree Trunk, 7 ½ x 9 ¾ In. | | 720 |
| **Water Cooler,** Cobalt Blue Lion, Deer, Bands, J. & E. Norton, c.1855, 3 Gal., 13 In. | | 63250 |

**BERLIN,** a German porcelain factory, was started in 1751 by Wilhelm Kaspar Wegely. In 1763, the factory was taken over by Frederick the Great and became the Royal Berlin Porcelain Manufactory. It is still in operation today. Pieces have been marked in a variety of ways.

| | | |
|---|---|---|
| **Plaque,** A Time For Roses, Courting Couple, Roses, Gilt Frame, 5 ½ x 3 ½ In. | | 345 |
| **Plaque,** Daphne, Bust, Flowing Hair, Oval, Signed, A. Bock, c.1900, 10 ½ x 8 ½ In. | | 1680 |
| **Plaque,** Gypsy Girl, Wearing Necklace, Oval Gilt Frame, c.1900, 5 x 7 ½ In. | | 288 |
| **Plaque,** Gypsy, Standing Next To Tree, Scrolling Pierced Wood Frame, 10 x 6 ½ In. | | 1955 |
| **Plaque,** Painted, Idyllic Scene, Maiden, Fairy Godmother, Multicolor, Frame, 15 x 11 In. | | 989 |
| **Plaque,** Woman, Cumean Sibyl, Turban, Oval Frame, Germany, c.1905, 5 x 8 In. | | 259 |
| **Tea Cozy,** Blue, White Chinoiserie, Beaded, c.1870 | | 420 |
| **Vase,** Courting Scenes, Blue, Flared Mouth, Shouldered, Goat Head Handles, c.1890, 7 In. | | 115 |

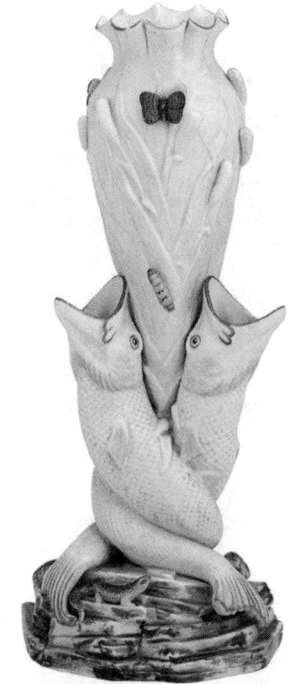

**Belleek,** Vase, Figural, Fish, Entwined, Butterflies, Marked, Ireland, 15 ¾ In.
$1,250

Rago Arts & Auction Center

**Bennington,** Cuspidor, Brown, Clubs, Diamonds, Hearts, Spades, Around Bowl
$60

Potter & Potter Auctions, Inc.

**Bennington,** Tobacco Jar, Flint Enamel, Glaze, Mottled Brown, Ribbed, Lug Handles, Lid, c.1850, 7 In.
$288

Jeffrey S. Evans & Assoc.

**Beswick,** Beatrix Potter, Figurine, 2 Gentleman Rabbits, Holding Christmas Stocking
$85

Potteries Specialist Auctions (PSA)

**Beswick,** Beatrix Potter, Figurine, 2 Gentleman Rabbits, Prim & Proper, Classic Jackets
$262

Potteries Specialist Auctions (PSA)

**Betty Boop,** Box, Candy Bar, Milk Nut Frappe, 5 Cents, Schutter-Johnson, 1931, 8 x 11½ In.
$548

Hake's Americana & Collectibles

---

**BESWICK** started making earthenware in Staffordshire, England, in 1936. The company is now part of Royal Doulton Tableware, Ltd. Figurines of animals, especially dogs and horses, Beatrix Potter animals, and other wares are still being made.

| | |
|---|---:|
| **Beatrix Potter,** Figurine, 2 Gentleman Rabbits, Holding Christmas Stocking .................*illus* | 85 |
| **Beatrix Potter,** Figurine, 2 Gentleman Rabbits, Prim & Proper, Classic Jackets ...............*illus* | 262 |
| **Beatrix Potter,** Figurine, Anna Maria, BP 3B .......... | 95 |
| **Beatrix Potter,** Figurine, Benjamin Bunny, BP 1A, 4 In. | 250 |
| **Beatrix Potter,** Figurine, Lady Mouse, BP 3B | 57 |
| **Beatrix Potter,** Figurine, Little Pig Robinson, BP 3C | 78 |
| **Beatrix Potter,** Figurine, Mr. Benjamin Benny, BP3 | 35 |
| **Beatrix Potter,** Figurine, Mrs. Tiggy Winkle, BP 1A, 3⅜ In. .......... | 175 |
| **Beatrix Potter,** Figurine, Old Woman In Shoe, BP 3B | 62 |
| **Beatrix Potter,** Figurine, Poorly Peter Rabbit, BP 3B. | 80 |
| **Beatrix Potter,** Figurine, Squirrel Nutkin, BP 3B | 75 |
| **Beatrix Potter,** Group, Flopsy, Mopsy & Cottontail, BP 2A, 2¾ x 3 In. | 165 |
| **Beatrix Potter,** Tom Kitten, BP 3B, 3¼ In. | 70 |
| **Figurine,** Chickadee, No. 929 | 85 |
| **Figurine,** Dog, Black Labrador, Seated, No. 2314, 13¼ In. | 130 |
| **Figurine,** Dog, Yorkshire Terrier, Standing, No. 3262 | 42 |
| **Figurine,** Elephant, No. 974 | 138 |
| **Figurine,** Fox, Seated, No. 2348, 12¼ In. | 431 |
| **Figurine,** Foxhound, Head Down, No. 2264. | 96 |
| **Figurine,** Gray Wagtail, No. 1041 | 60 to 77 |
| **Figurine,** Puma, On Rock, Matte Finish, No. 1702. | 212 |
| **Figurine,** Seal, No. 1534 | 135 |
| **Figurine,** Songthrush, No. 2308. | 142 |
| **Figurine,** Stonechat, On Branch, No. 2274. | 72 |
| **Figurine,** Tanager Bird, Red & Black, No. 928. | 125 |
| **Pitcher,** Hamlet Prince Of Denmark & Ghost, No. 1146, c.1970, 8 In. | 85 |
| **Toby Jug,** Midshipman, Seated, Playing Violin, 5 In. | 75 |
| **Toothbrush Holder,** Rabbit, Backpack, No. 665, 4¾ In. | 65 |
| **Vase,** Jumping Rabbits, Palm Trees, No. 667, 7¼ In. | 68 |
| **Vase,** Leaf Basket, Blue & Green Matte Glaze, No. 819, 11 x 10 In. | 78 |
| **Vase,** Ringed Pinch Pot, Urn Shape, Pastel Green, No. 347, 1930s, 4 In. | 49 |
| **Vase,** Ship, Stormy Sea, No. 1083, Peach, Mottled Turquoise, 6 In. | 65 |
| **Wall Pocket,** Straw Hat, Flowers, Yellow, No. 651. | 99 |

---

**BETTY BOOP,** the cartoon figure, first appeared on the screen in 1931. Her face was modeled after the famous singer Helen Kane and her body after Mae West. In 1935, a comic strip was started. Her dog was named Bimbo. Although the Betty Boop cartoons ended by 1938, there was a revival of interest in the Betty Boop image in the 1980s and new pieces are being made.

| | |
|---|---:|
| **Ashtray,** Betty & Bimbo, Porcelain, Iridescent, Japan, 1930s, 3 x 3 x 4 In. | 175 |
| **Box,** Candy Bar, Milk Nut Frappe, 5 Cents, Schutter-Johnson, 1931, 8 x 11½ In. ...........*illus* | 548 |
| **Doll,** Ballerina, Pink Tutu, Marty Toys, Box, c.1986, 12 In. | 55 |
| **Doll,** Bisque, Painted Side-Glancing Eyes, Jointed Arms, 1930s, 6 In. | 35 |
| **Doll,** Celluloid, Googly Eyes, Molded Hair, Jointed Shoulders, Japan, 8 In. | 38 |
| **Doll,** Cloth, Red Dress & Shoes, Fleischer Studio Inc., 1988, 39 In. | 20 |
| **Doll,** Cloth, Red Dress, Holding Roses, 11 In. | 19 |
| **Doll,** Wood, Painted Red Dress & Shoes, String Jointed, 1930s, 4½ In. | 110 |
| **Figurines,** Musicians, Drum, French Horn, Concertina, Violin, Box, 3¼ In., 4 Piece | 172 |
| **Nodder,** Bisque, Molded Hair, Jointed Shoulders, Japan, 1930s, 7 In. | 100 |
| **Pendant,** Betty, Holding Down Skirt, Sterling Silver, 2¾ x 1¼ In. | 115 |
| **Purse,** Betty, Holding Skirt, Stars, Tree, Lucite, Rhinestones, J. Massey, 1980s, 5 x 6 In. | 250 |
| **Puzzle Set,** 4 Puzzles, Boop, Fence, Tree, Bimbo, Box, 4 x 5½ In. | 172 |
| **Puzzle Set,** Movie-Land Cut Ups, 2 Puzzles, Horseback, Box, 7¼ x 8¼ In. | 225 |
| **Stand,** Figural, Waitress Pose, Tray, Red Dress, Red Heels, Black Round Base, 37 In. | 900 |
| **Toy,** Tea Set, Plates, Saucers, Teacups, Sugar & Creamer, 1930s, Box, 11 Pieces. | 316 |
| **Trinket Box,** Heart Shape, Betty Sitting, Hula Skirt, Vandor Sticker, 4 x 5 In. | 39 |
| **Wall Pocket,** Betty & Bimbo, Porcelain Lusterware, Fleischer Studios, 1930s | 110 |

---

**BICYCLES** were invented in 1839. The first manufactured bicycle was made in 1861. Special ladies' bicycles were made after 1874. The modern safety bicycle was not produced until 1885. Collectors search for all types of bicycles and tricycles. Bicycle-related items are also listed here.

| | |
|---|---:|
| **AMF,** Junior Roadmaster Spiderman, Solid Rubber Tires, Painted, Chrome, Decals, 1978, Child's. | 18 |

**B**

| | |
|---|---|
| **Baby Seat,** Iron Rod Frame, Black Paint, Fastens To Handlebars, Cloth Seat, c.1895, 11 x 9 In. . | 23 |
| **Bell,** Winged Wheel, Embossed Cast Top, Bristol Bell Co., c.1897, 1¾ In. | 176 |
| **Bicycle Scooter,** Hybrid, Red, White, Hard Rubber Tires, 53 In. | 180 |
| **Boneshaker,** J.B. Baker & Co., Iron, Wood Wheels, Leather Saddle, c.1870, 70 In. | 7200 |
| **Boneshaker,** Transitional High Wheel Ordinary, Bronze Oiler, Cast Pedals, Rear Brake, c.1870 . | 6143 |
| **Boneshaker,** Velocipede, Cast Iron, Wood, c.1860. | 2280 |
| **Bowden,** Spacelander, Painted Red, 2nd Generation, Bowdon Industries, c.1960 | 7605 |
| **Clothier & Burrows,** Roman, Racer, Fork-Mount Oil Lamp, c.1900, 22 In. | 995 |
| **Clown,** Square Wheels, 20th Century, 35 x 64 In. | 761 |
| **Columbia,** Standard High Wheel Ordinary, Open Head, Name Badge, Bell, c.1888, 56 In. | 4388 |
| **Comet,** Woman's, Wood Frame, Pneumatic Safety, Nickel Plate, Lucky Tread Tires, c.1898, 21 In. | 23400 |
| **Donaldson,** Tricycle, Jockey-Cycle, Red, Rubber Tires, White Spokes, 40 x 25 x 17 In. | 60 |
| **Galaxy,** Racer, Reynolds 531 Frame, Dawes, England, c.1970, 23 In. | 146 |
| **Gormully & Jeffery,** Safety, Woman's, Tangent Wheel, Hard Tire, Sprung Frame, c.1890, 20 In. | 4680 |
| **High Wheel,** Metal Frame, Leather Seat, Wood Handles, Pedals, Wheelmen Original, 41 x 53 In. | 4200 |
| **Huffy,** Radiobike, Cadmium Plated Rims, Bendix 2-Speed Rear Hub, White Wall Tires, 1955 | 3803 |
| **Huffy,** Radiobike, Red Paint, Blue & White Trim, Dayton, Ohio, c.1955, 41 x 70 In. ..........*illus* | 480 |
| **Indian Motorcycle Co.,** Pneumatic Safety, Horn, Electric Lamp, c.1915, 20½ In. | 7020 |
| **J.C. Higgins,** Boy's, Beehive Springer, Leather Seat, Batman Light, Sears, 1950s, 69 In. .....*illus* | 300 |
| **Jeunet,** Franche Comte, 10-Speed, Simplex Gears, Mafac Brakes, Grand Prix Saddle, c.1970, 23 In. | 70 |
| **Lozier Mfg. Co.,** Ice, Cleveland No. 4, Patented Feb. 4 1890, Dec. 30, March 17, 1891 | 11700 |
| **Mobo Minibike,** High Handlebars, Chain Guard, Training Wheels, 25 x 34½ In. ..............*illus* | 189 |
| **Poster,** Columbia Chainless Bicycle, A. Romes, J. Ottmann Lith. Co., 1800s, 87 x 40 In. | 5850 |
| **Poster,** Cycles Peugeot, Man, Woman, Bicycle, Tennis Court, E. Thelem, c.1897, 59 x 43 In. | 4608 |
| **Poster,** Swift World's Best Cycles, Man On Cycle, Frank Newbould, c.1935, 59 x 39 In. | 5500 |
| **Poster,** Victor Bicycles, Overman Wheel Co., Smiling Woman On Bike, H. Bradley, 1895, 41 x 13 In. | 6750 |
| **Rochester Cycle Mfg.,** Independent, Woman's, Wood Chain Guard, Brakes, c.1898, 22 In. | 614 |
| **Rollfast,** 2-Speed, Balloon, Spun Front Fork, Light, Horn Tank, Deluxe Model, Prewar | 1872 |
| **Schwinn,** Beach Cruiser, Springer Fork, Rack, Black, 26 In. | 330 |
| **Schwinn,** Black Phantom, Blue, c.1949 | 660 |
| **Schwinn,** Red Phantom, Leather Saddle, Horn, Fender Lights, 1959, 26 In. | 960 |
| **Schwinn,** Tandem, Town & Country, Middle Weight, Front & Rear Drum Brakes, c.1970 | 234 |
| **Schwinn,** Wasp, Balloon Cruiser, Painted Black, Chrome S-2 Rims, 1950s | 293 |
| **Shelby,** Flyer, Girl's, Blue, Red, White, Hand Grips, Bell, Front Fender Light, 26-In. Wheels | 157 |
| **St. Nicholas,** Transitional High Wheel Ordinary, Wood Spokes, Strap Steel Tire, 1876, 50 In. | 16380 |
| **Stearns,** Tandem, Male-Male, Yellow Fellow, Convertible Front Rider, c.1898, 23½ In. | 1112 |
| **Tricycle,** Foot Lever, Tiller, Metal Wheels, 22 x 46 In. | 234 |
| **Tricycle,** Hedstrom, Skyjet, Rear-Steering, Dark Red, White, Rectangular Handle, 30 In. | 60 |
| **Tricycle,** Horse, Wood, Carved, Painted, Hair Tail, 34 x 33 In. | 108 |
| **Tricycle,** Red & Green Stripes, Metal Rims, Wooden Spokes, Cloth Seat, Fringe, 44 In. | 4720 |
| **Tricycle,** Sky King, Airflow, Red & Cream, Orange, Calif., Reproduction ..............*illus* | 330 |
| **Tricycle,** Wood, Iron, Painted Red, Gilt Pinstriping, Turned Spool Pedals, 36 x 52 In. | 1599 |
| **Ward,** Quadracycle, Cushion Seat, J. Ward Coachmaker, c.1850, 42-In. Wheels, 84 x 32 In. | 28080 |

---

**BING & GRONDAHL** is a famous Danish factory making fine porcelains from 1853 to the present. Underglaze blue decoration was started in 1886. The annual Christmas plate series was introduced in 1895. Dinnerware, stoneware, and figurines are still being made today. The firm has used the initials *B & G* and a stylized castle as part of the mark since 1898. The company became part of Royal Copenhagen in 1987.

| | |
|---|---|
| **Figurine,** Goosegirl, No. 2254, 9 In. | 85 |
| **Figurine,** Ole, Holding Dachshund, No. 1747, 7 In. | 30 |
| **Figurine,** Polar Bear, Stamped In Green, 8 x 14 In. | 246 |
| **Figurine,** Who Is Calling, No. 2251, 6 In. | 73 |
| **Group,** 2 Friends, No. 1790, Boy, Hugging Bulldog, 4 x 5 In. | 300 |
| **Group,** Sleeping Monkey Family, No. 1581, Gray, Peach, Glazed, Marked, 4¾ In. | 236 |
| **Perfume Bottle,** Globe Shape, 7 x 5 In. | 69 |
| **Plate,** Christmas, 1908, Starlit Village, 7 In. | 18 |
| **Plate,** Christmas, 1972, Christmas In Greenland, 7 In. | 17 |
| **Plate,** Christmas, 1976, Christmas Welcome, Box, 7¼ In. | 30 |
| **Plate,** Christmas, 1977, Copenhagen Christmas, Box, 7¼ In. | 28 |
| **Plate,** Christmas, 1978, A Christmas Tale, Box, 7¼ In. | 22 |
| **Plate,** Christmas, 1979, White Christmas, Box, 7¼ In. | 30 |
| **Plate,** Christmas, 1980, Christmas In The Woods, 7¼ In. | 34 |
| **Plate,** Thanksgiving, 1987, The Pilgrims' Thanksgiving, Box | 45 |

**Bicycle,** Huffy, Radiobike, Red Paint, Blue & White Trim, Dayton, Ohio, c.1955, 41 x 70 In.
**$480**

Cowan's Auctions

**Bicycle,** J.C. Higgins, Boy's, Beehive Springer, Leather Seat, Batman Light, Sears, 1950s, 69 In.
**$300**

Morphy Auctions

**Bicycle,** Mobo Minibike, High Handlebars, Chain Guard, Training Wheels, 25 x 34½ In.
**$189**

Conestoga Auction Co., Inc.

**Bicycle,** Tricycle, Sky King, Airflow, Red & Cream, Orange, Calif., Reproduction
**$330**

Morphy Auctions

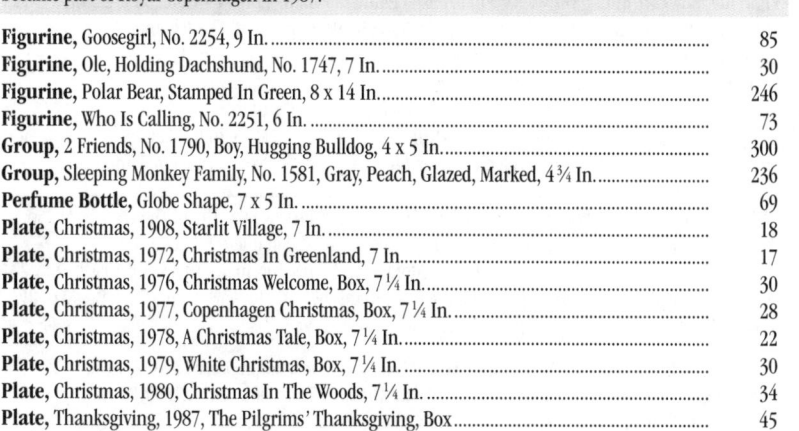

B

**Birdcage,** Wood, Pagoda, Tiered, Label, Made In China, 27 x 13 In.
$120

DuMouchelles Art Gallery

**Black,** Doll, Brown Cloth, Oil Painted Face, Stitch-Jointed, Varnish Finish, c.1900, 19 In.
$1,120

Theriault's

**Black,** Figure, Young Man, Dungarees, Bandanna, Hat, Cast Stone, c.1950, 44 x 15 In.
$593

James D. Julia Auctioneers

**BINOCULARS** of all types are wanted by collectors. Those made in the eighteenth and nineteenth centuries are favored by serious collectors. The small, attractive binoculars called opera glasses are listed in their own category.

| | |
|---|---|
| **Anchor Optical Corp.,** U.S. Navy, Mark 32, 7x50, 1943, Case, 7 x 3 x 7 In. | 207 |
| **Bausch & Lomb,** Leather Case | 45 |
| **Biascope,** Model E, Wollensak Optical Co., Bakelite, Green Swirl, Case | 35 |
| **Binolux,** Black, 7x35, Leather Case | 32 |
| **Busch,** Galilei, 8x56, Leather Case, 1930s, 7 x 5 In. | 75 |
| **Carpenter & Westley,** Tortoiseshell, Gilt Bronze, England, 1835-1914, 5 x 4 In. | 2706 |
| **Donkey Ears,** Telescope Stereoscopic No. 1B MK, Tripod, Case, 1953 | 950 |
| **E. Krauss & Co.,** Adjustable Sun Shades, Knob, France, 19 In. | 308 |
| **Legendre Grands Oculaires,** Night Hawk, 7x24, Paris, 1940s | 12 |
| **Merchant Marine,** Paris, Black Finish, 6¼ x 5 In. | 25 |
| **Negretti & Zambra,** London, Brass, 19th Century, 4¼ x 4 In. | 100 |
| **On Post,** Blue Paint, Coin-Operated, 62½ In. | 1200 |
| **San Streiffe,** No. 810, 7x35, Case, Japan | 49 |
| **Swarovski,** EL 10x52, Strap, Lens Caps, Case, Booklet, 6½ x 5½ In. | 2006 |
| **Zeiss,** 7x50, Leather Wrapped, Case, Germany, 6¾ In. | 431 |

**BIRDCAGES** are collected for use as homes for pet birds and as decorative objects of folk art. Elaborate wooden cages of the past centuries can still be found. The brass or wicker cages of the 1930s are popular with bird owners.

| | |
|---|---|
| **Bamboo,** Barrel Shape, Chinese, 25 x 10 In. | 420 |
| **Brass,** Regency Style, Round, Swing Perch, 1800s, 34 x 21 In. | 240 |
| **Brass,** Square, Rounded Corners, Onion Dome, Scrolled Feet, 2 Wells, Swing, 10 x 20 In. | 236 |
| **Mahogany,** Victorian Cathedral Shape, Turrets, Spires, On Stand With Drawer, 73 x 27 In. | 813 |
| **Metal,** House, Painted, Arched Window & Door, Late 19th Century, 24 x 21 x 20 In. | 600 |
| **Pine,** Victorian House, Windows, Gabled Roof, c.1890, 28½ x 21¾ In. | 381 |
| **Sewer Tile,** 8½ In. | 480 |
| **Softwood,** Crank, Rotating Bird, 19th Century, 4¾ In. | 147 |
| **Wirework,** Cone Shape, Round Base, 17 In. | 163 |
| **Wood,** Cathedral Shape, Stained, Black Highlights, Checkerboard Floor, Faux Rugs, 44 In. | 502 |
| **Wood,** House Shape, Wires, Pull-Out Tray, Red, 19th Century, American, 17½ x 15 In. | 810 |
| **Wood,** Pagoda, Tiered, Label, Made In China, 27 x 13 In. .................*illus* | 120 |
| **Wood,** Paint, Victorian, House Shape, Dome Turrets, Scrolled Stand, 62 x 28 In. | 313 |
| **Wood,** Victorian House, 2 Stories, Porch, Beaded Trim, Green, 1900s, 23 x 37 In. | 480 |
| **Wood,** Wire, Manor House, Turrets, Paint, France, c.1915, 35 x 40 In. | 938 |
| **Wood,** Wire, Windows, Wrap-Around Porch, Cupola, Folk Art, 21 x 31 x 15 In. | 118 |

**BISQUE** is an unglazed baked porcelain. Finished bisque has a slightly sandy texture with a dull finish. Some of it may be decorated with various colors. Bisque gained favor during the late Victorian era when thousands of bisque figurines were made. It is still being made. Additional bisque items may be listed under the factory name.

| | |
|---|---|
| **Bust,** Man, Woman, Feathery Hats, Period Attire, Blue Anchor Mark, 26 x 9 In., Pair | 3500 |
| **Dresser Box,** Figurine, Woman, Parade Drum, Feathered Cap, Ribbons, Germany, c.1875, 9 In. | 342 |
| **Dresser Box,** Figurine, Woman, Plaid Skirt, Molded Brown Hair, Pink Jacket, Germany, 9 In. | 171 |
| **Dresser Box,** Figurine, Woman, Sable Muff, Pink & White Skirt, Bonnet, Flowers, c.1860, 8 In. | 285 |
| **Figurine,** Boy, Girl, Sitting On Wicker Stool, Pastel Paint, Germany, 12 In., Pair | 123 |
| **Figurine,** Monkey, Human Like, Wearing Cap, Holding Bottle, Cup, 1800s, 13 x 6½ In. | 780 |
| **Figurine,** Women, Seated, Arrows, Wheat, Scythe, Cold Paint, Turquoise, 19 In., Pair | 531 |
| **Group,** Putto, On Goat, Oval Base, Continental, 8⅞ In. | 188 |
| **Mirror,** Dresser, Twig-Like Frame, Leaves, Painted White, 1900, 13 x 10 In. | 72 |
| **Plaque,** Betrothal, Pink, Blue, Cream Paint, Oval, Gilt Edge, Pucci, 13¾ x 10 In., Pair | 120 |
| **Vase,** September Morn, Figural Toddler, In Water, Shivering, Googly Eyes, G. Drayton, 7 In. | 392 |

**BLACK** memorabilia has become an important area of collecting since the 1970s. The best material dates from past centuries, but many recent items are also of interest. F & F is the mark used on plastic made by Fiedler & Fiedler Mold & Die Works, Inc. in the 1930s and 1940s. Objects that picture a black person may also be listed in this book under Advertising, Sign; Bank; Bottle Opener; Cookie Jar; Doll; Salt & Pepper; Sheet Music; Toy; etc.

| | |
|---|---|
| **Cane,** Maple, Figures, Horse's Head, Bird, Serpent Handle, Carved, Baltimore, c.1890, 38 In. | 115 |
| **Cane,** Maple, Rifles, Clasped Hands, Tobacco, United Order Of True Reformers, c.1890, 35 In. | 2645 |
| **Clicker,** Man With Monkey, Box, 4 In. | 175 |

**Cookie Jars** are listed in the Cookie Jar category.

**Dish,** Powder, Figural Lid, Josephine Baker, Dancing On Banana Bunch, Puff On Back, 4 In. ..... 4560
**Doll,** Boy & Girl, Cloth, Embroidered, Stitch-Jointed, Black Yarn Hair, c.1930s, 14 In., Pair ........ 336
**Doll,** Brown Cloth, Oil Painted Face, Stitch-Jointed, Varnish Finish, c.1900, 19 In. ..............*illus* 1120
**Doll,** Cloth, Make-Do, Lithograph, Cut Stuff Stitch, Printed Cotton, Slippers, c.1900, 16 In........ 224
**Doll,** Cloth, Oil Painted, Sewn-On Head, Brown Eyes, Eyeliner, Brown, Closed Mouth, 22 In....... 504
**Doll,** Cloth, Painted Features, Hair, Muslin, Columbian Doll Style, c.1890, 12 In. ........................ 336
**Doll,** Cotton, Painted Features, Elongated, Yarn Looped Hair, Stitch-Jointed, c.1910, 23 In......... 784
**Doll,** Cotton, Plump, Excelsior, Cloth, Painted Face, Wool Hair, Jointed Arms, c.1910, 23 In......... 952
**Doll,** Dancer, Woman, Brown Cloth Dress, Metal Rod, Clockwork, Key, c.1910, 4 x 7 In. .............. 1375
**Doll,** Julia Beecher, Missionary Rag Baby, Stockinet Head, Stitched Face, c.1890, 21 In.............. 4256
**Doll,** Make-Do, Rag Stuffed, Stockinet Head, Glass Eyes, Embroidered Features, c.1890, 20 In. ... 1904
**Doll,** Sateen, Embroidered Face, Bead Eyes, Lamb's Wool Hair, Stitch-Jointed, c.1900, 14 In. ...... 448
**Doll,** Stockinet, Button Eyes, Wool Yarn Cap Wig, Embroidered Features, Jointed, c.1890, 19 In.. 672
**Doll,** Witherspoon Rag, Cotton Sateen, Flat Dimensional Face, c.1900, 12 In........................... 2240
**Doll,** Wood, Carved Head, Painted Eyes, Sculpted Ears, Wiry Hair, Muslin, c.1890, 31 In. ............ 1344
**Doorstop,** Black Mammy, Holding 2 Babies, Multicolor, Cast Iron, 11 ½ In.............................. 390
**Doorstop,** Man, Banjo Player, Seated, Cast Iron, Spenser, 6 ½ In. ...................................... 780
**Figure,** Blackamoor, Carved, Painted, Yarn Hair, Cut-Off Shorts, Carved Base, 1800s, 18 In. ....... 615
**Figure,** Boy, Grass Shirt, Beating Drum, 4 In..................................................................... 25
**Figure,** Boy, Sitting, Eating Watermelon, 3 ½ In.................................................................. 51
**Figure,** Man, Carved, Painted, Dancing, Metal Wire, c.1875, 13 In........................................ 1150
**Figure,** Wood, Carved Head, Painted Eyes, Red Lips, Red Jacket, Articulated, c.1910, 15 In. ......... 615
**Figure,** Young Man, Dungarees, Bandanna, Hat, Cast Stone, c.1950, 44 x 15 In. .................*illus* 593
**Game,** Animal Grab, Black Child, Holding Umbrella, Tigers, Milton Bradley, Box, 7 ½ In............. 90
**Game,** Jolly Darkie Target, Cardboard, McLoughlin Bros., Box, 13 In...................................... 150
**Hearth Broom,** Walnut, Horsehair, Iron, Relief Carved, Grinning Blackface Holder, c.1825, 16 In... 494
**Inkwell,** Brass, Black Boy, In Hat, Head Is Hinged Lid, Glass Insert, Multicolor, 6 x 3 In. ............. 178
**Mask,** Minstrel Head, Papier-Mache, Painted, Top Hat, Red Lips, 19th Century, 16 x 13 In. .......... 1888
**Match Striker,** Green's August Flower German Syrup, Man, Wall, Die Cut, Cardboard, 8 In. ........ 308
**Nutcracker,** African Sailor's Head, Cast Iron, Old Paint, 19th Century, 8 In............................. 1680
**Painting,** Children Playing, Hydrant, Oil On Board, Shawmut Ave., Boston, A.R. Crite, 24 In. ..... 17080
**Poster,** Au Bal Negre, Josephine Baker, Nude, Man, Linen Mounted, 25 ½ x 31 In. ..................... 320
**Poster,** Minstrels, Neil O'Brien, Color Lithograph, c.1920, 24 x 16 ¼ In. ................................ 173
**Poster,** Movie, Black Gold, All Black Cast, Norman Studios, 1928, 27 x 41 In. ......................... 687
**Poster,** Uncle Tom's Cabin, Stage Play, Ackerman-Quigley Litho Co., c.1900, 23 x 30 In. ............ 475
**Recipe Box,** Aunt Jemima, Yellow, Black & Red Mammy Head, Fosta Product, 1950s................... 189
**Shoeshine Caddy,** Bellhop Figure, Wood, Painted, Red, Black, Faux Leather, c.1910, 8 In. ........... 474
**Sign,** Messet's Musical Entertainers, Black Man, Hat For Tips, Quigley Lith., Frame, 16 x 45 In. . 300
**Slave Tag,** Metal, Embossed No. 142 Porter Charleston 1858, 2 In.......................................... 1020
**Slave Transfer,** Father Deeds Slave Girl To Daughter, Shenandoah, Frame, 1823, 6 x 8 In. ........ 230
**Stringholder,** Butler, Yellow Tails, Top Hat, 2-Sided, Tray, Judd Co., 7 ½ In. ........................... 3600
**Thermometer,** Diaper Dan, Wood, Multi Product Co., Chicago, 1940s, 5 x 4 In. ........................ 32
**Walking Stick,** Man Wearing Hat, Walnut, Crop Jacket, Boots, Snake Encircles Shaft, 34 In....... 590
**Whirligig,** Man, Button-Front Vest, Top Hat, On Arrow, Wood, Painted, Folk Art Style, 43 In........ 660

---

**BLENKO GLASS COMPANY** is the 1930s successor to several glassworks founded by William John Blenko in Milton, West Virginia. In 1933, his son, William H. Blenko Sr., took charge. The company made tablewares and vases in classical shapes. In the late 1940s it hired talented designers and made innovative pieces. The company made a line of reproductions for Colonial Williamsburg. It is still in business and is best known today for its decorative wares and stained glass. All products are made to order.

*BLENKO HANDCRAFT*

**Ashtray,** Bowl Shape, Amber, Ruffled Rim, 3 x 6 In. ........................................................ 28
**Bookends,** Owl, Label, 7 In........................................................................................ 98
**Bowl,** Asymmetrical, Olive Green, 17 x 12 In.................................................................. 223
**Bowl,** Red-Orange To Yellow, Ruffled, 5 x 9 In............................................................... 95
**Bowl,** Yellow, Rough Texture, Scalloped, c.1960, 11 x 4 In. ............................................... 63
**Candleholder,** Emerald Green, Round Block, c.1950, 3 In. ................................................ 54
**Candlestick,** Amethyst, Foot Ring, Applied Punts, 3 In., Pair............................................. 132
**Centerpiece,** Trumpet Shape, Plum, Amber Foot, 7 ½ In. ................................................. 156
**Compote,** Ribbed, Azure, Emerald, 14 In. .................................................................... 112
**Decanter,** Red Air Trap Stopper, Yellow To Gold Shaped Body, c.1950, 16 ¼ In. ..................... 80
**Decanter,** Squat, Yellow, Stopper, 10 In........................................................................ 159
**Jug,** Amber, Crackle, Pontil, Kiwanis International Sticker, c.1971, 6 In.................................. 52
**Leaf Beaker,** Applied Leaves, Chartreuse, c.1936, 7 In...................................................... 51

**Boehm,** Snowy Owl, Pinecones & Branches, Rocky Base, c.1975, 39 x 29 In.
$2,375

Dallas Auction Gallery

---

**Bookends,** Dutch Boy & Girl, Painted Natural Colors, No. 332, Hubley, 4¾ In.
$118

Conestoga Auction Co., Inc.

---

**Bottle,** Barber, Blue Opalescent, Swirl, Genie Bottle Shape, Swollen Lip, c.1900, 7 In.
$149

Jeffrey S. Evans & Assoc.

**TIP**
*To dry a small-necked bottle, give it a last rinse with alcohol.*

# BLENKO

**Bottle,** Barber, Cranberry Opalescent, Fern, Melon Lobed Base, c.1890, 7 ⅛ In.
$177

Conestoga Auction Co., Inc.

**Bottle,** Barber, Cranberry To Clear, Flowers, Leaves, Panel Cut Neck, Silver Plate Cap, c.1870, 6 In., Pair
$1,380

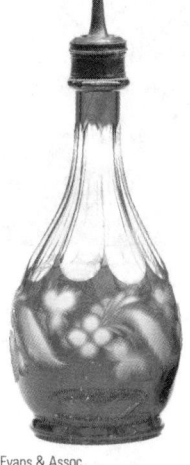

Jeffrey S. Evans & Assoc.

**Bottle,** Beer, Empire Bottling Co, Malt & Hops, Yellow Amber, Lightning Closure, 8 In.
$184

Glass Works Auctions

| | |
|---|---|
| **Paperweight,** Clear, Amber Shades, Bubbles, 4 In. | 46 |
| **Top Hat,** Ebony, 7 ¾ x 11 In. | 354 |
| **Vase,** Crackled, Turquoise Rosettes, Flared, 9 In. | 112 |
| **Vase,** Fish Shape, 1962, 12 x 9 In. | 98 |
| **Vase,** Heart Shape, Amethyst, 4 x 4 x 2 In. | 159 |
| **Vase,** Oval, Center Hole, Flat, Bubbles, Blue To Green, 6 x 10 x 3 In. | 80 |
| **Vase,** Purple Optic, Applied Leaf, 5 In. | 32 |
| **Vase,** Round, Green Optic, Ribbed, c.1952, 11 In. | 995 |
| **Vase,** Square, Ruffled Rim, Amber, 9 ½ In. | 150 |
| **Vase,** Trumpet, Canary Yellow, Corset Waist, Label, 22 In. | 86 |

**BLOWN GLASS**, *see Glass-Blown category.*

**BLUE GLASS**, *see Cobalt Blue category.*

**BLUE ONION**, *see Onion category.*

**BLUE WILLOW**, *see Willow category.*

**BOCH FRERES** factory was founded in 1841 in La Louviere in eastern Belgium. The wares resemble the work of Villeroy & Boch. The factory closed in 1985. M.R.L. Boch took over the production of tableware, but went bankrupt in 1988. Le Hodey took over Boch Freres in 1989, using the name Royal Boch Manufacture S.A. It went bankrupt in 2009. A new managing director is now running the company.

| | |
|---|---|
| **Vase,** Black, Yellow Stripes, Purple Flower, Tapered, 13 In. | 146 |
| **Vase,** Brown, Black Matte Glaze, Flowers, Green Ground, 7 ½ In. | 316 |
| **Vase,** Crackle Ware, Repeating Geometrics, Blued, Green, Yellow, Charles Catteau, 9 ¼ In. | 518 |
| **Vase,** Gourd, Catteau Harlequin, 6 ⅝ In. | 316 |

**BOEHM** is the collector's name for the porcelains of Edward Marshall Boehm. In 1953 the Osso China Company was reorganized as Edward Marshall Boehm, Inc. The company is still working in England and New Jersey. In the early days of the factory, dishes were made, but the elaborate and lifelike bird figurines are the best-known ware. Edward Marshall Boehm, the founder, died in 1969, but the firm has continued to design and produce porcelain. Today, the firm makes both limited and unlimited editions of figurines and plates.

| | |
|---|---|
| **2 Bluebirds,** Azalea Bush, 18 x 20 In. | 1971 |
| **Blue Grosbeak,** Oak Branch, Acorns, 11 ¼ In. | 246 |
| **Canada Goose,** Brown, Black, Gray, 7 x 4 ½ In., Pair | 60 |
| **Centerpiece,** Orchid & Hummingbird, Leaves, Tree Base, Green, Rose, 26 ½ In. | 2640 |
| **Common Tern,** Driftwood, Shells, Stines, 15 In. | 738 |
| **Crested Flycatcher,** Orange, Red Leaves, Branch, 18 ¼ In. | 338 |
| **Eagle,** Wings Outstretched, Rocky Base, c.1990, 20 x 19 In. | 1625 |
| **Foxes,** Standing, Sitting, By Tree Trunk, 12 In. | 277 |
| **Lion Cub,** Sitting, Signed, 5 In. | 60 |
| **Orchard Oriole,** Yellow Flower, Branch, 10 ¾ In. | 185 |
| **Owl,** Perched On Book, Signed, 9 In., Pair | 12 |
| **Parula Warblers,** Purple Morning Glory, Tree Trunk, 16 In. | 277 |
| **Raccoons,** On Tree, 12 In. | 310 |
| **Snowy Owl,** Pinecones & Branches, Rocky Base, c.1975, 39 x 29 In. ..........*illus* | 2375 |
| **Tumbler Pigeons,** White, Gray, 8 ¼ In., Pair | 90 |
| **Western Bluebirds,** Yellow Blossom Branch, 17 ½ In. | 984 |
| **Western Meadowlark,** Green Leaves, Yellow Flowers, 12 ¾ In. | 277 |
| **Woodcock,** Orange Beak, Green Leaf Oval Base, 10 ½ In. | 240 |
| **Yellow Bellied Sapsucker,** Pink Blossoms, Branch, 13 ½ In. | 660 |
| **Yellow Shafted Flicker,** On Branch, Wings Up, 13 ½ In. | 461 |
| **Yellowhammers,** Chicks, In Hawthorn, Oval Stand, 1973, 11 ¾ In. | 240 |

**BONE** includes those articles made of bone not listed elsewhere in this book.

| | |
|---|---|
| **Bodkin Case,** Carved, Fretwork Designs, Tubular, Rounded Ends, Vienna, 5 ½ In. | 1064 |
| **Box,** Carved, Medieval Style, Roundels On Sides, Bottom, Continental, 2 ¼ x 4 ½ In. | 219 |
| **Box,** Pantry, Oval, Copper Tacks, Whalebone Pegs, c.1840, 2 x 6 x 4 In. | 2160 |
| **Busk,** Baleen, Scratched American Shield, Memorial Scene, Trees, New England, c.1800, 14 In. | 369 |

| | |
|---|---|
| **Case,** Garden Table Shape, 6-Sided, Lidded, Jar Center, Wax, Bird, France, 2 ½ In. | 840 |
| **Model,** Guillotine, Napoleonic Prisoner Of War, France, c.1810, 9 In. | 2446 |
| **Oil Cask Measure,** Whalebone, Applied Metal Diamond Quarter Markers, 35 ½ In. | 1230 |
| **Toy,** 2 Acrobats, Balancing Bar, Articulated Joints, Carved, Leafy Base, Chinese, c.1860, 5 In. | 392 |
| **Watch Fob,** Gambler's Hand Holding Die, Square Base With Card Suits, 2 In. | 540 |

**BOOKENDS** have probably been used since books became inexpensive. Early libraries kept books in cupboards, not on open shelves. By the 1870s bookends appeared, especially homemade fret-carved wooden examples. Most bookends listed in this book date from the twentieth century. Bookends are also listed in other categories by manufacturer or material. All bookends listed here are pairs.

| | |
|---|---|
| **Bears,** Wearing Tall Hats, On Balls, Bronze, Tricolor Patination, Japan, 8 ¼ x 7 In. | 471 |
| **Buccaneer,** Bronze, Sword, Coiled Rope, Painted, Paul Herzel, 10 x 4 x 4 In. | 125 |
| **Cat,** Bronze, Arched Back, Verdigris Finish, Tiffany, Early 20th Century, 6 x 7 ¼ In. | 3567 |
| **Chinese Boy,** Girl, Stacked Books, Gold Finish, c.1930, 5 x 4 x 8 In. | 245 |
| **Dancer,** Arabesque, Cast Iron, Hubley, 6 In. | 575 |
| **Dog,** Bronze, Modernist Style Terriers, E. Nikolsky, France, c.1925, 6 ½ In. | 584 |
| **Dog,** English Setter, Cast Iron, Walking, 1930, 4 ½ In. | 46 |
| **Dog,** German Shepherd, Doghouse, Cast Iron, 6 ½ x 5 x 3 ½ In. | 350 |
| **Dog,** Greyhound, Seated, Looking Up, Marble Base, 11 x 6 ½ In. | 250 |
| **Dog,** Scottie, Cast Iron, White, 6 ½ In. | 23 |
| **Dog,** Scottie, On Fence, 4 ¾ In. | 154 |
| **Dolphins,** Bronze, Open Mouth, Tail Up, 15 x 6 In. | 300 |
| **Dutch Boy & Girl,** Painted Natural Colors, No. 332, Hubley, 4 ¾ In. ....................*illus* | 118 |
| **End Of Trail,** Bronze, 5 x 5 ½ In. | 125 |
| **Garden Gate,** Syroco Wood, Hanging Books, c.1935, 5 ⅝ x 5 ⅛ In. | 49 |
| **Globe,** Wood, Papier-Mache, Italy, c.1960, 6 ¼ x 6 x 3 ⅞ In. | 22 |
| **Goose,** In Flight, Cast Gray Metal, Jennings Brothers, c.1930, 5 x 6 In. | 125 |
| **Hammered,** Brass, Bronze, Roycroft, Marked, 3 ½ In. | 85 |
| **Horse Head,** Brass, 1900s, 7 In. | 430 |
| **Indian,** End Of Trail, Cast Iron, Spear Down, Painted, Hubley, 6 In. | 270 |
| **Indian,** On Horseback, Cast Iron, Painted, Shaped Base, 6 x 4 In. | 92 |
| **Indian,** Seated On Horse, Arms Out, Cast Iron, Hubley, 5 ½ In. | 210 |
| **Medallion,** Bronze, Hammered, Enamel, Bird, Radiating Plumage, Blue, Rebecca Cauman, 5 In. | 246 |
| **Pan,** Bronze, Kneeling On Rocks, Playing Pipe, B. Lillian Link, c.1915, 5 In. | 594 |
| **Parakeets,** On Branches, Bronze, Green Onyx Base, 4 ¾ In. | 406 |
| **Pushing Men,** Bronze, Harriet W. Frishmuth, Gotham Co., c.1930, 7 ½ x 4 ½ In. | 5760 |
| **Satyr,** Bronze, Playing Pipes, Stepped Base, c.1915, 6 In. | 563 |
| **Stylized Figure On Horseback,** Brass, Flat Scalloped Base, Flower, Hagenauer, 5 x 5 In. | 250 |
| **Stylized Figure,** Sitting, Brass, Wood, Hat, Arms Folded, Hagenauer Style, Austria, 6 In. | 188 |
| **Tomb Entrance,** Bronze, Egyptian Revival, 6 ½ x 5 ½ In. | 210 |
| **Virginia Creeper,** Bronze, Square, Open Center, 5 x 6 In. | 244 |
| **Whalemen,** Gold Colored, Boat, Waves, Spears, 7 In. | 132 |

**BOOKMARKS** were originally made of parchment, cloth, or leather. Soon woven silk ribbon, thin cardboard, celluloid, wood, silver, tortoiseshell, and metals were used. Examples made before 1850 are scarce, but there are many to be found dating before 1920.

| | |
|---|---|
| **Celluloid,** Die Cut, Cross, Violets, Lord Bless Thee, 1900s, 4 x 2 In. | 26 |
| **Celluloid,** Heron, Multicolor, 4 In. | 31 |
| **Embroidered,** Flowers, Butterfly, Oriental, 2 ½ x 9 In. | 7 |
| **Enameled,** Butterfly, 5 ½ x 2 In. | 12 |
| **Needlepoint,** Remember Me, 1800s, 8 x 4 In. | 16 |
| **Punch Paper,** Challis, Crucifix, Alphabet, Hand Sewn, 4 x 2 In. | 65 |
| **Punch Paper,** Lavender Cross, Green Ribbon, 4 x 2 In. | 20 |
| **Russian Silver,** Cabochon Sapphires, Faberge, Signed, 5 ½ In. | 8500 |
| **Silk,** Child Holding Cross, c.1880, 3 x 7 In. | 14 |
| **Sterling Silver,** Art Nouveau, Rectangular, Flowers, Pierced Splat, 11 ⅝ x 2 ½ In. | 246 |
| **Sterling Silver,** Cherub, Howard Sterling Co., c.1890, 5 ¼ In. | 183 |
| **Sterling Silver,** Dagger, 2 ½ In. | 25 |
| **Sterling Silver,** Man In The Moon, Star, 3 ½ In. | 45 |
| **Sterling Silver,** Open Book, Tiffany & Co., 2 ⅝ x 2 ¼ In. | 79 |
| **Sterling Silver,** Shell Shape, Monogram, Reed & Barton, c.1950, 1 ½ x 1 In. | 30 |
| **Sterling Silver,** Toad, 2 ¾ In. | 53 |
| **Thy Will Be Done,** Needlepoint, 8 x 2 In. | 5 |

**Barber Bottles**
Barber bottles are available in all kinds of glass: pressed, carnival, milk, cut, opalescent, overlay, and other art glass. Many have enameled designs or acid-etched decorations. They are sometimes labeled with the customer's name or with contents, such as "Bay Rum" or "Witch Hazel." They often come in pairs and occasionally have a matching vase for shaving paper. The vases are rare today.

**Bottle,** Bitters, Brown's Celebrated Indian Herb, Patented 1868, Amber, 12 ⅜ In.
$748

Glass Works Auctions

**Bottle,** Bitters, Dr. C.W. Roback's Stomach, Cincinnati, Barrel, Light Amber, 9 ¼ In.
$392

American Bottle Auctions

**Bottle,** Bitters, Dr. J. Hostetter's Stomach, Olive Amber, Sloping Collar, c.1870, 9¼ In.
**$575**

Glass Works Auctions

**Bottle,** Bitters, Dr. Petzold's Genuine German, Incept. 1862, Yellow Amber, Ribbed, 10½ In.
**$995**

Norman C. Heckler & Company

**Bottle,** Bitters, Globe Tonic, Semi-Cabin, Golden Amber, c.1870, 10 In.
**$1,610**

Glass Works Auctions

**BOSSONS** character wall masks (heads), plaques, figurines, and other decorative pieces were made by W.H. Bossons, Limited, of Congleton, England. The company was founded in 1946 and closed in 1996. Dates shown are the date the item was introduced.

| | |
|---|---|
| **Wall Mask,** Breton Woman, 5½ x 5 In. | 38 |
| **Wall Mask,** Emiliano Zapata, 7 In. | 215 |
| **Wall Mask,** Eskimo, 6½ In. | 48 |
| **Wall Mask,** Himalayan Man, c.1966, 5 In. | 72 |
| **Wall Mask,** King Henry VIII | 155 |
| **Wall Mask,** Kurd, c.1963, 5 x 4 In. | 75 |
| **Wall Mask,** Mr. Pickwick, c.1964, 4¾ x 3¼ In. | 25 |
| **Wall Mask,** Old Timer, 1960s, 6 x 6 In. | 125 |
| **Wall Mask,** Paddy, 5 In. | 40 |
| **Wall Mask,** Pancho, 1960s, 7¼ x 6½ In. | 65 |
| **Wall Mask,** Sea Captain, 1965, 5¼ In. | 50 |
| **Wall Mask,** Skipper, 6 x 3¾ In. | 95 |
| **Wall Plaque,** Custer & Sitting Bull, c.1989, 8 In. | 249 |
| **Wall Plaque,** Dog, English Setter, 5 In. | 95 |
| **Wall Plaque,** Dog, Golden Retriever, Collar, Gold Buckle, c.1968, 4 In. | 98 |
| **Wall Plaque,** Mountain Lion, On Limb, 16 x 6 In. | 60 |
| **Wall Plaque,** Poodle, White, Key Hook, c.1945, 5 x 4 In. | 50 |
| **Wall Plaque,** Raccoon, In Tree, 12¼ In. | 65 |
| **Wall Plaque,** Squirrel, Holding Acorn, On Leafy Branch, 7 In. | 30 |
| **Wall Plaque,** Woodpecker, Babies, c.1968, 12 In. | 75 |

**BOSTON & SANDWICH CO.** *pieces may be found in the Sandwich Glass category.*

**BOTTLE** collecting has become a major American hobby. There are several general categories of bottles, such as historic flasks, bitters, household, and figural. ABM means the bottle was made by an automatic bottle machine after 1903. Pyro is the shortened form of the word *pyroglaze,* an enameled lettering used on bottles after the mid-1930s. This form of decoration is also called ACL or applied color label. For more prices, go to kovels.com.

**Avon** started in 1886 as the California Perfume Company. It was not until 1929 that the name Avon was used. In 1939, it became Avon Products, Inc. Avon has made many figural bottles filled with cosmetic products. Ceramic, plastic, and glass bottles were made in limited editions.

| | |
|---|---|
| **Avon,** Bell, Emerald Green, Embossed, 1978, 6 x 3 In. | 30 |
| **Avon,** Canary, Yellow, 5 In. | 28 |
| **Avon,** Car, Chrysler Town & Country, Burgundy, Cream, 7 x 2 In. | 10 |
| **Avon,** Cruet, Ruby Red, Loop Handle, Paper Label, 5¼ In. | 15 |
| **Avon,** Foal, Resting, Amber, 1979, 5 x 3½ In. | 8 |
| **Avon,** Pipe, Leprechaun Head Bowl, 7 In. | 23 |
| **Avon,** Tepee, Amber, Plastic Cap, Paper Label, c.1974, 5 In. | 7 |
| **Barber,** Blue Opalescent, Fern, Melon Lobed Base, c.1894, 7 In. | 374 |
| **Barber,** Blue Opalescent, Swirl, Ceramic Stopper, c.1900, 9 x 2¾ In. | 196 |
| **Barber,** Blue Opalescent, Swirl, Genie Bottle Shape, Swollen Lip, c.1900, 7 In. .......*illus* | 149 |
| **Barber,** Cranberry Opalescent, Coral Reef, Tapered, Hobbs, Brockunier & Co., c.1890, 7 x 4 In. | 259 |
| **Barber,** Cranberry Opalescent, Fern, Melon Lobed Base, c.1890, 7⅛ In. ...........*illus* | 177 |
| **Barber,** Cranberry To Clear, Flowers, Leaves, Panel Cut Neck, Silver Plate Cap, c.1870, 6 In., Pair .*illus* | 1380 |
| **Barber,** Overlay, Ruby Cut To Clear, Ear Shape, Leaf Band, Screw Cap, 6½ In., Pair | 1380 |
| **Beer,** Baller Stout, Three Floyds Brewing Co. | 250 |
| **Beer,** C.D. Postel, S.F. Cal., Embossed Sheaf Of Wheat, Amber, Sloping Collar, 11½ In. | 560 |
| **Beer,** Empire Bottling Co., Malt & Hops, Yellow Amber, Lightning Closure, 8 In. .......*illus* | 184 |
| **Beer,** John Ryan Porter & Ale, Philada, XX, 1866, Blue, Sloping Double Collar | 224 |
| **Beer,** Soda, Albert Von Harten, Savannah, Ga., Teal, Blob Top | 146 |
| **Beer,** Wooden Hell, Flossmoor Station Restaurant & Brewery, 22 Oz. | 415 |
| **Bininger,** A.M. & Co., 375 Broadway, N.Y., Yellow, Topaz Tone, 9¾ In. | 1287 |
| **Bininger,** A.M. & Co., Old Dominion Wheat Tonic, Yellow Green, Arched Sides, 9¾ In. | 1680 |
| **Bitters,** Baker's, Orange Grove, Topaz, Sloping Collar, c.1870, 9½ In. | 920 |
| **Bitters,** Brown's Celebrated Indian Herb, Indian Maiden, Yellow Amber, 12 In. | 585 |
| **Bitters,** Brown's Celebrated Indian Herb, Patented 1868, Amber, 12⅜ In. ..........*illus* | 748 |
| **Bitters,** Brown's Iron, Honey Amber, Embossed, Paper Label, Double Collar, c.1890, 8⅝ In. ....... | 230 |
| **Bitters,** Caldwell's Herb, Great Tonic, Yellow Amber, 3-Sided, Tapered, Indented, 12 In. | 476 |
| **Bitters,** Cundurango, Amber, Indented Panels, Applied Square Collar, 9 In. | 1568 |
| **Bitters,** David Andrews' Vegetable Jaundice, Providence, R.I., Aqua, Tombstone, 8 In. | 2457 |

| | | |
|---|---|---|
| **Bitters,** Doctor Fisch's, Fish, Amber, Rounded Collar, 11 ½ In............................................... | | 246 |
| **Bitters,** Doyle's Hop, 1872, Amber, Square, c.1860, 9 ½ In............................................... | | 35 |
| **Bitters,** Dr. C.W. Roback's Stomach, Cincinnati, Barrel, Light Amber, 9 ¼ In. .....................*illus* | | 392 |
| **Bitters,** Dr. E.P. Eastman's Yellow Dock, Lynn, Mass., Aqua, Rectangular, Beveled, 7 ¾ In. ........... | | 2457 |
| **Bitters,** Dr. F. Woodbridge Headache, Red Amber, Square, Indented Panels, 9 In......................... | | 4680 |
| **Bitters,** Dr. J. Hostetter's Stomach, Olive Amber, Sloping Collar, c.1870, 9 ¼ In. .................*illus* | | 575 |
| **Bitters,** Dr. Loew's Celebrated Stomach & Nerve Tonic, Yellow Olive, Swirl Neck, 9 ¼ In. ............. | | 504 |
| **Bitters,** Dr. M.M. Fenner's Capitol, Fredonia, N.Y., Blue Aqua, Label, 9 In............................. | | 123 |
| **Bitters,** Dr. Petzold's Genuine German, Incept. 1862, Yellow Amber, Ribbed, 10 ½ In. ........*illus* | | 995 |
| **Bitters,** Dr. Soule's Hop, Amber, Embossed Monogram, Indented, 9 ½ In................................. | | 213 |
| **Bitters,** Dr. Wheeler's Tonic, Sherry Wine, 1849, Boston, Sea Green, Roped Corners, 9 ½ In......... | | 2691 |
| **Bitters,** Dr. Wonser's U.S.A. Indian Root, Aqua Tint, Fluted Shoulder, Rings, 10 ¾ In. ................. | | 1064 |
| **Bitters,** Drake's Plantation, 1860, 6 Log, Raspberry Puce, Sloping Collar 10 In......................... | | 187 |
| **Bitters,** Drake's Plantation, 1860, Amber, Cabin, Sloping Collar, c.1870, 10 In......................... | | 92 |
| **Bitters,** Globe Tonic, Semi-Cabin, Golden Amber, c.1870, 10 In. ...............................*illus* | | 1610 |
| **Bitters,** Greeley's Bourbon, Olive, Barrel, Applied Mouth, c.1870, 9 ⅜ In. .............................. | | 2185 |
| **Bitters,** Hall's, Barrel, Golden Yellow, Topaz Tone, Squared Collar, c.1870, 9 In. .............*illus* | | 527 |
| **Bitters,** Hierapicra, Extract Of Figs, California Botanical Society, Aqua Blue, 9 ⅝ In. ................... | | 1287 |
| **Bitters,** Jacob Pinkerton, Wahoo & Calisaya, Cabin, Golden Amber, Sloping Collar, 10 In........... | | 995 |
| **Bitters,** John Moffat, Phoenix, New York, Olive Green, Sloping Collar, c.1860, 5 ½ In.................. | | 863 |
| **Bitters,** John Moffat, Phoenix, Price 1 Dollar, Aqua Tint, Beveled, Rolled Rim, 5 ½ In.................. | | 280 |
| **Bitters,** John Root's, Buffalo, N.Y., Semi-Cabin, Blue Aqua, 10 ¼ In...................................... | | 560 |
| **Bitters,** Kelly's Old Cabin, Amber, Cabin Shape, 1863, 9 ⅜ In. ................................*illus* | | 1840 |
| **Bitters,** Maynard's Star, Shaded Amber, Square, Arched Panels, Sloping Collar, 9 In.................... | | 995 |
| **Bitters,** Morning Star, Inceptum, Amber, Tapered, Diagonal Ribs, Sloping Collar, 12 ½ In... | | 316 to 374 |
| **Bitters,** Moulton's Oloroso, Embossed Pineapple, Aqua, Mug Base, 11 ½ In. ......................... | | 420 |
| **Bitters,** National, Ear Of Corn, Amber, Sloping Double Collar, 12 ¼ In................................... | | 281 |
| **Bitters,** National, Ear Of Corn, Golden Amber, Applied Ring Mouth, c.1875, 12 ½ In. ............... | | 460 |
| **Bitters,** National, Ear Of Corn, Pink Puce, Sloping Double Collar, 12 ½ In............................... | | 3218 |
| **Bitters,** Old Hickory Celebrated Stomach, Amber, Case Gin Shape, 9 In................................. | | 308 |
| **Bitters,** Old Homestead Wild Cherry, Cabin, Amber, c.1870, 9 ½ In. ..........................*illus* | | 374 |
| **Bitters,** Pepsin, R.W. Davis Drug Co., Chicago, Lime Green, Fluted Shoulder, 8 In. .................... | | 157 |
| **Bitters,** Perrine's Apple Ginger, Philada., Cabin, Yellow Green, Roped Corners, 10 In.................. | | 2240 |
| **Bitters,** Pineapple, J.F.L. Capital On Base, Amber, Pink Iron Pontil, Applied Top ........................ | | 2464 |
| **Bitters,** Rising Sun, John C. Hurst, Philada, Yellow Amber, Square, Indented Panels, 9 ⅜ In. ...... | | 308 |
| **Bitters,** S.O. Richardson, Smooth Base ..................................................................... | | 90 |
| **Bitters,** Sazerac Aromatic, Milk Glass, Lady's Leg Neck, 10 In.............................................. | | 269 |
| **Bitters,** Simon's Centennial, G. Washington Bust, Aqua, Double Collar, 10 In............................ | | 748 |
| **Bitters,** Solomons' Strengthening & Invigorating, Savannah, Cobalt Blue, Paneled, 9 ¾ In......... | | 1638 |
| **Bitters,** Suffolk, Philbrook & Tucker, Boston, Pig, Yellow Amber, 10 In.................................... | | 819 |
| **Bitters,** Tyree's Chamomile, Amber, Square Mouth, c.1870, 6 ½ In. ..................................... | | 207 |
| **Bitters,** W.C. Brobst & Rentschler, Reading, Pa., Barrel, Amber, 10 ¾ In................................ | | 448 |
| **Bitters,** Warner's, Orange Amber, Applied Double Collar, c.1885, 9 ½ In. ............................... | | 1093 |
| **Bitters,** Wormser Bros., San Francisco, Amber, Double Roll Collar, Flask ............................... | | 728 |
| **Bitters,** Zingari, F. Rahter, Root Beer, Amber, Lady's Leg Neck, Square Collar, 12 ¾ In.............. | | 410 |
| **Black Glass,** Bulbous, Olive Green, Stippled, Andrew McCruther, 1866, 8 ¾ In. .............*illus* | | 234 |
| **Blown,** Amethyst, Vertical Ribs, Pontil, 6 ¾ In............................................................. | | 123 |
| **Blown,** Dutch Onion, Medium Olive Green, Kick-Up Base, 1700s, 7 In.................................... | | 104 |
| **Blown,** Globular, Amber, Cylindrical Neck, Squared Ring Lip, Pontil, 12 In.............................. | | 510 |
| **Blown,** Globular, Deep Olive Green, Squat, Flared Out Rim, 10 x 9 In. .................................. | | 497 |
| **Blown,** Globular, Yellow Olive, Bulbous, Flared Mouth, 3 In................................................ | | 3510 |
| **Coca-Cola** bottles are listed in the Coca-Cola category. | | |
| **Cologne,** 12-Sided, Canary Yellow, Outward Rolled Mouth, 9 ⅞ In....................................... | | 702 |
| **Cologne,** Bunker Hill Monument, Milk Glass, Obelisk Stopper, c.1870, 14 In. ...............*illus* | | 1035 |
| **Cologne,** Cut Glass, Amber Cut To Clear, Sterling Silver Mounted, c.1890, 6 In. ...............*illus* | | 6600 |
| **Cologne,** Monument, Cobalt Blue, Brick Texture, Tapered, Flared, 11 ¾ In. ............................ | | 896 |
| **Cologne,** Monument, Emerald Green, Square, Tapered, Flared Mouth, 12 In............................. | | 1287 |
| **Cologne,** Overlay, Chartreuse Cut To White, Vine & Berry, Pear Shape, Stem Stopper, 3 ¾ In....... | | 1610 |
| **Cologne,** Sandwich, Amethyst, 10-Sided, Hourglass, Flared Out Lip, c.1870, 6 ½ In. ................ | | 288 |
| **Cologne,** Sandwich, Style, Turquoise, Thumbprint Panels, Herringbone Corners, c.1870, 9 In.... | | 1495 |
| **Cosmetic,** Ayer's Hair Invigorator, Cobalt Blue, Shaped Stopper, Label, Box, 7 In. ..................... | | 235 |
| **Cosmetic,** Cram's Vegetable Hair Tonic, Boston, Square, Beveled Corners, 7 ⅝ In....................... | | 410 |
| **Cosmetic,** Fountain Of Youth Hair Restorer, Shaded Blue, Indented Panels, 7 ¾ In...................... | | 784 |
| **Cosmetic,** Laird's Bloom Of Youth, Milk Glass, Opalescent, c.1875, 4 ⅞ In. .......................*illus* | | 748 |
| **Cosmetic,** Rexall Hair Lotion, Amber, Metal Crown Cap, Label.............................................. | | 50 |
| **Cosmetic,** W.E. Hagan & Co., Troy, N.Y., 6-Sided, Cobalt Blue, Square Rim, 6 ¾ In. ................. | | 235 |

**Bottle,** Bitters, Hall's, Barrel, Golden Yellow, Topaz Tone, Squared Collar, c.1870, 9 In.
$527

Norman C. Heckler & Company

**Bottle,** Bitters, Kelly's Old Cabin, Amber, Cabin Shape, 1863, 9 ⅜ In.
$1,840

Glass Works Auctions

**Bottle,** Bitters, Old Homestead Wild Cherry, Cabin, Amber, c.1870, 9 ½ In.
$374

Glass Works Auctions

**Bottle,** Black Glass, Bulbous, Olive Green, Stippled, Andrew McCruther, 1866, 8¾ In.
$234

Norman C. Heckler & Company

**Bottle,** Cologne, Bunker Hill Monument, Milk Glass, Obelisk Stopper, c.1870, 14 In.
$1,035

Glass Works Auctions

**Bottle,** Cologne, Cut Glass, Amber Cut To Clear, Sterling Silver Mounted, c.1890, 6 In.
$6,600

DuMouchelles Art Gallery

56

| | |
|---|---|
| **Cure,** Babyhood Cough & Croup, For Infants & Children, Label, Box, 6½ In. ..................... | 168 |
| **Cure,** Cactus Blood, Alva's Brazilian Specific Co., Pat'd June 10, 1890, Cork, Box, 9 In. ......*illus* | 1792 |
| **Cure,** Foley's Kidney & Bladder, Chicago, USA, Amber, Label, 7 In. ..................................... | 90 |
| **Cure,** Harts' Honey & Horehound, Coughs, Colds, Croup, Harts Medicine, Il., Box, 7 In. ......*illus* | 123 |
| **Cure,** Kodol Dyspepsia, E.C. DeWitt & Co., Chicago, Aqua, Label, 9 In. ............................. | 62 |
| **Cure,** Wm. Radam's Microbe Killer, Cures All Diseases, Man Beating Skeleton, Amber, 10 In....... | 392 |
| **Decanter,** Backbar, Old Kirk Whiskey, Clear, Gold Trim, Cut Glass Stopper............................. | 179 |
| **Decanter,** Backbar, Willow Springs Bourbon, Monogram, Flared 8-Sided Neck, Gold Trim, 9 In. | 123 |
| **Decanter,** Figural, Walrus, Clear Glass, Hinged Gilt Brass Head, 10 x 14 In. ...................*illus* | 1434 |
| **Decanter,** Green Glass, Pewter, Stopper, A. Knox, J. Powell, Liberty & Co., Tudric, 14¼ In. .*illus* | 1875 |
| **Decanter,** Pillar Molded, Amethyst, 8 Vertical Ribs, Inverted Cone, Tooled Lip, 11 In. ........... | 702 |
| **Demijohn,** Amber, Blown, Applied Collar, Concave Base, 18¾ In. ...................................... | 570 |
| **Demijohn,** Amber, Pin-Etched, Sailboat, Flying Gulls, 3-Piece Mold, Sloping Collar, 18 In......... | 420 |
| **Demijohn,** Deep Yellow Amber, Globular, Sloping Collar, Pontil, 17 x 14 In. ...................... | 819 |
| **Demijohn,** Green, Applied Sloping Collar, Pontil, c.1820, 20 In. ...................................... | 900 |
| **Figural,** Cat, Hunched Back, Wide Eyes, Black, 5½ In. ................................................... | 390 |
| **Figural,** Gun, Jack Hearn, 561 Park Ave., East Oakland, Cal., Clear, Whiskey Sample ............... | 560 |
| **Figural,** Pig, Blind Folded, Holding Bottle, 5¾ In. ...................................................... | 252 |
| **Flask,** 18 Ribs, Swirled To Right, Amethyst, Sheared Mouth, Pontil, 5¼ In. ..................... | 1404 |
| **Flask,** 24 Vertical Ribs, Golden Amber, Yellow Tone, Sheared, Pontil, Pocket, 4¾ In.................. | 351 |
| **Flask,** Amethyst, Diamond Daisy, Flute, Stiegel Glass Works, c.1775, 5⅛ In. ..................... | 3250 |
| **Flask,** Chestnut, Olive Yellow, Applied Lip, 11¼ In. .................................................... | 1989 |
| **Flask,** Chestnut, Yellow Olive, Applied Collar, 7 In. ................................................... | 702 |
| **Flask,** Coffin, Chas. Langert, Importer, Tacoma, W.T., Clear, ½ Pt. ................................. | 1232 |
| **Flask,** Corn For The World, Baltimore & Monument, Amber, Blob Top, Qt., 8¾ In. ...........*illus* | 1680 |
| **Flask,** Corn For The World, Cornflower Blue, Square Collar, Qt. ...................................... | 527 |
| **Flask,** Corn For The World, Orange Amber, Double Collar, Qt. ....................................... | 2300 |
| **Flask,** Corn For The World, Yellow Amber, Double Collar, Qt. ....................................... | 2457 |
| **Flask,** Cornucopia & Urn, Blue Green, Sheared Mouth, Pontil, Pt. .................................. | 702 |
| **Flask,** Diamond Daisy, Amethyst, Flattened, Sheared Mouth, Pontil, 4⅜ In......................... | 1287 |
| **Flask,** Diamond Daisy, Amethyst, Sheared Mouth, Pocket, 5¼ In. ................................... | 2106 |
| **Flask,** Double Eagle, Aqua, c.1870, Qt., 9 In............................................................... | 127 |
| **Flask,** Double Eagle, Golden Amber, Ribbed Sides, Sheared Mouth, Qt..............................| 1521 |
| **Flask,** Double Eagle, Golden Amber, Sheared Mouth, Pontil, Pt. ..................................... | 5850 |
| **Flask,** Double Eagle, Olive Green, Square Collar, Qt. ................................................... | 281 |
| **Flask,** Double Eagle, Sapphire Blue, Applied Band, Pt. ................................................. | 4928 |
| **Flask,** Double Eagle, Yellow Amber, Squared Collar, Pt. ............................................... | 257 |
| **Flask,** Double Eagle, Yellow Green, Square Collar, Pt.................................................. | 819 |
| **Flask,** Double Eagle, Yellow Olive Amber, Tooled Lip, Granite Glass Works, c.1860, Qt............ | 690 |
| **Flask,** Eagle & Flag, Coffin & Hay, Aqua, Sheared Mouth, Qt........................................ | 187 |
| **Flask,** Eagle & Westford, Olive Amber, Double Collar, ½ Pt. ......................................... | 380 |
| **Flask,** Eagle & Willington, Olive Yellow, Double Collar, ½ Pt. ..............................*illus* | 1150 |
| **Flask,** Eagle & Willington, Yellow Amber, Double Collar, Pt........................................... | 497 |
| **Flask,** Eagle & Willington, Yellow Amber, Double Collar, Qt........................................... | 702 |
| **Flask,** Fish, Yellowware, Brown Glaze, 10 In............................................................... | 420 |
| **Flask,** Flora Temple, Harness Trot, Smoky Topaz, Applied Ring, c.1865, 1 Pt. .................... | 978 |
| **Flask,** For Pike's Peak, Prospector, Hunter, Olive Yellow, Ring Mouth, Pt. .................*illus* | 2185 |
| **Flask,** For Pike's Peak, Prospector, Old Rye, Blue Aqua, Applied Ring, c.1870, 1 Qt. ............ | 253 |
| **Flask,** Franklin & Dyott, Aqua, Pontil, Pt. ............................................................. | 497 |
| **Flask,** Franklin & Dyott, Kensington, Aqua, Tooled Lip, Pontil, Qt. .......................*illus* | 546 |
| **Flask,** Hunter & Fisherman, Calabash, Amber, Sloping Collar, Qt. .................................. | 364 |
| **Flask,** Jackson & Eagle, Aqua, Sheared Mouth, Pontil, Pt............................................. | 644 |
| **Flask,** Jenny Lind & Glasshouse, Calabash, Aqua, c.1870, Qt., 10 In. ............................. | 104 |
| **Flask,** Jenny Lind & Glasshouse, Calabash, Yellow Olive, Sloping Collar, Qt....................... | 2106 |
| **Flask,** Kossuth & Tree, Calabash, Yellow Olive, Sloping Collar, Qt................................... | 819 |
| **Flask,** Lafayette & Liberty, Yellow Amber, Sheared Mouth, Pontil, ½ Pt. .......................... | 995 |
| **Flask,** Lafayette & Liberty, Yellow Olive, Sheared, Pontil, ½ Pt...................................... | 644 |
| **Flask,** Lafayette & Masonic, Yellow Olive, Open Pontil & Iron Pontil, ½ Pt......................... | 1112 |
| **Flask,** Log Cabin & Flag, Blue Aqua, Ribs, Sheared, Pt................................................ | 5850 |
| **Flask,** Masonic & Eagle, Aqua, Sheared Mouth, Pontil, Pt............................................. | 1872 |
| **Flask,** Masonic & Eagle, Green Aqua, Flared Mouth, Pontil, Pt. ..................................... | 702 |
| **Flask,** Masonic & Eagle, Olive Amber, Sheared Mouth, Pontil, ½ Pt.................................. | 2925 |
| **Flask,** Masonic & Eagle, Olive Amber, Sheared Mouth, Pt............................................. | 269 |
| **Flask,** Masonic & Eagle, Yellow, Sheared Mouth, Pontil, Pt. ......................................... | 761 |
| **Flask,** McK G II-110, Eagle & Cornucopia, Aqua, Sheared Mouth, Pontil, ½ Pt..................... | 878 |
| **Flask,** McK G II-110, Eagle & Cunningham, Pittsburgh, Grass Green, Square Collar, Qt. ........... | 468 |

**Bottle,** Cosmetic, Laird's Bloom Of Youth, Milk Glass, Opalescent, c.1875, 4 7/8 In.
$748

**Bottle,** Cure, Cactus Blood, Alva's Brazilian Specific Co., Pat'd June 10, 1890, Cork, Box, 9 In.
$1,792

**Bottle,** Cure, Harts' Honey & Horehound, Coughs, Colds, Croup, Harts Medicine, Il., Box, 7 In.
$123

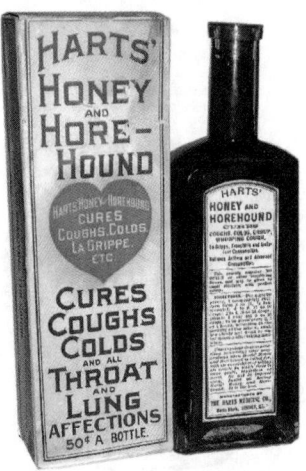

**Bottle,** Decanter, Figural, Walrus, Clear Glass, Hinged Gilt Brass Head, 10 x 14 In.
$1,434

**Bottle,** Decanter, Green Glass, Pewter, Stopper, A. Knox, J. Powell, Liberty & Co., Tudric, 14 1/4 In.
$1,875

**Bottle,** Flask, Corn For The World, Baltimore & Monument, Amber, Blob Top, Qt., 8 3/4 In.
$1,680

**Bottle,** Flask, Eagle & Willington, Olive Yellow, Double Collar, 1/2 Pt.
$1,150

**Bottle,** Flask, For Pike's Peak, Prospector, Hunter, Olive Yellow, Ring Mouth, Pt.
$2,185

**TIP**

*Do not keep wine and spirits in lead crystal decanters. The lead will leach out and go into the wine. It is unhealthy to drink liquid with lead.*

**Bottle,** Flask, Franklin & Dyott, Kensington, Aqua, Tooled Lip, Pontil, Qt.
$546

**Bottle,** Flask, Nailsea Type, Blue & White Looping, Clear Foot, Sheared Mouth, c.1850, 11 In.
$187

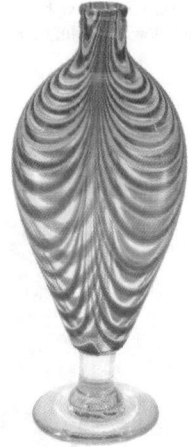

**Bottle,** Flask, Scroll, Green, Sheared Mouth, Open Pontil, Qt.
$2,464

**Bottle,** Flask, Scroll, JR & S, Aqua, Pontil, John Robinson & Son, 1830-34, ½ Pt.
$5,558

**Bottle,** Flask, Scroll, S. M'Kee, Flattened Pear Shape, Sheared Mouth, Aquamarine, U.S.A., c.1850
$5,850

**Bottle,** Flask, Sunburst, Clear Green, Sheared Lip, Tooled, Squared, Keene, c.1820, Pt.
$690

**Bottle,** Flask, Taylor & Corn For The World, Olive Yellow, Pontil, Pt.
$24,150

**Bottle,** Flask, Washington & Eagle, Aqua, Tooled Lip, Pontil, Pt.
$489

**Bottle,** Flask, Washington & Taylor, Little More Grape, Cobalt Blue, Qt., 8 In.
$4,480

| | |
|---|---|
| **Flask,** Nailsea Type, Blue & White Looping, Clear Foot, Sheared Mouth, c.1850, 11 In. .......*illus* | 187 |
| **Flask,** Newman's Colleges, San Francisco & Oakland, Golden Amber, Football Shape, 4 In.......... | 1232 |
| **Flask,** Olive Green, Double Roll Collar, ½ Pt.............................................................. | 364 |
| **Flask,** Pillar Molded, 8 Vertical Ribs, Sea Green, Triangular, Pontil, 5¾ In. ...................... | 585 |
| **Flask,** Pitkin Type, 30 Ribs, Swirled To Right, Forest Green, Tear Drop, Pontil, 3¾ In. ................. | 1872 |
| **Flask,** Pitkin Type, 32 Broken Ribs Swirled To Right, Blue Aqua, Tooled Lip, c.1825, 7 In. .......... | 690 |
| **Flask,** Pitkin Type, 32 Ribs, Swirled To Left, Blue Green, Sheared Mouth, 6¾ In.................... | 761 |
| **Flask,** Pitkin Type, 32 Ribs, Swirled To Right, Olive Green, Sheared, 7 In............................ | 2106 |
| **Flask,** Pitkin Type, 32 Ribs, Swirled To Right, Sea Green, Sheared, Pontil, 6⅜ In. ............... | 351 |
| **Flask,** Pitkin Type, 36 Ribs, Swirled To Left, Olive Yellow, Sheared, Pontil, 6⅝ In. ............... | 1638 |
| **Flask,** Pitkin Type, 36 Ribs, Swirled To Left, Yellow Olive, Sheared Mouth, Pontil, 5 In.... | 1289 to 2574 |
| **Flask,** Pitkin Type, 36 Ribs, Swirled To Right, Yellow Olive, Sheared, Pontil, 5 In............ | 761 to 995 |
| **Flask,** Pitkin Type, Swirled Ribs, Olive Green, Sheared Mouth, Open Pontil, 4¾ In. .......... | 2283 |
| **Flask,** Pumpkinseed, Electrical Bicycle Lubricating Oil, Embossed, Aqua, c.1890 ................ | 1008 |
| **Flask,** Pumpkinseed, Grand Central Saloon, San Francisco, Clear, ½ Pt. ............................ | 1456 |
| **Flask,** Pumpkinseed, Henry Koch, Los Angeles, Clear, Embossed, Pt. ................................. | 560 |
| **Flask,** Pumpkinseed, The Oberon, Brown & Gnesa, Santa Rosa Cal., Clear, Pt.................. | 420 |
| **Flask,** Sailor & Banjo Player, Yellow Olive, Sheared Mouth, ½ Pt. .................................... | 527 |
| **Flask,** Scroll, Amber, Sheared Mouth, Pontil, ½ Pt. .................................................... | 1170 |
| **Flask,** Scroll, Aqua, Sheared Mouth, Pontil, Qt. ........................................................ | 190 |
| **Flask,** Scroll, Blue Aqua, Sheared Mouth, Tubular Pontil, 2 Qt., 11 In. ............................ | 3510 |
| **Flask,** Scroll, Green, Sheared Mouth, Open Pontil, Qt. ..............................................*illus* | 2464 |
| **Flask,** Scroll, JR & S, Aqua, Pontil, John Robinson & Son, 1830-34, ½ Pt. .............*illus* | 5558 |
| **Flask,** Scroll, Light Green, Sheared Mouth, Iron Pontil, ½ Pt. ....................................... | 644 |
| **Flask,** Scroll, S. M'Kee, Flattened Pear Shape, Sheared Mouth, Aquamarine, U.S.A., c.1850 *illus* | 5850 |
| **Flask,** Sheaf Of Grain & Star, Yellow, Olive Tone, Sheared Mouth, ½ Pt......................... | 1170 |
| **Flask,** Silver, Copper, Hammered, Applied Flowers & Leaves, Whiting Mfg. Co., c.1900, 5 In. ........ | 969 |
| **Flask,** Soldier & Dancer, Baltimore, Blue Green, Ring Mouth, Pt................................... | 702 |
| **Flask,** Success To The Railroad, Aqua, Sheared Mouth, Pontil, Pt.................................. | 1755 |
| **Flask,** Success To The Railroad, Horse & Cart, Forest Green, Sheared, Pt.......................... | 1112 |
| **Flask,** Success To The Railroad, Horse & Cart, Olive Green, Pt...................................... | 468 |
| **Flask,** Summer & Winter, Deep Puce, Double Roll Collar, Qt............................................ | 1120 |
| **Flask,** Summer & Winter, Sapphire Blue, Rounded, Qt.................................................... | 819 |
| **Flask,** Sunburst, Clear Green, Sheared Lip, Tooled, Squared, Keene, c.1820, Pt. .................*illus* | 690 |
| **Flask,** Sunburst, Olive Green, Sheared Mouth, Keen, Pt................................................ | 1064 |
| **Flask,** Sunburst, Yellow Olive Green, Tooled Lip, c.1830, Pt. ........................................ | 1093 |
| **Flask,** Swirled Ribs, Amber, Sheared Mouth, Pontil, Pocket, 4¾ In. ............................... | 179 |
| **Flask,** Taylor & Corn For The World, Aqua, Sheared Mouth, Pontil, Pt............................ | 702 |
| **Flask,** Taylor & Corn For The World, Olive Yellow, Pontil, Pt. ..........................*illus* | 24150 |
| **Flask,** Teardrop, Spirits, Ribs, Swirled To Right, Orange Amber, Flattened, 9¼ In............. | 11115 |
| **Flask,** Traveler's Companion & Star, Ravenna, Golden Amber, Pt.................................... | 761 |
| **Flask,** Union, Clasped Hands & Cannon, Orange Amber, Neck Band, ½ Pt........................ | 4928 |
| **Flask,** Union, Clasped Hands & Cannon, Orange Amber, Squared Collar, Pt...................... | 351 |
| **Flask,** Union, Clasped Hands & Eagle, Amber, Applied Collar, ½ Pt. .............................. | 213 |
| **Flask,** Union, Clasped Hands & Eagle, Golden Yellow, Ring Mouth, Pt. ........................... | 439 |
| **Flask,** Union, Clasped Hands & Eagle, Light Green, Yellow Striations, Pt. ....................... | 322 |
| **Flask,** Union, Clasped Hands & Eagle, Yellow Amber, Rounded Shoulder, Pt...................... | 1287 |
| **Flask,** Union, Clasped Hands & Eagle, Yellow Green, Ring, Qt....................................... | 936 |
| **Flask,** Union, Clasped Hands & Eagle, Yellow Olive, Ring Mouth, c.1875, 1 Qt. ............... | 316 |
| **Flask,** Union, Oval, Fleckstein & Mayer, Portland, O., Amber, ½ Pt................................. | 308 |
| **Flask,** Washington & Eagle, Aqua, Tooled Lip, Pontil, Pt. ...........................*illus* | 489 |
| **Flask,** Washington & Jackson, Golden Amber, Sheared Mouth, Pt........................... | 936 |
| **Flask,** Washington & Lockport, Emerald Green, Double Collar, Pontil, Qt.................... | 12870 |
| **Flask,** Washington & Monument, Fells Point, Aqua, Sheared, Pontil, Pt.................... | 380 |
| **Flask,** Washington & Taylor, Blue Green, Double Collar, Pontil, Qt......................... | 2340 |
| **Flask,** Washington & Taylor, Cobalt Blue, Sheared Mouth, Pontil, Qt....................... | 4095 |
| **Flask,** Washington & Taylor, Cobalt Blue, Sheared, Tooled Lip, c.1855, Qt................. | 4025 |
| **Flask,** Washington & Taylor, Golden Amber, Bubbles, Double Collar, Qt................... | 5376 |
| **Flask,** Washington & Taylor, Little More Grape, Cobalt Blue, Qt., 8 In. ...............*illus* | 4480 |
| **Flask,** Washington & Taylor, Milky Aqua, Sheared Mouth, Pontil, Qt...................... | 819 |
| **Flask,** Washington & Taylor, Never Surrenders, Deep Claret, Square Collar, Qt........... | 2457 |
| **Flask,** Washington & Taylor, Never Surrenders, Sapphire Blue, Qt.......................... | 1904 |
| **Flask,** Washington & Taylor, Sapphire Blue Shaded To Teal, Blob Top, 8¾ In............ | 2464 |
| **Flask,** Washington & Taylor, Yellow, Olive Tone, Pt. ...................................... | 4680 |
| **Flask,** Wm. Wholey Dealer In Liquors, Staunton, Va., Aqua, Embossed, c.1880, 8 In. ......... | 460 |
| **Fruit Jar,** A. Stone & Co., Philada., Aqua, Cylindrical, Rolled Collar, Wax Seal Groove, Qt........... | 644 |

**Bottle,** Ink, J. & I.E.M., Igloo, Blue Green, Embossed 4, Tooled Lip, 1⅝ x 2¼ In.
$439

**Bottle,** Ink, Paperweight, Cylindrical, 3 Sections, Green, Rolled Rim, Blown Stopper, c.1850, 6⅞ In.
$497

**Bottle,** Ink, S.I. Comp., Pennslvania, Cottage, Aqua, Tooled Lip, c.1880, 2¾ In.
$115

This is an edited listing of current prices. Visit **Kovels.com** to check thousands of prices from previous years and sign up for free information on trends, tips, reproductions, marks, and more.

**Bottle,** Ink, Titcomb's, Ohio, 12-Sided, Aqua, Inward Rolled Lip, Pontil, c.1850, 2 ⅞ In.

$460

Glass Works Auctions

**Bottle,** Medicine, Apothecary, Pot. Bichrom, Green, Ribbed, Recessed Label, 7 ½ In.

$213

McMurray Antiques & Auctions

**Bottle,** Medicine, Bear's Oil, Rectangular, Beveled, Aquamarine, Rolled Rim, U.S.A., c.1850, 2 ¾ In.

$702

Norman C. Heckler & Company

| | |
|---|---:|
| **Fruit Jar,** Belle, Pat. Dec. 14th 1869, Aqua, Cylindrical, Ground Lip, 3 Round Feet, Qt. | 1638 |
| **Fruit Jar,** Bellerjeau's Simplicity, Patd. Mar. 31st 1868, Blue Aqua, Ground Lip | 1846 |
| **Fruit Jar,** Cunningham & Co., Pittsburgh, Pa., Aqua, 4-Piece Mold, Round Collar, 7 ⅝ In. | 258 |
| **Fruit Jar,** Cunningham & Co., Pittsburgh, Pa., Deep Aqua, Cylindrical, Square Collar, 6 In. | 1638 |
| **Fruit Jar,** Globe, Amber, Patented May 23, 1886, 8 ¾ In. | 86 |
| **Fruit Jar,** Globe, Aqua, Wide Mouth, 3-Piece Iron Clamp, c.1900, Pt. | 390 |
| **Fruit Jar,** Mason, Aqua, Pat. June 9, 1863, Wide Mouth, Insert, Hemingray, Qt. | 460 |
| **Fruit Jar,** Mason, Black Amber, Lugged Zinc Cap, Hemingray Glass Co., 1877, Qt. | 10350 |
| **Fruit Jar,** Mason's, Honey Amber, Boyd's Genuine Porcelain Lined, c.1860, Midget, Pt., 5 ½ In. | 219 |
| **Fruit Jar,** Millville, Hitall's Paten, Aqua, Rolled Collar, Glass Lid, Iron Yoke Clamp, ½ Pt. | 322 |
| **Fruit Jar,** Potter & Bodine's Air-Tight, Barrel, Aqua, Wax Seal Groove, Pontil, Qt. | 556 |
| **Fruit Jar,** R. Arthur's Patent, Jany 2nd 1855, Aqua, Cylindrical, Wax Sealer Groove, Pt. | 6435 |
| **Fruit Jar,** Van Vliet, Jar Of 1881, Aqua, 1881, 8 ¾ In. | 148 |
| **Household,** Blacking, Prepared By CA & LA Loomis, Blue Green, Oval, Rolled Lip, 4 ½ In. | 1053 |
| **Ink,** D.D. Thomlinson's Writing Fluid, Aqua, 6-Sided, Inward Rolled Lip, 2 ¾ In. | 460 |
| **Ink,** Estes's Metropolitan, Blue Aqua, Cone, Ribbed, Tapered Collar, c.1860, 7 ½ In. | 2530 |
| **Ink,** Geometric, Deep Amber, Fluted Base, Disc Mouth, 3-Piece Mold, Keen, N.H., 2 ⅜ In. | 308 |
| **Ink,** Harrison's Columbian, 8-Sided, Light Green, Flared Mouth, Master, 4 In. | 497 |
| **Ink,** Harrison's Columbian, 8-Sided, Sapphire Blue, Inward Rolled Mouth, Pontil, 2 In. | 527 |
| **Ink,** Harrison's Columbian, 12-Sided, Aqua, Applied Ring, c.1860, 7 ½ In. | 161 |
| **Ink,** Harrison's Columbian, 12-Sided, Aqua, Flared Mouth, Pontil, Master, 7 ½ In. | 234 |
| **Ink,** J. & I.E.M., Igloo, Blue Green, Embossed 4, Tooled Lip, 1 ⅝ x 2 ¼ In. .......... *illus* | 439 |
| **Ink,** J. & I.E.M., Igloo, Yellow, Offset Neck, Paneled Base, 1 ¾ In. | 936 |
| **Ink,** J.W. Seaton, Louisville, Ky., Umbrella, 10-Sided, Blue Green, Inward Rolled Lip, 2 In. | 1989 |
| **Ink,** Paperweight, Cylindrical, 3 Sections, Green, Rolled Rim, Blown Stopper, c.1850, 6 ⅞ In. *illus* | 497 |
| **Ink,** S.I. Comp., Pennslvania, Cottage, Aqua, Tooled Lip, c.1880, 2 ¾ In. ..........*illus* | 115 |
| **Ink,** Titcomb's, Ohio, 12-Sided, Aqua, Inward Rolled Lip, Pontil, c.1850, 2 ⅞ In. ....*illus* | 460 |
| **Ink,** Umbrella, 8-Sided, Amethyst, Sheared, Tooled Lip, Pebbly, c.1860, 2 In. | 4600 |
| **Ink,** Umbrella, 8-Sided, Sapphire Blue, Inward Rolled Lip, Pontil, 2 ½ In. | 1521 |
| **Ink,** Umbrella, 8-Sided, Tapered, Moss Green, Flared Lip, Master, 5 In. | 439 |
| **Ink,** Wood's Black, Portland, Cone, Aqua, Inward Rolled Lip, 2 ½ In. | 322 |
| **Jar,** Blue, 5-Point Star, Zinc Screw Band, c.1875, ½ Gal. | 92 |
| **Jar,** Canister, Amethyst, Cylindrical, Wide Mouth, Flared Rim, Pontil, 8 ¾ In. | 240 |
| **Jar,** Melon, Dark Aqua, Ribbed, Hemingray, 1860s, Qt. | 938 |
| **Jar,** Wax Sealer, Aqua, Iron Pontil, Ravenna Glass Works, 1850s, Qt. | 3155 |
| **Jar,** Yellow Olive, Cylindrical, Squat, Rounded Shoulder, Rolled Lip, Stoddard, 4 ⅞ In. | 3218 |
| **Medicine,** America Cough Drops, Tooled Flared Lip, c.1860, 5 ⅛ In. | 1380 |
| **Medicine,** Apothecary, Cobalt Blue, Globe Shape, Long Neck, Flared Rim, Stopper, 1800s, 15 In. | 177 |
| **Medicine,** Apothecary, Eagle, Cornucopia, Anchor, Gilt, White, Stamped, 1800s, 10 In., Pair | 210 |
| **Medicine,** Apothecary, Inscribed Mann, Elect, Peacocks, Fruit, Blue, White, Delft, Dutch, 1700s, 11 In. | 840 |
| **Medicine,** Apothecary, Lid, Amber, Round, Footed, Tiffin, 13 In. | 175 |
| **Medicine,** Apothecary, Lid, Clear, Footed, Tiffin, 9 ½ In. | 55 |
| **Medicine,** Apothecary, Lid, Columbia Swirl, Tiffin, 11 ½ In. | 45 |
| **Medicine,** Apothecary, Lid, Glass, Blown, Clear, Applied Blue Rings, Hollow Finial, c.1855, 13 In. | 518 |
| **Medicine,** Apothecary, Lid, Glass, Blown, Clear, Pinched Rim, Urn Shape, c.1870, 17 In. | 138 |
| **Medicine,** Apothecary, Liq. Arsenicalis, Green, Cylindrical, Ribbed, Stopper, 6 ½ In. | 106 |
| **Medicine,** Apothecary, Pot. Bichrom, Green, Ribbed, Recessed Label, 7 ½ In. ...............*illus* | 213 |
| **Medicine,** Apothecary, Spir. Amm. Aro., Cobalt Blue, Recessed Lug, Flat Stopper, 5 ½ In. | 123 |
| **Medicine,** Apothecary, U.S.A. Hosp. Dept., Olive Yellow, Double Collar, 9 ¼ In. | 761 |
| **Medicine,** Bear's Oil, Rectangular, Beveled, Aquamarine, Rolled Rim, c.1850, 2 ¾ In. *illus* | 702 |
| **Medicine,** Budwell's Emulsion Of Cod Liver Oil, Lynchburg, Va., Cobalt Blue, c.1920, 8 In. | 127 |
| **Medicine,** C. Brinkerhoff's Health Restorative, Price $1.00, Olive, Sticky Ball Pontil, 7 In. | 1344 |
| **Medicine,** Celebrated Burdock Blood Purifier, J.W.R. Parker, Basic City, Va., Aqua, c.1900, 7 In. | 150 |
| **Medicine,** Columbian Kidney & Liver Remedy, Dr. R.N. Mowry, 2 x 5 In. | 56 |
| **Medicine,** Dr. A.C. Daniels, Wonder Worker Lotion, Healing Liniment, Label, Contents, 9 In. | 700 |
| **Medicine,** Dr. A.C. McDill's Vermifuge, Aqua, Inward Rolled Lip, 4 ⅞ In. ..........*illus* | 1093 |
| **Medicine,** Dr. Brown's Ruterba, Monk Stirring Kettle, Amber, Square Rim, Label, 8 In. | 213 |
| **Medicine,** Dr. Fenner's Cough Cold Syrup, Aqua, Box, People's Remedies, 5 ¾ In. | 34 |
| **Medicine,** Dr. J.D. Freeman's Diarhea Syrup Or Cholera Mixture, St. Louis, Aqua, 5 In. .....*illus* | 1265 |
| **Medicine,** Dr. James Soothing Syrup Cordial, Cylindrical, Label, Wrapper, 5 In. | 336 |
| **Medicine,** Dr. Mintie's Nephreticum, San Francisco, Blue Aqua, Indented Panels, 7 In. | 224 |
| **Medicine,** Dr. Pinkham's Emmenagogue, Aqua, Square, Sloping Collar, 6 In. | 364 |
| **Medicine,** Dr. S.A. Weaver's Canker & Salt Rheum Syrup, Aqua Tint, Oval, 9 ½ In. | 269 |
| **Medicine,** Dr. Tebbetts' Physiological Hair Regenerator, Amethyst, Double Collar, c.1875, 7 In. | 633 |
| **Medicine,** Dr. Tebbetts' Physiological Hair Regenerator, Pink Puce, Double Collar, 7 ½ In. | 380 |
| **Medicine,** Dr. Thomas Eclectic Oil, Household Remedy, Label, Contents, Box, Hand, 5 In. | 123 |

| | |
|---|---|
| Medicine, Dr. W.S. Love's Vegetable Elixir, Baltimore, Olive Green, Collar, c.1860, 7⅜ In............ | 12650 |
| Medicine, Dr. Wyncoop's Iceland Pectoral, N.Y., Aqua Tint, Rolled Lip, Pontil, 5½ In. ................. | 336 |
| Medicine, Druggists, Purcell, Ladd & Co., Richmond Va., Aqua, c.1860, 6¼ In............................ | 127 |
| Medicine, G.W. Merchant Chemist, Lockport, N.Y., Green, Applied Top, 5¾ In. ...................*illus* | 224 |
| Medicine, George's Cough Balsam, Goffstown, N.H., Aqua, Label, Contents, 6¾ In........................ | 62 |
| Medicine, Gibb's Bone Liniment, Yellow Olive, 6-Sided, Sloping Double Collar, 6½ In. ............... | 819 |
| Medicine, Glover's Imperial Mange Remedy, H. Clay Glover Co., Amber, Tooled Lip, 7 In. ..*illus* | 56 |
| Medicine, Glycerine, Dr. W. Sawen's Medical Company, Yellow, Square Collar, 10 In. .................... | 168 |
| Medicine, H.H. Warner & Co., Tippecanoe, Log, Embossed Canoe, Amber, 9 In......................... | 556 |
| Medicine, Healy & Bigelow, Indian Sagwa, Kidney Renovator, Aqua, c.1890, 9 In. ............*illus* | 403 |
| Medicine, Hubbell, Sapphire Blue, Oval, Swollen Shoulder & Base, Square Collar, 10 In............. | 1053 |
| Medicine, John Hart & Co., Heart Shape, Amber, Double Collar, 7 In......................................... | 497 |
| Medicine, Lyon's Powder, B. & P.N.Y., Sloping Shoulder, Grape Puce, 4¼ In........................... | 420 |
| Medicine, Lyon's Powder, B. & P.N.Y., Sloping Shoulder, Yellow, Rolled Rim, 4¼ In.................. | 8000 |
| Medicine, Mrs. Winslow's Syrup, For Children Teething, Round, Cork, Yellow Wrapper, 5 In....... | 78 |
| Medicine, Myers' Rock Rose, New Haven, Blue Green, Square, Beveled, 9¼ In............................ | 2925 |
| Medicine, Ransom's Hive Syrup & Tolu, Croup Syrup, Beehive, Box, 4 In................................... | 90 |
| Medicine, Remedy, For All Domestic Animals, Label, Box, 6⅜ In. ....................................*illus* | 560 |
| Medicine, Rowand's Tonic Mixture, Green, Aqua, 6-Sided, Rolled Lip, c.1860, 5½ In................. | 196 |
| Medicine, Seaver's Joint & Nerve Liniment, Yellow Amber, Cylindrical, Stoddard, 4 In............... | 527 |
| Medicine, Shaker Asthma Cure, Price 1.00, Mt. Lebanon, Box, 1800s, 1½ x 3½ In..................... | 2583 |
| Medicine, Sulphate Of Morphine, Red Label, Skull & Crossbones, N.Y.Q. & C. Works, 3 In.......... | 62 |
| Medicine, Swaim's Panacea, Philada, Yellow Olive, Indented Panels, Ring Collar, 8 In. ............. | 497 |
| Medicine, Swift's Syphilitic Specific, Cobalt Blue, Rounded Shoulder, Square Collar, 9 In.......... | 616 |
| Medicine, U.S.A. Hosp. Dept., Cobalt Blue, Cylindrical, Square Collar, 9 In.............................. | 1680 |
| Medicine, U.S.A. Hosp. Dept., Yellow Olive, Cylindrical, Double Collar, 9¼ In......................... | 702 |
| Medicine, Warner's Log Cabin Extract, Amber, Metal Corkscrew, Label, Box, 8 In. ............*illus* | 504 |
| Medicine, Warner's Safe Diabetes Remedy, Aqua, Safe, Cork, Box, 9 In.................................... | 504 |
| Medicine, Warner's Safe Diuretic, Rochester, N.Y., Amber, 5 In............................................... | 157 |
| Milk, A.G.S. & Co., Patented April 5, 1989, Yellow Amber, Tapered Neck, Tin Handle, Qt............... | 4095 |
| Milk, Mount San Angelo Dairy, Sweet Briar, Va., Clear, Embossed, c.1940, Pt., 7¼ In............... | 207 |
| Mineral Water, Artesian Water, Chocolate Amber, Applied Sloping Collar, c.1860, 1 Pt............... | 1380 |
| Mineral Water, Bear Lithia Spring, Elkton, Va., Light Green, c.1870, ½ Gal., 10 In................... | 374 |
| Mineral Water, Congress & Empire Spring Co., Saratoga, N.Y., Emerald Green, Pt. ...................... | 878 |
| Mineral Water, Congress & Empire Spring, Columbian Water, Yellow Green, Pt. ........................ | 644 |
| Mineral Water, Congress Water, The Spa Phila, T.H.D., Yellow Olive, Sloping Collar, Pt............... | 995 |
| Mineral Water, Craig Healing Spring, Virginia, Aqua, Label, c.1920, ½ Gal., 10⅝ In................. | 259 |
| Mineral Water, Highrock Congress Spring, 1767, C & W, Saratoga, Yellow Amber, Pt. ........*illus* | 207 |
| Mineral Water, Highrock Congress Spring, C & W, Saratoga, N.Y., Teal Blue, Pt......................... | 995 |
| Mineral Water, J. Kennedy, Pittsburgh, Blue Green, Sloping Collar............................................ | 101 |
| Mineral Water, John Clarke, New York, Olive Green, Sloping Collar, c.1875, Pt., 7¼ In............... | 161 |
| Mineral Water, John H. Gardner & Son, Sharon Springs, N.Y., Teal, Sloping Collar, Pt............... | 322 |
| Mineral Water, Magee's Lithia Spring, Virginia, Aqua, Applied Lip, c.1890, ½ Gal., 10 In........... | 92 |
| Mineral Water, Quaker Springs, Old Saratoga, Blue Aqua, Applied Double Collar, c.1875.......... | 978 |
| Mineral Water, Roanoke, Virginia Springs, Clear, Applied Square Ring, c.1920, ½ Gal., 10 In.... | 115 |
| Mineral Water, Rockbridge, Va., Alum Water, Green, Sloping Collar, c.1870, Pt., 7¾ In............. | 46 |
| Mineral Water, Rockbridge, Va., Alum Water, Teal Blue, Square Ring, c.1880, 9⅝ In................. | 207 |
| Mineral Water, Rockbridge, Virginia, Alum Water, Aqua, Embossed Royal Figure, c.1885, 10 In. | 575 |
| Mineral Water, Rockbridge, Virginia, Alum Water, Green, Square Mouth, c.1880, ½ Gal., 9 In... | 748 |
| Mineral Water, Wampole's Elk Lithia, Elkton Va., Aqua, Embossed Elk, c.1885, ½ Gal., 10 In. ... | 150 |
| Mineral Water, White Sulpher Springs, W. Va., Teal Green, Embossed, c.1880, Qt., 9⅝ In.......... | 316 |
| Pepper Sauce, Cathedral, 6-Sided, Blue Aqua, Arched Panels, Long Neck, Rolled Rim, 8¾ In.... | 616 |
| Pepper Sauce, W.I., For Family Use, Cathedral, 6-Sided, Green Aqua, Label, 8¾ In. ..........*illus* | 616 |
| Perfume bottles are listed in their own category. | |
| Pickle, Cathedral, 4-Sided, Aqua, Indented Panels, Rolled Rim, 11 In........................................ | 258 |
| Pickle, Cathedral, 4-Sided, Blue Green, Arched Panels, Neck Ring, Rolled Rim, 13½ In.............. | 560 |
| Pickle, Cathedral, 4-Sided, Emerald Green, Arched Panels, Rolled Rim, 13½ In. ...................... | 1568 |
| Pickle, Cathedral, 4-Sided, Light Blue, Arched Panels, Medallions, Crosshatching, 14 In............ | 1456 |
| Pickle, Cathedral, Aqua, Square, Beveled Corners, Rolled Lip, Pontil, 14⅜ In............................ | 2223 |
| Pickle, Cathedral, Blue Aqua, Outward Rolled Lip, c.1865, 14 In. .....................................*illus* | 316 |
| Pickle, Cathedral, Blue Green, Rolled Mouth, Iron Pontil, c.1850, 11¾ In. ........................*illus* | 819 |
| Pickle, Cathedral, Green, Crosshatching, Rolled Lip, 14 In. ...........................................*illus* | 784 |
| Pickle, Cathedral, Teal Blue, Outward Rolled Lip, c.1860, 11½ In. ......................................... | 1265 |
| Pickle, Cylindrical, Paneled, Fluted Shoulder, Blue Green, Wm. Underwood, c.1850, 11⅜ In. *illus* | 1989 |
| Pickle, New England, Skilton Foote & Co., Amber, Applied Lip, Label, 13½ In. ..................*illus* | 190 |

**Bottle,** Medicine, Dr. A.C. McDill's Vermifuge, Aqua, Inward Rolled Lip, 4⅞ In.
$1,093

**Bottle,** Medicine, Dr. J.D. Freeman's Diarhea Syrup Or Cholera Mixture, St. Louis, Aqua, 5 In.
$1,265

### Slug Plates

Slug plates were invented in the late nineteenth century. A changeable metal sheet with embossed lettering was made to fit a section of an iron bottle mold. This meant many different customers could have bottles with their own molded name at a lower price. Slug plates leave a round or oval edge around the raised lettering in the glass bottle.

**Bottle,** Medicine, G.W. Merchant Chemist, Lockport, N.Y., Green, Applied Top, 5¾ In.
$224

**Bottle,** Medicine, Glover's Imperial Mange Remedy, H. Clay Glover Co., Amber, Tooled Lip, 7 In.
$56

**Bottle,** Medicine, Healy & Bigelow, Indian Sagwa, Kidney Renovator, Aqua, c.1890, 9 In.
$403

**Bottle,** Medicine, Remedy, For All Domestic Animals, Label, Box, 6⅜ In.
$560

**Bottle,** Medicine, Warner's Log Cabin Extract, Amber, Metal Corkscrew, Label, Box, 8 In.
$504

**Bottle,** Mineral Water, Highrock Congress Spring, 1767, C & W, Saratoga, Yellow Amber, Pt.
$207

**Bottle,** Pepper Sauce, W.I., For Family Use, Cathedral, 6-Sided, Green Aqua, Label, 8¾ In.
$616

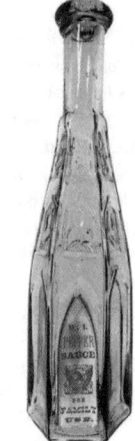

**Bottle,** Pickle, Cathedral, Blue Aqua, Outward Rolled Lip, c.1865, 14 In.
$316

**Bottle,** Pickle, Cathedral, Blue Green, Rolled Mouth, Iron Pontil, c.1850, 11¾ In.
$819

| | |
|---|---|
| **Pickle,** W.D. Smith, N.Y., Aqua, Cylindrical, Beaded Band, Rolled Collar, 11 ½ In. ....................... | 644 |
| **Poison,** Embossed Skull, Crossed Bones, Cobalt Blue, Flared Lip, Pat. Appl'd For, 3 In. ............... | 1872 |
| **Poison,** J.F. Hartz Co. Limited, Toronto, Blue, Embossed Hearts, Flared Lip, 6 In. ....................... | 560 |
| **Poison,** Lattice & Diamond, Moss Green, Flattened Lip, c.1900, 4 ½ In. ............................*illus* | 748 |
| **Poison,** Owl Drug Co., Owl Mortar & Pestle, Cobalt Blue, Triangular, c.1910, 9 ¾ In. ................... | 805 |
| **Poison,** Skull, Cobalt Blue, Crossed Bones Base, Flared Out Rim, 3 ½ In. ................................. | 4095 |
| **Sarsaparilla,** Dr. Townsend's, Albany, N.Y., Blue Green, Square, Sloping Collar, 9 ½ In. .............. | 2574 |
| **Sarsaparilla,** Dr. Townsend's, Emerald Green, Cloverleaf Iron Pontil, 9 ¼ In. .................*illus* | 863 |
| **Sarsaparilla,** Dr. Townsend's, Teal Blue, Applied Sloping Collar, c.1860, 9 ⅜ In. ...................... | 3163 |
| **Sarsaparilla,** Old Dr. Townsend's, New York, Emerald Green, Sloping Collar, c.1845, 9 ½ In. ...... | 345 |
| **Scent,** Cobalt Blue Glass, Thimble Lid, Figure, Pavilion, Shrubs, 2 ¾ x 1 ¼ In. ......................... | 7200 |
| **Scent,** Opalescent Glass, Hobnail, c.1930, 6 In. ................................................................... | 39 |
| **Scent,** Porcelain, Filbert, Nut Shape, Silver Lid, McIntyre & Co., c.1890, 1 ½ In. ....................... | 650 |
| **Seal,** All Souls Coll., C.R., Wine, Deep Olive Amber, 10 ¼ In. ................................................... | 1064 |
| **Seal,** Ambrosial, B.M. & E.A.W. & Co., Amber, Chestnut, Applied Handle, 9 In. ...................*illus* | 173 |
| **Seal,** S.B.P., Wine, Deep Yellow Olive, 3-Piece Mold, Sloping Collar, 7 ½ In. ............................ | 2691 |
| **Seltzer,** Dr Pepper, Pink, Etched, c.1910, 12 ½ In. ............................................................. | 360 |
| **Shoe Polish,** Topsy, Paper Label, Wooden Cap, Applicator Brush, Aqua, 5 In. ..................*illus* | 403 |
| **Snuff,** Agate, 5 Figures, Scroll, Tree, Coral & Metal Stopper, Chinese, c.1800, 3 ⅜ In. .........*illus* | 1599 |
| **Snuff,** Agate, Bird, Lotus Leaf, Red Stopper, Chinese, 2 ½ In. ................................................. | 438 |
| **Snuff,** Agate, Man, Toad, Coins, Flat Oval, Domed Stopper, Bone Spoon, Chinese, 2 ⅝ In. ........... | 308 |
| **Snuff,** Agate, Streaks, Brown, Beige, Oval Base, 3 ⅛ In. ........................................................ | 431 |
| **Snuff,** Amber, Carved, Flowering Trees, Double, Caps With Bone Spoons, 2 ¾ x 2 ½ In. ............... | 127 |
| **Snuff,** Amber, Monkeys, Picking Peaches, Oval, Carved, 3 In. ................................................. | 125 |
| **Snuff,** Celadon Jade, Purple Top, Carved, Rice Pattern, Chinese, 2 ⅝ In. ................................. | 4428 |
| **Snuff,** Cloisonne, Rectangular, Round Neck, Dragon, Phoenix, Multicolor, Chinese, 2 ¾ In. ....... | 2706 |
| **Snuff,** Cloisonne, Shishi Lions, Ruyi Scrolls, Multicolor, Chinese, Lid, 1644-1911, 3 ⅜ In. .......... | 2952 |
| **Snuff,** Dragons, Clouds, Black On White, Carnelian Stopper, Chinese, 3 ¼ In.  ...............*illus* | 59 |
| **Snuff,** Glass, 3 Dragons, Chasing, Ball, Carved Waves, Coral Stopper, Spoon, 3 ½ In. ............... | 480 |
| **Snuff,** Glass, Gilt Metal Overlay, Green Stone, Figural, Shell, 1900s, 2 In. ................................ | 150 |
| **Snuff,** Glass, White, Orange Cap, Chinese, 2 ¾ In. .............................................................. | 63 |
| **Snuff,** Hornbill, Carved Shou Lao, Holding Staff, Stag, Flattened, 3 In. .................................. | 3884 |
| **Snuff,** Jade, Black, White, Man On Horse, 2 Cottages On Reverse, Coral Stopper, 3 In.  ........*illus* | 3125 |
| **Snuff,** Jade, Carved Symbols, Jade Ball Stopper, Chinese, 2 ½ In. ........................................... | 920 |
| **Snuff,** Jade, Green, Figural, Melon, Vine, Chinese, 3 In. ....................................................... | 120 |
| **Snuff,** Jade, Man, Ox, Relief, Round, Gray, Black Collar, Brown Agate Stopper, 2 ⅝ In. ............... | 738 |
| **Snuff,** Jade, Phoenix, Dragon, Relief, Round, Flattened, Turquoise Stopper, Chinese, 2 ⅛ In. ...... | 984 |
| **Snuff,** Jade, Translucent Pale Green, Tourmaline Stopper, Chinese, c.1900, 2 In. ...............*illus* | 3851 |
| **Snuff,** Jade, White, Boy Riding Fish, Chinese, 2 ¾ In. ........................................................... | 150 |
| **Snuff,** Jadeite, Deer, Bird, Tree, Carved, Double Gourd, Carnelian Stopper, 4 x 2 ½ In. .............. | 178 |
| **Snuff,** Jadeite, Hand Shape, White, Carved, Green Spots, Stopper, 3 In. .................................. | 155 |
| **Snuff,** Jasper, Carnation, Carved, Double, Lids, Bone Spoons, Chinese, 2 ¾ x 3 In. .................... | 81 |
| **Snuff,** Lace Agate, Gold Fish Shape, Carved, Faux Pearl Stopper, 3 ¼ In. ................................ | 138 |
| **Snuff,** Lapis Lazuli, Phoenix, Peach, Relief Carved, Chinese, 20th Century, 2 In. ..................... | 60 |
| **Snuff,** Metal, White, Filigree, Jade Trim, Coral & Turquoise Cabochons, Mongolia, 4 In. ........... | 150 |
| **Snuff,** Scenes, Multicolor, Tapered, Flattened, Domed Stopper, Chinese, 2 ¾ x 1 ½ In. ............... | 173 |
| **Snuff,** Silver, Chased, Dragon's Head, Medallion, Coral, Turquoise, Elephant Handles, Tibet, 3 ½ In. | 870 |
| **Snuff,** Silver, Enameled, Multicolor, St. Petersburg Hallmark, Russia, 3 x 2 In. ....................... | 850 |
| **Snuff,** Turquoise, Mountains, Figures, Carved, Chinese, 2 ⅝ In. ............................................ | 205 |
| **Snuff,** Walnut Shell, Carved, c.1900, 2 ½ x 1 ¾ In. .............................................................. | 120 |
| **Snuff,** Yellow Glass, Buddha's Hand, Citron, Peaches, Pomegranate, Coral Stopper, 1900s, 4 In. | 246 |
| **Soda,** A.M. Farland, Philada., Blue Green, Sloping Collar, Blob Top ....................................... | 134 |
| **Soda,** Allen & Shaw, Staunton Va., Aqua, Applied Lip, c.1870, Pt., 6 ⅝ In. ............................... | 23 |
| **Soda,** Bay City, Blue, Blob Top .......................................................................................... | 146 |
| **Soda,** Carpenter & Cobb, Knickerbocker, Cobalt Blue, 10-Sided, Blob Top, c.1860, 7 ½ In. .......... | 1093 |
| **Soda,** Geo. Eagle, Blue Green, Diagonal Ribs, Sloping Collar, Iron Pontil, 6 ⅞ In. ..............*illus* | 288 |
| **Soda,** Howell's Grape Julep, Syrup, Clear, Metal Cap, Paper Label, c.1910, 12 ¼ In. ................... | 1140 |
| **Soda,** J. Rother, Black Amethyst, Sloping Collar, Round Bottom, Baltimore, c.1865 .................... | 4888 |
| **Soda,** Moriarity & Carroll, Waterbury Conn., Yellow Amber, Hutchinson, 7 ⅜ In. ...................... | 410 |
| **Soda,** P. Conway, Union Glass Works, Sapphire Blue, Mug Base, Sloping Collar, c.1860, 7 In. ...... | 374 |
| **Soda,** Stromeyer's Grape Punch, Syrup, Clear, Metal Cap, Paper Label, c.1910, 12 ¼ In. ............. | 660 |
| **Soda,** Wm. Russell, Balt., Yellow Olive, Torpedo Shape, Sloping Collar, 8 ¾ In.  .................*illus* | 633 |
| **Spirits,** Figural, Aspasia, Robin's-Egg Blue, Embossed Birds, c.1880, 10 In. .......................*illus* | 222 |
| **Target Ball,** G.A. Bastman, Stockholm, Diamond, Yellow Amber, c.1885, 2 ⅝ In. ...............*illus* | 1725 |
| **Target Ball,** Man, Shooting, Raised Circle, Diamond, Amethyst, c.1900, 2 ⅝ In. ....................... | 489 |

**Bottle,** Pickle, Cathedral, Green, Crosshatching, Rolled Lip, 14 In.
$784

**Bottle,** Pickle, Cylindrical, Paneled, Fluted Shoulder, Blue Green, Wm. Underwood, c.1850, 11 ⅜ In.
$1,989

**Bottle,** Pickle, New England, Skilton Foote & Co., Amber, Applied Lip, Label, 13 ½ In.
$190

**B**

**Bottle,** Poison, Lattice & Diamond, Moss Green, Flattened Lip, c.1900, 4½ In. $748

Glass Works Auctions

**Bottle,** Sarsaparilla, Dr. Townsend's, Emerald Green, Cloverleaf Iron Pontil, 9¼ In. $863

Glass Works Auctions

**Bottle,** Seal, Ambrosial, B.M. & E.A.W. & Co., Amber, Chestnut, Applied Handle, 9 In. $173

Glass Works Auctions

**Bottle,** Shoe Polish, Topsy, Paper Label, Wooden Cap, Applicator Brush, Aqua, 5 In. $403

Wm Morford Auctions

**Bottle,** Snuff, Agate, 5 Figures, Scroll, Tree, Coral & Metal Stopper, Chinese, c.1800, 3⅜ In. $1,599

Skinner Auctioneers & Appraisers

**Bottle,** Snuff, Dragons, Clouds, Black On White, Carnelian Stopper, Chinese, 3¼ In. $59

James D. Julia Auctioneers

**Bottle,** Snuff, Jade, Black, White, Man On Horse, 2 Cottages On Reverse, Coral Stopper, 3 In. $3,125

Garth's Auctioneers & Appraisers

**Bottle,** Snuff, Jade, Translucent Pale Green, Tourmaline Stopper, Chinese, c.1900, 2 In. $3,851

James D. Julia Auctioneers

**Bottle,** Soda, Geo. Eagle, Blue Green, Diagonal Ribs, Sloping Collar, Iron Pontil, 6⅞ In. $288

Glass Works Auctions

| | |
|---|---|
| Tonic, French Wine Coca, Ideal Nerve, Pemberton, Paper Label, 1880 ...............*illus* | 13750 |
| Whiskey, 26 Ribs, Swirled To Right, Red Amber, Ringed Mouth, Handle, c.1856, 8 ½ In.............. | 518 |
| Whiskey, Backbar, Kentucky Reserve, Clear, White Enamel Script, Sloping Collar, Qt............... | 134 |
| Whiskey, Backbar, Metropolis, Clear, White Enamel Letters, Cinched Waist, Fifth.................. | 123 |
| Whiskey, Backbar, Royal Velvet, Clear, White Enamel, Sloping Collar, Mug Base, Qt.................... | 157 |
| Whiskey, Brandy, Label Under Glass, Back Bar, Sloping Collar, Qt., 10 In. ......................*illus* | 316 |
| Whiskey, Casper's, Made By Honest North Carolina People, Cobalt Blue, 12 In.................. | 497 |
| Whiskey, Castle, O.K. Old Bourbon, F. Chevalier & Co. Sole Agents, Amber, Fifth ............. | 672 |
| Whiskey, Dr. Girard's London, Ginger Brandy, Amber, Double Collar Mouth, Seal, Handle, 9 In.. | 374 |
| Whiskey, E.G. Booz's Old Cabin, 120 Walnut St., Philadelphia, Cabin, Amber, 7 ¾ In. ........*illus* | 3450 |
| Whiskey, Figural, Clam Shell, Cobalt Blue, Threaded Neck, Tin Cap, c.1880, 5 ¼ In. ..........*illus* | 644 |
| Whiskey, Fine Old Rye, Yellow Amber, Label, Wicker Cover, c.1870, 11 ⅝ In. .....................*illus* | 380 |
| Whiskey, Griffith Hyatt & Co., Baltimore, Yellow Amber, Topaz Tone, Jug, 7 ¼ In........................ | 761 |
| Whiskey, Hildebrandt, Posner & Co., Monogram, Olive Amber, Sloping Collar, Fifth ................. | 1120 |
| Whiskey, J.F. Cutter, Extra Old Bourbon, Embossed Star & Shield, Amber, Fifth ................... | 280 |
| Whiskey, J.H. Cutter Old Bourbon, Amber, Coffin, ½ Pt.............................. | 504 |
| Whiskey, J.H. Cutter Old Bourbon, Amber, Coffin, Pt............................... | 1904 |
| Whiskey, J.H. Cutter, Old Bourbon, A.P. Hotaling & So., Amber, Long Neck, Fifth......................... | 2464 |
| Whiskey, J.H. Cutter, Old Bourbon, Milton J. Hardy, Embossed, Amber, 1873-79, Fifth ........*illus* | 308 |
| Whiskey, Jesse Moore & Co. Old Bourbon, Embossed Antlers & Stars, Amber, Fifth ..................... | 202 |
| Whiskey, Jockey Club, G.W. Chesley & Co., S.F., Light Amber, Fifth............................. | 5152 |
| Whiskey, Kellogg's Nelson County Extra Kentucky Bourbon, Red Amber, Embossed, Fifth........... | 728 |
| Whiskey, Label Under Glass, Pretty Woman, Drink, Red Dress, 11 ½ In. ......................*illus* | 784 |
| Whiskey, Lilienthal & Co. Distillers, Yellow Amber, 4-Piece Mold, 1874-80, Fifth ...............*illus* | 448 |
| Whiskey, Lilienthal & Co., S.F., Cognac, Yellow Amber, Flask, 6 ¾ In.......................... | 504 |
| Whiskey, P. Vollmer's Old Bourbon, Louisville, Red Amber, Fifth ....................... | 616 |
| Whiskey, Pig, Good Old Bourbon In A Hogs, Amber, Tooled Lip, c.1895, 6 ½ In....................... | 489 |
| Whiskey, Pioneer Bourbon, Braunschweiger & Co., San Francisco, Amber, Fifth ..................... | 2464 |
| Whiskey, Robinson & Lord, Lombard St., Baltimore, Barrel, Yellow Amber, 10 In. ................... | 1170 |
| Whiskey, Rum, Olive Amber, Blown, Applied Rim, Concave Bottom, c.1720, 5 ¾ In. ................. | 215 |
| Whiskey, Samuel Bros. & Co., San Francisco, Olive, Lady's Leg Neck, Double Collar, Fifth.......... | 504 |
| Whiskey, Simmond's Nabob, Pure Ky Bourbon, Embossed Nabob, Red Amber .......................... | 420 |
| Whiskey, Tea Kettle Old Bourbon, Embossed Teakettle, Shaded Amber, Fifth........................ | 1344 |
| Whiskey, Turner Brothers, New York, Barrel, Amber, Topaz Tone, Square Collar, 10 In. .............. | 1287 |
| Whiskey, Utah Liquor Co., Salt Lake City Ut., Clear, Megaphone Shape, 13 ¼ In......................... | 364 |
| Whiskey, Wharton's Whiskey, Chestnut Grove, Amber, Urn Shape, Handle, c.1865, 10 In........... | 863 |
| Wine, A.M. Smith's California Wind Depot, 321 Arch St., Philada., Amber, Tapered, 14 In........... | 2016 |
| Wine, Bell, Yellow Olive Green, Sheared Mouth, String Lip, c.1750, 6 ¾ x 4 In. ................... | 345 |
| Wine, Onion, Embossed Seal, Crouching Lion, Olive Green, Pontil, c.1700, 5 ¾ In. ............*illus* | 3218 |
| Wine, Onion, Olive Green, Pontil, Ring Lip, 8 ¼ In................................ | 420 |
| Wine, Wicker Covered, Globular, Olive Green, Sheared Mouth, c.1779, 9 ⅞ In. .................*illus* | 3803 |
| Zanesville, 15 Ribs, Yellow Amber, Applied Flattened Lip, Pontil, 7 In............................. | 120 |
| Zanesville, 24 Ribs, Swirled To Left, Amber, Globular, Flared Lip, 8 In.............................. | 615 |
| Zanesville, 24 Ribs, Swirled To Left, Yellow Amber, Globular, Pontil, 7 ⅞ In.......................... | 527 |
| Zanesville, 24 Swirled Ribs, Golden Amber, Bulbous, Applied Lip, Pontil, 7 ½ In. ................... | 861 |
| Zanesville, 24 Swirled Ribs, Root Beer Amber, Applied Lip, Pontil, 8 ¼ In. ......................... | 1046 |
| Zanesville, 24 Vertical Ribs, Amber, Chestnut, 5 In.............................. | 300 |
| Zanesville, 24 Vertical Ribs, Orange Amber, Flattened Chestnut, 8 In............................. | 702 |

**BOTTLE CAPS** for milk bottles are the printed cardboard caps used since the 1920s. Crown caps, used after 1892 on soda bottles, are also popular collectibles. Unusual mottoes, graphics, and caps from bottlers that are out of business bring the highest prices.

| | |
|---|---|
| **Amber-Glo Dairy Foods,** Half & Half, Blue, White, 2 In........................... | 4 |
| **Amber-Glo Dairy,** Pasteurized Grade A Milk, Yellow, Red, White, 2 In. ................. | 5 |
| **Brownie,** Chocolate Flavored Drink, Metal, Brown.......................... | 2 |
| **Clic-Quot Club Strawberry Cream Soda,** Red, White Metal ................. | 3 |
| **Cool Mountain,** Gourmet Soda, Indian Chief, Metal ........................ | 3 |
| **Crush,** Grapefruit Soda, Cork Lined, Yellow, Green, Metal.................... | 3 |
| **Donald Duck Ginger Ale,** Yellow, Green Metal ......................... | 9 |
| **Felix,** Orange Dry, Cat, Black, Orange, Metal ........................... | 14 |
| **Felix,** Orange Dry, Metal, 1 ¼ In................................ | 14 |
| **Kimberland Dairy,** Red, White, Blue, Paper, 2 ¼ In........................ | 5 |
| **Mellin's Food,** For Infants & Invalids, Paper, 1 ³/₁₆ In...................... | 10 |
| **Nichol's Creamery,** Pasteurized Milk, Red, White, Paper, 1 ⅝ In. ............... | 10 |
| **Old Red Eye,** Steer Head, Red, White, Cork Lined, Metal ...................... | 4 |

**Bottle,** Soda, Wm. Russell, Balt., Yellow Olive, Torpedo Shape, Sloping Collar, 8 ¾ In.
$633

**Bottle,** Spirits, Figural, Aspasia, Robin's-Egg Blue, Embossed Birds, c.1880, 10 In.
$222

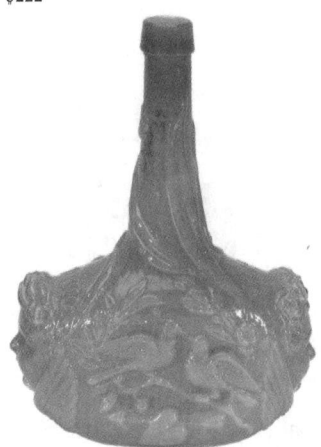

**Bottle,** Target Ball, G.A. Bastman, Stockholm, Diamond, Yellow Amber, c.1885, 2 ⅝ In.
$1,725

**Bottle,** Tonic, French Wine Coca, Ideal
Nerve, Pemberton, Paper Label, 1880
$13,750

Heritage Auction Galleries

**Bottle,** Whiskey, Brandy, Label Under
Glass, Back Bar, Sloping Collar, Qt., 10 In.
$316

Glass Works Auctions

**Bottle,** Whiskey, E.G. Booz's Old Cabin,
120 Walnut St., Philadelphia, Cabin,
Amber, 7¾ In.
$3,450

Glass Works Auctions

**BOTTLE OPENERS** are needed to open many bottles. As soon as the commercial bottle was invented, the opener to be used with the new types of closures became a necessity. Many types of bottle openers can be found, most dating from the twentieth century. Collectors prize advertising and comic openers.

| | |
|---|---|
| **Airplane,** Goodyear Aircraft Corp., Metal, 1¼ x 3⅛ In. | 115 |
| **Antler,** Corkscrew, Pat. 1906, 6⅞ In. | 150 |
| **Boy,** Alligator, Bronze | 53 |
| **Devil's Head,** Brass, 3¾ x 3½ In. | 28 |
| **Dog,** Pointer, Brown & Tan, Scott Products Co., 6 x 2 In. | 82 |
| **Dog,** Setter, Cast Iron, John Wright Co., 1950s, 4½ x 2½ In. | 115 |
| **Dolphin,** Chrome Finish, 6½ In. | 12 |
| **Drunk,** Street Sign, Skyline Drive, Va., Cast Iron, 4 In. | 25 |
| **Elephant,** Cast Iron, Gray Paint, 3¾ In. | 25 |
| **Fish,** Abalone, Mother-Of-Pearl, 1950s, 7½ In. | 129 |
| **Iguana,** Silver Plate, Articulated, Emilia Castillo, 11½ In. | 198 |
| **Lobster,** Cast Iron, Red Paint, 3½ In. | 12 |
| **Man's Head,** Top Hat, Wood, Anri, 2¼ In. | 45 |
| **Necktie,** Silver Plate, Princess House, Italy, 6⅝ In. | 22 |
| **Nude,** Art Deco, Bronze, Marked, 4¼ In. | 95 |
| **Owl,** Plastic, Sticker, Italy, c.1975, 6½ In. | 24 |
| **Parrot On Perch,** Multicolor, Cast Iron, John Wright Co., 5½ In. | 59 |
| **Parrot,** Art Deco, Pink, Blue, Yellow, Cast Iron, 1930s, 3½ In. | 167 |
| **Sterling Silver,** Amnesty Pattern, Web Weidlich, c.1940, 5½ In. | 24 |
| **Wood Handle,** Twisted, 6½ In. | 15 |
| **Zodiac Symbols,** Enamel, Brass, Made In Israel, 1960s, 5 In. | 40 |

**BOTTLE STOPPERS** are made of glass, metal, plastic, and wood. Decorative and figural stoppers are used to replace the original cork stoppers and are collected today.

| | |
|---|---|
| **Agate,** Angled, 1½ In. | 35 |
| **Bisque,** Clown, Movable Hat, Germany, 1920s, 4¼ In. | 65 |
| **Bisque,** Dog, Japanese Spaniel, Bow, 2⅜ In. | 15 |
| **Brass,** Couple, Cane, Parasol, 1930s, 6 In. | 45 |
| **Bronze,** Boar Head, Sailor Hat, c.1915, 2 In. | 450 |
| **Ceramic,** Naked Cave Man, Beard, Italy, 4 In. | 65 |
| **Glass,** Faceted, Oleg Cassini, 2½ In. | 10 |
| **Glass,** Scalloped Edge, Pressed Starburst, Amber, 1½ x 1¼ In. | 12 |
| **Papier-Mache,** Comedian Joe Penner, Cigar, Big Eyes, 1900s, 5½ In. | 40 |
| **Porcelain,** Moroccan Man, Mustache, Hat, Germany, 1940s, 3¼ In. | 35 |
| **Porcelain,** Old Man, Top Hat, Frown, Painted, 4 In. | 52 |
| **Porcelain,** Pierrot, Art Deco, 2 In. | 55 |
| **Porcelain,** Sea Captain, Pipe, 4 x 3 In. | 48 |
| **Sterling Silver,** Jigger, c.1960, 4½ x 2½ In. | 195 |
| **Sterling Silver,** Llama Head, Peru, 1930, 3⅞ In. | 175 |
| **Sterling Silver,** Punch & Toby, Marked, Louis Dee, c.1882, 4 In. | 2750 |
| **Sterling Silver,** Windmill, c.1900, 2¾ x 2 In. | 295 |
| **Wood,** Accordion Player, Mechanical, c.1926, 3½ In. | 48 |
| **Wood,** Bear, Glass Bead Eyes, c.1910, 2¼ In. | 132 |
| **Wood,** Bear, Upright, On Barrel, Shoebutton Eyes, c.1910, 4½ In. | 95 |
| **Wood,** Couple, Push Lever, Germany, 4 In. | 18 |
| **Wood,** Dog Head, Painted, c.1945, 3 x 2 In. | 68 |
| **Wood,** Drummer, Pull Lever To Play, Germany, 4¾ In. | 25 |
| **Wood,** Eagle, On Rock, Open Wings, Shoebutton Eyes, c.1920, 4¼ In. | 70 |
| **Wood,** Man, Hat, Rosy Cheeks, Coat, Vest, Anri, 4¾ In. | 30 |
| **Wood,** Ugly Woman, Movable Jaw, Swiss, 4 In. | 54 |

**BOXES** of all kinds are collected. They were made of thin strips of inlaid wood, metal, tortoiseshell, embroidery, or other material. Additional boxes may be listed in other sections, such as Advertising, Battersea, Ivory, Shaker, Tinware, and various Porcelain categories. Tea Caddies are listed in their own category.

| | |
|---|---|
| **Accessory,** Lacquer, Takamaki-E, Figures In Landscape, Interior Tray, Japan, 3⅜ x 8⅜ In. | 1353 |
| **Alms,** Cast Iron, Hexagonal Receiver, Post, Lower Keeper, Key, 49 In. | 300 |
| **Altar,** Elm, Pierced Sliding Panel Door, Chinese, 1800s, 28 x 24½ x 30½ In. | 250 |
| **Amulet,** Gau, Silver, Copper, Turquoise, Octagonal, Filigree, Tibet, 4¼ x 4¼ In. | 472 |
| **Anglo-Indian Style,** Bone Clad, Incised, Castle, Flower Borders, Scrollwork, 9 x 11½ In. | 984 |

| | |
|---|---|
| **Applewood,** Pine, Green, Red, White, Flowers, Scalloped, Pierced Sides, Pa., c.1830, 5½ x 10 In. | 10800 |
| **Arts & Crafts,** Copper, Riveted, Enameled, Fish, Seaweed, Green, Red, Blue, Black, 8 x 5 x 4 In.. | 1875 |
| **Bandbox,** Bentwood, Mother & Child, Wallpaper, Hannah Davis, New Hampshire, 1849, 16 x 19 In. | 1080 |
| **Bandbox,** Bentwood, Pink Flowers, Yellow Paint, Germany, c.1920, 1 x 4½ In. | 58 |
| **Bandbox,** Cardboard, Blue Wallpaper, Sailing Ships, Scrolling Flowers, c.1840, 11 x 17 In. | 615 |
| **Bandbox,** Cardboard, Floral Wallpaper, c.1850, 10 x 14 In. ............................*illus* | 570 |
| **Bandbox,** Cardboard, Wallpaper, Stagecoach Scene, Fitted Lid, c.1800, 11 x 16 In. .......*illus* | 533 |
| **Bandbox,** Lid, Bentwood, Wallpaper, Salmon & Blue Leaves & Stars, Oval, 13 x 19 In. | 720 |
| **Bandbox,** Orange Bird Design, Blue Ground, Oval, Pa., 13 x 17½ In. | 420 |
| **Bandbox,** Philadelphia, Boston, New York Scenes, Top Hat Shape, 1889, 8 In. | 120 |
| **Bandbox,** Wallpaper, Cylindrical, White Ground, Green Vines, 1800s, 3¾ x 5¾ In. | 59 |
| **Bandbox,** Wallpaper, Farm, Dated 1833, Hannah Davis, Oval, New Hampshire, 8 x 13 In. | 1200 |
| **Bandbox,** Wallpaper, Green, Yellow Flowers, Red Ground, Oval, 12 x 18 In. | 600 |
| **Bandbox,** Wallpaper, Lid, Cottage, Cows, Flowers, Blue, Pennsylvania, 1800s, 13 x 17 x 14 In. *illus* | 70 |
| **Basswood,** Dome Lid, Red, Yellow, Black Paint, New Eng., c.1820, 9 x 16 In. | 277 |
| **Bentwood,** Lid, Metal Tacks, Oval, Lap Seam, Old Red Paint, 2½ x 5½ x 9¾ In. | 240 |
| **Bentwood,** Lid, Oval, Tulips, Painted, Oval, Inscribed Ephrain Gochenour, c.1800, 4 x 11 In. | 196 |
| **Bentwood,** Lid, Potted Flower, Vines, Berries, Painted, Oval New England, 3 x 9 In. | 480 |
| **Bentwood,** Round, Upright Handle, Painted Cabin, Windmill Scene, c.1895, 5 x 3¾ In. | 104 |
| **Bentwood,** Stamped Designs, Oval, Scandinavia, c.1810, 14 x 22 In. | 120 |
| **Betel Nut,** Lid, Insert, Red, Black Lacquer, Incised Zodiac Images, Burma, c.1910, 7½ In. | 90 |
| **Bible,** Curly Maple, Poplar, Bracket Feet, 18th Century, 8 x 18 In. | 9600 |
| **Bible,** Flowers, Painted, Turned Feet, 11 x 19 In. | 1320 |
| **Bible,** Oak, Carved Leaves & Scrolls On Front, England, 17th Century, 8 x 27 In. | 570 |
| **Bible,** Oak, Hinged Top, Vine, Tulip Inlays, Ball Feet, c.1776, 9¾ x 23 In. | 575 |
| **Bible,** Painted, Tulip Decoration, 4 Ball Feet, Continental, 1700s, 6 x 13 In. | 738 |
| **Bible,** Pine, Black Over Red Paint, Carved, Stylized Leaves, Conn., c.1690, 24 x 17 In. | 8400 |
| **Bible,** Walnut, Strap Hinged Lid, Bracket Feet, Cutout Feet, c.1770, 9 x 18 In. | 1035 |
| **Blue & Black Grain Decoration,** Hinges, c.1850, 7½ x 17¾ In. | 400 |
| **Book Shape,** 2 Books, Fitted Interior, Slate Blue, 9½ In. | 1080 |
| **Bottle Case,** Pine, Red Wash, 6-Board, 4 Sections, Strap Hinges, Bracket Feet, 14 x 15 x 15 In.... | 2124 |
| **Bride's,** Bentwood, Laced Seams, Red, Flowers, Tulips, 5 x 12 In. | 420 |
| **Bride's,** Bentwood, Painted Scenes, Flower Band, German Text, Oval, 1928, 7 x 18 x 12 In. | 354 |
| **Bride's,** Lid, Fish, Painted, Oval, 9 x 5 In. | 205 |
| **Bride's,** Multicolor Paint, Flowers, Red Ground, Scandinavia, 1800s, 14 x 6½ In. | 68 |
| **Bride's,** Oval, Tulip Painted, Black Ground, Scandinavia, c.1810, 6 x 17 In. | 246 |
| **Bride's,** Pine, White Oak, Dome Lid, Multicolor Flowers, Leaves, c.1780, 5 x 2 In. | 2370 |
| **Bronze,** Jade, Carnelian Agate, Waves, Fish, Disc Base, Inscribed, 1920s, 2⅜ x 4¾ In. | 615 |
| **Camphorwood,** Brassbound, Inscribed P. Murray, Handles, c.1850, 12¾ x 31 In. | 330 |
| **Candle,** Drawer, Red Paint, Shaped Top, 18½ In. | 61 |
| **Candle,** Federal, Mahogany, Shell Inlaid, Pierced Back Crest, Line Inlay, 20 x 8 In. | 189 |
| **Candle,** Pine, Backsplash, Door, Smoke Painted, Mid-Atlantic, c.1900, 12 x 11 In. | 489 |
| **Candle,** Pine, Slide Lid, Green, Black Paint, Pa., 1800s, 6 x 11 In. | 111 |
| **Candle,** Pine, Slide Lid, Shenandoah Valley, c.1825, 12 x 26 In. | 403 |
| **Candle,** Poplar, Red, White Tulips, c.1810, 4½ x 8¼ In. | 3936 |
| **Candle,** Shaped Crest, Hinged Flap, Tapered, Flower Inlays, 19 In. | 360 |
| **Candle,** Slide Lid, Painted, Grapes, Leaves, Heart Shape Handle, Terry J. Graham, 7 x 15 In. | 212 |
| **Candle,** Slide Lid, Painted, Potted Plant, Squirrel On Table, Barbara Strawser, 3¼ x 13 In. | 106 |
| **Candle,** Spoon Rack, Pinwheel Design, Hanging, Signed, Matthew Austin, 28 x 15 In. | 130 |
| **Card,** Piano, Dancing, Guilloche, 14K Yellow Gold, Austria, c.1900, 3 x 2 x ½ In. | 4500 |
| **Cheese,** Lid, Bentwood, Gray Paint, c.1900, 22 In. | 86 |
| **Cherry,** Geometric Inlays, Drawer, Wooden Dice Lock, c.1880 | 224 |
| **Church Collection,** Comfort Box, Little Brown Church In The Dell, Hinged Lid, 15 x 21 In. | 380 |
| **Cigar,** Copper, Hammered, Riveted, Mahogany, Gustav Stickley, 7½ x 5 In. | 6100 |
| **Cigarette,** Marquetry, Circular Copper Lid, Masonic Emblem, 5 x 6 In. | 90 |
| **Coffer,** Fruitwood, Panels, Carved Architectural Patterns, Footed, Continental, 1700s, 25 x 54 In.. | 2337 |
| **Comb,** Hanging, Walnut, Cutout Tree Branches, Dark Stain, c.1870, 17 x 11 In. | 69 |
| **Cutlery,** Cherry, Hinged Lid, Heart Cutout Handle, Footed, Pa., c.1830, 10 x 16 In. | 677 |
| **Decanter Case,** Mahogany Veneer, Inlaid Butterfly Escutcheon, Fitted Interior, 8 x 10 In. | 480 |
| **Desk,** Hinged Top, Interior Compartments, Applied Molded Base, Blue Paint, 15 x 30 In. | 492 |
| **Desk,** Pine, Slant Lift Lid, 2 Inner Compartments, Well, Battens, Forged Handles, 1700s, 17 x 37 In. | 309 |
| **Desk,** Slant Top, Pine, Applied Molding, Painted, Green, Scrolls, c.1840, 6½ x 12 In. | 300 |
| **Desk,** Traveling, Enamel, Silver Gilt, Book Shape, Hinged, Enclosed Watch, 4¾ x 3¼ In. | 8400 |
| **Desk,** Walnut, Pine, Inlaid Trees, Birds, Fans, Eagles, 2-Sided, c.1880, 6 x 24 In. | 184 |
| **Document,** Burl Walnut, Brass Ring Pull, Mid-Atlantic, c.1840, 7 x 12 In. | 230 |
| **Document,** Dome Lid, Red, Green, Yellow Flowers, Berries, Tin, Connecticut, c.1820, 10 In. | 720 |

**Bottle,** Whiskey, Figural, Clam Shell, Cobalt Blue, Threaded Neck, Tin Cap, c.1880, 5¼ In.
$644

Norman C. Heckler & Company

**Bottle,** Whiskey, Fine Old Rye, Yellow Amber, Label, Wicker Cover, c.1870, 11⅝ In.
$380

Norman C. Heckler & Company

**Bottle,** Whiskey, J.H. Cutter, Old Bourbon, Milton J. Hardy, Embossed, Amber, 1873-79, Fifth
$308

American Bottle Auctions

67

B

**Bottle,** Whiskey, Label Under Glass, Pretty Woman, Drink, Red Dress, 11 ½ In. $784

American Bottle Auctions

**Bottle,** Whiskey, Lilienthal & Co. Distillers, Yellow Amber, 4-Piece Mold, 1874-80, Fifth $448

American Bottle Auctions

**Bottle,** Wine, Onion, Embossed Seal, Crouching Lion, Olive Green, Pontil, c.1700, 5 ¾ In. $3,218

Norman C. Heckler & Company

| | |
|---|---:|
| **Document,** Gilt, Bronze, Purple Leather Clad, Hinged Lid, Slotted Interior, 10 ½ In. | 313 |
| **Document,** Maple, Brass Bail Handle, c.1855, 6 x 17 In. | 188 |
| **Document,** Pine, Dovetailed, Lock, Blue & Brown Over Yellow, c.1830, 4 ¼ x 14 In. | 382 |
| **Document,** Pine, Geometric Designs, Black, Red Paint, 1800s, 7 ½ x 14 In. | 98 |
| **Document,** Pine, Green & Salmon Geometric Decoration, Rectangular, Wire Latch, 6 x 12 In. | 720 |
| **Document,** Pine, Oilcloth, Brass Tacks, Brass Handle, Paper Lined, 4 ½ x 9 In. | 150 |
| **Document,** Poplar, Molded Top, Dark Stain, 1700s, 8 x 22 In. | 161 |
| **Document,** Tiger Maple, Dovetailed Case, 1800s, 5 ½ x 16 ½ x 8 ¼ In. | 502 |
| **Document,** Wood, Dome Lid, Brass, Leather, Iron, Handle, c.1845, 6 x 12 In. | 161 |
| **Document,** Wood, Flower, Leaves, Hearts, Spades, Late 19th Century, 10 x 19 ¾ In. | 96 |
| **Dome Lid,** Grain Painted, Burnt Sienna, Ochre, New England, 10 ½ x 24 In. | 461 |
| **Dome Lid,** Hinged Lid, Wire Handle, Iron Latch, Multicolor Flowers, Birds, c.1810, 9 x 12 In. | 1046 |
| **Dome Lid,** Needlepoint Fox, Landscape Scene, 3 ½ x 7 ¾ In. | 153 |
| **Dome Lid,** Red, Yellow Sponge Paint, E.P.D. Monogram, New England, c.1845, 13 x 30 In. | 92 |
| **Double Candle,** Shaped Back, 2 Wells, Brown Paint, 21 x 11 In. | 2880 |
| **Dresser,** Art Nouveau, Bronze D'Ore, Serpentine, Relief Lily, Footed, Gilt, Benedict, 3 x 11 In. | 207 |
| **Dresser,** Bird's-Eye Maple, Inlaid Star Lid, c.1830, 5 x 12 In. | 240 |
| **Dresser,** Mahogany, Book Shape, Fitted Mirror Compartment, 1767, 4 x 3 In. | 450 |
| **Dresser,** Micro Mosaic, Etched Glass, Hexagonal, Flowers, White Ground, Hinged Lid, 4 x 5 In. | 600 |
| **Dresser,** Mixed Woods, Inlaid Bone Panels, Allegorical Scenes, Continental, 1800s, 6 x 9 In. | 2460 |
| **Dresser,** Pine, Lift Lid, Drawer, Green, Black, Yellow, c.1850, 7 x 16 x 7 In. | 1085 |
| **Dresser,** Porcelain, Gilt Metal, Oval Medallion Of Woman, Signed Wagner, 4 ¾ x 5 In. | 604 |
| **Dresser,** Wood, Lid Pinwheel, Leaf Carved Sides, Red, Brown Paint, Pa., c.1885, 5 x 12 In. | 92 |
| **Figural,** Rabbit, Coconut Body, Bronze Head & Legs, 6 ½ In. *illus* | 657 |
| **Fresian,** Chip Carved, Pinwheels, Triangles, Painted Green, Red, Slide Lid, 12 ¾ In. | 840 |
| **Gilt Bronze,** Bust Of Woman, Braided Hair, Onyx Base, France, 9 ⅜ In. | 1125 |
| **Gilt Lacquer,** Abalone Inlays, Moth Shape, Black Lid, 1800s, 8 x 11 ½ In. | 625 |
| **Gilt Metal,** Coffin Shape, Twig Finial, Hinged, Continental, 6 x 8 In. | 600 |
| **Gilt Silver,** Chased, Enameled Lid, Figures By Watershed, Sheep, Floral Cartouche, 3 x 2 In. | 495 |
| **Gilt,** Black Lacquer, Canted Corners, Hinged Lid, Paw Feet, Chinese, 15 x 12 In. | 677 |
| **Glass,** Casket, Cut Flowers & Starbursts, Silver Mount, Hinged Lid, CFM & Co., 10 x 5 In. | 1180 |
| **Glass,** Egg Shape, Swirled Ribs, Rainbow, Hinged, Rigaree Petals, Rose Branch Base, 8 In. | 944 |
| **Glass,** Swirled Ribs, Pink, Blue, Cream, Clear Handle & Feet, Gold Stencils, 9 ¾ In. | 649 |
| **Glove,** Ebonized, Pietra Dura, Inlay, 1800s, 13 ½ x 5 ½ In. | 293 |
| **Hat,** Leather, Stitched, Velvet Lined, Lock Flap, 10 x 13 ½ In. | 480 |
| **Humidor,** Brown Leather, Embossed, Crown, Cedar Lining, Tray, W. Bober, 6 x 14 x 10 In. | 345 |
| **Humidor,** Mahogany, Inlaid Hexagons, Chevron, Ormolu, Hinged Lid, Edwardian, 8 x 15 In. | 502 |
| **Ivory,** Ormolu, Woman's Portrait, 1700s Attire, 2 ½ x 3 ¼ In. | 150 |
| **Jewelry,** Art Nouveau, Bird's-Eye Maple, Metal Corners, Handle, Flared Base, c.1890, 4 x 13 In. | 480 |
| **Jewelry,** Black Forest, Silver Fittings, Mirrored Lid, 7 x 5 ½ In. | 53 |
| **Jewelry,** Brass, Inlay, Handle, Octagon Shape, Silk Interior, Scroll Feet, 3 ½ x 9 ½ In. | 150 |
| **Jewelry,** Gilt Bronze, Galleried Lid, Fitted, Flower Mounted, H.S. Karlsruhe, c.1850, 11 x 18 In. | 3750 |
| **Jewelry,** Leather, Gilt, Orangish Brown, Lift-Out Tray, Brass Button Feet, Italy, 15 x 11 x 4 In. | 210 |
| **Jewelry,** Mahogany, Maple, Inlays, 2 Drawers, Bracket, c.1800s, 11 x 15 In. | 460 |
| **Jewelry,** Marquetry, Flower Inlays, Stepped Casket Shape, Dutch, c.1890, 9 x 19 In. | 1080 |
| **Jewelry,** Mother-Of-Pearl Inlays, Dome Lid, Velvet Lined Interior, c.1940, 11 x 15 In. | 1152 |
| **Jewelry,** Rosewood, Mother-Of-Pearl Inlay, Fitted, 1886 Presentation, Continental, 12 x 12 In. | 563 |
| **Jewelry,** Silver, Hinged, Dome Lid, Flower, Scrolls, William Kerr, 1800-25, 8 ¼ x 5 ⅜ In. | 615 |
| **Jewelry,** Square Hinged Lid, Marquetry, Flower, Bird Inlays, Gilt Metal Mounted, 19 In. | 500 |
| **Jewelry,** Stacked Book Shape, Leather, 4 x 10 In. | 120 |
| **Jewelry,** Velvet Covered, Gilt Bronze Fittings, Putti, Pierced, Strapwork, c.1900, 18 x 14 In. | 1845 |
| **Jewelry,** Walnut, Carved, 6 x 13 x 8 In. | 120 |
| **Kindling,** Pine, Turned Stiles, Ball Finials, Footed, 24 x 18 In. | 570 |
| **Knife,** George III, Mahogany, Fitted Interior, c.1790, 14 x 9 In. | 510 |
| **Knife,** George III, Mahogany, Serpentine, Line Inlays, Handle, c.1820, 13 In. | 420 |
| **Knife,** George III, Mahogany, Slant Lid, Crossed Banded, England, c.1790, 15 x 12 In., Pair | 2125 |
| **Knife,** Inlaid, Mahogany, Pheasants, Seashells, Felt Lined Interior, 10 x 15 In. | 270 |
| **Knife,** Mahogany Veneer, Serpentine Front, Banded Inlay, Star, 15 x 10 In., Pair | 1440 |
| **Knife,** Mahogany, Hinged Lid, Brass Hasp, Brass Handles, 13 x 9 In. | 360 |
| **Knife,** Papier-Mache, Japanned, Bird, Girl, Flowers, Pink, 7 ½ x 12 ½ In. | 549 |
| **Knife,** Pine, Blue Green Paint, Scalloped Edges, Rectangular Base, Handle, 1800s, 9 x 13 In. | 1680 |
| **Knife,** Serpentine Front, Flame Mahogany Veneer, Hinged Lid, Stringing, c.1800, 15 x 11 In. | 184 |
| **Knife,** Shell Inlay, Medallion, Hinged, Sloped Lid, 13 ⅜ In. | 400 |
| **Knife,** Tiger Maple, Brass Ball Feet, Reeded Edge, Shaped Front, Fitted Interior, 16 x 11 ¾ In. | 1168 |
| **Knife,** Walnut, Inlaid, Divided Interior, Shaped Handle, Heart Cutout, 5 x 11 In. | 210 |
| **Lacquer,** Figures, Landscape, Gilt, Black, Octagonal, Brass Handles, Chinese, c.1805, 14 x 18 In. | 300 |

| | |
|---|---|
| **Lacquer,** Woman On Bicycle, Mountains, Rectangular, Rounded Corners, Hinged, 3 ½ In. | 46 |
| **Lap,** Rosewood, c.1860, 4 x 14 In. | 90 |
| **Leather,** Camphorwood, Flower Borders, Red Paint, Brass Mounted, Chinese, 10 x 25 In. | 1020 |
| **Letter,** Brass, Sloping Lid, Cutout Design, Flowers, Reticulated Letters, 1920s, 6 x 3 In. | 2271 |
| **Letter,** Oak, Bow Front, Slotted, Telegrams Plaque, England, 10 ¾ x 12 ½ In. | 150 |
| **Letter,** Papier-Mache, Mother-Of-Pearl Inlay, Exotic Scenes, Gilt, Serpentine Hinge Lid, 9 x 5 In. | 121 |
| **Letter,** Slant, Lid, Hinged, Interior Stationary Dividers, Lock, Key, c.1910, 10 ½ x 15 ½ In. | 177 |
| **Letter,** Walnut, Coffin Shape, Divided Interior, Gothic Revival, 8 ¼ x 10 In. | 900 |
| **Lock,** Oak, Carved Hunting Scenes, Germany, c.1900, 6 x 14 In. | 180 |
| **Mahogany Inlay,** Ebony, Bird's-Eye Maple, Fitted Interior, Compartments, Ball Feet, 14 x 11 In.. | 415 |
| **Mahogany,** Dome Lid, Georgian, Bail Handle, 1800s, 6 ½ x 10 In. | 200 |
| **Mahogany,** Relief Carved Hunting Dog, Carved From Single Piece Of Wood, 3 x 7 In. | 63 |
| **Mahogany,** Silver Chest, Inset Hinged Top, Drawer, Brass Plaque, 10 ½ x 19 ½ In. | 300 |
| **Mahogany,** Urn Inlay, Hinged Lid, Bail Handles, Ball Feet, England, c.1840, 7 ¾ x 11 In. | 425 |
| **Malachite,** Book Shape, Neoclassical Mount, Gilt Bronze, Russia, 12 ½ In. ........................*illus* | 1195 |
| **Marquetry,** Walnut, Hinged Lid, England, 1886, 14 ¾ x 8 ¾ In. | 313 |
| **Moravian,** Quilled Paper, Yellow Cottage, Red Roof, Landscape, Needlework, Oval, 1800s, 3 In. . | 1888 |
| **Nephrite,** Carved, Brass Rim, Hardstone Oak Leaves, Acorns, Russian Federation, 3 ½ x 2 In. | 587 |
| **Oak,** Dome Lid, Red, Black, Brown, Cream Ground, c.1800, 4 ½ x 10 x 4 In. | 323 |
| **On Stand,** 3 Leather-Bound Books, Turned Legs, Mahogany Base, Hinged Lid, 25 x 18 In. | 667 |
| **On Stand,** Geometric, Heart Design, Sweden, 18 x 25 In. | 438 |
| **Papier-Mache,** Furrowed, Oval & Starburst Relief, Chromolitho Landscape, 2 ¼ x 1 ½ In. | 115 |
| **Patch,** Papier-Mache, Rectangular, Jumping Horse, Rider, Landscape, 3 ⅜ x 2 In. | 300 |
| **Patch,** Papier-Mache, Round, Apsley House In London, 3 ⅜ In. | 180 |
| **Patch,** Papier-Mache, Round, Dark Brown, Hunting Dog, ¾ In. | 220 |
| **Patch,** Papier-Mache, Round, Horse-Drawn Coach, Town, 3 ¼ In. | 269 |
| **Patch,** Papier-Mache, Round, Huntsman, Dog Pack, 3 ⅝ In. | 330 |
| **Patch,** Papier-Mache, Round, Portrait, 2 Sisters, 3 ⅞ In. | 360 |
| **Pencil,** Green, Red, Tan, Curly Maple, Pine, Dove, Basket, Roses, Arrows, 3 ¾ x 10 ¼ In. | 3360 |
| **Pencil,** Slide Lid, Painted, Flowers, Yellow Ground, Signed S.B. Williams, 1840, 7 x 2 In. | 189 |
| **Pill,** Sulphide, Holy Mary, Cut Crystal, Sawtooth Edge, Baccarat, c.1820, 2 x 1 In. | 813 |
| **Pine,** Checkerboard Top, Lid, Leather Hinges, Paint, Va., c.1850, 11 x 20 In. | 230 |
| **Pine,** Cutout Handholds, Arched Ends, Brown Stain, 1800s, 9 ¾ x 10 ½ In. | 2706 |
| **Pine,** Dome Lid, Blue Paint, Dovetailed, Iron Hardware, 12 x 26 x 13 In. | 120 |
| **Pine,** Dome Lid, Blue, White Sponge Paint, New England, c.1845, 14 x 31 In. | 127 |
| **Pine,** Dome Lid, Painted Flowers, Black Ground, Red Scalloped Apron, 1832, 12 x 17 In. | 1080 |
| **Pine,** Dome Lid, Red Black Grain Paint, New England, 1800s, 11 x 27 In. | 185 |
| **Pine,** Dome Lid, Wrought Iron Strapping, Lock, Continental, c.1810, 10 ½ x 21 ½ In. | 450 |
| **Pine,** Gray Paint, Pa., c.1830, 9 x 14 In. | 369 |
| **Pine,** Hinged Dome Lid, Shenandoah Valley, c.1845, 9 x 11 In. | 345 |
| **Pine,** Hinged Lid, Grain Painted, Black Stenciled W. McG. 1859, New England, 12 x 21 In. | 150 |
| **Pine,** Iron Hinges, Green, Red Paint, c.1800, 11 x 9 In. | 288 |
| **Pine,** Monogram, Dated 1895, Yellow, Blue, Red Paint, Cantered, Lock, 7 x 17 In. | 185 |
| **Pine,** Painted Flower, Scandinavia, c.1850, 11 x 25 In. | 123 |
| **Pine,** Painted Putty, Red Striping, Green Border, Wire Hardware, Maine, c.1810, 9 ½ x 6 In. | 738 |
| **Pine,** Painted Red, Black Border, Eagle, Parcel Gilt, Hannah Miller, c.1810, 5 x 9 In. | 4920 |
| **Pine,** Painted Rider, Horse, Salmon, Bracket Feet, 2 Tombstone Panels, Pa., c.1790, 11 x 19 In.. | 10455 |
| **Pine,** Painted, Lid, Monogram MMC PA., c.1850, 9 x 16 In. | 111 |
| **Pine,** Painted, Stems With 5 Leaves, Stars, Dovetailed, Hinged Lid, Turned Feet, 7 x 10 x 6 In. | 5175 |
| **Pine,** Red Paint, Pa., c.1840, 10 ¾ x 11 ½ In. | 185 |
| **Pine,** Slant Lid, Red Paint, Pa., c.1810, 7 x 12 In. | 369 |
| **Pine,** Tulip Design, Painted, Slide Lid, Pinned, Pennsylvania, c.1810, 5 x 12 In. ...............*illus* | 840 |
| **Pine,** Wire Hasps, Military Officer On Horse, Handle, American, 1800-50, 31 In. | 600 |
| **Pipe,** Pine, Scrolled Backboard, Sides, Front Panel, Molded Drawer, Wood Pull, 1700s, 18 x 6 In. | 1230 |
| **Pipe,** Poplar, Maple, Lollipop Crest, Drawer, Red Paint, Inscribed, New Eng., c.1790, 20 x 6 In. ... | 2280 |
| **Pipe,** Wall, Cherry, Pine, Lollipop Hanger, Drawer, c.1800, 18 In. ........................*illus* | 840 |
| **Pipe,** Wall, George III, Mahogany, Whale's Tail Crest, Pierced With Heart, Sloped Lid, 20 In. | 480 |
| **Pipe,** Wall, Pine, Rosehead Nails, Dovetail, Drawer, Shaped Top, c.1775, 20 In. | 3525 |
| **Plaid,** Painted Red, Black, Green, Yellow, Lock, New England, 1800s, 7 ½ x 16 x 11 ½ In. | 1020 |
| **Playing Card,** English Monarchs, Glass Panels, Silver, Henry C. Davis, 1901, 4 ½ In. | 1188 |
| **Poplar,** Green Paint, Lock, New Eng., c.1800, 6 ½ x 16 ½ In. | 150 |
| **Poplar,** Slide Lid, Dovetailed, Spice, Divided Interior, Red Wash, 2 ¼ x 8 In. | 240 |
| **Razor,** Pine, Dovetailed, Leather Strap, Slide Lid, Red & Blue Paint, 19th Century, 2 x 11 In. | 1116 |
| **Regency,** Rosewood, Brassbound, Drawer, Inset Handle, c.1810, 5 x 11 In. | 600 |
| **Reliquary,** Copper, Embossed Scrolls, Face Reserves, 1800s, 6 ¾ x 12 In. | 330 |
| **Rosewood,** Penwork, Man, Woman, Garden, Birds, Geometric Borders, c.1820, 15 x 13 In. | 1680 |

**Bottle,** Wine, Wicker Covered, Globular, Olive Green, Sheared Mouth, c.1779, 9 ⅞ In.
$3,803

Norman C. Heckler & Company

**Box,** Bandbox, Cardboard, Floral Wallpaper, c.1850, 10 x 14 In.
$570

Garth's Auctioneers & Appraisers

**Box,** Bandbox, Cardboard, Wallpaper, Stagecoach Scene, Fitted Lid, c.1800, 11 x 16 In.
$533

James D. Julia Auctioneers

**TIP**
*To clean a veneered box or one made of porcupine quills or matchsticks, use a vacuum cleaner hose covered with a nylon stocking.*

**Box,** Bandbox, Wallpaper, Lid, Cottage, Cows, Flowers, Blue, Pennsylvania, 1800s, 13 x 17 x 14 In.
$70

Conestoga Auction Co., Inc.

**Box,** Figural, Rabbit, Coconut Body, Bronze Head & Legs, 6 ½ In.
$657

Neal Auction Co.

**Box,** Malachite, Book Shape, Neoclassical Mount, Gilt Bronze, Russia, 12 ½ In.
$1,195

Neal Auction Co.

| | |
|---|---:|
| **Round,** Flowers, Paint, Continental, Lid, 8 ½ x 9 ¾ In. | 63 |
| **Salt,** Pine, Poplar, Sulpher Inlaid, Slant Top, Lancaster, 7 x 12 In. | 210 |
| **Shoeshine,** Pine, Tin, Painted, Shoe Shape, 1900s, 8 ¼ x 17 ½ In. | 215 |
| **Shou Medallion Lid,** Animal Engravings, Wood, Mixed Metal, Korea, 5 In. | 1125 |
| **Stationary,** Famille Rose, Book Shape, Faux Embroidered Lid, Inscription, Chinese, 6 x 5 In. | 1230 |
| **Stationery,** Tooled Leather, S-Shape, Gilt Straps & Clasp, Jewels, c.1875, 5 In. | 1008 |
| **Storage,** Faux Painted, Fan, Dot Decorations, Molded Lid, Base, Ball Feet, 10 x 17 In. | 561 |
| **Storage,** Pine, Painted, Black Star, Green, Nail Accents, S. Wiley, New England, 11 x 24 In. | 210 |
| **Storage,** Pine, Painted, Green, Red, Star, Geometric Designs, Leaves, 1800s, 14 x 12 In. | 984 |
| **Storage,** Tea, Painted Red, Peonies, Bird, Greenery, Asia, 31 x 18 x 12 ¼ In. | 146 |
| **Storage,** Yellow Paint, Black Stripe, 15 x 39 In. | 240 |
| **Strong,** Forged Iron Clad, Top Locking Mechanism, Handles, Continental, 8 x 17 x 10 In. | 1896 |
| **Strong,** Oak, Iron-Bound, Lock & Key, Red Paint, Continental, 1700s, 12 ½ x 26 In. ..........*illus* | 1020 |
| **Strong,** Pine, Iron, Handles, Black Paint, c.1845, 11 x 19 In. | 259 |
| **Sulphide,** Woman, Victorian, Portrait, Brass, Openwork, Round, 2 ¼ In. | 129 |
| **Supply,** Carved Geometric Design, Drawer, Lift Lid, J. Risley, 1950s, 9 x 21 In. | 250 |
| **Tantalus,** Oak, 1 Drawer, Dovetailed, Silver Plate Decoration, 2 Ink Bottles, 13 x 16 In. | 210 |
| **Tantalus,** Wood, Brass, Mother-Of-Pearl Cartouches, 4 Decanters, 16 Cordials, 10 ½ x 13 In. | 360 |
| **Tinder,** Brass, Embossed, Dutch, c.1900, 16 x 24 x 13 In. | 210 |
| **Tobacco,** Walnut, Carved, Mastiff Shape, Glass Eyes, Hinged Top, Wells, 1800s, 7 x 9 In. | 837 |
| **Tote,** Square Handle, Green Sponge Painted, c.1920, 11 x 11 In. | 92 |
| **Trinket,** Blue Hardstone, Paneled, Gilded Brass Mounts, Ball Feet, 3 ½ x 2 In. | 219 |
| **Trinket,** Blue Jade, Hinged Lid, Brass Mountings, Drop Ring Handles, Ball Feet, 3 x 4 In. | 413 |
| **Trinket,** Blue, White, Faux Decoration, Karl Springer, Velvet Lined, 16 x 10 In. | 1342 |
| **Trinket,** Celluloid, Mother-Of-Pearl Inlay, Glass Insert, Amerith, 3 ¼ x 2 ¾ In. | 35 |
| **Trinket,** Lid, Agate, Dome Lid, 18K Gold, Diamonds, Russia, c.1950, 1 ½ x 2 In. .................*illus* | 1140 |
| **Trinket,** Round, Silver, Hardstone, Inlaid Turquoise & Coral, Lid, Tibet, 1900s, 6 In. Diam. *illus* | 1541 |
| **Tulip Design,** Painted, Slide Lid, Signed D. Elligner, 3 x 5 In. | 24 |
| **Vanity Case,** Motorist, Leather, Fitted Interior, Bottles, Handle, c.1930, 13 ½ x 8 ¾ In. | 500 |
| **Vanity,** Traveling, Victorian, Wood Veneer, Brass Edges, Lined, Compartments, 12 x 9 In. | 241 |
| **Wall,** Candle, Oak, Pierced, Shaped Hanger, England, c.1850, 19 ½ In. | 60 |
| **Wall,** Candle, Walnut, Slide Lid, Carved Flowers, France, c.1810, 19 In. | 215 |
| **Wall,** Pine, Grain Painting, Dovetailed, 2 Compartments, Slant Lid, 12 ½ x 16 ½ In. | 480 |
| **Wall,** Pine, Open, Tombstone Shape Back, Lollipop Crest, c.1750, 11 ½ x 8 x 6 In. ............*illus* | 830 |
| **Wall,** Salt, Cherry, Slant Lid, Divided Interior, Drawer, c.1840, 12 x 12 In. | 127 |
| **Wall,** Salt, Pine, Shaped Cutout Crest, Ochre Grain Paint, Pa., 1800s, 11 x 12 In. | 720 |
| **Wall,** Salt, Poplar, Scalloped Crest, Slanted Hinged Front, Pa., c.1865, 11 x 11 ½ In. | 360 |
| **Wall,** Walnut, Heart Cutout Crest, Pa., c.1810, 9 x 13 In. | 1200 |
| **Walnut,** Casket Shape, Deeply Carved, Italy, c.1700, 7 ⅝ x 24 In. | 438 |
| **Walnut,** Hinged Lid, Shenandoah Valley, c.1865, 4 x 12 In. | 316 |
| **Walnut,** Scalloped Back, Hinged Lid, Divided Interior, Drawer, Mid-Atlantic, c.1815, 11 x 12 In. | 518 |
| **William & Mary,** Oak, Carved Flowers, Scrolls, Lock, c.1700, 12 x 25 In. | 1020 |
| **Wood,** 3 Talking, Drinking Men, Carved, Welsh, 1800s, 3 x 4 In. | 500 |
| **Wood,** Blue Glass Panels, Brass, Scrolling Cartouche Shaped Feet, Lock, 6 ½ x 8 In. | 84 |
| **Wood,** Dome Lid, Rigged Ship, Whale, Star, Flower, Salmon Paint, Handles, 8 x 15 In. | 2006 |
| **Wood,** Dovetailed, Painted, Ivory Swirls, Blue Ground, Hinged Lid, 6 ¾ x 18 x 11 In. | 720 |
| **Wood,** Faux Tortoiseshell Patina, Painted Flower, Leaves, Handle, 2 x 4 ½ In. | 570 |
| **Wood,** Flowers, Red, Gilt Paint, Latch, Asian, 15 x 16 ½ In., Pair | 688 |
| **Wood,** Lacquer, Crossed Sword, Scabbard, 7 x 3 ¾ In. | 66 |
| **Wood,** Lift-Out Tray, Velvet Lining, Metal Label, Chickasaw Furniture Co., 10 x 7 ½ In. | 52 |
| **Work,** Oak, Hinged Lift Lid, 2 Interior Compartments, Drawer, Metal Mounts, 12 ½ x 8 In. | 115 |
| **Writing,** Checkerboard Top, Grain Painted, Drawer, Wavy Borders, Flowers, 8 x 16 In. | 540 |
| **Writing,** Rosewood, Satinwood Inlay, Mid 19th Century, 10 x 13 In. | 540 |

**BOY SCOUT** collectibles include any material related to scouting, including patches, manuals, and uniforms. The Boy Scout movement in the United States started in 1910. The first Jamboree was held in 1937. Girl Scout items are listed under their own heading.

| | |
|---|---:|
| **Backpack,** Canvas, Aluminum, Diamond Brand Canvas Craft, 1950s, 17 x 14 x 8 In. | 69 |
| **Badge,** First Class Patrol Leader, Be Prepared, Insignia, c.1915 | 350 |
| **Bugle,** Brass, Rexcraft Official Bugle, Be Prepared, Eagle Logo, 7 In. | 60 |
| **Camera,** Green Enamel, Black, Case, Eastman Kodak Vest Pocket, c.1930 | 245 |
| **Canteen,** Insignia, Mirro Co. | 20 |
| **Handbook For Boys,** Norman Rockwell, 1933, 7 x 5 In., 658 Pages | 24 |
| **Hatchet,** Scouting Emblem, Be Prepared, Genuine Plumb, 1920s, 12 In. | 35 |
| **Match Holder,** Cylindrical, Gold Plated, 3 In. | 75 |

| | |
|---|---|
| **Mug,** Covered Wagon, Multicolor, National Jamboree, Irvine Ranch Calif., 1953 | 35 |
| **Packbook,** Cub Master, 1943, 309 Pages, 4 ½ x 7 In. | 15 |
| **Pail,** Scouting Scene, Children, Seashore, Tin Lithograph, 4 x 5 In. ............*illus* | 403 |
| **Pin,** 100% Duty, Gold Plated, ¹¹⁄₁₆ x ⅝ In. | 75 |
| **Pin,** Red Enamel, Fleur-De-Lis, Eagle, Be Prepared, C-Clasp, ⅝ x ⅝ In. | 40 |
| **Scarf Slide,** Lion Head, Wood, 2 x 2 In. | 48 |
| **Spoon,** Fork, Knife, Stainless Steel, Logo, Case, 1950s | 24 |
| **Uniform,** Shirt, Pants, Garrison Hat, Neckerchief, Slide, Patches, 1960s | 30 |
| **Whistle,** Insignia, Nickel Plate, USA, 2 x 1 In. | 45 |

---

**BRADLEY & HUBBARD** is a name found on many metal objects. Walter Hubbard and his brother-in-law, Nathaniel Lyman Bradley, started making cast iron clocks, tables, frames, andirons, bookends, doorstops, lamps, chandeliers, sconces, and sewing birds in 1854 in Meriden, Connecticut. The company became Bradley & Hubbard Manufacturing Company in 1875. Charles Parker Company bought the firm in 1940. Bradley & Hubbard items may be found in other sections that include metal.

| | |
|---|---|
| **Andirons,** Hammered Sphere Finial, Cast Iron, Ct., 16 x 22 In. | 188 |
| **Chandelier,** 4-Light, White Cone-Shape Shades, Iron, Painted, Brass, c.1875, 43 x 35 In. | 173 |
| **Lamp,** Caramel Slag Glass Cone Shade, Metal Pane Dividers, 23 In. | 600 |
| **Lamp,** Domed Chipped Shade, Arts & Crafts Flowers, c.1910, 26 x 18 In. | 2500 |
| **Lamp,** Electric, Piano, Victorian, Brass, Marble, c.1890, 62 In. | 185 |
| **Lamp,** Fluid, Double Arm, Fluted Cranberry Shade, Electrified, 33 ½ x 30 In. | 224 |
| **Lamp,** Leaded Slag Glass Shade, Green, Orange Panels, Metal Base, c.1910, 21 x 19 In. | 1063 |
| **Lamp,** Oil, Brass, Glass, Painted Globe, 20 In. | 72 |
| **Lamp,** Paneled Slag Glass Shade, Prairie School, Cold Paint Metal, c.1910, 23 x 17 In. | 1625 |
| **Lamp,** Paneled Slag Glass Shade, Stylized Flowers, Cold Paint Metal, c.1910, 24 x 19 In. | 2000 |
| **Lamp,** Slag Glass Domed Shade, Owls, Green Panels, Cold Paint Metal, 11 x 7 In. | 1536 |
| **Lamp,** Slag Glass Shade, Red Medallions, Green Leaves, Geometric Overlay, 24 In. | 460 |
| **Mirror,** Beveled, Flowers, Round, Marked, 13 x 6 ¾ In. | 60 |
| **Mirror,** Impressed Frame, Pierced Crest, Brass, Round, Easel Back, 17 In. | 590 |
| **Smoking Set,** Brass, Dog's Heads, Boxer, Humidor, Ashtray, 14-In. Stand, 4 Piece | 375 |

---

**BRASS** has been used for decorative pieces and useful tablewares since ancient times. It is an alloy of copper, zinc, and other metals. Additional brass items may be found under Bell, Candlestick, Tool, or Trivet.

| | |
|---|---|
| **Basin,** Primitive, Bulbous, Handles, 3-Footed, 1800s, 16 In. | 24 |
| **Bed Warmer,** Banjo Shape, Punched Tulips, Turned Handle, 19th Century, 45 x 12 In. | 416 |
| **Bed Warmer,** Engraved Lid, Maple Handle, 19th Century, 45 In. | 90 |
| **Bed Warmer,** Pierced, Scrolls, Flowers, Wood Handle, Painted, 44 In. | 180 |
| **Bed Warmer,** Punched Bird Design, Turned Wood Handle, c.1860, 44 ½ In. | 180 |
| **Bed Warmer,** Punched Design, Wood Handle, c.1845, 43 ½ In. | 60 |
| **Bed Warmer,** Punched Star Design, Metal Handle, 1800s, 37 In. | 49 |
| **Bed Warmer,** Tooled Pan, Turned Wood Handle, New England, c.1835, 50 In. .........*illus* | 125 |
| **Blotter,** Block Handle, 2 Leaves, Curved Wood Base, D. Peche, Wiener Werkstatte, 6 In. | 188 |
| **Bookends,** Pierced, Daisies, Newcomb College, Rosalie Roos Wiener, 3 x 4 ½ In. ...........*illus* | 2868 |
| **Bowl,** Alms, Central Design, Gothic Letter Inscription, 1700s, 18 In. ...........*illus* | 618 |
| **Chandelier Chain,** Gilt, Pointing Hand, Grasping Ring, Rectangular Links, 1800s, 20 In. | 956 |
| **Coffee Set,** Blue Tiles, Curved Handles, Tray, Salvador Teran, Mexico, c.1960, 4 Piece ......*illus* | 563 |
| **Drop Spinner,** For Spinning Wool, Presentation Set, Lined Box, 1800s, 9 In. | 160 |
| **Ewer,** Shaped Rim, Bulbous Body, Scrolled Handle, Baluster Molded Base, 1700s, 7 ¼ In. | 369 |
| **Figurine,** Biplane, Working Wheels, Propeller, 18 ½ In. | 420 |
| **Figurine,** Cow, Reclining, Indian Style, Collar, Bells, Shaped Base, Cast, 5 ½ x 5 In. | 69 |
| **Figurine,** Koi, Open Mouth, Wavy Fins, Cast, 23 x 27 x 14 ½ In. | 236 |
| **Foot Warmer,** Pierced, Embossed Flowers, Handle, c.1790, 5 ¾ x 8 In. | 180 |
| **Humidor,** Textured Bark Finish, 2 Strap Handles, Arts & Crafts, 9 ½ x 8 x 6 In. | 250 |
| **Jardiniere,** Empire Style, Cup On 3 Dolphin Supports, 33 x 14 In. ...........*illus* | 492 |
| **Log Basket,** Arts & Crafts, Basket Weave Handle, Flower, Trellis, Sheet Iron, 18 x 18 ½ In. | 59 |
| **Mortar & Pestle,** Baroque Style, Concentric, Square Handle, c.1750, 6 In. | 250 |
| **Oil Can,** Hinged Lid, Angled Spout, 2 Handles, Polished, Oval, 12 x 5 x 10 In. | 185 |
| **Pitcher,** Stirrer, Tommi Parzinger, Mid-Century, 12 ½ In., 2 Piece | 980 |
| **Reliquary,** Gilt, Cut Crystal, Pineapple Finial, Applied Silver Surround, 1800s, 14 x 10 In. | 649 |
| **Sculpture,** Figure, Hound, Plated, Karl Hagenauer, c.1970, 16 ½ In. | 2952 |
| **Sculpture,** Ocean Waves, Clouds, Triangles, Steel Curves, C. Jere, 33 x 42 In. | 59 |
| **Sculpture,** Sailboat, C. Jere, 1976, 46 x 41 In. | 403 |
| **Stand,** Shoeshine, Stamped, Glass, 2 Drawers, 2-Tier Bins, 8 Bottles, Turkey, c.1900, 20 x 25 In. | 177 |

**Box,** Pine, Tulip Design, Painted, Slide Lid, Pinned, Pennsylvania, c.1810, 5 x 12 In.
$840

Garth's Auctioneers & Appraisers

**Box,** Pipe, Wall, Cherry, Pine, Lollipop Hanger, Drawer, c.1800, 18 In.
$840

**Box,** Strong, Oak, Iron-Bound, Lock & Key, Red Paint, Continental, 1700s, 12 ½ x 26 In.
$1,020

Garth's Auctioneers & Appraisers

**Box,** Trinket, Agate, Dome Lid,
18K Gold, Diamonds, Russia, c.1950,
1 ½ x 2 In.
$1,140

Cowan's Auctions

**Box,** Trinket, Round, Silver, Hardstone,
Inlaid Turquoise & Coral, Lid, Tibet,
1900s, 6 In. Diam.
$1,541

James D. Julia Auctioneers

**Box,** Wall, Pine, Open, Tombstone Shape
Back, Lollipop Crest, c.1750,
11 ½ x 8 x 6 In.
$830

James D. Julia Auctioneers

**Boy Scout,** Pail, Scouting Scene,
Children, Seashore, Tin Lithograph,
4 x 5 In.
$403

Wm Morford Auctions

| | |
|---|---:|
| **Standish,** Rococo Style, Cast, 2 Inkwells, Hinged Lids, Pen Holder On Gallery, 16 ½ x 8 In. | 75 |
| **Tea Set,** Carrier, Handle, Glass Holders, Pierced, Austria, c.1905, 8 ½ x 12 In., 7 Piece | 938 |
| **Tobacco Box,** Lid, Hinged Engraved, Flowers, Urns, Inscriptions, Dutch, 6 In. | 180 |
| **Tobacco Box,** Lid, Hinged, Engraved, Biblical Subjects, Leaves, Scrollwork, Dutch, 5 ⅜ In. | 600 |
| **Vase,** Flowers, Repousse, Butterflies, Dragonflies, Pokerwork Ground, 11 ⅜ In., Pair | 123 |
| **Vase,** Scalloped Rims, Repousse, Leaf, Berries, c.1918, 11 ⅛ In. | 154 |
| **Warming Pan,** Flower Engraved, Turned Wood Handle, 43 In. | 240 |

**BRASTOFF**, *see Sascha Brastoff category.*

**BREAD PLATE**, *see various silver categories, porcelain factories, and pressed glass patterns.*

**BRIDE'S BOWLS OR BASKETS** were usually one-of-a-kind novelties made in American and European glass factories. They were especially popular about 1880 when the decorated basket was often given as a wedding gift. Cut glass baskets were popular after 1890. All bride's bowls lost favor about 1905. Bride's bowls and baskets may also be found in other glass sections. Check the index at the back of the book.

| | |
|---|---:|
| **Blue Diamond Quilted,** Mother-Of-Pearl, Crimped Rim, Silver Plated, Pairpoint, 11 In. | 345 |
| **Carnival Glass,** Scrolling Flowers, 12 In. | 259 |
| **Cranberry Glass,** Opalescent, Silver Plated Frame, 1800s, 12 x 9 ½ In. | 154 |
| **Flowers,** Blue Interior, 6 Lobe Bowl, Fitted Metal Frame, c.1890, 14 x 9 ½ In. | 288 |
| **Glass,** Opalescent, Pink Edge, White, Silver Plated Frame, 1800s, 13 x 11 In. | 110 |
| **Glass,** Pink Edge, White, Ruffled, Silver Plated Frame, 1800s, 10 x 10 In. | 154 |
| **Glass,** Pink, Ruffled, Silver Plated Frame, 1800s, 7 ½ x 8 ½ In. | 154 |
| **Glass,** Pink, Striated, Silver Plated Frame, 1800s, 9 x 8 In. | 110 |
| **Glass,** Pink, Striated, Silver Plated Frame, 1800s, 10 x 10 In. | 123 |
| **Glass,** Pink, White, Silver Plated Frame, 14 x 13 In. | 110 |
| **Glass,** Satin, Double Basket, Pink Rim, Ruffled, Silver Plated Frame, 1800s, 13 x 16 In. | 308 |
| **Glass,** White, Blue Edge Ruffle, c.1800s, 11 x 12 In. | 185 |
| **Green Diamond Quilted,** Pink Interior, 4 Dolphin Base, 11 x 10 In. | 413 |
| **Lavender,** Satin Folded Rim, Silver Plated, Egyptian Man Holding Bowl, 9 ½ x 14 In. | 826 |
| **Mother-Of-Pearl Glass,** Air-Trap, Ruby To Clear, Blue Rim, c.1900, 4 ½ x 8 ½ In. | 184 |
| **Opalescent,** Ruby To Vaseline Glass, Crimped Rim, Metal Stand, c.1890, 10 x 13 In. | 150 |
| **Opaline,** Pink Interior, Gilt Dogwood Blossom, Webb, 11 ½ In. | 201 |
| **Peachblow,** Ruffled Rim, Scrolling, Leaves, 11 ½ In. | 115 |
| **Pink Satin Glass,** Herringbone Melon Ribs, Green Interior, Silver Frame, 10 x 16 In. | 2950 |
| **Pink,** White, Ruffled, Multicolor Butterfly, Flowers, Tufts Silver Frame, 9 x 9 In. | 531 |
| **Satin Glass,** Rainbow, Ruffled Rim, Quilted Body, Silver Mica, Silver Plated Frame, 12 In. | 920 |
| **Shaded Blue,** Enameled, Vaseline & Opal Crimped Rim, Silver Plated, Frame, 11 x 10 In. | 196 |
| **Silver,** Flower Engraved, Pierced Borders, Footed, Handle, 16 In. | 1750 |
| **Striped Cranberry Opalescent To Vaseline Glass,** Ruffled Rim, c.1890, 4 ¼ In. | 184 |
| **White,** Pink Jack-In-Pulpit, Ribbed, Frosted Rim, Rockford Silver Plated Frame, 10 x 14 In. | 531 |
| **Yellow Flowers,** Blue Ruffled Rim, Pairpoint Silver Frame, Cherubs, 14 In. ..................*illus* | 863 |

**BRISTOL** glass was made in Bristol, England, after the 1700s. The Bristol glass most often seen today is a Victorian, lightweight opaque glass that is often blue. Some of the glass was decorated with enamels.

| | |
|---|---:|
| **Biscuit Jar,** Courting Scene, White Ground, Pink Borders, Silver Plated Lid, Bail, 8 In. | 148 |
| **Decanter,** Stopper, Port, 13 Tumblers, c.1810, 5 In., 14 Piece | 593 |
| **Girl's Portrait In Cartouche,** Blue Ground, Silver Stencil, Round, Gilt Metal Base, 4 In. | 207 |
| **Lustres,** Opaline Glass, Pink Interior, Flowers, Crystal Prisms, 14 In., Pair | 230 |
| **Lustres,** Overlay Crystal, Prisms, 1800s, 13 In., Pair | 600 |
| **Vase,** Cranberry Ground, Painted Floral Reserves, Footed, Finial, 1800s, 16 In., Pair | 188 |

**BRITANNIA**, *see Pewter category.*

**BRONZE** is an alloy of copper, tin, and other metals. It is used to make figurines, lamps, and other decorative objects. Bronze lamps are listed in the Lamp category. Pieces listed here date from the eighteenth, nineteenth, and twentieth centuries.

| | |
|---|---:|
| **Ashtray,** Cigar Cutter, Hand Hammered, Ship's Wheel Shape, 7 ½ x 7 ⅜ x 6 In. | 154 |
| **Bas-Relief,** Dancing Maiden, Marked GW Parker, 1900-25, 28 x 16 In. | 1045 |
| **Bell Push,** Bergman, Woman's Bust, Erotic, Round Base, Painted, 1800s, 3 ½ In. | 2160 |
| **Blotter,** Dog, Onyx, 4 x 6 In. | 240 |
| **Bowl,** Centerpiece, Belle Epoque, Gilt, Cut Crystal, Molded Leaves, 9 x 14 In. | 1353 |

| | |
|---|---|
| **Bowl**, Crystal, Gilt, Woman Shape Handle, Flower Etched, Relief Socle, 19 In. | 676 |
| **Bowl**, Gurschner, G., Sack, Circles, Interlocking Knot Band, Black Base, Austria, c.1910, 7 In. | 2400 |
| **Box**, Jewelry, 2 Young Maidens, Holding Rectangular Trunk, c.1900, 5¾ In. | 3075 |
| **Bracket**, Gas, Venus Emerging From Shell, Glass Shades, Cornelius & Baker, c.1855, 18 In., Pair  *illus* | 2689 |
| **Brazier**, Overhung Interior Rim, Flower Shape Handles, Tripod Base, 7½ x 11⅜ In. | 590 |
| **Brush Holder**, Figures, Courtyard, Mountains, Round, Chinese, 4¾ In. | 480 |
| **Brush Wash**, Lily Pad Shape, Lotus Blossoms, Frog, Cast, Patina, 8¼ x 6¼ In. | 414 |
| **Bull**, Standing, Brown Patina, Marble Base, 1900s, 7 x 12 In. | 438 |
| **Bust**, Bouret, Eutrope, Cleopatra, Bichromatic, France, c.1872, 10 In. *illus* | 1098 |
| **Bust**, Brilliant, Fredda, Indian Girl, Braids, England, 1958, 22¾ In. | 1063 |
| **Bust**, Buddha, Cast, Verdigris, Fitted Carved Wood Stand, Painted, 12¼ x 9½ In. | 414 |
| **Bust**, Columbo, R., Napoleon, Hat, Military Coat, France, c.1900, 17½ In. | 2000 |
| **Bust**, Goodacre, G., Shoshone Brave, Signed, c.1955, 13 x 11½ In. | 2000 |
| **Bust**, Guanyin, Goddess Of Mercy, Crown, Head Covering, Hollow Cast, c.1890, 10 In. | 184 |
| **Bust**, Hood, Ethel, Portrait Of A Lady, 1939, 19 In. | 531 |
| **Bust**, Houdon, Jean-Antoine, Athena, Belle Epoque, Crescent In Hair, c.1900, 21 x 12 In. | 984 |
| **Bust**, Leroux, L., Man, Othello, Draped Attire, France, c.1920, 7½ In. | 6250 |
| **Bust**, Lucrece, ¾ Side Profile, Classical Gown, Tiara, 1880-1920, 21 In. | 1500 |
| **Bust**, MacDonald, James Wilson, George Washington, 1898, 19½ In. *illus* | 2706 |
| **Bust**, Man, Aviator, Jean Mermoz, Billowing Scarf, Green, Brown, c.1930, 11 x 22 In. | 4063 |
| **Bust**, Napoleon, Bicorn Hat, Gilt, Stepped Marble Base, 6½ In. | 344 |
| **Bust**, Nebel, Berthold, Head Of Kafka, 1915, 12¼ x 8 In. | 3120 |
| **Bust**, Old Man, Vietnam, 1900s, 9¼ x 9½ In. | 369 |
| **Bust**, Pouting Child, Stepped Base, Stamped Propriete Carpeaux, 11 x 7 x 5 In. | 584 |
| **Bust**, Proctor, A.P., Cowboy, c.1930, 11½ In. | 40800 |
| **Bust**, Schiele, E., Head, Upturned Gaze, Signed, Austria, 11 In. | 5625 |
| **Bust**, Van Der Straeten, La Demi-Mondaine, Inscribed, France, c.1915, 20 x 19 In. | 2214 |
| **Bust**, Woman, Byzance, Crown, Earrings, Brooch, Exposed Shoulder, 21½ In. | 3500 |
| **Bust**, Woman, Wearing Veil, Lace Trim, Marble Base, Continental, 12¾ In. | 1063 |
| **Candleholder**, Figural, Crane, On Turtle, Lotus, Chinese, 1800s, 12½ In. | 533 |
| **Candleholder**, Potpourri, Restauration, Gilt, Pierced Base, Caryatid Supports, 8 x 3½ In. | 1230 |
| **Casket**, Jewel, Napoleon III, Gilt, Fighting Stags, Blue Satin Liner, c.1875, 5½ x 8 In. | 861 |
| **Caviar Holder**, Dolphin Feet, Glass Liner, Marble Base, Continental, 1900, 6 x 8 In. | 1063 |
| **Censer**, Archaic Style, Cloisonne, Vented Lid, Tripod Base, Japan, 1800s, 10 x 6½ In., Pair | 215 |
| **Censer**, Carp Transforming Into Dragon, Ming Style, Chinese, c.1800, 11¾ x 4 x 8 In. | 1045 |
| **Censer**, Dragons, Oval Shape, Clouds, Figural Children Feet & Finial, Handles, c.1900, 9 x 7 In. *illus* | 830 |
| **Censer**, Elephant, Boy Rider, Painted, Japan, 1800s, 8 x 6½ In. *illus* | 119 |
| **Censer**, Embossed Neck Band, Lug Handles, Oval, Chinese, 2½ x 4¼ In. | 400 |
| **Censer**, Inlay, Elephant Trunk Handles, Signed Shih Siu, 2¼ x 5¼ In. | 1770 |
| **Censer**, Lion Mask Handles, 6 Character Hsuan Te Mark, Chinese, 1700s, 2 x 2 In. | 593 |
| **Censer**, Lion Mask Handles, Engraved, 8 Immortals, Patina, Mark, Chinese, 1800s, 7 In. | 474 |
| **Censer**, Lobed Kabocha Body, Leafy Branch Feet, Branch Handles, Japan, 17 x 17 In. | 777 |
| **Censer**, Mythical Animal, Lift-Off Shell On Back, Candle Pricket, c.1880, 6 x 6 In., Pair | 1353 |
| **Censer**, Pomegranate, Globe Shape, Open Work, Tripod Feet, Branch Handles, 8 In. | 178 |
| **Censer**, Resting On Flowing Dragon, Japan, c.1890, 9¾ In. *illus* | 600 |
| **Censer**, Sun Spot, Gold Splashes, Handles, 3-Footed, Hsuan Te Mark, c.1910, 5 In. | 1659 |
| **Censer**, Wooden Lid, Masks, 1796-1862, 13½ x 12⅜ In. | 3444 |
| **Centerpiece**, Art Nouveau, 2 Women, Leaf Base, Cold Paint, c.1920, 11½ In. | 688 |
| **Centerpiece**, Caldwell, J.E., Louis XV, Gilt, Tole Liner, Shells, Scrolls, Flowers, c.1890, 24 In. | 3250 |
| **Centerpiece**, Louis XVI Style, Divided Carnation Stems, Candlesticks, Vase, c.1945, 21 In. | 5000 |
| **Centerpiece**, Maiden's Heads, Moths, Sunflower Blossoms, Sinewy Feet, 4 x 10 x 7 In. | 2006 |
| **Centerpiece**, Napoleon III, Gilt, Festooned Boat, Swan, Putto, Cartouche Feet, 11 x 21½ In. | 3107 |
| **Centerpiece**, Standing Putto, Loose Cut Glass Bowl, Stepped Base, 15 In., Pair | 2250 |
| **Centerpiece**, Surtout De Table, Louis XVI Style, Gilt, Reticulated Gallery, 47 x 22 In. | 2988 |
| **Chalice**, Talon Stem, Castle Base, Incised, France, c.1910, 8 x 6 In. | 1500 |
| **Champagne Bucket**, Stand, Glass Bucket, Lion, Ring, 32½ In. | 2214 |
| **Door Knocker**, Masque, Headdress, Crane Crown, Cast Iron Plate, France, 10 x 5 In. *illus* | 861 |
| **Epergne**, Glass Bowls, Trumpet Shape, Scalloped Edge, Panels, Leaves, 18½ In. | 338 |
| **Ewer**, Leaves, Garland, Grapes, Gilt Lip & Handle, 12½ x 5¾ In., Pair | 1722 |
| **Garniture Set**, Gilt, Green Onyx, Urn Top, 5-Light Candelabra, 17-In. Clock, 3 Piece | 281 |
| **Garniture**, Chariot, Swan Drawn, Nosegay, Articulated Wheels, c.1910, 7½ x 5 In., Pair | 276 |
| **Girandole**, 3 Candleholders, Gilt, Prisms, Marble Base, c.1850, 21 x 18 In., Pair *illus* | 518 |
| **Humidor**, Standing Bear & 2 Dogs, Hinged Heads, Brass Inserts, 1800s, 15 x 10 In. | 7670 |
| **Incense Burner**, Handles, Chinese, 1800s, 6 x 4 In. | 180 |
| **Jardiniere**, 4 Panels, Bird, Stork, 4 Winged Feet, 8 In. | 90 |
| **Jardiniere**, Butterfly, Iris, Relief Decoration, 8½ x 9½ In. | 118 |

**Brass**, Bed Warmer, Tooled Pan, Turned Wood Handle, New England, c.1835, 50 In.
$125

Garth's Auctioneers & Appraisers

**Brass**, Bookends, Pierced, Daisies, Newcomb College, Rosalie Roos Wiener, 3 x 4½ In.
$2,868

Neal Auction Co.

**Brass**, Bowl, Alms, Central Design, Gothic Letter Inscription, 1700s, 18 In.
$618

James D. Julia Auctioneers

**Brass,** Coffee Set, Blue Tiles, Curved Handles, Tray, Salvador Teran, Mexico, c.1960, 4 Piece
$563

Heritage Auction Galleries

---

**Brass,** Jardiniere, Empire Style, Cup On 3 Dolphin Supports, 33 x 14 In.
$492

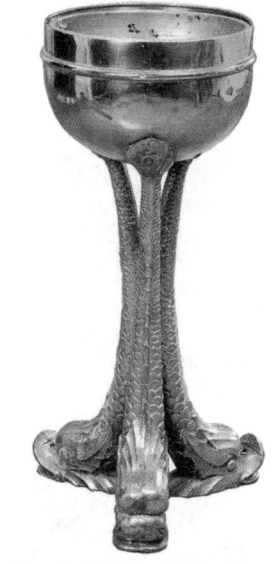

New Orleans Auction Galleries, Inc.

---

**Bride's Basket,** Yellow Flowers, Blue Ruffled Rim, Pairpoint Silver Frame, Cherubs, 14 In.
$863

Early Auction Co.

| | |
|---|---|
| **Jardiniere,** Dostal, Acanthus Leaves, Removable Brass Liner, Oval, Signed, 23 In. | 563 |
| **Jardiniere,** Napoleon III, Winged Female Handles, Cupid, Gilt, Patina, Oval, 17¼ In. | 1188 |
| **Larche,** Raoul, Tray, Lady Of The Pond, Art Nouveau, Seminude Woman, 12 x 13 In. | 330 |
| **Lequesne,** Eugene L., Dancing Faun, Cast, Brown Patina, Susse Freres, 11 In. | 748 |
| **Letter Opener,** Chenus, G.A., Seal, Art Nouveau, Gilt, Roses, Fitted Case, 9 x ¾ In. | 553 |
| **Letter Opener,** Owl Handle, Glass Eye, c.1900, 8 In. | 94 |
| **Mask,** Cherub, Winged, Gilt, Metal & Green Marble Base, 7¾ In. | 299 |
| **Mask,** Hagenauer, Stylized Face, Nickel Plated, Wien, Austria, 1930s, 11 x 7 In. ........*illus* | 10625 |
| **Medal,** Dammann, Paul-Marcell, Feriam Sidera, Art Nouveau, Nude, Winged Sandals, 1920, 3½ In. | 546 |
| **Medal,** Manship, Paul Howard, Victory Art War Relief, Base, Signed, 4 x 3½ In. | 1265 |
| **Medal,** Sailboat, Seas, Sea Monster, Tridents, Eastern Yacht Club, 1892, 3⅝ In. | 1046 |
| **Medallion,** Nini, Jean Baptiste, Benjamin Franklin, Profile, Frontier Hat, Round, Nini, 4½ In. | 840 |
| **Mirror,** Inset Painting Of Napoleon On Ivory, 10 In. | 188 |
| **Nutcracker,** Squirrel, Seated, Mouth Cracks Nut, 3 Sections, c.1925, 5¼ In. | 711 |
| **Plaque,** Death Of A Saint, Bas-Relief, 2 Angels, Italy, 15 x 9¼ In. | 738 |
| **Plaque,** Fraser, James Earle, Teddy Roosevelt, Bas-Relief, c.1920, 10 x 13 In. | 374 |
| **Plaque,** Luini, Costanzo, 4 Nymphs, Serenading, Female, 8½ x 17¼ In. | 224 |
| **Plaque,** Nymphes De La Fontain Des Innocents, Barbedienne Foundry, 17 x 9 In., Pair | 840 |
| **Plaque,** Zorach, William, Dance, 4 Dancers, Signed, 9 x 8¾ In. | 1320 |
| **Porringer,** Langworthy, L., Long Handle, 3-Footed, Marked, 1730, 16¾ x 7¼ In. .........*illus* | 9840 |
| **Posnet,** 3-Footed, Long Handle, Marked, Newport 1710, 19¾ x 8¾ In. ...........*illus* | 14760 |
| **Rain Drum,** Concentric Patterns, 4 Frogs, Elephants, Handles, Burma, 19¾ In. | 1936 |
| **Rain Drum,** Concentric Rings, Crouching Frogs, Loop Handles, Southeast Asia, 21 x 26 In. | 1673 |
| **Rhyton,** Ram's Head Shape, Footed, 19th Century, 7 x 6 x 5½ In. | 510 |
| **Sconce,** Regency Style, Hand Holding Torch, Flame Shape Glass Shade, 16 In., Pair ........*illus* | 2952 |
| **Sculpture,** 2 Classical Women Seated, Engineering, Agriculture Symbols, c.1900, 13 x 15 In. | 469 |
| **Sculpture,** 2 Dancers, Nude Women, Signed, 14 In. | 437 |
| **Sculpture,** 2 King Charles Spaniels, Resting, On Cushion, Gilt, Patina, c.1900, 3 x 8¾ In. | 1000 |
| **Sculpture,** 2 Men Wrestling, Triangle Base, Turtle Shape Feet, 3-Footed, 16 x 8½ In. | 2214 |
| **Sculpture,** 2 Wrestlers, Rocky Mound, Marble Pedestal, 35 x 27 In. | 10285 |
| **Sculpture,** Aitken, Robert Ingersol, Dancing Faun, 1908, 22 x 13⅞ In. | 2250 |
| **Sculpture,** Aizelin, Eugene-Antoine, Woman, At Harvest, Marble Pedestal, c.1895, 27 In. | 1250 |
| **Sculpture,** Albert-Ernest, Carrier-Beleuse, Maternal Love, Mother, 2 Children, 22 x 18 In. | 2337 |
| **Sculpture,** Allegory Of Spring, 2 Girls, Flowers, Basket, c.1900, 22 x 10 In. | 2091 |
| **Sculpture,** Alligator, Patina, 1900s, 26¼ In. .........*illus* | 1708 |
| **Sculpture,** Amerika, Indian Chief, Standing, Austria, c.1910, 19 In. | 9375 |
| **Sculpture,** Annie Oakley, Holding Rifle, 33 In. | 344 |
| **Sculpture,** Antinous As Deity, Grand Tour, 13½ x 18 In. | 4613 |
| **Sculpture,** Apollo Belvedere, Archer, Marble Base, Continental, 1800s, 24 In. | 956 |
| **Sculpture,** Arab, On Horseback, Barye, c.1990, 29 x 24 In. | 375 |
| **Sculpture,** Arabian Rug Merchant Displaying Rug, Cold Paint, Austria, 5 In. | 770 |
| **Sculpture,** Argentor, Boy, On Sled, Silvered, Stamped, 10 In. | 625 |
| **Sculpture,** Art Nouveau, Bacchanalian Nymph, Grapes, Gilt, Marble Base, 13 In. | 1722 |
| **Sculpture,** Bacchanal Procession, Lauchhammer Bildguss, Germany, 22¾ In. | 1476 |
| **Sculpture,** Bacchante, Riding Ram, Brown Patina, Oval Marble Base, c.1965, 20½ In. | 531 |
| **Sculpture,** Barbedienne, F., Pan, Playing Pipe, Lion Skin Cape, c.1890, 20¾ In. | 875 |
| **Sculpture,** Barbedienne, F., Venus De Milo, Inscribed, Late 1800s, 33½ In. | 2688 |
| **Sculpture,** Barbedienne, Jeane D'Arc, Seated, Hands Clasped, France, 26 In. | 1625 |
| **Sculpture,** Barbedienne, Joan Of Arc At Domremy, Green Marble, c.1900, 21 In. | 2625 |
| **Sculpture,** Barrias, Louis E., La Nature Se Devoilant Devant La Science, c.1900, 22 x 8 In. | 7800 |
| **Sculpture,** Barye, Antoine-Louis, Horse, Dog, Oval Base, c.1860, 6 x 6½ In. | 813 |
| **Sculpture,** Barye, Antoine-Louis, Rabbit, France, c.1845, 1¾ x 3 In. | 819 |
| **Sculpture,** Barye, Antoine-Louis, Seated Lion No. 2, 7⅜ x 5 In. | 3438 |
| **Sculpture,** Bastet, Antoine, Nude Woman, Brown Patina, 1899, 33½ In. | 3450 |
| **Sculpture,** Bauer, S., Woman, Carrying Water Jugs On Shoulder, 16 In. | 688 |
| **Sculpture,** Bayer, Panther In Tree, 57 x 46 In. | 1500 |
| **Sculpture,** Beach, Chester, Glint Of Sea, Nude Woman, Upraised Arms, Signed, 9¾ x 2 In. | 1179 |
| **Sculpture,** Beach, Chester, Glint Of Sea, Woman Standing, 7⅝ In. | 938 |
| **Sculpture,** Bennet, Tom, Nude Woman, Bending Backward, c.1970, 12 In. | 125 |
| **Sculpture,** Bergmann, Franz, Elephant, Huntsmen, Tiger, Painted, Signed, 9½ In. ..........*illus* | 13750 |
| **Sculpture,** Bergmann, Franz, Lizard, Cold Paint, Early 20th Century, 2½ x 8 In. | 2700 |
| **Sculpture,** Bertoia, Harry, Sonambient, 10 Straight Rods, Base, c.1970, 16 In. ..........*illus* | 20000 |
| **Sculpture,** Bertoia, Harry, Vertical Rods, Welded, Patina, Luminescent, 1970s, 15¼ x 5½ In. *illus* | 10625 |
| **Sculpture,** Bird, Art Deco, 3½ In. | 72 |
| **Sculpture,** Boisseau, Emile Andre, La Defense Du Foyer, c.1918, 25 In. | 2500 |
| **Sculpture,** Bonheur, J., Bull & Bear, Green Marble Base, Signed, 1900, 22 x 21½ In. .........*illus* | 1067 |

**Bronze,** Bracket, Gas, Venus Emerging From Shell, Glass Shades, Cornelius & Baker, c.1855, 18 In., Pair
$2,689

Neal Auction Co.

**Bronze,** Bust, Bouret, Eutrope, Cleopatra, Bichromatic, France, c.1872, 10 In.
$1,098

Neal Auction Co.

> **TIP**
> Scratches on bronze cannot be polished off without destroying the patina and lowering the value.

**Bronze,** Bust, MacDonald, James Wilson, George Washington, 1898, 19 ½ In.
$2,706

New Orleans Auction Galleries, Inc.

**Bronze,** Censer, Dragons, Oval Shape, Clouds, Figural Children Feet & Finial, Handles, c.1900, 9 x 7 In.
$830

James D. Julia Auctioneers

**Bronze,** Censer, Elephant, Boy Rider, Painted, Japan, 1800s, 8 x 6 ½ In.
$119

James D. Julia Auctioneers

**Bronze,** Censer, Resting On Flowing Dragon, Japan, c.1890, 9 ¾ In.
$600

Cowan's Auctions

**Bronze,** Door Knocker, Masque, Headdress, Crane Crown, Cast Iron Plate, France, 10 x 5 In.
$861

New Orleans Auction Galleries, Inc.

**Bronze,** Girandole, 3 Candleholders, Gilt, Prisms, Marble Base, c.1850, 21 x 18 In., Pair
$518

Cottone Auctions

**Bronze,** Mask, Hagenauer, Stylized Face, Nickel Plated, Wien, Austria, 1930s, 11 x 7 In.
$10,625

Rago Arts & Auction Center

75

**Bronze,** Porringer, Langworthy, L., Long Handle, 3-Footed, Marked, 1730, 16 ¾ x 7 ¼ In.
$9,840

Skinner Auctioneers & Appraisers

**Bronze,** Posnet, 3-Footed, Long Handle, Marked, Newport 1710, 19 ¾ x 8 ¾ In.
$14,760

Skinner Auctioneers & Appraisers

**Bronze,** Sconce, Regency Style, Hand Holding Torch, Flame Shape Glass Shade, 16 In., Pair
$2,952

New Orleans Auction Galleries, Inc.

**Bronze,** Sculpture, Alligator, Patina, 1900s, 26 ¼ In.
$1,708

Neal Auction Co.

**Bronze,** Sculpture, Bergmann, Franz, Elephant, Huntsmen, Tiger, Painted, Signed, 9 ½ In.
$13,750

Rago Arts & Auction Center

**Bronze,** Sculpture, Bertoia, Harry, Sonambient, 10 Straight Rods, Base, c.1970, 16 In.
$20,000

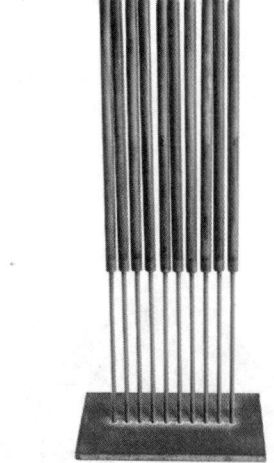

Los Angeles Modern Auctions (LAMA)

**Bronze,** Sculpture, Bertoia, Harry, Vertical Rods, Welded, Patina, Luminescent, 1970s, 15 ¼ x 5 ½ In.
$10,625

Rago Arts & Auction Center

**Bronze,** Sculpture, Bonheur, J., Bull & Bear, Green Marble Base, Signed, 1900, 22 x 21 ½ In.
$1,067

James D. Julia Auctioneers

**Bronze,** Sculpture, Buddha, Head, Sukhothai Style, Mounted, Wood Stand, Thailand, 21 x 16 In.
$1,968

Skinner Auctioneers & Appraisers

**Bronze,** Sculpture, Buddha, Manjusri, Seated, Flaming Sword, Gilt, Sino-Tibetan, 1800s, 9 In.
$1,845

New Orleans Auction Galleries, Inc.

| | |
|---|---|
| **Sculpture,** Bonheur, Rosa, Cow, Longhorn, Standing, c.1870, 3 x 6 In.............................. | 1375 |
| **Sculpture,** Bouret, Eutrope, Mercury, Seated, Marble Base, 34 In. | 6875 |
| **Sculpture,** Bracken, Clio Hinton Huneker, Sirene, Nude Woman, 1 ¾ x 6 In........................ | 738 |
| **Sculpture,** Buddha, Gilt, Seated, Hands In Lap, Robes, Leaves, 6 ¾ In............................. | 316 |
| **Sculpture,** Buddha, Head, Sukhothai Style, Mounted, Wood Stand, Thailand, 21 x 16 In. ..*illus* | 1968 |
| **Sculpture,** Buddha, Head, Wooden Stand, 18 ¾ In. | 984 |
| **Sculpture,** Buddha, Manjusri, Seated, Flaming Sword, Gilt, Sino-Tibetan, 1800s, 9 In. .....*illus* | 1845 |
| **Sculpture,** Buddha, Seated, Gilt, Manjushri, Chinese, 1800s, 7 In. ..................................*illus* | 1067 |
| **Sculpture,** Buddha, Seated, Removable Hat, Gilt, Engraved, Tibet, c.1800, 7 ¾ In.............. | 16520 |
| **Sculpture,** Buddha, Seated, Subduing Mudra, Gilt Trace, Thailand, 1900s, 21 x 15 In. ....... | 770 |
| **Sculpture,** Buddha, Standing, Lotus Blossom Base, Korea, c.1900, 9 ½ In........................... | 984 |
| **Sculpture,** Buddha, Standing, Obsidian Eyes, Hands In Calming Waters, Mundra, 1500s, 18 ½ In. *illus* | 2370 |
| **Sculpture,** Buddha, Vijrasana Position, Lotus Base, Gilt, Qing Dynasty, 1800s, 15 x 11 In.......... | 3936 |
| **Sculpture,** Buffalo Bill Cody, Holding A Rifle, 33 In. ....................................................... | 390 |
| **Sculpture,** Bull, Farm Hand Pulling, c.1920, 9 In. .......................................................... | 500 |
| **Sculpture,** Bullfrog, Crouching, 12 In............................................................................ | 146 |
| **Sculpture,** Bureau, Leon, Lion, On Rocky Base, c.1900, 23 x 25 In. ................................... | 3250 |
| **Sculpture,** Cahulka, Cowboy, On Rearing Horse, Signed, Onyx Base, c.1910, 11 In............... | 1140 |
| **Sculpture,** Callery, M., The Flirt, Wood Base, 1957, 15 In. .............................................. | 9375 |
| **Sculpture,** Carpenter, Hollow Cast, Wood Log, Japan, 1900s, 15 x 18 In. .......................... | 570 |
| **Sculpture,** Cartier, A., Woman, Allegorical Spring, Fall Figures, c.1890, 26 In., Pair ............... | 8125 |
| **Sculpture,** Catlett, Elizabeth, Woman, Arms On Head, 11 ½ In. ....................................... | 5625 |
| **Sculpture,** Causse, J., Reaper, Shirtless Laborer, Leaning On Scythe, Wheat, c.1905, 24 In. ......... | 2990 |
| **Sculpture,** Charles Lindbergh, Standing, Aviator Attire, 22 In. ........................................ | 1125 |
| **Sculpture,** Chevoux De Marly, Groom, France, c.1900, 22 ½ x 19 ½ In. ............................... | 1353 |
| **Sculpture,** Children At Play, Gilt, Wall, Dutch, 11 ½ In. ................................................ | 2813 |
| **Sculpture,** Children, Tree, Swing, 18 ¼ In. ................................................................... | 90 |
| **Sculpture,** Chiparus, D., Children, Wheelbarrow, Ivory, Marble Base, c.1900, 8 x 12 In. .....*illus* | 7187 |
| **Sculpture,** Chiparus, Demetre, Egyptian Dancer, 22 ⅜ In. ............................................. | 4248 |
| **Sculpture,** Chiparus, Demetre, Girl With Parrot, Kneeling, Signed, 14 x 19 In. .............*illus* | 1200 |
| **Sculpture,** Clodion, C.M., 2 Bacchantes, Satyr, France, 23 In. ......................................... | 2000 |
| **Sculpture,** Colleoni, B., Venetian Soldier, On Horse, Black Patina, Marble Base, 17 x 14 In......... | 2500 |
| **Sculpture,** Dallin, C.A., Appeal To Great Spirit, Brave, Horse, Arms Out, Signed, 20 In............. | 442 |
| **Sculpture,** Dalou, A., Homme Relevant Sa Manche, Signed, 5 ¾ In. ................................... | 687 |
| **Sculpture,** Dancing Satyr, Patina, Marble Base, Continental, 1800s, 14 ½ In....................... | 717 |
| **Sculpture,** Deity, Bodhisattva, Kneeling, Tiered Headdress, Gilt, Indonesia, c.1915, 32 In............ | 300 |
| **Sculpture,** Deity, Seated On Lotus, Hollow Cast, Gold Traces, Asia, 8 In. ........................... | 207 |
| **Sculpture,** Dog, Italian Greyhound, Marble Base, 8 ½ x 8 In........................................... | 350 |
| **Sculpture,** Dog, Pointer, Bone In Mouth, 7 ⅝ In........................................................... | 5228 |
| **Sculpture,** Drummer, Standing, Renaissance Dress, Eagle, Austria, 7 ½ In. ......................... | 615 |
| **Sculpture,** Durban, Arne, Nude Woman, Kneeling, Child, 12 In........................................ | 885 |
| **Sculpture,** Dying Gaul, Man Sitting, Bent Over, Roman Copy, Italy, 1800s, 3 x 6 In. .............. | 295 |
| **Sculpture,** Dying Gaul, Marble, Bronze Base, Continental, c.1900, 11 x 14 In. .................... | 640 |
| **Sculpture,** Eagle, 29-In. Wing Span, 16 In. ................................................................. | 224 |
| **Sculpture,** Egon, Weiner, Pillar Of Fire, c.1961, 19 In. .................................................. | 1080 |
| **Sculpture,** Elephant, Trunk Down, Austria, c.1890, 5 x 7 ¾ In......................................... | 813 |
| **Sculpture,** Equestrian, Classical Warrior, 2 Rearing Horses, c.1880, 15 ¾ In. ..................... | 2813 |
| **Sculpture,** Erte, Aphrodite, Woman, Standing, Holding Fan, c.1986, 18 In. ........................ | 2375 |
| **Sculpture,** Erte, Directoire, Standing Woman, Signed Base, 23 In. .................................... | 2700 |
| **Sculpture,** Erte, Elegance, Woman, Sleek Gown, Fur Wrap, Greyhound On Lead, 1980, 16 In..... | 3645 |
| **Sculpture,** Erte, Gala, Elegant Woman, Blue Gown, Draped Shawl, Signed, 15 ½ In. .........*illus* | 2126 |
| **Sculpture,** Erte, Soliel, Woman, Feather Bustier, Arched Headdress, Beaded Chains, 18 In.......... | 3645 |
| **Sculpture,** Fairy, Arms Out, Standing On Rayed Sun, Berlin, c.1899, 21 In. ........................ | 3300 |
| **Sculpture,** Falconer, Horse, Rider, Cyrillic Stamp, 19 x 16 In. ......................................... | 20000 |
| **Sculpture,** Fallen Bird, 3 ¼ x 5 ⅞ In. ......................................................................... | 360 |
| **Sculpture,** Faun, Dancing, Applied Patina, 30 ½ In. ...................................................... | 1188 |
| **Sculpture,** Female Satyr, Seated, 2 Children, Tambourine, Pipes, Marble Base, 12 x 13 In. ......... | 688 |
| **Sculpture,** Fiedler, Franz, Dancer, Nude Woman, Leg Up, Austria, 14 ¾ x 4 ½ In. ................... | 861 |
| **Sculpture,** Fremiet, Emmanuel, Young Satyr Playing With 2 Bear Cubs, Inscribed, 10 In........... | 732 |
| **Sculpture,** Game Bird, 7 ¾ x 10 ½ In. ........................................................................ | 813 |
| **Sculpture,** Gaudez, A.E., 2 Musicians, Le Duo Difficle, c.1900, 25 In. ............................... | 923 |
| **Sculpture,** Gaudez, Etienne, Pastorale Watteau, Woman, Lute Player, 28 In........................ | 1625 |
| **Sculpture,** Gennarelli A., Woman, Nude, Sitting, Lyre, 20 ½ In. ....................................... | 2304 |
| **Sculpture,** German Shepherd, Reclining, Base, c.1860, 7 x 15 x 7 In. ................................ | 660 |
| **Sculpture,** Girl, Dancing, Art Deco, Cold Paint, 24 ½ In.................................................. | 402 |
| **Sculpture,** Girl, Dress, Bare Feet, Grapevine, c.1990, 35 In............................................. | 469 |

**Bronze,** Sculpture, Buddha, Seated, Gilt, Manjushri, Chinese, 1800s, 7 In.
$1,067

James D. Julia Auctioneers

**Bronze,** Sculpture, Buddha, Standing, Obsidian Eyes, Hands In Calming Waters, Mundra, 1500s, 18 ½ In.
$2,370

James D. Julia Auctioneers

### Prevent Burglaries
Lock your doors and windows. In 65 percent to 82 percent of all home burglaries, the burglar enters through a door. Most often the doors were unlocked.

**Bronze,** Sculpture, Chiparus, D., Children, Wheelbarrow, Ivory, Marble Base, c.1900, 8 x 12 In.
$7,187

Cottone Auctions

**Bronze,** Sculpture, Chiparus, Demetre, Girl With Parrot, Kneeling, Signed, 14 x 19 In.
$1,200

Garth's Auctioneers & Appraisers

**Bronze,** Sculpture, Erte, Gala, Elegant Woman, Blue Gown, Draped Shawl, Signed, 15½ In.
$2,126

James D. Julia Auctioneers

**Bronze,** Sculpture, Helmet, Roman Images, Embossed Relief, Elkington & Co., c.1880
$2,013

James D. Julia Auctioneers

**Bronze,** Sculpture, Kelety, Alexandre, Children Sledding, Etling, Paris, 7 x 12 In.
$2,250

Rago Arts & Auction Center

**Bronze,** Sculpture, Le Verrier, Max, Woman, Glass Globe, Millefiori, Marble, 1900s, 31 In.
$704

Rago Arts & Auction Center

**Bronze,** Sculpture, Lobster, 10 Legs, Tentacles Pointing Up, Japan, 8½ x 14 In.
$1,298

Brunk Auctions

**Bronze,** Sculpture, Medicine Buddha, Seated, Gilt, Sino-Tibetan, 1800s, 9 x 7 In.
$2,706

New Orleans Auction Galleries, Inc.

**Bronze,** Sculpture, Pelican, Art Deco Style, Marble Base, A. Kelety, France, c.1930, 7 In.
$1,440

DuMouchelles Art Gallery

| | |
|---|---|
| Sculpture, Goodacre, Glenna, Bather, Marked, 1989, 57 In. | 1230 |
| Sculpture, Gorham Co., Forest Nymph, Seated, Squirrels, c.1920, 12 In. | 625 |
| Sculpture, Grefoire, Jean Louis, 2 Women Reading, Seated, Standing, c.1875, 16¾ In. | 615 |
| Sculpture, Gress Carlos Ayala, Dancing Nude Squaw, Eagle, Wood Base, 7½ In. | 420 |
| Sculpture, Greyhounds, Seated, Head Raised, Silvered, Green Marble Base, 11 In., Pair | 1500 |
| Sculpture, Habert, Alfred Louis, Terpsichore, Cast Signature, c.1900, 11 x 10 x In. | 615 |
| Sculpture, Hardy, Tom, Birds, Tall Grass, 1974, 36 x 36 In. | 580 |
| Sculpture, Harp, Gilt, Enamel, Multicolor Troubadours, Putti, c.1900, 5 x 2¾ In. | 676 |
| Sculpture, Helmet, Roman Images, Embossed Relief, Elkington & Co., c.1880 ............illus | 2013 |
| Sculpture, Hercules As Archer, Black Marble Base, 24 x 21 In. | 3444 |
| Sculpture, Hercules, Grand Tour, After The Antique, Tiered Marble Base, c.1890, 8 x 10¼ In. | 508 |
| Sculpture, Herrmann J., Race To The Sea, 19 Sea Turtle Hatchlings, Sand, Nest, 26 x 11 In. | 1035 |
| Sculpture, Hoffman III, L.F., Boy, Outstretched Arms, Raised Knee, 1967, 31½ In. | 1793 |
| Sculpture, Hoppins, Mark, Aviator, Turning Plane Propeller, 18 In. | 594 |
| Sculpture, Horse, Thoroughbred, Marble Base, W. Von Balluseck, 8 x 9 In. | 472 |
| Sculpture, Horses Jumping, Rider, Steeplechase, 12¼ In. | 472 |
| Sculpture, Hunter, Riding Elephant, Shooting Tiger, Cold Paint, Austria, c.1920, 10 x 9 In. | 10000 |
| Sculpture, Huntington, A., Panther, 8¾ In. | 3000 |
| Sculpture, Hyatt, Anna, Mountain Lioness, 2 Cubs, 1900s, 2½ x 6 In. | 3220 |
| Sculpture, Indian, On Rearing Horse, Austria, Onyx Base, c.1920, 7½ In. | 840 |
| Sculpture, Jacquemart, A., Dog With Turtle, 6 x 7½ In. | 3900 |
| Sculpture, Jaray, S., Nude Boy, Holding Roosters, Marble Base, c.1900, 15 x 6¼ In. | 2875 |
| Sculpture, Jockey, Riding Horse, Stepped Oval Base, 16 x 18 In. | 1500 |
| Sculpture, Kauba, Carl, Art Nouveau, Nudes, Tree Trunk, Gilt, Verdigris, 9½ In., Pair | 1438 |
| Sculpture, Kauba, Carl, Cheyenne, On Running Horse, Austria, 12¾ In. | 826 |
| Sculpture, Kauba, Carl, Treasure Seeker, Boy Digging, Nude Woman Under Lift Top, 7½ In. | 2700 |
| Sculpture, Kelety, Alexandre, Children Sledding, Etling, Paris, 7 x 12 In. .............illus | 2250 |
| Sculpture, Koi, Japan, c.1890, 12 In. | 570 |
| Sculpture, Kolbe, George, Nude, Kneeling, Arms Out To Side, Die Klage, 1974, 15 In. | 1000 |
| Sculpture, Korbel, Mario Joseph, Draped Nude, Marked, 1920, 23 In. | 13750 |
| Sculpture, Krause, Karl H., Nude, Standing, Hands To Hips, Wood Base, c.1970, 41 In. | 1200 |
| Sculpture, Krishna With Flute, 8⅛ In. | 431 |
| Sculpture, Le Faguays, Woman, Fan, Marble Base, Cold Paint, Etched Le Faguays, 28 In. | 5000 |
| Sculpture, Le Verrier, Max, Woman, Glass Globe, Millefiori, Marble, 1900s, 31 In. .............illus | 704 |
| Sculpture, Leopard, Seated, 31 x 21 In., Pair | 2700 |
| Sculpture, Lion Fish, Striped, Fanned Fins, On Rock, Patina, Verdigris, Modernist, 18 In. | 201 |
| Sculpture, Lion, Art Deco, Pouncing With Hind Legs, Extended Tail, 14¼ x 17½ In. | 1476 |
| Sculpture, Lion, Lying Down, Patina, 24 x 37 In., Pair | 1500 |
| Sculpture, Lobster, 10 Legs, Tentacles Pointing Up, Japan, 8½ x 14 In. .............illus | 1298 |
| Sculpture, Lobster, Articulated Limbs, Antennae, Japan, 1900s, 10½ In. | 3198 |
| Sculpture, MacMonnies, F.W., Bacchante, Infant Faun, 1894, 33 In. | 5000 |
| Sculpture, Marin, Joseph-Charles, Jeune Bacchante, Flowing Garb, Cup, Patina, 11½ In. | 690 |
| Sculpture, Marioton, Eugene, Femme Jouant De La Double Flute, Round Base, 32 In. | 2530 |
| Sculpture, Medicine Buddha, Seated, Gilt, Sino-Tibetan, 1800s, 9 x 7 In. .............illus | 2706 |
| Sculpture, Mene, P.J., Hunter With Bloodhound, Signed, 1879, 18¹¹⁄₁₆ In. | 3125 |
| Sculpture, Mene, Pierre Jules, L'Accolade, 2 Horses, Rocks, 26 x 8 In. | 1320 |
| Sculpture, Mercury, Winged Sandal, Seated On Rock, 20 In. | 750 |
| Sculpture, Modrow, Salome, John Baptiste Head, Germany, c.1900, 22 In. | 800 |
| Sculpture, Muller, Hans, Wrestler, Signed, Austria, 13 In. | 1063 |
| Sculpture, Muse Des Bois, Woman, Pipes To Mouth, Woodland Symbol, Marble Base, 29 In. | 2000 |
| Sculpture, Napes, Jabalino, Pan & Goat, c.1900, 14 In. | 1169 |
| Sculpture, Narcissus, Gilt, 24½ In. | 1434 |
| Sculpture, Narcissus, Raised Base, Italy, c.1850, 24 In. | 1375 |
| Sculpture, Neptune, Rearing Horse, Marble Base, 27 In. | 1125 |
| Sculpture, Nude Woman, Sash, Gold Wash, Standing On 1 Leg, Arm Raised, 1800s, 23 In. | 391 |
| Sculpture, Nude, Draped, Kneeling, Shell, Mythical Beast, France, c.1870, 12 In. | 1063 |
| Sculpture, Nude, Emerging From Shell, Rectangular Base, Art Nouveau, 12 x 20 In. | 1188 |
| Sculpture, Pandiana, Antonia, Dandy, Sword, Bi-Corner Hat, Italy, c.1900, 34 In. | 1750 |
| Sculpture, Panther, Crouching, On Incline, Silvered, Gilt, Black Base, c.1925, 9 x 22 In. | 3750 |
| Sculpture, Parsons, Edith Barretto Stevens, Lamb, 4⅜ In. | 625 |
| Sculpture, Parsons, Edith, Terrier, Every Dog Has Its Day, 5¾ In. | 1080 |
| Sculpture, Partridge, Leaf, Early 20th Century, 13 x 9½ In. | 1230 |
| Sculpture, Patlagean, Numa, Nun, Friar, Silver Plated, c.1945, 15½ x 19 In. | 1250 |
| Sculpture, Pegasus, Rearing, Green Patina, Round Base, 57 In. | 7380 |
| Sculpture, Pelican, Art Deco Style, Marble Base, A. Kelety, France, c.1930, 7 In. .............illus | 1440 |
| Sculpture, Perseus, Medusa, 42 In. | 923 |

**Bronze,** Sculpture, Stork, Cold Paint, Austria, c.1920, 5⅜ In. $1,046

Skinner Auctioneers & Appraisers

**Bronze,** Sculpture, Williams, Rene, Ruffian, Jockey, Racehorse, Marble, 1976, 11 x 15 In. $1,188

Garth's Auctioneers & Appraisers

**Bronze,** Vase, Elephants, Intertwined, c.1900, 6½ x 8 In.

$625

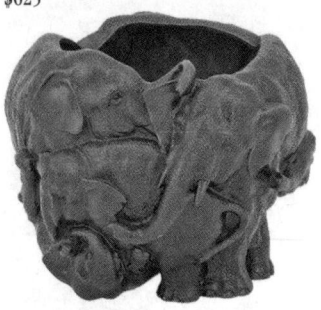

Rago Arts & Auction Center

---

**Brush,** Candlestick, Jeweled, Brush-McCoy, 7 In., Pair

$316

Humler & Nolan

---

**Buck Rogers,** Lunch Box, Thermos, Buck, Wilma Deering, Twiki & Dr. Huer, Metal, Aladdin, 1979, 7 In.

$158

Hake's Americana & Collectibles

---

**Buck Rogers,** Toy, Atomic Gun, Pressed Steel, Gold Paint, Popping Sound, Daisy, 10 In.

$236

Bertoia Auctions

| | |
|---|---:|
| **Sculpture,** Pheasant, Standing, Cold Paint, Multicolor, Gilt, 13 x 6 In. | 357 |
| **Sculpture,** Picault, Emile Louis, Satyr Youth With Goat, Staff, Gold Patina, 26 In. | 3220 |
| **Sculpture,** Pina, Alfredo, Kiss, Stamped Cire Perdue, 19¼ In. | 3933 |
| **Sculpture,** Plazzotta, Enzo, Arabesque, Patina, 16 x 16 In. | 1260 |
| **Sculpture,** Plazzotta, Enzo, Downfall, Falling, Man, Marble Base, 23 In. | 1599 |
| **Sculpture,** Plazzotta, Enzo, Study For Adam, Standing Man, Hand On Head, 24½ In. | 1476 |
| **Sculpture,** Poertzel, Otto, Woman, Nude, Standing, Gilt, Ivory Flowers, Marble Base, 17 In. | 3000 |
| **Sculpture,** Pollin, Pheasant, Standing, Marble Base, 26 In. | 375 |
| **Sculpture,** Pompon, Francois, Bird, Pintade, 7 In. | 469 |
| **Sculpture,** Puffin With Fish, Rock Base, 11 In. | 1440 |
| **Sculpture,** Putti Playing, Gilt, Marble Base, France, c.1890, 13 In., Pair | 554 |
| **Sculpture,** Retiarius, Roman Gladiator, Trident Held High, Fishing Net On Arm, 37 In. | 31125 |
| **Sculpture,** Roman Gladiator, Combat Pose, Shield, Sword, Yellow Marble Base, 6½ In. | 813 |
| **Sculpture,** Sailor, Waving Semaphore Flags, Stepped Wooden Base, 15 In. | 338 |
| **Sculpture,** Sander, S., African Courtship, 2 Elephants Mating, Marble Base, 1985, 17½ In. | 1440 |
| **Sculpture,** Satyr, Wineskin, Alabaster Base, Italy, 9 In. | 246 |
| **Sculpture,** Scarf, Bessie Potter Vannoh No. XII, Brown & Green Patina, c.1900, 13 In. | 11875 |
| **Sculpture,** Scherwerk, Woman, Nude, Hands Shackled, Gilt, Signed, c.1900, 22 In. | 420 |
| **Sculpture,** Scottish Fox Hunt, Horse, Man, Dogs, 1800-25, 13½ In. | 1722 |
| **Sculpture,** Shuler, Polished, Basset Kim, 15¼ In. | 271 |
| **Sculpture,** Siamese Cat, Seated, Verdigris Patina, 9½ In., Pair | 295 |
| **Sculpture,** Spanish Cowboy, On Mule, c.1890, 14 x 13 In. | 1500 |
| **Sculpture,** Sphinx Of Thebes, 1900s, 14½ x 18½ In. | 522 |
| **Sculpture,** Spring Poem, Reclining Nude Woman, Book, Marble Base, 1919, 6 x 12 In. | 270 |
| **Sculpture,** St. George Battling The Dragon, Renaissance Style, Marble Base, c.1900, 12¾ In. | 478 |
| **Sculpture,** Stagecoach, Horses, Marble Base, Vienna, 9¾ In. | 1200 |
| **Sculpture,** Stork, Cold Paint, Austria, c.1920, 5⅜ In. ......... *illus* | 1046 |
| **Sculpture,** Sykes, Charles, Spirit Of Ecstasy, Gilt, 20 x 13 In. | 540 |
| **Sculpture,** Terpsichore, Muse Of Dance, Lyre, After Jean-Louis Gregoire, Signed, 12 x 12 In. | 799 |
| **Sculpture,** Tourgueneff, P., Prussian Officer, On Horseback, 25 In. | 649 |
| **Sculpture,** Troubetzkoy, Paul, Cowboy On A Horse, 1911, 21 x 20 In. | 4500 |
| **Sculpture,** Uechitritz, C., Frederick The Great, On Horse, Oval Marble Base, c.1900, 5½ In. | 1750 |
| **Sculpture,** Vacossin, George Lucien, Puppy & Frog, Signed In Casting, 13 In. | 1694 |
| **Sculpture,** Valton, Charles, Lioness, Granite Base, Incised, 10 In. | 554 |
| **Sculpture,** Verkade, Kees, Swimmers, Netherlands, 1984, 16 x 9 In. | 2318 |
| **Sculpture,** Vidal, Henri, Lion Rigussant, Inscribed, 1900, 6½ In. | 478 |
| **Sculpture,** Villanis, Emmanuel, Bohemienne, Woman, Art Nouveau, 20 x 12 In. | 180 |
| **Sculpture,** Villarreal, V., Harry Vardon, Golfer, Back Swing, Knickers, 11¾ In. | 738 |
| **Sculpture,** Walrus, 2 Tons Of Love, Marble Base, 10 x 20 x 8 In. | 600 |
| **Sculpture,** Weems, Katherine W.L., Horse, Circus, Patina, Stepped Base, c.1945, 20 x 25 In. | 5760 |
| **Sculpture,** Williams, Rene, Ruffian, Jockey, Racehorse, Marble, 1976, 11 x 15 In. ......... *illus* | 1188 |
| **Sculpture,** Woman Holding 2 Basins, Patina, France, c.1900, 48 x 22 In. | 3567 |
| **Sculpture,** Woman, Allegorical, Seated, Le Histoire, Patina, 14 In. | 308 |
| **Sculpture,** Woman, Classical, Seated, c.1910, 13½ In. | 531 |
| **Sculpture,** Woman, Daneuse Arabe, Exotic Dancer, Round, Onyx Base, 37¾ In. | 3250 |
| **Sculpture,** Woman, Half Draped, Peacock, 10 In. | 875 |
| **Sculpture,** Woman, Hoop, Black Marble Base, 16 x 12½ In. | 518 |
| **Sculpture,** Woman, Kneeling, Doves On Outstretched Hands, Onyx Altar, c.1930, 13 x 9 In. | 469 |
| **Sculpture,** Woman, Nude, First Press, Bronze Base, Germany, 1930s, 11 In. | 1140 |
| **Sculpture,** Woman, Nude, Seated, Arms Raised, 48 In. | 1080 |
| **Sculpture,** Woman, Nude, Standing, Hand On Hip, Hand Raised, 16 In. | 2280 |
| **Sculpture,** Woman, Nude, Trumpeter, c.1920, 10½ In. | 469 |
| **Sculpture,** Woman, Russian, Holding Sacks, Signed, 15½ In. | 480 |
| **Sculpture,** Woman, Standing, Pedestal, Book, Lyre, France, c.1890, 16½ In. | 431 |
| **Sculpture,** Wyatt Earp, Holding 2 Revolvers, 33 In. | 390 |
| **Sculpture,** Zach, Bruno, Girl, Standing, Crossed Arms, Riding Crop, 14¾ In. | 5700 |
| **Sculpture,** Zach, Bruno, Hugger, Erotic Woman, Wrapped Around Phallus, Inscribed, 6½ In. | 1000 |
| **Sculpture,** Zach, Bruno, Woman On Horseback, Onyx Base, 17 x 18 In. | 7260 |
| **Sculpture,** Zajac, Jack, Dancer, Rough Shape, 1960, 10 x 9 In. | 1625 |
| **Smoker's Stand,** Man, Smoking Cigar, Foot On Ladder, Hat, Basket, Raised Base, 7¼ In. | 625 |
| **Stand,** Usubata, Round Tray Top, Samurai Relief, Gilt, Black, c.1890, Japan, 18½ In. | 1599 |
| **Tazza,** Women, Trees, Landscape, Bloom, 6¼ x 7 In., Pair | 140 |
| **Tieback,** Louis Philippe Style, Strap Shape, Raised Leaf Bands, 7 x 1¾ In., 16 Piece | 1168 |
| **Tray,** Gorham, Cat-O-Nine Tails, Birds, Butterfly, Hammered Border, Round Center, 5½ In. | 185 |
| **Tray,** Silvered, Mirror, 4 Sections, Leaves, Berries, Pierced Arcade, Rounded, 22 x 66 In. | 3444 |
| **Trinket Casket,** Cloisonne, Gilt, Red Overtones, Hinged Lid, Scrolled Feet, 5¾ x 3½ In. | 357 |

| | |
|---|---|
| **Urn,** Campana, Empire Style, Cut Glass, Strawberry Cut, Footed, c.1950, 13 x 7 In., Pair............ | 1168 |
| **Urn,** Caryatid Handles, Swags, Grotesque Masks, Socle Base, Verdigris, 26 x 13 In. ....................... | 2048 |
| **Urn,** Classical Figures, Grapevines, Twisting Vine Shape Handles, 12¾ In. ...................................... | 1331 |
| **Urn,** Egyptian Revival, Onyx, Figures Of Lamassu At Ends, Paw Feet, 1800s, 26 x 11 In............. | 4500 |
| **Urn,** Garniture, Empire Style, Patina, Gilt Bronze Mounts, Classical Figures, 17 x 4 In., Pair...... | 861 |
| **Urn,** Gilt, Black, Cherubs Astride Lion Masks, 9 x 7¼ In., Pair ................................................... | 610 |
| **Urn,** High Relief, Centaur, Cherub, Handles, Aubergine Marble Pedestal, 9½ In., Pair ................ | 569 |
| **Urn,** Lid, Moigniez, J., Pheasants, Hunting Dogs, Fox, Bird Finial, Tree Shape Foot, 9½ In. ........ | 308 |
| **Urn,** Louis XVI Style, Gilt, Cut Glass, Lid, Bouquet Finial, Mask Handles, 29 x 16 In., Pair .......... | 2768 |
| **Urn,** Louis XVI, Gadroon, Acanthus, Winged Caryatid, Ormolu, 19½ In., Pair .......................... | 2520 |
| **Urn,** Neoclassical, Scroll Handles, Portrait, Lion Masks, Footed, c.1865, 19 In., Pair................. | 594 |
| **Urn,** Potpourri, Restauration, Gilt, Turned, Pierced Lid, Pineapple Finial, 6 x 3 In....................... | 676 |
| **Urn,** Swimming Fish, Waves, Relief, Bulbous, 3 Elephant Feet, Japan, 1800s, 17 x 15 In. ............. | 488 |
| **Urn,** Vibert, Claude, Female Pechant, Art Nouveau, Branch Twist Handle, Nude, 16 In................. | 3068 |
| **Vase,** Arts & Crafts, Mounted Handle, Red Drip Glaze, c.1910, 20 In., Pair................................ | 615 |
| **Vase,** Birds, Relief, Handles, Stepped Socle, Round Base, Late 1900s, 30 In. .............................. | 503 |
| **Vase,** Cast Bamboo Root, Segmented, Japan, c.1900, 9 x 5½ In. .......................................... | 1353 |
| **Vase,** Domenech, S., Nude, Art Nouveau, Snail, Plant Shape Body, Face, c.1900, 12½ In............. | 3198 |
| **Vase,** Elephants, Intertwined, c.1900, 6½ x 8 In. ............................................................*illus* | 625 |
| **Vase,** Gilt, Strawberry Cut Crystal, Flared, Square Bases, Winged Paws, 12¼ x 8, Pair................. | 2214 |
| **Vase,** Gorham, Rhyton Shape, Patina, Griffins, Anthemion, Scroll Finial, c.1890, 10 x 14 In....... | 1599 |
| **Vase,** Iris Relief, Cylindrical, Pinched Rim, 3 Ball Feet, Patina, 7⅜ In. ................................... | 277 |
| **Vase,** Levasseur, H.L., Woman, Arms Raised, Standing By Urn, France, c.1930, 31 In. ................ | 1250 |
| **Vase,** Moreau, Auguste, Garden Scene, Child Sitting On Shoulder, Looking Down, 12 In............. | 661 |
| **Vase,** Sorenson, Carl, Flared, Footed, c.1910, 8 In. ........................................................... | 20 |
| **Vase,** Woven Basket Shape, Patina, High Handle, Japan, 20 In............................................... | 150 |
| **Vessel,** Li Shape, Archaic Decoration, Tao Tieh Masks, Chinese, 20th Century, 11 x 9½ In........... | 237 |
| **Vessel,** Wine, Archaic Style, Engraved Designs, Bands, Chinese, 1800s, 8¼ x 6¼ In. ............... | 1062 |
| **Wine Bottle Holder,** Louis XVI Style, Incised, Black, Gold Paint, c.1900, 7 x 5 In., Pair............. | 1000 |

---

**BROWNIES** were first drawn in 1883 by Palmer Cox. They are characterized by large round eyes, downturned mouths, and skinny legs. Toys, books, dinnerware, and other objects were made with the Brownies as part of the design.

| | |
|---|---|
| **Booklet,** Calendar, With Best Wishes, String Bound, 1895, 3½ x 4½ In........................ | 224 |
| **Cup,** Napoli, Dimpled, Postman, Policeman, Gold Tracery, Mt. Washington, 4 x 2½ In. ........... | 1725 |
| **Dish,** Gym, Loop Handle, 6 In........................................................................... | 185 |
| **Jam Jar,** Napoli, Dimpled, Rabbits, Turtle Finial, Mt. Washington, 3¼ In........................ | 3163 |
| **Mug,** 7 Brownies, Playing Leapfrog, 2½ In....................................................... | 48 |
| **Smoking Tobacco Pouch,** Smoking Brownie On Rail Fence, Ky., 4 Oz., 5 In. ...................... | 720 |
| **Toy,** Sleigh, Reindeer, 2 Drivers, Blue Paint, Cast Iron, Hubley, 16 In........................ | 4500 |

---

**BRUSH-MCCOY,** *see Brush category and related pieces in McCoy category.*

---

**BRUSH POTTERY** was started in 1925. George Brush first worked in 1901 in Zanesville, Ohio. He started his own pottery in 1907, but it burned to the ground soon after. In 1909 he became manager of the J.W. McCoy Pottery. In 1911, Brush and J.W. McCoy formed the Brush-McCoy Pottery Co. After a series of name changes, the company became The Brush Pottery in 1925. It closed in 1982. Old Brush was marked with impressed letters or a palette-shaped mark. Reproduction pieces are being made. They are marked in raised letters or with a raised mark. Collectors favor the figural cookie jars made by this company. Because there was a company named Brush-McCoy, there is great confusion between Brush and Nelson McCoy pieces. Most collectors today refer to Brush pottery as Brush-McCoy. See McCoy category for more information.

| | |
|---|---|
| **Candlestick,** Jeweled, Brush-McCoy, 7 In., Pair ................................................*illus* | 316 |
| **Candlestick,** Rockraft, Gray, Green Veining, 4⅞ In., Pair..................................... | 242 |
| **Figure,** Rabbit, Standing, Beige, 12½ In. .................................................. | 184 to 219 |
| **Vase,** Blue, Tan Stripe, White Ground, Cylindrical, 18½ In. ................................... | 127 |
| **Vase,** Onyx, Runny Blue, Purple Glaze, Gray Ground, Low Handles, 6¼ In. ...................... | 150 |
| **Vase,** Zuni, Horizontal Geometric Bands, Cylindrical, 4 In..................................... | 184 |

---

**BUCK ROGERS** was the first American science fiction comic strip. It started in 1929 and continued until 1967. Buck has also appeared in comic books, movies, and, in the 1980s, a television series. Any memorabilia connected with the character Buck Rogers is collectible.

| | |
|---|---|
| **Badge,** Chief Explorer, Solar Scouts, Highest Rank, Premium, Brass, Red Enamel, 1936, 2 In...... | 173 |
| **Costume,** Buck Rogers In 25th Century, Blue, Jumpsuit, 1979-80......................... | 347 |
| **Crayon Set,** Crayon Ship, Multicolor, 6 Pencils, Box, 2 x 4¾ In............................... | 203 |

**Buffalo Pottery,** Plaque, Friday, Monks At Table, 1914, 13¾ In.
$240

The Stein Auction Company

**Buffalo Pottery Deldare,** Charger, Fallowfield Hunt, The Start, P. Holland, 1908, 13⅝ In.
$142

Conestoga Auction Co., Inc.

# BUCK ROGERS

**Buffalo Pottery Deldare,** Humidor, Lid, Peg Leg Sailor, Ship, Portraits, 1909 $316

Humler & Nolan

**Buffalo Pottery Deldare,** Pitcher, The Hunt Supper, Fallowfield Hunt, 1909, 12 In. $222

The Stein Auction Company

**Burmese,** Lamp, Clock, Dome, Gas Run, Mt. Washington, Standard Novelty Co., Box, 6½ In. $7,475

Early Auction Co.

## TIP

*When going through the items in an old house be sure to shake every book, look for hidden drawers in desks and blanket chests, check hems of drapes and pillows, and check under the "dust protector" on the backs of pictures hung on the wall.*

| | |
|---|---:|
| **Game,** 3 Board Games In 1, 40 Illustrated Cards, 12 Play Pieces, Box, 1934 | 417 |
| **Gun,** Hero-Style Laser Pistol, 1979-81 NBC TV Series, Silver, 7¼ In. | 847 |
| **Gun,** Liquid Helium Water Pistol, Red, Yellow, Daisy, 1936, 7¼ In. | 407 |
| **Knife,** 2 Blades, Cockpit Scene, Cream, Spaceship Shape, Celluloid Grip, 3 x 2 In. | 800 |
| **Lunch Box,** Thermos, Buck, Wilma Deering, Twiki & Dr. Huer, Metal, Aladdin, 1979, 7 In. *illus* | 158 |
| **Ring,** Brass, Adjustable Band, Colorless Birthstone, Initial T, 1934 | 221 |
| **Ring,** Brass, Yellow Birthstone, M Initial, Coco Malt Premium, Adjustable, 1924 | 380 |
| **Ring,** Ring Of Saturn, White Plastic, Glow In Dark, Red Stone, Post Cereal Premium, 1946 | 173 |
| **Rocket Ship,** Futuristic, Graphics, Sparking, Tin Lithograph, Clockwork, Marx, 11½ In. | 561 |
| **Toy,** Atomic Gun, Pressed Steel, Gold Paint, Popping Sound, Daisy, 10 In. *illus* | 236 |
| **Toy,** Rocket, Tin Lithograph, Windup, Sparking Action, Marx, 12 In. | 384 |
| **Watch,** Copper Luster Lightning Bolt Hands, Chrome Case, Pocket, 2 In. | 347 |

**BUFFALO POTTERY** was made in Buffalo, New York, after 1902. The company was established by the Larkin Company, famous manufacturers of soap. The wares are marked with a picture of a buffalo and the date of manufacture. Deldare ware is the most famous pottery made at the factory. It has either a khaki-colored or green background with hand-painted transfer designs.

## BUFFALO POTTERY

| | |
|---|---:|
| **Bowl,** Cereal, Green Stripes, 5 In. | 26 |
| **Cup & Saucer,** Flowers, Blue, Lune, Restaurant | 32 |
| **Pitcher,** Geraniums, Cobalt Blue, 5¼ In. | 375 |
| **Pitcher,** Landing Of Roger Williams, Green, 1906, 7 x 7 In. | 104 |
| **Pitcher,** Roosevelt Bear, Paneled Sides, Brown Transfer, 1907, 8 x 8 In. | 604 |
| **Plaque,** Friday, Monks At Table, 1914, 13¾ In. *illus* | 240 |

## BUFFALO POTTERY DELDARE

| | |
|---|---:|
| **Bowl,** Fallowfield Hunt, Horse, Resting Dogs, Footed, 1909, 9 x 3 In. | 422 |
| **Candlestick,** Figures, Houses, Hexagonal, 8¾ In. | 255 |
| **Charger,** Fallowfield Hunt, The Start, P. Holland, 1908, 13⅝ In. *illus* | 142 |
| **Chop Plate,** An Evening At Ye Lion Inn, c.1908, 13½ In. | 268 to 350 |
| **Humidor,** Lid, Peg Leg Sailor, Ship, Portraits, 1909 *illus* | 316 |
| **Matchbox Holder & Tray,** Fallowfield Hunt, Olive, 3 x 6¼ In. | 288 |
| **Pitcher,** The Hunt Supper, Fallowfield Hunt, 1909, 12 In. *illus* | 222 |
| **Pitcher,** The Return, 8-Sided, c.1908, 8 In. | 378 |
| **Pitcher,** Vicar Of Wakefield, 8-Sided, c.1908, 9 In. | 399 |
| **Plate,** Bread & Butter, At Ye Lion Inn, Signed, c.1908, 6¼ In. | 225 |
| **Plate,** Dinner, Fallowfield Hunt, Breaking Cover, c.1909, 7½ In. | 180 |
| **Plate,** Dinner, Town Crier, c.1908, 9½ In. | 125 |
| **Plate,** Dinner, Ye Olden Times, Signed, c.1909, 9¼ In. | 90 |
| **Plate,** Dinner, Ye Town Crier, Building Border, 8½ In. | 90 |
| **Plate,** Emerald, Doctor Syntax Loses His Wig, Rat, Bed, 1911, 9¼ In. | 230 |
| **Sugar & Creamer,** Colonial Couple, Stone Walkway, c.1925 | 225 |
| **Sugar & Creamer,** Village Life Scenes, 5½ x 3½ In. | 63 |
| **Tankard,** 6 Mugs, Great Controversy, All You Have To Do, 12 In., 7 Piece | 374 |
| **Vase,** Landscape, Butterflies, Meadow, Flowers, Olive, 13½ x 5 In. | 690 |

**BURMESE GLASS** was developed by Frederick Shirley at the Mt. Washington Glass Works in New Bedford, Massachusetts, in 1885. It is a two-toned glass, shading from peach to yellow. Some pieces have a pattern mold design. A few Burmese pieces were decorated with pictures or applied glass flowers of colored Burmese glass. Other factories made similar glass also called Burmese. Related items may be listed in the Fenton category and under Webb Burmese.

| | |
|---|---:|
| **Base,** Optic Rib, Triangular Top, Amber Rim, 3 Reeded Feet, Mt. Washington, 7¼ In. | 1380 |
| **Bowl Set,** Tricorner, Gold Detail, Enameled Daisy Blossoms, Pairpoint Stand, 11½ In. | 748 |
| **Bowl,** Berry, Flowers, Pink To Yellow, c.1890, 3 In. | 118 |
| **Bowl,** Hawthorn, Beaded Enamel Rim, 4-Footed, Mt. Washington, 5 In. | 978 |
| **Bowl,** Optic Diamond, Scalloped Rim, Mt. Washington, 5 In. | 86 |
| **Bowl,** Ruffled Rim, Rectangular, Mt. Washington, 7½ x 10½ In. | 826 |
| **Bowl,** Scalloped Rim, 3 Reeded Feet, Oval, Raspberry Pontil, Mt. Washington, 5 In. | 403 |
| **Bowl,** White & Red Daisies, Pinched Waist, Mt. Washington, 3½ In. | 230 |
| **Condiment Set,** Glossy Finish, Ruffled Rim Bowls, Metal Caddy, 2 Spoons, 11 1n. | 518 |
| **Cruet,** Blue & White Daisies, Pillar Shape, Ribbed, Mt. Washington, 6¾ In. | 316 |
| **Cruet,** Stopper, Melon Ribbed, Mt. Washington, 6¾ In. | 173 |
| **Fairy Lamp,** Flower Shade, Pink Base, Marked Clarke, 5 In. | 826 |

| | |
|---|---|
| **Jar,** Cover, Amber Shaded To Rose, Bulbous, Mt. Washington, 10 In. | 1610 |
| **Lamp,** Chimney, Blossom, Leaf, Spider Web, Electrified, Mt. Washington, 18 ½ In. | 14160 |
| **Lamp,** Clock, Dome, Gas Run, Mt. Washington, Standard Novelty Co., Box, 6 ½ In. *illus* | 7475 |
| **Nappy,** 3 Raspberry Prunts, Folded Rim, Heart Shape, Loop Handle, 6 ½ In. | 1064 |
| **Pitcher,** Cream, Applied Amber Handle, Mt. Washington, 4 ¼ In. | 115 |
| **Pitcher,** Egyptian Scene, Chariot, Warrior, Square Mouth, 4 ½ In. *illus* | 518 |
| **Pitcher,** Egyptian Shape, Bronze Casing, Mt. Washington, 4 ½ In. | 40 |
| **Pitcher,** Egyptian, Applied Handle, Ivy, Charles Dickens Verse, Mt. Washington, 6 ¾ In. | 6325 |
| **Pitcher,** Tankard Shape, Bulbous, Bird Beak Rim, Mt. Washington, 7 ½ In. | 201 |
| **Pitcher,** Tankard Shape, Satin Finish, Mt. Washington, 9 In. | 460 |
| **Pitcher,** Water, Flowers, Thomas Hood Verse, Mt. Washington, 6 ½ In. *illus* | 5463 |
| **Plate,** Queen's Pattern, Pointillism Daisies, Mt. Washington, 6 In. | 460 |
| **Rose Bowl,** Shaded, Enameled Flowers, Inverted Crimped Rim, Mt. Washington, 3 In. | 144 |
| **Rose Bowl,** White & Blue Daisies, Folded Rim, Mt. Washington, 3 ½ In. | 144 |
| **Shaker,** Ribbed, Satin Finish, Rockford Silver Plated Caddy, Mt. Washington, 5 x 6 In., Pair | 201 |
| **Sugar & Creamer,** Satin, Bulbous, Squat, Mt. Washington, 5 In. | 86 |
| **Syrup,** Red Berries, Leafy Fall Branch, Embossed Metal Lid, Mt. Washington, 6 In. | 1725 |
| **Toothpick Holder,** Berries, Leaves, Hat Shape, Ruffled Rim, Mt. Washington, 2 ½ In. | 805 |
| **Toothpick Holder,** Blossoms, Bulbous, Cylindrical Neck, Squared Mouth, Mt. Washington, 3 In. | 173 |
| **Toothpick Holder,** Enameled Blossoms, Melon Ribbed, Pulled Finger Top, Mt. Washington, 2 In. | 144 |
| **Toothpick Holder,** White & Yellow Chrysanthemums, Squat, Square Neck & Rim, 2 ¾ In. | 288 |
| **Toothpick Holder,** Yellow Daisies, Rigaree Collar, Mt. Washington, 2 ¼ In. | 1035 |
| **Tumbler,** Shaded Yellow To Peach, Enamel Oxeye Daisy, Mt. Washington, 3 ¾ In. | 489 |
| **Vase,** Acid Finish, Trifold Rim, Mt. Washington, 23 ½ In. | 575 |
| **Vase,** Amber Shaded To Rose, Gold Moon, Ducks, Cascading Leaves, Cylindrical, 11 In. | 259 |
| **Vase,** Applied Ribbon Rigaree, Bag Shape, 4 In. | 207 |
| **Vase,** Bamboo Stalks, Gilt Enameled, Bulbous, Mt. Washington, 11 ½ In. | 590 |
| **Vase,** Bottle Shape, 4 Applied Feet, Raspberry Pontil, Mt. Washington, 8 In. | 230 |
| **Vase,** Daisies, Gold Stems, Bottle Shape, Squat, Narrow Neck, Mt. Washington, 8 In. | 978 |
| **Vase,** Enameled Flowers, Stippled, Double Bulbous, 8 In. *illus* | 460 |
| **Vase,** Fishnet, Coral, Green Ground, Gilt, Mt. Washington, 8 In. | 1298 |
| **Vase,** Flared Neck, 2 Curled Handles, Glossy Oval, Mt. Washington, 10 ½ In. | 1035 |
| **Vase,** Flowering Branches, Mt. Washington, 11 ½ In. | 1121 |
| **Vase,** Flowers, Pink Finish, Crimped Rim, Thomas Webb, c.1890, 3 In. | 161 |
| **Vase,** Lily, Fern, Trumpet Shape, White Dotted Foot, Trifold Rim, Mt. Washington, 12 In. | 1035 |
| **Vase,** Pink Blossom, Yellow Leaf, Bag Shape, Mt. Washington, 5 x 6 ½ In. | 2950 |
| **Vase,** Satin Glaze, Double Bottle Shape, Footed, Mt. Washington, 10 In. | 1725 |
| **Vase,** Seaweed, Trifold Rim, Bulbous Stick Shape, Mt. Washington, 10 ½ In. | 3565 |
| **Vase,** Stick, Bulbous, Trifold Rim, Yellow, White, Daisies, Gold Trim, 10 ½ In. *illus* | 1610 |
| **Vase,** Stick, Flowers, Vines, Gilt, Bulbous, 10 In. *illus* | 1265 |
| **Vase,** Stick, Gilt Rose Bush, Bulbous Base, Trifold Rim, Mt. Washington, 10 ½ In. | 1265 |
| **Vase,** Striped Wild Flowers, Pointillist, Bottle Shape, Mt. Washington, 10 ½ In. | 1495 |
| **Vase,** White Chrysanthemums, Green Stem, Gourd Base, Pencil Neck, 7 ½ In. | 345 |

---

**BUSTER BROWN,** the comic strip, first appeared in color in 1902. Buster and his dog, Tige, remained a popular comic and soon became even more famous as the emblem for a shoe company, a textile firm, and other companies. The strip was discontinued in 1920. Buster Brown sponsored a radio show from 1943 to 1955 and a TV show from 1950 to 1956. The Buster Brown characters are still used by Brown Shoe Company, Buster Brown Apparel, Inc., and Gateway Hosiery.

| | |
|---|---|
| **Bank,** Black Horse, Gold Horseshoe, Buster, Tige, Good Luck, 4 ¼ In. | 173 |
| **Button,** Buster Brown Shoes, Buster & Tige, W & H, 1 ½ In. *illus* | 173 |
| **Camera Box,** Cardboard, Color Lithograph, Instruction Books, Ansco Co., 4 ½ x 3 ¾ In. | 518 |
| **Doll,** Muslin, Lithograph, Printed Hair, Painted Face, Stitch Jointed, c.1900, 13 In. *illus* | 1064 |
| **Game,** Necktie Party, Oilcloth, Red, White, 1910, 25 ¼ x 29 ½ In. | 115 |
| **Sign,** Buster Brown Bread, Golden Sheaf Bakery, Embossed, Tin, 1920s, 22 x 30 In. *illus* | 1680 |
| **Tin,** Cigar, Man, Tige, Buster Brown, Cylindrical, 5 In. | 14000 |
| **Toy,** Bell, Buster Brown, Tige, Wagon, Paint, Cast Iron, Pull Toy, N.N. Hill, c.1905, 7 In. | 1920 |
| **Toy,** Buster & Tige, Hanging Bell, Clockwork, Lamp Post, 8 In. | 1920 |
| **Toy,** Buster Brown, Tige, Marble Rocker, Paint, Tin, Gunthermann, Germany, 9 ½ In. | 1140 |
| **Toy,** Horn, Paper, Plastic Mouthpiece, Tige, Blue, Red, 1920, 6 In. | 115 |

---

**BUTTER CHIPS,** or butter pats, were small individual dishes for butter. They were the height of fashion from 1880 to 1910. Earlier as well as later examples are known.

| | |
|---|---|
| **Azalea,** Gold Trim, Noritake, 1930-33, 3 ¼ In. | 59 |
| **Blue Willow,** Cobalt Blue, 3 In. | 17 |
| **Brown Aesthetic Transferware,** Melbourne, c.1883, 2 x 2 In. | 63 |

**Burmese,** Pitcher, Egyptian Scene, Chariot, Warrior, Square Mouth, 4 ½ In.
$518

Early Auction Co.

**Burmese,** Pitcher, Water, Flowers, Thomas Hood Verse, Mt. Washington, 6 ½ In.
$5,463

Early Auction Co.

**Burmese,** Vase, Enameled Flowers, Stippled, Double Bulbous, 8 In.
$460

Early Auction Co.

**Burmese,** Vase, Stick, Bulbous, Trifold Rim, Yellow, White, Daisies, Gold Trim, 10 ½ In.
**$1,610**

Early Auction Co.

**Burmese,** Vase, Stick, Flowers, Vines, Gilt, Bulbous, 10 In.
**$1,265**

Early Auction Co.

**Buster Brown,** Button, Buster Brown Shoes, Buster & Tige, W & H, 1 ½ In.
**$173**

Hake's Americana & Collectibles

| | |
|---|---:|
| **Brown Leaf Design,** Transfer, 3 ⅛ In. | 5 |
| **Daisy & Button,** Pressed Glass, Indented Corners, 2 x 2 In., 6 Piece | 39 |
| **Flow Blue,** 2 x 2 In. | 25 |
| **Flowers,** Pink, Blue, Gutherz & Carlsbad | 5 |
| **Flowers,** Stems, Leaves, Rounded Fluted Corners, Alfred Meakin, 5 x 5 In. | 40 |
| **Gold Bands,** Crown Staffordshire, 3 ½ In. | 22 |
| **Gold,** Green Leaves, Gilt Trim, Haviland Limoges | 13 |
| **Green Band,** Blue Flowers, Kyokaki-Fu Kinrande, Japan, 1982 | 7 |
| **Pink Luster Garland,** Enameled, 19th Century, 3 ½ In. | 45 |
| **Restaurant,** Kaiseki, Noritake, 3 x 2 In. | 10 |
| **Rose Sprays,** Gilt Trim, Scalloped, Haviland Limoges | 10 |
| **Strathmore Pattern,** Multicolor Flowers, Mason's Ironstone, 1940s | 3 |

---

**BUTTER MOLDS** *are listed in the Kitchen category under Mold, Butter.*

---

**BUTTON** collecting has been popular since the nineteenth century. Buttons have been used on clothing throughout the centuries, and there are millions of styles. Gold, silver, or precious stones were used for the best buttons, but most were made of natural materials, like bone or shell, or from inexpensive metals. Only a few types favored by collectors are listed for comparison.

| | |
|---|---:|
| **Abalone,** Carved, Owl's Face, c.1900, ⅝ In. | 10 |
| **Bakelite,** Clothespin Shape, Card, 6 Piece, 1937, 1 ⅜ In. | 62 |
| **Bakelite,** Feather, Petal Frame, Carved, Black, 1 ½ In. | 28 |
| **Bakelite,** Green, Marbled, 1 ⅛ x 1 ⅛ In., 2 Piece | 25 |
| **Bakelite,** Tomato Shape, Red, Shank Back, ¾ In. | 23 |
| **Boneshaker & Rider Image,** Metal, 1 In. | 117 |
| **Brass,** N.Y.C. Railroad Conductor, Loop Stud Back, 4 Piece | 36 |
| **Domed,** Paisley, Geometric Rim, Multicolor, Enameled, Art Deco, ⅞ In. | 40 |
| **Enamel,** Pink Roses, Black Ground, c.1890, ⅝ In. | 14 |
| **Leather,** Knot, Brown, Size 4, 1 ⅛ In. | 8 |
| **Mother-Of-Pearl,** Flowers, Pink, Green, ⅞ In. | 8 |
| **Turquoise Cabochon,** 18K Gold Filigree, Round, J. Lewis Goldsmith, Box, ⅜ In., 3 Piece | 104 |

---

**BUTTONHOOKS** have been a popular collectible in England for many years and are now gaining the attention of American collectors. The buttonhooks were made to help fasten the many buttons of the old-fashioned high-button shoes and other items of apparel.

| | |
|---|---:|
| **Celluloid,** Yellow, 6 ½ In. | 29 |
| **Gold Metal,** 6-Sided, 3 ¼ In. | 13 |
| **Mother-Of-Pearl,** 5 In. | 12 |
| **Silvertone,** Flowers, Art Nouveau, 5 ¼ In. | 10 |
| **Steel,** Folding Handle, Triangular, 1920s, 4 In. | 27 |
| **Sterling Silver,** Arts & Crafts, Shreve & Company, Monogram, c.1915, 8 In. | 195 |
| **Sterling Silver,** Baroque Scroll Handle, c.1890, 7 In. | 95 |
| **Sterling Silver,** Circular Oval Shape, S.M. & Co., c.1902, 2 x ⁷⁄₁₆ In. | 125 |
| **Sterling Silver,** Flowers, Scrolls, Monogram, c.1910, 8 ¾ In. | 95 |
| **Sterling Silver,** Mistletoe, Art Nouveau, France, 2 ½ In. | 85 |
| **Sterling Silver,** Repousse, Gorham, 4 ½ In. | 175 |
| **Sterling Silver,** Woman's Face, Flowing Hair, Art Nouveau, Marked, 7 ¾ In. | 75 |
| **Wood,** Cylindrical, 1920s, 5 ¼ In. | 16 |

---

**BYBEE POTTERY** of Bybee, Kentucky, was started by Webster Cornelison. The company claims it started in 1809, although sales records were not kept until 1845. The pottery is still operated by members of the sixth generation of the Cornelison family. The handmade stoneware pottery is sold at the factory. Various marks were used, including the name *Bybee*, the name *Cornelison*, or the initials *BB*. Not all pieces are marked. A mark shaped like the state of Kentucky with the words *Genuine Bybee* and similar marks were also used by a different company, Bybee Pottery Company of Lexington, Kentucky. It was a distributor of various pottery lines from 1922 to 1929.

| | |
|---|---:|
| **Vase,** Leaf Blades, Grey, Green, Brown Underglaze, 5 ⅝ In. | 259 |
| **Vase,** Purple, Blue Underglaze, Genuine Bybee Label, 7 ¾ In. | 259 |

---

**CALENDARS** made to hang on the wall or to be displayed on a desk top have been popular since the last quarter of the nineteenth century. Many were printed with advertising as part of the artwork and were given away as premiums. Calendars with guns, gunpowder, or Coca-Cola advertising are most prized.

| | | |
|---|---:|---:|
| **1896,** Garden City Bottling & Liquor Co., Litho, Girls, Kittens, Pabst's, 26 x 21 In. | *illus* | 390 |

**1899,** Greenwich Insurance Co., Crossing The Stream, Litho, Cardboard, Full Pad, 8 x 14 In...... 92
**1906,** Gustav Becker, Farm Machinery, Embossed, Cardboard, Die Cut, 9 x 16 In. ....................... 1680
**1906,** Lambertville Boots, Snag Proof, Trademark Girl Hunting, 12 x 8 In. ................................ 184
**1907,** Pretty Girl, Grape Leaves In Hair, Cardboard Litho, Die Cut, Frame, 25 x 26 In................. 104
**1908,** Schlitz Beer, Gus Broch & Son, Embossed Cardboard, Die Cut, 19 x 12 In. ..................... 46
**1909,** Butler Bros. Dentists, Embossed Cardboard, Die Cut, Frame, 15 x 19 In. ...................... 114
**1909,** Youths Companion, In Grandmother's Garden, Hollyhocks, Frame, 10 x 34 In. ............ 23
**1911,** Swartz' Bakery, St. Louis, Embossed, Die Cut, Full Pad, Frame, 11 x 17 In. .............*illus* 171
**1914,** Milwaukee Harvesting Machines, Friend Of The Forest, Dec., Spiegle, 13 x 21 In............... 1560
**1916,** Ford Sales Co., Flint, Mich., Couple, Full Pad, Frame, 15 x 26 In. ..........................*illus* 1200
**1917,** Hercules Gunpowder, Wild Turkeys, Paper Litho, Wild Turkeys, 29 x 12 In....................... 690
**1917,** Lambertville Rubber Footwear, Winter Scene, Cardboard, 12 x 8 In.  ........................*illus* 431
**1919,** Klund's Shoe Store, Selz Shoes Bloomer, Girl At Opera, Wisconsin, 11 x 38 In. ............... 81
**1920,** Yard Long, Selz Shoes, Woman, Pink Dress, W.R. Gregory, 42¼ In.  ..........................*illus* 390
**1923,** Orange Crush, Girl Seated, Orange Blouse, Frame, 32 x 19 In............................................ 660
**1924,** Hupmobile Auto, American Indian, Early Car, 30½ x 13 In............................................ 862
**1924,** Power Pumps, Water Systems, Spray Pumps, F.E. Myers, 20½ x 51 In................................. 720
**1925,** Imperial Ice Cream, Woman, Eating Ice Cream, Full Pad, 24 In........................................... 540
**1925,** Western Ammo, 2 Men, Dogs, Landscape, Paper Lithograph, 28 x 13 In............................ 1380
**1926,** Peters Cartridge Co., Birds In Field, 31 x 21 In................................................................... 1020
**1932,** Hercules Powder Co., Man, Gun, Boy, Dog, Frame, 32 x 22 In....................................... 570
**1935,** Eaton Transfer Company, Desk, Die Cut, Green, 3 x 6 In............................................... 57
**1936,** Roy Mack's Beverages, Pin Up, Nude Woman, Horse, Full Pad, 22 x 46 In.  ...............*illus* 420
**1937,** Black Motor Co., Dodge, Plymouth, Nude Woman, April To December, 15 x 20 In. ............. 480
**1950,** Metal, Thermometer, Fred M. Powell Co., Full Pad, Topeka, Kan. ................................. 12
**1953,** Orange Crush, 30 x 18 In.......................................................................................... 90
**1954,** Wrigley's Gum, Metal, Cardboard, 12½ x 14 In. ......................................................... 330

---

**CALENDAR PLATES** were popular in the United States as advertising giveaways from 1906 to 1929. Since then, a few plates have been made every year. A calendar and the name of a store, a picture of flowers, a girl, or a scene were featured on the plate.

**1909,** Yellow Roses, Purple Violets, Holly Berries, Carnation McNicol, 9 In................................. 55
**1910,** 4-Leaf Clover, Green, White, Dresden China, 8½ In................................................... 45
**1910,** Monk, Drinking, Steubenville, 9¼ In. ......................................................................... 15
**1911,** Arizona Country Scene, Marked, Dresden China, 8½ In............................................... 25
**1912,** Liberty Bell, American Flags, Grape Border, 8¼ In....................................................... 85
**1914,** Boy, Swiss Alps, Cobalt Blue Border, Faggard Grocery Co., 8¼ In................................. 50
**1953,** 4 Seasons, Gold On Blue, Homer Laughlin, 10 In............................................................. 24
**1954,** Zodiac Signs, Ivory, Signed, Fiesta, 10¼ In.................................................................... 90
**1961,** Dutch Scene, Taylor, Smith & Taylor, 10 In.................................................................. 29
**1965,** Pink Flowers, Gold Trim, 9¾ In................................................................................. 15
**1966,** Zodiac Signs, Central Bell, Alfred Meakin, 10 In............................................................. 18
**1968,** Sports Figures, Flower Border, 9 In............................................................................ 20
**1968,** USA, Eagle, Zodiac Signs, Swirled Border, Sheffield, 10 In......................................... 21
**1969,** Currier & Ives, Rimmed, Green, Royal China, 10 In..................................................... 30
**1972,** Animal Carnival, Zodiac Signs, Carousel, Wedgwood, 10 In......................................... 19
**1973,** God Bless Our House, Farmhouse, Scalloped Edge, Alfred Meakin, 9 In........................... 8
**1975,** 4 Seasons, White, Red, 10 In...................................................................................... 15
**1979,** Fair Store 90th Anniversary, Yellow, Black, 8 In. .......................................................... 6
**1980,** Home Of The Free, Abe Lincoln, Red, White, Blue, Spencer Gifts, 9 In............................ 5

---

**CAMARK POTTERY** started out as Camden Art Tile and Pottery Company in Camden, Arkansas. Jack Carnes founded the firm in 1926 in association with John Lessell, Stephen Sebaugh, and the Camden Chamber of Commerce. Many types of glazes and wares were made. The company was bought by Mary Daniel in the early 1960s. Production ended in 1983.

**Basket,** Yellow, Footed, Paper Label, 6 In. ....................................................................... 42
**Ewer,** Peach, Swirled Foot, 11 In. ...................................................................................... 42
**Sugar & Creamer,** Attached Tray, Ivory, Art Deco, 4½ x 2 In. ............................................. 45
**Vase,** Landscape, Iridescent, Multicolor, Tree, Mountains, Signed John Lessel, 12 In.................... 1150
**Vase,** Turquoise & Black, Pinched Neck, 5½ In. ................................................................ 36

---

**CAMBRIDGE GLASS COMPANY** was founded in 1901 in Cambridge, Ohio. The company closed in 1954, reopened briefly, and closed again in 1958. The firm made all types of glass. Its early wares included heavy pressed glass with the mark *Near Cut*. Later wares included Crown Tuscan, etched stemware, and clear and colored glass. The firm used a *C* in a triangle mark after 1920.

**Adonis,** Relish, 3 Sections, Oval, 12 In. ............................................................................ 64

**Buster Brown,** Doll, Muslin, Lithograph, Printed Hair, Painted Face, Stitch Jointed, c.1900, 13 In.
$1,064

Theriault's

**Buster Brown,** Sign, Buster Brown Bread, Golden Sheaf Bakery, Embossed, Tin, 1920s, 22 x 30 In.
$1,680

Morphy Auctions

**Calendar,** 1896, Garden City Bottling & Liquor Co., Litho, Girls, Kittens, Pabst's, 26 x 21 In.
$390

Morphy Auctions

**Calendar,** 1911, Swartz' Bakery, St. Louis, Embossed, Die Cut, Full Pad, Frame, 11 x 17 In.
$171

Showtime Auction Services

**Calendar,** 1916, Ford Sales Co., Flint, Mich., Couple, Full Pad, Frame, 15 x 26 In.
$1,200

Showtime Auction Services

**Calendar,** 1917, Lambertville Rubber Footwear, Winter Scene, Cardboard, 12 x 8 In.
$431

Wm Morford Auctions

| | |
|---|---:|
| **Alpine,** Ice Bucket, Bail Handle, 5 ¾ x 6 ½ In. | 42 |
| **Autumn,** Juice, 4 ⅜ In. | 13 |
| **Bacchus,** Decanter, 11 In. | 156 |
| **Beverly,** Goblet, 7 ⅞ In. | 34 |
| **Bijou,** Cordial, 4 ⅝ In. | 23 |
| **Bijou,** Goblet, 6 ½ In. | 13 |
| **Bijou,** Tumbler, 5 ⅝ In. | 18 |
| **Blossom Time,** Basket, Footed, 12 x 4 In. | 68 |
| **Blossom Time,** Compote, Gold, 6 x 7 In. | 67 |
| **Blossom Time,** Sherbet, 5 ¾ In. | 16 |
| **Blossom Time,** Sugar, Footed, 2 ⅜ In. | 21 |
| **Bookend,** Eagle, Spread Wings, 6 ⅜ In. | 45 |
| **Bookend,** Lion, 6 In. | 248 |
| **Broadmoor,** Goblet, 7 ⅛ In. | 27 |
| **Broadmoor,** Sherbet, 6 In. | 21 |
| **Buttercup,** Tumbler, Iced Tea, 6 ⅛ In. | 15 |
| **Caprice,** Bonbon, Moonlight Blue, Handles, 6 ½ In. | 60 |
| **Caprice,** Bowl, Moonlight Blue, Handle, 10 ½ In. | 95 |
| **Caprice,** Creamer, Moonlight Blue, 3 In. | 25 |
| **Caprice,** Plate, Salad, Cleo Blue, 7 In. | 22 |
| **Castleton,** Cocktail, 4 ⅝ In. | 8 |
| **Castleton,** Goblet, Water, 6 ½ In. | 8 |
| **Castleton,** Sherbet, 5 ⅜ In. | 7 |
| **Castleton,** Wine, 5 ¾ In. | 7 |
| **Century,** Cordial, 3 ⅞ In. | 28 |
| **Century,** Sherbet, 5 ¼ In. | 7 |
| **Century,** Wine, 5 ½ In. | 19 |
| **Charleston,** Compote, 4 ½ In. | 8 |
| **Charleston,** Goblet, 6 ½ In. | 6 |
| **Charleston,** Sherbet, 4 ⅞ In. | 10 |
| **Colonial,** Punch Bowl, 6 ⅞ In. | 168 |
| **Colonial,** Punch Cup | 23 |
| **Cordelia,** Goblet, 7 ½ In. | 31 |
| **Cordelia,** Plate, Salad, 7 In. | 19 |
| **Cordelia,** Tumbler, Juice, 4 ⅛ In. | 21 |
| **Corsage,** Plate, Luncheon, 8 In. | 12 |
| **Corsage,** Sherbet, 5 In. | 6 |
| **Corsage,** Tumbler, Iced Tea, 7 ⅝ In. | 8 |
| **Cranston,** Ice Bucket, Tab Handles, 4 ½ In. | 156 |
| **Croesus,** Cordial, 5 ⅛ In. | 24 |
| **Croesus,** Goblet, 8 ½ In. | 46 |
| **Croesus,** Plate, Salad, 8 ¼ In. | 28 |
| **Croesus,** Tumbler, Iced Tea, Footed, 7 ⅝ In. | 38 |
| **Decagon,** Bowl, Cereal, Pink, 6 ½ In. | 17 |
| **Decagon,** Compote, Pink, 3 ½ In. | 21 |
| **Decagon,** Cup & Saucer, Amber | 6 |
| **Decagon,** Nut Dish, Pink, 2 ½ In. | 13 |
| **Decagon,** Plate, Bread & Butter, 5 ⅞ In. | 7 |
| **Decagon,** Plate, Salad, Pink, 7 In. | 12 |
| **Decagon,** Tray, Center Handle, Amber, 10 ½ In. | 19 |
| **Festoon,** Goblet, 6 In. | 10 |
| **Festoon,** Sherbet, 4 ⅛ In. | 8 |
| **Festoon,** Tumbler, Iced Tea, 5 ¾ In. | 15 |
| **Festoon,** Tumbler, Juice, 4 ⅜ In. | 16 |
| **Figurine,** Bashful Charlotte, 6 ¾ In. | 98 |
| **Figurine,** Swan, Mandarin Gold, 5 ¾ In. | 190 |
| **Figurine,** Woman, Draped, Light Emerald, 8 In. | 339 |
| **Gadroon,** Candlestick, 2 ⅝ In. | 17 |
| **Gadroon,** Cup & Saucer | 19 |
| **Gadroon,** Plate, Salad, 8 ⅜ In. | 8 |
| **Gadroon,** Relish, 2 Sections, 6 In. | 9 |
| **Gadroon,** Relish, 3 Sections, 8 In. | 17 |
| **Gadroon,** Sherbet, 6 ⅜ In. | 14 |
| **Gadroon,** Sugar & Creamer | 26 |
| **Gadroon,** Tumbler, Iced Tea, Footed, 7 ⅝ In. | 16 |
| **Georgian,** Tumbler, Cobalt Blue, 12 Oz., 5 ¼ In. | 23 |

C

**Glendale,** Cordial, 4 ⅜ In. 37
**Glendale,** Plate, Salad, 7 ½ In. 15
**Glendale,** Tumbler, Iced Tea, 6 In. 14
**Glendale,** Wine, Sherbet, 5 ⅝ In. 7
**Golden Wheat,** Sherbet, 5 ¾ In. 16
**Heirloom,** Torte Plate, Amber, 12 ¾ In. 39
**Jar,** Underplate, Beehive Shape, Bee Finial, Pink, Silver Leaf Overlay, 5 x 6 In. 354
**Jefferson,** Sherbet, Amber, 3 ½ In. 8
**Jefferson,** Sherbet, Blue, 4 ⅞ In. 8
**Jefferson,** Sherbet, Pink, 4 ⅝ In. 8
**Jefferson,** Tumbler, Iced Tea, Pink, 5 ⅞ In. 14
**Jefferson,** Tumbler, Juice, Footed, Blue, 5 Oz., 4 In. 7 to 9
**Juliana,** Cordial, 4 ½ In. 31
**Juliana,** Goblet, 6 ⅝ In. 18
**Juliana,** Sherbet, 4 ¾ In. 17
**Juliana,** Tumbler, Iced Tea, 6 ¼ In. 12
**King Edward,** Celery Dish, 11 ¼ In. 36
**King Edward,** Cordial, 4 ½ In. 17
**King Edward,** Goblet, 6 ½ In. 17
**King Edward,** Sherbet, 4 ⅝ In. 8
**King Edward,** Wine, 5 ⅞ In. 26
**King George,** Cordial, 4 ½ In. 37
**King George,** Sherbet, 4 ⅞ In. 7
**King George,** Wine, 5 ¾ In. 21
**Larchmont,** Cordial, 3 ⅞ In. 43
**Larchmont,** Plate, Salad, 7 In. 9
**Laurel Wreath,** Cordial, 4 ½ In. 39
**Laurel Wreath,** Goblet, 6 ¾ In. 14
**Laurel Wreath,** Goblet, Iced Tea, 6 ¼ In. 9
**Laurel Wreath,** Sherbet, 4 ¾ In. 7
**Lily Of The Valley,** Cocktail, 3 ¾ In. 13
**Lily Of The Valley,** Plate, Salad, 7 ⅜ In. 12
**Lotus,** Sugar, Footed, 4 In. 33
**Lucia,** Plate, Salad, 7 ½ In. 31
**Lucia,** Tumbler, Iced Tea, 7 ⅝ In. 89
**Majestic,** Tumbler, Juice, 5 In. 21
**Marjorie,** Creamer, 2 ⅝ In. 36
**Marjorie,** Goblet, 7 ⅛ In. 22
**Marjorie,** Plate, Salad, 7 ⅞ In. 23
**Marjorie,** Punch Bowl, 12 ¼ In. 207
**Marjorie,** Saucer, 6 ¼ In. 11
**Marjorie,** Sherbet, 3 ⅜ In. 13
**Marjorie,** Sugar, 2 ⅝ In. 29
**Marjorie,** Tumbler, 4 In. 28
**Marjorie,** Wine, 5 ⅝ In. 46
**Minton Wreath,** Cordial, 4 ⅜ In. 17
**Minton Wreath,** Goblet, 6 ½ In. 14
**Minton Wreath,** Plate, Salad, 7 ½ In. 12
**Minton Wreath,** Sherbet, 4 In. 16
**Minton Wreath,** Tumbler, Juice, 4 ¼ In. 17
**Minton Wreath,** Wine, 5 ⅝ In. 43
**Minuet,** Cordial, 4 ⅜ In. 36
**Minuet,** Sherbet, 6 In. 10
**Moderne,** Plate, Bread & Butter, 6 ⅞ In. 8
**Mt. Vernon,** Tumbler, Flat, Amber, 12 Oz., 3 ⅞ In. 10
**Mt. Vernon,** Tumbler, Footed, Red, 2 Oz., 3 ¼ In. 19
**Near Cut,** Plate, 8 ½ In. 21
**Nudes,** Ashtray, Stemmed, Amethyst, 6 ⅜ In. 276
**Nudes,** Centerpiece, Shell Shape, Footed, Amber, 9 In. 2673
**Nudes,** Cocktail, Amber, 6 ½ In. 84
**Nudes,** Compote, Forest Green, 8 In. 254
**Nudes,** Cordial, Amber, 1 Oz., 5 ¾ In. 229
**Nudes,** Cordial, Amethyst, 1 Oz., 5 ¾ In. 449
**Nudes,** Wine, Amethyst, 7 ¾ In. 136
**Plaza,** Tumbler, Juice, 4 ¾ In. 13
**Plaza,** Wine, 5 ¾ In. 16



**Calendar,** 1920, Yard Long, Selz Shoes, Woman, Pink Dress, W.R. Gregory, 42 ¼ In.
$390

Showtime Auction Services

**Calendar,** 1936, Roy Mack's Beverages, Pin Up, Nude Woman, Horse, Full Pad, 22 x 46 In.
$420

Morphy Auctions

**TIP**

*Remember, hair spray, shaving lotion, skin creams, toothpaste, soap, antibiotic salves, antiseptics, and all cosmetics can damage paper.*

**Cambridge Pottery,** Vase, Otoe, Clover, Green Matte Glaze, Signed, 5 ¼ In. $316

Humler & Nolan

**Cameo Glass,** Vase, Flowers, White Over Red, Yellow Ground, Attributed To Webb, 8 ¾ In. $2,370

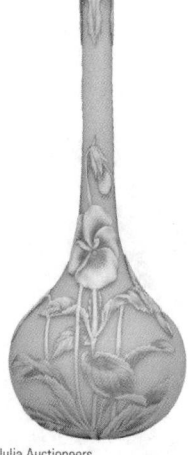

James D. Julia Auctioneers

**Cameo Glass,** Vase, Thistles Flowers, Leaves, Gilt Highlights, Burgun & Schverer, 7 In. $5,036

James D. Julia Auctioneers

| | |
|---|---:|
| **Plymouth,** Sherbet, 4 ⅝ In. | 29 |
| **Portia,** Relish, 5 Sections | 40 |
| **Pristine,** Cornucopia, Moonlight Blue, 7 ½ In. | 46 |
| **Radiant Rose,** Creamer, Footed, 2 ⅞ In. | 16 |
| **Radiant Rose,** Sherbet, 4 ⅝ In. | 8 |
| **Radiant Rose,** Sugar, Footed, 2 ⅞ In. | 15 |
| **Radiant Rose,** Tumbler, Iced Tea, 6 ¼ In. | 26 |
| **Radiant Rose,** Tumbler, Juice, 4 ⅞ In. | 14 |
| **Ravenna,** Sherbet, 5 ⅝ In. | 10 |
| **Regent,** Cordial, 4 ½ In. | 27 |
| **Regent,** Sherbet, 4 ¾ In. | 15 |
| **Regent,** Tumbler, Juice, 4 ¾ In. | 28 |
| **Rose Point,** Goblet, 8 ⅜ In. | 41 |
| **Rose Point,** Torte Plate, 3-Footed, 12 x 11 ½ In. | 28 |
| **Shelburne,** Goblet, 7 ⅝ In. | 11 |
| **Shelburne,** Sherbet, 6 In. | 9 |
| **Square,** Relish, 2 Sections, 6 ½ In. | 21 |
| **Sunnybrook,** Sherbet, 6 ⅝ In. | 8 |
| **Sunnybrook,** Tumbler, Iced Tea, 7 In. | 9 |
| **Symphony,** Sherbet, 6 ¼ In. | 10 |
| **Symphony,** Tumbler, Iced Tea, 7 ¼ In. | 9 |
| **Today,** Sherbet, 4 ½ In. | 22 |
| **Today,** Tumbler, Iced Tea, 5 ⅝ In. | 22 |
| **Today,** Wine, 4 In. | 38 |
| **Tomorrow,** Sherbet, 5 ⅝ In. | 6 |
| **Valencia,** Honey Pot, Lid, 7 In. | 187 |
| **Vase,** Green Matte Glaze, Angled Handles, 5 ⅞ In. | 92 |
| **Vesta,** Candlestick, 2-Light, 6 In. | 32 |
| **Victory Wreath,** Goblet, 8 ⅝ In. | 46 |
| **Victory Wreath,** Tumbler, Footed, 12 Oz., 7 In. | 12 |
| **Wetherford,** Bowl, Round, Pink, 9 In. | 25 |
| **Wetherford,** Creamer, Amber, 5 In. | 14 |

**CAMBRIDGE POTTERY** was made in Cambridge, Ohio, from about 1895 until World War I. The factory made brown glazed decorated artwares with a variety of marks, including an acorn, the name *Cambridge*, the name *Oakwood*, and the name *Terrhea*.

| | |
|---|---:|
| **Pitcher,** Yellow Flower, Standard Glaze, Stretched Neck, c.1895, 5 ½ In. | 125 |
| **Vase,** Otoe, Clover, Green Matte Glaze, Signed, 5 ¼ In. ..........................*illus* | 316 |
| **Vase,** Yellow Flower, Black Glaze, Footed, 6 In. | 90 |

**CAMEO GLASS** was made in much the same manner as a cameo in jewelry. Parts of the top layer of glass were cut away to reveal a different colored glass beneath. The most famous cameo glass was made during the nineteenth century. Signed cameo glass pieces are listed under the glasswork's name, such as Daum, Galle, Legras, Mt. Joye, Webb, and others.

| | |
|---|---:|
| **Bell,** Red, Frosted, Cascading Vine, Flower Handle, Corset Waist, 6 ½ In. | 3163 |
| **Jug,** Carved Flowers, Amber, Signed, Vertebrae D'Art De Lorraine, France, 6 In. | 3245 |
| **Lamp,** Barren Trees, Snowy Ground, Cylindrical, Mushroom Shade, 12 In. | 15405 |
| **Lamp,** Electric, Tricolor, Cut Glass, Mountainous River Scene, Brass, 12 x 7 In. | 357 |
| **Plate,** Flowers, Buds, Stems, Butterflies, 8 ½ In. | 474 |
| **Transparent,** Metallic, Cut, Etched, Thistle, France, c.1907, 14 ¼ In. | 3075 |
| **Vase,** Acid Cut, Back Patterned, Cranberry Flowers, Gilt Highlights, St. Louis, 8 In. | 308 |
| **Vase,** Amethyst Flowers, Frosted Ground, Squat, Cylindrical Neck, Pertusot, 4 In. | 29 |
| **Vase,** Bird, Bamboo, White, Red Ground, Teardrop Shape, 12 ½ In. | 165 |
| **Vase,** Blue Mottled Body, Grapevines, Fruit Clusters, A. Delatte, 7 ½ In. | 374 |
| **Vase,** Blue, White Dogwood Blossoms & Leaves, Shouldered, England, 7 ½ In. | 575 |
| **Vase,** Calla Lily, Stems, Leaves, Butterfly, Rose, Yellow Ground, 9 In. | 2962 |
| **Vase,** Carved White Blossom Overlay, Green To Yellow, England, 3 ¾ In. | 944 |
| **Vase,** Carved, Cranberry, White Flowers, 1800s, 6 In. | 540 |
| **Vase,** Chestnut Leaves, Orange, Cream, Footed, Cameo, 6 ½ x 12 In. | 3450 |
| **Vase,** Cranberry White Ivy Overlay, Green To Yellow, Bowling Pin Shape, 11 ½ In. | 5605 |
| **Vase,** Flared Rim, Red, Gold, Flowers, Gilt Highlights, Acid Cut, St. Louis, 10 In. | 338 |
| **Vase,** Flowers, Stems, Leaves, Compressed Globe, Light Green, 7 In. | 1777 |
| **Vase,** Flowers, White Over Red, Yellow Ground, Attributed To Webb, 8 ¾ In. .........*illus* | 2370 |
| **Vase,** Foxglove, Stems, Leaves, Blue Ground, Double Cameo Band At Foot, 7 In. | 1659 |
| **Vase,** Gold, Iridescent Wash, Ground Pontil, Signed, Gubisch, 9 ¾ In. | 150 |

| | |
|---|---|
| **Vase,** Long Neck, White, Yellow, Blossoms, Daylilies, Border, 16⅛ In. .......... | 1230 |
| **Vase,** Octopus, Ocean Scene, Green, Red, 6 In. .......... | 7800 |
| **Vase,** Pink Flower, Butterfly Overlay, Yellow Ground, England, 4½ In. .......... | 1888 |
| **Vase,** Pink, White Carved Flowers, Branch Overlay, Yellow Ground, 7 In. .......... | 5310 |
| **Vase,** Prussian Blue, Flowers, Dotted Border, Oval, Tapered, 7¼ In. .......... | 690 |
| **Vase,** Red & Orange Fiery Opalescent, Flowers, Leaves, Diamond Quilted, 7 In. .......... | 230 |
| **Vase,** Red Flowers, Bulbous Shape, Cream Ground, Signed, 12 In. .......... | 592 |
| **Vase,** Red Over White On Yellow, Cascading Dogwood Branch, 3¾ In. .......... | 144 |
| **Vase,** Red, White Branches & Leaves, Shouldered, Flared Rim, England, 4½ In. .......... | 748 |
| **Vase,** Red, White Daylilies, Shouldered Flared Neck, Flower Band, 8½ In. .......... | 1438 |
| **Vase,** Thistle, Stems, Leaves, Brown Ground 7 In. .......... | 2962 |
| **Vase,** Thistles Flowers, Leaves, Gilt Highlights, Burgun & Schverer, 7 In. ..........*illus* | 5036 |
| **Vase,** White Carved Cocks, Flowers Overlay, Handles, G.W., England 11 In. .......... | 5310 |
| **Vase,** White Carved Flowers, Insect Overlay, Pink To Orange, England, 5 In. .......... | 295 |
| **Vase,** White Over Citron, Bulbous Smokestack Shape, Flowers, Banded, 5 In. .......... | 288 |
| **Vase,** Yellow, Cranberry Tree, Mountains, P. Nicholas, Tapered Cylinder, 5½ In. .......... | 885 |

**CAMPAIGN** *memorabilia are listed in the Political category.*

**CAMPBELL KIDS** were first used as part of an advertisement for the Campbell Soup Company in 1904. The kids were created by Grace Drayton, a popular illustrator of the day. The kids were used in magazine and newspaper ads until about 1951. They were presented again in 1966; and in 1983, they were redesigned with a slimmer, more contemporary appearance.

| | |
|---|---|
| **Book,** Campbell Kids At Home, Cook Book, Rand McNally .......... | 27 |
| **Cookie Jar,** Figural, Boy, Holding Soup Can, 12½ In. .......... | 75 |
| **Dish,** Alphabet, Kids Playing, Transfer, 7½ In. .......... | 130 |
| **Doll,** Girl, Cloth, Side-Glancing Eyes, Ideal Corp., 1950s, 16 In. .......... | 40 |
| **Figurine,** Composition, Side-Glancing Eyes, E.I. Horseman Co., 1948, 12 In. .......... | 595 |
| **Lid,** Casserole, Kids, Eating Soup, Red, White, Pottery, 5 x 2 In. .......... | 18 |
| **Ornament,** Kids Ice Skating, Glass, White, 1987, 3½ In. .......... | 10 |
| **Postcard,** Thanksgiving Greeting, Dinner Table, Girl, Ringing Bell, c.1925 .......... | 8 |
| **Print,** Kids, Chalkboard, Tomato Is A Fruit, 8 x 10 In. .......... | 22 |
| **Print,** Paper, Kids Skating, 1970s, 8 x 10 In. .......... | 20 |
| **Salt & Pepper,** Kids, Aprons, Chef Hats, 1940s .......... | 64 |
| **Tray,** Metal, Kids, Bear, Sitting At Table, Red, 13 x 10 In. .......... | 25 |
| **Watch,** Windup, Girl Holding Umbrella, Swiss, Box, 8½ In. .......... | 40 |

**CANDELABRUM** refers to a candleholder with more than one arm to hold many candles; a candlestick is designed to hold one candle. The eccentricity of the English language makes the plural of candelabrum into candelabra.

| | |
|---|---|
| **2-Light,** Brass, Glass Hurricane Shade, Metal Center Pole, Denmark, 24½ In., Pair .......... | 420 |
| **2-Light,** Bronze, Egyptian Revival, Seated Winged Sphinx, Horus, Sun Finial, 17¾ In., Pair .......... | 2813 |
| **2-Light,** Bronze, Louis XVI Style, Putti, Cornucopia, Grape Bunches, 14¼ In. .......... | 531 |
| **2-Light,** Bronze, Marble, Putti, Fruit, Basket, Tambourine, 19¼ x 8¾ In., Pair .......... | 1045 |
| **2-Light,** Buds, Leaves, Berries, Twisted Branches, Urn Shape, Denmark, 10¼ In. .......... | 3900 |
| **2-Light,** Gilt Bronze, Eagle, Patinated, 9½ In., Pair .......... | 344 |
| **2-Light,** Gilt Bronze, Silver, Hermes & Aphrodite, Stone Base, c.1865, 11 x 6 In., Pair .......... | 500 |
| **2-Light,** Giltwood, Sconce, Louis XVI Style, Ribbons, Scrolls, 29 x 10 In., Pair .......... | 313 |
| **2-Light,** Metal, Cats, Dogs, Stylized, Half Circle, Round Base, Hegenauer, 9½ In. .......... | 4687 |
| **2-Light,** Porcelain, Green Bird Base, Flower Cups, Gilt Metal Arms, Italy, 10 In., Pair .......... | 375 |
| **2-Light,** Scroll Arms, Urn Shape Candlecups, Reeded, c.1900, 15⅜ In. .......... | 369 |
| **2-Light,** Silver Plate, Nude Woman Standard, Stepped Square Base, c.1920, 13 In., Pair .......... | 750 |
| **2-Light,** Silver, Mopane Tree, Elephants, Naturalistic, P. Mavros, Zimbabwe, 1994, 12 In. .......... | 2000 |
| **2-Light,** Silver, U Shape, Tapered Arms, Georg Jensen, c.1960, 7 In., Pair .......... | 11500 |
| **3-Light,** Brass, Candlecups Suspended, Round Base, Robert Riddle Jarvie, 7 x 11 In. .......... | 9150 |
| **3-Light,** Bronze, Marble Putto, Gilt Arms, 23¾ In., Pair .......... | 1230 |
| **3-Light,** Gilt Metal, Marble Base, Victorian, c.1860, 19 x 15 In. .......... | 60 |
| **3-Light,** Girandole, Silvered Bronze, Leather Stocking, Marble Base, 17½ In. .......... | 240 |
| **3-Light,** Iron, Crystal, Tree Shape, Flowers, Urn Shape Base, Italy, c.1800s, 39 In. .......... | 2500 |
| **3-Light,** Louis XV Style, Gilt Bronze, Marble, Putti, Bouquet Support, c.1890, 22 In., Pair .......... | 2304 |
| **3-Light,** Louis XV, Bronze, Porcelain, Parrots, Branches, Leaves, 23½ In., Pair .......... | 3025 |
| **3-Light,** Louis XVI Style, Tapered, Torch Standard, c.1920, 18 In., Pair .......... | 938 |
| **3-Light,** Metal, Art Nouveau Style, Patinated, 12 x 7 In. .......... | 150 |
| **3-Light,** Silver Plate, c.1900, 14 x 15 In., Pair .......... | 120 |
| **3-Light,** Silver Plate, c.1950, 19 x 19 In., Pair .......... | 750 |

**Candelabrum,** 7-Light, Silver, Scrolled Arms, Antonio Pineda, Taxco, c.1962, 15 In., Pair
$16,250

Heritage Auction Galleries

**Candlestick Brass,** Altar, Baluster Turned Squat Knop, Pricket, 3 Feet, c.1910, 44½ x 14 In.
$72

Gray's Auctioneers LLC

**Candlestick,** Brass, Spiral Turned, Drip Cups, England, 1800s, 20½ In., Pair
$250

Rago Arts & Auction Center

**Candlestick,** Copper, Hammered, Riveted Handle, G. Stickley, Stamped Als Ik Kan, 8½ In., Pair
$173

Humler & Nolan

**Candlestick,** Glass, Green Cut To Clear, Grape & Leaf, 1800s, 10 In., Pair
$560

Conestoga Auction Co., Inc.

**Candy Container,** Belsnickle, Yellow Robe, Pink & Aqua Fur Trim, Tree Sprig, Snow Mound, 12 In.
$8,260

Bertoia Auctions

| | |
|---|---|
| **3-Light,** Silver Plate, Scrolling Arms, Oval Foot, Ellis-Barker, c.1912, 17½ In., Pair | 598 |
| **3-Light,** Silver, Cambridge, Convertible, 4 Sections, Gorham, 15¼ In., Pair | 430 |
| **3-Light,** Silver, Converts To Candlesticks, London, 1925, 15 x 13 In., Pair | 1750 |
| **3-Light,** Silver, Corinthian Column, Swags, Mappin & Webb, 1895, 22 In., Pair | 2950 |
| **3-Light,** Silver, Curved Arms, Round Base, Interchangeable, Reed & Barton, 13 x 11 In., Pair | 265 |
| **3-Light,** Silver, Gorham, 15 In., Pair | 240 |
| **3-Light,** Silver, Putti, Flowers, Scrolls, Early 20th Century, 17¼ In., Pair | 6875 |
| **3-Light,** Silver, Scroll Arms, Weighted, Fisher, 10 In., Pair | 120 |
| **4-Light,** Bronze, Flower Shape Cup, Marble, Urn Shape, 20½ In., Pair | 1045 |
| **4-Light,** Bronze, Gilt, Marble, 3-Footed, Electric, c.1900, 22 In. | 4687 |
| **4-Light,** Bronze, Gilt, Rococo, Leaves, Scrolled, 20¾ x 14 In., Pair | 489 |
| **4-Light,** Bronze, Napoleon III, Winged Caryatids, Mounted As Lamp, 27 x 43 In., Pair | 5904 |
| **4-Light,** Bronze, Putti Holding Stem, France, 43 In. | 4305 |
| **4-Light,** Gilt Bronze, Louis XV Style, Column Standard, Petal Drip Cups, 20 In., Pair | 1063 |
| **4-Light,** Marble, Bronze, Urn Base, Gray, Lion Mask Handles, 18 In., Pair | 461 |
| **4-Light,** Silver, Gadrooned Urn, Shell & Scroll, Stepped Foot, Sheffield, c.1800, 32 In. | 1291 |
| **5-Light,** Brass, 2 Drip Pans, 1950s, 24 x 9 In. | 875 |
| **5-Light,** Brass, Aqua Gemstones, Urn, Multiple Stems, Leaves, Blossoms, 22 x 19½ In. | 127 |
| **5-Light,** Bronze, Central Sconce, Woman, Classical, Dress, Basket, 28½ In., Pair | 4920 |
| **5-Light,** Bronze, Column Shape, Draped Chains, Paw Feet, Griffin Finial, 30½ In. | 615 |
| **5-Light,** Bronze, Gilt, Marble, Leaf, Porcelain Plaques, 16½ x 15 In., Pair | 1599 |
| **5-Light,** Bronze, Red Marble, Leaves, Gilt, Urns, Bacchus, Paw Feet, 24 In., Pair | 1793 |
| **5-Light,** Capo-Di-Monte, Central Mask, 4-Part Base, Garlands, Ram Masks, 12 In. | 188 |
| **5-Light,** English Rose Pattern, 17⅛ In. | 1220 |
| **5-Light,** Faux Candlesticks, Figural Supports, Crystal Knop Stem, Electrified, 34 x 15 In. | 63 |
| **5-Light,** Gilt Bronze, Louis XV Style, Putto, Lamb, Scrolled Arms, Openwork, 31 In., Pair | 4250 |
| **5-Light,** Gilt Bronze, Neoclassical Style, Leaf & Mask Arms, 33 In. | 500 |
| **5-Light,** Gilt Bronze, Scroll Arms, Porcelain Base, Painted Scenes, 22½ In., Pair | 1250 |
| **5-Light,** Gilt, Patinated Bronze, Louis XV Style, Leaves, Putto, Flowers, c.1900, 26 In. | 1375 |
| **5-Light,** Gilt, Putti Dum, Reeded Pedestal, Candle Branches, Paw Feet, 44 In., Pair | 2952 |
| **5-Light,** Giltwood, Tole, Carved Baluster Stem, Flower Arms, Pedestal, 23 In., Pair | 500 |
| **5-Light,** Louis XVI Style, Crystal, Bronze, Fluted, Gilt Standards, 18 x 12 In., Pair | 2214 |
| **5-Light,** Silver, Baluster, Curved Arms, Round Base, Convertible, 12½ x 11½ In. | 207 |
| **5-Light,** Silver, Convertible, Durchin, 13¼ x 12¼ In., Pair | 219 |
| **5-Light,** Silver, Interlocking JLS Mark, Brazil, 18½ x 12½ In., Pair | 2596 |
| **5-Light,** Tin, Christmas Tree Shape, Multicolor, Mexico, 32½ In. | 82 |
| **6-Light,** Brass, Clear, Purple Glass Drop Pendants, 3 Tiers, c.1890, 23 In., Pair | 570 |
| **6-Light,** Bronze Dore, Pierced, Floral Swag Base, Silk Shade, 28 x 36 In., Pair | 1722 |
| **6-Light,** Bronze, Baroque Style, Ormolu, Patina, Putti, Branches, 27 x 15 In., Pair | 2588 |
| **6-Light,** Bronze, Regency, Three Part Base, Trophies, Paw Feet, c.1800, 40 In., Pair | 3444 |
| **6-Light,** Gilt Bronze, Louis XV Style, Bacchantes, Holding Branches, c.1945, 25 In., Pair | 1000 |
| **6-Light,** Ormolu, Tiered, Hung Clear Pendants, France, c.1900, 38½ In., Pair | 185 |
| **6-Light,** Patinated Gilt, Restauration Style, Upturned Branches, 1900s, 24 In., Pair | 750 |
| **6-Light,** Winged Goddess Of Victory, Cornucopia, Grapevines, 31¾ In. | 4880 |
| **7-Light,** Bronze, Empire Style, Winged Woman, Holding Arms, Wreath Base, 31 In. | 3250 |
| **7-Light,** Bronze, Gilt, Leaves, Flowers, France, 24½ x 17 In., Pair | 4687 |
| **7-Light,** Gilt Bronze, Acanthus, Flowers, Stems, Reed Supports, Masks, 17¾ In., Pair | 1465 |
| **7-Light,** Silver Plate, Leaves, Scrolls, c.1965, 28 x 22 In. | 938 |
| **7-Light,** Silver, Baroque, Fluted, 20th Century, 18¾ x 17½ In. | 2000 |
| **7-Light,** Silver, Knopped, Scrolls, Rocaille Designs, 25 In., Pair | 5000 |
| **7-Light,** Silver, Scrolled Arms, Antonio Pineda, Taxco, c.1962, 15 In., Pair _illus_ | 16250 |
| **9-Light,** Gilt, Bronze, Scrolled Arms, Sitting Putti, Scroll Base, 28 In. | 861 |
| **12-Light,** Bronze, Hanging Prism Pendants, Shaped Standard, Base, c.1885, 36 In., Pair | 300 |
| **12-Light,** Louis XV Style, Cut Glass, Brass, Clear Pendants, 33½ In. | 281 |
| **Brass,** 2-Light, Adjustable, Rope Twist Post, Finial, 3 Paw Feet, England, 14 In., Pair | 510 |
| **Brass,** Sconce, 2-Light, Sigismund III, Polish Arms, Pierced, c.1765, 12 In., Pair | 1140 |
| **Bronze,** Sconce, 2-Light, Bras De Lumiere, Louis XVI Style, Ormolu.c.1910, 23 In., Pair | 240 |
| **Silver,** 5 Fluted Arms, Leaf & Berry, Faceted Base, Georg Jensen, 17 In., Pair | 34220 |

**CANDLESTICKS** were made of brass, pewter, glass, sterling silver, plated silver, and all types of pottery and porcelain. The earliest candlesticks, dating from the sixteenth century, held the candle on a pricket (sharp pointed spike). These lost favor because in times of strife the large church candlesticks with prickets became formidable weapons, so the socket was mandated. Candlesticks changed in style through the centuries, and designs range from Classical to Rococo to Art Nouveau to Art Deco.

**Altar,** Fluted Column Stem, Leaves, Round Base, 3 Animal Paw Feet, 24 x 7½ In. ........ 167

| | |
|---|---:|
| **Brass,** Adjustable, Chinese Engraved, Butterfly Smoke Guard, 21½ In., Pair ............................... | 600 |
| **Brass,** Altar, Baluster Turned Squat Knop, Pricket, 3 Feet, c.1910, 44½ x 14 In. .................*illus* | 72 |
| **Brass,** Barley Twist Stem, Octagonal Base, Late 17th Century, 5¾ In. ........................................ | 210 |
| **Brass,** Capstan Foot, Banded Socle, Dutch, 5¼ In. ..................................................................... | 472 |
| **Brass,** Drip Pan, Late 17th Century, 11 In. ................................................................................ | 375 |
| **Brass,** Futuristic Cup, Round Base, Jessie Preston, 8 x 13 In., Pair ........................................... | 4270 |
| **Brass,** Grotto Style, Pricket, Spires, Trefoils, Arches, Crockets, 1800s, 58 In. ........................ | 307 |
| **Brass,** Paneled, Octagonal Base, Early 18th Century, 8½ In. ..................................................... | 120 |
| **Brass,** Petal Bases, Threaded Posts, Mid 18th Century, 4½ In. .................................................. | 540 |
| **Brass,** Round Base, Late 17th Century, 10 In. ............................................................................ | 375 |
| **Brass,** Spiral Turned, Drip Cups, England, 1800s, 20½ In., Pair .......................................*illus* | 250 |
| **Brass,** Theta, Impressed Signature, Robert Riddle Jarvie, 6 x 13½ In. .................................... | 1500 |
| **Bronze,** Art Nouveau, Nude, Holding Urn, On Sphere, Marble Base, McCartan, 18 In. ............. | 368 |
| **Bronze,** Gilt, Flared Foot, Scalloped Edge, Flowers, 19th Century, 10 In. ............................... | 400 |
| **Bronze,** Kneeling Winged Women, Holding Horns, France, c.1890, 15 In., Pair ...................... | 840 |
| **Bronze,** Leaves, Round Base, 18 In., Pair ................................................................................... | 984 |
| **Bronze,** Leaves, Thistles, Jessie Preston, 7 x 12 In. ................................................................... | 10370 |
| **Bronze,** Louis XV Style, Flowers, Scrolls, Shells, 21 In. ......................................................... | 438 |
| **Bronze,** Theta, Impressed Signature, Robert Riddle Jarvie, 6 x 13½ In. ................................. | 1464 |
| **Copper,** Hammered, Riveted Handle, G. Stickley, Stamped Als Ik Kan, 8½ In., Pair ...........*illus* | 173 |
| **Copper,** Square Domed Base, Charles Rohlfs, 7 x 14 In., Pair ................................................... | 3050 |
| **Enameled Brass,** Hardstone, Round Base, Thumbpiece, c.1890, 6⅜ In. .................................... | 123 |
| **Figural,** Crane, Decorated Candlecup, 16 In., Pair ...................................................................... | 140 |
| **Gilt Bronze,** Charles X, Basket Weave, Cast Base, Birds, Flowers, c.1830, 12 x 5 In., Pair ..... | 837 |
| **Gilt Bronze,** Louis XVI Style, Leaf Cast Stem, Fluted, Round Foot, 11 In., Pair ..................... | 3438 |
| **Gilt Bronze,** Neoclassical Style, Pricket, Fluted Shaft, Tripod Pedestal, Saints, 31 x 8 In., Pair.... | 120 |
| **Gilt Metal,** Neoclassical, Winged Caryatid Stem, Relief Decoration, 10¾ In., Pair ................ | 242 |
| **Giltwood,** Pricket, Paint, Tripart Base, Continental, 1700s, 22¾ In., Pair ............................... | 1250 |
| **Glass,** Amber, Baluster, Etched Flowers, Butterfly, Spider Web, 14 In., 4 Piece ....................... | 575 |
| **Glass,** Green Cut To Clear, Grape & Leaf, 1800s, 10 In., Pair .........................................*illus* | 560 |
| **Glass,** Yellow Olive Green, Striations, Pinched, Flattened Bulbous Base, 9 In. ....................... | 644 |
| **Iron,** Oscillating Top, Tripod Base, 22 In. .................................................................................. | 720 |
| **Iron,** S Shape Sections, Expanding Jamb, 6½ x 25 In. ................................................................ | 59 |
| **Iron,** Sconce, Shaped Hanging Crest, Pierced Gallery, 4 Penny Feet, 11 In. ............................ | 660 |
| **Majolica,** Flemish Style, Masks, Goat Head, Flowers, Leaves, Majolica, Minton, 15½ In. .......... | 861 |
| **Oak,** Openwork, Spiral Twist, 10 x 5¼ In. .................................................................................. | 120 |
| **Papier-Mache,** Gilt, Angle Holding Scrolled Stem, Plinth, 26¼ In., Pair ................................ | 984 |
| **Patinated Metal,** Seated Putti, Holding Cup, Marble Base, France, 20 x 12 In., Pair ............... | 250 |
| **Pewter,** Bulb Shape Base, American, 18th Century, 5 In., Pair ................................................... | 1125 |
| **Pewter,** Bulb Shape, Round Base, Mid 19th Century, 10 In., Pair .............................................. | 240 |
| **Pewter,** Painted, Village Scene, Tan Ground, Gilt Flowers, Leaves, 6¾ In., Pair ..................... | 47 |
| **Porcelain,** Blue & White, Bird, Butterfly, Flowers, Leaves, c.1900, 8 In. ................................ | 165 |
| **Silver Plate,** Edwardian, Tapering, Lobed Standard, Bobeche, 12 x 6 In., 4 Piece..................... | 246 |
| **Silver Plate,** Edwardian, William IV Style, Baluster Standard, Lobed Foot, 20 In., Pair ........... | 307 |
| **Silver Plate,** Lyre Shape, Reeded, Stepped, Base, 11⅜ In., Pair................................................. | 838 |
| **Silver,** Corinthian Column, Bobeche, Beaded, Gorham, 1915, 8 x 4 In., Pair .......................... | 799 |
| **Silver,** Figural, Amphora Shape Body, Scrolls, Flowers, Marked Wollenweber, 11 In. ............ | 750 |
| **Silver,** Flared, Fluted Stem, Stepped Base, Continental, c.1890, 7 In., Pair............................. | 369 |
| **Silver,** Flowers, Russia, 13½ In. ................................................................................................. | 540 |
| **Silver,** Fluted Column, Gadrooned Borders, William Davenport, c.1904, 6 In., Pair............... | 236 |
| **Silver,** George III, Neoclassical, Waisted, Square Base, Sheffield, 12 x 5 In., 4 Piece............. | 5412 |
| **Silver,** Georgian Style, Cylindrical, Fluted, Gorham, 1909, 10 In., 4 Piece .............................. | 1416 |
| **Silver,** Modern Style, Flared Base, Wind Drip Plate, Mark, Fisher, 1900s, 5 In., Pair............... | 354 |
| **Silver,** Octagonal Shape, Woodside, 8½ x 3½ In. ...................................................................... | 178 |
| **Silver,** Regency, Reeded Stem, Engraved Animals, Sheffield, c.1823, 12½ In. ......................... | 615 |
| **Silver,** Scroll, Leaves, Flowers, Hexagon Base, 17⅞ In. ............................................................ | 369 |
| **Silver,** Taper Stick, Turned Stem, Flared Round Foot, 3⅝ In., Pair .......................................... | 738 |
| **Silver,** Urn Shape, Vine Ribbons, Round Base, Marcus & Co., 10 In., 4 Piece......................... | 1125 |
| **Taper Jack,** Iron, Adjustable Drip Pan, Rope Twist Stem, Penny Feet, 11½ In. ........................ | 400 |
| **Wood,** Iron, Red Paint, 11⅞ In. .................................................................................................. | 540 |
| **Wrought & Sheet Iron,** Cutout Shaft, Square Pan Base, Splayed Feet, Hook, 9 In.................... | 805 |
| **Wrought Iron,** Tapered, 2 Adjustable Arms, Round Pans, Tripod, Penny Feet, 56 In.................. | 1495 |
| **Wrought Iron,** Torchere, Continental, 1800s, 75 In., Pair........................................................... | 330 |

**CANDLEWICK** *items may be listed in the Imperial Glass and Pressed Glass categories.*

**Candy Container,** Billiken, Glass, Painted, Metal Screw Cap
$44

Old Barn Auction

**Candy Container,** Halloween, Jack-O'-Lantern, Pumpkin, Glass, Wire Handle, 1920s, 2½ In.
$316

Hake's Americana & Collectibles

**Candy Container,** Moon Face, Smiling Man, Yellow, Dresden, 6½ In.
$354

Bertoia Auctions

**Candy Container,** Santa Claus, Banded Cloak, Glass, Old Paint
$66

Old Barn Auction

**Candy Container,** Santa Claus, Composition Head, Hands, Feet, Wooden Body, Rabbit Fur Beard, 11 In.
$826

Bertoia Auctions

**Candy Container,** Santa Claus, Composition, Rabbit Fur Beard, Bottle Brush Tree, 7 In.
$502

Bertoia Auctions

**CANDY CONTAINERS** have been popular since the late Victorian era. Collectors have long favored the glass containers, but now all types, including tin and papier-mache, are collected. Probably the earliest glass container sold commercially was the Liberty Bell made in 1876 for sale at the Centennial Exposition. Thousands of designs were made until the cost became too high in the 1960s. By the late 1970s, reproductions were being made and sold without the candy. Containers listed here are glass unless otherwise described. A Belsnickle is a nineteenth-century figure of Father Christmas. Some candy containers may be listed in Toy or in other categories.

| | |
|---|---:|
| **Baseball Player,** Bat, P On Jersey & Cap, Jar, Glass, Painted, Tin Lid, 4 In. | 1180 |
| **Belsnickle,** Blue Cape, Red Robe, Painted Face, Fur Beard, Germany, 16 In. | 2950 |
| **Belsnickle,** Composition, Silver Blue Robe, Feather Tree Sprig, Snowball Base, 6 In. | 649 |
| **Belsnickle,** Holding Tree, Red Hooded Robe, Cloth, Composition, 13 In. | 1534 |
| **Belsnickle,** Nodding, Gold Robe, Snow Flecked, Composition, Feather Tree, 7 In. | 944 |
| **Belsnickle,** Red Hooded Robe, Fir Tree, Long Beard, Germany, 12 In. | 2655 |
| **Belsnickle,** Robe, Composition, Rabbit Fur Beard, Feather Tree Sprig, 16 In. | 3245 |
| **Belsnickle,** Yellow Robe, Pink & Aqua Fur Trim, Tree Sprig, Snow Mound, 12 In. .............*illus* | 8260 |
| **Billiken,** Glass, Painted, Metal Screw Cap .............................................................................*illus* | 44 |
| **Boar's Head,** Silver, Red Silk Bag, Dresden Paper Trim, 2 ½ In. | 590 |
| **Boy,** Snowball, Bisque, Cotton Body, Side-Glancing Eyes, Germany, 5 ½ In. | 829 |
| **Bunny,** Brown, Crouching, Removable Base, Paper, 2 ½ In. | 472 |
| **Camera,** On Tripod, Clear, 1 ⅝ x 1 ⅞ x 2 ⅜ In. | 16 |
| **Cannon,** Clear, Red Metal Carriage, 4 ½ In. | 193 |
| **Car,** West Spec. Co., Limousine, Removable Top, Spoked Wheels, 2 ½ x 2 x 4 In. | 159 |
| **Dog,** Bulldog, Round Base, Painted, Tin Closure, 4 In. | 55 |
| **Doll,** Bisque, Green Silk Dress, Mohair, Brass Feet, 13 In. | 1093 |
| **Donkey & Cart,** Jeanette Glass, 1930s, 4 x 2 x 2 In. | 30 |
| **Duck On Basket,** Clear, Paint | 49 |
| **Easter Bunny,** Pushing Wheelbarrow, Bunny's Head Removes, 11 In. | 295 |
| **Father Christmas,** Blue Robe, Sled, Basket, Tin Litho, Meier, Germany, 4 In. | 6000 |
| **Father Christmas,** Composition, Fur-Like Robe, Tree, c.1900, 20 In. | 4977 |
| **Fire Engine,** Tin Spoked Wheels & Closure, Stough, 1914, 5 In. | 77 |
| **Gingerbread Man,** Papier-Mache, 2-Sided, Germany, 1940s, 8 x 6 In. | 295 |
| **Guitar,** Flower Decorated, Enclosure Card, 1904, 13 In. | 118 |
| **Halloween,** Cat, Arched Back, Black, Papier-Mache, 3 ¾ x 3 ½ In. | 65 |
| **Halloween,** Jack-O'-Lantern, Hat Box, Face On Lid, Painted, Germany, 1920, 3 x 2 In. | 285 |
| **Halloween,** Jack-O'-Lantern, Pumpkin, Glass, Wire Handle, 1920s, 2 ½ In. .............*illus* | 316 |
| **Horse,** Sparkplug, Painted Yellow Blanket, 3 x 1 ⅜ x 3 In. | 44 |
| **Independence Hall,** Clear, Coin Slot On Top, 7 ¼ In. | 38 |
| **Lighthouse,** Grayhead, Clear | 22 |
| **Locomotive,** Clear, 8 Red Wheels | 72 |
| **Moon Face,** Smiling Man, Yellow, Dresden, 6 ½ In. .............................................................*illus* | 354 |
| **Mr. & Miss Bunny,** Composition, Glass Eyes, Head Removes, Germany, 8 In., Pair | 118 |
| **Parrot Head,** Iridescent Multicolor, Silk Bag Base, Paper, Dresden, 2 In. | 1180 |
| **Pocket Watch,** Clear, Beaded Edge, Metal Ring, Tin Closure | 71 |
| **Rabbit,** Papier-Mache, Blue Cloth Coat, Striped Pants, Stars, Top Hat, 24 In. | 5605 |
| **Rabbit,** Standing On 4 Legs, Composition, Gold Trim, Germany, 14 x 17 In. | 3245 |
| **Ram's Head,** Curved Horns, Silver, Dresden, Germany, 2 ½ In. | 1121 |
| **Reindeer,** Composition, Flock Covering, Glass Eyes, Metal Antlers, Germany, 8 In. | 1416 |
| **Rocking Horse,** Clear, 3 x 2 ¼ x 4 ½ In. | 77 |
| **Rooster,** Crowing, Clear, Paint, 5 In. | 88 |
| **Santa Claus,** Banded Cloak, Glass, Old Paint .............................................................*illus* | 66 |
| **Santa Claus,** Banded Coat, Painted, 5 ¼ In. | 88 |
| **Santa Claus,** Composition Head, Hands, Feet, Wooden Body, Rabbit Fur Beard, 11 In. ......*illus* | 826 |
| **Santa Claus,** Composition, Rabbit Fur Beard, Bottle Brush Tree, 7 In. .........................*illus* | 502 |
| **Santa Claus,** Feather Tree, Orange, White Clothing, 7 In. | 270 |
| **Santa Claus,** Kaiser Cap, White Felt Robe, Blue Trim, Feather Tree, 8 In. | 1888 |
| **Santa Claus,** Paneled Coat, Clear, 5 ¼ In. | 66 |
| **Santa Claus,** Standing By Chimney, 3 ⅝ In. | 138 |
| **Soldier With Sword,** Glass, Painted .............................................................................*illus* | 220 |
| **St. Nicholas,** Blue Robe, White Trim, Composition, Cardboard, Feather Tree, 15 In. | 1298 |
| **Submarine,** Painted, Tin Sail & Closure, 2 x 1 ⅜ x 5 ½ In. | 143 |
| **Tank,** World War I Style, Painted, 2 ¼ x 1 ¾ x 4 ⅜ In. | 61 |
| **Toonerville Trolley,** Clear, 3 ½ In. | 297 |
| **Turkey,** Composition, Iridescent Feathers, Cardboard Base, Germany, 10 ¼ In. .................*illus* | 1062 |
| **Turkey,** Papier-Mache, Japan, 1920s, 4 ½ x 6 x 5 ½ In. | 125 |
| **Uncle Sam,** Smiling, Cardboard, Red, White, Blue, Fanny Farmer, 11 In. | 80 |
| **Veggie Man,** Pumpkin, Standing, Green Legs, Potato Feet, Composition, 7 In. | 1416 |

C

| | |
|---|---|
| **Victorian Girl,** Robe, Hood, Muff, Bisque Head, 1800s, 6½ In. | 595 |
| **Wheelbarrow,** Tin Front Wheel, 6 In. | 28 |
| **Windmill,** Pressed Glass, Tin Litho, Flag, Stripes, Tapered, West Bros, c.1914, 6 In. | 502 |

**CANES** and walking sticks were used by every well-dressed man in the nineteenth century, but by World War I the style had changed. Today canes are used by few but the infirm. Collectors prize old canes made with special features, like hidden swords, whiskey flasks, or risqué pictures seen through peepholes. Examples with solid gold heads or made from exotic materials are among the higher-priced canes. See also Scrimshaw.

| | |
|---|---|
| **Bone,** Chestnut, 2-Tone Handle, Mother-Of-Pearl, Dome Top, 5½ x 35½ In. | 59 |
| **Burl,** Nautical Fist Holding Baton, Ivory Ring, Hardwood Shaft, 1800s, 36 In. | 212 |
| **Deer Hoof,** Carved, Blued, Gilt Diamond Shape Blade, Rosewood Shaft, 1800s, 34 In. | 59 |
| **Dogwood,** Root Handle, Carved As Stag's Head, Metal Ferrule, c.1910, 35½ In. | 575 |
| **Ducks,** Bearded Lilies, Gilt Highlights, Silver Collar, Exotic Wood Shaft, 33 In. | 2880 |
| **Fist,** Clutching Snake, Silver Handle, Silver Handle, 36½ In. | 236 |
| **Horse Measuring,** Bamboo, Silver Handle, Retractable, 37 In. | 354 |
| **Ivory,** Handle, Nautical Theme, Ship Mast, Sail, Tackle, Rope, Walrus Head, 5 In. | 384 |
| **Lapis Lazuli,** Rock Crystal Rings, Mushroom Shape, Silver Collar, c.1895, 35½ In. | 900 |
| **Maple,** Snake, Lizard, Dog, Lady's Leg, Bird, Crescent Moon, Loudoun Co., Va., 35 In. | 2990 |
| **Oak,** Turned, Carved Names Of 55 Men Executed, Auburn Prison, c.1900, A. Lamb, 31 In. | 7339 |
| **Rock Crystal,** American Eagle, Polished Beak, Silver Collar, Ebony Shaft, 36 In. | 1900 |
| **Rock Crystal,** Faceted, Silver & Blue Enamel Stem, Christmas Holly, 36¾ In. | 700 |
| **Rosewood,** Horsehead Silver Top, Buccellati, c.1970, 36½ In. | 2125 |
| **Sailor's,** Whalebone, Baleen, Ivory, Relief Carved Heart, Angled Rings, 34 In. | 984 |
| **Silver,** Art Nouveau, Mucha Maidens, Snakewood, Ungar Brothers, 34¾ In. | 1300 |
| **Snake,** Green Spots, Red Mouth, Eyes, Paint, 37¾ In. | 300 |
| **Sword,** Ivory, Baleen, Silver Collar, Blue & Gilt Triangular Blade, 1700s, 36 In. | 1180 |
| **Sword,** Ivory, Carved, Faux Bamboo, Dragons, Monkeys, Frog, Butterflies, Flowers, 35 In. | 236 |
| **Walking Stick,** Applewood, Indian's Head In Relief, Lizard, c.1920, 35 In. | 575 |
| **Walking Stick,** Burl, Lapis Lazuli Handle, Gold Filigree Bands, Horn Tip, 36 In. | 649 |
| **Walking Stick,** Carved Eagle, G.A.R. Banner, Eagle, Civil War Generals' Busts, c.1890, 35 In. | 805 |
| **Walking Stick,** Carved Hand, Birds, Heart, Alligator, Va. | 633 |
| **Walking Stick,** Hickory, Carved Beavers, Hearts, Diamonds, c.1885, 39 In. | 489 |
| **Walking Stick,** Hickory, Red Paint, Coiled Rattlesnake, Carved Eyes, Faceted Handle, 36 In. | 518 |
| **Walking Stick,** Horse Head Handle, White Oak, Eagle, Frog, Coiled Snake, H.J., 1942, 35 In. | 633 |
| **Walking Stick,** Laminated Wood, Tapered, Loop Handle, N. Ditzel, Denmark, 1960s, 37 In. | 1125 |
| **Walking Stick,** Man Playing Flute Handle, Carved, Painted, Pa., c.1890, 30¾ In. | 510 |
| **Walking Stick,** Maple Branch, Carved Snake & Turtle, W.J. Ball, N.C., 1890s, 37 In. | 325 |
| **Walking Stick,** Maple, Bird In Hand Handle, Tack Eyes, Brass Ferrule, c.1880, 38 In. | 2415 |
| **Walking Stick,** Maple, Clover, Hearts, Fish, Coiled Snake, Carved, Old Paint, c.1890, 38 In. | 1840 |
| **Walking Stick,** Maple, Patriotic Carved Scenes, Zachariah Robinson, c.1865, 35 In. | 4888 |
| **Walking Stick,** Maple, Snake, Crosshatched, Brad Eyes, Hand Handle, c.1900, 40 In. | 518 |
| **Walking Stick,** Sterling Cap, Boat, Water, Palm Trees, c.1900, 36 In. | 375 |
| **Walking Stick,** Sterling Cap, Owl, Amber Eyes, Hardwood Shaft, c.1905, 30 In. | 365 |
| **Walking Stick,** Walnut, Zombie Face Handle, Georgia, 19th Century, 41½ In. | 354 |
| **Walking Stick,** Wrapped Snake Shaft, Carved, Painted, c.1900, 33 In. | 37 |
| **Wood Handle,** Shark's Vertebrae Shaft, Stacked, Tapered, Leather Rings, 36 In. | 360 |
| **Wood,** Carved, Bird, Red Glass Eyes, Bone Beak, Partidgewood, 34½ In. | 550 |
| **Wood,** Eagle Head Handle, Red Paint, Carved Textured Feathers, 1800s, 35½ In. | 215 |
| **Wood,** Stylized Dragon, Head & Neck Handle, Red Eyes, Exposed Teeth & Tongue, 36 In. | 185 |
| **Wood,** Whimsical, Glass Eyes, 24 In. | 210 |

**CANTON CHINA** is blue-and-white ware made near the city of Canton, in China, from about 1795 to the early 1900s. It is hand decorated with a landscape, building, bridge, and trees. There is never a person on the bridge. The "rain and cloud" border was used. It is similar to Nanking ware, which is listed in this book in its own category.

| | |
|---|---|
| **Cider Jug,** Lid, Foo Dog Finial, c.1850, 8½ In. | 2520 |
| **Cuspidor,** Wide Flared Mouth, c.1855, 6½ x 8 In. | 2160 |
| **Pitcher,** 1800s, 8¾ In. | 660 |
| **Pitcher,** Flared Base, c.1860, 12½ In. | 1440 |
| **Platter,** Boats, Buildings, Sea, Rounded Rectangle, c.1845, 17½ In. | 150 |
| **Platter,** Houses, Small Boats, Shaped Oval, c.1845, 16 In. | 313 |
| **Platter,** Landscape, 1800s, 18½ In. | 295 |
| **Platter,** Landscape, c.1900, 11¾ x 12½ In., Pair | 354 |
| **Platter,** Octagonal, Fishing Boats, Houses, 1800s, 16 In. ......*illus* | 150 |

Old Barn Auction

**Candy Container,** Soldier With Sword, Glass, Painted
$220

Bertoia Auctions

**Candy Container,** Turkey, Composition, Iridescent Feathers, Cardboard Base, Germany, 10¼ In.
$1,062

DuMouchelles Art Gallery

**Canton,** Platter, Octangular, Fishing Boats, Houses, 1800s, 16 In.
$150

**Canton,** Teapot, Landscape, Pagoda, Intertwining Handle, Pomegranate Finial, 1800s, 4½ In.
$200

Conestoga Auction Co., Inc.

**Capo-Di-Monte,** Trinket Box, Embossed, Battle & Hunt Scenes, Figures, Cherubs, Lid, 6 x 9¾ In.
$649

Conestoga Auction Co., Inc.

**Captain Marvel Pennant,** Standing Superhero, Felt, Frame, 16½ x 22½ In.
$120

Morphy Auctions

| | |
|---|---:|
| **Platter,** Oval, Landscape, 19th Century, 13½ In. | 120 |
| **Teapot,** Landscape, Pagoda, Intertwining Handle, Pomegranate Finial, 1800s, 4½ In. ......*illus* | 200 |
| **Teapot,** Lid, c.1850, 8 In. | 660 |
| **Tureen,** Sauce, Lid, Boats, Pagodas, Fish Mask Handles, c.1850, 13 In. | 688 |

**CAPO-DI-MONTE** porcelain was first made in Naples, Italy, from 1743 to 1759. The factory moved near Madrid, Spain, and operated there from 1771 until 1821. The Ginori factory of Doccia, Italy, acquired the molds and began using the crown and *N* mark. It eventually became the modern-day firm known as Richard Ginori, often referred to as Ginori or Capo-di-Monte. This company also used the crown and *N* mark. Richard Ginori was purchased by Gucci in 2013.

| | |
|---|---:|
| **Box,** Classical Mythological Scenes, Oval, 13 In. | 125 |
| **Charger,** Battle Scene, Putti, Fruit, Flower Garlands, 21 In. | 250 |
| **Clock,** Shelf, Charioteer, Dancing Muse, Tapered Case, Ram Masks, Griffin, 18 In. | 813 |
| **Figurine,** Boy Holding Garland, Girl Holding Bouquets, 21¾ In., Pair | 313 |
| **Figurine,** Monk, Holding Book, Staff, Painted, Gilt, Square Base, 6¼ In. | 63 |
| **Group,** 2 Seated Women, Arranging Flower Bouquets, 9¾ x 10 In. | 384 |
| **Group,** Horse Drawn Sleigh, 3 Figures, 1700s Attire, White, c.1900, 12 x 20 In. | 100 |
| **Jewelry,** Box, Relief Scenes, Goddess, Bacchanal Figures, Garlands, 3 x 9 In. | 288 |
| **Pedestal,** Porcelain, Cherubs, Landscape, 35¾ In. | 117 |
| **Pitcher,** Grapevine Handle, Satyrs, Putti Bands, 9 In., Pair | 250 |
| **Pitcher,** Playing Cherub Band, Mountain Man Handle, 16 In. | 60 |
| **Plaque,** Bacchus Drinking Scenes, Oval, c.1900, 2½ x 17½ In. | 460 |
| **Stein,** Cherubs, Nudes, Cherub On Goat Finial, Tongue Stuck Out, Handle, 11½ In. | 1003 |
| **Stein,** Relief, Julius Caesar Announced As Emperor, Crown N Mark, c.1885, 16 In. | 2940 |
| **Table Casket,** Hinged Lid, House Shape, Bail Handles, Figures, 14 In. | 1625 |
| **Tankard,** Hinged, Cherub, Mermaid, N & Crown Mark, 14 In. | 330 |
| **Tankard,** Multicolor, Entombment Of Christ, Angel Finial, Hinged, 9¼ In. | 461 |
| **Tea & Coffee Set,** Porcelain, Painted, 15 Piece | 720 |
| **Trinket Box,** Embossed, Battle & Hunt Scenes, Figures, Cherubs, Lid, 6 x 9¾ In. .....*illus* | 649 |
| **Tureen,** Handles, 3-Footed, Flower Lid, 17 x 11 x 15 In. | 95 |
| **Tureen,** Underplate, Toasting Youth Finial, Winged Women Handles, Bacchus, 13 In. | 313 |
| **Urn,** Lid, Classical Cherub Scene, Marked, 17 In. | 207 |
| **Urn,** Lid, Mermen Handles, Foot, Baluster Shape, 29 In. | 250 |
| **Urn,** Lid, Ram's Head Corners, Painted, Finial, 1900s, 11 In. | 210 |
| **Urn,** Lid, Satyr Finial, Ram Masks, Fleur-De-Lis, Flower Scrolls, 20½ In., Pair | 563 |
| **Urn,** Pedestal, Classical Scenes, Putti, Lovers Reserve, Gilt Accents, c.1950, 53 In. | 120 |
| **Vase,** Dome Lid, Urn Shape, Relief Figures, Animals, Finial, Multicolor, Gilt, 23 In. | 207 |
| **Vase,** Urn Shape, Dome Cover, Relief Figures, Animals, Horn Player Finial, 23 In. | 184 |

**CAPTAIN MARVEL** was introduced in February 1940 in Whiz comic books. An orphan named Billy Batson met the wizard, Shazam, and whenever he said the magic word he was transformed into a superhero. A movie serial was released in 1940. The comic was discontinued in 1954. A second Captain Marvel appeared in 1966, a third in 1967. Only the original was transformed by shouting "Shazam."

| | |
|---|---:|
| **Figure,** Mary, Yellow Emblem, Captain Marvel, Kerr, Resin, 1946, 5 In., Pair | 417 |
| **Membership Card,** Mary Marvel Club, 2-Sided, 1946, 2¾ x 4 In. | 201 |
| **Paper Doll,** Mary Marvel, Proof Pages, Outfits, c.1940, 17 x 23 In., 9 Piece | 575 |
| **Patch,** Colors, Felt, Shield Design, Standing, Hands On Hips, 3 x 4 In. | 115 |
| **Pennant,** Standing Superhero, Felt, Frame, 16½ x 22½ In. .....*illus* | 120 |
| **Puzzle,** Marvel Riding A Flaming Plane Engine, Box, 1941, 13 x 17 In. | 317 |
| **Soap Box,** Captain, Mary Marvel, Illustrated Soap Co., Inc., 1947, 6 x 6 In. | 886 |
| **Toy,** Cars, Orange, Yellow, Blue, Green, Windup, No.1, No. 2, No. 3, No. 4, 1947, 4 Pieces | 392 |

**CAPTAIN MIDNIGHT** began as a network radio show in September 1940. The first comic book appeared in July 1941. Captain Midnight was really the aviator Captain Albright, who was to defeat the Nazis. A movie serial was made in 1942 and a comic strip was published for a short time. The comic book version of Captain Midnight ended his career in 1948. Radio premiums are the prized collector memorabilia today.

| | |
|---|---:|
| **Badge,** Decoder, Brass, Pinback, 1940s, 1¾ x 2¼ In. | 70 |
| **Badge,** Decoder, Manuel, 1957 | 65 |
| **Badge,** Decoder, Mirro-Flash Code-O-Graph, Brass, Premium, 1946 | 65 |
| **Badge,** Flight Patrol, Skelly, Oil Gas Station, Propeller, 1938 | 34 |
| **Book,** Joyce Of The Secret Squadron, R.R. Winterbotham, 1942 | 18 |
| **Keychain Fob,** Skelly, Flight Patrol Membership, Brass, 1¼ In. | 21 |

| | |
|---|---|
| **Membership Card,** Secret Squadron, Ovaltine Premium, 1957 | 10 |
| **Patch,** Secret Squadron Emblem, Ovaltine Premium, 1957 | 12 |
| **Portrait,** Decal, Transfer, Premium, 1948, 4 x 4 In. | 78 |
| **Whistle,** Decoder, Celluloid, Red, Blue, 1947, 1¾ In. | 38 |

**CARAMEL SLAG,** *see Imperial Glass category.*

**CARDS** listed here include advertising cards (often called trade cards), baseball cards, playing cards, and others. Color photographs were rare in the nineteenth century, so companies gave away colorful cards with pictures of children, flowers, products, or related scenes that promoted the company name. These were often collected and stored in albums. Baseball cards also date from the nineteenth century, when they were used by tobacco companies as giveaways. Gum cards were started in 1933, but it was not until after World War II that the bubble gum cards favored today were produced. Today over 1,000 cards are issued each year by the gum companies. Related items may be found in the Christmas, Halloween, Movie, Paper, and Postcard categories.

| | |
|---|---|
| **Advertising,** Mercifulness Hudson's Soap, Smiling Black Face, 7½ In. | 60 |
| **Baseball,** Eddie Mathews, 3rd Base, Topps, 1964 | 482 |
| **Baseball,** Joe DiMaggio, Gourdey Heads Up, 1938, 9½ In. | 150 |
| **Baseball,** Tris Speaker, Hassan Cigarettes, Gold Border, 1911 | 93 |
| **Football,** Johnny Unitas, Baltimore Colts, Topps, No. 1, 1959 ............*illus* | 146 |
| **Football,** Sammy Baugh, Signed, Bowman, 1951 | 146 |
| **Greeting,** Valentine, Car, Fold-Out, Embossed, Honeycomb Inside, Die Cut, 14 In. ............*illus* | 118 |
| **Greeting,** Valentine, Cupid, Multicolor Flowers, Wreath, Verse, Paper Lace, c.1850, 11 x 9 In. | 142 |
| **Greeting,** Valentine, Cut Paper, Hearts, Crosses, Ink Inscriptions, Round, 1843, Frame, 12 In. | 1150 |
| **Greeting,** Valentine, Cutwork, Watercolor, Round, Crowns, Hearts, Lions, Flowers, Frame, 1700s, 13 In. | 2829 |
| **Greeting,** Valentine, Scherenschnitte, Heart Cutout, Red, Green Watercolor Trim, c.1810, 6 x 5 In. | 472 |
| **Greeting,** Valentine, Silver Dresden Paper Bird House, Fold-Out, Germany, 8 In. | 148 |
| **Playing,** Crow Brand, N.Y. Consolidated Card Co., c.1910 | 50 |
| **Playing,** Steamboat, A. Dougherty, Convex Corners, c.1905, Full Deck | 80 |
| **Playing,** Tiger Brand, Russell & Morgan, Round Corners, c.1885, Full Deck | 110 |
| **Valentine,** Love Token, Heart In Hand, Cut Paper, Woven Hair, Gilt Frame, c.1875, 6 x 5 In. | 2875 |
| **Victorian Girl,** Watt & Peterson, Embossed, Die Cut, Glitter, Litho, 16 x 30 In. | 345 |

**CARDER,** *see Aurene and Steuben categories.*

**CARLTON WARE** was made at the Carlton Works of Stoke-on-Trent, England, beginning about 1890. The firm traded as Wiltshaw & Robinson until 1957. It was renamed Carlton Ware Ltd. in 1958. The company went bankrupt in 1995, but the name is still in use.

| | |
|---|---|
| **Cup & Saucer,** Leaves, Red & Yellow Primroses, c.1945 | 45 |
| **Egg Cup,** Novelty, Mary Jane Shoes, Blue, 2⅜ In. | 38 |
| **Jug,** Black, Pink Flowers, Footed, c.1910, 6 In. | 110 |
| **Match Safe,** Trademark, Bird In Circle, c.1900, 2 x 3 In. | 90 |
| **Mug,** Advertising, Man Smoking, 5 In. | 45 |
| **Mug,** Wild Rose, Undulating, Crimped, c.1920 | 99 |
| **Plate,** Flowers, Cobalt Blue & Gold Trim, Scalloped Edge, c.1898, 6 In. | 24 |
| **Plate,** Islands, Pagoda, Flowers, Plants, Woman, Maroon Ground, 8 In. | 135 |
| **Tea Plate,** Pink Buttercup, 6 In. | 10 |
| **Tea Plate,** Yellow Water Lily, Swirled, 7 In., 2 Piece | 23 |
| **Toast Rack,** Foxglove Pattern, Yellow, 5 Bar, 4½ x 2¼ In. | 75 |
| **Tray,** Fruit Basket Handles, Yellow, 6 x 3¾ In. | 50 |

**CARNIVAL GLASS** was an inexpensive, iridescent pressed glass made from about 1907 to about 1925. More than 1,000 different patterns are known. In September 2014 an important collection was sold and resulted in very high prices. Some of them are included here. Carnival glass is currently being reproduced.

| | |
|---|---|
| **Acanthus,** Bowl, Ruffled Edge, Marigold, 8 In. | 38 |
| **Acorn Burrs,** Punch Set, Ice Blue, 7 Piece | 750 |
| **Acorn Burrs,** Punch Set, White, 8 Piece | 2200 |
| **Acorn,** Bowl, Ruffled Edge, Red, 7½ In. | 325 |
| **April Showers,** Vase, Amethyst, 11 In. | 15 |
| **April Showers,** Vase, Footed, Scalloped, Blue, 9½ In. | 15 |
| **Basketweave,** Basket, Open Edge, 2 Sides Up, Black Amethyst | 40 |
| **Big Butterfly,** Tumbler, Olive Green | 675 |
| **Big Fish,** Bowl, 3-In-1 Edge, Marigold, 7 In. | 575 |

**Card,** Football, Johnny Unitas, Baltimore Colts, Topps, No. 1, 1959
$146

Worthridge Auction

**Card,** Greeting, Valentine, Car, Fold-Out, Embossed, Honeycomb Inside, Die Cut, 14 In.
$118

Bertoia Auctions

**Carnival Glass,** Cherry, Bowl, Green, Millersburg, 7 In.
$83

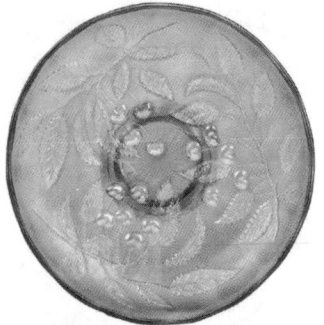

Conestoga Auction Co., Inc.

**Carnival Glass,** Goddess Of Harvest, Bowl, Blue, Candy Ribbon Edge, Fenton, 9 ½ In.
$52,500

Seeck Auctions

**Carnival Glass,** Grape & Cable, Hat Pin Holder, Amethyst, Northwood, 6 ½ In.
$118

Conestoga Auction Co., Inc.

| | |
|---|---:|
| **Big Fish,** Bowl, Ice Cream, Amethyst, Satin, 7 ¼ In. | 550 |
| **Bird & Grape,** Wall Pocket, Marigold | 10 |
| **Blackberry Block,** Pitcher, Water, Tankard Shape, Green | 1200 |
| **Blackberry Bramble,** Compote, Ruffled Edge, Green | 30 |
| **Blackberry Spray,** Hat, Ruffled Edge, Blue | 15 |
| **Blackberry Wreath,** Bowl, Green Satin, 16 Panels, Crimped Rim, Millersburg, 2 ⅜ x 8 ¾ In. | 58 |
| **Blackberry Wreath,** Bowl, Ice Cream, Amethyst, 7 In. | 20 |
| **Blossomtime,** Compote, Ruffled Edge, Green | 120 |
| **Blueberry,** Tumbler, Blue Silver | 40 |
| **Butterfly & Berry,** Vase, Flared, Ruffled Edge, Red, 8 ½ In. | 85 |
| **Cherries,** Sauce Bowl, Ruffled Edge, Peach Opal, Dugan | 10 |
| **Cherry Chain,** Plate, Marigold, 6 In. | 20 |
| **Cherry,** Bowl, Green, Millersburg, 7 In. *illus* | 83 |
| **Cherry,** Tumbler, Enameled, Blue | 100 |
| **Chesterfield,** Cake Plate, Red Stretch, 5 x 9 In. | 350 |
| **Christmas Snowflake,** Pickle Castor, Silver Plated Stand, Forks, L.G. Wright, 1900s, 3 x 5 In. | 184 |
| **Cone & Tie,** Tumbler, Purple | 675 |
| **Corinth,** Vase, Jack-In-The-Pulpit, Marigold On Milk Glass, 9 ½ In. | 325 |
| **Courthouse,** Bowl, Ruffled Edge, Amethyst, 8 In. | 650 |
| **Crackle,** Water Set, Pitcher, Tumbler, Marigold, 2 Piece | 90 |
| **Cut & Roses,** Rose Bowl, Green | 35 |
| **Dahlia,** Water Set, Pitcher, Tumblers, Marigold, 7 Piece | 550 |
| **Daisy & Little Flowers,** Tumbler, Enameled, Blue | 40 |
| **Daisy,** Tumbler, Enameled, Blue | 40 |
| **Dance Of The Veils,** Vase, Flared, Marigold, Footed | 450 |
| **Dandelion,** Water Set, Pitcher, Tankard Shape, Tumblers, White, 7 Piece | 1200 |
| **Diamond Point,** Vase, Flared, Purple, 9 ½ In. | 15 |
| **Diamond Point,** Vase, Green, 10 ½ In. | 25 |
| **Diamond Rib,** Vase, Squat, Whimsy Ruffled Edge, Green, 6 In. | 135 |
| **Double Daisy Variant,** Pitcher, Water, Enameled, Marigold | 500 |
| **Double Stem Rose,** Bowl, Domed Foot, White | 20 |
| **Dragon & Lotus,** Bowl, Blue, 9 In. | 20 |
| **Dragon & Lotus,** Bowl, Ruffled Edge, Aqua Opal, 9 In. | 2000 |
| **Dragon & Lotus,** Bowl, Ruffled Edge, Red, 9 In. | 1000 |
| **Dragon & Strawberry,** Bowl, Ice Cream, Marigold | 400 |
| **Drapery,** Tumbler, White | 800 |
| **Drapery,** Vase, Sapphire, 8 In. | 1100 |
| **Elk,** Nappy, Ruffled Edge, Purple | 7500 |
| **Embroidered Mums,** Bowl, Ribbed Back, Ruffled Edge, Aqua Opal | 3500 |
| **Farmyard,** Bowl, 3-In-1 Edge, Purple, 10 In. | 2500 |
| **Farmyard,** Chop Plate, Crimped Edge, Blue, Contemporary, 10 ½ In. | 30 |
| **Fashion,** Tumbler, Smoke | 25 |
| **Field Flower,** Tumbler, Purple | 130 |
| **Field Thistle,** Plate, Marigold, 6 In. | 40 |
| **Fine Rib,** Vase, Stick, Blue 15 In. | 20 |
| **Flowering Dill,** Dish, Hat Shape, Ruffled Edge, Marigold | 15 |
| **Forget-Me-Not,** Pitcher, Water, Tankard Shape, Enameled, 3 Banded, Blue | 550 |
| **Forget-Me-Not,** Pitcher, Water, Tankard Shape, Enameled, Marigold | 300 |
| **Forget-Me-Not,** Water Set, Tankard Shape, 3 Tumblers, 3 Banded, Amethyst, 3 Piece | 450 |
| **Forget-Me-Not,** Water Set, Tankard Shape, 4 Tumblers, 3 Banded, Green, 5 Piece | 450 |
| **Four Seventy Four,** Vase, Marigold, 10 In. | 500 |
| **Frolicking Bears,** Pitcher, Water, Green | 26000 |
| **Frolicking Bears,** Tumbler, Green | 4000 |
| **Fruits & Flowers,** Bonbon, Marigold | 25 |
| **Gay Nineties,** Tumbler, Marigold, Millersburg | 525 |
| **Gay Nineties,** Water Set, Pitcher, Tumbler, Amethyst, Millersburg, 7 Piece | 2100 |
| **God & Home,** Tumbler, Blue | 140 |
| **Goddess Of Harvest,** Bowl, Blue, Candy Ribbon Edge, Fenton, 9 ½ In. *illus* | 52500 |
| **Good Luck,** Bowl, Ruffled Edge, Ribbed Back, Ice Green, 8 ½ In. | 3000 |
| **Good Luck,** Bowl, Ruffled Edge, Ribbed Back, Marigold, 8 ½ In. | 75 |
| **Good Luck,** Plate, Ribbed Back, Ice Blue, 9 In. | 5500 |
| **Grape & Cable,** Cup, Amethyst, Northwood | 17 |
| **Grape & Cable,** Hat Pin Holder, Amethyst, Northwood, 6 ½ In. *illus* | 118 |
| **Grape & Cable,** Hatpin Holder, Aqua Opal | 21000 |
| **Grape & Cable,** Tumbler, Green | 15 |
| **Grape Arbor,** Pitcher, Water, Tankard Shape, Ice Green | 5500 |
| **Grape Arbor,** Tumbler, Blue | 170 |

| | | |
|---|---|---|
| **Grape Arbor,** Water Set, Pitcher, Tankard Shape, Tumbler, Ice Blue, 7 Piece | | 1200 |
| **Grapevine Lattice,** Tumbler Marigold | | 15 |
| **Grapevine Lattice,** Tumbler, Purple | | 325 |
| **Hanging Cherries,** Bowl, Hobnail Back, Ruffled Edge, Marigold, 10 In. | | 950 |
| **Hanging Cherries,** Bowl, Ice Cream, Marigold, Satin, 7 In. | | 100 |
| **Hanging Cherries,** Tumbler, Green, Millersburg | | 165 |
| **Hanging Cherries,** Tumbler, Straight Sided Base, Green, Millersburg | | 160 |
| **Hearts & Flowers,** Bowl, 3-In-1 Edge, Blue, Highlights, 8 ½ In. | | 575 |
| **Hearts & Flowers,** Bowl, Ruffled, Ribbed Back, Marigold, 8 ½ In. | | 180 |
| **Hearts & Flowers,** Plate, Ribbed Back, Marigold, 9 In. | | 275 |
| **Heavy Web,** Bowl, Ruffled Edge, Peach Opal, 11 In. | | 1200 |
| **Holly,** Bowl, 3-In-1 Edge, Marigold On Moonstone | | 500 |
| **Holly,** Bowl, Ruffled Edge, Blue Opal, 9 In. | | 21 |
| **Holly,** Bowl, Ruffled Edge, Red, 9 In. | | 800 |
| **Holly,** Plate, Aqua Opal, Fenton, 9 In. | *illus* | 22000 |
| **Holly,** Plate, Ice Green, 9 In. | | 16000 |
| **Holly,** Plate, Marigold, 9 In. | | 2550 |
| **Honeycomb & Beads,** Banana Boat, Peach Opal | | 15 |
| **Honeycomb & Hobstar,** Vase, Footed, Amethyst | | 4250 |
| **Horse Medallion,** Bowl, Blue, 7 In. | | 110 |
| **Horse Medallion,** Bowl, Ruffled Marigold, 7 In. | | 55 |
| **Imperial Grape,** Bowl, Ruffled Edge, Light Marigold, 11 In. | | 10 |
| **Imperial Grape,** Bowl, Ruffled Edge, Marigold, 11 In. | | 65 |
| **Imperial Grape,** Bowl, Ruffled Edge, Purple, 11 In. | | 25 |
| **Imperial Grape,** Decanter, Smoke | | 95 |
| **Inverted Feather,** Pitcher, Water, Tankard Shape, Marigold | | 1300 |
| **Inverted Strawberry,** Pitcher, Water, Tankard Shape, Amethyst | | 575 |
| **Leaf Chain,** Plate, Marigold, 7 In. | | 15 |
| **Lily Of The Valley,** Water Set, Pitcher, Tumbler, Blue, 6 Piece | | 4750 |
| **Little Beads,** Compote, Peach Opal | | 20 |
| **Little Flowers,** Bowl, Ruffled Edge, Amberina, 10 In. | | 650 |
| **Long Thumbprint,** Vase, Squat, Jack-In-The-Pulpit Shape, Green, 6 ½ In. | | 90 |
| **Lotus,** Bowl, Blue, Fenton, 8 ⅝ In. | *illus* | 59 |
| **Lotus,** Tumbler, Enameled, Marigold | | 10 |
| **Luster Rose,** Water Set, Pitcher, Tumbler, Purple | | 700 |
| **Luster Rose,** Whimsy, Flared, Powder Blue | | 180 |
| **Memphis,** Punch Set, Marigold, 8 Piece | | 350 |
| **Mitered Ovals,** Vase, Ruffled Edge, Green, Millersburg | | 11000 |
| **Morning Glory,** Vase, Funeral, Marigold, 12 ½ In. | | 625 |
| **Morning Glory,** Vase, Funeral, Purple | | 275 |
| **Morning Glory,** Vase, Funeral, Smoke | | 1350 |
| **Morning Glory,** Vase, Jack-In-The-Pulpit, Marigold, 9 ½ In. | | 75 |
| **Multi Fruits & Flowers,** Tumbler, Amethyst, Millersburg | | 425 |
| **Nautilus,** Vase, Whimsy, Purple, 8 In. | | 250 |
| **Nearcut,** Pitcher, Water, Marigold | | 110 |
| **Nine Sixteen,** Vase, Squat, Blue, Ruffled Edge, 7 ½ In. | | 25 |
| **Nippon,** Plate, Ribbed Back, Ice Green, Northwood, 9 In. | | 12000 |
| **Nugget,** Creamer, Blue, Contemporary | | 15 |
| **Open Rose,** Centerpiece, Footed, Smoke | | 450 |
| **Optic & Buttons,** Pitcher, Water, Marigold | | 300 |
| **Orange Tree,** Powder Jar, Blue | | 35 |
| **Oriental Poppy,** Pitcher, Water, Tankard Shape, Ribbed Interior, Ice Green | | 5000 |
| **Oriental Poppy,** Tumbler, Purple | | 45 |
| **Oriental Poppy,** Water Set, Pitcher, Tankard Shape, 6 Tumblers, White, Frosty, 7 Piece | | 700 |
| **Oriental Poppy,** Water Set, Purple, Pitcher, 6 Tumblers, Northwood, c.1915 | | 633 |
| **Palm Beach,** Berry Bowl, Gooseberry Interior, Honey Amber | | 30 |
| **Peach & Pear,** Banana Boat, Marigold | | 500 |
| **Peacock & Urn,** Bowl, Blue Fluted Edge, Fenton, 9 In. | *illus* | 47 |
| **Peacock & Urn,** Bowl, Ice Cream, Master, Aqua Opal, Northwood, 10 In. | *illus* | 34000 |
| **Peacock At The Fountain,** Bowl, Fruit, Ruffled Edge, Renninger Blue | | 800 |
| **Peacock At The Fountain,** Punch Set, Ruffled Edge, Purple, 10 Piece | | 950 |
| **Peacock At The Fountain,** Punch Set, White, 7 Piece | | 2000 |
| **Peacock At The Fountain,** Water Set, Blue, Pitcher, 6 Tumblers, c.1920, Pitcher, 8 In., 7 Piece. | | 518 |
| **Peacock Tail,** Dish, 3-Sided, Green, 7 In. | | 20 |
| **Peacock Urn,** Bowl, Ice Cream, Ice Green, Northwood, 10 In. | | 575 |
| **Peacocks On The Fence,** Bowl, Purple, Amethyst, Scalloped Rim, Northwood, c.1915, 2 x 9 In. | | 184 |
| **Peacocks On The Fence,** Plate, Flowers, Berries, Amethyst Plum, Northwood, 9 ½ In. | | 207 |

**Carnival Glass,** Holly, Plate, Aqua Opal, Fenton, 9 In.
$22,000

Seeck Auctions

**Carnival Glass,** Lotus, Bowl, Blue, Fenton, 8 ⅝ In.
$59

Conestoga Auction Co., Inc.

**Carnival Glass,** Peacock & Urn, Bowl, Blue Fluted Edge, Fenton, 9 In.
$47

Conestoga Auction Co., Inc.

97

**Carnival Glass,** Peacock & Urn, Bowl, Ice Cream, Master, Aqua Opal, Northwood, 10 In. $34,000

Seeck Auctions

**Carnival Glass,** Poppy Show, Plate, Aqua Opal, Pastel Iridescence, Northwood, 9 In. $24,000

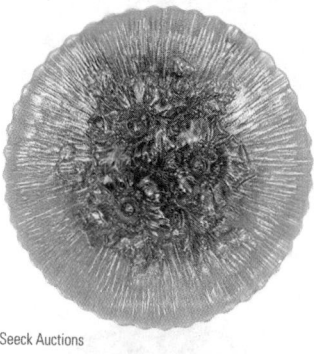

Seeck Auctions

**Carnival Glass,** Ski Star, Bowl, Peach, Scalloped Edge, Fluted, Dugan, 10½ In. $24

Conestoga Auction Co., Inc.

**Carnival Glass,** Water Lily, Bowl, Marigold, Footed, Fenton, 10 In., Pair $12

Conestoga Auction Co., Inc.

| | |
|---|---:|
| **Peacocks,** Bowl, 3-In-1 Edge, Ribbed Back, Ice Blue, 9 In. | 525 |
| **Peacocks,** Bowl, 3-In-1 Edge, Ribbed Back, Purple, 9 In. | 190 |
| **Peacocks,** Bowl, Ribbed Back, Aqua Opal, 9 In. | 550 |
| **Peacocks,** Bowl, Ruffled Edge, Ribbed Back, Blue, 9 In. | 250 |
| **Peacocks,** Plate, Ribbed Back, Ice Blue, 9 In. | 800 |
| **Pearly Dots,** Bowl, Ruffled, Amber, 8¼ In. | 15 |
| **Persian Garden,** Sauce Bowl, White | 25 |
| **Petal & Fan,** Bowl, Ruffled Edge, Purple, 10 In. | 375 |
| **Plume Panels,** Vase, Red, 10½ In. | 450 |
| **Poinsettia,** Tumbler, Green Opalescent, Northwood Glass, c.1910, 3⅞ In. | 219 |
| **Poppy Show,** Bowl, Ruffled Edge, Ice Blue, 9 In. | 275 |
| **Poppy Show,** Bowl, Ruffled Edge, Marigold, 9 In. | 120 |
| **Poppy Show,** Bowl, Ruffled Edge, White, 9 In. | 110 |
| **Poppy Show,** Plate, Aqua Opal, Pastel Iridescence, Northwood, 9 In. ...........*illus* | 24000 |
| **Poppy Show,** Plate, Ice Blue, 9 In. | 650 |
| **Poppy Show,** Plate, Marigold, 9 In. | 400 |
| **Poppy Show,** Plate, White, 9 In. | 225 |
| **Ragged Robin,** Bowl, Crimped Ruffled Edge, Blue, 8½ In. | 160 |
| **Ranger,** Tumbler, Marigold | 45 |
| **Ribbon Tie,** Bowl, Blue, 9 In. | 20 |
| **Ribbon Tie,** Bowl, Ice Cream, Marigold | 50 |
| **Ripple,** Vase, Green, 14½ In. | 20 |
| **Rose Column,** Vase, Marigold, Millersburg | 5500 |
| **Rose Show,** Bowl, Aqua Opal, Ruffled Edge, 8¾ In. | 750 |
| **Rose Show,** Bowl, Ice Blue, Ruffled Edge, 8¾ In. | 400 |
| **Rose Show,** Bowl, Lime Green Opal, Ruffled Edge, 8¾ In. | 1600 |
| **Rose Show,** Bowl, White, Ruffled Edge, 8¾ In. | 135 |
| **Rose Show,** Plate, Blue Iridescent, 9 In. | 400 |
| **Rose Show,** Plate, Blue, 9 In. | 500 |
| **Rose Show,** Plate, Emerald Green, 9 In. | 1100 |
| **Rose Show,** Plate, Marigold On Custard, 9 In. | 3750 |
| **Rose Show,** Plate, Marigold, 9 In. | 350 |
| **Rustic,** Vase, Crimped Edge, Blue, 9½ In. | 15 |
| **Rustic,** Vase, Funeral, Plunger Base, Blue, 22½ In. | 1150 |
| **Rustic,** Vase, Red | 2500 |
| **Rustic,** Vase, Squat, Marigold, 10 In. | 125 |
| **Scales & Greek Key,** Bowl, Domed Foot, Green, 8¾ In. | 10 |
| **Shell & Sand,** Bowl, Ruffled Edge, Purple, 8 In. | 250 |
| **Ski Star,** Bowl, Peach, Scalloped Edge, Fluted, Dugan, 10½ In. ...........*illus* | 24 |
| **Ski Star,** Bowl, Ruffled Edge, Peach Opal, 10½ In. | 25 |
| **Smooth Rays,** Bowl, Ruffled Edge, Purple, 8 In. | 70 |
| **Star Of David,** Bowl, Ruffled Edge, Domed Foot, Purple | 25 |
| **Stippled Grape & Cable,** Bonbon, 4-Sided, Peach Opal | 13000 |
| **Stippled Grape & Cable,** Bowl, Ribbed Back, 3-In-1 Edge, Aqua Opal | 800 |
| **Stippled Peacock,** Bowl, Renninger Blue | 1200 |
| **Stippled Peacock,** Bowl, Smoke Clambroth | 1300 |
| **Stippled Rays,** Bowl, 3-In-1 Edge, Purple | 275 |
| **Stippled Strawberry,** Bowl, Ribbed Back, Ruffled Edge, Aqua Opal | 12000 |
| **Strawberry Scroll,** Tumbler, Blue | 50 |
| **Strawberry,** Plate, Purple, 9 In. | 45 |
| **Thin Rib,** Vase, Flared, Ruffled Edge, Aqua Opal, Butterscotch, 12 In. | 2200 |
| **Three Row,** Vase, Bulbous, Marigold | 1700 |
| **Toothpick Holder,** White, Paper Label, Imperial, Contemporary, 2¼ In. | 12 |
| **Tree Bark,** Pitcher, Aqua | 25 |
| **Tree Trunk,** Vase, Aqua Opal, 11½ In. | 19000 |
| **Tree Trunk,** Vase, Blue, 9 In. | 100 |
| **Tree Trunk,** Vase, Blue, 9-Petal Rim, Flared, Northwood, c.1915, 16 x 4 In. | 115 |
| **Tree Trunk,** Vase, Funeral, Blue, 19 In. | 2400 |
| **Tree Trunk,** Vase, Funeral, Purple, Ruffled Edge, 17 In. | 625 |
| **Tree Trunk,** Vase, Ice Blue, Squat, 7 In. | 950 |
| **Tree Trunk,** Vase, Marigold, 11¾ In. | 80 |
| **Tree Trunk,** Vase, Renninger Blue, 15 In. | 4300 |
| **Tree Trunk,** Vase, Squat, Purple, 6½ In. | 160 |
| **Triands,** Vase, Marigold, 8 In. | 35 |
| **Trout & Fly,** Bowl, 3-In-1 Edge, Amethyst Satin, 8¾ In. | 400 |
| **Trout & Fly,** Bowl, 3-In-1 Edge, Green Satin, 8¾ In. | 375 |
| **Trout & Fly,** Bowl, Square, Marigold, 8¾ In. | 850 |

| | |
|---|---|
| **Twig,** Vase, Crimped Edge, Purple, 3 ¾ In. | 600 |
| **Twig,** Vase, Jack-In-The-Pulpit, Crimped Edge, Purple, 3 ½ In. | 550 |
| **Vintage,** Bowl, 3-In-1 Edge, Red, 9 In. | 1050 |
| **Vintage,** Bowl, Ice Cream, Hobnail Back, Green Satin | 375 |
| **Water Lily,** Berry Bowl, Footed, Marigold | 35 |
| **Water Lily,** Bowl, Marigold, Footed, Fenton, 10 In., Pair ...............*illus* | 12 |
| **Western Thistle,** Pitcher, Water, Amber | 205 |
| **Wild Strawberry,** Bowl, Ruffled Edge, Lime Green, 10 In. | 1800 |
| **Wild Strawberry,** Plate, Handgrip, Green, 7 In. | 50 |
| **Windflower,** Dish, Ice Cream, Marigold | 65 |
| **Wishbone,** Bowl, Green, 10 In. | 250 |

---

**CAROUSEL** or merry-go-round figures were first carved in the United States in 1867 by Gustav Dentzel. Collectors discovered the charm of the hand-carved figures in the 1970s, and they were soon classed as folk art. Most desirable are the figures other than horses, such as pigs, camels, lions, or dogs. A jumper is a figure that was made to move up and down on a pole; a stander was placed in a stationary position.

| | |
|---|---|
| **Camel,** Stander, Outside Row, Carved, Painted, Charles Dare, c.1890, 43 ½ x 55 In. | 5400 |
| **Dog,** Red Saddle, France, 40 In. | 2725 |
| **Elephant Head,** Wood, Carved, Downward Curving Trunk, Glass Eyes, 31 x 15 In. | 1304 |
| **Horse Head,** Carved, Painted, Glass Eyes, c.1900, 13 ½ In. | 600 |
| **Horse,** Jumper, Carved, Painted, c.1900, 38 x 55 In. | 2040 |
| **Horse,** Jumper, Cast Alloy, Pink, Red Mane, 48 In. | 242 |
| **Horse,** Jumper, Painted, Carved Mane, Glass Eyes, Flag Saddle, Horsehair Tail, 39 x 51 In. | 1845 |
| **Horse,** Jumper, Wood, Carved, Rearing Head, Glass Eyes, Paint, c.1945, 69 x 37 In. | 546 |
| **Horse,** Prancer, Brown, Brass Pole, Finial, c.1920, 74 In. | 660 |
| **Horse,** Prancer, White, Brown Saddle, Blue Bridle, Real Hair Tail, Brass Pole, 48 x 68 In. | 600 |
| **Horse,** Rearing, Open Mouth, Glass Eyes, Wood, Carved, Painted, Stand, 53 x 46 In. | 2360 |
| **Horse,** Running, Pine, Carved, Incised, c.1900, 24 ½ x 34 ½ In. | 840 |
| **Horse,** Stander, Foot Raised, Carved, Painted, Charles Looff, c.1890, 38 x 27 In. | 9440 |
| **Horse,** Stander, Wood, Carved, Painted, c.1900, 46 x 51 In. | 1080 |
| **Horse,** Walker, Flowers In Mane, Carved, Painted, Brass Pole, Wood Base, 68 x 47 In. | 1625 |
| **Lion,** Kiddie Ride, 1950s, 48 In. | 360 |
| **Ostrich,** Pine, Painted, Wood Base, Late 19th Century, 75 In. ...............*illus* | 1375 |
| **Ostrich,** Running, Saddle, Carved, Painted, Glass Eyes, c.1890, 65 ½ x 42 In. ...............*illus* | 8295 |
| **Panel,** Carved, Winged Beasts, Leaves, Multicolor Paint, Convex, c.1890, 83 In. | 431 |
| **Panel,** Lighted, Painted, Fairland Amusements, Lion's Head, c.1935, 50 x 33 In. ...............*illus* | 336 |
| **Rabbit,** Running, Carved Wood, Painted, Glass Eyes, Cast Iron Stand, c.1890, 32 In. .........*illus* | 3024 |
| **Rabbit,** Running, Wood, Carved, Painted, Bayol, France, 41 In. | 2360 |
| **Rounding Board,** Rhinoceros In The Veldt, Cartouche, Wood, Painted, Dentzel, 96 In. | 2006 |
| **Rounding Board,** Wood, Painted Elk, Scalloped Edge, Philadelphia, c.1880, 34 x 100 In. | 1610 |
| **Shield,** Lion's Head, Scrolls, High Relief, Wood, Painted, Herschell-Spillman, 33 x 18 In. | 413 |
| **Tiger,** Walker, Painted, Carved Saddle, Pad, Teeth Bared, Glass Eyes, c.1890, 50 x 73 In. | 17220 |

---

**CARRIAGE** means several things, so this category lists baby carriages, buggies for adults, horse-drawn sleighs, and even strollers. Doll-sized carriages are listed in the Toy category.

| | |
|---|---|
| **Baby Buggy,** Wicker, Bentwood Frame, Steel Wheels, Springs, Velvet Cushioned ...............*illus* | 480 |
| **Baby,** Wicker, Scrollwork, Padded, Early 1900s | 49 |
| **Blue Ribbon,** Durant-Dort Carriage Co., c.1900, 62 x 104 In. | 1200 |
| **Coach,** Mahogany, Brass Mounts, Windows, Doors, 70 In. | 1375 |
| **Foot Warmer,** Oak, Copper, Pierced Cutout Hearts, Drawer, Bail Handle, c.1870, 12 x 17 In. | 69 |
| **Pull Cart,** Painted Red, Yellow Pinstripes, 2 Wheels, 1800s, 21 x 55 In. | 330 |
| **Sleigh,** Cutter, Painted, Velour Upholstery, Wrought Iron, Cortland Wagon Co., 75 In. .......*illus* | 708 |
| **Sleigh,** Cutter, Victorian, Wicker, Wood, Iron, Painted, c.1890, 83 In. ...............*illus* | 2040 |
| **Stroller,** Rattan, Painted Green, Heywood-Wakefield, 13 x 26 x 16 ½ In. | 143 |
| **Sulky,** Child's, Wood, Black, Pinstripes, c.1900, 56 In. | 330 |
| **Wicker,** Double Facing, Cast Aluminum Wheels, 41 In. | 172 |

---

**CASH REGISTERS** were invented in 1884 because an eye on the cash was a necessity in stores of the nineteenth century, too. John and James Ritty invented a large model that resembled a clock and kept a record of the dollars and cents exchanged in the store. John Patterson improved the cash register with a paper roll to record the money. By the early 1900s, elaborate brass registers were made. More modern types were made after 1920.

| | |
|---|---|
| **Bronze,** Marble Coin Shelf, 3 Keys, 1907-08, 21 x 10 ½ In. | 948 |
| **Cash Register Co.,** Glass Tray, Brass Tray Dish, Wood, 20 ½ x 20 ½ In. | 2280 |

**Carousel,** Ostrich, Pine, Painted, Wood Base, Late 19th Century, 75 In. $1,375

Garth's Auctioneers & Appraisers

**Carousel,** Ostrich, Running, Saddle, Carved, Painted, Glass Eyes, c.1890, 65 ½ x 42 In. $8,295

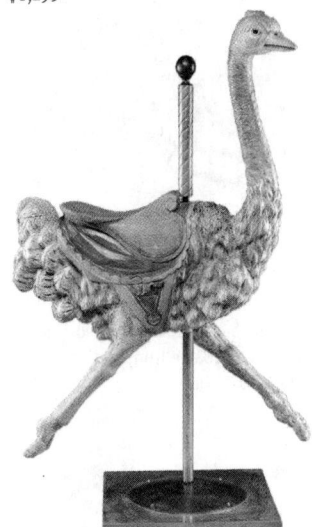

James D. Julia Auctioneers

**Carousel,** Panel, Lighted, Painted, Fairland Amusements, Lion's Head, c.1935, 50 x 33 In. $336

Mosby Auctions

This is an edited listing of current prices. Visit **Kovels.com** to check thousands of prices from previous years and sign up for free information on trends, tips, reproductions, marks, and more.

**Carousel,** Rabbit, Running, Carved Wood, Painted, Glass Eyes, Cast Iron Stand, c.1890, 32 In.
$3,024

Theriault's

**Carriage,** Baby Buggy, Wicker, Bentwood Frame, Steel Wheels, Springs, Velvet Cushioned
$480

Morphy Auctions

**Carriage,** Sleigh, Cutter, Painted, Velour Upholstery, Wrought Iron, Cortland Wagon Co., 75 In.
$708

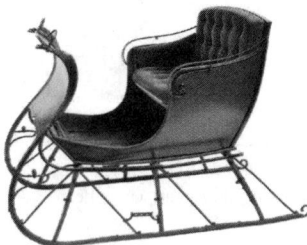

Conestoga Auction Co., Inc.

**Carriage,** Sleigh, Cutter, Victorian, Wicker, Wood, Iron, Painted, c.1890, 83 In.
$2,040

Garth's Auctioneers & Appraisers

| | |
|---|---:|
| **Hallwood,** Model 15, Brass, Curved Bell, 23 Keys | 660 |
| **Hallwood,** Model 16131, Nickel Plated Brass, Hallwood Co., Pat 1890s, 22 In. ......... *illus* | 360 |
| **Monitor,** Womden, Metal Tags, Amount Of Sale, 1 Drawer | 270 |
| **National,** Bohemian Model 522-EL-2C, Saloon, Oak, Brass, 2-Sided Top Sign | 1440 |
| **National,** Brass Design, Oak Base, 24 x 30 In. | 900 |
| **National,** Bronze, Cast, Amount Purchased, 2 Rows Of Keys, 19 In. | 554 |
| **National,** Model 12, Brass, Scrollwork, Keys, 9 x 20 In. | 1777 |
| **National,** Model 35 3/4, Embossed Brass, Marble Sill, 1917, 22 In. | 450 |
| **National,** Model 38, Embossed Brass, Original Marquee, 1909, 22 In. | 450 |
| **National,** Model 47, Brass, Dolphin Design, Marble Ledge, 27 Keys, 1885-1903 | 2700 |
| **National,** Model 97, Nickel Plated Bronze, c.1903, 21 x 25 ¼ In. | 575 |
| **National,** Model 130, Art Nouveau, Drink Coca-Cola In Bottles, Brass, 2-Sided Top Sign | 575 |
| **National,** Model 138, Nickel, Art Nouveau, Keys, 1903-04, 17 ½ x 20 In. | 592 |
| **National,** Model 250, Brass, Marble Sill, 1906, 20 In. | 510 |
| **National,** Model 311, Candy Store, Brass, Dolphin Design, Wood Base | 1080 |
| **National,** Model 313, Candy Store, Brass, Dolphin Pattern, Marble Till, c.1910 | 330 to 660 |
| **National,** Model 313, Candy Store, Brass, Nickel Plated Brass, Marble Ledge | 1440 |
| **National,** Model 313, Candy Store, Shoes Shined 5 Cents, Shoe Repair Sign, Embossed | 1200 |
| **National,** Model 313, Embossed Brass, Marble Sill, Oak Base, 1910, 17 In. | 330 |
| **National,** Model 313, Special Edition, Amount Purchase Top Sign, Reissue, 1984 | 840 |
| **National,** Model 356-G, Brass, Receipt Side Cage, Dolphin, 25 x 16 In. | 90 |
| **National,** Model 441-S, Receipt Side Cage, Crank, Empire, c.1912, 18 ½ x 19 In. | 120 |
| **National,** Model 442, Embossed Brass, 1909, 26 In. | 270 |
| **National,** Model 711, Mahogany, Metal Finish, 17 In. | 150 |
| **National,** Model 9112, 4 Drawer, Room, Cigar, Restaurant, 16 ½ x 18 In. | 780 |
| **National,** Wood Model, Brass Inlay, Clamshell Design, 25 Keys, 1879-1888 | 840 |
| **National,** Wood, Brass Inlay, 25 Keys, Clamshell, Brass Railing, 1879-91 | 2040 |
| **Wood,** 3 Drawers, Extended Stepped Base, Stand, 19th Century, 33 x 19 In. | 179 |
| **World,** Cast Iron, 23 Keys, Embossed, Sale, Record, SEE Logo | 443 |

**CASTOR JARS** for pickles are glass jars about six inches in height, held in special metal holders. They became a popular dinner table accessory about 1890. Each jar had a top that was usually silver or silver plate. The frame, also of a silver metal, had a handle that arched above the jar and a hook that held a pair of tongs. By 1900, the pickle castor was out of fashion. Many examples found today have reproduced glass jars in old holders. Additional pickle castors may be found in the various Glass categories.

| | |
|---|---:|
| **Pickle,** Blue Glass, Enameled Flowers, Footed Aurora Silver Plate Frame, 8 In. | 207 |
| **Pickle,** Blue Pressed Glass, Silver Plate, Monarch Silver Co., Tongs, 11 In. | 75 |
| **Pickle,** Blue Satin Peacock Tail Mother-Of-Pearl Glass, Silver Plate Frame, 12 In. | 944 |
| **Pickle,** Burmese Glass, Acorn, Branch Design, Webster Silver Plate Frame, 9 In. | 1298 |
| **Pickle,** Christmas Snowflake, Blue Opalescent, Pierced Holder, 12 In. | 201 |
| **Pickle,** Cranberry Glass, Inverted Thumbprint, Silver Plate, Tongs, c.1880, 8 In. | 225 |
| **Pickle,** Cranberry Glass, Silver Plate, Fluted Base, Twist Handle, Tongs, Marked, 11 In. | 94 |
| **Pickle,** Cranberry, Underwater Seaweed Pattern, 10 In. | 115 |
| **Pickle,** Fern, Green Opalescent, 4-Sided Holder, 10 ½ In. | 144 |
| **Pickle,** Green Mother-Of-Pearl Glass, Diamond Quilted, Yellow, Frame, 11 ½ In. | 633 |
| **Pickle,** Herringbone, Mother-Of-Pearl Glass, Pink Satin, 11 In. | 115 |
| **Pickle,** Millefiori, Silver Plate Frame, Tongs, 9 ½ In. | 236 |
| **Pickle,** Pigeon Blood Red, Enameled Flowers, Metal Frame, c.1905, 10 x 3 In. | 259 |
| **Pickle,** Silver Plate, Scrolls, Flowers, Etched Ferns, Tongs, Vanbergh Silver, 11 In. | 189 |
| **Pickle,** Snowflake, Cranberry Opalescent, Silver, Kate Greenaway, 9 ¾ In. | 1180 |
| **Pickle,** Spot Optic, Cranberry, Quadruple Stand, Lid, c.1890, 10 x 4 ½ In. | 115 |
| **Pickle,** Vaseline Button, Daisy Pattern, Barbour Silver Frame, 12 In. | 530 |

**CASTOR SETS** holding just salt and pepper castors were used in the seventeenth century. The sugar castor, mustard pot, spice dredger (shaker), bottles for vinegar and oil, and other spice holders became popular by the eighteenth century. These sets were usually made of sterling silver. The American Victorian castor set, the type most collected today, was made of silver plated Britannia metal. Colored glass bottles were introduced after the Civil War. The sets were out of fashion by World War I. Be careful when buying sets with colored bottles; many are reproductions. Other castor sets may be listed in various porcelain and glass categories in this book.

| | |
|---|---:|
| **3 Bottles,** Flower Vines, Earthenware, Metal, Lancaster & Sandland, c.1920, 5 x 6 In. | 63 |
| **3 Bottles,** Shakers, Cruet, Tray, Forget-Me-Nots, Blue Glass, Challinor & Taylor, c.1890 | 225 |
| **4 Bottles,** Etched Glass, Pedestal, Silver Plate, Pairpoint, c.1890 | 188 |

| | | |
|---|---|---|
| **4 Bottles,** Etched Glass, Pewter, Flower Handle, 9¾ In. | | 57 |
| **4 Bottles,** Shakers, Cruets, Cranberry Glass, Silver Plate, 16 x 7 In. | | 525 |
| **5 Bottles,** Etched Glass, Art Nouveau Filigreed Handle, Silver Plate, 17 In. | | 299 |
| **5 Bottles,** Oriental Landscape, Transferware, c.1850, 7¾ In. | | 295 |
| **5 Bottles,** Porcelain, Fruit Design, Wood Handle, 5¾ x 5¾ In. | | 49 |
| **6 Bottles,** Silver Stand, U Shape Handle, Medallion, Krider & Biddle, c.1865, 12 In. | *illus* | 1000 |
| **7 Bottles,** Silver Plate, Georgian, Cut Glass, 1800s, 9½ x 9 x 8 In. | | 469 |

**CAUGHLEY** porcelain was made in England from 1772 to 1814. Caughley porcelains are very similar in appearance to those made at the Worcester factory. See the Salopian category for related items. ℭ

| | | |
|---|---|---|
| **Asparagus Server,** Blue & White, Fisherman, c.1785, 2¾ In. | | 220 |
| **Bowl,** Blue & White, Chinese River Scene, Geometric Border, Fluted, c.1795, 6 In. | | 294 |
| **Cup & Saucer,** Ribbed, Blue & Gilt Trim, Interior Blue Band, c.1790 | | 84 |
| **Cup & Saucer,** Salopian, c.1795 | | 140 |
| **Jug,** Blue & White, Sprays, Blue Border, 7½ In. | | 325 |
| **Jug,** Cabbage Leaf, Mask Spout, Gilt Monogram, c.1790, 6½ In. | *illus* | 360 |
| **Pickle Dish,** Leaf Shape, Blue & White, Geisha, 8 x 9 In. | | 96 |
| **Sugar,** Blue, Gilt, Leaf Garland, Round, Knob Finial, Marked, c.1790 | | 360 |
| **Waste Bowl,** Fluted, Gilt Rope Design, Blue Band, Leaves, Scalloped Edge, c.1790, 6 In. | | 216 |

**CAULDON** Limited worked in Staffordshire, Great Britain, and went through many name changes. John Ridgway made porcelain at Cauldon Place, Hanley, until 1855. The firm of John Ridgway, Bates and Co. of Cauldon Place worked from 1856 to 1859. It became Bates, Brown-Westhead, Moore and Co. from 1859 to 1862. Brown-Westhead, Moore and Co. worked from 1862 to 1904. About 1890, this firm started using the words *Cauldon* or *Cauldon Ware* as part of the mark. Cauldon Ltd. worked from 1905 to 1920, Cauldon Potteries from 1920 to 1962. Related items may be found in the Indian Tree category.

| | | |
|---|---|---|
| **Bowl,** Porcelain Gold Ground, Turtle Scenes, Painted, Joseph Birbeck, c.1890, 4 Piece | | 1920 |
| **Game Plate,** Bird, Gilt Burgundy Border, Cauldon J. Birbeck Sen., c.1850, 8¾ In., 9 Piece | | 354 |
| **Plate,** Landscape Center, Wreath, Garland Swag Border, C. Pohl, 10¼ In., 12 Piece | | 2500 |

**CELADON** is the name of a velvet-textured green-gray glaze used by Chinese, Japanese, Korean, and other factories. This section includes pieces covered with celadon glaze with or without added decoration.

| | | |
|---|---|---|
| **Bowl,** Bell Shape, Wide Rim, Molded Rib Sides, Foot Ring, 11¾ x 4 In. | *illus* | 538 |
| **Bowl,** Crackle Glaze, Blue Ground, Brown Tones, Chinese, 2¼ x 10 In. | | 360 |
| **Bowl,** Kuan Style, Foliated Body, Scalloped Edge, 1900s, 6¼ In. | | 474 |
| **Bowl,** Oxblood Glaze, Applied Blossoms, Leaves, Footed, 1900s, 16 x 9 In. | | 127 |
| **Bowl,** Round, Green, Light Green, Footed, 10⅝ In. | | 861 |
| **Censer,** Crackle, Brown Gray, 3-Footed, Label, Yamanaka 1965 Kyoto, 5 x 4 In. | *illus* | 2370 |
| **Censer,** Round Body, Incised Decoration, 3-Footed, Chinese, c.1600s, 6¼ x 11 In. | | 1107 |
| **Charger,** Lily Pad, Lovers, 1800s, Chinese, 13¾ In. | | 615 |
| **Compote,** Domed Foot, Rolled Rim, Flowers, Chinese, 4½ x 8½ | *illus* | 460 |
| **Dish,** Flower Spray Center, Wide Turned Out Barbed Rim, Chinese, 14½ x 3½ In. | *illus* | 1315 |
| **Dish,** Leaf Rim, Flat Barbed Edge, Carved, Flower Medallion, Bands, 2¼ x 15¾ In. | | 976 |
| **Ginger Jar,** Blue, White, Cartouches, Happiness Symbols, 9⅕ In. | | 209 |
| **Jardiniere,** Mythical Animals, Wood Base, Pair | | 960 |
| **Plate,** Birds, Butterflies, Fruit, Leaves, Red, Yellow, Green, 19th Century, 7½ In. | | 120 |
| **Plate,** Small Flowers, Pink & Turquoise Cloud Border, 12 In. | | 210 |
| **Platter,** Blue, Chinese, 12 x 9¼ In. | | 60 |
| **Shaving Bowl,** Flowers, Birds, Butterflies, 10½ x 9 In. | | 219 |
| **Urn,** Blue, White Flowers, Tapered, Gilt Bronze Mounts, c.1905, 12 In., Pair | | 750 |
| **Vase,** Barrel Shape, Dotted Protrusion Design Bands, Incised Designs, Yung Cheng Marks, 4 In. | | 138 |
| **Vase,** Birds, Branches, Blossoms, Stick Neck, Multicolor, Chinese, 15 In. | | 1645 |
| **Vase,** Carved, Floral Scrolling, Mounted As Lamp, Chinese, 1800s, 13¾ In. | | 356 |
| **Vase,** Crackle Glaze, Round Brocade Stand, Fitted Box, Chinese, 7¾ In. | | 1200 |
| **Vase,** Dragon, Relief Flowers, Hexagonal, Footed, Chinese, 9 In. | | 236 |
| **Vase,** Gilt, Baluster, Multicolor, Courting Couples, 1800s, 23 In. | | 1434 |
| **Vase,** Long Neck, 9⅜ In. | | 270 |
| **Vase,** Red, Blue, Square Base, Porcelain, Marked, 1800s, 12 In. | *illus* | 474 |
| **Vase,** Tapered Sides, Banded, Edmund De Waal, c.1999, 4 x 3½ In. | | 308 |
| **Vase,** Yen-Yen, Trumpet Mouth, Flowers, Allover Crackling, Chinese, 19⅜ In. | *illus* | 6150 |
| **Water Dropper,** Cricket, Bamboo Form Handle, 2½ In. | | 52 |

**Cash Register,** Hallwood, Model 16131, Nickel Plated Brass, Hallwood Co., Pat 1890s, 22 In.
$360

Morphy Auctions

**Castor Set,** 6 Bottles, Silver Stand, U Shape Handle, Medallion, Krider & Biddle, c.1865, 12 In.
$1,000

Heritage Auction Galleries

**Caughley,** Jug, Cabbage Leaf, Mask Spout, Gilt Monogram, c.1790, 6½ In.
$360

DuMouchelles Art Gallery

**Celadon,** Bowl, Bell Shape, Wide Rim, Molded Rib Sides, Foot Ring, 11¾ x 4 In.
$538

Neal Auction Co.

**Celadon,** Censer, Crackle, Brown Gray, 3-Footed, Label, Yamanaka 1965 Kyoto, 5 x 4 In.
$2,370

James D. Julia Auctioneers

**Celadon,** Compote, Domed Foot, Rolled Rim, Flowers, Chinese, 4½ x 8½
$460

Cottone Auctions

**Celadon,** Dish, Flower Spray Center, Wide Turned Out Barbed Rim, Chinese, 14½ x 3½ In.
$1,315

Neal Auction Co.

**Celadon,** Vase, Red, Blue, Square Base, Porcelain, Marked, 1800s, 12 In.
$474

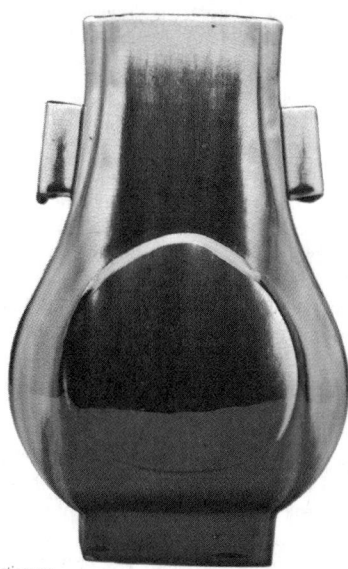

James D. Julia Auctioneers

**Celadon,** Vase, Yen-Yen, Trumpet Mouth, Flowers, Allover Crackling, Chinese, 19⅜ In.
$6,150

Skinner Auctioneers & Appraisers

**CELLULOID** is a trademark for a plastic developed in 1868 by John W. Hyatt. Celluloid Manufacturing Company, the Celluloid Novelty Company, Celluloid Fancy Goods Company, and American Xylonite Company all used celluloid to make jewelry, games, sewing equipment, false teeth, and piano keys. The name *celluloid* was often used to identify any similar plastic. Celluloid toys are listed under Toy.

| | |
|---|---:|
| **Barrette,** Rhinestones, Tortoise Color, c.1930, 1 ¾ In. | 22 |
| **Box,** Dresser, American Indian, Embossed Pattern, 3 ½ x 8 ¼ x 6 In. .............................*illus* | 207 |
| **Box,** Ivory, Flowers, Basket Weave, c.1892, Paper Sticker, 8 x 6 x 4 In. | 150 |
| **Hair Comb,** Egyptian Revival, Pharaoh, Red, 6 ½ x 3 ⅝ In. | 92 |
| **Hair Comb,** Green & Amber, Rhinestones, Fan Shape, 1900s, 5 In. | 75 |
| **Hat Pin,** Art Deco, Black, Ivory, 8 In. | 75 |
| **Purse,** Tubular, Art Deco, Flapper Girl, Green & Black Swirls, Velvet Ribbon, 3 ½ In. | 125 |

**CELS** *are listed in this book in the Animation Art category.*

**CERAMIC ART COMPANY** of Trenton, New Jersey, was established in 1889 by Jonathan Coxon and Walter Scott and was an early producer of American belleek porcelain. It became Lenox, Inc. in 1906. Do not confuse this ware with the pottery made by the Ceramic Arts Studio of Madison, Wisconsin.

| | |
|---|---:|
| **Stein,** Indian, Full Headdress, Mixed Metal Lid, Marked, Lenox, ½ Liter ..............................*illus* | 630 |
| **Tankard,** Footed, Green, Silver Lid, Marked, 1898 | 695 |
| **Vase,** American Indian, Oval, Shouldered, c.1900, 14 ⅜ In. | 2252 |
| **Vase,** Cylindrical, Tapered, Metallic Glazes, Marked, c.1900, 8 ⅞ In. | 279 |
| **Vase,** Oval, Seminude Woman, Waterfall, Marked, 8 In. | 1126 |
| **Vase,** Silver Leaves, Brown, Green Ground, Pinched Neck, 10 In. | 184 |

**CERAMIC ARTS STUDIO** was founded about 1940 in Madison, Wisconsin, by Lawrence Rabbett and Ruben Sand. Their most popular products were molded figurines. The pottery closed in 1955. Do not confuse these products with those of the Ceramic Art Co. of Trenton, New Jersey.

| | |
|---|---:|
| **Double Candleholder,** Girl, Seated, Holding Buckets, Flowers, c.1948, 5 In. | 85 |
| **Figurine,** Aphrodite, c.1953, 7 In. | 188 |
| **Figurine,** Chinese, Boy, 1940s, 4 ¼ In. | 15 |
| **Figurine,** Chipmunk, Holding Acorn, 2 ½ In. | 22 |
| **Figurine,** Dance Modern Woman, Green, 10 In. | 135 |
| **Figurine,** Little Miss Muffet, 4 ½ In. | 20 |
| **Figurine,** Peter Pan & Wendy, 5 ½ In., Pair | 275 |
| **Figurine,** Shelf Sitter, Ballerina, En Repos, 1940s, 3 ½ In. | 50 |
| **Figurine,** Shelf Sitter, Colonial Couple, 5 In. | 15 |
| **Figurine,** Shelf Sitter, Greg, 6 ½ In. | 65 |
| **Figurine,** Shelf Sitter, Sun-Li & Su-Lin, 1950s, 6 In., Pair | 75 |
| **Figurine,** Sultan & Woman, 4 In., Pair | 275 |
| **Head Vase,** Svea, Brown Pig Tails, Green Straps, c.1950, 6 In. | 165 |
| **Salt & Pepper,** Eskimos, c.1945, 3 ⅜ In. | 30 |

**CHALKWARE** is really plaster of Paris decorated with watercolors. One type was molded from Staffordshire and other porcelain models and painted and sold as inexpensive decorations in the nineteenth century. This type is very valuable today. Figures of plaster, made from about 1910 to 1940 for use as prizes at carnivals, are also known as chalkware. Kewpie dolls made of chalkware will be found in their own category.

| | |
|---|---:|
| **Bank,** Dove, On Hollow Stump, c.1880, 10 ¾ x 8 ½ In., Pair | 863 |
| **Bank,** Sheep, Standing, Painted, Oval Base, 1800s, 4 In. | 600 |
| **Church,** Multicolor Glass Windows, Hollow, White Paint, c.1920, 22 x 10 In. | 115 |
| **Compote,** Fruit, Lovebird Finial, 1800s, 11 In. | 584 |
| **Figurine,** Angel, Praying, 1800s, 11 ½ In. | 123 |
| **Figurine,** Calico Cat, Multicolor, 19th Century, 5 ½ In. | 923 |
| **Figurine,** Cat, Seated, Hollow Cast, Yellow Paint, Black, Spots, Stripes, 10 In. | 1560 |
| **Figurine,** Cat, Seated, Painted White, Smoke Design, Oval Base, c.1875, 15 In. | 575 |
| **Figurine,** Cat, Tabby, Brown, Black, 15 ¾ In. | 720 |
| **Figurine,** Deer, Resting, Hollow, Painted, c.1900, 15 x 16 In. | 92 |
| **Figurine,** Dog, Dalmatian, Seated, Dog Tag, 8-Sided Plinth, c.1890, 18 x 7 In. | 1599 |
| **Figurine,** Dog, Pug, Standing, Red Paint, c.1890, 9 ½ In. | 62 |
| **Figurine,** Dove, Cherry Branch, Stump Base, Painted Highlights, Pa., 1800s, 11 In. ..........*illus* | 266 |

**Celluloid,** Box, Dresser, American Indian, Embossed Pattern, 3 ½ x 8 ¼ x 6 In.
$207

Wm Morford Auctions

**Ceramic Art Co.,** Stein, Indian, Full Headdress, Mixed Metal Lid, Marked, Lenox, ½ Liter
$630

The Stein Auction Company

**Chalkware,** Figurine, Dove, Cherry Branch, Stump Base, Painted Highlights, Pa., 1800s, 11 In.
$266

Conestoga Auction Co., Inc.

**Charlie Chaplin,** Game, Chasing
Charlie, Gameboard, Spear Works, Box,
1920s, 7 x 10 In.
$139

Hake's Americana & Collectibles

**Charlie McCarthy,** Puppet, Composition
Head, Wire Monocle, Cloth Body, Tuxedo,
c.1938, 11 In.
$115

Hake's Americana & Collectibles

**Charlie McCarthy,** Toy, Charlie
McCarthy, Walker, Tin Lithograph, Key
Wind, Marx, 8¼ In.
$236

Bertoia Auctions

**Charlie McCarthy,** Toy, Private Car,
Charlie & Mortimer, Marx, 1939, 16 In.
$830

James D. Julia Auctioneers

| | |
|---|---|
| **Figurine,** Fireman, Standing, Holding Trumpet, Pedestal Base, c.1850, 14½ In. | 1020 |
| **Figurine,** Seated, Painted, Yellow Bow Collar, c.1900, 5¾ In. | 1062 |
| **Garniture,** Flowers, Multicolor Paint, 1800s, 12½ In., Pair | 2040 |
| **Garniture,** Fruit, Hollow, Red, Yellow, Green, Black Painted, c.1850, 13¾ In. | 720 |
| **Match Holder,** 2 Owls, On Perch, Brown, Red Trim, 1800s, 7½ In. | 90 |
| **Menu Holder,** Orange, Smile, c.1935, 6½ In. | 390 |
| **Phrenology Head,** Glazed, Fowlers & Wells, c.1890, 10½ In. | 369 |
| **Plaque,** Landscape, Castle, Clouds, Rich-Kraft, Frame, c.1950, 10½ x 9½ In. | 35 |

**CHARLIE CHAPLIN,** the famous comedian, actor, and filmmaker, lived from 1889 to 1977. He made his first movie in 1913. He did the movie *The Tramp* in 1915. The character of the Tramp has remained famous, and in the 1980s appeared in a series of television commercials for computers. Dolls, candy containers, and all sorts of memorabilia with the image of Charlie's Tramp are collected. Pieces are being made even today.

| | |
|---|---|
| **Box,** Pencil, Tin Litho, Charlie, Hands In Pocket, Signed Henry Clive, 8 x 2 In. | 49 |
| **Candy Container,** Figure Standing Next To Barrel, Glass, Tin, Painted, 4 In. | 148 |
| **Doll,** Little Tramp Attire, Cloth, Orange Cane, 6 In. | 300 |
| **Doll,** Walking, Composition Head & Arms, Clock Mechanism, 1914 | 245 |
| **Figurine,** Little Tramp, Lladro, 11¼ In. | 225 |
| **Game,** Chasing Charlie, Gameboard, Spear Works, Box, 1920s, 7 x 10 In. ..........*illus* | 139 |
| **Pendant,** Enamel, Hand In Pocket, Umbrella, 3 In. | 122 |
| **Photograph,** Charlie, Jackie Coogan Sitting In Doorway, From The Kid, 1921, 8 x 10 In. | 50 |
| **Portrait,** Oil On Canvas, Frame, Initialed, 16 x 20 In. | 3460 |
| **Print,** Woodblock, Black & White, Signed, Lavy Lee, 10 x 13 In. | 125 |
| **Purse,** Mesh, Charlie Profile, Star Series, Whiting Davis, 6 x 4 In., 13 In. Chain | 1150 |
| **Rag Doll,** 1 Hand In Pocket, Deans Rag Doll Co., 12½ In. | 35 |
| **Toy,** Charlie Chaplin, Cloth, Celluloid, Windup, Schuco, Box, 6½ In. | 944 |
| **Toy,** Charlie Chaplin, Walker, Cloth Outfit, Tin Shoes, Windup, 11½ In. | 325 |
| **Toy,** Charlie Chaplin, Walker, Tin, Composition Head, Clothing, Clockwork, c.1925, 9 In. | 403 |
| **Toy,** Tramp, Cane, Bowler, Tin Litho, Iron Shoes, Windup, Gunthermann, c.1920, 9 In. | 576 |
| **Watch,** Little Tramp, Silver Luster Case, Velvet Band, Bubbles, Inc., Box, 1972, 1 x 2 In. | 221 |

**CHARLIE McCARTHY** was the ventriloquist's dummy used by Edgar Bergen from the 1930s. He was famous for his work in radio, movies, and television. The act was retired in the 1970s. Mortimer Snerd, another Bergen dummy, is also listed here.

| | |
|---|---|
| **Bank,** Figural, Suitcase, Die Cast, Trap Bottom, 8 In. | 413 |
| **Doll,** Composition, Movable Jaw, Painted, 12½ In. | 47 |
| **Doll,** Hat, Monocle, Lapel Pin, Effanbee, 1937, 17 In. | 625 |
| **Paper Doll,** Formal Wear, Movable Mouth, 1930s, 15 In. | 200 |
| **Puppet,** Composition Head, Wire Monocle, Cloth Body, Tuxedo, c.1938, 11 In. ......*illus* | 115 |
| **Toy,** Benzine Buggy, Tin, Clockwork, Crazy Car Action, Marx, 8 In. | 207 to 325 |
| **Toy,** Charlie McCarthy, Arms, Cane Move, Tin Lithograph, Windup, Marx, 11 In. | 270 |
| **Toy,** Charlie McCarthy, In Convertible, Tin Lithograph, Windup, Marx, 7 In. | 270 to 330 |
| **Toy,** Charlie McCarthy, Walker, Tin Lithograph, Key Wind, Marx, 8¼ In. ......*illus* | 236 |
| **Toy,** Mortimer Snerd, Driving Car, Multicolor, Tin Litho, Windup, Marx, 8 In. | 360 |
| **Toy,** Mortimer Snerd, Walker, Tin, Windup, Marx, Box, 8½ In. | 246 |
| **Toy,** Private Car, Charlie & Mortimer, Marx, 1939, 16 In. ......*illus* | 830 |

**CHELSEA** porcelain was made in the Chelsea area of London from about 1745 to 1769. Some pieces made from 1770 to 1784 are called Chelsea Derby and may include the letter *D* for *Derby* in the mark. Ceramic designs were borrowed from the Meissen models of the day. Pieces were made of soft paste. The gold anchor was used as the mark, but it has been copied by many other factories. Recent copies of Chelsea have been made from the original molds. Do not confuse Chelsea porcelain with Chelsea Grape, a white pottery with luster grape decoration. Chelsea Keramic is listed in the Dedham category.

| | |
|---|---|
| **Candleholder,** Man, Woman, Seated, Multicolor, Gilt, Pair, 9¾ In. | 246 |
| **Candlestick,** Figural, Shepherd, Shepherdess, Flowers, 11 In., Pair | 75 |
| **Figurine,** Fruit Sellers, Man, Woman, Multicolor, Gilt, Anchor Mark, 7¼ In., Pair | 196 |
| **Figurine,** Women, Standing On Rococo Base, Bocage Tree, Gold Anchor, 8 x 4¼ In., Pair | 155 |
| **Plate,** Soup, Border, Cherries, Pomegranates, Insects, Multicolor, c.1750, 8½ & 8 In., Pair | 311 |

**CHELSEA GRAPE** pattern was made before 1840. A small bunch of grapes in a raised design, colored with purple or blue luster, is on the border of the white plate. Most of the pieces are unmarked. The pattern is sometimes called Aynsley or Grandmother. Chelsea Sprig is similar but has a sprig of flowers instead of the bunch of grapes. Chelsea Thistle has a raised thistle pattern. Do not confuse these Chelsea patterns with Chelsea Keramic Art Works, which can be found in the Dedham category, or with Chelsea porcelain, the preceding category.

| | |
|---|---|
| **Cup** | 17 |
| **Cup & Saucer,** Purple Luster, Paneled, c.1830 | 50 |
| **Plate,** Copper Luster, c.1860, 7 In. | 68 |
| **Plate,** Dessert, Copper Luster, Paneled, c.1840, 7 ¼ In. | 17 |
| **Plate,** Luncheon, Purple Luster, 8 ⅜ In. | 24 |
| **Platter,** Copper Luster, c.1830, 9 x 10 In. | 78 |
| **Saucer,** Purple Luster, 5 ½ In. | 15 |
| **Soup,** Bowl, 9 In. | 45 |
| **Sugar & Creamer,** Purple Luster, Footed, c.1920 | 56 |

**CHELSEA SPRIG** is similar to Chelsea Grape, a pattern made before 1840, but has a sprig of flowers instead of the bunch of grapes. Chelsea Thistle has a raised thistle pattern. Do not confuse these Chelsea patterns with Chelsea Keramic Art Works, which can be found in the Dedham category, or with Chelsea porcelain.

| | |
|---|---|
| **Bowl,** Footed, c.1875, 6 In. | 76 |
| **Plate,** Dinner, Octagonal, 8 ⅞ In. | 36 |
| **Teapot,** Lid, Copper Luster, Paneled, Footed, 9 In. | 45 |

**CHINESE EXPORT** porcelain comprises the many kinds of porcelain made in China for export to America and Europe in the eighteenth, nineteenth, and twentieth centuries. Other pieces may be listed in this book under Canton, Celadon, Nanking, Rose Canton, Rose Mandarin, and Rose Medallion.

| | |
|---|---|
| **Basin,** Famille Rose, Figures, Flowers, Turned-Out Rim, 1800s, 14 ⅝ In. .............*illus* | 598 |
| **Bowl,** Copper, Red, 3 x 7 In. | 201 |
| **Bowl,** Famille Rose, Armorial, Arms Of Box Impaling Smith, Bouquets, c.1880, 12 In. | 600 |
| **Bowl,** Famille Rose, Brass Dolphin & Dragon Shape Supports, 1900s, 13 x 17 In. | 780 |
| **Bowl,** Famille Rose, Enameled, Emperor, Harem, Landscape, Mark, 1900s, 4 x 22 In. | 295 |
| **Bowl,** Famille Rose, Pink & Yellow Flowers, White Ground, 4 ½ x 10 In. | 295 |
| **Bowl,** Famille Rose, Pink, Orange Flower Band, 11 ¼ In. | 188 |
| **Bowl,** Lion & Bird Panels, Geometric Ground, 2 x 6 In. .............*illus* | 246 |
| **Bowl,** Round Panels, Figures In Landscapes, Scalloped Edge, c.1800, 4 ½ x 10 In. | 2400 |
| **Bowl,** Salad, Lake Scene, Diapered Border, Notched Corners, 5 x 12 In. .............*illus* | 1230 |
| **Cann,** Cup, Famille Rose, Sprigs, Moths, Greek Key Border, Handles, 5 ½ x 3 ¼ In., Pair | 676 |
| **Card Box,** Lacquered, Red, Black, Gold Figures, Landscapes, 1800s, 14 x 12 In. | 1778 |
| **Celery Tray,** Multicolor Flowers, Butterfly, Gilt Highlights, c.1900, 11 ¾ In. | 6 |
| **Charger,** Famille Rose, Animals In Pastoral Landscape, 1700s, 13 ⅝ In. | 1680 |
| **Charger,** Famille Rose, Armorial, Songbirds, Peonies, Trellis Panels, c.1740, 15 In. | 1560 |
| **Charger,** Famille Rose, Sacred Bird, 1800s, 15 In. | 1722 |
| **Charger,** Famille Rose, Scalloped Gilt Rim, c.1820, 12 ¾ In. | 300 |
| **Charger,** Famille Verte, Birds, Flowering Branches, Green Flower Border, 14 In. | 1046 |
| **Charger,** Famille Verte, Bowl Shape, Flared Rim, Plated, Animals, 15 In., Pair | 4183 |
| **Charger,** Famille Verte, Vases Of Flowers, Rust Red, Cobalt Blue, White, 15 In. | 1408 |
| **Charger,** Warrior Scene, Castle, Flags, Characters, c.1890, 22 In. | 1722 |
| **Cider Jug,** Lid, Famille Rose, Court Scene, Couple, Drinking Tea, Canton, c.1820, 9 In. | 1440 |
| **Cistern,** Blue & White, Mythical Beast Knop, Ring Handles, Footed, 24 x 11 In. | 13743 |
| **Coffeepot,** Gilt Eagle & Shield, Lighthouse Form, Monogram, 10 In. | 768 |
| **Creamer,** Eagle, Shield, Banner, Don't Give Up The Ship, Helmet Form, 5 In. | 11875 |
| **Creamer,** Fitzhugh, Orange, Helmet, Monogram, Footed, 1800s, 5 In. | 480 |
| **Cup,** Famille Verte, Flared Stem, Multicolor Enamel, Bugs, Flowers, 4 ½ x 7 In. | 46 |
| **Dish,** Famille Rose, Immortals, Iris, Peaches, Quatrefoil Shape, Footed, 11 x 9 In. | 104 |
| **Dish,** Rose Spray, Gilt Rim, Oval, c.1800, 7 ⅝ x 10 ⅝ In., Pair | 922 |
| **Dish,** Shrimp, Famille Rose, Clobbered, c.1860, 9 ½ In., 3 Piece | 2160 |
| **Dish,** Vegetable, Pinecones, Trellis Diaper Band, Lid, c.1800, 5 ½ x 11 In., Pair | 861 |
| **Figurine,** Bird, Articulated, Multicolor Rock, Pierced, 19th Century, 22 In., Pair | 10762 |
| **Figurine,** Buddha, Blue, 5 ½ In. | 165 |
| **Figurine,** Court Woman, Famille Rose, Costumes, 1900s, 17 x 6 In., Pair | 2214 |
| **Figurine,** Phoenix Birds, Famille Rose, Ruyi Mushroom, Rocks, 9 ½ In., Pair | 357 |
| **Figurine,** Rooster, Pierced, Tree Trunks, Incised Feathers, c.1900, 16 x 9 In., Pair | 2460 |
| **Figurine,** Shoulao, Famille Rose, Crane, Carved Wood Stand, 1900s, 14 ¾ In. ........*illus* | 308 |
| **Flask,** Moon, Figures & Performers, Blue & White, Dragon Handles, 17 ¾ In., Pair | 2006 |
| **Jar,** Famille Rose, Gilt Foo Dog Lid Finial, Gardens, Birds, Wood Stand, 32 In., Pair | 6000 |
| **Jar,** Lid, Famille Verte, Baluster Body, Phoenix Birds, Rocks, Branches, 16 x 35 In. | 246 |

**Chinese Export,** Basin, Famille Rose, Figures, Flowers, Turned-Out Rim, 1800s, 14 ⅝ In.
**$598**

Neal Auction Co.

**Chinese Export,** Bowl, Lion & Bird Panels, Geometric Ground, 2 x 6 In.
**$246**

Skinner Auctioneers & Appraisers

**Chinese Export,** Bowl, Salad, Lake Scene, Diapered Border, Notched Corners, 5 x 12 In.
**$1,230**

New Orleans Auction Galleries, Inc.

### Chinese Export for Europe and America

The porcelains wanted in Europe and the United States were different from those made for Asians. The porcelain wasn't as thin and designs were usually distinctly European. Dishes with family coats of arms, figures in European clothes, American flags, ships, and biblical and mythological scenes were made for the European and American markets.

**Chinese Export,** Figurine, Shoulao, Famille Rose, Crane, Carved Wood Stand, 1900s, 14 ¾ In.
$308

**Chinese Export,** Plate, Rose Fitzhugh, Flowers & Moth Border, c.1800, 9 ½ In.
$7,703

James D. Julia Auctioneers

**Chinese Export,** Platter, Armorial, Flowers, Scrolling Leaves, Canted Corners, 9 x 13 In.
$300

DuMouchelles Art Gallery

**Chinese Export,** Tureen, Lid, Famille Rose, Flower, Leaves, Leaf Handles, Leafy Finial, Porcelain, 1700s
$1,195

Neal Auction Co.

**Chinese Export,** Tureen, Lid, Wheat & Grapes, Monogrammed WG, c.1800, 10 ½ x 7 ¾ In.
$3,444

New Orleans Auction Galleries, Inc.

**Chinese Export,** Umbrella Stand, Famille Rose, Narrative Scenes, c.1910, 23 x 9 In.
$704

Rago Arts & Auction Center

**Chinese Export,** Urn, Lid, Mandarin, Gilt, 2 Dragon Handles, Foo Dog Finial, c.1790, 10 ¼ In.
$4,720

Brunk Auctions

**Chinese Export,** Vase, Bottle Shape, Crackle Camellia-Leaf Green Glaze, Porcelain, 1900s, 12 In.
$729

James D. Julia Auctioneers

**Chinese Export,** Vase, Famille Rose, Flowers, Children, Dragon Handles, Marked, c.1900, 14 In.
$1,823

James D. Julia Auctioneers

C

| | |
|---|---|
| **Jar,** Tea, Blue & White, c.1800, 7 x 4 In. | 468 |
| **Jardiniere,** Famille Rose, Mazarin, Blue Porcelain, Globe Shape Body, 11 x 16 In. | 837 |
| **Joss Stick Holder,** Famille Rose, Foo Dog Shape, 2¾ x 5 In. | 840 |
| **Joss Stick Holder,** Famille Rose, Foo Dog Shape, Orange, Green, 1800s, 3 x 6 In., Pair | 960 |
| **Libation Cup,** Famille Rose, Petals, Stem Handles, Leaf Base, c.1908, 7 In. | 14145 |
| **Mug,** Famille Rose, Blue & White, Landscape Scenes, Loop Handle, 1800s, 4½ In. | 90 |
| **Mug,** Tobacco Leaf, Scalloped Rim, 1700s, 5½ In. | 2280 |
| **Pitcher,** House, Trees, Blue, Light Blue, Canton, 14 In. | 938 |
| **Plate,** Famille Rose, Aesop Fable, Fox & The Cat, Birds, Multicolor, c.1890, 9½ In. | 570 |
| **Plate,** Famille Rose, Court Scene, Women, Steps, c.1810, 9⅞ In. | 1320 |
| **Plate,** Famille Rose, Flowers, Multicolor, c.1800, 9 In., 7 Piece | 355 |
| **Plate,** Famille Rose, Millefiori Enamel, Footed, Flared Wide Border, Gilt, 10 In., Pair | 1058 |
| **Plate,** Famille Rose, Millefleur, Gilt Ground, 1800s, 10 In. | 489 |
| **Plate,** Famille Rose, Multicolor, Bird, Butterfly, Fruit, Fauna Border, 8¾ In. | 266 |
| **Plate,** Famille Rose, Multicolor, Center Flowers, Floral, Fruit Reserves, 8½ In. | 295 |
| **Plate,** Famille Rose, Octagonal, Arms Of Hunter, Inscription, Flower Border, c.1770, 9 In. | 420 |
| **Plate,** Famille Rose, Strolling Figures, Pavilions, River, c.1880, 9¾ In. | 840 |
| **Plate,** Famille Rose, Women, Pavilions, Dragons, Pearls, c.1820, 9¾ In. | 600 |
| **Plate,** Garden Scene, Birds, Floral & Leaf Scroll Rim, Octagonal, 1700s, 8½ In., Pair | 240 |
| **Plate,** Gilt Edge, Rural Landscapes, Armorial Crest, Mid-1700s, 8¾ In., Pair | 1476 |
| **Plate,** Grisaille Painted, Figures & Ox In Landscape, Shell Rim, 8-Sided, 10 In. | 1250 |
| **Plate,** Rose Fitzhugh, Flowers & Moth Border, c.1800, 9½ In. .....................*illus* | 7703 |
| **Platter,** Armorial Center, Unicorns, Lions, Floral Sprays, c.1810, 10 x 13 In., Pair | 984 |
| **Platter,** Armorial, Flared, Serpentine Rim, Multicolor Enamel, Octagon, 11½ x 8 In. | 242 |
| **Platter,** Armorial, Flowers, Scrolling Leaves, Canted Corners, 9 x 13 In. ...........*illus* | 300 |
| **Platter,** Famille Rose, Boy, Water Buffalo, Ducks, Scrolls, Oval, c.1750, 16⅞ In. | 3900 |
| **Platter,** Famille Rose, Flowers, Oval, Scalloped Edge, 18½ In. | 1125 |
| **Platter,** Famille Rose, Passion Flower, Rock Garden, Rectangular, c.1755, 14½ In. | 1320 |
| **Platter,** Famille Rose, Roundel, Figure On Elephant, Banding, c.1800s, 15 x 12 In. | 800 |
| **Platter,** Famille Rose, Royal Pavilion, Bird Border, Oval, c.1790, 19 In. | 1125 |
| **Platter,** Floral Sprigs, Flower Center, Birds, Insects, Multicolor, 13 x 9¼ In. | 237 |
| **Platter,** Rose Medallion, Multicolor Enamels, Gilt, 15 x 12 In. | 265 |
| **Punch Bowl,** Cabbage Leaf, Famille Rose, U Shaped, Floral Rim, 1800s, 5¾ x 14 In. | 837 |
| **Punch Bowl,** Famille Rose, Alternating Bird & Flower, Butterfly Panels, 7 x 16 In. | 956 |
| **Punch Bowl,** Famille Rose, Lotus In Gilt Reserve, Overlapping Lotus Petals, 11 In. | 2625 |
| **Punch Bowl,** Famille Rose, Pavilions, Palace, Dignitaries, c.1825, 14 In. | 3120 |
| **Punch Bowl,** Famille Rose, Peony, Fruit, Flower Spray, c.1790, 12 In. | 720 |
| **Punch Bowl,** Famille Verte, Hunt Scenes, Y Diapering, Red Ground, 4½ x 11 In. | 738 |
| **Punch Bowl,** Pictorial, Figures, Animals, Birds, Gilt Border, Teak Stand, 9 x 15 In. | 6765 |
| **Punch Bowl,** Raised Medallions, Houses, Boats, Mountains, Blue, White, 11 In. | 512 |
| **Rose Medallion,** Plate, E Monogram, Birds, Flowers, Pond, Canton, c.1865, 8½ In. | 390 |
| **Soap Dish,** Lid, Fitzhugh, Blue, Clobbered, Early 19th Century, 5½ In. | 570 |
| **Teapot Stand,** Famille Rose, British Shipping, c.1775, 5 In. | 960 |
| **Teapot,** Lid, Famille Rose, Woman, Children, Interior Scene, 11 In. | 750 |
| **Trinket Box,** Enamel On Copper, Multicolor, Child, Mother, Landscape, 4 x 2½ In. | 47 |
| **Tureen,** Boar's Head, Porcelain, Open Mouth, Tusks, Pink Tongue, c.1760, 14 In. | 23750 |
| **Tureen,** Famille Rose, Peony Blossoms, Flowers, Gold Trim, Dome Lid, 6 x 8 In. | 1250 |
| **Tureen,** Lid, Famille Rose, Boy, Water Buffalo, Ducks, Scrolls, Handles, c.1750, 16 In. | 3600 |
| **Tureen,** Lid, Famille Rose, Flower, Leaves, Leaf Handles, Leafy Finial, Porcelain, 1700s .....*illus* | 1195 |
| **Tureen,** Lid, Undertray, Scattered Flowers, Bud Knop, Shaped Rim, c.1810, 10 x 14 In. | 523 |
| **Tureen,** Lid, Wheat & Grapes, Monogrammed WG, c.1800, 10½ x 7¾ In. .......................*illus* | 3444 |
| **Umbrella Stand,** Famille Rose, Narrative Scenes, c.1910, 23 x 9 In. .....................*illus* | 704 |
| **Umbrella Stand,** Famille Verte, Urns, Animals, Flowers, Apple Green Ground, 24 In. | 2400 |
| **Urn,** Lid, Mandarin, Gilt, 2 Dragon Handles, Foo Dog Finial, c.1790, 10¼ In. .................*illus* | 4720 |
| **Vase,** Bottle Shape, Crackle Camellia-Leaf Green Glaze, Porcelain, 1900s, 12 In. .............*illus* | 729 |
| **Vase,** Bottle, Landscape, Figures, Birds, Blue, Iron Red, Dragon Handle, 11 In. | 1375 |
| **Vase,** Canteen Shape, Dragons, Blue, Pierced Handles, 13 In., Pair | 1062 |
| **Vase,** Famille Noir, Carved, Reticulated, Gourd Shape, Enameled, 11 In. | 590 |
| **Vase,** Famille Noir, Enameled, Bulbous Body, Long Neck, Marked, 18 In., Pair | 4956 |
| **Vase,** Famille Rose, Celadon, Gilt Foo Dog Handles, 3-Dimensional Design, 25 In. | 3304 |
| **Vase,** Famille Rose, Figures, Clouds, Flowers, Scrolled Handles, 25 In., Pair | 7080 |
| **Vase,** Famille Rose, Figures, Flowering Trees, Peacocks, Ring Handles, c.1900, 22 x 7 In. | 708 |
| **Vase,** Famille Rose, Figures, Flowers, Birds, Gilt Dragon Handles, c.1890, 12 In., Pair | 400 |
| **Vase,** Famille Rose, Figures, Landscape, Flowers, 11½ In., Pair | 1875 |
| **Vase,** Famille Rose, Flowers, Birds, Butterflies, c.1850, 16½ In., Pair | 1320 |
| **Vase,** Famille Rose, Flowers, Children, Dragon Handles, Marked, c.1900, 14 In. .................*illus* | 1823 |

**Chinese Export,** Vase, Famille Rose, Palace Scene, Court Officials, Ladies, 1800s, 22 In., Pair
$1,353

New Orleans Auction Galleries, Inc.

**Chinese Export,** Vase, Famille Rose, Raised Precious Objects, 19th Century, 13¾ In., Pair
$1,534

Brunk Auctions

**Chinese Export,** Vase, Famille Verte, Processional Scene, Porcelain, Marked, c.1800, 23½ In.
$5,333

James D. Julia Auctioneers

C

**Chinese Export,** Vase, Narrative Scenes, Flowers, Gilt, Enamel, 1900s, 73 x 24 In. $500

Rago Arts & Auction Center

---

### TIP
*Treat your antiques like your grandparents: Have proper respect for their age, but don't exaggerate their fragility.*

---

**Christmas,** Nodder, Santa Claus, Lantern, Sack, Celluloid, Windup, Marked, Japan, c.1930, 2½ In. $139

Hake's Americana & Collectibles

| | |
|---|---:|
| **Vase,** Famille Rose, Flowers, Exotic Birds, Phoenix, Red, 6 Characters, c.1870, 15 In. | 677 |
| **Vase,** Famille Rose, Gilt Mounts, Chinese, 1800s, 24 In., Pair | 6000 |
| **Vase,** Famille Rose, Gu Shape, Applied Bronze Rim & Base, 1800s, 20 In., Pair | 2596 |
| **Vase,** Famille Rose, Hundred Deer, Mountains, Animal Shape Handles, 7 x 5 In. | 719 |
| **Vase,** Famille Rose, Palace Scene, Court Officials, Ladies, 1800s, 22 In., Pair *illus* | 1353 |
| **Vase,** Famille Rose, Pink Flowers, White Ground, Calligraphy, 23 In., Pair | 885 |
| **Vase,** Famille Rose, Raised Precious Objects, 19th Century, 13¾ In., Pair *illus* | 1534 |
| **Vase,** Famille Rose, Yellow Ground, Double Gourd, Strap Handles, 8 In. | 826 |
| **Vase,** Famille Rose, Yellow Ground, Landscape, Panels, Hu Shape, 18 x 14 In. | 1180 |
| **Vase,** Famille Rose, Yellow Sgraffito, Bird, Branches, c.1835, 7½ In., Pair | 3840 |
| **Vase,** Famille Verte, Bottle Shape, Women In Garden, Birds, Branches, 7 In., Pair | 478 |
| **Vase,** Famille Verte, Enameled, 3-Dimensional Gourds, c.1900, 23 x 8½ In. | 1416 |
| **Vase,** Famille Verte, Processional Scene, Porcelain, Marked, c.1800, 23½ In. *illus* | 5333 |
| **Vase,** Lid, Prunus, Lotus Vines, 17 In., Pair | 1169 |
| **Vase,** Narrative Scenes, Flowers, Gilt, Enamel, 1900s, 73 x 24 In. *illus* | 500 |
| **Warming Dish,** Famille Rose, Figures, Pierced Oval Inset, 1800s, 18 x 15 In. | 1298 |
| **Watch Holder,** Domed Lid, White, Applied Flowers, Cylindrical, 7 x 5 In. | 832 |
| **Water Dropper,** Lotus Shape, Open Blossom, Pink Shaded To Rose, Stem, 8 In. | 2400 |

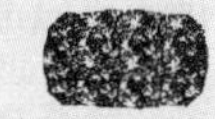

---

**CHINTZ** is the name of a group of china patterns featuring an overall design of flowers and leaves. The design became popular with English makers about 1928. A few pieces are still being made. The best known are designs by Royal Winton, James Kent Ltd., Crown Ducal, and Shelley. Crown Ducal and Shelley are listed in their own sections.

| | |
|---|---:|
| **Dorset,** Syrup, Underplate, Warwick, 4 In. | 35 |
| **Eleanor,** Jam, Lid, Underplate, 3 x 3 In. | 55 |
| **Evesham,** Dish, Square, Raised Edges, Scalloped Edge, Royal Winton, 4 x 5 In. | 156 |
| **Hazel,** Cup & Saucer, Royal Winton | 102 |
| **Pink Surprise,** Cup & Saucer, Footed, Royal Albert | 35 |

---

**CHOCOLATE GLASS,** sometimes mistakenly called caramel slag, was made by the Indiana Tumbler and Goblet Company of Greentown, Indiana, from 1900 to 1903. It was also made at other National Glass Company factories. Fenton Art Glass Co. made chocolate glass from about 1907 to 1915. More recent pieces have been made by Imperial and others.

| | |
|---|---:|
| **Bicentennial,** Bell, Fenton, 6¾ In. | 29 |
| **Cactus,** Compote, Greentown, 5½ In. | 73 |
| **Cactus,** Cruet, Paneled, Greentown, 5 x 3¼ In. | 93 |
| **Cactus,** Tumbler, Panels, Greentown, 4 In. | 14 |
| **Figurine,** Bulldog Pup, Imperial Glass, c.1969, 3 In. | 28 |
| **Figurine,** Scottish Terrier, Imperial Glass, 6 x 5 x 3 In. | 168 |
| **Scalloped Flange,** Vase, Trumpet, Footed, 6 In. | 55 |

---

**CHRISTMAS** collectibles include not only Christmas trees and ornaments listed below, but also Santa Claus figures, special dishes, and even games and wrapping paper. A Belsnickle is a nineteenth-century figure of Father Christmas. A kugel is an early, heavy ornament made of thick blown glass, lined with zinc or lead, and often covered with colored wax. Christmas cards are listed in this section under Greeting Card. Christmas collectibles may also be listed in the Candy Container category. Christmas trees are listed in the section that follows.

| | |
|---|---:|
| **Belsnickle,** Black Coat With Hood, Chalkware, 19th Century, 14¼ In. | 1722 |
| **Belsnickle,** Brown Robe, Fur Trim, Fur Beard, Feather Tree, Mica Snowball Base, 11 In. | 885 |
| **Belsnickle,** Composition, Fabric, Canvas Bag, Germany, 6½ In. | 590 |
| **Belsnickle,** Composition, Gold Flecked Yellow Robe, Feather Tree Sprig, Germany, 7 In. | 148 |
| **Belsnickle,** Composition, Open Red Coat, Glitter, Goose Feather Branch, Germany, 9 In. | 236 |
| **Belsnickle,** Composition, Yellow Speckled Robe, Feather Tree Sprig, Germany, 8 In. | 354 |
| **Belsnickle,** Gold Coat, Rabbit Fur, 9½ In. | 150 |
| **Candy Containers** are listed in the Candy Container category. | |
| **Display,** Santa, Composition, Red & White Coat, Black Boots, Twig Tree, Germany, 36 In. | 1888 |
| **Display,** Santa, Toy Shop, Rocking Horse, Animated, Cardboard, Litho, Clockwork, 24 In. | 10620 |
| **Doll,** Santa Claus, Cloth, Felt, 25 In. | 295 |
| **Group,** 3 Magi, On Horseback, Carved, Painted, Rectangular Base, 8 x 9½ In. | 240 |
| **Lantern,** Composition, Electrified, Japan, 11 In., Pair | 83 |
| **Lantern,** Santa Claus Head, Smiling, Composition, Red, White Paint, Bail Handle, 6 In. | 413 |
| **Nativity Figures,** Lambs, Wax, Box, Weihnchts-Schafchen, 4 To 5 In., 4 Piece | 118 |
| **Nodder,** Polar Bear, Santa Claus On Back, Glass Eyes, Composition, Feather Tree, 16 In. | 5605 |

| | |
|---|---|
| **Nodder,** Santa Claus, Composition Head, Wood, Fur Beard, Germany, 11 ½ In. | 592 |
| **Nodder,** Santa Claus, Composition, Brown Coat, Holding Tree, 9 ½ In. | 2725 |
| **Nodder,** Santa Claus, Lantern, Sack, Celluloid, Windup, Marked, Japan, c.1930, 2 ½ In. ....*illus* | 139 |
| **Pail,** Old Kris Kringle Smoking Tobacco, Kris Kringle Bust, Lid, Bail, 5 ½ In. | 120 |
| **Pin,** Santa Claus, I Am At Marshall Fields, Metal, c.1905, 1 ¼ In. | 316 |
| **Plate,** Girl, Doll, Necklace, Holly Border, C.D. Kenny Co., Tin, Round, 10 In. | 106 |
| **Plate,** Santa Claus Checking Sleeping Child, C.D. Kenny Co., Tin, 9 ½ In. | 236 |
| **Plates** that are limited edition are listed in the Collector Plate category or in the correct factory listing. | |
| **Postcard,** Cats, Holly, With Best Christmas Wishes, 1910 | 5 |
| **Postcard,** Falstaff Lemp Beer, Santa On Roof, Beer Case, Calendar, c.1931, 3 x 5 In. | 180 |
| **Postcard,** Santa Claus Uncle Sam, Hanging Cookie On Tree, Vertical, 3 x 5 In. | 720 |
| **Postcard,** Santa Claus Uncle Sam, Standing On Step, Holding Tree, Vertical, 3 x 5 In. | 660 |
| **Postcard,** Santa Claus, Black Robe, Chiostri, Art Deco, 3 x 5 In. | 240 |
| **Postcard,** Santa Claus, Brown Robe, Seated, Girl Whispering, Squeaker, 3 x 5 In. | 60 |
| **Postcard,** Santa Claus, Children, Whitney, 1920 | 9 |
| **Postcard,** Santa Claus, On Telephone, Changes Month, Day, Mechanical Shutter, 3 x 5 In. | 90 |
| **Postcard,** Santa Claus, Pink Suit, Changes To Winter Scene, Mechanical Shutter, 3 x 5 In. | 330 |
| **Postcard,** Santa Claus, Red Hat, Holly Trim, Real Hair Beard, Gifts, Kids, 3 x 5 In. | 60 |
| **Postcard,** Santa Claus, Red Suit, Mistletoe Beard, Girl, Whispering, Hold-To-Light, 3 x 5 In. | 300 |
| **Postcard,** Santa Claus, Red Suit, With Stars, Children, Vertical, 3 x 5 In. | 360 |
| **Postcard,** Santa Claus, Red, Gold Suit, 2 Children, Hold-To-Light, 3 x 5 In. | 360 |
| **Postcard,** Santa Claus, With Sack, Green Robe, Mechanical Shutter, 3 x 5 In. | 210 |
| **Santa Claus Suit,** Jacket, Hat, Whiskers, Boots, Belt, Cloth, Plastic, Ben Cooper, Inc. | 47 |
| **Santa Claus,** Cloth Body, Molded Face, Red Fabric Suit, Fur Trim, c.1940, 27 In. | 148 to 236 |
| **Santa Claus,** Molded Plastic, Red, Cream, Black, Lighted, 16 In. | 59 |
| **Santa Claus,** Red Suit, Staff, Basket, Feather Tree, Paint, Chalkware, c.1900, 17 In. | 1610 |
| **Santa Claus,** Red, White, Black, Fur Trim, Composition, Fabric, Steiff, 14 In. | 413 |
| **Santa Claus,** Reindeer, Sleigh, Blue, Cast Iron, Open Shell Shape, Wheels, Hubley, 15 In. | 443 |
| **Santa Claus,** Sleigh Driver, Reindeer, Runners, Wheels, Cast Iron, Kyser & Rex, 12 In. | 3300 |
| **Santa Claus,** Sleigh, 2 Reindeer, Green, Gold, Red Paint, Cast Iron, Hubley, 15 ½ In. | 1200 |
| **Santa Claus,** Sleigh, Papier-Mache, Loofah, 1940s, 8 x 5 In. | 275 |
| **Scarf,** Santa Claus, Snow, Black Attire, Toys, Linen, Frame, Oriental Print Co., 22 x 17 In. | 210 |
| **Stocking,** Child's, Cotton, Merry Christmas, Striped, 6 In., Pair ...........................*illus* | 24 |
| **Toy,** Christmas Morning, Children, Seated, Toys, Cat, Platform, Paint, Cast Iron, 10 In. | 20400 |
| **Toy,** Father Christmas, Blue Robe, Sled In Tow, Candy Tin, Lid, Meier, 3 ¾ In. | 6000 |
| **Toy,** Santa Claus On Scooter, Battery, Marked Illfelder Toy, Box | 89 |
| **Toy,** Santa Claus, Blue Robe, Composition, Fur Beard, Windup, Germany, 10 In. ...........*illus* | 354 |
| **Toy,** Santa Claus, Mechanical, Feather Tree, Sculpted Head, Fur Beard, c.1920, 27 In. | 1568 |
| **Toy,** Santa Claus, Red, White, Black, Cloth Body, Silk Suit, 25 In. | 177 |
| **Toy,** Santa Claus, Reindeer, Sleigh, Tin, Windup, Strauss, c.1921 | 1595 |
| **Toy,** Santa Claus, Roly Poly, Composition, Painted, Red, White, c.1930, 9 ¼ In. | 258 |
| **Toy,** Santa Claus, Roly Poly, Painted, Red, White, Green, Label, Schoenhut, 7 In. | 885 |
| **Toy,** Santa Claus, Sleigh, 2 Reindeer, Tin Litho, Windup, Key, Strauss, c.1923, 11 In. .........*illus* | 342 |
| **Toy,** Santa Claus, Sleigh, 2 Reindeer, Tin Lithograph Windup, Strauss, 11 ¼ In. | 1020 |
| **Toy,** Santa Claus, Sleigh, Toys, Bentwood, Loofah, Tin, Composition, Paint, Germany, 16 In. | 1416 |
| **Toy,** Santa Claus, Split Log Sleigh, Toys, Composition, Wire Form, Felt, Germany | 590 |
| **Toy,** Santa Claus, Standing, Toys, Platform, Bells, Spirit Paint, Cast Iron, Watrous, 6 In. | 1680 |
| **Toy,** Santa Claus, Walker, Jumping Jack, Tin Litho, Paint, Clockwork, Germany, 7 In. | 7080 |
| **Wreath,** Berry, Painted, 11 ½ In. | 106 |
| **Yule Log,** Paper, Multicolor Ribbons, Berries, Hatchet, Embossed, 12 In. | 177 |

**CHRISTMAS TREES** made of feathers and Christmas tree decorations of all types are popular with collectors. The first decorated Christmas tree in America is claimed by many states, including Pennsylvania (1747), Massachusetts (1832), Illinois (1833), Ohio (1838), and Iowa (1845). The first glass ornaments were imported from Germany about 1860. Paper and tinsel ornaments were made in Dresden, Germany, from about 1880 to 1940. Manufacturers in the United States were making ornaments in the early 1870s. Electric lights were first used on a Christmas tree in 1882. Character light bulbs became popular in the 1920s, bubble lights in the 1940s, twinkle bulbs in the 1950s, plastic bulbs by 1955. In this book a Christmas light is a holder for a candle used on the tree. Other forms of lighting include light bulbs. Other Christmas collectibles are listed in the preceding section.

| | |
|---|---|
| **Bulb Shade,** Popeye Cheers, Multicolor, Box, 1930s, 8 Piece | 183 |
| **Feather,** Goose, Green, Red Berries, Stenciled Wood Stand, 50 In. | 561 |
| **Feather,** New Growth Ends, Berry On Tips, Germany, 66 In. ...........................*illus* | 1770 |
| **Feather,** White Painted Block Base, Red, Green Stenciled Laurel Drape, 54 In. | 590 |
| **Feather,** White, Pressed Cotton Fruits, Vegetables, 2-Dimensional, 36 In. | 89 |

C

**Christmas,** Stocking, Child's, Cotton, Merry Christmas, Striped, 6 In., Pair
$24

Conestoga Auction Co., Inc.

**Christmas,** Toy, Santa Claus, Blue Robe, Composition, Fur Beard, Windup, Germany, 10 In.
$354

Bertoia Auctions

**Christmas,** Toy, Santa Claus, Sleigh, 2 Reindeer, Tin Litho, Windup, Key, Strauss, c.1923, 11 In.
$342

Showtime Auction Servicesa

**TIP**
*Don't wrap Christmas ornaments in newspaper. The ink may rub off. Don't store them in plastic bags. Moisture may condense and cause problems.*

C

**Christmas Tree,** Feather, New Growth Ends, Berry On Tips, Germany, 66 In.
$1,770

Bertoia Auctions

**Christmas Tree,** Feather, Wood Base, Germany, c.1910, 47 In.
$540

Garth's Auctioneers & Appraisers

**Christmas Tree,** Light Bulb, Figural, Santa Claus, Painted, Japan, 9 In.
$119

James D. Julia Auctioneers

**Christmas Tree,** Ornament, Alligator, Multicolor, Dresden, 4 In.
$767

Bertoia Auctions

**Christmas Tree,** Ornament, Glass, Kugel, Cluster Of Grapes, Germany, 3 In.
$885

Conestoga Auction Co., Inc.

**Christmas Tree,** Ornament, Lobster, Red, Claws, Feelers, Germany, Dresden, 4 In.
$443

Bertoia Auctions

**Christmas Tree,** Ornament, Monkey, Seated, Arms Outstretched, Silver, Dresden, Germany, 2½ In.
$826

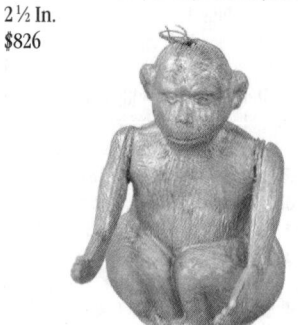

Bertoia Auctions

**Christmas Tree,** Ornament, Rocking Horse, Embossed Silver, Dresden, 2½ In.
$767

Bertoia Auctions

**Christmas Tree,** Ornament, Zeppelin, Blown Glass, Wire Wrapped, Paper Santa Rider, Basket, 6 In.
$207

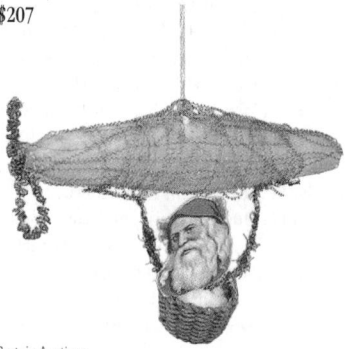

Bertoia Auctions

**Christmas Tree,** Ornament, Zeppelin, Swastika, Glass, 6½ In.
$168

The Stein Auction Company

| | |
|---|---|
| **Feather,** White, Wood Base, Tinsel, Beaded Garlands, Drops, Ornaments, c.1890, 45 In. | 840 |
| **Feather,** Wire Armature, Ornaments, Block Base, Germany, 41 In. | 304 |
| **Feather,** Wood Base, Charlie Brown Tree, 37 In. | 207 |
| **Feather,** Wood Base, Germany, c.1910, 47 In. *illus* | 540 |
| **Light Bulb,** Figural, Santa Claus, Painted, Japan, 9 In. *illus* | 119 |
| **Light Set,** Disneyana, Mickey Mouse, Silly Symphony, Mazda, 9¼ x 16½ In. | 189 |
| **Light Set,** Mickey Mouse, Minnie, Tree, Noma, 1930s, 16¼ x 6 In. | 229 |
| **Light Set,** Multiple Characters, Mazda, Box, 1954, 9½ x 13¼ In. | 208 |
| **Ornament Set,** Scotsman, Irishman, John Bull, Foxy Grandpa, Germany, 3 To 5 In. | 236 |
| **Ornament Set,** Snow White, Blown Glass, Multicolor, Box, 3½ In., 8 Piece | 172 |
| **Ornament,** Alligator, Multicolor, Dresden, 4 In. *illus* | 767 |
| **Ornament,** Bird Of Paradise, Red Feather Tail, Crest, Dresden, Germany, 4 In. | 118 |
| **Ornament,** Blue Icicles, Swirl Pattern, Blown Glass, Germany, 4 To 5 In., 10 Piece | 266 |
| **Ornament,** Cherub, Gold Scallop Shell, Silver Swan, Dresden, Germany, 4 In. | 236 |
| **Ornament,** Clown, Harlequin, Dresden, Germany, 3 In. | 1062 |
| **Ornament,** Elk, Hand Painted, Dresden, Germany, 3½ In. | 413 |
| **Ornament,** Frog, Multicolor Iridescent, Dresden, Germany, 2 In. | 384 |
| **Ornament,** Garland Chain, Alternating Silver & Gold Links, Dresden, Germany, 70 In. | 384 |
| **Ornament,** Go Fetch Dog, Running, Ears Back, Extended Tongue, Dresden, Germany, 3 In. | 118 |
| **Ornament,** Icicle, Blown Glass, 11½ In. | 12 |
| **Ornament,** Kugel, Cluster Of Grapes, Germany, 3 In. *illus* | 885 |
| **Ornament,** Kugel, Cobalt Blue, Round, 1¾ In. | 413 |
| **Ornament,** Kugel, Gold, Egg Shape, 4½ In. | 384 |
| **Ornament,** Kugel, Grape Cluster, Cobalt Blue, Blown Mold, 4¾ In. | 1003 |
| **Ornament,** Kugel, Grape Cluster, Glass, Cobalt Blue, Green, Metal Cap, 8 In., Pair | 413 |
| **Ornament,** Kugel, Green, 7½ In. | 330 |
| **Ornament,** Kugel, Green, Blown, 2½ In. | 83 |
| **Ornament,** Kugel, Purple, Round, 1¾ In. | 944 |
| **Ornament,** Kugel, Silver, Grape Bunch, 4½ In. | 271 |
| **Ornament,** Kugel, Silver, Royal Blue Band, Painted Flowers, 4¼ In. | 266 |
| **Ornament,** Kugel, Small, Various Colors, 1¼ To 2 In., 12 Piece | 826 |
| **Ornament,** Lobster, Maine, Claws, Feelers, Dresden, Germany, 4 In. | 531 |
| **Ornament,** Lobster, Red, Claws, Feelers, Germany, Dresden, 4 In. *illus* | 443 |
| **Ornament,** Man-In-The-Moon, Sunburst, Silver, Dresden, Germany, 2 & 4 In. | 413 |
| **Ornament,** Monkey, Seated, Arms Outstretched, Silver, Dresden, Germany, 2½ In. *illus* | 826 |
| **Ornament,** Parrot, Multicolor, Flat, Dresden, Germany, 7 In., Pair | 236 |
| **Ornament,** Peacock, Full Fan Tail, Iridescent, Dresden, Germany, 4 In. | 561 |
| **Ornament,** Polar Bear, Walking, Dresden, Germany, 4 In. | 413 |
| **Ornament,** Rocking Horse, Embossed Silver, Dresden, 2½ In. *illus* | 767 |
| **Ornament,** Royal British Lion, Dresden, Germany, 2½ In. | 561 |
| **Ornament,** Silver Chateau, 4-Story House, Dresden, Germany, 2 In. | 443 |
| **Ornament,** Silver, Gold, Raised Ribs, Round, Blown Mold, 2½ In. | 767 |
| **Ornament,** Sterling, Carousel, Flag Horse, Flirting Rabbit, Box, 4 x 3 In., 2 Piece | 242 |
| **Ornament,** Sterling, Various Snowflakes, Gorham, 3½ In., 12 Piece | 529 |
| **Ornament,** Wild Turkey, Painted Gold, Red, Dresden, Germany, 3 In. | 472 |
| **Ornament,** Zeppelin, Blown Glass, Wire Wrapped, Paper Santa Rider, Basket, 6 In. *illus* | 207 |
| **Ornament,** Zeppelin, L.Z. 129, Glass, 3¾ In. | 60 |
| **Ornament,** Zeppelin, Swastika, Glass, 6½ In. *illus* | 168 |
| **Stand,** Paint, Cast Iron, Hubley, 9¾ x 9¾ In. | 570 |
| **Stand,** Poinsettia, Green, Red, White Paint, 6 x 13 In. | 30 |
| **Stand,** Santa's Boots Shape, Cast Iron, Black Paint, 4 Fasteners, c.1925, 12 In. | 708 |

**CHROME** items in the Art Deco style became popular in the 1930s. Collectors are most interested in high-style pieces made by the Connecticut firms of Chase Brass & Copper Co., Manning-Bowman & Co., and others.

| | |
|---|---|
| **Ashtray,** Mack Truck Bulldog, Art Deco, 1930s, 5½ In. | 30 |
| **Ashtray,** Pincherette Pelican, Hamilton Products, 1950s, 5¾ In. Diam. | 27 |
| **Bottle Opener,** Nude, Germany, 1970s, 4¾ In. | 50 |
| **Cake Saver,** Plastic Handle, Lincoln Beauty Ware, 12 x 12 x 5 In. | 20 |
| **Canister Set,** Horizontal Ribs, Black Lid, Red Knob, Art Deco, 3 Piece | 65 |
| **Lamp,** 3-Light, Midcentury Modern, Acrylic Leaves, 20th Century, 26 x 21 In., Pair | 492 |
| **Lamp,** Electric, G. Kovacs, Demilune Base & Shade, Lucite Stem & Pulls, 1970s, 59 x 20 In. | 531 |
| **Lamp,** Electric, Stacked Orbs, Painted Black Metal Base, R. Sonneman, 1960s, 46 In. | 295 |
| **Lamp,** Enameled Steel, 4-Light, R. Sonneman, 1970s, 32 x 14 In. | 768 |
| **Lamp,** Midcentury Modern, Murano Glass, 3 Standards, Globe Shades, 57 x 12 In. | 984 |
| **Lamp,** Robert Sonneman Style, 3 Standards, White Globes, Steel Base, 54 x 12 In. | 120 |

**Cigar Store Figure,** Indian Maiden, Terry & Nobiling, Signed, In. A. Clong Ptr., c.1890, 80 In.
$22,800

Garth's Auctioneers & Appraisers

**Cinnabar,** Box, Trefoil, Carved, Landscape, Flowers, Marked, Chinese, 6¼ x 6¾ In.
$356

James D. Julia Auctioneers

**Cinnabar,** Plate, Peony Branch, Scholar's Rock, Flower Border, Wood Stand, c.1900, 12 In.
$676

New Orleans Auction Galleries, Inc.

**Civil War,** Cipher Disc, Brass, 2 Discs, Axle, Latin Alphabet, Confederate Secret Service
$18,000

Cowan's Auctions

**Civil War,** Log, Antietam, Shell Embedded In Log, 27 x 8 In.
$1,560

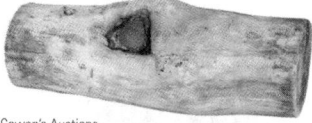

Cowan's Auctions

**Clarice Cliff,** Cafe-Au-Lait, Inkwell, Berries, 2 Cubes, Pen Holder, Square Handle Lids
$1,202

Bonhams

**Clarice Cliff,** Ophelia, Plate Set, Green, Flowers, Woven Vase, Royal Staffordshire, 10 ¾ In., 12 Piece
$546

Humler & Nolan

| | |
|---|---|
| **Lamp,** Sconce, Reggiani, 9 Convex Discs, Italy, 32 ½ x 26 In. | 3172 |
| **Lamp,** Sconce, Reggiani, 9 Convex Discs, Italy, 33 x 29 In. | 2928 |
| **Model Airplane,** Floor Stand, Full Bodied, Aluminum, Chromed Metal, 31 x 27 In. | 738 |
| **Sculpture,** Wall, Bottle Opener, C. Jere, 19 x 47 In. | 938 |
| **Sculpture,** Wall, Longhorn Steer Head, Streamlined Style, 20th Century, 23 x 34 In. | 345 |
| **Sculpture,** Wall, Raindrops, Flat & Convex Drops, C. Jere, 25 x 65 In. | 3294 |
| **Smoking Stand,** Black Swivel Top, Removable Ash Cup, Lazy Boy, W. Von Nessen, 21 In. | 854 |
| **Toothpick Holder,** Chick, Open Mouth, 1930s, 3 In. | 28 |
| **Vase,** Art Deco, 4-Tube, Bud, Centaur Mark, Chase, 1930s, 9 In. | 50 |
| **Vase,** Cone Shape, Stepped Base, Spiraling Lines, Art Deco, 1930s, 6 In. | 60 |
| **Wine Cooler,** 2 Bottle Holders, Center Ice Compartment, Oval Stepped Base, 9 x 13 In. | 90 |

**CIGAR STORE FIGURES** of carved wood or cast iron were used as advertisements in front of the Victorian cigar store. The carved figures are now collected as folk art. They range in size from counter type, about three feet, to over eight feet high.

| | |
|---|---|
| **Black Dandy,** Wide Brim Hat, Holding Cigars, Painted, c.1890, 55 x 72 In. | 33210 |
| **Black Man,** Smiling, Holding Tray, Red Coat, Yellow, Red Pants, Carved, Paint, 60 In. | 410 |
| **Boy,** Black, Barefoot, Striped Shirt, Kerchief, Visor Cap, Bagger Short Pants, c.1900, 26 In. | 3555 |
| **Brave,** Tree Stump, Tobacco Leaves, Cast Zinc, J.W. Fiske, c.1880, 63 In. | 14820 |
| **Chief,** Bow, Bear Claws, Marked, W. Demuth & Co., c.1875, 91 In. | 33000 |
| **Indian Maiden,** Feathered Headdress, Cigar Bundle, Raised Arm, Wood, 1900s, 67 In. | 13640 |
| **Indian Maiden,** Metal Headband, Holding Cigars, Painted, Countertop, 32 In. | 19680 |
| **Indian Maiden,** Painted, Inscribed, Cut Plug Snuff, Cast Iron, Tabletop, c.1900, 37 In. | 2640 |
| **Indian Maiden,** Standing, Raised Arm, Tobacco Leaf, Wood, Painted, 71 In. | 12650 |
| **Indian Maiden,** Terry & Nobiling, Signed, In. A. Clong Ptr., c.1890, 80 In. ...........*illus* | 22800 |
| **Indian Maiden,** Wearing Tunic, Holding Cigars, Painted, Cast Zinc, c.1871, 53 In. | 23370 |
| **Indian Princess,** Outstretched Hand, Holding Tobacco, Cigars, Painted, 57 x 72 In. | 92250 |
| **Indian Princess,** Tobacco Leaf, Wood, Carved, Stepped Base, 1800s, 72 x 20 x 17 In. | 36000 |
| **Indian Warrior,** Painted, Wood, Composition, Tabletop, 27 ½ In. | 3690 |
| **Indian,** Brave, Bow, Quiver, Arrows, Paint, c.1950, 47 x 12 In. | 431 |
| **Indian,** Coat, Sash, Moccasins, Headdress, Tobacco Leaf, Cigars, Mahogany, 40 In. | 738 |
| **Indian,** Fringed Garb, Leaning On Post, Holder For Cigars, Painted, c.1870, 43 In. | 2829 |
| **Indian,** Headdress, Braids, Medallion, Tunic, Cylindrical Base, 96 In. | 2160 |
| **Indian,** Headdress, Hatchet, Cigar 5 Cent, Multicolor | 480 |
| **Indian,** Headdress, Looking Pose With Hand Over Eye, Blue, Red, 72 In. | 4800 |
| **Indian,** Holding Knife & Tobacco, Gesso Over Wood, Red, White, 77 In. | 14640 |
| **Indian,** Standing, Zinc, Multicolor Paint, William Demuth & Co., c.1859, 65 In. | 2070 |
| **Punch,** Wood, Carved, Painted, Pedestal, Multicolor, 1800s, 69 ½ In. | 102600 |
| **Woman,** Classical Gown, Liberty Cap, Flowing Hair, Painted, c.1890, 47 x 16 In. | 20910 |

**CINNABAR** is a vermilion or red lacquer. Pieces are made with tens to hundreds of thicknesses of the lacquer that is later carved. Most cinnabar was made in the Orient.

| | |
|---|---|
| **Box,** Carved, Dragon Waves, Pearls, Shou Character, Chinese, 1900s, 6 ¾ In. | 356 |
| **Box,** Carved, Elders, Pagoda, Mountain Landscape, Black Interior, Peonies, 5 x 7 In. | 5900 |
| **Box,** Cylindrical, Dome Lid, Relief Carved, Dragon, Pearl Of Wisdom, Chinese, 3 ½ x 3 In. | 322 |
| **Box,** Trefoil, Carved, Landscape, Flowers, Marked, Chinese, 6 ¼ x 6 ¾ In. ...........*illus* | 356 |
| **Brush Pot,** Carved, Dragons, Waves, Thunder Meander Border, Chinese, 1800s, 6 x 6 In. | 356 |
| **Plate,** Peony Branch, Scholar's Rock, Flower Border, Wood Stand, c.1900, 12 In. ...........*illus* | 676 |
| **Snuff Bottle,** Lion Masks, 3 ¾ In. | 209 |
| **Stand,** Carved, Red, Black Underneath, Lotus & Key Fret, 4-Footed, Chinese, 4 In. | 121 |
| **Vase,** Overall Carved Scrolls, Leaves, Round Foot, 13 ½ x 6 ½ In. | 150 |

**CIVIL WAR** mementos are important collectors' items. Most of the pieces are military items used from 1861 to 1865. Be sure to avoid any explosive munitions.

| | |
|---|---|
| **Belt Plate,** Cartridge, Union Army, Brass, Eagle, Arrows, Olive Branch, Stamped | 236 |
| **Broadside,** Recruiting, Vosburgh Chasseurs, 53rd NY, Eagle Brigade, 1861, 38 x 24 In. | 2963 |
| **Broadside,** Robert E. Lee Farewell Address, April 10, 1865, Printed, Frame, 13 x 9 In. | 374 |
| **Cap,** Kepi, Dark Blue Broadcloth, Pennsylvania, Gold Galloon, Gold Tape, Visor | 492 |
| **Cipher Disc,** Brass, 2 Discs, Axle, Latin Alphabet, Confederate Secret Service ...........*illus* | 18000 |
| **Coat,** Medical Officer, Wool, Double Breasted, 7 Buttons, Gold Oak Leaves, Civil War | 3525 |
| **Drum,** Drumsticks, Holder, Rope Tension, Wooden, 19th Century, 12 x 16 ¾ In. | 400 |
| **Jacket,** Artillery, Wool, Red Trim, 12 Button, Pvt. Henry Thomas 8th NYHA | 3877 |
| **Log,** Antietam, Shell Embedded In Log, 27 x 8 In. ...........*illus* | 1560 |

| | |
|---|---|
| **Map,** United States Military Railroads, Confederate, J. Bien, 1862-66, 25 x 38 In. ......................... | 732 |
| **Pipe Bowl,** Carved, Chancellorsville & Frdksburg, Gettsyburg, c.1861, 3 In................................... | 3198 |
| **Plate,** Dinner, Lincoln's, White House, Alhambra, Scalloped Rim, Eagle, Shield, Limoges, 9 In.... | 9200 |
| **Rattle,** Wood, Carved J. Scrott, Turned Handle, c.1860, 8 In. ........................................................ | 518 |
| **Stool,** Camp, Wooden Frame, Carpet Seat, Marked G.H. Wright, c.1863, 35 x 16 In. .................. | 492 |
| **Sword,** Confederate Officer, Leather Wrapped Grip, Brass Hilt, c.1863, 35 In................................ | 22140 |
| **Sword,** US Army, NCO, Model 1840, Single Edge, Marked Ames Mfg., Chicopee, 1864, 32 In. ....... | 165 |

**CKAW,** *see Dedham category.*

---

**CLARICE CLIFF** was a designer who worked in several English factories, including A.J. Wilkinson Ltd., Wilkinson's Royal Staffordshire Pottery, Newport Pottery, and Foley Pottery after the 1920s. She is best known for her brightly colored Art Deco designs, including the Bizarre line. She died in 1972. Reproductions have been made by Wedgwood.

| | |
|---|---|
| **Bizarre,** Inkwell, Double Cube, Penholder, Berries, Cafe-Au-Lait, 3 ½ x 4 In. ......................... | 1376 |
| **Bizarre,** Plate, Tree, Flowers, Rectangular, Stamped, 10 ¼ x 8 ¼ In. ......................................... | 120 |
| **Cafe-Au-Lait,** Inkwell, Berries, 2 Cubes, Pen Holder, Square Handle Lids ...........................*illus* | 1202 |
| **Crocus,** Bizarre, Vase, Flat Rim, Smokestack Shape, 8 In. ........................................................ | 423 |
| **Figurine,** Lion, Resting, Next To Globe, Acorns, Plants, Marked, 10 x 4 In.............................. | 466 |
| **Ophelia,** Plate Set, Green, Flowers, Woven Vase, Royal Staffordshire, 10 ¾ In., 12 Piece .....*illus* | 546 |
| **Sunburst,** Bizarre, Teapot, Stamford, 6 In. .............................................................................. | 1800 |

---

**CLEWELL** was made in limited quantities by Charles Walter Clewell of Canton, Ohio, from 1902 to 1955. Pottery was covered with a thin coating of bronze, then treated to make the bronze turn different colors. Pieces covered with copper, brass, or silver were also made. Mr. Clewell's secret formula for blue patinated bronze was burned when he died in 1965.

| | |
|---|---|
| **Basket,** Molded Wavy Design, Copper Clad, 6 x 4 In..................................................................... | 671 |
| **Mug,** Copper Clad, Lizard Design, 3 Handles, Signed, 7 x 5 In. .......................................*illus* | 813 |
| **Mug,** Molded, Brown, 5 In....................................................................................................... | 184 |
| **Punch Bowl,** 12 Cups, Copper Clad Porcelain, Footed, Incised, Canton, 9 x 11 In., 13 Piece....... | 438 |
| **Vase,** Bowl, Lobed, Copper Clad, 4 ½ x 8 ½ In............................................................................. | 732 |
| **Vase,** Bud, Blue, Purple, Copper Clad, 7 ¼ In.............................................................................. | 274 |
| **Vase,** Bud, Copper Clad, 7 ½ In. ............................................................................................... | 183 |
| **Vase,** Bud, Copper Clad, 13 ½ In. .............................................................................................. | 488 |
| **Vase,** Copper Clad, Basket Shape, Molded Designs, 4 x 6 In. .................................................*illus* | 250 |
| **Vase,** Copper Clad, Carved Lily Design, Swollen, 3 ½ x 6 ½ In. ..........................................*illus* | 1000 |
| **Vase,** Copper Clad, Hexagonal, Tapered, 11 ½ x 4 ½ In.............................................................. | 1342 |
| **Vase,** Copper Clad, Purple, 9 x 4 In.......................................................................................... | 610 |
| **Vase,** Copper Clad, Red, Turquoise, 11 ¾ In. ............................................................................. | 2562 |
| **Vase,** Lilies, Swollen, Carved, Copper Clad, Marked, 6 ½ x 3 ½ In........................................... | 1000 |
| **Vase,** Mottled Bronze, Embossed Arts & Crafts Designs, 2 Inset Handles, 9 In. ......................... | 960 |
| **Vase,** Mottled Green Patina, Flared, Footed, 5 In. ...................................................................... | 360 |
| **Vase,** Squat, Copper Clad, Handles, 4 x 1 ¾ In. ......................................................................... | 183 |

---

**CLIFTON POTTERY** was founded by William Long in Newark, New Jersey, in 1905. He worked there until 1909 making lines that included Crystal Patina and Clifton Indian Ware. Clifton Pottery made art pottery until 1911 and then concentrated on wall and floor tile. By 1914, the name had been changed to Clifton Porcelain and Tile Company. Another firm, Chesapeake Pottery, sold majolica marked *Clifton Ware.*

| | |
|---|---|
| **Vase,** Green Glaze, Long Neck, Spreading Base, Signed, 1906, 4 ½ In. ..................................... | 125 |
| **Vase,** Green Matte Glaze, Bulbous, Elongated Neck, 1905, 10 ½ x 5 In. .................................. | 580 |
| **Vase,** Poppy, Green Matte Glaze, Oval, Impressed, c.1905, 8 In. .............................................. | 431 |

---

**CLOCKS** of all types have always been popular with collectors. The eighteenth-century tall case, or grandfather's, clock was designed to house a works with a long pendulum. The name on the clock is usually the maker but sometimes it is a merchant or other craftsman. In 1816, Eli Terry patented a new, smaller works for a clock, and the case became smaller. The clock could be kept on a shelf instead of on the floor. By 1840, coiled springs were used and even smaller clocks were made. Battery-powered electric clocks were made in the 1870s. A garniture set can include a clock and other objects displayed on a mantel.

| | |
|---|---|
| **Aaron Sellman,** Quarter Chiming, Carved Scrolls, Veneered Case, 25 In. .................................... | 4920 |
| **Advertising,** Call For Philip Morris, White, Red Lettering, Round, 15 ½ In................................ | 720 |

**Clewell,** Mug, Copper Clad, Lizard Design, 3 Handles, Signed, 7 x 5 In. $813

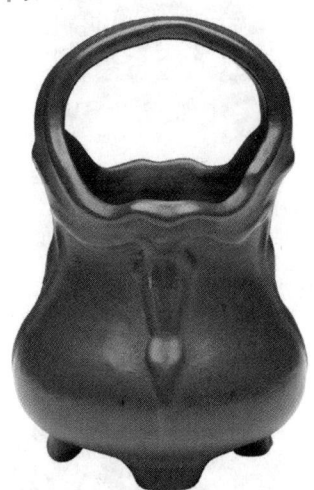

**Clewell,** Vase, Copper Clad, Basket Shape, Molded Designs, 4 x 6 In. $250

**Clewell,** Vase, Copper Clad, Carved Lily Design, Swollen, 3 ½ x 6 ½ In. $1,000

**Clock,** Advertising, Calumet Baking Powder, Regulator, Sessions Clock Co., Key, Pendulum, 38 In.
**$720**

Showtime Auction Services

---

**Clock,** Advertising, Whistle Soda, Painted, Die Cut, Electric, Phelps Mfg. Co., 24 x 24 In.
**$851**

James D. Julia Auctioneers

---

**Clock,** Archibald Knox, Tudric, Pewter, Enamel, Liberty & Co., c.1905, 7¾ x 4 In.
**$4,062**

Rago Arts & Auction Center

| | |
|---|---|
| **Advertising,** Calumet Baking Powder, Regulator, Sessions Clock Co., Key, Pendulum, 38 In. *illus* | 720 |
| **Advertising,** Dr Pepper, Deco Style, Good For Life, 5 Cents, 22 x 17 In. | 3025 |
| **Advertising,** It's Time To Drink, Thompson's Wild Cherry Bitters, Bronze, Cherubs, 17 In. | 1344 |
| **Advertising,** J & K Shoe For Women, Scalloped Rim, Red, Cream, Round, Electric, 12 In. | 150 |
| **Advertising,** J. & P. Coats, Oak, 31-Day, Sessions Clock Co., 17 x 26½ In. | 474 |
| **Advertising,** John Fitzer & Bros, Baird Clock Co., 31½ In. | 802 |
| **Advertising,** Kools Tobacco, Round, Electric, 15 In. | 720 |
| **Advertising,** Liberty Root Beer, 5 Cents, Roman Numerals, Marble, 25 In. Diam. | 150 |
| **Advertising,** Louis LeRoy, Crystal Regulator, Champleve Case, Portrait Pendulum, 12 x 8 In. | 1150 |
| **Advertising,** Moxie, Red, Cream, Electric, Square, 25½ In. | 600 |
| **Advertising,** Orange Crush, Wood Case, Glass Face, 38½ In. | 240 |
| **Advertising,** Packard, Round, Silver Rim, Light-Up, Neon, 20 In. | 1020 |
| **Advertising,** Parry Buggies, Gilt Pendulum Window, 17¼ x 26½ In. | 770 |
| **Advertising,** Red Goose Shoes, Metal, Glass, Electric, 15 In. | 210 |
| **Advertising,** Rockingham Poultry, It Is Time To Buy, Rooster, Pam Clock Co., c.1950, 15 In. | 460 |
| **Advertising,** Schwinn, Light-Up, Blue & Red Face, Dualite Corp., Electric, 16 In. | 702 |
| **Advertising,** Seidlitz Paints, Tinto Character, Red, Blue, Yellow, c.1945, 15 In. Diam. | 480 |
| **Advertising,** Stanton's Pain Relief, Household Remedy, Iron, Gold Paint, 1886, 12 x 11 In. | 1568 |
| **Advertising,** Thirsty Just Whistle, Whistle Soda, Masonite, 24 x 24 In. | 720 |
| **Advertising,** Weather-Bird Shoes, Rooster, Light-Up, 15 In. Diam. | 540 |
| **Advertising,** Whistle Soda, Painted, Die Cut, Electric, Phelps Mfg. Co., 24 x 24 In. *illus* | 851 |
| **Alarm,** Rhodium, Square, Quartz Movement, Switzerland, Tiffany & Co., 4 In. | 197 |
| **Ansonia,** Royal Bonn, Delft, Porcelain Face, Blue & Yellow Beveled Glass Door, 11 x 8 In. | 328 |
| **Archibald Knox,** Tudric, Pewter, Enamel, Liberty & Co., c.1905, 7¾ x 4 In. *illus* | 4062 |
| **Arnold & Lewis,** Shelf, Warrior Figure, Battle Dress, Spear, Bronze Patina, 24 x 20 In. | 316 |
| **Art Deco,** Marble, Gray Veins, Pink, 3 Sections, Shaped Top, Chevron Shapes, 14 x 9 In. | 94 |
| **Arts & Crafts,** Copper, Overhanging Top, Repousse Stylized Butterfly, c.1910, 10 x 10 In. | 369 |
| **Asa Munger,** Shelf, Mahogany, Ironing Board Top, Half Columns, Steel Dial, 1830s, 39 In. | 1438 |
| **Astroclock-Ological Time,** Carved, Gilt & Silver Wood, Pedro Friedeberg, 1960s, 22 x 18 In. *illus* | 4063 |
| **Baker,** Eleazer, Shelf, Federal, Mahogany, Eagle, Brass Finials, Columns, Bracket Feet, 27 In. | 1020 |
| **Banjo,** A. Willard, Federal, Mahogany, Gilt, Eglomise, Chariot Scene | 1800 |
| **Banjo,** A. Willard, Federal, Mahogany, White Painted Dial, c.1820, 33½ In. | 1020 |
| **Banjo,** A. Willard, Mahogany, Gilt Rope Twist, Glass Tablet, Woman In Garden, 35 In. | 5843 |
| **Banjo,** A. Willard, Mahogany, Gilt, Reverse-Painted Glass, Brass, 8-Day, c.1820, 34 In. *illus* | 2460 |
| **Banjo,** A. Willard, Mahogany, Reverse Painted Tablet, Country Scene, Alarm, c.1815, 33 In. | 11685 |
| **Banjo,** Chandler & Farley, Mahogany, Wooden Bezel, Brass, Alarm Movement, 33 In. | 1476 |
| **Banjo,** Colonial Revival, Mahogany Case, c.1900, 33½ x 10½ In. | 215 |
| **Banjo,** E. Howard, No. 5, Regulator, Rosewood, Grain Painted, 29 x 11 In. | 1298 |
| **Banjo,** Federal, Giltwood, Beaded Edge, Eagle Finial, Painted Tablet, Courting Couple, 43 In. | 1320 |
| **Banjo,** Foster Campos, Mahogany, Inlaid Frames, Ships, Eagle, Pendulum, 43 In. | 1230 |
| **Banjo,** Herschede, Hall Clock Co., Mahogany Case, Reverse Painted, c.1920, 34 In. | 1046 |
| **Banjo,** J.N. Dunning, Mahogany, Reverse Painted River Scene, Cottage, 8-Day, 32 In. | 1845 |
| **Banjo,** L. Curtis, Federal, Mahogany, Patriotic Panels, Gilt, c.1820, 38 In. | 1080 |
| **Banjo,** L. Curtis, Mahogany, Gilt Rope Molding, Mt. Vernon Tablet, Blue Moon Hands, 34 In. | 12300 |
| **Banjo,** Mahogany Veneer, Gilt Molding, Brass Eagle Finial, Chariot, 33 In. | 480 |
| **Banjo,** Mahogany Veneer, Gold Paint, Brass Ball Finial, Scenic Landscape, c.1815, 34 In. | 468 |
| **Banjo,** Plymouth Co., Mahogany, Painted Scene, Finial, c.1930, 29 In. | 270 |
| **Banjo,** Simon Willard & Son, Regulator, Mahogany, Tapered Neck, c.1820, 49 In. | 21600 |
| **Banjo,** T.E. Burleigh, Gilt, Eglomise Panel, Naval Battle, Don't Give Up The Ship, 42 In. | 2432 |
| **Banjo,** Waterbury Willard, Gilt Metal Trimmings, Marked Hull, Eagle, Pendulum, 44 In. | 523 |
| **Barnett,** Silver, 8-Sided, Canted Corners, Green Guilloche Enamel, Rectangular Base, 5 In. | 1250 |
| **Barometer,** Thermometer, Humidity Gauge, Onyx, Gold Wash, Desk Top Stand, 3 x 6 In. | 552 |
| **Birge & Fuller,** Shelf, Steeple, Mahogany, Painted Tablets, Wagon Spring, 8-Day, 27 In. | 2829 |
| **Birge & Fuller,** Steeple, Wagon Spring, Reverse Painted, 8-Day, c.1845, 26 In. *illus* | 6150 |
| **Birge,** Mallory & Co., Shelf, Triple Decker, Mahogany, Gilt, Fruit Basket, c.1845, 26½ In. | 400 |
| **Black Forest,** Cuckoo, Carved, Rabbit, Pheasant, Stag Head, 3-Weight, 30 x 59 In. *illus* | 6000 |
| **Black Forest,** Cuckoo, Stag Head, Guns, Hunting Horn, Rabbit & Bird Trophies, 39 x 29 In. | 2500 |
| **Blinking Eye,** Sambo, Banjo Player, Cast Iron, 30-Hour, Rectangular Base, 16 In. | 492 |
| **Boudoir,** Brass, Enamel, Maiden & Knight By Castle Clock Tower, 3 x 2 In. | 554 |
| **Boudoir,** Silver, Enamel, Blue Guilloche, Arched, Round Dial, Leafy Rim, Leather Case, 2 In. | 984 |
| **Bracket,** Gilt Bronze, Tempietto At San Pietro, Lionskin Of Hercules, Gong, 10 x 5 In. | 418 |
| **Bracket,** Gilt Bronze, Winged Griffins, Stepped Base, 8-Day Movement, c.1890, 20 x 9 In. | 2375 |
| **Bradley,** L., Shelf, Pillar & Scroll, Mahogany, Glass Tablet, Garden, 8-Day, 1825, 33 In. | 2583 |
| **Brass,** French, Porcelain Tiles, Cherub, Butterfly, Footed, PH Mourey, 1800s, 16 x 8 In. *illus* | 747 |

| | |
|---|---|
| **Brass,** Repousse, Cherub Border, Arabic Numbers, Engraved Dial, Pendulum, 18 In. | 86 |
| **Brewster & Ingraham,** Shelf, Gothic, Rosewood, Ogee, Spires, Etched Glass, 20 In. | 677 |
| **Brewster Manufacturing Co.,** Shelf, Rosewood, Column, Cornice, Tablet, 20 ½ In. | 308 |
| **Bronze,** Putti, Leaning, Architectural Symbols Of The Arts, Marble Base, France, 20 x 16 In. | 403 |
| **Brown,** J.C., Shelf, Mahogany, Ripple Front, 2 Spires, Tablet, Countryside, Zinc Dial, 20 In. | 738 |
| **Brown,** J.C., Shelf, Ogee, Rosewood, Spires, Ripple Front, Tablet, Gothic Arches, 20 In. | 1722 |
| **C. & N. Jerome,** Shelf, Mahogany Case, 8-Day, Brass, Pendulum, 22 In. | 185 |
| **Caldwell,** J.E., Aesthetic, Marble, Porcelain, Fans, Dragonflies, Birds, c.1879, 13 x 9 In. | 1722 |
| **Carriage,** Brass, Beveled Glass, Cornishe Case, Porcelain Dial, Handle, Tiffany & Co., 6 In. | 1046 |
| **Carriage,** Brass, Beveled Glass, Overlaid Friezes, Spade Hands, France, c.1900, 7 ½ In. | 738 |
| **Carriage,** Brass, Lapis Lazuli Panels, Hour Repeating, Alarm, France, c.1880, 7 In. ..........*illus* | 6765 |
| **Carriage,** Brass, Time & Strike, Beveled Glass, National Baby Week Inscription, c.1920, 9 In. | 414 |
| **Carriage,** Champleve, Brass, Beveled Glass, White, Flowers, Leaves, Handle, 7 In. | 2337 |
| **Carriage,** Enamel, Silver, Repeater, Gilt Banding, Case, Tiffany & Co., 3 ¼ In. ..................*illus* | 4305 |
| **Carriage,** L'Epee, Brass, Beveled Glass, Alarm, Handle, France, 20th Century, 7 In. | 984 |
| **Carriage,** M & S Woog, Brass, Alarm, Leather Carrying Case, Import, 7 ½ In. | 1046 |
| **Cartel,** Henry Dasson, Louis XVI Style, Gilt Bronze, Barometer, 1877, 35 In., Pair | 34375 |
| **Cartier,** Green Mottled Enameling, White Dial, Black Numerals, Fitted Box, 3 x 3 In. | 506 |
| **Cartier,** Travel, Stainless Steel, Gold Bands, Roman Numerals, Rectangular, 4 In. | 504 |
| **Chelsea,** Regulator, Weight Driven, Narrow Base, Step Molded, Round Face, c.1890, 36 In. | 1481 |
| **Congreave,** Rolling Ball, Brass, 4 Pillars, Tilt Table, Trefoil Hands, Cherry Stand, 22 In. | 1599 |
| **Cornu,** E., Shelf, Bronze Jar, Marble, Gilt, Twin Train, c.1875, 22 x 12 In. .........................*illus* | 3750 |
| **Cuckoo,** Black Forest, Oak, Walnut, Carved, Birds, Leaves, Pendulum, Germany, 31 x 19 In. | 1888 |
| **Cuckoo,** Black Forest, Spotted Cat, Blinking Eye, 2-Weight, Continental, c.1915, 16 x 10 In. | 688 |
| **Cuckoo,** Black Forest, Stag & Gun Crest, Dead Game By Dial, Carved, Germany, 40 In. | 492 |
| **Cuckoo,** Wood, Pheasant, Rabbit, Glass Eyes, Crossed Rifles, Stag, Germany, 19 x 12 In. | 150 |
| **Darice A. Paris,** Shelf, Empire, Portico, Brass, France, c.1859, 14 ½ In. | 439 |
| **Dent,** Mahogany, Silvered Sheet Brass, Brass Finials, Handles, Pendulum, c.1890, 17 In. | 2460 |
| **Desk,** Black Slate, Malachite, 3 Dials, Thermometer, Barometer, Brass Bezels, France, 9 In. | 492 |
| **Desk,** Bronze, Blue Globe, 3 Putti Holding Stem, Applied Stars, c.1900, 19 In. | 738 |
| **Desk,** Reed & Barton, Silver, Oval, Swivel, Acanthus Leaf Relief, Monogram, 9 x 9 In. | 874 |
| **Diorama,** Clock In Tower, Figural Landscape, Trees, Silver Plate, Glass Dome Lid, 6 In. | 2829 |
| **Eastman Clock Co.,** Girandole, Mahogany, White, Reverse Painted, Aurora, 45 In. | 3567 |
| **Elgin,** Wall, Sunburst, Rays, Black Dial, Arabic Numerals, Atomic Retro Style, 1960, 23 In. | 120 |
| **Eszeha,** Travel, 14K Yellow Gold, Rectangular, Blue Cabochon Thumbpiece, 1 ½ x 1 In. | 575 |
| **Eureka,** Balance Wheel, Electric, Mahogany, Satinwood, Glass, Enameled Dial, c.1910, 15 In. | 3444 |
| **Federal,** Tall Case, Broken Pediment, Turned Column, Shell Inlay, c.1810, 93 In. | 2714 |
| **Figural,** 4 Columns On Platform, Attendants Carrying, Gilt Metal, Lapis Lazuli, Jewels, 6 In. | 5535 |
| **Figural,** Atlas Holding Globe, Gilt Metal, Enamel, Cherub Finial, Paw Feet, Vienna, 13 In. | 9840 |
| **Figural,** Harp, Gilt Metal, Hinged Base Reveals Clock, Enamel Decoration, 7 In. | 4920 |
| **Figural,** Joe Louis, Boxer, Bronze Finish, White Metal, 12 ½ x 8 ½ In. ...............................*illus* | 288 |
| **Figural,** Mermaid Holding Round Case, Silver, Enamel, Rock Crystal Base, Vienna, 9 In. | 2952 |
| **Figural,** Rooster, Gem Set Case, Silver, Enamel, Rose Quartz Base, Vienna, 5 In. | 4305 |
| **Figural,** Satyr, On Stump, Holding Dial, Grapevines, Silver, Enamel, Rock Crystal, 7 In. | 3998 |
| **Figural,** Violinist, Silver, Enamel, Pearl, Raised Rectangular Base, Paneled, Vienna, 9 In. | 7955 |
| **Frankl,** P., Modernique, No. 431, Electric, Brass, Bakelite, Glass, Warren Telechron, 8 In. | 750 |
| **Frankl,** P., Telechron, Electric, Modernique, Chrome, Brass, Bakelite, c.1930, 8 x 6 In. ......*illus* | 1500 |
| **French Empire,** Mahogany, Pediment, Glass Door, Gothic Arch, Gridiron, 1840, 49 In. | 2091 |
| **French,** Mandarin Elder, Metal, Parasol Is Bell, Enamel Dial, Table Base, 10 x 5 In. .........*illus* | 1107 |
| **General Electric,** Shelf, Moderne, Streamline, Glass, Demilune, Black Dial, 7 x 15 In. | 240 |
| **Guibal,** Louis XVI, Gilt, Bronze Cupid, Holding Dial, Pink Marble, Paris, c.1895, 24 In. | 5938 |
| **Hammond,** Figural, 2 Standing Nudes, Octagonal Face, Footed Base, c.1930, 13 x 10 In. | 518 |
| **Horolovar,** Hickory Dickory Dock, Climbing Mouse, Wood Base, Germany, 1900s, 25 In. | 234 |
| **Howard & Co.,** E., Regulator, Mahogany Case, Black, Gold, 8-Day, c.1860, 50 In. | 4920 |
| **Howard & Davis,** Regulator, No. 1, Rosewood, Tapered Waist, 8-Day, c.1860, 50 In. | 14760 |
| **Howard & Davis,** Regulator, No. 3, Rosewood, Grain Paint, Zinc Dial, Damascene Bob, 38 In. | 9225 |
| **Howard Miller,** Ball, Brass Center & Spokes, Black Balls & Hands, G. Nelson, 1960s, 13 In. | 671 |
| **Howard Miller,** Ball, Windup Key, Nelson, 1949, 13 ¾ In. .........................................*illus* | 1125 |
| **Howard Miller,** Glass Tiles, Walnut, Enamel, G. Nelson, 1950s, 13 ½ x 13 ½ x 3 In. ...........*illus* | 938 |
| **Howard Miller,** Spikes, No. 2202-D, 1952, 18 In. | 1625 |
| **Howard Miller,** Sunflower, Birch Center, White Enamel Hands, G. Nelson, 29 In. | 1875 |
| **Howard Miller,** Teakwood, Painted Metal, 19 In. | 1200 |
| **Howard Miller,** Watermelon, Walnut, Brass, Elliptical, G. Nelson, c.1955, 5 x 8 In. | 1840 |
| **Howard,** E., No. 20, Marble Dial, c.1920, 28 In. | 2091 |

**Clock,** Astroclock-Ological Time, Carved, Gilt & Silver Wood, Pedro Friedeberg, 1960s, 22 x 18 In.
**$4,063**

Rago Arts & Auction Center

**Clock,** Banjo, A. Willard, Mahogany, Gilt, Reverse-Painted Glass, Brass, 8-Day, c.1820, 34 In.
**$2,460**

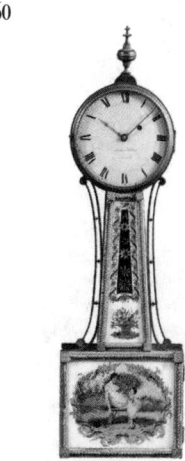

Skinner Auctioneers & Appraisers

**Clock,** Birge & Fuller, Steeple, Wagon Spring, Reverse Painted, 8-Day, c.1845, 26 In.
**$6,150**

Skinner Auctioneers & Appraisers

**Clock,** Black Forest, Cuckoo, Carved, Rabbit, Pheasant, Stag Head, 3-Weight, 30 x 59 In.
$6,000

Fox Auctions

**Clock,** Brass, French, Porcelain Tiles, Cherub, Butterfly, Footed, PH Mourey, 1800s, 16 x 8 In.
$747

Cottone Auctions

**Clock,** Carriage, Brass, Lapis Lazuli Panels, Hour Repeating, Alarm, France, c.1880, 7 In.
$6,765

Skinner Auctioneers & Appraisers

| | |
|---|---|
| **Howard,** E., Regulator, No. 7, Walnut, Figure 8, Scrolled, Cast Iron Weight, 8-Day, 58 In. | 28290 |
| **Howard,** E., Regulator, No. 75, Oak, Leaf, Maroon, Black & Gold Glass, 8-Day, 34 In. | 1845 |
| **Howard,** E., Wall, No. 20, Marble, Shaped, Roman Numerals, 8-Day, c.1920, 28 In. | 2091 |
| **Ingraham,** Regulator, School House, Calendar Dial, 1800s, 16 x 24½ In. | 205 |
| **Ingraham,** Shelf, 8-Day Brass Strike, Walnut, Reverse Painted Glass, Flowers, 16 x 9 In. | 92 |
| **Ithaca Calendar Clock Co.,** Skeleton, Walnut, Ebony Trim, Glass, 8-Day, 23 In. | 17220 |
| **Ithaca,** Regulator No. 2, Walnut, Zinc, Calendar, 8-Day, Time Only, c.1875, 44 In. *illus* | 1968 |
| **Junghans,** Wall, Ceramic, Blue, Glass Door, Timer, Teardrop, Max Bill, 1954, 10 x 7 In. | 531 |
| **Kroeber,** Noiseless Rotary No. 1, Derrick, Ebonized, Cone Pendulum, Glass Dome, 21 In. | 2091 |
| **L. Curtis,** Girandole, Gilt, Convex Glass, Aurora, Beaded Brass Bezel, 8-Day, 45 In. | 3321 |
| **Lantern,** Beech, Brass Dial, Steel Hands, Red, Gold, Finial, Arched Door, c.1725, 102 In. | 6765 |
| **Lantern,** Brass Case, Strapped Bell, Chapter Ring, Engraved Dial, c.1880, 16 In. | 861 |
| **Lantern,** Brass, Oak Case, Domed Bell, Baluster Posts, Weight Driven, c.1710, 78 In. | 2337 |
| **Lantern,** Thomas Swinnerton, Brass Case, Engraved Dial Plate, c.1690, 14 In. | 3321 |
| **LeCoultre,** Atmos, Brass, Glass, 9 x 7 In. | 660 |
| **LeCoultre,** Atmos, Brass, Glass Case, Visible Works, Swiss Movement, 9 x 8½ In. | 334 |
| **LeCoultre,** Atmos, Brass, Round Pendulum, 9¼ In. | 443 |
| **LeCoultre,** Atmos, Glass, Brass Case, Visible Mechanism, 8½ x 6½ x 9 In. | 529 |
| **LeCoultre,** Travel, Alarm, Nickel Plated Brass, 8-Day Mechanical Wind, 3¼ x 1 In. | 81 |
| **Leroy,** Shelf, Louis XV Style, Gilt Bronze, Flower Finial, Signed, Paris, c.1900, 16 In. | 1875 |
| **Louis Philippe,** Brass, Cathedral Shape, Gold Hands, Wooden Base, c.1840, 22½ In. | 2091 |
| **Louis Philippe,** Gilt Brass, Classical Woman, Seated, Lyre, Leaf Base, 16½ x 12 In. | 813 |
| **Lunette Shape,** Enameled, Bronze, Image Of Aurora, Continental, c.1900, 5 x 9 In. | 1476 |
| **Lyre,** E. Stennes, Mahogany, Reverse Painted Panel, Woman With Harp, 43 In. | 2214 |
| **Lyre,** Glass, Ormolu, Engine Turned Bezel, Pierced Hands, 8-Day, Gilt, France, 22 In. | 2460 |
| **Lyre,** J. Sawin, Mahogany, Leaf, Scroll, 8-Day, Reverse Painted Glass, Acorn Finial, 41 In. | 13530 |
| **Lyre,** Ovington Bros., Louis XVI Style, Putti, Garland, Gilt Bronze, Marble, 1884, 30 In. | 3840 |
| **Lyre,** Portrait Medallion, Leafy Trim, Silver, Enamel, Jewels, Vienna, 5½ In. | 1845 |
| **Marenzeller,** Ignatz, Regulator, Walnut, Peaked Crest, Vienna, 1800s, 54 In. | 3000 |
| **Marti Et Cie,** Shelf, Napoleon III, Marble, Bronze, Columns, 18 x 13 In. | 922 |
| **Marti,** Regulator, Crystal Palace, Guilloche Enamel, Rhinestones, Bronze, France, 12 x 8 In. | 1208 |
| **Marti,** S., Shelf, Black, Open Escapement, Pendulum Door, Scroll, 18½ In. | 366 |
| **Massoni,** Travel, Baby Fox, Figural, 18K Gold, Blue Enamel, Ruby Eyes, Diamonds, 2 In. | 3075 |
| **Munroe,** J., Shelf, Mahogany, Fretwork, Scalloped Skirt, 8-Day, Brass Finials, 40 In. | 30750 |
| **Musical,** Clock Tower Shape, Blue Enamel, Silver, Gilt Metal, Round Base, Pearls, 6 In. | 1169 |
| **Mystery,** Ceres, Holding Suspended Clock, Gilt, Pendulum, c.1890, 28 In. *illus* | 5843 |
| **Mystery,** Jefferson Electric, Golden Hour, Brass, Glass, c.1955, 9 x 7½ In. | 127 |
| **National Calendar Clock Company,** Shelf, Rosewood, Gold Dials, Tortoiseshell, 27 In. | 338 |
| **New Haven,** Shelf, Art Nouveau, Porcelain Face, Beveled Glass, Woman's Face, 14 x 7 In. | 115 |
| **P. Hansen,** L. & J.G. Stickley, Oak, Trapezoidal, Arts & Crafts, c.1910, 22 In. *illus* | 10880 |
| **Regency Style,** Brass Inlay, Fusee Movement, 16 x 6 In. | 719 |
| **Regulator,** Pinwheel, Mahogany, Crown & Dentil, Oval Glass, 8-Day, France, c.1890, 70 In. | 2583 |
| **Regulator,** Pinwheel, Walnut, Glass, Gridiron Pendulum, Brass Weight, 8-Day, France, 65 In. | 1353 |
| **Regulator,** Vienna, Wood Carved Case, Broken Swan Neck Case, c.1890, 46 In. | 240 |
| **Ripple,** Jerome, Shelf, Mahogany, Ripple Molded, Hinged Brass Bezel, Alarm, 13½ In. | 431 |
| **Royal Vienna Style,** Pedestal, Dome Top, Putti Painted Reserves, Porcelain, Gilt, 60 In. | 6250 |
| **Samuel Henry Leah,** Fusee Brass Inlay, Rosewood Case, Octagonal Shape, 17 In. | 604 |
| **Seth Thomas,** Calendar, No. 3, Peanut, Rosewood, Zinc Dial, Roman Numerals, 8-Day, 23 In. | 3567 |
| **Seth Thomas,** Metal, Patinated, Art Nouveau Nymph, Gilt Dragonflies, 21 In. *illus* | 922 |
| **Seth Thomas,** Pillar & Scroll, Federal, Eglomise Tablet, House In Landscape, 29 x 16 In. | 330 |
| **Seth Thomas,** Pillar & Scroll, Mahogany, Fruit Basket, Glass Tablet, Town Center, 32 In. | 923 |
| **Seth Thomas,** Pillar & Scroll, Mahogany, Garden House, 30-Hour Time & Strike, 29 In. | 2583 |
| **Seth Thomas,** Pillar & Scroll, Mahogany, Glass Tablet, Country House, 30-Hour, 32 In. | 3321 |
| **Seth Thomas,** Regulator, Birch, Mahogany, Weight Driven, 8-Day, Round Dial, 36 In. | 770 |
| **Seth Thomas,** Regulator, No. 1, Keyhole, Oak, Zinc Dial, Arabic Numerals, Tablet, 34 In. | 3690 |
| **Seth Thomas,** Regulator, Oak Case, Painted Dial, Key, Pendulum, Weight, 16 x 37 In. | 855 |
| **Seth Thomas,** Shelf, Art Nouveau, Metal, Standing Nymph, Dragonflies, c.1900, 21½ In. | 922 |
| **Seth Thomas,** Shelf, Mahogany, Ogee Cornice, Columns, Painted Panel, c.1860, 26 x 15 In. | 161 |
| **Seth Thomas,** Wall, Burled Walnut Veneer, Carved, Celtic Cross, c.1900, 36 In. *illus* | 180 |
| **Seth Thomas,** Walnut, Ebonized, Panel, Mountain Scene, Lake, Pendulum, 1890s, 25 x 15 In. | 144 |
| **Shelf,** Art Deco, Hexagonal Base, Round Face, 2 Bronze Women, France, c.1930, 10 x 16 In. | 492 |
| **Shelf,** Art Deco, Ormolu, Marble, Trapezoid Shape, Carved, Diamond Shape Face, 4 x 5 In. | 138 |
| **Shelf,** Art Nouveau, Figural, Nymph, In Garden, German Mercedes Clock, Bronze, 13 x 8 In. | 219 |
| **Shelf,** Arts & Crafts, Pine Trees, Cones, Triangular, Metal, Signed SGDG, c.1915, 12 x 17 In. | 840 |

**Clock,** Carriage, Enamel, Silver, Repeater, Gilt Banding, Case, Tiffany & Co., 3 ¼ In.
$4,305

Skinner Auctioneers & Appraisers

**Clock,** Cornu, E., Shelf, Bronze Jar, Marble, Gilt, Twin Train, c.1875, 22 x 12 In.
$3,750

Rago Arts & Auction Center

**Clock,** Figural, Joe Louis, Boxer, Bronze Finish, White Metal, 12 ½ x 8 ½ In.
$288

Wm Morford Auctions

**Clock,** Frankl, P., Telechron, Electric, Modernique, Chrome, Brass, Bakelite, c.1930, 8 x 6 In.
$1,500

Rago Arts & Auction Center

**Clock,** French, Mandarin Elder, Metal, Parasol Is Bell, Enamel Dial, Table Base, 10 x 5 In.
$1,107

New Orleans Auction Galleries, Inc.

**Clock,** Howard Miller, Ball, Windup Key, Nelson, 1949, 13 ¾ In.
$1,125

Los Angeles Modern Auctions (LAMA)

**Clock,** Howard Miller, Glass Tiles, Walnut, Enamel, G. Nelson, 1950s, 13 ½ x 13 ½ x 3 In.
$938

Rago Arts & Auction Center

**Clock,** Ithaca, Regulator No. 2, Walnut, Zinc, Calendar, 8-Day, Time Only, c.1875, 44 In.
$1,968

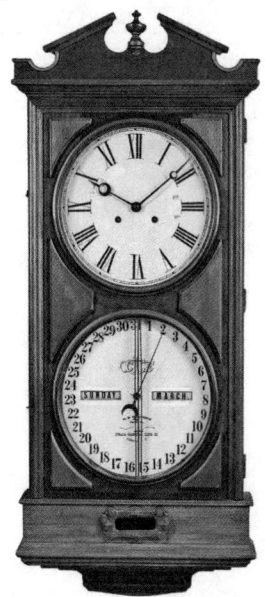

Skinner Auctioneers & Appraisers

**Clock,** Mystery, Ceres, Holding Suspended Clock, Gilt, Pendulum, c.1890, 28 In.
$5,843

Skinner Auctioneers & Appraisers

**Clock,** P. Hansen, L. & J.G. Stickley, Oak, Trapezoidal, Arts & Crafts, c.1910, 22 In. $10,880

Rago Arts & Auction Center

**Clock,** Seth Thomas, Metal, Patinated, Art Nouveau Nymph, Gilt Dragonflies, 21 In. $922

New Orleans Auction Galleries, Inc.

**Clock,** Seth Thomas, Wall, Burled Walnut Veneer, Carved, Celtic Cross, c.1900, 36 In. $180

Cowan's Auctions

**Clock,** Shelf, Bronze, Mythical Scene, Boulle Overlay, Gilt, Mynuel Movement, c.1750, 46 In. $15,405

James D. Julia Auctioneers

**Clock,** Shelf, Charles X, Gilt Bronze, Cut Crystal, Striking Bell Movement, c.1825, 21 In. $4,880

Neal Auction Co.

**Clock,** Shelf, Metal, Mother-Of-Pearl, Victorian, c.1880, 18 x 12 In. $300

DuMouchelles Art Gallery

**Clock,** Tall Case, Bushman, Burl Walnut, Brass Dial, 8-Day, Quarter Strike, c.1725, 93 In. $9,840

Skinner Auctioneers & Appraisers

**Clock,** Tall Case, Cherry, Inlay, Moon's Age, Quarter Columns, 8-Day, Weights, c.1810, 93 In. $2,337

Skinner Auctioneers & Appraisers

**Clock,** Tall Case, Chippendale, Walnut, 8-Day Movement, Moon Phase, Pa., c.1790, 99 In. $4,130

Conestoga Auction Co., Inc.

| | |
|---|---|
| **Shelf,** Boulle, Shaped Case, Footed, France, 15 x 10 In. | 277 |
| **Shelf,** Bronze Satyr Stem, Marble Globe Movement Case, France, c.1890, 15 In. | 300 |
| **Shelf,** Bronze, Mythical Scene, Boulle Overlay, Gilt, Mynuel Movement, c.1750, 46 In. ......*illus* | 15405 |
| **Shelf,** Charles X, Gilt Bronze, Cut Crystal, Striking Bell Movement, c.1825, 21 In. ...........*illus* | 4880 |
| **Shelf,** Crown, Columns, Mirror Tablet, c.1950, 27 In. | 123 |
| **Shelf,** Dresden Style, Porcelain, 4 Season Figures, Bell Chime, Pendulum, 19 x 12 In. | 219 |
| **Shelf,** Egyptian Revival Style, Marble, Reclining Sphinx, Granite Base, c.1900, 14 x 15 In. | 600 |
| **Shelf,** Empire Style, Bronze, Gilt Torches, Fruits, Garlands, Griffins, c.1850, 17 x 10 In. | 2125 |
| **Shelf,** Empire, Gilt Brass, Eagle, Enameled Dial, Flower Pendulum, Paw Feet, 24 x 21 In. | 295 |
| **Shelf,** Empire, Gilt Bronze, Torch, Swan Crest, Enamel Dial, Caryatid Supports, 1800s, 16 In. .... | 3750 |
| **Shelf,** Enameled, Round Dial, Yellow Scale Dolphin Surround, Stepped Onyx Base, 3 ½ In. ........ | 813 |
| **Shelf,** French Empire, Black Slate, Gilt Metal E Pluribus Unum Eagle, c.1820, 15 x 7 ½ In. ....... | 3840 |
| **Shelf,** Gilt Bronze, Artist, Easel, Urns, Wood Case, Round Enamel Dial, c.1895, 17 In. | 1320 |
| **Shelf,** Gilt Bronze, Figure Playing Lyre, Embossed Musical Scene, France, c.1985, 23 In. | 840 |
| **Shelf,** Gilt Bronze, Porcelain Dial, Urn Finial, Flowers, Scrolls, France, 1800s, 28 x 12 In. | 2000 |
| **Shelf,** Gilt, Patinated Bronze, Square, Round Dial, Putto Frieze, Austria, c.1910, 10 x 12 In. | 2250 |
| **Shelf,** Liberty & Co., Pewter, Tudric, Archibald Knox, c.1905, 6 ¼ x 9 In. | 1875 |
| **Shelf,** Lonsdale & Snelling, Cathedral Style, Carved Crest, Leaves, Quatrefoil, 58 x 10 In. | 1920 |
| **Shelf,** Louis IV Style, Bronze, Cherubs, 8-Day Time & Strike, 1800s, 31 x 15 In. | 2250 |
| **Shelf,** Louis XVI Style, Gilt Bronze, Love Birds, Arrows, Round Dial, Marble Base, 9 x 5 In. | 1375 |
| **Shelf,** Metal, Mother-Of-Pearl, Victorian, c.1880, 18 x 12 In. .......*illus* | 300 |
| **Shelf,** Neoclassical Style, Black Marble, Round White Enameled Dial, 10 x 17 In. | 188 |
| **Shelf,** Porcelain, Egg Shaped, Round Dial, Ormolu Mounts, Base, France, c.1890, 22 In. | 240 |
| **Shelf,** Reform Movement, Gilt Bronze, Multicolor Lacquer, W&M Dodge, c.1890, 17 x 12 In. | 1353 |
| **Shelf,** Regency, Mahogany, Arched, Porcelain Dial, Convex Glass Door, Bun Feet, 17 In. | 518 |
| **Shelf,** Restauration, Alabaster, Seated Woman, Carved, Round Brass Dial, c.1845, 17 In. | 875 |
| **Shelf,** Rococo Style, Gilt Bronze, Bouquet Crest, Scroll Feet, 16 In. | 625 |
| **Shelf,** Rococo, Seated Man & Woman, Flowers, Gilt, 20 ¾ x 11 ¼ In. | 922 |
| **Shelf,** Round, Glass Door, Champleve Enamel Rims, Japy Freres Movement, c.1900, 12 In. | 1750 |
| **Shelf,** Scroll Top, Columns, Lower Tablet, Rural Scene, 30-Hour, 31 In. | 677 |
| **Shelf,** Scrolling Arch, Hand-Painted Door, Stepped Base, 17 ½ In. | 70 |
| **Shelf,** Seth Thomas, Electric, Curved Wood Base, Brushed Silver, Art Deco, c.1950 | 49 |
| **Shelf,** Shreve Stanwood & Co., Alabaster Portico, Faux Marble Dial, France, c.1895, 17 In. | 215 |
| **Shelf,** Urn Shape, Porcelain, Gilt Bronze Lion Mask, Ring Handles, Amsterdam, c.1910, 16 In. .. | 1125 |
| **Shelf,** Walnut, Onyx, Dominic, Domed, Brass Dial, Paw Feet, Time & Strike, 19 In. | 1875 |
| **Ship's Bell,** Chelsea, Black Case, Ivory Arms, Quartz Clockwork, 8 In. | 70 |
| **Ship's Bell,** Chelsea, Brass, Round, Key, 7 In. | 390 |
| **Skeleton,** Brass, Gothic, Cathedral Shape, Pierced, Mahogany Case, 22 ½ In. | 1968 |
| **Skeleton,** Brass, Pierced, Masonic Symbols, Trowel, Mahogany Base, Glass Dome, 16 In. | 2091 |
| **Skeleton,** Brass, Pierced, Pendulum, Fusee, Quarter Strike, Ebonized, Glass Dome, 20 In. | 3321 |
| **Southern Calendar Clock Co.,** Shelf, Walnut, Urn Finials, Marked Fashion, c.1880, 33 In. | 923 |
| **Spenser & Wooster,** Shelf, Mahogany, Triple Decker, Country Home Panel, c.1850, 33 In. | 660 |
| **Stennes Elmer,** Girandole, Giltwood Case, Round Panels, 8-Day, c.1970, 44 x 11 In. | 2500 |
| **Tall Case,** A. Miller, Edinburgh, Mahogany, Dome Top, Columns, Door, 8-Day, 79 In. | 2952 |
| **Tall Case,** A. Miller, Queen Anne, Walnut, Bulbous Finials, 8-Day, Brass Face, c.1780, 99 In. | 11400 |
| **Tall Case,** Aaron Willard, Mahogany, Fret Top, Ship, Columns, Inlaid Door, 1806, 95 In. | 22140 |
| **Tall Case,** Andrew Lyon, Mahogany, Broken Pediment, Scotland, c.1800, 81 x 17 In. | 1320 |
| **Tall Case,** Arts & Crafts, Oak, Brass, Maple, Ebony, Shop Of Crafters, c.1906, 80 x 21 In. | 3690 |
| **Tall Case,** Arts & Crafts, Oak, Regina Music Box, 2-Weight Movement, 85 x 22 In. | 2952 |
| **Tall Case,** B. Willard, Cherry, Pagoda Top, Brass Finials, Roman Numerals, c.1770, 88 In. | 10455 |
| **Tall Case,** Bird's-Eye Maple, Scroll Top, Arched Door, French Feet, 8-Day, Alarm, 42 In. | 11685 |
| **Tall Case,** Bushman, Burl Walnut, Brass Dial, 8-Day, Quarter Strike, c.1725, 93 In. ..........*illus* | 9840 |
| **Tall Case,** Carved, Figural, Maiden, Garland, Putti, Scrolls, Roman Numerals, Germany, 98 In. .. | 2750 |
| **Tall Case,** Cherry, Inlay, Moon's Age, Quarter Columns, 8-Day, Weights, c.1810, 93 In. ......*illus* | 2337 |
| **Tall Case,** Chippendale, Walnut, 8-Day Movement, Moon Phase, Pa., c.1790, 99 In. ..........*illus* | 4130 |
| **Tall Case,** Chippendale, Walnut, Broken Arch Pediment, Carved, Column Supports, 103 In. ....... | 12390 |
| **Tall Case,** Cuckoo, Wood, Carved, Shaped Front, Flower Basket, Columns, 49 x 12 In. | 92 |
| **Tall Case,** David Williams, Mahogany, Iron Dial, Gilt, 8-Day, Pendulum, c.1800, 89 In. .....*illus* | 11070 |
| **Tall Case,** David Wood, Mahogany, Dome Top, Reeded Columns, c.1790, 80 In. | 1599 |
| **Tall Case,** E. Howard & Co., Oak, Regulator, Door, 8-Day, Pendulum, c.1890, 102 In. ........*illus* | 1845 |
| **Tall Case,** Elnathan Taber, Chippendale, Brass Finials, Enamel Dial, Footed, Roxbury, 91 In. ...... | 22800 |
| **Tall Case,** Federal, Cherry, Carved, Inlay, Moses Wing, Windsor, Conn., c.1800, 81 In. ........*illus* | 1680 |
| **Tall Case,** Federal, Mahogany, 8-Day, Roxbury Case, New England, c.1805, 94 ½ In. | 480 |
| **Tall Case,** Figured Mahogany, Scroll Top, Urn Finials, Painted Iron Dial, 8-Day, 100 In. | 4920 |

**Clock,** Tall Case, David Williams, Mahogany, Iron Dial, Gilt, 8-Day, Pendulum, c.1800, 89 In.
$11,070

Skinner Auctioneers & Appraisers

**Clock,** Tall Case, E. Howard & Co., Oak, Regulator, Door, 8-Day, Pendulum, c.1890, 102 In.
$1,845

Skinner Auctioneers & Appraisers

**Clock,** Tall Case, Federal, Cherry, Carved, Inlay, Moses Wing, Windsor, Conn., c.1800, 81 In.
$1,680

Cowan's Auctions

This is an edited listing of current prices. Visit **Kovels.com** to check thousands of prices from previous years and sign up for free information on trends, tips, reproductions, marks, and more.

**Clock,** Tall Case, French Country, Multicolor Flowers & Vines, Morbier Style Works, 1800s, 89 In. $500

Rago Arts & Auction Center

---

**Clock,** Tall Case, J.J. Elliot, Mahogany, Tubes, Westminster, Chimes, c.1890, 107 In. $13,743

Neal Auction Co.

---

**Clock,** Tall Case, Jacob Wolf, Mahogany, 8-Day, Anchor Escapement, c.1790, 97 In. $2,500

Rago Arts & Auction Center

| | |
|---|---:|
| **Tall Case,** Fisher, Federal, Cherry, Line Inlay, Painted Dial, 8-Day, French Feet, c.1805, 103 In.... | 2500 |
| **Tall Case,** Fowles-Kilmarnock, Mahogany, Flat Top Hood, Flowers, Birds, Bracket Feet, 83 In. .... | 500 |
| **Tall Case,** French Country, Multicolor Flowers & Vines, Morbier Style Works, 1800s, 89 In. *illus* | 500 |
| **Tall Case,** G. Hoff, Pine, Time & Strike, Lancaster, Pa., 84 In. ........................ | 1440 |
| **Tall Case,** George III, Japanned, 8-Day, Brass Face, Signed Jno Stokes, St. Ives, c.1790, 84 In. ... | 1920 |
| **Tall Case,** George III, Mahogany, Arched Hood, String Inlay, Painted Dial, c.1810, 87 In. ...... | 840 |
| **Tall Case,** George III, Mahogany, Banded Inlay, Time & Strike, 8-Day, c.1810, 94 x 29 In. ......... | 615 |
| **Tall Case,** George III, Mahogany, Mixed Wood Inlay, Broken Arch, c.1810, 93 x 20 In. ............. | 861 |
| **Tall Case,** Georgian, Mahogany, Silver Dial, Time & Strike Movement, Eng., c.1800, 87 In. ......... | 2375 |
| **Tall Case,** Grandmother's, Oak, Beading, Chime Movement, Continental, 1920s, 56 x 11 In. ...... | 585 |
| **Tall Case,** H. Mitchell, Federal, Mahogany, 8-Day, Fan Inlays, 3 Ball Finials, N.Y., c.1810, 94 In.. | 1800 |
| **Tall Case,** Hanson Clock Co., Colonial Revival, Mahogany, 5 Tubes, c.1920, 86 x 24 In............. | 1476 |
| **Tall Case,** Henry Taylor, Chippendale, Scroll Crest, Arched Panel Door, Philadelphia, 103 In. ..... | 4688 |
| **Tall Case,** Hepplewhite, Walnut, Eagle, Broken Arch Pediment, Columns, c.1790, 109 In. .......... | 7375 |
| **Tall Case,** Hoover & Smith, Mahogany, 8-Day, 8 Tubes, Philadelphia, c.1900, 96 In. ................. | 2625 |
| **Tall Case,** J. Elliot Works, Renaissance Revival, Oak, Carved, Shaped, c.1895, 106 In. ............. | 17500 |
| **Tall Case,** J.E. Caldwell, Mahogany, Broken Arch Pediment, Pendulum, 98 x 23 In. ................. | 1888 |
| **Tall Case,** J.J. Elliot, Mahogany, Tubes, Westminster, Chimes, c.1890, 107 In. ..............*illus* | 13743 |
| **Tall Case,** Jacob Wolf, Mahogany, 8-Day, Anchor Escapement, c.1790, 97 In. ..............*illus* | 2500 |
| **Tall Case,** James Butler, Mahogany, Brass Dial, Silvered Chapter Ring, 1700s, 86 x 22 In. ........... | 1840 |
| **Tall Case,** Joseph Mulliken, Cherry, Fluted Columns, Waist Door, Inlays, c.1800, 92 ½ In.... | 4920 |
| **Tall Case,** Kipp Stewart, Declaration, Rosewood, Enameled Metal, Drexel, 1960s, 60 x 14 In....... | 344 |
| **Tall Case,** Louis XV Style, Bombe, Mahogany, Ormolu, Angel, Brass Dial, France, 92 In........... | 4613 |
| **Tall Case,** Mahogany, Domed, Glass Door, Painted Moon Face Dial, Germany, 90 x 25 In......... | 2500 |
| **Tall Case,** Marti, French Style, Bombe Shape, Multicolor, Signed, c.1910, 68 x 17 In............. | 492 |
| **Tall Case,** Oak, Time & Strike 8-Day Movement, Painted Dial, England, c.1800, 91 x 20 In......... | 875 |
| **Tall Case,** Parquetry, 30-Hour Movement, Brass Face, Pewter Dial, Dutch, c.1780, 91 In.......... | 540 |
| **Tall Case,** Pine, Faux Mahogany Grain Paint, Mora, Sweden, 1800s, 78 In. ..................*illus* | 480 |
| **Tall Case,** Pine, Multicolor Painted Flowers, Sponge Design, Scandinavia, c.1848, 87 In............ | 2640 |
| **Tall Case,** Poplar, Broken Swan Crest, Paneled, Red Stain, 30-Hour Movement, c.1800, 90 In...... | 1800 |
| **Tall Case,** Queen Anne, Japanned, Signed Dial Sam Stanton, London, 97 x 18 In..................... | 5192 |
| **Tall Case,** Queen Anne, Pine, Flat Top Bonnet, Pinwheel Sound Holes, c.1756, 88 In. ........... | 14400 |
| **Tall Case,** R. Whiting, R. Cole, Figured Mahogany, Scroll Top, Stenciling, 30-Hour, 83 In. ......... | 5043 |
| **Tall Case,** R.J. Horner, Mahogany, Westminster Chimes, Brass Dial, 8-Day, c.1900, 103 In. ......... | 12000 |
| **Tall Case,** Renaissance Revival, Oak, Urn Finials, Landscapes, c.1890, 25 In. ..................... | 5843 |
| **Tall Case,** S. Hoadley, Paint Decorated, Arched, Pull-Up Movement, c.1830, 87 In.................. | 1722 |
| **Tall Case,** Shaker, Walnut, Panel Door, Hook & Eye Latch, Plinth Base, Union Village, 92 In. ..... | 19200 |
| **Tall Case,** Sheraton, Cherry, 30-Hour, Inscribed Henry Saledy, Bucks County, c.1830, 91 In. ...... | 1140 |
| **Tall Case,** T.F. Lancaster, George III, Mahogany, 8-Day, Brass Face, Fretwork, c.1789, 97 In......... | 5280 |
| **Tall Case,** Tiger Maple, Mahogany Veneer, Cornucopia, Moon's Age, 92 In......................... | 2214 |
| **Tall Case,** Turned Columns, Crown Molding, Bonnet, Finials, Black, Green, c.1810, 88 In.......... | 7110 |
| **Tall Case,** W. Barlow, Walnut, Fret Carved, Twist Pilasters, Gilt Brass Dial, 8-Day, 88 In. ............. | 2875 |
| **Tall Case,** W. Lewis Warren, Federal, Swan Neck Pediment, House, Trees, Red Wash, 87 In. ......... | 3600 |
| **Tall Case,** Walnut, Fretwork, Satinwood Inlay, Classical Figure, Lions, Flowers, 95 In. .......*illus* | 861 |
| **Tall Case,** Waltham, Oak, Carved, 3 Revelers, Musicians, Putti, Scrolls, Columns, 102 In. ......... | 10240 |
| **Tall Case,** Waterbury, Inlay, Miniature, 17 ½ In. ....................................... | 155 |
| **Tall Case,** Whiting Winchester, Flat Top, Wooden Works, Glazed, Painted Face, 85 x 14 In. ......... | 633 |
| **Tall Case,** Wm. Champ, Queen Anne, Japanned, Brass Dial, London, 1700s, 96 x 20 In............. | 2360 |
| **Terry & Andrews,** Shelf, Double Steeple, Stenciled, 2 Tablets, Reverse Painted, 25 In................. | 431 |
| **Terry,** Eli, Pillar & Scroll, Mahogany, Glass Tablet, Masonic Symbols, 30-Hour, 29 In. ................. | 3998 |
| **Terry,** Eli, Pillar & Scroll, Mahogany, Wood Dial, Arabic Numerals, 30-Hour, 2-Weight, 29 In. ..... | 431 |
| **Terry,** Eli, Shelf, Mahogany, Pillar & Scroll, Flower Face, Eglomise Landscape, Finials, 31 In...... | 1020 |
| **Terry,** Eli, Shelf, Walnut, Carved, Painted Flower Wood Dial, Eglomise, c.1850, 33 x 17 In.......... | 246 |
| **Terry,** S.B., Shelf, Mahogany, Reverse Painted, Church, Heart Opening, Brass Dial, 23 In. .......... | 984 |
| **Tiffany** clocks that are part of desk sets made by Louis Comfort Tiffany are listed in the Tiffany category. Clocks sold by the store Tiffany & Co. are listed here. | |
| **Time Card,** Wood, Cincinnati Time Recorder Co., 20 x 46 In........................................ | 325 |
| **Tower Form,** Mother-Of-Pearl, Crown Top, Leaves, Pierced Gallery Base, Vienna, 6 In. ............... | 2706 |
| **Tower Form,** Silver, 4 Owl-Topped Columns, Enamel Panels, Maidens, Vienna, 10 In. ............... | 6150 |
| **Tower Form,** Silver, Enamel Panels, Soldiers, Putti, Mythical Symbols, Vienna, 1880, 11 In. ....... | 8610 |
| **Trankle,** Joesph, Shelf, Mahogany, Pine, Boxwood Inlay, Porcelain Face, c.1880, 19 x 13 In........ | 891 |
| **Travel,** Blue Enamel, Gilt Dial, Pierced Hands, 8-Sided, France, c.1920, 3 ½ In. .................*illus* | 300 |
| **Travel,** Metal, Round Case, Roman Numerals On Bezel, Kickstand, Tiffany & Co., 1 x 1 In.......... | 230 |
| **Victorian,** Wall, Classical Pediment, Applied Brass Plaque, Allegorical Figures, c.1880, 48 In. ..... | 2185 |

| | | |
|---|---|---|
| **Vulliamy,** Bracket, Oak, No. 1868, Door, 8-Day, Time & Strike, c.1850, 18 In. | *illus* | 3321 |
| **Wadsworth & Turners,** Shelf, Pillar & Scroll, Brass Urn Finials, Landscape, Eglomise, 31 In. | | 1140 |
| **Wall,** Gothic Revival, Walnut, Carved Bracket Support, Arched Tracery, 42½ In. | | 1476 |
| **Waterbury,** Calendar, No. 27, Oak, Carved, Turned, Zinc Dials, 8-Day, Brass Pendulum, 45 In. | | 1353 |
| **Waterbury,** Kitchen, Gabled Crest, Stenciled Glass Door, 8-Day, Key Wind, 22 In. | *illus* | 300 |
| **Welch,** E.N., Wall Mount, Carved, Gold Flower, Glass Door, 31 In. | | 140 |
| **Welch,** Regulator, No. 5, Black Walnut, Turned Columns & Finials, Brass Bob, 52 In. | | 5535 |
| **Welch,** Shelf, Rosewood, Patti V.P., Turned Design, Zinc Dial, Glass Door, 8-Day, 19 In. | | 738 |
| **Willard,** A., Regulator, Mahogany, Painted Glass, Black, Gold, 8-Day, Trapezoidal, 50 In. | | 6150 |
| **Wm. L. Gilbert,** Shelf, Beehive, Mahogany, Alarm, Painted Glass Panel, 1800s, 18 x 10 In. | | 94 |

**CLOISONNE** enamel was developed during the tenth century. A glass enamel was applied between small ribbons of metal on a metal base. Most cloisonne is Chinese or Japanese. Pieces marked *China* are twentieth-century examples.

| | | |
|---|---|---|
| **Bowl,** 3 Dragon Head Legs, Multicolor, Red Dragons, Gilt, Chinese, 1900s, 7 x 11 In. | | 472 |
| **Bowl,** Kyoto Shippo, Roundels, Flowers, Brocade, Auspicious Emblems, 1800s, 4 x 7 In. | | 1185 |
| **Bowl,** Turquoise, 8 Immortals, Gilt Interior, Ching Tai Mark, 1900s, 7 In. | | 1363 |
| **Box,** Camel Shape, Reclining, Flowers, Turquoise Ground, Early 1900s, 6 x 4¾ In. | | 237 |
| **Box,** Incense, Figural, Goose Shape, Wing Opens To Interior, c.1890, 6¾ In., Pair | *illus* | 615 |
| **Box,** Jade Ornament, Red Ground, Double Happiness Character, c.1900, 4 x 6 In. | | 1230 |
| **Box,** White Jade, Carp In Lotus Pond, Egret, Chinese, 1¾ x 3 x 2½ In. | | 3075 |
| **Brush Pot,** Scrolling Leaves, Brass Ground, Turquoise Interior, 3-Footed, 4 x 2 In. | | 46 |
| **Candlesticks,** Knopped Stem, 4-Footed, Silver Gilt Ground, Russia, 5½ In., Pair | | 3690 |
| **Case,** Flowers, Leaves, Turquoise Beads, Russian Silver, Gilt, c.1900, 3 x 2 In. | *illus* | 3198 |
| **Censer,** Gilt Bronze, Tapered Bombe Body, Blue, Domed, 1900s, 4¾ x 5¼ In. | | 1315 |
| **Charger,** Bird, Fish, Flowers, Japan, c.1965, 18 In. | | 250 |
| **Cigarette Case,** Silver, Geometric Pattern, Medallion, Russia, 1875, 4 In. | | 984 |
| **Cup & Saucer,** Gold Washed, Pan-Slavic, Multicolor, Curved Handle, 4 x 4¾ In., Pair | | 403 |
| **Egg,** Multicolor Flowers, Wood Base, Chinese, 21 x 12 In. | | 600 |
| **Figurine,** Elephant, Brass, Painted, Gilt, Removable Seat, 13 x 17 In. | | 184 |
| **Figurine,** Fish, Koi, Applied Black Button Eyes, Open Mouth, Hollow Body, 10 x 3¼ In. | | 115 |
| **Figurine,** Horse, Cantering, Removable Saddle, Harness, Chinese, 1900s, 14 x 15 In., Pair | | 2032 |
| **Figurine,** Horse, Rearing, Hoof Up, Blue, Gilt, Chinese, 15½ In., Pair | | 677 |
| **Figurine,** Peacocks, Blue, Green, Standing, Gold Feet, 9 x 18 In., Pair | | 308 |
| **Figurine,** Rabbit, Brass, Flowers, Blue Gilt Ears, Eyes, 1900s, 3 x 5 In., Pair | | 236 |
| **Figurine,** Rhinoceros, Lapis Blue Ground, Multicolor Archaic Style Designs, 12½ x 20½ In. | | 644 |
| **Flask,** Moon, Landscapes, Gi Frame, Lotus Vining, Dragon Handles, Chinese, 15 In. | *illus* | 3600 |
| **Goblet,** Gold Washed Interior, Tapered, Pan-Slavic Design, Scroll, Grapes, Footed, 5 x 3 In. | | 575 |
| **Jar,** Dome Lid, Flowering Prunus, Oval, 1900s, 10¼ In. | | 120 |
| **Jar,** Lid, Symbols, Turquoise Ground, Tapered, Chinese, c.1950, 17 In. | | 406 |
| **Jardiniere,** Bronze, Blue, Yellow, Red, Flowers, 3-Footed, 12½ In. | | 2380 |
| **Jardiniere,** Turned In Rim, Floral Band, Globe Shape, Waisted Splayed Foot, 10 x 12 In. | | 149 |
| **Kovsch,** Multicolor, Leaves, Flowers, Leaves, Spoon, Dish, 3¼ x 5 In., 2 Piece | | 8610 |
| **Mythical Animals,** Horned, Blue, Turquoise, Gilt, Chinese, 1800, 10½ x 8 In., Pair | | 7703 |
| **Planter,** Key Fret Design, Gilt, Lotus, Lobed, Wide Rim, Carved, Footed, 3 x 5 x 4 In. | | 75 |
| **Spoon,** Gold Washed, Enamel, Floral Pan-Slavic, Multicolor, 8½ In. | | 138 |
| **Spoon,** Silver, Marked, Fedor Ruckert, Faberge, Russia, c.1900, 6⅜ In. | *illus* | 2875 |
| **Teapot,** Kyoto Shippo, Domed Base, Arched Shapes, Gilt Copper, Oval, 1800s, 6 In. | | 357 |
| **Teapot,** Lid, Pear Shape, Butterflies, Flowers, Rust Brown Ground, Fixed Handle, 5½ In. | | 184 |
| **Teapot,** Peach Shape, Flower, Prunus Fruit, Yellow Ground, Clouds, Gilt Leaves, 7 In. | | 172 |
| **Vase,** Baluster Shape, Flaring Lip, Base, Leaves, Vines, Zogan Jippo, 6-Sided, 12 In. | | 58 |
| **Vase,** Baluster Shape, Multicolor Flowers, Chinese, 31 x 16 In. | | 720 |
| **Vase,** Bird, Cherry Blossoms, Japan, c.1910, 58 In. | | 4688 |
| **Vase,** Blue Ground, Flared Copper Rim, Bird & Flower, Japan, c.1880, 47 In. | | 708 |
| **Vase,** Blue, Cherry Blossoms, Birds, Butterflies, Converted To Lamp, Pair | | 507 |
| **Vase,** Bottle Shape, 3 Standing Cranes, Lavender, Blue Ground, c.1900, 11¼ In. | | 2360 |
| **Vase,** Bottle Shape, Dragons, Scrolling, Turquoise, Marked, Chinese, 1900s, 18 x 10 In., Pair | | 1541 |
| **Vase,** Copper, Crane, Green, 4½ x 7½ In. | | 183 |
| **Vase,** Dragon, Flaming Pearl Of Wisdom, Green, Cylindrical, Gilt Wire, 12 x 4½ In. | | 207 |
| **Vase,** Flowers, Blue Red, Yellow Geometric Ground, Chinese, 1900, 12½ In., Pair | | 310 |
| **Vase,** High Shoulders, Flared Rim, Cherry Blossom, Dark Red, 9½ In. | | 140 |
| **Vase,** Kingfisher, Black, Lotus Blossoms, Leaves, Butterflies, Reeds, Japan, 9 In. | | 920 |
| **Vase,** Lid, Figural, Double Gourd, Blue, Waterfowl, Flowers, Metalwork, 8½ In., Pair | | 480 |

**Clock,** Tall Case, Pine, Faux Mahogany Grain Paint, Mora, Sweden, 1800s, 78 In. $480

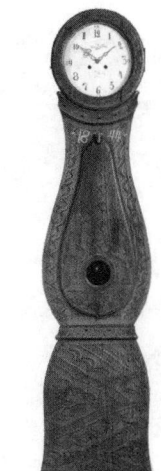

Garth's Auctioneers & Appraisers

**Clock,** Tall Case, Walnut, Fretwork, Satinwood Inlay, Classical Figure, Lions, Flowers, 95 In. $861

New Orleans Auction Galleries, Inc.

**Clock,** Travel, Blue Enamel, Gilt Dial, Pierced Hands, 8-Sided, France, c.1920, 3½ In. $300

DuMouchelles Art Gallery

# CLOISONNE

**Clock,** Vulliamy, Bracket, Oak, No. 1868, Door, 8-Day, Time & Strike, c.1850, 18 In.
**$3,321**

Skinner Auctioneers & Appraisers

---

**Clock,** Waterbury, Kitchen, Gabled Crest, Stenciled Glass Door, 8-Day, Key Wind, 22 In.
**$300**

DuMouchelles Art Gallery

---

**Cloisonne,** Box, Incense, Figural, Goose Shape, Wing Opens To Interior, c.1890, 6¾ In., Pair
**$615**

New Orleans Auction Galleries, Inc.

---

> **TIP**
> *Put shoe trees in vintage shoes to preserve the shape.*

---

| | |
|---|---:|
| **Vase,** Pigeon Blood Red, Stippled Embossed Foil, Birds, Fish, Japan, c.1945, 7½ In., Pair | 240 |
| **Vase,** Round, Lotus, Leaves, Light Blue, 22⅝ x 18½ In. | 7380 |
| **Vase,** Water Lily, Copper, Pink, Green, White, Flared Lip, Bulbous, 15¼ In. | 173 |
| **Water Coupe,** Peach Shape, Leaves, Millefleur, Bats, Chinese, c.1910, 6 x 5 In. *....illus* | 1659 |
| **Wine Pot,** Dome Lid, Duck Shape, Gilt Accents, Rust, White, Handle, 10¼ x 10 In. | 345 |

**CLOTHING** of all types is listed in this category. Dresses, hats, shoes, underwear, and more are found here. Other textiles are to be found in the Coverlet, Movie, Quilt, Textile, and World War I and II categories.

| | |
|---|---:|
| **Alb,** Silk Metallic Threading, Flowers, Cream Ground, c.1790, 53 x 112 In. | 531 |
| **Apron,** Red & Green Pattern, White Ground, Red Piping, 49¾ x 22 In. | 12 |
| **Apron,** Shaker, Silk, Brown, 3 Panels, 43 In. | 3068 |
| **Belt,** Snakeskin, Black, Goldtone Buckle, Onyx, Adjustable, Judith Leiber, ¾ x 39 In. | 143 |
| **Belt,** Snakeskin, White, Goldtone Buckle, Rose Quartz, Adjustable, J. Leiber, 1 x 38 In. | 167 |
| **Belt,** Sterling, Gold Overlay, Embossed Black Leather, Tan, Monogram, 1½ x 41 In. | 242 |
| **Belt,** Suede, Black, Art Deco Buckle, Judith Leiber | 185 |
| **Belt,** White, Silver Beads, Crystals, 1970s, 2½ x 20½ In. | 120 |
| **Blouse,** Cotton, Print, Front Button, Size 44 | 144 |
| **Boots,** Riding, Leather, Brown, New York, E. Vogel, Inc., 1900s, 21 x 12 In. | 60 |
| **Busk,** Carved, Chip Carved Geometric, Flowers, Hearts, Tapered, Copper Foil, c.1800, 13 In. | 369 |
| **Cape,** Mink, Galatoire, Chocolate Brown, Broad Collar, Hook Closure, Size 10, 46 In. | 2706 |
| **Cape,** Mongolian Lamb, Ivory, Lambskin, Label, Bergdorf Goodman, N.Y., 42 In. | 676 |
| **Chaps,** Leather, Fur, Child's, 26 In. | 150 |
| **Cloak,** Blue Wool, Hood, Silvered Thread Decoration, Canvas Undergarment, 53 In. | 480 |
| **Coat,** Ermine, Sable Collar, Vertical Pelts, Ecru Satin Lining, Pockets, Size 4-6, 43 In. | 2460 |
| **Coat,** Gentleman's, Kossack, Wool, Gold & Silver Braid, Open Sleeves, c.1890, 41 In. *....illus* | 486 |
| **Coat,** Jacket, Chinchilla, Notched Collar, Pockets, Silk Lining, 1960s, Size 6 | 1722 |
| **Coat,** Jacket, Leopard, Wing Collar, ¾ Sleeves, Hook Closure, 26 In. | 1599 |
| **Coat,** Leopard Skin, Fitted, Notched Collar, Inset Sleeves, Silk Lining, Size 6 | 6765 |
| **Coat,** Mink, Brown, Shawl Collar, Bias Pelts, Silk Lining, J. Tauben, c.1980, Size 8 | 3936 |
| **Coat,** Mink, Wing Lapels, Pockets, Maison Blanche, 1980s, Full Length, Size 10, 50 In. | 3936 |
| **Coat,** Ocelot, Black Fox Collar & Hem, Suede & Snakeskin Belt, 1970s, Size 4 | 799 |
| **Coat,** Sable Mink, Notched Lapels, Pockets, Brown Silk Lining, Dempster's, Size 4-6, 41 In. | 338 |
| **Coat,** Trench, Navy Blue, Wool Liner, Storm Flap, Epaulettes, Burberry, Size UK 8 | 345 |
| **Dress Coat,** Musician's, Woven Twill, Blue, Red Cuffs, Buttons, c.1861 | 1722 |
| **Dress,** Bob Bugnand, Paisley, Sequins, Long Sleeves, Dropped Waist, S. Friedlander, c.1970 | 82 |
| **Dress,** Chinese Style, Silk Brocade, Red, Mandarin Collar, Short Sleeves, 51 In. | 120 |
| **Dress,** Cocktail, Silk, Blue, Dynasty Peacock, Belt, ¾ Sleeves, 1960s, Size 14 | 60 |
| **Dress,** Coral, Long Sleeves, Cross-Over Bodice, Maxi, Robert-David Morton, 1970s, Size 6 | 96 |
| **Dress,** Evening, Chiffon, Aqua Blue, Empire Waist, Beaded Bodice, 1960s, Size 6 | 158 |
| **Dress,** Evening, Silk, Mauve, Gold Lace, Bead Trim, High Neck Bodice, Cuffs, c.1912 | 60 |
| **Dress,** Lace, Taffeta, Velvet, Blue, Cream, Sleeveless, J. Garfinckel & Co., c.1960, Size 4-6 | 508 |
| **Dress,** Sheath, Silk Animal Print, Sleeveless, Leather Armholes, Dolce & Gabbana, Size 8 | 184 |
| **Dress,** Silk, Pink, Mauve, White Swirl, E. Pucci, c.1960, Size 12 | 388 |
| **Dress,** Silk, Silk Chiffon, Embroidered Flowers, Phoenix, Multicolor, Chinese, 2 Piece | 960 |
| **Dress,** Strapless Sheath, Wool Crepe, Zipper, Christian Dior, France, 1970s, 49 In. | 443 |
| **Dress,** Wool, Blue, Short Sleeves, Knee Length, Vogue, c.1962 | 60 |
| **Ensemble,** Cotton, Multicolor, Sleeveless, Button, Knee Length, E. Pucci, c.1968, Size 12 | 96 |
| **Hat,** Black Wool, Red Satin, Rhinestone & Feather Trim, Whittall & Shon, 22 In. *....illus* | 60 |
| **Hat,** Cocktail, Black Beaded, Sequins, Pheasant & Ostrich Feathers | 276 |
| **Hat,** Cocktail, Black Felt, Jeweled Pheasant Feathers | 276 |
| **Hat,** Cocktail, Pheasant Feather, Fleur De Paris, New Orleans | 338 |
| **Hat,** Cocktail, Purple Felt, Jewel Trim, Pheasant Feathers, Net, Jack McConnell, N.Y. *....illus* | 215 |
| **Hat,** Cocktail, Riding Side Saddle To The Hounds, Black Wool, Net, Velvet Trim *....illus* | 676 |
| **Hat,** Cocktail, Steel Gray, Panne Velvet, Feathers, Beading | 246 |
| **Hat,** Cocktail, Top Hat, Veil, Strap, Printed Velvet, Zandra Rhodes, London | 215 |
| **Hat,** Fedora, Black Beaver Velour, Feather, Stetson, Box, 21½ In. | 225 |
| **Hat,** Stetson, Pins, Military Badges, Crossed Sabers, Lindbergh Plane *....illus* | 300 |
| **Hat,** Straw, Floppy Rim, The Winchester Store, Woman's *....illus* | 3900 |
| **Hat,** Straw, Lace Border, Flowers, Blue Bow, Frank Olive, I. Magnin, Woman's | 60 |
| **Hat,** Top, Beaver Skin, Black, D'Orsay Style, c.1880, 8 x 12½ In. | 295 |
| **Jacket,** Black Broadtail Lamb, Mink, ¾ Sleeves, Rolled Cuffs, Pockets, Gus Mayer, 24 In. | 861 |
| **Jacket,** Cotton, Wool, Brocade, White, Yves Saint Laurent, Rive Gauche, Size 38 | 269 |

| | |
|---|---|
| **Jacket,** Mink, Brown, Convertible Notched Collar, Set In ¾ Length Sleeves, Size 6-8, 22 In. | 799 |
| **Jumpsuit,** Nylon, Emilo Pucci, 1970s, Size 12 | 478 |
| **Kimono,** Blue, White Trim, Silk, Embroidery, Japan, c.1940, 40 In. | 127 |
| **Kimono,** Silk, Black, Embroidered, Silver, Gold Thread, Japan, c.1900, 64 In. | 461 |
| **Kimono,** Silk, Red Lining, Japan, c.1935, 52 In. .......................*illus* | 60 |
| **Kimono,** Wedding, Quilted, Silk, Woven Gold Threads, Embroidered Pine Motifs, 50 x 70 In. | 861 |
| **Kimono,** Wedding, Silk, Lavender, Floral Pattern, Batik Print, Multicolor, c.1945, 57 x 26 In. | 207 |
| **Mittens,** Wool, Woven, Diamond Shapes & 1845, Red, Blue, 10 x 6 In. ............*illus* | 1437 |
| **Obi,** Brocade, Silk, Gold Threads, Black Painted Frame, Japan, 62 ½ x 14 ¾ In. | 472 |
| **Pants,** Vest, Uncle Sam, Red, White, Stripes, Stars, c.1910, 22 In., Pants, 2 Piece | 62 |
| **Robe,** Black, Ivory, Embroidery Trim, Chinese, Woman's, 38 In. | 813 |
| **Robe,** Embroidery, Birds, Flowers, Black Ground, Chinese, c.1920, 53 In. | 1778 |
| **Robe,** Embroidery, Silk, Yellow, Fruit, Flowers, Chinese, Woman's, c.1910, 50 x 48 In. | 1185 |
| **Robe,** Flowers, Butterflies, Blue, Silk Embroidery, c.1900, 44 x 30 In. | 500 |
| **Robe,** Opera Warrior's, Peking, Embroidered, Metallic Threads, c.1910, 58 In. .........*illus* | 492 |
| **Robe,** Silk, Dragon, Red, Blue Border, Chinese, 38 x 64 In. | 535 |
| **Scarf,** Carousel, King Louis XIV Cavaliers, Horses, Blue, White, Silk, Hermes, 35 x 35 In. | 104 |
| **Scarf,** Cashmere, Blush Pink, Eyelash Fringe, Chanel Signature, 27 x 69 In. | 311 |
| **Scarf,** Cosmos, Silk, Hermes, 35 x 35 In. | 270 |
| **Scarf,** Diane, Hunt Theme, Arms, Burgundy, Henri De Linares, Hermes, c.1972, 35 x 35 In. | 213 |
| **Scarf,** Ecuries, Equestrian, Silk Twill, Burgundy, Black, P. Ledoux, Hermes, 1947, 35 x 35 In. | 219 |
| **Scarf,** India, Lakshmi, Orange, Yellow, Silk Twill, Caty Latham, Hermes, 1986, 35 x 35 In. | 293 |
| **Scarf,** Le Tarot, Silk Twill, Teal, Multicolor, Annie Faivre, Hermes, c.1991, 35 x 35 In. | 322 |
| **Scarf,** Le Timbalier, Silk, Francoise Heron, Hermes, 1961, 35 In. .......................*illus* | 518 |
| **Scarf,** Les Coupes, Modernist, Silk Twill, Francoise De La Perriere, 1971, 35 x 35 In. | 293 |
| **Scarf,** Les Fetes Du Roi Soleil, Silk Twill, Michel Duchene, Hermes, 1994, 35 x 35 In. | 224 |
| **Scarf,** Les Jardiniers Du Roy, Silk, Maurice Trenchant, Hermes, 1967, 35 In. .........*illus* | 330 |
| **Scarf,** Les Voitures A Transformation, Silk, Hermes, 35 x 35 In. | 246 |
| **Scarf,** L'Hiver, Village Life, Ledoux, Silk Twill, Hermes, 1968, 35 x 35 In. | 236 |
| **Scarf,** L'Opera, Silk, Art Deco Style, Erte, Italy, 34 x 32 In. | 236 |
| **Scarf,** Luna Park, Jacquard Silk, Multicolor, Black Ground, J. Metz, Hermes, 35 x 35 In. | 265 |
| **Scarf,** Nikko, Silk Twill, Yellow, Multicolor, V. Rybaltchenko, Hermes, c.1992, 35 x 35 In. | 207 |
| **Scarf,** Silk & Rayon, Pink & Gray Print, Beaded Fringe, Emilio Pucci, 67 x 12 In. .........*illus* | 88 |
| **Scarf,** Silk, Le Bien Aller, Hunt Scene, Navy Blue Ground, Hermes, 1979, 37 In. | 590 |
| **Scarf,** Silk, Orange, White Flowers, Green Leaves, Chanel, 38 x 38 In. | 154 |
| **Scarf,** Silk, Pink Purple Flower, Brown Leaves, Emilio Pucci, 35 x 35 In. | 84 |
| **Scarf,** Silk, Pink, Yellow Roses, Green Ground, Burgundy Border, Burberry, 34 x 34 In. | 36 |
| **Scarf,** Silk, Purses, Shoes, Pink, Black, Mauve, Rolled Edge, 21 x 21 In. | 18 |
| **Scarf,** Silk, Red & Green Stripes, Black Chain Ground, Square, Gucci, 30 In. | 75 |
| **Scarf,** Silk, Repeating FJ Logos, Pink, Black Letters, Square, Fendi, 40 In. | 25 |
| **Scarf,** Silk, Repeating Logos, Gray, Pink, White Ground, Square, Louis Vuitton, 30 In. | 100 |
| **Scarf,** Silk, Selles A Housse, Red, Gold, Saddles, Bridles, C. Vauzelles, Hermes, 34 x 35 In. | 167 |
| **Scarf,** Splendeur De Maharajas, Black, Multicolor, Silk Twill, Hermes, 1996, 35 x 35 In. | 380 |
| **Scarf,** Tibet, Yellow, Auburn, Green, Blue, Brown Ground, Caty Latham, Hermes, 35 x 35 In. | 207 |
| **Scarf,** Vendanges, Purple, Orange, Red, Silk Twill, V. Dawlat-Dumoulin, Hermes, 35 x 35 In. | 224 |
| **Shako,** Militia, Blue Broadcloth, Leather, Sunburst, Eagle, Massachusetts, 1850s, 11 In. | 1599 |
| **Shawl,** Black, Linen, Fringe, Va., c.1880, 53 x 59 In. | 104 |
| **Shawl,** Paisley, Black Center, Fringe, Silk, Wool, India, 62 x 63 In. | 82 |
| **Shawl,** Silk, Wool, Sequins, Red, Flower Embroidery, Black Ground, Flying Fig, 88 x 40 In. | 155 |
| **Shawl,** Wool, Cashmere, Paisley, Appliqued, Embroidered, Kashmir, c.1845, 66 In. .........*illus* | 615 |
| **Shoes,** Bootie Style, White Kid Leather, Heels, Louis Vuitton | 420 |
| **Shoes,** Heels, Flower Print, Bow, Stuart Weitzman, Size 6 ½ M | 48 |
| **Shoes,** Heels, Leather, Cream, Strap, Giorgio Armani, Box, Size 37 | 36 |
| **Shoes,** Heels, Patent Leather, Black, White, Bally, Jessica Shoes, Box, 7M | 24 |
| **Shoes,** Heels, Sling Backs, Silk, Pink, Black, Brown Geometrics, Prada, Size 38 ½ | 24 |
| **Shoes,** Lotus, For Bound Feet, Leather, Red, Chinese, c.1935, 4 ¾ In. | 391 |
| **Shoes,** Oxfords, Leather, Brown, Cream, Laces, Box, Size 37 | 42 |
| **Shoes,** Pumps, Heel, Gray Leather, Gold Bow, Ferragamo, Italy, Size 9 | 50 |
| **Shoes,** Victorian, Store Prop, Leather Soles, Uppers, Buttoned Kid Ankles, c.1880, 17 In. | 440 |
| **Skirt,** Blouse, Silk, Flowers, Puffy Sleeves, Miss O, Oscar De La Renta, 1980s, Size 4 | 84 |
| **Skirt,** Patchwork, Applique, Drawstring, Initials, Multicolor, Felt, Print, Silk, 1800s, 30 In. | 923 |
| **Skirt,** Silk, Kelly Green, Long, Lilly Pulitzer, Size 8 | 84 |
| **Surcoat,** Blue Silk, Couched Metallic Threads, Dragon, Phoenix Roundels, Chinese, 36 In. | 400 |

**C**

**Cloisonne,** Case, Flowers, Leaves, Turquoise Beads, Russian Silver, Gilt, c.1900, 3 x 2 In.
**$3,198**

Skinner Auctioneers & Appraisers

**Cloisonne,** Flask, Moon, Landscapes, Gi Frame, Lotus Vining, Dragon Handles, Chinese, 15 In.
**$3,600**

Garth's Auctioneers & Appraisers

**Cloisonne,** Spoon, Silver, Marked, Fedor Ruckert, Faberge, Russia, c.1900, 6 ⅜ In.
**$2,875**

Rago Arts & Auction Center

**Cloisonne,** Water Coupe, Peach Shape, Leaves, Millefleur, Bats, Chinese, c.1910, 6 x 5 In.
**$1,659**

James D. Julia Auctioneers

# CLOTHING

**Clothing,** Coat, Gentleman's, Kossack, Wool, Gold & Silver Braid, Open Sleeves, c.1890, 41 In.
$486

James D. Julia Auctioneers

**Clothing,** Hat, Black Wool, Red Satin, Rhinestone & Feather Trim, Whittall & Shon, 22 In.
$60

Garth's Auctioneers & Appraisers

---

**TIP**
*If a zipper is stuck on a vintage dress or old suitcase, try rubbing soap or a candle on the zipper teeth. It may help.*

---

**Clothing,** Hat, Cocktail, Purple Felt, Jewel Trim, Pheasant Feathers, Net, Jack McConnell, N.Y.
$215

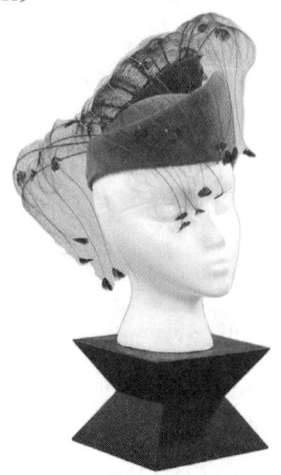

New Orleans Auction Galleries, Inc.

**Clothing,** Hat, Cocktail, Riding Side Saddle To The Hounds, Black Wool, Net, Velvet Trim
$676

New Orleans Auction Galleries, Inc.

**Clothing,** Hat, Stetson, Pins, Military Badges, Crossed Sabers, Lindbergh Plane
$300

Showtime Auction Services

---

**Clothing,** Hat, Straw, Floppy Rim, The Winchester Store, Woman's
$3,900

Santa Margarita Auction Barn

**Clothing,** Kimono, Silk, Red Lining, Japan, c.1935, 52 In.
$60

DuMouchelles Art Gallery

**Clothing,** Mittens, Wool, Woven, Diamond Shapes & 1845, Red, Blue, 10 x 6 In.
$1,437

Cottone Auctions

| | |
|---|---|
| **Swim Suit,** Wool, Blue Knit, Aqua Grosgrain Ribbon Trim, Jacket, Wood Buttons, Child's | 168 |
| **Top Hat,** Black, Leather Box, Dobbs & Co., 6 x 9½ In. | 188 |
| **Wrap,** Cashmere, Pink, Chanel, 60 x 68 In. | 478 |

**CLUTHRA** glass is a two-layered glass with small bubbles and powdered glass trapped between the layers. The Steuben Glass Works of Corning, New York, first made it in 1920. Victor Durand of Kimball Glass Company in Vineland, New Jersey, made a similar glass from about 1925. Durand's pieces are listed in the Durand category. Related items are listed in the Steuben category.

| | |
|---|---|
| **Vase,** Amethyst, Shouldered, Steuben, 8¼ In. ............*illus* | 460 |
| **Vase,** Blue Mottled, Opalescent Handles, Rolled Rim, Steuben, c.1920, 10⅝ In. | 1046 |
| **Vase,** Cluthra, White, Bulbous, Flared Rim, Steuben, 12 In. | 948 |
| **Vase,** Green, 6-Sided, Steuben, 4½ In. | 246 |
| **Vase,** Green, Shouldered, Steuben, 6¼ In. | 633 |

**COALBROOKDALE** was made by the Coalport porcelain factory of England during the Victorian period. Pieces are decorated with floral encrustations.

| | |
|---|---|
| **Basket,** Flowers, Multicolor, Handle, 10½ x 5 x 6 In. | 595 |
| **Vase,** Lid, Applied Flowers, Vines, Painted, Multicolor, Gilt, c.1850, 13 In. | 104 |
| **Vase,** Lid, Snowball Style, Footed, c.1820, 8 x 4½ In., Pair | 313 |

**COALPORT** ware was made by the Coalport Porcelain Works of England beginning about 1795. Early pieces were unmarked. About 1810–25 the pieces were marked with the name *Coalport* in various forms. Later pieces also had the name *John Rose* in the mark. The crown mark was used with variations beginning in 1881. The date 1750 is printed in some marks, but it is not the date the factory started. Coalport was bought by Wedgwood in 1967. Coalport porcelain is no longer being produced. Some pieces are listed in Indian Tree.

| | |
|---|---|
| **Bust,** Lord Nelson, Parian, Marked, c.1853, 9½ In. | 1125 |
| **Compote,** Lozenge Shape, Undulating Rim, Grape Cluster Relief, Pink, Gilt, 5 x 13 In. | 173 |
| **Cup & Saucer,** Demitasse, Fired Gold, Blue, Gold Interior, Scalloped Rim, Pair | 210 |
| **Plate,** Dessert, White, Turquoise Band, Gilt Rim, Mark, 8½ In., 12 Piece | 311 |
| **Plate,** Dinner, Burgundy Scalloped Rim, 10¼ In., 12 Piece | 375 |
| **Plate,** Pink, Gilt Monogram, Enameled Border, White Ground, c.1920, 10 In., 18 Piece | 1024 |
| **Teapot,** Diagonal Lined Green, Red Band, Tapered Oval, c.1800, 7⅜ In. | 69 |
| **Teapot,** Dome Lid, Red, Black, Gilt Flower Band, Straight White Sides, c.1826, 6 In. | 92 |
| **Teapot,** Lid, Stand, Red Leaves, Gilt Bands, Oval Shape, John Rose, c.1805, 7¼ In. | 115 |

**COBALT BLUE** glass was made using oxide of cobalt. The characteristic bright dark blue identifies it for the collector. Most cobalt glass found today was made after the Civil War. There was renewed interest in the dark blue glass in the late 1930s and dinnerware was made.

| | |
|---|---|
| **Sugar,** Lid, 16-Diamond Pattern, Stiegel Type, c.1820, 5¾ In. | 2160 |
| **Vase,** Urn Shape, Tooled Dore Rim, Footed, 5½ In., Pair | 460 |
| **Wine,** Cut, Rounded Bowl, Clear Tapered Stem, Flared Base, 8 x 3½ In., 6 Piece | 178 |
| **Witch Ball,** Holder, Blown, 1800s, 14¾ In., Pair | 1200 |

**COCA-COLA** was first served in 1886 in Atlanta, Georgia. It was advertised through signs, newspaper ads, coupons, bottles, trays, calendars, and even lamps and clocks. Collectors want anything with the word *Coca-Cola*, including a few rare products, like gum wrappers and cigar bands. The famous trademark was patented in 1893, the *Coke* mark in 1945. Many modern items and reproductions are being made.

| | |
|---|---|
| **Apron,** Vendor's, Pause, Refresh, White, Red, 1950s | 270 |
| **Ashtray,** Pullmatch, Bottle, 1930s, 7¼ In. | 1680 |
| **Ax,** Coca-Cola Decal, Metal Head, Carved Wood Handle, General Wear, 1920s, 13 In. | 360 |
| **Bag Of Marbles,** Sales Promotion, 1950s, 6½ In. | 36 |
| **Bicycle,** Huffy Promotion Beach Cruiser, c.1980, 41 x 68 In. | 240 |
| **Bookmark,** 1-Sided, Girl, White Dress, Urn, Drink Coca-Cola, 2⅜ x 5⅜ In. | 185 |
| **Bookmark,** Heart Shape, Celluloid, Vintage Woman, c.1900, 2¼ In. | 35 |
| **Bookmark,** Heart Shape, Drink Coca-Cola, 5 Cents, Celluloid, c.1899, 4½ In. | 540 |
| **Bottle,** Coca-Cola, Amber, Elkins, West Virginia, 7½ In. | 90 |
| **Bottle,** Coca-Cola, Amber, Huntsville, Alabama, 7¾ In. | 60 |
| **Bottle,** Coca-Cola, Amber, Toledo, Ohio, 8 In. | 60 |
| **Bottle,** Coca-Cola, Aqua, Atlanta, Georgia, 7½ In. | 60 |
| **Bottle,** Coca-Cola, Aqua, St. Andrew, Florida, 8 In. | 60 |
| **Bottle,** Coca-Cola, Aqua, Wilmington, North Carolina, 7½ In. | 120 |

**Clothing,** Robe, Opera Warrior's, Peking, Embroidered, Metallic Threads, c.1910, 58 In.
**$492**

Neal Auction Co.

**Clothing,** Scarf, Le Timbalier, Silk, Francoise Heron, Hermes, 1961, 35 In.
**$518**

DuMouchelles Art Gallery

**Clothing,** Scarf, Les Jardiniers Du Roy, Silk, Maurice Trenchant, Hermes, 1967, 35 In.
**$330**

DuMouchelles Art Gallery

**Clothing,** Scarf, Silk & Rayon, Pink & Gray Print, Beaded Fringe, Emilio Pucci, 67 x 12 In.
**$88**

Garth's Auctioneers & Appraisers

**Clothing,** Shawl, Wool, Cashmere, Paisley, Appliqued, Embroidered, Kashmir, c.1845, 66 In.
$615

Cowan's Auctions

**Cluthra,** Vase, Amethyst, Shouldered, Steuben, 8 ¼ In.
$460

Early Auction Co.

**Coca-Cola,** Calendar, 1896, Lady With Birds, April To December Pad, Frame, 15 x 18 In.
$105,000

Morphy Auctions

**TIP**

*Most Coca-Cola trays had green or brown borders in the 1920s, red borders in the 1930s.*

| | |
|---|---:|
| **Bottle,** Coca-Cola, Clear, Key West, Florida, 8 In. | 150 |
| **Bottle,** Coca-Cola, Faint Green, Buffalo, New York, 7¾ In. | 60 |
| **Bottle,** Coca-Cola, Green, Apallachicola, Florida, 7½ In. | 150 |
| **Bottle,** Coca-Cola, Green, Owensboro, Kentucky, 7½ In. | 30 |
| **Bottle,** Coca-Cola, Syrup, Peoples Drug Store Label, c.1945, 5 In. | 240 |
| **Bottle,** Coca-Cola, Syrup, Textured Color Label, Wreath, c.1915, 12½ In. | 720 |
| **Bottle,** Coca-Cola, Water, Green, Horses, Riders, Sloped, c.1945, 8¾ In. | 270 |
| **Bowl,** Coca-Cola Good With Food, White, Red, 1920s, 5¼ In. | 780 |
| **Box,** Shipping, Coca-Cola Gum, Wood, 6½ In. | 1320 |
| **Box,** Straw, Pause That Refreshes, Red, Bottle, 1930s, 9 In. | 420 |
| **Calendar,** 1896, Lady With Birds, April To December Pad, Frame, 15 x 18 In. ......*illus* | 105000 |
| **Calendar,** 1898, Girl, Blue Dress, Violets, 12 Months Pictures, 16 x 20 In. | 19200 |
| **Calendar,** 1901, Girl With Pansies At Soda Fountains, Feather Hat, ½ Pad, 16 x 20 In. | 5100 |
| **Calendar,** 1902, Girl With Feathered Hat, Drink Coca-Cola, 5 Cents, Full Pad, 16 x 20 In. | 2700 |
| **Calendar,** 1904, Lillian Nordica, White Gown, Formal Room, Frame, 15 x 8 In. | 360 |
| **Calendar,** 1908, Lady In Red, Red Dress, Hat, Frame, 14½ x 7 In. | 1560 |
| **Calendar,** 1912, Hamilton King, Delicious & Refreshing, Woman, Green Dress, Pad, 14 x 24 In. | 2700 |
| **Calendar,** 1914, Betty, Pink Dress, Lace, Bottle, Frame, 33 x 14 In. | 330 to 600 |
| **Calendar,** 1918, Beach Scene, 2 Girls, Umbrella, Sept.-Dec., Frame, 36½ x 18 In. ......*illus* | 1610 |
| **Calendar,** 1920, Golfer Girl, Yellow Dress, Wide Hat, Frame, 34 x 14½ In. | 3900 |
| **Calendar,** 1921, Autumn Girl, Blue Dress, Garden, Frame, 17 x 35 In. | 300 |
| **Calendar,** 1922, Summer Girl, Ballpark, 38½ x 19¾ In. | 575 |
| **Calendar,** 1925, Girl At Party, Blue Turban, White Fur Stole, Frame, 26 x 13 In. | 1020 |
| **Calendar,** 1928, Girl With Fur Stole, 13x 26 In. | 120 |
| **Calendar,** 1928, Girl, Lounging, Gold Gown, White Fur, Frame, 15 x 8½ In. | 480 |
| **Calendar,** 1929, Girl With Long String Of Pearls, Frame, 17 x 29 In. | 300 |
| **Calendar,** 1931, Barefoot Boy, Poem, Norman Rockwell, Frame, 25¾ x 13 In. | 510 |
| **Calendar,** 1935, Barefoot Boy, Out Fishin', Norman Rockwell, Frame, 25½ x 13 In. | 300 |
| **Calendar,** 1938, Girl At Shade, White Gown, Pink Hat, Bottle, Frame, 26 x 13 In. | 600 |
| **Calendar,** 1941, Skating Girl, Thirst Knows No Season, 14 x 20 In. | 390 |
| **Calendar,** 1943, Army Nurse, Blue Cape, Holding Bottle, 14 x 20 In. | 360 |
| **Calendar,** 1946, Boy Scout, Cub Scout, Tying Knots, Norman Rockwell, 16 x 33 In. | 1200 |
| **Calendar,** 1946, Sprite Boy, Cap Hat, Blue, 21 x 13 In. | 180 |
| **Calendar,** 1949, Seated Girl, Baseball Cap, 13 x 21 In. | 120 |
| **Cash Register,** National Cash Register, Model 711, Red, Drink Coca-Cola, Logos, 17 In. | 345 |
| **Cash Register,** National, Candy Store Model 313, Brass, Drink Coca-Cola In Bottles | 600 |
| **Cash Register,** National, Candy Store Model 316, Brass, Drink Coca-Cola In Bottles | 960 |
| **Cash Register,** National, Model 445A, Brass, Drink 5 Cent Coca-Cola, 1910 | 1320 |
| **Cigarette Case,** Frosted Glass, Yellow, 1936, 5 In. | 300 |
| **Clock Radio,** Cooler Shape, Drink Coca-Cola, Red, White, 1950s, 12½ In. | 1080 |
| **Clock,** Drink Coca-Cola, Neon, c.1935, 15 x 15 In. | 900 |
| **Clock,** Drink Coca-Cola, Plastic, Electric, Clock, 1940s, 15 In. | 180 |
| **Clock,** Electric, Cream, Red, Blue Numbers, Light-Up, 17 In. | 84 |
| **Clock,** Radio, Plastic, Convertible, General Electric, Battery Operated | 120 |
| **Clock,** Red, White, Electric, Wood Frame, Square, 1940s, 15 In. | 210 |
| **Cooler,** Drink Coca-Cola, 4 Tin Sides, Paint, Bottle Opener, Black, Red, 28 x 18 In. | 720 |
| **Cooler,** Insulated Tin, Red, Drink Coca-Cola In Bottles, 12 x 17½ In. | 237 |
| **Cooler,** Junior Picnic, Bail Handle, Opener, Stainless Steel, Kansas, c.1950, 14 x 12 In. | 173 |
| **Cooler,** Red, Embossed, Latching Lid, Handle, Bottle Opener, 17 x 6½ x 12 In. | 180 |
| **Cooler,** Wood, Drink Bottled Coca-Cola It's Better, Red Paint, 40 In. | 3600 |
| **Couch,** Cooler Shape, Red Metal Frame, White Leather Upholstery, Ice Cold, 69 x 32 In. | 1560 |
| **Crate,** 36-Bottle, Wood, Union City, Ind., c.1910, 17 In. | 720 |
| **Crate,** Plywood, 24-Bottle, c.1945, 17½ In. | 150 |
| **Dish,** Pretzel, Aluminum, 3 Coke Bottle Shape Feet, c.1935, 8 In. | 120 |
| **Dispenser,** Multiplex, Black Glass, Decal, 1920s, 22 In. | 3900 |
| **Display,** Cowboy, Lucite, Cardboard, 2-Sided, Motorized, Arms & Eyes Move, 1950s, 66 x 44 In. ...*illus* | 1200 |
| **Display,** Man On Phone, Meet Me At Soda Fountain, Cardboard, 1920s, 40 x 29 In. | 480 |
| **Door Handle,** Aluminum, 1940s, 8 In. | 60 |
| **Door Handle,** Bottle, Plastic, Metal, Have A Coke, Milton Sturm & Co., 1950s, 8 In. ......*illus* | 270 |
| **Door Push,** Buvez Glace, Porcelain, Orange, Red, French Canadian, 3 x 32 In. | 180 |
| **Door Push,** Come In!, Have A Coca-Cola, Red, Porcelain, Oval, 12 x 4 In. | 360 |
| **Figure,** Grocer, Holding Coca-Cola Bottle, c.1940s, 5½ In. | 1080 |
| **Glass Holder,** Pewter, Logo, Handle, c.1910, 3½ In. | 4200 |
| **Glass,** Drink Coca-Cola, Flared, Clear, Etched, 5 Cents, 4 In. | 600 |
| **Glass,** Soda, Flared Rim, Syrup Line, c.1904, 3¾ x 2 In. | 23 |

| | |
|---|---|
| Ice Tongs, Coca-Cola, Metal, 13 ½ In. | 510 |
| Jar, Coca-Cola Pepsin Gum, Lid, Clear, c.1915, 11 ½ In. | 570 |
| Jump Rope, Whistle, Pure As Sunlight On Handle, 1920s, 24 In. | 240 |
| Lamp, Bottle Shape, Iron Base, Embossed, Red, 1930s, 20 ¼ In. | 4200 |
| Lamp, Drink Coca-Cola, Globe, Hanging, Milk Glass, 1936, 14 In. | 420 |
| Match Strike Plate, Drink Coca-Cola, Red, Green, Porcelain, 1938, 46 x 60 In. | 1920 |
| Menu Card, Girl, Seated, Large Hat, Frame, 1902, 11 x 9 In. | 510 |
| Menu, Soda Fountain, Tin, 10 Strips, White, Red, 1950s, 62 In. | 2040 |
| Mirror, Girl, Holding Glass, Oval, Pocket, 1914, 3 In. | 660 |
| Mirror, Girl, Red Dress & Hat, Drinking Oval, Pocket, 1908, 3 In. | 780 |
| Mirror, Girl, Yellow Dress & Hat, Holding Bottle, Oval, Pocket, 1916, 2 ¾ In. | 1200 |
| Mirror, Pocket, Drink Delicious, Girl, Green Hat, Roses, 2 ¾ In. | 115 |
| Mirror, Pocket, Girl, Low Cut Gown, Holding Glass, Oval, 1907, 2 ¾ In. | 330 |
| Mirror, Pocket, Girl, Red Dress & Hat, Drinking, Oval, Pocket, 1908, 2 ¾ In. | 390 |
| Mirror, Pocket, Girl, Seated, Yellow Dress, Bottle, 1916, 2 ¾ In. | 480 |
| Panel, Bas-Relief, Bottle, Logo, Stylized Fronds, Cast Concrete, c.1930, 27 x 23 In. | 688 |
| Pin, Member Of Coca-Cola Bottle Club, Round, 1930s, 1 ¼ In. | 150 |
| Plaque, Coca-Cola Bottling Works, 3 Rosettes, Cast Iron, Brass, 1940s, 22 x 15 In. | 600 |
| Plate, Sandwich, Drink Coca-Cola, Yellow, Red, 1930s, 7 ¼ In. | 180 |
| Postcard, 1909, Girl, Black Hat, White Gown, Hamilton King, 3 x 5 In. | 840 |
| Postcard, Girl, Seated, Large Black Hat, Frame, 1910, 7 ¾ x 5 ¾ In. | 390 |
| Radio, Drink Coca-Cola, Red Paint, 1950s, 12 In. | 180 |
| Radio, Plastic, 2 Knobs, AM, 5 Tubes, Point Of Purchase Displays, Table | 360 |
| Rain & Wind Meter, Plastic, Metal, White, 1960s, 6 ½ In. | 48 |
| Salesman's Book, Red Cover, 1960s, 7 ½ In. | 36 |
| Scale, Model 724B, Fan, Red, Black Scoop, Bottle Sticker, The Pauses That Refreshes | 510 |
| Shopping Cart, Multicolor, 1950s, 20 In. | 360 |
| Sign, 6-Pack, Tin, Die Cut, 1951, 12 x 11 In. | 840 |
| Sign, Asian Landscape, Woven, Wood, Frame, c.1935, 31 x 12 ¾ In. | 1560 |
| Sign, Bottle Shape, Pressed Tin, Paint, c.1950, 16 x 5 In. | 195 |
| Sign, Bottle, White Ground, Porcelain, 1950s, 18 x 33 In. | 240 |
| Sign, Bottle, Yellow Ground, Tin, 1948, 32 x 14 In. | 240 |
| Sign, Cap, Bottle, Script Coca-Cola, Red Ground, Porcelain, 36 In. | 616 |
| Sign, Cap, Red, Round, 24 In. | 390 |
| Sign, Coca-Cola 6-Pack, Cutout, Tin, 13 In. | 1560 |
| Sign, Coca-Cola Bottle, Cutout, Tin, 36 In. | 420 |
| Sign, Coca-Cola Bottle, Porcelain, Die Cut, Brown, Green, 5 x 16 ½ In. | 176 |
| Sign, Coca-Cola Sold Here Ice Cold, Embossed Tin, 1932, 54 ½ x 18 In. | 3600 |
| Sign, Coca-Cola, Steel, Neon, Flexlume Electrical Advertising, 1930s, 117 x 62 In. | 12000 |
| Sign, Cowboy In Desert, Cardboard Lithograph, c.1941, 17 x 29 In. | 540 |
| Sign, Dec. 25, 1923 Bottle, Tin Lithograph, c.1930, 11 ⅜ x 34 ⅞ In. | 3565 |
| Sign, Delicious Coca-Cola Refreshing, Red, Round, Celluloid, Tin, c.1950 | 150 |
| Sign, Drink Coca-Cola Ice Cold, Flange, Tin, 1951, 22 x 18 In. | 660 |
| Sign, Drink Coca-Cola Ice Cold, Round, Arrow, Metal, Masonite, 1930s, 28 ¾ In. | 780 |
| Sign, Drink Coca-Cola In Bottles, White On Red, Porcelain Over Steel, 16 x 43 In. | 269 |
| Sign, Drink Coca-Cola, Bathing Girl, Green Swimsuit, Frame, 1938, 25 x 25 In. | 510 |
| Sign, Drink Coca-Cola, Bathing Girl, Red Swimsuit, Cardboard, Frame, 1940, 25 x 25 In. | 420 |
| Sign, Drink Coca-Cola, Bottles On Refrigerator Shelf, Cardboard, 1950s, 22 x 28 In. | 180 |
| Sign, Drink Coca-Cola, Delicious & Refreshing, Tin, 54 x 18 In. | 360 |
| Sign, Drink Coca-Cola, Diamond Shape, Masonite, 1946, 42 x 42 In. | 420 |
| Sign, Drink Coca-Cola, Embossed Tin, 1930s, 18 x 54 ½ In. | 1920 to 3600 |
| Sign, Drink Coca-Cola, Embossed Tin, 1936, 35 x 11 In. | 300 |
| Sign, Drink Coca-Cola, Girl, Parasol, Cardboard, Cutout Easel, Frame, 1931, 23 x 15 In. | 5700 |
| Sign, Drink Coca-Cola, Green Ground, Tin, 11 x 8 In. | 180 |
| Sign, Drink Coca-Cola, Hanging, 2-Sided, Round, Metal, Plastic, 1950s, 16 In. | 510 |
| Sign, Drink Coca-Cola, Light-Up, Round, Revolving Base, 1950s, 22 ½ In. | 2040 |
| Sign, Drink Coca-Cola, Please Pay When Served, Countertop, 1950s, 20 In. | 360 |
| Sign, Drink Coca-Cola, Please Pay When Served, Round, Green, Red, 1920s, 11 In. | 390 |
| Sign, Drink Coca-Cola, Policeman Crossing Guard, 2-Sided, Metal, 1950s, 60 In. | 2404 |
| Sign, Drink Coca-Cola, Shop Refreshed, Round, Halo Light-Up, 1950s, 16 In. | 720 |
| Sign, Entertain Your Thirst, c.1941, 17 x 29 In. | 480 |
| Sign, Extra Bright Refreshment, Housewife, Grocery Cart, c.1956, 35 x 63 In. | 480 |
| Sign, Fishtail Logo, Sign Of Good Taste, Marked, 1960-63, 15 x 18 In. | 322 |
| Sign, Fountain Service, Red, Green, DSP, 1934, 22 ¾ x 25 ½ In. | 1264 |

Coca-Cola, Calendar, 1918, Beach Scene, 2 Girls, Umbrella, Sept.-Dec., Frame, 36 ½ x 18 In.
$1,610

Wm Morford Auctions

Coca-Cola, Display, Cowboy, Lucite, Cardboard, 2-Sided, Motorized, Arms & Eyes Move, 1950s, 66 x 44 In.
$1,200

Morphy Auctions

**Coca-Cola,** Door Handle, Bottle, Plastic, Metal, Have A Coke, Milton Sturm & Co., 1950s, 8 In.
$270

Morphy Auctions

**Coca-Cola,** Sign, Policeman, Figural, Slow School Zone, Hand Up, Holding Sign, Blue, Yellow
$2,700

Morphy Auctions

**Coca-Cola,** Syrup Dispenser, 3 Sections, Reproduction, Markatron Of Atlanta, 1970s, 20 In.
$1,080

Morphy Auctions

| | |
|---|---|
| **Sign,** Fountain Service, Shield Shape, Red, Green, Porcelain, 26 x 23 In. | 3600 |
| **Sign,** Girl, Blue Dress, Sitting At Counter, Pause & Refresh, 27 x 44 In. | 1560 |
| **Sign,** Girl, Blue Lace Dress, Holding Bottle, Paper, Frame, 1905, 19 x 15 In. | 1560 |
| **Sign,** Girl, On Collar, Tennis Outfit, Play Refreshed, 30 x 50 In. | 510 |
| **Sign,** Girl, White Organdy Dress, Hat, Red Sash, Bottle, Paper, Frame, 27 x 21 In. | 3000 |
| **Sign,** Glass, Please Pay When Served, Metal Frame, Wood Backing, 11 ½ x 26 In. | 1200 |
| **Sign,** Good With Coke, Hamburger, Bun, Plastic, Size 11, 12 In. | 330 |
| **Sign,** Have A Coke, Cheerleader, White Sweater, Frame, Cardboard Litho, 26 x 42 In. | 660 |
| **Sign,** Hot Dog, Bottle, 1931, Frame, Paper, 22 x 13 In. | 780 |
| **Sign,** Ice Cold As Always 5 Cents, 12 x 15 In. | 180 |
| **Sign,** Ice Cold Coca-Cola In Bottles, Red, Green, Paper, Frame, 1920s, 16 x 25 In. | 1020 |
| **Sign,** Let's Have A Coke, Marching Band Baton Majorette, Coke Machine, 36 x 56 In. | 570 |
| **Sign,** McGuire Sisters, King Size, Be Really Refreshed, Cardboard, 36 x 20 In. | 173 |
| **Sign,** Pick Up 6, For Refreshment, Tin Lithograph, White, c.1954, 16 x 50 In. | 1680 |
| **Sign,** Policeman, Figural, Slow School Zone, Hand Up, Holding Sign, Blue, Yellow ...........*illus* | 2700 |
| **Sign,** Santa Claus, 1946, 12 ½ In. | 150 |
| **Sign,** Take Home A Carton Of Quality Refreshment, White, 16 x 41 In. | 450 to 780 |
| **Sign,** Take Home A Carton, Easy To Carry, Girl, Blue Dress, Frame, 1937, 36 x 19 In. | 1020 |
| **Sign,** Thing Go Better With Coke, Girl With Boating Cap, Cardboard, 1960s, 27 x 16 In. | 345 |
| **Sign,** Tin, Drink Coca-Cola, Enjoy That Refreshing New Feeling, Marked LRC, 54 x 18 In. | 620 |
| **Sign,** Tin, Pause, Drink Coca-Cola, Bottle, Painted Wooden Frame, 1939, 35 x 30 In. | 345 |
| **Sign,** Win A Visit From Anita Bryant, 1963, 35 x 23 In. | 180 |
| **Strawholder,** Chrome, Plastic Base & Sign, 1950s, 12 In. | 210 |
| **Stringholder,** Take Home Coca-Cola In Cartons, Metal, 16 In. | 210 |
| **Syrup Dispenser,** 3 Sections, Reproduction, Markatron Of Atlanta, 1970s, 20 In. ...........*illus* | 1080 |
| **Telephone,** Candlestick, Brass, Cord, Embossed, Notepad Holder, 1930s, 11 In. .........*illus* | 590 |
| **Thermometer,** Bottle Shape, 16 In. | 90 |
| **Thermometer,** Bottle Shape, Embossed, Tin, 1936, 16 ½ In. | 270 |
| **Thermometer,** Delicious & Refreshing, Intact Tube, c.1915, 5 x 21 In. | 150 |
| **Thermometer,** Delicious & Refreshing, Tin Litho, Intact Tube, c.1940, 7 x 16 In. | 300 |
| **Thermometer,** Dial, Things Go Better With Coke, Red, White, Green, 1960s, 18 In. Diam. | 270 |
| **Thermometer,** Drink Coca-Cola Delicious & Refreshing, 5 Cents, c.1905, 21 x 5 In. | 288 |
| **Thermometer,** Drink Coca-Cola Thirst Knows No Season, Porcelain, c.1935, 18 In. | 420 |
| **Thermometer,** Drink Coca-Cola, Masonite, 17 x 6 ¾ In. | 570 |
| **Thermometer,** Drink Coca-Cola, Red, White, Porcelain, 1950s, 36 In. | 1560 |
| **Thermometer,** Drink Coca-Cola, Sign Of Good Taste, Oval, Red & White, 30 In. | 157 |
| **Thermometer,** Drink Coca-Cola, Tan, Red, Green, Metal, c.1942, 15 ¾ In. | 300 |
| **Thermometer,** Tin, Embossed, Gold Bottle Shape, Box, 7 ⅝ x 2 ¼ In. | 92 |
| **Thermometer,** Wood, Carton Shape, 9 ½ In. | 48 |
| **Tip Tray,** 1906, Juanita, White Dress, Delicious, Refreshing, Round, 4 In. | 720 |
| **Tip Tray,** 1907, Drink Coca-Cola, Girl, Green Dress, Oval, 6 In. | 240 |
| **Tip Tray,** 1909, Exhibition Girl, Blue Dress, Summer Night Scene, Oval, Tin, 1909, 6 In. | 270 |
| **Tip Tray,** 1910, Coca-Cola Girl, Black Hat, White Dress, Oval, 1910, Tin, 6 In. | 180 |
| **Tip Tray,** 1913, Hamilton King, Girl, Black Hat, Oval, 6 ½ In. | 480 |
| **Tip Tray,** 1913, Hamilton King, Girl, Blond, Hat With Flower, Oval, 12 In. | 360 |
| **Tip Tray,** 1914, Betty, White Bonnet, Pink Dress, Oval, 6 In. | 125 to 270 |
| **Tip Tray,** 1916, Woman, Yellow Dress, Glass, Oval, 6 In. | 150 |
| **Tip Tray,** 1933, Frances Dee, Paramount Player, 13 ¼ x 10 ½ In. | 450 |
| **Tip Tray,** Girl, Yellow Dress, White Hat, Oval, Tin, 1920s, 6 ½ In. | 210 |
| **Towel,** Soda Fountain, Coca-Cola Delicious & Refreshing, Orange, Black, 19 x 8 In. | 24 |
| **Toy,** Car, Tin, Friction, Red, White, 10 ½ In. | 150 |
| **Toy,** Coca-Cola, Truck, Lincoln, Gray Paint, 1950s, 15 ½ In. | 210 |
| **Toy,** Coca-Cola, Truck, Red, Yellow Paint, Metalcraft, 1930s, 11 In. | 300 |
| **Toy,** Coca-Cola, Truck, Smitty, Paint, Cast Metal, 1940s, 14 In. | 240 |
| **Toy,** Coca-Cola, Truck, Yellow Paint, Metal, Smith-Miller, Box, 1980s, 13 In. | 1020 |
| **Toy,** Truck, 10 Glass Bottles, Metalcraft, 11 In. ...........*illus* | 420 |
| **Toy,** Truck, Delivery, Wood Blocks, Metal, Smitty Toys, Smith-Miller, 1940s, 14 In. | 300 |
| **Toy,** Truck, Delivery, Yellow, Round Signs On Doors, Tin Lithograph, Linemar, 1950s, 5 In. | 172 |
| **Toy,** Truck, Metalcraft, 1930s, 11 In. | 150 |
| **Trade Card,** Folding, Metamorphic, Girl Bathing, Girl Serving Drinks, c.1907, 6 x 5 ½ In. .*illus* | 180 |
| **Tray,** 1906, Juanita, Drink Coca-Cola, Girl, Drinking From Glass, Oval, 13 In. | 3300 |
| **Tray,** 1908, Topless, Wherever Ginger-Ale, Seltzer Or Soda, Tin, c.1908, 12 In. .........*illus* | 1680 |
| **Tray,** 1913, Hamilton King, Hat With Flower, Glass, 15 ¼ x 12 ½ In. | 300 |
| **Tray,** 1914, Betty, Tying Hat, Pink Bow, 13 ⅜ x 10 ⅝ In. | 420 |

| | |
|---|---|
| Tray, 1916, Elaine, Yellow Dress, 19 x 8 ½ In. | 120 to 246 |
| Tray, 1921, Girl, Blue Hat, Holding Glass, American Art Works, 13 ¼ x 10 ½ In. ...............*illus* | 390 |
| Tray, 1922, Summer Girl, Hat, Blue Ribbon, Holding Glass, 1922, 13 ¼ x 10 ½ In. | 480 |
| Tray, 1929, Girl In Yellow, Towel, 1929, 13 In. | 270 |
| Tray, 1934, Swimsuits, Holding Bottle, 13 In. | 360 |
| Tray, 1942, 2 Girls At Car, Green Convertible, Tin, 13 ¼ x 10 ½ In. | 150 |
| Tray, 1957, Girl With Umbrella, Holding Bottle, 13 ¼ x 10 ½ In. .................*illus* | 456 |
| Vase, Wall, Pressed Paper, Cardboard, c.1932, 9 x 12 In. | 270 |
| Vending Machine, Drink Coca-Cola, Metal, Red & White, 58 x 16 x 21 In. | 2240 |
| Vending Machine, Model 44, Drink Coca-Cola, Vendorlator Mfg., 58 x 16 In. | 3240 |
| Watch Fob, Drink Coca-Cola In Bottles, Brown, Swastika Shape, c.1915, 1 ½ In. | 780 |
| Watch Fob, Girl, Holding Bottle, Celluloid, Brass, 1910, 5 ¾ In. | 660 |

**COFFEE MILLS** are also called coffee grinders, although there is a difference in the way each grinds the coffee. Large floor-standing or counter-model coffee mills were used in the nineteenth-century country store. Small home mills were first made about 1894. They lost favor by the 1930s. The renewed interest in fresh-ground coffee has produced many modern electric mills and hand mills and grinders. Reproductions of the old styles are being made.

| | |
|---|---|
| Arcade Mfg., Imperial, Oak Case, Cast Iron Handle, Joint Construction, 10 x 6 ¾ In. | 59 |
| Arcade, Wood, Finger Jointed Case, Drawer, Top Crank, Cast Iron Top | 59 |
| Bell, Wall Mount, Grinder, Turning Crank, Glass Cup, 17 x 8 In. | 660 |
| Charles Parker, 2 Wheels, Grinder, Blue, Red, Gold, Flowers, 22 x 10 In. | 720 |
| Cherry, Grain Painted, Pewter Hopper, Iron Handle, Dovetail Case, 1800s, 9 ½ In. | 189 |
| Coles, 2 Wheels, Cast Iron, Tin Drawer, Wood Base, Turned Handle, 12 ½ In. ...............*illus* | 295 |
| Elgin National, 2 Wheels, Floor Model, Grinder, Red, Gold, Late 1800s, 64 x 28 In. | 1440 |
| Enterprise, 2 Tin Hoppers, Cast Iron, Electric, 25 x 16 In. | 64 |
| Enterprise, 2 Wheels, No. 2, Countertop, Wood Hand Grip, Drawer, Cast Iron, 9 In. | 502 |
| Enterprise, 2 Wheels, No. 5, Red Paint, Decals, Cast Iron, 17 In. | 413 |
| Enterprise, 2 Wheels, No. 7, Gold Shadow Lettering, Wood Drawer, 24 In. | 1416 |
| Enterprise, 2 Wheels, No. 16, Cast Iron, Red, 65 In. | 5400 |
| Enterprise, 2 Wheels, Red Paint, Eagle Finial, Cast Iron, c.1860, 29 In. | 176 |
| Enterprise, 2 Wheels, Red Paint, Handle, Cast Iron, 26 x 21 In. | 168 |
| Enterprise, 2 Wheels, Red, Blue, Eagle Finial, Cast Iron, 41 In. | 510 |
| Enterprise, 2 Wheels, Red, Blue, Yellow Paint, Drawer, 11 ½ In. | 472 |
| Enterprise, 2 Wheels, Red, Wood Base, 12 ½ In. | 502 |
| Enterprise, Single Wheel, No. 750, Countertop, Red, Blue, Gold, Cast Iron, 21 In. | 561 |
| Fairbanks Morse & Co., 2 Wheels, Grinder, No. 6, Red, Blue, Gold, 19 x 28 In. | 270 |
| Golden Rule, Metal Front Panel, Glass Shield, Blend Coffee, 17 ½ In. | 153 |
| Landers, Frary & Clark, Painted, Decals, Crown, 12 ½ In. .................*illus* | 510 |
| Lane Bros., 2 Wheels, No. 12, Swift, Painted Red, Decals, Pan, 14 x 9 In. | 570 |
| Lightning, No. 23, Green, Cast Iron, 7 In. | 480 |
| National Specialty, 2 Wheels, Grinder, Chrome Top, Eagle, Red, 22 x 12 In. | 720 |
| Pewter Hopper, Drawer, Dovetail & Nailed Construction Case, 1800s, 11 In. | 142 |
| Swift Mill Lane Brothers, 2 Wheels, Model 12, 1875, 12 x 13 ¾ In. .................*illus* | 450 |
| Universal, No. 20, 2 Wheels, Cast Iron, Eagle Finial, Green Paint, c.1880, 14 x 7 ½ In. .......*illus* | 344 |

**COIN SPOT** is a glass pattern that was named by collectors for the spots resembling coins, which are part of the glass. Colored, clear, and opalescent glass was made with the spots. Many companies used the design in the 1870–90 period. It is so popular that reproductions are still being made.

| | |
|---|---|
| Biscuit Jar, Cranberry, Copper Swing Handle, Lid | 81 |
| Bottle, Barber, Blue, Rolled Lip, 8 ½ In. | 68 |
| Lamp, Cobalt Blue, Cut To Clear, Marble & Bronzed Base, 20 ½ In. | 978 |
| Lamp, Oil, Blue, Milk Glass, Column, Base, 13 ½ In., Pair | 390 |
| Lamp, Oil, Cranberry Opalescent, 8 ½ In. | 220 |
| Lamp, Oil, Finger, Blue, Footed, c.1890, 5 In. | 299 |
| Pitcher, Water, Green, Candy Ribbon Rim, Clear Handles, 9 ¼ In., Pair | 92 |
| Pitcher, Water, Pink Satin, Mother-Of-Pearl Glass, 4 Dimples, 10 ½ In. | 207 |
| Pitcher, Water, Pink Satin, Mother-Of-Pearl Glass, Frosted Ribbed Handle, 7 In. | 236 |
| Rose Bowl, Blue Opalescent, Ruffled Top, c.1910, 4 x 4 In. | 135 |
| Sugar Shaker, Blue Opalescent, Paneled, Footed, 1800s, 4 ¾ In. | 275 |
| Sugar Shaker, Blue, Plated Lid, 4 ¾ In. | 47 |
| Tumbler, White, Cranberry Ground, 1800s, 3 ⅝ In. | 50 |
| Vase, Yellow To White, Raised Flowers, Hand Blown, Ruffled Rim, c.1900, 10 In. | 472 |

**Coca-Cola,** Telephone, Candlestick, Brass, Cord, Embossed, Notepad Holder, 1930s, 11 In.
**$590**

Morphy Auctions

**Coca-Cola,** Toy, Truck, 10 Glass Bottles, Metalcraft, 11 In.
**$420**

Mosby Auctions

**Coca-Cola,** Trade Card, Folding, Metamorphic, Girl Bathing, Girl Serving Drinks, c.1907, 6 x 5 ½ In.
**$180**

Morphy Auctions

**Coca-Cola,** Tray, 1908, Topless, Wherever Ginger-Ale, Seltzer Or Soda, Tin, c.1908, 12 In.
**$1,680**

Morphy Auctions

**Coca-Cola,** Tray, 1921, Girl, Blue Hat, Holding Glass, American Art Works, 13 ¼ x 10 ½ In. $390

Showtime Auction Services

**Coca-Cola,** Tray, 1957, Girl With Umbrella, Holding Bottle, 13 ¼ x 10 ½ In. $456

Showtime Auction Services

**Coffee Mill,** Coles, 2 Wheels, Cast Iron, Tin Drawer, Wood Base, Turned Handle, 12 ½ In. $295

Conestoga Auction Co., Inc.

**COIN-OPERATED MACHINES** of all types are collected. The vending machine is an ancient invention dating back to 200 B.C., when holy water was dispensed from a coin-operated vase. Smokers in seventeenth-century England could buy tobacco from a coin-operated box. It was not until after the Civil War that the technology made modern coin-operated games and vending machines plentiful. Slot machines, arcade games, and dispensers are all collected.

| | |
|---|---|
| Arcade, Baseball, Williams, 4 Bagger Deluxe, 10 Cent, c.1955, 65 ¾ In. ...............*illus* | 2400 |
| Arcade, Chicago Coin Steam Shovel, Floor Crane Digger, 25 Cents, Key, c.1956 ..............*illus* | 1440 |
| Arcade, Horse Kiddie Ride, 10 Cent, Bent Coin Release, Painted........................... | 708 |
| Arcade, Kiss-O-Meter, Exhibit Supply Co., c.1940, 22 x 78 In........................... | 510 |
| Arcade, Major League Baseball, Movable Base Runners, Williams, 1963, 72 In. ........................... | 672 |
| Arcade, Ray's Track Horseracing, 1930s, 45 ½ In........................... | 9600 |
| Arcade, Sculptoscope Viewer, Whiting, Countertop, Round........................... | 1320 |
| Arcade, Shuffleboard, 25 Cent, Marvel Manufacturing, 148 x 50 In........................... | 480 |
| Arcade, Skill, Victory, Basketball, Try Your Skill, Victor Vending, c.1950, 18 x 22 In. ..........*illus* | 780 |
| Arcade, Steam Shovel, Norway Steam Shovel, See It In Action, 1 Cent, Footed, Wood........................... | 5700 |
| Columbia, Slot, Blue Paint, Wood Base, 25 Cents, 19 In........................... | 720 |
| Dispenser, Cup, Dixie Cup Co., 32 ½ In........................... | 360 |
| Dispenser, Hand Dryer, Electric, Sani-Dry, Porcelain, Chicago Hardware, 47 In........................... | 1140 |
| Dispenser, Postage Stamps, 10 Cents, 5 Cents, Metal, Enamel, c.1974, 7 ½ x 16 In. ...........*illus* | 127 |
| Dispenser, Prophylactic, Brass, Metal, 20 ½ In........................... | 1080 |
| Fortune Teller, Crystal Gazer, 1 Cent, Esco, Exhibit Supply, c.1929, 10 x 27 In........................... | 1440 |
| Fortune Teller, Gaze Into Crystal For Your Fortune, Swami, Lights Up, 1930s........................... | 540 |
| Fortune Teller, Love Clinic, Don't Miss This, 5 Cent, Wood Cabinet........................... | 1560 |
| Fortune Teller, Swami, Wood Cabinet, 50 Cent, 27 x 80 In........................... | 1140 |
| Fortune Teller, Watling, Model 400, Porcelain, Mirror, c.1948, Floor Model........................... | 295 |
| Fortune Teller, Wizard, 1 Cent, Wood Cabinet, Keys........................... | 1020 |
| Fortune Teller, Wizard, Mills, Wood Case, Aluminum Front, 1920-30, 14 x 18 ½ In. ..........*illus* | 2370 |
| Fortune Teller, Wood Cabinet, Responds Verbally, 27 x 80 In........................... | 1680 |
| Gambling, Dice Cage Flipper, Chuck-A-Luck, 2 Die, Metal, 11 In........................... | 390 |
| Game, Bimbo, 3 Ring Circus, Dancing Clown, United Billiards, 69 x 27 In........................... | 644 |
| Game, Dutch Pool, Table Top Game, Carved Walnut, Metal Levers, c.1900, 9 x 25 In........................... | 2640 |
| Game, Table, Race Car, 1 Cent, National Advertising, 28 x 28 In........................... | 900 |
| Music Box, Criterion, Gumball, Crown Molding, Crank Arm, 80 ¾ In........................... | 5535 |
| Music Box, Regina, Disc, Oak, Artwork On Lid, 1-Cent, 1986........................... | 200 |
| Music Box, Sublime Harmonia, Mahogany, Dancing Dolls, 8 Tunes, Zither, 30 In........................... | 10445 |
| Music Box, Symphonium, Walnut Case, Music Lyre, Symphonion, 11 Discs, 25 In........................... | 1777 |
| Mutoscope, Beware Of Windows, 5 Cent, Laura La Plante, Indians........................... | 10200 |
| Mutoscope, Boxing, Hot Time In Hogan's Alley, Shell, Lion, 10 Cent........................... | 7200 |
| Mutoscope, Felix The Cat, Clamshell, Red, Cast Iron, c.1900, 49 In........................... | 3159 |
| Mutoscope, Welcome To Ft. Riley, Blue, 1 Cent........................... | 1440 |
| Pinball, 3 Deuces, Williams, 1955, 67 In........................... | 240 |
| Pinball, 4 Square, Gottlieb, c.1971........................... | 450 |
| Pinball, Bally Old Chicago, 52 x 70 x 30 In........................... | 314 |
| Pinball, Batting Practice, Irving Kaye, c.1968........................... | 1080 |
| Pinball, Beauty Contest, Bally, 1960, 65 In........................... | 90 |
| Pinball, Buccaneer, Gottlieb, 1948, 66 In........................... | 450 |
| Pinball, Captain Fantastic, Bally, 1976, 72 In........................... | 720 |
| Pinball, Daily Races, Playout, 5 Cents, D. Gottlieb, 1936, 53 In........................... | 720 |
| Pinball, Exhibit Mystery, 1947, 64 In........................... | 120 |
| Pinball, Fashion Show, Gottlieb, 1962, 71 In........................... | 360 |
| Pinball, Flying High, Gottlieb, 1953, 66 In........................... | 330 |
| Pinball, Follies Of 1940, Genco, c.1939........................... | 390 |
| Pinball, Ice Revue, 1965, 72 In........................... | 210 |
| Pinball, Just 21, Gottlieb, 1950, 66 In........................... | 420 |
| Pinball, Mars God Of War, Gottlieb, 1981, 75 In........................... | 420 |
| Pinball, Mr. & Mrs. Pac Man, 1984, 76 In........................... | 390 |
| Pinball, Nags Horse Race, Yellow, Williams, c.1960........................... | 2160 |
| Pinball, Niagara, Gottlieb, 1951, 65 In. .................................*illus* | 2700 |
| Pinball, Paradise, United, 1948, 66 In........................... | 570 |
| Pinball, Showboat, Gottlieb, 1967, 69 In........................... | 120 |
| Pinball, Southern Belle, Wayne Neyens, Gottlieb, 1955, 65 In........................... | 450 |
| Pinball, Space Ship, Lights Bulbs, Steve Kordek, Williams, 1961, 71 In........................... | 1560 |
| Pinball, Stage Coach, Gottlieb, 1954, 67 In........................... | 450 |
| Pinball, Target Alpha, Gottlieb, 1976, 73 In........................... | 270 |
| Pinball, Thriller, Kenney, 1939, 65 In........................... | 360 |

| | |
|---|---|
| **Pinball,** Wishing Well, Gottlieb, 1955, 65 In. ..................................*illus* | 300 |
| **Play Football,** Oak, Painted, Chester Pollard, c.1930, 73 x 28 x 46 In. ...... | 1215 |
| **Skill,** Baseball Play Ball, 1 Cent, 18½ In.................................................. | 840 |
| **Skill,** Grip Test, Metal, Green Paint, 14 In. ............................................. | 360 |
| **Skill,** Mutoscope, Punch-A-Bag, Strength Tester ..................................... | 6600 |
| **Skill,** Pink Elephant, Ride, Key ................................................................ | 1440 |
| **Skill,** Strength Tester, Caille, Uncle Sam, Hand Extended, Cast Iron, 28 In. .........................*illus* | 13035 |
| **Skill,** Target Practice, 1 Cent, Metal, Key, 12 x 16 x 7 In. ...............*illus* | 399 |
| **Slot,** Aristocrat, Black Bart Cowboy Stand, Golden Nugget, 76 In. ......... | 1440 |
| **Slot,** Bally, Jack Pot, 5 Cent, Dice, Key, c.1935, 18 In. ....................*illus* | 12600 |
| **Slot,** Caille, 5 Cent, 1933, Superior, 25 In. ............................................. | 900 |
| **Slot,** Caille, 25 Cent, Superior, 24 In...................................................... | 1200 |
| **Slot,** Caille, Musical, Puck, Upright, 5 Cent, c.1900, 63 x 28 In. ............. | 14400 |
| **Slot,** Caille, New Century Detroit, 5 Cent, Upright, 65 In. ....................... | 18000 |
| **Slot,** Chicago Club House, 5 Reels, Playing Cards, Art Deco, 13 x 11 x 8 In. ....... | 738 |
| **Slot,** High-Top Jackpot, Mermaid, Red, 25 Cent, Mills, c.1952 ................ | 748 |
| **Slot,** Jennings, 5 Cent, Front Vendor, Escalator Bell, Wood Stand, c.1933 ... | 1560 |
| **Slot,** Jennings, Little Duke Jackpot, 3 Wheel, 1 Cent, Coin Return, c.1932 ................ | 1534 to 3000 |
| **Slot,** Jennings, Riverside Model, Indian Design, 5 Cent, c.1930, 27½ x 18 In. ... | 625 |
| **Slot,** Jennings, Rock-Ola Jackpot, 5 Cent, 25 In. ................................... | 1020 |
| **Slot,** Jennings, Standard Chief, 3 Columns, Knob Handle, 25 Cent, 28 In. ... | 1344 |
| **Slot,** Jennings, Standard Chief, 25 Cent, Tic-Tac-Toe, 1946, 27 In. ........ | 1020 |
| **Slot,** Jennings, Sun Chief, Tic-Tac-Toe, Light-Up, 5 Cent, 1948, 28 In. .... | 1800 |
| **Slot,** Jennings, Tri-Plex Chief, Escalator Bell, Wood Pedestal, c.1938........ | 4500 |
| **Slot,** Melon High Top, Escalator Bell, Watermelon Reels, 5 Cent, c.1948 ...... | 1344 |
| **Slot,** Mills, 3-Reel, Cabinet, Gum Vendor, Wood Stand, c.1910 ............. | 7200 |
| **Slot,** Mills, 5 Cent, Club Bell, 3-Reel Jackpot, Green ............................. | 2280 |
| **Slot,** Mills, 5 Cent, Escalator Bell, Wood Pedestal Stand, c.1935 ........... | 4200 |
| **Slot,** Mills, 777, High Top, 10 Cent, 28 In. ........................................... | 900 |
| **Slot,** Mills, Baseball Front, Gooseneck Bell ............................................. | 4200 |
| **Slot,** Mills, Chicago 36, 5 Cent, Carved Oak Cabinet, Nickel Trim, c.1900 ... | 8400 |
| **Slot,** Mills, Chrome Diamond Front, 5 Cent, Cast Iron, 27 In. ............... | 960 |
| **Slot,** Mills, Dewey, Upright, Oak Case, Copper Trim, 5 Cent, c.1905, 67 In. .... | 16800 |
| **Slot,** Mills, Elk, 20 In. ........................................................................... | 4200 |
| **Slot,** Mills, Figural, Carved Indian, Headdress, 25 Cent, 3-Reel ............. | 6000 |
| **Slot,** Mills, Golf Ball Vendor, 3-Reel, Club Bell, Floor Console, c.1937 ...... | 6000 |
| **Slot,** Mills, High Top Blue Bell, 5 Cent, 27 In. ...................................... | 840 |
| **Slot,** Mills, Horsehead Bonus Bell, 25 Cent, Escalator, Key, c.1937 ........ | 2400 |
| **Slot,** Mills, Melon Bursting Cherry, 25 Cent, 26 In.................................. | 1020 |
| **Slot,** Mills, Novelty 25 Cent, Wood Grain Veneer, 60 In........................... | 1680 |
| **Slot,** Mills, Novelty Front, F.O.K. Jackpot, 5 Cent, Gooseneck Bell, c.1923 .... | 900 |
| **Slot,** Mills, Poinsettia, 5 Cent, 1929, 24 In............................................ | 840 |
| **Slot,** Mills, QT Bell, 4-Reel, Side Mint Vendor, Wood Stand, c.1935 ....... | 3600 |
| **Slot,** Mills, Red Eagle, 5 Cent, Yellow, Escalator Bell, c.1931............... | 1080 |
| **Slot,** Mills, Red Eagle, Yellow, 25 Cent, Escalator Bell, c.1933.............. | 900 |
| **Slot,** Mills, Silent War Eagle, Yellow, Escalator, Fortune Reels, 5 Cent, c.1931 ... | 1200 |
| **Slot,** Mills, Twenty-One, Jackpot Black & Red, High Top, 5 Cent, Keys, Bell, c.1950 .............*illus* | 1020 |
| **Slot,** Mills, Vest Pocket, 5 Cent, Key, 8 In............................................. | 390 |
| **Slot,** Pace, 10 Cent, Cherry Bell, Candle Change Light, Service Button, c.1945 ........ | 1800 |
| **Slot,** Pace, 10 Cent, Cherry Bell, Gooseneck Bell, Service Button, c.1945..... | 480 |
| **Slot,** Pace, Chrome, Silver Dollar, Top Candle Change Light, c.1945 ...... | 960 |
| **Slot,** Pace, Gooseneck Bell, Dark Gray, Bill's Casino Reels, c.1945 ........ | 2400 |
| **Slot,** Pace, Harrah's, 10 Cent, Cherry Bell, Gooseneck, Top Light, Service Button.......... | 780 |
| **Slot,** Pace, Wagon Wheel, 25 Cent, Top Change Light, Side Bell .......... | 660 |
| **Slot,** Sparks, 3 Cigarette Label Reels, Lever, Blue & Gold Washed Case, 13 In...... | 185 |
| **Slot,** Stand, Oak, Drawer, Open Shelves, 34 In. .................................... | 120 |
| **Slot,** Stand, Plywood Top, Cast Iron, 32 In............................................ | 300 |
| **Slot,** Watling, Big 6, 5 Cent, Upright Floor Wheel, Front Casting, 1800s ...... | 7800 |
| **Slot,** Watling, Blue Seal Jackpot, 5 Cent, 24 In. ................................... | 600 |
| **Slot,** Watling, Checkerboard Rol-A-Top, 25 Cent, 27 In.......................... | 2400 |
| **Slot,** Watling, Front Rol-A-Top, 5 Cent, 27 In......................................... | 1920 |
| **Slot,** Watling, Operators Bell, 1 Cent, Cast Iron, Countertop, Key, c.1910 ............*illus* | 5700 |
| **Slot,** Watling, Rol-A-Top Twin Jackpot, 25 Cent, Escalator Bell, 1935 ........ | 3600 |
| **Slot,** Watling, Torch Front, 5 Cent, 1933, 25 In. ................................... | 780 |
| **Slot,** Watling, Treasury Twin, 5 Cent Gooseneck Bell, c.1935................... | 1680 |
| **Slot,** Watling, Yellow Paint, 5 Cent, 26¼ In. ......................................... | 3300 |

**Coffee Mill,** Landers, Frary & Clark,
Painted, Decals, Crown, 12½ In.
$510

Showtime Auction Services

**Coffee Mill,** Swift Mill Lane Brothers,
2 Wheels, Model 12, 1875, 12 x 13¾ In.
$450

Cowan's Auctions

**Coffee Mill,** Universal, No. 20, 2 Wheels,
Cast Iron, Eagle Finial, Green Paint,
c.1880, 14 x 7½ In.
$344

Rago Arts & Auction Center

**Coin-Operated,** Arcade, Baseball, Williams, 4 Bagger Deluxe, 10 Cent, c.1955, 65¾ In. $2,400

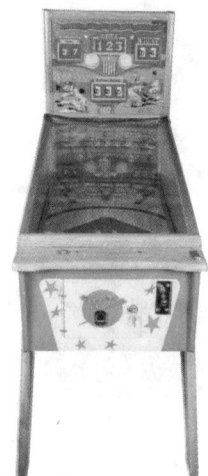

Morphy Auctions

**Coin-Operated,** Arcade, Chicago Coin Steam Shovel, Floor Crane Digger, 25 Cents, Key, c.1956 $1,440

Morphy Auctions

**Coin-Operated,** Arcade, Skill, Victory, Basketball, Try Your Skill, Victor Vending, c.1950, 18 x 22 In. $780

Morphy Auctions

**Coin-Operated,** Dispenser, Postage Stamps, 10 Cents, 5 Cents, Metal, Enamel, c.1974, 7½ x 16 In. $127

Hake's Americana & Collectibles

**Coin-Operated,** Fortune Teller, Wizard, Mills, Wood Case, Aluminum Front, 1920-30, 14 x 18½ In. $2,370

James D. Julia Auctioneers

**Coin-Operated,** Pinball, Niagara, Gottlieb, 1951, 65 In. $2,700

Morphy Auctions

**Coin-Operated,** Pinball, Wishing Well, Gottlieb, 1955, 65 In. $300

Morphy Auctions

**Coin-Operated,** Skill, Strength Tester, Caille, Uncle Sam, Hand Extended, Cast Iron, 28 In. $13,035

James D. Julia Auctioneers

**Coin-Operated,** Skill, Target Practice, 1 Cent, Metal, Key, 12 x 16 x 7 In. $399

Showtime Auction Services

| | |
|---|---|
| **Stand,** Slot, Wooden, Clawfoot, Owl Casting, Door, 19 x 34 In. ...........................*illus* | 390 |
| **Strength Tester,** Pull, Make Him Roar, Aluminum Tiger, Rope Tail, 28 x 57 In............. | 2700 to 5700 |
| **Trade Stimulator,** 1 Cent-25 Cent Reel, Blue Paint, 12 In. ........................................ | 330 |
| **Trade Stimulator,** Bicycle, Numbers On Spinning Wheels, Sun Mfg., 1890s, 17 In........ | 7670 |
| **Trade Stimulator,** Brownie, 5 Cent, Quarter Sawn Oak Cabinet, Mills, 21 x 29 In......... | 3510 |
| **Trade Stimulator,** Caille, Busy Bee, 5 Cent, 5 Way Wheel, Iron, Key, c.1901 ..........*illus* | 44400 |
| **Trade Stimulator,** Callie, Busy Bee, 5 Cent, Cast Iron, Nickel Finish, 13 In. ............. | 16800 |
| **Trade Stimulator,** Dandy Vendor Tavern, 12 ¼ In. ................................................ | 720 |
| **Trade Stimulator,** Fairest Wheel, Wood, Round Base, 15 x 22 In. ......................*illus* | 840 |
| **Trade Stimulator,** Horse Race, 3-Reel Countertop, Daval Mfg., c.1936...................... | 540 |
| **Trade Stimulator,** Jennings, Rock-Away, 1 Cent, 24 In........................................... | 1200 |
| **Trade Stimulator,** Kicker & Catcher, 5 Cent, 3 Balls, J.F. Frantz.............................. | 600 |
| **Trade Stimulator,** Lark Poker Card, 5-Reel, Supreme Vending, c.1932....................... | 540 |
| **Trade Stimulator,** Mills, 5 Cent, 6-Way Automatic Payout, c.1907............................ | 5400 |
| **Trade Stimulator,** Mills, Aluminum Puritan Bell, 5 Cent, Countertop, Key, Mills, c.1925.......... | 826 |
| **Trade Stimulator,** Mills, Puritan Bell, Oak, 11 ¼ In............................................... | 570 |
| **Trade Stimulator,** Novelty Jockey, 5 Cent, 5-Reel, Novelty Jockey, 1800s .................. | 6600 |
| **Trade Stimulator,** Over The Top, 1 Cent, Wall Mount, 20 ½ In................................. | 840 |
| **Trade Stimulator,** Pace, Whiz Ball, Flipball, 1 Cent, Countertop ........................*illus* | 420 |
| **Trade Stimulator,** Penny Drop Pin Field, 1 Cent, Wood, Glass, Little Coin-Op Shop ..... | 266 |
| **Trade Stimulator,** Penny Flip Trade, One Cent, Four Aces, 16 In.............................. | 1020 |
| **Trade Stimulator,** Pistol Target Skill, A.B.T. Mfg., 1930s-40s................................. | 450 |
| **Trade Stimulator,** Pok-O-Reel, 1-25 Cent, Orange, Groetchen 12 In. ........................ | 480 |
| **Trade Stimulator,** Puritan Bell, Marquee, Cast Iron, c.1907, 11 ½ In. ...................... | 1320 |
| **Trade Stimulator,** Reel Spot, 4-Reel, Selection Buttons, Daval Mfg., c.1937............... | 480 |
| **Trade Stimulator,** Rock-Ola, Roulette Wheel, Official Sweepstakes Horse Race, 1 Cent, c.1933.. | 1320 |
| **Trade Stimulator,** Wagon Wheels, Fruit Symbol Discs, 5 Cent, A.B.T. Mfg., 1930s........ | 330 |
| **Trade Stimulator,** World Champion, Baseball, Penny Flip, Tecumseh Sales, 17 In........ | 1560 |
| **Trade Stimulator,** Zipper Skill, 17 ½ In. ............................................................ | 210 |
| **Vending,** 1 & 5 Cent, Pistachio Nuts, Green, Chrome, Key, 2 Coin Flaps..................... | 840 |
| **Vending,** Ace Vendor, 1 Cent, Glass, 6-Sided Flared Base, Operators......................... | 600 |
| **Vending,** Candy Bar, Hershey, c.1930, 17 ¾ x 6 ¼ In. .......................................... | 240 |
| **Vending,** Change Machine, Arcade, Levers, Metal, 14 In......................................... | 780 |
| **Vending,** Chum Razor Blade, 10 Cent, Nickel Plated, Schermack.............................. | 720 |
| **Vending,** Cigar, Caille, 5 Cent, 3-Reel, Cast Iron.................................................. | 1326 |
| **Vending,** Cigar, Oak, Key, 7 ¾ x 24 ½ x 13 In..................................................... | 300 |
| **Vending,** Cigar, The Elm, Mirror Door, Oak, National Cash Registering Co., c.1899, 30 In. ......... | 2700 |
| **Vending,** Cigarette Dispenser, Dial-A-Smoke, 30 Cents, Elde Inc., 26 ½ In. .............. | 570 |
| **Vending,** Cigarette Gum, Centa-Smoke, 3-Reel, Daval Mfg., c.1936 .......................... | 600 |
| **Vending,** Cigarette, Blue, 1 Cent, 3-Reel, Countertop, Groetchen Tool, c.1939............. | 201 |
| **Vending,** Climax, 10 Cent, Burgundy, 20 In......................................................... | 2470 |
| **Vending,** Condom, Bear Skin Decals, 25 Cent, Restored, Key .................................. | 118 |
| **Vending,** Delicious Goodies Decal, Red, 1 Cent, Columbus Glass Globe ..................... | 270 |
| **Vending,** Dixie Cup, 1 Cent, Glass Globe, 32 ½ In................................................. | 450 |
| **Vending,** Gum, 1 Cent, Cast Iron, Superior, 14 ¼ In.............................................. | 450 |
| **Vending,** Gum, 1 Cent, Save Zeno Gum Wrappers, Wood Cabinet, Zeno .................... | 660 |
| **Vending,** Gum, 2 Column, Oak, Railway, 29 In...................................................... | 5925 |
| **Vending,** Gum, Baker Boy, Red Green, Manikan, 1930s, 16 In. ................................ | 5332 |
| **Vending,** Gum, Candy, Adams Chiclets, Dentyne, Porcelain, Label, 32 x 9 ¾ In. ....*illus* | 4255 |
| **Vending,** Gum, Flipball Skill, 1 Cent, Binks Industries, c.1954................................. | 480 |
| **Vending,** Gum, Glass Sides, Mansfield Automatic Clerk, c.1902, 16 In....................... | 1320 |
| **Vending,** Gum, Metal Lid, Tear Shape Globe, 1 Cent, Cast Iron, National Novelty Co.... | 460 |
| **Vending,** Gum, Oak Case, Embossed Tin, Key, 1 Cent, Zeno Mfg. Co., Pat. 1902 .....*illus* | 900 |
| **Vending,** Gum, Penny Drop, Oak, 1 Drawer, Smith Brothers, 14 x 20 ½ In.................. | 185 |
| **Vending,** Gum, Pepsin, Metal, Etched Glass, Mansfield, c.1920, 7 x 11 In. ................. | 180 |
| **Vending,** Gum, Pike's Peak, Skill Game, Groetchen Tool, c.1941.............................. | 420 |
| **Vending,** Gum, Pulver, Delivers A Tasty Chew, One Cent, Red, 20 ½ In. .............*illus* | 480 |
| **Vending,** Gum, Pulver, Yellow Kid, Key, Tall Case, 24 x 10 In. ..........................*illus* | 3000 |
| **Vending,** Gum, Winasmoke, 1 Cent, 12 In............................................................ | 375 |
| **Vending,** Gum, Wm. Wrigley Jr. Co., 5-Sided, Swivel Base...................................... | 270 |
| **Vending,** Gum, Yellow Kid, Red, Porcelain, Clockwork, Pulver, 1920s, 20 ½ In............ | 600 |
| **Vending,** Gum, Zeno, Yellow Porcelain, Clockwork, c.1908, 17 In. ............................ | 1440 |
| **Vending,** Gumball, 1 Cent, Bluebird, 1915............................................................ | 450 |
| **Vending,** Gumball, 1 Cent, Columbus Convention, Key, 15 In.................................. | 420 |
| **Vending,** Gumball, 21 Vender, Blackjack Hand, 5-Reel, Countertop, c.1934 ............... | 150 |

**Coin-Operated,** Slot, Bally, Jack Pot, 5 Cent, Dice, Key, c.1935, 18 In.
$12,600

Morphy Auctions

**Coin-Operated,** Slot, Mills, Twenty One, Jackpot Black & Red, High Top, 5 Cent, Keys, Bell, c.1950
$1,020

Morphy Auctions

**Coin-Operated,** Slot, Watling, Operators Bell, 1 Cent, Cast Iron, Countertop, Key, c.1910
$5,700

Morphy Auctions

**Coin-Operated,** Stand, Slot, Wooden, Clawfoot, Owl Casting, Door, 19 x 34 In. $390

Morphy Auctions

**Coin-Operated,** Trade Stimulator, Caille, Busy Bee, 5 Cent, 5 Way Wheel, Iron, Key, c.1901 $44,400

Morphy Auctions

**Coin-Operated,** Trade Stimulator, Fairest Wheel, Wood, Round Base, 15 x 22 In. $840

Showtime Auction Services

**Coin-Operated,** Trade Stimulator, Pace, Whiz Ball, Flipball, 1 Cent, Countertop $420

Morphy Auctions

**Coin-Operated,** Vending, Gum, Candy, Adams Chiclets, Dentyne, Porcelain, Label, 32 x 9¾ In. $4,255

Wm Morford Auctions

**Coin-Operated,** Vending, Gum, Oak Case, Embossed Tin, Key, 1 Cent, Zeno Mfg. Co., Pat. 1902 $900

Morphy Auctions

**Coin-Operated,** Vending, Gum, Pulver, Delivers A Tasty Chew, One Cent, Red, 20½ In. $480

Morphy Auctions

**Coin-Operated,** Vending, Gum, Pulver, Yellow Kid, Key, Tall Case, 24 x 10 In. $3,000

Showtime Auction Services

**Coin-Operated,** Vending, Gumball, Advanced Model D, 1 Cent, Acme Decal, Pat. 1912, 1917-1923 $150

Morphy Auctions

| | |
|---|---|
| **Vending,** Gumball, 33 Gum, Blue Porcelain, Key, Northwestern, c.1933 | 240 |
| **Vending,** Gumball, Advanced Model D, 1 Cent, Acme Decal, Pat. 1912, 1917-1923 *illus* | 150 |
| **Vending,** Gumball, Buckley, 1 Cent, Black Case, 3-Reel | 390 |
| **Vending,** Gumball, Climax 10, Maroon, Advance Machine Co., c.1915, 19 ½ In. | 1440 |
| **Vending,** Gumball, Countertop, 1 & 5 Cent, Northwestern De Luxe, c.1931 | 960 |
| **Vending,** Gumball, Derby Confection, 1 Cent, Electro-Serve, 14 ½ In. | 1944 |
| **Vending,** Gumball, Dome Glass, Vendex Co., c.1927, 12 ½ In. | 390 |
| **Vending,** Gumball, E-Z Machine, Marquee, Ad-Lee Novelty Co., c.1908, 21 In. | 600 |
| **Vending,** Gumball, Green, Ad-Lee E-Z, 5 Cent, Marquee Card, Box, 16 In. | 4148 |
| **Vending,** Gumball, Magic Vendor, 1 Cent, Red, Iron, Townsend, c.1939, 16 In. | 960 |
| **Vending,** Gumball, Master Penny Drop, Drop Pin Field, 1 Cent, Norris Mfg. | 1200 |
| **Vending,** Gumball, Mickey Mouse, 1 Cent, c.1938, 14 In. | 2346 |
| **Vending,** Gumball, Model A Red, Footed, Columbus, c.1910, 15 ½ In. | 300 |
| **Vending,** Gumball, Red, Foxy Grandpa, 1 Cent, Tasty Chew, 1915, 10 x 24 In. | 2640 |
| **Vending,** Gumball, Red, Traffic Officer, Tasty Chew, 1 Cent, 1930, 20 x 8 In. | 1320 |
| **Vending,** Gumball, Whirlwind, 1 Cent, Key, 13 In. *illus* | 1080 |
| **Vending,** Gumball, Yellow, Keys, Northwestern, 1 Cent, c.1919 | 430 |
| **Vending,** Hot Peanuts, Chained Lid, 21 x 12 ½ In. | 1920 |
| **Vending,** Match, Griffin Box, 1 Cent, Northwestern, 13 ½ In. | 1440 |
| **Vending,** Match, Krema, Model D, 1 Cent, Cast Iron Face, Wood Cabinet, 1920s | 345 |
| **Vending,** Mint Dispenser, Mill's F.O.K., 5 Cent, 4 Column, 25 In. | 960 |
| **Vending,** Mint, Honey Breath, 4 Glass Tubes, 4 For 1 Cent, Gravity, 13 ½ In. | 6075 |
| **Vending,** Morris Match, Safety Matches Light King, 1 Cent, Countertop | 180 |
| **Vending,** Nut, Bulk, Tray Base, 5 Cent, Atlas Bantam, c.1947 | 240 |
| **Vending,** Peanut, Big Mouth, Delicious Confections Decal, Advance, c.1925 | 270 |
| **Vending,** Peanut, Fresh Salted, 1 Cent, Hance Rex, c.1908-30 | 1440 |
| **Vending,** Peanut, Glass Globe, Cast Iron Stand, Sunflower Vending Co., 43 In. | 224 |
| **Vending,** Peanut, Gooseneck, 1 Or 5 Cent, Norris Master No. 2, Pat. 1923-24, 16 In. *illus* | 390 |
| **Vending,** Peanut, Green, Art Deco, 1 Cent, Keys, Northwestern, c.1933 | 330 |
| **Vending,** Peanut, Model 33, 1 Cent Black Octagon Base, Northwestern, c.1933 | 780 |
| **Vending,** Peanut, Red Star, Cast Iron, Griswold Mfg. Co, c.1914, 19 In. | 2700 |
| **Vending,** Peanut, Salted, Smilin' Sam From Alabam', 1 Cent, Prince Mfg. | 840 |
| **Vending,** Pencils, 5 Cent, Blue Porcelain, Sharpener, Harmon Machine Co. *illus* | 780 |
| **Vending,** Perfume Dispenser, Bull By Horns, 1 Cent, Cast Iron, T. Worth Martin, 16 In. | 6600 |
| **Vending,** Perfume Dispenser, Perfume Woman, Red Dress, Life Size | 5400 |
| **Vending,** Postage Stamp, Porcelain, Metal, 1940s, 20 In. | 150 |
| **Vending,** Postage Stamps, Cast Iron, Rotating, Schermack, c.1930, 7 x 8 ½ In. | 570 |
| **Vending,** Postage Stamps, Model 45, Schermack, 13 x 7 ½ In. | 330 |
| **Vending,** Pulver's Chocolate Cocoa, Gum, Foxy Grandpa, 10 ½ x 24 In. | 6600 |
| **Vending,** Too Choos, Pulver's, 1 Cent, Red Porcelain, Yellow Kid Character | 431 |
| **Vending,** U.S. Postage Stamp, 5 Cent, 10 Cent, Porcelain, Steel, 13 ¾ In. | 180 |
| **Vendor,** Baseball, Skills Stop, 5 Cent, Key, c.1929 | 10200 |

**COLLECTOR PLATES** are modern plates produced in limited editions. Some may be found listed under the factory name, such as Bing & Grondahl, Royal Copenhagen, Royal Doulton, and Wedgwood.

| | |
|---|---|
| **Bradford Exchange,** The Star, Central Bouquet, Pink, Yellow Blue, 7 x 7 In. | 45 |
| **Enoch Wedgwood,** Christmas, Christmas On The Farm, Box, 1973, 9 In. | 48 |
| **Enoch Wedgwood,** Christmas, Dashing Through The Snow, Box, 1979, 8 In. | 24 |
| **Franklin McMahan,** Chicago Collection, Sunday At Lincoln Park Zoo, 1973, 8 In. | 12 |
| **Franklin Mint,** Country Carnival, Jane Wooster Scott, 24K Gold Trim, 8 In. | 30 |
| **Franklin Mint,** Noah's Ark, Before The Rain, Bill Bell, 8 ¼ In. | 15 |
| **Franklin Mint,** Norman Rockwell, Christmas, The Carolers, Silver, 1972, 8 In. | 250 |
| **Gorham,** Nature Portraits Of America, October Cardinals, 10 ¾ In. | 49 |
| **Gorham,** Southern Landmark Series, Ashland, 1977, 10 In. | 15 |
| **Gorham,** Southern Landmark Series, Montpelier, 1973, 10 In. | 24 |
| **Holly Hobbie,** Christmas, Put A Song In Our Hearts, Japan, 1973, 10 In. | 18 |
| **John Wayne,** Man Of The Golden West, Lynell Endre Szabo, 1979, 10 ½ In. | 195 |
| **Knowles,** Annie Collector's Plate Series, Annie & Sandy, 8 ½ In. | 15 |
| **Knowles,** Gone With The Wind, Mammy Lacing Scarlett, 8 ½ In. | 40 |
| **Knowles,** King & I, Shall We Dance, 8 ½ In. | 15 |
| **Norman Rockwell,** A Day In The Life Of A Boy, 1981, 10 ⅞ In. | 30 |
| **Norman Rockwell,** Home Of The Brave, Reminiscing, 1981, 8 ½ In. | 23 |
| **Norman Rockwell,** Mother's Day, Cradle Of Love, 1980 | 20 |

**Coin-Operated,** Vending, Gumball, Whirlwind, 1 Cent, Key, 13 In.
$1,080

Morphy Auctions

**Coin-Operated,** Vending, Peanut, Gooseneck, 1 Or 5 Cent, Norris Master No. 2, Pat. 1923-24, 16 In.
$390

Morphy Auctions

**Coin-Operated,** Vending, Pencils, 5 Cent, Blue Porcelain, Sharpener, Harmon Machine Co.
$780

Morphy Auctions

C

| | |
|---|---:|
| **Reco,** Mother Goose, Little Miss Muffet, 8 ½ In. | 32 |
| **Royal Cornwall,** Royal Birds Of Tropique, Toco Toucan, 1981, 9 In. | 23 |
| **Schumann Imperial,** Christmas, 1980, Halleluja, Woman Playing Violin, 10 In. | 36 |
| **W.S. George,** Gone With The Wind, Burning Of Atlanta, 1988, 8 ½ In. | 24 |
| **Wedgwood,** Christmas, Enjoying The Night Before Christmas, Box, 1983, 9 In. | 48 |

**COMIC ART,** or cartoon art, includes original art for comic strips, magazine covers, book pages, and even printed strips. The first daily comic strip was printed in 1907. The paintings on celluloid used for movie cartoons are listed in this book under Animation Art.

| | |
|---|---:|
| **Cover,** Coloring Book, 3 Stooges, Various Outfits, Lowe, Frame, 1960, 17 x 21 In. .............*illus* | 2277 |
| **Illustration,** Eat It, Robert Crumb, Los Angeles Free Press, 1973, 6 ¾ x 3 ¾ In. | 335 |
| **Illustration,** Gahan Wilson, Bolster Shabby Little Theories, Bristol Board, 7 x 10 In. | 1315 |
| **Illustration,** Spy Vs. Spy, Plus Gray Spy, Antonio Prohias, 9 x 11 In. | 389 |
| **Page 5,** Vampirella, No. 100, 1981, 10 ½ x 15 In. | 5378 |
| **Page 14,** Uncle Scrooge, No. 60, Phantom Of Notre Duck, 1965, 16 x 23 In. | 5079 |
| **Page,** Creepy Magazine, No. 3, Howling Success, Page 4, Angelo Torres, 1965, 12 x 17 In. | 1135 |
| **Painting,** Donald Duck, Where Ducks & Antelopes Roam, Singing, Carl Barks, 1974, 8 x 10 In.. | 3107 |
| **Panel,** New Yorker, Charles Addams, That's Not A Real Hangman's Knot, 1941, 10 x 12 In. | 3734 |
| **Strip,** Barney Google, 3 Panels, Danny, Lucy, Belle, Sarah, India Ink, Signed, 1934, 4 x 16 In. .........*illus* | 329 |
| **Strip,** Donald Duck, Impetuous Donald, Al Taliaferro, 1934, 21 x 4 ½ In. | 3346 |
| **Strip,** Li'l Abner, Gold In Calif-Or-Ni-Ay, Al Capp, Art Board, 1940, 6 x 22 In. .........*illus* | 115 |
| **Strip,** Pogo, Walt Kelly, Deacon Mushrat Agrees With Boombah, 1960, 18 ¾ x 5 ¼ In. | 538 |
| **Sunday,** Dennis, Snow Prince, Sunday, H. Ketcham, Jan. 16, 1977, Frame, 17 x 15 In. | 187 |
| **Sunday,** Doonesbury, Garry Trudeau, Nov. 24, 1996, 21 x 14 ¼ In. | 1135 |
| **Sunday,** Garfield, Garfield & Odie Switch Places, Jim Davis, 1995, 19 x 13 In. | 1733 |
| **Sunday,** Li'l Abner, Shmoo, Nursery Songs, Al Capp, 1949, 21 ¾ x 19 In. | 2151 |
| **Sunday,** Peanuts, Snoopy Mealtime, 10 Panels, 1958, 22 ½ x 15 In. | 38838 |

**COMMEMORATIVE** items have been made to honor members of royalty and those of great national fame. World's Fairs and important historical events are also remembered with commemorative pieces. Related collectibles are listed in the Coronation and World's Fair categories.

| | |
|---|---:|
| **Bowl,** Thomas Hart Benton, White Ground, Black Pictures, 1889-1975, 12 In. | 125 |
| **Olympic Medal,** Stand, Paris, Discus Thrower, Torch, 1924, 2 ½ x 2 ½ In. | 52 |
| **Pitcher,** Parian, Battle Of Trafalgar, Lavender, Samuel Alcock, c.1850, 9 ¼ In. | 185 |
| **Plate,** Jimmy Carter, Portrait, Undulating Rim, 7 In. | 12 |
| **Spoon,** State Of Wyoming, Repousse, Sterling Silver, 5 ½ In. | 43 |
| **Tumbler,** Kansas Centennial, Wheat Sheaf, Airplane, Federal Glass Co., 1961, 5 In., Pair | 12 |

**COMPACTS** hold face powder. A woman did not powder her face in public until after World War I. By 1920, the beauty parlor, permanent waves, and cosmetics had become acceptable. A few companies sold cake face powder in a box with a mirror and a pad or puff. Soon the compact was designed by jewelers and made of gold, silver, and precious materials. Cosmetic companies began to sell powder in attractive compacts of less valuable metal or plastic. Collectors today search for Art Deco designs, famous brands, compacts from World's Fairs or political events, and unusual examples. Many were made with companion lipsticks and other fittings.

| | |
|---|---:|
| **14K Bicolor Gold,** Alternate Bands, Ribbed & Engraved, Diamond Monogram, 3 In. | 3690 |
| **14K Gold,** Half Moon Shape, Ribbed, Ruby & Diamond Accents, c.1940, 3 ¼ In. | 2250 |
| **14K Gold,** Platinum, Ribbed Squares, Arched Diamond & Sapphire Clasp, R. Yard, 3 In. | 3690 |
| **Cartier,** 14K Yellow Gold, Lapis Blue, Black Enamel, Black Onyx, Diamonds, Art Deco | 14760 |
| **Cartier,** Birds, Leaves, Pink Ground, Gold Border, Felt Sleeve, Box, 2 x 2 ¾ In. | 2350 |
| **Damsel & Suitor,** Incised, 18K Gold, Rubies, Diamonds, Kidskin Case, Austria, 3 In. ........*illus* | 5313 |
| **Enamel Silver Top,** Victorian Lovers, Pink Flowers Sides, 3 In. | 390 |
| **Enamel Silver,** Couple, Child Flying Kite, Shaped Sides, 3 ½ In. | 420 |
| **Enamel Silver,** Lavender Guilloche, Flowers, Hinged Mirror, 2 ¼ x 2 ¼ In. | 288 |
| **Enamel Silver,** Lovers In Landscape, Shaped Sides, 3 In. | 360 |
| **Georg Jensen,** Sterling, Acorn, Stylized Ornament, Oval, Interior Mirror, 3 ¼ x 2 ¼ In. | 81 |
| **Gold,** Diaper Engraving, Applied Flowers, Paperclip Chain, Edwardian | 1230 |
| **Gold,** Jade, Onyx & Diamond, Enamel Panels, Art Deco, 6 In. | 4613 |
| **Goldtone Metal,** Lucky Charms, 4-Leaf Clovers, Horseshoes, Wishbones, P. Flato, 1950s, 3 In. ... | 1599 |
| **Sterling Silver,** Green, Flowers, Cushion Shape, Mirror, Hinged, Art Deco, 2 ¼ x 2 ¼ In. | 115 |
| **Sterling,** Beveled Mirror, Lid, Starburst Scoring, Stylized Leaf Decoration, 2 ¾ x 2 ¾ In. | 138 |
| **Sterling,** Chased, Leaf Design, Applied Shield, Armor, Helmet, Hinged, 3 x 3 In. | 178 |
| **Sterling,** Ruby, Art Deco, 3 In. | 210 |
| **Van Cleef & Arpels,** 18K Gold, Polished & Ribbed Panels, Square Cut Sapphires, 3 In. | 9375 |

**Comic Art,** Cover, Coloring Book, 3 Stooges, Various Outfits, Lowe, Frame, 1960, 17 x 21 In. $2,277

Hake's Americana & Collectibles

**Comic Art,** Strip, Barney Google, 3 Panels, Danny, Lucy, Belle, Sarah, India Ink, Signed, 1934, 4 x 16 In. $329

Hake's Americana & Collectibles

**Comic Art,** Strip, Li'l Abner, Gold In Calif-Or-Ni-Ay, Al Capp, Art Board, 1940, 6 x 22 In. $115

Hake's Americana & Collectibles

**Compact,** Damsel & Suitor, Incised, 18K Gold, Rubies, Diamonds, Kidskin Case, Austria, 3 In. $5,313

Rago Arts & Auction Center

**CONSOLIDATED LAMP AND GLASS COMPANY** of Coraopolis, Pennsylvania, was founded in 1894. The company made lamps, tablewares, and art glass. Collectors are particularly interested in the wares made after 1925, including black satin glass, Cosmos (listed in its own category in this book), Martele (which resembled Lalique), Ruba Rombic (1928–32 Art Deco line), and colored glasswares. Some Consolidated pieces are very similar to those made by the Phoenix Glass Company. The colors are sometimes different. Consolidated made Martele glass in blue, crystal, green, pink, white, or custard glass with added fired-on color or a satin finish. The company closed for the final time in 1967.

| | |
|---|---|
| **Berry Bowl,** Crisscross, Opalescent, c.1888, 1 ½ x 4 ¼ In., 4 Piece | 127 |
| **Lemonade Set,** Pink, Beaded Swags, 9 ½-In. Pitcher, 5 Piece | 180 |
| **Perfume Bottle,** Ruba Rombic, Jade Green, Satin Finish, c.1928, 3 ¾ In. ..........*illus* | 2271 |
| **Vase,** Catalonian, Green, Triangular Shape, Bubble, Rough Pontil, 1930s, 6 x 4 In. | 27 |
| **Vase,** Lovebirds, Branches, Ruby Red, Molded, 11 In. | 2438 |
| **Vase,** Poppy, Beige On Custard, c.1945, 10 ½ In. | 150 |

**CONTEMPORARY GLASS**, *see Glass-Contemporary.*

**COOKBOOKS** are collected for various reasons. Some are wanted for the recipes, some for investment, and some as examples of advertising. Cookbooks and recipe pamphlets are included in this category.

| | |
|---|---|
| **Art Of Home Candy Making,** Softcover, 1909 | 5 |
| **Better Homes & Gardens,** Hardcover, Binder, 1946 | 13 |
| **Calumet Baking Powder,** Reliable Recipes, Paperback, 1912, 75 Pages | 187 |
| **Eggs In A Thousand Ways,** Adolphe Meyer, 1917, 153 Pages, 6 ½ x 3 ½ In. | 8 |
| **Household Ladies,** Hardcover, c.1829, 6 x 8 ½ In. | 20 |
| **Jell-O Ice Cream Powder,** Paperback, 1890, 11 Pages | 45 |
| **Jell-O,** America's Most Famous Dessert, Paperback, 1913, 16 Pages | 105 |
| **Lee's Priceless Recipes,** Paperback, 1895, 368 Pages, 4 x 5 In. | 7 |
| **Mackenzie's Five Thousand Recipes,** Leather Cover, 1829, 456 Pages, 5 x 8 In. | 90 |
| **Pillsbury,** Paperback, 1913, 120 Pages | 8 |
| **School & Home Cooking,** Hardcover, Greer, 1920 | 7 |
| **Sloan's Handy Hints & Up-To-Date Cook Book,** Paperback, 1901, 48 Pages | 150 |
| **White House,** Hardcover, 1905 | 16 |

**COOKIE JARS** with brightly painted designs or amusing figural shapes became popular in the mid-1930s. Many companies made them and collectors search for cookie jars either by design or by maker's name. Listed here are examples by the less common makers. Major factories are listed under their own names in other categories of the book, such as Abingdon, Brush, Hull, McCoy, Metlox, Red Wing, and Shawnee. See also the Disneyana category.

| | |
|---|---|
| **Aunt Jemima,** Mosaic Tile Co., 13 x 7 x 6 ½ In. | 274 |
| **Balloon Lady,** Ribbed Skirt, Cronin China, c.1940, 11 In. | 163 |
| **Chef,** Black, Figural, Painted, Ceramic, 10 In. | 104 |
| **Dog,** Paw Up, Bow, Toothache, American Bisque, c.1950, 14 In. | 495 |
| **Humpty Dumpty,** Sitting On Wall, Painted, Indented Handles, Ransburg, c.1935, 10 In. | 135 |
| **Moon Girl Head,** Closed Eyes, c.1940, 8 In. | 345 |
| **Pig,** Boy, Yellow, Blue, Black, Scarf, Bent Ear, American Bisque, c.1950 | 145 |
| **Pot O' Cookies,** Kettle Shape, Mottled Matte Glaze, Footed, Twin Winton, 7 x 8 In. | 59 |
| **Potbelly Stove,** Black, Red, American Bisque, c.1950, 11 x 8 x 7 In. | 85 |
| **Quaker Oats,** Cylindrical, Recipe, Regal China, 9 In. | 42 |
| **Tree Stump Trunk,** Cocker Spaniel Finial, California Originals, 1960s, 14 In. | 26 |
| **Zero Man,** Figural Head, Hat Is Lid, Eye Patch, Ceramic, Peter Max, Japan, 1989, 8 In. .....*illus* | 168 |

**COORS** ware was made by the Coors Porcelain Company of Golden, Colorado, a company founded with the help of the Coors Brewing Company. Its founder, John Herold, started the Herold China and Pottery Company in 1910. The company name was changed in 1920, when Herold left. Dishes were made from the turn of the century. Coors stopped making nonessential wares at the start of World War II. After the war, the pottery made ovenware, teapots, vases, and a general line of pottery, but no dinnerware—except for special orders. The company is still in business making industrial porcelain. For more prices, go to kovels.com.

| | |
|---|---|
| **Banana Boat,** Rust Trim | 8 |
| **Bowl,** Batter, Colorado Red, Handle, 9 In. | 85 |
| **Cookie Jar,** Rosebud Red, Twisted Handles, Lid | 75 |
| **Cookie Jar,** Rosebud White, Twisted Handles, Lid | 45 |

**Consolidated,** Perfume Bottle, Ruba Rombic, Jade Green, Satin Finish, c.1928, 3 ¾ In.
$2,271

Neal Auction Co.

**Cookie Jar,** Zero Man, Figural Head, Hat Is Lid, Eye Patch, Ceramic, Peter Max, Japan, 1989, 8 In.
$168

Hake's Americana & Collectibles

**Copeland,** Bust, Veiled Bride, Pedestal Base, Parian, Marked, c.1865, 14 ½ In.
$2,214

Skinner Auctioneers & Appraisers

**Copeland,** Figurine, Bust, Mother & Child, Signed, R. Monty, Parian, 1871, 14¾ In.
$356

James D. Julia Auctioneers

**Copper,** Bottle, Cover, Enameled, Molded Flowers, Buds & Scrollwork, Middle Eastern, 13 In.
$615

New Orleans Auction Galleries, Inc.

**Copper,** Box, Enamel Flower On Lid, Stylized Butterfly Mark, Arts & Crafts, 2 x 4 In.
$2,460

Skinner Auctioneers & Appraisers

| | |
|---|---:|
| **Mortar & Pestle,** Marked, 4¼ x 3 In. | 55 |
| **Mug,** Scottish Man, Blue, Red Green, c.1935, 4 In., 6 Piece | 75 |
| **Pitcher,** Lid, Square Knob, 8-Sided, Flowers, Stems, 7½ In. | 105 |
| **Plate,** Salad, Blue, 7 In. | 5 |
| **Vase,** Art Deco, White, Green Interior, Marked, c.1930, 6 In. | 65 |
| **Vase,** Blue Matte Glaze, Handles, Footed, 1930s, 10 In. | 135 |
| **Vase,** Brown Matte Glaze, Loop Handles, Globular, c.1930, 7¾ x 6¾ In. | 125 |
| **Vase,** Orange Matte Glaze, Bulbous, Stick Neck, 9 In. | 65 |

**COPELAND** pieces listed here are those that have a mark including the word *Copeland* used between 1847 and 1976. Marks include *Copeland Spode* and *Copeland & Garrett.* See also Copeland Spode, Royal Worcester, and Spode.

| | |
|---|---:|
| **Bust,** Juno, Parian, 20½ In. | 1353 |
| **Bust,** Veiled Bride, Pedestal Base, Parian, Marked, c.1865, 14½ In. ....................*illus* | 2214 |
| **Centerpiece,** Teal, Gilt, Still Life With Fruit & Bread, c.1870, 15½ x 18 In. | 1534 |
| **Charger,** Porcelain, Haunt Of Heron, Signed W. Yale, 16 In. | 176 |
| **Cup & Saucer,** Richmond, Grosvenor, Imari Colors, Gilt Trim, 3 x 5 In. | 40 |
| **Figurine,** Bust, Mother & Child, Signed, R. Monty, Parian, 1871, 14¾ In. ..........*illus* | 356 |
| **Figurine,** Go To Sleep, Girl, Lap Dog, Embossed Title, Parian, c.1878, 17½ In. | 861 |
| **Group,** Sleep Of Sorrow & Dream Of Joy, Floating Woman, c.1877, 18¼ In. | 3998 |
| **Plate,** Dinner, Gold Filigree, 10¼ In., 12 Piece | 313 |
| **Plate,** Hunting Scene, L. Edwards, Soane & Smith, c.1930, 10 In., 12 Piece | 4063 |
| **Plate,** Parcel Gilt Jeweled Rim, T. Good & Co., London, 1800s, 10¼ In., 12 Piece | 375 |
| **Plate,** Roses, Basket, Gold Shell, Urn Border, 9 In., 12 Piece | 295 |
| **Platter,** Greek Pattern, Black & Pink Luster, Transfer, Marked, c.1835, 16 x 21 In. | 1476 |
| **Vase,** Multicolor Scrolled Flowers, Deep Brown Ground, Double Lip, c.1860, 11 In. | 35 |

**COPELAND SPODE** appears on some pieces of nineteenth-century English porcelain. Josiah Spode established a pottery at Stoke-on-Trent, England, in 1770. In 1833, the firm was purchased by William Copeland and Thomas Garrett and the mark was changed. In 1847, Copeland became the sole owner and the mark changed again. W.T. Copeland & Sons continued until a 1976 merger when it became Royal Worcester Spode. The company was bought by the Portmeirion Group in 2009. Pieces are listed in this book under the name that appears in the mark. Copeland, Royal Worcester, and Spode have separate listings.

| | |
|---|---:|
| **Pitcher,** Chicago, Historical Scenes, Chicago Fire, White, Blue, Bulbous, 8 In. | 250 |
| **Plate,** Dinner, Red, Gilt Floral Wreath, c.1900, 10¼ In., 12 Piece | 799 |
| **Platter,** Fish, Spode's Tower, Blue, White, Bridge, Creek, 1894, 10¾ x 23 In. | 259 |
| **Platter,** Turkey Pattern, Blue, White, Landscape, Flower Border, 22½ In. | 130 |

**COPPER** has been used to make utilitarian items, such as teakettles and cooking pans, since the days of the early American colonists. Copper became a popular metal with the Arts & Crafts makers of the early 1900s, and decorative pieces, like desk sets, were made. Other pieces of copper may be found in Arts & Crafts, Bradley & Hubbard, Kitchen, Roycroft, and other categories.

| | |
|---|---:|
| **Bed Warmer,** Tooled, Pierced Flowers, Turned Wood Handle, c.1865, 40 In. | 62 |
| **Bottle,** Cover, Enameled, Molded Flowers, Buds & Scrollwork, Middle Eastern, 13 In. ........*illus* | 615 |
| **Bowl,** Original Patina, Low, Rounded Sides, Kalo Shop, 2 x 10 In. | 244 |
| **Box,** Enamel Flower On Lid, Stylized Butterfly Mark, Arts & Crafts, 2 x 4 In. ..............*illus* | 2460 |
| **Box,** Foil & Enamel, Peacock, Orange Sun, Yellow Sky, Hammered, Arts & Crafts, 3 x 7 In. | 1840 |
| **Box,** Lid, Hammered, Enamel, Flowers, Cylinder, F. Marshall, 5 x 4¼ In. | 610 |
| **Box,** Lid, Hammered, Enamel, Peacock, Square, F. Marshall, 5 x 4¼ In. | 4575 |
| **Box,** Twin Lizards, Scrolling Vines, Lid, Latch, Arts & Crafts, Hammered, 3 x 7¼ | 575 |
| **Chafing Dish,** Gothic, Hammered, Oak, Terra-Cotta, G. Stickley, 15 x 19 In. | 2318 |
| **Container,** Lid, Coiled Rope Pattern, Hammered, Wiener Werkstatte, 7 x 5 In. ...............*illus* | 403 |
| **Crucifix,** Christ Figure, Inscribed INRI, Gorham, 1929, 9⅛ In. ..............*illus* | 469 |
| **Dish,** Alms, Embossed Rampant Lion, Continental, c.1759, 21 In. | 584 |
| **Epergne,** Silvered, Cut Glass, 4 Arms, Late 1800s, 14½ x 11 In. | 438 |
| **Fern Dish,** 4 Curled Feet, Hammered, Onondaga, 3½ x 8¼ In. | 427 |
| **Figure,** Eagle On Orb, Outstretched Wings, c.1900, 21 x 29 In. | 438 |
| **Fish Poacher,** 19th Century, 9 x 31 In. | 780 |
| **Frame,** Scrolling Dragon & Leaves, Rectangular Off Center Opening, Arts & Crafts, 15 In. | 244 |
| **Hand Warmer,** Pivoting Bent Metal Handle, Pierced Lid, Angled Corners, Chinese, 4 x 6 In. | 120 |
| **Jardiniere,** Hammered, Riveted Base, 2 Handles, Onondaga Metal Shop, 13 x 12 In. | 1830 |
| **Jardiniere,** Hand Hammered, Handles, G. Stickley, 12½ x 11 In. | 9150 |

| | |
|---|---|
| **Kettle,** Apple Butter, Handle, c.1845, 14 ½ x 22 In. | 240 |
| **Kettle,** Apple Butter, Handle, c.1860, 19 x 28 In. | 210 |
| **Kettle,** Candy, Round, Riveted Iron Handles, c.1890, 7 x 15 In. | 184 |
| **Kettle,** Dovetailed, Marked, I. Dunn, Attributed to John Dunn & Sons, N.Y., 1831, 13 In. ....*illus* | 369 |
| **Kettle,** Dovetailed, Swing Handle, c.1890, 17 ½ In. | 360 |
| **Kettle,** Hearth, Brass Mushroom Finial, Handle, W. Morrison, N.Y., c.1810, 17 In. .............*illus* | 1599 |
| **Kettle,** Lid, Swing Handle, Curved Neck, Cyrillic Mark, Russia, 1800s, 11 In. | 360 |
| **Kettle,** Swing Handle, Stamped P. Schaum, Pa., c.1800, 13 In. | 800 |
| **Lavabo,** Bird, Branch, Spigots, Basin, Brass, 78 x 16 In. | 356 |
| **Lock,** 6 Levers, 2 ⅜ In. | 35 |
| **Measure,** Tapered, Flared Rim, Handle, Marked, Condemne, c.1800, 8 x 5 ¾ In. .............*illus* | 554 |
| **Mirror,** Repousse Stylized Onions In Corners, Arts & Crafts, 15 x 13 In. | 488 |
| **Molds** are listed in the Kitchen category. | |
| **Plaque,** Hammered, Repousse Stylized Pods, G. Stickley, Round, 19 ¾ In. | 8540 |
| **Pot,** Hammered, Round, Dovetail, Seams, Handles, 13 x 20 In. | 35 |
| **Pot,** Lid, Arts & Crafts, Handles, Brass, 15 x 13 In. | 1159 |
| **Pot,** Lid, Iron Handles, c.1870, 9 ¾ x 19 ½ In. | 338 |
| **Pot,** Tapered, Footed, Handles, 23 x 8 ½ In. | 70 |
| **Saucepan,** Spout, Side Handle, Thomas Mills & Brother, Phila., c.1890, 7 x 15 In. | 120 |
| **Sculpture,** Crayfish, Enamel, c.1970, Japan, 9 ½ In. | 1625 |
| **Sculpture,** Head, Avalokiteshvara, Crown, Inlaid Turquoise & Coral, Cabochons, c.1900, 17 In. *illus* | 2161 |
| **Sterilizer,** Lid, Riveted Brass Handles, Legry 2R Miromesnil, France, 1800s, 8 x 23 In. | 130 |
| **Teakettle,** Dome Lid, Gooseneck Spout, Trefoil Handle, Signed G. Reed, c.1800, 13 In. | 2990 |
| **Teakettle,** Dovetailed, Swing Handle, Stamped, C. Gillispie, c.1800, 11 In. | 1020 |
| **Teakettle,** Gooseneck Spout, Stationary Handle, c.1850, 8 In. | 230 |
| **Tray,** Arts & Crafts, Hammered, G. Stickley, c.1905, 20 ½ In. | 15860 |
| **Tray,** Hammered Bands, Chased Peacocks, Folded Up Sides, Flat Handles, 11 x 16 In. | 427 |
| **Urn,** Hot Water, Lid, Stepped Finial, Regency, Handles, 1800s, 17 In. | 123 |
| **Urn,** Inverted Bell Shape, Brass Handles, Pedestal Base, Round Foot, 32 x 23 In. | 483 |
| **Vase,** Arts & Crafts, Hammered, Shaped Rim, Applied Cornstalks, c.1910, 11 x 6 ½ In. | 300 |
| **Vase,** Blue, Bamboo Design, Ikora Dinanderie, WMF, c.1930, 8 ½ x 6 In. | 531 |
| **Vase,** Enamel, Flock Of Ducks, Signed, Henriette Marty, 12 x 7 ½ In. ...............*illus* | 1150 |
| **Vase,** Flower Shape, Marie Zimmerman, 5 ¾ In. | 780 |
| **Vase,** Hammered, 3 Antler Handles, WMF, c.1915, 9 ¼ x 10 In. ...............*illus* | 625 |
| **Vase,** Hammered, Lotus Shape, Secessionist, 7 ¼ In. | 295 |
| **Vase,** Thistle, Riveted, Cylindrical, Tapered, 3 Strap Handles, Arts & Crafts, 12 x 9 In. | 397 |
| **Wall Sconce,** Candle Cup, Brass, H. Aguilar, Taxco, c.1943, 9 ¾ In., Pair .........*illus* | 438 |

---

**CORALENE** glass was made by firing many small colored beads on the outside of glassware. It was made in many patterns in the United States and Europe in the 1880s. Reproductions are made today. Coralene-decorated Japanese pottery is listed in the Japanese Coralene category.

| | |
|---|---|
| **Pitcher,** Peachblow, Reeded Handle, Yellow Seaweed, 7 ¾ In. | 259 |
| **Pitcher,** Yellow, Pink Satin, 8 In. | 374 |
| **Vase,** Gilt Twig Shape Handle, Ruffled Rim, Brown To Yellow, Leaf Feet, 10 In. | 215 |

---

**CORDEY CHINA COMPANY** was founded by Boleslaw Cybis in 1942 in Trenton, New Jersey. The firm produced gift shop items. In 1969 it was acquired by the Lightron Corp. and operated as the Schiller Cordey Co., manufacturers of lamps. About 1950 Boleslaw Cybis began making Cybis porcelains, which are listed in their own category in this book.

| | |
|---|---|
| **Figurine,** Woman, Ball Gown, Flower Garland, Matching Hat, 8 In. | 275 |
| **Figurine,** Woman, Flowered Hat, Necklace, Ringlets, 11 In. | 145 |
| **Figurine,** Woman, Roses, Curls, Pitcher On Shoulder, 10 ½ In. | 75 |
| **Lamp,** Boudoir, Gentleman, Bust, Silk Shade, c.1930, 16 ½ In. | 40 |

---

**CORKSCREWS** have been needed since the first bottle was sealed with a cork, probably in the seventeenth century. Today collectors search for the early, unusual patented examples or the figural corkscrews of recent years.

| | |
|---|---|
| **Antler,** Sterling Silver Ends, John Hasselbring, c.1935, 6 In. | 325 |
| **Bartender,** Black Suit, Syroco, Carved, 1960s, 8 In. | 50 |
| **Bell Shape,** Chrome, Rosewood, c.1935, 6 ½ x 2 In. | 285 |
| **Boar's Tusk,** Carved Flowers, Leaves, Silver, Scrollwork, c.1900, 6 x 6 In. | 275 |
| **Bone Handle,** Sterling Silver Mounts, Gorham, Early 20th Century, 7 In. .........*illus* | 708 |
| **Brush Handle,** Bone, Carved, Brass, Victorian, Thomason, England, 10 In. ...........*illus* | 472 |
| **Cherry Wood,** Steel, 19th Century, 5 ¼ In. | 100 |

**Copper,** Container, Lid, Coiled Rope Pattern, Hammered, Wiener Werkstatte, 7 x 5 In.
$403

Humler & Nolan

---

**Copper,** Crucifix, Christ Figure, Inscribed INRI, Gorham, 1929, 9 ⅛ In.
$469

Heritage Auction Galleries

---

**Copper,** Kettle, Dovetailed, Marked, I. Dunn, Attributed to John Dunn & Sons, N.Y., 1831, 13 In.
$369

Garth's Auctioneers & Appraisers

C

**Copper,** Kettle, Hearth, Brass Mushroom Finial, Handle, W. Morrison, NY., c.1810, 17 In.
$1,599

Skinner Auctioneers & Appraisers

**Copper,** Measure, Tapered, Flared Rim, Handle, Marked, Condemne, c.1800, 8 x 5¾ In.
$554

Skinner Auctioneers & Appraisers

**Copper,** Sculpture, Head, Avalokiteshvara, Crown, Inlaid Turquoise & Coral, Cabochons, c.1900, 17 In.
$2,161

James D. Julia Auctioneers

| | |
|---|---:|
| **Deer Foot,** Steel, 5 x 4¼ In. | 34 |
| **Gnarled Burl Wood Handle,** Steel, 7½ In. | 120 |
| **Grapevine Handle,** Lacquered, Steel, France, 7¼ In. | 24 |
| **Key Shape,** Brass, Marked, Italy, 1930s, 7¼ In. | 95 |
| **Man,** Wood, Carved, Anri, Italy, 5½ In. | 50 |
| **Pierre,** Wine Waiter, Silver Plated, 2 Levers, Sommelier, A. Columbo, 1984, 8 In. | 78 |
| **Pig,** Corkscrew Tail, Open Mouth Bottle Opener, Chrome, 4¾ In. | 145 |
| **Scottie Dog,** Wood, Glass Eyes, Marked Depose, 4 In. | 40 |
| **Sterling Silver,** Repousse, 1950s, 3 In. | 143 |
| **Stump,** Woodpecker Handles, Painted, Multicolor, Signed, 1930s, 7 In. | 115 |
| **Tropical Nut,** Carved Monkey Head, Hat, Metal, Plastic, 1950s, 4¼ In. | 55 |

**CORONATION** souvenirs have been made since the 1800s. Pottery, glass, tin, silver, and paper objects with a picture of the monarchs and date have been sold at many coronations. The pieces that mention King Edward VIII, the king who was never crowned, are not rare; collectors should be sure to check values before buying. Related pieces are found in the Commemorative category.

| | |
|---|---:|
| **Ashtray,** Queen Elizabeth II, E II R, Wedgwood Jasper Ware, 1953, 4 In. | 50 |
| **Beaker,** King George VI, Elizabeth, Daughters, Blue, White, Wedgwood, 1937, 4½ In. | 220 |
| **Beaker,** King George VI, Elizabeth, Portraits, Oak Leaves, Acorns, England, 1937, 4 In. | 70 |
| **Beaker,** Tzar Nicholas II, Transfer, Enamel, Eagle, Cipher, Gilt, 1896, 4 x 3¾ In. | 368 |
| **Book,** King George VI, Queen Elizabeth, Hardcover, Daily Express, 1937, 12 x 10 In. | 70 |
| **Figurine,** Queen Elizabeth II, Royal Regalia, Scepter & Orb, Royal Doulton, 8 In. | 699 |
| **Jar,** Queen Elizabeth, Lid, Portrait, Crest, Oval, Gilt Trim, England, 1953, 5 In. | 60 |
| **Medal,** Emperor Alexander II, Profile, 1856, 2 In. | 4800 |
| **Mug,** Queen Elizabeth II, White, Embossed, England, 1953, 3 In. | 35 |
| **Napkin,** King Edward VIII, Linen, Castle, Hunters, Horse, Flags, 1937, 15 x 15 In. | 250 |
| **Photograph,** Tzar Nicholas II, Procession, May 14, 1896, 6 x 4 In. | 1200 |
| **Plate,** King Edward VII, Alexandra, Blue Border, Gilt, 1902, 8 In. | 95 |
| **Plate,** King Edward VII, Alexandra, Portraits, Scalloped Edge, 1902, 9½ In. | 150 |
| **Plate,** King Edward VIII, Gilt Edge, Crowned Shield, Lion, Unicorn, 1937, 10 In. | 175 |
| **Plate,** King George VI, Elizabeth, Portrait, Royal Flags, 1937, 10 In. | 175 |
| **Program,** King Edward VII, 6 Pages, June 1902, 7½ x 4¾ In. | 58 |
| **Serving Plate,** King George VI, Elizabeth, Long May They Reign, Handle, 1937, 8 In. | 85 |
| **Set,** Plate, Cup & Saucer, King Edward VIII, Crown, Flags, England, May 27th 1937 | 85 |
| **Tray,** Queen Elizabeth, Royal Purple, Tin, 1953, 12½ In. | 40 |

**COVERLETS** were made of linen or wool during the nineteenth century. Most of the coverlets date from 1800 to the 1880s. There was a revival of hand weaving in the 1920s and new coverlets, especially geometric patterns, were made. The earliest coverlets were made on narrow looms, so two woven strips were joined together and a seam can be found. The weave structures of coverlets can include summer and winter, double weave, overshot, and others. Jacquard coverlets have elaborate pictorial patterns that are made on a special loom or with the use of a special attachment. Quilts are listed in this book in their own category.

| | |
|---|---:|
| **4 Colors,** Floral Sunburst, Vines, Columns, Heart Border, J. Keagy, 75 x 82 In. | 106 |
| **Blue,** White, Red, Green, Flowers, Ettinger & Co., 88 x 83 In. | 270 |
| **Jacquard,** 9 Snowball, Signed John Brosey, 1853, 81 x 93 In. | 360 |
| **Jacquard,** Dark Blue, Grapevine Border, 83 x 91 In. | 469 |
| **Jacquard,** Flower Medallion, Eagle Corners, Red, White, Wool, Cotton, Pa., 79 x 91 In. | 300 |
| **Jacquard,** Green, Black, Flowers, Stars, Musselman, Bucks County, 1849, 96 x 70 In. | 120 |
| **Jacquard,** Green, Red, Birds Of Paradise, Urn, c.1840, 90 x 90 In. | 120 |
| **Jacquard,** Green, Red, Cream, Flowers, Fringe, Inscribed A. Brubaker, 1845, 81 x 96 In. | 480 |
| **Jacquard,** Green, Red, Cream, Flowers, Inscribed Emmanuel Ettinger, Pa., 1837, 78 x 92 In. | 450 |
| **Jacquard,** Red, Black, Cream, Flowers, Fringe, W. Steier, Pa., c.1845, 100 x 78 In. | 150 |
| **Jacquard,** Red, Blue, Cream, Inscribed Henry Keever Womelsdorf, 1841, 77 x 92 In. | 332 |
| **Jacquard,** Red, Blue, Cream, Star, Flowers, S.D. Sugarloaf, Pa., 1847, 94 x 80 In. | 180 |
| **Jacquard,** Red, Blue, Green, Bird, Berry Border, Pa., 82 x 96 In. | 600 |
| **Jacquard,** Red, Blue, Green, House Border, J. Witmer, Manor Township, 1845, 97 x 78 In. | 277 |
| **Jacquard,** Red, Blue, White, Eagles, Buildings, Triangles, Squares, 76 x 86 In. | 438 |
| **Jacquard,** Red, Blue, White, Rose Lily, Triple Border, 1842, 85 x 94 In. | 390 |
| **Jacquard,** Red, White Flowers, Pinwheel Corner Blocks, Wm. Ney, Pa., 62 x 83 In. | 71 |
| **Jacquard,** Red, White, Blue, Green, Pa., c.1840, 95 x 88 In. | 90 |
| **Jacquard,** Red, White, Green, Blue, Sunburst, Tulips, Stars, J. Lutz, Pa., 1855, 88 x 97 In. | 518 |
| **Jacquard,** Rose, Olive, Bird, Bush, Signed Corner Blocks, Daniel Lehr, 67 x 89 In. | 188 |
| **Jacquard,** Spreadwing Eagles, Lily Border, 4 Corner Courthouse Blocks, 78 x 92 In. | 600 |

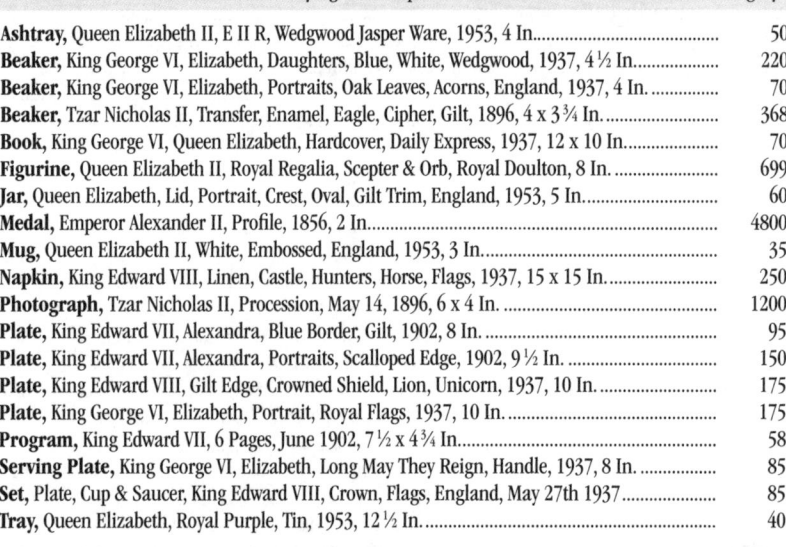

| | | |
|---|---|---:|
| **Jacquard,** Star, Flowers, Red, Blue, Cream, William Schnee, Freeburg, Pa., 1838, 94 x 82 In....... | | 150 |
| **Jacquard,** Stripes, Flowers, Signed & Dated Corner Blocks, 77 x 94 In.......................................... | | 720 |
| **Jacquard,** Sunburst, Floral Medallion, Spread Wing Eagle, Shield Corners, 77 x 83 In................ | | 118 |
| **Jacquard,** Thistle Border, Lily Border, Double Weave, Tile Centerfield, 74 x 92 In...................... | | 300 |
| **Jacquard,** Wool, Cotton, Flowers, Houses, Sailboats, Indiana, 1840, 74 x 92 In. ............... *illus* | | 570 |
| **Overshot,** 3 Colors, Geometric, Fringe, 70 x 74 In. ............................................................................ | | 106 |
| **Overshot,** Olive Green, Red, White Geometrics, Lover's Chain, Va., c.1875, 68 x 94 In................ | | 345 |
| **Overshot,** Red, White, Blue, 9-Star Block, Geometrics, Star Border, Fringe, c.1880, 78 x 93 In.... | | 316 |
| **Overshot,** Red, White, Snowball, Stars, Geometrics, Fringe, Appalachian, c.1890, 80 x 88 In. ..... | | 196 |
| **Starburst,** Eagle & Flower Border, J. & M. Ardener, Ohio, 1854, 72 x 85 In. .................. *illus* | | 384 |
| **Woven,** 4 Colors, Flowers, Geometric, A. Frey, Mt. Joy Lanc. Co. Pa., 1858, 84 x 74 In. ........*illus* | | 165 |
| **Woven,** Blue & White, Snowball Pattern, Pine Tree Border, c.1900....................................... | | 180 |
| **Woven,** Stenciled, Flowers, Urn, Hearts, Vines, Sarah Martin Ball, 87 x 75 In............................... | | 8850 |
| **Woven,** Stylized Flowers, Red On Blue Green, C. Wiand, Allentown, 1849, 101 x 92 In................. | | 575 |

**COWAN POTTERY** made art pottery and wares for florists. Guy Cowan made pottery in Rocky River, Ohio, a suburb of Cleveland, from 1913 to 1931. A stylized mark with the word *Cowan* was used on most pieces. A commercial, mass-produced line was marked *Lakeware*. Collectors today search for the Art Deco pieces by Guy Cowan, Viktor Schreckengost, Waylande Gregory, or Thelma Frazier Winter.

| | | |
|---|---|---:|
| **Bookends,** Partial Gear Shape, Stepped, Albert Jacobson, 1929, 5 In. ................................................. | | 8125 |
| **Bookends,** Push-Pull Elephant, Black Matte Glaze, Logo, 4⅝ In. ....................................................... | | 1035 |
| **Bowl,** Ivory Glaze, Yellow High Glaze Interior, Female Flower Figure, 11 In. .....................*illus* | | 184 |
| **Charger,** The Hunt, Fox Hunters, Dogs, High Glaze, V. Schreckengost, 11½ In. ................*illus* | | 1380 |
| **Figurine,** Bird On Wave, Egyptian Blue Glaze, Alexander Blazys, Marked, 12½ In. ................ | | 633 |
| **Figurine,** Peacock, Turquoise, Black, White Base, Waylande Gregory, 5 x 9¼ In. ...................... | | 805 |
| **Flower Frog,** Triumphant, Ivory Glaze, Logo, 15 In. ........................................................................ | | 1093 |
| **Jewelry Box,** Courting Couple, Hinged, Gilt Metal, Felt Lining, 4-Footed, Signed, 7 In. ............... | | 84 |
| **Paperweight,** Elephant, Ivory Glaze, Margaret Postgate, Logo, 4½ In. ............................................ | | 161 |
| **Sculpture,** Head, Woman, 1912-19, 11½ x 7 In. ............................................................................... | | 3250 |
| **Tea Set,** Teapot, Stand, Sugar, Creamer, 2 Cups, Saucers, Green, 7¾ In., 8 Piece......................... | | 161 |
| **Vase,** Oriental Red Glaze, Octagonal, Marked, 8¼ In................................................................. | | 94 |
| **Vase,** Peacock Blue Gloss Glaze, Double Handles, Fitted As Lamp Base, 9½ x 10 In. ...................... | | 138 |
| **Vase,** Teazels, Upside Down Designs & Signature, Waylande Gregory, 15 In. .....................*illus* | | 1840 |

**CRACKER JACK,** the molasses-flavored popcorn mixture, was first made in 1896 in Chicago, Illinois. A prize was added to each box in 1912. Collectors search for the old boxes, toys, and advertising materials. Many of the toys are unmarked.

| | | |
|---|---|---:|
| **Box,** Jack Saluting, Bingo, Red, White, Blue, 1920s, 6 x 2 x 1 In...................................................... | | 25 |
| **Collar Stud,** Baseball Player, Throwing Ball, Pot Metal, ⅞ x ⅝ x ¼ In. ....................................... | | 35 |
| **Pin,** Baseball Ki Ki Cuyler, c.1930, ¹³⁄₁₆ In. ..................................................................................... | | 95 |
| **Tin,** Baseball Scene, 1990, 8 x 6 In. .................................................................................................. | | 15 |
| **Toy,** Clever Clown, Circus Performer, Tub, Ladder, Chair, Schoenhut, Box, 8 In. .......................... | | 885 |
| **Toy,** Fortune Teller Disc, Jack, Bingo, Sheet Metal, 1930s, 1¾ In. .................................................. | | 75 |
| **Toy,** Game Table, Pot Metal, Gold Finish, Checkerboard Top, 1920s, 1¼ In. ................................. | | 20 |
| **Toy,** Pistol, Cast Metal, 1950s, 1¼ In. ............................................................................................. | | 10 |
| **Toy,** Pitcher, Metal, Celluloid Insert, c.1910, 1 In. ......................................................................... | | 35 |
| **Toy,** Plate, Plastic, Pink, Marbleized, Angel Fish, 1950s, 1½ In. ...................................................... | | 20 |
| **Toy,** Railroad Lantern, Pot Metal, Celluloid Insert, c.1910, 1⅜ In. ................................................. | | 35 |
| **Toy,** Ring, G Man, Shield, Brass, Size 4½ ........................................................................................ | | 35 |
| **Toy,** Shelf Clock, Eagle, Die Cast Metal, c.1905, 1⅜ In. ................................................................. | | 45 |
| **Toy,** Tray, Clown, Dog, Red, Yellow, Black, 2⅜ In. ........................................................................ | | 75 |
| **Toy,** Whistle, Owl, Multicolor, 1950s, 1½ In. .................................................................................. | | 21 |
| **Toy,** Zephyr Train, Tootsietoy, Red Paint, 1930s, 2¼ In.................................................................. | | 25 |

**CRANBERRY GLASS** is an almost transparent yellow-red glass. It resembles the color of cranberry juice. The glass has been made in Europe and America since the Civil War. It is still being made, and reproductions can fool the unwary. Related glass items may be listed in other categories, such as Rubina Verde.

| | | |
|---|---|---:|
| **Basket,** Russian, Cut To Clear, c.1880, 8 In........................................................................................ | | 3900 |
| **Bottle,** Stopper, Enameled, Bulbous, Thumbprint, Flared Rim, Multicolor, 8 In............................ | | 47 |
| **Bottle,** Water, Seaweed, Opalescent, Beaumont Glass Co., c.1890, 7½ In. ..................................... | | 345 |
| **Carafe,** Water, Lattice, Opalescent, Bulbous, c.1900, 8 x 5¾ In........................................................ | | 374 |

**Copper,** Vase, Enamel, Flock Of Ducks, Signed, Henriette Marty, 12 x 7½ In. $1,150

Humler & Nolan

**Copper,** Vase, Hammered, 3 Antler Handles, WMF, c.1915, 9¼ x 10 In. $625

Heritage Auction Galleries

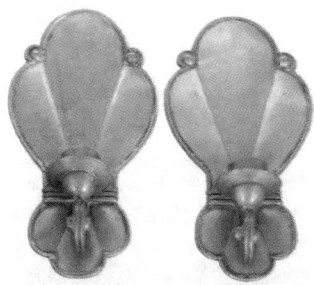

**Copper,** Wall Sconce, Candle Cup, Brass, H. Aguilar, Taxco, c.1943, 9¾ In., Pair $438

Heritage Auction Galleries

**TIP**
*If you have a mildew spot on a piece of fabric, soak it in buttermilk and let it dry in the sun. Then rinse and wash.*

**Corkscrew,** Bone Handle, Sterling Silver Mounts, Gorham, Early 20th Century, 7 In.
$708

Brunk Auctions

**Corkscrew,** Brush Handle, Bone, Carved, Brass, Victorian, Thomason, England, 10 In.
$472

Brunk Auctions

**TIP**

*Wash your hands before handling old textiles.*

**Coverlet,** Jacquard, Wool, Cotton, Flowers, Houses, Sail Boats, Indiana, 1840, 74 x 92 In.
$570

Garth's Auctioneers & Appraisers

| | |
|---|---|
| **Carafe,** Water, Opalescent, Bull's-Eye, c.1890, 7 x 6 In. | 115 |
| **Cologne Bottle,** Cut To Clear, Globular Stopper, c.1900, 6 In. | 540 |
| **Cologne Bottle,** Cut To Clear, Kirk Sterling Stopper, c.1900, 6¾ In. | 3600 |
| **Decanter,** Swirl Body, Multicolor Flowers, Flared, 9½ In. | 106 |
| **Dinner Bell,** Parisian, Cut To Clear, Dorflinger, c.1890, 6 In. | 3600 |
| **Finger Bowl,** Underplate, Opaque, Scalloped Edge, Stevens & Williams, 3 x 6 In. | 30 |
| **Ring Tree,** Cut To Clear, c.1880, 3 In. | 330 |
| **Syrup,** Windows, Opalescent, Handle, Metal Lid, Buckeye Glass Co., c.1890, 7 In. | 374 |
| **Tumbler,** Swirling Maze, Opalescent, Jefferson Glass Co., c.1905, 4 In. | 196 |
| **Vase,** Garniture, Silver Plate, Openwork, Renaissance Revival Flowers, 15 In., Pair | 575 |
| **Vase,** Paperweight, Cut To Clear, Bulbous, Flared, Scalloped Rim, c.1880, 9 In. | 4500 |
| **Water Set,** Opalescent Stars & Stripes, Clear Handle, 8½-In. Pitcher, 8 Piece | 518 |
| **Water Set,** Thumbprint, Flowers, Pitcher, 6 Tumblers, 9 In. | 201 |
| **Water Set,** Thumbprint, Frosted, Clear Frosted Handle, 4 Tumblers, Pitcher | 48 |

**CREAMWARE,** or queensware, was developed by Josiah Wedgwood about 1765. It is a cream-colored earthenware that has been copied by many factories. Similar wares may be listed under Pearlware and Wedgwood.

| | |
|---|---|
| **Cider Jug,** Glorious Defeat Of The French, Black Transfer, Staffordshire, c.1800, 9 In. | 863 |
| **Coffeepot,** Lid, Cornflowers, Tulips, White, Footed, Staffordshire, c.1850, 12 x 4 In. | 115 |
| **Compote,** Basket Weave, 3 Putti Support, Round Foot, England, 9 In. | 125 |
| **Creamer,** Cow, Girl Milking, Brown, Ocher, Sponged, England, c.1805, 5 x 6½ In. | 360 |
| **Creamer,** Figural, Cow, Cantered Base, c.1810, 6 x 6¾ In. | 690 |
| **Creamer,** Lafayette & Franklin, Eagle, Motto, Transferware, 6 In. | 944 |
| **Cup & Saucer,** Marbleized Slip, Mocha, Green Reeded Rims, c.1800, 2½ In. ...........*illus* | 1722 |
| **Jug,** Bands, Diamonds, Twigs, Reeds, Leaves, Blue, Mochaware, England, c.1820, 8 In. | 5700 |
| **Jug,** Mochaware, Wavy Bands, Cat's-Eyes Bands, Blue, Green, England, c.1830, 7 In. | 2160 |
| **Jug,** Presentation BC 1791, Farmhouse, Buildings, Brown, Green, Black, 8 In. | 540 |
| **Jug,** Ship, Sailors Launching Boat, Eagle, U.S. Seal, Black Transfer, c.1800, 11 In. | 600 |
| **Mug,** Brown, Orange, Blue Slip, Twigs, Black Bands, Mochaware, England, c.1820, 4 In. | 660 |
| **Plate,** Merchant Ship, Flag, Black Transfer, Hand Colored, Scalloped Edge, 10 In. | 185 |
| **Plate,** William V, Princess Wilhemina Busts, Red Cherry Border, England, 10 In. | 185 |
| **Sauceboat,** Catherine, Captain Edgerton, Black Transfer, 7 In. | 180 |
| **Teapot,** Lid, Red, Green, Yellow, Prince, Princess Portraits, England, c.1787, 4 In. | 570 |
| **Teapot,** Lid, Tortoiseshell Glaze, Blue, Gray, Crabstock Spout, Staffordshire, c.1765, 4 In. | 300 |
| **Teapot,** Lid, White Cauliflower, Leaves, Flower Knop, Staffordshire, c.1775, 4 In. | 240 |

**CROWN DERBY** is the name given to porcelain made in Derby, England, from the 1770s to 1935. Andrew Planche and William Duesbury established Crown Derby as the first china-making factory in Derby. Pieces are marked with a crown and the letter *D* or the word *Derby*. The earliest pieces were made by the original Derby factory, while later pieces were made by the King Street Partnerships (1848–1935) or the Derby Crown Porcelain Co. (1876–90). Derby Crown Porcelain Co. became Royal Crown Derby Co. Ltd. in 1890. It is now part of Royal Doulton Tableware Ltd.

| | |
|---|---|
| **Birds,** Flowering Branches, Blue & White, 9 In. | 135 |
| **Plate,** Blue Bird, On Branch, Aesthetic Flower Border, 9 In. | 209 |
| **Plate,** Corner, Roses, Garland, Scalloped Rim, Pierced Handle, 8 x 7 In. | 384 |
| **Plate,** Robin, Stretched Wings, Flower Border, c.1878, 9 In. | 209 |
| **Platter,** Gilt Rope Border, Enameled Flowers, c.1877, 11 x 8½ In. | 325 |
| **Vase,** Blue Birds, Rose Blossoms, Cartouches, Round Handles, c.1884, 6 In., Pair | 1499 |
| **Vase,** Flowers, Crisscross Bottom Ring, Teal Blue, 9 In. | 900 |
| **Vase,** Fluted, Flowers, Gilt Highlights, 9½ In. | 1399 |

**CROWN DUCAL** is the name used on some pieces of porcelain made by A.G. Richardson and Co., Ltd., of Tunstall and Cobridge, England. The name has been used since 1916. Crown Ducal is a well-known maker of chintz pattern dishes. The company was bought by Wedgwood in 1974.

| | |
|---|---|
| **Bowl,** Low, Pomegranates, Multicolor, Black Ground, 1930s, 10¼ In. | 95 |
| **Cup & Saucer,** Chintz, Marked | 59 |
| **Plate,** Central Flowers, Birds, Yellow Border, Octagonal, 8½ In. | 80 |
| **Plate,** Paul Revere's Ride, Blue & White, 9 In. | 30 |
| **Plate,** Raised Fruit & Flower Border, Pub Scene, 1932, 8¾ In., 6 Piece | 100 |
| **Plate,** Reticulated Sterling Border, Bouquet, 11 In. | 175 |
| **Vase,** Bird Of Paradise, Butterfly, Multicolored, Cream Ground, c.1927, 5 In. | 48 |
| **Vase,** Exotic Bird, Shouldered, c.1920, 7 In. | 32 |

| | |
|---|---|
| Vase, Pink Rose Swags, Black Ground, Oval, Footed, 1920s, 13 In. | 145 |
| Vase, Red Flowers, Black Ground, Oval, Marked, 6 In. | 46 |

**CROWN MILANO** glass was made by the Mt. Washington Glass Works about 1890. It was a plain biscuit color with a satin finish decorated with flowers and often had large gold scrolls. Not all pieces are marked.

| | |
|---|---|
| Biscuit Jar, Burmese Coloring, Acorns, Leaves, 6 In. | 144 |
| Biscuit Jar, Lid, Melon Ribbed, Blossoms, Berries, Silver Plate Handle, 6 In. .............*illus* | 920 |
| Bowl, Tricorner, Crimped, Enameled Pansies, Pairpoint Stand, 11 In. | 1380 |
| Bride's Basket, Cream, Crimson, Gold Leaves, Pairpoint Silver Stand, Marked, 12 In. | 575 |
| Bride's Bowl, Yellow, Ruffled Orange Rim, Silver Woman Stand, 15 x 13 In. | 826 |
| Cologne Bottle, Swirled, Leaves, Blossoms, Flame Shape Stopper | 288 |
| Jar, Enameled Duck In Flight, Sun, Gold Highlights, Handles, Lamp Base, 13 In. | 805 |
| Jar, Gilt Enamel Flowers, Opal, Melon Ribbed, Silver Plate Lid, c.1890, 5 x 6 In. | 184 |
| Jar, Lid, Gold Thread & Cupid, Steeple Shape Finial, Tapered, 11¾ In. | 2415 |
| Plate, Guba Duck, White, Yellow Trim, 8¾ In. | 295 |
| Rose Bowl, Leaves, Berries, 2½ In. | 230 |
| Syrup, Metal Lid, Melon Rib, Yellow Ground, Gilt Flowers, 5 In. | 863 |
| Vase, Multicolor Flowers, Opal, Gilt, Cylindrical, c.1890, 11 x 5 In. | 403 |
| Vase, Multicolor Flowers, White, Pink Ground, Pulled Ear Handles, 10 In. | 1062 |
| Vase, Opal Shaded To Blue, Cut Top, Dogwood Blossoms, Cylindrical, 7 In. | 1035 |
| Vase, Orchids, Bulbous, 3-Leaf Rim, Thorn Handles, 14 In. | 4600 |
| Vase, Pink Thistle, Brown Leaves, Gilt Webbing, Squat, Ruffled Rim, 14 In. | 972 |
| Vase, Shorebirds At Water's Edge, Gold Stylized Leaves, Bottle Form, 15 In. | 2066 |

**CRUETS** of glass or porcelain were made to hold vinegar, oil, and other condiments. They were especially popular during Victorian times and have been made in a variety of styles since the eighteenth century. Additional cruets may be found in the Castor Set category and also in various glass categories.

| | |
|---|---|
| Blue, Enameled Leaves, Berries, Applied Camphor Handles, Opal Interior, Victorian, 8 In., Pair | 58 |
| Cranberry, Enameled Flowers, 7 In., Pair | 115 |
| Cut Glass, Emerald Green Cut To Clear, Strawberry Diamond & Prism, Engraved, 7 In. | 300 |
| Mother-Of-Pearl, Glass, Diamond Quilted, Frosted Thorny Handle, Stopper, 4¾ In. | 345 |
| Mother-Of-Pearl, Glass, Diamond Quilted, Striated Rainbow, 7 In. | 374 |
| Silver, Pierced, Boat Shape, Charles Cathery, George III, Footed, 8 Bottles, c.1825, 7 In. | 540 |
| Yellow Satin Glass, Gilt Leafy Branch, Pink Inside, Clear Handle & Stopper, 6½ In. | 662 |

**CT GERMANY** was first part of a mark used by a company in Altwasser, Germany (now part of Walbrzych, Poland), in 1845. The initials stand for C. Tielsch, a partner in the firm. The Hutschenreuther firm took over the company in 1918 and continued to use the *CT*.

**C. T.**

| | |
|---|---|
| Serving Dish, Ribbed, Ruffled Edge, Flowers, Ferns, 12¼ x 6 In. | 65 |

**CUP PLATES** are small glass or china plates that held the cup while a diner of the mid-nineteenth century drank coffee or tea from the saucer. The most famous cup plates were made of glass at the Boston and Sandwich factory located in Sandwich, Massachusetts. There have been many new glass cup plates made in recent years for sale to gift shops or collectors of limited editions. These are similar to the old plates but can be recognized as new.

| | |
|---|---|
| Clear, Egg In The Sand, 3⁷⁄₁₆ In. | 20 |
| Clear, Hearts, Arrows, Scalloped Edge, Boston & Sandwich Glass Co., 3½ In. | 46 |
| Clear, Peacock Eye, Boston Sandwich Glass, c.1845, 4 In. | 40 |
| Glass, Amber, Double Hearts, Pierced, Lyre Border, Scalloped Edge, 3½ In. | 8 |
| Glass, Amethyst, Roman Rosette, Boston Sandwich Glass, c.1840, 5⅜ In. | 350 |
| Landscape, Figures, Cow, Castle, Blue Transfer, Sunderland Luster Rim, 4 In. .............*illus* | 35 |
| Majolica, Dogwood, 4¼ In. | 129 |
| Pearlware, Butterflies, Transferware, Blue Staffordshire, Scalloped Rim, c.1830, 3 In. | 60 |
| Pink Luster, Ribbons, Flowers, c.1800, 5½ In. | 30 |
| Porcelain, Castle Garden, Battery Park, Flow Blue, 3¾ In. | 325 |
| Porcelain, Palm Trees, Pagodas, Double Transfer, Flow Blue, Clews, c.1830, 4 In. | 125 |
| Porcelain, River, Boat, Transfer, Blue & White, Podmore, Walker & Co., c.1875, 4 In. | 100 |
| Porcelain, Sailing Ships, Brown & White, Transferware, c.1840, 3⅞ In. | 125 |
| Porcelain, Shirley House, String Border, Blue, Enoch Wood & Sons, c.1830, 4 In. | 250 |
| Porcelain, Worcester Cathedral, Dark Blue Staffordshire, c.1830, 3¾ In. | 145 |

**Coverlet,** Starburst, Eagle & Flower Border, J. & M. Ardener, Ohio, 1854, 72 x 85 In.
$384

Conestoga Auction Co., Inc.

**Coverlet,** Woven, 4 Colors, Flowers, Geometric, A. Frey, Mt. Joy Lanc. Co. Pa., 1858, 84 x 74 In.
$165

Conestoga Auction Co., Inc.

**Cowan,** Bowl, Ivory Glaze, Yellow High Glaze Interior, Female Flower Figure, 11 In.
$184

Humler & Nolan

**TIP**
*Coverlets made before the 1830s were done on a loom that was no more than 40 inches wide. Old coverlets are made of two panels joined at the center seam.*

C

**Cowan,** Charger, The Hunt, Fox Hunters, Dogs, High Glaze, V. Schreckengost, 11 ½ In.
$1,380

Humler & Nolan

**Cowan,** Vase, Teazels, Upside Down Designs & Signature, Waylande Gregory, 15 In.
$1,840

Humler & Nolan

**Creamware,** Cup & Saucer, Marbleized Slip, Mocha, Green Reeded Rims, c.1800, 2 ½ In.
$1,722

Skinner Auctioneers & Appraisers

**CURRIER & IVES** made the famous American lithographs marked with their name from 1857 to 1907. The mark used on the print included the street address in New York City, and it is possible to date the year of the original issue from this information. Earlier prints were made by N. Currier and use that name from 1835 to 1847. Many reprints of the Currier or Currier & Ives prints have been made. Some collectors buy the insurance calendars that were based on the old prints. The words *large*, *small*, or *medium folio* refer to size. The original print sizes were very small (up to about 7 x 9 in.), small (8.8 x 12.8 in.), medium (9 x 14 in. to 14 x 20 in.), large (larger than 14 x 20 in.). Other sizes are probably later copies. Other prints by Currier & Ives may be listed in the Card category under Advertising and in the Sheet Music category. Currier & Ives dinnerware patterns may be found in the Adams or Dinnerware categories.

| | |
|---|---:|
| **American Field Sports Chance For Both Barrels,** A.F. Tait, 1857, 32 x 40 In. | 1920 |
| **American Forest Scene,** Maple Sugaring, N. Currier, 1856, Large Folio | 2400 |
| **American Hunting Scenes,** Early Start, A.F. Tait, Frame, 1863, 33 x 42 In. | 13800 |
| **Arguing The Point,** A.F. Tait, Frame, 1855, 32 x 37 In. | 6900 |
| **Autumn Fruits,** Bird's-Eye Maple, Frame, 1861, 27 x 31 In. | 300 |
| **Brook Trout Fishing,** An Anxious Moment, A.F. Tait, Frame, 1862, 32 x 40 In. | 9600 |
| **Camping In The Woods,** Laying Off, 4 Men, Catch Of Fish, Large Folio, 22 x 30 In. ..........*illus* | 960 |
| **Cares Of A Family,** Chicks, Mother Bird, Nest, Frame, Small Folio | 270 |
| **Central Park,** Winter, Skating Pond, Lithograph, 1862, 19 x 26 In. | 660 |
| **Clipper Ship,** Comet, Hurricane, Lithograph, 1852, Large Folio | 720 |
| **Four Seasons Of Life,** Middle Age, Frame, 1868, 16 x 18 In. | 495 |
| **Futurity Race At Sheepshead Bay,** L. Maurer, Frame, 1888, 32 x 45 In. | 960 |
| **Garden Orchard & Vine,** Color Lithograph, 1867, 18 x 24 In. | 281 |
| **Gold Mining In California,** Miners By Stream, 1871, Small Folio | 2400 |
| **Great West,** Bird's-Eye Maple Frame, 1870, 20 x 24 In. | 600 |
| **Hudson Highlands,** Frame, 1857, Large Folio | 1020 |
| **In & Out Of Condition,** Satirical, Color Lithograph, 1879, 24 x 16 In. | 500 |
| **Life Of A Fireman,** Night Alarm, 1854, Large Folio | 900 |
| **Pacing Horse,** Billy Boyce Of St. Louis, Tho. Worth, J. Cameron, 1868, 33 x 40 In. | 1200 |
| **Rocky Mountains,** Emigrants Crossing The Plains, Fanny F. Palmer, 1866, 31 x 38 In. | 20040 |
| **Sleigh Race,** N. Currier, Maple Frame, 1848, 20 x 24 In. | 1020 |
| **The Road-Summer,** Horse, Wagon, N. Currier, Frame, 1853, Large Folio | 5760 |
| **U.S. Sloop Of War Kearsarge Sinking The Pirate Alabama,** 1884, Small Folio | 660 |
| **Wild Duck Shooting,** Good Day's Sport, A.F. Tait Painted, 1854, 33 x 39 In. | 2880 |
| **Winter Morning In The Country,** Horse Drawn Sleigh, 1873, Small Folio | 840 |
| **Winter Morning,** Bird's-Eye Maple Frame, 1861, 23 x 27 In. | 2280 |
| **Yacht Squadron At Newport,** Ships, Boats, Sea, Frame, 1872, Large Folio | 1920 |

**CUSTARD GLASS** is a slightly yellow opaque glass. It was made in England in the 1880s and was first made in the United States in the 1890s. It has been reproduced. Additional pieces may be found in the Cambridge, Fenton, and Heisey categories. Custard glass is called *Ivorina Verde* by Heisey and other companies.

| | |
|---|---:|
| **Argonaut Shell,** Sugar & Creamer, Footed, c.1895 | 75 |
| **Beaded Shell,** Mug, 8 Oz., 3 ⅞ In., Pair | 28 |
| **Daisy & Panel,** Bowl, Oval, Scalloped Rim & Foot, 8 In. | 36 |
| **Grape Arbor,** Toothpick Holder, Ruffled Rim, 2 ¾ In. | 110 |
| **Hobstar & Fan,** Toothpick Holder, Sawtooth Rim, 2 ½ In. | 23 |
| **Inverted Fan & Feather,** Toothpick Holder, Footed, 2 ½ In. | 35 |
| **Maize** is its own category in this book. | |

**CUT GLASS** has been made since ancient times, but the large majority of the pieces now for sale date from the American Brilliant period of glass design, 1875 to 1915. These pieces have elaborate geometric designs with a deep miter cut. Modern cut glass with a similar appearance is being made in England, Ireland, Poland, and the Czech and Slovak republics. Chips and scratches are often difficult to notice but lower the value dramatically. A signature on the glass adds significantly to the value. Other cut glass pieces are listed under factory names, like Hawkes, Libbey, and Sinclaire.

| | |
|---|---:|
| **Basket,** Hobstar, Notching, Double Notched Handle, 11 ½ x 11 ½ In. | 254 |
| **Basket,** Willow, Dorflinger, c.1900, 17 x 11 In. | 1680 |
| **Beaker,** Wedding, Gilded Body, 8 ¾ In. | 1921 |
| **Biscuit Jar,** Starburst, 9 In. | 48 |
| **Bowl,** 6-Point Star, Hobstars, 2 ¼ x 8 ¾ In. | 254 |
| **Bowl,** Arabesque, Hoare, 2 ¼ x 11 In. | 1582 |
| **Bowl,** Bateau Shape, Georgian Style, Diamond Cut, Footed, c.1875, 9 x 16 x 8 In. | 1107 |

| | |
|---|---|
| **Bowl,** Blowout Pattern, c.1890, 4 x 11 In. | 540 |
| **Bowl,** Cane Pattern, Diamond Points, Clear, Flared Rim, Oval, 4½ x 12 In. | 708 |
| **Bowl,** Cranberry To Clear, Hobstar, Cane, Nailhead Diamond, 3 x 8½ In. | 207 |
| **Bowl,** Cut Block, Diamond & Star, 2¼ x 8¾ In. | 75 |
| **Bowl,** Genoa, Rolled Rim, Signed Clark, 3 x 9 In. | 113 |
| **Bowl,** Grecian Pattern, c.1900, 4 x 10 In. | 780 |
| **Bowl,** Hobstar, Cane, Strawberry Diamond & Fan, Square, Scalloped, Notched Edge, 11 In. | 125 |
| **Bowl,** Hobstar, Cane, Vesica, Strawberry Diamond, Napoleon Hat Shape, 4 x 14 In. | 650 |
| **Bowl,** Hobstar, Hobstar Cluster & Vesica, 2 x 9 In. | 150 |
| **Bowl,** Hobstar, Strawberry Diamond & Cane, Trefoil Shape, 1¾ x 10 In. | 200 |
| **Bowl,** Hobstar, Strawberry Diamond, Flared, Oval, 3¼ x 9¾ In. | 102 |
| **Bowl,** Hobstar, Strawberry Diamond, Scalloped Border, Matching Base, 9 In., 2 Piece | 283 |
| **Bowl,** Hobstar, Vesica, Nailhead Diamond, Sterling Rim, Silver By Whiting, 4½ x 13 In. | 1582 |
| **Bowl,** Hobstar, Vesica, Nailhead, Strawberry Diamond, Silver Rim, 4 x 9 In. | 177 |
| **Bowl,** Hobstar, Vesica, Strawberry Diamond, 8 In. | 57 |
| **Bowl,** Navette Shape, Scalloped, Squared Ends, 16½ In. | 1652 |
| **Bowl,** Radiant, 9 x 3 In. | 29 |
| **Bowl,** Royal, 8-Sided, Hunt, 3½ x 9 In. | 102 |
| **Bowl,** Russian & Pillar, c.1890, 8 In. | 1320 |
| **Bowl,** Russian Center, Trellis Border, 2¾ x 8¾ In. | 4700 |
| **Bowl,** Russian, Round, Signed J. Hoare & Co., c.1910, 8 In. | 2478 |
| **Bowl,** Scalloped, Serrated Rim, Hobstars, Mitered Borders, c.1900, 4 x 9 In. | 300 |
| **Bowl,** Theodora, Meriden, c.1900, 8¼ In. | 660 |
| **Bowl,** Trellis Block, Alternating Hobstar & Strawberry Diamond, J. Hoare, 4 x 8 In. | 450 |
| **Bowl,** Triple Miter Trellis, Green Cased, c.1900, 7 In. | 2040 |
| **Bowl,** Vintage Pattern, Brilliant Cut, Sinclaire, c.1910, 4 x 11½ In. | 1080 |
| **Bowl,** Water Lily, Intaglio, 6 x 8½ In. | 400 |
| **Box,** Hobstar, Strawberry Diamond, Hinged Lid, C.F. Monroe, 3¾ x 9½ In. | 904 |
| **Box,** Lid, Cane, Red Cut To Clear, Round, Flame Finial, 3½ In. | 80 |
| **Bucket,** Champagne, Starred Button, Russian, Sawtooth Edge, 10 x 12 In. | 518 |
| **Butter,** Hobstar, Strawberry Diamond, Fan, 6½ x 9 In. | 170 |
| **Cachepot,** Neoclassical Style, Gilt Bronze Rim & Base, France, c.1915, 7 x 6 In. .............*illus* | 738 |
| **Cake Plate,** Nassau, Round, 3-Footed, J. Hoare, 10 In. | 175 |
| **Cake Stand,** Engraved Flowers, Pedestal Base, 6-Sided Stem, 5 x 10 In. | 125 |
| **Candlestick,** 6-Sided Stem, Prism Cut Corners, Faceted Ball, Rayed Base, 10 In. | 100 |
| **Candlestick,** Notched Teardrop Stem, Hobstar Base, 6 In. | 90 |
| **Carafe,** Crosscut Diamond Ring Neck, Dorflinger, 9 In. | 141 |
| **Carafe,** Water, Electra, Pinched Neck, Flared, Straus, 9¼ In. | 150 |
| **Celery Dish,** Harvard, Oblong, Brilliant Cut, 11¾ In. | 184 |
| **Celery Dish,** Hobstar, Crosscut Diamond & Pinwheel, Oval, 12 In. | 40 |
| **Celery Dish,** Lattice & Block, Castle Tooth Border, 12 In. | 80 |
| **Celery Vase,** Flashed Hobstar, Nailhead Diamond, Notched Fan, Hobstar Foot, 9 In. | 600 |
| **Celery Vase,** Strawberry Diamond & Fan, Angular Knop, Rayed Foot, 7½ In. | 176 |
| **Centerpiece,** Creswick, Eggington, 6⅓ x 8 In. | 254 |
| **Centerpiece,** Glenwood, Hobstar Base, Bergen, 7 x 12 In. | 509 |
| **Centerpiece,** Hobstar, Vesica, Nailhead Diamond, Strawberry Diamond, 7¼ x 9 In. | 198 |
| **Champagne Stem,** Cranberry, Intaglio, c.1910, 4½ In. | 1680 |
| **Champagne,** Flutes, Intaglio, Blue Cut To Clear, 3¾ In. | 135 |
| **Cheese Dish,** Domed Lid, Fontenoy, Unger Bros., 6¾ x 9¾ In. | 325 |
| **Cheese Dish,** Scalloped, Sawtooth Rim, Crosscut Diamond, Fans, c.1900, 8 x 10 In. | 46 |
| **Coffeepot,** Globe Shape Stopper, Harvard, c.1890, 15 In. | 39000 |
| **Coffeepot,** Turkish Hookah, Footed, Faceted Stopper, 16 In. | 1534 |
| **Cologne Bottle,** Hobstar, Vesica & Fan, Bulbous, Faceted Stopper, 6 In. | 80 |
| **Compote,** Hobstar, Nailhead Diamond, Strawberry Diamond, Teardrop Stem, 7 x 8 In. | 175 |
| **Compote,** Hobstar, Strawberry Diamond, Signed Pitkin & Brooks, 9 x 5 In. | 192 |
| **Compote,** Intaglio Fruit, Faceted Ball Stem, Petticoat Base, 8½ x 6 In. | 200 |
| **Compote,** Navette Shape, Scalloped Edge, Diamond Point, Lozenge, Anglo-Irish, 9 x 15 In. | 478 |
| **Compote,** Theodora, c.1900, 10 In. | 1926 |
| **Decanter,** Fredericka, Cut Gooseneck, Stopper, W.C. Anderson, 15 In. | 2260 |
| **Decanter,** Herringbone, Hobstar, Nailhead Diamond & Star, Elongated Neck, 14 In. | 650 |
| **Decanter,** Hobstar, Cane & Strawberry Diamond, Snake Handle, Wafer Base, 9 In. | 300 |
| **Decanter,** Hobstar, Strawberry Diamond, Double Notched Handle, Stopper, 8 In. | 226 |
| **Decanter,** Hobstar, Strawberry Diamond, Star & Fan, Goose Neck, Stopper, 12 In. | 125 |
| **Decanter,** Prism & Fish Scale, Elongated Neck, Hobstar Base, Pattern Stopper, 15 In. | 400 |
| **Decanter,** Strawberry, Mushroom Stopper, Pittsburgh, c.1820, 10¾ In. | 478 |

**Crown Milano,** Biscuit Jar, Lid, Melon Ribbed, Blossoms, Berries, Silver Plate Handle, 6 In.
$920

Early Auction Co.

---

**Cup Plate,** Landscape, Figures, Cow, Castle, Blue Transfer, Sunderland Luster Rim, 4 In.
$35

Conestoga Auction Co., Inc.

---

**Currier & Ives,** Camping In The Woods, Laying Off, 4 Men, Catch Of Fish, Large Folio, 22 x 30 In.
$960

Garth's Auctioneers & Appraisers

> ### TIP
> *Is it cut or pressed glass? Feel the edges of the design of the glass. Cut glass has sharp edges; pressed-glass designs are molded into the glass.*

# CUT GLASS

**Cut Glass,** Cachepot, Neoclassical Style, Gilt Bronze Rim & Base, France, c.1915, 7 x 6 In.
$738

New Orleans Auction Galleries, Inc.

---

**Cut Glass,** Pitcher, Cranberry Cut To Clear, Mounted Sterling Silver Lid & Handle, 1892, 11 In.
$33,000

DuMouchelles Art Gallery

---

**Cut Glass,** Pokal, Cobalt Blue, Arms Of Russia, 20½ x 6 In.
$923

New Orleans Auction Galleries, Inc.

| | |
|---|---:|
| **Dish,** Mayonnaise, Underplate, Hobstar & Prism, 2½ x 7 In. | 70 |
| **Dish,** Mayonnaise, Underplate, Monarch, J. Hoare | 80 |
| **Epergne,** 3 Parts, Hobstar, Strawberry Diamond, Fan, 19 x 11½ In. | 960 |
| **Epergne,** Lily, Intaglio Flowers, Flared Out Rim, Dish Base, W.C. Anderson, 10 x 8 In. | 350 |
| **Ewer,** Prism Cut Neck, Strawberry Diamond, Loop Handle, Anglo-Irish, 1800s, 12 In. | 538 |
| **Flask,** Russian, Star Cut Buttons, Silver Cap, 5 In. | 509 |
| **Girandoles,** Regency, Gilt Bronze, Vase Shape Standard, Prisms, 11½ In., Pair | 1107 |
| **Hair Receiver,** Hobstar, Intaglio Flowers | 50 |
| **Hookah,** Silver Plate, Leaf Decoration, Tassels, Vase Shape, 22 x 6½ In. | 598 |
| **Humidor,** Carolyn, Hobstar Lid, Ray Base, Hoare, 9 In. | 565 |
| **Humidor,** Monarch, Hobstar Lid, Ray Base, Hoare, 9½ In. | 508 |
| **Humidor,** Vertical Prisms, Silver Top, Embossed Acorns, Bailey, Banks & Biddle, 8 In. | 900 |
| **Ice Cream Tray,** Navette Form, Scalloped Sections, Notched Edge, 17¾ In. | 3776 |
| **Ice Cream Tray,** Newport, J. Hoare, 17 x 10½ In. | 600 |
| **Ice Tub,** Hindoo, Pedestal Base, J. Hoare, 6¾ x 6 In. | 450 |
| **Ice Tub,** Hobstar, Strawberry Diamond & Block, Pedestal, Scalloped Edge, 5 x 7 In. | 200 |
| **Jug,** Cranberry Cut To Clear, Silver Overlay, Gorham, 1892, 11 In. | 33000 |
| **Jug,** Whiskey, Hobstar, Strawberry Diamond, Double Notched Handle, 11 In. | 452 |
| **Jug,** Whiskey, Monarch, Signed J. Hoare, 11 In. | 961 |
| **Jugs,** Claret, Intaglio Cut, Green, Stevens & Williams, c.1900, 11 In., Pair | 10800 |
| **Knife Rest,** Facet Cut, 8-Sided, Turned Down Ends, 6 In. | 70 |
| **Pitcher,** Cranberry Cut To Clear, Mounted Sterling Silver Lid & Handle, 1892, 11 In. ........*illus* | 33000 |
| **Pitcher,** Hobstar, Cane, Star, Fan, Double Notched Handle, 7 In. | 102 |
| **Pitcher,** Hobstar, Vesica, Triple Notched Handle, 9 In. | 141 |
| **Pitcher,** Russian, Cranberry, c.1900, 6½ In. | 3000 |
| **Pitcher,** Triple Notched Handle, Rayed Base, J. Hoare, 10½ In. | 80 |
| **Pitcher,** Water, Hobstar, Strawberry Diamond, Prism & Window, 10 In. | 200 |
| **Plate,** Chrysanthemum, Hobstars, Double Fans, Sawtooth Rim, 13 In. | 1840 |
| **Plate,** Hobstar, Nailhead Diamond, Cane, Arch & Fan, 10 In. | 125 |
| **Plate,** Hobstar, Split Vesica, Cane & Fan, Square, Notched Edge, 7 In. | 50 |
| **Pokal,** Cobalt Blue, Arms Of Russia, 20½ x 6 In. ........*illus* | 923 |
| **Punch Bowl,** Cranberry Cut To Clear, Separate Base, Bergen Co., c.1898, 8 x 7½ In. ........*illus* | 10200 |
| **Punch Bowl,** Flashed Hobstars, Vesicas, Notched Prism Bands, Fry, 7 x 14 In. | 1265 |
| **Punch Bowl,** Hobstar, Strawberry Diamond, Prism, 2 Parts, 14½ x 14 In. | 735 |
| **Punch Bowl,** Interlocking Russian, Strawberry Diamond & Prism, Vesicas, Notched, 14 In. | 375 |
| **Punch Bowl,** Scalloped, Sawtooth Rim, Base, Hobstars, Diamonds, Stars, c.1900, 9¾ In. | 184 |
| **Punch Bowl,** Stand, Hobstar, Notched Prism, Cane, Vesica & Fan, 9 x 10 In. | 175 |
| **Punch Cup & Plate,** Strawberry Diamond, Cranberry, Dorflinger, c.1910 ........*illus* | 1080 |
| **Punch Set,** Flattened Diamond Point & Chain, Tray, Cups, Ladle, 10-In. Bowl, 14 Piece | 118 |
| **Punch Set,** Hobstars, Pinwheels, Fans, Flared Base, Brilliant, 9-In. Bowl, 5 Piece | 173 |
| **Rose Bowl,** Croesus Pedestal, J. Hoare, c.1890, 10 In. | 19200 |
| **Rose Bowl,** Cut In Tusks, Crosshatch, 6¾ In. | 495 |
| **Rose Bowl,** Hobstar, Strawberry Diamond & Fan, 6 x 8 In. | 125 |
| **Salt & Pepper,** Nailhead Diamond, Strawberry Diamond, Prism, Sterling, 4½ In. | 113 |
| **Spooner,** Hobstar, Strawberry Diamond, Prism & Fan, 4¾ In. | 60 |
| **Tankard,** 9 Large Hobstars, Nailhead Diamond, Fan, Sterling Collar, 14 In. | 508 |
| **Tankard,** Hobstar, Cane, Triple Notched Handle, Sterling Collar, Spout, Meriden, 14 In. | 396 |
| **Tazza,** Pattern 100, Rolled Rim, Elmira, 8 x 6½ In. | 141 |
| **Tray,** Diadem, Meriden, 14½ In. | 1469 |
| **Tray,** Expanding Star, Elite, 13½ In. | 3107 |
| **Tray,** Hobstar, Cane, Strawberry Diamond, Vesica & Fan, Round, Quatrefoil, 15 In. | 2600 |
| **Tray,** Hobstar, Circular Cane Bands, Strawberry Diamond, Round, 12 In. | 282 |
| **Tray,** Hobstar, Modified Hobstar, Round, Fan, Notched Fan, Thick Blank, 11¾ In. | 226 |
| **Tray,** Hobstar, Strawberry Diamond, 17¾ x 10½ In. | 622 |
| **Tray,** Hobstar, Strawberry Diamond, Nailhead Diamond & Star, Round, 12 In. | 225 |
| **Tray,** Ice Cream, Intaglio Flowers, Harvard, Navette, 14 x 7 In. | 125 |
| **Tray,** Star Of David, Trellis Cut, Hobstar, Strawberry Diamond, 13½ In. | 509 |
| **Tray,** Trellis Pattern, c.1900, 14 In. | 1080 |
| **Tumble Up,** Hobstar, Cane & Fan, Cranberry Cut To Clear, 7 In. | 2300 |
| **Tumbler,** Diamond Band, Sulphide Portrait, G. Washington, Pittsburgh, c.1825, 3¼ In. | 9375 |
| **Vase,** Alhambra, Tapered, Meriden, Monumental, c.1911, 21 In. | 10800 |
| **Vase,** Comet, Bulbous Base, Lady's Leg Neck, Flared Rim, 14 x 7 In. | 885 |
| **Vase,** Diamond Point Design, 20th Century, 15¾ x 9 In., Pair | 369 |
| **Vase,** Dore Bronze Neoclassical Mounts, Baluster, Winged Goddesses, 19 x 11 In. | 4658 |
| **Vase,** Feathered Prism, Crescent Moons, Hobstar & File, Bulbous, Cup Rim, 14 In. | 1700 |

C

| | |
|---|---|
| **Vase,** Feathered Star, Flared-Out Shape, 10¾ x 9½ In. | 400 |
| **Vase,** Flower, Monarch, Scallop Rim, Hobstar, Fans, J. Hoare & Co., c.1900, 10 In. | 288 |
| **Vase,** Flowers, Squat, Step Cut Neck, Flared Notched Edge, J. Hoare, 8 In. | 25 |
| **Vase,** Hobstar, Nailhead Diamond, Cane, Vesica & Fan, Bowling Pin Shape, 14 In. | 700 |
| **Vase,** Othello, High Shoulder Shape, Step Cut Neck, Clark, 19¼ In. | 1017 |
| **Vase,** Pinched Waist, Hobstar, Strawberry Diamond, 16 In. | 311 |
| **Vase,** Rose Cut Diamond, Pinched Waist, Meriden, 13¾ In. | 2147 |
| **Vase,** Sweet Pea, Hobstar & Strawberry Diamond, Step Cut Sides, 4½ x 8 In. | 50 |
| **Vase,** Trumpet, 46½ x 12 In. | 538 |
| **Water Set,** Cincinnati, J. Hoare, Tumblers, 8-In. Pitcher, 7 Piece | 125 |
| **Wine,** Green Cut To Clear, Crosscut Diamond, Strawberry Diamond, 4¾ In. | 622 |
| **Wine,** Marlboro, Cranberry Cut To Clear, Dorflinger, 5 In. | 850 |
| **Wine,** Overlay, Chartreuse To Clear, Flowers, Swags, Notched Stem, 7¾ In., Pair | 138 |
| **Wine,** Red Cut To Clear, 4⅞ In. | 315 |
| **Wine,** Red Cut To Clear, 5⅛ In. | 320 |

**CYBIS** porcelain is a twentieth-century product. Boleslaw Cybis came to the United States from Poland in 1939. He started making porcelains in Long Island, New York, in 1940. He moved to Trenton, New Jersey, in 1942 as one of the founders of Cordey China Co. and started his own company, Cybis Porcelains, about 1950. The firm is still working. See also Cordey.

CYBIS

| | |
|---|---|
| **Cup & Saucer,** Spatterware, Red Border, Rooster | 35 |
| **Dish,** Orchids, Leaves, Lavender, Green, 10¾ x 5½ In. | 100 |
| **Figurine,** Carousel Giraffe, Sir Cuthbert, Numbered, 1982, 14½ In. | 1400 |
| **Figurine,** Donkey Foal, Fitzgerald, 1964, 6¼ x 6⅞ In. | 90 |
| **Figurine,** Heidi, Holding Flowers, 7½ In. | 100 |
| **Figurine,** Lady Godiva, Woman, Horse, Signed, c.1950, 13 x 15 In. *illus* | 375 |
| **Figurine,** Lady Macbeth, 24K Gold Accents, Signed, Numbered, 1975, 13 In. | 899 |
| **Figurine,** Laughing Water, Indian Woman, Seating, Wood Base, c.1969 | 1450 |
| **Figurine,** Owl, Bisque, Painted, 4¼ In. | 71 |
| **Figurine,** Raccoon, Climbing Branch, Eating Cherries, 7 x 8¼ In. | 187 |
| **Figurine,** Rapunzel, Pink, 8½ In. | 650 |
| **Figurine,** Wendy, Holding Doll, Bisque, Multicolor, 7 In. | 48 |
| **Figurine,** Wildflower, Ladybug, Pink, Long Stem, 1940s, 7¾ In. | 165 |
| **Vase,** Blue Birds, Leaves, 9¾ In. | 200 |

**CZECHOSLOVAKIA** is a popular term with collectors. The name, first used as a mark after the country was formed in 1918, appears on glass and porcelain and other decorative items. Although Czechoslovakia split into Slovakia and the Czech Republic on January 1, 1993, the name continues to be used in some trademarks.

## CZECHOSLOVAKIA GLASS

| | |
|---|---|
| **Bowl,** Green Satin, Red Drips, Glass Inclusions, Garnet Handles, 5 x 11 In. | 161 |
| **Perfume Bottle,** Blue Stopper, Dabber, 6½ In. | 75 |
| **Perfume Bottle,** Blue, 6 In. | 75 |
| **Perfume Bottle,** Ingrid, Ruby Jeweled, Ivory Stopper | 9600 |
| **Vase,** Pale Pink, Cobalt Blue Leaf Design, Ball Shape, 7¾ In. | 80 |
| **Vase,** Pillow, Opal & Amethyst Waves, Oval, c.1930, 5½ x 4 In. | 46 |

## CZECHOSLOVAKIA POTTERY

| | |
|---|---|
| **Cup & Saucer,** Roses, Swag Border, Gilt Trim, 1930s | 35 |
| **Dish,** Lid, Fish Shape, Red, 5¾ x 3 In. | 49 |
| **Dish,** Swan Shape, Turned Head, 5 x 4¼ In. | 62 |
| **Double Vase,** Parrot, On Tree Branch, Multicolor, 9 In. | 32 |
| **Pitcher,** Bull's Head, Reddish Brown, Horns, Marked, 6 x 7½ In. | 195 |
| **Salt,** Hexagonal, Pearly White Luster Glaze, 2 In. | 10 |
| **Tray,** 2 Tiers, Central Handle, Fruit, 9½ In. | 25 |
| **Vase,** Multicolor Flowers, Scalloped Rim, Footed, Handles, 3½ In. | 29 |

**DANIEL BOONE,** a pre-Revolutionary War folk hero, was a surveyor, trapper, and frontiersman. A television series, which ran from 1964 to 1970, was based on his life and starred Fess Parker. All types of Daniel Boone memorabilia are collected.

| | |
|---|---|
| **Book,** Life Of Daniel Boone, Timothy Flint, Applegate Co., 252 Pages, 1856 | 40 |
| **Match Safe,** Profile, Brass, Hinged, Stamped GAR, c.1895, 2⅞ In. | 950 |
| **Spoon,** Kentucky Home, Sun, Mountains, Chickens, Sterling Silver, Watson Co., 5 In. | 49 |

**Cut Glass,** Punch Bowl, Cranberry Cut To Clear, Separate Base, Bergen Co., c.1898, 8 x 7½ In.
**$10,200**

DuMouchelles Art Gallery

**Cut Glass,** Punch Cup & Plate, Strawberry Diamond, Cranberry, Dorflinger, c.1910
**$1,080**

DuMouchelles Art Gallery

**Cybis,** Figurine, Lady Godiva, Woman, Horse, Signed, c.1950, 13 x 15 In.
**$375**

Rago Arts & Auction Center

147

D

**Daum,** Box, Lid, Leaves & Berries, Mottled Red Shaded To Yellow Ground, 2 x 3 In.
**$2,133**

James D. Julia Auctioneers

---

**Daum,** Lamp Shade, Cameo Glass, Ceiling, Dahlias, Leaves, Red, Brown, Signed, 19 In. Diam.
**$9,440**

Brunk Auctions

---

**Daum,** Vase, Daisies, Deep Blue To Sky Blue, Enamel, Inscribed, c.1910, 14 x 2 ½ In.
**$9,430**

Cottone Auctions

---

**D'ARGENTAL** is a mark used in France by the Compagnie des Cristalleries de St. Louis. The firm made multilayered, acid-cut cameo glass in the late nineteenth and twentieth centuries. D'Argental is the French name for the city of Munzthal, home of the glassworks. Later the company made enameled etched glass.

| | |
|---|---:|
| **Lamp,** Electric, Red Flowers, Brown Leaves, Domed Shade, Footed, 22 In. | 4148 |
| **Pitcher,** Landscape, Burgundy, Red, Yellow, Acid Etched, Cylindrical, Cameo, 9 In. | 492 |
| **Vase,** Blue, Applied Purple Flowers, Signed Base, 6 ¼ In. | 390 |
| **Vase,** Blue, Pink, Trees, Water, Landscape, Cylindrical, Cameo, 11 ⅜ In. | 615 |
| **Vase,** Carved Pine Tree, Lake Scene, White, Yellow Ground, 13 In. | 826 |
| **Vase,** Flared Rim, Cylindrical Base, Trumpet Flowers, Vines, 10 ½ In. | 800 |
| **Vase,** Landscape, Conifer Trees, Lake, Mountains, Oval Windows, Cameo, 12 In. | 1955 |
| **Vase,** Landscape, Wasenbourg, Tricolor, Flared Lip, Cameo, 12 ¾ In. | 1150 |
| **Vase,** Pedestal, Pink Roses, Leaves, Amber Band, Olive Border, Cameo, 6 ½ In. | 259 |
| **Vase,** Pink Maple Leaf Overlay, Pale Green Ground, Dome Neck, Tapered, 10 In. | 1003 |
| **Vase,** Yellow, Black, Mountain Scene, Tapered, c.1920, 6 ½ x 4 ½ In. | 469 |

**DAUM,** a glassworks in Nancy, France, was started by Jean Daum in 1875. The company, now called *Cristalleries de Nancy*, is still working. The *Daum Nancy* mark has been used in many variations. The name of the city and the artist are usually both included. The term *martele* is used to describe applied decorations that are carved or etched in the cameo process.

| | |
|---|---:|
| **Atomizer,** Art Nouveau, Acid Etched, Green Leaves, Amber, Plum, c.1900, 7 ½ In. | 531 |
| **Bowl,** Cobalt Blue & Orange Mottled, Shaded To Light Blue, Footed, Signed, 16 In. | 230 |
| **Bowl,** Grape Leaves Shape, Big Purple Grapes On Edges, Lizard, Signed, 12 ¾ In. | 2666 |
| **Bowl,** Leaves, Frosted, Rounded & Pulled Square, Brown Lip Wrap & Foot, 5 x 12 In. | 2300 |
| **Bowl,** Lily Pond, Blue, Cream, Orange Lilies, Padded, Carved, Cameo, Signed, 11 ½ In. | 6221 |
| **Bowl,** Peach, Applied Flowers, Dragon, Acid Texture, Cameo, Signed, 5 In. | 3910 |
| **Bowl,** Winter Scene, Trees, Snow, Mottled Orange & Yellow, Pinched Rim, 3 x 4 ½ In. | 1188 |
| **Bowl,** Yellow Flowers, Mottled Purple, Yellow & Cream Ground, Folded Rim, 3 x 4 ⅝ In. | 1067 |
| **Box,** Lid, Autumn Leaves, Mottled & Frosted Yellow Ground, Round, Squat, 3 x 5 ½ In. | ⁻55 |
| **Box,** Lid, Leaves & Berries, Mottled Red Shaded To Yellow Ground, 2 x 3 In. .......*illu* | |
| **Charger,** Yellow, Green, Seaweed, Blue Ground, 14 In. | |
| **Creamer,** Winter Scene, Snowy Forest, Mottled Orange, Rectangular, 5 In. | |
| **Cruet,** Amber, Gold Mistletoe, Oval, Clear Handle & Disc Stopper, 6 In. | |
| **Cruet,** Green Textured Glass, Gold Gingko Branches, Bulbous, Cameo, 5 ½ In. | |
| **Cruet,** Mottled Blue, Purple Iris, Green Stems, Gold Trim, Oval, Disc Stopper, 7 ½ In. | |
| **Decanter,** Stopper, Green, Incised Soucis Oublye, c.1900, 11 x 4 In. | |
| **Dresser Box,** Lid, Yellow & Brown Flowers, Green Leaves, Yellow, Round, Squat, 4 In. | |
| **Dresser Jar,** Lid, Yellow, Purple Mottled, Etched, Lady Slippers, Webs, c.1905, 3 x 6 In. | |
| **Ewer,** Vines, Leaves, Berries, Souvenir De L'Exposition 1900, Bands, Cameo, 12 In. | 5 |
| **Figurine,** Guitar, Green, Plum, Strings, Metal Keys, Pate-De-Verre, 23 ½ In. | 5 |
| **Figurine,** La Colombe, Pate-De-Verre, Marked PW Yenawine, c.1975, 10 x 11 In. | 8⁷⁵ |
| **Figurine,** Rabbit, Crouching, Crystal, 2 ½ x 3 ½ In. | 42 |
| **Group,** Horses, Cheval Harnache Pattern, Brown, Clear, Box, 17 ½ x 10 In. | 5748 |
| **Jar,** Lid, Purple & Orange Tulips, Green To Pink, Gold Trim, Knob Handle, 4 In. | 5333 |
| **Lamp Shade,** Cameo Glass, Ceiling, Dahlias, Leaves, Red, Brown, Signed, 19 In. Diam.......*illus* | 9440 |
| **Lamp,** Inverted Shade, Red Flowers, Yellow Ground, 15 In. | 8591 |
| **Lamp,** Red Shade, Wrought Iron Base, Twigs, Leaves, 13 In. | 554 |
| **Pitcher,** Blue Flowers, Blue Shaded To Mottled Green, Mottled Cream, 2 ½ In. | 1896 |
| **Pitcher,** Cameo, Pink Textured, Gilt Banded Neck, Handle, Iris, Signed, 5 In. | 2070 |
| **Plate,** Blue, Pate-De-Verre, Gold Design, S. Dali, France, c.1960, 10 ½ In. | 750 |
| **Rose Bowl,** Barren Trees, Snowy Ground, Bark, Mottled Yellow & Orange, 4 In. | 5925 |
| **Scent Bottle,** Water Lilies, Beds, Lily Pads, Gold Trim, Light Blue Ground, Cameo, 3 In. | 3258 |
| **Sculpture,** Flame Shape, Clear, Stepped Base, 22 ½ In. | 308 |
| **Table Plaque,** Camargue, Horse, Relief, Arched Ground, Purple, G. Petitfils, 1974, 17 In. | 800 |
| **Vase,** Autumn Leaves, Thorns, Grown, Green, Frosted Yellow Ground, Cameo, 12 In. | 9480 |
| **Vase,** Black Sailboats, Distant Shore, Dusk, 11 ½ In. | 2666 |
| **Vase,** Blackbirds, Gray Trees, Snowy, Frosted Blue Sky, Bulbous, Undulating Rim, 3 In. | 10665 |
| **Vase,** Blue Mottled Body, Lake Scene, Summer Trees, Cameo, Signed, 3 ¼ In. | 748 |
| **Vase,** Bottle, Green Glass, Silver Cap, Gilt Detail, Leaf, Vine, Berry, Signed, 4 In. | 651 |
| **Vase,** Brown Mottled Decoration At Base, Gold Flecks, Padded Discs, Cameo, 7 In. | 1540 |
| **Vase,** Bud, Amethyst Leaves, Flowers, Clear Ground, Silver Mounts, c.1900, 7 In., Pair | 2000 |
| **Vase,** Bud, Enameled Maroon Lilies, Green Stems, Leaves, c.1900, 4 ¾ In. | 1188 |
| **Vase,** Bud, Leaves, Stems, Pink Roses, Frosted Cream Ground, Cameo, 7 ¾ In. | 5036 |
| **Vase,** Bud, Square Shape, Purple Flowers, Stems, Leaves, Cameo, 3 ¾ In. | 1777 |
| **Vase,** Bud, Striated Yellow To Blue, Elongated Neck, 14 ¾ In. | 472 |

| | | |
|---|---|---|
| **Vase,** Bud, Yellow Neck, Enameled Red Berries, Green Leaves, Round Base, c.1900, 5 In. | | 1625 |
| **Vase,** Corset Diamond Shape, Textured Red & Green, Thistles, Gold Luster, Cameo, 5 In. | | 345 |
| **Vase,** Cranes, Lily Pond, Aquatic Plants, Green Textured, Gold Trim, Bulbous, 4 In. | | 4148 |
| **Vase,** Crimson Lake Scene, Yellow & Rose Mottled, Cylindrical, Cameo, 3½ In. | | 431 |
| **Vase,** Crocus, Carved Leaves, Mottled Yellow Shaded To Purple, Bulbous Foot, 12 In. | | 8888 |
| **Vase,** Cylindrical, Orange Mottled, Brown Tree Scene, Footed, Cameo, Signed, 10 In. | | 863 |
| **Vase,** Daisies, Deep Blue To Sky Blue, Enamel, Inscribed, c.1910, 14 x 2½ In. | *illus* | 9430 |
| **Vase,** Daisies, Leaves, Yellow To Raspberry To White, Cameo, Signed, 12 x 4 In. | *illus* | 7763 |
| **Vase,** Dark Pink Carved Flower, Yellow To Orange Ground, Footed, 9¾ In. | | 1770 |
| **Vase,** Dark Purple Flowers, Leaves, Frosted White Ground, Signed, 7½ In. | | 3555 |
| **Vase,** Enamel Pink Flowers, Mottled Yellow Ground, Etched, 4¾ In. | | 1755 |
| **Vase,** Fish, Wraps Around, Pate-De-Verre, Cobalt Blue To Orange, Footed, 7 x 5 In. | | 720 |
| **Vase,** Flowers, Blue To Yellow, Frosted High Handles, 11 In. | | 3300 |
| **Vase,** Flowers, Blue, Green To Purple To Blue To Sky Blue, Fire Polished, 11 x 3 In. | | 4485 |
| **Vase,** Flowers, Stems, Mottled, Green To Yellow To Cream, Bulbous, Lady's Leg Neck, 9 In. | | 1304 |
| **Vase,** Fuchsia Flowers, Stems, Leaves, Mottled Blue To White Ground, Cameo, 14 In. | | 3555 |
| **Vase,** Gilt Flowers, Mottled Amber To Rose, Green Flakes, Handles, France, c.1900, 8 x 5 In. | | 633 |
| **Vase,** Green Martele, Yellow Flowers, Leafy Stems, Mottled Blue Rim, Waisted, 20 In. | | 2415 |
| **Vase,** Green, Summer Landscape, Pillow, Signed, 4½ x 6 In. | | 4720 |
| **Vase,** Harbor, Ships, Silver, Rim, Leaf Foot, Cameo, 11½ In. | | 923 |
| **Vase,** Irises, Gilt, Cameo, 4¼ In. | | 461 |
| **Vase,** Leafless Trees, Snow, Amber Sky, Irregular Lip, Cameo, Signed, 9⅝ In. | | 7702 |
| **Vase,** Leafless Trees, Snow, Dutch Cabins, Windmills, White, Orange, Cameo, 4½ In. | | 2607 |
| **Vase,** Leafless Trees, Snow, Red Mottled Sky, Cameo, Signed, 10½ In. | | 7410 |
| **Vase,** Mottled Green, Gray, Wheat, Low Foot, 2¾ x 8¼ In. | | 545 |
| **Vase,** Mottled Orange Base, Applied Green Stalk, Gourd Shape, 11 In. | | 4080 |
| **Vase,** Mottled Purple & Pink, Blown Out, Majorelle, Iron Openwork Frame, 9¾ In. | *illus* | 1244 |
| **Vase,** Orange & Green Mottled, Fruit On Branch, Pillow Shape, Cameo, Signed, 4 x 5 In. | | 1610 |
| **Vase,** Pate-De-Verre Roses, Green Pink, Signed, 8½ In. | | 1230 |
| **Vase,** Pink Flowers, Green Leaves, Mottled White, Orange, Cameo, 3¼ In. | | 1540 |
| **Vase,** Pink, Purple Fuchsia, Green Leaves, 3-Sided Rim, Tapered, Footed, 13 In. | | 5557 |
| **Vase,** Purple, Gold Thistles, Flower Embossed Metal Rim, Cameo, Signed, 10 In. | | 805 |
| **Vase,** Rainbow, Thistles, Burgundy Enameled, Gold Highlights, Cameo, 5 In. | | 259 |
| **Vase,** Red & Pink, Flowers, Stems, Leaves, Mottled Orange Ground, Cameo, 6 In. | | 2844 |
| **Vase,** Red Anemones, Leaves, Vertical Stripe Cream & Rose Ground, Footed, 8 In. | | 8913 |
| **Vase,** Red Berries, Green Leaves, Purple Shaded To Yellow, Swollen Top, 6 In. | | 1840 |
| **Vase,** Red Berries, Green Leaves, Tapered Cylinder, Footed, 19 In. | | 1989 |
| **Vase,** Red Crocuses, Purple Ground, Signed, Cameo, 12⅛ In. | | 8295 |
| **Vase,** Red Flowers, Green Leaf Base, Long Neck, Flared Rim, Footed, 12 In. | | 3900 |
| **Vase,** Red Flowers, Yellow Ground, Cameo, 1915, 9¾ x 5¾ In. | | 984 |
| **Vase,** Red Foxgloves, Yellow Ground, Footed, Cross Of Lorraine, Cameo, 17 In. | | 2185 |
| **Vase,** Red Orange, Stylized Flowers, Mottled Stain Ground, Bulbous, Cameo, 6½ In. | | 1476 |
| **Vase,** Red Poppies, Mottled Cream Ground, Black Stems, Cameo, 7⅛ In. | | 8295 |
| **Vase,** Red Thistles, Green Leaves, Gold Trim, Signed, Cameo, 8½ In. | | 1066 |
| **Vase,** Roses, Pate-De-Verre, Etched Mark, Box, c.1970, 12 x 10½ In. | | 1320 |
| **Vase,** Sailboats In Harbor, Green Shaded To Mottled Yellow & Orange, Swollen, 8 In. | | 1778 |
| **Vase,** Scenic Rainy Landscape, Enameled Signature, France, c.1910, 11¾ In. | | 7670 |
| **Vase,** Sea Gull, Ocean, Gilt Sun, Sea Turtle, Cameo, Signed, 7½ In. | | 6636 |
| **Vase,** Sea Gull, Ocean, Sea Turtle, Gilt Setting Sun, Gilt Rim & Base, Cameo, 16 In. | | 10072 |
| **Vase,** Sea Gull, Ocean, Setting Sun, White Opalescent, Gray Enamel Accents, 8 In. | | 11850 |
| **Vase,** Spring Scene, Brown Trees, Green Leaves, Mottled Yellow, Pillow Form, 3 In. | | 2252 |
| **Vase,** Spring Scene, Foliage, Frosted Ground, Squared, France, c.1915, 5 x 3 In. | | 750 |
| **Vase,** Square Foot, Tapered, Brown, Orange, Green, Yellow, Striated, 24¼ In. | | 1422 |
| **Vase,** Square Shape, Violets, Green Stem, Leaves, White, Purple Ground, Cameo, 5 In. | | 3851 |
| **Vase,** Stick, Earth Tone Mottled, Bulbous Base, 6 In. | | 115 |
| **Vase,** Stylized Orange Flowers, Rust, Opaque Ground, Tapered, Signed, 8 In. | | 984 |
| **Vase,** Thistle, Brown, Textured Iridescent Ground, Squat Base, Tapered Neck, 4 In. | | 237 |
| **Vase,** Trees, Grass, Mountains In Distance, Squat Base, Elongated Neck, 6½ In. | | 3105 |
| **Vase,** Trees, Yellow, Orange, Leaves, Vines, Acid Etched, Cameo, 7½ In. | | 2706 |
| **Vase,** Tri-Pointed Rim, Tapered, Peach, White, Leaves, Etched, Circular Foot, 9 In. | | 1169 |
| **Vase,** Trumpet, Mottled Peach, White Ground, Squat Bulbous Bottom, 19 In. | | 1230 |
| **Vase,** Violet Flowers, Green Stems, Leaves, Mottled Cream To Purple, Cameo, 6½ In. | | 5036 |
| **Vase,** Violets, Green, Purple, White, Fire Polished, Square, Pinched Waist, 4½ x 3 In. | | 2185 |
| **Vase,** White Flowers, Brown Reeds, Blue Ground, Footed, 17⅜ In. | | 4680 |
| **Vase,** White Swan, On Pond, White Trees & Grasses, Gray Shading, Cylindrical, 9 In. | | 11850 |
| **Vase,** White, Lavender, Yellow, Iris, Green Leaf, Tulip Shape, Blue, Blown Out, 17 In. | | 885 |

**Daum,** Vase, Daisies, Leaves, Yellow To Raspberry To White, Cameo, Signed, 12 x 4 In.
**$7.763**

Humler & Nolan

---

**Daum,** Vase, Mottled Purple & Pink, Blown Out, Majorelle, Iron Openwork Frame, 9¾ In.
**$1,244**

James D. Julia Auctioneers

### Daum History

Cut and enameled glass was made by Daum. In 1885 Daum's sons Auguste (1853–1909) and Antonin (1864–1930) introduced Art Nouveau–style pâte-de-verre and cameo glass. Pieces were decorated with flowers, landscapes, and natural forms. In 1900 Daum joined Emile Gallé and Louis Majorelle to found the École de Nancy. Daum started making freeform clear glass in the 1950s. It reintroduced pâte-de-verre glass in 1966, using contemporary designs. Daum glass is still being made.

**De Vez,** Vase, Blue, Mountains, Trees, Lake, Cameo Cut, Star Shape Rim, 10¼ In.
$403

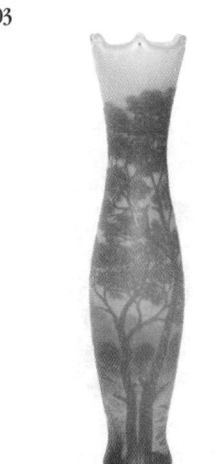

Early Auction Co.

**De Vez,** Vase, Oval, Pink, Sailors, Cameo, Signed, 6½ In.
$345

Early Auction Co.

**TIP**

*It is easy to glue pieces of broken china. Use a new fast-setting but not instant glue. Position the pieces correctly, then use tape to hold the parts together. If the piece needs special support, lean it in a suitable position in a box filled with sand.*

| | |
|---|---|
| **Vase,** Wine Barrel, Flowers, Stems, Leaves, Blue Staves, Green Ground, 8 In. | 4147 |
| **Vase,** Winter Church Scene, Blue, Birches, Snow, 7¾ In. | 4972 |
| **Vase,** Winter Scene, Barren Trees, Snowy Ground, Mottled Yellow, Tapered, 14 In. | 10665 |
| **Vase,** Winter Scene, Barren Trees, Snowy Ground, Orange & Brown, Pillow, 4¾ In. | 3200 |
| **Vase,** Winter Scene, Barren Trees, Snowy Ground, Yellow & Orange, 11 In. | 7110 |
| **Vase,** Winter Scene, Yellow, Signed, Cross Of Lorraine, c.1902, 4⅝ In. | 2829 |
| **Vase,** Yellow Flowers, Green Leaves, Stems, Yellow Ground, Signed, 10¾ In. | 2962 |
| **Vase,** Yellow, Green, Brown Trees, Grass, Mottled Purple, Cameo, Signed, 12 In. | 6517 |

**DAVENPORT** pottery and porcelain were made at the Davenport factory in Longport, Staffordshire, England, from 1793 to 1887. Earthenwares, creamwares, porcelains, ironstone, and other ceramics were made. Most of the pieces are marked with a form of the word *Davenport*.

DAVENPORT LONGPORT STAFFORDSHIRE

| | |
|---|---|
| **Bowl,** Ironstone, Flow Blue Amoy, 12-Sided, Flared, Round Base, c.1845, 4 x 7 In. | 173 |
| **Cachepot,** Pumpkin Ground, Orange Fruit, Leaves, Fish Head Handles, 5¼ In., Pair | 413 |
| **Ewer,** Basin, Amoy Pattern, Asian, Flower Scenes, Flow Blue, c.1850, 10 In., 12 In. | 374 |
| **Pitcher,** Bowl, Pink Luster, Muleteer, Black Transfer, Staffordshire, c.1830, 10 & 13 In. | 189 |
| **Pitcher,** Ironstone, Flow Blue Amoy, Hexagonal Paneled, c.1845, 8¼ In. | 460 |
| **Pot,** Pierced Lid, D-Shape, Tapered, Red, Black Flowers, Ring Handles, c.1805, 4 In. | 258 |
| **Tureen,** Soup, Lid, Ironstone, Flow Blue Amoy, Scroll Handles, Shell Finial, c.1845, 9 In. | 748 |
| **Warming Dish,** Flowers, Blue Applied Nozzle, Lobed, c.1835, 10½ In. | 23 |

**DAVY CROCKETT**, the American frontiersman, was born in 1786 and died in 1836. The historical character gained new fame in 1954 when the Walt Disney television show ran a series of episodes featuring Fess Parker as Davy Crockett. Coonskin caps and buckskins became popular and hundreds of different Davy Crockett items were made.

DAVY CROCKETT CONGRESSMAN

| | |
|---|---|
| **Clock,** Electric, Log Cabin Shape, Composition, Crocket, Handle, c.1955, 7 x 12 In. | 189 to 412 |
| **Game,** At The Alamo, Tin Litho Building, Plastic Figures, Walt Disney Prod., 11 x 23 In. | 413 |
| **Lamp,** Clock, Figural, Motion Light Cylinder, United Clock Corp., c.1955, 10½ In. | 233 |
| **Toy,** Cap Gun, 50-Shot Repeater, White Horse Head Grip, Nickel Plated, 1950s, 9 In. | 221 |
| **Toy,** Play Set, Davy Crockett At The Alamo, Box, Marx, 23 x 16 In. | 336 |

**DE VEZ** was a signature used on cameo glass after 1910. E. S. Monot founded the glass company near Paris in 1851. The company changed names many times. Mt. Joye, another glass by this factory, is listed in its own category.

*de Vez*

| | |
|---|---|
| **Vase,** Amber, Lake Scene, Flowering Branches, Signed, 8 In. | 805 |
| **Vase,** Blue, Mountains, Trees, Lake, Cameo Cut, Star Shape Rim, 10¼ In. ..............*illus* | 403 |
| **Vase,** Bulbous, Bottle Shape, Mountain Lake Scene, Sailing Shops, 7 In. | 518 |
| **Vase,** Cameo, Blue Ground, Black Flowers, Leaves, Bulbous, Waisted, c.1910, 5 In. | 270 |
| **Vase,** Landscape, House, Tapered, Purple, Red, Cream, 10¾ In. | 330 |
| **Vase,** Oval, Pink, Sailors, Cameo, Signed, 6½ In. ..............*illus* | 345 |
| **Vase,** Sailing Ships, Lake, Mountains, Red On Cream, Swollen, Tapered, 16 In. | 2415 |
| **Vase,** Scenic, Pine Trees, Lake, Mountains, Frosted Opalescent Ground, 10 In. | 729 |
| **Vase,** Trumpet, White, Brown Tree & Lake Scene, Tapered, Cup Rim, 7¼ In. | 374 |
| **Vase,** Yellow, Crimson Flowering Branch, Oval, Square Mouth, Signed, 4 In. | 144 |

**DECORATED TUMBLERS** *may be by maker or design or in Advertising, Coca-Cola, Pepsi-Cola, Sports, and other categories.*

**DECOYS** are carved or turned wooden copies of birds, fish, or animals. The decoy was placed in the water or propped on the shore to lure flying birds to the pond for hunters. Some decoys are handmade; some are commercial products. Today there is a group of artists making modern decoys for display, not for use in a pond. Many sell for high prices.

| | |
|---|---|
| **American Widgeon Hen,** Low Head, Stamped, William Quinn | 16100 |
| **American Widgeon,** Baldpate Drake, William H. Howell, Glass Eyes, Cork Body | 295 |
| **Black Duck,** Folk Art, Root, Paint, c.1875, 11 x 5½ In. | 155 |
| **Bluebill,** Delaware River, Glass Eyes, Hollow, Tony Bianco, 12 In. | 325 |
| **Brant,** Carved, Black, Gray, White Paint, New Jersey, c.1920, 18 In. | 148 |
| **Brant,** Carved, Painted, Harry V. Shourds, c.1900, 16¾ In. | 360 |
| **Brant,** Marked Fenmore, 16 In. | 219 |
| **Brant,** Shoot Scars, Charles Parker, American, 1800-50, 18 In. | 270 |
| **Canada Goose,** Carved Wing Detail, Original Paint, c.1950, 23 In. | 1046 |
| **Canada Goose,** Carved, Brown, Tan Paint, 11 x 20 In. | 120 |

| | | |
|---|---|---|
| **Canada Goose,** Carved, Painted, 11 x 20 In. | | 120 |
| **Canada Goose,** Feeding, Glass Eyes, Delaware Valley, c.1910, 26 x 7 In. | | 281 |
| **Canada Goose,** Hollow Carved, Glass Eye, Meredith & Thos. Chambers, 1870s | | 31050 |
| **Canada Goose,** Naive Swimming Form, Newfoundland, 27 In. | | 150 |
| **Canada Goose,** Pine, Painted, Turned Head, Glass Eyes, Carved, c.1890, 25 x 13 In. | | 1185 |
| **Canada Goose,** Swimming, Carved Wings, White, Black Paint, c.1970, 35 In. | | 160 |
| **Canada Goose,** Wood, Canvas Cover, Black, White, Yellow Paint, 14¾ x 20¾ In. | | 480 |
| **Canada Goose,** Wood, Canvas Cover, Paint, 13 x 31 In. | | 480 |
| **Canada Goose,** Wood, Canvas, 13 x 31 In. | | 480 |
| **Canada Goose,** Wood, Canvas, 16 x 28 In. | | 360 |
| **Canvasback Drake,** Red Head, Carved, Painted, Glass Eyes, Mason, c.1925, 7 x 14 In. | | 431 |
| **Canvasback Hen,** Carved, Glass Eyes, Painted Details, Mason Premier, Detroit, 15 In. | | 840 |
| **Canvasback,** Glass Eyes, Black Beak, 1950s, 15 In. | | 210 |
| **Canvasback,** Wood, Carved, Painted, c.1920, 17 In. | | 210 |
| **Crow,** Balsa, Carved, Black Paint, Wire Support, c.1965, 11½ In. | | 111 |
| **Dove,** Gray, Black Paint, Wood, 14½ In. | | 71 |
| **Duck,** Carved, Black Paint, 7 x 14½ In. | | 56 |
| **Duck,** Preening, Painted Eyes, Lead Weight, 1900s, 6 x 13 In. | | 374 |
| **Duck,** Wood, Cork, Carved, Painted, Connecticut, 7 x 18¾ In. | | 708 |
| **Duck,** Wood, Glass Eyes, Paint, Branded WJM, Mason, c.1925, 6 x 14 In. | | 690 |
| **Eider,** Carved, White, Black Paint, Maine, c.1900, 15¾ In. | | 330 |
| **Eider,** Wood, Canvas Covered, 12½ x 22½ In. | | 240 |
| **Fish,** Muskie, 7½ In. | | 154 |
| **Fish,** Sucker Fish, Wood, Carved, Painted, Copper Fins, Tack Eyes, Green Paint, 11 In. | | 660 |
| **Fish,** Trout, Wood, Carved, Painted, Oscar Peterson, Cadillac, Michigan, 9 In. | | 1680 |
| **Golden Eye Drake,** Wood, Carved, Painted, New England, 8 x 12 In. | | 708 |
| **Goose,** Canvas Over Wood Slat, Joseph Whiting, Lincoln, c.1930, 28 In. | | 1440 |
| **Goose,** Canvas, Over Wood Slat, c.1920, 28 In. | | 1440 |
| **Goose,** Canvas, Straw Filled, Weighted, c.1900 | | 425 |
| **Goose,** Cork, Carved, Painted, Madison Mitchell, c.1935, 11 x 25 In. | | 161 |
| **Heron,** Carved, Painted, c.1920, 58 x 36 In. | | 127 |
| **Hooded Merganser,** Paint, Glass Eyes, American, c.1950, 11 In. | | 738 |
| **Hooded Merganser,** Wood, Ringlet Neck, Tack Eyes, Lead Weight On Base, 6 x 18 In. | | 531 |
| **Long-Billed Curlew,** Carved, Painted, New Jersey, 8½ x 24 In. | | 2640 |
| **Mallard Drake,** Carved, Blue, Green, Black Paint, 11 x 22 In. | | 300 |
| **Mallard Drake,** Carved, Painted, 11 x 22 In. | | 300 |
| **Mallard,** Carved, Gray, Brown Paint, c.1915, 16 In. | | 123 |
| **Mallard,** Hollow, Charles Schoenheider, American, 1800-50, 17 In. | | 250 |
| **Mallard,** Wood, Paint, Glass Eyes, Alz & Co., 15 In. | | 21 |
| **Merganser,** Painted, American, 11 In. | | 123 |
| **Merganser,** Wood, Carved Wing Detail, Painted, Glass Eyes, c.1930, 19 In. | | 369 |
| **Owl,** Metal, Dimpled, Wood Beak & Ears, Glass Eyes, Steel Talons, Folk Art, 19 In. | | 390 |
| **Pintail,** Glass Eyes, Robert Ellison, 15½ In. | | 240 |
| **Redhead Drake,** Carved, c.1875, 12 In. | | 738 |
| **Ruddy Duck Drake,** Heders Inc., c.1893 | | 150 |
| **Sea Gull,** Carved, Glass Eyes, Gray, Black, Cream, Yellow, Red Paint, 17½ In. | | 240 |
| **Smew,** Blue, Gray, Signed Wilson Ditty | | 180 |
| **Snow Goose,** Hollow Carved, Jim Keefer, c.1985, 19 In. | | 180 |
| **Swan,** Carved, Paint, Lead Weight, c.1950, 17 x 26 In. | | 270 |
| **Swan,** Carved, Painted, 20th Century, 21 x 37 In. | | 689 |
| **Trumpeter Swan,** Carved, White, Gray Paint, M.J. Gray, Maine, c.1965, 12 x 23 In. | | 2640 |
| **Trumpeter Swan,** Sleeping, Carved, Painted, M.J. Gray, c.1950, 12 x 23½ In. | | 2640 |
| **Trumpeter Swan,** Sleeping, Carved, White, Black Paint, Chesapeake Bay, 32 In. | | 1140 |
| **Trumpeter Swan,** White, Black Paint, Glass Eyes, Carved, Chesapeake Bay, 32 In. | | 1140 |
| **Trumpeter Swan,** Wood, Hollow, Canvas Cover, Paint, E.W., 14 x 33 In. | | 300 |

**DEDHAM POTTERY** was started in 1895. Chelsea Keramic Art Works was established in 1872 in Chelsea, Massachusetts, by members of the Robertson family. The factory closed in 1889 and was reorganized as the Chelsea Pottery U.S. in 1891. The firm used the marks *CKAW* and *CPUS*. It became the Dedham Pottery of Dedham, Massachusetts. The factory closed in 1943. It was famous for its crackleware dishes, which picture blue outlines of animals, flowers, and other natural motifs. Pottery by Chelsea Keramic Art Works and Dedham Pottery is listed here.

| | | |
|---|---|---|
| **Chestnut,** Plate, Blue & White, 6 In., 2 Piece | | 189 |
| **Clover,** Vase, Adeline Gates, Chelsea Keramic, Signed, 1881, 4¼ x 4 In. | *illus* | 2500 |
| **Crab,** Plate, Blue & White, 8½ In. | | 369 |
| **Dolphin,** Plate, Blue & White, Marked, 1896-1928, 8½ In. | *illus* | 1169 |

**Dedham,** Clover, Vase, Adeline Gates, Chelsea Keramic, Signed, 1881, 4¼ x 4 In.
$2,500

Rago Arts & Auction Center

**Dedham,** Dolphin, Plate, Blue & White, Marked, 1896-1928, 8½ In.
$1,169

Skinner Auctioneers & Appraisers

**Dedham,** Polar Bear, Plate, Blue & White, Marked, 1896-1928, 10 In.
$923

Skinner Auctioneers & Appraisers

**Dedham,** Poppy, Plate, Central Poppy, Blue & White, Marked, 1896-1943, 8½ In.
$369

Skinner Auctioneers & Appraisers

**Delft,** Charger, Multicolor Flowers, Tin Glaze, 18th Century, 2 ½ x 13 ½ In. $472

Brunk Auctions

**Delft,** Tile, Ships In Battle Scene, Blue & White, 1800s, 6 x 6 In. Tiles, 24 Pieces $1,722

Skinner Auctioneers & Appraisers

**Delft,** Vase, Jacoba, Incised, Adolf LeComte, Holland, 1910, 15 In. $4,063

Rago Arts & Auction Centera

| | |
|---|---|
| **Double Moth,** Plate, Blue & White, 9 ¾ In. | 2091 |
| **Double Turtle,** Plate, 8 ½ In. | 1783 |
| **Fairbanks House,** Plate, Blue & White, 8 ¾ In. | 984 |
| **Fairbanks House,** Rabbit Border, Plate, 8 ¾ In. | 960 |
| **Grape,** Bowls, Blue & White, 6 ½ In., 2 Piece | 153 |
| **Grape,** Plate Set, Blue & White, 8 ½ In. | 443 |
| **Polar Bear,** Plate, Blue & White, Marked, 1896-1928, 10 In. ........*illus* | 923 |
| **Poppy,** Plate, Central Poppy, Blue & White, Marked, 1896-1943, 8 ½ In. ....*illus* | 369 |
| **Rabbit,** Bowl, 5 ¼ In., Pair | 165 |
| **Swan,** Plate, Blue & White, 9 ¾ In. | 215 |
| **Turtle,** Plate, Blue & White, 8 ½ In. | 215 |
| **Vase,** White Crackle Glaze, Bulbous, 4 ½ x 5 In. | 438 |

**DEGUE** is a signature acid-etched on pieces of French glass made by the Cristalleries de Compiegne in the early 1900s. Cameo, mold blown, and smooth glass with contrasting colored rims are the types most often found.

*Degué*

| | |
|---|---|
| **Chandelier,** 4-Light, Frosted, Metal, Brass Fittings, Signed, Bowl, 1930s, 30 x 22 In. | 704 |
| **Vase,** Pine Cone, Carved, Blue Mottled Pink Ground, Cameo, Signed, c.1920, 5 In. | 270 |
| **Vase,** Scenic, Camel, Red Matte Over Orange Mottled, Cameo, Signed, 8 ¼ In. | 345 |

**DELDARE**, *see Buffalo Pottery Deldare.*

**DELFT** is a special type of tin-glazed pottery. Early delft was made in Holland and England during the seventeenth century. It was usually decorated with blue on a white surface, but some was polychrome, decorated with green, yellow, and other colors. Most delftware pieces were dishes needed for everyday living. Figures were made from about 1750 to 1800, and are rare. Although the soft tin-glazed pottery was well-known, it was not named delft until after 1840, when it was named for the city in Holland where much of it was made. Porcelain became more popular because it was more durable and Holland gradually stopped making the old delft. In 1876 De Porceleyne Fles factory in Delft introduced a porcelain ware that was decorated with blue and white scenes of Holland that reminded many of old delft. It became popular with the Dutch and tourists. By 1990 all of the blue and white porcelain with Dutch scenes was made in Asia, although it was marked *Delft*. Only one Dutch company remains that makes the traditional old-style delft with blue on white or with colored decorations. Most of the pieces sold today were made after 1891, and the name *Holland* usually appears with the Delft factory marks. The word *Delft* appears alone on some inexpensive twentieth- and twenty-first-century pottery from Asia and Germany that is also listed here.

*Delft*

| | |
|---|---|
| **Bowl,** Blue & White, Peacock, Landscape, Leaves, London, c.1670, 10 In. | 660 |
| **Bowl,** Flowers, Footed, Fazackerly, c.1750, 4 x 9 In. | 431 |
| **Bowl,** Shaving, Tin Glazed, Multicolor Flowers, Leaves, White, Oval, 3 x 12 In. | 212 |
| **Centerpiece,** Blue, White, Ribbed Body, Allover Flowers, c.1750, 5 ½ x 10 In. | 900 |
| **Charger,** Adam & Eve, Tree With Serpent, Applies, Border Band, c.1710, 14 In. | 4012 |
| **Charger,** Adam, Eve, Snake, Tree, Multicolor, England, c.1760, 13 In. | 7200 |
| **Charger,** Blue, White, Flowers, c.1750, 13 ¾ In., Pair | 594 |
| **Charger,** Landscape, Blue, Leaf Border, Holland, 18th Century, 14 In. | 594 |
| **Charger,** Multicolor Flowers, Garlands, Tin Glaze, England, c.1810, 13 ½ In. | 300 |
| **Charger,** Multicolor Flowers, Tin Glaze, 18th Century, 2 ½ x 13 ½ In. ....*illus* | 472 |
| **Charger,** Royal Portrait, Blue, Green, Yellow, Dutch, c.1700, 14 x 14 In., Pair | 9600 |
| **Charger,** Tree, Woman, Cornucopia, Allegorical Plenty, Dutch, c.1755, 14 In. | 960 |
| **Charger,** Tulip, Lily, Leaves, Blue, Red, Yellow, England, c.1700, 13 In. | 6900 |
| **Console,** City, Earthenware, Octagon Shape, Handles, 15 ½ In. | 120 |
| **Ewer,** Blue & White, Bird, Perched On Rock, Flower Garden, 8 ½ In. | 480 |
| **Ewer,** Songbird, In Garden, Blue & White, Stripe & Dot Handle, c.1700, 8 ½ In. | 1320 |
| **Figurine,** Cow, Lying Down, Blue, White, Multicolor Flowers, c.1750, 5 ¼ In. | 600 |
| **Flower Brick,** Blue & White, Landscape, Pagoda, Houses, Recessed Foot, c.1750, 6 In. | 660 |
| **Garniture,** Seated Foo Dogs, Stylized Flowers, Scrolling, Octagonal, 16 In., Pair | 1652 |
| **Jar,** Blue & White Flowers, Leaves, Octagonal, Ribbed Body, 12 ¾ In. | 259 |
| **Jug,** Chinese Figure In Landscape, Blue, Iron Red, Holland, 18th Century, 7 ⅝ In. | 246 |
| **Panel,** Hunter & Squire, Blue & White, 42 Tiles, 34 x 35 In. | 1121 |
| **Plaque,** Painted, Windmill, Blue, White, 5 x 6 ¼ In. | 150 |
| **Plaque,** Pastoral Village Scene, Blue, White, Oval, Shaped, 23 x 19 In., Pair | 1000 |
| **Plaque,** Winter Harbor Scene, Gargoyle Mask, Scalloped Edge, Oval, c.1890, 23 x 19 In. | 474 |
| **Plate,** Blue, Urn, Peacock Feathers, Holland, 10 ½ In. | 180 |
| **Plate,** Chinese Woman, Tree, Diaperwork, Blue, Green, Yellow, Bristol, c.1750, 9 In., Pair | 720 |
| **Plate,** Couple, Landscape, Trellis Border, Blue, Green, Yellow, Purple, Dutch, c.1750, 12 ½ In. | 960 |
| **Plate,** Flowers, Insects, Blue, Green, Red, Bristol, c.1745, 13 In. | 1440 |

| | |
|---|---:|
| **Plate,** Peacock, Ocher, Green, Brown, Vase, Flower Border, De Vergulde Bloempot, 1700s, 9 In.... | 600 |
| **Plate,** Stag, Flower Borders, Multicolor, Continental, 18th Century, 9 In......... | 210 |
| **Posset,** Pot, Lid, Peacock, Grass, Bird, Flowers, Blue, White, Handles, England, c.1725, 8 In....... | 3240 |
| **Punch Bowl,** Multicolor Vines, Flowers, c.1820, 5 x 11 ½ In......... | 420 |
| **Punch Bowl,** Pagoda, Flowers, Scrolls, Bianco-Sopra-Bianco, England, 1760, 10 In. ........... | 3360 |
| **Puzzle,** Jug, Blue, White, Text, Hearts, Flowers, 7 In......... | 360 |
| **Stein,** Deer, Blue Ground, Pewter, Lid, Holland, 18th Century, 9 ½ In......... | 390 |
| **Tankard,** Hinged Lid, Loop Handle, Blue, Yellow, Red, Green, Signed, c.1800, 9 In......... | 230 |
| **Tea Canister,** Blue, White, Parrots, Flowers, Cone Top, England, c.1745, 6 In......... | 1320 |
| **Tile,** Ships In Battle Scene, Blue & White, 1800s, 6 x 6 In. Tiles, 24 Piece ...............*illus* | 1722 |
| **Vase,** Blue & White, Flared Rim, 18th Century, 9 ½ In......... | 225 |
| **Vase,** Jacoba, Incised, Adolf LeComte, Holland, 1910, 15 In......................*illus* | 4063 |
| **Vase,** Lid, Batavian Brown, Blue & White Flower, Octagonal, Holland, 7 In., Pair......... | 338 |
| **Vase,** Pierced Lid, Leaves, Framed Panels, Landscapes, Windmill, Lovers, 22 ½ In......... | 523 |
| **Vase,** Stick Neck, Blue & White Flowers, 6 ½ In., Pair......... | 42 |
| **Vase,** Tulip, 9 Openings, Blue, White, Dragon Handles, c.1960, 12 In., Pair ......... | 211 |
| **Wall Pocket,** Blue & White, Woman's Head, c.1790, 9 x 6 ½ In., Pair......... | 944 |

**DENTAL** cabinets, chairs, equipment, and other related items are listed here. Other objects may be found in the Medical category.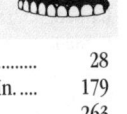

| | |
|---|---:|
| **Arnica Tooth Soap,** Tin, Hinged Lid, Pocket, 3 x 2 In......... | 28 |
| **Brown's Camphorated Saponaceous Dentifrice,** Bottle, Clear, Oval, Contents, Cork, 3 In. .... | 179 |
| **Cabinet,** 8 Graduated Drawers, Clear Knobs, Wood, American Cabinet, 12 x 39 In. ......... | 263 |
| **Chair,** Black Metal, Tan Upholstery, Head Rest, 19th Century, 47 x 29 In......... | 112 |
| **Chair,** Wood, Cast Iron, Red A's, Gold Stripes ......... | 1140 |
| **Dr. I.W. Lyon's Perfect Tooth Powder,** Tin, Woman, 25 Cents, Contents, Box, 3¾ In. ......... | 202 |
| **Drill,** Foot Pedal, Cast Iron, 1800s, 62 In......... | 180 |
| **Goettings Medicated Tooth Powder,** Bottle, Clear, Oval, 3¼ In. ......... | 95 |
| **Peroxigen Tooth Wash,** Bottle, 6-Sided, Embossed, Crown Glass Stopper, 5¼ In......... | 235 |
| **Sign,** Albumen Print, Man, Top Hat, Green Velvet Matte, Teeth, Bone, 31 x 22 In......... | 6728 |
| **Sign,** Dr. Hyman, Painless Dentist, Little Cost, Phila., Tin Arrow, Yellow, Red, 19 In. ......... | 150 |
| **Tod'Co Waxed Dental Floss,** Owl Drug Co., Tin, Round, Hole & Cutter On Top, 1 In......... | 22 |
| **Toothbrush,** Klenzo, White, United Drug Co., Boston, Box, 6¾ In......... | 50 |

**DENVER** is part of the mark on an American art pottery. William Long of Steubenville, Ohio, founded the Lonhuda Pottery Company in 1892. In 1900 he moved to Denver, Colorado, and organized the Denver China and Pottery Company. This pottery, which used the mark *Denver*, worked until 1905, when Long moved to New Jersey and founded the Clifton Pottery. Long also worked for Weller Pottery, Roseville Pottery, and American Encaustic Tiling Company. Do not confuse this pottery with the Denver White Pottery, which worked from 1894 to 1955 in Denver.

DENVER
C T &
P Co

| | |
|---|---:|
| **Vase,** Light Blue, White Trees, Signed, 6 In......... | 242 |
| **Vase,** Pinecones, Pine Boughs, Cream Ground, Green, Brown, 5⅝ In. ......... | 196 |

**DEPRESSION GLASS** is an inexpensive glass that was manufactured in large quantities during the 1920s and early 1930s. It was made in many colors and patterns by dozens of factories in the United States. Most patterns were also made in clear glass, which the factories called *crystal*. If no color is listed here, it is clear. The name *Depression glass* is a modern one and also refers to machine-made glass of the 1940s through 1970s. Sets missing a few pieces can be completed through the help of a matching service.

| | |
|---|---:|
| **Adam,** Bowl, Cereal, Pink, 5 In......... | 12 |
| **Adam,** Bowl, Pink, Lid, 9 In......... | 37 |
| **Adam,** Pitcher, Pink, 7 ½ In......... | 7 |
| **Adam,** Tumbler, Iced Tea, Pink, Footed, 5 ½ In......... | 40 |
| **Adam,** Tumbler, Pink, Square Footed, 1932-34, 4 ½ In., 4 Piece ......... | 148 |
| **Adam,** Vase, Pink, 7 In......... | 199 |
| **American Sweetheart,** Plate, Monex White, 12 In. ......... | 20 |
| **American Sweetheart,** Platter, Pink, 13 In......... | 65 |
| **Anniversary,** Creamer, Pink, Footed, 1947-49, 3¼ In. ......... | 18 |
| **Apple Blossom** pattern is listed here as Dogwood. | |
| **Aunt Polly,** Tumblers, Blue, 1920s, Pair ......... | 78 |
| **Aurora,** Creamer, Cobalt Blue, Hazel Atlas, 1935, 4⅜ In. ......... | 14 |
| **Aurora,** Cup & Saucer, Cobalt Blue, Late 1930s, 6 Piece ......... | 128 |
| **Ballerina** pattern is listed here as Cameo. | |
| **Bamboo Optic,** Creamer, Green......... | 8 |

D

**Derby,** Urn, 3 Figures, Boat, Castle, Cobalt Blue, Gold Trim, Handles, c.1800, 12½ In.
$450

DuMouchelles Art Gallery

**Dick Tracy,** Toy, B.O. Plenty, Waddles, Holds Baby, Tips Hat, Tin Lithograph, Windup, Marx, 8½ In.
$89

Bertoia Auctions

**Dick Tracy,** Toy, Burglar Alarm Kit, Flashlight, String Tags, Box, 1930s, 8 x 13 In.
$399

Hake's Americana & Collectibles

**Dinnerware,** Eva Zeisel, Casserole, Duck Head Cover, Great Western Stoneware, 1940s, 9 In.
$875

Rago Arts & Auction Center

**Dionne Quintuplets,** Doll, 5 Babies, Composition, Scooter, Madame Alexander, c.1935, 7 In. Dolls
$840

Theriault's

## Cherry Blossom

Cherry Blossom is one of the most popular Depression glass patterns. It was made by Jeannette Glass Company, Jeannette, Pennsylvania, from 1930 to 1939. Full dinner sets, serving pieces, and a child's set were made in a range of colors. Pieces were made in Crystal, Delphite (opaque blue), Green Jadite, Pink, and Red. Molds were changed, resulting in several shapes and styles for some pieces. Reproductions have been made.

| | |
|---|---:|
| **Block** pattern is listed here as Block Optic. | |
| **Block Optic,** Cup & Saucer, Pink, 2¼ x 6¼ In. | 5 |
| **Block Optic,** Sugar & Creamer, Pink, 1929-33 | 34 |
| **Block,** Cup & Saucer, Optic Green, Anchor Hocking | 13 |
| **Block,** Goblet, Optic Pink, Anchor Hocking, 9 Oz., 5¾ In. | 30 |
| **Block,** Sandwich Tray, Optic Pink, Anchor Hocking, 10¼ In. | 22 |
| **Block,** Tumbler, Optic Pink, Footed, Anchor Hocking, 9 Oz., 4¾ In. | 17 |
| **Bouquet & Lattice** pattern is listed here as Normandie. | |
| **Bowknot,** Custard, Cup, Green, 4¼ x 2½ In. | 10 |
| **Bowknot,** Tumbler, Green, Footed, 5 In. | 20 |
| **Bubble,** Berry Bowl, Anchor Hocking, 8⅜ In. | 7 |
| **Bubble,** Bowl, Cereal, Anchor Hocking, 5¼ In. | 5 |
| **Bubble,** Cup & Saucer, Anchor Hocking | 3 |
| **Bubble,** Relish, Leaf Shape | 4 |
| **Bubble,** Soup, Dish, Anchor Hocking, 7¾ In. | 8 |
| **Bullseye** pattern is listed here as Bubble. | |
| **Buttons & Bows** pattern is listed here as Holiday. | |
| **By Cracky,** Plate, Amber, L.E. Smith, 8 In., 10 Piece | 70 |
| **Cabbage Rose** pattern is listed here as Sharon. | |
| **Cameo,** Butter, Cover | 232 |
| **Cameo,** Decanter, Cameo, Satin Glass, 1930s, 10¼ x 5 In. | 75 |
| **Cameo,** Platter, Green, 13½ In. | 15 |
| **Cameo,** Sherbet, Green, 3⅛ In., 6 Piece | 118 |
| **Candlewick** pattern is listed in the Imperial Glass category. | |
| **Cape Cod,** Plate, Dinner, 10 In. | 22 |
| **Caprice** pattern is included in the Cambridge Glass category. | |
| **Catalonia,** Vase, Green, Trumpet, 5 In. | 52 |
| **Charm,** Cup & Saucer, Azurite, 1950-56, 8 Piece | 62 |
| **Cherry Blossom,** Berry Bowl, Pink | 2 |
| **Cherry Blossom,** Bowl, Cereal, Pink, 1¾ x 6 In., 3 Piece | 44 |
| **Cherry Blossom,** Bowl, Pink, 8½ x 2½ In. | 48 |
| **Cherry Blossom,** Cake Plate, Pink | 5 |
| **Cherry Blossom,** Cup & Saucer, Green | 27 |
| **Cherry Blossom,** Cup & Saucer, Pink | 32 |
| **Cherry Blossom,** Pitcher, Pink, 6½ In. | 10 |
| **Cherry Blossom,** Tumbler, Pink, Footed, 1930s, 4 Oz., 3¾ In., 4 Piece | 72 |
| **Chinex Classic,** Sherbet, 4¼ x 2⅜ In. | 5 |
| **Circle,** Goblet, Green, 5¾ x 3⅛ In., 4 Piece | 48 |
| **Cleo,** Ice Bucket, Green, Bail Handle, 5¾ x 5½ In. | 125 |
| **Cloverleaf,** Cup & Saucer, Pink, Hazel Atlas | 15 |
| **Cloverleaf,** Sherbet, Green | 8 |
| **Colonial Block,** Creamer, Pink, 3½ x 4 In. | 21 |
| **Colony,** Pitcher, Green, 6½ x 5½ In. | 30 |
| **Columbia,** Bowl, Ruffled Edge, 10½ In. | 17 |
| **Columbia,** Cup & Saucer | 7 |
| **Crackle,** Sherbet, Footed, 3 x 4 In., 4 Piece | 28 |
| **Cube** pattern is listed here as Cubist. | |
| **Cubist,** Sugar, Pink, Open, 2½ x 3½ In. | 9 |
| **Dancing Girl** pattern is listed here as Cameo. | |
| **Diamond** pattern is listed here as Miss America. | |
| **Diamond Quilted,** Creamer, Black | 12 |
| **Diamond Quilted,** Creamer, Pink | 18 |
| **Diana,** Bowl, Cereal, Pink, 5 In. | 6 |
| **Diana,** Creamer, Amber | 8 |
| **Diana,** Plate, Bead & Butter, Pink, 6 In. | 3 |
| **Diana,** Platter, Amber, Oval, 12 In. | 11 |
| **Diana,** Sugar & Creamer, Pink | 10 |
| **Dogwood,** Plate, Luncheon, Pink, 8 In. | 12 |
| **Doric & Pansy,** Plate, Green, 9⅛ In., 3 Piece | 65 |
| **Doric,** Pitcher, Green, 32 Oz., 5½ In. | 40 |
| **Doric,** Platter, Pink, Round, 12 In. | 4 |
| **Doric,** Salt & Pepper, Pink | 25 |
| **Dutch Rose** pattern is listed here as Rosemary. | |
| **English Hobnail,** Strawholder, 9¾ x 4 In. | 81 |
| **Fan Fold,** Napkin Holder, 4¼ x 4 In. | 34 |
| **Fine Rib** pattern is listed here as Homespun. | |

Flat Diamond pattern is listed in the Imperial Glass category.

| | |
|---|---:|
| **Floral,** Beverage Set, Pitcher, Cone Shape, Footed, Pink, 6 Tumblers, 8 & 5 In. | 275 |
| **Floral,** Cup, Pink | 21 |
| **Floral,** Salt & Pepper, Pink, 4 In. | 7 |
| **Floral,** Salt & Pepper, Pink, 6 In. | 8 |
| **Floral,** Vegetable, Divided, Pink | 6 |
| **Florentine No. 1,** Cup, Pink, Footed, 3 ½ x 2 ¼ In. | 10 |
| **Florentine No. 2,** Sugar & Creamer, Pink, 3 ¾ x 2 ¼ In. | 22 |
| **Forest Green,** Canister, Lid, Coffee, Diagonal Ridge, 40 Oz., 7 In. | 68 |
| **Forest Green,** Cordial, Footed, 3 ½ In. | 29 |
| **Forest Green,** Juice Set, 1952, 36 Oz. Pitcher, 6 Tumblers | 58 |
| **Forest Green,** Shaker, Diagonal Ridges, Metal Lid, 4 ½ In. | 19 to 35 |
| **Fortune,** Bowl, Dessert, Pink, Tab Handle, 5 x 1 ¼ In. | 12 |
| **Fortune,** Plate, Sherbet, Pink, 6 ¾ In. | 5 |
| **Fruits,** Berry Bowl, Green, 4 ½ x 1 ¾ In. | 45 |
| **Fruits,** Cup, Pink | 18 |
| **Georgian Lovebirds,** Berry Bowl, Green, 4 ½ In. | 8 |
| **Georgian,** Butter, Green | 54 |
| **Gracious Living,** Pitcher & Tumbler Set, Balloons, Stripes, 9 In. & 4 In., 9 Piece | 119 |

Hairpin pattern is listed here as Newport.

Hex Optic pattern is listed here as Hexagon Optic.

| | |
|---|---:|
| **Hexagon Optic,** Pitcher, Lemonade, 8 ½ In. | 65 |
| **Hobnail,** Saucer, Pink, 6 ⅜ In., Pair | 5 |
| **Holiday,** Candlestick, c.1950, 3 In., Pair | 130 |
| **Homespun,** Creamer, Pink, 1939-49, 3 ⅜ In. | 15 |
| **Homespun,** Pitcher, Tilt, Cobalt Blue, 32 Oz. | 52 |
| **Homespun,** Tumbler, Juice, Pink, Footed, 5 Oz., 4 In., 6 Piece | 86 |
| **Homestead,** Sugar, Pink, L.E. Smith, Late 1920s | 22 |

Honeycomb pattern is listed here as Hexagon Optic.

Horizontal Ribbed pattern is listed here as Manhattan.

Horseshoe pattern is listed here as No. 612.

Iris & Herringbone pattern is listed here as Iris.

| | |
|---|---:|
| **Iris,** Goblet, Cocktail, 1930s, 4 ½ Oz., 4 ¼ In. | 19 |
| **Iris,** Sugar, Lid, Iridescent, 5 ¾ x 5 ¾ In. | 25 |
| **Iris,** Vase, Marigold, 9 x 5 ½ In. | 28 |
| **Ivy,** Butter, Cover, Rectangular, 7 ¼ x 2 ¾ In. | 28 |
| **Jadeite,** Grease Jar, Tulip Floral Top, 1940s | 110 |
| **Jadeite,** Measuring Cup Set, Embossed Handles, 1930s, 4 Piece | 145 |
| **Jubilee,** Goblet, Water, Topaz, Lancaster Glass, 12 Oz., 6 In. | 127 |

Lace Edge pattern is listed here as Old Colony. There is also a pattern called Lace Edge listed in the Imperial Glass category.

| | |
|---|---:|
| **Leaf & Blossom,** Snack Set, Jade-Ite, Plate, Bowl | 48 |

Line 300 pattern is listed in the Paden City category as Peacock & Wild Rose.

| | |
|---|---:|
| **Lorain Basket,** Cup & Saucer, Yellow, c.1930 | 17 |

Lorna pattern is included in the Cambridge Glass category.

Lovebirds pattern is listed here as Georgian.

| | |
|---|---:|
| **Madrid,** Cookie Jar, Lid, Topaz, 7 ½ x 5 In. | 50 |
| **Madrid,** Cup & Saucer, Pink | 15 |
| **Madrid,** Plate, Luncheon, 8 ⅞ In. | 5 |
| **Madrid,** Sherbet, Cone Shape, Blue, 2 ⅞ In. | 11 |
| **Madrid,** Sugar & Creamer, Pink | 15 |
| **Manhattan,** Candleholder, 1 ¼ x 4 ¼ In., Pair | 21 |
| **Manhattan,** Candy Dish, Pink, Footed, Round, 2 ¼ x 6 ¼ In. | 14 |
| **Manhattan,** Relish, Handle, 4 Sections, 14 x 15 ¾ In. | 15 |
| **Manhattan,** Vase, 1938-43, 8 x 5 ¼ In. | 35 |

Martha Washington pattern is included in the Cambridge Glass category.

| | |
|---|---:|
| **Mayfair Open Rose,** Biscuit Jar, Lid, 14 In. | 12 |
| **Mayfair Open Rose,** Plate, Salad, Amber, 6 ¾ In. | 6 |
| **Mayfair Open Rose,** Salt & Pepper, Blue, Zinc Top, 4 ⅝ In. | 149 |
| **Mayfair Open Rose,** Salt & Pepper, Pink, Zinc Lids, 1930s, 4 ½ In. | 65 |
| **Mayfair Open Rose,** Serving Bowl, Pink, Handles, 1930s, 11 ½ In. | 28 |
| **Mayfair Open Rose,** Sugar, Rose Pink, Handles, Anchor Hocking | 24 |
| **Mayfair Open Rose,** Tray, Center Handle, Pink, 12 In. | 16 |
| **Miss America,** Bowl, Pink, 8 In. | 25 |
| **Miss America,** Compote, Pink, Square Foot | 17 |
| **Miss America,** Goblet, Water, Pink, Square Foot, 5 ½ In., 5 Piece | 70 |

**Dirk Van Erp,** Lamp, Copper, Hammered, 4-Panel Mica Shade, Stamped, c.1912, 21 ½ x 20 In.
$6,250

Rago Arts & Auction Center

**Disneyana,** Ashtray, Mickey Mouse, Mickey, Rag Style, Standing, Matchbox Block, c.1935, 3 x 4 In.
$173

Hake's Americana & Collectibles

**Disneyana,** Doll, Minnie Mouse, Stuffed, Skirt, Felt Flower, Pie-Eye Accents, Needleart Toys, 15 ½ In.
$3,479

Hake's Americana & Collectibles

**Disneyana,** Figurine, Fantasia, Nubian Centaurette, Ceramic, Vernon Kilns, Stamped, 1940, 8 In.
$385

Hake's Americana & Collectibles

**Disneyana,** Mold, Chocolate, Mickey Mouse, Anton Reiche, T.C. Weygandt, Germany, 6 x 11 In.
$265

Conestoga Auction Co., Inc.

**Disneyana,** Pail, Snow White & 7 Dwarfs, Handle, Tin Lithograph, Scene, Ohio Art, 1938, 8 In.
$285

Hake's Americana & Collectibles

| | |
|---|---:|
| **Miss America,** Pitcher, Pink, 7 In. | 90 |
| **Miss America,** Sugar & Creamer, Pink | 10 |
| **Miss America,** Tumbler, Pink, 4½ x 3 In. | 46 |
| **Moondrops** pattern is listed in the New Martinsville category. | |
| **Mt. Vernon** pattern is included in the Cambridge Glass category. | |
| **Newport,** Soup, Cream, Amethyst, 4¾ x 2¼ In., Pair | 34 |
| **No. 612,** Pitcher, Green, 8½ x 5 In. | 500 |
| **No. 612,** Sugar & Creamer, Open, Green, Square Base, 4⅜ & 4 In. | 60 |
| **No. 618,** Tumbler, 8 Oz., 4¼ In., 4 Piece | 90 |
| **Normandie,** Berry Bowl, Amber, 5 In. | 8 |
| **Normandie,** Sugar & Creamer, Iridescent, Federal, 3 x 3¾ In. | 20 |
| **Ocean Wave,** Sugar & Creamer, Green, 4 x 3⅛ In. | 24 |
| **Old Cafe,** Soup, Dish, Pink, Handle, 5 In. | 16 |
| **Old Cafe,** Vase, Flared, Vertical Ribs, 7¼ In. | 18 |
| **Old Colony,** Bowl, Cereal, Pink, 6⅜ In., Pair | 58 |
| **Old Colony,** Plate, Dinner, Pink, Anchor Hocking, 10 In. | 30 |
| **Old Colony,** Relish, Pink, Open Lace Trim, Divided, Round, 10⅜ In. | 12 |
| **Old Florentine** pattern is listed here as Florentine No. 1. | |
| **Open Lace** pattern is listed here as Old Colony. | |
| **Open Rose** pattern is listed here as Mayfair Open Rose. | |
| **Oyster & Pearl,** Relish, Pink, Divided, 12 x 7½ In. | 12 |
| **Parrot** pattern is listed here as Sylvan. | |
| **Patrician Spoke,** Creamer, Amber, Footed | 9 |
| **Patrician Spoke,** Cup & Saucer, Amber | 14 |
| **Patrician Spoke,** Cup & Saucer, Green | 17 |
| **Patrician Spoke,** Plate, Luncheon, Pink, 9 In. | 15 |
| **Patrician,** Grill Plate, Topaz, 11 In. | 10 |
| **Patrician,** Plate, Dinner, Amber, 1930s, 11 In. | 14 |
| **Patrician,** Tumbler, Green, 14 Oz., 5½ In. | 40 |
| **Peacock & Wild Rose** pattern is listed in the Paden City category. | |
| **Petal Swirl** pattern is listed here as Swirl. | |
| **Petalware,** Platter, Pink, Oval, 13 x 10 In. | 28 |
| **Pillar Optic,** Tumbler, Green, 4 In., 6 Piece | 118 |
| **Pineapple & Floral** pattern is listed here as No. 618. | |
| **Pinwheel** pattern is listed here as Sierra. | |
| **Poinsettia** pattern is listed here as Floral. | |
| **Poppy No. 1** pattern is listed here as Florentine No. 1. | |
| **Poppy No. 2** pattern is listed here as Florentine No. 2. | |
| **Pretty Polly Party Dishes,** see also the related pattern Doric & Pansy. | |
| **Princess,** Sherbet, Green, 1931-35, 4 Piece | 92 |
| **Princess,** Sherbet, Green, 2 Piece | 45 |
| **Princess,** Sugar, Yellow, Anchor Hocking | 8 |
| **Prismatic Line** pattern is listed here as Queen Mary. | |
| **Provincial** pattern is listed here as Bubble. | |
| **Queen Mary,** Cup, Pink, 1936-43 | 12 |
| **Queen Mary,** Tumbler, Pink, 1936-49, 5 Oz., 3½ In., 4 Piece | 58 |
| **Radiance** pattern is listed in the New Martinsville category. | |
| **Restaurant Ware,** Plate, Grill, Jade-Ite, 9⅝ In., 3 Piece | 126 |
| **Romanesque,** Console, Amber, L.E. Smith, 10½ In. | 48 |
| **Rose Of Sharon,** Bowl, Pink, Tapered, Federal Glass, 1930s, 10½ x 4 In. | 70 |
| **Rose Of Sharon,** Creamer, Pink, Federal Glass, 3¾ x 3½ In. | 35 |
| **Rosemary,** Soup, Cream, Amber, Handles, 6¼ x 4¾ In. | 18 |
| **Royal Lace,** Candy Dish, Lid, Pink, 5½ In. | 12 |
| **Royal Lace,** Creamer, 4¼ In. | 28 |
| **Royal Lace,** Cup & Saucer, 5¾ x 2⅝ In. | 16 |
| **Royal Lace,** Platter, Round, Pink, 13 In. | 10 |
| **Royal Lace,** Soup, Cream, Saucer, Blue, 4¾ x 6 In., 6 Piece | 425 |
| **Royal Lace,** Tumbler, Cobalt Blue, 9 Oz., 4¼ In. | 55 |
| **Royal Lace,** Tumbler, Pink, 9 Oz., 4¼ In., 3 Piece | 25 |
| **Sailboat** pattern is listed here as Sportsman Series. | |
| **Shake,** Plate, Green, 8¼ In. | 20 |
| **Sharon,** Cake Plate, Pink | 5 |
| **Sharon,** Salt & Pepper, Pink, 2½ In. | 17 |
| **Sharon,** Soup, Cream, Pink, Handles, 2¼ x 5 In. | 35 |
| **Sierra,** Bowl, Pink, 5¾ x 1¼ In., Pair | 12 |
| **Sphinx,** Vase, Topaz, Fluted Edge, 6¾ x 9 In. | 125 |
| **Sportsman Series,** Sailboat, Tumbler, White, Cobalt Blue, 8 Oz., 3⅜ In. | 79 |

| | | |
|---|---|---|
| **Sportsman Series,** Windmill, Roly Poly, Cobalt Blue, 5 Oz., 2½ x 2½ In. | | 5 |
| **Sunflower,** Cake Plate, Pink, 10 In. | | 17 |
| **Swirl,** Bonbon, Green, 2 Handles, 2⅜ x 7½ In. | | 10 |
| **Swirl,** Bowl, Cereal, Ultramarine, 5¼ In., 4 Piece | | 48 |
| **Swirl,** Bowl, Pink, Scalloped Lacy Edge, 5¼ In., Pair | | 12 |
| **Swirl,** Mold, Gelatin, Individual, Tapered, 2 x 3 In., 12 Piece | | 40 |
| **Sylvan,** Sherbet, Amber, Footed, 3 In., Pair | | 64 |
| **Tea Room,** Sugar & Creamer, Pink, 1926-31, Large | | 58 |
| **Thistle,** Wine, 5 x 3 In., 4 Piece | | 50 |
| **Thumbprint,** Cup & Saucer, Green | | 10 |
| **Thumbprint,** Cup, Green | | 7 |
| **Tiara,** Honey Bee, Dish, Lid, Pink, 5½ x 6 In. | | 48 |
| **Tulip,** Grease Jar, Lid, 6½ In. | | 68 |
| **Vertical Ribbed** pattern is listed here as Queen Mary. | | |
| **Wild Rose** pattern is listed here as Dogwood. | | |
| **Windmill** pattern is listed here as Sportsman Series. | | |
| **Windsor Diamond,** Cake Plate, Pink, 12½ x 10¼ In. | | 45 |
| **Windsor Diamond,** Tumbler, Pink, Flat, 5 Oz., 3¼ In. | | 25 |
| **Windsor,** Butter, Cover, Pink, Round, 4 x 6 In. | | 45 |
| **Woolworth Stippled Grape,** Bowl, Pink, 6 In. | | 3 |

**DERBY** has been marked on porcelain made in the city of Derby, England, since about 1748. The original Derby factory closed in 1848, but others opened there and continued to produce quality porcelain. The Crown Derby mark began appearing on Derby wares in the 1770s.

| | | |
|---|---|---|
| **Candlestick,** Cherub, Kneeling, Flowers, c.1770, 8½ In., Pair | | 780 |
| **Figure,** Milton, Leaning On Stack Of Books, Pedestal, Multicolor, c.1770, 11½ In. | | 250 |
| **Urn,** 3 Figures, Boat, Castle, Cobalt Blue, Gold Trim, Handles, c.1800, 12½ In. | *illus* | 450 |
| **Urn,** Campana, Satyr Mask Handles, Gilt Foliage, Cobalt Ground, Painted Birds, 17 In. | | 989 |

**DICK TRACY,** the comic strip, started in 1931. Tracy was also the hero of movies from 1937 to 1947 and again in 1990, and starred in a radio series in the 1940s and a television series in the 1950s. Memorabilia from all these activities are collected.

| | | |
|---|---|---|
| **Badge,** Secret Service Patrol, Inspector General, Die Cut, 1938, 2½ In. | | 301 |
| **Badge,** Secret Service Patrol, Sergeant, Star, Brass, 1938, 2¾ In. | | 50 |
| **Book,** Dick Tracy & The Phantom Ship, Big Little Book, No. 1434, 1940 | | 20 |
| **Book,** Dick Tracy & Wreath Kidnapping Case, Big Little Book, No. 1482, 1945 | | 14 |
| **Buckle,** Face, Detective Club, Relief, Brass, 1937, 3 x 2¼ In. | | 65 |
| **Game,** Playing Cards, Lithograph, Box, c.1937, 6½ x 5 In. | | 95 |
| **Game,** Target, Tin Lithograph Public Enemy No. 1, Marx, 15 x 15 In. | | 90 |
| **Knife,** 2 Blades, Dick Tracy On Front Handle, 1930s, 3 In. | | 86 |
| **Knife,** Single Blade, Dick Tracy On Front Handle, Imperial, 1930s, 2¾ In. | | 306 |
| **Puppet,** Flexi-Disc Record, Vinyl Hat, Cloth Body, Ideal, 1964 | | 221 |
| **Radios,** 2-Way Electric Wrist Set, Instruction Sheet, Remco, 1960, Box | | 126 |
| **Ring,** Compartment, Horseshoe, Clover, Brass, Adjustable, 1938 | | 75 |
| **Thermos,** Luna TV, Metal, Aladdin, 1967 | | 20 |
| **Toy,** B.O. Plenty, Waddles, Holds Baby, Tips Hat, Tin Lithograph, Windup, Marx, 8½ In. | *illus* | 89 |
| **Toy,** Burglar Alarm Kit, Flashlight, String Tags, Box, 1930s, 8 x 13 In. | *illus* | 399 |
| **Toy,** Dick Tracy Car, Blue, Green, 2 Riders, Tin Lithograph, Friction & Battery, Marx, 11 In. | | 180 |
| **Toy,** Police Station, Squad Car, Automatic, Doors Fly Open, 6 x 8¾ In. | | 379 |
| **Toy,** Squad Car, Siren, Electric Flashing Light, Windup, Box, 1949, 11 In. | | 316 |
| **Toy,** Squad Car, Windup, Lights, Marx, Box, 11 In. | | 195 |

**DICKENS WARE** *pieces are listed in the Weller category.*

**DINNERWARE** used in the United States from the 1930s through the 1950s is listed here. Most was made in potteries in southern Ohio, West Virginia, and California. A few patterns were made in Japan, England, and other countries. Dishes were sold in gift shops and department stores, or were given away as premiums. Many of these patterns are listed in this book in their own categories, such as Autumn Leaf, Azalea, Coors, Fiesta, Franciscan, Hall, Harker, Harlequin, Red Wing, Riviera, Russel Wright, Vernon Kilns, Watt, and Willow. For more prices, go to kovels.com. Sets missing a few pieces can be completed through the help of a matching service.

| | | |
|---|---|---|
| **Angelus Rose,** Cup & Saucer, Homer Laughlin | | 16 |
| **Apple Blossom,** Creamer, Edwin Knowles | | 38 |
| **Blue Bonnet,** Chop Plate, Harmony House, 12 In. | | 17 |

Disneyana, Plate, Baby's, Here's Something To Tickle You, Mickey Mouse, Pig, Dagger, c.1935, 6 x 8 In.
$403

Hake's Americana & Collectibles

Disneyana, Rug, Mickey Mouse Playing Accordion, Minnie Mouse, Donald Duck, 27 x 41 In.
$60

Morphy Auctions

### Mickey Is a Wagging Head Clock

An Ingersoll Mickey Mouse alarm clock was made with arms that were the hands that moved around the face of the clock and a head that bobs. The 1933 clock is called the "wagging head" clock.

Disneyana, Toy, Dopey, Dwarf, Walker, Tin Lithograph, Clockwork, Louis Marx, 8 In.
$236

Bertoia Auctions

## Soup Bowls

A soup bowl holds soup, but some dinner sets have many types of soup bowls. A cream soup (round, two-handled shallow bowl) held cream of tomato or other creamy soups. A bouillon cup (small, about 5 inches round, with handles) held clear soup. A coupe soup is a shallow pottery bowl about 7 inches in diameter.

**Disneyana,** Toy, Dumbo, Flip & Leap, Tin Litho, Windup, Marx, Walt Disney Prod., 1941, 4 In.
$148

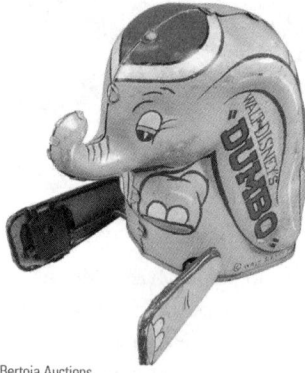

Bertoia Auctions

**Disneyana,** Toy, Ferdinand The Bull, Composition, Painted, Jointed Legs, Walt Disney, 9 In.
$89

Bertoia Auctions

**TIP**
*Don't use a repaired plate for food. It could be a health hazard.*

| | |
|---|---:|
| **Blue Bonnet,** Creamer, Harmony House, 3¾ In. | 23 |
| **Blue Heaven,** Mixing Bowl, Fire King, 1970s, 1½ Qt., 7¼ x 8¾ In. | 29 |
| **Bristol,** Soup Dish, Castleton, 5 In. | 20 |
| **Buttercup,** Plate, Bread & Butter, Knowles, 6 In. | 5 to 12 |
| **Carnation Windblown,** Bowl, Cereal, Tab Handles, Crooksville, 6¾ In. | 12 |
| **Carnation Windblown,** Cream & Sugar, Crooksville | 47 |
| **Carnation Windblown,** Cup & Saucer, Crooksville | 14 |
| **Carnation Windblown,** Plate, Dinner, Crooksville, 10 In. | 12 |
| **Carnation Windblown,** Platter, Tab Handles, Crooksville, 13½ In. | 32 |
| **Cattails,** Bowl, Vegetable, Divided, Round, Blue Ridge, 8½ In. | 40 |
| **Cattails,** Plate, Bread & Butter, Blue Ridge, 6⅜ In. | 10 |
| **Cattails,** Plate, Dinner, Blue Ridge, 10½ In. | 24 |
| **Chanticleer,** Cup & Saucer, Brock | 12 |
| **Chanticleer,** Plate, Bread & Butter, Brock, 6¾ In. | 8 |
| **Charm,** Plate, Luncheon, Azurite Blue, 1950s, 8⅜ x 8⅜ In., 4 Piece | 60 |
| **Country Lane,** Creamer, Brock | 22 |
| **Country Strawberry,** Plate, Dinner, Homer Laughlin, 10 In. | 12 |
| **Courtship,** Plate, Dinner, Alfred Meakin, 10 In. | 22 |
| **Crocus,** Cup & Saucer, Crooksville | 10 |
| **Crocus,** Plate, Bread & Butter, Crooksville, 6 In. | 6 |
| **Crocus,** Plate, Dinner, Crooksville, 9¼ In. | 10 |
| **Doe Eyes,** Creamer, Blue Ridge | 23 |
| **Eva Zeisel,** Casserole, Duck Head Cover, Great Western Stoneware, 1940s, 9 In. ...............*illus* | 875 |
| **Evening Flower,** Bowl, Cereal, Lugged | 10 |
| **Evening Flower,** Cup & Saucer | 14 |
| **Fantasy Apple,** Plate, Dinner | 8 |
| **Farmer In The Dell,** Bowl, Vegetable, Oval, Fluted Edge, Salem China | 28 |
| **Forsythia,** Cup & Saucer, Edwin Knowles | 12 |
| **Frageria,** Plate, Dinner, Blue Ridge, 1¼ In. | 12 |
| **Grapevine,** Plate, Dinner, Edwin Knowles, 10 In. | 10 to 16 |
| **Honey Hen,** Plate, Bread & Butter, Taylor, Smith & Taylor, 7 In. | 6 |
| **Irene,** Bowl, Cereal, Petalware, Lobed, 1930-50, 5¾ In., 4 Piece | 58 |
| **Lismore,** Berry Bowl, Alfred Meakin, 5½ In. | 10 |
| **Lismore,** Bowl, Vegetable, Alfred Meakin, 8½ In. | 45 |
| **Lismore,** Plate, Dinner, Alfred Meakin, 9¾ In. | 18 |
| **Lismore,** Platter, Alfred Meakin, 14¼ In. | 65 |
| **Madras,** Bowl, Vegetable, Handles, Lid, Alfred Meakin, 10 In. | 85 |
| **Madras,** Gravy Boat, Alfred Meakin, 8 In. | 38 |
| **Madras,** Platter, Alfred Meakin, 13 x 16 In. | 75 |
| **Old Ivory,** Cake Plate, No. 16, 11 In. | 119 |
| **Pink Magnolia,** Platter, Crooksville, 11½ In. | 28 |
| **Pink Magnolia,** Platter, Crooksville, 13¼ In. | 35 |
| **Plate,** Ellastone, Flowers, Serrated Rim, Rounded Square, Johnson Bros, c.1940, 7 In., 12 Piece | 35 |
| **Puritan,** Bowl, Vegetable, Lid, Edwin Knowles | 48 |
| **Severn,** Cup & Saucer, Alfred Meakin | 28 |
| **Severn,** Plate, Luncheon, Alfred Meakin, 9 In. | 22 |
| **Severn,** Plate, Salad, Alfred Meakin, 8 In. | 18 |
| **Silver Wheat,** Cup & Saucer, Harmony House | 12 |
| **Skytone,** Cup & Saucer, Homer Laughlin | 12 |
| **Spring Song,** Creamer, Homer Laughlin | 22 |
| **Spring Song,** Cup & Saucer, Homer Laughlin | 12 |
| **Spring Song,** Plate, Salad, Square, Homer Laughlin, 8 x 8 In. | 15 |
| **Spring Song,** Platter, Homer Laughlin, 15¼ In. | 48 |
| **Stanhome Ivy,** Gravy Boat, Blue Ridge | 35 |
| **Stanhome Ivy,** Plate, Bread & Butter, Blue Ridge, 6½ In. | 6 |
| **Stanhome Ivy,** Platter, Tab Handles, Blue Ridge, 13 x 11 In. | 45 |
| **Tea Leaf,** Gravy Boat, Alfred Meakin | 89 |
| **Tea Leaf,** Platter, Alfred Meakin, 14 In. | 50 |
| **Tom & Jerry,** Punch Bowl Set, Green, Red Snowflakes, White Ground, Fire-King, 7 Piece | 125 |
| **Tropical,** Berry Bowl, Blue Ridge, 5⅝ In. | 12 |
| **Tropical,** Bowl, Vegetable, Oval, Blue Ridge, 9⅜ In. | 35 |
| **Tropical,** Bowl, Vegetable, Round, Blue Ridge, 8⅞ In. | 38 |
| **Trotter,** Plate, Dinner, Crooksville, 10 In. | 42 |
| **Trousseau,** Cup, Castleton | 28 |
| **Tulip Eggshell Nautilus,** Bowl, Fruit, Homer Laughlin, 5⅜ In. | 6 |
| **Tulip Eggshell Nautilus,** Creamer, Homer Laughlin | 12 |

| | |
|---|---|
| Tulip Eggshell Nautilus, Cup & Saucer, Homer Laughlin | 11 |
| Tulip Eggshell Nautilus, Plate, Bread & Butter, Homer Laughlin | 5 |
| Tulip Eggshell Nautilus, Plate, Dinner, Homer Laughlin, 9 ⅞ In. | 12 |
| Turquoise, Sugar & Creamer, Fire-King, c.1957 | 42 |
| Wheat, Plate, Salad, Fire-King, 1962-66, 7 ⅜ In. | 48 |
| Yellow Nocturne, Cup & Saucer, Blue Ridge | 24 |
| Yellow Nocturne, Plate, Dinner, Blue Ridge, 10 ¼ In. | 22 |
| Yellow Nocturne, Platter, Blue Ridge, 13 In. | 35 to 48 |

**DIONNE QUINTUPLETS** were born in Canada on May 28, 1934. The publicity about their birth and their special status as wards of the Canadian government made them famous throughout the world. Visitors could watch the girls play; reporters interviewed the girls and the staff. Thousands of special dolls and souvenirs were made picturing the quints at different ages. Emilie died in 1954, Marie in 1970, Yvonne in 2001. Annette and Cecile still live in Canada.

| | |
|---|---|
| Apron, Quints, Crawling Up Stairs, Names, Linen, Child's, 17 x 11 In. | 40 |
| Book, Soon We'll Be Three Years Old, Whitman Publishing, 1936 | 24 |
| Calendar, 1943, Girls, On Beach, Frame, 13 x 16 In. | 60 |
| Doll, 5 Babies, Composition, Scooter, Madame Alexander, c.1935, 7 In. Dolls ...... *illus* | 840 |
| Dolls, 5 Babies, Hair Bow, Pink Blanket, Bisque, Japan, 1930, 10 x 4 In. | 125 |
| Dolls, Composition, Babies, Molded Hair, Effanbee, 1930s, 7 In., 5 Piece | 525 |
| Dolls, On Seesaw, Madame Alexander, 7 In. | 2799 |
| Mirror, Girls In Basket, Pocket, 1936 | 85 |
| Paper Dolls, 5 Dolls, Outfits, Story, 1930s, 9 ½ x 8 ½ In., Uncut | 45 |
| Postcard, Girls, In Chairs, Black & White, 1937, 3 x 5 In. | 20 |

**DIRK VAN ERP** was born in 1860 and died in 1933. He opened his own studio in 1908 in Oakland, California. He moved his studio to San Francisco in 1909 and the studio remained under the direction of his son until 1977. Van Erp made hammered copper accessories, including vases, desk sets, bookends, candlesticks, jardinieres, and trays, but he is best known for his lamps. The hammered copper lamps often had shades with mica panels.

| | |
|---|---|
| Bowl, Copper, Hammered, Oval, Footed, Closed Box Mark, 3 ½ x 16 In. | 813 |
| Box, Copper, Hammered, Rectangular, Swollen Lid, 2 x 6 In. | 1342 |
| Jardiniere, Copper, Hammered, Dirk Van Erp, 1910, 8 ½ x 10 In. | 5397 |
| Jardiniere, Copper, Hammered, Dirk Van Erp, 1910, 15 ½ x 11 ½ In. | 7500 |
| Lamp, Copper, Hammered, 4-Panel Mica Shade, Stamped, c.1912, 21 ½ x 20 In. ....... *illus* | 6250 |
| Match Holder, Copper, Hammered, Rolled Edge, Signed, c.1910, 5 x 5 In. | 425 |
| Tray, Silver Plate, Over Hammered Copper, c.1925, 15 x 15 In. | 896 |
| Vase, Copper, Hammered, Swollen, 8 ½ x 7 ½ In. | 2562 |
| Vase, Copper, Hammered, Tooled Flowers, Cylindrical, Stepped Foot, 5 ½ x 2 In. | 1063 |

**DISNEYANA** is a collectors' term. Walt Disney and his company introduced many comic characters to the world. Collectors search for examples of the work of the Disney Studios and the many commercial products modeled after his characters, including Mickey Mouse and Donald Duck, and recent films, like *Beauty and the Beast* and *The Little Mermaid*.

| | |
|---|---|
| Ashtray, Mickey Mouse, Art Deco, Torso Is Tray, White, Porcelain, Germany, 1932, 5 In. | 168 |
| Ashtray, Mickey Mouse, Metal, Attached 3 ½-In. Mickey, Germany, 4 ½ In. | 760 |
| Ashtray, Mickey Mouse, Mickey, Rag Style, Standing, Matchbox Block, c.1935, 3 x 4 In. ....... *illus* | 173 |
| Autograph, Walt Disney, Adventures Of Mickey Mouse, No. 3, Pencil, c.1949, 8 x 6 In. | 750 |
| Bank, Mechanical, Mickey Mouse, Folded Hands, Tin Litho, Saalheimer & Strauss, 1930s, 7 In. | 36000 |
| Bank, Mickey Mouse, Hands On Chest, Pull Ear, Tin Litho, Saalheimer & Strauss, c.1930, 7 In. | 33600 |
| Bank, Mickey Mouse, Hands On Hips, Coin Slot On Head, France, 1930s, 9 In. | 172 |
| Bank, Mickey Mouse, Leaning Against Yellow Treasure Chest, 1938, 6 In. | 253 |
| Bottle Stopper, Mickey Mouse, 5-Fingered Mickey, Cork Stopper, 5 ⅛ In. | 575 |
| Bowl, Mickey Mouse, 12-Sided, Minnie, Pluto, White, Faience, 6 ⅛ In. | 115 |
| Cel, see Animation Art category. | |
| Comic Book, Snow White, Movie Adaptation, Bob Grant Art, No. 49, July 1944 | 612 |
| Cookie Jar, Mickey Mouse, Hand On Chin, Drum, California Originals, c.1970, 11 In. | 285 |
| Creamer, Alice In Wonderland, King Of Hearts Shape, 1951, 7 In. | 139 |
| Doll, Donald Duck, Stuffed, Felt Beak, Applique Eyes, Middy Jacket, c.1935, 12 In. | 112 |
| Doll, Ferdinand & Matador, Black, Brown, Paint, Composition, Cloth, 1930s, 10 In., 9 In. | 1000 |
| Doll, Mickey & Minnie Mouse, Felt, Side-Glancing Eyes, Lenci, 15 In., Pair | 1344 |
| Doll, Mickey & Minnie Mouse, Muslin, Embroidered, Charlotte Clark, c.1935, 19 In. | 392 |
| Doll, Mickey Mouse, Cloth, Pie-Eyed, Tied Whiskers, Felt Ears, Knickerbocker, 11 In. | 660 |
| Doll, Mickey Mouse, Steiff Style, Cloth, Stand-Up, Velvet, Felt, 1930s, 6 ½ x 3 In. | 575 |
| Doll, Mickey Mouse, Tin, Windup, Linemar, 1950s, 5 ¾ In. | 150 |

Disneyana, Toy, Goofy, Riding Unicycle, Cloth Pants, Tin Litho, Clockwork, Linemar, Japan, 5 In.
$384

Bertoia Auctions

Disneyana, Toy, Mickey Mouse, Celluloid, Windup, Key, Germany, c.1930, 5 ¾ In.
$575

Hake's Americana & Collectibles

Disneyana, Toy, Mickey Mouse, Xylophone, Wood, Label, Pull Toy, Fisher-Price, 1939, 11 In.
$230

Hake's Americana & Collectibles

This is an edited listing of current prices. Visit **Kovels.com** to check thousands of prices from previous years and sign up for free information on trends, tips, reproductions, marks, and more.

**D**

# DISNEYANA

**Disneyana,** Toy, Pull, Mickey Mouse, Nephew, Wood, Paper, Bells, N.N. Hill, Brass, 1937, 11 In.
**$575**

Hake's Americana & Collectibles

**Doll,** Advertising, Buddy Lee, Hard Plastic, Jointed Arms, Sculpted Hair, c.1950, 12 In.
**$285**

Theriault's

## Dating China Head Dolls
The age of a china head doll can be determined from the hairstyle. The doll with curls on the neck was made about 1840, short curls about 1850, and the chignon style about 1860. Dolls with brown eyes are rare, and blue eyes can be found in various shades.

| | |
|---|---:|
| **Doll,** Mickey Mouse, Yellow Gloves, Red Shoes, Felt, Cloth, George Borgfeldt, 1930s, 19 In. | 1125 |
| **Doll,** Mickey, Minnie Mouse, Pie-Eyed, Composition, Cloth, Knickerbocker, 1930s, 10 In., 2 Piece | 750 |
| **Doll,** Minnie Mouse, Stuffed, Skirt, Felt Flower, Pie-Eye Accents, Needleart Toys, 15 ½ In. .....*illus* | 3479 |
| **Doll,** Pinocchio, Composition, Felt Outfit, Knickerbocker, Box, 1939, 13 ¼ In. | 2875 |
| **Doll,** Pinocchio, Fabric Bow, Composition, Box, Ideal, 1940, 11 In. | 466 |
| **Drinks Stand,** Mickey Mouse, 2-Sided, Round Tray, Paint, Wood, 25 ½ In. | 900 |
| **Figurine,** Donald Duck, Reading Comics, Sitting On Books, Capo-Di-Monte, 9 In. | 253 |
| **Figurine,** Fantasia, Nubian Centaurette, Ceramic, Vernon Kilns, Stamped, 1940, 8 In. .....*illus* | 385 |
| **Figurine,** Five Men In Funny Hats, Bandanna, Moustache, c.1938, 8 ¾ In. | 948 |
| **Figurine,** Five Men In Funny Hats, Sombrero, Flowers On Shirt, c.1938, 8 ½ In. | 3579 |
| **Figurine,** Five Men In Funny Hats, Top Hat, Green Coat, Scarf, c.1938, 8 ¾ In. | 942 |
| **Figurine,** Geppetto, Yellow Apron, Standing, Hand On Chin, c.1939, 8 In. | 757 |
| **Figurine,** Jiminy Cricket, Standing, Umbrella, Brayton Laguna, c.1939, 5 ½ In. | 306 |
| **Figurine,** Matador, From Ferdinand, Cape, Hat, Brayton, Laguna, 8 ¾ In. | 1020 |
| **Figurine,** Mickey Mouse, Hands On Hips, Green Buttons, 1930s, 2 ½ In. | 164 |
| **Figurine,** Mickey Mouse, Porcelain, Kettlebell, Rosenthal, Germany, 3 ⅜ In. | 575 |
| **Figurine,** Mickey Mouse, Porcelain, Throwing Discus, Rosenthal, 3 ¼ In. | 765 |
| **Figurine,** Mickey Mouse, Saxophone, Mandolin, Violin, Drum, 1 ½ In., 4 Piece | 115 |
| **Figurine,** Pinocchio, Seated, Leaning Forward, Brayton Laguna, 1940s, 4 In. | 581 |
| **Figurine,** Snow White, Musician Set, 2 ½ & 3 ½ In., Box, 8 Piece | 184 |
| **Figurine,** Snow White, Pottery, Box, 1947, 6-In. Dwarfs, 9-In. Snow White, 8 Piece | 230 |
| **Gumball Machine,** Mickey Mouse, Green, Crystal Bowl, Hamilton, 1938, 14 In. | 885 |
| **Honey Pot,** Happy, Wade Heath, Lid | 127 |
| **Hood Ornament,** Minnie Mouse, Red Face, Chrome Plated, Enamel, 1934, 4 In. | 345 |
| **Lip Balm Container,** Mickey Mouse, Mickey Unscrews At Waist, France, 2 In. | 139 |
| **Lunch Box & Thermos,** Dome Shape, Metal, School Bus, 1970s | 158 |
| **Mickey Mouse,** Velvet, Mother-Of-Pearl Buttons, c.1940, 7 In. | 1033 |
| **Mold,** Chocolate, Mickey Mouse, Anton Reiche, T.C. Weygandt, Germany, 6 x 11 In. .....*illus* | 265 |
| **Nodder,** Goofy, Composition, Japan, 1960s, 6 In. | 45 |
| **Nodder,** Pluto, Plastic, Yellow, Marx, 1960s, 1 ¾ x 2 ¾ In. | 35 |
| **Pail,** Mickey Mouse, Picnic, Tin Lithograph, Multicolor, Ohio Art Co., 1930s, 7 x 6 In. | 719 |
| **Pail,** Snow White & 7 Dwarfs, Handle, Tin Lithograph, Scene, Ohio Art, 1938, 8 In. .....*illus* | 285 |
| **Pencil Sharpener,** Mickey Mouse, Catalin Plastic, Brass Rim, Octagonal, 1930s, 1 In., Pair | 146 |
| **Pendant,** Mickey Mouse, Pave Diamond Ground, 14K Gold, Oval, Rope Twist Edge, 1 In. | 861 |
| **Pin,** Mickey Mouse's Head, Figural, Gold, Black Enamel Ears, Diamond Melee Star, 2 In. | 984 |
| **Pin,** Pinocchio, Red, White, Black, 1943, 1 ¼ In. | 30 |
| **Plate,** Baby's, Here's Something To Tickle You, Mickey Mouse, Pig, Dagger, c.1935, 6 x 8 In. .....*illus* | 403 |
| **Plate,** Mickey Mouse, Riding Train, Bavaria, 7 ½ In. | 92 |
| **Poster,** Movie, Daffy Duck, Walt Disney's Flying Jalopy, 1943, 41 x 27 In. | 1750 |
| **Radio,** Mickey Mouse, Emerson, Cream, Upright Bass, Green, Yellow, 5 ½ x 7 ¼ In. | 462 |
| **Radio,** Snow White & 7 Dwarfs, Wood, Embossed Figures, Emerson, 1939, 7 x 7 ½ In. | 1062 |
| **Ring,** Pinocchio, Tell The Truth, Plastic, Rubber Nose, Weatherbird Premium, 1953, ¾ In. | 173 |
| **Rug,** Hooked, Mickey Mouse, Train Engineer, Disney Characters, Multicolor, 46 x 57 In. | 59 |
| **Rug,** Mickey Mouse Playing Accordion, Minnie Mouse, Donald Duck, 27 x 41 In. .....*illus* | 60 |
| **Scissors,** Mickey Mouse, 2-Sided Die Cut Image, Plastic Coated Handles, 1 ¾ x 3 In. | 35 |
| **Shoes,** Mickey Mouse, White, Leather, Toddler, Moran, Box, 1930s | 115 |
| **Tankard,** Donald Duck, Kneeling, 9 ½ In. | 30 |
| **Tankard,** Mickey Mouse, Seated, Black Handle, 9 In. | 60 |
| **Toothbrush Holder,** Doc, Next To Barrel, Doc Says Brush Your Teeth, 6 In. | 68 |
| **Toy Box,** Mickey Mouse, Carousal, Japan, 1930, 3 x 5 ¾ In. | 347 |
| **Toy,** Donald Duck, Car, Donald Duck Driver, Wiggling Hat, Tin Lithograph, Windup, 6 In. | 210 |
| **Toy,** Donald Duck, Dipsy Car, Clockwork, Linemar, Japan, 5 ¼ In. | 295 |
| **Toy,** Donald Duck, Dipsy Car, Tin Lithograph, Windup, Linemar, Box, 6 In. | 510 |
| **Toy,** Donald Duck, Drummer, Tin Lithograph, Painted, Blue Shirt, Hat, Linemar, 5 ½ In. | 207 |
| **Toy,** Donald Duck, Drummer, Tin Lithograph, Windup, Linemar, Japan, 6 In. | 270 |
| **Toy,** Donald Duck, Duckling Pulled By Rope, Tin Lithograph, Linemar, Japan, 5 ½ In. | 120 |
| **Toy,** Donald Duck, Marionette, Madame Alexander, Controller Unit, Box, 11 In. | 385 |
| **Toy,** Donald Duck, Moving Legs, Yellow Cart, Pull Toy, c.1933, 12 In. | 649 |
| **Toy,** Donald Duck, Pull, Wood, Red Cart, 8 ¾ In. | 221 |
| **Toy,** Donald Duck, Race Car, Green, Rubber Wheels, 1936, 4 In. | 201 |
| **Toy,** Donald Duck, Trapeze, Celluloid, Tin Lithograph, Windup, Linemar, Japan, 13 In. | 180 |
| **Toy,** Donald Duck, Tricycle, Celluloid, Tin Lithograph, Clockwork, Linemar, 4 In. | 115 to 354 |
| **Toy,** Donald Duck, Tricycle, Cloth Pants, English Flag, c.1930, 5 ¾ In. | 236 |
| **Toy,** Donald Duck, Waddles, Opens Mouth, Germany, Schuco, 6 In. | 266 |
| **Toy,** Donald Duck, Whirl Tail, Umbrella, Tin Litho, Windup, Walt Disney Productions, Japan, 5 In. | 210 |
| **Toy,** Dopey, Dwarf, Walker, Tin Lithograph, Clockwork, Louis Marx, 8 In. .....*illus* | 236 |

| | |
|---|---|
| **Toy,** Dumbo, Flip & Leap, Tin Litho, Windup, Marx, Walt Disney Prod., 1941, 4 In. .............*illus* | 148 |
| **Toy,** Ferdinand The Bull, Composition, Painted, Jointed Legs, Walt Disney, 9 In. ..................*illus* | 89 |
| **Toy,** Ferris Wheel, Mickey Mouse, Donald Duck, Tin Lithograph, Windup, Chien, 17 In. ............. | 240 |
| **Toy,** Goofy Walker, Tail Spins, Tin, Linemar, 5 ½ In. ..................................................... | 196 |
| **Toy,** Goofy, Riding Unicycle, Cloth Pants, Tin Litho, Clockwork, Linemar, Japan, 5 In. .........*illus* | 384 |
| **Toy,** Jiminy Cricket, Blue Hat, Tin Lithograph, Battery, Remote Control, Marx, 6 In. ..................... | 60 |
| **Toy,** Jiminy Cricket, Walks, Umbrella, Clockwork, Linemar, Japan, 7 In. .................................... | 266 |
| **Toy,** Mickey Delivery Bicycle, Disney Scenes, Tin Lithograph, Friction, Marx, 5 ½ In. ................ | 240 |
| **Toy,** Mickey Mouse Car, Driver Mickey Wiggling Hat, Tin Lithograph, Windup, Marx, 6 In. .......... | 150 |
| **Toy,** Mickey Mouse Express With Overhead Plane, Marx, Box, c.1950, 9 In. ............................. | 443 |
| **Toy,** Mickey Mouse Hand Car, Mickey & Minnie, Red Car, Lionel, 8 In. .................................. | 300 |
| **Toy,** Mickey Mouse, Airplane, Donald Duck, Goofy, 1950s, 6 In. ......................................... | 431 |
| **Toy,** Mickey Mouse, Baby Rattle, Wraparound Cylinder, Instruments, Japan, 8 In. ....................... | 115 |
| **Toy,** Mickey Mouse, Bus, Wood, Cardboard, Gong Bell, Box, 19 ½ In. .................................... | 384 |
| **Toy,** Mickey Mouse, Car, Dipsy, Spring Neck, Open Car, Windup, Linemar, Japan, 5 In. ................ | 118 |
| **Toy,** Mickey Mouse, Celluloid, Windup, Key, Germany, c.1930, 5 ¾ In. ................................*illus* | 575 |
| **Toy,** Mickey Mouse, Christmas House, Brown, Minnie, Mickey, 1930s, 8 ½ x 7 In. ½ .................. | 126 |
| **Toy,** Mickey Mouse, Dancing Minnie, Hurdy-Gurdy, Tin Lithograph, Windup, Distler, 6 In. .......... | 5700 |
| **Toy,** Mickey Mouse, Doll, Pie-Eyed, String Whiskers, Tag, Needleart, 1930s, 10 In. .................. | 2656 |
| **Toy,** Mickey Mouse, Donald Duck, Googly, Flowers, Draped Ribbons, Yellow, 11 In. .................. | 347 |
| **Toy,** Mickey Mouse, Hobby Horse, Bouncing, Mickey Holds Reins, 1930s, 5 In. ......................... | 379 |
| **Toy,** Mickey Mouse, Multiple Characters, Sand Art Kit, Box, Toy Tinkers, 1938. ....................... | 115 |
| **Toy,** Mickey Mouse, Parade Car, 3 Characters, Tin Lithograph, Multicolor, Marx, 11 x 5 ½ In. ..... | 81 |
| **Toy,** Mickey Mouse, Pull, Train, Bell, Wood, 11 In. .......................................................... | 234 |
| **Toy,** Mickey Mouse, Race Car, Windup, Tin Lithograph, Green, Rubber Tires, Schneider, 4 In. ...... | 234 |
| **Toy,** Mickey Mouse, Sparkler, Black, White, Box, 5 ½ In. .................................................. | 383 |
| **Toy,** Mickey Mouse, Tricycle, Ringing Bell, Windup, Linemar, Box, 4 In. ............................... | 207 |
| **Toy,** Mickey Mouse, Umbrella, Multicolor, Japan, 1930s, 12 ¼ In. ...................................... | 569 |
| **Toy,** Mickey Mouse, Unicyclist, Tin Lithograph, Cloth Pants, Clockwork, Linemar, 5 In. .............. | 443 |
| **Toy,** Mickey Mouse, Washer, Crank, Wraparound Washing Scene, 7 ½ In. ............................... | 263 |
| **Toy,** Mickey Mouse, Whirligig, Windup, Multicolor, Balls, Japan, 1930s, 4 ½ In. ..................... | 1265 |
| **Toy,** Mickey Mouse, Xylophone, Articulated Axles, Pull Toy, Fisher-Price, 11 ½ In. ..................... | 177 |
| **Toy,** Mickey Mouse, Xylophone, Wood, Label, Pull Toy, Fisher-Price, 1939, 11 In. .................*illus* | 230 |
| **Toy,** Minnie Mouse, Knitting In Rocking Chair, Japan, Linemar, 6 ½ In. ................................. | 266 |
| **Toy,** Minnie Mouse, Sitting In Rocker, Knitting, Tin Lithograph, Windup, Marx, 7 In. ................. | 240 |
| **Toy,** Pinocchio, Tin Lithograph, Windup, Marx, 8 ½ In. .................................................... | 240 |
| **Toy,** Pinocchio, Tin Lithograph, Windup, Walt Disney Productions, Japan, 6 In. ........................ | 72 |
| **Toy,** Pinocchio, Walker, Tin Lithograph, Pronounced Nose, Windup, Marx, 8 ½ In. .................... | 295 |
| **Toy,** Pluto, Drum Major, Horn, Hat, Tin Litho, Windup, Walt Disney Production, 6 ½ In. .............. | 180 |
| **Toy,** Pluto, On Unicycle, Tin Lithograph, Clockwork Wheel, Linemar, Label, 5 ½ In. .................. | 354 |
| **Toy,** Pluto, On Unicycle, Yellow, Tin Lithograph, Windup, Marx, 5 ½ In. ............................... | 300 |
| **Toy,** Pluto, Rollover, Wire Tail, Tin Lithograph, Clockwork, Marx, c.1939, 8 In. ....................... | 118 |
| **Toy,** Pluto, Tricycle, Tin, Celluloid, Windup, Box, Linemar ................................................. | 595 |
| **Toy,** Professor Von Drake, Stick, Tin Lithograph, Windup, Box, Marx Linemar, 6 ½ In. ................. | 180 |
| **Toy,** Pull, Mickey Mouse, Nephew, Wood, Paper, Bells, N.N. Hill, Brass, 1937, 11 In...............*illus* | 575 |
| **Toy,** Ride-A-Rocket, 4 Rockets, 8 Riders, Tin Lithograph, Windup, J. Chein, 19 In. ........................ | 150 |
| **Toy,** Roller Coaster, Disney Scenes, Tin Lithograph, Windup, J. Chein, 18 In. ........................... | 150 |
| **Toy,** Santa Claus Driving Cart, Mickey Mouse In Sack, Tin, Pressed Steel, Lionel, 10 In.............. | 510 |
| **Toy,** Washing Machine, Footed, Mickey, Minnie, Pluto, Tin, Crank Handle, Ohio Art Co., 8 In. ..... | 75 |
| **Watch,** Three Little Pigs, Red Brick, Ingersoll, Box, 1934, Pocket ......................................... | 522 |
| **Wristwatch Set,** Donald Duck, Watch, Ring, Pen, Pink Case, Cake Shape, 4 ½ In. ..................... | 253 |
| **Wristwatch,** Cinderella, Pink, Green, Pumpkin Coach, Square Box, 1950 ................................. | 115 |
| **Wristwatch,** Cinderella, Pink, Yellow Plastic Case, 1972. .................................................. | 115 |
| **Wristwatch,** Mickey Mouse, Black Leather Band, Full Body, Presentation Box, 1955 .................. | 221 |
| **Wristwatch,** Mickey Mouse, Full Body, Box, Ingersoll, 1958 ............................................... | 212 |
| **Wristwatch,** Mickey Mouse, Red Leather Band, Ingersoll, Box, 1947 ..................................... | 189 |
| **Wristwatch,** Mickey Mouse, Second Hand Disc, 3 Small Images, Red Box, 1934 ...................... | 384 |
| **Wristwatch,** Minnie Mouse, Pink Skirt, Green Shoes, With Figure, Box, Ingersoll........................ | 341 |

**DOCTOR**, *see Dental and Medical categories.*

**DOLL** entries are listed by marks printed or incised on the doll, if possible. If there are no marks, the doll is listed by the name of the subject or country or maker. Notice that Barbie is listed under Mattel. G.I. Joe figures are listed in the Toy section. Eskimo dolls are listed in the Eskimo section and Indian dolls are listed in the Indian section. Doll clothes and accessories are listed at the end of this section. The twentieth-century clothes listed here are in mint condition.

| | |
|---|---|
| **A.M.,** 243, Topknot Googly, Bisque Head, Closed Mouth, Composition Body, 10 In........................ | 1680 |

**Doll,** Advertising, Dubble Bubble Gum, Cloth Body, Frank H. Fleer Corp., 21 In. $460

Wm Morford Auctions

**Doll,** American Character, Betsy McCall, Flirty Eyes, Vinyl, Dress, Coat, 20 In. $285

Theriault's

**Doll,** American Character, Betsy McCall, Vinyl, Birthday Party, 1958, 14 In. $855

Theriault's

**Doll,** American Character, Sweet Sue, Plastic, Silk & Tulle Gown, Wrist Tag, c.1955, 17 In. $456

Theriault's

**Doll,** American Character, Sweet Sue, Walker, Plastic, Lace, Tulle Gown, Tag, Box, 24 In. $285

Theriault's

D

| | |
|---|---|
| **A.M.,** 341-6K, Black Molded Head, 5 Piece Composition Body, Sleep Eyes, Painted Hair | 325 |
| **A.M.,** 390, Bisque Head, Composition Body, 22 In. | 60 |
| **A.M.,** 971, Socket Head, Mohair Wig, Paint, Blue Sleep Eyes, Composition, c.1913, 13 In. | 127 |
| **A.M.,** Bisque Head, Olive Tint, Glass Sleep Eyes, Composition, Oriental Baby, 13 In. | 668 |
| **A.M.,** Fany, Boy, Bisque, Blue Sleep Eyes, Chubby Pouty Face, Composition, Toddler, 14 In. | 3248 |
| **Advertising,** Buddy Lee, Hard Plastic, Jointed Arms, Sculpted Hair, c.1950, 12 In. *illus* | 285 |
| **Advertising,** Buddy Lee, Railroad Engineer, Cap, c.1925, 13 In. | 300 |
| **Advertising,** Ceresota Flour, Boy, Cloth, Lithograph, Stuffed, c.1900, 15 In. | 1232 |
| **Advertising,** Dubble Bubble Gum, Cloth Body, Frank H. Fleer Corp., 21 In. *illus* | 460 |
| **Alabama Baby,** Molded Head, Painted, 23 In. | 555 |
| **Alexander** dolls are listed in this category under Madame Alexander. | |
| **Alt,** Beck & Gottschalk, 896, Bisque Shoulder Head, Inset Eyes, Sculpted Blond Ringlets, 21 In. | 1904 |
| **American Character,** Betsy McCall, Flirty Eyes, Vinyl, Dress, Coat, 20 In. *illus* | 285 |
| **American Character,** Betsy McCall, Vinyl, Birthday Party, 1958, 14 In. *illus* | 855 |
| **American Character,** Sweet Sue, Plastic, Silk & Tulle Gown, Wrist Tag, c.1955, 17 In. *illus* | 456 |
| **American Character,** Sweet Sue, Plastic, Walker, Ding Dong School, c.1952, 18 In. | 456 |
| **American Character,** Sweet Sue, Plastic, Walker, Pink Gown, Wrist Tag, Box, 15 In. | 288 |
| **American Character,** Sweet Sue, Plastic, Walker, Wrist Booklet, Box, c.1952, 18 In. | 456 |
| **American Character,** Sweet Sue, Vinyl, High Society Costume, Tag, Box, 20 In. | 288 |
| **American Character,** Sweet Sue, Walker, Plastic, Lace, Tulle Gown, Tag, Box, 24 In. *illus* | 285 |
| **American Character,** Sweet Sue, Walker, Vinyl, Pink Taffeta Dress, Tag, Box, 31 In. *illus* | 342 |
| **American Character,** Toni, Ballerina, Vinyl, Sleep Eyes, Chignon, Tutu, Box, 20 In. *illus* | 342 |
| **American Character,** Toni, Vinyl, Love In Bloom, Tag, Wave Set, Box, 20 In. | 171 |
| **American Character,** Toni, Vinyl, Sleep Eyes, Dinner Date Costume, 1958, 10 In. *illus* | 171 |
| **Armand Marseille** dolls are listed in this category under A.M. | |
| **Automation,** Fashion, Ballerina, Tin Platform, 3 Wheels, Paperweight Eyes, 14 In. | 3341 |
| **Automaton,** Bear, Bootmaker, Hide Covered, Glass Eyes, Decamps, 12 ½ In. | 1298 |
| **Automaton,** Bisque Socket Head, Whip, Top, Musical, 13 In. | 2223 |
| **Automaton,** Bisque, Holding Marotte, Musical, 1890s, 17 In. | 2794 |
| **Automaton,** Boy Pulling Girl In Wooden Cart, Bisque, Mohair Wig, Simon Halbig, 1900 | 6160 |
| **Automaton,** Chinese Tea Server, Bisque, Wood, Silk, Upswept Hair, Turns Head, Pours, 19 In. | 11200 |
| **Automaton,** Concert In Garden, Papier-Mache, Wood, Painted, Phalibois, c.1865, 26 In. *illus* | 8550 |
| **Automaton,** Court Musician With Mandolin, Bisque Head, Windup, Music, c.1885, 16 In. | 5600 |
| **Automaton,** Girl, Playing Harp, Bisque Head, Arms & Head Move, Music Plays, 7 x 8 In. | 502 |
| **Automaton,** Girls, Maypole, Bisque Heads, Blue Glass Eyes, Wood, Composition, c.1900, 12 In. | 1888 |
| **Automaton,** Horse, Head & Tail Move, Horse Hair, Clockwork Motion, Key, 1880s, 30 x 28 In. | 720 |
| **Automaton,** Jester Seated On Cushion, Bisque, Wood, Velvet, Turns Head, Lifts Mirror, 12 In. | 9520 |
| **Automaton,** Jester, Bisque, White Mohair, Red & Gold Silk Costume, Strums Guitar, 16 In. | 3808 |
| **Automaton,** Kitten At Ironing Board, Papier-Mache, Wood, Fur, Yellow Glass Eyes, 13 In. | 1792 |
| **Automaton,** Ladies Drinking Tea, Violinist, Tin, Painted, Bing, Germany, 6 ½ x 9 In. | 4425 |
| **Automaton,** Little Girl At Toilette Table, Bisque, Wood, Silk, Blinks, Powders Nose, 20 In. | 5600 |
| **Automaton,** Little Girl, Piano, Bisque Bebe, Head & Hands Move, Music, France, 15 In. | 9520 |
| **Automaton,** Man, Performing Dogs, On Ferris Wheel, Painted Heads, c.1910, 13 x 13 ½ In. | 4720 |
| **Automaton,** Marotte, Musical, Bisque Shoulder Head, Blond Wig, Wood Handle, 14 In. | 177 |
| **Automaton,** Marquis Monkeys, Papier-Mache, Wood, Glass, Phalibois, 27 In. *illus* | 10640 |
| **Automaton,** Policeman, Felt, Uniform, Windup, Schuco, 1920s, 10 ½ In. | 2912 |
| **Automaton,** Punchinello, Organ Grinder, Dancer, Cloth Outfits, Composition Head, France, 21 In. | 3245 |
| **Automaton,** Schoolmaster & His Pupil, Dunce Cap, Music, Roullet Et Decamps, 18 In. | 7000 |
| **Automaton,** Steiner, Waltzing, Windup, Bisque Head, Teeth, Mohair Wig, 1867, 15 In. | 2016 |
| **Automaton,** Woman, Fruit, Flower Seller, Bisque Head, Straw Hat, Music Box, c.1900, 15 In. | 600 |
| **Averill,** Beloved Belindy, Brown Cloth, Button Eyes, Stitch-Jointed, c.1948, 15 In. *illus* | 896 |
| **Averill,** Bonnie Babe, Boy, Bisque, Swivel Head, Jointed, Blue Shoes & Costume, 7 In. | 616 |
| **Averill,** Puppy, Rags, Bisque, Swivel Head, Sleep Eyes, Loop-Jointed, c.1918, 5 In. *illus* | 1482 |
| **Babyland Rag,** Cloth, Hand Stitched Face, Painted Features, Stitch-Jointed, c.1890, 27 In. | 504 |
| **Babyland Rag,** Cloth, Litho Face, Muslin, Stitch-Jointed, Sateen Stocking Legs, c.1910, 13 In. | 336 |
| **Babyland Rag,** Laughing Child, Cloth, Silk Screen Litho Face, Muslin Head, c.1912, 15 In. | 728 |
| **Bahr & Proschild,** 1072, Bisque Socket Head, Mohair Wig, Hip Jointed, 15 In. | 560 |
| **Bahr & Proschild,** Bisque Socket Head, Mohair Wig, c.1910, 17 In. | 2464 |
| **Bahr & Proschild,** Bisque Socket Head, Upper Glancing Eyes, Ball-Jointed, 11 In. | 784 |
| **Barbie** dolls are listed in this category under Mattel. | |
| **Barrois,** Bisque Socket, Black, Teeth, Human Hair, Bunting With Babies, 15 In. | 7110 |
| **Baseball Player,** Bisque Shoulder Head, Moustache, Painted, Cotton Pinstripe Uniform, 6 In. | 472 |
| **Bisque Head,** Amber Complexion, Fully Jointed, Exotic, Late 19th Century, 15 In. | 2128 |
| **Bisque Head,** Performs Movements, Music Plays, Stage, Mirror Backdrop, Germany, c.1890 | 2006 |
| **Bisque Socket Head,** Inset Eyes, Mohair Wig, Composition, Jointed, 1888, 9 ½ In. | 7840 |
| **Bisque Swivel Head,** Blue Inset Eyes, Gusset-Jointed, Human Hair Wig, c.1875, 13 In. | 1120 |
| **Bisque,** Asian Baby, Sleep Eyes, Mohair, Loop-Jointed, Germany, c.1915, 7 In. *illus* | 741 |

| | |
|---|---|
| **Bisque**, Black, Closed Mouth, Leather, Gusset-Jointed, 14 In............................ | 2251 |
| **Bisque**, Man, Sculpted Hair, Painted Face, Muslin Body, Top Hat, Boots, c.1875, 13 In. ............... | 896 |
| **Bisque**, Swivel Head, Glass Eyes, Closed Mouth, Leather, Mohair, 17 In. ........................... | 3258 |
| **Black** dolls are also included in the Black category. | |
| **Boucher**, Dutch Girl, Metal, Jointed Boy, Cloth Outfit, Native Dutch Dress, 8 In........................... | 502 |
| **Boudoir**, Molded Resin, Painted Simian Face, White Wig, Wayne Kleski, 72 In. ............ | 368 |
| **Bru Jne**, Bebe Brevete, Bisque Swivel Head, Amber Glass Eyes, Blond, Kid, Wood, 19 In. .............. | 14000 |
| **Bru Jne**, Bebe, 10, Bisque Swivel Head, Paperweight Eyes, Kid, Gusset-Jointed, 26 In........*illus* | 28500 |
| **Bru Jne**, Bisque Swivel Head, Blue Inset Eyes, Dowel & Swivel-Jointed, c.1872, 15 In...... 2240 to | 4592 |
| **Bru Jne**, Bisque Swivel Head, Inset Eyes, Lamb's Wool Wig, Gusset-Jointed, c.1872, 20 In........... | 4480 |
| **Bru Jne**, Bisque Swivel Head, Paperweight Eyes, Open Mouth, Gusset-Jointed, 13 In.......... | 10640 |
| **Bru Jne**, Dark Brown Bisque Socket Head, Teeth, Mohair, Gusset-Jointed, c.1875, 14 In. ............. | 5600 |
| **Bru Jne**, Fashion, Depose Model, 2 Faces, Bisque, Painted Features, Wig, 15 In. ........................ | 6720 |
| **Bruno Schmidt**, 2048, Boy, Bisque, Sculpted Hair, 2 Teeth, Composition, Wood, Wool, 28 In...... | 952 |
| **Bye-Lo**, 2 Babies, In Woven Carriage, Bisque, Painted, Pink & Blue Shoes, 1923, 4 In.................. | 560 |
| **Chad Valley**, English Bobby, Felt, Swivel Head, Pressed, Painted, Glass Eyes, Jointed, 17 In................... | 504 |
| **Chad Valley**, Pressed, Felt, Swivel Head, Pressed Face, Mohair Wig, Guard Uniform, 1930s, 19 In.. *illus* | 224 |
| **Child**, Standing, Wood, Carved, Painted, Right Arm Out, Holding Cup, 18th Century, 15 In........ | 672 |
| **Cloth**, Black, Shoebutton Eyes, Calico Dress, Embroidered Face, Wool Hair, c.1905, 15 In........ | 385 |
| **Cloth**, Folk, Oil-Painted Face & Hair, Stitch-Jointed, Dress & Pinafore, 1920s, 21 In. ...........*illus* | 168 |
| **Cloth**, Oil Painted, Flat Dimensional Face, Muslin Head, Stitch-Jointed, c.1885, 21 In. ............... | 560 |
| **Cloth**, Painted Long Hair, Flat Dimensional Face, Stitch-Jointed, c.1885, 23 In. ............... | 1008 |
| **Cloth**, Punch & Judy, Lithographed, Multicolor, Cutout, Art Fabric Mills, c.1901, 22 In., Pair...... | 280 |
| **Cloth**, Puss-In-Boots, Stitched, Face, Jacket, Hat, Boots, Willoughby Ions, Va., c.1930, 28 In........ | 489 |
| **Cloth**, Stockinet, Bead Eyes, Floss Mouth, Red Checked Dress, c.1915, 12 In...................... | 29 |
| **Clown**, Bisque, Blue Glass Googly Eyes, Jointed, Colored Costumes, Boy, Girl, 5 In., Pair............. | 2240 |
| **Clown**, Cloth, Celluloid Head, Gund, 1940s, 19 In....................................................... | 65 |
| **Columbian**, Cloth, Stitched On Shoulder Plate Head, Muslin Form, Oil Paint, Hair, 30 In. ........ | 3584 |
| **Creeping Baby**, Composition, Wood, Metal, Painted, Linen, Lace, Clockwork, Ives, 11 In. .......... | 354 |
| **Dolly Dingle**, Bobby Blake, Composition, Googly Eyes, Drayton, Ideal, 9 In., Pair...............*illus* | 912 |
| **Door Of Hope**, Bride, Wood Head, Stuffed Muslin Body, Chinese, c.1910, 12 In..................*illus* | 21280 |
| **Door Of Hope**, Bride, Wood, Carved, Sculpted Face, Hair, Cloth Body, Red, c.1920, 12 In............ | 1008 |
| **Door Of Hope**, Carved Pear Wood, Silk Robe, 11 ½ In. .................................................. | 121 |
| **Door Of Hope**, Wood Head, Amber Skin, Wrinkles, Painted Hair, Cloth Body, 1925, 11 In. .......... | 504 |
| **Door Of Hope**, Wood Head, Human Hair, Smile, Muslin Body, Boy, 1920, 8 In............................ | 336 |
| **Door Of Hope**, Young Lady, Wood Head, Limbs, Stuffed Muslin Body, c.1920, 11 In. ...........*illus* | 448 |
| **Dressel & Kister**, Porcelain, Painted Eyes, Sculpted Curls, Apollo Knot, Muslin Body, 13 In. ........ | 952 |
| **Dressel**, Admiral Dewey, Glass Eyes, Molded Moustache, Hair, Clothing, Hat, 10 ½ In. ............ | 531 |
| **Dressel**, Bisque Socket Head, Mohair Lashes, Mohair Wig, Wood, Flapper, Heels, 14 In............... | 2128 |
| **Dressel**, Uncle Sam, Bisque Socket Head, Glass Eyes, Closed Mouth, c.1890, 15 In..............*illus* | 6840 |
| **Effanbee**, Honey Walker, Hard Plastic, Silver & Pink Gown, Parasol, c.1953, 26 In. ............ | 342 |
| **Effanbee**, Honey, Hard Plastic, Chignon, Schiaparelli Dress, Wrist Tag, Box, 18 In. .............*illus* | 2850 |
| **Elite**, Boy, Bisque, Blue Glass Side-Glancing Eyes, 12 In............................................... | 1111 |
| **Ella Smith**, Alabama Baby, Cloth, Painted, Closed Mouth, Stitch-Jointed, c.1910, 21 In. ........ | 840 |
| **Excelsior**, Bisque Socket Head, Blue Sleep Eyes, Brown Mohair Wig, c.1890, 28 In................... | 1568 |
| **Fashion**, Bisque Head, Blue Paperweight Eyes, Leather Stuffed Body, c.1880, 16 ½ In. .......... | 1495 |
| **Fashion**, Bisque Head, Mohair Wig, Paperweight Eyes, Leather, Cloth Body, 1880, 15 In............ | 403 |
| **Fashion**, Bisque, Paperweight Eyes, Leather Body, Jointed, Closed Mouth, Germany, 18 In. ........ | 1093 |
| **Fashion**, Bisque, Swivel Head, Glass Eyes, Mohair Wig, Kid, c.1870, 12 In..........................*illus* | 1904 |
| **Felt**, Hug Me Kiddie, Blue Side-Glancing Eyes, Smile, Shoulder & Hip-Jointed, 10 In.................. | 336 |
| **Felt**, Hug Me Kiddie, Blue Side-Glancing Eyes, Smile, Shoulder & Hip-Jointed, 12 In................... | 616 |
| **French**, Bisque Head, Arms, Open Mouth, Jointed Composite Body, Belton Type, c.1890, 18 In.... | 960 |
| **French**, Bisque Head, Carton Torso & Legs, Posed On Candy Container, c.1890, 9 In. ............... | 1120 |
| **French**, Bisque Socket Head, Closed Mouth, Lamb's Wool, Brown Eyes, Ball-Jointed, 12 In. ........ | 5890 |
| **French**, Bisque Socket Head, Curly Lashes, Fully Jointed, Mohair Wig, Bebe, 1885, 11 In. ........ | 8960 |
| **French**, Bisque Socket Head, Frowning, Auburn Mohair, Jointed, 1912, 9 In............................ | 2800 |
| **French**, Bisque Swivel Head, Blue Eyes, Closed Mouth, Human Hair, Wood, 1867, 19 In. ........ | 8120 |
| **French**, Bisque Swivel Head, Blue Eyes, Gusset-Jointed, 21 In........................................ | 2800 |
| **French**, Bisque Swivel Head, Blue Inset Eyes, Arched Eyebrow, Ball-Jointed, 4 ½ In...................... | 2464 |
| **French**, Bisque Swivel Head, Blue Inset Eyes, Blond Mohair Wig, c.1882, 5 ½ In. ...................... | 2912 |
| **French**, Bisque Swivel Head, Blue Inset Eyes, Blond Mohair Wig, Peg-Jointed, 5 In................... | 2128 |
| **French**, Bisque Swivel Head, Blue Inset Eyes, Dowel-Jointed, Brown Mohair Wig, 18 In............. | 7280 |
| **French**, Bisque Swivel Head, Brown Inset Eyes, Peg-Jointed Arms & Legs, c.1882, 6 In................ | 1568 |
| **French**, Bisque Swivel Head, Closed Mouth, Brown Mohair Wig, Stitch-Jointed, 15 In.................. | 1904 |
| **French**, Bisque Swivel Head, Painted Lashes, Mohair Wig, Sculpted Shoes, 17 In. ...................... | 8960 |
| **French**, Bisque Swivel Head, Peg-Jointed, Blue Eyes, c.1882, 5 In....................................... | 2128 |
| **French**, Papier-Mache Head, Glass Inset Eyes, Composition, Wood, 35 In. .........................*illus* | 6840 |

**Doll**, American Character, Sweet Sue, Walker, Vinyl, Pink Taffeta Dress, Tag, Box, 31 In.
$342

Theriault's

**Doll**, American Character, Toni, Ballerina, Vinyl, Sleep Eyes, Chignon, Tutu, Box, 20 In.
$342

Theriault's

**Doll**, American Character, Toni, Vinyl, Sleep Eyes, Dinner Date Costume, 1958, 10 In.
$171

Theriault's

**Doll,** Automaton, Concert In Garden, Papier-Mache, Wood, Painted, Phalibois, c.1865, 26 In.
**$8,550**

Theriault's

**Doll,** Automaton, Marquis Monkeys, Papier-Mache, Wood, Glass, Phalibois, 27 In.
**$10,640**

Theriault's

**Doll,** Averill, Beloved Belindy, Brown Cloth, Button Eyes, Stitch-Jointed, c.1948, 15 In.
**$896**

Theriault's

| | |
|---|---:|
| **French,** Papier-Mache Head, Human Hair, Gusset-Jointed, Separated Fingers, 1850, 15 In. | 1232 |
| **French,** Papier-Mache Shoulder Head, Human Hair Wig, Teeth, 1840, 32 In. | 1792 |
| **French,** Papier-Mache, Black Eyes, Open Mouth, Mohair Wig, Redskin Boots, 1850, 26 In. | 1792 |
| **French,** Papier-Mache, Smile, Red Cheeks, Brown Mohair Wig, Hinged Hips, 1910, 14 In. | 3472 |
| **French,** Wax, Shoulder Head, Painted, Brunette Widow's Peak, Wood Arms, Legs, 24 In. | 1904 |
| **Frozen Charlie,** Porcelain, 14 In. | 182 |
| **G. Borgfeldt,** Baby, Bisque, Sleep Eyes, 2 Teeth, Mohair, Composition, Bent Limb, 17 In. | 280 |
| **G. Borgfeldt,** Bisque, Gray Glass Eyes, Blond Mohair, Jointed Composition & Wood, 28 In. | 1120 |
| **G.I. Joe** figures are listed in the Toy category. | |
| **Gaultier,** Bebe, Bisque Socket Head, Brown Paperweight Eyes, 17 In. | 741 |
| **Gaultier,** Bisque Head, Blue Glass Eyes, Blond Mohair, Composition & Wood, 22 In. | 6160 |
| **Gaultier,** Bisque Socket Head, Blue Eyes, Leather, Gusset-Jointed, Mohair, 12 In. | 948 |
| **Gaultier,** Bisque Socket Head, Blue Paperweight Eyes, Wood Body, c.1880, 17 In. | 8120 |
| **Gaultier,** Bisque Socket Head, Hazel Paperweight Eyes, Ball-Jointed, c.1880, 16 In. | 6160 |
| **Gaultier,** Bisque Socket Head, Inset Eyes, Porcelain Teeth, Dimple, Jointed, 29 In. | 5320 |
| **Gaultier,** Bisque Swivel Head, Blue Eyes, Mohair, Gusset-Jointed, 1875, 14 In. | 5880 |
| **Gaultier,** Bisque Swivel Head, Blue Inset Eyes, Leather Body, Mohair, 1875, 14 In. | 2352 |
| **Gaultier,** Bisque Swivel Head, Blue Paperweight Eyes, Swivel-Jointed, c.1870, 21 In. | 5600 |
| **Gaultier,** Fashion, Bisque, Swivel Head, Kid Body, Brittany Bride, Ribbon, Lace, 15 In. | 3920 |
| **Gebruder Heubach** dolls may also be listed in this category under Heubach. | |
| **Gebruder Heubach,** Bisque Socket Head, 2 Faces, Ball-Jointed, c.1910, 18 In. | 2016 |
| **Gebruder Heubach,** Bisque Socket Head, Beaded Teeth, Laughing, Molded Hair, 14 In. | 504 |
| **Gebruder Heubach,** Bisque Socket Head, Blond Sculpted Hair, Bent Limb, c.1912, 8 In. | 224 |
| **Gebruder Heubach,** Bisque Socket Head, Blue Sleep Eyes, Teeth, Dimples, 25 In. | 2240 |
| **Gebruder Heubach,** Bisque Socket Head, Sculpted Bonnet, c.1915, 8 In. | 280 |
| **Gebruder Heubach,** Bisque Socket Head, Sculpted Bonnet, Sleep Eyes, Ball-Jointed, 10 In. | 672 |
| **Gebruder Heubach,** Bonnet Head Baby, Painted Face, Leather Body, Bisque Forearms, 17 In. | 1534 |
| **Gebruder Heubach,** Cat, Molded Bisque Head, 5 Piece Toddler Body, Painted, Boots, 6 In. | 1888 |
| **Gebruder Heubach,** Dolly Dimple, Bisque, Socket Head, Sleep Eyes, Mohair Wig, 28 In. | 1700 |
| **Gebruder Heubach,** Googly, Molded, Painted, Inverted V Shape Mouth, Composition, 10 In. | 1416 |
| **Gebruder Heubach,** Pink Bisque Socket Head, Blue Sleep Eyes, Ball-Jointed, c.1910, 13 In. | 951 |
| **Gebruder Heubach,** Pink Bisque Socket Head, Sculpted Hair, Ball-Jointed, 23 In. | 560 |
| **Gebruder Heubach,** Whistling Jim, Bisque Head, Swivel Neck, Cloth, Composition, 11 In. | 885 |
| **Gebruder Kuhnlenz,** Black Bisque Swivel Head, Loop-Jointed, Black Inset Eyes, 9 ½ In. | 2352 |
| **Gebruder Kuhnlenz,** Light Brown Bisque, Peg-Jointed, c.1890, 3 ½ In. | 504 |
| **Gebruder Ohlhaver,** Bisque Socket Head, Beaded Teeth, Ball-Jointed, 13 In. | 392 |
| **Gerbruder Heubach,** 7081, Bisque Socket Head, Sculpted Hair, Ball-Jointed, c.1910, 23 In. | 1232 |
| **German,** Baby, Bisque Socket Head, Smiles, Cries, Composition, Wood, Jointed, 13 In. | 728 |
| **German,** Baby, Seated, Porcelain, Sculpted, Blond Hair, Ruffled Cap, Smock, c.1885, 3 In. | 728 |
| **German,** Bisque Head, Mohair Lashes & Wig, Muslin Body, 1927, 18 In. | 3024 |
| **German,** Bisque Head, Plump Stomach, Painted White Stockings, Peg-Jointed, 8 In. | 84 |
| **German,** Bisque Shoulder Head, Glass Eyes, Sculpted Braids, Dresden Trim, Kid, 17 In. | 1904 |
| **German,** Bisque Socket Head, Admiral Dewey, Papier-Mache Body, 1898, 14 In. | 1112 |
| **German,** Bisque Socket Head, Blond Mohair Wig, Composition, Jointed, 16 In. | 4200 |
| **German,** Bisque Socket Head, Full Lips, Brown Mohair Wig, Ball-Jointed, 1910, 18 In. | 2352 |
| **German,** Bisque Socket Head, Mohair Lashes, Jointed, 1890s, 25 In. | 1904 |
| **German,** Bisque Socket Head, Mohair Wig, Composition, Jointed, 15 In. | 6160 |
| **German,** China Head, Shoulders, Black Molded Hair, Cloth Body, Plaid Dress, 31 In. | 360 |
| **German,** Girl, 3 Faces, Smiling, Crying, Sleeping, Bisque, Composition, Pull String, 12 In. | 1008 |
| **German,** Lady, Papier-Mache, Shoulder Head, Black Eyes, Muslin, Sculpted Chignon, 13 In. | 2016 |
| **German,** Medieval Lady, Bisque, Holding Bird, Painted, Mohair Wig, 13 In. | 1456 |
| **German,** Porcelain, Black Queen Victoria Coiffure, Painted, Closed Mouth, c.1850, 10 In. | 2240 |
| **German,** Renaissance Woman, Bisque, Painted Face, Closed Mouth, Mohair Wig, 12 In. | 1568 |
| **German,** Tauflinge Baby, Papier-Mache, Painted, Bellows, Turns Head, Cries Mama, 11 In. | 1680 |
| **German,** Wax Over Papier-Mache, Shoulder Head, Glass Eyes, Jointed Muslin, c.1875, 21 In. | 448 |
| **German,** Wood, Bedpost Shape Head, Painted Hair, Sculpted Ear, Dress, Grodner Tal, c.1850, 21 In. | 448 |
| **Gertrude Rollinson,** Character Boy, Cloth, Pressed, Painted Face, Stitch-Jointed, c.1920, 18 In. | 2464 |
| **Greiner,** Papier-Mache, Painted Blue Eyes, Molded Hair, Center Part, Child's Dress, 30 In. | 600 |
| **Greiner,** Papier-Mache, Painted Blue Eyes, Molded Hair, Center Part, Dress, Lace, 30 In. | 230 |
| **Grossman,** Bisque Head, Set Eyes, Composition & Wood, Ball-Jointed, Germany, 13 In. ......*illus* | 741 |
| **Half Dolls** are listed in the Pincushion Doll category. | |
| **Handwerck,** Bisque Head, Fixed Eyes, Open Mouth, Inscribed 6 ½, 30 In. | 240 |
| **Handwerck,** Incised Head, Blue Glass Sleep Eyes, Wig, 26 In. | 177 |
| **Hertel Schwab,** 165, Bisque, Googly Eyes, Composition, Wood, Jointed, 25 In. ......*illus* | 14820 |
| **Hertel Schwab,** 165, Blue Googly Eyes, Jointed Wood, Composition, Human Hair, 12 In. | 2161 |
| **Hertel Schwab,** Bisque Socket Head, Googly Sleep Eyes, Painted, Ball-Jointed, c.1915, 13 In. | 2464 |
| **Hertel Schwab,** Bisque Socket Head, Sleep Eyes, Ball-Jointed, c.1912, 16 In. | 3920 |

| | |
|---|---|
| Hertel Schwab, Jubilee, Bisque Socket Head, Smile, Mohair, Ball-Jointed, c.1916, 16 In. | 3080 |
| Heubach, see also Gebruder Heubach. | |
| Heubach Koppelsdorf, 310, Googly, Bisque Shoulder Head, Glass Eyes, Kid Toddler Body, 12 In. | 3584 |
| Heubach Koppelsdorf, 418, Boy, Bisque Head, Brown, Smile, Composition Toddler, 13 In. | 1344 |
| Heubach, 6970, Bisque, Head, Glass Sleep Eyes, Mohair, Composition, c.1912, 18 In. | 2100 |
| Heubach, Baby Bo-Kaye, Bisque Head, Brunette Mohair Bob, Composition, Toddler, 7 In. | 616 |
| Heubach, Bisque Socket Head, Sculpted Hair, Side-Glancing Eyes, Dimples, 7 In. | 896 |
| Heubach, Googly, Bisque Socket Head, Intaglio Eyes, Sculpted Forelock, Topknot, 6 In. | 448 |
| Heubach, Native American Woman, Bisque, Muslin, Intaglio Eyes, Beaded Costume, 13 In. | 3920 |
| Heubach, Pink Bisque Socket Head, Human Hair, Ball-Jointed, Wood, c.1912, 11 In. | 672 |
| Horsman, Bride, Composition, Ivory Satin Gown, Accessories, Tag, Box, 1940s, 14 In. .......illus | 627 |
| Horsman, Cindy, Bride, Brown Vinyl, Jointed, Satin Gown, Accessories, Tag, Box, 18 In. ......illus | 86 |
| Horsman, Cindy, Vinyl, Swivel Waist, Ponytail, Dress, Velveteen Coat, Box, 10 In................illus | 86 |
| Horsman, Tynie Baby, Bisque, Swivel Head, Sleep Eyes, Painted Hair, Jointed, 1924, 8 In. | 1456 |
| Huret, Fashion, Porcelain, Wood Body, Painted Face, Closed Mouth, Mohair Wig, c.1860, 17 In. | 14000 |
| Ideal, Miss Revlon, Hat, Blond Curls, Wrist Tag, 1957...........................................................illus | 840 |
| Ideal, Miss Revlon, Vinyl Head, Blond Curls, Deb Gown, Heels, Tag, Box, 18 In...................illus | 456 |
| Ideal, Miss Revlon, Vinyl Head, Blond Hair, Deb Gown, Tag, c.1957, 18 In............................illus | 456 |
| Ideal, Miss Revlon, Vinyl Head, Sleep Eyes, Evening Star Costume, 1957, 18 In. ..................illus | 399 |
| Ideal, Miss Revlon, Vinyl Socket Head, Auburn Saran Hair, Kissing Pink, Box, c.1957, 20 In..... | 438 |
| Ideal, Miss Revlon, Vinyl Socket Head, Auburn Saran Hair, Sleep Eyes, Deb, c.1957, 18 In. | 456 |
| Ideal, Miss Revlon, Vinyl Socket Head, Blond Saran Hair, Aqua Body, Box, c.1957, 10 In. | 228 |
| Ideal, Miss Revlon, Vinyl Socket Head, Blond Saran Hair, Cherries A La Mode, 1957, 20 In. | 313 |
| Ideal, Miss Revlon, Vinyl Socket Head, Blond Saran Hair, Kissing Pink, Box, c.1957, 18 In. | 342 |
| Ideal, Miss Revlon, Vinyl Socket Head, Saran Hair, Cherries A La Mode, c.1957, 22 In. | 375 |
| Ideal, Miss Revlon, Vinyl, Cherries A La Mode Series, Navy Dress, Tag, Box, 22 In. ..............illus | 342 |
| Ideal, Miss Revlon, Vinyl, Queen Of Diamonds Dress, Gold Brocade, Fur, 22 In. | 228 |
| Indian dolls are listed in the Indian category. | |
| Izannah Walker, Cloth, Pressed, Oil-Painted Features, 4 Ringlets, Stitch-Jointed, 19 In. | 17360 |
| J.D.K. dolls are also listed in this category under Kestner. | |
| Joel Ellis, Mannequin Type, Wood, Painted, Jointed, Springfield, Vermont, 15 In. | 425 |
| Jumeau, Bebe Triste, Bisque Socket Head, Paperweight Eyes, Ball-Jointed, c.1884, 22 In. | 10640 |
| Jumeau, Bebe, Bisque Head, Paperweight Eyes, Closed Mouth, Composition & Wood, 14 In. | 5040 |
| Jumeau, Bebe, Bisque Socket, Brown Paperweight Eyes, Mohair, 16 ½ In. | 4740 |
| Jumeau, Bebe, Blue Paperweight Eyes, Wood, Composition, Human Hair, 34 ½ In. | 1215 |
| Jumeau, Bisque Head, Inscribed Tete, Composition, Fixed Eyes, Red Dress, Cap, Lace, 19 In. | 3120 |
| Jumeau, Bisque Socket Head, Amber Paperweight Eyes, Mohair Wig, Jointed, 21 In. | 3920 |
| Jumeau, Bisque Socket Head, Amber Paperweight Eyes, Mohair, Jointed, c.1886, 15 In. | 3136 |
| Jumeau, Bisque Socket Head, Amber Paperweight Eyes, Mohair, Jointed, c.1888, 15 In. | 3640 |
| Jumeau, Bisque Socket Head, Blond Mohair, Jointed, 1880, 22 In. | 7000 |
| Jumeau, Bisque Socket Head, Blue Paperweight Eyes, Blond Mohair, Jointed, 11 In. | 5600 |
| Jumeau, Bisque Socket Head, Blue Paperweight Eyes, Jointed, Human Hair, 32 In. | 5040 |
| Jumeau, Bisque Socket Head, Blue Paperweight Eyes, Jointed, Human Hair, c.1888, 20 In. | 3360 |
| Jumeau, Bisque Socket Head, Blue Paperweight Eyes, Mohair Wig, Jointed, c.1892, 12 In. | 2240 |
| Jumeau, Bisque Socket Head, Brown Inset Eyes, Mohair Wig, Ball-Jointed, 1888, 14 In. | 5600 |
| Jumeau, Bisque Socket Head, Brown Paperweight Eyes, Ball-Jointed, c.1878, 14 ½ In. | 5880 |
| Jumeau, Bisque Socket Head, Closed Mouth, Blond Mohair Wig, Jointed, c.1888, 27 In. | 3584 |
| Jumeau, Bisque Socket Head, Closed Mouth, Pierced Eyes, Ball-Jointed, 1878, 15 In. | 6440 |
| Jumeau, Bisque Socket Head, Cork Pate, Blond Mohair Wig, Ball-Jointed, c.1877, 15 In. | 7280 |
| Jumeau, Bisque Socket Head, Hazel Paperweight Eyes, Blond Mohair Wig, c.1878, 15 In. | 5320 |
| Jumeau, Bisque Socket Head, Human Hair, Jointed, c.1888, 16 In. | 2240 |
| Jumeau, Bisque Socket Head, Inset Eyes, Mohair Wig, Ball-Jointed, c.1884, 18 In. | 3584 |
| Jumeau, Bisque Socket Head, Inset Eyes, Mohair Wig, Box, 1885, 17 In. | 8120 |
| Jumeau, Bisque Socket Head, Lamb's Wool Wig, Composition, Jointed, 19 In. | 6720 |
| Jumeau, Bisque Socket Head, Lamb's Wool Wig, Dimple, Ball-Jointed, 1878, 14 In. | 10360 |
| Jumeau, Bisque Socket Head, Paperweight Eyes, Closed Mouth, Mohair Wig, 16 In. | 7560 |
| Jumeau, Bisque Socket Head, Paperweight Eyes, Dimples, Mohair Wig, Jointed, 15 In. | 6160 |
| Jumeau, Bisque Socket Head, Paperweight Eyes, Wood, Composition Body, Wig, 26 In. | 1519 |
| Jumeau, Bisque Swivel Head, Blue Eyes, Mohair Wig, Gusset-Jointed, Fingers, 1875, 15 In. | 4480 |
| Jumeau, Bisque Swivel Head, Blue Inset Eyes, Mohair Wig, Gusset-Jointed, c.1870, 17 In. | 2240 to 2464 |
| Jumeau, Bisque Swivel Head, Brown Inset Eyes, Human Hair Wig, Gusset-Jointed, 17 In. | 2240 |
| Jumeau, Bisque, Amber Paperweight Eyes, Ball-Jointed, Skin Wig, 17 ½ In. | 5467 |
| Jumeau, Bisque, Brown Paperweight Eyes, Closed Mouth, Mohair, 24 In. | 2666 |
| Jumeau, Bisque, Jointed, Human Hair, Blond, 26 In. | 2666 |
| Jumeau, Bisque, Paperweight Eyes, Pierced Earlobes, Leather, Mohair, 21 In. | 4444 |
| Jumeau, Bisque, Papier-Mache, Walker, Hunter, 13 ½ In. | 592 |
| Jumeau, Fashion, Bisque, Swivel Head, Glass Eyes, Blond Mohair Wig, Signed, 13 In..........illus | 3080 |

**Doll,** Averill, Puppy, Rags, Bisque, Swivel Head, Sleep Eyes, Loop-Jointed, c.1918, 5 In.
$1,482

Theriault's

**Doll,** Bisque, Asian Baby, Sleep Eyes, Mohair, Loop-Jointed, Germany, c.1915, 7 In.
$741

Theriault's

**Doll,** Bru Jne, Bebe, 10, Bisque Swivel Head, Paperweight Eyes, Kid, Gusset-Jointed, 26 In.
$28,500

Theriault's

**Doll,** Chad Valley, Pressed, Felt, Swivel Head, Pressed Face, Mohair Wig, Guard Uniform, 1930s, 19 In.
$224

**Doll,** Dolly Dingle, Bobby Blake, Composition, Googly Eyes, Drayton, Ideal, 9 In., Pair
$912

Theriault's

Theriault's

**Doll,** Door Of Hope, Bride, Wood Head, Stuffed Muslin Body, Chinese, c.1910, 12 In.
$21,280

**Doll,** Door Of Hope, Young Lady, Wood Head, Limbs, Stuffed Muslin Body, c.1920, 11 In.
$448

**Doll,** Cloth, Folk, Oil-Painted Face & Hair, Stitch-Jointed, Dress & Pinafore, 1920s, 21 In.
$168

Theriault's

Theriault's

Theriault's

| | |
|---|---|
| **Jumeau,** Jointed, Wood, Composition, Paperweight Eyes, V Lip, 13 ½ In. | 3523 |
| **Jumeau,** No. 201, Bisque Head, Paperweight Eyes, Composition, Wood, Jointed, 24 In. ........*illus* | 280000 |
| **Jumeau,** Paperweight Eyes, Open Mouth, Teeth, Jointed, Composition, Wood, Hair, 20 In. | 829 |
| **Jumeau,** Young Marquis, Bisque Head, Brown Paperweight Eyes, Open Mouth, Jointed, 33 In. | 2800 |
| **Just Me,** Sleep Eyes, 5 Piece Composition Body, Wig, Bisque Body, Germany, 7 ½ In. | 944 |
| **K * R,** 22, Bisque Head, Character, Blue Fixed Eyes, Painted, Composition, c.1929, 17 In. | 460 |
| **K * R,** 80, Bisque Head, Sleep Eyes, Open Mouth, Blond Curls, Purple Bonnet, Dress, 30 In. | 240 |
| **K * R,** 100, Kaiser, Bisque Head, Composition Body, 14 In. | 165 |
| **K * R,** 101, Bisque Socket Head, Brown Sleep Eyes, Pout, Mohair Wig, c.1912, 18 In. | 4480 |
| **K * R,** 101, Wood, Composition, Curly Mohair, 21 In. | 948 |
| **K * R,** 101/50, Marie, Bisque, Socket Head, Pout, Face, Mohair Wig, Jointed, c.1910, 20 In. | 4480 |
| **K * R,** 114, Bisque Socket Head, Mohair Wig, Ball-Jointed, c.1910, 9 In. | 672 |
| **K * R,** 114, Boy, Blue Painted Eyes, Wood, Composition, 1910 Sailor Suit, 21 ½ In. | 729 |
| **K * R,** 114, Brown Sleep Eyes, Wood, Composition, Human Hair, 18 In. | 1777 |
| **K * R,** 115A, Phillip, Bisque, Brown Sleep Eyes, Pouty Lips, Mohair, Toddler, 13 In. | 2352 |
| **K * R,** 117A, Bisque Head, Mohair Lashes & Wig, Ball-Jointed, 1912, 18 In. | 3080 |
| **K * R,** 117A, Mein Liebling, Bisque Head, Sleep Eyes, Human Hair Ringlets, 27 In. | 3920 |
| **K * R,** 119, Bisque Socket Head, 5 Piece Body, Painted Shoes & Socks, c.1910, 7 In. | 1064 |
| **K * R,** 126, Bisque Socket Head, Brown Sleep Eyes, 2 Porcelain Teeth, Ball-Jointed, 28 In. | 560 |
| **K * R,** 127, Toddler Boy, Bisque, Composition, Sleep Eyes, 2 Teeth, Tyrolean Suit, 17 In. | 2352 |
| **K * R,** 127, Toddler, Bisque, Painted Hair, Socket Head, Sleep Eyes, Open Mouth, c.1912, 23 In. | 1008 |
| **K * R,** Parasol, Bisque Head, Teeth, Leg Handgrip, Pink Skirt, c.1910, 11 In. | 840 |
| **Kallus,** 1394, Bisque Head, Curly Lashes, Bo-Kaye, Pouting Lips, Sculpted Hair, 1927, 18 In. | 1120 |
| **Kampes,** Cloth, Swivel Head, Blue Eyes, Human Hair Wig, Stitch-Jointed, c.1930, 18 In. | 1456 |
| **Kathe Kruse,** Boy, Cloth Face, Human Hair, 20 In. | 1659 |
| **Kathe Kruse,** Boy, Cloth, Blue Eyes, Jointed Arms, Blond, Original Clothes, c.1914, 16 In. | 1725 |
| **Kathe Kruse,** Cloth, Oil Painted Face, Pouting, Brown Hair, Flowered Dress, c.1915, 17 In. | 4750 |
| **Kathe Kruse,** Doll I Face, Stitched Fingers, Swivel Hip Joints, 17 In. | 1185 |
| **Kathe Kruse,** Girl, Blond, Knit Hat, Print Dress, Brown Shoes, Cloth, Composition, 17 In. | 1750 |
| **Kathe Kruse,** Girl, Cloth, Disc Swivel Joints, Human Hair, 20 In. | 972 |
| **Kathe Kruse,** Linen & Cloth, Blond Wig, Wreath, Peggy, Wrist Tag, Box, c.1945, 17 In. | 2133 |
| **Kathe Kruse,** Linen, Evelyn, Wrist Tag, Germany, US Zone, Box, 1940s, 14 In. | 2133 |
| **Kathe Kruse,** Pressed Felt, Cloth, Swivel Hip Joints, 17 In. | 1185 |
| **Kestner,** 150, Bisque Head & Torso, Brown Sleep Eyes, Jointed, 1910, 5 In. | 224 |
| **Kestner,** 150, Bisque Head & Torso, Teeth, 1910, 9 In. | 336 |
| **Kestner,** 156, Bisque Socket Head, Blue Sleep Eyes, 4 Porcelain Teeth, Ball-Jointed, 29 In. | 504 |
| **Kestner,** 185, Bisque Socket Head, Smile, Teeth, Mohair, Composition, Ball-Jointed, 11 In. | 1568 |
| **Kestner,** 190, Child, Multi-Head Set, Bisque, Socket Head, Mohair Wig, c.1910, 15 In. .........*illus* | 3420 |
| **Kestner,** 192, Bisque Head, Sleep Eyes, Brunette Braids, Wool & Velvet Coat & Hat, 18 In. | 10080 |
| **Kestner,** 211, Baby, Bisque Head, Brown Glass Eyes, Brunette Mohair Bob, Sailor Suit, 23 In. | 1064 |
| **Kestner,** 221, Bisque Head, Blue Googly Eyes, Composition, Jointed, Toddler, 12 In. ............*illus* | 4560 |
| **Kestner,** 221, Bisque, Googly Eyes, Jointed Wood, Composition, Blond Mohair, 14 ½ In. | 1518 |
| **Kestner,** 221, Bisque, Side-Glancing Googly Eyes, Watermelon Slice Smile, Toddler, 15 In. | 5600 |
| **Kestner,** 237, Blue Sleep Eyes, 2 Upper Teeth, 5 Piece Composition, Baby, 16 In. | 850 |
| **Kestner,** 237, Hilda, Bisque, Sleep Eyes, Wood, Composition, Mohair, Toddler, 16 ½ In. | 1362 |
| **Kestner,** 243, Asian Baby, Bisque, Composition, Brown Eyes, Smile, Headdress, Pearls, 16 In. | 2800 |
| **Kestner,** 260, Boy, Bisque, Blue Sleep Eyes, 4 Teeth, Brunette Hair, Jointed, Sailor Suit, 40 In. | 2576 |
| **Kestner,** Bisque Head & Body, Sleep Eyes, Blond Mohair Wig, Loop-Jointed, 9 In. | 392 |
| **Kestner,** Bisque Head, Boy, Character, Sleep Eyes, Composition Body, Jointed, c.1820, 16 In. | 259 |
| **Kestner,** Bisque Socket Head, Blue Sleep Eyes, Blond Mohair, Pointed Teeth, 1885, 12 In. | 3248 |
| **Kestner,** Bisque Socket Head, Blue Sleep Eyes, Human Hair, Jointed, c.1885, 7 In. | 1232 |
| **Kestner,** Bisque Socket Head, Brown Inset Eyes, Brown Human Hair, Jointed, 24 In. | 1344 |
| **Kestner,** Bisque Socket Head, Brown Sleep Eyes, Pout, Ball-Jointed, c.1885, 21 In. | 1456 |
| **Kestner,** Bisque Socket Head, Brown Sleep Eyes, Teeth, Dimples, Brown Mohair Wig, 18 In. | 2800 |
| **Kestner,** Bisque Socket Head, Closed Mouth, Blond Mohair Wig, Ball-Jointed, 11 In. | 1232 |
| **Kestner,** Bisque Socket Head, Plump, Closed Mouth, Mohair Wig, Ball-Jointed, 14 In. | 1232 |
| **Kestner,** Bisque Socket Head, Side-Glancing Eyes, Smile, Ball-Jointed, 1912, 13 In. | 3472 |
| **Kestner,** Bisque Socket Head, Side-Glancing Eyes, Smile, Ball-Jointed, 1912, 16 In. | 7840 |
| **Kestner,** Bisque Swivel Head, Blue Sleep Eyes, Loop-Jointed, Bare Feet, c.1915, 8 In. | 224 |
| **Kestner,** Bisque Swivel Head, Brown Sleep Eyes, Loop-Jointed, Brown Mohair Wig, 9 In. | 224 |
| **Kestner,** Bisque, Blue Glass Eyes, Blond Mohair Braid, Peg-Jointed, Knitted Dress, 6 In. | 1904 |
| **Kestner,** Blue Sleep Eyes, 2 Porcelain Teeth, Ball-Jointed, Hilda, c.1915, 23 In. | 2240 |
| **Kestner,** Gibson Girl, Bisque Shoulder Head, Sleep Eyes, Mohair Lashes & Wig, Kid, 16 In. | 1792 |
| **Kestner,** Gibson Girl, Bisque Shoulder Head, Uptilted Pose, Mohair, Kid, Jointed, 20 In. | 2240 |
| **Kestner,** Hilda, Bisque, Sleep Eyes, 2 Teeth, Mohair, Composition, Bent Limb Baby, 23 In. | 2800 |
| **Kewpie** dolls are listed in the Kewpie category. | |

**Doll,** Dressel, Uncle Sam, Bisque Socket Head, Glass Eyes, Closed Mouth, c.1890, 15 In.
$6,840

Theriault's

**Doll,** Effanbee, Honey, Hard Plastic, Chignon, Schiaparelli Dress, Wrist Tag, Box, 18 In.
$2,850

Theriault's

**Doll,** Fashion, Bisque, Swivel Head, Glass Eyes, Mohair Wig, Kid, c.1870, 12 In.
$1,904

Theriault's

D

167

**Doll,** French, Papier-Mache Head, Glass Inset Eyes, Composition, Wood, 35 In. $6,840

Theriault's

**Doll,** Grossman, Bisque Head, Set Eyes, Composition & Wood, Ball-Jointed, Germany, 13 In. $741

Theriault's

**Doll,** Hertel Schwab, 165, Bisque, Googly Eyes, Composition, Wood, Jointed, 25 In. $14,820

Theriault's

| | |
|---|---:|
| **Kley & Hahn,** 133, Baby, Bisque Head, Sleep Eyes, Tongue, 2 Teeth, Composition, 9 In. | 392 |
| **Kley & Hahn,** 536, German, Intaglio Eyes, Dimples, Wood, Composition, 12 ½ In. | 1540 |
| **Leather,** Cloth, Oil Painted Features, Dimples, Blond Human Hair, Stitched Details, 17 In. | 728 |
| **Leather,** Glass Eyes, Gusset-Jointed Hips, 14 In. | 1778 |
| **Lenci,** 1500 Series, Felt Swivel Head, Plump, Brown Mohair Braids, 1926, 18 In. | 1568 |
| **Lenci,** Character, Girl, Swivel Head, Painted, Side-Glancing Eyes, Series 1500, 17 In. ...*illus* | 4275 |
| **Lenci,** Chinese Girl, Dschang-Go, Felt, Swivel Head, Painted Face, Human Hair, 23 In. ...*illus* | 6840 |
| **Lenci,** Girl, Benedetta, Felt, Swivel Head, Painted, Braids, Jointed, Plaid Dress, 19 In. | 2800 |
| **Lenci,** Girl, Felt, Pressed, Painted, Side-Glancing Eyes, Blond Mohair, Organdy Dress, 13 In. | 840 |
| **Lenci,** Hu San, Felt, Swivel Head, Painted Face, Mohair Wig, Opium Pipe, 1924, 21 In. ...*illus* | 2850 |
| **Lenci,** Italian Felt Character Girl, No. 450, Painted Face, Red Ensemble, c.1930, 14 In. | 2240 |
| **Lenci,** Torino, Boy, Ethnic Clothes, Tall Hat With Feather, 11 In. | 72 |
| **Leontine Rohmer,** Bisque Socket Head, Plump, Mohair Wig, Leather, Porcelain, 1860, 16 In. | 7560 |
| **Limbach,** Bisque Socket Head, Blue Sleep Eyes, Composition Bent Limb, c.1915, 11 In. | 560 |
| **Little Red Riding Hood,** Cloth, Litho, Carrying Basket, Arnold Print Works, c.1892, 17 In. | 168 |
| **M. Milliere,** Flapper, Plaster, Painted, Head Turned, Brunette Wig, Lace Dress, Veil, 16 In. | 1120 |
| **Madame Alexander,** Cissette, Plastic, Jointed, Curly Updo, Box, c.1957, 10 In. | 285 |
| **Madame Alexander,** Cissette, Plastic, Jointed, Sleep Eyes, Box, c.1961, 10 In. | 285 |
| **Madame Alexander,** Glamour Girl, Plastic, Walker, Velvet, Taffeta Gown, c.1953, 18 In. ...*illus* | 4332 |
| **Madame Alexander,** Godey Bridegroom, Plastic, Gold Cloverleaf Tag, c.1950, 14 In. ...*illus* | 1482 |
| **Madame Alexander,** Judy, Plastic, Jointed, Sleep Eyes, Rhinestone Beauty Mark, 20 In. | 6555 |
| **Madame Hendron,** Dolly Dingle, Cloth, Painted, Stitch-Jointed, Label, c.1930, 16 In. ...*illus* | 684 |
| **Marseille,** 240, Bisque Socket Head, Sculpted Top Knot, Hip-Jointed, 1915, 10 In. | 1680 |
| **Marseille,** 241, Bisque Socket Head, Plump Cheeks, Side-Glancing Eyes, 1915, 10 In. | 2352 |
| **Marseille,** Bisque Socket Head, Side-Glancing Eyes, Mohair, Papier-Mache, c.1925, 7 In. | 280 |
| **Marseille,** Floradora, Bisque Socket Head, Sleep Eyes, Painted, Mohair Wig, Jointed, 17 In. | 392 |
| **Martha Chase,** Character Boy, Stockinet, Pressed, Painted Face, Stitch-Jointed, c.1910, 20 In. | 560 |
| **Martha Chase,** Cloth, Brown Eyes, Bobbed Hair, Painted Face, Hair, Jointed, c.1915, 16 In. | 1008 |
| **Mattel,** Barbie, Ash Blond Bubble Cut, Red Swimsuit, Stand, Shoes | 90 |
| **Mattel,** Barbie, Blond Bubble Cut, No. 992 Golden Elegance, Box, 11 In. ...*illus* | 285 |
| **Mattel,** Barbie, Blond Ponytail, No. 963 Resort Sct, Original Box, c.1960, 11 In. ...*illus* | 1824 |
| **Mattel,** Barbie, Blond Ponytail, White & Black Striped Knit Maillot, Box, Booklet, c.1961 | 285 |
| **Mattel,** Barbie, Blond, Red Swimsuit, Stand, Wrist Bracelet, Booklet, Box, c.1963 | 342 |
| **Mattel,** Barbie, Brunette Bubble Cut, Red Swimsuit, Pearl Earrings, Shoes, Stand, Box | 158 |
| **Mattel,** Barbie, Brunette Ponytail, Apple Print Sheath, Peep Toe Shoes, Box, c.1960 | 627 |
| **Mattel,** Barbie, Brunette Side Swirl Ponytail, Side-Glancing Eyes, Yellow Knit, c.1964 | 399 |
| **Mattel,** Barbie, Brunette Swirl Ponytail, Red Swimsuit, Shoes, Stand, Box | 158 |
| **Mattel,** Barbie, Elizabeth Taylor, Violet Eyes, Black Dress, Gold Label Silkstone | 124 |
| **Mattel,** Barbie, Elizabeth Taylor, White Diamonds, White Dress, Gold Label, Silkstone, Box | 102 |
| **Mattel,** Barbie, Japanese American, Brunette Side-Part Hair, Swimsuit, Shoes | 791 |
| **Mattel,** Barbie, Japanese Costume, Franklin Lim Liao Couture | 158 |
| **Mattel,** Barbie, Japanese, Red Bubble Cut, 5 Kimonos, Shoes | 1413 |
| **Mattel,** Barbie, No. 1, Blond Ponytail, Swimsuit, Peg Stand, Box, c.1959, 11 In. ...*illus* | 4788 |
| **Mattel,** Barbie, No. 3, Brunette Ponytail, Striped Swimsuit, Sunglasses, Box | 424 |
| **Mattel,** Barbie, No. 4, Blond Ponytail, Wearing Midnight Blue Gown, No. 1617 | 136 |
| **Mattel,** Barbie, No. 5, Brunette Ponytail, Black & White Striped Swimsuit, Box | 136 |
| **Mattel,** Barbie, No. 5, Titian Ponytail, Let's Dance Dress, No. 978 | 1124 |
| **Mattel,** Barbie, Talking, Wearing Romantic Ruffles Outfit, No. 1871 | 158 |
| **Mattel,** Barbie, Twist 'N' Turn, Titian Hair, Swimsuit, Wrist Tag | 283 |
| **Mattel,** Julia, Nurse's Outfit, Cap, Shoes, Stand | 45 to 51 |
| **Mattel,** Ken, Brown Flocked Hair, Bathing Shorts, Jacket, Sandals, Box, c.1961, 12 In. ...*illus* | 114 |
| **Mattel,** Midge, Blond, Flip-Curled Bob, 2 Piece Swimsuit, Wrist Tag, Box, c.1963 | 114 |
| **Mattel,** Skipper Fashion Boutique, Doll, 4 Outfits, Display Case, 1970s | 1130 |
| **Mattel,** Skipper, Growing Up, Make Her Grow, Red & White Outfit, Box | 136 |
| **Mattel,** Walking Jamie, Brown Hair, Original Outfit, Box | 181 |
| **Nancy Ann Storybook,** Hard Plastic, Blond Hair, Lavender & Lace, Box, 1950s, 18 In. ...*illus* | 1254 |
| **Nancy Ann Storybook,** Hard Plastic, Old-Fashioned Bouquet, White Lace, 1950s, 18 In. ...*illus* | 2964 |
| **Neapolitan,** 3 Wish Men, Hemp Wrapped Bodies, Early 1800s, 14 In. | 5600 |
| **Neapolitan,** Baby Goat, Earthenware, Sculpted, Child, 1800s, 9 In. | 1008 |
| **Neapolitan,** Earthenware Head, Sculpted Hair, Hemp Wrapped Body, 1800s, 14 ½ In. | 1008 |
| **Neapolitan,** Earthenware, Angel, Wood Wings, Sculpted Curls, Bare Feet, 1800s, 12 In. | 1568 |
| **Neapolitan,** Earthenware, Hemp Wrapped Body, Inset Eyes, Side Curls, Boy, 1800s, 8 In. | 1344 |
| **Neapolitan,** Earthenware, Hemp Wrapped Body, Sculpted Head, Smile, 1800s, 14 In. | 1232 |
| **Neapolitan,** Sculpted Hair, Hemp Wrapped Body, Herder With Goat, 13 In. | 1904 |
| **Nodder,** German, Bisque, Green Costumes, Side-Glancing At Each Other, c.1915, 5 In., Pair | 224 |
| **O. Hitt,** No. 22, Bisque Head, Glass Googly Eyes, Muslin, Composition, Toddler, 13 In. ...*illus* | 23940 |

**Doll,** Horsman, Bride, Composition, Ivory Satin Gown, Accessories, Tag, Box, 1940s, 14 In.
$627

Theriault's

**Doll,** Horsman, Cindy, Bride, Brown Vinyl, Jointed, Satin Gown, Accessories, Tag, Box, 18 In.
$86

Theriault's

**Doll,** Horsman, Cindy, Vinyl, Swivel Waist, Ponytail, Dress, Velveteen Coat, Box, 10 In.
$86

Theriault's

**Doll,** Ideal, Miss Revlon, Hat, Blond Curls, Wrist Tag, 1957
$840

Theriault's

**Doll,** Ideal, Miss Revlon, Vinyl Head, Blond Curls, Deb Gown, Heels, Tag, Box, 18 In.
$456

Theriault's

> ### TIP
> *Save your doll's packaging, tags, and inserts. These can triple the price when the doll is sold.*

**Doll,** Ideal, Miss Revlon, Vinyl Head, Blond Hair, Deb Gown, Tag, c.1957, 18 In.
$456

Theriault's

**Doll,** Ideal, Miss Revlon, Vinyl Head, Sleep Eyes, Evening Star Costume, 1957, 18 In.
$399

Theriault's

**Doll,** Ideal, Miss Revlon, Vinyl, Cherries A La Mode Series, Navy Dress, Tag, Box, 22 In.
$342

Theriault's

**Doll,** Jumeau, Fashion, Bisque, Swivel Head, Glass Eyes, Blond Mohair Wig, Signed, 13 In.
$3,080

Theriault's

**TIP**

*An old cotton sock is a good polishing cloth. So is an old cloth diaper.*

| | |
|---|---:|
| **Oilcloth Shoulder Head,** Cloth Dress, Bonnet, Body, c.1910, 25 In. | 489 |
| **Orsini,** Didi, Bisque Head & Torso, Mohair Wig, Loop-Jointed, Bent Elbows, c.1920, 5 In. | 784 |
| **Orsini,** Mimi, Bisque, Mohair Wig, Jointed Arms, Legs, Label, Germany, c.1920, 5 In. ......*illus* | 896 |
| **Orsini,** Vivi, Bisque Head & Torso, Mohair Wig, Loop-Jointed, Bent Elbows, c.1920, 5 In. | 896 |
| **Paper** dolls are listed in their own category. | |
| **Papier-Mache,** Kid, Shoulder Head, Wood Arms & Legs, Original Clothes, Germany, 15 In. | 748 |
| **Papier-Mache,** Moritz, Mechanical, Sculpted Hair, Painted Face, c.1900, 9 In. | 224 |
| **Papier-Mache,** Shoulder Head, Painted, Inset Eyes, Stitch-Jointed, Germany, c.1840, 29 In. | 952 |
| **Papier-Mache,** Shoulder Head, Sculpted Curls, Flower Garland, Red Rose, 24 In. | 1792 |
| **Papier-Mache,** Surprise Skirt, Kitchen Ware, Utensils, Inset Eyes, Germany, c.1870, 14 In. | 4760 |
| **Pincushion** dolls are listed in their own category. | |
| **Porcelain,** Arms In Front, Pink Tinted Complexion, Painted Hair, Germany, c.1880, 15 In. ..*illus* | 616 |
| **Porcelain,** Brown Eyes, Lashes, Shoulder Head, Sculpted Hair, Muslin, Leather, c.1860, 24 In. | 1344 |
| **Porcelain,** Frozen Charlotte, Folded Fists, Painted Eyes, Closed Mouth, c.1880, 16 In. | 672 |
| **Porcelain,** Shoulder Head, Sculpted Hair, Painted Eyes, Muslin, Stitch-Jointed, c.1870, 13 In. | 672 |
| **Rabery & Delphieu,** Mohair, Paperweight Eyes, Wood, Composition, Dimple, 15 In. | 2370 |
| **Rabery & Delphieu,** Socket Head, Paperweight Eyes, Wood, Composition, Wig, Jointed, 18 In. .. | 889 |
| **Raggedy Ann & Andy,** Cloth, Stitch-Jointed, Volland, Shoebutton Eyes, c.1920, 16 In. | 840 |
| **Raggedy Ann,** Cloth, Shoebutton Eyes, Yarn Hair, Patent Stamp 1975, 16 In. | 432 |
| **Raggedy Ann,** Cloth, Yarn Hair, Cardboard Heart, Volland, c.1930, 16 In. ............*illus* | 784 |
| **Raggedy Ann,** Cloth, Yarn Hair, Shoebutton Eyes, Shoes, Volland, c.1920, 16 In. .........*illus* | 728 |
| **Recknagel,** Googly, Composition Head, Painted Eyes, Sculpted Hair & Bonnet, 9 In. | 616 |
| **S & H** dolls are also listed here as Simon & Halbig. | |
| **S.F.B.J.,** 233, Crying Girl, Bisque Head, Blue Glass Eyes, Teeth, Composition Baby Body, 15 In. | 2016 |
| **S.F.B.J.,** 252, Toddler, Bisque, Pouty, Sleep Eyes, Blond Mohair, Composition, Wood, 13 In. | 2352 |
| **S.F.B.J.,** Bisque Socket Head, 2 Faces, Smile, Scowl, Teeth, Mohair Wig, Jointed, 17 In. | 5600 |
| **S.F.B.J.,** Bisque Socket Head, 2 Porcelain Teeth, Human Hair Wig, Twirp, c.1912, 18 In. | 1064 |
| **Santon,** Carved Bone Head, Dowel-Jointed, Toes, Painted Sandals, Late 18th Century, 16 In. | 616 |
| **Schoeneau & Hoffmeister,** Princess Elizabeth, Bisque Head, Composition, Toddler, 20 In. *illus* | 2508 |
| **Schoenhut,** 308, Wood Socket Head, Mohair Wig, Spring-Jointed, c.1912, 19 In. | 448 |
| **Schoenhut,** Boy, Carved Hair, Intaglio Eyes, 1910 Style Costume, 16 In. | 472 |
| **Schoenhut,** Boy, Wood Socket Head, Carved Hair, Forelock, Spring-Jointed, 1911, 16 In. | 1064 |
| **Schoenhut,** Boy, Wood Socket Head, Mohair Wig, Spring-Jointed, 1915, 19 In. | 392 |
| **Schoenhut,** Boy, Wood, Somber Expression, Painted Eyes, Spring-Jointed, Green Suit, 14 In. | 207 |
| **Schoenhut,** Girl, Pouty, Wood, Painted, Intaglio Eyes, Spring-Jointed, Cotton Dress, 16 In. | 266 |
| **Schoenhut,** Girl, Wood, Painted, Intaglio Eyes, 2 Teeth, Human Hair, Dress, Bonnet, 16 In. | 561 |
| **Schoenhut,** Girl, Wood, Socket Head, Painted, Intaglio Eyes, Mohair, Jointed, 1911, 18 In. | 1344 |
| **Schoenhut,** Toddler, Spring-Jointed, Molded, Painted, Cotton Romper Suit, 11 In. | 236 |
| **Schoenhut,** Wood Socket Head, Carved, Bobbed Wig, Spring-Jointed, 1912, 22 In. | 784 |
| **Schoenhut,** Wood, Carved Socket Head, Sculpted Bonnet, Painted, Jointed, c.1911, 16 In. | 3360 |
| **Shirley Temple** dolls are included in the Shirley Temple category. | |
| **Simon & Halbig,** 612, Bisque Socket Head, Mohair Lashes, Porcelain Teeth, 1915, 20 In. | 896 |
| **Simon & Halbig,** 886, Bisque, Sleep Eyes, 4 Teeth, Peg Jointed Limbs, Silk Dress, 9 In. .......*illus* | 1482 |
| **Simon & Halbig,** 908, Bisque Head, Jointed Composition & Wood, Silk Dress, 15 In. | 6720 |
| **Simon & Halbig,** 949, Bisque Socket Head, 2 Upper Teeth, Mohair Wig, Ball-Jointed, 16 In. | 672 |
| **Simon & Halbig,** 1159, Flapper, Bisque Socket Head, Mohair Wig, Ball-Jointed, 13 In.........*illus* | 1120 |
| **Simon & Halbig,** 1329, Asian Child, Bisque Head, Sleep Eyes, Black Mohair, Kimono, 14 In. | 1456 |
| **Simon & Halbig,** 1358, Black, Socket Head, Sleep Eyes, Open Mouth, c.1900, 20 In. | 5600 |
| **Simon & Halbig,** 1358, Ebony Bisque, Sleep Eyes, Black Wig, Homespun Costume, 21 In. | 22400 |
| **Simon & Halbig,** 1358, Girl, Brown Bisque, Sleep Eyes, Black Mohair Curls, 16 In. | 3640 |
| **Simon & Halbig,** 1488, Bisque Head, Blue Sleep Eyes, Blond Mohair Curls, Toddler, 23 In. | 4032 |
| **Simon & Halbig,** Bisque Socket Head, Brown Sleep Eyes, 2 Teeth, Ball-Jointed, 14 In. | 784 |
| **Simon & Halbig,** Bisque Socket Head, Inset Eyes, Closed Mouth, Ball-Jointed, 10 In. | 2016 |
| **Simon & Halbig,** Bisque Socket Head, Open Mouth, Teeth, Human Hair, Ball-Jointed, 42 In. | 3136 |
| **Simon & Halbig,** Bisque Socket Head, Sculpted Curls, Ball-Jointed, 1910, 13 In. | 8064 |
| **Simon & Halbig,** Brown Glass Eyes, 4 Teeth, Ball-Jointed Arms, c.1900, 16 In. | 560 |
| **Simon & Halbig,** Parian, Bisque Shoulder Plate, Cloth Body, 10 In. | 948 |
| **Sonneberg,** 15, Bisque Socket Head, Human Hair, Pull-String Crier, Jointed, 1885, 25 In. | 3024 |
| **Sonneberg,** 136, Bisque Socket Head, Blue Inset Eyes, Closed Mouth, Jointed, 14 In. | 1792 |
| **Sonneberg,** 136, Bisque Swivel Head, Red Cheeks, Gusset-Jointed, Lamb's Wool Wig, 15 In. | 1456 |
| **Sonneberg,** Bisque Socket Head, Inset Eyes, Mohair Wig, Ball-Jointed, c.1885, 16 In. | 896 |
| **Sonneberg,** Bisque Socket Head, Plump, Blond Mohair Wig, Composition, Wood, 17 In. | 3024 |
| **Steiff,** Anton, Felt Swivel Head, Center Seam, Jointed Shoulders & Hips, c.1910, 11 In. | 1792 |
| **Steiff,** Felt Swivel Head, Center Seam, Glass Eyes, Jointed Arms & Legs, c.1910, 11 In. | 2576 |
| **Steiff,** Felt Swivel Head, Center Seam, Unruly Mohair Wig, Chubby, c.1915, 11 In. | 2016 |
| **Steiff,** Felt Swivel Head, Felt Uniform, Metal Sword, Center Seam, c.1915, 12 In. | 1568 |

D

**Doll,** Jumeau, No. 201, Bisque Head, Paperweight Eyes, Composition, Wood, Jointed, 24 In.
$280,000

**Doll,** Lenci, Character, Girl, Swivel Head, Painted, Side-Glancing Eyes, Series 1500, 17 In.
$4,275

Theriault's

Theriault's

**Doll,** Lenci, Chinese Girl, Dschang-Go, Felt, Swivel Head, Painted Face, Human Hair, 23 In.
$6,840

Theriault's

**Doll,** Kestner, 190, Child, Multi-Head Set, Bisque, Socket Head, Mohair Wig, c.1910, 15 In.
$3,420

**Doll,** Kestner, 221, Bisque Head, Blue Googly Eyes, Composition, Jointed, Toddler, 12 In.
$4,560

**Doll,** Lenci, Hu San, Felt, Swivel Head, Painted Face, Mohair Wig, Opium Pipe, 1924, 21 In.
$2,850

Theriault's

Theriault's

Theriault's

171

**Doll,** Madame Alexander, Glamour Girl, Plastic, Walker, Velvet, Taffeta Gown, c.1953, 18 In.
$4,332

Theriault's

**Doll,** Madame Alexander, Godey Bridegroom, Plastic, Gold Cloverleaf Tag, c.1950, 14 In.
$1,482

Theriault's

**Doll,** Madame Hendron, Dolly Dingle, Cloth, Painted, Stitch-Jointed, Label, c.1930, 16 In.
$684

Theriault's

**Doll,** Mattel, Barbie, Blond Bubble Cut, No. 992 Golden Elegance, Box, 11 In.
$285

Theriault's

**Doll,** Mattel, Barbie, Blond Ponytail, No. 963 Resort Set, Original Box, c.1960, 11 In.
$1,824

Theriault's

**Doll,** Mattel, Barbie, No. 1, Blond Ponytail, Swimsuit, Peg Stand, Box, c.1959, 11 In.
$4,788

Theriault's

**Doll,** Mattel, Ken, Brown Flocked Hair, Bathing Shorts, Jacket, Sandals, Box, c.1961, 12 In.
$114

Theriault's

**Doll,** Nancy Ann Storybook, Hard Plastic, Blond Hair, Lavender & Lace, Box, 1950s, 18 In.
$1,254

Theriault's

**Doll,** Nancy Ann Storybook, Hard Plastic, Old-Fashioned Bouquet, White Lace, 1950s, 18 In.
$2,964

Theriault's

| | |
|---|---|
| **Steiff,** Felt, Jointed Hips & Shoulders, Oversized Feet, Stitched Ears, Original Button, 17 In......... | 1344 |
| **Steiff,** Felt, Soldier, Center Seam Face, Button Eyes, 1909-18, 11 In. ............................ | 1422 |
| **Steiff,** Sailor, Pressed Felt, Painted, Bead Eyes, Mohair Beard, Felt Costume, 15 In. .............*illus* | 3024 |
| **Steiff,** Soldier, Felt, Swivel Head, Bead Eyes, Painted, Jointed, Ear Button, c.1910, 10 In. ......... | 1792 |
| **Steiner,** Bebe, Bisque Head, Blue Glass Eyes, Closed Mouth, Blond Curls, Jointed, 14 In............... | 8400 |
| **Steiner,** Bebe, Bisque Socket Head, Glass Paperweight Inset Eyes, Closed Mouth, Mohair, 18 In.. | 5040 |
| **Steiner,** Bisque Head, Blue Inset Eyes, Open Mouth, Teeth, Bebe Gigoteur, 1875, 17 In. ............. | 5040 |
| **Steiner,** Bisque Socket Head, Blue Eyes, Curly Lashes, Mohair, Fully Jointed, 1875, 14 In. .......... | 3584 |
| **Steiner,** Bisque Socket Head, Blue Paperweight Eyes, Blond Mohair Wig, Jointed, 20 In. ............. | 3920 |
| **Steiner,** Bisque Socket Head, Blue Paperweight Eyes, Composition, Jointed, c.1899, 16 In.......... | 3920 |
| **Steiner,** Bisque Socket Head, Blue Paperweight Eyes, Mohair Wig, c.1890, 12 In. ......................... | 1120 |
| **Steiner,** Bisque Socket Head, Blue Side-Glancing Eyes, Mohair, 5-Piece Body, 7 In...................... | 336 |
| **Steiner,** Bisque Socket Head, Brown Inset, Ringlets, Jointed, 28 In...................................... | 6160 |
| **Steiner,** Bisque Socket Head, Inset Eyes, Closed Mouth, Mohair Wig, 1885, 39 In. ................ | 10640 |
| **Steiner,** Bisque Socket Head, Inset Eyes, Human Hair Wig, Jointed, 39 In............................. | 9520 |
| **Steiner,** Gliding Lady, Bisque, Kid, Blond Mohair, Wheels, Arms Wave, Cries Mama, 15 In. .......... | 5880 |
| **Stockinet,** Dark Brown Complexion, Shoebutton Eyes, Yarn Hair Cap, Sateen, 20 In. .............. | 840 |
| **Stockinet,** Stitch Shape Nose, Shoebutton Eyes, Embroidered Features, c.1880, 21 In. ......... | 504 |
| **Tete Jumeau,** Paperweight Eyes, Open Mouth, Jointed Wood, Composition, France, 30 In. ......... | 1062 |
| **Topsyturvy,** Cloth, Painted Faces, White Girl, Black Girl, Babyland Rag, c.1895, 12 In. .......*illus* | 224 |
| **Topsyturvy,** Cloth, Pressed Mask Face, White, Black Heads, Albert Bruckner, c.1915, 11 In..*illus* | 224 |
| **Topsyturvy,** Muslin, Lithograph Printed Face, Black & White, c.1890, 10 In. ............................. | 616 |
| **Uneeda,** Betsy McCall, Soft Vinyl, Jointed, Green Tunic, Tights, Box, c.1964, 11 In...............*illus* | 114 |
| **Vivandiere,** Bisque Head, Sculpted Hair, Painted, Muslin Body, Germany, c.1865, 16 In. ............. | 3808 |
| **Walker,** Papier-Mache, Kid, Shoulder Head, Painted, 3-Wheel Tin Base, France, 11 In. ............. | 1792 |
| **Walker,** Throws Kisses, Bisque Head, Open Mouth, Glass Eyes, Composition Body, 21 In............ | 413 |
| **Walkure,** Bisque Head, Glass Eyes, Brown Hair, Jointed Composite Body, Plaid Dress, 34 In. ....... | 450 |
| **Wislizensus,** Bisque Socket Head, High Forehead, Teeth, Tongue, Hip-Jointed, 25 In. ................. | 1232 |
| **Woman,** Wood, Carved, Articulated Body, Brown Enamel Eyes, Painted, Dress, 28 In. .................. | 2688 |
| **Wood Peg,** Painted Face & Hair, Raised Nose, Jointed, c.1890, 11 ½ In. ....................................... | 145 |
| **Wood,** Carved, 1-Piece Head, Torso, Painted Face, Brocade Costume, 1700s, 22 In. ...................... | 3360 |

## DOLL CLOTHES

| | |
|---|---|
| **Barbie,** Debutante Ball, No. 1666.......................................................................................... | 228 |
| **Barbie,** Evening Gown, Blue Strapless, Sequins, 9 In.............................................................. | 16 |
| **Barbie,** Evening Splendor, Dress & Coat, No. 961, c.1960 .......................................... | 39 to 113 |
| **Barbie,** Gay Parisienne, No. 964.......................................................................................... | 537 |
| **Barbie,** Graduation Gown, Cap, Collar, Scroll, Black.......................................................... | 35 |
| **Barbie,** Jacket, Resort Set, Red, Mattel, No. 963................................................................. | 10 |
| **Barbie,** Ken, Pajamas, Slippers, No. 781, 1963.................................................................... | 42 |
| **Barbie,** Picnic Set, Jeans, Checkered Shirt, Hat, Purse, c.1960 ............................................ | 25 |
| **Barbie,** Tennis Anyone, No. 941, Skirt, Jacket, Racket, White .............................................. | 30 |
| **Barbie,** Western Outfit, Pants, Jacket, Hat, Boots, Box, 1981 .............................................. | 20 |
| **Bru Bebe,** Bru Jne, Shoes, Kidskin, Ankle Strap, Brass Buckle, 5 In. ......................*illus* | 1368 |
| **Coat,** Vinyl, Mod, Yellow, Orange, Red, 1969, 11 In............................................................ | 20 |
| **Totsy,** Dress, Pink, Lace Overlay, White Flats, Box, 1960s, 9 In.......................................... | 24 |
| **Tutti,** Clowning Around, Mattel, Dress, Yellow, Black Checks, Box, c.1965......................... | 85 |

**DONALD DUCK** *items are included in the Disneyana category.*

**DOORSTOPS** have been made in all types of designs. The vast majority of the doorstops sold today are cast iron and were made from about 1890 to 1930. Most of them are shaped like people, animals, flowers, or ships. Reproductions and newly designed examples are sold in gift shops.

| | |
|---|---|
| **2 Footmen,** Standing, Hands At Sides, Red Paint, Cast Iron, Anne Fish, Hubley, 12 In................. | 660 |
| **5 Puppies,** Fence, Cast Iron, Black, White, Brown, 8 x 10 x 3 In.......................................... | 48 |
| **Ann Hathaway Cottage,** Thatched Roof, Pastel, Garden, Hubley, 6 ½ x 8 ⅜ In. .............. | 180 to 295 |
| **Basket,** Apple Blossoms, Branch, Cast Iron, Blue, Hubley, 7 x 5 ½ In........................................ | 177 |
| **Basket,** Lily Of The Valley, Multicolor, Cast Iron, Hubley, 10 ¼ In. ........................................ | 95 |
| **Basket,** Narcissus, Footed, Cast Iron, Hubley, 7 ½ x 7 In....................................................... | 225 |
| **Basket,** Petunias, Daisies, Cast Iron, Hubley, No. 120, c.1920............................................. | 145 |
| **Basket,** Tulips, Pink, Yellow, Wicker Basket, Cast Iron, Hubley, 13 In. .................................... | 540 |
| **Bathing Beauties,** 2 Women Seated, Sharing Umbrella, Cast Iron, Fish, Hubley, 11 In.. | 660 to 960 |
| **Bear,** Standing, Holding Honey Pot, Licking Lips, Paint, Cast Iron, 15 In.................................... | 3000 |
| **Bellhop,** Standing At Attention, Green, Yellow, Judd Co., 8 x 4 In......................................... | 826 |
| **Boy,** Hands & Feet Crossed, Crossword Puzzle Books, Cast Iron, 7 ⅜ In................................... | 1560 |

**Doll,** O. Hitt, No. 22, Bisque Head, Glass Googly Eyes, Muslin, Composition, Toddler, 13 In.
$23,940

Theriault's

**Doll,** Orsini, Mimi, Bisque, Mohair Wig, Jointed Arms, Legs, Label, Germany, c.1920, 5 In.
$896

Theriault's

**Doll,** Porcelain, Arms In Front, Pink Tinted Complexion, Painted Hair, Germany, c.1880, 15 In.
$616

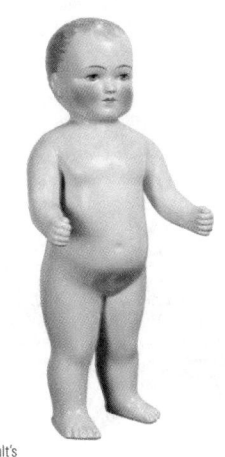

Theriault's

**Doll,** Raggedy Ann, Cloth, Yarn Hair, Cardboard Heart, Volland, c.1930, 16 In. $784

Theriault's

**Doll,** Raggedy Ann, Cloth, Yarn Hair, Shoebutton Eyes, Shoes, Volland, c.1920, 16 In. $728

Theriault's

**Doll,** Schoeneau & Hoffmeister, Princess Elizabeth, Bisque Head, Composition, Toddler, 20 In. $2,508

Theriault's

| | | |
|---|---|---|
| **Boy,** Hands In Pockets, Cast Iron, H.L. Judd Co., c.1920, 10¾ In. | *illus* | 593 |
| **Boy,** Holding Fruit Basket, Yellow Top Hat, Cast Iron, 9 In. | | 390 |
| **Boy,** Messenger, Blue Uniform, Holding Bouquet, Paint, Cast Iron, Fish, Hubley, 10 In. | | 1920 |
| **Boy,** Swimsuit, Beach Ball, Full Body, Cast Iron, c.1920, 9½ In. | | 2074 |
| **Cat,** Black, Sitting, Red, Green Paint, Cast Iron, c.1920, 8 x 6 In. | | 92 |
| **Cat,** Black, Sitting, Red, White Paint, c.1840, 6 x 5 In. | | 138 |
| **Cat,** Cast Iron, 11¾ In. | | 188 |
| **Cat,** Curled Up, Ribbon Collar, Hollow, Japanned Finish, National Foundry, 10 In. | | 384 |
| **Cat,** Sitting, Black, Cast Iron, Stepped Wedge, Spencer, Guilford, Conn., 7⅝ In. | | 2280 |
| **Cat,** Sitting, Tilted Head, Black, Hollow, Hubley, c.1925, 10 In., 2 Piece | | 364 |
| **Cat,** Sleeping, Curled Up, Orange, Black, Cast Iron, 5 x 14 In. | | 1080 |
| **Cat,** Sleeping, Hollow, Cast Iron, Black, Gilt, National Foundry, c.1920, 3½ x 9½ In. | | 593 |
| **Charleston Dancers,** Couple Dancing, Cast Iron, Marked Fish On Base, Hubley, 8¼ In. | *illus* | 1778 |
| **Charleston Dancers,** Man, Woman, Intertwined, Cast Iron, Anne Fish, Hubley, 8½ In. | | 570 |
| **Clown,** Scottie Dog, Painted, Cast Iron, c.1920, 7½ In. | *illus* | 593 |
| **Colonial Man,** Holding Flower Bouquets, Cast Iron, 9 In. | | 360 |
| **Colonial Woman,** Cast Iron, Blue, Pink Flowers, 4¾ x 3 In. | | 135 |
| **Cornucopia,** Multicolor Paint, Cast Iron, Hubley, 7⅜ In. | | 270 |
| **Cottage,** Cape Cod, 2 Pathways, Paint, Cast Iron, 5½ In. | | 180 |
| **Cottage,** Cape Cod, Trees, Cast Iron, Hubley, 8 In. | | 60 |
| **Cottage,** Cast Iron, Signed Hiram Powers' Birthplace, Vt., 10 In. | | 330 |
| **Cottage,** Curtains, Path, Brick Steps, Marked CJO 1283, 4½ x 8½ In. | | 384 |
| **Cottage,** Flowers On Wall, Doorway, Cast Iron, 7¾ In. | | 120 |
| **Cottage,** Women, Flowers, Picket Fence, Cast Iron, Marked Pingree House, Salem, 6 In. | | 1560 |
| **Cow,** Flat Back, Black, White, Green Base | | 47 |
| **Dog,** Boston Terrier, Begging, Paint, Cast Iron, 8¾ In. | | 540 |
| **Dog,** Boston Terrier, Brown, White, Cast Iron, Early 20th Century, 10 x 10 In. | | 150 |
| **Dog,** Boston Terrier, Painted Black, White, 1900s, 9 x 11 In. | | 263 |
| **Dog,** Boston Terrier, Paw Up, Seated, Cast Iron, 10 In. | | 570 |
| **Dog,** Boston Terrier, Standing, Head Turned, Skoog, Dutka Liebl Foundry, Mass., 7 In. | | 240 |
| **Dog,** Boston Terrier, Standing, Rubber Bumpers, Cast Iron, Bradley & Hubbard, 10 In. | | 510 |
| **Dog,** Boxer, Standing, Paint, Cast Iron, 8 In. | | 660 |
| **Dog,** Cocker Spaniel, Standing, Cast Iron, Hubley, 4½ In. | | 150 |
| **Dog,** Dachshund, Standing, Cast Iron, Hubley, 6¼ In. | | 600 |
| **Dog,** Doberman Pincher, Show Stance, Cast Iron, Hubley, 8 In. | | 510 to 900 |
| **Dog,** English Bulldog, Standing, Cast Iron, Hubley, 5½ In. | | 900 |
| **Dog,** Fox Terrier, Standing, Cast Iron, Hubley, 10 In. | | 330 |
| **Dog,** French Bulldog, Seated, Cast Iron, Hubley, 8 In. | | 420 |
| **Dog,** Laddie Boy, President Harding's Dog, Cast Iron, 8½ In. | | 390 |
| **Dog,** Mutt, Bone, 8½ In. | | 212 |
| **Dog,** Pekingese, Brown, 14 In. | | 826 |
| **Dog,** Pekingese, Paint, Cast Iron, 9¾ In. | | 1800 |
| **Dog,** Pup, With Duck, Paint, Cast Iron, 1924, 10 In. | | 600 |
| **Dog,** Saint Bernard, Pack, Collar, White, Brown, 8 In. | | 354 |
| **Dog,** Scottie, Black, 8 In. | | 53 |
| **Dog,** Scottie, White, Wilton Products, 8 In. | | 94 |
| **Dog,** Setter, Pointing, Black, White Paint, c.1920, 9 x 16 In. | | 161 |
| **Dog,** Spaniel, Black & White Paint, Cast Iron, Hubley, 6¾ In., Pair | | 270 |
| **Dog,** Spaniel, Tawny Brown Paint, Cast Iron, Japan, c.1945, 9 x 5 In. | | 173 |
| **Dog,** Terrier, Painted, Hubley, 8¼ x 7½ In. | | 245 |
| **Dog,** Wirehaired Fox Terrier, Running, Cast Iron, Marked Spencer, Conn., 7 In. | | 1320 |
| **Dolly Dimple,** Full Figure, Yellow Dress, Cast Iron, Hubley, 7¾ In. | | 150 |
| **Dolphin,** Cast Metal, Verdigris Finish, 11½ x 6 In. | | 276 |
| **Dolphin,** Classical Style, Gilt, Cast Iron, 1800s, 14 x 9¼ In. | | 230 |
| **Drum Major,** Holding Baton, Red, White, Littco Products, 12¾ x 3⅝ In. | | 236 to 300 |
| **Duck,** Plant, Beetle, Paint, Cast Iron, 7⅝ In. | | 1560 |
| **Duck,** Seated, Yellow Paint, Wedge Style, Cast Iron, Hubley, 5½ In. | | 210 |
| **Dutch Boy,** Hands In Pocket, Hat, Blue, Littco Co., 11 x 3½ In. | | 266 |
| **Dutch Boy,** Hands In Pocket, Wedge Base, Cast Iron, 6 In. | | 90 |
| **Dutch Girl,** Hands On Hips, Blond Braid, Cast Iron, Albany Foundry, 4¼ In. | | 120 |
| **Elf,** Digging For Gold, Foot On Shovel, Green, Red, Cast Iron, Spencer, Conn., 13 In. | | 150 |
| **Fence,** Brick Path, Urn Finial, Shrubs, Roses, Cast Iron, Sarah Symonds, 8 In. | | 1080 |
| **Fisherman,** Hat, Jacket, 6½ In. | | 70 |
| **Fisherman,** Standing, Yellow Slicker, Blue, Cast Iron, Eastern Spec. Co., c.1910, 15 In. | | 1003 |
| **Flower Basket,** Multicolor, French Basket, Cast Iron, Hubley, 11 In. | | 90 |
| **Flower,** Poinsettia, Red Paint, Cast Iron, Judd Co., 9¾ In. | | 270 |

D

| | |
|---|---|
| **Flowers,** Calla Lilies, White, Yellow, Urn Base, Cast Iron, Hubley, 7 In. | 180 |
| **Flowers,** Daisies, Multicolor, Cast Iron, Hubley, 6¾ In. | 60 |
| **Flowers,** French Basket, Fallen Rose, Cast Iron, National Foundry, 10 In. | 60 |
| **Flowers,** Goldenrod, Green Leaves, Cast Iron, Hubley, 7 In. | 180 |
| **Flowers,** Petunias & Asters, Wicker Basket, Cast Iron, Hubley, 9½ In. | 90 |
| **Flowers,** Poppies, Cornflower, Ribbed Pot, Cast Iron, Hubley, 7 In. | 180 |
| **Flowers,** Red Poppies, Slant Handle Basket, Cast Iron, Marked C.H.F. Co., 10 In. | 360 |
| **Flowers,** Tiger Lilies, White, Green Leaves, Cast Iron, Hubley, 10¾ In. | 330 |
| **Foundry Man,** Hill Clutch, Gloves, Cap, Goggles, Paint, Cast Iron, 6 In. | 2040 |
| **Fox & Grapes,** Black, Green, Purple Paint, Cast Iron, c.1935, 11½ x 6 In. | 173 |
| **Frog,** Cast Iron, Early 1900s, 3 x 5½ In. | 210 |
| **Fruit Basket,** Multicolor, Cast Iron, 10⅜ In. | 90 |
| **Fruit Basket,** Multicolor, Twisted Handle, Cast Iron, 12⅝ In. | 60 |
| **Galleon Ship,** Sailing Ship, Cast Iron, A.A. Richardson, 1927, 7½ In. | 270 |
| **Geisha,** Wearing Kimono, Cast Iron, Hubley, 10 In. | 510 |
| **George Washington,** Standing, Cast Iron, 12 In. | 47 |
| **Giraffe,** Standing, Painted, Cast Iron, 14 In. | 900 |
| **Giraffe,** Viney Leaves, Cast Iron, Hubley, 10½ x 5¾ In. | 1003 |
| **Girl In Canoe,** Water, Trees, Cast Iron, National Foundry, 10 In. | 330 |
| **Girl,** Holding Flower Basket, Pink Dress, Cast Iron, 9 In. | 120 |
| **Girl,** Kicking Flower, Holding Flower, Polka-Dot Dress, Cast Iron, 9¾ In. | 1560 |
| **Girl,** Leaning On Shaggy Dog, Cast Iron, Bronze Products Inc., 7 In. | 780 |
| **Gnome,** Lantern, Keys, Paint, Cast Iron, 10 In. | 120 |
| **Golfer,** Cast Iron, Painted, Red Jacket, Tan Breeches, Cast Iron, Hubley, No. 34, 8 In. | 345 |
| **Graf Zeppelin,** Docked, Cast Iron, c.1925, 8¾ x 13 In. | 345 |
| **Graf Zeppelin,** Mooring Tower, Silver Paint, Lights Up, Cast Iron, 8 In. | 450 |
| **Grapes,** Purple, Cast Iron, Albany Fdry. Co., 1926, 7⅞ In. | 120 |
| **Happy Hooligan,** Standing, Sunday Comic Character, Cast Iron, c.1930, 11½ In. | 960 |
| **Heron,** Painted, Cast Iron, Albany Foundry, N.Y., c.1920, 7½ x 5 In. ..........*illus* | 474 |
| **Horse,** Bay Color, Cast Iron, Hubley, 12 In. | 360 |
| **Horse,** Old Gray Mare, Harness, Blinkers, 7 In. | 780 |
| **Huck Finn,** Standing On Fishing Bank, Cast Iron, Bradley & Hubbard, 9¾ In. | 600 |
| **Humpty Dumpty,** Sitting On Stone Wall, Cast Iron, 4½ In. | 120 |
| **Huntsman,** On Horse, Tipping Hat, Dog, Cast Iron, National Foundry, 5⅝ In. | 1560 |
| **Jonquils,** Blowing, Yellow, Hubley, 7 x 6 In. | 207 |
| **Judy,** Standing, Holding Little Punch, Paint, Cast Iron, 11¾ In. | 300 |
| **Kitten,** Resting, Head Up, Black, Cast Iron, National Foundry, 9 In. | 600 |
| **Lighthouse,** Cape Hatteras, Half Round Hollow Cast Iron, Wire, Painted, c.1920, 22 In. | 3555 |
| **Lighthouse,** Cottage, Iron, Painted, Hollow, National Foundry, Mass., c.1920, 6 In. | 296 |
| **Lion,** Holding Shield, Cast Iron, Stepped Base, 1800s, 15 x 10 In. | 75 |
| **Little Red Riding Hood,** Basket, Cast Iron, Grace Drayton, Hubley, 7⅜ In. | 90 |
| **Mammy,** Hands On Hips, Red & Blue Dress, White Apron, Littco Foundry, c.1920, 13½ In. | 474 |
| **Mary Quite Contrary,** Holding Bouquet, Rake, Water Can, Cast Iron, 15 In. | 1320 |
| **Old Salt With Fishing Net,** Black, Tan Paint, Cast Iron, c.1940, 11 x 4 In. | 230 |
| **Olive Picker,** Hollow Cast Iron, Painted, Multicolor, Donkey, Hubley, c.1920, 7 x 7 In. | 1541 |
| **Owl,** On Books, Wide Eyed, Black, Yellow, Cast Iron, Eastern Specialty Mfg., 9¼ In. | 540 to 561 |
| **Pan,** Flute, Landscape, Cast Iron, 7½ In. | 53 |
| **Parlor Maid,** Serving Cocktails, Paint, Cast Iron, Fish, Hubley, 9 In. | 1680 |
| **Parrot On Stump,** Red, Green, Black Paint, Cast Iron, c.1930, 12 x 5 In. | 288 |
| **Peacock,** Spread Feathers, Paint, Cast Iron, Albany Foundry Co., 6 In. | 210 |
| **Penguin,** Standing, Head Turned To Right, Paint, Cast Iron, 8 In. | 1020 |
| **Pheasant,** Paint, Cast Iron, Hubley, 8½ In. | 390 |
| **Pied Piper,** Albany Foundry Co., 7¼ In. | 120 |
| **Pirate,** With Sack, Hollow, Paint, Cast Iron, c.1930, 12 x 10 In. | 575 |
| **Pirate,** Woman, Holding Sword, Paint, Cast Iron, Albany Fdry. Co. | 840 |
| **Punch,** Cast Iron, Painted, 12 In. | 480 |
| **Punch,** Dog Toby, Paint, Cast Iron, 12 In. | 270 |
| **Punch,** Dog, Multicolor Paint, Cast Iron, c.1890, 12 In. | 118 |
| **Puss In Boots,** Yellow Cat, Climbing From Boot, Marked Creations Co., 1930, 8 In. | 1320 |
| **Rabbit,** Begging, Paint, Cast Iron, Bradley & Hubbard, 15 In. | 2160 |
| **Rabbit,** Fence, Carrots, Cast Iron, Albany Foundry, 8 In. | 300 |
| **Rabbit,** In Top Hat, Cast Iron, National Foundry., 10 In. | 420 |
| **Rabbit,** Seated, White Paint, Cast Iron, 9½ In. | 150 |
| **Rabbit,** With Top Hat, Cast Iron, Painted, Multicolor, Albany Foundry, c.1920, 10 x 5 In. | 1600 |
| **Red Riding Hood,** Wolf, Basket, Cast Iron, Albany Foundry Co., 7⅜ In. | 840 |
| **Rhumba Dancer,** Stylized Green Dress, Hands On Hips, Red Turban, Cast Iron, 11 In. | 1440 |

**Doll,** Simon & Halbig, 1159, Flapper, Bisque Socket Head, Mohair Wig, Ball-Jointed, 13 In.
$1,120

Theriault's

**Doll,** Simon & Halbig, 886, Bisque, Sleep Eyes, 4 Teeth, Peg Jointed Limbs, Silk Dress, 9 In.
$1,482

Theriault's

**Doll,** Steiff, Sailor, Pressed Felt, Painted, Bead Eyes, Mohair Beard, Felt Costume, 15 In.
$3,024

Theriault's

**Doll,** Topsyturvy, Cloth, Painted Faces, White Girl, Black Girl, Babyland Rag, c.1895, 12 In.
$224

Theriault's

**Doll,** Topsyturvy, Cloth, Pressed Mask Face, White, Black Heads, Albert Bruckner, c.1915, 11 In.
$224

Theriault's

**Doll,** Uneeda, Betsy McCall, Soft Vinyl, Jointed, Green Tunic, Tights, Box, c.1964, 11 In.
$114

Theriault's

| | |
|---|---|
| **Rooster,** Crowing, Paint, Cast Iron, 13 ½ In. | 360 |
| **Rooster,** Crowing, Painted, Cast Iron, 11 In. | 146 |
| **Sailor,** Bell Bottom Pants, White Shirt, Barrel, Hands On Hips, Cast Iron, 11 ½ In. | 271 |
| **Sailor,** Holding Rope, Hands On Hips, Art Deco Shape, Cast Iron, Littco Products, 11 In. | 1800 |
| **Santa Claus,** Green Robe, Cast Iron, Germany, 1909, 4 In. | 259 |
| **Scotsman,** Paint, Cast Iron, Albany Foundry Co., 11 ⅞ In. | 780 |
| **Ship,** Storm Tossed, Painted, Cast Iron, Albany Foundry, c.1925, 9 ½ In., Pair | 360 |
| **Skier,** Woman, Standing, Legs Crossed, Holding Skies, Blue, Red, Cast Iron, 12 In. | 450 |
| **Skunk,** Black, Cast Iron, 6 ⅜ In. | 960 |
| **Snooper,** Man, Magnifying Glass, 13 In. | 330 |
| **Soldier,** French, Standing, Red Uniform, Cast Iron, William Bullock & Co., 16 In. | 2700 |
| **Squirrel,** Holding Nut, Rubber Bumpers, Cast Iron, Bradley & Hubbard, 11 ¾ In. | 4500 |
| **Squirrel,** Stump, Nut On Stump, 9 ½ In. | 570 |
| **Stagecoach,** Cast Iron, 5 ½ x 4 ½ In. | 105 |
| **Stork,** Standing, Paint, Cast Iron, Hubley, 13 In. | 1200 |
| **Stork,** Wedge, Green, Red, Black Paint, Cast Iron, Hubley, 5 ½ In. | 180 |
| **Tiger,** Cast Iron, Stylized Ringmaster, Top Hat, Hubley, c.1920, 9 ¼ x 4 In. | 1778 |
| **Totem Pole,** Multicolor, Cast Iron, 8 ½ In. | 180 |
| **Totem Pole,** Yellow Paint, Hollow, ½ Round, Wedge Base, Cast Iron, c.1920, 6 In. .......*illus* | 474 |
| **Troubadour,** Guitar, Paint, Cast Iron, Candlestick Co., 11 In. | 1020 |
| **Turkey,** Rubber Bumpers, Paint, Cast Iron, Bradley & Hubbard, 12 ½ In. | 3300 |
| **Wine Merchant,** Apron, Holding Red, White Wines, Paint, Cast Iron, 9 ¾ In. | 1080 to 1800 |
| **Wine Merchant,** Cast Iron, Man Carrying Multiple Wine Bottles, Painted, 9 ¾ x 7 In. | 1778 |
| **Woman In Hoop Skirt,** Cast Iron, National Foundry, 6 In. | 30 |
| **Woman Riding Sidesaddle,** Jumping Fence, Hunt Attire, Cast Iron, National Foundry, 7 In. | 450 |
| **Woman,** Art Deco, Outstretched Arms Hold Flowing Gown, Cast Iron, 9 ¼ In. | 431 |
| **Woman,** Flapper, Big Hair, Paint, Cast Iron, E.G.M. Co., Toledo, 12 In. | 600 |
| **Woman,** Fruit Basket On Head, Painted, Red Dress, Floral Apron, Cast Iron, 11 ½ In. | 234 |

**DOULTON** pottery and porcelain were made by Doulton and Co. of Burslem, England, after 1882. The name *Royal Doulton* appeared on the company's wares after 1902. Other pottery by Doulton is listed under Royal Doulton.

| | |
|---|---|
| **Bowl,** Salad, Servers, Stoneware, Flower Medallions, Drapery Swags, Lambeth, 7 In. | 123 |
| **Candlesticks,** Stoneware, Brass Mounts, Incised, Multicolor, Leaves, Lambeth, 8 In. | 431 |
| **Ewer,** Stoneware, Birds, Branch, Lambeth, 9 ½ In. | 338 |
| **Ewer,** Stoneware, Chicks, Grass, Lambeth, c.1902, 10 In. | 923 |
| **Ewer,** Stoneware, Running Horses, Gray Ground, Beaded Trim, Lambeth, 1883, 12 In. | 615 |
| **Figurine,** Nude Woman, Bather, Stoneware, Lizard, 4 Frog Feet, Lambeth, 12 In. | 1230 |
| **Figurine,** Shylock, Gilded, Enamel, Signed, Charles Noke, Burslem, c.1893, 16 ½ In. .......*illus* | 3198 |
| **Figurine,** Stoneware, Boy, Tambourine, Octagonal Pedestal, 4 ⅜ In. | 1046 |
| **Figurine,** Stoneware, Queen Victoria, Brown Glaze, Lambeth, c.1901, 11 ½ In. | 8610 |
| **Jug,** Stoneware, Bottle Shape, Heron, Grass, Leaf Borders, Lambeth, c.1873, 9 In. | 800 |
| **Jug,** Stylized Leaves, Blue Wash, Buff Ground, Silver Rim, Hinged Lid, 7 ½ In. | 185 |
| **Menu Holder,** 2 Mice, Playing Harp, Horn, Tinworth, Lambeth, c.1885, 3 ¾ In. .......*illus* | 3075 |
| **Menu Holder,** Mice, Sculpting Bust Of Mouse, G. Tinworth, Lambeth, 1880s, 3 ¾ In. .......*illus* | 2583 |
| **Pitcher,** Cartouche, Horse, Leaf Borders, Hinged Silver Lid, Lambeth, 9 ¾ In. | 861 |
| **Pitcher,** Stoneware, Brown Flowers, Blue Ground, Leaves, Lambeth, c.1885, 12 In. | 461 |
| **Pitcher,** Stoneware, Center Band, Scrolled Leaves, Black, Beading, Lambeth, 13 In. | 461 |
| **Pitcher,** Stoneware, Deer Grazing, Leaves, Raised Flowers, Lambeth, 1874, 9 ½ In. | 523 |
| **Pitcher,** Stoneware, Raised Beadwork, Silver Rim, Hinged Lid, Lambeth, 8 In. | 369 |
| **Plaque,** Terra-Cotta, Gate Of Samaria, A Time To Get 2 Kings, Lambeth, 8 x 14 In. | 2337 |
| **Plaque,** Terra-Cotta, Thou Shall No More Be Termed Forsaken, 1880s, 11 x 18 In. | 3690 |
| **Preserve Pot,** Lid, Barrel Shape, Pate-Sur-Pate Birds, Handle, F. Barlow, c.1880, 5 x 6 In. | 211 |
| **Punch Bowl,** Green Transfer Flowers, Leaves, Vining, Green Border, Gilt, Footed, 8 x 14 In. | 354 |
| **Punch Bowl,** Hunt Scene Transfer, Riders On Horseback, Hounds, Footed, 8 x 14 In. | 1770 |
| **Spoon Rest,** Boar, Leaves, Curled Tail Handle, c.1885, 8 In. | 2583 |
| **Tile,** Terra-Cotta, Luke Chapter 22, Angel, 2 Men, Lambeth, 8 ⅜ In. | 738 |
| **Umbrella Stand,** White Ground, Sunflowers, Flowers, Burslem, 24 In. | 345 |
| **Vase,** 2 Cows, Rural Landscape, Rounded Shoulder, Flared Rim, C. Hopkins, Burslem, 13 In. | 633 |
| **Vase,** 2 Handles, Faience, Flowers, Leaves, Yellow Ground, Lambeth, 17 In. | 800 |
| **Vase,** Aesthetic Period, Blue, Green, Geometric Bands, Short Neck, Lambeth, 1882, 9 In. | 104 |
| **Vase,** Bead Framed Oval Cartouches, Birds, Lambeth, 1883, 9 In. | 677 |
| **Vase,** Birds On Branches, Impasto, Florence Lewis, Lambeth, c.1885, 14 In., Pair .......*illus* | 1107 |
| **Vase,** Birds Perched On Line, Florence Barlow, Lambeth, c.1905, 10 ½ In. .......*illus* | 492 |
| **Vase,** Bottle Shape, Birds, Scrolled Leaves, Stippled Ground, 12 ¼ In. | 492 |

| | | |
|---|---|---|
| **Vase,** Cattle Scene Incised, Oval, Hannah Barlow, Lambeth, c.1880, 18 In. | | 466 |
| **Vase,** Cattle, Central Band, Wide Borders, Flowers, Lambeth, 18 ½ In., Pair | | 1845 |
| **Vase,** Flowers, Pale Green, Lambeth, c.1885, 12 ⅝ In., Pair | | 431 |
| **Vase,** Hexagonal Cartouches, Birds, Branches, Beaded Frames, Lambeth, 1879, 9 ½ In. | | 861 |
| **Vase,** Landscape, Horses, Green Ground, White, Black, Hannah Barlow, c.1890, 9 ½ In. *illus* | | 1353 |
| **Vase,** Old Man, Holmes, Small Mouth, Flow Blue, Signed H.G. Theaker, Burslem, 7 In. | | 472 |
| **Vase,** Porcelain, Blue Flowers, Ruffled Lip, Brown Ground, 19th Century, 8 In. | | 58 |
| **Vase,** Red To Dark Brown, Flared Cylinder, Burslem, c.1932, 5 ⅞ In. | | 81 |
| **Vase,** Scroll Leaf Molded, Green, Ocher, Frill Sides, J. Broad, Lambeth, c.1909, 2 x 9 In. | | 46 |
| **Vase,** Silicon Ware, Flowers, Long Neck, Simmance, Lambeth, 10 ¾ In., Pair | | 369 |
| **Vase,** Stoneware, Beaded Brown Leaves, 8 ¼ In., Pair | | 1353 |
| **Vase,** Stoneware, Bottle Shape, Central Band, Deer Grazing, Landscape, Lambeth, 12 In. | 738 to | 1046 |
| **Vase,** Stoneware, Bottle Shape, Goats, Landscape, Lambeth, 7 ¾ In. | | 400 |
| **Vase,** Stoneware, Bottle Shape, Handle, Cranes, Lambeth, 11 In. | | 338 |
| **Vase,** Stoneware, Cartouche, Bull, Horse, Donkey, Flowers, Lambeth, c.1885, 16 In. | | 1353 |
| **Vase,** Stoneware, Cattle, Stippled Ground, Hannah Barlow, Lambeth, 1887, 10 In. *illus* | | 984 |
| **Vase,** Stoneware, Central Band, Horses, Leaves, Palmettes, Barlow, 8 ⅜ In. | | 677 |
| **Vase,** Stoneware, Central Band, Sheep Grazing, Leaves, Barlow, Lambeth, c.1885, 21 In. | | 431 |
| **Vase,** Stoneware, Central Band, Sheep, Landscape, Leaves, Lambeth, 11 ¼ In. | | 1169 |
| **Vase,** Stoneware, Central Band, Sheep, Landscape, Leaves, Lambeth, 14 ½ In. | | 861 |
| **Vase,** Stoneware, Circular Cartouches, Birds, Leaves, Lambeth, c.1885, 17 ⅜ In., Pair | | 2583 |
| **Vase,** Stoneware, Cows Grazing, Gray Ground, Lambeth, c.1890, 13 ½ In. | | 738 |
| **Vase,** Stoneware, Cows Grazing, Lambeth, c.1884, 9 ¼ In., Pair | | 1230 |
| **Vase,** Stoneware, Green, Brown, Lambeth, 13 ¾ In. | | 554 |
| **Vase,** Stoneware, Griffin Handles, Bands, Leaves, Flowers, Beading, Lambeth, 10 ⅜ In. | | 1599 |
| **Vase,** Stoneware, Horses, Donkeys, Cows, Grass, Lambeth, 16 In., Pair | | 1476 |
| **Vase,** Stoneware, Horses, Leaves, Lambeth, 11 ½ In. | | 677 |
| **Vase,** Stoneware, Mottled Green, White Ground, Leaves, Lambeth, 10 ¼ In. | | 1476 |
| **Vase,** Stoneware, Oval Panels, Birds, Marked, 8 ½ In. | | 338 |
| **Vase,** Stoneware, Raised Flowers, Beadwork, Blue, Cream, Lambeth, 15 ¼ In. | | 677 |
| **Vase,** Stoneware, Sheep Grazing, Leaves, Lambeth, 1884, 6 ⅞ In. | | 1046 |
| **Vase,** Stoneware, Stylized Leaves, Beadwork, Late 1800s, 10 ½ In., Pair | | 369 |
| **Wash Set,** Bowl, Chamber Pot, Mug, Hunt Scene, Transfer, Multicolor, Pot 14 In. | | 180 |

**DRESDEN** and Meissen porcelain are often confused. Porcelains were made in the town of Meissen, Germany, beginning about 1706. The town of Dresden, Germany, has been home to many decorating studios since the early 1700s. Blanks were obtained from Meissen and other porcelain factories. Some say porcelain was also made in Dresden in the early years. Decorations on Dresden are often similar to Meissen, and marks were copied. Some of the earliest books on marks confused Dresden and Meissen, and that has remained a problem ever since. The Meissen "AR" mark and crossed swords mark are among the most forged marks on porcelain. Meissen pieces are listed in this book under Meissen. German porcelain marked "Dresden" is listed here. Irish Dresden and Dresden made in East Liverpool, Ohio, are not included in this section.

| | | |
|---|---|---|
| **Box,** Painted Courting Scenes, Classical Landscape, Gilt Scrolls, c.1885, 5 x 7 In. | | 423 |
| **Candelabrum,** 2-Light, Man, Woman, Tree With Flowers & Pears, C. Theime, 8 x 10 In., Pair | | 500 |
| **Candelabrum,** 5-Light, Flowers, Figure, Fruit, Scrolled Tripart Base, 26 ¾ In. | | 500 |
| **Centerpiece,** Rococo, Blossoms, Lattice, Column, Cupids, 4 Seasons, Domed Foot, 11 In. | | 375 |
| **Figurine,** Cockatoo, Multicolored Feathers, On Tree Stump, 9 In. | | 130 |
| **Frame,** Baroque Style, Painted, Angels, Psyche, Among Clouds, Heart Shape, 1800s | | 242 |
| **Frame,** Painted Angels, Baroque Style, Heart Shape, Multicolor, Gilt, Marked, 1800s | | 161 |
| **Garniture Set,** Cherubs, Flower Garlands, Leafy Scrolled Handles, Rococo Base, 3 Piece | | 920 |
| **Group,** 2 Women Dressing, Porcelain-Dipped Lace, Rococo Mirror & Table, 15 x 14 x 9 In. | | 960 |
| **Group,** 4 Putti, Holding Reticulated Tray, Applied Flowers & Fruit, 6 ½ x 12 In. | | 375 |
| **Group,** Classical Figures, At Banquet, c.1950, 22 In. | | 531 |
| **Group,** Count's Tailor, On Goat, Raised Base, 1890s, 11 ½ In. | | 250 |
| **Group,** Musical Scene, Harp, Piano, Violin, Children Dancing, Scrolled Base, 13 x 22 In. | | 2875 |
| **Group,** Sitzendorf Horse Couch, Royal Woman Passenger, 2 Men, Blue, White, Oval Base, c.1960, 20 In. | | 531 |
| **Mirror,** Girandole, Cartouche Frame, Flowers, Putti, Scrolls, Electric Candle, 58 x 32 In. | | 1500 |
| **Pitcher,** Putti Playing In Garden, Wine, Wine Barrel, Gold & Green Ground, 8 ¾ In. | | 250 |
| **Plate Set,** Armorial, Earl Of Craven, Banner, c.1910, 9 ½ In., 5 Piece | | 531 |
| **Plate,** Queen Louise Of Prussia, Jeweled, Gilt Blue Border, 10 In. | | 1000 |
| **Tray,** Gilt Rococo Edge, Flowers, Multicolor, c.1800, 5 x 7 In. | | 145 |
| **Urn,** Dome Lid, Musicians In Landscape, Applied Flowers, Socle Base, 25 x 9 In. | | 938 |
| **Urn,** Lid, Cobalt Blue, Gilt, Oval Reserve, Romantic Couple, Handles, 9 In. | | 167 |
| **Urn,** Lid, Crown Finial, Applied Flowers, Women, Cupids, Classical Figures, c.1950, 33 In. | | 1188 |

**D**

**Doll Clothes,** Bru Bebe, Bru Jne, Shoes, Kidskin, Ankle Strap, Brass Buckle, 5 In. $1,368

Theriault's

**Doorstop,** Boy, Hands In Pockets, Cast Iron, H.L. Judd Co., c.1920, 10 ¾ In. $593

James D. Julia Auctioneers

**Doorstop,** Charleston Dancers, Couple Dancing, Cast Iron, Marked Fish On Base, Hubley, 8 ¼ In. $1,778

James D. Julia Auctioneers

D

**Doorstop,** Clown, Scottie Dog, Painted, Cast Iron, c.1920, 7½ In.
**$593**

James D. Julia Auctioneers

**Doorstop,** Heron, Painted, Cast Iron, Albany Foundry, N.Y., c.1920, 7½ x 5 In.
**$474**

James D. Julia Auctioneers

**Doorstop,** Totem Pole, Yellow Paint, Hollow, ½ Round, Wedge Base, Cast Iron, c.1920, 6 In.
**$474**

James D. Julia Auctioneers

| | |
|---|---:|
| **Urn,** Lid, Orange Ground, Flower Bouquets, Leaves, Handles, 16½ x 10¾ In., Pair | 597 |
| **Urn,** Lid, Paneled Wreath, Ribbon, Flowers, Vine, Pink, Green, 14 In., Pair | 215 |
| **Urn,** Stand, Crown Finial, Putti, Women Handles, Courting Couple Reserve, 23 In. | 1750 |
| **Vase,** Bottle, Watteau, Amorous Couples, Elongated Neck, 12 In., Pair | 236 |
| **Vase,** Courting Couples, 1820s Attire, Gold Ground, Gilt Bands, Tapered Oval, 7½ In. | 344 |
| **Vase,** Gilt, Greek Key, Landscape, Figures, Garden, Leaves, Grapes, c.1900, 7 In. | 213 |
| **Vase,** Marie Antoinette, Portrait, Gilt Accents, Richard Klemm, c.1920, 6¼ In. | 316 |
| **Vase,** Portrait, Maiden, Lavender, Gold Trim, Cylindrical, Germany, 8⅜ In. | 177 |
| **Wall Bracket,** D-Shape Top, Pierced Basket, Flowers, Cherub, Karl Thieme, 8 x 12 In. | 196 |

**DUNCAN & MILLER** is a term used by collectors when referring to glass made by the George A. Duncan and Sons Company or the Duncan and Miller Glass Company. These companies worked from 1893 to 1955, when the use of the name *Duncan* was discontinued and the firm became part of the United States Glass Company. Early patterns may be listed under Pressed Glass.

| | |
|---|---:|
| **Basket,** Fruit, White Lace, Footed, 13 x 6 x 8 In. | 46 |
| **Button Arches,** Pitcher, Syrup, Ruby, Etched Band, c.1875, 6½ In. | 115 |
| **Candy Dish,** Amber, Footed, Lid, 8 x 4 In. | 65 |
| **Canterbury,** Dish, Divided, Lavender, Tab Handles, 6 In. | 15 |
| **Canterbury,** Relish, 3 Sections, 8¼ x 8 In. | 10 |
| **Caribbean,** Pitcher, 6 In. | 35 |
| **Caribbean,** Plate, Snack, Blue, 9½ In. | 24 |
| **Fern,** Relish, 3 Sections | 10 |
| **First Love,** Lamp, Hurricane, Etched, Footed, c.1937, 15½ In., Pair | 330 |
| **Hobnail,** Bowl, Flared, Handles, Footed, c.1930, 7 In. | 13 |
| **Hobnail,** Juice, Clear, 3½ In. | 11 |
| **Indian Tree,** Vase, Cornucopia, c.1940, 8¾ In. | 20 |
| **Mardi Gras,** Creamer, 3⅛ In. | 20 |
| **Ripple,** Tumbler, Black Amethyst, Footed, c.1925, 3½ In. | 50 |
| **Sandwich,** Iced Tea, Tumbler, 5⅜ In. | 19 |
| **Sandwich,** Plate, Luncheon, 8¼ In., 2 Piece | 15 |
| **Teardrop,** Sugar & Creamer | 12 |

**DURAND** art glass was made from 1924 to 1931. The Vineland Flint Glass Works was established by Victor Durand and Victor Durand Jr. in 1897. In 1924 Martin Bach Jr. and other artisans from the Quezal glassworks joined them at the Vineland, New Jersey, plant to make Durand art glass. They called their gold iridescent glass Gold Luster.

| | |
|---|---:|
| **Bowl,** Blue Luster Iridescent, White Heart & Vine, Signed, 5 In. | 431 |
| **Ginger Jar,** Lid, Blue Iridescent, White Hearts & Vines, Amber Prunt Finial, 9 In. | 3081 |
| **Goblet,** Prussian Blue, Optic Rib, Spanish Yellow Standard, 8½ In. | 81 |
| **Lamp Base,** Red & White Crackle, Clear Ground, Brass, Fleur-De-Lis Feet, 26 In., Pair | 178 |
| **Lamp,** Electric, Desk, Crackle Design, Iridescent, Bronze Base, c.1910, 17½ In. ............*illus* | 750 |
| **Plate,** Luncheon, Deep Amethyst, Optic Ribbing, 8½ In., 4 Piece | 460 |
| **Shade,** Aurene, Threaded Glass, Hearts, Bell Shape, Flared Rim, 2¾ x 3 In., Pair | 63 |
| **Torchere,** Blue & Yellow Leaves, Cream Ground, Gold Threading, 9¼ In. | 237 |
| **Urn,** Lid, King Tut, Iridescent Marigold, Blue Swirls, Gold, Label, 10 x 8½ In. ..............*illus* | 2070 |
| **Urn,** Lid, King Tut, Iridescent, Yellow, Orange, Rose, 10 x 8½ In. | 2070 |
| **Vase,** Ambergris, Iridescent Amber, Intaglio Flower Band, 13½ In. | 288 |
| **Vase,** Ambergris, Translucent Green, Opalescent Pulled Feathers, Cut Flowers, 10 In. | 460 |
| **Vase,** Blue Iridescent, 6 x 3½ In. | 196 |
| **Vase,** Blue Luster, Blue, Iridescent, White Hearts & Vines, 6 In. | 748 |
| **Vase,** Blue Luster, Hanging Hearts & Vine Design, Flared Mouth, Base, 9 In. | 1440 |
| **Vase,** Bottle, Blue Iridescent, Bulbous, Elongated Tapered Neck, 12 In. | 608 |
| **Vase,** Brown Iridescent, Long Flared Neck, 1920s, 16 x 9 In. | 1024 |
| **Vase,** Cluthra, Mottled Yellow & Red Swirls, Bulbous, Flared Rim, 10 In. | 948 |
| **Vase,** Cobalt Blue, Pulled Feathers, Round Base, 11¾ In. | 984 |
| **Vase,** Crackle, Gold & Gold Iridescent, Vertical Crackle Ribs, Bulbous, 7 In. | 304 |
| **Vase,** Gold Luster, Black, Hanging Hearts & Vine Design, Flared Mouth, Base, 9 In. | 1440 |
| **Vase,** Gold Luster, Heart, Vine Design, Flared Lip, Bulbous, Signed, 7 In. | 1080 |
| **Vase,** Gold Luster, Magenta, Straight Tapered Sides, 6 x 4½ In. | 288 |
| **Vase,** Gold, Iridescent, Bulbous Body, Flared Cylindrical Neck, Signed, 12¼ In. | 592 |
| **Vase,** Green Coil Design, Pulled Blue, Silver Highlights, Signed, 1948, 6 In. | 1560 |
| **Vase,** Heart & Vine, Silver Blue Luster, Opalescent, Signed, c.1931, 6½ In. | 633 |
| **Vase,** Iridescent Platinum, Heart & Vine, Cobalt Blue Ground, Rolled Flared Rim, 7 In. | 2251 |
| **Vase,** Iridescent, Bright Blue, White, Heart & Vine, Applied Gold Foot, 10 In. | 711 |
| **Vase,** Iridescent, Vine, Leaves, Orange To Clear, Early 20th Century, 12 In. | 1845 |
| **Vase,** King Tut, Blue & Bronze Iridescent, Platinum Highlights, 9½ In. ............................*illus* | 1955 |

| | |
|---|---|
| **Vase,** King Tut, Blue Iridescent, Green Ground, Orange To Yellow Inside, Oval, Footed, 8 In. | 1185 |
| **Vase,** King Tut, Blue, Coil Design, Opal, Blue Iridescence, Undulating Rim, 6 ½ In. | 1380 |
| **Vase,** King Tut, Blue, Gold, Bulbous Body, Flared Cylindrical Neck, 9 ½ In. | 1955 |
| **Vase,** King Tut, Gold Orange Luster, Apple Green, Applied Foot, Signed, c.1931, 8 In. | 748 |
| **Vase,** King Tut, Green Ground, Oval, 9 In. | 1035 |
| **Vase,** King Tut, Green, Iridescent Coiling, Marigold Interior, Shouldered, Signed, 7 In. | 1380 |
| **Vase,** King Tut, Platinum Iridescent, Green Ground, Tapered, Flattened Foot, 14 In. | 1185 |
| **Vase,** King Tut, Platinum, Mint Green Ground, Spherical, Gold Iridescent Foot, 6 In. | 2133 |
| **Vase,** Lady Gay Rose, Iridescent Luster, Gold Coil King Tut, Cylindrical, 9 In. | 586 |
| **Vase,** Moorish Crackle, Blue & White, 1920s, 8 ½ x 4 ½ In. .............................................*illus* | 1125 |
| **Vase,** Moorish Crackle, Pink & White, 1920s, 9 x 6 In. | 1125 |
| **Vase,** Ribbed Iridescent, Green, Gold Interior, Cylindrical, Shouldered, Signed, 18 In. | 1380 |
| **Vase,** Squat Body, Trumpet Neck, Blue Bands, Marked, 5 ⅝ x 7 In. | 633 |
| **Vase,** Threaded Pulled Feather, Tapering, Tall Shoulder, Iridescent, Yellow Interior, 10 In. | 862 |

**ELVIS PRESLEY,** the well-known singer, lived from 1935 to 1977. He became famous by 1956. Elvis appeared on television, starred in twenty-seven movies, and performed in Las Vegas. Memorabilia from any of the Presley shows, his records, and even memorials made after his death are collected.

| | |
|---|---|
| **Concert Tickets,** Market Square Arena, Indiana, June 26, 1977, 3 Piece | 125 |
| **Doll,** White Jumpsuit, World Doll Co., Box, 1980, 21 In. | 139 |
| **Guitar Pick,** Letter E, Yellow, 1 ⅜ In. .......................................................................*illus* | 3125 |
| **Knife,** Pocket, King Of Rock 'N' Roll, Plastic, 2 Blades, 3 ½ In. | 19 |
| **Movie Poster,** Viva Las Vegas, Linen Mounted, Argentina, 1964, 29 x 42 In. | 115 |
| **Pin,** Laminated Cellulose Acetate, Elvis Playing Guitar, Lea Stein, 2 ¾ In. | 130 |
| **Pin,** You're Nothin' But A Houn' Dog, Red, White, Green Duck Co., 1956, ⅞ In. | 28 |
| **Plate,** '68 Comeback Special, Delphi, 1990, 8 In. | 26 |
| **Plate,** Elvis At The Gates Of Graceland, Bruce Emmett, 1988, 8 ½ In. | 10 |
| **Scarf,** Elvis, Dog, Singing, Silk, Elvis Presley Enterprises, c.1956, 30 x 30 In. | 145 |

**ENAMELS** listed here are made of glass particles and other materials heated and fused to metal. In the eighteenth and nineteenth centuries, workmen from Russia, France, England, and other countries made small boxes and table pieces of enamel on metal. One form of English enamel is called *Battersea* and is listed under that name. There was a revival of interest in enameling in the 1930s and a new style evolved. There is now renewed interest in the artistic enameled plaques, vases, ashtrays, and jewelry. Enamels made since the 1930s are usually on copper or steel, although silver was often used for jewelry. Graniteware is a separate category, and enameled metal kitchen pieces may be included in the Kitchen category. Cloisonne is special type of enamel and is listed in its own category.

| | |
|---|---|
| **Box,** Arts & Crafts, Silver, Butterfly, Frank G. Hale, Marked, 6 ¼ x 4 ¼ In. ...................*illus* | 6765 |
| **Box,** Lid, Woman, Flowers, Leaves On Side, Round, France, 5 ½ In. | 375 |
| **Box,** Red, Cartouche, Cameo, Woman, Pearls, White Enamel Border, Vienna, 4 In. | 1599 |
| **Box,** Silver, Guilloche Ocher, Cobalt Blue, Geometric Pattern, Blue Cabochon, 3 ½ x 2 In. | 633 |
| **Box,** Silver, Painted Roses, Lid, Continental, 4 ¼ In. | 270 |
| **Box,** Silver, Ship, Water, Stylized Dolphins, Mildred Watkins, c.1950, 1 ⅛ In. ..............*illus* | 15990 |
| **Letter Opener,** Dagger Shape, Silver Gilt Mounts, Teal, Sheath, Agate, Seed Pearls, 12 In. | 529 |
| **Lipstick Holder,** Romantic Scene, Engraved, Scrolling, Lapis Glass, 2 ¼ x ¾ In. | 104 |
| **Plaque,** Arts & Crafts, Goldfish, Signed, F.G. Hale, Frame, Limoges, 5 ½ x 3 ½ In. .............*illus* | 4305 |
| **Plaque,** Christ Standing On Rock, Red Robe, Signed Sarlandie, Limoges, Frame, 13 x 10 ½ In. | 118 |
| **Plaque,** Copper, Musician, Interior, Limoges, Jean-Paul Loup, Frame, 7 x 5 In. | 188 |
| **Plaque,** Copper, Woman, Profile, Long Auburn Hair, Limoges, Frame, 6 ½ x 4 ½ In. | 594 |
| **Plaque,** Profile, Woman, Lace Bonnet, Round, Limoges, Frame, P. Bonnaud, c.1907, 18 x 16 ½ In. | 688 |
| **Plaque,** Psyche, Seated, Branches, Gown, Turquoise, Gold, Wings, c.1900, 8 ¾ x 7 ½ In........*illus* | 615 |
| **Plaque,** Roman Centurion, Multicolor, Limoges, Gilt Frame, 1800s, 5 ½ x 4 In. | 702 |
| **Plate,** Old Jerusalem, Dome Of The Rock, On Copper, Gilt Wood Frame, 20 x 24 In. | 311 |
| **Plate,** Peacock Feather, Flower, Red, Green, Blue, Black, Arts & Crafts, 8 In. | 610 |
| **Profile,** Woman, Laurel Wreath, Convex, Multicolor, Gilt, Bronze Dore Frame, 8 x 6 In. | 633 |
| **Triptych,** Rectangular Central Plaque, Limoges, 2 Roundels, Tooled Leather Frame | 2583 |

**ERPHILA** is a mark found on Czechoslovakian and other pottery and porcelain made after 1920. This mark was used on items imported by Ebeling & Reuss, Philadelphia, a giftware firm that was founded in 1866 and out of business sometime after 2002. The mark is a combination of the letters *E* and *R* (Ebeling & Reuss) and the first letters of the city, Phila(delphia). Many whimsical figural pitchers and creamers, figurines, platters, and other giftwares carry this mark.

| | |
|---|---|
| **Bird,** Blue, Pink Breast, Yellow Beak, White Tree Shape Base, 5 ¼ x 4 ¾ In. | 30 |
| **Biscuit Barrel,** Children, Goat, Grass, Black, White, Silhouette | 50 |

**Doulton,** Figurine, Shylock, Gilded, Enamel, Signed, Charles Noke, Burslem, c.1893, 16 ½ In.

$3,198

**Doulton,** Menu Holder, 2 Mice, Playing Harp, Horn, Tinworth, Lambeth, c.1885, 3 ¾ In.

$3,075

**Doulton,** Menu Holder, Mice, Sculpting Bust Of Mouse, G. Tinworth, Lambeth, 1880s, 3 ¾ In.

$2,583

This is an edited listing of current prices. Visit **Kovels.com** to check thousands of prices from previous years and sign up for free information on trends, tips, reproductions, marks, and more.

E

**Doulton,** Vase, Birds On Branches, Impasto, Florence Lewis, Lambeth, c.1885, 14 In., Pair
$1,107

Skinner Auctioneers & Appraisers

**Doulton,** Vase, Birds Perched On Line, Florence Barlow, Lambeth, c.1905, 10½ In.
$492

Skinner Auctioneers & Appraisers

**Doulton,** Vase, Landscape, Horses, Green Ground, White, Black, Hannah Barlow, c.1890, 9½ In.
$1,353

Skinner Auctioneers & Appraisers

| | |
|---|---|
| **Candlesticks,** Couple Seated On Cushions, Yellow, Pink, Green, White, 8 In., Pair | 35 |
| **Creamer,** Applied Cat, Climbing, Looking Over Rim, Yellow | 50 |
| **Dish,** Turquoise, Applied Birds, White, 5¼ x 3¾ In. | 9 |
| **Teapot,** Figural, Dog, Beagle, Brown, Cream, Paw Shape Spout, 8 In. | 25 to 64 |
| **Teapot,** Figural, Rabbit, Reddish Brown, Cream, Paw Shape Spout, 8 In. | 98 |

**ES GERMANY** porcelain was made at the factory of Erdmann Schlegelmilch from 1861 to 1937 in Suhl, Germany. The porcelain, marked *ES Germany* or *ES Suhl*, was sold decorated or undecorated. Other pieces were made at a factory in Saxony, Prussia, and are marked *ES Prussia*. Reinhold Schlegelmilch made the famous wares marked *RS Germany*.

| | |
|---|---|
| **Basket,** Yellow Roses, Gilt Handle, 4¾ x 5⅜ In. | 89 |
| **Berry Bowl,** Roses, Stems, Green, Suhl, 5 In. | 16 |
| **Cake Plate,** Ribbon & Jewel Mold, Green, Pink & Peach Roses, Suhl, 10½ In. | 185 |
| **Charger,** Grouse, Woodland, Scalloped & Gilt Rim, 11½ In. | 100 |
| **Creamer,** Transfer, Three Graces, 2¾ In. | 49 |
| **Cup & Saucer,** Classical Group, Column, Green, Gold, Demitasse, Suhl | 15 |
| **Cup & Saucer,** Classical Group, Landscape, Green, Gold, Demitasse, Suhl | 40 |
| **Cup & Saucer,** Pink Flowers, Scallop Shell Shape, c.1880 | 98 |
| **Ewer,** Sparrows, Stick Neck, c.1861, 10¼ In. | 350 |
| **Lemon Server,** Flowers, Gold Ring Handle, Signed, 6¼ In. | 52 |
| **Pillow Vase,** Oval Vignette, Woman, Scarf, Bird, Nest, Green, Handles, Suhl, 8¼ In. | 95 |
| **Plate,** 3 Goddesses, Cherub, Olive Branch, Gilt, 9¾ In. | 700 |
| **Plate,** 3 Maidens, Seated, Tree, Garland Border, Transfer, 9½ In. | 85 |
| **Plate,** Tea Roses, Leaves, Suhl, 8½ In. | 20 |
| **Powder Shaker,** Roses, Leaves, Yellow, Green Ground, Suhl, 5 x 3 In. | 10 |
| **Trinket Dish,** Mother-Of-Pearl Glaze, Gold Lines, 4 In. | 24 |

**ESKIMO** artifacts of all types are collected. Carvings of whale or walrus teeth are listed under Scrimshaw. Baskets are in the Basket category. All other types of Eskimo art are listed here. In Canada and some other areas, the term *Inuit* is used instead of Eskimo.

| | |
|---|---|
| **Figurine,** Eskimo, Outstretched Arms, Soapstone, Stone Base, 10 x 7 In. | 184 |
| **Figurine,** Polar Bear, Carved, Whalebone, 28 In. | 984 |
| **Figurine,** Soapstone, Man Hunter, Dressed In Winter Clothing, Holding Bone Knife, 8½ In. | 120 |
| **Figurine,** Walrus, Soapstone, Walrus, Initialed E.F., 4 x 10 In. | 120 |
| **Mask,** Spirit, Ivory, Carved, Traditional Appendages, c.1970, 6¼ x 7 In. | 546 |
| **Pouch,** Inuit, Sealskin, Beaded, 1800s, 12 In. | 245 |
| **Sculpture,** Inuit, Man & Stylized Walrus, Soapstone, 10 In. .....................*illus* | 308 |
| **Snow Goggles,** Inuit, Wood, Carved, Braided Sinew Cord, 1800s, 4¾ In. | 3180 |

**FABERGE** was a firm of jewelers and goldsmiths founded in St. Petersburg, Russia, in 1842, by Gustav Faberge. Peter Carl Faberge, his son, was jeweler to the Russian Imperial Court from about 1870 to 1917. The rare Imperial Easter eggs, jewelry, and decorative items are very expensive today.

| | |
|---|---|
| **Creamer,** Silver, Matte Finish, Tapered Cylinder, c.1895, 3 In. | 1063 |
| **Cuff Links,** Triangular, Raised Crown, 14K Gold, Silver, Diamond, Red Enamel, Box, c.1860, 1 In. | 5520 |
| **Figurine,** Draft Horse, Agate, Naturalistic, Semiprecious Stone Eyes, Gold Rims, 3 x 3 In. | 1250 |
| **Vodka & Caviar Set,** Figural, Egg, Cobalt Glass, Decanter, Shot Glasses, Dish, 5 Piece | 1440 |

**FAIENCE** refers to tin-glazed earthenware, especially the wares made in France, Germany, and Scandinavia. It is also correct to say that faience is the same as majolica or Delft, although usually the term refers only to the tin-glazed pottery of the three regions mentioned.

| | |
|---|---|
| **Bowl,** Allover Flowers, Blue, Green, Orange, 1800s, 12 In. | 46 |
| **Bowl,** Carved Leaves, Turquoise Interior, Blue Applied Exterior, California, 3¼ x 7½ In. | 230 |
| **Bowl,** Funerary, Blue Glaze, Flat Bottom, Incised Bands, Rome, 7½ In. | 127 |
| **Charger,** Birds, Nest, Signed, E. Lachenal, 1878, 19¾ In. | 2375 |
| **Charger,** Red & Cream Flowers, Butterfly, Turquoise Ground, T. Deck, c.1880, 15 In. | 3198 |
| **Garniture Urns,** Classic Style, Putti Panels, Faux Marble Base, c.1770, 15 x 6 In., Pair | 1845 |
| **Jardiniere,** Turquoise Glaze, Column Form Pedestal, England, 1855, 42 In. | 708 |
| **Tankard,** Fisherman, Nets, River, Multicolor, Pewter Lid, Foot, Engraved A.W., 1700s, 7 In. | 219 |
| **Tile,** Grapes, Leaves, Matte Glaze, Flint Faience Tile Co., 8⅜ x 10 In. ...................*illus* | 863 |
| **Tureen,** Duck Shape, Multicolor Glaze, Green, Yellow, White, Rose, 1800s, 9 x 8½ In. | 69 |
| **Urn,** Painted, Geometric, Flowers, Scrolled Handles, Footed, Continental, 5½ x 7 In. | 90 |
| **Vase,** Blue, White, Tree, House Landscape, Bulbous, To Tapered Base, 18 In. | 277 |
| **Vase,** Round Body, Flared Neck, Curved Handles, Blue, Ocher, Yellow, 1700s, 9 x 5 In. | 161 |

**FAIRINGS** are small souvenir boxes and figurines that were sold at country fairs during the nineteenth century. Most were made in Germany. Reproductions of fairings are being made, especially of the famous *Twelve Months after Marriage* series.

| | |
|---|---|
| **Box,** Dome Lid, Multicolor Tulip, Zigzag, Dots, Tin Hinges, Hasp, c.1800, 2⅝ x 5 In. | 12980 |
| **Box,** Gilt Metal, Beveled Glass Panels, Cast Metal Framework, Bird Finial, 8 x 5 In. | 414 |
| **Box,** Pine, Flowers, Yellow Ground, Paint, J. Webster, Pa., c.1850, 2½ x 4½ In. | 5166 |
| **Box,** Poplar, Flower Decoupage, Green Ground, J. Lehn, c.1850, 6 x 5 In. | 5760 |
| **Figurine,** 3 Girls, Bonnets, Staffordshire, 3 In. | 39 |
| **Figurine,** A Mouse A Mouse, Conta Boehme, 19th Century, 3½ x 3¼ In. | 40 |
| **Figurine,** Boy, Sleeping On Dog, c.1860, 3 x 3 x 2 In. | 135 |
| **Figurine,** Dog Biting Boy, Germany, 1900s, 3½ x 2½ In. | 69 |
| **Figurine,** Dresser, Dog, Keg, Gloves, Victorian, 4¾ x 1½ x 3 In. | 55 |
| **Figurine,** Last In To Bed, Porcelain, c.1875, 4 x 3 x 3½ In. | 150 |
| **Figurine,** Modesty, Man Holding Bathroom Door Closed, England, c.1880, 3 x 2 In. | 225 |
| **Figurine,** Pig, Outhouse Phone Booth, Engaged, Germany, c.1900, 4 x 2 x 2 In. | 70 |
| **Figurine,** Sailor, Hands In Pocket, Germany, 4 In. | 46 |
| **Figurine,** Twelve Months After Marriage, Bed Scene, Conta Boehme, 3½ x 3¼ In. | 45 |
| **Figurine,** Wedding Night, Couple In Front Of Fireplace, Germany, c.1890, 3¾ x 3½ In. | 40 |
| **Figurine,** Who Is Coming, Woman Dressing Behind Screen, Conta Boehme, 3½ x 3¾ In. | 60 |
| **Trinket Box,** 18th Century Lady, Scrolled Base, Multicolor, Germany, 4 x 3 x 3 In. | 89 |
| **Trinket Box,** 3 Girls, Muffs, Conta Boehme, c.1890, 4¾ x 3 x 2½ In. | 79 |
| **Trinket Box,** Basketweave, Bird Laying On Back, Bisque, 19th Century, 4 x 2 x 2 In. | 125 |
| **Trinket Box,** Figural, Toddler In Basket, Horn, Doll, Staffordshire, 2¼ In. | 59 |
| **Trinket Box,** Lid, Figural, 3 Women, Victorian Dresses, Staffordshire, 3 In. ...............*illus* | 35 |
| **Trinket Box,** Preening Swan, Branches, Conta Boehme, 2 x 2 x 1 In. | 95 |

**FAIRYLAND LUSTER** *pieces are included in the Wedgwood category.*

**FAMILLE ROSE,** *see Chinese Export category.*

**FANS** have been used for cooling since the days of the ancients. By the eighteenth century, the fan was an accessory for the lady of fashion and very elaborate and expensive fans were made. Sticks were made of ivory or wood, set with jewels or carved. The fans were made of painted silk or paper. Inexpensive paper fans printed with advertising were giveaways in the late nineteenth and early twentieth centuries. Electric fans were introduced in 1882.

| | |
|---|---|
| **Advertising,** 7Up, Pinup Girl, Bathing Suit, Lithograph, Multicolor, 1931, 9 x 9¼ In. | 125 |
| **Advertising,** Dr. Morse's Indian Root Plus, Indian, On Horse, Bear, Cardboard, 13 x 8 In. | 149 |
| **Advertising,** Drink A Bite To Eat, Pumpkin Head Man, 2-Sided, Cardboard, 1930s, 7 In. | 300 |
| **Black & Red Translucent Sticks,** Pierced, Painted Flowers, Black Lace, 9 x 17 In. | 115 |
| **Bone Brise,** Pierced Painted Sticks, Flower, Leaf Design, Girl's, c.1900, 4¾ In. | 47 |
| **Bone,** Goose, Peacock Feather, Flowers, Woman, Painted, Red, Green Tassels, Chinese, 13 In. | 826 |
| **Bone,** Lace, Gold Decoration, Inset Piques, Brass Rope Twist Ring, Child's, 4 In. | 62 |
| **Bone,** Paper, Carved, Reticulated, Chromolithograph, Silver, Gilt, 1800s, 14 x 22 In. | 529 |
| **Bone,** Parchment, 2-Sided, Painted Couples, Flowers Scene, France, c.1820, 9½ In. | 130 |
| **Bone,** Pierced, Paper, 2-Sided, Paper Leaves, Sheep Scene, Flowers, 10½ In. | 35 |
| **Bone,** Pierced, White Satin, Painted Swags, Swirls, Silver Foil Inlay, Brass Loop, 10 In. | 172 |
| **Bone,** Satin, Red, Painted Bird, Reeds, Bone Sticks, Cotton Tassel, 14 In. | 53 |
| **Bone,** Silk, Louis XVI Style, Courting Couple, Frame, 1800s, 17¾ In. | 438 |
| **Brise,** Leather, Red, Gold Leaf Monogram, Velvet Ribbon, 9 In. | 70 |
| **Brise,** Shell, Brown, Yellow Leaves, Monogram, Metal Loop, Cotton Tassel, 1800s, 9¼ In. | 767 |
| **Brise,** Shell, Mottled Brown, Plain Sticks, 8¼ In. | 413 |
| **Celluloid,** Fixed, Woman, Goat, Dog, Cat, Blue, White, Metal Handle, Rene De Garam, 1924, 9 In. | 83 |
| **Cherry Smash,** Our Nation's Beverage, Plantation, c.1920, 16 In. | 90 |
| **Coin-Operated,** Black, 5 Cent, National Prepayment Fan Co., 18½ x 13 In. | 1800 |
| **Electric,** Desk, Oscillating, 5 Cent, General Electric, 18 In. | 480 |
| **Electric,** Emerson, Metal, 4 Blades, Spread Base, Table..................................*illus* | 72 |
| **Electric,** General Electric, Model A00, Maroon, Brass, 20 x 17 In. | 180 |
| **Electric,** General Electric, Vortalex, Multi-Speed, 4 Aluminum Blades, Trailing Tip, 20 In. | 120 |
| **Electric,** Partner, Double, Wire Frame, Robbins & Myers, Springfield, Ohio, 13 x 17 x 10½ In. | 2280 |
| **Electric,** Westinghouse, Metal, Brass, 1900s, 18 x 12½ In. | 192 |
| **Electric,** Winchester, 4 Blades, Logo, 10¾ x 8 In. | 750 |
| **Faux Tortoiseshell,** Black Lace, Maidens, Cupids, Doves, Shadowbox Frame, c.1900, 17 x 30 In. | 94 |
| **Giltwood,** Paper, Children, Landscape, Frame, c.1800, 14 x 23 In. | 188 |
| **Horn,** Paper, Lithograph, 3 Vignettes, Family Group, Gilt Horn Guards & Sticks, Birds, 10 In. | 246 |
| **Horn,** Pierced, Paper, 2-Sided, Harem Scene, Gold Foil Edges, Gold Foil Inlay, 10½ In. | 59 |

**Doulton,** Vase, Stoneware, Cattle, Stippled Ground, Hannah Barlow, Lambeth, 1887, 10 In.
$984

Skinner Auctioneers & Appraisers

**Durand,** Lamp, Electric, Desk, Crackle Design, Iridescent, Bronze Base, c.1910, 17½ In.
$750

Rago Arts & Auction Center

**Durand,** Urn, Lid, King Tut, Iridescent Marigold, Blue Swirls, Gold, Label, 10 x 8½ In.
$2,070

Humler & Nolan

**F**

**Durand,** Vase, King Tut, Blue & Bronze Iridescent, Platinum Highlights, 9 ½ In. $1,955

James D. Julia Auctioneers

---

**Durand,** Vase, Moorish Crackle, Blue & White, 1920s, 8 ½ x 4 ½ In. $1,125

Rago Arts & Auction Center

---

## TIP

*A glass flower frog, a holder for the flower stems in an arrangement, can be useful. Look for the round glass holders with many holes. Each hole can hold a marble so a group of about 5 to 15 can be displayed in different sizes of flower frogs.*

---

**Elvis Presley,** Guitar Pick, Letter E, Yellow, 1 ⅜ In. $3,125

Graceland Auctions

| | |
|---|---:|
| **Ivory,** 31 Pierced Sticks, Heraldic Shield Design, Ferns, Flowers, 19th Century, 8 ¼ In. | 460 |
| **Ivory,** Brise, Pierced Figures, Landscape, Mother-Of-Pearl Washer, 7 ½ In. | 502 |
| **Ivory,** Mother-Of-Pearl Inlay, Vellum, Frigate, Caged Bird, Flowers, 11 ¾ In. | 885 |
| **Ivory,** Net, Fontage, Painted Daffodil Basket, Ribbon Edge, Brass Loop, c.1890, 15 In. | 142 |
| **Ivory,** Painted Floral Vignette, 20 Peacock Feathers, 19th Century, 12 x 21 In. | 201 |
| **Ivory,** Paper, Metal, 2 Women, Floating In Shell Boat, Lithograph, c.1805, 8 ½ In. | 118 |
| **Ivory,** Parchment Leaf, Muses, Shepherd, Sheep, Peasant Woman, Folding, c.1720, 11 In. | 1770 |
| **Ivory,** Parchment, 2-Sided, Figures, Bubbles, Birds, Flowers, Instruments, Italy, 1700s, 11 In. | 944 |
| **Ivory,** Pierced, Beige Lace, 19th Century, 12 ¾ In. | 201 |
| **Ivory,** Vellum, Country Scene, Instruments, Flower, Vines, Scrolls, Painted, 1700s, 10 In. | 413 |
| **Ivory,** Vernis Martin Style, Picnic Scene, Flute Player, Pierced Flower, Bird Border, 1700s, 8 In. | 142 |
| **Kerosene,** J.H. Strong, Lake Breeze Motor, Iron, Scrolls, 4 Blades, Copper Oil Lamp Base, 41 In. | 4130 |
| **Mahogany,** Pink, White, Feathers, Hummingbird, Beetle, Feather Cockade Center, Handle, c.1890, 13 In. | 200 |
| **Mother-Of-Pearl,** Chiffon, Lace, Lady, Flower, Putti, 9 ½ In. | 94 |
| **Mother-Of-Pearl,** Chromolitho, Lohengrin, Figures, Swan, Landscape, Case, 9 ½ x 17 ¾ In. | 1162 |
| **Mother-Of-Pearl,** Courting Scene In Garden, Cartouches, Birds, Gilt Trim, 12 In. | 345 |
| **Mother-Of-Pearl,** Gray Silk, Silver Netting Drape, Spangles, Sequins, Loop, 8 ½ In. | 266 |
| **Mother-Of-Pearl,** Paper, Lithograph, Harvest, Bacchus, Fruit, c.1850, 10 In. | 221 |
| **Mother-Of-Pearl,** Paper, Roman Warrior, Flowers, Scrolls, Openwork, Frame, 1800s, 20 ¼ In. | 375 |
| **Mother-Of-Pearl,** Paper, Women Bowing To Goddesses, Putti, Clouds, Swag, Birds, 10 In. | 246 |
| **Mother-Of-Pearl,** Pierced, Carved, Paper, 2-Sided, Women, Courtier, Italy, c.1890, 10 ½ In. | 200 |
| **Mother-Of-Pearl,** Pierced, Gilt, Court Garden Scene Border, Metal Handle, Tassel, 11 In. | 259 |
| **Mother-Of-Pearl,** Satin, Daisy Spray, Peach, Ivory, Painted, 13 ¾ In. | 224 |
| **Mother-Of-Pearl,** Silk Moire, 2 Vignettes, Lovebirds, Garland, Tassel, 10 In. | 308 |
| **Mother-Of-Pearl,** Silk, Mesh Insets, Flowers, Sequins, Horns, Swags Painted, Brass Loop, 8 In. | 70 |
| **Oil Lamp,** J.H. Strong, Lake Breeze, Metal, Scroll Feet, 23 x 43 In. ...... *illus* | 1320 |
| **Papier-Mache,** Courting Scenes, Scalloped Rim, Carved Handle, c.1890, 15 x 10 In. | 92 |
| **Papier-Mache,** Mica, 2 Women, Etched, Cotton Fringe, c.1690, Pair | 153 |
| **Papier-Mache,** Mother-Of-Pearl, Villa, Church, Painted, Wood Handles, 1800s, 8 x 10 In., Pair. | 118 |
| **Shell,** Lace Netting, Chiffon, Couple, Seated, Black, c.1850, 9 ¾ In. | 70 |
| **Shell,** Paper, Couples On Horseback, Castle, Birds, 9 ½ In. | 59 |
| **Silk,** Mother-Of-Pearl, Man, 2 Women, Country Scene, Louis XVI Style Frame, 1800s, 19 In. | 188 |
| **Wood,** Ballroom Scene, Lithograph, Black, Gold Frame, France, 1800s, 10 x 18 In. | 230 |
| **Wood,** Chiffon, Black, Spangles, Sequins, Mother-Of-Pearl, 9 ½ In. | 35 |
| **Wood,** Lace, Black, Netting, Sequins, c.1905, 13 ¾ In. | 212 |
| **Wood,** Pierced, Black, Silk, Lacquer, Embroidery, 2 Cranes Flying, Heart Shape, Chinese, 1900s, 14 ½ In. | 106 |
| **Wood,** Red Satin, Painted Leaves & Berries, Red Marabou Feathers, Gilt, 12 ½ In. | 135 |
| **Wood,** Rice Paper, Large Butterfly, Purple, Blue, Metal, Cotton Tassel, 8 ½ In. | 118 |
| **Wood,** Silk Netting, Silver Sequins, Pierced, Black, c.1950, 9 ½ In. | 30 |

---

**FAST FOOD COLLECTIBLES** *may be included in several categories, such as Advertising, Coca-Cola, Toy, etc.*

---

**FEDERZEICHNUNG**, *see Loetz category.*

---

**FENTON ART GLASS COMPANY** was founded in 1905 in Martins Ferry, Ohio, by Frank L. Fenton and his brother, John W. Fenton. They painted decorations on glass blanks made by other manufacturers. In 1907 they opened a factory in Williamstown, West Virginia, and began making glass. The company stopped making art glass in 2011 and assets were sold. A new division of the company makes handcrafted glass beads and other jewelry. Copies are being made from leased original Fenton molds by an unrelated company, Fenton's Collectibles. The copies are marked with the Fenton mark and Fenton's Collectibles mark. Fenton is noted for early carnival glass produced between 1907 and 1920. Some of these pieces are listed in the Carnival Glass category. Many other types of glass were also made. Spanish Lace in this section refers to the pattern made by Fenton.

| | |
|---|---:|
| **Amberina,** Slipper | 23 |
| **Aqua Crest,** Compote, 5 ½ In. | 25 |
| **Bicentennial,** Plate, Milk Glass, 1976, 8 In. | 9 |
| **Burmese,** Bell, Ruffled Rim, Flower Enameling, Signed, 1982, 7 In. | 29 |
| **Butterfly & Berry,** Basket, 7 ½ In. | 34 |
| **Coin Dot,** Perfume Bottle, White Opalescent, King's Crown Top, 1940s, 4 ½ x 4 In. | 199 |
| **Coinspot,** Barber Bottle, Cranberry, Stopper, 8 ½ In. | 85 |
| **Coinspot,** Basket, Ruffled Rim, Blue Green, Milk Glass Interior, 1970s, 8 ½ In. | 66 |
| **Crystal Crest,** Relish, Silver, Handle | 36 |
| **Crystal Crest,** Vase, Honey Comb, Green, 5 ¼ In. | 35 |
| **Crystal Velvet,** Basket, 5 ½ In. | 35 |

| | |
|---|---:|
| **Daisy & Button,** Candlestick, 2-Light, Milk Glass | 20 |
| **Daisy & Button,** Creamer, Milk Glass, 2 ¾ In. | 12 |
| **Daisy & Button,** Rose Bowl, Amber, 5 In. | 20 |
| **Daisy & Button,** Top Hat, Milk Glass, 3 ¼ In. | 15 |
| **Daisy & Button,** Vase, Footed, Scalloped Rim, Milk Glass, 10 ¼ In. | 63 |
| **Diamond Lace,** Epergnette, Milk Glass, 9 In., 4 Piece | 92 |
| **Diamond Optic,** Plate, Salad, Green, 8-Sided, 7 ⅝ In. | 8 |
| **Dolphin,** Bonbon, Pink, 6 ½ In. | 27 |
| **Dolphin,** Bowl, Flower Intaglio, Crimped, Round, 9 In. | 20 |
| **Dolphin,** Candlestick, Pink, 3 ½ In. | 18 |
| **Dolphin,** Compote, Blue Opalescent, Oval, 5 In. | 109 |
| **Dragons & Lotus,** Bowl, Master Ice Cream, Scalloped Trim, Cobalt Blue Iridescent, 2 x 8 In. | 58 |
| **Drapery,** Pitcher, Water, Green Opalescent, Globe Shape, Crimped Rim, c.1910, 9 In. | 104 |
| **Dusty Rose,** Basket, 7 In. | 34 |
| **Dusty Rose,** Vase, Crimped, Draped, 8 In. | 30 |
| **Dusty Rose,** Votive, Double Candle, Footed, 4 ¼ In. | 12 |
| **Elizabeth,** Plate, Luncheon, Black, 8 In. | 27 |
| **Elizabeth,** Saucer, Black | 11 |
| **Emerald Crest,** Plate, 10 ⅜ In. | 89 |
| **Favrene,** Vase, Shouldered, 6 ¾ In. | 298 |
| **Figurine,** Duckling, Lavender Petals, 3 ½ In. | 28 |
| **Figurine,** Hummingbird, Green Iridescent | 22 |
| **Fine Cut & Block,** Compote, Milk Glass, 3 In. | 19 |
| **Gilded Star Flowers,** Basket, 7 In. | 36 |
| **Gilded Star Flowers,** Bowl, Flared, 8 In. | 24 |
| **Gold Crest,** Top Hat, Double Crimped | 15 |
| **Gold Crest,** Vase, Double Crimped, Footed, 9 In. | 32 |
| **Gold Crest,** Vase, Footed, Double Crimped, 4 In. | 27 |
| **Gold Crest,** Vase, Melon, Double Crimped, 6 In. | 29 |
| **Good Luck,** Heart & Horseshoe, Bowl, Ruffled Edge, Marigold | 2200 |
| **Grape & Cable,** Centerpiece, 3-Footed, Flared, Red, 14 In. | 2700 |
| **Hobnail,** Banana Boat, Milk Glass, 9 ½ x 12 x 3 ¾ In. | 40 |
| **Hobnail,** Basket, Blue Marble, 6 ½ In. | 38 |
| **Hobnail,** Basket, Milk Glass, Crimped Edge, c.1953, 10 In. | 39 |
| **Hobnail,** Bell, Milk Glass, 6 In. | 18 |
| **Hobnail,** Bonbon, Cranberry Opalescent, Triangular, 6 In. | 29 |
| **Hobnail,** Bonbon, Double Crimped, Blue Opalescent | 45 |
| **Hobnail,** Bonbon, Double Crimped, Milk Glass, 5 ⅝ In. | 15 |
| **Hobnail,** Bonbon, Ruby, Ruffled Rim, 7 ½ x 2 ¼ In. | 26 |
| **Hobnail,** Boot, Lid, Blue Marble, 1970s, 5 ¾ x 7 In. | 54 |
| **Hobnail,** Bottle Stopper, Blue Opalescent, 1940s, 1 ⅛ In. | 5 |
| **Hobnail,** Bowl, Candle, Footed | 12 |
| **Hobnail,** Bowl, Dessert, Milk Glass, 4 x 4 In. | 10 |
| **Hobnail,** Bowl, Double Ruffled, Milk Glass, 10 x 4 In. | 42 |
| **Hobnail,** Bowl, Milk Glass, 3 In. | 12 |
| **Hobnail,** Bowl, Oval, 4-Footed, Milk Glass, 8 In. | 35 |
| **Hobnail,** Butter, Cover, Round, Milk Glass | 25 to 28 |
| **Hobnail,** Candleholder, Cranberry Opalescent, Loop Handle, 3 In. | 74 |
| **Hobnail,** Candleholder, Milk Glass, Footed, 1960s, 2 x 4 In. | 35 |
| **Hobnail,** Candlestick, Amber, 8 ⅞ In. | 28 |
| **Hobnail,** Compote, Blue Marble | 22 |
| **Hobnail,** Compote, Olive Green, Ruffled Rim | 15 |
| **Hobnail,** Compote, Ruby, Ruffled Rim, 6 In. | 21 |
| **Hobnail,** Compote, Ruffled, Crimped Rim, Milk Glass | 75 |
| **Hobnail,** Creamer, Blue Opalescent | 15 |
| **Hobnail,** Creamer, Footed, Milk Glass | 18 |
| **Hobnail,** Cruet, Cranberry, Prism Stopper, 6 In. | 70 |
| **Hobnail,** Cruet, Light Blue, Stopper, 4 ¾ In. | 35 |
| **Hobnail,** Dish, 3-Toed, Scalloped Rim, Milk Glass, 5 ½ x 3 In. | 30 |
| **Hobnail,** Epergnette, Turquoise, 4 Piece, 6 ⅝ In. | 137 |
| **Hobnail,** Saltshaker, Black | 20 |
| **Hobnail,** Slipper, Milk Glass, c.1955, 5 In. | 15 |
| **Hobnail,** Sugar & Creamer, Milk Glass | 25 |
| **Hobnail,** Sugar, Cranberry Opalescent, 3 ⅝ In. | 89 |
| **Hobnail,** Sugar, Lid, Milk Glass | 22 |

**Enamel,** Box, Arts & Crafts, Silver, Butterfly, Frank G. Hale, Marked, 6 ¼ x 4 ¼ In.
$6,765

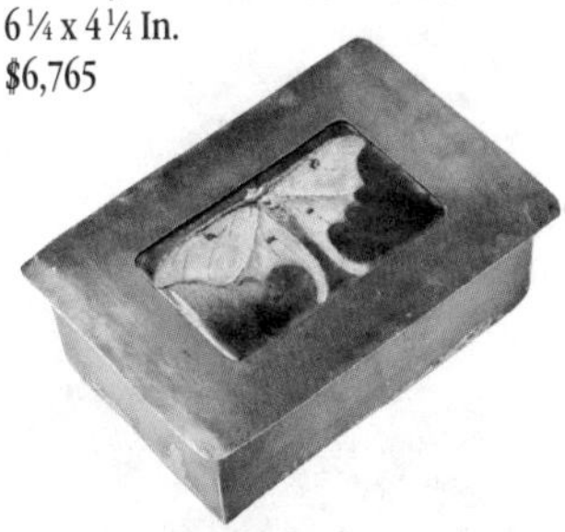

Skinner Auctioneers & Appraisers

**Enamel,** Box, Silver, Ship, Water, Stylized Dolphins, Mildred Watkins, c.1950, 1 ⅛ In.
$15,990

Skinner Auctioneers & Appraisers

**Enamel,** Plaque, Arts & Crafts, Goldfish, Signed, F.G. Hale, Frame, Limoges, 5 ½ x 3 ½ In.
$4,305

Skinner Auctioneers & Appraisers

**Enamel,** Plaque, Psyche, Seated, Branches, Gown, Turquoise, Gold, Wings, c.1900, 8 ¾ x 7 ½ In.
$615

New Orleans Auction Galleries, Inc.

**Eskimo,** Sculpture, Inuit, Man & Stylized Walrus, Soapstone, 10 In.
**$308**

Skinner Auctioneers & Appraisers

**Faience,** Tile, Grapes, Leaves, Matte Glaze, Flint Faience Tile Co., 8⅜ x 10 In.
**$863**

Humler & Nolan

**Fairing,** Trinket Box, Lid, Figural, 3 Women, Victorian Dresses, Staffordshire, 3 In.
**$35**

Conestoga Auction Co., Inc.

> **TIP**
> *Folding fans should be stored closed.*

| | |
|---|---:|
| **Hobnail,** Sugar, White Opalescent, 2 Handles, Footed | 13 |
| **Hobnail,** Top Hat, Blue, 2½ In. | 12 |
| **Hobnail,** Vase, Blue Opalescent, Crimped, 5½ In. | 22 |
| **Hobnail,** Vase, Fluted, Milk Glass, Bud, 8 In. | 20 |
| **Hobnail,** Vase, Ruffled Edge, Footed, Milk Glass, 5½ x 5½ In. | 35 |
| **Hobnail,** Vase, Violet, Milk Glass, 2⅜ x 4¼ In. | 15 |
| **Hobnail,** Vase, White Opalescent, Footed, Ruffled | 10 |
| **Hobnail,** Wine, Ruby, 4⅝ In. | 31 |
| **Lacy Edge,** Bowl, Milk Glass, 8 In. | 19 |
| **Lacy Edge,** Compote, Milk Glass, 5½ In. | 21 |
| **Lincoln Inn,** Goblet, Wine, Flared, Ruby Red, 6 Oz., 5¾ In. | 31 |
| **Lincoln Inn,** Sherbet, 4¼ In. | 8 |
| **Lincoln Inn,** Tumbler, Footed, Flared, Ruby Red, 6 Oz., 5⅛ In. | 36 |
| **Milk Glass,** Compote, Double Crimped, 6 In. | 25 |
| **Mosaic,** Vase, Multicolor Splashes, Black Ground, 5½ x 6½ In. ...................*illus* | 1154 |
| **Mother's Day,** Plate, Blue Satin, Madonna, Child, Blue Satin, 7 In. | 11 |
| **Orange Tree,** Loving Cup, Amethyst, 5¾ In. | 476 |
| **Orange Tree,** Mug, Marigold, 3½ In. | 27 |
| **Orange Tree,** Sherbet, Marigold, 3⅛ In. | 17 |
| **Peach Crest,** Bowl, Double Crimped, 10 In. | 83 |
| **Peach Crest,** Jug, Beaded, 6¼ In. | 47 |
| **Peach Crest,** Vase, Stick Neck, Ruffled Rim, 8 In. | 36 |
| **Pineapple,** Goblet, Water, Colonial Blue, 6⅛ In. | 23 |
| **Pink Blossoms,** Basket, Crimped Rim, 7⅛ In. | 68 |
| **Pink Blossoms,** Bell, Medallion, 6 In. | 32 |
| **Pink Blossoms,** Fawn, Reclining, 3⅝ In. | 39 |
| **Plymouth,** Iced Tea, Ruby, 12 Oz., 6 In. | 24 |
| **Priscilla,** Goblet, Water, 6⅛ In. | 20 |
| **Priscilla,** Sherbet, 4⅛ In. | 12 |
| **Rose Crest,** Vase, Crimped, Bulbous, 11 In. | 157 |
| **Rose Overlay,** Bowl, Double Crimped, 7 In. | 20 |
| **Rose Overlay,** Vase, Double Crimped, 5½ In. | 21 |
| **Rose,** Compote, Milk Glass, Scalloped Rim, 6¼ In. | 18 |
| **Rose,** Slipper, Milk Glass, 4 In. | 21 |
| **Rose,** Slipper, Petal Pink, 4 In. | 12 |
| **Rose,** Vase, 3-Toed, Milk Glass, 4 In. | 14 |
| **Silver Crest,** Banana Boat, Footed | 37 |
| **Silver Crest,** Basket, Clear Handle, Ruffled Rim, 6 In. | 25 |
| **Silver Crest,** Basket, Handle | 18 |
| **Silver Crest,** Bonbon, Double Crimped, 6 In. | 9 |
| **Silver Crest,** Bowl, Double Crimped, 10 In. | 30 |
| **Silver Crest,** Compote | 15 |
| **Silver Crest,** Compote, Lid | 36 |
| **Silver Crest,** Compote, Ruffled | 26 |
| **Silver Crest,** Cornucopia, 6 In. | 23 |
| **Silver Crest,** Plate, 10¾ In. | 82 |
| **Silver Crest,** Salt & Pepper, Footed | 145 |
| **Silver Crest,** Tumbler, Footed, 9 Oz., 6 In. | 97 |
| **Spiral Optic,** Basket, Oval, Clear Handle, French Opalescent, 9 In. | 54 |
| **Spiral Optic,** Cruet, Cranberry Opalescent, 5 In. | 27 |
| **Spiral,** Decanter, Cranberry Opalescent, Crimped Handle, Hobnail Stopper, c.1950, 12 In. | 104 |
| **Spruce Green,** Rose Bowl, 3½ In. | 22 |
| **Stag & Holly,** Bowl, Crimped, 3-Toed, Marigold, 11 In. | 97 |
| **Swirl,** Salt & Pepper, Milk Glass, 3⅜ In. | 36 |
| **Thumbprint,** Ashtray, Oval, Colonial Green, 4½ In. | 13 |
| **Thumbprint,** Basket, Ruffled Rim, Black, 8 In. | 32 |
| **Thumbprint,** Bowl, Amber, Ruffled, 2 x 7 In. | 15 |
| **Thumbprint,** Candy Dish, Lid, Oval, Colonial Blue, 3-Toed, 6 In. | 35 |
| **Thumbprint,** Compote, Amber, Ruffled, 6⅛ In. | 15 |
| **Thumbprint,** Compote, Blue, Ruffled, 6⅛ In. | 18 |
| **Thumbprint,** Compote, Double Crimped, Milk Glass | 25 |
| **Thumbprint,** Compote, Green, Ruffled, 6¼ In. | 15 |
| **Thumbprint,** Creamer, Amber, 4⅛ In. | 14 |
| **Thumbprint,** Creamer, Colonial Blue, 4⅛ In. | 16 |
| **Thumbprint,** Creamer, Colonial Pink, 4⅛ In. | 24 |

F

| | |
|---|---|
| Thumbprint, Goblet, Water, 6 5/8 In. | 28 |
| Thumbprint, Goblet, Water, Ruby, 10 Oz., 6 5/8 In. | 21 |
| Thumbprint, Nappy, Footed, Crimped, Milk Glass, 5 In. | 14 |
| Thumbprint, Plate, Amber, 8 5/8 In. | 14 |
| Thumbprint, Salt & Pepper, Colonial Green | 13 |
| Thumbprint, Sherbet, Colonial Blue, 4 1/4 In. | 7 |
| Thumbprint, Sherbet, Colonial Green, 4 1/4 In. | 7 |
| Thumbprint, Tumbler, Footed, Colonial Green, 13 Oz., 6 3/8 In. | 16 |
| Thumbprint, Tumbler, Footed, Ruby, 13 Oz., 6 3/8 In. | 46 |
| Thumbprint, Vase, Handkerchief, Amber, Footed, 8 In. | 21 |
| Thumbprint, Vase, Oval, Footed, Colonial Orange, 15 In. | 11 |
| Twilight Blue, Slipper, 3 In. | 29 |
| Valencia, Creamer, Amber, 2 5/8 In. | 15 |
| Vase, Pinecones, Branch, White Over Green, Baluster, K. Murphy & R. Bokamp, 9 In. | 384 |
| Violets In The Snow, Cake Stand, 13 In. | 243 |
| Violets In The Snow, Top Hat, 5 In. | 64 |
| Water Lily, Basket, Crystal Velvet, 7 In. | 32 |
| Water Lily, Rose Bowl, Crystal Velvet, 3 1/8 In. | 18 |
| White Satin, Candlestick, 3 1/4 In. | 19 |
| Wreath Of Roses, Punch Cup, Marigold, 2 3/4 In. | 11 |

**FIESTA**, the colorful dinnerware, was introduced in 1936 by the Homer Laughlin China Co., redesigned in 1969, and withdrawn in 1973. It was reissued again in 1986 in different colors and is still being made. New colors, including some that are similar to old colors, have been introduced. One new color is introduced in March every year. The simple design was characterized by a band of concentric circles beginning at the rim. Cups had full-circle handles until 1969, when partial-circle handles were made. Harlequin and Riviera were related wares. For more prices, go to kovels.com.

*fiesta*

| | |
|---|---|
| Apricot, Cup | 7 |
| Apricot, Gravy Boat | 46 |
| Apricot, Plate, Salad, 7 1/4 In. | 12 |
| Apricot, Platter, 11 1/2 In. | 25 |
| Apricot, Saucer | 4 |
| Chartreuse, Eggcup | 102 |
| Chartreuse, Plate, Dinner, 10 In. | 65 |
| Chartreuse, Saucer | 5 |
| Cobalt Blue, Syrup | 276 |
| Gray, Plate, 9 In. | 11 |
| Green, Plate, 6 In. | 4 |
| Ivory, Bowl, Cereal, 6 1/4 In. | 45 |
| Ivory, Plate, 6 In. | 4 |
| Ivory, Plate, 10 In. | 18 |
| Ivory, Tumbler, Juice, 3 1/2 In. | 15 |
| Turquoise, Cup & Saucer | 14 |
| White, Bowl, Cereal, 6 7/8 In. | 3 |
| Yellow, Cup & Saucer | 13 |
| Yellow, Plate, Dinner, 10 In. | 15 to 26 |
| Yellow, Saucer | 4 |
| Yellow, Sugar, Lid | 10 |

**FINCH**, *see Kay Finch category.*

**FINDLAY ONYX AND FLORADINE** are two similar types of glass made by Dalzell, Gilmore and Leighton Co. of Findlay, Ohio, about 1889. Onyx is a patented yellowish white opaque glass with raised silver daisy decorations. A few rare pieces were made of rose, amber, orange, or purple glass. Floradine is made of cranberry-colored glass with an opalescent white raised floral pattern and a satin finish. The same molds were used for both types of glass.

| | |
|---|---|
| Bowl, Floradine, Red, Opal Leaves & Blossoms, Crimped Rim, 6 In. | 403 |
| Bowl, Onyx, Opal, Silver Inclusions, Scalloped Rim, 8 In. | 173 |
| Bowl, Pink, Raspberry Flower & Leaf Inclusions, Rounded Sides, 1 3/4 In. | 1035 |
| Creamer, Floradine, Red, Opal Flower & Leaf Inclusions, Applied Camphor Handle, 5 In. | 460 |
| Creamer, Onyx, Opal, Silver Flower Inclusions, Fluted Neck, Clear Handle, 4 3/4 In. | 58 |
| Mustard Pot, Onyx, Opal, Iridescent Silver Inclusions, 3 3/4 In. | 29 |
| Shaker, Purple, Silver Inclusions, Bulbous, Fluted Neck, 5 1/2 In. | 4600 |

**Fan,** Electric, Emerson, Metal, 4 Blades, Spread Base, Table
$72

Gray's Auctioneers LLC

**Fan,** Oil Lamp, J.H. Strong, Lake Breeze, Metal, Scroll Feet, 23 x 43 In.
$1,320

Showtime Auction Services

**Fenton,** Mosaic, Vase, Multicolor Splashes, Black Ground, 5 1/2 x 6 1/2 In.
$1,154

James D. Julia Auctioneers

**Findlay,** Toothpick Holder, Floradine, Scalloped Rim, 2 ¼ In. $1,093

Early Auction Co.

**Firefighting,** Alarm Box, Cast Iron, Flip Open Door, Faraday, No. 2022, c.1925, 7 x 5 In. $124

James D. Julia Auctioneers

**Firefighting,** Bucket, Leather, Black Paint, R.C. Searle, New England, c.1810, 13 x 8 In. $770

James D. Julia Auctioneers

| | |
|---|---:|
| **Shaker,** Shaded Pink & Opal, Red Flower Inclusions, Bulbous, Fluted Neck, 5 ½ In. | 633 |
| **Spooner,** Floradine, Red Satin, White Flowers, 4 ½ In. | 403 |
| **Spooner,** Floradine, Red, Opal Inclusions, Swirls Over All, Fluted Neck, 4 ½ In. | 288 |
| **Sugar Shaker,** Onyx, Ivory, Platinum Flowers, Dalzell, Gilmore & Leighton Co., c.1900, 5 In. | 316 |
| **Toothpick Holder,** Floradine, Scalloped Rim, 2 ¼ In. .........*illus* | 1093 |
| **Toothpick Holder,** Onyx, Silver Inclusions, Ruffled Rim, 2 ½ In. | 29 |

**FIREFIGHTING** equipment of all types is wanted, from fire marks to uniforms to toy fire trucks. It is said that every little boy wanted to be a fireman or a train engineer 75 years ago and the collectors today reflect this interest.

| | |
|---|---:|
| **Alarm Annunciator Panel,** Wood Panel, 6 Station Knob, 5 Brass Bells, 24 In. | 1020 |
| **Alarm Box,** Cast Iron, Flip Open Door, Faraday, No. 2022, c.1925, 7 x 5 In. .........*illus* | 124 |
| **Alarm,** ADT, Industrial, Red, Cast Iron, Wall Mount, 1908, 8 x 6 x 5 In. | 70 |
| **Ax,** Metal, Wood Handle, 1800s, 32 In. | 135 |
| **Ax,** Steel Blade, Wood Handle, 1930s, 34 In. | 30 |
| **Bell,** Brass, Tapered Wood Handle, Muffin, 10 In. | 300 |
| **Bell,** Firehouse, Bronze, Nickel Plated, Period Mount, c.1965, 21 In. | 354 |
| **Belt,** Leather, No. 4, Wrapped Hose Buckle | 270 |
| **Bucket,** Leather, Black Paint, C.S. Thompson No. 2, 7 ¾ x 12 In. | 425 |
| **Bucket,** Leather, Black Paint, R.C. Searle, New England, c.1810, 13 x 8 In. .........*illus* | 770 |
| **Bucket,** Leather, Blue, Hose, Gilt, 12 ½ In. | 840 |
| **Bucket,** Leather, Columbian Eagle Fire Society, Eagle, Banner, No. 2, Fiero, 12 In. | 1800 |
| **Bucket,** Leather, Elisha & Folger, 1813, Pair | 330 |
| **Bucket,** Leather, Green, Yellow, Iron, Marked L. Chappotin, No. 1, 1790, 18 In. | 1067 |
| **Bucket,** Leather, Inscribed Captain Jacob 1775, Medallions, Swing Handle, 13 In. | 3600 |
| **Bucket,** Leather, No. 2, J. Meacham, Yellow, Black Paint, 18 ¾ In. | 420 |
| **Bucket,** Leather, No. 16 Washington Fire Club, J. McCausland, Yellow, Black, 1825, 20 In. | 840 |
| **Bucket,** Leather, Painted Band, George Washington, Woven Handle, 12 x 10 In. | 110 |
| **Bucket,** Leather, Painted Eagle, Banners, Franklin Fire Society, Shattuck, 1830, 14 x 8 In. | 3259 |
| **Bucket,** Leather, Painted Red, Eagle, Shield, Banner, Mechanic Fire Society, c.1815, 13 In. | 800 |
| **Bucket,** Leather, Painted, D. Thomas, No. 89, Iron, Handle, c.1810, 18 ½ In. .........*illus* | 1235 |
| **Bucket,** Leather, Painted, Inscribed Benjin Cresson & Co., Philadelphia, c.1800, 11 ½ In. | 338 |
| **Bucket,** Leather, Red, R.H. Parker Phoenix Fire Society, Exeter, N.H., 1932, 20 In., Pair | 3360 |
| **Bucket,** Leather, Yellow, Wheeler, 1794, 13 In. | 960 |
| **Call Box,** Stand, Cast Iron, Steel Column, Iron Base, Red Paint, Kellogg, 66 In. | 420 |
| **Extinguisher,** Floafoam, Copper Case, Model 833, General Detroit Corp., 24 In. .........*illus* | 150 |
| **Extinguisher,** Foamite, Nickel Plated, Leather Strap, American LaFrance, 26 In., 2 ½ Gal. | 360 |
| **Fire Mark,** Hydrant, Hose, F A, Cast Iron, Fire Assoc., Philadelphia, c.1875, 11 ½ x 7 In. .........*illus* | 356 |
| **Grenade,** Harden's Hand, Blue, Diamond Diaper, 4 Flattened Panels, Flared Rim, 6 ¾ In. | 120 |
| **Grenade,** Harkness Fire Destroyer, Cobalt Blue, Horizontal Ribs, c.1880, 6 ¼ In. .........*illus* | 460 |
| **Grenade,** Heatman's Swift, Gasoline Color, Sheared Lip, Plug, Embossed, c.1900, 6 In. | 1725 |
| **Grenade,** London Fire Appliance Co., Yellow Amber, Tooled Lip, c.1900, 9 In. | 3450 |
| **Hat,** Parade, Red, Hose 1, Gold Sunburst, Philadelphia, J.F.F., Germantown, 1848, 6 In. | 13800 |
| **Hat,** Wood, 2 Hose, Bullard, 9 ½ In. | 60 |
| **Helmet,** Brass, Embossed Symbols, Leaves, France, c.1905 | 90 |
| **Helmet,** Leather, Grattacap, High Eagle, Brown, Merrimac, No. 3, 14 In. | 360 |
| **Helmet,** Leather, No. 3, Black, Rounded, c.1810, 11 In. | 780 |
| **Helmet,** Leather, White, Lynn, Massachusetts, 1st Foreman, High Eagle, 15 In. | 600 |
| **Helmet,** Metal, Brass Shield, Top Comb, Chin Strap, France, 11 In. | 210 |
| **Helmet,** Tin, Chaplin PFD, White, Cairns & Brother, Clifton, New Jersey, 15 In. | 761 |
| **Lantern,** Dietz, King, Steel Body, Copper Base, Water Shield, Glass, Handle, 19 In. | 150 |
| **Lantern,** Wrist, Etched Charles Phelps Lens, c.1890, 10 ½ In. | 360 |
| **Mask,** Fireman's, Leather, Wool, Nickel, Vajen-Bader Head Protector, c.1900, 18 In. .........*illus* | 780 |
| **Model,** Fire Pumper, Friendship, Cast Iron, Clark Ship Model Co., c.1930, 8 ¾ x 15 In. | 960 |
| **Nozzle,** Brass, Cord Wrapped, Elkhart Mfg. Co., 18 In. .........*illus* | 60 |
| **Nozzle,** Brass, Leather Strap, U.S.R. Co. Eureka Fire Hose Div., 11 In. | 90 |
| **Relay Panel,** Walnut, 12 In. | 120 |
| **Sign,** Granite State Fire Insurance, Tin, Portsmouth, N.H., 23 ½ x 15 In. | 86 |
| **Sign,** Wood, Painted, A.F.D., Athol Fire Department, Black Molded Frame, 1893, 43 x 35 In. | 1845 |
| **Siren,** Fire Truck Siren, Federal Signal, Model Q2B, 15 In. | 300 |
| **Torch,** Silver Plate, 26 In., Pair | 120 |
| **Trumpet,** Fire, Silver Plate, 1800s, 20 ½ In. | 240 |
| **Trumpet,** Silver Plate, Relief Trees & Flowers, Eagle Holding Leather Strap, 23 In. | 1140 |

F

**Trumpet,** Silver, Repousse, Flowers, Haddock, Lincoln & Foss, Boston, c.1860, 25 In.................... 6765
**Uniform,** Firefighter's, Embroidered, Wool Coat, Leather Cap, Jacket, Logo, Japan, c.1890 .......... 240

**FIREPLACES** were used to cook food and to heat the American home in past centuries. Many types of tools and equipment were used. Andirons held the logs in place, firebacks reflected the heat into the room, and tongs were used to move either fuel or food. Many types of spits and roasting jacks were made and may be listed in the Kitchen category.

| | |
|---|---|
| **Andirons,** Bell Metal, Curled Wrought Iron, Continental, c.1690, 16 In............... | 780 |
| **Andirons,** Brass, Acorn Top, Hexagonal Columns, Arch Support, Ball Feet, 22 x 20 In. ............ | 480 |
| **Andirons,** Brass, Anchor Shape, Rostand Manufacturing, c.1950, 17 x 14 In. ........... | 472 |
| **Andirons,** Brass, Chippendale Style, Urn Finial, Pedestal Form, 19 x 9 ¼ In. ......... | 86 |
| **Andirons,** Brass, Chippendale, Ball Finials, Vase Shape Standard, c.1780, 22 In. ......... | 840 |
| **Andirons,** Brass, Chippendale, Garland Wrapped Columns, Flowers, Phila., c.1770, 26 In........... | 11400 |
| **Andirons,** Brass, Chippendale, Urn Finial, c.1790, 27 In.................. | 1063 |
| **Andirons,** Brass, Classical, Ball Finial, Boston, c.1825, 12 x 22 ½ In............ | 344 |
| **Andirons,** Brass, Classical, Ball Finial, John Molineux, Boston, c.1820, 15 x 25 In. ......... | 688 |
| **Andirons,** Brass, Classical, Beehive Shape, S-Scroll Legs, c.1850, 21 In............ | 359 |
| **Andirons,** Brass, Federal, Lemon Top, c.1815, 19 In., Pair....... | 180 |
| **Andirons,** Brass, Federal, Oval Top, c.1820, 22 In............ | 180 |
| **Andirons,** Brass, Lemon Finial, Arched Legs, Ball Feet, c.1800, 20 In............ | 266 |
| **Andirons,** Bronze, Ball Finial, Corinthian Capitals, Columnar Body, 1800s, 23 ¾ In.......... | 115 |
| **Andirons,** Bronze, Cherub, Ram's Head, Baroque Style, Serpent Base, c.1890, 34 In........ | 938 |
| **Andirons,** Bronze, Classical Revival, Cabriole Legs, Reeded, Urn Finial, c.1900, 26 x 12 x 18 In. | 1168 |
| **Andirons,** Bronze, Corinthian Column, Ball Finial, Cabriole Legs, 30 x 10 ¾ In.......... | 9222 |
| **Andirons,** Bronze, Iron, Seahorse, William Van Erp, 1930s, 18 x 14 In. .......... | 6400 |
| **Andirons,** Bronze, Louis XVI Style, Leaf Design, On Quivers, 24 In........... | 938 |
| **Andirons,** Bronze, Polished, Lion Mask Base, Ring, Ball & Fleur-De-Lis Design, 21 x 24 In. ........ | 288 |
| **Andirons,** Bronze, Putti On Dragon's Head, Heraldic Lions, Pyramid Shape, 35 In.......... | 3280 |
| **Andirons,** Bronze, Renaissance Style, Patinated, Putto, Ram's Heads, Dragons, 37 x 21 In. ........ | 4063 |
| **Andirons,** Cast Iron, Black Dancers, Hands On Knees, c.1820, 17 x 21 In. ............ | 633 |
| **Andirons,** Cast Iron, Bulldog, Seated, Black Paint, New York, 15 ½ x 22 In. ....... | 720 |
| **Andirons,** Cast Iron, Cat Shape, Stepped Base, Green Glass Eyes, c.1910, 19 x 17 In. ......... | 236 |
| **Andirons,** Cast Iron, Dog, Labrador, 13 ⅜ x 15 ½ In. .......... | 720 |
| **Andirons,** Cast Iron, Dog, Seated, Stamped Liberty Fdy., St. Louis, Mo., 13 ½ x 18 ½ In............ | 300 |
| **Andirons,** Cast Iron, Dragon, Log Supports, Bradley & Hubbard, c.1910, 26 In...................*illus* | 850 |
| **Andirons,** Cast Iron, Figural Sun, Serpentine Sun Base, Bradley & Hubbard, 16 ½ x 10 In......... | 400 |
| **Andirons,** Cast Iron, George Washington, Figural, 15 In.......... | 60 |
| **Andirons,** Cast Iron, George Washington, Figural, Hinged Log Rests, 18 x 7 In. ........ | 270 |
| **Andirons,** Cast Iron, Hessian Soldiers, 19 ¾ In. .......... | 500 |
| **Andirons,** Cast Iron, Hessian, Paint, c.1850, 19 ½ In. .......... | 720 |
| **Andirons,** Cast Iron, I Beams, 9 ½ x 16 ¼ In. .......... | 90 |
| **Andirons,** Cast Iron, Masted Ship Finial, Anchor Base, Cast Iron, 18 x 17 In. .......... | 510 |
| **Andirons,** Cast Iron, Mother Goose, Facing Right, Glass Eyes, Yellow Bonnets, 15 In. ............. | 923 |
| **Andirons,** Cast Iron, Openwork Medallion, Scrolling Flowers In Vase, Polished Brass, 23 In. ...... | 923 |
| **Andirons,** Cast Iron, Oval Finial, Penny Foot, c.1770, 23 ½ In., Pair.......... | 2640 |
| **Andirons,** Cast Iron, Pagoda Shape, 1800s, 14 x 15 In.......... | 123 |
| **Andirons,** Cast Iron, Soldier, Painted, 20 x 16 In. .......... | 285 |
| **Andirons,** Classical, Ball Top, Faceted Standard, Spur Feet, 1800s, 20 ½ x 12 x 26 In.................. | 299 |
| **Andirons,** Column Form, Urn Finials, Ball & Claw Feet, 29 In. .......... | 2040 |
| **Andirons,** Composite, Columns, Ball Finial, Scrolling Base, 51 x 21 x 31 In. ............ | 719 |
| **Andirons,** Fox & Horn, 13 x 21 ½ In. .......... | 281 |
| **Andirons,** Iron, Arts & Crafts, Scrolled, Drop Rings, Twisted Chain, Ball, Black Paint, 28 In. ...... | 83 |
| **Andirons,** Iron, Baroque, Acorn Finial, Leaves, Scrolling, Italian, 32 x 16 In. .......... | 345 |
| **Andirons,** Iron, Brass, Baroque Style, Pierced Rosette Finial, Scrolled Feet, c.1900, 23 In........... | 236 |
| **Andirons,** Iron, Gold Paint, Stacked Geometrics, 1978, 13 x 11 In........ | 7800 |
| **Andirons,** Iron, Hessian Soldier, Painted, c.1920, 20 ¼ x 19 In. .......... | 660 |
| **Andirons,** Iron, Knife Blade, Faceted Brass Finials, c.1800, 21 In. .......... | 300 |
| **Andirons,** Iron, Sun Shape, Face, Serpentine Bases, Stamped B & H, 16 ½ x 10 In. .......... | 800 |
| **Andirons,** Mixed Metal, Rooster, Sitting On Horseshoes, c.1910 .......... | 3900 |
| **Andirons,** Rustic Upright Log, Forged Legs, Welded Tubular Body, 16 ½ In.......... | 889 |
| **Andirons,** Snake Shape, Repurposed Railroad Rails, 23 In.......... | 180 |
| **Andirons,** Stylized Cats, Seated, Brass, Chrome Plating Co. Of Tenn., 20 In. .............*illus* | 390 |
| **Andirons,** Tool Set, Cast Iron, Marching Hessian Soldier Handles, Red, Yellow, 19 x 21 In........... | 900 |
| **Andirons,** Tool Set, Cast Iron, Owls, Glass Eyes, c.1900, 15 x 17 x 9 In., 5 Piece.......... | 1095 |

**F**

**Firefighting,** Bucket, Leather, Painted, D. Thomas, No. 89, Iron, Handle, c.1810, 18 ½ In.
$1,235

James D. Julia Auctioneers

**Firefighting,** Extinguisher, Floafoam, Copper Case, Model 833, General Detroit Corp., 24 In.
$150

DuMouchelles Art Gallery

**Firefighting,** Fire Mark, Hydrant, Hose, F A, Cast Iron, Fire Assoc., Philadelphia, c.1875, 11 ½ x 7 In.
$356

James D. Julia Auctioneers

**Firefighting,** Grenade, Harkness Fire Destroyer, Cobalt Blue, Horizontal Ribs, c.1880, 6 ¼ In.
**$460**

Glass Works Auctions

**Firefighting,** Mask, Fireman's, Leather, Wool, Nickel, Vajen-Bader Head Protector, c.1900, 18 In.
**$780**

Garth's Auctioneers & Appraisers

**Firefighting,** Nozzle, Brass, Cord Wrapped, Elkhart Mfg. Co., 18 In.
**$60**

Showtime Auction Services

| | |
|---|---:|
| **Andirons,** Tool Set, Iron, Brass Urn Finials, Federal, Tongs, Shovel, c.1800, 22 ½ In. | 960 |
| **Andirons,** Wrought Iron, Arts & Crafts, Tapered Shaft, Faceted Finial, 24 x 21 In. | 469 |
| **Andirons,** Wrought Iron, Continental, c.1760, 33 In. | 570 |
| **Andirons,** Wrought Iron, Continental, c.1860, 34 In. | 120 |
| **Andirons,** Wrought Iron, Gooseneck Shaft, Applied Hearts, Spit Hooks, c.1800, 19 In. *illus* | 3690 |
| **Andirons,** Wrought Iron, Notched Dog, Rope Twisted Mouth Insert, 1900s, 9 ½ In. | 150 |
| **Andirons,** Wrought Iron, Oval Loop, Circular Craftsman Stamp, c.1910, 16 x 13 x 19 In. | 1875 |
| **Andirons,** Wrought Iron, Penny Feet, Brass Finials, 1800-50, 16 In. | 420 |
| **Andirons,** Wrought Iron, Shield, Fleur-De-Lis, Scroll Feet, 29 In. | 750 |
| **Andirons,** Wrought Iron, Swan Neck Terminal, Punched-Out Eyes, Long Bill, c.1920, 22 x 10 In. | 92 |
| **Andirons,** Wrought Iron, Winged Dragon Shape, Holding Twisted Ring, c.1900, 34 x 16 In. | 1770 |
| **Bellows,** Apple, Flower Design, Grain Paint, c.1820, Pair | 165 |
| **Bellows,** Carved Wood, Leather, Scroll Design, 19 x 7 ¾ x 2 In. | 60 |
| **Bellows,** Mask Handles, Eagle, Bronze Nozzle, Baroque, 30 In. | 590 |
| **Bellows,** Pine, Green, Red Flowers, Brass Nozzle, Leather, c.1820, 18 In. | 81 |
| **Bellows,** Red Paint, Wood, c.1845, 24 In. | 105 |
| **Bellows,** Stenciled Fruit, Mustard Ground, 19th Century, 18 In. | 60 |
| **Bellows,** Stenciled, Flowers, Mustard Ground, 19 In. | 180 |
| **Bellows,** Turtleback, White Paint, Gilt, Carved Lenox, Brass Nozzle, 17 In. | 360 |
| **Bellows,** Wood, Carved, Man's Face, Woman's Bust On Handle, Scrollwork, 26 In. | 120 |
| **Brazier,** Mixed Metal, Dragons On Ends, Oval, Stepped Platform Base, Electric, 17 x 28 In. | 1093 |
| **Chenets,** Andirons, Bronze, Acanthine, Rail, Lion's Head, Lamb's Tongue, Putto, 17 ¼ In. | 4780 |
| **Chenets,** Andirons, Bronze, Central Bar, Urns, Rams, Ribbons, Swags, Putti, Owl, 18 ¾ x 21 In. | 10000 |
| **Chenets,** Andirons, Bronze, Gilt, Fender, France, 16 ½ x 30 In. | 813 |
| **Chenets,** Andirons, Bronze, Gilt, Neptune, Minerva, Stamped Bouhon, 17 x 19 In. | 7500 |
| **Chenets,** Andirons, Bronze, Gilt, Reclining Figure, Scrollwork Base, 14 x 14 In. | 1230 |
| **Chenets,** Andirons, Bronze, Lion's Heads, Swags, Egg & Dart Borders, 15 x 17 In. | 460 |
| **Chenets,** Andirons, Bronze, Louis XVI Style, Putti, Warming Hands, Torches, 11 x 15 x 4 In. | 1968 |
| **Chenets,** Andirons, Bronze, Napoleon III, Shell Molded Base, Putti, Wine Cup, 16 x 11 In. | 1230 |
| **Chenets,** Andirons, Cast Bronze, Rococo Style, Polished Finish, Iron Leg, France, 17 x 10 In. | 150 |
| **Chenets,** Andirons, Fender Set, Bronze, Louis XV Style, Pierced, 1900s, 15 ½ x 32 ½ In. | 215 |
| **Chenets,** Andirons, Gilt Bronze, Renaissance Style, Griffins, Portrait Medallions, 14 x 28 In. | 1464 |
| **Chenets,** Andirons, Gilt Metal, Louis XV, Finial, Top Shape Feet, 14 x 17 In. | 2813 |
| **Chenets,** Andirons, Iron, Tole, Acanthine Finial, Twisted Supports, Scrolled Legs, 36 x 22 In. | 1076 |
| **Chenets,** Andirons, Silvered Bronze, Louis XVI Style, Obelisk Standards, c.1875, 17 x 11 In. | 738 |
| **Coal Bucket,** Cast Iron, Porcelain, Painted Flowers, White Ground, Hinged Lid, Footed | 35 |
| **Coal Bucket,** Footed, Ring In Lion's Mouth Handles, Brass, c.1850, 15 x 14 In. | 146 |
| **Coal Scuttle,** Brass, Bright Finish, Removable Interior, Ring Handles, 12 x 13 In. | 121 |
| **Coal Scuttle,** Brass, Pierced Flowers, Handle, Raised Feet, 18 In. | 188 |
| **Coal Scuttle,** Brass, Pierced, Wreath, Garlands, 2 Handles, Flame Finial, 22 x 16 In. | 115 |
| **Coal Scuttle,** Copper, Hammered, Wrought Iron, G. Stickley, 14 x 24 In. | 7320 |
| **Coal Scuttle,** Oak, Slant Front, Arched Sides, Brass Handle & Knob, England, 15 x 18 In. | 58 |
| **Coal Scuttle,** Repousse, Engraved Flowers, Handle, Brass, 1800s, 18 In. | 325 |
| **Coal Scuttle,** Tin, Painted Flowers, Applied Iron Handles, Paw Feet, Liner, 23 ½ In. | 35 |
| **Coal Scuttle,** Tole, Hinged Flap, Flower Clusters, 19 x 13 In. | 420 |
| **Coal Scuttle,** Tole, Red, Rope Twist Handles, Lion's Paw Feet, 18 ¼ x 22 ¼ In. | 90 |
| **Ember Tongs,** Wrought Iron, Brass Inlaid Bands, Signed C. Gross, c.1890, 21 In. | 180 |
| **Fender,** Bell Metal, Georgian Style, Pierced, Serpentine, 6 x 55 In. | 720 |
| **Fender,** Brass, Curved, Pierced, 9 ¼ x 40 ½ In. | 25 |
| **Fender,** Brass, Georgian, Serpentine, Pierced, 6 ¾ x 47 In. | 300 |
| **Fender,** Brass, Horizontal Rods, Bulbous Posts, Acorn Finials, 10 ¾ x 42 In. | 94 |
| **Fender,** Brass, Iron Feet, Lion's Paw, Flower, Pierced Leaf Bands, 42 ½ x 13 In. | 288 |
| **Fender,** Brass, Louis XVI, Openwork Gallery, Sunflowers, Dolphins, c.1950, 9 x 59 In. | 594 |
| **Fender,** Brass, Pierced, Curvy, England, c.1870, 5 ¼ x 50 In. | 60 |
| **Fender,** Brass, Pierced, England, 1800s, 53 In. | 375 |
| **Fender,** Brass, Wire, Federal, Serpentine, Ball Steeple Finial, New York, c.1820, 17 x 55 In. | 546 |
| **Fender,** Brass, Wire, Serpentine Front, Straight-Sided, England, 8 ½ x 37 x 11 In. | 738 |
| **Fender,** Gilt Bronze, Restauration, Gilt Bronze, End Plinths, Cornucopia, c.1830, 11 x 42 In. | 584 |
| **Fender,** Hearth, Club Style, Brass Rail Frame, Button & Tack Leather Seat, 19 x 62 In. | 944 |
| **Fender,** Iron, Urn Finials, American, Late 19th Century, 28 x 50 In. | 60 |
| **Fender,** Leather Trim, Brass Spindles, Frame, 25 ½ x 63 In. | 344 |
| **Fender,** Mesh Wire & Iron Molding, Rail, Finials, Early 1800s, 15 x 54 In. | 836 |
| **Fender,** Nickel Plated Steel, Finial Posts, Rosettes, Stepped Base, W.H. Jackson, 62 x 13 In. | 63 |
| **Fire Screen,** Bronze, Louis XV Style, Early 20th Century, 31 x 25 In. | 338 |
| **Fire Screen,** Copper, Cast Iron, Art Nouveau, Hammered Edge, Embossed Leaves, c.1910, 32 In. | 246 |

| | |
|---|---|
| Fire Screen, Iron, Copper, Rooster, Scrolling Frame, Scroll Feet, c.1910, 33 x 23 In. | 948 |
| Fire Screen, Iron, Wire, Ducks In Flight Scene, c.1950, 34 x 48 In. | 240 |
| Fire Screen, Mahogany, Faceted Columns, Mirror, Carved Ram, Crest, 45 x 29 In. | 60 |
| Fire Screen, Mahogany, Glass, Lead, Roses, Leaves, Tobey Furniture, 38½ x 14 In. | 5795 |
| Fire Screen, Mahogany, Needlework, 50½ x 27 In. | 240 |
| Fire Screen, Mahogany, Upholstered Panel, Corinthian Columns, 48 x 33 In. | 120 |
| Fire Screen, Oak, Leather, Brass, G. Stickley, 31 x 35 In. | 2806 |
| Fire Screen, Palm Trees, Islands, Ships, Harbor, 3 Sections, Virginia Pena, 30 x 42 In. | 266 |
| Fire Screen, Rosewood, Brass Mounted, Needlework, William IV, Paw Feet, 1800s, 60 x 18 In. | 177 |
| Fireback Panel, Iron, Soul Of Sunflower, Center For Tripartite, Elihu Vedder, 31 x 28 In. | 1968 |
| Fireback, Cast Iron, Shaped Crest, Courting Couple, Easel, 1800s, 31 x 24 In. | 538 |
| Fireback, Cast Iron, The Scales, Cast Iron, Pa., 1700s, 24 x 20 In. | 125 |
| Fireback, Iron, Cast, Thick Panel, Raised Arms Of England, 23 x 29 In. | 300 |
| Fireback, Men On Horses, Iron, 31 x 33 In. | 708 |
| Footman, Forged Iron, Crescent Moons, Hearts, Cutout Handle, 11¾ x 16 In. | 59 |
| Fork, Wrought Iron, Heart Handle, American, 19th Century, 30 In. | 63 |
| Grate, Adams Style, Reticulated Apron, Finials, Engraved Brass, Cast Iron, 31 x 32 In. | 2040 |
| Hearth Broom, Federal, Stenciled, Painted, Horsehair, 1800s, 20½ In. | 531 |
| Hearth Plate, Fire Grate, Cast Iron, Arched, Putti, Scroll Feet, 1697, 29 x 17½ In. | 836 |
| Insert, Coal, Arts & Crafts, Iron, Brass, Flowers, Oak Leaf Decoration, 23½ In. | 90 |
| Insert, Pine, Wallpaper, Brown Geometrics, Orange Flower Border, c.1850, 32 x 42 In. | 184 |
| Log Basket, Brass, Ring Handle, Curve Shaped Disc, Paw Footed, 13 x 23 In. | 84 |
| Log Caddy, Brass, Lion & Shield Relief Design, Hinged Handles, 4-Footed, 16 x 17 In. | 368 |
| Log Holder, Iron, Tan Leather, Folding, Brushed Exterior, 20 x 21 In. | 88 |
| **Mantel** is listed in the Architectural category. | |
| Screen, Aesthetic Revival, Gilt Bronze, Needlework, Adjustable, Faux Bamboo, c.1890, 47 In. | 1168 |
| Screen, Arts & Crafts, Copper, Hammered, Fruit Trees, c.1910, 35 x 28 In. ...........*illus* | 1534 |
| Screen, Brass Frame, Flower Pattern Fabric, Splayed Legs, Paw Feet, 44 In. | 188 |
| Screen, Brass, Fan Shape, Reticulated, Figural Stem Handle, Victorian, 34 x 47 In. | 127 |
| Screen, Brass, Pierced, Fan Shape, Allegorical Animal Base, c.1890, 25 x 8 In. | 50 |
| Screen, Federal, Mahogany, Adjustable, Urn Finial, Tripod Base, Shield Screen, 57 In. | 561 |
| Screen, French Rococo Style, Gilt Metal Leaf Frame, 25 x 28 In. | 375 |
| Screen, French Style, Walnut, Carved, Needlepoint, c.1900, 38 x 23 In. | 180 |
| Screen, Louis XV Style, Carved Giltwood Frame, Flower Fabric, Scrolled Feet, 62 x 33 In. | 375 |
| Screen, Louis XV Style, Rococo & Flowers, Carved, Needlepoint, c.1930, 39 x 36 In. | 200 |
| Screen, Louis XVI Style, Blue, Gilt Embroidered Landscape, Flame Finials, 40 In. | 250 |
| Screen, Louis XVI Style, Gilt Bronze, Torch Appliques, Quivers, c.1900, 30 x 28 In. | 1353 |
| Screen, Louis XVI Style, Gilt Carved, Embroidered, c.1901, 44 x 28½ In. | 160 |
| Screen, Mahogany, Needlepoint, Octagonal, Swivel, Turned Supports, 1900s, 32 x 22 In. | 180 |
| Screen, Mahogany, Pierced Leaves, Turned Finials, Velvet, Napoleon Profile, 47 x 25 In. | 265 |
| Screen, Painted Frame, Black & Gold, Vase Of Flowers, c.1940, 40 x 30 In. | 72 |
| Screen, Peacock Shape, Fold-Out Fan, Urn Finial, 27½ x 37½ In. | 531 |
| Screen, Pole, Mahogany, Embroidery, Carved Tripod Base, c.1860, 61 x 19 In. | 344 |
| Screen, Pole, Needlepoint Image, Silk, Carved Wood, Adjustable, Tripod Base, 58 x 19 In. | 362 |
| Screen, Queen Anne, Mahogany, c.1981, 46 In. | 36 |
| Screen, Rococo Style, Bronze Dore, Flourishes, Metal Screening, 29 x 31 In. | 633 |
| Screen, Stained Glass, 3-Panel, Garden Flowers, Butterfly, Multicolor, 97 In. | 259 |
| Screen, Tapestry, Louis XVI Style, Gilt, Woman, Flowers, c.1910, 42 x 25 In. | 150 |
| **Screens** are also listed in the Architectural and Furniture categories. | |
| Shovel, Tongs, Hearth, Wrought Iron, c.1800, 28 x 7½ In. | 215 |
| Shovel, Wrought Iron, Heart Shape Handle, 19th Century, American, 28 In. | 120 |
| Spit Jack, Brass, Tin Reflector Oven, Stand, c.1810, 52 In. | 1320 |
| Surround, Cast Iron, Wreath, Leaves, S. Thompson, c.1880, 35 In. | 313 |
| Tongs, Federal, Brass, Iron, 19th Century, 28 In. | 84 |
| Tool Rests, Gilt Metal, Orb, 2 Arms, 3-Footed, 1800, 8 In., Pair | 120 |
| Tool Set, Brass, Glass, Brush, Shovel, Stand, Fontana Arte, 1950s, 11 x 7 In., 3 Piece | 793 |
| Tool Set, Steel, Cast Bronze, Satyr Finials, Tongs, Shovel, Pitchfork, Hook, Stand, 36 In. | 633 |
| Trammel, Hearth, Adjustable, Sawtooth, Wrought Iron, Curl, 1700s, 38 x 55 In. | 46 |
| Trammel, Sawtooth, Steel, Swivel Loop Hanger, Bone Pull, Brass, 1800s, 16 In. | 554 |
| Trammel, Steel, Flat, Adjustable, Sawtooth Edge, Hook, Brass Inlaid IC, 1780, 27 In. ...........*illus* | 984 |
| Trammel, Wrought Iron, Adjustable, Sawtooth Edge, Rooster Finial, 9½ x 16½ In. | 767 |

FISCHER porcelain was made in Herend, Hungary, by Moritz Fischer. The factory was founded in 1839 and is still in business. The wares are sometimes referred to as Herend porcelain.

**MF**

| | |
|---|---|
| Bowl, Salad, Rothschild Bird Pattern, White, Birds, Insects, Square, 10 In. | 403 |

Fireplace, Andirons, Cast Iron, Dragon, Log Supports, Bradley & Hubbard, c.1910, 26 In.
$850

James D. Julia Auctioneers

Fireplace, Andirons, Stylized Cats, Seated, Brass, Chrome Plating Co. Of Tenn., 20 In.
$390

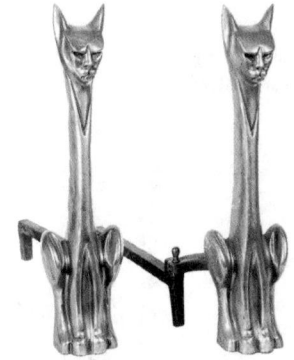

Garth's Auctioneers & Appraisers

Fireplace, Andirons, Wrought Iron, Gooseneck Shaft, Applied Hearts, Spit Hooks, c.1800, 19 In.
$3,690

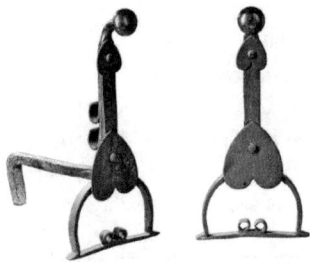

Skinner Auctioneers & Appraisers

**Fireplace,** Screen, Arts & Crafts, Copper, Hammered, Fruit Trees, c.1910, 35 x 28 In.
$1,534

Conestoga Auction Co., Inc.

**Fireplace,** Trammel, Steel, Flat, Adjustable, Sawtooth Edge, Hook, Brass Inlaid IC, 1780, 27 In.
$984

Skinner Auctioneers & Appraisers

### Fishing Lures

Lures are popular with collectors. Names to look for in fishing lures: Heddon, South Bend, Creek Chub, Paw Paw, Shakespeare, and Pflueger.

**Fischer,** Vase, Flowers, Gold Trim, Scrolled Leaf Handles, Herend, c.1950, 10 ½ x 7 In.
$72

DuMouchelles Art Gallery

| | |
|---|---:|
| **Box,** Lid, Rothschild Bird, 4 ¾ x 5 ½ In. | 120 |
| **Candelabrum,** 2-Light, Rothschild Birds, Insects, 20th Century, 9 In., Pair | 600 |
| **Chop Plate,** Rothschild Bird Pattern, Gold Trim, Round, Branch Handles, 14 In. | 460 |
| **Figurine,** Cat, Tail Up, Blue & White Fishnet, 5 In. | 295 |
| **Figurine,** Dancers, Man, Woman, Upraised Arms, Painted, Herend, 12 In. | 96 |
| **Figurine,** Elephant, Painted, Raised Trunk, 20th Century, 10 In. | 1230 |
| **Figurine,** German Shepard, Lying Down, 11 x 7 ½ In. | 269 |
| **Figurine,** Panda, Eating Leaves, Black Fishnet, Herend, Blue Mark, 5 In. | 495 |
| **Figurine,** Parrot, Stump Bases, Fruit, Multicolor, Signed, 6 ½ & 5 In., 2 Piece | 237 |
| **Plate,** Rothschild, Basket Weave Border, Birds, Butterflies, Gilt Trim, Herend, 10 In. | 121 |
| **Platter,** Blue Garland, White, Blue Flowers, Scalloped Edge, Herend, 1900s, 11 In. | 154 |
| **Platter,** Green, Chinese Bouquet, Round, Handles, Basket Weave Border, 13 x 12 In. | 121 |
| **Platter,** Rothschild Pattern, 5 Sections, Undertray, 9 ½ In. | 563 |
| **Relish,** Rothschild Bird Pattern, 3 Sections, Bird Handle, Herend, 12 In. | 201 |
| **Sculpture,** Kneeling Nude, Horvathgeza, Herend, 18 In. | 300 |
| **Serving Dish,** Rothschild, Scalloped Border, Bird, Butterfly, Gilt Border, 7 x 5 In., Pair | 138 |
| **Tea & Coffee Set,** Rothschild Bird, Sugar & Creamer, Cup & Saucer, Tray, 7 Piece | 1750 |
| **Tea Set,** Rothschild Bird, White, Birds, Insects, Rose & Lemon Finials, 4 Piece | 230 |
| **Tea Set,** Tray, Open Handles, Pitcher, Bowls, Lids, Creamer, Herend | 630 |
| **Tray,** Rothschild's Bird, Pierced Handles, Insects, Branches, Herend, 19 ½ x 7 In. | 299 |
| **Tureen,** Birds On Branch, Bird Finial, Lid, Underplate, Herend, 13 x 17 In. | 1180 |
| **Tureen,** Lid, Green Chinese Bouquet, Bird Finial, Handles, Herend, c.1950, 15 In. | 690 |
| **Tureen,** Tray, Rothschild Bird, Handles, Lemon Knob, Herend, Miniature, 4 x 5 ⅜ In. | 540 |
| **Tureen,** Underplate, Flowers, Fish Finial, Blue Fish Scale Bands, 12 ½ In. | 750 |
| **Vase,** Flowers, Gold Trim, Scrolled Leaf Handles, Herend, c.1950, 10 ½ x 7 In. ....*illus* | 72 |
| **Vase,** Pate-Sur-Pate Style, Calla Lily, Easter Lilies, Herend, c.1902, 19 ½ In., Pair | 2070 |
| **Vase,** Square, Base, Scrolled Leaf Handles, Painted Flowers, 10 ½ x 7 In. | 72 |
| **Vase,** Urn Shape, Footed, Birds, Butterflies, White Ground, Gilt, Handles, 1900s, 9 In., Pair | 472 |

**FISHING** reels of brass or nickel were made in the United States by 1810. Bamboo fly rods were sold by 1860, often marked with the maker's name. Lures made of metal, or metal and wood, were made in the nineteenth century. Plastic lures were made by the 1930s. All fishing material is collected today and even equipment of the past thirty years is of interest if in good condition with original box.

| | |
|---|---:|
| **Bobber,** White, Yellow, Black, 8 ¼ In. | 1028 |
| **Creel,** Birch Bark, Twig, c.1930-40, 12 ¼ x 6 ¾ In. | 666 |
| **Creel,** E. Robichaud, Wood, Carved Brook Trout, 7 ¼ x 15 In. | 1080 |
| **Hook,** Wrought Iron, Wood Mount, 1800s, 29 x 14 In. | 46 |
| **Lure,** Heddon Gamefisher, Red Head, White Body | 302 |
| **Lure,** Shakespeare, Revolution, Box, Kalamazoo, Michigan | 1476 |
| **Lure,** Slade's, Moveable Cone Shaped Head, 1930s, 4 In. | 194 |
| **Minnow Trap,** Glass, Lid, Wire, C.F. Orvis. | 87 |
| **Reel,** Fly Casting Bas-Kit, Brass, Elmer Sellers, Kutztown, Pennsylvania, 3 ½ In. | 960 |
| **Reel,** Fly Casting Bas-Kit, Chromium, Elmer Sellers, Kutztown, Pennsylvania, 3 ½ In. | 420 |
| **Reel,** Kopf, Free Spool, Silver Sliding Click Switch, 1900, 2 ⅝ In. | 968 |
| **Rod,** Tycoon Tackle Co., Bimini King, Trolling Rod, Chrome Plated Roller, 6 Ft. 10 In. | 1936 |
| **Tackle Box,** American Angler, Turned Wooden Handle, 13 ½ x 5 ½ In. | 121 |
| **Tackle Box,** Rudolph's, Green, Gold, 9 ¼ x 6 ¾ In. | 424 |

**FLAGS** *are included in the Textile category.*

**FLASH GORDON** appeared in the Sunday comics in 1934. The daily strip started in 1940. The hero was also in comic books from 1930 to 1970, in books from 1936, in movies from 1938, on the radio in the 1930s and 1940s, and on television from 1953 to 1954. All sorts of memorabilia are collected, but the ray guns and rocket ships are the most popular.

| | |
|---|---:|
| **Button,** Chicago Herald & Examiner, Portrait, Red, White, 1 ⅛ In. | 115 |
| **Comic Book,** King Comics, No. 8, September 1967 | 8 |
| **Comic Book,** King Comics, No. 9, October 1967 | 5 |
| **Toy,** Holding Gun, Seated In Cockpit, Tin Lithograph, Clockwork, Louis Marx, 12 In. | 354 |
| **Toy,** Knife, Whistle, Spaceship, Red, Yellow, Plastic, Camco, 1950s | 65 |
| **Toy,** Rocket Fighter Ship 5, Sparkling, Tin Litho, Windup, Marx, c.1935, 12 In. ....*illus* | 518 |
| **Toy,** Rocket Fighter Ship, Red, Yellow Stripe, Flash In Cockpit, Windup, 5 In. | 470 |

**FLORENCE CERAMICS** were made in Pasadena, California, from World War II to 1977. Florence Ward created many colorful figurines, boxes, candleholders, and other items for the gift shop trade. Each piece was marked with an ink stamp that included the name *Florence Ceramics Co.* The company was sold in 1964 and although the name remained the same, the products were very different. Mugs, cups, and trays were made.

| | |
|---|---|
| Figurine, Abigail, Green Dress, 8 ½ In. | 120 |
| Figurine, Amelia, Ruffled, Low Cut, 8 ¾ In. | 127 |
| Figurine, Clarissa, Gray Dress, Hat & Muff, Gilt Trim, 7 ½ In. | 120 |
| Figurine, Clarissa, Maroon Dress, Marked, 7 ¾ In. | 330 |
| Figurine, Delia, Blond, Burgundy & Gray Dress, Muff, c.1940, 7 ¾ In. | 145 |
| Figurine, Delia, Maroon Dress, Muff, Marked, 7 ¾ In. | 253 |
| Figurine, Elizabeth, Sitting, Stamped, 1940s | 243 |
| Figurine, Ethel, Blue Dress & Hat, White Cape | 176 |
| Figurine, Louis XVI, White, Gilt, Marked, c.1945, 10 ¼ In. | 333 |
| Figurine, Matilda, Blue Dress, 8 ½ In. | 95 |
| Figurine, Matilda, Red Dress, 8 ½ In. | 75 |
| Figurine, Melanie, Blond, Gray Dress, Pink Hat, 7 ¾ In. | 45 |
| Figurine, Parakeet, On Stump, Multicolor, 7 ¼ In. | 245 |
| Figurine, Pat, Girl, Hat, Scarf, Muff, Marked, 6 In. | 240 |
| Figurine, Peter, Turquoise, Tuxedo, Hat, Marked, 9 ¼ In. | 430 |
| Figurine, Rita, Beige Dress, Flowers, 9 ½ In. | 135 |
| Figurine, Sarah, Gray Dress, Green Hat & Purse, 7 ½ In. | 101 |
| Figurine, Sue Ellen, Green Dress, Gilt, Marked, 8 ½ In. | 140 |
| Figurine, Victoria, Red Dress, Seated, Sofa, 7 x 8 In. | 175 |
| Planter, Girl, White, Pink & Brown Accents, 6 In. | 45 |
| Plaque, Woman, Muffler, Umbrella, Mauve, Green, 9 x 6 In., Pair | 135 |

**FLOW BLUE** was made in England and other countries about 1830 to 1900. The dishes were printed with designs using a cobalt blue coloring. The color flowed from the design to the white body so that the finished piece has a smeared blue design. The dishes were usually made of ironstone china. More Flow Blue may be found under the name of the manufacturer.

| | |
|---|---|
| Bowl, Lid, Manila Pattern, Ironstone, Octagonal Foot, Carlyle F. West, c.1845, 9 In. | 184 |
| Bowl, Vegetable, Ironstone, Snowflake, 7 ⅝ In. | 148 |
| Cake Stand, Shell Molded, Scalloped Edges, Flared Foot, Staffordshire, c.1885, 4 ½ In. | 207 |
| Centerpiece, La Belle China, Scalloped Rim, 3-Footed, Wheeling Pottery, c.1900, 13 x 11 In. | 138 |
| Coffeepot, Lid, La Belle China, Flared Cylinder, Scroll Handle, c.1900, 9 ⅞ In. | 316 |
| Creamer, Ironstone, Snowflake, 4 In. | 118 |
| Cup & Saucer, Ironstone, Snowflake, 6 In., 16 Piece | 177 to 189 |
| Ewer, Basin, Ironstone, Scinde, Paneled Sides, J. & G. Alcock, c.1845, 11 In., 13 In. | 920 |
| Gravy Boat, Ironstone, Strap Handle, Marked, c.1845, 5 ⅜ In. | 69 |
| Jardiniere, Flower Panels, Tapered, La Belle China, Wheeling, c.1910, 8 In. | 316 |
| Jardiniere, Lid, Yellow Rose Transfer, Embossed, Shell, Leaf, Scroll, Gold Highlights, 8 In. | 30 |
| Pitcher, Ironstone, Nankin Pattern, Children, Octagonal Panels, R. H. & L. English, c.1845, 8 In. | 92 |
| Platter, Ironstone, Scinde, Blue Grapevines, J. & G. Alcock, c.1840, 13 x 10 ½ In. | 259 |
| Platter, Ironstone, Transfer, Kin-Shan, 13 In. | 189 |
| Serving Bowl, Scinde Pattern, Reticulated Border, J. & L. Alcock, c.1850, 4 x 13 ½ In. | 1035 |
| Serving Dish, White To Blue, Dark Blue Rim, Flowers, Scalloped, 12 In. | 60 |
| Sugar, Lid, Ironstone, Snowflake, 8 ½ In. | 130 |
| Teapot, Lid, Ironstone, Snowflake, 8 ½ In. | 295 |
| Tureen, Flowers, Oriental Theme, Lid, Ashworth, c.1870, 13 x 8 In. | 95 |

**FOLK ART** is also listed in many categories of this book under the actual name of the object. See categories such as Box, Cigar Store Figure, Paper, Weather Vane, Wooden, etc.

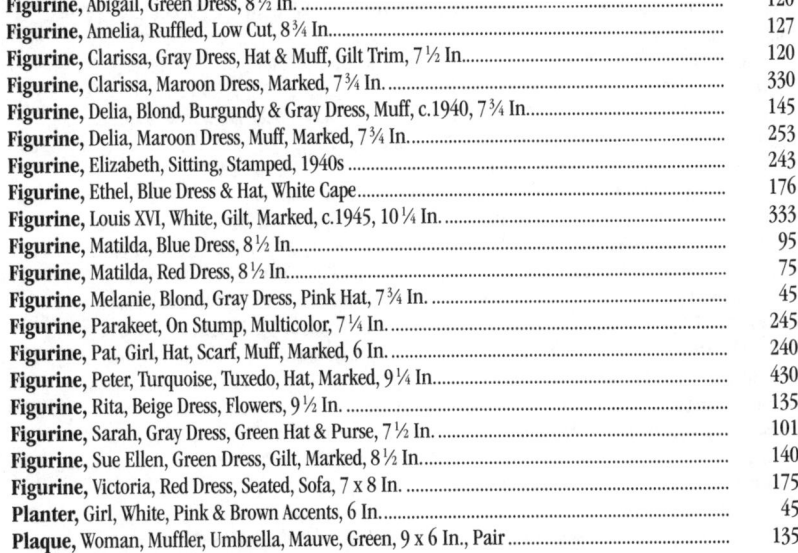

| | |
|---|---|
| Alligator, Wood, Carved, Green, Red Paint, Signed Ballard 1994, 54 In. | 420 |
| Banjo, Bentwood, Carved, Nails, Open Back, Appalachian, c.1880, 33 ½ In. | 978 |
| Bear Ass, Bear Dipping Paw In Honeypot, Man With Moonshine Jug, Pottery, B.H., 8 In. | 325 |
| Bird Tree, Wood, 10 Songbirds, Wire Legs, Copper Leaves, Fence, Painted, c.1880, 36 In. | 960 |
| Bird, On Perch, Wood, Carved, Brown, Cream, Orange Paint, W. Gottshall, 1979, 6 In. | 461 |
| Bird, Red-Headed Woodpecker, Perched On Branch, Weathered Wood Base, 13 In. | 1035 |
| Bird, Wood, Parrot, Spread Wing, Paint, 1900s, 15 x 12 In. | 920 |
| Birdhouse, Metal, Red Paint, c.1890, 24 x 21 In. | 600 |
| Birdhouse, Pine, Old Yellow Paint, Shake Roof, 4 Wings, Windows, Perches, 31 x 26 In. | 900 |
| Birdhouse, Sheet Iron, Painted Green, 2 Chimneys, 4 Arched Perch Openings, 13 x 21 In. | 805 |
| Box, Coffin Form, Red Paint, Striped Bird, Cutout Scalloped Molding, c.1830, 8 x 13 In. | 489 |

**Flash Gordon,** Toy, Rocket Fighter Ship 5, Sparkling, Tin Litho, Windup, Marx, c.1935, 12 In.
$518

Hake's Americana & Collectibles

**F**

**Folk Art,** Whirligig, Man, Carved, Glass Eyes, Mounted On Stepped Base, c.1890, 12 ¾ In.
$5,843

Skinner Auctioneers & Appraisers

**Folk Art,** Whirligig, Sailor, Painted, Wood, Nantucket, Massachusetts, c.1900, 13 x 11 In.
$2,370

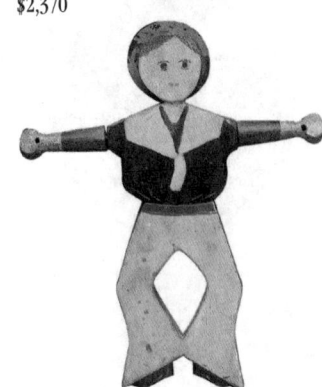

James D. Julia Auctioneers

**Folk Art,** Whirligig, Soldier, Carved, Kepi Hat, Painted, Paddle Arms, c.1950, Figure 12 In.
$119

James D. Julia Auctioneers

**Foot Warmer,** Openwork Hinged Lid, Bail Handle, Iron, Victorian, 4½ x 11½ x 7½ In.
$24

Conestoga Auction Co., Inc.

**Fraternal,** Kiwanis, Sign, Metal, K Logo, Round, 30 In.
$90

Morphy Auctions

---

**TIP**

*Don't keep identification on your key ring. If it is lost, it's an invitation for burglars to visit.*

---

| | |
|---|---:|
| **Box,** Faux Book, Snake In A Box, Snake, 5½ x 4 x 1 In. | 330 |
| **Cat,** On Oval Rug, Wood, Carved, Red, Peach, Green Paint, Walter Gottshall, 1988, 5 x 10 In. | 400 |
| **Chicken,** Pine, Red, Black, 19 In. | 60 |
| **Chipmunk,** On Hind Legs, Hardwood, Silvio Zoratti, 1965, 10½ In. | 189 |
| **Deer Head,** Wood, Real Antlers, Red Paint, Incised Eyes, Nostrils & Lips, 17 In. | 540 |
| **Diorama,** Hunter, Dog Pursuing Deer, Wood, Carved, Painted, 10 x 16 In. | 480 |
| **Dog,** Great Dane, Standing, Pine, Cream Coat, Brown Features, Collar, 10½ x 12½ In. | 720 |
| **Doll,** Wood, Carved Head, Jointed Arms & Legs, 19th Century, 14½ In. | 461 |
| **Dulcimer,** Wood, Painted, Double-Bouted, Cutout Hearts, Scrolled End, 3 Strings, c.1885, 35 In. | 4600 |
| **Eagle,** Federal Shield, Wood, Carved, 27 x 10 In. | 351 |
| **Eagle,** Spread Wing, Perched, Wood, Carved, Green, Orange, Keith Collis, 1982, 16 x 34 In. | 1353 |
| **Eagle,** Spread Wing, Wood Carving, Painted, W. Schimmel, c.1875, 9 x 12 In. | 72000 |
| **Eagle,** Spread Wing, Wood, Carved, Red Paint, Daniel Strawser, 1975, 15 x 22 In. | 677 |
| **Eagle,** Standing, Spread Wing, Crisscross, Red, Yellow, Wood, D. Strawser, 1987, 13 x 22 In. | 738 |
| **Eagle,** Wood Carving, Schimmel Type, Painted, Multicolor, Jonathan Bastian, 20 x 35 In. | 236 |
| **Flask,** Coconut Shell, Carved, 4 Cartouches, Instruments, Arrows, Lion, Mouth Opening, 5 In. | 180 |
| **Fox,** Wood, Carved, Red, White, Black Paint, Signed Minnie Adkins, 2000, 44 In. | 738 |
| **Frame,** Pine, Carved Snake & Date, April 15th 1900, Red Paint, c.1900, 10 x 7 In. | 546 |
| **Frame,** Wood, Round, Handle, Relief Carved Bust, Varnished, Painted, c.1925, 14 x 6 In. | 978 |
| **George Washington,** Horseback, Painted, Carved, P. Tyson, Bicentennial, 1976, 14 x 11 In. | 1440 |
| **Giraffe,** Salt Glaze, Cobalt Trim & Dots, B.H., 1947, 13 In. | 708 |
| **Hand Holding Red Orb,** Wood, Carved, Old Paint, Wood Base, 13 In. | 531 |
| **Horse,** Standing, Alligatored White & Gray Paint, Wood, Ned Jurran Jr., 12¼ In. | 2040 |
| **Horse,** Wood, Old White Paint, Wearing Woven Plaid Blanket, c.1900, 16 In., Pair | 6900 |
| **House Boat,** American Flag, Railing, Portholes, 23 x 22 In. | 348 |
| **Hunter,** Standing Along Fence Post, Holding Rifle & Rabbit, Wood, 11½ In. | 270 |
| **Lady Liberty,** Raised Torch, Stars & Stripes Dress, Carved, Wood, Ballard, 1999, 30 In. | 234 |
| **Man,** Standing, Hat, Carved, Wood, Painted, Stand, c.1920, 11½ In. | 288 |
| **Mirror,** Abalone Shell Border, Round, 43 In. | 500 |
| **Parrot,** Carved, c.1920, 18 In. | 360 |
| **Paul Revere,** Cornered Hat, Galloping Spotted Horse, Wood, Rhinestone Eyes, 9 x 12 In. | 12500 |
| **Pelican,** Gray, White, Stamped Metal Band, Blue Base, Silvio Zoratti, 11½ In. | 72 |
| **Picture,** Fully Rigged Ship, Jigsaw, 13 x 20½ In. | 60 |
| **Pipe Flue,** Dragon, Metal, Applied Legs, Tail & Spine, 28 In. | 1200 |
| **Policeman,** Rusted Sheet Metal, Wood, Paint, 56 In. | 1080 |
| **Potted Flower,** 2 Leaves, Wood, Planted In Tin Can With Concrete, Painted, 14 In. | 600 |
| **Rattlesnake,** Wood, Carved, Painted, Orange, Black Spots, D. Rawlings, 20 In. | 60 |
| **Retablo,** Church, Oxen, Man, Blue, Clouds, Oil, Canvas, Mexico, 16⅝ x 13⅛ In. | 259 |
| **Retablo,** Madonna, Recessed, Flowers, Leaves, Mexico, 19th Century, 15 x 9½ In. | 129 |
| **Robot,** Iron, Movable Arms, Rectangular Legs, 5¼ In. | 180 |
| **Rooster,** Wood, Carved, Standing On Base, Red Paint, 32 In. | 185 |
| **Scarecrow,** Repurposed Clothesline Poles, Fence Boards, Maine, 70 In. | 840 |
| **Sculpture,** Wall, Horseshoe, Applied Metal Roses, Stems & Leaves, Painted, 8 x 10 In. | 120 |
| **Shark,** Cross-Cut Saw Blade, Applied Eye & Fins, Weathered Wood Base, 13 x 44 In. | 472 |
| **Snuffbox,** Burl, Carved, Rounded Corners, Hinged Paneled Lid, 19th Century, 3 In. | 270 |
| **Squirrel,** Standing, Wood, Carved, Bead Eyes, Shaped Base, 19th Century, 8 In. | 62 |
| **Stand,** Oak & Rhododendron Root, 2 Shelves, 20 Carved Figures, Animals, c.1925, 38 x 31 In. | 3738 |
| **Table,** Inlaid Wood, Stars, Geometrics, Diagonals, Shaped Shelf, Ball In Cage Legs, 32 In. | 1150 |
| **Top Hat,** Tin Anniversary, Tin Hat Band, 19th Century, 6½ In. | 1560 |
| **Uncle Sam,** Composition, Patriotic Costume, 11½ In. | 360 |
| **Uncle Sam,** Full Profile, Red, White, Blue, Wood, 65 x 59 In. | 1440 |
| **Wedding Globe,** Blown Glass, Bisque Angel, Gilt, Mirrors, Dove, c.1880, 19 In. | 448 |
| **Whale,** Wood, Carved, Black, Pink, Paint, 18 In. | 720 |
| **Whirligig,** 4 Sailboats, Central Arm, White, Red Paint, Wood, 35 In. | 1200 |
| **Whirligig,** Airplane, Wood, Red, White Paint, Hat On Wing, Caged Bird, c.1915, 21 x 20 In. | 70 |
| **Whirligig,** Bearded Soldier, Red Coat, Gold Collar, Blue Hat, Carved, Painted, 1800s, 11 In. | 1080 |
| **Whirligig,** Blacksmith, Grinding Ax, Man, Sawing Log, Tin Blades, Paint, 1900s, 21 x 28 In. | 288 |
| **Whirligig,** Cyclist, Cast Aluminum, 15 x 22 In. | 468 |
| **Whirligig,** Ducks, Wood, Carved, Painted, Metal Rod, Base, 12½ x 12 In. | 263 |
| **Whirligig,** Gentleman Sawing Wood, Pine, Yellow, White, Black Paint, c.1965, 33 In. | 74 |
| **Whirligig,** Horse, Sheet Iron, Painted, c.1890, 20 In. | 92 |
| **Whirligig,** Indian Man, In Canoe, Paddle Arms, Headdress, Wood, c.1910, 12 x 31 In. | 800 |
| **Whirligig,** Maggie & Jigs, Sawing Wood, Pine, Cutout, 20th Century, 22½ In. | 60 |
| **Whirligig,** Man Sawing Wood, Trees, Propeller, Wood, Paint, 23 In. | 90 |
| **Whirligig,** Man, Black, In Canoe, Wood, Paint, c.1945, 12 x 13 In. | 230 |
| **Whirligig,** Man, Carved, Glass Eyes, Mounted On Stepped Base, c.1890, 12¾ In. ...............*illus* | 5843 |
| **Whirligig,** Man, Cutting Wood, Painted, Falcon Wooden Novelties, c.1940, 15 x 17 In. | 196 |

| Whirligig, Man, On High Wheeler Bike, Coat, Tails, Stand, c.1930, 20 x 20 In. | 1840 |
|---|---|
| Whirligig, Man, Sawing, Black Hat, Windmill, Red, Green, Black Paint, Wood, 18 x 27 In. | 234 |
| Whirligig, Nantucket Sailor, Carved, Black, White Paint, Tin, Wood Stand, 12¾ In. | 2640 |
| Whirligig, Nantucket Sailor, White, Black Paint, Wood, c.1890, 13 In. | 960 |
| Whirligig, Nantucket Sailor, Wood, Painted Moustache, Sailor Suit, 13 In. | 960 |
| Whirligig, Policeman, Bobby Cap, Blue & Silver Paint, Tin Nose, 19th Century, 18 In. | 4200 |
| Whirligig, Policeman, Wood, Painted Multicolor, Arms Spin, 25 In. | 35 |
| Whirligig, Sailboat, 4 Sailboats, Crossed Supports, Wood, Painted, Cloth Sails, 35 In. | 1200 |
| Whirligig, Sailor, Painted, Wood, Nantucket, Massachusetts, c.1900, 13 x 11 In. .......illus | 2370 |
| Whirligig, Soldier, Cap, Sword, Carved, Wood, Red, Blue, Black Paint, c.1910, 27 In. | 840 |
| Whirligig, Soldier, Carved, Kepi Hat, Painted, Paddle Arms, c.1950, Figure 12 In. .......illus | 119 |
| Whirligig, Soldier, Civil War, Wood, Carved, Painted, c.1870, 25 x 6½ In. | 3555 |
| Whirligig, Uncle Sam, Flag, Machines, Red, White, Blue Paint, Wood, 30 In. | 12600 |

**FOOT WARMERS** solved the problem of cold feet in past generations. Some warmers held charcoal, others held hot water. Pottery, tin, and soapstone were the favored materials to conduct the heat. The warmer was kept under the feet, then the legs and feet were tucked into a blanket, providing welcome warmth in a cold carriage or church.

| Brass & Copper, Needlepoint Top, Flowers, Round, 9½ x 5 In. | 188 |
|---|---|
| Brass, Footed, Handles, 1800s, 11½ x 15 x 13 In. | 650 |
| Copper, Brass Handle & Cap, Oval, West Germany, 10 x 7 x 5 In. | 50 |
| Iron, Star & Circle Cutouts, Handle, c.1860, 10 x 8 x 5 In. | 145 |
| Openwork Hinged Lid, Bail Handle, Iron, Victorian, 4½ x 11½ x 7½ In. .......illus | 24 |
| Slide Lid, Pine, Stone Block, Holes, Handle, Painted, Pa., c.1800, 8 x 10 In. | 120 |
| Stoneware, Jug, White, 9 x 4 x 4 In. | 25 |
| Tin, Hinged, Pierced Heart & Circles, 7 x 6 x 4 In. | 43 |
| Tin, Pierced Hearts, Diamonds & Flowers, 1800s, 7 x 6 x 4 In. | 60 |
| Tole, Stenciled, Flowers, 1800s, 5 x 7 x 7 In. | 100 |
| Wood, Tin, Whale Oil, Soldered Edge, c.1850, 7¾ x 6¾ x 5 In. | 250 |

**FOOTBALL** collectibles may be found in the Card and the Sports categories.

**FOSTORIA** glass was made in Fostoria, Ohio, from 1887 to 1891. The factory was moved to Moundsville, West Virginia, and most of the glass seen in shops today is a twentieth-century product. The company was sold in 1983; new items will be easily identifiable, according to the new owner, Lancaster Colony Corporation. Additional Fostoria items may be listed in the Milk Glass category.

| American, Ashtray, Square, 2 In. | 9 |
|---|---|
| American, Bowl, Cupped, 7 In. | 36 |
| American, Pitcher, Ice Lip, 2 Qt., 6 x 9 In. | 19 |
| American, Plate, Salad, 7 In. | 6 |
| American, Rose Bowl | 9 |
| American, Sherbet, Low, Footed, Flared | 5 |
| American, Tumbler, Flared, 8 Oz. | 12 |
| American, Vase, Milk Glass, Footed, Flared, 8½ In. | 30 |
| Baroque, Bowl, Azure Blue, Ruffled Rim, Handles, 8 x 2⅜ In. | 45 |
| Baroque, Saucer | 2 |
| Betsy Ross, Basket, Peach, 11½ In. | 54 |
| Beverly, Serving Bowl, Amber, 10¾ x 3⅜ In. | 65 |
| Brocade, Saucer | 2 |
| Brocade, Sweetmeat, Blue | 30 |
| Camellia, Plate, Luncheon, 8½ In. | 11 |
| Celestial, Bowl, 5 In. | 7 |
| Century, Cup & Saucer | 6 |
| Century, Plate, Dinner, 9½ In. | 11 |
| Chintz, Sugar | 12 |
| Coin Glass, Ashtray, 4 Coins, Blue, 7½ In. | 35 |
| Coin Glass, Ashtray, Ruby, 7½ In. | 15 |
| Coin Glass, Compote, Amber, 4 In. | 10 |
| Coin Glass, Nappy, Handle, Amber | 11 |
| Colony, Goblet, Water, 5¼ In. | 9 |
| Colony, Plate, Salad, 7 In. | 6 |
| Colony, Relish, 3 Sections, 10½ In. | 17 |
| Colony, Sugar & Creamer | 12 |
| Coronet, Bowl, Flared, 12 In. | 65 |

**Fraternal,** Masonic, Watch, Rolex, Silver, Sapphires, Mother-Of-Pearl Dial, 18 Jewel, c.1930, 2 In. $6,300

Garth's Auctioneers & Appraisers

**Fulper,** Doorstop, Dog, Bulldog, Bum The Pup, Blue Flambe Over Tan, 8¼ In. $805

Humler & Nolan

**Fulper,** Vase, Bottle Shape, Famille Rose Glaze, Footed Stand, 18½ x 6 In. $3,750

Rago Arts & Auction Center

**Fulper,** Vase, Copper Dust Crystalline & Mirror Black Flambe Glaze, Buttressed, 11 x 8 In.
**$2.625**

Rago Arts & Auction Center

---

**TIP**
*Don't keep a house key in an obvious spot in the garage.*

---

**Furniture,** Baby Tender, Windsor, 15 Spindles, Built-In Seat, Tray, c.1810, 20 x 12 x 25 In.
**$780**

Cowan's Auctions

---

**Furniture,** Bed, Renaissance Revival, Gilt Incised, Ebonized, c.1890, 79 x 58 In.
**$4,575**

Neal Auction Co.

---

| | |
|---|---:|
| **Coronet,** Sugar & Creamer | 40 |
| **Fairfax,** Bowl, Ice, Green, Liner | 32 |
| **Fairfax,** Cup | 3 |
| **Fairfax,** Cup, Blue, Footed | 10 |
| **Fairfax,** Cup, Green, After Dinner | 15 |
| **Fairfax,** Cup, Topaz, Footed | 4 |
| **Fairfax,** Plate, Luncheon, Pink, 8¾ In., 6 Piece | 24 |
| **Fairfax,** Plate, Salad, Green, 7½ In. | 3 |
| **Fairfax,** Sugar & Creamer, Blue | 24 to 27 |
| **Fairfax,** Sugar & Creamer, Topaz | 22 |
| **Fairfax,** Tumbler, Pink, Footed, 4½ In. | 16 |
| **Fascination,** Sherbet, Lilac, 4¾ In. | 15 |
| **Fascination,** Tumbler, Lilac, Footed, 4¼ In. | 9 |
| **Flame,** Candelabra, 2-Light, 7 x 10 In. | 55 |
| **Heather,** Cup & Saucer | 13 |
| **Heather,** Tumbler, Footed, 4 In. | 18 |
| **Heirloom,** Bowl, Blue Opalescent, 10 In. | 65 |
| **Heirloom,** Bowl, Blue Opalescent, Oval, 13 In. | 70 |
| **Heirloom,** Bowl, Red, 7 In. | 35 |
| **Heirloom,** Bowl, Red, Crimped, 11 In. | 65 |
| **Heirloom,** Vase, Blue Opalescent, Stick, 13½ In. | 55 |
| **Hermitage,** Tumbler, Blue 3 In. | 18 |
| **Horizon,** Sugar, Cinnamon | 12 |
| **Jamestown,** Goblet, Water, Blue, 5⅞ In. | 10 |
| **Jamestown,** Tumbler, Blue, Footed, 6 In. | 18 |
| **Jenny Lind,** Cologne, Flask, 10¾ In. | 125 |
| **Jenny Lind,** Cologne, Milk Glass, 8 In. | 60 |
| **Kashmir,** Plate, Dinner, Azure, Blue, 9 In. | 30 |
| **Lafayette,** Relish, 2 Sections | 9 |
| **Lafayette,** Sugar & Creamer, Regal Blue | 55 |
| **Lido,** Plate, Luncheon, 7 In. | 6 |
| **Navarre,** Creamer, 1937-80, 4⅛ In. | 14 |
| **No. 2315,** Grapefruit, Orchid, 6¾ In. | 22 |
| **No. 2324,** Candlestick, Pink, 3¼ In. | 26 |
| **No. 2362,** Candlestick, Orchid, 3½ In. | 26 |
| **No. 2372,** Candlestick, Amber, Dome Shape, 1⅝ In. | 21 |
| **No. 2374,** Nut Dish, Amber, 2⅜ In. | 5 |
| **No. 2375,** Nut Dish, Swirled, Blue, 1½ In. | 10 |
| **No. 2394,** Candlestick, Blue, 3-Footed, 2¼ In. | 13 |
| **No. 2447,** Candlestick, Topaz, 2-Light, 5 In. | 28 |
| **No. 2519,** Cologne Bottle, Stopper, Milk Glass, 5½ In. | 64 |
| **No. 4101,** Sherbet, Azure Blue, 3¼ In. | 17 |
| **No. 4101,** Tumbler, Footed, Azure Blue, 9 Oz., 4¾ In. | 21 |
| **No. 5082,** Tumbler, Footed, Gold Rose Rim, 5 Oz., 4⅛ In. | 25 |
| **No. 5083,** Tumbler, Iced Tea, Green, Spiral Optic, 5½ In. | 23 |
| **No. 5083,** Tumbler, Water, Green, Spiral Optic, 7⅜ In. | 22 |
| **No. 6056,** Goblet, Water, Tear Drop Stem, 5½ In. | 11 |
| **No. 6056,** Juice, Teardrop Stem, 4⅞ In. | 15 |
| **No. 805,** Optic, Goblet, Water, 6¾ In. | 18 |
| **Priscilla,** Plate, Luncheon, Amber, 8 In. | 6 |
| **Romance,** Sugar & Creamer | 19 |
| **Sprite,** Cup & Saucer | 22 |
| **Wisteria,** Candlestick, 2-Light, Alexandrite, 7 In., Pair | 122 |

**FOVAL**, *see Fry category.*

**FRAMES** *are included in the Furniture category under Frame.*

**FRANCISCAN** is a trademark that appears on pottery. Gladding, McBean and Company started in 1875. The company grew and acquired other potteries. It made sewer pipes, floor tiles, dinnerware, and art pottery with a variety of trademarks. It began using the trade name *Franciscan* in 1934. In 1936, dinnerware and art pottery were sold under the name *Franciscan Ware*. The company made china and cream-colored, decorated earthenware. Desert Rose, Apple, El Patio, and Coronado were best sellers. The company became Interpace Corporation and in 1979 was purchased by Josiah Wedgwood & Sons. The plant was closed in 1984, but a few of the patterns are still being made. For more prices, go to kovels.com.

| | |
|---|---|
| **Acacia,** Chop Plate, 13 In. | 73 |
| **Amapola,** Baker, 14¾ In. | 32 |
| **Amapola,** Bowl, Fruit, 5⅝ In. | 8 |
| **Amapola,** Bowl, Vegetable, 9 In. | 35 |
| **Amapola,** Creamer | 10 |
| **Amapola,** Cup & Saucer | 8 |
| **Amapola,** Plate, Bread & Butter, 6¾ In. | 5 |
| **Amapola,** Plate, Dinner, 10¾ In. | 10 |
| **Amapola,** Plate, Salad, 8¾ In. | 6 |
| **Amapola,** Platter, 14 In. | 26 |
| **Antiqua,** Bowl, Vegetable, Divided, 11 In. | 25 |
| **Antiqua,** Plate, Bread & Butter, 6⅛ In. | 3 |
| **Antiqua,** Plate, Dinner, 10⅜ In. | 8 |
| **Antiqua,** Plate, Salad, 8¼ In. | 8 |
| **Antiqua,** Sugar, Lid | 3 |
| **Antique Green,** Plate, Bread & Butter, 6¼ In. | 12 |
| **Antique Green,** Saucer | 3 |
| **Apple,** Ashtray, 9 In. | 64 |
| **Apple,** Bowl, Fruit, 5¼ In. | 12 |
| **Apple,** Bowl, Vegetable, Divided, 10¾ In. | 26 |
| **Apple,** Butter, Cover, Lb. | 55 |
| **Apple,** Candlestick, 2⅝ In. | 39 |
| **Apple,** Chop Plate, 12½ In. | 34 |
| **Apple,** Eggcup | 21 |
| **Apple,** Gravy Boat, Underplate | 32 |
| **Apple,** Grill Plate, 10¾ In. | 90 |
| **Apple,** Plate, Bread & Butter, 6⅜ In. | 5 |
| **Apple,** Plate, Dinner, 10⅝ In. | 21 |
| **Apple,** Platter, 14 In. | 35 |
| **Apple,** Relish, 3 Sections, 11⅞ In. | 40 |
| **Apple,** Salt & Pepper | 21 |
| **Apple,** Sugar & Creamer | 28 |
| **Arcadia,** Bowl, Vegetable, Oval, 9⅛ In. | 65 |
| **Arcadia,** Cup & Saucer | 10 |
| **Arcadia,** Plate, Bread & Butter, 6⅜ In. | 7 |
| **Arcadia,** Plate, Salad, 8⅜ In. | 7 |
| **Arcadia,** Platter, 16 In. | 80 |
| **Autumn,** Ashtray, 4¾ In. | 5 |
| **Autumn,** Bowl, Vegetable, Divided, 13¾ In. | 16 |
| **Autumn,** Butter, Cover, Lb. | 23 |
| **Autumn,** Coffeepot, Lid, 10¼ In. | 45 |
| **Autumn,** Gravy Boat, Underplate | 20 |
| **Autumn,** Plate, Bread & Butter, 6½ In. | 4 |
| **Autumn,** Plate, Dinner, 10½ In. | 20 |
| **Autumn,** Salt & Pepper | 35 |
| **Beverly,** Cup & Saucer, After Dinner | 21 |
| **Beverly,** Platter, Round, 14 In. | 80 |
| **Beverly,** Salt & Pepper | 44 |
| **Bird 'N Hand,** Cup & Saucer | 5 |
| **Bird 'N Hand,** Plate, Dinner, 10¼ In. | 15 |
| **Bird 'N Hand,** Plate, Salad, 8¼ In. | 12 |
| **Blanc,** Bowl, Vegetable, Divided, 10¾ In. | 21 |
| **Blue Dawn,** Dinner, Plate, 10¾ In. | 15 |
| **Blue Dawn,** Plate, Salad, 8¾ In. | 10 |
| **Blueberry,** Bowl, Fruit, 5¼ In. | 8 |
| **Bountiful,** Bowl, Cereal, 6 In. | 15 |
| **Bountiful,** Cup & Saucer | 11 |
| **Bountiful,** Plate, Dinner, 10⅝ In. | 33 |
| **Cameo,** Cup & Saucer | 8 |
| **Cameo,** Plate, Bread & Butter, 6⅜ In. | 8 |
| **Cameo,** Plate, Dinner, 10¾ In. | 10 |
| **Cantata,** Bowl, Vegetable, 8¼ In. | 21 |
| **Cantata,** Cup & Saucer | 8 |
| **Cantata,** Plate, Bread & Butter, 6⅛ In. | 4 |
| **Cantata,** Plate, Dinner, 10⅜ In. | 9 |
| **Cantata,** Teapot, Lid, 4⅞ In. | 25 |

**F**

**Furniture,** Bed, Rococo Revival, Rosewood, Carved, Head & Footboard, c.1850, 93 x 66 x 87 In.
$1,845

New Orleans Auction Galleries, Inc.

**Furniture,** Bed, Sleigh, Mahogany, Marquetry, Paneled, Scrolled, Dutch, c.1840, 59 x 94 In.
$2,091

New Orleans Auction Galleries, Inc.

**Furniture,** Bench, Bucket, Plank Construction, Lower Shelf, Arched Cutout Feet, Pa., 28 x 40 In.
$502

Conestoga Auction Co., Inc.

**Furniture,** Bench, Window, George III Style, Mahogany, Inlay, Cylindrical Arms, 27 x 48 In.
$598

Neal Auction Co.

**Furniture,** Bookcase, Arts & Crafts, 2 Glass Doors, Shelves, Stepped Cornice, c.1910, 60 x 52 In. $375

Garth's Auctioneers & Appraisers

**Furniture,** Bookcase, Corner, Esherick, Poplar, Sculpted, Stained, Painted, c.1954, 78 x 54 In. $10,625

Rago Arts & Auction Center

**Furniture,** Bookcase, Ettore Sottsass, Casablanca, Laminates, Memphis, Milano, 1981, 90 In. $8,750

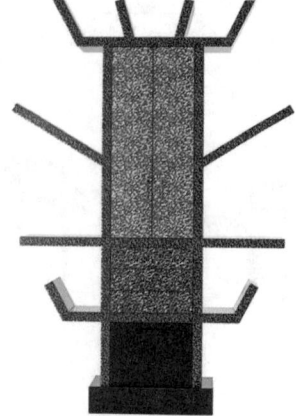

Rago Arts & Auction Center

| | |
|---|---:|
| **Canton,** Plate, Dinner, 10 In. | 36 |
| **Capri,** Cup & Saucer | 6 |
| **Capri,** Gravy Boat | 32 |
| **Cloud Nine,** Plate, Bread & Butter, 6⅛ In. | 5 |
| **Cloud,** Cup & Saucer | 8 |
| **Cloud,** Plate, Dinner, 10¼ In. | 12 |
| **Corinthian,** Plate, Bread & Butter, 6 In. | 12 |
| **Corinthian,** Plate, Dinner, 10¾ In. | 28 |
| **Corinthian,** Plate, Dinner, 10 In. | 28 |
| **Creole,** Plate, Dinner, 10¾ In. | 13 |
| **Creole,** Plate, Salad, 8¾ In. | 7 |
| **Daisy,** Bowl, Vegetable, Divided | 13 |
| **Daisy,** Butter | 15 |
| **Daisy,** Gravy Boat, Underplate | 14 |
| **Daisy,** Mug, 2⅞ In. | 15 |
| **Daisy,** Plate, Bread & Butter, 6½ In. | 4 |
| **Daisy,** Relish, 12 In. | 13 |
| **Daisy,** Salt & Pepper | 25 |
| **Desert Rose,** Cup & Saucer | 17 |
| **Desert Rose,** Jam Jar, Lid, 4½ In. | 89 |
| **Dogwood,** Bowl, Fruit, 5⅝ In. | 12 |
| **Dogwood,** Plate, Dinner, 10⅝ In. | 15 |
| **Fan Tan,** Creamer | 7 |
| **Fan Tan,** Cup & Saucer | 7 |
| **Fruit,** Cup | 5 |
| **Fruit,** Plate, Salad, 8⅜ In. | 15 |
| **Fruit,** Serving Bowl, 9⅜ In. | 42 |
| **Happy Talk,** Bowl, Vegetable, 8¼ In. | 20 |
| **Happy Talk,** Plate, Bread & Butter, 6⅛ In. | 3 |
| **Larkspur,** Plate, Bread & Butter, 6½ In. | 4 |
| **Larkspur,** Platter, 14 In. | 20 |
| **Mesa,** Chop Plate, 13¼ In. | 85 |
| **Mesa,** Cup & Saucer | 8 |
| **Mesa,** Soup, Dish | 30 |
| **Monaco,** Plate, Dinner, 10½ In. | 23 |
| **Montecito,** Platter, 13¼ In. | 35 |
| **Pink-A-Dilly,** Bowl, Vegetable, Divided, 11⅛ In. | 21 |
| **Pink-A-Dilly,** Butter, Cover, Lb. | 25 |
| **Pink-A-Dilly,** Plate, Bread & Butter, 6⅛ In. | 4 |
| **Poppy,** Bowl, Vegetable, 8¼ In. | 65 |
| **Poppy,** Butter, Cover, Lb. | 160 |
| **Poppy,** Chop Plate, 12 In. | 52 |
| **Poppy,** Gravy Boat, Underplate | 125 |
| **Poppy,** Plate, Bread & Butter, 6¼ In. | 10 |
| **Rossmore,** Plate, Bread & Butter, 6⅜ In. | 5 |
| **Rossmore,** Plate, Dinner, 10⅝ In. | 8 |
| **Rossmore,** Soup, Dish, 8¼ In. | 24 |
| **Silver Pine,** Creamer | 40 |
| **Springsong,** Creamer | 8 |
| **Springsong,** Plate, Dinner, 10⅛ In. | 12 |
| **Springsong,** Saucer | 3 |
| **Sweet Pea,** Cup | 5 |
| **Sycamore,** Casserole, Lid, 1¾ Qt. | 44 |
| **Sycamore,** Creamer | 15 |
| **Sycamore,** Gravy Boat, Underplate | 28 |
| **Sycamore,** Relish, 2 Sections | 25 |
| **Sycamore,** Salt & Pepper | 22 |
| **Tiger Flower,** Plate, Luncheon, 9¼ In. | 21 |
| **Tulip Time,** Butter, Cover, Lb. | 21 |
| **Tulip Time,** Coffeepot, 7⅜ In. | 45 |
| **Tulip Time,** Mug, 4⅛ In. | 25 |
| **Winsome,** Bowl, Fruit, 5 In. | 13 |
| **Winsome,** Plate, Dinner, 10⅛ In. | 12 |
| **Winsome,** Saucer | 2 |
| **Woodlore,** Platter, 16½ In. | 40 |
| **Woodlore,** Relish, 3 Sections, 6 In. | 12 |

**FRANKART INC.** , New York, New York, mass-produced nude "dancing lady" lamps, ashtrays, and other decorative Art Deco items in the 1920s and 1930s. They were made of white lead composition and spray-painted. *Frankart Inc.* and the patent number and year were stamped on the base.

| | |
|---|---:|
| **Bookends,** Dog, Hunting, Bird In Mouth, Signed, 1930s, 9 ½ x 4 ½ In. | 175 |
| **Bookends,** Nude, Kneeling In Circle Of Leaves, Cast Iron, White, 5 In. | 200 |
| **Bookends,** Sailor Boy, Dog, Bronze Finish, Marked, 6 x 5 x 3 In. | 180 |
| **Bookends,** Scottie Dog, Cast Metal, Bronze Finish, c.1921, 5 x 6 x 3 In. | 175 |
| **Bust,** Woman, Flowered Headband, Long Hair, Marked, Pat Applied For, 6 x 5 In. | 120 |
| **Candlestick,** Nude, Sitting, Arms Around Knees, Looking Up, 4 ½ In., Pair | 550 |
| **Figurine,** Ballerina Girl, On Toes, Stackable Trays As Tutu, Marked, 10 In. | 950 |
| **Lamp,** Nude, Bucket On Shoulder, Electrified, 1922, 12 In. | 525 |
| **Lamp,** Nude, Green, Dancing Nymph Plate Shade, Signed, 13 x 8 In. | 1650 |
| **Lamp,** Nude, Seated, Fluted Column, Staring At Globe, 1930s, 8 ½ x 6 In. | 950 |
| **Vase,** Nude, Arms Around Vase, Marked, c.1930, 12 In. | 1205 |

**FRANKOMA POTTERY** was originally known as The Frank Potteries when John F. Frank opened shop in 1933. The factory is now working in Sapulpa, Oklahoma. Early wares were made from a light cream-colored clay from Ada, Oklahoma, but in 1956 the company switched to a red clay from Sapulpa. The firm made dinnerware, utilitarian and decorative kitchenwares, figurines, flowerpots, and limited edition and commemorative pieces. John Frank died in 1973 and his daughter, Joniece, inherited the business. Frankoma went bankrupt in 1990. The pottery operated under various owners for a few years and was bought by Joe Ragosta in 2008. It closed in 2010. The buildings, assets, name, and molds were sold at an auction in 2011.

| | |
|---|---:|
| **Creamer,** Green, Plainsman | 18 |
| **Cup,** Green, Prairie, 2 ½ In. | 8 |
| **Honey Pot,** Lid, Green, Plainsman, 5 ½ In. | 12 |
| **Salt & Pepper,** Brown & Beige, Handles, 1950s | 20 |
| **Vase,** Candle, Oval, Brown, Plainsman, 7 ¼ In. | 45 |

**FRATERNAL** objects that are related to the many different fraternal organizations in the United States are listed in this category. The Elks, Masons, Odd Fellows, and others are included. Also included are service organizations, like the American Legion, Kiwanis, and Lions Club. Furniture is listed in the Furniture category. Shaving mugs decorated with fraternal crests are included in the Shaving Mug category.

| | |
|---|---:|
| **Eastern Star,** Ring, Filigree, 14K White Gold, Onyx, Enamel, Art Deco, Size 5 ¼ | 132 |
| **Kiwanis,** Sign, Metal, K Logo, Round, 30 In. .................................................*illus* | 90 |
| **Knights Of Pythias,** Sword, Ceremonial, Sheath, Knight's Head Pommel, Lion, 37 x 5 In. | 132 |
| **Lioness Club,** Sign, Blue, White, Logo, 30 In. | 90 |
| **Masonic,** Apron, Eye In Sun, Compass, Square, White Leather, Blue Velvet Edge, 16 x 20 In. | 59 |
| **Masonic,** Apron, G. Washington, Gavel, Scroll, Carved, Frame Signed S. Levy, c.1950, 21 In. | 2040 |
| **Masonic,** Apron, Royal Arch, Symbols, Flowers, White Silk, Pink Trim, Frame, 21 x 20 In. | 472 |
| **Masonic,** Apron, Symbols, Eye In Sun, Blue, Black, White Leather, Frame, 1800s, 22 x 20 In. | 266 |
| **Masonic,** Fob, 32nd Degree, Medallion, 14K Yellow Gold, Enamel, 1921, 1 ½ x 1 In. | 736 |
| **Masonic,** Jug, Chart, Symbols, Verse, Black Transfer, Creamware, England, c.1805, 11 In. | 1560 |
| **Masonic,** Medal, District Deputy Grand Masters, Silver Gilt, J. Bennett, 3 ½ In. | 352 |
| **Masonic,** Ring, 10K Yellow Gold, Diamond, Size 9 ½ | 375 |
| **Masonic,** Ring, 14K Yellow Gold, Pink Synthetic Sapphire, Insignia, Man's, Size 8 | 345 |
| **Masonic,** Watch, Rolex, Silver, Sapphires, Mother-Of-Pearl Dial, 18 Jewel, c.1930, 2 In. ....*illus* | 6300 |
| **Match Safe,** Odd Fellows, Symbols, Banner, Hendrick Hudson Hotel | 117 |
| **Moose,** Watch Fob, Moose Image Pendant, 14K Yellow Gold, Diamond, Engraved I.O.O.M. | 719 |
| **Odd Fellows,** Emblem, Cutwork, Repeating 3-Link Chains, 10-Point Star, 38 x 38 In. | 923 |
| **Odd Fellows,** Mug, Symbols, 3-Link Chain, Initials F.L.T.E. Hitchcock, 1900s, 3 ½ In. | 35 |
| **Odd Fellows,** Staff, Carved, Gilt, Painted Red Heart, Open Hand, c.1890, 66 In. | 2460 |
| **Optimists International,** Sign, Blue, Yellow, Round, 30 In. | 60 |
| **Rotary International,** SSP, Frame, 30 In. | 60 |

**FRY GLASS** was made by the H.C. Fry Glass Company of Rochester, Pennsylvania. The company, founded in 1901, first made cut glass and other types of fine glasswares. In 1922 it patented a heat-resistant glass called Pearl Ovenglass. For two years, 1926–1927, the company made Fry Foval, an opal ware decorated with colored trim. Reproductions of this glass have been made. Depression glass patterns made by Fry may be listed in the Depression Glass category. Some pieces of cut glass may also be included in the Cut Glass category.

**FRY**

| | |
|---|---:|
| **Plate,** Duquesne, 9 ¾ In. | 565 |

**Furniture,** Bookcase, George III, Mahogany, Glazed Doors, 2 Lower Doors, c.1785, 111 x 64 In.
$4,674

New Orleans Auction Galleries, Inc.

**Furniture,** Bookcase, George III, Mahogany, Satinwood, Glass Doors, 3 Lower Doors, 89 x 55 In.
$2,000

Rago Arts & Auction Center

**Furniture,** Breakfront, Chippendale Style, Mahogany, Mullions, Hickory & White, c.1980, 98 x 78 In.
$480

Garth's Auctioneers & Appraisers

F

**Furniture,** Bureau, Empire, Cherry, Bird's-Eye Maple, Step Back, 6 Drawers, 48 x 44 In.
$384

Conestoga Auction Co., Inc.

**Furniture,** Cabinet, Art Nouveau, Walnut, Oak, Curved Frame, Leaded Glass, France, 50 x 54 In.
$885

Brunk Auctions

**Furniture,** Cabinet, Baker's, Pine, Possum Belly, 2 Sections, 56 x 48 In.
$150

Rich Penn

| | |
|---|---:|
| **Tray,** Trojan, Heart Shape, Cut, 13¼ x 11½ In. | 254 |
| **Vase,** Jack-In-The-Pulpit, Delft Blue Rim, Polished Pontil Mark, c.1922, 10¼ In. | 173 |

**FRY FOVAL**

| | |
|---|---:|
| **Tea Set,** Teapot, Sugar & Creamer, Cup & Saucer, Silver Band, Blue Handles | 300 |
| **Vase,** Trumpet Shape, Jade Connector, Foot, 9¼ x 5 In. | 374 |
| **Vase,** Trumpet, Jade Connector & Foot, Polished Pontil Mark, 9¼ In. | 374 |

**FULPER POTTERY COMPANY** was incorporated in 1899 in Flemington, New Jersey. It made art pottery from 1909 to 1929. The firm had been making bottles, jugs, and housewares from 1805. Doll heads were made about 1928. The firm became Stangl Pottery in 1929. Stangl Pottery is listed in its own category in this book.

| | |
|---|---:|
| **Basket,** Lid, Flower Finial, Multicolor, Handle, 9½ In. | 77 |
| **Bookends,** Mission Verde Matte Glaze, Aztec, Face, Triangular, c.1915, 5½ x 5¾ In. | 469 |
| **Bowl,** Black, Tan & Blue Flambe Glaze, Rounded Overlapping Lobes, 3 x 13 In. | 219 |
| **Bowl,** Fish, Verde Antique, Green, Copper Dust Crystalline Glaze, c.1910, 11½ In. | 540 |
| **Bowl,** Flared, 4-Footed, Marked, 7⅜ In. | 173 |
| **Doorstop,** Cat, Standing, Arched Back, Ears Back, Green Crystalline Glaze, 6¾ In. | 460 |
| **Doorstop,** Dog, Bulldog, Bum The Pup, Blue Flambe Over Tan, 8¼ In. ...............*illus* | 805 |
| **Figurine,** Duck, Glass Eyes, White, Brown, Green Gloss Glaze, Impressed, 4½ x 9 In. | 259 |
| **Flower Frog,** Castle Shape, Bridge, Road, Landscape, 4¾ x 5⅜ In. | 184 |
| **Flower Frog,** Turtle Shape, Brown Glaze, 4¼ In. | 71 |
| **Jug,** Brown, Fade To Green, Ivory Flambe, c.1915, 11 x 6 In. | 320 |
| **Lamp,** Cat's-Eye Flambe, Flemington Green, Cucumber Crystalline Glaze, 20½ In. | 5750 |
| **Tile,** Acorn, Leaf, Blue, Green, Oak Frame, 1996, 13¼ In. | 46 |
| **Vase,** Bell Pepper, Green, c.1910, 4 x 4½ In., Pair | 3200 |
| **Vase,** Blue & Brown Crystalline Glaze, Oval, 4 Curled Handles On Shoulder, 13 In. | 549 |
| **Vase,** Blue Crystalline Glaze, Squat, Handles, 6 x 8 In. | 230 |
| **Vase,** Blue Drip Glaze, Early 20th Century, 7½ In. | 60 |
| **Vase,** Blue Matte Glaze, 4 Handles, c.1918, 8 x 9 In. | 1920 |
| **Vase,** Blue Matte Glaze, Blue Flambe Drip, Snowflake Crystals, 3 Handles, 7¼ In. | 138 |
| **Vase,** Blue Matte, Horizontal Ribbing, 6¾ In. | 40 |
| **Vase,** Blue Snowflake Crystalline Glaze, Buttress Handles, 8½ In. | 518 |
| **Vase,** Blue, 4 Handles, 8¼ x 9 In. | 1920 |
| **Vase,** Blue, Loop Rim Handles, 6 In. | 161 |
| **Vase,** Blue, Yellow Glaze, Squat, 10¾ x 7½ In. | 167 |
| **Vase,** Bottle Shape, Famille Rose Glaze, Footed Stand, 18½ x 6 In. ..............*illus* | 3750 |
| **Vase,** Brown Over Green, Speckled, Oval, 12 x 7 In. | 225 |
| **Vase,** Bud, Blue, Squat Base, 5¾ In. | 270 |
| **Vase,** Buttress, Green Crystalline Over Famille Rose, Vertical Racetrack Stamp, 8¼ In. | 259 |
| **Vase,** Chinese Blue Glaze, Drippy, Bulbous Shoulder, 12 x 12 In. | 1159 |
| **Vase,** Chinese Blue To Mahogany To Ivory Flambe Glaze, c.1916, 10 x 7 In. | 863 |
| **Vase,** Copper Dust Crystalline & Mirror Black Flambe Glaze, Buttressed, 11 x 8 In..............*illus* | 2625 |
| **Vase,** Copper Dust, 2 Handles, Vertical Racetrack Ink Stamp, 7½ In. | 173 |
| **Vase,** Cylindrical, Cast Geometric Design At Rim, Mahogany, Green Flambe, 6½ In. | 288 |
| **Vase,** Flambe Glaze, Black, Brown, Blue, Green, Raised Dots On Shoulder, 7 In. | 230 |
| **Vase,** Flower, Blue Snowflake Crystals, Holes For Stems, Marked, 8 In. | 345 |
| **Vase,** Grecian, Blue Matte Glaze, Over Blue Flambe Glaze, Handles, 10¾ In. | 184 |
| **Vase,** Green & Light Blue Flambe, Crystalline Highlights, Horizontal Ribs, 2 Handles, 10 In. | 244 |
| **Vase,** Green Crystalline Glaze, Open Glaze Bubbles, 12 In. | 230 |
| **Vase,** Green Crystalline Glaze, Ring Handles, 12½ In. | 173 |
| **Vase,** Green Crystalline Over Tan Gloss Glaze, Handles, Incised, 8 In. | 207 |
| **Vase,** Green Flambe Glaze, Over Mustard Glaze, 6 In. | 150 |
| **Vase,** Green Flambe Over Drip Tan Flambe Glaze, Handles, 4¾ In. | 81 |
| **Vase,** Green Matte Glaze, Speckled, Streaked, Bulbous, Handles, c.1930, 8 In. | 150 |
| **Vase,** Green Mottled Gloss Glaze, Shaded To Darker Green, Applied Handles, 7¾ x 6 In. | 150 |
| **Vase,** Green Snowflake Crystalline Glaze, Handles, 9 In. | 127 |
| **Vase,** Green, Over Blue Flambe, Tapered, 6¾ x 7¾ In. | 230 |
| **Vase,** Green, Tan Mottled Glaze, Round, Marked, 5½ In. | 200 |
| **Vase,** Ivory Flambe Over Mustard Matte Glaze, 3¾ In. | 138 |
| **Vase,** Leopard Skin Crystalline Glaze, Handles, Racetrack Ink Stamp, 6¼ In. | 184 |
| **Vase,** Matte Blue, Green, Blue, Flambe Glazes, Flared, c.1920, 13½ x 6 In. | 1063 |
| **Vase,** Micro Crystalline Black Glaze, Handles, 9 x 6 In. | 150 |
| **Vase,** Mirror Black Over Copper Dust Crystalline Glazes, 7⅝ x 8 In. | 1725 |

| | |
|---|---|
| **Vase,** Mirror Black, Mahogany, Ivory Flambe, Shape 483, 7 ½ In. | 173 |
| **Vase,** Pink Flambe Over Blue Drip Glaze, Handles, Raised Vertical Mark, 9 ¼ In. | 184 |
| **Vase,** Plum Flambe Over Blue Glaze, Racetrack Ink Stamp, 7 ¾ In. | 81 |
| **Vase,** Purple, Yellow, 7-Sided Cylinder, Prank Mark, 8 ¾ In. | 35 |
| **Vase,** Shell, Blue Ruffled Rim, Marked, 11 ½ In. | 29 |
| **Vase,** Trumpet, Blue Glaze, 8 ½ In. | 58 |
| **Vase,** Urn Shape, Mahogany Glaze, Chinese Blue Flambe, 8 In. | 460 |
| **Vase-Bowl,** Mustard Glaze, Green Flambe, 5 In. | 288 |

**FURNITURE** of all types is listed in this category. Examples dating from the seventeenth century to the 1970s are included. Prices for furniture vary in different parts of the country. Oak furniture is most expensive in the West; large pieces over eight feet high are sold for the most money in the South, where high ceilings are found in the old homes. Condition is very important when determining prices. These are NOT average prices but rather reports of unique sales. If the description includes the word *style*, the piece resembles the old furniture style but was made at a later time. It is not a period piece. Small chests that sat on a table or dresser are also included here. Garden furniture is listed in the Garden Furnishings category. Related items may be found in the Architectural, Brass, and Store categories.

| | |
|---|---|
| **Altar,** Baroque, Walnut, Carved Columns, Stepped Base, Hinged Lid, 1700s, 41 x 30 In. | 590 |
| **Altar,** Gilt, Red Lacquer, Chinese, 36 x 66 In. | 400 |
| **Armchairs** are listed under Chair in this category. | |
| **Armoire,** Art Deco, White Paint, Mirrored Door, Applied Designs, 1920s, 42 x 54 In. | 82 |
| **Armoire,** Art Nouveau, Oak, Arched, Mirror Doors, Drawer, c.1900, 81 x 50 In. | 244 |
| **Armoire,** Art Nouveau, Walnut, Arched, Beveled Mirror Doors, Drawer, 83 x 50 In. | 275 |
| **Armoire,** Cherry, Inlay, Molded Cornice, Frieze, Monogram, Paneled Doors, 83 x 56 In. | 21510 |
| **Armoire,** Cherry, Vernacular, Beaded Drawers, Scalloped Apron, Doors, c.1825, 85 x 55 In. | 6457 |
| **Armoire,** Desk, Mahogany, Paneled Doors, Molded Cornice, 74 x 47 In. | 330 |
| **Armoire,** Esherick, Cherry, Vertical Boards, Painted, 80 x 63 x 20 In. | 4375 |
| **Armoire,** Fruitwood, Carved Leaves, Scrolls, 2 Panel Doors, France, c.1790, 83 x 52 In. | 960 |
| **Armoire,** Louis XV Style, Mahogany, Arched Top, Carved Cartouche, Mirrors, 105 x 58 In. | 615 |
| **Armoire,** Louis XV Style, Scrolling Leaf Cartouche, Mirror Doors, Apron, 105 x 89 In. | 600 |
| **Armoire,** Louis XV, Fruitwood, 2 Panel Doors, c.1770, 82 x 51 In. | 600 |
| **Armoire,** Louis XV, Fruitwood, Carved, Door, Arched Top, c.1780, 81 x 35 In. | 1722 |
| **Armoire,** Louis XVI Style, 2 Mirror Doors, Gilt Accents, Gray Paint, c.1875, 91 x 70 In. | 1500 |
| **Armoire,** Majorelle, Art Nouveau, Walnut, Mirror, 2 Side Doors, Flower Carved, 97 x 74 In. | 4375 |
| **Armoire,** Neoclassical, Mahogany, Flared Cornice, Paneled Doors, 86 x 76 In. | 5378 |
| **Armoire,** Neoclassical, Walnut, Cyma Molded Cornice, Doors, Bracket Feet, 93 x 63 In. | 1722 |
| **Armoire,** Oak, 2 Doors, 2 Drawers, Late 19th Century, 23 x 16 ½ In. | 390 |
| **Armoire,** Panel Door, Flowers Bouquets, Green Paint, 1854, 73 x 51 In. | 1375 |
| **Armoire,** Provincial, Louis XV Style, Walnut, Molded Cornice, Carved Frieze, 90 x 55 In. | 1722 |
| **Armoire,** Provincial, Louis XV, Walnut, Cornice, Doors, Shaped Panels, c.1800, 85 x 5 In. | 861 |
| **Armoire,** Rococo, Rosewood, Carved, Beaded Cornice, Mirrored Doors, 109 x 72 In. | 5975 |
| **Armoire,** Rosewood, 2 Panel Doors, Raised Bracket Feet, 89 x 69 In. | 688 |
| **Armoire,** Victorian, Cherry, 2 Doors, Beveled Mirror, c.1900, 81 x 48 In. | 360 |
| **Armoire,** Walnut, Arch Crest, Beveled Mirror, Drawer, 103 In. | 183 |
| **Armoire,** Walnut, Fruitwood, Parquetry, 2 Doors, Urn Carvings, Italy, 89 x 70 In. | 1625 |
| **Baby Tender,** Windsor, 15 Spindles, Built-In Seat, Tray, c.1810, 20 x 12 x 25 In. ...............*illus* | 780 |
| **Banquette,** Mies Van Der Rohe, Chrome, Walnut, Leather, Tufted Bolster, 77 x 39 In. | 2032 |
| **Bar Cart,** Brushed Metal, Glass Shelves, Tray Top, Casters, Maison Jansen, 33 x 33 In. | 336 |
| **Bar Cart,** Teak, Black Laminate Top, Casters, L. Pontoppidan, 25 x 27 In. | 244 |
| **Bar,** Dry, Art Deco Style, Rosewood, Fold-Open Top, Fitted Interior, Drawers, 36 x 30 In. | 738 |
| **Bar,** Globe, Zodiac, Rotating, Interior Shelf, Brown, Stretcher, c.1950s, 40 In. | 458 |
| **Bar,** Tage Frid, Rosewood, 2 Burl Doors, Shelves, Drawers & Sink Inside, 40 x 65 In. | 1150 |
| **Bar,** Victorian, Mahogany, Lift Top, Frieze Drawer, 2 Shelves, England, 37 x 24 In. | 1560 |
| **Barstool,** Black Wavy Seat, 4 Metal Legs, 27 In., Pair | 96 |
| **Barstool,** Curved Wood Slat Seat, Backrest, Tubular Frame, Brown Paint, 42 In., 4 | 253 |
| **Barstool,** Roy McMakin, Domestic Furniture Co., c.1886, 20 x 14 In., Pair | 1625 |
| **Bed Backrest,** Federal, Walnut Frame, Cushioned, Upholstered, Adjustable, c.1850, 24 x 22 In. | 270 |
| **Bed Steps,** Georgian, Mahogany, Leather, 3 Treads, Top Step Lifts, c.1800, 28 x 27 In. | 1586 |
| **Bed Steps,** Regency, Mahogany, c.1804, 26 x 27 In. | 523 |
| **Bed,** Baroque Revival, Oak, Walnut, Carved, Headboard, Footboard, 98 In. | 11250 |
| **Bed,** Cannonball, Tiger Maple, Headboard, Rolling Pin Top, Posts, c.1810, 52 x 56 In. | 2370 |
| **Bed,** Canopy, Mahogany, Carved, Turreted Corners, Paneled Headboard, c.1850, 118 x 80 In. | 11590 |
| **Bed,** Canopy, Transitional Classical To Rococo Revival, Walnut, c.1850, 112 x 59 In. | 3444 |

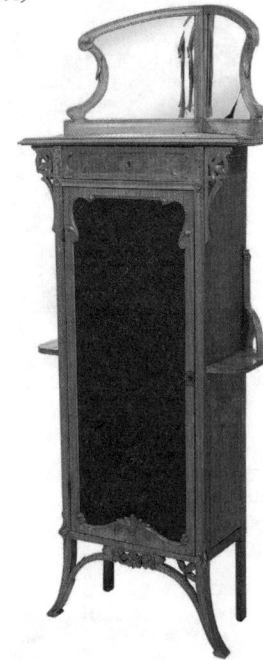

**Furniture,** Cabinet, Corner, Art Nouveau, Chestnut, Carved, Stained Glass, c.1900, 70 x 28 In.
**$649**

Brunk Auctions

**Furniture,** Cabinet, Corner, Glass Door, Wood Grill, Lower Door, Shelves, England, 71 x 26 In.
**$120**

DuMouchelles Art Gallery

**Furniture,** Cabinet, Display, French, 2 Doors, Painted Scene, Gilt Metal Trim, 71 x 43 In.
$2,750

Woody Auction

**Furniture,** Cabinet, Display, French, Mahogany, Bowfront, Glass, Mirror Back, Inlay, 66 x 40 In.
$125

Woody Auction

**Furniture,** Cabinet, Display, Louis XVI Style, Gold Paint, Glass Shelves, France, 55 In.
$563

Garth's Auctioneers & Appraisers

**Furniture,** Cabinet, Elm, Lacquer, Gilt Dragon Scene, 2 Doors, Drawers, Chinese, 81 x 50 In.
$1,320

Garth's Auctioneers & Appraisers

**Furniture,** Cabinet, Frankl, Skyscraper, Wood, Lacquer, Drawers, Mirror, 1920s, 66 x 36 In.
$3,750

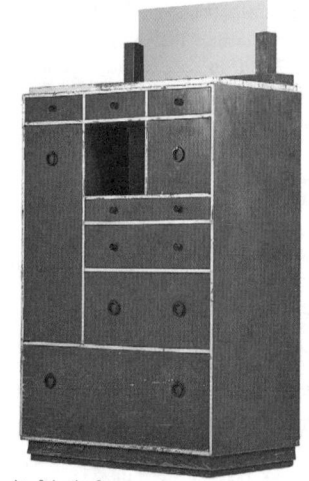

Rago Arts & Auction Center

**Furniture,** Cabinet, Kingwood, Mahogany, Inlay, Gilt, Mounts, France, 1800s, 39 x 21 In.
$2,460

Neal Auction Co.

**Furniture,** Cabinet, Letter File, Quartersawn Oak, Cardboard Drawers, 1868-1903, 66 x 35 In.
$1,416

Conestoga Auction Co., Inc.

**Furniture,** Cabinet, Louis XV Style, Doors, Faux Marble Top, Urn Frieze, c.1890, 34 x 47 In.
$1,968

New Orleans Auction Galleries, Inc.

**Furniture,** Cabinet, Neogrecque, Ebonized, Inlay, Pietra Dura, Doors, Gilt, c.1870, 41 x 60 In.
$13,530

New Orleans Auction Galleries, Inc.

| | |
|---|---|
| Bed, Four-Poster, Cherry, Carved, Shaped Headboard, Mahogany Panel, 89 x 77 In...... | 1673 |
| Bed, Four-Poster, Federal, Mahogany, Rice & Spiral Carving, Charleston, 1820, 81 x 60 In. ......... | 8260 |
| Bed, Four-Poster, Mahogany, Scroll Headboard, Pineapple Finials, 66 x 56 In............... | 154 |
| Bed, Four-Poster, Maple, Pine, Red Paint, American, 81 x 51 In...... | 469 |
| Bed, Four-Poster, Neoclassical, Mahogany, Cherry, Carved, Brass Ball Feet, 60 x 80 In........ | 4182 |
| Bed, Frankl, Wood, Stained, Enameled, Silvered Waves, 1920s, 52 x 47 x 90 In. ........ | 8125 |
| Bed, Geoffrey Warner, Cherry, Beech, Turned Post, Paneled, Chip Carved, c.1999, 94 x 84 In...... | 4305 |
| Bed, Half-Tester, Rococo, Mahogany, Flower, Shell, Arched Headboard, 93 x 61 In. | 948 |
| Bed, Maple, Green, Shaped Headboard, Turned Posts, Rope, c.1830, 74 x 36 In............ | 2596 |
| Bed, Renaissance Revival, Gilt Incised, Ebonized, c.1890, 79 x 58 In......................*illus* | 4575 |
| Bed, Renaissance Revival, Walnut, Burl Walnut, High Back, Carved, 77 x 92 In............ | 984 |
| Bed, Rococo Revival, Rosewood, Carved, Head & Footboard, c.1850, 93 x 66 x 87 In..........*illus* | 1845 |
| Bed, Rococo Revival, Walnut, Figured Walnut, Paneled, Fluted Posts, c.1850, 91 x 59 In. | 1353 |
| Bed, Sleigh, Day, Empire Revival, Mahogany, Tapered Legs, Plank Rail, 30 x 80 In........ | 854 |
| Bed, Sleigh, Empire, Mahogany, Parcel Gilt, 39 x 43 In. | 687 |
| Bed, Sleigh, Mahogany, Marquetry, Paneled, Scrolled, Dutch, c.1840, 59 x 94 In. ............*illus* | 2091 |
| Bed, Sleigh, Neoclassical, Figured Mahogany, Veneer, Shaped Rails, France, 1800s, 42 x 91 In. .... | 295 |
| Bed, Walnut, Arched Crest, Oak Rails, Arched Footboard, Square Legs, 95 x 57 In............ | 183 |
| Bedroom Set, Renaissance Revival, Carved, Walnut, Bed, Bureau, Washstand, 60 x 122 In. ...... | 9560 |
| Bench, Art Nouveau, Quartersawn Oak, Applied Carvings, Bronzed Cast Iron, 83 x 29 In. ........ | 325 |
| Bench, Bootjack, Molded Top, Scalloped Apron, 4 x 16 In. | 205 |
| Bench, Bucket, 3 Shelves, Green Paint, c.1850, 46 x 44 In. | 720 |
| Bench, Bucket, Pine, 2 Open Shelves, Carved Feet, Pennsylvania, c.1860, 31 x 42 In. | 615 |
| Bench, Bucket, Pine, 3 Drawers, Open Shelf, 2 Panel Doors, c.1860, 49 x 43 In. ...... | 360 |
| Bench, Bucket, Pine, 3 Open Shelves, Green Paint, Pa., 49 x 34 In. | 2040 |
| Bench, Bucket, Pine, 3 Shelves, Scalloped Ends, Pa., 46 x 48 In. ...... | 1200 |
| Bench, Bucket, Pine, 4 Shelves, c.1850, 41 x 36 In...... | 308 |
| Bench, Bucket, Pine, Green Paint, Tenon Construction, 5 Shelves, Shaped Ends, 61 x 42 In........ | 1800 |
| Bench, Bucket, Plank Construction, Lower Shelf, Arched Cutout Feet, Pa., 28 x 40 In..........*illus* | 502 |
| Bench, Bucket, Red Paint, Scalloped Back, Cutout Slab Sides, 3 Shelves, 42 x 56 In..................... | 2125 |
| Bench, Chippendale Style, Walnut, Carved, Upholstered, Acanthus Cabriole Legs, 22 x 25 In. ...... | 418 |
| Bench, Cinema, P. Jeanneret, 2 Seats, Teak, Cane, Brass, 1950s, 34 x 43 ½ In............ | 6250 |
| Bench, Continental, Oak, Rounded Top, Pierced Carved Trestle Base, 1800s, 29 x 59 In........... | 1500 |
| Bench, Deacon's, Red Paint, Shaped 3 Sections Back, 20 Spindles, Scroll Arms, 35 x 77 In. ........ | 420 |
| Bench, H. Bertoia, Slat, Oak, Chrome Steel Base, Knoll, 1970s, 16 x 72 In............ | 1500 |
| Bench, H. Bertoia, Wood Slats, Black Enamel Frame, c.1965, 16 x 82 In. | 661 |
| Bench, Hardwood, Carved, Reticulated Crest, Back, Dragon, Pierced Seat Rail, 44 x 51 In.......... | 5079 |
| Bench, Kilim Upholstery, Padded Top, Brass Tack Accents, Bulbous Legs, 1900s, 31 x 49 In........ | 676 |
| Bench, Knight's, Ebonized Wood, Brass, H. Probber, 1950s, 21 x 27 In......... | 875 |
| Bench, Leather, Chromed Steel, Undulating X-Shape Base, Cecchini, Italy, 36 In., Pair ............ | 2875 |
| Bench, Louis XV Style, Painted, Antiqued, Turned Wood Base, Upholstered, 25 x 21 In. ........ | 253 |
| Bench, Louis XVI Style, Multicolor, Padded Top, Ribbed, Tapered, 1900s, 20 x 29 In.......... | 584 |
| Bench, Louis XVI Style, Padded Seat, Fluted Legs, Top Shape Feet, c.1910, 17 x 53 In., Pair........ | 1230 |
| Bench, Louis XVI, Cream Paint, High Sides, 34 x 45 In. | 450 |
| Bench, Maple, Ash, Splayed Legs, Red Paint, c.1810, 22 x 29 In........ | 10455 |
| Bench, Meetinghouse, Quaker, Pine, Shaped Crest Rail, Medial Slat, Plank Seat, 34 x 118 In. ... | 369 |
| Bench, Neoclassical Style, Cream Paint, X-Shape Seat, Lion Masks, Paw Feet, 20 x 23 In., Pair... | 615 |
| Bench, Neoclassical Style, Silver Wood, Silk Upholstery, Ferguson Copeland, 58 x 30 In. ............ | 8125 |
| Bench, Oak, Mortised Legs, Skirt On 2 Sides, Arched Cutout Feet, c.1900, 18 x 69 In. | 94 |
| Bench, Oak, Shell-Carved Panels, High Arms, Back, England, c.1900, 36 ½ x 44 In........ | 720 |
| Bench, P. Jeanneret, Teak, Slats, Inverted V Legs, 1950s, 16 x 60 In. | 7500 |
| Bench, Pine, Cutout Diagonal Supports, Salmon Orange Paint, c.1840, 17 x 74 In........ | 4920 |
| Bench, Pine, Cutout Feet, Green Paint, 1800s, 19 x 51 In. | 115 |
| Bench, Pine, Green Paint, Shaped Cutout Legs, c.1880, 18 x 58 x 12 In............... | 489 |
| Bench, Pine, Green Paint, Splayed Legs, Pennsylvania, c.1860, 7 ½ x 37 In. ....... | 246 |
| Bench, Pine, Low Stretcher, c.1855, 22 x 54 In. | 240 |
| Bench, Pine, Open, Horizontal Splats, Painted, c.1850, 32 x 75 In. | 270 |
| Bench, Pine, Paneled Back, Arms, Pennsylvania, 37 x 52 In....... | 210 |
| Bench, Pine, Scalloped Supports, c.1810, 19 x 85 x 13 In. ...... | 120 |
| Bench, Pine, Spindle Back, Plank Seat, Splayed Legs, Brown Paint, Sweden, 35 x 56 In............ | 1140 |
| Bench, Pine, Yellow Paint, c.1910, 16 x 57 In......... | 374 |
| Bench, Pine, Yellow Paint, Solid Back, Shaped Ends, 1800s, 37 x 80 In. ........ | 540 |
| Bench, Queen Anne Style, Mahogany, Pierced Corner Brackets, 21 x 64 In. ............ | 861 |
| Bench, Regency Style, Wood, Gilt Mythical Head Arm Ends, Black Paint, Tassels, 39 In. ............ | 594 |
| Bench, Regency, Rosewood, Brass, Scrolled Armrests & Feet, X-Stretcher, c.1820, 51 In. ............ | 4375 |

**Furniture,** Cabinet, Richard Neutra, 10 Drawers, Cutout Handles, Overhang Top, 1956, 36 x 50 In.
$3,750

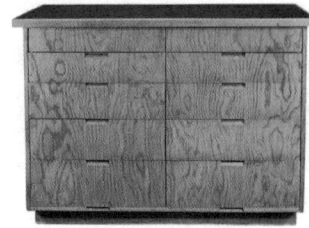

Los Angeles Modern Auctions (LAMA)

**Furniture,** Cabinet, Tobacco, Oak, Door Over Door, Shaped Mirror, Old Judge Cigarettes Ad, 62 In.
$780

Garth's Auctioneers & Appraisers

**Furniture,** Cabinet, Walnut, Doors, Shelves, Pullout Board, France, c.1900, 84 x 83 In.
$1,180

Brunk Auctions

**Furniture,** Cabinet, Wormley, Bleached Mahogany, Walnut, Brass, Dunbar, 1940s, 38 x 70 In.
**$4,063**

Rago Arts & Auction Center

---

**Furniture,** Candlestand, Walnut, Tilt Top, Birdcage Support, Ring-Turned Post, Pa., c.1790, 28 In.
**$2,583**

Skinner Auctioneers & Appraisers

---

**Furniture,** Cellarette, Hepplewhite Style, Mahogany, 6-Sided, Tapered Legs, Inlay, c.1890, 24 In.
**$281**

Garth's Auctioneers & Appraisers

---

**TIP**

*When waxing intricately carved furniture apply paste wax with a stenciling brush. Use a shoe brush to buff the wax.*

---

| | |
|---|---:|
| **Bench,** Regency, Style, Wood Frame, Scroll Arms, 29 x 51 In. | 344 |
| **Bench,** Renaissance Revival, Mahogany, Pierced, Figural Carved, 51 x 57 In. | 1063 |
| **Bench,** Rustic, Hardwood, Stretchers, France, 1800s, 20 x 69 In., Pair | 600 |
| **Bench,** Shaker, Chair Taping, Oak, Maple, Pine, Swiveling Vises, c.1850, 27 x 28 In. | 1416 |
| **Bench,** Shaker, Pine, Diagonal Supports, Cutout Feet, New Lebanon, c.1830, 16 x 48 In. | 3690 |
| **Bench,** Shaped Apron, Bootjack Ends, Gray Paint, 18 x 33 In. | 660 |
| **Bench,** Softwood, Bootjack Ends, Folksy Landscape, 19th Century, 19 x 73 In. | 570 |
| **Bench,** Teak, Slat, Yugoslavia, c.1955, 16 x 72 In. | 438 |
| **Bench,** Thayer Coggin, Platform, Rosewood Top, Black Painted Platform Base, 9 x 106 In. | 960 |
| **Bench,** Victorian, Mahogany, Scrolled Ends, Reeded Legs, John Lamb, c.1875, 54 x 15 In. | 4688 |
| **Bench,** Window, Chippendale Style, Mahogany, Upholstered, Scrolled Arms, 26 x 58 x 21 In. | 2100 |
| **Bench,** Window, Edwardian, Satinwood, Low Openwork Back, Painted, Cane Seat, 22 x 36 In. | 813 |
| **Bench,** Window, George III Style, Mahogany, Inlay, Cylindrical Arms, 27 x 48 In. *illus* | 598 |
| **Bench,** Window, Louis XVI Style, Pickled Fruitwood, Caning, c.1930, 26 x 40 In. | 984 |
| **Bench,** Windsor, Arrow Back, Green Paint, Cut Corner Crest Rail, 37 x 49 x 16 In. | 540 |
| **Bench,** Windsor, Bamboo Turnings, 3-Section Spindle Back, Arms, 66 In. | 1320 |
| **Bench,** Wood, Barley Twist Stretchers, Turned & Cut Legs, Cushion, 19 x 24 In., Pair | 690 |
| **Bench,** Wood, Gray Paint, Bootjack Ends, 1800s, 60 x 11 x 17 In. | 117 |
| **Bin,** Feed, Pine, Painted, Pennsylvania, 1800s, 53 ½ x 41 In. | 467 |
| **Bin,** Feed, Softwood, Yellow, Slant Top, Iron Strap Hinges, Hasp, Bracket Base, 38 x 44 In. | 266 |
| **Bookcase,** Anglo-Colonial Style, Mahogany, Carved, Reeded Surround, Shelves, 89 x 55 In. | 956 |
| **Bookcase,** Art Nouveau, Fruitwood, Open Compartment, Flowers, 2 Glass Doors, 63 x 34 In. | 1599 |
| **Bookcase,** Art Nouveau, Mahogany, Arched, Leaves, Glazed Doors, 75 x 41 In. | 915 |
| **Bookcase,** Arts & Crafts Style, Walnut, Gallery, Diamond Cutouts, 12-Pane Door, 65 x 40 In. | 295 |
| **Bookcase,** Arts & Crafts, 2 Glass Doors, Shelves, Stepped Cornice, c.1910, 60 x 52 In. *illus* | 375 |
| **Bookcase,** Arts & Crafts, Oak, Glass Pane Door, c.1915, 48 x 26 In. | 896 |
| **Bookcase,** Bureau, George III Style, Burl Walnut, Broken Pediment, Doors, 97 x 40 In. | 2440 |
| **Bookcase,** Cabinet, Pine, Ogee Pediment, 3 Paneled Doors, Egg & Dart Border, 89 x 80 In. | 575 |
| **Bookcase,** Corner, Esherick, Poplar, Sculpted, Stained, Painted, c.1954, 78 x 54 In. *illus* | 10625 |
| **Bookcase,** Eastlake, Mahogany, Oak, Doors, Side Panels, 2 Drawers, 63 x 46 In. | 444 |
| **Bookcase,** Ettore Sottsass, Casablanca, Laminates, Memphis, Milano, 1981, 90 In. *illus* | 8750 |
| **Bookcase,** Federal, Mixed Wood, Inlay, 2 Glass Doors, Tambour Doors, c.1805, 78 x 40 In. | 4800 |
| **Bookcase,** G. Stickley, Arts & Crafts, Oak, Gallery Top, 2 Glass Doors, c.1910, 56 x 48 In. | 4800 |
| **Bookcase,** G. Stickley, Arts & Crafts, Through Tenon Construction, 45 x 39 In. | 4484 |
| **Bookcase,** George III Style, Inlaid Mahogany, Molded Cornice, Glazed Doors, 85 x 46 In. | 836 |
| **Bookcase,** George III Style, Mixed Wood, 3 Stepped Shelves, Drawer, c.1890, 5 x 26 In., Pair | 2125 |
| **Bookcase,** George III Style, Regency, Mahogany, Glazed Doors, Drawers, c.1900, 85 x 73 In. | 1968 |
| **Bookcase,** George III, Mahogany, Glazed Doors, 2 Lower Doors, c.1785, 111 x 64 In. *illus* | 4674 |
| **Bookcase,** George III, Mahogany, Inlay, Molded Cornice, Shelves, 1700s | 2988 |
| **Bookcase,** George III, Mahogany, Satinwood, Glass Doors, 3 Lower Doors, 89 x 55 In. *illus* | 2000 |
| **Bookcase,** George IV, Mahogany, 2 Glass Doors, 3 Lower Drawers, c.1830, 88 x 44 In. | 1063 |
| **Bookcase,** Gilt Bronze, Mahogany, 3 Sections, Bird Mounts, 3 Doors, Mask, 59 x 72 In. | 2091 |
| **Bookcase,** Gothic Revival, Bird's-Eye Maple, Arched Gallery, Glazed Doors, 87 x 54 In. | 3198 |
| **Bookcase,** Gothic Revival, Walnut, Crenellated Crest, Inscription, Glazed Doors, 82 x 43 In. | 13145 |
| **Bookcase,** L. & J.G. Stickley, 2 Glass Pane Doors, c.1912, 56 x 52 In. | 3750 |
| **Bookcase,** L. & J.G. Stickley, Oak, Gallery Top, Mullioned Glass Doors, c.1910, 55 x 49 In. | 3198 |
| **Bookcase,** L. & J.G. Stickley, Oak, Open Style, Key & Tenon, Slab Sides, 54 x 34 In. | 1422 |
| **Bookcase,** L. & J.G. Stickley, Oak, Panel Backboards, Key & Tenon, c.1910, 55 x 53 In. | 1185 |
| **Bookcase,** Library, Renaissance, Walnut, 3 Glass Doors, Hart Malone & Co., 117 x 79 In. | 3286 |
| **Bookcase,** Louis Philippe, Rosewood, Molded Cornice, Glazed, Paneled Doors, 70 x 53 In. | 2135 |
| **Bookcase,** Louis XVI Style, Gray Paint, Ribboned Crest, Garland, Open Shelves, 92 x 58 In. | 1845 |
| **Bookcase,** Louis XVI Style, Mahogany, 2 Glass Doors, Shaped Feet, 87 x 50 In. | 1875 |
| **Bookcase,** Mitchell & Rammelsberg, Walnut, Arched Crest & Doors, 1800s, 107 x 48 In. | 1400 |
| **Bookcase,** Mixed Wood, 2 Glass Doors, Drop Drawer, Interior, 3 Drawers, c.1825, 95 x 43 In. | 1380 |
| **Bookcase,** Mummy Case Shape, Composition, Foil Gilt, Red & Black Paint, 75 x 22 In. | 886 |
| **Bookcase,** Neoclassical, Mahogany, Molded Top, 4 Shelves, Fluted Pilasters, 51 x 60 In. | 178 |
| **Bookcase,** Neoclassical, Mahogany, Shell-Carved Crest, Glass Doors, c.1840, 113 x 143 In. | 2460 |
| **Bookcase,** Oak, 2 Doors, 3 Book Spine Shape Drawers, Dutch, 26 x 20 In. | 344 |
| **Bookcase,** Oak, 3 Sections, Early 20th Century, 47 x 35 In. | 420 |
| **Bookcase,** Oak, Gallery, Gargoyle Crest, Glazed Doors, Shelves, Drawers, 78 x 48 In. | 708 |
| **Bookcase,** Open, Edwardian Style, Mahogany Inlay, c.1950, 71 x 44 In. | 307 |
| **Bookcase,** Regency, Walnut, Stand, 2-Sided, 3 Shelves, Saber Legs, Stretcher, 55 x 32 In. | 1560 |
| **Bookcase,** Revolving, Mahogany, Stenciled Danner, 32 In. | 165 |
| **Bookcase,** Risom, 5 Shelves, Label, 1955, 57 x 36 In. | 750 |
| **Bookcase,** Rococo, Mahogany, Molded Cornice, Glazed Doors, Fretwork, 96 x 85 In., Pair | 5185 |
| **Bookcase,** Secretary, Rococo Revival, Cabochon Leaf & Carved Crest, Shelf, 75 x 37 In. | 3198 |

| | |
|---|---|
| **Bookcase,** Stacking, Mahogany, 4 Sections, Glass Panes, 61 x 34 In. | 236 |
| **Bookcase,** Stacking, Oak, Globe-Wernicke Co., 12 x 9 ½ In., 5 Piece | 375 |
| **Bookcase,** Stacking, Quartersawn Oak, 4 Sections, Glass Panes, J.C. Widman & Co., 58 x 34 In. | 236 |
| **Bookcase,** Stickley, Arts & Crafts, Slat Sides, 5 Shelves, Brand, 48 x 36 In. | 531 |
| **Bookrack,** L. & J.G. Stickley, Oak, Open, Slat Sides, 42 x 21 In. | 863 |
| **Bookrack,** Wood, Carved, Owl Ends, Resin Eyes, R. Sachs, Cincinnati Art, 7 x 19 In. | 854 |
| **Bookstand,** Wood, Grain Painted, Yellow, Blue, V-Shape, Scrolled Skirt, 10 x 12 In. | 780 |
| **Bookstand,** Wood, Yellow, Black, Red, Blue Paint, c.1850, 10 x 12 ½ In. | 780 |
| **Bracket,** Chippendale Style, Ho-Ho Birds, Gilt, Composition, c.1950, 17 x 13 In., Pair | 246 |
| **Bracket,** Hardwood, Carved, Birds, Flowers, Leaves, Continental, 15 x 11 ½ In., Pair | 1353 |
| **Bracket,** Venetian Style, Composition, Blackamoor, Multicolor, 16 x 14 In., Pair | 922 |
| **Breakfront,** Biedermeier, Burl Mahogany, Ebonized, Glazed Top, Victor, 87 x 70 In. | 1180 |
| **Breakfront,** Chippendale Style, Mahogany, Mullions, Hickory & White, c.1980, 98 x 78 In... *illus* | 480 |
| **Breakfront,** George III Style, Chinoiserie, Pediment, Doors, Scenes, c.1900, 89 x 78 x 18 In. | 1722 |
| **Breakfront,** Regency, Mahogany, Glass Paned Doors, Panel Doors, Baker Furniture, 78 x 60 In. | 1440 |
| **Buffet A Deux Corps,** Provincial, Molded, Dentil, Frieze, Paneled Doors, c.1860, 97 x 47 In. | 3444 |
| **Buffet,** French Provincial, Deux Corp, 2 Grill Inset Doors, 2 Cupboard Doors, 94 x 52 In. | 1125 |
| **Buffet,** French Provincial, Fruitwood, Banded, Drawers, Cupboard, 38 x 51 In. | 1107 |
| **Buffet,** John Richard, Argente, Mirrored Glass, Painted, Fold-Out Desk, c.1970, 39 x 60 In. | 3690 |
| **Buffet,** Louis XV Style, Cherry, Canted Corners, Drawers, Cupboard Doors, 43 x 66 In. | 1599 |
| **Buffet,** Louis XV Style, Multicolor, Bowed Front, 4 Frieze Drawers, Panels, 42 x 80 In. | 5412 |
| **Buffet,** Louis XV Style, Oak, Fruitwood, 3 Drawers, Cupboard, 40 x 77 In. | 1845 |
| **Buffet,** Louis XV Style, Provincial, Fruitwood, Drawers, Cupboard Doors, 1800s, 37 x 53 In. | 1722 |
| **Buffet,** Louis XV, Fruitwood, 2 Drawers, 2 Doors, Carved Panels, 39 x 57 In. | 2250 |
| **Buffet,** Provincial, Walnut, Fruitwood, Drawers, Diamond Center Panel, 1700s, 42 x 64 In. | 2006 |
| **Bureau,** Biedermeier, Mahogany, Cylinder, Stepped, Roll Top, Block Feet, c.1825, 46 x 44 In. | 1722 |
| **Bureau,** Biedermeier, Mahogany, Roll Top, Pullout Desk, Cupboard, 48 x 40 In. | 738 |
| **Bureau,** Edwardian, Mahogany, Tambour Cylinder, Candle Arms, c.1910, 51 x 54 In. | 4674 |
| **Bureau,** Empire, Cherry, Bird's-Eye Maple, Step Back, 6 Drawers, 48 x 44 In. *illus* | 384 |
| **Bureau,** Federal, Cherry, Bird's-Eye Maple, Beaded Drawers, Elliptical Front, c.1810, 38 x 40 In. | 2091 |
| **Bureau,** Hepplewhite, Mahogany, 5 Drawers, Splayed Feet, England, 44 x 38 In. | 885 |
| **Bureau,** Louis XVI Style, Kingwood, Gilt Bronze, Arched, Candleholders, 48 x 57 In. | 2510 |
| **Bureau,** Mahogany, Bowed, 5 Drawers, Cock-Beaded, Bracket Feet, c.1790, 40 x 42 In. | 443 |
| **Bureau,** Secretary, Drop Front, Mahogany, 9 Drawers, 71 x 23 In. | 875 |
| **Cabinet,** 2 Sliding Doors, Glass Top, Drawers, 43 x 51 In. | 236 |
| **Cabinet,** Art Deco, Calamander, Maple, Serpentine Front, Doors, Inlay, c.1950, 33 x 51 In. | 984 |
| **Cabinet,** Art Nouveau, Mirror Door, Mahogany, 3 Drawers, c.1900, 90 x 57 In. | 5900 |
| **Cabinet,** Art Nouveau, Walnut, Oak, Curved Frame, Leaded Glass, France, 50 x 54 In. *illus* | 885 |
| **Cabinet,** Arts & Crafts, Oak, 2 Panel Doors, Carved Sides, Iron Hardware, Legs, 49 x 61 In. | 563 |
| **Cabinet,** Arts & Crafts, Oak, Metal, Glass, Motto, Shelf, Panel Doors, 69 x 30 In. | 861 |
| **Cabinet,** Baker's, Pine, Possum Belly, 2 Sections, 56 x 48 In. *illus* | 150 |
| **Cabinet,** Bar, Rosewood, Laminate, Brass, 2 Doors, Casters, Denmark, 1960s, 34 x 60 In. | 1152 |
| **Cabinet,** Baroque, Walnut, Carved, Drawer, Door, Bluet Pilasters, Italy, 37 x 29 In. | 2360 |
| **Cabinet,** Biedermeier, Beech, Ebonized Trim, Drawer, Tapered Feet, c.1820, 34 x 18 In. | 920 |
| **Cabinet,** Black Lacquer, 4 Doors, Painted Landscapes, Chinese, c.1930, 22 x 49 In. | 360 |
| **Cabinet,** Bowfront Top, 2 Doors, Painted Women, 1700s Attire, Eng., c.1850, 42 x 42 In. | 2750 |
| **Cabinet,** Burl, Brass Fittings, Chinese, 20 x 21 In. | 120 |
| **Cabinet,** Carved, Painted, Drawers, Doors, Chinese, c.1910, 34 x 34 In. | 472 |
| **Cabinet,** China, Mahogany, 3 Doors, 6 Drawers, Shelves, 85 x 71 In. | 900 |
| **Cabinet,** China, Oak, Curved Glass, Lion's Heads & Paw Feet, c.1890, 64 x 40 In. | 522 |
| **Cabinet,** China, Quartersawn Oak, Bowfront, Mirrored Gallery, Paw Feet, 69 x 39 In. | 266 |
| **Cabinet,** Collector's, Mahogany, Door, Fitted Interior, Brass Bail Handle, 16 x 11 In. | 720 |
| **Cabinet,** Colonial Revival, Oak, 2 Panel Doors, Fitted Interior, c.1790, 49 x 69 In. | 1750 |
| **Cabinet,** Corner, 3 Open Shelves, Door, Man, Woman, Putti Painted, Italy, c.1790, 59 x 20 In. | 1750 |
| **Cabinet,** Corner, Art Nouveau, Chestnut, Carved, Stained Glass, c.1900, 70 x 28 In. *illus* | 649 |
| **Cabinet,** Corner, Cherry, Pine, Glass Door, Drawer, Panel Door, c.1850, 92 x 49 In. | 625 |
| **Cabinet,** Corner, Dutch Style, Inlaid Mahogany, Bronze Mounted, c.1910, 33 x 26 In. | 338 |
| **Cabinet,** Corner, Federal, Walnut, Arched Glass Door, 2 Panel Doors, c.1845, 86 x 41 In. | 2160 |
| **Cabinet,** Corner, Glass Door, Wood Grill, Lower Door, Shelves, England, 71 x 26 In. *illus* | 120 |
| **Cabinet,** Corner, Rococo Style, Marquetry, Arched Glass Door, Curved Door, 77 x 31 In. | 688 |
| **Cabinet,** Corner, Walnut, Carved, Arched Doors, Raised Panels, 3 Shelves, 88 x 48 In. | 9225 |
| **Cabinet,** Corner, Walnut, Marble Top, Curved Front, Fluted Frieze, 2 Panel Doors, 41 x 25 In. | 840 |
| **Cabinet,** Directoire Style, Walnut, Demilune, Inlaid Panel Door, 20 x 14 In. | 240 |
| **Cabinet,** Display, French, 2 Doors, Painted Scene, Gilt Metal Trim, 71 x 43 In. *illus* | 2750 |
| **Cabinet,** Display, French, 4-Leaf Clover Shape, Courting Scene, Shelves, Lighted, 56 x 24 In. | 400 |
| **Cabinet,** Display, French, Flower Baskets, Mirror, Lighted, 2 Sections, c.1875, 86 x 74 In. | 5500 |

**Furniture,** Cellarette, Hepplewhite, Mahogany, Eagle Inlay, Dovetailed, c.1815, 36 x 22 In.
$1,778

James D. Julia Auctioneers

**Furniture,** Cellarette, Regency, Mahogany, Ebonized, Lead-Lined, Casters, c.1810, 21 x 26 In.
$2,032

Neal Auction Co.

**Furniture,** Chair Set, Leon Frost, Lucite, Metal, Upholstery, Lion In Frost, Arms, c.1970, 32 x 22 In., 4
$1,600

Palm Beach Modern Auctions

**Furniture,** Chair, A. Branzi, Beech, Back Becomes Arms, Cassina, 1900s, 30 In. $400

Garth's Auctioneers & Appraisers

**Furniture,** Chair, Aalto, Paimio 41, Birch, Enameled Plywood Seat, Arms, Finland, 1990s, 26 x 33 In. $1,152

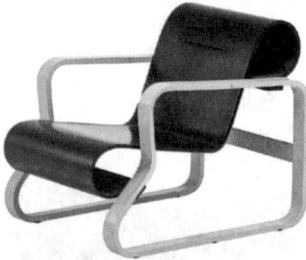

Rago Arts & Auction Center

**TIP**

*Use an electrostatic cloth, the kind used for computer screens, to dust fine furniture. It draws the dust off with little rubbing.*

**Furniture,** Chair, Anglo-Indian, Rosewood, Cane, Carved, Scroll Arms, Rear Paw Feet, c.1810, 34 In. $1,353

Skinner Auctioneers & Appraisers

| | |
|---|---|
| **Cabinet,** Display, French, Mahogany, Bowfront, Glass, Mirror Back, Inlay, 66 x 40 In. .........*illus* | 125 |
| **Cabinet,** Display, Louis XVI Style, Gold Paint, Glass Shelves, France, 55 In. ....................*illus* | 563 |
| **Cabinet,** Display, S Front, Lake Scene, Painted, Glass Shelves, 48 x 39 In. ................................. | 850 |
| **Cabinet,** Display, Woman, Cherubs, Flowers, Ram's Head Columns, Mirror, 72 x 38 In. .............. | 3000 |
| **Cabinet,** Drop Front, Wood, Carved, Continental, 34 x 18 x 60 In. .............................................. | 380 |
| **Cabinet,** Dunbar, Rosewood, Chromed Steel, 3 File Drawers, R. Sprunger, 1970s, 27 x 61 In. ....... | 1750 |
| **Cabinet,** Elm, Lacquer, Gilt Dragon Scene, 2 Doors, Drawers, Chinese, 81 x 50 In. ...............*illus* | 1320 |
| **Cabinet,** Elm, Mortised Construction, Open Shelves, Lacquered, Chinese, c.1910, 35 x 58 In. ..... | 240 |
| **Cabinet,** Empire Style, Yellow, Marble Top, Gilt Bronze, Mahogany, 4 Doors, 35 x 65 In. ............. | 625 |
| **Cabinet,** Enameled Wood, Brass, 3 Doors, Ceramic Medallions, P. Mendoza, 31 x 54 In. .............. | 5625 |
| **Cabinet,** File, Oak, 40 Drawers, 38 x 58 x 16 In. .......................................................................... | 513 |
| **Cabinet,** Filing, Mahogany, 48 Drawers, Index Card Size, Brass Pulls, c.1920, 31 x 53 In. .......... | 1125 |
| **Cabinet,** Filing, Oak, 4 Drawers, Paneled, Raised On Base, 58 x 24 In. ....................................... | 420 |
| **Cabinet,** Filing, Oak, Tambour Front, 15 Drawers, 74 x 14 In. ..................................................... | 1250 |
| **Cabinet,** Filing, Walnut, Roll Top, 12 Drawers, Amberg's Patent Letter File, 35 x 31 In. .............. | 649 |
| **Cabinet,** Folio, Renaissance Revival, Walnut, Felt Top Slide, 4 Drawers, 33 x 39 In. ................... | 2375 |
| **Cabinet,** Frankl, Skyscraper, Wood, Lacquer, Drawers, Mirror, 1920s, 66 x 36 In.................*illus* | 3750 |
| **Cabinet,** Frieze Drawer, 2 Doors, Figural Stiles, Paw Feet, 36 x 27 In. ......................................... | 1464 |
| **Cabinet,** G. Nakashima, Cherry, Sliding Doors, 72 x 20 In. ......................................................... | 10000 |
| **Cabinet,** G. Nakashima, Hanging, Walnut, Sliding Doors, Slats, 18 ½ x 104 In. ........................... | 4650 |
| **Cabinet,** G. Nakashima, Walnut, Padanus Cloth, Sliding Doors, Vertical Slats, 32 x 84 In. .......... | 16250 |
| **Cabinet,** G. Nelson, Drop Front, Fitted Interior, 3 Drawers, Herman Miller, c.1955, 41 x 56 In..... | 1300 |
| **Cabinet,** G. Nelson, Teak, 4 Drawers, Aluminum Knobs, Hairpin Legs, 35 x 34 In., Pair............... | 3660 |
| **Cabinet,** Geoffrey Warner, Cherry, Beech, Folding Doors, 7 Drawers, c.1999, 77 x 43 In. ............ | 2583 |
| **Cabinet,** George I, Green Japanned, Gilt Figures, 2 Mirror Doors, Slant Front, 89 x 39 In. .......... | 28125 |
| **Cabinet,** George III Style, 2 Glass Doors, 2 Scrolled Drawers, 2 Doors, Mirrors, 90 x 52 In. ......... | 1250 |
| **Cabinet,** George III, Mahogany, Line Inlay, Glass Doors, Panel Doors, c.1800, 94 x 45 In. ........... | 3125 |
| **Cabinet,** George III, Mahogany, Trapezoid, Brass Astragal Paired Doors, c.1790, 42 x 34 In. ....... | 1230 |
| **Cabinet,** Georgian Style, Mahogany, Mirrored Back, Drawer, 66 x 22 In., Pair............................ | 270 |
| **Cabinet,** Gio Ponti, Walnut, Brass, 1950s, 30 x 72 In.................................................................. | 1920 |
| **Cabinet,** Gothic Revival, Fretwork, Arched Drops, Drawer, Carved Head Pulls, 60 x 80 In. ......... | 995 |
| **Cabinet,** Gothic Revival, Oak, Iron Mounts, Door, Arch, Leaf Carved, Open Shelf, 55 x 34 In....... | 1000 |
| **Cabinet,** Hanging, Make Do, Pine, Old Red Paint, 6 Shelves, American, 62 x 23 In...................... | 720 |
| **Cabinet,** Hanging, Walnut, Putto On Door, Serpentine Top, Germany, c.1800, 23 x 25 In. ............ | 375 |
| **Cabinet,** Highline, Oak, Stainless Steel Veneer, Jamie Herzlinger, 2000, 30 x 100 In. ................. | 3000 |
| **Cabinet,** J. Adnet, Rosewood, Block Legs, Nickeled Brass Plates, 1940s, 35 x 79 In. ................... | 8125 |
| **Cabinet,** Jacobean Style, Side Columns, Carved Doors, Stretcher Shelf, c.1910, 42 x 54 In........... | 1067 |
| **Cabinet,** Kingwood, Mahogany, Inlay, Gilt, Mounts, France, 1800s, 39 x 21 In. ...................*illus* | 2460 |
| **Cabinet,** Kingwood, Marble Top, Doors, Drawers, Inlay, Millwork, 55 x 24 In. ............................ | 2460 |
| **Cabinet,** Kyoto, Faux Parchment, Lacquered Wood, N.Y., 1970s, 33 x 76 In.................................. | 2750 |
| **Cabinet,** Letter File, Quartersawn Oak, Cardboard Drawers, 1868-1903, 66 x 35 In.............*illus* | 1416 |
| **Cabinet,** Louis XV Style, Doors, Faux Marble Top, Urn Frieze, c.1890, 34 x 47 In. .................*illus* | 1968 |
| **Cabinet,** Louis XVI Style, Hardwood, 2 Crisscross Panel Doors, Stacked, 62 x 30 In. ................... | 350 |
| **Cabinet,** Magazine, Arts & Crafts, Oak, Vertical Slat, 3 Shelves, Splayed Legs, 36 x 18 In. ............ | 300 |
| **Cabinet,** Mahogany, Marquetry, Domed Cornice, Arched Doors, Mother-Of-Pearl, 96 x 74 In. ...... | 5904 |
| **Cabinet,** Map, Maple, 4 Drawers, Chrome Pulls, Streamlined, Wheels, 30 x 37 x 48 In................. | 805 |
| **Cabinet,** McCobb, Rolling, Maple, Drawer, Shelf, Metal Pull, Wheels, 37 x 24 In........................ | 288 |
| **Cabinet,** Mirrored, 2 Doors, Lion Mask Handles, Tapered Legs, 32 x 25 In., Pair........................ | 2750 |
| **Cabinet,** Mixed Wood, Marble Top, Gilt Metal Frieze Drawer, Inlaid Door, c.1985, 33 x 38 In....... | 688 |
| **Cabinet,** Music, Edwardian Style, 2 Doors, Musical Inlay, Medial Shelf, c.1955, 43 x 22 In. ......... | 625 |
| **Cabinet,** Napoleon III, Black Lacquer, Gilt, Brass Mounts, 3 Glass Doors, 42 x 60 In.................... | 813 |
| **Cabinet,** Napoleon III, Bronze Mounted, Inlaid Walnut, Figural, Shaped Top, 44 x 71 In. ........... | 6573 |
| **Cabinet,** Napoleon III, Gilt Metal, Pietra Dura, Ebonized, Lily, Cherry Branches, 48 x 46 In........ | 6250 |
| **Cabinet,** Napoleon III, Mahogany, Carved, Marble, Cupboard Doors, c.1890, 37 x 71 In. ............. | 10762 |
| **Cabinet,** Nelson, Wood Laminate, Herman Miller, 1946, 40 x 56 In. ........................................... | 3125 |
| **Cabinet,** Neoclassical Style, Oak, Marble Top, Pedestal Shape, 38 x 15 In....................................... | 1375 |
| **Cabinet,** Neoclassical, Figured Walnut, Shelves, Stepped Hinged Top, 33 x 29 In. ........................ | 354 |
| **Cabinet,** Neogrecque, Ebonized, Inlay, Pietra Dura, Doors, Gilt, c.1870, 41 x 60 In..............*illus* | 13530 |
| **Cabinet,** Open Center Shelves, Carved Doors, Open Turned Legs, Distressed Paint, 58 x 86 In..... | 338 |
| **Cabinet,** P. Evans, Cityscape, Chrome Plated Steel, Brass, Directional, 1970s, 24 x 24 In............... | 1845 |
| **Cabinet,** Pine, 2 Panel Doors, c.1860, 37 x 41 In. ...................................................................... | 439 |
| **Cabinet,** Pine, Poplar, Mustard Paint, 12 Doors, Metal Slide Latches, 42 x 51 x 15 In.................... | 960 |
| **Cabinet,** Pine, Stripped, 2 Glass Doors, 2 Drawers, Ireland, 1980s, 79 x 56 In. ............................ | 518 |
| **Cabinet,** Portfolio, Rosewood, Carved, Needlepoint Panel, Fretwork, c.1845, 66 x 26 In.............. | 3585 |
| **Cabinet,** Queen Anne, Oyster Veneer, 2 Doors, 4 Beaded Drawers, 65 x 48 In............................. | 6875 |
| **Cabinet,** Regency Style, Demilune Marble Top, Carved Door, 42 x 36 In....................................... | 275 |

F

| | |
|---|---:|
| **Cabinet,** Regency, Mahogany, Mirror Back, Gallery, Drawer, Doors, J. Zonon, 51 x 36 In. | 780 |
| **Cabinet,** Regency, Rosewood, Brass Mounts, 2 Doors, 38 x 55 In. | 1500 |
| **Cabinet,** Renaissance Revival, Walnut, 3 Tiers, Glazed Doors, Fitted Interior, 80 x 40 In. | 584 |
| **Cabinet,** Renaissance Revival, Walnut, Bronze, Marquetry, Paneled Doors, c.1865, 58 x 56 In. | 2706 |
| **Cabinet,** Renaissance Revival, Walnut, Paneled Doors, Fluted Stiles, c.1800, 33 x 35 In. | 1220 |
| **Cabinet,** Revolving, F. Armijo, Walnut, Chip Carved, Sculpted, 1970s, 44 x 17 In. | 4687 |
| **Cabinet,** Revolving, Walnut, Multicolor Pedestal Base, Phil Powell, 1960s, 40 x 35 In. | 8125 |
| **Cabinet,** Richard Neutra, 10 Drawers, Cutout Handles, Overhang Top, 1956, 36 x 50 In.......*illus* | 3750 |
| **Cabinet,** Side-By-Side, Oak, Drop Center, Drawers, Glazed Doors, c.1910, 56 x 48 In. | 413 |
| **Cabinet,** Spice, 16 Drawers, Arched Sides, Galley, Painted, 23 x 21 In. | 1440 |
| **Cabinet,** Spice, Cherry, Metal Pulls, 13 Drawers, 19th Century, 18 ¼ x 15 ½ In. | 306 |
| **Cabinet,** Spice, Hepplewhite, Mahogany, Fitted Interior, Pa., c.1810, 23 x 20 In. | 660 |
| **Cabinet,** Spice, Neoclassical, Walnut, Satinwood, Inlay, 2 Doors, Fitted, c.1850, 11 x 15 In. | 360 |
| **Cabinet,** Spice, Oak, 10 Drawers, 14 x 10 ½ In. | 213 |
| **Cabinet,** Spice, Pine, Dovetailed, 6 Interior Compartments, Sliding Incised Lid, 5 x 13 In. | 180 |
| **Cabinet,** Spice, Poplar, 12 Marked Drawers, Brown Paint, Pa., c.1890, 21 x 13 In. | 1200 |
| **Cabinet,** Spice, Walnut, 7 Drawers, c.1800, 11 x 25 In. | 450 |
| **Cabinet,** Tobacco, Oak, Door Over Door, Shaped Mirror, Old Judge Cigarettes Ad, 62 In.......*illus* | 780 |
| **Cabinet,** Under Stairway, Softwood, Tan & Cream Paint, Paneled Doors, 1800s, 68 x 57 In. | 1180 |
| **Cabinet,** Walnut, Birch, Brass, Glass, Inlaid Fish, E. Busche, Stuttgarter, 1940s, 35 x 68 In. | 4375 |
| **Cabinet,** Walnut, Doors, Shelves, Pullout Board, France, c.1900, 84 x 83 In. ....................*illus* | 1180 |
| **Cabinet,** Walnut, Gilt Bronze, Parquetry, Marble Top, Drawer, Dasson, c.1880, 43 x 17 In. | 6875 |
| **Cabinet,** William IV, Mahogany, Carved Supports, Paneled Doors, c.1810, 43 x 135 In. | 4481 |
| **Cabinet,** William IV, Rosewood, 2 Silk-Lined Doors, c.1835, 36 x 39 In. | 2000 |
| **Cabinet,** Wine, Cherry, 10 Sliding Drawers, 8 Oak Slots, France, c.1890, 57 x 36 In., Pair | 5333 |
| **Cabinet,** Wine, Directoire Style, Burl Walnut Veneer, 37 x 28 In. | 276 |
| **Cabinet,** Wormley, Bleached Mahogany, Walnut, Brass, Dunbar, 1940s, 38 x 70 In. ............*illus* | 4063 |
| **Cabinet,** Wormley, Mahogany, Lacquered, Woven Front, Brass Accents, 30 x 81 In. | 3250 |
| **Cabinet-On-Stand,** Edwardian, Mahogany, Arched Crest, Astragal Glazed Doors, 70 x 29 In. | 549 |
| **Cabinet-On-Stand,** Gilt Wood, Reverse Painted Mirror Door, Coat Of Arms, 63 x 35 In. | 885 |
| **Caddy,** On Stand, Baker Furniture, Georgian Style, Mahogany, Shaped Rim, 26 x 28 In. | 759 |
| **Cafe Set,** Gehry, Table, 5 Chairs, Hat Trick, Signature, 1992, 29 x 40 In. | 5313 |
| **Candle Screen,** Gothic Revival, William IV Day, Patent, Telescopic Shaft, 9 ½ In., Pair | 610 |
| **Candleholder,** Wrought Iron, Adjustable, Tripod Base, Penny Feet, Contemporary, 25 ½ In. | 123 |
| **Candlestand,** 2-Light, Tapered Shaft, Penny Feet, Adjustable, c.1790, 22 x 18 In. | 1610 |
| **Candlestand,** 2-Light, Wood, Adjustable, Crossed Shoe Feet, 1700s, 25 ½ In. | 1140 |
| **Candlestand,** 2-Light, Wrought Iron, Adjustable, Tripod Base, Penny Feet, 44 In. | 1298 |
| **Candlestand,** Cherry, Oval Top, Cabriole Legs, New England, c.1820, 28 x 22 In. | 633 |
| **Candlestand,** Cherry, Oval Top, Scrolled Legs, Conn., c.1810, 28 x 20 In. | 956 |
| **Candlestand,** Cherry, Round Dish Top, Tripod Base, New England, 26 x 14 In. | 660 |
| **Candlestand,** Cherry, Round Top, Shaped Standard, Cabriole Legs, Pa., 1800s, 28 x 15 In. | 185 |
| **Candlestand,** Cherry, Round Top, Spiral Carved Standard, 3 Legs, c.1890, 29 x 13 ½ In. | 150 |
| **Candlestand,** Cherry, Square Top, Inlay, Tripod Base, New England, 26 x 15 In. | 480 |
| **Candlestand,** Chippendale Style, Maple, Tilt Top, Shaped Edge, Splayed Legs, 27 x 22 In. | 156 |
| **Candlestand,** Chippendale, Cherry, Round Top, Late 18th Century, 16 In. | 360 |
| **Candlestand,** Chippendale, Cherry, Shaped Top, 19th Century, 27 In. | 1125 |
| **Candlestand,** Chippendale, Mahogany, Tilt Top, Round, Tripod Base, c.1775, 28 x 21 In. | 1610 |
| **Candlestand,** Chippendale, Mahogany, Tilt Top, Tripod Base, c.1760, 24 x 19 In. | 1750 |
| **Candlestand,** Chippendale, Walnut, Tilt Top, Square, Inlay, Cabriole Legs, 28 In. | 1920 |
| **Candlestand,** Classical Style, Mahogany, Tilt Top, Spiral Twist Urn Standard, 27 x 21 In. | 300 |
| **Candlestand,** Federal, Birch, Round Top, 3-Footed, 19th Century, American, 26 In. | 360 |
| **Candlestand,** Federal, Birch, Spider Legs, 27 x 23 In. | 210 |
| **Candlestand,** Federal, Cherry, Pine, Round Top, Drawer, Snake Feet, 24 In. | 720 |
| **Candlestand,** Federal, Cherry, Tilt Top, Baluster Shaft, Tripod Base, c.1800, 30 In. | 277 |
| **Candlestand,** Federal, Mahogany, Serpentine Top, Carved, Paw Feet, 28 x 19 In. | 1140 |
| **Candlestand,** Federal, Mahogany, Tilt Top, Urn Shaft, 1815-30, 28 In. | 330 |
| **Candlestand,** Federal, Maple, Arched Legs, 29 x 19 In. | 660 |
| **Candlestand,** Federal, Maple, Square Top, Brown, 27 In. | 600 |
| **Candlestand,** Federal, Maple, Tilt Top, Turned Standard, Spider Legs, c.1810, 29 x 21 In. | 240 |
| **Candlestand,** Federal, Painted, Round Top, Gameboard, Incised Tripod Base, 28 x 19 In. | 4688 |
| **Candlestand,** Federal, Tiger Maple, Round Top, Turned Post, Tripod Base, c.1810, 28 x 18 In. | 923 |
| **Candlestand,** Federal, Tiger Maple, Tilt Top, Twist Carved Stem, Tripod Base, c.1800 | 384 |
| **Candlestand,** Federal, Walnut, Round Tilt Top, Barber Pole Inlay, Pa., c.1800, 28 x 10 In. | 600 |
| **Candlestand,** George II, Mahogany, Round Top, Turned Standard, c.1760, 28 x 15 In. | 450 |
| **Candlestand,** Green, Brown Paint, Round, Bulbous Turned Shaft, 4 Arched Feet, 25 x 14 In. | 2375 |
| **Candlestand,** Hepplewhite, Cherry, Line Inlay, Turned Post, c.1800, 29 x 17 x 25 In. | 215 |

**Furniture,** Chair, Arts & Crafts, Morris, Oak, Adjustable, Carved Mark, Roycroft, c.1912, 45 In.
$1,968

Skinner Auctioneers & Appraisers

**Furniture,** Chair, Arts & Crafts, Oak, 3-Slat Back, Carved Flowers, 37 x 16 ½ In.
$431

Cottone Auctions

**Furniture,** Chair, Bugatti, Wood, Copper, Brass, Pewter, Vellum, Upholstered, Arms, c.1900, 66 ½ In.
$8,750

Rago Arts & Auction Center

**Furniture,** Chair, Campeche, Walnut, Leafy Crest, Shaped Arms, Louisiana, c.1850, 40 x 25 In.
$9,261

Neal Auction Co.

**Furniture,** Chair, Cockfighting, Continuous Arm, Vinyl, Nailheads, England, 1800s, 31 In.
$250

Garth's Auctioneers & Appraisers

**Furniture,** Chair, Commode, Caned, Hinged Lid, Wood Seat, c.1920, 38 x 19 In.
$180

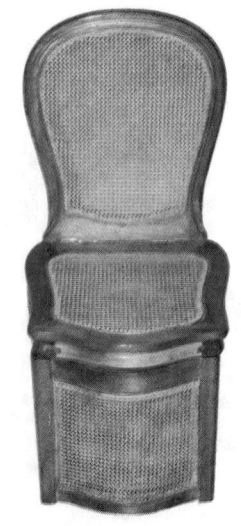

DuMouchelles Art Gallery

| | |
|---|---|
| **Candlestand,** Iron, Tabletop, Revolving, Forged, Arched Snakefoot Legs, 1700s, 23 In. | 1422 |
| **Candlestand,** Mahogany, Tilt Top, c.1850, 18 x 25 In. | 146 |
| **Candlestand,** Maple, Round Tray, 2 Arms, Tripod Base, Adjustable, c.1900, 37 x 16 In. | 115 |
| **Candlestand,** Neoclassical, Tilt Top, Notched, Paw Feet, New York, c.1810, 23 x 29 In. | 146 |
| **Candlestand,** Pine, Ash, Green Paint, Peg Leg, Chamfered Edge Top, Cleat, c.1750, 13 In. | 2133 |
| **Candlestand,** Pine, Maple, Chestnut, Baluster Pedestal, Brown Wash, c.1680, 25 x 14 In. | 2370 |
| **Candlestand,** Pine, Painted, Round 2-Board Top, Turtle Base, 4 Arched Feet, 30 x 16 In. | 2415 |
| **Candlestand,** Queen Anne Style, Mahogany, Tilt Top, Round, Turned Pedestal, 24 x 19 In. | 142 |
| **Candlestand,** Queen Anne, Cherry, Dish Top, N.Y., Round Top, Cabriole Legs, 25 x 15 In. | 180 |
| **Candlestand,** Queen Anne, Mahogany, Tilt Top, Column Pedestal, Pa., c.1760, 29 x 20 In. | 5463 |
| **Candlestand,** Queen Anne, Tiger Maple, Round Top, Tapered Pedestal, c.1790, 27 x 17 In. | 345 |
| **Candlestand,** Queen Anne, Walnut, Round Top, Birdcage Support, Pa., c.1770, 28 x 20 In. | 2880 |
| **Candlestand,** Ratchet, Walnut, Pine, 2 Arms, Screw Stem, 3 Splayed Legs, 40 In. | 1046 |
| **Candlestand,** Salmon Paint, Ring-Turned Support, Tripod Cabriole Legs, 27 x 17 In. | 338 |
| **Candlestand,** Square Top, Cabriole Legs, Snake Feet, Black Paint, New England, 25 x 15 In. | 600 |
| **Candlestand,** Walnut, Adjustable, Tripod Base, Walnut, Pa., 1800s, 37 In. | 523 |
| **Candlestand,** Walnut, Round Top, Barley Twist Standard, c.1850, 30 x 25 In. | 360 |
| **Candlestand,** Walnut, Tilt Top, Birdcage Support, Ring-Turned Post, Pa., c.1790, 28 In. *illus* | 2583 |
| **Candlestand,** Wrought Iron, Adjustable, Double, Round Base, Tripod Base, 16 In. | 443 |
| **Canterbury,** English Style, Rosewood, Turned Uprights, 18 x 20 In. | 210 |
| **Canterbury,** Georgian, Mahogany, Balusters, Turned Spindles, Drawer, c.1810, 21 x 20 In. | 1169 |
| **Canterbury,** Mahogany, 5 Pierced Dividers, Drawer, Ball Finials, 19 x 15 In. | 540 |
| **Canterbury,** Mahogany, Drawer, England, c.1890, 20 x 19 ½ In. | 325 |
| **Canterbury,** Mahogany, Drawer, Turned Legs, England, c.1950, 21 x 20 ½ In. | 125 |
| **Canterbury,** Regency, Mahogany, 4 Compartments, Ring-Turned Legs, 1800s, 27 x 22 In. | 1125 |
| **Canterbury,** Rosewood, 4 Divisions, Drawer, Wood Pulls, Brass Casters, 25 x 24 In. | 1020 |
| **Canterbury,** Sheraton, Rosewood, 3 Compartments, Beaded Drawer, 21 x 20 In. | 840 |
| **Canterbury,** Victorian, Gilt, Black Lacquer, Turned Spindles, Urn Finials, 21 x 24 In. | 250 |
| **Canterbury,** Victorian, Mahogany, 5 Dividers, Turned Legs, 20 In. | 200 |
| **Canterbury,** Victorian, Walnut, 2 Compartments, Openwork Panels, Turned Legs, 18 x 23 In. | 375 |
| **Canterbury,** Wood, Carved, Leaf Decoration On Knees, Handle, Cabriole Legs, 22 x 18 In. | 483 |
| **Case,** Display, Oriental Style, Carved Case, Hinged Glass Door, Mirror Back, 32 x 20 In. | 299 |
| **Cassone,** Multicolor Paint, Hinged Lid, Paneled, Carved Border, Bracket Feet, 35 x 75 In. | 2091 |
| **Cellarette,** Chippendale, Mahogany, Dovetailed, Hinged Lid, Bracket Feet, Va., 17 x 26 In. | 2360 |
| **Cellarette,** Federal, Walnut, Line Inlaid Front, Coastal N.C., 1800s, 30 x 18 In. | 6490 |
| **Cellarette,** George III Style, Mahogany, Brass, Hexagonal, Pierced Brackets, 27 x 19 In. | 750 |
| **Cellarette,** Georgian, Mahogany, Brass Bound, Octagonal Font, Tinned Interior, 19 x 27 In. | 1185 |
| **Cellarette,** Hepplewhite Style, Mahogany, 6-Sided, Tapered Legs, Inlay, c.1890, 24 In. *illus* | 281 |
| **Cellarette,** Hepplewhite, Mahogany, Eagle Inlay, Dovetailed, c.1815, 36 x 22 In. *illus* | 1778 |
| **Cellarette,** On Stand, Federal, Inlaid Mahogany, Lift Top, Shell, Drawer, 1800s, 36 x 21 In. | 6710 |
| **Cellarette,** On Stand, Hepplewhite, Mahogany Inlay, 6 Compartments, c.1800, 25 x 16 In. | 2607 |
| **Cellarette,** On Stand, Mahogany, Tapered Legs, Handles, 1780-1820, 30 x 16 In. | 1080 |
| **Cellarette,** Regency Style, Rosewood, Brass Inlay, Casket Shape, Drawer, 18 x 24 In. | 750 |
| **Cellarette,** Regency, Mahogany, Divided Interior, Raised Pedestal, c.1845, 27 x 24 In. | 345 |
| **Cellarette,** Regency, Mahogany, Ebonized, Lead-Lined, Casters, c.1810, 21 x 26 In. *illus* | 2032 |
| **Cellarette,** Regency, Mahogany, Hinged Lid, Divided Interior, Octagonal, c.1810, 22 x 29 In. | 978 |
| **Cellarette,** Regency, Mahogany, Metal Interior, Lion's Head Handles, c.1810, 22 x 30 In. | 3438 |
| **Cellarette,** Stand, Federal, Walnut, Inlay, Hinged Bottle Case, Stand Drawer, c.1800, 8 x 14 In. | 3105 |
| **Cellarette,** Stand, George III, Mahogany, Brass Fittings, c.1780, 22 ½ x 16 In. | 660 |
| **Chair Set,** Aesthetic Revival, Gilt, Bamboo Turning, Reticulated Back, Stretcher, c.1900, 3 | 369 |
| **Chair Set,** Arne Jacobsen, Lily, Shaped Back, Fritz Hansen, Denmark, 30 In., 6 | 1440 |
| **Chair Set,** Arts & Crafts, Oak, Carved, Upholstered Seat, Carved Leaves, 46 x 20 In., 8 | 1150 |
| **Chair Set,** Arts & Crafts, Oak, Leather Seat & Back, Brass Tacks, Arms, c.1900, 36 In., 8 | 369 |
| **Chair Set,** Baker Furniture, Gov. Winthrop, Black Lacquer, Pierced, Gilt, Cane Seat, 33 In., 6 | 2588 |
| **Chair Set,** Chippendale, Mahogany, Cross-Eyed Owl Splats, Square Legs, Pad Seat, Mass., 6 | 5400 |
| **Chair Set,** Chippendale, Mahogany, Ribbonback, Salesman Sample, 7 ¼ In., 6 | 2962 |
| **Chair Set,** Chrome, Frame, Leather, Miles Van Der Rohe, Knoll, 1970s, 32 x 19 In., 8 | 750 |
| **Chair Set,** Classical Revival, Mahogany, 2 Armchairs, 6 Chairs, c.1900, 39 ½ In., 8 | 1045 |
| **Chair Set,** Contemporary, Suede, Teak, Armed, De La Espada, 32 In., 4 | 430 |
| **Chair Set,** Eames, Soft Pad, Aluminum, Steel, Leather, 5 Wheels, Herman Miller, 33 In., 6 | 4688 |
| **Chair Set,** Fancy, Neoclassical, Painted, Tablet Crest, Beehive, Reticulated Slats, Rush Seat, 8 | 2390 |
| **Chair Set,** Federal, Birch, Mahogany, Carved Crest, Gothic Arch Splats, J. & T. Seymour, 3 | 7500 |
| **Chair Set,** Federal, Mahogany, Carved, Molded Frame, Burl Walnut Backrest, 35 In., 4 | 5310 |
| **Chair Set,** Folding, Chrome Frame, Lucite Seat & Back, Plia, G. Piretti, Italy, 30 In., 4 | 502 |
| **Chair Set,** G. Nakashima, Walnut, Curved Crest, Grass Seat, 27 x 23 In., 6 | 13750 |
| **Chair Set,** G. Stickley, 3 Curved Back Rails, Leather, Brass Tacks, c.1910, 38 In., 4 | 923 |

F

**Furniture,** Chair, Corner, Queen Anne, Maple, Turned Legs, New England, 1800s, 30 In.
$240

Garth's Auctioneers & Appraisers

**Furniture,** Chair, Dan Johnson, Upholstered, Metal, Wood Arms, 1950s, 28 x 30 In., Pair
$3,125

Los Angeles Modern Auctions (LAMA)

**Furniture,** Chair, Finn Juhl, Chieftan, Teak, Leather, Baker Furniture, Denmark, 1970s, 37 x 38 In.
$6,875

Rago Arts & Auction Center

**Furniture,** Chair, Finn Juhl, Niels Vodder, Teak, Leather, Arms, Marked, 1960s, 33 In.
$15,360

Rago Arts & Auction Center

---

**TIP**
*Fifties aluminum chairs and other brushed aluminum can be cleaned with a paste silver polish or a metal cleaner.*

---

**Furniture,** Chair, Finn Juhl, Upholstered, France & Son, Denmark, c.1953, 28 In.
$1,250

Los Angeles Modern Auctions (LAMA)

**Furniture,** Chair, Folding, Walnut, Leather Sling, Arms, Army & Navy Stores Plaque, c.1900
$1,434

Neal Auction Co.

**Furniture,** Chair, Frank Lloyd Wright, Plywood, Meeting House, 1951, 27 x 21 In.
$2,500

Los Angeles Modern Auctions (LAMA)

---

**Furniture,** Chair, G. Nelson, Coconut, Chromed Steel, Upholstered, Herman Miller, 41 In.
$1,280

Rago Arts & Auction Center

**Furniture,** Chair, Gehry, Power Play Club, Maple, Interwoven Strips, Knoll, 1992, 32 x 32 In.
$2,500

Los Angeles Modern Auctions (LAMA)

**Furniture,** Chair, Gondola, Carved, Gilt, Burnished Red Ground, Rotating, Venetian, 1800s
$1,952

Neal Auction Co.

**Furniture,** Chair, Gothic Revival, Walnut, Bobbin-Turned Back, Needlepoint Seat, c.1890, Child's
$239

Neal Auction Co.

**Furniture,** Chair, Gothic Revival, Walnut, Cathedral Window Rondel, Arches, Meeks, 58 In.
$922

New Orleans Auction Galleries, Inc.

**Furniture,** Chair, Hepplewhite, Mahogany, Shieldback, Inlay, Upholstered Seat, Arms, c.1810, 37 In.
$2,520

Garth's Auctioneers & Appraisers

| | |
|---|---:|
| **Chair Set,** George III, Mahogany, Carved, Serpentine Leaf Carved Crest Rail, Splat, c.1790, 4 | 1076 |
| **Chair Set,** George IV, Mahogany, Concave Top Rail, Reeded Stiles, Upholstered, c.1825, 6 | 5000 |
| **Chair Set,** Georgian Style, Mahogany, Carved, Needlepoint Upholstery, 14 | 17925 |
| **Chair Set,** Gothic Revival, Walnut, Carved, Padded Back, Seat, Mask Terminals, 1800s, 4 | 149 |
| **Chair Set,** H. Bertoia, Diamond, Black Enameled Steel Wire, Knoll, 30 In., 4 | 1035 |
| **Chair Set,** Hepplewhite Style, Oval Back, Upholstered Seat, Back, Open Arms, 1900s, 6 | 660 |
| **Chair Set,** Heywood-Wakefield, Dog Bone, Champagne Tone, Orange Cloth Seat, 32 In., 8 | 575 |
| **Chair Set,** Inlaid, Arched Crest, Seat Centering Compass Star, Leaf Tapered Legs, 4 | 1195 |
| **Chair Set,** Iron, Painted, Wings, Stretcher, Ball Finials, Arms, Padded Seat, Back, 4 | 469 |
| **Chair Set,** Jacobean Style, Oak Frame, Upholstered, Turned Legs, Bracket Stretcher, 43 In., 8 | 2082 |
| **Chair Set,** Leaf Pierced Crest, Plain Splat, Padded Seat, Stretcher, Pad Feet, 45 In., 8 | 615 |
| **Chair Set,** Leon Frost, Lucite, Metal, Upholstery, Lion In Frost, Arms, c.1970, 32 x 22 In., 4 *illus* | 1600 |
| **Chair Set,** Limbert, Arts & Crafts, Oak, Leather, Upholstered Seat, c.1910, 37 In., 5 | 1353 |
| **Chair Set,** Louis XVI Style, Fruitwood, Line Carved, Square Back, Leather Upholstery, 4 | 1125 |
| **Chair Set,** Louis XVI Style, Gilt, Padded Back, Fluting, Flower Block Capital, 38 In., 6 | 922 |
| **Chair Set,** Louis XVI, Side, Oval Back, Upholstered Seat, Fluted Legs, c.1920, 37 In., 4 | 1440 |
| **Chair Set,** Lucite, Continuous Back To Arms To Legs, Tufted Seat, C.H. Jones, 29 In., 4 | 531 |
| **Chair Set,** Lucite, Tubular Chrome, Squared, Bucket Seat, Purple Cushions, 30 In., 6 | 590 |
| **Chair Set,** M. Bellini, Cab, Black Leather, Continuous Arm, Cassina, 1970s, 32 In., 4 | 3125 |
| **Chair Set,** Mies Van Der Rohe, Chrome, Suede, Knoll, 32 x 23 In., 8 | 2242 |
| **Chair Set,** Mies Van Der Rohe, Knoll, 31 ½ x 22 ½ In., 8 | 5000 |
| **Chair Set,** Mira Nakashima, Sap Cherry, Curved Crest Rail, 8 Spindles, Arms, 38 In., 8 | 6150 |
| **Chair Set,** Office, C. Pollock, Black Leather, Chrome, Swivel, Knoll, 1900s, 33 x 27 In., 4 | 738 |
| **Chair Set,** P. Evans, Directional, Cityscape, Chromed Steel, Upholstered, Casters, 34 In., 8 | 8125 |
| **Chair Set,** Paint Decorated, Salmon, Flowers, Bootjack Splats, 33 In., 6 | 660 |
| **Chair Set,** Plank Seat, Shaped Back Rail, Flowers, Yellow Paint, J. Swint, Lancaster, 6 | 1800 |
| **Chair Set,** Regency, Rosewood, Oval Backrest, Parcel Gilt, Cane Seat, c.1810, 4 | 6875 |
| **Chair Set,** Renaissance, Oak, Carved, Arched Flowers Crests, Shaped Seat Rails, 1800s, 8 | 1554 |
| **Chair Set,** Sheraton, Mahogany, 1 Armchair, Padded Seat, 8 | 480 |
| **Chair Set,** Tage Frid, Walnut, Mortise & Tenon, Leather Pad Seat, 1956, 32 x 19 In., 8 | 4025 |
| **Chair Set,** Tiger Maple, Rush Seat, Horizontal Slat Back, c.1875, 6 | 900 |
| **Chair Set,** Tulip, Eero Saarinen, Fiberglass, Enameled Aluminum, Knoll, c.1998, 32 In., 4 | 492 |
| **Chair Set,** Wegner, The Chair, Teak, Vinyl, Denmark, 1960s, 30 x 25 In., 8 | 23750 |
| **Chair Set,** Wegner, Wishbone, Oak, Continuous Arm, Woven Seat, 1949, 29 In., 4 | 738 |
| **Chair Set,** Wegner, Wishbone, Oak, Curved Back, Paper Cord Seat, 28 In., 6 | 2500 |
| **Chair Set,** Wicker, Donghia, 1980s, 36 x 19 In., 4 | 688 |
| **Chair Set,** Windsor, Bird's-Eye Maple, Shaped Crest, Inlay, Spindle Back, N.H., 6 | 3900 |
| **Chair Set,** Windsor, Carved Seat, Turned Posts, Scrolling Back Rail, 1800s, 46 In., 7 | 4148 |
| **Chair Set,** Windsor, Fanback, 25 ½ In., 4 | 625 |
| **Chair,** 5-Slat Arched Back, Rush Seat, Delaware River Valley, c.1790, 46 x 23 In. | 127 |
| **Chair,** A. Branzi, Beech, Back Becomes Arms, Cassina, 1900s, 30 In. *illus* | 400 |
| **Chair,** Aalto, Birch Frame, Plywood, Painted, Artek, Finland, 1990s, 26 x 33 In. | 1152 |
| **Chair,** Aalto, Lounge, Birch Bentwood, 1900s, 35 x 24 In. | 120 |
| **Chair,** Aalto, Paimio 41, Birch, Enameled Plywood Seat, Arms, Finland, 1990s, 26 x 33 In. *illus* | 1152 |
| **Chair,** Acadian Walnut, Acorn Finials, Ladder Back, 3 Slats, Woven Seat, 28 In., Child's | 956 |
| **Chair,** Acrylic Legs, Reeded Acrylic Back, Dorothy Draper, 35 In., Pair | 2834 |
| **Chair,** Adam Style, Cane Back, Seat, Turned Legs, Cushion, 38 x 23 In. | 472 |
| **Chair,** Adam Style, Carved Back, Painted Flowers, Black, Cane Seat, Arms, 1800s, 34 x 19 In. | 288 |
| **Chair,** Adam Style, Painted, Scrolled Back, Arms, Vase Shape Splat, Saber Legs, 1900s | 657 |
| **Chair,** Adrian Pearsall, Lounge, Walnut, High, Triangular Back, Kraft, 1960s, 40 x 34 In. | 1216 |
| **Chair,** Aesthetic Revival, Mahogany, Upholstered, Padded Back, Seat, Arms, Casters, c.1890 | 478 |
| **Chair,** Aesthetic Revival, Walnut, Carved Plum Tree Branches, Upholstered, c.1890, Pair | 180 |
| **Chair,** American Gothic Revival, Mahogany, Arched Crest, Openwork, Upholstered, Arms | 594 |
| **Chair,** Anglo-Indian, Rosewood, Cane, Carved, Scroll Arms, Rear Paw Feet, c.1810, 34 In. *illus* | 1353 |
| **Chair,** Art Deco, Green Velvet, Tufted Back, Fringe, c.1930, 35 x 30 x 36 In., Pair | 1250 |
| **Chair,** Art Deco, Palisander Wood Frame, Black Upholstery, Open Arms, c.1935, Pair | 1200 |
| **Chair,** Art Deco, Tassel Trim, 8-In. Fringe Skirt, 33 x 30 In. | 549 |
| **Chair,** Art Nouveau, Curved, Crest, Ribbed Arms Terminals, E. Gaillard, France, c.1900 | 1625 |
| **Chair,** Art Nouveau, Mahogany, Flower Carved, Crest, Upholstered, Straight Arms, c.1910 | 3125 |
| **Chair,** Art Nouveau, Walnut, Oak, Upholstered Seat, c.1900, 32 ½ In. | 531 |
| **Chair,** Arts & Crafts, Ladder Back, Concave, Tenon, Oak, 38 ½ x 21 ½ In., Pair | 300 |
| **Chair,** Arts & Crafts, Morris, Oak, Adjustable, Carved Mark, Roycroft, c.1912, 45 In. *illus* | 1968 |
| **Chair,** Arts & Crafts, Oak, 3-Slat Back, Carved Flowers, 37 x 16 ½ In. *illus* | 431 |
| **Chair,** Baker Furniture, Padded Back, Seat, Carved Legs, Arms, 41 In., Pair | 480 |
| **Chair,** Bamboo, Outswept Arms, Geometric Back, Chinese, 20th Century, 38 In. | 60 |
| **Chair,** Banana, Wicker Enameled Iron, 1980s, 32 x 32 In. | 1280 |

| | |
|---|---|
| **Chair,** Banister Back, Rush Seat, Ebonized, New England, c.1750, 46 x 23 In. | 1500 |
| **Chair,** Banister Back, Shaped Crest Rail, Vase & Ring Turnings, Arms, 1700s, 45 x 17 In. | 584 |
| **Chair,** Barcelona, Chrome, White Leather, 1900s, 31 x 35 In. | 430 |
| **Chair,** Baroque, Mahogany, Scroll Arms, Shaped Legs, Needlepoint Upholstery, 45 In. | 300 |
| **Chair,** Baroque, Walnut, Figural Carved, Putti Carved Crest, Arms, Paw Feet, Italy, 31 x 30 In. | 472 |
| **Chair,** Belter, Rococo, Rosalie, Rosewood, Carved, Laminated, Padded Back, Seat, c.1850 | 1098 |
| **Chair,** Belter, Rosewood, Openwork Carved Frame, Upholstered, c.1860, Pair | 1476 |
| **Chair,** Bergere, Cane Sides, Back, Curved Wood Frame, Closed Arms, Chinese, Pair | 2880 |
| **Chair,** Bergere, Carved Frame, Boxed Seat Cushion, Leather, Closed Arms, 37 In., Pair | 989 |
| **Chair,** Bergere, Empire, Cream Paint, Parcel Gilt, Closed Arms, Upholstered, c.1810 | 1076 |
| **Chair,** Bergere, Louis XV Style, Gilt, Tufted Upholstery, Closed Arms, 36¾ In. | 469 |
| **Chair,** Bergere, Louis XV Style, Oak, Carved, Arched Floral Crest, Closed Arms, Pair | 1195 |
| **Chair,** Bergere, Louis XVI Style, Mahogany, Fluted Legs, Padded Closed Arms, 36 In., Pair | 1230 |
| **Chair,** Bergere, Louis XVI Style, Oval Back, Upholstered, Closed Arms, c.1890, 33 x 32 In. | 350 |
| **Chair,** Bergere, Louis XVI, Upholstered, Fluted Carved Frame, Closed Arms, 33½ In. | 813 |
| **Chair,** Bergere, Restauration, Fruitwood, Padded Back, Carved, Closed Arms, 36 In., Pair | 1476 |
| **Chair,** Biedermeier, Ebonized, Parcel Gilt Shield Crest, Straight Rail, 35 In., Pair | 313 |
| **Chair,** Biedermeier, Fruitwood, Ebonized Splats, Griffins On Crests, 37½ In., Pair | 180 |
| **Chair,** Biedermeier, Satinwood, Carved Dome Crest Rail, Triangular Seat, 35 In., Pair | 750 |
| **Chair,** Black Lacquer, Gilt, Raised Legs, Open Arms, 36½ In., Child's | 125 |
| **Chair,** Black Paint, Rush Seat, Banister Back, Turned Stretcher, Arms, 1700s, 16 x 43 In. | 544 |
| **Chair,** Bugatti, Wood, Copper, Brass, Pewter, Vellum, Upholstered, Arms, c.1900, 66½ In. *illus* | 8750 |
| **Chair,** Campaign, Mahogany, Black Leather, Adjustable, Side Lifts, Folds, Arms, c.1810 | 840 |
| **Chair,** Campeche, Iron, Scroll Backs, Arms, Curule Base, Cushions, 1900s, 31 In., Pair | 360 |
| **Chair,** Campeche, Walnut, Leafy Crest, Shaped Arms, Louisiana, c.1850, 40 x 25 In. *illus* | 9261 |
| **Chair,** Carved, Grotesque Mask, Shaped Rail, Upholstered, Griffin Arms, 53 x 27 In. | 426 |
| **Chair,** Castilian Spanish, Mahogany, Embroidered Back Rails, Scroll Arms, 1600s, 40 In., Pair | 1599 |
| **Chair,** Charles I Style, Walnut, Carved, Shaped Crest Rail, Flat Arms, 50 x 35 In. | 180 |
| **Chair,** Charles X, Birch, Marquetry, Upholstered, Casters, c.1830, 43 x 26 In. | 625 |
| **Chair,** Chippendale Style, Mahogany, Carved Cabriole Leg, Upholstered, Ireland, 40 In. | 875 |
| **Chair,** Chippendale Style, Mahogany, Carved, Serpentine Crest, Splat, Arms, Stretcher | 878 |
| **Chair,** Chippendale Style, Mahogany, Carved, Square Back, Padded Arms | 179 |
| **Chair,** Chippendale Style, Mahogany, Leaf Carved Crest, Pierced Splat, Open Arms, 37 In. | 406 |
| **Chair,** Chippendale Style, Mahogany, Vase Shape Splat, Carved Crest, c.1950, 40 In., Pair | 522 |
| **Chair,** Chippendale, Cherry, Arched, Pierced Slats, Slip Seat, New England, c.1780, 39 In. | 104 |
| **Chair,** Chippendale, Cross-Eyed Owl Splat, Slip Seat, Mass., Pair | 1800 |
| **Chair,** Chippendale, Mahogany, Blind Fretwork Legs, Open Arms, Chinese, c.1790 | 1680 |
| **Chair,** Chippendale, Mahogany, Carved Cabriole Legs, Upholstered, Ireland, 40 x 29 In. | 2500 |
| **Chair,** Chippendale, Mahogany, Carved Ribbonback, Rosettes, Maryland, c.1820, 36 x 17 In. | 633 |
| **Chair,** Chippendale, Mahogany, Carved Splat, Serpentine Crest Rail, Slip Seat, Pair | 240 |
| **Chair,** Chippendale, Mahogany, Cupid's Bow, Shell Crest, Fluted Ears, Diamond Splats, Mass. | 1020 |
| **Chair,** Chippendale, Mahogany, Damask Upholstery, Carved Arms, 40 x 28 In. | 11800 |
| **Chair,** Chippendale, Mahogany, Gothic Splat, Ball & Claw Feet, Arms, John Folwell, c.1770 | 2400 |
| **Chair,** Chippendale, Mahogany, Ladder Back, Pierced Crest Rail, Needlepoint Seat, 39 In. | 711 |
| **Chair,** Chippendale, Mahogany, Ribbonback, Rosettes, Serpentine Apron, Phila., c.1780, Pair | 2952 |
| **Chair,** Chippendale, Mahogany, Shell Carved Crests, Owl-Eye Splat, c.1780, Pair | 1416 |
| **Chair,** Chippendale, Pierced Splat, Leather Seat, Arms, Ball & Claw Feet, c.1800, 41 In. | 1875 |
| **Chair,** Chippendale, River Birch, Square Rail Crest, Pierced Splat, Va., c.1770, 37 x 15 In. | 4888 |
| **Chair,** Chippendale, Tiger Maple, Serpentine Crest Rail, Vase Shape Splat, 38 In. | 948 |
| **Chair,** Chippendale, Walnut, 3 Carved Shells, Ball, Claw Feet, Pa., c.1770 | 984 |
| **Chair,** Chippendale, Walnut, Curved Crest, Spiral Ends, Pierced Splat, Virginia, 1780, 38 In. | 9440 |
| **Chair,** Chippendale, Walnut, Serpentine Crest, Vase Shape Splat, Slip Seat, c.1770, 39 In. | 3321 |
| **Chair,** Chippendale, Walnut, Shaped Crest Rail, Scrolled Ears, Vase Shape Splat, Arms, 41 In. | 14222 |
| **Chair,** Club, Edwardian, Leather, Arched Tufted Back, Padded Arms, Casters, c.1900, Pair | 4880 |
| **Chair,** Club, Fruitwood, Tufted Upholstery, 1950s, 26 x 31 In., Pair | 500 |
| **Chair,** Club, Green Upholstery, Rounded Arms, Mayo, 1957, 34 x 28 In. | 200 |
| **Chair,** Club, Leather, Casters, 29 x 21 In., Pair | 900 |
| **Chair,** Cockfighting, Continuous Arm, Vinyl, Nailheads, England, 1800s, 31 In. *illus* | 250 |
| **Chair,** Commode, Caned, Hinged Lid, Wood Seat, c.1920, 38 x 19 In. *illus* | 180 |
| **Chair,** Commode, Chippendale, Mahogany, Removable Pot Seat, Shaped Splat, c.1780 | 180 |
| **Chair,** Commode, Pine, Cutout Heart, Red Paint, Pa., c.1850, 21 In. | 123 |
| **Chair,** Commode, Wainscot, Oak, Paneled Back, Crest, Wings, 48 In. | 438 |
| **Chair,** Continental, Walnut, Carved, Ram's Head Armrests, Upholstered, 1800s, Pair | 1250 |
| **Chair,** Copacabana, Enameled Iron, Leather, M. Mategot, France, 1950s, 30 In., Pair | 8125 |
| **Chair,** Corner, Chippendale, Fruitwood, Pierced Splats, Scrolled Hand Grip Ends, 32 In. | 354 |
| **Chair,** Corner, Chippendale, Mahogany, Gothic Pierced Splats, Leather Seat, 32 In. | 472 |

**Furniture,** Chair, Hvidt, Birch, Leather Upholstery, Branded, Fritz Hansen, Denmark, 30 x 24 In.
$531

Rago Arts & Auction Center

**Furniture,** Chair, Ico Parisi, Folding, Enameled Steel, Leather, Buckles, c.1950, 28 x 30 In.
$2,500

Rago Arts & Auction Center

**Furniture,** Chair, J. Hoffmann, Bentwood, Leather Upholstery, Button Banding, c.1904, 39 In.
$30,680

Brunk Auctions

**Furniture,** Chair, Jean Prouve, Standard, Shaped Back Legs, Arched Back, c.1950, 32 In.
**$9,063**

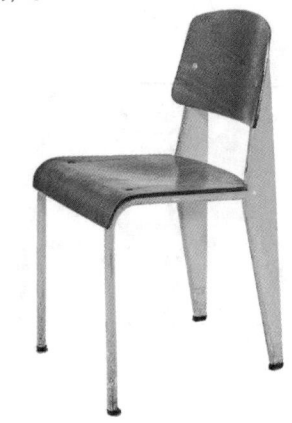

Los Angeles Modern Auctions (LAMA)

**Furniture,** Chair, Ladder Back, 3 Arched Slats, Painted, Splint Seat, Arms, 1700s, 38 In.
**$120**

Garth's Auctioneers & Appraisers

**Furniture,** Chair, Ladder Back, Maple, Green, Turned Finials, Rush Seat, Arms, 1700s, 47 In.
**$780**

Garth's Auctioneers & Appraisers

| | |
|---|---|
| **Chair,** Corner, George II, Mahogany, Line Inlay, Ring & Baluster Supports, 33 x 27 In. | 236 |
| **Chair,** Corner, George III, Mahogany, Heart Splats, Molded Legs, Skirt, 32 In. | 390 |
| **Chair,** Corner, Georgian, Elm, Shaped Splats, Needlepoint Seat, Arms, 1700s | 359 |
| **Chair,** Corner, Jacobean Style, Oak, Triangular Seat, Carved Stretchers, Legs, Arms | 180 |
| **Chair,** Corner, Queen Anne, Maple, Turned Legs, New England, 1800s, 30 In. *illus* | 240 |
| **Chair,** Corner, Queen Anne, Walnut, 2 Wavy Splats, Woven Seat, Pa., c.1750 | 1440 |
| **Chair,** Corner, Queen Anne, Walnut, Continuous Arm, Shaped Splats, c.1760, 18 x 31 In. | 2124 |
| **Chair,** Corner, Rosewood, Rococo Carved, Pierced, Slip Seat, Portugal | 3840 |
| **Chair,** Corner, Roycroft, Mahogany, Leather, Tacks, c.1905, 33 x 21 x 21 In. | 2875 |
| **Chair,** Corner, Shaped Splat, Ring Turned, Stretchers, Brown Paint, 32 x 17 In. | 1107 |
| **Chair,** Corner, Smoking, Chippendale, Mahogany, Carved, Arm Rail, Va., c.1790, 33 In. | 16100 |
| **Chair,** Corner, William & Mary, Turned Baluster & Block Legs, Stretchers, c.1750 | 1320 |
| **Chair,** Corner, William IV Style, Mahogany, Tufted, Round Tapered Legs, Ball Feet, 31 In. | 1230 |
| **Chair,** D. Chadwick, Lounge, Plastic, Upholstered, Herman Miller, 27 x 28 In., Pair | 938 |
| **Chair,** Dan Johnson, Upholstered, Metal, Wood Arms, 1950s, 28 x 30 In., Pair *illus* | 3125 |
| **Chair,** Deck, Folding, Rosewood, Mahogany, Arms, Pierced Adjustable Legs, c.1910, 42 In. | 923 |
| **Chair,** Deck, Rosewood, Vertical Slats, Folding, Pair | 500 |
| **Chair,** DeSede, Leather, Chrome Frame, Stendig, 25 x 35 In., Pair | 4175 |
| **Chair,** Desk, Le Corbusier, LC7, Chrome Frame, Swivel, Cassina, 1928, 28 x 24 In. | 767 |
| **Chair,** Duchesse Brisee, Louis XV, Walnut, Molded Frame, Upholstered, c.1800, 41 x 84 In. | 8750 |
| **Chair,** Dunbar, Lounge, Bleached Mahogany, Upholstered, Barrel Back, 1940s, 27 x 27 In. | 563 |
| **Chair,** Eames, Bikini, Metal Grid, Green Cloth, Wood Legs, Herman Miller, 1951, 32 In. | 443 |
| **Chair,** Eames, Fiberglass, Enameled Steel Frame, Herman Miller, 1940s, 28 x 25 In. | 313 |
| **Chair,** Eames, LAX, Fiberglass, Metal, Rubber, Molded Seat, Glider Feet, c.1954, 26 In. | 615 |
| **Chair,** Eames, Lounge, Ottoman, Rosewood, Tufted, 32 x 33 In. | 2375 |
| **Chair,** Eames, Shell, Pale Yellow, Fiberglass, Zinc Legs, Herman Miller, 31 x 24 In. | 472 |
| **Chair,** Eames, Shell, Wire Base, Sage Leather, Herman Miller, 25 In., Pair | 1770 |
| **Chair,** Eames, Wire Seats, Black Paint, Eiffel Tower Base, c.1955, 32 In., Pair | 492 |
| **Chair,** Eames, Zenith, Fiberglass, Gray, Herman Miller, 1950s, 31 x 23 In., Pair | 460 |
| **Chair,** Eastlake Style, Gentleman's, Lady's, Carved Crest, 1 Armchair, Upholstered, Pair | 120 |
| **Chair,** Edwardian, Mahogany, Arched Crest, Shieldback, Swag, Feathers, Cane Seat, Pair | 875 |
| **Chair,** Eero Aarnio, Ottoman, Rattan, Red Leather Cushions, c.1961, 26 x 33 & 11 x 20 In. | 984 |
| **Chair,** Eero Saarinen, Womb, Upholstered Back, Arms, Seat, Chromed Legs, 36 x 42 In., Pair | 3360 |
| **Chair,** Empire Style, Gilt, Padded Back, Carved Frame, Sphinx Uprights, 1900s, 37 In. | 1476 |
| **Chair,** Empire Style, Mahogany, Gilt Metal Mounts, Lyre Shape Splat, Pad Seat | 625 |
| **Chair,** Empire Style, Mahogany, Ormolu, Upholstered, Open Arms, c.1890, 36 x 23 In. | 480 |
| **Chair,** Empire Style, Wood, Gilt Trim, Ormolu, Sphinx Legs, Griffin, Upholstered, 40 x 28 In. | 518 |
| **Chair,** Empire, Mahogany, Shaped Splat, Needlepoint Seat, c.1840, Pair | 210 |
| **Chair,** Eva, B. Mathsson, Bentwood, Canvas, 33 x 19 In., Pair | 960 |
| **Chair,** F. Albini, Rattan, Round, Concave Seat, 1950s, 15 x 25 In. | 397 |
| **Chair,** F. Kayser, Rosewood, Cushions, Tapered Legs, V. Lenestolfabrikk, Norway, 28 x 28 In. | 625 |
| **Chair,** F. Kayser, Rosewood, Upholstered, Open Arms, c.1960, 28 x 27 In., Pair | 550 |
| **Chair,** Fauteuil, Acanthus Scroll, Stretchers, Open Upholstered Arms, 44 In. | 122 |
| **Chair,** Fauteuil, Carved, Gilt, Arched Crest, Oval Back, Padded Arms, Fluted Legs, Pair | 976 |
| **Chair,** Fauteuil, Empire, Fruitwood, Scrolled Top Rail, Upholstered, c.1810, Pair | 1125 |
| **Chair,** Fauteuil, Henredon, Wood, Carved, Cane Backs, Arms, Seat Cushion, 37 In., Pair | 299 |
| **Chair,** Fauteuil, Louis XIII/XIV Style, Walnut, Carved, Arched Crest, Arms, 42 In., Pair | 1830 |
| **Chair,** Fauteuil, Louis XV Style, Carved, Upholstered, 39 x 25 In., Pair | 687 |
| **Chair,** Fauteuil, Louis XV Style, Cream, Parcel Gilt, Upholstered, Open Arms, 1800s, Pair | 2032 |
| **Chair,** Fauteuil, Louis XV Style, Gilt Frame, Upholstered, Open Arms, c.1945, Pair | 250 |
| **Chair,** Fauteuil, Louis XV Style, Gilt, Carved, Upholstered, Open Arms, Cabriole Legs, Pair | 836 |
| **Chair,** Fauteuil, Louis XVI Style, Square Back, Ribbon Crest, Carved, Leaf Toes, c.1900, 48 In., Pair | 1845 |
| **Chair,** Fauteuil, Louis XV, Upholstered, Padded Arms, Shaped Frame, c.1790, 32 In. | 313 |
| **Chair,** Fauteuil, Louis XVI Style, Fruitwood, Carved Frame, Needlepoint Upholstery, Pair | 500 |
| **Chair,** Fauteuil, Louis XVI Style, Gilt, Domed Back, Seat, Top Shape Feet, c.1890, 38 In., Pair | 1353 |
| **Chair,** Fauteuil, Louis XVI Style, Straight Crest, Upholstered, Open Arms, Pair | 938 |
| **Chair,** Fauteuil, Louis XVI Style, Upholstered, Open Arms, Flute Legs, 35 In., Pair | 861 |
| **Chair,** Fauteuil, Louis XVI Style, Upholstered, Open Arms, Molded Frame, 34 In., Pair | 1230 |
| **Chair,** Fauteuil, Louis XVI, Gilt, Upholstered, Floral Aubusson, Open Arms, c.1910, 37 In. | 399 |
| **Chair,** Fauteuil, Louis-Philippe, Mahogany, Carved, Upholstered, Open Arms, Pair | 1673 |
| **Chair,** Fauteuil, Napoleon III, Ebonized, Medallion Back, Open Arms, 38 In., Pair | 1599 |
| **Chair,** Fauteuil, Regency Style, Walnut, Upholstered, Flat Back, Arms, c.1810, 47 In. | 738 |
| **Chair,** Fauteuil, Regency, Cane Back, Seat, Open Arms, c.1745 | 531 |
| **Chair,** Federal, Mahogany, Arched Crest Rail, 4 Carved Stiles, Boxed Stretcher, Mass., Pair | 480 |
| **Chair,** Federal, Mahogany, Line Inlay, Upholstered, Open Arms, c.1800, 26 x 30 In. | 1920 |
| **Chair,** Federal, Mahogany, Serpentine Crest, Upholstered, Shaped Turned Arms, c.1840 | 6250 |

F

| | | |
|---|---|---|
| **Chair,** Federal, Mahogany, Shieldback, Heart, Oval, Serpentine Seat, 37 In., Pair | | 625 |
| **Chair,** Federal, Urn Slat, Painted, John Seymour Jr., Boston, c.1790, 35 In. | | 944 |
| **Chair,** Finn Juhl, Chieftain, Teak, Oval Tan Leather Pads, c.1949, 36 x 40 In. | | 55000 |
| **Chair,** Finn Juhl, Chieftain, Teak, Leather, Baker Furniture, Denmark, 1970s, 37 x 38 In. | *illus* | 6875 |
| **Chair,** Finn Juhl, Lounge, France & Son, Denmark, 1954, 31 x 28 In., Pair | | 2250 |
| **Chair,** Finn Juhl, Niels Vodder, Teak, Leather, Arms, Marked, 1960s, 33 In. | *illus* | 15360 |
| **Chair,** Finn Juhl, Upholstered, France & Son, Denmark, c.1953, 28 In. | *illus* | 1250 |
| **Chair,** Flaming Urn Finial, Crest, Dragon Brackets, Padded Back, Seat, Allen & Bro., Pair | | 549 |
| **Chair,** Flemish Style, Round Cane Back, Seat, Carved, Arms, Stretcher, 39 x 28 In. | | 178 |
| **Chair,** Folding, Aluminum, Nylon, Multicolor Panels, Adjustable, Italy, 1990s, 32 x 17 In. | | 1000 |
| **Chair,** Folding, Continental, Mahogany, Concave Rail, Leather Seat, Crossed Legs, 1800s | | 500 |
| **Chair,** Folding, Walnut, Leather Sling, Arms, Army & Navy Stores Plaque, c.1900 | *illus* | 1434 |
| **Chair,** Footstool, Woven Back, Seat, Branch Frame, Hickory, 24 x 16 In., Stool, 21 x 19 In. | | 234 |
| **Chair,** Frank Lloyd Wright, Plywood, Meeting House, 1951, 27 x 21 In. | *illus* | 2500 |
| **Chair,** French Provincial, Ladder Back, Oak, Curved Crest & Arms, Rush Seat, 38 In., Pair | | 259 |
| **Chair,** Fruitwood, Cartouche Shape, Cane Back, Cushion Seat, Fluted Legs, Italy, 1900s, Pair | | 956 |
| **Chair,** G. Nakashima, Captain's, Walnut, 28 x 24 In., Pair | | 2750 |
| **Chair,** G. Nakashima, Lounge, Ottoman, Walnut, 2 Piece | | 8750 |
| **Chair,** G. Nakashima, Lounge, Walnut, Slats, Arms, c.1950, 30 x 33 x 30 In., Pair | | 6250 |
| **Chair,** G. Nelson, Coconut, Chromed Steel, Upholstered, Herman Miller, 41 In. | *illus* | 1280 |
| **Chair,** G. Stickley, Oak, Leather Seat, V-Shape Crest, Slat Back, Arms, c.1910, 38 x 26 In. | | 704 |
| **Chair,** G. Stickley, Oak, Spindles, Continuous Arm, Back, Cushion, c.1908, 30 x 28 In. | | 2625 |
| **Chair,** Gehry, Power Play Club, Maple, Interwoven Strips, Knoll, 1992, 32 x 32 In. | *illus* | 2500 |
| **Chair,** George II Style, Mahogany, Leather, Carved Knees, Arms, 1900s, 34 x 33 In., Pair | | 540 |
| **Chair,** George II Style, Walnut, Upholstered, Open Arms, Dolphin Feet, 1800s, 42 x 32 In. | | 5192 |
| **Chair,** George II, Mahogany, Shaped Crest Rail, Pierced Splat, Serpentine Arms, c.1750 | | 1195 |
| **Chair,** George II, Mahogany, Shaped Splat, Slip Seat, c.1760 | | 185 |
| **Chair,** George II, Walnut Frame, Wing, Upholstered, c.1800, 38 x 29 In. | | 1000 |
| **Chair,** George II, Walnut, Pierced Vase Back, Slip Seat, c.1745, 37 x 20 In. | | 275 |
| **Chair,** George III Style, Mahogany, Padded Back, Seat, Square Legs, c.1890, 40 In., 6 | | 1476 |
| **Chair,** George III Style, Mahogany, Padded, c.1890, 41 x 23 In., Pair | | 2250 |
| **Chair,** George III Style, Mahogany, Silk Damask Upholstery, 36 In. | | 2091 |
| **Chair,** George III Style, Satinwood, Cane, Pierced Crest, Painted Flowers, Open Arms, Pair | | 1500 |
| **Chair,** George III, Mahogany, Barrel Back, Green Leather, Brass Tacks, c.1790 | | 1800 |
| **Chair,** George III, Mahogany, Carved, Openwork Splat, Carved Knees, 1700s, 39 In. | | 480 |
| **Chair,** George III, Mahogany, Carved, Shaped Crest, Swags, Pierced Splat, Arms, 1700s | | 1556 |
| **Chair,** George III, Mahogany, Chinese Chippendale, Lattice Back, Arms, Pair | | 4920 |
| **Chair,** George III, Mahogany, Leather, Continuous Curved Back To Arms, c.1800 | | 3438 |
| **Chair,** George III, Mahogany, Upholstered, Arms, 1700s, 39 x 29 In. | | 5625 |
| **Chair,** George III, Mahogany, Upholstered, Open Arms, c.1750, 37 x 27 In. | | 1375 |
| **Chair,** George III, Pakouk Wood, Square Back, Serpentine Crest, Splats, Slip Seat, c.1790 | | 1107 |
| **Chair,** George III, Pierced Trelliswork Back, Cane Seat, Open Arms, Gillows, c.1795, Pair | | 1375 |
| **Chair,** Georgian Style, Mahogany, Carved, Upholstered, Arms, Pair | | 360 |
| **Chair,** Georgian Style, Walnut, Carved, Arms, 40 x 22 In., Pair | | 246 |
| **Chair,** Georgian, Walnut, Arched Crest, Scrolled Acanthus Arms, Trapezoid Seat, 1700s | | 1076 |
| **Chair,** Gilt, Carved Frame, Upholstered, Arms, c.1890, 44 In. | | 813 |
| **Chair,** Gilt, Flowers, Painted Frame, Cabriole Legs, Upholstered, Italy, c.1750, Pair | | 1125 |
| **Chair,** Gio Ponti, Lounge, Walnut, Velvet, Angular Arms, Singer, 1950s, 32 In., Pair | | 5313 |
| **Chair,** Gio Ponti, Polished Steel, 2 Horizontal Slats, Black Plastic Woven Seat, 32 In. | | 384 |
| **Chair,** Gondola, Carved, Gilt, Burnished Red Ground, Rotating, Venetian, 1800s | *illus* | 1952 |
| **Chair,** Gondola, Neoclassical Style, Green Paint, Parcel Gilt, Padded Back, Seat, Pair | | 1845 |
| **Chair,** Gothic Revival, Carved Back, Apron, 42 In., Pair | | 468 |
| **Chair,** Gothic Revival, Mahogany, Arched, Pierced Crest, Stiles, Pad Back, Seat, c.1870 | | 438 |
| **Chair,** Gothic Revival, Oak, Pierced Carved Crest Rail, Pad Seat, 34 In., Pair | | 225 |
| **Chair,** Gothic Revival, Pierced Crest, Stiles, Upholstered, c.1890, 46 In. | | 213 |
| **Chair,** Gothic Revival, Walnut, Bobbin-Turned Back, Needlepoint Seat, c.1890, Child's | *illus* | 239 |
| **Chair,** Gothic Revival, Walnut, Cathedral Window Rondel, Arches, Meeks, 58 In. | *illus* | 922 |
| **Chair,** Gothic Revival, Walnut, Pierced Quatrefoil Crest, Arms, 1800s, 30 x 83 In. | | 717 |
| **Chair,** Grecian Style, Painted, Scrolled Tablet Back, Vase Shape Splat, 32 x 18 In. | | 246 |
| **Chair,** Green Paint, Urn Splat, Tapered Posts, Shaped Back Legs, Arms, Woven Seat, 41 In. | | 119 |
| **Chair,** Gueridon, Neoclassical Style, Bronze Dore, Inset Specimen Marble, 27 x 12 In., Pair | | 4305 |
| **Chair,** H. Bertoia, Diamond, Steel, Black Powder Coated, 1960s, 30 x 34 In., Pair | | 767 |
| **Chair,** H. Olsen, Fried Egg, Rounded Shape, Orange Upholstery, 4 Teak Legs, c.1956, 40 In. | | 4720 |
| **Chair,** Hall, Gothic Revival, Mahogany, Carved, Arched Tracery Back, Spool Turned, c.1890 | | 123 |
| **Chair,** Hepplewhite, Mahogany, Shieldback, Inlay, Upholstered Seat, Arms, c.1810, 37 In. | *illus* | 2520 |
| **Chair,** Herman Miller, Shaped Upholstered Back, Aluminum, Casters, 31 ½ In. | | 240 |

**Furniture,** Chair, Louis XV, Walnut, Cane Back, Seat, Carved, Cabriole Legs, 36 In., Pair
$615

Skinner Auctioneers & Appraisers

**F**

**Furniture,** Chair, Lounge, Milo Baughman, Chrome, Chenille, Thayer Coggin, 1970s, 26 x 28 In., Pair
$4,375

Rago Arts & Auction Center

**Furniture,** Chair, Mahogany, Fruitwood, Branded, Sumner Greene His True Mark, 1911, 40 In.
$32,500

Rago Arts & Auction Center

**TIP**

*Don't move a bed all by yourself unless the bed is on wheels. You may cause stress on one of the bed's joints and break it. Of course, you could also stress your own joints.*

**F**

**Furniture,** Chair, Oak, Cow Horns, Upholstered, Arms, c.1890, 34 x 30 In. $1,652

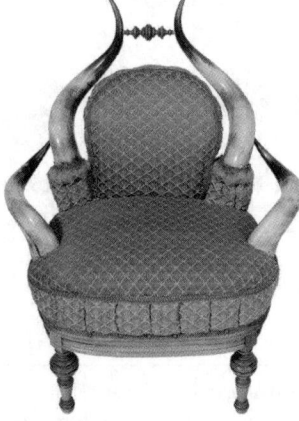

Brunk Auctions

**Furniture,** Chair, P. Evans, Metal, Bronze, Sculptured, Curved Back, 1970s, 32 x 29 In., Pair $21,250

Rago Arts & Auction Center

**Furniture,** Chair, Paulin, Butterfly, Leather, Metal Frame, 1966, 31 x 29 In. $1,125

Los Angeles Modern Auctions (LAMA)

| | |
|---|---:|
| **Chair,** Heywood-Wakefield, Deck, Folding, Adjustable, Label, 55 In., Pair | 819 |
| **Chair,** High Square Back, Open Arms, Wood Frame, Upholstered, France, c.1965, Pair | 840 |
| **Chair,** High Square Back, Wood Frame, Toile Fabric, 20 x 39 In. | 293 |
| **Chair,** Hollywood Regency, Ebonized, Upholstered Crest, Ormolu Mounted, 34 In., Pair | 799 |
| **Chair,** Horseshoe Back, Splat, Carved Dragons, Scrolling, Arms, 1700s, 41 In., Pair | 830 |
| **Chair,** Hvidt, Birch, Leather Upholstery, Branded, Fritz Hansen, Denmark, 30 x 24 In. *illus* | 531 |
| **Chair,** Ico Parisi, Folding, Enameled Steel, Leather, Buckles, c.1950, 28 x 30 In. *illus* | 2500 |
| **Chair,** Invalid, Oak, Cane Back, Leg Supports, Wheels, Adjustable, 1900s | 47 |
| **Chair,** Irish Georgian, Mahogany, Round Back, Center Ball, R. Strahan, Dublin, 36 In., Pair | 1770 |
| **Chair,** J. Donahue, Winnipeg, Mohair, Naugahyde, Oak Arms, Tubular Legs, 1950s, 29 In. | 885 |
| **Chair,** J. Hoffmann, Bentwood, Leather Upholstery, Button Banding, c.1904, 39 In. *illus* | 30680 |
| **Chair,** J. Risley, King, Queen, Enameled Iron, 54-In. King, 50-In. Queen, Pair | 3750 |
| **Chair,** Jean Prouve, Standard, Shaped Back Legs, Arched Back, c.1950, 32 In. *illus* | 9063 |
| **Chair,** Joe, De Pas, D'Urbino, Lomazzi, Baseball Glove, Leather, Casters, c.1970, 33 x 56 In. | 4613 |
| **Chair,** Kem Weber, Chromed Metal, 1900s, 28 x 19 In., Pair | 180 |
| **Chair,** King Tut, Ebonized Frame, Yellow, Black, Brass Panels, Arms, c.1985, 37 x 21 In. | 4063 |
| **Chair,** L. & J.G. Stickley, Morris, Dark Wide Frame, 2 Cushions, Adjustable, 29 x 35 In. | 1053 |
| **Chair,** L. & J.G. Stickley, Morris, Oak, Adjustable Back, Upholstered, Arms, 38 x 34 x 37 In. | 1080 |
| **Chair,** L. & J.G. Stickley, Morris, Open Arms, Leather Cushions, c.1910, 40 x 30 In. | 1625 |
| **Chair,** Ladder Back, 3 Arched Slats, Painted, Splint Seat, Arms, 1700s, 38 In. *illus* | 120 |
| **Chair,** Ladder Back, 5 Arched Slats, Delaware Valley, c.1800 | 369 |
| **Chair,** Ladder Back, Arched Splats, Flame Finials, Arms, Rush Seat, 23 In., Child's | 180 |
| **Chair,** Ladder Back, Maple, Green, Turned Finials, Rush Seat, Arms, 1700s, 47 In. *illus* | 780 |
| **Chair,** Ladder Back, Maple, Splint Seat, Arm | 77 |
| **Chair,** Ladder Back, Mushroom Hand Grips, Carved, Connecticut | 840 |
| **Chair,** Le Corbusier, LC3, Chrome Frame, Leather Upholstery, Arms, 1928, 24 x 39 x 29 In. | 590 |
| **Chair,** Leather, Bentwood, Round, Padded Seat, Back, Arms, Mexico, 36 In., Pair | 180 |
| **Chair,** Leather, Tufted, Slingback, Rolled Arms, Tacks, 41 x 27 ½ In. | 840 |
| **Chair,** Limbert, Arts & Crafts, Oak, Curved, Notched Crest Rail, 3 Slats, c.1912, 36 x 27 In. | 154 |
| **Chair,** Lolling, Chippendale Style, Mahogany, Padded Back, Seat, c.1950, 43 In., Pair | 369 |
| **Chair,** Lolling, Federal Style, Mahogany, Upholstered, Open Scroll Arms, Box Stretcher, Pair | 1080 |
| **Chair,** Louis XIV Style, Walnut, High Back, Scroll Arms, Upholstered, Seat, Pair | 625 |
| **Chair,** Louis XV Style, Carved, Caned, Open Arms, 38 x 23 In., Pair | 354 |
| **Chair,** Louis XV Style, Ebonized, Ormolu Mounted, Shaped Padded Back, Shell Crest, 39 In. | 522 |
| **Chair,** Louis XV Style, Fruitwood, Carved, Serpentine Crest, Tapestry Upholstery | 360 |
| **Chair,** Louis XV Style, Gilt Wood, Carved Frame, Shaped Back, Upholstered, 34 x 19 In. | 98 |
| **Chair,** Louis XV Style, Mahogany, Upholstered, Carved, Painted, Open Arms, c.1955, Pair | 1375 |
| **Chair,** Louis XV Style, Painted, Flower-Carved Frame, Barrel Shape Back, Curved Arms, Pair | 200 |
| **Chair,** Louis XV, Beech, Canes, Carved, Leather Cushion, Open Arms, c.1750 | 1500 |
| **Chair,** Louis XV, Leaf-Carved Frame, Upholstered, Open Arms, 37 In. | 750 |
| **Chair,** Louis XV, Shaped Frame, Green, Upholstered Seat, Open Arms, c.1750, Pair | 2250 |
| **Chair,** Louis XV, Walnut, Cane Back, Seat, Carved, Cabriole Legs, 36 In., Pair *illus* | 615 |
| **Chair,** Louis XVI Style, Gilt, Arched Back, Rose Carved Crest, Arms, Upholstered | 563 |
| **Chair,** Louis XVI Style, Gilt, Floral Crest, Padded Back, Scrolling Arms, 39 In., Pair | 1476 |
| **Chair,** Louis XVI, Ribbon Crest, Upholstered, Carved, Open Arms, France, 42 x 29 In., Pair | 425 |
| **Chair,** Lounge, Milo Baughman, Chrome, Chenille, Thayer Coggin, 1970s, 26 x 28 In., Pair *illus* | 4375 |
| **Chair,** Lounge, Ottoman, Snowshoe, Bent Ash, Woven Sinew, Brass, c.1900, 37 x 42 In. | 474 |
| **Chair,** Lounge, Walnut, Upholstered, Ernst Schwadron, 1950s, 31 x 33 In. | 813 |
| **Chair,** Lounge, Wood, Steel, Red Leather, Ligne Roset, France, 1990s, 32 x 36 In. | 1280 |
| **Chair,** Mademoiselle, White, Tapered Spindle Back, Edsby Verken, Sweden, 1961, 29 In. | 594 |
| **Chair,** Mahogany, Carved, Adelphia, Oval Pierced Back, Arms, Adams, 1700s, 55 In., Pair | 1416 |
| **Chair,** Mahogany, Carved, Pierced Slat Back, Upholstered Seat, c.1790, 38 In., Pair | 431 |
| **Chair,** Mahogany, Fruitwood, Branded, Sumner Greene His True Mark, 1911, 40 In. *illus* | 32500 |
| **Chair,** Mahogany, Inlay, 4 Back Stiles, Upholstered Seat, Reeded Arms, 1800s, 20 x 35 In. | 351 |
| **Chair,** Mahogany, Leather, Carved Legs, Bird's Head Arm Terminals, England, 39 x 31 In. | 700 |
| **Chair,** Mahogany, Panel Crest, Brass Mounts, Upholstered, Open Arms, c.1870, Pair | 625 |
| **Chair,** Mahogany, Serpentine Crest, Shaped Sided, Scrolling Arms, c.1790, 48 x 18 In. | 1230 |
| **Chair,** Marcel Breuer, Wassily, Chrome Steel Frame, Leather, Knoll, 1982, 29 x 31 In., Pair | 1216 |
| **Chair,** McCobb, Lounge, High Back, Squared Arms, Upholstered, 42 x 30 In. | 173 |
| **Chair,** Mies Van Der Rohe, Brno, Polished Steel, Knoll International, 22 ½ x 21 In., Pair | 1353 |
| **Chair,** Milo Baughman, Egg, Upholstered, 2 Cushions, Swivel, Rocks, Thayer Coggin, 46 In. | 826 |
| **Chair,** Milo Baughman, Scoop, Enameled Metal, Vinyl, Broyhill, 1960s, 29 x 26 In., Pair | 1188 |
| **Chair,** Milo Baughman, Steel, Upholstered, Tufted, Continuous Arm, 1970s, 27 x 30 In., Pair | 2125 |
| **Chair,** Milo Baughman, Swivel, Tilt, Thayer Coggin, 1970s, 29 x 48 In. | 1625 |
| **Chair,** Milo Baughman, Swivel, Walnut, Upholstered, Thayer Coggin, 1970s, 24 x 30 In., Pair | 4375 |
| **Chair,** Ming Style, Padded Seat, Shaped Crest Rail, Arms, Huanghuali, Chinese, 40 In., Pair | 1320 |

| | |
|---|---|
| **Chair,** Modern, Birch, Functionalist, Upholstered, Arms, Sweden, 33 In., Pair | 1722 |
| **Chair,** Music, Swivel, Curved Back, Round Seat, Upholstered, Silvertone Stubs, 35 In., Pair | 219 |
| **Chair,** N. Ditzel, Barrel, Stained & Lacquered Beech, Vinyl, Selig, 27 x 30 In., Pair | 6250 |
| **Chair,** Nakashima, Cone Shape, Black Walnut, Hickory, Flat Arms, 36 x 34 In. | 3584 |
| **Chair,** Nakashima, Lounge, Walnut Hickory, Spindle Back, Saddle Seat, 1965, 33 In. | 3075 |
| **Chair,** Neoclassical Style, Brown, Gold Paint, Upholstered, Open Arms, 37 x 29 In. | 354 |
| **Chair,** Neoclassical Style, Mahogany, Gilt, Eagle Head Crest, Back, Carved, Russia, c.1850, Pair.. | 1750 |
| **Chair,** Neoclassical, Duncan Phyfe, Mahogany, Crest, Medallion, Saber Legs, c.1810, Pair | 3884 |
| **Chair,** Neoclassical, Mahogany, Tablet Crest, Scrolled Supports, Saber Legs, c.1810 | 359 |
| **Chair,** O. Borsani, Lounge, Steel, Wool Upholstery, Adjustable, Tecno, 1970s | 1250 |
| **Chair,** Oak, Carved, Barleycorn Twist Construction, Vertical Spindles, Crest, 1900s, 37 In. | 486 |
| **Chair,** Oak, Cow Horns, Upholstered, Arms, c.1890, 34 x 30 In. ...illus | 1652 |
| **Chair,** Oak, Slat Back, Woven Seat, Blue Paint, c.1900, 22 In. | 308 |
| **Chair,** Opium, Hardwood, Carved, Pullout Footstool, Reclining, Chinese, c.1800, 33 x 40 In. | 1534 |
| **Chair,** Ottoman, Art Nouveau, Fruitwood, Curved, Leaf Detail Ormolu Finials, 41 x 27 In. | 1722 |
| **Chair,** Ottoman, Danish Modern, Shaped Crest, Spindle Back, Upholstered, 1960s, 37 In. | 420 |
| **Chair,** Ottoman, H. Bertoia, White Diamond, 39 x 39 x 33 In. | 840 |
| **Chair,** Ottoman, Lexington, Walnut, Upholstered, Arms | 150 |
| **Chair,** Ottoman, Mies Van Der Rohe, Barcelona, Chrome, Leather, Tufted, X-Shape Legs | 854 |
| **Chair,** Ottoman, Papa Bear, Wegner, Wool Upholstery, Teak, c.1960, 38 In. | 9840 |
| **Chair,** Ottoman, Saarinen, Womb, Knoll, 34 ½ x 38 ½ & 17 x 25 In. | 2125 |
| **Chair,** Ottoman, Sleepy Hollow, Tufted Upholstery, Carved Legs, Carl Forslund, 33 x 33 In. | 270 |
| **Chair,** Oval Openwork Roundel Carved Back, Trapezoid Seat, 36 x 25 In., Pair | 200 |
| **Chair,** P. Evans, Metal, Bronze, Sculptured, Curved Back, 1970s, 32 x 29 In., Pair...illus | 21250 |
| **Chair,** P. Jeanneret, Lounge, Teak, Cane, Cushion, 30 x 20 ¼ In., Pair | 8750 |
| **Chair,** Patio, Salterini, Tempestini, Orange Slice, Wrought Iron, Elliptical, Curved, 26 In., Pair.. | 403 |
| **Chair,** Patio, Salterini, Wicker, Petal Shape Back, Iron Frame, Legs, 34 x 34 In., Pair | 1107 |
| **Chair,** Paul Laszlo, Paddle Arms, Loose Cushion, Upholstered, 1946, 32 x 35 In., Pair | 15000 |
| **Chair,** Paul Volther, Steel Frame, Plywood, Foam, Naugahyde, Venni, 35 x 32 In., Pair | 2106 |
| **Chair,** Paulin, Butterfly, Leather, Metal Frame, 1966, 31 x 29 In. ...illus | 1125 |
| **Chair,** Pine, Painted Flowers, Fruit, Bootjack Back, Brown Ground, Pa., c.1890, 21 In. | 677 |
| **Chair,** Plantation, Anglo-Colonial, Hardwood, Scrolled Back, Caned, Stretchers, Pair | 1434 |
| **Chair,** Plantation, Anglo-Indian, Folding, Carved, Cane Seat, Back, c.1890, 56 In. ...illus | 590 |
| **Chair,** Plantation, Teak, Shaped Arms, Woven Diamonds, British Colonial, 37 x 48 In. | 708 |
| **Chair,** Porter's, Louis XVI Style, Fruitwood, Domed Back, Cane, Carved Arms, 1900s, 57 In..illus | 1353 |
| **Chair,** Potty, Georgian, Mahogany, Fluted Column, Hinged, Pullout Footrest, 18 In. | 86 |
| **Chair,** Poul Kjaerholm, PK11, Steel Frame, Ash, Leather, 26 x 25 In. | 1064 |
| **Chair,** Poul Volther, Corona, Steel, Upholstered, Erik Jorgensen, 1964, 38 x 34 In.....illus | 1750 |
| **Chair,** Queen Anne, Black, Vase Shape Back, Turned Stretcher, 1700s, 17 ½ In. | 688 |
| **Chair,** Queen Anne, Cupid Bow's Crest, Urn Splat, Turned Stiles, Rush Seat, N.Y. | 600 |
| **Chair,** Queen Anne, Maple, Carved Crest, Shaped Splat, Rush Seat, Mass., Pair | 1080 |
| **Chair,** Queen Anne, Maple, Openwork Splat, Turned Stretcher, 40 ½ In., Pair | 600 |
| **Chair,** Queen Anne, Maple, Shaped Crest Rail, Urn Splat, Scroll Arms, Spanish Feet, 43 In. | 889 |
| **Chair,** Queen Anne, Walnut, Carved Shell Crest, Slip Seat, Philadelphia, c.1780, 38 x 18 In. | 1875 |
| **Chair,** Queen Anne, Walnut, Pierced Flared Splat, Upholstered Slip Seat, 39 In. ...illus | 384 |
| **Chair,** Queen Anne, Walnut, Pierced Splats, Deep, Scalloped Apron, New England | 720 |
| **Chair,** Queen Anne, Walnut, Pierced, Curled Splat, Shell Carved Knees, Pa., c.1760 | 1560 |
| **Chair,** Ralph Lauren, Club, Tufted Barrel Back, Rolled Arms, Bun Feet | 1680 |
| **Chair,** Ralph Lauren, Wing, Wicker, Allover Braided Cable Pattern, Cushions, 40 In. | 767 |
| **Chair,** Rattan, Seat & Back Upholstered Cushions, Wings Sides, Arms, 1900s, 33 In. | 105 |
| **Chair,** Regency Style, Faux Rosewood, Barrel Back, Painted Splat, c.1945, 35 In., Pair | 938 |
| **Chair,** Regency Style, Mahogany, Cane Seat, Open Arms, X-Stretcher, 33 x 21 In., Pair | 425 |
| **Chair,** Regency Style, Mahogany, Caned, Shaped Back, Padded Arms, Seat, c.1910 | 671 |
| **Chair,** Regency Style, Mahogany, Carved Back Stiles, Oval, Velvet Seat, 38 x 21 In. | 100 |
| **Chair,** Regency, Mahogany, Crest Rail, Medial Rail, 3 Reeded Stiles, c.1800 | 478 |
| **Chair,** Regency, Rosewood, Concave Crest Rail, Reticulated Splat, Carved, c.1810, Pair | 2510 |
| **Chair,** Regency, Round Legs, Open Arms, Gilt, Black Ground, 34 In. | 450 |
| **Chair,** Renaissance Revival, Ornate Crest, Openwork Splat, Pad Seat, Arms, 54 In. | 500 |
| **Chair,** Renaissance Revival, Walnut, Carved Back, Upholstered Seat, Open Arms, 52 In. | 1000 |
| **Chair,** Renaissance Style, Brass, Patinated Metal, Cushion, c.1965, 35 x 23 In., Pair | 1000 |
| **Chair,** Renaissance Style, Walnut Hill, Ebonized, Inlaid, Carved, Italy, c.1850, Pair | 1195 |
| **Chair,** Renaissance Style, Walnut, Carved, c.1865, 46 x 17 In. | 406 |
| **Chair,** Risom, Lounge, Walnut, Gingham Upholstery, 29 In. | 185 |
| **Chair,** Robert Venturi, Sheraton, Knoll International, 1984, 34 x 23 In., Pair.....illus | 4063 |
| **Chair,** Robsjohn-Gibbings, Bleached Walnut, Upholstered, Arms, Widdicomb, 1970s, 35 In. | 750 |
| **Chair,** Rocker, is listed under Rocker in this category. | |

**Furniture,** Chair, Plantation, Anglo-Indian, Folding, Carved, Cane Seat, Back, c.1890, 56 In.
$590

Brunk Auctions

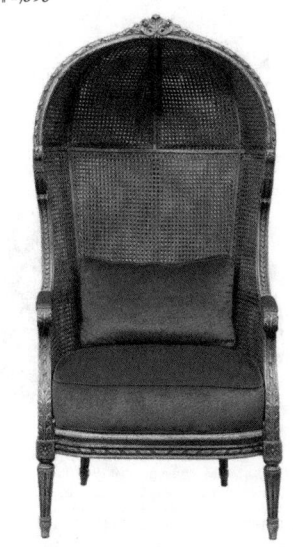

**Furniture,** Chair, Porter's, Louis XVI Style, Fruitwood, Domed Back, Cane, Carved Arms, 1900s, 57 In.
$1,353

New Orleans Auction Galleries, Inc.

**Furniture,** Chair, Poul Volther, Corona, Steel, Upholstered, Erik Jorgensen, 1964, 38 x 34 In.
$1,750

Rago Arts & Auction Center

# FURNITURE

**Furniture,** Chair, Queen Anne, Walnut, Pierced Flared Splat, Upholstered Slip Seat, 39 In.
$384

Conestoga Auction Co., Inc.

**Furniture,** Chair, Robert Venturi, Sheraton, Knoll International, 1984, 34 x 23 In., Pair
$4,063

Los Angeles Modern Auctions (LAMA)

**Furniture,** Chair, Rosewood, Inset Dreamstones, Chinese, c.1800, 37 In., Pair
$1,778

James D. Julia Auctioneers

**Furniture,** Chair, Serpentine Crest, Pierced Splat, Rush Seat, New England, c.1775, 40 In.
$523

Skinner Auctioneers & Appraisers

**Furniture,** Chair, Shaker, Ladder Back, Maple, Woven Seat, Tilters, Canterbury, c.1830, 40 In.
$1,239

Willis Henry Auctions, Inc.

**Furniture,** Chair, Slipper, Gothic Revival, Arched Crest, Horsehair, Needlepoint, c.1850
$538

Neal Auction Co.

**Furniture,** Chair, Spratling, Oak, Leather, Carved, Scroll Arms, c.1940, 32 x 22 In.
$1,563

Heritage Auction Galleries

**Furniture,** Chair, Stool, Arne Jacobsen, Metal, Curved, Egg Shape, Upholstered, 1958, 43 x 32 In.
$9,375

Los Angeles Modern Auctions (LAMA)

**Furniture,** Chair, Tub, Art Nouveau, Majorelle, Gilt, Carved Ferns, c.1900, 32 In.
$590

Brunk Auctions

| | |
|---|---|
| Chair, Rococo, Green, Slip Seat, Cabriole Legs, Italy, c.1860, 42 x 20 In., Pair | 625 |
| Chair, Rohde, Tubular Chrome, 1900s, 29 x 20 In., Pair | 120 |
| Chair, Ron Arad, Mold Formed, Orange, Moroso, c.2000, 28 x 28 In., Pair | 480 |
| Chair, Rosewood, Gilt, Carved Crest & Apron, Fluted Legs, Tufted Upholstery, c.1890, Pair | 240 |
| Chair, Rosewood, Inset Dreamstones, Chinese, c.1800, 37 In., Pair.....................*illus* | 1778 |
| Chair, Roycroft, Mahogany, Leather Seat, High Back, Vertical Splat, c.1908, 44 x 17 In. | 1375 |
| Chair, Roycroft, Meditation, Wood, Leather, Straddle, T-Shape Back, 34 x 24 In. | 2074 |
| Chair, Saarinen, Black Wood Frame, Woven Upholstery, Arms, Knoll, 32 In. | 776 |
| Chair, Salon, Louis XV, Gilt, Early 20th Century, 38 In., Pair | 338 |
| Chair, Sam Maloof, Walnut, Sculpted, Crest & Curved Arms, 1980, 31 x 22 In. | 11875 |
| Chair, Savonarola Style, Walnut, Carved, Ram's Heads, Hoof Feet, c.1910, 39 x 25 In. | 1722 |
| Chair, Scandinavian Modern, Swivel, Aluminum, Upholstered, Carl Klote, 1960s, 27 x 30 In., Pair | 483 |
| Chair, Scissor, Pierre Jeanneret, Birch, Upholstered, Chrome Plated Steel, c.1955, 30 In., Pair | 2829 |
| Chair, Sculptura, Enameled Steel Mesh, Cantilevered, R. Woodward, 1960s, 32 x 33 In., Pair | 938 |
| Chair, Sedan, Painted Courting & Landscape Scenes, Scrolling Leaves, 70 x 31 In. | 3900 |
| Chair, Serpentine Crest, Pierced Splat, Rush Seat, New England, c.1775, 40 In.................*illus* | 523 |
| Chair, Sgabelli, Walnut, Carved, Shaped Backrest & Legs, Octagonal Seat, c.1780, Pair | 813 |
| Chair, Shaker, 3 Slats, Cantaloupe Paint, Woven Seat, Union Village, 40 x 20 In. | 1200 |
| Chair, Shaker, Cherry, Tilt, Rush Seats, Harvard Community, 43¾ In., Pair | 5428 |
| Chair, Shaker, Ladder Back, 3 Arched Slats, Curved Arms, Tape Seat, 28 In. | 480 |
| Chair, Shaker, Ladder Back, Maple, Woven Seat, Tilters, Canterbury, c.1830, 40 In..............*illus* | 1239 |
| Chair, Shaker, Slat Back, Armless, Swivel, Curved Base, Mt. Lebanon | 5040 |
| Chair, Shaker, Tiger Maple, Tilter, 3 Horizontal Slats, Woven Seat, c.1850 | 570 |
| Chair, Shaker, Tilter, 3 Arched Slats, Rush Seat, Red Stain, New Lebanon, c.1830, 14½ In. | 3567 |
| Chair, Shaker, Walnut, 4 Slats, Acorn Finials, Tape Seat, c.1880, 14 In., Pair | 1416 |
| Chair, Sheraton Style, Mahogany, Upholstered, Open Scroll Arms, c.1875, 44 In., Pair | 625 |
| Chair, Sheraton, Mahogany, Padded Back, Seat, Arms, 1800s, 35 In., Pair | 625 |
| Chair, Sheraton, Mahogany, Reeded Arm Supports, Inlaid Crest, Upholstered, 1800s, 39 In. | 240 |
| Chair, Sheraton, Mahogany, Swivel, Upholstered, c.1820 | 600 |
| Chair, Sheraton, Paint Decorated, Rush Seat, Scroll Arms, Stretchers, 1800s, 34 In. | 205 |
| Chair, Sheraton, Painted, Gold Highlights, Swans, Curved Seat Rail, Splat, c.1815, 33 In., Pair | 178 |
| Chair, Slat Back, 6 Arched, Onion Finials, Rush Seat, Turned Legs, Pa., 51 In. | 1280 |
| Chair, Slipper, Aesthetic Revival, Mahogany, Carved, Mother-Of-Pearl, Griffin Stiles, c.1890 | 359 |
| Chair, Slipper, Belter, Rosewood, Pad Seat, Pierced Back, c.1860, 43 x 20 In. | 625 |
| Chair, Slipper, Gothic Revival, Arched Crest, Horsehair, Needlepoint, c.1850.....................*illus* | 538 |
| Chair, Sno-Sho, Ash, Gut, Enameled Steel, Woven Seat, Arms, W.F. Tubbs Co., c.1962 | 1750 |
| Chair, Spanish Style, Wood, Relief Carved, Snake Arms, 1800s, 57 x 29 In. | 250 |
| Chair, Spindle Back, Headrests, Black, 18th Century, 46 In., Pair | 480 |
| Chair, Spratling, Oak, Leather, Carved, Scroll Arms, c.1940, 32 x 22 In.....................*illus* | 1563 |
| Chair, Spring, Rococo, Cast Iron, Centripetal, Head Rest, Arms, American Chair, 1800s | 598 |
| Chair, Stool, Arne Jacobsen, Metal, Curved, Egg Shape, Upholstered, 1958, 43 x 32 In........*illus* | 9375 |
| Chair, Theater, Iron, Wood, 4 Connected Seats, Upholstered, c.1910, 34 x 80 In. | 120 |
| Chair, Throne, Gothic Revival, Oak, Pierced Canopy, Carved Crown, 95 x 30 In. | 540 |
| Chair, Tub, Art Nouveau, Majorelle, Gilt, Carved Ferns, c.1900, 32 In......................*illus* | 590 |
| Chair, Tub, Pine, Red Paint, 1800s, 27 In. | 840 |
| Chair, Tub, Victorian, Curved Open Back, Leather Upholstery, Brass Casters, Pair | 625 |
| Chair, V. Panton, Adjustable Peacock, Bright Red, 7 Cushions, Metal, 15½ In. | 1220 |
| Chair, V. Panton, Molded Polyurethane Foam, Glossy Red Lacquer, Vitra, 1960s, 33 In. | 472 |
| Chair, Van Keppel & Green, Lounge, 2 Ottomans, c.1950 | 500 |
| Chair, Victorian, Balloon Back, Velvet Tufted, 36 x 21 In., Pair | 100 |
| Chair, Victorian, Mahogany, Shaped Back, Open Arms, Spindle Gallery, c.1870, 37 In. | 799 |
| Chair, Victorian, Walnut, Carved, Inlay, Arms, 46 x 27 In......................*illus* | 281 |
| Chair, Wainscot, Oak, Carved Back, Turned Legs, Shoe Feet, Continental, c.1890, 52 In. | 390 |
| Chair, Walnut Frame, Acanthus, Needlepoint, Forest Landscape, France, 43 In. | 1150 |
| Chair, Walnut, Carved, Twisted Legs, Flower, Leaf, 46 x 27 In., Pair | 210 |
| Chair, Walnut, Carved, Upholstered, Inward Curved Arms, c.1940, 42 x 46 In. | 720 |
| Chair, Walnut, High Back, Carved, Needlepoint Upholstery, Continental, 1800s, Pair | 1673 |
| Chair, Walnut, Oak, Fishtail Crest, Wainscot Back, Turned Arm Supports, Pa., c.1720 | 9600 |
| Chair, Walnut, Serpentine Crest, Carved Shell, Pierced Splat, Upholstered Seat, 38 In., Pair | 4920 |
| Chair, Walnut, Shaped Crest, Splat Back, Arm Supports, Padded Seat, Skirt, 1700s, 48 In. | 2714 |
| Chair, Walnut, Shaped, Carved Crest Rail, Upholstered, Cabriole Legs, Open Arms, 35½ In. | 625 |
| Chair, Walnut, Upholstered, Barrel Back, Shaped Arms, Tapered Legs, 28 In., Pair | 246 |
| Chair, Wegner, Sawbuck, Oak, Green Leather Seat & Back, C. Hansen, 1960s, 30 In. | 2250 |
| Chair, Wegner, Swivel, Wood, Casters, Johannes Hansen, Denmark, 1955, 29 In.................*illus* | 17500 |
| Chair, Wegner, Teak, Cord Back, Seat, Tapered Legs, Denmark, 28 x 28 In. | 1625 |
| Chair, Wegner, Valet, Oak, Teak, Sculpted, Leather, J. Hansen, 1960s, 37½ x 20 In. | 10625 |

**Furniture,** Chair, Victorian, Walnut, Carved, Inlay, Arms, 46 x 27 In.
**$281**

Rago Arts & Auction Center

**Furniture,** Chair, Wegner, Swivel, Wood, Casters, Johannes Hansen, Denmark, 1955, 29 In.
**$17,500**

Los Angeles Modern Auctions (LAMA)

**Furniture,** Chair, William & Mary Style, Cane Back, Carved Medallion, Arms, 1800s, 36 In.
**$330**

DuMouchelles Art Gallery

F

**Furniture,** Chair, Windsor, Comb Back, Mixed Wood, 5 Over 7 Spindles, Arms, 1800s, 45 In.
$660

Cowan's Auctions

**Furniture,** Chair, Wing, Roy McMakin, Extended Seat & Arms, 1989, 41 x 37 In.
$3,750

Los Angeles Modern Auctions (LAMA)

**Furniture,** Chair, Writing Arm, Neoclassical, Mahogany, Leather, Drawer, c.1850, 38 In.
$500

Garth's Auctioneers & Appraisers

**Furniture,** Chair-Table, Pine, Rectangular Top Over Bench, Green, 1800s, 30 x 66 In.
$900

Garth's Auctioneers & Appraisers

**Furniture,** Chest, Blanket, Painted, Tombstones, Jonestown, Lebanon Co., Pa., c.1810, 23 x 50 In.
$2,006

Conestoga Auction Co., Inc.

**Furniture,** Chest, Blanket, Walnut, Inlay, Carved, Dovetailed, Till, 2 Drawers, Pa., c.1810, 28 x 49 In.
$984

Skinner Auctioneers & Appraisers

**Furniture,** Chest, Bombe Style, Inlay, Drawers, Hairy Paw Feet, Dutch, c.1900, 35 x 43 In.
$1,375

Rago Arts & Auction Center

**Furniture,** Chest, Campaign, Mahogany, Brass Mounted, Drawers, England, 1900s, 42 x 39 In.
$1,342

Neal Auction Co.

**Furniture,** Chest, Chiffonier, Louis XVI, Mahogany, Brass Gallery, Fluting, Drawers, 59 x 24 In.
$2,337

Skinner Auctioneers & Appraisers

**Furniture,** Chest, Chippendale, Cherry, Drawers, Bracket Feet, New England, 1700s, 34 x 40 In.
$1,128

Rago Arts & Auction Center

| | |
|---|---|
| Chair, Welsh, Spindle Back, Arms, Rush Seat, 1800s, 40 x 16 In. | 345 |
| Chair, William & Mary Style, Cane Back, Carved Medallion, Arms, 1800s, 36 In. .................*illus* | 330 |
| Chair, William & Mary Style, Wood Frame, Arms, Pierced Apron, Needlepoint, 40 x 26 In. | 886 |
| Chair, William & Mary, Black, Heart & Crown, Rush Seat, Arms, Thomas Salmon, c.1735 | 6000 |
| Chair, William & Mary, Ladder Back, Black, Shaped Arms, Turned Legs, Stretchers, c.1750 | 600 |
| Chair, William & Mary, Maple, Banister Back, Rush Seat, Bulbous Stretcher, New Hampshire | 3840 |
| Chair, William & Mary, Oak, 4 Shaped Slats, Turned Stiles, Rush Seat, N.Y., c.1700 | 1968 |
| Chair, William & Mary, Walnut, Pierced Splat, Plank Seat, Square Legs, Pa., c.1740 | 360 |
| Chair, William IV, Mahogany, Back, Arm, Upholstered Seat, Tapered Legs, 35 In. | 1063 |
| Chair, William IV, Mahogany, Oval Back, Painted Shield, Triangle Seat, 35 In. | 875 |
| Chair, Windsor, 6 Spindles, Saddle Seat, Curved Arms, Splayed Legs, Cincinnati, 44 In. | 3240 |
| Chair, Windsor, 7 Spindles, Mixed Wood, Writing Arm, Drawer, 33 In. | 180 |
| Chair, Windsor, 7 Spindles, Saddle Seat, Turned Legs, c.1880, 19 x 37 In. | 117 |
| Chair, Windsor, Arrow Back, Green Paint, Va., c.1850, 24 x 13 In. | 288 |
| Chair, Windsor, Bamboo Turnings, Serpentine Crest Rail, Painted, New England, Pair | 900 |
| Chair, Windsor, Birdcage, 7 Spindles, Bamboo Turnings, 25 In., Child's | 900 |
| Chair, Windsor, Bow Back, Red Paint, c.1800, Pair | 431 |
| Chair, Windsor, Bow Back, Red Paint, c.1820, 18 x 38 In. | 325 |
| Chair, Windsor, Bow Back, Saddle Seat, Splayed Legs, W. MacBride | 600 |
| Chair, Windsor, Captain's, Mahogany, Rounded Crest, Scroll Arms, Spindles, 31 In., Pair | 922 |
| Chair, Windsor, Comb Back, 9 Spindles, Black Paint, Carved Crest, Scroll Arms, 48 In. | 800 |
| Chair, Windsor, Comb Back, Black Paint, Arms, Pa., c.1790 | 2040 |
| Chair, Windsor, Comb Back, Continuous Arm, Saddle Seat, Splayed Legs, c.1800, 42 In. | 748 |
| Chair, Windsor, Comb Back, Mixed Wood, 5 Over 7 Spindles, Arms, 1800s, 45 In. ..........*illus* | 660 |
| Chair, Windsor, Comb Back, Red Paint, Scrolled Ears, Arms, Philadelphia, c.1780 | 1200 |
| Chair, Windsor, Comb Back, Scrolled Crest, Carved Ears, Spindles, Knuckle Arms, New England | 840 |
| Chair, Windsor, Fanback, Arms, 1900s, Pair | 369 |
| Chair, Windsor, Fanback, Black, Shaped Concave Crest, Pine Seat, c.1780, 45 In. | 1837 |
| Chair, Windsor, Fanback, Voluted Ears, Pa., c.1800, Pair | 1140 |
| Chair, Windsor, Fanback, Wavy Back Rail, New England, 1700s, 37 In. | 146 |
| Chair, Windsor, High Spindle Back, Crossed Stretchers, c.1860, 45 In. | 384 |
| Chair, Windsor, Knuckle Arms, Rounded Back, Black Paint, 17 x 40 In. | 322 |
| Chair, Windsor, Low Back, Splayed Legs, Arms, Philadelphia, c.1790 | 738 |
| Chair, Windsor, Low Back, Writing Arm, Drawer, Candle Slide, Black, Pa., c.1780 | 738 |
| Chair, Windsor, Mixed Wood, Pierced Splat, Turned Legs, Arms, 1800s, 44 In. | 450 |
| Chair, Windsor, Mixed Wood, Spindle Back, Arms, Bucks County, c.1820, 34 x 21 In. | 688 |
| Chair, Windsor, Nutting, Sack Back, Mixed Wood, 7 Spindles, Baluster Legs, 46 In. | 750 |
| Chair, Windsor, Oak, Arms, Spindle, Shaped Seat, 32 In. | 313 |
| Chair, Windsor, Oak, Spindle Back, Arched Crest Rail, Arms, 36 In. | 250 |
| Chair, Windsor, Pine, Spindle Back, Plank Seat, 36 In. | 100 |
| Chair, Windsor, Raked Back, Stepped Crest Rail, Bamboo Turnings, Scroll Arms, 35 In. | 153 |
| Chair, Windsor, Rod Back, Square Top, Faux Bamboo, 7 Spindles, Shaped Seat, 34 In. | 120 |
| Chair, Windsor, Rounded Back Frame, Stamped A.D. Allen, c.1840, 19 x 37 In. | 293 |
| Chair, Windsor, Sack Back, 7 Spindles, Continuous Arm, Turned Legs, Pa., 35 In. | 633 |
| Chair, Windsor, Sack Back, Arms, Black Paint, New England, c.1800 | 720 |
| Chair, Windsor, Sack Back, Black Paint, Turned Legs, New York, c.1800, 35 In. | 813 |
| Chair, Windsor, Sack Back, Shaped Arms, 7 Spindles, Saddle Seat, 35 In. | 240 |
| Chair, Windsor, Walnut, Knuckle Arms, Footrest, Curved Back, Pa., c.1790, 44 In. | 360 |
| Chair, Windsor, Writing Arm, Birdcage Back, Tablet Crest Rail, Green, c.1820, 39 In. | 3105 |
| Chair, Wing, Chippendale Style, Mahogany, Butternut Leather, Stretcher Base, c.1950, 43 In. | 875 |
| Chair, Wing, Chippendale, Mahogany, High Back, Leather Upholstery, c.1910, 60 In. | 3000 |
| Chair, Wing, George III Style, Mahogany, Padded Back, Scrolled Arms, c.1910, 45 In., Pair | 984 |
| Chair, Wing, George III Style, Mahogany, Shaped Sides, Outswept Arms, c.1890, 41 In. | 1045 |
| Chair, Wing, Georgian Style, Mahogany, Upholstered, Pair | 563 |
| Chair, Wing, Hepplewhite, Mahogany, Pegged H-Stretcher, Upholstered, c.1800, 42 In. | 492 |
| Chair, Wing, Queen Anne Style, Leather, Arms, Cabriole Legs, c.1910, 49 x 31 In., Pair | 6457 |
| Chair, Wing, Regency, Walnut, Scalloped Sides, Upholstered, Brass Tacks, Arms, c.1790 | 1080 |
| Chair, Wing, Roy McMakin, Extended Seat & Arms, 1989, 41 x 37 In. ..................*illus* | 3750 |
| Chair, Wire, Russell Woodard, Sculptura, Arms, c.1950, Pair | 450 |
| Chair, Wormley, Mahogany, Brown Herringbone Upholstery, Dunbar, 36 In., Pair | 1121 |
| Chair, Writing Arm, Neoclassical, Mahogany, Leather, Drawer, c.1850, 38 In. .............*illus* | 500 |
| Chair, Wrought Iron, Brass, Arms, Grillwork Seat, Upholstered, Cushion, c.1900, 33 x 25 In. | 236 |
| Chair, Yngve Ekstrom, Lounge, Sheepskin, High Back, Arms, Sweden, 39 x 27 In. | 840 |
| Chair, Yoked Crest, Vase Shape Splat, Vase & Ring Turnings, Red Paint, Arms, c.1760, 39 In. | 369 |
| Chair, Rocker, is listed under Rocker in this category. | |
| Chair-Table, Pine, Drawer, Adjustable, 1700s, 27 x 54 In. | 240 |

**Furniture,** Chest, Federal, Tiger Maple, 5 Cock-Beaded Drawers, Dovetailed, Columns, 42 x 43 In.
**$590**

Conestoga Auction Co., Inc.

F

**Furniture,** Chest, Mahogany, Inlaid, Turned Columns, Claw Feet, 20 x 16 x 12 In.
**$4,830**

Cottone Auctions

**Furniture,** Chest, Money, Hardwood, Iron Strapwork, Handles, Chinese, 1800s, 32 x 36 x 15 In.
**$1,500**

Rago Arts & Auction Center

**TIP**

*To hide a scratch on wooden furniture, rub it with a matching shade of shoe polish. A child's wax crayon might also work.*

**Furniture,** Chest, Mule, Pine, 4 Drawers, 2 Faux, Vinegar Decoration, c.1810, 39 x 42 In.
**$1,680**

Garth's Auctioneers & Appraisers

---

**TIP**

*If your dark furniture has a scratch, you can make it less obvious by rubbing half a shelled walnut on it. This will stain the light scratch mark.*

---

**Furniture,** Chest, Mule, Pine, Hinged Lid, Dovetailed Drawer, Painted, Scene, 1800s, 33 x 42 In.
**$720**

Cowan's Auctions

---

**Furniture,** Chest, Neoclassical, Cherry, Apple Burl, Drawers, Paw Feet, c.1830, 55 x 47 In.
**$750**

Garth's Auctioneers & Appraisers

| | |
|---|---:|
| **Chair-Table,** Pine, Oval Top, Drawer, Red Paint, c.1810, 27 x 43 In. | 600 |
| **Chair-Table,** Pine, Rectangular Top Over Bench, Green, 1800s, 30 x 66 In. ...........*illus* | 900 |
| **Chair-Table,** Pine, Red Paint, Shoe Feet, Round Top, c.1750, 27 x 44 In. | 1800 |
| **Chaise Longue,** B. Mathsson, Model T-108, Birch, Laminated Beech, 1943, 36 x 69 In. | 214 |
| **Chaise Longue,** Baroque, Scroll Carved Crest, Cane Seat, Back, Spanish Feet, 40 In. | 900 |
| **Chaise Longue,** Biedermeier, Scrolling Back, Curved Legs, Flowers, 27 x 68 In. | 600 |
| **Chaise Longue,** Contour, Vinyl Upholstery, Lime Green, 64 x 27 In. | 384 |
| **Chaise Longue,** Louis XV Style, Cream Paint, Carved Shell Crest, Barrel Back, 33 x 59 In. | 418 |
| **Chaise Longue,** McCobb, Lacquered Wood, Brass, Upholstered, c.1955, 32 x 51 In. | 3840 |
| **Chest,** 1-Board, 5 Drawers, Turned Feet, c.1830, 14 x 11 In. | 3105 |
| **Chest,** 6-Board, Blue, Flower Urn, Scrolling Vines, Hinged Top, N.Y., c.1810, 19 x 42 In. | 3075 |
| **Chest,** 6-Board, Green, Cutout Ends, New England, c.1810, 26 x 42 In. | 5535 |
| **Chest,** 6-Board, Red Umber, Molded Lift Top, Cutout Bracket Base, 28 x 51 In. | 492 |
| **Chest,** Art Deco, Mahogany, Bowfront, 3 Drawers, Stepped Feet, c.1950, 33 x 19 In. | 95 |
| **Chest,** Art Nouveau, Marquetry, Man With Wood, Sloping Lid, Fluted Pilasters, 26 x 35 In. | 1422 |
| **Chest,** Bachelor's, Mahogany, 4 Drawers, c.1910, 31 ½ In. | 125 |
| **Chest,** Bachelor's, Pine, Serpentine Front, 4 Drawers, Bracket Feet, 1800s, 32 x 36 In. | 938 |
| **Chest,** Baker Furniture, Mahogany, Historic Charleston, 4 Drawers, 33 In. | 840 |
| **Chest,** Biedermeier, Birch, 3 Drawers, 39 x 21 In. | 938 |
| **Chest,** Biedermeier, Satinwood, 4 Drawers, Patinated Inlay, c.1850, 35 x 34 In. | 431 |
| **Chest,** Biedermeier, Walnut, Ebonized Columns, Gilt Blackamoor Capitals, c.1840, 31 x 34 In. | 780 |
| **Chest,** Blanket, Blue Paint, New England, c.1820, 19 x 43 In. | 184 |
| **Chest,** Blanket, Blue, Brown, Triple Tombstone Design, Interior Till, 1800s, 22 x 49 In. | 472 |
| **Chest,** Blanket, Cherry, 6-Board, Dovetailed, Fish Tail Hinges, Till, N.C., c.1825, 19 x 48 In. | 708 |
| **Chest,** Blanket, Cherry, Walnut, Lid, Stenciled Front, Drawer, Ocher Paint, c.1950, 25 x 37 In. | 138 |
| **Chest,** Blanket, Chestnut, Pie Board Top, Interior Till, Iron Strap Hinges, 1700s, 23 x 51 In. | 649 |
| **Chest,** Blanket, Chippendale, Pine, 3 Lower Drawers, Chevron Decoration, 31 x 50 In. | 5520 |
| **Chest,** Blanket, Chippendale, Pine, Iron Strap Hinges, Dovetail, c.1800, 28 x 50 x 20 In. | 1652 |
| **Chest,** Blanket, Chippendale, Tiger Maple, 3-Drawer Base, Pa., c.1800, 22 x 54 In. | 660 |
| **Chest,** Blanket, Chippendale, Walnut, Hinged Lid, 3 Drawers, Bracket Feet, c.1775, 48 In. | 1080 |
| **Chest,** Blanket, Chippendale, Walnut, Lift Top, Bracket Feet, c.1800, 26 ½ x 48 In. | 840 |
| **Chest,** Blanket, Chippendale, Walnut, Pine, Bracket Base, Shenandoah Valley, c.1810, 15 x 24 In. | 1265 |
| **Chest,** Blanket, Double Tombstone Panels, Breadboard Top, Ball Feet, Green, 22 x 52 In. | 593 |
| **Chest,** Blanket, Esherick, Figured Walnut, Poplar, Leather, Brass, 24 x 48 x 16 In. | 31250 |
| **Chest,** Blanket, Federal, Cherry, Candle Box, Serpentine Skirt, 43 x 19 In. | 458 |
| **Chest,** Blanket, Federal, Walnut, Inlaid, Star In Shaped Reserves, Maryland, 26 x 52 In. | 625 |
| **Chest,** Blanket, Federal, Walnut, Inlaid, Wrought Iron Hinges, Piedmont, 24 x 46 In. | 531 |
| **Chest,** Blanket, George I, Pine, Recessed Panels, 2 Drawers, Bun Feet, c.1730, 31 x 47 In. | 1200 |
| **Chest,** Blanket, Grain Painted, Inner Till, New England, 23 x 42 In. | 938 |
| **Chest,** Blanket, Grain Painted, Turned Feet, 1800s, 26 x 50 In. | 406 |
| **Chest,** Blanket, Hinged Top, 3 Drawers, Green Paint, Pa., c.1890, 26 x 52 In. | 1188 |
| **Chest,** Blanket, James Adams Anno Domus 1800, Chinese Elders, Scandinavia, 16 x 28 In. | 308 |
| **Chest,** Blanket, Lehn, Painted, Portraits, Flowers, Hinge Lid, Base Molding, Feet, Miniature | 1534 |
| **Chest,** Blanket, Lift Top, 2 Drawers, Bracket Feet, Grain Painted, New England, 40 x 42 In. | 3000 |
| **Chest,** Blanket, Lift Top, 2 Drawers, Sponge Painted, Pennsylvania, c.1850, 30 x 48 In. | 510 |
| **Chest,** Blanket, Lift Top, Bracket Feet, Red Umber, Fruit Trees, 6-Board, 24 x 42 In. | 5843 |
| **Chest,** Blanket, Lift Top, Green Paint, Splayed, Bootjack Ends, 48 In. | 720 |
| **Chest,** Blanket, Lift Top, Painted Vines, 2 Drawers, Bun Feet, Mass., c.1650, 42 x 39 In. | 938 |
| **Chest,** Blanket, Maple, Single Board Top, Bootjack Legs, New England, 23 x 46 In. | 210 |
| **Chest,** Blanket, Painted, Green, Stippled, Arched Reserves, Vases Of Flowers, 24 x 46 In. | 3250 |
| **Chest,** Blanket, Painted, Landscape, Blue Ground, T.E.H. 1834, Hinged, Ohio, 25 x 46 In. | 1375 |
| **Chest,** Blanket, Painted, Rows Of Waves, Arched Sides, Shaped Apron, 19 x 31 x 13 In. | 1200 |
| **Chest,** Blanket, Painted, Strap Hinges, Flower Panels, Carved, 1794, 37 x 60 In. | 1375 |
| **Chest,** Blanket, Painted, Tombstones, Jonestown, Lebanon Co., Pa., c.1810, 23 x 50 In. ....*illus* | 2006 |
| **Chest,** Blanket, Pine, 2 Drawers, 2 False Drawers, Snipe Hinges, Turnip Feet, 39 x 34 In. | 360 |
| **Chest,** Blanket, Pine, 6-Board, Painted, Medallions, Birds, Strap Hinges, 1823, 24 x 48 In. | 708 |
| **Chest,** Blanket, Pine, 6-Board, Red Paint, Bootjack Ends, 1814, 23 x 39 In. | 600 |
| **Chest,** Blanket, Pine, 6-Board, Teal Paint, Bracket Feet, Hudson Valley, 20 x 40 In. | 660 |
| **Chest,** Blanket, Pine, Ball Feet, Ochre Paint, Pa., c.1860, 22 x 44 In. | 240 |
| **Chest,** Blanket, Pine, Breadboard Ends, 2 Low Drawers, Fish Tail Hinges, N.C., 25 x 60 In. | 649 |
| **Chest,** Blanket, Pine, Dovetailed, Graining, Strap Hinges, Painted, CFI, 1819, 26 x 49 In. | 300 |
| **Chest,** Blanket, Pine, Dovetailed, Green, Yellow, Horse, House, Trees, 10 ½ x 17 ½ In. | 1063 |
| **Chest,** Blanket, Pine, Flower, Leaf Painted Panels, Red Ground, c.1830, 27 x 47 In. | 2300 |
| **Chest,** Blanket, Pine, Green Paint, Drawer, Lift Top, New England, c.1830, 36 x 42 In. | 510 |
| **Chest,** Blanket, Pine, Iron Side Handles, Base Molding, Blue Paint, c.1850, 43 x 20 In. | 259 |
| **Chest,** Blanket, Pine, Iron Strap Hinges, Painted, Pa., c.1800, 20 x 51 In. | 518 |

| | |
|---|---|
| **Chest,** Blanket, Pine, Lift Top, Bun Feet, Yellow, Green Paint, c.1830, 25 x 31 In. | 7475 |
| **Chest,** Blanket, Pine, Lift Top, Painted Flowers, Black Ground, Continental, 1873, 30 x 46 In. | 270 |
| **Chest,** Blanket, Pine, Nailed, Brown, American, 18th Century, 41 x 21 In. | 188 |
| **Chest,** Blanket, Pine, Nailed, Turned Feet, Yellow, Miniature | 375 |
| **Chest,** Blanket, Pine, Orange, Yellow Sponged Paint, Pa., c.1835, 26 x 39 In. | 2400 |
| **Chest,** Blanket, Pine, Painted Ground, Flower Baskets, Cartouches, Bracket Feet, 20 x 49 In. | 240 |
| **Chest,** Blanket, Pine, Painted Panels, Man With Fire Hook, Flowers, 18 x 43 In. | 563 |
| **Chest,** Blanket, Pine, Paneled, Shoe Feet, Blue, 25 x 52 In. | 360 |
| **Chest,** Blanket, Pine, Poplar, Inset Tombstone Panels, Shaped Skirt, 28 x 47 In. | 1840 |
| **Chest,** Blanket, Pine, Poplar, Red Paint, Black Diagonal Stripes, Lift Top, 24 x 43 In. | 1380 |
| **Chest,** Blanket, Pine, Raised Panels, Green Paint, Signed G.F., M.G., Va., 1852, 25 x 40 In. | 5750 |
| **Chest,** Blanket, Pine, Salmon Paint, Iron Strap Hinges, c.1800, 27 x 47 In. | 360 |
| **Chest,** Blanket, Pine, Sponge Painted, Pa., c.1830, 27 x 51 In. | 748 |
| **Chest,** Blanket, Pine, Stenciled Flowers, Red Ground, Pa., c.1840, 13 x 15 In. | 1920 |
| **Chest,** Blanket, Pine, Walnut, Red Paint, c.1820, 23 x 45 In. | 115 |
| **Chest,** Blanket, Poplar, Dovetailed, Hinged Lid, Turned Feet, 9 ½ x 16 ¾ In. | 570 |
| **Chest,** Blanket, Poplar, Dovetailed, Red, Stencils, Leaves, Yellow, 25 x 44 ½ In. | 1200 |
| **Chest,** Blanket, Poplar, Faux Mahogany Graining, Stencil, J.F., 1853, 24 x 43 In. | 720 |
| **Chest,** Blanket, Poplar, Grain Painted, Pa., c.1850, 26 x 42 In. | 500 |
| **Chest,** Blanket, Poplar, Hinged Lid, 2 Drawers, Painted, New England, 1800s, Miniature | 374 |
| **Chest,** Blanket, Poplar, Hinged Lid, Bracket Base, Scrolled, Mid-Atlantic, c.1820, Miniature | 748 |
| **Chest,** Blanket, Poplar, Nailed, Molded Lid, Blue, American, 24 x 45 In. | 1063 |
| **Chest,** Blanket, Poplar, Painted, 2 Drawers, M.W. 1860, Soap Hollow, Pa., 29 x 50 In. | 1440 |
| **Chest,** Blanket, Poplar, Sponge Painted, Turned Feet, Pa., 23 ¾ x 42 In. | 570 |
| **Chest,** Blanket, Poplar, Tree, Riders, Horses, Red Grain Painted, c.1820, 27 x 47 In. | 5904 |
| **Chest,** Blanket, Poplar, Yellow Sponge Paint, Pa., c.1850, 24 x 45 In. | 420 |
| **Chest,** Blanket, Queen Anne, Lift Top, 2 Drawers, Scalloped Apron, New England, 48 x 39 In. | 420 |
| **Chest,** Blanket, Queen Anne, Tiger Maple, Drawers, Hinged Top, Bracket Feet, 38 x 43 In. | 1440 |
| **Chest,** Blanket, Red Paint, Snipe Hinges, Scalloped Apron, c.1780, 43 x 22 In. | 351 |
| **Chest,** Blanket, Red, Ocher Black, Grain Painted, 19 x 39 In. | 1200 |
| **Chest,** Blanket, Shaker, Cherry, Pine, Lift Top, Beaded Drawer, Glass Knobs, 28 x 41 In. | 1680 |
| **Chest,** Blanket, Sheraton, Softwood, Mahantongo Valley Style, D. Ellinger, 21 x 32 x 19 In. | 2950 |
| **Chest,** Blanket, Tulips, Painted Panels, Blue, Bracket Feet, Germany, c.1800, 31 x 51 In. | 1000 |
| **Chest,** Blanket, Walnut, 4 Raised Panels, Reeded Trim, Turned Feet, Va., c.1830, 31 x 43 In. | 649 |
| **Chest,** Blanket, Walnut, Inlay, Carved, Dovetailed, Till, 2 Drawers, Pa., c.1810, 28 x 49 In....*illus* | 984 |
| **Chest,** Blanket, Walnut, Lift Top, Pa., c.1800, 27 x 49 In. | 738 |
| **Chest,** Blanket, Walnut, Painted, Blue, Bowtie Decoration, Dovetailed, Till, 28 x 49 In. | 1680 |
| **Chest,** Blanket, White Pine, Lift Top, Drawer, Cupboard Door, New England, 32 x 30 In. | 148 |
| **Chest,** Blanket, William & Mary, Bun Feet, Pa., c.1730, 23 x 48 In. | 600 |
| **Chest,** Blanket, William & Mary, Maple, 2 Drawers, Well, Ball Feet, 41 x 38 In. | 1200 |
| **Chest,** Blanket, William & Mary, Maple, Red Stain, Lift Top, 2 Drawers, c.1720, 44 x 36 In. | 660 |
| **Chest,** Blanket, Wood, Hinged Drop Front, Iron, 3 Drawers, Korea, c.1890, 30 x 28 In. | 275 |
| **Chest,** Blanket, Wood, Peaked Lid, Eastern Continental, c.1850, 41 x 31 In. | 205 |
| **Chest,** Blanket, Yellow, Red, Scroll, Vase, Roses, Teal Ground, 46 x 19 ½ In. | 10800 |
| **Chest,** Bombe Style, Inlay, Drawers, Hairy Paw Feet, Dutch, c.1900, 35 x 43 In.............*illus* | 1375 |
| **Chest,** Bottle, Oak, Handles, England, c.1800, 12 x 17 In. | 120 |
| **Chest,** Bowfront, Banded, 4 Graduated Drawers, Bracket Feet, 35 x 41 In. | 1375 |
| **Chest,** Bowfront, Federal, Figured Maple, String Inlay, 4 Graduated Drawers, 36 x 36 In. | 3000 |
| **Chest,** Bride's, Painted Flower Panels, Red, Fitted Interior, Scandinavia, 19 x 42 In. | 840 |
| **Chest,** British Colonial Style, Mahogany, 5 Drawers, Handles, Bun Feet, 36 x 39 In. | 790 |
| **Chest,** Butler's, Neoclassical, Mahogany, Bookmatched, 5 Drawers, 55 x 46 In. | 767 |
| **Chest,** Campaign Style, Mahogany, 3 Drawers, Footed, 35 x 42 In. | 210 |
| **Chest,** Campaign, Anglo-Indian, Camphorwood, Brass, Lift Top, c.1810, 19 x 36 In. | 777 |
| **Chest,** Campaign, Camphorwood, Brass Trim, 6 Drawers, c.1955, 34 x 36 In., Pair | 813 |
| **Chest,** Campaign, Hardwood, Brass, 4 Drawers, c.1870, 34 x 48 In. | 1875 |
| **Chest,** Campaign, Mahogany, Brass Mounted, Drawers, England, 1900s, 42 x 39 In. ..........*illus* | 1342 |
| **Chest,** Campaign, Mahogany, Hinged Top, Drawer, Fitted Interior, Brass, 1800s, 45 x 36 In. | 8400 |
| **Chest,** Camphorwood, Brass, Butler Desk Drawer, 3 Lower Drawers, c.1850, 43 x 39 In. | 1169 |
| **Chest,** Camphorwood, Brass, Chinese, 1800s, 22 x 41 In. | 1200 |
| **Chest,** Camphorwood, Brassbound, c.1850, 14 x 36 In. | 480 |
| **Chest,** Carpenter's, Pine, Mixed Wood, Green, Black Paint, 1800s, 22 x 38 In. | 130 |
| **Chest,** Charak Furniture Co., Tiger Maple, Serpentine, 4 Graduated Drawers, 33 x 39 In. | 840 |
| **Chest,** Charles II, Oak, Pin & Nailhead, 4 Graduated Drawers, Ball Feet, 38 x 35 In. | 2596 |
| **Chest,** Cherry, 2 Sections, 2 & 3 Drawers, Line & Checkerboard Inlay, Ogee Feet, 52 x 45 In. | 523 |
| **Chest,** Cherry, 8 Graduated Drawers, c.1800, 55 x 39 In. | 840 |
| **Chest,** Cherry, Tiger Maple, Bowfront, Reeded Crest Board, Drawers, c.1820, 43 x 41 In. | 1121 |

**Furniture,** Chest, Neoclassical,
Mahogany, Ogee Drawer, Columns,
Miniature, c.1810, 14 In.
$610

Neal Auction Co.

**Furniture,** Chest, Oak, 2 Sections,
Drawers, Geometric Designs, Bun Feet,
c.1700, 40 x 38 In.
$2,040

Garth's Auctioneers & Appraisers

**Furniture,** Chest, Oak, Metal Strapwork,
Arts & Crafts, England, c.1905, 18 x 55 In.
$1,353

Skinner Auctioneers & Appraisers

**Furniture,** Chest, Semanier, Painted, 7 Drawers, Incised Gilt Decoration, c.1885, 59 x 28 In.
$3,198

New Orleans Auction Galleries, Inc.

**Furniture,** Chest, Shaker, Yellow Pine, Dovetailed, 9 Drawers, 73 x 30 In.
$5,900

Willis Henry Auctions, Inc.

| | |
|---|---|
| **Chest,** Chiffonier, Louis XVI Style, Kingwood, 18 Drawers, Bracket Feet, c.1890, 75 x 46 In. | 2500 |
| **Chest,** Chiffonier, Louis XVI, Mahogany, Brass Gallery, Fluting, Drawers, 59 x 24 In. ...........*illus* | 2337 |
| **Chest,** Chinoiserie, Faux Mahogany, 3 Drawers, Bracket Feet, Gilt, c.1770, 27 x 25 In. | 1586 |
| **Chest,** Chippendale, Birch, Pine, 6 Drawers, Bracket Feet, 51 ½ x 42 In. | 3000 |
| **Chest,** Chippendale, Cherry, 3 Graduated Drawers, Bracket Feet, 35 x 40 In. | 1200 |
| **Chest,** Chippendale, Cherry, 4 Drawers, Ball, Claw Feet, New England, c.1790, 37 x 41 In. | 1020 |
| **Chest,** Chippendale, Cherry, 6 Graduated Drawers, Bracket Feet, New England, 50 x 38 In. | 1320 |
| **Chest,** Chippendale, Cherry, Chestnut, 4 Drawers, Cross Band Inlaid, 44 x 36 In. | 6000 |
| **Chest,** Chippendale, Cherry, Drawers, Bracket Feet, New England, 1700s, 34 x 40 In...........*illus* | 1128 |
| **Chest,** Chippendale, Cherry, Pine, Poplar, 4 Drawers, Claw Feet, 38 ½ x 37 In. | 250 |
| **Chest,** Chippendale, Cherry, Poplar, Ball & Claw Feet, 6 Drawers, 51 x 41 In. | 3600 |
| **Chest,** Chippendale, Cherry, Shell Carved, 7 Drawers, Ball & Claw Feet, c.1790, 78 x 38 In. | 8750 |
| **Chest,** Chippendale, Curly Maple, 4 Drawers, Bracket Feet, New England, c.1760, 36 x 39 In. | 4375 |
| **Chest,** Chippendale, Mahogany, 4 Drawers, Ogee Bracket Base, c.1770, 38 x 10 In. | 593 |
| **Chest,** Chippendale, Mahogany, 4 Graduated Drawers, Bracket Feet, 30 x 33 ½ In. | 1680 |
| **Chest,** Chippendale, Mahogany, 4 Graduated, Beaded Drawers, Portsmouth, 31 x 39 In. | 18000 |
| **Chest,** Chippendale, Mahogany, Bowed 4 Drawers, Brass Handles, Mass., c.1790, 34 x 41 In. | 6900 |
| **Chest,** Chippendale, Mahogany, Carved Columns, 6 Drawers, Ball Feet, Pa., 41 x 39 In. | 900 |
| **Chest,** Chippendale, Mahogany, Fluted Columns, 4 Drawers, Ball Feet, c.1770, 32 x 36 In. | 11250 |
| **Chest,** Chippendale, Mahogany, Gadroon Trim, 4 Drawers, Ball & Claw Feet, c.1775, 33 x 36 In. | 7500 |
| **Chest,** Chippendale, Mahogany, Oxbow, 4 Drawers, Ball & Claw Feet, c.1750, 37 x 39 In. | 3750 |
| **Chest,** Chippendale, Mahogany, Serpentine, 4 Drawers, Bracket Feet, 32 x 39 In. | 3900 |
| **Chest,** Chippendale, Maple, 8 Drawers, Bracket Feet, Rhode Island, 58 x 40 In. | 2100 |
| **Chest,** Chippendale, Maple, 9 Drawers, Bracket Feet, New England, 72 x 38 In. | 15600 |
| **Chest,** Chippendale, Maple, Graduated Drawers, Bracket Feet, New England, c.1800, 39 x 22 In. | 438 |
| **Chest,** Chippendale, Satinwood, Mixed Wood, Inlay, 4 Drawers, c.1790, 39 x 39 In. | 2040 |
| **Chest,** Chippendale, Walnut, 2 Parts, 10 Drawers, Raised Legs, c.1775, 77 x 40 In. | 900 |
| **Chest,** Chippendale, Walnut, 4 Drawers, Carved Bracket Base, 33 x 31 In. | 246 |
| **Chest,** Chippendale, Walnut, 4 Drawers, Massachusetts, c.1760, 33 x 41 In. | 3438 |
| **Chest,** Chippendale, Walnut, Fluted Columns, 4 Drawers, Bracket Feet, c.1775, 33 x 36 In. | 780 |
| **Chest,** Chippendale, Walnut, Fluted Columns, Bracket, Pa., 36 x 38 In. | 2640 |
| **Chest,** Chippendale, Walnut, Reeded Columns, 8 Drawers, Pa., c.1780, 78 x 39 In. | 8400 |
| **Chest,** Chippendale, Walnut, Reeded Quarter Columns, 8 Drawers, c.1790, 64 x 42 In. | 1625 |
| **Chest,** Collector's, Lockside, 8 Graduated Shallow Drawers, Hinged Slats, 27 x 20 In. | 9200 |
| **Chest,** Colonial Revival, Hardwood, Brass Strapwork, Fixtures, 1900s, 33 x 49 x 34 In. | 125 |
| **Chest,** Continental, Elm, Burl, Marble Top, 2 Drawers, 32 x 33 In. | 2813 |
| **Chest,** Continental, Pine, Chip Carved, Shaped Base, 1780, 26 x 53 In. | 1000 |
| **Chest,** Dower, Chippendale, Softwood, Pie Board Ends, Till, Strap Hinges, c.1800, 34 x 51 In. | 472 |
| **Chest,** Dower, Chippendale, Walnut, Pie Board Molded Lid, Till, Drawers, 28 x 51 In. | 5015 |
| **Chest,** Dower, Dome Lid, Painted, Scandinavian Decorations, 1849, 30 x 49 x 25 In. | 780 |
| **Chest,** Dower, Pine, 3 Arched Panels, Rider, Horse, Blue Ground, Pa., c.1795, 22 x 49 In. | 11070 |
| **Chest,** Dower, Pine, 3 Flower Panels, Green Ground Paint, Ball Feet, c.1850, 26 x 48 In. | 720 |
| **Chest,** Dower, Pine, Painted Diamonds, Ocher Sponge Ground, Drawers, c.1810, 29 x 51 In. | 2640 |
| **Chest,** Dower, Pine, Painted, Flowers, Sarah Draper 1789, Snipe Hinges, 27 x 42 In. | 25000 |
| **Chest,** Dower, Poplar, Diamond Border, Red, Gold Paint, Lebanon, Pa., 25 x 54 In. | 780 |
| **Chest,** Dower, Poplar, Potted Tulip Panels, Hearts, Eefa Dunckels, Pa., 1785, 26 x 48 In. | 21600 |
| **Chest,** Dower, Softwood, Painted, Molded Lid, Till, Iron Strap Hinges, c.1793, 24 x 49 In. | 153 |
| **Chest,** Dower, Walnut, Inlaid Stars, Lattice, Vines & 1771, 2 Drawers, 15 x 23 In. | 3375 |
| **Chest,** Eastlake, Mahogany, 3 Drawers, Beveled Mirror, Carved, c.1890, 52 x 25 In. | 322 |
| **Chest,** Eastlake, Mahogany, Backsplash, Brass Pulls, 1880s, 44 x 40 In. | 152 |
| **Chest,** Eastlake, Walnut, Fruit & Leaf Pulls, Casters, c.1890, 43 x 35 In. | 275 |
| **Chest,** Empire Style, Mahogany, Gray Marble Top, 4 Drawers, Columns, 34 x 48 In. | 938 |
| **Chest,** Empire, Mahogany, 4 Graduated Drawers, 39 x 37 In. | 205 |
| **Chest,** Empire, Mahogany, Shaped Backsplash, Sides, 4 Drawers, 1800s, 48 x 23 In. | 210 |
| **Chest,** Empire, Paint Decorated, 4 Drawers, Rolled Feet, 1800s, 45 x 18 x 46 In. | 176 |
| **Chest,** Federal, Cherry, Eagle Inlay, 4 Beaded, Drawers, Splayed Legs, 36 x 43 In. | 3840 |
| **Chest,** Federal, Cherry, Figured Maple, 4 Graduated Drawers, Line Strung, 37 x 47 In. | 1722 |
| **Chest,** Federal, Cherry, Inlay, Eagle Embossed Brasses, 8 Drawers, Pa., c.1810, 67 x 42 In. | 3936 |
| **Chest,** Federal, Mahogany, 3 Graduated Drawers, Reeded Pilasters, c.1820, 21 x 20 In. | 5000 |
| **Chest,** Federal, Mahogany, 4 Drawers, Turned Feet, c.1850, 13 x 11 In. | 1750 |
| **Chest,** Federal, Mahogany, Bowfront, 4 Drawers, c.1800, 37 x 42 In. | 406 |
| **Chest,** Federal, Mahogany, Bowfront, 4 Drawers, Reeded Stiles, c.1870, 39 x 41 In. | 2500 |
| **Chest,** Federal, Mahogany, Carved Sides, 5 Drawers, Mass., c.1820, 49 x 44 In. | 750 |
| **Chest,** Federal, Mahogany, Inlay, 4 Graduated Drawers, Beading, c.1810, 36 x 42 In. | 1093 |
| **Chest,** Federal, Mahogany, Line Inlay, 4 Drawers, Pa., c.1810, 33 x 40 In. | 660 |
| **Chest,** Federal, Mahogany, Line Inlay, French Feet, Graduated Drawers, c.1800, 45 x 45 In. | 1125 |

| | |
|---|---|
| **Chest,** Federal, Maple, Cherry, 4 Drawers, Scalloped Apron, c.1830, 23 x 19 In., Child's | 2530 |
| **Chest,** Federal, Mixed Wood, 4 Drawers, French Feet, Portsmouth, c.1810, 38 x 40 In. | 14400 |
| **Chest,** Federal, Tiger & Bird's-Eye Maple, Bowfront, Graduated Drawers, c.1810, 44 x 24 In. | 1912 |
| **Chest,** Federal, Tiger Maple, 5 Cock-Beaded Drawers, Dovetailed, Columns, 42 x 43 In. .......*illus* | 590 |
| **Chest,** Federal, Tiger Maple, Bird's-Eye Maple, 4 Drawers, Paneled, Turned Feet, 46 x 42 In. | 944 |
| **Chest,** Federal, Walnut, 4 Drawers, Ball & Claw Feet, c.1800, 34 x 38 In. | 270 |
| **Chest,** Federal, Walnut, 4 Drawers, Brass Pulls, N.C., 1800s, 37 x 43 In. | 2242 |
| **Chest,** Federal, Walnut, 4 Graduated Drawers, Turned Feet, Va., c.1830, 24 x 11 In., Child's | 920 |
| **Chest,** Federal, Walnut, Ebonized Columns, Scalloped Skirt, 7 Drawers, c.1840, 52 x 21 In. | 1840 |
| **Chest,** Federal, Walnut, Lift Top, Stenciled Lyre, c.1820, 15 x 21 In. | 748 |
| **Chest,** Federal, Walnut, Pine, Barber Line Pole Inlay, 6 Drawers, N.C., c.1810, 47 x 38 In. | 6490 |
| **Chest,** Figured Maple, Raised Back, 7 Drawers, Rolled Feet, 1800s, 43 x 21 x 51 In. | 468 |
| **Chest,** French Provincial, Oak, 3 Drawers, Block Feet, 1800s, 30 x 45 In. | 915 |
| **Chest,** French Provincial, Walnut, Marble Top, 3 Graduated Drawers, c.1810, 33 x 43 In. | 443 |
| **Chest,** French Provincial, Walnut, Parquetry, Steel Pulls, Cabriole Legs, 32 x 40 In. | 84 |
| **Chest,** G. Stickley, Oak, 5 Drawers, Hammered Iron Pulls, c.1910, 43 x 37 In. | 2040 |
| **Chest,** G. Stickley, Oak, Brass Hardware, 5 Drawers, Mirror, Pegged, 1910, 48 x 66 In. | 7703 |
| **Chest,** Gentleman's, John Kapel, Walnut, 2 Doors, Mirror, Drawers, c.1960, 70 x 42 In. | 615 |
| **Chest,** George I, Mahogany, 6 Drawers, Bracket Feet, c.1760, 43 x 38 In. | 1080 |
| **Chest,** George I, Pine, Scalloped Apron, 6 Drawers, Raised Legs, c.1750, 54 x 36 In. | 660 |
| **Chest,** George I, Walnut, 5 Drawers, Bracket Feet, 1700s, 38 x 37 In. | 1625 |
| **Chest,** George II, Burl, 3 Drawers, Bun Feet, 33 x 41 In. | 1875 |
| **Chest,** George II, Walnut, 11 Drawers, Bun Feet, 66 ¾ x 42 In. | 3000 |
| **Chest,** George II, Walnut, Molded Cornice, 9 Drawers, Bracket Feet, 71 x 41 In. | 6875 |
| **Chest,** George III Style, Mahogany, 4 Drawers, Bracket Feet, c.1880, 33 x 37 In. | 1080 |
| **Chest,** George III Style, Mahogany, Serpentine Front, 5 Drawers, c.1800, 34 x 47 In. | 813 |
| **Chest,** George III Style, Mahogany, Serpentine Top, 3 Drawers, c.1910, 37 x 45 In. | 861 |
| **Chest,** George III Style, Mahogany, Serpentine, Gadrooned, Fretwork, 1800s, 38 x 51 In. | 2460 |
| **Chest,** George III Style, Rosewood, Beech, 3 Drawers, Continental, c.1900, 12 x 12 In. | 375 |
| **Chest,** George III, Inlaid Mahogany, 2 Over 2 Drawers, 35 x 35 In. | 1195 |
| **Chest,** George III, Mahogany, Bowfront, 3 Drawers, 33 x 36 In. | 750 |
| **Chest,** George III, Mahogany, Bowfront, 5 Beaded Drawers, Splayed Feet, 42 x 42 In. | 625 |
| **Chest,** George III, Mahogany, Bowfront, 5 Drawers, 40 x 20 In. | 688 |
| **Chest,** George III, Mahogany, Bowfront, 8 Drawers, c.1790, 84 x 42 In. | 1353 |
| **Chest,** George III, Mahogany, Bowfront, Line Overlay, Shaped Skirt, c.1790, 39 x 45 In. | 554 |
| **Chest,** George III, Mahogany, Carved Crest, Bracket, 9 Drawers, 61 x 22 In. | 2500 |
| **Chest,** George III, Mahogany, Cock-Beaded, 5 Drawers, c.1785, 35 x 38 In. | 875 |
| **Chest,** George III, Mahogany, Line Inlay, Bowfront, Apron, 6 Drawers, c.1800, 40 x 43 In. | 2800 |
| **Chest,** George III, Mahogany, Walnut, 5 Drawers, 30 ½ x 25 In. | 1500 |
| **Chest,** George III, Oak, Fruitwood, Short & Long Drawers, Bracket Feet, c.1790, 38 x 38 In. | 984 |
| **Chest,** Hepplewhite, Mahogany, Inlay Serpentine Front, 4 Drawers, c.1800, 37 x 44 In. | 1188 |
| **Chest,** Hepplewhite, Mahogany, Reeded Edge, 4 Graduated Drawers, French Feet, 40 In. | 1080 |
| **Chest,** Hepplewhite, Maple Inlay, 4 Beaded Banded Drawers, 39 x 39 ½ In. | 8160 |
| **Chest,** Hepplewhite, Sawtooth Inlaid Edge, 5 Drawers, Flared Feet, England, 42 x 41 In. | 120 |
| **Chest,** Hepplewhite, Tiger Maple, 4 Graduated Drawers, c.1820, 39 x 42 In. | 1320 |
| **Chest,** Inlay, 3 Carved Drawers, Cabriole Legs, Italy, c.1750, 34 x 50 In. | 312 |
| **Chest,** Inlay, Carved, Gadrooned Top, 6 Drawers, Scrolling Feet, c.1880, 63 x 33 In. | 2726 |
| **Chest,** Jacobean, Oak, Pine, 4 Drawers, Geometric Panels, Applied Bosses, c.1800, 35 x 39 In. | 540 |
| **Chest,** Jacobean, Oak, Pine, 5 Drawers, Geometric Facades, Bun Feet, 37 In. | 1440 |
| **Chest,** Jacobean, Pine, 4 Paneled Drawers, c.1710, 37 x 39 In. | 1320 |
| **Chest,** Kuramata, Side One, Ebonized Ash, Laminate, S-Shape, 18 Drawers, 1992, 67 x 24 In. | 10000 |
| **Chest,** Lingerie, Burl, Marble Top, 7 Drawers, France, c.1900, 54 x 19 In. | 1200 |
| **Chest,** Lingerie, Contemporary, Art Deco Style, Mirrored, 51 x 20 In. | 246 |
| **Chest,** Lingerie, Hepplewhite Style, Figured Mahogany, 5 Drawers, c.1900, 36 x 18 In. | 413 |
| **Chest,** Louis Philippe, Mahogany, Marble Top, Stepped Base, Bracket Feet, 36 x 45 In. | 861 |
| **Chest,** Louis Philippe, Walnut, Marble Top, Dolphin Pulls, Stepped Feet, 37 x 48 In. | 676 |
| **Chest,** Louis XV Style, Cherry, Bowfront, Cabriole Legs, 4 Drawers, 33 x 24 In. | 244 |
| **Chest,** Louis XV Style, Cherry, Gilt Brass Pulls, Cabriole Legs, c.1910, 34 x 45 In. | 397 |
| **Chest,** Louis XV Style, Fruitwood, Shaped Top, 2 Drawers, 26 ½ x 18 In., Pair | 1000 |
| **Chest,** Louis XV Style, Pine, Carved Flowers, Scrolls, Flowers, Italy, 32 x 52 In. | 1722 |
| **Chest,** Louis XV, Fruitwood, Serpentine, Carved Apron, 3 Drawers, c.1750, 38 x 47 In. | 3438 |
| **Chest,** Louis XVI Style, Mahogany Inlay, Turreted Top, 3 Drawers, Turned Feet, 12 x 11 In. | 657 |
| **Chest,** Louis XVI Style, Mahogany, 8 Drawers, Fluted Sides, c.1890, 39 x 15 In. | 1250 |
| **Chest,** Louis XVI, Cookie Corner Marble Top, Ormolu, 5 Drawers, c.1910, 35 x 45 In. | 1476 |
| **Chest,** Mahogany, 4 Drawers, Bracket Feet, 1800s, 17 x 16 In. | 210 |
| **Chest,** Mahogany, 4 Graduated Beaded Drawers, Bracket Feet, c.1770, 31 x 19 In. | 633 |

**Furniture,** Chest-On-Chest, George III, Oak, 7 Drawers, 2 Sections, England, 73 x 39 In.
$780

Garth's Auctioneers & Appraisers

**Furniture,** Coffer, Oak, Carved, Panels, Molding, Hinged, Lock, England, c.1700, 27 x 50 In.
$8,591

James D. Julia Auctioneers

**Furniture,** Commode, Louis XVI, Drop Front, Marquetry, Marble Top, Drawers Inside, 33 x 35 In.
$2,242

Brunk Auctions

**Furniture,** Commode, Walnut, Ebony & Bone Inlay, Scrolls, 3 Drawers, Italy, 38 x 55 In. $3,690

New Orleans Auction Galleries, Inc.

**Furniture,** Cupboard, Corner, Chippendale, Pine, Doors, Shelves, Painted, Virginia, c.1790, 83 In. $11,800

Brunk Auctions

**Furniture,** Cupboard, Corner, Chippendale, Walnut, Glass, 2 Sections, c.1900, 95 x 63 In. $6,490

Brunk Auctions

| | |
|---|---:|
| Chest, Mahogany, 5 Drawers, French Feet, 19th Century, 43 x 20 x 42 In. | 410 |
| Chest, Mahogany, 5 Drawers, Ogee Bracket Feet, c.1810, 26 x 28 In. | 460 |
| Chest, Mahogany, Bone Pulls, 4 Drawers, Salesman Sample, 16 x 14¾ In. | 652 |
| Chest, Mahogany, Bowfront, 4 Drawers, England, c.1850, 36 x 36 In. | 1100 |
| Chest, Mahogany, Bowfront, 4 Drawers, Twist-Carved Columns, Mass., c.1810, 40 x 38 In. | 468 |
| Chest, Mahogany, Bowfront, Line Inlay, 4 Graduated Drawers, Bracket Feet, 36 x 40 In. | 1168 |
| Chest, Mahogany, Cherry, 3 Drawers, Turned Feet, c.1835, 15 x 17 In. | 403 |
| Chest, Mahogany, Drawer, Fitted Bottle Drawer, Bracket Feet, 1800s, 22 x 24 In., Pair | 431 |
| Chest, Mahogany, Inlaid, Turned Columns, Claw Feet, 20 x 16 x 12 In. *illus* | 4830 |
| Chest, Mahogany, Shaped Apron, 4 Drawers, Flared Feet, 36½ x 41 In. | 720 |
| Chest, Mahogany, Twist Columns, 4 Drawers, Brass Fitted, 40 x 45 In. | 938 |
| Chest, Maple, 5 Graduated Thumb-Molded Drawers, Bracket Feet, c.1790, 50 x 36 In. | 738 |
| Chest, Marquetry Inlay, Fitted Interior, Bombe, Lid Handle, Dutch, c.1750, 17 x 22 In. | 563 |
| Chest, Money, Hardwood, Iron Strapwork, Handles, Chinese, 1800s, 32 x 36 x 15 In. *illus* | 1500 |
| Chest, Mule, Cherry, Drop Front, 2 Drawers, Fan Carved, Scrolls, c.1790, 40 x 38 In. | 1140 |
| Chest, Mule, Chippendale, Cherry, Red Paint, 2 Faux Drawers & 2 Drawers, 45 x 37 In. | 900 |
| Chest, Mule, Chippendale, Pine, Red Paint, 3 Faux & 3 Drawers, c.1790, 52 x 37 In. | 1020 |
| Chest, Mule, Pine, 4 Drawers, 2 Faux, Vinegar Decoration, c.1810, 39 x 42 In. *illus* | 1680 |
| Chest, Mule, Pine, Drop Front, 2 Drawers, Painted, New England, c.1800, 39 x 41 In. | 550 |
| Chest, Mule, Pine, Hinged Lid, Dovetailed Drawer, Painted, Scene, 1800s, 33 x 42 In. *illus* | 720 |
| Chest, Mule, Pine, Red Paint, Lift Top, 2 Drawers, Snipe Hinges, Bootjack Ends, 36 x 39 In. | 1440 |
| Chest, Neoclassical Style, Mahogany, 5 Paneled Drawers, Brass Inlay, c.1890, 40 x 36 In. | 1353 |
| Chest, Neoclassical Style, Painted Flowers, Garlands, 4 Drawers, 3 Doors, 51 x 37 In. | 125 |
| Chest, Neoclassical, Cherry, Apple Burl, Drawers, Paw Feet, c.1830, 55 x 47 In. *illus* | 750 |
| Chest, Neoclassical, Cherry, Maple, Carved, Outset Drawer Over 3 Drawers, 44 x 45 In. | 657 |
| Chest, Neoclassical, Mahogany, Ogee Drawer, Columns, Miniature, c.1810, 14 In. *illus* | 610 |
| Chest, Neoclassical, Multicolor, Raised Scrolling Leaves, 3 Drawers, c.1810, 34 x 34 In. | 1045 |
| Chest, Oak, 2 Sections, Drawers, Geometric Designs, Bun Feet, c.1700, 40 x 38 In. *illus* | 2040 |
| Chest, Oak, 3 Banded Drawers, Bun Feet, 32 x 41 In. | 375 |
| Chest, Oak, 3 Carved Drawers, Flowers, France, c.1820, 24 x 29 In. | 584 |
| Chest, Oak, 4 Graduated Drawers, c.1820, 37 x 36 In. | 570 |
| Chest, Oak, Diamond Shape Panels, Lift Top, Lock, England, 23½ x 34¾ In. | 413 |
| Chest, Oak, Lift Top, Carved Case, Drawers, Stile Feet, Hadley, c.1700, 46 x 46 In. | 9840 |
| Chest, Oak, Lift Top, Panels, Architectural Front, Knight, Queen, Gothic Arches, 31 x 54 In. | 891 |
| Chest, Oak, Metal Strapwork, Arts & Crafts, England, c.1905, 18 x 55 In. *illus* | 1353 |
| Chest, Oak, Pine, Carved, Hinged Top, Cleated Ends, Recessed Panels, 1600s, 25 x 44 In. | 1230 |
| Chest, Painted, Base Molding, Red Ground, Black Comb Grained, Dots, c.1800, 19 x 43 In. | 948 |
| Chest, Painted, Lift Top, Interior Till, 4 Drawers, Plinth, 1800s, 37 x 42 x 16 In. | 1076 |
| Chest, Parquetry, Metal Mounts, 6 Drawers, Marble Top, c.1890, 57 x 22 In., Pair | 2500 |
| Chest, Peter Hunt, Pine, Painted, Folk Art Style, 4 Drawers, 1944, 32 x 23 In. | 1610 |
| Chest, Pine, 4 Drawers, Cutout Skirt, Blue Paint, 33 x 37 In. | 403 |
| Chest, Pine, 4 Drawers, Red Paint, c.1850, 34 x 46 In. | 480 |
| Chest, Pine, 5 Drawers, Bracket Base, Salmon Paint, 1800s, 46 x 48 In. | 115 |
| Chest, Pine, 5 Drawers, Green Banding, Grain Painted, England, 35 x 41 In. | 885 |
| Chest, Pine, Lift Top, Shoe Feet, Green Paint, Va., c.1775, 25 x 52 In. | 431 |
| Chest, Pine, Paint, Drawers, Cock-Beaded, Scalloped Apron, Cutout Feet, c.1810, 42 x 40 In. | 2706 |
| Chest, Pine, Painted, 3 Graduated Drawers, 2-Drawer Facade, Shaped Skirt, 42 x 42 In. | 510 |
| Chest, Pine, Painted, Stenciled, Flowers, Eli Phillippi 1867, 5 Drawers, 46 In. | 1080 |
| Chest, Poplar, Red Paint, 2 Deep Drawers, Button Knobs, Demilune Ends, 30 x 38 In. | 1020 |
| Chest, Provincial, Painted, Marble Top, 3 Drawers, 28 x 24 In. | 150 |
| Chest, Queen Anne, Birch, Red Paint, 6 Graduated Drawers, Peter Bartlett, 58 x 39 In. | 8400 |
| Chest, Queen Anne, Walnut, 6 Drawers, Scalloped Apron, Raised Legs, c.1770, 66 x 40 In. | 5280 |
| Chest, Queen Anne, Walnut, 7 Graduated Drawers, Pa., c.1750, 51 x 38 In. | 1320 |
| Chest, Queen Anne, Walnut, Step Back, 9 Drawers, Fan Carving, Cabriole Legs, 72 x 35 In. | 1063 |
| Chest, Renaissance Style, Walnut, Hinged Top, Carved Bishops, Linenfold, 29 x 60 In. | 1188 |
| Chest, Rosewood, Walnut, Marble Serpentine Top, 3 Drawers, Cabriole Legs, 36 x 43 In. | 2000 |
| Chest, Sacred Jewels, Flowers, Leaf Painted, Orange, Gilt, Wood, Tibet, 1800s, 18 x 34 In. | 812 |
| Chest, Seed, Incised Flower-Carved Backsplash, 20 Pinstriped Drawers, c.1870, 21 x 21 In. | 2400 |
| Chest, Seed, Poplar, Red, Slant Lid, 12 Drawers, Shaped Carved Crest, c.1890, 22 x 16 In. | 1440 |
| Chest, Semanier, Painted, 7 Drawers, Incised Gilt Decoration, c.1885, 59 x 28 In. *illus* | 3198 |
| Chest, Shaker, Drawer, Hinges Signed T. Clark, 49 x 36½ In. | 2360 |
| Chest, Shaker, Pine, Poplar, Red Stain, 8 Drawers, Turned Pulls, 42 x 44 In. | 7670 |
| Chest, Shaker, Red Stain, 4 Drawers, Dovetailed, 34 x 15 In. | 5015 |
| Chest, Shaker, Seed, Pine, Poplar, Blue, Dovetailed, 12 Drawers, Brass Pulls, 7 x 24 In. | 4484 |
| Chest, Shaker, Yellow Pine, Dovetailed, 9 Drawers, 73 x 30 In. *illus* | 5900 |
| Chest, Sheraton, Birch, Bowfront, Column Corners, 5 Drawers, c.1810, 39 x 43 In. | 593 |

| | |
|---|---|
| Chest, Sheraton, Cherry, 4 Drawers, Ball Feet, John Gould, Jr., New Hampshire, 39 x 42 In. | 1200 |
| Chest, Sheraton, Cherry, 8 Drawers, Turned Legs, Pennsylvania, c.1830, 67 x 40 In. | 1320 |
| Chest, Sheraton, Cherry, Figured Maple, Turret Corners, 4 Drawers, Crossbanded, 35 x 41 In. | 474 |
| Chest, Sheraton, Grain Painted, 4 Drawers, c.1835, 44 x 40 In. | 1500 |
| Chest, Sheraton, Mahogany Inlay, Bowed Front, Banded Fronts, c.1820, 43 x 42 In. | 4148 |
| Chest, Sheraton, Mahogany, Bowfront, 4 Drawers, New England, c.1815, 35 x 37 In. | 360 |
| Chest, Sheraton, Mahogany, Bowfront, Columns, 4 Drawers, c.1820, 40 x 42 In. | 750 |
| Chest, Sheraton, Mahogany, Inlay, 4 Drawers, Reeded Columns, Mass., c.1810, 41 x 44 In. | 2640 |
| Chest, Sheraton, Walnut, 4 Drawers, Newtown Bucks County, Pa., c.1810, 40 x 41 In. | 677 |
| Chest, Sheraton, Walnut, Poplar, 4 Drawers, Turned Legs, Vine Inlay, 45 ½ x 43 In. | 4063 |
| Chest, Softwood, Feather Grain Painted Dome Lid, Pieboard Ends, Ohio, 1800s, 11 x 7 In. | 531 |
| Chest, Sugar, Walnut, Compartments, Molded Frame, Turned Legs, 1800s, 33 x 31 In. | 3567 |
| Chest, Sugar, Walnut, Hinged Top, Divided Well, Drawer, Tapered Legs, N.C., 32 x 24 In. | 863 |
| Chest, Sycamore, 6 Drawers, Bracket Base, New England, c.1750, 39 x 21 In. | 1053 |
| Chest, Tiger Maple, 4 Graduated Drawers, 40 x 32 In. | 625 |
| Chest, Tiger Maple, Walnut, 4 Banded Drawers, Spiral Carved Feet, c.1840, 44 x 43 In. | 510 |
| Chest, Vanity, Oak, Upper Gallery Shelf, Mirror, Side Folding Mirrors, Drawers, 65 x 39 In. | 178 |
| Chest, Victorian, Walnut, Glove Drawers On Top, 4 Graduated Drawers, 48 x 42 In. | 480 |
| Chest, Walnut, Carved, Fruit, Leaf, Pulls, Keyholes, 3 Drawers, c.1880, 30 x 32 In. | 270 |
| Chest, Walnut, Line Inlay, 5 Drawers, Pa., 59 x 42 In. | 1080 |
| Chest, Wellington, Regency, Walnut, 7 Graduated Drawers, Plinth Base, 50 x 22 x 16 In. | 2100 |
| Chest, Wellington, William IV, Walnut, Drop Front, 7 Drawers, 1800s, 51 x 24 In. | 1845 |
| Chest, William & Mary Style, Oyster Veneer, Inlaid, 5 Drawers, Bun Feet, 37 x 43 In. | 885 |
| Chest, William & Mary, Mahogany, 4 Drawers, Spanish Brushed Feet, c.1730, 38 x 36 In. | 2400 |
| Chest, William & Mary, Pine, Panel Sides, 11 Drawers, Raised Turned Legs, Pa., 66 x 39 In. | 5280 |
| Chest, William & Mary, Pine, Red Paint, Batwing Brasses, 6 Drawers, 48 x 44 In. | 2359 |
| Chest, William & Mary, Rust Color Paint, Molded Top, 5 Drawers, Bun Feet, 27 x 38 In. | 2640 |
| Chest, Wrought Iron, Oak, Dome Lid, Strap Hinges, Handles, 1700s, 27 x 17 In. | 615 |
| Chest-On-Chest, Chippendale Style, Mahogany, Drawers, Shell Carvings, c.1970, 89 x 41 In. | 2125 |
| Chest-On-Chest, Chippendale, Cherry, Bonnet Top, Pinwheel Carving, c.1775, 89 x 42 In. | 9000 |
| Chest-On-Chest, Chippendale, Cherry, Bonnet Top, Spiral Finials, 11 Drawers, 88 x 38 In. | 9600 |
| Chest-On-Chest, Chippendale, Maple, Fan Carved, 9 Drawers, Bracket Feet, 80 x 39 In. | 3360 |
| Chest-On-Chest, Chippendale, Tiger Maple, Cornice, Graduated Drawers, c.1790, 81 x 42 In. | 11800 |
| Chest-On-Chest, E. Spence, Beech, Carved, Metal Loop Feet, 1950s, 46 x 42 In. | 5625 |
| Chest-On-Chest, E. Spence, Walnut, Beech, Carved, Sweden, 1950s, 46 ½ x 20 In. | 1625 |
| Chest-On-Chest, George III, Mahogany, Oak, 2 Sections, 5 Drawers, 1700s, 81 x 45 In. | 1320 |
| Chest-On-Chest, George III, Oak, 7 Drawers, 2 Sections, England, 73 x 39 In. .....*illus* | 780 |
| Chest-On-Chest, Georgian, Mixed Wood, Fretwork Frieze, Drawers, Bracket Feet, 77 x 42 In. | 1080 |
| Chest-On-Chest, Mahogany, 6 Drawers, Cock-Beaded Bracket Feet, Eng., c.1780, 72 x 24 In. | 649 |
| Chest-On-Chest, Mahogany, 8 Graduated Drawers, Bracket Feet, Eng., c.1800, 74 x 44 In. | 875 |
| Chest-On-Chest, Queen Anne, Burl Walnut, Oak, 5 Drawers, 19th Century, 61 x 31 In. | 1320 |
| Chest-On-Chest, Queen Anne, Maple, Chestnut, 6 Drawers, Cabriole Legs, 71 x 40 In. | 4320 |
| Chest-On-Chest, Walnut, Inlay, 9 Drawers, Bracket Base, c.1790, 76 x 43 In. | 2000 |
| Chest-On-Chest, Walnut, Line Inlay, 8 Drawers, c.1760, 68 x 40 In. | 1024 |
| Chest-On-Chest, William & Mary, Maple, 7 Drawers, Stretchers, 62 x 42 In. | 840 |
| Chest-On-Frame, Bone, Mother-Of-Pearl, Inlaid Oak, Drawers, Twist Legs, 37 x 34 In. | 2153 |
| Chest-On-Frame, Oak, Iron Handles, Lock, Carved Legs, c.1700s, 24 x 27 In. | 813 |
| Chest-On-Frame, Pine, Green Paint, 1800s, 32 x 33 In. | 184 |
| Chest-On-Frame, Vargueno Style, Marquetry, Stepped Molding, Drawers, 1800s, 66 x 47 In. | 948 |
| Chiffonier, Regency Style, Rosewood, 2 Brass Gallery Shelves, Mirror Back, c.1890, 55 x 42 In. | 1300 |
| Chiffonier, William IV, Mahogany, Leaf Carved Backsplash, Mount, Eng., c.1840, 56 x 48 In. | 594 |
| Chifforobe, Modern, Black Lacquer, 7 Chrome Drawers, Door, 1970s, 57 In. | 649 |
| Clothespress, Mahogany, Line Inlay, 2 Doors, 5 Drawers, c.1790, 90 x 51 In. | 9375 |
| Coat Rack, Wood, 3 Bears, Climbing Tree, 6 Coat Hooks, 4-Footed | 563 |
| Coffer, Oak, Burl Veneer, Parquetry Panels, Floral Designs, Shaped Feet, 1700s, 22 x 41 In. | 300 |
| Coffer, Oak, Carved, Geometric, Scrolling Vines, Set In Panels, 17th Century, 42 x 20 In. | 633 |
| Coffer, Oak, Carved, Panels, Molding, Hinged, Lock, England, c.1700, 27 x 50 In. .....*illus* | 8591 |
| Coffer, Oak, Carved, Shield, Arched Panels, Figures, Iron Handles, 1600s, 30 x 60 In. | 1845 |
| Commode, Art Nouveau, Walnut, Compartments, 5 Drawers, Flowers, c.1905, 36 x 34 In. | 10000 |
| Commode, Baker Furniture, Pecan, 2 Doors, Contemporary Far East Style, 32 x 40 In., Pair | 420 |
| Commode, Biedermeier, Birch, Ebonized, Columns, 3 Drawers, 37 x 43 In. | 4000 |
| Commode, Biedermeier, Fruitwood, Drawer, 2 Doors, Blocked Feet, 33 x 33 In. | 330 |
| Commode, Bombe Shape, 3 Drawers, Painted Flower, Carved Apron, Italy, 34 x 37 In. | 625 |
| Commode, Bombe, Figured Walnut, Inlay, 4 Drawers, Banding, c.1800, 32 x 47 In. | 657 |
| Commode, Bombe, Olivewood, Serpentine Front, 3 Drawers, Cabriole Legs, 38 x 47 In. | 1968 |
| Commode, Bombe, Walnut, Shaped Apron, 3 Drawers, France, 29 x 28 In., Pair | 270 |

F

**Furniture**, Cupboard, Corner, Pine, Glass Panel Doors, Carved, Delaware, c.1810, 87 x 60 In.
$10,200

Garth's Auctioneers & Appraisers

**Furniture**, Cupboard, Shaker, Butternut, Interior Shelves, Drawers, Mt. Lebanon, 1860, 66 x 46 In.
$123,000

Skinner Auctioneers & Appraisers

**TIP**
*Make sure your nightstand, the small table next to the bed that usually holds a lamp and a phone, is large enough. Find a vintage or antique table that is 28 to 31 inches high to use next to the bed. A small desk will also work.*

# FURNITURE

**Furniture,** Cupboard, Step Back, Pine, Scraped Surface, Multiple Paint Layers, c.1890, 76 x 42 In.
$360

Replacements, Ltd.

**Furniture,** Cupboard, Step Back, Poplar, Glass Doors, Drawer Over Door, Pa., 1800s, 80 x 41 In.
$813

Garth's Auctioneers & Appraisers

**Furniture,** Daybed, Queen Anne, Maple, Rush Seat, Reclining, Turned Legs, New Eng., c.1750, 66 In.
$480

Garth's Auctioneers & Appraisers

**Furniture,** Desk Organizer, Slant Front, Burl Veneer, Doors, Compartments, Eng., c.1900, 13 x 11 In.
$360

Garth's Auctioneers & Appraisers

**Furniture,** Desk, Chippendale, Tiger Maple, Slant Front, Fitted Interior, c.1750, 40 x 43 In.
$2,963

James D. Julia Auctioneers

**Furniture,** Desk, Davenport, Slant Front, Walnut, Rosewood, 4 Drawers, c.1890, 34 x 21 In.
$563

Rago Arts & Auction Center

**Furniture,** Desk, Edwardian, Mahogany, Leather, Neoclassical Inlay, Maple & Co., 39 x 45 In.
$923

Skinner Auctioneers & Appraisers

**Furniture,** Desk, Hepplewhite, Slant Front, Curly Maple, Fitted Interior, c.1810, 45 x 41 In.
$1,320

Garth's Auctioneers & Appraisers

**Furniture,** Desk, Lacquer, Gilt, Tray, Fitted Interior, Chinese Export, c.1815, 55 In.
$615

New Orleans Auction Galleries, Inc.

| | |
|---|---|
| **Commode,** Burl, Walnut, Marble Top, 2 Incised Doors, Splayed Legs, Italy, 38 x 55 In. | 1625 |
| **Commode,** Empire Style, Mahogany, Gilt Mount, Marble Top, 3 Drawers, 35 x 21 In., Pair | 1250 |
| **Commode,** Empire Style, Mahogany, Marble Top, Conforming Case, 1800s, 36 x 51 In. | 1476 |
| **Commode,** Empire, Mahogany, Marble Top, Ebonized Pilaster, Drawers, Scroll, 30 x 34 In. | 1599 |
| **Commode,** Flame Mahogany Veneer, Marble Top, 4 Drawers, Bracket Feet, 38 x 46 In. | 834 |
| **Commode,** French Provincial, Green, Marble Top, 27 ½ x 25 In. | 1912 |
| **Commode,** George III, Mahogany, Enamel Chamber Pot, Tambour Door, Drawers, 34 x 22 In. | 2988 |
| **Commode,** Georgian, Mahogany, 2 Upper Doors, Lid Seat, Fluted Case, c.1800, 33 x 17 In. | 738 |
| **Commode,** Green Paint, Chinoiserie Parcel Gilt, Bombe Shape, Venice, 29 x 18 In., Pair | 1750 |
| **Commode,** Hepplewhite Style, Figured Mahogany, Marble Top, Beacon Hill, 36 x 23 In. | 450 |
| **Commode,** Kingwood, Marble Top, Paneled, Lattice Pattern Parquetry, c.1810, 36 x 37 In. | 4182 |
| **Commode,** Louis Philippe, Burl, 3 Drawers, Bracket Feet, 41 x 47 In. | 875 |
| **Commode,** Louis XV Provincial, Walnut, Serpentine Front, 3 Drawers, 34 x 48 ½ In. | 7500 |
| **Commode,** Louis XV Style, Black Lacquer, Marble, Drawers, Japanese Scenes, c.1950, 33 x 39 In. | 1125 |
| **Commode,** Louis XV Style, Floral Marquetry, Marble Top, Drawers, 34 x 22 x 53 In. | 960 |
| **Commode,** Louis XV Style, Marquetry, Inlaid Mahogany, 25 x 14 In., Pair | 720 |
| **Commode,** Louis XV Style, Parquetry, Bronze Mounted, Marble Top, 3 Drawers, 32 x 27 In. | 472 |
| **Commode,** Louis XV Style, Parquetry, Marble Top, Gilt Bronze, Bombe Case, 35 x 38 In. | 5250 |
| **Commode,** Louis XV Style, Parquetry, Serpentine Top, 2 Drawers, Splayed Legs, 29 x 25 In. | 375 |
| **Commode,** Louis XV Style, Walnut, Inlay, Metal Mounts, Marble Top, c.1975, 33 x 36 In. | 469 |
| **Commode,** Louis XV, Gilt Bronze Parquetry, Marble Top, 2 Drawers, c.1790, 36 x 50 In. | 2500 |
| **Commode,** Louis XV, Tulipwood Veneer, 3 Drawers, Ormolu Hardware, 35 x 16 In. | 1169 |
| **Commode,** Louis XV, Walnut, 2 Drawers, Carved Apron, 34 x 42 In. | 563 |
| **Commode,** Louis XV, Walnut, Gilt Bronze, Inlay, Marble Top, 2 Drawers, 34 x 50 In. | 3750 |
| **Commode,** Louis XVI Style, Kingwood, Mahogany, Parquetry, Marble Top, 33 x 36 In. | 584 |
| **Commode,** Louis XVI Style, Kingwood, Rouge Marble Top, Blocked Case, 32 x 31 In. | 1230 |
| **Commode,** Louis XVI Style, Mahogany, Marble Top, Turreted Corners, Figures, 34 x 47 In. | 1230 |
| **Commode,** Louis XVI Style, Multicolor, Drawer, Laurel Wreath Carving, 28 x 36 In. | 3198 |
| **Commode,** Louis XVI Style, Parquetry, Marble Top, Gilt Metal Mounts, c.1900, 34 x 46 In. | 1063 |
| **Commode,** Louis XVI, Drop Front, Marquetry, Marble Top, Drawers Inside, 33 x 35 In. ......*illus* | 2242 |
| **Commode,** Louis XVI, Walnut, Banded, Turreted Corners, Frieze Drawer, 1700s, 33 x 51 In. | 1845 |
| **Commode,** Mahogany, Marble Top, England, c.1870, 37 ½ x 16 In. | 246 |
| **Commode,** Napoleon III, Walnut Parquetry, Bronze, Serpentine Marble Top, 40 x 63 In. | 5378 |
| **Commode,** Neoclassical Style, Painted, Parcel Gilt, Drawers, Italy, 36 x 49 In. | 615 |
| **Commode,** Neoclassical, Inlaid Fruitwood, Banded Top, 3 Drawers, c.1800, 35 x 49 In. | 2868 |
| **Commode,** Neoclassical, Walnut, Parcel Ebonized, 3 Drawers, Italy, c.1820, 34 x 49 In. | 3198 |
| **Commode,** Painted Bombe Case, 2 Drawers, Italy, 31 x 26 In. | 750 |
| **Commode,** Rococo Style, Painted, Parcel Gilt, Marble Top, Germany, c.1900, 35 x 38 In. | 625 |
| **Commode,** Rococo, Serpentine, Painted, 2 Drawers, Cabriole Legs, Italy, c.1800, 32 x 30 In. | 813 |
| **Commode,** Rococo, Walnut, Brass, Crossbanded Drawers, Bombe Shape, 30 x 25 In., Pair | 1750 |
| **Commode,** Walnut, 3 Drawers, Bun Feet, Germany, 33 x 38 In. | 875 |
| **Commode,** Walnut, Ebony & Bone Inlay, Scrolls, 3 Drawers, Italy, 38 x 55 In. .....................*illus* | 3690 |
| **Commode,** Walnut, Flower, Swag Inlay, Square Corners, 4 Drawers, 1800s, 45 x 65 In. | 3750 |
| **Commode,** Walnut, Gray Marble Top, 3 Drawers, Brass Pulls, 32 x 48 In. | 780 |
| **Commode,** Walnut, Inlay, 4 Graduated Drawers, Continental, c.1850, 40 x 51 In. | 1750 |
| **Commode,** Walnut, Variegated Marble Top, 3 Drawers, Block Feet, 1800s, 32 x 38 In. | 598 |
| **Counter,** Shaker, Pine, Overhanging Top, Mt. Lebanon, c.1830, 31 x 33 In. | 7380 |
| **Cradle,** Cherry, Brown Paint, Arched Headboard, Footboard, Heart Cutouts, 1800s, 23 x 46 In. | 24 |
| **Cradle,** Curly Maple, Dovetailed, Hood, Cutouts, c.1850, 31 x 41 In. | 240 |
| **Cradle,** Field, Bentwood Basket, Sled Shape Frame, Iron Wheels, 1800s, 26 x 48 In. | 118 |
| **Cradle,** Mahogany, Hooded, 41 In. | 118 |
| **Cradle,** Neoclassical, Yew, Curved Canopy, Lyre Supports, 40 x 42 In. | 240 |
| **Cradle,** Pine, Hooded, Turned Finials, Blue, Red Paint, c.1850, 27 x 34 In. | 115 |
| **Cradle,** Rocking, Cherry, Curved Legs, Spool Spindles, Swan Head, c.1890, 64 x 52 In. | 119 |
| **Cradle,** Rocking, Oak, Slatted, Oval, Swan's Neck Support, Splayed Feet, Victorian, 55 In. | 201 |
| **Cradle,** Rocking, Wrought Iron, Wire Construction, Scroll Base, 1800s, 37 x 48 In. | 72 |
| **Cradle,** Walnut, Hooded, Shaped Rockers, 1800s, 27 ½ x 39 ½ In. | 60 |
| **Credenza,** Baroque, Walnut, Carved, 2 Doors, Bracket Feet, Italy, 39 x 49 In. | 840 |
| **Credenza,** Edwardian Style, Satinwood, 6 Side Open Shelves, 2 Doors, 32 x 48 In. | 281 |
| **Credenza,** M. Villency, Teak, 3 Sliding Doors, 4 Stacked Drawers, Denmark, c.1965, 30 x 79 In. | 492 |
| **Credenza,** Tuscan, Walnut, Drawers, 3 Compartments, Interior Shelves, 1600s, 47 x 60 In. | 6440 |
| **Crib,** Oak, Pine, Southern, 1800s, 26 x 30 In. | 35 |
| **Crib,** Sheraton, Tiger Maple, Hinged Side, Spindles, 35 x 42 In. | 540 |
| **Crib,** Wood Carved, Cutout Side Handles, Loop Head Crest, Scandinavia, c.1780, 17 x 31 In. | 120 |
| **Cupboard,** 2 Glass Doors, 3 Drawers, Bracket Feet, Pa., c.1750, 83 x 65 In. | 2500 |
| **Cupboard,** 2 Panel Doors, Shelf Interior, Carved Molding, Bun Feet, c.1950, 72 x 42 In. | 280 |

**F**

**Furniture,** Desk, Moore, Renaissance Revival, Walnut, Maple, Inlay, Plaque, 1878, 56 x 32 In.
$43,050

Skinner Auctioneers & Appraisers

**TIP**
*Touching up gilding does not change value if it is done by an expert.*

**Furniture,** Desk, Partners, V. Kagan, Y-Shape, Drawers, 1950, 28 x 99 x 84 In.
$7,500

Los Angeles Modern Auctions (LAMA)

**Furniture,** Desk, Queen Anne Style, Slant Front, Mahogany, Oak, Shaped Interior, c.1900, 40 x 30 In.
$240

Garth's Auctioneers & Appraisers

**Furniture,** Desk, Queen Anne, Maple, Slant Front, Drawer, Fitted Interior, c.1750, 40 x 32 In.
$5,629

James D. Julia Auctioneers

**Furniture,** Desk, R.J. Horner, Faux Bamboo, Bird's-Eye Maple, Leather, c.1880, 53 x 32 In.
$2,625

Rago Arts & Auction Center

| | |
|---|---:|
| **Cupboard,** 2 Panel Doors, Yellow Grain Painted, Bracket Feet, c.1890, 26 x 26 In. | 263 |
| **Cupboard,** 3 Shelves, 4 Doors, Red Flower Panels, Blue, Scandinavia, c.1865, 76 x 44 In. | 677 |
| **Cupboard,** 9 Open Cubicle Shelves, 9 Drawers, Green Paint, c.1900, 60 x 22 In. | 540 |
| **Cupboard,** Anglo-Indian, Paint Decorated, Elephant Cutout Door Panels, 30 x 48 In. | 176 |
| **Cupboard,** Bench, Pine, Painted, Raised Panel Door, Shaped Base, c.1850, 29 x 32 In. | 1610 |
| **Cupboard,** Blue Paint, 2 Doors, 2-Board, Arched Bracket Feet, 85 x 51 In. | 720 |
| **Cupboard,** Canning, Pine, Painted, Green Scrubbed, Pennsylvania, 1800s, 56 x 29 In. | 369 |
| **Cupboard,** Chimney, Pine, Flat Door, Blue Paint, c.1875, 70 x 30 In. | 570 |
| **Cupboard,** Chimney, Queen Anne, Tombstone Arched Doors, Shelf, Cutouts, 74 x 21 In. | 10073 |
| **Cupboard,** Chimney, Softwood, Ivory Paint, Cornice, 4-Panel Door, c.1890, 76 x 24 In. | 325 |
| **Cupboard,** Chippendale, Walnut, 2 Doors, 4 Drawers Over 2 Panel Doors, Va., c.1800, 86 In. | 2185 |
| **Cupboard,** Corner, 2 Stacked Panel Doors, Flame Grain Painted, Pa., c.1830, 86 x 40 In. | 2400 |
| **Cupboard,** Corner, 3 Open Shelves, 2 Paneled Doors, Shaped Base Apron, c.1950, 76 x 36 In. | 173 |
| **Cupboard,** Corner, Arched Glass Door, 3 Drawers, 2 Panel Doors, Pa., c.1850, 92 x 55 In. | 3120 |
| **Cupboard,** Corner, Blue Paint, 4 Paneled Doors, Fluted Sides, Shelves Inside, 84 x 42 In. | 2500 |
| **Cupboard,** Corner, Cherry, 2 Glass Doors, 2 Panel Doors, 1800s, 87 x 46 In. | 800 |
| **Cupboard,** Corner, Cherry, 2 Glass Doors, 3 Drawers, 2 Panel Doors, Pa., c.1830, 90 x 58 In. | 900 |
| **Cupboard,** Corner, Cherry, 4 Doors, Kentucky, c.1810, 85 x 40 In. | 1080 |
| **Cupboard,** Corner, Chippendale, Mahogany, 2 Glass Doors, Barrel Back, Va., c.1800, 94 x 49 In. | 18400 |
| **Cupboard,** Corner, Chippendale, Mahogany, Salesman Sample, c.1920, 14 x 7 In. | 2962 |
| **Cupboard,** Corner, Chippendale, Pine, 2 Arched Doors, 2 Lower Doors, c.1800, 85 x 52 In. | 1000 |
| **Cupboard,** Corner, Chippendale, Pine, Doors, Shelves, Painted, Virginia, c.1790, 83 In. *illus* | 11800 |
| **Cupboard,** Corner, Chippendale, Pine, Glass Door, 2 Panel Doors, Blue, c.1810, 91 x 46 In. | 2415 |
| **Cupboard,** Corner, Chippendale, Walnut, Glass, 2 Sections, c.1900, 95 x 63 In. *illus* | 6490 |
| **Cupboard,** Corner, Chippendale, Walnut, Inlay, 4 Paneled Doors, 2 Drawers, 85 In. | 2006 |
| **Cupboard,** Corner, Curly Maple, 9-Pane Glazed Door, Raised Panel Doors, 72 In. | 1080 |
| **Cupboard,** Corner, Federal, Cherry, 2 Panel Doors Over Flat Door, Shaped Apron, 79 x 43 In. | 375 |
| **Cupboard,** Corner, Federal, Cherry, Carved, Broken-Arch Crest, Pilasters, 90 x 47 In. | 2151 |
| **Cupboard,** Corner, Federal, Cherry, Glass Door, 2 Panel Doors, c.1805, 85 x 40 In. | 1800 |
| **Cupboard,** Corner, Federal, Softwood, Molded Dentil, 8 Pane, Glazed, c.1800, 82 x 36 In. | 767 |
| **Cupboard,** Corner, Federal, Walnut, 4 Paneled Doors, Southern U.S., 85 x 44 In. | 649 |
| **Cupboard,** Corner, George III, Mahogany, 2 Sections, Mullion Glazed Doors, 84 x 45 In. | 3776 |
| **Cupboard,** Corner, Grain Painted, Arched Glazed Doors, John Rupp, 93 x 64 In. | 2478 |
| **Cupboard,** Corner, Hanging, Georgian, Mahogany, Arched Door, H Hinges, Shelves, 31 In. | 236 |
| **Cupboard,** Corner, Hanging, Maple, Raised Panel Door, Drawer, Lebanon County, Pa., 36 In. | 640 |
| **Cupboard,** Corner, Hanging, Oak, Carved Panel Door, England, c.1750, 39 x 28 In. | 390 |
| **Cupboard,** Corner, Hanging, Pine, Red Paint, Panel Door, 1800s, 24 x 25 In. | 234 |
| **Cupboard,** Corner, Hanging, Poplar, Gray Paint, Double Arched Door, Michigan, 51 x 32 In. | 420 |
| **Cupboard,** Corner, Hanging, Poplar, Tombstone Panel Door, Pa., c.1780, 38 x 30 In. | 960 |
| **Cupboard,** Corner, Hanging, Walnut, 3 Open Shelves, 2 Carved Doors, c.1890, 35 x 15 In., Pair. | 688 |
| **Cupboard,** Corner, Maple, Glass Door, 2 Panel Doors, Shaped Bracket Feet, 88 x 44 In. | 1440 |
| **Cupboard,** Corner, Pine, Alligatored Cream Paint, 12-Pane Door, 2 Paneled Doors, 84 In. | 2640 |
| **Cupboard,** Corner, Pine, Arched Glass Door, 2 Panel Doors, Pa., c.1845, 76 x 41 In. | 748 |
| **Cupboard,** Corner, Pine, Arched, Molded, Blue, 3 Shelves, Paneled Door, 85 x 47 In. | 24600 |
| **Cupboard,** Corner, Pine, Glass Door, 2 Drawers, Blue, Salmon, Pa., c.1800, 85 x 48 In. | 4320 |
| **Cupboard,** Corner, Pine, Glass Door, 2 Panel Doors, Black, Salmon, Pa., c.1810, 88 x 39 In. | 5040 |
| **Cupboard,** Corner, Pine, Glass Door, 2 Panel Doors, Ocher, Grain Paint, Pa., c.1830, 83 x 42 In. | 2337 |
| **Cupboard,** Corner, Pine, Glass Panel Doors, Carved, Delaware, c.1810, 87 x 60 In. *illus* | 10200 |
| **Cupboard,** Corner, Pine, Step Back, 4 Panel Doors, c.1850, 78 x 51 In. | 390 |
| **Cupboard,** Corner, Pine, Yellow Paint, 2 Over 2 Paneled Doors, Bracket Base, 79 x 41 In. | 6325 |
| **Cupboard,** Corner, Poplar, 2 Sections, Glass Door, 2 Drawers, Panel Door, c.1860, 86 x 45 In. | 720 |
| **Cupboard,** Corner, Poplar, Bittersweet Paint, 2 Panel Doors, 81 x 39 In. | 2666 |
| **Cupboard,** Corner, Poplar, Glass Door, 2 Panel Doors, White Paint, Pa., c.1865, 86 x 48 In. | 300 |
| **Cupboard,** Corner, Queen Anne, Glass Door, Pilasters, Carved Flowers, New England, 83 x 51 In. | 2640 |
| **Cupboard,** Corner, Red Stain, 3 Open Shelves, Shaped Sides, Paneled Door, Conn., 77 In. | 1750 |
| **Cupboard,** Corner, Walnut, 4 Panel Doors, 2 Beaded Drawers, Shaped Apron, 83 x 43 In. | 1080 |
| **Cupboard,** Corner, Walnut, Dentil Cornice, Glass Door, Panel Doors, Pa., c.1800, 90 x 43 In. | 1140 |
| **Cupboard,** Corner, Walnut, Dentil Molding, 4 Panel Doors, Pa., c.1790, 89 x 43 In. | 984 |
| **Cupboard,** Cornice, Lozenge Molded Doors, Green Paint, Marbleized, 1800s, 79 x 50 In. | 2500 |
| **Cupboard,** Court, Charles I Style, Carved, 1800s, 73 x 36 x 24 In. | 840 |
| **Cupboard,** Door, Pine, Mustard Yellow Paint, 82 x 38 In. | 330 |
| **Cupboard,** Dutch Baroque, Rosewood, Carved, 2 Doors, 2 Drawers, 1800s, 91 x 90 In. | 2400 |
| **Cupboard,** Dutch, Federal, Cherry, Cover Molded Cornice, Drawers, c.1850, 93 x 61 In. | 2360 |
| **Cupboard,** Dutch, Walnut, Glass Door, Pie Shelf, Fluted Pilasters, 3 Drawers, 84 x 69 In. | 3600 |
| **Cupboard,** English Oak, Molded Cornice, Paneled Doors, Block Feet, 1700s, 89 x 34 In. | 1230 |
| **Cupboard,** Federal, Cherry, Step Back, 2 Sections, Glazed Doors, Paneled Doors, 78 x 48 In. | 2749 |

| | | |
|---|---|---|
| **Cupboard,** Hanging, Blue, Orange, Yellow Painted Designs, Scandinavia, 1816, 32 x 12 In. ...... | 1140 |
| **Cupboard,** Hanging, Chippendale Style, Mahogany Pediment, Glass Door, c.1845, 43 x 29 In. .... | 345 |
| **Cupboard,** Hanging, Door, Apple Green Paint, c.1850, 16 x 9 ½ In. ............................ | 263 |
| **Cupboard,** Hanging, George III, Mahogany, Glass Pane Door, c.1790, 42 x 22 In. ............. | 780 |
| **Cupboard,** Hanging, Mahogany, Ormolu Mounts, c.1910, 21 x 22 In. ........................... | 120 |
| **Cupboard,** Hanging, Panel Door, Painted Flowers, Black Ground, Sweden, 29 x 26 In........... | 540 |
| **Cupboard,** Hanging, Pine, 2 Panel Doors, Base Drawer, c.1850, 36 x 36 In. .................. | 210 |
| **Cupboard,** Hanging, Pine, Door, Sunken Navel, Lancaster Co., c.1790, 29 x 21 In. .......... | 1320 |
| **Cupboard,** Hanging, Pine, Flat Door, Gray Paint, c.1865, 23 x 19 In. ..................... | 570 |
| **Cupboard,** Hanging, Pine, Painted Door, Hinged, Scandinavia, c.1810, 23 x 14 In. ......... | 510 |
| **Cupboard,** Hanging, Pine, Panel Door, Pennsylvania, c.1780, 34 x 22 In. ................... | 277 |
| **Cupboard,** Hanging, Pine, Poplar, Gray Paint, 4-Panel Door, Drawer, 26 x 17 In. .......... | 840 |
| **Cupboard,** Hanging, Pine, Red Paint, 2 Panel Doors, Continental, c.1800, 22 x 21 In. ..... | 360 |
| **Cupboard,** Hanging, Softwood, Blue Paint, Blind Door, Paneled Door, 48 x 30 In. .......... | 384 |
| **Cupboard,** Hanging, Softwood, Blue, Sponged Panel, Cornice, c.1800, 43 x 28 In............ | 649 |
| **Cupboard,** Hanging, Walnut, Panel Door, Scalloped Relief Carving, Pa., 32 x 25 In......... | 1800 |
| **Cupboard,** Hanging, Walnut, Panel Door, Shelf, Carved, Chester Co., c.1780, 29 x 18 In. ... | 16800 |
| **Cupboard,** Hanging, Walnut, Paneled Door, c.1945, 28 x 27 In................................ | 150 |
| **Cupboard,** Hanging, Walnut, Pine, Old Red Paint, 4-Pane Door, 35 x 28 In.................... | 1440 |
| **Cupboard,** Hanging, Walnut, Pine, Panel Door, Base Molding, c.1880, 28 x 30 In. ........... | 2070 |
| **Cupboard,** Hutch, Pine, Poplar, Step Back, Shelf, Spoon Rack, 78 x 39 In. ................. | 767 |
| **Cupboard,** Jelly, Backsplash, 2 Top Drawers, 2 Panel Doors, c.1850, 53 x 59 In. .......... | 498 |
| **Cupboard,** Jelly, Grain Painted, Wood, 2 Panel Doors, Bracket Feet, c.1850, 40 x 38 In. ... | 938 |
| **Cupboard,** Jelly, Pine, 2 Doors, Gray Paint, c.1890, 49 x 38 In........................... | 420 |
| **Cupboard,** Jelly, Pine, 2 Drawers, 2 Doors, Red Paint, Pa., c.1865, 45 x 43 In. .......... | 450 |
| **Cupboard,** Jelly, Pine, Green Paint, 2 Drawers, 2 Doors & 4 Short Drawers, 52 x 51 In. .... | 7475 |
| **Cupboard,** Jelly, Raised Panel Door, Old Red Paint, 18th Century, 78 x 33 In. ............ | 1020 |
| **Cupboard,** Jelly, Softwood, Green Paint, Backsplash, Shaped Sides, Drawers, 56 x 42 In...... | 266 |
| **Cupboard,** Jelly, Walnut, 2 Panel Doors, c.1820, 47 x 42 In. ............................. | 660 |
| **Cupboard,** Mahogany, 4 Panel Doors, 84 x 26 In., Pair ..................................... | 750 |
| **Cupboard,** Maple, Step Back, Projecting Cornice, Glazed Doors, Paneled Doors, 81 x 49 In. ...... | 2040 |
| **Cupboard,** Milk, Softwood, Red Paint, Sunken Panel Door, Cutout Feet, 1800s, 41 In. ....... | 1652 |
| **Cupboard,** Milk, Softwood, Scrubbed Surface, Plank Top, Scalloped Skirt, 1800s, 47 x 55 In. ..... | 590 |
| **Cupboard,** Mixed Wood, 2 Panel Doors, 5 Drawers, Black Paint, c.1845, 64 x 38 In. ......... | 1625 |
| **Cupboard,** Mixed Wood, 4 Open Shelves, Step Back, Lower Door, c.1845, 78 x 45 In. ......... | 938 |
| **Cupboard,** Mixed Wood, Top Open Shelf, 5 Panel Doors, 3 Drawers, c.1720, 77 x 54 In. ...... | 1125 |
| **Cupboard,** Painted Wood, Aqua, White Trim, 2 Paneled Doors, Continental, 48 x 76 In. ...... | 614 |
| **Cupboard,** Paneled Door, Drawer, Green Paint, 1900s, 19 x 35 ½ In............................ | 70 |
| **Cupboard,** Pantry, Pine, Green Paint, 1-Plank Door, Wood Latch, New England, 75 x 30 In...... | 948 |
| **Cupboard,** Pewter, Oak, Step Back, Shaped Cornice, 2 Tombstone Panel Doors, Welsh, 77 In. .... | 708 |
| **Cupboard,** Pewter, Pine, Chestnut, Shelves, Drawers, Doors, North Shore, 1700s, 92 x 77 In...... | 1200 |
| **Cupboard,** Pine, 2 Panel Doors, Blue Paint, Bracket Feet, 47 x 40 In...................... | 4320 |
| **Cupboard,** Pine, 2 Panel Doors, Bracket Feet, c.1850, 58 x 67 In. ........................ | 500 |
| **Cupboard,** Pine, 4 Shelves, Bracket Feet, c.1855, 52 ½ x 42 ½ In.......................... | 180 |
| **Cupboard,** Pine, Paneled Doors, Shelves, Late 18th Century, 71 x 57 In. .................. | 1750 |
| **Cupboard,** Pine, Raised Panel Door, Shaped Skirt, Gray Paint, 29 x 32 x 13 In............. | 2280 |
| **Cupboard,** Pine, Step Back, 3 Open Shelves, 2 Drawers, Door, 71 x 59 In. ................. | 500 |
| **Cupboard,** Pine, Step Back, 3 Open Shelves, Flat Door, Red Paint, Pa., c.1865, 80 x 31 In. ..... | 720 |
| **Cupboard,** Pine, Step Back, 3 Panel Doors, Pa., 77 ¾ x 45 ½ In............................ | 369 |
| **Cupboard,** Pine, Step Back, 4 Open Shelves, Carved, New England, c.1750, 80 x 49 In. ...... | 1188 |
| **Cupboard,** Pine, Step Back, 4 Plank Doors, White Paint, c.1890, 60 x 41 In................ | 374 |
| **Cupboard,** Pine, Step Back, Pie Shelf, Crown Molding, Drawers, c.1810, 77 x 42 In. ....... | 356 |
| **Cupboard,** Pine, Step Back, Yellow Paint, c.1850, 61 x 30 In.............................. | 2760 |
| **Cupboard,** Poplar, Scalloped Open Shelf, Step Back, Paneled Doors, 1900s, 78 x 60 In........ | 531 |
| **Cupboard,** Ribbon Case, Oak, 4 Glass Doors, A.N. Russell, c.1900, 27 x 28 In. ............ | 480 |
| **Cupboard,** Salmon Paint, Pinned Mortise & Tenon, 2 Doors, Bucket Bench, 77 x 48 In. ....... | 9225 |
| **Cupboard,** Shaker, Butternut, Interior Shelves, Drawers, Mt. Lebanon, 1860, 66 x 46 In. ....*illus* | 123000 |
| **Cupboard,** Shaker, Door, Inset Panel, Turned Pull, 9 x 15 In. ............................ | 826 |
| **Cupboard,** Shaker, Hanging, Pine, Raised Panel Door, c.1825, 42 x 19 In.................... | 7552 |
| **Cupboard,** Shaker, Pine, 2 Panel Doors, Fitted Interior, Red Paint, c.1800, 81 x 38 In. .... | 4920 |
| **Cupboard,** Shaker, Pine, 6 Shelves, c.1830-1840, 86 x 42 In. ............................. | 10030 |
| **Cupboard,** Shaker, Pine, Door, Interior, Red Paint, New Lebanon, c.1820, 25 x 32 In. ...... | 738 |
| **Cupboard,** Shaker, Pine, Tulip, 3 Doors, 16 Drawers, Cherry Pulls, 75 x 86 In............. | 8260 |
| **Cupboard,** Slant Back, 4 Shelves, Molded Surround, Paneled Base, Doors, Painted, 87 x 57 In... | 7380 |
| **Cupboard,** Softwood, Blind Door, Red Paint, Panel Doors, Pie Shelf, 1800s, 78 x 52 In...... | 1003 |
| **Cupboard,** Step Back, 2 Glass Doors, 2 Drawers, 2 Panel Doors, 85 x 49 In................. | 600 |

**Furniture,** Desk, Robsjohn-Gibbings, Walnut, 3 Drawers, File Separators, Widdicomb, 29 x 46 In.
$1,098

Palm Beach Modern Auctions

**Furniture,** Desk, Rohlfs, Drop Front, Drawers, Cutouts, Pivoting Base, c.1898, 56 x 25 In.
$255,750

F

Rago Arts & Auction Center

**Furniture,** Desk, Schoolmaster's, Mixed Wood, Cutout Gallery Top, 61 x 31 In.
$840

Garth's Auctioneers & Appraisers

**Furniture,** Desk, Walnut, Slant Front, Ring-Turned Legs, Pa., 1800s, 52 x 24 In. $1,230

Skinner Auctioneers & Appraisers

**Furniture,** Desk, Wegner, 2 Drawers, Organizer, Johannes Hansen, 1954, 76 x 35 In. $50,000

Los Angeles Modern Auctions (LAMA)

**Furniture,** Desk, Widdicomb, Campaign Style, Double Pedestal, Burl Walnut, 30 x 52 In. $960

Garth's Auctioneers & Appraisers

### TIP
*If there are two handles on a drawer, open the drawer using both handles. It lessens the strain on the joints.*

| | |
|---|---:|
| **Cupboard,** Step Back, 2 Glass Doors, 2 Drawers, 2 Panel Doors, Yellow, c.1900, 48 x 82 In. | 205 |
| **Cupboard,** Step Back, 2 Open Shelves, 2 Drawers, 2 Raised Paneled Doors, 77 x 40 In. | 1800 |
| **Cupboard,** Step Back, 4 Shelves, Hinged Lift Top, Door, Gray Paint, 78 x 24 In. | 1169 |
| **Cupboard,** Step Back, Black Paint, 2 Glazed Doors, Doors, c.1850, 41 x 22 In. | 492 |
| **Cupboard,** Step Back, Chippendale, Walnut, 9 Pane Doors, Fluted, c.1775, 87 x 74 In. | 6000 |
| **Cupboard,** Step Back, Faux Tiger Grain, Glass Doors, 6 Drawers, Flat Doors, 41 In., Child's | 330 |
| **Cupboard,** Step Back, Pine, Scraped Surface, Multiple Paint Layers, c.1890, 76 x 42 In. ...... *illus* | 360 |
| **Cupboard,** Step Back, Poplar, Glass Doors, Drawer Over Door, Pa., 1800s, 80 x 41 In. ........ *illus* | 813 |
| **Cupboard,** Wall, Faux Grain Painted, Multicolor Flowers, Scandinavia, 1800, 79 x 35 In. | 1800 |
| **Cupboard,** Walnut, Poplar, Step Back, 2 Glazed Doors, 3 Drawers, Ohio, 81 In. | 1500 |
| **Cupboard,** Walnut, Shaped Backsplash, Drawers, Paneled Doors, Ball Feet, 41 x 39 In. | 418 |
| **Cupboard,** Walnut, Step Back, 2 Glass Doors, 2 Drawers, c.1920, 38 x 20 In., Child's | 360 |
| **Daybed,** Cast Iron, Green Paint, Yellow Trim, c.1890, 30 x 74 In. | 130 |
| **Daybed,** Empire Style, Mahogany, Gilt Mounts, Tubular Crest Rail, Supports, 35 x 60 In. | 375 |
| **Daybed,** Empire, Karelian Birch, c.1850, 42 x 50 In. | 1063 |
| **Daybed,** G. Nakashima, Plank, Walnut, Free Edge Back & Armrest, c.1960, 35 x 92 In. | 17080 |
| **Daybed,** G. Nelson, Wood, Zinc Plated Metal, Cushions, Herman Miller, 1950s, 28 x 75 In. | 1000 |
| **Daybed,** George I, Walnut, Cane Seat, Back, Pierced Crest & Side Stretcher, 42 x 70 In. | 960 |
| **Daybed,** Louis XVI, Cornucopia Shape Rail, Fluted Feet, 37 x 80 In. | 1599 |
| **Daybed,** Queen Anne Style, Maple, Adjustable Cane Back, Yoke Crest Rail, Splat, 42 x 69 In. | 239 |
| **Daybed,** Queen Anne, Maple, Rush Seat, Reclining, Turned Legs, New Eng., c.1750, 66 In. ... *illus* | 480 |
| **Daybed,** Queen Anne, Walnut, Shaped Crest, Carved Ears, Pierced Vase Shape, 37 x 77 In. | 1920 |
| **Daybed,** Restauration, Plum Pudding Mahogany, Paneled, France, 1800s, 42 x 36 x 65 In. | 400 |
| **Daybed,** William & Mary Style, Maple, Rush Seat, Flat Slat Back, Slanted, 76 In. | 510 |
| **Desk Organizer,** Slant Front, Burl Veneer, Doors, Compartments, Eng., c.1900, 13 x 11 In. *illus* | 360 |
| **Desk,** Accountant's, Red Paint, Partial Backsplash, 3 Drawers, H-Stretcher Base, 39 x 72 In. | 474 |
| **Desk,** Anglo-Indian, Slant Front, Mixed Wood, Parquetry, 35 x 22 In. | 1625 |
| **Desk,** Art Deco, Mahogany, Ebonized, Blond, Double Pedestal, 6 Drawers, 28 x 68 In. | 531 |
| **Desk,** Art Nouveau, Dovetailed Drawers, Brass Pulls, c.1900, 84 x 48 In. | 3304 |
| **Desk,** Arts & Crafts, Slant Front, Oak, 2 Shelves, Shoefoot Base, 1910s, 29 x 42 x 31 In. | 117 |
| **Desk,** Baker Furniture, Italian Style, Tapered Fluted Legs, Leather Inset, 60 x 27 In. | 431 |
| **Desk,** Biedermeier, Fruitwood, Ebonized Banding, 5 Drawers, c.1820, 31 x 55 In. | 625 |
| **Desk,** Burl Veneer, 4 Door, 6 Drawer Top Over 3 Drawers, Continental, c.1900, 36 x 41 In. | 677 |
| **Desk,** Butler's, Biedermeier, Walnut, 4 Drawers, Fitted Interior, c.1830, 41 x 50 In. | 1169 |
| **Desk,** Butler's, Federal, Mahogany, Fitted, 3 Drawers, Claw Feet, N.Y., c.1810, 44 x 43 In. | 1063 |
| **Desk,** Butler's, George III, Mahogany, Satinwood Veneers, 5 Drawers, 48 x 46 In. | 1298 |
| **Desk,** Butler's, Hepplewhite, Cherry, Mahogany Banding, 6 Drawers, c.1810, 47 x 22 In. | 515 |
| **Desk,** Cabinet, Display, Victorian, Mahogany, Curved Glass, Drawers, Mirror, 71 x 44 In. | 720 |
| **Desk,** Chair, A. Vodder, Danish Modern, Shaped Back, Vinyl Upholstery, 29 x 20 In., 2 Piece | 960 |
| **Desk,** Chair, McCobb, 2 Left-Facing Drawers, Curved Crest Rail, Tapered Legs, 30 In., 2 Piece | 660 |
| **Desk,** Chippendale, Drop Front, Walnut, Fitted Interior, 4 Drawers, c.1800, 41 x 43 In. | 374 |
| **Desk,** Chippendale, Slant Front, Cherry, 4 Drawers, Bracket Feet, 44 x 36 In. | 1320 |
| **Desk,** Chippendale, Slant Front, Cherry, Fitted Interior, Bracket Feet, c.1790, 42 x 36 In. | 1125 |
| **Desk,** Chippendale, Slant Front, Cherry, Graduated Drawers, New England, c.1780, 42 x 38 In. .. | 1845 |
| **Desk,** Chippendale, Slant Front, Curly Maple, Cherry, 4 Drawers, c.1770, 44 x 39 In. | 2880 |
| **Desk,** Chippendale, Slant Front, Walnut, Broken-Arch Pediment, 2 Doors, c.1800, 83 x 36 In. .. | 4080 |
| **Desk,** Chippendale, Slant Front, Walnut, Center Shell-Carved Door, c.1790, 44 x 40 In. | 3186 |
| **Desk,** Chippendale, Slant Front, Walnut, Drawer, Raised Legs, Pa., c.1790, 34 x 36 In. | 1356 |
| **Desk,** Chippendale, Tiger Maple, Slant Front, Fitted Interior, c.1750, 40 x 43 In. .............. *illus* | 2963 |
| **Desk,** Chippendale, Walnut, Slant Front, Fitted, Carved Interior, c.1775, Pa., 43 x 38 In. | 1046 |
| **Desk,** Colonial Revival, Drop Front, Mahogany, Brass Gallery, 3 Drawers, c.1920, 42 x 26 In. | 138 |
| **Desk,** Davenport, Slant Front, Burl Walnut, Pull-Out Surface, Drawers, c.1870, 36 x 23 In. | 1845 |
| **Desk,** Davenport, Slant Front, Gillow, Burl Veneer, Brass Gallery, c.1845, 33 x 20 In. | 1476 |
| **Desk,** Davenport, Slant Front, Walnut, Rosewood, 4 Drawers, c.1890, 34 x 21 In. ................ *illus* | 563 |
| **Desk,** Davenport, Victorian, Slant Front, Mahogany, Gallery Top, Inset Leather, 35 x 22 In. | 750 |
| **Desk,** Davenport, Victorian, Slant Front, Walnut, Pierced Gallery, Leather Inset, 34 x 22 In. | 305 |
| **Desk,** Davenport, Victorian, Slanted Lift Top, Burl, Inlay, 4 Side Drawers, 32 x 21 In. | 344 |
| **Desk,** Davenport, Victorian, Walnut, Shaped Crest, Gallery, Curved Lift Top, 26 x 45 In. | 300 |
| **Desk,** Davenport, Walnut, Leather Inset, England, 1800s, 35 x 24 In. | 300 |
| **Desk,** Directoire Style, Mahogany, Leather Inset, Drawers, 1900s, 30 x 25 x 26 In. | 780 |
| **Desk,** Double Pedestal, Birch Plywood, 9 Drawers, Paul Goldman, Plycraft, 1950s, 30 x 46 In. | 448 |
| **Desk,** Ebonized Hardwood, Carved Vernacular Design, Drawer, Japan, c.1910, 55 x 50 In. | 352 |
| **Desk,** Edwardian, Mahogany, Leather, Neoclassical Inlay, Maple & Co., 39 x 45 In. ............. *illus* | 923 |
| **Desk,** Edwardian, Roll Top, Marquetry, Rosewood, Pullout Surface, c.1910, 38 x 25 In. | 584 |
| **Desk,** Empire Style, Lady's, Mahogany, Brass Bands, Tambour Drawer, 34 x 26 In. | 750 |
| **Desk,** Empire Style, Mahogany, Leather Inset, Frieze Pull-Out Slide, c.1880, 56 x 28 In. | 1722 |

| | |
|---|---|
| **Desk,** Empire Style, Mahogany, Leather Top, 3 Drawers, 31 x 64 In. | 1125 |
| **Desk,** Executive, Mount Vernon, Sheraton Style, Mahogany, Tapered Legs, 35 x 65 In. | 799 |
| **Desk,** Federal Mahogany, Inlay, 2 Tambour Doors, Writing Surface, c.1820, 50 x 40 In. | 4375 |
| **Desk,** Federal Style, Mahogany, 2 Tambour Doors, 4 Drawers, c.1950, 48 x 36 In. | 750 |
| **Desk,** Federal, Cherry, Slant Front, 4 Drawers, Inlay, 43 x 39 In. | 540 |
| **Desk,** Federal, Mahogany, Beaded Edge, Interior Compartments, Drawer, c.1810, 29 x 24 In. | 1845 |
| **Desk,** Federal, Mahogany, Drawers, Handles, Pa., c.1810, 13 x 14 In. | 660 |
| **Desk,** G. Nakashima, Walnut, Floating Top, Sap Streak Pedestals, Pegged, 1977, 29 x 60 In. | 18450 |
| **Desk,** G. Stickley, Arts & Crafts, Slant Front, Oak, Flat Stretcher, Decal, 44 x 30 In. | 413 |
| **Desk,** G. Stickley, Chalet, Drop Front, Oak, Fitted Interior, c.1902, 46 x 24 In. | 3625 |
| **Desk,** G. Stickley, Slant Front, Oak, Interior Letter Rack, Shoefoot, 46 x 25 In. | 690 |
| **Desk,** George II Style, Mahogany, Kneehole, 7 Drawers, Panel Door, 30 x 37 In. | 563 |
| **Desk,** George II Style, Walnut, 3 Drawers, c.1905, 31 x 67 In. | 1250 |
| **Desk,** George III, Drop Front, Mahogany, Fitted Interior, 4 Drawers, c.1800, 42 x 37 In. | 800 |
| **Desk,** George III, Mahogany, Pedestal, 9 Drawers, c.1805, 30 x 54 In. | 5625 |
| **Desk,** George III, Slant Front, Burl, 4 Graduated Drawers, Bracket Feet, c.1770, 40 x 37 In. | 2125 |
| **Desk,** Henredon, Burl, Kingwood Inlay, Center Medallion, Tapered Legs, Gilt, 31 x 75 In. | 1680 |
| **Desk,** Hepplewhite, Slant Front, Curly Maple, Fitted Interior, c.1810, 45 x 41 In. ...............*illus* | 1320 |
| **Desk,** Hooker, Mainline, Walnut, Kneehole, 3 Drawers, Sliding Woven Panel, 30 x 54 In. | 708 |
| **Desk,** Italian Rococo, Slant Front, Burl Walnut, Fitted Interior, 5 Drawers, c.1830, 45 x 47 In. | 1000 |
| **Desk,** Jens Quistgaard, Oak, Cubbyholes, 4 Lateral Drawers, Lovig, Dansk, c.1967, 34 x 64 In. | 2813 |
| **Desk,** Lacquer, Gilt, Tray, Fitted Interior, Chinese Export, c.1815, 55 In. ...............*illus* | 615 |
| **Desk,** Louis XVI Style, Roll Top, Fruitwood, Musical Marquetry, 40 x 30 x 18 In. | 1020 |
| **Desk,** Louis XVI Style, Roll Top, Mahogany, Brass Gallery, 5 Drawers, 1945, 59 x 31 In. | 500 |
| **Desk,** Mackenzie & Mitchell, George III Style, Mahogany, c.1910, 31 x 42 In. | 369 |
| **Desk,** Mahogany, 9 Drawers, Swing Out, Kidney Shape, c.1940 | 150 |
| **Desk,** Mahogany, Slant Front, Inlaid Edge Banding, Shell, 3 Drawers, 29 x 38 In. | 265 |
| **Desk,** Marquetry, Brass, 8 Drawers, 2 Doors, 3 Drawers, Kidney Shape, c.1910, 38 x 41 In. | 1020 |
| **Desk,** Moore, Renaissance Revival, Walnut, Maple, Inlay, Plaque, 1878, 56 x 32 In.............*illus* | 43050 |
| **Desk,** Napoleon III, Rosewood, Fruitwood, Bone Inlay, Drawer, c.1850, 31 x 36 In. | 688 |
| **Desk,** Oak, Overhang Top, Lion & Paw Foot Supports, Drawers, 1800s, 48 x 29 x 30 In. | 614 |
| **Desk,** On Frame, Pine, Slant Front, Red Paint, Drawers, Stretcher, c.1810, 42 x 36 In. | 660 |
| **Desk,** On Stand, Chippendale, Slant Front, Figured Walnut, Fitted, Shaped Skirt, 43 In. | 472 |
| **Desk,** P. Protzman, Zebrawood, Chromed Steel, 2 Drawers, Herman Miller, c.1970, 30 x 65 In. | 896 |
| **Desk,** Partners, 2 Pedestals, George III Style, Mahogany, Inset Leather Top, 1900s, 32 x 67 In. | 1414 |
| **Desk,** Partners, 4 Drawers, Turned Legs, Leatherette Top, 48 x 36 x 30 In. | 87 |
| **Desk,** Partners, Aesthetic Revival, Satinwood, Mahogany, Reeded Legs, c.1900, 62 x 45 In. | 1599 |
| **Desk,** Partners, Dansk, Teak, Fitted Top, Flip Desk Top, 4 Drawers, 1970s, 34 x 64 In. | 2375 |
| **Desk,** Partners, Majorelle, Art Nouveau, Mahogany, 3 Drawers, c.1900, 57 x 31 In. | 1750 |
| **Desk,** Partners, Pine, Mahogany Stain, Leather Top, Gilt, 9 Drawers, England, 31 x 55 In. | 1438 |
| **Desk,** Partners, V. Kagan, Y-Shape, Drawers, 1950, 28 x 99 x 84 In.......................*illus* | 7500 |
| **Desk,** Pedestal, Oak, Leather Inset, 9 Drawers, England, 1800s, 28 x 47 In. | 313 |
| **Desk,** Pedestal, Walnut, Pierced Brass, Galley, 9 Drawers, England, 30 x 48 In. | 1000 |
| **Desk,** Pine, Hinged Lid, Divided Well, c.1850, 25 x 18 In. | 127 |
| **Desk,** Plantation, Drop Front, Paneled, Walnut, Molded Cornice, Fitted Interior, 58 x 39 In. | 615 |
| **Desk,** Plantation, Federal, Walnut, Paneled Fallboard, Fitted, 58 x 35 In. | 708 |
| **Desk,** Plantation, Gothic Revival, Mahogany, 2 Glass Doors, 3 Drawers, c.1870, 86 x 46 In. | 546 |
| **Desk,** Plantation, Pine, Grain Painted, 2 Glazed Doors, Slant Front, 85 x 42 In. | 780 |
| **Desk,** Ponti, Walnut, Brass, Black Glass, 1950s, 59 x 29 ¾ In. | 1920 |
| **Desk,** Quartersawn Oak, Carved, Curved Base, Compartment Pulls Out, Drawers, 42 x 27 In. | 163 |
| **Desk,** Queen Anne Style, Slant Front, Mahogany, Oak, Shaped Interior, c.1900, 40 x 30 In...*illus* | 240 |
| **Desk,** Queen Anne, Cherry, Slant Front, 4 Graduated Drawers, New England, 40 x 40 In. | 813 |
| **Desk,** Queen Anne, Maple, Pine, Slant Front, Dovetailed, 4 Drawers, 41 x 35 In. | 1140 |
| **Desk,** Queen Anne, Maple, Slant Front, Drawer, Fitted Interior, c.1750, 40 x 32 In. ..............*illus* | 5629 |
| **Desk,** Queen Anne, Walnut, Line Inlay, Slant Front, 5 Drawers, Pa., c.1740, 40 x 34 In. | 1440 |
| **Desk,** Queen Anne, Walnut, Slant Front, Fitted Interior, 4 Drawer, c.1735, 43 x 38 In. | 4375 |
| **Desk,** R.J. Horner, Faux Bamboo, Bird's-Eye Maple, Leather, c.1880, 53 x 32 In. ...............*illus* | 2625 |
| **Desk,** Regency Style, Mahogany, Leather Top, 6 Side Drawers, Kneehole, c.1900, 29 x 50 In. | 1063 |
| **Desk,** Regency Style, Roll Top, Figured Mahogany, Leather, 7 Drawers, 42 x 54 In. | 531 |
| **Desk,** Robsjohn-Gibbings, Walnut, 3 Drawers, File Separators, Widdicomb, 29 x 46 In. ........*illus* | 1098 |
| **Desk,** Rococo Revival, Kingwood, Gilt Bronze Trim, Ram's Heads, Germany, c.1750, 54 In. | 2875 |
| **Desk,** Rococo Revival, Painted, Slant Front, Stepped Interior, Venice, 42 x 43 In. | 4183 |
| **Desk,** Rohlfs, Drop Front, Drawers, Cutouts, Pivoting Base, c.1898, 56 x 25 In. ............*illus* | 255750 |
| **Desk,** Roll Top, Art Nouveau, Fruit & Nut Woods, Veneer, Fitted Interior, 51 x 44 In. | 1230 |
| **Desk,** Roll Top, Mahogany, Fitted Interior, 2 Drawers, 1800s, 38 ¾ x 36 In. | 325 |
| **Desk,** Roll Top, Wood, Carved, Floral Scenes, Marked M, Compartments, 59 x 52 In. | 360 |

**Furniture,** Desk, Wooton, Renaissance Revival, Walnut, Maple, Burl, Parcel Gilt, 1874, 81 x 43 In.
$58,425

Skinner Auctioneers & Appraisers

**Furniture,** Desk, Wooton, Walnut, Cylinder, Ebonized, Gilt Incised, House Shape Crest, c.1876, 64 x 56 In.
$20,910

New Orleans Auction Galleries, Inc.

**Furniture,** Dresser, Dorothy Draper, Espana, Lacquer, Gilt, Henredon, 1950s, 32 x 38 In., Pair
$3,625

Rago Arts & Auction Center

**Furniture,** Dresser, Herter Bros., Aesthetic Revival, Rosewood, Marble, c.1885, 84 x 50 In.
$2,460

Skinner Auctioneers & Appraisers

**Furniture,** Dresser, Mastercraft, 3 Drawers, Asian Inspired Handles, 29½ x 32 In.
$2,562

Palm Beach Modern Auctions

**Furniture,** Dresser, Shaker, Pine, 4 Drawers, 4 Larger Drawers, c.1830, 71 x 36 In.
$86,100

Skinner Auctioneers & Appraisers

| | |
|---|---|
| **Desk,** Schoolmaster's, Mixed Wood, Cutout Gallery Top, 61 x 31 In. .....................................*illus* | 840 |
| **Desk,** Schoolmaster's, Poplar, Slant Front, Fitted Interior, Mid-Atlantic, c.1850, 43 x 37 In. ........ | 374 |
| **Desk,** Schoolmaster's, Softwood, Grain Painted, Tabletop, Slant Front, 27 x 25 In. ..................... | 266 |
| **Desk,** Serpentine Stretcher, Ormolu Mounts, 2 Drawers, France, c.1890, 31 x 52 In. ................. | 1440 |
| **Desk,** Sheraton, Drop Front, Cherry, Birch Panels, Reeded Legs, Portsmouth, 35 x 34 In. ........... | 2400 |
| **Desk,** Slant Front, Cherry, 4 Drawers, Bracket Feet, 39 x 36 In. .............................................. | 1000 |
| **Desk,** Slant Front, Chippendale, Birch, 4 Drawers, Bracket Feet, New England, 41 x 39 In. .......... | 840 |
| **Desk,** Slant Front, Chippendale, Mahogany, Fitted Interior, Ox-Bow, New England, c.1775, 44 In. | 4313 |
| **Desk,** Slant Front, Chippendale, Walnut, 4 Drawers, Carved Columns, Pa., c.1780, 45 x 42 In. ..... | 36000 |
| **Desk,** Slant Front, Chippendale, Walnut, Fitted Interiors, 3 Drawers, Pa., c.1770, 42 x 40 In. ........ | 780 |
| **Desk,** Slant Front, Chippendale, Walnut, Star Inlay, Fitted Interior, c.1795, 43 x 39 In. .............. | 2375 |
| **Desk,** Slant Front, Curly Maple, 4 Graduated Drawers, Fitted, Bracket Feet, c.1790, 39 In. .......... | 4313 |
| **Desk,** Slant Front, Federal, Cherry, Maple, Fitted Interior, Splayed Legs, c.1850, 42 x 39 In. ....... | 1500 |
| **Desk,** Slant Front, George III, Burl Walnut, Fitted Interior, Bracket Feet, 21 x 19 In., Child's....... | 1046 |
| **Desk,** Slant Front, Maple, 4 Drawers, Bracket Feet, 40 x 39 In. .............................................. | 813 |
| **Desk,** Slant Front, Poplar, Tulip, Figures, Stars, Drawers, Turned Feet, Pa., c.1830, 44 x 38 In. ..... | 66000 |
| **Desk,** Slant Front, Walnut, Line & Bellflower Inlay, Drawer, Fitted Interior, 39 x 42 In. .............. | 1003 |
| **Desk,** Slant Front, Writing Panel, 4 Drawers, Turned Reed Legs, 47 x 33 In. ............................. | 176 |
| **Desk,** Standing, William & Mary Style, Burl Veneer, Baize, 1800s, 48 x 33 In........................... | 590 |
| **Desk,** Tabletop, Green, Cherry, Poplar, Nailed Construction, 1800s, 11 x 28½ In. ..................... | 344 |
| **Desk,** Tabletop, Slant Front, Pine, Old Green Paint, Tall Gallery, Pa., 27 x 27 In. ..................... | 360 |
| **Desk,** Tabletop, Walnut, Drop Front, Bun Feet, Pa., c.1790, 16 x 25 In. ................................. | 330 |
| **Desk,** Tiger Maple, Slant Front, Interior Compartments, Drawers, Conn., c.1790, 40 x 35 In. ....... | 5843 |
| **Desk,** Travel, Anglo-Indian, Inlay Rosewood, Brass Handles, Lift Top, Foldover, 7 x 16 In. .......... | 1554 |
| **Desk,** Trestle, Figured Maple Faux Paint, 3 Drawers, Gallery, Stretcher, 1800s, 32 x 47 In. ........ | 531 |
| **Desk,** Victorian, Burl, Oak, Gallery Back, Shelves, Drawers, Slanted Top, 1800s, 45 x 56 In.......... | 1691 |
| **Desk,** Victorian, Campaign, Ebonized, Brass Mounts, Kneehole, 9 Drawers, 30 x 53 In. ............. | 1062 |
| **Desk,** Walnut, Slant Front, 3 Drawers, England, 1700s, 36 x 31 In. ........................................ | 1560 |
| **Desk,** Walnut, Slant Front, Ring-Turned Legs, Pa., 1800s, 52 x 24 In. ..........................*illus* | 1230 |
| **Desk,** Wegner, 2 Drawers, Organizer, Johannes Hansen, 1954, 76 x 35 In. ....................*illus* | 50000 |
| **Desk,** Widdicomb, Campaign Style, Double Pedestal, Burl Walnut, 30 x 52 In. ..................*illus* | 960 |
| **Desk,** William & Mary, Chinoiserie, Figures, Kneehole, Writing Slide, 7 Drawers, 30 x 32 In. ........ | 43200 |
| **Desk,** William IV, Mahogany, Leather Top, 3 Drawers, Turned Legs, 31 x 72 In. ......................... | 1500 |
| **Desk,** William IV, Oak, Carved, Tooled Leather Panels, Turned Legs, 1800s, 85 x 48 In. .............. | 4880 |
| **Desk,** Wooton, Mixed Wood, 2 Doors, Fitted Interior, Carved Crest, Pat. 1875, 43 x 70 In. .......... | 8190 |
| **Desk,** Wooton, Renaissance Revival, Walnut, Maple, Burl, Parcel Gilt, 1874, 81 x 43 In. .......*illus* | 58425 |
| **Desk,** Wooton, Walnut, Cylinder, Ebonized, Gilt Incised, House Shape Crest, c.1876, 64 x 56 In.......*illus* | 20910 |
| **Desk,** Wooton, Walnut, Maple, Pierced Crest, 2 Curved Paneled Doors, c.1885, 72 x 43 In. ........ | 6250 |
| **Desk-Bookcase Top,** Curly Maple, Cherry, Turned Legs, Fitted, Ohio, 82 x 44 In......................... | 720 |
| **Desk-Bookcase,** Cherry, Drop Front, Molded Cornice, Dentil, Gadroon Carving, 82 x 42 In. ........ | 5843 |
| **Desk-Bookcase,** Chippendale, Cherry, Pine, 7 Drawers, 83 x 37 In................................. | 8400 |
| **Desk-Bookcase,** Federal, Cherry, Cornice, Cupboards, Drawers, Slant Front, 1845, 81 x 42 In.... | 2124 |
| **Desk-Bookcase,** Georgian, Mahogany, Oak, 4 Drawers, 2 Shelves, Glass, 81 x 32 In. .................. | 1200 |
| **Desk-Bookcase,** Victorian, Drop Front, Walnut, 3 Sections, Scalloped Crest, 94 x 44 In. ............. | 295 |
| **Dining Set,** Federal Style, Mahogany, 8 Chairs, Charleston Line, Baker Furniture, 1900s, 9 Piece | 2160 |
| **Dining Set,** Henredon, Mahogany, 3 Leaves, Table, 8 Chairs, 72 x 44 In., 9 Piece ...................... | 600 |
| **Dining Set,** James Mont, Art Deco, Green, Glass Top, Upholstered Chair, 90-In. Table, 9 Piece .... | 863 |
| **Dining Set,** Knoll, Table, White Laminate, Metal X-Legs, Plastic Chairs, c.1960, 3 Piece............. | 2400 |
| **Dining Set,** Mahogany, 4 Turned Posts As Center Pedestal, 6 Chairs, 7 Piece ......................... | 840 |
| **Display Case,** Gilt Bronze Frame, X-Stretcher, Spiral Tapered Legs, Mirror, 33 x 32 In. .............. | 4612 |
| **Display Case,** Veneered, Glass Front, Shelves, Hinged Door, Ball Feet, France, 54 x 41 In. .......... | 2329 |
| **Dog Bed,** Empire Style, Pine, Ebonized Trim, Continental, c.1900, 16 x 27½ In. ..................... | 469 |
| **Dresser,** Acrylic, Laminate, Chrome Steel, Red, White, Rougier, Canada, 1970s, 50 x 22 In. ........ | 1000 |
| **Dresser,** Barbara Barry, Diamonds, Gold Leaf, 2 Doors, 2 Shelves, 36 x 49 In........................... | 1952 |
| **Dresser,** Cherry, 4 Drawers, 19th Century, 36 x 44 In................................................ | 210 |
| **Dresser,** Dorothy Draper, Espana, Lacquer, Gilt, Henredon, 1950s, 32 x 38 In., Pair ............*illus* | 3625 |
| **Dresser,** G. Nakashima, Double, Walnut, 6 Drawers, Indented Handles, 1978, 32 x 60 In. .......... | 10625 |
| **Dresser,** G. Nakashima, Walnut, 4 Drawers, Slab Feet, 1963, 32 x 36 In........................... | 7500 |
| **Dresser,** G. Stickley, Mirror, Red Decal & Paper Label, c.1908, 65 x 48 x 22 In. ..................... | 3250 |
| **Dresser,** George III, Oak, Crossbanded, 6 Drawers, 2 Doors, c.1790, 35 x 73 In. ..................... | 4688 |
| **Dresser,** Herter Bros., Aesthetic Revival, Rosewood, Marble, c.1885, 84 x 50 In..................*illus* | 2460 |
| **Dresser,** Mastercraft, 3 Drawers, Asian Inspired Handles, 29½ x 32 In. ........................*illus* | 2562 |
| **Dresser,** Neils Vodder, 8 Drawers, 6 Legs, H-Frame, Denmark, 32 x 78 In. ......................... | 891 |
| **Dresser,** Neoclassical, Mahogany, Inlay, Mirror, Marble Top, 4 Drawers, c.1820, 79 x 44 In. ........ | 1076 |
| **Dresser,** Pine, Molded Cornice, Scalloped Frieze, Open Shelves, Wales, c.1890, 86 x 59 In. ........ | 615 |
| **Dresser,** Shaker, Pine, 4 Drawers, 4 Larger Drawers, c.1830, 71 x 36 In. .........................*illus* | 86100 |

| | |
|---|---|
| **Dresser,** Victorian, Walnut, Applied Carvings, Mirror, 3 Drawers, Tramp Art, 77 x 40 In............... | 1000 |
| **Dresser,** Walnut, 6 Drawers, Bracket Feet, Shaped Apron, North Carolina, c.1800, 59 x 38 In...... | 313 |
| **Dresser,** Welsh Style, Oak, Inlay, Brown Patina, Carved, Shaped Apron, c.1800, 32 x 74 In.......... | 3068 |
| **Dresser,** Welsh, Oak, 3 Open Shelves, 2 Side Doors, Shelf Stretcher, 1800s, 78 x 75 In.............. | 2250 |
| **Dresser,** Welsh, Oak, 4 Open Shelves, 6 Drawers, 2 Doors, Bracket Feet, c.1800, 88 x 71 In......... | 2000 |
| **Dresser,** Welsh, Oak, Base Shelf, 5 Drawers, 31 x 56 In..................................... | 344 |
| **Dresser,** William & Mary, Oak, Carved, Bun Feet, 3 Drawers, England, c.1650, 32 x 38 In. .......... | 1375 |
| **Dressing Table,** Mirror, Curved Supports, 3 Drawers, Tapered Legs, c.1910, 64 x 51 In............... | 344 |
| **Dressing Table,** Mirror, Shelves, 4 Drawers, Carved Colorado Sayings, 50 x 40 In................... | 600 |
| **Dry Sink,** Oak, 2 Panel Doors, Yellow Grain Painted, c.1945, 30 x 48 In. ....................... | 2375 |
| **Dry Sink,** Pine, Backsplash, 3 Drawers, 2 Panel Doors, 1800s, 36 x 53 In. ..................... | 480 |
| **Dry Sink,** Pine, Blue Paint, Deep Well, Bootjack Ends, 35 x 38 In. ........................... | 570 |
| **Dry Sink,** Pine, Dovetailed Drawers, Painted Flowers, Scandinavia, 1850s, 39 x 39 In.........*illus* | 210 |
| **Dry Sink,** Pine, Ocher Grain Painted, Pa., c.1865, 33 x 39 In. .............................. | 984 |
| **Dry Sink,** Pine, Open Frame Top, 2 Drawers, 2 Panel Doors, 1800s, 34 x 68 In. ................... | 720 |
| **Dry Sink,** Pine, Red, Gray Paint, Door, c.1850, 30 x 35 In................................. | 1062 |
| **Dry Sink,** Poplar, 2 Panel Doors, Scalloped Apron, Grain Painted, Pa., 32 x 47 In................. | 720 |
| **Dry Sink,** Softwood, Grain Painted, Backsplash, Drawer, Panel Doors, c.1890, 38 x 48 In. .......... | 295 |
| **Dry Sink,** Softwood, Walnut, Red Paint, Hinged Top, 2 Doors, Panels, 32 x 39 In. ................. | 1003 |
| **Dry Sink,** Tiger Maple, Backsplash, Paneled Doors, Pa., 1800s, 44 x 51 In. ..................... | 600 |
| **Dry Sink,** Walnut, Poplar, Red Wash, 2 Doors, 30 x 42 x 17 In. .............................. | 1140 |
| **Dumbwaiter,** George III, Mahogany, 3 Tiers, Carved, 3 Cabriole Legs, c.1760, 41 In. ............... | 780 |
| **Dumbwaiter,** George III, Mahogany, 3 Tiers, Shaped Rims, Pad Feet, 41 x 23 In. .................. | 1298 |
| **Dumbwaiter,** George III, Mahogany, 3 Tiers, Tripod Base, c.1800, 43 In. ........................ | 175 |
| **Dumbwaiter,** Georgian Style, Mahogany, 3 Graduated Shelves, Tripod Base, 43 x 23 In. ............. | 299 |
| **Dumbwaiter,** Queen Anne, Mahogany, 2 Tiers, Revolving, Cabriole Legs, 1700s, 36 In. .............. | 240 |
| **Easel,** Carved, Black Paint, Geometric Carving, 6 Applied Hearts, c.1890, 66 x 23 In. ............. | 215 |
| **Easel,** Oak, 19th Century, 78 x 24 In. ............................................... | 531 |
| **Easel,** Pine, 74 x 25 In. ........................................................ | 300 |
| **Easel,** Wood, Carved Leaf Crest, Ledge, 70 In. ........................................ | 82 |
| **Etagere,** Art Nouveau, Mahogany, Shelves, Mirror, c.1900, 60 x 28 x 17 In. ..................... | 240 |
| **Etagere,** Corner, Mahogany, 4 Shelves, Drawer, 65 x 23 In. ................................ | 150 |
| **Etagere,** Mahogany, 4 Tiers, Turned Supports, c.1850, 53 x 21 In. ........................... | 344 |
| **Etagere,** Rococo Revival, Rosewood, Broken-Arch Cornice, c.1855, 107 x 62 In. ...........*illus* | 44813 |
| **Etagere,** Rosewood, 2 Tiers, Drawer, Spiral Carved Supports, England, 41 x 25 In................. | 1000 |
| **Etagere,** Rosewood, Turned Legs, Drawer, Early 20th Century, 50 x 18 In...................... | 180 |
| **Etagere,** Sheraton, Mahogany, Carved, Tray Top, 4 Shelves, Drawer, c.1810, 60 In..........*illus* | 1708 |
| **Etagere,** Victorian, Mahogany, 3 Open Shelves, Twist Column Supports, c.1900, 48 x 47 In. ....... | 938 |
| **Etagere,** Victorian, Mahogany, Gallery, 3 Shelves, Turned Tapered Feet, 38 x 20 In. ............. | 185 |
| **Etagere,** Victorian, Rosewood, Carved Crest, Shelves, Marble Top, Mirrors, 97 x 56 In. ........... | 2000 |
| **Etagere,** Walnut, Carved, 5 Shelves, 80 x 48 In. ....................................... | 488 |
| **Etagere,** William IV, Mahogany, 3 Shelves, Turned Supports, Drawer, c.1845, 50 x 20 In. ......... | 1375 |
| **Folio Stand,** Burl Walnut, Pierced, Hinged, Adjustable, Slots, Shelves, Ormolu, 45 x 30 In.......... | 4674 |
| **Folio Stand,** Renaissance Revival, Walnut, Ebonized, Parcel Gilt, Hinged Panel, 50 In............... | 625 |
| **Footrest,** Shaker, Sister's, Pine, 2 Step, Hinged Lid, Compartment, 1860, 11 x 15 In...........*illus* | 2214 |
| **Footstool,** Abercrombie & Fitch, Horse, Leather, Dimitri Omersa, 28 In.......................... | 1000 |
| **Footstool,** Chippendale Style, Mahogany, Label, E.P. Wilkerson, Atlanta, 17 ½ x 22 In., Pair ....... | 246 |
| **Footstool,** French Style, Wood Frame, Needlepoint Upholstery, 13 x 9 In......................... | 293 |
| **Footstool,** Neoclassical, Mahogany, Curule, Turned Stretcher, Figured, New York, c.1810............ | 418 |
| **Footstool,** Neoclassical, Mahogany, Horsehair, Linen, Frieze, Block Feet, c.1830, Pair............... | 1554 |
| **Footstool,** Pine, Carved, Angled, Old Dark Stain, Cutout Star, Rustic, c.1890, 8 x 13 In............ | 345 |
| **Footstool,** Pine, Red Grain Paint, Book Jack Ends, Pa., 1800s, 8 x 14 In......................... | 111 |
| **Footstool,** Queen Anne, Mahogany, Turned Stretcher, Upholstered, England, 18 x 20 In. ........... | 1080 |
| **Footstool,** Victorian, Wrought Iron, Shaped Top, Openwork Apron, Paw Feet, 1800s, 8 x 13 In. ...*illus* | 72 |
| **Footstool,** Walnut, Bull's-Eye Center, Oval, Turned Legs, Va., c.1850, 9 x 12 In................... | 403 |
| **Footstool,** Walnut, Carved, Needlepoint Top, 7 x 9 x 12 In..................................... | 96 |
| **Footstool,** Wood, Carved, Waisted Panel Top, Cloud Scrolls, Footed, Chinese, 26 x 13 In............. | 179 |
| **Frame,** Arts & Crafts Style, Carved, Line Drawing Detail, 79 x 52 In............................ | 234 |
| **Frame,** Baroque, Giltwood, Carved, c.1750, 26 x 20 In. ..................................... | 875 |
| **Frame,** Birch, Bark Covered, Crossed Corners, c.1975, 14 x 16 In. .....................*illus* | 90 |
| **Frame,** Bois Durci, Oval Opening, Black Metal, Leaf Relief, Victorian, 9 x 7 In. ................. | 104 |
| **Frame,** Brass, Art Nouveau, Curvilinear, Openwork, Vines, Berries, Multicolor, 12 x 8 In. .......... | 1476 |
| **Frame,** Ebonized Wood, Gilt, Belgium, c.1970, 28 x 25 ½ In. ................................ | 1188 |
| **Frame,** Giltwood, Flowers, Fruit, Leaves, 1800s, 17 ⅜ In................................. | 1434 |
| **Frame,** Giltwood, Rococo Scrolls, Shells, Continental, 47 x 40 In. ............................ | 875 |
| **Frame,** Giltwood, Rococo Style Carved, Tanous Fine Art Frames, 25 x 46 In................. | 117 |

F

**Furniture,** Dry Sink, Pine, Dovetailed Drawers, Painted Flowers, Scandinavia, 1850s, 39 x 39 In.
**$210**

Rich Penn

**Furniture,** Etagere, Rococo Revival, Rosewood, Broken-Arch Cornice, c.1855, 107 x 62 In.
**$44,813**

Neal Auction Co.

**Furniture,** Etagere, Sheraton, Mahogany, Carved, Tray Top, 4 Shelves, Drawer, c.1810, 60 In.
**$1,708**

Neal Auction Co.

**Furniture,** Footrest, Shaker, Sister's, Pine, 2 Step, Hinged Lid, Compartment, 1860, 11 x 15 In.
**$2,214**

Skinner Auctioneers & Appraisers

---

**Furniture,** Footstool, Victorian, Wrought Iron, Shaped Top, Openwork Apron, Paw Feet, 1800s, 8 x 13 In.
**$72**

Gray's Auctioneers LLC

---

**Furniture,** Frame, Birch, Bark Covered, Crossed Corners, c.1975, 14 x 16 In.
**$90**

Garth's Auctioneers & Appraisers

---

> ## TIP
> *Examine the back of any cabinet, desk, sideboard, or highboy you are thinking of buying. It is easy to spot replaced backboards and you can check further for unseen repairs. Put the piece on its side to look for replaced feet.*

| | | |
|---|---|---|
| **Frame,** Giltwood, Scroll, Leaf Carved, 25 ½ x 35 ½ In. | | 585 |
| **Frame,** Green Variegated Enamel, Green Jewels, Jay Strongwater, 6 ½ x 4 In. | | 58 |
| **Frame,** Louis XV Style, Giltwood, Scroll Shell Carved, 26 x 25 ½ In. | | 344 |
| **Frame,** Mahogany, Yellow Pine, Painted, c.1860, 24 x 14 In. | | 288 |
| **Frame,** Redware, Molded Oval, Anthony W. Baecher, Va., 1800s, 14 x 13 In. | | 2640 |
| **Frame,** Tiger Maple, Raised Corner Blocks, Beaded Interior Edge, 1800s, 20 x 13 ⅜ In. | | 177 |
| **Glider,** Adirondack, Double Woven Seat, Back, Branch Frame, Adjustable, 64 x 21 In. | | 1404 |
| **Gueridon,** Empire Style, Gilt Metal, Round Composite Top, Starburst, c.1910, 28 x 20 In. | | 799 |
| **Gueridon,** Regency, Mahogany, Carved, Marble Top, Column, Lotus, Stretcher, 32 x 24 In. | | 1342 |
| **Gueridon,** Rococo, Cast Iron, Marble Top, Scrolled 3-Section Support, Hexagon, 20 x 21 In. | | 1195 |
| **Gun Safe,** Neoclassical Style, Mahogany Veneer, Hinged Lid, Door, Felt Lined, 62 x 33 In. ...*illus* | | 2006 |
| **Hall Seat,** Art Nouveau, Mahogany, Scalloped Crown, Leaves, Gilt Hooks, 75 In. | | 356 |
| **Hall Seat,** Oak, Spindled Back & Sides, Paper Label, Michigan Chair Co., c.1908, 36 x 42 In...*illus* | | 2750 |
| **Hall Stand,** Aesthetic Revival, Rosewood, Burl Maple, Mirror, Umbrella Holder, 109 x 68 In. | | 1830 |
| **Hall Stand,** Art Deco, Wrought Iron, Hat Rack, 4 Hooks, Beveled Mirror, 75 x 21 In. | | 213 |
| **Hall Stand,** Arts & Crafts, Oak, Horn Hooks, Scalloped Edge, Mirror, c.1912, 85 x 27 In. | | 492 |
| **Hall Stand,** Cast Iron, Painted, Oval Mirror Back, Coat Hooks, Umbrella Stand, 65 x 40 In. | | 295 |
| **Hall Stand,** Oak, Mirror, Seat, Storage, 4 Hooks, 81 In. | | 570 |
| **Hall Stand,** Rococo Style, Cast Iron, Fruit Basket Finial, Scrolled Standard, Mirror, 79 x 27 In. | | 478 |
| **Hall Stand,** Victorian, Cast Iron, Mirror, Brass Rods, Marble Top, c.1890, 92 In. .................*illus* | | 4428 |
| **Hall Stand,** Victorian, Mahogany, 3-Panel, Carved, Drawer, 93 x 50 In. | | 540 |
| **Hall Stand,** Victorian, Oak, Mirror, Hooks, Lift Seat, Carved Splat, 76 In. | | 234 |
| **Hall Stand,** Victorian, Shaped Mirror Plate, Drawer, Scrolls Legs, c.1890, 84 x 45 In. | | 1063 |
| **Hall Stand,** Victorian, Walnut, 3-Pane Mirror, Marble Shelf, Brass Hooks, c.1900, 76 x 34 In. | | 1125 |
| **Hall Tree,** Geometric Crest, Hat Hooks, Umbrella Rack, France, 1900s, 82 x 32 In. | | 2280 |
| **Hall Tree,** Oak, Carved Crest, 4 Metal Hooks, Lyre Shape Stem, Seat, c.1920, 82 x 26 In. | | 330 |
| **Hall Tree,** Victorian, Cast Iron, Painted, England, c.1860, 83 x 22 In. | | 594 |
| **Hat Rack,** Wrought Iron, Mirror, 4 Hooks, Rose, Leaves, Early 1900s, 22 x 27 In. | | 153 |
| **Headboard,** Empire Style, Mahogany, Gilt, Arched, Downturned Swan Heads, 62 x 65 In. | | 375 |
| **Headboard,** P. Evans, Cityscape, Chrome Plated Steel, Brass, Directional, 1970s, 36 x 80 In. | | 5652 |
| **Highboy,** Chippendale, Maple, 10 Drawers, Ball, Claw Feet, c.1750, 67 x 39 In. | | 2375 |
| **Highboy,** Chippendale, Walnut, 8 Graduated Drawers, Delaware, 74 x 47 In. | | 4063 |
| **Highboy,** Federal, Walnut, 2 Drawers, Peaked Skirt, Hinged Lid, N.C., 29 x 45 In. | | 8260 |
| **Highboy,** Mahogany, 10 Drawers, c.1900, 69 x 42 In. | | 840 |
| **Highboy,** Maple, 9 Drawers, Fan Carved, 2 Pendant Finials, Cabriole Legs, 72 In. | | 1875 |
| **Highboy,** Queen Anne, Cherry, Inlay, Swan's Neck Crest, Flame Finials, 86 x 39 In. | | 12600 |
| **Highboy,** Queen Anne, Fruitwood, 7 Drawers, Shaped Apron, c.1750, 71 x 32 In. | | 2625 |
| **Highboy,** Queen Anne, Maple, 13 Drawers, Bonnet Top, Fan Carved, Connecticut, 20 x 40 In. | | 2040 |
| **Highboy,** Queen Anne, Maple, Bonnet Top, 9 Drawers, Cabriole Legs, 83 x 43 In. | | 2400 |
| **Highboy,** Queen Anne, Walnut, Feather Banded, 7 Drawers, Cabriole Legs, c.1760, 65 x 37 In. | | 3120 |
| **Highboy,** Queen Anne, Walnut, Oak, Short & Long Drawers, Banded, 1700s, 55 x 39 In. | | 1476 |
| **Highboy,** Split Swan-Neck Pediment, Applied Carving, Ball & Claw Feet, 1900s, 90 x 47 In. | | 1869 |
| **Highboy,** William & Mary Style, Curly Maple, 8 Drawers, Base Stretcher, Carved, 64 x 37 In. | | 246 |
| **Highboy,** William & Mary, Maple Veneer, 7 Drawers, Stretcher Base, 1700s, 62 x 41 In. | | 1625 |
| **Highboy,** William & Mary, Molded Cornice, Short & Long Drawers, 1700s, 57 x 42 In. | | 584 |
| **Highboy,** William & Mary, Walnut, Fitted, Drawers, Herringbone Band, 1600s, 66 x 38 In. | | 1722 |
| **Highchair,** 2-Slat Back, Woven Seat, Red Paint, 1800s, 31 x 11 In. | | 46 |
| **Highchair,** 2 Spindles, Mixed Wood, Black Paint, Woven Seat, Splayed Legs, 36 In. | | 420 |
| **Highchair,** Adirondack, Shaped Back, Arms, Stretchers, c.1900, 32 In. | | 180 |
| **Highchair,** Bentwood, Turned Spindles, Split Seat. | | 240 |
| **Highchair,** Ladder Back, Red Paint, 2 Splats, Tapered Seat, Splayed Base, 37 In. | | 240 |
| **Highchair,** Ladder Back, Red Paint, Arms, Rush Seat, Stretchers, 1700s. | | 720 |
| **Highchair,** Mighty Mouse, Red, White, Vinyl, Lift-Up Tray. | | 120 |
| **Highchair,** Rustic, Pine, Stained, Slat Back, American, 1800s, 31 x 15 In. | | 115 |
| **Highchair,** Windsor, Bow Back, Mixed Wood, Splayed Legs, New England, c.1800, 37 x 13 In. | | 750 |
| **Highchair,** Windsor, Bow Back, Spindles, Green Paint, Philadelphia, c.1790, 36 In. | | 1375 |
| **Highchair,** Windsor, Horseshoe Shape Spindle Back, Splayed Legs, Red Wash, 1800s. | | 239 |
| **Highchair,** Windsor, Spindle Back, Bamboo Turned, Footrest, 33 In. | | 71 |
| **Huntboard,** Federal, Mahogany, 3 Drawers, Paneled Sides, Tapered Legs, 44 x 44 In. | | 688 |
| **Huntboard,** Federal, River Birch, Maple, Yellow Pine, Iron Locks, S.C., 1800s, 44 x 53 In. | | 2360 |
| **Huntboard,** Victorian, Pine, 3 Drawers, 4 Doors, Marble Top, Scrolls, Fruit, Masks, 85 x 81 In. | | 1521 |
| **Huntboard,** Yellow Pine, 2-Board Top, 2 Drawers, Ebonized Knobs, Georgia, 41 x 59 In. | | 9775 |
| **Hutch,** South German Baroque, Oak, Carved, Grotesque Masks, 95 x 60 In. | | 748 |
| **Jardiniere,** William IV, Mahogany, Brass Liner, Flared, Footed, Carved, c.1845, 20 x 34 In. | | 1560 |
| **Kas,** Gumwood, 2 Panel Doors, Drawer, Removable Bun Feet, N.Y., c.1740, 72 x 54 In. | | 8400 |
| **Kas,** William & Mary, Stepped Cornice, Paneled Doors, Banded Pilasters, Drawer, 76 x 75 In. | | 6000 |

F

| | | |
|---|---|---|
| **Kneeler,** Prie Dieu, Italian Baroque, Walnut, Drawer, Door, 37 x 25 In. | | 625 |
| **Kneeler,** Prie Dieu, Walnut, Door, Carved, Scrolled Feet, Italy, c.1770, 34 x 27 In. | | 2125 |
| **Kneeler,** Prie-Dieu, Baroque Revival, Walnut, Pierced Leaf Splat, c.1880, 34 In. | | 183 |
| **Lap Desk,** Bird's-Eye Maple, Lid, 5 x 13 In. | | 390 |
| **Lap Desk,** Camphorwood, Hinged Roll Top, Chinese, c.1865, 9¾ x 19½ In. | | 300 |
| **Lap Desk,** Rosewood, Hinged Lid, Fitted Interior, England, 14 x 9 In. | | 123 |
| **Lap Desk,** Rosewood, Mother-Of-Pearl Inlay, 2 Ink Bottles, Straight Edge, 5 x 13 In. | | 106 |
| **Lap Desk,** Stand, Burl, Hinged Top, Fitted Interior, Side Drawer, England, 14 In. | | 750 |
| **Lap Desk,** Tiger Maple, Hinged Lid, Compartments, Drawer, Brass Bail Handles, 22 x 11 In. | | 354 |
| **Lectern,** Neoclassical Style, Oak, Carved, Column Pedestal, 44 x 19 In. | | 250 |
| **Lectern,** Printed, Wrought Iron Candleholder Attachment, 1800s, 33 In. | | 763 |
| **Lectern,** Shaker, Pine, Maple, Red Paint, Adjustable, Canted Top, 32 To 53 In. | | 767 |
| **Library Ladder,** Oak, 6 Steps, Square Supports, England, 1800s, 57 In. | | 531 |
| **Library Ladder,** Oak, 9 Steps, Casters, Early 1900s, 117 In. | | 246 |
| **Library Ladder,** Pine, 6 Steps, Stretcher Base, England, 19th Century, 40 In. | | 230 |
| **Library Steps,** Mahogany, 4 Treads, Ring-Turned Supports, 69 In. | | 1063 |
| **Library Steps,** Metal, Painted, Folding, 35 x 43 In. | | 625 |
| **Library Steps,** Neoclassical Style, Green, Tan Paint, Gilt, 3 Steps, 31 x 17 In. | | 201 |
| **Library Steps,** Regency Style, Mahogany, 3 Steps | | 540 |
| **Library Steps,** Regency Style, Wood, 4 Steps, Leather Covered, England, 67 In. | | 813 |
| **Linen Press,** Cherry, Poplar, Ogee Molded, Paneled Doors, Drawers, c.1835, 88 x 42 In. | | 4484 |
| **Linen Press,** Chippendale, Cherry, 2 Panel Doors, 4 Drawers, c.1860, 86 x 48 In. | | 3250 |
| **Linen Press,** Chippendale, Cherry, Panel Doors, Drawers, Bracket Feet, c.1790, 75 x 47 In. | | 1250 |
| **Linen Press,** Chippendale, Mahogany, Panel Doors, Fitted, Drawers, Va., c.1800, 78 x 53 In. | | 3335 |
| **Linen Press,** Empire Style, Drawer, Doors, Columnar Pilasters, Animal Feet, 1900s, 62 x 40 In. | | 500 |
| **Linen Press,** Federal, Walnut, Stepped Cornice, 3 Drawers, 2 Doors, c.1790, 75 x 43 In. | *illus* | 2950 |
| **Linen Press,** George III Style, Mahogany, Paneled Doors, Shelves, Drawers, 1800s, 83 x 50 In. | | 984 |
| **Linen Press,** George III, Mahogany, 2 Doors, 2 Drawers, Dentil Molding, c.1800, 74 x 48 In. | | 2000 |
| **Linen Press,** George III, Mahogany, 2 Doors, Fitted Interior, 5 Drawers, c.1790, 90 x 103 In. | | 1375 |
| **Linen Press,** George III, Mahogany, Drawers, Oval Door Inlay, c.1800, 90 x 49 In. | | 1534 |
| **Linen Press,** George IV, Mahogany, Doors, Drawers, Arched Pediment, c.1830, 85 x 50 In. | | 750 |
| **Linen Press,** Georgian, Mahogany, Panel Doors, Fitted Interior, Drawers, c.1840, 80 x 49 In. | | 575 |
| **Linen Press,** Mahogany, Carved, Breakfront Case, Paneled Doors, 4 Drawers, 47 x 92 In. | | 2868 |
| **Linen Press,** Mahogany, Paint Decorated, Inlay, Paneled Doors, 1800s, 79 x 49 In. | *illus* | 3660 |
| **Linen Press,** Shaker, Walnut, Pinned, Paneled Door, 2 Drawers, Union Village, 50 x 46 In. | | 3480 |
| **Linen Press,** Walnut, 2 Sections, 2 Paneled Doors Over 2 Over 3 Drawers, 80 x 47 In. | | 1920 |
| **Liquor Set,** Napoleon III, Boulle, Crystal, Bronze, Serpentine Case, Lift-Out Tray, 10 x 13 In. | | 2460 |
| **Love Seat,** Empire, Mahogany, Eagle Crest Rail, Carved, Upholstered, c.1840, 34 x 57 In. | | 720 |
| **Love Seat,** G. Stickley, Branded Mark, c.1912, 37½ x 48 In. | *illus* | 1625 |
| **Love Seat,** Louis XV Style, Walnut Frame, Cushion, Carved Legs, c.1970, 33 x 40 In. | | 288 |
| **Love Seat,** Victorian Style, Mahogany, Medallion Back, Tufted Upholstery, 38 x 51 In. | | 71 |
| **Love Seat,** Victorian, Camelback, Carved Frame, Tufted Upholstery, 38 x 79 In. | | 375 |
| **Lowboy,** Chippendale Style, Mahogany, Drawers, Cabriole Legs, c.1850, 33 x 41 In. | | 500 |
| **Lowboy,** Chippendale, Walnut, Carved, 4 Drawers, Pa., 30 x 31 In. | | 4560 |
| **Lowboy,** Chippendale, Walnut, Drawers, Fan, Shell, Carved, c.1770, 31 x 33 In. | | 14400 |
| **Lowboy,** George II Style, Burl Veneer, 4 Drawers, 28 x 32 In. | | 200 |
| **Lowboy,** Queen Anne Style, Mahogany, 4 Drawers, Drop Finials, Fan Carved, 31 x 35 In. | | 780 |
| **Lowboy,** Queen Anne Style, Walnut, 3 Drawers, Scalloped Apron, c.1820, 30 x 39 In. | | 550 |
| **Lowboy,** Queen Anne, Cherry, 4 Drawers, Shaped Apron, 1700s, 35 x 41 In. | | 625 |
| **Lowboy,** Queen Anne, Oak, Carved, Molded, Notched Corners, Drawers, c.1710, 27 x 30 In. | | 1793 |
| **Lowboy,** Queen Anne, Walnut, 5 Drawers, Shaped Apron, Cabriole Legs, 30 x 30 In. | | 8400 |
| **Lowboy,** Queen Anne, Walnut, Long & Short Drawers, Cabriole Legs, c.1760, 28 x 34 In. | | 2242 |
| **Mirror,** 2-Headed Eagle, Carved, Giltwood, Continental, 1800s, 34 x 24 In. | *illus* | 717 |
| **Mirror,** 8-Point Star, Gold Leaf, Florentine, c.1920, 18 In., Pair. | *illus* | 480 |
| **Mirror,** Adirondack, Rustic, Branches, Stained, Entwined Roots, Sapling, 75 x 54 In. | | 1150 |
| **Mirror,** Aesthetic Revival, Walnut, Giltwood Outset Corners, Crest, c.1880, 45 x 34 In. | | 4063 |
| **Mirror,** Art Deco, Chrome Steel, 4 Hooks, France, 1930s, 20 x 19 In. | | 563 |
| **Mirror,** Art Deco, Oscar Bach, Patina, Pierced Scrollwork, Leaves, Flapper Crest, 40 x 22 In. | | 799 |
| **Mirror,** Art Deco, Tragedy Mask, Bronze, Iron, Scrolling, Fruit, Leaves, O. Bach, 38 x 22 In. | | 575 |
| **Mirror,** Art Nouveau Style, Serpentine, Flowers, Leaves, 46 x 32 In. | | 2706 |
| **Mirror,** Arts & Crafts, Copper, Wood, Repousse, Beveled, 17½ x 14⅜ In. | | 1476 |
| **Mirror,** Arts & Crafts, Pewter, Octagonal, Geometrics, 2 Ceramic Inserts, 20 x 28 In. | | 750 |
| **Mirror,** Baker Furniture, Convex, Starburst, Giltwood, Radiating Spikes, 47 In. | | 2013 |
| **Mirror,** Baroque, Brass Repousse Crest, Spandrels, Beveled, 57 x 36 In. | | 236 |
| **Mirror,** Baroque, Gilt Bronze, Shaped Pane, Leaf Carved Frame, Spain, 1900s, 30 x 22 In. | | 188 |
| **Mirror,** Baroque, Shell, Leaf Carved Frame, Divides Pane, Italy, 62 x 31 In. | | 1000 |

**Furniture,** Gun Safe, Neoclassical Style, Mahogany Veneer, Hinged Lid, Door, Felt Lined, 62 x 33 In.
**$2,006**

Brunk Auctions

**Furniture,** Hall Seat, Oak, Spindled Back & Sides, Paper Label, Michigan Chair Co., c.1908, 36 x 42 In.
**$2,750**

Rago Arts & Auction Center

**Furniture,** Hall Stand, Victorian, Cast Iron, Mirror, Brass Rods, Marble Top, c.1890, 92 In.
**$4,428**

New Orleans Auction Galleries, Inc.

**Furniture,** Linen Press, Federal, Walnut,
Stepped Cornice, 3 Drawers, 2 Doors,
c.1790, 75 x 43 In.
$2,950

Brunk Auctions

**Furniture,** Linen Press, Mahogany,
Paint Decorated, Inlay, Paneled Doors,
1800s, 79 x 49 In.
$3,660

Neal Auction Co.

**Furniture,** Love Seat, G. Stickley,
Branded Mark, c.1912, 37½ x 48 In.
$1,625

Rago Arts & Auction Center

| | |
|---|---:|
| **Mirror,** Beadwork, King, Queen, Castles, Satin Ground, England, c.1690, 34 x 28 In. | 18000 |
| **Mirror,** Belle Epoque, Parcel Giltwood & Lacquer Gesso, Crest, c.1890, 61 x 39 In. | 213 |
| **Mirror,** Beveled, Giltwood, Bird's-Eye Maple, Ribbon Shape Inlay, c.1810, 43 x 33 In. | 240 |
| **Mirror,** Beveled, Shell Frame, Giltwood, Flowerhead Corners, Belgium, 1800s, 40 x 32 In. ..*illus* | 1722 |
| **Mirror,** Black Forest, Bear, Holding Oval Pane, Continental, c.1900, 20 x 11 In. | 875 |
| **Mirror,** Bone, Round, Gesso, Enamel, Jimeco, c.1980s, 48 x 52 In. | 750 |
| **Mirror,** Brass Frame, Serpentine Shape, Fontana Arte, Italy, 1950s, 43 x 26 In. | 5313 |
| **Mirror,** Bull's-Eye, Giltwood Sunburst Frame, Convex Carved Rays, 29 x 29 In. | 2400 |
| **Mirror,** Bull's-Eye, Giltwood, Eagle, Leaf Carved Crest, Convex, c.1790, 36 x 25 In. | 1500 |
| **Mirror,** Burl, Inlay, Ebonized, Ripple Molded Frame, Flanders, 36 x 28 In. | 1476 |
| **Mirror,** C. Jere, Metal, Round, Raindrops, Circles, Signed, 1970s, 35 In. Diam. ............*illus* | 5625 |
| **Mirror,** Carved Wood, Caribou Antlers, 71 x 34 In. | 1750 |
| **Mirror,** Carved, Giltwood, Overlapping Flowers, Albert Suckow, Berlin, c.1900, 45 x 52 In. | 200 |
| **Mirror,** Carved, Shaped Pane, c.1870, 41 x 28 In. | 677 |
| **Mirror,** Cheval, Brass, 68 x 33 In. | 390 |
| **Mirror,** Cheval, Column Sides, Ormolu Mounts, Trestle Base, 75 x 45 In. | 10200 |
| **Mirror,** Cheval, Edwardian, Mahogany, Mother-Of-Pearl Inlay, Swivel, Footed, 72 x 32 In. | 826 |
| **Mirror,** Cheval, Empire, Mahogany, Gothic Columns, Candleholder, 46 x 22 x 81 In. | 644 |
| **Mirror,** Cheval, Victorian, Mahogany, Carved, c.1850, 66½ x 31 In. ..............*illus* | 688 |
| **Mirror,** Cheval, Walnut, Shaped Pane, Carved Harp Stand, 69 x 29 In. | 275 |
| **Mirror,** Chinoiserie, Giltwood, Bamboo, Blue, Gilt Reverse Painted Mat, 47 x 39 In. | 399 |
| **Mirror,** Chippendale Style, Giltwood, Carved Scrolls, Leaves, Chinese, 49 x 26 In. | 1000 |
| **Mirror,** Chippendale Style, Giltwood, Garlands, Vining, 70 x 44 In. | 1560 |
| **Mirror,** Chippendale Style, Mahogany, Parcel Gilt, Plume Crest, 47 x 29 In. | 325 |
| **Mirror,** Chippendale Style, Tiger Maple, Scrolled, Crest, Apron, 29 x 17 In. | 540 |
| **Mirror,** Chippendale, Mahogany Veneer, Beveled Edge, c.1750, 30 x 17 In. | 270 |
| **Mirror,** Chippendale, Mahogany, Cutout Crest, Giltwood, Leaves, Carved, c.1790, 39 In. | 480 |
| **Mirror,** Chippendale, Mahogany, Gilt Scrolls, Leaves, Phoenix Crest, 57 x 26 In. | 1110 |
| **Mirror,** Chippendale, Mahogany, Giltwood, Carved Crest, 34 x 17 In. | 360 |
| **Mirror,** Chippendale, Mahogany, Prince Of Wales Feather Crest, Gilt, c.1800, 36 x 18 In. | 300 |
| **Mirror,** Chippendale, Mahogany, Swan Neck Pediment, Arches, Eagle, 58 x 29 In. | 4994 |
| **Mirror,** Chippendale, Walnut Veneer, Cutout Crest, c.1790, 30½ In. | 330 |
| **Mirror,** Circular, Cupid, Ball, Jewelry Box, 3 Drawers, Brass Base, 21 In. | 615 |
| **Mirror,** Continental, Giltwood, Pierced, Carved Leaves, M. Grieve Co., 53 x 44 In. | 1500 |
| **Mirror,** Convex, Giltwood, Eagle, Scrolls Crest, c.1845, 41 x 24 In. | 531 |
| **Mirror,** Convex, Giltwood, Seahorse Carved Crest, Eagle Base, c.1820, 48 In., Pair | 7200 |
| **Mirror,** Convex, Giltwood, Winged Seahorse, Flanking Carp On Rocks, c.1850, 31 x 18 In. | 1888 |
| **Mirror,** Copper, Warty Surface, 4 Repousse Mounts, Oval, Arts & Crafts, 16 x 22 In. | 275 |
| **Mirror,** Courting, Reverse Glass Paneled Frame, Flowers, Pine, c.1800, 18 x 13 In. | 210 |
| **Mirror,** Dressing, Baltic Neoclassical, Rosewood, Inlaid Ivory, 24 x 23 In. | 281 |
| **Mirror,** Dressing, Cast Iron, Scroll, Leaves, Flowers, Tripod Base, Signed Chinnock, 66 In. | 1404 |
| **Mirror,** Dressing, Hardwood, Carved, Trestle, Lion Finials, Reticulated Crossbar, 21 x 21 In. | 123 |
| **Mirror,** Dressing, Louis XV Style, Gilt Bronze, Putti, 19 x 10 In. | 461 |
| **Mirror,** Dressing, Queen Anne, Mahogany, Flower Inlay, Drawers, Bracket Feet, 24 x 16 In. | 300 |
| **Mirror,** Eastlake, Walnut, Incised, c.1890, 45 x 26½ In. | 123 |
| **Mirror,** Empire, Burl Mahogany, Veneer, Ogee Frame, 32½ x 26½ In. ...............*illus* | 130 |
| **Mirror,** Empire, Mahogany, Square Pane, Caryatid Mounts, Drawer, Splayed Feet, 23 x 16 In. | 375 |
| **Mirror,** Etched Glass, Rectangular, Venice, 44 x 31 In. | 625 |
| **Mirror,** Federal Style, Giltwood, Carved, 1800s, 45 x 24 In. | 300 |
| **Mirror,** Federal Style, Giltwood, Convex, c.1865, 34¼ In. | 1375 |
| **Mirror,** Federal Style, Giltwood, Salt Box House, Riverscape Panel, 20 x 14 In. | 275 |
| **Mirror,** Federal Style, Mahogany, Giltwood, Swan Neck Crest, Urn, 57 x 24 In. | 563 |
| **Mirror,** Federal, Burl Mahogany, Ebony, Eagle Inlay, Molded Cornice, 42 x 15 In. | 472 |
| **Mirror,** Federal, Carved, Giltwood, Lyre, Leaves, Paw Feet, c.1800, 62 x 30 In. | 767 |
| **Mirror,** Federal, Convex, Giltwood, Carved Eagle, Leaves, Round, c.1810, 32 x 20 In. | 1896 |
| **Mirror,** Federal, Giltwood, Carved, Reverse Painted Panel, c.1815, 50 x 19 In. | 480 |
| **Mirror,** Federal, Giltwood, Convex, Carved Eagle Crest, Flowers, c.1810, 44 In. | 1652 |
| **Mirror,** Federal, Giltwood, Fruit Bowl Reverse Painted Panel, c.1830, 31 x 14 In. | 180 |
| **Mirror,** Federal, Giltwood, Reverse Painted Panel, c.1812, 54 x 27 In. | 2625 |
| **Mirror,** Federal, Giltwood, Shells, Acorn Drops, Floral Columns, 20 x 42 In. | 322 |
| **Mirror,** Federal, Giltwood, Woman, By Shore, Reverse Painted, New England, 33 In. | 1080 |
| **Mirror,** Federal, Reverse Painted, Giltwood, U.S. Frigate, 32 x 15 In. | 5540 |
| **Mirror,** Federal, Reverse Painted, House & Tree Scene, Pa., c.1850, 19 x 12 In. ......*illus* | 165 |
| **Mirror,** Federal, Walnut, Architectural Scene, Reverse Painted, 20 x 18 In. | 35 |
| **Mirror,** Federal, Wood, Black, Gilt, c.1830, 48 x 23 In. | 480 |
| **Mirror,** Florentine Style, Giltwood, Pierced Scrollwork, Leaf Crest, Oval, 27 x 18 In. | 492 |

| | | |
|---|---|---|
| **Mirror,** Flower, Leaf Engraved Glass Frame, Octagonal, c.1970, 54 x 42 In. ................................. | 2813 | |
| **Mirror,** Frame, Beaded Mosaic, Canvas, Animals, Trees, Lacquer, c.1790, 19 x 18 In............*illus* | 7995 | |
| **Mirror,** Frank Lloyd Wright, Taliesin Design, Heritage Henredon, 20 x 16 In. ............................. | 688 | |
| **Mirror,** Franz Hagenauer, Stylized Hands, Brass, Tabletop, Stamped, 26 x 15 In..................*illus* | 4063 | |
| **Mirror,** French Rococo Style, Parcel Gilt, Ebonized, Carved Leaf, 52 x 29 In. ........................... | 1000 | |
| **Mirror,** George II Style, Giltwood, Carved Leaves, Flowers, 54 x 47 In. ..................................... | 625 | |
| **Mirror,** George II Style, Parcel Gilt, Mahogany, Broken Swan Neck Crest, 58 x 26 In..................... | 1188 | |
| **Mirror,** George II, Carved Giltwood, 18th Century, 44 x 26 In. ................................................... | 1968 | |
| **Mirror,** George II, Giltwood, Carved, Rope Twist, Leaf, Openwork Crest, c.1790, 52 x 22 In.......... | 600 | |
| **Mirror,** George II, Green Japanned, Parcel Gilt, Swan Neck Crest, c.1735, 57 x 30 In. ................... | 46875 | |
| **Mirror,** George II, Mahogany, Giltwood, Carved, Flower, Leaf, Pane Crest, c.1760, 40 x 19 In. ...... | 1560 | |
| **Mirror,** George II, Parcel Gilt, Flower Pediment, Carved, c.1790, 66 x 30 In. .............................. | 3800 | |
| **Mirror,** George II, Walnut, Parcel Gilt, Shell Cornice, Carved, c.1765, 53 x 27 In. ...................... | 1125 | |
| **Mirror,** George III Style, Marble Top, Bowfront, Urn, Green Paint, 33 x 37 In., Pair .................... | 10625 | |
| **Mirror,** George III, Giltwood, Carved, Pierced Crest, Leaves, Oval, c.1760, 45 x 27 In. ................ | 1375 | |
| **Mirror,** George III, Giltwood, Divided Panes, Beaded, Leaf Carved, c.1790, 39 x 27 In. ................. | 3750 | |
| **Mirror,** Gilt Bronze, Kneeling Putto Support, Etched Glass, Column Base, France, 14 x 5 In. ....... | 281 | |
| **Mirror,** Gilt Gesso, Shell Shape Shield, Bead & Flower Frieze, 106 x 36 In.................................. | 889 | |
| **Mirror,** Gilt Iron, Sunburst Shape, Round Plate, 24 x 41 In. ..................................................... | 2250 | |
| **Mirror,** Giltwood, 2 Cornucopia Crest, Carved, Braided Design, c.1835, 34 x 17 In. ................... | 1200 | |
| **Mirror,** Giltwood, Carved Crest, France, 41 x 24 In. ............................................................... | 1500 | |
| **Mirror,** Giltwood, Carved Flowers, Columns, Angels, Continental, c.1720, 23 x 14 In. ................ | 469 | |
| **Mirror,** Giltwood, Carved Putti Scroll Crest, Leaf, Flowers, Continental, 72 x 40 In. ................... | 3500 | |
| **Mirror,** Giltwood, Carved, Flower Reticulated, c.1910, 37 x 41 In. ............................................. | 118 | |
| **Mirror,** Giltwood, Circular, Reeded Border, Scrolled Candle Arms, Eagle, 44 In........................... | 2460 | |
| **Mirror,** Giltwood, Cove Molded, c.1840, 28 x 18 ½ In............................................................... | 403 | |
| **Mirror,** Giltwood, Eagle, Urns, Swags, Rosettes, Fluted Column Sides, 72 x 31 In. ...................... | 6875 | |
| **Mirror,** Giltwood, George III, Oval, Scroll, Flower Crest, c.1775, 60 x 50 In. .............................. | 23750 | |
| **Mirror,** Giltwood, Mosaic Arch Crest, Lion, Stars, Flowers, Blue, Gold, 59 x 35 In. ..................... | 13750 | |
| **Mirror,** Giltwood, Rectangular, Fluted Columns, Putti, Leaves, 52 x 29 ½ In. ............................. | 492 | |
| **Mirror,** Giltwood, Ribbon Crest, Recessed Panel, Classical Figure, 39 x 18 In............................. | 142 | |
| **Mirror,** Giltwood, Rococo Style, Oval, Flower, Scroll, Putto, Carved, 39 x 32 In., Pair ................ | 850 | |
| **Mirror,** Giltwood, Round Plate, Leaves, Masks, Scrolls, 54 x 44 In............................................. | 1875 | |
| **Mirror,** Giltwood, Tole, Shaped, Wood Back, Black, Metal Relief, Beveled, 53 x 36 In. ................. | 184 | |
| **Mirror,** Girandole, Aesthetic Revival, Black, Giltwood, Oval, 35 x 19 In., Pair ............................ | 2000 | |
| **Mirror,** Girandole, Federal, Giltwood, Eagle, Sphere, Star, c.1880, 47 x 28 In. ............................ | 5625 | |
| **Mirror,** Girandole, George III, Giltwood, Carved, Shelves, Bird Crest, 32 x 15 In. ....................... | 276 | |
| **Mirror,** Girandole, Giltwood, Eagle Crest, 2 Glass Bobeche, c.1820, 32 x 19 In............................. | 1265 | |
| **Mirror,** Girandole, Giltwood, Eagle Crest, Garlands, c.1825, 37 x 27 In. ..................................... | 1280 | |
| **Mirror,** Girandole, Giltwood, Eagle, Convex Round Plate, Prisms, c.1820, 32 x 19 In.................... | 1265 | |
| **Mirror,** Girondole, Federal, Giltwood, Eagle, 2 Candles, Round Frame, c.1800, 17 x 17 In...*illus* | 2596 | |
| **Mirror,** Gothic Revival, Mahogany, Round, Carved, Leaves, Flowers, c.1875, 37 x 37 In. .............. | 500 | |
| **Mirror,** Grain Painted Frame, 1900s, 24 ½ x 20 ½ In................................................................ | 35 | |
| **Mirror,** Gray Paint, Parcel Gilt, Shell, Leaf Crest, Italy, 49 x 28 In., Pair.................................... | 1800 | |
| **Mirror,** Hall, G. Stickley, Hooks, Paper Label, c.1908, 28 x 26 In. ............................................. | 2125 | |
| **Mirror,** Hall, Victorian, Giltwood, c.1850, 31 x 82 In. ............................................................. | 819 | |
| **Mirror,** Iron, Giltwood, La Barge, c.1960, 48 x 29 In. ............................................................. | 540 | |
| **Mirror,** J. Adnet, Wood, Brass, Stars, 33 x 19 In......................................................*illus* | 3172 | |
| **Mirror,** Louis Philippe, Giltwood, Molded Frame, Gilt Flowers, c.1850, 60 x 32 In. ..................... | 1722 | |
| **Mirror,** Louis Philippe, Giltwood, Molded, Incised Flowers, Tooled, 61 x 39 In............................ | 1968 | |
| **Mirror,** Louis Philippe, Parcel Gilt, Rounded Corners, Painted, 74 x 50 In. ................................ | 625 | |
| **Mirror,** Louis Philippe, Rococo Style, Pierced Crest, Scrollwork, 80 x 47 In.................................. | 1476 | |
| **Mirror,** Louis XIV, Gilt Gesso, Flowers, Leaves, Urns, c.1880, 72 x 43 In..................................... | 610 | |
| **Mirror,** Louis XV Style, Courting Couple Panel, Painted, c.1950, 63 x 45 In. ............................... | 625 | |
| **Mirror,** Louis XV Style, Gilt Gesso, Crest, Flowers, Leaves, 42 x 27 In. ...................................... | 153 | |
| **Mirror,** Louis XV Style, Giltwood, Beveled, Gadrooned, Serpentine Crest, c.1890, 63 x 39 In. ....... | 1845 | |
| **Mirror,** Louis XV Style, Giltwood, Flowers, Carved, France, c.1860, 59 x 44 In. ........................... | 1063 | |
| **Mirror,** Louis XV Style, Giltwood, Leaf, Flower Carved, Oval Plate, 55 x 41 In............................. | 1500 | |
| **Mirror,** Louis XV Style, Giltwood, Openwork Crest, Urn & Scroll, c.1920, 47 x 50 In. .................. | 431 | |
| **Mirror,** Louis XV Style, Giltwood, Pierced Scrollwork, Shell Finial, Oval, 48 x 27 In. ................... | 553 | |
| **Mirror,** Louis XV Style, Giltwood, Shaped Pane, 50 x 34 In., Pair .............................................. | 1062 | |
| **Mirror,** Louis XV Style, Outdoor Banquet Scene Panel, Painted, 87 x 38 In. ................................ | 625 | |
| **Mirror,** Louis XV Style, Pierced, Fruit, Flowers, Filtwood, Silver, c.1850, 71 x 30 In...................... | 2091 | |
| **Mirror,** Louis XV, Gilt Gesso, Relief Scroll, Leaves, 33 x 56 In.................................................... | 369 | |
| **Mirror,** Louis XVI Style, Bronze Frame, Swags, Crest, Blue Enamel, 48 x 28 In. .......................... | 937 | |
| **Mirror,** Louis XVI Style, Carved, Giltwood, Swag Crest, Bellflowers, Dolphins, 53 x 29 In. ........... | 1230 | |

**Furniture,** Mirror, 2-Headed Eagle, Carved, Giltwood, Continental, 1800s, 34 x 24 In.
$717

Neal Auction Co.

**Furniture,** Mirror, 8-Point Star, Gold Leaf, Florentine, c.1920, 18 In., Pair
$480

DuMouchelles Art Gallery

**Furniture,** Mirror, Beveled, Shell Frame, Giltwood, Flowerhead Corners, Belgium, 1800s, 40 x 32 In.
$1,722

Skinner Auctioneers & Appraisers

**Furniture,** Mirror, C. Jere, Metal, Round, Raindrops, Circles, Signed, 1970s, 35 In. Diam.
$5,625

Rago Arts & Auction Center

---

**Furniture,** Mirror, Cheval, Victorian, Mahogany, Carved, c.1850, 66 ½ x 31 In.
$688

Rago Arts & Auction Center

---

**Furniture,** Mirror, Empire, Burl Mahogany, Veneer, Ogee Frame, 32 ½ x 26 ½ In.
$130

Conestoga Auction Co., Inc.

| | |
|---|---:|
| **Mirror,** Louis XVI Style, Figures, Landscape, Ribbon & Bow Crest, c.1875, 58 x 44 In. | 2952 |
| **Mirror,** Louis XVI Style, Gilt Carved, 3 Panels, c.1900, 30 x 46 In. | 84 |
| **Mirror,** Louis XVI Style, Gilt Gesso, Stepped Ribbon Twist, c.1920, 64 x 40 In. | 214 |
| **Mirror,** Louis XVI Style, Giltwood, Carved, Pierced Crest, Torchere & Wreath, 69 x 41 In. | 1968 |
| **Mirror,** Louis XVI Style, Giltwood, Divided, Blue Grisaille, Putti, Garland, 50 x 72 In. | 2500 |
| **Mirror,** Louis XVI Style, Giltwood, Landscape Panel, Carved, 61 x 32 In., Pair | 2125 |
| **Mirror,** Louis XVI Style, Giltwood, Openwork Carvings, Beaded, c.1895, 80 x 49 In. | 938 |
| **Mirror,** Louis XVI Style, Giltwood, Openwork Urn, Leaf Crest, Divided, 59 x 41 In. | 3125 |
| **Mirror,** Louis XVI Style, Parcel Gilt, Carved Ribbons, Flowers, Painted, 63 x 37 In. | 625 |
| **Mirror,** Louis XVI, Carved, Giltwood, Arched Crest, Leaf Cartouche, 45 x 31 In. | 1554 |
| **Mirror,** Louis XVI, Giltwood, Rope Twist Edges, Beveled, 58 x 34 In. | 366 |
| **Mirror,** Mahogany, Gilt, Broken Pediment Crest, 49 x 24 In. | 72 |
| **Mirror,** Mahogany, Parcel Giltwood Bird, Cutout Crest, c.1845, 34 x 18 In. | 188 |
| **Mirror,** Mahogany, Swivel, Oval, Curved Stretcher, Base, c.1865, 28 x 29 In. | 90 |
| **Mirror,** Midcentury Modern, Arched, Venice, 48 x 36 In. | 1188 |
| **Mirror,** Napoleon III, Lattice, Shell & Leaf Crest, c.1850, 71 x 50 ½ In. | 1968 |
| **Mirror,** Neoclassical Style, Fluted Cornice, Masque Crest, Garlands, Oval, 89 x 57 In. | 5228 |
| **Mirror,** Neoclassical, Giltwood, Carved, Baluster, Rosettes, Divided, 50 x 25 In. | 837 |
| **Mirror,** Neoclassical, Giltwood, Carved, Rosette, Fluted, Isaac Platt, c.1830, 53 x 27 In. | 1434 |
| **Mirror,** Neoclassical, Giltwood, Guilloche Frame, Pierced Flowers, c.1900, 48 x 25 In. | 1107 |
| **Mirror,** Neoclassical, Giltwood, Leaves, Rope Turned Border, 24 x 38 In. | 209 |
| **Mirror,** Neoclassical, Giltwood, Phoenix, Carved, Openwork Crest, Italy, c.1810, 65 x 32 In. | 2813 |
| **Mirror,** Octagonal, Divided Panes, Etched Flowers, Venice, c.1950, 50 In. | 677 |
| **Mirror,** Optical, Ebonized Frame, Round, England, c.1940, 33 In. | 2000 |
| **Mirror,** Pier, Biedermeier, Walnut, Ebony Columns, Gilt Mounts, 1800s, 72 x 45 In. | 875 |
| **Mirror,** Pier, French Empire, Mahogany, Gilt Mounts, Columns, 1800s, 92 x 33 In. | 625 |
| **Mirror,** Pier, French Style, Painted, Gilt Beaded Surround, 67 x 40 In. | 425 |
| **Mirror,** Pier, George III, Giltwood, Urn, Scrolls, Beaded Frame, c.1790, 62 x 33 In. | 2250 |
| **Mirror,** Pier, Giltwood, Allegorical Panel, Green Paint, 50 x 40 In. | 688 |
| **Mirror,** Pier, Giltwood, Composition, Village, Rope Twist Columns, c.1890, 62 x 35 In. | 625 |
| **Mirror,** Pier, Giltwood, Eagle, Serpent, Twist Carved Columns, c.1890, 108 x 32 In. | 1250 |
| **Mirror,** Pier, Giltwood, Split Spindle Frame, Rosette Corners, 38 x 26 In., Pair | 1200 |
| **Mirror,** Pier, Louis XVI, Giltwood, Trophy Crest, Openwork, Masks, 76 x 36 In. | 2125 |
| **Mirror,** Pier, Parcel Gilt, Half Pilasters, Painted Still-Life Panel, 62 x 55 In. | 518 |
| **Mirror,** Pier, Victorian, Giltwood, Fan, Scroll Carved Crest, c.1800, 53 x 27 In. | 500 |
| **Mirror,** Pine, Carved Scroll Supports, Oval Pane, Drawer, Grain Painted, 26 x 13 In. | 123 |
| **Mirror,** Pine, Divided Frame, Half Turnings, Scrolling Vines, c.1890, 22 x 17 In. ...... *illus* | 240 |
| **Mirror,** Porcelain, Arched Crest, Cherubs, Flowers, Meissen, c.1890, 76 ½ x 48 ½ In. ...... *illus* | 13145 |
| **Mirror,** Queen Anne, Black & Gold, Japanned, Divided, Etched Glass, c.1750, 42 x 18 In. | 960 |
| **Mirror,** Queen Anne, Chinoiserie Decorated, Shaped Top, Boston, c.1710, 17 x 9 In. | 3360 |
| **Mirror,** Queen Anne, Pine, Scalloped Crest, Blue Japanned Paint, c.1740, 21 x 12 In. | 4080 |
| **Mirror,** Queen Anne, Pine, Walnut, Etched Glass, Crest, 15 x 9 ½ In. | 900 |
| **Mirror,** Queen Anne, Walnut, Giltwood, Molded, Shaped, Pierced, Carved, 34 x 17 In. | 240 |
| **Mirror,** Queen Anne, Walnut, Giltwood, Scrolled Crest, Leaf Roundel, 48 x 18 In. | 1020 |
| **Mirror,** Queen Anne, Walnut, Scrolled Crest, c.1750, 24 x 15 In. | 1320 |
| **Mirror,** Queen Anne, Walnut, Scrolled, Cutout Crest, 47 x 18 In. | 600 |
| **Mirror,** Regency Style, Giltwood, Scroll, Plume, Bird Crest, Carved, 1700s, 58 x 30 In. | 2000 |
| **Mirror,** Regency, Bull's-Eye, Round, Convex, Giltwood, Eagle Crest, 37 x 23 In. | 748 |
| **Mirror,** Regency, Convex, Dolphins, Leaf, Candle Cups, Eagle, c.1800, 55 x 47 In. | 11070 |
| **Mirror,** Regency, Convex, Giltwood, Round, Spherules, Beaded, c.1820, 33 In. | 5000 |
| **Mirror,** Reverse Painted, Half Turnings, Panel, Child & Shoe, c.1815, 25 x 13 In. ...... *illus* | 180 |
| **Mirror,** Reverse Painted, Landscape, Ruins, Wood, Composition, c.1800, 40 x 21 In. | 295 |
| **Mirror,** Rococo Style, Carved, Gesso, C-Scrolls, Gold Paint, 1800s, 49 x 30 In. | 461 |
| **Mirror,** Rococo Style, Giltwood, Mid 20th Century, 62 x 36 In. | 300 |
| **Mirror,** Rococo Style, Giltwood, Molded Frame, Shells, Flowers, 38 x 31 In. | 676 |
| **Mirror,** Rococo Style, Giltwood, Openwork Frame, Carved, Oval, 59 x 31 In. | 406 |
| **Mirror,** Rococo Style, Green Paint, Parcel Gilt, Venice, 1800s, 66 x 36 In. | 2196 |
| **Mirror,** Rococo Style, Pine, Openwork Scrolls, Fruit, Carved, Stained, c.1845, 26 x 20 In. | 162 |
| **Mirror,** Rococo Style, Softwood, Carved Scrollwork, Gilt, c.1900, 54 x 43 In. | 420 |
| **Mirror,** Rococo Style, Syroco, Carved Crest, Beveled Glass, 1900s, 59 x 38 In. | 120 |
| **Mirror,** Rococo, Gilt, Group, Acanthus Crest, 50 x 29 In. | 240 |
| **Mirror,** Rococo, Giltwood, Carved, Cherubs, Scrolls, Beaded, Shaped, 42 x 26 In. | 4200 |
| **Mirror,** Rococo, Giltwood, Shield Shape, Leaves, Pendants, Italy, 1700s, 44 x 26 In. | 1434 |
| **Mirror,** Shaker, Hanging, Walnut, Pine, Hinged Box Container, 18 x 12 In. | 2950 |
| **Mirror,** Shaker, Holder, Cherry, Pine, Label, 19 x 11 In. | 6195 |
| **Mirror,** Shaker, Maple, 2 Peg Holes, Shelf, Brass Pins, 25 ½ x 14 In. ...... *illus* | 1845 |

**Furniture,** Mirror, Federal, Reverse Painted, House & Tree Scene, Pa., c.1850, 19 x 12 In. $165

Conestoga Auction Co., Inc.

**Furniture,** Mirror, Frame, Beaded Mosaic, Canvas, Animals, Trees, Lacquer, c.1790, 19 x 18 In. $7,995

Skinner Auctioneers & Appraisers

**Furniture,** Mirror, Franz Hagenauer, Stylized Hands, Brass, Tabletop, Stamped, 26 x 15 In. $4,063

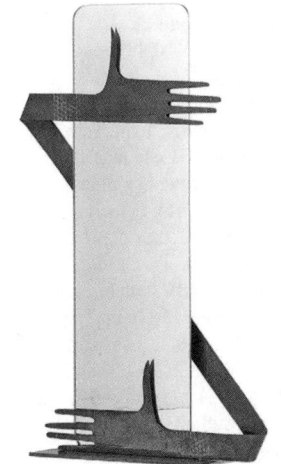

Rago Arts & Auction Center

**Furniture,** Mirror, Girondole, Federal, Giltwood, Eagle, 2 Candles, Round Frame, c.1800, 17 x 17 In. $2,596

Brunk Auctions

**Furniture,** Mirror, J. Adnet, Wood, Brass, Stars, 33 x 19 In. $3,172

Palm Beach Modern Auctions

**Furniture,** Mirror, Pine, Divided Frame, Half Turnings, Scrolling Vines, c.1890, 22 x 17 In. $240

Garth's Auctioneers & Appraisers

**Furniture,** Mirror, Porcelain, Arched Crest, Cherubs, Flowers, Meissen, c.1890, 76½ x 48½ In. $13,145

Neal Auction Co.

**Furniture,** Mirror, Reverse Painted, Half Turnings, Panel, Child & Shoe, c.1815, 25 x 13 In. $180

Garth's Auctioneers & Appraisers

**Furniture,** Mirror, Shaker, Maple, 2 Peg Holes, Shelf, Brass Pins, 25½ x 14 In. $1,845

Skinner Auctioneers & Appraisers

F

**Furniture,** Mirror, Shaving, Webb Burmese, 2 Fairy Lamps, Ruffled Bowl, 21½ In.
**$1,725**

Early Auction Co.

---

**Furniture,** Mirror, Sheraton, Giltwood, Reverse Painted, Carved, Columns, 43 x 25 In.
**$1,422**

James D. Julia Auctioneers

---

**Furniture,** Mirror, Venetian Glass Panels, Etched, Scrolled, 1900s, 36 x 54 In.
**$1,000**

Rago Arts & Auction Center

| | |
|---|---:|
| **Mirror,** Shaving, Empire, Mahogany, Swivel Base, c.1850, 32 x 21 In. | 150 |
| **Mirror,** Shaving, Georgian Style, Pivoting, Rectangular Base, Footed, 16 x 22 In. | 24 |
| **Mirror,** Shaving, Mahogany Veneer, Bowfront, Drawer, Turned Posts, c.1800, 19 x 16 In. | 120 |
| **Mirror,** Shaving, Victorian, Walnut, Round, Carved Crest, Roll Top, c.1890, 22 x 12 In. | 30 |
| **Mirror,** Shaving, Walnut, Oval, Pivoting, Drawers, England, 25 x 24 In. | 120 |
| **Mirror,** Shaving, Webb Burmese, 2 Fairy Lamps, Ruffled Bowl, 21½ In. ............*illus* | 1725 |
| **Mirror,** Sheraton, Gilt, Overhanging Top, Carved, Acorns, Drops, Rosettes, 34 x 21 In. | 415 |
| **Mirror,** Sheraton, Giltwood, Reverse Painted, Carved, Columns, 43 x 25 In. ......*illus* | 1422 |
| **Mirror,** Sheraton, Giltwood, Washington Memorial, Reverse Painted, N.Y., c.1810, 34 x 14 In. | 4375 |
| **Mirror,** Shield Shape, Flowers, Urn Crest, Gilt Metal, Mahogany Panel, 30 x 20 In. | 127 |
| **Mirror,** Shield Shape, Giltwood, Ribbon & Garland, Gilt Gesso, Wire Work, 32 In. | 356 |
| **Mirror,** Silver, Rectangular, Putti, Masks, Beasts, Leaves, Scrollwork, 35 x 44 In. | 615 |
| **Mirror,** Spanish Baroque, Giltwood, Pierced Scrollwork, c.1900, 35 x 24 In. | 1107 |
| **Mirror,** Tabernacle, Neoclassical, Giltwood, Marc Antony, Chariot, c.1800, 43 x 25 In. | 861 |
| **Mirror,** Tooled Leather, Oval Pane, Bow Carved Crest, 37 x 28 In. | 60 |
| **Mirror,** Vanity, Neoclassical Style, Oval, Gilt Metal, 21 x 17¾ In. | 438 |
| **Mirror,** Venetian Glass Panels, Etched, Scrolled, 1900s, 36 x 54 In. .............*illus* | 1000 |
| **Mirror,** Venetian, Leaf Crest, Cartouche Shape, 83 x 47 In. | 500 |
| **Mirror,** Venetian, Parcel Gilt, Leaves, Arched Crown, Beveled Plate, 51 x 43 In. | 275 |
| **Mirror,** Victorian, Giltwood, Oval, Pierced Scrolled Carvings, c.1850, 55 x 37 In. | 406 |
| **Mirror,** Victorian, Giltwood, Pierced, Leaf Crest, Carved Scrolled Base, 103 x 40 In. | 625 |
| **Mirror,** Victorian, Giltwood, Shell, Leaf Carved, Oval, 28 x 25 In. | 500 |
| **Mirror,** Walnut, Carved, Cherubs, Full Relief, Flower Basket Crest, 14 x 11 In. | 300 |
| **Mirror,** Walnut, Moon Crest, Needlework Country Scenes, Courtship, 47 x 26 In. | 4444 |
| **Mirror,** Walnut, Parcel Gilt, Scrolled Crest, Molded, c.1710, 39 x 17 In. | 369 |
| **Mirror,** Wrought Iron, Arched Panels, Square Panes, 7 Curved Panes, 45 x 34 In. | 270 |
| **Ottoman,** Contemporary, Red Leather, Tufted, Ebonized Base, 48 x 48 In. | 615 |
| **Ottoman,** Louis XVI Style, Giltwood, 4 Acanthus Leaf Posts, Cushion, 26 x 30 In. | 1500 |
| **Ottoman,** Upholstered, Round, Painted Ceramic Feet, Mackenzie-Childs, c.1980, 20 In. | 500 |
| **Ottoman,** William IV Style, Mahogany, Upholstered, 17 x 39 In. | 250 |
| **Overmantel Mirror,** see Architectural category. | |
| **Parlor Set,** Louis XVI Style, Giltwood, Padded Back, Arms & Seat, c.1910, 4 Piece | 1353 |
| **Parlor Set,** Louis XVI Style, Mahogany, Caned, Settee, 2 Armchairs, 1900s, 38 x 55 In. | 738 |
| **Pedestal Stand,** Art Deco Style, Mahogany, Paneled, c.1960, 36 In. | 979 |
| **Pedestal,** Adam Style, Inlaid Mahogany, Bronze Mounted, Tapered, 43 x 12 In., Pair | 2629 |
| **Pedestal,** Aesthetic Revival, Ebonized Wood, Gilt Metal, Octagonal Top, 41 x 12 In. | 813 |
| **Pedestal,** Agate, Column Shape, Stepped Base, Square Foot, 4 Sections, 32 x 14 In. | 489 |
| **Pedestal,** Belle Epoque, Ebonized, Gilt, Round Top, Swans, 38 x 15 In. | 1315 |
| **Pedestal,** Blackamoor, Giltwood, Carved, Figures, Painted, c.1885, 40 In., Pair ..........*illus* | 14760 |
| **Pedestal,** Cellarette, Biedermeier, Mahogany, Cupboard, Lined Interior, 44 x 18 In., Pair | 1968 |
| **Pedestal,** Chinese Style, Teak, Marble Top, c.1920, 32 x 14 In. | 240 |
| **Pedestal,** Classical Style, Marble, 8-Sided Stepped Base, Fluted Column, 41 x 21 In. | 460 |
| **Pedestal,** Classical Style, Marble, Spiral Twist, 5 Sections, 1900s, 39 x 14 In. | 1045 |
| **Pedestal,** Classical Style, Patinated Bronze, c.1910, 48 x 13 In. | 676 |
| **Pedestal,** Column, Alabaster, Marble, Champleve, Enamel, Porcelain, France, 44 In. ..........*illus* | 6457 |
| **Pedestal,** Doric Style, Faux Marble, Parcel Gilt, 50 x 18 In., Pair | 984 |
| **Pedestal,** Edwardian, Burl, Painted Flowers, 51 In., Pair | 688 |
| **Pedestal,** Egyptian Style, Aesthetic Revival, Carved, Incised, Ebonized, Square, 41 x 15 In. | 2214 |
| **Pedestal,** Folk Art, Blackamoor Standing On Head, Tray On Feet, Venice, 35 In. | 4375 |
| **Pedestal,** Fruitwood, Carved, Old Man Balancing Tray On Head, Venice, c.1900, 10 In. | 3125 |
| **Pedestal,** Gilt Wood, Carved, Gilt Finish, Fluted Column, Acanthus Base, 35 x 13 In. | 196 |
| **Pedestal,** Giltwood, Faux Onyx, Dog Standard, Round Top Tray, 28 x 9 In., Pair | 875 |
| **Pedestal,** Louis XV Style, Burl Walnut, Gilt Bronze, Bombe, Masks, Swags, 57 x 18 In., Pair | 1434 |
| **Pedestal,** Louis XVI Style, Gilt Bronze, Winged Woman, Appliques, Footed, 51 x 14 In., Pair | 956 |
| **Pedestal,** Louis XVI Style, Green Onyx, Enamel, Bronze Mounts, Stepped Base, 43 x 10 In. | 1625 |
| **Pedestal,** Louis XVI Style, Mahogany, Gilt Metal Mounts, Stretcher, c.1960, 41 x 16 In. | 750 |
| **Pedestal,** Mahogany, Carved, Dolphin Stem, Round Base, c.1900, 15¼ In. | 2091 |
| **Pedestal,** Marble, Tapered, Fluted, Beading, Spiral, Square Top, Italy, 1800s, 44 x 11 In. | 399 |
| **Pedestal,** Neoclassical, Green Onyx, Swivel Top, Metal Base, Continental, c.1900, 46 In. ......*illus* | 390 |
| **Pedestal,** Neoclassical, Rouge Marble, Bronze Mounted, Columnar, Plinth, 40 x 16 In., Pair | 1912 |
| **Pedestal,** Neoclassical, Satinwood, Figural Frieze, Paneled Standard, c.1910, 42 x 13 In., Pair | 3444 |
| **Pedestal,** Pine, Grain Painted, Faux Marble, Stepped Base, 1800s, 23½ In. | 123 |
| **Pedestal,** Renaissance Revival, Bronze, Patina, Scrolled Angular Legs, 34 x 23 In. | 984 |
| **Pedestal,** Verde Marble, Gilt Bronze, Corinthian Capitals, Rings, Italy, 48 x 23 In., Pair | 984 |
| **Pedestal,** Victorian Style, Greyhound, Round Tray On Head, Iron, c.1920, 28 x 13 In., Pair | 2625 |
| **Pedestal,** Victorian, Marble, Canted Corners, Columnar Standard, 8-Sided Base, 40 x 11 In. | 307 |

| | |
|---|---|
| **Pedestal,** Victorian, Marble, Carved, Columnar, Fluted, Plinth Base, 40 x 9 ¼ In. | 598 |
| **Pedestal,** Wood, Carved, Corinthian Column, Marble Top, 16 x 42 In. | 374 |
| **Peg Rail,** Shaker, Pine, 4 Turned Pegs, Blue Gray Paint, 1800s, 3 x 55 In. | 984 |
| **Pie Safe,** Cherry, Frieze Drawer, Doors, Punched Tin Panels, 1800s, 55 x 39 In. | 896 |
| **Pie Safe,** Curly Maple, Shaped Backsplash, 2 Doors, Screens, 4 Shelves, 51 x 53 In. | 738 |
| **Pie Safe,** Pierced, Door, Green Paint, Tin, Wood, 1800s, 33 x 28 In. | 660 |
| **Pie Safe,** Pine, Curved Backsplash, Drawer, 2 Doors, Tin Panels, Leaves, 57 In. | 300 |
| **Pie Safe,** Pine, Doors, Punched Tin Panels, Diamond Pattern, Va., c.1859, 43 x 42 In. | 2990 |
| **Pie Safe,** Pine, Poplar, 2 Paneled Doors, Punched Tin Panels, Doves, Branches, 56 In. | 4025 |
| **Pie Safe,** Pine, Poplar, 6 Punched Tin Panels, Stars, Leaves, Parrots, 53 x 42 In. | 5750 |
| **Pie Safe,** Pine, Poplar, Old Paint, 2 Punched Tin Panels, 2 Paneled Doors, Va., 72 x 42 In. | 590 |
| **Pie Safe,** Pine, Poplar, White Paint, Punched Tin Panels, Stars, 55 x 66 In. | 1320 |
| **Pie Safe,** Pine, Stain, Drawers, Hinged Doors, Punched Tin Stars, 44 x 50 In. | 150 |
| **Pie Safe,** Pine, Star Punched Tins, 2 Doors, 2 Drawers, Green Paint, Pa., 1800s, 71 x 48 In. | 1845 |
| **Pie Safe,** Poplar, 2 Doors, Drawers, Punched Tin Panels, Ohio, c.1850, 81 In. ...........*illus* | 960 |
| **Pie Safe,** Poplar, Lift Top, 2 Doors, 4 Punched Tin Panels, 49 x 46 In. | 1020 |
| **Pie Safe,** Poplar, Yellow Paint, 2 Punched Tin Panels On Doors & Sides, 61 x 42 In. | 1680 |
| **Pie Safe,** Softwood, Bead-Board Top, 8 Punched Tin Panels, 1800s, 48 In. .............*illus* | 1003 |
| **Pie Safe,** Tiger Maple, Drawers, Doors, Punched Tin Panels, Urns, Rosettes, 52 In. | 3738 |
| **Pie Safe,** Walnut, 6 Punched Tin Panel Doors, 2 Drawers, 61 x 46 In. | 1353 |
| **Pie Safe,** Walnut, Poplar, Painted Eagle, Punched Tin Panels, c.1830, 49 x 39 In. | 7800 |
| **Pie Safe,** Wood, 2 Shelves, Green Paint, Wire Mesh Sides, 1900s, 16 ½ x 28 In. | 527 |
| **Pie Safe,** Wood, Punched Tin Panels, Green Paint, 19th Century, 33 x 28 x 20 In. | 660 |
| **Planter,** Oak, Caned Box, Stretcher, Carved Edges, Spiral Legs, 32 x 32 In. | 351 |
| **Print Rack,** Victorian, Walnut, Adjustable, Carved Supports, 44 ½ x 26 In. | 1800 |
| **Rack,** Baking, Iron, Brass, 3 Shelves, Openwork Scrolls, c.1950, 91 x 65 In. | 240 |
| **Rack,** Baking, Wrought Iron, Curved Front, 4 Shelves, Scroll Supports, 79 In. | 660 |
| **Rack,** Bread, French Provincial, Mahogany, Cherry, Carved, Shaped Crest, Finials, 32 x 29 In. | 2091 |
| **Rack,** Drying, Shaker, Pine, 3 Bars, Chamfered Trestle Feet, 48 x 27 In. | 826 |
| **Rack,** Drying, Shaker, Tiger Maple, 3 Bars, Arched Trestle Feet, 33 x 27 ½ In. | 1298 |
| **Rack,** Hanging, Fruitwood, Welsh Style, 4 Shelves, Shaped Sides, 45 x 55 x 7 In. | 295 |
| **Rack,** Magazine, Bentwood, V-Shape, c.1950, 15 x 16 In. | 375 |
| **Rack,** Magazine, Brass, Tubular, Casters, c.1950, 18 x 18 x 12 In. ...........*illus* | 48 |
| **Rack,** Pegs, Wood, Carved, Painted, Scalloped, Birds, Hearts, Flowers, 12 x 4 In. | 474 |
| **Rack,** Plate, Hanging, Victorian, Mahogany, Carved, Animals, Open Shelves, 28 x 49 In. | 120 |
| **Rack,** Plate, Oak, Eagle & Scroll Carved Sides, 1800s, 24 x 43 In. | 270 |
| **Rack,** Quilt, Green Paint, 3 Rails, 44 x 30 In. | 118 |
| **Rack,** Quilt, Old Red Paint, 3 Sets Of Racks, Splayed Legs, 51 x 28 In. | 60 |
| **Rack,** Quilt, Pine, 19th Century, 41 x 51 In. | 135 |
| **Rack,** Quilt, Pine, Folding, 3 Panels, 4 Cross Bars, Iron Hardware, 70 x 98 In. | 180 |
| **Rack,** Shaker, Herb, Poplar, Through Tenon & Peg, 3 Rails, Arched Feet, 1800s, 43 x 15 In. | 277 |
| **Rack,** Spoon, Oak, 2 Bars, Deep Shelf, Scalloped Crest, England, c.1800, 24 x 14 In. | 154 |
| **Rack,** Spoon, Pine, Hanging, Lollipop Finial, Pinwheel, Sawtooth Detail, 26 x 13 In. | 10200 |
| **Rack,** Towel, Gentleman's, Brass, 2 Tiers, Tripod Base, Twisted Rope Arms, 49 x 30 In. | 270 |
| **Rack,** Wall, Forged, 6 Hooks, Decorative Nail Detail, 25 x 15 In. | 117 |
| **Rack,** Wine, Cherry, 10 Drawers, Locking Mechanism, France, 1900s, 36 x 57 In. | 474 |
| **Recamier,** Gilt Wood, White Paint, Fluted Legs, Rolled Back, Foot, 32 x 69 In. | 357 |
| **Recamier,** Neoclassical, Rosewood, Mahogany, Carved, Upholstered, c.1830, 35 x 82 In., Pair | 4956 |
| **Recamier,** Regency, Partial Back, Outscrolled Arms, Splayed Legs, c.1810, 76 In. .............*illus* | 1845 |
| **Recamier,** Victorian, Caned, Wood Supports, 63 x 23 In. | 205 |
| **Rocker,** A. Pearsall, Walnut, Upholstered, Craft Assoc., 1960, 31 x 27 In. | 688 |
| **Rocker,** Arts & Crafts, Oak, Bent Arm, Cushion Seat & Back, Harden, c.1910, 38 x 36 In. | 767 |
| **Rocker,** Arts & Crafts, Oak, Curved Crest Rail, Vertical Slats, Harden, c.1912, 35 x 28 In. | 215 |
| **Rocker,** Bench, Mammy's, Pine, Horizontal Slated Holder, New England, c.1890, 48 In. | 300 |
| **Rocker,** Cherry, Swollen Spindles, Woven Seat, Straight Arms, Mushroom Terminals, 38 In. | 390 |
| **Rocker,** Chrome Frame, Cowhide Upholstery, Arched Arms | 875 |
| **Rocker,** Finn Juhl, Beech, Cushions, France & Sons, Denmark, 1960s, 26 x 27 In. .............*illus* | 813 |
| **Rocker,** G. Nakashima, Spindles, Walnut, Hickory, Slab Arm, 1976, 33 x 33 In. | 5938 |
| **Rocker,** G. Nakashima, Walnut, Hickory, 1 Slab Arm, 1978, 34 x 32 In. | 6875 |
| **Rocker,** G. Nakashima, Walnut, Hickory, Spindles, Shaped Seat, Armrest, 1965, 34 In. | 4613 |
| **Rocker,** Hickory, Shaped Crest, Curved Arms, Splint Seat, Appalachian, 24 In. | 1150 |
| **Rocker,** Hunzinger, Spiral Carved Frame, Upholstered Back, Seat, 44 x 27 In. | 325 |
| **Rocker,** Knoll, Ebonized Wood Frame, Upholstered, Carlos Riart, 1982, 39 x 40 In. | 608 |
| **Rocker,** Ladder Back, 4 Slats, Woven Seat, Cutout Scroll Armrests, Va., c.1860, 41 x 16 In. | 460 |
| **Rocker,** Ladder Back, 5 Graduated Arched Slats, Splint Seat, Shaped Arms, Pa., 42 In. | 469 |
| **Rocker,** Ladder Back, Curved Slats, Woven Seat, Open Arms, Delaware Valley, c.1780 | 123 |

**Furniture,** Pedestal, Blackamoor, Giltwood, Carved, Figures, Painted, c.1885, 40 In., Pair
$14,760

New Orleans Auction Galleries, Inc.

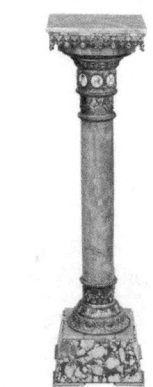

**Furniture,** Pedestal, Column, Alabaster, Marble, Champleve, Enamel, Porcelain, France, 44 In.
$6,457

New Orleans Auction Galleries, Inc.

**Furniture,** Pedestal, Neoclassical, Green Onyx, Swivel Top, Metal Base, Continental, c.1900, 46 In.
$390

Cowan's Auctions

**Furniture,** Pie Safe, Poplar, 2 Doors, Drawers, Punched Tin Panels, Ohio, c.1850, 81 In.
**$960**

Garth's Auctioneers & Appraisers

**Furniture,** Pie Safe, Softwood, Bead-Board Top, 8 Punched Tin Panels, 1800s, 48 In.
**$1,003**

Conestoga Auction Co., Inc.

**Furniture,** Rack, Magazine, Brass, Tubular, Casters, c.1950, 18 x 18 x 12 In.
**$48**

DuMouchelles Art Gallery

| | |
|---|---|
| **Rocker,** Ladder Back, Rush Seat, Black Paint, Delaware Valley, c.1800 | 240 |
| **Rocker,** Limbert, Oak, Upholstered, Vertical Splats, Arms, 41 x 28 In. | 416 |
| **Rocker,** Limbert, Slats, Cutouts, Cushion Seat, Paper Label, c.1905, 36 x 31 In. ...... *illus* | 1750 |
| **Rocker,** Lounge, Upholstered, Bronze Composite, A. Pearsall, 1960s, 30 x 58 In. | 1625 |
| **Rocker,** Maple, Walnut Stain, 3 Slats, Taped Seat, Green, c.1890, 28 In., Child's | 1062 |
| **Rocker,** Milo Baughman, Thayer Coggin, c.1970, 31 x 42 In. | 3125 |
| **Rocker,** Neoclassical, Mahogany, Scrolled Back, Serpentine Seat, Upholstered, Arms, c.1850 | 478 |
| **Rocker,** Oak, 2-Slat Back, Splint Seat, Green Paint, Va., c.1875, 19 x 8 In., Child's | 230 |
| **Rocker,** Potty, Cherry, Pilgrim, Shaped Crest, Heart Cutout, 25 In., Child's | 165 |
| **Rocker,** Rococo, Mahogany, Carved, Molded Back, Scroll Arms, Serpentine Seat, Child's | 246 |
| **Rocker,** Sam Maloof, Walnut, Ebony, Curved Slat Back, 1985, 42 x 46 In. ......... *illus* | 37500 |
| **Rocker,** Shaker, Bar, Arched Slats, Woven Seat, Armless, Mt. Lebanon, c.1880, 34 In. | 14760 |
| **Rocker,** Shaker, Ladder Back, 4 Slats, Tape Seat, Label, Mt. Lebanon, c.1810, 46 In. ...... *illus* | 18450 |
| **Rocker,** Shaker, No. 6, Maple, 4 Horizontal Slats, Button Arms, Woven Seat, 42 In. | 431 |
| **Rocker,** Shaker, No. 7, Mt. Lebanon, New York | 300 |
| **Rocker,** Shaker, Sewing, Orange Tape Seat & Back, Armless, 41 x 23 In. | 120 |
| **Rocker,** Thonet, Bentwood, 20th Century, 41 x 22 x 38 In. | 60 |
| **Rocker,** Wegner, Oak, Upholstered Seat, Denmark, c.1957, 32 ¼ In. ...... *illus* | 861 |
| **Rocker,** Windsor, Birdcage Back, Bamboo Turnings, Cheese Cutter Rockers, 31 In. | 12 |
| **Rocker,** Windsor, Sack Back, H-Stretcher, Continuous Arm, Lancaster County, Pa., 37 ½ In. *illus* | 83 |
| **Schrank,** Chippendale, Walnut, Inlay, 3 Drawers, 2 Doors, 1785, 81 x 69 In. | 1750 |
| **Schrank,** Chippendale, Walnut, Ogee Cornice, Tombstone Panel Doors, c.1770, 81 x 60 In. | 6240 |
| **Schrank,** Contemporary, Pine, Paint, Raised Panels, Dentil Molding, Charles Putt, 80 x 63 In. | 864 |
| **Screens** are also listed in the Architectural and Fireplace categories. | |
| **Screen,** 2-Panel, Full Moon, Bamboo, Gold Ground, Japan, 68 x 71 In. | 277 |
| **Screen,** 3-Panel, Bayou Landscape, Egret, Cherry Tree, Charles Reineke, 70 x 51 In. | 1353 |
| **Screen,** 3-Panel, Belle Epoque, Giltwood, Glass, Fabric, Ribbon Finials, c.1900, 60 x 53 In. | 1168 |
| **Screen,** 3-Panel, Belle Epoque, Giltwood, Mirror, Frosted, Damask, c.1900, 65 x 58 In. | 1200 |
| **Screen,** 3-Panel, Birds, Flowering Branches, Multicolor, 69 x 66 In. | 6875 |
| **Screen,** 3-Panel, Dressing, Giltwood, Shaped Open Panels, Green, France, c.1970, 66 x 56 In. | 210 |
| **Screen,** 3-Panel, Folding, Arched Tops, Leather Upholstery, Nailhead Trim, 78 x 45 In. | 288 |
| **Screen,** 3-Panel, Gilt, Mirrored, Carved Berry Vine, 78 x 48 In. | 300 |
| **Screen,** 3-Panel, Oval, Lafayette, On Horseback, Harbor, Oil On Panel, c.1845, 69 x 55 In. | 1680 |
| **Screen,** 3-Panel, Painted, Oil, On Canvas, Flowers, Vines, Leather Trim, 71 x 60 In. | 510 |
| **Screen,** 3-Panel, Vanity, French Style, Caned, Upholstered, 62 x 72 In. | 234 |
| **Screen,** 3-Panel, Victorian, Decoupage Chinoiserie Figures, 3 Finials, 76 x 78 In. | 1020 |
| **Screen,** 4-Panel, Black Lacquer, Hardstone Inlay, Birds, Chinese, 72 x 63 In. ...... *illus* | 1168 |
| **Screen,** 4-Panel, Black Wood, Porcelain Inserts, Landscapes, Chinese, 1800s, 78 In. ...... *illus* | 7703 |
| **Screen,** 4-Panel, Chinese, Pine, Reticulated Upper Sections, 103 x 92 In. | 480 |
| **Screen,** 4-Panel, Chinoiserie, Figures, Landscape, Painted, 67 x 84 In. | 1125 |
| **Screen,** 4-Panel, Continental, Leather, Domed, Medallions, Fruit, Flowers, 1800s, 70 x 60 In. | 4674 |
| **Screen,** 4-Panel, Coromandel, Lacquered, Carved, Paint, Figures, Garden, 1900s, 73 x 64 In. | 338 |
| **Screen,** 4-Panel, Gold Leaf, Hand Painted, Pavilions, Silk Lining, Japan, 56 x 96 In. | 1800 |
| **Screen,** 4-Panel, Lacquer, Mother-Of-Pearl, Hardstone, Japan, 72 x 64 In. ......... *illus* | 330 |
| **Screen,** 4-Panel, Leather, Painted, Chinese Landscape, Birds, Figures, 71 x 84 In. | 325 |
| **Screen,** 4-Panel, Neoclassical, Canvas, Center Medallion, 67 x 48 In. | 984 |
| **Screen,** 4-Panel, Regency, Chinoiserie, Red Flower Band, c.1825, 78 x 72 In. | 4688 |
| **Screen,** 4-Panel, Resin, Wood, Holes, Twigs & Leaves, 1970s, 84 x 80 In. ...... *illus* | 625 |
| **Screen,** 4-Panel, Silk, Embroidery, Linen, Gold Thread, Flowers, Stripes, 72 x 99 In. | 1464 |
| **Screen,** 5-Panel, Hand Painted Wallpaper, Trees, Flowers, 93 x 90 In. | 720 |
| **Screen,** 6-Panel, Carved Scroll Frame, Painted Lakeside Scene, c.1850, 77 x 150 In. | 2125 |
| **Screen,** 6-Panel, Figures, Terrace, Garden, Black Lacquer, 84 x 96 In. | 175 |
| **Screen,** 6-Panel, Flowering Tree, Folding, Silkworm Border, Chinese, c.1850, 37 x 110 In. | 677 |
| **Screen,** 6-Panel, Folding, Canal Scenes, Landscape, Blue, Gray, Chinese, 96 x 108 In. | 6150 |
| **Screen,** 12-Panel, Wood, Black Lacquered, Carved, Multicolor, Gilt, 110 x 228 In. | 2400 |
| **Screen,** Eames, Birch Plywood, Red Dye, Canvas Webbing, Folds, 67 x 59 In. | 4375 |
| **Screen,** Hardwood, Carved, Mother-Of-Pearl Inset, Chinese, c.1880, 64 x 70 In. | 590 |
| **Screen,** Louis XVI, Giltwood, Carved, Fabric Inset, Shaped Crest, 40 x 29 In. | 650 |
| **Screen,** Pole, Victorian, Rosewood, Silk Panel, Carved Legs, c.1850, 51 x 21 In. | 375 |
| **Secretary,** 2 Doors, Writing Surface Slide, Drawer, Painted Figures, Flowers, Venice, 66 In. | 1125 |
| **Secretary,** Aesthetic Revival, Drop Front, Walnut, Frieze Drawer, c.1870, 56 x 40 In. | 922 |
| **Secretary,** Arts & Crafts, Oak, Glass Doors, Drop Front, Drawer, Danner, c.1915, 63 In. | 416 |
| **Secretary,** Biedermeier, Fruitwood, Drop Front, Fitted Interior, Drawers, c.1850, 58 x 39 In. | 750 |
| **Secretary,** Biedermeier, Mahogany, Veneer, Roll Top, Shelves, Drawers, 1835, 83 In. ......... *illus* | 3998 |
| **Secretary,** Butler, Federal, Salesman Sample, 5 Drawers, 18 x 9 ½ In. | 4147 |
| **Secretary,** Chippendale, Mahogany, Drop Front, Glass Doors, Drawers, 89 x 40 In. ...... *illus* | 1003 |
| **Secretary,** Chippendale, Slant Front, Cherry, Flowers, Glass Doors, Drawers, c.1790, 100 In. | 28800 |

| | |
|---|---|
| **Secretary,** Chippendale, Slant Front, Walnut, Panel Doors, Bracket Feet, Pa., 1785, 87 x 40 In.... | 2952 |
| **Secretary,** Drexel, Biedermeier, Fruitwood, Drop Front, 3 Drawers, 60 x 14 x 34 In...................... | 390 |
| **Secretary,** Drop Front, Fruitwood, 2 Doors, Fluted Trim, c.1860, 55 x 26 In............................. | 561 |
| **Secretary,** Empire Style, Drop Front, Fruitwood, Fitted, Drawers, c.1810, 58 x 38 In...........*illus* | 1045 |
| **Secretary,** Federal Style, Mahogany Inlay, Tambour, c.1910, 78 x 36 In. | 215 |
| **Secretary,** Federal, Drop Front, Cherry, 2 Shaped Panel Doors, 4 Drawers, 44 In. | 1320 |
| **Secretary,** George III, Mahogany, Carved, 2 Parts, Mirror Doors, c.1790, 87 x 41 In...........*illus* | 1434 |
| **Secretary,** George III, Mahogany, Cornice, Glazed Doors, Drawers, 90 x 42 In. | 3286 |
| **Secretary,** Hepplewhite Style, Mahogany, Inlay, Tambour Doors, 3 Drawers, 48 In. | 575 |
| **Secretary,** Mahogany, Drop Front, Tambour Doors, Drawers, Columns, 54 x 43 In. | 875 |
| **Secretary,** Mahogany, Walnut, Carved Crest, Doors, Drawer, c.1850, 99 x 48 In...................*illus* | 5175 |
| **Secretary,** Napoleon III, Rosewood, Carved Crest, Drawers, Fold-Out, 1800s, 53 x 41 In............ | 553 |
| **Secretary,** Neoclassical, Mahogany, 3 Doors, Bronze, Paw Feet, P.A. Wood, 57 x 41 In. ............. | 960 |
| **Secretary,** Oxbow, Chippendale, Mahogany, 2 Shaped Panel Doors, 4 Drawers, 82 In. ................ | 6250 |
| **Secretary,** Queen Anne, Burl, 2 Arches Top, Gothic Doors, Fitted, c.1760, 38 x 84 In............... | 2192 |
| **Secretary,** Renaissance Revival, Walnut, Molded Cornice, Glazed Doors, Doors, 95 x 83 In........ | 799 |
| **Secretary,** Sheraton, Drop Front, Walnut, Glass Doors, Ring-Turned Legs, c.1850, 82 x 42 In..... | 360 |
| **Secretary,** Slant Front, Walnut, Bookcase Top, 3 Drawers, Fitted, Va., 1841, 71 x 48 In. | 3450 |
| **Secretary,** Walnut, Marquetry, Slant Front, 2 Doors, Dutch, 1800s, 84 In...................*illus* | 2214 |
| **Semainier,** Burl, Ebonized Columns, 7 Drawers, 63 x 18 In. | 1250 |
| **Semainier,** Empire Style, Mahogany, Marble, Ebonized Paw Feet, 1800s, 58 x 37 x 17 In. ........... | 2460 |
| **Semainier,** Louis XV Style, Fruitwood, Marble, Top, 48 x 16 ½ In. | 250 |
| **Semanier,** Louis XV Style, Kingwood, Gilt Bronze, Marble Top, c.1910, 40 x 16 In., Pair............. | 359 |
| **Semanier,** Louis XV Style, Walnut, Molded Edge, Fitted, Cabriole Legs, 59 x 26 In. | 615 |
| **Server,** Art Deco, Carved, Marble Top, c.1930, 50 x 18 In........................................ | 330 |
| **Server,** Art Nouveau, Walnut, Carved Trees, Flowers, France, c.1900, 71 x 65 In. ..................*illus* | 1534 |
| **Server,** Country French, Cherry, 3 Drawers, Overhang Top, Scalloped Apron, 36 x 34 In............ | 420 |
| **Server,** Empire, Shaped Front Legs, Drawers, Lower Shelf, Mirrored Back, 35 x 68 In. ................ | 460 |
| **Server,** Federal, Bowfront, Beaded Drawers, Oval Panels, Apron, c.1800, 46 x 50 x 28 In. ........... | 799 |
| **Server,** Federal, Cherry, Mahogany, 3 Drawers, Spiral Turned Legs, Ky., c.1845, 35 x 21 In. ......... | 1035 |
| **Server,** Federal, Mahogany, 3 Drawers, Low Shelf, Reeded Turned Legs, c.1845, 36 x 36 In........... | 6875 |
| **Server,** Federal, Mahogany, 4 Drawers, 2 Doors, Reeded Stiles, Boston, c.1820, 44 x 46 In. ......... | 2813 |
| **Server,** Federal, Mahogany, Splashboard, Turned Stiles, Drawers, New England, 48 x 45 In. ....... | 2040 |
| **Server,** George III Style, Mahogany, Inlay, Bowed Top, 2 Doors, 3 Drawers, 42 x 34 In. | 313 |
| **Server,** Hepplewhite Style, Mahogany, Serpentine, 3 Drawers, Beaded Inlay, 35 x 73 In. ............ | 3360 |
| **Server,** Hepplewhite, Mahogany, Bird's-Eye Maple, Serpentine Front, Inlay, 26 x 71 In............. | 3555 |
| **Server,** Louis XVI Style, Mahogany, Marble Top, 3 Drawers, Mirror, Gilt Mounts, 38 x 63 In. ....... | 3125 |
| **Server,** Louis XVI Style, Multicolor, Marble Top, Leaf Carved Frieze, Shells, 35 x 86 In. | 2706 |
| **Server,** Mahogany, 4 Drawers, 4 Paneled Doors, Tapered Legs, 37 x 86 In. | 4025 |
| **Server,** Mahogany, 4 Drawers, Reeded Tapered Legs, 1800s, 35 x 38 In. | 3750 |
| **Server,** Mahogany, Openwork Gallery, Scroll Carved Apron, Stretcher, 53 x 38 In. | 176 |
| **Server,** Regency, Mahogany, Tambour Door, Drawers, Bowed Front, 39 x 51 In. | 1180 |
| **Server,** Salterini, Wrought Iron, Marble Top, Glass, 34 x 17 In................................. | 449 |
| **Server,** Sheraton, Birch, 8 Banded Drawers, Reeded Feet, Vermont, 46 x 48 In.......................... | 900 |
| **Server,** Sheraton, Mahogany, Drawers, Backsplash, Rosettes, Turned Legs, c.1810, 34 x 35 In..... | 2360 |
| **Server,** William IV, Mahogany, Bowfront, Drawer, Turned Legs, England, c.1850, 36 x 54 In. ...... | 438 |
| **Serving Cart,** Louis XVI Style, Mahogany, Silver Mounted, Roller Dome, 44 x 35 In. ................ | 2460 |
| **Settee,** American Rustic, Twig, 3-Arch Back, Arms, c.1910, 40 x 67 In...................*illus* | 16250 |
| **Settee,** Art Nouveau, Shaped Crest Rail, Upholstered, c.1890, 49 In. | 300 |
| **Settee,** Biedermeier, Fruitwood, Slat Back, Straight Arms, 1800, 60 In......................... | 594 |
| **Settee,** Chippendale Style, Camelback, Upholstered, Stretchers, 30 x 44 In. | 180 |
| **Settee,** Classical Revival, Mahogany, Carved Pierced Frame, Upholstered, c.1890, 72 In. ............ | 406 |
| **Settee,** Domed Back, Outscrolled Arms, Carved, Cabriole Legs, Italy, c.1890, 36 x 54 In. | 1845 |
| **Settee,** Dux, 4 Cushions, Upholstered, Teak Frame, Sweden, c.1950, 27 x 50 In. ................. | 308 |
| **Settee,** Federal, Mahogany, Upholstered, Arched Crest, c.1810, 77 In. ......................... | 1188 |
| **Settee,** Federal, Mahogany, Upholstered, Carved Crest Rail, Reeded Frame, c.1810, 78 In. ......... | 5625 |
| **Settee,** French Empire Style, Mahogany, Brass Winged Sphinx, Upholstered, Open Arms, 45 In. . | 2125 |
| **Settee,** G. Nakashima, Black Walnut, c.1955, 30 ¼ x 78 x 33 In.................................. | 5900 |
| **Settee,** George III Style, Mahogany, Double Chairback, Carved, Arms, c.1810, 38 x 62 In............ | 2952 |
| **Settee,** George III Style, Multicolor, 4 Shield Shape Backs, Fan Design, c.1890, 36 x 72 In......... | 1230 |
| **Settee,** George III, Mahogany, Domed Back, Downswept Arms, Fluted Legs, c.1775, 37 x 71 In... | 2952 |
| **Settee,** LC2, Tubular Steel, Leatherette, Quilted Back, Cushion, After Le Corbusier, 32 x 59 In..... | 1845 |
| **Settee,** Louis XV Style, Fruitwood, Barrel Back, Upholstered, Early 1900s, 34 x 60 In. ................ | 522 |
| **Settee,** Louis XV Style, Fruitwood, Flower Crest, Carved, Painted, Upholstered, 53 In................... | 625 |
| **Settee,** Louis XV Style, Fruitwood, Molded Cartouche, Cabriole Legs, Upholstered, 54 In............. | 480 |
| **Settee,** Louis XVI Style, Giltwood, Carved Crest, Aubusson Upholstery, Arms, c.1890, 60 In. ........ | 469 |
| **Settee,** Louis XVI Style, Mahogany, Bronze Mounted, c.1910, 43 x 70 In....................... | 522 |

**Furniture,** Recamier, Regency, Partial Back, Outscrolled Arms, Splayed Legs, c.1810, 76 In.
$1,845

New Orleans Auction Galleries, Inc.

**Furniture,** Rocker, Finn Juhl, Beech, Cushions, France & Sons, Denmark, 1960s, 26 x 27 In.
$813

Rago Arts & Auction Center

**Furniture,** Rocker, Limbert, Slats, Cutouts, Cushion Seat, Paper Label, c.1905, 36 x 31 In.
$1,750

Rago Arts & Auction Center

**F**

## TIP

*The "tilters," balls held in a special mount on Shaker chair legs, were not meant as rockers or to tilt the chair back. They were used to keep the chair from scratching the floor when it was dragged to a new spot.*

**Furniture,** Rocker, Sam Maloof, Walnut, Ebony, Curved Slat Back, 1985, 42 x 46 In. $37,500

Los Angeles Modern Auctions (LAMA)

**Furniture,** Rocker, Shaker, Ladder Back, 4 Slats, Tape Seat, Label, Mt. Lebanon, c.1810, 46 In. $18,450

Skinner Auctioneers & Appraisers

**Furniture,** Rocker, Wegner, Oak, Upholstered Seat, Denmark, c.1957, 32 ¼ In. $861

Skinner Auctioneers & Appraisers

| | |
|---|--:|
| **Settee,** Louis XVI Style, Mahogany, Out-Curved Ends, Ribbed Frame, c.1890, 37 x 63 In. | 1476 |
| **Settee,** Mahogany, Marquetry, Shaped & Padded Back, Outswept Arms, c.1850, 36 x 76 In. | 1045 |
| **Settee,** Mahogany, Medallion, Tufted, Green, Grape Crest, Late Victorian, 40 x 61 In. | 185 |
| **Settee,** Mahogany, Scrolled Back, Armrests, Upholstered, Carved, c.1850, 46 x 64 In. | 1250 |
| **Settee,** Neoclassical Style, Mahogany, Chairback, Tablet Crest, Interlaced Splat, 35 x 41 In. | 1315 |
| **Settee,** Neoclassical, Gilt Stencils, Cane Seat, Roll Arms, Turned Legs, Baltimore, 82 In. | 900 |
| **Settee,** Neoclassical, Rosewood, Upholstered, Scroll Arms, Carved Seat Rail, c.1845, 83 In. | 469 |
| **Settee,** Oak, Carved Back, Plank Seat, Ball & Claw, c.1920, 42 x 47 In. | 875 |
| **Settee,** Openwork Crest Rail, 3 Urn Shape Splats, Striped Upholstery, Italy, c.1800, 59 In. | 4500 |
| **Settee,** Painted, Faux Rosewood, Red, Black, Green & Yellow Grapes, c.1830, 33 x 72 In. | 1440 |
| **Settee,** Queen Anne, Walnut, Serpentine Crest Back, Open Arms, Tapestry Upholstery | 5700 |
| **Settee,** Restauration, Fruitwood, Back Scrolled Crest, Cushioned Seat, 38 x 70 In. | 1722 |
| **Settee,** Rococo Revival, Rosewood, Crests, Flowering Urn, Orange Silk, 51 x 70 In. | 533 |
| **Settee,** Rococo Style, Carved, Pierced Crest, Gilt Painted, Upholstered, Germany, 53 In. | 1875 |
| **Settee,** Sheraton Style, Mahogany, X-Splats, Reed Open Arms, Pad Seat, 35 x 52 In. | 1046 |
| **Settee,** Sheraton, 3-Part Back, Gilt Harp, Instruments, Cane Seat, Arms, Portsmouth, 54 In. | 7680 |
| **Settee,** Sheraton, Plank Seat, Brown Ground, Flowers, Leaves, Pa., 34 x 74 In. | 177 |
| **Settee,** Steer Horns, Shaped Cushion, Flared Legs, Upholstered, c.1885, 38 x 56 In. .............*illus* | 1968 |
| **Settee,** Tiger Maple, Green, Cream Tape Weave, 50 x 57 In. | 295 |
| **Settee,** Victorian, Walnut, Carved, Upholstered, Caned Frame, Fluted Legs, 1800s, 43 x 64 In. | 295 |
| **Settee,** Walnut Frame, Loose Cushion Seat, Upholstered Back, Carved Crest Rail, Italy, 72 In. | 600 |
| **Settee,** William & Mary, Oak, Carved Panels, Arms, Hinged Seat, England, c.1750, 57 x 52 In. | 1500 |
| **Settee,** Windsor, Half Spindle, Arrow Rail, 3 Sections, Green Paint, Kentucky, c.1830, 78 In. | 1955 |
| **Settee,** Windsor, Triple Chairback, Knuckle Arms, c.1780, 38 x 70 In. | 16800 |
| **Settle,** Arts & Crafts, Oak, Canted Back, Vertical Slats, Even Arms, c.1912, 32 x 65 In. | 738 |
| **Settle,** Arts & Crafts, Oak, Even Slat Back, Sides, Arms, Cushion, c.1910, 39 x 71 In. | 2125 |
| **Settle,** Arts & Crafts, Oak, Slat Back, Brown Leather Upholstery, 33 x 72 In. | 708 |
| **Settle,** Bed, Tuck-Away, Wood, Green Paint, Flowers, Scandinavia, 1800s, 35 x 67 In. | 1353 |
| **Settle,** Elm, Ornate Carved Back, Apron, Lion's Paw Feet, Arms, c.1910, 67 x 56 In. | 354 |
| **Settle,** English Oak, Paneled Back, Wood Seat, Padded, Arms, 1800s, 56 x 85 In. | 1353 |
| **Settle,** George II, Oak, High Panel Back, Open Arms, c.1740, 40 x 76 In. | 720 |
| **Settle,** George II, Oak, Panel Back, Open Arms, Carved, c.1760, 43 x 72 In. | 600 |
| **Settle,** Grain Painted, Plank Back, Spindle Center Hinged Seat, Cushion, 79 In. | 469 |
| **Settle,** Oak, 4-Panel Back, Stretcher Base, Cushion, England, 47 x 72 In. | 625 |
| **Settle,** Pine, Brown Paint, Paneled Back, Shaped Wing Arms, c.1760, 47 x 49 In. | 1800 |
| **Settle,** Pine, Lift Top, Pullout Bed, Red, Yellow, 1820-40, 30 x 40 ½ In. | 2250 |
| **Settle,** Pine, Red Paint, New England, 63 x 50 In. | 4080 |
| **Settle,** Softwood, Beaded Support Board, Shaped Sides, Arms, c.1800, 65 x 20 In. | 767 |
| **Settle,** Stickley Bros., Even Arm, Thin Slats, Canted Sides, 36 x 84 In. | 4375 |
| **Settle,** Walnut, Spindle Back, Carved, Painted, Arms, Continental, c.1790, 40 x 48 In. | 1125 |
| **Shelf,** Corner, Wood, Blue, Daffodil, 3 Shelves, Cobbs, Hamilton Co., 1930s, 18 x 4 In. | 32 |
| **Shelf,** Corner, Wood, Turned Spool Supports, 5 Shelves, Gallery, Footed, 1900s, 49 In. | 205 |
| **Shelf,** Hanging, Wood, 3 Open Shelves, Cutout Sides, c.1850, 27 x 25 In. | 288 |
| **Shelf,** Louis XV, 3 Open Shelves, Carved Crest, Apron, Raised Feet, 34 x 38 In. | 875 |
| **Shelf,** Mahogany, Whale Ends, New England, c.1810, 32 x 28 In. | 461 |
| **Shelf,** Metal, Scrolled Sides, 2 Tiers, Red Paint, Musical Decal, 1950s, 16 x 9 In. | 46 |
| **Shelf,** Pantry, Pine, Freestanding, Bootjack Ends, 4 Shelves, Applied Trim, 62 x 49 In., Pair | 948 |
| **Shelf,** Pine, Grain Painted, Rounded Ends, 3 Stylized Brackets, 19th Century, 72 In. | 600 |
| **Shelf,** Pine, Scrolled Bracket, White Paint, 15 ½ x 24 In. | 492 |
| **Shelf,** Shaker, Hanging, Pine, 2 Tiers, Pierced, c.1880, 31 x 12 ⅜ In. | 400 |
| **Shelf,** Shaker, Pine, 6 Tiers, Cutout Feet, 1800s, 62 ¾ x 20 In. | 2583 |
| **Shelf,** Wall, Pine, 3 Open Shelves, Triangular, Red Paint, England, c.1850, 25 x 28 In. | 180 |
| **Shelving Unit,** Danish Modern, 3 Cabinets, Desk, Drop Front, Drawers, Shelves, 80 x 126 In. | 960 |
| **Sideboard,** Aesthetic Revival, Burl Inlay, Ebonized, Bronze, Fluted Columns, 107 x 74 In. | 2460 |
| **Sideboard,** Arts & Crafts, Roycroft Style, Mirror, Leaded Glass, Doors, 64 x 51 In. | 840 |
| **Sideboard,** Baltimore Style, Bellflower Inlay, Mahogany, 38 x 65 In. | 461 |
| **Sideboard,** Berkey & Gay, Hepplewhite Style, Ebony, Drawers, Cabinets, 52 x 90 In. | 1035 |
| **Sideboard,** Cherry, Poplar, Red Wash, Scrolled Backsplash, N.C., 1830s, 50 x 62 In. | 3540 |
| **Sideboard,** D. Deskey, White Lacquer, Mahogany, Lime Green Inside, 28 x 84 In. .............*illus* | 1770 |
| **Sideboard,** Danish Modern, Tambour Door, Adjustable Shelves, 1960s, 31 x 65 In. | 1298 |
| **Sideboard,** Danish Modern, Teak, Tambour Doors, 4 Drawers Each Side, J. Anderson, 94 In. | 1652 |
| **Sideboard,** Directoire Style, Pine, Distress Paint, 33 x 99 In. | 922 |
| **Sideboard,** Empire, Mahogany, 3 Carved Drawers, 3 Cabinet Doors, Columns, 68 x 25 In. | 259 |
| **Sideboard,** Federal Style, Mahogany, Bellflower Inlay, Bowed, Drawers, c.1920, 40 x 73 In. | 518 |
| **Sideboard,** Federal Style, Mahogany, Line Inlay, Serpentine, 5 Drawers, c.1945, 36 x 72 In. | 438 |
| **Sideboard,** Federal, Figured Mahogany, Drawers, Cellarette Dividers, S.C., 1810, 40 x 69 In. | 8260 |
| **Sideboard,** Federal, Mahogany, Birch Veneer, Drawers, Portsmouth, c.1810, 43 x 71 In. | 2400 |

**Furniture,** Rocker, Windsor, Sack Back, H-Stretcher, Continuous Arm, Lancaster County, Pa., 37½ In.
$83

Conestoga Auction Co., Inc.

**Furniture,** Screen, 4-Panel, Black Lacquer, Hardstone Inlay, Birds, Chinese, 72 x 63 In.
$1,168

New Orleans Auction Galleries, Inc.

**Furniture,** Screen, 4-Panel, Black Wood, Porcelain Inserts, Landscapes, Chinese, 1800s, 78 In.
$7,703

James D. Julia Auctioneers

**Furniture,** Screen, 4-Panel, Lacquer, Mother-Of-Pearl, Hardstone, Japan, 72 x 64 In.
$330

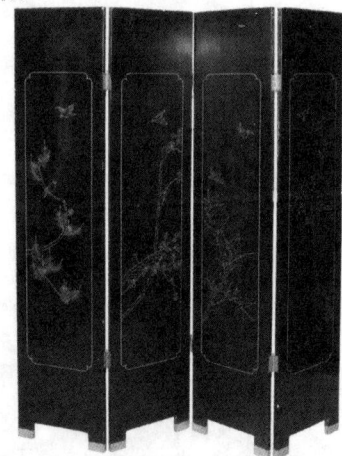

DuMouchelles Art Gallery

**Furniture,** Screen, 4-Panel, Resin, Wood, Holes, Twigs & Leaves, 1970s, 84 x 80 In.
$625

Rago Arts & Auction Center

**Furniture,** Secretary, Biedermeier, Mahogany, Veneer, Roll Top, Shelves, Drawers, 1835, 83 In.
$3,998

Skinner Auctioneers & Appraisers

**Furniture,** Secretary, Chippendale, Mahogany, Drop Front, Glass Doors, Drawers, 89 x 40 In.
$1,003

Conestoga Auction Co., Inc.

**Furniture,** Secretary, Empire Style, Drop Front, Fruitwood, Fitted, Drawers, c.1810, 58 x 38 In.
$1,045

New Orleans Auction Galleries, Inc.

**Furniture,** Secretary, George III, Mahogany, Carved, 2 Parts, Mirror Doors, c.1790, 87 x 41 In.
$1,434

Neal Auction Co.

**F**

**Furniture,** Secretary, Mahogany, Walnut, Carved Crest, Doors, Drawer, c.1850, 99 x 48 In.
$5,175

Cottone Auctions

**Furniture,** Secretary, Walnut, Marquetry, Slant Front, 2 Doors, Dutch, 1800s, 84 In.
$2,214

New Orleans Auction Galleries, Inc.

**Furniture,** Server, Art Nouveau, Walnut, Carved Trees, Flowers, France, c.1900, 71 x 65 In.
$1,534

Brunk Auctions

**TIP**

*When moving a heavy chest of drawers, take all the drawers out first. The cabinet frame will be easier to move and you are less likely to loosen the parts.*

**Furniture,** Settee, American Rustic, Twig, 3 Arch Back, Arms, c.1910, 40 x 67 In.
$16,250

Rago Arts & Auction Center

**Furniture,** Settee, Steer Horns, Shaped Cushion, Flared Legs, Upholstered, c.1885, 38 x 56 In.
$1,968

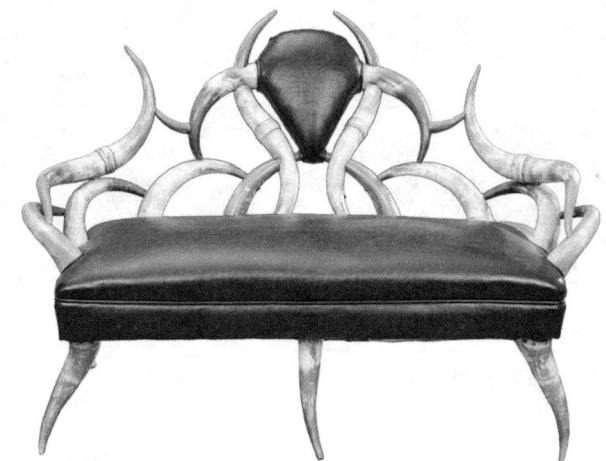

New Orleans Auction Galleries, Inc.

**Furniture,** Sideboard, D. Deskey, White Lacquer, Mahogany, Lime Green Inside, 28 x 84 In.
$1,770

Brunk Auctions

| | |
|---|---|
| Sideboard, Federal, Mahogany, Flower Inlay, 5 Drawers, 2 Doors, 81 x 26 In. | 2500 |
| Sideboard, Federal, Mahogany, Line Inlay, Serpentine, c.1800, 39 x 57 In. | 2460 |
| Sideboard, Federal, Mahogany, Poplar, Inlay, 3 Drawers, 6 Legs, 40 x 25 In. | 3375 |
| Sideboard, Federal, Mahogany, Shaped Top, Shelf, Drawers, Doors, c.1800, 38 x 64 In. | 923 |
| Sideboard, Federal, Tiger Maple, Poplar, Fan Backsplash, 3 Drawers, 3 Doors, 61 In. | 2950 |
| Sideboard, Federal, Walnut, Marble Top, Doors, Drawers, Mid-Atlantic, c.1810, 39 x 67 In. | 1200 |
| Sideboard, French Provincial, Oak, 3 Panel Doors, 2 Sliding Doors, Drawers, 58 x 59 In. | 625 |
| Sideboard, G. Stickley, 8 Legs, Doors, Drawers, c.1906, 50 x 70 x 25 ½ In. | 6875 |
| Sideboard, G. Stickley, Butterfly Insets, Through Tenons, c.1901, 40 x 50 In. ..............illus | 20000 |
| Sideboard, G. Stickley, Oak, Slated Backsplash, 4 Drawers, 2 Doors, 46 x 48 In. | 1875 |
| Sideboard, George III Style, Mahogany, 2 Drawers, 2 Doors, 38 x 64 In. | 1000 |
| Sideboard, George III Style, Mahogany, Bowfront, Brass Rail, Urn Finials, 53 x 77 In. | 2460 |
| Sideboard, George III Style, Mahogany, Serpentine, 3 Drawers, 4 Doors, 40 x 73 In. | 500 |
| Sideboard, George III, Mahogany, Bowfront, Inlay, Drawers, Tambour Door, c.1790, 75 In. | 4063 |
| Sideboard, George III, Mahogany, Drawer, 2 Doors, c.1810, 36 x 72 In. | 500 |
| Sideboard, George III, Mahogany, Inlay, Bowfront, Drawers, Tapered Legs, c.1790, 74 In. | 2500 |
| Sideboard, George III, Mahogany, Marquetry Urns, Swags, Doors, Drawers, c.1775, 82 In. | 4375 |
| Sideboard, George III, Mahogany, Serpentine, 5 Drawers, c.1790, 35 x 64 In. | 1875 |
| Sideboard, Georgian Style, Beaded Edges, 3 Paneled Doors, France, 35 x 64 In. | 1837 |
| Sideboard, Georgian, Mahogany, Fan, Oval Inlay, 5 Drawers, c.1840, 36 x 60 In. | 2000 |
| Sideboard, Hardwood, Drawers, Cabinet, Inlay, Heal & Son Ltd., c.1935, 61 In. | 431 |
| Sideboard, Hepplewhite Style, Mahogany Veneer, Oak, Shaped, String Inlay, 38 x 56 In. | 738 |
| Sideboard, Hepplewhite Style, Mahogany, 2 Drawers, 2 Doors, Henkel Harris, 39 x 66 In. | 1020 |
| Sideboard, Hepplewhite Style, Mahogany, Flowers, Bellflower & Swag, 40 x 69 In. | 2596 |
| Sideboard, Hepplewhite, Inlaid Mahogany, Drawer, False Drawers, c.1800, 36 x 78 x 26 In. | 1180 |
| Sideboard, Hepplewhite, Mahogany, 4 Doors, Drawer, Raised Legs, N.Y., c.1800, 39 x 73 In. | 2040 |
| Sideboard, Hepplewhite, Mahogany, Fan Inlay, 3 Drawers, 4 Doors, New England, 41 x 72 In. | 2160 |
| Sideboard, Hepplewhite, Mahogany, Inlay, Banding, Drawer, 4 Doors, Mass., 37 x 73 In. | 1680 |
| Sideboard, Hepplewhite, Mahogany, Serpentine Front, Inlay, c.1820, 42 x 71 In. | 1500 |
| Sideboard, Kipp Steward, 2 Drawers, 4 Paneled Doors, Drexel, 1900s, 31 x 61 In..............illus | 540 |
| Sideboard, Mahogany, Bird's-Eye Maple, Inlay, Step Back Doors, Baltimore, 44 x 68 In. | 1148 |
| Sideboard, Mahogany, Splashboard, Doors, Carved Columns, Vermont, 1825, 53 x 48 In. | 1020 |
| Sideboard, McCobb, Bifold Doors, Fitted Drawer, Brass Legs, Stretchers, 34 x 36 In. | 1599 |
| Sideboard, McCobb, Drawers, Leather-Covered Doors, 37 x 66 In. | 805 |
| Sideboard, Mirror Backsplash, 3 Drawers, 2 Doors, Pagoda Shape, c.1905, 49 x 43 In. | 1440 |
| Sideboard, Neoclassical, Carved, Backsplash, Cove Molded Pedestals, c.1830, 53 x 76 In. | 956 |
| Sideboard, Neoclassical, Mahogany, Poplar, 3 Drawers, Doors, Columns, c.1820, 42 x 73 In. | 840 |
| Sideboard, Oak, 2 Tambour Doors, B. Schaefer, Mid-Century, 36 x 85 x 21 In. | 240 |
| Sideboard, Red Paint, Silvered Wood, Brass Gallery, 33 x 98 In. | 344 |
| Sideboard, Regency Style, Mahogany, 5 Drawers, c.1910, 39 x 55 In. | 2250 |
| Sideboard, Renaissance Revival Style, Walnut, Scalloped Backsplash, c.1910, 50 x 86 In. | 687 |
| Sideboard, Robsjohn-Gibbings, Bowed, 3 Drawers, Widdicomb, 20 x 66 In. | 633 |
| Sideboard, Sheraton, Mahogany, Birch, Bowed, Drawers, Turned Legs, New England, 37 x 46 In. | 9600 |
| Sideboard, Teak, Tambour Doors, Shelves, Denmark, 31 ½ x 65 ½ In. | 529 |
| Sideboard, Victorian Style, Walnut, Carved, Marble Top, Paneled Doors, 85 x 52 In. | 142 |
| Sideboard, Victorian, Marble Top, Serpentine Front, Doors, Cutout Panels, 37 x 74 In. | 604 |
| Sideboard, Walnut, Serpentine Backsplash, 4 Drawers, 2 Doors, c.1920, 66 In. | 244 |
| Sideboard, William IV, Mahogany, Pedestal, Center Section, Cupboards, c.1830, 45 x 94 In. | 861 |
| Sideboard, Wormley, Mahogany, 3 Drawers, 3 Sliding Doors, Woven Fronts, 61 In. | 976 |
| Sideboard, Wormley, Walnut, Pine, Maple, Drawer, Sliding Doors, c.1956, 36 x 71 In. | 3998 |
| Silver Chest, Queen Anne, Mahogany, 3 Drawers, 6 Handles, Stretchers, 38 x 24 In. | 270 |
| Sleigh Chair, Walter Lamb, Ottoman, End Table, c.1950, 29 x 30 In. | 2813 |
| Sofa, 1 Arm, Half Back, Upholstered, William Haines, 1960, 29 x 97 x 36 In. | 12500 |
| Sofa, Aesthetic Revival, Rosewood, Inlay, Brass, 3-Part Back, Arms, c.1885, 72 In. | 922 |
| Sofa, Anglo-Colonial, Rosewood, Carved, Serpentine Crest Rail, Scroll Arms, 41 x 93 In. | 2629 |
| Sofa, Art Deco, Mahogany, High Back, Arms, Upholstered, Carved, c.1920, 36 x 76 In. | 390 |
| Sofa, Art Deco, Mahogany, Upholstered, Padded Dome Back, c.1910, 38 x 68 In. | 1107 |
| Sofa, Baroque, Walnut, Carved, Shaped Crest, Leaf Cartouche, Scroll Arms, 42 x 85 In. | 956 |
| Sofa, Biedermeier, Fruitwood, Outcurved Arms, Upholstered, c.1835, 39 x 103 In. | 338 |
| Sofa, Biedermeier, Fruitwood, Paneled Crest Back, Outswept Arms, c.1825, 41 x 82 x 27 In. | 1722 |
| Sofa, Chesterfield, Blue Leather, Tufted Back, Arms, Seat, Brass Nailhead Trim, 26 x 78 In. | 3107 |
| Sofa, Chesterfield, Button Tufting, 3 Cushions, Leather Upholstery, 86 x 35 In. | 805 |
| Sofa, Chippendale Style, Shaped Back, Outcurved Arms, Upholstered, c.1970, 34 x 81 In. | 120 |
| Sofa, Contemporary, Lawson, Upholstered, 3 Cushions, Arms, 88 In. | 180 |
| Sofa, Curran, Contemporary, Deco Style, Exposed Wood, Century, 90 x 90 In. | 661 |
| Sofa, Curved Ornate Frame, Carved, Tufted Upholstery, 51 x 37 In. | 439 |
| Sofa, Eames, Black Steel, Wool Upholstery, Chromed Tubular Legs, 1954, 35 x 73 In. | 738 |

**Furniture,** Sideboard, G. Stickley, Butterfly Insets, Through Tenons, c.1901, 40 x 50 In.
**$20,000**

Rago Arts & Auction Center

**Furniture,** Sideboard, Kipp Steward, 2 Drawers, 4 Paneled Doors, Drexel, 1900s, 31 x 61 In.
**$540**

Garth's Auctioneers & Appraisers

**Furniture,** Sofa, Eames, Compact, Metal Legs, Herman Miller, 1954, 36 x 72 In.
**$2,500**

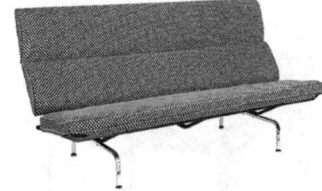

Los Angeles Modern Auctions (LAMA)

**Furniture,** Sofa, Irish Chippendale Style, Carved Leaf & Rosette Arms, 38 x 80 In.
**$1,298**

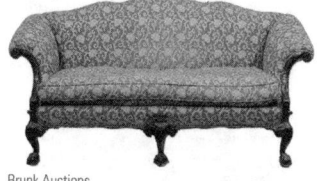

Brunk Auctions

**TIP**
*Push your antique sofa against the wall if the back seems loose. It will keep large friends from sitting down with a thud against the weak back.*

**Furniture,** Sofa, Wormley, Dunbar, Upholstered, c.1955, 29 x 91 In. $3,750

Los Angeles Modern Auctions (LAMA)

**Furniture,** Stand & Chair, Telephone, Oscar Bach Style, Iron, Marble Top, Brass, 1900s, 41 In. $450

Cowan's Auctions

**Furniture,** Stand, Bird's-Eye Maple, Mahogany, Drawer, Brass Ring Pull, c.1825, 29 x 16 ½ In. $400

Skinner Auctioneers & Appraisers

| | | |
|---|---|---|
| **Sofa,** Eames, Compact, Metal Legs, Herman Miller, 1954, 36 x 72 In. | *illus* | 2500 |
| **Sofa,** Eames, Compact, Upholstered Back, Seat, Chrome Plated Steel Legs, 35 x 73 In. | | 1200 |
| **Sofa,** Empire Style, Figured Veneer, Upholstered, Bulbous Legs, Brass Casters, 34 x 90 In. | | 345 |
| **Sofa,** Empire Style, Mahogany, Scalloped Back, Carved, Upholstered, 37 x 79 In. | | 270 |
| **Sofa,** Federal, Mahogany, Arched Back, Scroll Arms, c.1800, 38 x 25 In. | | 3105 |
| **Sofa,** Federal, Mahogany, High, Straight Back, c.1820, 36 x 77 In. | | 1380 |
| **Sofa,** Federal, Mahogany, Inlay, Brocade Upholstery, Sloped Arms, New England, c.1810 | | 2880 |
| **Sofa,** Federal, Mahogany, Inlay, Upholstered Back, Crest, Sloping Arms, c.1810, 78 x 25 In. | | 1778 |
| **Sofa,** Federal, Mahogany, Reeded Crest, Downswept Arms, Baltimore, 35 x 78 In. | | 2375 |
| **Sofa,** French Style, Carved, Triple Camelback, Cabriole Legs, Upholstered, 42 x 76 In. | | 1581 |
| **Sofa,** G. Nakashima, Walnut, 3 Cushions, 6-Footed, 72 x 34 In. | | 4312 |
| **Sofa,** George II Style, Mahogany, Silk Upholstery, c.1910, 35 x 81 In. | | 813 |
| **Sofa,** George II, Mahogany, Camelback, Upholstered, c.1750, 32 x 84 In. | | 875 |
| **Sofa,** George II, Mahogany, Upholstered, High Back, Flared Arms, c.1770, 43 x 64 In. | | 900 |
| **Sofa,** George III, Mahogany, Camelback, Rolled Arms, Inlaid Legs, c.1800, 38 x 78 In. | | 413 |
| **Sofa,** Georgian Style, Camelback, Cabriole Legs, Scrolled Feet, Upholstered, 40 x 84 In. | | 661 |
| **Sofa,** Georgian, Mahogany, Camelback, Outward Scrolling Arms, Upholstered, 77 In. | | 2400 |
| **Sofa,** Gio Ponti, Painted Wood, Silk, Curved Back, Tufted, 3 Cushions, 1938, 30 x 83 In. | | 6250 |
| **Sofa,** Irish Chippendale Style, Carved Leaf & Rosette Arms, 38 x 80 In. | *illus* | 1298 |
| **Sofa,** Knoll, Chromed Steel, Upholstered, 1970s, 28 x 83 In. | | 2176 |
| **Sofa,** Louis XV Style, Pickled Wood, Upholstered, Carved Apron, c.1950, 33 x 74 In. | | 676 |
| **Sofa,** Louis XV Style, Walnut, Scroll Arms, Scalloped Apron, Cabriole Legs, 35 x 24 In. | | 553 |
| **Sofa,** Mae West Lips, Pop Art Style, Red Velvet, c.1970, 34 x 70 In. | | 690 |
| **Sofa,** Mid-Century Modern, Denim Upholstery, Tufted, Box Shape, 1960s, 28 x 98 In. | | 1230 |
| **Sofa,** Mid-Century Modern, Fruitwood, Box Shape, Tapered Legs, 35 x 88 In. | | 676 |
| **Sofa,** Milo Baughman, Curved Form, 2 Sections, Purple Velour, Thayer Coggin, 31 x 130 In. | | 2300 |
| **Sofa,** Modular, Upholstered, Metal, 3 Corners, 6 Sections, M. Bellini, Cassina, 1970s, 139 x 138 In. | | 2500 |
| **Sofa,** Neoclassical, Carved, Painted Flowers, Scrolls, Silk, Curved Arms, c.1875, 39 x 72 In. | | 1680 |
| **Sofa,** Neoclassical, Mahogany, Crest Rail, Acanthine Scrolls, Dolphin Arms, 34 x 92 In. | | 956 |
| **Sofa,** Neoclassical, Mahogany, Gilt Mounts, Continuous Back, Arms, c.1830, 35 x 79 In. | | 3738 |
| **Sofa,** Neoclassical, Mahogany, Paneled Crest Rail, Carved Dolphins, Arms, 38 x 84 In. | | 1912 |
| **Sofa,** Neoclassical, Mahogany, Scroll Arms, Leaf-Carved Crest Rail, Paw Feet, 36 x 87 In. | | 615 |
| **Sofa,** Neoclassical, Mahogany, Serpentine Crest Rail, Brackets, Scroll Arms, 35 x 89 In. | | 837 |
| **Sofa,** Non Stop, Ueli Berger, Heinz Ulrich, Eleonore Peduzzi-Riva, Stendig, 1972, 29 x 180 In. | | 15000 |
| **Sofa,** Ottoman, Le Corbusier, LC3, Chrome, Leather, 26 x 82 In. & 26 x 26 In. | | 1792 |
| **Sofa,** Pottier & Stymus, Renaissance Revival, Ebonized, Gilt Bronze, c.1865, 37 x 71 In. | | 4780 |
| **Sofa,** Rococo Revival, Rosewood Laminate, Rosalie Without Grapes Pattern, 42 x 73 In. | | 1230 |
| **Sofa,** Salterini, Tempestini, Wrought Iron, 3 Triple Loop Sections, Cushions, 1950s, 72 In. | | 519 |
| **Sofa,** Sheraton, Mahogany, Carved, Reeded Scrolling Arms, Upholstered, 38 x 80 In. | | 885 |
| **Sofa,** Sheraton, Mahogany, Cushion, Fluted Legs, c.1805, 36 x 71 In. | | 938 |
| **Sofa,** V. Kagan, Cloud, Red Microfiber, Acrylic, Curved, Directional, 1970s, 93 In. | | 5313 |
| **Sofa,** Victorian, Walnut, Carved, Molded Medallion Back, Upholstered, 43 x 72 In. | | 83 |
| **Sofa,** Walnut, Upholstered, Splayed Legs, A. Pearsall, Kraft, 1960s, 30 x 112 In. | | 2000 |
| **Sofa,** William IV, Mahogany, Rolled Back, Carved, Bulbous Feet, c.1825, 39 x 74 x 29 In. | | 1845 |
| **Sofa,** Wormley, Dunbar, Upholstered, c.1955, 29 x 91 In. | *illus* | 3750 |
| **Sofa,** Wormley, Gondola, Walnut, Tufted Back, Continuous Arms, c.1956, 111 x 32 In. | | 15990 |
| **Stand & Chair,** Telephone, Oscar Bach Style, Iron, Marble Top, Brass, 1900s, 41 In. | *illus* | 450 |
| **Stand,** Bible, Iron, Scrolling, Flowers, 28 ½ In. | | 47 |
| **Stand,** Bird's-Eye Maple, Mahogany, Drawer, Brass Ring Pull, c.1825, 29 x 16 ½ In. | *illus* | 400 |
| **Stand,** Chinese, Rosewood, Marble Top, Scalloped, Carved Apron, c.1900, 23 x 15 In. | | 593 |
| **Stand,** Curly Maple, Bowed Drawer, Block & Turned Legs, 29 x 19 x 17 In. | | 180 |
| **Stand,** Eastlake, Walnut, Carved, Molded Marble Top, Fan Shape Supports, 31 x 30 In. | | 153 |
| **Stand,** Federal, Cherry, Bird's-Eye Maple, Tiger Maple, Back Splash, Drawer, 36 x 21 In. | | 142 |
| **Stand,** Federal, Mixed Wood, Drawer, Shaped Backsplash, Skirt Drawer, 33 x 23 In. | | 59 |
| **Stand,** Federal, Overhanging Square Top, Drawer, Tapered Legs, 27 x 19 In. | | 780 |
| **Stand,** Federal, Walnut, Poplar, Well Lid, 2 Drawers, Va., c.1840, 31 x 22 In. | | 1725 |
| **Stand,** Fern, Spiral Carved Shaft, Leaf Capital, Base, Tripod, Claw Carved Feet, 55 x 10 In. | | 127 |
| **Stand,** Fern, Victorian, Cast Iron, 4-Footed, Darted Edge Gadrooned Bowl, 55 x 21 In. | | 288 |
| **Stand,** Fern, Wire, Classical Column Form, Ionic Capital, Victorian, 29 x 10 In. | | 277 |
| **Stand,** Flower, 2-Tier Shelf, Oval Top, Red Paint, Shaped Handle, Va., c.1890, 43 x 32 In. | | 633 |
| **Stand,** Folio, Aesthetic Revival, Marquetry, Ebonized, Pictorial, Carved, c.1870, 66 x 42 In. | | 1875 |
| **Stand,** Folio, Victorian, Walnut, Gilt Bronze, Scroll Supports, Adjustable, c.1890, 45 x 29 In. | | 2000 |
| **Stand,** Forged Iron, Adjustable, Round Platform Top, Double Sliding Shaft, 1700s, 53 x 10 In. | | 237 |
| **Stand,** Hardwood, Carved, Marble Top, Shelves, Pierced Apron, Chinese, 1800s, 19 x 19 In. | | 960 |
| **Stand,** Hepplewhite, 2-Board Top, Splayed Base, Red Paint, Tapered Square Legs, 26 x 23 In. | | 215 |
| **Stand,** Hepplewhite, Birch, Drawer, Medial Shelf, New Hampshire, 17 x 16 ½ In. | | 720 |
| **Stand,** Hepplewhite, Mahogany, Corner, Bowfront, Basin Well Shelf, Lid, 40 x 22 In. | | 330 |

| | |
|---|---|
| **Stand,** Jardiniere, Georgian Style, Mahogany, Brass Liner, Saber Legs, 37 x 15 In., Pair | 369 |
| **Stand,** Lamp, Art Deco, Stainless Steel, Aluminum, Glass, Airplane Shape, c.1940, 67 In., Pair | 738 |
| **Stand,** Louis XV Style, Rosewood, Inset Black Marble Top, Parquetry, 33 x 16 In. | 214 |
| **Stand,** Louis XV Style, Walnut, Inset Rouge Marble Top, Parquetry, 33 x 16 In. | 185 |
| **Stand,** Magazine, Brass, Looped Handle, Glass Sides, Etched Stars, 24 x 18 In. | 531 |
| **Stand,** Magazine, Fornasetti, Books, Shelf, Enameled Metal, Flared, 1950s, 15 x 17 In. | 2250 |
| **Stand,** Magazine, L. & J.G. Stickley, Oak, Decal, Paper Label, c.1905, 42 x 19 In. .............*illus* | 1750 |
| **Stand,** Magazine, Mahogany, Fruitwood Inlay, 3 Slots, Footed, 1900s, 40 x 16 In. | 210 |
| **Stand,** Magazine, Revolvers, Brown Ground, 1960s, 15¼ x 17 In. | 2000 |
| **Stand,** Magazine, Wormley, Tree, Bleached Mahogany, Dunbar, 1947, 27 x 24 In. ..........*illus* | 8125 |
| **Stand,** Mahogany, 3 Tiers, Drawer, Brass Gallery Top, 35 x 16 In. | 153 |
| **Stand,** Majorelle, Art Nouveau, Walnut, Inlay, 3 Drawers, c.1900, 20 In. | 590 |
| **Stand,** Maple, Drawer, Tapered Legs, c.1850, 27 x 22 In. | 115 |
| **Stand,** Maple, Round Top, Turned Post, Split Baluster, 25 x 15 In. | 615 |
| **Stand,** Music, Aesthetic Revival, Drawer, Shelves, Marquetry Inlay, c.1900, 43 x 29 In. | 313 |
| **Stand,** Music, Baroque, Walnut, Curved, Scroll Support, Leaves, Tripod Base, 50 x 25 In. | 708 |
| **Stand,** Music, Empire Style, Mahogany, Giltwood, Pierced, Lyre Shape, c.1900, 54 In. | 246 |
| **Stand,** Music, Wendell Castle, Ash, Sculpted, Signed, 1965, 51½ x 26 In. ..........*illus* | 43750 |
| **Stand,** Music, William IV, Walnut, Openwork Carved, 31 x 21 In. | 875 |
| **Stand,** Napoleon III, Parcel Ebony, Marquetry, Drawer, c.1870, 30 x 19 In. | 875 |
| **Stand,** Pine, Drawer, Stained, Pa., c.1850, 28 x 16 In. | 270 |
| **Stand,** Pine, Poplar, 2 Drawers, Ring-Turned Legs, Orange Paint, c.1850, 28 x 19 In. | 259 |
| **Stand,** Plant, 4 Ascending Shelves, Blue Paint, New England, c.1870, 35 x 38 In. | 369 |
| **Stand,** Plant, 5 Steps, Scrolled, Green Paint, New England, 1800s, 51 x 41 In. ..........*illus* | 1659 |
| **Stand,** Plant, Brass, Onyx, 3 Legs, c.1880, 33 In. | 360 |
| **Stand,** Plant, Empire, Parcel Gilt, Wrought Iron, Marble Top, Arrows, 42½ In. | 244 |
| **Stand,** Plant, Mahogany, Round Top, Paw Feet, 17 x 27 In. | 105 |
| **Stand,** Plant, Mica, Leaves, M. Zimmerman, 15 x 9 In. | 366 |
| **Stand,** Plant, Oak, Pine, Iron, Stepped Shelves, Scroll, Green Paint, c.1890, 37 x 40 In. | 460 |
| **Stand,** Plant, Painted White, 9 Pot Trays, Tripod Base, Cast Iron, 42 x 18 In. | 72 |
| **Stand,** Plant, Pine, 4 Tiers, Green Paint, Carved, 1800s, 54 x 60 In. | 840 |
| **Stand,** Plant, Pine, Painted, 3 Tiers, c.1910, 29 x 39 In. | 554 |
| **Stand,** Plant, Pine, Square Support, Oval Shelves, Black Paint, Rectangular Base, 48 In. | 420 |
| **Stand,** Plant, White, Arched & Looped Designs, 3 Demilune Tiers, Wire, 19 x 17 In. | 360 |
| **Stand,** Planter, Bronze, Vertical Slats, Tripod Base, Satyrs, Paw Feet, 37 x 19 In. | 5192 |
| **Stand,** Poplar, Black, Checkerboard, Drawer, 28½ x 21 In. | 660 |
| **Stand,** Portfolio, William IV, Rosewood, Carved, Casters, c.1850, 42 x 29 In. ..........*illus* | 1434 |
| **Stand,** Shaker, Bowfront, Cherry, Dovetailed, Pinned, Drawer, Brass Knob, 28 x 18 In. | 600 |
| **Stand,** Shaker, Maple, Cherry, Dovetailed Drawers, Pedestal, Label, c.1850, 26 x 22 In. ........*illus* | 52275 |
| **Stand,** Shaker, Pine, Maple, Drawers, Rectangular Top, Tripod Base, c.1840, 24 x 17 In. | 28290 |
| **Stand,** Shaving, Bamboo Turnings, Pine, Mirror, Drawer, Finials, c.1870, 32 x 17 In. | 1003 |
| **Stand,** Shaving, Regency, Mahogany, Shield Shape Mirror, 3 Splayed Legs, 54 In. | 313 |
| **Stand,** Shaving, Wood, Carved Crest, Dragons, Mirror, Hinged Legs, Holds Bowl, c.1880, 66 x 26 In. *illus* | 474 |
| **Stand,** Sheraton, Cherry, Drawer, Turned Legs, Pa., c.1835, 29 x 24 In. | 210 |
| **Stand,** Sheraton, Mahogany, Satinwood, Drawer, Reeded Legs, 27¾ x 17 In. | 2040 |
| **Stand,** Sheraton, Maple, Inlay, Beaded, Scalloped Gallery, Portsmouth, 28 x 18 In. | 1440 |
| **Stand,** Sheraton, Maple, Turned Legs, Drawer, Dovetail, c.1800, 24 x 19 x 18 In. | 330 |
| **Stand,** Sheraton, Pine, 2 Drawers, Drop Leaves, Red, Black Paint, c.1830, 29 x 17 In. | 960 |
| **Stand,** Sheraton, Tiger Maple, 2 Drawers, c.1830, 29 x 22 In. | 1107 |
| **Stand,** Sheraton, Tiger Maple, Drop Leaves, 2 Drawers, Pa., c.1850, 29 x 17 In. | 360 |
| **Stand,** Sheraton, Tiger Maple, Mahogany, Drawers, Reeded Legs, Mass., c.1820, 28 x 19 In. | 2880 |
| **Stand,** Smoking, Boston Terrier On Ashtray, Iron, Brass Stand, Bradley & Hubbard, 32 In. | 420 |
| **Stand,** Softwood, Gallery Top, Drawer, Shelf, 19th Century, 33 x 25 x 21 In. ..........*illus* | 83 |
| **Stand,** Tiger Maple, 2 Drawers, Wood Pulls, Turned Legs, New England, 28 In. | 590 |
| **Stand,** Tiger Maple, Cherry, Drawers, Turned Legs, Pa., c.1830, 30 x 18 In. | 369 |
| **Stand,** Torchere, Venetian, Blackamoor, Painted, Gilt, Extended Arm, 1800s, 46 In. ..........*illus* | 1195 |
| **Stand,** Victorian, Bamboo, Decoupage Fish, Lower Shelf, England, c.1880, 28 x 20 In. ........*illus* | 600 |
| **Stand,** Victorian, Walnut, Carved, Molded Marble Oval Top, 30 x 29 In. | 94 |
| **Stand,** Whatnot, Victorian, Oak, Adjustable Top, 8 Shelves, Wheeled Base, 36 x 21 In. | 492 |
| **Stand,** Work, Federal, Cherry, Tiger Maple, Drop Leaf, Pullout Supports, c.1835, 32 x 19 In. | 885 |
| **Stool,** Concave Seat, Tripod Base, Red Paint, c.1820, 12 x 11 In. | 58 |
| **Stool,** Drum Shape, Inset Marble Plaque Top, Chinese, c.1900, 20 x 18 In., Pair | 711 |
| **Stool,** Egg, Arne Jacobsen, 1958, 16¼ x 22¼ In. | 1125 |
| **Stool,** Empire Style, Fruitwood, Tasseled Cushion, Crossed Sword Legs, c.1985, 26 x 33 In. | 344 |
| **Stool,** Empire Style, Multicolor, Tasseled Cushion Top, X-Shape Supports, 19 x 22 In., Pair | 369 |
| **Stool,** G. Nakashima, Fitch, Walnut, Grass Seat, c.1954, 12 x 20½ In. | 1250 |
| **Stool,** Jacobean Style, Beech, Upholstered, Shaped Apron, Scroll Stretchers, 15 x 19 In. | 120 |

**Furniture,** Stand, Magazine, L. & J.G. Stickley, Oak, Decal, Paper Label, c.1905, 42 x 19 In.
$1,750

Rago Arts & Auction Center

**Furniture,** Stand, Magazine, Wormley, Tree, Bleached Mahogany, Dunbar, 1947, 27 x 24 In.
$8,125

Wright (Chicago)

**Furniture,** Stand, Music, Wendell Castle, Ash, Sculpted, Signed, 1965, 51 ½ x 26 In. $43,750

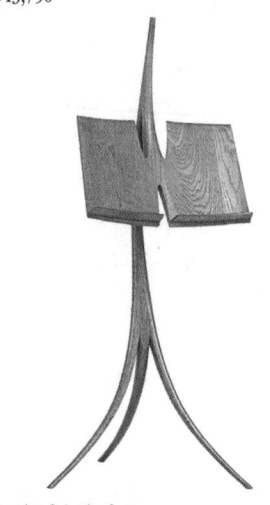

Rago Arts & Auction Center

**Furniture,** Stand, Plant, 5 Steps, Scrolled, Green Paint, New England, 1800s, 51 x 41 In. $1,659

James D. Julia Auctioneers

**Furniture,** Stand, Portfolio, William IV, Rosewood, Carved, Casters, c.1850, 42 x 29 In. $1,434

Neal Auction Co.

| | |
|---|---:|
| **Stool,** Jacobean Style, Jointed, Baluster Legs, Box Stretcher, Red Stain, c.1950, 22 In. | 150 |
| **Stool,** Jacobean, Oak, Carved Apron, Base Stretcher, 22 In. | 250 |
| **Stool,** Louis XVI Style, Carved, Painted, Upholstered, c.1890, 16 ½ x 15 In., Pair | 406 |
| **Stool,** Neoclassical, Mahogany, Carved, Needlepoint Seat, Molded Frame, Curule Base, 1800s | 657 |
| **Stool,** Oak, Carved, Turned Supports, Stretchers, England, 17 In. | 270 |
| **Stool,** Oak, Trestle Style, Carved Legs, 22 x 17 In. | 299 |
| **Stool,** Piano, Giltwood, Carved, Round Needlepoint Seat, France, c.1905, 19 In. | 185 |
| **Stool,** Piano, Mahogany, Demilune Back, Scrolling Inlay, Petal Shape Edge, 1800s, 33 In. | 922 |
| **Stool,** Piano, Maple, Hinged Seat, Cloth, 19th Century, 17 x 19 x 10 In. | 50 |
| **Stool,** Piano, Regency, Mahogany, Oak, Adjustable, Damask Upholstery, Stretcher, 19 x 16 In. | 236 |
| **Stool,** Piano, Venetian, Grotto, Walnut, Shell-Carved Swivel Seat, Turned Support | 1076 |
| **Stool,** Piano, Walnut, Revolving, Shell Seat, Dolphin Supports, Italy, 1800s, 26 In. ...........*illus* | 2689 |
| **Stool,** Pine, Apron Drawer, Landscape, Resting Dog, Red Paint, c.1830, 8 x 12 In. | 2160 |
| **Stool,** Pine, Flowers, Drawer, Red, Blue, Yellow Paint, Pa., c.1840, 6 x 11 In. | 570 |
| **Stool,** Poplar, Walnut, Plank Seat, 3 Legs, T-Stretcher, c.1830, 32 x 13 In. | 288 |
| **Stool,** Shaker, Revolving, Pine, Oak, Round Seat, Cast Iron Screw, 37 To 42 In. | 4425 |
| **Stool,** Shoeshine, Lift Top, Carved, Leather Top, Turned Legs, 1900s, 15 x 14 x 19 In. | 59 |
| **Stool,** Step, 2 Treads, Blue Paint, c.1850, 18 x 20 In. | 173 |
| **Stool,** Step, Pine, 3 Treads, Yellow Paint, c.1900, 29 x 26 In. | 259 |
| **Stool,** Step, Shaker, Butternut, Red Stain, Arched Support, 10 ½ x 10 ½ In. | 2596 |
| **Stool,** Tractor Seat, Pierced Saddle, Champion, Iron Shaft, Round Base, 22 x 18 In. | 58 |
| **Stool,** Tuffet, Burled Walnut, Inlaid, Needlepoint, Faux Ivory Feet, 11 In., Pair..................*illus* | 312 |
| **Stool,** Walnut, Round, Adjustable, Leather Seat, France, 27 In. | 138 |
| **Stool,** William & Mary, Oak, Base Stretcher, c.1720, 22 x 18 In. | 720 |
| **Stool,** William & Mary, Oak, Molded Rails, Turned Legs, Box Stretcher, Eng., 22 x 18 In. | 1440 |
| **Stool,** William & Mary, Rush Seat, Turned Stretchers, Pad Feet, c.1850, 16 x 21 In. | 590 |
| **Storage Unit,** Eames, Plywood, Walnut, Herman Miller, 1952, 59 x 47 In...............*illus* | 17500 |
| **Storage Unit,** G. Nelson, 5-Bay, Enameled Steel, Aluminum, Walnut, Herman Miller, 1960s, 102 x 162 In. | 11250 |
| **Table Desk,** Florence Knoll, Oval, 28 x 96 x 54 In. | 2500 |
| **Table,** 6-Tile Top, Golden Gate Bridge, Seaplane, Taylor, 1920s, 17 x 24 In.............*illus* | 2750 |
| **Table,** Abolitionist, Cast Iron, Marble Top, Cabriole Legs, Britannia Busts, Shelf, 30 x 28 In. | 956 |
| **Table,** Adam Style, Satinwood, Crossbanded, Carved Legs, Painted, 32 x 37 In., Pair | 550 |
| **Table,** Adirondack, Multi-Board Top, Canted, Entwined Branches, 30 x 78 In. | 1150 |
| **Table,** Albert Tirbo, Round Top, Tapered Standard, 3-Part Metal Base, Sweden, 17 x 18 In. | 584 |
| **Table,** Alligator Motif, Signed R. Ferguson, c.1975, 60 x 36 In. | 7320 |
| **Table,** Altar, Carved Apron, Rolled Ends, Chinese, c.1910, 33 ¾ x 65 In. | 3360 |
| **Table,** Altar, Cedar, Linear Carvings, Chinese, 1700s, 36 x 79 In. | 1063 |
| **Table,** Altar, Chinese, Hardwood, Carved Skirt, Stylized Bats, Characters, 30 x 36 In. | 354 |
| **Table,** Altar, Rosewood, Pierced, Carved, Lingzhi Shapes, Chinese, 1800s, 33 x 16 In. | 1353 |
| **Table,** Arne Jacobsen, Round, Laminated Birch, Aluminum, 4-Prong Base, c.1960, 23 x 19 In. | 360 |
| **Table,** Art Deco Style, Wood Frame, Waterfall Legs, Blue Glass Top, Shelf, 1940s, 17 x 32 In. | 35 |
| **Table,** Art Deco, Figured Onyx, Oval, Square Legs, Muller, Mexico, 1960s, 31 x 142 In. | 2596 |
| **Table,** Arts & Crafts, Oak, Gateleg, Drop Leaves, Drawers, c.1912, 27 x 14 In. | 523 |
| **Table,** Arts & Crafts, Oak, Leather Top, Round Medial Shelf, Top, c.1910, 26 x 19 In. | 295 |
| **Table,** Arts & Crafts, Walnut, Octagonal, Pierced Tapered Legs, Stretchers, Shelf, 25 x 22 In. | 360 |
| **Table,** Bamboo Turned Legs, Round Top, Stretchers, 22 x 15 In., Pair | 480 |
| **Table,** Bamboo, Scrolled Shape, 30 x 59 In. | 1125 |
| **Table,** Baroque, Mahogany, Fluted Frieze, X-Stretcher, Column Legs, A. Smitt, Russia, 30 x 42 In. | 2000 |
| **Table,** Baroque, Oak, Scallop Carved Stretcher, Spain, c.1790, 33 x 65 In. | 2500 |
| **Table,** Baroque, Walnut, Drawer, Italy, c.1690, 27 x 40 In. | 1625 |
| **Table,** Baroque, Walnut, Drawer, Turned Legs, X-Shape, Stretcher, 29 x 39 In. | 750 |
| **Table,** Bedside, Mahogany, Adjustable, Rectangular Top, Turned Standard, 28 x 30 In. | 200 |
| **Table,** Bench, Pine, Drawers In Lower Shelf, Wheeled Base, New England, c.1810, 28 x 71 In. | 1200 |
| **Table,** Bench, Walnut, Drawer, Overhanging Top, Carved Apron, c.1870, 58 x 36 In. | 240 |
| **Table,** Biedermeier, Birch, Ebonized, Banded Top, Tripart Base, 18 x 32 In. | 625 |
| **Table,** Biedermeier, Bird's-Eye Maple, Round, Marquetry Fruitwood, 28 x 25 In. | 2390 |
| **Table,** Biedermeier, Walnut, Round, Recessed Apron, 3 Column Supports, 29 x 45 In. | 1375 |
| **Table,** Birch, Toothpick Cactus, Round Top, Lawrence Laske, Knoll, N.Y., 1993, 20 x 20 In. | 768 |
| **Table,** Black Lacquer, Mother-Of-Pearl Inlay, Scholars, Poem, Chinese, 1700s, 20 x 11 In....*illus* | 830 |
| **Table,** Black Wash, 2-Board Top, Flush Skirt, Tapered Legs, N.C., c.1850, 27 x 30 x 24 In. | 266 |
| **Table,** Bracket, Carved, Shaped Top, Curved Dragon Legs, Pickled Finish, 26 x 20 In., Pair | 184 |
| **Table,** Brass, Marble, Oval Mirror, 2 Hammered Drawers, 60 x 35 In. | 295 |
| **Table,** Bronze, Figural Base, Nude Woman, Glass Top, 17 x 54 x 21 In.................*illus* | 3952 |
| **Table,** Bronze, Glass Top, X-Stretcher, Ilana Goor, 17 x 36 In. | 1250 |
| **Table,** Burl Roots, Corner, Black Lacquer Slabs, Asia, 20th Century, 32 x 44 In. | 270 |
| **Table,** Burl Walnut, Bookmatched, Oval, Pedestal Base, Victorian, 21 x 54 x 41 In. | 354 |
| **Table,** Burl, Gilt Gallery, 3 Open Shelves, Cabriole Legs, 31 x 20 In. | 188 |

**Furniture,** Stand, Shaker, Maple, Cherry, Dovetailed Drawers, Pedestal, Label, c.1850, 26 x 22 In.
$52,275

**Furniture,** Stand, Shaving, Wood, Carved Crest, Dragons, Mirror, Hinged Legs, Holds Bowl, c.1880, 66 x 26 In.
$474

**Furniture,** Stand, Softwood, Gallery Top, Drawer, Shelf, 19th Century, 33 x 25 x 21 In.
$83

**Furniture,** Stand, Torchere, Venetian, Blackamoor, Painted, Gilt, Extended Arm, 1800s, 46 In.
$1,195

**Furniture,** Stand, Victorian, Bamboo, Decoupage Fish, Lower Shelf, England, c.1880, 28 x 20 In.
$600

**Furniture,** Stool, Piano, Walnut, Revolving, Shell Seat, Dolphin Supports, Italy, 1800s, 26 In.
$2,689

**Furniture,** Stool, Tuffet, Burled Walnut, Inlaid, Needlepoint, Faux Ivory Feet, 11 In., Pair
$312

**Furniture,** Storage Unit, Eames, Plywood, Walnut, Herman Miller, 1952, 59 x 47 In.
$17,500

**Furniture,** Table, 6-Tile Top, Golden Gate Bridge, Seaplane, Taylor, 1920s, 17 x 24 In.
$2,750

Rago Arts & Auction Center

**Furniture,** Table, Black Lacquer, Mother-Of-Pearl Inlay, Scholars, Poem, Chinese, 1700s, 20 x 11 In.
$830

James D. Julia Auctioneers

**Furniture,** Table, Bronze, Figural Base, Nude Woman, Glass Top, 17 x 54 x 21 In.
$3,952

New Orleans Auction Galleries, Inc.

**Furniture,** Table, Card, Federal, Mahogany, Hinged Top, Inlay, Massachusetts, c.1810, 30 x 37 In.
$1,185

James D. Julia Auctioneers

**TIP**
*Brown shoe polish is good to cover scuffs and slight damage on furniture.*

| | |
|---|---:|
| **Table,** Calling Card, Inset Marble, Suspended Prisms, Brass, c.1875, 31 x 14 In. | 130 |
| **Table,** Card, Chippendale, Birch, Hinge Top, Drawer, Red Paint, New England, 29 x 35 In. | 240 |
| **Table,** Card, Chippendale, Mahogany, Beaded Drawer, Carved Pockets, 30 x 33 In. | 840 |
| **Table,** Card, Federal, Mahogany, Foldover, Carved Legs, New England, c.1815, 31 x 37 In. | 1680 |
| **Table,** Card, Federal, Mahogany, Hinged Top, Inlay, Massachusetts, c.1810, 30 x 37 In.....*illus* | 1185 |
| **Table,** Card, Federal, Mahogany, Inlay, Banding, Ring-Turned Legs, 31 x 34 In. | 1476 |
| **Table,** Card, Federal, Mahogany, Inlay, Foldover Top, 1800s, 29 x 36 In. | 938 |
| **Table,** Card, Foldover, Mahogany, Inlay, Banding, Ball Feet, Boston, 1800s, 30 x 36 In. | 938 |
| **Table,** Card, Hepplewhite Style, Mahogany, Pine, Demilune, Banded Inlay, c.1900, 30 In. | 120 |
| **Table,** Card, Hepplewhite, Inlaid Mahogany, Demilune Top, New Hampshire, 30 x 36 In. | 780 |
| **Table,** Card, Hepplewhite, Mahogany, Line Inlay, England, c.1800, 29 x 36 In. | 215 |
| **Table,** Card, Hepplewhite, Mahogany, Line Inlay, Flower, Foldover Top, c.1790, 30 x 36 In. | 2875 |
| **Table,** Card, Hepplewhite, Vine, Line Inlay, Tapered Legs, New England, c.1800, 29 x 36 In. | 780 |
| **Table,** Card, Lift Top, Mahogany, Drawer, Turned & Fluted Legs, 10th Century, 31 x 51 In. | 531 |
| **Table,** Card, Mahogany, Foldover Top, Oval Frieze Inlay, Rope-Twist Legs, 30 x 35 In. | 813 |
| **Table,** Card, Mahogany, Foldover Top, Reeded Dolphin Supports, c.1825, 29 x 37 In. | 13750 |
| **Table,** Card, Regency, Mahogany, Folding, Drawer, England, c.1820, 30 x 38 In. | 120 |
| **Table,** Card, Sheraton, Mahogany, Geometric Inlay, Serpentine Top, 30 x 35 In. | 1680 |
| **Table,** Card, Sheraton, Mahogany, Tiger Maple Veneer, Hinged Top, Bowed, Mass., 29 x 35 In. | 3600 |
| **Table,** Card, Tiger Maple, Foldover Top, Drawer, Rhode Island, c.1790, 29 x 35 In. ......*illus* | 7380 |
| **Table,** Carved Frieze, Green Paint, Tapered Fluted Legs, 30 x 40 In. | 313 |
| **Table,** Carved, Rose Medallion Insert, Round Stretcher, Gilt, Chinese, c.1890, 30 x 26 In. | 2400 |
| **Table,** Center, Anglo-Indian, Hardwood, Flared Apron, Snake Entwined Shaft, 30 x 29 In. | 690 |
| **Table,** Center, Carved Frieze, Flowers, Leaves, X-Shape Stretcher With Urn, 43 x 28 In. | 1169 |
| **Table,** Center, Edwardian Style, Mahogany, Triple Banded, Bulbous Standard, 30 x 60 In. | 799 |
| **Table,** Center, Louis XVI Style, Giltwood, Marble Top, Stretcher Shelf, c.1910, 30 x 28 In. | 369 |
| **Table,** Center, Neoclassical, Burl Walnut, Walnut, Mirror Plate Inset, Fluted Legs, 31 x 42 In. | 1599 |
| **Table,** Center, Neoclassical, Mahogany, Carved, Segmented Top, Bulbous Stem, 29 x 25 In. | 2151 |
| **Table,** Center, Neoclassical, Mahogany, Crossbanded, Ebony Stringing, c.1825, 28 x 35 In. | 2214 |
| **Table,** Center, Neoclassical, Mahogany, Molded Frieze, Urn Shape Support, 30 x 41 In. | 717 |
| **Table,** Center, Regency, Plum Pudding Mahogany, Tilt Top, Molded Frieze, 29 x 42 In. | 1434 |
| **Table,** Center, Renaissance Revival, Shell & Rosewood Inlay, Bronze, c.1870, 30 x 54 In......*illus* | 25092 |
| **Table,** Center, Rococo Revival, Rosewood, Marble Top, Flowers, c.1855, 29 x 38 In. ......*illus* | 86638 |
| **Table,** Center, Victorian, Walnut, Marble Top, Scrolled Base, c.1890, 26 x 27 In. | 180 |
| **Table,** Center, Walnut, Ebonized, Banded Oval, Flower Inlay, Drawer, c.1800, 30 x 37 x 25 In. | 2706 |
| **Table,** Chair, Round Top, Horizontal Rails, Ring-Turned Legs, Painted, Stretcher, 27 x 54 In. | 3998 |
| **Table,** Charles X, Mahogany, Gilt Bronze, Dished Marble Top, Triangular Base, 28 x 32 In. | 1599 |
| **Table,** Cherry, Drop Leaf, Rectangular, Stretcher, 29 x 42 In. | 120 |
| **Table,** Cherry, Maple, 3 Drawers, Turned Legs, c.1830, 28 x 22 In. | 219 |
| **Table,** Cherry, Tuckaway, Drop Leaf, Ring-Turned Legs, Stretcher, 1700s, 27 x 30 In. | 2337 |
| **Table,** Chinese, Carved Elm, Rose Marble Inset, c.1910, 19 x 18 In. | 192 |
| **Table,** Chinese, Rosewood, Carved, Marble Top, Cabriole Legs, Apron, Stretcher, 28 x 19 In. | 178 |
| **Table,** Chinoiserie, Painted, Lacquered, Rectangular Top, Phoenix, Dragons, 19 x 48 In. | 717 |
| **Table,** Chippendale, Mahogany, Drop Leaves, Shaped Apron, New England, 1700s, 28 x 17 In. | 1000 |
| **Table,** Chippendale, Mahogany, Round Dish Top, 3 Cabriole Legs, c.1790, 29 x 29 In. | 375 |
| **Table,** Chippendale, Maple, Curly Maple, Drop Leaves, c.1780, 28 x 42 In. | 649 |
| **Table,** Chippendale, Walnut, Round Tilt Top, Birdcage Support, Pa., c.1780, 29 x 35 In. | 900 |
| **Table,** Chromed Steel, Leather, Double X-Stretcher, 2 Drawers, c.1990, 28 x 48 In. | 313 |
| **Table,** Classical Scene, Inlay, Papier-Mache, Mother-Of-Pearl, England, 28 x 23 In. ......*illus* | 413 |
| **Table,** Cocktail, Burl Veneer, Square Top, Conforming Base, c.1970, 10 x 48 x 48 In. | 570 |
| **Table,** Cocktail, Coromandel, Chinese, 17 x 40 In. | 2091 |
| **Table,** Cocktail, I. Noguchi, Free Style, Plate Glass Top, Black Base, 17 x 50 In. | 1200 |
| **Table,** Cocktail, Neoclassical Style, Gilt Bronze, Mirrored Top, Leaf Frame, 18 x 52 In. | 1845 |
| **Table,** Cocktail, Oval Glass Top, 6-Footed, Hooves, 65 x 20 In. | 180 |
| **Table,** Coffee, Baker Gilt, Metal Rope Twist, Glass Top, 20th Century, 18 x 42 x 28 In. | 450 |
| **Table,** Coffee, Black Lacquer, Painted Flowers, Gilt, Scalloped, Maitland Smith, 24 x 39 In. | 230 |
| **Table,** Coffee, Charak Modern Cherry, Lazy Susan Top, Pedestal, Boston, 1957, 18 x 48 In. | 406 |
| **Table,** Coffee, Cherry, Stack Laminated, 3 Cone Shape Pedestals, 65 x 39 In......*illus* | 2875 |
| **Table,** Coffee, Contemporary, Cast Bronze, Plate Glass, P.E. Guerin, 16 x 48 In. | 1168 |
| **Table,** Coffee, Contemporary, Glass, Round Top, Free-Form Base, Laurel Fyfe, 17 x 39 In. | 450 |
| **Table,** Coffee, Contemporary, Neoclassical Style, Gilt Metal, Beveled Glass, 21 x 42 In. | 338 |
| **Table,** Coffee, Contemporary, Steel, Anodized, Brushed, Round, 20 x 42 In. | 584 |
| **Table,** Coffee, French Brittany, Oak, 3 Planks, Double Lyre, Trestle, Stretcher, 33 x 21 In. | 118 |
| **Table,** Coffee, G. McCabe, Glass, 2 V-Shape Supports, c.1968, 17 x 40 In......*illus* | 344 |
| **Table,** Coffee, G. Nakashima, Black Walnut, Rosewood, Free-Form, 1976, 66 x 34 In. | 29520 |
| **Table,** Coffee, G. Nakashima, Slab, Black Walnut, Rosewood, 1967, 14 x 75 In. | 23750 |
| **Table,** Coffee, Gio Ponti, Walnut, Brass, Glass Top, X-Support, 1950s, 15 x 40 In. | 9375 |

| | |
|---|---|
| **Table,** Coffee, I. Noguchi, IN-50, Birch, Glass, Triangular, Herman Miller, 1940s, 60 x 36 In........ | 1625 |
| **Table,** Coffee, I. Noguchi, Mid-Century Modern, Organic Shape, Herman Miller, 16 x 50 In. ....... | 949 |
| **Table,** Coffee, Louis XIII, Oak, Rectangle, Wide Skirt, Barley Twist Legs, 39 x 19 In. ..................... | 338 |
| **Table,** Coffee, Maple, Burl, Natural Form, Glass Top, c.1900, 19 x 39 In..............................*illus* | 1046 |
| **Table,** Coffee, Mid-Century Modern, Recessed Base, Metal Mosaic, Square, 15 x 36 In.................. | 299 |
| **Table,** Coffee, Modern, Lucite, Chrome, Glass Top, 16 x 60 In. ................................................ | 354 |
| **Table,** Coffee, Oak, Textured Mosaic Tiles, Signed Tue, 16 x 61 x 32 In........................*illus* | 2214 |
| **Table,** Coffee, P. Evans, Glass Top, Steel, Welded, Signed, 1967, 18 ½ x 42 In........................*illus* | 9375 |
| **Table,** Coffee, P. Powell, Walnut, Rosewood, Rustic Form, 13 x 61 x 22 In................................ | 3250 |
| **Table,** Coffee, Philip & Kelvin LaVerne, Chan, Bronze, Pewter, 1960s, 39 x 35 In.................*illus* | 5000 |
| **Table,** Coffee, Pietra Dura Round Top, Black, White Painted Geometrics, c.1905, 17 x 37 In. ...... | 832 |
| **Table,** Coffee, Pietro Chiesa, Crystal, Brass, Fontana Arte, Italy, 1940s, 18 x 49 In.................*illus* | 9375 |
| **Table,** Coffee, Poul Kjaerholm, Steel, Glass Top, Square, Hansen, 1999, 13 x 33 In...................... | 1000 |
| **Table,** Coffee, Robsjohn-Gibbings, Burch, Free-Form Top, 3 Legs, Widdicomb, 41 In.................. | 4375 |
| **Table,** Coffee, Robsjohn-Gibbings, Mid-Century Modern, Walnut, Boat Shape, 17 x 73 In............ | 1610 |
| **Table,** Coffee, Rustic, Burl, Free-Form, 16 x 54 x 45 In. ......................................................... | 720 |
| **Table,** Coffee, Tree Trunk, Burl Cypress, Cross Cut, 74 x 36 In. ............................................... | 553 |
| **Table,** Coffee, V. Kagan, Boomerang, Walnut, Travertine Top, 1950s, 14 x 51 In...................*illus* | 8750 |
| **Table,** Coffee, V. Kagan, Glass, Oval Top, Lucite, Enameled Wood Base, 1970s, 14 x 60 In. ......... | 875 |
| **Table,** Coffee, W. Platner, Nickeled Steel, Glass, Plastic Base, Round, 1970s, 15 x 36 In............. | 875 |
| **Table,** Coffee, Walnut, Birds-Eye-Maple, Puzzle Piece Top, R. Whitley, c.1982, 17 x 39 In......... | 900 |
| **Table,** Coffee, Walnut, Glass Top, Arden Riddle, 18 x 43 ½ In. ................................................ | 354 |
| **Table,** Coffee, Wormley, Burl, 5-Sided, Mahogany Trim, Dunbar, 17 x 50 In. ............................ | 1000 |
| **Table,** Coffee, Wormley, Walnut, Natzler Ceramic Inserts, Dunbar, 17 x 77 In. .......................... | 6250 |
| **Table,** Conference, Teak, Rectangular, Canted Corners, Double Pedestal, 1960s, 108 In. ............. | 590 |
| **Table,** Conservatory, Travertine, Iron, Molded, Scroll Supports, c.1910, 31 x 76 In. ................... | 922 |
| **Table,** Conservatory, Victoria, Multicolor Metal, Marble Top, Palmetto Frieze, 31 x 49 In............ | 2337 |
| **Table,** Console, Anglo-Colonial, Carved, Reticulated, Pierced Scrollwork, 1800s, 42 x 51 In. *illus* | 3944 |
| **Table,** Console, Anglo-Indian, Fan-Carved Back, Scrolled Supports, Paw Feet, 37 x 38 In. ........... | 263 |
| **Table,** Console, Art Nouveau, Mahogany, Demilune, Marble Top, Frieze, c.1905, 34 x 38 In......... | 4375 |
| **Table,** Console, Corner, Louis XV Style, Giltwood, Marble Top, Scroll Supports, 34 x 32 In. .......... | 359 |
| **Table,** Console, Demilune, Marble Top, Ebonized, Pietra Dura Inlay, Gilt Trim, 35 x 43 In. .......... | 1500 |
| **Table,** Console, Empire Style, Onyx, Bronze Cupids, Quivers, Stepped Base, 30 x 36 In................ | 1125 |
| **Table,** Console, Empire, Marble Top, Shelf Stretcher, Gilt Mounts, France, c.1830, 35 x 50 In...... | 1968 |
| **Table,** Console, Faux Marble Top, White Paint, 34 x 81 In........................................................ | 480 |
| **Table,** Console, George II Style, Carved, Gilt, Eagle, Marble, William Kent, 34 x 48 In., Pair........ | 15860 |
| **Table,** Console, George III, Mahogany, Demilune, 28 ¾ x 48 In., Pair...................................... | 563 |
| **Table,** Console, Kittinger, Mahogany, Demilune, Square Tapered Legs, 29 x 48 x 24 In. .............. | 275 |
| **Table,** Console, Louis Philippe Style, Amaranth, Burr Elm, Gothic, c.1900, 35 x 43 In., Pair........ | 2706 |
| **Table,** Console, Louis XV Style, Hardwood, Marble Top, Gilt Bronze, Drawers, 35 x 51 In. .......... | 10625 |
| **Table,** Console, Louis XVI Style, Carved Frieze, Marble Top, Demilune, c.1950, 34 x 48 In........... | 1125 |
| **Table,** Console, Louis XVI Style, Gilt, Marble Top, 39 x 51 In. ................................................ | 960 |
| **Table,** Console, Louis XVI Style, Gilt, Marble Top, Carved Frieze, Fluted Legs, 33 x 46 In. ........... | 1875 |
| **Table,** Console, Louis XVI Style, Gilt, Marble Top, Leaf Frieze, X-Stretcher, c.1950, 32 x 41 In. ...... | 375 |
| **Table,** Console, Maple, Drawer, X-Stretcher, England, 32 x 42 In., Pair ................................... | 531 |
| **Table,** Console, Neoclassical Style, Iron, Egyptian Style, Marble Top, 1800s, 32 x 59 In. ............. | 1968 |
| **Table,** Console, Neoclassical, Mahogany, Carved Pedestal, Paw Feet, c.1830, 28 x 46 In., Pair ..... | 3936 |
| **Table,** Console, Regency, Japanned, Chinoiserie, Pierced Apron, Column Supports, 37 x 60 In..... | 9225 |
| **Table,** Console, William IV Style, Mahogany, Tapered Legs, Low Shelf, 1900s, 34 x 102 In............ | 615 |
| **Table,** Console, Wrought Iron, Gilt, Black Paint, Green Variegated Marble Top, 35 x 56 In............ | 1534 |
| **Table,** Console, Wrought Iron, Marble Top, Scrolls, Flower Shapes, 33 x 42 In. ......................... | 345 |
| **Table,** Contemporary, Silvered Metal, Glass Top, Round, 16 x 33 In. ...................................... | 875 |
| **Table,** Continental, Wrought Iron, Wood, Openwork Scrolls, Bowfront, c.1790, 36 x 56 In. ......... | 531 |
| **Table,** Corner, Dutch Neoclassical Style, Mahogany, Marquetry Inlay, 2 Shelves, 31 x 31 In. ...... | 750 |
| **Table,** Corner, Federal, Walnut, Cherry, Drop Front Drawer, Shelf, Va., c.1850, 29 x 30 In. ......... | 259 |
| **Table,** Cypress Stump, Organic Form, Mid-Century, 29 x 39 In. ............................................. | 345 |
| **Table,** Dining, Arts & Crafts, Oak, Round, Octagonal Columns, Plank Feet, c.1912, 29 x 60 In.... | 1353 |
| **Table,** Dining, Baker Furniture, Fruitwood, Brass Stringing, Molding, c.1980, 29 x 102 In. ......... | 1230 |
| **Table,** Dining, Blue Enameled Wood, 2 Leaves, Oval, Karl Springer, 1980s, 30 x 72 In................. | 1625 |
| **Table,** Dining, Drop Leaf, Chippendale, Mahogany, 1700s, 19 ½ x 48 x 28 In. ........................... | 234 |
| **Table,** Dining, Drop Leaf, Federal, Mahogany, Sheraton Style, Reeded, Fly Leg, 46 x 86 In. .......... | 2214 |
| **Table,** Dining, Drop Leaf, Queen Anne, Walnut, Gateleg, N.C., 28 x 42 In............................... | 502 |
| **Table,** Dining, Drop Leaf, Queen Anne, Walnut, Pa., c.1770, 29 x 43 In................................... | 840 |
| **Table,** Dining, Drop Leaf, Queen Anne, Walnut, Va., c.1750, 30 x 42 In................................... | 489 |
| **Table,** Dining, Drop Leaf, Sheraton, Mahogany, 2 Piece, c.1825, 45 x 81 In........................*illus* | 344 |
| **Table,** Dining, Empire, Mahogany, Pedestal, Scroll Feet, c.1850, 53 In. .........................*illus* | 840 |
| **Table,** Dining, Expansion, Salesman Sample, 5 ½ In. ........................................................... | 593 |

**F**

**Furniture,** Table, Card, Tiger Maple, Foldover Top, Drawer, Rhode Island, c.1790, 29 x 35 In.
**$7,380**

Skinner Auctioneers & Appraisers

**Furniture,** Table, Center, Renaissance Revival, Shell & Rosewood Inlay, Bronze, c.1870, 30 x 54 In.
**$25,092**

Neal Auction Co.

**Furniture,** Table, Center, Rococo Revival, Rosewood, Marble Top, Flowers, c.1855, 29 x 38 In.
**$86,638**

Neal Auction Co.

**Furniture,** Table, Classical Scene, Inlay, Papier-Mache, Mother-Of-Pearl, England, 28 x 23 In.
$413

Brunk Auctions

---

**Furniture,** Table, Coffee, Cherry, Stack Laminated, 3 Cone Shape Pedestals, 65 x 39 In.
$2,875

Cottone Auctions

---

> **TIP**
> *Brown shoe polish is good to cover scuffs and slight damage on furniture.*

---

**Furniture,** Table, Coffee, G. McCabe, Glass, 2 V-Shaped Supports, c.1968, 17 x 40 In.
$344

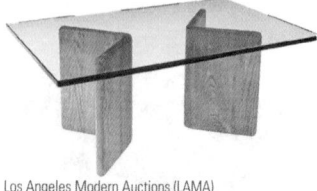

Los Angeles Modern Auctions (LAMA)

---

| | |
|---|---:|
| **Table,** Dining, French Provincial, Serpentine Skirt, Trestle Stretcher, 29 x 67 In. | 296 |
| **Table,** Dining, G. Nakashima, Walnut, Free Edge, Stretchers, 1956, 28 x 84 In. | 20060 |
| **Table,** Dining, G. Stickley, 5-Legged Cross Stretcher, 6 Leaves, Stamped, c.1904, 30 x 54 In. *illus* | 9375 |
| **Table,** Dining, Gateleg, William & Mary, Walnut, 2 Drawers, Pa., c.1740, 29 x 19 In. | 228 |
| **Table,** Dining, George III Style, Mahogany, 2 Pedestals, Splayed Legs, Henredon, 45 x 72 In. | 984 |
| **Table,** Dining, George III Style, Mahogany, 3 Pedestals, Splayed Legs, Casters, 48 x 169 In. | 2952 |
| **Table,** Dining, George III, Double Pedestal, 2 Leaves, c.1810, 28 x 66 In. | 8750 |
| **Table,** Dining, George III, Mahogany, Demilune Ends, Tapered Legs, Casters, 40 x 42 In. | 717 |
| **Table,** Dining, Glass Top, Brass Base, Mastercraft, 1980s, 29 x 96 In. | 5313 |
| **Table,** Dining, Jacobean, Ebonized, Patina, 4 Leaves, Twist-Carved Legs, 94 x 44 In. | 311 |
| **Table,** Dining, Louis XV Style, Walnut, Oval Top, Banded, Pull-Up Leaf, 43 x 99 In. | 1353 |
| **Table,** Dining, Louis XVI Style, Mahogany, Drop Leaf, Brass Banding, c.1890, 29 x 51 In. | 1045 |
| **Table,** Dining, M. Graves, Wood, Brass, Plastic, Glass Top, 1980s, 48 In. Diam. *illus* | 3840 |
| **Table,** Dining, Majorelle, Art Nouveau, Walnut, 4 Leaves, France, c.1900, 131 In. | 11210 |
| **Table,** Dining, Marble Top, Oval, Brass Plated Steel Standard, Italy, 1960s, 29 x 70 In. | 1500 |
| **Table,** Dining, Mid-Century Modern, Glass Top, Stainless Steel Base, 28 x 60 In. | 96 |
| **Table,** Dining, Mid-Century Modern, Teak, Boat Shape, 2 Pedestal, Denmark, 65 x 42 In. | 1006 |
| **Table,** Dining, Neoclassical Style, Fruitwood, Carved, Garlands, Italy, 1900s, 31 x 62 12 In. | 125 |
| **Table,** Dining, Neoclassical, Burl, Elm, Mahogany, 3 Pedestals, Demilune, c.1930, 23 x 46 In. | 2074 |
| **Table,** Dining, P. Evans, Directional, Sculptured Steel, Glass Top, c.1968, 84 x 44 In. *illus* | 10000 |
| **Table,** Dining, Pine, Stripped, Plank Top, Apron, Turned Legs, Ireland, 1980s, 95 x 45 In. | 1058 |
| **Table,** Dining, Pine, Wide Barley Twist Legs, Bun Feet, 5 Leaves, American, 27 x 43 In. | 420 |
| **Table,** Dining, Regency Style, Birch, Fluted Frieze, Turned Legs, c.1910, 29 x 72 In. | 354 |
| **Table,** Dining, Regency Style, Mahogany, 2 Pedestals, Leaf Carved, Saber Legs, 78 x 30 In. | 1800 |
| **Table,** Dining, Renaissance Revival, Walnut, Ebonized, 2 Leaves, c.1850, 58 x 58 In. *illus* | 2214 |
| **Table,** Dining, Robsjohn-Gibbings, Walnut, Saber Legs, 1950s, 29 x 68 In. | 1408 |
| **Table,** Dining, Roger Sprunger, Rosewood, Chromed Steel, Dunbar, 1970s, 96 x 44 In. *illus* | 2688 |
| **Table,** Dining, Sheraton, Mahogany, Spiral Twist Legs, c.1825, 29 x 48 In. *illus* | 600 |
| **Table,** Dining, Victorian, Mahogany, Griffin Legs, Leaves, 12 Chairs, c.1890, 54 x 102 In. | 4920 |
| **Table,** Drafting, Chippendale, Mahogany, Hinged Top, 2 Drawers, Shelf, England, 31 x 34 In. | 1800 |
| **Table,** Drafting, George III, Mahogany, Adjustable, Sliding Panel, c.1800, 32 x 23 In. | 1800 |
| **Table,** Drafting, George III, Mahogany, Leather Top, Ratchet Supports, c.1780, 30 x 42 In. | 1375 |
| **Table,** Drafting, Mechanical, Mahogany, Cock-Beaded Drawer, Ratchet Support, 29 x 24 In. | 3335 |
| **Table,** Drafting, Walnut, Adjustable, 2 Drawers, Iron Pedestal, c.1890, 39 x 28 In. *illus* | 188 |
| **Table,** Dressing, Baker Furniture, Italian Style, 3 Drawers, Brass Trim, c.1970, 30 x 36 In. | 270 |
| **Table,** Dressing, Chippendale, Mahogany, Drawers, Scrolled, Pierced Skirt, 29 x 32 In. | 590 |
| **Table,** Dressing, Empire Style, Oval Swivel Mirror, Gallery Drawers, 58 x 32 In. | 625 |
| **Table,** Dressing, George II, Oak, 3 Drawers, c.1750, 29 x 29 In. | 570 |
| **Table,** Dressing, George III, Satinwood, Fold-Out Top, Ivory Knobs, 30 x 26 In. *illus* | 1680 |
| **Table,** Dressing, Georgian, Walnut, Oak, Ball, Claw Feet, 3 Drawers, 29 x 29 In. | 270 |
| **Table,** Dressing, Louis XVI, Mahogany, Brass Mounted, 3 Drawers, 29 x 37 In. | 875 |
| **Table,** Dressing, Painted, Mirror, 2 Drawers, 2 Sections, c.1825, 58 x 38 In. *illus* | 3998 |
| **Table,** Dressing, Queen Anne, Cabriole Legs, Drawer, Mid 18th Century, 28 x 37 In. | 625 |
| **Table,** Dressing, Queen Anne, Mahogany, Carved, Drawers, Brass, c.1770, 30 x 37 In. | 8260 |
| **Table,** Dressing, Queen Anne, Walnut, 5 Drawers & 1 Concealed, Boston, c.1765, 34 x 20 In. *illus* | 4740 |
| **Table,** Dressing, Queen Anne, Walnut, Carved, Shells, Trifid Feet, c.1770, 32 x 37 In. | 2640 |
| **Table,** Dressing, Regency, Mahogany, 2 Drawers, Shaped Backsplash, c.1820, 31 x 36 In. | 400 |
| **Table,** Dressing, Rococo Revival, Rosewood, Mirror, Wishbone Frame, Marble Top, 69 x 49 In. | 984 |
| **Table,** Dressing, Sheraton, Maple, Tiger Maple, Bird's-Eye Maple, 2 Tiers, Drawers, 36 x 29 In. | 224 |
| **Table,** Dressing, Sheraton, Tiger Maple, Glove Box, Splash Guard, c.1840, 40 x 34 In. | 889 |
| **Table,** Dressing, William & Mary Style, Walnut, Burl Veneer, 30 x 30 In. | 738 |
| **Table,** Dressing, William & Mary, Mahogany, Turned Drop Finials, c.1790, 29 x 31 In. | 688 |
| **Table,** Drop Leaf, George I, Mahogany, Demilune Leaves, 28 ½ x 60 In. | 1063 |
| **Table,** Drop Leaf, Handkerchief, Edwardian, Rosewood, Inlay, c.1900, 27 x 33 In. *illus* | 799 |
| **Table,** Drop Leaf, Handkerchief, George II, Mahogany, Turned Legs, 1700s, 27 x 35 In. | 500 |
| **Table,** Drop Leaf, Handkerchief, Mahogany, Gateleg, Pad Feet, 27 x 36 In. | 531 |
| **Table,** Drop Leaf, Louis Philippe, Walnut, Oval, Wide Skirt, Ring-Turned Legs, 51 In. | 178 |
| **Table,** Drop Leaf, Neoclassical, Mahogany, Rosewood, Brass, Venetian, c.1830, 54 x 26 In. *illus* | 4900 |
| **Table,** Drop Leaf, Pine, Drawer, Pad Feet, 27 x 31 In. | 250 |
| **Table,** Drop Leaf, Queen Anne, Cherry, Pa., c.1780, 29 x 45 In. | 540 |
| **Table,** Drop Leaf, Queen Anne, Mahogany, Pine, Cabriole Legs, 46 ½ In. Open *illus* | 660 |
| **Table,** Drop Leaf, Reeded Legs, 2 Drawers, Pullout Writing Slide, c.1850, 28 x 17 In. | 200 |
| **Table,** Drop Leaf, Regency, Mahogany, 2 Apron Drawers, c.1800, 28 x 54 In. | 600 |
| **Table,** Drop Leaf, Rounded, Turned Legs, Ball Feet, Salesman's Sample, 16 x 10 In. | 200 |
| **Table,** Drop Leaf, Sheraton, Birch, Drawer, Turned Legs, 1800s, 20 x 29 In. | 176 |
| **Table,** Drop Leaf, Sheraton, Birch, New England, 29 x 60 In. | 1200 |
| **Table,** Drop Leaf, Sheraton, Rectangular, Turned Legs, Casters, Pa., c.1850, 30 x 72 In. | 30 |

| | |
|---|---|
| **Table,** Drop Leaf, Sheraton, Tiger Maple, Square Leaves, New England, 29 x 44 In. | 1080 |
| **Table,** Drop Leaf, Sheraton, Tiger Maple, Turned Legs, c.1820, 30 x 40 In. | 1534 |
| **Table,** Drop Leaf, Walnut, D-Shape Leaves, Stretcher Brass Bowl, 30 x 20 In. | 1250 |
| **Table,** Drop Leaf, Walnut, Rounded Corners, 6 Legs, Gateleg, Spade Feet, 30 x 51 In. | 259 |
| **Table,** Drop Leaf, William & Mary, Oak, Turned Supports, Box Stretcher, 29 x 35 In. | 600 |
| **Table,** Drop Leaf, Work, Neoclassical, Mahogany, Carved, Drawer, c.1810, 30 x 22 In. | 427 |
| **Table,** Drum, Hardwood, Arched Splat, 2 Turned Supports, Woven Seat, Africa, 32 In. | 200 |
| **Table,** Drum, Regency, Mahogany, Leather Top, Carved, Drawers, Carved Legs, 30 x 48 In. | 6000 |
| **Table,** Duncan Phyfe Style, Lyre Standard, Rectangular Top, Splayed Legs, 30 x 20 In. | 250 |
| **Table,** Dutch Neoclassical Style, Mahogany, Inlay, Foldover, 30 x 31 In. | 313 |
| **Table,** Eastlake, Mahogany, Marble Top, Carved Skirt, 4-Footed Base, 18 x 27 x 19 In. | 154 |
| **Table,** Eastlake, Mahogany, Pink Marble Top, Oblong, 28 x 29 x 20 In. | 240 |
| **Table,** Eastlake, Walnut, Marble Top, Reeded Skirt, 20 x 20 In. | 207 |
| **Table,** Eastlake, Wood, Carved, Marble Top, Splayed Legs, 29 x 21 In. | 163 |
| **Table,** Ebonized, Gilt, Oval Top, Figural Blackamoor Column Support, Italy, 22 x 25 In. | 826 |
| **Table,** Ebonized, Parcel Gilt, Pietra Dura, Sunburst Inlay, Stretcher, c.1910, 30 x 26 In. | 1722 |
| **Table,** Edwardian, Amboyna, Burl Veneer, Inlaid Banding, Tilt Top, Oval, 29 x 54 In. | 2596 |
| **Table,** Edwardian, Mahogany, Satinwood, Vitrine Top, X-Stretcher, 29 x 25 In. | 281 |
| **Table,** Eero Saarinen, Tulip, Marble Top, Enameled Metal Base, Knoll, 2000, 20 x 23 In. | 1625 |
| **Table,** Eero Saarinen, Tulip, Steel, Walnut, Round, Knoll, 1960s, 28 x 48 In. | 1188 |
| **Table,** Eileen Grey, Chrome, Glass, 1930s, 25 x 19 In., Pair | 450 |
| **Table,** Empire Style, Mahogany, Drop Leaf, Pedestal, Scrolled Feet, 30 x 42 In. | 118 |
| **Table,** Empire Style, Mahogany, Gilt Bronze, Male Supports, Round, c.1905, 29 x 35 In. | 1875 |
| **Table,** Empire Style, Mahogany, Gilt Metal, Feather Mounts, Turned Stretcher, 31 x 23 In. | 250 |
| **Table,** Empire Style, Mahogany, Marble Top, 2 Drawers, Columns, 30 x 20 In. | 750 |
| **Table,** Empire Style, Quarter-Matched Veneers, Round Top, Caryatid Legs, Shelf, 28 x 20 In. | 357 |
| **Table,** Empire, Gilt Metal, Mixed Wood, Round Top, Hairy Paw Legs, 34 x 47 In. | 12550 |
| **Table,** Empire, Mahogany, Bronze Mounts, Drawer, Columns, Stretcher, c.1810, 30 x 32 In. | 1125 |
| **Table,** Empire, Mahogany, Parcel Gilt, Marble Round, 3-Part Base, c.1810, 29 x 30 In. | 5313 |
| **Table,** Empire, Mahogany, Rectangular Top, Claw Feet, Phila., 1800s, 29 x 40 In. | 1800 |
| **Table,** Empire, Mahogany, Round Top, Cylindrical Support, c.1860, 29 x 60 In. | 1750 |
| **Table,** Farm, 3-Board Top, 3 Apron Drawers, Turned Legs, Pa., c.1810, 71 x 37 In. | 1067 |
| **Table,** Farm, Drop Leaves, Red Paint, Pine, Maple, Birch, New England, c.1850, 25 x 60 In. | 1755 |
| **Table,** Farm, Pine, Butcher Block Top, 2 Drawers, Blue Paint, 36 x 72 In. | 330 |
| **Table,** Farm, Poplar, Turned Legs, Box Stretcher, 29 x 94 In. | 390 |
| **Table,** Federal Style, Mahogany, Inlay, Foldover, Serpentine Top, 30 x 31 In. | 688 |
| **Table,** Federal, Cherry, Maple, Scalloped Skirt, Ring-Turned Legs, c.1840, 29 x 18 In. | 546 |
| **Table,** Federal, Cherry, Overhanging Top, Drawer, New England, c.1800, 29 x 18 In. | 500 |
| **Table,** Federal, Drop Leaf, Bird's-Eye Maple, c.1905, 28 x 19 In. | 2160 |
| **Table,** Federal, Drop Leaf, Mahogany, Dovetailed, Pedestal, c.1840, 23 x 39 In. ...............*illus* | 165 |
| **Table,** Federal, Maple, Mixed Wood, Drawer, New England, c.1825, 30 x 16 In. | 288 |
| **Table,** Federal, Square Legs, Va., c.1820, 28 x 28 In. | 805 |
| **Table,** Federal, Tiger Maple, Drawer, Straight Skirt, Tapered Legs, c.1810, 29 x 31 In. | 1353 |
| **Table,** Federal, Walnut, Fan Inlay, Drawer, c.1820, 30 x 35 In. | 1200 |
| **Table,** Federal, Walnut, Square Legs, Hinged Leaves, c.1820, 29 x 43 In. | 219 |
| **Table,** Figured Walnut Veneer, 2 Drawers, Tapered Legs, Overhang Top, 29 x 32 In. | 11800 |
| **Table,** Florence Knoll, Mid-Century Modern, Walnut, Chrome, Round Top, 28 x 54 In. | 1722 |
| **Table,** Fornasetti, Side, Wood, Transfer, Steel Base, Label, 1950s, 15 x 20 In. ...............*illus* | 2875 |
| **Table,** Frankl, Side, Lacquered Cork, Mahogany, Brass, Johnson Furniture, 24 x 24 In.........*illus* | 5000 |
| **Table,** French Provincial, Cherry, 2 Drawers, Stretcher, 78 x 29 In. | 793 |
| **Table,** French Provincial, Fruitwood, Drawers, Shaped Top, 28 x 39 In. | 531 |
| **Table,** French Provincial, Fruitwood, Shaped Frieze, Drawers, c.1960, 35 x 121 In. | 1107 |
| **Table,** French Provincial, Fruitwood, Tray Top, Drawer, Cabriole Legs, 24 x 17 In. | 799 |
| **Table,** French Provincial, Mahogany, Fan, Square Legs, 36 x 25 In. | 651 |
| **Table,** French Provincial, Molded Edge, D Ends, Decoupage Top, Stretcher, 46 x 105 In. | 2214 |
| **Table,** French Provincial, Oak, Carved, Marble Top, Cabriole Legs, 27 x 30 In. | 1434 |
| **Table,** French Provincial, Oak, Fruitwood, 3-Board Top, Drawers, c.1810, 31 x 76 In. | 2562 |
| **Table,** French Style, Classical Details, Gold Paint, Marble Top, Fluted Legs, 30 x 20 In. | 288 |
| **Table,** French Style, Satinwood, 2 Tiers, Shaped Round Tops, 3 Cabriole Legs, c.1940 | 300 |
| **Table,** French Style, Walnut, Marble Top, Carved Skirt, Wall Mount, 35 x 28 x 16 In. | 130 |
| **Table,** Fruitwood, Inlay, Gilt Metal, Geometric Top, Stretcher, France, c.1910, 28 x 15 In. | 210 |
| **Table,** Fruitwood, Round Top, Carved Apron, 28 x 29 In. | 719 |
| **Table,** Fruitwood, Tilt Top, Round, Curved Supports, Stepped Base, Art Deco, 25 x 47 In. | 840 |
| **Table,** G. Nakashima, Side, Walnut, Triangular Top, Tripod Base, c.1963, 21 x 18 In. | 6250 |
| **Table,** G. Nakashima, Walnut, Ash, Overhanging Top, Slatted Shelf, 20 x 28 x 29 In. | 2125 |
| **Table,** G. Nakashima, Walnut, Round, Pedestal Base, 1966, 29 ¾ x 48 In. | 3124 |
| **Table,** G. Nakashima, Wohl, Walnut, Triangular, 3 Legs, 1966, 21 x 27 x 20 In. | 2500 |

**Furniture,** Table, Coffee, Maple, Burl, Natural Form, Glass Top, c.1900, 19 x 39 In.
**$1,046**

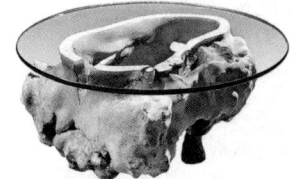

Skinner Auctioneers & Appraisers

**Furniture,** Table, Coffee, Oak, Textured Mosaic Tiles, Signed Tue, 16 x 61 x 32 In.
**$2,214**

Skinner Auctioneers & Appraisers

**Furniture,** Table, Coffee, P. Evans, Glass Top, Steel, Welded, Signed, 1967, 18 ½ x 42 In.
**$9,375**

Rago Arts & Auction Center

---

**TIP**

*Concrete furniture is a modern idea and designers are changing the formula with modern materials like fiberglass or reinforcing microfibers. Then they can mold tables, chairs, clocks, bowls, candelabra, and even "cushions" from cement to be used indoors and in the garden. A chair by a known designer can cost as much as $3,000. Old cement tables, chairs, and planters made for a yard sell for a few hundred dollars.*

**F**

**Furniture,** Table, Coffee, Philip & Kelvin LaVerne, Chan, Bronze, Pewter, 1960s, 39 x 35 In.
$5,000

Rago Arts & Auction Center

**Furniture,** Table, Coffee, Pietro Chiesa, Crystal, Brass, Fontana Arte, Italy, 1940s, 18 x 49 In.
$9,375

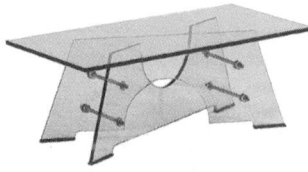

Rago Arts & Auction Center

**Furniture,** Table, Coffee, V. Kagan, Boomerang, Walnut, Travertine Top, 1950s, 14 x 51 In.
$8,750

Rago Arts & Auction Center

**Furniture,** Table, Console, Anglo-Colonial, Carved, Reticulated, Pierced Scrollwork, 1800s, 42 x 51 In.
$3,944

Neal Auction Co.

| | |
|---|---:|
| **Table,** G. Nelson, Rosewood Veneer, Round, Nickel Plated Base, Adjustable, 30 x 42 In. | 478 |
| **Table,** G. Stickley, Oak, Grueby Tile Top, X-Stretcher, c.1905, 22 x 17 In. .............................*illus* | 19520 |
| **Table,** G. Stickley, Oak, Tile Top, Pegged Arched Apron, Medial Shelf, 29 x 20 In. | 6000 |
| **Table,** Galle, Oak, Mixed Wood, Molded Edge, Inlay, Landscape, c.1900, 29 x 27 x 18 In. | 2460 |
| **Table,** Game, Backgammon, Cribbage, Regency, Rosewood, Frieze, c.1810, 30 x 18 In. | 922 |
| **Table,** Game, Baker Furniture, Burl Walnut, Leather Flip Top, Ebony Inlay, 29 x 36 In. | 805 |
| **Table,** Game, Baroque, Giltwood, Chess, Tilt Top, 3 Carved Scroll Feet, 31 x 26 In. | 3750 |
| **Table,** Game, Blackjack, Lucky Ladies, Colorado Belle Hotel, Galaxy Gaming, 72 x 38 In. | 354 |
| **Table,** Game, Bouillotte, Louis XVI Style, Mahogany, Marble Top, Brass, c.1875, 29 x 25 In. | 861 |
| **Table,** Game, Chess, G. Stickley, Leather Top, Square, Stretcher, No. 419, 39 x 26 In. | 14640 |
| **Table,** Game, Chippendale, Walnut, Flip Top, Rectangular, 2 Drawers, Va., 28 x 32 In. | 2360 |
| **Table,** Game, Dovetailed Skirt Drawer, Bellflower Inlay, Tapered Legs, 30 x 36 x 18 In. | 236 |
| **Table,** Game, Edwardian, Mahogany, Hinged Top, Oval Medallion, c.1900, 30 x 39 In. | 984 |
| **Table,** Game, Empire, Burl Mahogany, Veneer, Lyre Base, 27 x 34 In. ................................*illus* | 142 |
| **Table,** Game, Federal Style, Mahogany, String Inlay, Center Drawer, 28 x 38 In. | 150 |
| **Table,** Game, Federal, Cuban Mahogany, Foldover, Reeded Edge, c.1810, 30 x 35 In. | 598 |
| **Table,** Game, Federal, Pine, Sponge Painted, Elliptical Front, Drawer, c.1810, 30 x 37 In. | 461 |
| **Table,** Game, Fruitwood, Folding, Floral Marquetry, Ormolu, Leather Top, 31 x 34 In. | 3300 |
| **Table,** Game, George II Style, Mahogany, Felt Top, Eared Corners, 1800s, 29 x 34 In. | 438 |
| **Table,** Game, George III Style, Mahogany, Foldover Top, c.1750, 28 x 36 In. | 150 |
| **Table,** Game, George III, Mahogany, Foldover, Satinwood, Swing Legs, c.1790, 29 x 37 In. | 1315 |
| **Table,** Game, George III, Mahogany, Hinged Top, Drawer, Tapered Legs, 29 x 36 In. | 1045 |
| **Table,** Game, George III, Mahogany, Round, 4 Drawers, 2 False, c.1810, 29 x 22 In. | 500 |
| **Table,** Game, George III, Mahogany, Shell-Carved Knees, 29 x 33 In. | 1046 |
| **Table,** Game, Hepplewhite, Mahogany, Foldover, Inlaid Capitals, 29 x 41 In. | 308 |
| **Table,** Game, Louis Philippe, Inlaid Satinwood, Mahogany, Trestle Base, 29 x 36 In. | 354 |
| **Table,** Game, Louis XVI Style, Mahogany, Hinged Top, Bronze Mounts, c.1895, 30 x 33 In. | 1875 |
| **Table,** Game, Mahogany, Rounded Corners, Cabriole Legs, Hekman, c.1950, 28 x 33 In. | 270 |
| **Table,** Game, Middle Eastern Style, Exotic Woods, Flip Over, Mother-Of-Pearl, 32 x 32 In. | 1481 |
| **Table,** Game, Napoleon III, Kingwood, Exotic Wood, Scrolling Leaf, Flower Inlay, 30 x 35 In. | 2952 |
| **Table,** Game, Neoclassical, Mahogany, Flip Top, Concave Pedestal, Serpentine, c.1825, 28 x 35 In. | 2444 |
| **Table,** Game, Neoclassical, Mahogany, Foldover Top, Carved, Baluster Standard, 29 x 36 In. | 366 |
| **Table,** Game, Neoclassical, Mahogany, Foldover, Carved, Swivel Top, Satinwood, 29 x 28 In. | 2829 |
| **Table,** Game, Neoclassical, Mahogany, Foldover, Column Support, Curved Plinth, 29 x 36 In. | 359 |
| **Table,** Game, Neoclassical, Mahogany, Gilt Bronze, Rosettes, Plinth, Saber Legs, 30 x 34 In. | 598 |
| **Table,** Game, Regency, Bird's-Eye Maple, Foldover, Ebonized, Shelf, c.1825, 29 x 38 In. | 1230 |
| **Table,** Game, Regency, Rosewood, Flip Top, Drawer, Slide, X-Shape Base, 29 x 21 In. | 688 |
| **Table,** Game, Rococo Revival, Rosewood, Foldover, Drawer, Baudouine, 51 x 36 In. | 1722 |
| **Table,** Game, Sheraton, Mahogany, Flip Top, Serpentine, Ormolu, c.1825, 30 x 38 In. .........*illus* | 984 |
| **Table,** Game, Tooled Leather, Glass Top, Fluted Tapered Legs, 4 Chairs, 36 x 19 In. | 489 |
| **Table,** Game, Walnut, Checkers, Backgammon, Cribbage, Drawer, c.1850, 29 x 25 In. | 354 |
| **Table,** Game, Walnut, Gilt, Inlaid Checkerboard, Figural Game, Pedestal, 31 In. | 2460 |
| **Table,** Gateleg, William & Mary, Cherry, Maple, Drop Leaf, Drawer, N.Y., 27 x 39 In. | 1020 |
| **Table,** Gateleg, William & Mary, Oak, Drop Leaf, Drawer, Oval, England, c.1650, 27 x 57 In. | 875 |
| **Table,** Gateleg, William & Mary, Walnut, Drawer, Baluster Legs, Stretcher, c.1740, 27 x 36 In. | 5520 |
| **Table,** Gateleg, William & Mary, Walnut, Drawer, Carved, 29 x 48 In. | 540 |
| **Table,** Gateleg, William & Mary, Walnut, Oak, Drop Leaf, Turned Base, 30 x 46 In. | 948 |
| **Table,** George I Style, Parcel Gilt, Walnut, Marquetry, Carved Apron, 32 x 43 In. | 938 |
| **Table,** George II Style, Mahogany, Scalloped Apron, 3 Drawers, 27 x 30 In. | 406 |
| **Table,** George II, Mahogany, Green Marble Top, c.1750, 32 x 40 In. | 5000 |
| **Table,** George II, Mahogany, Tilt Top, Square, Tripod Base, 27 x 20 In. | 625 |
| **Table,** George II, Triple Top, Chip Wells, Leather Board, Ireland, c.1759, 29 x 34 In. | 938 |
| **Table,** George III Chinese Chippendale, Mahogany, Fretwork Apron, 1800s, 31 x 58 In. | 2040 |
| **Table,** George III Style, Mahogany, 3 Pedestals, Downswept Legs, 2 Leaves, 29 x 155 In. | 3438 |
| **Table,** George III Style, Mahogany, Double Pedestal, 3 Leaves, 30 x 68 In. | 625 |
| **Table,** George III Style, Mahogany, Serpentine, Beaded Drawers, Tapered Legs, 37 x 69 In. | 1375 |
| **Table,** George III, Mahogany, Drop Leaf, c.1790, 15 x 48 In. | 510 |
| **Table,** George III, Mahogany, Scalloped Tilt Top, Ball & Claw Feet, 28 x 32 In. | 375 |
| **Table,** George III, Mahogany, Tripod Base, c.1790, 31 x 33 In. | 840 |
| **Table,** George III, Satinwood, Banding, Top & Side Drawers, c.1790, 35 x 18 In. | 1125 |
| **Table,** George III, Satinwood, Mixed Wood, Banded, Demilune, c.1780, 33 x 43 In. | 531 |
| **Table,** George III, Wood, Octagonal, Leather, Drawers, Carved Legs, c.1805, 30 x 52 In. | 1000 |
| **Table,** George IV, Mahogany, Bronze, Octagonal, Reeded, Tripart Base, 24 x 16 In., Pair | 1875 |
| **Table,** George IV, Rosewood, Gilt, Round, Flared Standard, Paw Feet, 28 x 48 In. | 4375 |
| **Table,** Georgian Style, Mahogany, Marble Top, Frieze Drawers, Carved, 36 x 77 In. | 1845 |
| **Table,** Georgian Style, Sunderland, Mahogany, c.1905, 30 x 36 x 33 In. | 344 |
| **Table,** Georgian, Inlaid Mahogany, Pedestal, Drawers, Brass Casters, 30 x 24 In. | 590 |

| | |
|---|---|
| **Table,** Gilt Steel, Round Glass Top, Sheaf Shape Base, 1960s, 24 x 27 In. | 544 |
| **Table,** Gilt, Lacquer, Sparrows, Flowering Tree, Square, Gallery, Shaped Feet, 5 x 13 In. | 976 |
| **Table,** Giltwood, Round, Napoleon Porcelain Insert, Bronze Base, Pierced, 29 x 18 In. | 3000 |
| **Table,** Giltwood, Silvered, Painted, Tapered Legs, X-Shape Stretcher, 32 x 47 In. | 1625 |
| **Table,** Gio Ponti, Compass, Walnut, Glass, Brass Center, c.1950, 15 x 39 In. *illus* | 6765 |
| **Table,** Gio Ponti, Walnut, Shaped Top, 3 Tapered Legs, 18 x 31 x 19 In., Pair | 8125 |
| **Table,** Gothic Revival Style, Mahogany, Marquetry Star, Footed, 30 x 32 In., Pair | 1625 |
| **Table,** Gothic Revival Style, Wood, Flowers, White Paint, Cutouts, 25 x 22 In., Pair | 344 |
| **Table,** Guard Room, Spanish, Walnut, Iron, Shaped Supports, Scroll, c.1800s, 31 x 78 In. | 4674 |
| **Table,** Handkerchief, Mahogany, Marquetry, Opens To Felt Surface, Edwardian, 29 In. *illus* | 984 |
| **Table,** Hardwood, Allover Carving, Chinese, 21 x 49 In. | 2500 |
| **Table,** Hardwood, Marble, Column, Carved Dragons, Tripod Base, c.1900, 31 x 22 In. | 6250 |
| **Table,** Harvest, Pine, Drop Leaf, Tapered Legs, 30 x 72 In. | 325 |
| **Table,** Heywood-Wakefield, Modern, Drawer, Shelf, Splayed Tapered Legs, 24 x 20 In., Pair | 270 |
| **Table,** Hunt, Mahogany, Oval Drop Leaves, 6 Chamfered Legs, Ireland, 30 x 70 In. | 984 |
| **Table,** Huntboard, Pine, Drawer, 60 x 17 ½ In. | 146 |
| **Table,** Ice Cream Parlor Set, 4 Chairs, Table, Bent Wire, Copper, Wood Seats, 1905-20, 35 In. | 720 |
| **Table,** Invalid's, Edwardian, Oak, Brass, Adjustable, Telescoping Support, c.1900, 35 x 27 In. | 299 |
| **Table,** Italian Baroque, Walnut, Shaped Supports, 45 In. | 1000 |
| **Table,** Italian Renaissance Revival Style, Walnut, Trestle Supports, 1800s, 29 x 140 In. | 4063 |
| **Table,** Italian Style, Wood, Carved, Gilt, Leaves, Green Marble Top, 17 x 17 In. | 529 |
| **Table,** Jacobean Style, Oak, Barley Twist Legs, Gateleg, 29 x 34 In. | 123 |
| **Table,** Jacobean Style, Oak, Parquetry, Carved Legs, 20 x 126 In. | 1800 |
| **Table,** Jacobean Style, Round Top, Spool Turned, Drop Leaf, 30 x 48 In. | 1080 |
| **Table,** James Bearden, Sky Dwelling, Glass, Bronzed Steel, Signed, 2014, 23 x 18 In. *illus* | 1125 |
| **Table,** Kitchen, Enamel Top, Flowers, Wood Apron, Drawer, Metal Legs, 32 x 42 In. | 117 |
| **Table,** Kitchen, Formica Top, Chrome Trim & Legs, 12-In. Leaf, 1950s, 36 x 47 x 39 In. | 105 |
| **Table,** Kittinger, Pembroke, Federal Style, Mahogany, Bowfront, Tapered Legs, 1900s, 38 In. | 240 |
| **Table,** L. & J.G. Stickley, Oak, Butterfly, Arched Apron, c.1980, 26 x 20 In. | 360 |
| **Table,** L. & J.G. Stickley, Tabouret, Square, Clipped Corners, c.1912, 18 x 16 In. *illus* | 625 |
| **Table,** Lacemaker's, Cherry, 3-Board Top, Demilune Leaves, Stretchers, c.1890, 30 x 96 In. | 2133 |
| **Table,** Library, Arts & Crafts Style, Chestnut, Trestle Base, 30 x 88 x 41 In. | 531 |
| **Table,** Library, Arts & Crafts, Quartersawn Oak, Drawer, Flat Stretcher, 31 x 45 In. | 354 |
| **Table,** Library, Biedermeier, Fruitwood, Frieze Drawer, Stretcher, 1800s, 31 x 47 In. | 861 |
| **Table,** Library, Burl Walnut, Drawer, Spool-Turned Front Legs, 30 x 38 In. | 165 |
| **Table,** Library, G. Stickley, 2 Drawers, Red Decal, Paper Label, c.1906, 30 x 42 x 29 In. | 1625 |
| **Table,** Library, G. Stickley, Arts & Crafts, Oak, Copper, Drawers, Corbel Support, 30 x 42 In. | 1169 |
| **Table,** Library, G. Stickley, Oak, Trestle, Medial Shelf, N.Y., c.1915, 29 x 48 In. | 1536 |
| **Table,** Library, Jacobean Style, Oak, Carved, Gadrooned, Turned Legs, Ball Feet, 31 x 48 In. | 830 |
| **Table,** Library, Regency, Mahogany, Inset Leather Blotter, Drawer, Trestle, c.1840, 30 x 48 In. | 584 |
| **Table,** Library, Regency, Mahogany, Rosewood, Brass Stringing, Curule Supports, 29 x 72 In. | 1230 |
| **Table,** Library, Rosewood, 2 Tiers, Turned Supports, Scrolled Tripod Base, 1800s, 29 x 28 In. | 506 |
| **Table,** Library, Spanish Style, Walnut, X-Stretcher Base, 30 x 46 In. | 780 |
| **Table,** Library, William IV, Mahogany, Carved, Leather Top, c.1810, 31 x 72 In. | 4880 |
| **Table,** Library, William IV, Mahogany, Leather Top, Drawers, Turned Legs, c.1820, 32 x 60 In. | 1375 |
| **Table,** Limbert, Arts & Crafts, Oak, 2 Drawers, Stretcher Shelf, c.1910, 30 x 48 In. | 438 |
| **Table,** Limbert, Turtle Top, Shaped, Blind Drawer, Slab Sides, Cutouts, 29 x 48 x 30 In. | 4270 |
| **Table,** Lloyd Loom, Rolling, Wicker, Glass, Green Paint, Shelf, Casters, 37 x 34 In. | 76 |
| **Table,** Louis XV Style, Black Lacquer, Gilt Metal Mounts, Leather Top, 1900s, 30 x 48 In. | 2500 |
| **Table,** Louis XV Style, Fruitwood, Gilt Bronze Masks, Leather Top, c.1970, 31 x 69 In. | 1063 |
| **Table,** Louis XV Style, Fruitwood, Inset Leather Top, Gilt Bronze Masks, 31 x 55 In. | 1500 |
| **Table,** Louis XV Style, Giltwood, Marble Top, Cabriole Legs, X-Stretcher, c.1860, 31 x 53 In. | 6000 |
| **Table,** Louis XV Style, Giltwood, Serpentine Marble Top, Carved, c.1890, 35 x 47 In. | 900 |
| **Table,** Louis XV Style, Inlay, Metal Mounts, Quatrefoil, Flowers, Cabriole Legs, 30 x 25 In. | 125 |
| **Table,** Louis XV Style, Kingwood, Bronze, Serpentine, Leather Top, Drawers, 30 x 65 In. | 4183 |
| **Table,** Louis XV Style, Kingwood, Veneer, Marble Top, Bronze Mounts, 1910, 29 x 31 In. | 338 |
| **Table,** Louis XV Style, Mahogany, Round, Ormolu Mounts, 1900s, 40 x 15 In., Pair | 300 |
| **Table,** Louis XV Style, Marble Top, Giltwood, Pendant Apron, Urn Stretcher, 48 In. | 861 |
| **Table,** Louis XV Style, Mixed Wood, Marble Top, Brass, Drawer, c.1920, 26 x 26 In. | 2250 |
| **Table,** Louis XV Style, Mixed Wood, Parquetry, Leather, Drawers, Gilt, c.1945, 30 x 45 In. | 3125 |
| **Table,** Louis XV Style, Walnut, Drawer, Hoof Feet, 33 x 23 In. | 1554 |
| **Table,** Louis XV, Gilt, Round, Inlay, Venus, Flower, Relief Busts, c.1860, 30 In. | 1476 |
| **Table,** Louis XV, Walnut, Round, Flower Serpentine Skirt, Cabriole Legs, 27 In. | 119 |
| **Table,** Louis XVI Style, 2 Drawers, Gallery, Inset Marble Top, 25 x 16 In., Pair | 1063 |
| **Table,** Louis XVI Style, Faux Malachite, Multicolor, Inset Top, Glazed, 25 x 25 In., Pair | 1722 |
| **Table,** Louis XVI Style, Fruitwood, Bronze, Leather Top, Round, c.1950, 30 x 20 In. | 338 |
| **Table,** Louis XVI Style, Hardwood, Brass Mounts, 1800s, 59 x 30 In. | 1062 |

**Furniture,** Table, Dining, Drop Leaf, Sheraton, Mahogany, 2 Piece, c.1825, 45 x 81 In.
$344

Garth's Auctioneers & Appraisers

**Furniture,** Table, Dining, Empire, Mahogany, Pedestal, Scroll Feet, c.1850, 53 In.
$840

Garth's Auctioneers & Appraisers

**Furniture,** Table, Dining, G. Stickley, 5-Legged Cross Stretcher, 6 Leaves, Stamped, c.1904, 30 x 54 In.
$9,375

Rago Arts & Auction Center

**Furniture,** Table, Dining, M. Graves, Wood, Brass, Plastic, Glass Top, 1980s, 48 In. Diam.
$3,840

Rago Arts & Auction Center

F

**Furniture,** Table, Dining, P. Evans, Directional, Sculptured Steel, Glass Top, c.1968, 84 x 44 In.
$10,000

Los Angeles Modern Auctions (LAMA)

**Furniture,** Table, Dining, Renaissance Revival, Walnut, Ebonized, 2 Leaves, c.1850, 58 x 58 In.
$2,214

Neal Auction Co.

**Furniture,** Table, Dining, Roger Sprunger, Rosewood, Chromed Steel, Dunbar, 1970s, 96 x 44 In.
$2,688

Rago Arts & Auction Center

**Furniture,** Table, Dining, Sheraton, Mahogany, Spiral Twist Legs, c.1825, 29 x 48 In.
$600

Garth's Auctioneers & Appraisers

> **TIP**
> Never use spray polish on antique furniture. It will leave a gray haze and attracts dirt.

| | |
|---|---:|
| **Table,** Louis XVI Style, Kingwood, Gilt Metal, Brass, Leather, Drawers, 30 x 60 In. | 2000 |
| **Table,** Louis XVI Style, Landscape Inlay, Round Top, Drawers, Writing Slide, 30 x 32 In. | 1188 |
| **Table,** Louis XVI Style, Mahogany, 2 Graduated Tiers, Banded, Parquetry Inlay, 30 x 19 In. | 1230 |
| **Table,** Louis XVI Style, Mahogany, 3 Drawers, Low Shelf, 29 x 20 In. | 406 |
| **Table,** Louis XVI Style, Mahogany, Inlay, Gilt Bronze, Leather Top, Drawers, 30 x 51 In. | 2151 |
| **Table,** Louis XVI Style, Mahogany, Marble Top, Ormolu, Gallery Shelf, 30 x 26 In. | 799 |
| **Table,** Louis XVI Style, Parquetry, Gilt Metal, Leather Top, Drawers, 1950s, 31 x 51 In. | 4250 |
| **Table,** Louis XVI, Marble Top, Demilune, Gray Paint, 35 x 43 In. | 2000 |
| **Table,** Louis XVI, Walnut, Gilt Metal, Leather Book Spine Front, Shelf, 26 x 24 In. | 365 |
| **Table,** Louis XVI, Walnut, Medallion Carved Skirt, Ring-Turned Legs, 30 x 47 In. | 244 |
| **Table,** Low, G. Nakashima, Walnut, Black Soapstone, 1956, 11 ½ x 24 In., Pair | 4375 |
| **Table,** Mahogany, 2 Drawers, Turned Legs, England, 29 x 18 In. | 375 |
| **Table,** Mahogany, 2 Drawers, Turned, Carved Legs, c.1850, 29 x 23 In. | 1125 |
| **Table,** Mahogany, 3 Pedestals, Rounded, Reeded Downswept Legs, England, 30 x 94 In. | 688 |
| **Table,** Mahogany, Carved Columns, Knees, Paw Feet, England, 1800s, 28 x 33 In. | 461 |
| **Table,** Mahogany, Carved Lace Tablecloth Top, Lion Feet, Portugal, 44 x 33 In. | 205 |
| **Table,** Mahogany, Carved Rim, Shaped, Iron Standard, 28 x 22 ½ In., Pair | 563 |
| **Table,** Mahogany, Carved, Plaque, Under Glass, Dolphin Feet, c.1970, 21 x 23 In. | 127 |
| **Table,** Mahogany, Drop Leaf, Inlaid, Drawers, Turned Stretcher, England, 28 x 36 In. | 500 |
| **Table,** Mahogany, Gallery Top, Tripod Base, Robert Irwin, c.1950, 29 x 29 In. | 180 |
| **Table,** Mahogany, Glass Top, Inlay, c.1905, 30 x 35 In. | 156 |
| **Table,** Mahogany, Horn, Inlay, Decagonal, Stars & W.H.T. Ehle, 1892, 28 x 26 In. ............ *illus* | 9840 |
| **Table,** Mahogany, Marble Top, Wide Skirt, Bead Carved, 4-Footed, 18 x 41 In. | 244 |
| **Table,** Mahogany, Octagonal, Pierced, Bird, Flower Carved, Lion Supports, 44 x 33 In. | 293 |
| **Table,** Mahogany, Oval Leaves, Drawer, Tapered Legs, c.1820, 28 x 42 In. | 300 |
| **Table,** Mahogany, Rope Turned, Round, Pedestal, Leaf Carved, 6 Leaves, 30 x 54 In. | 1188 |
| **Table,** Mahogany, Round, Tapered Column, Carved, Legs, c.1950, 29 x 47 In. | 375 |
| **Table,** Mahogany, Round, Tripart Base, c.1850, 29 x 40 In. | 123 |
| **Table,** Mahogany, Round, Wide Skirt, Hexagonal Pedestal, c.1880, 34 In. | 336 |
| **Table,** Mahogany, Square Tilt Top, Tripod Base, c.1800, 28 x 18 In. | 120 |
| **Table,** Maple, Overhanging Top, Drawer, X-Stretcher, 27 ½ x 16 In. | 500 |
| **Table,** Maple, Pine, Overhanging Top, Drawer, Square Legs, Stretchers, 25 x 61 In. | 2214 |
| **Table,** Maple, Pine, Overhanging Top, Tilting, Shoefoot Base, New England, 29 x 47 In. | 1800 |
| **Table,** Maple, Pine, Round, Lazy Susan, Rotating, Square Legs, c.1880, 33 x 57 In. | 1265 |
| **Table,** Marble Top, Round, 3 Caryatid Bronze Supports, 31 x 13 In., Pair | 688 |
| **Table,** Marble, Pietra Dura Top, Starfish, Seahorse, Brass Legs, 1900s, 17 x 26 In. | 106 |
| **Table,** Marquetry, Chariot Scene, Shelf, Oval Top, Drawer, Hoof Feet, 32 x 30 In. | 3250 |
| **Table,** McCobb, Directional 8706, Walnut, Blond Stain, Steel, 2 Drawers, 15 x 71 In. | 1888 |
| **Table,** Meret Oppenheim, Bird's Feet, Cast Bronze, Gold Leaf, 1970s, 25 x 27 In. ......... *illus* | 5625 |
| **Table,** Metal, Glass, Round Top, 3 Legs, Wheels, Ward Bennett, 1900s, 28 x 60 In. | 360 |
| **Table,** Mid-Century Modern, Chrome Plated, Spiral Design, Glass Top, Pace, 18 x 14 In. | 776 |
| **Table,** Mid-Century Modern, Rectangular, Round Tapered Legs, Medial Shelf, 22 x 26 In. | 120 |
| **Table,** Mid-Century Modern, Vinyl Cover, Splayed Tapered Legs, Shelf, 35 x 30 In. | 120 |
| **Table,** Mixed Wood, Inlaid Leaves, Harp, Drawers, Shaped Stretcher, Carved, 29 x 40 In. | 500 |
| **Table,** Mixed Wood, Leaf, Vine, Gilt Metal, Round Marble Top, Stretcher, c.1950, 31 x 27 In. | 375 |
| **Table,** Mixed Wood, Parquetry, Round, Tilt Top, 3 Scrolled Legs, c.1910, 30 x 54 In. | 3750 |
| **Table,** Mixed Wood, Pine Top, Stretcher Base, Drawers, c.1800, 54 x 43 In. | 413 |
| **Table,** Mixed Wood, Trestle Base, c.1850, 29 x 30 In. | 1000 |
| **Table,** Mosaic Glass Top, Neptune, Fish, Enamel, Varreny, Mexico, 1950s, 28 x 31 In. | 2125 |
| **Table,** Napoleon III, Interior Tray, Flower Marquetry, Cabriole Legs, 33 x 24 In. | 2460 |
| **Table,** Napoleon III, Walnut, Louis XV Style, Pierced Brass Gallery, Ormolu, 31 x 29 In. | 799 |
| **Table,** Neoclassical Style, Birch, Drawer, Square, Tapered Legs, 27 x 21 In., Pair | 313 |
| **Table,** Neoclassical Style, Chinoiserie, Bronze, Bird, Prunus, Stretcher, Paw Feet, 28 x 30 In. | 1434 |
| **Table,** Neoclassical Style, Mahogany, Gilt Figural Supports, Oval Top, Shelf, 31 x 32 In. | 500 |
| **Table,** Neoclassical Style, Mahogany, Gilt, Round Swivel Top, Tapered, c.1955, 19 x 30 In. | 125 |
| **Table,** Neoclassical Style, Walnut, Marble Top, Column Support, c.1950, 29 x 26 In., Pair | 594 |
| **Table,** Neoclassical, Fruitwood, Round Top, Drawer, Lyre Standard, c.1890, 29 x 20 In. | 200 |
| **Table,** Neoclassical, Giltwood, Marble Top, Carved Scrolls, Italy, 1700s, 34 x 46 In. | 3438 |
| **Table,** Neoclassical, Mahogany, Faux Marble, Spiral Turned Legs, c.1830, 29 x 39 In. | 956 |
| **Table,** Neoclassical, Mahogany, Round, Leaves, Carved, Winged Beast Supports, 29 x 41 In. | 3750 |
| **Table,** Neoclassical, Multicolor, Marble Top, Carved Swags, Urns, Italy, c.1810, 36 x 48 In. | 2337 |
| **Table,** Neoclassical, Tulipwood, Drawer, Banded, Fluted Sides, Dutch, 29 x 40 In. | 2813 |
| **Table,** Neoclassical, Walnut, Round Top, Brass Bound, Drawer, France, 31 x 32 In. | 923 |
| **Table,** Neoclassical, Walnut, Sunburst Inlay, Round, Low Shelf, Drawer, 20 x 29 In. | 1250 |
| **Table,** Nesting, Art Nouveau, Mahogany, Marquetry Branches, Majorelle, c.1900, 4 Piece | 1845 |
| **Table,** Nesting, Danish Modern, Teak, Round Tapered Legs, Stretchers, 20 To 15 In., 3 Piece | 480 |
| **Table,** Nesting, Edwardian, Mahogany, Maple Inlay, c.1910, 7 x 19 In., 4 Piece .............. *illus* | 418 |

| | |
|---|---|
| Table, Nesting, Louis XV, Walnut, Fruitwood, Inlay, Glass, 24 x 23 In., 3 Piece | 180 |
| Table, Nesting, Travertine, Rectangular, Top Transitions Into Legs, 22 To 14 In., 3 Piece | 420 |
| Table, Nesting, Vernis Martin Style, Painted, Woman In Sedan Chair, 22 x 16 In., 4 Piece | 805 |
| Table, Oak, Barley Twist, Upholstered, Gateleg, Carved, Arms, c.1900, 29 In. | 215 |
| Table, Oak, Carved Apron, England, 25 x 21 In. | 406 |
| Table, Oak, Divided Open Shelf, Oval, Michigan Chair Co., c.1915, 29 x 44 In. | 448 |
| Table, Oak, Drawer, Griffin Supports, X-Shape Stretcher, Urn Finial, 30 x 52 In. | 813 |
| Table, Oak, Drop Leaf, Round, Baluster Turned Supports, England, 47 x 60 In. | 1625 |
| Table, Oak, Drop Leaf, Spiral Carved Legs, 30 x 60 In. | 406 |
| Table, Oak, Leather Top, 4-Part Pedestal Supports, c.1900, 30 x 36 In. | 150 |
| Table, Oak, Oval Drop Leaves, Ring Carved, Gateleg, England, 10 x 28 In. | 380 |
| Table, Oak, Pedestal, Flower Carved Frieze, Tripod Base, 29¾ x 49 In. | 2000 |
| Table, Oak, Trestle, Continental, 30 x 83 In. | 1250 |
| Table, Oak, Trestle, Mouse Hole, 2 Leaves, 1990s, 31 x 76 In. | 688 |
| Table, Onyx, Champleve, Octangular Top, Baluster Support, Flowers, 31 x 18 In. | 1250 |
| Table, Oval Drop Leaves, Base Stretcher, Gateleg, Continental | 1375 |
| Table, Overhanging Oval Top, Frieze Drawer, Box Stretcher, New England, 25 x 35 In. | 1920 |
| Table, P. Evans, Directional, Olive Burl, Chromed Steel, Blocks, 1970s, 29 x 48 In. | 3500 |
| Table, P. Powell, Amoeba, Marble, Walnut, 3 Legs, 1959, 16 x 46 x 29 In. | 3750 |
| Table, Parquetry, Round Top, Tripod Base, England, 1800s, 29 x 28 In. | 594 |
| Table, Parquetry, Shaped Apron, Dancer's Legs Base, Black Shoes, 31 x 27 In. | 7200 |
| Table, Parsons Style, Faux Burl, Drawer, Sleigh Base, Stepped Panel, 24 x 24 In., Pair | 150 |
| Table, Pastry, Iron, Marble Top, Brass Flower Apron, Leaf, Scroll Base, 31 x 51 In. | 4500 |
| Table, Paul Laszlo, Drawer, Open Tapered Leg Frames, c.1940, 22 x 21 In., Pair .......*illus* | 3125 |
| Table, Pedestal, Contemporary, Square Top, Laurel Fyfe, 36 x 19 In. | 540 |
| Table, Pedestal, Empire, Burl Walnut, Round Top, Base Stretcher, 29 x 15 In. | 1500 |
| Table, Pedestal, G. Nelson, Laminated Round Top, Aluminum Base, 22 x 17 In. | 300 |
| Table, Pedestal, Walnut, Carved, Shaped Apron, Round Top, 29 x 26 In. | 120 |
| Table, Pembroke, Chippendale, Mahogany, Cock-Beaded Drawer, c.1790, 28 x 21 In. | 277 |
| Table, Pembroke, Chippendale, Mahogany, Drawer, Pierced Stretcher, c.1790, 28 x 19 In. | 531 |
| Table, Pembroke, Chippendale, Walnut, Drawer, Inlay, Crossed Stretcher, Pa., 29 x 30 In. | 300 |
| Table, Pembroke, Federal, Mahogany, Inlay, Bellflower Inlay, c.1845, 28 x 20 In. | 625 |
| Table, Pembroke, Federal, Mahogany, Inlay, Drawer, c.1820, 29 x 34 In. | 863 |
| Table, Pembroke, Federal, Mahogany, Shell, Flower Inlay, c.1800, 29 x 19 In. | 1920 |
| Table, Pembroke, Federal, Mahogany, Tapered, 1800s, 29 x 29 In. | 688 |
| Table, Pembroke, George III Style, Mahogany, Banded, Drawer, c.1860, 27 x 20 In. | 840 |
| Table, Pembroke, George III, Mahogany, Banded Top, Drawer, c.1790, 33 x 29 In. | 799 |
| Table, Pembroke, George III, Mahogany, Drawer, Oval, Casters, c.1790, 28 x 30 In. | 1342 |
| Table, Pembroke, George III, Mahogany, Oval Leaves, Square Legs, c.1775, 26 x 39 In. | 1168 |
| Table, Pembroke, George III, Satinwood, Inlay, c.1800, 29 x 20 In. | 1152 |
| Table, Pembroke, Hepplewhite, Mahogany, Crotch Top, c.1800, 28 x 40 x 30 In. | 900 |
| Table, Pembroke, Hepplewhite, Mahogany, Drop Leaves, 2 Drawers, X-Stretcher, 27 x 15 In. | 1320 |
| Table, Pembroke, Hepplewhite, Mahogany, Shaped Leaves, New England, 28 x 32 In. | 840 |
| Table, Pembroke, Hepplewhite, Tiger Maple, Square Legs, New England, 28 x 35 In. | 2280 |
| Table, Pembroke, Mahogany Inlay, D-Shape Ends, Bead-Molded Edge, c.1800, 28 x 35 In. | 2074 |
| Table, Pembroke, Mahogany, Drawer, Square Legs, Rounded Leaves, 29 x 20 x 37 In. | 295 |
| Table, Pembroke, Mahogany, Drawer, X-Stretcher, 29 x 33 In. | 420 |
| Table, Pembroke, Walnut, Drawer, Tapered Legs, 28 x 33 In. | 360 |
| Table, Pier, Biedermeier, Fruitwood, Mahogany, Drawers, Scrolled Supports, 32 x 44 In. | 799 |
| Table, Pier, Empire, Mahogany, Egyptian Style, Mirror Back, Rolled Columns, 42 x 19 In. | 936 |
| Table, Pier, Empire, Mahogany, Marble Top, Ogee Frieze, Scroll Supports, 37 x 44 In. | 1334 |
| Table, Pier, Figured Mahogany, Lyre Shape, Mirror Back, Scrolled Feet, c.1830, 40 x 36 In. | 708 |
| Table, Pier, Mahogany, Marble Top & Columns, Gilt, Ormolu Frieze, c.1825, 39 x 40 In. | 1875 |
| Table, Pier, Mahogany, Marble Top, Mirror Back, Columns, Stretcher, c.1840, 36 x 41 In. | 813 |
| Table, Pier, Mahogany, Marble Top, Scroll Carved Legs, Crest, Stretcher, c.1860, 29 x 37 In. | 720 |
| Table, Pier, Neoclassical, Gilt Bronze, Brass Inlay, Mahogany, Burl Ash, Mirror, 38 x 51 In. | 3585 |
| Table, Pier, Neoclassical, Mahogany, Carved, Marble Top, Scroll Supports, 35 x 42 In. | 1912 |
| Table, Pier, Neoclassical, Mahogany, Classical, Arched Frieze, Columns, Shelf, 37 x 35 In. | 1793 |
| Table, Pier, Neoclassical, Mahogany, Marble Top, Friezes, Scroll Supports, Plinth, 32 x 31 In. | 359 |
| Table, Pier, Neoclassical, Mahogany, Marble Top, Scroll Supports, c.1825, 40 x 45 In. | 3705 |
| Table, Pier, Neoclassical, Walnut, Carved, Shaped Apron, Blue, Italy, 1800s, 36 x 43 In. | 885 |
| Table, Pine, Drawer, Blue Paint, New England, c.1840, 28 x 71 In. | 805 |
| Table, Pine, Drawer, Carved Frieze, Flowers, Paint, New England, c.1820, 32 x 18 In. | 2415 |
| Table, Pine, Drawer, Scalloped Apron, Stretcher, Turned Legs, c.1750, 24 x 36 In. | 840 |
| Table, Pine, Drawer, Square Legs, Red Paint, c.1845, 32 x 22 In. | 575 |
| Table, Pine, Drawer, Tapered Legs, Red Paint, New England, c.1840, 28 x 35 In. | 403 |
| Table, Pine, Lift Top, Trestle Sides, Arched Cutouts, 31 x 72 In. | 1560 |

**Furniture,** Table, Drafting, Walnut, Adjustable, 2 Drawers, Iron Pedestal, c.1890, 39 x 28 In.
$188

Garth's Auctioneers & Appraisers

**Furniture,** Table, Dressing, George III, Satinwood, Fold-Out Top, Ivory Knobs, 30 x 26 In.
$1,680

DuMouchelles Art Gallery

**Furniture,** Table, Dressing, Painted, Mirror, 2 Drawers, 2 Sections, c.1825, 58 x 38 In.
$3,998

Skinner Auctioneers & Appraisers

# FURNITURE

**Furniture,** Table, Dressing, Queen Anne, Walnut, 5 Drawers & 1 Concealed, Boston, c.1765, 34 x 20 In.
$4,740

James D. Julia Auctioneers

**Furniture,** Table, Drop Leaf, Handkerchief, Edwardian, Rosewood, Inlay, c.1900, 27 x 33 In.
$799

New Orleans Auction Galleries, Inc.

**Furniture,** Table, Drop Leaf, Neoclassical, Mahogany, Rosewood, Brass, Venetian, c.1830, 54 x 26 In.
$4,900

Neal Auction Co.

**Furniture,** Table, Drop Leaf, Queen Anne, Mahogany, Pine, Cabriole Legs, 46 ½ In. Open
$660

Garth's Auctioneers & Appraisers

---

**TIP**

Vintage furniture sells well if it is Danish Modern style (1960s) or an elaborate adaptation of William & Mary style made in the 1930s. Look for tables that can also be used as desks, buffets, or cabinets that can hold a large screen television set, or unusual framed mirrors that can be decorative as well as useful. Be sure the piece is made with real wood and has no loose arms, legs, or badly fitted drawers.

**Furniture,** Table, Federal, Drop Leaf, Mahogany, Dovetailed, Pedestal, c.1840, 23 x 39 In.
$165

Conestoga Auction Co., Inc.

**Furniture,** Table, Fornasetti, Side, Wood, Transfer, Steel Base, Label, 1950s, 15 x 20 In.
$2,875

Rago Arts & Auction Center

**Furniture,** Table, Frankl, Side, Lacquered Cork, Mahogany, Brass, Johnson Furniture, 24 x 24 In.
$5,000

Rago Arts & Auction Center

| | |
|---|---|
| Table, Pine, Maple, Overhanging Top, Red Paint, New England, c.1860, 28 x 72 In. | 923 |
| Table, Pine, Maple, Round, Turned Legs, New England, c.1790, 24 x 29 In. | 420 |
| Table, Pine, Oak, Drawer, Black Paint, 1800s, 25 x 15 In. | 127 |
| Table, Pine, Overhanging Top, Drawer, Black Paint, New England, c.1820, 28 x 38 In. | 316 |
| Table, Pine, Overhanging Top, Drawer, Turned Legs, c.1910, 23 x 26 In. | 270 |
| Table, Pine, Overhanging Top, Drawer, Turned Legs, Stretcher, c.1820, 30 x 61 In. | 384 |
| Table, Pine, Painted, Medial Shelf, Branded PEB, 29 x 73 In. | 570 |
| Table, Pine, Slate Top, 2 Drawers, Base Stretcher, Red Stain, Pa., c.1810, 29 x 54 In. | 6765 |
| Table, Pine, Turned Legs, Red Paint, c.1830, 29 x 19 In. | 518 |
| Table, Pine, Walnut, Drawer, New England, c.1770, 25 x 30 In. | 420 |
| Table, Plank Top, Molding, Carved Drawer, Forged Hardware, Stretcher, c.1800, 24 x 33 In. | 1185 |
| Table, Poplar, Scrubbed 2-Board Top, 2 Drawers, Stretcher Base, 29 x 55 x 33 In. | 1169 |
| Table, Poplar, Scrubbed Top, 3 Drawers, Turned Legs, Old Cream Paint, 29 x 63 In. | 600 |
| Table, Queen Anne Style, Birch, Maple, Drawer, Overhanging Top, New England, 27 x 30 In. | 1320 |
| Table, Queen Anne Style, Cherry, Tray Top, Shaped Apron, Cabriole Legs, 29 x 32 In. | 344 |
| Table, Queen Anne Style, Maple, 4 Drawers, Cutout Apron, c.1850, 34 x 41 In. | 938 |
| Table, Queen Anne, Cherry, Butterfly, Rosehead Nails, Conn., 1700s, 28 x 14 x 40 In. | 11800 |
| Table, Queen Anne, Cherry, Drop Leaf, Oval, Delaware Valley, c.1750, 28 x 44 In. | 750 |
| Table, Queen Anne, Maple, Drop Leaf, Bowed Ends, Carved Apron, 27 x 43 In. | 2280 |
| Table, Queen Anne, Maple, Overhanging Top, Beaded Rim, c.1770, 26 x 29 In. | 690 |
| Table, Queen Anne, Maple, Round, Tilt Top, Pedestal Base, 28 x 35 In. | 118 |
| Table, Queen Anne, Maple, Scalloped, Carved Apron, Cabriole Legs, Drawers, 29 x 38 In. | 1625 |
| Table, Queen Anne, Tiger Maple, Porringer Top, Overhang, Turned Legs, c.1765, 25 x 26 In. | 12000 |
| Table, Queen Anne, Walnut, Overhanging Top, 3 Drawers, Pa., c.1765, 29 x 55 In. | 2880 |
| Table, Refectory, Baroque, Walnut, 2 Drawers, Square Stretchers, Turned Legs, 31 x 79 In. | 1888 |
| Table, Refectory, English Oak, Turned Legs, Stretchers, Clock Feet, 1700s, 38 x 134 In. | 6150 |
| Table, Refectory, Spanish, Walnut, Carved, Plank Top, Frieze Drawers, Trestle, 32 x 60 In. | 1912 |
| Table, Refectory, Trestle Base, Relief Edge Banded Top, Stretcher, c.1900, 72 x 24 In. | 891 |
| Table, Refectory, Walnut, Baluster Supports, Sledge Feet, Italy, 1600s, 32 x 98 In. | 9375 |
| Table, Refectory, Walnut, Foldover Leaves, Carved Apron, Stretcher, c.1690, 34 x 79 In. | 3360 |
| Table, Regency Style, Hardwood Inlay, Round Top, Carved Standard, 31 x 24 In., Pair | 275 |
| Table, Regency Style, Kingwood, Inset Leather, Ormolu Banding, Drawers, 32 x 70 In. | 399 |
| Table, Regency Style, Mahogany, Inlay Bands, Downswept Legs, 30 x 36 In. | 250 |
| Table, Regency Style, Mahogany, Triple Pedestal, Saber Legs, 2 Leaves, 28 x 48 In. | 4800 |
| Table, Regency, Mahogany, Brass Inlay, Round Top, 19 x 38 In. | 813 |
| Table, Regency, Mahogany, Double Pedestal, Saber Legs, 3 Leaves, c.1820, 29 x 49 In. | 1140 |
| Table, Regency, Mahogany, Drop Leaves, 2 Frieze Drawers, Trestle, England, 28 x 35 In. | 540 |
| Table, Regency, Mahogany, Leather Top, 2 Drawers, 2 Fake Drawers, c.1815, 42 x 30 In. | 4063 |
| Table, Regency, Mahogany, Round Top, Saber Legs, England, 1800s, 30 x 46 In. | 406 |
| Table, Regency, Mahogany, Satinwood, Drop Leaf, 4 Drawers, England, 1800s, 32 x 29 In. | 351 |
| Table, Regency, Mixed Wood, Drop Leaf, Banded, Drawers, Trestle Base, c.1810, 28 x 58 In. | 3125 |
| Table, Regency, Rosewood, Brass Banding, Round Top, c.1860, 29 x 52 In. | 1063 |
| Table, Regency, Sheet Metal, Scalloped Apron, Paint, Folding, Oval, 1800s, 30 x 25 In. | 120 |
| Table, Regency, Walnut, Carved, Cyr Stone Top, Cabriole Legs, Hoof Feet, 28 x 34 In. | 1464 |
| Table, Regency, Walnut, Serpentine, Carved, Shells, Flowers, Drawers, c.1890, 30 x 51 In. | 3360 |
| Table, Renaissance Revival Style, Iberian Trestle, Plank Top, Iron Braces, 31 x 104 In. | 7768 |
| Table, Renaissance Revival, Walnut, Carved, Marble Top, Hoof Feet, c.1890, 29 x 20 In. | 244 |
| Table, Renaissance Revival, Walnut, Drawer, Man's Head Pull, Shaped Supports, 25 x 25 In. | 1000 |
| Table, Rent, Mahogany, Burl Veneer, Round, Drawer Rimmed, England, 1900s, 28 x 30 In. | 330 |
| Table, Restauration, Burl, Marble Top, Scrolled Supports, c.1840, 31 x 36 In. | 688 |
| Table, Restauration, Mahogany, Carved, Round Marble Top, Reeded, France, 31 x 40 In. | 1554 |
| Table, Restauration, Mahogany, Marble Top, Frieze Drawer, Paw Feet, 1800s, 32 x 46 In. | 1476 |
| Table, Rococo Style, Blue, Red Paint, Scalloped Apron, 58 ½ x 29 In. | 250 |
| Table, Rococo Style, Burl Walnut, Carved, Leaves, Drawer, Cabriole Legs, c.1895, 30 x 53 In. | 625 |
| Table, Rococo Style, Giltwood, Glass Top, Leaf Carved Frame, Round, France, 22 x 30 In. | 325 |
| Table, Rococo Style, Mauve, Gray Marble Top, Pierced Apron, 20 x 45 In. | 750 |
| Table, Rococo, Giltwood, Marble Top, Shell Carved, Cabriole Legs, 1700s, 36 x 57 In. | 1375 |
| Table, Rosewood, Mother-Of-Pearl, Flower Inlay, Drawer, Carved, c.1890, 32 x 21 In. | 188 |
| Table, Round, Man-Made Marble Top, 3-Footed, Scroll, X-Shape Stretcher, 48 In. | 915 |
| Table, Saarinen, Mid-Century Modern, Tulip, Enamel, Carrara Marble Top, 20 x 16 In. | 506 |
| Table, Sawbuck, Pine, Brown Stain, Breadboard Ends, 29 x 72 In. | 443 |
| Table, Sawbuck, Pine, Walnut, c.1800, 30 x 40 In. | 210 |
| Table, Sewing, Cherry, Drawers, Turned Columns, Pedestal, c.1835, 30 x 20 In. ...............*illus* | 240 |
| Table, Sewing, Chestnut, Lift Top, Mirror, Fitted Interior, England, 1800s, 30 x 19 In. ...........*illus* | 404 |
| Table, Sewing, Federal, Mahogany, 2 Drawers, Turned Legs, c.1800, 28 x 19 In. | 1080 |
| Table, Sewing, Federal, Mahogany, Shaped Top, Drawers, Turned Legs, c.1800, 27 x 18 In. | 1080 |
| Table, Sewing, George III, Mahogany, Lift Top, Cabriole Feet, c.1800, 30 x 20 x 14 In. | 154 |

F

**Furniture,** Table, G. Stickley, Oak, Grueby Tile Top, X-Stretcher, c.1905, 22 x 17 In.
**$19,520**

Treadway Toomey Galleries

**Furniture,** Table, Game, Empire, Burl Mahogany, Veneer, Lyre Base, 27 x 34 In.
**$142**

Conestoga Auction Co., Inc.

**Furniture,** Table, Game, Sheraton, Mahogany, Flip Top, Serpentine, Ormolu, c.1825, 30 x 38 In.
**$984**

New Orleans Auction Galleries, Inc.

This is an edited listing of current prices. Visit Kovels.com to check thousands of prices from previous years and sign up for free information on trends, tips, reproductions, marks, and more.

**Furniture,** Table, Gio Ponti, Compass, Walnut, Glass, Brass Center, c.1950, 15 x 39 In.
$6,765

Skinner Auctioneers & Appraisers

**Furniture,** Table, Handkerchief, Mahogany, Marquetry, Opens To Felt Surface, Edwardian, 29 In.
$984

New Orleans Auction Galleries, Inc.

**Furniture,** Table, James Bearden, Sky Dwelling, Glass, Bronzed Steel, Signed, 2014, 23 x 18 In.
$1,125

Rago Arts & Auction Center

**Furniture,** Table, L. & J.G. Stickley, Tabouret, Square, Clipped Corners, c.1912, 18 x 16 In.
$625

Rago Arts & Auction Center

| | |
|---|---:|
| **Table,** Sewing, Mahogany, Oval, Hinged, Drawers, 3-Part Base, Baltimore, 26 x 26 In. | 1625 |
| **Table,** Sewing, Maple, Square, Needlepoint Lift Lid, 4 Arched Leg Stand, 31 x 17 In. | 210 |
| **Table,** Sewing, Neoclassical, Mahogany, 2 Drop Leaves, 3 Drawers, Well, c.1825, 19 x 20 In. | 316 |
| **Table,** Sewing, Parquetry Inlay, Exotic Wood, Oval Panel Top, Drawers, c.1810, 20 x 17 In. | 1185 |
| **Table,** Sewing, Pincushion Top, Mahogany, 2 Drawers, Glass Knobs, 1870, 11 x 10 In. | 660 |
| **Table,** Sewing, Regency, Tortoiseshell, Fitted Interior, c.1800, 25 x 14 In. | 2988 |
| **Table,** Sewing, Shaker, Birch, Red Stain, Drawer, Dovetailed, 17 ½ x 14 In. | 1180 |
| **Table,** Sewing, Shaker, Birch, Single-Board Top, Drawer, Brass Pull, 27 x 17 In. | 1416 |
| **Table,** Sewing, Shaker, Cherry, 2 Short Drawers, 1 Deep Drawer, Union Village, 29 x 22 In. | 2640 |
| **Table,** Sewing, Shaker, Cherry, Pine, Drawer, Dovetailed, Turned Pull, 27 x 20 In. | 2124 |
| **Table,** Sewing, Tiger Maple, D-Shape Leaves, Drawers, Ring-Turned Legs, c.1810, 29 x 18 In. | 2726 |
| **Table,** Sewing, Victorian, Mahogany, Octagonal, Hinged Top, Mirrored Lid, 29 x 19 In. | 295 |
| **Table,** Sewing, Walnut, Pine, Drawer, Turned Pull, Tapered Legs, 24 x 19 In. | 5664 |
| **Table,** Sewing, Wicker, Lift Top, 2 Shelves, 19th Century, 30 x 12 x 12 In. | 90 |
| **Table,** Shaker, Birch, Pine, Oval Top, Square, Tapered Legs, Alfred, c.1830, 27 x 30 In. | 11685 |
| **Table,** Shaker, Cherry, Drop Leaf, Red Paint, Sabbathday Lake, 28 ¾ x 33 ¾ In. | 4920 |
| **Table,** Shaker, Drop Leaf, Birch, Maple, Red Paint, 2 Leaves, 42 x 12 In. | 2655 |
| **Table,** Shaker, Herb Drying, Gallery Top, Tapered Legs, Vermont, 19th Century, 30 x 97 In. | 354 |
| **Table,** Shaker, Pine, Birch, Overhanging Top, Drawer, Canterbury, c.1840, 26 x 30 In. | 2460 |
| **Table,** Shaker, Trestle, Walnut, 1-Board Top, Arched Feet, Union Village, 29 x 74 In. | 2640 |
| **Table,** Shaker, Walnut, 3-Board Top, Drawer, Tapered Legs, Union Village, 29 x 54 x 36 In. | 780 |
| **Table,** Shaker, Work, Drop Leaf, Tiger Maple, Tapered Legs, c.1840, 28 x 32 In. .............*illus* | 9145 |
| **Table,** Shaker, Work, Maple, Square To Round Tapered Legs, Skirt, c.1830, 31 x 24 In. | 2950 |
| **Table,** Shaker, Work, Walnut, Overhang Top, Drawer, Union Village, Ohio, 29 x 32 In. | 7800 |
| **Table,** Sheraton Style, Maple, Drawer, Ring-Turned Legs, 1900s, 30 x 19 In., Pair | 720 |
| **Table,** Sheraton, Birds-Eye, Tiger Maple, Graduated Drawers, Turned Legs, c.1810, 18 x 28 In. | 688 |
| **Table,** Sheraton, Drawer, Turned Legs, 28 x 16 In. | 360 |
| **Table,** Sheraton, Drop Leaf, Red Paint, Turned Legs, c.1830, 29 x 42 In. | 660 |
| **Table,** Sheraton, Mahogany, Birch Veneer, Drawers, Reeded Legs, Salem, 21 x 18 In. | 5400 |
| **Table,** Sheraton, Mahogany, Drop Leaf, Swing-Out Supports, Turned Legs, Pa., 29 x 32 In. | 189 |
| **Table,** Sheraton, Mahogany, Inlay, Hinged Top, Banded, Reeded Legs, 29 x 37 In. | 1080 |
| **Table,** Sheraton, Maple, Drop Leaf, 4 Drawers, Turned Legs, New England, 30 x 25 In. | 900 |
| **Table,** Sheraton, Maple, Scrubbed Top, Skirt Drawer, Turned Legs, Pa., 44 x 32 In. | 354 |
| **Table,** Sheraton, Mixed Wood, Inlay, Turned Legs, New England, c.1810, 29 x 36 In. | 3750 |
| **Table,** Sheraton, Overhanging Top, Turned Legs, Red Paint, 27 x 20 In. | 300 |
| **Table,** Sheraton, Satinwood, Line Inlay, 2 Drawers, c.1810, 30 x 15 In. | 750 |
| **Table,** Sheraton, Tiger Maple, Drawer, Turned Legs, Pa., c.1825, 28 ½ x 19 ¾ In. | 1680 |
| **Table,** Sheraton, Walnut, Round, Reeded Legs, Accordion Action, c.1810, 30 x 48 In. | 1680 |
| **Table,** Side, Art Nouveau, Walnut, Leather, Leaf, Bellflower, c.1903, 29 ½ x 19 In. | 590 |
| **Table,** Side, Galle, Art Nouveau, Inlay, Iris, Dragonfly, Moth, Shelf, c.1900, 29 x 24 In. ........*illus* | 1298 |
| **Table,** Side, George II Style, Parcel Gilt, Multicolor, Demilune, 1800s, 33 x 60 In. | 1968 |
| **Table,** Side, George III Style, Mahogany, Demilune, Foldover, Inlay, 30 x 40 In. | 1353 |
| **Table,** Side, Giltwood, Multicolor, Marble, Paneled Frieze, Fluted Legs, c.1810, 30 x 43 In. | 2214 |
| **Table,** Side, Neoclassical, Drop Leaf, Mahogany, c.1850, 29 x 19 x 38 In., Pair | 1476 |
| **Table,** Side, O. Borsini, Walnut, Rectangle Top, Apple Core Shape Pedestal, 23 ½ In. | 5625 |
| **Table,** Side, Renaissance Revival Style, Walnut, Dovetailed, Italy, c.1600s, 25 x 22 In. .........*illus* | 2370 |
| **Table,** Sinbad, Wood, Demilune, Triangular Base, Cassina, Italy, 15 x 73 In., Pair | 177 |
| **Table,** Southwestern, Mesquite, Tenon Construction, 2-Board Top, 1800s, 29 x 42 In. | 295 |
| **Table,** Spanish Baroque, Oak, Iron, Carved Trestle Base, c.1860, 30 x 62 In. | 1800 |
| **Table,** Spanish Baroque, Walnut, Figured, Carved, Molded, Drawers, 1700s, 34 x 70 In. | 2311 |
| **Table,** Stacking, Regency Chinoiserie, Quartetto, Gilt, Black Lacquer, c.1810, 29 x 22 In. | 1434 |
| **Table,** Stainless Steel, Glass Top, Tubular Legs, c.1950, 21 x 30 x 30 In. | 695 |
| **Table,** Stand, Wicker, Brown, Box Top, Hinged Lid, Shelf, Swivel Handle, 26 x 12 x 14 In. | 37 |
| **Table,** Sugar, Walnut, Drawer, Crotch Walnut, Turned Legs, c.1830, 29 x 26 x 20 In. | 1200 |
| **Table,** Swag-Carved Apron, Cream Paint, Italy, 33 x 40 In. | 1000 |
| **Table,** Tabouret, Hardwood, Carved, Famille Rose, Tile Inset, Stretcher, 29 x 16 In., Pair | 800 |
| **Table,** Tap, Queen Anne, Oval, Shaped Skirt, 25 x 32 In. | 360 |
| **Table,** Tavern, Birch, Drawer, Overhanging Top, New England, c.1810, 28 x 43 In. | 492 |
| **Table,** Tavern, Black Paint, Oval, Splayed Legs, Pad Feet, New England, 27 x 20 x 31 In. | 704 |
| **Table,** Tavern, Drop Leaf, Maple, D-Shape Leaves, Vase-Turned Legs, 27 x 31 In. | 938 |
| **Table,** Tavern, English Style, Oak, Shaped Apron, Stretchers, 21 x 21 In., Pair | 210 |
| **Table,** Tavern, Fruitwood, Carved, Drawers, Columnar Supports, c.1790, 58 x 34 In. | 956 |
| **Table,** Tavern, Mahogany, Frieze Drawers, Splayed Turned Legs, Stretcher, 1700s | 793 |
| **Table,** Tavern, Maple, Pine, Overhang Top, Drawer, Turned Legs, Button Feet, 26 x 30 In. | 1125 |
| **Table,** Tavern, Maple, Rectangular, Breadboard Ends, Drawer, Turned Legs, 27 x 42 In. | 500 |
| **Table,** Tavern, Mixed Wood, Overhang Top, Drawer, Box Stretcher, c.1800, 28 ½ x 47 In. | 510 |

**Furniture,** Table, Mahogany, Horn, Inlay, Decagonal, Stars & W.H.T. Ehle, 1892, 28 x 26 In. $9,840

New Orleans Auction Galleries, Inc.

**Furniture,** Table, Meret Oppenheim, Bird's Feet, Cast Bronze, Gold Leaf, 1970s, 25 x 27 In. $5,625

Los Angeles Modern Auctions (LAMA)

**Furniture,** Table, Nesting, Edwardian, Mahogany, Maple Inlay, c.1910, 7 x 19 In., 4 Piece $418

Neal Auction Co.

**Furniture,** Table, Paul Laszlo, Drawer, Open Tapered Leg Frames, c.1940, 22 x 21 In., Pair $3,125

Los Angeles Modern Auctions (LAMA)

**Furniture,** Table, Sewing, Cherry, Drawers, Turned Columns, Pedestal, c.1835, 30 x 20 In. $240

Garth's Auctioneers & Appraisers

### TIP
*Vintage furniture with a Danish modern look is selling quickly at shows, auctions, and secondhand furniture stores. The Danish modern china cabinet is useful as a cabinet or a bar. Tables can be office desks, and you can put a large flat-screen TV on a large, strong buffet.*

**Furniture,** Table, Sewing, Chestnut, Lift Top, Mirror, Fitted Interior, England, 1800s, 30 x 19 In. $404

Cowan's Auctions

**Furniture,** Table, Shaker, Work, Drop Leaf, Tiger Maple, Tapered Legs, c.1840, 28 x 32 In. $9,145

Willis Henry Auctions, Inc.

**Furniture,** Table, Side, Galle, Art Nouveau, Inlay, Iris, Dragonfly, Moth, Shelf, c.1900, 29 x 24 In. $1,298

Brunk Auctions

# FURNITURE

**Furniture,** Table, Side, Renaissance Revival Style, Walnut, Dovetailed, Italy, c.1600s, 25 x 22 In.
$2,370

**Furniture,** Table, Tea, Tilt Top, Chippendale, Cherry, Birch, New England, 1700s, 28 x 34 In.
$1,200

**Furniture,** Table, Tea, Tilt Top, Chippendale, Mahogany, Birdcage, Carved, c.1775, 48 x 30 In.
$8,888

**Furniture,** Table, Tea, Tilt Top, Queen Anne, Mahogany, Carved, Dish Top, c.1750, 24 x 28 In.
$1,778

**Furniture,** Table, Tea, Tilt Top, Victorian, Papier-Mache, Mother-Of-Pearl Inlay, c.1890
$130

**Furniture,** Table, Tilt Top, Painted, Gilt, Pedestal, Chinese Export, c.1850, 31 x 35 In.
$1,168

**Furniture,** Table, Tray, Papier-Mache, Birds, Bamboo-Turned Base, England, c.1835, 19 x 30 In.
$1,107

**Furniture,** Table, Wendell Castle, Side, Curly Maple, Carved, Painted Base, 1987, 23 x 20 In.
$2,645

**Furniture,** Table, Wendell Castle, Walnut, Laminated, Single Socket, Signed, 1969, 51 x 20 In.
$135,750

| | |
|---|---:|
| **Table,** Tavern, Overhanging Top, Red Painted Base, 1800s, 27 x 54 In. | 780 |
| **Table,** Tavern, Pine, Cut Corner Overhang Top, Drawer, Stretcher, c.1730, 30 x 75 In. | 1230 |
| **Table,** Tavern, Pine, Hickory, Overhang Top, Drawer, Stretcher Base, 28 x 47 x 31 In. | 590 |
| **Table,** Tavern, Pine, Overhang Top, Block & Turned Legs, New England, 21 x 28 x 18 In. | 540 |
| **Table,** Tavern, Pine, Painted, Single Overhanging Board, Drawer, c.1800, 28 x 43 In. | 1495 |
| **Table,** Tavern, Queen Anne, Mixed Wood, Oval Top, Column Legs, 1700s, 25 x 26 In. | 374 |
| **Table,** Tavern, Queen Anne, Walnut, Drawer, Scalloped Apron, Pa., 30 x 40 In. | 600 |
| **Table,** Tavern, Walnut, Oval, Overhang Top, Drawer, Stretcher, Pa., c.1770, 25 x 37 In. | 1920 |
| **Table,** Tavern, Walnut, Pine, Turned Legs, Stretcher, Drawer, 1790-1910, 31 x 34 In. | 1680 |
| **Table,** Tavern, William & Mary, Scalloped, Drawer, Box Stretcher, Mass., 1700s, 27 x 38 In. | 9600 |
| **Table,** Tea, Art Nouveau, Mahogany, France, c.1900, 33 x 21 In. | 4484 |
| **Table,** Tea, Chippendale Style, Mahogany, Reticulated Gallery, Fretwork, 29 x 34 In. | 837 |
| **Table,** Tea, Chippendale Style, Mahogany, Scalloped Gallery, Blind Key Fret, 29 x 33 In. | 1294 |
| **Table,** Tea, Chippendale Style, Mahogany, Serpentine, Edward & Roberts, c.1900, 28 x 28 In. | 676 |
| **Table,** Tea, G. Stickley, Round Top, Key & Tenon, 4 Flared Legs, 24 x 24 In. | 4270 |
| **Table,** Tea, George II, Mahogany, Round Piecrust Edge, c.1760, 28 x 27 In. | 240 |
| **Table,** Tea, George III Style, Mahogany, Pierced Gallery, Round, Carved, 31 x 19 In. | 437 |
| **Table,** Tea, George III Style, Mahogany, Tray Top, Cabriole Legs, Carved Brackets, 28 x 28 In. | 2125 |
| **Table,** Tea, George III, Mahogany, Shaped Gallery, Pierced Frieze, X-Stretcher, 30 x 30 In. | 2460 |
| **Table,** Tea, George III, Rectangular Gallery Top, X-Stretcher, c.1750, 29 x 33 In. | 3375 |
| **Table,** Tea, Louis XVI Style, Bronze Mounted, Kingwood, Parquetry, Handles, 34 x 34 In. | 615 |
| **Table,** Tea, Mahogany, 2 Tiers, Glass Tray, Brass Handles, X-Shape Stretcher, 27 In. | 123 |
| **Table,** Tea, Mahogany, Marquetry, Dished Edge, Crimped Corners, c.1790, 29 x 31 In. | 1845 |
| **Table,** Tea, Mahogany, Tray Top, Cabriole Legs, Slipper Feet, Newport, c.1750, 27 x 30 In. | 31200 |
| **Table,** Tea, Maple, Tray Top, Serpentine Gallery, Rectangular, Spade Feet, 30 x 33 x 22 In. | 1250 |
| **Table,** Tea, Queen Anne Style, Ebonized, Scalloped Apron, c.1920, 30 x 35 In. | 1440 |
| **Table,** Tea, Queen Anne Style, Mahogany, Inlay, Dish Top, 28 x 16 In. | 1003 |
| **Table,** Tea, Queen Anne, Cherry, Scalloped Apron, Connecticut, 27 x 31 In. | 20400 |
| **Table,** Tea, Queen Anne, Mahogany, Oak, End Drawers, Cabriole Legs, 28 x 33 In. | 1020 |
| **Table,** Tea, Queen Anne, Walnut, Dish Top, Cabriole Legs, Pa., c.1770, 28 x 33 In. | 2460 |
| **Table,** Tea, Queen Anne, Walnut, Dish Top, Drawers, Cabriole Legs, 1700s, 28 x 31 In. | 922 |
| **Table,** Tea, Tilt Dish Top, Walnut, Sunburst Inlay, Tripod Base, Tennessee, 30 x 29 In. | 944 |
| **Table,** Tea, Tilt Top, Chippendale, Cherry, Birch, New England, 1700s, 28 x 34 In. ...............*illus* | 1200 |
| **Table,** Tea, Tilt Top, Chippendale, Mahogany, Birdcage, Carved, c.1775, 48 x 30 In. ...........*illus* | 8888 |
| **Table,** Tea, Tilt Top, Chippendale, Mahogany, Piecrust, Fluted Standard, 28 x 30 In. | 1320 |
| **Table,** Tea, Tilt Top, Chippendale, Walnut, Round, Birdcage Support, c.1780, 31 x 36 In. | 180 |
| **Table,** Tea, Tilt Top, George III, Mahogany, Carved, Molded, Tripod Base, 1700s, 28 x 27 In. | 2684 |
| **Table,** Tea, Tilt Top, Mahogany, Piecrust Edge, Turned Pedestal, Tripod, c.1760, 31 x 21 In. | 415 |
| **Table,** Tea, Tilt Top, Queen Anne, Mahogany, Carved, Dish Top, c.1750, 24 x 28 In. .........*illus* | 1778 |
| **Table,** Tea, Tilt Top, Queen Anne, Mahogany, Dish Top, Leaves, Baluster Shaft, 28 x 33 In. | 180 |
| **Table,** Tea, Tilt Top, Queen Anne, Square, Mahogany, Cabriole Legs, England, 27 x 25 In. | 600 |
| **Table,** Tea, Tilt Top, Victorian, Papier-Mache, Mother-Of-Pearl Inlay, c.1890 ...................*illus* | 130 |
| **Table,** Tea, Tilt Top, Walnut, Dish Top, Birdcage Platform, Turned Post, c.1790, 30 x 34 In. | 2091 |
| **Table,** Tea, Walnut, Rectangular Top, Baluster Standard, England, 30 x 22 In. | 250 |
| **Table,** Tiger Maple, Queen Anne Style, Octagonal, Eldred Wheeler, 25 x 24 In. | 649 |
| **Table,** Tilt Top, Baker Furniture, Mahogany, Piecrust Top, Tripod Base, c.1940, 29 x 33 In. | 180 |
| **Table,** Tilt Top, Chinoiserie, Goldtone, Painted, Green, Tripod Base, 26 x 19 In. | 167 |
| **Table,** Tilt Top, Federal, Mahogany, Molded Edge, Cabriole Legs, Mass., 39 x 24 In. | 1440 |
| **Table,** Tilt Top, George II Style, Mahogany, Octagonal, 3 Scrolled Legs, 28 x 28 In. | 3125 |
| **Table,** Tilt Top, George III Style, Round Top, Carved Support, 29 x 52 In. | 863 |
| **Table,** Tilt Top, George III, Mahogany, Piecrust Top, Tripod Base, Paw Feet, 28 x 21 In. | 238 |
| **Table,** Tilt Top, Inlay, Geometric, Kingcome, 1880, Salesman's Sample, 4 ½ In. | 1481 |
| **Table,** Tilt Top, Mahogany, Tripod Base, c.1810, 29 x 37 In. | 633 |
| **Table,** Tilt Top, Painted, Gilt, Pedestal, Chinese Export, c.1850, 31 x 35 In. .........................*illus* | 1168 |
| **Table,** Tilt Top, Papier-Mache, Black Lacquer Side Chairs, England, 1800s, 4 Piece | 330 |
| **Table,** Tilt Top, Queen Anne Style, Mahogany, Round, Turned Pedestal, c.1800, 30 x 40 In. | 161 |
| **Table,** Tilt Top, Queen Anne, Mahogany, Round, Urn Standard, Cabriole Legs, 28 x 33 In. | 1020 |
| **Table,** Tilt Top, Queen Anne, Oak, Round Top, Tripod Base, England, 29 x 31 In. | 230 |
| **Table,** Tilt Top, Round, Radial Parquetry, Tripod Base, 30 x 40 In. | 4750 |
| **Table,** Tilt Top, Tripod Base, Cabriole Legs, 1800s, 27 x 27 In. | 230 |
| **Table,** Tilt Top, Victorian, Chinoiserie Designs, Green, Pedestal Standard, c.1890, 27 x 20 In. | 250 |
| **Table,** Tilt Top, Victorian, Papier-Mache, Turtle Top, Mother-Of-Pearl Inlay, Tripod, 1890 | 130 |
| **Table,** Tilt Top, Wrought Iron, Marble Top, Pietra Dura, Leaf & Flower, c.1890, 21 x 14 In. | 708 |
| **Table,** Tray, Mahogany, Pierced Folding Handles, Brass Hinges, 24 In., Pair | 400 |
| **Table,** Tray, Papier-Mache, Birds, Bamboo-Turned Base, England, c.1835, 19 x 30 In. .........*illus* | 1107 |
| **Table,** Trestle, Pine, Drawer, Wide Stretcher, Continental, c.1800, 29 x 67 In. | 600 |
| **Table,** Trestle, Sawbuck, Pine, Cross Leg, 2-Board Top, X-Stretcher, 1700s, 71 x 33 In. | 1659 |

**Furniture,** Table, William & Mary, Oak, Ebonized, Drawer, Rosehead Nails, 25 x 24 In.
**$1,298**

Brunk Auctions

**Furniture,** Table, Work, Sheraton, Mahogany, Satinwood, 2 Drawers, Casters, c.1815, 32 x 19 In.
**$2,489**

James D. Julia Auctioneers

**Furniture,** Table, Wormley, Bedside, Janus, Natzler Tiles, Dunbar, 1956, 25 x 20 In., Pair
**$4,375**

Los Angeles Modern Auctions (LAMA)

### TIP
*To make a new marble tabletop look old, wipe it with vinegar a few times. The dull finish of old tops came from repeated washings.*

**Furniture,** Table, Wormley, Marble, Rosewood, Brass, X Base, Dunbar, 1954, 25½ x 23 In. $2,032

Wright (Chicago)

**Furniture,** Table, Z-Shape, Brown Leather Upholstery, White Stitching, 23 x 17 In., Pair $1,003

Brunk Auctions

**Furniture,** Tea Cart, Aalto, 900, Birch, Tile Top, Rattan Basket, 24 x 35 In. $1,220

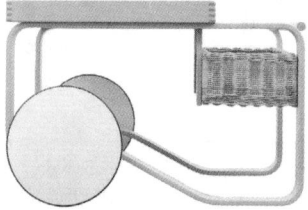

Palm Beach Modern Auctions

**Furniture,** Tete-A-Tete, Mahogany, Carved, Off-White Upholstery, 34½ x 50 In. $300

DuMouchelles Art Gallery

| | |
|---|---:|
| **Table,** Tripod, George III, Mahogany, Tilting Round Top, Birdcage Support, 29 x 33 In. | 615 |
| **Table,** Twig, Adirondack, Scalloped Top, Medial Shelf, c.1900, 29 x 29 In. | 120 |
| **Table,** Victorian, Burl Veneer Top, Pedestal Base, Oval, c.1850, 29 x 40 In. | 891 |
| **Table,** Victorian, Cherry, Dolphin Supports, Talon & Ball Feet, Carved, 28 x 24 In. | 550 |
| **Table,** Victorian, Faux Bamboo, Medial Shelf & Gallery, 21 x 30 In. | 322 |
| **Table,** Victorian, Mahogany, Carved, Shaped Supports, Marble Top, 29 x 29 In. | 210 |
| **Table,** Victorian, Mahogany, Drawer, Spiral Carved Legs, c.1900, 31 x 40 In. | 531 |
| **Table,** Victorian, Oak, 2 Drawers, Turned Legs, 42 x 31 In. | 199 |
| **Table,** Victorian, Rosewood, Mother-Of-Pearl, Canted Top, Octagonal Base, 32 x 20 In. | 2250 |
| **Table,** Victorian, Tilt Top, Rosewood, Oval, Leaf Carved, Arched Legs, 29 x 54 In. | 531 |
| **Table,** Victorian, Walnut, Marble Top, Bowfront, Carved, Shelf Stretcher, 29 x 48 In. | 750 |
| **Table,** Victorian, Walnut, Marble Top, Trestle, Carved, Thomas Brooks, c.1870, 32 x 24 In. | 1323 |
| **Table,** W. Platner, Beveled Glass Over Nickel Plated Wire Base, Round, 16 x 36 In. | 1464 |
| **Table,** Wake, Cherry, Drop Leaves, Tapered Round Legs, Pad Feet, England, 31 x 82 In. | 861 |
| **Table,** Walnut, 2 Drawers, Line Inlaid Border, Sides, Ohio River Valley, c.1840, 28 x 21 In. | 4313 |
| **Table,** Walnut, 3 Drawers, Overhanging Top, Pennsylvania, c.1770, 29 x 40 In. | 390 |
| **Table,** Walnut, Base, X-Stretcher, Carved, Frieze, Italy, 1800s, 63 x 31 In. | 3125 |
| **Table,** Walnut, Cherry, Overhanging Top, Drawer, Splayed Legs, Va., 28 x 19 In. | 1495 |
| **Table,** Walnut, Drop Leaf, Oak, Turned Legs, England, 23 x 34 In. | 2375 |
| **Table,** Walnut, Inlay, Drawer, American Of Martinsville, Mid-Century, 19 x 20 In. | 173 |
| **Table,** Walnut, Inlay, Scalloped Skirt, Drawer, Squared Legs, American, 27 x 29 In. | 1121 |
| **Table,** Walnut, Overhang Top, 3 Drawers, Base Stretcher, Pa., c.1820, 29 x 60 In. | 615 |
| **Table,** Walnut, Overhang Top, 3 Drawers, Pennsylvania, c.1790, 28 x 72 In. | 510 |
| **Table,** Walnut, Overhang Top, Drawer, Turned Legs, X-Stretcher, c.1780, 30 x 42 In. | 1250 |
| **Table,** Walnut, Overhang Top, Frieze Drawer, Turned Legs, Continental, 1700s, 40 In. | 531 |
| **Table,** Walnut, Pedestal, Dog, Stag, Fence, Black Forest, Carved, Marble Inset, 36 In. | 1000 |
| **Table,** Walnut, Pine Top, 2 Drawers, Turned Legs, Pa., 53 x 33 In. | 369 |
| **Table,** Walnut, Star Inlay, Tilt Top, Baluster Support, Tripod Base, c.1830, 27 x 28 In. | 861 |
| **Table,** Walnut, Trestle Base, Scalloped Carved Supports, c.1950, 30 x 84 In. | 420 |
| **Table,** Walnut, X-Base Stretcher, Continental, 32 x 39 In., Pair | 2000 |
| **Table,** Wendell Castle, Side, Curly Maple, Carved, Painted Base, 1987, 23 x 20 In. ...............*illus* | 2645 |
| **Table,** Wendell Castle, Walnut, Laminated, Single Socket, Signed, 1969, 51 x 20 In. ...........*illus* | 135750 |
| **Table,** William & Mary, Oak, Ebonized, Drawer, Rosehead Nails, 25 x 24 In. ................*illus* | 1298 |
| **Table,** William & Mary, Pine, Maple, Turned Legs, Box Stretcher, New England, 26 x 40 In. | 360 |
| **Table,** William & Mary, Pine, Maple, Turned Legs, Stretcher, New England, c.1810, 28 x 29 In. | 313 |
| **Table,** William & Mary, Walnut, 2 Drawers, Column Legs, Pa., 28 x 72 In. | 960 |
| **Table,** William & Mary, Walnut, Demilune, Foldover Top, Frieze Drawers, 29 x 30 In. | 938 |
| **Table,** William & Mary, Walnut, Drawer, Turned Legs, Carved Stretchers, 28 x 34 In. | 1750 |
| **Table,** William & Mary, Walnut, Drawer, Turned Legs, Stretcher, England, c.1710, 29 x 33 In. | 625 |
| **Table,** William & Mary, Walnut, Round, Cross Frame, Turned Legs, Pa., c.1740, 30 x 25 In. | 1560 |
| **Table,** William IV, Tilt Top, Rosewood, Round, Flared Standard, Tripart Plinth, 29 x 51 In. | 281 |
| **Table,** Wine, Adams, Satinwood, Gallery Top, Bellflowers, c.1800, 28 x 12 In. | 480 |
| **Table,** Wine, Tilt Top, Oval, c.1810, 30 x 51 In. | 700 |
| **Table,** Wood, Demilune, Flip Top, Tapered Legs, Pad Feet, 27 x 19 In. | 163 |
| **Table,** Wood, Round Top, Stacked Squares, Spiral Twisted, Clear Lucite Base, 23 x 15 In. | 345 |
| **Table,** Work, Federal, Cherry Inlay, Banded Edge, Drawer, Tapered Legs, c.1830, 26 x 15 In. | 178 |
| **Table,** Work, Federal, Mahogany, Veneer, Carved, Oval, Drawers, Bag Drawer, 28 x 22 In. | 1599 |
| **Table,** Work, Georgian, Oak, Drawer, c.1850, 28 x 33 In. | 338 |
| **Table,** Work, Maple, Hinged Top, Fitted Tray, Square Stretchers, c.1890, 28 x 13 In. | 150 |
| **Table,** Work, Neoclassical, Mahogany, Beaded, Drawer, Upholstered Bag, c.1810, 30 x 19 In. | 461 |
| **Table,** Work, Neoclassical, Mahogany, Duncan Phyfe Style, Drawers, Octagonal, 30 x 20 In. | 1195 |
| **Table,** Work, Pine, Painted, Heart Shape Ends, V-Shape Shelf, Shoe Feet, 31 x 36 In. | 360 |
| **Table,** Work, Sheraton, Mahogany, Satinwood, 2 Drawers, Casters, c.1815, 32 x 19 In..........*illus* | 2489 |
| **Table,** Work, Sheraton, Tiger Maple, Cherry, Single-Board Top, Drawer, Reeded Legs, 28 In. | 270 |
| **Table,** Wormley, Bedside, Janus, Natzler Tiles, Dunbar, 1956, 25 x 20 In., Pair.............*illus* | 4375 |
| **Table,** Wormley, Mahogany, Lacquered, Extends, Murano Glass Tile Ends, 44 In. | 4375 |
| **Table,** Wormley, Marble, Rosewood, Brass, X Base, Dunbar, 1954, 25 ½ x 23 In...........*illus* | 2032 |
| **Table,** Writing, Federal, Walnut, Pierced Gallery, Drawer, 32 x 25 x 20 In. | 2124 |
| **Table,** Writing, Louis Philippe, Mahogany, Inset Leather Slide, Drawers, c.1860, 31 x 51 In. | 492 |
| **Table,** Writing, Louis XIII, Walnut, Drawer, Barley Twist Legs, Stretcher, 39 x 23 In. | 397 |
| **Table,** Writing, Napoleon III, Gilt, Bird's-Eye Maple, Satinwood, Leather, c.1875, 29 x 63 In. | 2460 |
| **Table,** Writing, Pine, Bamboo Turning, Grained, Tooled Leather Panel, c.1810, 31 x 42 In. | 948 |
| **Table,** Writing, Regency, Burl Maple, Inset Leather Top, Paneled Frieze, Trestle, 29 x 36 In. | 1434 |
| **Table,** Z-Shape, Brown Leather Upholstery, White Stitching, 23 x 17 In., Pair......................*illus* | 1003 |
| **Tabouret,** Louis XVI Style, Walnut, Carved, Gilt, Cushion Top, c.1910, 21 x 24 In. | 120 |
| **Tabouret,** Renaissance Revival, Reticulated, Floral Top, Scrolled Legs, Iron, 31 x 16 In., Pair | 478 |

F

| | |
|---|---|
| **Tantulus,** Rosewood, Serpentine, Flower, Scroll Inlay, c.1860, 12 x 13 In. | 123 |
| **Tea Cart,** Aalto, 900, Birch, Tile Top, Rattan Basket, 24 x 35 In. ..........*illus* | 1220 |
| **Tea Cart,** Brass, Mahogany, Glass Tray Top, Reticulated Gallery, Columns, 36 x 20 In. | 366 |
| **Tea Cart,** Dessert, Mahogany, Shaped Backsplash, Shelf, Carved Legs, 49 x 48 In. | 1875 |
| **Tea Cart,** Ico & Luisa Parisi, Shaped Handle, Wood & Glass Trays, Splayed Legs, 35 x 24 In. | 360 |
| **Teapoy,** Regency, Mahogany, Carved, Fitted Interior, 3-Section Base, c.1820, 31 x 15 In. | 738 |
| **Teapoy,** Rosewood, Sarcophagus, Round Column, Carved, Platform Base, c.1830, 32 x 16 In. | 891 |
| **Tete-A-Tete,** Louis XV Style, Giltwood, Carved, Tufted Backs, Serpentine Seats, 24 x 60 In. | 1912 |
| **Tete-A-Tete,** Mahogany, Carved, Off-White Upholstery, 34½ x 50 In. .........*illus* | 300 |
| **Tete-A-Tete,** Rustic, Pine, Stained, Arched Slats, Woven Reed Seat, 36 x 30 In. | 86 |
| **Tete-A-Tete,** Salterini, Wrought Iron, 2 Clamshell Chairs, Center Table, 1950s, 68 In. | 1188 |
| **Tray,** Conforming Stand, Regency, Gilt, Black Papier-Mache, c.1810, 26 x 20 In. | 2074 |
| **Tray,** On Stand, Chinoiserie, Mother-Of-Pearl Inlay, Cartouche Shape, Gilt, 20 x 29 In. | 295 |
| **Trolley,** Cheese, Mahogany, Curved, Divided, Applied Half Turnings, England, 6 x 16 In. | 120 |
| **Umbrella Stand,** Bear, On Hind Legs, Carved Wood, Glass Eyes, 26 In. | 748 |
| **Umbrella Stand,** Black Forest, Walnut, Carved, Dog, Paws On Holder, 32 x 10 In. | 3198 |
| **Umbrella Stand,** Brass, 27 x 24 In. | 500 |
| **Umbrella Stand,** Bronze, 3 Boots, Gilt, Patinated, England, 1900s, 32 In. ...*illus* | 3585 |
| **Umbrella Stand,** Carved, Incised, Gilt, Ebonized, Brass Deer Hoof Handle, 48 In. | 1195 |
| **Umbrella Stand,** Figural, Woman, Long Green, Peach Gown, Painted, Wood, 14 x 34 In. | 211 |
| **Umbrella Stand,** Fornasetti, Dog Shape, Boxer, Enamel, Metal, Milan, c.1990, 32 x 18 In. | 1875 |
| **Umbrella Stand,** Oak, Stick & Ball, Scrolled Design, Pan, 12 x 28 In. ......*illus* | 228 |
| **Umbrella Stand,** Victorian, Brass, Handle, 3-Column Shape, Leaf Repousse, 30 In. | 188 |
| **Valance Board,** Painted Landscape, Scrolling, Gilt Stenciled, 9 x 46 In. | 480 |
| **Valet,** 3 Legs, Johannes Hansen, 1953, 37 x 20 x 20 In. | 11875 |
| **Valet,** Brass, Ball Finial, Shaped Coat Rack, Circular Base, Scroll Feet, 55 In. | 120 |
| **Vanity,** Eastlake Style, Teardrop Pulls, Widdicomb, c.1900, 86 In. ..........*illus* | 210 |
| **Vanity,** Limbert, Oak, Mirror, Drawer, c.1920, 56 x 36 In. | 960 |
| **Vasselier,** French Provincial, Louis Philippe, Fruitwood, Cupboard, 1800s, 89 x 57 In. | 1722 |
| **Vasselier,** French Provincial, Multicolor, Molded Cornice, Pierced Frieze, Shelves, 76 x 48 In. | 2091 |
| **Vitrine,** Gilt, Glass Panels, Shelves, Painted Panels, France, c.1900, 59 x 29 In. ...*illus* | 1495 |
| **Vitrine,** Glass Door, Side Panels, Couple Courting, Paint, France, c.1910, 55 x 25 In. | 450 |
| **Vitrine,** Hardwood, Glazed Door, Arched Scrolled Legs, Shelf, Chinese, 55 x 24 In. ...*illus* | 478 |
| **Vitrine,** Louis XV Style, Bronze, Hinged Top, Mirror, 13 x 18 In. | 1625 |
| **Vitrine,** Louis XV Style, Glass Door, Gilt Metal Mounts, Vernis Martin, 71 x 27 In. | 2125 |
| **Vitrine,** Louis XV Style, Mahogany, Marquetry, Hinged Top, Brass Banding, 16 x 24 In. | 688 |
| **Vitrine,** Louis XVI Style, Kingwood, Bronze Mounts, Lift Top, Stretcher, 31 x 30 In. | 5795 |
| **Vitrine,** Mahogany, Glass, Ormolu Mounts, France, c.1910, 39 x 28 In. | 1080 |
| **Vitrine,** Rococo Revival, Painted, Carved, Gilt, Velvet Lined, c.1800, 80 In. .........*illus* | 3585 |
| **Vitrine,** Walnut, Wreath, Ribbon Inlay, 2 Doors, Ormolu Mounts, France, 89 x 56 In. | 250 |
| **Vitrine,** Wood, Ormolu Mounts, Cabriole Legs, France, c.1910, 31 x 29 In. | 270 |
| **Wall Brackets,** Danish Modern, Teak, Drawer, Twin Supports, Stretcher, 8½ x 16 In., Pair | 210 |
| **Wall Rack,** Multicolor Paint, Carved, Iron Hooks, 10 x 27 In. | 527 |
| **Wall Unit,** Andrea Branze, Beech, 3 Shelves, Drawer, Round Table, Cassina, 44 x 53 In. | 431 |
| **Wall Unit,** McCobb, Mid-Century, Walnut, Shelves, Doors, Drawers, 80 x 64 In., 3 Units | 900 |
| **Wall Unit,** Mid-Century Modern, Dark Wood, Shelves, Storage, Denmark, 80 x 67 In. | 403 |
| **Wall Unit,** Poul Cadovius, Rosewood, 7 Supports, 12 Shelves, 4 Cabinets | 3552 |
| **Wall Unit,** Poul Cadovius, Teak, 5 Supports, 9 Shelves, 1 Cabinet, Mid-Century | 1342 |
| **Wardian Case,** Stand, Cast Iron, Finials, Glass Panels, Trestle, England, 46 x 31 In. .........*illus* | 2583 |
| **Wardrobe,** Art Nouveau, Oak, 3 Glass & Paneled Doors, Arched Crest, c.1900, 88 x 60 In. | 720 |
| **Wardrobe,** Arts & Crafts, Oak, Copper, Glass & Panel Doors, Drawers, c.1910, 82 x 88 In. | 9375 |
| **Wardrobe,** Double, Walnut, Paneled Doors, Fitted, Secret Drawer, Ohio, 1848, 80 x 66 In. | 1560 |
| **Wardrobe,** Lacquer, Gilt, Calligraphy, Butterfly Hardware, Doors, Chinese, c.1910, 71 In. | 600 |
| **Wardrobe,** Mahogany, 2 Paneled Doors, Fitted Interior, Paw Feet, Philadelphia, 88 x 68 In. | 1536 |
| **Wardrobe,** Pine, Cornice, Painted, Urn, Flower, Janarin, Paneled Doors, c.1829, 74 x 60 In. | 1680 |
| **Wardrobe,** Pine, Lift-Off Cornice, Painted, Drawers, Flowers, Saints, 1826, 78 In. ...........*illus* | 615 |
| **Wardrobe,** Pine, Painted, Red, Brown, Pennsylvania, 77 x 42½ In. | 258 |
| **Wardrobe,** Pine, Poplar, 2-Panel Doors, Red Paint, Va., c.1840, 73 x 47 In. | 633 |
| **Wardrobe,** Pine, Red Paint, Ebonized Feet, Pa., c.1830, 53 x 39 In., Child's | 3600 |
| **Washstand,** Corner, Federal, Cherry, 3 Holes, Backsplash, Drawer, Pa., c.1820, 38 x 22 In. | 92 |
| **Washstand,** Corner, Federal, Mahogany, 2 Drawers, Glass Knobs, Open Center, 30 x 26 In. | 150 |
| **Washstand,** Corner, Georgian, Mahogany, Arch Crest, Scalloped Shelf, c.1845, 49 x 25 In. | 375 |
| **Washstand,** Curly Maple, Walnut Drawer & Arched Door Panels, 32 x 30 In. | 308 |
| **Washstand,** Federal, Corner, Mahogany, Stepped Backsplash, 2 False Drawers, 41 x 27 In. | 885 |
| **Washstand,** Federal, Mahogany, Marble, Backsplash, Drawers, Bidet, c.1810, 32 x 25 In. | 2390 |
| **Washstand,** George III, Mahogany, Flip Top, Shaped Skirt, Shelf, Drawer, c.1800, 34 In. | 120 |

**Furniture,** Umbrella Stand, Bronze, 3 Boots, Gilt, Patinated, England, 1900s, 32 In.
$3,585

Neal Auction Co.

**Furniture,** Umbrella Stand, Oak, Stick & Ball, Scrolled Design, Pan, 12 x 28 In.
$228

Showtime Auction Services

**Furniture,** Vanity, Eastlake Style, Teardrop Pulls, Widdicomb, c.1900, 86 In.
$210

DuMouchelles Art Gallery

**Furniture,** Vitrine, Gilt, Glass Panels, Shelves, Painted Panels, France, c.1900, 59 x 29 In.
$1,495

Cottone Auctions

**Furniture,** Vitrine, Hardwood, Glazed Door, Arched Scrolled Legs, Shelf, Chinese, 55 x 24 In.
$478

Neal Auction Co.

**Furniture,** Vitrine, Rococo Revival, Painted, Carved, Gilt, Velvet Lined, c.1800, 80 In.
$3,585

Neal Auction Co.

| | |
|---|---:|
| **Washstand,** George III, Mahogany, Tiers, Drawer, c.1800, 33 x 18 In. | 236 |
| **Washstand,** Oak, Soapstone, Towel Bars, Beveled Mirror, 1800s, 18 x 13 In. | 420 |
| **Washstand,** Shaker, Pine, Splashboard, Panel Doors, Yellow, Mt. Lebanon, c.1820, 36 x 25 In. | 9225 |
| **Washstand,** Sheraton, Backsplash, Pinstriping, Red, Green, Yellow Paint, 34 x 19 In. | 720 |
| **Washstand,** Sheraton, Mahogany, 2 Drawers, 2 Doors, Carved Backsplash, c.1850, 37 x 28 In. | 270 |
| **Washstand,** Walnut, Painted, ¾ Gallery, Straight Frieze, Turned Supports, Shelf, 31 x 27 In. | 610 |
| **Whatnot Shelf,** Regency, Rosewood, Brass Mounts, 3 Tiers, Pierced Gallery, 30 x 36 In. | 3776 |
| **Whatnot Shelf,** Regency, Rosewood, Brass, 3 Tiers, England, 1800s, 31 x 17 In., Pair | 2596 |
| **Window Seat,** Biedermeier, Walnut, Upholstered, Shaped, Splay Feet, 1800s, 33 ½ In. | 250 |
| **Window Seat,** Curule, Renaissance Revival, Carved, Gilt, Masque Terminals, 1800s, Pair | 5378 |
| **Window Seat,** Empire Style, Giltwood, Padded, Fluted Rail, Ram's Heads, 26 x 33 In. | 1107 |
| **Window Seat,** Federal, Mahogany, Upholstered, Inlay, Reeded Legs, N.Y., 29 x 53 In. ...........*illus* | 5535 |
| **Window Seat,** Louis XVI Style, Giltwood, Bow Shape, Padded Back, c.1910, 24 In. | 584 |
| **Window Seat,** Neoclassical Style, Multicolor, Paw Feet, 1900s, 22 ½ x 31 In. | 430 |
| **Wine Cooler,** George III, Mahogany, Brass Mounts, Octagonal, c.1760, 28 x 20 In. | 1250 |
| **Wine Cooler,** George IV, Mahogany, Canted Corners, Tapered, Paw Feet, Handles, 20 x 30 In. | 1500 |
| **Wine Cooler,** Georgian Style, Mahogany, Brass, Lion's Head Pulls, c.1890, 22 x 26 In. | 550 |
| **Wine Cooler,** Mahogany, Brass, Parcel Gilt, Metal Lines, Tapered, Victorian, 17 x 35 In. | 875 |
| **Wine Cooler,** Table, Neoclassical Style, Mahogany, 2 Wells, Medial Shelf, 29 x 48 In. | 125 |

---

**G. ARGY-ROUSSEAU** is the impressed mark used on a variety of glass objects in the Art Deco style. Gabriel Argy-Rousseau, born in 1885, was a French glass artist. In 1921, he formed a partnership that made pate-de-verre and other glass. The partnership ended in 1931 and he opened his own studio. He worked until 1952 and died in 1953.

G-ARGY-ROUSSEAU

| | |
|---|---:|
| **Bowl,** Orange Anemone, Black Stems, Mottled Yellow & Cream Ground, 3 x 4 In. | 3851 |
| **Jar,** Lid, Pate-De-Verre, Red, Pink, Black, c.1920, 3 x 3 In. | 640 |
| **Nightlight,** Purple, Green, Arched, 3-Sided Panels, Overlapping Leaves, Ribs, 7 In. | 5036 |
| **Vase,** Amber, Panels, Wild Cat Faces, Pate-De-Verre, c.1920, 8 ½ In. ...........*illus* | 4320 |

---

**GALLE** was a designer who made glass, pottery, furniture, and other Art Nouveau items. Emile Galle founded his factory in France in 1874. After Galle's death in 1904, the firm continued to make glass and furniture until 1931. The *Galle* signature was used as a mark, but it was often hidden in the design of the object. Galle glass is listed here. Pottery is in the next section. His furniture is listed in the Furniture category.

*Gallé*

| | |
|---|---:|
| **Atomizer,** Flattened, Round, Landscape, Plum, Trees, Mountains, c.1900, 7 ¼ In. | 500 |
| **Atomizer,** Flattened, Round, Plum, Blue, Flower, Leaves, Cream Ground, c.1900, 6 In. | 750 |
| **Atomizer,** Globular, Pond Lilies, Cattails, Shoots, Gilt Metal, Acid Etched, Cameo, 6 ½ In. | 500 |
| **Atomizer,** Plum Over Amber, Berry, Branches, Tendrils, Leaves, c.1900, 9 In. | 469 |
| **Bowl,** Cameo, Lobed, Amber, Frosted, Vining, Signed, 8 In. | 230 |
| **Box,** Lid, Thorny Vines, Blue, Purple, Cameo, Frosted Opalescent, Signed, 4 ¾ In. ...........*illus* | 3851 |
| **Creamer,** Variegated Red, Brown, Free-Form Branching Handle, Flower, Signed, 3 ½ In. | 1840 |
| **Cruet,** Optic Rib, Enameled, Insects, Leaves, Signed, 8 In. | 288 |
| **Decanter,** Crystal, Enamel, Gold Grasshoppers, Spiders, Beetles, Ribbed Stopper, 8 In. | 575 |
| **Jar,** Lid, Blue Flowers, Yellow, Metal Band, Round, 4 In. | 2040 |
| **Lamp,** Electric, 3-Light, Domed Shade, Blossoms, Leafy Branches, Lighted Base, 12 ½ In. | 6900 |
| **Perfume Bottle,** Flattened, Round, Landscape, Plum Tree, Yellow Lake, Cameo, 6 In. | 469 |
| **Perfume Bottle,** Green Triangular Stopper, Applied Orange, Pink Flowers, 4 ⅜ In. | 3360 |
| **Pitcher,** Crimped Handle, Enameled Crustacean, Grasshopper, Leaf Ground, c.1900, 6 In. | 738 |
| **Pitcher,** Lavender Carved Flowers, Vines, Aqua Ground, Lobed, Curled Handle, France, 8 In. | 3540 |
| **Pitcher,** Smoky Purple, Gilded, Embossed Woman, Text, Ribbed, Signed E. Galle, 6 In. | 4500 |
| **Powder Box,** Green Leaves, Seed Pods, Round, Squat, Lid With Boat In Pond, Trees, 6 In. | 356 |
| **Shade,** Domed, Brown Berries, Vines, Cameo, 7 ½ In. | 123 |
| **Vase,** Banjo Shape, Frosted Yellow, Red Stemmed Leaves, Signed In Cameo, 6 ¾ In. | 748 |
| **Vase,** Banjo, Brown Lily Pond, Dragonfly, Yellow Ground, Cameo, Signed, 6 ½ In. | 2547 |
| **Vase,** Banjo, Trees, Olive Green, Light Blue Shaded To Yellow Ground, 6 ¾ In. | 2126 |
| **Vase,** Berries On Branches, Green, Pink, Yellow Ground, Bulbous, 7 x 7 In. | 2070 |
| **Vase,** Black Thistle, Amber Ground, Bulbous, c.1900, 10 x 4 In. | 1700 |
| **Vase,** Bleeding Heart, Frosted To Amber Ground, Tapered, Signed, 10 In. | 944 |
| **Vase,** Bleeding Hearts, Blue, Pink, Waisted, Signed, 22 x 5 In. | 3712 |
| **Vase,** Bleeding Hearts, Red, Creamy Yellow Ground, Bulbous, Flared Navette Rim, 8 ½ In. | 4740 |
| **Vase,** Blue & Green, Cobalt Blue Leaves, Cameo, Bulbous, Stick Shape, Singed, 6 In. | 173 |
| **Vase,** Blue Hydrangea Blossoms, Leafy Stems, Pale Blue Frosted Ground, Tapered, 8 ½ In. | 805 |
| **Vase,** Blue Mountains, Pine Trees, Rocks, Pond, Yellow Sky, Cameo, Signed, 10 In. | 4443 |
| **Vase,** Blue Mountains, Purple Pine Trees, Shaded Yellow Sky, Shouldered, 10 In. | 3555 |

| | |
|---|---|
| Vase, Blue Trees, Yellow Ground, Shouldered, 5 In. | 633 |
| Vase, Blue, Green Mottled Highlights, Fish Jumping, Frosted Ground, Triangular, 10 In. | 14160 |
| Vase, Blue, Indigo, Berries, Leaves, Branches, Cream Ground, Cameo, 13 5/8 In. | 374 |
| Vase, Brown Grapevines, Leaves, Pink To Cream Ground, Cameo, 9 1/2 In. | 1066 |
| Vase, Bud, Cameo, Orange Fuchsia Flowers, Vines, Yellow Ground, Signed, 10 1/4 x 3 1/4 In. | 615 |
| Vase, Bud, Flowers, Leaves, Purple, Lavender, Green, Cylindrical, Bulbous Base, 23 In. | 1888 |
| Vase, Bud, Stick Neck, Amber, Over Lime Green, Frosted Pink Ground, c.1900, 6 3/4 In. | 531 |
| Vase, Burgundy Leaves, Clear & Shaded Yellow Ground, Swollen Shape, Cameo, 10 3/8 In. | 800 |
| Vase, Carved Scroll, Flowers, Frosted Amber, Yellow, Knight, Princess Toasting, 9 In., Pair | 24780 |
| Vase, Clematis, Fire Polished Purple & Blue, Frosted Ground, Tapered, 14 In. | 3050 |
| Vase, Cream Ground, Red Leaves Overlay, Cameo, Early 20th Century, 2 1/2 In. | 300 |
| Vase, Crimson Crocus, Blown Out, Yellow Ground, Oval, Flared Rim, 8 1/2 In. | 4600 |
| Vase, Dark Green Trees, Green & Yellow Pond, Distant Shore, Yellow Ground, 14 1/2 In. | 1185 |
| Vase, Dark Purple, Lily Pond, Aquatic Plants, Frosted Yellow Ground, Cameo, 11 In. | 1422 |
| Vase, Double Gourd Shape, Aquatic Vegetation, Bubbles, Cameo, 8 In. | 1185 |
| Vase, Enameled Leaf, Flowers, Tortoiseshell Highlights, Green Ground, Cristallerie, 8 In. | 3835 |
| Vase, Etched Mermaid, Riding Dolphin, Silvery Clear, Scrolled Base Band, Signed, 3 1/2 In. | 18000 |
| Vase, Etched Rust Red Poppies, Gray Ground, Tapered, France, c.1900, 8 x 4 In. | 100 |
| Vase, Flared Rim, Acid-Etched Flowers, Brown, Cameo, France, 8 3/4 In. | 1599 |
| Vase, Flowering Branch, Amber Over Pale Blue, Tapered Cylinder, Cameo, 9 1/2 In. | 313 |
| Vase, Flowering Branches, Frosted, Amber, Plum, Tapered, c.1900, 15 1/2 In. | 1500 |
| Vase, Flowers, Tan Mushrooms, Green Cylinder, Ringed Base, 11 In. | 3000 |
| Vase, Flowers, Tan, Pink, Mottled Blue Shaded To Cream Ground, Oval, Flared Rim, 3 5/8 In. | 652 |
| Vase, Frosted Peach Body, Cascading Cameo Cut Branch, Blossoms, Signed, 9 In. | 375 |
| Vase, Gold, Enameled Nasturtiums, Gilt Trim, Cameo Signed, 8 1/2 x 7 In. | 1168 |
| Vase, Grape Leaves, Tendrils, Blue To Light Blue, Mauve Ground, Squat, 7 x 7 1/2 In. | 3450 |
| Vase, Green Ferns, Crimson & Frosted Ground, Banjo Form, 6 3/4 In. | 863 |
| Vase, Green Leaves, Seed Pods, White To Peach Ground, Cylindrical, Signed, 24 1/2 In. | 2596 |
| Vase, Green Leaves, Shaded To Pink, Cameo, Cylindrical Neck, Bulbous Base, Signed, 22 In. | 1722 |
| Vase, Green Mottled, Acid Etched Cameo, Violet Flowers, Green Leaves, Ground, 5 3/4 In. | 369 |
| Vase, Green, Carved Flowers, Stick Neck, Signed, 5 In. | 649 |
| Vase, Iris, White, Lavender Green, Signed, 10 In. | 1121 |
| Vase, Ivory & Yellow Ground, Purple Poppies, Leaves, Cameo, Handles, c.1910, 8 x 7 In. | 1560 |
| Vase, Lake Scene, Cobalt Blue Trees, Blue Mountains, Yellow Ground, Shouldered, 5 In. | 1725 |
| Vase, Lake Scene, Evergreen Trees, Shaded Dark To Light Green To Blue, Ball Shape, 5 In. | 920 |
| Vase, Landscape, Narcissus, Green, Orange, Amber, Cameo, Heart Shape, Footed, 8 x 7 In. | 1610 |
| Vase, Landscape, Scenic Landscape, Cameo, Pillow Shape, Pedestal Base, 1960s, 13 x 9 In. | 3795 |
| Vase, Landscape, Trees, Pond, Purple, Yellow, Cameo, Signed, 10 In. | 2962 |
| Vase, Lavender Carved Morning Glory, Vine Overlay, Green Ground, Long Neck, 15 In. | 3800 |
| Vase, Lavender Ground, Flowers, Leaves, France, c.1905, 3 3/4 x 2 1/2 In. | 492 |
| Vase, Leaves, Turk's Cap, Green, Cameo, c.1900, 2 In. | 599 |
| Vase, Lilac, Hydrangea, Leaves, White Ground, Footed, Cameo, 6 In. | 546 |
| Vase, Mold-Blown, Plums, Stems, Leaves, Amber, Cameo, 7 1/4 In. | 4613 |
| Vase, Mountain Landscape, Plum, Over Amber, Blue, Cameo, c.1900, 8 3/4 In. | 2500 |
| Vase, Multicolor, Shaded Green To Peach, Leaves, Cameo, Squat Base, c.1900, 17 1/2 x 6 In. | 1320 |
| Vase, Oak Leaves, Acorns, Cameo, Signed, c.1930, 4 3/4 x 5 1/2 In. | 1845 |
| Vase, Olive, Lime Flowers, Blossoms, Frosted Pink, Cylindrical, Brown Base, c.1900, 13 In. | 1250 |
| Vase, Opal, Shaded, Amethyst Branches, Tapering, 10 1/2 In. | 920 |
| Vase, Orange Day Lilies, Cameo, Tapered To Round Foot, Signed, c.1910, 17 3/8 In. | 861 |
| Vase, Orange Leaves, Cameo, Frosted, Oval, Shouldered, Signed, 3 In. | 374 |
| Vase, Oxblood, Incised Designs, Curled Black Rim, c.1900, 7 x 4 In. | 20000 |
| Vase, Pale Yellow, Amber Overlay, Branches, Cameo, c.1900, 17 1/2 In. | 1500 |
| Vase, Pink Peach Ground, Purple & Green Flowers, Cameo, Signed, 10 In. | 1003 |
| Vase, Pink, Orange Embossed Flowers, Tan Mottled Ground, Triangular, Footed, 8 1/2 In. | 6600 |
| Vase, Plum, Amber, White, Grapevine, Cameo, Signed Galle, 17 1/4 In. | 1750 |
| Vase, Plum, On Amber Grapes, Vines, Frosted, Flared, Tapered Cylinder, c.1910, 14 In. | 1500 |
| Vase, Purple Flowers, Pink Ground, Mold Blown, Signed In Cameo, 6 3/4 In. | 6813 |
| Vase, Purple Iris, Frosted Cylinder, Pinched Top, 8 1/2 In. | 1320 |
| Vase, Purple Striated Neck, Opalescent Base, Flower, Cameo, 10 3/4 In. | 900 |
| Vase, Purple, Blue, Flowers, Cameo, 8 1/2 In. | 223 |
| Vase, Red Flowers, Over Pale Orange, Frosted Yellow, Cameo, c.1900, 11 3/4 In. | 750 |
| Vase, Red Flowers, Stems, Leaves, Frosted Cream Ground, Cameo, Signed, 8 In. | 1185 |
| Vase, Scenic, Mountains, Trees, Cameo, Incised, Amethyst, Blue, Yellow Ground, 12 In. | 1840 |
| Vase, Square, Acid Etched, Poppies, Pink, Green, Blue, 8 1/8 In. | 492 |
| Vase, Thistle, Green, Frosted Pink Ground, Squat Base, Elongated Neck, 10 In. | 593 |
| Vase, Trees, Fruit, Green, Blue, Yellow, c.1900, 8 x 6 In. | 938 |

**Furniture,** Wardian Case, Stand, Cast Iron, Finials, Glass Panels, Trestle, England, 46 x 31 In.
$2,583

**Furniture,** Wardrobe, Pine, Lift-Off Cornice, Painted, Drawers, Flowers, Saints, 1826, 78 In.
$615

**Furniture,** Window Seat, Federal, Mahogany, Upholstered, Inlay, Reeded Legs, N.Y., 29 x 53 In.
$5,535

G

**G. Argy-Rousseau,** Vase, Amber, Panels, Wild Cat Faces, Pate-De-Verre, c.1920, 8½ In.
$4,320

DuMouchelles Art Gallery

## Jokers Date Cards
Jokers were added to decks of cards in the 1890s.

**Galle,** Box, Lid, Thorny Vines, Blue, Purple, Cameo, Frosted Opalescent, Signed, 4¾ In.
$3,851

James D. Julia Auctioneers

**Galle Pottery,** Figurine, Cat, Seated, Yellow, Blue, Faience, Signed, c.1890, 13 x 11 In.
$2,750

Rago Arts & Auction Center

| | |
|---|---:|
| **Vase,** White, Yellow, Carved Flowers, Long Neck, Bulbous Base, Signed, 15¾ In. | 4720 |
| **Vase,** Wisteria, Leaves, Petals, Lilac Over Opal Frost, Cameo, Slender Neck, 17 x 6 In. | 1150 |

**GALLE POTTERY** was made by Emile Galle, the famous French designer, after 1874. The pieces were marked with the initials *E. G.* impressed, *Em. Galle Faiencerie de Nancy*, or a version of his signature. Galle is best known for his glass, listed above.

| | |
|---|---:|
| **Centerpiece,** Raised Flowers & Checkerboard, Brown, Orange, Yellow, 6 x 12 In. | 1180 |
| **Decanter,** Lid, Parrot Shape, Flowers, Insects, Birds, Red, Handle, Signed, c.1880, 13 In. | 633 |
| **Figurine,** Cat, Seated, Yellow, Blue, Faience, Signed, c.1890, 13 x 11 In. ...............*illus* | 2750 |
| **Vase,** Incised Flowers, Cobalt, Gilt, Silver Leaf, 2 High Handles, Art Nouveau, 8 In. | 708 |
| **Vase,** Oriental Design, Flat Body, Applied Tree Trunk Feet, Signed, 9 In. .................*illus* | 2126 |
| **Vase,** Pinched Waist, Free Flowing, Flying Insect, Flowers, Signed, 5½ In. .................*illus* | 1035 |

**GAME** collectors like all types of games. Of special interest are any board games or card games. Transogram and other company names are included in the description when known. Other games may be found listed under Card, Toy, or the name of the character or celebrity featured in the game.

| | |
|---|---:|
| **Above The Clouds,** Milton Bradley, Zeppelin, Board, 1927, 11 x 7 In. | 150 |
| **Baseball Game,** 2-Sided, Red, Yellow, Paint, Board, Wood, 17¾ x 17¾ In. | 23 |
| **Board,** 2-Sided, Checkers & Parcheesi, Wood, Paint, c.1900, 23 x 23 In. | 615 |
| **Board,** 2-Sided, Moldings, Incised Stars, Triangles, Red, Black Paint, c.1925, 24 x 24½ In. | 1150 |
| **Board,** Captain's Wheel Shape, Multicolor Paint, Folk Art, 20 In. | 117 |
| **Board,** Carrom, 2-Sided, Wood, Model 95, Ludington, Michigan, 1961 | 80 |
| **Board,** Checkers & Parcheesi, Red, Black Paint, 18 x 17 In. | 7800 |
| **Board,** Checkers, Paint, Red Leaves, Reverse Parcheesi, c.1890, 20 x 20 In. ...........*illus* | 3690 |
| **Board,** Chinese Checkers, Carved, Pine Frame, New England, c.1890, 18 x 16 In. .........*illus* | 948 |
| **Board,** Chinese Checkers, Pine, Red, Blue, White Paint, c.1920, 30 x 21 In. | 160 |
| **Board,** Cribbage, Walnut, Bone, c.1850, 13 In. | 130 |
| **Board,** Darts, Baseball Diamond, Wood, Green, Yellow, Red, Black, c.1910, 17 x 17 In. | 1169 |
| **Board,** Papier-Mache, Mother-Of-Pearl, Gilt, Book Shape, View Of Wales, c.1850, 16 In. | 956 |
| **Board,** Parcheesi, 3-Board Construction, Original Paint, c.1900, 39 x 25½ In. ...........*illus* | 1353 |
| **Board,** Parcheesi, Pine, Painted, Scenic Home Square, Hinge, c.1850, 20 x 21½ In. ..........*illus* | 1235 |
| **Board,** Parcheesi, Red, Yellow, Black Paint, 25 x 25 In. | 4080 |
| **Board,** Parcheesi, Walnut, 2-Sided, Yellow, Green Paint, Carved, c.1900, 17 x 17 In. | 403 |
| **Board,** Parquetry, Red, Black, c.1905, 29 x 19 In. | 431 |
| **Board,** Pine, 2-Sided, 2 Side Trays, Red, Cream, Black Paint, c.1860, 25 x 14 In. | 210 |
| **Board,** Pine, 2-Sided, Red, White Green Paint, 14¾ x 14 In. | 325 |
| **Board,** Pine, Red, Black Paint, Initialed SPT, 17½ x 14½ In. | 154 |
| **Board,** Red, Black Paint, Wood, c.1910, 20 x 19½ In. | 633 |
| **Board,** Slate, Green, White, Black, c.1900, 22 In. | 104 |
| **Board,** Slate, Octagonal Frame, Red, Black, Yellow Paint, c.1890, 22 x 22 In. | 154 |
| **Box,** Bone, Prisoner-Of-War, Domed Openwork, Cribbage Board, Footed, 9 x 3 In. | 708 |
| **Camelot,** Painted, Gilt, Black, Red, Stars, Spandrels, Board, c.1890, 25 x 15 In. | 1353 |
| **Checkerboard,** Black, Cream, c.1900, 16 x 21 In. | 90 |
| **Checkerboard,** Painted, Brown, Ivory, Frame Edge, Maine, c.1850, 11 x 11 In. | 711 |
| **Checkerboard,** Painted, Red, Black, Applied Frame, c.1890, 12¼ x 12 In. | 923 |
| **Checkerboard,** Pine, Painted, EJW, Meriden, N.H., Dec. 12th, 1876, 14½ x 15¼ In. | 660 |
| **Checkerboard,** Pine, Red, Black Paint, 1800s, 29 x 20¾ In. | 180 |
| **Checkerboard,** Pine, Slide Lid Compartments, Black, Yellow Paint, c.1850, 23 x 13 In. | 1020 |
| **Checkerboard,** Reverse Painted Glass, Marbleized Squares, c.1875, 21 x 21 In. | 123 |
| **Checkerboard,** Reverse Painted Glass, Storks, Hound, Stag, Wood Frame, c.1900, 19 In. | 308 |
| **Checkerboard,** White, Drinking Game, 2-Sided, Raised Edges, Red Paint, 25 x 16 In. | 1020 |
| **Chess Pieces,** American Revolution Figures, Silver & Gilt, J. Goodbrand, London, 32 Piece | 7380 |
| **Chessboard,** Wood, Drawer, Paneled, Painted, Footed, Maitland-Smith | 270 |
| **Chiromagica,** Hand Of Fate, Lithograph Paper, Box, McLoughlin Bros., Board, 1875, 12 In. | 531 |
| **Chuck-A-Luck,** Metal Wire Hourglass Cage, Dice, Wood Base, 15 In. | 240 |
| **Cows In The Corn,** Graphic Cover, Wood Board, Parker Bros., Box, 14 x 13¾ In. | 115 |
| **Dartboard,** Cork, Bull's-Eye, Painted, Red, Purple, White, Green, Blue, Yellow, 1900s, 18 In. | 923 |
| **Fish Pond,** 4 Fishing Poles, Board, McLoughlin Bros., N.Y., 18 x 9 In. .................*illus* | 88 |
| **Football Game,** Footballs, Field, Players With Balls, Board, Linoleum, 17 x 17 In. | 94 |
| **Fox & Geese,** Carved, Painted Red, Octagonal Panel, Pierced Hanger, Board, 12 x 8¼ In. | 984 |
| **Gambling,** Keno Goose, Mahogany Balls, Turned Wood, Supports, c.1880, 22½ In. | 540 |
| **Lottery,** Doll, Gambling Wheel, Prizes, Lithographed Paper, France, c.1890, 11 In. | 826 |
| **New Pretty Village Toy Town,** Cardboard Village Pieces, Box, c.1897, 21 x 15 In. | 150 |
| **Punchboard,** Pin-Up Girl, Jackpot, 25 Dollars, 10 Dollars, 5 Dollars, 1900s, 21 In. ..........*illus* | 270 |

| | |
|---|---:|
| **Puzzle,** Chrysler Building, Wood, Painted, Skyline Series, Box, Kawin Mfg. Co., 1930s, 14 In. | 1062 |
| **Race,** Wood Mast, Composition Sailors, Climbing Rig, Jack Scales, Box | 492 |
| **Racing Game,** Bicycle Riders, Railed Track, Paint, Tin, Clockwork, France, c.1900, 9½ In. | 2400 |
| **Skittles,** Clown, Composition Figures, Multicolor, Various Poses, Wood Base, 9 Pins, 5¼ In. | 1298 |
| **Skittles,** Frog, Papier-Mache, Full Figure, Standing, 9 Pins, Ball | 1652 |
| **Sociable Snake,** For Home Circle, Paper, Watercolor Ink, Snake, Board, c.1880, 22 In. | 2070 |
| **Table,** Gambling, Craps, Chip Set, Dice, Markers, Case, Chip Rack, Wood, 84 x 42 In. | 2700 |
| **Target,** Shooting Gallery, 6 Swiveling Animal Figures, Cast Iron, c.1900, 35 x 79 In. | 4920 |
| **Target,** Shooting Gallery, Bell Ringer, Cast Iron, Red, Round, Bird On Top, c.1890, 14 In. | 1107 |
| **Target,** Shooting Gallery, Round, 8 White Painted Hinged Stars, Cast Zinc, c.1890, 24 In. | 2583 |
| **Target,** Shooting Gallery, Tin, Wood, Painted, Mechanical, Early 20th Century, 11½ In. | 180 |
| **Voyage Through The Clouds,** Zeppelin, 6 Pieces, Trifold Board, Spears, 1910, 8 x 11 In. | 443 |
| **Watermelon Patch,** Lithograph Slotted Box Base, Box, McLoughlin, c.1890, 10 x 19½ In. | 708 |
| **Wheel,** Gambling, Big 6, Pole Stand, Wood, Glass, Metal Spokes, H.C. Evans, 60 x 84 In. | 960 |
| **Wheel,** Gambling, Black Numbers, Green Panels, Orange Borders, Arrow, c.1910, 15 In. | 1046 |
| **Wheel,** Gambling, Brass, Oak Pedestal, c.1900, 79 x 38¾ In. | 2250 |
| **Wheel,** Gambling, Numbers, Blue, White Paint, Square Base, 30 In. | 293 |
| **Wheel,** Gambling, Painted, Numbers 1-15, 1930s, 40 x 40 In. | 1600 |
| **Wheel,** Gambling, Poker High Hand, Spins, Green, White Paint, 11 In. | 330 |
| **Wheel,** Gambling, Wood, 2-Sided, Cutout Hearts, Painted, Red, Gold Numbers, Scrolls, 30 In. | 561 |
| **Wheel,** Gambling, Wood, Painted, Star, Numbers, Alternating Red & Yellow, 24 In. | 502 |
| **Wheel,** Gambling, Wood, Wire Spokes, Paint, c.1900, 33 In. | 172 |
| **Wheel,** Horse Racing Game, Odds Meter, 3-Part Base, 34 In. | 960 |
| **Wheel,** Roulette, Spins, Wood, Paint, 17 In. | 480 |

**GAME PLATES** are plates of any make decorated with pictures of birds, animals, or fish. The game plates usually came in sets consisting of twelve dishes and a serving platter. These sets were most popular during the 1880s.

| | |
|---|---:|
| **Deer,** In Meadow, Transfer, Reticulated Border, Gilt, 7⅜ In., 3 Piece | 50 |
| **Octagonal,** Pink Border, Marked, Wedgwood, 8¼ x 8¾ In., 12 Piece | 350 |
| **Rabbits,** Wooded Scene, Rosenthal, c.1920, 7 In., 6 Piece | 225 |
| **Shore Birds,** Rococo Rim, Rose Swags, Marsh & Prairie Scenes, Limoges, 8 In., 3 Piece | 149 |

**GARDEN FURNISHINGS** have been popular for centuries. The stone or metal statues, urns and fountains, sundials, small figurines, and wire, iron, or rustic furniture are included in this category. Many of the metal pieces have been made continuously for years.

| | |
|---|---:|
| **Bench & Chair Set,** Fern Pattern, Cast Iron, 33 x 54½ In. | 5412 |
| **Bench,** French Provincial, Beech, White, Leaves, Flowers, 2 Doors, 40 x 38 In. | 276 |
| **Bench,** Gothic Revival Style, White Paint, Cast Iron, 1900s, 34 x 56 In., Pair | 2625 |
| **Bench,** Metal, Slatted, Scrolled Armrests, Apron, Stretcher, 32¼ x 59 In. | 1320 |
| **Bench,** Neoclassical Style, Sienna Marble, Curved Seat, Leaf Carved Supports, 72 x 18 In. | 1875 |
| **Bench,** Openwork, Arms, White Paint, Iron, 54 In., Pair | 1500 |
| **Bench,** Pierced, Scrolled Back, Arms, Black Paint, Iron, 35 In. | 469 |
| **Bench,** Scrolled Grape & Vine, Black, Cast Iron, Kramer Bros., Ohio, c.1890, 32 x 42 In. | 2124 |
| **Bench,** Stoneware, Winged Sphinx Ends, Wood Slats, Doulton Lambeth, c.1900, 35 x 79 In. | 1440 |
| **Bench,** Victorian, Light Green, Iron, Kramer Bros., Late 19th Century, 34 x 43 In. | 1440 |
| **Birdbath,** Putti, Holding Shell, c.1900, 29 In. | 492 |
| **Birdhouse,** Victorian, White, Green Roof, Many Windows, Wide Door, 24 x 18 In. | 263 |
| **Boot Scraper,** Armadillo, Cast Iron, Flattened, c.1940, John Wright Foundry, 7 x 16½ In. | 1185 |
| **Boot Scraper,** Bird, Cast Iron, BB Foundry Mark, Boot Jack | 239 |
| **Boot Scraper,** Cast Iron, 20th Century, 21 In. | 258 |
| **Boot Scraper,** Cat, Arched Back, Curled Tail, Iron, 12 x 7 In. | 94 |
| **Boot Scraper,** Dachshund, Curly Tail, Painted, Iron, 7½ x 21 In. | 330 |
| **Boot Scraper,** Duck, Square Frame, Cast Iron, c.1920, 8 x 9 In. | 288 |
| **Boot Scraper,** Horse, Standing, c.1900, 10 x 10¼ In. *illus* | 188 |
| **Boot Scraper,** H-Shape, Scroll Terminals, Iron, Limestone Block, c.1865, 12½ x 18 In. | 374 |
| **Boot Scraper,** Pierced Diamonds, Scrolled Uprights, Iron, Mass., c.1885, 11 x 14 In., Pair | 2000 |
| **Boot Scraper,** Tray, Raised Flared Border, Iron, 8-Sided, c.1900, 10 x 16 In. *illus* | 590 |
| **Boot Scraper,** Victorian, Scrolls, Iron, 1880s, 6½ x 6½ In. | 100 |
| **Chair Set,** Lyre & Rose, Black, Cast Iron c.1840, 32½ x 21 In. | 1107 |
| **Chair,** Lounge, Aluminum, Nylon, Adjustable Backrest, R. Schultz, 1977, 27 x 74 In., Pair | 2074 |
| **Chair,** Lounge, White, Bronze Or Copper Tubing, Roping, Walter Lamb, 22 x 36 In. | 2572 |
| **Chair,** Lyre Splat, Pierced Seat, White Paint, Arms, Cast Iron, Philadelphia, 1800s *illus* | 598 |
| **Chaise Lounge,** White, Bronze Tubing, Roping, Walter Lamb, 23 x 67 In., Pair | 6737 |
| **Chaise Lounge,** White, Bronze Tubing, Roping, Walter Lamb, 23 x 76 In. | 2572 |

**Galle Pottery,** Vase, Oriental Design, Flat Body, Applied Tree Trunk Feet, Signed, 9 In.
$2,126

James D. Julia Auctioneers

**G**

**Galle Pottery,** Vase, Pinched Waist, Free Flowing, Flying Insect, Flowers, Signed, 5½ In.
$1,035

Early Auction Co.

**Game,** Board, Chinese Checkers, Carved, Pine Frame, New England, c.1890, 18 x 16 In.
$948

James D. Julia Auctioneers

**TIP**
*Printed game boards from the 1940s–60s fade very quickly. Older printing seems to be damaged less by exposure to ultraviolet light*

**Game,** Board, Parcheesi, 3-Board
Construction, Original Paint, c.1900,
39 x 25 ½ In.
$1,353

Garth's Auctioneers & Appraisers

**Game,** Board, Checkers, Paint, Red
Leaves, Reverse Parcheesi, c.1890,
20 x 20 In.
$3,690

Skinner Auctioneers & Appraisers

**Game,** Board, Parcheesi, Pine, Painted,
Scenic Home Square, Hinge, c.1850,
20 x 21 ½ In.
$1,235

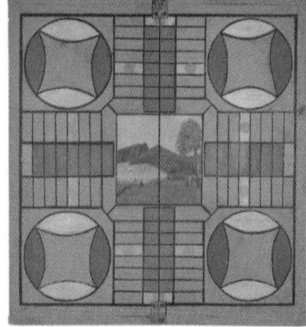

James D. Julia Auctioneers

| | |
|---|---:|
| **Dining Table & Benches,** H-Shape Supports, Stretchers, 95 x 30 ½ In. | 938 |
| **Faucet,** Squirrel Handle, Bronze, Green Patina, 2 In. | 48 |
| **Fernier,** Mahogany, Line Inlay, Oval, Medial Shelf, 3 Legs, c.1920, 38 x 13 In. | 62 |
| **Figure,** 2 Boys, Bird, Rocks, Stump, White Marble, 38 In. | 885 |
| **Figure,** 2 Naked Children Riding On Tortoise, Bronze, 26 ½ In. | 615 |
| **Figure,** 4 Nudes, Outstretched Arms, Circular Track, Cast Iron, 39 In. | 1700 |
| **Figure,** Asian Scholar, Standing, Shaped Top, Granite, 24 In. | 59 |
| **Figure,** Bacchus, Pouring Wine From Ewer, Cast Iron, c.1900, 72 In. | 2500 |
| **Figure,** Bird, Metal, 35 x 50 In. | 420 |
| **Figure,** Bull, Standing, Black, Cast Iron, 29 ½ In. | 1476 |
| **Figure,** Crane, Standing, 1 Head Up, 1 Down, Metal, Patina, Japan, 46 In., 2 Piece | 875 |
| **Figure,** Doe, Cast Metal, Rectangular Base, 38 In., Pair | 4250 |
| **Figure,** Dog, Boston Terrier, Stand, 2-Sided Cast Iron, 12 ¼ In. | 830 |
| **Figure,** Dolphin Shape, Cast Iron, 27 ¾ In. | 200 |
| **Figure,** Eagle, Lead, c.1905, 19 ½ In. | 780 |
| **Figure,** Egrets, Cast Iron, 1900s, 28 ½ In. | 1159 |
| **Figure,** Fountain, Bronze, Big Duck, Verdigris, Edith Parsons, 35 In. | 7200 |
| **Figure,** Fountain, Putto, Pursed Lips, Metal, Patina, 27 In. | 540 |
| **Figure,** Lamb, Concrete, Painted Plinth, 20 x 8 ½ In., Pair | 826 |
| **Figure,** Lion, Resting, Cast Iron, c.1900, 19 ½ x 42 In., Pair | 3500 |
| **Figure,** Lion, Seated, With Shield, Cast Stone, 34 In., Pair | 625 |
| **Figure,** Man, Ganymede, Standing, Eagle, Cast Metal, 70 In. | 3750 |
| **Figure,** Merman, Blowing Conch Horn, Cast Metal, 36 In. | 1125 |
| **Figure,** Pineapple, Iron, Black Paint, 23 In. | 688 |
| **Figure,** Putto, Sphere, Stone, Carved, 39 In. | 780 |
| **Figure,** Snow Goose, Spread Wings, White Paint, Wood, Carved, c.1945, 25 x 24 In. | 885 |
| **Figure,** Turtle, Welded Steel, Georgia Gerber, 67 x 67 In. | 2880 |
| **Figure,** Woman, Standing, Half Draped, Post, Cast Metal, 53 ½ In. | 1188 |
| **Figure,** Young Golfer, Shorts, T-Shirt, Untied Shoes, Bronze, Patinated, 41 In. | 649 |
| **Figurine,** Lion, Standing, Black, Cast Iron, 29 In. | 1080 |
| **Fontaine De Cygne,** French Empire, Swan Neck, Shell Shape Tazza, Column, Iron, 47 In. | 8365 |
| **Fountain,** Aquarium, 3 Storks On Base, Paneled Roof, Posts, Iron, Fiske, 1800s, 84 In. | 10073 |
| **Fountain,** Bronze, Frog, Costume, Lily Pad, 30 x 18 In. | 569 |
| **Fountain,** Child, Holding Water Pitcher, 3 Swans, Iron, 1900s, 49 x 36 In. .............*illus* | 1830 |
| **Fountain,** Child, Water Pitcher, Swans, Green, Iron, 49 In. | 130 |
| **Fountain,** Egret, Fish In Beak, Bronze, Patinated, 26 ¾ In. | 1195 |
| **Fountain,** Figural, Boy & Girl Playing, Naturalistic Base, Nino Venezia, 34 In. | 2596 |
| **Fountain,** Frog, Leaping, Lily Pad Base, Bronze, Patina, 25 x 18 In. | 657 |
| **Fountain,** Shell Shape Basin & Back, Mask, Inset Rouge, Marble, Carved, 66 x 39 In. | 9600 |
| **Fountain,** Swans, Cast Iron, J.W. Fiske, 1800s, 39 x 70 In. ....................*illus* | 4025 |
| **Fountain,** Town, Basin Wall, French Provincial Style, Cast Stone, 4-Sided, 79 x 85 In. | 4182 |
| **Fountain,** Wall, Bronze, Baroque, Scallop Cast Rim, Dolphins, Acanthus, 85 x 45 In. | 5127 |
| **Fountain,** Wall, French Style, Lion Masque Spigot, Demilune Bowl, Pump, 53 x 44 In. | 1353 |
| **Fountain,** Wall, Rococo Style, Scrolled Acanthus Water Spigot, Carrara Marble, 1900s | 2271 |
| **Frog,** On Ball, Painted, Cast Iron, 11 In. | 1560 |
| **Hitching Post Finial,** Horse Head, Ring, Iron, c.1900, 13 x 10 In. ...............*illus* | 1020 |
| **Hitching Post,** Chinese Man, Holding Fan, Ring, Iron, J.L. Mott Iron Works, N.Y., 43 ½ In. | 9000 |
| **Hitching Post,** Horse Head, Iron, 22 In. | 195 |
| **Hitching Post,** Horse Head, Rings, Lion's Masks, Iron, J.W. Fiske, 1800s, 41 In. ...........*illus* | 738 |
| **Hitching Post,** Jockey, Black Boy, Fishing, Painted, 16 In. | 144 |
| **Hitching Post,** Jockey, Black, Blue Jacket, White Hat, Cast Iron, 39 In. | 2200 |
| **Hitching Post,** Man, Smoking, Cap, Cigar, Bowtie, Stand, Cast Iron, c.1890, 16 ½ In. | 2460 |
| **Hitching Post,** Scalloped Base, Red Paint, Cast Iron, 1800s, 48 x 16 In. ............*illus* | 915 |
| **Hitching Post,** Woman, Upraised Hand, Flaming Torch, 32 In. | 1121 |
| **Hose Reel,** Industrial Design, Iron, Early 1900s, 37 x 44 In. | 59 |
| **House Marker,** Sunflower, Leaves, Cast & Wrought Iron, Painted, c.1890, 50 x 20 In.........*illus* | 2337 |
| **Jardiniere,** Putti Bacchus, Arm Holding Bowl, Terra-Cotta, 69 ¾ In., Pair | 2500 |
| **Jardiniere,** Putti, Carved, Scrolled Supports, Marble, 27 x 38 In. | 2813 |
| **Jardiniere,** Putto, Holding Basket Weave Vase On Head, Cast Iron, 31 In. | 313 |
| **Jardiniere,** Stone, Gray, Carved Celtic Knots, 12 ½ In., Pair | 1353 |
| **Jardiniere,** Vertical Lines, Marble, Continental, 22 In., Pair | 1375 |
| **Lavabo,** Rococo Style, Lion's Head Spout, Cast Iron, Continental, 1800s, 33 ¼ x 24 In. | 390 |
| **Pagoda,** Stone, Cast, 3 Parts, Early 20th Century, 56 ½ In. | 1314 |
| **Patio Set,** Iron, White Paint, Pierced, Scrolls, P. Timmes Son, 1895, 44-In. Settee, 3 Piece | 2360 |
| **Patio Set,** Table, 4 Armchairs, Lyre & Rose Pattern, Cast Iron, c.1920, 26 x 38 In. & 32 In. | 3444 |
| **Patio Set,** Table, Chairs, Molded, White, Fiberglass, Douglas Deeds, c.1971 | 2500 |

G

**Game,** Fish Pond, 4 Fishing Poles, Board, McLoughlin Bros., N.Y., 18 x 9 In.
$88

Showtime Auction Services

**Game,** Punchboard, Pin-Up Girl, Jackpot, 25 Dollars, 10 Dollars, 5 Dollars, 1900s, 21 In.
$270

Morphy Auctions

**Garden,** Boot Scraper, Horse, Standing, c.1900, 10 x 10¼ In.
$188

Garth's Auctioneers & Appraisers

**Garden,** Boot Scraper, Tray, Raised Flared Border, Iron, 8-Sided, c.1900, 10 x 16 In.
$590

Brunk Auctions

**Garden,** Chair, Lyre Splat, Pierced Seat, White Paint, Arms, Cast Iron, Philadelphia, 1800s
$598

Neal Auction Co.

**Garden,** Fountain, Child, Holding Water Pitcher, 3 Swans, Iron, 1900s, 49 x 36 In.
$1,830

Neal Auction Co.

**Garden,** Fountain, Swans, Cast Iron, J.W. Fiske, 1800s, 39 x 70 In.
$4,025

Cottone Auctions

**Garden,** Hitching Post Finial, Horse Head, Ring, Iron, c.1900, 13 x 10 In.
$1,020

DuMouchelles Art Gallery

**Garden,** Hitching Post, Horse Head, Rings, Lion's Masks, Iron, J.W. Fiske, 1800s, 41 In.
$738

Neal Auction Co.

**Garden,** Hitching Post, Scalloped Base, Red Paint, Cast Iron, 1800s, 48 x 16 In. **$915**

Neal Auction Co.

**Garden,** House Marker, Sunflower, Leaves, Cast & Wrought Iron, Painted, c.1890, 50 x 20 In. **$2,337**

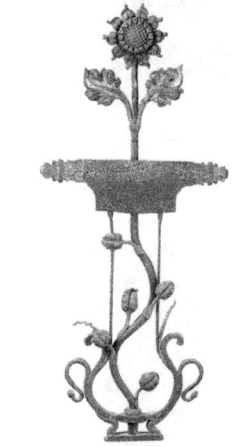

Skinner Auctioneers & Appraisers

**Garden,** Settee, Gothic, Triple Back, Iron, John F. Gaul, Wm. Adams, c.1890, 40 x 46 In. **$1,540**

James D. Julia Auctioneers

| | |
|---|---:|
| **Patio Set,** Table, Urn Shape Pedestal, 6 Chairs, 2 With Arms, Scrolling, Aluminum, 52 In. | 308 |
| **Patio Set,** Wrought Iron, Table, 4 Chairs, 2 Tables, Settee, 3 Armchairs, Upholstered, Woodard | 840 |
| **Plant Stand,** see Furniture, Stand, Plant | |
| **Planter,** Adirondack, Stick Basket, Scalloped Twig Edge, Painted Blue Green, 1930s, 40 In. | 35 |
| **Planter,** Bronze, Maidens, Putti, 4 Seasons, Pio Fedi, 12 In. | 461 |
| **Planter,** Copper, Raised Iron Legs, Applied Fleur-De-Lis, 26 x 21 In., Pair | 246 |
| **Planter,** Lobed, Footed, Cast Iron, France, 1800s, 14 In., Pair | 240 |
| **Planter,** Napoleon III Style, Square, Ogee Ribbed Sides, Cast Iron, 19 ½ x 18 In., 4 Piece | 1476 |
| **Planter,** Neoclassical Style, Marble, Leaves, Corbel Shape Base, Putti, Crests, 28 x 38 In. | 3690 |
| **Rocking Chair,** White, Bronze Or Copper Tubing, Roping, Walter Lamb, 21 x 32 In. | 1960 |
| **Seat,** Blue & White, Pierced Medallions, Flowers, Octagonal, 1900s, 20 x 13 ½ In. | 236 |
| **Seat,** Famille Rose, Octagonal, Chinese, c.1945, 18 ½ In. | 1375 |
| **Seat,** Rose Medallion, 6-Sided, Pierced Top, Sides, 18 ½ In. | 1353 |
| **Settee,** Gothic, Triple Back, Iron, John F. Gaul, Wm. Adams, c.1890, 40 x 46 In. ...........*illus* | 1540 |
| **Sprinkler,** Alligator, Raised Head, Cast Iron, 10 ½ In. | 443 |
| **Sprinkler,** Drake, Cast Iron, Wood, Signed Nuyda, 13 In. | 3300 |
| **Sprinkler,** Frog, Green Glaze, Hardware In Mouth, Burley Winter, 12 x 11 ½ In. | 575 |
| **Sprinkler,** Frog, On Ball, Cast Iron, 8 ½ In. | 767 |
| **Sprinkler,** Frog, Seated, Green, Black, Brown, Robinson Ransbottom, 12 In. | 518 |
| **Sprinkler,** Squirrel, Acorn In Mouth, Lead Alloy, 7 ¾ In. | 148 |
| **Sprinkler,** Turtle, Cast Iron, 10 In. | 600 |
| **Sprinkler,** Turtle, Cast Iron, 14 ½ In. | 413 |
| **Stand,** Fernier, Masks, Scrolls, 3-Part Stem, Paw Feet, Bronze, France, 1800s, 36 x 17 In. | 3600 |
| **Statue,** Dog, Seated, Lead, c.1890, 24 In. ...........*illus* | 1020 |
| **Sundial,** Charioteer, 3 Horses, Rising Sun, Bronze, Patina, Louis F. Ragot, 17 x 18 In. | 1845 |
| **Sundial,** Gnome, Compass Points, Engraved, Brass, John Margas, Dublin, 5 ¼ x 8 ⅝ In. | 2596 |
| **Sundial,** Golfer, Slow Back Time Right, Bronze, Stone, E.E. Codman, c.1900, 19 x 13 In. | 3120 |
| **Sundial,** Robed Woman On Dial, Fluted Pedestal, Bronze, Cast Stone, 47 x 25 In. | 2160 |
| **Sundial,** Silver, Equinoctial, Hinged, Case, Dolland, London, c.1850, 2 ½ In. | 1845 |
| **Sundial,** Zodiac Signs, Ye Are Born Under A Good Star, Bronze, Louis F. Ragot, 1917, 12 In. | 492 |
| **Table,** Dining, Bronze Tubing, Stone, Walter Lamb, 29 x 48 In. | 2082 |
| **Table,** Side, White, Bronze Tubing, Glass Top, Walter Lamb, 23 x 18 In., Pair | 2450 |
| **Topiary Frame,** Victorian, Obelisk Shape, Pedestal, Metal Wire, 1800s, 55 x 14 In. | 277 |
| **Topiary Frame,** Victorian, Urn Shape, Pedestal, Metal Wire, 1800s, 48 ½ x 28 In. | 960 |
| **Urn,** Baluster, Gadrooned Border, Cast Iron, c.1900, 21 In. | 225 |
| **Urn,** Bust Shape Handles, White Paint, Aluminum, c.1900, 44 In., Pair. | 625 |
| **Urn,** Campana Shape, Figural Design, Handles, Black, Cast Iron, 38 In., Pair. | 875 |
| **Urn,** Campana Shape, Stylized Leaves, Rolled Rim, Pedestal Base, Stone, 39 x 24 In., Pair | 2832 |
| **Urn,** Flared & Fluted Basin, Stepped Base, Cast Iron, 28 In., Pair | 840 |
| **Urn,** Flared & Lobed Basin, Mask Head Handles, Stepped Base, Cast Iron, 38 ½ In., Pair | 1920 |
| **Urn,** Lead, Finials, Fluted Bodies, Reeded Base, 22 x 14 ¼ In., Pair. | 2260 |
| **Urn,** Neoclassical Style, Footed, Ribbed, Handles, Metal, 29 In., Pair. | 1188 |
| **Urn,** Neoclassical, Campana Shape, White Marble, 20 In., Pair. | 1187 |
| **Urn,** Pedestal Base, Cast Iron, c.1890, 19 In., Pair. | 234 |
| **Watering Can,** White Ground, Pink, Blue Flowers, Curved Handle, Tin, Ohio Art, 13 x 6 In. | 26 |

**GAUDY DUTCH** pottery was made in England for the American market from about 1810 to 1820. It is a white earthenware with Imari-style decorations of red, blue, green, yellow, and black. Only sixteen patterns of Gaudy Dutch were made: Butterfly, Carnation, Dahlia, Double Rose, Dove, Grape, Leaf, Oyster, Primrose, Single Rose, Strawflower, Sunflower, Urn, War Bonnet, Zinnia, and No Name. Other similar wares are called Gaudy Ironstone and Gaudy Welsh.

| | |
|---|---:|
| **Cup & Saucer,** Butterfly, Handleless, 5 ½ In. | 826 |
| **Plate,** Cup, Handleless, Rose, Blue Vine Borders, 9 ¾ In. | 212 |
| **Plate,** Oyster, Cobalt Blue, Orange, Green, 8 ¼ In. ...........*illus* | 649 |
| **Plate,** Sunflower, Blue Zigzag Border, 7 ⅜ In. | 266 |
| **Plate,** Urn Pattern, 8 ¼ In. | 295 |
| **Plate,** Urn, 8 ⅜ In. | 666 |
| **Soup,** Dish, Double Rose, 8 ⅞ In. ...........*illus* | 590 |
| **Waste Bowl,** Urn, 3 ¼ x 6 ⅜ In. | 968 |

**GAUDY IRONSTONE** is the collector's name for the ironstone wares with the bright patterns similar to Gaudy Dutch. It was made in England for the American market after 1850. There may be other examples found in the listing for Ironstone or under the name of the ceramic factory.

| | |
|---|---:|
| **Basin,** Painted, c.1820, 20 x 8 In. | 251 |
| **Coffeepot,** Floral & Fern, Pomegranate Finial, Loop Handle, Ring Foot, 10 ½ In. ...........*illus* | 413 |
| **Coffeepot,** Morning Glory, Strawberry, Paneled, 10 ½ In. | 325 |

| | |
|---|---:|
| **Pitcher,** Blue, Flowers, Lobed, Scalloped Waist, Twig Handle, Silver Lid, 8 In. | 127 |
| **Pitcher,** Strawberry, Paneled, Cock's Comb Handle, 6 ¼ In. | 413 |
| **Plate,** Dinner, Floral & Fern, Niagara Shape, 9 ½ In., Pair | 83 |
| **Plate,** Strawberry, Paneled, 9 ¾ In. | 133 |
| **Sugar & Creamer,** Flowers & Fern, Pomegranate Finial, E. Walley, 7 In. | 177 |
| **Toddy Plate,** Seeing Eye Pattern, Paneled Shape, Scalloped Border, 5 ½ In. ...........*illus* | 84 |

**GAUDY WELSH** is an Imari-decorated earthenware with red, blue, green, and gold decorations. Most Gaudy Welsh was made in England for the American market. It was made from 1820 to about 1860.

| | |
|---|---:|
| **Ewer,** Grapes, Llanberis, Blue, Red, Green, Wavy Mouth, Scroll Handle, Staffordshire, 11 In. | 92 |
| **Pitcher,** Blue, Orange, Green, Scalloped Rim, Waisted Shape, Scroll Handle, c.1845, 8 In. | 81 |
| **Pitcher,** Eryri Pattern, Red, Blue, Green, Pink, Scroll Handle, Octagonal, c.1845, 5 ¾ In. | 46 |
| **Plate,** Strawberry Pattern, Paneled, 8 ¼ In., 6 Piece | 531 |
| **Plate,** Toddy, Seeing Eye Pattern, Paneled, Scalloped Border, 5 ½ In. | 83 |
| **Sugar,** Strawberry Pattern, Paneled, Leaf Handles, 8 ¼ In. | 1062 |
| **Teapot,** Lid, Nebula Pattern, Round, Footed, Scroll Handle, c.1840, 7 In. | 35 |

**GEISHA GIRL** porcelain was made for export in the late nineteenth century in Japan. It was an inexpensive porcelain often sold in dime stores or used as free premiums. Pieces are sometimes marked with the name of a store. Japanese ladies in kimonos are pictured on the dishes. There are over 125 recorded patterns. Borders of red, blue, green, gold, brown, or several of these colors were used. Modern reproductions are being made.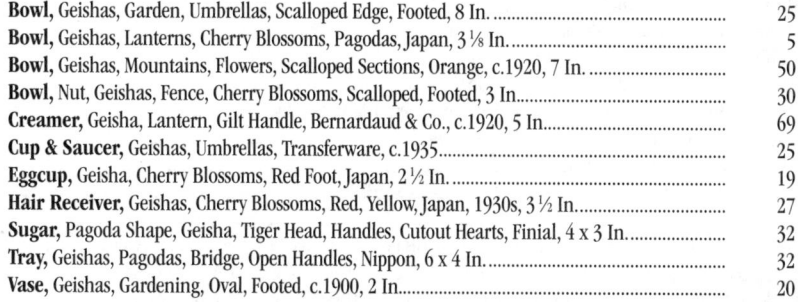

| | |
|---|---:|
| **Bowl,** Geishas, Garden, Umbrellas, Scalloped Edge, Footed, 8 In. | 25 |
| **Bowl,** Geishas, Lanterns, Cherry Blossoms, Pagodas, Japan, 3 ⅛ In. | 5 |
| **Bowl,** Geishas, Mountains, Flowers, Scalloped Sections, Orange, c.1920, 7 In. | 50 |
| **Bowl,** Nut, Geishas, Fence, Cherry Blossoms, Scalloped, Footed, 3 In. | 30 |
| **Creamer,** Geisha, Lantern, Gilt Handle, Bernardaud & Co., c.1920, 5 In. | 69 |
| **Cup & Saucer,** Geishas, Umbrellas, Transferware, c.1935 | 25 |
| **Eggcup,** Geisha, Cherry Blossoms, Red Foot, Japan, 2 ½ In. | 19 |
| **Hair Receiver,** Geishas, Cherry Blossoms, Red, Yellow, Japan, 1930s, 3 ½ In. | 27 |
| **Sugar,** Pagoda Shape, Geisha, Tiger Head, Handles, Cutout Hearts, Finial, 4 x 3 In. | 32 |
| **Tray,** Geishas, Pagodas, Bridge, Open Handles, Nippon, 6 x 4 In. | 32 |
| **Vase,** Geishas, Gardening, Oval, Footed, c.1900, 2 In. | 20 |

**GENE AUTRY** was born in 1907. He began his career as the "Singing Cowboy" in 1928. His first movie appearance was in 1934, his last in 1958. His likeness and that of the Wonder Horse, Champion, were used on toys, books, lunch boxes, and advertisements.

| | |
|---|---:|
| **Book,** Gene Autry & Redwood Pirates, Hardcover, Whiteman, 1946, 5 x 8 In., 248 Pages | 36 |
| **Cap Gun,** 50-Shot Repeater, Nickel Plated, Horse Head Grips, Box, 1940s, 9 x 4 ½ In. | 172 |
| **Cap Gun,** Horse Head Grip, Leather Holster, 1950s, 9 ½ In. | 100 |
| **Cap Pistol,** Repeater, Orange Plastic Grips, Nickel Plated Cast Iron, Kenton, Box, 1940s, 6 In. | 173 |
| **Lobby Card Set,** Back In The Saddle, 1941, 11 x 14 In., 8 Piece | 215 |
| **Official Ranch Outfit,** Holster, Cord Lasso, Bandanna, Box, 1941, 7 ¾ x 11 ¼ In. | 115 |
| **Toy,** Guitar, Automatic Chord Player, Plastic, Image, Emenee, Box, 1950s, 13 x 33 In. | 139 |
| **Toy,** Guitar, Cowboy Girl, Plastic, 4 Strings, Holster, Steer, Signature, Emenee, 1955, 32 In. | 225 |
| **Toy,** Gun & Holster Set, Leather Belt, Horseshoe Buckles, 12 Bullets, 2 Cap Guns | 252 |
| **Toy,** Pistol, 50-Shot Repeater, Gold Finish, Leslie Henry, 9 x 4 ¾ In. | 390 |
| **Wristwatch,** Multicolor Portrait, White Ground, Leather Band, Box, 5 x 5 In. | 189 |
| **Wristwatch,** Six-Shooter, Multicolor Portrait, Second Hand, 3 x 6 ½ In. | 253 |

**GIBSON GIRL** black-and-blue decorated plates were made in the early 1900s. Twenty-four different 10 ½-inch plates were made by the Royal Doulton pottery at Lambeth, England. These pictured scenes from the book *A Widow and Her Friends* by Charles Dana Gibson. Another set of twelve 9-inch plates featuring pictures of the heads of Gibson Girls had all-blue decoration. Many other items also pictured the famous Gibson Girl.

| | |
|---|---:|
| **Plate,** Here Winning New Friends, 10 ½ In. | 80 |
| **Plate,** Mr. Waddles Arrives Late, 10 ½ In. | 90 to 95 |
| **Plate,** Mrs. Diggs Is Alarmed, 10 ½ In. | 85 |
| **Plate,** She Becomes A Trained Nurse, 10 ½ In. | 105 |
| **Plate,** She Contemplates The Cloister, 10 ½ In. | 90 |
| **Plate,** She Decides To Die In Spite Of Dr. Bottles, 10 ½ In. | 76 |

**Garden,** Statue, Dog, Seated, Lead, c.1890, 24 In.
$1,020

Garth's Auctioneers & Appraisers

**Gaudy Dutch,** Plate, Oyster, Cobalt Blue, Orange, Green, 8 ¼ In.
$649

Conestoga Auction Co., Inc.

**Gaudy Dutch,** Soup, Dish, Double Rose, 8 ⅞ In.
$590

Conestoga Auction Co., Inc.

G

**Gaudy Ironstone,** Coffeepot, Floral & Fern, Pomegranate Finial, Loop Handle, Ring Foot, 10 ½ In.
**$413**

Conestoga Auction Co., Inc.

**Gaudy Ironstone,** Toddy Plate, Seeing Eye Pattern, Paneled Shape, Scalloped Border, 5 ½ In.
**$84**

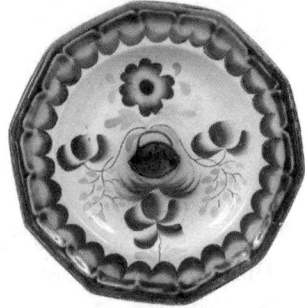

Conestoga Auction Co., Inc.

**Gibson Girl,** Plate, She Looks For Relief Among Old Ones, Royal Doulton, 10 ½ In.
**$125**

Merriman Auction Gallery

**Glass-Art,** Bowl, Green, Garnet Handles, Red Drizzle, Oblong, Saucer Foot, Czechoslovakia, 5 x 11 ½ In.
**$161**

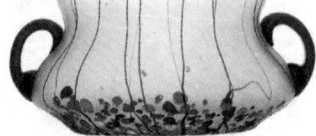

Humler & Nolan

| | |
|---|---|
| **Plate,** She Finds Some Consolation In The Mirror, 10 ½ In. | 95 |
| **Plate,** She Looks For Relief Among Old Ones, Royal Doulton, 10 ½ In. .............*illus* | 125 |
| **Plate,** They All Go Skating, 10 ½ In. | 103 |
| **Postcard,** Forget Me Not | 8 |

**GILLINDER** pressed glass was first made by William T. Gillinder of Philadelphia in 1863. GILLINDER The company had a working factory on the grounds at the Centennial and made small, marked pieces of glass for sale as souvenirs. It made a variety of decorative glass pieces and tablewares.

| | |
|---|---|
| **Figurine,** Horse Head, Red, 6 x 4 x 2 In. | 75 |
| **Lamp,** Electric, Dog, Brown, Gray, 1920s | 230 |
| **Plate,** Children, Seesaw, Dogs, Scalloped Rim, Commemorative, c.1880, 10 In. | 65 |
| **Sherbet,** Stag, Bison, Cabin, Mountains, 1879, 4 In. | 45 |

**GIRL SCOUT** collectors search for anything pertaining to the Girl Scouts, including uniforms, publications, and old cookie boxes. The Girl Scout movement started in 1912, two years after the Boy Scouts. It began under Juliette Gordon Low of Savannah, Georgia. The first Girl Scout cookies were sold in 1928.

| | |
|---|---|
| **Backpack,** Aluminum, Canvas, Green, Insignia, 1970s, 27 x 14 In. | 59 |
| **Badge,** Bronze, Adult Tenderfoot, Trefoil, 1 ⁵⁄₁₆ In. | 85 |
| **Barrette,** Yellow, Plastic, Emblem, 1 ½ In. | 8 |
| **Bracelet,** Spring-Loaded Hinge, Trefoils, G & S, Gold Tone, c.1957 | 38 |
| **Charm,** Disc, Logo, Sunbeams, Metal, ¾ In. | 65 |
| **Cup,** Collapsing, Aluminum, Insignia, 2 x 2 In. | 22 |
| **Handbook,** Green Hardcover, First Impression, N.Y., N.Y., 1940, 694 Pages, 7 x 5 In. | 35 |
| **Handbook,** Green, 20th Edition, 1959, 8 x 5 In. | 22 |
| **Knife,** Pocket, Green, Emblem, 1950s, 3 ½ In. | 43 |
| **Locket,** Trefoil GS, Gold Plated, c.1960, 1 In. | 25 |
| **Photo Album,** Girl Scout Snap Shots, Emblem, Green, 1920s, 11 Pages, 11 x 7 In. | 35 |
| **Postcard,** 50th Anniversary, Leader & Scout, 1962 | 14 |
| **Ring,** Insignia, Sterling, Adjustable | 42 |
| **Uniform Dress,** Green, Size Small, 1950s | 24 |

**GLASS** factories that are well known are listed in this book under the factory name. This category lists pieces made by less well-known factories. Additional pieces of glass are listed in this book under the type of glass, in the categories Glass-Art, Glass-Blown, Glass-Bohemian, Glass-Contemporary, Glass-Midcentury, Glass-Venetian, and under the factory name.

| | |
|---|---|
| **Bowl,** Internal Bubbles, Multicolor, Leon Applebaum, 6 ¾ In. | 246 |
| **Figurine,** Nude, Ena Rottenberg, 1937, 13 x 6 In. | 1500 |
| **Flask,** Alligator, Removable Silver Cap, Walker & Hall, 7 ¼ In. | 154 |
| **Vase,** Pink To Cream, Swirling Ribs, Domed Foot, Flower Shape, Victorian, 6 In. | 355 |
| **Water Set,** Cara Nome, Frosted White, 7 Piece | 225 |

**GLASS-ART.** Art glass means any of the many forms of glassware made during the late nineteenth or early twentieth century. These wares were expensive when they were first made and production was limited. Art glass is not the typical commercial glass that was made in large quantities, and most of the art glass was produced by hand methods. Later twentieth-century glass is listed under Glass-Contemporary, Glass-Midcentury, or Glass-Venetian. Even more art glass may be found in categories such as Burmese, Cameo Glass, Tiffany, and other factory names.

| | |
|---|---|
| **Biscuit Jar,** Multicolor Flowers, White Opalescent Ground, Silver Plate Lid, Bail, 6 In. | 30 |
| **Bowl,** Emerald Frog, Green Cut To Frosted Glass, Signed, Correia, 7 ¾ x 3 In. | 104 |
| **Bowl,** Green, Garnet Handles, Red Drizzle, Oblong, Saucer Foot, Czechoslovakia, 5 x 11 ½ In... *illus* | 161 |
| **Bowl,** Ruffled Pink To White, Victorian, 5 x 12 In. | 72 |
| **Bowl,** Sterling Clad, Art Nouveau, Matte Finish, Gilt Trim, France, c.1900, 5 ¼ x 3 ¾ In. | 584 |
| **Butter,** Cover, Canary, Red Spatterware, Leaf Mold, 5 ½ In. | 604 |
| **Dresser Bottle,** Pulled Swirls, Green, White, Silver Cap, Repousse, c.1910, 6 ½ In., Pair | 384 |
| **Ewer,** Frosted, Gilt, Purple & Pink Flowers, Shell Shape Lid, Collar, Saglier, 11 In., Pair | 677 |
| **Pitcher,** Blue Crackle, Bulbous, Cylindrical Neck, Clear Rose Handle, Victorian, 6 ½ In. | 29 |
| **Pitcher,** Enamel, Stylized Applied Handle, Persian Style, Joseph Brocards, 10 ½ In. | 1840 |
| **Pitcher,** Mottled Red, Blue, Yellow & White Glaze, Marked, Dalpayrat, 9 ½ x 7 In. | 793 |
| **Pitcher,** Water, Yellow, Painted Pink & White Flowers, Green Stems, Victorian, 8 ½ In. | 86 |
| **Plate,** Mottled Blue, Red & Tan Glaze, Dalpayrat, 9 ½ In. | 549 |
| **Rose Bowl,** Blue Aventurine, Gold Foil Inclusions, 6 ½ In. | 122 |
| **Sweetmeat,** Enamel Flowers, Green Opaque, Silver Plate Lid, Bail Handle, 3 In. | 59 |

| | |
|---|---:|
| **Tumbler,** Blue Grape Cluster, Green Stemmed, Amber Leaves, 5 In. | 230 |
| **Vase,** Amber, Etched, Flowers, Leaves, Pulled Feathers, 7 In. | 510 |
| **Vase,** Applied Fish, Seaweed, Orange, Black, Green, Black, Tapered, 9½ In. | 450 |
| **Vase,** Art Deco, Blue Overlay, Acid Etched, Stylized Leaf, Chevron, Charles Catteau, 10 In. | 923 |
| **Vase,** Art Nouveau, Silver Overlay, Quilted Green Glass, La Pierre, 5⅜ In. | 437 |
| **Vase,** Abstract Design, 13 In. | 183 |
| **Vase,** Bud, Ruffled, Verre De Soie, 12½ In. | 125 |
| **Vase,** Diamond Quilted, Mother-Of-Pearl, Peach, Blue Flowers, Yellow, Cylindrical, 7 In. | 144 |
| **Vase,** Etched, Blue Overlay, Stags, Pedestal Base, Germany, c.1830, 7 In., Pair ..........*illus* | 270 |
| **Vase,** Fan, Green, Gilt, Acid Etched, Birds, Flowers, Footed, DeVilbiss, c.1910, 8¾ x 7 In. | 518 |
| **Vase,** Green, King On Horseback Scene, Black Enameled Scrolls, Wavy Rim, c.1900, 14 In. | 750 |
| **Vase,** Iridescent Gold Damascene Pattern, Green Ground, Blue Highlights, 5½ In. | 770 |
| **Vase,** Jugendstil, Copper Mounted, Ribbed, c.1910, 10 x 4¼ In. | 522 |
| **Vase,** Lilac Poppies, Green Leaves, Enameled, Attributed To Honesdale, 11 In. ..........*illus* | 80 |
| **Vase,** Loetz Style, Iridescent Splashes, Textured, Blue Ground, 1900s, 6½ In. ..........*illus* | 62 |
| **Vase,** Multicolor Matte Glazes, Bulbous, Tapered, Dalpayrat, 2 In. | 366 |
| **Vase,** Opal, Gold Iridescent Coiling, Gold Interior, Martin Bach, 10½ In. | 633 |
| **Vase,** Oval, Black Silhouettes, Dancing Nudes, Woods, Turquoise, c.1950, 22 In. | 1500 |
| **Vase,** Paperweight, Undersea Design, Angelfish, Aquatic Plants, Orient & Flume, 7 In. | 259 |
| **Vase,** Purple Flowers, Leaves, Frosted Ground, Yellow Highlights, Delatte, c.1900, 8 In. | 750 |
| **Vase,** Red Iridescent, White Threading, Squat Base, Swollen Rim, Palme-Konig, 5 In. | 61 |
| **Vase,** Stoneware, Crystalline Glaze, Stamped Mark, Dalpayrat, c.1905, 17 x 6½ In. ..........*illus* | 1063 |
| **Vase,** Stylized Flowers, Leaves, Art Deco, Frosted & Clear, A. Hunebelle, France, 6 In. ......*illus* | 184 |
| **Vase,** Tapered, Tripod Base, Green Iridescent, Bronze Footed, c.1900, 13 In. | 590 |
| **Vase,** Yellow Iridescent, Silver Overlay, c.1910, 4 In. | 531 |

**GLASS-BLOWN.** Blown glass was formed by forcing air through a rod into molten glass. Early glass and some forms of art glass were hand blown. Other types of glass were molded or pressed.

| | |
|---|---:|
| **Basket,** White Lattice Ribbons, Flameworked Fruit, Handle, St. Louis, 3¼ In. | 948 |
| **Bottle,** Chestnut Form, Deep Olive Amber, Tooled Collar, Pontil, 9 In. | 439 |
| **Bottle,** Olive, Applied Rim, Green, c.1800, 11½ In. | 570 |
| **Bowl,** Aqua, Flared Rolled Rim, c.1850, 7½ x 9½ In. | 240 |
| **Bowl,** Aqua, Flared, Outward Rolled Rim, Pontil, c.1850, 6½ x 6½ In. ..........*illus* | 184 |
| **Bowl,** Fish, Globular, Clear, Footed, c.1850, 13½ In. | 720 |
| **Bowl,** Pale Green, Folded Rim, American, 19th Century, 8¼ In. | 1260 |
| **Compote,** Pear Shape, Baluster Stem, Disc Foot, Conical Lid, Bulbous Knob Finial, 13 In. | 338 |
| **Creamer,** Emerald Green, c.1850, 4⅜ In. | 420 |
| **Cuspidor,** Cobalt Blue, Bulbous, Flared & Folded Rim, Applied Handle, Miniature, 3¼ In. | 300 |
| **Cuspidor,** Emerald Green, Bulbous, Squat, Flared Rim, 5¾ x 7 In. | 510 |
| **Decanter,** Diamond Diaper Band, Olive Green, Tooled Lip, N.H., 9 In. ..........*illus* | 2300 |
| **Demijohn,** Olive, Bulbous Base, c.1759, 19 In. | 600 |
| **Dish,** Swirl Molded, Enameled, Plants, Iznik Style, Middle Eastern, 9¾ In. | 430 |
| **Figurine,** Dog, Seated, On Pedestal, Green, 7 In. | 35 |
| **Fishbowl,** Round, Flared Rim, Pontil, 10½ x 10¼ In. | 240 |
| **Fishbowl,** Round, Tapered & Spread Foot, 19th Century, 13½ In. | 720 |
| **Goblet,** Amber Stem, Stacked Rings, Student Shield, 7 In. | 98 |
| **Goblet,** Amber, Student Fraternal Shield, 2 Spheres Stem, 7 In. | 123 |
| **Goblet,** Blue, Red, Gold, Wheel Cut Borders, Faceted Stem, 7 In. | 148 |
| **Goblet,** Coat Of Arms, Wheel Engraved, Student Society, 1900, 11 In. ..........*illus* | 108 |
| **Goblet,** Green, Grape, Leaf, 7 In. | 283 |
| **Hat,** Flip, Yellow Amber, Pulled Down Brim, New England, c.1860, 3¾ x 6 In. | 207 |
| **Hourglass,** Center Iron Ring, Wooden Cage, 19th Century, 8¾ In. | 2760 |
| **Hourglass,** Oak, Maple Frame, 2 Green Bulbs, 1700s, 8 x 5 In. | 489 |
| **Jar,** Apothecary, Bulbous Teardrop Form, Bulbous Teardrop Finials, 32 In. | 720 |
| **Jar,** Pale Green, Folded Rim, American, 19th Century, 10½ In. | 1320 |
| **Pitcher,** Blue, Type I Lily Pad, Reeded Neck, Black Foot, N.Y., c.1850, 6 In. | 10800 |
| **Pitcher,** Fiery Opalescent Milk Glass, Bulbous, Flared, Footed, 2¼ In. | 1404 |
| **Pitcher,** Olive Green, Oval Base, Flared Neck & Rim, Shaped Handle, 10½ In. | 351 |
| **Pitcher,** Yellow Olive Amber, 5 Applied Lily Pads, Threading, Ear Handle, Foot, 6 In. | 1755 |
| **Salt,** Amethyst, Flared & Flattened Rim, Pedestal Base, Master, Pontil, 2¾ In. | 210 |
| **Shade,** Hurricane Shape, Emerald Green, c.1850, 20½ In. | 1560 |
| **Shade,** Hurricane, 3 Bands Of Etched Flowers, 23½ x 9 In. | 570 |
| **Syrup,** Pillar, Curved Handle, Tapered, 8 Panels, Thumbprints, Britannia Nozzle, 5¾ x 3 In. | 173 |
| **Vase,** Bulbous, Rounded Lip, Undulating Sides, Peacock Blue Iridescent, 5¾ In. | 368 |

**Glass-Art,** Vase, Etched, Blue Overlay, Stags, Pedestal Base, Germany, c.1830, 7 In., Pair
**$270**

**Glass-Art,** Vase, Lilac Poppies, Green Leaves, Enameled, Attributed To Honesdale, 11 In.
**$80**

**Glass-Art,** Vase, Loetz Style, Iridescent Splashes, Textured, Blue Ground, 1900s, 6½ In.
**$62**

G

**Glass-Art,** Vase, Stoneware, Crystalline Glaze, Stamped Mark, Dalpayrat, c.1905, 17 x 6½ In.
$1,063

Rago Arts & Auction Center

**Glass-Art,** Vase, Stylized Flowers, Leaves, Art Deco, Frosted & Clear, A. Hunebelle, France, 6 In.
$184

Humler & Nolan

**Glass-Blown,** Bowl, Aqua, Flared, Outward Rolled Rim, Pontil, c.1850, 6½ x 6½ In.
$184

Glass Works Auctions

**Glass-Blown,** Decanter, Diamond Diaper Band, Olive Green, Tooled Lip, N.H., 9 In.
$2,300

Glass Works Auctions

**Glass-Blown,** Goblet, Coat Of Arms, Wheel Engraved, Student Society, 1900, 11 In.
$108

The Stein Auction Company

**Glass-Blown,** Vase, Witch's Ball Stopper, Clear, White Looping, c.1850, 9⅜ In.
$633

Glass Works Auctions

**Glass-Bohemian,** Goblet, Green, Enameled Flowers, Applied Punts, Myers Neffe, 10 In., Pair
$324

Fox Auctions

**Glass-Contemporary,** Basket, Dale Chihuly, 1981, 5 x 16 x 15 In., 5 Piece
$10,000

Rago Arts & Auction Center

**Glass-Contemporary,** Bowl, Cobalt Blue, Coiled, Signed, Mark Peiser, 5 x 15¼ In.
$2,006

Brunk Auctions

**Glass-Contemporary,** Bowl, Macchia, Chartreuse Lip Wrap, Signed, Dale Chihuly, 1986, 14 x 21 In.
$23,750

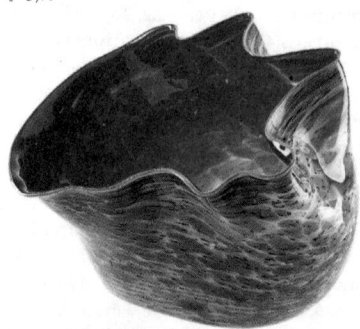

Rago Arts & Auction Center

| | |
|---|---|
| **Vase,** Hyacinth, Sapphire Blue, Cupped Mouth, c.1850, 8 ¾ x 2 ½ In. | 403 |
| **Vase,** Pilsner, Student Shield, Pewter, Relief Base, Van Hauten, 12 In. | 431 |
| **Vase,** Trumpet, Amethyst, Inward Folded Rim, Footed, c.1870, 10 x 4 In., Pair | 978 |
| **Vase,** Trumpet, Parade, Yellow, End Of Day, c.1885, 31 In. | 180 |
| **Vase,** Witch's Ball Stopper, Clear, White Looping, c.1850, 9 ⅜ In. ...............*illus* | 633 |
| **Witch's Ball,** Marbrie Loop, Rose Loopings, Boston & Sandwich Glass Co., c.1875, 4 In. | 219 |
| **Witch's Ball,** Stand, Red Amber, Flared, Squat Knop, Conical Base, Stoddard, 10 In. | 1638 |

**GLASS-BOHEMIAN.** Bohemian glass is an ornate overlay or flashed glass made during the Victorian era. It has been reproduced in Bohemia, which is now a part of the Czech Republic. Glass made from 1875 to 1900 is preferred by collectors.

| | |
|---|---|
| **Bowl,** Flashed, Engraved Flowers, Amber, Blue, White Enamel, Footed, c.1910, 5 ¼ In. | 127 |
| **Bowl,** Ruby, Swirling Star & Sunburst, Geometric Border, 9 x 4 In. | 52 |
| **Centerpiece,** Blue, Teal, Green, Iridescent Glass, Attributed To Loetz, Bronze, 12 In. | 1230 |
| **Chalice,** Blue Cut To Clear Top, Stags In Forest, Faceted Stem, Star Foot, 9 ½ In. | 3555 |
| **Claret Jug,** Enamel Overlay, Opaline Panel, Scrollwork, Ruby Glass, Gilt, 13 ¼ x 5 ¼ In. | 369 |
| **Cologne,** Bottle, Cranberry, 6-Sided, Raised Cartouches, Gilt Leaves & Scrolls, 5 In., Pair | 213 |
| **Compote,** Etched Grapevine, Scalloped Rim, Flared, Paneled, 8 x 9 In., Pair | 210 |
| **Decanter,** Gilt, Cut Glass, Flowers, Leaves, Teardrop Shape, 3 Neck Bands, 24 In., Pair | 144 |
| **Decanter,** Gilt, Teardrop, 3 Bands At Neck, Cut Flowers, Spike Shape Stopper, 24 In., Pair | 201 |
| **Decanter,** Goblets, Cobalt Blue, To Clear, Etched Grapes, Leaves, 16 x 14 In., 8 Piece | 125 |
| **Decanter,** Spire Stopper, Etched Arabesques, Flowers, Green, Ring Neck, 1800s, 13 In. | 500 |
| **Decanter,** Spire Stopper, Etched Arabesques, Ruby, Ringed Neck, 1800s, 13 ½ In. | 875 |
| **Ewer,** Red, Etched White Flowers, c.1875, 13 ½ In. | 344 |
| **Goblet,** Cartouche, Flower, Maiden, Leaves, Etched, 1800s, 13 ¼ In. | 338 |
| **Goblet,** Clear, Grape Cluster, Intaglio Clear, Green Stem, Amber Leaves, Harrach, 5 In. | 748 |
| **Goblet,** Cobalt Blue, Frosted Flowers, Footed, 19th Century, 6 In. | 300 |
| **Goblet,** Green, Enameled Flowers, Applied Punts, Myers Neffe, 10 In., Pair .........................*illus* | 324 |
| **Goblet,** Soldiers, Inscription Above Cartouches, Metal Foot, 9 ¼ In. | 338 |
| **Jar,** Dresser, Panels, Grape & Vine, Ruby, 19th Century, 6 ¾ In., Pair | 110 |
| **Pitcher,** Green, Free-Form Handle, 7 ½ In. | 246 |
| **Pokal,** Ruby Cased, Cut, Engraved, Gabriel, Water Lilies, Landscape, 15 x 4 ¾ In., Pair | 615 |
| **Pokal,** Ruby Stain, Engraved, Deer, Landscape, Cut Bull's Eyes, Scrolling, 14 x 5 In., Pair | 738 |
| **Urn,** Cobalt Blue Cut To Clear, Gilt Metal Rim, Double Handle, Pedestal, 8 ¼ In., Pair | 1277 |
| **Vase,** 5 Gilt Panels, Intaglio Flowers, Scrolls, Folded Form, Bubble Ball Stem, 11 In. | 237 |
| **Vase,** Bulbous, Tapered Neck, Footed, Crackle, 6 ½ In. | 100 |
| **Vase,** Cobalt Blue Cut To Clear, 12 x 7 In. | 150 |
| **Vase,** Cranberry Cased, Trumpet Shape, Tapered, Outward Rim Pink Border, 7 x 12 ½ In. | 178 |
| **Vase,** Double Overlay Beaker, Green To White, Paneled, Punty Designs, c.1900, 6 x 4 In. | 115 |
| **Vase,** Engraved Griffins, Urns, Flowers, Flared Rim, Handles, J. & L. Lobmeyr, c.1870, 10 In. | 1920 |
| **Vase,** Faceted, Pierced, Scrolled Handles, Crenulated Edge, c.1850, 14 x 7 ½ In., Pair | 369 |
| **Vase,** Gilt Scrolls, Cream Outline, Stylized Flowers, Rigaree, Tapered, Footed, 18 In. | 1519 |
| **Vase,** Green Cut To Clear, Paneled, 4 Deer In Woodland, Bulbous, Scalloped, 5 In. | 474 |
| **Vase,** Green, Dimpled Spiral Ribbing, Tapered Cylinder, Gilt Rim, c.1900, 10 In., Pair | 375 |
| **Vase,** Green, Gilt Leaves, Tapered, Flared & Flattened Rim, Art Nouveau, 13 In. | 413 |
| **Vase,** Green, Square, Classical Woman Bust, Applied Gilt, c.1920, 8 x 2 ¾ In. | 161 |
| **Vase,** Icicle, Enameled Branches, Raised Gilt Bird, Gilt, c.1880, 14 x 6 ½ In. | 369 |
| **Vase,** Molded Forest Scene, Clear, Frosted, Barolac, 10 x 7 ½ In. | 305 |
| **Vase,** Pale Iridescent, Pulled Feather, Tapered, c.1900, 12 In. | 184 |
| **Vase,** Scales, Pinch, Cobalt Blue, Urn Shape, Kralik, c.1910, 6 ¼ x 3 In. | 345 |
| **Vase,** Threaded Glass, Cobalt Blue, 12 In. | 215 |
| **Vase,** Translucent Cobalt Blue, Oil Spots, Tendrils, Silver Overlay, c.1900, 10 In. | 688 |
| **Vase,** White Opalescent, Green Threading, Double Gourd Form, Kralik, 10 In. | 531 |
| **Wine,** Cranberry Flash, Gilt Designs, c.1910, 7 ½ In., 10 Piece | 704 |
| **Wine,** Green Enamel, Gilt Design, c.1930, 6 ¼ In. | 544 |

**GLASS-CONTEMPORARY** includes pieces by glass artists working after 1970. Many of these pieces are free-form, one-of-a-kind sculptures. Paperweights by contemporary artists are listed in the Paperweight category. Earlier studio glass may be found listed under Glass-Midcentury or Glass-Venetian.

| | |
|---|---|
| **Basket,** Dale Chihuly, 1981, 5 x 16 x 15 In., 5 Piece.................................*illus* | 10000 |
| **Basket,** Plum, Cylinder, Threaded, Shard Drawing, Chihuly, 7 ½ In. | 4305 |
| **Basket,** Untitled No. 1, Green Lip, Mottled, D. Chihuly, 1988, 17 x 15 In. | 4750 |
| **Bowl,** Cast Glass, John Lewis, 1989, 14 In. | 3250 |
| **Bowl,** Cobalt Blue, Coiled, Signed, Mark Peiser, 5 x 15 ¼ In..............................*illus* | 2006 |

**Glass-Contemporary,** Bowl, Woven Thread, Engraved R. Rackham, '84 Vortex, Sweden, 7 ¼ In.
**$127**

Humler & Nolan

**Glass-Contemporary,** Plaque, Abstract, Birds, Grass, Plants, Sun, Frame, Higgins, 17 ½ x 13 ½ In.
**$366**

G

Palm Beach Modern Auctions

**TIP**

*Shallow nicks and rough edges on glass can sometimes be smoothed off with fine emery paper.*

**Glass-Contemporary,** Sculpture, 2 Piece, H. Littleton, 1981, 19 In.
**$21,240**

Brunk Auctions

**Glass-Contemporary,** Sculpture, Cut Eye, Blown & Cut, Label, Harvey Littleton, 9 x 6 In. $2,944

Rago Arts & Auction Center

**Glass-Contemporary,** Sculpture, Persian, Yellow, Black Lip Wrap, Dale Chihuly, 1997, 9 x 13 In. $3,625

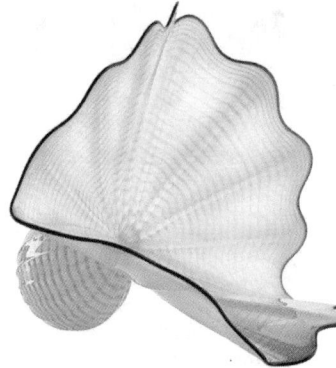

Rago Arts & Auction Center

**Glass-Contemporary,** Sculpture, Sea Kingdom, Signed, Dominick Labino, 6 x 5 In. $2,875

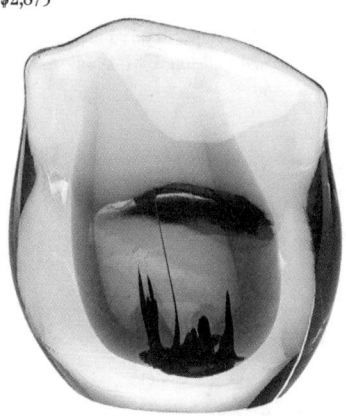

Rago Arts & Auction Center

**Glass-Contemporary,** Teapot, Checkerboard Murrine, Richard Marquis, 1985, 7 ½ x 5 ¾ In. $9,375

Rago Arts & Auction Center

**Glass-Contemporary,** Vase, Red Shard, Pilchuck Glass School, William Morris, 1980, 14 x 10 In. $5,000

Rago Arts & Auction Center

**Glass-Contemporary,** Vase, Clear Blue, Yellow & White Flower Buds, Dominick Labino, 1980, 5 ⅞ In. $633

Humler & Nolan

**Glass-Contemporary,** Vase, Flame, Blue, Red, Gold Foil Inclusions, Etched Dale Chihuly, 16 In. $2,963

James D. Julia Auctioneers

**Glass-Contemporary,** Vase, Internal Yellow Swirl, Bulbous, Labino, 1971, 3 ¾ In. $420

DuMouchelles Art Gallery

**Glass-Contemporary,** Vase, Noble Effort, Triangular, Murrine, Richard Marquis, 1980, 9 x 6 ¾ In. $875

Rago Arts & Auction Center

| | |
|---|---|
| **Bowl,** Iridescent, Ribbed, Gold Applied Banding, Dark Stipple, Signed, Lundberg, 4¾ In. | 173 |
| **Bowl,** Macchia, Chartreuse Lip Wrap, Signed, Dale Chihuly, 1986, 14 x 21 In. ...........*illus* | 23750 |
| **Bowl,** Multi Flora, Yellow & Pink Iridescent, Flowers, Signed Charles Lotton, 10 x 7 In. | 805 |
| **Bowl,** Patinated Copper, Cast Glass, John Lewis, 1987, 14½ x 6½ In. | 3250 |
| **Bowl,** Red, Flared Rim, Stretched Gold Iridescent Finish, Black Foot, Lotton, 1983, 6 x 3 In. | 265 |
| **Bowl,** Woven Thread, Engraved R. Rackham, '84 Vortex, Sweden, 7¼ In. ...........*illus* | 127 |
| **Clarinet,** Clear, Signed, Scott Darlington, 1993, 24¾ In. | 960 |
| **Figurine,** Frog, Nygren, Marked, 9 In. | 854 |
| **Panel,** Sun Over Stylized Green Hills, Pyramid Form, M. Peiser, 1986, 10 x 5 In. | 4956 |
| **Penholder,** Paperweight, Crown, Blue, Green, St. Louis, 1992, 6½ In. | 651 |
| **Penholder,** Paperweight, Crown, Blue, Yellow, St. Louis, 1992, 6½ In. | 651 |
| **Penholder,** Paperweight, Crown, Red, Green, St. Louis, 1992, 6½ In. | 651 |
| **Perfume Bottle,** Multi Flora, Amber, White Flowers, Green Leaves, Oval, 1978 | 403 |
| **Plaque,** Abstract, Birds, Grass, Plants, Sun, Frame, Higgins, 17½ x 13½ In. ...........*illus* | 366 |
| **Plaque,** Lily Pond, Signed S. Stelz, 9 x 15¾ In. | 2370 |
| **Sconce,** Amber, Opalescent, Streamers, Gourds, Attributed To D. Chihuly | 5904 |
| **Sculpture,** 2 Piece, H. Littleton, 1981, 19 In. ...........*illus* | 21240 |
| **Sculpture,** Abstract, Green Glass, Metal, Claire Falkenstein, 20th Century, 9 In. | 7080 |
| **Sculpture,** Cut Eye, Blown & Cut, Label, Harvey Littleton, 9 x 6 In. ...........*illus* | 2944 |
| **Sculpture,** Hill On The Hill, Red, Cast Glass, Jindrich Dolezal, 17 x 12 In. | 1500 |
| **Sculpture,** Interlock, Frosted, Pink Square Shape, Kreg Kallenberger, 7 x 8 In. | 2160 |
| **Sculpture,** Jockey, Green, Signed Dan Dailey, 9¾ x 8 In. | 4062 |
| **Sculpture,** Obelisk, Organic Shape, Enclosed Air Bubbles, Amber, Rose, 13 In. | 207 |
| **Sculpture,** Persian, Yellow, Black Lip Wrap, Dale Chihuly, 1997, 9 x 13 In. ...........*illus* | 3625 |
| **Sculpture,** Sea Kingdom, Signed, Dominick Labino, 6 x 5 In. ...........*illus* | 2875 |
| **Sculpture,** Seaform, Shaded Yellow, Wavy Bands, Red Lip Wrap, Chihuly, 18 In. | 8750 |
| **Sculpture,** Stranded, Cast Glass, Granite, Bertil Vallien, 5½ x 15¾ In. | 1125 |
| **Tankard,** Neo Deco, Clear, Cobalt Blue Marbles, George Ponzi, 8½ In. | 104 |
| **Teapot,** Checkerboard Murrine, Richard Marquis, 1985, 7½ x 5¾ In. ...........*illus* | 9375 |
| **Vase,** Applied Leaves, Trumpet Shape, Green Iridescent Oil Spot, Dennis Mullen, 13 In. | 713 |
| **Vase,** Blue Opal Leaves, Yellow Vines, Beige Lip Wrap, Lotton, 1977, 7½ In. | 288 |
| **Vase,** Blue, Red, Pulled, Charles Lotton, 1982, 4½ In. | 215 |
| **Vase,** Bottle Shape, Tall Neck, Amber, Plum, Signed, Dominick Labino, 10½ In. | 483 |
| **Vase,** Clear Blue, Yellow & White Flower Buds, Dominick Labino, 1980, 5⅞ In. ...........*illus* | 633 |
| **Vase,** Cosmic, Panoramic Milky Way Galaxy, Cobalt Blue Ground, Kent Ispen, 10 In. | 316 |
| **Vase,** Cylindrical, Frosted, Blue Oil Spots, Signed Eicholt, 1993, 9½ In. | 86 |
| **Vase,** Cylindrical, Gold Iridescent, White Millefiori, Purple Stem, 10½ In. | 173 |
| **Vase,** Diffused Designs, Red, Orange, Green, Yellow, Herb Babcock, 5½ x 5 In. | 450 |
| **Vase,** Filet-De-Verre, Fused, Thermoformed Color Threads, Toots Zynsky, 1994, 7 x 16 In. | 9840 |
| **Vase,** Flame, Blue, Red, Gold Foil Inclusions, Etched Dale Chihuly, 16 In. ...........*illus* | 2963 |
| **Vase,** Gold Iridescent, Pulled Lines, King Tut Design, Orient & Flume, 1981, 8 In. | 173 |
| **Vase,** Gold Iridescent, Pulled Peacock Feather, Signed Lundberg, 8 x 5½ In. | 230 |
| **Vase,** Gold Pulls, Purple Feather, Ivory, Pinched Clover Shape Rim, Lotton, 7 In. | 1035 |
| **Vase,** Green, Ivory Split Leaves, Green, Blue, Silver, Lotton, 6¾ In. | 288 |
| **Vase,** Internal Yellow Swirl, Bulbous, Labino, 1971, 3¾ In. ...........*illus* | 420 |
| **Vase,** Iridescent, Gold, Tree, White Flowers, Zellique, 1996, 10 In. | 120 |
| **Vase,** Iridescent, Green, Pulled, Orient & Flume, 1983, 11 In. | 215 |
| **Vase,** Jack-In-The-Pulpit, Yellow, Raspberry Pull Feather, Orient & Flume, 12½ In. | 403 |
| **Vase,** Lava, Blue Aurene Organic Design, Amber & Red Marbling, Lotton, 5½ In. | 431 |
| **Vase,** Mandarin Red, Bulbous, Pinched Neck, Signed Lotton, 4 In. | 460 |
| **Vase,** Multi Flora, Dogwood, Leaves, Striated, Blue Shaded To Aqua, Lotton, 7¾ In. | 633 |
| **Vase,** Multi Flora, Pink Luster Flowers, Green, Blue Stems, Lotton, 10½ In. | 3450 |
| **Vase,** Noble Effort, Triangular, Murrine, Richard Marquis, 1980, 9 x 6¾ In. ...........*illus* | 875 |
| **Vase,** Olive Opal, Metallic Blue, Gloss Applied Prunts, Labino, 5¼ In. | 288 |
| **Vase,** Orange, Marbled Green, Blue, Melon Rib Swirl Base, Labino, 5¾ x 4¾ In. | 489 |
| **Vase,** Paperweight, Bird Of Paradise, Calla Lilies, Blue Stalks, Orient & Flume, 8½ In. | 196 |
| **Vase,** Paperweight, Orange, Variegated Leaves, Pink Flowers, Lotton, 7 x 12 In. | 1840 |
| **Vase,** Purple, Footed, V. Zecchin, Italy, 1900s, 9 x 4 In. | 1125 |
| **Vase,** Red, Blue Cascading Feather, Oval, Signed Lotton, 1975, 3¼ In. | 403 |
| **Vase,** Red, Blue, Chemically Treated, Jon Kuhn, 1982, 16 x 12 In. | 1375 |
| **Vase,** Red, Gold Split Leaves, Lotton, 1983, 7 In. | 317 |
| **Vase,** Red Shard, Pilchuck Glass School, William Morris, 1980, 14 x 10 In. ...........*illus* | 5000 |
| **Vase,** Seaform, Chihuly, 7½ x 7¾ In. | 5000 |
| **Vase,** Spherical, Matte & Glossy Ground, Striped Canes, George Thiewes, c.1984, 6 x 6 In. | 308 |
| **Vase,** Swirl Designs, Brown Tones, Black Spots, Richard Ritter, 5 x 4½ In. | 180 |
| **Vase,** Swirl Rib Body, Red Zipper Pattern, Orient & Flume, 14⅜ In. | 431 |

**Glass-Midcentury,** Charger, Geometric Shapes, Shades Of Green, Higgins, 22 In. $720

DuMouchelles Art Gallery

**G**

**Glass-Venetian,** Bowl, Murrine Opache, Irregular Dots, Carlo Scarpa, Venini, 1940s, 7½ In. $12,500

Rago Arts & Auction Center

**Glass-Venetian,** Figurine, Bird, Wire Feet, Alessandro Pianon, Vistosi, 1962, 12 x 5¾ In. $4,688

Los Angeles Modern Auctions (LAMA)

**Glass-Venetian,** Vase, Applied Elements, Oxidized Finish, Seguso Vetri D'Arte, Murano, 16 x 10 In.
$1,625

Rago Arts & Auction Center

**Glass-Venetian,** Vase, Blue Reticello, Oval, Grafted Glass, Giampaolo Seguso, 12 x 8 In.
$288

Humler & Nolan

**Glass-Venetian,** Vase, Intarsio, Air Bubbles, Murano, Ercole Barovier, 1960s, 7½ x 4½ In.
$1,625

Rago Arts & Auction Center

| | |
|---|---:|
| **Vase,** Teapot, Crazy Quilt, Pulled Checkerboard, R. Marquis, 1979, 6 In. | 4600 |
| **Vase,** Trees, Blue Millefiori Flowers, White Ground, Orient & Flume, 15 In. | 403 |
| **Vase,** White, Cobalt Chain, Green Combed Pattern, Gold Rim, Orient & Flume, 4 x 5½ In. | 115 |

**GLASS-CUT,** *see Cut Glass category.*

**GLASS-DEPRESSION,** *see Depression Glass category.*

**GLASS-MIDCENTURY** refers to art glass made from the 1940s to the early 1970s. Some glass factories, such as Baccarat or Orrefors, are listed under their own categories. Earlier glass may be listed in the Glass-Art and Glass-Contemporary categories. Italian glass may be found in Glass-Venetian.

| | |
|---|---:|
| **Charger,** Geometric Shapes, Shades Of Green, Higgins, 22 In. ...............................*illus* | 720 |
| **Creamer,** Soreno, Avocado Green, 1966-70, 4 In. | 9 |
| **Plaque,** Owl, Red Moon, Fused, M. & F. Higgins, Metal Clad Frame, 12 x 13 In. | 976 |
| **Sherbet Set,** Boopie, Desert Gold, c.1960, 3½ In., 6 Piece | 72 |
| **Tumbler,** Swing Yer Ma, Couple, Square Dancing, Red, Black, White, 1950s, 5 In. | 14 |
| **Vase,** Blue, Dark Blue Swags, Burgundy Zipper, Lundberg, 7¼ In. | 432 |
| **Vase,** Metallic, Sand, Cream, Samuel Herman, 1971, 8 In. | 150 |

**GLASS-PRESSED,** *see Pressed Glass category.*

**GLASS-VENETIAN.** Venetian glass has been made near Venice, Italy, since the thirteenth century. Thin, colored glass with applied decoration is favored, although many other types have been made. Collectors have recently become interested in the Art Deco and fifties designs. Glass was made on the Venetian island of Murano from 1291. The output dwindled in the late seventeenth century but began to flourish again in the 1850s. Some of the old techniques of glassmaking were revived, and firms today make traditional designs and original modern glass. Since 1981, the name *Murano* may be used only on glass made on Murano Island. Other pieces of Italian glass may be found in the Glass-Contemporary and Glass-Midcentury categories of this book.

| | |
|---|---:|
| **Bottle,** Stopper, Red, Clear, Paolo Venini, 1952, 8¼ x 4 In. | 750 |
| **Bowl,** Acid Stencil, Clear, Green, Venini, 1953, 8 x 4 In. | 3437 |
| **Bowl,** Finestre, Yoichi Ochira, 1997, 4¼ x 5½ In. | 4688 |
| **Bowl,** Green, Blue, Murrine, Venini, 10¾ In. | 1250 |
| **Bowl,** Honey, Green Swirl, Murano, c.1940, 3½ In., 4 Piece | 180 |
| **Bowl,** Murrine Opache, Irregular Dots, Carlo Scarpa, Venini, 1940s, 7½ In. ................*illus* | 12500 |
| **Bowl,** Yellow, Fazzoletto, Lino Tagliapietra, 1986, 11 x 14 In. | 2000 |
| **Coffee Set,** Green, Gilt, Flowers, 10 Cups & Saucers, A. Nason, 23 Piece | 246 |
| **Cruet,** Fused Lip & Handle, Gilt, 1900s, 6¾ In. | 295 |
| **Decanter,** Stopper, Cenedese, Murano, 1900s, 7⅜ x 4½ In. | 132 |
| **Duck,** Blown, White Mottled, Turquoise, Black, Yellow, Formia Murano, 5 x 12 In. | 173 |
| **Ewer,** Iridescent, Blown, Flared Neck, Fluted Rim, Spout, Twisted Handle, 14 x 5 In. | 92 |
| **Figurine,** Bird, Blue, Clear Wings, Taking Flight, 12 In., Pair | 210 |
| **Figurine,** Bird, Wire Feet, Alessandro Pianon, Vistosi, 1962, 12 x 5¾ In. ...............*illus* | 4688 |
| **Figurine,** Bodice With Bikini, Clear, Aubergine & White, F. Bianconi, c.1950, 15 In. | 14375 |
| **Goblet,** Lavender, Cone Shape, Inverted Cone Foot, L. Tagliapietra, 12¾ In. | 1750 |
| **Plate,** Red Clear Glass, Enamel, Gilt, Muse Center, Flowers, 7¼ In., 4 Piece | 92 |
| **Scent Bottle,** Hourglass Shape, White & Pink Swirl Stripe, Brass Lid, Chain, 2 In. | 115 |
| **Sculpture,** Bird, Chick, Orange, Copper, A. Pianon, Murano, 1950s, 5 x 8 In. | 3660 |
| **Sculpture,** Block, Aquarium, Goldfish, Seaweed, 1960s, 4¾ x 6½ In. | 625 |
| **Sculpture,** Fish, Red, Blue, Pino Signoretto, Murano, 14½ x 17 In. | 1220 |
| **Vase,** A Fili, Lino Tagliapietra, 1992, 7½ x 6 In. | 1250 |
| **Vase,** Amphora Shape, Applied Prunts, Handles, Scavo, Seguso, Italy, 1900s, 12 x 3½ In. | 369 |
| **Vase,** Applied Elements, Oxidized Finish, Seguso Vetri D'Arte, Murano, 16 x 10 In. ............*illus* | 1625 |
| **Vase,** Blue Reticello, Oval, Grafted Glass, Giampaolo Seguso, 12 x 8 In. ................*illus* | 288 |
| **Vase,** Blue, Clear, Archimede Seguso, 1990, 12½ In. | 2000 |
| **Vase,** Blue, Gold, Giulio Radi, 1948, 7 x 4¼ In. | 1375 |
| **Vase,** Blue, Martinuzzi, 1933, 13 x 9½ In. | 4375 |
| **Vase,** Blue, Yellow & Red Spots, Versace, 6½ x 10 In. | 1875 |
| **Vase,** Bulbous, Applied Violet Design, Blush Mottled Body, Murano, 9 x 3½ In., Pair | 121 |
| **Vase,** Bulbous, Slender Neck, Black, Swirling Brown Lines, Tagliapietra, 10 In. | 1777 |
| **Vase,** Burgundy, Clear, Ercole Barovier, 1960s, 7¼ In. | 1625 |
| **Vase,** Clear Glass, Vertical Panels, Dark Red, Signed Lino Tagliapietra, 9⅞ In. | 2073 |
| **Vase,** Controlled Bubbles, Applied Decorations, Murano, Barovier & Toso, c.1950, 13 x 11 In. | 207 |

| | |
|---|---|
| **Vase,** Green Cut Layers, Bird Figure Stopper, Gino Cenedese Sommerso, 1969, 11 x 7 In. | 2280 |
| **Vase,** Green Iridescent, Controlled Air Bubbles, Sea Urchin Shape, Murano, 3 x 5¾ In. | 63 |
| **Vase,** Handkerchief, Clear, Vertical Green & White Stripes, Venini, 4 In. | 275 |
| **Vase,** Incalmo, Horizontal Band Of Diagonal Lines, Squat, Tagliapietra, 9 x 10 In. | 1625 |
| **Vase,** Incalmo, Lino Tagliapietra, 1988, 14½ x 6¼ In. | 1024 |
| **Vase,** Incalmo, White, Pink Band, Tapered, Squat, Tagliapietra, 10 x 12 In. | 1250 |
| **Vase,** Intarsio, Air Bubbles, Murano, Ercole Barovier, 1960s, 7½ x 4½ In. ............*illus* | 1625 |
| **Vase,** Interior Rub, Milky Glass Bowl, Broad Rim, Applied Blue Handle, 8 x 9 In. | 104 |
| **Vase,** Iridized, Michele Burato, 9 x 8 In. | 625 |
| **Vase,** Millefiori, Bulbous, Matte Finish, Pontil, 5½ In. | 55 |
| **Vase,** Murrine, Aventurine, Renzo Pavanello, Murano, 13 x 6½ In. ............*illus* | 1088 |
| **Vase,** Pezzato, Checkerboard, White & Clear, Controlled Bubbles, Barovier, 8 x 6 In. | 1250 |
| **Vase,** Pezzato, Patchwork, Fulvio Bianconi, Venini, Murano, c.1950, 9¼ In. ......*illus* | 3690 |
| **Vase,** Pink, Rolled Collar, Signed Lino Tagliapietra, 11½ In. | 711 |
| **Vase,** Purple, Blue, Venini, 1985, 8½ x 9 In. | 750 |
| **Vase,** Rust, Blue Swirl, Opaque Trim, Long Neck, 9 In. | 130 |
| **Vase,** Sommerso, Blue In Yellow, Rectangular, F. Tosi, Cenedese, 1959, 9 x 6 In. | 625 |
| **Vase,** Threaded, Fulvio Bianconi, Murano, 1970s, 10¾ x 5½ In. ............*illus* | 1875 |
| **Vase,** Trumpet Shape, Silvered, Green Flowers, Street Scene, 8 x 3¼ In. | 150 |
| **Vase,** White, Murrini, Richard Marquis, 1979, 12½ x 3½ In. | 3750 |

**GLASSES** for the eyes, or spectacles, were mentioned in a manuscript in 1289 and have been used ever since. The first eyeglasses with rigid side pieces were made in London in 1727. Bifocals were invented by Benjamin Franklin in 1785. Lorgnettes were popular in late Victorian times. Opera Glasses are listed in the Opera Glass category.

| | |
|---|---|
| **Coin Silver,** Oval Lenses, Adjustable Slides, Loop Ends, J.A., c.1810, 4⅜ In. ............*illus* | 266 |
| **Folding,** Round Lenses, Gold Filled, Chain, Case, c.1850 | 30 |
| **Lorgnette,** Edwardian, Platinum, Diamond Mounting, Spring Opening Mechanism, 3¼ In. | 1150 |
| **Lorgnette,** Sterling Silver, Scroll Design, Silver Chain, Lozenge Shape Sections, 3¼ x 29 In. | 242 |
| **Sunglasses,** Black Plastic, Wide Arms, Interlocking CCs, Chanel | 385 |
| **Sunglasses,** Oval Lenses, Black Frame, Large Gs, Gucci, Italy | 58 |

**GLIDDEN POTTERY** worked in Alfred, New York, from 1940 to 1957. The pottery made stoneware, dinnerware, and art objects.

| | |
|---|---|
| **Casserole,** Boston Spice, Handled, Lid, 8¼ x 5½ In. | 225 |
| **Planter,** Brown & Black Speckle Glaze, 4 x 4 x 3 In. | 28 |
| **Plate,** Clown, Lifting Weights, Abstract, Marked, 5 x 5 In., Pair | 25 |
| **Tray,** Turquoise, 5 Sections, 14 x 11 In. | 95 |
| **Vase,** Mesa, Green, Stylized Rim, Speckled Glaze, Ringed, Incised, Stamp, 7 In. ....*illus* | 288 |
| **Vase,** Serpentine Shape, Turquoise Mottled, 7 x 3 In. | 65 |
| **Vase,** Squat, Pillow, Turquoise Speckle Glaze, 9 x 6 x 5 In. | 75 |

**GOEBEL** is the mark used by W. Goebel Porzellanfabrik of Oeslau, Germany, now Rodental, Germany. The company was founded by Franz Detleff Goebel and his son, William Goebel, in 1871. It was known as F&W Goebel. Slates, slate pencils, and marbles were made. Soon the company began making porcelain tableware and figurines. Hummel figurines were first made by Goebel in 1935 and are now being made by another company. Goebel is still in business. Old pieces marked *Goebel Hummel* are listed under Hummel in this book.

| | |
|---|---|
| **Bell,** Cardinal Tuck, Red Robe, 6½ In. | 225 |
| **Creamer,** Friar Tuck, 2⅜ In. | 30 |
| **Dresser Box,** Chinese Boy With Teapot, Black Ground, Flowers, Red Teapot, 1920s, 6 In. | 171 |
| **Egg Cup,** Footballer, Kicking Ball, 2½ In., Pair | 90 |
| **Egg,** Daffodil, Yellow, White, Porcelain, 1982, 3⅛ x 2 In. | 10 |
| **Figurine,** Cat, Black, White | 32 |
| **Figurine,** Dog, German Shepherd, Standing, 14 x 11 In. | 150 |
| **Figurine,** Dog, Sheepdog, Sitting, 1970s, 4 In. | 48 |
| **Figurine,** Dog, St. Bernard, 12 x 19 In. | 140 |
| **Figurine,** Duckling, Green, 2 In. | 20 |
| **Figurine,** Flight Into Egypt, Joseph, Mary, Jesus, 2 Piece | 29 |
| **Figurine,** Girl, Nightgown, Dog, 2 Fingers, White | 6 |
| **Figurine,** Marie Antoinette, White, Blue, Pink | 11 |
| **Figurine,** Peasant Girl, Wash Basket, 1978, 4½ In. | 57 |
| **Pitcher,** Figural, Clown, Blue Buttons, Yellow Collar, 7½ In. | 95 |
| **Plate,** Little Fiddler, 1984, 4 In. | 25 |

**Glass-Venetian,** Vase, Murrine, Aventurine, Renzo Pavanello, Murano, 13 x 6½ In.
$1,088

**Glass-Venetian,** Vase, Pezzato, Patchwork, Fulvio Bianconi, Venini, Murano, c.1950, 9¼ In.
$3,690

**Glass-Venetian,** Vase, Threaded, Fulvio Bianconi, Murano, 1970s, 10¾ x 5½ In.
$1,875

**Glasses,** Coin Silver, Oval Lenses, Adjustable Slides, Loop Ends, J.A., c.1810, 4⅜ In.
$266

Conestoga Auction Co., Inc.

**Glidden,** Vase, Mesa, Green, Stylized Rim, Speckled Glaze, Ringed, Incised, Stamp, 7 In.
$288

Humler & Nolan

**Goldscheider,** Figurine, Chloe, Maiden, Terra-Cotta, c.1890, 37 x 11 In.
$1,320

DuMouchelles Art Gallery

| | |
|---|---|
| **Salt & Pepper,** Owl, Orange Beak, White | 30 |
| **Sugar,** Friar Tuck, 4¾ In. | 58 |

**GOLDSCHEIDER** was founded by Friedrich Goldscheider in Vienna in 1885. The family left Vienna in 1938 and the factory was taken over by the Germans. Goldscheider started factories in England and in Trenton, New Jersey. The New Jersey factory started in 1940 as Goldscheider–U.S.A. In 1941 it became Goldscheider-Everlast Corporation. From 1947 to 1953 it was Goldcrest Ceramics Corporation. In 1950 the Vienna plant was returned to Mr. Goldscheider and the company continues in business. The Trenton, New Jersey, business, called Goldscheider of Vienna, imports all of the pieces.

| | |
|---|---|
| **Boy,** Terra-Cotta, Fishing Pole, 17 x 22¼ In. | 2187 |
| **Bust,** Black Skin, Bronze Curls, Pearl Necklace, 6⅜ In. | 62 |
| **Bust,** Terra-Cotta, Banjo Player, Black Skin, Hat, 29½ In. | 6400 |
| **Figure,** Terra-Cotta, Man, Black Skin, Straw Hat, White Shirt, Tray, 27½ x 17 In. | 5313 |
| **Figurine,** Boy, Standing, Hands In Pockets, Terra-Cotta, Marked, c.1900, 20 In. | 423 |
| **Figurine,** Butterfly Girl, Signed Lorenzl, 12 In. | 2040 |
| **Figurine,** Chloe, Maiden, Terra-Cotta, c.1890, 37 x 11 In. .................................*illus* | 1320 |
| **Figurine,** Dog, Borzoi, Gray, White, Lying Down, Crossed Legs, Marked, 6½ x 13 In. | 148 |
| **Figurine,** Playing Piano, 27¾ In. | 531 |
| **Vase,** Earthenware, Gourd, Branches, Nude Girl, Shell, Infant, 35 In. | 1599 |
| **Vase,** White, Black, Blue Flowers, Cherubs, 5½ In. | 61 |

**GOLF,** *see Sports category.*

**GONDER CERAMIC ARTS, INC.,** was opened by Lawton Gonder in 1941 in Zanesville, Ohio. Gonder made high-grade pottery decorated with flambe, drip, gold crackle, and Chinese crackle glazes. The factory closed in 1957. From 1946 to 1954, Gonder also operated the Elgee Pottery, which made ceramic lamp bases.

| | |
|---|---|
| **Ewer,** Turquoise, Art Deco, 8 x 6 In. | 25 |
| **Jar,** Lid, Chinese Dragon, Gold Crackle, Base, 9¼ In. | 160 |
| **Planter,** Blue, 10¾ x 5 In. | 40 |
| **Vase,** Figural, Peacock, Gold Luster, 11¼ In., Pair | 29 |
| **Vase,** Flower Shape, Green, Round Base, 9 In. | 11 |
| **Vase,** Purple, Flower Shape, 8 x 6 In. | 8 |
| **Vase,** Sponge Blue, 7 In. | 30 |

**GOOFUS GLASS** was made from about 1900 to 1920 by many American factories. It was originally painted gold, red, green, bronze, pink, purple, or other bright colors. Many pieces are found today with flaking paint, and this lowers the value.

| | |
|---|---|
| **Bowl,** Gold & Red Grapes, Impressed, Footed, Scalloped, 7½ In. | 21 |
| **Bowl,** Gold, Red, Strawberries, Vining, Scalloped Edge, 9¾ x 2½ In. | 42 |
| **Bowl,** Grapes & Leaves, Sawtooth Edge, Footed, c.1900, 10 x 5 In. | 18 |
| **Bowl,** Roses In Snow, Lattice, c.1900, 9 In. | 20 |
| **Nappy,** Heart Shape, Red Roses, Loop Handles, 6 x 6 x 1 In. | 27 |
| **Plate,** Gold & Red, Cherries, Leaves, c.1910, 11 In. | 45 |
| **Powder Jar,** Puffy Roses, Gold, 3½ In. | 15 |
| **Powder Jar,** Red, Gold, Cameo, 3½ In. | 38 |
| **Rose Bowl,** Puffy Rose, Milk Glass, Pink, Green, 5½ In. | 38 |
| **Rose Bowl,** Red, Gold Trim, c.1900, 3 x 8½ In. | 46 |
| **Sugar,** Red & Gold, Leaves, Sawtooth Rim, Square, 5 x 5 x 2 In. | 43 |
| **Vase,** Bird On Grape, Oval, c.1910, 9 In. | 63 |
| **Vase,** Peacock, Gold, Black, Red, Oval, Flared Rim, 10½ In. | 65 |
| **Vase,** Pink & Gold, Open Rose, Pinched Neck, c.1924, 9½ In. | 40 |
| **Vase,** Red & Gold, Grapes, Paneled, Geometric Design, 7 In. | 35 |

**GOUDA,** Holland, has been a pottery center since the seventeenth century. Two firms, the Zenith pottery, established in the eighteenth century, and the Zuid-Hollandsche pottery, made the brightly colored art pottery marked *Gouda* from 1898 to about 1964. Other factories followed. Many pieces featured Art Nouveau or Art Deco designs. Pattern names in Dutch, listed here, seem strange to English-speaking collectors.

| | |
|---|---|
| **Ashtray,** Rosario Pattern, Windmill, Sails Turn, 4¼ In. | 81 |
| **Candlestick,** Red, Blue, Marked, 156, Purdah, 1920s, 19⅞ In., Pair. | 127 |
| **Charger,** Stylized Flowers, Leaves, Multicolor, Henri Breetvelt, c.1925, 16½ In. ..............*illus* | 288 |
| **Charger,** Thistle, Green, Blue, Dark Red, Gold, Gloss Glaze, Impressed, c.1899, 12 In. | 431 |

| | |
|---|---|
| **Vase,** Beige Ground, Flowers, Leaves, Gloss Glaze, Long Neck, Tapered, Holland, 13 In. | 369 |
| **Vase,** Blue Mums, Leaves, Marked, Jana, Holland, c.1922, 16¾ In. | 208 |
| **Vase,** Double Gourd, Rust, Cobalt Blue, Amber, Green Mottled Bands, Marked, 21½ In. | 127 |
| **Vase,** Flowers, Leaves, Blue, Green, Ivory, 2 Handles, c.1906, 10¾ In. ...............*illus* | 246 |
| **Vase,** Pansies, Multicolor, Incised Mark, O.J., 12¼ In. | 230 |
| **Vase,** Regina Chryso, Painted, Rust Red Mums, Multicolor Patches, Hoop Handle, 11¼ In. | 288 |
| **Vase,** Winter Scene, Canal, Barge, Windmill, Glossy, Handles, Signed Nil. Apol., 12 In. | 173 |

**GRANITEWARE** is enameled tin or iron used to make kitchenware since the 1870s. Earlier graniteware was green or turquoise blue, with white spatters. The later ware was gray with white spatters. Reproductions are being made in all colors. There is a second definition of the word *graniteware* meaning a blue speckled pottery. Only the metal graniteware is listed here.

| | |
|---|---|
| **Coffeepot,** Blue, White Swirl, Hinged Lid, 9¼ In. | 200 |
| **Coffeepot,** Gray, Gray Swirls, Hinged Lid, 8½ In. | 45 |
| **Coffeepot,** Green & White Swirl, Tapered Body, Hinged Lid, 9¼ In. ...........*illus* | 248 |
| **Coffeepot,** Green, White, Hinged Lid, 10 In. | 265 |
| **Double Boiler,** Cream & Green, Lid, 5½ x 8¾ In. | 25 |
| **Funnel,** Robin's-Egg Blue, White Interior, Rolled Edge, 6 In. | 45 |
| **Grater,** Robin's-Egg Blue, White Speckled, Wire Legs & Handle, 8 In. | 65 |
| **Kettle,** Lid, Berlin Style, Green & White, Bail Handle, 5½ In. ...........*illus* | 142 |
| **Measure,** Cobalt Blue, White Swirl, 4¼ x 5½ In. | 135 |
| **Mixing Bowl,** Blue & White Swirl, 9¾ x 4¾ In. | 52 |
| **Pail,** Brown, White Speckled, Bail Handle, Ridges, 4 x 4½ In. | 32 |
| **Pitcher,** Water, Red & White Swirl, Handle ...........*illus* | 3600 |
| **Roasting Pan,** Black, White Speckled, Lid, 16 x 12 x 7 In. | 70 |
| **Slop Bucket,** Bail Handle, White, Black Trim, Label, Flintstone, 15 In. | 90 |
| **Spoon,** Robin's-Egg Blue, White Speckled, Hole For Hanging, 6 In., 6 Piece | 35 |
| **Strainer,** Black, White Speckled, 10¾ In. | 39 |
| **Strainer,** Gray, Handle, 6¼ In. Diam., 4-In. Handle | 27 |
| **Strainer,** White, Speckled, 3-Footed, 8 x 3 In. | 20 |
| **Tub,** Brown, Gray Interior, Handles, Pedestal Base, 18 x 13 In. | 98 |
| **Water Can,** Blue & White, Raised Star, Top & Side Handle, 15 In. | 95 |

**GREENTOWN** glass was made by the Indiana Tumbler and Goblet Company of Greentown, Indiana, from 1894 to 1903. In 1899, the factory became part of National Glass Company. A variety of pressed glass was made. Additional pieces may be found in other categories, such as Chocolate Glass, Holly Amber, Milk Glass, and Pressed Glass.

| | |
|---|---|
| **Austrian,** Compote, Scalloped Rim, 7 x 8 In. | 70 |
| **Cactus,** Compote, Scalloped Rim, Chocolate, 5½ In. | 73 |
| **Cactus,** Cruet, Chocolate, Paneled, 5 In. | 85 |
| **Cactus,** Tumbler, Chocolate, 4 In. | 14 |
| **Dewey,** Mug, Amber, Footed, 3½ In. | 16 |
| **Holly Amber,** Dish, Opalescent, 7½ In. | 201 |
| **Leaf Bracket,** Dish, 3-Footed, Handle, 3⅝ In. | 48 |
| **Wildrose & Bowknot,** Tumbler, Footed, Frosted, 3 In. | 72 |

**GRUEBY FAIENCE COMPANY** of Boston, Massachusetts, was founded in 1894 by William H. Grueby. Grueby Pottery Company was incorporated in 1907. In 1909, Grueby Faience went bankrupt. Then William Grueby founded the Grueby Faience and Tile Company. Grueby Pottery closed about 1911. The tile company worked until 1920. Garden statuary, art pottery, and architectural tiles were made until 1920. The company developed a green matte glaze that was so popular it was copied by many other factories making a less expensive type of pottery. This eventually led to the financial problems of the pottery. Cuerda seca and cuenca are techniques explained in the Tile category. The company name was often used as the mark, and slight changes in the form help date a piece.

| | |
|---|---|
| **Jardiniere,** Green Matte, 19 x 12½ In. | 10980 |
| **Scarab,** Green Mottled Matte Glaze, 3 x 4 In. | 1830 |
| **Tile,** Blue Jay, Frame, 6 x 6 In. | 2074 |
| **Tile,** Geese, Entwined, On Island, Green Trees, Cuenca, Metal Mount, 4 x 4 In. | 1080 |
| **Tile,** House, Cypress Trees, Sky, Green, Blue, Yellow, Ocher, Cream, Square, 4¼ In. | 1625 |
| **Tile,** Musician, Yellow, Blue, 6 In. | 489 |
| **Tile,** The Pines, Landscape, Trees, Blue Mountains, Boston, c.1910, 1¼ x 6 In. | 875 |
| **Tile,** Tulip, Leaves, Yellow Green, c.1905, 6 x 6 In. | 687 |
| **Tile,** Turtle Under Leaf Garland, Yellow, Brown, Green, Cuenca, Kichi Yamada, 6 x 6 In. | 1476 |
| **Tile,** Viking Ship, Green, White, Frame, 8 x 8 In. | 2875 |

G

**Gouda,** Charger, Stylized Flowers, Leaves, Multicolor, Henri Breetvelt, c.1925, 16½ In. $288

Humler & Nolan

**Gouda,** Vase, Flowers, Leaves, Blue, Green, Ivory, 2 Handles, c.1906, 10¾ In. $246

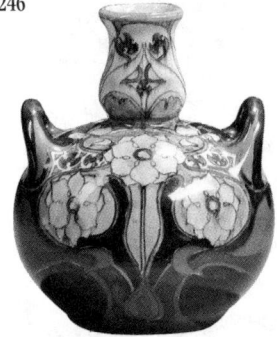

Skinner Auctioneers & Appraisers

**Good Gouda**

Potteries in the Gouda area include ADCO, Ed. Antheunis, Arnhem, Brantjes, De Distel, De Jong, De Kroon, De Porceleyne Fles, De Rozenboom, De Ysel, De Zwing, Flora, GeWi, Goedewaagen, Haga, Huisenga, Ivora, Kennermerland, Kohler, Mobach, Nieuw Rozenburg, PBD, Purmerend, Ram, Regina, Rembrandt, Rijn, Rozenburg, Schoonhoven, St. Lukas, Talos, Tiko, Zaalberg, and Zenith.

**Graniteware,** Coffeepot, Green & White Swirl, Tapered Body, Hinged Lid, 9¼ In. $248

Conestoga Auction Co., Inc.

**Graniteware,** Kettle, Lid, Berlin Style, Green & White, Bail Handle, 5½ In. $142

Conestoga Auction Co., Inc.

**Graniteware,** Pitcher, Water, Red & White Swirl, Handle $3,600

> ### TIP
> *Graniteware pieces made in the 1950s were lighter in weight and brighter in color than early-nineteenth-century wares.*

| | |
|---|---:|
| **Trivet,** Pottery, Green Matte, Gilt Bronze, 7 x 7 In. | 1464 |
| **Vase,** Ball Shape, Leaves, Green Glaze, c.1905, 3¾ x 4 In. | 3750 |
| **Vase,** Blue Glaze, Tapered, Impressed Mark, 12 In. | 1150 |
| **Vase,** Daffodil, 2 Color, 5½ x 11 In. | 7000 |
| **Vase,** Green Matte Glaze, Alligatored, Impressed Mark, 9¾ In. | 1304 |
| **Vase,** Green Matte Glaze, Leaves, Buds, Pinched Rim, Partial Paper Label, c.1904, 7¼ In. | 1169 |
| **Vase,** Green Matte Glaze, Leaves, Yellow Buds, Pinched Rim, W. Post, Boston, c.1910, 8 In. | 1920 |
| **Vase,** Green Matte Glaze, Round, Impressed Logo, 4½ In. | 920 |
| **Vase,** Green Matte, Bulbous, Leaves, 10 x 8½ In. | 7320 |
| **Vase,** Green Matte, Leaves, Sprouts, 9⅕ x 13 In. | 6710 |
| **Vase,** Green Matte, Water Lily, Garlic Mouth, c.1900, 8 In. | 1440 |
| **Vase,** Irises, Carved, Curdled Blue Glaze, Ruth Erickson, c.1905, 14¾ x 9 In. ......*illus* | 32500 |
| **Vase,** Kendrick, Leaf Green Matte Glaze, Florence S. Liley, 11¾ In. | 8338 |
| **Vase,** Lobed, Yellow Buds, Green Ground, 1905, 8¼ x 4½ In. | 2000 |
| **Vase,** Mustard Matte Glaze, Flared, Inward Folded Rim, 3 x 5½ In. | 458 |
| **Vase,** Mustard Matte, George Kendrick, 8 x 12 In. | 14640 |
| **Vase,** Overlapping Leaves, Green Matte Glaze, Marie Seaman, c.1905, 12 x 8 In. ......*illus* | 8125 |
| **Vase,** Yellow Buds, Lobed, Green, Scalloped Rim, c.1905, 8 x 4½ In. | 2000 |
| **Vase,** Yellow Matte Glaze, Alternating Leaves, Buds, Pinched Rim, Marie Seaman, 7 In. | 2280 |

**GUN,** *see Toy.*

**GUSTAVSBERG** ceramics factory was founded in 1827 near Stockholm, Sweden. It is best known to collectors for its twentieth-century artwares, especially Argenta, a green stoneware with silver inlay. The company was sold in the 1990s.

Gustafsberg

| | |
|---|---:|
| **Dish,** Flower Inlay, Argenta, Scalloped Edge, 4 In. | 65 |
| **Figurine,** Girl, Mei, Lisa Larson, Foil Label, 1970s, 3¾ In. | 98 |
| **Tray,** Bouquet Inlay, Argenta, 5 In. Diam. | 100 |
| **Vase,** Blood Red, Green Speckled, Shouldered, Marked, 8 x 5 In. | 850 |
| **Vase,** Blue Flambe Glaze, 3 Inlay Crowns, Argenta, 5 x 3 x 3 In. | 75 |
| **Vase,** Flower Inlay, Argenta, Flared, Footed, 5 In. | 250 |
| **Vase,** Hashtag Inlay, Argenta, Cylindrical, 3½ In. | 80 |
| **Vase,** Stylized Fish, Blue Matte Glaze, Paper Label, Kage, 5 In. | 293 |
| **Vase,** Variegated Brown Glaze, Striped, Shouldered, S. Lindberg, 4 In. | 167 |

**HAEGER POTTERIES, INC.,** Dundee, Illinois, started making commercial artwares in 1914. Early pieces were marked with the name *Haeger* written over an *H*. About 1938, the mark *Royal Haeger* was used in honor of Royal Hickman, a designer at the factory. The firm is still making florist wares and lamp bases. See also the Royal Hickman category.

Haeger

| | |
|---|---:|
| **Ashtray,** Green Matte, Open Mouth Rim, Eyes, Teeth, 6¾ In. | 52 |
| **Bowl,** Aqua, Curved, c.1949, 4 x 15 In. | 20 |
| **Bowl,** Lid, Green Matte, Frog Shape, 6¾ In. | 92 |
| **Bowl,** Pedestal, Black, Orange, Yellow, Red, Abstract Striping, 4¼ x 8¼ In. | 12 |
| **Figurine,** Gazelle, Light Blue, c.1986, 19 In. | 83 |
| **Figurine,** Intertwined Couple, Arched Backs, Gown, White, 16½ x 9 In. | 48 to 60 |
| **Figurine,** Leopard, Brown Mottled, Green, 8¾ In. | 96 |
| **Flower Frog,** Mushrooms, Frog, Light Blue, 10½ x 17 In. | 738 |
| **Vase,** Amethyst Crackle, c.1961, 11 In. | 24 |
| **Vase,** Art Deco, Doe, Leaping Over Tall Grass, Marked, 15 In. ......*illus* | 108 |
| **Vase,** Brown Abstract Swirled Splotches, Orange Ground, Cylindrical, 12 In. | 35 |
| **Vase,** Cornucopia, Girl, Blue, Green, 8 x 7¼ In. | 18 |
| **Vase,** Sailfish, Marked, Brown Drip Glaze, 1942, 13 x 8 In. | 35 |
| **Vase,** Seashell, Wave, Mauve, Blue, c.1940, 7¾ In. | 47 |
| **Vase,** Stoneware, Brown, White Swirl, 1950s, 9½ In. | 18 to 48 |
| **Vase,** Tropical Leaf, Relief, Foil Label, Peach Glaze, 7 x 8 In. | 105 |
| **Vase,** Wide Flaring Rim, Orange Peel Glaze, Cylindrical, c.1970, 9¼ Diam. | 49 |

**HALF-DOLL,** *see Pincushion Doll category.*

**HALL CHINA COMPANY** started in East Liverpool, Ohio, in 1903. The firm made many types of wares. Collectors search for the Hall teapots made from the 1920s to the 1950s. The dinnerware of the same period, especially Autumn Leaf pattern, is also popular. The Hall China Company merged with Homer Laughlin China Company in 2010. Autumn Leaf pattern dishes are listed in their own category in this book.

HALL'S SUPERIOR QUALITY KITCHENWARE

| | |
|---|---:|
| **Arizona,** Bowl, Vegetable, 8 x 8 In. | 31 |

G

| | |
|---|---|
| **Arizona,** Creamer, 6 Oz., 3 In. ................................................... | 21 |
| **Arizona,** Plate, Dinner, 11 ⅛ In. ............................................. | 8 |
| **Blue Garden,** Casserole, Lid, 8 In. ........................................ | 48 |
| **Cactus,** Coffeepot, Lid, 10 Cup, 7 ¾ In. ................................ | 47 |
| **Cameo Rose,** Creamer, 6 Oz., 3 In. ...................................... | 14 |
| **Cameo Rose,** Cup & Saucer .................................................. | 8 |
| **Cameo Rose,** Gravy Boat, Underplate.................................. | 30 |
| **Cameo Rose,** Plate, Dinner, 10 ¼ In. .................................. | 29 |
| **Cameo Rose,** Plate, Salad, 7 ⅜ In. ....................................... | 10 |
| **Cameo Rose,** Platter, Oval, 11 ½ In. ............................ | 31 to 35 |
| **Cameo Rose,** Salt & Pepper................................................. | 43 |
| **Dutch Couple,** Coffeepot, Lid, 8 Cup, 5 ¼ In. ................... | 35 |
| **Frost Flowers,** Cup & Saucer, Footed. ............................... | 7 |
| **Golden Glo,** Casserole, Lid, Basketweave, 8 In. ................. | 95 |
| **Golden Glo,** Casserole, Lid, Basketweave, 9 In. ................. | 95 |
| **Hallcraft White,** Cup & Saucer, Footed.............................. | 15 |
| **Hallcraft White,** Eggcup, Double, 4 ¼ In. .......................... | 41 |
| **Hallcraft White,** Plate, Dinner, 11 ⅛ In. ........................... | 55 |
| **Harlequin,** Platter, 17 ¼ In. ................................................ | 82 |
| **Harlequin,** Platter, 18 ⅛ In. ................................................ | 65 |
| **Harlequin,** Platter, Round, 15 In. ....................................... | 65 |
| **Harlequin,** Platter, Round, 17 In. ....................................... | 82 |
| **Heirloom Pink,** Plate, Bread & Butter, 6 ⅝ In. .................. | 5 |
| **Heirloom Pink,** Sugar & Creamer........................................ | 33 |
| **Moderne Ivory,** Teapot, Lid, 6 Cup .................................... | 65 |
| **Mt. Vernon,** Bowl, Vegetable, Lid, Oval, 9 ¼ In. ................ | 18 |
| **Mt. Vernon,** Cup & Saucer, Footed ..................................... | 12 |
| **Mt. Vernon,** Plate, Bread & Butter, 6 ⅜ In. ...................... | 6 |
| **Mt. Vernon,** Plate, Dinner, 10 ⅛ In. ................................... | 15 |
| **Mt. Vernon,** Platter, 13 ½ In. .............................................. | 28 |
| **Mulberry,** Platter, Oval, 17 In. ........................................... | 47 |
| **Old Rose,** Creamer, 7 Oz., 3 ¼ In. ...................................... | 12 |
| **Orange Poppy,** Sugar & Creamer ........................................ | 90 |
| **Pinecone,** Creamer, 8 Oz., 4 In. .......................................... | 28 |
| **Pinecone,** Cup & Saucer, Footed ......................................... | 23 |
| **Pinecone,** Jug, 40 Oz., 5 ¾ In. ............................................ | 27 |
| **Pinecone,** Plate, Dinner, 11 ⅛ In. ....................................... | 58 |
| **Pinecone,** Platter, 12 ¾ In. .................................................. | 60 |
| **Pinecone,** Soup, Dish, Lugged, 9 In. .................................. | 16 |
| **Refrigerator Ware,** Bowl, Lid, Blue, Yellow, Westinghouse, 1950s, 2 ¾ x 3 ¾ In.......................... | 20 |
| **Rose Parade,** Bowl, Vegetable, 9 In. ................................... | 52 |
| **Rose Parade,** Casserole, Lid, Tab Handles, 2 ½ Qt. ............ | 62 |
| **Rose Parade,** Casserole, Round, Lid, 2 ½ Qt....................... | 41 |
| **Rose Parade,** Casserole, Tab Handles, 2 Qt. ....................... | 62 |
| **Rose Parade,** Drip Jar, Lid, Tab Handles, 2 ½ In. .............. | 33 |
| **Rose Parade,** Sugar & Creamer............................................ | 200 |
| **Rose Parade,** Teapot, 6 Cup ................................................ | 64 |
| **Rose White,** Casserole, Lid, 8 In. ........................................ | 21 |
| **Rose White,** Jug, 5 In........................................................... | 41 |
| **Rose White,** Saltshaker, 4 In. .............................................. | 14 |
| **Rose White,** Sugar ............................................................... | 25 |
| **Royal Rose,** Bean Pot, Lid, 4 ¼ In. ..................................... | 20 |
| **Royal Rose,** Casserole, Lid, 2 Qt. ....................................... | 54 |
| **Royal Rose,** Salt & Pepper................................................... | 41 |
| **Royal Rose,** Teapot, Lid, 3 Cup, 4 ¾ In. ............................ | 98 |
| **Serenade,** Bowl, Vegetable, 9 In. ........................................ | 35 |
| **Serenade,** Cup & Saucer, Footed ........................................ | 20 |
| **Serenade,** Gravy Boat ......................................................... | 25 |
| **Serenade,** Plate, Bread & Butter, 6 ¼ In. ........................... | 7 |
| **Serenade,** Platter, Oval, 11 In. ........................................... | 39 |
| **Silhouette,** Coaster, 3 In. .................................................... | 7 |
| **Silhouette,** Mug.................................................................. | 41 |
| **Silhouette,** Sugar................................................................ | 21 |
| **Silhouette,** Teapot, Banded, 8 Cup.................................... | 128 |
| **Springtime,** Cup & Saucer, Footed ..................................... | 7 |
| **Springtime,** Gravy Boat....................................................... | 21 |

**Grueby,** Vase, Irises, Carved, Curdled Blue Glaze, Ruth Erickson, c.1905, 14 ¾ x 9 In.
$32,500

Rago Arts & Auction Center

**Grueby,** Vase, Overlapping Leaves, Green Matte Glaze, Marie Seaman, c.1905, 12 x 8 In.
$8,125

Rago Arts & Auction Center

**Haeger,** Vase, Art Deco, Doe, Leaping Over Tall Grass, Marked, 15 In.
$108

Capo Auction

H

**Hall,** Teapot, Automobile, Art Deco, Marked Hall's Superior Quality Kitchenware, 4 ½ x 9 x 4 In. $300

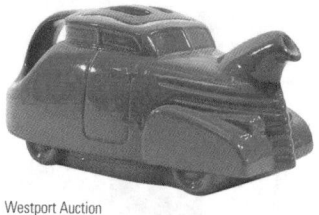

Westport Auction

**Halloween,** Basket, Candy, Pumpkin Head, Glass, Painted, 7 ½ In. $118

Morphy Auctions

**Halloween,** Toy, Witch, Composition, Black Hat & Cape, Tin Base, Wheels, Windup, 5 In. $413

Bertoia Auctions

| | |
|---|---:|
| **Springtime,** Plate, Bread & Butter, 6 ¼ In. | 4 |
| **Springtime,** Soup, Dish, 8 ½ In. | 7 |
| **Teapot,** Automobile, Art Deco, Marked Hall's Superior Quality Kitchenware, 4 ½ x 9 x 4 In. ...*illus* | 300 |
| **Teapot,** Rhythm, Pink, Lid, 6 In. | 62 |
| **Tomorrow's Classic,** Bowl, Cereal, 6 In. | 12 |
| **Tulip,** Bowl, Vegetable, Oval, 10 In. | 15 |
| **Tulip,** Creamer, 8 Oz., 3 In. | 33 |
| **Tulip,** Platter, Oval, 13 In. | 23 |

**HALLOWEEN** is an ancient holiday that has changed in the last 200 years. The jack-o'-lantern, witches on broomsticks, and orange decorations seem to be twentieth-century creations. Collectors started to become serious about collecting Halloween-related items in the late 1970s. The papier-mache decorations, now replaced by plastic, and old costumes are in demand.

| | |
|---|---:|
| **Banner,** Cat Faces, Black, Orange, Die Cut, 7 x 7-In. Faces, 50 In. | 135 |
| **Basket,** Candy, Pumpkin Head, Glass, Painted, 7 ½ In. ...*illus* | 118 |
| **Candy Holder,** Cardboard, Girl, Costume, Rosen Of Rhode Island, c.1940, 4 x 3 In. | 65 |
| **Cookie Cutter,** Tin, Box, 6 Piece | 20 |
| **Costume,** Archie, Jumpsuit Style, Red, Yellow, Blue, Rayon, Size Small | 30 |
| **Costume,** Owls, Witches, Black Cats, Orange, Full Length, 40 In. | 207 |
| **Decoration,** Friendly Ghost, House, Mouse, Jack-O'-Lantern, Die Cut, c.1960, 12 x 9 In. | 16 |
| **Decoration,** Witch's Hat, Witch On Broom, Cat, Lithographed, Tassel, USA, c.1935, 15 In. | 35 |
| **Eye Glasses,** Pumpkins, Witches, Foster Grant, 1950s | 35 |
| **Game,** Crystal Fortunes, Fortune Telling, Cardboard, Luhrs Co., 12 x 4 ½ In. | 70 |
| **Jack-O'-Lantern,** Parade, Tin, Painted Orange, Black, Green, Ohio Art Co., 8 ½ In. | 767 |
| **Jack-O'-Lantern,** Witch, Grinning, Black Hat, Insert Eyes, Composition, Germany, 5 In. | 1121 |
| **Jiggler,** Rubber, Pumpkin Man, Orange, Black, Ben Cooper, Marked, 1973, 7 In. | 68 |
| **Lantern,** Grinning Log Face, Composition, Round, Slide Back, c.1920, 5 x 3 In. | 173 |
| **Lantern,** Pumpkin, Papier-Mache, F.N. Burt Co., 5 ½ x 6 In. | 160 |
| **Lantern,** Tabby Cat, Composition, Painted Features, Paper Insert Eyes, Mouth, 4 In. | 1888 |
| **Mask,** Butterfly, Papier-Mache, Green, c.1950. | 49 |
| **Noisemaker,** Rattle, Cats, Pumpkins, Lithograph, USA | 28 |
| **Nut Cup,** Pumpkin Shape, Papier-Mache, Orange, 2 ½ In. | 35 |
| **Placecard Holder,** Black Cat, Arched Back, Celluloid, Japan, 2 ½ x 1 ½ In. | 48 |
| **Postcard,** Baby, Green Sleep Attire, Jack-O'-Lantern, Check Border, Freixas, Winsch, 3 x 5 In. | 90 |
| **Postcard,** Black Fur Cat, Girl, Riding Broom | 90 |
| **Postcard,** Boy, Girl Holding Broom, Pumpkins, Winsch, 1915 | 90 |
| **Postcard,** Frightened Black Children, Ghost, Pumpkin At Window | 240 |
| **Postcard,** Girl, Pumpkin Creatures, Dark Rose Border, Schmucker, Winsch, c.1913 | 1140 |
| **Postcard,** Hallowe'en Gambols, Clown, Witch, Frogs Jumping Rope, Winsch, c.1913, 3 x 5 In. | 150 |
| **Postcard,** Hallowe'en Gambols, Masks, Girl, Big Orange Bow, Winsch, c.1913, 3 x 5 In. | 270 |
| **Postcard,** Hallowe'en Jollity, Witch In Car, Owls, Yellow, Check Border, Winsch, c.1913 | 150 |
| **Postcard,** Hallowe'en Surprises, Jack-In-The-Box, 2 Clowns, Winsch, c.1913, 3 x 5 In. | 300 |
| **Postcard,** Pumpkin Girls, Googly Eyes, Holding Broom, Barton & Spooner, Germany | 49 |
| **Postcard,** Woman, White Cloak, Pumpkin Faces, Winsch, 1912 | 300 |
| **Skeleton,** Composition, Glass Eyes, Spring Arms & Legs, c.1950, 7 In. | 95 |
| **Squeaker,** Man, Jack-O'-Lantern Head, Pressed Feet, Head, Germany, 8 ½ In. | 708 |
| **Tambourine,** Witch, Face, Tin, Kirchhoff Co., 1930s, 6 ¼ In. | 65 |
| **Tea Set,** Cup & Saucer, Teapot, Sugar & Creamer, Bisque, Japan, 1920s, 13 Piece | 325 |
| **Toy,** Witch, Composition, Black Hat & Cape, Tin Base, Wheels, Windup, 5 In. ...*illus* | 413 |

**HAMPSHIRE** pottery was made in Keene, New Hampshire, between 1871 and 1923. Hampshire developed a line of colored glazed wares as early as 1883, including a Royal Worcester–type pink, olive green, blue, and mahogany. Pieces are marked with the printed mark or the impressed name *Hampshire Pottery* or *J.S.T. & Co., Keene, N.H.* Many pieces were marked with city names and sold as souvenirs.

| | |
|---|---:|
| **Bowl,** Blue Matte Ground, White Leaf, 6 In. | 94 |
| **Bowl,** Green Matte Glaze, Handles, 2 ¾ x 4 ½ In. | 218 |
| **Bowl,** Low, Green Matte, Inserted Rim, 5 ¾ In. | 80 |
| **Chamberstick,** Green Matte Glaze, Keene, N.H., 1904-16, 6 ½ In., Pair | 330 |
| **Lamp,** Leaves, Buds, Green, c.1910, 27 x 9 In. | 2250 |
| **Vase,** Arts & Crafts, Field Corn, Husk, Raised, Green, 5 ⅞ In. | 288 |
| **Vase,** Blue Matte Glaze, Arched Lines, Impressed, 9 In. | 420 |
| **Vase,** Blue Mottled Matte Glaze, Cylinder, 7 x 4 In. | 240 |
| **Vase,** Cornhusk, Green Matte Glaze, Impressed, 5 ¾ x 5 ½ In. | 288 |
| **Vase,** Dark Blue Matte Glaze, Geometric Designs, 6 ½ In. | 330 |

| | |
|---|---|
| Vase, Embossed, Green Matte Glaze, Marked, 8 x 7 In. | 520 |
| Vase, Green Matte Glaze, Bulbous Base, Narrow Neck, 9 ½ In. | 360 |
| Vase, Green Matte Glaze, Long Neck, Molded Leaves, Incised, c.1910, 9 In. | 420 |
| Vase, Green Matte Glaze, Lug Handles, 7 ½ In. | 420 |
| Vase, Green Matte Glaze, Relief Leaves, Marked M With Circle, 6 ¾ In. | 338 |
| Vase, Green Matte Glaze, Stylized Leaves, Inscribed, c.1910, 7 x 4 In. | 426 |
| Vase, Leaves, Buds, Blue Glaze, 7 In. | 422 |
| Vase, Molded Leaves, Green Matte Glaze, Impressed, M In Circle Mark, 4 ¼ In. | 316 |
| Vase, Olive Green Glaze, Arrowhead Leaves, Drop Shape, Cadmon Robertston, 3 ½ In. | 219 |

HANDEL glass was made by Philip Handel working in Meriden, Connecticut, from 1885 and in New York City from 1893 to 1933. The firm made art glass and other types of lamps. Handel shades were made not only of leaded glass in a style reminiscent of Tiffany but also of reverse painted glass. Handel also made vases and other glass objects.

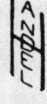

| | |
|---|---|
| Chandelier, 3-Light, Diamond Border, Slag Glass Shade, Metal Overlay, c.1910, 9 x 22 In. | 3000 |
| Lamp, 2-Light, Chipped Ice Shade, Enameled Mosserine, Green, Ivy Rim, Bronze Base, 14 In. | 3220 |
| Lamp, 3-Light, Art Deco, Black, Orange, Amber, Yellow, Wavy Bands, 20 ¾ In. | 2488 |
| Lamp, 3-Light, Leaded Ruby Flowers, Leaves, Bronze, Narrow Base, Acorn Pulls, 19 x 23 In. | 2242 |
| Lamp, 3-Light, Sailboats, Dusk, Sun, Water, Reflections, Gargoyles On Base, 17 ¾ In. | 7702 |
| Lamp, 3-Light, Twilight & Flowers Shade, 16 In. | 1968 |
| Lamp, 5-Light, Shade, Cone Shape, Striated Green & Brown, Leaf Shape Panels, 24 ⅜ In. | 3555 |
| Lamp, Bamboo Overlay, Slag Glass, Fabric Label, c.1910, 13 x 12 In. | 1375 |
| Lamp, Birds Of Paradise Domed Shade, Signed, 3 Legs, Leaf Feet, 24 ½ In. | 9480 |
| Lamp, Bronze Water Lily Base, 3 Slag Glass Shades, 2 Bud Shades, Signed, c.1910, 16 In. | 4182 |
| Lamp, Bronze, Enameled Mosserine Shade, 57 In. | 1652 |
| Lamp, Carmel Slag Glass, 8-Panel, Pine Needles, Metal Overlay, 18 ¼ In. | 2284 |
| Lamp, Chipped Glass, Domed Shade, Copper, Stamped, c.1910, 25 x 18 In. ...........illus | 3000 |
| Lamp, Chipped Ice Shade, Multicolor Flower Band, Gold Ground, Cloth Label, 23 ¼ x 18 In. | 2760 |
| Lamp, Chipped Ice Shade, Multicolor Flowers, 2 Butterflies, Acanthus Leaf Vase, 24 In. | 11850 |
| Lamp, Chipped Ice Shade, Overlapping Leaves, Tapered, Patinated Metal Base, 18 In. | 5192 |
| Lamp, Chipped Ice Shade, Windmills, Shore At Sunset, Spread Foot Base, 15 In. | 1458 |
| Lamp, Cone Shape Shade, Green Leaves, Green & Blue Ground, 18 In. | 6792 |
| Lamp, Daisy, Pansy Band, Yellow Domed Shade, Metal Base, c.1910, 22 x 14 In. | 3250 |
| Lamp, Desk, Beach Sunset, 6 Panels, Orange, Green, Palm Tree Overlay, Curved Arm, 13 In. | 1422 |
| Lamp, Desk, Swivel Tilt Roof Top Shade, Glass Inserts, Brass Base, 16 x 8 In. ............illus | 2645 |
| Lamp, Domed Glass Shade, Flowers, Lobed, Metal Base, C. Norbet, c.1910, 21 x 14 In. | 2875 |
| Lamp, Domed Milk Glass Shade, Pink, Poppy Embossed, Metal Base, c.1920, 14 x 7 In. | 313 |
| Lamp, Domed Shade, Dusk, Bird, Landscape, Metal Base, c.1910, 21 x 15 In. | 3250 |
| Lamp, Domed Shade, Frosted Flowers, Metal Base, Harvard Co-Operative, c.1920, 18 In. | 390 |
| Lamp, Domed Shade, Jungle Birds, Flowers, Ribbed, Stepped Flower Base, 22 In. | 14812 |
| Lamp, Domed Shade, Paperwhites, Metal Base, Conn., c.1910, 21 x 14 In. | 6080 |
| Lamp, Domed Shade, Wavy Orange Sections, Green Rim, Metal Base, c.1920, 24 x 20 In. | 1500 |
| Lamp, Exotic Birds, Black, Prisms, 3-Leg Standard, Spelter, Broggi, c.1924, 18 x 24 In. | 8125 |
| Lamp, Exotic Birds, Leaves, Iridescent Gold, Hanging, 24 ½ In. | 2073 |
| Lamp, Floor, Geometric Shade, Adjustable, c.1910, 58 x 19 In. | 2625 |
| Lamp, Floor, Glass Shade, Bronze, Patina, c.1890, 55 ½ In. | 688 |
| Lamp, Floor, Green Enamel Mosserine Shade, c.1910, 57 x 14 In. | 960 |
| Lamp, Floor, Landscape Overlay Slag Glass Shade, Patinated Metal, c.1910, 66 ½ x 25 In. | 7500 |
| Lamp, Flowers, Bronze Base, 18 In. Diam. Shade. ...........illus | 9000 |
| Lamp, Frosted Glass Shade, Paneled, Metal, Adjustable, c.1910, 26 x 15 In. | 1000 |
| Lamp, Geometric Slag Glass Shade, Bronze, Footed Base, 55 ½ In. | 1230 |
| Lamp, Glass Shade, Maidenhair Fern, Patinated Metal, Adjustable, c.1910, 14 x 15 In. | 2125 |
| Lamp, Glass Woodland Shade, Cone Shape, Metal Tree Trunk Base, c.1910, 24 x 18 In. | 688 |
| Lamp, Glass, Brown, White Bands, Flowers, Bronzed Metal, 10 x 14 ½ In. | 1159 |
| Lamp, Glass, Landscape, Bronzed Metal, 11 x 14 In. | 3416 |
| Lamp, Glass, Landscape, Sunset, Bronzed Metal, 11 x 14 In. | 3416 |
| Lamp, Glass, Pink, Flowers, Round Shade, Bronzed Metal, 18 x 23 In. | 3416 |
| Lamp, Green Glass Shade, Metal Base, Teroma, c.1910, 27 x 18 In. | 4063 |
| Lamp, Green Slag Glass, 4 Lily Shape Shades, Green, White, 15 In. | 2099 |
| Lamp, Hawaiian Sunset, Orange & Green Slag, Palm Tree Overlay, Ribbed Base, 26 In. | 5468 |
| Lamp, Hexagonal Shade, Stylized Flower Panels, Textured, Patina, Base, 22 x 16 In. | 1320 |
| Lamp, House On Bluff, Ocean, Rocky Shore, Sunset, Hexagonal Base, 19 In. | 729 |
| Lamp, Ivy Painted Leaded Glass Shade, Bronze Base, Signed, c.1920, 18 ½ x 13 ¾ In. | 518 |
| Lamp, Leaded Glass Shade, Chipped Ice, Reeded, Oil Lamp Base, c.1910, 21 x 13 In. | 5625 |
| Lamp, Leaded Glass Shade, Gulls, Black, White, Trumpet Shape, Metal Standard, 18 x 24 In. | 7020 |

**Handel,** Lamp, Chipped Glass, Domed Shade, Copper, Stamped, c.1910, 25 x 18 In.
$3,000

Rago Arts & Auction Center

**Handel,** Lamp, Desk, Swivel Tilt Roof Top Shade, Glass Inserts, Brass Base, 16 x 8 In.
$2,645

Humler & Nolan

## Handel Marks

Handel lamp bases are marked with the word *Handel*. The glass shades usually have a four-digit number on the inside near the rim. It is a design number and can be looked up in several books about the lamps. A few are marked on the inside of the glass shade with the name of an artist— Palme, Runge, or Parlow.

H

**Handel,** Lamp, Flowers, Bronze Base, 18 In. Diam. Shade
$9,000

DuMouchelles Art Gallery

**Harlequin,** Maroon, Butter, Cover, ½ Lb.
$91

Strawser Auction Group

**Haviland,** Vase, Landscape, Fisherman, Mother, Child, Dragonflies, E. Chaplet, c.1885, 17 In.
$4,375

Rago Arts & Auction Center

---

**TIP**

*Dust your antiques regularly but carefully. Dust leads to mold growth and attracts insects.*

---

| | |
|---|---:|
| **Lamp,** Leaded Glass Shade, Ivy Painted, Bronze Base, c.1920, 19 x 14 In. | 518 |
| **Lamp,** Mountainscape Domed Glass Shade, Metal, c.1910, 15 x 7 In. | 3625 |
| **Lamp,** Obverse, Reverse Painted Glass Shade, Snow Scene, Adjustable, c.1910, 13 x 14 In. | 2000 |
| **Lamp,** Piano, Frosted Shade, Chipped Finish, Metal Base, 8 ½ In. | 863 |
| **Lamp,** Student, Enameled Mosserine Shade, Green, Ivy Leaf, Adjustable, c.1910, 13 x 11 In. | 875 |
| **Lamp,** Teroma, Cone Shape, Landscape Glass Shade, Metal, c.1910, 24 x 18 In. | 3750 |
| **Lamp,** Teroma, Palm Tree & Sunset Shade, Slag Glass, Bronze Tree Trunk Base, 24 In. | 1610 |
| **Lamp,** Tropical Overlay Slag, Glass Shade, Basketweave Metal Base, c.1910, 26 x 20 In. | 2625 |
| **Lamp,** Windmills At Sunset, Orange To Purple To Gray, Copper Patina, 19 In. | 3341 |
| **Lamp,** Yellow Shade, Metal Standard, c.1910, 22 x 13 In. | 832 |
| **Vase,** Woods, Trees, Birds, Blue Ground, 11 In. | 2160 |

**HARDWARE,** *see Architectural category.*

---

**HARKER POTTERY COMPANY** was incorporated in 1890 in East Liverpool, Ohio. The Harker family had been making pottery in the area since 1840. The company made many types of pottery but by the Civil War was making quantities of yellowware from native clays. It also made Rockingham-type brown-glazed pottery and whiteware. The plant was moved to Chester, West Virginia, in 1931. Dinnerware was made and sold nationally. In 1971 the company was sold to Jeannette Glass Company, and all operations ceased in 1972. For more prices, go to kovels.com.

| | |
|---|---:|
| **Alpine,** Bowl, Vegetable, Round, 8 ¾ In. | 15 |
| **Alpine,** Chop Plate, 11 ¼ In. | 16 |
| **Alpine,** Salt & Pepper | 14 |
| **Amy,** Bean Pot | 6 to 12 |
| **Amy,** Sugar | 28 to 32 |
| **Amy,** Utility Bowl | 32 |
| **Blue Dane,** Cup & Saucer | 7 |
| **Blue Mist,** Platter, 13 In. | 56 |
| **Chesterton,** Cup & Saucer, Olive Green | 14 |
| **Coronet,** Bowl, Vegetable, Round, 9 In. | 15 |
| **Coronet,** Cup & Saucer | 7 |
| **Coronet,** Plate, Bread & Butter, 6 ½ In. | 7 |
| **Coronet,** Salt & Pepper | 13 |
| **Currier & Ives,** Plate, Bread & Butter, 6 ¼ In. | 8 |
| **Currier & Ives,** Plate, Dinner, 9 In. | 12 |
| **Daisy Lane,** Plate, Bread & Butter, 6 ⅛ In. | 7 |
| **Everglades,** Plate, Salad, 7 ¼ In. | 8 |
| **Everglades,** Platter, Oval, 13 In. | 25 |
| **Everglades,** Soup, Dish | 14 |
| **Forest Flower,** Cup & Saucer | 5 |
| **Forest Flower,** Plate, Dinner, 10 ⅛ In. | 6 |
| **Forest Flower,** Salt & Pepper | 16 |
| **Forest Flower,** Soup, Dish, Lugged, 7 ½ In. | 7 |
| **Garden Trail,** Coaster, 4 ¾ In. | 6 |
| **Garden Trail,** Creamer | 16 |
| **Golden Dawn,** Cup & Saucer | 5 |
| **Golden Dawn,** Plate, Dinner, 10 ⅛ In. | 7 |
| **Lemon Tree,** Bowl, Fruit, 5 ⅛ In. | 8 |
| **Lemon Tree,** Bowl, Vegetable, Round, 8 In. | 15 |
| **Lemon Tree,** Cup & Saucer | 6 |
| **Lemon Tree,** Plate, Dinner, 10 ½ In. | 14 to 18 |
| **Lemon Tree,** Platter, Oval, 13 In. | 17 |
| **Magnolia,** Platter, Oval, 13 In. | 34 |
| **Pate Sur Pate,** Gravy Boat, Underplate, Chartreuse, 8 In. | 18 |
| **Pate Sur Pate,** Plate, Dinner, Green, 10 ½ In. | 10 |
| **Peacock Alley,** Bowl, Vegetable, Divided, Oval, 10 In. | 43 |
| **Peacock Alley,** Creamer | 8 |
| **Peacock Alley,** Cup & Saucer | 5 |
| **Peacock Alley,** Plate, Salad, 7 ¾ In. | 7 |
| **Peacock Alley,** Salt & Pepper | 33 |
| **Persian Key,** Bowl, Dessert, 5 ¾ In. | 8 |
| **Persian Key,** Bowl, Vegetable, Oval, Divided, 10 ⅜ In. | 16 |
| **Persian Key,** Cup & Saucer | 9 |
| **Persian Key,** Gravy Boat | 22 |
| **Persian Key,** Mug, 3 ½ In. | 5 |

| | |
|---|---|
| **Persian Key,** Plate, Bread & Butter, 6 In. | 3 |
| **Shell Pink,** Bowl, Cereal, Rim, 6½ In. | 11 |
| **Shell Pink,** Bowl, Dessert, 5¼ In. | 4 |
| **Shell Pink,** Creamer, 8 Oz., 3⅝ In. | 15 |
| **Shell Pink,** Gravy Boat | 18 |
| **Shell Pink,** Platter, Oval, 13 In. | 41 to 63 |
| **Snowleaf,** Cup & Saucer | 6 |
| **Snowleaf,** Platter, Oval, 11 In. | 14 |
| **Springtime,** Tray, 2 Tiers | 38 |
| **Sun Glow,** Bowl, Vegetable, Round, 8 In. | 15 |
| **Sun Glow,** Cup & Saucer | 8 |
| **Sun Glow,** Platter, Oval, 11 In. | 18 |
| **White Cap,** Bowl, Fruit, 5 In. | 5 |
| **White Cap,** Bowl, Vegetable, Divided, Oval, 10 In. | 16 |
| **White Cap,** Creamer, 8 Oz., 3⅝ In. | 14 |
| **White Cap,** Cup & Saucer | 9 |
| **White Daisy,** Plate, Dinner, 10½ In. | 19 |
| **White Rose,** Plate, Bread & Butter, Blue, 6¼ In. | 10 |
| **Woodsong,** Bowl, Soup, Coupe, Gray, 7¾ In. | 8 |
| **Woodsong,** Cup & Saucer, Gray | 8 |

**HARLEQUIN** dinnerware was produced by the Homer Laughlin Company from 1938 to 1964, and sold without trademark by the F. W. Woolworth Co. It has a concentric ring design like Fiesta, but the rings are separated from the rim by a plain margin. Cup handles are triangular in shape. Seven different novelty animal figurines were introduced in 1939. For more prices, go to kovels.com.

| | |
|---|---|
| **Chartreuse,** Bowl, 5 In. | 35 |
| **Chartreuse,** Cup & Saucer | 26 |
| **Chartreuse,** Pitcher, 24 Oz., 4⅞ In. | 80 |
| **Forest Green,** Bowl, 7⅜ In. | 28 |
| **Forest Green,** Cup | 16 |
| **Forest Green,** Cup & Saucer | 10 to 14 |
| **Forest Green,** Saucer | 5 |
| **Forest Green,** Teapot, Lid, 3 Cup, 4⅞ In. | 199 |
| **Gray,** Cup | 5 |
| **Gray,** Cup & Saucer | 16 |
| **Gray,** Plate, 6¾ In. | 5 |
| **Green,** Cup | 16 |
| **Light Green,** Cup | 16 |
| **Light Green,** Cup, After Dinner | 96 |
| **Light Green,** Plate, 6¾ In. | 5 |
| **Maroon,** Butter, Cover, ½ Lb. ........................*illus* | 91 |
| **Maroon,** Cup, After Dinner | 90 |
| **Mauve Blue,** Bowl, Dessert, 5⅝ In. | 14 |
| **Mauve Blue,** Cup & Saucer | 12 |
| **Mauve Blue,** Cup, Dinner | 60 |
| **Mauve Blue,** Figurine, Duck | 225 |
| **Mauve Blue,** Nut Dish, Basketweave, 3 In. | 18 |
| **Mauve Blue,** Pitcher, Ball, Tilt | 49 |
| **Mauve Blue,** Plate, Salad, 7¼ In. | 13 |
| **Mauve Blue,** Platter, Oval, 13 In. | 38 |
| **Medium Green,** Bowl, Dessert | 36 |
| **Medium Green,** Cup | 13 |
| **Medium Green,** Gravy Boat | 28 |
| **Medium Green,** Plate, Luncheon, 9¼ In. | 44 |
| **Red,** Nut Dish, Basketweave, 3 In. | 15 |
| **Red,** Pitcher, Ball | 60 |
| **Red,** Tumbler, 9 Oz., 4¼ In. | 30 |
| **Rose,** Butter, Cover, ½ Lb. | 149 |
| **Rose,** Cup | 10 |
| **Rose,** Cup & Saucer | 8 to 12 |
| **Rose,** Cup & Saucer, After Dinner | 67 |
| **Rose,** Plate, Bread & Butter, 6 In. | 9 |
| **Rose,** Sugar & Creamer | 48 |
| **Rose,** Teapot, Lid, 3 Cup, 4⅞ In. | 126 |

**Heintz Art,** Humidor, Cigar, Copper, Silver On Bronze Overlay, Deer & Hounds, 6 In.
$316

Cottone Auctions

**Heintz Art,** Vase, Applied Leaves, Sterling On Bronze, Squat, Marked, 5¾ x 5¼ In.
$118

Burchard's Galleries

**Heisey,** Animal, Plug Horse, Oscar, 1940s, 4 In.
$50

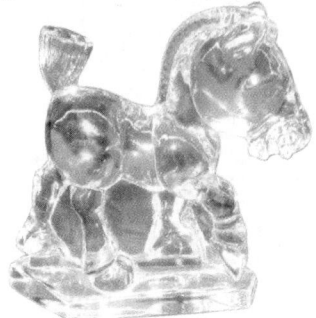

Homestead Auctions

**Heisey,** Locket On Chain, Cruet, Faceted Stopper, 1896-1904, 5 ½ In. $138

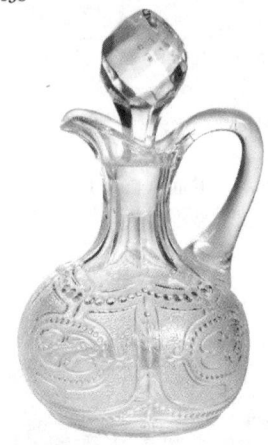

Jeffrey S. Evans & Assoc.

**Heisey,** Pineapple & Fan, Toothpick Holder, Ruby Stained, c.1898, 2 In. $345

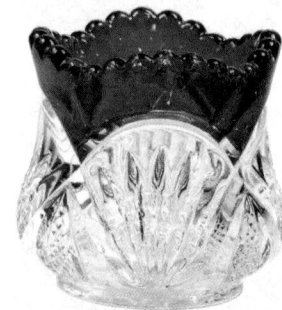

Jeffrey S. Evans & Assoc.

**Heisey,** Queen Anne, Toothpick Holder, Signed, c.1907, 2 ¼ In. $150

Jeffrey S. Evans & Assoc.

**TIP**
*Wash art glass in lukewarm water with a little softening agent and some mild dishwashing soap.*

| | |
|---|---:|
| **Spruce Green,** Cup & Saucer, After Dinner | 119 |
| **Spruce Green,** Figurine, Penguin | 169 |
| **Spruce Green,** Pitcher, Ball, 80 Oz., 7 ½ In. | 94 |
| **Spruce Green,** Teapot, 3 Cup, 4 ⅞ In. | 158 |
| **Turquoise,** Creamer, 7 Oz., 2 ⅝ In. | 15 |
| **Turquoise,** Cup | 5 to 7 |
| **Turquoise,** Cup, After Dinner | 24 |
| **Turquoise,** Pitcher, Tankard, 24 Oz., 4 ⅞ In. | 104 |
| **Turquoise,** Sugar & Creamer | 39 |
| **Turquoise,** Teapot | 129 |
| **Turquoise,** Tumbler, 9 Oz., 4 ¼ In. | 32 |
| **Yellow,** Ashtray, Basketweave, 4 In. | 32 |
| **Yellow,** Bowl, Dessert, 5 ⅝ In. | 8 |
| **Yellow,** Bowl, Vegetable, 9 In. | 65 |
| **Yellow,** Creamer | 42 |
| **Yellow,** Cup | 9 |
| **Yellow,** Cup & Saucer | 10 |
| **Yellow,** Cup & Saucer, After Dinner | 57 |
| **Yellow,** Dish, Vegetable, 8 In. | 25 |
| **Yellow,** Figurine, Duck | 180 |
| **Yellow,** Gravy Boat | 24 |
| **Yellow,** Plate, Luncheon, 9 ¼ In. | 12 |
| **Yellow,** Salt | 14 |
| **Yellow,** Salt & Pepper | 45 |
| **Yellow,** Sugar | 50 |
| **Yellow,** Sugar, Lid | 70 |
| **Yellow,** Teapot, Lid, 3 Cup, 4 ⅞ In. | 148 |
| **Yellow,** Tumbler, 9 Oz., 4 ¼ In. | 28 |

**HATPIN** collectors search for pins popular from 1860 to 1920. The long pin, often over four inches, was used to hold the hat in place on the hair. The tops of the pins were made of all materials, from solid gold and real gemstones to ceramics and glass. Be careful to buy original hatpins and not recent pieces made by altering old buttons.

| | |
|---|---:|
| **Brass,** Glass, Enamel, Bird, Cattail, Fan, Pink, Blue, Victorian, 12 In. | 148 |
| **Dragonfly,** Multicolored Rhinestones, Steel, Goldtone, c.1920, 10 In. | 288 |
| **Glass Beads,** Turquoise, Spherical, c.1905, 7 ¾ In. | 39 |
| **Glass,** Faux Tortoiseshell, Rhinestones, 6 In. | 22 |
| **Gold,** 9K White, Dragons Breath, Art Deco, 7 ¾ In. | 150 |
| **Rhinestone,** Ball, 7 ¼ In. | 15 |
| **Rhinestone,** Star, Domed, c.1910, 12 In. | 158 |
| **Rhinestone,** Steel, Snake, c.1920, 10 In. | 58 |
| **Silver,** Figural, Flower, Mexico, 8 In. | 50 |
| **Silver,** Figural, Golf Club, c.1908, 10 In. | 195 |
| **Silver,** Filigree, Chinese Bird, Spread Wings, c.1880, 8 In. | 225 |
| **Silver,** Glass, Green, Faceted, c.1915, 6 ½ In. | 42 |
| **Sterling Silver,** New York University, Perstare Et Praestare, 1880, 10 In. | 95 |

**HATPIN HOLDERS** were needed when hatpins were fashionable from 1860 to 1920. The large, heavy hat required special long-shanked pins to hold it in place. The hatpin holder resembles a large saltshaker, but it often has no opening at the bottom as a shaker does. Hatpin holders were made of all types of ceramics and metal. Look for other pieces under the names of specific manufacturers.

| | |
|---|---:|
| **Bisque,** Cowgirl Angel Fairy, 4 In. | 35 |
| **Brass,** Portrait, Art Nouveau, Monogram, c.1900, 8 In. | 40 |
| **Brass,** Roosters, 9 x 1 In. | 28 |
| **Clay,** Red, Greek Key Design, Rounded Corners, Dome Lid, Japan, 5 x 2 x 2 In. | 49 |
| **Glass,** Black, Diamond Design, Beaded, 5 ½ In. | 25 |
| **Glass,** Stretch Base, Treebark Pattern, Gold Ribbon, 7 In. | 145 |
| **Gunmetal,** Victorian Mourning, Egg Shape, 19th Century, 11 In. | 125 |
| **Porcelain,** Cornucopia, Multicolor Flowers, c.1890, 6 ¾ In. | 430 |
| **Porcelain,** Cream, Gold Roses, Nippon, 4 ¾ In. | 24 |
| **Porcelain,** Elfinware, Flowers, Pink, Blue, Germany, 3 Sections, c.1900, 4 In. | 125 |
| **Porcelain,** Figural, 2 Faces, Black Curly Hair, c.1850, 3 ½ x 3 In. | 475 |
| **Porcelain,** Figural, Clown, Art Deco, White, Black, Yellow, Germany, 1920s, 7 In. | 350 |
| **Porcelain,** Flower, Petals, Lustered, 3 Handles, RS Prussia, 4 In. | 239 |

H

| | |
|---|---:|
| **Porcelain,** Flowers, Scalloped Edges, Gilt Trim, 4 ½ In. | 89 |
| **Porcelain,** Geishas, Child, Footed, 6 ¼ In. | 69 |
| **Porcelain,** Ostriches Scenic Design, RS Prussia, 4 ½ In. | 2006 |
| **Porcelain,** Rose, Gilt Trim, Footed, Royal Bavaria, 4 ¼ In. | 62 |
| **Porcelain,** Violets, 6-Sided, Beyer & Bock, 5 In. | 24 |
| **Pot Metal,** Branch, Oak Leaves, Victorian, c.1890, 5 In. | 55 |
| **Pottery,** Green, Blue, Yellow, Torquay, 4 ½ In. | 135 |

**HAVILAND** china has been made in Limoges, France, since 1842. The factory was started by the Haviland Brothers of New York City. Pieces are marked *H & Co.,* *Haviland & Co.,* or *Theodore Haviland.* It is possible to match existing sets of dishes through dealers who specialize in Haviland china. Other factories worked in the town of Limoges making a similar chinaware. These porcelains are listed in this book under Limoges.

**HAVILAND & CO.**

| | |
|---|---:|
| **Bone Dish,** Norma, Pink & Yellow Flowers, 6 In. | 21 |
| **Bouillon Cup,** Cloverleaf Pattern, Gold Handles | 25 |
| **Bowl,** Dessert, Multicolor Berries, Flowers, Scalloped Edge, Yellow Border, 7 In., 12 Piece | 59 |
| **Bowl,** Pink Flowers, Leaves, Brown Border, Footed, 5 In. | 75 |
| **Bowl,** Vegetable, Branford, Oval, 9 In. | 92 |
| **Bowl,** Vegetable, Lid, Cream Band, Blue Leaves, Blossoms, Star Center, 10 In. | 65 |
| **Bowl,** Vegetable, Tray, Gold Handles, c.1920, 2 Piece | 42 |
| **Butter,** Cover, Pink Rose Clusters, Leaves, Bow Tail Handle, 7 In. Diam. | 55 |
| **Chop Plate,** Cornflower Pattern, 12 In. | 149 |
| **Cup & Saucer,** Astoria, Inner Gold Band | 14 |
| **Cup & Saucer,** Black Band, Hanging Baskets, Flowers, Gilt Trim | 40 |
| **Cup & Saucer,** Cornflower, Yellow, Purple & Blue Flower Band, Footed | 60 |
| **Cup & Saucer,** Footed, Bel Air, Dots & Leaves, Green | 12 |
| **Cup & Saucer,** Norma Pattern, Pink Flowers | 25 |
| **Dinner Service,** Winefield, Center Flower Spray, Gilt Rim, 8 Place Settings, c.1945, 70 Piece | 259 |
| **Gravy Boat,** Astoria, Attached Underplate | 138 |
| **Oyster Plate,** 7 Wells, Shell Decoration, Turquoise Ground, Lemon Center, 9 In., Pair | 250 |
| **Plate,** Bread & Butter, Multicolor Border, 6 ⅜ In. | 8 |
| **Plate,** Dinner, Branford, Gilt Trim, 9 In. | 38 |
| **Plate,** Dinner, Rose Border, Central Rose Cluster, 9 ⅝ In. | 40 |
| **Plate,** Salad, Pink & White Sprays, 7 ⅜ In. | 15 |
| **Platter,** Branford, Gilt Trim, Oval, 14 In. | 154 |
| **Platter,** Cornflower, Flower Band, Oval, 15 In. | 59 |
| **Platter,** Pink & Blue Flowers, Scalloped Edge, 10 ¾ x 8 ¾ In. | 18 |
| **Platter,** Pink Apple Blossom Sprays, Scalloped Edge, Gold Trim, 17 x 12 In. | 215 |
| **Platter,** Yellow Edge, Roses, Gilt Trim, 16 In. | 125 |
| **Soup,** Cream, Bows, Flower Scrolls, Gold, Handles, 5 ⅜ In. | 100 |
| **Sugar,** Lid, Astoria, Inner Gold Band | 43 |
| **Sugar,** Lid, Branford | 74 |
| **Sugar,** Lid, Cornflower, Multicolor Flowers | 58 |
| **Tray,** Dresser, Painted, Cherubs, Flower Ribbon Border, Scalloped Edge, c.1890, 8 x 11 In. | 84 |
| **Tureen,** Lid, Handles, White, Gold, Oval, 1870, 6 x 10 ½ In. | 84 |
| **Vase,** Blue, White Flowers, Brown Incised Leaves, E. Chaplet, c.1882, 15 x 14 In. | 1408 |
| **Vase,** Landscape, Fisherman, Mother, Child, Dragonflies, E. Chaplet, c.1885, 17 In. ........*illus* | 4375 |
| **Vase,** Oxblood Glaze, Bottle Shape, France, c.1900, 10 x 6 In. | 1063 |
| **Vase,** Oxblood Glaze, Tapered, E. Chaplet, c.1885, 16 x 12 ½ In. | 6250 |
| **Vase,** Tyrol, Farmers, Country Scene, Gilt Stoneware, Incised, E. Chaplet, 1883, 12 x 12 In. | 2176 |
| **Vase,** White Chrysanthemums, Glazed, Incised, Gilt, E. Chaplet, 1880s, 10 x 8 In. | 2500 |

**HAVILAND POTTERY** began in 1872, when Charles Haviland decided to make art pottery. He worked with the famous artists of the day and made pottery with slip glazed decorations. Production stopped in 1885. Haviland Pottery is marked with the letters *H & Co.* The Haviland name is better known today for its porcelain.

**H&C?**

| | |
|---|---:|
| **Vase,** Applied Flowers, Cobalt Blue, Footed, c.1890, 9 ½ x 5 In. | 2750 |
| **Vase,** Bird, Tab Handles, Green Glaze, Marked, c.1880, 12 x 10 In. | 2800 |
| **Vase,** Oval, Flat, Trees, River, Marked, c.1870, 17 x 11 x 5 In. | 4850 |

**HAWKES** cut glass was made by T. G. Hawkes & Company of Corning, New York, founded in 1880. The firm cut glass blanks made at other glassworks until 1962. Many pieces are marked with the trademark, a trefoil ring enclosing a fleur-de-lis and two hawks. Cut glass by other manufacturers is listed under either the factory name or in the general Cut Glass category.

| | |
|---|---:|
| **Bowl,** Columbia, Brilliant Cut, Scalloped Rim, c.1880, 12 In. | 7200 |

**H**

**Heubach,** Candy Container, Child, Football Attire, Bisque Head, Large Snowball, 5 In.
**$443**

Bertoia Auctions

**Hochst,** Group, Family Picking Grapes, Grass, Rocks, Marked, c.1910, 8 ⅝ In.
**$236**

Brunk Auctions

**Hopalong Cassidy,** Ring, Brass, Removable Hat, Compass, Post Cereal Premium, 1952
**$190**

Hake's Americana & Collectibles

**H**

**Horn,** Drinking Horn, Lid, Brass Mounts, Vines, Touchmarks, 28 x 17 In. $360

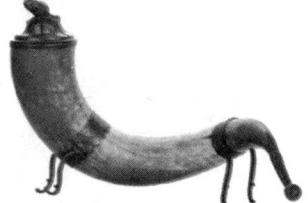

The Stein Auction Company

**Howdy Doody,** Ring, Flashlight, Howdy Doody Face, Plastic, Brass Ring, 1950s $115

Hake's Americana & Collectibles

**Hull,** Little Red Riding Hood, Wall Pocket, 1940s, 9 In. $23

Strawser Auction Group

| | |
|---|---:|
| **Bowl,** Gravic, Engraved Flowers, Scalloped Edge, 3 ½ x 8 In. | 60 |
| **Bowl,** Grecian, Rolled Rim, American Brilliant, 4 x 12 In. | 2655 |
| **Bowl,** Hobstar, Cane, Strawberry Diamond & Fan, Square, Notched Edge, 3 x 9 ½ In. | 100 |
| **Bowl,** Kensington, Round, Notched Edge, 4 x 8 ¾ In. | 175 |
| **Bowl,** Napoleon, 6 In. | 85 |
| **Bowl,** Queen's, Brilliant Cut, Scalloped Edge, c.1890, 9 In. | 450 |
| **Bucket,** Aberdeen, 4 ¾ x 6 ¼ In. | 141 |
| **Candleholder,** Hollow Cut Crystal, Leaves, Frosted Areas, 16 In., Pair | 431 |
| **Carafe,** Valencian, 9 ½ In. | 1130 |
| **Card Tray,** Kohinoor Center, Shaped Rim, 6 ½ In. | 25 |
| **Claret Jug,** Stopper, Queen's, Brilliant Cut, c.1900, 14 In. | 1200 |
| **Cologne Bottle,** Chrysanthemum, Embossed Gorham Silver Stopper, 6 ¼ In. | 450 |
| **Cologne Bottle,** Florence, 4 ¾ In. | 68 |
| **Cologne Bottle,** Stopper, Florence, Signed, 6 ½ In. | 311 |
| **Compote,** Armanda, Brilliant Cut, c.1880, 8 x 10 In. | 660 |
| **Cruet,** Hobstar & Crosscut Diamond, Squat, Faceted Stopper, 6 ¼ In. | 80 |
| **Dish,** Blow Out, Brilliant Cut, c.1900, 9 ¼ In. | 420 |
| **Fernier,** Palmero, 3-Footed, 4 x 7 ¾ In. | 70 |
| **Finger Bowl,** Underplate, Engraved Flowers & Scrolls, American Brilliant | 100 |
| **Goblet Set,** Miters & Fruits, 6 ½ In., 12 Piece | 1020 |
| **Goblet,** Verre De Soie, Cut, Floral Swags, Ribbons, Blossoms At Foot, 6 In., 8 Piece | 863 |
| **Hatpin Holder,** Naomi, Hobstar Base, 8 ½ In. | 240 |
| **Ice Cream Set,** Chrysanthemum, 15 x 11 In. Tray, 11 Piece | 600 |
| **Ice Cream Tray,** Gladys, 15 ½ x 10 ½ In. | 350 |
| **Jar,** Victoria, Hobstar Lid, 5 ¾ In. | 735 |
| **Lamp,** Queen's, Brilliant Cut, Mushroom Shape Shade, c.1910, 15 In. | 6000 |
| **Mustard,** Holland, Hobstar Lid, 3 ½ In. | 80 |
| **Pitcher,** Muddler, Silver, Pheasant, 19 ¼ In., 2 Piece | 180 |
| **Pitcher,** Navarre, Notched Handle, Signed, 11 In. | 198 |
| **Pitcher,** North Star, Cylindrical, Shaped Edge, 8 ¾ In. | 300 |
| **Plate,** Brunswick, Scalloped Notched Edge, 10 In. | 600 |
| **Plate,** Panel, Signed, 8 ½ In. | 4238 |
| **Powder Box,** Chrysanthemum, Gravic, Round, Gorham Engraved Silver Lid, 3 x 5 In. | 250 |
| **Relish,** Chrysanthemum, Rolled Rim, 9 ¾ x 6 In. | 330 |
| **Rose Bowl,** Lid, Brunswick, Brilliant Cut, Footed, c.1900, 8 ½ In. | 420 |
| **Rose Bowl,** Teutonic, 5 x 5 In. | 350 |
| **Tankard,** Lemonade, Wheel Carved, Sterling Hinged Cover, Strainer Spout, 9 ¼ In. | 173 |
| **Tray,** Albany, Oval, Scalloped Notched Edge, 12 x 10 In. | 12000 |
| **Tray,** Queens, 10 In. | 565 |
| **Tray,** Queens, Oval, Signed, 15 ½ x 10 ½ In. | 1243 |
| **Tray,** Strawberry, Gravic, Signed, 11 In. | 396 |
| **Tray,** Willow, Lattice, Rosette, Signed, 13 ½ x 8 In. | 7062 |
| **Vase,** Crosscut Diamond, Hobstar, Strawberry Diamond & Fan Border, Ruffled, 14 In. | 250 |
| **Vase,** Green Shaded To Clear, Dragon, Gilt Rim, Flared Rim, Cylindrical, c.1925, 10 In. | 277 |
| **Vase,** Iris, Flared, Bubble Knop, Silver Pedestal Base, 14 In. | 150 |
| **Vase,** Trumpet, Brunswick, 14 In. | 500 |
| **Vase,** Turquoise, Tapered, Short Neck, Everted Raised Rim, Etched Scrolling, 8 ½ x 5 ½ In. | 127 |

**HEAD VASES,** generally showing a woman from the shoulders up, were used by florists primarily in the 1950s and 1960s. Made in a variety of sizes and often decorated with imitation jewelry and other lifelike accessories, the vases were manufactured in Japan and the U.S.A. Less elaborate examples were made as early as the 1930s. Religious themes, babies, and animals are also common subjects. Other head vases are listed under manufacturers' names and can be located through the index in the back of this book.

| | |
|---|---:|
| **Boy,** Blond Hair, Cap, Blue, 5 ½ In. | 65 |
| **Girl,** Blond Hair, Hat, Turquoise, Blue, Yellow, Glossy, 6 In. | 56 |
| **Girl,** Blond Hair, Miss Bashful, c.1955, 5 ¾ In. | 45 |
| **Girl,** Bonnet, Roses, Blue, 6 In. | 65 |
| **Teen,** Blond Hair, Bobbed, Green Bowl, Earrings, Napco, 7 In. | 78 |
| **Woman,** Blond Hair, Closed Eyes, 5 ½ In. | 18 |
| **Woman,** Burgundy Hat & Dress, Ruffled, Gold Accents, 1960s, 8 In. | 89 |
| **Woman,** Dark Hair, Demure Face, Flowers In Hair, Japan, 4 In. | 60 |
| **Woman,** Girl, Blond Hair, Braids, Bangs, Scarf, 1950s, 5 ¾ In. | 38 |
| **Woman,** Tilted Hat, Curls, Ivory Glaze, 1940s, 8 In. | 88 |

**HEDI SCHOOP** Art Creations, North Hollywood, California, started about 1945 and was working until 1954. Schoop made ceramic figurines, lamps, planters, and tablewares.

*Hedi Schoop S*

| | |
|---|---|
| **Figurine,** Chinese Couple, Green, Flowers, Branches, Hat, Fan, 11 In. | 60 |
| **Figurine,** Dutch Couple, Dancing, Blond, c.1950, 11 In. | 175 |
| **Figurine,** Senorita, Blue Dress, Baskets, 12¾ In. | 125 |
| **Pitcher,** White, Pink & Gold Ridges, Pillow Shape, Loop Handle, 6 x 6 x 3 In. | 45 |
| **Vase,** Shell Fan Shape, Gilt & White, c.1945, 7 x 11 In. | 52 |

**HEINTZ ART METAL SHOP** used the letters *HAMS* in a diamond as a mark. In 1902, Otto Heintz designed and manufactured copper items with colored enamel decorations under the name Art Crafts Shop. He took over the Arts & Crafts Company in Buffalo, New York, in 1903. By 1906 it had become the Heintz Art Metal Shop. It remained in business until 1930. The company made ashtrays, bookends, boxes, bowls, desk sets, vases, trophies, and smoking sets. The best-known pieces are made of copper, brass, and bronze with silver overlay. Similar pieces were made by Smith Metal Arts and were marked *Silver Crest*. Some pieces by both companies are unmarked.

| | |
|---|---|
| **Box,** Bronze, Sterling On Bronze, Geometric Design On Lid, Rectangular, 8 x 3 x 2 In. | 375 |
| **Candlestick,** Bronze, Flared Cup, Baluster, Sterling On Bronze, Flower, 11 x 4 In., Pair | 688 |
| **Frame,** Sterling On Bronze, c.1910, 10 x 8 In. | 300 |
| **Humidor,** Cigar, Bronze, Patina, Cylindrical, Sterling On Bronze, Leaves, Monogram, 7 In. | 854 |
| **Humidor,** Cigar, Copper, Silver on Bronze, Deer & Hounds, 6 In. *illus* | 316 |
| **Humidor,** Cigar, Copper, Sterling On Bronze, Hinged Lid, Ball Feet, Wood, 1912, 3 x 10 In. | 354 |
| **Lamp,** Bronze, Green Patina, Sterling On Bronze, Vs, Drum Shade, Floral Cutouts, 15 In. | 2250 |
| **Lamp,** Electric, Bronze Dore, Cattail, Silver, Mica, 11 In. | 875 |
| **Lamp,** Electric, Bronze, Silver, Mica, Drum Shade, 13 In. | 1875 |
| **Lamp,** Jonquil Mushroom, Bronze, Silver, 14¼ x 16½ In. | 12200 |
| **Lamp,** Pine Needle, Bronze, Silver, 8¾ x 10½ In. | 1037 |
| **Lamp,** Vine, Black, Bronze, Silver, 12¾ x 9¼ In. | 976 |
| **Tray,** Bronze, Sterling On Bronze, Grapevines, 7 In. | 344 |
| **Vase,** Applied Leaves, Sterling On Bronze, Squat, Marked, 5¾ x 5¼ In. *illus* | 118 |
| **Vase,** Arabesque, Cylinder, Brown, Silver, Bronze, 10 x 4 In., Pair | 915 |
| **Vase,** Bronze, Sterling On Bronze, Birds In Trees, Brown Mottled, c.1912, 8 x 3 In. | 138 |
| **Vase,** Bronze, Sterling On Bronze, Fuchsia Design, 11¾ x 4 In. | 366 |
| **Vase,** Bronze, Sterling On Bronze, Windmill Landscape, Flared Rim & Base, 12 In. | 813 |
| **Vase,** Climbing Rose, 10¾ In. | 793 |
| **Vase,** Mottled Iced Finish, Sterling On Bronze, Wild Rose, Tapered, c.1912, 5¾ In. | 236 |
| **Vase,** Rose, Bronze, Silver, 17½ In. | 610 |
| **Vase,** Swallows, Bronze, Silver On Bronze, 12¼ In. | 732 |
| **Vase,** Thistle, Bronze, Silver On Bronze, 12 In. | 343 |
| **Vase,** Verdigris Patina, Sterling On Bronze, Daffodils, 10 x 4 In. | 671 |

**HEISEY** glass was made from 1896 to 1957 in Newark, Ohio, by A. H. Heisey and Co., Inc. The Imperial Glass Company of Bellaire, Ohio, bought some of the molds and the rights to the trademark. Some Heisey patterns have been made by Imperial since 1960. After 1968, they stopped using the *H* trademark. Heisey used romantic names for colors, such as Sahara. Do not confuse color and pattern names. The Custard Glass and Ruby Glass categories may also include some Heisey pieces.

| | |
|---|---|
| **Animal,** Bull | 750 |
| **Animal,** Colt, Standing | 55 |
| **Animal,** Geese, Wings Up, Wing Down, 8½ In., Pair | 100 |
| **Animal,** Plug Horse, Oscar, 1940s, 4 In. *illus* | 50 |
| **Banded Flute,** Punch Cup | 12 |
| **Baroque,** Candlestick, 2-Light, Pair | 40 |
| **Coarse Rib,** Plate, Luncheon, 7⅜ In. | 4 |
| **Cobel,** Cocktail Shaker, 462 Fox Chase Etch, 2 Qt. | 180 |
| **Colonial,** Nappy, Scalloped, 8 In. | 20 |
| **Country Club,** Soda, 517 Winchester Etch, 12 Oz. | 120 |
| **Crocus,** Candlestick, 2-Light | 90 |
| **Crystolite,** Bowl, Cereal, 5⅜ In. | 12 |
| **Crystolite,** Candlestick, 3-Light | 27 |
| **Crystolite,** Champagne | 8 |
| **Crystolite,** Cup & Saucer | 15 |
| **Crystolite,** Nut Dish, Swan, Individual | 20 |
| **Crystolite,** Sugar & Creamer | 44 |

**Hummel,** Figurine, No. 7/II, Merry Wanderer, Last Bee, 10 In. $236

Conestoga Auction Co., Inc.

**Hummel,** Figurine, No. 152/IIB, Umbrella Girl, Goebel Bee, 7¾ In. $384

Conestoga Auction Co., Inc.

**Hummel,** Figurine, No. 170/II, School Boys, Goebel Bee, 9¾ In. $201

Conestoga Auction Co., Inc.

**H**

**Hummel,** Figurine, No. 406, Pleasant Journey, Missing Bee, Box, 6½ In.
$236

Conestoga Auction Co., Inc.

**Icon,** Devotion Scene, Tempera On Wood, Silver Riza, Marked, Russia, 8¾ x 7 In.
$600

Cowan's Auctions

**Imari,** Bowl, Dragon & Flaming Pearl, Flowers, Ming Wanli Mark, Japan, 6 x 13 In.
$738

New Orleans Auction Galleries, Inc.

| | |
|---|---:|
| **Crystolite,** Vase, Flared, Footed, 5 In. | 32 |
| **Double Rib & Panel,** Basket, Flamingo, 8¼ x 6 In. | 235 |
| **Empress,** Candlestick, Alexandrite | 250 |
| **Empress,** Nut Dish, Alexandrite | 80 |
| **Empress,** Sugar & Creamer, Tray, Marked, Individual | 25 |
| **Empress,** Tumbler, Marked | 60 |
| **Fancy Loop,** Cruet | 25 |
| **Fancy Loop,** Dish, 8½ In. | 25 |
| **Fancy Loop,** Punch Cup | 15 |
| **Fern,** Plate, 8 In. | 25 |
| **Flamingo,** Toddy, Marked | 100 |
| **Flat Panel,** Toothpick Holder, Tray, Medium | 25 |
| **Flower Frog,** Hawthorne | 50 |
| **Greek Key,** Punch Bowl, 2 Cups, Flamingo, c.1925, 7½ In. Bowl | 161 |
| **Greek Key,** Sugar & Creamer, Marked, Individual | 25 |
| **Half Circle,** Sugar & Creamer, Marked, Individual | 40 |
| **Koors,** Water Lamp, Flamingo | 620 |
| **Lariat,** Candlestick, 4 In. | 14 |
| **Lariat,** Cologne Bottle, Stopper | 25 |
| **Lariat,** Creamer | 14 |
| **Lariat,** Nut Dish, 4 In. | 13 |
| **Lariat,** Relish, 3 Sections, 11 In. | 24 |
| **Locket On Chain,** Cruet, Faceted Stopper, 1896-1904, 5½ In. ...............*illus* | 138 |
| **Maytime,** Juice | 30 |
| **Mercury,** Candlestick, 1-Light | 15 |
| **Moon Gleam,** Basket, Double Rib & Panel | 95 |
| **Moon Gleam,** Compote, 8 In. | 95 |
| **Old Colony,** Bowl, Dolphin Feet, 10⅞ x 4 In. | 65 |
| **Old Dominion,** Soda, 447 Empress Etch, Footed, Flamingo, 12 Oz. | 35 |
| **Old Sandwich,** Wine, Flamingo | 25 to 30 |
| **Orchid Etch,** Candlestick, 1-Light | 32 |
| **Orchid Etch,** Dish, Flared, 11 x 4 In. | 60 |
| **Orchid Etch,** Vase, Crimped Top, 7 In. | 125 |
| **Orchid Etch,** Vase, Fan Shape, 7 x 6 In. | 100 |
| **Patrician,** Candlestick, 9 In., Pair | 40 |
| **Patrician,** Candlestick, Toy, Gold Decor, Marked, 4½ In. | 15 |
| **Pillows,** Salt & Pepper | 55 |
| **Pineapple & Fan,** Toothpick Holder, Ruby Stained, c.1898, 2 In. ...............*illus* | 345 |
| **Pinwheel & Fan,** Sugar & Creamer | 45 to 60 |
| **Plantation,** Bowl, Flower, 12 In. | 72 |
| **Plantation,** Compote, 9½ In. | 30 |
| **Pleat & Panel,** Compote, Lid, 8 In. | 30 |
| **Prince Of Wales Plumes,** Punch Cup | 12 |
| **Prison Stripe,** Butter, Cover, Marked | 100 |
| **Prison Stripe,** Jelly, Footed, Marked | 26 |
| **Prison Stripe,** Punch Cup | 18 |
| **Prison Stripe,** Tumbler, Marked | 80 |
| **Punty & Diamond Point,** Punch Cup | 15 |
| **Puritan,** Bonbon, 9½ In. | 80 |
| **Quator,** Sugar & Creamer, Marked, Individual | 25 |
| **Queen Anne,** Toothpick Holder, Signed, c.1907, 2¼ In. ...............*illus* | 150 |
| **Regency,** Candlestick, 2-Light | 20 |
| **Ridgeleigh,** Ice Bucket, Handles, 6½ x 4½ In. | 65 |
| **Ridgeleigh,** Nappy, 9 x 9 In. | 32 |
| **Ridgeleigh,** Sugar & Creamer | 19 |
| **Ridgeleigh,** Sugar & Creamer, Marked, Individual | 15 |
| **Rooster Head,** Cocktail, 980 Moonglow Cutting | 55 |
| **Rose,** Candlestick, 2-Light, Pair | 85 |
| **Rose,** Goblet | 30 |
| **Rose,** Plate, Salad, 8 In. | 18 |
| **Rose,** Sherbet | 15 |
| **Rose,** Tumbler, Footed | 40 |
| **Seahorse,** Cocktail | 70 |
| **Sunburst,** Bowl, Oval, Underplate, Marked | 50 |
| **Sunburst,** Compote, Round, Marked, 10 In. | 35 |

| | | |
|---|---|---:|
| **Sunburst,** Nappy, 9 ½ In. | | 25 |
| **Sunburst,** Nappy, Marked, 8 In. | | 30 |
| **Sunburst,** Punch Cup | | 18 |
| **Sunburst,** Toothpick Holder, Marked | | 30 to 40 |
| **Teardrop,** Bowl, Flowers, Hawthorne | | 320 |
| **Tom Thumb,** Candlestick, Toy, Marked | | 15 |
| **Toujours,** Sugar & Creamer, Marked, Individual | | 35 |
| **Twist,** Bonbon, 7 In. | | 10 |
| **Twist,** Celery Dish, 13 In. | | 25 |
| **Twist,** Mustard, Lid, Underplate, Flamingo, Marked | | 55 |
| **Twist,** Mustard, Lid, Underplate, Moongleam, Marked | | 55 |
| **Warwick,** Vase, 5 In. | | 12 |
| **Waverly,** Celery Dish, 12 x 4 x 2 In. | | 24 |
| **Waverly,** Relish, 4 Sections, Swirl Handles, 9 In. | | 38 |
| **Waverly,** Sugar & Cream, 515 Rose Etch, Marked, Individual | | 30 |
| **Whirlpool,** Sugar & Creamer | | 25 |
| **Yeoman,** Banana Split, Footed, Flamingo, Marked | | 25 |
| **Yeoman,** Salt, Flamingo, Individual | | 30 |
| **Zodiac,** Sugar & Creamer, Paper Label | | 55 |

**HEREND,** *see Fischer category.*

**HEUBACH** is the collector's name for Gebruder Heubach, a firm working in Lichten, Germany, from 1840 to 1925. It is best known for bisque dolls and doll heads, the principal products. The company also manufactured bisque figurines, including piano babies, beginning in the 1880s, and glazed figurines in the 1900s. Piano Babies are listed in their own category. Dolls are included in the Doll category under Gebruder Heubach and Heubach. Another factory, Ernst Heubach, working in Koppelsdorf, Germany, also made porcelain and dolls. These will also be found in the Doll category under Heubach Koppelsdorf.

| | | |
|---|---|---:|
| **Candy Container,** Child Sitting On Snowball, Bisque Head, Cotton, Mica, 7 In. | | 649 |
| **Candy Container,** Child, Football Attire, Bisque Head, Large Snowball, 5 In. | *illus* | 443 |
| **Figurine,** Cyclist, Hand To Head, Looking In Distance, Painted, Gold Detail, c.1898, 14 ¼ In. | | 205 |
| **Vase,** Woman's Portrait, Clementine, Blue Enamel, Gold Flowers, Wagner, 5 ½ In. | | 1725 |

**HISTORIC BLUE,** *see factory names, such as Adams, Ridgway, and Staffordshire.*

**HOBNAIL** glass is a style of glass with bumps all over. Dozens of hobnail patterns and variants have been made. Clear, colored, and opalescent hobnail have been made and are being reproduced. Other pieces of hobnail may also be listed in the Duncan & Miller and Fenton categories.

| | | |
|---|---|---:|
| **Basket,** Amber, Crimped, Ruffled Rim, 5 x 7 In. | | 20 |
| **Bowl,** Fluted Edge, 8 x 5 x 2 In. | | 43 |
| **Candleholder,** Sawtooth Rim, Footed, 3 x 6 ½ In. | | 17 |
| **Dish,** Black, c.1950, 5 In. | | 13 |
| **Egg Plate,** Indiana Glass, 1970s, 11 In. Diam. | | 21 |
| **Goblet,** Water, Amber, 6 In. | | 15 |
| **Sugar & Creamer,** Moonstone, Opalescent | | 39 |
| **Tumbler,** Marigold, Millersburg | | 275 |
| **Vase,** Milk Glass, Flared, Anchor Hocking, 5 ½ In. | | 10 |
| **Vase,** Milk Glass, Trumpet, Footed, 9 ½ In. | | 12 |

**HOCHST,** or Hoechst, porcelain was made in Germany from 1746 to 1796. It was marked with a six-spoke wheel. Be careful when buying Hochst; many other firms have used a very similar wheel-shaped mark. Copies have been made from the original molds.

| | | |
|---|---|---:|
| **Group,** Family Picking Grapes, Grass, Rocks, Marked, c.1910, 8 ⅝ In. | *illus* | 236 |

**HOLLY AMBER,** or golden agate, glass was made by the Indiana Tumbler and Goblet Company of Greentown, Indiana, from January 1, 1903, to June 13, 1903. It is a pressed glass pattern featuring holly leaves in the amber-shaded glass. The glass was made with shadings that range from creamy opalescent to brown-amber.

| | | |
|---|---|---:|
| **Bowl,** Flared, Greentown, 3 x 7 ½ In. | | 325 |
| **Toothpick Holder,** Greentown, 2 ½ In. | | 345 |

**Imari,** Bowl, Scalloped, Bands, Goldfish Center, Marked, c.1900, 14 ¼ In.
$308

Cowan's Auctions

**Imari,** Jar, Dome Lid, Ribbed Body, Foo Dog Finial, c.1890, 25 ¼ In., Pair
$1,180

Brunk Auctions

**Imari,** Platter, Flowers, Foo Dog Corners, Peony Border, Barbed Rim, Japan, 12 ½ In.
$472

Brunk Auctions

**H**

**TIP**

*Be careful where you put a fresh pumpkin or gourd at Halloween or Thanksgiving. Put a plastic liner underneath it. A rotting pumpkin will permanently stain wood or marble.*

295

**Imari,** Tureen, Lid, Underplate, Riverscape, Boar Head Handles, Japan, 1800s, 15¼ In.
$4,375

Rago Arts & Auction Center

**Imari,** Umbrella Stand, Iron Red Underglaze, Blue Flowers, 1800s, 24¼ x 8¾ In.
$799

New Orleans Auction Galleries, Inc.

**Indian,** Bag, Plateau, Beaded, Contour Style, Girl Figure, Handle, c.1890, 8 x 8¾ In.
$1,265

Allard Auctions

> **TIP**
> *Never restore a stamp.*
> *It lowers the value.*

---

**HOLT-HOWARD** was an importer that started working in New York City in 1949 and moved to Stamford, Connecticut, in 1955. The company sold many types of table accessories, such as condiment jars, decanters, spoon holders, and saltshakers. Its figural pieces have a cartoon-like quality. The company was bought out by General Housewares Corporation in 1969. Holt-Howard pieces are often marked with the name and the year or *HH* and the year stamped in black. The *HH* mark was used until 1974. The company also used a black and silver paper label. Holt-Howard production ceased in 1990. Similar pieces are being made today by Grant Holt, one of the founders, and are marked *GHA*.

| | |
|---|---:|
| **Bowl,** Pineapple, Brown, Yellow, 1960s, 8 In. | 9 |
| **Ice Cream Set,** Handles, Stackable, Fruit Finials, c.1959, 6 Piece | 135 |
| **Jar,** Cocktail Olives, Pixieware, Green Head, Winking, 1958, 5½ In. | 125 |
| **Jar,** Instant Coffee, Blue Stripes, 3 In. | 40 |
| **Jar,** Jam 'N Jelly, Pixieware, Rosy Checks, Smiling, 1958, 5½ In. | 60 |
| **Jar,** Ketchup, Pixieware, Red Head, Smiling, c.1958, 5½ In. | 45 |
| **Jar,** Mustard, Pixieware, Yellow Flat Head, Annoyed Face, c.1958 | 60 |
| **Mug,** Coq Rouge Rooster, Sticker, 1964, 3½ In. | 12 |
| **Napkin Holder,** Holly Berries, 1962, 2¾ x 3¾ In. | 7 |
| **Salt & Pepper,** Coiled Spring, c.1959 | 80 |
| **Salt & Pepper,** Tomato Shape, Red, 2¾ In. | 20 |

**HOPALONG CASSIDY** was a character in a series of twenty-eight books written by Clarence E. Milford, first published in 1907. Movies and television shows were made based on the character. The best-known actor playing Hopalong Cassidy was William Lawrence Boyd. His first movie appearance was in 1919, but the first Hopalong Cassidy film was not made until 1934. Sixty-six films were made. In 1948, William Boyd purchased the television rights to the movies, then later made fifty-two new programs. In the 1950s, Hopalong Cassidy and his horse, named Topper, were seen in comics, records, toys, and other products. Boyd died in 1972.

| | |
|---|---:|
| **Cap Pistol,** Gold Plated, Wyandotte, Box, 9½ x 3¾ In. | 390 |
| **Dental Kit,** Smiling Cassidy, Metal Toothpaste, Toothbrush, Clear Glass Tube, Box, 8 x 9 In. | 161 |
| **Doll,** Black Hat, Shirt, Pants, Rubber, Stuffed Cloth Torso, Ideal, c.1950, 25 In. | 493 |
| **Game,** Hopalong Cassidy Shooting Gallery, Board, Tin, Windup, Box, Automatic Toy Co. | 35 |
| **Gun & Theater Set,** Boy, Metal Picture Gun To Project Film, Cardboard, c.1950, 8 x 13 In. | 196 |
| **Hamper,** Tin Lithograph, 22½ In. | 35 |
| **Holster Set,** Gold Plated Metal Cap Gun, All Metal Products, 1955, 7 x 12 In. | 403 |
| **Mug,** Red Image, Milk Glass, Hazel Atlas | 28 |
| **Radio,** Arvin, Electric, Tabletop, Red Metal, Scene, Front Dial, Knob, c.1950, 8 x 4 x 5 In. | 300 |
| **Ring,** Brass, Removable Hat, Compass, Post Cereal Premium, 1952 ........ *illus* | 190 |
| **Toy,** Hoppy Riding Horse, Lasso, Rocker Base, Tin Litho, Key Wind, Marx, 11¼ In. | 210 to 472 |
| **Watch,** Black Border, Cord Fob, Photo Portrait, 2 In., Pocket | 191 |
| **Wristwatch,** Photo Portrait, Branding Symbols, Red Box, 1950s, 4 x 7 In. | 126 |

**HORN** was used to make many types of boxes, furniture inlays, jewelry, and whimsies.

| | |
|---|---:|
| **Cup,** Brass Mounted, Embossed Metal Ends, Stand, Inscription Plaque, 1901, 21 In. | 120 |
| **Cup,** Tumbler, Curved, Tapered, Woman, Portrait, Inscribed Brig Rose 1873, 5 In. | 188 |
| **Drinking Horn,** Bird Shape, Soviet Russia Silver Mounts, Sickle In Star Mark, c.1970, 9 In. | 180 |
| **Drinking Horn,** Brass Mounts, Inscribed, Internationaler Tisch Zu Peine Juli, 1889, 22 In. | 660 |
| **Drinking Horn,** Lid, Brass Mounts, Vines, Touchmarks, 28 x 17 In. ........ *illus* | 360 |
| **Footstool,** 12 Horns, 4 Splayed Legs, 2 Stretchers, Leather Upholstery Top, 11 x 12 x 12 In. | 236 |

**HOWARD PIERCE** began working in Southern California in 1936. In 1945, he opened a pottery in Claremont. He moved to Joshua Tree in 1968 and continued making pottery until 1991. His contemporary-looking figurines are popular with collectors. Though most pieces are marked with his name, smaller items from his sets often were not marked.

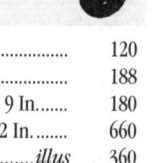

Howard Pierce

| | |
|---|---:|
| **Figurine,** Dog, Droopy Ears, Brown, Tan, 8 & 6 In., Pair | 150 |
| **Figurine,** Frog, On Stone, 5¼ x 4¼ In. | 95 |
| **Figurine,** Goose, Raised Head, Brown, Purple Accents, 4 x 2 In. | 40 |
| **Figurine,** Rabbit, Sitting Up, Brown, 4 In. | 65 |
| **Figurine,** Roadrunner, Brown Matte Glaze, 12 In. | 100 |
| **Figurine,** St. Francis, Holding Bird, 14 In. | 56 |
| **Vase,** Flamingo, Tall Grass, Speckled Chartreuse, 8¾ x 5 In. | 125 |
| **Vase,** Flared Mouth, Brown To Tan, 6¼ In. | 25 |
| **Vase,** Quails, On Branch, 1960s, 9 In. | 75 |

**HOWDY DOODY** and Buffalo Bob were the main characters in a children's series televised from 1947 to 1960. Howdy was a redheaded puppet. The series became popular with college students in the late 1970s when Buffalo Bob began to lecture on campuses.

| | |
|---|---|
| **Ring,** Flashlight, Howdy Doody Face, Plastic, Brass Ring, 1950s .........................*illus* | 115 |
| **Store Display,** Hey Kids 2 Big Offers, Yellow, c.1954, 29¾ x 31 In. | 382 |
| **Store Display,** Standing, NBC-TV, Multicolor, 1950s................................ | 569 |
| **Toy,** Band, Howdy Dancing, Bob Smith At Piano, Tin Litho, Key Wind, Unique Art, 5 In. . | 767 to 944 |
| **Toy,** Duet, Howdy Doody, Bob Smith, Piano, Tin Litho, Windup, Unique Art Mfg. Co., 9 In........... | 660 |
| **Toy,** Howdy Doody Acrobat, Striped Bars, Kagran, West Germany, Box, 16 In. .................. | 118 to 270 |
| **Toy,** Ring, Poll Parrot, Red Plastic, Yellow Top, Jack-In-The-Box, Premium, 1950s...................... | 115 |

**HULL** pottery was made in Crooksville, Ohio, from 1905. Addis E. Hull bought the Acme Pottery Company and started making ceramic wares. In 1917, A. E. Hull Pottery began making art pottery as well as the commercial wares. For a short time, 1921 to 1929, the firm also sold pottery imported from Europe. The dinnerware of the 1940s (including the Little Red Riding Hood line), the matte wares of the 1940s, and the high gloss artwares of the 1950s are all popular with collectors. The firm officially closed in March 1986.

| | |
|---|---|
| **Bank,** Corky Pig, Pink, Blue, 1957, 7¼ In. .......................................... | 35 to 69 |
| **Bank,** Corky Pig, Pink, Bow, c.1940 .................................................. | 48 |
| **Bank,** Corky Pig, Yellow, 1957, 7¾ In. ............................................. | 69 |
| **Bow Knot,** Basket, Scalloped Flared Rim, Handle, 11¾ In. ..................... | 118 |
| **Bow Knot,** Bowl, Red Border, Scalloped Wide Rim, Tapered, Footed, Marked, 14 In...................... | 40 |
| **Bow Knot,** Jardiniere, Wavy Blue Rim, Round, Pink Handles, 7¾ In............... | 63 |
| **Bow Knot,** Pitcher, Marked, Blue Border, 14 In..................................... | 138 |
| **Bow Knot,** Plate, Wall, Flowers, Blue Border, Marked, 10⅛ In.................... | 276 |
| **Bow Knot,** Vase, Blue Petal Mouth, Footed, 6 In. ............................... | 14 |
| **Bow Knot,** Vase, Blue Scalloped Rim Border, 12¾ In............................. | 86 |
| **Bow Knot,** Vase, Blue, White, Scalloped, Flared Rim, Handles, 8⅝ In........... | 115 |
| **Bow Knot,** Vase, Pink, Blue Flowers, 8½ In. ...................................... | 46 |
| **Bow Knot,** Vase, Scalloped Cutout Blue Rim, 11 In. ........................... | 127 |
| **Butterfly,** Basket, Flowers, White, 3-Part Handle, 1956, 10 In. .............. | 35 |
| **Butterfly,** Vase, White, Triangular Shape, Raised 3-Part Base, 1956, 10½ In. ............... | 52 |
| **Dachshund,** Planter, Marked, 13¼ In.................................................. | 21 |
| **Dogwood,** Cornucopia, Peach, Marked, 12 In. ................................... | 28 |
| **Dogwood,** Planter, Round, Scalloped Rim, Lug Handles, 7½ In.................. | 25 |
| **Dogwood,** Vase, Flowers, Pink, Small Handles, 5 In. ......................... | 46 |
| **Dogwood,** Vase, Rose To Blue, Wavy Rim, Shaped Handles, Marked, 6⅝ In. ....... | 46 |
| **Dogwood,** Vase, Suspended, Scalloped Rim, 7¼ In.............................. | 69 |
| **Granada,** Pitcher, Peach To Rose, Split Rim, 10¾ In........................... | 17 |
| **Imperial,** Planter, Frog Shape, Green, Marked, 6¼ In.......................... | 16 |
| **Iris,** Console, Scalloped Rim, Peach, 12 In. .................................... | 22 |
| **Little Red Riding Hood,** Wall Pocket, 1940s, 9 In. ......................*illus* | 23 |
| **Magnolia,** Console, Matte, Pink To Blue, Oval, Loop Handles, 13¾ In.......... | 23 |
| **Magnolia,** Pitcher, Flowers, Peach To Pale Yellow, Matte Finish, 5 In. ....... | 25 |
| **Magnolia,** Vase, Asymmetrical Scalloped Rim, Handles, Footed, 9 In......... | 22 |
| **Magnolia,** Vase, Matte, Blue, Yellow, Pink, Swan Handles, Marked, 12½ In..... | 86 |
| **Magnolia,** Vase, Tassel, Pink To Blue, Marked, 12⅞ In........................ | 86 |
| **Open Rose,** Vase, Peachy Tan, Flared Rim, Looped Handles, Marked, 5½ In. ... | 17 |
| **Orchid,** Vase, Bud, Peach To Rose, Handles, 6¾ In........................... | 40 |
| **Orchid,** Vase, Flowers, Pale Pink, Handles, 4⅞ In. ........................... | 17 |
| **Orchid,** Vase, Pink, Yellow Flowers, Blue Ground, Handles, 8⅞ In. ........... | 18 |
| **Pig,** Planter, Bust, Eyes Closed, Pale Peach, 6 In. ........................... | 14 |
| **Serenade,** Basket, Flowers, Slanted, Lobed Rim, 12½ In. ..................... | 35 |
| **Serenade,** Bowl, Flowers, Angled Rim, Blue, Mark, 12½ In..................... | 17 |
| **Serenade,** Pitcher, Pink Blossoms, Yellow Ground, Scoop Spout, 10½ In....... | 40 |
| **Serenade,** Planter, Hat Shape, Pink, 5⅜ In. ................................... | 40 |
| **Serenade,** Planter, Pink, Deep Rose Flowers, Top Hat Shape, 5⅜ In............ | 12 |
| **Serenade,** Vase, Blue, Divided Rim, Mark, 8½ In............................... | 20 |
| **Siamese Cat,** Planter, Kitten On Back, Resting, Tan, Brown, 11½ In. ....... | 35 |
| **Thistle,** Vase, Pink, Waist Handles, 6½ In....................................... | 19 |
| **Thistle,** Vase, Squat Base, Long Handles, 6¾ In................................ | 12 |
| **Tokay,** Basket, Round, Cone On Handle, Base, 10¾ In......................... | 16 |
| **Tropicana,** Pitcher, Black Man Rowing, White, Ground, 12½ In............... | 173 |
| **Tulip,** Basket, Pink, Shaded To Blue, Shaped Handle, 7¾ In.................. | 92 |
| **Tulip,** Jardiniere, Pink, Flowers, Tapered, 9 In.............................. | 35 |

**Indian,** Bag, Plateau, Hide & Cloth, Beaded, Horse, Flowers, Border, c.1925, 12½ x 11 In.
$1,968

Skinner Auctioneers & Appraisers

**Indian,** Bag, Wasco, Sally, Lid, Soft Weave, Figures, Condors, Deer, c.1880, 10 x 6 In.
$4,313

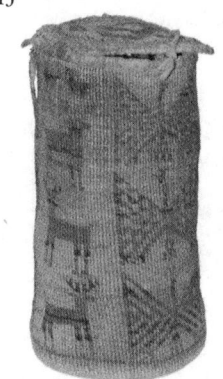

Allard Auctions

**Indian,** Bandolier, Chippewa, Beaded Cloth, Flowers, Fringe, c.1910, 44 x 14 In.
$875

Rago Arts & Auction Center

**Indian,** Basket, Apache, Bowl Shape, Banded, Human Figures, Animals, c.1910, 5 x 14¼ In.
$3,198

Skinner Auctioneers & Appraisers

**Indian,** Basket, Maidu, Vertical Rows, Stacked Design, Single Rod, Early 1900s, 4 x 7¼ In.
$316

Allard Auctions

**Indian,** Basket, Ojibway, Basket Shape, Birch, Embroidered, Margaret Hill, 1970s, 2¼ x 9¼ In.
$316

Allard Auctions

**Indian,** Basket, Woodlands, Lid, Birch Bark, Quills, Flowers, c.1950, 2 x 6½ In.
$489

Allard Auctions

| | |
|---|---|
| **Tulip,** Jardiniere, Rose To Cream, Blue, Tapered, 9 In. | 40 |
| **Tulip,** Pitcher, Flowers, Cream To Blue, Scroll Handle, 13½ In. | 173 |
| **Tulip,** Pitcher, Vase, Bud, Cream To Blue, 6¾ In. | 18 |
| **Tulip,** Vase, Cream To Blue, Flared, Tapered, High Handles, 10½ In. | 29 |
| **Tulip,** Vase, Flowers, Cream To Blue, Deep Scallop Rim, Triple Loop Handles, 9 In. | 29 |
| **Tulip,** Vase, Flowers, Cream To Blue, Wing Handles, 6⅞ In. | 25 |
| **Tulip,** Vase, Suspended, U-Shape Frame, Pink, To Blue, Flowers, 7 In. | 63 |
| **Water Lily,** Jardiniere, Pink, Green, Round, 8⅝ In. | 28 |
| **Water Lily,** Vase, Brown, Divided Rim, Arched Handles, 9½ In. | 46 |
| **Water Lily,** Vase, Lobed, Petal Rim, Base Handles, Footed, Marked, 8¾ In. | 22 |
| **Wildflower,** Basket, Pink, Wavy Rim, 7¾ In. | 150 |
| **Wildflower,** Console, Wavy Rim, Rose Interior, 12½ In. | 27 |
| **Wildflower,** Pitcher, Horizontal Ribbed, Green, Mossy Blue, Red Panels, 13½ In. | 81 |
| **Wildflower,** Vase, Yellow Petal Mouth, Handles, 5½ In. | 23 |
| **Woodland,** Cornucopia, Double, Gloss, Green, To Red, Tapered, Footed, 8⅞ In. | 17 |
| **Woodland,** Cornucopia, Green Footed Base, Swirl Handle, Marked, 11¼ In. | 29 |
| **Woodland,** Ewer, Red Flower, Gilt Trim, 6⅞ In. | 18 |
| **Woodland,** Vase, Matte, Lobed, Flared, Base Green Handles, 8⅞ In. | 46 |
| **Woodland,** Vase, Suspended, Green Frame, Yellow Scalloped Bowl, c.1945, 7⅝ In. | 58 |
| **Woodland,** Wall Pocket, Green, Yellow, Marked, 7⅞ In. | 86 |

**HUMMEL** figurines, based on the drawings of the nun M.I. Hummel (Berta Hummel), were made by the W. Goebel Porzellanfabrik of Oeslau, Germany, now Rodental, Germany. They were first made in 1935. The *Crown* mark was used from 1935 to 1949. The company added the *bee* marks in 1950. The *full bee* with variations was used from 1950 to 1959; *stylized bee*, 1957 to 1972; *three line mark*, 1964 to 1972; *last bee*, sometimes called *vee over gee*, 1972 to 1979. In 1979 the V bee symbol was removed from the mark. *U.S. Zone* was part of the mark from 1946 to 1948; *W. Germany* was part of the mark from 1960 to 1990. The Goebel *W. Germany* mark, called the *missing bee* mark, was used from 1979 to 1990; *Goebel, Germany*, with the crown and *WG*, originally called the *new mark*, was used from 1991 through part of 1999. A new version of the bee mark with the word *Goebel* was used from 1999 to 2008. A special *Year 2000* backstamp was also introduced. Porcelain figures inspired by Berta Hummel's drawings were introduced in 1997. These are marked *BH* followed by a number. They were made in the Far East, not Germany. Goebel discontinued making Hummel figurines in 2008 and Manufaktur Rodental took over the factory in Germany and began making new Hummel figurines. Hummel figurines made by Rodental are marked with a yellow and black bee on the edge of an oval line surrounding the words *Original M.I. Hummel Germany.* The words *Manufaktur Rodental* are printed beneath the oval. Manufaktur Rodental was sold in 2013 and new owners have taken over. Hummel Manufaktur GmbH is the new company. Other decorative items and plates that feature Hummel drawings have been made by Schmid Brothers, Inc., since 1971.

| | |
|---|---|
| **Figurine,** Harmony In 4 Parts, 4 Boys Singing, Lantern, Missing Bee, 9¾ x 9 In. | 1200 |
| **Figurine,** No. 2/II, Little Fiddler, Goebel Bee, 11 In. | 266 |
| **Figurine,** No. 2/II, Little Fiddler, Last Bee, 11 In. | 83 |
| **Figurine,** No. 3, Festival Harmony Mandolin Player, Stylized Bee, 10½ In. | 177 |
| **Figurine,** No. 3/II, Bookworm, Goebel Bee, 9½ In. | 130 |
| **Figurine,** No. 7/I, Merry Wanderer, Crown Mark, 7½ In. | 192 |
| **Figurine,** No. 7/II, Merry Wanderer, Last Bee, 10 In. ............*illus* | 236 |
| **Figurine,** No. 12/II, Heavenly Angel, Last Bee, 8¾ In. | 83 |
| **Figurine,** No. 47, Goose Girl, Last Bee, 7¾ In. | 35 |
| **Figurine,** No. 71, Stormy Weather, Full Bee, 6½ In. | 30 |
| **Figurine,** No. 88, Heavenly Protection, Angel, Over 2 Children, 9½ In. | 150 |
| **Figurine,** No. 89/II, Figure Hear Ye, Hear Ye, Last Bee, 7½ In. | 47 |
| **Figurine,** No. 126/V, Friends, Last Bee, 11 In. | 354 |
| **Figurine,** No. 143, Boots, Hummel Mark, 7 In. | 47 |
| **Figurine,** No. 152/IIB, Umbrella Girl, Goebel Bee, 7¾ In. ............*illus* | 384 |
| **Figurine,** No. 170/II, School Boys, Goebel Bee, 9¾ In. ............*illus* | 201 |
| **Figurine,** No. 177/III, School Girls, Hummel Mark, 9½ In. | 236 |
| **Figurine,** No. 226, Mail Is Here, Last Bee, 4¾ x 6¾ In. | 83 |
| **Figurine,** No. 331, Crossroads, Last Bee, 6½ In. | 47 |
| **Figurine,** No. 340, Letter For Santa, Missing Bee, 7¼ In. | 47 |
| **Figurine,** No. 347, Adventure Bound, Missing Bee, 7⅛ In. | 1495 |
| **Figurine,** No. 348, Ring Around The Rosie, Full Bee, 6½ In. | 177 |
| **Figurine,** No. 348, Ring Around The Rosie, Missing Bee, 7 In. | 805 |
| **Figurine,** No. 406, Pleasant Journey, Missing Bee, Box, 6½ In. ............*illus* | 236 |
| **Figurine,** No. 416, Jubilee, 50 Year Anniversary, Box, Missing Bee, 6¼ In. | 83 |
| **Figurine,** No. 471, Harmony In 4 Parts, Goebel, Missing Bee, 10¼ In. | 600 |
| **Figurine,** No. 487, Let's Tell The World, Box, Missing Bee, 10½ In. | 212 |

H

| | |
|---|---|
| **Figurine,** No. 635, Welcome Spring, Box, Hummel Mark, 12 ½ In. | 265 |
| **Figurine,** No. 757, A Tuneful Trio, Goebel, Germany, Box, 6 ¾ In. | 153 |
| **Lamp,** No. 228, Good Friend, 15 In. | 59 |
| **Tree Topper,** No. 755, Heavenly Angel, Stand, Box, 8 ¾ In. | 130 |

**HUTSCHENREUTHER PORCELAIN FACTORY** was founded by Carolus Magnus in Hohenburg, Bavaria, in 1814. A second factory was established in Selb, Germany, in 1857. The company made fine quality porcelain dinnerware and figurines. The mark changed through the years, but the name and the lion insignia appear in most versions. Hutschenreuther became part of the Rosenthal division of the Waterford Wedgwood Group in 2000. Rosenthal was bought by Sambonet Paderno Industries, headquartered in Orfento, Novaro, Italy, in 2009.

| | |
|---|---|
| **Bowl,** Lid, Blue, Silver Overlay Flowers, Melon Shape, Green Finial, 8 x 6 In. | 63 |
| **Figurine,** Art Deco Nude, Plinth Base, Stamp Logo, Paper Label, 8 ⅝ In. | 161 |
| **Figurine,** Nude Woman, Raised Arms, White, Standing, Foot On Gold Ball, 13 In. | 300 |
| **Group,** Bremen Town Musicians, Donkey, 3 Animals On Each Other, 7 ½ In. | 150 |
| **Milk Set,** Cup, Dome Lid, Handles, Underplate, Etched Gilt, Flowers, c.1910, 5 In. | 104 |
| **Plaque,** Woman, Long Brown Hair, Oval, Frame, c.1910, 5 x 4 In. | 720 |
| **Plate,** Flower, 2 Green Bands, Wide Gilt Bands, c.1930, 10 ¾ In., 12 Piece | 403 |
| **Plate,** Flower, Scroll, Allover Gilt, c.1930, 10 ¾ In., 12 Piece | 431 |
| **Plate,** Service, Art Deco, Raised Gilt Borders, Shagreen Ground, 11 In., 6 Piece | 276 |
| **Plate,** Service, White Center, Green, Ivory, Gilt Floral Rim, 10 ⅝ In., 11 Piece | 295 |

**ICONS,** special, revered pictures of Jesus, Mary, or a saint, are usually Russian or Byzantine. The small icons collected today are made of wood and tin or precious metals. Many modern copies have been made in the old style and are being sold to tourists in Russia and Europe and at shops in the United States. Rare, old icons have sold for over $50,000. The riza is the metal cover protecting the icon. It is often made of silver or gold.

| | |
|---|---|
| **4 Patron Saints,** Christ, Russia, c.1900, 8 x 7 In. | 492 |
| **Annunciation,** Angel Gabriel, Mary, Cyrillic Text, Painted Giltwood, Russia, 12 x 11 In. | 1088 |
| **Archangel Michael,** Red Pegasus, 4 Saints, Jesus Christ, Russia, 13 ½ x 12 In. | 615 |
| **Christ,** Silver, Oil On Panel, St. Petersburg Mark, E. Brandenburg Assayer, c.1855, 7 x 6 In. | 400 |
| **Devotion Scene,** Tempera On Wood, Silver Riza, Marked, Russia, 8 ¾ x 7 In. *illus* | 600 |
| **Kazan Mother Of God,** Mother & Child Beneath Chased Riza, Silver Oklad, 1880, 7 x 6 In. | 938 |
| **Kazan Mother Of God,** Traveling, Triptych, Saints, Blue, White Enamels, Russia, 4 x 4 ½ In. | 92 |
| **Mother & Child,** Silver, Pierced Brass Surround, Oklad, Russia, c.1885, 11 x 9 In. | 300 |
| **Nativity Of The Mother Of God,** 19th Century, Russia, 12 ¼ x 10 In. | 369 |
| **Prophet Elijah & Fiery Chariot,** Cyrillic Text, Painted Giltwood, Russia, 13 x 12 In. | 1536 |
| **Resurrection,** Feast Days, Brown Border, 2 Saints, Composite, Russia, 43 ½ x 35 ½ In. | 3321 |
| **St. Anna,** Standing, Blue Enamel, Silver, Inset Stone, Russia, 8 In. | 10625 |
| **St. George Slaying Dragon,** Cast Bronze, Traveling, Triptych, Blue, White Enamel, 4 x 5 In. | 127 |
| **St. George,** Dragon, Silver Plate Riza, Scroll, Leaves, Gilt Halo, Russia, 11 ¾ x 10 In. | 677 |
| **St. George,** On Horseback, Slaying Dragon, Tempera On Wood, Gold Ground, 10 x 7 ½ In. | 259 |
| **St. Nicholas,** Bishop's Robes, Gospels, Cloisonne Brass Riza, Velvet, Russia, 8 ½ x 6 ¾ In. | 923 |
| **St. Nicholas,** Silver Mounter, Halo, Oak Frame, 10 ½ x 8 ¼ In. | 840 |
| **St. Sergius Of Radonezh,** Traveling, Silver, Enamel, Russia, 3 ½ x 2 ¼ In. | 960 |
| **Virgin Of Kazan,** Sterling, Enamel Riza, Nicolay Kemper, c.1900, 3 ½ x 2 ⅞ In. | 13420 |
| **Vladimir Mother Of God,** Madonna & Child, Egg Tempera On Wood, Gold Leaf, 13 x 10 In. | 1438 |

**IMARI** porcelain was made in Japan and China beginning in the seventeenth century. In the eighteenth century and later, it was copied by porcelain factories in Germany, France, England, and the United States. It was especially popular in the nineteenth century and is still being made. Imari is characteristically decorated with stylized bamboo, floral, and geometric designs in orange, red, green, and blue. The name comes from the Japanese port of Imari, which exported the ware made nearby in a factory at Arita. Imari is now a general term for any pattern of this type.

| | |
|---|---|
| **Bowl,** Barber's, Flowers, Iron Red, Cobalt Blue, 2 ½ x 10 ⅝ In. | 984 |
| **Bowl,** Blue, Rose, Flowers, Ormolu Bird Mounts, Stand, Chinese, 5 x 11 ½ In. | 240 |
| **Bowl,** Blue, White, Flowers, Leaves, Scalloped Edge, Japan, c.1900, 11 In., 2 Piece | 185 |
| **Bowl,** Dragon & Flaming Pearl, Flowers, Ming Wanli Mark, Japan, 6 x 13 In. *illus* | 738 |
| **Bowl,** Flowers, Gilt, Stylized Bat, Japan, 5 x 11 ¼ In. | 885 |
| **Bowl,** Gilt Rim, Japan, Wooden Stand, 9 ½ x 15 ¾ In. | 120 |
| **Bowl,** Napoleon III, Gilt Bronze, U-Shape, Angular Handles, Loops, Swag Rim, 12 x 18 In. | 1912 |
| **Bowl,** Round, Scalloped, Flowers, Red, Blue, Japan, 1800s, 2 x 6 In. | 154 |
| **Bowl,** Scalloped, Bands, Goldfish Center, Marked, c.1900, 14 ¼ In. *illus* | 308 |
| **Charger,** Cobalt Blue, Iron Red, Green, Gold, Footed, Japan, 16 x 2 ¼ In. | 63 |
| **Charger,** Crane, Leaves, 12 In. | 189 |

**Indian,** Belt, Navajo, 6 Conchas, Silver, Repousse Spider Buckle, 1950s, 41 In.
$1,035

Allard Auctions

**Indian,** Belt, Navajo, 6 Conchas, Silver, Turquoise Stone, Butterfly Spacers, Conchas 4 x 3 In.
$2,829

Skinner Auctioneers & Appraisers

**Indian,** Blanket, Navajo, Rows Of Serrated Diamonds, Crosses, 1890-1910, 98 x 55 In.
$1,180

Brunk Auctions

This is an edited listing of current prices. Visit **Kovels.com** to check thousands of prices from previous years and sign up for free information on trends, tips, reproductions, marks, and more.

**Indian,** Blanket, Rug, Navajo, Wool, Serrated Diamonds, Red Ground, 76 x 51 In.

$2,460

Skinner Auctioneers & Appraisers

**Indian,** Bottle, Paiute, Glass, Woven Bead Lid, Fully Beaded, c.1950, 11½ x 3¼ In.

$196

Allard Auctions

**Indian,** Bowl, Pomo, Coiled Basket, Brown, Oval, Geometric & Zigzag Design, c.1880, 4 x 12 In.

$2,337

Skinner Auctioneers & Appraisers

| | |
|---|---:|
| **Charger,** Flowers, Bonsai, Landscape, Panels, 18 In. | 266 |
| **Charger,** Leaves, Chrysanthemum Shape, Japan, 1868-1912, 18 In. | 478 |
| **Charger,** Paneled, Exotic Birds, Green, Gilt Accents, Japan, c.1930, 18 In. | 150 |
| **Charger,** Reserves, Flowers, Landscapes, 2 Blue Rings Reverse, Wood Stand, 18½ In. | 369 |
| **Charger,** Round, Scalloped, Panels, Flowers, Landscapes, Red, Blue, Japan, 15¼ In. | 800 |
| **Charger,** Round, Scalloped, Panels, Flowers, Orange, Red, Blue, Japan, 1800s, 18 In. | 338 |
| **Charger,** U-Shape Body, Flared Rim, Pinwheels, Leaves, Flowers, c.1700, 15 In., Pair | 837 |
| **Dish,** Chrysanthemum, Shallow, Petal Lobed Sides, Landscape, Brocade Panels, 12 In. | 122 |
| **Dish,** Falcons, Phoenixes, Landscape, Flowers, Round Foot, Blue Rim, 14 In., Pair | 708 |
| **Footbath,** Flowers, Leaves, Branch Handles, c.1850, 21 x 9 In. | 212 |
| **Inkwell,** Molded Tray, Red, Blue, White, 2 Inkpots, 3¾ x 8¾ In. | 615 |
| **Jar,** Dome Lid, Lotus Finials, Flowers, 15¼ In., Pair | 1180 |
| **Jar,** Dome Lid, Ribbed Body, Foo Dog Finial, c.1890, 25¼ In., Pair ........*illus* | 1180 |
| **Jar,** Lid, Finials, Hexagons, Flowers, Birds, c.1900, 26¾ In. | 2032 |
| **Jar,** Lid, Flowers, Flying Pheasants Reserves, Blue, Orange, Lobed, Japan, c.1910, 27 In. | 875 |
| **Landscape,** Blue, White, Red, Japan, c.1920, 43 In. | 2625 |
| **Plate,** Gilt, Koi, Fruit Trees, Phoenixes, Early 20th Century, 10⅜ In., 12 Piece | 236 |
| **Platter,** Flowers, Foo Dog Corners, Peony Border, Barbed Rim, Japan, 12½ In. .......*illus* | 472 |
| **Punch Bowl,** Leaf Reserves, Blue Exotic Birds, Orange Fronds, Flower Urn, c.1900, 8 x 18 In. | 2015 |
| **Tray,** Black, Cream, Shell Shape Handles, 18¼ x 12 In. | 780 |
| **Tureen,** Lid, Underplate, Riverscape, Boar Head Handles, Japan, 1800s, 15¼ In. .......*illus* | 4375 |
| **Umbrella Stand,** Blue, Orange, Japan, 24 In. | 1750 |
| **Umbrella Stand,** Iron Red Underglaze, Blue Flowers, 1800s, 24¼ x 8¾ In. ........*illus* | 799 |
| **Urn,** Lid, Orange, Blue Flowers, Foo Dog Finial, Japan, c.1890, 20 In. | 1375 |
| **Vase,** Blue & Red Enamel, Gilt Accents, Scrolling Vine Inner Lip, c.1890, 37 x 17 In. | 3690 |
| **Vase,** Cobalt Blue, Iron Red, Gilding, Japan, c.1900, 4 x 2¾ In., Pair | 369 |
| **Vase,** Dragon, Enameled, 3-Dimensional, Applied Dragon, Hardwood Stand, 20 x 25 In. | 236 |
| **Vase,** Horizontal Bands, Fruit, Flower Heads, Branches, Gilt, Japan, 13 x 8½ In. | 900 |
| **Vase,** Iron Red, Cobalt Blue, Leaf Designs, 16 x 18 In., Pair | 242 |
| **Vase,** Iron Red Enamel, Foo Dog, Butterfly, Mums, Bottle Shape, Chinese, c.1750, 11¾ In. | 960 |
| **Vase,** Navy, Iris, Chrysanthemum, Japan, 4⅝ x 2 In., Pair | 1800 |
| **Vase,** Stand, Red Cobalt, Flowers, 9 In., Pair | 259 |
| **Vase,** Urn Shape, Carved Pierced Dome, Ruyie Style, Figures, Landscape, 17 x 11 In. | 633 |

**IMPERIAL GLASS CORPORATION** was founded in Bellaire, Ohio, in 1901. It became a subsidiary of Lenox, Inc., in 1973 and was sold to Arthur R. Lorch in 1981. It was sold again in 1982, and went bankrupt in 1984. In 1985, the molds and some assets were sold. The Imperial glass preferred by the collector is freehand art glass, carnival glass, slag glass, stretch glass, and other top-quality tablewares. Tablewares and animals are listed here. The others may be found in the appropriate sections.

IMPE
RIAL

| | |
|---|---:|
| **Ashtray,** Snuffy Smith, Multicolor Gloss, Copyright 1946, 6 x 3¾ In. | 58 |
| **Candlewick,** Cocktail, 3½ x 5¼ In. | 28 |
| **Candlewick,** Cordial, Ruby Red, 3½ In., 4 Piece | 80 |
| **Candlewick,** Sugar & Creamer | 19 |
| **Candlewick,** Whiskey Sour Glass, 3 Bead Stem, 2⁷⁄₁₆ x 5½ In., Pair | 35 |
| **Cape Cod,** Goblet, Water, 5½ In. | 4 |
| **Cape Cod,** Juice, 4¼ In. | 7 |
| **Cape Cod,** Plate, Salad, 8 In. | 6 |
| **Cape Cod,** Relish, 4-Part, Handles, Round | 21 |
| **Cape Cod,** Sugar | 12 |
| **Cathay,** Urn, Lid, Bamboo, Azalea, Cranberry Satin, c.1965, 9½ In. | 69 |
| **Dresser Box,** Daisy Mae, Seated, On Lid, Marked, 4¼ In. | 127 |
| **Free Hand,** Candlestick, Orange & Blue Drag Loop, 11 In. | 173 |
| **Free Hand,** Vase, Blue & Orange Drag Loops, 3 Cobalt Blue Feet, Lip Wrap, 8 In. | 920 |
| **Grape No. 473,** Punch Bowl, Green, Scalloped Rim, Pedestal, c.1920, 9½ x 12 In. | 104 |
| **Grape,** Bowl, Green Iridescent, Scalloped Rim, 6-Sided, 9 x 3½ In. | 38 |
| **Lace Edge,** Vase, Katy Blue, Lid, Footed, 5¼ x 3½ In. | 45 |
| **Lamp Base,** Dagwood, Standing By Tree, Multicolor Glaze, 8¼ In. | 115 |
| **Vase,** Cobalt Blue, White Opal Leaves, Vines, Flaring Rim, Marigold Luster, 7¾ In. | 316 |
| **Vase,** Leaf & Vine, Cream Mottled, Mirror Bronze Ground, Rolled Rim, 3 Handles, 11 In. | 1244 |

**INDIAN** art from North and South America has attracted the collector for many years. Each tribe has its own distinctive designs and techniques. Baskets, jewelry, pottery, and leatherwork are of greatest collector interest. Eskimo art is listed under Eskimo in this book.

| | |
|---|---:|
| **Awl Case,** Apache, Stepped Design, Tin Cone Danglers On Fringe, c.1885, 13 In. | 1230 |

| | |
|---|---|
| **Ax,** Bronze Head, Wood Handle, Trade, 18 ¾ In................................................ | 960 |
| **Backrest,** Blackfoot, Willow Rods, Hide Fastener, Beaded, Child, c.1865, 42 x 28 ½ In................ | 2460 |
| **Bag,** Medicine, Apache, Beaded, Tanned Deer Hide, Drawstring Closure, 3 ½ x 2 ½ In.............. | 104 |
| **Bag,** Plateau, Beaded, Contour Style, Girl Figure, Handle, c.1890, 8 x 8 ¾ In.................*illus* | 1265 |
| **Bag,** Plateau, Beaded, Heart Shape, Buckskin, Flowers, Handles, 1920s, 12 ½ x 11 In.............. | 518 |
| **Bag,** Plateau, Beaded, Tradecloth, Red Flower, Leaves, 1930s, 12 x 10 In.......................... | 259 |
| **Bag,** Plateau, Hide & Cloth, Beaded, Horse, Flowers, Border, c.1925, 12 ½ x 11 In.............*illus* | 1968 |
| **Bag,** Tobacco, Sioux, Hide, Geometric Beadwork, Quillwork, Fringe, 36 In....................... | 2478 |
| **Bag,** Wasco, Sally, Lid, Soft Weave, Figures, Condors, Deer, c.1880, 10 x 6 In..............*illus* | 4313 |
| **Bandolier,** Chippewa, Beaded Cloth, Flowers, Fringe, c.1910, 44 x 14 In.....................*illus* | 875 |
| **Bandolier,** Woodlands, Beaded, Traditional Flowers, Chippewa Strap, c.1910, 40 x 14 In........... | 1093 |
| **Basket Lid,** Northeast Woodland, Split Ash, Rectangular, Painted, 11 x 17 x 10 In................. | 720 |
| **Basket,** Achumawi, Globe Shape, Serrated Chevrons, c.1910, 5 ¾ x 10 ½ In....................... | 805 |
| **Basket,** Algonquian, Picnic, 2-Tier Lid, Swing Handles, c.1900, 11 x 19 In...................... | 86 |
| **Basket,** Apache, Bowl Shape, Banded, Human Figures, Animals, c.1910, 5 x 14 ¼ In..........*illus* | 3198 |
| **Basket,** Apache, Bowl Shape, Coiled, 5-Point Star, Animals, c.1920, 16 In....................... | 800 |
| **Basket,** Apache, Geometrics, Central Flower, c.1920, 5 x 15 In................................. | 1024 |
| **Basket,** Burden, Cherokee, White Oak, Walnut & Bloodroot Dyes, Curls, Flared, 4 x 3 In.......... | 413 |
| **Basket,** Cherokee, River Cane, Double Weave, Eva Wolfe, Swain Co., N.C., 15 x 12 In............. | 4012 |
| **Basket,** Cherokee, River Cane, Dyed, Red Bands, Diamonds, Square Base, 13 In.................... | 708 |
| **Basket,** Hupa, Bowl Shape, Serrated Triangle, Beige, Brown, Black, 5 ½ x 8 In................... | 748 |
| **Basket,** Klickitat, Cooking, Hard Sided, Overlapping Geometric Design, c.1910, 11 x 12 In........ | 690 |
| **Basket,** Lid, Cherokee, River Cane, Double Weave, Rowena Bradley, 14 x 10 x 10 In............... | 6490 |
| **Basket,** Maidu, Bowl Shape, Geometric Pattern, Early 1900s, 3 x 8 ½ In.......................... | 690 |
| **Basket,** Maidu, Vertical Rows, Stacked Design, Single Rod, Early 1900s, 4 x 7 ¼ In...........*illus* | 316 |
| **Basket,** Navajo, Storage Jar, Woven, Geometric Design, c.1900, 11 x 12 In....................... | 360 |
| **Basket,** Navajo, Storage Jar, Woven, Geometric Design, c.1900, 14 In............................ | 600 |
| **Basket,** Northern California, Lid, Geometric Designs, Round, c.1925, 3 ½ x 5 ¼ In................ | 360 |
| **Basket,** Ojibway, Basket Shape, Birch, Embroidered, Margaret Hill, 1970s, 2 ¼ x 9 ¼ In.......*illus* | 316 |
| **Basket,** Papago, Greek Key Design, Tapered, Arizona, c.1900, 4 x 14 ½ In........................ | 420 |
| **Basket,** Papago, Lid, Butterfly, Star, Arizona, 5 x 6 ½ In...................................... | 210 |
| **Basket,** Papago, Round, Tapered, Geometric Design, 6 x 14 In................................... | 120 |
| **Basket,** Papago, Tray, 4-Petal Flower Interior, c.1955, 11 ½ In................................. | 120 |
| **Basket,** Pima, Bowl Shape, Coiled, Brown, Black, c.1920, 14 In................................. | 338 |
| **Basket,** Pima, Horsehair, Multicolor, Friendship Figured Band, Wedding Design, c.1970, 5 In..... | 489 |
| **Basket,** Pima, Oval, Men, 4 x 7 ¾ In.......................................................... | 234 |
| **Basket,** Pima, Papago, Horses, 4 x 7 In....................................................... | 205 |
| **Basket,** Tohona O'Odham, Burden, Woven, Flying Ducks, Scalloped Edge, 1950s, 14 In............. | 300 |
| **Basket,** Trinket, Karuk, Lid, ½ Twist Overlay, Bear Grass, Maidenhair Fern, 1970s, 6 x 5 In........ | 489 |
| **Basket,** Trinket, Papago, Lid, Square Braided Knob, c.1955, 5 In................................ | 60 |
| **Basket,** Woodlands, Lid, Birch Bark, Quills, Flowers, c.1950, 2 x 6 ½ In.....................*illus* | 489 |
| **Basket,** Woodlands, Round, Black, Orange Paint, c.1890, 12 ½ x 18 In............................ | 390 |
| **Basket,** Yokuts, Bowl, Rattlesnake, Zigzag, Diamond Bands, c.1900, 6 ¾ x 13 In.................. | 960 |
| **Basket,** Yokuts, Jar, Coiled, 3 Figure Rows, Multicolor, Tapered, c.1900, 4 ¾ x 7 In............. | 8400 |
| **Basket,** Yokuts, Woven, 2-Tone Triangle Design, Tapered, Flat Shoulder, c.1900, 4 x 7 In......... | 1020 |
| **Belt,** Navajo, 6 Conchas, Silver, Repousse Spider Buckle, 1950s, 41 In......................*illus* | 1035 |
| **Belt,** Navajo, 6 Conchas, Silver, Turquoise Stone, Butterfly Spacers, Conchas 4 x 3 In........*illus* | 2829 |
| **Belt,** Navajo, Concha, Silver, Wrought, Buckle, Stacy Gishal, 1980s, 56 x 2 ½ In................ | 978 |
| **Belt,** Plateau, Leather, Beaded Section, Crosses, Stripes, Brass Tacks, 37 x 2 ¼ In.............. | 288 |
| **Blanket,** Chimayo, Woven, Multicolor Stripes, Red Wool Tasseled Ends, c.1920, 55 x 100 In....... | 356 |
| **Blanket,** Navajo, Chief's, Cross Decoration, Tan, Red, Black, 36 x 64 In........................ | 3660 |
| **Blanket,** Navajo, Double Saddle, Gray, Red, Central Panels, Crosses, Stripes, 54 x 31 In.......... | 4305 |
| **Blanket,** Navajo, Rows Of Serrated Diamonds, Crosses, 1890-1910, 98 x 55 In.................*illus* | 1180 |
| **Blanket,** Navajo, Tres Nos Pattern, Red Mesa Outline, Gray, Black, 78 x 42 In................... | 908 |
| **Blanket,** Navajo, Triangular Pattern, Red, Gray, White, Black, c.1950, 56 x 46 In................ | 563 |
| **Blanket,** Rug, Navajo, Wool, Serrated Diamonds, Red Ground, 76 x 51 In.....................*illus* | 2460 |
| **Bolo,** Zuni, Turquoise, Silver, Chief Dancer, Carved, Barrel Drums, 1970s, 46 x 5 ¼ In........... | 748 |
| **Bottle,** Paiute, Glass, Woven Bead Lid, Fully Beaded, c.1950, 11 ½ x 3 ¼ In..................*illus* | 196 |
| **Bowl,** Apache, 3 x 11 ½ In................................................................... | 526 |
| **Bowl,** Columbia River, Burl, Carved, Handles, c.1890, 11 ¼ x 9 ½ In............................ | 1380 |
| **Bowl,** Eastern Woodlands, Burl, Incised Ring, c.1820, 9 x 18 In................................ | 1265 |
| **Bowl,** Hopi Tewa, Round, Brown, Black, Tapered, Annie Healing, c.1930, 3 x 6 In................ | 185 |
| **Bowl,** Hopi, Multicolor On Buff, Incurve Rim, Signed Carol Namoki, c.1960, 3 x 6 ½ In........... | 115 |
| **Bowl,** Laguna, Pottery, Mimbres Style, Black On White, Bats, Kanteena, 1980s, 4 ½ In............ | 184 |
| **Bowl,** Pomo, Coiled Basket, Brown, Oval, Geometric & Zigzag Design, c.1880, 4 x 12 In......*illus* | 2337 |
| **Bowl,** San Ildefonso, Blue Corn, Blackware, Carved, Avanyu Serpent, 1960s, 2 ¾ x 4 In........... | 374 |

**Indian,** Box, Glove, Birch Bark, Camp Scenes, Animals, Tomah Joseph, 11 x 3 ½ In.
$1,230

**Indian,** Cape, Great Lakes, Cloth, Feathers, Crescent Shape, Long Tabs, c.1850, 27 In.
$1,476

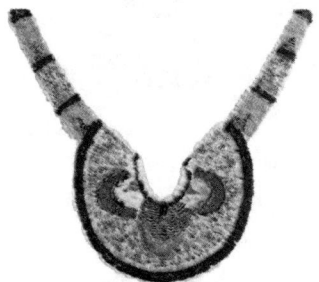

**Indian,** Cradle, Lakota, Beaded, Hide, Geometric Designs, White Ground, c.1880, 22 In.
$9,225

# INDIAN

**Indian,** Doll, Cree, Hide Face &
Moccasins, Beaded Outfit, 1940s, 13 ½ In.
$403

Allard Auctions

**Indian,** Doll, Skookum, Buckskin
Moccasins, Bully Good Label, 1900s,
19 In.
$230

Allard Auctions

**Indian,** Doll, Skookum, Papier-Mache,
Painted Face, Mohair Wig, Mary McAboy,
c.1925, 71 In.
$2,508

Theriault's

302

| | |
|---|---|
| **Bowl,** San Ildefonso, Swirling Wing, Black On Black, Maria & Julian Martinez, 3 ½ In. | 210 |
| **Bowl,** Santa Clara, Melon Shape, Fluted Sides, Polished Blackware, c.1930, 9 In. | 120 |
| **Bowl,** Santa Clara, Round, Tapered, Margaret Tafoya, 4 x 5 ¼ In. | 150 |
| **Bowl,** Woodlands, Oval, Cutout Handles, c.1805, 22 x 16 In. | 9600 |
| **Box,** Glove, Birch Bark, Camp Scenes, Animals, Tomah Joseph, 11 x 3 ½ In. *illus* | 1230 |
| **Box,** Northwest Coast, Painted, Tribal Decorations, c.1910, 5 x 5 ½ In. | 1250 |
| **Bracelet,** Navajo, Cuff, Burst Design, Turquoise, Sterling, Signed JW MS, 2 ½ x 2 In. | 322 |
| **Canoe Cup,** Iroquois, Hole In Handle, c.1775, 5 ¾ x 2 ⅝ In. | 350 |
| **Cape,** Great Lakes, Cloth, Feathers, Crescent Shape, Long Tabs, c.1850, 27 In. *illus* | 1476 |
| **Cradle,** Lakota, Beaded, Hide, Geometric Designs, White Ground, c.1880, 22 In. *illus* | 9225 |
| **Cradleboard,** Shoshone, Basketry, Woven Willow, Root, Buckskin, Beads, c.1950, 13 x 29 In. | 374 |
| **Doll,** Cree, Hide Face & Moccasins, Beaded Outfit, 1940s, 13 ½ In. *illus* | 403 |
| **Doll,** Skookum, Buckskin Moccasins, Bully Good Label, 1900s, 19 In. *illus* | 230 |
| **Doll,** Skookum, Papier-Mache, Painted Face, Mohair Wig, Mary McAboy, c.1925, 71 In. *illus* | 2508 |
| **Dress,** Woodlands, Jingle, Black Cloth, Rolled Cones, Tin Conchas, c.1910, Medium | 805 |
| **Drum,** Gaming, Northwest Coast, Bentwood, Rawhide, Wolf Figure, 1970s, 13 In. *illus* | 173 |
| **Fetish,** Plains, Turtle, Beaded, Tin Cone Feather Danglers, c.1885, 11 ½ x 5 ¾ In. | 2091 |
| **Figure,** Chiriqui, Shaman, Male, Crown, Headdress, Holding Rattles, 14K Gold, 2 ¼ In. *illus* | 3075 |
| **Gauntlets,** Beaded Tops, Flower Designs, Fringe, c.1910, Size Medium *illus* | 2588 |
| **Gloves,** Plateau, Beaded, Floral Cuff & Backhand Designs, Long, c.1950, Medium | 460 |
| **Hat,** Navajo, Silver Concha, Hat Band, Stetson Hat, Wrought, c.1950, 29 In. | 489 |
| **Iron Head,** Falcon, Leaves, Gold Overlay, Leather Grip, Horseman's, 1700s | 2300 |
| **Jar,** Acoma, Multicolor, Geometric, Volute, White Ground, 7 x 8 ½ In. | 984 |
| **Jar,** Acoma, Multicolor, Pottery, Bird, Leaves, Geometric, White Ground, 7 ½ x 10 In. | 615 |
| **Jar,** Acoma, Stylized Geometric Designs, 1930s, 8 ½ x 11 ½ In. *illus* | 1353 |
| **Jar,** Hopi Tewa, Eagle Designs, Fannie Lesou Polacca, c.1940, 6 In. | 720 |
| **Jar,** Lid, 4 Indian Portraits, Black Ground, Rick Wisecarver, 1982, 20 In. | 1380 |
| **Jar,** Olla, Anasazi, Black On White, Checkered Medallions, Socorro, 12 ½ x 15 In. | 3738 |
| **Jar,** San Ildefonso, Feathered, Black On Black, c.1940, 6 In. | 210 |
| **Jar,** Santa Clara, Black, Handles, c.1930, 9 In. | 120 |
| **Jar,** Zia, Pottery, 4 Colors, Birds, Leaves, Scallops, White Ground, 10 x 11 In. | 2460 |
| **Katsina,** Crow, Dancing Position, Feather Headdress, Carved Wood, 21 x 11 In. | 85 |
| **Katsina,** Hopi, Antelope Dancer, Carved, Painted, 1970s, 15 x 8 In. | 138 |
| **Katsina,** Hopi, Crow, Dance Pose, Carved, Painted, R. Mitchell, 1970s, 16 ½ x 10 In. | 138 |
| **Katsina,** Hopi, Wood, Carved, Black, White, Purple, Hemis Maiden, Jimmy Koots, 11 In. | 1230 |
| **Katsina,** Hopi, Wood, Carved, Multicolor, 10 In. *illus* | 2091 |
| **Mat,** Navajo, Burnt Water, Brown, Tan, White Geometrics, Border, Tassels, 21 x 19 In. | 69 |
| **Moccasins,** Assiniboine, Beaded Geometrics, Blue Ground, c.1930, 11 In. | 300 |
| **Moccasins,** Beaded, Flowers, Cream, High Top, Brass Buttons, Leather, 9 In. | 180 |
| **Moccasins,** Beaded, Hide, Geometric Design, Youth, c.1880, 8 ½ In. *illus* | 615 |
| **Moccasins,** Cheyenne, Beaded, Lazy Stitch, Red Crosses, Blue Field, Hard Sole, c.1950, 10 In. | 374 |
| **Moccasins,** Cheyenne, Geometric Beadwork, Lazy Stitch, Buckskin, c.1910, Size 10 | 415 |
| **Moccasins,** Crow, Painted, Parfleche Soles, Partially Beaded, Multicolor, c.1885, 11 In. | 738 |
| **Moccasins,** Lakota, Green, Buffalo Tracks, c.1885, 10 ½ In. | 615 |
| **Moccasins,** Lakota, Multicolor On White, Geometric, c.1885, Child's, 5 ¾ In. | 1599 |
| **Moccasins,** Lakota, White Beaded, Multicolor Geometrics, Sitting Bull, 1800s, 9 In. | 9174 |
| **Moccasins,** Plains, Hide, Multicolor Translucent & Opaque Beads, c.1910, 9 ½ In. | 84 |
| **Moccasins,** Sioux, Beads, Blue, Red Yellows, Child's, 6 ½ In. | 978 |
| **Necklace,** Crow, Beaded Loop, Brass Tacks, Yellow, c.1885, 14 In. | 2952 |
| **Necklace,** Earrings, Navajo, Zuni, Turquoise, Silver, Squash Blossom, 1970s, 27 x 2 In. | 460 |
| **Necklace,** Navajo, 14 Squash Blossoms, Silver, Turquoise, Stamped Naja, 26 In. | 1845 |
| **Necklace,** Navajo, Silver, Traditional Beads, Joe H. Quintana, c.1970, 25 In. | 805 |
| **Necklace,** Navajo, Squash Blossom, Silver, Coral, 24 In. | 230 |
| **Necklace,** Navajo, Squash Blossom, Silver, Turquoise, 1970s, 31 In. *illus* | 575 |
| **Necklace,** Turquoise, Heishi Jocla Style, Coral Nugget, c.1950, 18 In. | 207 |
| **Olla,** Acoma, Squat, Red, Black & Cream, Abstract Design, c.1900, 11 In. Diam. *illus* | 2214 |
| **Olla,** Apache, Basketry, Vertical Stepped Design, Shouldered, c.1915, 13 x 11 In. | 1440 |
| **Olla,** Papago, Woman, With Pole, Hitting Saguaro Fruit, Bird Flying, c.1950, 13 In. | 180 |
| **Olla,** Zuni, Red, Painted Geometrics, Applied Frogs On Shoulder, c.1900, 7 ½ x 8 In. | 4313 |
| **Peyote Box,** Plains, Rattle, Silver Pins, Wood, Ritual Objects, c.1825, 15 x 4 x 4 | 1476 |
| **Pipe Bag,** Lakota, Beaded, Crosses, Flags, White, Tin Cone Horsehair, c.1885, 35 In. | 2460 |
| **Pipe Bag,** Pipe, Sioux, 3-Sided, Beads, File-Branded Ash, Elbow Horn, c.1885, 18 In. | 3075 |
| **Pipe,** Cherokee, Steatite, Figural, Seated Man, Bear Holding Frog, Marked, 6 ⅞ x 2 ¼ In. *illus* | 1320 |
| **Pipe,** Paiute, Soapstone, Carved, Straight, Wood Stem, Tradecloth, Ervin Lent, 9 ½ In. | 460 |
| **Plant Stand,** Woodland, Oak Strips, Green, Double Arched Rim, 4 Arched Feet, 34 x 12 In. | 295 |
| **Pot,** Ildefonso, Blackware, Geometric Design, Signed Maria Martinez, 1920-25, 5 ½ In. | 1718 |

**Indian,** Drum, Gaming, Northwest Coast, Bentwood, Rawhide, Wolf Figure, 1970s, 13 In. $173

**Indian,** Figure, Chiriqui, Shaman, Male, Crown, Headdress, Holding Rattles, 14K Gold, 2 ¼ In. $3,075

**Indian,** Gauntlets, Beaded Tops, Flower Designs, Fringe, c.1910, Size Medium $2,588

**Indian,** Jar, Acoma, Stylized Geometric Designs, 1930s, 8 ½ x 11 ½ In. $1,353

**Indian,** Katsina, Hopi, Wood, Carved, Multicolor, 10 In. $2,091

**Indian,** Moccasins, Beaded, Hide, Geometric Design, Youth, c.1880, 8 ½ In. $615

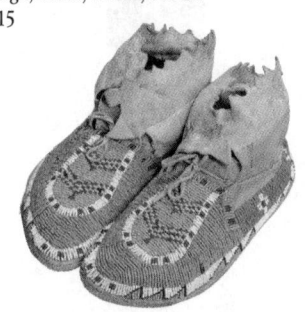

**Indian,** Necklace, Navajo, Squash Blossom, Silver, Turquoise, 1970s, 31 In. $575

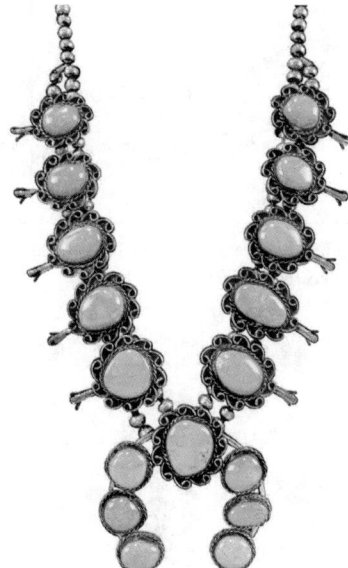

**TIP**

*Old iron heating grates have a new use. Put them on the outdoor mat to be used as mud scrapers.*

**Indian,** Olla, Acoma, Squat, Red, Black & Cream, Abstract Design, c.1900, 11 In. Diam. $2,214

**Indian,** Pipe, Cherokee, Steatite, Figural, Seated Man, Bear Holding Frog, Marked, 6 ⅞ x 2 ¼ In. $1,320

# INDIAN

**Indian,** Purse, Hupa, Antler, Bone Lid, Incised & Painted, Geometric Lines, c.1885, 4 ⅛ In.
$1,476

**Indian,** Rug, Navajo, 2 People, Black & Red, White Ground, 1930s-1940s, 30 x 13 In.
$184

**Indian,** Rug, Navajo, Ganado, Geometric Design, Black, White, Gray, Burgundy, 24 x 33 In.
$161

**Indian,** Sheath, Cheyenne, Beaded, Hide, Geometric Designs, Knife, c.1860, 9 In.
$5,535

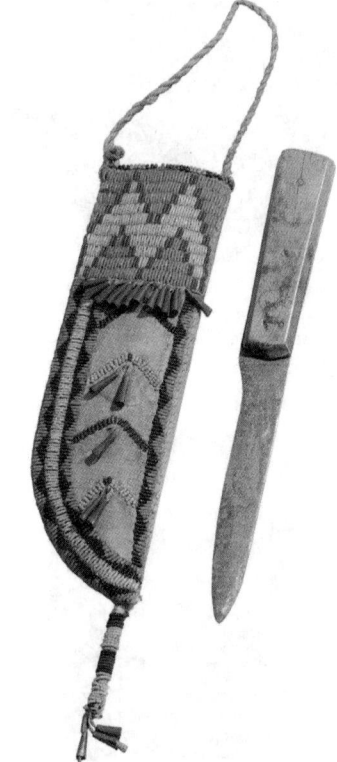

**Indian,** Totem Pole, Haida, Argillite, Human & Animal Figures, 13 ½ In.
$1,476

**Indian,** Tray, Yavapai, Basketry, Flower Design, Multicolor, c.1920, 12 ½ In.
$677

**Indian,** Vase, Hopi, Corn Maiden, Abstract Pottery Figure, Al Qoyawayma, 1985, 11 ½ In.
$1,320

**Indian,** Vest, Lakota, Beaded, Hide, Geometric Designs, Flags, Quilt Lined, c.1880, 19 ½ x 18 In.
$6,150

| | |
|---|---|
| **Pouch,** Apache, Strike-A-Light, Tin Cone Danglers, Silver Button, Beading, c.1885, 6 In............. | 984 |
| **Pouch,** Arapaho, Beaded Hide Paint, Tab-Bottom Shape, Red, Yellow, c.1885, 10 In................... | 584 |
| **Pouch,** Plateau, Beaded, 2-Sided, Buffalo, Warrior, Horseback, Strap, c.1920, 12 x 8 In............. | 1107 |
| **Purse,** Hupa, Antler, Bone Lid, Incised & Painted, Geometric Lines, c.1885, 4⅛ In..............*illus* | 1476 |
| **Rug,** Navajo, 2 Figures, Corn, Blue & Dark Red U-Shape Border, 38 x 38 In. ........................... | 259 |
| **Rug,** Navajo, 2 Gray Hills, Geometric Pattern, 1970s, 32 x 45½ In. ....................................... | 431 |
| **Rug,** Navajo, 2 People, Black & Red, White Ground, 1930s-40s, 30 x 13 In.......................*illus* | 184 |
| **Rug,** Navajo, Concentric Diamonds, Terraced Border, Gray Ground, c.1940, 75 x 40 In. ........... | 270 |
| **Rug,** Navajo, Double Arrow Medallion, Ivory Ground, Gray Border, c.1920, 80 x 36 In. ............ | 840 |
| **Rug,** Navajo, Ganado, Geometric Design, Black, White, Gray, Burgundy, 24 x 33 In.............*illus* | 161 |
| **Rug,** Navajo, Horizontal Stripe, Multicolor, Hook Corners, 60 x 30 In. .................................. | 150 |
| **Rug,** Navajo, Klagetoh Style, Optical Pattern, c.1950, 41 x 63 In. ......................................... | 431 |
| **Rug,** Navajo, Pictorial, Homespun Wool, Thunderbirds, Arrows, Crosses, 64 x 32 In. .............. | 1599 |
| **Rug,** Navajo, Repeating Squares, Striped Ground, Brown, White, Black, 50 x 30 In. ................ | 210 |
| **Rug,** Navajo, Runner, Stacked Trapezoids, White, Black, Red, Brown, c.1940, 65 x 30 In............ | 330 |
| **Rug,** Navajo, Striped, Red, Tan, Black, 20th Century, 66 x 57 In. .......................................... | 2091 |
| **Rug,** Navajo, Wool, Gray, Orange, Triangle Border, 1880-1920, 79½ x 45 In. ........................ | 1599 |
| **Rug,** Navajo, Wool, Multicolor, Diamonds, Orange, Gray, 84½ x 54 In. ................................ | 1700 |
| **Rug,** Navajo, Zigzag Diamonds, Black, White, Red, Transitional, 41 x 66 In. .......................... | 500 |
| **Rug,** Navajo, Zigzag Diamonds, Red, Orange, Brown, Wool, c.1950, 36 x 68 In. ...................... | 360 |
| **Rug,** Navajo, Zigzag, Diamonds, White Field, Gray, Cranberry, c.1940, 60 x 40 In. ................. | 180 |
| **Rug,** Yei, 4 Figures, Brown Ground, White, Tan, 59 x 38 In. ................................................ | 236 |
| **Sand Painting,** Navajo, Multicolor, Masonite, Cardinal Points, Symbols, 1900s, 16 x 24 In........ | 250 |
| **Sash,** Hopi, Ceremonial, Woven, Red, Yellow, Blue, 1800s, 104 In. ...................................... | 1040 |
| **Sheath,** Cheyenne, Beaded, Hide, Geometric Designs, Knife, c.1860, 9 In. ...........................*illus* | 5535 |
| **Sheath,** Gun, Sioux, Buffalo Hide, Beaded, 41 In................................................................ | 770 |
| **Snowshoes,** Penobscot, Bentwood, Laced Rawhide, Red Wool Tufts, c.1890, 34 x 11½ In. .......... | 690 |
| **Tomahawk Head,** Pipe, Pierced Heart In Blade, Wrought Iron, 8 In........................................ | 660 |
| **Tomahawk,** Brass Pipe, Wire-Wrapped Wooden Handle, c.1875, 18 x 8 In............................... | 2990 |
| **Tomahawk,** Wooden Pipe Shaft, Cast Iron, 20 In. ............................................................. | 236 |
| **Totem Pole,** Haida, Argillite, Human & Animal Figures, 13½ In................................*illus* | 1476 |
| **Totem Pole,** Kwakiutl, Carved, Bird, Animal, Multicolor, c.1910, 19½ In. ............................ | 563 |
| **Totem Pole,** Northwest Coast, Standing Bear, On Turtle, Painted, c.1910, 13½ In. ............... | 431 |
| **Totem Pole,** Northwest, Carved, Dry Painted Design, c.1900, 18¼ In. ................................. | 750 |
| **Tray,** Apache, Basketry, Coiled, Double Flower Design, Figures, Animals, c.1900, 14 In............. | 1380 |
| **Tray,** Huron, Birch Bark, Hair Embroidered, Flowers, Bees, Brown, c.1850, 10 x 8 In. ............. | 308 |
| **Tray,** Yavapai, Basketry, Flower Design, Multicolor, c.1920, 12½ In.............................*illus* | 677 |
| **Vase,** Hopi, Corn Maiden, Abstract Pottery Figure, Al Qoyawayma, 1985, 11½ In............*illus* | 1320 |
| **Vase,** San Ildefonso, Pueblo, Serpent Design, Black On Black, Incised Marie, 9 In. ................ | 805 |
| **Vest,** Lakota, Beaded, Hide, Geometric Designs, Flags, Quilt Lined, c.1880, 19½ x 18 In.......*illus* | 6150 |
| **War Club,** Woodland, 1700s, 17¼ In............................................................................ | 1650 |
| **Weaving,** Human Figures, Abstract Birds, 2 Panels, 34½ x 33 In. ......................................... | 1599 |
| **Weaving,** Navajo, Homespun Wool, Stacked Diamonds, Stylized Figures, 90 x 39 In............*illus* | 1968 |
| **Weaving,** Navajo, White Ground, Spider Woman Crosses, Black, Red, 78 x 54 In. ................... | 861 |
| **Weaving,** Navajo, Yei, 28 Dancers, Multicolor, Brown Ground, Zigzag Border, 86 x 59 In............. | 7995 |
| **Weaving,** Navajo, Yei, Feathers, Birds, Arrows, Double Border, Wool, 80 x 48 In.................... | 4305 |
| **Weaving,** Rio Grande, Concentric Serrate Diamond Center, Multicolor, 69 x 40 In...................... | 2706 |

**INDIAN TREE** is a china pattern that was popular during the last half of the nineteenth century. It was copied from earlier Indian textile patterns that were very similar. The pattern includes the crooked branch of a tree and a partial landscape with exotic flowers and leaves. Green, blue, pink, and orange were the favored colors used in the design. Coalport, Spode, Johnson Brothers, and other firms made this pottery.

| | |
|---|---|
| **Ashtray,** Scalloped Edge, Geometric Border, Coalport, 4 x 4 In. ......................................... | 20 |
| **Cake Plate,** Tab Handles, Scalloped Edge, Coalport, 9 x 10 In............................................ | 50 |
| **Creamer,** Coalport, 4½ In. ......................................................................................... | 25 |
| **Cup & Saucer,** Coalport, Demitasse, 2⅜ In. .................................................................. | 90 |
| **Cup & Saucer,** Meakin, c.1912................................................................................... | 60 |
| **Cup & Saucer,** Ribbed, Spode Copeland, c.1925 ............................................................. | 30 |
| **Dish,** Sweetmeat, Ruffled Edge, Coalport, 5 x 4 In. ......................................................... | 45 |
| **Eggcup,** Greek Key Border, England, 1930s, 1¾ In. ......................................................... | 18 |
| **Plate,** Bread & Butter, Aynsley, 7 In. ........................................................................... | 9 |
| **Plate,** Dinner, Coalport, 8¾ In. .................................................................................. | 45 |
| **Plate,** Dinner, Hope & Carter, c.1880, 10 In. ................................................................ | 85 |
| **Plate,** Dinner, Purple, G.L. Ashworth Bros., c.1870, 10 In.................................................. | 50 |

**Indian,** Weaving, Navajo, Homespun Wool, Stacked Diamonds, Stylized Figures, 90 x 39 In.
$1,968

Skinner Auctioneers & Appraisers

**I**

### A Standish

A *standish* is an inkstand. Most are figural with inkwells and containers for pens, blotting material, sealing wax, or other things needed to write a letter in the nineteenth century.

**Inkwell,** Bronze, Egyptian Bust, Stylized Disc, Marble Base, Patina, c.1900, 9 x 8 In.
$538

Neal Auction Co.

**Inkwell,** Glass, Benjamin Franklin Bust, Teakettle, Cobalt Blue, c.1880, 3 In. $196

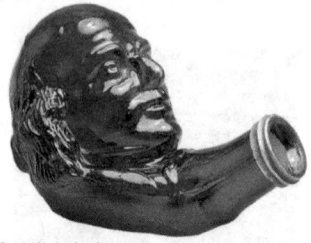

Glass Works Auctions

**Inkwell,** Stoneware, Frog, Molded, Manganese Glaze, Round Base, 1800s, 2½ x 4 In. $24

Conestoga Auction Co., Inc.

**Iron,** Boot Scraper, Figural, Unicorn, Reclining, 16 x 24 x 10 In. $593

James D. Julia Auctioneers

### New or Old Iron

New cast-iron copies of old doorstops, toys, and other collectibles are not as well-made as originals. The parts of the old ones fit together with no empty space between joints. It is said that you cannot fit even a piece of paper into a joint. Old cast-iron pieces are held together with flat-head screws, not Phillips-head screws. Rust on old pieces is dark brown. Rust on new pieces is reddish brown. Old cast iron has a smooth surface; newer pieces are rough and slightly bumpy.

| | |
|---|---:|
| **Plate,** Dinner, Ridgway, c.1865, 10¼ In. | 125 |
| **Plate,** Luncheon, Shenango China Of New Castle, Pa., 8¾ In. | 45 |
| **Platter,** John Maddock & Sons, c.1900, 16¾ In. | 69 |
| **Platter,** Keeling & Co., c.1920, 14 x 11 In. | 65 |
| **Platter,** Oval, Johnson Brothers, 1960s, 12 x 9 In. | 35 |
| **Platter,** Scalloped Edge, Silver Trim, Burgess & Leigh, c.1890, 21 x 18 In. | 395 |
| **Soup,** Cream, Saucer, Handles, Coalport, c.1900 | 55 |
| **Sugar & Creamer,** Gold Border, Pickard, c.1920 | 145 |
| **Tankard,** H.W. Wood, 5 In. | 40 |
| **Teapot,** Fluted, Coalport, 6½ In. | 325 |
| **Trinket Box,** Egg Shape, Coalport, 1¼ x 1 In. | 40 |
| **Tureen,** Footed, Finial, Handles, Coalport, c.1910, 11 x 7 x 7 In. | 90 |

**INKSTANDS** were made to be placed on a desk. They held some type of container for ink, and possibly a sander, a pen tray, a pen, a holder for pounce, and even a candle to melt the sealing wax. Inkstands date to the eighteenth century and have been made of silver, copper, ceramics, and glass. Additional inkstands may be found in these and other related categories.

| | |
|---|---:|
| **Bronze,** Resting Mother Bear, Climbing Cub, Hinged Lid, Onyx Base, 8½ x 20 In. | 2500 |
| **Gilt Bronze,** Bell Shape Wells, Domed, Eagle Finial, Napoleon III Bust, Onyx, 9 x 16 In. | 313 |
| **Gilt Bronze,** Louis XV Style, 2 Urn Wells, Lids, Scrolls, Dolphin Heads, Doors, 7 x 18 In. | 625 |
| **Gilt Bronze,** Louis XVI, Cross Arrow Filled Quiver, Torch, Swag, 3¾ x 12 In. | 438 |
| **Jasperware,** Ormolu-Mounted, Rope Twist Handles, Octagonal Wells, 9½ x 5¼ In. | 2040 |
| **Porcelain,** Painted Feathers, Urn Shape Pots, Flight, Barr & Barr, c.1815, 10 In. | 1500 |
| **Redware,** Pierced, Applied Dog, c.1850, 4¼ x 6¼ In. | 9200 |
| **Rosewood,** Standish Case, England, c.1870, 6 x 11 In. | 210 |
| **Silver,** 3 Fitted Pots, Bird Finial, Tray, Beaded Border, Engraved Swags, Spain, 10 In., 7 Piece | 420 |
| **Silver,** Boat Shape Bowl, Pierced & Lidded, Reeded Feet, N.N. & Co., 1905, 2⅛ x 8 In. | 240 |
| **Silver,** Cut Glass, Rococo, 2 Wells, Pierced Feet, Bradbury & Sons, Sheffield, c.1854, 12 In. | 438 |
| **Silver,** Set, Cut Glass Inkwell, Letter Clip, Letter Opener, Blotters, Gorham, 1907, 12 In. | 563 |
| **Silver,** Trophy, Pen Reservoir, 4-Footed, Larchmont, 10 In. | 246 |
| **Tortoiseshell Veneer,** Rolled Side Handles, 2 Glass Wells, Pen Well, Paw Feet, 4 x 10 In. | 690 |

**INKWELLS,** of course, held ink. Ready-made ink was first made about 1836 and was sold in bottles. The desk inkwell had a narrow hole so the pen would not slip inside. Inkwells were made of many materials, such as pottery, glass, pewter, and silver. Look in these categories for more listings of inkwells.

| | |
|---|---:|
| **Amethyst Glass,** Fluted Sides, Ground Spout, 1800s, 2 In. | 472 |
| **Brass,** Art Nouveau, Maiden, Head, Hinged Wells, Quill Penholder, 3¼ x 9 In. | 230 |
| **Brass,** Cast, Masks, Roses, Pierced Sides, Handles, Hinged Lid, Eagle Finial, 8 x 7 x 7 In. | 144 |
| **Brass,** Garland, Flowers, Scrolls, 3 x 3 x 3½ In. | 165 |
| **Brass,** Griffin Handles, c.1920, 9 x 17 In. | 185 |
| **Brass,** Locomotive, Flanged Wheels, Track Base, Drawer In Boiler, Pot Under Dome, 6 In. | 354 |
| **Bronze Dore,** Art Nouveau, Acanthus Leaf Shape, Flowers, Square Beveled Well, 3-Footed, 5 In. | 40 |
| **Bronze Dore,** Rococo Style, Shell Shape, Round Glass Well, Hinged Lid, France, 9 x 7 In. | 115 |
| **Bronze,** Egyptian Bust, Stylized Disc, Marble Base, Patina, c.1900, 9 x 8 In. ........................*illus* | 538 |
| **Bronze,** Gnome, Tree Trunk, Mushrooms, 4½ In. | 295 |
| **Bronze,** Pierced, Red Marble, Figure Of Lorenzo, 2 Urns, 2 Inkpots, 16¾ x 16 In. | 2460 |
| **Clear Bottle,** Brass Lid, 2 Stag Horns, Stepped Oval Wood Base, 19 x 8½ In. | 293 |
| **Double,** Copper, Roses, Verdigris, Pyramidal, Glass Inserts, Carence Crafters, 3 x 12 In. | 375 |
| **Double,** Sang-De-Boeuf, Turquoise Glaze, Metal Lid, c.1900, 3 x 6½ x 6 In. | 1500 |
| **Enamel,** Harbor Scene, Fisherman, Blue, Staffordshire, Sander, 2 x 4 In. | 390 |
| **Faience,** 2 Wells, 2 Holes, Flower Painted, Yellow Ground, France, 3 x 5½ In. | 90 |
| **Gilt Bronze,** Figural, Lion, Standing, Gilt Bronze, Pen Tray, France, 1800s, 3 x 9½ In. | 184 |
| **Gilt Metal,** Cherub, Standing, Arms Out, Column Base, 12 x 6 In. | 281 |
| **Glass,** Benjamin Franklin Bust, Teakettle, Cobalt Blue, c.1880, 3 In. ........................*illus* | 196 |
| **Glass,** Blue, White Enameled Flowers, Squared, Faceted Lid, 2½ x 2½ In. | 266 |
| **Glass,** Green, Pulled Platinum Iridescent Designs, Metal Poppies, Kralik, 4 x 4 In. | 458 |
| **Iron,** Car Shape, Roof Flips For Ink Pad, Tin Tires, Guntherman, Germany, 8¾ In. | 720 |
| **Liner,** Flower Stack Lid, 3 Quill Holder, Drum Shape, Staffordshire, c.1830, 3½ In. | 69 |
| **Malachite,** Ormolu, Round, Hinged Lid, Chain Links, 7 In. | 431 |
| **Papier-Mache,** Black, 2 Glass Inkwells, 13 x 8½ In. | 180 |
| **Porcelain,** Figural, Honeydew Melon, Attached Leafy Base, Green, 2¼ x 3¾ In., 8 Piece | 480 |
| **Porcelain,** Spaniels, Red, White, Lying Down, Seated, Blue Well, Staffordshire, c.1850, 7 In. | 104 |
| **Porcelain,** Woman, Cat, Rococo Style Desk, 6 x 5 In. | 225 |
| **Porcelain,** Yellow, Dome Shape, Silver Mount, Jadeite Finial, Edward Farmer, 4 x 5 In. | 7670 |

| | |
|---|---|
| **Standish,** Bird, Flower Reserve, Yellow Ground, Wells, Pot, Lid, France, c.1900, 5 ½ In. | 83 |
| **Standish,** Stepped, Acorn Finial, Crest, Silver Plate, 4 Bun Feet, 7 ¼ x 4 ¼ In. | 75 |
| **Stoneware,** Frog, Molded, Manganese Glaze, Round Base, 1800s, 2 ½ x 4 In. .....*illus* | 24 |

**INSULATORS** of glass or pottery have been made for use on telegraph or telephone poles since 1844. Thousands of styles of insulators have been made. Most common are those of clear or aqua glass; most desirable are the threadless types made from 1850 to 1870.

| | |
|---|---|
| **A. Tel. & Tel Co.,** Jade Green Milk | 40 |
| **Brookfield B & O,** Aqua | 50 |
| **Brookfield,** No. 2, Beehive, Blue Green, 4 In. | 11 |
| **CD,** 181, Pluto, Aqua, c.1890 | 3920 |
| **CD,** 699, L'Electro Verre, Green, French National Railway | 532 |
| **CEW,** No. 120, Aqua | 70 |
| **CNW Telegraph Co.,** Pale Aqua Green | 15 |
| **Diamond,** No. 102, Amber Black | 25 |
| **Diamond,** No. 102, Dark Yellow Green | 20 |
| **Embossed Patent,** Octagonal Cone, Olive Green, Bulbous Neck Ring, 5 ⅝ In. | 702 |
| **Hemingray,** No. 41-41, CSA, Clear Glass, 4 In. | 8 |
| **Lapp,** No. 1929, Glossy Cocoa Brown, Telephone, Porcelain, 3 ¾ x 3 In. | 12 |
| **Maydwell,** No. 164, Milk Glass | 8 |
| **McLaughlin,** No. 20, Olive Black Glass | 29 |
| **No Name,** Royal Purple, Canadian Pony | 45 |
| **O.V.G. Co.,** Celery Green | 25 |
| **U 983,** Threadless, Domed, Panel Skirt, Brown Rockingham Glaze, c.1855, 4 ⅜ In. | 2400 |

**IRISH BELLEEK,** *see Belleek category.*

**IRON** is a metal that has been used by man since prehistoric times. It is a popular metal for tools and decorative items like doorstops that need as much weight as possible. Items are listed here or under other appropriate headings, such as Bookends, Doorstop, Kitchen, Match Holder, or Tool. The tool that is used for ironing clothes, an iron, is listed in the Kitchen category under Iron and Sadiron.

| | |
|---|---|
| **Aquarium Holder,** Frog, Dancing, Tails, Top Hat, Deco Shape, Painted, Spencer, 8 x 7 In. | 330 |
| **Boot Scraper,** Figural, Unicorn, Reclining, 16 x 24 x 10 In. .....*illus* | 593 |
| **Bootjack,** Stylized Devil Shape, Openwork, 10 ½ In. | 240 |
| **Broiler,** Revolving, Ogee Edge, Heart Handle, Acorn Finial, Continental, 1800s, 25 x 14 In. | 1845 |
| **Card Tray,** Figural, Bellman, Painted, Molded Base, 1920s, 37 ½ In. .....*illus* | 854 |
| **Cigar Cutter,** Eastern Box Turtle, Back Hold, Movable Head, Green, Germany, 6 In. | 1680 |
| **Cigar Cutter,** Lighter, Elephant Shape, Lamp, Red Globe Shade, Cast, 11 ½ x 12 In. | 2565 |
| **Cork Press,** Figural, Reclining Dog, 10 In. | 235 |
| **Corn Grinder,** Black Wheel, Red Funnel, Wood Crank, Enterprise Mfg., Phila., 21 In. | 240 |
| **Cuspidor,** Figural, Dragon Turtle, Marked, 9 ½ x 12 ½ x 6 In. | 250 |
| **Cuspidor,** Figural, Turtle, Bronze Wash, Step On Head To Raise Shell, 4 x 14 x 11 In. | 161 |
| **Cuspidor,** Figural, Turtle, Hammered Copper, Step On Head To Raise Shell, 5 x 13 In. | 633 |
| **Cuspidor,** Top Hat Shape, Porcelain Lined, Painted, 8 x 10 x 10 In. | 1007 |
| **Dog,** Whippet, Laying Down, Head Up, 17 ½ x 26 ½ In., Pair | 4320 |
| **Figure,** Cat Head, On Stand, Flat, Blue Paint, c.1890, 11 ¾ x 11 In. .....*illus* | 14760 |
| **Figure,** Frog, Cast, Painted, Marked Frederick Iron & Steel, 1900s, 5 In., Pair | 295 |
| **Figure,** Frog, Painted, Glass Eyes, R.H. Rich, East Hampton, Conn., c.1920, 6 ½ In. .....*illus* | 153 |
| **Figure,** Gargoyle Head, Pointed Ears, Wide Grin, Painted Gray, c.1890, 8 ½ In. | 185 |
| **Figure,** Hen, Seated, Molded, c.1920, 14 In., Pair | 71 |
| **Figure,** Labrador, Reclining, White Paint, 9 In. | 380 |
| **Figure,** Lighthouse, Cast, Black & White, Horizontal Stripes, Rock Base, 15 In. | 84 |
| **Figure,** Lion Resting, Polished, 26 ½ In. | 1063 |
| **Figure,** Lion, Standing, Paw On Ball, Rectangular Base, 7 x 9 ¼ In. | 63 |
| **Figure,** Lion's Head, Paint Trace, Stand, c.1890, 17 In. | 615 |
| **Figure,** Mermaid, Seated, Holding Starfish, 12 In. | 110 |
| **Figure,** Monk, Seated On Lotus Base, Paint Trace, Chinese, c.1900, 11 ¾ In. | 120 |
| **Figure,** Rabbit, Standing, Brown, White Paint, 17 ½ In., Pair | 187 |
| **Figure,** Snake, Hammered Plates, Hinged Jaw, Moving Tongue, Marked, Muneyoshi, 39 In. ...*illus* | 119000 |
| **Figure,** Woman, Classical, White Draped Dress, Blue Painted Base, c.1890, 25 In. | 369 |
| **Helmet,** Burgonet, Hinged Ear Flaps & Visor, Linen Liner, 17th Century, 12 In. | 2829 |
| **Herb Grinder,** Wheel, Carved Hardwood Handle, Marked, C.B. Rogers, 1810-85, 18 In. ...*illus* | 1845 |
| **Horse Head,** Mounted, Paint, 15 x 7 ¼ In., Pair | 469 |
| **Incense Burner,** Inlaid Gold, Peacocks, Peonies, Marked, Chinese, c.1700, 5 In. .....*illus* | 2489 |

**Iron,** Card Tray, Figural, Bellman, Painted, Molded Base, 1920s, 37 ½ In.
**$854**

Neal Auction Co.

**Iron,** Figure, Cat Head, On Stand, Flat, Blue Paint, c.1890, 11 ¾ x 11 In.
**$14,760**

Skinner Auctioneers & Appraisers

**Iron,** Figure, Frog, Painted, Glass Eyes, R.H. Rich, East Hampton, Conn., c.1920, 6 ½ In.
**$153**

Conestoga Auction Co., Inc.

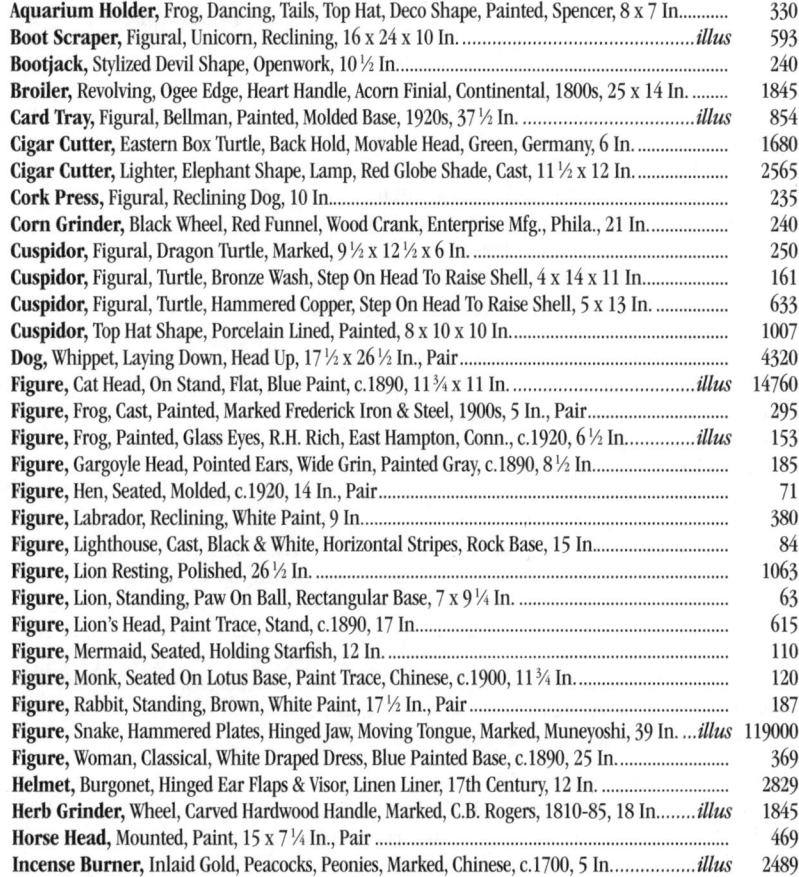

**Iron,** Figure, Snake, Hammered Plates, Hinged Jaw, Moving Tongue, Marked, Muneyoshi, 39 In.
**$119,000**

Rago Arts & Auction Center

**Iron,** Herb Grinder, Wheel, Carved Hardwood Handle, Marked, C.B. Rogers, 1810-85, 18 In.
**$1,845**

Skinner Auctioneers & Appraisers

**Iron,** Incense Burner, Inlaid Gold, Peacocks, Peonies, Marked, Chinese, c.1700, 5 In.
**$2,489**

James D. Julia Auctioneers

| | |
|---|---:|
| **Match Striker,** Basket Shape, Curved Handles, Forged, 4 ½ In. | 152 |
| **Oven Door,** Beehive Shape, Strap Handle, Footed, 15 x 16 In. | 338 |
| **Paperweight,** Hubley, Duck, Atta Boy, Dapper Suit, Hat, Paint, 5 In. | 240 |
| **Paperweight,** Hubley, Flapper Duck, Rain Gear, Paint, 4 In. | 270 |
| **Plaque,** Sun God, Bas-Relief, E. Vedder, 23 ½ x 31 ½ In. | 5490 |
| **Rack,** Drying, 2 Revolving Rings, 12 Hooks, c.1800, 19 x 19 In. | 1107 |
| **Rack,** Drying, Wine Bottle, Prongs, Flared, France, 51 In. | 1080 |
| **Rondel,** Horse Head, Braided Bar, Relief Cast, 15 ½ In. | 1320 |
| **Safe,** Allover Strap & Raised Bosses, 2 Handles, Fitted Interior, J. Delano, N.Y., 25 x 19 In. | 826 |
| **Sculpture,** Horse Head, Bit, Wooden Wall Plaque, 12 In. | 281 |
| **Seat,** Plow, Oliver Chilled, Plow Works, Green Paint, Cast. *illus* | 264 |
| **Seat,** Tractor, IOWO Racine, Red, Black, Yellow Paint, Cast. *illus* | 2255 |
| **Star,** 8-Point, Mounting Bar, Black Paint, c.1910, 8 ¾ x 21 In., Pair | 159 |
| **Target,** Leaping Dog, Stand, Gray Paint, 13 x 26 In. | 4613 |
| **Target,** Shooting Gallery, Woman, Full Body, Paint, Wurflein, c.1900, 63 x 19 In. *illus* | 43050 |
| **Tobacco Cutter,** Boy, Holding Cigar, c.1875, 7 ½ x 13 In. | 147 |
| **Tobacco Cutter,** Iron Blade, Virginia, 19th Century, 13 ½ In. | 60 |
| **Windmill Weight,** Bobtail Horse, Red Paint, Dempster Mill, Nebraska, c.1910, 17 In. | 210 to 570 |
| **Windmill Weight,** Bull, 18 x 24 In. | 450 |
| **Windmill Weight,** Bull, Fairbury, Nebr., Red Paint, Wood Base, c.1910, 20 x 27 In. *illus* | 510 |
| **Windmill Weight,** Flattened Full Body, Painted Red, c.1900, 10 ½ x 15 ½ In. | 1185 |
| **Windmill Weight,** Horse, Dempster Mill Mfg., c.1910, 18 ½ x 17 ½ In. | 603 to 984 |
| **Windmill Weight,** Horse, Running, White Wood Base, c.1900, 12 ½ x 21 In. | 338 |
| **Windmill Weight,** Rooster, 19 ½ x 21 In. | 497 |
| **Windmill Weight,** Rooster, Painted White, Red, c.1890, 15 ½ x 17 In. | 738 |
| **Windmill Weight,** Rooster, Rectangular Base, c.1890, 18 ½ x 16 ½ In. | 984 |
| **Windmill Weight,** Steer, Red Paint, Embossed Letters, Fairbury, Nebr., c.1925, 18 x 24 In. | 4600 |

**IRONSTONE** china was first made in 1813. It gained its greatest popularity during the mid-nineteenth century. The heavy, durable, off-white pottery was made in white or was decorated with any of hundreds of patterns. Much flow blue pottery was made of ironstone. Some of the decorations were raised. Many pieces of ironstone are unmarked, but some English and American factories included the word *Ironstone* in their marks. Additional pieces may be listed in other categories, such as Chelsea Grape, Chelsea Sprig, Flow Blue, Gaudy Ironstone, Mason's Ironstone, Moss Rose, Staffordshire, and Tea Leaf Ironstone.

| | |
|---|---:|
| **Coffeepot,** Copper Luster, Morning Glory, Elsmore & Forster, c.1860, 10 In. *illus* | 47 |
| **Cooler,** Flowers, Gold Trim, Animal Heads, Mask Handles, 11 In., Pair. *illus* | 4248 |
| **Figurine,** Bird, Salt Glazed, Rust, Brown, Blue Glaze, 1800s, 4 ¼ In., Pair. | 130 |
| **Jug,** Dolphin Handle, Squared, England, c.1885, 8 ¼ x 8 In. | 155 |
| **Jug,** Flow Blue Mask & Trim, Octagonal Paneled, c.1860, 4 ¾ In. | 173 |
| **Pitcher,** Flow Blue, Trellis, Flowers, Hexagonal Panels, Impressed c.1845, 6 ¾ In. | 196 |
| **Pitcher,** Lid, China Fort, Blue Spatter, Paneled Shape, 5 ½ In. | 242 |
| **Plate,** Hospital Near Poissy, France, Blue Transfer, R. Hall, 6 ½ In. *illus* | 48 |
| **Plate,** Soup, Ashworth, Asian Pattern, Black, White, Orange, Marked, c.1845, 10 In. | 81 |
| **Plate,** Toddy, Alphabet, Transfer, Crusoe Finding The Footprints, 7 ¼ In. | 118 |
| **Platter,** Flow Blue Transfer, Chen-Si, Signed Maddock, 10 In. | 71 |
| **Platter,** Flow Blue, Shapoo Pattern, 11 ¾ x 15 ⅜ In. | 142 |
| **Platter,** Siam Pattern, Blue Transfer, J. Clementson, 14 ¼ x 18 In. *illus* | 35 |
| **Punch Bowl,** Gilt, Footed, Imari, Flowers, 1800s, 6 In. | 123 |
| **Sugar,** Lid, China Fort, Blue Spatter, Paneled Shape, Open Handles, 7 ¼ In. | 121 |
| **Teapot,** Lid, Lobelia Pattern, Geometrics, Flowers, G. Phillips, c.1840, 10 ½ In. | 81 |
| **Tureen,** Lid, Jackson, Red, Blue, 12 ¾ x 14 In. | 600 |
| **Tureen,** Soup, Wheat Pattern, Underplate, Ladle, Red Cliff, 11 ½ In. | 138 |
| **Tureen,** Stand, Imari Design, Acanthus, Masque Handles, Hicks & Meigh, 14 In. *illus* | 1168 |
| **Tureen,** Tray, Flowers, 19th Century, 9 ½ x 12 In. | 210 |

**ISPANKY** figurines were designed by Laszlo Ispanky, who began his American career as a designer for Cybis Porcelains. In 1966, he established his own studio in Pennington, New Jersey; since 1976, he has worked for Goebel of North America. He works in stone, wood, or metal, as well as porcelain. The first limited edition figurines were issued in 1966.

| | |
|---|---:|
| **Bust,** 2 Donkeys, Sidekicks, 1966, 6 ½ In. | 250 |
| **Figurine,** Artist Girl, Seated, Drawing, 1967, 10 ½ In. | 395 |
| **Figurine,** Autumn, Sitting On Stump, Bowl Of Fruit, Pumpkin, 7 In. | 65 |
| **Figurine,** Cinderella, Kneeling, Washing Floor, Signed, Numbered, 12 x 8 In. | 650 |

| | | |
|---|---|---|
| **Figurine,** Girl, On Wave, Seminude, 14½ In. | | 108 |
| **Figurine,** Maria, Raised Arm, Flying Hair, Purple Dress, c.1966, 18 In. | | 425 |
| **Figurine,** Tiger, Top Hat, Vest, 7¾ In. | | 350 |
| **Figurine,** Winter, Long Dress, Cape, c.1983, 9 In. | | 60 |
| **Vase,** Seminude, Long Braid, Skirt, Numbered, 11 In. | | 150 |

**IVORY** from the tusk of an elephant is thought by many to be the only true ivory. To most collectors, the term *ivory* also includes such natural materials as walrus, hippopotamus, or whale teeth or tusks, and some of the vegetable materials that are of similar texture and density. Other ivory items may be found in the Scrimshaw and Netsuke categories. Collectors should be aware of the recent laws limiting the buying and selling of elephant ivory and scrimshaw.

| | | |
|---|---|---|
| **Box,** Carved, Woman's Portrait, Continental, 3 In. | | 236 |
| **Bust,** Woman, Renaissance Attire, Hands Crossed, Continental, 5 In. | | 750 |
| **Fan,** Figural Medallion, Gilt, Birds, Leaves, Vines, Cover, 12 In. | *illus* | 177 |
| **Figurine,** 12 Signs Of Lunar Zodiac, Rooster, Inlaid Stone Eyes, Chinese, 1800s, 6 x 6 In. | | 1968 |
| **Figurine,** Bird, Fish In Beak, White, Boxwood Perch, 4¾ In. | | 720 |
| **Figurine,** Emperor, Consort, Sword, Multicolor, Stand, Chinese, 14¼ x 3¾ In., Pair | | 1722 |
| **Figurine,** Hotei, Seated, Wood Base, Carved, Ink, Red Incised Marking, 6½ x 3¼ In. | | 369 |
| **Figurine,** Kannon, Goddess Of Mercy, Standing, Lotus Base, Headpiece, Robes, c.1900, 5 In. | *illus* | 1896 |
| **Figurine,** Man, Holding Basket, Large Bird, Signed, Asian, 7 In. | | 540 |
| **Figurine,** Man, Holding Staff, Large Bird, Asian, 5 In. | | 510 |
| **Figurine,** Stag, Monkeys, Ormolu Flowers, Gilt Bronze Base, Late 1800s, 10 In. | | 3998 |
| **Figurine,** Travels In The West, Scenic, Fossil, Chinese, c.1890, 23 In. | | 1968 |
| **Figurine,** Woman, Standing, Bonnet, 1820s Attire, Continental, 4½ In. | | 500 |
| **Group,** Courting Couple, Column Base, Continental, 8 In. | | 1500 |
| **Group,** Men Launching Boat From Shore, Japan, c.1890, 17 In. | | 1169 |
| **Group,** Venus, Cupid, Art Nouveau, Raised Base, 12 In. | | 3250 |
| **Group,** Woman, On Water Buffalo, Playing Flute, Chinese, c.1890, 4 x 6 In. | | 1320 |
| **Knife,** Paper, Silver, Gorham Mfg. Co., 12½ In. | | 625 |
| **Knife,** Paper, Tapered, Rounded, Engraved, Virtue Et Veritas Vincuni, Monogram, 18 In. | | 86 |
| **Page Turner,** Figures On Handle, Carved, 12 x 1½ In. | | 138 |
| **Seal,** Agate Intaglio, Yellow Gold Scrolling, Winged Dragon, Monogram, 3½ x 1¼ In. | | 196 |
| **Tankard,** Battle Scene, Silver Plate, Soldier On Horse Finial, c.1880, 13½ In. | *illus* | 5220 |
| **Tusk,** Carved, Man, Woman, Ebonized Base, 1900s, 19 In., Pair | | 610 |

**JACK-IN-THE-PULPIT** vases, shaped like trumpets, resemble the wildflower named jack-in-the-pulpit. The design originated in the late Victorian years. Vases in the jack-in-the-pulpit shape were made of ceramic or glass.

| | | |
|---|---|---|
| **Vase,** Enameled Flowers, Frosted Ground, Pink Ruffled Top, 9½ In. | | 35 |
| **Vase,** Peachblow, Crimped Rim, Yellow & White Daisies, Mt. Washington, 7 In. | | 1610 |

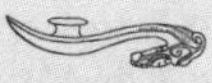

**JADE** is the name for two different minerals, nephrite and jadeite. Nephrite is the mineral used for most early Oriental carvings. Jade is a very tough stone that is found in many colors from dark green to pale lavender. Jade carvings are still being made in the old styles, so collectors must be careful not to be fooled by recent pieces. Jade jewelry is found in this book under Jewelry.

| | | |
|---|---|---|
| **Archer's Ring,** White, Stamped Characters, Silver Lining, Asia, 1900s, 1½ In. | | 2583 |
| **Ax Shape,** Mother-Of-Pearl Inlay, Wood Handle, Figural, 17 In. | | 660 |
| **Bowl,** Dragons, Relief, 15¼ In. | | 2723 |
| **Bowl,** Green Mottled, Black & White Flecks, Everted Rim, Footed, Chinese, 4 x 2 In., Pair | | 150 |
| **Bowl,** Variegated, Footed, 3½ x 8¾ In. | | 984 |
| **Boy,** On Buffalo, Green Mottled, Spiral Wood Stand, Chinese, 3 x 6 In. | | 1107 |
| **Buddha,** Seated, Carved Wood Base, 4½ In. | | 200 |
| **Cat,** Sleeping, On Lotus Leaf, White, Translucent Gray, 1¾ x 1 In. | | 63 |
| **Censer,** Floral Carving, Pierced Lid, Footed, Chinese, 1800s, 6½ x 8 In. | | 8610 |
| **Censer,** White, Lid, Flowers, Pierced, Foot, Chinese, 6½ In. | | 3750 |
| **Centerpiece,** Orchid Flower, Coral, Carved Buds, Brown Leaves, Chinese, 14 In. | | 561 |
| **Coin,** Replica Of Spanish Coin, King Carolus V, 1806, Box, 2 In., Pair | | 3125 |
| **Figurine,** Buffalo, Reclining, Chicken Bone Jade, Ivory, Lavender, Chinese, 2 x 3 In. | *illus* | 7670 |
| **Figurine,** Foo Dog, Nephrite, Stand, 4¾ x 6½ In. | | 389 |
| **Figurine,** Lion, White, Laying Down, Clenching Scroll, Ribbon, 2 x 5 In. | | 840 |
| **Finial,** Gray Stone, Black Markings, Carved, Pierced, Deer, Leaves, c.1910, 1 In. | | 1304 |
| **Foo Dog,** Lying Down, Pearl In Front Paws, Ram's Head, Branching Tail, White, 2 x 3 In. | | 649 |
| **Foo Dogs,** White, Pierced Wood Stand, Chinese, 2⅜ x 7 In. | | 2460 |
| **Hair Ornament,** Knot Of Chang, White Jade, Carved, Chinese, 3 x 2 In. | *illus* | 25960 |

**Iron,** Seat, Plow, Oliver Chilled, Plow Works, Green Paint, Cast
$264

Arus Auctions

**Iron,** Seat, Tractor, IOWO Racine, Red, Black, Yellow Paint, Cast
$2,255

Arus Auctions

**Iron,** Target, Shooting Gallery, Woman, Full Body, Paint, Wurflein, c.1900, 63 x 19 In.
$43,050

Skinner Auctioneers & Appraisers

**Iron,** Windmill Weight, Bull, Fairbury, Nebr., Red Paint, Wood Base, c.1910, 20 x 27 In.

**$510**

Garth's Auctioneers & Appraisers

**Ironstone,** Coffeepot, Copper Luster, Morning Glory, Elsmore & Forster, c.1860, 10 In.

**$47**

Conestoga Auction Co., Inc.

**Ironstone,** Cooler, Flowers, Gold Trim, Animal Heads, Mask Handles, 11 In., Pair

**$4,248**

Brunk Auctions

**Ironstone,** Plate, Hospital Near Poissy, France, Blue Transfer, R. Hall, 6½ In.

**$48**

DuMouchelles Art Gallery

| | |
|---|---|
| **Magnifying Glass,** Belt Buckle Handle, Repousse, Dragon, Green, 8⅞ In. | 8610 |
| **Mountain,** Scholar's, Openwork Carving, Pierced Holes, Wood Stand, 4 In. | 4800 |
| **Pendant,** Low Relief, Figure, Bridge, Text, 2¾ In. | 156 |
| **Perfume Box,** Coin Stopper, Clover Shape, Ruby Cabochon Clasp, 1½ x 2⅜ In. | 6000 |
| **Plaque,** Carved, Figures Of Children, Chinese, 20th Century, 3 In. | 615 |
| **Plaque,** Carved, White Translucent, Landscape, Inscription, Chinese, 2 x 1½ In. | 3555 |
| **Rabbit,** Crouching, White, Chinese, 1800s, 2 In. | 375 |
| **Scepter,** Ruyi, Openwork Carving, Wood Stand, 1900s, 13 In. | 1250 |
| **Screen,** Table, Panel, Painted, Figures In Garden, Gilt, Carved Rosewood Stand, 12 x 7 In. | 1896 |
| **Sculpture,** Branch, Leaves, China, c.1900, 5⅞ In. | 5228 |
| **Urn,** Foo Dog Finial, Carved, Ring Handles, Lamp Mounted, c.1910, 15 In. | 500 |
| **Urn,** Lid, Green, Incised, Prunus, Bamboo, Chinese, 1900s, 6½ In. | 1230 |
| **Vase,** Carved, Taotie Masks, Grayish White, Brown, Dragon Handles, Chinese, 1800s, 6 In. | 5036 |
| **Vase,** Hanging, Spinach Jade, Carved, Rosewood Stand, Chain, Chinese, 11¾ In. ........*illus* | 1062 |
| **Wrist Rest,** Bamboo Shape, Celadon Color Stone, Markings, Chinese, 1800s, 5¾ In. ......*illus* | 3259 |

**JAPANESE WOODBLOCK PRINTS** *are listed in this book in the Print category under Japanese.*

**JASPERWARE** can be made in different ways. Some pieces are made from a solid-colored clay with applied raised designs of a contrasting colored clay. Other pieces are made entirely of one color clay with raised decorations that are glazed with a contrasting color. Additional pieces of jasperware may also be listed in the Wedgwood category or under various art potteries.

| | |
|---|---|
| **Cake Plate,** Lid, Acorn Finial, Classical Figures, Wedgwood Style, 8 x 11 In. | 188 |
| **Cheese Dish,** Lid, Green, White, Hunt Scene, Dogs, Horses, 1800s, 10 x 11 In. ........*illus* | 390 |
| **Cheese Dome,** Blue Matte, White Cameo Figures, Leafy Vine Border, 11 x 10 In. .......*illus* | 250 |
| **Cheese Keeper,** Figures, Leaves, Acorns, Lyres, Late 19th Century, 9 In. | 420 |
| **Plaque,** Classical, Woman, Cherub, Poppy Border, Blue, White, Oval, 12 In. | 649 |
| **Plaque,** Stork, Babies, Lily Of The Valley, Cattails, Green, 5½ In. | 125 |

**JEWELRY,** whether made from gold and precious gems or plastic and colored glass, is popular with collectors. Values are determined by the intrinsic value of the stones and metal and by the skill of the craftsmen and designers. Victorian and older jewelry has been collected since the 1950s. More recent interests are Art Deco and Edwardian styles, Mexican and Danish silver jewelry, and beads of all kinds. Copies of almost all styles are being made. American Indian jewelry is listed in the Indian category. Tiffany jewelry is listed here.

| | |
|---|---|
| **Armlet,** Horse's End, Gold Vermeil, Hermes, 7⅞ In. | 1476 |
| **Barrette,** Abstract Rectangle, 14K Gold, Hammered, 2½ In. | 800 |
| **Belt Buckle,** Dragon's Head, Monkeys, Peach, 4⅛ In. | 9840 |
| **Belt Buckle,** Jade, Carved Relief, Chih Lung, Chinese, c.1800, 4¼ x 2 In. | 8295 |
| **Belt Buckle,** Jade, Dragon, Carved, Chinese, 1800s, 1 x 4 In. | 250 |
| **Belt Buckle,** Roman Soldier Profile, Curled Bands, Silver, Gold, Shiebler, c.1880, 3 In. | 500 |
| **Belt Buckle,** Shield Shape, Applied Chrysanthemums, Dragonfly, Shiebler, c.1880, 3 In. | 375 |
| **Belt Buckle,** Silver, Armadillo Pattern, Over Laying Links, Mexico, c.1953, 4¾ In. | 531 |
| **Belt Buckle,** Stirrup & Buckle, Gold Plated, Marked, Mimi Di Niscemi, 1989, 5½ x 3 In. | 145 |
| **Belt Buckle,** Sun, Crescent Moon, Copper, Silver, Spratling, Taxco, c.1944, 3½ In. .......*illus* | 812 |
| **Belt Hook,** Jade, Carved, Dragon Head Terminal, Polished, Chinese, 4½ In. | 437 |
| **Bracelet & Earrings,** Daisies, Clusters, White Enamel, Goldtone, Charel, 7¼ In. & 1½ In. | 45 |
| **Bracelet & Earrings,** Mesh, Goldtone, Baguettes, Rhinestones, Clip-On, Emmons, 1960s | 51 |
| **Bracelet & Earrings,** Micro Mosaic, 6 Panels, Rome Sights, Oval, Gold Mount, 7¼ In. | 3075 |
| **Bracelet & Earrings,** Scrolls, White Enamel, Faux Pearls, Goldtone, Clip-On, Hargo | 275 |
| **Bracelet,** 3 Charms, Greek Emblems, Motto, Diamonds, Seed Pearls, Gold Link, 1949, 7 In. | 3186 |
| **Bracelet,** 5 Ladybugs, Red Enamel, 18K Gold, Circular Links, Cartier, 7 In. | 6150 |
| **Bracelet,** 5 Plaques, Busts Of Classical Figures, Silver, Etruscan Style, G. Shiebler, 7 In. | 677 |
| **Bracelet,** 12 Slides, Gemstones, 14K Gold, Victorian, 7¼ In. | 2360 |
| **Bracelet,** 15 Amethysts, Emerald Cut, Diamond Spacers, 14K Gold, Cartier | 4600 |
| **Bracelet,** Alhambra, 5 Quatrefoils, Mother-Of-Pearl, 18K Gold, Van Cleef & Arpels, 7 In. | 4613 |
| **Bracelet,** Balls, Twisted Scroll, Link, Silver, Pin & Chain Closure, Aguilar, c.1940, 6 In. | 437 |
| **Bracelet,** Bangle, 12 Emeralds, Square Cut, 96 Round Diamonds, 20th Century, 7¼ In. | 1080 |
| **Bracelet,** Bangle, 3 Amethysts, 14K Gold Allover Scrolling, Art Nouveau, 7⅜ In. | 3198 |
| **Bracelet,** Bangle, Amethyst, Gold, Scrolling, Art Nouveau, Whiteside & Blank, 7⅝ In. ......*illus* | 1476 |
| **Bracelet,** Bangle, Birds, Black Enamel, 15K Gold, Safety Chain, Late 1800s, ¾ In. | 1159 |
| **Bracelet,** Bangle, Bypass, 22K Polished Gold, Round, Cartier, 8 In. | 8125 |
| **Bracelet,** Bangle, Bypass, Blue Chalcedony Cabochon Ends, Smoky Quartz, Gold, Adelline | 861 |
| **Bracelet,** Bangle, Bypass, Ram's Head, 18K Granulated Gold Wire & Bead, c.1870, 6 In. | 11250 |
| **Bracelet,** Bangle, Cameo, Coral, 14K Gold, Engraved, Aesthetic, c.1890 | 1107 |

J

| | |
|---|---|
| Bracelet, Bangle, Cinnabar, Carved, Chinese, c.1950 .......................................... | 44 |
| Bracelet, Bangle, Crazy Twist, 18K Gold, Schlumberger Studios, 6 In............... | 5843 |
| Bracelet, Bangle, Hinged, 18K Gold, Polished, Fluted, Chirico, Italy, 6 ½ In. | 2560 |
| Bracelet, Bangle, Hinged, Basket Weave Pattern, 22K Gold, Hilat, Istanbul, 6 In. | 2214 |
| Bracelet, Bangle, Hinged, Silver, Onyx, Marked, Grosse, Germany, 1975............ | 108 |
| Bracelet, Bangle, Irish Christian Symbols, Silver, Gilt, Garnets, Dublin, 1870s, 7 In. | 1353 |
| Bracelet, Bangle, Lion, Sapphire In Mouth, Diamond Eye, 14K Gold, Art Nouveau | 598 |
| Bracelet, Bangle, Lucite, Frosted, Torque Shape, P. Von Musulin, c.1980, 8 In. | 148 |
| Bracelet, Bangle, Rope Twist, 18K Gold, Van Cleef & Arpels, 6 ½ In................. | 4613 |
| Bracelet, Bangle, Twisted Wire, 4 Double Roundels, Gold, Hinged, Italy, 6 ¾ In............*illus* | 660 |
| Bracelet, Charm, Chain Link, Letters, Spell Chanel, Logo, Goldtone, 7 In. ......... | 374 |
| Bracelet, Charm, Oval Links, 15 Charms, 14K & 18K Gold, 7 ⅜ In...............*illus* | 6150 |
| Bracelet, Chatelaine Medallion, Medieval Women, Guitar, Chain, Gothic Revival, 7 In............ | 1476 |
| Bracelet, Chrysoprase Beads, 5 Strands, Textured Gold & Diamond Links, E. Rand, 7 ⅜ In......... | 1968 |
| Bracelet, Cuff, 3 Openwork Curves, Silver, Hinged, Mexico, 7 In. ..................... | 369 |
| Bracelet, Cuff, Bone, Silver, Elsa Peretti, Tiffany & Co., Pouch, Box, 1978, 2 x 1 ¾ In. | 541 |
| Bracelet, Cuff, Braided Bands, Silver, Copper, Mexico, c.1940, 1 ⅜ x 2 ⅝ In. | 812 |
| Bracelet, Cuff, Brass On Copper, Hour Glass Shape, Art Smith, 2 ½ In................ | 1830 |
| Bracelet, Cuff, Etruscan Revival, 15K Gold, Barnet Henry Joseph, 1885, ¾ In............*illus* | 2091 |
| Bracelet, Cuff, Hinged, Lion Relief, 18K Gold, Marked, David Webb, 6 In. .....*illus* | 15375 |
| Bracelet, Cuff, Hinged, Pierced, Silver, Applied Balls, C. Friedell, c.1940, 2 ¼ In....*illus* | 594 |
| Bracelet, Cuff, Hinged, Tiger, Raised, Oxidation, Mexico, 2 ¾ In. ................... | 656 |
| Bracelet, Cuff, Icicle, Brass, Cutout, Flared Ends, Art Smith, 2 ½ x 3 ½ In. ......... | 3660 |
| Bracelet, Cuff, Plastic, Black, White Coco Signature, Chanel, 2 ½ In. ............... | 213 |
| Bracelet, Cuff, Silver, Amethyst Inset, Art Deco, Taxco, c.1940, 1 ¾ In............... | 131 |
| Bracelet, Cuff, Silver, Ribbed, Turquoise, Pin & Chain Closure, Aguilar, Mexico, c.1955, 2 In...*illus* | 1625 |
| Bracelet, Cuff, Stylized Hunting Figures, Pierced, Mexico, c.1955, 2 ⅜ In. ......... | 625 |
| Bracelet, Cuff, Tiffany & Co. Address, Inscribed, Silver, Stamped 1997, ¾ x 2 ½ In........ | 132 |
| Bracelet, Cuff, Wavy Shape, Pearls In Indents, 18K Gold, Van Cleef & Arpels, 6 In. | 3690 |
| Bracelet, Cuff, Woven, Herringbone, Silver, Dome Ends, A. Cummings, 6 ½ In., Pair ........ | 861 |
| Bracelet, Dolphin, Flexible Braid, Gold, 6 In.........................................*illus* | 3936 |
| Bracelet, Enamel, Taille D'Epargne, 14K Gold, ½ Pearl Slide, Victorian, Pair .............. | 4183 |
| Bracelet, Juste Un Clou, Just A Nail, Curved Nail, Flattened Head, Gold, Cartier, 6 ¼ In. | 6765 |
| Bracelet, Link, 36 Diamonds, 34 Rubies, 18K Gold, Foxtail Chain, 1900s, 7 In. | 1920 |
| Bracelet, Link, Alternating Quatrefoil Flowers & Leaves, Box Clasp, Georg Jensen, 7 ½ In. | 1046 |
| Bracelet, Link, Anchor Chain, A.G.A. Correa & Son, 8 ½ In........................... | 1722 |
| Bracelet, Link, Bars & Circles, Art Deco, Platinum, Diamonds, 7 In................... | 8260 |
| Bracelet, Link, Black Onyx Medallions, Silver Scrolled Frame, Felch & Co., 1950s ........ | 195 |
| Bracelet, Link, Concave, Square, Hinged, Box Clasp & Chain, Pineda, Mexico, c.1953, 3 In. ....... | 812 |
| Bracelet, Link, Diamond Shape, Silvertone, Marked, Coro, 7 ½ In. ................... | 75 |
| Bracelet, Link, Florentine Textured Metal, Aurora Borealis Rhinestones, Mode Art, 7 ¼ In......... | 59 |
| Bracelet, Link, Jade Bars, Chinese Characters, 14K Gold End Caps, Oval Clasp, 1960s, 7 In........ | 590 |
| Bracelet, Link, Silver, Birds, Blossoms, Cabochon Moonstones, Georg Jensen, 7 In.............*illus* | 1046 |
| Bracelet, Link, Silver, Jadeite, Box Clasp, Chain, Antonio Pineda, Taxco, c.1953, 3 In..........*illus* | 748 |
| Bracelet, Link, Splayed, Silver, Box Clasp, Hector Aguilar, Mexico, c.1940, 8 ¾ In. | 312 |
| Bracelet, Link, White Gold, Baguette Diamond Rows, 20th Century, 7 ¾ In. ......... | 840 |
| Bracelet, Mesh, Rope Style, 14K Gold, Hidden Box Clasp, 1900s, 7 In. ............. | 369 |
| Bracelet, Palomino's Head, Green Eyes, Textured Goldtone Band, Clamp Closure, Pauline Rader | 150 |
| Bracelet, Pearl, 2 Strands, 3 Diamond Spacers, 14K White Gold, Tiffany & Co., 7 ¾ In. ............ | 1250 |
| Bracelet, Pink Rhinestones, Silvertone Leaves, Foldover Clasp, D. Lisner, c.1959, 6 ½ In. ......... | 36 |
| Bracelet, Plaques, Platinum, Graduated, European & Full Cut Diamonds, Art Deco, 8 In. ......... | 3000 |
| Bracelet, Plaques, Reverse Painted Glass, Horse, Foxes, Gold Stirrup Bit & Links, 7 In. | 1968 |
| Bracelet, Puzzle, Silver, 17 Fitted Links, Concealed Hinges, A. Pineda, 2 ¼ In. | 1464 |
| Bracelet, Sapphires, 3 Lozenge, Diamonds, 14K White Gold Filigree, Art Deco, 7 In. | 357 |
| Bracelet, Silver, 8 Links, Pin Clasp, Marked, William Spratling, Mexico, c.1950, 7 In. | 615 |
| Bracelet, Silver, Double Curb Link, Textured Plaque, Toggle, Lois Hill, Indonesia, 7 x 1 In......... | 167 |
| Bracelet, Silver, Enameled Leaves & Berries, Margot De Taxco, 1950s, 7 In........*illus* | 360 |
| Bracelet, Silver, Link, 5 Stylized Knots, Alternating Beads, H. Aguilar, 2 In.......... | 1125 |
| Bracelet, Silver, Links, Barrel, Geometric Decoration, Lobster Clasp, Spratling, 8 ½ In. .......... | 293 |
| Bracelet, Silver, Panels, Curved & Peaked, Hematite Centers, A. Pineda, 6 ½ In. ......... | 1003 |
| Bracelet, Snake, Silver, Green Enamel, Articulated, M. De Taxco, 2 ½ In.............. | 1375 |
| Bracelet, Sunburst, Lion's Head, Chains, Goldtone, Chanel, 7 In...................... | 380 |
| Bracelet, Victorian, Bangle, Rhinestone, Gold Filled, Raised Crescent, Scrolling, 2 ¾ In............. | 153 |
| Bracelet, Watch Fob, T-Bars, Curb Link Bracelet, Gold, Hardstones, 8 ½ In............ | 1476 |
| Brooch, Jade, Butterfly, Gold, 14K ........................................................... | 321 |
| Buckle, Celtic Designs, 18K Gold, Multicolored Enamel, Edwardian, c.1903, 4 x 2 In.......... | 3220 |

**Ironstone,** Platter, Siam Pattern, Blue Transfer, J. Clementson, 14 ¼ x 18 In.
$35

Conestoga Auction Co., Inc.

**Ironstone,** Tureen, Stand, Imari Design, Acanthus, Masque Handles, Hicks & Meigh, 14 In.
$1,168

New Orleans Auction Galleries, Inc.

**Ivory,** Fan, Figural Medallion, Gilt, Birds, Leaves, Vines, Cover, 12 In.
$177

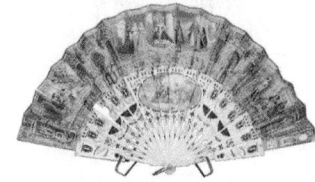

Ahlers & Ogletree Auction Gallery

**Ivory,** Figurine, Kannon, Goddess Of Mercy, Standing, Lotus Base, Headpiece, Robes, c.1900, 5 In.
$1,896

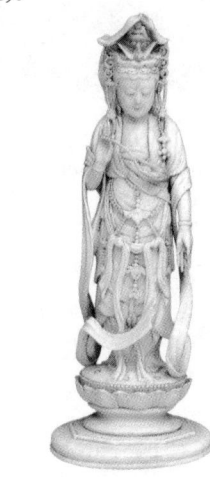

James D. Julia Auctioneers

**Ivory,** Tankard, Battle Scene, Silver Plate, Soldier On Horse Finial, c.1880, 13½ In. $5,220

The Stein Auction Company

**TIP**

*Ivory expands and contracts in heat and cold, so it can crack or craze if the temperature and humidity do not remain moderate.*

**Jade,** Figurine, Buffalo, Reclining, Chicken Bone Jade, Ivory, Lavender, Chinese, 2 x 3 In. $7,670

Brunk Auctions

**Jade,** Hair Ornament, Knot Of Chang, White Jade, Carved, Chinese, 3 x 2 In. $960

Brunk Auctions

| | |
|---|---:|
| **Buckle,** C-Scrolls, Repousse, 14K Gold, Art Nouveau, 2¼ x 1½ In. | 518 |
| **Buckle,** Ship, 2 Sails, Enamel On Silver, Arts & Crafts, F.G. Hale, 3¼ In. | 3075 |
| **Buckle,** Silver, Guilloche, Blue & Green Enamel, c.1896, 3 x 2 In. | 121 |
| **Buckle,** Silver, Turquoise, Applied Leaves, Dots, Cabochon, Oval, 3½ x 3 In. | 311 |
| **Charm,** Car, Model T, 10K Gold, 20th Century, 1¼ In. | 270 |
| **Charm,** Globe, 18K Gold, Green Enamel, Italy, 1 In. .................................................. *illus* | 180 |
| **Charm,** Poodle's Head, Stone Drop, Pull To See Eyes & Tongue, Gold, Enamel, Retro, 1 In. | 738 |
| **Charm,** Royal Carriage, 18K Gold, Sapphires, Rubies, Rope Twist Accent, Wheels Turn, 1 In. | 500 |
| **Charm,** Silver, Heart, Puffy, Padlock, Scotland, c.1885, 1⅛ In. | 795 |
| **Charm,** Steamer Trunk, Smoky Quartz, Citrine, 18K Gold, Louis Vuitton, 1¼ In. | 661 |
| **Chatelaine,** Belt Hook, Silver, Carved, Embossed Flower, Leaves, Tiffany, 3 x 4½ In. | 115 |
| **Chatelaine,** Ormolu, Leaf & Scroll, Gilt Brass, Mother-Of-Pearl, Belt Loop, c.1850, 10 In. | 1680 |
| **Chatelaine,** Plaques, Mythological Scenes, Gilt Metal, Sewing Tools, Belt Loop, 11 In. | 3640 |
| **Cigar Cutter,** 14K Gold, Ruby, 6 Diamonds, 1¼ In. ................................................ *illus* | 360 |
| **Cigarette Box,** Silver Plate, Belt Buckle Detail, Maria Pergay, 1970s, 10 x 3 In. | 1125 |
| **Cigarette Case,** 14K Gold, Engraved, Map Of South America, Cartier, 4 In. | 10455 |
| **Cigarette Case,** 14K Gold, Polished, Rose Gold Hinge Detail, Durand & Co., 4 In. | 3690 |
| **Cigarette Case,** Chased Dragon Design, Playing With Pearl, 4 x 3 In. | 362 |
| **Cigarette Case,** Engine Turned Stripes, Enamel Plaque, Nude Woman, 3¼ In. | 350 |
| **Cigarette Case,** Silver, 14K Gold, Musical Staff, F, James E. Blake, c.1900, 4¾ In. | 300 |
| **Cigarette Case,** Silver, Blue Enamel, Geometric Border, Jeweled Clasp, 5¼ x 3¼ In. | 154 |
| **Cigarette Case,** Silver, Celluloid, Man, Scantily Clad Woman, Toasting, England, 4 In. | 369 |
| **Cigarette Case,** Silver, Celluloid, Nude Woman, Bearded Man, England, 1919, 4 In. | 197 |
| **Cigarette Case,** Silver, Enameled Lid, Racy Semi-Clad Woman, England, 1917, 3½ In. | 369 |
| **Cigarette Case,** Silver, Enameled Lid, Woman Riding Dragonfly, Birmingham, 1918, 4 In. | 400 |
| **Cigarette Case,** Silver, Engraved Scrolling, Monogram, Hinged, 3 x 3 In. | 109 |
| **Cigarette Case,** Silver, Etched Floral Scrolling, Oak Leaf Closure, Italy, c.1950, 4 x 3 In. | 109 |
| **Cigarette Case,** Silver, Monogram, Vertical Flower Stripes, Blue Enamel, 4 x 3¼ In. | 265 |
| **Cigarette Case,** Silver, Painted Lid, Reclining Woman In Negligee, England, 1919, 5 In. | 400 |
| **Cigarette Case,** Silver, Rose Gold, Geometric Ribbing, Blue Cabochon, 3¾ x 2¾ In. | 334 |
| **Cigarette Case,** Silver, Stylized Leaping Animals, Leaves, 20th Century, 3 x 5¼ In. | 308 |
| **Cigarette Holder,** Amber, Gold Collar, Sheffield Silver Case, c.1910, 2½ In. | 253 |
| **Clasp,** Purse, Flower Basket, Coral & Diamond Flowers, Emeralds, Enamel, Platinum, 1 In. | 9225 |
| **Clip,** Bow, Diamonds, Platinum, Lacy Openwork, Gubelin, 3 In., 2 Piece | 12300 |
| **Clip,** Fur, Faux Moonstone Cabochon, Grapes, Bow Loops, Goldtone, Coro, 1940s, 2½ In. | 80 |
| **Clip,** Fur, Unicorn, 18K Gold, Sapphire Horn, Ruby Eyes, Diamond Mane, c.1940, 3½ In. *illus* | 5625 |
| **Clip,** Jade, Carved Bamboo, Gold Mount, Split Pearls, Arts & Crafts, F.G. Hale, 1½ In. | 1845 |
| **Clip,** Leaf, Textured, Scrollwork, Raised Beads, Marked, Rice Weiner Co., 1 x 3 In., Pair | 155 |
| **Clip,** Turquoise, Citrine, Jade, Ruby, Diamond Melee, 14K Gold, Seaman Schepps, 1 In. | 1968 |
| **Comb,** Hair, Tortoiseshell, Rectangular, Engraved Lines, 14 Tines, 19th Century, 5 In. | 58 |
| **Comb,** Stylized Figure Shape, Sterling Silver, Art Smith, 2 x 6 In. | 1000 |
| **Cuff Links,** Amethyst, Oval, Gold Beaded Mount, Arts & Crafts, F.G. Hale | 1476 |
| **Cuff Links,** Barbell Shape, 14K Gold, Tiffany & Co., Box | 615 |
| **Cuff Links,** Briefcase Shape, Silver, Fitted With Toggles, Tiffany & Co., ⅝ x ⅜ In. | 299 |
| **Cuff Links,** Coin, Gold Sicilian, 18K White Gold Toggle Mount, Bulgari, ⅞ In. | 1534 |
| **Cuff Links,** Disc, 18K Gold, Green & Black Enamel, Cartier, ½ In. | 3304 |
| **Cuff Links,** Dog, Scottish Terrier, Reverse Painted Glass, Round, 14K Gold Frame | 431 |
| **Cuff Links,** Fish, Silver, Antonio Pineda, Taxco, c.1962, 1¾ In. ................................. *illus* | 325 |
| **Cuff Links,** Hat, Professor Higgins, Enamel, Rhinestones, B. Steinberg, Kaslo, 1 x 1¾ In. | 43 |
| **Cuff Links,** Knot, 18K Gold, Rope Twist, Ralph Lauren, Tiffany | 861 |
| **Cuff Links,** Knot, Malachite, Ribbed 14K Gold, ¾ In. | 523 |
| **Cuff Links,** Lobster, 14K Gold, Hinged Tail & Claws, Ruby Eyes, Toggle Closure, A.G., 1 In. | 708 |
| **Cuff Links,** Man In The Moon, Coral, Carved, 18K Gold, Round | 1169 |
| **Cuff Links,** Mother-Of-Pearl Tablets, Oval, Pearl Center, Platinum Over Gold, Larter | 369 |
| **Cuff Links,** Mother-Of-Pearl, 10K Gold, Oval, ¾ In. | 120 |
| **Cuff Links,** Prince Of Wales Feather Design, 18K Gold, Oval, Tiffany & Co., ¾ In. | 767 |
| **Cuff Links,** Satyr Head, Relief, Round, 18K Gold, 1 In. | 861 |
| **Cuff Links,** Shamrocks, Silver, Green, Enamel, Marked, France | 195 |
| **Cuff Links,** Silver, Round, Stylized Flowers, Georg Jensen, ¾ In. | 288 |
| **Cuff Links,** Silver, Square, Angled Oxidized Decoration, Kalo, ¾ In. | 313 |
| **Cuff Links,** Stirrup, 18K Gold, Marked, Hermes, 1½ In. ...................................... *illus* | 3000 |
| **Cuff Links,** Taurus The Bull, 18K Gold, Textured Ground, Square | 431 |
| **Cuff Links,** Toad On Lily Pad, 18K Gold, Emerald Eyes, Tiffany & Co. | 3998 |
| **Dress Set,** Man's, Acorn, 18K Gold, Hematite Balls, Schlumberger, 5 Piece | 2337 |
| **Dress Set,** Man's, Bloodstone Tablet, Silver Mount, Cuff Links, Studs, G. Jensen, 8 Piece | 677 |
| **Dress Set,** Man's, Discs, Mother-Of-Pearl, Diamonds, Platinum Over Gold, Edwardian, 5 Piece | 1107 |

| | |
|---|---|
| **Dress Set,** Man's, Onyx, Pearl, Platinum Over Gold, Carrington, Tiffany, 9 Piece ...............*illus* | 1625 |
| **Earrings,** Black Beads, 3 Dangling Strands, Goldtone, Clip-On, Christian Lacroix, 1980s, 4 In... | 72 |
| **Earrings,** Bow, Emeralds, Gold, Rampant Lion Mark, Portugal, 1700s, 2 In......................*illus* | 5938 |
| **Earrings,** Cameo, Hardstone, Woman's Profile, Black & White, 14K Gold Frame, 1½ In. .......... | 920 |
| **Earrings,** Checkerboard, 18K Gold, Inlaid Mother-Of-Pearl, A. Cummings, ⅝ In. ...................... | 2091 |
| **Earrings,** Cube, Black Jade, Mother-Of-Pearl Sides, 18K Gold, A. Cummings, ½ In. ...................... | 1230 |
| **Earrings,** Dome, 18K Gold, Hammered, Paloma Picasso, Tiffany & Co., 1 In. ...................... | 1722 |
| **Earrings,** Drop, 18K Textured Gold, Tiffany & Co., 1 In. ...................... | 800 |
| **Earrings,** Drop, Gripoix, Cobalt Blue, Red, Goldtone, Clip-On, Chanel, 1993, 2 In. ...................... | 538 |
| **Earrings,** Faux Pearl, Rhinestone, Round, Miriam Haskell, 1 In....................................... | 84 |
| **Earrings,** Half Hoop, Coral, Graduated Egg Shaped, Stones, Hargo Creations, 1 x ¾ In. ..... | 69 |
| **Earrings,** Half Hoop, Rose Ceramic, Seed Pearls, Hearts, Goldtone, Avon ...................... | 17 |
| **Earrings,** Hoop, 18K Gold, Silver, Pierced, Cartier, ¾ In. ...................... | 660 |
| **Earrings,** Jacks, 3 Stick & Ball Shapes, Brass, Art Smith, 2½ In....................................... | 915 |
| **Earrings,** Leaf & Ball, Silver, Screwback, Bond Boyd, ¾ x ½ In....................................... | 19 |
| **Earrings,** Leaf, 14K Textured Gold, Aquamarine Water Drop, Clip-On, Retro, 1¼ In............ | 360 |
| **Earrings,** Leaf, Goldtone, Clear & Emerald Green Rhinestones, Clip-On, Ciro, c.1940 ............ | 25 |
| **Earrings,** Leaf, Ribbed, Raised Center Vein, Goldtone, Clip-On, Boucher, 1 x ⅞ In. ...................... | 20 |
| **Earrings,** Leaf, Veins, Pierced, Silvertone, Clip-On, B. Seinberg-Kaslo, B.S.K., ¾ In. ...................... | 15 |
| **Earrings,** Leaves, 18K Textured Gold, Emerald Blossom, M. Buccellati, 1 x ½ In. ...................... | 1783 |
| **Earrings,** Leaves, Yellow Enamel, Faux Pearls, Clip-On, Charel ...................... | 15 |
| **Earrings,** Link, Mariner, 18K Gold Plated, Clip-On, Gucci, 1950s...................................... | 165 |
| **Earrings,** Pendant, Spiral, Spinel Center, 18K Gold, Gubelin, 1⅜ In. ...................... | 1046 |
| **Earrings,** Pink Tourmaline, Hammered 18K Gold Mount, Beaded, E. Locke, 1 In...................... | 2829 |
| **Earrings,** Red Cabochon, Round, Vermeil Mount, Hermes, ½ In....................................... | 215 |
| **Earrings,** Rhinestones, Pearls, Blue Center, Marked, Mimi Di Niscemi, 1 In. ...................... | 50 |
| **Earrings,** Scarab, Turquoise, Silvertone Rim, Amber Rhinestones, Chico's ...................... | 21 |
| **Earrings,** Scribble, 18K Gold, Paloma Picasso, Tiffany & Co., 1⅜ In. ...................... | 554 |
| **Earrings,** Shell, 18K White Gold, Gem Set, Citrines, Gold Studs, Trianon, 1¼ In. ...................... | 1599 |
| **Earrings,** Spiral, Copper, Trapped Marble, Art Smith, 2 In. ...................... | 610 |
| **Earrings,** Stylized Leaf, Brass, Oxidation, Screwback, Art Smith, 2 In. ...................... | 594 |
| **Earrings,** Toad, Silver, Clip-On, Tiffany & Co., 1 x 1 In....................................... | 437 |
| **Earrings,** Triangles, Fluted, Faceted 18K Gold, Clip-On, Henry Dunay, 1¼ In. ...................... | 2048 |
| **Earrings,** Wreath, Teal Aurora Borealis Rhinestones, Clip-On, 1950s, 1 In....................................... | 32 |
| **Hair Comb,** Interwoven Organic Shape, Open Prongs, Silver, Cummings, 2½ In., Pair.............. | 861 |
| **Hatpins** are listed in this book in the Hatpin category. | |
| **Jabot,** Playful Puppy & Agitated Cat, Diamonds, Platinum, Beaded, Art Deco, France ................ | 1722 |
| **Key Chain,** Gold, Leather, Gucci, Box, 1979 ...................................... | 72 |
| **Lavaliere,** Abalone Pearl, Diamond & Platinum Link Chain, c.1900, 15 In......................*illus* | 2750 |
| **Leaves,** Scrolls, Pin, Green Tourmaline, Silver, Gold, 3-Sided, Arts & Crafts, F.G. Hale, 1 In.......... | 5843 |
| **Locket,** 23 Diamonds, Quilted Grid, Oval, Rope Chain, 18K Gold, Germany, 1995, 30 In. ...................... | 1625 |
| **Locket,** Miniature Portrait Of Girl, Watercolor, 10K Gold Chain, c.1850, 33 In............................. | 1476 |
| **Locket,** Star Center, Pave Set, Turquoise, Split Pearls, Diamonds, 15K Gold, Victorian.........*illus* | 896 |
| **Locket,** Tricolor Gold, Beaded, Ropework, Applied Leaves & Acorns, 2¾ In. ........................*illus* | 861 |
| **Necklace & Bracelet,** Silver, Cabochons, Curved Ribbed Links, Kalo, 17-In. Necklace............... | 1220 |
| **Necklace & Earrings,** Blue Glass Beads, Rhinestones, 4 Strands, M. Haskell, 16-In. Necklace.... | 295 |
| **Necklace & Earrings,** Bobble, Pink Glass, Aurora Borealis Rhinestones, Clip-On, Mode Art, 16 In | 125 |
| **Necklace & Earrings,** Leaves, Swirls, Vines, Rhinestones, Screwback, Bond Boyd, 18 In. ............ | 185 |
| **Necklace & Earrings,** Medallions, Leaf Design, Goldtone, Clip-On, Reja...................... | 244 |
| **Necklace & Earrings,** Open Loops, 18K Gold, Cartier, 50-In. Necklace, 2-In. Earrings ............. | 11800 |
| **Necklace & Earrings,** Pendant, 2-Headed Eagle, Enamel, Goldtone, Joan Rivers, c.1989, 25 In. | 40 |
| **Necklace & Earrings,** Silver, Hematite, 3 Strands, Mignon Faget, 22 In. ...................... | 369 |
| **Necklace,** 12 Plaques, Bronze, 4 Stones, Rhinestones, Marked, Chanel, Box, 1997, 24 In............ | 2390 |
| **Necklace,** 18K Gold, Amethyst, Sapphires, Diamonds, Krauss, c.1970, 16 In......................*illus* | 2750 |
| **Necklace,** Alhambra, Cat's-Eye Quatrefoils, 18K Gold Chain, Van Cleef & Arpels, 17 In............... | 6250 |
| **Necklace,** Amethyst Drops, Boomerang-Shaped Links, Box Closure, Mexico, 16 In...................... | 1875 |
| **Necklace,** Aquamarine Drops, 3 Swags, 18K Gold Paperclip Chain, Edwardian, 14 In.................. | 2337 |
| **Necklace,** Bead, Emerald, Carved, Graduated, 14K Gold, Toggle Clasp, 19 In. ......................*illus* | 1968 |
| **Necklace,** Bead, Glass, 3 Strands, Faceted, Round, Marked, Christian Dior, 1958, 17½ In. .......... | 270 |
| **Necklace,** Beads, Hematite, 5 Strands, 18K Gold Dove Clasp, P. Picasso, c.1981, 15¾ In. .......... | 1169 |
| **Necklace,** Beads, Hematite, 6 Strands, Silver Panther Head Center, P. Von Musulin, 15 In. .......... | 175 |
| **Necklace,** Berlin Ironwork, 7 Cameos, Gadroon & Rococo Links, c.1815, 18½ In. ...............*illus* | 4688 |
| **Necklace,** Blue Rhinestones, Marquise & Round, Dangling Strands, Marked, Weiss, 15 In. .......... | 122 |
| **Necklace,** Bone, Turquoise, Indian, Pueblo, New Mexico, c.1930, 22½ In. ...................... | 180 |
| **Necklace, Bracelet & Earrings,** Abstract, Silver, Champleve, Margot De Taxco, c.1955 .........*illus* | 3750 |
| **Necklace, Bracelet & Earrings,** Amethysts, Oval, Silver, Antonio Pineda, c.1951 .................*illus* | 4063 |

**Jade,** Vase, Hanging, Spinach Jade, Carved, Rosewood Stand, Chain, Chinese, 11¾ In.
$1,062

J

**Jade,** Wrist Rest, Bamboo Shape, Celadon Color Stone, Markings, Chinese, 1800s, 5¾ In.
$3,259

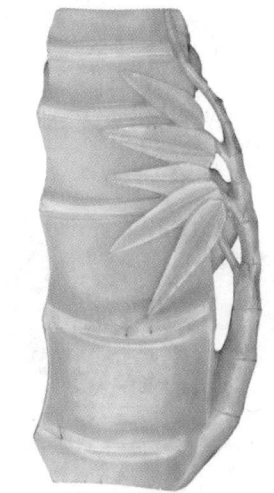

**Jasperware,** Cheese Dish, Lid, Green, White, Hunt Scene, Dogs, Horses, 1800s, 10 x 11 In.
$390

**Jasperware,** Cheese Dome, Blue Matte, White Cameo Figures, Leafy Vine Border, 11 x 10 In.
$250

Rago Arts & Auction Center

---

### TIP
*When putting on earrings in front of the bathroom mirror, be sure the sink stopper is closed. Don't risk dropping the jewelry down the drain.*

---

**Jewelry,** Belt Buckle, Sun, Crescent Moon, Copper, Silver, Spratling, Taxco, c.1944, 3½ In.
$812

Heritage Auction Galleries

---

**Jewelry,** Bracelet, Bangle, Amethyst, Gold, Scrolling, Art Nouveau, Whiteside & Blank, 7⅝ In.
$1,476

Skinner Auctioneers & Appraisers

| | |
|---|---:|
| Necklace, Bracelet & Earrings, Lucite Disks, White, Rhinestones, Charel, 16-In. Necklace | 65 |
| Necklace, Bracelet, Earrings & Ring, Serpent, Green Champleve, Margot De Taxco, c.1948. *illus* | 4375 |
| Necklace, Chain, Diamond, Seed Pearl, 14K Gold, Scroll Mount, Victorian, 16 In. | 153 |
| Necklace, Chain, Looped, Faux Pearls, Goldtone, Boucher, 17 In. | 70 |
| Necklace, Chains, Goldtone, Removable 3-In. Tassel, Emmons Jewelers, 1970s, 26 In. | 45 |
| Necklace, Charm, 27 Equestrian Charms, Link Chain, 14K Gold, 1950 | 3250 |
| Necklace, Choker, Faux Baroque Pearl, 4 Strand, Chanel, 1980s, 15 x 1¾ In. | 866 |
| Necklace, Choker, Mesh, Goldtone, Pave Rhinestone Center, Dior, 16 x ¼ In. | 69 |
| Necklace, Choker, Silver, Shark's-Tail Design, 9 Pieces, Flattened, J.M. Puig Doria | 400 |
| Necklace, Citrines, 3 Oval, Silver Frames, Paperclip Chain, Kalo Shop, 16 In. | 1159 |
| Necklace, Cleopatra Style, Goldtone Wings, Chain Tassel, Hook Clasp, Avon, 18 In. | 30 |
| Necklace, Coin, 20 Dollar, 14K Gold, St. Gaudens, Double Eagle, 1914D, Link Chain, 26 In. *illus* | 2500 |
| Necklace, Coin, Roman, 18K Gold Curb Link Chain, Monete, Bulgari, 14 In. | 5843 |
| Necklace, Collar, Arched Links, Silver, Amethyst Drops, A. Pineda, De Taxco, 15 In. | 2583 |
| Necklace, Collar, Hinged, 18K Textured Gold, Abstract Shape, Ed Weiner, 8 x 6 In. | 8050 |
| Necklace, Collar, Kinetic, Acrylic, Metal Rings, C. Kriegman, c.1965, 17 x 10 In. | 1250 |
| Necklace, Collar, Leaves, Textured 18K Gold, Mario Buccellati, 16 In. | 9840 |
| Necklace, Collar, Pointed, Half Woven & Beaded, Half Plain, Mexico, c.1950, 14 In. | 175 |
| Necklace, Collar, Silver, Garnet Bead Connector, Biomorphic, Art Smith | *illus* 2640 |
| Necklace, Collar, Tubogas, 14K Gold, Coral Cabochon Enhancer, Forstner, 14 In. | 3690 |
| Necklace, Coral Beads, Graduated, 14K Gold Clasp, c.1950, 33½ In. | 5535 |
| Necklace, Cross, Cobalt Blue Enamel, Diamonds, Rubies, 18K Gold, Faberge, 2 x 18 In. | 3508 |
| Necklace, Faux Pearl, 2 Strands, Flower Pendant, Miriam Haskell, 14 In. | 240 |
| Necklace, Faux Pearl, 3 Strands, Pyramid Spacers, Egyptian, Mimi Di Niscemi, 1960s, 17 In. | 159 |
| Necklace, Faux Pearl, Glass Bead, Bezel Set, Royal Blue, Emerald, Kenneth Jay Lane, 20 In. | 150 |
| Necklace, Faux Pearl, Strands, Knotted, Goldtone, Pave Clasp, Joan Rivers, 34 In. | 58 |
| Necklace, Festoon Medallion, Rose Glass, Rhinestones, Hollywood Style, Warner, 18 In. | 125 |
| Necklace, Festoon, Flower Pendant, Seed Pearls, Green Gemstones, Art Nouveau, 15 In. | 915 |
| Necklace, Figaro, Silver, 18K Gold, D. Yurman, 32 In. | 738 |
| Necklace, Fish, Champleve Enamel, Silver, Margot De Taxco, c.1948, 21 In. | 812 |
| Necklace, Flowers, Yellow Rhinestones, Frosted Marquise, Goldtone, Weiss, 16 In. | 188 |
| Necklace, Gripoix Glass, Emerald, Chain Link, Goldtone Metal, Chanel, 1983, 32 In. | 368 |
| Necklace, Human Tooth, Drilled, On Sennit Cord, Box Frame, Fiji Islands, c.1800, 18 x 16 In. | 7794 |
| Necklace, Knot, Ribbon Shape, Woven 14K Gold, Grosse, Cartier, Germany, 1962, 16½ In. | 1625 |
| Necklace, Lariat, Pearl, Round Cut Diamonds, 18K White Gold, Mikimoto, 18 In. | 546 |
| Necklace, Lily Pads, Silver, Felch & Co., Danecraft, c.1945, 15½ In. | 205 |
| Necklace, Link, 18K Gold, Chain, Slide In Clasp, Piaget, 16 In. | 3335 |
| Necklace, Link, Alternating Amethyst & Silver, Fred Davis, Mexico, c.1950, 15¼ In. *illus* | 2257 |
| Necklace, Link, Concave Circles, Silver, Pearl Centers, Robert Lee Morris, 15 In. | 492 |
| Necklace, Link, Emerald, Round Cut Diamonds, 14K Gold, 81 In. | 6600 |
| Necklace, Link, Nuggets, Polished, 18K Gold, Chiampesan, Italy, 17½ In. | 3250 |
| Necklace, Link, Silver, Oval, Open, Stamped, Weiss, 925, 16 In. | 210 |
| Necklace, Links, Curls, Silvertone, Pink & Lavender Rhinestones, Lisner, c.1960, 16 In. | 60 |
| Necklace, Locket, Applied Bead, Ropework, Link Chain, Pearls, Gold, 17 In. *illus* | 1599 |
| Necklace, Locket, Leaf, Silver Chain, Felch & Co., Danecraft, 1950s, 24 In. | 210 |
| Necklace, Negligee, Platinum, Diamonds, 14K White Gold Chain, Art Deco, 1¾ x 18 In. | 1047 |
| Necklace, Pearls, 109 Graduated, Platinum & Diamond Clasp, Art Deco, 18 In. | 4920 |
| Necklace, Pearls, 14K Gold Clasp, Mikimoto, 14½ In. | 354 |
| Necklace, Pearls, 3 Strands, Graduated, Silver Clasp, Mikimoto, 19 In. | 1230 |
| Necklace, Pearls, Single Strand, 98 Cultured, Graduated, Rose Tone, Mikimoto, 17½ In. | 800 |
| Necklace, Pearls, Single Strand, Pearls, 14K Gold, 24 In. | 300 |
| Necklace, Pendant, 18K Gold Bar, Suspended From Tension Collar, Cartier, 15 In. | 1770 |
| Necklace, Pendant, 1904 20 Dollar Gold Coin, Bead Chain, 10K Gold, 1926, 14½ In. | 1375 |
| Necklace, Pendant, Amber Stone, Marked, Danish Standards | 95 |
| Necklace, Pendant, Amethyst, Pear Shape, Beaded Bezel, 14K Gold, Curb Links, Kohn, 16 In. | 920 |
| Necklace, Pendant, Amethyst, Pearls, Enamel, Gold, Renaissance Revival, C. Giuliano, 15 In. *illus* | 17220 |
| Necklace, Pendant, Blister Pearl, Pear Shape, Silver Openwork Vine, Chain, Art Deco, 17 In. | 344 |
| Necklace, Pendant, Coin, 10 Dollar, Gold, 1912, Open Scrolled Bezel, Rope Twist Chain, 24 In. | 1121 |
| Necklace, Pendant, Cross, Amethysts, Silver Mount, Thick Link Chain, Spratling, 2¾ In. | 523 |
| Necklace, Pendant, Diamond Shape, Rhinestones, Art Deco Style, Avon, 20 In. | 26 |
| Necklace, Pendant, Disc, Metal, Black Leather Cord, Modernist, Chico's, 2¾ In. | 45 |
| Necklace, Pendant, Dog Tag, Silver, Marked, Gucci, 20 In. | 150 |
| Necklace, Pendant, Flower, Blue Grass, Silvertone Frame, Geometric, Chico's, 15 In. | 28 |
| Necklace, Pendant, Flower, Leaves, Silvertone, Blanch-Ette, 2 In. Diam. | 23 |
| Necklace, Pendant, Gourds, Carved Jade, Diamonds, Pearls, Link Chain, Art Deco, 16 In. | 1230 |
| Necklace, Pendant, Heart, Chalcedony, Pearls, Moonstones, Silver Leaves, Sandheim, 26 In. | 976 |

J

**Jewelry,** Bracelet, Bangle, Twisted Wire, 4 Double Roundels, Gold, Hinged, Italy, 6¾ In.
$660

Cowan's Auctions

**Jewelry,** Bracelet, Charm, Oval Links, 15 Charms, 14K & 18K Gold, 7⅜ In.
$6,150

Skinner Auctioneers & Appraisers

**Jewelry,** Bracelet, Cuff, Etruscan Revival, 15K Gold, Barnet Henry Joseph, 1885, ¾ In.
$2,091

New Orleans Auction Galleries, Inc.

**Jewelry,** Bracelet, Cuff, Hinged, Lion Relief, 18K Gold, Marked, David Webb, 6 In.
$15,375

New Orleans Auction Galleries, Inc.

**Jewelry,** Bracelet, Cuff, Hinged, Pierced, Silver, Applied Balls, C. Friedell, c.1940, 2¼ In.
$594

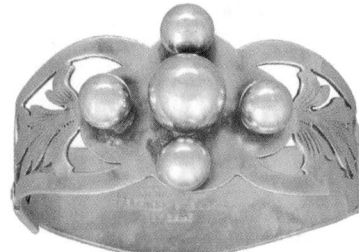

Heritage Auction Galleries

**Jewelry,** Bracelet, Cuff, Silver, Ribbed, Turquoise, Pin & Chain Closure, Aguilar, Mexico, c.1955, 2 In.
$1,625

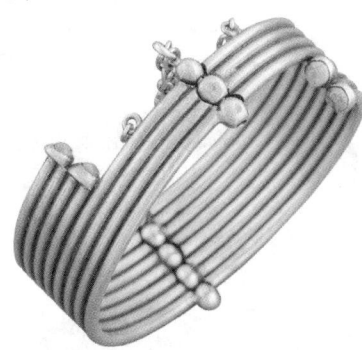

Heritage Auction Galleries

**Jewelry,** Bracelet, Dolphin, Flexible Braid, Gold, 6 In.
$3,936

Skinner Auctioneers & Appraisers

**Jewelry,** Bracelet, Link, Silver, Birds, Blossoms, Cabochon Moonstones, Georg Jensen, 7 In.
$1,046

Skinner Auctioneers & Appraisers

**Jewelry,** Bracelet, Link, Silver, Jadeite, Box Clasp, Chain, Antonio Pineda, Taxco, c.1953, 3 In.
$748

Heritage Auction Galleries

**Jewelry,** Bracelet, Silver, Enameled Leaves & Berries, Margot De Taxco, 1950s, 7 In.
$360

Cowan's Auctions

**Jewelry,** Charm, Globe, 18K Gold, Green Enamel, Italy, 1 In.
$180

DuMouchelles Art Gallery

**Jewelry,** Cigar Cutter, 14K Gold, Ruby, 6 Diamonds, 1 ¼ In.
$360

Cowan's Auctions

**Jewelry,** Clip, Fur, Unicorn, 18K Gold, Sapphire Horn, Ruby Eyes, Diamond Mane, c.1940, 3 ½ In.
$5,625

Rago Arts & Auction Center

**Jewelry,** Cuff Links, Fish, Silver, Antonio Pineda, Taxco, c.1962, 1 ¾ In.
$325

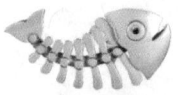 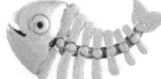

Heritage Auction Galleries

> **TIP**
> *Perfume and hair spray will damage amber beads and pearls.*

**Jewelry,** Cuff Links, Stirrup, 18K Gold, Marked, Hermes, 1 ½ In.
$3,000

Rago Arts & Auction Center

**Jewelry,** Dress Set, Man's, Onyx, Pearl, Platinum Over Gold, Carrington, Tiffany, 9 Piece
$1,625

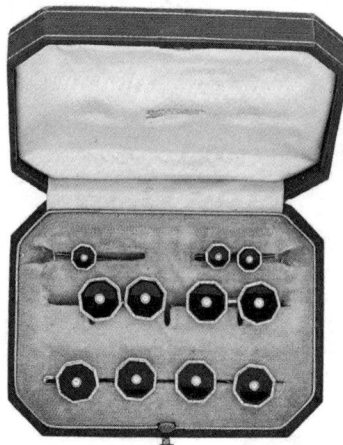

Rago Arts & Auction Center

**Jewelry,** Earrings, Bow, Emeralds, Gold, Rampant Lion Mark, Portugal, 1700s, 2 In.
$5,938

Rago Arts & Auction Center

**Jewelry,** Lavaliere, Abalone Pearl, Diamond & Platinum Link Chain, c.1900, 15 In.
$2,750

Rago Arts & Auction Center

**Jewelry,** Locket, Star Center, Pave Set, Turquoise, Split Pearls, Diamonds, 15K Gold, Victorian
$896

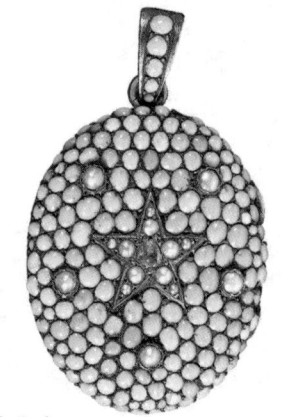

Neal Auction Co.

**Jewelry,** Locket, Tricolor Gold, Beaded, Ropework, Applied Leaves & Acorns, 2 ¾ In.
$861

Skinner Auctioneers & Appraisers

| | | |
|---|---|---|
| **Necklace,** Pendant, Leaf, Matte & Polished 18K Gold, Link Chain, A. Cummings, 19 In. | | 768 |
| **Necklace,** Pendant, Loupe Monocle, Braided Chain, Pinch Clasp, Logo, Chanel, 37 x 2 In. | | 575 |
| **Necklace,** Pendant, Medallion, Square Links, Filigree Balls, Goldtone, Pauline Rader, 30 In. | | 145 |
| **Necklace,** Pendant, Scarab, Blue & Green Enamel, 2 Chains, C. Horner, 1911, 18 In. | | 1037 |
| **Necklace,** Pendant, Watch, Blue Enamel, Diamonds, Pearls, 18K Gold, c.1880, 2 In. | *illus* | 10625 |
| **Necklace,** Pink Cabochon, Pearl Drop, Gold Scroll Mount, Swag Chain, Arts & Crafts, 17 In. | | 2091 |
| **Necklace,** Rhinestones, Goldtone, Button Clasp, Attwood & Sawyer, 16 In. | | 225 |
| **Necklace,** Sautoir, Chicklet, Gripoix, Blue, Goldtone Metal, Chanel, 1981, 62 In. | | 1093 |
| **Necklace,** Sautoir, Rubies, Diamonds, Platinum, Palmettes, Pearl Strap, 22 In. | *illus* | 8610 |
| **Necklace,** Sautoir, Seed Pearls Braid, Amethysts, Tassels, Silver & Ruby Caps, 48 In. | | 1722 |
| **Necklace,** Serpent, 15K Gold, Turquoise Enamel, Diamonds, Victorian, 15 In. | *illus* | 3500 |
| **Necklace,** Silver, Alternating Beads, Geometric S-Shape Links, Hector Aguilar, 15 In. | | 874 |
| **Necklace,** Silver, Arts & Crafts Style, Hans Hansen, 16 In. | | 177 |
| **Necklace,** Silver, Link, V-Shape, Blue Champleve, Los Castillo, Mexico, c.1950, 16 In. | *illus* | 313 |
| **Necklace,** Slide, Charmian, Step-Cut Blue Glass Stone, Goldtone Flower, Coro, 15 ½ In. | | 40 |
| **Necklace,** Star Sapphire, Diamonds, Platinum Mount, Tiffany & Co., 16 In. | | 861 |
| **Necklace,** Swag, 2 Tiers, Peridot, Pearl & Enamel Links, Gold Chain, Art Nouveau, 16 In. | | 3198 |
| **Necklace,** Swag, 5 Ropetwist Chains, Diamond Ties, 14K Gold, Grosse, Germany, 15 In. | | 2583 |
| **Necklace,** Swag, Amethysts, 18K Gold, Pink Enamel, Victorian, 16 In. | | 5313 |
| **Necklace,** Twisted Wire, Textured White Gold, Gold & Blue Enamel Slide, Wellendorf, 17 In. | | 6875 |
| **Pendant,** 14K Gold, Peridots, Rose Cut Diamonds, Russia, Art Nouveau, 2 ½ In. | | 805 |
| **Pendant,** Amber Teardrop, Silver Mount, Paolo Romeo, Italy, 18 In. | | 420 |
| **Pendant,** Boulder Opal, Wrapped In Platinum Chain, 1 x ½ In. | *illus* | 954 |
| **Pendant,** Buddha's Hand, Jadeite, Diamonds, 14K Gold, Chinese, 1900s, 1 ½ In. | *illus* | 6518 |
| **Pendant,** Cameo, Classical Maiden In Flowing Dress, Hardstone, 18K Gold Ropework, 3 In. | | 2214 |
| **Pendant,** Coin, 1910 Liberty Indian Head, 5 Dollar | | 431 |
| **Pendant,** Coin, Krugerrand, 14K Gold Mount, Bail, South Africa, 1975, 1 ¼ In. | | 1476 |
| **Pendant,** Cross, Amethyst, Faceted, Anchor Link Chain, 15K Gold, Victorian | | 2032 |
| **Pendant,** Cross, Flared, Hardstones, Silver, Hammered, Mexico, 5 ¼ In. | | 1000 |
| **Pendant,** Edelweiss, Green, Red, Pate-De-Verre, Silk Cord, G. Argy-Rousseau, 2 ½ In. | | 1185 |
| **Pendant,** Fleur-De-Lis, Seed Pearls, 14K Gold, Victorian, 1 ¼ x 1 In. | | 167 |
| **Pendant,** Flower, Orange, Yellow, Pate-De-Verre, Oval, Rousseau, 2 ½ x 1 ⅞ In. | | 600 |
| **Pendant,** Flowers, Pate-De-Verre, Multicolor, Rousseau, 2 ⅜ x 1 ¾ In. | | 600 |
| **Pendant,** Glass, Molded, Abstract, Brown Shaded To Amber, Brown Cord, Lalique, 2 ½ In. | *illus* | 984 |
| **Pendant,** Gold Coin, 10 Dollar, American, 14K Gold, Bezel Set | | 900 |
| **Pendant,** Heart, 14K Gold, 110 Diamonds, 1900s, 1 ½ In. | | 720 |
| **Pendant,** Horse's Head, 18K Gold, Hammered Ground, David Webb, ⅞ In. | | 492 |
| **Pendant,** Iris, Art Nouveau Maiden's Head & Arm, Gold, Enamel, Link Chain, Rambour, 1 In. | | 9840 |
| **Pendant,** Jade, Carved, Grape Bunch Shape, Greenish White, Chinese, 20th Century, 2 In. | | 119 |
| **Pendant,** Jade, Carved, Scholar, Attendant, Calligraphy, 1900s, 2 ¼ In. | | 240 |
| **Pendant,** Jade, Fingering Piece, White, Oval, Entwined Fish, ½ x 3 ¾ In. | | 5795 |
| **Pendant,** Jade, Green Oblong Bead, Pink Tourmaline Melon Shape, Chinese, 1800s, 1 In. | | 1659 |
| **Pendant,** Jade, Green, Foo Dog In Scrolling Leaves, Rectangular, 2 In. | | 1230 |
| **Pendant,** Jade, Woman, 4 Children, Flowers, Rectangular, Openwork, 2 ¼ x 1 ½ In. | | 3198 |
| **Pendant,** Key, 18K White Gold, Pave Diamonds, Trace Link Chain, Asprey, 2 ⅜ In. | | 1968 |
| **Pendant,** Ladybug, Red, Black, Yellow, Pate-De-Verre, Oval, Rousseau, 2 ½ x 1 ⅞ In. | | 600 |
| **Pendant,** Mourning, 14K Gold, Cobalt Blue Enamel, Woven, Blond Hair, c.1810 | | 239 |
| **Pendant,** Mourning, Child's Portrait On Ivory, Gold Bead & Scroll Frame, Hair Curl, 2 In. | | 177 |
| **Pendant,** Onyx Plaque, Intaglio, Cupid, Navette Shape, 18K Gold, Beaded Edge, E. Locke, 2 In. | | 2337 |
| **Pendant,** Pin, Gold, Horloge A La Langue, Clock Face, Picasso, Pierre Hugo, 2 In. | *illus* | 12300 |
| **Pendant,** Pin, Lion's Face, Chain, Miriam Haskell, 2 ¼ x 26 In. | | 180 |
| **Pendant,** Psyche, Hardstone, Intaglio, Gold, Scalloped Frame, Peridot, 2 ⅜ In. | *illus* | 923 |
| **Pendant,** Puffed Heart, 18K Gold, Blue Enamel, Gold Shamrock, Faberge, 18 In. | | 719 |
| **Pendant,** Skeleton Key, Platinum, Round Diamonds, Tiffany & Co., 1 ¼ x ½ In. | | 2645 |
| **Pendant,** Skull, Steer, Horns, Dipped In 24K Gold, 14K Gold Chain, 18 In. | | 369 |
| **Pendant,** Stylized Flower, Turquoise, Silver, John Lauritzen, 1 ¾ In. | | 47 |
| **Pendant,** Stylized Roman Soldier, Marked Bellone, Bicolor Gold, 1 In. | | 265 |
| **Pendant,** Stylized Starburst, Arched Rays, Copper, Brass, Art Smith, 3 ½ In. | | 1220 |
| **Pendant,** Sulphide, Pewter, Goddess Diana, Intaglio, Cut, 1 ½ In. | | 42 |
| **Pendant,** Sulphide, Sterling, Butterfly Wings, Woman, White Dress, Blue Ground, 1 ½ In. | | 199 |
| **Pendant,** Swirled, Fluted Sides, Silver, 14K Gold Center, Bale, David Yurman, 1 x ¾ In. | | 121 |
| **Pendant,** Turquoise Sections, Silver Seed Pearls, 14K Gold, Victorian, 1 ¼ x ½ In. | | 178 |
| **Pendant,** Woman, Flowing Hair, Revolving Disc, Riches, Sorrow, Glory, Art Nouveau, 1 In. | | 188 |
| **Pendant,** Woman's Portrait, Thermoplastic, Marked, Amerith, 1920s, 1 ½ x 2 In. | | 15 |
| **Pendant,** Woman's Profile, 14K Gold, Shell Shape, Box Link Chain, Art Nouveau Style, 18 In. | | 293 |

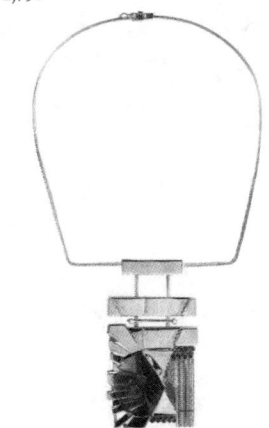

**Jewelry,** Necklace, 18K Gold, Amethyst, Sapphires, Diamonds, Krauss, c.1970, 16 In.
$2,750

Rago Arts & Auction Center

**Jewelry,** Necklace, Bead, Emerald, Carved, Graduated, 14K Gold, Toggle Clasp, 19 In.
$1,968

New Orleans Auction Galleries, Inc.

**Jewelry,** Necklace, Berlin Ironwork, 7 Cameos, Gadroon & Rococo Links, c.1815, 18 ½ In.
$4,688

Rago Arts & Auction Center

J

**TIP**
*Never dip a piece of rhinestone jewelry in water. It will cause damage.*

**Jewelry,** Necklace, Bracelet & Earrings, Abstract, Silver, Champleve, Margot De Taxco, c.1955
$3,750

Heritage Auction Galleries

**Jewelry,** Necklace, Bracelet & Earrings, Amethysts, Oval, Silver, Antonio Pineda, c.1951
$4,063

Heritage Auction Galleries

**Jewelry,** Necklace, Bracelet, Earrings & Ring, Serpent, Green Champleve, Margot De Taxco, c.1948
$4,375

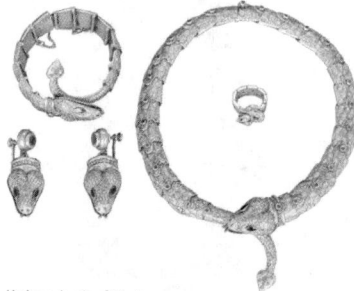

Heritage Auction Galleries

**Jewelry,** Necklace, Coin, 20 Dollar, 14K Gold, St. Gaudens, Double Eagle, 1914D, Link Chain, 26 In.
$2,500

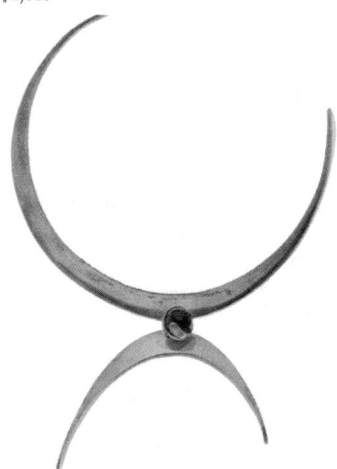

Rago Arts & Auction Center

**Jewelry,** Necklace, Collar, Silver, Garnet Bead Connector, Biomorphic, Art Smith
$2,640

Cowan's Auctions

**Jewelry,** Necklace, Link, Alternating Amethyst & Silver, Fred Davis, Mexico, c.1950, 15¼ In.
$2,257

Heritage Auction Galleries

**Jewelry,** Necklace, Locket, Applied Bead, Ropework, Link Chain, Pearls, Gold, 17 In.
$1,599

Skinner Auctioneers & Appraisers

**Jewelry,** Necklace, Pendant, Amethyst, Pearls, Enamel, Gold, Renaissance Revival, C. Giuliano, 15 In.
$17,220

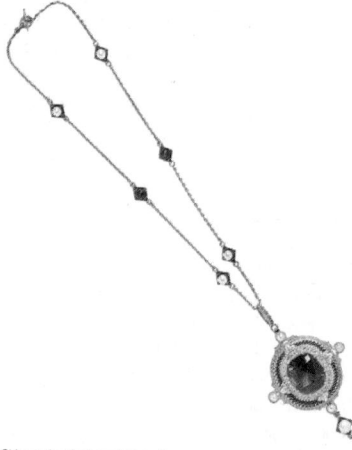

Skinner Auctioneers & Appraisers

**Jewelry,** Necklace, Pendant, Watch, Blue Enamel, Diamonds, Pearls, 18K Gold, c.1880, 2 In.
$10,625

Rago Arts & Auction Center

| | | |
|---|---|---:|
| **Pin & Earrings,** Blossom, Pearls, Rhinestones, Goldtone Metal, Schiaparelli, 2-In. Pin. | | 531 |
| **Pin & Earrings,** Blue Rhinestone Cluster, Silvertone, Marked, Clip-On, Weiss, 1 ¾ In. & 1 In. | | 75 |
| **Pin & Earrings,** Circle, Open, Gray Rhinestones, Silvertone, Clip-On, Warner, 1 ¾ In. | | 50 |
| **Pin & Earrings,** Fish, Green Rhinestones, Navette & Round, Clip-On, Blanch-Ette, 1 x ¾ In. | | 72 |
| **Pin & Earrings,** Flowers, Pietra Dura, Inlaid Hardstone, Gold, c.1850, 2-In. Pin | *illus* | 780 |
| **Pin & Earrings,** Moonstone, Step Cut Tourmalines, 14K Bicolor Gold, Retro, 2-In. Pin | | 1476 |
| **Pin & Earrings,** Rainbow Starburst, Rhinestone, Pearl Center, Clip-On, Emmons, 1965. | | 39 |
| **Pin & Earrings,** Silver, Scrolling Leaves, Gemstones, Arts & Crafts, E. Oakes, 2-In. Pin | | 3998 |
| **Pin & Earrings,** Windmill, Green Lucite Center, Openwork, Goldtone, Clip-On, Hargo, 2 In. | | 125 |
| **Pin,** 180 Diamonds, Pierced Geometric Mount, Art Deco, c.1920, 1 ½ x 2 ⅜ In. | | 3200 |
| **Pin,** 2 Butterflies, On Moonlight Blossoms, Silver, Round, G. Jensen, c.1950, 2 In. | | 488 |
| **Pin,** 2 Flowers, Round Faceted Rubies, 18K Gold, Tiffany & Co., 1 ¾ x 1 In. | | 575 |
| **Pin,** 2 Lovebirds, Branch, Diamonds, Emerald Eyes, Platinum, 18K Gold, Cartier, 1 ¼ In. | | 9225 |
| **Pin,** 2 Triangles, Overlapping, Elongated, Cutouts, Brass, Art Smith, 4 ½ In. | | 854 |
| **Pin,** Abstract, Curved Design, Rhinestones, Goldtone, Boucher, 1 ¾ In. | | 145 |
| **Pin,** Amethysts, Split Pearls, Gold Discs, Silver Navette Mount, Dorrie Nossiter, 1 ½ In. | | 677 |
| **Pin,** Arrow, Silver, 18K Gold, Snakeskin Pattern, Oval, Arts & Crafts, John Hardy, 3 x 1 ¼ In. | | 184 |
| **Pin,** Ballerina, Silver, Felch & Co., Danecraft, 1 ¾ x 1 ¾ In. | | 125 |
| **Pin,** Bar, 7 Pearls, Diamonds, Platinum & Gold, Shaped Openwork Mount, Edwardian, 3 In. | | 492 |
| **Pin,** Bar, Amethyst, 14K Gold Frame, Split Pearls, Enameled Greek Key, Art Nouveau, 1 In. | | 861 |
| **Pin,** Bar, Amethysts, Rose Cut, Pear Shape Center Drop, 14K Gold, 2 In. | | 190 |
| **Pin,** Bar, Clover Leaf, 3 Diamonds, 15K Granulated Gold, Etruscan, 1 ¾ In. | | 179 |
| **Pin,** Bar, Diamonds, Platinum, Navette Shape, Pierced Scrolls, Edwardian, 1 ¾ In. | | 3250 |
| **Pin,** Bar, Emeralds, 14K Gold, Scrolling Wirework, Beaded, Marcus & Co., 2 ¼ In. | | 1107 |
| **Pin,** Bar, Etruscan Revival, 18K Gold, Granulated, Pearl, Victorian, 2 In. | | 155 |
| **Pin,** Bar, Gold, 3 Pronged Basket Settings, Colored Stones, c.1900, 2 ½ In. | | 240 |
| **Pin,** Bar, Lapis Lazuli, Silver Saw Cut Mount, Tre-O Shop, Art Deco, 2 ½ In. | | 793 |
| **Pin,** Bar, Platinum, Art Deco, 3 European Cut, 20 Round Cut, Brilliant Cut Diamonds | | 1298 |
| **Pin,** Bar, Turquoise Enamel, Inset Star, Rose Cut Diamonds, Coral, 15K Gold | | 598 |
| **Pin,** Bar, Walrus Tusk, Carved, Gold Nugget Border, Marked, Suter's, Alaska, 2 In. | *illus* | 1107 |
| **Pin,** Beetle, Emerald, Pear Shape, Garnet Eyes, 14K Gold, 1 In. | *illus* | 123 |
| **Pin,** Bird, Diamonds, Blackened Gold, Diamond Suspended From Beak, 3 In. | *illus* | 2706 |
| **Pin,** Bird, In Flight, Plique-A-Jour, Blue & Green Panels, Gold, Pave Diamond Head, 3 In. | | 1230 |
| **Pin,** Bird, On Branch, Goldtone, Silvertone, Garnet, Turquoise, Jomaz, 1 ¾ In. | | 72 |
| **Pin,** Bird, Standing On 1 Leg, Goldtone, Marked, Charel, 4 ½ In. | | 75 |
| **Pin,** Birds, On Branch, Enamel, Multicolor, Rhinestones, Trifari, 1 ¾ x 1 ¾ In. | | 550 |
| **Pin,** Blackamoor Bust, 18K Gold, Aquamarine, Engraved, G. Nardi, 2 In. | *illus* | 2091 |
| **Pin,** Blackamoor, Enamel, Gold, Malachite Turban, Ruby Collar, Pearl, Aventurine, 2 In. | | 738 |
| **Pin,** Bow, 3 Round Faceted Rubies, 2 Accent Diamonds, Retro, 2 x ¾ In. | | 207 |
| **Pin,** Bow, Diamonds, Onyx, Beaded Accents, Art Deco, 2 ½ In. | *illus* | 3198 |
| **Pin,** Bow, Peridot, 18K Gold, 4 Peridot Drops, Tiffany & Co., Made In Italy, 1 ¾ In. | | 1968 |
| **Pin,** Bow, Ruby & Diamond Flower, 14K Bicolor Gold, 3 In. | | 1968 |
| **Pin,** Bow, Ruby & Diamond Knot, 14K Gold, Tiffany & Co., 1 ½ In. | | 575 |
| **Pin,** Bow, Sapphire, Diamond, Gold, Platinum, Baroque Pearl Drop, Edwardian, 1 ¼ In. | | 1440 |
| **Pin,** Branch, Twisted Wire, 18K Gold, 3 Suspended Leaf Caps With Pearls, Tiffany, 2 In. | | 1180 |
| **Pin,** Branches, Intertwined, Red Rhinestones, D. Lisner, Marked, 2 In. | | 75 |
| **Pin,** Buddha, Coral, Carved, Blue Enamel Ground, Oval, 14K Gold Mount, 2 In. | | 554 |
| **Pin,** Bug, Open Wings, Red & Clear Rhinestones, Ciro, 1 x 1 ¾ In. | | 100 |
| **Pin,** Bust, Moretto, Ebony, Pierced Gold, Ruby & Diamond Fringe, Nardi, 2 In. | *illus* | 6875 |
| **Pin,** Butterfly, Enameled Copper Tone Metal, Rhinestones, Joan Rivers, 2 In. | | 35 |
| **Pin,** Butterfly, Faux Turquoise Beads, Milk Glass Cabochons, Goldtone, Pauline Rader, 2 In. | | 62 |
| **Pin,** Butterfly, Multicolor Enamel, Filigree, Goldtone, Mode Art, 1 ¾ x 2 In. | | 49 |
| **Pin,** Butterfly, Silver, Bezel Set Opals, Antonio Pineda, Mexico, c.1953, 4 In. | *illus* | 813 |
| **Pin,** Camel, Woman, Carved, Silver, c.1900, 1 ¼ x 1 ½ In. | | 120 |
| **Pin,** Cameo, 3 Graces, Revolving Center, Pinchbeck, c.1850 | | 448 |
| **Pin,** Cameo, Coral, Carved, 14K Gold Scroll Mount, 1800s, 2 x 2 ¼ In. | | 357 |
| **Pin,** Cameo, Glass, Classical Beauty, Fringe, 14K Gold, Victorian, 3 ¼ x 1 ½ In. | | 414 |
| **Pin,** Cameo, Hardstone, Classical Maiden Profile, 18K Gold Garland, Pearls, 2 In. | | 923 |
| **Pin,** Cameo, Shell, Gold Filled, Victorian, 2 x 1 ½ In. | | 295 |
| **Pin,** Cameo, Shell, Woman On Horseback, Gold Frame, Pinback, Swivel Bail, 2 ¼ In. | *illus* | 108 |
| **Pin,** Cameo, Victorian Woman, 14K Bicolor Gold Frame, 18 Pearls, 1864, Box, 2 In. | *illus* | 1007 |
| **Pin,** Cat, Sitting, Rhinestones, Metal Whiskers & Tail, Marked, Warner, 1 ½ In. | | 40 |
| **Pin,** Chalcedony Cabochon, Plique-A-Jour Enamel, Organic Silver Mount, T. Fahrner, 1 In. | | 2583 |
| **Pin,** Chi Rho, X Over P, Heart End, Emeralds, 18K Gold, Rope Edge, Castellani, c.1860, 2 In. | | 22500 |
| **Pin,** Christmas Tree, Goldtone, Enamel, Ribbon, Ornaments, Rhinestones, Attwood & Sawyer, 5 In. | | 95 |
| **Pin,** Circle, 3 Sections Of Repeating Lines, Silver, Kalo, 1 ¼ In. | | 153 |

**Jewelry,** Necklace, Sautoir, Rubies, Diamonds, Platinum, Palmettes, Pearl Strap, 22 In.
$8,610

Skinner Auctioneers & Appraisers

**Jewelry,** Necklace, Serpent, 15K Gold, Turquoise Enamel, Diamonds, Victorian, 15 In.
$3,500

Rago Arts & Auction Center

**Jewelry,** Necklace, Silver, Link, V-Shape, Blue Champleve, Los Castillo, Mexico, c.1950, 16 In.
$313

Heritage Auction Galleries

This is an edited listing of current prices. Visit **Kovels.com** to check thousands of prices from previous years and sign up for free information on trends, tips, reproductions, marks, and more.

**Jewelry,** Pendant, Boulder Opal, Wrapped In Platinum Chain, 1 x ½ In. $954

Skinner Auctioneers & Appraisers

**Jewelry,** Pendant, Buddha's Hand, Jadeite, Diamonds, 14K Gold, Chinese, 1900s, 1 ½ In. $6,518

James D. Julia Auctioneers

**TIP**

*Always make sure the repairs to jewelry are made with matching solder—gold on gold, platinum on platinum. Lead solder will lower the value of any piece of jewelry.*

| | |
|---|---:|
| **Pin,** Circle, Moonstones, Heart Shape, Sapphires, Diamonds, Palladium, R. Yard, 2 In. | 4305 |
| **Pin,** Circle, Multicolor Rhinestones, Pearls, Thief Of Bagdad, Rice-Weiner Co., 2¾ In. | 225 |
| **Pin,** Circle, Open, Sapphires, Seed Pearls, C-Clasp, 15K Gold, Arts & Crafts, 1 x 1 In. | 173 |
| **Pin,** Circles, Interlocking, 14K Gold, Tiffany & Co., 1¾ x 1¼ In. | 230 |
| **Pin,** Citrine, Silver Mount, Repousse Thistle, Round, Scotland, 1910, 2 In. | 123 |
| **Pin,** Clip, Dress, Platinum, Marquise-Cut Diamonds, 18K Gold, Art Deco, 3 In. ............*illus* | 10762 |
| **Pin,** Crescent, Alternating Sapphires & Seed Pearls, 14K Gold, Single Pin Stem, 3¼ In. | 708 |
| **Pin,** Cricket, 18K Gold, Green Enamel, Diamond Accents, Tiffany & Co., 1¾ In. | 1476 |
| **Pin,** Daisies, Rhinestone Petals & Bow, Stems, Rhodium, Ciro, 2½ x 1¼ In. | 32 |
| **Pin,** Diamond, 18K Gold, Black Enamel, France, c.1875, 7 x 1 In. | 1920 |
| **Pin,** Diamond, Baguette Cut, Platinum Over Gold, c.1950, 1¾ In. | 937 |
| **Pin,** Diamonds, Platinum Openwork Mount, 3 Shaped Sides, Drop, Edwardian, 1½ In. | 2074 |
| **Pin,** Diamonds, Round Cut, Platinum, Filigree, Oval, Safety Catch, Edwardian, 2 x 1 In. | 3623 |
| **Pin,** Dog, Terrier, 14K Textured Gold, Enamel Collar, Sloan & Co., 1 In. | 246 |
| **Pin,** Dogwood Blossom, Silver, Oval Mount, Arts & Crafts, 2⅜ In. | 61 |
| **Pin,** Donkey, Silver, Sapphire Eyes, Bezel Set, Gold, Tiffany & Co., 1½ x 1¾ In. | 173 |
| **Pin,** Dove, Silver, Georg Jensen, c.1940, 1¾ In. | 270 |
| **Pin,** Dragon, 18K Gold, Engraved Scales, Sapphire Navettes, Coral Head, E. Giansanti, 3 In. | 2706 |
| **Pin,** Dragonfly, 18K Bicolor Gold, Plique-A-Jour, c.1900, 2¼ x 3¾ In. | 3198 |
| **Pin,** Dragonfly, 18K Gold, Diamonds, Peridot, Emeralds, Ruby, Victorian, 1¾ In. | 2006 |
| **Pin,** Dragonfly, Diamond, Emerald, Peridot, Platinum Over Gold, c.1910, 3 In. | 13750 |
| **Pin,** Drop Pendant, Oval, Turquoise Center, Seed Pearls, Pauline Rader, 2 In. | 110 |
| **Pin,** Duck, 18K Gold, Coral Beak, Emerald Eye, Chalcedony & Diamond Wing, Cartier, 1 In. | 5843 |
| **Pin,** Eagle, Holding Arrows, Red Rhinestone Eye, Goldtone, c.1942, 2½ In. | 125 |
| **Pin,** Eagle, Pave Diamonds, Marquise Cut Tail, 18K Gold, Ruby Eye, McTeigue, 2 In. | 3198 |
| **Pin,** Eagle, Spread Wings, Perched On Branch, 14K Gold, Tiffany & Co., 2 In. | 1046 |
| **Pin,** Elephant, 14K Gold, Pave Diamond & Ruby Accents, 20th Century, ¾ In. | 120 |
| **Pin,** Emerald, Diamond Ribbon Loop, 14K Gold, August Hollming, Faberge, 1 x ¼ In. | 1783 |
| **Pin,** Etruscan Style, 14K Gold, Amethyst Cabochons, Seed Pearls, Victorian, 1¾ x 1¼ In. | 357 |
| **Pin,** Etruscan, Medallion, Pave, Diamonds, 15K Gold, Persian Turquoise, Victorian, c.1850 | 896 |
| **Pin,** Eye Of Time, Enamel, Diamonds, Cabochon, Platinum, Gold, Kaston, Dali, 1½ In. ......*illus* | 24600 |
| **Pin,** Faux Pearls, Enamel Cabochons, Pierced Logo, Goldtone Metal, Chanel, 2 In. ...........*illus* | 270 |
| **Pin,** Filigree, 14K White Gold, 2 European Cut Diamonds, Art Deco, 2⅛ In. | 201 |
| **Pin,** Flag, 17 Rubies, 24 Sapphires, 13 Rhinestones, 14K Gold, Retro, ¾ In. | 374 |
| **Pin,** Flower Bouquet, Enameled Leaves, Rhinestones, Marked, Reja, 2¾ In. | 366 |
| **Pin,** Flower Bouquet, Faux Moonstones, Rhinestones, Rose Gold Finish, Coro, 4 In. | 50 |
| **Pin,** Flower Spray, Moonstones, Sapphires, 18K Gold Ribbon, Diamond Knot, R. Yard, 2 In. | 2706 |
| **Pin,** Flower, 10K Gold, Pastel Enamel, Diamond, Art Nouveau, 1 x 1 In. | 345 |
| **Pin,** Flower, 18K Gold, Florentine Finish, Turquoise Cabochon Accents, Retro, 1¼ In. | 1063 |
| **Pin,** Flower, 18K Yellow Gold, Diamond, Tiffany, c.1900, 1 In. | 5400 |
| **Pin,** Flower, 5 Enamel Petals, Diamond Center, 14K Gold, Whiteside & Blank, 1¼ In. | 861 |
| **Pin,** Flower, 5 Petals, Old Mine Diamonds, Black Enamel Stamens, S.J. Phillips, 2 In. | 10625 |
| **Pin,** Flower, Art Glass, Faux Pearls, Rhinestone Center, Goldtone, Blanch-Ette, 2½ In. | 50 |
| **Pin,** Flower, Carved Turquoise, Silver Pearl Center, Diamonds, Grasso, 2½ In. | 3625 |
| **Pin,** Flower, Layered Cluster, Red & Clear Rhinestones, Marked, Weiss, 1½ In. | 10 |
| **Pin,** Flower, Openwork Petals, Orange Center, Mode Art, 2¾ x 3 In. | 65 |
| **Pin,** Flower, Seed Beads, Rhinestones, Glass Petals, Marked, Miriam Haskell, 3½ In. | 1560 |
| **Pin,** Flower, Stem, Reeds, Rhinestone Center, Bronze Finish, Reja, 4 In. | 125 |
| **Pin,** Flower, Textured Petals, Rhinestone Center Tendril, B. Steinberg-Kaslo, B.S.K., 2½ In. | 196 |
| **Pin,** Flower, Textured Petals, Stems, Rhinestone, Hargo Creations, 2 x 3 In. | 60 |
| **Pin,** Flowers, Drooping 14K Gold Stems, 2 Amethyst Buds, Seaman Schepps, 1½ In. | 584 |
| **Pin,** Flowers, Spiked, Cultured Pearl, Goldtone, Boucher, 1950s, 2½ x 2¼ In. | 40 |
| **Pin,** Fluted Wave Design, Rhinestones, Half Ball, Clip-On, Reja, 1¾ In. | 188 |
| **Pin,** Fox, Running, Diamonds, Platinum, Art Deco, 1⅜ In. | 738 |
| **Pin,** Frog, Enamel, Green, 18K Gold, Protrusions, Ruby Cabochon Eyes, D. Webb, 1 In. | 2706 |
| **Pin,** Fruiting Branch, Puffy Design, Silver, Kalo, 2 In. | 244 |
| **Pin,** Golf Club, 18K White Gold, Pearl Ball, Baguette Diamonds, Raymond Yard, 2¼ In. | 1200 |
| **Pin,** Harp, Scroll Top, 7 Strings, 18K Gold, 7 Diamonds, 9 Pearls, Mikimoto, 2 In. | 875 |
| **Pin,** Hat, Goldtone, Chanel, c.1875, 2 In. | 299 |
| **Pin,** Head, Jasper, Gold Headdress, Bead & Ropework Mount, Egyptian Revival, 2 In. | 861 |
| **Pin,** Horseshoe, Natural Pearl, 14K Gold, Victorian, 1 x 1 In. | 63 |
| **Pin,** HOT, Diamonds, Platinum, Rectangular Garland Border, Art Deco, 1 In. | 984 |
| **Pin,** Infinity, Silver, Twisted Wire, Free-Form, Art Smith, 3 x 2 In. ............*illus* | 600 |
| **Pin,** Iris, Figural, 18K Gold, Green Enamel Stem, Pearl Petals, Marcus & Co., 2 In. | 7380 |
| **Pin,** Jabot, Jade, Diamond, Art Deco, Lacloche Freres, c.1925, 3¼ In. | 1320 |

**Jewelry,** Pendant, Glass, Molded, Abstract, Brown Shaded To Amber, Brown Cord, Lalique, 2½ In.
$984

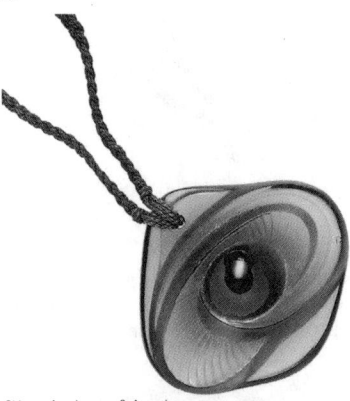

**Jewelry,** Pendant, Pin, Gold, Horloge A La Langue, Clock Face, Picasso, Pierre Hugo, 2 In.
$12,300

**Jewelry,** Pendant, Psyche, Hardstone, Intaglio, Gold, Scalloped Frame, Peridot, 2⅜ In.
$923

### Taxco Mark

I went to a flea market recently and searched the costume jewelry boxes. I found a hinged bracelet marked "sterling, 925, TCH 10" with a gold buckle and thin onyx inlay for $20. There is a small one on eBay for $65 so I bought a bargain. But the mark tells me only that it was made in Taxco, Mexico, after 1980.

**Jewelry,** Pin & Earrings, Flowers, Pietra Dura, Inlaid Hardstone, Gold, c.1850, 2-In. Pin
$780

**Jewelry,** Pin, Bar, Walrus Tusk, Carved, Gold Nugget Border, Marked, Suter's, Alaska, 2 In.
$1,107

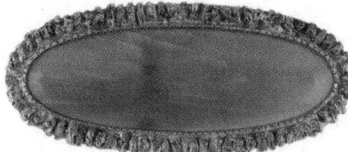

**Jewelry,** Pin, Beetle, Emerald, Pear Shape, Garnet Eyes, 14K Gold, 1 In.
$123

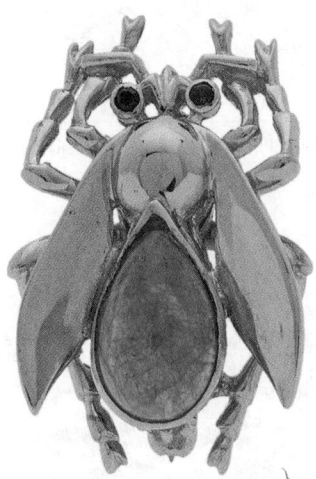

**Jewelry,** Pin, Bird, Diamonds, Blackened Gold, Diamond Suspended From Beak, 3 In.
$2,706

**Jewelry,** Pin, Blackamoor Bust, 18K Gold, Aquamarine, Engraved, G. Nardi, 2 In.
$2,091

**Jewelry,** Pin, Bow, Diamonds, Onyx, Beaded Accents, Art Deco, 2½ In.
$3,198

J

**Jewelry,** Pin, Bust, Moretto, Ebony, Pierced Gold, Ruby & Diamond Fringe, Nardi, 2 In.
$6,875

**Jewelry,** Pin, Butterfly, Silver, Bezel Set Opals, Antonio Pineda, Mexico, c.1953, 4 In.
$813

**Jewelry,** Pin, Cameo, Shell, Woman On Horseback, Gold Frame, Pinback, Swivel Bail, 2 ¼ In.
$108

**Jewelry,** Pin, Cameo, Victorian Woman, 14K Bicolor Gold Frame, 18 Pearls, 1864, Box, 2 In.
$1,007

**Jewelry,** Pin, Clip, Dress, Platinum, Marquise-Cut Diamonds, 18K Gold, Art Deco, 3 In.
$10,762

**Jewelry,** Pin, Eye Of Time, Enamel, Diamonds, Cabochon, Platinum, Gold, Kaston, Dali, 1 ½ In.
$24,600

**Jewelry,** Pin, Faux Pearls, Enamel Cabochons, Pierced Logo, Goldtone Metal, Chanel, 2 In.
$270

**Jewelry,** Pin, Infinity, Silver, Twisted Wire, Free-Form, Art Smith, 3 x 2 In.
$600

**Jewelry,** Pin, Landscape, Painted Under Glass, Gold Filled Frame, c.1850, 2 In.
$120

**Jewelry,** Pin, Lips, Rubies, Pearl Teeth, 18K Gold, Henryk Kaston, Dali, 2 In.
$12,300

**Jewelry,** Pin, Lover's Eye, Painted, Braided Hair & Enamel Borders, Gold Beaded Frame, 2 In.
$2,375

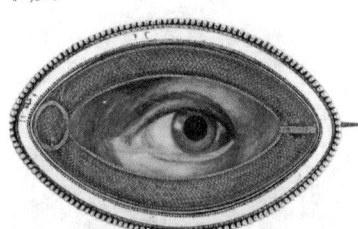

| | |
|---|---|
| **Pin,** Knot, Blue & White Enamel Cabochons, 18K Gold Lattice, Tiffany & Co., 2 In. ...................... | 3444 |
| **Pin,** Knot, Goldtone, Rhinestones, Marked, Attwood & Sawyer, 2 x ⅝ In. | 55 |
| **Pin,** Lady's Hat, 18K Bicolor Gold, Turquois, Ruby & Diamond Flowers, Marchak, 2 In. .............. | 8125 |
| **Pin,** Landscape, Painted Under Glass, Gold Filled Frame, c.1850, 2 In. ...................*illus* | 120 |
| **Pin,** Lapel, Jade, Egg Shape, 14K Gold, Lotus Flower Mount, c.1900, 2¾ In. | 59 |
| **Pin,** Leaf, 18K Textured Gold, Tiffany & Co., 2½ In. | 923 |
| **Pin,** Leaf, Red Rhinestones, Round & Teardrop, Japanned Metal, D. Lisner, 1 x 2 In. ............. | 45 |
| **Pin,** Leopard, Black Enamel Spots, Rhinestones, 18K Gold Plate, Attwood & Sawyer, 2 x 1 In. ...... | 79 |
| **Pin,** Lips, Rubies, Pearl Teeth, 18K Gold, Henryk Kaston, Dali, 2 In. ...................*illus* | 12300 |
| **Pin,** Lover's Eye, Painted, Braided Hair & Enamel Borders, Gold Beaded Frame, 2 In. .........*illus* | 2375 |
| **Pin,** Micro Mosaic, Insect, Oval, 18K Gold, Bead & Ropework Mount, 1¼ In. .............................. | 492 |
| **Pin,** Micro Mosaic, Landscape, Trees, Goldstone Border, Gold Mount, Oval, 2 In. | 531 |
| **Pin,** Micro Mosaic, Pantheon, Rome, Onyx Tablet, Gold Frame, C-Hook Bar Pin, 2 x 1½ In. ....... | 403 |
| **Pin,** Micro Mosaic, Spaniel & Game Birds In Landscape, Gold & Black Oval Mount, 2 In. | 2706 |
| **Pin,** Moss-In-Snow Jade, Diamonds, 18K Textured Gold, Abstract Frame, Ed Weiner, 3 In. ........... | 3450 |
| **Pin,** Musicians, Playing Lyre, Intaglio, Emerald, Citrine Surround, 18K Gold, c.1890, 2¼ In. ..... | 1062 |
| **Pin,** Nosegay, 18K Gold, Multicolor Enamel, Gucci, 3¼ In. | 1722 |
| **Pin,** Opal, 14K Gold Frame, Egyptian Symbols, Enamel Details, Marcus & Co., 2¾ In. | 9840 |
| **Pin,** Opal, Oval, Navette Mount, 14K Gold, Applied Grapes & Flowers, Art Nouveau, 3 In. | 984 |
| **Pin,** Orchid, Enamel, Diamonds, 14K Gold, 1 In. ...................*illus* | 1888 |
| **Pin,** Park Bench, 18K Gold Slats, 2 Coral & Diamond Hearts, Cartier, 1 In. | 11070 |
| **Pin,** Pear, Red, Green Leaves, Rhinestones, Joan Rivers, 1¾ In. | 75 |
| **Pin,** Pendant, Butterfly, Rhinestones, Goldtone, Ciro, 1980s, 2½ In. | 89 |
| **Pin,** Pendant, Flower, 18K Gold, Van Cleef & Arpels, ¾ In. | 360 |
| **Pin,** Pendant, Vase Of Flowers, Tassel, Silver, Glass, Art Deco, Bond-Boyd, c.1943, 2¼ In. ........... | 125 |
| **Pin,** Peridot, Pink Tourmaline, Blue Topaz, 18K Gold, Bulgari, 1⅝ In. ...................*illus* | 2583 |
| **Pin,** Photo, 3 Children, 9K Gold, Opals, Victorian, 1¼ In. | 155 |
| **Pin,** Pinwheel, Flower Ends, Rhinestones, Silver, Bond-Boyd, 2 In. | 100 |
| **Pin,** Plique-A-Jour Enamel, Diamonds, Peridot Drop, Marcus & Co., Art Nouveau, 2½ In. ....*illus* | 10455 |
| **Pin,** Portrait, Geisha, Enamel, 14K Gold, Pearl & Diamond Rim, 1¼ In. ...................*illus* | 861 |
| **Pin,** Portrait, Woman Wearing Feathered Hat, Gold Frame, Oval, 1¾ In. | 177 |
| **Pin,** Portrait, Woman, Painted, 14K Gold Frame, Pearls, Turquoise Beads, France...............*illus* | 180 |
| **Pin,** Purse, Quilted, Flap Top, Goldtone, Chanel, 1½ x 1 In. | 207 |
| **Pin,** Rabbit, Twisted Wire, 18K Gold, Emerald, Ruby, Diamonds, Van Cleef & Arpels, 1½ In. ........ | 4375 |
| **Pin,** Raccoon, Matte & Blackened Gold, Ruby Eyes, Diamonds, On Coral Branch, 3 In. .............. | 1875 |
| **Pin,** Reindeer, Leaping, 18K Gold, Ruby Nose, Diamond Collar, Tiffany & Co., 2 In. | 4305 |
| **Pin,** Renaissance Woman Profile, Painted, Diamond Tiara, Enamel, Gold, Limoges, 1 In. ........... | 800 |
| **Pin,** Rhinestone Crackle Glass Cabochons, Multicolor, Countess Cissy Zoltowska, 1960s, 3 In. .... | 330 |
| **Pin,** Ribbon, Curled, 14K Gold, Citrine & Ruby Accents, Retro, 2¾ In. | 2337 |
| **Pin,** Rooster, Diamond Melee Head & Comb, Ruby Eye, 18K Gold, Tiffany, 1¼ In. | 984 |
| **Pin,** Sacred Frog, Agate, Turquoise, Zuni Indian, 3¼ In. | 240 |
| **Pin,** Sailboat, Sailor, Kalo Shop, Felt Bag, 1½ In. | 305 |
| **Pin,** Sailfish, Platinum, Diamond Melee, Blue Enamel Fins, 2¼ In. ...................*illus* | 1599 |
| **Pin,** Sailfish, Split Pearls, 14K Gold, Blue Enamel Fins, Sloan & Co., 1¼ In. | 584 |
| **Pin,** Salamander, 14K Gold, Demantoid Garnets, Diamonds, Hedges, c.1910, 2 In. .............*illus* | 1625 |
| **Pin,** Sapphire, Ruby, 18K Gold, Platinum, Diamond, Retro, 2½ x 2¼ In. ...................*illus* | 5904 |
| **Pin,** Scarab, Hardstone, Diamonds, Serpents, Gold, Enamel Wings, Egyptian Revival, 3⅝ In....*illus* | 2706 |
| **Pin,** Scarab, Iridescent Favrile Glass, Shaped Silver Mount, Tiffany & Co., 1⅝ In. | 738 |
| **Pin,** Schooner, Mother-Of-Pearl Sails, 18K Gold, Diamonds On Hull, c.1890, 1⅜ In. | 1476 |
| **Pin,** Scribble, 18K Gold, Diamond Tail, P. Picasso, Tiffany & Co., 2 In. | 523 |
| **Pin,** Seal, Pave Diamonds, Peridot Belly, 18K White Gold, Bulgari, 1½ x 1¾ In. | 4613 |
| **Pin,** Seashell, Pave Rhinestone Center, Satin Goldtone, B. Steinberg-Kaslo, B.S.K., 2 In. | 18 |
| **Pin,** Signature Jacket, Felt, Black, Cream, Pearl Necklace, Buttons, Logo, Wardrobe Box, 3 x 4 In. | 184 |
| **Pin,** Silver, Amber, Georg Jensen, 1915-27, 3½ x 2 In. ...................*illus* | 6250 |
| **Pin,** Silver, Flower Band, Engraved Script, Martha May 10th 1911, Oval, Unger Bros., 2 In. ......... | 115 |
| **Pin,** Silver, Green Glass, Potter Studio, Art & Crafts, 1⅞ In. ...................*illus* | 861 |
| **Pin,** Spiral, Elongated, Silver, Art Smith, 3¼ In. | 976 |
| **Pin,** Starburst, 14K Gold, Seed Pearls, Opal Cabochon, Victorian, 1 In. | 132 |
| **Pin,** Starflower, Stem With Leaf, Blue & Purple Rhinestones, Blanch-Ette Inc., 3 In. | 110 |
| **Pin,** Stylized Bird, On Amethyst Orb, Silver, William Spratling, c.1935, 2¾ In. | 875 |
| **Pin,** Stylized Bow, 18K Gold, Diamond Pave Band, Van Cleef & Arpels, 2 In. | 2430 |
| **Pin,** Stylized Fan, 18K Gold, Crimped, Sprinkled With Rubies, Gubelin, 1½ In. | 861 |
| **Pin,** Stylized Feather, 18K Textured Gold, Diamond Melee Shaft, Retro, 3½ In. | 1230 |
| **Pin,** Stylized Mermaid, Amethyst Cabochon Face, Silver, H. Harmon, 2¼ In. | 750 |
| **Pin,** Stylized Pinwheel, Inset Opal, Art Smith, 2 In. | 732 |

**Jewelry,** Pin, Orchid, Enamel, Diamonds, 14K Gold, 1 In.
**$1,888**

Brunk Auctions

**Jewelry,** Pin, Peridot, Pink Tourmaline, Blue Topaz, 18K Gold, Bulgari, 1⅝ In.
**$2,583**

Skinner Auctioneers & Appraisers

**Jewelry,** Pin, Plique-A-Jour Enamel, Diamonds, Peridot Drop, Marcus & Co., Art Nouveau, 2½ In.
**$10,455**

Skinner Auctioneers & Appraisers

**Jewelry,** Pin, Portrait, Geisha, Enamel, 14K Gold, Pearl & Diamond Rim, 1 ¼ In.
$861

Skinner Auctioneers & Appraisers

**Jewelry,** Pin, Portrait, Woman, Painted, 14K Gold Frame, Pearls, Turquoise Beads, France
$180

Cowan's Auctions

**Jewelry,** Pin, Sailfish, Platinum, Diamond Melee, Blue Enamel Fins, 2 ¼ In.
$1,599

Skinner Auctioneers & Appraisers

**Jewelry,** Pin, Salamander, 14K Gold, Demantoid Garnets, Diamonds, Hedges, c.1910, 2 In.
$1,625

Rago Arts & Auction Center

| | |
|---|---:|
| **Pin,** Stylized Wings, Plique-A-Jour, Purple, Green, 2 Amethysts, Levinger & Bissinger, 1 In. | 427 |
| **Pin,** Sun, Facial Features, Rhinestone Eyes, Goldtone, Avon, 2 ½ In. | 25 |
| **Pin,** Sunflower, 18K Textured Gold, Asprey, 1 ¼ In. | 984 |
| **Pin,** Swan, Freshwater Pearl Body, Diamond Neck, Platinum Over Gold, Edwardian, 1 In. | 2583 |
| **Pin,** Thistle, 18K Tricolor Gold, Textured, Marked, Mario Buccellati ......................*illus* | 1560 |
| **Pin,** Tiger Shere Khan, 3 Heads, Turquoise Beads, Silvertone, Rice-Weiner Co., 3 ½ In. | 215 |
| **Pin,** Tree, Open Leaves, Rhinestones, Emmons, 1 ¼ In. | 40 |
| **Pin,** Woman's Profile, Flowing Hair, Pearls, Sapphire, Goldtone Disc, Art Nouveau, 1 x 1 In. | 173 |
| **Pin,** Wood, Carved, Curved Shape, Yellow Sapphire Rim, Seaman Schepps, 2 In. | 1845 |
| **Pin,** Wreath, Seed Pearls, Goldtone Frame, Mimi Di Niscemi, 1983, 1 ¼ In. | 45 |
| **Pin,** Zebra, 18K Gold, Ruby Eyes, Diamond On Hoof, 1 ½ x 1 ¾ In. .....................*illus* | 625 |
| **Ring & Earrings,** Sputnik, Aquamarines, Tourmalines, Citrines, 18K Gold, H. Stern, 1950s | 1298 |
| **Ring & Earrings,** Torchon, Arched Links, 18K Gold, Florentine, Buccellati, ¾-In. Earrings | 3198 |
| **Ring,** 6 Diamonds, 3 Round Rubies, Flower Shape, Size 8 ½ ..................................*illus* | 1180 |
| **Ring,** 18K Gold, Geometric Black Opal Inlay, Marked, Asach Grossbardt, Size 9 ½ | 403 |
| **Ring,** 18K Gold, Persian Oval Turquoise, Diamonds, Victorian | 837 |
| **Ring,** Amber Cabochon, Crystalline Inclusions, Silver Leafy Mount, Art Nouveau, 1 ¾ In. | 92 |
| **Ring,** Amethyst, Silver, Flared & Folded Mount, Art Smith, 1 ½ In. | 1220 |
| **Ring,** Angelskin Coral, 4 Rubies, Diamonds, 18K Gold Mount, Emis, Size 5 ¾ | 1476 |
| **Ring,** Aquamarine, Cushion Cut, 4-Prong Basket Setting, 2 Diamonds, Size 5 ½ In. | 3120 |
| **Ring,** Aquamarine, Diamond, 18K Gold, Edwardian, Size 7 | 2242 |
| **Ring,** Aquamarine, Oval, 20 Round Diamonds, 1900s, 14K White Gold, Size 8 | 600 |
| **Ring,** Aquamarine, Oval, 30 Round, 12 Baguette Diamonds, 14K Gold, 1900s, Size 10 | 780 |
| **Ring,** Baltic Amber, Oval Cabochon, Diamonds, 14K Gold, 1 ¾ x 2 ¼ In., Size 8 | 1800 |
| **Ring,** Band, Atlas, 18K Gold Band, Tiffany & Co., Size 8 ½ | 633 |
| **Ring,** Band, Diamonds, 3 Round Cut, Van Cleef & Arpels, Size 6 | 805 |
| **Ring,** Band, Diamonds, 6 Rows, White Gold Mount, Garrard, Italy, Size 7 ½ | 2714 |
| **Ring,** Band, Diamonds, 9 Round, 14K White Gold, 1900s, Size 6 ¾ | 840 |
| **Ring,** Band, Diamonds, Baguette, 14 Square Rubies, 14K Gold, Size 5 ½ ..............*illus* | 180 |
| **Ring,** Band, Eternity, 14K White Gold, 1900s, Size 6 ¼ | 720 |
| **Ring,** Band, Garland Of Leaves, 18K Gold, M. Buccellati, Size 7 | 1230 |
| **Ring,** Band, Platinum, Marked, Harry Winston, Size 6 | 357 |
| **Ring,** Belt, Mesh, 14K Gold Brickwork Links, Sapphire & Diamond Buckle, Tiffany, 3 In. | 1845 |
| **Ring,** Black Crystal, Dome Shape, Marked, Lalique, Size 6 ¼ | 150 |
| **Ring,** Black Diamonds, Round Cut, Coin Silver, Domed Beveled Mount, Roberto, Size 7 | 230 |
| **Ring,** Black Opal, Diamond Frame, 18K White Gold Shank, Gubelin, Size 5 ½ | 9840 |
| **Ring,** Blue Topaz, Emerald Cut, Round Diamonds, 18K White Gold, Fochtmann, Size 7 | 1150 |
| **Ring,** Blue Topaz, Fantasy Cut, 56 Diamonds, 14K Gold, 1900s, Size 6 ½ | 840 |
| **Ring,** Cameo, Cat's Eye, 10K Gold, Man's, Box, 1900s, Size 10 | 96 |
| **Ring,** Cameo, Maiden, Renaissance, Hardstone, Gold, Scrolling Leaves, Art Nouveau | 369 |
| **Ring,** Cameo, Maiden, Upswept Hair, Bird On Shoulder, Hardstone, 18K Gold, Pearls, Size 8 | 861 |
| **Ring,** Cameo, Tiger's Eye, Classical Woman, Square Gold Mount, 1894, Size 11 | 148 |
| **Ring,** Cat & Mouse Playing Chess, Figural, 14K Gold, Silver, Malachite Board, Size 9 ¾ | 1230 |
| **Ring,** Cat's Eye Chrysoberyl, Round, Baguette Diamonds, 1900s, Size 5 ¾ | 900 |
| **Ring,** Citrine, Round, 14 Round Diamonds, 14K Gold, 1900s, Size 8 | 510 |
| **Ring,** Citrine, Squared Oval, 18K Gold Bezel Mount, Paloma Picasso, Size 5 ¼ | 1845 |
| **Ring,** Cluster, Diamonds, 12 Marquise Cut, 10 Baguette, 14K Gold, 1900s, Size 9 | 360 |
| **Ring,** Cluster, Diamonds, 25 Round, 14K Bicolor Gold, 1900s, Size 6 ½ | 780 |
| **Ring,** Cluster, Diamonds, 14K Gold, Rolex Style, c.1980, Size 8 | 360 |
| **Ring,** Cocktail, Angel Skin Coral, Pierced Flower, Scrolls, 14K Gold ......................*illus* | 360 |
| **Ring,** Cocktail, Step Cut, Blue Topaz, 14K Gold, Prong Set, Size 8 ½ ..................*illus* | 540 |
| **Ring,** Cocktail, Citrine, Oval, 14K Gold ....................................................................*illus* | 360 |
| **Ring,** Cocktail, Coral Cabochons, 7 Oval, Prong Set, 18K Granulated Gold, 1950s | 780 |
| **Ring,** Cocktail, Coral, Oval, 14K Gold .....................................................................*illus* | 420 |
| **Ring,** Cocktail, Dome, Cluster, Pink Sapphires, 14K Gold, Size 4 ¾ ...................*illus* | 270 |
| **Ring,** Cocktail, Dome, Multicolored Gemstones, 18K Gold, Size 6 ¼ ..................*illus* | 480 |
| **Ring,** Cocktail, Emerald, Square, Star, Diamonds, 18K Gold, c.1940, Size 7 | 720 |
| **Ring,** Coin, Medusa, Owl, Lizard On Reverse, 18K Gold Abstract Mount, Rubies | 861 |
| **Ring,** Coin, Roman, Bronze, 18K Gold, Continental, 1900s, Size 10 | 660 |
| **Ring,** Coin, Silver, Wolf, Textured 18K Gold Mount, Size 6 ½ | 984 |
| **Ring,** Diamond Solitaire, 14K Gold, Scroll Designs, Victorian, Size 7 ¾ | 184 |
| **Ring,** Diamond, Asscher Cut & Round, Platinum, Art Deco, Size 4 ¼ | 2415 |
| **Ring,** Diamond, Platinum Filigree Mount, Art Deco, 1920, Size 7 | 2415 |
| **Ring,** Diamond, Round Brilliant Cut, Channel Set, 14K White Gold, 1900s, Size 9 | 720 |
| **Ring,** Diamond, Round Cut, 14K Gold, Victorian, Size 5 ¼ In. | 380 |

J

**Jewelry,** Pin, Sapphire, Ruby, 18K Gold, Platinum, Diamond, Retro, 2 ½ x 2 ¼ In.
$5,904

New Orleans Auction Galleries, Inc.

**Jewelry,** Pin, Scarab, Hardstone, Diamonds, Serpents, Gold, Enamel Wings, Egyptian Revival, 3 ⅝ In.
$2,706

Skinner Auctioneers & Appraisers

**Jewelry,** Pin, Silver, Amber, Georg Jensen, 1915-27, 3 ½ x 2 In.
$6,250

Rago Arts & Auction Center

**Jewelry,** Pin, Silver, Green Glass, Potter Studio, Art & Crafts, 1 ⅞ In.
$861

Skinner Auctioneers & Appraisers

**Jewelry,** Pin, Thistle, 18K Tricolor Gold, Textured, Marked, Mario Buccellati
$1,560

Cowan's Auctions

**Jewelry,** Pin, Zebra, 18K Gold, Ruby Eyes, Diamond On Hoof, 1 ½ x 1 ¾ In.
$625

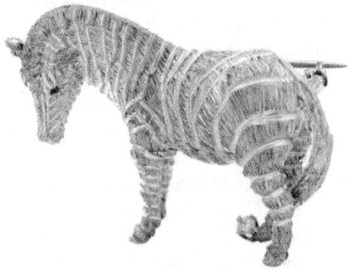

Garth's Auctioneers & Appraisers

**TIP**
*Porcelain breaks, so jewelry set with porcelain insets should be handled with care. If you drop the piece, it may break.*

**Jewelry,** Ring, 6 Diamonds, 3 Round Rubies, Flower Shape, Size 8 ½
$1,180

Brunk Auctions

**Jewelry,** Ring, Band, Diamonds, Baguette, 14 Square Rubies, 14K Gold, Size 5 ½
$180

Cowan's Auctions

**Jewelry,** Ring, Cocktail, Angel Skin Coral, Pierced Flower, Scrolls, 14K Gold
$360

DuMouchelles Art Gallery

**Jewelry,** Ring, Cocktail, Step Cut, Blue Topaz, 14K Gold, Prong Set, Size 8 ½
$540

DuMouchelles Art Gallery

**J**

**Jewelry,** Ring, Cocktail, Citrine, Oval, 14K Gold
$360

DuMouchelles Art Gallery

**Jewelry,** Ring, Cocktail, Coral, Oval, 14K Gold
$420

DuMouchelles Art Gallery

**Jewelry,** Ring, Cocktail, Dome, Cluster, Pink Sapphires, 14K Gold, Size 4¾
$270

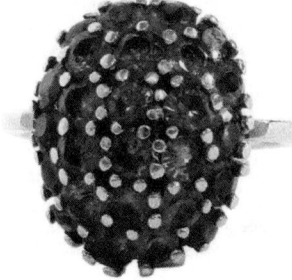

DuMouchelles Art Gallery

| | |
|---|---:|
| **Ring,** Diamond, Round, 18 Bead Set Diamonds, Platinum, Art Deco | 227 |
| **Ring,** Diamond, Round, 18K Gold, Platinum, Tiffany, Size 4½ | 1438 |
| **Ring,** Diamonds, Opal, Oval, 18K Gold, England, Victorian | 538 |
| **Ring,** Diamonds, Opals, 14K Gold, 20th Century, Size 7¼ | 900 |
| **Ring,** Diamonds, Platinum Filigree Mount, Art Deco, Size 4¼ In. | 546 |
| **Ring,** Diamonds, Platinum, Pierced & Beaded Mount, Edwardian, Size 7 | 3712 |
| **Ring,** Diamonds, Retro Style, Platinum, Diamonds, H.W. Beattie & Sons, Size 4¾ | 4083 |
| **Ring,** Dome, 14K Gold, Woven, Blue & Green Enameled Bands, c.1960, Size 6½ | 531 |
| **Ring,** Dome, Old European Diamonds, Beaded Platinum Mount, Art Deco, Size 5½ | 2706 |
| **Ring,** Dragon Heads, Conjoined, Green & Red Stone Eyes, 14K Textured Gold, c.1900 | 390 |
| **Ring,** Emerald, Pave Diamonds, 14K White Gold, 1900s, Size 6½ | 2160 |
| **Ring,** Emeralds, Oval, 22 Round Diamonds, 14K Gold, Size 7 | 1440 |
| **Ring,** Eternity Band, Platinum Band, Rectangular Cut Diamonds, Tiffany, Size 7½ | 2358 |
| **Ring,** Eternity, Platinum, Round Brilliant Cut Diamonds, Tiffany & Co., Size 7 | 2875 |
| **Ring,** Jade, Oval Cabochon, Platinum, Tiered Diamond Surround, Art Deco, c.1940, Size 7 | 1000 |
| **Ring,** Jadeite, Oval Cabochon, Bezel Set, 14K Gold, Marcus & Co., Size 6½ | 11070 |
| **Ring,** Kinetic, Cube, 2 Square Spinners, 14K Gold, 2 Diamonds, N. Teufel, 1975, Size 4½ | 561 |
| **Ring,** Knot, 18K Gold Textured Twist, Cartier, Size 5¼ | 1353 |
| **Ring,** Knot, Blue & Green Enamel, 18K Gold, Tiffany, Size 7½ | 472 |
| **Ring,** Knot, Woven, Diamonds, 14K Gold, Melee, Valobra, Size 7 | 2706 |
| **Ring,** Labradorite Cabochon, Silver Mount, Flowers, Arts & Crafts, Size 6½ | 92 |
| **Ring,** Lapis, 14K Gold, Stamped, Kalo, c.1910, Size 6 ........*illus* | 2875 |
| **Ring,** Lemon Quartz, Oval, Faceted, 18K Gold Mount, Adelline, Size 7¼ | 615 |
| **Ring,** Lemon Quartz, Triangular Cut, 40 Round Diamonds, 14K Gold, 1900s, Size 7 | 480 |
| **Ring,** Love, Single Screw Shape, 18K Gold, Marked, Cartier, Size 7½ | 1035 |
| **Ring,** Marquise Diamond, 52 Princess Cut Diamonds, 14K Gold, 1900s, Size 9 | 1080 |
| **Ring,** Mourning, Gold, Enamel, Eliza Hickey, 14 Years, Portsmouth, 1783, 1 In. | 5040 |
| **Ring,** Onyx Cylinder, Ribbed 18K Gold Bezel & Shank, Cartier, Size 5½ | 2214 |
| **Ring,** Peacock, Opal, Oval, Diamond Tail, Garnets, 14K Gold, Art Nouveau, Walton, 1 In. | 2952 |
| **Ring,** Peridot, 14K Gold, Diamond Jacket, 20th Century, Size 7 | 270 |
| **Ring,** Pink Sapphire, Oval, 44 Princess Cut Diamonds, 18K Gold, 1900s, Size 6 | 1800 |
| **Ring,** Platinum, Marquise Diamond, 24 Channel Set Baguette Diamonds, 1900s, Size 6 | 4200 |
| **Ring,** Poison, Emerald, Enamel, Swirls, Steer Heads, 18K Gold, Size 9 ........*illus* | 1185 |
| **Ring,** Poison, Hardstone Tablet, Compartment, 8-Sided 14K Gold Mount, Size 9¾ | 1230 |
| **Ring,** Raised Scrolls, Coral Cabochon, Clear Stones, Rose Gold, Retro, Size 8½ | 253 |
| **Ring,** Rings, Graduated, Fluted, Faceted 18K Gold, Henry Dunay, Size 7½ | 1625 |
| **Ring,** Sapphire, Oval, 18K Gold Dome Mount, Marcus & Co., Size 3 | 584 |
| **Ring,** Seed Pearls, 2 Round Diamonds, Oval Openings, 14K White Gold, Beattie, Size 5½ | 368 |
| **Ring,** Signet, West Point, Intaglio, 18K Gold Mount, Inscribed, 1872, Size 6 ........*illus* | 531 |
| **Ring,** Smoky Quartz, Rectangular, Buff Top, 18K Gold Mount, Adelline, 1¼ x 1 In. | 492 |
| **Ring,** South Sea Pearl, Diamond, 18K Gold Ring, Asia, 1900s, Size 8 | 960 |
| **Ring,** Star Sapphire, Round, Platinum, Diamonds, Ring Guard, Art Deco Style, 1900s, Size 6 | 1800 |
| **Ring,** Sugarloaf Emerald, Pave Diamond Surround, 18K Gold, Bailey, Banks & Biddle, Size 5 | 13750 |
| **Ring,** Tanzanite, Baguette Diamond Ground, White Gold Mount, Van Cleef & Arpels, Size 8 | 5192 |
| **Ring,** Topaz, Blue, Emerald Cut, 58 Diamonds, 18K Gold, 1900s, Size 8 | 480 |
| **Ring,** Tourmaline, Pink, Oval, 54 Round Diamonds, 18K White Gold, 1900s, Size 8 | 960 |
| **Ring,** Trinity, Interlocking Bands, 18K Tricolor Gold, Cartier, Size 5½ | 531 |
| **Ring,** Trinity, Interlocking, 18K Tricolor Gold, Le Must De Cartier, Size 5¼ | 633 |
| **Ring,** Turquoise Ball, 18K Gold, Swirled Prongs, Woman's, M & Co., Size 7¾ | 552 |
| **Ring,** Yellow Sapphire, Oval Cut, Diamond Shoulders, 14K Gold, S.O. Peabody, Size 6 | 3444 |
| **Rosary,** Amber, Carved Pendant, 3 Peaches, Birds, Chinese, 1800s, 2½ x 2 In. Pendant ........*illus* | 4740 |
| **Seal,** Wax, Stamp, Citrine, Gold, Inscribed, The Grove, Victorian, 2¼ In. | 900 |
| **Slide,** Mermaid, Leaf Mount, 18K Bicolor Gold, Diamonds, 6 Pearls, Art Nouveau, 3 In. | 885 |
| **Stickpin,** Banded Agate, Oval Cabochon, 4 Split Pearl Accents, 18K Gold | 738 |
| **Stickpin,** Diamond, European Cut, Sapphire, 14K Bicolor Gold, Art Deco, 2½ In. | 81 |
| **Stickpin,** Dog, Bullmastiff, Reverse Painted Glass, Gold Beaded Border, ¾ In. | 523 |
| **Stickpin,** Fan, Enamel Veins, 14K Gold, 2½ In. | 584 |
| **Stickpin,** Man In The Moon Face, Smoking Fat Cigar, Diamond Melee Tip, 14K Gold | 738 |
| **Stickpin,** Owl Head, Gold, Silver, Old Mine-Cut Diamond Eyes, Tiffany & Co. | 2706 |
| **Stickpin,** Pearl, Diamond Surround, 14K Gold, Platinum, Tiffany & Co., 2½ In. | 406 |
| **Stickpin,** Peridot, 14K Yellow Gold, White Gold Overlay, Diamond, Edwardian, 2½ In. | 184 |
| **Stickpin,** Scarab, Enamel, Oval Gold Mount, Arts & Crafts, F.G. Hale | 431 |
| **Stickpin,** Seahorses, Faceted Cut Peridot, Accent Pearl, 14K Gold, Victorian, 2¼ In. | 132 |
| **Stickpin,** Snake, Opal Bead, Diamond, 14K Gold, Platinum, J.E. Caldwell, 2¾ In. | 1024 |
| **Tiara & Earrings,** Pearls, Half Pearls, 15K Gold, Fitted Case, London, Edwardian | 2562 |
| **Toothpick,** 14K Gold Textured Case, Retractable, 1¾ In. | 207 |

**Vinaigrette,** Bird, Butterfly, Leaves, Gold, Enamel, Fan Shape, Scalloped, Link Chain, 19 In....... 6150
**Watches** are listed in their own category.
**Wristwatches** are listed in their own category.

---

**JOHN ROGERS** statues were made from 1859 to 1892. The originals were bronze, but the thousands of copies made by the Rogers factory were of painted plaster. Eighty different figures were created. Similar painted plaster figures were produced by some other factories. Rights to the figures were sold in 1893, and the figures were manufactured for several more years by the Rogers Statuette Co. Never repaint a Rogers figure because this lowers the value to collectors.

**Group,** Checkers Up At Farm, c.1875, 12 x 24 In.................................................. 395
**Group,** One More Shot, Wounded Soldier, Inscribed, c.1864, 20 In. ......................*illus* 2583
**Group,** Uncle Ned's School................................................................................ 1200
**Group,** Weighing Baby, Mother Baby, Doctor, Sibling, c.1876................................ 900

---

**JOSEF ORIGINALS** ceramics were designed by Muriel Joseph George. The first pieces were made in California from 1945 to 1962. They were then manufactured in Japan. The company was sold to George Good in 1982 and he continued to make Josef Originals until 1985. The company was then sold to Southland Corporation. The name is now owned by Applause, and the Birthday Girl series is still being made.

**Bell,** Angel, Strumming Harp, Ponytail, 4 ½ In.................................................... 24
**Bell,** Church Belle, Holding Bible, Lavender Dress & Hat, Little Belle Series, 3 ½ In. ... 55
**Bell,** School Belle, Holding Apple & Books, Yellow Dress, Little Belle Series, 3 In. ...... 52
**Figurine,** Angel Serenade, Playing Violin, Sitting On Cloud, 4 In. .......................... 55
**Figurine,** Angel, Blue & White Dress, Gold Stars, 3 ⅝ In. .................................... 27
**Figurine,** Birthday Angel, Age 3, Blond, Yellow Dress, Holding Bucket, 3 ¼ In. ....... 15
**Figurine,** Birthday Angel, Age 6, Holding Cake, Pink Dress, 4 In. ........................ 25
**Figurine,** Birthday Girl, Age 15, Yellow Dress, 6 ⅛ In. ...................................... 32
**Figurine,** Birthday Girl, Age 19, Pink Dress, Bird, 6 In. ..................................... 24
**Figurine,** Birthday Girl, February, Blond, Purple, Amethyst Stone, 4 In. ............... 15
**Figurine,** Elf, Kneeling, Green, Present, Foil Label, 4 In. ................................... 12
**Figurine,** France, Pink Dress, Apron, International Series, Hang Tag, 3 ½ In. ......... 45
**Figurine,** Japanese Sandman, Closed Eyes, Wings, 4 x 3 ½ In. ........................... 58
**Figurine,** Mother Ostrich & Baby, White, Yellow, 5 ½ In. ................................... 25
**Figurine,** Secret Pal, Pale Green Dress, Fan, 1960s, 3 ¼ In. ............................... 36
**Figurine,** Shaggy Dog, Sitting, Foil Label, 1960s, 3 ¾ In. .................................. 22
**Head Vase,** Closed Eyes, Long Lashes, Brown Hair, Green Collar, 4 ¾ In. ............. 89
**Music Box,** 50th Anniversary, Pink & Blue Gown, Shawl, I Love You Truly, Sticker, 7 In. .. 33
**Music Box,** Santa, Playing Mandolin, Plays Jingle Bells, Paper Label, 7 In. ............ 34
**Pie Bird,** Yellow, Marked, 1950s, 3 ½ In. ......................................................... 52

---

**JUDAICA** is any memorabilia that refers to the Jews or the Jewish religion. Interests range from newspaper clippings that mention eighteenth- and nineteenth-century Jewish Americans to religious objects, such as menorahs or spice boxes. Age, condition, and the intrinsic value of the material, as well as the historic and artistic importance, determine the value.

**Box,** Fish Shape, Silver, 2 ½ In. ........................................................................ 120
**Candlestick,** Sabbath, Brass, Engraved Flowers, Jakubowski & Jarra, Warsaw, 14 In., Pair......... 142
**Container,** Etrog, Silver, Leafy Branch Base, Gilt Interior, Germany, c.1900, 7 x 4 In...........*illus* 1476
**Marriage Belt,** Silvered Gilt Metal, 10 Rectangular Links, Gilt Figures, Urn, 1661, 50 In. .......... 2040
**Menorah,** 7-Light, Brass, c.1900, 17 ½ x 12 In. ................................................ 72
**Menorah,** Gilt Bronze, Red Marble Base, Face, Salvador Dali, 20 x 13 In. ............. 5748
**Menorah,** Hands, Rotating Arms, Brass, Germany, 1800s, 25 x 22 In...................*illus* 270
**Menorah,** Rococo, Repousse, Domed Foot, Baluster Stem, Scroll Arms, A. Meyer, 10 x 11 In. ...... 874
**Menorah,** Silver Plate, Rococo, S-Scroll Branches, 22 In. .................................. 281
**Menorah,** Silver, Filigree, Tapering Stem, Hexagonal Base, Israel, 16 In. .............. 4375
**Menorah,** Sterling Silver, Hammered, Flowers, Buccellati, Round Base, 15 ¼ x 15 In. .. 5625
**Menorah,** Tin, Cylindrical Candle Cups, Arched Support, Domed Base, 7 x 8 In. ...... 1625
**Menorah,** Tin, Flared Legs, 8 Oil Wells, Hinged, Servant Lamp, c.1800, 7 x 3 In.................*illus* 1599
**Mezuzah,** Frosted Glass, Metal, Symbols, Lalique, France, Box, 5 ½ x 1 ½ In............. 390
**Pendant,** Hebrew Letter, Hai, 14K Gold, 1 In., 20-In. Flat Link Chain ..................... 767
**Pendant,** Torah Scroll, 14K Yellow Gold Filigree, Blue Enamel, Citrine, Pearls, 1 x 1 In. ....... 322
**Pin,** Winged Lion Of Judah, Paw On Ten Commandments, Pietra Dura, 14K Gold...............*illus* 300
**Torah Finial,** Bells, Embossed Metal, Wood Stand, 9 In., Pair.................................. 105
**Torah Pointer,** Silver, Cast, Chased, Hand, Pointed Finger, c.1875, 12 In. .............. 395
**Torah Scroll Case,** Silver, Eagle Finial, Repousse, Continental, 1800s, 12 ½ In............ 800

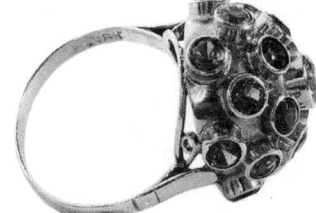

**Jewelry,** Ring, Cocktail, Dome, Multicolored Gemstones, 18K Gold, Size 6 ¼
$480

DuMouchelles Art Gallery

**Jewelry,** Ring, Lapis, 14K Gold, Stamped, Kalo, c.1910, Size 6
$2,875

Rago Arts & Auction Center

**Jewelry,** Ring, Poison, Emerald, Enamel, Swirls, Steer Heads, 18K Gold, Size 9
$1,185

James D. Julia Auctioneers

**Jewelry,** Ring, Signet, West Point, Intaglio, 18K Gold Mount, Inscribed, 1872, Size 6
$531

Brunk Auctions

**Jewelry,** Rosary, Amber, Carved Pendant, 3 Peaches, Birds, Chinese, 1800s, 2½ x 2 In. Pendant
$4,740

James D. Julia Auctioneers

**John Rogers,** Group, One More Shot, Wounded Soldier, Inscribed, c.1864, 20 In.
$2,583

Skinner Auctioneers & Appraisers

**Judaica,** Container, Etrog, Silver, Leafy Branch Base, Gilt Interior, Germany, c.1900, 7 x 4 In.
$1,476

New Orleans Auction Galleries, Inc.

| | |
|---|---:|
| **Tray,** 3 Jewish Men, Karlsbad, Porcelain, Czechoslovakia, 6 x 3 ½ In. .......................*illus* | 324 |
| **Tzedakah Box,** Mixed Metal, Ginger Jar Shape, Architectural Details, Arched, Door, 11 In. ......... | 414 |

**JUGTOWN POTTERY** refers to pottery made in North Carolina as far back as the 1750s. In 1915, Juliana and Jacques Busbee set up a training and sales organization for what they named Jugtown Pottery. In 1921, they built a shop at Jugtown, North Carolina, and hired Ben Owen as a potter in 1923. The Busbees moved the village store where the pottery was sold to New York City. Juliana Busbee sold the New York store in 1926 and moved into a log cabin near the Jugtown Pottery. The pottery closed in 1959. It reopened in 1960 and is still working near Seagrove, North Carolina.

| | |
|---|---:|
| **Creamer,** Green, Frogskin, 4 ½ In. ...................... | 59 |
| **Duck,** Applied Eyes, Cobalt Blue Accents, Pierced For Shaker, Sander, c.1930, 4 x 5 ½ In............ | 345 |
| **Jug,** Salt Glaze, Cobalt Blue Flowers, Small Neck, 10 In. ...................... | 90 |
| **Mixing Bowl,** Gray Salt Glaze, Bird, 6 x 11 In. ...................... | 120 |
| **Vase,** Blue, Green, Red, Shouldered, 4 In. ...................... | 357 |
| **Vase,** Gray, Cobalt Blue Flowered Band, 8 In. ...................... | 75 |
| **Vase,** Gray, Green Spots, Pinched Ribbons, 6 ¼ x 5 In. ...................... | 180 |
| **Vase,** Persian Blue, 12 ½ In. ...................... | 885 |

**JUKEBOXES** play records. The first coin-operated phonograph was demonstrated in 1889. In 1906 the Automatic Entertainer appeared, the first coin-operated phonograph to offer several different selections of music. The first electrically powered jukebox was introduced in 1927. Collectors search for jukeboxes of all ages, especially those with flashing lights and unusual design and graphics.

| | |
|---|---:|
| **Aireon,** Multicolor, Mosaic, Wood Veneer, 1200A, c.1949 ...................... | 480 |
| **AMI,** Model D40, Music For You, Domed Front, Light-Up, 60 x 26 In. ...................... | 784 |
| **AMI,** Model WRD-200, Remote, Wall Box, Rowe International, Triangle Ind., Grand Rapids........ | 118 |
| **Rock-Ola,** Model 432, GP160, Blue ...................... | 360 |
| **Rock-Ola,** Model 1426, Multi-Coin, Etched Glass, Grill, 1950s, 59 x 30 In.................*illus* | 2280 |
| **Rock-Ola,** Nostalgia CD-6B, Wood, Chrome, Glass, Peacocks, Torches, Satyrs, Arched, 64 In....... | 2588 |
| **Rock-Ola,** Nostalgia Model 1000, Phonograph, Serial No. 49735, Key ...................... | 767 |
| **Seeburg,** Mardi Gras, Arched Design, Flashing Lights, Multicolor, c.1977, 54 x 40 In.............. | 46 |
| **Seeburg,** Model 100, Select-O-Matic, 100 Selection, c.1952 ...................... | 1680 |
| **Seeburg,** Model 148ML, Symphonola, Yellow, Red, 20 Selections, c.1948, 34 x 58 In.............. | 1020 |
| **Seeburg,** Model DS160, Select-O-Matic, c.1960 ...................... | 270 |
| **Seeburg,** Model M100C, Select-O-Matic, 45 RPM Records, 100, c.1952...................... | 1920 |
| **Speaker,** Seeburg, Model RS2-12, Remote, Teardrop, Red, Treble Clef Grill, 17 x 30 In.............. | 660 |
| **Wurlitzer,** Model 42, Harlequin, 24 Selections, c.1942, 36 x 66 In. ...................... | 1560 |
| **Wurlitzer,** Model 71, Countertop, 56 In. ...................... | 4500 |
| **Wurlitzer,** Model 81, Stand, 23 In. ...................... | 15000 |
| **Wurlitzer,** Model 412, Tortoiseshell Finish, Column Sides, 1930s, 51 x 32 In...................... | 672 |
| **Wurlitzer,** Model 780, Wagon Wheel, 78 Selections, c.1941, 38 x 60 In...................... | 3000 |
| **Wurlitzer,** Model 800, Restored, 61 In.................................*illus* | 6600 |
| **Wurlitzer,** Model 1015, External Speaker, Cream, Red, 69 In., 2 Piece...................... | 8400 |
| **Wurlitzer,** Model 1100, Phonograph, Rainbow, 30 x 58 In. ...................... | 6600 |
| **Wurlitzer,** Model 1250, Multi-Selector, c.1950 ...................... | 1560 |
| **Wurlitzer,** Model 3000, Cusimano Stereo Console, Multi-Selector, c.1966...................... | 177 |
| **Wurlitzer,** Remote Selector, 12 x 8 In. ...................... | 90 |

**KATE GREENAWAY,** who was a famous illustrator of children's books, drew pictures of children in high-waisted Empire dresses. She lived from 1846 to 1901. Her designs appear on china, glass, napkin rings, and other pieces.

| | |
|---|---:|
| **Book,** Almanack, 1928, 4 ½ x 3 ¼ In. ...................... | 183 |
| **Book,** Birthday Book For Children, Hardcover, c.1886, 3 ½ x 3 ¾ In. ...................... | 176 |
| **Cutout Cloth Dolls,** Lithograph, Brother & Sister, 14 & 12 In. ...................... | 50 |
| **Doll,** Jack & Molly, Wool Felt, Yellow, Blue, 8 ½ In., Pair ...................... | 695 |
| **Figurine,** Girl, Basket, Hand On Hip, Pink, Yellow, Porcelain, c.1875, 9 In. ...................... | 250 |
| **Match Safe,** Boy & Girl, Fence, Umbrella, c.1890, 3 x 1 ½ x ½ In. ...................... | 132 |
| **Napkin Ring,** Figural, Child, Pushing Ring, Toronto Silver Plate, c.1885 ...................... | 235 |
| **Pitcher,** Girls, On Fence, Toad, Transfer, Blue, White, Bulbous, 11 In. ...................... | 128 |
| **Plate,** 2 Girls, Holding Bucket, Aquarius, Royal Doulton, 1977, 8 ¼ In...................... | 15 |
| **Plate,** Girls, Holding Hands, Gemini, Royal Doulton, 1977, 8 ¼ In...................... | 15 |
| **Salt & Pepper,** Boy & Girl, Porcelain, Gilt, 1800s, 3 In. ...................... | 155 |
| **Tray,** Pewter, Engraved, Characters, c.1885, 7 In. ...................... | 155 |

**KAY FINCH CERAMICS** were made in Corona del Mar, California, from 1935 to 1963. The hand-decorated pieces often depicted whimsical animals and people. Pastel colors were used.

*Kay Finch*
CALIFORNIA

| | |
|---|---|
| Figurine, Baby Cottontail, Pink, White, 3 In. | 62 |
| Figurine, Dog, Pekingese, Rose, Black, Cream, 1930s, 14 x 5 x 5 ½ In. | 385 |
| Figurine, Lamb, Prancing, Flower Collar, 10 ½ In. | 155 |
| Figurine, Mama Duck, Blue, Green, 5 ½ In. | 325 |
| Figurine, Mermaid, Blond, 6 ½ In. | 1250 |
| Figurine, Monkey, Jocko, Socko, Multicolor, 3 ½ In., Pair | 76 |
| Shaker, Cat, Green Collar, 6 ¼ In. | 250 |

**KAYSERZINN,** *see Pewter category.*

**KELVA** glassware was made by the C. F. Monroe Company of Meriden, Connecticut, about 1904. It is a pale, pastel-painted glass decorated with flowers, designs, or scenes. Kelva resembles Nakara and Wave Crest, two other glasswares made by the same company.

**KELVA**

| | |
|---|---|
| Box, Tulips, Blown-Out Design, Orange, Peach, Cream, Green Ground, 6-Sided, Lid, 2 ½ In. | 122 |
| Dresser Box, Hinged, Blue Mottled, Enamel Blossoms, Gold Interior, Mirror, 3 ½ x 8 In. | 575 |
| Dresser Box, Lid, Green Mottled Panels, Amethyst, Pink Blossoms, Marked, 6 ½ In. ......*illus* | 403 |

**KENTON HILLS POTTERY** in Erlanger, Kentucky, made artwares, including vases and figurines that resembled Rookwood, probably because so many of the original artists and workmen had worked at the Rookwood plant. Kenton Hills opened in 1939 and closed during World War II.

| | |
|---|---|
| Vase, Blue Matte Glaze, Leaves, Oval, Shouldered, W. Hentschel, 6 ⅜ In. | 156 |
| Vase, Iris, Leaves, Yellow, Green, Glossy, Marked, c.1939, 12 ½ In. | 1190 |
| Vase, Magnolias, Beige, Flared Rim, c.1940, 13 In. | 295 |
| Vase, Tulips, Bulbous, Glossy Glaze, Alza Stratton, 6 In. | 495 |

**KEW BLAS** is the name used by the Union Glass Company of Somerville, Massachusetts. The name refers to an iridescent golden glass made from the 1890s to 1924. The iridescent glass was reminiscent of the Tiffany glass of the period.

**KEW-BLAS**

| | |
|---|---|
| Finger Bowl, Underplate, Gold Iridescent, Ribbed, Ruffled, 5-In. Bowl, 7-In. Plate | 156 |
| Rose Bowl, Green & Gold Pulled Feather, Opaque Tan Ground, Signed, 3 x 5 In. | 775 |
| Vase, Black Iridescent, Butterscotch Opalescent, Oval, 6 In. | 800 |
| Vase, Blue Iridescent, Cylindrical, Flared Base & Rim, 8 x 3 ¾ In. | 150 |
| Vase, Flower Shape, Scalloped Rim, Footed, Green Accents, c.1900, 12 In. | 1750 |
| Vase, Globular Shape, 4 Green Pulled Feathers, Gold Highlights, Rolled Rim, 4 ¼ In. | 316 |
| Vase, Gold Iridescent, Cinched Rim, Footed, Signed, 12 In. | 230 |
| Vase, Gold Pulled Feather, Iridescent, Signed, c.1900, 6 In. | 489 |
| Vase, Green Iridescent, Diagonal Shading, Cylindrical, Flared Base & Rim, 8 x 4 In. | 182 |
| Vase, Pulled Feather, Gold, Ivory Iridescent, Signed, 4 In. | 800 |
| Vase, Pulled Feather, Green & Gold Highlights, Oval, Pinched Neck, 7 In. | 1000 |
| Vase, Pulled Feather, Squat, Round Footed, Raised Neck, Gold, Iridescent, 2 x 4 In. | 595 |
| Vase, Quad Dimpled Base, Blue Iridescent, Gold, Purple, Signed, c.1900, 5 In. | 350 |
| Vase, White Zipper Pattern, Gold Iridescent, Undulating Rim, Signed, 3 x 4 In. | 475 |
| Wine, Gold Iridescent, Baluster Stem, Flared Rim, Flattened Foot, 4 ¾ In. | 148 |

**KEWPIES,** designed by Rose O'Neill, were first pictured in the *Ladies' Home Journal*. The figures, which are similar to pixies, were a success, and Kewpie dolls and figurines started appearing in 1911. Kewpie pictures and other items soon followed. Collectors search for all items that picture the little winged people.

| | |
|---|---|
| Bisque Head, Composition Body, Wooden Ball Joints, Rose O'Neill, Germany, 11 In. ......*illus* | 3990 |
| Bisque Head, Side-Glancing Eyes, Composition Body, Kestner, c.1910, 11 In. ......*illus* | 3920 |
| Bisque, Brown Left-Glancing Eyes, Blond, Kestner, 11 In. | 3087 |
| Bisque, Jointed Arms, Porcelain Wreath, Italy, 11 In. | 1422 |
| Bisque, Reading, Chair, Side-Glancing Eyes, 1910, 5 In. | 1904 |
| Bisque, Side-Glancing Eyes, Smiling, Closed Mouth, Jointed, Paper Label, c.1913, 7 In. | 175 |
| Bisque, Side-Glancing Eyes, Umbrella, Doodle Dog, Wings, c.1912, 3 ½ In. | 700 |
| Bisque, Sitting, Playing Mandolin, c.1914, 2 In. | 225 |
| Bisque, Socket Head, Glass Eyes, Composition Body, Kestner, c.1912, 14 In. | 7420 |
| Chocolate Mold, Tin, Hinged, 11 In., 2 Piece | 94 |
| Pincushion Doll, Bisque Head, Silk Costume, Jointed Arms, Germany, c.1915, 4 ½ In. | 336 |

**KING'S ROSE,** *see Soft Paste category.*

**Judaica,** Menorah, Hands, Rotating Arms, Brass, Germany, 1800s, 25 x 22 In.
$270

DuMouchelles Art Gallery

**Judaica,** Menorah, Tin, Flared Legs, 8 Oil Wells, Hinged, Servant Lamp, c.1800, 7 x 3 In.
$1,599

Skinner Auctioneers & Appraisers

**Judaica,** Pin, Winged Lion Of Judah, Paw On Ten Commandments, Pietra Dura, 14K Gold
$300

DuMouchelles Art Gallery

**Judaica,** Tray, 3 Jewish Men, Karlsbad, Porcelain, Czechoslovakia, 6 x 3 ½ In.
$324

The Stein Auction Company

**Jukebox,** Rock-Ola, Model 1426, Multi-Coin, Etched Glass, Grill, 1950s, 59 x 30 In. $2,280

Morphy Auctions

**Jukebox,** Wurlitzer, Model 800, Restored, 61 In.
$6,600

Morphy Auctions

**Kelva,** Dresser Box, Lid, Green Mottled Panels, Amethyst, Pink Blossoms, Marked, 6½ In.
$403

Early Auction Co.

**KITCHEN** utensils of all types, from eggbeaters to bowls, are collected today. Handmade wooden and metal items, like ladles and apple peelers, were made in the early nineteenth century. Mass-produced pieces, like iron apple peelers and graniteware, were made in the nineteenth century. Also included in this category are utensils used for other household chores, such as laundry and cleaning. Other kitchen wares are listed under manufacturers' names or under Advertising, Iron, Tool, or Wooden.

| | |
|---|---:|
| **Bin,** Grain, Pine, Beadboard Construction, Red Paint, 37 x 29 x 18 In. | 540 |
| **Blender,** Eskimo Whiz Mix, Nesbitt's, Embossed, It's Frozen, Cup, Electric | 120 |
| **Board,** Cutting, Set, Pig, Cutout, c.1900, Various Sizes, Largest 19 In., 6 Piece | 234 |
| **Bottle Filler,** Shaker, Funnels, Tin, Glass, Witch Hazel, Rose Balm, 13½ x 12 In. | 1770 |
| **Bowl Set,** Polly-Flex, Best Money Can Buy, Red, Plastic, 1954, 6, 7½, 10 In., 3 Piece | 28 |
| **Bowl,** Burl, Flared, c.1825, 2½ x 13 In. | 3335 |
| **Bowl,** Burl, Silver Beech, Naturalistic, Wayne Robinson, New Zealand, 18 In. | 173 |
| **Bowl,** Burl, Turned Rim, Footed, c.1825, 6 x 13½ In. | 1840 |
| **Bowl,** Dough, Maple, 1800s, 6⅝ x 22¾ In. | 185 |
| **Bowl,** Hawaiian Koa, Oval, 16 In. | 1003 |
| **Box,** Cutlery, Walnut, Dovetailed Drawer, Open Center Handle, 10 x 12 In. | 984 |
| **Broiler,** Fish, Wrought Iron, 4-Footed, 10 Hooks, Hinged Handle, c.1800, 31 x 15 In. | 277 |
| **Broiler,** Heart Handle, Wrought Iron, Bent Foot, 12½ In. | 180 |
| **Broiler,** Iron, Forged, Rotating, Footed, 28 In. | 129 |
| **Broiler,** Scottish, Black, Cast Iron, 12 In. | 234 |
| **Broiler,** Standing, Horseshoe Shape, Scrolls, 3 Legs, Iron, J. Conway, c.1800, 18 In. | 6150 |
| **Broiler,** Wrought Iron, Circular Gridiron, Spiral, 1800s, 3-Footed, 3 x 13 x 8 In. | 308 |
| **Broiler,** Wrought Iron, Revolving Gridiron, 3-Footed, Curved Handle, 20 x 7 x 12 In. | 154 |
| **Butcher Block,** Bird's-Eye Maple Burl, Round, 4 Hickory Legs, 24 x 13 In. | 540 |
| **Butcher Block,** Mixed Wood, 24 x 33½ In. | 439 |
| **Butter Mold,** look under Mold, Butter in this category. | |
| **Butter Paddle,** Wood, Carved, Painted, Heart, Garland, Animals, Germany, 1823, 12 In. | 390 |
| **Butter Press,** Wood, Strawberry & Fern, 3¼ In. | 145 |
| **Butter Print,** Sheaf Of Wheat, Turned Wood, Pennsylvania, 1800s, 4¼ In. ...............*illus* | 71 |
| **Butter Stamp,** Double Rose, Maple, 1800s, 4⅜ In. | 142 |
| **Butter Stamp,** Pine, Carved, 6-Lobe Radial, Star, 1⅜ x 3½ In. | 83 |
| **Butter Stamp,** Pineapple, Leaves, Rope Edge, Pine, Demilune, Handle, c.1850, 7 x 3½ In. | 474 |
| **Butter Stamp,** Potted Flower, Leaves, Double Sided, Round, 1879, 3¼ In. | 266 |
| **Butter Stamp,** Stylized Tulip, Initials, C.D., Walnut, Handle, 3¾ x 6¾ In. ...............*illus* | 354 |
| **Cabbage Cutter,** Heart Shape Cutout, 4 Legs, 19th Century, 5 x 17 In. | 63 |
| **Cabbage Cutter,** Walnut, Lollipop End, Pa., 41 In. | 37 |
| **Cake Breaker,** Red Bakelite Handle, C.J. Schneider Mfg., Box, c.1932, 10 x 3¾ In. | 32 |
| **Cake Plate,** Lid, Pennsylvania Dutch, Metal, Red, White, Green, 11½ In. | 32 |
| **Carpet Sweeper,** Sanitary, Push Model, The Winchester Store .................................*illus* | 2000 |
| **Casserole,** Chicken, Mexico, 1950s | 135 |
| **Chafing Dish,** Terra-Cotta, Copper & Wood Stand, Benedict Studios, 14 x 15 In. | 375 |
| **Cheese Dish,** Agateware, Brass Finial, 10 x 11 In. | 840 |
| **Cheese Press,** Oak, Red Paint, 1800s, 36 x 23 In. | 92 |
| **Chopper,** Curved Blade, Forged Metal, Figured Maple Handle, 19th Century, 6½ In. | 60 |
| **Churn,** Cobalt Blue Flowers, Applied Handles, Cylindrical, 1½ Gal., 12½ In. | 325 |
| **Churn,** Cylindrical, Wood, 24 In. | 146 |
| **Churn,** Mechanical, Champion Churn, Toledo, Ohio, c.1868, 44 x 38 In. | 374 |
| **Churn,** Pine, Barrel, Stave, Iron Band, Handle, Blue Paint, c.1860, 14 x 25 In. | 259 |
| **Churn,** Pine, Blue Paint, c.1860, 22 In. | 200 |
| **Churn,** Wood, Barrel Shape, 5 Bands, Blue Paint, 19th Century, 22 In. | 360 |
| **Churn,** Wood, Cylindrical, Splay Sided, Staved Construction, Iron Bands, 17½ In. | 59 |
| **Cleanser Holder,** Cameo Emblem, Cream, Black, Holds Can, 1950s | 34 |
| **Coffee Grinders** are listed in the Coffee Mill category. | |
| **Coffee Mills** are listed in their own category. | |
| **Colander,** Redware, Loop Side Handles, 9½ x 5 In. | 117 |
| **Condiment Dispenser,** Red, Yellow, Air-Seal Cap, Lustro-Ware, 4½ x 5½ In., Pair | 48 |
| **Cookie Cutter,** Bird, Tin, Sheet Iron, 1800s, 6¾ In. | 1560 |
| **Cookie Cutter,** Bird, Tin, Sheet Iron, 1800s, 7¾ In. | 150 |
| **Cookie Cutter,** Deer Running, Tin, Sheet Iron, 1800s, 8 In. | 369 |
| **Cookie Cutter,** Eagle, Flying, Tin, Sheet Iron, 1800s, 6¾ In. | 150 |
| **Cookie Cutter,** Elephant, Tin, 5 x 7¼ In. .........................................................*illus* | 106 |
| **Cookie Cutter,** Gentleman, Tin, Sheet Iron, 1800s, 10 In. | 185 |
| **Cookie Cutter,** Horse Running, Tin, Sheet Iron, 1800s, 9¼ In. | 360 |
| **Cookie Cutter,** Horse, Tin, Sheet Iron, 1800s, 11¼ In. | 369 |

K

| | |
|---|---|
| Cookie Cutter, Man, On Horse, Tin, Sheet Iron, 1800s, 8 ¼ In. ........................................ | 677 |
| Cookie Cutter, Man, Walking, Arm Out, Large Eye, Sheet Metal, Penn., 1800s, 9 ¾ x 6 In. .......... | 546 |
| Cookie Cutter, Native American, Headdress, Tomahawk, Tin, Sheet Iron, 1800s, 9 In................. | 390 |
| Cookie Cutter, Preacher Shape, Tin, Sheet Iron, 1800s, 9 ¾ In. ...................................... | 120 |
| Cookie Cutter, Rabbit, Tin, Sheet Iron, 1800s, 8 ½ In. ............................................. | 150 |
| Cookie Cutter, Rooster, Tin, Sheet Iron, c.1860, 6 In. ............................................. | 270 |
| Cookie Cutter, Soldier, Long Coat, Stripes On Arm, Sheet Metal, Tab, Penn., 17 x 7 In. ........... | 1035 |
| Cookie Cutter, Stag, Tin, Sheet Iron, 1800s, 8 ¼ In. ............................................... | 584 |
| Cookie Press, Aluminum, Maid Of Honor, Sears Roebuck & Co., Box, 19 Piece.......................... | 38 |
| Cutlery Tray, Mahogany, 2 Sections, 16 ¾ x 9 ½ In. ................................................. | 180 |
| Dipper, Coconut, Wood Handle, Whale's Tooth, 13 ¼ In. .............................................. | 277 |
| Dough Blender, Cutter, Red Wood Handle, Androck, 1920s.............................................. | 12 |
| Dough Box, Grain Painted, Splayed Legs, 1800s, 39 x 21 In.......................................... | 212 |
| Dough Box, Lid, Softwood, Red, Dovetailed, Wood Peg, Key, Lancaster County, 8 x 17 In.............. | 1416 |
| Dough Box, Pine, Lid, Splayed Legs, Stand, Pa., c.1850, 28 x 46 In. ................................ | 390 |
| Dough Box, Pine, Lift Top, Splayed Legs, Red Grain Painted, Pa., c.1810, 29 x 37 In. .............. | 840 |
| Dough Box, Pine, Tiger Maple, Single Board, Canted Sides, Splayed Leg Stand, 28 x 38 In. ......... | 748 |
| Dough Box, Stand, Oval Top, Tapered Bin, Splayed Legs, Green Paint, 33 x 38 In. ................... | 1200 |
| Dough Scraper, Steel, Heart Piercing, 19th Century, 4 ½ In......................................... | 375 |
| Dough Stand, 2 Shelves, Lid, Shaped Handle, Painted, W. Va., c.1850, 33 x 31 In. ................. | 460 |
| Drying Rack, Wrought Iron, Arched Legs, Penny Feet, 8 ½ x 12 In. ................................... | 266 |
| Eggbeater, Jiffy Whip, Whips Any Quantities Of Eggs, Batters, Cream, Wood Handle, c.1950 ...... | 38 |
| Eggbeater, Keystone, No. 20, Glass Churn, 12 ½ In. ................................................. | 130 |
| Eggcup, Wood, Multicolor, Salmon, Yellow Interiors, Strawberries, Lehn, Pair, 2 ⅝ In............... | 413 |
| Eggcup, Wood, Painted, Strawberries, Salmon Ground, Yellow, Red, Green, Blue, 2 ¾ In. ............ | 2006 |
| Feed Bin, Pine, Slant, Hinged Top, Blue, Green Paint, Pa., 34 x 40 In. ............................ | 2280 |
| Fish Roaster, Frame, 4 Hooks, Lollipop Hanger, Iron, Incised, c.1805, 35 ½ In. ...............illus | 923 |
| Fish Roaster, Wrought Iron, Lollipop Hanger, 3 Hooks, 2-Footed, 1800s, 27 In. ..................... | 338 |
| Fish Roaster, Wrought Iron, Lollipop Hanger, 5 Hooks, 2-Footed, c.1800, 38 In. ................... | 431 |
| Flour Sifter, Blood's, Pat. Sept. 17 1861, Stenciled, Wood, Nails, 13 x 9 x 11 In..............illus | 153 |
| Flour Sifter, Duplex, 2 Lids, Uneek Utilities Corp., c.1922, 5 Cup, 6 ⅝ In.......................... | 44 |
| Flour Sifter, Hand-I-Sift, Metal, Painted White, Wheat, Baked Goods, Androck, 1952................. | 29 |
| Food Chopper, Glass Jar, Red Bullet Shape Handle, Hazel Atlas, 1 ½ Cup............................. | 32 |
| Food Chopper, Pierced Heart Blade, Iron, Copper, Maple Handle, c.1750, 12 x 5 In. ...........illus | 948 |
| Fork, Carving, Host, Lifetime Chrome Finish, Caramel Brown Swirl Bakelite Handle, Box........... | 32 |
| Fork, Meat, Wrought Iron, Brass Inlay, Punch Decorated, Pierced Heart End, 18 In. ................. | 1750 |
| Fork, Meat, Wrought Iron, Shaped Handle, Punched, Inlaid Brass Diamonds, 19 In. ................... | 1188 |
| Fork, Spit, Wrought Iron, Brass, Curled Heart End, Samuel Yellin, 1920s, 35 x 4 In. .............. | 11250 |
| Fork, Wrought Iron, 2 Tines, Inscribed A.M.T. Schmit, 1866, 22 In. ................................ | 566 |
| Griddle, Iron, Cast, Oblong, Double Heart Handles, 23 In........................................... | 180 |
| Griddle, Iron, Cast, Round, Footed, Heart Handle, 23 In. .......................................... | 375 |
| Gridiron, Wrought Iron, Round, Rotating, Raise Shaped Handle, 3 Legs, 7 x 26 X13 In .............. | 189 |
| Grill, Revolving, Pierced, Wrought Iron, Handle, 24 ½ In. .......................................... | 180 |
| Grinder, Ice, Little Giant, Model 23, Cast Iron, Red Wheel, 18 In.................................. | 90 |
| Herb Chopper, Hand Forged, Cut Out Heart, 18th Century, 6 In. ..................................... | 275 |
| Herb Chopper, Steel, Heart Piercings, 19th Century, 7 In.......................................... | 625 |
| Herb Crusher, Cast Iron, Boat Shape Trough, Round Wheel, Wood Handles, 3 ½ x 17 ¾ In........ | 649 |
| Holster, Butcher's, 4 Knife Slots, Punched, Heart, Pig, Tin, Wood, 1860, 9 x 7 In. ............... | 431 |
| Horseradish Grinder, Oak, Iron, Brass, Crank, Fly Wheel, Drawer, c.1895, 14 x 14 In. ............. | 195 |
| Ice Cream Cone Display Jar, Polished Brass Lid, c.1915, 14 In...................................... | 180 |
| Ice Cream Maker, Hand Crank, Steel, Wood, Ward Way, c.1913, 12 Qt., 24 In. ........................ | 46 |
| Ice Shaver Machine, Polar, Brass, Hand Crank, Cup Holder, Marble Base ............................. | 1200 |
| Icebox, Oak, 2 Doors, Cavalier Model, Tennessee Furniture Co., c.1920, 35 x 20 In. ............... | 259 |
| Icebox, Oak, 3 Paneled Doors, Hardware, Zinc Lined, c.1900, 57 x 40 In. ........................... | 173 |
| Icebox, Wood, Zinc, Old White & Green Paint, Octagonal, Door, Lift Lid, 39 x 32 In. .............. | 450 |
| Iron, Coleman, Model 4A, Self-Heating, Instant-Lite, Blue, Box, Measuring Can, 12 x 8 In. ........ | 46 |
| Iron, Wafer, Wrought Iron, Scenic Views, Animals, Flowers, 21 ½ In. ............................... | 165 |
| Jar, Apple Butter, Green Mottled Glaze, Redware, c.1855, 5 In. .................................... | 126 |
| Juicer, Black & White, Sunkist Junior, Milk Glass Dish, A.C. Gilbert Co., 10 ½ x 6 ¾ In. ............ | 120 |
| Kettle Tilter, Wrought Iron, Handle, Mushroom Finial, Spring Lock, c.1800, 16 x 13 In............. | 308 |
| Kettle, Butchering, 2 Ear Handles, 3 Raised Feet, Cast Iron, c.1905, 17 x 27 In. ................. | 46 |
| Kettle, Copper, Dovetailed, 10 ½ In.................................................................. | 531 |
| Kettle, Copper, Squared Shape, Gooseneck Spout, Shaped Handle, John Wolf, 12 ¾ In. ............... | 720 |
| Kettle, Copper, Squat, Gooseneck Spout, Dome Lid, Brass Finial, Bail Handle, J. Resor, 7 In........ | 1560 |
| Kettle, Hearth, Bail Handle, Footed, Iron, Sampson & Tisdale, N.Y., 7 ½ x 12 In.............illus | 369 |
| Kettle, Hearth, Iron, 3-Part Mold, 3-Footed, Swivel Hanging Loop, c.1800, 7 x 12 In................ | 523 |

Kewpie, Bisque Head, Composition Body, Wooden Ball Joints, Rose O'Neill, Germany, 11 In.
$3,990

Theriault's

Kewpie, Bisque Head, Side-Glancing Eyes, Composition Body, Kestner, c.1910, 11 In.
$3,920

Theriault's

Kitchen, Butter Print, Sheaf Of Wheat, Turned Wood, Pennsylvania, 1800s, 4 ¼ In.
$71

Conestoga Auction Co., Inc.

K

331

## Smooth Iron Pans

Vintage cast-iron pans were hand-cast in sand, while modern pieces are made by a different method that leaves a rough surface. The old ones bring the highest prices.

**Kitchen,** Butter Stamp, Stylized Tulip, Initials, C.D., Walnut, Handle, 3¾ x 6¾ In.
$354

Conestoga Auction Co., Inc.

**Kitchen,** Carpet Sweeper, Sanitary, Push Model, The Winchester Store
$2,000

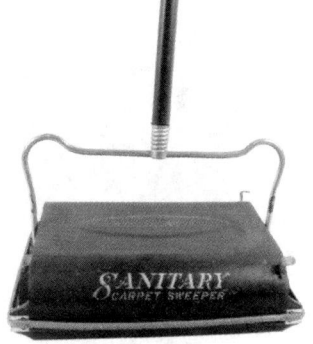

Santa Margarita Auction Barn

**Kitchen,** Cookie Cutter, Elephant, Tin, 5 x 7¼ In.
$106

Conestoga Auction Co., Inc.

> ### TIP
> *Some people say you should shine the chrome on your 1940s toaster with club soda or lemon juice.*

| | |
|---|---:|
| **Kettle,** Iron, Tilter Stand, Turned Handle, 13-In. Kettle, 14-In. Stand | 420 |
| **Kettle,** Sugar, Everted Rim, Cast Iron, Louisiana, 1800s | 1830 |
| **Kettle,** Tilting, Iron, Leaf Embossed, Gooseneck Spout, Lid, Handle, 3-Footed, 1834, 14 In. | 5463 |
| **Knife Holder,** Art Deco, Wood, White, Red, Daffodil, 5 Slots, Nuway, 1930s | 26 |
| **Knife Sharpener,** For Carving Knives & Other Household Cutlery, Red Handle, Norton Co. | 28 |
| **Knife Sharpener,** Lil Sharpy, Red, White, Milwaukee File Co., c.1950, 5 x 1¼ In. | 22 |
| **Knife,** Antler Handle, Walnut Box, Heart Cutout, 12 In. | 180 |
| **Knife,** Bird's Eye Maple, Carved Heart, 19th Century, 16¾ In. | 180 |
| **Lemon Press,** Wood, 2-Part, c.1900, 10¾ In. | 25 |
| **Match Holders** can be found in their own category. | |
| **Match Safes** can be found in their own category. | |
| **Mixer,** Hand Crank, Iron, Tin, Cylindrical, Crandall & Godley, N.Y., c.1900, 12 In. | 90 |
| **Mixer,** Milk Shake, Coles Shaker, Hand Crank, 1880s-90s | 1920 |
| **Mixer,** Milk Shake, Hamilton & Beach Manufacturing Co., 18 x 8 In. | 240 |
| **Mixer,** Milk Shake, Hamilton Beach, 3 Heads, Green Porcelain, Stainless Steel Cup, 20 In. | 330 |
| **Mixer,** Milk Shake, Myers Bullet, Soda Fountain, Chrome, Black, c.1940 | 3300 |
| **Molds** may also be found in the Pewter and Tinware categories. | |
| **Mold,** Butter, Double Hearts, Feathers, Cross Hatch Border, Treen, 1800s, 4 x 3 In. | 2070 |
| **Mold,** Butter, Lyre, Stars, Leaf Carved, Serrated Edge, Treen, Mid-Atlantic, 1800s, 7 x 5 In. | 2300 |
| **Mold,** Butter, Redware, Manganese, Lead Glaze, Spread Eagle, Handle, c.1900, 2 x 4 In. | 161 |
| **Mold,** Butter, Wood, Crisscross, Dovetail, c.1900, 5 x 3 x 3 In. | 58 |
| **Mold,** Cake, Copper, Tin-Lined, Swirled Frond, Oval, Italy, 1900s, 12 In. | 360 |
| **Mold,** Cake, Redware, Glazed, Impressed John Bell Waynesboro, Pa., 1¼ x 10 In. | 210 |
| **Mold,** Cake, Redware, Manganese Sponging, Orange, 1800s, 5¾ In. | 86 |
| **Mold,** Cake, Redware, Sponged Manganese, J. Bell, Pa., c.1840, 3¾ x 8¾ In. | 546 |
| **Mold,** Candle, see Tinware category. | |
| **Mold,** Cheese, Heart Shape, Tin, Pierced, Applied Loop Handles, Ring Feet, 4 In., Pair .......*illus* | 354 |
| **Mold,** Cheese, Tin, Heart Shape, Punched Geometric, Applied C-Shape Handle, 4¼ In. | 189 |
| **Mold,** Chocolate, Car, Metal, Cluydts Antwerp, 5½ x 2 In. | 105 |
| **Mold,** Chocolate, Car, Metal, Marked Van Emden New York, 5½ x 2½ In. | 105 |
| **Mold,** Chocolate, Teddy Roosevelt, 3 x 4 x 2 In. | 80 |
| **Mold,** Chocolate, Train Engine, Metal, 6 x 5 In. | 205 |
| **Mold,** Cookie, Redware, Man, Trumpet, Colonial Attire, On Horse, c.1820, 6 x 5¾ In. | 861 |
| **Mold,** Food, Fish Shape, Redware, Mottled Glaze, Scales, Fins, Trestle Legs, Pa., 1800s, 12 In. | 165 |
| **Mold,** Food, Fish Shape, Tin, 1800s, 11¼ In. | 209 |
| **Mold,** Food, Grapes, Oval, Mottled, Glazed, Pa., Redware, 1800s, 3 x 9 In. | 142 |
| **Mold,** Food, Oak, Royalty, Armorial Carvings, c.1855, 7 x 6⅝ In. | 180 |
| **Mold,** Springerle, Wood, Figure, Cone Shape Hat, Reverse Dough Wells, 1800s, 48 x 8½ In. | 47 |
| **Mold,** Sugar, Lamb, Stoneware, c.1850, 1½ In., Pair | 450 |
| **Mold,** Sugar, Maple, Heart Shape, Beveled Edge, Leather Strap, c.1810, 6 x 5 In. | 356 |
| **Mortar & Pestle,** Blue Paint, 1800s, 7 In. | 266 |
| **Mortar & Pestle,** Burl, Brown Paint, 6 In. | 177 |
| **Mortar & Pestle,** Turned Base, Blue Paint, Treen, c.1865, 8 x 6 In. | 805 |
| **Mortar & Pestle,** Turned Elm Mortar, Oak Pestle, 6⅛ x 6¾ In., 2 Piece | 270 |
| **Oven,** Reflector, Tin, 1800s, 18½ x 22 In. | 74 |
| **Oven,** Reflector, Tin, Flared Sides, Meat Hooks, Applied Handles, Rotating Lid, 11 x 7 In. | 325 |
| **Oven,** Roasting, Barrel Shape, Spit, Handles, Tin, 1800s, 18 x 21 In.................*illus* | 240 |
| **Oven,** Roasting, Hinged Door, Lid, Grease Pan, Punched Tin Star Frame, 1800s, 52 In. | 360 |
| **Oven,** Roasting, Sheet Iron, Box Shape, 4 Splayed Wire Legs, 9 Hooks, 18 x 18 In. | 185 |
| **Oven,** Roasting, Tin, Demilune Shape, Spit, 19th Century, 21 x 19½ In. | 210 |
| **Pantry Box,** 1-Finger, Lid, Painted Maltase Crosses, Flowers, Oval, New England, 3 x 11 In. | 180 |
| **Pantry Box,** Bentwood, Painted Red Rooster, Yellow Ground, 1800s, 3½ x 8 In. | 86 |
| **Pantry Box,** Lapped Joints, Lid, Oval, Olive Green, New England, 2 x 6 In. | 180 |
| **Pantry Box,** Maple, Bentwood, Glued Seam, Red, White, Blue, 19th Century, 5¼ In. | 323 |
| **Pantry Box,** Mixed Woods, Vinegar Decoration, Brown, Yellow, Round, c.1835, 12½ In. | 294 |
| **Pantry Box,** Oval, Blue Paint, Lid, c.1850, 21 x 9 In. | 117 |
| **Pantry Box,** Pine, Lid, Handle, 1800s, 7 x 13 In. | 135 |
| **Pantry Box,** Pine, Semicircle, Ship, Gray, Green, Hinged, c.1800, 9¼ In. | 353 |
| **Pantry Box,** Round, Blue Paint, Lid, Handle, c.1850, 11 x 6 In. | 205 |
| **Pantry Box,** Wood, Oval, Green Paint, Lid, 1800s, 5½ In. | 236 |
| **Peel,** Wrought Iron, Diamond Shape Handle, c.1800, 59 x 11 In. | 308 |
| **Peeler,** Apple, Cast Iron, Hudson Parring Co. | 85 |
| **Peeler,** Apple, Mixed Wood, Leather Belt, Crank Handle, Penn., 13 x 24 In.................*illus* | 94 |
| **Pepper Mill,** Brass, Iron Mounts, Treen, c.1845, 3¾ In. | 259 |
| **Pie Crimper,** Brass, Heart Handle, 19th Century, 8½ In. | 570 |
| **Pie Crimper,** Walnut, Monogram, Bird, Heart Crosshatch Handle, 1777, 6 In. | 1560 |

K

**Kitchen,** Fish Roaster, Frame, 4 Hooks, Lollipop Hanger, Iron, Incised, c.1805, 35 ½ In.
$923

Skinner Auctioneers & Appraisers

**Kitchen,** Flour Sifter, Blood's, Pat. Sept. 17 1861, Stenciled, Wood, Nails, 13 x 9 x 11 In.
$153

Conestoga Auction Co., Inc.

**Kitchen,** Food Chopper, Pierced Heart Blade, Iron, Copper, Maple Handle, c.1750, 12 x 5 In.
$948

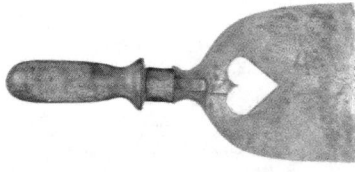

James D. Julia Auctioneers

**Kitchen,** Kettle, Hearth, Bail Handle, Footed, Iron, Sampson & Tisdale, N.Y., 7 ½ x 12 In.
$369

Skinner Auctioneers & Appraisers

**Kitchen,** Mold, Cheese, Heart Shape, Tin, Pierced, Applied Loop Handles, Ring Feet, 4 In., Pair
$354

Conestoga Auction Co., Inc.

**Kitchen,** Oven, Roasting, Barrel Shape, Spit, Handles, Tin, 1800s, 18 x 21 In.
$240

Garth's Auctioneers & Appraisers

**Kitchen,** Peeler, Apple, Mixed Wood, Leather Belt, Crank Handle, Penn., 13 x 24 In.
$94

Conestoga Auction Co., Inc.

**TIP**

*Clean a cast-iron pot the right way. Don't soak it. Don't put it in the dishwasher. Clean it with coarse salt and a sponge. Rinse, dry. If you use other methods, you may remove the pan's seasoning.*

**Kitchen,** Pot, Red Paint, Bail Handle, 3-Footed, Iron, Polley Bates, Mansfd., Z.L, c.1801, 6 x 8 In.
$2,583

Skinner Auctioneers & Appraisers

**Kitchen,** Scoop, Ice Cream Sandwich, 1920s, 9 In.
$300

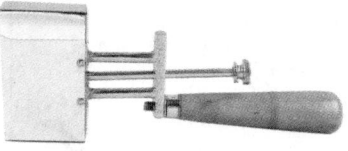

Morphy Auctions

**Kitchen,** Scoop, Ice Cream, Clipper No. 5, F.S. Co., Troy, N.Y., 1910s, 10 ½ In.
$120

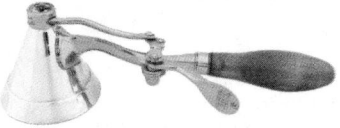

Morphy Auctions

**Kitchen,** Spatula, Pierced, Flower, Circles, Iron, Incised Line, Marked MMK 1818, 24 In.
$7,380

Skinner Auctioneers & Appraisers

K

**Kitchen,** Strawholder, Green Glass, Embossed, Gold Highlights, 12½ In. $1,800

Morphy Auctions

**Kitchen,** Toaster, Rotary, Twisted Double-Arch Grill, Scrolled Foot, Iron, WP, c.1817, 21¾ In. $646

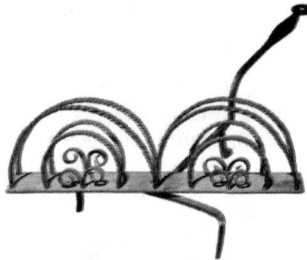

Skinner Auctioneers & Appraisers

**Knife,** Dagger, Third Reich, SS, Steel Scabbard, Wood Handle, 1940-42, 14½ In. $7,440

The Stein Auction Company

| | |
|---|---|
| **Pie Crimper,** Wrought Iron, Bird Finial, Fork Terminal, Pa., c.1945, 8 In. | 2706 |
| **Pitcher,** Lid, Ice Retainer, White, Yellow, Lustro-Ware, 1950s, 6½ x 4 x 6¾ In. | 32 |
| **Plate,** Bread, Beech, Raised Lip, Treen, 1800s, 7 In., Pair | 119 |
| **Pot Hanger,** Cast Iron, Half Dome, 27 x 19 In. | 86 |
| **Pot,** Cast Iron, Straight-Sided, 3-Footed, DT Over Sunburst, 1800s, 3½ In. | 369 |
| **Pot,** Lid, Eagle, Round Flat Base, Iron, 6 x 3½ In. | 82 |
| **Pot,** Lid, Peacock, Round Flat Base, Iron, 5½ x 3½ In. | 205 |
| **Pot,** Lid, Rooster, Round Flat Base, Iron, 5½ x 3½ In. | 94 |
| **Pot,** Red Paint, Bail Handle, 3-Footed, Iron, Polley Bates, Mansfd., Z.L, c.1801, 6 x 8 In. ...... *illus* | 2583 |
| **Potato Masher,** Stainless Steel, Round, Red Bakelite Handle, 8¼ x 3 In. | 28 |
| **Pudding Steamer,** Cylindrical, Lid, Tin, c.1900, 6½ In. | 39 |
| **Rack,** 4 Skewers, Heart Shape Back, Lollipop Hanger, Wrought Iron, 5½ x 6 In. | 443 |
| **Rack,** Utensil, Pine, Scalloped Top, Wrought Iron Hooks, c.1845, 30¾ In. | 300 |
| **Rack,** Utensil, Wrought Iron, Heart Crest, Scrolling, 7 Hooks, 1800s, 15 In. | 320 |
| **Ramekin Set,** Yellow, White Interior, Pyrex, Rectangular, 7 Oz., 3½ In., 4 Piece | 48 |
| **Reamers** are listed in their own category. | |
| **Recipe Box,** Metal, Geometric Shapes, Green, Red, Blue, Syndicate Mfg., 3½ x 5½ In. | 12 |
| **Refrigerator,** Steel, Monitor Top, Electric, Single Door, G.E., c.1930, 49¾ x 24 In. | 708 |
| **Roaster,** Bird, Wrought Iron, Double Tines, 2 Shaft Legs, Ring Tip Handle, c.1820, 4 x 20 In. | 316 |
| **Roaster,** Chestnut, Brass, Pierced, England, c.1875, 18 In. | 92 |
| **Roaster,** Chestnut, Iron, Wood Handle, Cylindrical, Sliding Hatch Door, c.1800, 53 x 7 In. | 123 |
| **Roasting Oven,** Hearth, Sheet Iron, Open Handles, Hinged Door, c.1850, 16 x 19 In. | 35 |
| **Rolling Pin,** Blown Glass, Olive, Amber, White Mottled, Knob Handles, c.1810, 15½ In. | 123 |
| **Rolling Pin,** Cherry, c.1900, 20½ In. | 25 |
| **Rolling Pin,** Treen, Draal-Hus, Fitted Handle, Pa., c.1830, 7 x 17 In. | 184 |
| **Salad Tongs,** Tupperware, Green Plastic, Service-Talented, Separate For Mixing, Box, c.1958 | 28 |
| **Salt & Pepper Shakers** are listed in their own category. | |
| **Salt Bowl,** Spoon, Wood, Round Bowl, Shouldered, Long Handle, Incised Rim, 2 & 3 In. | 474 |
| **Scoop,** Ice Cream Sandwich, 1920s, 9 In. *illus* | 300 |
| **Scoop,** Ice Cream, Clipper No. 5, F.S. Co., Troy, N.Y., 1910s, 10½ In. *illus* | 120 |
| **Scoop,** Ice Cream, Nickel Plated Brass, Wood, F.S. Co., Troy, N.Y., c.1915, 10¾ In. | 185 |
| **Scoop,** Ice Cream, Plastic, Aqua, Scoop Master | 6 |
| **Sifter,** Portland Ash, Hinged, Tapered Lid Box, Red, Stenciling, Crank, 19 x 19 In. | 260 |
| **Skewer Set,** Lollipop Hanger, 8 Skewers, Urn Shape, Iron, 1800s, 7 x 9 In. | 4613 |
| **Skillet,** Griswold, No. 3. | 28 |
| **Skillet,** Griswold, No. 9. | 28 |
| **Skillet,** Griswold, No. 10. | 39 |
| **Skillet,** Griswold, No. 14. | 77 |
| **Skillet,** Griswold, No. 80, Double, c.1935, 10 In. | 125 |
| **Skillet,** Lid, Cast Iron, 3-Footed, Straight Handle, c.1800, 16 x 9 In. | 246 |
| **Skillet,** Posnet, Bronze, 3-Footed, Marked Austin & Crocker Boston, c.1793, 17 x 7 In. | 6150 |
| **Skillet,** Sidney, No. 8. | 11 |
| **Skillet,** Wagner Ware, No. 4, Sidney, O | 22 |
| **Skillet,** Wagner, No. 5 | 17 |
| **Spatula,** Heart Cutout, Wrought Steel, 21 In. | 570 |
| **Spatula,** Iron, Heart Cutout Blade, Rounded, Flattened Handle, Hook, 19 In. | 649 |
| **Spatula,** Pierced, Flower, Circles, Iron, Incised Line, Marked MMK 1818, 24 In. *illus* | 7380 |
| **Spatula,** Wrought Iron, D-Shape, Pierced Tulips & Hearts, Ram's Horn Finial, 20 In. | 1063 |
| **Spice Box,** 8 Drawers, Green Paint, Bracket Feet, 17 x 13 In. | 413 |
| **Spice Box,** Oak, Wall, Carved Backsplash, 8 Drawers, c.1900, 17¾ x 11 In. | 60 |
| **Spice Grinder,** Trough, Incised Pinwheel, 2-Handle Wheel, Serrated, 1800s, 6 x 14 In. | 230 |
| **Spice Holder,** Stacking, 5 Sections, Lithograph Label, Locking, Treen, 8 x 3 In. | 1422 |
| **Spice Rack,** Wooden, Roosters, 9 Shakers, Shafford Type, 1950s | 75 |
| **Spoon Drip Plate,** Plastic, Yellow, 3 Spoon Hollows, Hanging Hook, 8¼ x 5¼ In. | 16 |
| **Spoon Rack,** Wood, Hanging, 3 Levels, Scrolled Cutouts, Red Paint, c.1845, 31 x 28 In. | 219 |
| **Spoon Rack,** Wood, Hanging, Pine, Lollipop, Pinwheel, Blue, Red Paint, 1800s, 26 x 13 In. | 10200 |
| **Spoon,** Wood, Incised Tulip, Fish Toggle Handle, Bead Eyes, 19th Century, 10 In. | 180 |
| **Spoon,** Wrought Iron, Pointed Bowl, Rattail Handle, Notched, Punch Dots, 18 In. | 1188 |
| **Spreader,** Stainless Steel, Serrated, Butterscotch Bakelite Handle, Burns Mfg. | 24 |
| **Stand,** Cheese Wheel, Blond Wood, Pedestal, 7½ x 17 In. | 480 |
| **Strainer,** Greaser, Yellow Wood Handle, Foley Mfg., c.1950 | 22 |
| **Strawholder,** Green Glass, Embossed, Gold Highlights, 12½ In. *illus* | 1800 |
| **Sugar Cutter,** Iron, Walnut Base, Wood Handle, 6 x 15 In. | 201 |
| **Sugar Nippers,** Punched & Engraved Decoration, Iron, R. Timmins & Sons, 10½ In. | 288 |
| **Sugar Nippers,** Steel, c.1825, 9 In. | 360 |
| **Syrup Dispenser,** Spring-Loaded Metal Sliding Lid, Red Bakelite Handle, c.1932 | 28 |

K

| | |
|---|---|
| **Tea Strainer,** Porcelain, Gilt, Rococo, Over-The-Cup Design, 6 In. | 120 |
| **Teakettle,** Griswold No. 8, Cast Aluminum, Coil Handle, Erie, c.1880, 5 Qt. | 50 |
| **Timer,** Pink, Black Numbers, Silver Stripe On Dial Handle, Lux Minute Minder, 1950s | 78 |
| **Timer,** Portable, Metal, White, Black Lettering, Numbers, Westclox, 1950s | 32 |
| **Toaster,** Crescent Shape, Iron, 3 Scrolled Feet, Hardwood Handle, c.1800, 15 x 10 In. | 154 |
| **Toaster,** Hearth, Iron, Revolving Center Shaft, Scrolled Arches, 2 Forks, c.1800, 7 x 16 In. | 316 |
| **Toaster,** Hearth, Iron, Revolving Rack, Scrolled Double Arches, 3-Footed, c.1800, 7 x 17 In. | 259 |
| **Toaster,** Rotary, Iron, Tripod Base, Shaped Handle, Lollipop Hanger, c.1802, 14 x 13 In. | 123 |
| **Toaster,** Rotary, Twisted Double-Arch Grill, Scrolled Foot, Iron, WP, c.1817, 21¾ In. ......*illus* | 646 |
| **Toaster,** Rotary, Wrought Iron, Grill Frame, Scrolled Heart, Tripod, c.1800, 16 x 12 In. | 431 |
| **Toaster,** Wrought Iron, Heart & Pinwheel Piercings, c.1840, 22 In. | 330 |
| **Trammel,** Hook End, Wrought Iron, c.1850, 22 In. | 120 |
| **Tray,** Metal, Red, Yellow, Black Barbeque Scene, Scalloped Edges, 1960s, 20½ x 16 In. | 24 |
| **Trencher,** Wood, Dugout, 52 x 17 In. | 117 |
| **Trencher,** Wood, Oval, c.1865, 10 x 46 In. | 150 |
| **Trencher,** Wood, Oval, c.1900, 22 In. | 98 |
| **Trencher,** Wood, Red Paint, 1800s, 22 In. | 266 |
| **Trencher,** Wood, Red Paint, Extended Handles, 1800s, 23 x 12¼ In. | 153 |
| **Trencher,** Wood, Wide Edge, 27 x 12 In. | 59 |
| **Trivet,** see Trivet category. | |
| **Utensil Set,** Parer, 2 Forks, Slotted Spoon, Wood Handles, Samson Stainless Steel, 1950s | 36 |
| **Wafer Iron,** Great Seal Of The United States, Eagle, Scissor Shape, Wire Latch, 27 In. | 660 |
| **Waffle Iron,** Scroll Design, American Eagle, 23½ In. | 210 |
| **Waffle Iron,** Wrought Iron, Stamped, 19th Century, 28 In. | 420 |
| **Washing Machine,** Easy Model M, Vacuum Copper, Wringer, 53 x 24 In. | 420 |
| **Washing Machine,** Glory, Pine, Stenciled, Splayed Legs, Patented 1898, 32 x 33½ In. | 480 |
| **Washing Machine,** Perfect Washer, Wood, Tin, Iron, W.H. Whetzel, Va., c.1870, 44 x 36 In. | 345 |
| **Water Heater,** Copper, William Vulcodisc Valves, John Van Range Co. | 210 |

**KNIFE** collectors usually specialize in a single type. In the 1960s, the United States government passed a law that required knife manufacturers to mark their knives with the country of origin. This seemed to encourage the collectors, and knife collecting became an interest of a large group of people. All types of knives are collected, from top quality twentieth-century examples to old bone- or pearl-handled knives in excellent condition.

| | |
|---|---|
| **Adolphus Busch,** Corkscrew, Leather Pouch, Box, 6 In. | 1560 |
| **Adolphus Busch,** Red & Black Enameling, Brass Highlights, Peephole, 1890s, 2½ In. | 360 |
| **Bowie,** Brass Guard, Serpent, Inset Glass Eyes, Fangs | 875 |
| **Bowie,** Clipped Point, Oval Fighting Guard, Stag Antler Scale Grips, 5½ In. | 185 |
| **Bowie,** Confederate, D Guard, Single Edge, c.1863, 27 In. | 369 |
| **Bowie,** Ivory Handle, Silver Trim, Capt. Thomas P. Leathers, SS Natchen, 1870, 1½ In. | 385 |
| **Bowie,** Wood Grip, Sheath, Imperial Sword Co., London, 12⅝ In. | 248 |
| **Dagger,** Single Edge Blade, Bone Hilt, Inlaid Stones, Shell, Silver Sheath, Persia, 13 In. | 450 |
| **Dagger,** Third Reich, SS, Steel Scabbard, Wood Handle, 1940-42, 14½ In. ......*illus* | 7440 |
| **Fish Shape Handle,** Revolving Steel Blade, Attached S Hook, 1 x 5½ In. | 236 |
| **Pocket,** File, Silver, Stamped Latama, Italy, 2-In. Blade, 3 In. | 161 |
| **Stag Horn,** Turquoise & Malachite Stones, 13 In. | 350 |
| **Swiss Army,** Wenger, Streamamerica, 7 Tools, Silver Case, Tiffany, 3¼ x 1 In. | 299 |
| **Trapper,** Babe Ruth, Facsimile Signature, Yellow Composition Handle, c.1988, 4½ In. | 206 |

**KNOWLES,** *Taylor & Knowles items may be found in the KTK and Lotus Ware categories.*

**KOSTA,** the oldest Swedish glass factory, was founded in 1742. During the 1920s through the 1950s, many pieces of original design were made at the factory. Kosta and Boda merged with Afors in 1964 and created the Afors Group in 1971. In 1976, the name Kosta Boda was adopted. The company merged with Orrefors in 1990 and is still working.

**W KOSTA**

| | |
|---|---|
| **Bowl,** Blue & Green Swirls, Warff, Signed, 1964, 2 x 3 In. | 126 |
| **Bowl,** Clear Swirls, Goran Warff, Marked, 8 x 6 x 4 In. | 750 |
| **Bowl,** Couple Dancing, Under Trees, K. Engman, 4 x 5 In. | 75 |
| **Bowl,** Green, Blue Orange, Signed, Goran Warff, 10¼ x 2 In. | 317 |
| **Bowl,** Inclusions, Gold Foil, Twist Canes, Confetti, Blue, B. Vallien, 8 In. | 125 |
| **Bowl,** Opus, Round, Signed, Goran Warff, 5 In. | 178 |
| **Charger,** Swirls, Warff, c.1976, 10 In. | 632 |
| **Pitcher,** Rooster, Signed, V. Lindstrand, c.1958, 10½ In. | 325 |
| **Sculpture,** Fish, Signed, V. Lindstrand, 1958, 8½ In. | 525 |
| **Sculpture,** Koala Bear, Signed, Mats Jonasson, 3 In. | 30 |

**Kosta,** Vase, Clear, Etched Nude Woman, Tapered, Vicke Lindstrand, Signed, 11¾ In.
$354

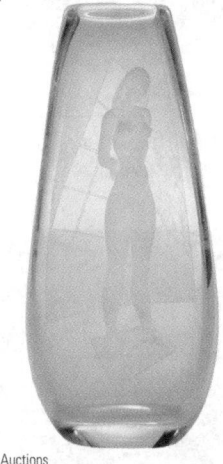

Brunk Auctions

**KPM,** Centerpiece, Berlin Bowl, Flowers, Handles, Marked, c.1890, 10½ x 21 In.
$4,688

Rago Arts & Auction Center

**KPM,** Plaque, 3 Fates, Carved & Gilded Frame, Scepter Mark, Signed, 13 x 7¾ In.
$4,140

Cottone Auctions

**K**

**KPM,** Plaque, Epheu, Young Woman, Ivy Wreath, Signed, Wagner, Frame, 13⅜ In. $7,380

Skinner Auctioneers & Appraisers

**KPM,** Plaque, Miriam & Moses, Hand Painted, Frame, 25 x 29 In. $14,400

Fox Auctions

**KPM,** Vase, Snowy Forest, Theodore Schmuz-Baudiss, Cross Mark, 1910, 17 x 9½ In. $6,250

Rago Arts & Auction Center

| | |
|---|---:|
| **Sculpture,** Lion, Erik Hoglund, 1970s, 3 x 5 In. | 55 |
| **Sculpture,** Panther Under Glass, B. Vallien, 4 x 7 In. | 266 |
| **Vase,** Clear, Black Swirls, Oval, Signed, V. Lindstrand, 1959, 4 In. | 275 |
| **Vase,** Clear, Etched Nude Woman, Tapered, Vicke Lindstrand, Signed, 11¾ In. ............*illus* | 354 |
| **Vase,** Pink, Green Design, 3 x 3½ In. | 150 |
| **Vase,** Textured, Iridized Finish, Applied Drops, Oval, B. Vallien, 8½ In. | 175 |
| **Vase,** Threaded, Oval, V. Lindstrand, c.1959, 11 In. | 525 |

KPM refers to Berlin porcelain, but the same initials were used alone and in combination with other symbols by several German porcelain makers. They include the Konigliche Porzellan Manufaktur of Berlin, initials used in mark, 1823–47; Meissen, 1723–24 only; Krister Porzellan Manufaktur in Waldenburg, after 1831; Kranichfelder Porzellan Manufaktur in Kranichfeld, after 1903; and the Krister Porzellan Manufaktur in Scheibe, after 1838.

*K.P.M.*

| | |
|---|---:|
| **Centerpiece,** Berlin Bowl, Flowers, Handles, Marked, c.1890, 10½ x 21 In. ...........*illus* | 4688 |
| **Compote,** Flowers, Gilt, 4-Footed Pedestal, c.1890, 9½ x 3 In. | 495 |
| **Cup,** Imperial General, On Horse, Green, Gilt Band, 3 Paw Feet, Leaf Handle, c.1900, 5 In. | 196 |
| **Figurine,** Europa Riding Bull, White, Marked, Amberg, 16 x 16 In. | 518 |
| **Figurine,** Gladiator, Multicolor, Gilt, Silver Gilt, Marked, 6¾ In. | 132 |
| **Figurine,** Westphalian Buckeburgerian, Woman In Native Dress, Apples, Signed, 10 In. | 633 |
| **Group,** Geschichte & Mars, Military Allegory, God, Woman, Standing, Draped, 17½ In. | 1375 |
| **Jardiniere,** Enameled Flowers, Fruit, Putti, Gilt Crabstock Handles, Paw Feet, c.1865, 9⅝ In. | 1063 |
| **KPM,** Lithophane, see also Lithophane category. | |
| **Plaque,** 3 Fates, Carved & Gilded Frame, Scepter Mark, Signed, 13 x 7¾ In. ..........*illus* | 4140 |
| **Plaque,** 3 Fates, Porcelain, Signed Werner, 9¾ x 7½ In. | 6875 |
| **Plaque,** Banishment Of Ishmael, Porcelain, Hager, Frame, c.1890, 10 x 7½ In. | 5000 |
| **Plaque,** Children In Hay Cart, Scenic, Frame, Impressed, J.O. Moss, c.1890, 19 x 15 In. | 6300 |
| **Plaque,** Epheu, Young Woman, Ivy Wreath, Signed, Wagner, Frame, 13⅜ In. .........*illus* | 7380 |
| **Plaque,** Erbluth, Half-Dressed Woman, Brown Hair, Signed Maltz, c.1890, 13 x 10 In. | 6960 |
| **Plaque,** Fairy, On Lily, Carved Giltwood Frame, Berlin, 8½ x 6 In. | 4750 |
| **Plaque,** Flowers, Birds, Insects, Rococo Style, Painted, Gilt, 22 x 15½ In. | 891 |
| **Plaque,** Girl Holding Candlestick, Red Skirt, 9 x 6¼ In. | 2300 |
| **Plaque,** Hansel & Gretel, 2 Children, Lost In Forest, Painted, Frame, c.1900, 7 x 5 In. | 1188 |
| **Plaque,** Mary Magdalena, Reading Book, Prone, Oval, Scepter Mark, Wood Frame, 9 In. | 1380 |
| **Plaque,** Miriam & Moses, Hand Painted, Frame, 25 x 29 In. ....................*illus* | 14400 |
| **Plaque,** Mother, Child, Velvet Lined, Carved Giltwood Frame, 11 x 7½ In. | 1375 |
| **Plaque,** Mother, Holding Crowned Infant, Oval, Marked E. Sturm 1870, Frame, 22 In. | 6490 |
| **Plaque,** Nude Maiden, Arms Raised, Hovering Above Lily Pond, Gilt Frame, 9½ x 6½ In. | 11850 |
| **Plaque,** Portrait, Woman, Pensive, In Turban, Holding Paper, Oval, Convex, 3¼ x 2¾ In. | 127 |
| **Plaque,** Queen Louise & Prince Wilhelm Of Prussia, L. Scherf, 10¾ x 8 In. | 12500 |
| **Plaque,** Rembrandt's Mother, Old Woman, Fur Coat, Frame, Oval, 20 x 16 In. | 2600 |
| **Plaque,** Ruth, Porcelain, Signed R. Dittrich, Frame, 13 x 8 In. | 4063 |
| **Plaque,** The Secret, 2 Children, 2 Boys Whispering, Signed Wagner, c.1900, 9 x 16 In. | 4688 |
| **Plaque,** Woman, 1700s Attire, Hat, Porcelain, Impressed, Frame, c.1900, 7 x 5 In. | 1375 |
| **Plaque,** Woman, Long Dark Hair, Porcelain, Frame, c.1900, 10 x 7½ In. | 2625 |
| **Plaque,** Woman, Profile, Half Nude, Giltwood Frame, 13 x 10¾ In. | 12500 |
| **Plate,** Landscapes, Figures, Maroon Border, Gold Trim, 9¾ In., 12 Piece | 3245 |
| **Salt,** Putto, Standing Over 2 Oval Bowls, Butterfly, Flowers, Blue, Red, White, 4⅞ In. | 375 |
| **Scent Bottle,** Lid, Flowers, Gilt, Tapered Rectangle, 4¾ In. | 75 |
| **Tureen,** Dome Lid, Putto Finial, Underplate, Flowers, Basket Weave, Twig Handles, 15½ In. | 563 |
| **Urn,** Lid, Flower Panels, Gilt Handles, Signed Aulich, c.1850, 22 In. | 4688 |
| **Urn,** Lid, Putto, Landscape, Flower Sprays, Gilt, Ram Mask Handles, 27 In. | 1625 |
| **Vase,** Lid, 18th Century Figures In Garden, Latticework, Scrolls, Hexagonal Base, 47 In. | 86500 |
| **Vase,** Lid, Lattice, Yellow Ground, Venus, Eros, Pedestal Base, Putti, 2 Handles, 24 In. | 3250 |
| **Vase,** Painted Tasseled Loop, Bottle Shape, 11 In., Pair | 369 |
| **Vase,** Snowy Forest, Theodore Schmuz-Baudiss, Cross Mark, 1910, 17 x 9½ In. .........*illus* | 6250 |

KTK are the initials of the Knowles, Taylor & Knowles Company of East Liverpool, Ohio, founded by Isaac W. Knowles in 1853. The company made many types of utilitarian wares, hotel china, and dinnerware. It made the fine bone china known as Lotus Ware from 1891 to 1896. The company merged with American Ceramic Corporation in 1928. It closed in 1934. Lotus Ware is listed in its own category in this book.

*K.T.&K. CHINA*

| | |
|---|---:|
| **Pitcher,** Flowers, Pastel, Bamboo Handle, 7 x 4 In. | 795 |
| **Pitcher,** Milk, Moss Rose, Gilt Trim, 6½ x 7 In. | 75 |
| **Platter,** Pink To Red Flowers, Gilt Trim, 12 x 15 In. | 79 |

| | |
|---|---|
| **Tureen,** Lid, Pink Roses, Blue Vertical Stripes, Handles, 11 ½ In. | 32 |
| **Vase,** Flower, Stem, Teal, Plum, 5 x 3 ½ In. | 28 |

**KU KLUX KLAN** items are now collected because of their historic importance. Literature, robes, and memorabilia are seen at shows and auctions. Laws passed in 1870 and 1871 caused the decline of the Klan. A second group calling itself the Ku Klux Klan emerged in 1915. There are still local groups using the name.

| | |
|---|---|
| **Ballot Box,** Mahogany, Brass Slot, Kentucky, 1920s, 11 x 20 In. | 17900 |
| **Comic Book,** Batman Vs. Ku Klux Klan, DC Comics, 1989 | 6 |
| **Gavel,** Oak, Carved KKK, Painted Klan Star, Stone Mountain, Ga., c.1930, 12 In. | 1295 |
| **Membership Book,** Kreed, 1917, 7 x 3 ½ In. | 36 |
| **Photo,** Capitol Building, Washington, D.C., 1925, 8 x 10 In. | 15 |
| **Photo,** Parade, Rhode Island, September 13, 1926, 8 x 10 In. | 10 |
| **Postcard,** Rider, Horse, Red Robe, Stripe Hat, Regalia Of Grand Cyclops, Ala., 1908, 3 x 5 In. | 300 |
| **Sheet Music,** Ku Klux Klan Fox Shimmy, Klansman, Statue Of Liberty, 10 x 13 In., 8 Pages | 191 |

**KUTANI** porcelain was made in Japan after the mid-seventeenth century. Most of the pieces found today are nineteenth-century. Collectors often use the term *Kutani* to refer to just the later, colorful pieces decorated with red, gold, and black pictures of warriors, animals, and birds.

| | |
|---|---|
| **Bowl,** Iron Red, Figures, Scrolls, Decorated Inside Rim, c.1890, 11 ¼ In. | 390 |
| **Bowl,** Straight-Sided, Lip, Footed, Fisherman, Dragon, Leaves, Gilt, 1900s, 18 x 3 In. | 69 |
| **Charger,** Iron Red, Black, Brown, Gold, Immortal, Raised Arm, Phoenix, 1 ¾ x 13 ⅜ In. | 219 |
| **Plate,** Rooster, Flowers, Red Ground, Greek Key Band, Gilt Scrolls, c.1900, 9 ⅝ In. | 46 |
| **Vase,** Applied Fruit, Berry Handles, Vignettes, On Gilt & Orange Ground, 25 x 8 In., Pair | 531 |

**L.G. WRIGHT** Glass Company of New Martinsville, West Virginia, started selling glassware in 1937. Founder "Si" Wright contracted with Ohio and West Virginia glass factories to reproduce popular pressed glass patterns like Rose & Snow, Baltimore Pear, and Three Face, and opalescent patterns like Daisy & Fern and Swirl. Collectors can tell the difference between the original glasswares and L.G. Wright reproductions because of colors and differences in production techniques. Some L.G. Wright items are marked with an underlined *W* in a circle. Items that were made from old Northwood molds have an altered Northwood mark—an angled line was added to the *N* to make it look like a *W*. Collectors refer to this mark as "the wobbly W." The L.G. Wright factory was closed and the existing molds sold in 1999.

| | |
|---|---|
| **Daisy & Button,** Bowl, Amber, 4 ⅛ In. | 8 |
| **Daisy & Button,** Bowl, Oval, Amber, 5 In. | 12 |
| **Daisy & Button,** Bowl, Star Shape, Blue, 5 ¼ In. | 14 |
| **Daisy & Button,** Goblet, 6 In. | 15 |
| **Daisy & Button,** Plate, Salad, 7 x 7 In. | 10 |
| **Daisy & Button,** Plate, Salad, Pink, 7 x 7 In. | 10 |
| **Daisy & Button,** Plate, Salad, Yellow, 7 x 7 In. | 10 |
| **Daisy & Button,** Toothpick Holder, Blue | 10 |
| **Daisy & Cube,** Goblet, Forest Green, Etched, 5 ¾ In. | 35 |
| **Eyewinker,** Bowl, Fruit, Amber, 4 In. | 10 |
| **Eyewinker,** Goblet, 6 In. | 14 |
| **Eyewinker,** Sauce, Amber, 2 x 3 In. | 10 |
| **Eyewinker,** Toothpick Holder, Amber, 2 ⅜ In. | 9 |
| **Eyewinker,** Wine | 10 |
| **Grape & Cable,** Plate, Nutmeg, Custard Glass, c.1910, 7 ½ In. | 100 |
| **Moon & Stars,** Champagne, Dark Amber | 34 |
| **Moon & Stars,** Compote, Blue, Lid, 12 ½ In. | 82 |
| **Moon & Stars,** Compote, Green, 6 ¼ x 4 In. | 18 |
| **Moon & Stars,** Fairy Lamp, Amber | 25 |
| **Moon & Stars,** Goblet, Amber, 5 ⅝ In. | 12 |
| **Moon & Stars,** Goblet, Green, 5 ⅞ In. | 15 |
| **Moon & Stars,** Goblet, Milk Glass, 5 ⅞ In. | 21 |
| **Moon & Stars,** Sauce Bowl, Amberina, Footed, 3 ⅞ In. | 21 |
| **Moon & Stars,** Sugar, Lid, Red | 60 |
| **Moon & Stars,** Tumbler, Iced Tea, Green, 5 ⅜ In. | 41 |
| **Paneled Grape,** Goblet, Red, 6 In. | 35 |
| **Paneled Thistle,** Goblet, 5 ½ In. | 22 |
| **Wild Rose,** Goblet, Blue, 6 ⅜ In. | 18 |
| **Wild Rose,** Goblet, Yellow, 6 ⅜ In. | 15 |
| **Wild Rose,** Wine, Ruby, 5 In. | 30 |

**Lacquer,** Box, Document, Chrysanthemums, Plum Blossoms, Checkerboard, Japan, 9 In. $400

Skinner Auctioneers & Appraisers

**TIP**
*Lalique glass made before 1945 will fluoresce yellow under a black light. Glass made after 1945 does not.*

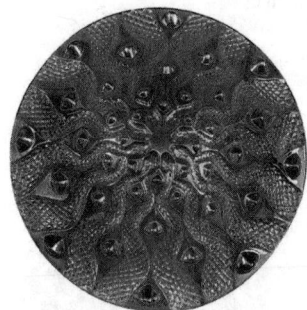

**Lalique,** Bowl, Serpentine, Red, Snakes, Geometric Design, Box, 15 ¾ In. Diam. $2,390

Neal Auction Co.

**Lalique,** Clock, Moineaux, Sparrows, Frosted, 6 ½ x 8 ½ In. $1,708

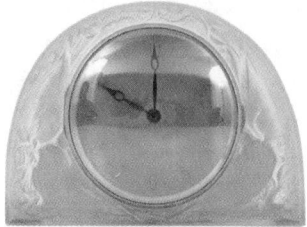

Palm Beach Modern Auctions

L

**Lalique,** Figurine, Tete D'Aigle, Eagle Mascot, Head, Amber, Signed, 4½ In. $918

James D. Julia Auctioneers

**Lalique,** Figurine, Victorie Mascot, Woman's Head, Frosted, R. Lalique France, 9½ x 6 In. $7,110

James D. Julia Auctioneers

**Lalique,** Perfume Bottle, Worth, Dans La Nuit, Blue Enamel, Molded Stopper, 1924, 10 x 6 In. $1,500

Rago Arts & Auction Center

---

**TIP**

*Use coasters under glasses and flower vases on marble-topped tables. Marble can stain easily.*

---

**LACQUER** is a type of varnish. Collectors are most interested in the Chinese and Japanese lacquer wares made from the Japanese varnish tree. Lacquer wares are made from wood with many coats of lacquer. Sometimes the piece is carved or decorated with ivory or metal inlay.

| | |
|---|---|
| **Bowl,** Shallow, Scalloped Sides, Red, Black Exterior, Chinese, 1700s, 11 In. | 230 |
| **Box,** Document, Chrysanthemums, Plum Blossoms, Checkerboard, Japan, 9 In. ...............*illus* | 400 |
| **Box,** Lid, Black, Mother-Of-Pearl Inlay, Symbols, Chrysanthemum, Red Interior, 3 x 7¾ In. | 69 |
| **Inro,** Gilt Horse, Black Ground, 4 Compartments, Cherry Branch Netsuke, Japan, c.1900, 3 In. | 461 |
| **Knife Box,** Hinged, Black, Gilt, Flowers, Fruits, Bail Handles, Japan, 1800s, 14 x 8¾ In. | 480 |
| **Tray,** Faux Bamboo Stand, Extension Leaves, England, c.1890, 19 x 27 In. | 390 |
| **Tray,** Pine & Prunus Trees, Lake, Gilded Clouds, Black Bottom, Japan, c.1870, 10¼ x 13 In. | 738 |

**LADY HEAD VASE,** *see Head Vase.*

**LALIQUE** glass and jewelry were made by Rene Lalique (1860-1945) in Paris, France, **R.LALIQUE** between the 1890s and his death in 1945. Beginning in 1921 he had a manufactuing plant in Alsace. The glass was molded, pressed, and engraved in Art Nouveau and Art Deco styles. Most pieces were marked with the signature *R. Lalique.* Lalique glass is still being made. Most pieces made after 1945 bear the mark *Lalique.* After 1980 the registry mark was added and the mark became *Lalique ® France.* In the prices listed here, this is indicated by Lalique (R) France. Some pieces that are advertised as ring dishes or pin dishes were listed as ashtrays in the Lalique factory catalog and are listed as ashtrays here. Jewelry made by Rene Lalique is listed in the Jewelry category.

| | |
|---|---|
| **Ashtray,** Tokio, Chrysanthemums, Signed, 5½ x 2 In. | 350 |
| **Bookends,** Kneeling Nude, Reverie, 9 In. | 1800 |
| **Bowl,** Cannes, Frosted, 2¼ x 7½ In. | 120 |
| **Bowl,** Cernuschi, Roses, Floral Rim, Clear To Frosted, R. Lalique, c.1927, 5 x 10¾ In. | 413 |
| **Bowl,** Chataignier, Geometric Leaf, Signed, 4 In. | 4600 |
| **Bowl,** Dauphins, Fish In Waves, Opalescent, Frosted, Flared, R. Lalique, 1932, 9 In. | 1062 |
| **Bowl,** Luxembourg, Cherubs, Frosted, 8 x 12 In. | 2360 |
| **Bowl,** Nemours, Flower Heads, Acid Etched, Round, 4 x 10 In. | 450 to 540 |
| **Bowl,** Nemours, Flower Heads, Molded, Frosted, Flowers, Black Centers, 10 In. | 400 |
| **Bowl,** Pinsons, Finches, Frosted, Birds Nesting Relief, Fern Fronds, Engraved, 9¼ In. | 472 |
| **Bowl,** Serpentine, Red, Snakes, Geometric Design, Box, 15¾ In. Diam. ...............*illus* | 2390 |
| **Box,** Coppelia, Rose Garlands, Frosted, 3 x 7 In. | 230 |
| **Box,** Lid, Cigales, Stylized Cicadas, Amber, 5 Panels, Round, 10¼ In. | 3559 |
| **Box,** Lid, D'Orsay, 3 Dancing Nudes, Flower Band, Red Patina, Round, 3¾ In. | 770 |
| **Candlestick,** Diamond Shape, Palm Leaves, Silver Candle Cups, 8 x 10¾ In., Pair | 1195 |
| **Champagne Flute,** Roxanne, Frosted Nude On Stem, 9 In., 12 Piece | 1298 |
| **Clock,** Moineaux, Sparrows, Frosted, 6½ x 8½ In. ...............*illus* | 1708 |
| **Compote,** Elisabeth, Frosted, Molded Birds, Leaves, Branches, Square Foot, 5½ In. | 308 |
| **Compote,** Moineau, Sparrow, Bird, Leaf, Signed, 5¼ x 5¼ In. | 201 |
| **Cordial,** Six Figurines, Women, In Panels, Clear, Frosted, 3¾ In., 6 Piece | 3000 |
| **Decanter,** Langeais, Frosted, Ribbed, Oval, Clear Flared Rim & Ball Stopper, 10 In. | 649 |
| **Decanter,** Parme, Circles, Disc Shape, 10½ In. | 600 |
| **Figurine,** Caroline, Turtle, Amber, 5¾ In. | 270 |
| **Figurine,** Chats Couche, Reclining Cat, Smoky Crystal, 1900s, 4¼ x 8½ In., Pair | 354 |
| **Figurine,** Cockatoo, Frosted, Crystal, 11½ x 10½ In. | 540 to 748 |
| **Figurine,** Gregoire, Toad, Green, 3½ x 4½ In. | 450 |
| **Figurine,** Tete D'Aigle, Eagle Mascot, Head, Amber, Signed, 4½ In. ...............*illus* | 918 |
| **Figurine,** Tete De Cheval, Horse's Head, 15 x 7 In. | 7680 |
| **Figurine,** Victorie Mascot, Woman's Head, Frosted, R. Lalique France, 9½ x 6 In. .........*illus* | 7110 |
| **Group,** Groupe De Six Moineaux, 6 Chicks, Signed, 11⅝ In. | 2250 |
| **Hood Ornament,** Coq Nain, Rooster, Molded, Frosted, 8 x 5 In. | 385 |
| **Ice Bucket,** Stand, Free-Form Pebbles, Clear & Frosted, 2 Handles, Engraved R. Lalique, 5 In. | 608 |
| **Invitation,** Invitation Pour Visiter, Birds, Reflections, Frame, 9½ x 10½ In. | 1185 |
| **Jardiniere,** Acanthes, Acanthus Leaves, Frosted, Boat Shape, Engraved R. Lalique, 18 In. | 668 |
| **Lamp,** Cariatides, Nudes Around Stem, Domed Shade, Stylized Leaf Ribs, Frosted, 13 In. | 17775 |
| **Lamp,** Hokkaido, Birds, Frosted, Fan Shape, Box, c.1900, 16¾ x 21¾ In. | 4375 |
| **Luminaire,** Suzanne, Nude Woman, Arms Out, Hanging Shawl, Bronze Peacock Base, 11 In. | 18960 |
| **Paperweight,** Bison, Clear, Frosted, 3¾ In., Pair | 246 |
| **Paperweight,** Chat, Cat, Seated, Paw Raised, 6 In. | 270 |
| **Paperweight,** Eagle Head, Tet D'Aigle, France, 1900s, 4¼ In. | 277 |
| **Perfume Bottle,** Amphitrite, Shell, Green, Stopper, Nude Kneeling, Etched R. Lalique, 4 In. | 8888 |
| **Perfume Bottle,** Amphitrite, Shell, Purple, Stopper, Nude Kneeling, Etched R. Lalique, 4 In. | 8888 |
| **Perfume Bottle,** Cactus, Frosted, Molded, Black Accents, 3¾ In. | 52 |
| **Perfume Bottle,** Dahlia, Black Enameled Center, Flower Shape, Satin Finish, 8 In. | 185 |

L

| | | |
|---|---|---:|
| **Perfume Bottle,** Dans La Nuit, Cobalt, Round Shape, Incised Worth, Lalique, 5 ¼ In. | | 210 |
| **Perfume Bottle,** Double Poppy Flowers, Signed, 4 x 3 ½ In. | | 265 |
| **Perfume Bottle,** Duncan, Art Deco Style, 3 Graces, Frosted, Acid Etched Signed, 8 x 3 ¾ In. | | 403 |
| **Perfume Bottle,** Flacon, Six Danseuses, 6 Dancing Nudes, Garland, Flattened Stopper, 4 In. | | 21330 |
| **Perfume Bottle,** LeJade, Bird & Branches, Pierced Scrolls, Stopper, Roger Et Gallet, 3 x 2 In. | | 3125 |
| **Perfume Bottle,** Panier De Roses, Trellis, Roses, Puffy Rose Band, Engraved R. Lalique, 4 In. | | 4148 |
| **Perfume Bottle,** Phalene D'Heraud, Butterfly, Nude With Wings, Amberina, Signed, 4 In. | | 10665 |
| **Perfume Bottle,** Worth, Dans La Nuit, Blue Enamel, Molded Stopper, 1924, 10 x 6 In. .......*illus* | | 1500 |
| **Perfume Burner,** Sirenes, Mermaids, Sepia Opalescent Tint, Dome Lid, 6 ¾ In. | | 1380 |
| **Plaque,** Masque De Femme, Woman's Face, Griffin Dolphins, 12 ½ x 12 ½ In. | 1840 to | 5625 |
| **Plate Set,** Annual, Clear & Frosted, 1965 Through 1976, 8 ¼ In., 12 Piece | | 1094 |
| **Plate,** Cote D'Or, 3 Women Dancers, Grapes, Conforming Border, Frosted, c.1985, 16 In. | | 1875 |
| **Scent Bottle,** Stopper, Female Nudes, c.1930, 7 In. | | 554 |
| **Sculpture,** Deux Poissons, 2 Fish, Clear & Frosted, Circular, Signed Lalique, France, 11 In. | | 2006 |
| **Sculpture,** Trophee, Ice Skating, Frosted, Clear, 12 ½ In. | | 1952 |
| **Statue,** Deux Poissons, 2 Fish, Molded, Frosted, 11 In. | | 2214 |
| **Tray,** Perdrix, 5 Partridge Birds, Leaves, Crystal, Signed, 12 x 17 In. | | 840 |
| **Vase,** 2 Nude Females, Frosted Green, Clear, Long Hair, 9 In. | | 1230 |
| **Vase,** Acanthes, Acanthus Leaves, Blue, Plain Shoulder, Globular, R. Lalique, 11 In. | | 17775 |
| **Vase,** Aigrettes, Egrets, In Flight, Reeds, Clear, Oval, c.1935, 10 In. | | 2813 |
| **Vase,** Amiens, Smoked Glass, Applied Scrolls, Signed R. Lalique, c.1905, 7 In. | | 1750 |
| **Vase,** Aras, Macaws, Berries, Branches, Clear, Frosted, Tapered Round, Green Patina, 9 In. | | 3750 |
| **Vase,** Archers, Red, Oval, 10 ½ In. | | 2666 |
| **Vase,** Avallon, Birds, Vine & Berries, Frosted, Opalescent, Blue Stain, Straight Sides, 6 In. | | 2596 |
| **Vase,** Bacchantes, Encircling Females Nudes, Footed, 7 ½ In. | | 2640 |
| **Vase,** Bacchantes, Frieze Of Nudes, Frosted, Tapered Cylinder, 9 ½ In. | 2125 to | 3198 |
| **Vase,** Bacchantes, Gray, Crystal, Nude Dancing, Maenads, 9 ½ In. | | 4481 |
| **Vase,** Bagatelle, Bird, Leaves, Frosted, 6 ¾ x 4 ¼ In. | 200 to | 288 |
| **Vase,** Beautrellis, Clear, Frosted, Flared Rim, Honeycomb Foot, R. Lalique, c.1927, 6 In. | | 575 |
| **Vase,** Biskra, Long Leaves, Zipper Feathers, Raised, Vertical, Amber, Melon Shape, 11 In. | | 3555 |
| **Vase,** Borneo, Elephants, Molded Glass, 12 In. | | 1029 |
| **Vase,** Bougainvillier, Flowers, Straight-Sided, Molded, 7 x 2 ½ In. | | 180 |
| **Vase,** Camarque, 4 Raised Panels Of Rearing Horses, Ruffled Band, Signed, 11 ½ In. | | 1836 |
| **Vase,** Chardons, Thistle Leaves, Melon Shape, Chamfered Corners, Frosted, c.1922, 6 x 7 In. | | 1500 |
| **Vase,** Charmilles, Overlapping Leaves, Gray, Molded, Impressed R. Lalique, c.1926, 14 In. ....*illus* | | 3068 |
| **Vase,** Cherubs, Frosted, Wavy Lines, Raised Dots, Clear Windows, Signed, 7 ⅝ In. | | 948 |
| **Vase,** Chevreuse, 5 Flower Bands, Ribs, Flared & Stepped Shape, Etched R. Lalique, 6 In. | | 1896 |
| **Vase,** Chrysalide, Winged Female Fairies, Smoky To Clear, Flared, 12 x 9 In. | | 4012 |
| **Vase,** Clematites, Clematis, Amethyst, Clear, Opalescent, Flowers, 6 ¾ In., Pair | | 1159 |
| **Vase,** Courges, Pears, Blue, Bulbous, Teardrop, Signed, Lalique, France, 7 ½ In. ....*illus* | | 15405 |
| **Vase,** Dampierre, Relief Sparrows, Garlands, Satin Finish, Footed, 4 ¾ In. | | 185 |
| **Vase,** Danaides, Nude Water Carriers, Clear & Frosted, Oval, Engraved R. Lalique, 7 In. | | 4688 |
| **Vase,** Desna, Cherubs, Flowers, Clear & Frosted, Wide Mouth, R. Lalique, 7 x 6 ¾ In. | | 360 |
| **Vase,** Domremy, Thistles, Smoky Gray, Orange Patina, R. Lalique, 1926, 8 ¼ In. ....*illus* | | 1625 |
| **Vase,** Druide, Mistletoe Branches, Opalescent Berries, Impressed Stems, c.1924, 7 x 7 In. | | 1000 |
| **Vase,** Escargot, Snail Shell, White Opalescent, Disc Form, Etched R. Lalique, 8 ⅜ In. | | 2006 |
| **Vase,** Espalion, Ferns, Opalescent, Narrow Mouth, Bulbous, Marked R. Lalique, 7 In. | | 461 |
| **Vase,** Formose, Swirling Carp, Amber, Molded R. Lalique, 1924, 6 ½ x 6 In. ....*illus* | | 6875 |
| **Vase,** Frosted Body, Birds, Leaves, Clear Neck, Signed, 4 ¾ In. | | 325 |
| **Vase,** Gui, Mistletoe, Turquoise, Opalescent Foot, Round, Etched R. Lalique, 7 In. | | 1718 |
| **Vase,** Guirlandes De Roses, Rose Garlands, Frosted, Wide Rim, 1935, 8 ¼ x 7 ¾ In. | | 1500 |
| **Vase,** Herblay, Fan-Shaped Flowers, Oval, Stamped R. Lalique, 7 ¼ In. | | 1062 |
| **Vase,** Ispahan, Roses, Red Crystal, Embossed, Original Box, 9 ⅜ In. | | 2318 |
| **Vase,** Laurier, Molded Leaf, Berry, Opalescent, R. Lalique, 7 In. | | 1046 |
| **Vase,** Le Mans, Stylized Roosters, Amber Glass, c.1930, 4 ¼ In. | | 2460 |
| **Vase,** Lezard, Lizard, Frosted Amber, Clear, Round Shape, Round Foot, 8 ½ In. | | 4182 |
| **Vase,** Macao, 2 Cockatoos, Frosted Amber To Clear, Original Box, 13 In. | | 5676 |
| **Vase,** Marrakech, Palm Leaves, Dark Amber, 12 In., Pair | | 1845 |
| **Vase,** Marrakech, Palm Leaves, Shaded Amber, Topaz, Wing-Like Sides, 1980s, 12 ½ In. | | 863 |
| **Vase,** Monnaie Du Pape, Money Plant, Sepia Patina, Ovoid, Signed R. Lalique, 9 In. | | 4148 |
| **Vase,** Mures, Blackberries, Opalescent, Flared Rim, c.1930, 7 ½ In. | 3600 to | 4236 |
| **Vase,** Orchidee, Orchid, Clear, Opalescent, Tapered, Purple, Blue, 6 ½ In. | | 976 |
| **Vase,** Orchidee, Orchid, Opalescent Flowers, 6 ½ x 8 In. | | 540 |
| **Vase,** Perroquet, Parrot, Flowering Branches, Frosted, 9 ½ In. | | 460 |
| **Vase,** Perruches, Parakeets, Red, Yellow, Molded R. Lalique, 1919, 10 x 8 ½ In. ....*illus* | | 4688 |
| **Vase,** Poissons, School Of Fish, Amber, Footed, R. Lalique France, 9 ½ In. ....*illus* | | 4148 |

**Lalique,** Vase, Charmilles, Overlapping Leaves, Gray, Molded, Impressed R. Lalique, c.1926, 14 In.
$3,068

Brunk Auctions

**Lalique,** Vase, Courges, Pears, Blue, Bulbous, Teardrop, Signed, Lalique, France, 7 ½ In.
$15,405

James D. Julia Auctioneers

L

**Lalique,** Vase, Domremy, Thistles, Smoky Gray, Orange Patina, R. Lalique, 1926, 8 ¼ In.
$1,625

Rago Arts & Auction Center

This is an edited listing of current prices. Visit Kovels.com to check thousands of prices from previous years and sign up for free information on trends, tips, reproductions, marks, and more.

# LALIQUE

**Lalique,** Vase, Formose, Swirling Carp, Amber, Molded R. Lalique, 1924, 6 ½ x 6 In.
**$6,875**

Rago Arts & Auction Center

**Lalique,** Vase, Perruches, Parakeets, Red, Yellow, Molded R. Lalique, 1919, 10 x 8 ½ In.
**$4,688**

Rago Arts & Auction Center

**Lalique,** Vase, Poissons, School Of Fish, Amber, Footed, R. Lalique France, 9 ½ In.
**$4,148**

James D. Julia Auctioneers

---

**TIP**

*A small chip in a glass goblet or vase can be ground off by a glass-repair expert, but there is little that can be done for cracks.*

---

| | |
|---|---:|
| **Vase,** Poseidon, Seahorses, Aqua, Label, Lalique, Paris, Fitted Box, 11 ½ x 14 In. ...............*illus* | 2091 |
| **Vase,** Rampillon, Cabochons & Flowers, Opalescent, Green, Etched R. Lalique, 5 In. ...........*illus* | 1422 |
| **Vase,** Renes, Antelope, Curling Horns, Leaves, Opalescent Foot, 4 ⅞ In. ................................ | 2310 |
| **Vase,** Ronces, Briars, Intertwining, Emerald Green, Molded, Marked, 9 ½ In. ...............*illus* | 11210 |
| **Vase,** Ronces, Thorny Branches, Short Neck, Molded, France, 1921, 9 ¼ In. ......................... | 800 |
| **Vase,** Saint Francois, Finches On Branches, Cone Shape, Flared Rim, c.1930, 6 ½ x 7 In. ......... | 3800 |
| **Vase,** Sandrift, Molded, Frosted, Etched Signature, 8 x 6 In. .................................................. | 265 |
| **Vase,** Sauge, Sage Leaves, Frosted Amber, Leaves, Bulbous Base, Narrow Neck, 10 In. ............... | 8625 |
| **Vase,** Sauge, Sage Leaves, Green Patina, Pear Shape, Etched R. Lalique, 10 In. ........................ | 1422 |
| **Vase,** Sauterelles, Grasshoppers, Frosted Glass, Signed, Box, 10 ¾ In. ................................... | 2214 |
| **Vase,** Six Figures Et Masques, 6 Nudes & Masks, Frosted, Oval, 9 ½ In. ................................. | 1534 |
| **Vase,** Tanega, Green Leaf, Frosted, Clear, Tapered, Molded Leaves, 14 ½ In. ........................... | 4780 |
| **Vase,** Tanzania, Zebras, Black Glass, c.1965, 8 ½ In. ........................................................... | 3750 |
| **Vase,** Tourbillons, Whirlwind, Molded Swirls, Cobalt Blue, Etched Lalique, France, 8 x 7 In. ....... | 5700 |
| **Vase,** Tulipes, Tulips, Molded Opalescent Glass, Round, Marcilhac, c.1930, 8 ¼ In. ................ | 3125 |
| **Vase,** Turquoise, Foraging Deer, Leaves, Bushes, 6 ⅝ x 5 ½ In. ........................................... | 748 |
| **Wine Cooler,** Clos Sainte-Odile, Woman & Grapevines, Signed R. Lalique, c.1925, 8 ½ In. .......... | 1750 |

---

**LAMPS** of every type, from the early oil-burning Betty and Phoebe lamps to the recent electric lamps with glass or beaded shades, interest collectors. Fuels used in lamps changed through the years; whale oil (1800–40), camphene (1828), Argand (1830), lard (1833–63), turpentine and alcohol (1840s), gas (1850–79), kerosene (1860), and electricity (1879) are the most common. Other lamps are listed by manufacturer or type of material.

| | |
|---|---:|
| **Aladdin,** B-63, Kerosene, Clear Short Lincoln Drape ............................................................ | 4600 |
| **Aladdin,** Blue Moonstone, Short Lincoln Drape.................................................................... | 300 |
| **Aladdin,** Electric, G-79, Rooster, Clear, c.1936.................................................................... | 3900 |
| **Aladdin,** G-16, Gowned Lady, Flowers Around Neck, Green ................................................... | 4500 |
| **Aladdin,** G-79, Rooster, Clear, 1936................................................................................... | 3900 |
| **Aladdin,** Kerosene, B-63, Short Lincoln Drape, Clear Glass.................................................... | 4600 |
| **Alpine,** Rush, Combination, Candle Socket, Curved Handle, Twisted Stem, Iron, 9 ¼ In.............. | 413 |
| **Argand,** 2-Light, Gilt Bronze, 2-Tier Prisms, Flower Stem, B. Gardiner, c.1835, 25 In................. | 1375 |
| **Argand,** Bronze, Etched, Frosted Flared Shade, c.1850, 16 ½ In., Pair...................................... | 240 |
| **Argand,** Bronze, Patinated, Multifunctional, 13 ½ x 5 ½ In. ................................................. | 1830 |
| **Astral,** Brass, Frosted Shade, Brilliant Meteor Brenner, R. Ditmar, Wien, c.1825, 32 In., Pair....*illus* | 5079 |
| **Astral,** Marble, Brass, Prisms, Glass Shade, Stepped Base, c.1850, 28 In. ................................. | 563 |
| **Bouillotte,** Brass Tole, Painted, 20th Century, 26 ½ x 15 In. ................................................. | 168 |
| **Bradley & Hubbard Lamps** are included in the Bradley & Hubbard category. | |
| **Chandelier,** 1-Light, Brass, Grapes, Leaves, Crosses, 43 x 12 In............................................... | 360 |
| **Chandelier,** 2-Light, Arts & Crafts, Slag Glass, Monk Head Design, Verdigris, 14 x 19 In............. | 293 |
| **Chandelier,** 2-Light, Glass Rosettes, Brass, Barovier Style, Murano, 1930s, 15 In. Diam. ............. | 3125 |
| **Chandelier,** 3-Light, Art Glass, Amber, Muller Freres, c.1925, 33 In. ....................................... | 861 |
| **Chandelier,** 3-Light, Bronze, Lantern Shape, Hexagon, 32 In.................................................. | 600 |
| **Chandelier,** 3-Light, Bronze, Spherical, Swans, Pinecone, 17 In.............................................. | 1968 |
| **Chandelier,** 3-Light, Cranberry Glass, Bell Shape, Folded Rim, Chains, c.1830, 24 x 12 In.......... | 2760 |
| **Chandelier,** 3-Light, Gilt, Patinated Metal, Urn Shape, Applied Swans, 18 x 17 In. ..................... | 2125 |
| **Chandelier,** 3-Light, Iron, Lantern, Glass Shade, Copper, 1890s, 33 x 14 In. ......................*illus* | 649 |
| **Chandelier,** 3-Light, Raised Flowers, Sand Filled Center, Green, 19th Century, 15 In. ................ | 540 |
| **Chandelier,** 3-Light, Tin, Green, 13 In............................................................................... | 1020 |
| **Chandelier,** 3-Light, Tole, Gilt Stencil, Reflective Shades, Drip Pans, c.1840, 18 x 16 ½ In. ......... | 2460 |
| **Chandelier,** 4-Light, Antler, Caribou, 39 In......................................................................... | 813 |
| **Chandelier,** 4-Light, Brass, Prism, Ribbed Glass Stem, 20th Century, 22 x 13 In. ...................... | 584 |
| **Chandelier,** 4-Light, Copper, Patina, Slag Glass, Guanine & Hilarity, c.1905, 31 x 21 In............. | 22500 |
| **Chandelier,** 4-Light, Cut Glass, Gilt Metal, Louis XVI, 37 x 25 In............................................ | 1063 |
| **Chandelier,** 4-Light, Gilt Metal, Empire Style, Clear Drop Prisms, France, 18 x 21 In. ................ | 250 |
| **Chandelier,** 4-Light, Metal, Ethan Allen, 28 x 24 In.............................................................. | 120 |
| **Chandelier,** 4-Light, Metal, Secessionist, Glass, 3 Parts, Hammered, Austria, c.1900, 46 In. ........ | 1590 |
| **Chandelier,** 4-Light, Silver Plate, Regency Style, Round Canopy, J.E. Caldwell, c.1900, 20 In. ...... | 2988 |
| **Chandelier,** 4-Light, Wood, Mermaid, Antlers, Chains, Black Forest, 41 x 40 In. ....................... | 9375 |
| **Chandelier,** 4-Light, Wood, Woman, Antlers, Gesso, Lusterweibchen, 20 x 27 In. ...............*illus* | 2100 |
| **Chandelier,** 5-Light, Brass, Busts, Angels, Opalescent Coin Dot Shades, 36 x 30 In., Pair............ | 2952 |
| **Chandelier,** 5-Light, Gilt Bronze, Neoclassical Style, Frosted Glass Flame Shades, 39 x 25 In...... | 922 |
| **Chandelier,** 5-Light, Gilt Metal, Leaf Standard, Petal Candlecups, 28 x 20 In. ........................... | 598 |
| **Chandelier,** 5-Light, Gilt Metal, Louis XVI Style, Beaded Glass, c.1950, 34 x 15 In. ................... | 563 |
| **Chandelier,** 5-Light, Glass Clear Prisms, Chains, Scroll Candlearms, 23 x 25 In. ........................ | 281 |
| **Chandelier,** 5-Light, Iron, Art Deco, Pierced Corona, Hammered Canopy, 49 x 25 In.................. | 984 |

| | |
|---|---|
| **Chandelier,** 5-Light, Iron, Pigtail Hanger, Twisted Shaft, Candlecups, c.1830, 30 x 21 In. ............ | 2370 |
| **Chandelier,** 5-Light, Venetian Glass, Blue Flowers, 33 x 29 In. ..................................................... | 3438 |
| **Chandelier,** 6-Light, Brass, Dutch Baroque Style, 17 x 20 In. ........................................................ | 960 |
| **Chandelier,** 6-Light, Cast Glass, Chromed Steel, Murano, Italy, 12 ½ x 30 ½ In. ............................ | 2000 |
| **Chandelier,** 6-Light, Copper, Arts & Crafts, Hammered, Slag Glass Panels, Chain, 15 x 16 In. ...... | 748 |
| **Chandelier,** 6-Light, Crystal Swags, Silvered Metal Frame, c.1930, 40 x 20 In. ....................*illus* | 1020 |
| **Chandelier,** 6-Light, Cut Glass, Georgian, Prism Hung, Glass Bead Swags, 44 In. ........................ | 1968 |
| **Chandelier,** 6-Light, Gilt Bronze, Louis XVI Style, 3 Caryatids, Leafy Swags, Rosettes, 24 In. ....... | 2125 |
| **Chandelier,** 6-Light, Gilt Bronze, Louis XVI Style, Crystal Basket, Prism Swags, c.1915, 26 x 19 In. .. | 1968 |
| **Chandelier,** 6-Light, Gilt Metal Bands, 4 Tiers, Wedding Cake Shape, c.1900, 29 x 24 In. ............. | 5312 |
| **Chandelier,** 6-Light, Gilt Metal, Hot Air Balloon Shape, Glass Beads, Prisms, 27 x 112 In. ........... | 861 |
| **Chandelier,** 6-Light, Gilt Metal, Neoclassical, Glass, Prism, Beaded, Sweden, 36 x 24 In. ............. | 422 |
| **Chandelier,** 6-Light, Gilt, Enamel, Urn, Ball Finial, Cornucopia Branches, Masks, 27 x 24 In. ..... | 2000 |
| **Chandelier,** 6-Light, Gilt, Metal, Empire Style, Patina, Chain, 30 x 20 In. .................................. | 281 |
| **Chandelier,** 6-Light, Glass, Georgian Style, Prisms, 31 x 27 In. .................................................. | 313 |
| **Chandelier,** 6-Light, Glass, Porcelain, Metal, Flowers, Multicolor, 28 x 23 In. ............................ | 938 |
| **Chandelier,** 6-Light, Iron, Tudor Style, Leaf & Vine Decoration, 34 x 32 In. ............................... | 173 |
| **Chandelier,** 6-Light, Iron, Twisted, 19th Century, 8 x 20 In. ..................................................... | 900 |
| **Chandelier,** 6-Light, Louis XV Style, Urn Standard, Flowers, Putti, c.1900, 23 x 20 In. ................. | 1353 |
| **Chandelier,** 6-Light, Murano Glass, Grape Cluster Shades, Metal Frame, c.1950, 28 x 28 In. ....... | 3936 |
| **Chandelier,** 6-Light, Rolled Sheet Iron, Pigtail Forged Hanger, Downswept Arms, 19 x 30 In. ...... | 1422 |
| **Chandelier,** 6-Light, Urn Shape Shaft, Scrolling Arms, Crystal Swags, 34 x 26 In. ........................ | 780 |
| **Chandelier,** 8-Light, Baroque Style, Wood, Carved, Painted, Gilt, Electrified, 58 In. ............*illus* | 1845 |
| **Chandelier,** 8-Light, Brass, Cast, Molded Leaves, Tassel Finial, c.1900, 24 x 20 In. ..................... | 461 |
| **Chandelier,** 8-Light, Bronze, French Empire Style, Arms & Chains, Alabaster Shade, 36 In. ......... | 1560 |
| **Chandelier,** 8-Light, Bronze, Louis XV Style, Porcelain, Painted Couple, 33 x 26 In. ................... | 1722 |
| **Chandelier,** 8-Light, Bronze, Molded Gilt Bronze Arms, Chains, 33 ½ In. ................................... | 3444 |
| **Chandelier,** 8-Light, Cast Iron, Antler, Deer, Shaft, 34 ½ In. ..................................................... | 517 |
| **Chandelier,** 8-Light, Chrome Plated, Sputnik, Blown Glass Spirals, 49 ¼ In. ............................... | 799 |
| **Chandelier,** 8-Light, Cut Glass, Faceted, Teardrops, Pendalogues, 1900s, 35 x 26 In. ................. | 1353 |
| **Chandelier,** 8-Light, Enamel, Brass, Gilt Leaves, Phoenix Birds, c.1915, 42 x 23 In. ............*illus* | 5166 |
| **Chandelier,** 8-Light, Gilt Bronze, Neoclassical Style, Cone Basket, Figures, 50 x 26 In. .............. | 6765 |
| **Chandelier,** 8-Light, Gilt, Palm Frond, Leaf Shape Cups, Crystal Beads, Swags, 38 In. ............... | 3025 |
| **Chandelier,** 8-Light, Glass, Round Shade, Flanking Candlearms, 46 In. ...................................... | 1952 |
| **Chandelier,** 8-Light, Iron, Rope Twist, Spanish Colonial, Octagonal Frame, 44 x 31 In. .............. | 1045 |
| **Chandelier,** 8-Light, Iron, Wrought, 4 Bar Supports, 50 x 37 In. ............................................... | 1625 |
| **Chandelier,** 8-Light, Wrought Metal, Composition, Italy, 43 x 50 In. ......................................... | 600 |
| **Chandelier,** 9-Light, Gilt, Bronze, Empire Style, Anthemion Corona, 1800s, 28 x 27 In. ............. | 3107 |
| **Chandelier,** 9-Light, Gilt, Empire Style, Pierced, Patinated Metal, 31 x 23 In. ........................... | 875 |
| **Chandelier,** 10-Light, Brass, Cut Glass, Cherubs, Grape Prisms, Green Leaves, 51 ½ In. ............. | 738 |
| **Chandelier,** 10-Light, Tole, Scroll Arms, Leaves On Vine, Cut Glass Buds, 36 x 30 In. ................. | 768 |
| **Chandelier,** 12-Light, Brass, Baroque Style, Baluster Turned Standard, 27 x 27 In. .................... | 1200 |
| **Chandelier,** 12-Light, Bronze, 4 Cherubim, C-Scroll Supports, Acanthine Shades, 48 In. ............ | 1875 |
| **Chandelier,** 12-Light, Bronze, Gilt, Ribbons, Twisted Rods, Urn Shape Base, 52 x 32 In. ............. | 8125 |
| **Chandelier,** 12-Light, Chromed Steel, Sputnik, White Glass Globes, 1960s, 24 In. ..................... | 688 |
| **Chandelier,** 12-Light, Cut Glass, Waterford Style, Cut Bowl, Ball Finial, Prisms, 51 x 33 In. ........ | 1045 |
| **Chandelier,** 12-Light, Gilt Bronze, Crystal Stem, Beads, Swags, Drop Prisms, 42 In. .................. | 2178 |
| **Chandelier,** 12-Light, Glass, 2 Tiers, Scrolls, Beaded Branches, Prisms, c.1965, 35 x 33 In. ........ | 469 |
| **Chandelier,** 12-Light, Glass, Georgian Style, Prisms, 25 x 32 In. ............................................... | 250 |
| **Chandelier,** 13-Light, Brass, Cut Crystal, Scroll, Bowl, Prisms, 31 ½ In. .................................... | 1015 |
| **Chandelier,** 15-Light, Belle Epoque, 3-Part Standard, Scrollwork, 38 x 28 In. ........................... | 2460 |
| **Chandelier,** 15-Light, Gilt Bronze, Louis XVI Style, Clear Prisms, 2 Tiers, 48 x 31 In. ................. | 11250 |
| **Chandelier,** 16-Light, Gilt Bronze, Belle Epoque, Pinecone Finial, 36 x 35 In. ........................... | 7995 |
| **Chandelier,** 16-Light, Gilt Metal, Beads, Scroll Branches, Basket Shape, c.1970, 40 x 30 In. ....... | 500 |
| **Chandelier,** 85-Light, Rody Graumans, Bulbs, Wires, Connectors, Droog, 1993, 35 In., Pair....*illus* | 3000 |
| **Chandelier,** Brass Frame, Lucite Prisms, Ribbon, Inverted Arch Form, 21 x 19 In. ...................... | 354 |
| **Chandelier,** Bronze Canopy, Art Deco, Frame, Etched Glass Panels, c.1935, 60 x 24 In. ............. | 5335 |
| **Chandelier,** Empire, Cut Glass Beaded Chains, Prisms, Brass Leaf Mount, Tent & Bag, 38 In. ...... | 1664 |
| **Chandelier,** Gold Colored, 100 Plus Burst Light, Emil Stejnar, 16 x 26 In. .................................. | 7625 |
| **Chandelier,** Leaded Glass, Fleur-De-Lis, Gold, Duffner & Kimberly, c.1910, 14 x 23 In. .............. | 1375 |
| **Chandelier,** Nickel, Brushed, Art Deco, Perforations, Fronds, Etched Glass, 1930s, 30 x 26 In. ..... | 1220 |
| **Chandelier,** Wood, Woman, Shield, Antlers, Paint, Germany, c.1860, 32 x 28 In. ........................ | 2000 |
| **Combination,** Betty, Candle Socket, Iron, Shaft, Ball Finial, Brass Rosette, 3 Legs, 17 ¾ In. ......... | 443 |
| **Electric,** 2-Light, Directoire Style, Bronze, Bowknot & Tassel, Backplate, 17 x 8 In., Pair............ | 430 |
| **Electric,** 2-Light, Empire Style, Green Ground, Gilt, 19 In., Pair ............................................... | 660 |
| **Electric,** 2-Light, Reverse Painted, 6-Panel Lighted Base, Autumnal Scene, 19 x 23 In. ............... | 891 |

**Lalique,** Vase, Poseidon, Seahorses, Aqua, Label, Lalique, Paris, Fitted Box, 11 ½ x 14 In.
**$2,091**

New Orleans Auction Galleries, Inc.

**Lalique,** Vase, Rampillon, Cabochons & Flowers, Opalescent, Green, Etched R. Lalique, 5 In.
**$1,422**

James D. Julia Auctioneers

**Lalique,** Vase, Ronces, Briars, Intertwining, Emerald Green, Molded, Marked, 9 ½ In.
**$11,210**

Brunk Auctions

L

**Lamp,** Astral, Brass, Frosted Shade, Brilliant Meteor Brenner, R. Ditmar, Wien, c.1825, 32 In., Pair
$5,079

Neal Auction Co.

**Lamp,** Chandelier, 3-Light, Iron, Lantern, Glass Shade, Copper, 1890s, 33 x 14 In.
$649

Brunk Auctions

**Lamp,** Chandelier, 4-Light, Wood, Woman, Antlers, Gesso, Lusterweibchen, 20 x 27 In.
$2,100

The Stein Auction Company

**Lamp,** Chandelier, 6-Light, Crystal Swags, Silvered Metal Frame, c.1930, 40 x 20 In.
$1,020

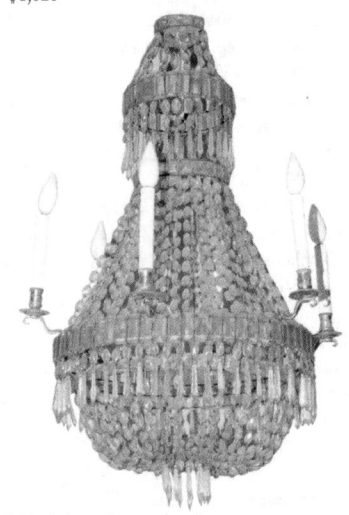

DuMouchelles Art Gallery

**Lamp,** Chandelier, 8-Light, Baroque Style, Wood, Carved, Painted, Gilt, Electrified, 58 In.
$1,845

New Orleans Auction Galleries, Inc.

**Lamp,** Chandelier, 8-Light, Enamel, Brass, Gilt Leaves, Phoenix Birds, c.1915, 42 x 23 In.
$5,166

New Orleans Auction Galleries, Inc.

**Lamp,** Chandelier, 85-Light, Rody Graumans, Bulbs, Wires, Connectors, Droog, 1993, 35 In., Pair
$3,000

Rago Arts & Auction Center

**Lamp,** Electric, Angelo Lelli, Green Domed Shade, Arredoluce, Italy, 1950s, 14 x 13 In.
$5,313

Los Angeles Modern Auctions (LAMA)

**Lamp,** Electric, Arts & Crafts, Oak, Brass, Leaded Glass, c.1910, 19½ x 14 In.
$1,000

Rago Arts & Auction Center

L

| | | |
|---|---|---|
| **Electric,** 2-Light, Slag Glass Panels, Gilt Metal Frame, Glass Paneled Base | | 270 |
| **Electric,** 3-Light, Glass, Opal, Blue, Green, Ruffled Shade, Rainbow, J. Lotton, 22 In. | | 259 |
| **Electric,** 3-Light, Spelter, Art Nouveau, Nymph, On Fish, Flower Shape Shades, 35 x 18 In. | | 633 |
| **Electric,** 5-Light, Bronze, Seminude Woman, Art Glass Shade, After Moreau, 43 In. | | 1080 |
| **Electric,** 11-Light, Brass, Spiral Ribbon, Round Marble Base, 64½ x 15 In., Pair | | 5937 |
| **Electric,** A. Hart, Leaded Glass, Flowers, Cone Shape Shade, Blue, Yellow, Green, 18 x 23 In. | | 3555 |
| **Electric,** Acrylic, Chromed Steel, Aluminum, Lobed Petals, Rougier, Canada, 1970s, 35 x 19 In. | | 938 |
| **Electric,** Agate Disc, Bronze Cattails, Landscape Form Base, 35 x 9½ In. | | 1837 |
| **Electric,** Angelo Lelli, Green Domed Shade, Arredoluce, Italy, 1950s, 14 x 13 In. | *illus* | 5313 |
| **Electric,** Archimede Seguso, Blown Glass, Ribbed Twist, Mauve, Italy, 28½ In., Pair | | 1470 |
| **Electric,** Arco, Achille & Pier Giacomo Castiglioni, Chrome Shade, Flos, 1962, 96 x 88 In. | | 1063 |
| **Electric,** Arco, Polished Steel, Curved Stem, Dome Shade, Marble Base, Flos, 1960s, 72 In. | | 518 |
| **Electric,** Arredoluce, Steel, Chromed Shade, Enamel Pole, Marble Base, 68 x 12 In. | | 2500 |
| **Electric,** Arredoluce, Triennale, 3 Adjustable Arms, Nickeled Brass, Tripod, 76 In. | | 5000 |
| **Electric,** Art Deco, Figural, Kneeling Woman, Holding Glass Vase, Metal, Marble, 15 x 10 In. | | 540 |
| **Electric,** Art Deco, Figural, Woman, Amber Glass Sphere, White Metal, c.1910, 16 x 4 In. | | 150 |
| **Electric,** Art Moderne, Rock Crystal, Graduated Sphere, Plinth Base, 19 x 5 In., Pair | | 2390 |
| **Electric,** Art Nouveau, Nautilus Shade, Bronzed Reclining Nude, Signed C. Bonnefond, 12 In. | | 1534 |
| **Electric,** Art Nouveau, Seminude Woman, Alabaster Shade, Patinated Metal, c.1910, 21 In. | | 738 |
| **Electric,** Arteluce, Balance Shade, Disc Foot, Italy, c.1950, 58 In. | | 1875 |
| **Electric,** Arts & Crafts, 8 Panes, Striated Caramel Slag Glass, Cast Metal, 25 x 20 In. | | 492 |
| **Electric,** Arts & Crafts, Oak Base, Copper, Green Slag Glass Shade, Curved Support, 16 x 7 In. | | 210 |
| **Electric,** Arts & Crafts, Oak, Brass, Leaded Glass, c.1910, 19½ x 14 In. | *illus* | 1000 |
| **Electric,** Arts & Crafts, Pierced Metal Shade, Patinated Copper, Tapered, c.1915, 22 x 13 In. | | 125 |
| **Electric,** B. Lacroix, Steel, Brass, Red, Blue, White, Rectilinear Spiral Base, 63¾ In. | | 6250 |
| **Electric,** Barovier & Toso, Blown Glass, White, Metal, Wood, Opaline, Italy, 36 In., Pair | | 1464 |
| **Electric,** Barovier & Toso, Bright Blue, Spherical, Bronzed Metal, Wheat, 22 In., Pair | | 1194 |
| **Electric,** Beaded Gilt Metal Basket, Glass Fruit, Czechoslovakia, c.1930, 10 In. | *illus* | 660 |
| **Electric,** Bellova, Acid Etched, Gold Design, Flowers, Scrolls, Czechoslovakia, 10 In. | *illus* | 1540 |
| **Electric,** Bellova, Black Medallion, Pink Flowers, Alternating Blue & Opal Bands, 21 In. | | 115 |
| **Electric,** Bisque, Figurine, Masquerade, Couple, 1800s, 24 In., Pair | *illus* | 805 |
| **Electric,** Bitossi, Modernist Style Fish, Multicolor, Terra-Cotta Ground, c.1950, 39 x 6½ In. | | 240 |
| **Electric,** Black Forest, Carved Wood Bear Support, c.1900, 17 In. | | 234 |
| **Electric,** Blown Glass, Blue, Metal, Lucite, Italy, 25 In., Pair | | 2440 |
| **Electric,** Boudoir, Cut Glass, Domed Shade, Hanging Prisms, c.1910, 19 In. | *illus* | 625 |
| **Electric,** Brass, Black Enameled Metal, Silk Shade, 1950s, 40 x 19 In., Pair | | 1375 |
| **Electric,** Brass, Leaf Shape Shade, Square Stepped Base, 20½ x 7¼ In. | | 660 |
| **Electric,** Bronze Oak Leaf, Acorn Base, Floral Mushroom Shade, Etched Glass, 1900s, 20 In. | | 300 |
| **Electric,** Bronze, Cloisonne, Japan, c.1910, 75 x 33 In. | *illus* | 832 |
| **Electric,** Bronze, Cold Painted, Man, Headdress, Rifle, Teepee, Tree, 24¾ x 8 In. | | 2091 |
| **Electric,** Bronze, Gilt, Blown Glass, Moorish Designs, 3-Footed, c.1850, 28 In. | | 2952 |
| **Electric,** Bronze, Orchid Petal Shade, Stem Relief, Shaped Stem, Stepped Base, 1920s, 15 In. | | 891 |
| **Electric,** Bronze, P. Tereszczuk, Loie Fuller Dancing, Signed, Austria, 15¾ In. | | 4629 |
| **Electric,** Bronze, Patinated, Cloisonne, Vase Shape Standard, Opaque Glass Shade, 70 x 15 In. | | 1135 |
| **Electric,** C. Jere, Brass, Rectangular Base & Shade Design, 34 x 21 In. | | 1750 |
| **Electric,** Casella Lighting Co., Brass, Rectangular Column, Marked, 72½ x 11½ In. | | 520 |
| **Electric,** Ceiling, Flush Mounted, Gold Tone, 3-Tiered Sockets, Blown Glass, 1960s, 18 In. | | 984 |
| **Electric,** Cenedese, Blown Glass, Bulb Shape, Smooth, Pink To Coral, 32½ In., Pair | | 1163 |
| **Electric,** Ceramic, Quail, Tree, 24 In., Pair | | 90 |
| **Electric,** Charles Lotton, White Flowers, Green Leaves, Iridescent Glass, Wavy Shade, 23 In. | | 3335 |
| **Electric,** Cold-Painted Metal, Scribe, Courtyard, Carpet, Austria, c.1914, 13½ x 6½ In. | | 2952 |
| **Electric,** Crystal Urn Shape, Bronze Dore Handles, Base, Cap, Cut Crystal Finial, 40 In. | | 127 |
| **Electric,** D. Lotton, Glass, Blue, Pink Flowers, Fern Leaves, 12¾ In. | | 345 |
| **Electric,** David Weeks, Tripod 303, Black, Adjustable, 3 Shades, 73 x 27 In. | | 2327 |
| **Electric,** Desk, Art Nouveau, Bronze, Flaring Scalloped Shade, 15 In. | | 185 |
| **Electric,** Desk, Opal Glass Shade, Red Looping, Silvered Bronze Stem & Foot, 15 In., Pair | | 2370 |
| **Electric,** Desk, W. A. Forge, Pinecone Design, Stepped Base, 1920s, 16 x 18 In. | | 688 |
| **Electric,** Dino Martens, White, Brown, Stripe, Mezza Filligrana, Midcentury, 28 In. | | 398 |
| **Electric,** Domed Shade, Amber Glass Border, 4 Buttressed Handles, c.1915, 19 x 16 In. | | 640 |
| **Electric,** Duffner & Kimberly, Leaded Glass, Owl's Head Band, Green, Amber, Bronze, 22 In. | | 5096 |
| **Electric,** Duffner & Kimberly, Leaded Glass, Purple, Green Slag, Shield Shape Border, 13 In. | | 415 |
| **Electric,** Duffner & Kimberly, Leaded, Glass, 4-Sided, Green Fish Scale, Owl, 22 In. | | 3705 |
| **Electric,** Duffner & Kimberly, Leaded, Glass, Hanging, Green Striated Vine, 45 In. | | 5332 |
| **Electric,** Enameled Steel, Aluminum, Brass, Wiring, Angle, 1970s, 81 x 38 In. | | 2375 |
| **Electric,** Figural, Nude Woman, Bronze, Spelter, 3-Light, Stained Glass, c.1905, 57 In. | *illus* | 3900 |
| **Electric,** Floor, M. Gilmartin, Fir Wood, Curved, Glass Shade, 1984, 79 x 50 In. | *illus* | 2250 |

**Lamp,** Electric, Beaded Gilt Metal Basket, Glass Fruit, Czechoslovakia, c.1930, 10 In.
$660

DuMouchelles Art Gallery

**Lamp,** Electric, Bellova, Acid Etched, Gold Design, Flowers, Scrolls, Czechoslovakia, 10 In.
$1,540

James D. Julia Auctioneers

**Lamp,** Electric, Bisque, Figurine, Masquerade, Couple, 1800s, 24 In., Pair
$805

Cottone Auctions

343

**Lamp,** Electric, Boudoir, Cut Glass, Domed Shade, Hanging Prisms, c.1910, 19 In. $625

Rago Arts & Auction Center

**Lamp,** Electric, Bronze, Cloisonne, Japan, c.1910, 75 x 33 In. $832

Rago Arts & Auction Center

**Lamp,** Electric, Figural, Nude Woman, Bronze, Spelter, 3-Light, Stained Glass, c.1905, 57 In. $3,900

DuMouchelles Art Gallery

| | |
|---|---|
| **Electric,** Floor, Mahogany, Draped Woman, Finger Shade, Continental, c.1890, 68 In. | 584 |
| **Electric,** Floor, Mermaid, Composition, Fringe Shade, Italia Cruise Ship, 60 x 49 In. | 1500 |
| **Electric,** Floor, Queen Anne Style, Chinoiserie Decoration, 20th Century, 64 x 16 In. | 216 |
| **Electric,** Floor, Victorian, Brass, Turned Center Column, Green Marble Base, 59 x 16 In. | 175 |
| **Electric,** Francois Raoul Larche, Loie Fuller, Gilt Bronze, c.1900, 17 ½ x 9 In. | 22140 |
| **Electric,** G. Aulenti, Pipistrello, White Enameled Metal, Lobed Plastic Shade, 28 x 22 In. | 875 |
| **Electric,** G. Magnusson Grossman, Enameled Steel & Aluminum, Tripod Base, 1950s, 50 In. | 10625 |
| **Electric,** G. Nelson, Bubble, Pendant, Sprayed Fiberglass, Round Metal Frame, c.1960, 25 In. | 62 |
| **Electric,** Gambone, Ceramic, Blue, White Threads, Italy, 1960s, 31 In. | 3000 |
| **Electric,** Gilt Metal Mounted, Porcelain, Green, Yellow, Flowers, 29 In., Pair | 3198 |
| **Electric,** Glass Shade, Blue, Flowers, Signed Charles Lotton, 26 In. | 2962 |
| **Electric,** Glass Shade, Red, Flowers, Signed Charles Lotton, 26 In. | 4147 |
| **Electric,** Glass, Nickeled Brass, Metal, Vase Shape, Sweden, 1960s, 14 ½ x 5 In., Pair | 1792 |
| **Electric,** Gold Iridescent Shade, King Tut Pattern, Bronze Art Nouveau Base, Leaf Foot, 19 In. | 3259 |
| **Electric,** Gone With The Wind, Brass Base, Ball Feet, Milk Glass Cover, Flowers, 23 In. | 144 |
| **Electric,** Gone With The Wind, Brass Base, Round Glass Hurricane, Milk Glass, 23 In. | 92 |
| **Electric,** Gone With The Wind, Floral Transfer, Brass Leaf Cast, Hurricane Shade, 20 In. | 12 |
| **Electric,** Gorham Metal Base, Domed Shade, Leaded Glass, Roses, Vines, 21 In. ....._illus_ | 1215 |
| **Electric,** Gorham, Leaded Glass, Daffodils, Yellow, Swirled Bronze, Knotted Stem, 24 In. | 8295 |
| **Electric,** Green Shade, 2 Candlearms, 28 In. | 60 |
| **Electric,** Grosfeld House, Ceramic, Black, Seated Classical Figure, Gilt, 32 x 8 ⅕ In., Pair | 854 |
| **Electric,** Hall Lantern, Aesthetic, Gilt Bronze, Globe Shade, Scrolled Chains, 33 x 13 In. | 492 |
| **Electric,** Hanging, Cranberry Coin Dot, Victorian, 14 x 8 In. ....._illus_ | 96 |
| **Electric,** Hanging, Green Slag Glass, 4 Panels, Copper Frame, c.1920, 8 x 7 In. | 115 |
| **Electric,** Hanging, Suess, Leaded Glass, Geometric Panels, Colors, Brass, 49 In. ....._illus_ | 593 |
| **Electric,** Hollywood Regency, Giltwood, Scrollwork Shape, Italy, c.1950, 16 x 26 In., Pair | 799 |
| **Electric,** I. Noguchi, Parchment Shade, 3 Tapered Cherry Supports, Knoll, 16 x 7 In. | 1188 |
| **Electric,** Ikora Shade, Oil Spot Clouds, Mottled Tan, Bronze Base, Austria, 21 In. ....._illus_ | 3259 |
| **Electric,** Imari Style Urn, Multicolor, Red, Green, White, Dragon, Bronze Base, 31 In., Pair | 1476 |
| **Electric,** Industrial Style, 2-Light, Metal, Domed Shade, Hanging, 50 x 34 In. | 813 |
| **Electric,** Industrial Style, Metal, Wall Mounted, Reflector Shade, Expansion Arm, 25 x 20 In. | 344 |
| **Electric,** J. Adnet, Black Leather, Brass, Bamboo Design, Tripod, Paper Shade, 64 In., Pair | 11875 |
| **Electric,** J. Cook, Glass, Blue, Aurene, Pulled Swag, 18 In. | 403 |
| **Electric,** Jean Besnard, Ceramic, Brown, Orange, Linen Shade, France, 1930s, 17 x 10 In. ...._illus_ | 3250 |
| **Electric,** John Dickinson, Tree Shape, c.1975, 24 x 10 In. ....._illus_ | 5000 |
| **Electric,** John Morgan & Sons, Leaded Glass, Rose Flowers, Wilkinson Base, 29 In. ....._illus_ | 8888 |
| **Electric,** K. Springer, Sculpture, Brass, Block Base, Quarter Round Shade, 1970s, 24 In., Pair | 9375 |
| **Electric,** K. Versen, Copper, Nickel-Plated Brass, Angular, Frosted Glass Shade, 1930s, 14 In. | 3375 |
| **Electric,** Karl Springer, Blue, White, Faux Decoration, Midcentury, Shade, 27 ½ In. | 2583 |
| **Electric,** Karl Springer, Lucite, Square Mirror Base, Black Shades, 64 In., Pair | 9760 |
| **Electric,** Koch & Lowy, Floor, Brass, Adjustable, 1960s, 48 x 9 In., Pair | 1375 |
| **Electric,** Leaded Glass, Suess Green Ground, Poppies, 3-Light, 24 ¾ In. | 7110 |
| **Electric,** Leaded, Glass, Flowers, Red, Pink, Green, Acanthus Base, 29 ½ In. | 2099 |
| **Electric,** Louis XV Style, Lapis Lazuli, Gilt Bronze, Rocaille Scrollwork, 30 x 8 In., Pair | 6150 |
| **Electric,** Louis XV Style, Napoleon & Josephine Shade, Bronze Openwork, Rey, 28 In. | 875 |
| **Electric,** Lundberg Studios, Glass, Blue, Gold Pulled Feathers, Aurene, 15 ½ In. | 374 |
| **Electric,** M. Fantoni, Bronzed Steel, Glass, Italy, 1960s, 17 ½ x 8 In. | 1500 |
| **Electric,** Marble Corinthian Column, Composite Base, Dore, 47 In. | 288 |
| **Electric,** Mauser Bolt Action Rifle Attached To Base, Civil War Shade, c.1960, 66 In. | 123 |
| **Electric,** Mercury Glass, Tiered Column Standard, Domed Foot, 18 In., Pair | 1500 |
| **Electric,** Michael Adams, Marti Palmer, 4-Panel Leaded Glass Shade, Oswego, 1990s, 62 x 19 In. | 1375 |
| **Electric,** Mid-Century Modern, Egg Shape, White, 20 x 13 In. | 360 |
| **Electric,** Mid-Century Modern, Figural, Dancing Couple, c.1950, 24 x 36 In., Pair | 150 |
| **Electric,** Mid-Century Modern, Glass, Cone Shape Base, Painted, Textured, Clown, 36 ½ In. | 12 |
| **Electric,** Mid-Century Modern, Wood, Bottle Shape, Black Leather Base, Enamel, 34 In. | 98 |
| **Electric,** Miller Lamp Co., Openwork Shade, Blue Glass Panels, Iron Case, c.1930, 24 x 20 In. | 403 |
| **Electric,** Miller, Reverse Painted Glass, 23 x 18 In. | 540 |
| **Electric,** Modern, Wood, Plastic, Pillar Shape, 58 x 6 ½ In. | 240 |
| **Electric,** Moe Bridges, Reverse Painted Shade, Ocean, Palm Trees, Sunset, Black Base, 23 In. | 2126 |
| **Electric,** Murano Glass, Black, Gray, Teardrop Shape, Chromed Metal, 34 In. | 2688 |
| **Electric,** Murano Glass, Blue Sphere, Brassy Leaves, Blue Flowers, c.1950, 43 In. | 270 |
| **Electric,** Murano Glass, Blue, Gold Aventurine, Wheat Stalks, Metal, 22 In., Pair ....._illus_ | 976 |
| **Electric,** Murano Glass, White, Teardrop Shape, Chromed Metal, Silk Shades, 34 In. | 1216 |
| **Electric,** Murano, Blown Glass, Ribbed, Metal, 31 In., Pair | 1464 |
| **Electric,** Nova Art, Bakelite, Clear, Frosted Glass, Enameled Metal, Saturn Shape, 7 x 7 In. | 1188 |
| **Electric,** Nude Woman, Bronze, Crackle Glass Globe, Max LeVerrier, c.1925, 24 In. ....._illus_ | 3000 |

**Lamp,** Electric, Floor, M. Gilmartin, Fir Wood, Curved, Glass Shade, 1984, 79 x 50 In. $2,250

**Lamp,** Electric, Hanging, Suess, Leaded Glass, Geometric Panels, Colors, Brass, 49 In. $593

**Lamp,** Electric, John Dickinson, Tree Shape, c.1975, 24 x 10 In. $5,000

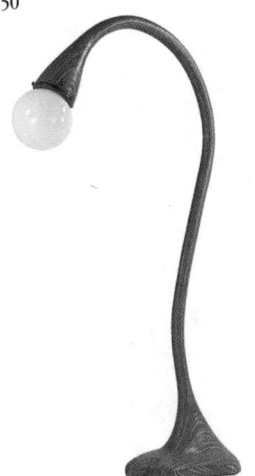

Rago Arts & Auction Center

James D. Julia Auctioneers

Los Angeles Modern Auctions (LAMA)

**Lamp,** Electric, Gorham Metal Base, Domed Shade, Leaded Glass, Roses, Vines, 21 In. $1,215

**Lamp,** Electric, Ikora Shade, Oil Spot Clouds, Mottled Tan, Bronze Base, Austria, 21 In. $3,259

**Lamp,** Electric, John Morgan & Sons, Leaded Glass, Rose Flowers, Wilkinson Base, 29 In. $8,888

James D. Julia Auctioneers

James D. Julia Auctioneers

James D. Julia Auctioneers

**Lamp,** Electric, Hanging, Cranberry Coin Dot, Victorian, 14 x 8 In. $96

**Lamp,** Electric, Jean Besnard, Ceramic, Brown, Orange, Linen Shade, France, 1930s, 17 x 10 In. $3,250

**Lamp,** Electric, Murano Glass, Blue, Gold Aventurine, Wheat Stalks, Metal, 22 In., Pair $976

DuMouchelles Art Gallery

Rago Arts & Auction Center

Palm Beach Modern Auctions

L

**Lamp,** Electric, Nude Woman, Bronze, Crackle Glass Globe, Max LeVerrier, c.1925, 24 In. $3,000

DuMouchelles Art Gallery

**Lamp,** Electric, P. Laszlo, Maria Kipp Shades, Royal Copenhagen, c.1946, 27 In., Pair $5,625

Los Angeles Modern Auctions (LAMA)

**Lamp,** Electric, Paul Evans, Cityscape, Brass, Chrome, Double Headed, Floor, 30 x 22 In. $1,708

Palm Beach Modern Auctions

**Lamp,** Electric, Pepe Mendoza, Brass, Leafy Stalk, Ceramic Inlays, 41 In. $4,514

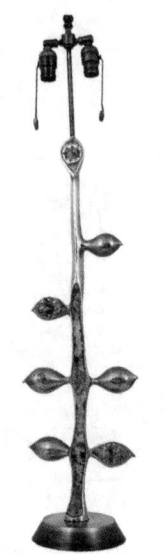

Palm Beach Modern Auctionsa

**Lamp,** Electric, Student, Plume & Atwood, 2-Light, Pink Shades, 1800s, 18 x 21 In. $2,990

Cottone Auctions

**Lamp,** Electric, Wilkinson, Flowers, Leaded Glass Shade, 29 x 22 In. $3,335

Cottone Auctions

**Lamp,** Electric, William Haines, Chinese Figures, Tree, 1960, 28 ½ In. $2,000

Los Angeles Modern Auctions (LAMA)

**Lamp,** Fluid, Frosted, Etched, Drop Prisms, Blue, White, Brass Pedestal, Marble Base, 26 In. $1,003

Conestoga Auction Co., Inc.

**Lamp,** Gasolier, 8-Light, Curved Arms, Etched Glass Shades, Electrified, c.1890, 30 In. $359

Neal Auction Co.

L

| | |
|---|---|
| Electric, Osten Kristiansson, Luxus, Adjustable Black Enameled Shade, Tripod, c.1960, 51 In. ... | 1722 |
| Electric, P. Laszlo, Maria Kipp Shades, Royal Copenhagen, c.1946, 27 In., Pair..................*illus* | 5625 |
| Electric, Parchment Shade, 3-Legged Support, Round Base, Mid 20th Century, 55 In.................. | 123 |
| Electric, Paul Evans, Cityscape, 40-In. Pedestal, 33 In. .................................................... | 726 |
| Electric, Paul Evans, Cityscape, Brass, Chrome, Double Headed, Floor, 30 x 22 In..............*illus* | 1708 |
| Electric, Paul Evans, Cityscape, Patchwork Column, Chrome & Brass Squares, 18 x 7 In........... | 531 |
| Electric, Peacock, Bronze, Glass, Oval Pierced Base, Fanned Beaded Tail, 17 x 16 In. ................. | 1150 |
| Electric, Pepe Mendoza, Brass, Leafy Stalk, Ceramic Inlays, 41 In.........................*illus* | 4514 |
| Electric, Pierre Cardin, Brass, Curled Base, France, 1970s, 29 x 16 In. ........................... | 594 |
| Electric, Pierre Casenove, Bronze, Bird, Gilt, Midcentury, France, 18 In. ........................... | 1952 |
| Electric, Pierre Casenove, Bronze, Gilt, Midcentury, France, 20 ½ x 5 In., Pair.................... | 3430 |
| Electric, Pittsburg Lamp Co., Dome Shade, Windmills, Lake, Iron Base, c.1920, 19 x 13 In........ | 230 |
| Electric, Pittsburgh, Reverse Painted Shade, Maple Leaves, Chipped Ice, Owl Base, 22 In........... | 4148 |
| Electric, Pittsburgh, Reverse Wave Domed Shade, Owl Metal Base, 1920s, 22 x 18 In.............. | 4375 |
| Electric, Plafonnier, Ceiling, Dome Shape, Cut Glass Drops, Gilt Floral Swags, 13 x 15 In......... | 250 |
| Electric, Porcelain, Figural Group, Man Wooing Woman, Painted, Footed, 20 x 6 ½ In. ................. | 52 |
| Electric, Porcelain, Painted, Globe Shade, Germany, 18 x 13 In................................ | 120 |
| Electric, Porcelain, Reticulated Brass Base, Squared Vase Shape, Figures, Chinese, 37 In......... | 587 |
| Electric, Poul Henningsen, Charlottenborg, Pendant, White, Midcentury, 16 x 26 In...... 643 to 793 | |
| Electric, Pricket Shape, Parcel Gilt, Carved Leaves, Tripod Base, Italy, 1800s, 67 In...................... | 1250 |
| Electric, Pricket, Ecclesiastical, Brass, Scrolls, Masks, Continental, c.1800, 32 In., Pair .............. | 360 |
| Electric, Puffy, Reverse Painted, Multicolor, White Metal Base, Bronze, 19 x 14 In. ....................... | 58 |
| Electric, Pukeberg, Cast Glass, Rectangular, Faceted, Travertine Base, 13 x 6 ¼ In., Pair............ | 750 |
| Electric, Ralph Lauren, Midcentury Modern, Chrome, Leather, Fiber Shade, 31 x 14 In. .............. | 253 |
| Electric, Renaissance Style, Giltwood, Carved, Fluted, Triangle Base, c.1940, 26 In., Pair ........... | 563 |
| Electric, Reverse Painted Domed Shade, Patinated Metal Frame, c.1920, 6 ½ In. ................. | 480 |
| Electric, Reverse Painted Shade, House On Lake, 3 Supports, 3-Part Platform Base, 23 In......... | 729 |
| Electric, Rock Crystal, Graduated Orbs, Silvered Metal Base, 26 In., Pair ........................ | 1815 |
| Electric, Rococo Style, Bronze Dore, 2-Light Candleholder, Marbleized Shade, 20 In. ................. | 213 |
| Electric, Rococo Style, Gilt Carved, Dolphin Base, Floor, 20th Century, 61 x 13 In. ................ | 330 |
| Electric, Roman Foot, Leg & Foot Wearing Leather Sandal, Wood, Black Plinth Base, 33 In........ | 690 |
| Electric, Sabino, Fountain, Frosted, Molded Shade, Metal Base, Chevron Stem, 24 x 8 In............ | 2300 |
| Electric, Shafran & Glucksman, White Marble, Column, 1980s, 19 x 7 In......................... | 173 |
| Electric, Slag Glass Panels, Caramel, Blue, 2-Light, Pull Chains, 23 In. .......................... | 1064 |
| Electric, Slag Glass Shade, Grapevines, Metal Overlay, 4 Panels, Twisted Vine Base, 22 In......... | 2370 |
| Electric, Slag Glass, Domed Shade, Flowers, Leaves, Double Sockets, c.1910, 25 x 20 In. ............. | 649 |
| Electric, Slag Shade, Egyptian Scene Border, Metal Base, 1920s, 27 x 16 In. ...................... | 625 |
| Electric, Spelter, Deco Woman, Holding Glass Shade, Marble Base, Germany, c.1930, 27 In. ......... | 938 |
| Electric, Stiffel, Cream, Brown, Metal, 39 ½ In.................................................. | 366 |
| Electric, Student, Plume & Atwood, 2-Light, Pink Shades, 1800s, 18 x 21 In.....................*illus* | 2990 |
| Electric, Symfoni, Ceiling, Steel, Paper, Navy, White, Denmark, 1960s, 17 ½ x 8 In., Pair ............ | 1500 |
| Electric, T. Barbi, Brass, Vertical Leaf Shade, Coiled Base, 1970s, Italy, 25 x 9 In. ................ | 438 |
| Electric, Tommaso Barbi, Double Headed, Flower Shape Shade, Brass, Marble, 68 In................. | 1952 |
| Electric, Tommaso Barbi, Single Leaf Shape, Brass, 67 In. ....................................... | 1952 |
| Electric, Tommi Parzinger, Pierced Brass Shades, Hand Shaped, Wood, 73 In., Pair ................... | 7930 |
| Electric, Vetri Murano, White, Curved Cone Shape, Striped, 23 ½ In., Pair......................... | 1041 |
| Electric, Vetri Murano, White, Egg Shape, 11 ½ In., Pair ........................................ | 732 |
| Electric, Water Lily Base, Gilt Metal, Art Deco Metal Mesh Shade, Paneled, 23 x 17 In. ............... | 266 |
| Electric, Whaley, Leaded Glass, White Flowers, Green, Yellow, 3-Socket, 24 ½ In. ................ | 2223 |
| Electric, Whaley, Leaded, Glass, 8 Panels, Flower, Leaves, Caramel Ground, 26 In....................... | 2370 |
| Electric, White, Flowers, 6-Sided, Square Shade, William Haines, 1960s, 19 x 17 x 13 In., Pair... | 1125 |
| Electric, Wilkinson, Flowers, Leaded Glass Shade, 29 x 22 In..............................*illus* | 3335 |
| Electric, Wilkinson, Hollyhock, Slag Glass, Bronze Patina, Tree Trunk Base, 30 x 20 In. ............. | 2013 |
| Electric, Wilkinson, Leaded Glass Shade, Roses, Pink Ground, Blue Starburst, 9 In. ................... | 6517 |
| Electric, William Haines, Chinese Figures, Tree, 1960, 28 ½ In......................*illus* | 2000 |
| Electric, William Haines, Turquoise, Square, Oriental Flowers, 1960s, 32 ½ x 12 In. ............. | 2000 |
| Electric, Wood Can, Model T, Underhay Oil Co., 18 ½ In........................................ | 185 |
| Electric, Zeppelin, Crescent Moon, Chrome, Tube & Bead Dangles, Art Deco, 17 x 16 In. ............. | 1298 |
| Fairy, Nailsea Shade, White Loops, Red Ground, Pressed Glass Base, S. Clarke, 5 In. ................. | 165 |
| Fat, Double Font, Rooster, Tulip, Cross, Arrowhead Pierced, Loop Ring, Iron, c.1790, 12 In. ......... | 948 |
| Fluid, Double Cut Glass, Blue To White To Clear, Stepped Marble Base, c.1850, 22 In. ................. | 330 |
| Fluid, Frosted, Etched, Drop Prisms, Blue, White, Brass Pedestal, Marble Base, 26 In...........*illus* | 1003 |
| Fluid, Make Do, Cherry, Etched Glass, 1800s, 7 ¾ In.......................................... | 123 |
| Fluid, Overlay, Cut White To Green, Geometrical, Elongated Peg Font, Brass Stem, 11 ½ In......... | 1093 |
| Fluid, Peg, Free Blown, Engraved, Cylinder Shape, Berry & Leaf, c.1860, 12 In. ..................... | 92 |
| Fluid, Pottery, Multicolor Enamel Glaze, Brass Base, Reservoir, Glass Hurricane Shade, 20 In. ... | 118 |

**Lamp,** Hubley, Dolly Dimple, Grace Drayton Design, Iron, Doorstop, Cloth Shade, 16 ¾ In.

$35

Conestoga Auction Co., Inc.

**Lamp,** Kerosene, Arabian Scenes, Setting Sun, Palm Trees, Brass Foot, Royal Flemish, 18 In.

$7,110

James D. Julia Auctioneers

**Lamp,** Kerosene, Gone With The Wind, Glass Globes, Painted Flowers, Brass, Late 1800s, 28 In.

$150

DuMouchelles Art Gallery

**Lamp,** Oil, Bronze, Figural, Boy Riding Ram's Head, Grand Tour, 1800s, 4⅜ x 6½ In.
$239

Neal Auction Co.

**Lamp,** Oil, Bronze, Fish, Swallowing Another Fish, Pierced Handle, 1800s, 3 x 6½ In.
$329

Neal Auction Co.

**Lamp,** Rushholder, Pivoting Jaw, Counterweight, Tripod Base, Iron, c.1800, 11¼ In.
$554

Skinner Auctioneers & Appraisers

**Lamp,** Solar, Webster & Co., Enamel, Round Glass Shade, Embossed, c.1870, 18½ In.
$492

Neal Auction Co.

| | |
|---|---:|
| **Fluid,** Pressed Glass, Blue, Ribbed Font, Embossed Flowers, Hurricane Shade, 19½ In. | 30 |
| **Gas,** Arts & Crafts, Oak, Pyramid Shade, Striated Caramel Slag Glass Panes, 23 x 15 In. | 338 |
| **Gas,** Bronze, Urn Shape, Wood Base, Cornucopia, Frosted Ball Shade, 22½ In., Pair | 1599 |
| **Gas,** Miller Gas Burner, Gone With The Wind, Globular, Red Satin Glass, Scrollwork, 24 In. | 144 |
| **Gas,** Victorian, Opalescent Swirl, Glass Shade, Brass Ornate Frame, 21 In. | 71 |
| **Gasolier,** 6-Light, Brass, Enamel, Winged Gargoyles, Scrolls, Etched Glass Shades, 46 x 44 In. | 5000 |
| **Gasolier,** 8-Light, Curved Arms, Etched Glass Shades, Electrified, c.1890, 30 In. *illus* | 359 |
| **Grease,** Betty Lamp, Slide Top, Pole, Hook, Iron, 5 In. | 94 |
| **Grease,** Betty, Copper, Wrought Iron Hook, On Turned Wood Tidy, 8 In. | 510 |
| **Grease,** Betty, Iron, Marked On Lid W. Iameson, 1800s, 5 In. | 308 |
| **Grease,** Betty, Iron, Rooster Knop, Turned Stand, Threaded Shaft, 17 In., 3 Piece | 813 |
| **Grease,** Betty, Tin, Ipswich Type, Crimped Pan, Saucer Base, 14 In. | 240 |
| **Grease,** Betty, Wrought Iron, 1800s, 2½ In. | 800 |
| **Grease,** Betty, Wrought Iron, Copper Bird Finial, John Long, Pennsylvania, 4½ In. | 660 |
| **Grease,** Betty, Wrought Iron, Swivel Cover, Bird Finial, Hanging Hook, Wick Pick, Pa., 7 In. | 1150 |
| **Grease,** Betty, Wrought Iron, Twisted Rat Tail Pick, 9 In. | 360 |
| **Grease,** Glazed Pottery, Yellow, Brown Sponge Dots, Signed James Seagreaves, 10 In. | 71 |
| **Grease,** Pottery, Double Spout, Brown Glaze, c.1840, 5¼ In. | 1169 |
| **Handel Lamps** are included in the Handel category. | |
| **Hanging,** 3-Light, Cast Glass, Grapes, Vines, Honey Amber, Verdun, Signed, 1930s, 17 In. | 1507 |
| **Hanging,** Art Deco, Spelter, Opalescent Glass, Metal Casing, Shells, c.1930, 19 x 52 In. | 461 |
| **Hanging,** Bigelow & Kennard, Pinecone, Shade, Multicolor, Link Chain, c.1910, 14 x 29 In. | 4920 |
| **Hanging,** Claus Bonderup & Torsten Thorup, 1967, 14½ x 27½ In. | 875 |
| **Hanging,** Gio Ponti, Brass, Glass Disc, 6-Light, Fontana Arte, Italy, 1950s, 34 x 26 In. | 3250 |
| **Hanging,** Hollyhocks, Pink, Lavender, Mottled White & Green Glass, Bronze Rim, 18 In. | 593 |
| **Hanging,** Lillian Palmer, Copper, Cone Shape, Mica Panels, c.1915, 12 x 24 In. | 1500 |
| **Hanging,** Morgan & Sons, Grape Clusters, Leaves, Caramel Opalescent, 12 x 27 In. | 2952 |
| **Hanging,** Mother-Of-Pearl Swirl Glass, Melon Ribbed, Electrified | 472 |
| **Hanging,** Poul Henningsen, Tiered, Enameled Metal, Purple, White, Red, c.1960, 10 x 20 In. | 308 |
| **Hanging,** Swag, Globe Shape, Acrylic Armature, Monofilament, Chain, 1960s, 19 In. | 265 |
| **Hanging,** V. Panton, Moon, White Enamel Concentric Rings, 1960s, 14 In. Diam. | 549 |
| **Hubley,** Dolly Dimple, Grace Drayton Design, Iron, Doorstop, Cloth Shade, 16¾ In. *illus* | 35 |
| **Hurricane,** Regency Style, Cut Glass, Pineapples, Latticed Rondels, 11½ x 7¼ In., Pair | 984 |
| **Kerosene,** Arabian Scenes, Setting Sun, Palm Trees, Brass Foot, Royal Flemish, 18 In. *illus* | 7110 |
| **Kerosene,** Banquet, Brass, Stepped Marble Base, Cut & Frosted Mushroom Shade, 27 In. | 142 |
| **Kerosene,** Banquet, Pink Nailsea Glass, Oval Font, Ruffled Shade, 3 Clear Reeded Feet, 15 In. | 3555 |
| **Kerosene,** Bronze, Griffin, Putti, Mask, 36¾ In. | 676 |
| **Kerosene,** Centennial Bell, Figural Stem, Frosted, Acid Etched Petals, c.1876, 18½ In. | 805 |
| **Kerosene,** Cobalt Blue, White Vine, Flower Carved Cameo Glass, England, 17½ In. | 8400 |
| **Kerosene,** Cut Glass, Crosscut Diamond Shade & Font, Red Cut To Clear, 16 In. | 1700 |
| **Kerosene,** Gone With The Wind, Glass Globes, Painted Flowers, Brass, Late 1800s, 28 In. *illus* | 150 |
| **Kerosene,** Gone With The Wind, Old Climbing Rose Pattern, Painted Flowers, 16 In. | 96 |
| **Kerosene,** Gone With The Wind, Porcelain, Painted Globe, Gilt Base, 19th Century, 28 In. | 480 |
| **Kerosene,** Green Satin Glass, Raindrop Spots, Squat Font, Ball Shade, 8 In. | 547 |
| **Kerosene,** Marbrie Ruby Loop, Pyriform Font, Brass Stem, Marble Base, c.1859, 15 In. | 1495 |
| **Kerosene,** Parade, Tin, Cylinder Shape, Double Wick, Swivel Handle, 1800s, 13½ In. | 53 |
| **Kerosene,** Pink Glass Font, Pink Rolled & Ruffled Shade, Green Flower Form Foot, 15 In. | 2489 |
| **Kerosene,** Rainbow Satin Glass, Diamond Quilted, Pinched Sides, Crimped Shade, 14 In. | 1215 |
| **Kerosene,** White Satin Glass, Raindrop Spots, Squared Ruffled Shade, 5 Frosted Feet, 9 In. | 326 |
| **Kettle,** Brass, Cylinder Reservoir, Wick Holder, Iron Trunnion Frame, Saucer Base, 9¾ In. | 590 |
| **Kettle,** Iron, Brass, Gimbaled, Chain, Peter Derr, 1856, 9½ In. | 7200 |
| **Kettle,** Iron, Cylindrical Shade, Banded Stem, Saucer Base, Wick Tweezers, 8½ In. | 3840 |
| **Lamp Base,** Electric, Red Marble, Gilt Bronze, 2 Swan Shape Handles, 16½ In., Pair | 615 |
| **Lamp Base,** Iridescent Platinum Pulled Feather, Cobalt Blue Ground, Cream Neck, 13 In. | 1066 |
| **Lard,** Argand, Tole, Lamp Shade Style Reservoir, Wick Holder, Applied Handle, 7 x 6 In. | 177 |
| **Mantel,** Cream, Gold Iridescent Fishnet, Bulbous, Silver Stepped Foot, 7½ In., Pair | 1067 |
| **Oil,** Blown, Cut Honeycomb, Compressed Globular Font, Panel Cut, Stem, c.1875, 8 In., Pair | 345 |
| **Oil,** Brass Base, Milk Glass Globe, Painted, Victorian, c.1886, 19 In. | 90 |
| **Oil,** Brass, Column Base, Pattern Glass Well, Milk Glass Shade, 22 In. | 92 |
| **Oil,** Brass, Horizontal Cylinder, 3 Wick Tubes, Covers, Pan Tray | 118 |
| **Oil,** Bronze, Figural, Boy Riding Ram's Head, Grand Tour, 1800s, 4⅜ x 6½ In. *illus* | 239 |
| **Oil,** Bronze, Fish, Swallowing Another Fish, Pierced Handle, 1800s, 3 x 6½ In. *illus* | 329 |
| **Oil,** Copper, Serpent Handles, Spout, Champleve Flowers, Patina, Kashmir, 6 x 4 In. | 242 |
| **Oil,** G. Stickley, Wrought Iron, Wood, Hammered Copper Font, Basket Shade, 25 In. | 2074 |
| **Oil,** Gilt Metal, Marble, Cut Glass, Shield & Star Decoration, Cut Leaf Shades, 21 In., Pair | 598 |

L

| | |
|---|---|
| **Oil,** Hobbs, Brockunier, Glass, Blue, White Hobnail, Opalescent Wafer Base, 10½ In. | 1440 |
| **Oil,** Miner's, Iron, Round Reservoir, Hinged Lid, Heart Handle, Adjustable, 1800s, 6 x 4 In. | 259 |
| **Oil,** Raised On Stem, Base, Connected To Lamp, Persia, 4½ x 3¾ In. | 17 |
| **Pairpoint Lamps** are in the Pairpoint category. | |
| **Rush,** Acorn Finial, Forged Iron, Pincer Shaft, Counterbalance Arm, c.1750, 10 In. | 432 |
| **Rush,** Combination, Candle Socket, Drip Tray, Iron, Burl Base, Scissor Shape, 11 In. | 384 |
| **Rush,** Combination, Candleholder, Wrought Iron, Burl Base, Scissor Jaws, 16½ In. | 236 |
| **Rush,** Penny Foot, Forged Iron, Pincer Holder, Counterbalance Arm, Rolled Rim Cup, 12 In. | 533 |
| **Rush,** Spring, Iron, Tripod Base, 9 In. | 354 |
| **Rush,** Wrought Iron, Wood Turned Base, Scissor Type Jaws, Counter Weight, 11 In. | 325 |
| **Rushholder,** Pivoting Jaw, Counterweight, Tripod Base, Iron, c.1800, 11¼ In. ...........*illus* | 554 |
| **Rushholder,** Wrought Iron, Wooden Base, 19th Century, 32 In. | 420 |
| **Sconce,** 1-Light, Bronze, Swan, Dragonflies, Leaves Backplate, 20 In., Pair | 3750 |
| **Sconce,** 1-Light, Oak, Arm, Protruding From Mask's Mouth, Carved, 16½ In. | 438 |
| **Sconce,** 1-Light, Poulsen, Concave Disc, Denmark, 1980s, 9 x 17¾ In. | 1875 |
| **Sconce,** 1-Light, Tin, Mirror Tiles, Round, 1800s, 14½ In., Pair. | 1800 |
| **Sconce,** 1-Light, Tin, Oval, Mirrored Back, Crimped Candle Sockets, 14 In., Pair | 480 |
| **Sconce,** 2-Light, Armorial Backplate, Crest, Saucer Drip Pans, 19¼ x 13¾ In., Pair | 597 |
| **Sconce,** 2-Light, Art Deco, Bronze, Metal, Glass, Leaves, Enameled Vines, 26 x 13 In., Pair | 2706 |
| **Sconce,** 2-Light, Art Nouveau, Amber Art Glass Ball Shades, Gilt, c.1910, 11½ x 10 In., Pair | 1968 |
| **Sconce,** 2-Light, Brass, Eagle Pediment, Oval Frame, Star, Mirror, 16 x 11 In., Pair | 550 |
| **Sconce,** 2-Light, Chinoiserie, Wood, Porcelain, Bronze, Tole Vines, c.1900, 12 x 10 In., Pair | 1968 |
| **Sconce,** 2-Light, Copper, Hand Hammered, G. Stickley, 12½ x 5 In., Pair | 6100 |
| **Sconce,** 2-Light, Gilt Bronze, Clear Prisms, 26 x 16 In., Pair | 2500 |
| **Sconce,** 2-Light, Gilt Metal, Faux Rock Crystal, Bird, Branches, Leaves, 19 x 9¾ In., Pair | 1968 |
| **Sconce,** 2-Light, Gilt Metal, Glass, Bird, Leaves, 1900s, 22¾ In., Pair | 4500 |
| **Sconce,** 2-Light, Louis XVI Style, Gilt Bronze, Pierced Backplate, 24 x 10 In., Pair | 984 |
| **Sconce,** 2-Light, Neoclassical Style, Silvered Bronze, Twisted Leaf Swag, 25 x 14 In., Pair | 472 |
| **Sconce,** 2-Light, Roycrofters, Copper, Hammered, 11 x 6 In. | 1586 |
| **Sconce,** 3-Light, Belle Epoque, Bronze, Bow Knot, Branches, c.1900, 21 x 11 In., Pair | 799 |
| **Sconce,** 3-Light, Belle Epoque, Bronze, Cupids, Leaf, Scroll, 21 x 5¼ In. | 1722 |
| **Sconce,** 3-Light, Gilt Bronze, Louis XVI Style, Flower Urn Finial, Tapered, 19 In., Pair | 344 |
| **Sconce,** 3-Light, Gilt Bronze, Scrolled Flowers, Bow, France, c.1920, 12 x 17 In., Pair | 360 |
| **Sconce,** 3-Light, Giltwood, Metal, Shell Carved, Continental, c.1950, 26 x 19 In., Pair | 750 |
| **Sconce,** 3-Light, Iron Mounted, Giltwood, Crown, Scroll, Early 1900s, 23¾ x 20¾ In. | 359 |
| **Sconce,** 3-Light, Louis XV, Scrolled Backplate, Gilt, Leaves, 23 x 15 In. | 976 |
| **Sconce,** 3-Light, Mirror Back, Arched Sawtooth Crest, Tin, 20 In. | 176 |
| **Sconce,** 3-Light, Parcel Gilt, Metal, Neoclassical, Italy, c.1950, 31½ x 11¾ In., Pair | 399 |
| **Sconce,** 3-Light, Tole, Silvered, Beaded, Feathers, 27 x 9½ In., 4 Piece | 10200 |
| **Sconce,** 5-Light, Tole, Faux Bamboo Style, Red Paint, 28 x 15 In., Pair | 625 |
| **Sconce,** 6-Light, Brass, Gothic Revival, c.1900, 20 x 12 In., Pair | 140 |
| **Sconce,** 8-Light, Parcel Gilt, Metal, Neoclassical Style, 47 x 24 In. | 184 |
| **Sconce,** Art Deco, 3 Panels, Cone Shape Frames, 15¼ In. | 615 |
| **Sconce,** Bronze, Reeded, Domed Backplates, Torch Shape, 23 x 24 In., Pair | 1230 |
| **Sconce,** Double Socket, Reflector Back, Folded Edge, Step Lobed, Crimped Crest, 13 In. | 889 |
| **Sconce,** Giltwood, Cupid Masks, Cornucopia Candle Mounts, 17 x 14 In., Pair | 175 |
| **Sconce,** Gothic Style, Cast Metal, Matte Black, Frosted Glass Inserts, Italy, 20 x 10 In. | 587 |
| **Sconce,** Marc D'Haens, Mica, Metal, Abstract, Signed, Belgium, 25 x 7 In. | 1837 |
| **Sconce,** Marc D'Haens, Quartz, Metal, Abstract, Leaf, Seed, Signed, Belgium, 32 x 10 In. | 1837 |
| **Sconce,** Mathieu Mategot Style, Multicolor Cones, Metal, 34 In. | 673 |
| **Sconce,** Medieval Style, 1-Light, Gilt Caps, Wrought Iron, 33½ In., Pair | 123 |
| **Sconce,** Moorish Style, Outdoor, Copper, Brass, Gold Patina, Iron, 1800s, 45 x 11 In., Pair | 633 |
| **Sconce,** P. Hamburger, Swing Arm, Chromed Steel, Lucite, Knoll, 1970s, 36 x 13 In., Pair | 1375 |
| **Sconce,** Plaster, White Paint, Hands Holding Vase, R. Etts, 1974, 13 x 10 In. | 1088 |
| **Sconce,** Tin, Crimped Arched Crest, Mirror Back, 3 Candleholders, 18 In. | 570 |
| **Sconce,** Tin, Round, Pressed Silvered Tin Reflectors Under Glass, Crimped Cups, 9 In., Pair | 6875 |
| **Sconce,** Wall, 2-Light, Louis XV, Rococo Style, Gilt Metal, 16 x 14 In., Pair | 300 |
| **Sconce,** Wall, Punched Tin, Hearts, Arched Back, D-Shape Gallery, 2 Candleholders, 14 In. | 295 |
| **Sinumbra,** Gilt Brass, Bronze, Reticulated Band, Plinth Base, Etched Glass Shade, 32 x 13 In. | 1793 |
| **Sinumbra,** Gilt Brass, Cut Glass Shade, Gothic Tower Shape, Cornelius & Co., c.1845, 40 In. | 1500 |
| **Sinumbra,** Gilt Brass, Etched Shade, Tapered Stem, Leaf Mounts, Stepped Base, c.1845, 34 In. | 3125 |
| **Sinumbra,** Gilt, Patina Bronze, Column Standard, Stepped Foot, Blown Globe, 17 x 6 In. | 1793 |
| **Solar,** Brass, Marble, Baluster, Geo. Washington Bust, Etched Glass Shade, c.1860, 30 In. | 875 |
| **Solar,** Gilt Lacquer, Brass, Banding, Column Standard, 20 In., Pair | 984 |
| **Solar,** Gilt Metal, Etched Glass Shade, Female Mask, Stepped Marble Base, c.1895, 23 In. | 500 |

**Lamp,** Taper Jack, Spring-Action Nippers, Spool, 4 Penny Feet, Iron, c.1800, 5¼ x 6¼ In.
$2,460

Skinner Auctioneers & Appraisers

**Lamp,** Torchere, Figural, Woman, Amphora, Spelter, Signed, A. Carrier, c.1890, 66 In., Pair
$7,670

Brunk Auctions

**Lantern,** Hall, Regency Style, Bell Shape, Etched Glass, 3 Arms, Electrified, 21 In.
$717

Neal Auction Co.

L

349

**Lantern,** Hanging, Arts & Crafts, Hammered Brass, Green Glass Panels, Electrified, 8 x 6 In.
$84

DuMouchelles Art Gallery

**Lantern,** Hanging, Copper, Enamel, Hexagonal, Stepped, Multicolor Glass Inserts, Middle East, 21 x 10 In.
$738

New Orleans Auction Galleries, Inc.

**Le Verre Francais,** Vase, Azurettes, Cobalt Blue, Turquoise, Engraved, 4 x 2¾ In.
$345

Humler & Nolan

---

**TIP**

*Have an inventory of your collections and adequate insurance.*

---

| | |
|---|---:|
| **Solar,** Gilt, Lacquered Brass, Bronze, Etched Gothic Shade, Chimney, Dietz Brother, 35 In. | 1599 |
| **Solar,** Hanging, Gilt Brass, Bronze, Font In Circlet, Scrolled Arms, Chains, 28½ In. | 717 |
| **Solar,** Webster & Co., Enamel, Round Glass Shade, Embossed, c.1870, 18½ In. .......*illus* | 492 |
| **Student,** Double Arm, Brass, Red Shades, c.1890, 24½ In. | 192 |
| **Student,** Red Tole, Stenciled, Pineapple Finial, Cylindrical Burner, Shade, 19 In. | 179 |
| **Taper Jack,** Spring-Action Nippers, Spool, 4 Penny Feet, Iron, c.1800, 5¼ x 6¼ In. ...*illus* | 2460 |
| **Tiffany Lamps** are listed in the Tiffany category. | |
| **Torchere,** 5-Light, Neoclassical, Composition, Reeded Column, Metal Base, 77 In. | 588 |
| **Torchere,** 6-Light, Wrought Metal, Tripod Base, Electrified, c.1900, 11 x 79 In., Pair | 360 |
| **Torchere,** Blackamoor Woman, Robes, Raised Pedestal Base, Carved, Painted, Venice, 83 In. | 1875 |
| **Torchere,** Carved Wood, Gesso, Young Men, Long Hair, Tunics, Leggings, 75 In. | 6250 |
| **Torchere,** Classical, Woman Depicting Summer, Copper, Patinated, Electrified, 1900s, 79 In. | 1125 |
| **Torchere,** Column, 6 Lucite Tubes, Brass Rods & Capital, Stepped Black Acrylic Base, 71 In. | 173 |
| **Torchere,** Electric, Metal, Painted, Composite, Gilt Tracery, Cream Mottled, 73 In., Pair | 834 |
| **Torchere,** Figural, Woman, Amphora, Spelter, Signed, A. Carrier, c.1890, 66 In., Pair. .......*illus* | 7670 |
| **Torchere,** J. Salterini, Inverted Pyramid Shade, Frosted Glass Panes, 1930s, 67 In., Pair | 1230 |
| **Torchere,** Wrought Iron, Brass Standard, Pricket, Scroll Iron Feet, Toes, 69 x 14 In., Pair | 1353 |
| **Trammel,** Hanging, 4-Light, c.1820, 25 In. | 1920 |
| **Urn,** Baroque Style, Silver Gilt, Pierced Handles, Giltwood, 24 In., Pair | 1722 |
| **Whale Oil,** Blown Molded, 12-Panel Font, Opalescent, Pyriform Font, Footed, c.1847, 7 In. | 1265 |
| **Whale Oil,** Pressed Glass, Ring & Oval, Violet Blue, Inverted Pyriform Font, c.1860, 7½ In. | 2415 |
| **Whale Oil,** Sandwich, Blown Glass, Globular Font, Saucer Base, Flared Rim, 4½ In. | 322 |
| **Whale Oil,** Spout, Mixed Metal, Tin, Cone Shape, Swirl Base, Brass Cap, 8 In. | 201 |

---

## LAMPSHADE

| | |
|---|---:|
| **Aladdinite No. 681** | 300 |
| **Blue Iridescent Glass,** Lily Form, Vertical Ribs, Ruffled Rim, Silver Holder, 6 In. | 61 |
| **Dome,** Orange Overlapping Arches, Lobed Blue Iridescent Glass Standard, 17 In. | 344 |
| **Dome,** Reverse Painted, Lake Scene, 13½ In. | 288 |
| **Leaded Glass,** Greek Key Band, Red, Amber Granite Glass Geometric Ground, 24 In. | 356 |
| **Reverse Painted,** Frosted Glass, Cylindrical, 7 Scenes, 10¼ In. | 120 |
| **Slag Glass,** Flower Border, Red & Pink, Green Ground, Shaped Rim, Unique Art, 20 In. | 851 |
| **Slag Glass,** Flower Border, Yellow, Green, Caramel, Domed, Shaped Rim, Unique Art, 20 In. | 729 |

---

**LANTERNS** are a special type of lighting device. They have a light source, usually a candle, totally hidden inside the walls of the lantern. Light is seen through holes or glass sections.

| | |
|---|---:|
| **Blizzard,** Dietz, No. 2, Bail Handle, 1900s, 14 In. | 6 |
| **Brass,** Leather, Glass, Green, Hermes, 1950s, 11 x 3¾ In. | 3250 |
| **Bronze,** 12-Light, Gilt, Hexagonal, Scrolling Surmount, Acanthus, 40 x 17 In., Pair | 3328 |
| **Candle,** Wood, Glass, Wire Bail Handle, 16 x 11½ In. | 840 |
| **Cast Metal,** Frosted Glass, Lion Mask Mounts, Hexagonal, Tapered, c.1910, 39 In., Pair | 1000 |
| **Dietz,** No. 30, Tin, Handle, 1800s, 15 In. | 74 |
| **Gigging,** Tin, 12 Tubes, Conical Center, Handle, 18 x 23 In. | 360 |
| **Glass,** Wire Guards, Glass, Punched Tin, American, 19th Century, 11½ In. | 270 |
| **Hall,** Bronze, Hexagonal, Gothic Piercing, Scroll Molded Chains, 65½ In. | 615 |
| **Hall,** Regency Style, Bell Shape, Etched Glass, 3 Arms, Electrified, 21 In. ...........*illus* | 717 |
| **Hanging,** Arts & Crafts, Hammered Brass, Green Glass Panels, Electrified, 8 x 6 In. ......*illus* | 84 |
| **Hanging,** Chinese Pagoda, 11¼ x 7¾ In., Pair | 240 |
| **Hanging,** Copper, Enamel, Hexagonal, Stepped, Multicolor Glass Inserts, Middle East, 21 x 10 In. ...*illus* | 738 |
| **Iron,** Gothic Revival, Strapwork Designs, 26 In. | 125 |
| **Oil,** Brass, Copper, E. Thomas & Williams, 1895, 12 In. | 250 |
| **Onion,** Globe Shape, Green Glass, Metal Cage, Vented, Bail Ring, Perkins, 20 x 12 In. | 200 |
| **Onion,** Globe Shape, Red Glass, Metal Cage, Vented, Bail Ring, Perkins, No. 8, 16 x 12 In. | 300 |
| **Porcelain,** Famille Rose, Pierced, Brocade Pattern, Children, Flowers, 8-Sided, 1800s, 14 In. | 593 |
| **Skater's,** Brass, Stepped Font, Fitted Glass Shade, Hanging Chain & Loop Handle, 9 In. | 185 |
| **Skater's,** Tin, Dome Vent Cap, Hanging Chain, Ring, Glass Globe, Molded Base, 10 In. | 94 |
| **Tin,** Onion Globe, Blue Glass, Black Paint, Hanging Ring, Punched, Wire Guard, 17½ In. | 1107 |
| **Tin,** Onion Globe, Pierced Frame, Cranberry Glass Fluid Lamp, Oil Burners, 14 In. | 523 |
| **Tin,** Onion Globe, Pierced Frame, Glass Fluid Lamp, Oil Burners, 1800s, 8½ In. | 492 |
| **Tin,** Pierced, Cylindrical, Loop Strap Handle, Cone Shape Top, 1800s, 17 In. | 1046 |
| **Tin,** Pierced, Glass Door, ½ Cylindrical, Loop Strap Handle, 1800s, 15¼ In. | 923 |
| **Train,** Tay Bridge, Inscribed, Ruby & Cobalt Blue Glass Sides, 1879, 4¼ x 8½ x 6 In. | 240 |
| **Wooden,** Loop Handles, Tin, Paneled, Tin, Lid, 14 In. | 1123 |

**LE VERRE FRANCAIS** is one of the many types of cameo glass made by the Schneider *Le Verre Francais* Glassworks in France. The glass was made by the C. Schneider factory in Epinay-sur-Seine from 1918 to 1933. It is a mottled glass, usually decorated with floral designs, and bears the incised signature *Le Verre Francais*.

| | |
|---|---:|
| **Bowl,** Footed, Primerolles, Brown, Orange, Yellow, Signed, 9 In. | 1125 |
| **Lamp,** Art Deco, Flowers, Pink, Orange, 1918-22, 15 ½ In. | 2370 |
| **Lamp,** Electric, Stylized Plant, Honeycomb, Blue To Orange, 16 In. | 6221 |
| **Vase,** Azurettes, Cobalt Blue, Turquoise, Engraved, 4 x 2 ¾ In. ............*illus* | 345 |
| **Vase,** Bulbous, Long Neck, Amethyst, Mottled Clear, 10 ¼ In. | 726 |
| **Vase,** Campanules, Brown Flowers, Mottled Yellow Ground, 12 In. | 1540 |
| **Vase,** Dahlias, Purple & Lilac, Mottled Pink Ground, Bulbous, Footed, 10 In. | 593 |
| **Vase,** Digitales, Charles Schneider, c.1930, 14 ¼ In. | 1250 |
| **Vase,** Digitalis, Orange Flowers, Pink Ground, 12 In. | 1185 |
| **Vase,** Groseilles, Brown Berries, Yellow Ground, Base, 8 ¼ In. | 592 |
| **Vase,** Groseilles, Currants, Acid Etched, Signed, c.1930, 22 ¼ In. ........*illus* | 1920 |
| **Vase,** Lauriers, Brown Flowers, Amber Ground, 10 ¼ In. | 651 |
| **Vase,** Marrons, Acid Etched, Design, Signed, c.1920, 12 ½ x 8 In., Pair | 1216 |
| **Vase,** Mirettes, Blue Foot, Yellow Ground, Orange Flowers, 18 ½ In. | 2370 |
| **Vase,** Mottled Purple, Pink Art Deco Flowers, Bulbous, Signed, 3 In. | 403 |
| **Vase,** Orange Flower, Green Leaves, Yellow, Marked Chardes, France, c.1910, 8 In. | 750 |
| **Vase,** Orange Yellow Flowers, Mottled Ground, Signed, 4 ½ x 7 ½ In. | 344 |
| **Vase,** Papillons, Butterflies, Mottled Cream Shaded To Blue, 14 In. ......*illus* | 2489 |
| **Vase,** Pivoines, Orange Flowers, Mottled Brown Leaf Base, Tapered, 10 In. | 2666 |
| **Vase,** Round, Orange, Iris, Leaf, Mottled Yellow Ground, 8 ½ In. | 1210 |
| **Vase,** Stylized Flowers, Brown Honeycomb, Mottled Orange To Yellow, 12 In......*illus* | 1541 |
| **Vase,** Stylized Mushrooms, Rolled Rim, Cameo, 15 In. ...................*illus* | 862 |

**LEATHER** is tanned animal hide and has been used to make decorative and useful objects for centuries. Leather objects must be carefully preserved with proper humidity and oiling or the leather will deteriorate and crack. This damage cannot be repaired.

| | |
|---|---:|
| **Bag,** Tooled, Horse, Button, c.1810, 14 ½ x 14 ¾ In. | 270 |
| **Basket,** Key, Incised Geometric Designs, Oval, Handle, Va., c.1860, 6 x 3 In. | 2185 |
| **Basket,** Tooled Flowers, Shark Skin Sides, Red Inside, Shaped Rim, Arched Handle, 5 x 8 In. | 1610 |
| **Basket,** Tooled Hearts, Stars & Diamonds, Red Inside, Oval, Arched Handle, c.1850, 7 x 8 In. | 29900 |
| **Basket,** Tooled, Gray Canvas Inside, Oval, Arched Handle, Brass Tacks, c.1870, 7 x 8 x 4 In. | 1725 |
| **Hat Box,** Top Hat Shape, Straps, Buckles, Handle, I & W Lowndes, London, 10 x 14 In. | 90 |
| **Knapsack,** Ralph Lauren, 19 x 16 In. | 420 |
| **Riding Crop,** Stitched, Wrapped, Cream, Loop Strap, 20th Century | 30 |
| **Rug,** Hide, Cow, Brown, White, 82 x 90 In. | 281 |
| **Saddle,** Camel, High Back, Oval Seat, Hide, Brass Fittings, Middle East, c.1950, 36 In..........*illus* | 120 |
| **Saddle,** Embroidered, Repousse Silver Horn & Trim, D. Lozano, Mexico, c.1870................*illus* | 10350 |
| **Saddle,** McClellan, Brass Hardware, Medallion, 12-In. Seat, 20th Century | 300 |
| **Saddle,** Nickeled Breastplate, Engraved Silver Mounts, c.1930, 45 x 29 In. | 2500 |
| **Saddle,** Tooled, Eastern Style, Stitched, Engraved Design, Metal Studs................*illus* | 288 |
| **Saddle,** Western Seat, Silver & Gold Steer Conchas, Silver Gullet, Stand, 14 ¾ In. | 4500 |
| **Saddle,** Western Seat, Tooled, Brown, 15 ¾ In. | 813 to 1125 |
| **Saddlebags,** Stitched Straps, c.1900, 22 x 12 In. | 58 |
| **Sporran,** Pouch, Embossed Scrolls, Leaves, Gilt Leaf Trim, Scotland, 1900 | 120 |
| **Traveling Bar,** Leather, Brown, 4 Bottles, 4 Tumblers, Spoons, Germany, c.1905, 9 x 16 In. | 1250 |
| **Wallet,** Men's, Alligator, Bifold, Interior Compartments, Clasp, 4 ¼ In. | 44 |
| **Wig Powderer,** Wood, Brass Nozzle, Triangular, 1700s, 4 x 10 In. | 81 |

**LEEDS** pottery was made at Leeds, Yorkshire, England, from 1774 to 1878. Most Leeds ware was not marked. Early Leeds pieces had distinctive twisted handles with a greenish glaze on part of the creamy ware. Later ware often had blue borders on the creamy pottery. A Chicago company named Leeds made many Disney-inspired figurines. They are listed in the Disneyana category.     **LEEDS POTTERY**

| | |
|---|---:|
| **Bowl,** Blue, Mustard, Flowers, Leaf Rim, 4 x 12 ¼ In. | 266 |
| **Bowl,** Pearlware, Flowers, Leaves, Multicolor, 4 ¼ x 9 ¼ In. | 201 |
| **Chop Plate,** Green Rim, Trees, Leaves, 13 ¼ In. | 59 |
| **Coffeepot,** Dome Lid, 5-Color Flowers, Gooseneck Spout, Pearlware, 9 ½ In. .........*illus* | 177 |
| **Cup & Saucer,** Handless, Flowers, Multicolor, Impressed Adams, 5 ⅜ In. | 189 |
| **Jug,** Bacchantes, Head, Strap Handle, Painted, Highlights, Soft Paste, c.1810, 5 ½ In. ..........*illus* | 224 |
| **Mug,** Pearlware, Cylindrical Body, Loop Handle, Painted, Seed Band, Flowers, 5 ¾ In. | 413 |
| **Mug,** Pearlware, Cylindrical, Loop Handle, Flower & Leaf Band, Bocage Designs, 6 In. | 165 |

**Le Verre Francais,** Vase, Groseilles, Currants, Acid Etched, Signed, c.1930, 22 ¼ In. $1,920

Rago Arts & Auction Center

**TIP**

*To remove powdery mildew stains from leather, wipe them with a mixture of equal parts rubbing alcohol and water. When the leather dries, rub it with a conditioner like neat's-foot oil or castor oil.*

**Le Verre Francais,** Vase, Papillons, Butterflies, Mottled Cream Shaded To Blue, 14 In. $2,489

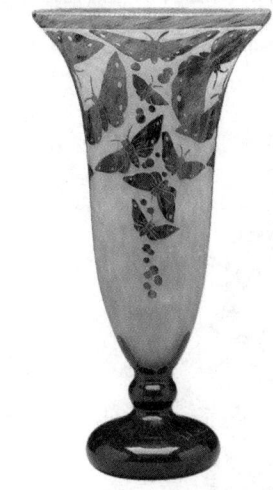

James D. Julia Auctioneers

**Le Verre Francais,** Vase, Stylized Flowers, Brown Honeycomb, Mottled Orange To Yellow, 12 In.
$1,541

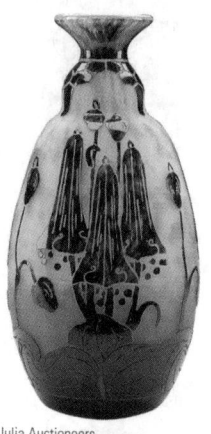

James D. Julia Auctioneers

**Le Verre Francais,** Vase, Stylized Mushrooms, Rolled Rim, Cameo, 15 In.
$862

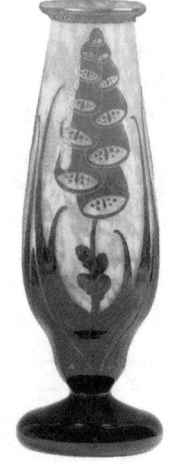

Cottone Auctions

**Leather,** Saddle, Camel, High Back, Oval Seat, Hide, Brass Fittings, Middle East, c.1950, 36 In.
$120

Garth's Auctioneers & Appraisers

| | | |
|---|---|---:|
| **Mug,** Pearlware, Cylindrical, Loop Handle, Painted, Flower Sprays, 4¼ In. | | 177 |
| **Mug,** Pearlware, Painted, Flowers, Leaf Band, Winchester Measure, Scroll Handle, 5¼ In. | | 560 |
| **Plate,** Blue Feather Edge, Soft Paste, Multicolor Flowers, Leaves, 8¼ In. | | 472 |
| **Plate,** Pineapple, Yellow, Green Leaves, Brown, Blue Sprig Border, 7¼ In. | | 266 |
| **Platter,** Blue Feather Edge, Soft Past, Embossed Flowers, Leaves, Wreath, 13 In. | | 24 |
| **Platter,** Blue Feather Edge, Pearlware, 19th Century, 17½ x 14 In. | | 245 |
| **Platter,** Soft Past, Blue Feather Edge, Daisy & Fleur-De-Lis Leaf Embossed Border, 12 x 15 In. | | 47 |
| **Platter,** Soft Paste, Feather Edge, Blue, Embossed Flowers, Leaves, 14 x 17½ In. | | 158 |
| **Platter,** Soft Paste, Feather Edge, Green, Impressed Wood, 11 x 13½ In. | | 158 |
| **Platter,** Soft Paste, Feather Edge, Green, Impressed Wood, 14 x 18 In. | | 194 |
| **Platter,** Sprays, Blue Feather Edge, 19th Century, 11½ x 15½ In. | | 450 |
| **Platter,** White Rim, Green Border, Oval, c.1845, 19 In. | | 94 |
| **Teapot,** Grape & Leaf, Soft Paste, Globe Shape, 7½ In. | | 130 |
| **Toddy Plate,** Flowers, Tan, Brown, Blue, Pearlware, Soft Paste, 6⅝ In. ...............*illus* | | 106 |
| **Tureen,** Lid, Pearlware, Feather Edge, Bamboo Handles, Footed, Flower Finial, 9 x 14 In. | | 354 |

**LEFTON** is a mark found on pottery, porcelain, glass, and other wares imported by the Geo. Zoltan Lefton Company. The company began in 1941. George Lefton died in 1996 and the company was sold in 2001. The company mark has changed through the years, but because marks have been used for long periods of time, they are of little help in dating an object.

| | | |
|---|---|---:|
| **Ashtray,** Holly | | 22 |
| **Bell,** Figural, Boy, Angel, Slingshot, c.1956, 3 In. | | 15 |
| **Cake Plate,** Cabbage Roses, c.1950, 9 In. | | 35 |
| **Card Holder,** Roses, Gilt Trim, c.1960, 2¼ x 3 In. | | 20 |
| **Cookie Jar,** Miss Dainty, 1950s, 7 In. | | 93 |
| **Figurine,** Angel Of The Month, August, Foil Label, Marked, 4 In. | | 22 |
| **Figurine,** Grouse, Ruffled, Marked, c.1975, 5½ In. | | 18 |
| **Figurine,** Old Man & Woman, Kitchen, Pouring Tea, c.1960, 7 In. | | 90 |
| **Figurine,** Roadrunner, c.1948, 4½ x 9 In. | | 24 |
| **Pitcher,** Holly, Swirled Rib, 8 In. | | 48 |
| **Sugar & Creamer,** Heavenly Rose | | 85 |
| **Teapot,** Festival, Grapes, Lid, 7¼ In. | | 150 |

**LEGRAS** was founded in 1864 by Auguste Legras at St. Denis, France. It is best known for cameo glass and enamel-decorated glass with Art Nouveau designs. Legras merged with Pantin in 1920 and became the Verreries et Cristalleries de St. Denis et de Pantin Reunies.

| | | |
|---|---|---:|
| **Vase,** Art Deco, Black Daisy Petals, Mottled White, Pink & Yellow Ground, 6¼ In. | | 173 |
| **Vase,** Blue, Green, Birds, Grapevines, Frosted, 12¼ In., Pair | | 177 |
| **Vase,** Cameo Glass, Orange, Winter Scene, Oval, Signed, 4½ In. | | 748 |
| **Vase,** Cameo, Green, Mountain Lake Scene, Cylindrical, Footed, Signed, 8½ In. | | 288 |
| **Vase,** Lake Scene, Cylinder, France, c.1910, 6¾ x 2½ In. | | 256 |
| **Vase,** Opaque, Coral, Cream Ground, 6½ In. | | 188 |
| **Vase,** Swans On Lake, Summer Trees, Green, Yellow, Tapered Cylinder, Cameo, 9¾ In. | | 288 |
| **Vase,** Trees In Landscape, Brown, Green, Cream, Tapered, 13½ In. | | 403 |
| **Vase,** Trees, Autumn, Oval, Square Rim, Enamel, Cameo, 5½ In. | | 1195 |
| **Vase,** Trees, Autumn, Yellow, Coral, Irregular Rim, Cameo, 5 In. | | 345 |
| **Vase,** Triangular Shape, Forest Scene, Brown, Green, Purple, Yellow, Cameo, 3½ In. | | 948 |

**LENOX** porcelain is well-known in the United States. Walter Scott Lenox and Jonathan Coxon founded the Ceramic Art Company in Trenton, New Jersey, in 1889. In 1896 Lenox bought out Coxon's interest, and in 1906 the company was renamed Lenox, Inc. The company makes porcelain that is similar to Irish Belleek. In 2009, after a series of mergers, Lenox became part of Clarion Capital Partners. The marks used by the firm have changed through the years, so collectors can date the ceramics. Related pieces may also be listed in the Ceramic Art Co. category.

| | | |
|---|---|---:|
| **Bowl,** Opalescent, Seashells, Crashing Waves, Signed, c.1940, 13¾ In. | | 58 |
| **Bust,** The Gold Mask Of Tutankhamun, Fired Gold, 1978, 7 In. | | 174 |
| **Centerpiece,** Cream, Figural, Folded Cabbage, Applied Twigs, Artichokes, 7 x 12 In. | | 123 |
| **Clock,** Shelf, Flower Bouquets, Scroll Shape Edges, 16 In. | | 215 |
| **Coffee Set,** Cobalt Blue, Silver, Lock-On Lid, Creamer, Side Wood Handles, 2 Piece | | 484 |
| **Compote,** Aquarius Centerpiece, Shell Shape Bowl, Dolphins, Fired Gold, 6½ In. | | 308 |
| **Cup & Saucer,** 6 Porcelain Liners, 6 Silver Demitasse Cups, 6 Saucers, Bouillon Cup | | 400 |
| **Cup & Saucer,** Silver Overlay, Presentation Case, 12 Piece | | 424 |
| **Ginger Jar,** Silver Overlay, Dark Red, Flowers, Leaves, 20th Century, 5¼ In. | | 185 |
| **Lamp,** Electric, White, Urn Shape, Double Flower Shape Handles, Green, 11¾ In., Pair | | 338 |

| | |
|---|---:|
| **Plate,** Boehm Bird, 10¾ In., 12 Piece | 221 |
| **Plate,** Dinner, Autumn, 10½ In., 12 Piece | 540 |
| **Plate,** Dinner, Cream Color, Multicolor Floral, Gilt Accents, 10½ In., 12 Piece | 207 |
| **Plate,** Exhibition, Duomo From Ponte Vecchio, W.H. Morley, 10½ In. | 313 |
| **Plate,** Exhibition, Harbour Gateway, W.H. Morley, 10½ In. | 276 |
| **Plate,** Gold, Cobalt Blue, Rims, Flower Vine, c.1930, 10¼ In., 12 Piece | 276 |
| **Platter,** Vienna, Red, Blue, Birds, Flowers, Fired Gold, 12½ In. | 71 |
| **Stein,** Lid, Monk, Apron, Wine Cellar, Barrels, Basket, Brown | 308 |
| **Tea Set,** White, Silver, Inlaid, Teapot, Sugar & Creamer, 3 Piece | 484 |
| **Tobacco Jar,** Green, Landscape, Golfers, Silver Lid, Monogram, 6 In. | 1875 |
| **Tray,** Peachtree, Purple, Flowers, Leaves, Silver Mounted, 14¾ In., Pair | 276 |
| **Vase,** 5 Geishas, Umbrellas, Under Wisteria, Painted, Baldwin, Belleek, 16 In. | 920 |
| **Vase,** Cream, Spring, Doves, Dogwood Flowers, Fired Gold Rim, 7 x 7¾ In. | 69 |
| **Vase,** Wisteria, Birds, Green, Blue, Belleek, A. Bowers, 16 x 5⅜ In. | 205 |

**LETTER OPENERS** have been used since the eighteenth century. Ivory and silver were favored by the well-to-do. In the late nineteenth century, the letter opener was popular as an advertising giveaway and many were made of metal or celluloid. Brass openers with figural handles were also popular.

| | |
|---|---:|
| **Brass,** Birds, Harlequin Clown, Flowers, 8 In. | 210 |
| **Brass,** Cannon Handle, 10¼ In. | 24 |
| **Brass,** Clown Face, Flowers, Birds, Branches, 7 In. | 98 |
| **Soapstone,** Fish Handle, c.1930, 7½ In. | 25 |
| **Sterling Silver,** Francis I Pattern, Reed & Barton, c.1907, 7¾ In. | 35 |
| **Wood,** Monkey Handle, Carved, 10½ In. | 12 |

**LIBBEY** Glass Company has made many types of glass since 1888, including the cut glass and tablewares that are collected today. The stemwares of the 1930s and 1940s are once again in style. The Toledo, Ohio, firm was purchased by Owens-Illinois in 1935 and is still working under the name Libbey Inc. Maize is listed in its own category. *Libbey*

| | |
|---|---:|
| **Bowl,** Clear, Round, Swirling Ribs, Marked, 8¼ In. | 122 |
| **Bowl,** Cut Glass, Scalloped Edge, c.1900, 2½ x 7 In. | 60 |
| **Bowl,** Delphos, Brilliant Cut, Scalloped Rim, c.1890, 8 In. | 660 |
| **Bowl,** Delphos, Cut, 2¾ x 8¾ In. | 565 |
| **Bowl,** Fredericka, Cut, W.C. Anderson, 3¾ x 9 In. | 141 |
| **Bowl,** Geometric Garland, Shooting Star, Flared, Engraved Ivy Border, 3 x 8 In. | 125 |
| **Bowl,** Glenda, Cut, Hobstar Base, Signed Libbey, 6 x 9½ In. | 141 |
| **Bowl,** Intaglio Cut, Sterling Rimmed Bowl, J.E. Caldwell, c.1900, 12 In. | 7800 |
| **Bowl,** Loretta Matt, 2¾ x 9¾ In. | 101 |
| **Bowl,** Neola, 8-Sided, Shaped Notched Edge, 2 x 9½ In. | 275 |
| **Bowl,** Regis, Star Base, Notched Edge, 4 x 8 In. | 100 |
| **Bowl,** Wisteria, Lovebirds, Intaglio Cut, Hexagonal, c.1920, 8¼ In. | 600 |
| **Celery Dish,** Ellsmere, Folded, 11¾ In. | 500 |
| **Cologne Bottle,** Hobstar, Strawberry Diamond & Prism, Round, Ball Stopper, 5½ In. | 50 |
| **Compote,** Glenda, Cut Glass, Signed, 7½ x 7 In. | 509 |
| **Compote,** Vintage Pattern, Cut, Etched, 8 x 7¾ In. | 3000 |
| **Console,** Strawberry Diamond, Elliptical Vesicas, Black Cut To Clear, Flared, 3 x 9 In. | 400 |
| **Decanter,** Pattern Cut Ring Neck, Hobstar Base, Signed, 13 In. | 875 |
| **Jug,** Rum, Cut Glass, Hobstar, Strawberry Diamond, Triple Notched Handle, 6½ In. | 509 |
| **Jug,** Stopper, Ellsmere, Brilliant Cut, c.1900, 11¼ In. | 1680 |
| **Jug,** Whiskey, Star & Feather, Triple Notched Handle, Hobstar & Diamond Stopper, 8½ In. | 150 |
| **Perfume Bottle,** Cobalt Blue Cut To Clear, Peacock, Clear Stopper, Footed, 8½ In. | 1080 |
| **Pitcher,** Cut Glass, Neck Bands, Diamond Diaper, Notched Edge, Brilliant Period, 7¾ In. | 118 |
| **Pitcher,** Imperial Pattern, Brilliant Cut, Bulbous, c.1890, 7½ In. | 1320 |
| **Plaque,** Engraved Libbey, Round, Stand, c.1933, 5½ In. | 960 |
| **Punch Bowl,** Hobstar, Crosscut Diamond, Strawberry Diamond, Star & Fan, 7 x 12 In. | 400 |
| **Tray,** Oval, Kimberly, Cut Glass, Clear Blank, 10 x 7¾ In. | 113 |
| **Vase,** Amberina, Jack-In-The-Pulpit, Optic Ribbed, Acid Stamp, 5 In. | 460 |
| **Vase,** Engraved, Footed, Paneled, Scalloped Edge, c.1900, 13½ In. | 840 |
| **Vase,** Intaglio Carved, Flowers, Flared Base, Fern Fronds, Notched Rim, 11¾ x 2½ In. | 207 |
| **Vase,** Nash Spot-Optic, Blue Threading, Footed, Signed, 8½ x 6 In. | 173 |
| **Vase,** Sweet Pea, Engraved, Flared Rim, Scalloped Edge, Flowers, c.1900, 4 x 5½ In. | 180 |
| **Vase,** Trumpet, Amberina, 7 In. *illus* | 118 |
| **Vase,** Trumpet, Fluted Panel & Cane Button, 15 In. | 100 |
| **Water Bottle,** Maize, Custard, Brown & Green Stained Leaves, c.1890, 8 In. | 316 |

**Leather,** Saddle, Embroidered, Repousse Silver Horn & Trim, D. Lozano, Mexico, c.1870
$10,350

James D. Julia Auctioneers

**Leather,** Saddle, Tooled, Eastern Style, Stitched, Engraved Design, Metal Studs
$288

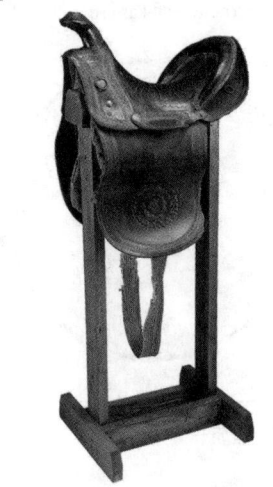

James D. Julia Auctioneers

**Leeds,** Coffeepot, Dome Lid, 5-Color Flowers, Gooseneck Spout, Pearlware, 9½ In.
$177

Conestoga Auction Co., Inc.

L

**Leeds,** Jug, Bacchantes, Head, Strap Handle, Painted, Highlights, Soft Paste, c.1810, 5 ½ In. $224

Conestoga Auction Co., Inc.

**Leeds,** Toddy Plate, Flowers, Tan, Brown, Blue, Pearlware, Soft Paste, 6 ⅝ In. $106

Conestoga Auction Co., Inc.

**Libbey,** Vase, Trumpet, Amberina, 7 In. $118

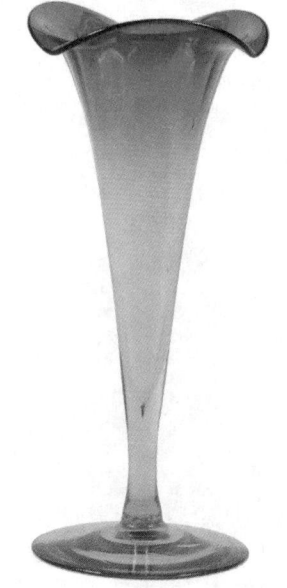

Conestoga Auction Co., Inc.

| | |
|---|---:|
| **Water Set,** Mignon, Cut Glass, American Brilliant, Goblets, 10-In. Pitcher, 7 Piece | 500 |
| **Water Set,** Star & Feather, Triple Notched Handle, 8 ½-In. Pitcher, 7 Piece | 100 |

**LIGHTERS** for cigarettes and cigars are collectible. Cigarettes became popular in the late nineteenth century, and with the cigarette came matches and cigarette lighters. All types of lighters are collected, from solid gold to the first of the recent disposable lighters. Most examples found were made after 1940. Some lighters may be found in the Jewelry category in this book.

| | |
|---|---:|
| **Bulgari,** 18K Yellow Gold, Guilloche Enamel, Gas, Plunger Activated, 2 ¼ x 1 ¼ In. | 1845 |
| **Cartier,** Gold Plated, Box, 2 ¾ x 1 In. | 354 |
| **Cartier,** Gold Plated, Cream Color Enameling, 2 ¾ x 1 In. | 144 |
| **Cartier,** Silver Plate, Engine Turned, Grid Pattern, Marked | 210 |
| **Cartier,** Woven, 18K Bicolor Gold, Flint Wheel Rotates, Butane, 3 In. *illus* | 660 |
| **Cigar Cutter,** Lighter, Art Bouquet, Painted Scene, Nude Women, 1902, 10 x 10 ½ In. | 3300 |
| **Cigar,** Blackamoor, Bird Talon Base, Bronze, 10 In. | 1020 |
| **Cigar,** Cherub, Green Glass Globe, Gas Valve, Burner, Metal, c.1900, 18 In. | 450 |
| **Cigar,** Devil Head, Bird Talon Base, 9 In. | 450 |
| **Cigar,** Dukes Cigarettes Mirror, Black Globe, Wicks, 22 ½ In. | 1920 |
| **Cigar,** F.B. Richards & Co., Red Globe, Acorn Wicks, Metal, c.1890, 11 In. | 960 |
| **Cigar,** John Karl, Red Globe, Woman's Image, Wicks, c.1890, 14 In. | 2160 |
| **Cigar,** Jump Spark Style, National Selling Co., Pa., Salesman's Sample, c.1900, 7 In. | 2400 |
| **Cigar,** Nobleman, Blue Glass Globe, Gas Valve, Burner, Metal, c.1900, 19 In. | 390 |
| **Cigar,** Silver, Art Deco Linear, Flower Etched, Square Base, J. Knewite, c.1900, 6 In. | 360 |
| **Cigar,** Tip Cutter, Bloomer Club 5 Cent Cigar, Scene, Panel, 7 x 17 x 9 In. *illus* | 4560 |
| **Cigar,** Woman's Head, Mouth Opening, Metal, Electric, c.1920, 7 ½ In. | 270 |
| **Cigarette,** Woman's Head, Gold Paint, Red Lips, Art Deco, 6 ½ In. *illus* | 143 |
| **Column,** Lions, Gold Washed Silver, 3 Flames, Pineapple Finials, Sheffield, 5 x 4 In. | 590 |
| **Gold Plated,** Red Lacquer, Hinged, Cartier, 2 ¾ In. | 180 |
| **Gold,** 14K Yellow & Rose, Applied Coat Of Arms, Monogram, 2 x 2 In. | 1107 |
| **Ship's Lamp Form,** Banner, Starboard, Sterling Silver, Green Glass, S. Jacob, London, 3 In. | 1476 |
| **Tinder,** Iron, Pistol Grip, Continental, c.1790, 7 In. | 720 |

**LIGHTNING RODS AND LIGHTNING ROD BALLS** are collected. The glass balls were at the center of the rod that was attached to the roof of a house or barn to avoid lightning damage. The balls were made in many colors and many patterns.

| | |
|---|---:|
| **Copper,** Iron, Twisted, Tripod Stand, Amber Ball, c.1890, 62 x 21 In. | 195 |
| **Iron,** Twisted, 5-Spikes, Screw On Tree Branch, 60 In. | 36 |

**LIMOGES** porcelain has been made in Limoges, France, since the mid-nineteenth century. Fine porcelains were made by many factories, including Haviland, Ahrenfeldt, Guerin, Pouyat, Elite, and others. Modern porcelains are being made at Limoges. The word *Limoges* as part of the mark is not an indication of age. Haviland, one of the Limoges factories, is listed as a separate category in this book.

| | |
|---|---:|
| **Bowl,** Berries, Blue, Green, Pink Ground, Footed, Gold Trim, Signed S. Ray, 1912, 6 x 9 In. | 148 |
| **Cachepot,** Pink Roses, Green, Brown Ground, Tapered Globe, c.1920, 9 x 11 In. | 288 |
| **Casket,** Hinged Lid, Bright Metal Trim, Painted Flowers, Lobed Corners, 8 ½ x 6 ½ In. | 184 |
| **Centerpiece,** Underplate, Fruit, Multicolor Paint, Gilt Trim, 9 x 14 In. | 1560 |
| **Charger,** Cranes, Pond, Scalloped Edge, 12 In. | 25 |
| **Charger,** Flowers, Landscape, Multicolor Ground, Signed Brahic, 12 In. | 60 |
| **Charger,** Landscape, Woman, Mandolin, Putti, Bushes, Multicolor, 18 In. | 1035 |
| **Charger,** Maiden, Pate-Sur-Pate, Thistle Border, Signed Riffaterre, c.1900, 15 ½ In. | 1375 |
| **Charger,** Pheasant Scene, Gold Scalloped Rim, Signed Baptiste, 15 ¾ In. | 826 |
| **Charger,** Pink Roses, Multicolor Ground, 12 In. | 55 |
| **Chocolate Service,** Light Blue, Pink Roses, Rococo, Cups & Saucers, Tray, 14 Piece | 500 |
| **Egg,** Faberge Style, Blue, Lovebirds Interior, 4 In. | 185 |
| **Egg,** Faberge Style, Pink, Gold Crosses, Ballet Slipper Interior, 4 ½ In. | 246 |
| **Fish Set,** Fish, Swimming, Watery Ground, Gold Rim, Platter, Plates, Sauce, 14 Piece | 1380 |
| **Fish Set,** Raised Gilt Border, Ruffled Rim, c.1900, 24-In. Platter, 7 8 ½-In. Plates | 399 |
| **Ice Bucket,** Painted, Chinese Fisherman, Flowers, Bands, Raynaud & Co., c.1970, 9 In., Pair | 900 |
| **Plate,** Art Nouveau, White, Stylized Flower Border, 8 In., 6 Piece | 36 |
| **Plate,** Charles Ahrenfeldt, 9 ¾ In, 12 Piece | 120 |
| **Plate,** White, Center Star, Green, Gold Border, Charles J. Ahrenfeldt, 9 ¾ In., 12 Piece | 450 |
| **Platter,** Fish, Pink Border, Blue Center, Life-Like Fish, G. Demartine, c.1900, 24 In. | 86 |
| **Punch Bowl,** Pink Flowers, Marked Tressemann & Voght, c.1905, 6 ¼ x 14 In. | 92 |

| | |
|---|---|
| **Sculpture,** Head, Hat, Visage, White, Signed, A. Bourdelle, c.1916, 8 x 10 In. | 1250 |
| **Standish,** Multicolor, Oriental Style, 1800s, 10 ½ x 7 ½ In. | 130 |
| **Tea Service,** Floral, Painted Twig Handles, Pot, Sugar & Creamer, 11 Cups & Saucers | 354 |
| **Tray,** Gilt, Blue, White, Japanese Musicians, Warrior, Free-Form, c.1870, 17 ¾ In. | 344 |
| **Tray,** Red Poppy Spray, Cream, Orange, Oval, 15 x 9 In. | 472 |
| **Vase,** Columbine, Lavender, Gold Band, Bernardaud, Stamped B & Co. France, 15 In. | 345 |
| **Vase,** Scenic, Castle, Footbridge, Trees, Stream, Multicolor Gloss Glaze, 11 x 4 In. | 1265 |
| **Water Set,** Pitcher, 6 Cups, Poppy, Orange, Gold Border, Osborne, 8-In. Pitcher, 7 Piece | 590 |

**LINDBERGH** was a national hero. In 1927, Charles Lindbergh, the aviator, became the first man to make a nonstop solo flight across the Atlantic Ocean. In 1932, his son was kidnapped and murdered, and Lindbergh was again the center of public interest. He died in 1974. All types of Lindbergh memorabilia are collected.

| | |
|---|---|
| **Autograph,** Spirit Of St. Louis Dust Jacket, 1953 | 625 |
| **Model Kit,** Airplane, Bristol Bulldog, 1982 | 29 |
| **Plate,** Flight Scenes, Commemorative, Limoges, 8 ¾ In. | 66 |
| **Toy,** Airplane, Lindy, Cast Iron, Black, Red Wings, Hubley, c.1930, 10-In. Wingspan | 3555 |
| **Toy,** Airplane, Lindy, Cast Iron, Ribbed Cabin, Gray, Pull Toy, Hubley, 13 ¼-In. Wingspan | 1896 |
| **Toy,** Airplane, Lindy, Cast Iron, Ribbed Cabin, Red, Pull Toy, Hubley, 10-In. Wingspan | 1481 |
| **Toy,** Airplane, Lindy, Embossed, Disc Wheels, Cast Iron, Hubley, 1920s, 9 In. | 826 |
| **Toy,** Airplane, Spirit Of St. Louis, Pressed Steel, Gendron, c.1928, 24-In. Wingspan ...*illus* | 2124 |
| **Ukulele,** Perfecto Cigar Box, Lindbergh In Heart Shape Sound Hole, Folk Art, c.1930, 21 In. | 431 |
| **Wristwatch,** Lone Eagle, 14K Gold Filled, Corner Cut, Bulova, Case, 1924 | 4513 |

**LITHOPHANES** are porcelain pictures made by casting clay in layers of various thicknesses. When a piece is held to the light, a picture of light and shadow is seen through it. Most lithophanes date from the 1825–75 period. A few are still being made. Many lithophanes sold today were originally panels for lampshades.

| | |
|---|---|
| **Plaque,** Boy, Petting Dog, Oval, c.1860, 3 ⅝ In. | 75 |
| **Plaque,** Couple Dining, Beggars, Cap In Hand, Child Watching, 4 x 5 In. | 349 |
| **Plaque,** Hunters, Grouse In Tree, Mountains, c.1875, 5 x 3 In. | 150 |
| **Plaque,** Girl Holding Lamb, Iron Frame, Stand, KPM, c.1890, 9 ¼ In. ...*illus* | 598 |
| **Plaque,** Portrait, Woman, Laura, Marked, c.1845, 5 ¾ x 7 ¼ In. | 225 |

**LIVERPOOL**, England, has been the site of many pottery and porcelain factories since the eighteenth century. Color-decorated porcelains, transfer-printed earthenware, stoneware, basalt, figurines, and other wares were made. Sadler and Green made print-decorated wares starting in 1756. Many of the pieces were made for the American market and feature patriotic emblems, such as eagles and flags. Liverpool pitchers are called Liverpool jugs by collectors.

| | |
|---|---|
| **Jug,** Black Transfers, Ship, Washington In Glory, Indians, c.1800, 10 In., Pair | 1375 |
| **Jug,** Washington, Franklin, Ship, Patriotic Symbols, Black, Green Transfer, 9 ½ In. | 400 |
| **Pitcher,** American Ship, Figure Of Hope, Transfer, 1800s, 8 In. | 984 |
| **Pitcher,** Ship, 3 Masts, Flags, Blue Grisaille Transfer, 8 ¼ In. | 236 |

**LLADRO** is a Spanish porcelain. Brothers Juan, Jose, and Vicente Lladro opened a ceramics workshop in Almacera in 1951. They soon began making figurines in a distinctive, elongated style. In 1958 the factory moved to Tabernes Blanques, Spain. The company makes stoneware and porcelain figurines and vases in limited and unlimited editions. Dates given are first and last years of production. Marks since 1977 have the added word "Daisa," the acronym for the company that holds the intellectual property rights to LLadro figurines.

| | |
|---|---|
| **Figurine,** Attorney, Next To Cabinet, No. 5213, 1984-98, 13 In. | 180 |
| **Figurine,** Avoiding The Goose, Girl, Boy, No. 5033, 1979-94, 10 In. | 108 |
| **Figurine,** Ballet Blue, No. 1359, 9 ¼ In. | 105 |
| **Figurine,** Cat Nap, Girl Holding Sleeping Cat, Quieting Dog, No. 5640, 1990, 5 ½ In. | 72 |
| **Figurine,** Children Praying, No. 4770, 8 ½ In. | 45 |
| **Figurine,** Cinderella & Her Fairy Godmother, No. 7553, 1994-95 In. | 300 |
| **Figurine,** Clown, Lying On Stomach, Foot On Ball, Glossy, No. 4618, 1970-92, 13 ¾ In. | 100 |
| **Figurine,** Dancer, Flowing Dress, No. 5050, 12 In. ...*illus* | 180 |
| **Figurine,** Food For Ducks, Girl Kneeling, 2 Ducks, No. 4849, 1973-92, 9 In. | 89 |
| **Figurine,** Friday's Child, No. 6020, Box, 1993-98, 6 In. | 73 |
| **Figurine,** Gabriela, Girl Holding Puppy, No. 2355, 1997, 13 x 8 In. | 1020 |
| **Figurine,** Girl With Goat, No. 4756, 1971-81, 10 ½ In. | 89 |
| **Figurine,** Great Expectations, Woman & Child, No. 5650, Box, 1990-94, 10 In. | 177 |

**Lighter,** Cartier, Woven, 18K Bicolor Gold, Flint Wheel Rotates, Butane, 3 In. $660

Cowan's Auctions

**Lighter,** Cigar, Tip Cutter, Bloomer Club 5 Cent Cigar, Scene, Panel, 7 x 17 x 9 In. $4,560

Showtime Auction Services

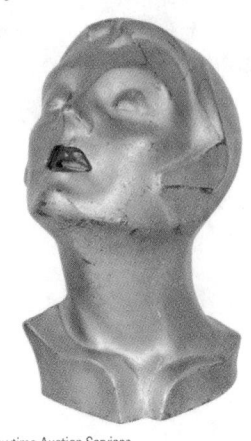

**Lighter,** Cigarette, Woman's Head, Gold Paint, Red Lips, Art Deco, 6 ½ In. $143

Showtime Auction Services

L

# LLADRO

**Lindbergh,** Toy, Airplane, Spirit Of St. Louis, Pressed Steel, Gendron, c.1928, 24-In. Wingspan
$2,124

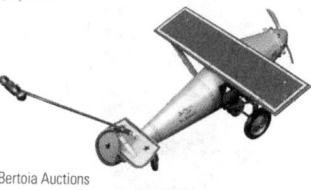

Bertoia Auctions

**Lithophane,** Plaque, Girl Holding Lamb, Iron Frame, Stand, KPM, c.1890, 9¼ In.
$598

Neal Auction Co.

**Lladro,** Figurine, Dancer, Flowing Dress, No. 5050, 12 In.
$180

DuMouchelles Art Gallery

| | |
|---|---:|
| **Figurine,** Here Comes The Bride, Bride, No. 1446, 1983-97, 13¾ In. | 142 |
| **Figurine,** I Am Don Quixote, No. 1522, Salvador Furio, 1987, 29 In. | 1680 |
| **Figurine,** I Feel Pretty, Girl On Bench, Holding Brush & Mirror, No. 5678, 1990-98, 6¼ In. | 177 |
| **Figurine,** Japanese Girl Flower Decorating, No. 4840, 1973-98, 8 In. | 180 |
| **Figurine,** Kitty Confrontation, Cat, Frog, Staring At Each Other, No. 1442, 1983, 4 In. | 96 |
| **Figurine,** Litter Of Fun, No. 5364, 8½ In. | 140 |
| **Figurine,** Lovers From Verona, No. 1250, 1974, 15¼ In. | 320 |
| **Figurine,** Madame Butterfly, Woman In Pink Kimono, No. 4991, 1978-2005, 12 In. | 84 |
| **Figurine,** Madonna, Bust, Blue, Taupe, No. 4649, 1970-2003, 8½ In. | 229 |
| **Figurine,** Message Of Peace, Dove, No. 6587, Box, 1998, 10½ In. | 59 |
| **Figurine,** My Little Treasure, Mother, Holding Baby, No. 6503, 1998-2005, 9 In. | 177 |
| **Figurine,** Nuns, No. 4611, 1970, 13¼ In. | 118 |
| **Figurine,** Organ Grinder, No. 5046, 1980-81, 13 In. | 210 |
| **Figurine,** Oriental Spring, Woman With Parasol, No. 4988, 1978-96, 11½ In. | 84 |
| **Figurine,** Our Cozy Home, Dogs In Bed, No. 6469, 1987-2007, 4½ In. | 150 |
| **Figurine,** Palace Dance, No. 6373, 1997-2000, 15½ x 9 In. | 480 |
| **Figurine,** Petals Of Love, Girl, Holding Bouquet, No. 6346, 1997-2007, 10 In. | 118 |
| **Figurine,** Poodle, No. 6337, 1997-2001, 5¾ x 6½ In. | 142 |
| **Figurine,** Rosey Posey, Ballerina, Sitting, No. 6690, 2000-05, 5 In. | 88 |
| **Figurine,** Sweet Dreams, Boy, Holding Puppies, No. 1535, 1988-92, 4 In. | 60 to 147 |
| **Group,** Trimming The Tree, No. 5897, 13 x 10 In. ...........................*illus* | 240 |

**LOETZ** glass was made in many varieties. Johann Loetz bought a glassworks in Klostermuhle, Bohemia (now Klasterky Mlyn, Czech Republic), in 1840. He died in 1848 and his widow ran the company; then in 1879, his grandson took over. Most collectors recognize the iridescent gold glass similar to Tiffany, but many other types were made. The firm closed during World War II.

*Loetz Austria*

| | |
|---|---:|
| **Bowl,** Diaspora, Honeycomb, Green Iridescent, Crimped Rim, 1900s, 3¾ x 5 In. | 92 |
| **Bowl,** Greenish Blue Iridescent, Oil Spot, Pinched Rim, 4 In. | 531 |
| **Bowl,** Phanomen, Blue Iridescent Oil Spot Band Over Yellow, Flared, Footed, 6 x 10 In. | 1007 |
| **Box,** Lid, Blue Flowers & Leaves, Yellow Ground, Blue Knob Handle, Round, 4 In. | 230 |
| **Inkwell,** Medici, Red Iridescent Oil Spots, Cream Ground, Blue Thread Loops, 2¾ In. | 711 |
| **Lamp,** Blue Iridescent Domed Shade, Platinum Spot, Bronze Heat Cap, Acorn Finial, 19 In. | 6221 |
| **Lamp,** Hanging, Gold Iridescent, Acorn Shape, Brass Chain & Cap, Cypriot, 28 In. | 533 |
| **Rose Bowl,** Federzeichnung, Brown, Octopus, Blue, White Scrolls, Ruffled, 3-Footed, 5 In. | 3220 |
| **Rose Bowl,** Titania, Green Graduating To Blue, Platinum Glaze, Oval, Trifold Rim, 5 In. | 2070 |
| **Sprinkler,** Rosewater, Amber, Platinum Looping, Bulbous, Pinched, Stretched Lip, 10 In. | 2734 |
| **Vase,** Argus, Amber, Blue & Platinum Iridescent, Vining, Bulbous, Squat, Folded, 4½ In. | 2126 |
| **Vase,** Art Deco, 3 Black Handles, Purple Butterflies, Mums, White Ground, Cameo, 6¼ In. | 575 |
| **Vase,** Astral, Gourd, Silver Honey Gold, Pulled Ruffled Rim, Dimples, 10½ In. | 546 |
| **Vase,** Ausfuhrung 36, Green, Blue & Platinum Horizontal & Vertical Threading, 8 In. | 1094 |
| **Vase,** Ausfuhrung 237, Multicolor, Green Ground, c.1918, 5 In. | 540 |
| **Vase,** Blue, Purple, Green Gloss Glaze, Bulbous, Narrow Cylindrical Neck, 5¼ x 3¼ In. | 240 |
| **Vase,** Bulbous, Ruffled Rim, Iridescent Purple, Gold Spots, Signed Loetz Austria, 5½ In. | 7998 |
| **Vase,** Cameo, Opal Purple, Green Leaves, Bottle Shape, 6¼ In. | 374 |
| **Vase,** Carved Flowers, Yellow, Green, Long Neck, Signed La Loetz, 10 In. | 826 |
| **Vase,** Cobalt Blue Papillon, Allover Oil Spot Design, Shouldered, c.1900, 11 In. | 1320 |
| **Vase,** Cobalt Papillon, Oil Spot, Pear Shape, Footed, Bohemian Glass House, c.1900, 13 In. | 1440 |
| **Vase,** Creta Silberiris Rusticana, Blue Aurene, Gold Highlights, Slender, 9¼ In. | 259 |
| **Vase,** Cytisus, Pinched Shoulder, Light Green To Copper, Iridescent, Silver Oil Spots, 7 In. | 5332 |
| **Vase,** Cytisus, Silver Flower Overlay, Amber To Purple, Iridescent Oil Spots, 5 In. | 2470 |
| **Vase,** Cytisus, Yellow, Green Iridescent Waves, Oil Spots, Silver Overlay, Waisted, 6 In. | 6518 |
| **Vase,** Diaspora Iridescent Gold, Green, Rose, Nautilus Shape, Footed, 7½ x 7 In. | 590 |
| **Vase,** Empire, Clear To Amethyst, Rainbow Iridescent, Ribbed, Gold Wreaths, Oval, 6 In. | 790 |
| **Vase,** Federzeichnung, Brown Mother-Of-Pearl, Octopus, Gold Tracery, 8 In. | 978 |
| **Vase,** Federzeichnung, Globular, Yellow Mother-Of-Pearl, Air Trap Octopus, Gold Tracery, 5½ In. | 2300 |
| **Vase,** Federzeichnung, Octopus, Brown, Bubble Lines, Gilt, Ruffled Rim, 6 In. .....................*illus* | 1067 |
| **Vase,** Federzeichnung, Octopus, Brown, Gold Enamel, 6 In. .....................*illus* | 1150 |
| **Vase,** Federzeichnung, Octopus, Citrus, Opal, Enameled Gold, Marked, 8½ In. .....................*illus* | 3163 |
| **Vase,** Federzeichnung, Octopus, Gold Ground, Trefoil Top, 4½ x 5½ In. | 1380 |
| **Vase,** Federzeichnung, Oval, Brown Mother-Of-Pearl, Gold Tracery, Ruffled Rim, 7 In. | 1495 |
| **Vase,** Gold, Iridescent, Green & Blue Swirls, Chalice Shape, Silver Overlay, 6½ In. | 5332 |
| **Vase,** Green Creta Mimosa, Crackle Finish, Pinched Rim, c.1907, 9 In. | 660 |
| **Vase,** Green Iridescent Spiral, Brass Textured Lip, 8 In. | 127 |

| | |
|---|---|
| **Vase,** Green Luster, Candia Diaspora Design, Iridized, Blue Over Green Sheen, c.1900, 10 In. | 720 |
| **Vase,** Green, Oil Spot Decoration, Oval, Pinched, Flared Rim, 6 x 6 In. | 854 |
| **Vase,** Iridescent, Pulled Feathers, Austria, 1900s, 12 x 5 In. | 2000 |
| **Vase,** Iridescent, Silver Flower, Leaf Overlay, Austria, c.1910, 7 In. | 2875 |
| **Vase,** Jade Green, Swirl Pattern, Ausfuhrung 237, 4 In. | 316 |
| **Vase,** Jugendstil, Marmoriete, Amethyst, Baluster Shape, Pearlescent Pink, 7 x 4 In. | 529 |
| **Vase,** Lava, Bulbous, Green, Iridescent, Purple Highlights, Pinched Sides, 6 ¾ In. | 651 |
| **Vase,** Lava, Green Iridescent, Textured, Bulbous, Flared Rim, 4 In. | 1422 |
| **Vase,** Martele, Green Iridescent, Folded Rim, Signed, 7 ¼ In. | 531 |
| **Vase,** Medici, Bronze Iridescent, Blue Iridescent Oil Spots, Folded Rim, 7 In. | 948 |
| **Vase,** Medici, Stylized Oil Spot, Iridescent, Shouldered, Signed, 7 ¼ In. | 805 |
| **Vase,** Papillon, Candia, Wide Shoulder, 3 Handles, c.1898, 5 ½ In. | 431 |
| **Vase,** Papillon, Double Gourd, Silvery Gold Crackle, Waisted, 6 In. | 316 |
| **Vase,** Papillon, Pinched Rim, 7 Openings, Blue & Platinum, Iridescent, 10 In. ...............*illus* | 889 |
| **Vase,** Papillon, Platinum Iridescent, Double Gourd, 8 ¾ In. | 1067 |
| **Vase,** Papillon, Yellow, Blue Iridescent, Platinum Accents, Quatrefoil, Pinched, 6 In. | 2734 |
| **Vase,** Phanomen Genre 299, Tricolor, Polished Pontil, c.1910, 6 In. | 2415 |
| **Vase,** Pinched Sides, Astraea, Gold Iridescent Oil Spots, Blue Flashes, 6 ½ In. .........*illus* | 3259 |
| **Vase,** Pink Blue Pattern, Pulled Feathers, Shaped Cylinder, c.1905, 10 In. | 3300 |
| **Vase,** Poppies Silver Overlay, Shouldered, Flared Rim, Green, Purple, Iridescent, 4 In. | 1777 |
| **Vase,** Purple Iridescent Spots, Pulled At Shoulder, Yellow Striated Ground, 16 ½ In. | 296 |
| **Vase,** Purple Iridescent, Applied Thread, Pinched, Bulbous, 7 x 6 In. | 265 |
| **Vase,** Rainbow, Crimson, Green Iridescent, Gilt Cascading Flower, Bulbous, 6 In. | 115 |
| **Vase,** Rainbow, Ribbed Swirl, Folded Rim, 6 ½ In. | 531 |
| **Vase,** Ruffled Rim, Green, Speckled, Iridescent, 5 ½ In | 246 |
| **Vase,** Ruffled Rim, Green, Speckled, Iridescent, Compressed, 6 In. | 369 |
| **Vase,** Scrolled Silver Overlay, Green, White Streaked Orange Ground, 8 ½ In. | 4500 |
| **Vase,** Shaped Panels, Cranberry, Green, Coils, Turquoise Flowers, Oval, Silver Overlay, 7 In. | 1458 |
| **Vase,** Swan Shape, White, Amber Bill, Gold Iridescent Oil Spots, Green Base, 12 In. | 2370 |
| **Vase,** Tango Glass, Flared, Dagobert Peche, c.1900, 5 x 6 In. .........*illus* | 512 |
| **Vase,** Titania, Green Hooked Feather, Silver Striated Ground, Tapering, 7 In. | 3851 |
| **Vase,** Titania, Green, Blue, Waves, Iridescent, Cigar Shape, 11 In. | 2370 |
| **Vase,** Titania, Orange & Silver, Brown Pulled Feather, Ruffled Top, 5 In. | 2074 |
| **Vase,** Titania, Pulled Threads, Silver Overlay, Art Nouveau Vine & Leaves, 12 In. .........*illus* | 7110 |
| **Vase,** Titania, Vase, Globe, Green To Silver Waves, Cobalt Blue Inside, 6 ½ In. | 3555 |
| **Vase,** Titania, Wide Mouth, Tapered, Green, Pulled Brown & Silver, 5 ¼ In. | 5628 |
| **Vase,** Titania, Yellow Green, Pulled Gray Loop, Silver Overlay, Leaves, Buds, 9 ½ In. | 8295 |
| **Vase,** Titania, Yellow Green, Pulled Gray Loop, Silver Overlay, Roses, Pinched Sides, 10 In. | 7110 |
| **Vase,** Vase, Gourd Shape, Orange, Speckled, Iridescent, 8 In. | 185 |
| **Vase,** Yellow, Iridescent, Red Oil Spot, Squat, 5 ½ In. | 201 |

**LONE RANGER,** a fictional character, was introduced on the radio in 1932. Over three thousand shows were produced before the series ended in 1954. In 1938, the first Lone Ranger movie was made. The latest movie was made in 2013. Television shows were started in 1949 and are still seen on some stations. The Lone Ranger appears on many products and was even the name of a restaurant chain for several years.

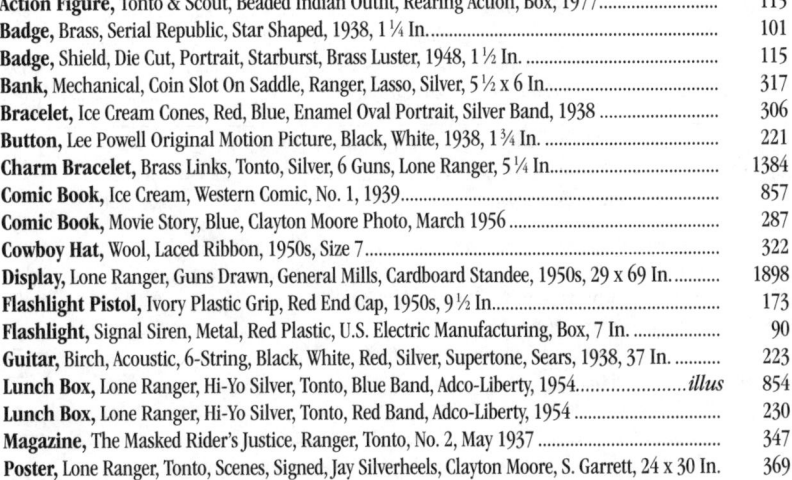

| | |
|---|---|
| **Action Figure,** Tonto & Scout, Beaded Indian Outfit, Rearing Action, Box, 1977 | 115 |
| **Badge,** Brass, Serial Republic, Star Shaped, 1938, 1 ¼ In. | 101 |
| **Badge,** Shield, Die Cut, Portrait, Starburst, Brass Luster, 1948, 1 ½ In. | 115 |
| **Bank,** Mechanical, Coin Slot On Saddle, Ranger, Lasso, Silver, 5 ½ x 6 In. | 317 |
| **Bracelet,** Ice Cream Cones, Red, Blue, Enamel Oval Portrait, Silver Band, 1938 | 306 |
| **Button,** Lee Powell Original Motion Picture, Black, White, 1938, 1 ¾ In. | 221 |
| **Charm Bracelet,** Brass Links, Tonto, Silver, 6 Guns, Lone Ranger, 5 ¼ In. | 1384 |
| **Comic Book,** Ice Cream, Western Comic, No. 1, 1939 | 857 |
| **Comic Book,** Movie Story, Blue, Clayton Moore Photo, March 1956 | 287 |
| **Cowboy Hat,** Wool, Laced Ribbon, 1950s, Size 7 | 322 |
| **Display,** Lone Ranger, Guns Drawn, General Mills, Cardboard Standee, 1950s, 29 x 69 In. | 1898 |
| **Flashlight Pistol,** Ivory Plastic Grip, Red End Cap, 1950s, 9 ½ In. | 173 |
| **Flashlight,** Signal Siren, Metal, Red Plastic, U.S. Electric Manufacturing, Box, 7 In. | 90 |
| **Guitar,** Birch, Acoustic, 6-String, Black, White, Red, Silver, Supertone, Sears, 1938, 37 In. | 223 |
| **Lunch Box,** Lone Ranger, Hi-Yo Silver, Tonto, Blue Band, Adco-Liberty, 1954 ...............*illus* | 854 |
| **Lunch Box,** Lone Ranger, Hi-Yo Silver, Tonto, Red Band, Adco-Liberty, 1954 | 230 |
| **Magazine,** The Masked Rider's Justice, Ranger, Tonto, No. 2, May 1937 | 347 |
| **Poster,** Lone Ranger, Tonto, Scenes, Signed, Jay Silverheels, Clayton Moore, S. Garrett, 24 x 30 In. | 369 |

**Lladro,** Group, Trimming The Tree, No. 5897, 13 x 10 In.
$240

DuMouchelles Art Gallery

**Loetz,** Vase, Federzeichnung, Octopus, Brown, Bubble Lines, Gilt, Ruffled Rim, 6 In.
$1,067

James D. Julia Auctioneers

**Loetz,** Vase, Federzeichnung, Octopus, Brown, Gold Enamel, 6 In.
$1,150

Early Auction Co.

357

Loetz, Vase, Federzeichnung, Octopus, Citrus, Opal, Enameled Gold, Marked, 8 ½ In.
$3,163

Early Auction Co.

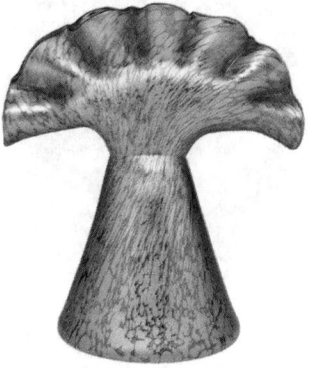

Loetz, Vase, Papillon, Pinched Rim, 7 Openings, Blue & Platinum, Iridescent, 10 In.
$889

James D. Julia Auctioneers

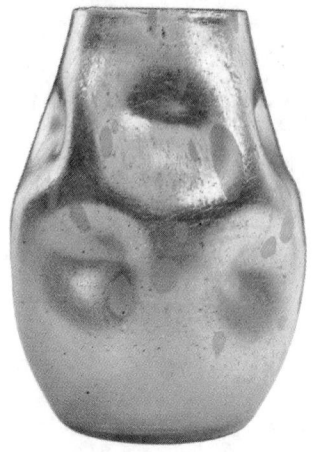

Loetz, Vase, Pinched Sides, Astraea, Gold Iridescent Oil Spots, Blue Flashes, 6 ½ In.
$3,259

James D. Julia Auctioneers

| | | |
|---|---|---|
| **Punch-Out Book,** Lone Ranger, Horse, Multicolor, Cardboard, Whitman, 1940, 10 x 15 In., 4 Pages | | 528 |
| **Radio,** Airline, Molded Plastic, White, Relief Lone Ranger, Red Dial, 7 ½ x 8 In. | | 379 |
| **Radio,** Lone Ranger, On Silver, Celluloid Window, Brown, Bakelite, Pilot, 1940s, 7x 15 In. | | 288 |
| **Record Player,** Relief Lone Ranger, Western Image Case, 12 ½ x 10 ¾ In. | | 172 |
| **Ring,** Navy Insignia, Compartment, Anchor, Horse, Kellogg's Premium, c.1952 | | 285 |
| **Toy,** Gun & Holster Set, 2 Cap Pistols, Chrome Luster, White Grips, Box, 1966 | | 328 |
| **Toy,** Gun, 2 Painted Silver Guns, Leather Holsters, Canvas Belt, Rivets, 1942 | | 115 |
| **Toy,** Hi-Yo Silver, Lone Ranger, Tin Litho, Windup, Marx, Box, Copyright 1938, 8 In. | | 570 |
| **Toy,** Hi-Yo Silver, Lone Ranger, Tin Lithograph, Windup, Marx, 11 In. | 148 to 354 | |
| **Toy,** Holster Set, Leather, Metal Horseshoes, Cowboy, Cap Guns, 1950s, 35 In. | | 702 |
| **Toy,** Lone Ranger, Rearing Silver, Wire Lasso, Pistol, Lithograph, 1938, 6 ½ In. | | 290 |
| **Toy,** Play Set, Lone Ranger Ranch, Animals, Figures, Cabin, Plastic, Box, 9 x 22 In. | | 230 |
| **Toy,** Saddle, Pony, Brown Leather, Tassels, Lone Ranger, Silver, TLR Inc., 1940s, 14 x 20 In. | | 986 |
| **Watch,** Lone Ranger With Fob & Gun, Box, Lapel | | 278 |

**LONGWY WORKSHOP** of Longwy, France, first made ceramic wares in 1798. The workshop is still in business. Most of the ceramic pieces found today are glazed with many colors to resemble cloisonne or other enameled metal. Many pieces were made with stylized figures and Art Deco designs. The factory used a variety of marks.

| | |
|---|---|
| **Champagne Bucket,** Flowers, Berries, Tab Handles, Paper Label, 1920s, 5 ½ x 4 ½ In. | 375 |
| **Charger,** Armorial, Coat Of Arms, Rising Sun, Faience, 1800s, 18 In. | 595 |
| **Charger,** Elephants, Faience, Stamped, 1920s, 15 In. | 1875 |
| **Cup & Saucer,** Flowers, Multicolor, Blue Ground, Faience | 195 |
| **Inkwell,** Flowers, Blue Ground, 3-Sided, c.1920 | 2225 |
| **Match Holder,** Flowers, Red, Yellow, Brown Rim, 2 ½ x 1 ¼ In. | 135 |
| **Plate,** Flowers, Central Cartouche, Spray, Multicolor, Octagonal, 7 In. | 195 |
| **Plate,** Outdoor Celebration, Bowling, Dancing, 8 ¼ In. | 86 |
| **Plate,** Peacock, Blue Border, c.1920, 12 ½ In. | 2950 |
| **Plate,** Village Life Scenes, Whimsical, c.1885, 8 ½ In. | 62 |
| **Vase,** Egret, Palm Tree, Beach, Flowers, Cylindrical, c.1880, 10 In., Pair | 2450 |
| **Vase,** Flowers, Multicolor, Cylindrical, 5 In. | 325 |
| **Vase,** Flowers, Multicolor, Globular, 10 x 10 In. | 1650 |
| **Vase,** Green & Brown Glaze, Gourd Shape, Footed, 8 x 6 In. | 235 |

**LONHUDA POTTERY COMPANY** of Steubenville, Ohio, was organized in 1892 by William Long, W. H. Hunter, and Alfred Day. Brown underglaze slip-decorated pottery was made. The firm closed in 1896. The company used many marks; the earliest included the letters *LPCO*.

LONHUDA

| | |
|---|---|
| **Ewer,** 4-Sided, Blackberry, Squat, Brown, Orange, Ruffled Rim, 6 ¼ In. | 288 |
| **Vase,** Nasturtium, Molded, Green Matte Glaze, Mushroom Form, 5 x 6 In. | 1586 |

**LOTUS WARE** was made by the Knowles, Taylor & Knowles Company of East Liverpool, Ohio, from 1890 to 1900. Lotus Ware, a thin porcelain that resembles Belleek, was sometimes decorated outside the factory. Other types of ceramics that were made by the Knowles, Taylor & Knowles Company are listed under KTK.

| | |
|---|---|
| **Bowl,** Shell, Gold, White, c.1891, 8 In. | 64 |
| **Sugar & Creamer,** Cream, Gold, Marked, 2 Piece | 283 |
| **Sugar & Creamer,** Venice Mold, Flowers, Double Handle, Marked, 2 Piece | 99 |
| **Teapot,** Venice Mold, Flowers, Gold, Double Handle, 1890s, 7 x 4 ¼ In. | 399 |
| **Urn,** Lid, Beading, Finial, Porcelain, White, Gold Pate-Sur-Pate, 7 ½ In. | 2184 |

**LOW** art tiles were made by the J. and J. G. Low Art Tile Works of Chelsea, Massachusetts, from 1877 to 1902. A variety of art and other tiles were made. Some of the tiles were made by a process called "natural," some were hand-modeled, and some were made mechanically.

J.&J.G.LOW

| | |
|---|---|
| **Tile,** Child, Kneeling, Dark Blue Glaze, c.1884, 6 x 6 In. | 85 |
| **Tile,** Portrait, Gladiator, Amber, c.1880, 6 x 6 In. | 195 |
| **Tile,** Portrait, Woman, Wheat Sheaves In Hair, 3 ⅛ In. Diam. | 156 |
| **Tile,** Scrolls, Reddish Brown Glaze, c.1881, 6 x 3 In. | 130 |
| **Tile,** Stylized Dragon, Open Mouth, Swirling Leaves, 6 x 6 In. | 75 |
| **Tile,** Sunburst, Caramel Glaze, 6 x 6 In. | 77 |
| **Tile,** Victorian Woman Profile, Majolica, 1880s, 6 x 6 In. | 129 |

**LOY-NEL-ART,** *see McCoy category.*

**LUNCH BOXES** and lunch pails have been used to carry lunches to school or work since the nineteenth century. Today, most collectors want either early tobacco advertising boxes or children's lunch boxes made since the 1930s. These boxes are made of metal or plastic. Boxes listed here include the original Thermos bottle inside the box unless otherwise indicated. Movie, television, and cartoon characters may be found in their own categories. Tobacco tin pails and lunch boxes are listed in the Advertising category.

| | | |
|---|---|---|
| **Astronauts,** Spaceships, Dome, Metal, American Thermos Products, c.1960 | | 330 |
| **Barbie,** Costume Images, Blond Ponytail Head, Blue Vinyl, Mattel, 1962, 8 ½ In. ......*illus* | | 230 |
| **Barnum Bailey Circus,** Tiger, 2-Sided, Vinyl, King-Seeley, 1970 | | 275 |
| **Bonanza,** Characters, Metal, c.1964 | | 120 |
| **Bus Shape,** Red, White, Plastic, Omni-Graphics, 1960 | | 795 |
| **Campus Queen,** Couple, Formal Outfit, 2-Sided, Metal, King-Seeley, 1967 | | 142 |
| **Dagwood & Blondie,** Characters, Multicolor, Metal, 1969 | | 89 |
| **Dome,** Black, Metal, Stamped, King-Seeley Thermos Co. | | 20 |
| **Gremlins,** Gizmo, Mystical Box, Metal, 1980s | | 60 |
| **Gunsmoke,** Western Scene, Embossed, Aladdin, 1972 | | 275 |
| **Hogan's Heroes,** Metal, Dome, Lithograph, Bing Crosby Productions, Aladdin, 1966 | | 176 |
| **Jurassic Park,** Logo, Van, Plastic | | 110 |
| **Man From U.N.C.L.E.,** Agents, Metal, 1967 | | 150 |
| **Raggedy Ann & Andy,** Holding Hands, Carrying Lunch Box, Vinyl, 1970s | | 125 |
| **Spot The Dog,** Red, Yellow, Plastic, Bluebird Toys, c.1980 | | 65 |
| **Thermos,** Suzette, Poodle, Black, Pink, Eiffel Tower, Aladdin, c.1970 | | 46 |
| **Tin,** Bail Handle, Wood Grip, 9 x 10 ½ In. | | 62 |
| **Tom Corbett,** Space Cadet, Spaceships, Metal, 1952 | | 85 |

**LUNEVILLE,** a French faience factory, was established about 1730 by Jacques Chambrette. It is best known for its fine biscuit figures and groups and for large faience dogs and lions. The early pieces were unmarked. The firm was acquired by Keller and Guerin and is still working.

| | | |
|---|---|---|
| **Candlestick,** Old Strasbourg Pattern, Baluster, 8 ¾ In. | | 75 |
| **Cup & Saucer,** Strasbourg Tulip Pattern | | 20 |
| **Tureen,** Rose Pattern, Basketweave Edge, Branch Handles, Underplate, Lid, 11 x 7 In. | | 100 |

**LUSTER** glaze was meant to resemble copper, silver, or gold. The term *luster* includes any piece with some luster trim. It has been used since the sixteenth century. Some of the luster found today was made during the nineteenth century. The metallic glazes are applied on pottery. The finished color depends on the combination of the clay color and the glaze. Blue, orange, gold, and pearlized luster decorations were used by Japanese and German firms in the early 1900s. Fairyland Luster was made by Wedgwood in the 1900s. Tea Leaf pieces have their own category.

| | | |
|---|---|---|
| **Chocolate Pot,** Dome Lid, Pink, Cottage, Footed, Cone Shape, Handle, 1800s, 9 In. | | 130 |
| **Cranberry Glass,** Cased, Enameled, Bohemia, 1900s, 10 ¼ x 5 ½ In., Pair | | 246 |
| **Fairyland Luster** is included in the Wedgwood category. | | |
| **Jug,** 2 Faces, Man Smiling, Angry Face, c.1810, 5 ¾ In. ......*illus* | | 236 |
| **Mug,** Canary Yellow, Transfer, Sheep, A Present For Mary, Child's, 2 In. ......*illus* | | 177 |
| **Mug,** Pink Highlights, Shepherds, Sheep Herd, c.1810, 5 ⅜ In. | | 325 |
| **Plate,** Toddy, Windmill, Tower, Embossed Multicolor Floral Borders, 7 ⅜ In. | | 106 |
| **Sunderland Luster** pieces are in the Sunderland category. | | |
| **Watch Hutch,** Temple Shape, Reclining Lion, 11 x 7 ¾ In. | | 1121 |

**LUSTRES** are mantel decorations or pedestal vases with many hanging glass prisms. The name really refers to the prisms, and it is proper to refer to a single glass prism as a lustre. Either spelling, luster or lustre, is correct.

| | | |
|---|---|---|
| **Cobalt Blue,** Overlay Crystal, Prisms, Gilt Decoration, England, 1800s, 14 In. | | 18 |
| **Cranberry Glass,** Roses, Clear Prisms, 12 ½ In., Pair | | 950 |
| **Cranberry,** Prisms, Flowers, Flower Form, Round Base, 14 In., 2 Pair | | 1762 |
| **Cut Glass,** Panel Cut, Spear Point Prisms, Anglo-Irish, 1800s, 11 x 5 ¾ In. | | 430 |
| **Gilt,** Enamel, Etched Shades, Spear Point Prisms, France, 1800s, 20 x 5 ¼ In., Pair | | 1195 |
| **Green Enameled Cut To Clear,** Roses, Spearpoint Prisms, 9 x 5 ½ In., Pair | | 1476 |
| **Ruby Glass,** Pink, White & Gilt Flowers, 2 Rows Cut Spear Prisms, 14 In., Pair | | 425 |
| **White Cut To Cranberry,** Cut Prisms, Trumpet Shape, Gilt, 14 ¾ In. | | 932 |

**MACINTYRE,** *see Moorcroft category.*

**Loetz,** Vase, Tango Glass, Flared, Dagobert Peche, c.1900, 5 x 6 In. $512

Rago Arts & Auction Center

**Loetz,** Vase, Titania, Pulled Threads, Silver Overlay, Art Nouveau Vine & Leaves, 12 In. $7,110

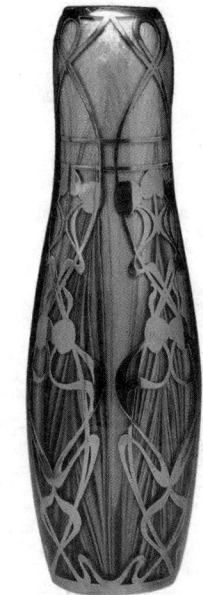

James D. Julia Auctioneers

**Lone Ranger,** Lunch Box, Lone Ranger, Hi-Yo Silver, Tonto, Blue Band, Adco-Liberty, 1954 $854

Hake's Americana & Collectibles

This is an edited listing of current prices. Visit **Kovels.com** to check thousands of prices from previous years and sign up for free information on trends, tips, reproductions, marks, and more.

**Lunch Box,** Barbie, Costume Images, Blond Ponytail Head, Blue Vinyl, Mattel, 1962, 8 ½ In.
$230

Hake's Americana & Collectibles

---

**Luster,** Jug, 2 Faces, Man Smiling, Angry Face, c.1810, 5 ¾ In.
$236

Conestoga Auction Co., Inc.

---

**Luster,** Mug, Canary Yellow, Transfer, Sheep, A Present For Mary, Child's, 2 In.
$177

Conestoga Auction Co., Inc.

---

**MAIZE** glass was made by W.L. Libbey & Son Company of Toledo, Ohio, after 1889. The glass resembled an ear of corn. The leaves were usually green, but some pieces were made with blue or red leaves. The kernels of corn were light yellow, white, or light green.

| | |
|---|---:|
| **Celery Vase,** Gold Iridescent, Blue Leaves, c.1900, 6 In. | 162 |
| **Rose Bowl,** Cranberry, Husks, Kernels, Ruffled, 5 ¼ x 6 ¾ In. | 90 |
| **Vase,** Translucent Green Leaves, Oval, c.1890, 6 In. | 132 |

**MAJOLICA** is a general term for any pottery glazed with an opaque tin enamel that conceals the color of the clay body. It has been made since the fourteenth century. Today's collector is most likely to find Victorian majolica. The heavy, colorful ware is rarely marked. Some famous makers include Minton; Griffen, Smith and Hill (marked *Etruscan*); and Chesapeake Pottery (marked *Avalon* or *Clifton*). Majolica made by Wedgwood is listed in the Wedgwood category.

| | |
|---|---:|
| **Bowl,** Fruit, Grapes, Cherries, Brown, Purple, 5 ¾ x 17 ¾ In. | 104 |
| **Bowl,** Mafra Palissy Style, Grass, Salamanders, Snake, Portugal, c.1890, 3 x 12 In. | 374 |
| **Bowl,** Palissy Style, Swamp Grass, Alligator, Toad, Beetle, Portugal, c.1890, 3 x 8 In. | 259 |
| **Bowl,** Pigeon, Scalloped, Wicker, Oak Branches, Blue Interior, Minton, 9 ¼ In. | 923 |
| **Box,** Hatching Chicks Lid, Basket Weave Exterior, Yellow, Brown, Green, c.1890, 8 x 8 In. | 184 |
| **Centerpiece,** Pierced, White Flower Band, Green Interior, c.1870, 23 In. | 530 |
| **Centerpiece,** Shell, Nude Woman, Dark Blue, Turquoise, Mythological Supports, 1800s, 13 In. | 266 |
| **Charger,** Abduction Of Women, Forest, Signed L. Poecheron, Italy, c.1900, 19 ¾ In. | 2250 |
| **Charger,** Bacchus, Companions, Lion, Chariot, Putti, Italy, 24 In. | 1875 |
| **Charger,** Depicting Victorious Roman General, Multicolor, Italy, Late 1800s, 20 In. | 250 |
| **Charger,** Figures At Well, Sheep, Armorial Crest, Hanger, Italian Renaissance, 18 In. | 354 |
| **Charger,** Italian Renaissance Style, Istoriato, Bible Scene, Cupids, Leaf Border, 1800s, 20 In. | 1000 |
| **Charger,** Italian Renaissance Style, Tin Glaze, Allegory, Women Bathing, Man, c.1890, 18 ⅝ In. | 300 |
| **Cheese Dish,** Lid, Barrel Slats, Vines, Brown, Green, George Jones, 12 ¼ In. | 246 |
| **Cheese Keeper,** Dome Lid, Arched Panels, Dogwood, Handle, Marked, 11 x 9 ½ In. ............*illus* | 649 |
| **Cheese Keeper,** Tray, Seaweed, Fish, Blue, J. Roth, c.1880, 10 In. | 726 |
| **Compote,** Boat Shape, Griffin Handle, Bacchanalian Mask Spout, Satyr, 15 ⅝ In. | 308 |
| **Compote,** Lion Masks, Allegorical Handles, Raised Foot, H. Lonitz, Austria, c.1890, 16 x 9 In. | 406 |
| **Dish,** Fox Peering Over Edge, Raised Leaves, Coiled Tail, George Jones, 10 In. | 400 |
| **Ewer,** Barrel Shape, Flat Sides, Bacchanalian Children, Grapevines, Minton, 15 In. | 1230 |
| **Ewer,** Lid, Painted, Yellow, White Bands, Painted Flowers, Scroll Handle, Deruta, Italy, 15 In. | 120 |
| **Figurine,** Boy, Resting On Basket, Grapevines, Minton, 1865, 9 ½ In. ...............................*illus* | 246 |
| **Figurine,** Grecian Maiden, Plinth Base, George Jones, c.1880, 16 In. ...........................*illus* | 984 |
| **Figurine,** Rooster, Cobalt Blue, Red, Yellow, Green, c.1925, 17 In. | 876 |
| **Figurine,** Woman, Flower Basket, Man, Bicorn Hat, Book, Period Attire, 24 ⅗ In., Pair | 563 |
| **Garden Seat,** Barrel Shape, Fruit, Vine, Cobalt Blue Ground, 17 x 14 ½ In., Pair | 1599 |
| **Jardiniere,** Blue, Black, Female Head, Flowers, Classical, George Jones, c.1875, 7 In. | 615 |
| **Jardiniere,** Bulbous, Gadroon, Lower Border, 3 Gargoyle Feet, Doulton, 13 ¼ In. | 400 |
| **Jardiniere,** Bulbous, Pierced Neck, Winged Caryatid Handles, Multicolor, 25 In. | 750 |
| **Jug,** Unruly Tavern Figures, Minton, 1866, 10 In. | 800 |
| **Oyster Plate,** Round, 6 Scalloped Wells, Fish, Purple, Blue, Victorian ...............................*illus* | 3868 |
| **Pedestal,** Eagle, Mottled Brown, Green Glaze, Square Top, c.1895, 39 x 12 In. | 594 |
| **Pedestal,** Square Capital, Faces, Hairy Paw Feet, Sweden, 1800s, 46 In. | 2629 |
| **Pitcher,** Orchid, Leaf Shape Handle, Flowers, George Jones, 7 ½ In. | 363 |
| **Pitcher,** Salmon Form, Green, Tan, Seaweed Foot, 10 ½ In. | 148 |
| **Planter,** Tree Trunk, Flower Handles, Leaves, Blue Interior, George Jones, c.1875, 7 In. | 492 |
| **Plaque,** Four Fish In The Waves, Choisy Le Roi, Impressed Mark, c.1875, 16 x 24 In. | 2460 |
| **Plate,** Green & Brown Mottled, Ivy Borders, 9 In., 8 Piece | 799 |
| **Plate,** Green, Leaf Pattern, 1900s, 9 ¼ In., 6 Piece | 188 |
| **Plate,** Lobster, Mussel Shells, Curly Parsley, Seaweed, Palissy Style, Portugal, 13 In. | 345 |
| **Platter,** Choisy Le Roi Palissy Style, Algae, Sand, Sardines, Oval, France, 11 ½ In. | 288 |
| **Salt Cellar,** Dog, Upper Body, Peering Over Edge, c.1875, 2 ⅝ In. | 492 |
| **Sardine Box,** Stand, Fish, Ocean Vegetation, Leaves, Green, Blue, George Jones, 8 ½ In. | 431 |
| **Tray,** Branch Handles, Overlapping Leaves, Green, Blue, George Jones, 14 ¼ In. | 1149 |
| **Tray,** Butterfly, Bee, Wheat Stalks, Basket Weave Rim, George Jones, c.1875, 12 ½ In. | 605 |
| **Tray,** White Orchids, Leaves, Butterflies, Mottled Ground, George Jones, 10 ¾ In. | 847 |
| **Umbrella Stand,** Molded Blooming Flowers, Multicolor, 20 ¼ x 10 ½ In. | 150 |
| **Urn,** Mythical Scenes, Multicolor, Grotesque Mask Handles, Tapered, Footed, Italy, 42 In. | 438 |
| **Urn,** Winged Females, Multicolor, 4-Footed, Italy, 49 ½ In. | 1875 |
| **Vase,** Art Nouveau, Grass, Flowers, White Lilies, Yellow, Green, 12 ¾ In., Pair | 195 |
| **Vase,** Art Nouveau, Green To Turquoise Glazes, Multicolor Flowers, 12 ½ In. | 184 |
| **Vase,** Bottle Shape, Art Nouveau, Leaves, Applied Birds, Handles, Incised, 1900s, 28 x 11 In. | 1434 |
| **Vase,** Climbing Frog, Green, Brown, Impressed Weller, 3 ⅞ In. | 1495 |

M

# HOW TO SELL
## Profits and Pitfalls

"I'm moving to a new job overseas in three months and have to decide where to go
and how much to charge to sell my collections quickly."

"When grandma died we planned a house sale. Distant relatives suddenly remembered
a teapot and painting that were promised to them at a very low price.
What would you sell them for?"

"All five of us, the children of the deceased, want objects in the estate.
How is this sort of problem handled so no one feels cheated and angry?"

These are the kind of questions we get from our readers. *Kovels Antiques and Collectibles Price Guide 2016* is filled with prices, pictures and, descriptions that can help you get an idea of the value of your items. But it doesn't tell you where you can sell things—this report will. Two things are required for a sale: an attractive item and a low enough price. There are places to sell very expensive antiques and other places that want certain types of low-priced collectibles. Networking can be helpful if you or your friends know the shops and collectors in the area and you understand the level of pricing. Prices are determined by condition (is it unrestored and perfect?), location (will it be expensive to ship?), rarity (only a few are known), history (did it belong to a celebrity?), and emotion (several bidders remember one just like it from their childhood). In the past five years, condition has become the most important feature in a sale. It used to be rarity or even age or beauty. To sell an antique or collectible you must see things like the buyer and forget what it cost, childhood memories, and how popular it was 25 years ago. Most of today's buyers never heard of Haviland china or frakturs and they think Chippendale desks and other "brown furniture" are ugly, old-fashioned, and not useful in a modern home. Our listings report actual sales last year, things that are popular with today's collectors, often things only 25 years old.

But selling is tricky. The rule is THE MORE YOU KNOW ABOUT THE PIECE, THE MORE ACCURATE THE PRICE AND THE EASIER THE SALE. The selling price should be a little lower than fair

*Jonah and the Whale mechanical bank, original paint*

so your pieces will sell more quickly. An iron mechanical bank with all original paint and the original box might sell in a well-advertised auction for thousands of dollars. The same bank with very little original paint still showing and no box should sell for only a few hundred dollars. Unless you are a dealer or a very serious, studious collector, you can't be sure what price is fair. But for average antiques and collectibles in used condition, there are a few rules to help you sell. Each type of sale calls for a slightly different pricing and selling strategy.

## WHAT TO DO BEFORE YOU DECIDE WHAT TO SELL WHERE

Don't panic when you first realize there may be hundreds of things to sell if you are downsizing, moving, or just cleaning the attic. Don't have a dealer who calls to "help" see what you have for sale. He or she will try to buy the very best things and if you decide to have a house sale or auction there will be little left to attract buyers. Our deceased neighbor's out-of-town daughter asked me to help her after she had sold things to a mall dealer. She was delighted with the $478 she got for 21-pieces or cut glass, part of a collection, a set of sterling silverware, and two carved wooden chairs. She had planned to throw away the nine leftover cut glass pieces. I suggested she donate them to a charitable auction. That donation was worth at least $600. I wonder how much her hurry to sell cost her.

Be sure you search for hidden money and jewelry. Look in purses, drapery hems, cans with false bottoms, pillows, the back of pictures, and underneath drawers where papers may be taped. Don't throw anything away before you have decided how you want to sell your things. Just put all the "trash" in a corner so you can reclaim it if it is needed. Many collections seem strange to others. Electric fans working or broken, telephone insulators, talcum powder tins, fast food toys, pencil sharpeners, tattoo patterns, tractors (toy or full-sized), auto license plates, maps, comic books, vintage rock 'n roll posters, milk bottle caps, twenty-first-century sneakers, and vintage ski clothes are just a few.

If you have records of the past history of the things you want to sell, you have an important clue. But very few average collectors record the cost, place purchased, year, cost of repairs, history of previous owners, etc. You need some of this information to determine what taxes you must pay. Antiques are like stocks—there is a capital gains tax, and original price and cost of upkeep is important. And it may help you decide how to sell to get the most money. Be sure the history is with the piece when you sell it. An interesting history encourages a quick sale.

You should decide how much time you have to sell things. The pieces must be displayed where there are prospective buyers, photographed and listed if the sale is online, and packed, shipped, and insured. And then there is "customer service" if a buyer is unhappy or a dish breaks. There is also an emotional price to pay if you are selling things you loved for years. And if you are selling family things, you may risk resentment from relatives or close friends. Collections are a form of money when they are to be sold and money can cause arguments.

There are nine ways to sell your antiques and collectibles and each have profits and pitfalls.

### FRIEND OR RELATIVE

Friends and relatives often say they would like to have something you are selling. If it is an estate, there may be rules that make special sales a problem. If you are downsizing, it might be nice to give your friend a gift if it is a low-cost item. If you sell to a friend, try to learn the wholesale price. It's easy if you are having a house sale since the person running the sale will price the items. If you think the item is very valuable, explain that it is being sold at auction and they can bid, or that they can buy ahead for the marked price at the house sale.

Watch out for the relative who wants to "reclaim" a valuable painting from grandma or a piece of gem-set jewelry for "sentimental reasons." It's all cash when you are selling.

## PRIVATE SALE TO COLLECTOR

If you have inherited or have enjoyed your special collection, you might want it to go to a "loving family" or collector buddy. But the best place to sell a special collection like ink bottles or KPM plaques is to a member of the collector club. Search for a club related to your item and see if you can put an ad in their bulletin. This type of private sale takes time, negotiating, wrapping, and shipping. Some eager buyers will drive to your home to pick up the purchase and see what else is for sale. You may not get highest price because not many prospective buyers will see it. But it will be in safe hands.

Beware of newspaper ads by "collectors," especially traveling hotel groups that buy for cash. Some give very low "appraisals" so they can buy at a low price. It is never a good idea to sell to the appraiser. In fact, those who are members of the official appraiser groups agree not to buy what they appraise.

If you use a local ad like Craigslist, be careful. Don't let anyone who contacts you inside your house if you are alone. Don't agree to meet a prospective buyer anywhere if you are alone.

## ESTATE SALE

An estate sale (also called a house sale) is a good way to sell if the house is empty. You can run the sale yourself, but it is a lot of work. Rearrange furniture, display like items together, dishes on the dining room table, clothes on the bed, or hung in the closet, toys, and baby things in a special place or room, books on shelves, etc. Everything must be priced to sell, and since many of your customers are dealers, they can pay half of retail or less. And you will need some expert advice on how to set the price. Customers at an estate sale go for a bargain but expect to pay higher prices than at a garage sale, because the sale has higher quality items.

If there is a house full of furniture, paintings, and accessories, it is best to hire someone who runs sales locally. The list of customers, where to place ads, how to write ads, extra trained help, and how to avoid theft and bad checks, etc., are all things you probably don't know. Of course there is a charge, but that is negotiable and is usually based on how much money is made at the sale. You should also have references, a written contract, a set date for the sale, and a description of the number of days to set up, the number of helpers, and the type of security. Also be sure you or the sale group have liability insurance. Be sure the floors are covered if it is raining, and that nothing is done to damage floors, walls, or the house while the sale is in session. The house should be left clean, ready to be sold, and all windows and doors should be locked.

A good sale has lots of people for several days and selling prices are low. But you can sell everything, even garbage cans, half-filled tin spice boxes in the kitchen, clothes, toys, gardening tools, and electronics equipment at the same time. You don't have to work or to figure out the right selling price and you get the money on the last day of the sale.

*Mother Dawson spice tin*

## GARAGE SALE

A garage sale is like a house sale but more manageable and you probably can do it without hiring others to set prices. You must put low prices (using hang tags, stickers, or markers) on everything before the sale starts. You can have a box that says "Anything-$2" full of Beanie Babies or political buttons. Keep the cash in a box you never leave unattended. Start with change and be careful about accepting checks. On the second day of the sale, sell the leftovers by moving prices down. If a customer wants a group of things, get the sale by lowering price and negotiating.

The best sellers at a garage sale are low-priced things useful to young families—clothes, baby stuff, toys, garden furniture, pots and pans, etc. Sort by type of item and get friends to help. You might even have a group sale and share expenses of ads, etc. There are sites online or local newspaper leaflets that can help you do this. Set low prices, well below half of retail. You don't want leftovers because prices were high.

Notify city hall that you are having a sale if you think there might be a traffic problem or if there is a need for a permit. Be sure you can legally sell everything. Avoid guns, including toy cap guns and BB guns, old cribs, cradles or car seats, liquor, and ivory.

## ANTIQUES SHOP OR MALL

Pick a shop that sells things like yours, perhaps small pieces of antique furniture, designer scarves, good crystal, or prints. Notice the prices. Your pieces should be sold to the owner for one-third or one-half the retail price. Take pictures of your belongings and show them to the shop owner. If the dealer thinks your things can be sold in the shop, you probably will be asked what you want to sell it for. Prepare ahead—use this book, other sources we mention at the end of this report, and ask knowledgeable friends who are collectors. Then negotiate prices or commissions and see if it is best to sell or consign your things. Commissions are usually 10% to 30% of the sold price and it takes time for a sale and a payment—we have waited as long as two years. Be sure you have the necessary paperwork about the item you are selling and state the condition of the piece, commission, and any other charges. If not sold in a set amount of time, you can take it back.

*Cow horn chair, reupholstered, 32 x 22 inches*

## INTERNET SITES

Online selling is not as easy as many think. If an item is well-known, in useable condition, not too large, can be described in a paragraph, and is easy to recognize in a photograph, it probably can be sold on the internet. But if it is one of many groups of collectibles that are now out of favor, especially the made-to-order limited editions, it may not find a buyer.

A buyer must be able to identify your collectibles from the pictures and descriptions. Often two to four different pictures are needed. For pottery, a picture must show all sides and the bottom mark. If there is a flaw, it should also be described and photographed. Minor flaws lower the price, but rare, valuable pieces with chips can be sold if priced low enough. Some dealers claim pictured flaws seem more serious, so they do not try to sell anything with damage on the internet. And many say the social media sites are not creating sales.

Describe the color, size, any decoration, marks, unique features, use and history if it adds information about age or possible origin. For example, "This chair was made from cow horns in the 1890s. The Western look was popular and some firms used horns saved at slaughter houses to make horn furniture. The legs, arms and back are curved horns of the necessary size and shape. The seat has replaced upholstery in good condition. Size: 32 by 22 inches. Price: $600 plus shipping." But would this be enough without a photograph? A maker's name or a reference to a similar piece pictured online or in a book would help.

It is very time consuming work to sell on the internet. Each item requires the time to learn the rules (you can't sell guns, liquor, ivory, eagle feathers, rhinoceros horns, or many other things covered by laws), contact the site, write the ad, place the ad, take the pictures, answer any inquiries, cash the check, pack the item, take it to be mailed or sent some other way—and perhaps more special requirements for some things.

## AUCTION HOUSE

If you have very expensive paintings, bronzes, antique Chinese jade or ceramics, Shaker furniture and accessories, or some name brands that are always expensive like Tiffany lamps and glass, Ohr pottery, Judith Leiber purses, Hermes purses and scarves, Cartier jewelry, furniture by Nakashima, Wendell Castle, Paul Evans and other designers working since 1950, and rare toys, advertising, glass or jewelry, you might want to sell at an auction.

There are thousands of auctions in the United States and most take bids online, by phone or in the room. Small "farm auctions" often just take bids from those attending the sale. If you own an internationally popular painting or work of art, there are also auctions overseas that have international bidding. Some large U.S. auctions only sell things worth $5,000 or more. Sometimes if you are selling expensive paintings, toys or lamps, the auction house will take more of your things, like a collection of Dedham

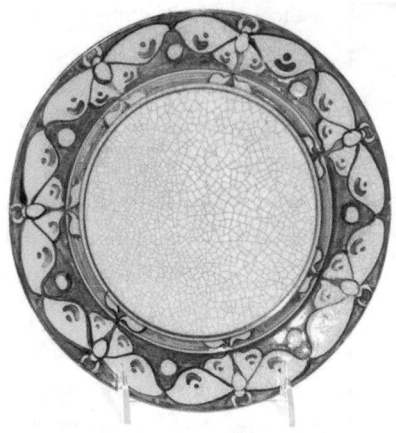

*Dedham Pottery plate, Moth pattern,*
*8½ inches*

pottery plates, and sell them as a group in one numbered auction catalog lot. There are listings for auction galleries in many places online or in antiques publications like *Maine Antiques Digest, Antique Week, Antique Trader,* and *Antiques and the Arts Weekly.* Read the ads, see what they are selling, and find an auction house that would like your kind of antique or collectible.

Check the history of the auction house, perhaps call the Better Business Bureau to be sure there are no reported problems. Call, send a letter, or email with some pictures. You might be more comfortable if you first talk to someone you know who had experience consigning things to the auction house. Ask to see some catalogs of past sales.

If you are selling a few things, you may have to ship them to the auction house. If you are selling a lot of things and a lot of money is involved, the auction staff will pack everything and take it to the auction site. Be sure you keep a photograph and description of each piece that will be sold. If you know there are some historic connections or other interesting facts about the piece, be sure to write them down and send them with your items. Keep copies of everything.

Many things are negotiable for an auction: the commission you pay, charges for storage, photographs, reserve prices, if sales tax is charged, who has insurance, and what happens if the piece gets no bids. Read the printed contract before you sign it to know about any extra costs. Also, get the tentative date for your sale and information on how long it takes to be paid. You should be paid the sale price minus the commissions and other charges about six weeks after the sale. Things that did not sell might be kept for another sale or sent back. You should decide what you want to do before the sale if possible. There is a charge for storage if you don't have the unsold lots you want back removed in a short time, sometimes less than a week.

## Pitfalls

You must decide if there is to be a reserve. That means the piece cannot be sold for less than the amount specified by you but it also means you may miss a chance to sell the piece and there is a charge for the reserve. Buyers do not like to bid on pieces that have been left behind from earlier auctions. There is a suspicion that there is something "wrong" that has not been explained in the catalog. If you are settling an estate, you probably don't want reserves. Added time means added legal fees and a reserve means another sale and months of delay. Discuss the suggested price with the

*Rhinoceros horn libation cup, never picked up by bidder*

auctioneer before the sale and ask for an opinion. Of course, the auctions like a reserve-free sale. They have put time and money into the advertising and preparation to sell the item. And if you take the antique back, they will have lost money.

Sometimes all of your items don't sell. Deciding what to do with the leftovers can be complicated. At a sale of designer clothing, almost none of the men's suits sold. The out-of-town consigner decided to have the auction house give them to a charitable resale shop rather than ship them back across the country. Most auctions will try to sell unsold lots in the weeks following the sale. Some even list the things that are available on their website. Of course, the prices are low.

## Appraisals

Lawyers and well-meaning friends often ask you about the appraisals of the things you want to sell. You do not need a formal appraisal to sell an antique. You might need one to settle a division of property in a divorce or an estate with several heirs. But appraisers are expensive, some as much as $250 an hour, and an appraisal is an estimate, not a guarantee that it will be the sold price. There are horror stories about estates taxed on very high appraisals, only to find later that the estate antiques sold for much less money.

Do not hire an appraiser who offers to buy your things. In extreme cases with estates, you might need a trained person to help determine what things are worth so each heir can get about the same value from the estate. Many antiques dealers can do this without writing a formal appraisal for each item. There are also some companies that advertise that they will help you empty a house, and give advice on where and how to sell. Be careful. Some of these companies are more interested in their profit than giving the best service to you. But if you are unable or unwilling to tackle the job of turning collections into money, ask local antiques enthusiasts to tell you who has the best reputation for helping close estates or help with downsizing.

These are the main appraisal associations in the United States. They can give you the names of their close members

## Appraisers

American Society of Appraisers
11107 Sunset Hills Rd.
Suite 310
Reston, VA 20190
800-ASA-VALU
(800-272-8258) or
703-478-2228
appraisers.org

Appraisers Association
  of America, Inc.
212 West 35th Street
11th Floor South
New York, NY 10000
212-889-5404 Ext. 10
appraisersassociation.org

International Society of
  Appraisers
225 West Wacker Drive
Suite 650
Chicago, Illinois 60606
312-981-6778
isa-appraisers.org

## DONATION TO MUSEUM OR NON-PROFIT

If you can use the tax deduction, a donation can be more profitable than selling. The tax deduction for charitable giving is usually the approved retail price. When you sell, you get wholesale price minus charges, so it is sometimes worthwhile to give things away. You're doing a good deed, the museum or non-profit will be delighted with the donation, and you and your family will probably be mentioned at a meeting or in a report. And you get a tax deduction that is as good as getting cash. Consider a donation to a charitable auction or a non-profit museum. The Cleveland public television station raises hundreds of thousands of dollars each year with a four-day on-air auction of donated goods. It is not difficult to find a charitable auction that wants donations or a museum that might want a special painting or historic letter. You can always donate to Goodwill (Goodwill.org/wp-content/uploads/2010/12/Donation_Valuation_Guide.pdf), Salvation Army (SATruck.org/donation-value-guide) or Volunteers of America (VOAGo.org/Give-a-Gift/Donate-Your-Used-Goods/Donation-Value-Guide). They will give you a list of suggested values. Think of the donation as a special type of sale because you do end up with extra cash in the form of an income tax deduction. Your only work is doing the bookkeeping and delivering the item. You should get the acknowledgment in one or two months, the extra cash at tax refund time.

## OTHER WAYS TO SELL FOR PROFIT

Many jewelry stores will buy silver or gold. If you have silver or gold items, you can sell at the going melt-down price set by the store. Gold was at $1,380 an ounce in 2014, a little over $1,100 in 2015. Silver high was about $21 in June 2015 at $15-$16.

If you are moving, you might be able to sell some things to the new owners of your house. Often rugs, drapes, special stained glass windows made to fit the space, antique light fixtures and chandeliers, antique iron gates, andirons, and other hard to find architectural pieces in a special size might be a good buy for the new owners. But be careful, the house buyer may ask you to include all these things in the sale price of the house. Replace valuable antiques attached to walls before you put the house up for sale.

There are companies that match dinner sets or silverware or even parts for toys or antique autos. They have to buy the things they sell, so you might be able to sell some of your things to them. Search online for these replacement companies and email or write a description of your dishes, silver, or jewelry to see if they are interested. The prices they list when selling are often three or four times the price they will pay you.

# MORE TIPS

Don't expect selling your antiques to be easy. It is a full-time job for hundreds of dealers.

Prices have gone down for many things since 2008, and you will not make a profit on everything you sell. You may not even be able to sell some things that are now out of style.

If you are selling, be sure to check all legal restrictions. To be safe, always be with a friend when large sums of money are involved.

Remember—anyone who sells antiques to the public must get the antiques somewhere, so you might be able to sell to them.

# RESOURCES

## BEST TO SELL ONLINE

Some antiques are very easy to sell online, some are much harder, and some just don't seem to attract any online buyers. Here is a list of 14 antiques and collectibles that sell quickly online if the descriptions and photographs are inviting.

Advertising trays and signs, especially those made of metal

Antique toys in good condition

Art pottery with makers' marks or artists' signatures

Coca-Cola bottles and advertising

Costume jewelry

Designer handbags

Elvis Presley belongings

Maps

One-of-a-kind eccentric items, like an artificial leg

Royalty items

Star Trek (early)

Tiffany anything

Unusual vintage Christmas ornaments

World's Fair memorabilia

*Christmas lantern, Santa Claus head, composition, paper, Germany, 10 inches*

## ALMOST WORTHLESS COLLECTIBLES THAT WILL SELL
## FOR LESS THAN WHOLESALE (IF AT ALL)

It's almost impossible to sell some collectibles that were popular in the 1970s and later. Limited editions and other collectibles that were made as parts of series were made by more and more companies. By 2010, series collectors lost interest and prices fell and then plummeted. Also listed are things that never were popular with most collectors, like family Bibles.

Baseball cards in less than mint condition, unless very old and rare

Beanie Babies

Bradford Exchange collectibles

Christmas plates (except for rare years of Danish plates)

Danbury Mint

Encyclopedias

Family Bibles

Family photographs

Franklin Mint sets

Hess trucks

Hummel figurines

Incomplete Haviland china sets

Royal Doulton figurines, commemorative plates and character jugs made in the 20th and 21st centuries

Silver ingots (sell for melt down value)

Single pieces of dinnerware made after 1920

Thomas Kinkaid enhanced "paintings"

## SOME CLUB PUBLICATIONS THAT TAKE FOR SALE ADS

There are hundreds of clubs devoted to collectibles. Members meet, discuss their favorites, and publish newsletters that inform members about events, research, and each other. Some have ads offering to buy or sell the collectible. This is a short list of some of the clubs that run ads in their newsletter. It is a good spot to list pieces of your collection that are "for sale."

**American Bell Association International**
americanbell.org

**Antique Doll Collector**
antiquedollcollector.com

**Fostoria Glass Society of America**
fostoriaglass.org

**National Cambridge Collectors Inc.**
cambridgeglass.org

**National Imperial Glass Collectors Society**
imperialglass.org

**Novelty Salt & Pepper Shakers Club**
saltandpepperclub.com

**Open Salt Collectors**
opensalts.info

**Red Wing Collectors Society**
redwingcollectorssociety.org

**Wagner & Griswold Society**
wag-society.org

## SOME ONLINE MALLS AND SPECIALTY SITES

Look for online malls and special sites that are selling your type of antique or collectible. Dealers first buy, then sell items listed on the site. If you have a collection of 50 sets of bookends, you might save time by offering it to an online dealer. Of course, you will get a lower price because the dealer has to make money and can't pay retail prices. This is just a sample of what you can find online.

### Malls
rubylane.com
icollect247.com
tias.com
trocadero.com

### Bottles
**Antique Bottle Collector's Haven**
antiquebottles.com

### Dinnerware, Silverware, Tableware & Glassware
**Replacements. Ltd.**
replacementsltd.com

### Cookie Jars
**The Cookie Jar Net**
thecookiejar.net;
click on the link to Marketplace

### Glass & Pottery
**Glass & Pottery Sellers' Association**
glassandpotterysellers.org

### Silver Flatware
**Nancy's Silver Shop**
nancysilver.com

## SOME SITES THAT SELL ITEMS THAT MAY ALSO BUY

### Antique & Vintage Bookends, Sculptures, Desk, Dresser & Library Accessories
**Antique Bookend Shoppe**
antiquebookendshoppe.com

### Pedal Cars, Tricycles, Bicycles, Scooters, Planes, Go-Karts, Trains, Tractors & Classic Ride-On Toys
**Pedal Car Planet**
pedalcarplanet.com

### Political Items
**USAmericana**
usamericana.com

### Jewelry
**Morning Glory Antiques & Jewelry**
morninggloryjewelry.com

**Vintage Treasures**
vintagejewelry.com

**Aged and Opulent Jewelry**
agedandopulentjewelry.com

### Art Deco Furniture & Lighting
**DecoDame.com**
decodame.com

### Pottery
**Just Art Pottery**
justartpottery.com

**Watt Pottery**
wattpotteryshop.com

**Franciscan and other California Pottery**
hillhousewares.com

### Glassware
**Kejaba Treasures Store**
kejabatreasures.com

### Perfume Bottles
**Passion For Perfume**
passionforperfume.com

# SOME SPECIALTY AUCTIONS

**Allard Auctions**
PO Box 1030
St. Ignatius, MT 59865
*American history, western, Indian*

**American Bottle Auctions**
915 28th St.
Sacramento, CA 95816
*Bottles, glass, marbles*

**American Glass Gallery**
PO Box 227
New Hudson, MI 48165
*Bottles, glass*

**Anderson Americana**
PO Box 644
Troy, OH 45373
*Political*

**Bertoia Auctions**
2141 DeMarco Dr.
Vineland, NJ 08360
*Advertising, banks, toy, doll*

**Brown Tool Auctions**
9325 Dwight Boyer
Watervliet, MI 49098
*Tools*

**Copake Auction**
266 East Main St.
Copake, NY 12516
*Bicycles*

**Cowan's Auctions Inc.**
6270 Este Ave.
Cincinnati, OH 45232
*American history, Western, firearms,
contemporary art pottery*

**Crocker Farm**
15900 York Rd.
Sparks, MD 21152
*Stoneware, ceramics*

**Early American History Auctions**
P.O. Box 3507
Rancho Santa Fe, CA 92067
*American history, Western*

**Early Auction Co.**
123 Main St
Milford, OH 45150
*Glass, lamps & art pottery*

**Garth's Auctioneers & Appraiser**
P.O. Box 369
Delaware, OH 43015
*Folk art*

**Glass Discoveries Auction**
P.O. Box 628
Parkman, OH 44080
*Bottles, glass*

**Glass Works Auctions**
PO Box 180
East Greenville, PA 18041
*Bottles, glass*

**Hake's Americana & Collectibles**
P.O. Box 12001
York, PA 17402
*Advertising, toy, doll, political, ephemera*

**Heritage Auctions**
3500 Maple Ave, 17th Flr.
Dallas, TX 75219
*Advertising, toy, comic books, designer purses,
historical, political*

**High Noon LA Inc.**
9929 Venice Blvd.
Los Angeles, CA 90034
*American history, Western*

**Humler & Nolan**
225 E. 6th St., 4th FL
Cincinnati, OH 45202
*Glass, lamps & art pottery*

**James D. Julia, Inc.**
203 Skowhegan Rd.
Fairfield, ME 04937
*Doll, firearms, glass, lamps, toy, art pottery*

**Jeffrey S. Evans & Associates**
P.O. Box 2638
Harrisonburg, VA 22801
*Glass, lamps, art pottery, stoneware, ceramics*

**John Toomey Gallery**
818 North Blvd
Oak Park, IL 60301
*Mid-Century Modern, Arts & Crafts*

**LA Modern Auctions**
16145 Hart St.
Van Nuys, CA 91406
*Mid-Century Modern, Arts & Crafts,*
*contemporary*

**Lang's Auction, Inc.**
663 Pleasant Valley Rd
Waterville, NY 13480
*Fishing tackle*

**Lloyd Ralston Gallery**
549 Howe Ave
Shelton, CT 06484
*Trains, toys, soldier*

**Martin J. Donnelly Antique Tools**
5223 County Road 8
Avoca, NY 14809
*Tools*

**McMasters Harris**
Apple Tree Doll Auctions
1625 West Church St.
Newark, OH 43055
*Dolls, toys*

**Morphy Auctions**
2000 N. Reading Road
Denver, PA 17517
*Advertising, toys, marbles,*
*movie props, firearms*

*Tiffany lamp, Venetian pattern,*
*green jewels, 18 inches, $103,500*

**Noel Barrett Vintage Toys at Auction**
P.O. Box 300
Carversville, PA 18913
*Advertising, toys, dolls*

**Norman C. Heckler & Co.**
79 Bradford Corner Rd.
Woodstock Valley, CT 06282
*Bottles, glass*

**Old West Show Events**
3201 Zafarano Dr., Ste. C585
Santa Fe, NM 87507
*American history, Western*

**Past Tyme Pleasures**
5424 Sunol Blvd., #10-242
Pleasanton, CA 94566
*Advertising, country store*

**Rago Arts & Auction Center**
333 North Main St.
Lambertville, NJ 08530
*Mid-Century Modern, Arts & Crafts,
contemporary pottery*

**Rich Penn Auctions**
Box 1355
Waterloo, IA 50704
*Advertising, country store*

**RSL Auctions**
295 US HWY 22 East, Ste. 204 West
Whiehouse Station, NJ 08889
*Toys, banks, soldiers*

**Seeck Auctions**
PO Box 377
Mason City, IA 50402
*Carnival glass, stoneware*

**Showtime Auction Services**
22619 Monterey Dr.
Woodhaven, MI 48183
*Advertising*

**Swann Galleries**
104 E. 25th St
New York, NY 10010
*Paper, photographs*

**Theriault's**
PO Box 151
Annapolis, MD 21404
*Dolls, childhood items*

**Treadway Gallery**
2029 Madison Rd.
Cincinnati, OH 45208
*Mid-Century Modern, Arts & Crafts, art pottery*

**Woody Auction**
PO Box 618
Douglass, KS 67039
*Glass, lamps, art pottery, carnival glass*

*Ohr art pottery vase,
9 inches*

| | |
|---|---|
| **Vase,** Flowers, Bottle Shape, Applied Dolphin Handles, 12 In. | 125 |
| **Vase,** Plum Ground, Leaves, Yellow Flower Applied, Tapered Cylinder, Art Nouveau, 16 In. | 250 |
| **Vase,** Putto, Bird, Leaves, Fruit, Double Handled, c.1920, 14 x 12 In. | 210 |
| **Vase,** Swan & Bulrush, Trumpet Shape, Pierced Rim, Copeland, 1800s, 8½ In. .................*illus* | 2380 |
| **Vase,** Tree Trunk, Applied Branches, Oak Leaves, Blue, Green, Brown, 11 x 6 In. | 1392 |

 **MALACHITE** is a green stone with unusual layers or rings of darker green shades. It is often polished and used for decorative objects. Most malachite comes from Siberia or Australia.

| | |
|---|---|
| **Box,** Figural Scene On Lid, Footed, Russia, 1989, 4¾ x 9 In. | 1250 |
| **Box,** Gilt Bronze Anthemion Shape Feet, Bezel, Hinge Lie, France, 5 x 11 In. | 4674 |
| **Candlestick,** Louis XV Style, Gilt Bronze, Russia, 10 x 5½ In., Pair | 1230 |
| **Figurine,** Budai, Happy, Seated, Open Robes, Wood Stand, Chinese, 1900s, 3½ x 4¼ In. | 179 |
| **Figurine,** Crocodile, Baby On Back, Carved, Wood Stand, 6 x 3 In. | 92 |
| **Snuff Bottle,** Flask Shape, Relief Carved Rose, Leaves, c.1900s, 2¼ In. | 142 |
| **Vase,** Winged Beast, Stand, Chinese, 2½ x 3 In. | 140 |

 **MAPS** of all types have been collected for centuries. The earliest known printed maps were made in 1478. The first printed street map showed London in 1559. The first road maps for use by drivers of automobiles were made in 1901. Collectors buy maps that were pages of old books, as well as the multifolded road maps popular in this century.

| | |
|---|---|
| **Africa,** Libia Ulterior, Color, Cosmography & Geography, R. Blome, 1600s, 11⅜ x 15¼ In. | 295 |
| **Alexandria,** Virginia, Bird's-Eye View, Print, Frame, c.1900, 14 x 23 In. | 184 |
| **Atlas To Adam's Geography,** Engraved, Paper Wrappers, Lincoln & Edmands, 1820, 85 x 69 In. | 313 |
| **Charleston,** Plan Of Charles Town From Survey Of Edwd. Crisp, James Akin, 1704, 9 x 11½ In. | 413 |
| **City Of Salisbury,** Close Church, River, William Naish, Saurm, Benj Colins, Printer, 1751, 24 x 18 In. .. | 354 |
| **Eastern U.S.,** C.F. Weiland, Weimar Geographic Institute, Germany, 1835, Frame, 32 x 28 In. | 502 |
| **Eastern U.S.,** Virginia, Marylandia Et Carolina, Johann Baptist Homann, Frame, 1700s, 20 x 23 In. | 1888 |
| **England & Ireland,** H. Jaillot, Watercolor, Engraved Title, Frame, 1700s, 23 x 26 In. .........*illus* | 356 |
| **Florida,** Seminoles, Inset Maps, Cedar Keys, Key West, 1846, 42¼ x 39 In. | 717 |
| **France,** Engraving, Laid Paper, Nico Las D'Abbeville, Duchy Of Cleves, 1679, 18 x 22 In. | 44 |
| **Georgia,** Florida, Louisiana, Part Of Carolina, S. Bowen, 1748, 14 x 18¾ In. | 2987 |
| **Globe,** Celestial, Constellations, Brass Median Ring, Mahogany Tripod, Cary, c.1815, 24 In. | 1845 |
| **Globe,** Celestial, Wood, Mythological Figures, 4 Turned Legs, 8 In. | 492 |
| **Globe,** Terrestrial, 12 Gores, Brass Median Ring, Ebonized Stand, Donaldson's, 1830, 18 In. | 800 |
| **Globe,** Terrestrial, 12 Gores, Cartouche, Pierced Hour Hand, Brass Base, Clock, Philip's, 12 In. | 3567 |
| **Globe,** Terrestrial, 12 Printed Gores, Brass Hour Circle, Cast Iron Tripod, Gilman Joslin, 23 In. .. | 492 |
| **Globe,** Terrestrial, Cast Iron Tripod Base, Loring, 1851, 12 x 41½ In. | 5938 |
| **Globe,** Terrestrial, Celestial Medial Stand, Kittinger, T.H. Costello, c.1898, 21 In. .................*illus* | 780 |
| **Globe,** Terrestrial, Celestial, Ebonized, Cast Iron Tripod Stand, Lothian, 1828, 35 x 9 In., Pair.... | 25000 |
| **Globe,** Terrestrial, Celestial, Mahogany Tripod Stand, J. & W. Cary, London, 12 x 25½ In., Pair.. | 11250 |
| **Globe,** Terrestrial, Fruitwood Stand, Josiah Loring, Boston, 15 x 9 In. | 1875 |
| **Globe,** Terrestrial, H.B. Nims & Co., Mahogany, Cast Iron Stand, c.1885, 41 In. .................*illus* | 1353 |
| **Globe,** Terrestrial, Patinated Metal Stand, France, c.1865, 13 x 6 In. | 1250 |
| **Globe,** Terrestrial, Plaster, 24 Printed Gores, Tripod Base, Dudley Adams, c.1800, 40 In. | 6150 |
| **Globe,** Terrestrial, Rand McNally Co., Chicago, Bronze Tripod Stand, c.1925, 19 In. | 300 |
| **Globe,** Terrestrial, Turned Wood Stand, Carey, London, c.1810, 12 x 18 In. | 2125 |
| **Globe,** W. & A.K. Johnston, Celestial, Cartouche, Classical, Brass Meridian, 4-Footed, 18 In. | 800 |
| **Globe,** Wire Overlay Continents, Square Base, Metal, 23 x 8 In. | 90 |
| **Hartford,** Connecticut, Lithograph, Survey & Drawn By Marcus Smith, 1850, 45 x 31 In. | 2750 |
| **Hooker's Pocket Plan City Of New York,** Engraved, Folding, Lower Manhattan, Color, 1828, 12 x 15 In. | 423 |
| **Isle Of Man,** Engraved, Color, Drayton, Frame, 9½ x 12 In. | 180 |
| **Louisiana,** Mississippi, Alabama, Panorama Of The Seat Of War, J. Bachmann, 23 x 33 In. | 2868 |
| **Mediterranean,** Engraved, Joannes Deutecum, 16th Century, 15 x 20 In. | 885 |
| **Missionary,** Island Mission, Colored, Chinese, 1905, 18 x 21 In. | 30 |
| **Mississippi River,** Copper, Engraving, Hand Colored, Lieutenant J. Ross, 1762, 46 x 21 In. | 3107 |
| **Mitchell's Travelers Guide Through United States,** Engraved, Folding, Color, 18 x 21 In., 77 Pages. | 406 |
| **Nautical Chart,** Maine Coast, Burl Frame, Eldridge, 1924, 36 x 55 In. | 600 |
| **New Mexico,** Old Territory & Military Dept., W.H. Dougal, 1859, 23¾ x 34¼ In. | 836 |
| **New Netherlands,** Engraved, Hand Colored, Justus Danckerts, Frame, 1656, 29 x 33 In. | 3450 |
| **New Orleans,** Plan, Thomas Jefferys, c.1760, 13 x 19 In. | 1434 |
| **New Orleans,** Wood Cut, Harper's Weekly, C. Graham, c.1884, 21¼ x 32¼ In. | 717 |
| **Norfolk & Essex,** John Speed, 17th Century, Frame, 15½ x 20½ In. | 950 |
| **North & South Carolina,** Indian Frontiers, Henry Mouzon, Color Outlines, 2 Sheets, 22 x 56 In. | 9600 |
| **North Pole,** Emanuel Bowen, London Engraving, On Paper, c.1752, 18 x 20 In. | 1800 |

**Majolica,** Cheese Keeper, Dome Lid, Arched Panels, Dogwood, Handle, Marked, 11 x 9½ In.
$649

**Majolica,** Figurine, Boy, Resting On Basket, Grapevines, Minton, 1865, 9½ In.
$246

**M**

**Majolica,** Figurine, Grecian Maiden, Plinth Base, George Jones, c.1880, 16 In.
$984

**Majolica,** Oyster Plate, Round, 6 Scalloped Wells, Fish, Purple, Blue, Victorian
$3,868

Clars Auction Gallery

**Majolica,** Vase, Swan & Bulrush, Trumpet Shape, Pierced Rim, Copeland, 1800s, 8 ½ In.
$2,380

Clars Auction Gallery

**Map,** England & Ireland, H. Jaillot, Watercolor, Engraved Title, Frame, 1700s, 23 x 26 In.
$356

James D. Julia Auctioneers

| | |
|---|---|
| **Northeast U.S.,** New York, Novi Belgii Novaeque Angliae Nec, 1600s, 18 x 21 ¼ In. ..................... | 3540 |
| **Palestine,** Robinson & Smith, Inset Maps Jerusalem, Linen Backed, 1856, 44 x 30 ½ In.............. | 478 |
| **Portsmouth,** J.G. Hales, Boston, Frame, 1813, 30 x 41 In. ..................... | 1320 |
| **Railroad,** Michigan, George Cram, Frame, 1878, 38 x 29 In. ..................... | 720 |
| **River Yazoo,** Part Of Mississippi, Copperplate Engraved, 15 ¾ x 24 In........... | 6273 |
| **San Francisco,** William M. Eddy, 1840, 24 ¾ x 19 In. ..................... | 427 |
| **Southern United States,** Laurie & Whittle, 1794, 19 ½ x 25 In. ..................... | 2270 |
| **State Of New Jersey,** Mathew Carey, Pocket, Folding, 20 x 13 In. ..................... | 531 |
| **Tennessee,** Engraved, Towns, Indian Sites, Payne's Geography, 1799, 16 ¼ x 8 ¼ In. .......... | 1416 |
| **Tennessee,** Formerly Part Of North Carolina, Trifold, 1795 9 ¼ x 16 ¼ In........... | 1180 |
| **United States,** 2-Sided, Topographical Railway Map, J.T. Lloyd, 1867, 37 x 49 ½ In. ....... | 854 |
| **United States,** Color, Cram's, c.1940, 40 x 50 In. ..................... | 180 |
| **Virginia,** Nova Virginia Tabula, Willum Blaeu, c.1635, 16 x 20 In. ..................... | 2640 |

**MARBLE** collectors pay highest prices for glass and sulphide marbles. The game of marbles has been popular since the days of the ancient Romans. American children were able to buy marbles by the mid-eighteenth century. Dutch glazed clay marbles were least expensive. Glazed pottery marbles, attributed to the Bennington potteries in Vermont, were of a better quality. Marbles made of pink marble were also available by the 1830s. Glass marbles seem to have been made later. By 1880, Samuel C. Dyke of South Akron, Ohio, was making clay marbles and The National Onyx Marble Company was making marbles of onyx. The Navarre Glass Marble Company of Navarre, Ohio, and M. B. Mishler of Ravenna, Ohio, made the glass marbles. Ohio remained the center of the marble industry, and the Akron-made Akro Agate brand became nationally known. Other pieces made by Akro Agate are listed in this book in the Akro Agate category. Sulphides are glass marbles with frosted white figures in the center.

| | |
|---|---|
| **Agate,** Guinea Clone, Micro, Christensen, ⅝ In........... | 420 |
| **Agate,** Guinea, Cobalt Blue Base, Multicolor, Christensen, ⅝ In........... | 300 |
| **Agate,** Guinea, Multicolor, Christensen, ⅝ In........... | 270 to 360 |
| **Agate,** Guinea, Red, Blue, Yellow, Christensen, ⅝ In........... | 270 |
| **Agate,** Submarine, Clear, Mint Green, Salmon, White, Color Looping, Christensen, ¹¹⁄₁₆ In. ........ | 660 |
| **Agate,** Submarine, Emerald Green, Orange, Christensen, ¹¹⁄₁₆ In........... | 960 |
| **Agate,** Tricolor Flame, Red, Yellow Tip, White Base, Christensen, ⅝ In. ..................... | 150 |
| **Akro Agate,** Corkscrew, Oxblood, Yellow Base, ¾ In........... | 150 |
| **Akro Agate,** Hybrid Popeye, Clear, Red, Green Blue Corkscrew, ⅝ In........... | 120 |
| **Akro Agate,** Hybrid Popeye, Red, Yellow, White, Green, ⅝ In........... | 330 |
| **Akro Agate,** Hybrid Popeye, Yellow, Green, Blue, White, Orange, ¹¹⁄₁₆ In........... | 150 |
| **Akro Agate,** Oxblood Corkscrew, White Base, ¾ In........... | 150 |
| **Akro Agate,** Popeye, White, Green, Yellow, Orange, ⅝ In........... | 270 |
| **Aventurine Swirl,** Open Ridge Core, 3 Ribbons, Yellow, Orange, Green, ⅝ In........... | 210 |
| **Banded,** Loops, Blue, Red, Brown, Green, Opaque, ¹¹⁄₁₆ In........... | 390 |
| **Chidy,** Pinwheel, Pink, Blue Leafs, Green Wreath Center, 1 ½ In........... | 510 |
| **Clambroth,** Black Opaque Base, White Lines, 1 ¾ In........... | 1080 |
| **Clambroth,** Black, Opaque, Mark Matthews, 1993, 1 ¾ In........... | 210 |
| **Cloud,** Yellow, Red, Green, Single Pontil, ⅝ In........... | 150 |
| **Cobalt Blue Sponging,** Bristol Slip Ground, c.1890, 1 ¾ In........... | 259 |
| **Double Helix Ribbon Swirl,** 2 White Latticinio Threads, ¹¹⁄₁₆ In........... | 360 |
| **End Of Day,** 3 Mossy Panels, Blue, White, Green, Yellow, 2 ⁵⁄₁₆ In........... | 2040 |
| **End Of Day,** Blue, White, Single Pontil, 2 ⅛ In. ..................... | 840 |
| **End Of Day,** Yellow, Green Torch-Like Interior, Single Pontil, ²⁹⁄₃₂ In........... | 180 |
| **Gooseberry,** Amber, White, Yellow Bands, ²¹⁄₃₂ In........... | 120 |
| **Indian Swirl,** Black Opaque Base, Blue, Green, Red, Orange Yellow, ²⁹⁄₃₂ In. ........... | 210 |
| **Joseph's Coat,** Red, Orange, Green, Blue, White, Swirl, ⅞ In. ..................... | 180 |
| **Joseph's Coat,** White, Yellow, Green, Blue, 1 ⁷⁄₁₆ In........... | 660 |
| **Lightning Bolt,** Semiopaque, White, Red, Green, 1 ²¹⁄₃₂ In........... | 2280 |
| **Lutz,** Amber, White Ribbon, Wide Banding, ²⁵⁄₃₂ In........... | 150 |
| **Lutz,** Black Opaque Bands, ¹³⁄₁₆ In........... | 90 |
| **Lutz,** Black Opaque, Blue, Twisted Bands, ⅞ In........... | 780 |
| **Lutz,** Black Opaque, Orange Bands, 2 ³⁄₁₆ In........... | 120 |
| **Lutz,** Blue, Lavender Bands, ¾ In. ..................... | 540 |
| **Lutz,** Brown, Blue Bands, 1 ⁷⁄₁₆ In........... | 180 |
| **Lutz,** Clear Base, 3 Latticinio Threads, ⅞ In........... | 480 |
| **Lutz,** Green Base, Blue, Bands, 1 ⁹⁄₁₆ In........... | 1920 |
| **Lutz,** Green Semiopaque, Banded, Green, Blue, ²³⁄₃₂ In........... | 450 |
| **Lutz,** Honey Amber, White Ribbon, ⁹⁄₁₆ In........... | 60 |

| | |
|---|---|
| **Lutz,** Orange Ribbon, ¾ In. | 120 |
| **Lutz,** Orange Ribbon, Wide Lutz Band, ⅞ In. | 180 |
| **Lutz,** Red Orange Band, 1 ¹⁷⁄₃₂ In. | 240 |
| **Lutz,** White Opaque, Yellow Band, ²⁵⁄₃₂ In. | 390 |
| **Lutz,** White Ribbon, Blue, Gold, ²¹⁄₃₂ In. | 180 |
| **Lutz,** Yellow Onionskin, ¾ In. | 270 |
| **Maglight Indian,** Transparent Purple Body, Blue, Green, Red Panels, 1 ¹⁷⁄₃₂ In. | 600 |
| **Mica,** Blue Cased, Clear, 1 ¹⁹⁄₃₂ In. | 7800 |
| **Mica,** Blue, 2 ³⁄₃₂ In. | 270 |
| **Mica,** Clear Base, 1 ²⁵⁄₃₂ In. | 900 |
| **Mica,** Peppermint, Red, White, Wide Blue Band, 1 ⁵⁄₃₂ In. | 840 |
| **Mica,** Red, ¾ In. | 390 |
| **Mist,** Banded Submarine, Green, White, Yellow, 1 ¹⁄₁₆ In. | 270 |
| **Navarre,** Swirl, Purple, White Loops, 1 ¹⁵⁄₃₂ In. | 210 |
| **Onionskin,** 2 Opposite Panels, Pink, Yellow, White, Blue, Red, 2 ½ In. | 3900 |
| **Onionskin,** 4 Panels, Lobed, Red, Yellow, Green, Faceted Pontil, 1 ¹⁹⁄₃₂ In. | 1020 |
| **Onionskin,** Clown, White Base, Multicolor, Mica Highlights, ²³⁄₃₂ In. | 240 |
| **Onionskin,** Lutz, Pink, White, ¾ In. | 300 |
| **Onionskin,** Lutz, Yellow, Blue, White, Pink, ¾ In. | 210 |
| **Onionskin,** Mica, Shrunken Core, Blue, White, Pink, 1 ³⁄₃₂ In. | 1140 |
| **Onionskin,** Mica, Shrunken Core, Orange, Yellow, 1 ⅛ In. | 2280 |
| **Onionskin,** Mica, Shrunken Core, White, Red, Blue, 1 ⁹⁄₁₆ In. | 660 |
| **Onionskin,** Multicolor, Mica, Faceted Pontil, ²¹⁄₃₂ In. | 360 |
| **Onionskin,** Paneled, Pink, White, Turquoise, 1 ½ In. | 270 |
| **Onionskin,** Paneled, Red, White, Yellow, Blue, 2 ¹⁄₃₂ In. | 780 |
| **Onionskin,** Paneled, Turquoise, White, Yellow, Red, 1 ¹³⁄₃₂ In. | 270 |
| **Onionskin,** Shrunken Core, Yellow, Orange, Mica, 1 ⅛ In. | 2040 |
| **Onionskin,** Turquoise, Mica Flakes, ²⁵⁄₃₂ In. | 210 |
| **Onionskin,** Twisted, Pink, White, Mica, ¹¹⁄₁₆ In. | 300 |
| **Onionskin,** White, Red, Blue Bands, Mica, 2 ¹⁄₃₂ In. | 180 |
| **Onionskin,** White, Turquoise, 2 ⁷⁄₁₆ In. | 240 |
| **Onionskin,** Yellow, Blue Spotting, 1 ⁹⁄₁₆ In. | 270 |
| **Opaque,** Blue Fern, White Base, 1 ¹⁷⁄₃₂ In. | 1800 |
| **Opaque,** Pin, Faceted Pontil, 1 ³⁄₁₆ In. | 390 |
| **Peewee Peppermint,** Wide Blue Band, Mica Chunks, ¹⁵⁄₃₂ In. | 1200 |
| **Peltier Golden Rebel,** Yellow, Red Black Aventurine, ⅝ In. | 300 |
| **Peltier,** Golden Rebel, Yellow, Black Aventurine, Red, ¾ In. | 960 |
| **Peltier,** Superman, Blue, Red, Yellow, ²⁵⁄₃₂ In. | 150 |
| **Peltier,** Swirl, Golden Rebel, Red, Black, ¾ In. | 300 |
| **Ridge Core,** Orange, Blue Bands, 1 ⁵⁄₃₂ In. | 180 |
| **Submarine Indian,** Green Transparent Base, Red, White Bands, ¹⁷⁄₃₂ In. | 360 |
| **Sulphide,** Amber, Girl Bathing, Bonnet, Seated, 2 ³⁄₁₆ In. | 510 |
| **Sulphide,** Baby In Basket, 1 ³¹⁄₃₂ In. | 240 |
| **Sulphide,** Child Sitting On Rock, 1 ⁷⁄₁₆ In. | 180 |
| **Sulphide,** Clear, Boy Praying, 1 ²³⁄₃₂ In. | 180 |
| **Sulphide,** Clear, Boy With Sailboat, Fleabites, 1 ²³⁄₃₂ In. | 180 |
| **Sulphide,** Clear, Court Jester, Spread Legs, 1 ²¹⁄₃₂ In. | 3900 |
| **Sulphide,** Clear, Jenny Lind, Bust, 1 ¹⁷⁄₃₂ In. | 300 |
| **Sulphide,** Clear, Numeral 1, 1 ²³⁄₃₂ In. | 150 |
| **Sulphide,** Clear, Numeral 3, 1 ¹⁵⁄₃₂ In. | 180 |
| **Sulphide,** Clear, Numeral 8, 1 ⁹⁄₁₆ In. | 240 |
| **Sulphide,** Clear, Seated Man, Hat, Hands On Chin, Air Bubbles, 1 ²⁷⁄₃₂ In. | 180 |
| **Sulphide,** Green, Boy On Rocking Horse, Blowing Horn, Holding Boat, 2 ¹⁄₁₆ In. | 2400 |
| **Sulphide,** Green, Man Playing Mandolin, Leaning On Tree Stump, 1 ⅜ In. | 600 |
| **Sulphide,** Large Fish, 2 ³⁄₁₆ In. | 60 |
| **Sulphide,** Numeral 2, 1 ¹⁷⁄₃₂ In. | 240 |
| **Sulphide,** Papoose, 1 ⅞ In. | 180 |
| **Sulphide,** Rooster, 2 ¹⁄₁₆ In. | 60 |
| **Sulphide,** Walking Horse, 1 ¹³⁄₁₆ In. | 270 |
| **Swirl Core,** 3-Stage Ribbon, Red, White, Yellow, Blue, ⅞ In. | 270 |
| **Swirl,** Blue Ridge Cone, White, Banded, 1 ⁹⁄₁₆ In. | 240 |
| **Swirl,** Blue, Yellow, Orange, Solid Core, 1 ⁹⁄₁₆ In. | 780 |
| **Swirl,** Butterscotch Transparent Base, Red, White, Pink Opaque Stripes, ⅞ In. | 120 |
| **Swirl,** Divide Core, Blue, Green, White Latticinio, 2 ³⁄₁₆ In. | 780 |
| **Swirl,** Divided Core, White, Green, Green, Yellow Bands, 2 ¼ In. | 120 |

**Map,** Globe, Terrestrial, Celestial Medial Stand, Kittinger, T.H. Costello, c.1898, 21 In.
$780

**Map,** Globe, Terrestrial, H.B. Nims & Co., Mahogany, Cast Iron Stand, c.1885, 41 In.
$1,353

**Marble Carving,** Bust, Antinous, After Mondragone, Continental, 1800s, 20 ¼ In.
$3,444

**M**

**Marble Carving,** Bust, Classical Maiden, Inscribed, Baratta Fecit, 1852, 25 In.
$3,294

Neal Auction Co.

**Marblehead,** Tile, Scenic, Trees, Arthur Baggs, Ship Mark, c.1910, 9 ½ x 6 In.
$30,000

Rago Arts & Auction Center

**Marblehead,** Vase, Sea Gulls, Waves, Arthur Baggs, Ship Mark, c.1915, 9 ¾ x 8 ½ In.
$15,000

Rago Arts & Auction Center

| | |
|---|---:|
| **Swirl,** Divided Core, Yellow, Green, Red Bands, 2 ¹/₃₂ In. | 210 |
| **Swirl,** End Of Cane Ribbon, Yellow, Orange, Green, ⅞ In. | 540 |
| **Swirl,** Joseph's Coat, Yellow, Orange, Blue, White, 1 ½ In. | 780 |
| **Swirl,** Multicolor, Solid Core, Yellow Latticinio Threads, 2 In. | 510 |
| **Swirl,** Navarre, Blue Loop, 1 ½ In. | 120 |
| **Swirl,** Navarre, Chocolate Brown Base, No. 9, ⅞ In. | 180 |
| **Swirl,** Orange, Yellow, White, 1 ⅞ In. | 360 |
| **Swirl,** Peewee Blue, Birdcage White Latticinio Threads, ½ In. | 720 |
| **Swirl,** Peppermint, Blue Band, Mica, ⁹/₁₆ In. | 270 |
| **Swirl,** Red, Blue, Green, 3 Yellow Latticinio Threads, 1 ¹³/₁₆ In. | 300 |
| **Swirl,** Red, Green, White Latticinio, 1 ⁵/₁₆ In. | 1320 |
| **Swirl,** Red, White Ribbons, ⅞ In. | 60 |
| **Swirl,** Solid Core, Orange, White, Yellow Bands, 1 ⁵/₃₂ In. | 300 |
| **Swirl,** Solid Core, Orange, Yellow, Blue White, 1 ⅜ In. | 270 |
| **Swirl,** Solid Core, Red, Aqua, White, 2 ¹/₁₆ In. | 300 |
| **Swirl,** Solid Yellow Core, Red, White, Green Bands, 1 ⅜ In. | 1920 |
| **Swirl,** White Core, Green, Blue, Red, Yellow Latticinio Bands, 1 ⅝ In. | 90 |
| **Swirl,** White Latticinio, Red Bands, 2 ¹/₃₂ In. | 210 |
| **Swirl,** Yellow Latticinio, Blue, Green, Red Bands, 2 ⅜ In. | 390 |
| **Swirl,** Yellow Latticinio, Green, Orange, White, Blue Bands, 2 ⁵/₁₆ In. | 1080 |
| **Swirl,** Yellow Latticinio, Orange, White, Blue Bands, 2 ⁷/₁₆ In. | 450 |
| **Toronto,** Pink, Green, Yellow, White, Swirl, 1 ⅝ In. | 108 |

**MARBLE CARVINGS,** such as large or small figurines, groups of people or animals, and architectural decorations, have been a special art form since the time of the ancient Greeks. Reproductions, especially of large Victorian groups, are being made of a mixture using marble dust. These are very difficult to detect and collectors should be careful. Other carvings are listed under Alabaster.

| | |
|---|---:|
| **Bust,** Antinous, After Mondragone, Continental, 1800s, 20 ¼ In. ...............*illus* | 3444 |
| **Bust,** Carrara, Diana, Classical Style, Cloak, 19 ⅜ In. | 1169 |
| **Bust,** Cipriani, A., Woman, Cloth Cap, 24 ½ In. | 1770 |
| **Bust,** Classical Maiden, Inscribed, Baratta Fecit, 1852, 25 In. ...............*illus* | 3294 |
| **Bust,** Curled Hair, Evening Attire, White, Socle Base, 28 In. | 1875 |
| **Bust,** Girl, Feeding Bird, Grape Cluster, Green & Black Marble Socle, c.1890, 19 x 11 In. | 690 |
| **Bust,** Greek Statesman, Curly Beard, Diadem On Head, Carrara, 20 ¾ In. | 3690 |
| **Bust,** Man, Wearing Toga, Continental, 23 In. | 438 |
| **Bust,** Mother, Child, Arms Around Neck, Signed E. Fiaschi, 16 In. | 885 |
| **Bust,** Napoleon, Inscribed, Green Marble Platform, 9 ½ x 5 In. | 425 |
| **Bust,** Peasant Woman, Head Scarf, Tunic, 13 ½ x 15 ¼ In. | 472 |
| **Bust,** Roman Statesman, Italy, c.1850, 22 ½ In. | 1625 |
| **Bust,** Soldier, Classical, Helmet, White, 23 In. | 527 |
| **Bust,** Woman, 1700s Dress, Updo Hair, Ringlets, Pedestal Base, France, 1800s, 24 In. | 1560 |
| **Bust,** Woman, Bacchus Maid, Grapes In Hair, Continental, 22 In. | 500 |
| **Bust,** Woman, Flower Garland At Chest, 22 In. | 625 |
| **Bust,** Woman, Long Wavy Hair, Rose On Bodice, c.1890, 26 In. | 1375 |
| **Bust,** Woman, Pink Dress, Cement Base, 43 In. | 240 |
| **Bust,** Woman, Plumed Military Helmet, A. Frilla, c.1900, 23 ½ In. | 3750 |
| **Bust,** Woman, Shawl, Hair Wrapped In Scarf, Continental, 23 In. | 1063 |
| **Bust,** Woman, Smiling, Long Curly Hair, c.1890, 18 ½ x 18 In. | 406 |
| **Bust,** Woman, Turned Socle, L. McDonald, England, c.1844, 17 ¾ In. | 6000 |
| **Bust,** Woman, Upswept Hair, White, Gray Dress, Socle Base, 24 x 17 In. | 633 |
| **Bust,** Woman, Victorian Ruffled Dress, Hair In Bun, 1889, 24 In. | 1230 |
| **Bust,** Young Caesar, Italian, 19th Century, 21 ½ In., Pair | 2337 |
| **Classical Architectural Ruin,** Columns, Pediment, Steps, Dore Bronze, 14 x 11 In. | 776 |
| **Fireplace Corbel,** Cherub Head, Inset Rouge & Black Detail, Italy, 25 x 15 In., Pair | 4800 |
| **Foot,** Variegated White To Gray, Rectangular Plinth, 10 x 20 x 9 In. | 236 |
| **Fountain,** Lion Head, 17 In. | 375 |
| **Garniture,** Oval, Pineapple Finial, Bronze Mounts, Handles, France, c.1910, 18 In. | 120 |
| **Group,** 2 Bacchantes, Tambourine, Grapevine, 20 In. | 1750 |
| **Group,** Man, Woman, Rising From Stump, Carrier Belleuse, c.1875, 33 ½ In. | 2250 |
| **Jardiniere,** Coffin Shape, Lion's Mask Handles, Paw Feet, 11 In., Pair | 2748 |
| **La Grande Taeur,** Parian Moreau, Signed, Auguste Moreau, 23 x 8 x 9 In. | 625 |
| **Obelisk,** Multicolor, Black Grout, 20th Century, 40 In., Pair | 1694 |
| **Obelisk,** Neoclassical Style, Multicolor Specimens, Plinth Base, 22 x 6 ¼ In., Pair | 1107 |

| | |
|---|---|
| **Obelisk,** Neoclassical Style, Specimen, Raised Plinth Base, 1900s, 40 x 8 In., Pair | 3660 |
| **Pedestal,** Classical, Urn, Acanthus, Fluted Column, c.1900, 43 In. | 180 |
| **Pedestal,** Gilt Bronze Mounts, Tapered, Stepped Base, France, c.1850, 46¾ In. | 4000 |
| **Pedestal,** Green, Column Standard, Round Base, c.1910, 41 In. | 185 |
| **Pedestal,** Louis XV, Woman, Cherub, Quadripartite Capital, 43¾ In., Pair | 4840 |
| **Pedestal,** Louis XVI Style, Rouge Griotte, Gilt Bronze, Tapered, Stepped Base, 42 x 11 In. | 5625 |
| **Pedestal,** Neoclassical Style, Verdigris, 48 x 8 In. | 1230 |
| **Pedestal,** Ring-Turned Column Standard, Octagonal Base, Continental, 40 In. | 225 |
| **Pedestal,** Urn, Square Handles, Tapered, Italy, c.1910, 56 In. | 185 |
| **Plaque,** Composition, Putti, Trophies, Rococo Gilt Frame, After Bertaux, Italy, 21 x 17 In. | 399 |
| **Plaque,** Lion, Relief Carved Head, Weathered, c.1890, 19 x 19 In. | 540 |
| **Profile,** Relief, Man, Oval, Parcel Gilt Frames, 28¾ x 25½ In., Pair | 10200 |
| **Relief,** Roman Emperors, Augustus, Claudius, Ortho, Vesparsian, 1900s, 15 x 14 In. | 3050 |
| **Statue,** Art Deco, Figural, Seated Woman, Classical Style Stool, c.1935, 13¼ x 9½ In. | 720 |
| **Statue,** Boy, Standing, Praying, Pietro Guarnerio, Italy, c.1850, 35 In. | 4063 |
| **Statue,** Bust, Diana, Profile, Chignon Hairstyle, White, 23¾ In. | 1000 |
| **Statue,** Crouching Venus, Amphora, After The Antique, 25 x 13 In. | 690 |
| **Statue,** Crouching Venus, Carrara, 31½ In. | 2390 |
| **Statue,** Diana, Houdon Style, Stampe Eumene Baratta, 1800s, 21½ In. | 875 |
| **Statue,** Dying Gaul, Green Serpentine, 10 x 19½ In. | 469 |
| **Statue,** Eagle, Pedestal, Inset Glass Eyes, Pedestal, Italy, c.1890, 15 x 38 In. | 489 |
| **Statue,** Girl, Dog, 31½ In. | 4688 |
| **Statue,** Go To Sleep, Young Girl, Holding Dog, Signed J. Durham London, 33 In. | 9375 |
| **Statue,** Lion, Seated, Open Mouth, Raised Paw On Shield, 44½ In., Pair | 3776 |
| **Statue,** Nude, Half Draped, Reclining, 37 In. | 1250 |
| **Statue,** Putti Holding A Dove, Petro Vandevelde, 23¼ In. | 2360 |
| **Statue,** Right Foot, Antique Style, Variegated White Marble, Plinth, 10 x 20 In. | 649 |
| **Statue,** Selena, Moon, Goddess, Scantily Clad, 23½ In. | 1107 |
| **Statue,** Winged Victory Of Samothrace, Continental, c.1920, 29 x 22 In. | 2952 |
| **Statue,** Woman, Holding Dove, Italy, c.1890, 32 In. | 431 |
| **Statue,** Woman, Reclining, Next To Water Jug, Signed E.T. Falconnet, France, 13 x 22 In. | 5625 |
| **Statue,** Woman, Watering Flowers, Stepped Base, 60 x 15 In. | 1000 |
| **Tablet,** Carrara, Urn, Leaves, Griffins, 18½ x 8 In. | 1373 |
| **Tazza,** Sienna, Bronze, Stepped Pedestal, 1800s, 10⅛ x 8½ In. | 1586 |
| **Tazza,** Variegated, Lobed Body, Molded Socle Base, Square Plinth, 15½ x 20 In., Pair | 1912 |
| **Urn,** Louis XVI, Ram Mask, Festoon Gilt Bronze Mounts, 28½ In., Pair | 2750 |
| **Urn,** Neoclassical Style, Gray, White, Satyr Masks, Blossoms, Square Handles, 20 In. | 313 |
| **Urn,** Ram's Head Mounts, Floral Swag, 27½ In., Pair | 1452 |
| **Urn,** Rouge Griotte, Gilt Bronze, Neoclassical Style, 15½ x 20¼ In. | 6250 |

**MARBLEHEAD POTTERY** was founded in 1904 by Dr. J. Hall as a rehabilitative program for the patients of a Marblehead, Massachusetts, sanitarium. Two years later it was separated from the sanitarium and it continued operations until 1936. Many of the pieces were decorated with marine motifs.

| | |
|---|---|
| **Bowl,** Blue, Leaves, Berries, c.1905, 2 x 6½ In. | 704 |
| **Bowl,** Gray Matte Glaze, Round, Inward Folded Sides, 4 x 8 In. | 438 |
| **Bowl,** Poinsettia, A. Hennessey, 8 x 2 In. | 1220 |
| **Tile,** Geese, Blue, Gray, Frame, 6¼ x 6¼ In. | 2440 |
| **Tile,** Potted Trees, Green, Tan, Blue, Frame, 6½ x 6½ In. | 5185 |
| **Tile,** Potted Trees, Matte Glaze, Square, Frame, 6½ In. | 3965 |
| **Tile,** Scenic, Trees, Arthur Baggs, Ship Mark, c.1910, 9½ x 6 In. ............*illus* | 30000 |
| **Tile,** Silhouetted Oak Trees, Green Matte Glaze, Square, 6 In. | 1342 |
| **Vase,** Berries, Vine, Gray, Blue, Flared, A. Baggs, c.1910, 6 x 5 In. | 4800 |
| **Vase,** Blue Matte Glaze, 8 x 6 In. | 325 |
| **Vase,** Blue Matte Glaze, Tapered, Impressed, 3⅝ In. | 138 |
| **Vase,** Blue, Incised, Flower Band Rim, Ship Logo, 4 In. | 1150 |
| **Vase,** Cobalt Blue, Impressed With Marblehead Ship Logo, 5¼ In. | 259 |
| **Vase,** Flared Rim, Gray Matte Glaze, Purple Interior, Marked, 5½ x 9¾ In. | 288 |
| **Vase,** Gray Matte Glaze, Blue Matte Glaze Interior, Impressed Logo, 5½ In. | 184 |
| **Vase,** Green Matte Glaze, Geometric Pattern On Shoulder, 5 In. | 2000 |
| **Vase,** Lavender, Cylinder, 9 In. | 46 |
| **Vase,** Parrot, 4 Colors, 1915-25, 11⅝ In. | 3600 |
| **Vase,** Prowling Panther Band, Yellow, Black, Green, Paper Label, 7 In. | 12000 |
| **Vase,** Sea Gulls, Waves, Arthur Baggs, Ship Mark, c.1915, 9¾ x 8½ In. ............*illus* | 15000 |

**Marblehead,** Vase, Stylized Trees, Cylindrical, Swollen Top, Arthur Hennessey, Sarah Tutt, c.1915, 7 In.
$5,000

Rago Arts & Auction Center

**Mardi Gras,** Dance Card, Scenes From Shakespeare, Mistick Krewe Of Comus, 1898
$597

Neal Auction Co.

**Mardi Gras,** Inkwell, Glass Ink Pot, Arts & Sciences, Rex, 1911
$800

Neal Auction Co.

**Mardi Gras,** Invitation, Ball, Knights Of Momus, Envelope, Ramayana, 1882, 2 Piece
$1,673

Neal Auction Co.

**Mardi Gras,** Necklace, Green Paste Jewels, Double Chain, Flowers, c.1880
$418

Neal Auction Co.

**Mardi Gras,** Pin, A Night In Japan, Sterling Silver Gilt, Enamel, Twelfth Night Revelers, 1905
$896

Neal Auction Co.

**Mardi Gras,** Pin, Carnival Of Venice, Elves Of Oberon, Ball Favor, c.1925
$800

Neal Auction Co.

| | |
|---|---|
| **Vase,** Stylized Apple Trees, Gray, Cylindrical, H. Tutt, Mass., 1910, 10 ½ x 5 ½ In. | 21250 |
| **Vase,** Stylized Flowers, Brown, Blue Matte Glaze, Bulbous, Tapered, 6 x 5 In. | 2440 |
| **Vase,** Stylized Trees, Cylindrical, Swollen Top, Arthur Hennessey, Sarah Tutt, c.1915, 7 In. ..*illus* | 5000 |
| **Vase,** Tapered, Fruiting Ivy, Stamped, c.1910, 6 x 5 In. | 4800 |

**MARDI GRAS,** French for "Fat Tuesday," was first celebrated in seventeenth-century Europe. The first celebration in America was held in Mobile, Alabama, in 1703. The first krewe, a parading or social club, was founded in 1856. Dozens have been formed since. The Mardi Gras Act, which made Fat Tuesday a legal holiday, was passed in Louisiana in 1875. Mardi Gras balls, carnivals, parties, and parades are held from January 6 until the Tuesday before the beginning of Lent. The most famous carnival and parades take place in New Orleans. Parades feature floats, elaborate costumes, masks, and "throws" of strings of beads, cups, doubloons, or small toys. Purple, green, and gold are traditional Mardi Gras colors. Mardi Gras memorabilia ranges from cheap plastic beads to expensive souvenirs from early celebrations.

| | |
|---|---|
| **Badge,** Rex Organization, 1983, 1 ½ In. | 35 |
| **Bracelet,** Athenians, Rose Medallions, Sterling Silver, 1958, 7 In. | 100 |
| **Bridge Card Set,** Elves Of Oberon Logo, Box, 1950s, 5 x 3 In. | 36 |
| **Dance Card,** Pencil, Smiling Mask, Consus, Shakespeare & His Creations, 1901 | 427 |
| **Dance Card,** Scenes From Shakespeare, Mistick Krewe Of Comus, 1898 ..........*illus* | 597 |
| **Doubloon,** Krewe Of Iris, 1983 | 75 |
| **Inkwell,** Glass Ink Pot, Arts & Sciences, Rex, 1911 ..........*illus* | 800 |
| **Invitation,** 2 Envelopes, Dance Card, Krewe Of Proteus, Hindoo Heavens, 1889 | 7015 |
| **Invitation,** Ball, Envelope, 2 Admit Cards, Nippon, Land Of Rising Sun, Junnie Wilde, 1892 | 1037 |
| **Invitation,** Ball, Envelope, Admit Card, Twelfth Night Revelers, Domino, 1885 | 478 |
| **Invitation,** Ball, Envelope, Dance Card, Krewe Of Nereus, Coral Groves & Grottoes, 1897 | 717 |
| **Invitation,** Ball, Envelope, Dance Card, Pencil, Knights Of Momus, Language Of Flowers, 1911 | 1793 |
| **Invitation,** Ball, Knights Of Momus, Envelope, Ramayana, 1882, 2 Piece ..........*illus* | 1673 |
| **Invitation,** Ball, Mystick Krewe Of Comus, Spencer's Faerie Queen, 1871 | 478 |
| **Medallion,** Krewe Of Rex, Ribbon, Purple, Yellow, Green, 1972, 3 In. | 90 |
| **Necklace,** Green Paste Jewels, Double Chain, Flowers, c.1880 ..........*illus* | 418 |
| **Parade Bulletin,** 1903, Mystick Krewe Of Comus, Leaf From Mahabharata, 28 x 42 In. | 538 |
| **Parade Bulletin,** 1905, Rex, Idealistic Queen, Lithographer Walle & Co., 28 x 42 In. | 598 |
| **Parade Bulletin,** February 3, 1910, Winged World Theme, Walle & Co., 28 x 42 In. | 549 |
| **Parade Bulletin,** February 3, 1913, Adventures Of Telemachus Theme, 28 x 42 In. | 554 |
| **Parade Bulletin,** February 15, 1904, Alphabet Theme, Walle & Co., 28 x 42 In. | 598 |
| **Parade Bulletin,** February 20, 1912, Cathay Theme, Walle & Co., 28 x 42 In. | 657 |
| **Parade Bulletin,** February 26, 1906, Proteus Theme, Fitzwilliam & Co., 28 x 42 In. | 549 |
| **Parade Bulletin,** Knights Of Momus, Language Of Flowers, Walle & Co., 1911, 28 x 42 In. | 956 |
| **Pin,** A Night In Japan, Sterling Silver Gilt, Enamel, Twelfth Night Revelers, 1905 ..........*illus* | 896 |
| **Pin,** Carnival Of Venice, Elves Of Oberon, Ball Favor, c.1925 ..........*illus* | 800 |
| **Pin,** High Priests Of Mithras, Favor, Silver, Gilt | 388 |
| **Pin,** High Priests Of Mithras, Snowflake Shape, Gold Plate, Enamel, 1985, 1 In. | 55 |
| **Pin,** Izdubar Theme, Krewe Of Comus, Favor, 1904 | 448 |
| **Pin,** Knights Of Momus, Jatakamala Tales Of Buddha's Lives, Favor, 1924 | 359 |
| **Pin,** Knights Of Momus, Sterling Gilt, Enamel, Visions Of World's Vanities, 1904 ..........*illus* | 538 |
| **Pin,** Krewe Of Proteus, Lamppost, Street Signs, Favor, 1985, 1 ¾ In. | 65 |
| **Pin,** Krewe Of Proteus, Queen Of The Serpents, Favor, 1907 | 717 |
| **Pin,** Mistick Krewe Of Comus, Lost Pleiad, Favor, 1905 | 1016 |
| **Pin,** The Rubaiyat Theme, Krewe, Favor, 1905 | 328 |
| **Pincushion,** In Utopia Theme, Purple Velvet, 1906 | 448 |
| **Postcard,** Crowds On Canal Street, E.C. Kropp Co., 1910 | 13 |
| **Token,** Aluminum, Elk's Club, Lodge 30, Building, 1967, 1 ½ In. | 9 |
| **Trumpet Vase,** Gilt, Box, Rex, Idealistic Queens, 1905 | 359 |

**MARTIN BROTHERS** of Middlesex, England, made Martinware, a salt-glazed stoneware, *Martin Bro London* between 1873 and 1915. Many figural jugs and vases were made by the three brothers. Of special interest are the fanciful birds, usually made with removable heads. Most pieces have the incised name of the artists plus other information on the bottom.

| | |
|---|---|
| **Bowl,** Stoneware, Flowers, Leaves, Incised R.W. Martin & Bro, 2 ⅝ In. | 308 |
| **Jar,** Lid, Bird, Wally, Glazed Stoneware, Wood Base, Signed, 1882, 11 In. ..........*illus* | 31980 |
| **Jug,** Face, 2-Sided, Glaring, England, 1911, 9 x 7 ½ In. | 8125 |
| **Jug,** Face, 2-Sided, Smiling, England, 1898, 8 x 7 In. | 8125 |
| **Jug,** Face, 2-Sided, Smiling, England, 1902, 7 x 6 ½ In. | 6875 |
| **Jug,** Face, 2-Sided, Smirky Smile, c.1910, 8 x 6 In. | 2375 |
| **Jug,** Face, Curled Judge Wig, 2-Sided, Cream, White, Stoneware, England, c.1910, 7 x 6 In. | 10625 |

**Mardi Gras,** Pin, Knights Of Momus, Sterling Gilt, Enamel, Visions Of World's Vanities, 1904
$538

Neal Auction Co.

**Martin Brothers,** Jar, Lid, Bird, Wally, Glazed Stoneware, Wood Base, Signed, 1882, 11 In.
$31,980

Skinner Auctioneers & Appraisers

**Martin Brothers,** Jug, Face, 2-Sided, Smiling, Molded, Strap Handle, c.1890, 4 ¾ In.
$2,832

Brunk Auctions

**Martin Brothers,** Tobacco Jar, Bird, Glazed, Inscribed Lid, Restored, 9 In.
$60,950

Cottone Auctions

**Martin Brothers,** Tobacco Jar, Bird, Glazed, Stoneware, Signed, 1905, 8¾ x 4 In.
$18,750

Rago Arts & Auction Center

**Martin Brothers,** Vase, Leaves, Incised, Pierced Stars, Tan Glaze, Folded, c.1900, 8 In.
$1,920

Rago Arts & Auction Center

M

**Mary Gregory,** Vase, Girl, Bird, Optic Rib, Prussian Blue, 16 In., Pair $460

Early Auction Co.

**Mason's,** Tureen, Lid, Underplate, Imari, Gilt, Shell Work Handles, 14 x 14½ In. $956

Neal Auction Co.

**Massier,** Vase, Desert Scene, Camels, Palm Trees, Clement Massier, c.1900, 24 In. $4,688

Rago Arts & Auction Center

| | |
|---|---|
| **Jug,** Face, 2-Sided, Smiling, Molded, Strap Handle, c.1890, 4¾ In. .................................*illus* | 2832 |
| **Tobacco Jar,** Bird, Glazed, Inscribed Lid, Restored, 9 In. .................................................*illus* | 60950 |
| **Tobacco Jar,** Bird, Glazed, Stoneware, Signed, 1905, 8¾ x 4 In. ...................................*illus* | 18750 |
| **Tobacco Jar,** Bird, Wally, Glazed Stoneware, Signed R.W. Martin, 6½ In. ..................... | 25200 |
| **Vase,** Face, 4-Sided, Brown, Pinched Top, c.1900, 7 x 6 In. ........................................... | 10625 |
| **Vase,** Leaves, Incised, Pierced Stars, Tan Glaze, Folded, c.1900, 8 In. .......................*illus* | 1920 |
| **Vase,** Stoneware, Incised Leaves, Black Ground, Footed, 1890, 7⅝ In........................... | 738 |

**MARY GREGORY** is the name used for a type of glass that is easily identified. White figures were painted on clear or colored glass as the decoration. The figures chosen were usually children at play. The first glass known as Mary Gregory was made in about 1870. Similar glass is made even today. The traditional story has been that the glass was made at the Boston & Sandwich Glass Company in Sandwich, Massachusetts, by a woman named Mary Gregory. Recent research has shown that none was made at Sandwich. In fact, all early Mary Gregory glass was made in Bohemia. Beginning in 1957, the Westmoreland Glass Co. made the first Mary Gregory–type decorations on American glassware. These pieces had simpler designs, less enamel paint, and more modern shapes. France, Italy, Germany, Switzerland, and England, as well as Bohemia, made this glassware. Children standing, not playing, were pictured after the 1950s.

| | |
|---|---|
| **Basket,** Deep Red Glass Inset, Children, Egg, Silver Plated Frame, Swing Handle, 9½ x 10 In..... | 338 |
| **Dresser Box,** Mottled Rose, Blue Satin, Round, Silver Plated Frame, 6 In........................... | 403 |
| **Lamp,** Oil, Brown, Girl With Bird, Stippled Accents, Stepped & Tapered, 13 In................... | 86 |
| **Perfume Bottle,** Glass, Stopper, Girl, Trees, 4 In. .......................................................... | 35 |
| **Pitcher,** Enamel, Woman, Landscape Scene, Lavender, Marigold Foot, Handle, 12 In. ........ | 266 |
| **Pitcher,** Girl Jumping Rope, Amber, Olive Green, Applied Turquoise Handle, 13 In............... | 148 |
| **Pitcher,** Water, Girls, White Dresses, Inscribed Atlantic City 1892 Annie M. Johnson, 8 In. .......... | 62 |
| **Stein,** Rib Optic, Blue, White Enameled Child, Hinged Lid, c.1910, 5¾ In......................... | 81 |
| **Vase,** Boy, Raking Leaves, Dog, Tree, White, Black Ground, 7½ In................................... | 25 |
| **Vase,** Girl, Bird, Optic Rib, Prussian Blue, 16 In., Pair ..........................................*illus* | 460 |

**MASONIC,** *see Fraternal category.*

**MASON'S IRONSTONE** was made by the English pottery of Charles J. Mason after 1813. Mason, of Lane Delph, was given a patent for this improved earthenware. He usually called it *Mason's Patent Ironstone China.* It resisted chipping and breaking, so it became popular for dinnerware and other table service dishes. Vases and other decorative pieces were also made. The ironstone was decorated with orange, blue, gold, and other colors, often in Japanese-inspired designs. The firm had financial difficulties, but the molds and the name *Mason* were used by many owners through the years, including Francis Morley, Taylor Ashworth, George L. Ashworth, and John Shaw. Mason's joined the Wedgwood group in 1973 and the name was used for a few years and then dropped.

| | |
|---|---|
| **Cooler,** Wine, Campana Shape, Shepherd, Livestock, Family, Dog, c.1820, 9½ In., Pair .............. | 3540 |
| **Inkstand,** Lid, 2 Trays, Dish, Foot, Imari Colors, c.1830, 13¼ In. ..................................... | 472 |
| **Jar,** Lid, Enameled, Hexagonal, Multicolor, Gilt, Dragon Finial, Handles, c.1825, 23 In. ............... | 1888 |
| **Jug,** Ale, Chinese Lions, Medallions, Clouds, Red, Orange, Hydra Shape, 7 In. ..................... | 495 |
| **Plate,** Flowers, Birds, Scalloped Edge, c.1900, 10 In................................................... | 123 |
| **Platter,** Flowers, Ironstone, c.1850, 16½ In. .......................................................... | 94 |
| **Tureen,** Lid, Underplate, Imari, Gilt, Shell Work Handles, 14 x 14½ In ......................*illus* | 956 |
| **Vase,** Griffin, Figural, Slender Neck, Gilt, Applied Foot, Base, 8¾ In., Pair........................ | 2124 |
| **Vase,** Ho Ho, Lid, Blue Overgilt, Zigzags, Hexagonal, Paneled, Waisted, c.1820, 27 In......... | 1180 |
| **Vase,** Lid, Pineapple Finial, Printed, Painted Scenic Views, Reserves, c.1840, 38 In. ......... | 885 |

**MASSIER,** a French art pottery, was made by brothers Jerome, Delphin, and Clement Massier in Vallauris and Golfe-Juan, France, in the late nineteenth and early twentieth centuries. It has an iridescent metallic luster glaze that resembles the Weller Sicardo pottery glaze. Most pieces are marked J. Massier. Massier may also be listed in the Majolica category.

| | |
|---|---|
| **Bowl,** Woman Drifting, Ocean, Iridescent, Green, Pink, 5 x 17 In...................................... | 3450 |
| **Ewer,** Slip Blooming Irises, Metallic Glaze, Nude Woman Handle, 23 In............................. | 6325 |
| **Plaque,** Landscape, Iridescent Blue, Green Rose, c.1900, 16 x 18 In. ............................... | 10625 |
| **Vase,** Bacchus, Embracing Couple, Signed, J. Vibert, c.1900, 12 x 8 In. ............................ | 4063 |
| **Vase,** Butterfly, Iridescent Glaze, Pinched & Folded Rim, Golfe-Juan Ami, 8¾ In. .................... | 944 |
| **Vase,** Cone Shape, Iridescent, Flowers, Walking Person, 9¼ In...................................... | 345 |
| **Vase,** Desert Scene, Camels, Palm Trees, Clement Massier, c.1900, 24 In. .....................*illus* | 4688 |
| **Vase,** Fish, Multicolored Iridescent Glaze, Golfe-Juan, 17 x 10 In. ...........................*illus* | 3625 |
| **Vase,** Flowers, Iridescent Green, Blue, Long Neck, Squat, Luster, Clement Massier, 15 In. ............. | 3177 |
| **Vase,** Iridescent Glaze, Long Neck, Flared Base, Signed Clement Massier, 10 In............................ | 540 |

| | |
|---|---|
| **Vase,** Leaves, Berries, Iridescent Glaze, Signed CM, Golfe-Juan, 3 ⅛ In. | 230 |
| **Vase,** Scenic, Iridescent, Trees, Lake, Foothills, Marked, 8 In. .....*illus* | 403 |

## MATCH HOLDERS

**MATCH HOLDERS** were made to hold the large wooden matches that were used in the nineteenth and twentieth centuries for a variety of purposes. The kitchen stove and the fireplace or furnace had to be lit regularly. One type of match holder was made to hang on the wall, another was designed to be kept on a tabletop. Of special interest today are match holders that have advertisements as part of the design.

| | |
|---|---|
| **Charter Oakes Stoves,** Leaf Shape, Acorn, Cast Iron, 7 x 5 x 1 In. | 316 |
| **Crystal,** Brass, Rooster, Glass Eyes, c.1890, 7 In. | 1101 |
| **Devil,** Head, Hands, Legs Protruding, Metal, Painted, Hanging, 6 ½ x 3 ⅝ In. | 920 |
| **Haberle Brewing,** Blue, Cone Shape, White's Utica Pottery Co., 4 x 6 In. | 374 |
| **Horse,** Bridle, Reins, Fence, Brass Over Copper, 3 x 3 In. | 80 |
| **Moxie,** Bottle Shape, Tin Lithograph c.1905, 7 In. | 660 |
| **Peasant Woman,** Pointed Hat, Holding Bucket, Paint, Tin, c.1850, 14 In. | 600 |
| **Red Raven Splits,** Medicinal Waters, Bird, Bottle, Die Cut, 2-Sided, 3 ⅝ x 5 In. ......*illus* | 374 |
| **Richard H. Adams & Co.,** Fly, Embossed, Wings Lift, Cast Iron, 2 x 3 In. | 460 |
| **Shoe Shape,** Sewer Tile, Incised Bessie, 1800s, 3 x 4 ½ In. | 118 |

## MATCH SAFES

**MATCH SAFES** were designed to be carried in the pocket. Early matches were made with phosphorus and could ignite unexpectedly. The matches were safely stored in the tightly closed container. Match safes were made in sterling silver, plated silver, or other metals. The English call these "vesta boxes."

| | |
|---|---|
| **Apples,** Cherries, Tin, Drawer At Bottom, 1940s | 28 |
| **Ballerina,** Painted, Enameled, Silver, Silver Gilt, Gorham, c.1892, 2 ⅜ In. | 1250 |
| **Bear,** Hugging Tree, F.S. Gilbert, c.1905, 2 ½ In. | 325 |
| **Cleopatra,** Hammered Silver, Cigar Cutter | 300 |
| **Cowboy,** Horseback, Pine Trees, Sky, Sterling Silver | 390 |
| **Elk Head,** Silver & Silver Gilt, Battin & Co., 2 ⅜ In. | 275 |
| **Fireman's Pants,** Wrinkles, Suspenders, Lead, 2 ¾ In. | 148 |
| **Football Players,** Enamel, Silver, Reed & Barton, c.1900, 2 ⅝ In. | 437 |
| **George Washington,** Sterling Silver, Embossed, Gorham, 1 ½ x 2 ½ In. ......*illus* | 314 |
| **Gold,** Incised, Scroll, Leaves, Rectangle, Horace Woodward, 1 x 1 ½ In. | 450 |
| **Golfer,** Swinging Club, Sterling Silver, Watrous Mfg. Co., c.1900, 2 ⅜ In. | 300 |
| **Hunters,** Game, Deer Head, Hunt Horn, Cast Iron, 10 ½ In. | 94 |
| **Indian Profile,** Chased Repousse, Silver, Unger Bros., c.1901, 2 ⅜ In. | 625 |
| **Lobster Form,** Lying On Seaweed Base, Yellowware, 19th Century, 6 In. | 300 |
| **Mask,** Silver & Bone, Gorham, c.1887, 2 In. | 5937 |
| **Metal,** Cream, Green Fruit, Leaves, Shelf At Bottom | 18 |
| **Nude Female,** Sterling Silver, Enamel, High Relief, Gorham, 1 ⅜ x 2 ⅜ In. ......*illus* | 1710 |
| **Peasant's Shoe,** Sterling Silver, 19th Century, 2 ¾ x 1 ½ In. | 475 |
| **Plaid,** 14K Gold, Sliding Lid, Engraved, c.1920. | 495 |
| **Punch,** Sterling Silver, Multicolor, Cameo, Marked SS, 1 x 1 ½ In. | 627 |
| **Queen Of Hearts,** Sterling Silver, Webster Co., c.1900, 2 ¼ In. | 625 |
| **Sultan's Favorite,** Exotic Woman, Celluloid, Heron Iron Bedstead Co., 2 ¼ x 1 ½ In. | 219 |
| **Swedish Coat Of Arms,** Gold Wash Sterling, Azure Enamel, c.1920, 2 ¼ x 1 ½ In. | 75 |
| **The Farmers Friend Stacker,** Celluloid, Bearded Man, Farmers Hat, 1 ½ x 2 ¾ In. ......*illus* | 180 |
| **Victorian Woman,** Safety Bicycle, Silver, 2 ¼ x 1 ½ In. | 205 |
| **Woman,** Fisherman, Brass, Hinged Lid, Enamel, 1 ¾ x 1 ¼ In. | 150 |

## MATT MORGAN

**MATT MORGAN,** an English artist, was making pottery in Cincinnati, Ohio, by 1883. His pieces were decorated to resemble Moorish wares. Incised designs and colors were applied to raised panels on the pottery. Shiny or matte glazes were used. The company lasted less than two years.

| | |
|---|---|
| **Charger,** Dragon, Waves, Bronzed Glaze, High Relief, Stamped, 16 In. | 748 |
| **Charger,** Yellow Finch, Blooming Branch, Limoges Style, Stamped, 16 ½ In. | 960 |

## McCOY

**McCOY** pottery was made in Roseville, Ohio. Nelson McCoy and J.W. McCoy established the Nelson McCoy Sanitary and Stoneware Company in Roseville, Ohio, in 1910. The firm made art pottery after 1926. In 1933 it became the Nelson McCoy Pottery Company. Pieces marked McCoy were made by the Nelson McCoy Pottery Company. Cookie jars were made from about 1940 until December 1990, when the McCoy factory closed. Since 1991 pottery with the McCoy mark has been made by firms unrelated to the original company. Because there was a company named Brush-McCoy, there is great confusion between Brush and Nelson McCoy pieces. See Brush category for more information.

| | |
|---|---|
| **Cookie Jar,** Bananas | 165 |

**Massier,** Vase, Fish, Multicolored Iridescent Glaze, Golfe-Juan, 17 x 10 In. $3,625

Rago Arts & Auction Center

**Massier,** Vase, Scenic, Iridescent, Trees, Lake, Foothills, Marked, 8 In. $403

Humler & Nolan

**M**

**Match Holder,** Red Raven Splits, Medicinal Waters, Bird, Bottle, Die Cut, 2-Sided, 3 ⅝ x 5 In. $374

Wm Morford Auctions

**TIP**

*If you have unopened bottles of drugs or other pharmaceuticals, be sure to check for ether or picric acid. These can explode spontaneously and are dangerous to keep.*

# McCOY

**Match Safe,** George Washington, Sterling Silver, Embossed, Gorham, 1 ½ x 2 ½ In.
$314

Showtime Auction Services

**Match Safe,** Nude Female, Sterling Silver, Enamel, High Relief, Gorham, 1 ⅜ x 2 ⅜ In.
$1,710

Showtime Auction Services

**Match Safe,** The Farmers Friend Stacker, Celluloid, Bearded Man, Farmers Hat, 1 ½ x 2 ¾ In.
$180

Showtime Auction Services

| | |
|---|---:|
| **Cookie Jar,** Barrel Shape, Nabisco, 9 ⅜ x 7 ⅝ In. | 99 |
| **Cookie Jar,** Lid, Happy Dog, 10 ¾ In. | 23 |
| **Cookie Jar,** Wishing Well, 9 ⅜ x 7 ⅝ In. | 89 |
| **Jardiniere,** Leaves, Diamond Pattern, 7 ½ x 10 ½ In. | 34 |
| **Mug,** Brown Drip, 4 ¾ In. | 15 |
| **Planter,** Attached Underplate, Applied Flowers, Cream Ground, Signed Leslie Cope, 5 x 8 In. | 58 |
| **Planter,** Duck, Long Bill, Egg, White, Blue, 1940s, 5 ½ x 7 In. | 28 |
| **Planter,** Spinning Wheel, Dog, On Leash, Cat, 1950s, 7 x 6 ¾ x 4 In. | 36 |
| **Vase,** Grapes, White, Purple, Marked, 14 ⅜ In. | 81 |
| **Vase,** Poppy, Red, Green, 8 ⅜ In. | 65 |
| **Vase,** Triple Calla Lily, Yellow, c.1950, 7 In. | 90 |

**McKEE** is a name associated with various glass enterprises in the United States since 1836, including J. & F. McKee (1850), Bryce, McKee & Co. (1850 to 1854), McKee and Brothers (1865), and National Glass Co. (1899). In 1903, the McKee Glass Company was formed in Jeannette, Pennsylvania. It became McKee Division of the Thatcher Glass Co. in 1951 and was bought out by the Jeannette Corporation in 1961. Pressed glass, kitchenwares, and tablewares were produced. Jeannette Corporation closed in the early 1980s. Additional pieces may be included in the Custard Glass and Depression Glass categories.

| | |
|---|---:|
| **Basket,** Martec, Milk Glass, 5 In. | 38 |
| **Bowl,** Feather Pattern, 1800s, 4 In. | 45 |
| **Bowl,** Fruit, Laurel, Jade Green, 4 In. | 27 |
| **Bowl,** Toltec, Milk Glass, 3-Toed, 7 In. | 32 |
| **Bread Tray,** Deer & Pine, Amber, Handles, 13 x 7 In. | 115 |
| **Butter,** Cover, Aztec Sunburst, Round, c.1910, 7 x 5 In. | 45 |
| **Butter,** Cover, Hickman, Round, 7 ⅝ In. | 43 |
| **Butter,** Cover, Rock Crystal, Bell Shape, Teardrop Finial | 319 |
| **Candlestick,** 3-Light, Rock Crystal, 6 In. | 30 |
| **Candlestick,** Plymouth Thumbprint, 3 ½ In. | 14 |
| **Candlestick,** Ray, Milk Glass, 7 ¾ In. | 30 |
| **Champagne,** Rock Crystal, 6 Oz., 4 ¾ In. | 10 |
| **Compote,** Nortec, 7 ¾ In. | 23 |
| **Compote,** Quintec, 8-Sided Foot, Crimped Rim, 6 ½ In. | 25 |
| **Compote,** Yutec, 4 ½ In. | 18 |
| **Cordial,** Rock Crystal, c.1894, 4 In. | 12 |
| **Creamer,** Laurel, Ivory, Footed, 4 In. | 14 |
| **Creamer,** Plymouth Thumbprint, Milk Glass, 4 ½ In. | 6 |
| **Creamer,** Quintec, 3 In. | 65 |
| **Creamer,** Toltec, Milk Glass, 3 ½ In. | 6 |
| **Cup & Saucer,** Laurel, Jade Green | 30 |
| **Cup & Saucer,** Rock Crystal | 20 |
| **Grill Plate,** Jade, 3 Sections, 9 In. | 42 |
| **Pickle Tray,** Quintec, Scalloped Sawtooth Edge, c.1910, 8 x 3 In. | 24 |
| **Pitcher,** Fentec, Applied Handle, c.1900, 54 Oz., 9 ¼ x 7 ¾ In. | 49 |
| **Pitcher,** Home, Footed, 48 Oz., 9 In. | 58 |
| **Pitcher,** Majestic, Footed, 64 Oz., 9 ½ In. | 37 |
| **Pitcher,** Rock Crystal, Scalloped, Squat, 54 Oz., 7 In. | 219 |
| **Pitcher,** Rock Crystal, Tankard Shape, 54 Oz., 8 ½ In. | 248 |
| **Plate,** Dinner, Laurel, Ivory, Scalloped, 9 ⅛ In. | 15 |
| **Plate,** Salad, Opal, 7 ¼ In. | 8 |
| **Plate,** Salad, Rock Crystal, Scalloped, 7 In. | 16 |
| **Punch Bowl,** Aztec, 13 In. | 162 |
| **Punch Bowl,** Hickman, 15 ¼ In. | 148 |
| **Punch Bowl,** Sextec, 13 ¾ In. | 199 |
| **Punch Cup,** Aztec, Footed, 2 ¼ In. | 6 |
| **Punch Cup,** Martec, 2 ¼ In. | 7 |
| **Punch Cup,** Sextec, 1 ⅝ In. | 18 |
| **Punch Cup,** Teutonic, 2 ¼ In. | 8 |
| **Relish,** Rock Crystal, 6 Sections, 14 In. | 34 |
| **Rose Bowl,** Snappy, 3-Toed, 7 In. | 48 |
| **Salt & Pepper,** Puritan, Milk Glass, 4 ¼ In. | 16 |
| **Salt & Pepper,** Roman Arches, Black, 4 ½ In. | 60 |
| **Serenade,** Plate, Brown Glass, c.1900, 6 ¼ In. | 35 |
| **Sherbet,** Laurel, Ivory, 3 ½ In. | 12 |
| **Sherbet,** Lenox, Green, 4 ⅞ In. | 19 |

| | |
|---|---|
| **Sherbet,** Toltec, 3 In. | 8 |
| **Spoon Tray,** Fentec, Gilt Trim, c.1900, 7 ½ x 4 ½ In. | 25 |
| **Sugar,** Heart Band Ruby Flash, Handles, 2 ¾ In. | 12 |
| **Torte Plate,** Wiltec, 19 ¾ In. | 94 |
| **Tray,** Innovation, c.1916, 12 x 5 In. | 50 |
| **Tray,** Rock Crystal, Amber, Center Handle, 10 ⅝ In. | 60 |
| **Tumbler,** Barberry, 5 ⅞ In. | 30 |
| **Tumbler,** Bellflower, 6 In. | 34 |
| **Tumbler,** Cane, 6 In. | 17 |
| **Tumbler,** Deer & Pine Tree, 6 ⅝ In. | 62 |
| **Tumbler,** Feather, 4 In. | 49 |
| **Tumbler,** Feather, 5 ¾ In. | 50 |
| **Tumbler,** Opal, 5 ¼ In. | 7 |
| **Tumbler,** Queen, 6 In. | 23 |
| **Tumbler,** Rock Crystal, 8 Oz., 6 ⅜ In. | 14 |
| **Tumbler,** Rock Crystal, 9 Oz., 7 In. | 18 |
| **Tumbler,** Rock Crystal, Amber, Concave, 4 ⅜ In. | 26 |
| **Tumbler,** Rock Crystal, Curved, 8 Oz., 4 ½ In. | 15 |
| **Tumbler,** Stippled, 5 ⅞ In. | 24 |
| **Vase,** Champion, Trumpet, Footed, 12 In. | 20 |
| **Wine,** Feather, 4 In. | 24 |

**MECHANICAL BANKS** *are listed in the Bank category.*

**MEDICAL** office furniture, operating tools, microscopes, thermometers, and other paraphernalia used by doctors are included in this category. Veterinary collectibles are also included here. Medicine bottles are listed in the Bottle category. There are related collectibles listed under Dental.

| | |
|---|---|
| **Anatomical Study,** Head & Shoulders, Papier-Mache, Glass, Wood, Multicolor, c.1910, 14 In. | 3670 |
| **Anti-Sunstroke Device,** Sponge, Silvered Case, Fits Inside Hat, A. Richardson, 1872, 2 In. | 134 |
| **Atomizer,** Magic Oil, No. 47, Davol Rubber Co., Providence, Glass, Rubber, Box, 6 In. | 73 |
| **Atomizer,** Oil, Whitall-Tatum & Co., No. 37, Glass, Metal, Rubber Bulb, Box, 3 x 4 In. | 62 |
| **Atomizer,** Steam, Acme, No. 1, Brass, Glass, Tubes, Lamp, Whitall, Tatum & Co., Box, 7 In. | 213 |
| **Blood Letting Kit,** 3 Bleeders, Mahogany Fitted Case, 6 Glass Bowls, Plunger, 1800s, 13 x 12 In. | 266 |
| **Bowl,** Leech, Glass, Round, Wide Flared-Out Rim, 3 ¼ x 6 In. | 84 |
| **Box,** Apothecary, Mahogany, Fitted Interior, Glass Bottles, 9 x 10 In. | 246 |
| **Cabinet,** Apothecary, 20 Drawers, Spice Names, Green Paint, c.1850, 58 x 50 In. | 2808 |
| **Cabinet,** Apothecary, Black Paint, 5 Upper Compartments, 20 Drawers, c.1810, 71 x 37 In. | 2706 |
| **Cabinet,** Apothecary, Chestnut, Pine, Blue Paint, 25 Small Drawers, 25 x 22 In. | 960 |
| **Cabinet,** Apothecary, Elmwood, Brass Mounts, Cubby Drawers, Block Feet, 1800s, 57 ½ x 34 In. ....*illus* | 830 |
| **Cabinet,** Apothecary, Fruitwood, 30 Drawers, Triangular Shape, 57 x 37 In. | 660 |
| **Cabinet,** Apothecary, Mahogany, Fruitwood, 12 Drawers, Labels, 31 ½ x 36 In. | 1159 |
| **Cabinet,** Apothecary, Pine, 32 Drawers, Bracket Base, c.1945, 76 x 36 In. | 345 |
| **Cabinet,** Apothecary, Pine, Painted, 4 Shelves, 30 Graduated Drawers, 66 x 51 In. | 4920 |
| **Cabinet,** Apothecary, Poplar, Painted, 40 Labeled Drawers, Shaped Feet, 1800s, 33 x 74 In. | 2952 |
| **Chair,** Vibratory, Wood, Leather, Metal, Motorized, Battle Creek, Quackery, 1900s, 62 x 36 In. | 4648 |
| **Chest,** Apothecary, Mahogany, Compartments, Bottles, Drawers, Brass Top Bail, 1800s, 8 x 9 In. | 1180 |
| **Chest,** Apothecary, Traveling, 2 Upper Doors, 23 Bottles, Drawers, 1800s, 18 x 13 In. | 1298 |
| **Chest,** Apothecary, William IV, Mahogany, Drawers, Pull-Out Tray, c.1830, 54 x 48 In. .......*illus* | 3383 |
| **Chest,** Apothecary, Wood Frame, White Paint, Glass Sides, Mirror Back, Drawer, Lock | 47 |
| **Cork Press,** Figural, Alligator, Cast Iron, c.1890, 12 In. ....*illus* | 258 |
| **Dissection Kit,** Microscopic Section Cutter, Scalpels, Probes, Tweezers, Case, Bausch & Lomb.... | 60 |
| **Field Surgical Set,** Capital, Mahogany Case, Brassbound, Snowden & Brother, 1860s, 17 x 9 In.. | 2952 |
| **Forceps,** Obstetric, Stainless Steel, Sklar. | 30 |
| **Glass Eye,** Various Colors, Velvet Lined Case, England, c.1890, 50 Piece | 6500 |
| **Indicator,** Poison Bottle, Devil's Head Skull, Rubber, Metal Corkscrew, 1 ¾ In. | 392 |
| **Instrument Set,** Surgical, Ebony Handles, Rosewood Case, W. Snowden, c.1880, 30 Piece | 5535 |
| **Jar,** Apothecary, Aq. Destill, Label Under Glass, Cobalt Blue, Stopper, 15 In. .......*illus* | 257 |
| **Lancet,** Brass, Steel Spring, Dome Case, c.1870, 4 ½ x 2 ½ In. | 173 |
| **Lancet,** Spring, Single Steel Blade, Brass Case, Leather Box, 19th Century, 2 In. | 123 |
| **Medicine Cabinet,** Corner, Oak, Wall Mount, Beveled Mirror, 16 ½ x 17 ¼ x 12 In. | 30 |
| **Model,** Anatomical, Composite, ¾ Size, Removable Layers, Labeled, Auzoux, 1800s, 54 In. | 15290 |
| **Model,** Medical School, Proctology, Latex, Medical Products, Skokie, Ill., c.1950, 24 x 16 In. | 3180 |
| **Mold,** Tablet, Whitall Tatum, No. 10, Hard Rubber, Box, Directions, 6 x 2 ½ In. | 73 |
| **Nasal Spray,** Drs. Starkey & Palen Compound Oxygen, Glass, Rubber, Cork, Box, 4 x 6 In. | 213 |

**Medical,** Cabinet, Apothecary, Elmwood, Brass Mounts, Cubby Drawers, Block Feet, 1800s, 57 ½ x 34 In.
$830

James D. Julia Auctioneers

**Medical,** Chest, Apothecary, William IV, Mahogany, Drawers, Pull-Out Tray, c.1830, 54 x 48 In.
$3,383

Neal Auction Co.

**TIP**

*Civil War re-enactors have been warned that some old medical instruments could still carry germs or viruses that are infectious. Be very careful when handling any old medical items. They should be carefully disinfected.*

**Medical,** Cork Press, Figural, Alligator, Cast Iron, c.1890, 12 In.
$258

McMurray Antiques & Auctions

**Medical,** Jar, Apothecary, Aq. Destill, Label Under Glass, Cobalt Blue, Stopper, 15 In.
$257

Showtime Auction Services

**Meissen,** Figurine, Putto, Winged, Tree Trunk Base, Crossed Swords, 12 In., Pair
$7,670

Brunk Auctions

**Meissen,** Group, 3 Putti, Wings, Painting Portrait, Crossed Swords Mark, c.1900, 7½ In.
$2,360

Brunk Auctions

| | |
|---|---|
| **Otoscope,** National Electrical Instrument Co., Ribbed Bakelite, Box | 123 |
| **Phrenology Head,** Ivory Cane, Numbered Sections, Pillar Base, 19th Century, 7 In. | 3360 |
| **Phrenology Head,** Porcelain, Descriptive Detail About Brain, L.N. Fowler, 12 In. | 30 |
| **Pill Counter,** Wooden, Paddle Shape, 50 Pill Indents, Flat Handle, 10½ In. | 56 |
| **Pillbox,** Enamel, Gold, Jockey Hat, Red, Cream, 1⅝ In. | 600 |
| **Pillbox,** Figural, Articulated Fish, 14K Gold, Cabochon Red Stone Eyes, 3 In. | 1420 |
| **Scalpel,** Fitted Mahogany Case, Bone Fishtail Handles, Dr. Griswald, 1800s, 7 In. | 324 |
| **Shock Box,** Quack Medical Device, 7 x 10 In. | 296 |
| **Springbleeder,** Silver Plate, Engraved Dr. Holiday, Slip Case, c.1835, 2¼ x 2¾ In. | 184 |
| **Stretcher,** Canvas, Wood Rails, Mine Safety Appliance Co., c.1900, 90 In. | 330 |
| **Surgeon's Field Kit,** Instruments, Folding, Case, Charriere Collin & Cie, France, 3½ x 6 In. | 460 |
| **Surgical Kit,** 18 Ebony Handled Tools, c.1962, 17 In. | 720 |
| **Tin,** Porous Belladonna Plaster, On Scarlet Felt, One Yard, Cylindrical, 8 In. | 62 |
| **Wet Drug Jar,** Delft Blue, White, c.1730, 7¾ In. | 1200 |

**MEISSEN** is a town in Germany where porcelain has been made since 1710. Any china made in the town can be called Meissen, although the famous Meissen factory made the finest porcelains of the area. The crossed swords mark of the great Meissen factory has been copied by many other firms in Germany and other parts of the world. Pieces of Meissen dinnerware in the Onion pattern are listed in their own category in this book.

| | |
|---|---|
| **Basket,** Reticulated, Applied Flowers, c.1890, 4¾ x 11 In., Pair | 240 |
| **Bottle,** Figural, Harlequin, Kaendler, Germany, 1800s | 3900 |
| **Bowl,** Center Flowers, Embossed, Gold Decorated Leaf Border, 12 In. | 266 |
| **Bowl,** Flower Sprays, Reticulated, Open Lattice, Oval, Gilt Handles, Raised Feet, 17 In. | 360 |
| **Bread Tray,** Oval, Gilt, Marked, c.1900, 12 In. | 94 |
| **Bust,** 2 Cupids, Flowers, Kiss, Curly Hair, Gilt, 11¼ In. | 3428 |
| **Bust,** Woman, Classical Dress, Gold Necklace, 8 In. | 531 |
| **Cachepot,** Satyr Mask Handles, Landscape, 8 Panels, Tooled Gilt Bands, 4⅛ In. | 677 |
| **Candelabrum,** Rococo, 2 Seated Putti, Multicolor, Baskets, Gilt, 13¾ In., 2 Piece | 1625 |
| **Centerpiece,** Basket, Pink, Blue, Reticulated, Leaf Column, Ring Base, c.1890, 13 In. | 600 |
| **Centerpiece,** Courting Couple Standard, 1800s Attire, Top Flower Bowl, c.1920, 19 x 14 In. | 2125 |
| **Clock,** Classically Dressed Dancers, Musicians, Eagle, Flowers, Key, 24½ In. | 6785 |
| **Compote,** Group, Multicolor, Ring Around The Rosie, 12⅝ In. | 2091 |
| **Compote,** Pierced Lattice Bowl, Flowers, Palm Tree Base, 4 Dancing Figures, 12 x 9 In. | 1408 |
| **Cup & Saucer,** Diamonds, Gilt Panels, White Bands, Leaf Handle, c.1810, 4⅝ In. | 69 |
| **Dispenser,** Liquor, Barrel Shape, Grapevines, Drunk Hussar, Putti, c.1850, 17 In. | 748 |
| **Dresser Box,** White, Flowers, Multicolor, Round, Crossed Swords Mark, 2 x 4 In. | 86 |
| **Figurine,** Angel, Rose Garlands Draped, 7½ In. | 1000 |
| **Figurine,** Apollo In Chariot, Holding Bow, Clouds, Lightning Bolts, Wheels Turn, 9 In. | 2750 |
| **Figurine,** Archer, Crossbow, Standing By Column, c.1890, 6 In. | 400 |
| **Figurine,** Aristocratic Woman, Purple Underskirt, Flower Dress, Fan, 8 In. | 688 |
| **Figurine,** Atlanta, Robed Figure, Golden Apple, Crossed Swords Mark, 11 In. | 688 |
| **Figurine,** Bathsheba, Bathing, Removing Sandals, Round Base, c.1910, 17 In. | 2500 |
| **Figurine,** Bearded Man, Warming Hands By Fire, Winter Allegory, 8¾ In. | 1625 |
| **Figurine,** Bird, Black, Yellow, White, c.1900, 6½ In. | 197 |
| **Figurine,** Boy, Crying, Holding Book, Seated On Chair, 5⅜ In. | 438 |
| **Figurine,** Bull, Striding, Brown, White, 11 x 15 In. | 438 |
| **Figurine,** Cherub, Grape Leaf Crown, Holding Grapevine Swag, 5 In. | 173 |
| **Figurine,** Cockatoo, Perched On Tree Stump, 9¾ In. | 472 |
| **Figurine,** Count Bruhl's Tailor, Riding Goat, Iron In Mouth, Impressed, c.1900, 8 In. | 1016 |
| **Figurine,** Cupid, Caught In Trap, Crossed Swords Mark, c.1900, 8 In. | 800 |
| **Figurine,** Cupid, Forging Heart, Hammer, Apron, Round Base, 1900s, 8 In. | 259 |
| **Figurine,** Cupid, Holding Flaming Heart, Lovebird, Love Letter, 12 In. | 1625 |
| **Figurine,** Cupid, Plumed Hat, Bow, Arrow, Socle Base, c.1920, 6 In. | 1375 |
| **Figurine,** Cupid, Standing, Leaning On Column, c.1920, 8 In. | 1250 |
| **Figurine,** Eagle, On Rocky Perch, 16 In. | 1180 |
| **Figurine,** Finch, On Droopy Bud, Pedestal, c.1910, 5 In. | 104 |
| **Figurine,** Girl, Hat, Lace Necklace, Holding Garland, 7 In. | 595 |
| **Figurine,** Girl, Holding Cards, Table, White Hat, Flowers, 6½ In. | 875 |
| **Figurine,** Girl, Holding Toy Animal, Impressed, 6 In. | 438 |
| **Figurine,** Girl, Seated, Holding Ribbon, Marked, 5 In. | 625 |
| **Figurine,** Girl, Seated, Sniffing Flowers, 5 Senses Series, 5½ In. | 1250 |
| **Figurine,** Girl, Sheep, Kerchief, Bouquet, Square Base, 6¼ In. | 1230 |
| **Figurine,** Grape Harvester, Marked, 3¾ In. | 375 |
| **Figurine,** Man, Dandy, Macaroni Style Dress, Round Base, c.1900, 9¾ In. | 431 |

| | | |
|---|---|---|
| **Figurine,** Monkey Conductor, Curled White Wig, Raised Baton, Impressed, c.1850, 7 In. | | 593 |
| **Figurine,** Parrot, On Tree Stump, Multicolor Plumage, Crossed Swords Mark, 16 In. | | 2124 |
| **Figurine,** Pauper Boy, Peg Leg, Torn Shirt, Hat In Hand, Round Base, 8¾ In. | | 813 |
| **Figurine,** Putto, Winged, Tree Trunk Base, Crossed Swords, 12 In., Pair | *illus* | 7670 |
| **Figurine,** Tanzer, Male Dancer, Blue Jacket, Check Pants, Germany, c.1905, 9½ x 9 In. | | 3375 |
| **Figurine,** Turkish Hunter, Turban, Purple Coat, Bow, Arrow, 1800s, 8¾ In. | | 431 |
| **Figurine,** Winter Allegory, Puce Cape, By Fire, c.1900, 9 In. | | 316 |
| **Figurine,** Woman, Gathering Flowers In Apron, Lamb At Feet, 10½ In. | | 384 |
| **Figurine,** Woman, Playing Cards, Dress, Lace, Crossed Swords Mark, 6 In. | | 900 |
| **Figurine,** Woman, Seated, Book, Table, Marked, Crossed Swords, 7 In. | | 369 |
| **Figurine,** Woman, Seated, Mirror, Representing Sight, 5 Senses Series, 5½ In. | | 625 |
| **Figurine,** Woman, Seated, Napping, Marked, 7¼ In. | | 813 |
| **Figurine,** Woman, Tricorn Hat, Rifle, Marked, 3 In. | | 200 |
| **Group,** 2 Winged Putti, Bird & Cage, Flower Encrusted Base, Sheaf Of Wheat, 6 x 7 In. | | 375 |
| **Group,** 3 Putti, Wings, Painting Portrait, Crossed Swords Mark, c.1900, 7½ In. | *illus* | 2360 |
| **Group,** Angels, Flowers, Marked, 6¼ In. | | 750 |
| **Group,** Apollo, Daphne, Reaching, Purple Robe, 14½ In. | | 4000 |
| **Group,** Boy, Girl, Cage, Flowers, Impressed, 6 In. | | 750 |
| **Group,** Broken Bridge, Gentleman Helping Woman Over Stream, 2 Putti, 10 In. | | 1476 |
| **Group,** Calydonian Boar Hunt, 6 Fitted Sections, Ebonized Wood Base, 13 x 16 In. | | 18000 |
| **Group,** Capture Of Infant Triton, Mythological Scene, 11⅝ In. | | 2125 |
| **Group,** Courting Couple, Musician, Putti, Goat, 1700s Attire, c.1925, 13¾ In. | | 2250 |
| **Group,** Courting Couple, Shepherds, Column, Crossed Swords Mark, 9½ In. | | 1188 |
| **Group,** Cupid, Standing, Holding Rose Wreath, c.1920, 7¾ In. | | 1375 |
| **Group,** Cupids, Tree, Tricorn Hat, Basket, Hearts, Sharpening Arrow, c.1800, 7 In. | | 345 |
| **Group,** Europa, On Bull, 2 Women Attendants, Garlands, c.1900, 8¼ In. | | 1625 |
| **Group,** Hunter, Shepherdess, Courting, Trees, Rocks, c.1890, 10¾ In. | | 1375 |
| **Group,** Leda, Pink Cape, Swan, Cupid, c.1960, 6¾ In. | | 1375 |
| **Group,** Man Standing, Grapes In Basket, Man & Woman With Barrel, 9 In. | | 875 |
| **Group,** Man, Woman, Young Satyr, Marked, 5⅞ In. | | 563 |
| **Group,** Mercury, Chariot, Pulled By Ravens, Blue Crossed Swords, 12 x 17 In. | *illus* | 5700 |
| **Group,** Mother, Girl, Boy, Blue Coat, 18th Century Attire, Chair, Stool, 6¾ In. | | 1250 |
| **Group,** Mother, Seated, 3 Children, Climbing On Her, Marked, 8½ In. | | 1750 |
| **Group,** Nymphs, Bull, Crossed Swords Mark, 9 In. | | 1625 |
| **Group,** Persistent Lover & Dog, Blue Crossed Swords Mark, 5¼ In. | | 708 |
| **Group,** Putti With Cannon, Gilt Trim, Naturalistic Base, Scrollwork, 5¼ In. | | 738 |
| **Group,** Shepherd, Shepherdess, Resting By Tree, 9¼ In. | | 800 |
| **Group,** Shepherd, Shepherdess, Seated, Sheep, Applied Flowers, 7⅜ In. | | 554 |
| **Group,** Shepherd, Shepherdess, Sheep, Fountain, Dog, c.1910, 9¾ In. | | 1375 |
| **Group,** Shepherdess, Beau, Seated, Sharing Grapes, c.1900, 8 In. | | 953 |
| **Group,** Shepherdess, Goat, c.1950, 6 In. | | 688 |
| **Group,** Spring & Fall, 2 Playful Putti, Wheat Sheaf, Grapes, Naturalistic Base, 9½ In. | | 1125 |
| **Group,** Venus & Cupid, Chariot, Marked, c.1880, 7 x 6¾ In. | *illus* | 1169 |
| **Group,** Woman Holding Book, Putto, Lyre, Round Base, 12¼ In. | | 1599 |
| **Group,** Woman, Mandolin, Man, Flute, Pink Settee, Pug Dog, 5¾ x 9 In. | | 1230 |
| **Plaque,** Madonna, Child, Blue, Red, Cream, Painted, Giltwood Frame, c.1910, 26 x 23 In. | | 7500 |
| **Plate,** Dessert, Blue, Red, Bird, Flowering Branches, Armorial Design, 8 In., 12 Piece | | 1000 |
| **Plate,** Figures, Horses, Cobalt Blue Ground, 9¼ In., Pair | | 2125 |
| **Plate,** Flowers, Gilt, Green Scalloped Rim, 1800s, 8½ In., 10 Piece | | 360 |
| **Plate,** Japanese Design, Kakiemon, Marked, c.1740, 9⅛ In. | *illus* | 7670 |
| **Plate,** Leaf Border, Scrolls, 10 In. | | 50 |
| **Plate,** Turquoise Ground, Center Courting Scene, Gilt Rim, 7¼ In., Pair | | 240 |
| **Plate,** Venus Gilt Highlights, Pierced Rim, c.1850, 9½ In. | | 5938 |
| **Plate,** Woman, Cherubs, Book, Lute, Marked, c.1900, 9½ In. | | 4500 |
| **Plate,** Young Lovers In Landscape, Cobalt Blue & Gilt Borders, Greek Key, 9¾ In. | | 189 |
| **Platter,** Serpentine Rim, Footed, Relief Border, Central Medallion, Gilt, 11 In. | | 127 |
| **Stand,** Sweetmeat, Mermaid Holding Shell, Putti, Blue Crossed Swords, 14 In. | *illus* | 3444 |
| **Stein,** Flowers, Yellow Ground, Inlaid Lid, Crown Thumblift, Crossed Swords Mark, 6 In. | | 720 |
| **Tray,** Dresser, Painted, Yellow Floral Bouquets, Landscape, Figures, 11 x 15 In. | | 345 |
| **Tray,** Shell Handles, Green Fish Scale Border, Musical Instruments, 20½ In. | | 1353 |
| **Tureen,** Lid, Putto Finial, Flowers, Oval, Handles, 2-Footed, 1800s, 9 In. | | 184 |
| **Urn,** Lid, Season Allegorical Reserves, Blue, Gilt Ground, Beast Tip Handles, 16 In., Pair | | 68500 |
| **Urn,** Lid, Yellow Bird Finial, Allover Blossoms, Schneeballen, 1900s, 12 In. | | 2500 |
| **Urns,** Lid, Putti Panels, Pate-Sur-Pate, Gilt Snake Handles, c.1900, 10½ In., Pair | | 16250 |
| **Vase,** Lid, Potpourri, Gilded, Flowers, Fruits, Woman, Flowers, Blue Mark, 28 In. | | 5228 |
| **Vase,** White Blossoms, Robin Redbreast, Green Stems & Leaves, 9¾ In., Pair | | 3438 |

### Old Onion

The Blue Onion pattern of Meissen dinnerware was designed in 1739 and is still being made.

**Meissen,** Group, Mercury, Chariot, Pulled By Ravens, Blue Crossed Swords, 12 x 17 In.
$5,700

Garth's Auctioneers & Appraisers

**Meissen,** Group, Venus & Cupid, Chariot, Marked, c.1880, 7 x 6¾ In.
$1,169

Neal Auction Co.

**Meissen,** Plate, Japanese Design, Kakiemon, Marked, c.1740, 9⅛ In.
$7,670

Brunk Auctions

**Meissen,** Stand, Sweetmeat, Mermaid Holding Shell, Putti, Blue Crossed Swords, 14 In.
$3,444

New Orleans Auction Galleries, Inc.

**Mettlach,** Ewer, Applied Cupid, Leaves, Silver Trim, Rope Twist Handle, Marked, 13 In.
$701

The Stein Auction Company

**Mettlach,** Jardiniere, No. 3107, Cameo, Women, Cherubs, Swags, 5 x 11 In.
$264

The Stein Auction Company

---

**MERCURY GLASS,** or silvered glass, was first made in the 1850s. It lost favor for a while but became popular again about 1910. It looks like a piece of silver.

| | |
|---|---:|
| **Butler's Ball,** c.1850, 10 x 19 In. | 850 |
| **Candlestick,** Baluster, c.1875, 8 In. | 75 |
| **Cordial,** Funnel Bowl, Double Twist Stem, Cone Shape Foot, 6 ½ In. | 1675 |
| **Ornament,** Car, c.1940, 3 In. | 19 |
| **Ornament,** Flower Basket, c.1900, 2 ½ In. | 16 |
| **Perfume Bottle,** Elephant Shape, White Tusks, Black Eyes, 2 ¼ In. | 60 |
| **Tieback,** Pewter Collar, 19th Century, 2 ½ x 3 ¾ In., Pair | 165 |
| **Vase,** Cylindrical, Pedestal, 1900s, 15 In., Pair | 425 |
| **Vase,** Spiral Ribbed, Pinched Neck, Footed, 9 In. | 195 |

**MERRIMAC POTTERY** Company was founded by Thomas Nickerson in Newburyport, Massachusetts, in 1902. The company made art pottery, garden pottery, and reproductions of Roman pottery. The pottery burned to the ground in 1908.

| | |
|---|---:|
| **Bowl,** Unglazed From Roman Molds, Massachusetts, 6 ½ In. | 615 |
| **Mug,** Green Glaze, Handle, Impressed, 6 ⅞ In. | 438 |

**METLOX POTTERIES** was founded in 1927 in Manhattan Beach, California. Dinnerware was made beginning in 1931. Evan K. Shaw purchased the company in 1946 and expanded the number of patterns. Poppytrail (1946–89) and Vernonware (1958–80) were divisions of Metlox under E.K. Shaw's direction. The factory closed in 1989.

| | |
|---|---:|
| **Aztec,** Gravy Boat, Underplate | 45 |
| **Bandero,** Bowl, Vegetable, Divided, Round, 9 ½ In. | 22 |
| **Bandero,** Cup & Saucer | 12 |
| **Blueberry Provincial,** Cup & Saucer | 15 |
| **Blueberry Provincial,** Platter, Oval, 11 In. | 40 |
| **California Rose,** Creamer, 3 ½ In. | 19 |
| **California Rose,** Platter, Oval, 13 ½ In. | 37 |
| **Cape Cod,** Cup & Saucer | 6 |
| **San Clemente,** Bowl, Cereal, Spanish Yellow | 12 |
| **San Clemente,** Cup & Saucer, Spanish Yellow | 14 |
| **San Clemente,** Platter, Spanish Yellow, 13 ½ In. | 26 |
| **San Fernando,** Bowl, Vegetable, Round, 9 In. | 24 |
| **San Fernando,** Chop Plate, 14 ¼ In. | 48 |
| **San Fernando,** Cup & Saucer | 8 |
| **Sculptured,** Grape, Bowl, Vegetable, Round, Divided, 9 ½ In. | 55 |
| **Sculptured,** Grape, Butter, Cover | 22 |
| **Sculptured,** Grape, Platter, 12 ½ In. | 38 |
| **Sculptured,** Grape, Salt & Pepper | 35 |
| **Sculptured,** Grape, Trail, Gravy Boat, Attached Underplate | 48 |
| **Tropicana,** Cup & Saucer | 13 |

**METTLACH,** Germany, is a city where the Villeroy and Boch factories worked. Steins from the firm are marked with the word *Mettlach* or the castle mark. They date from about 1842. *PUG* means painted under glaze. The steins can be dated from the marks on the bottom, which include a date-number code. Other pieces may be listed in the Villeroy & Boch category.

| | |
|---|---:|
| **Ashtray,** No. 2838, 6-Sided, Etched, 2 In. | 168 |
| **Ashtray,** No. 2907, Art Nouveau, Cream, Blue, Tan, Etched, 4 ½ In. | 162 |
| **Bowl,** Lid, For King Ludwig II Of Bavaria, Swan Finial, 8 ½ In. | 187 |
| **Ewer,** Applied Cupid, Leaves, Silver Trim, Rope Twist Handle, Marked, 13 In. ........*illus* | 701 |
| **Jardiniere,** No. 3107, Cameo, Women, Cherubs, Swags, 5 x 11 In. ........*illus* | 264 |
| **Pass Cup,** No. 2236, Couple, Musician, Handles, H. Schlitt, 6 In. | 312 |
| **Pitcher,** No. 1217, Knights In Reserves, Etched, 14 In. | 614 |
| **Pitcher,** No. 3321, Art Nouveau, Etched, 6 ½ In. ........*illus* | 240 |
| **Plaque,** Castle, Mountain Scene, Round, 17 In., Pair | 550 |
| **Plaque,** No. 1044/147, Lichtenstein, Castle On Hill, 14 In. | 156 |
| **Plaque,** No. 1044/5195, Delft, 17 ¼ In. | 168 |
| **Plaque,** No. 1770, Wilhelm Tell, Etched, 14 ½ In. | 960 |
| **Plaque,** No. 2196, Stolzenfels Castle On Rhine River, Painted, 1896 | 270 |
| **Plaque,** No. 2322, Man Trying To Kiss Woman, Cupid With Bow & Arrow, Etched, 14 In. | 420 |
| **Plaque,** No. 2533, Godesburg Castle, Etched, Gold, 17 ¼ In. ........*illus* | 540 |
| **Plaque,** No. 2597, Etched, Girl Eating Cherry, Art Nouveau, 16 In. ........*illus* | 720 |

| | |
|---|---|
| **Plaque,** No. 9029/1044, Dog, Painted, 14 In............................................ | 276 |
| **Plate,** No. 3096, Cream, Blue, Tan, Etched, Octagonal, 7 ¼ In., 8 Piece............ | 120 |
| **Punch Bowl Set,** No. 3360, 12 Goblets, 8 Liter, 5 In................................... | 1260 |
| **Punch Bowl,** No. 989, Print Under Glaze, H. Schlitt................................... | 312 |
| **Punch Bowl,** No. 2087, Relief Drinking Scene, Blue Ground, Double Dolphin Finial, 14 In....... | 148 |
| **Punch Bowl,** Underplate, Lid, Gnomes Making, Drinking Wine, Scroll Handles, 16 x 17 In....... | 413 |
| **Stein,** 4 White Wigged Gentlemen, Drinking In Tavern, Pewter Flip Lid, 16 In........ | 649 |
| **Stein,** King, Queen Playing Cards, Steins, Die Fighting, Pewter Lid, Gnome Handle, 20 In......... | 1003 |
| **Stein,** No. 240, Hunter, PUG, Pewter Lid, ½ Liter................................... | 196 |
| **Stein,** No. 284, Stag, Pewter Lid, ½ Liter......................................... | 173 |
| **Stein,** No. 328, Earlyware, Inlaid Lid, ½ Liter.................................... | 216 |
| **Stein,** No. 588, Barmaid, PUG, Pewter Lid, ½ Liter................................. | 92 |
| **Stein,** No. 612, Munich Child, PUG, Pewter Lid, ½ Liter............................ | 230 |
| **Stein,** No. 812, Relief, Figures, Horn Shape Handle, Pewter Lid, 1 ½ Liter.......... | 420 |
| **Stein,** No. 1033, Gnomes, PUG, Pewter Lid, ¼ Liter................................. | 1090 |
| **Stein,** No. 1037, Girl On Safety Bicycle, PUG, Pewter Lid, Thumblift, 8 ½ In........ | 263 |
| **Stein,** No. 1072, Mosaic, Etched, Pewter Lid, ½ Liter.............................. | 1080 |
| **Stein,** No. 1121, Stylized Flower & Fan, Mosaic, Inlaid Lid, ⅓ Liter............... | 192 |
| **Stein,** No. 1154, 4 Hunter Panels, Liter, 1803..................................... | 180 |
| **Stein,** No. 1394, German Cards, Etched, 1884, ½ In Liter........................... | 300 |
| **Stein,** No. 1395, Card Duits, Heart, Spade, Diamond, Club, Etched, Inlaid Lid, ½ Liter .... | 370 to 570 |
| **Stein,** No. 1519, Sculling, Etched, Inlaid Lid, ½ Liter............................. | 504 |
| **Stein,** No. 1526, Munich Child, Bavaria, Pewter Lid, ½ Liter....................... | 390 |
| **Stein,** No. 1526, Munich Child, PUG, Pewter Lid, ¼ Liter........................... | 161 |
| **Stein,** No. 1526/1271, Black Silhouette, Drunk In Wheelbarrow, PUG, 1 Liter .........*illus* | 192 |
| **Stein,** No. 1562, Cavalier In Reserve, Stoneware, Tapered, Pewter Lid & Lift, 22 In......... | 1080 |
| **Stein,** No. 1819, Masonic Symbols, Etched, Inlaid Lid, ½ Liter..................... | 660 |
| **Stein,** No. 1850, Mosaic, Inlaid Lid, ¼ Liter...................................... | 207 |
| **Stein,** No. 1932, Cavaliers Drinking, Etched, Inlaid Lid, ½ Liter .............*illus* | 264 |
| **Stein,** No. 1946, 1600s Courting Scene, Etched, ½ Liter, 1906...................... | 240 |
| **Stein,** No. 1956, Wilhelm I, Pewter Mounted, c.1910, 1 Liter, 10 ¼ In.............. | 1750 |
| **Stein,** No. 1963, Vining, Leaves, Mosaic, Inlaid Lid, ¼ Liter...................... | 528 |
| **Stein,** No. 2001B, Book Spines, Medicine, Relief, Inlaid Lid, ½ Liter.............. | 252 |
| **Stein,** No. 2005, 1600s Tavern Scene, 4 Drinkers, Signed H.D., 1901, ½ Liter....... | 270 |
| **Stein,** No. 2007, Black Cat, Etched, Inlaid Lid, F. Stuck, ½ Liter................. | 810 |
| **Stein,** No. 2015, Relief Decoration, Pewter Lid, ½ Liter........................... | 1440 |
| **Stein,** No. 2024, Shield, Coat Of Arms, Berlin, Etched, Inlaid Lid, ½ Liter........ | 240 |
| **Stein,** No. 2049, Chessboard, Knight, Etched, Inlaid Lid, Pewter Thumblift, Hupp, ½ Liter.......... | 2400 |
| **Stein,** No. 2090, Tavern, Nicer The Tavern, Worse It Is For The Wife, Etched, Schlitt, 1 Liter ....... | 390 |
| **Stein,** No. 2099, Art Nouveau, Flowers, Mosaic, Inlaid Lid, ⅓ Liter............... | 180 |
| **Stein,** No. 2140/769, Infanterie Regt. Nr. 36, PUG, Pewter Lid, ½ Liter........... | 228 |
| **Stein,** No. 2211, Bowling, Relief, Inlaid Lid, ¼ Liter............................. | 86 |
| **Stein,** No. 2277, View From Hill, Heidelberg, Etched, Inlaid Lid, ⅓ Liter......... | 180 |
| **Stein,** No. 2281, Etched, 23rd Armory, American Flags, Rifles, Drum, Inlaid Lid, ½ Liter .....*illus* | 1344 |
| **Stein,** No. 2324, American Football Game, Pewter Mounted Lid, c.1910, 9 ½ In....... | 438 |
| **Stein,** No. 2382, Etched, H. Schlitt, Inlaid Lid, ½ Liter.......................... | 431 |
| **Stein,** No. 2388, Pretzels, Inlaid Lid, Pretzel Handle, ½ Liter.................... | 312 |
| **Stein,** No. 2530, Mythological Figures, Cameo, Inlaid Lid, ½ Liter................. | 240 |
| **Stein,** No. 2583, Egyptian Hieroglyphic Symbols, Inlaid Lid, F. Quidenus, 8 In..... | 600 |
| **Stein,** No. 2728, Occupational, Brewer, Bucket With Wheat, Utensils, O. Hupp, ½ Liter............ | 1320 |
| **Stein,** No. 2778, Castle, Jesters, Entertainers, Feasting, Schlitt, Stoneware, Inlaid Lid, 7 In.......... | 480 |
| **Stein,** No. 2796, Heidelberg Scene, Pewter & Pottery Lid, 14 ¾ In.................. | 677 |
| **Stein,** No. 2796, Heidelberg View, Painted, 3 Liter, 1903.......................... | 900 |
| **Stein,** No. 2887, Knights At Table, Tankards, Etched, Inlaid Lid, ½ Liter.......... | 450 |
| **Stein,** No. 2917, Munich Child, Munich, Lion & Shield, Lid, Relief, ½ Liter .........*illus* | 1080 |
| **Stein,** No. 2921, Men By Campfire, Etched, Inlaid Lid, 2.8 Liter .............*illus* | 300 |
| **Stein,** No. 2934, Art Nouveau, Etched, Inlaid Lid, ½ Liter......................... | 600 |
| **Stein,** No. 2935, Art Nouveau, Etched, Inlaid Lid, ¼ Liter......................... | 462 |
| **Stein,** No. 2937, Night Watchman, Lantern, Staff, Etched, Lid, F. Quidenus, ½ Liter...... | 264 |
| **Stein,** No. 3089, Monk In Barrel, Etched, Inlaid Lid, H. Schlitt, 1 Liter.......... | 540 |
| **Stein,** No. 3090, Man With Guitar, Women Dancing, Etched, Inlaid Lid, H. Schlitt, 1 Liter .......... | 660 |
| **Stein,** No. 5002, Delft, Cavalier, Pewter Lid, ½ Liter............................. | 480 |
| **Stein,** Pate-Sur-Pate, 7 Men, Dog, Capturing Boar, Rabbit, 8 In., ½ Liter.......... | 345 |
| **Tray,** Villeroy & Boch Factory, Sepia Image, White Ground, Shaped Rim, 5 x 7 In...... | 226 |
| **Vase,** Black Forest Woman, Pinched Waist, Stand Up Pinecone Rim, 11 In............. | 228 |
| **Vase,** Iris, Etched, Tapered, Stand-Up Rim, Art Nouveau, 13 In.................... | 240 |

**Mettlach,** Pitcher, No. 3321, Art Nouveau, Etched, 6 ½ In.
$240

The Stein Auction Company

**Mettlach,** Plaque, No. 2533, Godesburg Castle, Etched, Gold, 17 ¼ In.
$540

The Stein Auction Company

**Mettlach,** Plaque, No. 2597, Etched, Girl Eating Cherry, Art Nouveau, 16 In.
$720

M

Fox Auctions

**TIP**

*An auction staff member examined a blanket chest that might be in a coming sale. He found a hidden compartment filled with valuable historical documents. Another reminder to search for secret compartments in antiques.*

**Mettlach,** Stein, No. 1526/1271, Black Silhouette, Drunk In Wheelbarrow, PUG, 1 Liter
$192

**Mettlach,** Stein, No. 1932, Cavaliers Drinking, Etched, Inlaid Lid, ½ Liter
$264

**Mettlach,** Stein, No. 2281, Etched, 23rd Armory, American Flags, Rifles, Drum, Inlaid Lid, ½ Liter
$1,344

**Mettlach,** Stein, No. 2917, Munich Child, Munich, Lion & Shield, Lid, Relief, ½ Liter
$1,080

**Mettlach,** Stein, No. 2921, Men By Campfire, Etched, Inlaid Lid, 2.8 Liter
$300

**Mettlach,** Vase, No. 2913, Art Nouveau, Etched, 14½ In.
$690

### TIP
*Do not put water in a pottery container with an unglazed interior. The water will be absorbed and eventually stain the container.*

**Mettlach,** Vase, No. 2977, Art Nouveau, Etched, 14 In.
$450

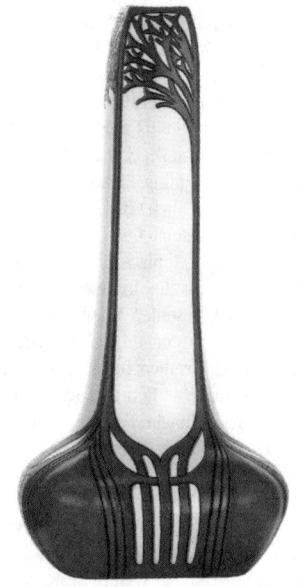

**Mettlach,** Vase, No. 5424, Dutch Girl, Delft, 13½ In.
$168

| | |
|---|---|
| **Vase,** No. 1829, Oval, Flared Rim, Etched, 9 In. | 161 |
| **Vase,** No. 1862, Mosaic, Shouldered, Handles, 15 In. | 390 |
| **Vase,** No. 2017, Mosaic, Globular, Footed, Fish Neck, 12 In. | 360 |
| **Vase,** No. 2495, Glazed, Elephant Handles, 5 In. | 299 |
| **Vase,** No. 2851, Etched, Blue Ground, Stylized Flowers, Elephant Handles, 13¾ In. | 181 |
| **Vase,** No. 2913, Art Nouveau, Etched, 14½ In. *illus* | 690 |
| **Vase,** No. 2977, Art Nouveau, Etched, 14 In. *illus* | 450 |
| **Vase,** No. 3006, Stick Neck, 2 Handles, Cameo, 13 In. | 265 |
| **Vase,** No. 3357, Etched Circle Band, Blue Fluted Base, Cream Top, Swollen, Art Deco, 12 In. | 510 |
| **Vase,** No. 5424, Dutch Girl, Delft, 13½ In. *illus* | 168 |

**MILK GLASS** was named for its milky white color. It was first made in England during the 1700s. The height of its popularity in the United States was from 1870 to 1880. It is now correct to refer to some colored glass as blue milk glass, black milk glass, etc. Reproductions of milk glass are being made and sold in many stores. Related pieces may be listed in the Cosmos, Vallerysthal, and Westmoreland categories.

| | |
|---|---|
| **Box,** Entwined Horseshoes, Whip, Bugle, c.1900, 2 x 2 In. | 92 |
| **Butter,** Cover, Pyrex, 1960s, 6 x 3 In. | 14 |
| **Butter,** Cover, Winburn, Fostoria, Round, 1950s, 8 x 6 In. | 50 |
| **Cake Stand,** Pedestal, Grapes, Paneled Rim, Anchor Hocking, 11 x 9¾ In. | 25 |
| **Candlestick,** Octagonal, Loop Handle, 4¾ In., Pair | 18 |
| **Candy Dish,** Boat Shape, 6½ x 3½ In. | 85 |
| **Candy Dish,** Hobnail, Lid, Round, 6 x 4 In. | 34 |
| **Centerpiece,** Lacy Rim, Footed, 11¾ In. | 24 |
| **Dish,** Strawberry Shape, Raised Seeds, 7 x 6 In., Pair | 17 |
| **Dish,** Swan, Imperial Glass, 9 x 5 x 5 In. | 20 |
| **Figurine,** Cat, Licking Paw, 1940s, 2¼ In. | 25 |
| **Fox On Basket,** Lattice Rim, Atterbury Glass, c.1900, 8 x 6 x 7 In. | 100 |
| **Goblet,** Paneled, Grapes, Pedestal, 5¾ x 3 In. | 8 |
| **Lamp,** Hurricane, Ruffled Chimney, Finger Hole Handle, 8 x 5 In. | 34 |
| **Mug,** Bird On Branch, Wheat, Angled Handle, Atterbury Glass Co., c.1885, 3 In. | 36 |
| **Mug,** Man Playing Mandolin, Woman, Flower, Germany, 4⅝ In. | 35 |
| **Plate,** Eagles, Flags, Fleur-De-Lis Border, c.1903, 8¾ In. | 55 |
| **Relish,** 4 Sections, Grapes, Leaves, Handles, Jeanette Glass, c.1955, 12 x 13 In. | 38 |
| **Salt & Pepper,** Diamond Quilt, Pedestal, 5 In. | 7 |
| **Shaker,** Figural, Man, Tuxedo, Atterbury, c.1872, 6½ In. | 125 |
| **Shaker,** Flour, McKee, 5 x 2 x 2 In. | 28 |
| **Shaker,** Layered Look, 3 In. | 35 |
| **Sock Darner,** Pontil, c.1900, 7 In. | 70 |
| **Top Hat,** Buttons & Bows, 2¼ x 3¼ In. | 15 |
| **Vase,** Diamond Quilt Pattern, Bulbous, Stick Neck, 9 In. | 10 |

**MILLEFIORI** means, literally, a thousand flowers. Many small pieces of glass resembling flowers are grouped together to form a design. It is a type of glasswork popular in paperweights and some are listed in that category.

| | |
|---|---|
| **Bowl,** Crimped Rim, Green, Blue, 7½ x 2 In. | 270 |
| **Fairy Lamp,** Cone Shape, Multicolor, Italy, 1960s, 5½ x 5⅝ In. | 303 |
| **Figurine,** Duck, Pink, Gold Head, Cane Eye, 5½ In. | 65 |
| **Figurine,** Purse Shape, Red Handle, 8 x 7 In. | 45 |
| **Lamp,** Multicolor, Gourd Shape, 9 x 5 In. | 199 |
| **Lighter,** Blue Ground, Ball Shape, Brass, 1960s, 3 x 3 In. | 28 |
| **Tumbler,** Pink, White, Italy, 3½ x 2¾ In. | 60 |
| **Vase,** Bulbous, Flared Rim, Pink, Green, Fratelli Toso, 1900s, 4⅜ In. | 129 |
| **Vase,** Bulbous, Stick Neck, Ruffled Lip, Multicolor, Art Nouveau, c.1915, 7 In. | 219 |

**MINTON** china has been made in the Staffordshire region of England from 1793 to the present. The firm became part of the Royal Doulton Tableware Group in 1968, but the wares continued to be marked *Minton*. In 2009 the brand was bought by KPS Capital Partners of New York and became part of WWRD Holdings. The company no longer makes Minton china. Many marks have been used. The word *England* was added in 1891. Minton majolica is listed in this book in the Majolica category.

| | |
|---|---|
| **Biscuit Jar,** Blue Willow, Blue, White, Silver Plated Lid, Bail, Marked, 6 In. | 325 |
| **Charger,** Stylized Leaves, Concentric Bands, Light Blue, Light Yellow Ground, 13¾ In. | 177 |
| **Cup & Saucer,** Raised Gilt, 4 Oval Reserves, Landscapes, Marked, c.1872 | 472 |

**Minton,** Plate, Birds, Apple Blossoms, Faience, Stamped, 1880s, 13½ In.
$1,188

Rago Arts & Auction Center

**Minton,** Plate, Burgundy Border, Raised Gilt Design, c.1902, 8¾ In., 8 Piece
$307

New Orleans Auction Galleries, Inc.

**M**

**Minton,** Vase, Double Gourd, Stencil Design, Thistles, Leaves, Brown Transfer, 10½ In.
$173

Humler & Nolan

**Mocha,** Mixing Bowl, Earthworm, Zigzag, Blue, Opaque White, Brown, 3¼ x 6¼ In.
$236

Conestoga Auction Co., Inc.

**Mocha,** Pitcher, Earthworm, Double Bulbous, Applied Handle, 8¼ In.
$413

Conestoga Auction Co., Inc.

**TIP**
*Don't scrub gilding and gold edges on porcelains.*

**Moorcroft,** Ginger Jar, Eventide, Trees, Sterling Silver Shreve Lid, Marked, c.1922, 14¾ In.
$6,250

Rago Arts & Auction Center

| | |
|---|---|
| **Figurine,** Dorothea, Parian, John Bell, 1800s, 14 In. | 108 |
| **Figurine,** Parian, Daniel Webster, Standing, Hand In Jacket, Books, 26 In. | 2460 |
| **Garden Seat,** Gilt, Cobalt Blue, Bulbous, Gold, Silver Flowers, Bows, 18 x 13 In., Pair | 625 |
| **Group,** Nude Ariadne, Parian, Panther, c.1862, 14¼ x 11¼ In. | 1845 |
| **Jardiniere,** Underplate, Ram's Head Mask, Garlands, Turquoise, c.1870, 15 x 17 In., Pair | 1875 |
| **Jug,** Medieval Tower, 4 Dancing Figures, Vines, Leaves, Vine Handle, 9½ In. | 484 |
| **Plaque,** Tile, Classical Man, Carrying Birdcage, Glaze, c.1884, 17 x 7 In. | 390 |
| **Plate,** Birds, Apple Blossoms, Faience, Stamped, 1880s, 13½ In. ............*illus* | 1188 |
| **Plate,** Blue Border, Flower Swags, Gilt, W. H. Plummer & Co, 10 In., 12 Piece | 1063 |
| **Plate,** Burgundy Border, Raised Gilt Design, c.1902, 8¾ In., 8 Piece ............*illus* | 307 |
| **Plate,** Dinner, Montrose, Pink Flowers, Blue Ribbon, Gold Trim, Scalloped, 10 In., 12 Piece | 86 |
| **Plate,** Raised Gilt Medallions, Scrollwork, Green, Mark, c.1927, 10 In., 12 Piece | 922 |
| **Teapot,** Three Friends, Bamboo, Branches, Flowers, Green, Tan, Blue, 5¾ In. | 726 |
| **Tile,** Courting, Palace Scenes, Blue, White, Wood Frame, 5½ x 5½ In., 4 Piece | 120 |
| **Tile,** Goat, Kid, Transferware, Brown On White, c.1870, 6 x 6 In. | 250 |
| **Urn,** Classical Figures Reserve, Cobalt Blue, Gilt Base, Ram's Head Handles, 13¼ In. | 188 |
| **Vase,** Double Gourd, Stencil Design, Thistles, Leaves, Brown Transfer, 10½ In. ............*illus* | 173 |
| **Vase,** Moon Flask, Blue, Chinoiserie Flowers, Gilt Mounts, c.1900, 12 x 10 In. | 4688 |
| **Vase,** Moon Flask, Woman, Plumed Hat, Pearls, 2 Ring Handles, S.H. Elis, c.1875 | 1376 |
| **Vase,** Women Portraits, Pate-Sur-Pate, Angled Gilt Handles, c.1900, 8 In., Pair | 1375 |

---

**MIRRORS** *are listed in the Furniture category under Mirror.*

---

**MOCHA** pottery is an English-made product that was sold in America during the early 1800s. It is a heavy pottery with pale coffee-and-cream coloring. Designs of blue, brown, green, orange, black, or white were added to the pottery and given fanciful names, such as Tree, Snail Trail, or Moss. Mocha designs are sometimes found on pearlware. A few pieces of mocha ware were made in France, the United States, and other countries.

| | |
|---|---|
| **Bowl,** Earthworm, Gray, 1800-25, 7 In. | 420 |
| **Bowl,** Geometrics, 9¾ In. | 2607 |
| **Bowl,** Marbleized, Tan Ground, 1800-25, 5½ In. | 240 |
| **Mixing Bowl,** Earthworm, Zigzag, Blue, Opaque White, Brown, 3¼ x 6¼ In. ............*illus* | 236 |
| **Mug,** Bands, Tan, Brown, Black Line, Loop Handle, 4¼ In. | 333 |
| **Mug,** Blue Seaweed, Straight-Sided, Yellowware, Applied Loop Handle, 1800s, 3¾ In. | 325 |
| **Mug,** Cat's-Eye, Green Band, Leaf Handle, 1800-25, 4¾ In. | 660 |
| **Mustard Pot,** Bands, Tan, Leaf Handle, c.1800, 4 In. | 246 |
| **Pitcher,** 2 Double Earthworms, Tooled Shoulder Bands, c.1875, 8 In. | 1020 |
| **Pitcher,** Earthworm Band, Sage Ground, Blue Bands, 7⅛ In. | 363 |
| **Pitcher,** Earthworm, Cabled Cat's-Eye, Twigs, Blue Bands, Black Accents, 8¼ In. | 2185 |
| **Pitcher,** Earthworm, Double Bulbous, Applied Handle, 8¼ In. ............*illus* | 413 |
| **Pitcher,** Green Seaweed, Red Bands, Tapered, Shell Handhold, Yellowware, 10½ In. | 1560 |
| **Pitcher,** Seaweed, 2-Tone Band, Leaf Handle, 5½ In. | 240 |
| **Pitcher,** Tooled Bands, Leaf Handle, 3-Color Leaves, c.1875, 7 In. | 390 |
| **Salt & Pepper,** Cat's-Eye, Seaweed, c.1825 | 780 |
| **Salt Pot,** Bands, White, Shaped Back, Hanging Holder, Label, 6 In. | 30 |

---

**MONMOUTH POTTERY COMPANY** started working in Monmouth, Illinois, in 1892. The pottery made a variety of utilitarian wares. It became part of Western Stoneware Company in 1906. The maple leaf mark was used until 1930. If *Co.* appears as part of the mark, the piece was made before 1906.

| | |
|---|---|
| **Ashtray,** Advertising, Western Stoneware Co., Maple Leaf, c.1900, 4 In. Diam. | 35 |
| **Bowl,** Brown Glaze, 8½ x 3¾ In. | 35 |
| **Bowl,** Ribbed, Brown Glaze, 10 In. | 21 |
| **Bowl,** Spongeware, Yellow, Ribbed, Marked, 9 In. | 28 |
| **Jug,** Brown, Yellow Rose, Transfer, Strap Handles, 7 x 4 In. | 45 |
| **Urn,** Light Green Glaze, Footed, Handles, Sawtooth Rim, 6 In. | 23 |
| **Vase,** Band Of Leaves, Footed, Flared, Green Matte Glaze, 11 In. | 120 |

---

**MONT JOYE,** *see Mt. Joye category.*

---

**MOORCROFT** pottery was first made in Burslem, England, in 1913. William Moorcroft had managed the art pottery department for James Macintyre & Company of England from 1898 to 1913. The Moorcroft pottery continues today, although William Moorcroft died in 1945. The earlier wares are similar to the modern ones, but color and marking will help indicate the age.

M

| | |
|---|---:|
| **Bowl,** Rouge Flambe Glaze, Flared-Out, Liberty Label, c.1925, 2 x 11 In. | 281 |
| **Candlestick,** Wisteria, Cobalt Blue Ground, Impressed Cobridge, 6 ½ In. | 345 |
| **Chalice,** 2 Handles, Signed, 9 In. | 8190 |
| **Ginger Jar,** Eventide, Trees, Sterling Silver Shreve Lid, Marked, c.1922, 14¾ In. ...............*illus* | 6250 |
| **Jam Jar,** Moonlit Blue, Trees, Mottled Green Blue, Dark Blue Ground, Silver Lid, 4 In. | 594 |
| **Jam Jar,** Pomegranate, Metal Lid, Handle, Burslem, 2¾ In. | 316 |
| **Jug,** Florian Ware, Blue Flowers, White Ground, Macintyre, England, c.1910, 6½ x 5 In. | 576 |
| **Lamp Base,** Orchid, Cobalt Blue Ground, Purple, Cream, Green, c.1945, 12½ In. | 230 |
| **Loving Cup,** Lid, Art Nouveau, Flowers, Gilt, Handles, Marked, 8½ x 4 In. .........................*illus* | 1652 |
| **Tankard,** Tulips, Green, Blue, Gold, Macintyre, Florian, 1902-13, 14 In. | 1725 |
| **Tea Service,** Flamminian, Teapot, Sugar, Creamer, Silver Overlay, c.1905, 7 x 6 ½ In. | 938 |
| **Teapot,** Smokestack Shape, Arch Handle, Green, Flowers, Signed, 10 x 5 ½ In. ..................*illus* | 1265 |
| **Vase,** Blue Cornflower, Signed, 8 In. | 1111 |
| **Vase,** Blue Cornflower, Signed, 10 In. | 1228 |
| **Vase,** Blue, Cream, Amethyst Wisteria, Burslem, Green Slip Signature, 8 In. | 546 |
| **Vase,** Claremont, Blue Green, Toadstools, Tapered Oval, c.1925, 10 In. | 5931 |
| **Vase,** Claremont, Flambe, Toadstools, Impressed, Rim To Waist Handles, 1932, 8 In. | 3813 |
| **Vase,** Cornflower, Florian Ware, 2-Tone Blue, Long, Flared Neck, c.1900, 11 In. | 1059 |
| **Vase,** Dark Blue Green Ground, Red Fruit, Leaves, Marked, 13 In. | 840 |
| **Vase,** Dawn, Blues, Abstract Landscape, Chevron Border, 4⅝ In. | 1035 |
| **Vase,** Eventide, Flared Rim, Liberty & Co. Tudric Foot, 6⅜ In. | 748 |
| **Vase,** Eventide, Trees, Mountains, Signed, c.1923, 11½ x 6½ In. | 9375 |
| **Vase,** Fish, Blue Ground, Chalice Form, Footed, c.1930, 4 x 3 In. | 519 |
| **Vase,** Freesia, Painted Flowers, Flambe, 7 In. | 529 |
| **Vase,** Grape & Leaf, Mottled Green Ground, Bulbous, c.1930, 10 x 6½ In. | 488 |
| **Vase,** Green Over Blue Gloss Glaze, Crystalline, 4 In. | 213 |
| **Vase,** Iris, Mottled Red, Flambe, Tapered, 6 In. | 423 |
| **Vase,** Macintyre Florian, Blue, Flowers, Butterflies, W.M., Des, 8¾ In. | 430 |
| **Vase,** Macintyre Florian, Bottle Shape, Green, Blue, Brown Transfer Logo, 10⅛ In. | 430 |
| **Vase,** Moonlit Blue Ground, Green Trees, 3½ In. | 590 |
| **Vase,** Moonlit Blue Landscape, Stamped, 1928-49, 10 x 8½ In. .........................*illus* | 4063 |
| **Vase,** Moonlit Blue, Green Tree, c.1924, 6 In. | 1271 |
| **Vase,** Moonlit Blue, Landscape, Bulbous, Flared Foot, Marked, 6½ x 4 In. | 1125 |
| **Vase,** Orchid, Band Of Flowers, Blue Ground, c.1940, 12 In. | 1059 |
| **Vase,** Orchid, Dark Blue Ground, Oval, 15 x 9 In. | 750 |
| **Vase,** Orchid, Mottled Green Ground, Bulbous, c.1945, 10 x 7 In. | 488 |
| **Vase,** Orchids, Cream Ground, c.1950, 6 In. | 200 |
| **Vase,** Pansies, Cream, Green Ground, Impressed, 9 In. | 1376 |
| **Vase,** Pansies, Mottled Blue Ground, Squat Base, Elongated Neck, c.1935, 12 x 8 In. | 671 |
| **Vase,** Pansy, Cream Ground, Silver Plated Rim, Marked, Macintyre, c.1912, 4 In. | 381 |
| **Vase,** Plums, Blue Ground, Marked, Signed William Moorcroft, 4 x 3¼ In. | 72 |
| **Vase,** Pomegranate, Flared, Footed, Impressed, c.1915, 17 In. | 1059 |
| **Vase,** Pomegranate, Mottled Blue Ground, Swollen, c.1918, 11½ x 8½ In. | 549 |
| **Vase,** Pomegranate, Mottled Green Ground, Flared, 2 Handles, 12 x 9 In. | 1952 |
| **Vase,** Pomegranate, Multicolor, Burslem, Cobridge Factory, c.1916, 10⅝ In. | 633 |
| **Vase,** Poppies, Flambe Glaze, Red, Green, Gold, Impressed, 9⅜ In. | 3220 |
| **Vase,** Red Flowers, Green Leaves, Handles, 1912, 8 x 7 In. | 5313 |
| **Vase,** Strawberry Thief, Incised, Painted, Blue Ground, Birds, 7¾ In. | 230 |
| **Vase,** Toadstool Blue, Green, Stamped, Claremont, c.1920, 7 x 3½ In. | 3125 |
| **Vase,** Trees, Blue, Green, Macintyre, Signed, 12 In. | 4370 |
| **Vase,** Tribute To Chas. Rennie Mackintosh, 8 In. | 210 |
| **Vase,** Trumpet Shape, Pomegranate, Signed, 10 In. | 3627 |
| **Vase,** Tulips, Orange, Cobalt Blue, Squat, 4 x 5¼ In. | 173 |

---

**MORGANTOWN GLASS WORKS** operated in Morgantown, West Virginia, from 1900 to 1974. Some of their wares are marked with an adhesive label that says *Old Morgantown Glass*.

| | |
|---|---:|
| **Bell,** American Beauty, Pink, 8 In. | 30 |
| **Candleholder,** Jacobi, Blue Ritz, Crystal Foot, 4⅛ x 3 In. | 89 |
| **Iced Tea,** Fairwin, 7 In. | 9 |
| **Tumbler,** Blue, Crinkle, 10 Oz., 4 In. | 15 |
| **Tumbler,** Green, Crinkle, 10 Oz., 4 In. | 15 |
| **Vase,** Peachblow, Blown Glass, Cased, Graduated Color, Glossy Glaze, 8 In. | 690 |
| **Wine,** Cathay, 6 In. | 17 |

**Moorcroft,** Loving Cup, Lid, Art Nouveau, Flowers, Gilt, Handles, Marked, 8½ x 4 In.
$1,652

Brunk Auctions

---

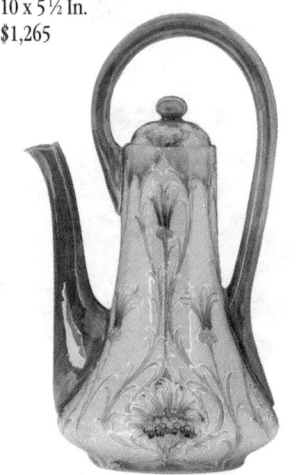

**Moorcroft,** Teapot, Smokestack Shape, Arch Handle, Green, Flowers, Signed, 10 x 5½ In.
$1,265

Cottone Auctions

---

**Moorcroft,** Vase, Moonlit Blue Landscape, Stamped, 1928-49, 10 x 8½ In.
$4,063

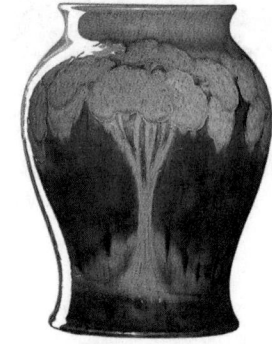

Rago Arts & Auction Center

---

This is an edited listing of current prices. Visit **Kovels.com** to check thousands of prices from previous years and sign up for free information on trends, tips, reproductions, marks, and more.

M

**Moriage,** Biscuit Jar, Slip Decorated, Electroplated Lid, Rim, James Dixon, Nippon, 5 ½ In.
$96

Waterford's Art & Antiques Auctioneer

**Moriage,** Vase, Copper, Enamel, Flowering Trees, Ando, Japan, 1900s, 11 ½ x 9 ¾ In.
$2,460

New Orleans Auction Galleries, Inc.

**Moser,** Dresser Box, Cobalt Blue, Birds, Flowers, Brass Handles, Lock, Footed, 4 ½ x 5 In.
$2,370

James D. Julia Auctioneers

**MORIAGE** is a special type of raised decoration used on some Japanese pottery. Sometimes pieces of clay were shaped by hand and applied to the item; sometimes the clay was squeezed from a tube in the way we apply cake frosting. One type of moriage is called Dragonware by collectors.

| | |
|---|---:|
| **Biscuit Jar,** Slip Decorated, Electroplated Lid, Rim, James Dixon, Nippon, 5 ½ In. .............*illus* | 96 |
| **Bowl,** Gods, Court Officials, Flower Border, Multicolor, c.1900, 7 x 3 In. .................................... | 95 |
| **Bowl,** Leaves, Flowers, Scalloped Edge, Handles, Blue, Gold, 10 In. ........................................... | 89 |
| **Cup & Saucer,** Goddess Of Mercy, Immortals, Dragonware ........................................................ | 22 |
| **Cup & Saucer,** Lid, Geisha......................................................................................................... | 125 |
| **Dresser Box,** Scrolling Design, Blue, Green, c.1900, 2 ½ x 1 ¼ In. ............................................. | 75 |
| **Figurine,** Buddha, Seated, Satsuma, Japan, 4 In........................................................................ | 30 |
| **Humidor,** Pink Flower Spray, Nippon, c.1895, 6 x 5 x 5 In........................................................ | 110 |
| **Pitcher,** 3-Footed, Oriental Couple By River, 3 In. .................................................................... | 90 |
| **Pitcher,** Windmill, Winding Road, Nippon, 5 ¾ In..................................................................... | 50 |
| **Tray,** Man Reading, Man Playing Instrument, Shaped Edge, Gold, 1800s, 12 x 10 In. .................. | 975 |
| **Vase,** Copper, Enamel, Flowering Trees, Ando, Japan, 1900s, 11 ½ x 9 ¾ In. .........................*illus* | 2460 |
| **Wall Pocket,** Bird, Spread Wings, On Branches, Blue, White, Japan, c.1950, 8 In. ...................... | 35 |

**MOSAIC TILE COMPANY** of Zanesville, Ohio, was started by Karl Langerbeck and Herman Mueller in 1894. Many types of plain and ornamental tiles were made until 1959. The company closed in 1967. The company also made some ashtrays, bookends, and related giftwares. Most pieces are marked with the entwined MTC monogram.

| | |
|---|---:|
| **Card Tray,** Terrier, Black & White, c.1935, 5 x 7 In......................................................................... | 142 |
| **Tableau,** Flock Of Geese, Multicolor Gloss Glaze, 26 x 13 In., 18 Piece ....................................... | 230 |
| **Tile Picture,** Windmill, Lake, Multicolor Gloss Glaze, 21 ½ x 13 In., 15 Piece............................... | 230 |

**MOSER** glass is made by a Bohemian (Czech) glasshouse founded by Ludwig Moser in 1857. Art Nouveau-type glassware and iridescent glassware were made. The most famous Moser glass is decorated with heavy enameling in gold and bright colors. The firm, Moser Glassworks, is still working in Karlovy Vary, Czech Republic. Few pieces of Moser glass are marked.

| | |
|---|---:|
| **Basket,** Clear, Gold Leaf Ground, Scrolls, Applied Flowers & Red Jewels, Flared, 9 In.................... | 425 |
| **Basket,** Raised Rectangular Cabochons, Ruby, Gilt Handle, c.1910, 4 x 5 ¼ In. ........................... | 199 |
| **Bowl,** Dark Red, Flowers, Scrolls, Fish Scale Border, 9 ¼ In........................................................ | 355 |
| **Bowl,** Gilt, Red, Wheels, Bellflowers, 16 x 7 ⅜ In....................................................................... | 474 |
| **Bowl,** Green, Stylized Flowers In Lattice, Shaped Gold Coraline Border, 4-Footed, 7 x 9 In........... | 593 |
| **Bowl,** Underplate, Cranberry, 4 Gilt Beaded Panels, Cherubs, Flowers, Undulating Rims, 6 In..... | 652 |
| **Casket,** Cranberry Glass, Enameled, Gilt, Ormolu, Hinged Lid, 4 Ball Feet, 4 ½ x 3 ¼ In. ............ | 385 |
| **Casket,** Jewelry, Blue Glass, Gilt Jeweled Design, Footed, c.1900, 7 ¾ x 10 x 6 ½ In................... | 2176 |
| **Chalice,** Amber, Grape Leaves & Vines, Applied Clusters, Insects, Drippy Gold Rim, 9 ¾ In.......... | 1778 |
| **Chalice,** Green, Gilt Persian Decoration, Vines, Flowers, Applied Prunts, Spread Foot, 16 In......... | 4740 |
| **Chalice,** Green, Gold & Platinum Grapevine, 2 Saints With Halos, Prunts, Spread Foot, 13 In. ... | 889 |
| **Cordial Set,** Aqua, Gold & Platinum, Lattice, Flowers, Gold Handle & Stopper, Tray, 10 Piece..... | 1363 |
| **Cordial Set,** Blue, Cornucopia, Decanter, Mugs, Fern, Brass Frame, 9 x 7 In., 7 Piece................. | 741 |
| **Cornucopia,** Lid, Prussian Blue Enamel, Acorns, Leaves, Gold Accent, Footed, 19 x 4 ½ In. ........ | 2530 |
| **Creamer,** Cranberry Glass, 3 Open Windows, Gold Scrolls & Geometrics, Ladder Handle, 4 In. ... | 356 |
| **Creamer,** Ruby, Painted Leaves, Acorn Jewels, 2 ¼ In. ............................................................... | 173 |
| **Cruet,** Cranberry, Peacock Eyes, Acanthus Scrolling, 6 ½ In........................................................ | 345 |
| **Cup & Saucer,** Cranberry Cup, Green Underplate, Ruffled Top, Gilt Scrolling, Flowers, 6 In. ....... | 86 |
| **Cup,** Horn Of Plenty, Acorns, Multicolor Leaves, 2 ½ In. ........................................................... | 29 |
| **Decanter,** Amber, Applied Grapevines, Bird, Insects, Gilt Rigaree, Aqua Handle, 15 In. .............. | 7110 |
| **Decanter,** Amberina, Green Leaves, Purple Grape Clusters, Bird, Insects, Rigaree Collar, 15 In... | 7110 |
| **Decanter,** Blue To Clear, Ferns, Red Berries, Applied Gilt Salamander, Rim & Stopper, 11 In....... | 1778 |
| **Decanter,** Crackle, Iridescent, Gold & Orange Vines, Flowers, Gold Rim, Domed Foot, Stopper, 14 In. | 237 |
| **Dresser Box,** Amethyst, Enameled Flowers, Birds, Brass Handles, Collar & Lock, 5 x 54 In.......... | 1701 |
| **Dresser Box,** Cobalt Blue, Birds, Flowers, Brass Handles, Lock, Footed, 4 ½ x 5 In. .............*illus* | 2370 |
| **Dresser Box,** Cranberry, Gilt Panels & Scrollwork, Grapes, Crosses, Jewels, Footed, 8 x 5 In........ | 593 |
| **Dresser Box,** Emerald Green, Enameled Flowers, Brass Handles, Collar, Lock & Feet, 5 In.......... | 889 |
| **Dresser Box,** Enameled, Oval, Blue, White, Gold Cross Hatch, Hearts, Fleur-De-Lis, 4 In............ | 144 |
| **Dresser Box,** Prussian Blue Glass, Metal, Gilt, White Medallion, Enamel Flowers, 4 In. ............. | 86 |
| **Epergne,** Shaded Pink Opalescent, Gold Vines, Applied Grapes, Flower Form, Ruffled, 11 In. ....... | 711 |
| **Ewer,** Cobalt Blue, Allover Gold Birds Nestled In Leaves, Elongated Handle, Star Foot, 10 In. ...... | 474 |
| **Ewer,** Cranberry, Applied Hawk, Oak Leaves, Acorns, Gilt Handle, Rim & Foot, 15 ¾ In. .............. | 3259 |
| **Ewer,** Cut & Applied Poppies, Clear Ground, Bulbous, Faceted Stopper, 9 x 6 In.......................... | 575 |

| | |
|---|---|
| **Ewer,** Green, Parrots On Tree Limb, Oak Leaves, Applied Acorns, Clear Handle, 17 In., Pair......... | 5333 |
| **Ewer,** Red, Gilt Collar, Flowers, Leaves, Vines, 10 In. ..................................................... | 371 |
| **Goblet,** Amethyst Stain, Gilt Stylized Flowers, Applied Opalescent Glass Jewel, 8 In., 4 Piece........ | 365 |
| **Goblet,** Champagne, Octagonal, Blue Oval Medallions, Gilt, Tracery, 6 In., 12 Piece .................. | 748 |
| **Goblet,** Prussian Blue, Multicolor Leaves, Fruit, 4½ In................................................ | 115 |
| **Jar,** Cover, Flower Sprays, Gilded Panels, Stems, Leaves, Finial, Footed, 22½ In. .................*illus* | 2074 |
| **Juice Set,** Cranberry, Branches, Insects, Bulbous, Pinched Sides, Reeded Handle, 3 Piece............ | 1541 |
| **Lamp,** Cranberry Glass, Gilded Panels, Applied Flowers, Leaves, Scrolling, 24 In. ..............*illus* | 10665 |
| **Lemonade Set,** Cranberry, Gilt & White Forest Scene, Coralene Bands, 13-In. Pitcher, 5 Piece ... | 593 |
| **Letter Holder,** Amber, Bird, Oak Leaves, Acorns, Insect, Gilt Trim & Reeded Feet, 7¼ In. ........... | 2666 |
| **Letter Rack,** Dark Red, Gold Decoration, Leaf, Vine, 3-Footed, 9¼ In. ................................ | 494 |
| **Perfume Bottle,** Gilt Etched, Baluster Shape, Rounded Foot, Flared Collar, 8½ x 2¾ In. ............ | 121 |
| **Pitcher,** Blue Translucent, Blossoms, Gold Scrolling, Trifold Mouth, Applied Shell Handle, 6½ In... | 489 |
| **Pitcher,** Cranberry, Amber, Bird, Grape Leaves, Jeweled Grapes, Egg Shape, Square Rim, 4 In..... | 1380 |
| **Pitcher,** Cranberry, Fall Colored Oak Leaves, Raised Acorn Jewels, 2¾ In................................ | 115 |
| **Sugar & Creamer,** Stylized Heart Shape Cartouches, Gilt Panels, Flowers, 3½ In. ................... | 1778 |
| **Urn,** Green, Stylized Butterflies, Flowers, Leaves, 2 Handles, 8 In. ....................................*illus* | 316 |
| **Vase,** Amethyst Shaded To Clear, Intaglio Blossoms, Optic Ribbed, Pinched Waist, 13 In............. | 115 |
| **Vase,** Animor, Amber, Cranberry, Cameo Cut Elephant Scene, Palms, Gold Enamel, Signed, 8 In. | 1840 |
| **Vase,** Aqua Opalene, Brown Stems, Green Leaves, Pink Flowers, Dragonfly, Oval, 4-Footed, 13 In. | 4740 |
| **Vase,** Aquarium, Amber, Applied Glass Minnows, Enameled, Coral Reef, 4¼ In. ......................... | 230 |
| **Vase,** Beaker, Purple, Gilt Panels, Flowers, Scrolls, Beading, 22¼ In.................................... | 1235 |
| **Vase,** Blown Glass, Applied Lizards, Enamel Flowers, 8 In., Pair .....................................*illus* | 660 |
| **Vase,** Blue & White Spatter, Pink Enameling, Luster, Fern Wreath, Melon, Ribbed, 7 In.............. | 173 |
| **Vase,** Blue, Applied Salamander, Enamel Ferns & Flowers, Crackled Foot & Cover, 9 In. ............ | 356 |
| **Vase,** Blue, Multicolor Flowers, Gilt, 4 Applied Snakes Crisscross To Form Feet, 10 In. ............... | 593 |
| **Vase,** Blue, Multicolor, Bird, Branches, Flowers, Footed, 16 In......................................... | 652 |
| **Vase,** Cameo Glass, Dark Red, Vines, Grapes, Acid Texture, Cream Ground, Signed, 10 In. ........ | 474 |
| **Vase,** Cobalt Blue, Allover Gold & Platinum Leaves, Orange Enamel Beads, Baluster, 9 In. ........ | 593 |
| **Vase,** Cranberry Iridescent, Gold Scrolls, Flowers, Birds, Vertical Ribs, Ruffled, Squat, 5 In........ | 304 |
| **Vase,** Cranberry Shaded To Clear, Oak Leaves, Applied Acorns & Bumblebee, 5 In. .............*illus* | 948 |
| **Vase,** Cranberry To Clear Glass, Hollow Cylinder Stem, Spike & Star Pinched Foot, 12¾ In........ | 276 |
| **Vase,** Cranberry Vase, Bulbous Base, Enamel, Tapered Neck, 9 In. ...................................... | 240 |
| **Vase,** Cranberry, Trumpet Shape, Gold Enamel Grapevine, Jeweled Grapes, 8 In. ...................... | 460 |
| **Vase,** Eagle On Branch, Oak Leaves, Applied Acorns, Clear Shaded To Green, Oval, 19 In............ | 4063 |
| **Vase,** Enamel Fish, Flowers, Bugs, Gilt Ripples, Smoky Ground, 7¾ In............................... | 325 |
| **Vase,** Enamel Flowers, Scrolls, Rubina To Clear, Green Accents, Flared, Tapered, c.1900, 17½ In. | 142 |
| **Vase,** Gilt, Green Windows, Flowers, Leaves, Scrolls, 4-Sided, Gold Rim & Base, 24 In. ........ | 4148 |
| **Vase,** Glass, Gold Paint, Purple, 6 x 8½ In. ...................................................... | 305 |
| **Vase,** Gold Leaf, 5-Petal Flowers Cut To Clear, Orange Beading, Tapered Square, 12 In. ............. | 356 |
| **Vase,** Green Shaded To Clear, Applied Parrot, Oak Branches, 4-Sided, Swollen, 8 In. .................. | 2963 |
| **Vase,** Green Shaded To Clear, Marquetry Blossom, Cut Stems & Leaves, Swollen, 7 In. ............... | 1840 |
| **Vase,** Green, Applied Ducks, Tree Stumps, Trees, Pond, 4-Sided, Swollen, Marked, 8 In............... | 2193 |
| **Vase,** Green, Gold & Platinum Roman Chariot Scene, Faceted Top & Bottom Borders, 8 In. ........ | 304 |
| **Vase,** Green, Gold Decoration, Panels, Flowers, Beading, 4 In. .......................................... | 177 |
| **Vase,** Green, Ribbed, Gilt Flowers, Scrolls, Gilt Lip, Foot, 11¼ In. ....................................... | 592 |
| **Vase,** Intaglio Flamingos & Palm Trees, Cranberry Cut To Clear, Faceted, Flared Neck, 10 In. ..... | 830 |
| **Vase,** Intaglio Flowers, Green, Gold, Flowers, Scrolls, Melon Ribbed, Long Neck, Ruffled, 15 In... | 830 |
| **Vase,** Intaglio Flowers, Shaded Amethyst, Optic Ribbed, Cylindrical, Waisted, 13 In..................... | 230 |
| **Vase,** Intaglio Leaves, Pink Shaded To Clear, Orange & Yellow Poppy, Tapered, Ruffled, 18 In. ..... | 4740 |
| **Vase,** Marquetry Flower, Leaves, Applied Green Thread, Clear To Green, 15½ In........................ | 4444 |
| **Vase,** Melon Shape, Ribbed, Green To Clear, Gold Leaves, Gilt Ruffled Rim, 5½ In. ..................... | 177 |
| **Vase,** Multicolor Roman Battle Scenes, Cobalt Blue, Goblet Shape, 9½ In............................. | 510 |
| **Vase,** Pansies, Amethyst Shaded To Clear, Pinched Waist, Swollen Top, 13 In., Pair .................... | 1035 |
| **Vase,** Pansies, Opal Shaded To Clear, Optic Ribbed, Gold Flecked Rim, Tapered, 13 In................. | 288 |
| **Vase,** Pillow, Amber, Applied Bird Of Prey, Oak Leaves, Acorns, Gilt, 4 Reeded Curled Feet, 8 In.... | 2666 |
| **Vase,** Pillow, Amber, Bird, Flower Sprays, Oak Leaves, Applied Gilded Acorns, 9¾ In. ..........*illus* | 3555 |
| **Vase,** Pillow, Pink Opalescent, Hawk, Gold Clouds, Rigaree & Reeded Feet, 7½ In. ................... | 2074 |
| **Vase,** Rainbow, Multicolor Oak Leaves On Shoulder, Cut Gold Rim, Ribbed, 10 In. ................... | 431 |
| **Vase,** Ribbed Body, White Enameled Poppy, Bud, Burgundy Leaves, 8¼ In. ................................ | 518 |
| **Vase,** Ruby, Bulbous, 3 Gilt Scrolling Feet, Grape Leaves, Insects, Fan Shape, Footed, 5½ In........ | 288 |
| **Vase,** Stick, Turquoise Shaded To Green, Gilt Grapevines, Cream Outlines, Elongated, 25 In. ...... | 593 |
| **Vase,** Trumpet, Cranberry, Footed, Enamel Flowers, Rigaree Rim, Applied Gilt Thorny Handle, 9 In..... | 345 |
| **Water Set,** Cranberry, Gold Coralene Flowers, White Stems & Flowers, Clear Handle, 6 Piece ..... | 1007 |

**Moser,** Jar, Cover, Flower Sprays, Gilded Panels, Stems, Leaves, Finial, Footed, 22½ In.
$2,074

James D. Julia Auctioneers

**Moser,** Lamp, Cranberry Glass, Gilded Panels, Applied Flowers, Leaves, Scrolling, 24 In.
$10,665

James D. Julia Auctioneers

**Moser,** Urn, Green, Stylized Butterflies, Flowers, Leaves, 2 Handles, 8 In.
$316

Early Auction Co.

M

**Moser,** Vase, Blown Glass, Applied
Lizards, Enamel Flowers, 8 In., Pair
$660

Fox Auctions

**Moser,** Vase, Cranberry Shaded To Clear,
Oak Leaves, Applied Acorns & Bumblebee,
5 In.
$948

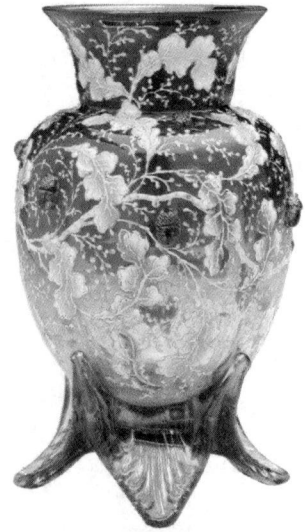

James D. Julia Auctioneers

**Moser,** Vase, Pillow, Amber, Bird, Flower
Sprays, Oak Leaves, Applied Gilded
Acorns, 9¾ In.
$3,555

James D. Julia Auctioneers

**MOSS ROSE** china was made by many firms from 1808 to 1900. It has a typical moss rose pictured as the design. The plant is not as popular now as it was in Victorian gardens, so the fuzz-covered bud is unfamiliar to most collectors. The dishes were usually decorated with pink and green flowers.

| | |
|---|---:|
| **Bowl,** Pedestal, Sterling Silver, Rosenthal, 4 x 9½ In. | 99 |
| **Bowl,** Scalloped Rim, Ironstone, Meakin, 9 In. | 96 |
| **Cup & Saucer,** Handleless, Ridgway & Morley, c.1850 | 125 |
| **Cuspidor,** Transfer, Haviland & Co. Limoges, c.1880, 6 x 7 In. | 350 |
| **Eggcup,** Double, Pink, Swing Shape, Homer Laughlin, 1940s, Pair | 56 |
| **Jewelry Tree,** 4 Branches, Japan, 4 In. | 23 |
| **Pitcher,** Knowles, Taylor & Knowles, c.1870, 6½ In. | 75 |
| **Plate,** Pink Border, Homer Laughlin, c.1942, 6¼ In. | 8 |
| **Platter,** Bow Handles, Gilt Trim, England, 9 x 10 In. | 38 |
| **Salt & Pepper,** Gourd Shape, Royal Albert, 3 In. | 52 |
| **Soap Dish,** Lid, Haviland & Co., Limoges, c.1865, 3 x 4⅞ x 3¾ In. | 175 |
| **Tray,** Central Handle, Scalloped Edge, Japan, 1960s, 9 In. | 18 |
| **Trinket Dish,** Butterfly Shape, Gilt Trim, Japan, 1950s, 4¾ In. | 16 |

**MOTHER-OF-PEARL GLASS,** or pearl satin glass, was first made in the 1850s in England and in Massachusetts. It was a special type of mold-blown satin glass with air bubbles in the glass, giving it a pearlized color. It has been reproduced. Mother-of-pearl shell objects are listed under Pearl.

| | |
|---|---:|
| **Biscuit Jar,** Blue Diamond Quilted, Pansy Design, Silver Lid, Bail, 8 In. | 236 |
| **Biscuit Jar,** Gold Enamel Flowers, Acorn, Leaves, Silver Lid, Bail, Round, 6 In. | 826 |
| **Biscuit Jar,** Pink Diamond Quilted, White Branch, Blossom, Fly, Silver Lid, Bail, 8 In. | 236 |
| **Biscuit Jar,** Pink Herringbone, Gold Enamel Flower, Branch, Silver Lid, Bail, 7 In. | 354 |
| **Bowl,** Blue Satin Diamond Quilted, Ruffled, Footed, Green Interior, 5 x 8 In. | 885 |
| **Bowl,** Gold Enamel Flowers, Branch, Blue Satin, Interior White, 4 x 8 In. | 236 |
| **Bowl,** Opal Shaded To Cranberry, Windows, Opal Inside, Trifold Rim, 5 In. | 86 |
| **Card Case,** Diamond Design, Flowers, Red Velvet, England, c.1840, 4 x 3 In. | 200 |
| **Ewer,** Rainbow, Herringbone, Handle, 10 In. *illus* | 633 |
| **Finger Bowl,** Scallop Rimmed Underplate, Rainbow Satin Swirl, Pair | 1298 |
| **Pitcher,** Cream, Blue, Herringbone Pattern, Melon Ribbed, 6 In. | 115 |
| **Pitcher,** Peach, Thumbprint, Swollen Neck, Camphor Handle, Ruffled Rim, 6 In. | 58 |
| **Pitcher,** Rainbow, Diamond Quilted, Applied Handle, 5¾ In. *illus* | 805 |
| **Pitcher,** Water, Diamond Quilted, Pink, 8¼ In. | 230 |
| **Potpourri,** Lid, Internal Decoration, Gilt Floral Highlights, 6½ In. | 1250 |
| **Sugar & Creamer,** Pink, Diamond Quilted, Flowers, Ruffled Rim | 316 |
| **Toothpick Holder,** Pink, Ruffled Rim, Diamond Quilted, Maude Feld Paper Label, 6¼ In. | 403 |
| **Tray,** Rosewood, Inlay, Floral Springs, 1800s, 13½ x 8½ In. | 237 |
| **Vase,** Blue Flower, Acorn Design, Pink, Satin Glass, Dimpled, 7½ In. | 1416 |
| **Vase,** Blue Swirled Body, Bird, Flowering Branch, Gold Tracery, Hexagonal, 8¾ In. | 172 |
| **Vase,** Cranberry, Raindrop, Ruffled Rim, Opal Interior, 5 In. | 173 |
| **Vase,** Indigo, Raindrop Design, Pinched Sides, Bulbous, Stick Shape, 13 In. | 1265 |
| **Vase,** Lemon Yellow, Flowers, Bulbous, Squat, Pinched Neck, Trifold Rim, 4 In. | 230 |
| **Vase,** Peach, Shaded, Moire Pattern, Shouldered, 5¼ In. | 63 |
| **Vase,** Pink, Diamond Quilted, Song Bird, Lily, Tapered, 11 In. | 230 |
| **Vase,** Rainbow Stripe, Blue Coralene Seaweed, Diamond Quilted, 11 In. | 29 |
| **Vase,** Rainbow, Diamond Quilted, Bulbous, Smokestack Shape, Cut Top, 8½ In. | 230 |
| **Vase,** Rainbow, Trifold Rim, Herringbone, 6 In. *illus* | 575 |
| **Vase,** Raindrop, Cylindrical, Pinched Sides, Caramel, Scalloped Rim, 15 In., Pair | 1208 |
| **Vase,** Spiral, 16 Vertical Ribs, Shaded Bronze, Peach Inside, c.1890, 7 In. | 460 |
| **Vase,** Stick, Cranberry Shaded To Opal, Coin Spot, Gold Branches, 7¼ In. | 201 |
| **Vase,** Stick, Herringbone, Rainbow, Bulbous, Trifold Rim, 6¼ In. | 288 |
| **Vase,** Yellow Herringbone Pattern, Applied Ornament, 6¼ In. | 259 |

**MOTORCYCLES** and motorcycle accessories of all types are being collected today. Examples can be found that date back to the early twentieth century. Toy motorcycles are listed in the Toy category.

| | |
|---|---:|
| **Belt,** Leather, Black, 3 Buckles, 1950s, 36 In. | 75 |
| **Bracelet,** Harley-Davidson, Chain Links, Sterling Silver, c.1978, 8 In. | 270 |
| **Cap,** Leather, Fur Trim, Brown, Aviator, Chin Strap, 1940s | 65 |
| **Charm,** 14K Yellow Gold, ⅞ x 7/16 In. | 110 |
| **Harley-Davidson,** Sidecar, 1000cc, 1923 | 57500 |

M

| | |
|---|---|
| **Indian Chief,** Black, Green Accents, 1948 | 23000 |
| **License Plate,** CAL, Blue, Yellow, PS 74, Steel, 1980, 4 x 7 In. | 30 |
| **License Plate,** Pennsylvania, 1915, White Number, Blue Ground, Porcelain, 4 x 8 In. | 90 |
| **Mirror,** Indian, Model 101, Hand Painted, Beveled, Oak Frame, 24 x 24 In. | 177 |
| **Motorcycle Goggles,** Steampunk, Safety Screen, c.1930 | 68 |
| **Motorcycle Lamp,** Carbide, Gloria, c.1900, 5 x 6 In. | 105 |
| **Oil Can,** Indian Oil, Indian Chief, Tin Lithograph, 5 x 2 x 1 In. | 161 |

**MOUNT WASHINGTON**, *see Mt. Washington category.*

**MOVIE** memorabilia of all types are collected. Animation Art, Games, Sheet Music, Toys, and some celebrity items are listed in their own section. A lobby card is usually 11 by 14 inches, but other sizes were also made. A set of lobby cards includes seven scene cards and one title card. An American one sheet, the standard movie poster, is 27 by 41 inches. A three sheet is 40 by 81 inches. A half sheet is 22 by 28 inches. A window card, made of cardboard, is 14 by 22 inches. An insert is 14 by 36 inches. A herald is a promotional item handed out to patrons. Press books, sent to exhibitors to promote a movie, contain ads and lists of what is available for advertising, i.e., posters, lobby cards. Press kits, sent to the media, contain photos and details about the movie, i.e., stars' biographies and interviews.

| | |
|---|---|
| **Costume Design,** My Fair Lady, Pencil On Paper, Cecil Beaton, Frame, 1964, 15 x 19 In. | 1875 |
| **Costume Design,** The Sting, Robert Redford, Watercolor, Pencil, Edith Head, 1973, 15 x 20 In. | 937 |
| **Lobby Card,** Each Dawn I Die, 2 Convicts, Man With Gun, Paper, 1939, 11 x 14 In. | 139 |
| **Lobby Card,** Love On A Pillow, Bridgette Bardot, 1962, 20½ x 17½ In. | 175 |
| **Lobby Card,** Rin Tin Tin, Seated, Photograph, Warner Bros., 1920s, 22 x 19 In. | 375 |
| **Lobby Card,** Werewolf Of London, Henry Hull, Hobson, Byington, Universal, 1935, 11 x 14 In. ...*illus* | 2150 |
| **Postcard,** Tarzan's Secret Treasure, Weissmuller Yelling, Black & White Photo, c.1942, 3 x 5 In. | 90 |
| **Poster,** Adventures Of Buffalo Bill, Starring William F. Cody, 1914, 46 x 32 In. ...*illus* | 4800 |
| **Poster,** Battling-Geo (Toboggan), George Carpentier, France, 1934, 65 x 49 In. | 690 |
| **Poster,** Bullet, Steve McQueen, Gun Aimed, Car Chase Scene, Italy, 1968, 39 x 55 In. | 253 |
| **Poster,** Butch Cassidy & The Sundance Kid, Paul Newman, Robert Redford, 1969, 41 x 27 In. | 47 |
| **Poster,** Chelsea Girls, Andy Warhol, 1st Edition, 1966, 29 x 23 In. | 625 |
| **Poster,** Chinatown, Roman Polanski, Paramount, 1974, 41 x 81 In. | 687 |
| **Poster,** Dimples, Shirley Temple, 1936, 40½ x 26½ In. | 1066 |
| **Poster,** Four Feathers, 1939, 40½ x 26¾ In. | 432 |
| **Poster,** Irving Berlin, There's No Business Like Show Business, 1954, 41 x 27 In. | 234 |
| **Poster,** Kabaret, Red, Legs In Swastika Shape, Liza Minnelli Face In Center, 22¾ x 33 In. | 695 |
| **Poster,** King Creole, Elvis Presley, Rene Chateau, 47 x 63 In. | 187 |
| **Poster,** Lady In The Lake, Robert Montgomery, 1947, 27 x 41 In. | 437 |
| **Poster,** Lone Defender, Rin-Tin-Tin, Stagecoach Holdup, 27 x 41 In. | 180 |
| **Poster,** Mildred Pierce, Joan Crawford, Jack Carson, 1945, 27 x 41 In. | 562 |
| **Poster,** Monkey Business, Cary Grant, Ginger Rogers, 20th Century Fox, 1952, 40 x 30 In. | 375 |
| **Poster,** Moon Over Miami, 35½ x 13½ In. | 2593 |
| **Poster,** My Fair Lady, Audrey Hepburn, Rex Harrison, Warner Bros., 1964, 39 x 55 In. | 375 |
| **Poster,** On The Bowery, Brooklyn Bridge, 3 Sheet, 38½ x 81¾ In. | 10072 |
| **Poster,** Peck's Bad Boy, Sitting On Barrel, Theater Lobby, Frame, 43 x 29 In. | 480 |
| **Poster,** Pulp Fiction, John Travolta, Samuel L. Jackson, Miramax, 1994, 27 x 41 In. | 525 |
| **Poster,** Raging Bull II, De Niro, United Artists, 1980, 27 x 41 In. | 525 |
| **Poster,** Rebecca Of Sunnybrook, Shirley Temple, 1938, 40¼ x 26½ In. | 711 |
| **Poster,** Silk Stockings, Fred Astaire, Cyd Charisse, Metro-Goldwyn-Mayer, 1957, 27 x 41 In. | 687 |
| **Poster,** Smashing The Vice Trust, 1937, 37½ x 72¼ In. | 556 |
| **Poster,** Some Like It Hot, Marilyn Monroe, Red, 1959, 27 x 41 In. | 974 |
| **Poster,** Sunset Boulevard, William Holden, Gloria Swanson, Paramount, 1950, 27½ x 41¾ In. | 5000 |
| **Poster,** The Big Sleep, Humphrey Bogart, Lauren Bacall, Warner Bros., 1954, 41 x 81 In. | 625 |
| **Poster,** The Blue Dahlia, 1946, 40½ x 26¾ In. | 3087 |
| **Poster,** The Great Escape, International United Artists, 1964, 27 x 41 In. | 1125 |
| **Poster,** The Incredible Shrinking Man, Grant Williams, Randy Stuart, Universal, 1957, 14 x 36 In. | 150 |
| **Poster,** The Killers, Burt Lancaster, Ava Gardner, 1956, 27 x 41 In. | 750 |
| **Poster,** The Quiet Man, John Wayne, Carrying Maureen O'Hara, Farm, 1957, 27 x 41 In. ...*illus* | 115 |
| **Poster,** Titanic, Barbara Stanwyck, Clifton Webb, 20th Century Fox, 1953, 40 x 30 In. | 375 |
| **Poster,** Under Two Flags, 1936, 27 x 40½ In. | 617 |
| **Poster,** Wake Of The Red Witch, John Wayne, 75 x 37 In. | 178 |
| **Poster,** Wee Willie Winkie, Shirley Temple, 1937, 40 x 26½ In. | 1185 |
| **Scene Study,** Jumbo, Billy Rose, Gouache On Board, MGM, 1962, 12 x 22 In. | 125 |
| **Scene Study,** The Nutty Professor, Watercolor, Pencil, Ink, R. Ayres, Paramount, 1963, 28 x 20 In. | 500 |
| **Screenplay,** Courtship Of Eddie's Father, John Gay, MGM, 1962, 134 Pages | 375 |
| **Screenplay,** Thin Man Goes Home, Yellow Cover, Dwight Taylor, MGM, 1944, 167 Pages | 937 |
| **Theatre Speakers,** Drive-In, Co-Op, Pedestal Base, Restored, 2 Piece | 443 |

**Mother-Of-Pearl,** Ewer, Rainbow, Herringbone, Handle, 10 In.
$633

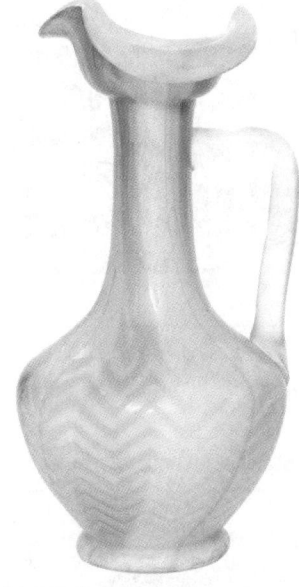

Early Auction Co.

**Mother-Of-Pearl,** Pitcher, Rainbow, Diamond Quilted, Applied Handle, 5¾ In.
$805

Early Auction Co.

**Mother-Of-Pearl,** Vase, Rainbow, Trifold Rim, Herringbone, 6 In.
$575

Early Auction Co.

M

**Movie,** Lobby Card, Werewolf Of London, Henry Hull, Hobson, Byington, Universal, 1935, 11 x 14 In.
$2,150

Hake's Americana & Collectibles

**Movie,** Poster, Adventures Of Buffalo Bill, Starring William F. Cody, 1914, 46 x 32 In.
$4,800

Morphy Auctions

**Movie,** Poster, The Quiet Man, John Wayne, Carrying Maureen O'Hara, Farm, 1957, 27 x 41 In.
$115

Hake's Americana & Collectibles

384

**MT. JOYE** is an enameled cameo glass made in the late nineteenth and twentieth centuries by Saint-Hilaire Touvier de Varraux and Co. of Pantin, France. This same company made De Vez glass. Pieces were usually decorated with enameling. Most pieces are not marked.

| | |
|---|---|
| **Bowl,** Cameo, Violet Daisies, Gold Detail, Jack Frost, Fleur-De-Lis Rolled Rim, 4 x 7 ½ In. | 288 |
| **Vase,** Handkerchief, Crystal To Sea Green, Pink Flowers, Shaped Gold Rim, 9 ½ In. | 173 |
| **Vase,** Iris, Green Enamel Texture, Square Shape, c.1905, 6 In. | 211 |
| **Vase,** Irises, Etched, Gold Enamel, 16 ¼ In. | 457 |
| **Vase,** Milk Glass Cut To Clear Green, Scenic, Lemon Tree, Roses, Leaves, Gilt, 7 In. | 472 |
| **Vase,** Poppies, Gold, Frost To Amethyst, Drip Pattern, Cameo, 7 ½ x 7 In. | 345 |
| **Vase,** Raised Acorn Design, Green Cylinder Body, Signed L.P., 11 In. | 450 |
| **Vase,** Round, Stick Neck, Green Aventurine, Mistletoe, Cabochons, c.1900, 7 In. | 355 |
| **Vase,** Stylized Thistle Flowers, Gilt, Purple Enamel, Amethyst Glass, Cylindrical, c.1900, 10 ½ In. | 461 |
| **Vase,** Yellow, Blue Pansy Flowers, Lavender, To Clear Ground, 11 ¾ In. | 826 |

**MT. WASHINGTON** Glass Works started in 1837 in South Boston, Massachusetts. In 1870 the company moved to New Bedford, Massachusetts. Many types of art glass were made there until 1894, when the company merged with Pairpoint Manufacturing Co. Amberina, Burmese, Crown Milano, Cut Glass, Peachblow, and Royal Flemish are each listed in their own category.

| | |
|---|---|
| **Berry Bowl Set,** Burmese Glass, Daisies, Pairpoint Silver Plated Stand, 19 In. ...............*illus* | 3220 |
| **Biscuit Jar,** Branches, Flowers, Tan Leaves, Mottled, Lid, 8 ½ In. | 532 |
| **Biscuit Jar,** Green Ground, Man Courting Woman Panel, Colonial Ware, Silver Bail, Lid, 6 In. .. | 177 |
| **Biscuit Jar,** Pink, Pansies, Silver Rim, Bail, 6 In. | 207 |
| **Celery Vase,** Rose Amber, Scalloped Rim, 6 ½ In. | 173 |
| **Creamer,** Rose Amber, Baby Coin Spot, 4 In. ...............*illus* | 316 |
| **Pitcher,** Burmese, Plush, Applied Handle, 1800s, 6 ¾ In. | 207 |
| **Pitcher,** Burmese, Roses, Thomas Hood Verse, 7 ¾ In. | 5900 |
| **Pitcher,** Cider, Bulbous, Squat, Angular Handle, 9 ½ In. | 236 |
| **Rose Bowl,** Hawthorne Pattern, Trifold, 3 ½ In. | 345 |
| **Shaker,** Cranberry Glass, Painted Flowers, Egg Shape, 4 In. | 1380 |
| **Shaker,** Custard Shaded To Brown, Enameled Seaweed, Egg Shape, 4 ½ In. | 144 |
| **Shaker,** Egg Shape, Pastel Enamel, Blossoms, Pierced Lids, 4 ½ In. | 144 |
| **Shaker,** Opal, Flowers On Lobed Panels, Silver Plated Cap, 3 In., Pair | 29 |
| **Shaker,** Sugar, Yellow Shaded To Salmon, Enameled Flowers, Ribbed, 4 In. | 173 |
| **Sugar & Creamer,** Burmese, Shaded Yellow, Orange Inside, Pedestal Base | 118 |
| **Sugar & Creamer,** Flower Sprays, Blue, Cream Ground, Silver Plated Rim, Lid | 148 |
| **Sugar Shaker,** Egg, Flowers, Opal, Yellow Cream Ground, c.1890, 4 In. | 138 |
| **Sweetmeat,** Gold Enamel Leaf, Yellow To Peach Shading, Jewel Accents, Melon Ribbed, 4 In. .... | 1298 |
| **Syrup,** Leaves, Shaded Caramel Ground, Melon Ribbed, Silver Plated Collar, 6 In. | 525 |
| **Tumbler,** Burmese Glass, Queen's Pattern, Stylized Flowers, 3 ⅝ In. | 948 |
| **Vase,** Albertine, Peacock, Raised Gold Enamel Scrollwork, 16 In. ...............*illus* | 7763 |
| **Vase,** Cream Body, Pastel Enamel Blossoms, Pinched Neck, Flaring Mouth, 10 ¼ In. | 575 |
| **Vase,** Flaring Cut Top, Gold, Green Enamel, Frosted & Clear Body, Signed, Verona, 9 ¾ In. | 2300 |
| **Vase,** Jack-In-The-Pulpit, Burmese, Pleated Rim, 15 ¼ In. | 119 |
| **Vase,** Lava, Black Ground, Pink, Gray, Green, Blue & White Shards, Squat, 5 In. | 1778 |
| **Vase,** Lava, Patches, Gold Trim, Bulbous, Flared, Looped Reeded Handles, 5 ⅝ In. | 3218 |

**MULBERRY** ware was made in the Staffordshire district of England from about 1850 to 1860. The dishes were decorated with a reddish brown transfer design, now called mulberry. Many of the patterns are similar to those used for flow blue and other Staffordshire transfer wares.

| | |
|---|---|
| **Compote,** Farmers, Animals, c.1800, 8 x 5 In. | 61 |
| **Creamer,** Paneled, Trees, Pagodas, Footed, 5 In. | 150 |
| **Plate,** Pagoda, Garden, Purple, Transferware, 9 ½ In. | 50 |
| **Plate,** People, Shore Bank, Stairway, Transferware, Black & White, 10 In. | 117 |
| **Platter,** Washington Vase, Ironstone, Podmore & Walker & Co., 15 ¾ In. ...............*illus* | 118 |

**MULLER FRERES,** French for Muller Brothers, made cameo and other glass from about 1895 to 1933. Their factory was first located in Luneville, then in nearby Croismare, France. Pieces were usually marked with the company name.

| | |
|---|---|
| **Bowl,** Sheep, Shepherd, Landscape, Orange, Black, 3 ¾ x 8 In. | 554 |
| **Box,** Egg Shape, Orange, Red & Blue Mottled, Ormolu Mounts, Hinged Lid, Ring Handles, 6 x 4 In.. | 230 |
| **Chandelier,** 4-Light, Multicolor Frosted Central Dome, 3 Flower Shades, Chain, 1910, 27 x 14 In. | 759 |
| **Pitcher,** Cream, Cameo, Amber Glass, Leaves, Insects, Signed, 6 In. | 1495 |
| **Vase,** Anemone Flowers, Burgundy, Mottled Pin, Blue & Yellow Ground, Oval, 15 In. | 8260 |

| | | |
|---|---|---|
| **Vase,** Art Deco, Red, Orange, Signed, c.1925, 9 x 5 In. | | 615 |
| **Vase,** Art Nouveau, Red Flowers, Green Leaves, Cameo, c.1900, 6½ In. | | 211 |
| **Vase,** Bird On Branch, Mottled Red & Yellow Ground, Oval, 8 In. | | 920 |
| **Vase,** Broken Pine, Trees & Mountains, Crimson & Brown, Pilgrim Form, 8 In. | | 920 |
| **Vase,** Bud, Landscape, Flared, Cameo, c.1900, 4½ In. | | 232 |
| **Vase,** Cameo Glass, Urn Shape, Frosted, Red Over Yellow Leaves, Footed, Signed, 4¾ In. | | 144 |
| **Vase,** Carved Pink Morning Glory Flowers, White Ground, Long Neck, Signed Croisemare, 11 In. | | 1298 |
| **Vase,** Flat Sided, Crimson Blossoms, Leaves, Cameo, Signed, 7¾ In. | *illus* | 1610 |
| **Vase,** Landscape, Yellow Ground, Mottled & Frosted, Cylindrical, Tripart Rim, 8 In. | | 1098 |
| **Vase,** Luneville, Enameled Thistle, Bee, Honeycomb, White, Blue, Orange Ground, Signed, 5½ In. | | 1180 |
| **Vase,** Mountain Landscape, Trees, Shaded Amethyst, Cream Ground, Shouldered, 6 In. | | 920 |

---

**MUNCIE** Clay Products Company was established by Charles Benham in Muncie, Indiana, in 1922. The company made pottery for the florist and giftshop trade. The company closed by 1939. Pieces are marked with the name *Muncie* or just with a system of numbers and letters, like *1A*.

MUNCIE

| | | |
|---|---|---|
| **Bookends,** Monkey, Stork Feeding, Peachskin Glaze, 4¾ x 6⅞ In., Pair | *illus* | 207 |
| **Lamp,** Scarf Dancers, 5 Panels, Pink Matte Glaze, Nude Finial, 10 In. | | 425 |
| **Pitcher,** Slate Matte Glaze, Arts & Crafts, 10½ x 6 In. | | 75 |
| **Pitcher,** Triangular Mouth, Jaunty Handle, Green Over Mauve Glaze, 7½ In. | | 68 |
| **Rose Bowl,** Blue Matte Glaze, 2¾ x 5 In. | | 125 |
| **Vase,** Eggshell Matte Glaze, Mauve To Moss, Variegated, Bud, Bulbous, 10 In. | | 145 |
| **Vase,** Green Over Yellow Matte Glaze, Pinched Waist, 9 In. | | 85 |
| **Vase,** Ruba Rombic, Green Over Purple, Matte Glaze, Marked, 4 In. | *illus* | 345 |

---

**MURANO**, *see Glass-Venetian category.*

---

**MUSIC** boxes and musical instruments are listed here. Phonograph records, jukeboxes, phonographs, and sheet music are listed in other categories in this book.

| | | |
|---|---|---|
| **Accordion,** Button Keys, Opposing Keyboard, Red Plastic Case, Case, Hohner, Germany | | 167 |
| **Accordion,** Piano, Excelsior, Case, 17¼ In. | | 384 |
| **Accordion,** Wood, Metal, Reticulated Box, Mother-Of-Pearl Keys, Case, Alfred L. Fischer, 1950s | | 70 |
| **Banjo,** 4-String, Mother-Of-Pearl Inlay, Inscribed Mousketeer, Case, 1900s, 33½ In. | | 360 |
| **Banjo,** 4-String, Rubber Body, Hide Drum, Fiddle, Wood Peg Head | | 94 |
| **Banjo,** Fender FB 5-String, Mahogany, Rosewood, Case, c.1970, 39 In. | | 184 |
| **Banjo,** Gibson, Mastertone, Mother-Of-Pearl Inlay On Head & Neck, Gold Trim, Strap | | 1020 |
| **Banjo,** Tenor, 4-String, Bird's-Eye Panel, Gordon, 33 In. | | 180 |
| **Box,** 3 Birds, Birdcage, Rounded, Coin-Operated, c.1920, 23 In. | | 2800 |
| **Box,** Black Female Magician, Voodoo Priestess, Headdress, Tree, Dried Flowers, 24 In. | | 869 |
| **Box,** Black Man, Raises Top Hat, Cane, Nods Head, Owl, Dog, Oak Barrel, France, 22 In. | | 1599 |
| **Box,** Brass, Cylinder, Start Stop Switch, Rosewood Case, 11¾ In. | | 338 |
| **Box,** Cabinet, 21 Discs, Queen Anne Style, Carved Leaf Panel, Cherubs, Clouds | | 2100 |
| **Box,** Cherry, Interchangeable Cuffs, 15 x 11 In. | | 2370 |
| **Box,** Cherry, Winter Scene, Interchangeable Cuffs, 15 x 11 In. | | 2370 |
| **Box,** Chocolate Dispenser, Clockwork, Painted Glass, Chromed Metal, Edelweiss, c.1950, 13 In. | | 652 |
| **Box,** Crosley Musix Wurks, Wood, 19th Century Ballroom Dancers, Glass | | 150 |
| **Box,** Cylinder, 3 Bell, Single Comb, Change/Repeat Levers, 8 Tunes, c.1890, Case, 16 In. | | 554 |
| **Box,** Cylinder, 6 Tunes, Flower Carving, Jacot & Son, 12½ x 25½ In. | | 2037 |
| **Box,** Cylinder, Brass, Zither Attachment, Tune Sheet, Change Switch, 8 Tunes, 17 In. | | 277 |
| **Box,** Cylinder, Forte Piano, 6 Tunes, Geneva, Switzerland, 19th Century, 20 x 6½ In. | | 563 |
| **Box,** Cylinder, Marquetry Inlays, 12-Tune Movement, 5 Bells, Swiss, c.1885, 10 x 26 In. | | 1140 |
| **Box,** Cylinder, Orchestral, 8 Tunes, 3 Bells, Drum, Single Comb, Tune Sheet, 17 In. | | 677 |
| **Box,** Cylinder, Rosewood, Nickel-Plated, Single Comb, 8 Tunes, 17½ In. | | 584 |
| **Box,** Cylinder, Single Comb, Lever-Wind, Tune Sheet, 8 Tunes, Wood Case, 16 In. | | 308 |
| **Box,** Egg, Baby Doll Hatches, Net, 2 Butterflies, 3-Legged Stool, Windup, 17 In. | | 554 |
| **Box,** Female Flower Vendor, Purple Dress, Bonnet, Baskets, R. Aldridge, 26 In. | | 492 |
| **Box,** Female Magician, Blue Ruffled Dress, Tree, Flowers, Rabbit Jumps, Windup, 20 In. | | 984 |
| **Box,** Ideal Piccolo, 3 Cylinders, Late 19th Century, Thomas Jay Bleason, 11 x 29 In. | | 3444 |
| **Box,** Jacot Patented Ideal Piccolo, 3 Cylinders, Interchangeable, Oak Case, Swiss, c.1890, 28 x 13 In. | | 260 |
| **Box,** Mermod Freres, Cylinder, Oak, Triple Comb, Drum, Castanet, Bells, Fly Hammers, 29 In. | | 2214 |
| **Box,** Monopol, Walnut, Double Comb, Crank, 38 Discs, Germany, c.1900, 20½ x 16 In. | *illus* | 1200 |
| **Box,** Paillard, Burl Maple, Ebonized, Interchangeable Cylinders, 2-Drawer Stand, 44 In. | | 13530 |
| **Box,** Piccolo, Single Comb, Zither Attachment, 6 Tunes, Brass Bed Plate, c.1890, 28 In. | | 738 |
| **Box,** Polyphon, Burl Walnut, Putti Playing Instruments, 37 Discs, c.1900, 8 x 17 In. | *illus* | 480 |
| **Box,** Regina, Concertina, Mahogany, Brass Bed Plate, Double Comb, Scalloped Lid, 34 In. | | 7380 |
| **Box,** Regina, Double Comb, Cherry Case, 12½ x 22½ In. | | 1422 |

**Mt. Washington,** Berry Bowl Set, Burmese Glass, Daisies, Pairpoint Silver Plated Stand, 19 In.
$3,220

Early Auction Co.

**Mt. Washington,** Creamer, Rose Amber, Baby Coin Spot, 4 In.
$316

Early Auction Co.

**Mt. Washington,** Vase, Albertine, Peacock, Raised Gold Enamel Scrollwork, 16 In.
$7,763

Early Auction Co.

M

**TIP**
*Never try to play a disc on your music box that was not made for that box. The machine will be damaged and the disc ruined.*

Mulberry, Platter, Washington Vase, Ironstone, Podmore & Walker & Co., 15¾ In.
$118

Conestoga Auction Co., Inc.

Muller Freres, Vase, Flat Sided, Crimson Blossoms, Leaves, Cameo, Signed, 7¾ In.
$1,610

Early Auction Co.

Muncie, Bookends, Monkey, Stork Feeding, Peachskin Glaze, 4¾ x 6⅞ In., Pair
$207

Humler & Nolan

Muncie, Vase, Ruba Rombic, Green Over Purple, Matte Glaze, Marked, 4 In.
$345

Humler & Nolan

| | |
|---|---|
| Box, Regina, Mahogany, Barley Twist Pressure Bar, Monochrome Lid Print, 21¾ In. | 1169 |
| Box, Regina, No. 25907, Mahogany, Single Comb, Starwheel Assembly, 30 Discs, 22 In. ...... *illus* | 2337 |
| Box, Regina, No. 44917, Walnut, Barley Twist Bar, 25 11-In. Discs, Hinged Lid, Cabinet, 41 In. ... | 2214 |
| Box, Regina, Walnut, Disc, Gothic, Rosettes, Arches, Goddesses, Dual Combs, 18 x 11½ In. ......... | 1230 |
| Box, Rocking Horse, Doll, White, Pink, Lace, Rotating Torso, Arms, Legs, Rattle, Doll, 11½ In. ... | 461 |
| Box, Singing Bird, Brass Cage, Perch, Feathers, Chirps, Beak Opens, Tail Wags, 11 In. | 502 |
| Box, Singing Bird, Brass Wire Cage, Chinoiserie, Urn Finial, Footed, Key, 12 x 6 In. | 1725 |
| Box, Singing Bird, Clock, Tree, Rocky Outcrop, Waterfall, Plants, Silk, Wool, France, 1860s, 24 x 12 In. | 11500 |
| Box, Singing Bird, Gold Colored Metal Cage, Red, Yellow Birds, Germany, 11 x 6 In. | 299 |
| Box, Singing Bird, Lapis Lazuli, Gilt, Key Wind, 2 x 4⅜ In. | 3776 |
| Box, Singing Bird, Twisted Wire Birdcage, Carved Giltwood Base, France, 23 x 15 In. | 4780 |
| Box, Stella, Disc, Mahogany, 29½ X14 In. | 2370 |
| Box, Stella, No. 3668, Wood, Green Stain, Single Comb, 36 17-In. Discs, 38 In. | 2706 |
| Box, Swiss Reuge, Cylinder, Burl Walnut, Tulip, Rosewood, 5 x 17 In. | 840 |
| Box, Swiss, Cylinder, Mahogany Lid, Faux Grained Case, Marquetry, c.1905, 22 In. | 420 |
| Box, Symphonion, Burl Walnut, 6¾ x 11 x 11 In. | 480 |
| Box, Table Shape, Gilt Metal, Enameled Romantic Pastoral Scene Inset, Swiss, 4 x 3 In. | 426 |
| Box, Wood, Carved, Flared, Windup, 3 -Footed, Swiss, c.1890, 4 x 9½ In. | 104 |
| Box, Wood, Inlay, Medallion, Drums, Bells, Castanets, Hinged Lid, 37 x 17 In. | 4800 |
| Buglet, 4-Turn, Applied Silver Shield, Keat | 351 |
| Clarinet, Boxwood, Bone, Stamped E. Riley, New York, c.1840, 19 In. | 230 |
| Coronet, Imperial, Silver Plated, Case, Boosey & Hawkes, England | 120 |
| Drum, Hobo Band, Pipe Smoking Hobo, Signed E.S. Howard, Pottstown Pa., 32 In. | 1080 |
| Drum, Rhumba, Mahogany, Carved Figures, Tapered, Cuba, 1941, 40 x 13½ In. | 750 |
| Drum, Snare, Military Style, Brass, Painted Wood Hoops, Signed, Frank King, 1800s ......... *illus* | 403 |
| Drum, Snare, Touch Tone, Hinger, 6½ x 14 In. | 1000 |
| Drum, Snare, Wood Shell, Brass Tack Design, Painted, Sticks, c.1800, 16 x 16 In. | 861 |
| Dulcimer, 3-String, Mixed Woods, c.1910, 34 In. | 295 |
| Dulcimer, Dovetail, Self-Cased, 13 x 45 In. | 142 |
| Dulcimer, Rosewood, Carved, Case, 1800s, 42 x 18 In. | 94 |
| Fiddle, Cherry, Notch Carved Scroll Piece, c.1965, 24 In. | 224 |
| Fiddle, Concert Soprano, Everet Lasoo Tucker 1873 Label, Mixed Woods, 24 In. | 295 |
| Fife, Maple, Brass Holes, Carved With Dates, c.1819, 14¾ In. | 800 |
| Flute, Silver, Headjoint, Crown, Body, Footjoint, Cleaning Rod, Gemeinhardt, Bag, 27½ In. | 702 |
| French Horn, Martin, Engraved, Handcraft, Elkhart, Ind., c.1970, 15 x 11¼ In. | 130 |
| Glockenspiel, No. 1229, Marimba, Round Top, Deagan, 1¼ In. Keys, Wood Case | 1680 |
| Grand Harmonicon, Mahogany, Bird's-Eye Maple, Gothic Panels, 25 Glass Vessels, 39 x 39 In. | 3585 |
| Guitar, 6-String, Acoustic, Ovation, Hand Shell Case, 41¼ In. | 153 |
| Guitar, Acoustic, Tara No. FG823, 6-String | 35 |
| Guitar, Child's, Regal, 1930s, 21 In. | 125 |
| Guitar, Electric, Gibson, 100th Anniversary, Ebony, Diamonds, Gold, Mother-Of-Pearl, 18 x 14 In. | 13200 |
| Guitar, Electric, Gibson, Sunburst Finish, Mother-Of-Pearl Fret, Mahogany, 41 In. | 10030 |
| Guitar, Electric, Lyle Trini Lopez Style, Rose Wood Neck, Block Inlay, c.1972, 42 In. | 130 |
| Guitar, Electric, Stratocaster, Fender, Ash, Maple Neck | 2124 |
| Guitar, Gibson, Map Of U.S.A. Shape, Stars & Stripes Painted, 1984 | 2714 |
| Guitar, Peavey Wolfgang, EVH, Flat Top, Masked Faux Binding, Custom Painted, 1998, 36½ In. ...*illus* | 696 |
| Harmonica, Chromatic S-45, Non Lever, Japan, c.1960, 18 x 3 x 2 In. | 199 |
| Harmonica, Hohner Melodica Soprano, Germany, Box | 300 |
| Harp, Giltwood, Maple, Carved, 44 Strings, 7 Pedals, Leaf Decoration, M.C. Stahl, c.1910, 69 x 35 In. | 1464 |
| Harp, J.F. Broune & Co., Gilt, Paint, c.1885, 70 x 38 In. | 2375 |
| Harp, Parcel Gilt, Bird's-Eye Maple, French Gothic, c.1850, 70½ In. | 2400 |
| Harp, Regency Style, Maple, Spruce, Ebonized, Parcel Gilt, Carved, Pedal, 66½ In. | 1063 |
| Horn, Long, Wood, Tin Ornamentation, Mouthpiece, Tapered, Collapsible, Tibet, 28½ In. | 263 |
| Lyre, 12-String, Mixed Woods, c.1920, 29 In. | 531 |
| Mandolin, 8-String, Stella, Case, 1900s, 25 In. | 744 |
| Marimba, Bentwood, M-30, Musser | 1100 |
| Organ, Roller, Walnut, Drop Down Door, 2 Drawers, Crank, Carved Scrolls, c.1900, 46 x 26 In.... | 175 |
| Piano Forte, Rosewood, Reeded, Banded Inlay, Stencils, Loud Brothers, Philadelphia, 70 In. | 2944 |
| Piano, Baby Grand, Baldwin, Black Ebony, 39 x 56 x 60 In. | 3900 |
| Piano, Baby Grand, Steinway, Walnut, No. 171869, Bench, c.1915, 64½ In. | 6250 |
| Piano, Baby Grand, Walnut Case, Model M, Steinway & Sons, 1928, 67 In. | 7500 |
| Piano, Baldwin, Grand, Model M, Ebonized Case, Square Tapered Legs, 1960s, 38 x 56 In. | 1625 |
| Piano, Concert Grand, No. 200 Opus, Bench, A. Bosendorfer, 1914, 78 x 59 In. | 9375 |
| Piano, Grand, Baldwin, Louis XV Style, White, Parcel Gilt, Bench, 68 x 56 In. | 1250 |
| Piano, Grand, Steinway & Sons, No. 211919, Parquetry, Scroll Bronze Mounts, c.1925, 75 x 63 In. | 40000 |
| Piano, Grand, Steinway, Ribbon Mahogany, Player, New York, 40 x 58 x 77 In. .................*illus* | 16605 |

**Music,** Box, Monopol, Walnut, Double Comb, Crank, 38 Discs, Germany, c.1900, 20½ x 16 In.
$1,200

DuMouchelles Art Gallery

**Music,** Box, Polyphon, Burl Walnut, Putti Playing Instruments, 37 Discs, c.1900, 8 x 17 In.
$480

DuMouchelles Art Gallery

**Music,** Box, Regina, No. 25907, Mahogany, Single Comb, Starwheel Assembly, 30 Discs, 22 In.
$2,337

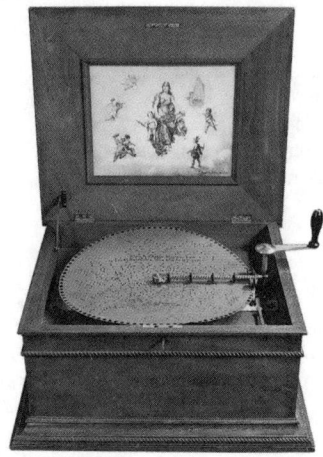

Skinner Auctioneers & Appraisers

### 78 Records

Old 78 records were made of shellac. Vinyl 78s were introduced around 1951. The records that followed were all vinyl.

**Music,** Drum, Snare, Military Style, Brass, Painted Wood Hoops, Signed, Frank King, 1800s
$403

James D. Julia Auctioneers

**Music,** Guitar, Peavey Wolfgang, EVH, Flat Top, Masked Faux Binding, Custom Painted, 1998, 36½ In.
$696

Hake's Americana & Collectibles

**Music,** Piano, Grand, Steinway, Ribbon Mahogany, Player, New York, 40 x 58 x 77 In.
$16,605

New Orleans Auction Galleries, Inc.

**Music,** Piano, Grand, Steinway, Satin Ebony, Music Room Grand, Bench, 1982, 83 x 57½ In.
$29,520

New Orleans Auction Galleries, Inc.

**Music,** Piano, Orchestrion, Player, Coin-Operated, Stained Glass, Style O Roll, 55 x 60 In.
$6,600

Morphy Auctions

M

**Nanking,** Dish, Blue & White, Scalloped, Gilt Rim, Landscape, Pagoda, Tree, Water, c.1790, 7¾ In., Pair
$390

Cowan's Auctions

**Napkin Ring,** Figural, Triton, Blowing Conch Shell Horn, Rectangular Base, Silver, 5 In.
$600

Morphy Auctions

**Napkin Ring,** Figural, Winged Cherub, Playing Flute, Book, Oval Footed Base, Silver, 4½ In.
$1,560

Morphy Auctions

| | | |
|---|---|---|
| **TIP** | | |

*If possible, handle silver with cotton gloves. Fingerprints will sometimes leave a mark.*

| | |
|---|---|
| **Piano,** Grand, Steinway, Satin Ebony, Music Room Grand, Bench, 1982, 83 x 57½ In. ........*illus* | 29520 |
| **Piano,** Grand, Steinweg, Rosewood, Scrolling Music Support, c.1862, 55 x 79 In. | 4200 |
| **Piano,** Orchestrion, Player, Coin-Operated, Stained Glass, Style O Roll, 55 x 60 In. .....*illus* | 6600 |
| **Piano,** Player, Wurlitzer, Auto Roll Changer, 6 Rolls & Pipes, c.1917, 60 x 82 In. | 10200 |
| **Symphonion Brevete,** Disc Player, 4 Discs, Decal, 13½ x 13½ In. | 546 |
| **Trombone,** Brass Director, Mouthpiece, Carrying Case, Conn. | 98 |
| **Ukelin,** Shoulder, 32-String, Hollow Wood Body, c.1900, 23 In. | 118 |
| **Violin,** Bow, Marked Joseph Guarnerius Fecit Violine, Case, Germany, 1778, 24 x 8½ In. | 288 |
| **Violin,** Case, 2 Bows, Label, August Gemunder & Sons, c.1880, 23½ In. | 590 |
| **Violin,** Caussin School, Bow, Wood Case, France, c.1890 | 275 |
| **Violin,** Copy Of Stradivarius, Carrying Case, Kiso Suzuki Violin Co. | 46 |
| **Violin,** G.A. Pfretzschner, Bow, Germany, 14 x 28½ In. | 1375 |
| **Violin,** J.B. Schweitzer, Black Case, Velvet Lining, Glasser Bow, 19th Century, 23 In. | 460 |
| **Violin,** Student, Tiger Maple, Silver, Mother-Of-Pearl, Germany, Bow, Case, c.1900 | 300 |
| **Violin,** Tiger Maple, Spruce Wood Top, Model Antonius Stradivarius, Josef Metzner, 1920, 14 x 23 In.. | 1007 |
| **Xylophone,** Painted Wood Base, Red, Yellow, Green, 9 Graduated Metal Bars, Mallet, 31 In. | 146 |

**MUSTACHE CUPS** were popular from 1850 to 1900 when the large, flowing mustache was in style. A ledge of china or silver held the hair out of the liquid in the cup. This kept the mustache tidy and also kept the mustache wax from melting. Left-handed mustache cups are rare but are being reproduced.

| | |
|---|---|
| **Blue Flowers,** Raised, Footed, 3 In. | 75 |
| **Cherries,** Peach, Walnut, Saucer, Left Handed | 490 |
| **Flowers,** Leaves, Relief, Multicolor, Germany | 21 |
| **Flowers,** Pink, White, Double Handle, Germany, 19th Century | 16 |
| **Flowers,** Remember Me, Gilt, 3 In. | 25 |
| **Gay 90s,** Couple On Bike, Gilt Trim, 3½ In. | 20 |
| **Ivory & Pink Lusterware,** Paneled, c.1900, 2¾ In. | 35 |
| **Pink Roses,** Green Base, 3½ In. | 22 |
| **River,** Trees, Gilt, Left Handed, Saucer, c.1870 | 120 |
| **Rose & Rope,** Saucer, Majolica | 485 |
| **Shells,** Fish Net, Turquoise, Majolica, Coral, Fielding Co. | 295 |
| **Stripes,** Swirled, Scroll Handle, Germany, 3½ In. | 71 |
| **Violets,** Gilt Trim, Saucer | 150 |

**MZ AUSTRIA** is the wording on a mark used by Moritz Zdekauer on porcelains made at his works in Altrolau, Austria, from 1884 to 1909. The mark was changed to MZ *Altrolau* in 1909, when the firm was purchased by C.M. Hutschenreuther. The firm operated under the name Altrolau Porcelain Factories from 1909 to 1945. It was nationalized after World War II. The pieces were decorated with lavish floral patterns and overglaze gold decoration. Full sets of dishes were made as well as vases, toilet sets, and other wares.

*MZ Austria*

| | |
|---|---|
| **Bonbon,** Roses, Leaves, Curved Rim, Handles, Pearl Luster, 7½ In. | 60 |
| **Bowl,** Scalloped, Blackberries, 4-Footed, 8 x 7 x 4 In. | 189 |
| **Cake Plate,** Poppies, Enameled Outlines, Handles, c.1890, 10½ In. | 49 |
| **Creamer,** Lid, Rose Swags, Gilt Arch, Scalloped Foot, 4 In. | 30 |
| **Dish,** Flowers, Sea Foam Green, Ruffled, Asymmetrical, c.1905, 12 x 5 In. | 79 |
| **Salt & Pepper,** Forget-Me-Nots, Bulbous, 2¾ In. | 42 |
| **Sugar & Creamer,** Pink Roses, Intertwined Branches, c.1900 | 65 |
| **Vase,** Cylindrical, Trailing Roses, Gilt Trim, 11 In. | 225 |

**NAKARA** is a trade name for a white glassware made about 1900 by the C. F. Monroe Company of Meriden, Connecticut. It was decorated in pastel colors. The glass was very similar to another glass, called Wave Crest, made by the company. The company closed in 1916. Boxes for use on a dressing table are the most commonly found Nakara pieces. The mark is not found on every piece.

**NAKARA**

| | |
|---|---|
| **Box,** Bishop's Hat, Blue, Flowers, 6½ In. | 160 |
| **Box,** Lid, Blue, 6-Sided, Hinged, Pink Flowers, Gilt, 4 x 4in. | 266 |
| **Card Receiver,** Pink, White Flowers, 4 x 2½ In. | 58 |
| **Dresser Box,** Pink Tulip S, Pink, Green Ground, Clover Shape, Hinged, 5 x 7½ In. | 767 |
| **Jewelry Box,** Embossed Pink Pansy, Blue, Cream Ground, Hinged, Round, 3½ In. | 266 |
| **Ring Box,** Hinged, Pink, Yellow, Woman, Man, Courting, 2½ x 2½ In. | 944 |
| **Toothpick Holder,** Blue, White Dots, Gilt Metal, 2¼ In. | 295 |
| **Vase,** Blue, Pink Flowers, 11 In. | 413 |
| **Vase,** Bud, Orange, Cherub, Cymbal, Gilt Metal Base, Rim, 4½ In. | 95 |

M

**NANKING** is a type of blue-and-white porcelain made in China from the late 1700s to the early 1900s. It was shipped from the port of Nanking. It is similar to Canton wares listed in that category, but it is of better quality. The blue design was almost the same, a landscape, building, trees, and a bridge. But a person was sometimes on the bridge on a Nanking piece. The "spear and post" border was used, sometimes with gold added. Nanking sells for more than Canton.

| | |
|---|---|
| **Bowl,** Lid, Footed, Handles, Thumb Rests, Pagodas, c.1830, 2 ¼ x 5 ¼ In. | 195 |
| **Dish,** Blue & White, Scalloped, Gilt Rim, Landscape, Pagoda, Tree, Water, c.1790, 7 ¾ In., Pair .... *illus* | 390 |
| **Gravy Dish,** Scalloped, Crimped Edge, Water, Mountains, Handle, c.1880, 7 x 3 In. | 265 |
| **Monteith,** Blue, White, Petal Edge, Lobed, Chinese, c.1860, 6 x 10 In. | 1680 |
| **Plate,** Pagoda, Bridge & Spear Border, c.1800, 7 ½ In. | 165 |
| **Plate,** River, Boat, Serpentine Edge, Oval, 18th Century, 5 x 3 In. | 175 |

**NAPKIN RINGS** were in fashion from 1869 to about 1900. They were made of silver, porcelain, wood, and other materials. They are still being made today. The most popular rings with collectors are the silver plated figural examples. Small, realistic figures were made to hold the ring. Good and poor reproductions of the more expensive rings are now being made and collectors must be very careful.

| | |
|---|---|
| **Bakelite,** Chick, Lime Green, Art Deco, c.1930, 2 ⅝ x 3 In. | 75 |
| **Figural,** Silver Plate, Baseball Player, Bat, Glove, Throwing Ball, Pairpoint Mfg., c.1900, 3 ½ In. | 3300 |
| **Figural,** Silver Plate, Cherub, Drinking Wine, Sitting On Holder, Grapevines, Wilcox Silver, 4 In. | 480 |
| **Figural,** Silver Plate, Cherub, Playing Flute, Book Shape Ring, 4 ½ In. | 1560 |
| **Figural,** Silver Plate, Cherub, Sitting Cross-Legged, Pairpoint Mfg., 5 In. | 780 |
| **Figural,** Silver Plate, Cherub, Wings, Cartouche, Swags, Flowers, 1800s, 1 ¾ In. | 45 |
| **Figural,** Silver Plate, Elves, Scrolled Pedestal, Reed & Barton, c.1875, 4 In. | 850 |
| **Figural,** Silver Plate, Fireman Hat, Eagle On Top, Pairpoint Mfg., 3 In. | 1440 |
| **Figural,** Silver Plate, Giraffe, Palm Tree, Acorn Feet, Rockford Silver Plate Co., 4 ¾ In. | 600 |
| **Figural,** Silver Plate, Horse Drawn, Movable Wheel, Victorian, 1800s, 2 ¾ x 3 ¼ In., Pair | 472 |
| **Figural,** Silver Plate, Horseshoe Frame, Engraved, Bonheur, 4 Ball Feet, James W. Tufts, 2 ½ In.. | 150 |
| **Figural,** Silver Plate, Man, Pushing Woman In Sleigh, c.1850, 2 In. | 45 |
| **Figural,** Silver Plate, Squirrel, Eating Nut, Engraved, Barbour, 2 ¼ In. | 150 |
| **Figural,** Silver Plate, Triton, God Of Sea, Blowing Conch Shell, 5 In. | 600 |
| **Figural,** Silver Plate, Well Dressed Youth, Top Hat, Silver Plate, Barbour, c.1875, 3 ½ In. | 218 |
| **Figural,** Silver Plate, Woman, Long Gown, Hat, On Toboggan, Wilcox Silver Plate Co., 4 ½ In. | 780 |
| **Figural,** Silver Plate, Woman, Seated, Leaning Against Ring, Wilcox Silver Plate Co., 2 ½ In. | 150 |
| **Figural,** Sterling Silver, Butterfly, Leaves, Flowers, 1 ½ In. | 50 |
| **Figural,** Sterling Silver, Dog, Collar, c.1885 | 485 |
| **Figural,** Sterling Silver, Horn, Shield, c.1913, 1 ⁵⁄₁₆ In. | 110 |
| **Figural,** Triton, Blowing Conch Shell Horn, Rectangular Base, Silver, 5 In. | 600 |
| **Figural,** Winged Cherub, Playing Flute, Book, Oval Footed Base, Silver, 4 ½ In. | 1560 |
| **Silver Plate,** Bird, On Wishbone, Engraved, Barbour, c.1875, 2 In. | 98 |
| **Silver,** Applied Medallion, Marked, Coin, 1 ¾ In. | 148 |
| **Silver,** Farmhouse, Fence, Trees, River, Bulbous, Striked Rim, Coin, 1 ½ In. | 290 |
| **Silver,** Octagonal, Beaded Border, Vines, Leaves, Coin, c.1850, 1 ¾ In. | 59 |
| **Sterling Silver,** Triangular, Bird, Flower, Engraved | 153 |
| **Tartanware,** Plaid, Red, Blue, Wallace, 1 ⅝ x 1 ¾ In. | 75 |

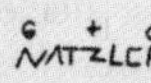

**NATZLER** pottery was made by Gertrud Amon and Otto Natzler. They were born in Vienna, met in 1933, and established a studio in 1935. Gertrud threw thin-walled, simple, classical shapes on the wheel, while Otto developed glazes. A few months after Hitler's regime occupied Austria in 1938, they married and fled to the United States. The Natzlers set up a workshop in Los Angeles. After Gertrud's death in 1971, Otto continued creating pieces decorated with his distinctive glazes. Otto died in 2007.

| | |
|---|---|
| **Bottle,** Long Neck, Blue Crystalline Glaze, Signed, c.1959, 10 ½ x 4 ½ In. ...........*illus* | 8125 |
| **Bottle,** Teardrop, Green Lava Glaze, Signed, 1962, 9 x 3 ¾ In. ...........*illus* | 9000 |
| **Bowl,** Blue Crystalline Glaze, Flared, Footed, 2 x 6 In. | 2318 |
| **Bowl,** Blue, Signed, 1961, 3 ½ x 5 ½ In. | 1250 |
| **Bowl,** Brown Crater Glaze, Signed, 1957, 6 ¾ x 7 In. | 3750 |
| **Bowl,** Brown, Turned Rim, Signed, 1965, 3 x 6 ½ In. | 813 |
| **Bowl,** Gray & Blue Glaze, Red Clay, Signed, 2 x 4 ¼ In. | 1188 |
| **Bowl,** Gray Celadon Reduction Glaze, 1961, 3 x 4 ¼ In. | 4375 |
| **Bowl,** Gray Crater Glaze, Flared, 3 ½ x 6 In. | 2375 |
| **Bowl,** Gray, Tan Rim, 1953, 7 ¾ x 5 ¼ In. | 2250 |
| **Bowl,** Green Glaze, Low, Marked, 11 In. | 1000 |
| **Bowl,** Green, Blue, 4 x 6 In. | 3250 |

**Natzler,** Bottle, Long Neck, Blue Crystalline Glaze, Signed, c.1959, 10 ½ x 4 ½ In.
$8,125

**Natzler,** Bottle, Teardrop, Green Lava Glaze, Signed, 1962, 9 x 3 ¾ In.
$9,000

**Natzler,** Bowl, Lapis Lazuli Glaze, Paper Label, 1966, 3 x 4 ½ In.
$1,250

N

**Natzler,** Bowl, Nocturne Glaze, Wide Rim, Red, Tan, Signed, Gertrud & Otto, 1962, 2 x 4 ½ In.
$4,063

Los Angeles Modern Auctions (LAMA)

**Natzler,** Vase, Gray Green Lava Glaze, Signed, Paper Label, 1970, 8 ½ x 4 ¾ In.
$8,125

Rago Arts & Auction Center

**Nautical,** Bell, Brass, Dolphin Supports, 19th Century, 18 x 16 In.
$500

Garth's Auctioneers & Appraisers

| | | |
|---|---|---|
| **Bowl,** Lapis Lazuli Glaze, Paper Label, 1966, 3 x 4 ½ In. | *illus* | 1250 |
| **Bowl,** Mystic Blue, Tan Rim, Late 1940s, 5 ¼ x 5 In. | | 6250 |
| **Bowl,** Nocturne Glaze, Wide Rim, Red, Tan, Signed, Gertrud & Otto, 1962, 2 x 4 ½ In. | *illus* | 4063 |
| **Bowl,** Verdigris Volcanic Glaze, Straight Sides, O. & G. Natzler, 4 x 5 In. | | 5313 |
| **Chalice,** Green Black Gunmetal Glaze, 7 x 3 ¾ In. | | 7500 |
| **Plate,** Flame Red Glaze, O. & G., 8 In. | | 2375 |
| **Sculpture,** Green Drip Glaze, On Plinth, Square Opening, 1977, 3 ¼ x 2 ¾ In. | | 690 |
| **Tray,** Thick Walled, Unglazed Rim, Blue Glass Fill, Signed Natzler, 1940s, 3 ⅞ Diam. | | 2813 |
| **Vase,** Gray Green Lava Glaze, Signed, Paper Label, 1970, 8 ½ x 4 ¾ In. | *illus* | 8125 |
| **Vase,** Green Crystalline Glaze, Narrow Neck, Flattened Rim, 1960, 8 ¼ x 4 ¼ In. | | 3438 |
| **Vase,** Iridescent Sang Nocturne Glaze, Melt Fissures, Teardrop, 10 In. | | 15000 |
| **Vase,** Light Blue, Tan Trim, c.1940s, 5 x 5 ⅞ In. | | 1500 |
| **Vase,** Sky & Clouds Glaze, Signed Natzler, 5 x 2 In. | | 6250 |

**NAUTICAL** antiques are listed in this category. Any of the many objects that were made or used by the seafaring trade, including ship parts, models, and tools, are included. Other pieces may be found listed under Scrimshaw.

| | | |
|---|---|---|
| **Anchor,** Brass, Inscribed H.B. Nevins, City Island, 32 In. | | 540 |
| **Anchor,** Ship's, Brass, Polished, 2 Wide Flukes, Hoisting Ring, 39 x 19 In. | | 326 |
| **Ax,** Boarding, Iron, Wood, c.1850, 19 In. | | 480 |
| **Ax,** Boarding, Iron, Wood, Stitched Leather Sheath, 16 In. | | 660 |
| **Bar,** Oak, Brass Trim, Gallery Top, Doors, Drawers, Straights Steamship Co., 1900s, 49 x 54 In. | | 3835 |
| **Bell Clock,** Ship's, Hinged Case, 8-Day, Brass Case, Mahogany, Seth Thomas, c.1920, 11 In. | | 480 |
| **Bell,** Brass, Dolphin Supports, 19th Century, 18 x 16 In. | *illus* | 500 |
| **Bell,** Ship's, Cast Bronze, 2 Bands, Chain Link, Iron Handle, 10 ½ In. | | 180 |
| **Bell,** Ship's, SS President Wilson, Bronze, Knotted Rope, 1900s, 10 ¾ In. | | 531 |
| **Bell,** Ship's, Steamer Continental, Bronze, Engraved, Mounted On Bracket, 1902, 10 In. | | 1020 |
| **Billet Head,** Scroll Terminal, Spray Of Leaves, Carved, Yellow, Green Paint, 1800s, 19 In. | | 540 |
| **Billet Head,** Wood, Fish Scale Panel, Scroll Carved, Yellow Paint, c.1860, 19 x 15 In. | | 1800 |
| **Binnacle,** Brass Compass, Mahogany Base, Balls, Side Lights, Kelvin & Hughes, c.1920, 50 In. | | 1770 |
| **Binnacle,** Compass, Brass, Wood, Henry Hughes & Sons, c.1900, 43 In. | | 1500 |
| **Binnacle,** Yacht, Divided Windows, Lantern, Mahogany Base, J. Ferguson, c.1825, 11 In. | | 984 |
| **Binnacle,** Yachting, Brass, Domed Top, Kelvin & Wilfred O. White Co., Boston, 10 x 9 In. | | 425 |
| **Canoe,** Wood, Ribbed, Caned Seats, Green Paint, Old Town Label, c.1942, 17 Feet | | 1695 |
| **Chart Chest,** Sailor's, Pine, Green Paint, Rope Handles, 10 ½ x 49 In. | | 360 |
| **Chest,** Diving Equipment, Cedar, Hinged Lid, Bronze Hasp, Morse Diving Co., 43 x 23 In. | | 775 |
| **Chest,** Sailor's Chart, Walnut, Inlays, Black, Blue Paint, Stenciled, Hinckley's, c.1850, 12 x 54 In. | | 240 |
| **Chest,** Sea, Camphorwood, Leather Handle, Side Metal Handles, c.1855, 6 x 12 In. | | 120 |
| **Chest,** Sea, Interior Lid Scene, Ship, Painted, New England, 18 x 42 In. | | 510 |
| **Chest,** Sea, Painted Eagle, Flag, Rope Handles, New England Steamship Co., 1879, 21 x 37 In. | | 2640 |
| **Chest,** Sea, Pine, Distressed Finish, Dovetailed, Hinged Lid, Rope Handles, c.1900, 18 x 44 In. | | 100 |
| **Chest,** Sea, Pine, Lid, Painted Ship, Iron Handles, c.1850, 19 x 36 ½ In. | | 360 |
| **Chest,** Sea, Pine, Ropewalk Beckets, Lift Top, Fitted Interior, 1800s, 16 x 37 In. | | 944 |
| **Chest,** Sea, Strap Iron Handles, Blue Paint, New England, c.1820, 17 x 45 In. | | 230 |
| **Chronometer Pocket Watch,** No. 22, Hamilton Watch Co, Wood Case, 5 x 6 In. | | 720 |
| **Chronometer,** 2-Day, Brass Bowl, Silvered Dial, J. Fletcher, London, Box, 7 In. | | 3690 |
| **Chronometer,** 2-Day, Damascened Nickel, Silvered Dial, Elgin, No. 600, U.S. Navy, Box | | 2583 |
| **Chronometer,** 2-Day, Mahogany, Brass Bound, Marine, Hamilton, 3 ⅞ In. Diam. | | 2250 |
| **Chronometer,** 8-Day, Brass Bowl, Damascened, Mahogany Box, Mercer, 8 In. | | 2091 |
| **Chronometer,** 8-Day, Mahogany, Brass Bound, Marine, Thomas Mercer, 3 ⅞ In. Diam. | | 3125 |
| **Chronometer,** Break-Circuit Contacts, Metal Bowl, c.1942, 6 x 8 ½ In. | | 1599 |
| **Chronometer,** Mahogany Case, Waltham, 7 ½ x 9 In. | | 1363 |
| **Chronometer,** Waltham, Silvered Dial, Mahogany, Brass Plates, 7 ½ In. | | 1968 |
| **Chronometer,** Yacht's, Mahogany Case, Swiss, c.1949, 5 x 6 In. | | 590 |
| **Clock,** Chelsea Shipstrike, Brass, Mahogany Stand, 7 ¾ In. | | 420 |
| **Clock,** Commodore Model, Brass, Chelsea Clock Co., Boston, 9 ⅜ In. | | 1320 |
| **Clock,** Ship's, Barometer, Waterbury, Brass, 8-Day Time & Strike, Key, 1900s, 8 x 4 In. | | 472 |
| **Clock,** Ship's, Chelsea, Brass, Round, Stepped Base, Millennium, Box, 12 ½ In. | | 1476 |
| **Clock,** Ship's, Chelsea, Nickel Plated, Round, Teak Back, 10 In. | | 1534 |
| **Clock,** Ship's, U.S. Navy, Chelsea Black Metal, Scalloped Wood Case, c.1905, 9 In. | | 277 |
| **Compass,** Binnacle, Brass, Liberty Ship, Lights Up, 1940s | | 1140 |
| **Compass,** Captain Paines' Tell-Tale, Yacht Calypso, Brass, TS & JD Negus, 8 In. | | 720 |
| **Compass,** Marine, Mahogany, Brass, E.S. Ritchie & Sons, Boston, Hinged Box, 7 In. | | 259 |
| **Compass,** Ship's, Brass, Dome Cylindrical Case, Oil Lamp Compartment, 10 ½ In. | | 375 |
| **Compass,** Ship's, Brass, G. Welford & Sons, London, c.1900, 10 x 8 In. | | 120 |

N

| | |
|---|---|
| **Desk,** Sea Captain, Pine, 2 Panel Doors, c.1860, 48 x 37 In. | 540 |
| **Diorama,** Ship Rose, Tugboat Amy, Shadowbox, Carved, Painted, c.1930, 22 x 32 ½ In. | 840 |
| **Diorama,** Ship, 3-Masted, Black, American Flag, Landscape, Painted Water, 18 x 23 In. | 540 |
| **Diorama,** Ship, Whaling Scene, Glass Case, Wood Base, 1900s, 8 x 21 In. | 120 |
| **Dipper,** Sailor's, Coconut, Brass, Heart Shape Handle Plate, 15 In. | 420 |
| **Ditty Box,** Pine, Carved Bone Hearts, Sunbursts, Hinged Lid, Brass Scroll Latch, 3 x 7 x 4 In. | 510 |
| **Ditty Box,** Pine, Fitted Interior, Wood Handles, Rope, George O. Tobey, c.1890, 9 x 16 In. | 360 |
| **Diver's Flashlight,** Nickel Plated, Glass Lens, 4 Posts Extend From Bezel, Siebe Gorman. | 190 |
| **Diving Boots,** Canvas Upper, Brass Sole & Toe Cap, Rope Laces, Hering. | 325 |
| **Diving Helmet,** Philadelphia Harbor Police, Copper, Morse, Mark V, 1942. | 11000 |
| **Diving Helmet,** Shallow Water, Copper, Brass, Top Handle, A.J. Morse & Son, Boston. | 1801 |
| **Diving Helmet,** U.S. Navy, Mark V, Copper, Brass, 12 Bolt Collar, Schrader, Scovill, 1944. | 7000 |
| **Eagle,** Pilot House, Wings Out, Giltwood, Stand, c.1860, 55 x 24 In. | 1989 |
| **Eel Spear,** Cast Iron, Stamped H.E. Barrus, Barnstable Mass, c.1945, 14 In. | 130 |
| **Fid,** Sailor's, Whalebone, Rosewood, 12 In. | 180 |
| **Figurehead,** Hardwood, Nude Woman, Mounted On Stand, c.1800, 47 In. | 4404 |
| **Figurehead,** Lord Nelson, Pine, Carved, Full Body, Outstretched Hand, Mounted, 70 In. | 6518 |
| **Figurehead,** Turkish Woman, Coiled Curls, Crescent Moon, Plume, Black Paint, 1800s, 7 In. | 480 |
| **Figurehead,** Viking, Beard, Helmet With Horns, Wood Carving, Painted, 24 x 12 In. | 210 |
| **Figurehead,** Woman, Brown Hair, Looking Up, Lace Collar, Painted, c.1840, 22 x 13 In. | 7995 |
| **Foghorn,** Air Pump, Brass Trumpet, Leather Bellows, Brass Hardware, Siebe Gorman. | 400 |
| **Foghorn,** Brass, Engraved John Leadbetter, 18 In. | 300 |
| **Frame,** Sailor's Knot, Lithograph Steamship Inside, 8 x 9 ½ In. | 308 |
| **Funnel,** Lamp Oil, Brass, U.S. Lighthouse Staten Island, 6 In. | 885 |
| **Gig Tiller Yoke,** Captain's, Brass, Double Anchor, Rope Shape, Backboard, c.1870, 19 In. | 1560 |
| **Half-Model,** Hull, Belle Of The West, Backboard Mount, Massachusetts, 23 ¾ In. | 1200 |
| **Half-Model,** Schooner, Mahogany, Black, Green, 2 Stubbed Masts, Planked Deck, 9 x 34 In. | 185 |
| **Half-Model,** Schooner, Ursula, Varnished & Painted, Cherry Backboard, 11 x 46 In. | 2000 |
| **Half-Model,** Ship's, Hull, Side Wheel, Single Wood Piece, 1800s, 13 x 91 In. | 2714 |
| **Half-Model,** Steamship, SS Saint Patrick, Black, Salmon, Binnacle, Helm, 1903, 60 In. | 2800 |
| **Half-Model,** Whale Ship, Black, White, Salmon Paint, Wood Backboard, 28 In. | 1800 |
| **Knife Box,** Sailor's, Satinwood, Mahogany, Ebonized, Drawer, Carved, c.1850, 7 x 11 In. | 2400 |
| **Lamp,** Diving, U.S. Navy, Mark V, Type JS-1, Metal, Old Paint, Handle | 50 |
| **Lamp,** Ship's, Brass, Perko-Perkins, 18 x 23 In. | 720 |
| **Lantern,** Port, Starboard, Brass, Bars, Curved Red & Green Glass Lenses, 12 In., Pair. | 426 |
| **Lantern,** Port, Starboard, Steel, Red & Green Glass Lenses, Vented, Loop, 15 x 9 In., Pair. | 650 |
| **Lantern,** Ship's, Black Paint, Tin, Porcelain, c.1900, 16 ½ In., Pair | 117 |
| **Lantern,** Ship's, Bulkhead, Painted, Glass Chimney, Perko, Brooklyn, 17 x 10 In., Pair. | 400 |
| **Lantern,** Ship's, Port, Starboard, Copper, Top Handle, 1910, 14 In. | 325 |
| **Lantern,** USS Constitution, Nickel Plated Brass, Squared, Domed, 27 In., Pair | 1440 |
| **Lazy Susan,** Sailor's, Mahogany, Parquetry, Stars, Octagonal Base, 1800s, 7 x 12 In. | 780 |
| **Letter Bag,** USS Saratoga, Letters For The U.S. Squadron Africa, Canvas, 26 x 20 In. | 5400 |
| **Light,** Masthead, Copper, Brass, Davey & Co., c.1905, 13 In. | 236 |
| **Lunch Box,** Brass, Lift Top, Square Handle, U.S.L.H. Lamp Shop Station, c.1910, 12 ½ In. | 1180 |
| **Lunette,** Freedom Of The Sea, Maid Of Eastport, Paint, Gilt, 1852, 35 x 66 In. | 7200 |
| **Mask,** Grotesque, Pine, Ship's Cathead Shape, 8 x 7 In. | 240 |
| **Mirror,** Sailor's, Shellwork, Flower Heads, Plant Ground, Oval, c.1850, 15 x 13 In., Pair | 120 |
| **Model,** 1924 Yacht Yankee, Half-Hull, 11 Lifts, Francis Herreshoff, Backboard 13 In. | 900 |
| **Model,** Battleship, Black, Papier-Mache, Composition, Guns, Cannons, Lifeboats, 46 ½ In. | 370 |
| **Model,** Cabin Cruiser, Delta Dawn, Carved, Painted, New Orleans, 17 x 38 In. | 480 |
| **Model,** Canoe, Cast Iron, Double Ended, Raised Lip, 1900s, 6 ½ x 24 In. | 770 |
| **Model,** Clipper, Flying Cloud, Wood, Copper, Planked Deck, Rigged, Case, 69 x 55 In. | 3000 |
| **Model,** Dutch Lempster Barge, Juliana, Oak, Hardwood, Single Mast, 44 x 55 In. | 1888 |
| **Model,** Gunship, Daphne, Wood, 1900s, 29 x 37 In. | 118 |
| **Model,** Launch, Meteor, Wood, Open Compartment, Steam Engine, Stand, 16 In. | 561 |
| **Model,** Le Superbe, Napoleonic 74-Gun, Ship-Of-The-Line, 32 x 40 In. | 1800 |
| **Model,** Louisiana Shrimper, Fancy Dancer, Wood, Paint, Angola Prison, 21 x 25 In. | 300 |
| **Model,** Sailboat, Green, Red, Black Hull, Mahogany Cradle, 1800s, 53 x 55 In. | 472 |
| **Model,** Sailboat, Mahogany, Canvas Sails, Brass Fittings, 63 x 50 In. | 325 |
| **Model,** Schooner, 3-Masted, Pine Cradle, 18 x 20 In. | 189 |
| **Model,** Ship In Bottle, 3-Masted, Wood Stand, A.G. Barnes, Philadelphia, 7 ¾ In. | 92 |
| **Model,** Ship-Of-The-Line, 74-Gun, Rigged, Figurehead, 32 x 33 In. | 600 |
| **Model,** Ship, 3-Masted, Riggings, Painted Sails, 20 ½ x 34 In. | 188 |
| **Model,** Ship, 3-Masted, Riggings, Parcel Ebonized Hull, 28 ½ x 34 In. | 313 |
| **Model,** Ship, Steamer, Paddle, Portland, Lifeboats, Wheelhouse, Mahogany Base, 18 x 39 In. | 701 |
| **Model,** Sloop, Cloth Sails, Carved Eagle Figurehead, Laminated Deck, Stand, c.1910, 34 In. | 2583 |

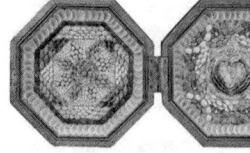

**TIP**

*Look through the wrong end of a telescope you plan to buy. If it can be focused, all of the parts are there.*

**Nautical,** Sailor's Valentine, Shellwork, Compass, Seahorse, Mahogany, 1800s, 9 x 9 In.
**$1,778**

James D. Julia Auctioneers

**Nautical,** Ship's Wheel, Wood, Spindle Spokes, Metal Wheel & Hub, Green Paint, 38 In.
**$240**

DuMouchelles Art Gallery

N

**Nautical,** Sign, Ship Chandler, Sextant, 3-D, Pine, Iron Hanging Ring, c.1890, 31 x 30 ½ In.
**$1,185**

James D. Julia Auctioneers

**TIP**

*A gummed tags can be removed by heating it with a hair dryer, then loosening it with a knife.*

**Netsuke,** Ivory, Demons, Playing
Instruments, Seated Priest, Signed,
Kogyoku, 1800s, 1⅛ In.
$2,091

Skinner Auctioneers & Appraisers

---

**Netsuke,** Ivory, Dragon, Emerging From
Egg, Signed, Hidekazu, 1700s,
1⅝ x 1⅞ In.
$1,599

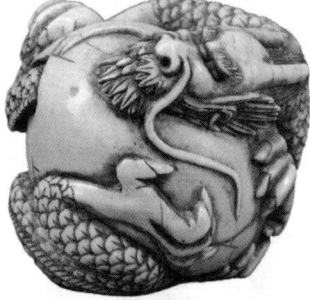

Skinner Auctioneers & Appraisers

---

**Netsuke,** Ivory, Oni, Acrobatic Pose,
Drum, Carrying Satchel, 1800s, 1¾ In.
$1,230

Skinner Auctioneers & Appraisers

---

**Newcomb,** Vase, Blossoms, Lily Pads,
Blue, Green, Yellow, Amelie Roman, 1903,
4⅜ In.
$7,469

Neal Auction Co.

---

| | |
|---|---:|
| **Model,** Sloop, Marconi Rigged, Green Hull Stripes, c.1945, 79 x 51 In. | 295 |
| **Model,** Speedboat, Pine, Hollowed Out Hull, Rub Rails, Decking, 36 In. | 266 |
| **Model,** Steamer Ferry, Frank Jones, Carved, Painted, Mahogany Base, 20½ In. | 480 |
| **Model,** Steamer, Ferry, Paddle, Island Home, Martha's Vineyard, Nantucket, 31 x 67 In. | 2200 |
| **Model,** Tugboat, Black Hull, Red Bottom, Wood, c.1905, 8½ x 16½ In. | 153 |
| **Model,** Tugboat, Cleveland, Pilot House, Erie Emblem, Lifeboat, Flags, c.1890, 21 x 33 In. | 2074 |
| **Model,** Tugboat, G.H. Wilson, 4-Masted, 48-Star U.S. Flag, Glass & Wood Case, 12 x 24 In. | 390 |
| **Model,** Tugboat, Inscribed US Army Port Pusan, Black, White, Red Paint, Stand, 29 In. | 360 |
| **Model,** USS Hartford, 22 November 1858, Naval Architect's Project, c.1920, 14½ x 66 In. | 1440 |
| **Model,** Warship, 3-Masted, Carved Stern Galleries, Pierced Gunports, Cannons, 27 x 35 In. | 351 |
| **Model,** Whaleboat, On Davits, Oars, Masts, Carved, Painted, 8 x 14¾ In. | 720 |
| **Model,** Yacht, Columbia, Pond, Wood, Blue, Maroon, Gaff-Rigged, Linen Sails, 43 In. | 1800 |
| **Model,** Yacht, Wood, Painted, Stained, Battery Powered, Abercrombie & Fitch, 1910, 32 In. | 413 |
| **Money Box,** Steel, Chest Shape, Birds, Flowers, Lock, Key, Handles, c.1700, 9 x 15 In. | 3068 |
| **Paddle Box,** Lid, Eagle, Carved, Painted, Side Wheel Steamer, 1800s, 35 x 60 In. | 1800 |
| **Parade Banner,** Kearsarge & Alabama Cherbourg, Muslin, Fringe, France, 1864, 72 x 54 In. | 1560 |
| **Pipe Box,** Applewood, Carved Crest, Open Pocket, R. Swain, Nantucket, 1814 | 720 |
| **Plaque,** Don't Give Up The Ship Banner, Eagle, Carved, Painted, 27½ In. | 2040 |
| **Pond Boat,** Mahogany, 2 Sails, 42 x 42 In. | 420 |
| **Pond Boat,** Metal, Painted Wood, 1940s, 101 x 72 In. | 960 |
| **Pond Boat,** Single Mast Schooner, Stand, 35¾ x 37 In. | 420 |
| **Pond Boat,** Yacht, Varnished Hull, Gaff-Rigged, 5 Sails, Rudder, Tiller, c.1925, 90 x 83 In. | 2200 |
| **Porthole Cover,** USS Maine, Framed, 24 x 24 In. | 1800 |
| **Porthole,** Ship, Brass, Glass, Round, 14 In. | 259 |
| **Pump,** Diver's Air, Wood Frame, Cylinder, Pressure Gauge, 2-Position Handle, 36 In. | 300 |
| **Quadrant,** Black Lacquer, Mahogany Case, Spencer Barrett & Co., c.1858, 13¾ In. | 840 |
| **Rope Beckets,** Braided, Black Paint, 10 In., Pair. | 300 |
| **Rudder Head,** Bust, Woman, Flowers In Hair, Necklace, Carved, Painted, 1820, 22 In. | 4320 |
| **Sailor's Valentine,** Double Shellwork, Blossom, Star, Octagonal, 1850, 9¾ In. | 4200 |
| **Sailor's Valentine,** Double Shellwork, Remember Me, Heart, Flower, Octagonal, 1850, 9 In. | 3600 |
| **Sailor's Valentine,** Double, Shellwork, Remember Me, Heart, Octagonal, c.1905, 9 x 9 In. | 2124 |
| **Sailor's Valentine,** Multicolor Shells, Heart, Think Of Me, 8-Sided, 8½ x 8½ In. | 2460 |
| **Sailor's Valentine,** Shellwork, Compass, Seahorse, Mahogany, 1800s, 9 x 9 In. ...............*illus* | 1778 |
| **Sailor's Valentine,** Shellwork, Double, Heart, Star, Octagonal Frame, Barbados, 1800s, 14 In. | 1840 |
| **Sailor's Valentine,** Shellwork, Watercolor Of Military Officer, France, c.1830, 6 x 8 In. | 2460 |
| **Sextant,** Brass, Ebony, Leaf, Bird, Folding Mirror, Pine Case, T.S. Bowles, c.1805, 18 In. | 1080 |
| **Sextant,** Brass, Marked Robert Young & Sons, Glasgow, Case, 10 In. | 224 |
| **Sextant,** Degree Scale, Ebonized Wood Frame, G. Lowther, Newcastle On Tyne, 1800s | 295 |
| **Sextant,** Navigational, Brass, Ebony, Inlaid Scale, Captain Richard Emms, 1777, 16 In. | 1320 |
| **Shadowbox,** 2 Ships, Pilot Boat, Entering Harbor, Carved, Painted, 22 x 42 In. | 2040 |
| **Ship Model,** see Nautical, Model. | |
| **Ship's Wheel,** 8 Wood Spokes, Iron Hull, c.1900, 57 In. | 354 |
| **Ship's Wheel,** Mahogany, Brass Inlays, 8 Spokes, Turned Posts, White Base, 1800s, 49 x 37 In. | 3600 |
| **Ship's Wheel,** Oak, Iron, 1800s, 66½ In. | 600 |
| **Ship's Wheel,** Walnut Spokes, c.1920, 84 In. | 1250 |
| **Ship's Wheel,** Wood, Brass, Iron Hub, 10 Spokes, 66 In. | 236 |
| **Ship's Wheel,** Wood, Spindle Spokes, Metal Wheel & Hub, Green Paint, 38 In. ...............*illus* | 240 |
| **Ship's Wheel,** Yacht, Mixed Wood, 8 Spokes, Brass Hub, 37 In. | 130 |
| **Ship's Wheel,** Yacht, Wood, Inlaid Frame, 6 Turned Spokes, Brass Hub, 34 In. | 575 |
| **Sign,** Diver Going Down, Clock, Metal, Black & White Paint, Red Movable Hands | 550 |
| **Sign,** Ship Chandler, Sextant, 3-D, Pine, Iron Hanging Ring, c.1890, 31 x 30½ In. ...........*illus* | 1185 |
| **Signal Light,** Boat, Brass, Loop Handles, Kerosene, c.1870, 8½ In. | 212 |
| **Signal Light,** Brass, 8-In. Lens Opening, Footed, Electric, 28 In. | 4800 |
| **Spyglass,** Wood Tube, Beveled, Single Draw, 1800s, 26 In. | 212 |
| **Steam Whistle,** Ship's, Brass, 14 In. | 150 |
| **Stern Board,** Frigate Le Seduisant, Fish, Garlands, Carved, Paint, France, 1800s, 21 x 103 In. | 4200 |
| **Sundial & Compass,** Silver, Engraved Landscape, Bird, Marked Bion A Paris, 2½ In. | 2360 |
| **Sundial,** Universal Equinoctial Pocket, Brass, Leather Case, J. Schrettegger, c.1750, 2½ In. | 720 |
| **Telegraph,** Ship's, Brass, A. Robinson & Co., 1900s, 36 In. | 1003 |
| **Telegraph,** Ship's, Donkin & Co., Brass Head, White Dial, Single Level Bell, 38½ In. | 461 |
| **Telegraph,** Ship's, Polished Brass, Glass, J.W. Ray & Co., Liverpool, 46 x 18 In. | 2901 |
| **Telegraph,** Ship's, Twin Hammerhead Design, Siemens Bros., London, 49 x 17 In. | 3500 |
| **Telescope,** 10 Sides, Long, Single Draw, Mahogany, Brass, Sailor's Rope, 52 In. | 1320 |
| **Telescope,** Brass, Tripod Base, Table Mounted, Jesse Ramsden, London, c.1795 | 2040 |
| **Telescope,** Brass, U.S. Navy, Maeiz Masy & John Munchen, c.1865, 31 In. | 118 |
| **Telescope,** Tabletop, Mahogany, Brass, J.P. Cutts, Sutton & Son, c.1858, 27 x 22 In. | 660 |

| | |
|---|---:|
| **Telescope,** Tripod, Brass, E. Troughton, W. Simms, England, c.1850 | 1080 |
| **Trunk,** Camphorwood, Brass Bound, 18 x 39 In. | 1020 |
| **Trunk,** Canvas Cover, Blue Paint, TH Initials, Rope Becket Handles, 17 x 32 In. | 1800 |
| **Trunk,** Seaman's, Camphorwood, Brass Bound, c.1890, 19 x 35 In. | 649 |
| **Trunk,** Seaman's, Iron Strap Hinges, Green Paint, Turk's Head, Rope Handles, 17 x 41 In. | 600 |
| **Trunk,** Seaman's, Pine, Blue Green Paint, Initials C.E., Bail Handles, 16 x 29 In. | 480 |
| **Watch,** Deck, Brass, Matte Silver 24-Hour Dial, Blue Spade Hands, Longines, Box, 6 In. | 1046 |
| **Whistle,** Boatswain's, Sterling Silver, Nussbaum & Hunold, c.1910, 5 ½ In. | 179 |

**NETSUKES** are small ivory, wood, metal, or porcelain pieces used as toggles on the end of the cord that held a Japanese money pouch or inro. The earliest date from the sixteenth century. Many are miniature carved works of art. This category also includes the ojime, the slide or string fastener that was used on the inro cord.

| | |
|---|---:|
| **Boxwood,** Chokaro Sennin, Standing, Drinking, Horse, Signed Hideyuki, 1 ½ In. | 1375 |
| **Boxwood,** Toad, Bulging Eyes, Signed Jyu Kyo, Straw Mat, 1 ½ In. | 1573 |
| **Coral,** Monkey, Seated, Hands Over Mouth, 1 ¾ In. | 354 |
| **Hornbill,** Ox, Lying Down, Calf, 1 ½ In. | 1250 |
| **Ivory,** 2 Frogs, Green Lily Pad, 3 ¼ x 1 ¼ In. | 554 |
| **Ivory,** 2 Rats, Crawling On Human Skull, Japan, c.1890, 1 ⅜ In. | 480 |
| **Ivory,** 3 Rats, Mother, 2 Babies, Applied Pigment, Signed, 1 ¼ x 1 In. | 219 |
| **Ivory,** 5 Horses, Openwork, Partially Stained, 1 x 1 ¾ In. | 1599 |
| **Ivory,** Bridge, Man, Carried By Devils, Signed Senzai, c.1900, 1 ½ In. | 750 |
| **Ivory,** Demons, Playing Instruments, Seated Priest, Signed, Kogyoku, 1800s, 1 ⅛ In. ........._illus_ | 2091 |
| **Ivory,** Dragon, Emerging From Egg, Signed, Hidekazu, 1700s, 1 ⅝ x 1 ⅞ In. ......_illus_ | 1599 |
| **Ivory,** Fish, Inlaid Pearl, 1800s, 1 ¾ In. | 861 |
| **Ivory,** Mammoth, Erotic, Foursome, Seated, Standing, Red Hat, 2 x 3 In. | 510 |
| **Ivory,** Man, Seated, Hat Pulled Back On Shoulder, Applied Pigment, 1800s, 1 x 1 ¼ In. | 46 |
| **Ivory,** Octopus, Crawling Out Of Vase, Bamboo Leaves, Signed Masanao, 1 ¾ In. | 431 |
| **Ivory,** Oni, Acrobatic Pose, Drum, Carrying Satchel, 1800s, 1 ¾ In. ......._illus_ | 1230 |
| **Ivory,** Quail, On Basket, Stylized Feathers, Leaves, Applied Pigment, 1800s, 1 ¼ x 1 ¼ In. | 81 |
| **Ivory,** Seven Lucky Gods, Treasure Ship, Crane, Waves, Signed Masatoshi, 1 ½ In. | 1230 |
| **Ivory,** Street Performer, Monkey, Signed Kaigyokusai Masatsugu, 1 ½ x 1 ¼ In. | 3750 |
| **Ivory,** Turtles, Board, 1 ½ In. | 1140 |
| **Jade,** White, Child, Embracing Gourd, Chinese, c.1845, 2 In. | 531 |
| **Wickerwork,** Gourd, Brass Bound, ¾ In. | 120 |
| **Wood,** Cottage, Man, Horse, Signed Ouchi Sosui, 1900s, 1 ¼ x 2 In. | 9375 |
| **Wood,** Devil, Taiko Drum, Stick, 1800s, 1 ½ In. | 1500 |
| **Wood,** Fox Holding Baby, Signed Masakazu, 1 ½ In. | 2057 |
| **Wood,** Lotus, Signed Kita Tamekata, 1 ¾ In. | 420 |
| **Wood,** Rooster, Seated, Detailed Feathers, Signed Masatani | 6250 |
| **Wood,** Seated Tanuki, Robe, Inlaid Eyes, Robe Clasp, Signed Masakazu, 1 ½ In. | 1028 |
| **Wood,** Skull, 6 Teeth, Signed Hogen Tadashige, c.1850, 1 ¾ In. | 6655 |
| **Wood,** Sumo Wrestlers, Signed Shozan, 1 ½ In. | 1500 |
| **Wood,** Surprise, In 3 Parts, Box, Palace, Grounds, c.1900, 1 ½ x 1 ¾ In. | 4063 |
| **Wood,** Trumpet Mushrooms, 1 ½ In. | 875 |
| **Wood,** Woman, Child, Nursing, Right Breast, Signed Tatekawa, 2 In. | 5445 |

**NEW MARTINSVILLE** Glass Manufacturing Company was established in 1901 in New Martinsville, West Virginia. It was bought and renamed the Viking Glass Company in 1944. In 1987 Kenneth Dalzell, former president of Fostoria Glass Company, purchased the factory and renamed it Dalzell-Viking. Production ceased in 1998.

| | |
|---|---:|
| **Candlewick,** Bowl, Green Satin, 11 In. | 41 |
| **Candlewick,** Punch Cup | 5 |
| **Cornucopia,** Candlestick, 3 ½ In. | 30 |
| **Elegant Arms,** Candelabra, 3-Light | 55 |
| **Epic,** Bowl, Blue, Spiked, 3 In. | 15 |
| **Epic,** Bowl, Blue, Spiked, 4 x 6 In. | 16 |
| **Epic,** Bowl, Spiked, Amber, 4 x 6 In. | 12 |
| **Epic,** Candy Dish, Blue, Footed, Lid, 7 In. | 20 |
| **Epic,** Compote, Avocado, Ruffled Rim, 10 In. | 21 |
| **Epic,** Compote, Blue, 7 In. | 22 |
| **Epic,** Compote, Persimmon, 7 ½ In. | 21 |
| **Epic,** Vase, Avocado, Stick Neck, Footed, 12 ½ In. | 15 |
| **Georgian,** Sherbet, Ruby, 3 In. | 15 |
| **Janice,** Candlestick, 2-Light, 6 In. | 82 |

**Newcomb,** Vase, Cone Flowers, Tall Stems, Green, Blue, Gray, Harriet Joor, 1902, 11 ½ In.
$51,250

Rago Arts & Auction Center

**Newcomb,** Vase, Cotton, Blue, Gray, Marie De Hoa LeBlanc, 1902, 11 x 6 In.
$23,750

Rago Arts & Auction Center

**Newcomb,** Vase, Freesia, Blue, Green, White, Semimatte Glaze, A.F. Simpson, 1911, 10 ⅜ In.
$11,950

Neal Auction Co.

**Newcomb,** Vase, Irises, Matte Glaze, Blue, Green, Pink, White, Joseph Meyers, 1915, 11¾ In.
$19,120

Neal Auction Co.

**Newcomb,** Vase, Moon & Moss, Blue, Trumpet Rim, 1928, 7 In.
$7,170

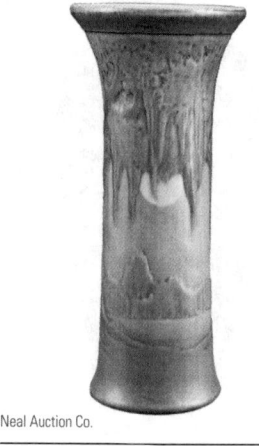

Neal Auction Co.

**Newcomb,** Vase, Stylized Thistle, Blue, Green, Marked, Harriet C. Joor, 1901, 12 In.
$11,950

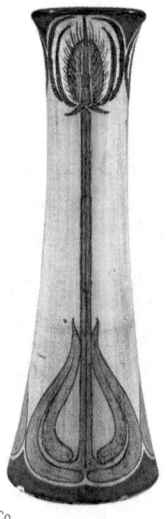

Neal Auction Co.

| | |
|---|---:|
| **Janice,** Candlestick, 5 In., Pair | 50 |
| **Marshall,** Candlestick, 2-Light, 5 In. | 82 |
| **Radiance,** Sugar & Creamer, Ruby | 25 |

**NEWCOMB POTTERY** was founded at Sophie Newcomb College, New Orleans, Louisiana, in 1895. The work continued through the 1940s. Pieces of this art pottery are marked with the printed letters *NC* and often have the incised initials of the artist and potter as well. A date letter code was printed on pieces made from 1901 to 1941. Most pieces have a matte glaze and incised decoration.

| | |
|---|---:|
| **Bowl,** Art Deco Stylized Leaves, Blue, Green, Pink, Yellow Matte Glaze, 2 x 5 In. | 598 |
| **Bowl,** Carved Narcissus, Blue, Green, White Matte Glaze, Mark, 1927, 4½ x 10 In. | 956 |
| **Bowl,** Morning Glories, Blue, Green, Pink, H. Davidson Bailey, 1927, 4½ In. | 1342 |
| **Charger,** High Glaze, Blue, Woman, Lilies, Harriet C. Joor, c.1900, 9¾ In. | 8066 |
| **Creamer,** Gardenias, Blue, Green, A.F. Simpson, 1909, 3¼ In. | 2151 |
| **Inkwell,** Lid, Syringa Flowers To Neck, Blue, M. Morel, c.1910, 2 x 4 In. | 1063 |
| **Jar,** Lid, Abstract Plants, Carved, Baluster, Lota Lee Troy, 5¾ x 4½ In. | 1230 |
| **Jardiniere,** Cobalt Blue Tulips, Leaves, Ivory Ground, 1902, 10 In. | 3936 |
| **Mailbox,** Brass, Wrought Sheeting, Monogram, Scrolls, Alice Leigh Moise, 1915, 12 x 9 In. | 478 |
| **Mug,** Alamanda Flowers, Let Us Be Happy, Blue, Green, Joor, 7¼ In. | 7995 |
| **Mug,** Artichokes, Blue, Green, M. De Hoa LeBlanc, 1902, 5⅞ In. | 2032 |
| **Mug,** Blue Designs, German Drinking Inscription, Gladys Bartlett, 1902, 4¼ x 5 In. | 1188 |
| **Mug,** Flower Buds, Low Relief, Blue, Green, A. Wilt, 1902, 4⅛ In. | 2988 |
| **Mug,** German Inscription, Blue, White, 1902, 4⅓ x 3½ In. | 1188 |
| **Pitcher,** Espagnol, Blue, Green Gloss Glaze, Sadie Irvine, 1929, 5 In. | 956 |
| **Pitcher,** Iridescent, Black, Stylized Handle, Narrow Spout, 7¾ In. | 98 |
| **Plate,** Green, Blue, Yellow Glazes, Incised Linear Design, 8½ In. | 1476 |
| **Tile,** Nursery Rhyme, Gloss Glaze, Leona Nicholson, Frame, 4½ x 5 In. | 1093 |
| **Trivet,** Daffodils, Low Relief, Blue, Green, Yellow Matte Glaze, Sadie Irvine, 1916, 5¾ In. | 1195 |
| **Trivet,** Oak Trees, Moss, Full Moon, Anna F. Simpson, 1928, 6 In. Diam. | 1875 |
| **Trivet,** Silver, Stylized BB Monogram At Center, c.1920, 8¼ x 6⅛ In. | 1016 |
| **Trivet,** Spiderwort Flower, Blue, Round, 1916, 5½ In. | 1750 |
| **Vase,** Blossoms, Lily Pads, Blue, Green, Yellow, Amelie Roman, 1903, 4⅜ In. *illus* | 7469 |
| **Vase,** Blue, Green Glazed, Incised Design, Narrow Mouth, Bulbous, Sadie Irvine, 2¾ In. | 400 |
| **Vase,** Blue, Jonquils, Squat, 4½ In. | 1380 |
| **Vase,** Bulbous Body, Narrow Neck, Daffodils, Sabina Wells, 10¾ In. | 5000 |
| **Vase,** Cone Flowers, Tall Stems, Green, Blue, Gray, Harriet Joor, 1902, 11½ In. *illus* | 51250 |
| **Vase,** Cotton, Blue, Gray, Marie De Hoa LeBlanc, 1902, 11 x 6 In. *illus* | 23750 |
| **Vase,** Crocus, Repeating Design, Painted, High Glaze, Flared, 4½ x 2½ In. | 3416 |
| **Vase,** Daffodil Band, Blue, Squat, Round, A. Simpson, c.1914, 4 x 6 In. | 1024 |
| **Vase,** Daffodils, Blue, Green, Pink Matte Glaze, S. Irvine, 8¾ In. | 5795 |
| **Vase,** Freesia, Blue, Green, White, Semimatte Glaze, A.F. Simpson, 1911, 10⅜ In. *illus* | 11950 |
| **Vase,** High Glaze, 7 Yellow Irises, 1908, 12⅜ In. | 8912 |
| **Vase,** High Glaze, Blue, Green, Incised, Alamanda Blossoms, Lily Pads, 1903, 4 In. | 7469 |
| **Vase,** High Glaze, Incised Alamanda Blossoms, Blue, Green, c.1904, 9½ x 7 In. | 20740 |
| **Vase,** Hollyhocks, Blue Striated Glaze, Shouldered, A.F. Simpson, 5½ x 3½ In. | 1098 |
| **Vase,** Irises, Matte Glaze, Blue, Green, Pink, White, Joseph Meyers, 1915, 11¾ In. | 19120 |
| **Vase,** Irises, Semimatte Glaze, Blue, Green, Pink, Yellow, Sadie Irvine, 1928, 9 x 6 In. | 5378 |
| **Vase,** Jonquils, Blue, Green, 1911, 8 In. | 2185 |
| **Vase,** Landscape, Full Moon, Hills, Oak Trees, Moss, 1930, 5½ In. | 2990 |
| **Vase,** Laurel Blossoms, Molded, Blue, Green Glaze, Marie De Hoa LeBlanc, 7 In. | 1434 |
| **Vase,** Live Oaks, Full Moon, Anna Simpson, 1922, 6¼ x 8½ In. | 3250 |
| **Vase,** Live Oaks, Spanish Moss, Full Moon, Blue, S. Irvine, 1927, 7 x 3½ In. | 4063 |
| **Vase,** Live Oaks, Spanish Moss, Moon, Tapered Base, A.F. Simpson, 1922, 6 x 8 In. | 3250 |
| **Vase,** Moon & Moss, Blue, Trumpet Rim, 1928, 7 In. *illus* | 7170 |
| **Vase,** Narcissus, Semimatte Glaze, Multicolor, Mark, Joseph Meyer, 1913, 5 In. | 1673 |
| **Vase,** Oak Trees, Pink Sky, Spanish Moss, Sadie Irvine, 1917, 3½ x 3 In. | 3125 |
| **Vase,** Overlapping Leaves, Blue, Tapered Cylinder, A. Arbo, 1932, 9½ x 4 In. | 2375 |
| **Vase,** Palm Trees, Semimatte Glaze, Blue, Green, Sadie Irvine, 1913, 14 x 7 In. | 17328 |
| **Vase,** Persimmon Band, Incised, Blue, Green Underglaze, Leona Nicholson, 1905, 6 In. | 4880 |
| **Vase,** Pine Trees, Full Moon, Blue, S. Irvine, 1916, 6 x 3 In. | 4375 |
| **Vase,** Pinecones, Carved & Painted, Blue Glaze, Bulbous, 4½ x 4 In. | 1342 |
| **Vase,** Pink Blossoms, Stylized Leaves, Blue, 1925, 9 x 5 In. | 3000 |
| **Vase,** Plum Ground, Mauve Relief, Stems, Flowers, 4 Handles, Blue Rim, 4¾ In. | 799 |
| **Vase,** Purple Iris, Shouldered, Alma Mason, 12 In. | 9200 |
| **Vase,** Raised Bats, Blue, Gray, L. Nicholson, New Orleans, 1913, 13 x 8 In. | 50000 |
| **Vase,** Rose, Orange Art Deco Neck Designs, Blue Matte, Marie Chalaron, 8 In. | 2700 |

N

| | | |
|---|---|---|
| **Vase,** Row Of Buds, Variegated Blue, Drip, Vellum Glaze, c.1931, 35 x 5 In. | | 1230 |
| **Vase,** Runny Green, Pink Band, Blue, S. Irvine, 1929, 3¾ x 3½ In. | | 1500 |
| **Vase,** Sable Palm, Blue & Green Underglaze, Sadie Irvine, 1913, 13¾ In. | | 17328 |
| **Vase,** Sea Green, White Flambe Glaze, Cipher, 5½ In. | | 369 |
| **Vase,** Stylized Blue Flower Band, Gray, I. B. Keep, 1902, 12 x 7 In. | | 8750 |
| **Vase,** Stylized Buds, Leaves, Blue, Green, White, H. Bailey, 1929, 5½ In. | | 2440 |
| **Vase,** Stylized Pepper Band, Blue, Green, Marked, Marie De Hoa LeBlanc, 1903, 6 In. | | 6274 |
| **Vase,** Stylized Thistle, Blue Glaze, Bulbous, Flared Neck, G.R. Smith, 3½ x 2½ In. | | 5185 |
| **Vase,** Stylized Thistle, Blue, Green, Marked, Harriet C. Joor, 1901, 12 In. *illus* | | 11950 |
| **Vase,** Tulips, Low Relief, Blue & Green Underglaze, 1909, 10⅝ In. | | 15535 |
| **Vase,** Turtles, Blue, White, E. De Hoa, c.1902, 2 x 2½ In. | | 9375 |
| **Vase,** Turtles, Blue, White, Emilie LeBlanc, 1902, 2 x 2½ In. | | 9375 |
| **Vase,** White Blossoms Band, Blue, Green, L. Nicholson, 1907, 3½ x 4½ In. | | 2625 |
| **Vase,** White Stylized Daffodil Band, Blue, Tapered, M. LeBlanc, 1905, 5 x 5 In. | | 1875 |
| **Vase,** White, Yellow Daffodils, Long Neck, Bulbous, Sabrina Wells, 1904, 11 x 5 In. | | 5000 |
| **Vase,** Yellow Freesia Band, Gray, Flared Base, M. LeBlanc, 1904, 10 x 4 In. | | 2625 |
| **Vase,** Yucca, Blue, White Underglaze, Marked, Mazie T. Ryan, 9¾ In. | | 8953 |
| **Vase,** Zephyr Lily, Blue, Green, Relief Carved, Anna Simpson, Marked, 1915, 8⅜ In. *illus* | | 5975 |
| **Wall Pocket,** Relief Blossoms, Blue, Green, White, Marked, 1901, 10½ x 3 In. | | 9560 |

**NILOAK POTTERY** (*Kaolin* spelled backward) was made at the Hyten Brothers Pottery in Benton, Arkansas, between 1910 and 1947. Although the factory did make cast and molded wares, collectors are most interested in the marbleized art pottery line made of colored swirls of clay. It was called Mission Ware. By 1931 the company made castware, and many of these pieces were marked with the name *Hywood*.

NILOAK

| | | |
|---|---|---|
| **Planter,** Squirrel Shape, Ozark Dawn, Marked, 4¾ In. | | 69 |
| **Vase,** Buttress, Green Matte Glaze, c.1940, 3½ x 2¾ In. | | 69 |
| **Vase,** Marbleized, Blue, Brown, Cream, Marked, 4½ In. | | 52 |
| **Vase,** Marbleized, Blue, White, Gray, Burgundy, Impressed Name, 10 In. | | 316 |
| **Vase,** Marbleized, Tan, Brown, Red, Blue, Marked, 8 In. | | 75 |

**NIPPON** porcelain was made in Japan from 1891 to 1921. *Nippon* is the Japanese word for "Japan." A few firms continued to use the word *Nippon* on ceramics after 1921 as a part of the company name more than as an identification of the country of origin. More pieces marked *Nippon* will be found in the Dragonware, Moriage, and Noritake categories.

Hand Painted
NIPPON

| | | |
|---|---|---|
| **Charger,** Peafowl, Berry Branches, Bird, Beaded Gilt Rim, c.1900, 11 In. | | 92 |
| **Cup & Saucer,** Maple Leaves, Translucent, Double Loop Handle, Gold Trim | | 15 |
| **Plaque,** Elk, Stream, Molded Relief, Hand Painted, 10¾ In. | | 230 |
| **Urn,** Lid, Urn Knop, Red, Pink, Yellow, Flowers, Gilt Handles, Footed, c.1910, 24 In. | | 1725 |
| **Vase,** Art Nouveau, Flowers, Fired Gold Handles, c.1900, 12 x 7 In. | | 150 |
| **Vase,** Irises, Coralene, Flaring Rim, 3 Ornaments At Base, 8¼ In. | | 2300 |
| **Vase,** Landscape, Lake, Trees, Coral Sky, Birds, Monument, Multicolor, 13⅛ In. | | 230 |
| **Vase,** Large Poppy, Brown Ground, Footed, Handles, Gold, Green Wreath Mark, 8 In. | | 94 |
| **Vase,** Lavender Flowers, Green Ground, Handles, Tapered, 10 In. | | 83 |
| **Vase,** Poppies, Raised, Multicolor, Gold Beaded Necklace At Rim, Handle, 8½ In. | | 546 |
| **Vase,** Roses, Gilt Trim, Hand Painted, Handles, 7⅜ In. | | 63 |
| **Vase,** Urn, Pine Forest, Bolted, Handled, Lake, Hills, Gold Trim, 16¼ In. | | 690 |
| **Vase,** Woman, Doves, Jeweled, Gilt Canopy, 12 In. | | 885 |

**NODDERS,** also called nodding figures or pagods, are figures with heads and hands that are attached to wires. Any slight movement causes the parts to move up and down. They were made in many countries during the eighteenth, nineteenth, and twentieth centuries. A few Art Deco designs are also known. Copies are being made. A more recent type of nodder is made of papier-mache or plastic. These often represent sports figures or comic characters. Sports nodders are listed in the Sports category.

| | | |
|---|---|---|
| **Andy Gump,** Blue Jacket, Yellow Pants & Hat, Bisque, 1930s, 4 In. | | 40 |
| **Angel,** Holding Tree, Porcelain, Germany, 3⅜ In. | | 75 |
| **Bowler,** Girl, Blond Hair, Red, White, Blue, Composition, 1950s, 5 In. | | 45 |
| **Boy & Girl,** Sculpted Features, Bisque, Germany, c.1915, 5 In., Pair *illus* | | 224 |
| **Dog,** Seated, Seated On Punch Magazines, Ruffled Collar, Porcelain, c.1885, 3½ In. | | 81 |
| **Dutch Girl,** Holding Skirt, Basket, Bisque, Germany, 6¼ In. | | 75 |
| **Gnome,** Yellow Jacket, Green Pointed Hat, Papier-Mache, c.1910, 10 x 6½ In. | | 185 |
| **Goose,** Celluloid, c.1925, 3½ In. | | 25 |
| **Hariko Doll,** Multicolor, Papier-Mache, 1950s, 2 x 3 In. | | 89 |

**Newcomb,** Vase, Zephyr Lily, Blue, Green, Relief Carved, Anna Simpson, Marked, 1915, 8⅜ In.
$5,975

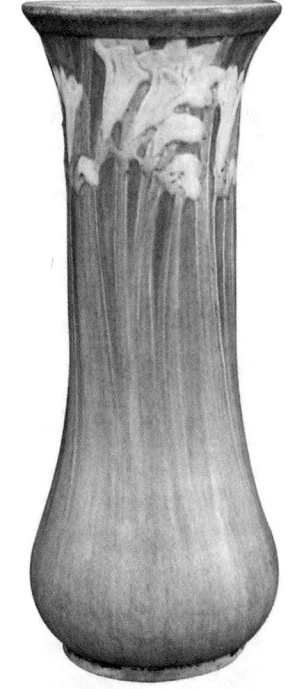

Neal Auction Co.

**Nodder,** Boy & Girl, Sculpted Features, Bisque, Germany, c.1915, 5 In., Pair
$224

Theriault's

**Nodder,** Man & Woman, Nodding Head, Hands, Porcelain, Japan, 1900s, 8 In., Pair
$237

James D. Julia Auctioneers

N

**Nodder,** Moon Face, Arms & Hat, Composition, Molded, Painted, Germany, 7 ½ In.
$443

Bertoia Auctions

**Noritake,** Vase, Boulder, Fall Grape Leaves, Fruit Pods, Green M In Wreath, 9 ¾ In.
$403

Humler & Nolan

**Norse,** Vase, Dragon Around Shoulder, Impressed, 12 In.
$805

Humler & Nolan

| | |
|---|---:|
| **Hound Dog,** Brown & White, Ceramic, Japan, 3 x 4 In. | 20 |
| **Hula Girl,** Hands On Head, Grass Skirt, Rubber, Hong Kong, 7 ½ In. | 21 |
| **Hula Girl,** Playing Guitar, Composition, 9 ½ In. | 89 |
| **Keystone Cop,** Nightstick, Bisque, 4 ½ In. | 60 |
| **Man & Woman,** Nodding Head, Hands, Porcelain, Japan, 1900s, 8 In., Pair ......*illus* | 237 |
| **Monkey,** Sitting, Blue Robe, Holding Fruit, Glass Eyes, Porcelain, Japan, 6 In. | 395 |
| **Moon Face,** Arms & Hat, Composition, Molded, Painted, Germany, 7 ½ In. ......*illus* | 443 |
| **Mule,** Pull Tail, Head Nods, Cast Iron, Painted, 11 In. | 798 |
| **Pop Jenks,** Bowtie, Vest, Striped Pants, Bisque, Carl Ed, Germany, c.1930, 3 ½ In. | 35 |
| **Roly Poly,** Boy, Blond Hair, Red Jacket, White Collar, Composition, c.1900, 7 ½ In. | 123 |
| **Salt & Pepper** shakers are listed in the Salt & Pepper category. | |
| **Turtle,** Pincushion, Velvet, Rhinestone Eye, Florenza, c.1945, 3 ½ x 2 In. | 29 |
| **Uncle Bim,** Bisque, Cardboard Base, Germany, 6 In. | 175 |
| **Woman,** Polka Dot Dress, Hair Up, Red Lips, Germany, 4 In. | 95 |

**NORITAKE** porcelain was made in Japan after 1904 by Nippon Toki Kaisha. The best-known Noritake pieces are marked with the *M* in a wreath for the Morimura Brothers, a New York City distributing company. This mark was used until the early 1950s. There may be some helpful price information in the Nippon category, since prices are comparable. Noritake Azalea is listed in the Azalea category in this book.

| | |
|---|---:|
| **Bowl,** Cereal, Angela, 6 In. | 21 |
| **Bowl,** Cereal, Berries N' Such, 5 ½ In. | 14 |
| **Bowl,** Cereal, Blue Haven, 6 ½ In. | 15 |
| **Bowl,** Cereal, Bright Side, 5 ½ In. | 8 |
| **Bowl,** Cereal, Desert Flowers, 6 ⅝ In. | 8 |
| **Bowl,** Cereal, Flower Time, 5 ½ In. | 12 |
| **Bowl,** Cereal, Mardi Gras, 6 ½ In. | 12 |
| **Bowl,** Cereal, Marguerite, 6 ¼ In. | 12 |
| **Bowl,** Cereal, Sunny Side, 6 ½ In. | 13 |
| **Bowl,** Fruit, Century, 5 ½ In. | 8 |
| **Bowl,** Fruit, Daisy, 5 ½ In. | 10 |
| **Bowl,** Fruit, Homecoming, 5 ⅝ In. | 8 |
| **Bowl,** Fruit, September Song, 5 ½ In. | 8 |
| **Bowl,** Fruit, Springfield, 5 ⅝ In. | 7 |
| **Bowl,** Fruit, Tisdale, 5 ½ In. | 12 |
| **Bowl,** Vegetable, Blue Moon, 9 ¾ In. | 26 |
| **Bowl,** Vegetable, Divided, Marguerite, 10 ⅛ In. | 18 |
| **Bowl,** Vegetable, Homecoming, 9 In. | 21 |
| **Bowl,** Vegetable, Lid, Isabella, 8 ¼ In. | 90 |
| **Bowl,** Vegetable, Oval, Selby, 10 ⅝ In. | 35 |
| **Bowl,** Vegetable, Round, Blue Haven, 8 ½ In. | 40 |
| **Bowl,** Vegetable, Up-Sa Daisy, 9 ¾ In. | 15 |
| **Butter,** Cover, Madrigal | 22 |
| **Butter,** Cover, Mardi Gras | 21 |
| **Butter,** Cover, Up-Sa Daisy | 32 |
| **Casserole,** Lid, Handles, Blue Haven, 2 ½ Qt. | 80 |
| **Casserole,** Lid, Handles, Melanie, 1 ½ Qt., 9 In. | 80 |
| **Casserole,** Lid, Palos Verde, 2 ½ Qt. | 75 |
| **Creamer,** Blue Haven | 13 |
| **Creamer,** Blue Moon | 12 |
| **Creamer,** Colburn | 17 |
| **Creamer,** Desert Flowers | 5 |
| **Creamer,** Laurel | 18 |
| **Creamer,** Mardi Gras | 15 |
| **Creamer,** Milburn | 14 |
| **Creamer,** Palos Verde | 12 |
| **Creamer,** Provincial | 12 |
| **Creamer,** September Song | 14 |
| **Creamer,** Sunny Side | 15 |
| **Creamer,** Tressa | 12 |
| **Creamer,** Up-Sa Daisy | 12 |
| **Cup & Saucer,** Angela | 13 |
| **Cup & Saucer,** Blue Haven | 8 |
| **Cup & Saucer,** Blue Moon | 8 |
| **Cup & Saucer,** Colburn | 15 |

N

| | | |
|---|---|---:|
| **Cup & Saucer,** Desert Flowers | .................... | 7 |
| **Cup & Saucer,** Homecoming | .................. | 7 |
| **Cup & Saucer,** Mardi Gras | .................. | 8 |
| **Cup & Saucer,** Marguerite | .................. | 7 |
| **Cup & Saucer,** Miyoshi | .................. | 12 |
| **Cup & Saucer,** September Song | .................. | 8 |
| **Cup & Saucer,** Sunny Side | .................. | 7 |
| **Cup & Saucer,** Up-Sa Daisy | .................. | 8 |
| **Cup,** Prelude | .................. | 11 |
| **Cup,** Selby | .................. | 8 |
| **Cup,** Spell Binder | .................. | 20 |
| **Dessert Set,** Milton, White, Gold Rim, Teapot 7 ¼ In., 20 Piece | .................. | 25 |
| **Gravy Boat,** Belda | .................. | 40 |
| **Gravy Boat,** Homecoming | .................. | 21 |
| **Gravy Boat,** Mardi Gras | .................. | 17 |
| **Gravy Boat,** Pacific | .................. | 25 |
| **Gravy Boat,** Tressa | .................. | 18 |
| **Gravy Boat,** Underplate, Dutch Treat | .................. | 28 |
| **Gravy Boat,** Up-Sa Daisy | .................. | 21 |
| **Plate,** Bread & Butter, Arabesque, 6 ⅜ In. | .................. | 7 |
| **Plate,** Bread & Butter, Blue Haven, 6 ⅜ In. | .................. | 4 |
| **Plate,** Bread & Butter, Blue Moon, 6 ⅜ In. | .................. | 4 |
| **Plate,** Bread & Butter, Bright Side, 6 ¼ In. | .................. | 8 |
| **Plate,** Bread & Butter, Century, 6 ¼ In. | .................. | 5 |
| **Plate,** Bread & Butter, Daisy, 6 ¼ In. | .................. | 4 |
| **Plate,** Bread & Butter, Homecoming, 6 ⅜ In. | .................. | 4 |
| **Plate,** Bread & Butter, Isabella, 6 ⅜ In. | .................. | 5 |
| **Plate,** Bread & Butter, Mardi Gras, 6 ⅜ In. | .................. | 5 |
| **Plate,** Bread & Butter, Miyoshi, 6 ½ In. | .................. | 6 |
| **Plate,** Bread & Butter, Orange County, 6 ⅜ In. | .................. | 5 |
| **Plate,** Bread & Butter, Tressa, 6 ⅜ In. | .................. | 5 |
| **Plate,** Bread & Butter, Up-Sa Daisy, 6 ⅜ In. | .................. | 4 |
| **Plate,** Dinner, Belda, 10 ⅝ In. | .................. | 15 |
| **Plate,** Dinner, Berries N' Such, 10 ½ In. | .................. | 15 |
| **Plate,** Dinner, Blue Haven, 10 ⅜ In. | .................. | 20 |
| **Plate,** Dinner, Blue Moon, 10 ⅜ In. | .................. | 17 |
| **Plate,** Dinner, Century, 10 ⅜ In. | .................. | 16 |
| **Plate,** Dinner, Daisy, 10 ⅜ In. | .................. | 21 |
| **Plate,** Dinner, Desert Flowers, 10 ⅝ In. | .................. | 11 |
| **Plate,** Dinner, Isabella, 10 ½ In. | .................. | 17 |
| **Plate,** Dinner, Mardi Gras, 10 ⅜ In. | .................. | 14 |
| **Plate,** Dinner, Miyoshi, 10 ⅝ In. | .................. | 31 |
| **Plate,** Dinner, Springfield, 10 ⅜ In. | .................. | 17 |
| **Plate,** Dinner, Up-Sa Daisy, 10 ¾ In. | .................. | 18 |
| **Plate,** Dinner, Willowbrook, 10 ⅝ In. | .................. | 35 |
| **Plate,** Salad, Springfield, 8 ¼ In. | .................. | 10 |
| **Plate,** Salad, Tara, 7 In. | .................. | 8 |
| **Plate,** Salad, Willowbrook, 8 ⅜ In. | .................. | 19 |
| **Platter,** Belda, 15 ⅜ In. | .................. | 45 |
| **Platter,** Desert Flowers, 14 ¼ In. | .................. | 20 |
| **Platter,** Flower Time, 13 In. | .................. | 21 |
| **Platter,** Homecoming, 13 ¼ In. | .................. | 15 |
| **Platter,** Isabella, 12 In. | .................. | 41 |
| **Platter,** Isabella, 16 In. | .................. | 52 |
| **Platter,** Melanie, 14 In. | .................. | 30 |
| **Platter,** Orange County, 13 ¼ In. | .................. | 35 |
| **Platter,** Serving, Oval, Blanche, 16 In. | .................. | 26 |
| **Platter,** Serving, Oval, Fontana, 12 In. | .................. | 28 |
| **Platter,** Sunny Side, 13 ⅜ In. | .................. | 15 |
| **Platter,** Up-Sa Daisy, 13 ¾ In. | .................. | 24 |
| **Salt & Pepper,** Blue Moon | .................. | 28 |
| **Salt & Pepper,** Mardi Gras | .................. | 21 |
| **Salt & Pepper,** Sunny Side | .................. | 21 |
| **Salt & Pepper,** Up-Sa Daisy | .................. | 21 |
| **Sugar & Creamer,** Sunny Side | .................. | 27 |
| **Teapot,** Lorenzo, 5 ⅝ In. | .................. | 65 |

**North Dakota,** Tile, Tea, Prairie Chicken, Purple Glaze, Huckfield, c.1936, 4 ⅝ In.
$161

Humler & Nolan

**North Dakota,** Vase, Blue, Brown Drip Glaze, Marked U.N.D., 1912, 8 x 4 In.
$1,000

Rago Arts & Auction Center

**Office,** Adding Machine, 10-Digit, Metal Stand, Electric, c.1950, 41 ½ x 15 In.
$90

Garth's Auctioneers & Appraisers

N

**Office,** Calculator, W.F. Stanley, Wood, Sliding Paper Label, Case, London, c.1910, 17 In. $250

Garth's Auctioneers & Appraisers

**Office,** Ticker Tape Machine, Stock, Edison, Early 20th Century, 11 In. $2,460

Pook & Pook, Inc.

| | |
|---|---|
| **Vase,** Boulder, Fall Grape Leaves, Fruit Pods, Green M In Wreath, 9¾ In. .........................*illus* | 403 |
| **Vase,** Cobalt Blue Ground, Samurait, Chikaramachi, Satsuma, Moriage, 6 In., Pair ................. | 288 |
| **Wall Pocket,** Tree In Meadow, Blue Luster ....................................................................... | 115 |

**NORSE POTTERY COMPANY** started in Edgerton, Wisconsin, in 1903. In 1904 the company moved to Rockford, Illinois. The company made a black pottery, which resembled early bronze relics of the Scandinavian countries. The firm went out of business in 1913.

| | |
|---|---|
| **Candleholder,** Hammered Metal Finish, Handle, Marked Norse 69, 5⅞ In. ............................. | 518 |
| **Vase,** Dragon Around Shoulder, Impressed, 12 In. .......................................................*illus* | 805 |

**NORTH DAKOTA SCHOOL OF MINES** was established in 1898 at the University of North Dakota. A ceramics course was established in 1910. Students made pieces from the clays found in the region. Although very early pieces were marked *U.N.D.,* most pieces were stamped with the full name of the university. After 1963 pieces were only marked with students' names.

| | |
|---|---|
| **Figurine,** Coyote, Light Green, 3⅜ In. ............................................................................... | 431 |
| **Tile,** Tea, Prairie Chicken, Purple Glaze, Huckfield, c.1936, 4⅝ In. ...............................*illus* | 161 |
| **Vase,** Aqua, Carved Wheat Around Shoulder, Flora Huckfield, c.1932, 2 In. ....................... | 288 |
| **Vase,** Bentonite, Flying Ducks, Reddish Brown, 3¼ In. ..................................................... | 863 |
| **Vase,** Blue, Brown Drip Glaze, Marked U.N.D., 1912, 8 x 4 In. .....................................*illus* | 1000 |
| **Vase,** Blue, Incised Shoulder Leaves, Flora Huckfield, Indigo Stamp, 5 x 4 In. .................... | 438 |
| **Vase,** Blue, Oak Leaf Incised, Julia Mattson, 6¼ x 6½ In. ................................................ | 1088 |
| **Vase,** Brown Over Green, Blue Green Interior, Round Stamp Logo, 8½ In. ......................... | 230 |
| **Vase,** Brown, Green Matte Glaze, Incised, M. Cable, 1934, 8 In. ........................................ | 518 |
| **Vase,** Brown, Purple, Green, Rabbits, Hand Carved, E. Bready, 1934, 3½ In. ....................... | 633 |
| **Vase,** Dark Blue Gloss, Tapered, Marked, 3⅞ In. ............................................................... | 184 |
| **Vase,** Dark Blue, Plum, Shouldered, Julia Mattson, 5½ x 6½ In. ........................................ | 184 |
| **Vase,** Ducks, Brown, Hand Carved, 3¾ In. ....................................................................... | 633 |
| **Vase,** Dutch Boys & Girls, Brown Matte Glaze, Florence Gregoire, c.1951, 4 In. .................. | 546 |
| **Vase,** Green, Coin Spot Design, Signed Jarvis, 8¼ In. ...................................................... | 570 |
| **Vase,** Green, Geometric Band At Shoulder, Marked, 4⅛ In. ................................................ | 575 |
| **Vase,** Grey, Incised Morning Glories, Myrtle Ellensen, 1927, 5⅞ In. .................................. | 690 |
| **Vase,** Meadow Lark, Green Semigloss Over Brown, Margaret Cable, 3 x 6 In. ...................... | 575 |
| **Vase,** Pale Purple, Squat, Tapered, Signed Huck & Evans, 5½ In. ....................................... | 92 |
| **Vase,** Pine Trees, Green, Tapered Cylinder, Signed, Cooley Huck, c.1930, 9 In. .................... | 3510 |
| **Vase,** Tan, Green, Brown, Band, Cowboys Holding Hands, 5 In. .......................................... | 690 |
| **Vase,** Wolf Silhouettes In Panels, Blue, Gray, Oval, 3½ x 4 In. .......................................... | 580 |

**NORTHWOOD** glass was made by one of the glassmaking companies operated by Harry C. Northwood. His first company, Northwood Glass Co., was founded in Martins Ferry, Ohio, in 1887 and moved to Ellwood City, Pennsylvania, in 1892. The company closed in 1896. Later that same year, Harry Northwood opened the Northwood Co. in Indiana, Pennsylvania. Some pieces made at the Northwood Co. are marked "Northwood" in script. The Northwood Co. became part of a consortium called the National Glass Co. in 1899. Harry left National in 1901 to found the H. Northwood Co. in Wheeling, West Virginia. At the Wheeling factory, Harry Northwood and his brother Carl manufactured pressed and blown tableware and novelties in many colors that are collected today as custard, opalescent, goofus, carnival, and stretch glass. Pieces made between 1905 and about 1915 may have an underlined *N* trademark. Harry Northwood died in 1919, and the plant closed in 1925.

| | |
|---|---|
| **Aurora,** Toothpick Holder, Cranberry Opalescent, Ring Neck Mold, 1895, 2 In. ................... | 345 |
| **Basketweave,** Peacock Feather, Bowl, Ice Blue Iridescent, Ruffled Rim, 8½ In. .................. | 150 |
| **Blackberry,** Compote, Daisy & Plume Bottom, 3-Footed, 4¼ x 8¼ In. ............................... | 115 |
| **Blue Swirl,** Vase, Yellow, White Pulled Feathers, Scalloped Rim, Round, 3 x 4 In. ............... | 2242 |
| **Blue Twist,** Tumbler, Opalescent, Blown, Polished Rim, c.1898, 4 In. ................................ | 92 |
| **Brocade Spanish Lace,** Sugar Shaker, Blue, c.1905, 4⅝ In. ............................................. | 104 |
| **Christmas Snowflake,** Cranberry, Tumbler, Opalescent, c.1895, 3¾ In. ........................... | 161 |
| **Christmas Snowflake,** Tumbler, Blue Opalescent, Dugan Glass, c.1895, 4 In. .................... | 161 |
| **Chrysanthemum Swirl,** Butter, Cover, Blue Opalescent, 1890, 5¼ x 6 In. ......................... | 196 |
| **Chrysanthemum Swirl,** Toothpick Holder, Opalescent, Blue, c.1893, 2 In. ........................ | 173 |
| **Coinspot,** Pitcher, Water, Green Opalescent, Ruffled Rim, Handle, c.1900, 9 In. ................. | 288 |
| **Coinspot,** Sugar Shaker, 9 Panels, Bittersweet Opalescent, Metal Lid, c.1894, 5 In. ............ | 11 |
| **Cora Nome,** Tumbler, Enameled, Green .......................................................................... | 50 |
| **Daffodil,** Pitcher, Water, Tankard Shape, Green Opalescent, Handle, 1903, 12 In. ................ | 1035 |
| **Daffodil,** Sugar Shaker, Opalescent, Metal Lid, c.1903, 5 In. ............................................ | 161 |
| **Daffodil,** Tumbler, Green Opalescent, c.1910, 3⅞ In. ....................................................... | 184 |

N

| | |
|---|---|
| **Grape Arbor,** Vase, Custard Glass, Cylindrical, Ruffled Rim, 4 In. | 58 |
| **Jar,** Metal Lid, White Body, Ribbed, Rainbow Pull-Up Feathers, 5 In. | 201 |
| **Leaf Umbrella,** Biscuit Jar, Topaz Lemon Glossy, Clear Finial, 1900, 8 x 5 In. | 1035 |
| **Leaf Umbrella,** Celery Vase, Turquoise Glossy, c.1900, 5 In. | 489 |
| **Leaf Umbrella,** Pitcher, Water, Topaz, Handle, Feather Design, c.1900, 9 In. | 184 |
| **Leaf Umbrella,** Tumbler, Opal & Cranberry Spatter, c.1889, 4 In. | 173 |
| **Poinsettia,** Tumbler, Vaseline Glass, Opalescent, c.1903, 3¾ In. | 173 |
| **Pull-Up,** Biscuit Jar, Cased Red, White, Yellow Stile, Silver Lid, Bail, 10 In. | 295 |
| **Pull-Up,** Bowl, Yellow, Pink, White, Swirled, Rolled Rim, 2¾ x 7½ In. | 2124 |
| **Royal Ivy,** Sugar Shaker, Rubina, Swirls, Metal Lid, c.1900, 4½ In. | 92 |
| **Royal Oak,** Toothpick Holder, Clear, Frosted, c.1891 | 95 |
| **Shell,** Toothpick Holder, Green Opalescent, c.1900.2 In. | 259 |
| **Swirl,** Biscuit Jar, Pink, White, Blue, Silver Lid, Bail, 7 In. | 295 |
| **Swirl,** Sugar Shaker, Cranberry Opalescent, Metal Lid, c.1905, 4½ In. | 104 |
| **Vase,** Chartreuse, Blue, Green Pulled Feather Design, 5 In. | 295 |
| **Verre D'Or Grape,** Bowl, Emerald Green, Gilt, 3 Scroll Feet, c.1906, 3 x 11 In. | 115 |

**NUTCRACKERS** of many types have been used through the centuries. At first the nutcracker was probably strong teeth or a hammer. But by the nineteenth century, many elaborate and ingenious types were made. Levers, screws, and hammer adaptations were the most popular. Because nutcrackers are still useful, they are still being made, some in the old styles.

| | |
|---|---|
| **Bill Sykes,** Chromed Brass, 4¾ In. | 75 |
| **Brass,** Engraved, Ornate, 6 In. | 58 |
| **Chimney Sweep,** Ladder, Brush, Erzgebirge, DDR, 13¾ In. | 79 |
| **Clothespin,** Walnut, c.1910, 8½ In. | 215 |
| **Dog Head,** Wood, Carved, Black Forest, Glass Eyes, 19th Century, 8 In. | 75 |
| **Dog,** Metal, Wood Base, c.1950, 5 x 7 In. | 145 |
| **Dog,** Retriever, Brass, c.1900, 5 x 12 x 2 In. | 175 |
| **Elephant,** Boy On Head, Brass, Chrome Plated, 6¾ In. | 106 |
| **Gnome,** Wood, Carved, Attached Bowl, Folk Art, c.1930, 9 In. | 145 |
| **Legs,** Woman's, Wood, Walnut, Carved, c.1900, 7 In. | 86 |
| **Monkey,** Wood, Carved, Black Forest, Germany, c.1900, 8 In. | 320 |
| **Night Watchman,** Beard, Lantern, Horn, Dog, Wood, Carved, Germany, 13 In. | 215 |
| **Parrot,** Green, Cast Iron, Orange Paint, 5¾ In. | 150 |
| **Punch & Judy,** Brass, England, 1920s, 5 In. | 112 |
| **Rooster,** Wood, Multicolor, Anri, Italy, 8½ In. | 595 |
| **Silver Plate,** Sheffield, 1900s, 7½ In. | 35 |
| **Trusty Servant,** Town Coat Of Arms, Brass, Marked, Peerage, 5½ In. | 107 |
| **Walnut,** Wood, Carved, Folk Art, 8¼ In. | 35 |
| **Wild Boar,** Wood, Glass Eyes, Black Forest, 6 In. | 370 |

**NYMPHENBURG,** *see Royal Nymphenburg.*

**OCCUPIED JAPAN** was printed on pottery, porcelain, toys, and other goods made during the American occupation of Japan after World War II, from 1947 to 1952. Collectors now search for these pieces. The items were made for export. Ceramic items are listed here. Toys are listed in the Toy category in this book.

| | |
|---|---|
| **Berry Bowl,** Montana Rose, Monarch China, 5½ In. | 8 |
| **Bowl,** Central Bouquet, Reticulated Rim, 5 In. | 39 |
| **Bowl,** Fruit, Virginia, Meito, 5½ In. | 12 |
| **Bowl,** Vegetable, Roslyn, Diamond China, 9⅛ In. | 50 |
| **Cigarette Box,** Ashtray Lid, Roses, 6-Footed, 3 x 2 x 2 In. | 34 |
| **Creamer,** Cobalt Blue, Pagodas | 5 |
| **Cup & Saucer,** Pagoda, Mountain, Scrolled Gilt Trim, Corona. | 75 |
| **Cup & Saucer,** Pink Flower, Green Ground, Merit | 35 |
| **Cup & Saucer,** Roslyn, Diamond China | 18 |
| **Dish,** Butterfly Shape, Multicolor, 6 x 5 In. | 36 |
| **Figurine,** Boy, Holding Flower, Begging Dog, 5 In. | 38 |
| **Figurine,** Couple, Playing Mandolin, Seated, 5 In. | 12 |
| **Figurine,** Puppy, Long Hair Terrier, Black & White, 3 x 5 In. | 38 |
| **Figurine,** Woman, Black Hat, Striped Umbrella, 5½ In. | 45 |
| **Figurine,** Woman, Holding Dress, Hand On Hat, 8 In. | 95 |
| **Flower Frog,** Multicolor Dots, White Ground, Footed, 4¼ In. | 18 |

**Ohr,** Inkwell, Mule's Head, Pottery, Black & Olive Brown Glaze, Grooved Base, 3 x 5 In.
$1,150

Glass Works Auctions

**TIP**
*Display groups of at least three of your collectibles to get decorating impact.*

**Ohr,** Mug, Teal Glaze, Incised, Drink To My Health, J. Jefferson, Stamped, 3¾ x 4 In.
$2,125

Rago Arts & Auction Center

**Ohr,** Vase, Pink & Purple Volcanic Glaze, In-Body Twist, Ruffled Rim, Stamped, 5½ x 5 In.
$68,750

Rago Arts & Auction Center

**Ohr,** Vase, Yellow, Dragon, Wings, Carved, Glazed, Stamped, c.1888, 10 ½ x 6 ¾ In. **$25,000**

Rago Arts & Auction Center

**Onion,** Tray, Molded Border, Meissen, 1860-1924, 17 ¾ In. **$276**

New Orleans Auction Galleries, Inc.

**Opera Glasses,** Mother-Of-Pearl, Signed, Lefils, Paris, Leather Case, 4 In. **$35**

Conestoga Auction Co., Inc.

| | |
|---|---:|
| **Gravy Boat,** Roslyn, Underplate, Diamond China | 48 |
| **Incense Burner,** Red Feet & Handles, Trefoil Shape, Buddhist Finial, 5 x 5 x 3 In. | 295 |
| **Lemon Server,** Pink & Orange Flowers, Tashiro Shoten Ltd., 5 x 5 In. | 35 |
| **Match Holder,** Couple, Holding Basket, Bisque China, 7 x 4 In. | 28 |
| **Mug,** For A Little Angel, Bouquet, 3 ¼ In. | 14 |
| **Planter,** Asian Children, Water Buckets, 6 x 7 In. | 40 |
| **Planter,** Girl On Swing, Tree Branch, Green Dress, 8 In. | 42 |
| **Plate,** Dinner, Virginia, Meito, 10 ⅛ In. | 22 |
| **Plate,** Women, Cherub, Pierced Rim, 8 In. | 53 |
| **Relish,** Roslyn, Diamond China, 9 x 6 In. | 22 |
| **Salt & Pepper,** Butterfly On Rosebud, Branch Handle Tray | 18 |
| **Salt & Pepper,** Roses, Gilt Trim, Ball Shape, Handles | 22 |
| **Sugar,** Montana Rose, Monarch China | 35 |
| **Toast Rack,** Pink & Gold Accents, 2-Slice, 2 ½ x 2 In. | 15 |
| **Tureen,** Flowers, Leaves, Ivory Ground, Handles, Aladdin, 11 x 6 In. | 30 |
| **Vase,** Figural, Angel, Playing Accordion, Bud, 4 In. | 12 |
| **Vase,** Figural, Crescent Moon, Cherub Playing Flute, Bud, 3 ½ In. | 15 |

**OFFICE TECHNOLOGY** includes office equipment and related products, such as adding machines, calculators, and check-writing machines. Typewriters are in their own category in this book.

| | |
|---|---:|
| **Adding Machine,** 10-Digit, Metal Stand, Electric, c.1950, 41 ½ x 15 In. .........................*illus* | 90 |
| **Adding Machine,** Burroughs, No. 3, 9 Row Keyboard, Collapsible Side Table, c.1910, 42 In. | 185 |
| **Arithmometer,** Burkhardt, 8 Slides, Mahogany Case, 23 In. | 738 |
| **Calculator,** The Millionaire, 16-Digit, Oak Case, Slide, Metal Stand, Hans Egli, 25 In. | 923 |
| **Calculator,** W.F. Stanley, Wood, Sliding Paper Label, Case, London, c.1910, 17 In. .........*illus* | 250 |
| **Coin Changer,** Staats, Cast Iron, c.1890, 11 x 10 In. | 180 |
| **Slide Rule,** Wood Case, Bethlehem Steel, Kauffel & Esser, 6 ½ x 24 In. | 480 |
| **Stapler,** Bronze Color, Swingline, c.1938, 6 x 4 In. | 22 |
| **Stapler,** Hotchkiss No. 1, National Cash Register, Nickel Finish, 1898, 4 x 5 x 2 In. | 180 |
| **Ticker Tape Machine,** Stock, Edison, Early 20th Century, 11 In. ...........................*illus* | 2460 |
| **Time Clock,** Pendulum, Bundy, 18 x 52 In. | 240 |

**OHR** pottery was made in Biloxi, Mississippi, from 1883 to 1906 by George E. Ohr, a true eccentric. The pottery was made of very thin clay that was twisted, folded, and dented into odd, graceful shapes. Some pieces were lifelike models of hats, animal heads, or even a potato. Others were decorated with folded clay "snakes." Reproductions and reworked pieces are appearing on the market. These have been reglazed, or snakes and other embellishments have been added.

| | |
|---|---:|
| **Bowl,** Crumpled, Pink Volcanic Glaze, Green Spots, 1895, 2 ¼ x 4 In. | 5312 |
| **Bowl,** Orange, Green, Black, Red Mottled Glaze, Pinched, Folded Rim, Impressed, 2 In. | 3450 |
| **Candlestick,** Unglazed, Triple Knops Shaft, Strap Handle, Signed, c.1900, 4 ½ x 5 In. | 489 |
| **Flower Frog,** Green, Gunmetal Glaze, Signed, c.1900, 9 x 6 In. | 1375 |
| **Inkwell,** Black Glaze, Artist's Palette, Paint Brush, Paint Tubes, c.1900, 6 x 5 ¼ In. | 805 |
| **Inkwell,** Cabin, Trees, Marked, Glazed, c.1895, 2 ¾ x 7 x 5 ¼ In. | 1500 |
| **Inkwell,** Mule's Head, Pottery, Black & Olive Brown Glaze, Grooved Base, 3 x 5 In. ............*illus* | 1150 |
| **Loving Cup,** Twisted Cylinder, Shaped Handles, Redware, Brown Glaze, Marked, 6 In. | 7670 |
| **Mug,** Ear Shape Handles, Speckled Brown & Green Glaze, c.1900, 4 x 6 In. | 2750 |
| **Mug,** Puzzle, Arts & Crafts, Cylindrical, Holes Near Rim, Decorated Handle, 3 ⅝ In. | 400 |
| **Mug,** Puzzle, Brown Glaze, Rabbit's Head Handle, Impressed, 3 ½ x 4 ¾ In. | 799 |
| **Mug,** Puzzle, Manganese Glaze, Rope-Like Handle, Signed, c.1890, 3 x 3 In. | 575 |
| **Mug,** Speckled Green Blue & Mauve Glaze, Oval, Twin Loop Handle, 4 x 5 In. | 1875 |
| **Mug,** Teal Glaze, Incised, Drink To My Health, J. Jefferson, Stamped, 3 ¾ x 4 In. ..........*illus* | 2125 |
| **Pitcher,** Bisque, In-Body Twist, Curled Ribbon Handle, c.1900, 8 ¾ x 5 In. | 5938 |
| **Pitcher,** Bisque, Ribbon Handle, Twist, 1887-1900, 8 ¾ In. | 5937 |
| **Pitcher,** Green, Brown Sponged Glaze, 2 Inset Holes Handle, c.1892, 2 ¾ x 4 ½ In. | 5938 |
| **Pitcher,** Gunmetal Glaze, Olive Inside, Folded, Crimped, Integrated Handle, 5 x 6 In. | 2375 |
| **Pitcher,** Moss Green Glaze, Pinched, Cutout Handle, c.1895, 3 x 3 ¹14 In. | 3750 |
| **Shoe,** Novelty, Brown Mottled Glaze, High Button Heel, c.1900, 3 ½ x 2 ¾ In. | 3750 |
| **Teapot,** Gunmetal Glaze, Ribbon Curled Handle, c.1895, 4 x 7 In. | 3750 |
| **Teapot,** Ribbon, Gunmetal, 4 x 7 In. | 3750 |
| **Vase,** 2-Tone Brown, Punched Sides, Signed G.E. Ohr Biloxi, 5 In. | 1440 |
| **Vase,** Bisque, Crimped, Folded Rim, Scroddled, c.1910, 3 ¾ x 4 ½ In. | 4063 |
| **Vase,** Bisque, Pierced In-Body Twist, Footed, c.1905, 5 x 5 In. | 1000 |

| | |
|---|---|
| **Vase,** Brown Matte Gunmetal Glaze, Bulbous, Crimped Base, Uneven Rim, 3 x 4 In. .................... | 875 |
| **Vase,** Brown, Green, Ocher Sponged Glaze, c.1900, 6 x 4 In. ........................................................ | 1152 |
| **Vase,** Brown, Tan, Green, Blue Sponged Glaze, Squat, c.1895, 1¾ x 4½ In........................... | 938 |
| **Vase,** Folded Rim, Speckled Green Glaze, Stamped, c.1900, 4¼ x 4¼ In.............................. | 3000 |
| **Vase,** Green, Black, Dimpled Body, Melt Fissures, c.1900, 2¼ x 4¼ In................................ | 1125 |
| **Vase,** Green, Brown Glaze, In-Body Twist, c.1895, 4½ x 2¾ In............................................. | 3250 |
| **Vase,** Green, Gunmetal, Sponged, Twisted Body, Ruffled Rim, c.1900, 4 x 4 In. ................... | 5313 |
| **Vase,** Indigo Glaze, In Body Twist, Stamped, 4½ x 4 In...................................................... | 5000 |
| **Vase,** Indigo, Twist, 1897-1900, 4½ In............................................................................ | 5000 |
| **Vase,** Mottled Brown & Green Matte Glaze, Bulbous, Pinched, Signed, 3 x 3¾ In................ | 1342 |
| **Vase,** Mottled Brown, Green, Yellow, Signed, 4 In............................................................... | 960 |
| **Vase,** Mottled Orange, Black Glaze, c.1895, 2¾ x 5 In....................................................... | 832 |
| **Vase,** Mug, Puzzle, Brown, Handle, Rim Spout, Bottom Hole, Signed, 3½ In........................ | 720 |
| **Vase,** Multicolor, Mottled, Crimped, Stamped, 3 In............................................................. | 1680 |
| **Vase,** Ocher, Brown Speckled Glaze, Ruffled Rim, Wide Neck, c.1897, 3½ x 4 In. ............... | 3750 |
| **Vase,** Orange, Olive & Brown Speckled Glaze, Dimpled, Stand-Up Rim, 3 x 4 In................. | 1250 |
| **Vase,** Oval, Footed, Blue, Green Streaks, Tapered, Biloxi, c.1890, 5½ In. .......................... | 1035 |
| **Vase,** Pink & Purple Volcanic Glaze, In-Body Twist, Ruffled Rim, Stamped, 5½ x 5 In. ........*illus* | 68750 |
| **Vase,** Pink Volcanic Glaze, Green Speckled, Ruffled Rim, Stamped, c.1895, 2 x 4 In. .......... | 5313 |
| **Vase,** Redware, Pinched Neck, Cinched Cylinder, Green Glaze, Stamped, c.1900, 5 In.......... | 1800 |
| **Vase,** Round, Twisted, Crimped & Folded Top, Redware, Mottled Brown Glaze, 3 In. .......... | 2124 |
| **Vase,** Swirled 2-Tone Orange To Red, Crimped, Folded Shape, 3½ In................................ | 2040 |
| **Vase,** Twisted & Folded Rim, Speckled Ocher Glaze, Stamped, c.1897, 5 x 4½ In. .............. | 4062 |
| **Vase,** Yellow, Dragon, Wings, Carved, Glazed, Stamped, c.1888, 10½ x 6¾ In. ............*illus* | 25000 |

**OLD PARIS**, *see Paris category.*

**OLD SLEEPY EYE**, *see Sleepy Eye category.*

**ONION PATTERN**, originally named bulb pattern, is a white ware decorated with cobalt blue or pink. Although it is commonly associated with Meissen, other companies made the pattern in the late nineteenth and the twentieth centuries. A rare type is called *red bud* because there are added red accents on the blue-and-white dishes.

| | |
|---|---|
| **Bowl,** Blue & White, Meissen, 14 In.............................................................................. | 212 |
| **Cake Stand,** Blue Pedestal Base, Meissen, 20th Century, 12½ In. ...................................... | 207 |
| **Cup & Saucer,** Blue, Scalloped Rim, Meissen ..................................................................... | 89 |
| **Platter,** Blue, Scalloped Rim, Meissen, Oval, 19¼ x 14 In. ................................................ | 127 |
| **Rolling Pin,** Wood Handles, Blue, White, 14 In................................................................. | 432 |
| **Salt,** Blue, Man, Woman, Reclining, Holding Bowl, Meissen, 7 In., Pair................................ | 1063 |
| **Salt,** Master, Reclining Male, Offering A Basin, Blue Onion, Meissen, 7 In. .......................... | 338 |
| **Sauceboat,** Underplate, Blue, Serpentine Rim, Handles, Meissen, 10 x 7 In........................ | 121 |
| **Standish,** Blue, 2 Inkwells, Underplate, Serpentine Rim, Flared Collar, Meissen, 11 x 7 In.......... | 178 |
| **Sweetmeat Set,** Blue, 7 Sections, Mahogany Pedestal Base, Meissen, 7 x 18 In. ................ | 375 |
| **Tray,** Molded Border, Meissen, 1860-1924, 17¾ In. ......................................................*illus* | 276 |

**OPALESCENT GLASS** is translucent glass that has the tones of the opal gemstone. It originated in England in the 1870s and is often found in pressed glassware made in Victorian times. Opalescent glass was first made in America in 1897 at the Northwood glassworks in Indiana, Pennsylvania. Some dealers use the terms *opaline* and *opalescent* for any of these translucent wares. More opalescent pieces may be listed in Hobnail, Pressed Glass, and other glass categories.

| | |
|---|---|
| **Alhambra,** Tumbler, Blue Opalescent, Model Flint Glass Co., c.1894, 3¾ In.......................... | 489 |
| **Brocade,** Spanish Lace, Creamer, Cranberry, Clear Handle, c.1900, 4½ In.......................... | 127 |
| **Brocade,** Spanish Lace, Tumbler, Bittersweet, Tapered, c.1900, 3⅞ In............................... | 288 |
| **Brocade,** Spanish Lace, Water Carafe, Cranberry c.1900, 8 In.......................................... | 374 |
| **Bubble Lattice,** Cruet, Cranberry, Clear Stopper, c.1910, 7¼ In........................................ | 259 |
| **Bubble Lattice,** Syrup, Cranberry, Buckeye Glass Co., c.1890, 6¾ In. .............................. | 633 |
| **Coin Spot,** Pitcher, Water, White, 8½ In.......................................................................... | 29 |
| **Daisy & Fern,** Sugar Shaker, Cranberry, Parian Swirl, c.1905, 4 In. ................................. | 115 |
| **Fern,** Pitcher, Water, Cranberry, 4-Lobe Rim, West Virginia Glass Co., c.1894, 9 In............. | 546 |
| **Lattice,** Pitcher, Water, Cranberry, Crimped Rim, Clear Handle, c.1900, 9 In...................... | 316 |
| **Opal Lattice,** Pitcher, Water, Cranberry, Wavy Rim, c.1905, 10 In.................................... | 316 |
| **Scottish Moor,** Tumbler, Bittersweet, Gilt Outlining, c.1890, 3¾ In. ................................. | 633 |
| **Seaweed,** Pitcher, Water, Blue, Crimped Rim, Hobbs, Brockunier & Co., c.1900, 9 In. ......... | 805 |

# OPALESCENT GLASS

**Orrefors,** Vase, Ariel, Cobalt Blue & Clear, Square, Low, Signed, 3¼ x 5½ In.
$295

**Orrefors,** Vase, Ariel, Floating Crystal Windows, Sapphire Blue, Ingeborg Lundin, 4⅝ x 7 In.
$575

**Overbeck,** Bowl, Exotic Flowers, Brown, Mauve, Teal & Cream, OBK, 3¼ In.
$3,450

O

**TIP**
*When changing an antique by rewiring a lamp or reupholstering a chair seat keep the old pieces and parts you remove. When you sell your antique the new owner will pay more if the old parts are part of the history. I am saving horsehair fabric and seaweed stuffing from an 1875 sofa we recovered and the pull chains with the acorn shaped tips from a Handel lamp.*

**Owens,** Wall Pocket, Turnip Man, Green Matte Glaze, Impressed Owensart, 11 x 6 In.
**$748**

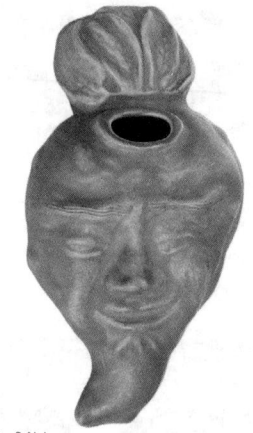

Humler & Nolan

**Oyster Plate,** 5 Wells, Crescent Plate, Oriental Design
**$272**

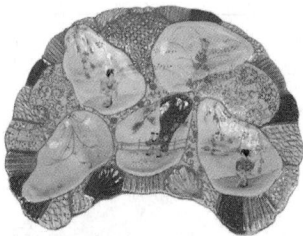

Strawser Auction Group

**Oyster Plate,** 5 Wells, Neptune & Mermaid, Round, 9 In.
**$206**

Strawser Auction Group

| | |
|---|---:|
| **Spanish Lace,** Syrup, Opaline Brocade, Ball Shape, Blue, Reeded Handle, c.1900, 6 In. | 196 |
| **Swastika Diamonds & Clubs,** Water, Pitcher, Clear, 1904, 11 In. | 374 |
| **Swirling Maze,** Water Pitcher, Cranberry, Crimped, Jefferson Glass Co., c.1905, 10 In. | 489 |
| **Thistle,** Biscuit Jar, Blue, Brass Rim, Handle, c.1900, 6 1/4 x 5 In. | 403 |

**OPALINE,** or opal glass, was made in white, green, and other colors. The glass had a matte surface and a lack of transparency. It was often gilded or painted. It was a popular mid-nineteenth-century European glassware.

| | |
|---|---:|
| **Bowl,** Blue & Pink Flowers, 4 Folded & Crimped Sides, Translucent Blue Lip Wrap, 8 In. | 58 |
| **Bowl,** Blue & White Ruffled Rim, Wallace Silver Plate Stand, 11 In. | 86 |
| **Bowl,** Centerpiece, Gilt Bronze, Pierced, Scrolled Feet, France, 20 x 8 3/4 In. | 2214 |
| **Lamp,** Lotus, 4 Tiers, Murano, Attributed To Carlo Nason, Mazzega, Italy, 1960s, 20 In. | 5166 |
| **Vase,** Pink Flowers, White Ground, Gilt Rim & Base, c.1890, 13 3/4 In. | 2500 |

**OPERA GLASSES** are needed because the stage is a long way from some of the seats at a play or an opera. Mother-of-pearl was a popular decoration on many French glasses.

| | |
|---|---:|
| **Enamel,** Painted 1700s Women, Adjustable Handle, Lemoire, France, 4 In. | 438 |
| **Gilt Brass,** Multicolor Flowers, Cobalt Blue Ground, Gilt Stars, Lemoire, 4 x 2 In. | 230 |
| **Gilt Brass,** Multicolor Flowers, Cream Ground, Gilt Stars, Lemoire, 3 3/4 x 2 1/4 In. | 230 |
| **Mother-Of-Pearl,** Brass, Enamel, Portraits, Cherubs, Lemoire, 4 In. | 659 |
| **Mother-Of-Pearl,** Brass, Tiffany & Co., New York, c.1920, 4 In. | 210 |
| **Mother-Of-Pearl,** Brass, Turquoise Glaze Enamel, Flowers, 3 1/2 x 4 1/4 In. | 460 |
| **Mother-Of-Pearl,** Guilloche Enamel, Painted Flowers, Gilt Stars, c.1900, 4 x 4 In. | 1845 |
| **Mother-Of-Pearl,** Signed, Lefils, Paris, Leather Case, 4 In. ..........................*illus* | 35 |
| **Mother-Of-Pearl,** Violet Enamel, Gilt Accents, Signed Paris La Princesse, 3 x 2 In. | 460 |

**ORPHAN ANNIE** first appeared in the comics in 1924. The last strip ran in newspapers on June 13, 2010. The redheaded girl, her dog Sandy, and her friends were on the radio from 1930 to 1942. The first movie based on the strip was produced in 1932. A second movie was produced in 1938. A Broadway musical that opened in 1977, a movie based on the musical and produced in 1982, and a made-for-television movie based on the musical produced in 1999 made Annie popular again, and many toys, dishes, and other memorabilia have been made. A new adaptation of the movie based on the musical opened in 2014.

| | |
|---|---:|
| **Bank,** Register, Save A Dime A Day, Lithograph, Annie & Sandy, Artists, 1936 | 225 |
| **Book,** Orphan Annie & The Big Town Gunman, Whitman Publishing, 1936, 7 x 5 In. | 20 |
| **Book,** Orphan Annie In The Circus, Hardcover, Cupples & Leon, 1927, 7 x 8 In. | 38 |
| **Button,** At R.K.O. Ritz Theater, Yellow Curls, White Ground, 1 1/4 In. | 319 |
| **Doll,** Composition, Jointed, Cloth Dress, Famous Artists Syndicates, 1930s, 10 In. | 165 |
| **Doll,** Composition, Red Hair & Dress, 25 x 11 In. | 90 |
| **Doll,** Porcelain, Velvet Dress, Applause, Box, 1980, 10 In. | 36 |
| **Mug,** Annie & Sandy, D Handle, Glasbake | 10 |
| **Mug,** Lid, Plastic, Annie, Sandy, Decal, Ovaltine, Green, 1930s, 4 In. | 35 |
| **Necklace,** Annie & Sandy, Painted Under Glass, Brass Chain, 1960s, 14 In. | 125 |
| **Necklace,** Pendant, Heart, I Love You, Goldtone, Avon, Box, c.1980, 16 In. | 65 |
| **Paper Doll Book,** Annie & Sandy, Happy House, 1982 | 16 |
| **Pin,** Brass, Orphan Annie's Radio Secret Society, 1 In. | 23 |
| **Pin,** Decoder, Metal, 1935, 1 1/4 In. | 30 |
| **Pin,** Radio Orphan Annie Secret Society, Raised Design, Metal, 1 In. | 10 |
| **Punch Out,** All-Star Action Show, Big Top Circus Scene, 1935, 10 x 14 1/2 In. | 143 |
| **Ring,** Secret Guard, Magnifying, Quaker Cereals, Portrait, SG On Sides | 519 |
| **Toy,** Sandy, Dog, Walks, Tin, Windup, 5 In. | 104 |
| **Toy,** Stove, White, Red, Pressed Tin, Lithograph 2 Ovens, 3 Burners, Graphics, 10 In. | 12 |

**ORREFORS** Glassworks, located in the Swedish province of Smaaland, was established in 1898. The company is still making glass for use on the table or as decorations. There is renewed interest in the glass made in the modern styles of the 1940s and 1950s. In 1990, the company merged with Kosta Boda. Most vases and decorative pieces are signed with the etched name *Orrefors*.

*Orrefors*

| | |
|---|---:|
| **Bowl,** Cobalt Blue, Clear Banded Rim, Round, 7 1/2 In. | 18 |
| **Vase,** Ariel Faces, Blue Cased In Clear, Cylindrical, Flared Rim, Ingeborg Lundin, c.1969, 7 In. | 3198 |
| **Vase,** Ariel, Cobalt Blue & Clear, Square, Low, Signed, 3 1/4 x 5 1/2 In. ...............*illus* | 295 |
| **Vase,** Ariel, Floating Crystal Windows, Sapphire Blue, Ingeborg Lundin, 4 5/8 x 7 In. ...........*illus* | 575 |
| **Vase,** Blue To Clear, Bubbles, Bulbous, Flared, Ingeborg Lundin, 7 1/2 x 6 1/2 In. | 1062 |
| **Vase,** Fish, Seaweed, Green, Black, Bulbous, Graal, Edvard Hald, 1940s, 4 1/4 In. | 826 |

**OTT & BREWER COMPANY** operated the Etruria Pottery at Trenton, New Jersey, from 1871 to 1892. It started making belleek in 1882. The firm used a variety of marks that incorporated the initials *O & B*.

| | | |
|---|---|---|
| **Bowl,** Vegetable, Stemmed Flowers, Gilt, 1880s, 9 x 6 In. | | 32 |
| **Charger,** Fluted, Blue Poppies, 10 In. | | 78 |
| **Cup & Saucer,** Twig Handle, Veined Leaves, Gilt Trim, c.1875 | | 56 |
| **Pitcher,** Droopy Stemmed Flower, Blue, Gilt, c.1885, 4¾ In. | | 345 |
| **Pitcher,** Lotus Leaves, Branch Handle, Marked, c.1883, 8¾ In. | | 1925 |
| **Punch Bowl,** Pink & Purple Flowers, Leaves, Crimped, Footed, 10 x 18 In. | | 3899 |
| **Sugar & Creamer,** Scalloped Edge, c.1885 | | 395 |
| **Vase,** Tree Trunk Shape, Gold Oak & Ivy Leaves, c.1888, 5 In. | | 150 |

**OVERBECK POTTERY** was made by four sisters named Overbeck at a pottery in Cambridge City, Indiana. They started in 1911. They made all types of vases, each one-of-a-kind. Small, hand-modeled figurines are the most popular pieces with today's collectors. The factory continued until 1955, when the last of the four sisters died.

| | | |
|---|---|---|
| **Bowl,** Exotic Flowers, Brown, Mauve, Teal & Cream, OBK, 3¼ In. | *illus* | 3450 |
| **Figurine,** Big-Eyed Creature, 4 Legs, Pink, Green, Blue, Tan, 2 x 2½ In. | | 427 |
| **Figurine,** Dodo Bird, Turquoise, Black, Exaggerated Features, 4 x 4½ In. | | 793 |
| **Figurine,** Goose, 5 x 3½ In. | | 750 |
| **Figurine,** Goose, Exaggerated Beak & Feet, Yellow, White, 3½ x 5 In. | | 549 |

**OWENS POTTERY** was made in Zanesville, Ohio, from 1891 to 1928. The first art pottery was made after 1896. Utopian Ware, Cyrano, Navarre, Feroza, and Henri Deux were made. Pieces were usually marked with a form of the name *Owens*. About 1907, the firm began to make tile and discontinued the art pottery wares.

| | | |
|---|---|---|
| **Jardiniere,** Arts & Crafts Style, Green Matte Glaze, Handles, 4-Footed, c.1910, 13 x 15 In. | | 296 |
| **Tankard,** Lotus, Tree, Shore Landscape, Boats, Flared Cylinder, 13⅝ In. | | 661 |
| **Tile,** Scarab, Raised, Matte Glazes, Impressed, Oak Frame, 11¾ x 11¾ In. | | 460 |
| **Vase,** Flowers, Matte Glaze, Long Flared Neck, 13 In. | | 92 |
| **Vase,** Gourd, Cattails, 5⅞ In. | | 747 |
| **Vase,** Green Matte Glaze, Arched Handles, 4-Footed, 7⅝ In. | | 230 |
| **Vase,** Green Matte Glaze, Carved Geometric Design, Stamped, 6 In. | | 240 |
| **Vase,** Green Matte, Arts & Crafts Designs, 7 x 8 In. | | 242 |
| **Vase,** Henri Deux, Art Nouveau Woman, Black Ground, Flared Base, 8¼ In. | | 184 |
| **Vase,** Henri Deux, Gold Irises, Dark Ground, Tapered Cylinder, 10 In. | | 242 |
| **Vase,** Lotus, Berries, Leaves, Gray Blue Ground, 10¼ In. | | 253 |
| **Vase,** Parchment Lotus, Carnations, Yellow To Purple Ground, 11 In. | | 403 |
| **Vase,** Squeezebag Design, Orange Ground, Flared Base, 16 In. | | 374 |
| **Vase,** Tan, Matte Glaze, Rounded, 7¾ In. | | 184 |
| **Vase,** Utopian, Blue, Incised Yellow Flowers, Tapered, 13 In. | | 345 |
| **Vase,** Utopian, Brown, Orange Flowers, Sara Timberlake, 7 In. | | 98 |
| **Vase,** Women's Faces, Flowers, Red, Blue Yellow Blended Glazes, 11¾ In. | | 345 |
| **Wall Pocket,** Turnip Man, Green Matte Glaze, Impressed Owensart, 11 x 6 In. | *illus* | 748 |

**OYSTER PLATES** were popular from the 1880s. Each course at dinner was served in a special dish. The oyster plate had indentations shaped like oysters. Usually six oysters were held on a plate. There is no greater value to a plate with more oysters, although that myth continues to haunt antiques dealers. There are other plates for shellfish, including cockle plates and whelk plates. The appropriately shaped indentations are part of the design of these dishes.

| | | |
|---|---|---|
| **5 Wells,** Brown, Gold, Net Ground, c.1890, 8¾ In., 10 Piece | | 590 |
| **5 Wells,** Cobalt Blue, Gilt, Round, Haviland, 8¼ In. | | 395 |
| **5 Wells,** Crescent Plate, Oriental Design | *illus* | 272 |
| **5 Wells,** Haviland, Presidential, Rutherford B. Hayes, Blue, Brown, c.1800, 8½ In. | | 3660 |
| **5 Wells,** Neptune & Mermaid, Round, 9 In. | *illus* | 206 |
| **5 Wells,** Rose Shading White, Gilt Weimar Porzellan, Germany, 8⅜ In., 12 Piece | | 163 |
| **5 Wells,** Tulip Pattern, Luneville, Marked, c.1892, 9½ In. | | 65 |
| **5 Wells,** Turkey, Gilt Trim, 9 In. | | 395 |
| **6 Wells,** Fan Shape, Ribbed, Lavender, Pink, 10 x 9 In. | | 395 |
| **6 Wells,** Indian Pattern, Red, Blue, S. Fielding & Co., c.1880, 9½ In. | | 595 |
| **6 Wells,** Pale Flowers, Raised Scrolling, Gilt, Excelsior, Germany, c.1895, 8½ In. | | 120 |
| **6 Wells,** Pink, Yellow, Oscar & Edgar Gutherz, Limoges, c.1890, 8 In., 6 Piece | | 960 |

**Painting,** Oil On Wood, Bull, Standing, Gilt Frame, 1900s, 9 x 12 In.
$660

Garth's Auctioneers & Appraisers

**Painting,** Reverse On Glass, Man, 3 Women, In Front Of Temple, Chinese, Frame, c.1900, 24 x 19 In.
$120

Cowan's Auctions

**Painting,** Tibetan, Bodhisattva, Buddha, Deities, Brocade Silk Borders, Metal Frame, 1800s, 32½ x 24 In.
$236

Brunk Auctions

**Pairpoint,** Lamp, Puffy, 4 Roses, Trellis
Ground, Tree Trunk Base, 10¾ In.
$2,726

James D. Julia Auctioneers

**Pairpoint,** Lamp, Puffy, Apple Blossoms,
Bees, Butterflies, Tree Trunk Base, c.1910,
23 In.
$23,040

Rago Arts & Auction Center

**PADEN CITY GLASS MANUFACTURING COMPANY** was established in 1916 at Paden City, West Virginia. The company made over twenty different colors of glass. The firm closed in 1951. Paden City Pottery may be listed in Dinnerware.

| | |
|---|---|
| **Biscayne,** Berry Bowl, 5⅜ In. | 8 |
| **Biscayne,** Bowl, Vegetable, 8¾ In. | 28 |
| **Biscayne,** Cup & Saucer | 12 |
| **Biscayne,** Plate, Dinner, 10 In. | 12 |
| **Buttercup,** Cup & Saucer | 18 |
| **Buttercup,** Plate, Dinner, 10 In. | 15 |
| **Buttercup,** Plate, Salad, Square, 8 x 8 In. | 16 |
| **Crow's Foot,** Compote, Red, 3½ x 6 In. | 54 |
| **Gadroon,** Ashtray, Mulberry, 10 In. | 34 |
| **Gadroon,** Bowl, Mulberry, Oval, 10 In. | 35 |
| **Gadroon,** Cup & Saucer, Mulberry | 30 |
| **Gadroon,** Plate, Mulberry, 6⅜ In. | 9 |
| **Gazebo,** Bowl, Flat Edge, 13 In. | 35 |
| **Ivy,** Bowl, Vegetable, 8¾ In. | 38 |
| **Ivy,** Cup & Saucer, Square Base | 12 |
| **Ivy,** Platter, 13¾ In. | 35 |
| **Ivy,** Soup, Dish, Square, 8 x 8 In. | 14 |
| **Lela Bird,** Vase, Ebony, Elliptical, 1930s, 8 x 5½ In. | 165 |
| **Lido,** Plate, Salad, 7¼ In. | 16 |
| **Modern Orchid,** Bowl, Vegetable, Lid, 9 In. | 85 |
| **Modern Orchid,** Gravy Boat | 38 |
| **Modern Orchid,** Platter, 13⅞ In. | 45 |
| **Modern Orchid,** Salt & Pepper | 45 |
| **Party Line,** Tumbler, Pink, 5 In. | 17 |
| **Provincial,** Cup & Saucer | 18 |
| **Tree,** Toothpick Holder, c.1918 | 34 |

**PAINTINGS** listed in this book are not works by major artists but rather decorative paintings on ivory, board, or glass that would be of interest to the average collector. Watercolors on paper are listed under Picture. To learn the value of an oil painting by a listed artist, you must contact an expert in that area.

| | |
|---|---|
| **Acrylic On Canvas,** Camels Sold Here, Wook Kyung Choi, c.1968, 26 x 25 In. | 6765 |
| **Acrylic On Canvas,** Liberty Head, Peter Max, Frame, 51 x 51 In. | 12000 |
| **Acrylic On Canvas,** Lipstick On My Man, George Rodrigue, 2004, 20 x 16 In. | 23370 |
| **Miniature,** Oil On Ivory, Child, Blue Dress, Pinafore, Gilt Case, Oval, Mrs. M. Russell, 3 In. | 625 |
| **Miniature,** Oil On Ivory, Woman, Bonnet, Round Frame, Courtois, 1784, 2¾ In. | 188 |
| **Miniature,** Oil On Ivory, Woman, Oval Gilt Metal Frame, 2⅝ x 1¼ In. | 250 |
| **Miniature,** Oil On Ivory, Woman, Ruffled Collar, Round Frame, Lucas, 1½ In. | 250 |
| **Oil On Board,** Bay Thoroughbred In Stable, Gilbert Cattley, 1946, 12½ x 17 In. | 120 |
| **Oil On Board,** Bell Bank Covered Bridge, Winter Landscape, D.K. Park, 13 x 24 In. | 338 |
| **Oil On Board,** Children Playing In Grass, H. Massmann, 1940, 26 x 29 In. | 660 |
| **Oil On Board,** Glass Factory, Landscape, Frame, 1800s, 12 x 19 In. | 1180 |
| **Oil On Board,** Harem Scene, Fred Green Carpenter, Frame, 15 x 18 In. | 7500 |
| **Oil On Board,** Interior Of Artists Studio, Gustav Goetsch, 1962, 7 x 9 In. | 850 |
| **Oil On Board,** Landscape, Stream, Fall, Edmund Wuerpel, 12 x 14 In. | 600 |
| **Oil On Board,** Missouri Cottage, Frank Nuderscher, 12 x 16 In. | 800 |
| **Oil On Board,** Moonlight, Mountains, Frank Nuderscher, 8 x 10 In. | 1200 |
| **Oil On Board,** Nude, Sitting On Rock, Ocean, Joseph Tomanek, 10 x 14 In. | 2000 |
| **Oil On Board,** Old Toll Bridge From Portsmouth To New Castle, 1882, 8 x 10 In. | 4800 |
| **Oil On Canvas,** 2 Cows, Creek, Landscape, Carved Frame, c.1900, 14 x 21 In. | 277 |
| **Oil On Canvas,** 3 Children, Frame, c.1840, 30 x 25 In. | 780 |
| **Oil On Canvas,** Apple Blossoms Over New England Farm, c.1940, 24 x 36 In. | 1003 |
| **Oil On Canvas,** Atop Of World, Barefoot Boy, On Hill, J.F. Sloan, c.1930, 24 x 20 In. | 4320 |
| **Oil On Canvas,** Basket, Fruit, Frame, c.1850, 24 x 32 In. | 960 |
| **Oil On Canvas,** Boy, Holding Grape Cluster, New Eng., Frame, c.1830, 25 x 21 In. | 720 |
| **Oil On Canvas,** Boy, Holding Sword, Dog, Landscape, Joseph Goodhue, 40 x 30 In. | 8610 |
| **Oil On Canvas,** Boys, Swimming, Boat, Carl Vilhelm Larsen, Frame, 1916, 8 x 11 In. | 270 |
| **Oil On Canvas,** Captain Pym, John Hoppner, 29 x 24 In. | 2250 |
| **Oil On Canvas,** Classical Allegory, George Herzog, Ebony Frame, 38 x 68 In. | 7680 |
| **Oil On Canvas,** Cottage, Sheep, Heinrich Steinike, Frame, 34 x 42 In. | 10000 |
| **Oil On Canvas,** Cow, Head Over Fence, c.1890, 36 x 28 In. | 688 |
| **Oil On Canvas,** Cows In Summer Pasture, C. Loveridge, Carved Frame, 1894, 18 x 24 In. | 1560 |

| | |
|---|---|
| **Oil On Canvas,** Cows, Max Stern, c.1925, 15 7/8 x 24 1/2 In. | 594 |
| **Oil On Canvas,** English Border Collie, Pointing, 1900s, 20 x 24 In. | 450 |
| **Oil On Canvas,** Fishing Boat Entering Harbor, Stormy Water, Frame, 23 x 35 In. | 1920 |
| **Oil On Canvas,** Gentleman, England, c.1810, 30 x 25 In. | 390 |
| **Oil On Canvas,** Gentleman, Frame, c.1810, 28 3/4 x 24 1/2 In. | 390 |
| **Oil On Canvas,** Gentleman, Seated, c.1840, Gilt Frame, 27 1/2 x 45 In. | 461 |
| **Oil On Canvas,** Girl With Music By The Sea, Waldo Pierce, c.1945, 30 x 25 In. | 4720 |
| **Oil On Canvas,** Girl, Standing, White Dress, Frame, c.1820, 48 x 36 In. | 875 |
| **Oil On Canvas,** Girl, White Dress, England, Frame, c.1890, 30 x 25 In. | 461 |
| **Oil On Canvas,** Green-Eyed Cat Beside Tree, C. Hughes, c.1900, 12 x 10 In. | 660 |
| **Oil On Canvas,** Guitar Player, R. Emmett Owen, c.1945, 50 x 40 In. | 2125 |
| **Oil On Canvas,** Hayfield, Covered Bridge, G. Miesse, 1891, 11 1/2 x 24 In. | 100 |
| **Oil On Canvas,** Indian Village Scene, George Biddle, Frame, 1960, 25 x 30 In. | 688 |
| **Oil On Canvas,** Island Camp, Evening, Nathaniel Berry, Frame, c.1915, 10 x 14 In. | 540 |
| **Oil On Canvas,** Japanese Cherry Blossoms, Gustav Goetsch, 1951, 22 x 18 In. | 450 |
| **Oil On Canvas,** Judgment Of Paris, Louis Grell, 1937, 55 1/2 x 48 1/2 In. | 2300 |
| **Oil On Canvas,** King Edward VII Coronation Run, Nautical, Frame, 1902, 24 x 36 In. | 1375 |
| **Oil On Canvas,** Landscape Meadow, Stream, c.1860, 7 3/4 x 9 In. | 300 |
| **Oil On Canvas,** Landscape, E. Masters, Giltwood Frame, c.1895, 16 x 12 In. | 390 |
| **Oil On Canvas,** Landscape, Sheep, C.W. Oswald, Giltwood Frame, c.1895, 10 x 8 In. | 240 |
| **Oil On Canvas,** Little Red Riding Hood, Wolf, Forest, Cal Distel, 1924, 10 x 7 In. | 246 |
| **Oil On Canvas,** Lobstering, Boat, Sea, Clouds, Walter Franklin Lansil, 14 x 24 In. | 2280 |
| **Oil On Canvas,** Monks, Drinking, Around Table, G. Schills, Frame, 22 x 18 In. | 452 |
| **Oil On Canvas,** Moonlit Water, Classical Buildings, Gondola, Marie, 34 x 45 In. | 230 |
| **Oil On Canvas,** Quarry, New Hope, Pa., Frame, 1949, 30 x 25 In. | 1875 |
| **Oil On Canvas,** Sisters, Kitten In Parlor, Elliott Daingerfield, 1883, 16 x 24 In. | 7930 |
| **Oil On Canvas,** Snow On Washington Square, New York, Bela DeTirefort, 1938, 14 x 11 In. | 518 |
| **Oil On Canvas,** St. Nicholas, Fireplace, Bag Of Toys, Frame, c.1900, 36 x 24 In. | 390 |
| **Oil On Canvas,** Sunset, M.K. Hurley, 1900s, 23 x 35 In. | 738 |
| **Oil On Canvas,** The Dogana, Venice, Alfred Pollentine, 16 x 24 In. | 3200 |
| **Oil On Canvas,** Venetian Canal, Warren Sheppard, c.1920, 20 x 30 In. | 3125 |
| **Oil On Canvas,** View Of The Bay Of Naples, Neapolitan School, c.1900, 20 x 31 In. | 3750 |
| **Oil On Canvas,** Whaleback Light With Passing Sailboats, Black Frame, 1927, 12 x 19 In. | 900 |
| **Oil On Canvas,** Woman In Gold Beige Chiffon Dress, c.1920, 35 x 25 In. | 1020 |
| **Oil On Canvas,** Woman, Cows, Landscape, Giltwood Frame, c.1895, 27 x 22 In. | 215 |
| **Oil On Canvas,** Woman, Seated, Book, Dog, Bridge, Continental, Frame, 19 3/4 x 12 In. | 560 |
| **Oil On Canvas,** Yellow Cottage, James Michalopoulos, Frame, 1991, 24 x 30 In. | 5166 |
| **Oil On Canvas,** Yellows, Flowers, Still Life, LRC, 24 x 25 In. | 263 |
| **Oil On Canvas,** Young Boy With Spaniel, Frame, 22 x 20 In. | 2400 |
| **Oil On Canvas,** Young Boy, Seated, Peeling Apple, c.1860, 36 x 31 In. | 660 |
| **Oil On Canvas,** Young Woman In Black, Frame, c.1830, 33 x 28 In. | 600 |
| **Oil On Cloth,** Thangka, Buddha, Attendants, Holding Varja, Nepal, 1800s, 35 x 21 In. | 81 |
| **Oil On Leather,** Orpheus, British School, Gilt, Glazed, Frame, 10 3/4 x 7 In. | 584 |
| **Oil On Linen,** Autumn Landscape, Karl A. Buehr, Gilt Frame, 1923, 25 x 30 In. | 1673 |
| **Oil On Masonite,** Drought, Dried Field, Man Kneeling, Joseph Paul Vorst, 30 x 25 In. | 25000 |
| **Oil On Masonite,** Salvatore, Valparaiso, Emil Eugen Holzhauer, 1965, 27 x 14 In. | 657 |
| **Oil On Panel,** 5 Nuns Strolling On Normandy Coast, A. Gautier, France, 9 x 13 In. | 2300 |
| **Oil On Panel,** Landscape, Indians, Hudson River School, Octagonal Frame, 9 x 8 In. | 1250 |
| **Oil On Panel,** Still-Life With Grapes, W. Youkins, c.1960, 5 x 7 In. | 420 |
| **Oil On Panel,** Winter In Quebec City, C. Anthony Law, c.1980, 14 x 17 In. | 1320 |
| **Oil On Paper,** Portrait Of A Man, Guy Pene Du Bois, c.1940, 22 x 18 In. | 8750 |
| **Oil On Tin,** Gentleman, Wood Frame, c.1860, 12 1/2 x 10 1/2 In. | 300 |
| **Oil On Wood,** Bull, Standing, Gilt Frame, 1900s, 9 x 12 In. ..............................*illus* | 660 |
| **Oil On Wood,** Le Vieux Carre, New Orleans Harbor, Armorials, c.1950, 36 x 36 In. | 6457 |
| **Panel,** Oil On Canvas, Louis XVI Style, Instruments, Flowers, 1900s, 44 x 12 In., Pair | 676 |
| **Reverse On Glass,** Man, 3 Women, In Front Of Temple, Chinese, Frame, c.1900, 24 x 19 In. *illus* | 120 |
| **Tibetan,** Bodhisattva, Buddha, Deities, Brocade Silk Borders, Metal Frame, 1800s, 32 1/2 x 24 In. ....*illus* | 236 |

**PAIRPOINT** Manufacturing Company started in 1880 in New Bedford, Massachusetts. It soon joined with the glassworks nearby and made glass, silver-plated pieces, and lamps. Reverse-painted glass shades and molded shades known as "puffies" were part of the production until the 1930s. The company reorganized and changed its name several times but is still working today. Items listed here are glass or glass and metal. Silver-plated pieces are listed under Silver Plate.

| | |
|---|---|
| **Bell,** Peachblow, Applied Swirled Handle, Blown Teardrop, 1973, 11 1/2 In. | 104 |
| **Biscuit Jar,** Flowers, Maroon Body, 6-Sided, Silver Base, Rim, Lid, 8 1/2 In. | 177 |

---

---

**Pairpoint,** Lamp, Puffy, Rose & Butterfly, Signed, 22 x 14 In.
$5,175

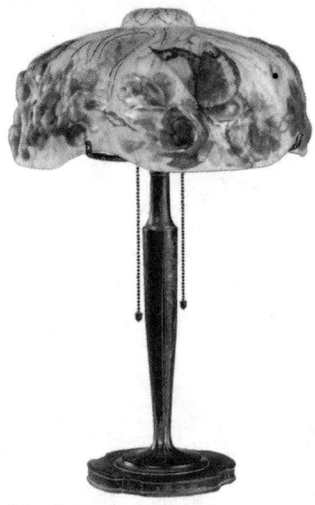

Cottone Auctions

---

**Pairpoint,** Lamp, Sailing Ships, Patina, Signed, 15 x 8 1/2 In.
$1,208

Cottone Auctions

P

**Pairpoint,** Pickle Castor, Silver Plate, Enamel, Cranberry Glass, Marked, c.1880, 12 In.
$313

Heritage Auction Galleries

**Paper,** Book, Nurse Nancy, Little Golden Book, Kathryn Jackson, Johnson & Johnson Band-Aids, 1952
$400

Aleph-Bet Books

**Paper,** Book, Pop-Up, Little Black Sambo, Hardcover, Blue Ribbon Press, 1934, 4 x 5 In., 60 Pages
$411

WITH "POP-UP" PICTURE

Hake's Americana & Collectibles

| | |
|---|---:|
| **Bowl,** Amethyst, Applied Foot, Controlled Bubble Stem, c.1930, 6¼ x 12 In. | 138 |
| **Bowl,** Cut Glass, 32-Point Hobstars, 3¾ x 8½ In. | 395 |
| **Box,** Lid, Flowers, Hinge, 6 In. | 160 |
| **Candle Lamp,** Puffy, Pansies, Wooden Baluster Base, 10¼ In. | 518 |
| **Cologne Bottle,** Nevada, Cut, 5 In. | 85 |
| **Compote,** Cut Prisms, Fans, Fluted Center, Notched, Sawtooth Edge, 6½ x 11 In. | 230 |
| **Compote,** Undulating Bowl, Ruby Swirl Extending From Center, Clear Foot, 5 x 8 In. | 174 |
| **Finger Bowl,** Underplate, Gloss Glaze, Burmese, 6 In. | 144 |
| **Goblet,** Water, Green Faceted, Ribbon & Flower Swag, Stemmed, 9¾ In., 8 Piece | 690 |
| **Ladle,** Silver Plate, Cut Glass Handle, Engraved Stem, Lobed Bowl, c.1900, 13½ In. | 62 |
| **Lamp,** 2-Light, Bombay Shade, Nautical Scene, Sails, Shells, Ribbed Base, 22 x 16 In. | 1353 |
| **Lamp,** Canada Geese, Silvered Metal, Copper, Round Shade, 16 x 20 | 2125 |
| **Lamp,** Electric, Flowered Vassar Shade, 4-Sided, Cupid Style Base, Metal, Marble, 15 In. | 403 |
| **Lamp,** Lansdowne Shade, Horses, Wagon, Farm, Church, Trees, Copper Base, 20 In. | 1215 |
| **Lamp,** Mantel, Coraline Bluebirds, Pond, Blue To Clear, Walnut Base, 19 In., Pair | 1541 |
| **Lamp,** Painted, Trees, Birds, Butterflies, Metal Urn, 21 In. | 1777 |
| **Lamp,** Puffy Flowers, Pink, Yellow, Hummingbird, Ribbed White Ground, 22½ In. | 2370 |
| **Lamp,** Puffy Tulips, Red, Yellow, White, Green Ground, Gold Trim, Signed, 15 In. | 9480 |
| **Lamp,** Puffy, 4 Roses, Trellis Ground, Tree Trunk Base, 10¾ In. *illus* | 2726 |
| **Lamp,** Puffy, Apple Blossoms, Bees, Butterflies, Tree Trunk Base, c.1910, 23 In. *illus* | 23040 |
| **Lamp,** Puffy, Butterflies, Daisies, Mottled Red, Green & Purple, Gold Metal Base, 12 In. | 2133 |
| **Lamp,** Puffy, Devonshire, Roses, Hummingbirds, Gilt Metal Base, 23 x 14 In. | 2125 |
| **Lamp,** Puffy, Flowers, Pink Purple, Reverse Painted Trellis, 23½ In. | 1896 |
| **Lamp,** Puffy, Reverse Painted Shade, Flowers, Frosted, Gilt Stem, c.1910, 7 x 14 In. | 5938 |
| **Lamp,** Puffy, Reverse Painted, Yellow, Pink, Flowers, Black Ground, 14½ In. | 2133 |
| **Lamp,** Puffy, Rose & Butterfly, Signed, 23 x 14 In. *illus* | 5175 |
| **Lamp,** Puffy, Rose Tree, Butterflies, Domed, Baluster Base, Spread Foot, 16 In. | 1840 |
| **Lamp,** Puffy, Rose, Green Leaf Ground, Silver Plated Base, 23 In. | 9480 |
| **Lamp,** Reverse Painted Glass, Winter Forest, Amber Sky, Bronze Base, 18 In. | 1035 |
| **Lamp,** Reverse Painted Shade, Figures, Landscape, Cinched Waist, Tapered Base, 22 In. | 1150 |
| **Lamp,** Reverse Painted Shade, Garden Of Allah, Bronze 3-Part Base, 22 In. | 2645 |
| **Lamp,** Reverse Painted Shade, Parrot, Tulip, Metal Base, 1920s, 18½ x 13 In. | 1250 |
| **Lamp,** Reverse Painted, Autumn Landscape, Domed Shade, W. Macy, 1920s, 22 x 18 In. | 2750 |
| **Lamp,** Reverse Painted, Bird, Flowers, Leaves, Berries, Black Ground, 22¼ In. | 3258 |
| **Lamp,** Reverse Painted, Brown, Ships, Sea, Sunset, Wooden Base, 20¾ In. | 1540 |
| **Lamp,** Reverse Painted, Glass Domed Shade, Bronze Base, Signed, c.1910, 17½ In. | 896 |
| **Lamp,** Reverse Painted, Melon Ribbed Shape, White, Roses, Artichoke Base, 21½ In. | 2370 |
| **Lamp,** Reverse Painted, Sailing Ships, Sea, Clouds, Signed F. Mayo, 22 In. | 4147 |
| **Lamp,** Reverse Painted, Seville Shade, Tropical Scene, Signed Hirshel, c.1910, 27 x 16 In. | 1476 |
| **Lamp,** Reverse Painted, Shepherd, Sheep, Landscape, Village, Ocean, 23½ In. | 2014 |
| **Lamp,** Reverse Painted, Sunflower, Leaves, Button Form, Tapered Base, 4-Footed, 20 In. | 1067 |
| **Lamp,** Sailing Ships, Patina, Signed, 15 x 8½ In. *illus* | 1208 |
| **Lamp,** Turino Shade, Venetian Harbor, Oriental Carpet, 4 Spider Arms, Square Base, 22 In. | 5036 |
| **Perfume Bottle,** Figural, Globular, Controlled Bubbles, Elongated Bird Stopper, 12 In. | 259 |
| **Pickle Castor,** Silver Plate, Enamel, Cranberry Glass, Marked, c.1880, 12 In. *illus* | 313 |
| **Pitcher,** Duck, Landscape, Tan Ground, Gold Enamel Highlights, 12 In. | 150 |
| **Vase,** Dark Blue, Flared Rim, Pedestal, Clear Sphere, 14 In. | 300 |
| **Vase,** Peachblow, Trumpet, Scalloped Rim, White Rigaree, 11¾ In. | 58 |
| **Vase,** Rib Optic, Green, Clear Bubble Ball, c.1940, 11 In., Pair | 92 |

**PALMER COX,** *Brownies, see Brownies category.*

**PAPER** collectibles, including almanacs, catalogs, children's books, some greeting cards, stock certificates, and other paper ephemera, are listed here. Paper calendars are listed separately in the Calendar category. Paper items may be found in many other sections, such as Christmas and Movie.

| | |
|---|---:|
| **Birth & Baptism,** Printed, Illuminated, Frame, Wm. Maybaugh, Lancaster, Pa., 1832, 16 x 13 In. | 59 |
| **Birth Record,** Pen, Ink, Watercolor, Angels, Dove, Book, Roswell Putnam, 1840, 9 x 7 In. | 180 |
| **Birth Record,** Pen, Watercolor, Edmund Gebert, Multicolor, Geometric, 1835, 6¾ x 9 In. | 142 |
| **Book,** Little Golden Book, Little Red Hen, 1954, 8 x 6¾ In. | 11 |
| **Book,** Nurse Nancy, Little Golden Book, Kathryn Jackson, Johnson & Johnson Band-Aids, 1952 *illus* | 400 |
| **Book,** Pop-Up, Little Black Sambo, Hardcover, Blue Ribbon Press, 1934, 4 x 5 In., 60 Pages *illus* | 411 |
| **Bookplate,** Hasty Pudding Library, Harvard, Book, Theodore Lyman, 1809, 5 x 4 In., Pair | 360 |
| **Bookplate,** Pen, Ink, Alphabet, Birds, Flower, Inscribed Jacob Kolb March 14, 1821, 4 x 7 In. | 270 |
| **Bookplate,** Pen, Ink, Watercolor, Stylized Tulip, 1828, 6½ x 3½ In. | 3840 |

| | |
|---|---|
| **Bookplate,** Watercolor, Ink, Heart, Flowers, Arches, Barbara Horner, 6 ½ x 3 ¾ In. ....................... | 750 |
| **Bookplate,** Watercolor, Ink, Nancy K. Horst, March 18th, 1885, Frame, 5 ¾ x 4 In. ....................... | 94 |
| **Bookplate,** Watercolor, Ink, Property Of Ann Mariah Kintzer, Bucks County, Pa., 1827, 7 In. ...... | 938 |
| **Bookplate,** Watercolor, Orange, Brown Designs, Signed Christian Rayer, 1786, Frame, 6 x 4 In.. | 300 |
| **Broadside,** Clearing Out At Cost, Chester, January 7, 1885, 22 x 13 In. ..................................... | 59 |
| **Calligraphy,** Couplet, Cursive, Gilt, Yu Youren, Framed, Glazed, Chinese, 52 x 12 In................... | 593 |
| **Certificate,** Birth & Baptismal, Printed, Illuminated, Scrivener, 1812, 13 x 16 In. .................... | 1416 |
| **Certificate,** Membership, Salem Marine Society, Peabody, 1863, Framed, 15 x 17 In. ................ | 270 |
| **Certificate,** Reward Of Merit, Printed, Multicolor, Bird, Flowers, 1857, 8 ¼ x 5 ¾ In................ | 153 |
| **Comic Book,** Incredible Hulk, No. 1, May 1962, First Appearance, Marvel Comic ..............*illus* | 4877 |
| **Confirmation Record,** German Text, Jacob Heller, Frame, 1838, 9 ½ x 7 ½ In. .......................... | 49 |
| **Cutwork,** 2 Horses, Under Trees, Paper Backing, Rollo Custer, Aged 13 Years, 10 In. ............... | 1610 |
| **Cutwork,** Circles, Stylized Stars, Pineapples, Round, 8-Scallop Edge, Frame, c.1850, 9 ½ In...... | 288 |
| **Cutwork,** Farmhouse, 2 Story, Wraparound Porch, Trees, Black, White, Frame, 8 x 9 In. ........... | 575 |
| **Cutwork,** House, Gothic Style, 2 Trees, Birds, Dogs, Paper Backing, Gilt Frame, 9 x 11 In. ....... | 575 |
| **Cutwork,** Love Token, Heart In Hand, Blue & Green Woven Accents, Frame, c.1880, 7 x 6 In. ...... | 690 |
| **Etching,** La Galerie Notre-Dame, Signed, Charles Meryon, c.1845, 15 ⅝ x 10 ⅝ In. ................ | 594 |
| **Fares,** Family Record, Temple, Trees, Hairwork, Evansville, Indiana, Watercolor, 16 x 11 In........ | 360 |
| **Fraktur,** Angels, Heart, Verse, Yellow, Watercolor, Ink, Meritta Miller, 1823, 12 x 15 In............. | 1625 |
| **Fraktur,** Arches, Topiary, Verse, Watercolor, Ink, Jacob McNulty, 1787, 11 x 18 In. ................ | 12500 |
| **Fraktur,** Bird, Flower Branch, Heart Stem, Watercolor, Pen & Ink, Pa., c.1820, 3 x 3 In............. | 570 |
| **Fraktur,** Birth Of Christ, Watercolor, Ink, John F.W. Stahr, Pa., Frame, 1835, 16 x 12 In............ | 2640 |
| **Fraktur,** Birth Record, Ink, Watercolor, Jacob Heinle, 1797, 8 x 13 In. .............................. | 1200 |
| **Fraktur,** Birth Record, Multicolor Flower Reserves, Verse, 1829, 7 ½ x 5 ½ In. ...................... | 443 |
| **Fraktur,** Birth Record, Printed, Colored, Catharina Mauerlin, 1792, Maryland, 13 x 16 In.......... | 3840 |
| **Fraktur,** Birth Record, Tulips, Parrots, Watercolor, Ink, E. Wissler, Frame, c.1802, 13 x 16 In..... | 6600 |
| **Fraktur,** Birth Record, Watercolor, Clarissa J. Swallow, 1814, 10 x 8 In.............................. | 360 |
| **Fraktur,** Birth, Baptism, Turkeys, Tulips, Watercolor, A. Scherertz, Va., 1819, 13 x 8 In............ | 27600 |
| **Fraktur,** Birth, Baptism, Watercolor, David Alder, Hearts, Angels, 1792, 12 x 14 In. ................ | 3220 |
| **Fraktur,** Birth, Blousy Angel, Ink, Watercolor, Johan Georg Schliger, Pa., 1794, 13 x 17 In......... | 2040 |
| **Fraktur,** Birth, Death, Birds, Flowers, Watercolor, Gold Leaf, John Kelley, 1847, 10 x 8 In. .......... | 32200 |
| **Fraktur,** Bookplate, Bird, Flowers, Leaves, Watercolor, Lancaster County, 1826, 5 x 3 In. ......... | 1770 |
| **Fraktur,** Eagle, Spread Wing, Watercolor, Pa., c.1830, 3 ⅝ x 6 ½ In................................... | 1620 |
| **Fraktur,** Geometrics, Vining, Watercolor, Ink, Christina Knisley, 1803, 7 ½ x 13 In................ | 1375 |
| **Fraktur,** House Blessing, Watercolor, Ink, George & Catherine Gundrum, Pa., c.1835, 11 x 9 In. | 704 |
| **Fraktur,** Marriage, Family Record, Sun, Watercolor, J. Van Minian, Pa., c.1816, 15 x 12 In. ........ | 345 |
| **Fraktur,** Monstrous Great Snake, Anaconda, Watercolor, Pen, Pa., c.1824, 15 x 15 In. .............. | 3300 |
| **Fraktur,** Parrot, Watercolor, Pen & Ink, Pennsylvania, Frame, c.1820, 4 x 3 In. .......................... | 2640 |
| **Fraktur,** Red House, Flowers, Birds, Watercolor, Schwenkfelder, 12 x 7 ⅜ In......................... | 1298 |
| **Fraktur,** Religious Text, Birds, Hearts, Watercolor, Ink, Pa., Frame, 1824, 12 x 10 In. ............ | 5040 |
| **Fraktur,** Tulip, Watercolor, Ink, Caroline Clutter, Born Aug 29th 1830, Frame, 10 x 8 In. ........ | 3738 |
| **Illustration,** Death Of Buddha, Mourning Followers, Gold, India, Frame, 21 x 15 In. ............... | 242 |
| **Indenture,** Ink On Vellum, Berks County Pa., 1760, 19 ½ x 26 In.................................... | 90 |
| **Manuscript Page,** Courtly Scene, Prince, Attendants, Full Moon, India, Frame, 11 x 7 In. ......... | 299 |
| **Memorial,** Death, Watercolor, Angus Dei Lamb, Angels, Elisabeth Schumann, 13 x 13 In. .......... | 270 |
| **Moravian Love Note,** Watercolor, Ink, Fr. Ritter, Frame, 1837, 3 ½ x 5 In.................................. | 375 |
| **Page,** Book Of Hours, Dragon, Pen, Ink, Paint, Gilding, Vellum, Frame, c.1350, 12 x 10 In......... | 600 |
| **Sign,** Girl, Snow, Cardboard, Die Cut, Embossed, Multicolor, Germany, Victorian, 34 In............. | 502 |

**PAPER DOLLS** were probably inspired by the pantins, or jumping jacks, made in eighteenth-century Europe. By the 1880s, sheets of printed paper dolls and clothes were being made. The first paper doll books were made in the 1920s. Collectors prefer uncut sheets or books or boxed sets of paper dolls. Prices are about half as much if the pages have been cut.

| | |
|---|---|
| **Baby Tender Love,** Doll, Outfits, Whitman, 1971, Uncut.................................... | 10 |
| **Barbie,** Super Star, Doll, 4 Pages Of Clothing, Whitman, 1970s, Uncut.................... | 40 |
| **Bride,** Whitman, 1970s, 12 x 9 ½ In., Uncut................................................ | 26 |
| **Brother Dan,** Knickers, Suspenders, 2-Sided, 6 ¾ In. ...................................... | 10 |
| **Bugs Bunny & Honey Bunny,** 18 Outfits, Golden, 1983, Uncut ............................. | 25 |
| **Bundle Of Love,** 6 Pages Of Clothes, Whitman, 1959, Uncut............................... | 45 |
| **Dennis The Menace,** Backyard Picnic, Whitman Publishing, 1960 .......................... | 42 |
| **Doris Day,** Magic Stay On Clothes, Sportswear, Bathing Suit, Folder, 1957................ | 40 |
| **Jayne's Doll,** Blond, Brunette, Jayne's Tonic Vermifuge, Pat. July 30, 1895............... | 35 |
| **Little Nurse & Little Doctor,** Outfits, Reuben H. Lija & Co., 1949, 14 In., Uncut....... | 85 |
| **Mother Goose,** Saalfield No. 4409, 5 Dolls, 1957, 13 ½ x 10 ½ In. ...................... | 49 |
| **Old Woman,** Lives In Shoe, 9 Dolls, Outfits, 14 Pages, Saalfield, 1960..................... | 19 |

**Paper,** Comic Book, Incredible Hulk, No. 1, May 1962, First Appearance, Marvel Comic
$4,877

Hake's Americana & Collectibles

**TIP**
*A quick way to keep newspaper clippings is to photocopy them on acid-free paper.*

**Paperweight,** Lundberg, Orange Flower, Leafy Scroll, Purple, Blue, Engraved, 1974, 2 In.
$80

Humler & Nolan

**Paperweight,** Pinchbeck, Gold Scene, Man, Horse, Man & Woman Seated, Dog, Oval, 3 ¼ In.
$304

James D. Julia Auctioneers

P

**Paperweight,** St. Louis, Amber Glass, 5 Faceted Windows, Clematis, Leaves, Stem, 2½ In.
$8,888

James D. Julia Auctioneers

**Paperweight,** St. Louis, Pear, Clear Square Base, 3 In.
$2,133

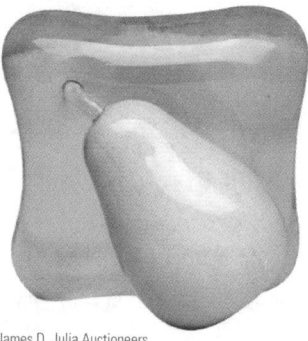

James D. Julia Auctioneers

**Paperweight,** Stankard, Paul, Glass, Raspberries, Roots, 1988, 5¼ x 2¾ In.
$5,000

Rago Arts & Auction Center

| | |
|---|---:|
| **Patty Duke,** 2 Dolls, 41 Pieces Of Clothes, Whitman, 1965 | 25 |
| **Peggy & Peter,** Queen Holden, Big Paper Doll Book, No. 9041, 1962, 19 x 12 In. | 65 |
| **Skipper,** Super Teen, 4 Pages, 1980, 12¾ x 10 In., Uncut | 26 |
| **Terri & Tonya,** The Duo-Tones, Outfits, Saalfield Co., Artcraft Co., 1961, Uncut | 35 |
| **Trixie Belden,** 32-Piece Wardrobe, Whitman, Box, Punch-Out, 1979 | 20 |

**PAPERWEIGHTS** must have first appeared along with paper in ancient Egypt. Today's collectors search for every type, from the very expensive French weights of the nineteenth century to the modern artist weights or advertising pieces. The glass tops of the paperweights sometimes have been nicked or scratched, and this type of damage can be removed by polishing. Some serious collectors think this type of repair is an alteration and will not buy a repolished weight; others think it is an acceptable technique of restoration that does not change the value. Baccarat paperweights are listed separately under Baccarat.

| | |
|---|---:|
| **Advertising,** Albers Cereals & Flours, Miner Cooking, 3½ In. | 834 |
| **Advertising,** Sewer Pipe, Portland Pipe, Strongest In Market, Sewer Tile, 3 In. | 540 |
| **Advertising,** Tower Grove Brick Works, St. Louis, Eagle, Banner, Brick, Round, 4 In. | 360 |
| **Apple Shape,** Blues, Blown, Elongated Stem, Signed Hal David Berger, 8 x 4 In. | 150 |
| **Ayotte,** Rick, Blue Bird, Leaves, 1983, 3¼ In. | 1380 |
| **Ayotte,** Rick, White Flowers, Brown Bird, 1989, 3½ In. | 690 |
| **Banford,** Bob, Coral, 3 Fish, Signed, c.1885, 3¼ In. | 230 |
| **Banford,** Bob, Strawberries, c.1975, 3 In. | 460 |
| **Banford,** Bob, Sunflowers, Blue Ground, c.1995, 3½ In. | 431 |
| **Banford,** Bob, Violet Pansy, Latticinio, c.1980, 3 In. | 546 |
| **Banford,** Ray, Pink Rose, Crosshatch Cut Base, c.1980, 3½ In. | 196 |
| **Blake,** Jennie, Glass, Round, Blue Flower, 1892, 3 In. | 70 |
| **Bronze,** Foo Dog, Cub, Brocade Ball, Chinese, c.1900, 2 x 2 In. | 119 |
| **Buzzini,** Charles, Flowers, Multicolor, Signed, 1995, 3¼ In. | 920 |
| **Buzzini,** Charles, Pink Orchids, Green Striped Caterpillar, Signed, 1996, 3¼ In. | 805 |
| **Buzzini,** Chris, Blue Flowers, Signed, 1995, 3¼ In. | 575 |
| **Buzzini,** Chris, Lavender, Yellow Flower, Clear Ground, 1994, 3⅜ In. | 546 |
| **Clichy,** Circles, Green, Red, White, Pink & Blue Millefiori, 2½ In. | 1245 |
| **Clichy,** Millefiori, Canes, Pink, Blue, Green, Star Cut Base, 2¾ In. | 2251 |
| **Clichy,** Purple, White, Green, Blue Ground, Stardust, Bull's-Eye, France, 3 In. | 2370 |
| **Cristal D'Albert,** Sulphide, Jenny Lind, Scalloped Edge, 3 x 1 In. | 75 |
| **DePalma,** Anthony, Frosted Rose, 1985, 3¼ In. | 259 |
| **Glass,** Blown, Green, 2 Flowers, Vase, 4¼ In. | 60 |
| **Grubb,** Randall, Raspberries, Clear Ground, 1995, 3 In. | 518 |
| **Hand,** Pen Holding Pose, Molded, Redware, c.1880, 2 x 4½ In. | 196 |
| **Heilman,** Chris, Angelfish, Coral, Signed, 1996, 4¾ In. | 288 |
| **Kaziun,** Charles, Heart, Green Ground, Clear, Stepped Base, 2 x 1¼ In. | 219 |
| **Kaziun,** Charles, Pansy, Purple, Millefiori Ring, Blue Ground, c.1970, 2½ In. | 460 |
| **Kaziun,** Charles, Pink, Red Rose, Petals, Green Leaves, Pedestal, c.1945, 2¾ In. | 413 |
| **Kaziun,** Charles, Yellow, Red Snakes, Flowers, Blue Ground, c.1970, 2½ In. | 489 |
| **Lundberg,** Orange Flower, Leafy Scroll, Purple, Blue, Engraved, 1974, 2 In. ...............*illus* | 80 |
| **Lundberg,** Steven, Coral, Sea Scene, Twisted Blue Shell Shape, c.1975, 4 x 5 In. | 546 |
| **Lundberg,** Steven, Green Fish, Seaweed, Dots, Iridescent Ground, 1982, 3 In. | 92 |
| **Lundberg,** Steven, Yellow Dahlias, 1991, 3 In. | 460 |
| **Lundberg,** Steven, Yellow Rose, Rose Ground, 1994, 2¾ In. | 316 |
| **Murano,** Millefiori, Blue, Green, 3 x 2 In. | 159 |
| **Murano,** Millefiori, Cane Flowers, Bubbles, Gold Base, Foil Label, Italy, 2 In. | 79 |
| **Orient & Flume,** Earth Tone, Grape Pod, Snakes, 3¼ In. | 184 |
| **Parsely,** John, White Dogwood Flowers, Blue Ground, 1989, 2½ In. | 1150 |
| **Parsely,** John, Yellow, White Flowers, White Ground, 1989, 2½ In. | 748 |
| **Perthshire,** Bouquet, Multicolor, Latticinio, c.1980, 3 In. | 316 |
| **Perthshire,** Green, Yellow Parrots, Signed, 2000, 2¼ In. | 345 |
| **Perthshire,** Horse, Rider, Millefiori, Blue Ground, 1987, 3½ In. | 403 |
| **Pinchbeck,** Gold Scene, Man, Horse, Man & Woman Seated, Dog, Oval, 3¼ In. ................*illus* | 304 |
| **Reindeer,** Crystal, Emerald Green, Oland, Norway, 4¾ x 3½ In. | 65 |
| **Ritter,** Richard, Starry Night, 1970s, 5 x 5 In. | 281 |
| **Rosenfeld,** Ken, Flowers, Leaves, Multicolor, 1992, 3¼ In. | 1265 |
| **Rosenfeld,** Ken, Jonquils, Ladybugs, Clear Ground, 1997, 4¼ In. | 230 |
| **Rosenfeld,** Ken, Purple Grapes, Signed, 1996, 3¼ In. | 288 |
| **Rosenfeld,** Ken, Red Rose, Green Black Ground, Pedestal, 2000, 2½ In. | 259 |
| **Rosenfeld,** Ken, Sunflowers, Red Ground, 1998, 3¼ In. | 374 |

P

| | |
|---|---|
| **Satava,** Rick, Jellyfish, Crystal Dome, 4 ½ In. | 403 |
| **Smith,** Gordon, Purple Flowers, Desert Scene, 1997, 3 In. | 920 |
| **St. Louis,** Amber Glass, 5 Faceted Windows, Clematis, Leaves, Stem, 2 ½ In. ..............*illus* | 8888 |
| **St. Louis,** Blue, White Swirl, Foil Label, 2 ¼ x 3 ¼ In. | 161 |
| **St. Louis,** Concentric Mushroom, Blue, Green, White, Red, Lattice, 2 ½ In. | 3851 |
| **St. Louis,** Concentric Mushroom, Blue, White, Red, Lattice, 2 ¾ In. | 1066 |
| **St. Louis,** Crown, Alternating Green, White, Red, Blue, Ribbon Twists, Pedestal, 5 In. | 988 |
| **St. Louis,** Crown, White, Blue, Green, White, Lattice Ribbon Twists, 3 ⅛ In. | 1066 |
| **St. Louis,** Encased Bouquet, Red, Cobalt, Blue, Brown Overlay, 2 ¾ In. | 2962 |
| **St. Louis,** Fish Flowers, Faceted, Blue Ground, 1998, 3 In. | 863 |
| **St. Louis,** Honeycomb, Red & White, Signature Cane Center, S.L. 1974, 3 In. | 851 |
| **St. Louis,** Millefiori Flowers, Chartreuse Base, Faceted, 1997, 3 ¼ In. | 978 |
| **St. Louis,** Millefiori, Blue, Pink, Double Overlay, Green, White, Fitted Box, 3 In. | 711 |
| **St. Louis,** Millefiori, Diamond Pattern, Blue, Central Green Cane, 3 In. | 2370 |
| **St. Louis,** Mushroom, Millefiori, Spiral Rose, Latticinio Torsade, 3 In. | 2248 |
| **St. Louis,** Pansies, Millefiori Ring, Faceted, 1997, 3 ¼ In. | 690 |
| **St. Louis,** Pansy, Green Leaves, Millefiori, Star Cut Ground  2 In. | 2963 |
| **St. Louis,** Pear, Clear Square Base, 3 In. ................................................*illus* | 2133 |
| **St. Louis,** Pink White Spiral, Red, Green Ground, 1988, 3 In. | 518 |
| **St. Louis,** Red Flowers, Latticinio Basket, Signed Handle, 1997, 3 ¾ In. | 1035 |
| **St. Louis,** Scattered Canes, Blue, Pink, Green, White Stardust Canes, 3 ½ In. | 1777 |
| **St. Louis,** Star Millefiori, Double Overlay, Red, White, Fitted Box, 3 In. | 829 |
| **Stankard,** Paul, Flowers, Red, White, Blue, Roots, Root People, 1987, 6 In. | 7110 |
| **Stankard,** Paul, Glass, Raspberries, Roots, 1988, 5 ¼ x 2 ¾ In. ..........................*illus* | 5000 |
| **Stankard,** Pink Flower, Black Ground, 1972, 1 ¾ x 2 ½ In. | 625 |
| **Sulphide,** Eleanor Roosevelt, Amethyst, Faceted, 1971, 2 ½ In. | 79 |
| **Sulphide,** Lafayette, Bust, Star, Marked, c.1955, 2 In. | 75 |
| **Sulphide,** Lion, Seated, Pedestal, End Of Day Glass, Purple, Yellow, 4 ¾ In. | 119 |
| **Tarsitano,** Debbie, Butterfly, Flowers, Sand Base, c.1980, 3 ½ In. | 863 |
| **Tarsitano,** White Flowers, Circle Of Red Ladybugs, c.1990, 2 ¾ In. | 633 |
| **Trabucco,** Victor, Blue Flowers, Pink Ground Faceted, 1987, 3 ¼ In. | 403 |
| **Trabucco,** Victor, Flowers, Purple, Pink, Signed, 1996, 4 In. | 805 |
| **Ward,** Mayauel, Purple Flowers, Black Pedestal, c.1980, 3 In. | 259 |
| **Yellow Flower,** Banding, Lattice, Perthshire, Crieff, Scotland, 1 ½ x 2 ½ In. | 132 |
| **Ysart,** Paul, Pink Flower, Basket, Lattice, 2 ¾ In. | 829 |

---

**PAPIER-MACHE** is made from paper mixed with glue, chalk, and other ingredients, then molded and baked. It becomes very hard and can be painted. Boxes, trays, and furniture were made of papier-mache. Some of the nineteenth-century pieces were decorated with mother-of-pearl. Papier-mache is still being used to make small toys, figures, candy containers, boxes, and other giftwares. Furniture made of papier-mache is listed in the Furniture category.

| | |
|---|---|
| **Bust,** Milliner's Head, Woman, Roses, Stars On Cheeks, 1920, 15 In. | 330 |
| **Figure,** Blackamoor, Turbaned Man, Striped Rolled Up Pants, 68 In. | 1000 |
| **Figure,** Cherub, Gilt Painted, Inscribed, George V. Dureau, 1984, 44 x 20 In. | 1107 |
| **Figure,** Eagle, Spread Wings, 19th Century, 20 x 39 x 16 In. | 270 |
| **Head,** Carnival, Man, Painted Black Hair, Red Lips, Brown Eyes, 1900s, 15 In. | 205 |
| **Pen Case,** Kalamkar Lacquer, Multicolor Flowers, Gilt, Kashmir, 1800s, 11 In. | 59 |
| **Tray,** Black Lacquer, Flower Sprays, Oval, Stand, c.1850, 19 x 31 In. | 250 |
| **Tray,** Gilt, Mother-Of-Pearl, Eagle, Bamboo Turned Stand, 19 ½ x 31 In. | 308 |
| **Tray,** Horse & Rider, Hunting Dogs, Raised Gold Sphere Border, 23 In. | 400 |
| **Tray,** Painted, Black, Exotic Bird, Branches, Gilt Vines, Shaped, 32 x 25 In. | 345 |
| **Tray,** Painted, Peacock, Flowers, Gilt, Jennes & Bettridge, c.1850, 31 x 24 In. | 1063 |
| **Tray,** Painted, Peacocks, Fountain, Flowers, Gilt Scrolls, Serpentine, 31 x 22 In. | 805 |
| **Tray,** Victorian, Oval, Gilt, Mother-Of-Pearl Inlays, 30 In. | 125 |

---

**PARASOL,** *see Umbrella category.*

---

**PARIAN** is a fine-grained, hard-paste porcelain named for the marble it resembles. It was first made in England in 1846 and gained in favor in the United States about 1860. Figures, tea sets, vases, and other items were made of Parian at many English and American factories.

| | |
|---|---|
| **Bust,** Putto, Integral Stepped Base, 10 ¾ x 4 ½ x 5 ¾ In. | 154 |
| **Bust,** Shakespeare, Cubed Base, Impressed Numbers, 9 ¼ x 6 ½ In. | 155 |
| **Figurine,** 4 Senses, Classical Maiden, Cherub, Symbolic Object, 11 ¼ In., 4 Piece | 299 |

**Paris,** Cocoa Pot, Card Game & Mother & Child Scenes, Dog Head Spout, 10 ½ In. $182

James D. Julia Auctioneers

**Paris,** Vase, Classical Scene, Reserves, 3 Figures, Ebonized Ground, Gilt Highlights, 1800s, 20 In. $544

P

Rago Arts & Auction Center

**Pate-De-Verre,** Vase, Roses, Green, Lavender Rim, Signed, Daum, 11¾ In. $2,160

DuMouchelles Art Gallery

## Goldilocks

Goldilocks wasn't part of the story of The Three Bears until the 1880s. The story started in 1831 as a poem about three male bears and a witch. About 1850 the witch became a girl named "Silverhair." Later, she became "Goldenhair," then "Goldenlocks," and finally Goldilocks in 1888.

**Patent Model,** Washing Machine, Wood, G.M. Harris Washing Machine July 12th, 1864, 9 x 11 In. $2,250

Garth's Auctioneers & Appraisers

| | |
|---|---:|
| **Figurine,** Boy & Dog, Period Dress, Naturalistic Base, 12 In. | 150 |
| **Figurine,** Boy, Hat, Playing Cricket, Robinson & Leadbetter, c.1860, 14 In. | 475 |
| **Figurine,** Cleopatra, Nude, Snake On Arm, c.1849, 9½ In. | 175 |
| **Figurine,** Model Of Colin Minton Campbell, Standing, Hand On Compote, 19 In. | 861 |
| **Figurine,** Napoleon On Horseback, Leaf Base, Multicolor, 14½ x 13½ x 7 In. | 122 |
| **Figurine,** Woman, Seated, Arms Out, Garden, 27 In. | 711 |
| **Group,** 2 Young Children Asleep On Armchair, Titled Croisy, 15¼ In. | 1476 |
| **Group,** Cupid & Psyche, Round Base, 1800s, 6¼ x 2⅜ x 2 In. | 123 |
| **Group,** Rebekah & Isaac, England, c.1850, 22 x 15 In. | 813 |

**PARIS,** Vieux Paris, or Old Paris, is porcelain ware that is known to have been made in Paris in the eighteenth or early nineteenth century. These porcelains have no identifying mark but can be recognized by the whiteness of the porcelain and the lines and decorations. Gold decoration is often used.

| | |
|---|---:|
| **Basket,** Hexagonal, Gilt, Flowers, 6 Splayed Legs, 1800s, 9¼ x 9 In. | 185 |
| **Bowl,** Exterior River Scene, Interior Roses, Gilt Trim, 7 x 15 In. | 130 |
| **Bowl,** Metal Base, Pierced Gilt Rim, Handles, 3-Footed, Chateau De Longpre, 4 x 6 In. | 63 |
| **Centerpiece,** Corbeille, Flared Basket, 3 Raised Paw Feet, Gilt Trim, c.1850, 3¾ In. | 173 |
| **Charger,** Warriors, Fighting, Red & Black Geometric Border, 19th Century, 13 In. | 60 |
| **Cocoa Pot,** Card Game & Mother & Child Scenes, Dog Head Spout, 10½ In. *illus* | 182 |
| **Coffee & Tea Set,** Gothic Style, Cobalt Blue, Gilt, Gothic Tracery, c.1810, 4 Piece | 1159 |
| **Jug,** Children Playing, Gilt Trim, Oval, c.1800, 5 In. | 211 |
| **Lamp,** Urn Shape, Gilt, White Ground, Leaves, Flowers, Silk Shades, 27 In., Pair | 288 |
| **Plate,** Botanical, Gilt Border, Marked Iron Red Darte, 9 In., 6 Piece | 478 |
| **Plate,** Dessert, Bird, Landscape, Wide Gilt Band, Flowers, Swags.c.1810, 8 In., Pair | 258 |
| **Urn,** Couples, Balcony, Landscape, Hand Painted, Scrolled Handles, Gilt, 17⅕ In., Pair | 1875 |
| **Urn,** Multicolor Flowers, Gilt Trim, Campana Shape, Socle Foot, Raised Base, 14 In., Pair | 480 |
| **Urn,** Presentation, Topographical, City Scenes, Mask Handles, c.1839, 13 x 10 In., Pair | 1793 |
| **Vase,** Classical Scene, Reserves, 3 Figures, Ebonized Ground, Gilt Highlights, 1800s, 20 In. *illus* | 544 |
| **Vase,** Flowers, White Ground, Claret, Gilt Neck, Rim & Foot, 11 In. | 375 |
| **Vase,** Gilt Leaf Handles, Scenic Reserves, Couple Finding Cupid, Gilt Overlay, 15½ x 8 In. | 127 |
| **Vase,** Gothic Style, Gilt Tracery, Figures, Green Ground, Gilt, Handles, 1800s, 30 x 5 In., Pair | 1586 |
| **Vase,** La Faincee Du Aoede Garbe, Painted Scenes With Figures, 2 Handles, 14¼ In., Pair | 944 |
| **Vase,** Matte Lapis Lazuli Blue, Petal Rim, Pink Blossoms, Bottle Shape, c.1850, 13 In., Pair | 344 |
| **Vase,** Men, Rowboats, Waves, Whale, Bears, Flowers, Gilt Highlights, c.1850, 7 In., Pair | 480 |
| **Vase,** Painted Landscape, Bisque Woman With Flowers, Bird, Flared, Gilt Rim, 17 In. | 438 |
| **Vase,** Painted, Figure, Landscape, Champleve Base, Cover, Gilt Bronze Mounts, V. Berz, 10 In. | 437 |
| **Vase,** Rose, Waisted Necks, Grape Leaf Handles, Children Playing, 17¼ In, Pair | 418 |
| **Vase,** Snowball, Oval, Flower Encrusted, Birds, Fruit, Gilt Handles, J. Petit, 9 x 6 In., Pair | 1500 |
| **Vase,** Spill, Flowers, Cobalt Blue Ground, Gilt Trim, Scroll Base, 1800s, 13 In., Pair | 123 |
| **Vase,** Spill, Flowers, Gilt Arabesques & Handles, Deep Ruffles, Rococo Stand, 11 In., Pair | 201 |

**PATE-DE-VERRE** is an ancient technique in which glass is made by blending and refining powdered glass of different colors into molds. The process was revived by French glassmakers, especially Galle, around the end of the nineteenth century.

| | |
|---|---:|
| **Bowl,** Vines, Footed, Rousseau, 1½ x 3⅞ In. | 600 |
| **Toothpick Holder,** Blossom, Leaf, Blue, White Mottled Ground, 1¾ In. | 649 |
| **Vase,** Flowers, Pink, Green, Footed, Daum, 7 In. | 900 |
| **Vase,** Roses, Green, Lavender Rim, Signed, Daum, 11¾ In. *illus* | 2160 |

**PATENT MODELS** were required as part of a patent application for a United States patent until 1880. In 1926 the stored patent models were sold as a group by the U.S. Patent Office, and individual models are now appearing in the marketplace.

| | |
|---|---:|
| **Clothes Dryer,** Folding, Rosewood, Turned Center, Late 19th Century, 8 In. | 185 |
| **Deep Sea Diver,** Denayrouze, 3-Bolt, Regulator, Copper, Brass, 15 x 14 In. | 16940 |
| **Dental Chair,** Elevating, Mahogany, Cranking Mechanism, 1869, 16 In. | 968 |
| **Desk,** School, Wood, Cast Iron, J.W. Child's, c.1876, 11 x 11 In. | 575 |
| **Disappearing Hitching Post,** Elmer Sellers, 1898 Letter U.S. Patent Office, 17½ In. | 1200 |
| **Flour Sifter,** Walnut, Metal, James Coyle, 3 x 12 In. | 787 |
| **Plow,** Wrought Iron, Wood, 1800s, 5½ x 14 In. | 3751 |
| **Rubber Press,** George Miller, 16 x 14 In. | 1815 |
| **Washing Machine,** Cherry, Metal, Levi Holderman, c.1873, 10 x 9½ In. | 1573 |
| **Washing Machine,** Henry Yost, Dovetailed, Pine, 8 x 12 In. | 2178 |
| **Washing Machine,** Wood, G.M. Harris Washing Machine July 12th, 1864, 9 x 11 In. *illus* | 2250 |

**P**

**PATE-SUR-PATE** means paste on paste. The design was made by painting layers of slip on the ceramic piece until a relief decoration was formed. The method was developed at the Sevres factory in France about 1850. It became even more famous at the English Minton factory about 1870. It has since been used by many potters to make both pottery and porcelain wares.

| | |
|---|---|
| **Cup & Saucer,** Blue, White, Cherubs, 2 In. | 123 |
| **Ginger Jar,** Lid, Blue, Flowers, 11¾ In., Pair | 500 |
| **Lamp,** Electric, 2-Light, Female Figures, 14 In. | 1784 |
| **Plate,** Cobalt Blue, Jumping Fish, Gilt Highlights, Footed, Serpentine Border, 1800s, 9 In. | 230 |
| **Urn,** Purple, Blue, White Flower Sprays, Converted To Lamp, 14 In., Pair | 4096 |
| **Vase,** Celadon, Flowers, Ferns, 9 x 13½ In. | 677 |
| **Vase,** Crane, Green, Gold, Pieced Base, 14⅛ In., Pair | 1197 |
| **Vase,** Green, Muses, 3-Footed, Gilt, 8 In. | 1890 |

**PAUL REVERE POTTERY** was made at several locations in and around Boston, Massachusetts, between 1906 and 1942. The pottery was operated as a settlement house program for teenage girls. Many pieces were signed *S.E.G.* for Saturday Evening Girls. The artists concentrated on children's dishes and tiles. Decorations were outlined in black and filled with color.

| | |
|---|---|
| **Bowl,** Black Pond Lily, Slate Blue, White, Lili Shapiro, 4¼ In. | 295 |
| **Bowl,** Geese, Cuerda Seca, Fannie Levine, S.E.G., 1914, 5 x 11½ In. ................................*illus* | 9375 |
| **Bowl,** Green Matte Glaze, Incised Interior Flower Band, S.E.G., 1½ x 5 In. | 374 |
| **Bowl,** Landscape Band, A. Mangini, S.E.G., 1915, 3 x 8 In. | 1586 |
| **Bowl,** Landscape, Trees, Yellow, White, Green, Eva Geneco, 6½ In. | 325 |
| **Bowl,** Lotus Blossom Band, Cuerda Seca, Blue, S.E.G., 2½ x 8½ In. | 938 |
| **Bowl,** Rabbits, Standing, Initials, MLR, Marked, S.E.G., 6 In. ................................*illus* | 345 |
| **Bowl,** Turquoise, Semimatte, Round, Low, Marked S.E.G., 1920s, 8½ In. | 161 |
| **Bowl,** Unglazed Outline, Lotus Blossoms, Blue, White, 2½ x 8½ In. | 938 |
| **Cup & Saucer,** AM Monogram, Blue, Black Glaze, S.E.G., 5¾ In. | 81 |
| **Jar,** Lid, Underplate, Clover, Signed, 1912, 4¾ x 5½ In. | 3000 |
| **Tea Caddy,** White Glaze, Green Trees, Blue Band, 6-Sided, S.E.G., 1919, 4¼ In. | 1107 |
| **Teapot,** Blue, Tree Reserve, S.E.G, 8¾ In. | 322 |
| **Trivet,** Cottage, Trees, Round, Tan Rim, S.E.G., 4⅜ In. | 161 |
| **Trivet,** House In Landscape, Cuerda Seca, Marked, JDM, S.E.G., 5½ In. ................................*illus* | 1125 |
| **Tumbler,** Tree & Mountain Band, Tapered Cylinder, S.E.G., 4 In. | 610 |
| **Vase,** Blue Green Crystalline Glaze, S.E.G., 6½ In. | 161 |
| **Vase,** Blue, Flecking, Oval, Marked, c.1924, 4½ In. | 225 |
| **Vase,** Green, Drip Glaze, Boston, c.1938, 8 x 3¾ In. | 250 |
| **Vase,** Semimatte Dark Blue, Tapered, 12½ In. | 288 |
| **Vase,** Tree Band, Cuerda Seca, Blue, Cylindrical, S. Galner, S.E.G., 1917, 11 x 6 In. | 6080 |
| **Vase,** Yellow Semigloss, Eva Geneco, S.E.G., 4⅛ In. | 115 |

**PEACHBLOW** glass was made by several factories beginning in the 1880s. New England peachblow is a one-layer glass shading from red to white. Mt. Washington peachblow shades from pink to bluish-white. Hobbs, Brockunier and Company of Wheeling, West Virginia, made Coral glass that it marketed as Peach Blow. It shades from yellow to peach and is lined with white glass. Reproductions of all types of peachblow have been made. Related pieces may be listed under Webb Peachblow.

| | |
|---|---|
| **Bottle,** Wild Rose, Globular, Stick, Narrow Pinched Collar, New England, 5½ In. | 518 |
| **Bowl,** Glossy, Squat, Undulating 5-Fold Rim, 7½ In. | 230 |
| **Bowl,** Satin, Ruffled Rim, New England, 5 In. | 173 |
| **Bowl,** White & Red Daisy Clusters, Rounded, Scalloped Edge, Mt. Washington, 5 In. | 920 |
| **Bride's Basket,** Yellow Shaded To Red, Exaggerated Undulating Ribs, Gold Trim, 11 In. | 115 |
| **Castor,** Matte White Shaded To Pink, Large Hobnail, Silver Plated Frame, 12 In. | 4140 |
| **Celery Vase,** Cylindrical, Crimped Top, Gloss Glaze, New England, 6½ In. | 201 |
| **Celery Vase,** Glossy, Pinched Waist, Wheeling, 6½ In. | 345 |
| **Creamer,** Satin, Bulbous, Square Mouth, Amber Satin Handle, Wheeling, 4 In. | 288 |
| **Creamer,** Yellow To Peach, White Interior, Wheeling, 4 In., Pair | 236 |
| **Cruet,** Amber Faceted Stopper, Reeded Handle, Hobbs, Wheeling, 7 In. ................................*illus* | 460 |
| **Decanter,** Ship's Bottle Shape, Conical, Ring Neck, Wheeling, 8¼ In. | 431 |
| **Fairy Lamp,** Leaf Bird Design, Clarke's Candleholder, Square Base, 6 In. | 590 |
| **Goblet,** Satin Finish, Gundersen, 5½ In. | 29 |
| **Jug,** Claret, Amber Rigaree, Reeded Handle, Hobbs, Brockunier, 10 In. | 1610 |
| **Pitcher,** Cream, Amber Handle, Wheeling, 3 In. | 58 |
| **Pitcher,** Milk, Glossy, Oval, Reeded Handle, 4-Sided Pinched Rim, 6½ In. | 518 |
| **Pitcher,** Satin, Bulbous, Square Mouth, Amber Satin Handle, Wheeling, 5¾ In. | 345 |

**Paul Revere,** Bowl, Geese, Cuerda Seca, Fannie Levine, S.E.G., 1914, 5 x 11½ In.
$9,375

Rago Arts & Auction Center

**Paul Revere,** Bowl, Rabbits, Standing, Initials, MLR, Marked, S.E.G., 6 In.
$345

Humler & Nolan

**Paul Revere,** Trivet, House In Landscape, Cuerda Seca, Marked, JDM, S.E.G., 5½ In.
$1,125

Rago Arts & Auction Center

**P**

**Marbleized Wares**

Marbleized wares have been made for centuries. Recent potteries like Silver Springs or Niloak, nineteenth-century pieces like Doulton Rix ware, and eighteenth-century Whieldon are all made from colored clays pressed together and then squeezed into shapes so the streaks of colored clay form the design. The Japanese call it Nerikomi technique.

# PEACHBLOW

**Peachblow,** Cruet, Amber Faceted Stopper, Reeded Handle, Hobbs, Wheeling, 7 In.
$460

Early Auction Co.

**Peachblow,** Rose Bowl, Oval, Quadrafold Rim, 4 Crimped Feet, Mt. Washington, 7 In.
$805

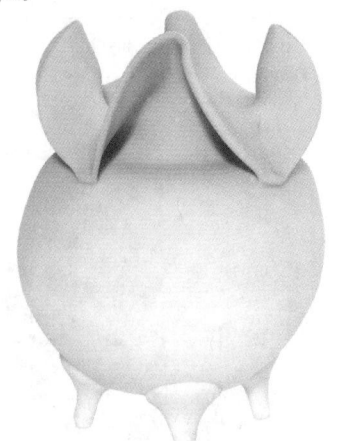

Early Auction Co.

**Peachblow,** Vase, Double Gourd, Fuchsia Shaded To Amber, 7 In.
$356

James D. Julia Auctioneers

**Peachblow,** Vase, Morgan, Satin Finish, Hobbs, Brockunier, Wheeling, c.1890, 8 In.
$413

Conestoga Auction Co., Inc.

**Peachblow,** Vase, Queen's Pattern, Tricorner Top, Applied Feet, Mt. Washington, 7 ¾ In.
$8,295

James D. Julia Auctioneers

**Peachblow,** Vase, Rose To Pink, Gilt, Enamel, Urn Shaped, c.1880, 4 ½ In.
$288

Jeffrey S. Evans & Assoc.

**Peachblow,** Vase, Trumpet, Swirled Foot, Venetian Bulb, Optic Ribbed, Mt. Washington, 13 ¾ In.
$2,586

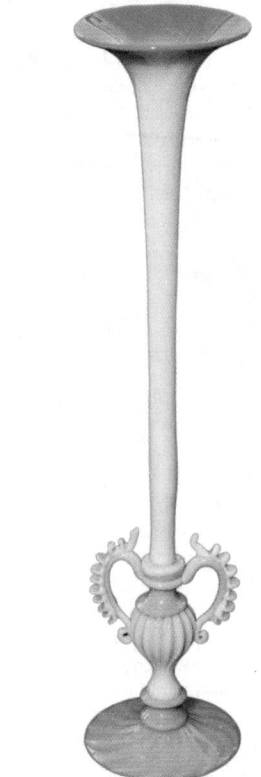

Early Auction Co.

**Peachblow,** Vase, Wild Rose, Deep Pink To Opal, Gold Circles, 10 In.
$2,750

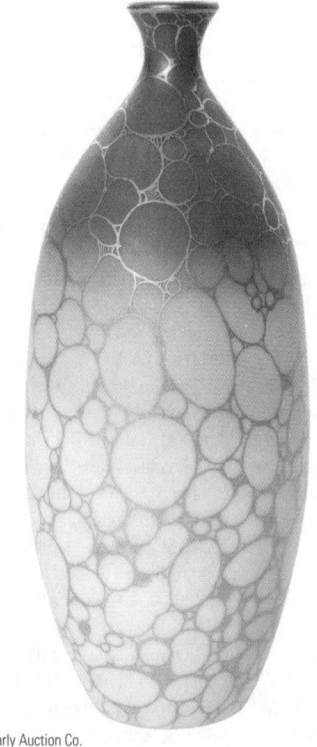

Early Auction Co.

| | |
|---|---|
| **Pitcher,** Satin, Tankard, Cylindrical, Frosted Amber Handle, 8 ¾ In. | 1380 |
| **Pitcher,** Smokestack Tankard, Reeded Amber Handle, Hobbs, Brockunier, 10 In. | 4312 |
| **Pitcher,** Water, Satin, Glossy Handle, Oval, Mt. Washington, 5 ½ In. | 805 |
| **Punch Cup,** Satin, Applied Amber Handle, Wheeling, 2 ½ In. | 173 |
| **Rose Bowl,** Oval, Quadrafold Rim, 4 Crimped Feet, Mt. Washington, 7 In. .............*illus* | 805 |
| **Salt & Pepper,** Wild Rose, Mold Blown, White To Ivory To Lavender Rose, 3 ¾ x 4 In. | 354 |
| **Shakers,** Wild Rose, Silver-Plated Caddy, New England, 5 ½ In. | 288 |
| **Spittoon,** Lady's, Glossy, Flared & Ruffled Rim, 5 ¼ In. | 144 |
| **Spooner,** Pinched Waist, Wheeling, 4 ¼ In. | 662 |
| **Toothpick Holder,** Blue Berries, Autumn Leaves, Mt. Washington, 2 In. | 2415 |
| **Toothpick Holder,** Squat, Smokestack Shape, 2 ½ In. | 489 |
| **Vase,** Double Gourd, Fuchsia Shaded To Amber, 7 In. .............*illus* | 356 |
| **Vase,** Double Gourd, Gloss Glaze, Wheeling, 7 ¼ In. | 1610 |
| **Vase,** Jack-In-The-Pulpit, Opal, Wild Rose Inside, Ribbed, Flared Ruffled Rim, 6 In., Pair | 35 |
| **Vase,** Melon Ribbed, Narrow Neck, Widened Rim, Mt. Washington, 4 ¾ In. | 288 |
| **Vase,** Morgan, Custard To Mahogany, Gloss Glaze, Bulbous, Stick Shape, Wheeling, 8 In. | 431 |
| **Vase,** Morgan, Satin Finish, Hobbs, Brockunier, Wheeling, c.1890, 8 In. .............*illus* | 413 |
| **Vase,** Morgan, Tapered, Narrow Neck, 7 ¾ In. | 316 |
| **Vase,** Optic Diamond, Stemmed Daisies, Mt. Washington, 2 ¾ In. | 1955 |
| **Vase,** Queen's Pattern, Tricorner Top, Applied Feet, Mt. Washington, 7 ¾ In. .............*illus* | 8295 |
| **Vase,** Rose To Pink, Gilt, Enamel, Urn Shaped, c.1880, 4 ½ In. .............*illus* | 288 |
| **Vase,** Satin, Coralene Branch Overlay, Stand-Up Rim, 5 ½ In. | 177 |
| **Vase,** Satin, Double Gourd Shape, Wheeling, 7 ½ In. | 1035 |
| **Vase,** Stick, Bulbous, Stain Gloss, Hobbs, Brockunier, Wheeling, 10 ½ In. | 460 |
| **Vase,** Stick, Double Bulbous, Mt. Washington, 7 In. | 518 |
| **Vase,** Stick, Glossy Glaze, Bulbous, 9 In. | 345 |
| **Vase,** Stick, Glossy, Rigaree Collar, Wheeling, 8 ½ In. | 920 |
| **Vase,** Stick, Queen's Pattern, Mt. Washington, Daisies, Pointillism Style, 8 In. | 5750 |
| **Vase,** Stick, Satin, Squat Bulbous Base, Tapered Neck, Wheeling, 10 ½ In. | 805 |
| **Vase,** Stick, Wheeling, 8 ¼ In. | 345 |
| **Vase,** Stick, White To Pink Stain, Mt. Washington, 8 In. | 345 |
| **Vase,** Stick, Wild Rose, Glossy, Gilt Flowers & Leaves, 8 ½ In. | 230 |
| **Vase,** Trumpet, Swirled Foot, Venetian Bulb, Optic Ribbed, Mt. Washington, 13 ¾ In. ..........*illus* | 2586 |
| **Vase,** Wild Rose, Deep Pink To Opal, Gold Circles, 10 In. .............*illus* | 2750 |

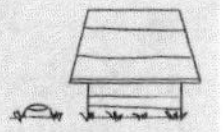

---

**PEANUTS** is the title of a comic strip created by cartoonist Charles M. Schulz (1922–2000). The strip, drawn by Schulz from 1950 to 2000, features a group of children, including Charlie Brown and his sister Sally, Lucy Van Pelt and her brother Linus, Peppermint Patty, and Pig Pen, and an imaginative and independent beagle named Snoopy. The Peanuts gang has also been featured in books, television shows, and a Broadway musical.

| | |
|---|---|
| **Bottle,** Shampoo, Plastic, Charlie Hugging Snoopy, Avon, c.1950, 8 In. | 9 |
| **Bracelet,** Charm, Characters, Goldtone Metal, Taiwan, 7 In. | 32 |
| **Cookie Cutter,** Charlie Brown, Plastic, Red, United Features Syndicate, 4 In. | 12 |
| **Date Book,** Snoopy, Spiral, 1973-74 | 24 |
| **Mug,** Charlie, Snoopy, Woodstock, Christmas Tree, 1977, 4 x 3 In. | 24 |
| **Mug,** Lucy, Musical, Pink, Paper Label, Japan, 1971 | 45 |
| **Music Box,** Schroeder, Grand Piano, Plays Leitmotiv Kaiserkonzert, Anri, 1968, 5 x 4 In. | 99 |
| **Nodder,** Lucy, Composition, 1952, 3 ½ In. | 59 |
| **Ornament,** Snoopy, Viking, Ceramic, United Features, Japan, 1966, 4 In. | 29 |
| **Telephone,** Snoopy, Push Button, 1985 | 35 |
| **Tie,** Charlie Brown & Snoopy, Playing Golf, Silk, 4 x 57 In. | 37 |
| **Toy,** Boat, Snoopy, Lucy, Red, White, Blue, Plastic, Hong Kong, 1972, 3 ½ In. | 18 |
| **Toy,** Snoopy, Cowboy, Hat, Badge, Rubber, Taiwan, 1970s, 5 ½ In. | 14 |
| **Trinket Box,** Marcie & Sally, Reading Paper, In Grass, Flambro, 3 x 1 x 3 In. | 16 |
| **Watch,** Charlie Brown, Outstretched Arms, Brown Band, Quartz, 8 In. | 50 |
| **Wristwatch,** Snoopy, Hero-Time, Plastic, Embroidered Patch, Box, 1971, 2 Piece ..............*illus* | 153 |

---

**PEARL** items listed here are made of the natural mother-of-pearl from shells. Such natural pearl has been used to decorate furniture and small utilitarian objects for centuries. The glassware known as mother-of-pearl is listed by that name. Opera glasses made with natural pearl shell are listed under Opera Glasses.

| | |
|---|---|
| **Card Case,** Diamond-Shaped Tiles, 4 ¼ x 2 ¾ In. | 91 |
| **Card Case,** Late 19th Century, Hinges, Fabric Interior, 4 In. | 121 |
| **Card Case,** Mother-Of-Pearl Inlay, Tortoiseshell, 4 ¼ In. | 363 |
| **Caviar Knives,** Silk Fabric Holder, 6 Piece | 20 |

**Peanuts,** Wristwatch, Snoopy, Hero-Time, Plastic, Embroidered Patch, Box, 1971, 2 Piece
$153

Hake's Americana & Collectibles

---

**Pearlware,** Bust, Woman, Rosy Red Cheeks, Square Base, Painted, c.1800, 6 x 5 In.
$677

Cowan's Auctions

---

**Peking Glass,** Snuff Bottle, Flattened, 3 Layers, Flower, Cloisonne Stopper, Marked, 2 ⅝ In.
$523

Skinner Auctioneers & Appraisers

P

**Peking Glass,** Snuff Bottle, Xuantong Portrait, Reverse Painted, Jasper Stopper, c.1910, 3 ¾ In.
$1,599

Skinner Auctioneers & Appraisers

**Pencil Sharpener,** El Casco, Goldtone Metal, Black, Lever Mechanism Locks Onto Table, 6 In.
$113

Leonard Auction

**Pencil Sharpener,** Perfect Pencil Pointer, Goodelle Co., c.1890, 3 ½ x 10 In.
$195

Dirk Soulis Auctions

**Pfefferminz**
PEZ (the candy) is the shortened form of the German word *pfefferminz* (peppermint).

**Caviar Plate,** Figural, Fish, Scales, 6 ½ In. .......... 30
**Dessert Service,** Mother-Of-Pearl Handle, Silver Collar, 12 Knives, 12 Forks, 24 Piece .......... 224
**Magnifying Glass,** Mother-Of-Pearl & Rolled Gold Handle, 15 In. .......... 121

## Pearl

**PEARLWARE** is an earthenware made by Josiah Wedgwood in 1779. It was copied by other potters in England. Pearlware is only slightly different in color from creamware and for many years collectors have confused the terms. Wedgwood pieces are listed in the Wedgwood category in this book. Most pearlware with mocha designs is listed under Mocha.

**Basket,** Chestnut, Eastern Street, Blue, Octagon, Handles, J. Riley, Staffordshire, c.1825, 11 x 7 In. 230
**Basket,** Oval, Reticulated Band, Green Rope Twist Borders & Handles, 5 x 9 In. .......... 259
**Bowl,** Blue, White Asian Style, England, c.1800, 3 x 8 In. .......... 154
**Bowl,** Peafowl, Geometric, Flower Bands, Staffordshire, c.1800, 4 x 11 In. .......... 633
**Bust,** G. Washington, Blue Coat, Wig, Scarf, Inscribed, Enoch Wood, 1818, 8 In. .......... 2640
**Bust,** Man, Head Covering, Arthur Vernay, Paper Label, 10 In. .......... 300
**Bust,** Woman, Rosy Red Cheeks, Square Base, Painted, c.1800, 6 x 5 In. .......... *illus* 677
**Charger,** Scalloped Rim, Berries, Vines, Rural Landscape, Staffordshire, c.1800, 14 In. .......... 1725
**Coffeepot,** Blue, Yellow Flowers, England, 11 ¼ In. .......... 210
**Coffeepot,** Dark Blue Transfer, Staffordshire, c.1815, 10 ½ In. .......... 420
**Coffeepot,** Lid, Baluster, Scroll Handle, Multicolor Flowers, c.1820, 11 x 5 In. .......... 230
**Cup & Saucer,** Handless, Strawberry, 5 ⅜ In. .......... 94
**Figurine,** Charity, Woman, Children, Multicolor Enamel, Staffordshire, c.1800, 10 In. .......... 600
**Figurine,** Ram, Reclining, Tan & Green Glaze, c.1800, 4 ½ In. .......... 240
**Figurine,** Ram, Reclining, White, Yellow, Blue, England, c.1820, 4 ¾ x 6 In. .......... 660
**Figurine,** Woman, Classical Attire, Leaning On Urn, c.1800, 8 ¾ In. .......... 92
**Group,** Sacrifice At Lystra, Multicolor, Staffordshire, 1800s, 11 x 13 In. .......... 3360
**Jug,** Brown, Blue, Looping, Orange Field, Brown, Green Bands, England, c.1830, 7 In. .......... 1680
**Jug,** Brown, Niagara Falls, Decatur, Black Transfer, Pink Luster, Staffordshire, 6 In. .......... 1080
**Jug,** Chinoiserie, Blue Speckled Slip, Flower Rim Band, c.1780, 5 ¾ In. .......... 240
**Jug,** Green, Leaves, Bearded Mask Spout, Leaf Handle, Staffordshire, c.1800 .......... 420
**Jug,** Green, Overlapping Leaves, Stippled Ground, Staffordshire, c.1800, Qt., 6 In. .......... 720
**Jug,** House, Bird, Fence, Inscribed, Staffordshire, 1803, 9 ½ In. .......... 1495
**Jug,** Mocha, Brown Slip Grid, White, Cobalt Blue Bands, Baluster, 7 ¾ In., c.1800 .......... 2520
**Jug,** Neck Band, Peafowl, Vines, Inscribed, Staffordshire, 1797, 8 In. .......... 1955
**Jug,** Peafowl, Blue Dentil Rim, Sponged Leaves, Staffordshire, c.1805, 5 In. .......... 518
**Jug,** Swags, Farm Tools, Wheat Sheaves, Inscribed Spout, Staffordshire, 1800, 11 In. .......... 4888
**Lazy Susan,** Buds, Flowers, Leaves, Vine Border, 4 Curved Sections, 1800s, 18 In .......... 83
**Mug,** Orange, Green, Black Bands, Reeded Border, Mocha, England, c.1820, 6 In. .......... 600
**Mug,** Peafowl, Large Handles, Round, Staffordshire, c.1790, 5 In. .......... 546
**Mug,** Wolverine, Flower, Scroll Border, Blue Transfer, Staffordshire, c.1815, 2 ⅜ In. .......... 1020
**Pitcher,** Flowers, Cat's-Eye Band, Waisted Baluster, Staffordshire, 1800s, 7 x 5 In. .......... 173
**Pitcher,** Flowers, Green Incised Bands, Baluster, Staffordshire, 1800s, 7 x 5 In. .......... 374
**Pitcher,** Red, Green Flowers, Leaves, Bands, Arched Handle, Staffordshire, 1825, 5 In. .......... 184
**Plate,** Soft Paste, Burnt Orange Castle, Landscape Transfer, Green Band Border, 6 Piece .......... 94
**Punch Bowl,** Blue & White Transfer, Fisherman, Pavilion, Cell & Diaper Band, 5 x 11 In. .......... 58
**Sash Window Stop,** William Shakespeare, Painted, 1820-30, 3 ½ In., 4 Piece .......... 1080
**Sauce,** Orange Transfer, Shepherd & Landscape, 4 ⅝ In. .......... 6
**Stirrup Cup,** Hare's Head, c.1825, 6 ¼ In. .......... 1770
**Teapot,** Lid, Blue Bands, Peafowl, Staffordshire, c.1800, 4 ¾ In. .......... 403

**PEKING GLASS** is a Chinese cameo glass first made popular in the eighteenth century. The Chinese have continued to make this layered glass in the old manner, and many new pieces are now available that could confuse the average buyer.

**Bowl,** Cameo Cut, Blue & White, Geese, Flowering Plants, 1900s, 5 ¼ In. .......... 237
**Bowl,** Yellow, Carved Leaves, c.1845, 1 ¼ x 3 ¾ In. .......... 125
**Jar,** Lid, Cameo, Red Over White, Multicolor Blossoms, 8 In. .......... 121
**Jar,** White, Carved, Bird Of Paradise, Chrysanthemums, Lotus Lid, Wood Stand, 9 x 5 In. .......... 213
**Platter,** Turquoise, Carved Relief, Phoenixes, Peonies, 1800s, 4 x 4 ¾ In. .......... 474
**Snuff Bottle,** 3 Layers, Blue, Yellow Phoenix, Ceramic Stopper, 1900s, 2 ¾ In. .......... 180
**Snuff Bottle,** Double Overlay, Man, Pink, White, 2 ⅞ In. .......... 308
**Snuff Bottle,** Flattened, 3 Layers, Flower, Cloisonne Stopper, Marked, 2 ⅝ In. .......... *illus* 523
**Snuff Bottle,** Multicolor Overlay, Opaque White Glass, Squirrels, Fruit, 1800s, 3 In. .......... 1888
**Snuff Bottle,** Xuantong Portrait, Reverse Painted, Jasper Stopper, c.1910, 3 ¾ In. .......... *illus* 1599
**Snuff Bottle,** Yellow, Blue, Figures, Raised Oval Base, 2 ½ In. .......... 1599
**Vase,** Amber, Inscription Near Rim, Matte Finish Geometric Fan, 6 ½ x 6 ½ In. .......... 345

| | |
|---|---|
| **Vase,** Blue, Fruit, Flowers, Branches, Carved, 11 In. | 120 |
| **Vase,** Peonies, Phoenix, Black Overlay, White Ground, 8½ In. | 738 |

**PENS** replaced hand-cut quills as writing instruments in 1780, when the first steel pen point was made in England. But it was 100 years before the commercial pen was a common item. The fountain pen was invented in the 1830s but was not made in quantity until the 1880s. All types of old pens are collected. Float pens that feature small objects floating in a liquid as part of the handle are popular with collectors. Advertising pens are listed in the Advertising section of this book.

### PEN

| | |
|---|---|
| **Montblanc,** Fountain, 14K Nib, Leather Traveler Set, 5 Cartridges, Monogram, 5¾ In. | 259 |
| **Montblanc,** Fountain, Blue, Retractable Nib, Black Resin Body, Blue Gemstone, 4 In. | 380 |
| **Montblanc,** Fountain, Meisterstuck, Black Resin Body, 14K Gold Clip, Banding, 4810 Nib | 240 |
| **Montblanc,** Fountain, Sterling Silver, 18K Gold Nib, Clip Monogram, 5¼ In. | 403 |
| **Montblanc,** Meisterstuck, 18K Goldtone Cap, 5¾ In. | 840 |
| **Montblanc,** Meisterstuck, Hemingway, Ballpoint, Fountain Pen, 18K Gold Nib, Box, 5 In. | 1770 |
| **Parker 21,** Red, Box | 140 |
| **Parker,** Fountain, Sonnet, Cisele, Silver, 18K Gold Nib, 5¼ In. | 266 |
| **Pelikan Toledo M900,** Enamel, Elephants, Case | 800 |
| **Tiffany & Co.,** Ballpoint, Sterling, Retractable, Signed, Box, Pouch, 4½ In. | 86 |
| **Tiffany,** Ballpoint, Bamboo Style, 14K Yellow Gold, Marked, Blue Box, 4¼ In. | 529 |
| **Tiffany,** Ballpoint, Silver, Embossed, 2 Inserts, 4 In. | 155 |
| **Waterman,** Fountain, Bicentenaire Edition, 18K Gold Nib, Black Shaft, 3 Birds, 5¾ In. | 177 |
| **Waterman,** Fountain, Ideal, 18K Gold, Case | 240 |
| **Wipes,** Rooster, Hen, Wool, Felt Capes, On Round Penny Rugs, c.1880, 5 In., 4 Piece | 1200 |

### PEN & PENCIL

| | |
|---|---|
| **Anson,** Sterling Silver, Box, 1960s | 55 |
| **Bradley Astramatic,** Goldtone, Box, 1970s | 22 |
| **Cross,** Ballpoint, Mechanical Pencil, Chrome, Ireland, Box | 24 |
| **Ever-Ready,** Marbled Celluloid, Green, Box, c.1925 | 150 |
| **Eversharp,** Skyline, Command Performance, 14K Gold, Monogram, Box, c.1948, 5½ In. | 546 |
| **Pierre Cardin,** Ballpoint Pen, Mechanical Pencil, Chrome, Gold Accents | 41 |
| **Tiffany & Co.,** Fountain Pen, Mechanical Pencil, Sterling Silver, Marked | 140 |
| **Wearever,** Fountain Pen, Mechanical Pencil, Green Marbled Celluloid, Box, 1900s | 95 |

**PENCILS** were invented, so it is said, in 1565. The eraser was not added to the pencil until 1858. The automatic pencil was invented in 1863. Collectors today want advertising pencils or automatic pencils of unusual design. Boxes and sharpeners for pencils are also collected. Advertising pencils are listed in the Advertising category. Pencil boxes are listed in the Box category.

### PENCIL

| | |
|---|---|
| **14K Gold,** Engraved Script Monogram, Loop End, Tiffany & Co., 6 In. | 197 |
| **Chatelaine,** 14K Yellow Gold, Mabie Todd, c.1850, 2 In. | 390 |
| **Eversharp,** Mechanical, 14K Yellow Gold, Engraved Scrolling, Chain Bail, 4 In. | 213 |
| **Faberge,** Retractable, 14K Gold, Silver, Diamond, Amethyst, Flower Handles, Russia, c.1890, 4 In. | 3840 |
| **Mechanical,** Marbleized, Hershey Derby Conn, 2½ In. | 35 |
| **Mechanical,** Sterling Silver, Repose, 3 In. | 159 |
| **Propelling,** 18K Yellow Gold, Zurich Jeweler Meister, 3⅝ In. | 825 |
| **Propelling,** Gold, S. Mordan & Co., 1932, 4¼ In. | 439 |
| **Propelling,** Sterling Silver, L & S, Birmingham, 1908, 6 In. | 120 |
| **Wahl,** Eversharp, Mechanical, Sterling Silver, 2 Piece | 180 |

### PENCIL SHARPENER

| | |
|---|---|
| **Apsco,** Adjustable, 6 Sizes, Gray | 18 |
| **Bakelite,** Green, Chain, 1930s, 1 x ¾ In. | 25 |
| **Bakelite,** Green, Keychain, c.1930, 1 x ¾ In. | 25 |
| **Binoculars,** Metal, Gold Paint, Germany, 1¼ x 1¼ In. | 85 |
| **Camera,** Metal, China, Box, 1980s, 2½ x 2 In. | 21 |
| **Cash Register,** Contado, Die Cast, 2¼ x 2 In. | 24 |
| **Coffee Mill,** Die Cast, Spain, 3 x 1¾ In. | 24 |
| **Egg Shape,** Retro, Orange, Electric, Boston, 5 In. | 95 |
| **El Casco,** Goldtone Metal, Black, Lever Mechanism Locks Onto Table, 6 In. *illus* | 113 |
| **Gypsy,** Dancing, Tambourine, Lead, Germany, c.1925, 2 In. | 68 |
| **Pelican,** Celluloid, Yellow, Black, Orange, 3 In. | 60 |
| **Perfect Pencil Pointer,** Goodelle Co., c.1890, 3½ x 10 In. *illus* | 195 |
| **Pinocchio,** Bakelite, 1⅝ In. | 29 |
| **Pistol,** White Metal, Gray Paint, Hinged, Germany, 2 x 1 In. | 38 |

**Pepsi-Cola,** Calendar, 1909, Woman, Green Dress, Large Hat, 19 x 10 In. $1,920

Morphy Auctions

**Pepsi-Cola,** Clock, Neon, Ice Cold, Drink Pepsi-Cola, 5 Cent, 18 In. $270

Morphy Auctions

**Pepsi-Cola,** Dispenser, Syrup, Urn, Lid, Ceramic, Trees, Art Nouveau, c.1900, 18 In. $69,000

Morphy Auctions

P

**Pepsi-Cola,** Sign, Drink Pepsi-Cola, Delicious-Healthful, Double Dash, 15 x 7 In.
**$240**

Morphy Auctions

**Pepsi-Cola,** Sign, Slow School Zone, Boy Crossing Guard, 2-Sided, Stout Sign Co., 51 In.
**$840**

Morphy Auctions

**Pepsi-Cola,** Stringholder, Join The Swing To, 5 Cents, 1930s, 16 In.
**$270**

Morphy Auctions

| | |
|---|---:|
| **Pump,** Handled, Die Cast, 3 ½ x 2 In. | 29 |
| **Sewing Machine,** Die Cast, Spain, 2 ¼ x 1 ½ In. | 28 |
| **Tank,** Bakelite, US Army, Olive Green, 1940s, 1 ⅞ x 1 In. | 50 |
| **World Globe On Stand,** Die Cast, Spain, 3 x 3 In. | 20 |

**PENNSBURY POTTERY** worked in Morrisville, Pennsylvania, from 1950 to 1971. Full sets of dinnerware as well as many decorative items were made. Pieces are marked with the name of the factory.

*Pennsbury Pottery*

| | |
|---|---:|
| **Amish,** Cookie Jar, 7 In. | 98 |
| **Bookends,** Eagle, Spread Wings, 5 x 6 In. | 232 |
| **Dutch Tulip,** Creamer, 4 In. | 7 |
| **Eagle,** Pitcher, Spread Wings, 6 In. | 20 |
| **Hex,** Plate, 10 In. | 18 |
| **Red Rooster,** Dip & Chip, 11 ½ In. | 75 |

**PEPSI-COLA,** the drink and the name, was invented in 1898 but was not trademarked until 1903. The logo was changed from an elaborate script to the modern block letters in 1963. Several different logos have been used. Until 1951, the words *Pepsi* and *Cola* were separated by two dashes. These bottles are called "double dash." In 1951 the modern logo with a single hyphen was introduced. All types of advertising memorabilia are collected, and reproductions are being made.

**PEPSI-COLA**

| | |
|---|---:|
| **Calendar,** 1909, Woman, Green Dress, Large Hat, 19 x 10 In. ............................*illus* | 1920 |
| **Calendar,** 1947, Boy Scouts, Norman Rockwell, December, 16 x 33 In. ................ | 840 |
| **Clock,** Neon, Ice Cold, Drink Pepsi-Cola, 5 Cent, 18 In. ...........................*illus* | 270 |
| **Cooler,** Handle, Blue, Metal, 13 x 18 In. | 210 |
| **Dispenser,** Syrup, Urn, Lid, Ceramic, Trees, Art Nouveau, c.1900, 18 In. ...........*illus* | 69000 |
| **Display Bottle,** Salesman's Sample, 20 In. | 180 |
| **Door Plate,** Tin, Drink Pepsi-Cola, 5 Cents, Bottle, Yellow, Red, 1930s, 13 x 3 In. | 780 |
| **Door Pull,** Black, Red, White, Metal, 1940s, 12 In. | 390 |
| **Sign,** Bottle, Reputation Follows High Quality, 5 Cents, Cardboard, Frame, 16 x 8 In. | 45 |
| **Sign,** Buy Pepsi Here, Double Dash, Tin Lithograph, 12 x 16 In. | 720 |
| **Sign,** Die Cut, 2-Sided, Flange, Tin, 15 x 14 In. | 780 |
| **Sign,** Drink Pepsi-Cola, Delicious-Healthful, Double Dash, 15 x 7 In. ...........*illus* | 240 |
| **Sign,** Drive Slow Please, Boy, Stout Sign Co., 44 x 18 In. | 420 |
| **Sign,** Fish, Bottle Cap, Bigger, Better, Cardboard, 1940s, 11 x 27 In. | 195 |
| **Sign,** Pepsi's Best, Take No Less, Pretty Girl, Bottle, Yellow Roses, 21 x 29 In. | 180 |
| **Sign,** Porcelain, Door Push, c.1950, 3 x 32 In. | 240 |
| **Sign,** Red, White, Blue, Round Logo, Embossed, Self-Framed, Tin, Stout Sign Co., 31 x 12 In. | 72 |
| **Sign,** Say Mix Mine With Pepsi, Cardboard, Easel Back, 12 x 6 In. | 450 |
| **Sign,** Say Pepsi Please, Tin, Embossed Frame, Tin Lithograph, 1965 | 126 |
| **Sign,** Slow School Zone, Boy Crossing Guard, 2-Sided, Stout Sign Co., 51 In. ...........*illus* | 840 |
| **Stadium Carrier,** Metal Wire, Logo Panel, 25 ¾ x 17 ½ In. | 22 |
| **Store Display,** Rack, Drink Pepsi Ice Cold, Bottle Cap Sign, 17 x 66 In. | 180 |
| **Straw Dispenser,** Can Shape, Bottle Cap Logo, 1930s, 9 ¼ In. | 3900 |
| **Stringholder,** Join The Swing To, 5 Cents, 1930s, 16 In. ...........................*illus* | 270 |
| **Syrup Drum,** Double Dash, Bigger & Better, Red, White, c.1945, 5 Gal. | 150 |
| **Thermometer,** Bottle Cap Logo, White, Any Weather's Pepsi Weather, 8 x 26 ½ In. | 150 |
| **Thermometer,** Say Pepsi Please, Tin, Glass, 9 x 9 In. | 120 |
| **Toy,** Pedal Car, Blue, Red Wheels, c.1999, 34 x 15 In. | 390 |
| **Toy,** Truck, Tin, Friction, Driver, Japan, 9 In. | 270 |
| **Tray,** Bigger & Better, Coast To Coast, Map Of America, Bottle, Tin, 13 x 10 In. | 240 |
| **Vending Machine,** Blue, Double Dash, Model 1-55, Hinged Lid, c.1950, 43 x 34 In. | 420 |
| **Watch Fob,** Nickeled Brass, Obverse U.S. Capitol Building, c.1910, 1 ½ x 1 ¾ In. | 127 |

**PERFUME BOTTLES** are made of cut glass, pressed glass, art glass, silver, metal, enamel, and even plastic or porcelain. Although the small bottle to hold perfume was first made before the time of ancient Egypt, it is the nineteenth- and twentieth-century examples that interest today's collector. DeVilbiss Company has made atomizers of all types since 1888 but no longer makes the perfume bottle tops so popular with collectors. These were made from 1920 to 1968. The glass bottle may be by any of many manufacturers even if the atomizer is marked *DeVilbiss*. The word *factice*, which often appears in ads, refers to store display bottles. Glass or porcelain examples may be found under the appropriate name such as Lalique, Czechoslovakia, Glass-Bohemian, etc.

| | |
|---|---:|
| **Amethyst Cut Crystal,** Shaped Stoppers, Intaglio Fairies, 1900s, 6 ½ In., Pair | 123 |
| **Blown Glass,** Cobalt Blue & White Enamel, Concave, Long Neck, Atar Myosotis, 5 In. | 30 |
| **Blown Glass,** Cobalt Blue, Swirl Pattern, 3 In. | 83 |

| | |
|---|---|
| **Blue To Green Iridescent,** Cylindrical, Tapered, Ball Stopper, Mark Peiser, 1977, 4½ In. | 480 |
| **Cologne,** 16 Ribs, Swirled Left, Amethyst, Stopper, Toilet Water, c.1830, 6½ In. ..............*illus* | 556 |
| **Cut Glass Panels,** Sulphide Portraits, Notched Stopper, France, c.1850, 6 In. .............*illus* | 2100 |
| **Cut Glass,** Flowers, Starburst, Hexagonal, Guilloche Enamel Stopper, 5 x 3 In. | 253 |
| **Cut Glass,** Russian Pattern, Tusk Shape, Laydown, Silver Twist Cap & Tip, 7½ In. | 413 |
| **DeVilbiss,** Atomizer, Acid Cut Back, Gold, Birds, Flowers, Ebony Acorn Finial, 10 In. | 230 |
| **DeVilbiss,** Iridescent Gold Body, Metal Neck, Black Glass Stopper, Footed, 7 In. | 144 |
| **Glass,** Faux Tortoiseshell, Gilt Mount, Faceted Stopper, Art Deco, France, 8 In. | 295 |
| **Glass,** Iridescent, Blue, Green, Cream, Flame Finial, Lundberg, 1980, 6 In. ............*illus* | 150 |
| **Glass,** Ruby, Bronze Mounts, Stopper, Architectural Scene On Cap, 4½ In. | 82 |
| **Nina Ricci,** 2 Frosted Lovebirds On Lid, Hand Blown, France, 8 In. | 180 |
| **Nina Ricci,** Factice, Clear Swirled Bottle, Frosted Dove Stopper, Lalique, 12 In. | 500 |
| **Paperweight Base,** St. Louis, Millefiori, Upset Muslin, Blue Rim, 8½ In. | 2725 |
| **Pink Cut Crystal,** Bronze Mounted, Shield Form, Paw Foot Base, 7½ In. | 1845 |
| **Van Cleef & Arpel,** 18K Yellow Gold, Tubular, Engraved Flowers, Sapphires, Diamond | 1150 |

**PETERS & REED POTTERY COMPANY** of Zanesville, Ohio, was founded by John D. Peters and Adam Reed in 1897. Chromal, Landsun, Montene, Pereco, and Persian are some of the art lines that were made. The company, which became Zane Pottery in 1920 and Gonder Pottery in 1941, closed in 1957. Peters & Reed pottery was unmarked.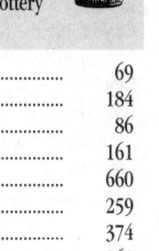

| | |
|---|---|
| **Doorstop,** Cat, Seated, Black Glaze, 10 In. | 69 |
| **Doorstop,** Lion, Resting, Marbleized, Green, Orange, 9 In. | 184 |
| **Jardiniere,** Aztec, Green Accents, 7 x 6 In. | 86 |
| **Jardiniere,** Egyptian, Figures, Geometrics, Green, Flared Rim, 10 x 9 In. | 161 |
| **Jardiniere,** Pedestal, Green Moss Aztec, Grapes, Leaves, 36 In. | 660 |
| **Umbrella Stand,** Ivory, Carved Scrolls, Lines, Tan, Orange, 20½ In. | 259 |
| **Umbrella Stand,** Moss Aztec, Orange, Green, Carved Vines, 19½ In. | 374 |
| **Vase,** Blue, Brown, Landscape, Bridge, River, Trees, Boulders, 12⅞ In. | 863 |
| **Vase,** Chromart, Blue, River Landscape, 19 In. | 115 |
| **Vase,** Embossed Flowers, Standard Glaze, Squared Opening, c.1920, 5¾ In. | 95 |
| **Vase,** Flowers, Ivory Ground, Flared, 8 In. | 69 |
| **Vase,** Frog Shape, Brown Gloss Glaze, Wide Mouth, Marked, 3¾ In. | 35 |
| **Vase,** Green, Yellow Flower Band, Tapered, 8 In. | 219 |
| **Vase,** Italia Antique, Multicolor Art Nouveau Designs, Orange Ground, Flared, 9 In. | 75 |
| **Vase,** Italia, Antique, Handles, Pink, Green, Blue Designs, Brown Ground, 5¼ In. | 92 |
| **Vase,** Landscape, Trees, Mountains, Stream, 9 In. ............*illus* | 199 |
| **Vase,** Landsun, River Landscape, Bridge, Blue, Tan, 13 In. | 489 |
| **Vase,** River, Shoreline, c.1910, 13 In. | 675 |
| **Vase,** Scenic Chromart, Snow Covered Canyon, Shrubs, Clouds, 7¼ In. | 259 |
| **Vase,** Scenic, Yellow, Brown, Green, Cylindrical, 7 In. | 40 |
| **Wall Pocket,** Marbleized, 9 In. | 81 |

**PEWABIC POTTERY** was founded by Mary Chase Perry Stratton in 1903 in Detroit, Michigan. The company made many types of art pottery, including pieces with matte green glaze and an iridescent crystalline glaze. The company continued working until the death of Mary Stratton in 1961. It was reactivated by Michigan State University in 1968.

| | |
|---|---|
| **Bowl,** Luster Shell, Blue, Red, Scalloped, 8¼ In. | 374 |
| **Bowl,** Short Foot, Iridescent Glaze, Early 20th Century, 5 In. Diam. | 360 |
| **Bowl,** Turquoise, Variegated Burgundy, Paper Label, 12 x 4 In. ............*illus* | 330 |
| **Box,** Fish Swimming, Green, Turquoise, 1¾ x 4¾ In. | 360 |
| **Plate,** Rabbits, Trees, Bushes, Green, Cream, 10 In. | 2125 |
| **Plate,** Repeating Landscape Border, Green Trees, Blue Sky, Beige Ground, 10 In. | 1037 |
| **Plate,** Repeating Rabbit & Tree Border, Tan, Green, 10½ In. | 732 |
| **Plate,** Repeating Rabbit Border, Green, Yellow, Blue, 11 In. | 793 |
| **Plate,** Repeating Stylized Chicken Border, Brown, Beige Ground, 10 In. | 458 |
| **Tile,** Black, White Floral Designs, 7 In. | 108 |
| **Trivet,** Octagonal, 8 Circles, Gold, 5¼ In. | 215 |
| **Vase,** Brown Glaze, Yellow & Green Drip, Squat Bowl Form, 3 x 4 In. | 549 |
| **Vase,** Brown, Tan Drip, High Shoulder, 9 x 11 In. | 7320 |
| **Vase,** Bulbous, Stepped Neck, Yellow, Gold Metallic Glaze, 2 In. | 1232 |
| **Vase,** Deep Blue Glaze, Shouldered, 3 Flattened Handles, 10 x 10½ In. | 2000 |
| **Vase,** Drippy Red, Green & Yellow Metallic Glaze, Low, Shouldered, 2 x 3 In. | 500 |
| **Vase,** Gold, Green & Turquoise Metallic Glaze, Bulbous Base, Cylindrical Neck, 3 x 2 In. | 469 |
| **Vase,** Gray & Black Metallic Glaze, Bulbous, 7½ x 6 In. | 1464 |
| **Vase,** Gray, Speckled Green & Tan Metallic Glaze, Bulbous, Inward Folded Rim, 3 x 3 In. | 488 |

**Perfume Bottle,** Cologne, 16 Ribs, Swirled Left, Amethyst, Stopper, Toilet Water, c.1830, 6½ In.
$556

Norman C. Heckler & Company

**Perfume Bottle,** Cut Glass Panels, Sulphide Portraits, Notched Stopper, France, c.1850, 6 In.
$2,100

DuMouchelles Art Gallery

**Perfume Bottle,** Glass, Iridescent, Blue, Green, Cream, Flame Finial, Lundberg, 1980, 6 In.
$150

DuMouchelles Art Gallery

This is an edited listing of current prices. Visit **Kovels.com** to check thousands of prices from previous years and sign up for free information on trends, tips, reproductions, marks, and more.

**Peters & Reed,** Vase, Landscape, Trees, Mountains, Stream, 9 In.
$199

Humler & Nolan

---

**Pewabic,** Bowl, Turquoise, Variegated Burgundy, Paper Label, 12 x 4 In.
$330

DuMouchelles Art Gallery

---

**Pewabic,** Vase, Luster Glaze, Persian Blue Drip, Bulbous, 11 x 10 In.
$27,500

Rago Arts & Auction Center

> **TIP**
> Many collectors want pewter that has darkened with age even though it was shiny when new.

| | |
|---|---:|
| **Vase,** Green Luster Glaze, Over Gray, Round Stamp, 6 In. | 374 |
| **Vase,** Green Metallic, Drip, 6 x 7¾ In. | 3965 |
| **Vase,** Green, Gray, Red, Metallic, 10 x 20 In. | 8540 |
| **Vase,** Indigo & Purple Iridescent Glaze, Baluster, Ribbed, Rolled Rim, 11½ x 7 In. | 3660 |
| **Vase,** Iridescent Gray, Pear Shape, Flared Foot, Early 20th Century, 13¼ In. | 2160 |
| **Vase,** Luster Glaze, Persian Blue Drip, Bulbous, 11 x 10 In. .........*illus* | 27500 |
| **Vase,** Mottled Blue Metallic Glaze, Horizontal Ribs, Bulbous, Tapered, 13 x 6 In. | 3300 |
| **Vase,** Multicolor Gloss Glaze, Globe Shape, 3 x 4 In. | 540 |
| **Vase,** Red & Turquoise Metallic Glaze, Bulbous, Horizontal Ribs, 8 x 6 In. | 3965 |
| **Vase,** Red, Lavender, Metallic, Globe, 7 x 7 In. | 3172 |
| **Wall Pocket,** Orange Micro Crystalline Glaze, Triangular, 8 In. | 196 |

**PEWTER** is a metal alloy of tin and lead. Some of the pewter made after 1840 has a slightly different composition and is called Britannia metal. This later type of pewter was worked by machine; the earlier pieces were made by hand. In the 1920s pewter came back into fashion and pieces were often marked *Genuine Pewter*. Eighteenth-, nineteenth-, and twentieth-century examples are listed here.

| | |
|---|---:|
| **Basin,** Providence, Rhode Island, Touchmark, Early 19th Century, 8 In. | 300 |
| **Basket,** Handle, Stamped Tudric, Archibald Knox, Liberty & Co., c.1900, 12 x 8¾ In. | 1125 |
| **Biscuit Box,** Tudric, Enamel Buttons, Archibald Knox, Liberty & Co., c.1905, 5 x 4 In. ......*illus* | 1625 |
| **Bowl,** Art Nouveau, Flower Handle, Plate, Tulips, Stamped, Kayserzinn, 9 x 11 In. | 184 |
| **Bowl,** Hammered, 2 Handles, Green Glass Insert, Liberty & Co., 2½ x 11½ In. | 976 |
| **Bowl,** Hammered, 3-Petal Flowers, Green Glass Insert, 3 Round Feet, Liberty, 3 x 5 In. | 610 |
| **Bowl,** Hammered, Flared, Tudric, Liberty & Co., 10 In. | 75 |
| **Bowl,** Shallow, Wide Flat Rim, 9⅝ In., 8 Piece | 360 |
| **Candelabrum,** 3-Light, Ovals Border, Marked Tudric, Liberty & Co., 12 In., Pair | 1080 |
| **Candlestick,** Baluster, Engraved Flowers, Flagg & Homan, Cincinnati, 10 In., Pair | 252 |
| **Candlestick,** Enameled Copper Cabochons, Tundric, Liberty, England, c.1900, 9 x 6 In., Pair | 960 |
| **Chamberstick,** Cylindrical, Dish Base, Loop Handle, Lewis & Cowles, 4¼ In. | 450 |
| **Charger,** Alexander Cleeve, London, 23 In. | 528 |
| **Charger,** England, Partial Touchmark, 22 In. | 270 |
| **Charger,** Spencer Stafford, N.Y., c.1800, 13½ In. | 360 |
| **Charger,** Touchmark, Nathanial Austin, 1763-1800, 13½ In. | 219 |
| **Charger,** Touchmark, Thomas Badger, 15 In. | 750 |
| **Charger,** Wrigglework Tulip, C. Baldwin, England, c.1735, 12⅝ In. | 123 |
| **Coffee Set,** Coffeepot, Sugar & Creamer, Tray, Wood Handle, P.E. Raymor, 1950s | 2000 |
| **Coffee Set,** Paul Evans, Raymor, Coffeepot, Sugar & Creamer, 1950s, 13 In., 3 Piece .........*illus* | 1375 |
| **Coffeepot,** Ball Finial, Dome Lid, Baluster, Curved Handle, Boardman & Co., 12 In., Pair | 180 |
| **Coffeepot,** Dome Lid, S-Scroll Handle, G. Richardson, Rhode Island, c.1835, 9¾ In. .........*illus* | 224 |
| **Coffeepot,** Tankard Shape, Scroll Handle, Issac Lewis, Meriden, Conn., c.1840, 11 In. | 277 |
| **Dinner Gong,** Tabletop, Hammered, Arched Stand, Tudric, Liberty & Co., 17 x 20 In. | 1342 |
| **Dish,** Deep, Boardman & Hart, New York, 9⅜ In. | 180 |
| **Dish,** John Andrew Brunstrom, Philadelphia, c.1780, 1½ x 13 In. | 240 |
| **Dish,** S. Hamlin, Rhode Island, c.1890, 13½ In. | 120 |
| **Dish,** Wide Rim Band, Thomas Boardman, Hartford, Connecticut, 10¾ In. | 94 |
| **Flagon,** Lid, Tapered, Zinn Schnabelkanne, 3 Claw Feet, c.1950, 18½ In. .........*illus* | 84 |
| **Lamp,** Whale Oil, W.H. Parmenter, Chamber, Geo. Carr's Patent, 9 In. | 180 |
| **Mold,** Candle, 23 Tubes, Pine Frame, 3 Wick Rods, 16 x 19 In. | 510 |
| **Mold,** Candle, 24 Pewter Tubes, Pine Frame, 18 x 24 In. | 660 |
| **Mold,** Candle, 24 Tubes, Pine Frame, 1800s, 16 x 21½ In. .........*illus* | 594 |
| **Ornament,** Furniture, Center Mask, Dolphins, Curvilinear Scrolls, Frame, c.1800, 12 x 5 In. | 242 |
| **Pitcher,** Green Glass, A. Knox, J. Powell, Liberty & Co., c.1905, 14 x 5 In. | 1125 |
| **Pitcher,** Green Glass, Archibald Knox, Liberty & Co., 13½ x 5¼ In. | 1125 |
| **Pitcher,** Green Glass, Stamped Tudric, A. Knox, J. Powell, Liberty & Co., c.1905, 8 x 6 In. | 1500 |
| **Pitcher,** Oval, Applied Handle, Geometric & Flower Designs, Marked, 8¼ In. | 845 |
| **Pitcher,** Zinn Schnabelstitze, Touchmarks, Eger, Czech Republic, c.1831, 9¾ In. | 84 |
| **Plate,** Love, Lovebirds & Spurious London Mark, 1700s, 7¾ In. .........*illus* | 200 |
| **Plate,** Wavy Rim, Joseph Spackman, English, c.1765 | 195 |
| **Plates,** Hebrew Letters, Partial Hallmarks, 9½ In. | 63 |
| **Porringer,** Samuel Hamlin, 5 In. | 266 |
| **Tankard,** Green Glass, Archibald Knox, Liberty & Co., 8 x 6 In. | 1500 |
| **Tankard,** Green Glass, Pope's Money Pattern, Archibald Knox, Liberty & Co., c.1905, 15 x 7 In. | 2000 |
| **Tankard,** Soldier, Helbard, Flowers, Geometric Engraved, 17th Century, 12 In. | 595 |
| **Tankard,** Tulip, Impressed Crown WR, England, c.1920, 6½ In. | 60 |

P

| | |
|---|---|
| **Tea Set,** Sugar & Creamer, Waste, 6 Cups & Saucers, Spoons, Box, Child's, 5 x 12 In. | 1375 |
| **Tea Urn,** Tapered Brass Top, 3 Scroll Legs, Wood Ball Feet, Germany, c.1820, 16 In. | 192 |
| **Teapot,** Bailey & Putnam, Touchmark, c.1840, 8 ½ In. | 390 |
| **Teapot,** Footed, Black Scrolled Handle, Dixons & Sons, England, 13 In. | 70 |
| **Teapot,** Hinged Lid, Wooden Wafer, Scroll Handle, Footed, Signed J. Danforth, 10 In. | 212 |
| **Teapot,** Pear Shape, Bone Finial, Richardson, Boston, 7 ½ In. | 443 |
| **Teapot,** Wood Handle, Samuel Ellis, London, c.1790, 5 ¾ In. | 375 |
| **Tray,** Marriage Record, 1766, Round, Scalloped Rim, 13 In. | 192 |
| **Tray,** Nude Woman, Lying On Beach, Putti, Fish, Signed J. Jouant, 12 ½ x 16 ¼ In. | 115 |
| **Urn,** Lid, Spice Container, c.1735, 4 In. | 142 |
| **Urn,** Scrolled Legs, Trefoil Base, Wooden Feet, Urn Finial, 18th Century, 16 In. | 125 |
| **Vase,** Art Nouveau, Pelican & Iris, Palm Leaf Handles, Kayserzinn, 23 In. | 360 |
| **Vase,** Bottle, Incised Stylized Leaves, A. Knox, Liberty & Co., 7 x 3 In. | 519 |
| **Vase,** Ceramic Top, Stylized Trees, Blue & Green, Flared Base, Tudric, c.1900, 9 In. | 1770 |
| **Vase,** Dragonflies, Water Lilies, Signed, Etian Fin Garanta, 19 ¼ In. | 288 |
| **Vase,** Hammered, Rocket Shape, 3 Buttressed Handles, A. Knox, Liberty & Co., 12 In. | 1220 |
| **Vase,** Organic Form, Blue & Green Enameled Heart, Liberty & Co., 6 x 3 In., Pair | 1159 |

---

**PHOENIX GLASS** Company was founded in 1880 in Pennsylvania. The firm made commercial products, such as lampshades, bottles, and glassware. Collectors today are interested in the "Sculptured Artware" made by the company from the 1930s until the mid-1950s. Some pieces of Phoenix glass are very similar to those made by the Consolidated Lamp and Glass Company. Phoenix made Reuben Blue, lavender, and yellow pieces. These colors were not used by Consolidated. In 1970 Phoenix became a division of Anchor Hocking, which was sold to the Newell Group in 1987. The factory is still working.

| | |
|---|---|
| **Finger Bowl,** Drape, Cranberry Opalescent, Scalloped Rim, c.1888, 5 In. | 58 |
| **Pitcher,** Spot-Optic, Rose Opalescent, Square Rim, Reeded Handle, c.1888, 7 In. | 173 |
| **Pitcher,** Spot-Optic, Spatter, Blue & Opal Flakes, Crimped Rim, c.1888, 5 ½ In. | 69 |
| **Pitcher,** Stripe-Optic, Multicolor Flowers, Birds, Ball Shape, Handle, c.1888, 6 In. | 138 |
| **Pitcher,** Water, Diamond Optic Craquelle, Clear Opalescent, c.1885, 7 ⅜ In. | 259 |
| **Toothpick Holder,** Coin Spot, Blue Opalescent, Footed, c.1888, 2 ¾ In. | 207 |
| **Vase,** Dancing Nudes, Pan, Blue, c.1945, 11 ½ x 9 In. | 288 |
| **Vase,** Draped, Crimped, Cased, Shading From Red To Pearl, 7 ½ In. | 58 |
| **Vase,** Lovebirds, Ivory, Brown, Frosted Glass, Pa., 1930, 10 x 8 ½ In. | 480 |
| **Vase,** Owl, Bittersweet, Blue, Cream, Brown, c.1910, 6 In. | 94 |
| **Vase,** Relief Geese, Pale Blue, 9 ½ In. | 266 |

---

**PHONOGRAPHS,** invented by Thomas Edison in 1877, have been made by many firms. This category also includes other items associated with the phonograph. Jukeboxes and Records are listed in their own categories.

| | |
|---|---|
| **Columbia,** Graphophone BX, Cylinder, Horn, Portable, Lid, Wood Case | 600 |
| **Columbia,** Graphophone, Brass Horn, Cast Handle, 13 x 9 In. | 864 |
| **Edison,** Amberola, Model B-5, Cylinder, Mahogany | 600 |
| **Edison,** Cylinder Player, Oak Case, Tabletop, Pat. 1896-98 ............................. *illus* | 330 |
| **Edison,** Diamond Disc, Floor, Mahogany | 1600 |
| **Edison,** Home, C Reproducer, Cylinder, Cover, Crank | 275 |
| **Edison,** Home, Horn, Lid, Oak Case, c.1910, 12 ½ x 16 In. ....................... *illus* | 500 |
| **Edison,** Home, Oak Case, Black Morning Glory Horn, 19 Cylinders, 32 In. ........ *illus* | 531 |
| **Edison,** Model C, Cylinder, Portable, Lid, Horn, Crank, Wood Case | 510 |
| **Edison,** Model VIII, Cylinder, Black Cygnet Horn | 700 |
| **Edison,** Standard, Cygnet Horn, Crank, c.1920, 12 x 13 In. | 1063 |
| **Edison,** Suitcase Model, Brass Horn, 12 x 16 In. | 415 |
| **Gramophone Company,** His Master's Voice, 2-Door, 3 Compartment, 33 x 30 In. | 600 |
| **Gramophone Company,** No. 4, Mahogany, c.1920, 13 x 15 x 18 In. | 240 |
| **Grundig,** Record Player, Console Model, Wood, Sliding Doors, 33 x 44 In. | 390 |
| **Modernola,** Cylindrical Floor Console, Lamp, Fringe Shade, Storage, 47 In. | 1560 |
| **Victor E,** Disc, Brass Bell Horn | 825 |
| **Victor II,** Disc, Oak, Brass Bell Horn | 600 |
| **Victor V,** Disc, Wooden Horn, Spruce | 1600 |
| **Victor Victrola,** Model VE-405, Floor Console, Gold, c.1924, 34 x 37 In. | 660 |
| **Victor Victrola,** Model VV-VIII, Tabletop, 3 Shelves, c.1916 | 330 |
| **Victor,** E, Horn, Oak, 11 x 11 In. | 556 |
| **Victor,** External Horn, Tin, Oak, Knobs, Nipper Decal, c.1910, 30 In., 19-In. Horn | 403 |

**Pewter,** Biscuit Box, Tudric, Enamel Buttons, Archibald Knox, Liberty & Co., c.1905, 5 x 4 In.
$1,625

Rago Arts & Auction Center

**Pewter,** Coffee Set, Paul Evans, Raymor, Coffeepot, Sugar & Creamer, 1950s, 13 In., 3 Piece
$1,375

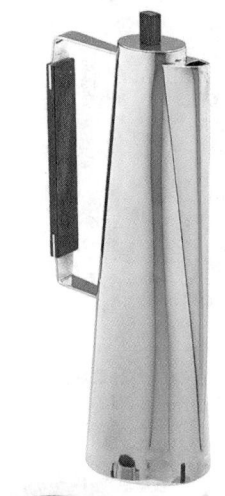

Rago Arts & Auction Centera

**Pewter,** Coffeepot, Dome Lid, S Scroll Handle, G. Richardson, Rhode Island, c.1835, 9 ¾ In.
$224

Conestoga Auction Co., Inc.

**Pewter,** Flagon, Lid, Tapered, Zinn Schnabelkanne, 3 Claw Feet, c.1950, 18 ½ In.
$84

The Stein Auction Company

**Pewter,** Mold, Candle, 24 Tubes, Pine Frame, 1800s, 16 x 21 ½ In.
$594

Garth's Auctioneers & Appraisers

**Pewter,** Plate, Love, Lovebirds & Spurious London Mark, 1700s, 7 ¾ In.
$200

Conestoga Auction Co., Inc.

| | |
|---|---:|
| **Victor,** Talking Machine, Type D, Carved Oak Case, c.1907, 25 x 28 ¾ In. ...............*illus* | 1320 |
| **Victor,** Talking Machine, Wood Cabinet, Fluted Horn, 31 x 16 In. | 1750 |
| **Victor,** Upright, VV-110, Mahogany, Victrola No. 2 Reproducer, 47 In. | 90 |
| **Wood,** Decorative Cutout Front, Metal Lid, 2 Glass Sides, Tabletop | 120 |

**PHONOGRAPH NEEDLE CASES** of tin are collected today by music and phonograph enthusiasts and advertising addicts. The tins are very small, about 2 inches across, and often have attractive graphic designs lithographed on the top and sides.

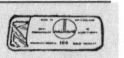

| | |
|---|---:|
| **Electro-Phonic,** Records, Paper, 1 x 2 In. | 15 |
| **Elkah 200,** Green Hinged, Tin, 1 ⅜ x 1 ¹³⁄₁₆ In. | 24 |
| **Golden Pyramid,** Pyramid Shape, Gold, Blue, Tin, 2 ½ In. | 145 |
| **Goldentone Soloist,** Red, White, 2 ¾ x 1 ¾ In. | 14 |
| **Imperial,** Horned Phonograph, Green, Red, Tin, Germany, 1 ⅞ x 1 ⅜ In. | 42 |
| **Nelson,** Oil Tempered Steel, Black & White, Tin, 2 ⅞ x 1 ¾ In. | 25 |
| **Sem Needles,** Couple Dancing, Tin, 2 ¾ x 1 ¼ In. | 50 |
| **Shadowgraph,** Paper, Yellow, Black, 2 ¼ x 3 ½ In. | 18 |
| **Soft Tone,** His Master's Voice, Nipper, Victor Logo, Paper, 1 ⅝ x 1 ¼ In. | 15 |
| **Songster Needles,** Bird On Branch, Blue, Gold, Tin, 1 ⅞ x 1 ⅜ In. | 48 |
| **Taj Mahal,** Extra Loud, Black, Red, Yellow, Tin, 1 ⅞ x 1 ⅜ In. | 55 |
| **Verona Needles,** Nude Woman, Tin, 1 ½ x 1 ½ In. | 50 |

**PHOTOGRAPHY** items are listed here. The first photograph was a view from a window in France taken in 1826. The commercially successful photograph started with the daguerreotype introduced in 1839. Today all sorts of photographs and photographic equipment are collected. Albums were popular in Victorian times. Cartes de visite, popular after 1854, were mounted on 2 ½-by-4-inch cardboard. Cabinet cards were introduced in 1866. These were mounted on 4 ¼-by-6 ½-inch cards. Stereo views are listed under Stereo Card. Stereoscopes are listed in their own section.

| | |
|---|---:|
| **Albumen,** A Sharpshooter's Last Sleep, A. Gardener, 7 x 9 In. | 1320 |
| **Albumen,** Grand Canyon, Wheeler Expedition, Timothy O'Sullivan | 1680 |
| **Albumen,** Interior Of Breastworks On Round Top, A. Gardener, 6 ¾ x 9 In. | 510 |
| **Ambrotype,** Civil War Soldier, 10th Army Patch, Union Case, 9th Plate ...............*illus* | 330 |
| **Ambrotype,** Confederate Lt. Bassett Atkinson Marsden, Civil War | 5400 |
| **Cabinet Card,** Annie Oakley, Little Sure-Shot, England, 1890s ...............*illus* | 4800 |
| **Cabinet Card,** Sitting Bull, Traditional Dress, Standing, G. Spencer | 492 |
| **Camera,** Bell & Howell, Auto Load, 16 mm, Size 4.5, Leather Handle, Case, 7 ½ In. | 60 |
| **Camera,** Brown Scout, 620 Flash, c.1933 | 5 |
| **Camera,** Brownie, Kodak No. 3A, Maroon Bellows | 15 |
| **Camera,** Canon, EOS 650 | 35 |
| **Camera,** Cine-Kodak, Model K 3/5, Carry Case, Hand Crank Power, c.1930 | 120 |
| **Camera,** Graphex, 135 mm, Case | 60 |
| **Camera,** J.A. Sinclair, Una, Mahogany, Brass, Quarter Plate, 3 Holders, Case, London, c.1930 | 1230 |
| **Camera,** Kodak, Ektar 127 mm, Burke & James | 30 |
| **Camera,** Korona, Speed Graphic, Series No. 2 | 75 |
| **Camera,** Leica, M3 Double Stroke, Summicron Lens, c.1955, Germany | 1046 |
| **Camera,** Leica, M3 Double Stroke, Summicron Lens, c.1957, Germany | 1230 |
| **Camera,** Leitz 21 mm Superangulon-R Lens, Leica R Mount, Leather Case, Germany | 584 |
| **Camera,** Leitz Thambar, 9 cm, Soft Focus, Leica Screw Mount | 1845 |
| **Camera,** Leitz, Summarex, M Mount Lens, Leitz UV Filter, Lens Shade, Leather Case | 984 |
| **Camera,** Mahogany, Bellows, Tailboard Plate, Voigtlander Lens, Tripod, c.1890 ...............*illus* | 185 |
| **Camera,** Minolta SRT 101, Rokkorph 58 mm Lens | 5 |
| **Camera,** Motion Picture, Junior Professional, Eberhard Schneider, c.1900, 10 x 12 In. | 10625 |
| **Camera,** Nikon, FE, Bushnell 28 mm Lens, c.1978 | 30 |
| **Camera,** Studio, Steel, Mahogany Case, Adjustable Stand, Swift & Son, London, 58 In. | 1250 |
| **Carte De Visite,** Famished Andersonville Prison Survivor, Albumen | 1046 |
| **Carte De Visite,** Gen. Joseph J. Bartlett, Signed | 441 |
| **Carte De Visite,** Gen. Wm. W. Belknap, Signed | 300 |
| **Carte De Visite,** General George A. Custer, Arms Crossed, 1865 | 1645 |
| **Carte De Visite,** General Henry E. Davis, Signed | 240 |
| **Carte De Visite,** General Joseph Mower, Shoulder-Length Portrait | 264 |
| **Carte De Visite,** General Rutherford B. Hayes, Vignette | 4112 |
| **Carte De Visite,** Lt. Colonel Charles R. Mudge, Seated At Table | 2160 |
| **Carte De Visite,** U.S. Grant As Lt. General, Vignette, Signed | 2702 |
| **Carte De Visite,** Union Gen. James D. Morgan, Signed ...............*illus* | 210 |
| **Carte De Visite,** Union General David A Russell, Signed | 1046 |

**Phonograph,** Edison, Cylinder Player, Oak Case, Tabletop, Pat. 1896-98
$330

Morphy Auctions

**Phonograph,** Edison, Home, Horn, Lid, Oak Case, c.1910, 12½ x 16 In.
$500

Rago Arts & Auction Center

**Phonograph,** Edison, Home, Oak Case, Black Morning Glory Horn, 19 Cylinders, 32 In.
$531

Brunk Auctions

**TIP**

*Do not use photo albums with plastic or black paper pages. These will damage the photos in time.*

**Phonograph,** Victor, Talking Machine, Type D, Carved Oak Case, c.1907, 25 x 28¾ In.
$1,320

DuMouchelles Art Gallery

**Photography,** Ambrotype, Civil War Soldier, 10th Army Patch, Union Case, 9th Plate
$330

Cowan's Auctions

**Photography,** Cabinet Card, Annie Oakley, Little Sure-Shot, England, 1890s
$4,800

Cowan's Auctions

**Photography,** Camera, Mahogany, Bellows, Tailboard Plate, Voigtlander Lens, Tripod, c.1890
$185

Skinner Auctioneers & Appraisers

**Photography,** Carte De Visite, Union Gen. James D. Morgan, Signed
$210

Cowan's Auctions

**Photography,** Daguerreotype, Odd Fellows Member, Gold-Tinted Apron, Half Case, ½ Plate
$1,560

Cowan's Auctions

P

Photography, Photograph, Lauren Bacall, Black & White, Inset Autograph, Mat, Frame, 13 x 8 In.
$84

DuMouchelles Art Gallery

Photography, Photograph, Marilyn Monroe, Hollywood Hills, George Barris, July 1962, 13 x 10 In.
$523

Skinner Auctioneers & Appraisers

| | |
|---|---:|
| **Carte De Visite,** Union General Gabriel R. Paul, Arms Folded | 2880 |
| **Carte De Visite,** Union General James S. Negley, Signed | 300 |
| **Carte De Visite,** Union General Thomas H. Neill, Signed | 1440 |
| **Carte De Visite,** Union General William H. Morris, Signed | 720 |
| **Daguerreotype,** Odd Fellows Member, Gold-Tinted Apron, Half Case, ½ Plate _illus_ | 1560 |
| **Gelatin Silver Print,** Portrait Of Dr. Eloesser, Signed, Edward Weston, c.1929, 5 x 5 In. | 3125 |
| **Lithograph,** Shakers, New Lebanon, Dancing, Inside, c.1845, 9½ x 13¾ In. | 2583 |
| **Magic Lantern,** Ernst Plank, Tin, Copper, Paper Cover, Vulcan, 10 Slides, Box, 13 x 8 In. | 413 |
| **Newspaper Acting Picture Machine,** Flicker Action, Tin Lithograph, Crank, c.1919, 5 In. | 561 |
| **Panotype,** General Thomas Crook Sullivan, Leather | 185 |
| **Photograph,** Abraham Lincoln, Bust Profile, Matthew Brady, c.1864, 3¾ x 2¼ In. | 2963 |
| **Photograph,** Alys, Lisa Conrad, Color Print, Glazed, Aluminum Frame, 54 x 48 In. | 2460 |
| **Photograph,** Brooklyn Bridge, Al Macy, Estate Stamp, 1950s, 8 x 10 In. | 135 |
| **Photograph,** Fatima Candles, Portugal, Nan Goldin, Cibachrome, Frame, 1998, 30 x 40 In. | 7995 |
| **Photograph,** Greta Garbo, Gelatin Silver Print, Signed, George E. Hurrell, 15½ x 19 In. | 480 |
| **Photograph,** Janis Joplin, On Sofa, Southern Comfort Bottle, J. Marshall, 1968, 11 x 14 In. | 812 |
| **Photograph,** Jimi Hendrix, ¾-Length Portrait, Elliott Landy, 1968, 18¾ x 12 In. | 295 |
| **Photograph,** Lauren Bacall, Black & White, Inset Autograph, Mat, Frame, 13 x 8 In. _illus_ | 84 |
| **Photograph,** Marilyn Monroe, Hollywood Hills, George Barris, July 1962, 13 x 10 In. _illus_ | 523 |
| **Photograph,** Nan Goldin Portrait, David Armstrong, Gelatin Silver Print, Frame, 21 x 18 In. | 799 |
| **Photograph,** Silver Gelatin Print, David Lynch, Isabella Rossellini, Helmut Newton, 1988, 19 x 19 In. | 2988 |
| **Tintype,** 9 Civil War Soldiers, Uncased, Lightly Tinted, Sabers, ½ Plate | 461 |
| **Tintype,** Indian Brave, Wife, 2 Children, Gutta Percha Case, 3¾ In. | 550 |

**PIANO BABY** is a collector's term. About 1880, the well-decorated home had a shawl on the piano. Bisque figures of babies were designed to help hold the shawl in place. They range in size from 6 to 18 inches. Most of the figures were made in Germany. Reproductions are being made. Other piano babies may be listed under manufacturers' names.

| | |
|---|---:|
| **Baby,** Crawling, Sucking Thumb, c.1915, 3 In. | 50 |
| **Baby,** Holding Toes, Sweet Face, Germany, 3 In. | 40 |
| **Baby,** Sucking Toes, Nude, Gebruder Heubach, 5 In. | 850 |
| **Boy,** Crawling, Intaglio Eyes, Finger Over Mouth, 5 x 3½ In. | 150 |
| **Boy,** Crawling, Rabbit, Kitten, 6¼ x 2⅜ In. | 135 |
| **Boy,** Lying On Back, Holding Shell, Blue Romper, 3 x 6¾ In. | 135 |
| **Girl,** Crying, Hands Over Eyes, White Gown, 5½ In. | 125 |
| **Girl,** Kneeling, Rattle, c.1900, 2½ x 4 In. | 90 |
| **Girl,** Lying, Holding Ring, Resting Head On Hand, White & Pink Dress, 6 x 2 In. | 35 |
| **Girl,** Lying, Playing With Toes, Bonnet, Romper, Pink Trim, 3½ In. | 100 |
| **Girl,** Reaching Out, Blond, Pigtails, Nude, 9 In. | 48 |
| **Girl,** Sitting, Blond Hair, Straight Legs, Porcelain, 6½ In. | 86 |
| **Girl,** Sitting, Blond, Bonnet, 4 In. | 25 |
| **Girl,** Sitting, Legs Crossed, Holding Bottle, Flowered Romper, 3¾ In. | 100 |

**PICKARD** China Company was started in 1893 by Wilder Pickard. Hand-painted designs were used on china purchased from other sources. In the 1930s, the company began to make its own china wares in Chicago, Illinois. The company now makes many types of porcelains, including a successful line of limited edition collector plates.

| | |
|---|---:|
| **Ashtray,** Floral Chintz, 3 In. Diam. | 21 |
| **Cup & Saucer,** Brocade, Footed | 23 |
| **Pitcher,** Art Nouveau Lotus Blossoms, Watery Background, Signed Keates, 5 In. | 230 |
| **Pitcher,** Berries, Leaves, Yellow, Green Ground, Gold Trim, 7¾ In. | 354 |
| **Pitcher,** Strawberry, Gold Trim, Squat, Signed Beitler, 7¾ In. | 413 |
| **Plate,** Dinner, Greenbriar, 10 In. | 32 |
| **Plate,** Poppies, Cream Center, Gold Border, 9½ In. | 325 |
| **Tankard,** Monk, Seated, Peeling Turnips, Signed Gasper, 13¾ In. | 472 |
| **Tankard,** Orange Tree, Green Ground, Gold Handle, 10¾ In. | 266 |
| **Tankard,** Plums, Cream, Rust, Green Ground, Gold Trim, Signed Deroy, 10¾ In. | 767 |
| **Vase,** Blue, Scenic, Gold Scalloped Rim, Cylindrical, Signed, 6½ In. | 357 |
| **Vase,** Hummingbirds, Gold Flower Etched Body, Angled Handles, 10 In. | 413 |
| **Vase,** Large Poppy, Green Ground, Waisted Shape, Signed Kiefus, 13½ In. | 531 |
| **Vase,** Painted, Tropical Waterscape, Palm Trees, Full Moon, Signed Hames, c.1915, 7 In. | 236 |
| **Vase,** Roses, Flowers, Gilt, Tapered, Footed, Marked, 5⅝ In. | 60 |
| **Vase,** Vellum, Birch Trees, Snow Covered Mountain, Curtis H. Marker, c.1919, 8 In. | 546 |
| **Vase,** Vellum, Moonlit Florida Scene, Handles, Curtis H. Marker, c.1935, 9⅝ In. | 546 |
| **Water Set,** Pitcher, Cup, Tray, Flowers, Bands, Square Handle, H.L. Lang, c.1910, 8 x 12 In. | 431 |

**PICTURES**, silhouettes, and other small decorative objects framed to hang on the wall are listed here. Some other types of pictures are listed in the Print and Painting categories.

| | |
|---|---|
| **Chalk,** Pastel, Union Civil War Soldier, Tall Musket, Long Saber, Painted Frame, Oval, 25 In....... | 303 |
| **Collection Of Artifacts,** 46 Points, Scrapers, Blades, On Red Felt, Frame, 27 x 20 In. .........*illus* | 138 |
| **Color Screenprint,** Hommage Au Carre, Josef Albers, Signed, Frame, c.1965, 19 x 15 In. ........... | 3438 |
| **Crayon,** On Paper, Black & White Cat, Eddie Arning, c.1980, 12 x 18 In. ....................................... | 275 |
| **Drawing,** Nymphs Of The Garden, Birds, Childe Hassam, Matted, c.1923, 4¾ x 11½ In............... | 1195 |
| **Engraving,** Brooklyn Bridge, Multicolor, Oct. 6, 1929, 10¾ x 15¾ In........................................... | 175 |
| **Etching & Aquatint,** Farm House, Chickens, Gustav Goetsch, 1946, 7 x 9 In.............................. | 50 |
| **Etching,** On Paper, Pair Of Yellowlegs, Signed Frank Benson, 1916, 3½ x 4 In............................ | 1440 |
| **Etching,** On Paper, The Constitution, Charles Woodbury, 1932, 11½ x 14¾ In. ........................... | 720 |
| **Etching,** Self-Portrait, Hat, Gustav Goetsch, 1951, 5 x 3½ In. .................................................... | 75 |
| **Gouache,** On Paper, Roses On Ledge, Raoul Maucherat De Longpre, France, c.1870, 21 x 28 In. | 4375 |
| **Gouache,** On Paper, Sailing Ship, Initialed, American School, Frame, 1800s, 8 x 9 In. .......*illus* | 630 |
| **Graphite,** Charcoal, On Paper, Self-Portrait, Dr. Atl, Bearded Man, Mexico, c.1945, 23 x 17 In... | 7200 |
| **Ink & Colors,** On Paper, Grocer's Shop, Frame, Chinese Export, c.1830, 17 x 13 In. ...........*illus* | 533 |
| **Ink,** Color, On Paper, Beauty Beneath The Waterfall, Watanabe Shiko, 43 x 17 In. .................... | 1494 |
| **Ink,** Gouache, On Paper, Mandarin Portrait, Brocade Border, Chinese, 37 x 21 In. ................... | 207 |
| **Ink,** On Paper, Leaping Stag, Pond, Swan, J. Henry Hoffman In Banner, Frame, c.1885, 32 In..... | 1495 |
| **Lithograph,** New England Farm, Thomas Hart Benton, c.1951, 9 x 13¾ In..................................... | 3250 |
| **Lithograph,** Oil Barges, Joe Jones, 13 x 18½ In................................................................................ | 650 |
| **Lithograph,** Pretty Girl, Dressed In Early 1900s Style Fancy Dress, Frame, 12 x 28 In............... | 300 |
| **Lithograph,** Sandstone House, Cottonwood Trees, Birger Sandzen, 10 x 12 In. ......................... | 400 |
| **Lithograph,** Tough Guy, Cap, Pipe, Hands In Pocket, Joe Jones, 17 x 12 In. ................................ | 250 |
| **Miniature,** Porcelain, Enamel, George IV, Prince Regent, Signed, HB, 1½ In. ....................*illus* | 2706 |
| **Miniature,** Watercolor, On Ivory, Child, Frame, Etched, Stones, Signed, M. Bost, 1½ In. ......*illus* | 923 |
| **Miniature,** Watercolor, On Ivory, Girl, White Dress, Rose, Mrs. Moses Russell, c.1850, 4 In......... | 6875 |
| **Miniature,** Watercolor, Profile, Man, Cravat, Waistcoat, Frame, R. Porter, c.1870, 4 x 3 In. ......... | 1560 |
| **Mixed Media,** On Paper, Circle, Section Series: Reach, John Pearson, Frame, 25 x 37 In............. | 127 |
| **Mourning Print,** Memory Of George Willis Who Departed This Life 1848, 1800s, 12 x 8 In........ | 61 |
| **Needlework,** Adam & Eve, Tree With Snake, 1776, Silk On Linen, Frame, 17 x 12 In. .................. | 3304 |
| **Needlework,** Berlin Work, Tulip, Initials, M.B. 1863, Frame, 5 x 4½ In......................................... | 71 |
| **Needlework,** Chenille, Linen, Church, Bird On Steeple, Landscape, Frame, c.1910, 7 x 7 In........ | 35 |
| **Needlework,** Flora Temple, Running Horse, House, c.1890, 17 x 18 In. ........................................ | 840 |
| **Needlework,** Floral Vine, Squirrel, Stag, Butterfly, Wool, On Linen, Frame, 1700s, 19 x 15 In. .... | 960 |
| **Needlework,** Flower Basket, 3 Birds, Metal Beads, Gilt Molded Frame, 1800s, 27 x 28 In. .......... | 295 |
| **Needlework,** Hot Air Balloon, Copper, Clear & Red Beads, Butterfly, Waves, 13 x 9 In. .............. | 123 |
| **Needlework,** Panel, Macaw, Dogs, Mrs. Jeremiah Smith Of Rye, Frame, c.1900, 36 x 26 In. ........ | 472 |
| **Needlework,** Silk, Woman, Cornucopia, Flowers, Watercolor, c.1810, 13 x 11 In. ...............*illus* | 265 |
| **Needlework,** Stumpwork, Charles II, Royal Couple, Trees, Animals, Birds, Frame, 9 x 15 In. ....... | 9600 |
| **Needlework,** Stumpwork, Hunters, Charles I, Forest Animals, Frame, c.1700, 10 x 16 In. ........... | 2880 |
| **Needlework,** Watercolor, On Silk, Memorial, Woman, Garden, Frame, c.1810, 16 x 13 In. ..*illus* | 920 |
| **Needlework,** Watercolor, On Silk, Mourning Scene, Not Lost, Oval Mat, Frame, 12 x 15 In. ......... | 780 |
| **Needlework,** Watercolor, On Silk, Silk Threads, Shepherdess, Flock, Frame, 20 x 16 In. ............ | 600 |
| **Needlework,** Wool, 6-Mast Paddle Wheeler, Blue Ground, England, 16 x 28 In. ........................ | 1200 |
| **Needlework,** Wool, Old Stone House, Gen. G. Washington, Headquarters, 1892, 20 x 18 In........ | 4600 |
| **Needlework,** Wool, On Linen, House, Church, Trees, Berlin Work, N.H., 1884, 18 x 21 In. ........... | 978 |
| **Needlework,** Yarn Work, Fruit, Flowers, Wreath, Walnut Shadowbox, Victorian, 20 x 23 In. *illus* | 94 |
| **Panel,** Egyptian Style, Gilt, Linen Back, Acrylic Display Box, 14 x 14 In........................................ | 246 |
| **Panel,** Painted, Carved, Woman, Apron, Man, Uniform, Flowers, Conn., c.1920, 21 x 12 In., Pair | 750 |
| **Panel,** Plaster, Anna Pavlova & Mikhail Mordkin, Bacchanale, 46 x 61 In., 9 Piece...................... | 1920 |
| **Pastel,** Child, In Chair, Orange Dress, Coral Necklace, Holding Flowers, c.1810, 25 x 18 In. ........ | 1920 |
| **Pastel,** On Paper, Family, On Beach, Gustav Goetsch, 1958, 11 x 15 In. ....................................... | 950 |
| **Pencil,** On Paper, Self-Portrait, Gustav Goetsch, 1960, 5½ x 3¾ In............................................. | 100 |
| **Sandpaper,** Town, Waterfall, Dam, Mill, Bridge, New England, Wood Frame, 15 x 21 In............. | 2414 |
| **Scherenschnitte,** Lovebirds, Within Heart, Watercolor, Cut Out, G.B. French, 10 x 9½ In. ......... | 197 |
| **Scherenschnitte,** Vining Flowers, Blue, Green, Red, Foil, J.B. Walker, Frame, 16 x 13 In. ...*illus* | 600 |
| **Scherenschnitte,** Watercolor, Birds, On Urn, Claudia Hopf, 1986, 10 x 6½ In. .......................... | 74 |
| **Scroll,** Hanging, Deities, 3 Rows, Ink, Paint, On Silk, Chinese, 1800s, 58 x 30 In. ..................... | 711 |
| **Scroll,** Paper, Ink, Color, Recluse In Mount Hua, Hanging, Chinese, 1900s, 36 x 20 In............... | 474 |
| **Silhouette,** Reverend Thomas Barnard, Cut Paper, Frame, Salem, Ma., 6 x 5¼ In................... | 660 |
| **Silhouette,** Woman In Rocking Chair, Black, Gold Highlights, c.1810, 13 x 8¼ In..................... | 295 |
| **Silhouette,** Woman With Flower Sprig, Puffy Sleeves, Watercolor, New England, 5 x 4 In............ | 2625 |
| **Tempora On Board,** Meadow Lark No. 3, Bird On Child's Blocks, A.R. Saalburg, 18 x 13 In....... | 540 |
| **Thangka,** Depicting A Deity, 6-Armed Center Figure, Lotus Throne, c.1810, 30 x 22 In. ............. | 240 |

**Picture,** Collection Of Artifacts, 46 Points, Scrapers, Blades, On Red Felt, Frame, 27 x 20 In.
$138

Allard Auctions

**Picture,** Gouache, On Paper, Sailing Ship, Initialed, American School, Frame, 1800s, 8 x 9 In.
$630

Garth's Auctioneers & Appraisers

**P**

**Picture,** Ink & Colors, On Paper, Grocer's Shop, Frame, Chinese Export, c.1830, 17 x 13 In.
$533

James D. Julia Auetioneers

# PICTURE

**Picture,** Miniature, Porcelain, Enamel, George IV, Prince Regent, Signed, HB, 1 ½ In.
$2,706

Skinner Auctioneers & Appraisers

**Picture,** Miniature, Watercolor, On Ivory, Child, Frame, Etched, Stones, Signed, M. Bost, 1 ½ In.
$923

Skinner Auctioneers & Appraisers

**Picture,** Needlework, Silk, Woman, Cornucopia, Flowers, Watercolor, c.1810, 13 x 11 In.
$265

Conestoga Auction Co., Inc.

**Picture,** Needlework, Watercolor, On Silk, Memorial, Woman, Garden, Frame, c.1810, 16 x 13 In.
$920

Cottone Auctions

**Picture,** Needlework, Yarn Work, Fruit, Flowers, Wreath, Walnut Shadowbox, Victorian, 20 x 23 In.
$94

Conestoga Auction Co., Inc.

**Picture,** Scherenschnitte, Vining Flowers, Blue, Green, Red, Foil, J.B. Walker, Frame, 16 x 13 In.
$600

Garth's Auctioneers & Appraisers

**Picture,** Watercolor, On Paper, Polo Match, Women Watching, Jac B 1906, 14 ½ x 18 In.
$531

Garth's Auctioneers & Appraisers

**Picture,** Watercolor, On Paper, Portrait, Mary Stevens, Inscription, Joseph Davis, Frame, 1837, 10 x 8 In.
$3,198

Skinner Auctioneers & Appraisers

**Picture,** Watercolor, Silhouette, Cutwork, Gentleman, Frederick Firth, 1851, 13 x 8 ¾ In.
$474

James D. Julia Auctioneers

P

424

| | | |
|---|---|---|
| **Thangka,** Depicting Yama Holding Karmic Wheel Of Life, 53 x 39 In. | | 480 |
| **Thangka,** Oil, On Cloth, Buddhist Imagery, Multiple Figures, Frame, Tibet, c.1910, 41 x 28 In. | | 360 |
| **Theorem,** Appliqued Cotton, Flowers, Vase, Handles, Virginia, Frame, c.1840, 9¾ x 13 In. | | 3220 |
| **Theorem,** Castle, Deerfield Academy, Hillside Landscape, Bridge, Couple, 1820s, 16 x 22 In. | | 584 |
| **Theorem,** Flowers, Classical Urn, Butterflies, Watercolor, Frame, 19th Century, 20 x 15 In. | | 123 |
| **Theorem,** Fruit In Stylized Bowl, Gold Leaf Frame, c.1830, 12¼ x 14¼ In. | | 2370 |
| **Theorem,** Fruit, Marble Plinth, 6 Column Supports, 19th Century, 21 x 23 In. | | 1560 |
| **Theorem,** Fruit, On Column Supports, Frame, 1800s, 21 x 23 In. | | 1560 |
| **Theorem,** Oil, On Velvet, Basket Of Fruit, Multicolor, Frame, 15½ x 18½ In. | | 1680 |
| **Theorem,** Oil, On Velvet, Cat In Basket, With Ball, G.B. French, Frame, 12¾ x 14 In. | | 234 |
| **Theorem,** Stag, Reclining, Evergreen Trees, Mountains, Frame, Ellinger, 14 x 14 In. | | 1298 |
| **Theorem,** Still Life, Bowl Of Fruit, Watercolor, Emma Jane Cade, Gilt Frame, 14 x 16 In. | | 2370 |
| **Theorem,** Urn, Tulips, Roses, Posies, Butterfly, Velvet, Frame, c.1830, 20 x 15 In. | | 711 |
| **Theorem,** Watercolor, Ink, Velvet, Woman, 3 Birds, Flowers, Verse, Affection, 26 x 23 In. | | 2000 |
| **Theorem,** Watercolor, On Paper, Flowers, Fruit, Table, Great Grandmother, Frame, 6 x 8 In. | | 420 |
| **Theorem,** Watercolor, On Velvet, Parrot, Grapes, Fruit Basket, Frame, 1838, 22 x 34 In. | | 44560 |
| **Wallpaper,** Hudson River Scene, People Walking, Horse, Pierre Francois, 1800s, 60 x 88 In. | | 995 |
| **Watercolor,** Bird, Multicolor Feathers, On Branch, Tulips, Leaves, 1875, 3¾ x 3¼ In. | | 212 |
| **Watercolor,** Blue Bird, Grass, By My Great Grandmother Mary King Smith Tyler, 12 x 10 In. | | 115 |
| **Watercolor,** Broken Cinch, Cowboy Tumbling Off Horse, Steer, L. Reddy, c.1945, 15 x 18 In. | | 840 |
| **Watercolor,** Exotic Bird, Tree Stump, Turned Wood Frame, 19th Century, 15 x 12 In. | | 330 |
| **Watercolor,** Flowers In Urn, Red, Yellow, Leaves, Walnut Frame, 1800s, 9 x 6 In. | | 201 |
| **Watercolor,** Girl, Blue Dress, Holding Doll, Miniature, c.1840, 8 x 6 In. | | 840 |
| **Watercolor,** Girl, Next To Table, Frank Nelson Wilcox, Signed, 1925, 21 x 14½ In. | | 1200 |
| **Watercolor,** Ink, On Paper Cutout, Basket Of Flowers, Birds, Samuel Eberly 1828, 5 x 3 In. | | 330 |
| **Watercolor,** Ink, On Paper, Dauntless, Sailing Ships Off Southampton, c.1950, 12 x 20 In. | | 469 |
| **Watercolor,** Ink, On Paper, Flower Wreath, Blessing, Frame, c.1885, 16 x 20 In. | | 575 |
| **Watercolor,** Ink, On Paper, Fraktur, Heart, David Huber Birth, Germany, c.1810, 7⅞ In. | | 4313 |
| **Watercolor,** Ink, On Paper, Perched Birds, Floral Branch, Frame, Garrett B. French, 9 x 7 In. | | 94 |
| **Watercolor,** Lithograph, Memorial, Landscape, In Memory Of Our Departed, 1810, 9 x 12 In. | | 652 |
| **Watercolor,** Mourning Card, Memorial, German Blessing, Willow Tree, 1800s, 6¼ x 4 In. | | 71 |
| **Watercolor,** On Board, Allegorical Figure, Landscape, Louis Oscar Griffith, c.1917, 14 x 7 In. | | 777 |
| **Watercolor,** On Board, Edge Of Night, Signed, Viktor Schreckengost, Frame, 39 x 49 In. | | 1380 |
| **Watercolor,** On Paper, Abstract, Geometric Shapes, Yellow, Orange, Black, Gray, 22 x 25 In. | | 431 |
| **Watercolor,** On Paper, Birds, Flowers, Black Frame, Signed Fanny Wenger, 1826, 6 x 8 In. | | 2400 |
| **Watercolor,** On Paper, Coat Of Arms, Frame, 26 x 23 In. | | 150 |
| **Watercolor,** On Paper, Family Record, 12 Stages Of Human Life, Figures, Verse, 17 x 14 In. | | 9600 |
| **Watercolor,** On Paper, Iron Trail, Paul A. Rossi, 1978, 6½ x 7 In. | | 175 |
| **Watercolor,** On Paper, Jackson House, Portsmouth, Frame, c.1890, 17½ x 19 In. | | 720 |
| **Watercolor,** On Paper, Miss Smith, Woman's Profile, Hair Up, J. Maentel, Frame, 5 In. | | 2760 |
| **Watercolor,** On Paper, Polo Match, Women Watching, Jac B 1906, 14½ x 18 In. ............*illus* | | 531 |
| **Watercolor,** On Paper, Portrait Of Tess, Girl, Wearing Jumper, William Sommer, 18 x 12 In. | | 600 |
| **Watercolor,** On Paper, Portrait, Mary Stevens, Inscription, Joseph Davis, Frame, 1837, 10 x 8 In. *illus* | | 3198 |
| **Watercolor,** On Paper, Tugboat Portsmouth, Alvaro Acores, Frame, c.1920, 16 x 20 In. | | 1200 |
| **Watercolor,** On Paper, View Of Royal Street, Rolland Harve Golden, 1958, 17¾ x 22¾ In. | | 598 |
| **Watercolor,** On Paper, Woman In Lavender, Signed E. Percy Moran, 18 x 12 In. | | 563 |
| **Watercolor,** Peaches, Basket, Frame, 9½ x 11½ In. | | 123 |
| **Watercolor,** Pencil, On Paper, Henry, 2nd Duke Of Cleveland, Horse, Frame, c.1800, 20 x 18 In. | | 1200 |
| **Watercolor,** Portrait, Girl, In Blue Dress, Coral Necklace, Basket, c.1840, 7¼ x 5½ In. | | 840 |
| **Watercolor,** Silhouette, Cutwork, Gentleman, Frederick Firth, 1851, 13 x 8¾ In. ............*illus* | | 474 |
| **Watercolor,** Springtime, Canada Geese, Goslings, Signed, Donald Paterson, Frame, 21 x 28 In. | | 357 |
| **Watercolor,** Stylized Flower, Tiger Maple Frame, Carved Rosettes, 1846, 8 x 7 In. | | 443 |
| **Watercolor,** Woman, Black Dress, Blue Bonnet, Bird's-Eye Maple Frame, 1800s, 13 x 11 In. | | 300 |
| **Wax Relief,** George Washington, Patience Wright, Gilt Frame, c.1785, 15 x 13 In. ............*illus* | | 1888 |
| **Wax,** Admiral Lord Richard Howe, Bust, Black & Gilt Frame, 19th Century, 5 x 4 In. ..........*illus* | | 77 |
| **Yarn Work,** Stag, Brown Velour, Gilt Molded Frame, 1800s, 28 x 24 In. ..............*illus* | | 70 |

**PICTURE FRAMES** *are listed in this book in the Furniture category under Frame.*

**PIERCE***, see Howard Pierce category.*

**PIGEON FORGE POTTERY** was started in Pigeon Forge, Tennessee, in 1946. Red clay found near the pottery was used to make the pieces. Molded or thrown pottery with matte glaze and slip decoration was made. The pottery closed in 2000.

*The Pigeon Forge Pottery Pigeon Forge Tenn*

| | | |
|---|---|---|
| **Bowl,** Ocher, Light & Gray Glaze, Marked, c.1960, 8½ In. | | 115 |

**Picture,** Wax Relief, George Washington, Patience Wright, Gilt Frame, c.1785, 15 x 13 In.
**$1,888**

Conestoga Auction Co., Inc.

**Picture,** Wax, Admiral Lord Richard Howe, Bust, Black & Gilt Frame, 19th Century, 5 x 4 In.
**$77**

Conestoga Auction Co., Inc.

**Picture,** Yarn Work, Stag, Brown Velour, Gilt Molded Frame, 1800s, 28 x 24 In.
**$70**

**P**

Conestoga Auction Co., Inc.

# PIGEON FORGE

**Pilkington,** Vase, Lancastrian Luster, Sea Maidens, Ships, Crane, Mycock, c.1904, 10 x 7½ In. $10,625

Rago Arts & Auction Center

**Pilkington,** Vase, Lid, Blue Gray Drizzled Over Red, Beige, Impressed, 1940, 11½ In. $863

Humler & Nolan

**Pilkington,** Vase, Ships, Red Flambe Glaze, Royal Lancastrian, W. Mycock, 1920s, 14 x 10 In. $4,375

Rago Arts & Auction Center

| | |
|---|---|
| **Coaster,** Slate Blue, Yellow, Animals, Birds, 5 Piece | 45 |
| **Group,** Bear Family, Tax, 5¾ In. | 24 |
| **Planter,** Dogwood, Blue Interior, 2¾ x 5⅜ In. | 30 |
| **Sculpture,** Abstract, Brown Drips, Tapered Base, Marked, 10 x 3 x 4 In. | 40 |
| **Vase,** Blue, Runny Brown Glazed Rim, Sloped Triangular, Douglas Ferguson, 8 In. | 17 |
| **Vase,** Crater Glaze, Brown White, Bulbous, Stick Neck, Bud, 6½ In. | 50 |
| **Vase,** Dogwood, Bulbous, Footed, Marked, 3 x 2 In. | 35 |
| **Vase,** Mottled Cocoa Brown, Blue Incised Lines, 1961, 5 In. | 176 |
| **Vase,** Seed Pod, Brown Crystalline Glaze, Signed, 10 x 8 In. | 295 |

**PILKINGTON TILE AND POTTERY COMPANY** was established in 1892 in England. The company made small pottery wares, like buttons and hatpins, but soon started decorating vases purchased from other potteries. By 1903, the company had discovered an opalescent glaze that became popular on the Lancastrian pottery line. The manufacture of pottery ended in 1937. Pilkington's Tiles Ltd. has worked from 1938 to the present.

| | |
|---|---|
| **Tile,** Art Nouveau, Yellow Cyclamen, Buds, Leaves, c.1901, 6 x 6 In. | 62 |
| **Vase,** Lancastrian Luster, Sea Maidens, Ships, Crane, Mycock, c.1904, 10 x 7½ In. *illus* | 10625 |
| **Vase,** Lid, Blue Gray Drizzled Over Red, Beige, Impressed, 1940, 11½ In. *illus* | 863 |
| **Vase,** Royal Lancastrian, Red Pomegranates, Luster Glaze, Gladys Rogers, 7⅜ In. | 1035 |
| **Vase,** Royal Lancastrian, Repeating Flowers, Luster Glaze, Richard Joyce, 1925, 4½ In. | 403 |
| **Vase,** Ships, Red Flambe Glaze, Royal Lancastrian, W. Mycock, 1920s, 14 x 10 In. *illus* | 4375 |

**PILLIN** pottery was made by Polia (1909–1992) and William (1910–1985) Pillin, who set up a pottery in Los Angeles in 1948. William shaped, glazed, and fired the clay, and Polia painted the pieces, often with elongated figures of women, children, flowers, birds, fish, and other animals. Pieces are marked with a stylized Pillin signature.

W+P Pillin

| | |
|---|---|
| **Bowl,** Pinched Rim, Woman, Horses, 8 In. | 1350 |
| **Box,** 2 Dancers, 4⅞ x 3⅝ In. | 699 |
| **Plate,** 2 Female Figures, Bird, Multicolored, 7¾ In. | 281 |
| **Vase,** 3 Women, Dancing, Multicolored, Gray, 6⅜ In. | 374 |
| **Vase,** Brown, Bird, Woman, Dress, Horse, Multicolored, Signed, 7 In. | 805 |
| **Vase,** Bulbous, Stick Neck, Yellow, Girl, Signed, 5½ In. | 1000 |
| **Vase,** Cylindrical, Stylized Woman, Horse, Bird, Stippled Glaze, 4½ In. | 495 |
| **Vase,** Galloping White Horses, Multicolored Ground, Bottle Shape, 9 In. | 688 |
| **Vase,** Long Neck, Squat Body, Woman, Multicolored, 6½ In. | 335 |
| **Vase,** Prancing Horses, Multicolored, Signed, 9 In. | 230 |
| **Vase,** Small Birds, Multicolored Concentric Rings, 7 In. | 660 |
| **Vase,** Tapered, 2 Women, Heads Down, 3 x 2 In. | 375 |
| **Vase,** Turquoise, 4-Sided, Woman, Tree, Horse, Woodpecker, Signed, 13⅛ In. | 862 |
| **Vase,** Woman, Bird, High Glaze, Signed, 7¼ In. *illus* | 403 |
| **Vase,** Woman, White Gloves, Balloons, Galloping White Horse, 8½ x 5 In. | 488 |
| **Vase,** Yellow & Red Volcanic Glaze, Round, Squat, 6½ x 10 In. | 2500 |

**PINCUSHION DOLLS** are not really dolls and often were not even pincushions. Some collectors use the term "half-doll." The top half of each doll was made of porcelain. The edge of the half-doll was made with several small holes for thread, and the doll was stitched to a fabric body with a voluminous skirt. The finished figure was used to cover a hot pot of tea, powder box, pincushion, whiskbroom, or lamp. They were made in sizes from less than an inch to over 9 inches high. Most date from the early 1900s to the 1950s. Collectors often find just the porcelain doll without the fabric skirt.

| | |
|---|---|
| **Child,** Blue Dress, Purple Flower In Hair, Extended Arm, Germany, 5 In. | 4275 |
| **Child,** Dutch Cap, Magenta, Brown Curls, Holding White Cloth, Germany, 4 In. | 399 |
| **Woman,** Bonnet, Blue Polka Dot Dress, Holding Flower, Japan, 5 In. | 34 |
| **Woman,** Hand On Head & Hip, Fan In Hair, Germany, c.1900, 6 In. | 88 |
| **Woman,** Holding Tea Tray, Sculpted Bonnet, Blue & White, Delft, Goebel, 4 In. | 285 |
| **Woman,** Nude, Gray Bonnet, Flower, Holding Red Lipstick, Germany, c.1920, 6 In. | 285 |
| **Woman,** Nude, Jeweled Gold Helmet, Bent Arm Holds Fan, Kister, c.1900, 5 In. | 1596 |
| **Woman,** Red & White Plaid Ruffled Cape, Bonnet, Germany, c.1915, 4½ In. | 342 |
| **Woman,** With Basket Of Dresden Flowers, Buxom, Gray Hair, Magenta Cap, 5 In. | 570 |
| **Woman,** With Basket Of Flowers & Cherub On Head, D. Kister, Germany, c.1900, 5 In. | 11115 |
| **Woman,** With Ribbon-Tied Papers, Brown Ringlets, Charlotte Cap, Flowers, Papers, 7 In. | 5700 |

**PINK SLAG** *pieces are listed in this book in the Slag Glass category.*

## PIPES

**PIPES** have been popular since tobacco was introduced to Europe by Sir Walter Raleigh. Carved wooden, porcelain, ivory, and glass pipes and accessories may be listed here.

| | |
|---|---:|
| **Bowl,** Skull, Porcelain, Black Stem, 36 In. | 216 |
| **Calabash,** State, Silver Mounts, Adolph Frankau & Co., England, 1907, 8 ½ In. | 83 |
| **Case,** Wood, Mythical Creature, White Eyes, Japan, 8 x 1 ½ In. | 240 |
| **Meerschaum,** Black Sultan's Head, Bakelite Mouthpiece, 6 In. | 225 |
| **Meerschaum,** Carved, Battle Scene, Men, Horses, Silver, c.1825, 32 In. | 1440 |
| **Meerschaum,** Carved, Kaiser Wilhelm, Fitted Case, 7 ¼ In. | 469 |
| **Meerschaum,** Dinosaur, Bakelite Mouthpiece, 7 In. | 75 |
| **Meerschaum,** Distinguished Man's, Bakelite Mouthpiece, 6 In. | 1100 |
| **Meerschaum,** Fisherman Smoking Corncob Pipe, Bakelite Mouthpiece, 6 In. | 125 |
| **Meerschaum,** Genie's Head, 13 In. | 175 |
| **Meerschaum,** Hand Holding Bowl, Bakelite Mouthpiece, 10 In. | 300 |
| **Meerschaum,** Lion's Head, Case, 6 ½ In. | 70 |
| **Meerschaum,** Mountain Goats, Carved Bands, Bakelite Mouthpiece, 6 In. | 100 |
| **Meerschaum,** Napoleon's Head, Bakelite Mouthpiece, 6 In. | 350 |
| **Meerschaum,** Nude Woman, Curly Hair, Case, Austria, c.1900, 14 In. | 6875 |
| **Meerschaum,** Nude Woman, Flowing Hair, Bakelite Mouthpiece, Turkey, 1979, 12 In. | 200 |
| **Meerschaum,** Nude Women, Long Hair, Carved, Case, 12 In. .......*illus* | 2400 |
| **Meerschaum,** Old Bearded Man, Bakelite Mouthpiece, 6 In. | 125 |
| **Meerschaum,** Queen Victoria, Bakelite Mouthpiece, 6 In. | 350 |
| **Meerschaum,** Royal Lady, Big Hat, Ruffled Collar, Silver Band, Bakelite Mouthpiece, 9 In. | 400 |
| **Meerschaum,** Skull, Carved, 7 ½ In. | 145 |
| **Meerschaum,** Soldier, In Civil War Uniform, Holding Saber, c.1890, 3 ½ x 4 In. | 288 |
| **Meerschaum,** Turk's Head, 9 ½ In. | 47 |
| **Silver,** Engraved DH, Scrolling, Composite Stem, Fitted Case, 1800s, 8 ¼ In. | 354 |
| **Wood,** Black Forest, Marked Bruyere, Carved, Germany, 9 In. | 23 |
| **Wood,** Man's Head, Painted, Folk Art Style, Brass Collar, c.1925, 2 x 6 In. | 115 |

## PIRKENHAMMER

**PIRKENHAMMER** is a porcelain manufactory started in 1803 by Friedrich Holke and J. G. Lilst. It was located in Bohemia, now Brezova, Czechoslovakia. The company made tablewares usually decorated with views and flowers. Lithophanes were also made. The mark of the crossed hammers is easy to remember as the Pirkenhammer symbol.

| | |
|---|---:|
| **Bowl,** Peasant, Flowers, Leaves, c.1837, 4 In. | 54 |
| **Bowl,** Vegetable, Luise Rose, Handles, Lid | 125 |
| **Cup & Saucer,** Birds & Butterflies, Gilt Handle, Demitasse | 75 |
| **Figurine,** Dog, Setter, Black, White, 8 x 3 In. | 390 |
| **Group,** Women, Seated, Dog, Flowered Dresses, c.1850, 5 ½ x 3 ½ In. | 575 |
| **Plate,** Crane, Applied Butterflies, Water, Gilt, 8 In. | 195 |
| **Plate,** Crane, Butterfly, Gilt Trim, 8 In. | 195 |
| **Teapot,** Shell, Salamander Handle, Brown, Orange, 7 In. | 1000 |
| **Vase,** Figural, Tree Trunk, Retriever, Pheasant, Rabbit, c.1846, 8 In. | 525 |

## PISGAH FOREST POTTERY

**PISGAH FOREST POTTERY** was made in North Carolina beginning in 1926. The pottery was started by Walter B. Stephen, who had been making pottery in that location since 1914. The pottery continued in operation after his death in 1961. The most famous kinds of Pisgah Forest ware are the cameo type with designs made of raised glaze and the turquoise crackle glaze wares.

| | |
|---|---:|
| **Pitcher,** Covered Wagon, Prairie Scene, 1950s | 357 |
| **Vase,** Brown Shaded To Turquoise Gloss Glaze, c.1950s, 6 In. | 72 |
| **Vase,** Rolled Rim, Sang De Boeuf Glaze, c.1930, 10 ½ x 5 In. .......*illus* | 448 |
| **Vase,** Sailboat, Cameo, Green, Cobalt Glaze, c.1936 | 1045 |
| **Vase,** Sang De Boeuf, Impressed, c.1930, 10 ½ x 5 In. | 448 |
| **Vase,** Turquoise To Aubergine, 1941, 9 In. | 360 |
| **Vase,** Turquoise, Purple, Marked, 3 ½ In. | 46 |

## PLANTERS PEANUTS

**PLANTERS PEANUTS** memorabilia are collected. Planters Nut and Chocolate Company was started in Wilkes-Barre, Pennsylvania, in 1906. The Mr. Peanut figure was adopted as a trademark in 1916. National advertising for Planters Peanuts started in 1918. The company was acquired by Standard Brands, Inc., in 1961. Standard Brands merged with Nabisco in 1981. Some of the Mr. Peanut jars and other memorabilia have been reproduced and, of course, new items are being made.

| | |
|---|---:|
| **Bank,** Vendor, Mr. Peanut Head, Plastic, Yellow, Battery Operated, 1950s, 7 x 5 In. | 374 |
| **Bookmark,** Hand On Hip, Cardboard, 6 ¼ In. | 43 |

**Pillin,** Vase, Woman, Bird, High Glaze, Signed, 7 ¼ In.
$403

Humler & Nolan

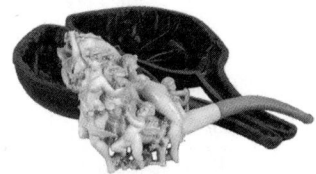

**Pipe,** Meerschaum, Nude Women, Long Hair, Carved, Case, 12 In.
$2,400

Morphy Auctions

**Pisgah Forest,** Vase, Baluster, Rolled Rim, Sang De Boeuf Glaze, c.1930, 10 ½ x 5 In.
$448

Rago Arts & Auction Center

P

# PLANTERS PEANUTS

**Planters Peanuts,** Costume, Mr. Peanut, Papier-Mache, 1930s, 48 In.
$1,800

**Planters Peanuts,** Figurine, Mr. Peanut, Metal, Standing, Square Base, 7 In.
$840

**Planters Peanuts,** Standee, Mr. Peanut, Petey Planters, Cardboard, 1950s, 6 ½ x 14 In.
$197

**Planters Peanuts,** Tin, Salted Peanuts, Pennant, Mr. Peanut, 5 Lbs.
$60

**Plastic,** Figure, Mr. Wink, Cosmos Ball, Eyes, Faces, Takashi Murakami, Marked, 10 In.
$2,813

**Plated Amberina,** Punch Cup, Amber To Rose, Amber Handle, 2 ½ In.
$3,105

**Plated Amberina,** Tumbler, Mahogany To Custard, 3 ¾ In.
$2,070

**Political,** Badge, Ulysses S. Grant, Portrait, Painted Metal Frame, 1868, 1 ¼ In.
$5,250

**Political,** Band Box, W. H. Harrison Campaign, Block-Printed Paper, 1840, 11 x 16 In.
$5,700

**Political,** Broadside, Confederate, Lt. James Clay, Kentucky, October, 1862, Frame, 9 x 12 In.
$8,400

P

| | | |
|---|---|---:|
| **Bowl,** Enameled, Mr. Peanut, Peanut Border, 1939, 3 In., 3 Piece...... | | 25 |
| **Costume,** Mr. Peanut, Papier-Mache, 1930s, 48 In. | *illus* | 1800 |
| **Display,** Mr. Peanut Head, Plastic, 13 x 9 In.................... | | 35 |
| **Figurine,** Mr. Peanut, Metal, Standing, Square Base, 7 In. | *illus* | 840 |
| **Letter Opener,** Figural Peanut Handle, Metal, 9 In............. | | 241 |
| **Mr. Peanut,** Cast Iron, Monocle, Cane, 38 In........................ | | 660 |
| **Mr. Peanut,** Light-Up, Papier-Mache Blinker, 25 In. .......... | | 2280 |
| **Spoon,** Measuring, Red, Mr. Peanut Shape Handle, Cups For ¼ Tsp. To 1 Tbsp..... | | 14 |
| **Standee,** Mr. Peanut, Petey Planters, Cardboard, 1950s, 6½ x 14 In. | *illus* | 197 |
| **Tin,** Salted Peanuts, Pennant, Mr. Peanut, 5 Lbs. | *illus* | 60 |
| **Toy,** Racer, Mr. Peanut, Plastic, Yellow, Red Wheels, Box, 2⅛ x 5½ x 2¼ In. ..... | | 138 |

**PLASTIC** objects of all types are being collected. Some pieces are listed in other categories; gutta-percha cases are listed in the Photography category. Celluloid is in its own category.

| | | |
|---|---|---:|
| **Bowl,** Vegetable, Divided, Green Speckled, Melmac, Kenro Corp., 9 x 2½ In. | | 16 |
| **Box,** Lid, Recipes, Green, Mammy Head On Side, Red & White Scarf, 5 In.... | | 56 |
| **Canister Set,** Red, White Top, Handle, Spout, Flour, Sugar, Coffee, 5⅝ x 4⅝ In., 3 Piece .......... | | 58 |
| **Coaster Set,** Wagon Wheel, Multicolor, Caddy, Tupperware, 1966, 3¾ x 3 In.......... | | 28 |
| **Figure,** Mr. Wink, Cosmos Ball, Eyes, Faces, Takashi Murakami, Marked, 10 In. | *illus* | 2813 |
| **Ice Bucket,** Lid, Orange, Bolero, Therm-O-Ware, 1960s, 11 x 5½ In. | | 32 |
| **Jug,** Juice & Water, Handi-Kanter, Lid, No-Spill Cap, Plastic Dispenser Inc., 36 Oz., 9 In..... | | 18 |

**PLATED AMBERINA** was patented June 15, 1886, by Joseph Locke and made by the New England Glass Company. It is similar in color to amberina, but is characterized by a cream colored or chartreuse lining (never white) and small ridges or ribs on the outside.

| | | |
|---|---|---:|
| **Creamer,** Amber Loop Handle, 2 In........................ | | 2696 |
| **Cruet,** Bulbous, Lobed, Amber Handle, Faceted Amber Stopper, 7 In. ......... | | 1093 |
| **Cruet,** Faceted Amber Stopper, Handle, New England, 7 In........... | | 2990 |
| **Horn Glass,** Opal Cased Rose To Amber, Tapered, 12 Vertical Ribs, c.1886, 5 x 2¾ In......... | | 2185 |
| **Lemonade Cup,** Cylindrical, Ribbed, Amber Low Handle, 5 In. .......... | | 2990 |
| **Pitcher,** Water, Lobed, Trifold Rim, Amber Handle, 6½ In. ......... | | 9775 |
| **Punch Cup,** Amber To Rose, Amber Handle, 2½ In. | *illus* | 3105 |
| **Punch Cup,** Mahogany Shaded To Custard, 9 Ribs, Applied Amber Handle, 2½ In. .... | | 1725 |
| **Spittoon,** Lady's, Squat, Pinched Waist, Ribbed, 3½ In........ | | 4025 |
| **Spooner,** Shading Amber To Rose, New England, 4¼ In........ | | 1725 |
| **Sugar Shaker,** Light Green To Amber To Rose, Ribbed, Pinched Waist, 6 In............ | | 14900 |
| **Tumbler,** Mahogany To Custard, 3¾ In. | *illus* | 2070 |
| **Vase,** Lily, Translucent Amber Base, Trumpet Shape, Trifold Rim, New England, 9½ In. .......... | | 3105 |
| **Vase,** Squared Form, Pinched Sides, Opal Inside, Ruffled Rim, 4½ In........... | | 575 |

**PLIQUE-A-JOUR** is an enameling process. The enamel is laid between thin raised metal lines and heated. The finished piece has transparent enamel held between the thin metal wires. It is different from cloisonne because it is translucent.

| | | |
|---|---|---:|
| **Bowl,** Lobed, Round, Flowers, Blue, Cream, Red, Green, 1800s, 3 x 6 In............ | | 360 |
| **Bowl,** White Flower, Blue, Green Scale Design, Stand, Chinese, c.1910, 2¾ x 6 In. ..... | | 210 |
| **Dresser Box,** Silver Gilt, Cut Glass, Enamel Cover, Flowers, Patterns, Rope Edge, 8 x 3 In. ......... | | 1150 |
| **Rosary,** 14K Yellow Gold Cross, Bone Beads, Gold Saint Stations, 18 In. ......... | | 495 |

**POLITICAL** memorabilia of all types, from buttons to banners, are collected. Items related to presidential candidates are the most popular, but collectors also search for material related to state and local offices. Memorabilia related to social causes, minor political parties, and protest movements are also included here. Many reproductions have been made. A jugate is a button with photographs of both the presidential and vice presidential candidates. In this list a button is round, usually with a straight pin or metal tab to secure it to a shirt. A pin is brass, often figural, sometimes attached to a ribbon.

| | | |
|---|---|---:|
| **Badge,** Mechanical, Harrison, Presidential Chair Who Shall Occupy It, Brass, 1888, 1½ In. ...... | | 411 |
| **Badge,** Ulysses S. Grant, Portrait, Painted Metal Frame, 1868, 1¼ In. | *illus* | 5250 |
| **Band Box,** W. H. Harrison Campaign, Block-Printed Paper, 1840, 11 x 16 In. | *illus* | 5700 |
| **Bandanna,** Portrait, I Like Ike, Win With Ike, Red, White, Blue, 26 x 26 In. ............ | | 98 |
| **Bandanna,** Theodore Roosevelt, Hat In Ring, 1912 National Progressive, Red, Silk, 17 x 26 In.. | | 370 |
| **Banner,** Roosevelt For President, Canvas, Portrait, Red, Blue, Sweeney Litho, 58 x 39 In............ | | 995 |
| **Broadside,** Confederate, Lt. James Clay, Kentucky, October, 1862, Frame, 9 x 12 In. ..........*illus* | | 8400 |
| **Button,** A Winning Team, Stevenson, Kefauver, Headshots, Blue, Cream, Oval, 2¼ In. ........ | | 230 |

**Political,** Button, Abraham Lincoln, Inscription, Ambrotype, Metal Frame, c.1860, 3 x 2 In.
$9,225

Skinner Auctioneers & Appraisers

**Political,** Button, Cox & Roosevelt, Browntones, Whitehead & Hoag, Jugate, 1920, ⅞ In.
$27,552

Hake's Americana & Collectibles

**Political,** Button, Hello Al, Goodbye Cal, 1¼ In.
$250

Heritage Auction Galleries

**P**

**Political,** Button, McKinley, Roosevelt, A Full Dinner Bucket, Jugate, 1 ¼ In.
$115

Hake's Americana & Collectibles

**Political,** Button, Parker, Davis, Uncle Sam's White Elephant, Celluloid, 1904, 1 ½ In.
$304

Hake's Americana & Collectibles

**Political,** Button, Peter Max, Peace Symbol, Hippies, Doves, Anti-War, 1960s, 2 ½ In.
$288

Hake's Americana & Collectibles

**Political,** Button, The Winner, Portrait, Theodore Roosevelt, 2 In.
$750

Heritage Auction Galleries

**Political,** Button, Vote Dewey For President, Portrait In Shield, 1 ¾ In.
$115

Hake's Americana & Collectibles

**Political,** Button, Wallace In '48, Portrait, Henry Wallace, 1948, ⅞ In.
$656

Heritage Auction Galleries

**Political,** Dumb Stove, George Washington, Cast Iron, J.L. Mott Iron Works, c.1870, 48 In.
$8,610

Skinner Auctioneers & Appraisers

**Political,** Flag, McKinley, Patriotism-Protection & Prosperity, Portrait, Stars, 1896, 12 x 18 In.
$316

Hake's Americana & Collectibles

**Political,** Flask, Whiskey, Presented To Gen. Ulysses S. Grant From A.L., Pewter Top, Bottom, 1863, 9 In.
$7,475

James D. Julia Auctioneers

### Political Ribbons
Mass-produced printed ribbons for political campaigns were first manufactured in the United States in 1813.

| | | |
|---|---|---|
| **Button,** Abraham Lincoln, Hannibal Hamlin, Ferrotype, Brass, 1860, 2 In. | | 4025 |
| **Button,** Abraham Lincoln, Inscription, Ambrotype, Metal Frame, c.1860, 3 x 2 In. ............*illus* | | 9225 |
| **Button,** America Forward March, Celluloid, Whitehead & Hoag Co., 1931, ⅞ In. | | 48 |
| **Button,** Bryan, Labor, United We Stand, 1¼ In. | | 9375 |
| **Button,** Cox & Roosevelt, Browntones, Whitehead & Hoag, Jugate, 1920, ⅞ In. ...............*illus* | | 27552 |
| **Button,** Eugene Debs, War No, ⅞ In. | | 2750 |
| **Button,** Hello Al, Goodbye Cal, 1¼ In. .................................................*illus* | | 250 |
| **Button,** I'm With Harry, Challenger 5¼-In. Ribbon, White, Blue, 3 In. | | 1669 |
| **Button,** Inauguration Of Harry S. Truman, Jan. 20, 1949, 4 In. | | 253 |
| **Button,** Jack Once More In 64, Red, White, Blue, Headshot, 4 In. | | 7028 |
| **Button,** Kennedy, Election Night, Press, 3½ In. | | 1267 |
| **Button,** Kennedy, Our Next President, Headshot, Flag, Red Border, 4 In. | | 287 |
| **Button,** McKinley, Roosevelt, A Full Dinner Bucket, Jugate, 1¼ In. ...............*illus* | | 115 |
| **Button,** Our President, Dwight Eisenhower, Celluloid, 1953, 4 In. | | 55 |
| **Button,** Parker, Davis, Uncle Sam's White Elephant, Celluloid, 1904, 1½ In. ........*illus* | | 304 |
| **Button,** People To People For Ford, Portrait, Celluloid, 1976, 3 In. | | 29 |
| **Button,** Peter Max, Peace Symbol, Hippies, Doves, Anti-War, 1960s, 2½ In. .........*illus* | | 288 |
| **Button,** Shoeworkers For Kennedy, Headshot, Red, White, Emress, 3½ In. | | 449 |
| **Button,** Taft, Wood, Ribbon, Big Stick, Red, White, Blue, 1908, 3 x 3½ In. | | 115 |
| **Button,** Texas For Roosevelt & Truman, Lithograph, Green Duck Co., 1944, ⁹⁄₁₆ In. | | 65 |
| **Button,** The Winner, Portrait, Theodore Roosevelt, 2 In. .........................*illus* | | 750 |
| **Button,** Truman & Barkley Inauguration, 5-In. Ribbon, 1949, 2¼ In. | | 460 |
| **Button,** Truman, Vote Truman For President, 3½ In. | | 1840 |
| **Button,** Vote Dewey For President, Portrait In Shield, 1¾ In. ...................*illus* | | 115 |
| **Button,** Vote The Kennedy Ticket, Red, White, 4 In. | | 640 |
| **Button,** Wallace In '48, Portrait, Henry Wallace, 1948, ⅞ In. .....................*illus* | | 656 |
| **Button,** Washington Wants Hillary's Husband For President, Celluloid, 1992, 1¾ In. | | 4 |
| **Button,** William Jennings Bryan, Celluloid, 1900, 1¾ In. | | 75 |
| **Button,** Win With Wilson & Marshall, Cello, 1912, ⅞ In. | | 42 |
| **Cane,** Grover Cleveland, Photo Under Convex Glass, Bamboo, Pewter Mount, 33 In. | | 325 |
| **Cane,** Walking Stick, William Jennings Bryan, Next President, Embossed, c.1900, 35 In. | | 230 |
| **Change Purse,** President Harding, Flags, Leather, c.1922, 2½ x 3½ In. | | 65 |
| **Cigar Label,** Lt. General Grant 1864, Black & White, 5 x 7 In. | | 127 |
| **Clothing Brush,** William Henry Harrison, 1840 | | 2070 |
| **Cup,** Lincoln & Hamlin, Walnut, Carved, Square, Flared Rim, c.1860, 2½ In. | | 4613 |
| **Dish,** President McKinley, Portrait, Flower Border, Germany, c.1900, 4 x 5 In. | | 68 |
| **Dumb Stove,** George Washington, Cast Iron, J.L. Mott Iron Works, c.1870, 48 In. ............*illus* | | 8610 |
| **Figurine,** Cat, Bisque, I Want My Vote, 5 In. | | 460 |
| **Figurine,** Cat, Ceramic, Votes For Women, Germany, c.1915, 3¼ In. | | 245 |
| **Flag,** McKinley, Patriotism-Protection & Prosperity, Portrait, Stars, 1896, 12 x 18 In. ........*illus* | | 316 |
| **Flask,** Theodore Roosevelt, Suffer-E'Get, Dressed As Woman, Holding Umbrella, 6 In. | | 2185 |
| **Flask,** Whiskey, Presented To Gen. Ulysses S. Grant From A.L., Pewter Top, Bottom, 1863, 9 In. *illus* | | 7475 |
| **Hand Fan,** Cleveland, Thurman, Wooden Handle, Jugate, c.1888, 12 In. | | 230 |
| **Hand Fan,** Coolidge, Farmington, Maine On Reverse, 6½ In. | | 62 |
| **Hand Fan,** Harrison, Morton, Wooden Handle, Jugate, c.1888, 12 In. | | 230 |
| **Handkerchief,** Harris, Reid, Silk, White, 1892, 17 x 17 In. | | 72 |
| **Handkerchief,** Henry Clay, Tariff, Clay, Union, Harry Of The West, Frame, c.1850, 25 x 26 In. | | 1440 |
| **Handout,** Buchanan, Fremont, Comic Portraits, Cardboard, 3 In., 2 Piece ........*illus* | | 300 |
| **Hat,** GOP Campaign, Harrison, Reid, Felt, Leather, Ribbon, Jugate, 1892, 7 In. | | 278 |
| **Jug,** Arms Of The United States, Free Trade, Sailors Rights, Yellow Neck Band, c.1810, 7 In. | | 3438 |
| **Jug,** Blaine & Logan, Stoneware, Angular Shape, 1884, 4¾ In. | | 330 |
| **License Plate,** Repeal 18th Amendment, Prohibition, Red, White, Blue, Metal, 12 In. | | 120 |
| **License Plate,** Roosevelt & Repeal, Supports Anti Prohibition, Metal, 12¼ In. | | 150 |
| **License,** Plate Attachment, Roosevelt, Garner, Happy Days, Donkey, Aluminum, 1932, 5 x 7 In. | | 221 |
| **Lunch Bucket,** McKinley & Roosevelt, Full Dinner Pail, Tin, Wood Handle, 1900, 6 x 8 In. | | 506 |
| **Match Safe,** McKinley, Head Shape, Brass, Spring-Loaded Cover, 2 x 3 In. | | 211 |
| **Medal,** Polk, Dallas, Metal, Rim Hold, Leonard DeWitt, c.1844, 1⅝ In. | | 835 |
| **Mug,** Gen. Dwight Eisenhower, 5-Star General Uniform, c.1952, 6 x 7 In. | | 139 |
| **Newspaper,** Dewey Defeats Truman, Chicago Tribune, Nov. 3, 1948, Sections 1 & 2, 17 x 24 In. | | 822 |
| **Panel,** Harrison & Reform, Portrait, Log Cabin, Hard Cider Barrel, 1840, 11 x 12 In. .........*illus* | | 173 |
| **Paperweight,** Zachary Taylor, Military Portrait, Sulphide, Glass, 2 x 2¾ In. | | 569 |
| **Parade Horn,** Cleveland, Stevenson, Triangular, Paint, Tin, 1892, 14 In. | | 288 |
| **Parade Torch,** Benjamin Harrison, Hat Shape, Bail, Metal, 5 x 6 In., 24-In. Wood Pole | | 278 |
| **Pennant,** Freedom March, Washington D.C., August 1963, Abraham Lincoln, 22½ In. | | 271 |
| **Pennant,** Taft, Photograph, Tinted, Felt, 1912, 22 In. | | 158 |
| **Pennant,** Woodrow Wilson, Flag, Multicolor, Felt, 2 Streamers, 24 In. | | 443 |

**Political,** Handout, Buchanan, Fremont, Comic Portraits, Cardboard, 3 In., 2 Piece
$300

Heritage Auction Galleries

### Reproduction Political Memorabilia

Beware of copies of political buttons, pins, and other political memorabilia. The 1972 Hobby Protection Act requires reproduction and fantasy political items to be marked with the word "reproduction" and the year of manufacture. Not all are.

**Political,** Panel, Harrison & Reform, Portrait, Log Cabin, Hard Cider Barrel, 1840, 11 x 12 In.
$173

Hake's Americana & Collectibles

**Political,** Pin, Campaign, Harrison & Reform, Glass, Sulphide, 1840
$550

Heritage Auction Galleries

P

**Political,** Pitcher, Garfield, Born 1831, President 1881, Eagle, J. Wedgwood, 9 In. $759

Hake's Americana & Collectibles

### Collector's Lament

Here's a quote that really speaks to us: A lifelong collector said he "gravitates toward four categories: broken, large, heavy, and useless."

**Political,** Pitcher, James Garfield Profile, Flags, Eagle, Matte Glaze, Rookwood, 11 In. $600

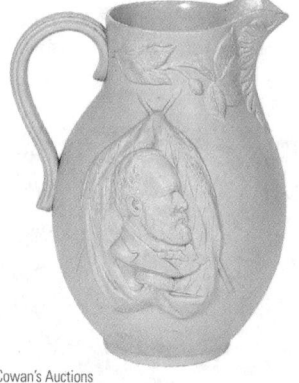

Cowan's Auctions

**Political,** Pitcher, William Henry Harrison, Copper Luster, Transfer Images, 1840, 5½ In. $2,717

James D. Julia Auctioneers

| | |
|---|---|
| **Photograph,** Harpo Marx, In Kennedy Johnson Stickered Cart, Autograph, Black, White, 7 x 9 In. | 312 |
| **Pin,** Boycott Nazi Goods, N.S.A.N.L., Eagle, Gripping Snake, Blue, Cream, c.1936, ⅞ In. | 316 |
| **Pin,** Campaign, Harrison & Reform, Glass, Sulphide, 1840 ...........................................*illus* | 550 |
| **Pin,** McKinley, Hobart, Brass, Bug, Jugate, 1½ x 1⅝ In. | 177 |
| **Pin,** McKinley, Railroad Boxcar Shape, Brass, 1900, 2 In. | 190 |
| **Pin,** Rail Splitter Honest Abe, Ax Blade, Handle, Brass, 1860, 1⁷⁄₁₆ In. | 2070 |
| **Pitcher,** Garfield, Born 1831, President 1881, Eagle, J. Wedgwood, 9 In. ...............*illus* | 759 |
| **Pitcher,** James Garfield Profile, Flags, Eagle, Matte Glaze, Rookwood, 11 In. .......*illus* | 600 |
| **Pitcher,** James Garfield, Portrait, Relief, Bennington Style, Brown, c.1880, 7½ In. | 255 |
| **Pitcher,** William Henry Harrison, Copper Luster, Transfer Images, 1840, 5½ In. ........*illus* | 2717 |
| **Plaque,** Bust, Al Smith, Top Hat, Copper, 1928, 9 x 5½ In. | 80 |
| **Plaque,** Theodore Roosevelt, Bronzed Iron, Bas Relief Profile, J. Fraser, 1920, 10 x 13 In. | 316 |
| **Postcard,** Bryan & Taft, Mechanical Roller Wheels, Green, Black, White, 3 x 5 In. | 210 |
| **Poster,** Kennedy For President, Leadership For The 60s, Photograph, 27 x 41 In. | 168 |
| **Poster,** Mao, Liberator Scenes, Communist Era, Multicolor, Chinese, 20 x 30 In. | 138 |
| **Poster,** McCarthy Peace, Dove, Lithograph, Signed, Ben Shahn, Frame, 1968, 38 x 25 In. | 461 |
| **Poster,** McKinley, Bryan, U.S. Mint, Uncle Sam, 1896, 18¾ x 25½ In. | 948 |
| **Poster,** McKinley, Roosevelt, Flag, 1900, 42½ x 27½ In. | 3555 |
| **Poster,** Ronald Reagan, Jelly Bean Kid, Caricature, Dressed As Cowboy, 1981, 33 x 21 In. | 47 |
| **Ribbon Badge,** Reception, T.R., Grant, Lincoln, McKinley In Clover Frame, 1905, 6 In. | 202 |
| **Ribbon,** Gen. J.A. Garfield, Center Portrait, Blue Silk, Gold Lettering, c.1880, 6 x 3 In. | 132 |
| **Seat Cushion,** Smith, Get On The Smith Band Wagon, 14 x 17 In. | 805 |
| **Sheet Music,** Cox, Democratic Campaign March Song, Pages, 6 x 9 In. | 759 |
| **Shot Glass,** Bryan, Bust, Black, White, Gilt Accents, 1¾ x 2¼ In. | 115 |
| **Snuffbox,** Wm. H. Harrison 9th President Of United States, Papier-Mache, Round, 3½ In. | 575 |
| **Spoon,** Equality, Unity, Liberty Bell, Independence Hall, William Penn, 4 In. | 190 |
| **Spoon,** Susan B. Anthony, Bust, Political Equality, Sterling Silver, 1890s, 5⅝ In. | 395 |
| **Statue,** Washington, Standing, Black & White, Gilt Trim, Staffordshire, 1800s, 16 In. | 531 |
| **Stickpin,** Garfield, Ferrotype, Brass Frame, 1⅛ In. | 748 |
| **Stud,** McKinley, Coffin Shape, Billy Bryan Inside, Brass, Silver, 1896, 1⅛ In. | 173 |
| **Teapot,** W.H. Harrison, Portrait, Log Cabin, Hard Cider Barrel, 1840, 7 x 11 In. .................*illus* | 570 |
| **Toy,** Elephant, Landon-Knox GOP Button, Mohair, Iron Wheels, 13 In. | 1008 |
| **Toy,** Teddy Roosevelt, Bear On String Riding Bike, Mechanical, Color Litho, 4¼ x 6¾ In. | 184 |
| **Tray,** McKinley, Roosevelt, Great Eastern Clothing House, Tin Litho, 1900, 13 x 16 In. ........*illus* | 506 |
| **Tray,** Theodore Roosevelt, 1903 Sargent Portrait, Life Scenes Border, Oval, Tin, 14 x 17 In. | 316 |
| **Watch Fob,** Davis, Sepia Photo Celluloid, Eagle, 1924, 1¹⁵⁄₁₆ In. | 287 |
| **Watch Fob,** Socialist Party, Debs & Seidel, Celluloid, Leather, Jugate, 1912, 1½ In. ............*illus* | 2500 |
| **Wood Carving,** Al Smith In Derby Hat, Former Mayor Of NYC, Bust, Painted, 5¾ In. | 531 |

**POMONA** glass is a clear glass with a soft amber border decorated with pale blue or rose-colored flowers and leaves. The colors are very, very pale. The background of the glass is covered with a network of fine lines. It was made from 1885 to 1888 by the New England Glass Company. First grind was made from April 1885 to June 1886. It was made by cutting a wax surface on the glass, then dipping it in acid. Second grind was a less expensive method of acid etching that was developed later.

| | |
|---|---|
| **Bowl,** Fluted, Amber Stain, 1st Grind, c.1885, 5½ x 2½ In. | 125 |
| **Toothpick Holder,** Pink, Frosted, Translucent Tricornered Rim, 1st Grind | 73 |
| **Tumbler,** Frosted, Inverted Diamond Guilt, Cornflower, Fern, 2nd Grind, 3 In., 6 Piece | 210 |

**PONTYPOOL,** *see Tole category.*

**POOLE POTTERY** was founded by Jesse Carter in 1873 in Poole, England, and has operated under various names since then. The pottery operated as Carter & Co. for several years and established Carter, Stabler & Adams as a subsidiary in 1921. The company specialized in tiles, architectural ceramics, and garden ornaments. Tableware, bookends, candelabra, figures, vases, and other items have also been made. The name *Poole Pottery Ltd.* was taken in 1963. The company went bankrupt in 2003 but is in business today with new owners.

| | |
|---|---|
| **Bowl,** Yellow, Brown, Orange, Flowers, c.1975, 10 In. | 68 |
| **Casserole,** Lid, Cornflower Blue, Retro, Pea Pods, Leaves, c.1950, 8 x 2 In. | 55 |
| **Pin Dish,** Flowers, Dotted Rim, 4 In. | 32 |
| **Plate,** Aegean, Green, Orange, 1970s, 8 In. | 59 |
| **Plate,** Central Leaf, Marked, Brown, Orange, 8 In. | 55 |
| **Plate,** Delphis, Orange, Green, Yellow, Oval, 1970s, 12 x 8 In. | 78 |
| **Tray,** Aegean Pattern, Green, Brown, 1970s, 7 x 4 In. | 45 |
| **Trinket Box,** Galaxy Pattern, Black Matte Ground, Round, Lid, 5 In. Diam. | 45 |

P

| | |
|---|---|
| **Vase,** Oval, Red, Orange, Black, Flambe, 8 In. | 78 |
| **Wall Pocket,** Wild Poppy, Yellow, Orange, Turquoise Highlights, 10 x 11 In. | 153 |

**POPEYE** was introduced to the Thimble Theatre comic strip in 1929. The character became a favorite of readers. In 1932, an animated cartoon featuring Popeye was made by Paramount Studios. The cartoon series continued and became even more popular when it was shown on television starting in the 1950s. The full-length movie with Robin Williams as Popeye was made in 1980. KFS stands for King Features Syndicate, the distributor of the comic strip.

| | |
|---|---|
| **Badge,** Popeye Navy Admiral, In Uniform, Brass, 1930s, 1 9/16 In. | 115 |
| **Bank,** Dime Register, Tin Litho, White, Black, Red, Popeye Holding Coins, 1929, 3 x 3 In. | 85 |
| **Bank,** Mechanical, Tin Litho, Straits Mfg., c.1929, 4 3/4 In. | 540 |
| **Bank,** Popeye The Knockout, Nickel Figures, Bluto, Straits, 4 1/2 In. | 443 |
| **Book,** Popeye & His Friends, Hardcover, Dust Jacket, Glossy Full Color, Whitman, 1937, 9 x 11 In. *illus* | 115 |
| **Corkscrew,** Popeye, Flexing Muscles, c.1938, 5 1/2 In. | 675 |
| **Doll,** Popeye, Composition, Wooden Pipe, Green Pants, Blue Shirt, Ideal, 1935, 14 In. | 885 |
| **Doll,** Popeye, Composition, Wooden Pipe, Green Pants, Jointed Arms, Ideal, 1935, 11 1/2 In. | 436 |
| **Doorstop,** Popeye, Cast Iron, Hubley, 1929, 9 In. | 600 |
| **Game,** Bagatelle, Popeye Holding Tomatoes, Metal Frame, 14 x 23 In. | 298 |
| **Game,** Pinball, Tabletop, Popeye Image, Menu, 14 x 24 In. *illus* | 330 |
| **Lamp,** Shade, 8 1/2-In. Popeye Holds Base, Chase Scene On Shade, 11 1/2 In. | 316 |
| **Lunch Box,** Arm Wrestling, Brutus, Olive Oil, Metal, Aladdin | 199 |
| **Pencil Sharpener,** Popeye Holding Pencil, Bakelite, 1 3/4 In. | 45 |
| **Soap,** Trio, Popeye, Well Blow Me Down Here I Yam, Box, 3 Piece | 115 |
| **Toothbrush Holder,** Figural, Bisque, Painted, 5 In. *illus* | 59 |
| **Toy,** Air-O-Plane, Popeye The Pilot, 8-In. Wingspan, Windup, 8 1/2 In. | 556 |
| **Toy,** Airport, Blow Me Down, 1930s, 9 In. | 510 |
| **Toy,** Barrel Walker, Tin Lithograph, Clockwork, Chein, 1932, 7 In. | 384 |
| **Toy,** Boat Fleet, Celluloid Sheet Sails, Box, 1930s, Box, 8 1/4 x 12 1/8 In., 4 Piece | 612 |
| **Toy,** Brutus In Cart, Tin Lithograph, Windup, Marx, Box, 7 In. | 590 |
| **Toy,** Bubble Blower, Tin Litho, Battery, Linemar, Japan, 11 3/4 In. | 561 |
| **Toy,** Dippy Dumper Dump Truck, Brutus, Celluloid, Tin Litho, Clockwork, Marx, 9 In. | 502 |
| **Toy,** Lantern, Popeye, Rubber Pipe, Tin Lithograph, Windup, Linemar, Japan, 7 1/2 In. | 240 |
| **Toy,** Popeye Boxing, Tin Lithograph, Windup, Chein, 7 In. | 270 to 390 |
| **Toy,** Popeye Cyclist, Riding Tike, Celluloid Arms, Tin Lithograph, Windup, Linemar, 4 In. | 270 |
| **Toy,** Popeye Express, Popeye Pushing Wheelbarrow, 8 In. | 270 |
| **Toy,** Popeye Heavy Hitter, Hammer, Windup, Chein, 11 3/4 In. | 1180 |
| **Toy,** Popeye Pilot, Tin Lithograph, Windup, Marx, 1920s, 5 1/2 x 8 1/4 In. *illus* | 1006 |
| **Toy,** Popeye, Bag Puncher, Tin, Windup, Chein, c.1930, 9 1/2 In. | 1416 |
| **Toy,** Popeye, Baggage, Wheelbarrow, Parrot, Trunk, Tin Litho, Clockwork, Marx, 8 1/2 In. | 531 |
| **Toy,** Popeye, Barrel Walker, Orange Shoes, Tin Lithograph, Windup, J. Chein, 7 In. | 300 to 502 |
| **Toy,** Popeye, Basketball Player, Tin Lithograph, Ball Goes Through Hoop, Linemar, 9 In. | 708 to 826 |
| **Toy,** Popeye, Boom Boom, Drum, Paper, Wood, Pull Toy, Fisher-Price, 1929, 9 1/2 In. | 1560 |
| **Toy,** Popeye, Carrying Parrot Cages, Blue Shirt, Tin Lithograph, Clockwork, Chein, 8 In. | 354 |
| **Toy,** Popeye, Carrying Parrot Cages, Tin Litho, Windup, Marx, Box, 8 1/2 In. | 1800 |
| **Toy,** Popeye, Carrying Parrot Cages, Tin, Windup, Marx, 8 1/2 In. | 291 |
| **Toy,** Popeye, Express, Blow Me Down Airport, Circling Plane, Train, Tin Litho, Marx, 9 In. | 2360 |
| **Toy,** Popeye, Floor Puncher, Tin Litho, Celluloid Punching Bag, Windup, Chein, 7 In. | 767 to 1121 |
| **Toy,** Popeye, Motorcycle Patrol, Paint, Cast Iron, Hubley, c.1955, 9 In. | 480 |
| **Toy,** Popeye, Olive Oyl, Jigger, Dancing, Playing Accordion, Tin Litho, Box, Marx, 9 1/2 In. | 1652 |
| **Toy,** Popeye, Olive Oyl, Juggling Olive Oyl In Chair, Linemar, Box, 9 In. | 2360 |
| **Toy,** Popeye, Rocket Ride, Wooden Popeye, Metal Spring-Mounted Base, Rocks, 37 x 36 In. | 1888 |
| **Toy,** Popeye, Roller Skater, Tin Litho, Windup, Linemar, Box, c.1950, 6 5/8 x 4 1/2 In. *illus* | 688 |
| **Toy,** Popeye, Roof Dancing, Tin Lithograph, Windup, Marx, 10 1/2 In. | 360 |
| **Toy,** Popeye, Tin Lithograph, Windup, A26 Chein, 6 In. | 210 |
| **Toy,** Spinach Cart, Removable Popeye Figure, Embossed, Cast Iron, Red Paint, Hubley, 5 1/4 In. | 531 |
| **Toy,** Turnover Tank, Tin Lithograph, Die Cut Popeye, Windup, Linemar, Japan, 4 In. | 210 to 266 |
| **Wristwatch,** Popeye, Other Portraits, Chrome, Link Band, New Haven Clock, 1935 *illus* | 288 |

**PORCELAIN** factories that are well known are listed in this book under the factory name. This category lists pieces made by the less well-known factories. Additional pieces of porcelain are listed in this book in the categories Porcelain-Contemporary, Porcelain-Midcentury, and under the factory name.

| | |
|---|---|
| **Bell Push,** Gilt Metal Mounts, Multicolor, Pink Roses, Leaves, Strawberries, 2 3/4 In. | 104 |
| **Biscuit Barrel,** Painted, Oriental Style Scenes, Continental, c.1900, 6 1/2 x 5 In. | 42 |

**Political,** Teapot, W.H. Harrison, Portrait, Log Cabin, Hard Cider Barrel, 1840, 7 x 11 In.
$570

Hake's Americana & Collectibles

**Political,** Tray, McKinley, Roosevelt, Great Eastern Clothing House, Tin Litho, 1900, 13 x 16 In.
$506

Hake's Americana & Collectibles

**Political,** Watch Fob, Socialist Party, Debs & Seidel, Celluloid, Leather, Jugate, 1912, 1 1/2 In.
$2,500

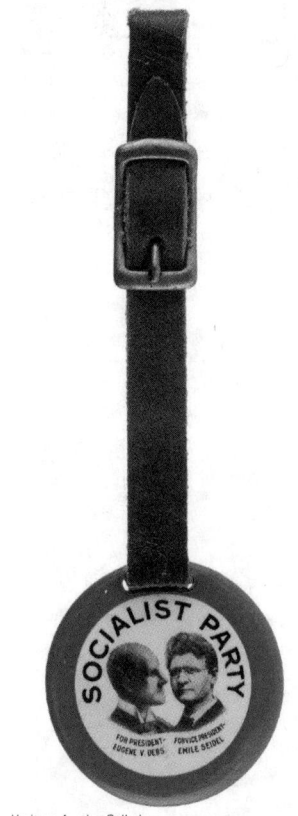

Heritage Auction Galleries

**Popeye,** Book, Popeye & His Friends, Hardcover, Dust Jacket, Glossy Full Color, Whitman, 1937, 9 x 11 In.
$115

Hake's Americana & Collectibles

**Popeye,** Game, Pinball, Tabletop, Popeye Image, Menu, 14 x 24 In.
$330

Showtime Auction Services

---

**TIP**

*Several types of glue are needed to repair broken pottery and porcelain. Commercial glues found in a local hardware store are often satisfactory. Read the labels. Some types work only with pieces that are porous, others only with pieces that are not porous. Instant glue is difficult to use if the break is complicated.*

---

| | |
|---|---:|
| **Bottle,** Wine, White Ground, Blue Dragons, Clouds, Korea, 1800s, 12 x 7 In. | 1185 |
| **Bowl,** Feet, Cobalt Blue Floral Border, Paneled Landscape Scene, 1800s, 14 ½ In. | 71 |
| **Bowl,** Figural, Luster, 2 Women Holding Hands, Dancing, Skirts Form Bowl, Wahliss, 6 In. | 748 |
| **Bowl,** Ruby Enameled Ground, Multicolor Flowers, White Translucent Glaze, 2 ¾ x 6 In. | 767 |
| **Box,** Boy On Chair With Teddy Bear Cover, Brown, Pink Blanket, Germany, c.1925, 5 In. | 171 |
| **Box,** Pigeon Shape, Green, Pink, Orange Paint, Continental, c.1900, 5 x 8 In. | 81 |
| **Bust,** Hindenburg, Man, Cap On Head, Mustache, Medal On Chest, Fraureuth, 13 In. | 92 |
| **Cachepot,** Famille Noire Style, Gilt Bronze, Rococo Style Stand, 11 ½ x 12 ¾ In. | 215 |
| **Candlestick,** Rococo Style, Urn Shape, Scroll Work, Painted Flowers, Gilt, 5 ½ In., Pair | 92 |
| **Centerpiece,** Basket, Pierced, Applied Flowers, Germany, c.1900, 5 x 16 In. | 60 |
| **Charger,** Blue, White, Flowers, Panels, Japan, 13 In. | 185 |
| **Charger,** Japanese Style, Blue Transfer, Cherry Blossoms, Poppies, 13 ½ In. | 58 |
| **Charger,** Shaped Gilt Rim, Flowers, Lowestoft, 18th Century, 13 In. | 720 |
| **Charger,** Woman, Court Attire, Blue, Gilt, Creil Et Montereau, France, c.1885, 13 In. | 150 |
| **Chargers,** Scalloped Gilt, Shepherdess, Sheep, Signed A. Princann, 13 ⅛ In., Pair | 215 |
| **Chocolate Cup & Saucer,** Fairy, Wild Rose Vines, Blue, Pouyat Limoges, c.1900 | 250 |
| **Chocolate Pot,** Lid, Flowers, Stippled, 3-Footed, Handle, Cream Pont-Aux-Choux, c.1780, 8 In. | 1140 |
| **Compote,** Flowers, Multicolor, Gilt Trim, Bronze Frame, Sevres Style, 10 In. | 215 |
| **Compote,** Lid, Painted Flowers, Leaves, Dog Finial, Square Handle, Footed, c.1790, 5 x 5 In. | 360 |
| **Compote,** Viste Allegre, Pierced, White, Gilt, 9 In., Pair | 90 |
| **Cup & Saucer,** Bleu Celeste, Pentagonal Saucer, Vincennes, 2 ½ x 5 ½ In. | 4500 |
| **Cup & Saucer,** Raised Gilt, Gothic Style, Roses, Pastels, Demitasse, Adderley, 1890s | 450 |
| **Dish,** Condiment, Duck, Dove, Blue, Purple, Russian Imperial Exhibit, 7 ½ & 8 ¼ In., Pair | 415 |
| **Dish,** Figural Lid, Woman With Cigarette, Powder Puff Skirt, Red Art Deco Base, 7 In. | 570 |
| **Dresser Box,** Figurine Top, Snake Charmer, Exotic Woman, Geometric, Round, 6 In. | 1140 |
| **Dresser Box,** Flapper, Yellow Dress, Holding Red Parrot, Turquoise Stripes, France, 8 In. | 456 |
| **Dresser Box,** Harlequin Figure, Pink, Black & Yellow Diamonds, Art Deco, France, 5 In. | 228 |
| **Dresser Jar,** Chubby Boy Boxer, Orange Tank Suit, Side-Glancing Eyes, 7 In. | 171 |
| **Figurine,** Dancers, Man, Woman, Tambourines, Period Dress, 16 In., Pair | 121 |
| **Figurine,** Hindu Goddess Bodhisattva, Blanc De Chine, Applied Figures, c.1900, 22 x 8 In. | 590 |
| **Figurine,** Horse Drawn Carriage, 4 Horses, 2 Women, Cherub, Multicolor, 18 ¼ In. | 1230 |
| **Figurine,** Lipizzaner Horse, Rider, Rearing, Augarte Wein, Austria, 11 In. | 213 |
| **Figurine,** Man, Woman, Leaning, Blue Attire, Vion & Baury, c.1900, 23 x 21 In., Pair. | 600 |
| **Figurine,** Military Man, On Rearing Horse, Multicolor, Gold Trim, Sitzendorf, 11 ½ In., Pair | 460 |
| **Figurine,** Peacock, Gilt, Enameled, On Rock, Pine Tree, Stream, Japan, c.1912, 14 x 7 In. | 2214 |
| **Figurine,** Samantabhadra, Elephant, Blanc De Chine, Gold Parcel Gilt, 1800s, 10 x 8 In. | 2125 |
| **Figurine,** Woman, Flowers, Man, Blowing Horn, Bocage, 11 ½ In., Pair | 375 |
| **Flask,** Pretzel Shape & Color, Salt Added, Hard Paste, 1800s, 5 ½ In. *illus* | 106 |
| **Footbath,** Flower Reserve, Apple Green Ground, Gilt, Lug Handle, England, c.1820, 20 In. | 625 |
| **Garniture,** Figural Putti & Flowers, 18-In. Clock On Stand, Sitzendorf, 4 Piece | 590 |
| **Ginger Jar,** Blue & White, Painted Scene, Magistrates, Architecture, Garden, c.1920, 5 In. | 58 |
| **Ginger Jar,** Hunting Scenes, Lattices, c.1890, Gilt, Germany, 21 In., Pair | 2337 |
| **Ginger Jar,** Lid, Famille Rose, Bird, Text, c.1900, 9 In. | 60 |
| **Group,** Classically Dressed Men, Women, On Rising Ledge, France, 21 In. | 472 |
| **Icer,** Hinged Lid, Cherubs, Flowers, Gold Trim, Egg Shape, Gilt Metal Mount, 14 In. | 826 |
| **Jar,** Dome Lid, Multicolor, Baluster Shape, Birds, Flowers, Crackle Ground, 18 In. | 461 |
| **Jar,** Lid, Lapis Blue Glaze, Gilding At Base, Flowers, Vines, 1800s, 4 ¾ In. | 178 |
| **Knife Rest,** Figural, Asparagus, Blue Bow, 1 ⅝ x 1 ½ In. | 60 |
| **Pitcher,** Tucker & Hemphill, Flower, Gilt Wreath, Andrew C. Walker, c.1832, 9 In., Pair | 32400 |
| **Pitcher,** Tucker, Cottage Scenes, Grisaille Landscape, Gilt, Philadelphia, c.1830, 9 In. | 1250 |
| **Plaque,** Man, Buying Melon From Woman, Painted, M.E. Taylor, c.1895, 12 x 9 In. | 492 |
| **Plaque,** Painted, 3 Dutch Girls, c.1920, 7 x 16 In. | 24 |
| **Plaque,** Raucher, Smoker, Portrait, Painted, Frame, c.1910, 8 ¾ x 5 ⅜ In. | 2000 |
| **Plaque,** Woman, 4 Children, Seminude, Frame, Frz. X. Thallmaier Munchen, 14 x 12 In. *illus* | 5036 |
| **Plaque,** Woman, Chin In Hands, c.1920, 3 In. Diam. | 165 |
| **Plate,** Luncheon, Pink, Green Border, Gilt, Kornilow Bros, Russia, 10 In., 12 Piece | 1236 |
| **Plate,** Russian Imperial, 2-Headed Eagle, Gilt Rim, Nicholas II Period, 9 In., 12 Piece | 3690 |
| **Plate,** Service, Beaux Arts Style, Raised Gilt Border, Henrich & Co., 11 In., 8 Piece | 1045 |
| **Platter,** Blue White, Map Of Japan, Scalloped Edge, Rectangular, Hizen, Japan, 11 In. | 137 |
| **Platter,** Painted Flowers, Leaves, Cobalt Blue Border, Gilt Scrolling, George Davis, 19 In. | 83 |
| **Potpourri,** Lid, Birds, Flower Borders, Pierced, Stamped, Aerozon, Germany, 7 In. *illus* | 115 |
| **Powder Box,** Flapper Cover, Blue Dress, Cushion Base, Blue Tassels, Sitzendorf, 8 In. | 456 |
| **Powder Jar,** Asian Woman Figure, Holds Fan, Yellow Flowered Skirt, France, 7 In. | 285 |
| **Powder Jar,** Figural Cover, Art Deco Dancer, Holding Red Ball, Marbleized Base, 7 In. | 342 |
| **Powder Jar,** Figural, Bathing Beauty On Conch Shell, Blue Swimsuit, Parasol, 6 In. | 228 |
| **Powder Jar,** Figural, Flapper Seated In Chair, Blue Dress, Pink Boa, Germany, 1920s, 8 In. | 1368 |

| | |
|---|---|
| Powder Jar, Woman, Pink 18th Century Gown, Ruffles, Hair Plumes, Sitzendorf, 10 In. | 513 |
| Teapot, Lid, Multicolor Geometric & Leaf Design, Lotus, Vines, 4 ½ In. | 483 |
| Tray, Landscape, 18th Century Figures, Pond, Fountain, Steps, 2 Handles, 23 x 17 In. | 512 |
| Tureen, Underplate, Meissen Style, Flowers, Couples, Applied Flower Handles, 6 x 8 In. | 484 |
| Urn, Gilt, Berliner Dom Cathedral, Westerkerk Cathedral, 16 x 5 ¾ In., Pair | 1049 |
| Urn, Lid, Bronze Mounted, Crackled Turquoise Ground, Pineapple Finials, 17 x 10 In., Pair | 944 |
| Urn, Lid, Stand, Birds, Flowers, Gilt Grim, Signed, Jacob Petit, c.1850, 16 ½ In., Pair .........illus | 2214 |
| Urn, Neoclassical, Woman, Putti, Orange, Gilt Lid, Handles, J.A. & Co., France, 19 In., Pair | 300 |
| Urn, Sevres Style, Venus, On Dolphin, Cupids, Bronze Mounts, Footed Stand, c.1900, 28 In. | 2375 |
| Urn, Venus, Cupids, Reverse Side With 4 Youths, Scroll Handles, 18 In. .....................illus | 920 |
| Vase, Blue & White, Footed, Flared Rim, Petal Border, Japan, 12 In. | 132 |
| Vase, Bottle Shape, Copper Red Mottled Glaze, Globular, Tall Neck, 9 ¾ In. | 1195 |
| Vase, Bottle Shape, White Ground, Blue Foo Dogs, Brocade Balls, Clouds, 10 ½ In. | 356 |
| Vase, Crystalline Glaze, Adelaide Robineau, Marked, 3 ¾ x 4 ¼ In. .....................illus | 20000 |
| Vase, Fukagawa, Chrysanthemum, Blue Flowers, Red Ground, Gilt, Japan, 7 ½ x 7 ¼ In. | 173 |
| Vase, Imperial Yellow, Blue, Turquoise, Hardwood Lid & Base, Chinese, 10 In. .............illus | 1652 |
| Vase, Lid, Landscape, Quail, Brown, White, Blue, Applied Monkeys, Japan, 17 In. | 1140 |
| Vase, Painted Thistles, Gilt Metal Winged Mask Handles, Paw Feet, Victorian, 13 ½ In. | 375 |
| Vase, Palace, Figures, Crossing River, Red Scroll Handles, Japan, 30 In. | 360 |
| Vase, Peachbloom, Glazed, Apple Shape, Copper Red, Green Mottled Glaze, 1800s, 4 In. | 448 |
| Vase, Potpourri, Pierced Lid, Flowers, Gilt Trim, Bird Knop, c.1850, 5 ½ In., Pair | 2214 |
| Vase, Sang De Boeuf Glaze, 1800s, 17 x 8 In. | 288 |
| Vase, Spring Maid, Flowers, Apples, Green, Pink, Footed, Continental, c.1900, 19 In., Pair | 1093 |
| Vase, Textured Glaze, Brother Thomas Bezanson, Symbol, 9 ¼ x 5 ½ In. .....................illus | 7500 |
| Vase, Underglaze Blue, Garden Scene, High Shoulders, 8 Paneled Sides, 1900s, 8 x 4 In. | 161 |
| Water Coupe, Beehive Shape, Red Glaze, 1800s, 3 ½ x 3 In. | 119 |
| Wine Barrel, Flowers, Figural Bacchus With Goblet, Grapevine, Gilt Bands, 14 x 10 In. | 576 |

**PORCELAIN-CHINESE** is listed here. See also Canton, Chinese Export, Imari, Moriage, Nanking, and other categories.

| | |
|---|---|
| Base, Bottle Shape, Long Neck, Bulbous Body, Peony Blossoms, 1900s, 16 x 8 In. | 861 |
| Basin, Turquoise Ground, Bats, Butterflies, Blossoms 1900s, 5 x 15 In. | 3444 |
| Bowl, Bats, Clouds, Sgraffito, Turquoise Interior, c.1910, 5 ¾ In. .....................illus | 593 |
| Bowl, Blue, White, Bird, Flowers, c.1985, 11 In. | 120 |
| Bowl, Blue, White, River Scene, Figures, Reticulated Border, 11 In. | 185 |
| Bowl, Branches, Flowers, Figures, Gilt, Green Ground, c.1890, 5 x 11 In. | 246 |
| Bowl, Crackle Glaze, Unglazed Rim, Cone Shape, 1 ½ x 3 ¼ In. | 123 |
| Bowl, Dice, Scrolling Lotus, Footed, Xuande Reign Mark, 15th Century, 11 ½ In. | 1599 |
| Bowl, Eggshell, Blue Glazed, White Interiors, 1 ¾ x 4 In., Pair | 984 |
| Bowl, Eggshell, Translucent Wedding Bowl, Peaches, Bats, Gilt, 2 x 4 In., Pair | 738 |
| Bowl, Gilt Rim, Immortals At A Feast, 2 ⅝ x 4 ¾ In. | 492 |
| Bowl, Lapis Lazuli, Slip Dragons, Pearls, Cone Shape, 1800s, 7 In. | 711 |
| Bowl, Lid, Stem, Iron Red, 9 Dragons Chasing Flaming Pearl, 12 In. | 1342 |
| Bowl, Ming Style, Underglaze Blue Flowers, 1800s, 12 ¾ In. | 593 |
| Bowl, Orange Glaze, Gilt Scrolls, Leaves, Lotus, Turquoise, Footed, 2 x 5 In. | 1955 |
| Bowl, Reserves, Fruits, Flowers, Sgraffito Ruby Ground, 1800s, 7 ⅛ In. | 6518 |
| Bowl, Reserves, Scholar, Wine, Woman, Green Border, 1900s, 11 In., Pair | 237 |
| Bowl, Rice, Yellow Ground, Tapered, c.1790, 2 ½ x 6 In. | 660 |
| Bowl, Rice, Yellow, Incised Dragons, Clouds, Buddhist Symbol, 2 x 4 In. | 649 |
| Bowl, Ruby Sgraffito, Scrolls, Flowers, Landscape Reserves, Famille Rose, 6 x 3 In. | 2133 |
| Bowl, Tou Tsai, White Ground, Flower Bouquets, Yellow Rim, 6 In. | 9480 |
| Bowl, Women, Picking Cherries, Basket, Dog, c.1865, 9 In. | 120 |
| Box, Painted, Mille Fleur, Turquoise Interior, Round, 1900s, 4 x 2 In. | 948 |
| Cachepot, Cover, Blue & White, Short Neck, Handles, Foo Dog Finial, 8 x 7 In. | 259 |
| Censer, Blue, White, Square, Lid, Foo Dog Finial, Landscape, c.1890, 4 x 3 In. | 625 |
| Charger, Blue & White, Fruit, Flowers, Leaves, White Ground, 1700s, 12 In. | 296 |
| Charger, Blue & White, Grape & Vine Design, 41 In. | 330 |
| Charger, Blue & White, Molded Floral Vignettes, Scalloped Rim, c.1910, 14 In. | 413 |
| Charger, Dragon, Leaf Designs, Green, Orange, c.1890, 16 In. | 510 |
| Charger, Dragon, Phoenix, Pearl, Yellow, Blue Border, Chinese, c.1900, 18 In. | 1168 |
| Charger, Grapefruit Center, Blossoms, Blue, White, 14 In. | 1600 |
| Charger, Yellow, Brown, Purple, Green, Dragons, Lotus Scrolls, 15 In. .....................illus | 7110 |
| Cider Jug, Lid, Foo Dog Finial, Blue, White, Twist Handle, c.1850, 11 In. | 780 |
| Compote, Flowers, Pomegranate, Green Bat Symbols, 3 ¾ x 9 ½ In. | 270 |
| Cricket Cage, Orange Glaze, Gilt Melons, Leaves, Butterflies, 1800s, 5 ½ In. | 2489 |

**Popeye,** Toothbrush Holder, Figural, Bisque, Painted, 5 In.
$59

### Popeye in the Grocery Store

Popeye has long been the logo on brands of fresh and canned spinach. There have also been Popeye iron-fortified white bread, Wimpy hamburger buns, Olive Oyl hot dog buns, and Swee'pea wheat bread.

**Popeye,** Toy, Popeye Pilot, Tin Lithograph, Windup, Marx, 1920s, 5 ½ x 8 ¼ In.
$1,006

**Popeye,** Toy, Popeye, Roller Skater, Tin Litho, Windup, Linemar, Box, c.1950, 6⅝ x 4½ In.
$688

Rago Arts & Auction Center

**Popeye,** Wristwatch, Popeye, Other Portraits, Chrome, Link Band, New Haven Clock, 1935
$288

Hake's Americana & Collectibles

| | |
|---|---:|
| **Cup,** Painted, Cats, Flowering Plants, 2½ In., Pair | 1896 |
| **Cup,** Tea, Lid, Stand, Famille Rose, Birds, Trees, Yellow Ground, Late 1800s, 4½ In. | 296 |
| **Dish,** Dragon, Red, Flaming Pearl Amid Flames, Bowl, 1900s, 4 x 16 In. | 478 |
| **Dish,** Orange Reticulated Border, Grisaille Landscape, 10 x 11 In. | 800 |
| **Figurine,** Bird, Green, Orange Glaze, c.1850, 10½ In., Pair | 677 |
| **Figurine,** Buddha, Rosary, Famille Rose, Marked, 10 In. ..........................*illus* | 1230 |
| **Figurine,** Foo Dog, Famille Verte, Green Coat, Gilt, White Spots, 17th Century, 9 In. | 1920 |
| **Figurine,** Geese, Turquoise, Purple, Yellow Glaze, c.1910, 13 In., Pair ............*illus* | 830 |
| **Figurine,** Guanyin, Blanc De Chine, Seated, On Lotus Blossom Throne, c.1910, 15 In. | 90 |
| **Figurine,** Guanyin, Blanc De Chine, Seated, Royal Ease Position, Chignon, 13 In. | 4900 |
| **Figurine,** Hotai, Seated, Multicolor, Marked China, Oval Stamp, Platform, 10½ In. | 638 |
| **Figurine,** Parrot, Green, Orange, Hunched, On Stump, 8 In., Pair | 240 |
| **Figurine,** Parrot, Green, Yellow Talons, Reticulated Base, c.1890, 10 In., Pair | 2160 |
| **Figurine,** Priest Lohan, Leaning On Book Pile, Painted, 12½ In. | 96 |
| **Figurine Set,** Zodiac, Blue & White, c.1900, 13¼ x 4 In., 12 Piece | 2706 |
| **Fishbowl,** Blue & White, Greek Key, Dragons, Clouds, 18½ & 19½ In., Pair | 590 |
| **Flask,** Moon, Red & Blue Leaves, Dragons, Copper Underglaze, c.1900, 16 x 12 In. | 1500 |
| **Jar,** Baluster, Landscape, Underglaze Blue, Brass Mounts, Lock Plate 1800s, 25 In. | 889 |
| **Jar,** Baluster, Mythical Beast Panels, Flower Head Ground, Multicolor, 17 In., Pair | 369 |
| **Jar,** Horses, Waves, Swirls, Wutsai, 5 Colors, c.1650, 12 x 9½ In. ................*illus* | 4029 |
| **Jar,** Lid, Famille Verte, Children Playing, Chinese, 1800s, 6 x 5 In. | 119 |
| **Jar,** Lid, Flowering Prunus, Blue Underglaze, Stand, 1800s, 9 x 13 In. ..........*illus* | 593 |
| **Jar,** Stand, Blue Water Plant, White Ground, Signed Hirado, 4 x 1¾ In. | 305 |
| **Jar,** Temple, Blue & White, Foo Dog Knob, Reserves, Pheasant, Birds, 64 x 24 In. | 1476 |
| **Jar,** Temple, Lid, Brown Black Monochrome Glaze, Baluster, 14 x 8 In. | 58 |
| **Jardiniere,** Blue Ground, White Designs, 15 x 17 In. | 300 |
| **Jardiniere,** Stand, Famille Verte, Battle Figure, Fish, Water Plants, c.1900, 14 x 25 In. | 6457 |
| **Mirror,** Hand, Enameled Leaves, Birds, 11 In. | 120 |
| **Pedestal,** Elephant, White, Red, Black, 20th Century, 19½ x 12 In. | 74 |
| **Pillow,** Boy Embracing Fish, Painted, 1900s, 10 x 15 In. | 108 |
| **Pillow,** Underglaze Blue Fish, Aquatic Plants, Clouds, 1800s, 5½ x 10½ In. | 326 |
| **Plaque,** Bodhidharma In Cave, Frame, Bone Inlay, 13 x 9 In. | 1778 |
| **Plate,** Blue & White Koi, Flowers, 4 Character Kangzi Mark, 1700s, 11½ In. | 984 |
| **Plate,** Blue, White, Man, Woman, Standing, Landscape, c.1790, 10 In. | 300 |
| **Plate,** Blue, White, Octagonal, c.1800, 9⅜ In., Pair | 240 |
| **Plate,** Governor Winthrop Coat Of Arms, Silver, Green, Black Paint, c.1905, 8½ In., Pair | 1020 |
| **Plate,** Sacred Bird & Butterfly Pattern, Peachy Gold, White, c.1870, 7¾ In., 12 Piece | 1440 |
| **Plate,** Tobacco Leaf Pattern, Multicolor, c.1810, 6 In. | 1140 |
| **Platter,** Octagonal, Blue, White, 12 x 8 In. | 236 |
| **Platter,** Tobacco Leaf, Multicolor, Oval, Scalloped, c.1790, 13¾ x 16¾ In. | 11400 |
| **Platter,** Yellow, Flower Sprays, Fruit, Oval, c.1815, 17 In. | 420 |
| **Roof Tile,** Dignitary, On Horse, Green, Brown Glaze, 1700s, 13 In. | 120 |
| **Teapot,** Acorn Finial, Cobalt Blue Borders, Armorial Spout, c.1780, 10 In. | 438 |
| **Teapot,** Blue Pinwheel, Flowers, White Ground, c.1800, 9½ In. | 154 |
| **Teapot,** Lid, Blanc De Chine, Pagoda Relief, Mythical Beast, Waisted Oval Shape, 9 x 9 In. | 92 |
| **Teapot,** Lid, Purple, Orange, Brown Flowers, Ribbons, Gilt, Barrel Shape, c.1780, 6 In. | 115 |
| **Tray,** Pink, Peony, Lotus, Flower Spray, Silver Shape, c.1780, 15½ In. | 600 |
| **Tureen,** Lid, Flower Knop, Fitzhugh, Blue, White, Reeded Strap Handles, c.1855, 14 In. | 300 |
| **Urn,** Famille Rose, Flower Basket, Dragon Shape Handles, 1800s, 14 In., Pair | 3584 |
| **Vase,** Blanc De Chine, Carved, Leaves, Flowers, Flared Rim, Footed, c.1800, 12 In. | 8850 |
| **Vase,** Blanc De Chine, Molded Deer, Pine, Prunus Branch Handles, Border, c.1910, 9 In. | 119 |
| **Vase,** Blue & White, Coral, Courtiers In Garden Scene, Baluster, 9½ In. | 399 |
| **Vase,** Blue & White, Flowers, Figures, Round, Handles, 8½ In. | 600 |
| **Vase,** Blue & White, Landscape, Rocks, Fishermen, Bottle Shape, 8¼ In. | 874 |
| **Vase,** Blue & White, Scholars, 1900s | 1107 |
| **Vase,** Blue Glaze, Taoist Masks, Footed Base, 4¾ x 4¾ In. | 219 |
| **Vase,** Blue Ground, Relief Enameled Dragons, Bottle Shape, Long Neck, 1900s, 11¾ In. | 590 |
| **Vase,** Blue Monochrome, Flared Neck, 16 In. | 219 |
| **Vase,** Blue Monochrome, Squared Shoulders, Flared Rim, 8 x 3 In. | 104 |
| **Vase,** Blue, White, Dragons, Clouds, Scrolls, Bulbous Base, 14¾ In., Pair | 1200 |
| **Vase,** Blue, White, Flared Rim, Fitzhugh, c.1855, 15 In. | 480 |
| **Vase,** Bottle Shape, Blue Glaze, Gilt Dragons, Flaming Pearl, Clouds, 1800s, 15 In. | 7380 |
| **Vase,** Bottle Shape, Millefleur, Gilt Ground, Turquoise Interior, Late 1800s, 15 In. | 948 |
| **Vase,** Bottle, Lilac Flambe Glaze, Mottled Milky Blue Drip, Pear Shape, 18 In. | 1298 |
| **Vase,** Chicken Blood, Double Handles, Tapered Neck, Footed, 16½ In. | 720 |
| **Vase,** Clair De Lune Flambe Gloss Glaze, Green Streaks, Calligraphy Marks, 11 In. | 69 |

**Porcelain,** Flask, Pretzel Shape & Color, Salt Added, Hard Paste, 1800s, 5 ½ In.
$106

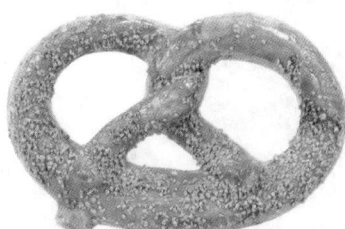

Conestoga Auction Co., Inc.

**Porcelain,** Plaque, Woman, 4 Children, Seminude, Frame, Frz. X. Thallmaier Munchen, 14 x 12 In.
$5,036

James D. Julia Auctioneers

**Porcelain,** Potpourri, Lid, Birds, Flower Borders, Pierced, Stamped, Aerozon, Germany, 7 In.
$115

Humler & Nolan

**Porcelain,** Urn, Lid, Stand, Birds, Flowers, Gilt Grim, Signed, Jacob Petit, c.1850, 16 ½ In., Pair
$2,214

New Orleans Auction Galleries, Inc.

**Porcelain,** Urn, Venus, Cupids, Reverse Side With 4 Youths, Scroll Handles, 18 In.
$920

Humler & Nolan

**Porcelain,** Vase, Crystalline Glaze, Adelaide Robineau, Marked, 3 ¾ x 4 ¼ In.
$20,000

Rago Arts & Auction Center

**Porcelain,** Vase, Imperial Yellow, Blue, Turquoise, Hardwood Lid & Base, Chinese, 10 In.
$1,652

Brunk Auctions

**Porcelain,** Vase, Textured Glaze, Brother Thomas Bezanson, Symbol, 9 ¼ x 5 ½ In.
$7,500

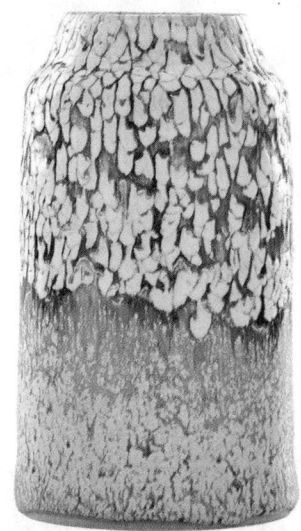

Rago Arts & Auction Center

**Porcelain-Chinese,** Bowl, Bats, Clouds, Sgraffito, Turquoise Interior, c.1910, 5 ¾ In.
$593

James D. Julia Auctioneers

P

**Porcelain-Chinese,** Charger, Yellow, Brown Purple, Green, Dragons, Lotus Scrolls, 15 In. $7,110

James D. Julia Auctioneers

**Porcelain-Chinese,** Figurine, Buddha, Rosary, Famille Rose, Marked, 10 In. $1,230

New Orleans Auction Galleries, Inc.

**Porcelain-Chinese,** Figurine, Geese, Turquoise, Purple, Yellow Glaze, c.1910, 13 In., Pair $830

James D. Julia Auctioneers

**Porcelain-Chinese,** Jar, Horses, Waves, Swirls, Wutsai, 5 Colors, c.1650, 12 x 9 ½ In. $4,029

James D. Julia Auctioneers

**Porcelain-Chinese,** Jar, Lid, Flowering Prunus, Blue Underglaze, Stand, 1800s, 9 x 13 In. $593

James D. Julia Auctioneers

**Porcelain-Chinese,** Vase, Famille Rose, Farmers, Foo Dog Jump Rings, Square, 1800s, 18 In. $593

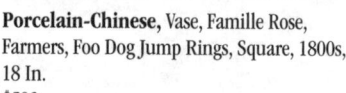

James D. Julia Auctioneers

**TIP**

*You can cover up a small chip in an enamel or even a piece of porcelain with a bit of colored nail polish. It comes in almost every color now.*

| | |
|---|---|
| **Vase,** Clair De Lune, Flared Rim, Concentric Rings, 8 In. | 196 |
| **Vase,** Coral Ground, Blue & Yellow Flowers, Inscribed Poetry, 1900s, 8 x 4 In., Pair | 369 |
| **Vase,** Dome Lid, Famille Rose, Millefleur, Baluster, Wood Stand, 4 x 5 In., Pair | 615 |
| **Vase,** Dragon, Phoenix, Pearl, Gilt, Multicolor, Kui Dragon Handles, 19 x 9 In. | 984 |
| **Vase,** Famille Noire, Tapered, White Ground Reserves, Landscapes, 1800s, 19 x 5 In. | 3444 |
| **Vase,** Famille Rose, Faceted, Foo Dog Handles, Emblems, Pink Ground, 17 x 18 In. | 738 |
| **Vase,** Famille Rose, Farmers, Foo Dog Jump Rings, Square, 1800s, 18 In. .............................*illus* | 593 |
| **Vase,** Famille Rose, Millefleur, Double Gourd, Turquoise Base, c.1890, 9 In. | 1067 |
| **Vase,** Famille Rose, Yellow Leaves, Millefleur Border, c.1900, 14 ½ x 7 ½ In. | 492 |
| **Vase,** Famille Verte, Figures, Calligraphy, Cylindrical, Flared Rim, 11 x 5 In., Pair | 236 |
| **Vase,** Famille Verte, Prunus Branch, Birds, Green Ground 8 x 5 In. | 69 |
| **Vase,** Figures, Blossoming Trees, Republic Period, 17 ¾ In. | 1020 |
| **Vase,** Figures, Flower Vines, Green, Blue, Orange Glaze, 11 In., Pair | 3120 |
| **Vase,** Flambe Glaze, Narrow Mouth, 6 ⅝ In. .............................................................*illus* | 2829 |
| **Vase,** Flowers, Cinnabar, Lobed Bodies, c.1850, 12 In., Pair | 615 |
| **Vase,** Flowers, White Ground, Black Red Bands, c.1940, 13 ¾ In., Pair | 600 |
| **Vase,** Lid, Foo Dog Finial, Women, Garden, Blue, White, c.1850, 10 ¾ In., Pair | 1125 |
| **Vase,** Lid, Foo Dog Knop, Flowers, Vines, Squirrels, Dragon Handles, c.1785, 14 In. | 840 |
| **Vase,** Mallet, Copper Red, Stylized Phoenix Birds, 7 x 9 In. | 3050 |
| **Vase,** Mei Po, Sang De Boeuf, Glazed, Flared Turned-Out Rim 6 ¼ In. | 219 |
| **Vase,** Ming Style, Pear Shape, Flower Panels, Hexagonal, 21 ½ In. | 413 |
| **Vase,** Ming Style, Sang, Elephant Feet, Bird Finials, Green, Brown, 1900s, 6 x 8 x 7 In. | 148 |
| **Vase,** Painted, Warriors, Mask Handles, Blue, c.1910, 10 In., Pair | 677 |
| **Vase,** Pomegranate Tree, White Ground, Republic, c.1947, 24 x 15 In. | 7500 |
| **Vase,** Robin's-Egg Blue, Sculpted Dragon, Acanthus Leaf Rim, 1800s, 7 ¾ In. | 474 |
| **Vase,** Sang De Boeuf, Long Neck, c.1860, 13 In. | 1169 |
| **Vase,** Sang De Boeuf, Tall Neck, Flared Rim, 1900s, 22 ¼ In., Pair | 2091 |
| **Vase,** Turquoise, Dog Head Ring Handles, Incised, Dragon, Phoenix, Marked, 1911-49, 14 In. *illus* | 732 |
| **Vase,** White, Flower Shape, Incised Petal Shape Rim, Leaf Panels, 10 In. | 6490 |
| **Water Pot,** Peach Blossom, Clouds, Pierced Stand, Chinese, 3 x 5 In. | 15600 |
| **Wine Cup,** Imperial Yellow, Flared Sides, Wide Rim, Flared Stem, 3 x 3 ½ In. | 178 |

**PORCELAIN-CONTEMPORARY** lists pieces made by artists working after 1975.

| | |
|---|---|
| **Moonpot,** Rattle, Glazed, Signed, Toshiko Takaezu, 5 ¼ x 4 ¼ In. .............................*illus* | 1625 |
| **Teapot,** 2 Half Circles, Cone Top, Michael Duvall, 1989, 10 ¼ x 10 ½ In. .............................*illus* | 960 |
| **Vase,** Raku Filled, Harvey Sadow, 1981, 9 x 11 In. | 625 |
| **Vase,** Sgraffito Design, Menage A Trois, R. Duffy, Ca., 1989, 30 x 19 In. | 500 |

**PORCELAIN-MIDCENTURY** includes pieces made from the 1940s to about 1975.

| | |
|---|---|
| **Bowl,** Blue, Folded Rim, Interior Fish Design, B. Stevenson, 1950s, 3 x 6 In. | 125 |
| **Figurine,** Seated Child, Holding Flower, Karl Ens, 10 ¼ In. | 281 |
| **Figurine,** Young Woman, Bird Perched On Her Hand, A. Borsato, 6 In. .............................*illus* | 48 |
| **Moonpot With Rattle,** White, Glaze, N.J., 1967, 4 x 4 ½ In. | 938 |
| **Vase,** Egg Shape, Navy, Brother Thomas Benzason, 12 ½ x 6 In. | 3125 |
| **Vase,** Oxblood Glaze, Spherical, Small Top Opening, Gerry Williams, 1973, 5 In. | 369 |

**POSTCARDS** were first legally permitted in Austria on October 1, 1869. The United States passed postal regulations allowing the card in 1872. Most of the picture postcards collected today date after 1910. The amount of postage can help to date a card. The rates are: 1872 (1 cent), 1917 (2 cents), 1919 (1 cent), 1925 (2 cents), 1928 (1 cent), 1952 (2 cents), 1958 (3 cents), 1963 (4 cents), 1968 (5 cents), 1971 (6 cents), 1973 (8 cents), 1975 (7 cents), 1976 (9 cents), 1978 (10 cents), March 1981 (12 cents), November 1981 (13 cents), 1985 (14 cents), 1988 (15 cents), 1991 (19 cents), 1995 (20 cents), 2001 (21 cents), 2002 (23 cents), 2006 (24 cents), 2007 (26 cents), 2008 (27 cents), 2009 (28 cents), 2011 (29 cents), 2012 (32 cents), 2013 (33 cents), 2014 (34 cents). While most postcards sell for low prices, a small number bring high prices. Some of these are listed here.

| | |
|---|---|
| **Baseball,** 1919 Cincinnati Red Legs, Team Photo, Hooven & Allison, 3 x 5 In. | 1320 |
| **Baseball,** Boston Bloomer Girls Baseball Team, c.1908, 3 x 5 In. | 180 |
| **Baseball,** Chicago White Sox, 1906, 3 x 5 In. | 150 |
| **Baseball,** Frank Chase, Cubs, Fielding A Ball, Photo, Black & White | 330 |
| **Baseball,** New York Giants Team, 1912, Cancelled, 3 x 5 In. | 780 |
| **Baseball,** Ty Cobb, At Bat, Photo, Black, White, H.M. Taylor, 1908, 3 x 5 In. | 1320 |
| **Budweiser Bar Beer Wagon,** Photo, Venice, Ill., Ox Driven Wagon, 3 x 5 In. | 120 |
| **Buffalo Bill Cody,** Portrait Photo, Black & White, 1909, 3 x 5 In. | 150 |
| **Cat,** Gray, Black, Louis Wains Annual Advertising, 1905 | 450 |

**Porcelain-Chinese,** Vase, Flambe Glaze, Narrow Mouth, 6 ⅝ In.
$2,829

Skinner Auctioneers & Appraisers

**Porcelain-Chinese,** Vase, Turquoise, Dog Head Ring Handles, Incised, Dragon, Phoenix, Marked, 1911-49, 14 In.
$732

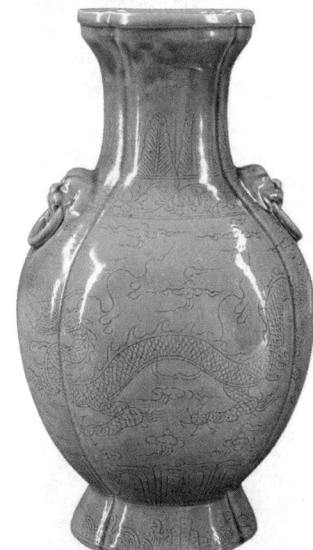

Neal Auction Co.

**P**

**TIP**

*Maroon and yellowish chrome-green were colors never used to decorate porcelain during the eighteenth century.*

439

**Porcelain-Contemporary,** Moonpot, Rattle, Glazed, Signed, Toshiko Takaezu, 5 ¼ x 4 ¼ In.
$1,625

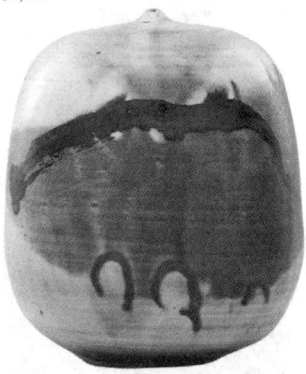

Rago Arts & Auction Center

**Porcelain-Contemporary,** Teapot, 2 Half Circles, Cone Top, Michael Duvall, 1989, 10 ¼ x 10 ½ In.
$960

Cowan's Auctions

**Porcelain-Midcentury,** Figurine, Young Woman, Bird Perched On Her Hand, A. Borsato, 6 In.
$48

DuMouchelles Art Gallery

**P**

| | |
|---|---:|
| **Girl,** Kissing Santa, Embossed, 1914, 5 ½ x 3 ½ In. | 15 |
| **Halloween,** Pretty Witch, Goblins, Winsch Publisher, 1912 | 125 |
| **Happy Thanksgiving,** Corn On Cob, Turkey, M.W. Taggart, N.Y., 1908 | 8 |
| **Home Interior,** Woman, Cat, Carl Krenek, Wiener Werkstatte, No. 908 | 330 |
| **Horse Drawn Medicine Wagon,** Seelye's Was-A-Tusa The Great Healer, Photo, 3 x 5 In. | 150 |
| **International Expo Of Illustrated Postcards,** Italy, 1899, 3 x 5 In. | 90 |
| **Junkins Ride To Gallows,** Photo, Horse & Wagon, Minister, 3 x 5 In. | 60 |
| **Motorboat,** Icy Lake Keuka N.Y., Black & White Photo, 3 x 5 In. | 210 |
| **New York State,** Woman, Holding Empire State Building, 1910 | 9 |
| **Organ Grinder,** One Leg, Horse, England, Photo, 1904, 3 x 5 In. | 60 |
| **R.M.S. Titanic,** Color, J. Salmon, England, 3 x 5 In. | 150 |
| **Rodeo Cowgirls,** Sheridan, Wyoming, Photo, Black & White, O'Neill Photo Co, 3 x 5 In. | 150 |
| **Rural Mail Wagon,** Postman, Mailbags, His Family, Black & White Photo, 3 x 5 In. | 120 |
| **St. Patrick's Day,** Baby Irish, International Art Pub. Co., 1912 | 8 |
| **The Plaza,** New York City, 1972 | 5 |
| **Train Depot,** Kearney Nebraska, Photo, Black & White, 3 x 5 In. | 60 |
| **Woman In The Gazebo,** Blue, Green, Black, Oskar Kokoschka, Wiener Werkstatte, No. 152 | 900 |
| **Yacht Club,** Falstaff Lemp Beer, Woman By Railing, Fade Away, Sandberg, 3 x 5 In. | 150 |

**POSTERS** have informed the public about news and entertainment events since ancient times. Nineteenth-century advertising and theatrical posters and twentieth-century movie and war posters are of special interest today. The price is determined by the artist, the condition, and the rarity. Other posters may be listed under Movie, Political, and World War I and II.

| | |
|---|---:|
| **1928,** Munich, Home & Technology Expo, Man Woman Workers, Cardboard, 13 In. | 60 |
| **About Paris,** Moulin Rouge, 2 Black Cats, E. Penfield, Harper & Bros., 1895, 15 x 10 In. | 6250 |
| **Bally,** Black, Red-Headed Stylized Woman, Bernard Villemot, c.1920, 66 x 49 In. | 316 |
| **Buffalo Bill,** Portrait Weiners Ch. Wall, Paris, c.1905, 39 x 29 In. | 14080 |
| **Buffalo Bill's Wild West,** 3 Horsemen, 40 ½ x 29 In. | 1852 |
| **Buffalo Bill's Wild West,** Train Robbery, 38 ¼ x 29 In. | 5214 |
| **Burlesque,** Anne Howe, Roxy Theatre, Photograph, Wood Panel, 62 x 42 In. | 201 |
| **Burlesque,** Petite Frenchie Colette, Roxy Theatre, Photo, Wood Panel, 62 x 42 In. | 230 |
| **Carter The Great,** Modern Priestess Of Delphi, 74 ¾ x 38 ¼ In. | 888 |
| **Carter The Great,** World's Weird Wonderful Wizard, Cards, Imps, 74 ½ x 38 ¼ In. | 1481 |
| **Chairman Mao,** Chinese Propaganda, Shining Sun, Red Ground, 40 x 30 ½ In. | 362 |
| **Circus,** Barnum & Bailey, Arrivee Dans Les Ports De Mers, 1902, 75 x 28 In. | 1500 |
| **Circus,** Barnum & Bailey, German, Linen, Strobridge & Co., 1895, 40 x 31 In. .........*illus* | 530 |
| **Circus,** Barnum & Bailey, Gorilla, c.1938, 41 ½ x 27 ½ In. | 1235 |
| **Circus,** Ringling Bros. & Barnum & Bailey, Girls, Performing Cats, 28 ½ x 41 In. | 196 |
| **Circus,** Ringling Bros. Barnum & Bailey, Monkeys, c.1960, 41 x 27 In. | 95 |
| **Circus,** Ringling Bros., Cinderella, Ballerinas, Medieval Parade, 1916, 55 x 38 In. | 1152 |
| **Circus,** Ringling Bros., Tiger Head, Green, Red, Paper, Frame, 1958, 36 x 22 In. | 240 |
| **Concert,** Grateful Dead, Fillmore West, Purple, Green, Orange, 1966, 14 x 22 In. | 375 |
| **Concert,** Grateful Dead, Jerry Garcia Photograph, 1966, Black, White, B. Graham, 20 x 28 In. | 625 |
| **Continental,** Fire Insurance Co., Indians, Horse Fleeing Wildfire, Chromolitho, 31 x 37 In. | 184 |
| **Dartmouth Winter Carnival,** Feb. 10-11, 1939, Dom Lupo, 34 x 22 In. | 2006 |
| **Dartmouth Winter Carnival,** Feb. 5-6, 1954, 34 x 22 In. | 1416 |
| **Dylan,** Portrait, Multicolor Hair, Milton Glaser, Signed, 1967, 33 x 22 In. .........*illus* | 305 |
| **Eastern Maine State Fair,** Racing Scene, Mounted On Linen, 1888, 28 x 38 In. | 600 |
| **Expert Tattooing Done Here,** Reclining Tattooed Lady, Lithograph, Friedlander, 24 x 38 In. | 4840 |
| **Exposition Universelle Palais De L'Optique,** Woman, Moon, G. Leroux, 1900, 31 x 23 In. | 1152 |
| **Fete Des Fleurs,** Women, Pelting Men With Flowers, Lithograph, 1892, 49 x 35 In. | 1063 |
| **Fur Seal's Tooth,** Begun In Harper's Young People, E. Penfield, 1894, 18 x 13 In. | 438 |
| **Kar-Mi,** Swallows Loaded Gun Barrel, Hallsworth, Paper, Frame, 41 x 28 In. .........*illus* | 456 |
| **L'Arc En Ciel,** Folies-Bergere, Mat, Frame, Signed, Jules Cheret, 49 x 34 In. .........*illus* | 1230 |
| **L'Emeraude,** Alphonse Mucha, Lithograph, Frame, c.1900, 38 x 16 In. | 4012 |
| **Magic,** Cirque Palmarium, La Guillotine, Chromolitho, Frame, 1930, 62 x 46 In. | 1468 |
| **Miller Bros. 101 Ranch Real Wild West,** Edith Tantlinger, Apples, 1912, 19 x 20 In. | 3081 |
| **Mistinguett,** Woman, Long Blue Dress, Landscape, D. DeLosques, c.1900, 78 x 44 In. | 123 |
| **Nude,** For Sunshine & Surfing, Swimmers, Seashore, A.R. Baler, 1935, 40 x 25 In. | 875 |
| **Olympics,** 1914, Paris, Des Jeux Olympiques, Victor, Horse, E. Elzingre, 40 x 28 In. | 3072 |
| **Olympics,** 1920, Antwerp, Ville Olympiade Anvers, Olympian, City, Van Der Ven, 34 x 24 In. | 1250 |
| **Olympics,** 1924, Paris, Poster, Jeux Olympiques, Draped Men, Hands Raised, Jean Droit, 40 x 30 In. | 7500 |
| **Olympics,** 1956, Melbourne, Olympic City, Winking Sportsman, Forbes, 39 x 24 In. | 1375 |
| **Paratrooper,** Last Step Toward Becoming A Man, Planes, c.1974, 18 x 24 In. | 58 |
| **Pennsylvania Railroad,** Delightful Summer Travel, Penguins, A.P. Lefton, 46 x 30 In. | 1625 |

**Poster,** Circus, Barnum & Bailey, German, Linen, Strobridge & Co., 1895, 40 x 31 In.
$530

Mosby Auctions

**Poster,** Dylan, Portrait, Multicolor Hair, Milton Glaser, Signed, 1967, 33 x 22 In.
$305

Palm Beach Modern Auctions

**Poster,** Kar-Mi, Swallows Loaded Gun Barrel, Hallsworth, Paper, Frame, 41 x 28 In.
$456

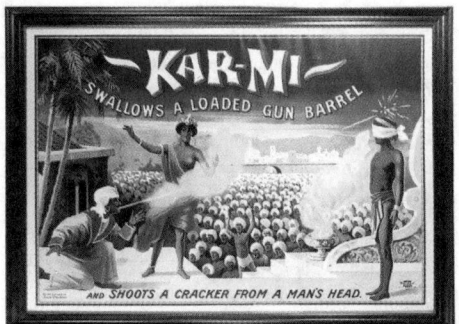

Showtime Auction Services

**Poster,** L'Arc En Ciel, Folies-Bergere, Mat, Frame, Signed, Jules Cheret, 49 x 34 In.
$1,230

New Orleans Auction Galleries, Inc.

**Poster,** Thurston, Kellar's Successor, Greatest Magician, Devils, Frame, 1908, 31 x 55 In.
$510

Morphy Auctions

**Poster,** Woodstock, White Bird, Guitar, 3 Days Of Peace & Music, 1969, 25 x 35 In.
$510

Morphy Auctions

**Pottery,** Decanter, Gentleman, Brick Wall, Relief, Dumler & Breiden
$72

Fox Auctions

**Pottery,** Figurine, Dog, Seated, Logan Pottery, Inscribed, Bill White, c.1910, 8½ In.
$300

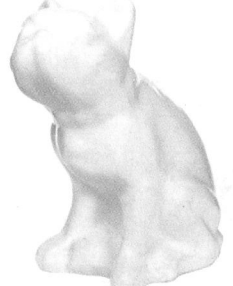

Garth's Auctioneers & Appraisers

**Pottery,** Plate, Birds, Flowers, Leaves, Puebla Talavera, Mexico, 1960s, 18 In.
$150

Allard Auctions

**Pottery,** Urn, Marriage Scene, Dumler & Breiden, Relief, 19 In.
$570

Fox Auctions

| | |
|---|---:|
| **Rosemary & Rue,** Woman Playing Lyre, Brown, Red, W.W. Denslow, c.1896, 25 x 20 In. | 688 |
| **Sarah Bernhardt American Tour,** Lithographic, Multicolor, Alphonse Mucha, 1896, 76 x 28 In. | 2300 |
| **Sunset Carson,** On Stage, Broadway, Virginia Theatre, Frame, c.1940, 28 x 22 In. | 104 |
| **Theatre De La Gaite,** Siamese Twins, Rosa-Josepha, Chromolitho, Frame, 45 x 31 In. | 2447 |
| **Thurston,** Kellar's Successor, Greatest Magician, Devils, Frame, 1908, 31 x 55 In. ..........*illus* | 510 |
| **Thurston,** The Great Magician, Red Imps, Cardboard, 35¾ x 23 In. | 2073 |
| **Travel,** Antibes, Beach, Women, Umbrella, Roger Broders, Paris, c.1928, 43 x 31 In. | 10625 |
| **Travel,** Australia Fly Qantas, Umbrellas, On Beach, F. Nanninga, 1950s, 38 x 24 In. | 2000 |
| **Travel,** Avignon, Sea, Buildings, Roger Broders, 1922, 42 x 30 In. | 1250 |
| **Travel,** Belgian Watering Place, Mother, Children, By Beach, c.1920, 40 x 25 In. | 1500 |
| **Travel,** Berck Plage, Woman, Bathing Suit, Beach, C. Belletre, c.1900, 42 x 30 In. | 500 |
| **Travel,** Brunnen Suisse, Spa On Lake Lucerne, G. Meunier, France, c.1900, 42 x 28 In. | 832 |
| **Travel,** Bulgaria, Land Of Roses, Mountains, Healing Waters, Germany, 1930s, 40 x 25 In. | 180 |
| **Travel,** Cabourg, Woman, Bathing Suit, Surf, Maurice Milliere, France, 1928, 46 x 32 In. | 7750 |
| **Travel,** California, This Summer, Woman, Sitting On Wall, Valley Below, c.1933, 41 x 27 In. | 5500 |
| **Travel,** Canne, Woman Golfer, Sea View, Georges Goursat, c.1930, 40 x 28 In. | 625 |
| **Travel,** Corse, Woman On Donkey, View Of Seaport, David Dellepiane, c.1910, 41 x 30 In. | 750 |
| **Travel,** Dunbar, Rocky Sea Scenes, Eric Lander, c.1928, 39 x 25 In. | 563 |
| **Travel,** Family Pulling Raft To Sea, Paignton, British Railways, London, c.1956, 40 x 25 In. | 594 |
| **Travel,** Hawaii Pan American, Boat Scene, Within Lei, A. Amspoker, c.1950, 35 x 22 In. | 1250 |
| **Travel,** Hawaii, Pan Am, Surfer, Within Sun, 1960s, 42 x 28 In. | 813 |
| **Travel,** La Place De Monte Carlo, Trellis, Bay, Stylized, Michel Bouchaud, 1929, 46 x 31 In. | 3750 |
| **Travel,** Monaco 24 Grand Prix Automobile, Michael Turner, 1966, 24 x 16 In. | 2750 |
| **Travel,** Monaco, Race Cars, Geo Ham, 1936, 47 x 31 In. | 11875 |
| **Travel,** Passy Mont Blanc, Rogers Broders, 1932, 39 x 24 In. | 2125 |
| **Travel,** Rainier National Park, Gustav W. Krollmann, 1930, 40 x 30 In. | 2750 |
| **Travel,** Santa Barbara Old Spanish Days, Padre, Roy E. Lawhorne, 1939, 41 x 27 In. | 1188 |
| **Travel,** See Bermuda, You Are Almost There When You Go To The Fair, c.1939, 40 x 25 In. | 813 |
| **Travel,** Sun Valley Idaho, Summer Holiday, Riders, Wm. Willmarth, 1939, 38 x 25 In. | 3072 |
| **Travel,** Tahiti, Fly Teal, Matt Chote & Co., New Zealand, 38 x 24 In. | 531 |
| **Travel,** Vichy, Woman, Holding Sports Equipment, Lefor-Openo, c.1960, 39 x 24 In. | 344 |
| **Travel,** Wild Australia, Cowboys, Cowgirls, Bucking Bronco, Bull, c.1925, 30 x 20 In. | 1188 |
| **Village Parson Paper Show,** People In Formals, U.S. Lithograph, Frame, 1903, 42 x 28 In. | 208 |
| **Woodstock,** White Bird, Guitar, 3 Days Of Peace & Music, 1969, 25 x 35 In. ..........*illus* | 510 |

**POTLIDS** are just that, lids for pots. Transfer-printed potlids had their heyday from the 1840s to the early 1900s. The English Staffordshire potteries made ceramic containers with decorative lids for bear's grease, shrimp or meat paste, cold cream, and toothpaste. Printed advertising and pictures of historical events, portraits of famous people, or scenic views were designed in black and white or color. Reproductions have been made.

| | |
|---|---:|
| **Bale's Savoury Mushroom,** Brown, Transfer, England, 3⅛ In. | 126 |
| **Bazin's Ambrosial Shaving Cream,** Eagle, Flowers, Purple Transfer, Stoneware, 3 In. | 110 |
| **Cherry Toothpaste,** Cherry Blossoms, Staffordshire, 1880s, 3 In. | 126 |
| **Children Of Flora,** Boys, Wreaths On Heads, Cart, 6½ In. | 200 |
| **Circassian Beauty Cream,** Black Transferware, Woman's Portrait, c.1890, 2 In. | 250 |
| **Glysophate For The Hair,** Black Transferware, c.1885, 3¾ In. | 203 |
| **Potted Tongue,** Black Transferware, c.1885, 4¼ In. | 158 |
| **The Rivals,** 2 Men, Maiden, c.1850, 5¾ In. | 220 |
| **Thistles,** Transferware, 5½ In. | 32 |
| **Windsor Castle,** Men On Horses, Dogs, Ceramic, 5 In. | 135 |
| **Wright's Gold Medal Saponaceous Shaving Compound,** Porcelain, 3 In. | 439 |

**POTTERY** and porcelain are different. Pottery is opaque; you can't see through it. Porcelain is translucent. If you hold a porcelain dish in front of a strong light, you will see the light through the dish. Porcelain is colder to the touch. Pottery is softer and easier to break and will stain more easily because it is porous. Porcelain is thinner, lighter, and more durable. Majolica, faience, and stoneware are all pottery. Additional pieces of pottery are listed in this book in the categories Pottery-Art, Pottery-Contemporary, Pottery-Midcentury, and under the factory name. For information about pottery makers and marks, see *Kovels' Dictionary of Marks—Pottery & Porcelain: 1650–1850* and *Kovels' New Dictionary of Marks—Pottery & Porcelain: 1850 to the Present.*

| | |
|---|---:|
| **Biscuit Jar,** Lid, Multicolor, Flowers, Butterflies, Black Ground, Silver Frame, Royal Sydney, 7 In. | 118 |
| **Bottle,** Crackle, Brown, White, Stoneware, J. Besnard, Signed, 1930s, 8 In. | 2750 |
| **Bowl,** Blue, Green, Yellow, Black, White Ground, Star Center, Morocco, 1800s, 3 x 10 In. | 81 |
| **Decanter,** Gentleman, Brick Wall, Relief, Dumler & Breiden ..........*illus* | 72 |
| **Figurine,** Dog, Seated, Logan Pottery, Inscribed, Bill White, c.1910, 8½ In. ..........*illus* | 300 |

**Pottery,** Vase, Bamboo, Low Relief, Blue, Gilt Swirls, Fukagawa, Arita, Japan, c.1925, 13 In. $400

**Pottery,** Vase, Wild Roses, Painted, John Bennett, Signed, 1882, 7 x 4 In. $1,125

**Pottery,** Vase, Yellow Irises, Brown Ground, Marked, Bretby, England, c.1910, 27 In. $777

**Pottery-Art,** Bottle, Pinched Waist, Enameled, Prunus, Theodore Deck, Signed, 1880s, 14 x 6 In. $4,688

**Pottery-Art,** Bowl, Butterflies, Incised Mark, Zark, c.1908, 2½ x 9 In. $2,375

**Pottery-Art,** Bowl, Crystalline Glaze, Brown Tones, Fred Robertson, Stamped, 3 x 6 In. $2,875

**Pottery-Art,** Charger, Faience, Birds, Edmond Lachenal, France, 1887, 17 In. $1,188

**Pottery-Art,** Charger, Putti On Sea Creature, Pink Luster, W. DeMorgan, c.1880, 14¼ In. $2,460

**Pottery-Art,** Dish, Bird With Worm, Partial Glaze, Pablo Picasso, c.1952, 6¼ In. $523

**Pottery-Art,** Figurine, Flower Vendor, Woman, Holding Child, Basket, Charles Vyse, c.1930, 10 In. $2,963

**P**

**Pottery-Art,** Figurine, Head Of A Child, Glazed, Waylande Gregory, c.1932, 15 In. $17,500

Rago Arts & Auction Center

**Pottery-Art,** Figurine, Head Of Baby, Bib, Green, Signed, Ozark, 4 ⅛ In. $403

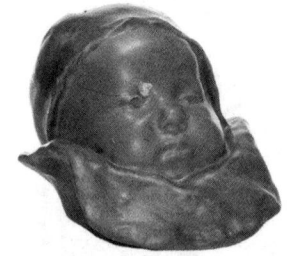

Humler & Nolan

**Pottery-Art,** Figurine, Work Horse, Stable Hand, Show Bridle, Charles Vyse, c.1930, 11 In. $4,740

James D. Julia Auctioneers

**Pottery-Art,** Group, Scholars, Red, Mustard, Blue, Hardwood Stand, Chinese, 3 x 3 ½ In. $472

Brunk Auctions

| | |
|---|---|
| **Figurine,** Rooster, Standing, Brown, Orange, Chinese, 12 In., Pair | 4688 |
| **Group,** Standing Man, Sitting Woman, Blue, 13 x 8 In. | 1625 |
| **Humidor,** Monkey Head Shape, Hat Lid, Bow Tie Pipe Holders, Multicolor, 1800s, 8 x 6 In. | 717 |
| **Jar,** Shigaraki, Tapered Bulbous Body, Flared Neck, Turned Out Rim, 1800s, 15 In. | 1912 |
| **Pedestal,** Earthenware, Elephant Shape, Multicolor, Chinese, 1900s, 23 x 18 In. | 72 |
| **Plate,** Birds, Flowers, Leaves, Puebla Talavera, Mexico, 1960s, 18 In. ...... *illus* | 150 |
| **Plate,** Sun, Pink, Yellow, White Ground, Henry Poor, 1920s, 8 ½ In. | 1375 |
| **Stirrup Cup,** Hound's Head, English Glaze, 8 ¾ In. | 3540 |
| **Teapot,** Caneware, Brown Slip Neck, Cock Fighting, Impressed Turner, 1780-1820, 6 ¼ In. | 390 |
| **Umbrella Holder,** Blue Ground, Multicolor Flowers, White Band, Red Rim, Chinese, 24 In. | 48 |
| **Urn,** Marriage Scene, Dumler & Breiden, Relief, 19 In. ...... *illus* | 570 |
| **Vase,** Bamboo, Low Relief, Blue, Gilt Swirls, Fukagawa, Arita, Japan, c.1925, 13 In. ...... *illus* | 400 |
| **Vase,** Branches, Iris, Flower Band, Turquoise Glaze, Ceil Et Montereau, c.1895, 15 In., Pair | 600 |
| **Vase,** Fish Swimming, Multicolor, Handles, Foley Intarsio, Wileman & Co. Logo, 3 x 4 In. | 403 |
| **Vase,** Fish, Turquoise Blue Glaze, Black Figures, Sea Fronds, Persia, c.1800, 12 x 9 In., Pair | 978 |
| **Vase,** Flower Band, Mottled Glaze, Flared Cylinder, California Faience, 1920s, 8 x 4 In. | 1125 |
| **Vase,** Glazed Earthenware, Honey Color, Footed, T. Sam Haile, 12 x 4 ½ In. | 615 |
| **Vase,** Globe Shape, Rising Wind, Zenji Miyashita, 7 ¼ x 12 ¾ In. | 1652 |
| **Vase,** Hanging Leaves, Red Berries, Yellow Ground, Foley Pottery, England, 11 In. | 840 |
| **Vase,** Wild Roses, Painted, John Bennett, Signed, 1882, 7 x 4 In. ...... *illus* | 1125 |
| **Vase,** Yellow Irises, Brown Ground, Marked, Bretby, England, c.1910, 27 In. ...... *illus* | 777 |

**POTTERY-ART.** Art pottery was first made in America in Cincinnati, Ohio, during the 1870s. The pieces were hand thrown and hand decorated. The art pottery tradition continued until the 1930s when studio potters began making the more artistic wares. American, English, and Continental art pottery by less well-known makers is listed here. Most makers listed in *Kovels' American Art Pottery*, such as Arequipa, Ohr, Rookwood, Roseville, and Weller, are listed in their own categories in this book. More recent pottery is listed under the name of the maker or in another pottery category.

| | |
|---|---|
| **Basket,** Yellow, Green, Pie Crimped Ends, Arched Handle, North Carolina, c.1930, 12 x 12 In. | 150 |
| **Bottle,** Pinched Waist, Enameled, Prunus, Theodore Deck, Signed, 1880s, 14 x 6 In. ...... *illus* | 4688 |
| **Bowl,** Burgundy, Black Leaves, Vines, Frosted Handles, Trifold Rim, Pallme-Konig, 4 x 9 In. | 403 |
| **Bowl,** Butterflies, Incised Mark, Zark, c.1908, 2 ½ x 9 In. ...... *illus* | 2375 |
| **Bowl,** Crystalline Glaze, Brown Tones, Fred Robertson, Stamped, 3 x 6 In. ...... *illus* | 2875 |
| **Bowl,** Geometric Pattern, Robert & Edna Tenorio, Santo Domingo, 6 ½ In. | 489 |
| **Bowl,** Green Enameled Scroll, Black, Emile Kenoble, Choisey-Le-Roi, c.1930, 3 x 10 In. | 1250 |
| **Bowl,** Incised Leg, Seraphim Soudbinne, 1910, 2 x 10 ½ In. | 1500 |
| **Charger,** Faience, Birds, Edmond Lachenal, France, 1887, 17 In. ...... *illus* | 1188 |
| **Charger,** Putti On Sea Creature, Pink Luster, W. DeMorgan, c.1880, 14 ¼ In. ...... *illus* | 2460 |
| **Charger,** Terra-Cotta, Landscape, Riverbank, Haviland, 13 ⅜ In. | 523 |
| **Dish,** Bird With Worm, Partial Glaze, Pablo Picasso, c.1952, 6 ¼ In. ...... *illus* | 523 |
| **Figurine,** Flower Vendor, Woman, Holding Child, Basket, Charles Vyse, c.1930, 10 In. ...... *illus* | 2963 |
| **Figurine,** Head Of A Child, Glazed, Waylande Gregory, c.1932, 15 In. ...... *illus* | 17500 |
| **Figurine,** Head Of Baby, Bib, Green, Signed, Ozark, 4 ⅛ In. ...... *illus* | 403 |
| **Figurine,** Pigeon, Primavera France, 18 In. | 531 |
| **Figurine,** Work Horse, Stable Hand, Show Bridle, Charles Vyse, c.1930, 11 In. ...... *illus* | 4740 |
| **Flask,** Hungarian Faience Style, Flowers, Leaves, Gold Trim, William Dell, 1891, 8 ⅝ In. | 196 |
| **Group,** Scholars, Red, Mustard, Blue, Hardwood Stand, Chinese, 3 x 3 ½ In. ...... *illus* | 472 |
| **Humidor,** Earth Tones, Wood Fired, Karen Karnes, Black Mountain College, 5 ¾ In. | 489 |
| **Jar,** Lid, Arts & Crafts, Cream, Hawk Relief, Early 20th Century, 9 In. | 185 |
| **Jug,** Water, Fish, Orange, Black, Loop Top Handle, Pablo Picasso, France, 1952, 5 x 8 In. ...... *illus* | 4375 |
| **Pitcher,** Blue, White Daisies, Red Berries, Brown, A. Dammouse, c.1900, 13 x 9 In. | 1500 |
| **Plate,** Face No. 202, Signed, Pablo Picasso, 1963, 9 ¾ In. ...... *illus* | 10625 |
| **Plate,** Stag, Purple, William Diederich, 1930s, 4 x 13 In. | 3750 |
| **Platter,** Art Nouveau, Shell Shape, Waterscape, Metal Twig Rim, Snail Shape Pot, Bronze Lid, 15 x 9 In. | 615 |
| **Sculpture,** 2 Men, Holding Lamb, Glazed, Grace Luse, 1930s, 14 ¾ x 7 In. ...... *illus* | 1024 |
| **Sculpture,** Bust, Magic Flute, Girl With Flute, Metal Stand, Signed, Ugo Lucerni, 21 ½ In. . *illus* | 2000 |
| **Sculpture,** Mermaid & Fish, Maurice Gensoli, Stamped, France, 1930s, 9 x 9 ¼ In. ...... *illus* | 3250 |
| **Sculpture,** Nude Woman, In Oyster Shell, M. Blondat, E. Lachenal, France, 1898, 9 x 9 In. | 4688 |
| **Sculpture,** Nude Woman, Seated, C. Besnard-Dubray, c.1900, 16 x 7 In. | 3125 |
| **Sugar & Creamer,** Dogwood Blossom | 165 |
| **Urn,** Lid, Flower, Cream, Green, 4-Footed, Pauline Pottery, 7 ½ x 20 In. | 671 |
| **Vase,** 4 Seasons, Faience, Max Laeuger, Stamped, Geschutzt, c.1900, 15 x 7 In. ...... *illus* | 875 |
| **Vase,** Abstract Design, 2 Handles, Wieselthier, Wiener Werkstatte, 1920s, 7 In. ...... *illus* | 813 |
| **Vase,** Andromeda, Figural Handle, Pierre-Adrien Dalpayrat, Jean Coulon, c.1900, 12 In. ...... *illus* | 9375 |
| **Vase,** Applied Bats, Green, White, Lantern Shape, E. Lachenal, c.1900, 11 x 8 In. | 11250 |

P

**Pottery-Art,** Jug, Water, Fish, Orange, Black, Loop Top Handle, Pablo Picasso, France, 1952, 5 x 8 In.
$4,375

Rago Arts & Auction Center

**Pottery-Art,** Plate, Face No. 202, Signed, Pablo Picasso, 1963, 9 ¾ In.
$10,625

Rago Arts & Auction Center

**Pottery-Art,** Sculpture, 2 Men, Holding Lamb, Glazed, Grace Luse, 1930s, 14 ¾ x 7 In.
$1,024

Rago Arts & Auction Center

**Pottery-Art,** Sculpture, Bust, Magic Flute, Girl With Flute, Metal Stand, Signed, Ugo Lucerni, 21 ½ In.
$2,000

Rago Arts & Auction Center

**Pottery-Art,** Sculpture, Mermaid & Fish, Maurice Gensoli, Stamped, France, 1930s, 9 x 9 ¼ In.
$3,250

Rago Arts & Auction Center

**Pottery-Art,** Vase, 4 Seasons, Faience, Max Laeuger, Stamped, Geschutzt, c.1900, 15 x 7 In.
$875

Rago Arts & Auction Center

**Pottery-Art,** Vase, Abstract Design, 2 Handles, Wieselthier, Wiener Werkstatte, 1920s, 7 In.
$813

Rago Arts & Auction Center

**Pottery-Art,** Vase, Andromeda, Figural Handle, Pierre-Adrien Dalpayrat, Jean Coulon, c.1900, 12 In.
$9,375

Rago Arts & Auction Center

**Pottery-Art,** Vase, Art Deco, Plant Sprigs, Stars, Raised Borders, Impressed Fritz Pohl, 7 x 8 In.
$138

Humler & Nolan

**Pottery-Art,** Vase, Blackberries, Pierced Neck, Impressed Pauline Pottery, 8 ¾ In.
$1,093

Humler & Nolan

**Pottery-Art,** Vase, Blackberry Blossoms, Leaves, Jersey City Pottery, Ivory White Ware, 1887, 9 ⅜ In.
$345

Humler & Nolan

**Pottery-Art,** Vase, Celadon Crystalline Glaze, Adelaide Robineau, 1921, 5 ½ x 3 ¼ In.
$5,000

**Pottery-Art,** Vase, Daisies, Squeezebag, Glossy, Vance Avon, 6 In.
$288

Humler & Nolan

**Pottery-Art,** Vase, Faience, Nude Woman, Enamel, Rene Buthaud, France, 1918-28, 11 x 5 ½ In.
$4,375

Rago Arts & Auction Center

**Pottery-Art,** Vase, Flambe Crystalline Drip Glaze, Handles, Auguste Delaherche, c.1901, 18 x 11 In.
$5,000

Rago Arts & Auction Center

**Pottery-Art,** Vase, Flame Painted, Ribbed, Flame Mark, T. Brouwer, Middle Lane, 1900s, 12 x 8 In.
$8,750

Rago Arts & Auction Center

**Pottery-Art,** Vase, Hydrangea Blossoms, Red & Blue Splashes, Incised, G. Foudji, Stamped, 19 In.
$1,955

Humler & Nolan

**Pottery-Art,** Vase, Nude Male Figures, Glazed, Rene Buthaud, France, 1930s, 12 x 10 In.
$5,000

Rago Arts & Auction Center

**P**

Rago Arts & Auction Center

| | |
|---|---|
| **Vase,** Art Deco, Plant Sprigs, Stars, Raised Borders, Impressed Fritz Pohl, 7 x 8 In. ............*illus* | 138 |
| **Vase,** Bisque, Gray Mottled Glaze, Sculpted Lines, Pond Farm, Marguerite Wildenhain, 7 In........ | 460 |
| **Vase,** Blackberries, Pierced Neck, Impressed Pauline Pottery, 8¾ In. ...................*illus* | 1093 |
| **Vase,** Blackberry Blossoms, Leaves, Jersey City Pottery, Ivory White Ware, 1887, 9⅜ In. ......*illus* | 345 |
| **Vase,** Blue Drips, Crystalline Glaze, Tapered, Dalpayrat, c.1905, 14 x 5 In............................ | 1625 |
| **Vase,** Blue, Nude Woman, Peacocks, Flask Shape, Primavera, France, 12 In., Pair...................... | 3000 |
| **Vase,** Burgundy, Cut Rim, Palm Handles, Crimped Ridges, Dimpled, Pallme-Konig, 14 x 7 In..... | 805 |
| **Vase,** Celadon Crystalline Glaze, Adelaide Robineau, 1921, 5½ x 3¼ In. ...................*illus* | 5000 |
| **Vase,** Copper Crystalline Glaze, A. Delaherche, France, c.1900, 13 x 8 In. ......................... | 4688 |
| **Vase,** Daisies, Squeezebag, Glossy, Vance Avon, 6 In. ...................*illus* | 288 |
| **Vase,** Earthenware, Flambe Glazed, Baluster Shape, Variegated Lavender, c.1900, 11 In. ............ | 531 |
| **Vase,** Enameled Birds, Prunes, France, c.1875, 10 x 6 In., Pair......................................... | 768 |
| **Vase,** Faience, Nude Woman, Enamel, Rene Buthaud, France, 1918-28, 11 x 5½ In. .........*illus* | 4375 |
| **Vase,** Flambe Crystalline Drip Glaze, Handles, Auguste Delaherche, c.1901, 18 x 11 In. ......*illus* | 5000 |
| **Vase,** Flambe Crystalline Glaze, 4 Handles, Tapered, A. Delaherche, c.1898, 11 x 8 In.................. | 6875 |
| **Vase,** Flambe Crystalline Glaze, Tapered, Handles, A. Delaherche, France, c.1890, 16 x 11 In. ..... | 8750 |
| **Vase,** Flame Painted, Ribbed, Flame Mark, T. Brouwer, Middle Lane, 1900s, 12 x 8 In. ........*illus* | 8750 |
| **Vase,** Flowers, Gilt, Faience, Flared Neck, Branch Shape Handle, Footed, William Dell, 9 In......... | 23 |
| **Vase,** Flowers, Leaves, Tapered, A. Delaherche, c.1893, 12 x 7 In. ............................. | 1875 |
| **Vase,** Fruit, Branches, Oxblood & Indigo, Tapered, A. Delaherche, France, c.1890, 14 x 11 In. ..... | 4688 |
| **Vase,** Green, Impressed Design, Chicago Crucible, 7 In.............................................. | 600 |
| **Vase,** Hydrangea Blossoms, Red & Blue Splashes, Incised, G. Foudji, Stamped, 19 In. .........*illus* | 1955 |
| **Vase,** Incised Scrolls, Black, Emile Lenoble, c.1930, 11 x 10 In. ................................. | 10625 |
| **Vase,** Jugendstil, Amphora Style, Gilt Webbing, Stones, Holly Panel, c.1900, 15 x 7 In. ........... | 1152 |
| **Vase,** Mottled Glaze, Bulbous, Swirled, Splashed Glazed Inside, Dalpayrat, 4¾ In. ...................... | 472 |
| **Vase,** Nude Male Figures, Glazed, Rene Buthaud, France, 1930s, 12 x 10 In. .........*illus* | 5000 |
| **Vase,** Oxblood Drip Glaze, Handles, Emile Decoeur, France, c.1915, 10 x 12 In. ..................... | 5625 |
| **Vase,** Piercings, Green Glass Glaze, Rust Streaking, Ferock, 4 In. ................................. | 489 |
| **Vase,** Purple Matte, Curved Handles, Marked Pickfull, 21¾ In. .................................... | 403 |
| **Vase,** Rabbits, Leaves, Blue, White, Luster, Passenger, DeMorgan, c.1900, 9 x 5 In.................... | 6875 |
| **Vase,** Red Dragon, Olive Ground, Flambe Glaze, Bernard Moore, 4 In. ............................ | 288 |
| **Vase,** Sang De Boeuf & Turquoise Glazes, Bulbous, Dalpayrat, Art Nouveau, 8 In. ...................... | 2596 |
| **Vase,** Sang De Boeuf Glaze, Frederick Rhead, 1914-17, 3¼ x 2½ In. ...................*illus* | 1000 |
| **Vase,** Secessionist, Purple, Bronze Overlay, Opal Cabochons, Austria, 8⅝ In. ...................... | 633 |
| **Vase,** Shamrocks, Mottled Blue, Thin Neck, Scrolled Handles, Della Robbia, c.1895, 15 In........... | 1059 |
| **Vase,** Stylized Buds, Carved, Reticulated, F.H. Rhead, W.P. Jervis, c.1910, 8 In. ..................*illus* | 3500 |
| **Vase,** Stylized Flowers, Pink Luster, F. Passenger, Bushy Heath, c.1925, 7½ In. ...................*illus* | 615 |
| **Vase,** Summer Landscape, Flowering Topiary Trees, R. Dean, Impressed, Wardle, 5 In. ............... | 288 |
| **Vase,** Tan Glazed, Squat, Adelaide Robineau, c.1900, 4½ x 5 In. .................................. | 875 |
| **Vase,** Tan, Blue Drip Glaze, Tapered, A. Delaherche, c.1920, 11 x 5 In. ........................... | 2500 |
| **Vase,** Turquoise Blue, Flowers, Slender Neck, Theodore Deck, c.1890, 12½ In. ...................*illus* | 2596 |

**POTTERY-CONTEMPORARY** lists pieces made by artists working about 1975 and later.

| | |
|---|---|
| **Bottle,** Earthenware, Gold Luster, Handle, Spout, B. Wood, c.1980, 5½ x 6 In.............................. | 2460 |
| **Bowl,** Copper Red, Scalloped Edge, Cut Wing, Elsa Rady, 1980, 2¼ x 6¾ In............................. | 336 |
| **Bowl,** Earthenware, Luster, Beatrice Wood, c.1985, 3½ x 11¾ In.......................................... | 2829 |
| **Bowl,** Figures Holding Hands, Luster Glaze, Beatrice Wood, c.1985, 8 x 10 In. .....................*illus* | 3125 |
| **Bowl,** Flared, White Combed, Brown Ground, Footed, Rupert Spira, c.1990, 13 In....................... | 3177 |
| **Bowl,** Stoneware, Salt Glaze, Blue Stylized Nude Inside, K. Ferguson, 5 x 11 In........................ | 875 |
| **Charger,** Glazed Stoneware, Signed, Peter Voulkos, 1973, 4 x 19 In. ...................*illus* | 4688 |
| **Charger,** Unglazed, Incisions, Signed, 1975, 4 x 20 In........................................... | 2125 |
| **Ewer,** Handbuilt, John Gill, 16 x 12 In. ......................................................... | 2000 |
| **Jar,** Lid, Earth Tones, Glazed, Signed, Clyde Burt, 17 x 7 In. ...................*illus* | 1750 |
| **Jar,** Stoneware, Beige, Double Gourd, Stamped, Paul Chaleff, 8 x 6 In. ............................ | 270 |
| **Jar,** Stoneware, Brown, Applied Strokes, Paul Chaleff, 16 x 13 In................................. | 720 |
| **Jar,** Stoneware, Brown, Undulating Edge, Paul Chaleff, 16 x 18 In................................. | 720 |
| **Jug,** Face, Dark Alkaline Glaze, Open Mouth, China Teeth, Ear Handles, 16 In......................... | 590 |
| **Jug,** Face, Olive Glaze, Open Mouth, China Teeth, B.B. Craig, Vale N.C., 7 In......................... | 325 |
| **Jug,** Face, Orange Glaze, Open Mouth, Teeth, Question Mark Ears, B.H., 9 In........................... | 354 |
| **Moonpot With Rattle,** Round, Streaked Glaze, T. Takaezu, 5 In. ..................................... | 1875 |
| **Moonpot,** Brown, Toshiko Takaezu, 12 x 9 In. ................................................... | 2875 |
| **Moonpot,** Rattle, Drip Glaze, Signed, TT, Toshiko Takaezu, 6 x 5 In. ...................*illus* | 1536 |
| **Mug,** Night Cup, Glazed, Happy's Curios Series, Ken Price, 1970s, 3 In. ...................*illus* | 5625 |
| **Pitcher,** Brown, Tan, Signed Claude Conover, 15 x 6¾ In............................................ | 1250 |
| **Pitcher,** Pillow, Jelly Bean, Glazed, Betty Woodman, 1983, 17½ x 23 In. ...................*illus* | 10625 |

**Pottery-Art,** Vase, Sang De Boeuf Glaze, Frederick Rhead, 1914-17, 3¼ x 2½ In.
$1,000

Rago Arts & Auction Center

**Pottery-Art,** Vase, Stylized Buds, Carved, Reticulated, F.H. Rhead, W.P. Jervis, c.1910, 8 In.
$3,500

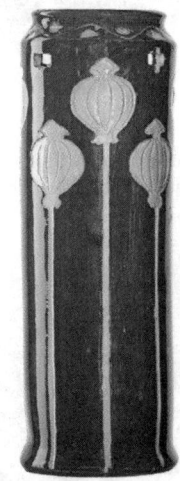

Rago Arts & Auction Center

**Pottery-Art,** Vase, Stylized Flowers, Pink Luster, F. Passenger, Bushy Heath, c.1925, 7½ In.
$615

Skinner Auctioneers & Appraisers

P

**Pottery-Art,** Vase, Turquoise Blue, Flowers, Slender Neck, Theodore Deck, c.1890, 12 ½ In.
$2,596

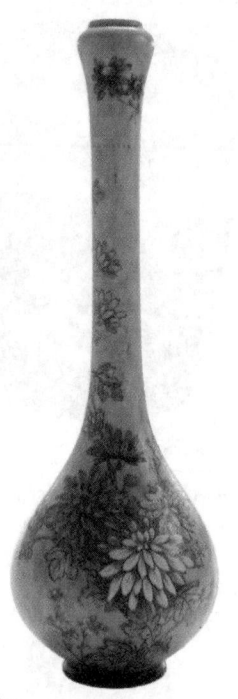

Brunk Auctions

**Pottery-Contemporary,** Bowl, Figures Holding Hands, Luster Glaze, Beatrice Wood, c.1985, 8 x 10 In.
$3,125

Los Angeles Modern Auctions (LAMA)

**Pottery-Contemporary,** Charger, Glazed Stoneware, Signed, Peter Voulkos, 1973, 4 x 19 In.
$4,688

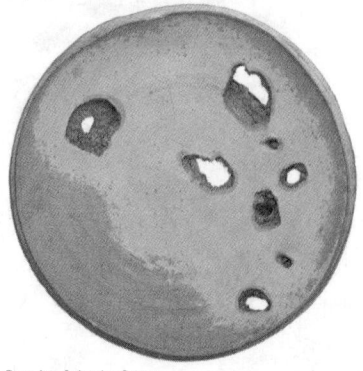

Rago Arts & Auction Center

**Pottery-Contemporary,** Jar, Lid, Earth Tones, Glazed, Signed, Clyde Burt, 17 x 7 In.
$1,750

Rago Arts & Auction Center

**Pottery-Contemporary,** Moonpot, Rattle, Drip Glaze, Signed, TT, Toshiko Takaezu, 6 x 5 In.
$1,536

Rago Arts & Auction Center

**Pottery-Contemporary,** Mug, Night Cup, Glazed, Happy's Curios Series, Ken Price, 1970s, 3 In.
$5,625

Rago Arts & Auction Center

**Pottery-Contemporary,** Pitcher, Pillow, Jelly Bean, Glazed, Betty Woodman, 1983, 17 ½ x 23 In.
$10,625

Rago Arts & Auction Center

**Pottery-Contemporary,** Sculpture, Stack Pot, Glazed, Peter Voulkos, 1962, 23 x 11 x 7 In.
$21,250

Rago Arts & Auction Center

**Pottery-Contemporary,** Teapot, Female, Nude, Glazed, Akio Takamori, 11 x 14 ½ In.
$6,250

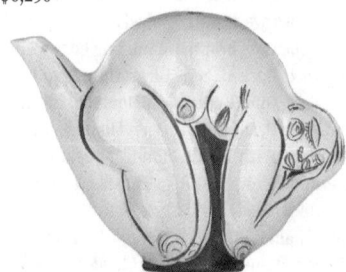

Rago Arts & Auction Center

| | |
|---|---|
| **Plaque,** Raku, Green, Pink, Signed Paul Soldner, 22 x 15¼ In. .................... | 1000 |
| **Plate,** Abstract Design, Blue, Black, Orange, P. Voulkos, 1960, 3 x 13 In. .... | 2375 |
| **Plate,** Naked Women, Ropes, Bondage, Signed Nevadomi, 1982, 15 In. ...... | 998 |
| **Plate,** Stoneware, White Matte Glaze, Ruth Duckworth, c.1968, 2½ x 9½ In. | 492 |
| **Sculpture,** Brown, Wouter Dam, 11 x 12 In. ........................................... | 875 |
| **Sculpture,** Garbage Can, Small Pail, Victor Spinski, 15 x 12 In. ................ | 2944 |
| **Sculpture,** Green, Wouter Dam, 12½ x 11 In. ........................................ | 1750 |
| **Sculpture,** It's About Time, Building, Jack Earl, 1983, 21 x 16¾ In. ........... | 10625 |
| **Sculpture,** Owl, On Log, Mushrooms At Base, Rick Wisecarver, 1982, 9½ In. | 253 |
| **Sculpture,** Photo Negative & Ashtray, Glass, J. Melchert, 1968, 18 x 20 In. | 4305 |
| **Sculpture,** Rocky, Hand-Built, Peter Vandenberge, 1977, 52 x 21 In. ......... | 2250 |
| **Sculpture,** Stack Pot, Glazed, Peter Voulkos, 1962, 23 x 11 x 7 In. .....................*illus* | 21250 |
| **Teapot No. 38,** Signed John Gill, 7½ x 14 In. ........................................ | 1188 |
| **Teapot,** Brown, C.O.D. Shipping Box Shape, M. Harvey, c.1995, 5¾ In....... | 35 |
| **Teapot,** Female, Nude, Glazed, Akio Takamori, 11 x 14½ In. ................*illus* | 6250 |
| **Teapot,** Multicolor, Abstract Dog Shape, P. Shire, 1982, 15¾ x 17½ ...... | 3125 |
| **Teapot,** Organic Twisted, Green, Peter Stark, c.2005, 6 x 7 In. ............... | 480 |
| **Teapot,** Woman's Face, Reeded Handle, R. Meyers, c.1990, 8½ x 13 In. ...*illus* | 840 |
| **Totem,** Whiteware, Carved, Multicolor, Christine Federighi, c.1995, 68 x 6½ In. ..... | 1020 |
| **Vase,** 2 Stacked Squat Rectangles, Glazed, Claude Conover, 19 x 16 In..... | 4688 |
| **Vase,** Ashes Of Roses Glaze, Teardrop Shape, Brother T. Bezanson, 6 x 5 In. | 3000 |
| **Vase,** Blue Shaded, Abstract Shape, Incised, Alison Britton, 1987, 14 In. ... | 1059 |
| **Vase,** Blue Volcanic Glaze, Cylinders, 3 Figures On Shoulder, Beatrice Wood, 13 In..... | 3125 |
| **Vase,** Chrysanthemum Glaze, Cylindrical, Brother T. Bezanson, 10 x 4 In. . | 5937 |
| **Vase,** Coil, Bulbous, Tan & Brown Glaze, White Band, C. Conover, 1970s, 20 In.......... | 5625 |
| **Vase,** Copper Red Glaze, Cylindrical, Flattened Rim, Brother T. Bezanson, 12 In....... | 8750 |
| **Vase,** Crouching Cat, Blue Ground, Sargent, Santa Barbara Ceramic Design, 1983, 7 In..... | 196 |
| **Vase,** Cunha, Textured, White Bands, Round, Claude Conover, 18 In........... | 4480 |
| **Vase,** Earthenware, Black Flared Rim, M. Odundo, 1991, 14½ x 12¼ In. ... | 30000 |
| **Vase,** Feelie, Earth Tones, Karen Karnes, c.1998, 10 x 8¾ In. ............*illus* | 1845 |
| **Vase,** Fern, Green, Yellow, Cylindrical, Marked Tim Eberhardt, 1999, 12 In. | 196 |
| **Vase,** Fish, Cutthroat, T-Shape, Signed, Rudy Autio, 1980, 15 x 17½ In. .....*illus* | 5440 |
| **Vase,** Flowers, Blue, Brown, Iridescent, Cylindrical, Tim Eberhardt, 1998, 17¼ In. .... | 403 |
| **Vase,** Flowers, Blue, Green, Cylindrical, Handles, Marked, Tim Eberhardt, 1999, 12 In. | 288 |
| **Vase,** Housepot No. 1, Lines, Geometric Designs, John Gill, 1986, 16 x 10 In. ......*illus* | 1625 |
| **Vase,** Incised, Underwater Scene, Green Glaze, V. Schreckengost, 11 x 7 In. | 4375 |
| **Vase,** Kaxab, Glazed Stoneware, Signed, Claude Conover, 1970s, 23 x 10 In. ......*illus* | 4688 |
| **Vase,** Lid, Stoneware, Teardrop Rows, H. McIntosh, c.1995, 7½ x 7½ In.... | 1920 |
| **Vase,** Light Gatherer, Porcelain, Carved, Rudolph Straffel, 1984, 4 x 3½ In. | 1230 |
| **Vase,** Luster Glaze, Figure, 2 Side Wells, Beatrice Wood, c.1980, 10 x 10½ In. .....*illus* | 6250 |
| **Vase,** Owl, Blue Green Ground, Marked FraMae, 1981, 10¾ In............... | 23 |
| **Vase,** Salt Glaze, Stamped Woodman, 1980, 12 x 9¼ In. ...................... | 1125 |
| **Vase,** Square Shape, Stoneware, Blue, Black, Albert Green, c.1980, 9½ In. . | 960 |
| **Vase,** Tiger Lilies, Long Neck, Santa Barbara Ceramic Design, 1981, 9 In. . | 109 |
| **Vase,** White, Signed, Robert Turner, 1990, 8 x 7¾ In. ........................ | 2250 |
| **Vase,** Yellow To Green, Flared, Signed Tina Reutenberg, 1990s, 25 In........ | 1125 |

**POTTERY-MIDCENTURY** includes pieces made from the 1940s to about 1975.

| | |
|---|---|
| **Bottle,** Stoneware, J. Besnard, Signed, 1930s, 13¼ In........................ | 2750 |
| **Bowl,** Apple Green Reduction Glazed, Flame Mark, Signed, 1962, 3 x 9 In... | 3750 |
| **Bowl,** Duck Lid, Microcrystalline Glaze, Eva Zeisel, Great Western, 1940s, 8 x 9 In. .......*illus* | 3500 |
| **Bowl,** Geometric, Earth Tones, Myrton Purkiss, c.1950, 3¾ x 16 In.......... | 3125 |
| **Bowl,** Handbuilt, Orange Drip Glaze, Glen Lukens, 1940s, 4¾ x 6 In........ | 5312 |
| **Bowl,** Red & Copper, Horizontal Ribs, Gold Trim, V. Schreckengost, 5 x 10 In....... | 1875 |
| **Bowl,** Turquoise Lava Glaze, Marked Beato, Beatrice Wood, 1950s, 9 x 7 In. .......*illus* | 677 |
| **Bowl,** White, Brown, Flattened, Flared, Dame Lucy Rie, c.1955, 6 In......... | 1271 |
| **Bust,** Young Man, Lilian Swann Saarinen, 1956, 16 x 12½ In. ............... | 531 |
| **Candleholder,** Eagle Shape, Molded, Blue Speckled Glaze, James Seagreaves, 6 In..... | 130 |
| **Charger,** Adam, Eve & Serpent, Signed, E. & M. Scheier, 1991, 16¾ In. :........*illus* | 1750 |
| **Charger,** Birds, White Ground, Signed Ralph Bacerra, 23 In. ................ | 1875 |
| **Charger,** Green Corrida, Bullfighting, Black, P. Picasso, 1949, 14 In........ | 6875 |
| **Charger,** Modernist Cityscape, Crackled Glaze, Myrton Purkiss, 16 In. ...*illus* | 3125 |
| **Charger,** Raku, Iridescent Glaze, Evan Kahn, 1965, 12 In..................... | 108 |
| **Charger,** Speckled Iridescent Glaze, Beatrice Wood, 3 x 19 In............... | 10625 |
| **Figure,** Mother & Child, Green & Black Glaze, Susi Singer, 12 x 3 In. ...... | 1220 |

**Pottery-Contemporary,** Teapot, Woman's Face, Reeded Handle, R. Meyers, c.1990, 8½ x 13 In.
$840

Cowan's Auctions

**Pottery-Contemporary,** Vase, Feelie, Earth Tones, Karen Karnes, c.1998, 10 x 8¾ In.
$1,845

Cowan's Auctions

**Pottery-Contemporary,** Vase, Fish, Cutthroat, T-Shape, Signed, Rudy Autio, 1980, 15 x 17½ In.
$5,440

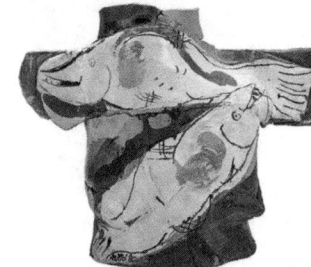

Rago Arts & Auction Center

**P**

**TIP**

*Put ceramic saucers or glass or plastic plant holders under vases of flowers or potted plants. There are inexpensive throwaway plastic dishes that have a rim and are exactly the right size and shape for a plant.*

**Pottery-Contemporary,** Vase, Housepot No. 1, Lines, Geometric Designs, John Gill, 1986, 16 x 10 In.
$1,625

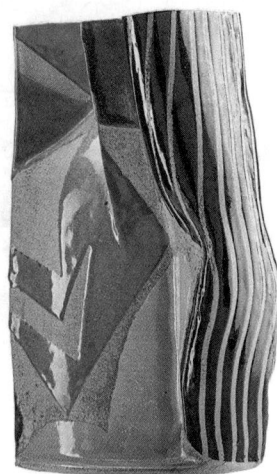

Rago Arts & Auction Center

**Pottery-Contemporary,** Vase, Kaxab, Glazed Stoneware, Signed, Claude Conover, 1970s, 23 x 10 In.
$4,688

Rago Arts & Auction Center

**Pottery-Contemporary,** Vase, Luster Glaze, Figure, 2 Side Wells, Beatrice Wood, c.1980, 10 x 10½ In.
$6,250

Los Angeles Modern Auctions (LAMA)

**Pottery-Midcentury,** Bowl, Duck Lid, Microcrystalline Glaze, Eva Zeisel, Great Western, 1940s, 8 x 9 In.
$3,500

Rago Arts & Auction Center

**Pottery-Midcentury,** Bowl, Turquoise Lava Glaze, Marked Beato, Beatrice Wood, 1950s, 9 x 7 In.
$677

Skinner Auctioneers & Appraisers

**Pottery-Midcentury,** Charger, Adam, Eve & Serpent, Signed, E. & M. Scheier, 1991, 16¾ In.
$1,750

Rago Arts & Auction Center

**Pottery-Midcentury,** Charger, Modernist Cityscape, Crackled Glaze, Myrton Purkiss, 16 In.
$3,125

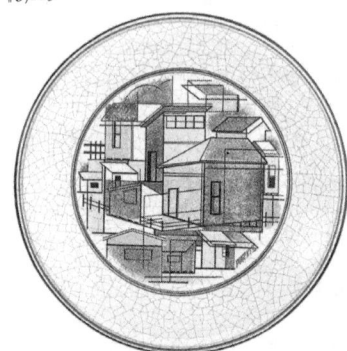

Rago Arts & Auction Center

**Pottery-Midcentury,** Figurine, Fish, Glass Fused, Waylande Gregory, Marked, 12 x 18 x 5 In.
$3,680

Humler & Nolan

**Pottery-Midcentury,** Figurine, Polynesian Fisherman & Woman, Glazed, T. Winter, 14 In., Pair
$640

Rago Arts & Auction Center

**Pottery-Midcentury,** Jar, Cover, Stoneware, Green Glaze, Reticulated Knob, H. McIntosh, 9 In.
$2,304

Rago Arts & Auction Center

P

| | |
|---|---|
| **Figurine,** Anteater, Gordon Newell, c.1958, 8 x 27 x 6 In. | 4063 |
| **Figurine,** Fish, Glass Fused, Waylande Gregory, Marked, 12 x 18 x 5 In. ...............*illus* | 3680 |
| **Figurine,** Owl, Glazed, Platform, Marked Pennsylvania, James Seagreaves, 9 In. ................ | 295 |
| **Figurine,** Pigeon, White Glass Glaze, Gold, Waylande Gregory, 6 x 10 In., Pair ................ | 184 |
| **Figurine,** Polynesian Fisherman & Woman, Glazed, T. Winter, 14 In., Pair ..............*illus* | 640 |
| **Jar,** Cover, Stoneware, Green Glaze, Reticulated Knob, H. McIntosh, 9 In. .............*illus* | 2304 |
| **Jar,** Lid, Applied Handles, Gerry Williams, c.1969, 7 ½ x 7 ¾ In. | 615 |
| **Pitcher,** Bearded Man's Wife, Black, Green, Gray, Picasso, Madoura, 15 In. ................ | 21275 |
| **Pitcher,** Black, Horse, Rider, P. Picasso, Madoura, 1952, 5 ½ In. | 3125 |
| **Pitcher,** Blue, White, Face, G. Jouve, 1950s, 8 x 5 ¾ In. | 2250 |
| **Pitcher,** Chope Visage, Face, Blue, Orange, Picasso, Madoura, 1959, 8 In. | 5192 |
| **Pitcher,** Devil Face, Grotesque, Glazed, Signed, James Seagreaves, 7 ¼ In. | 2360 |
| **Pitcher,** Face, Cream, Green, Brown, P. Picasso, Madoura, 1969, 12 ¼ In. | 8125 |
| **Pitcher,** Little Wood Owl, Blue, White Ground, Pablo Picasso, 1949, 5 In. | 4425 |
| **Pitcher,** Sculpted Figures, Iridescent Glaze, Beatrice Wood, 9 In. .......................*illus* | 2250 |
| **Pitcher,** Seized Handle Pitcher, Bird, Pablo Picasso, 1953, 7 In. .......................... | 7050 |
| **Planter,** Cylindrical, Green, Blue Glaze, David Cressey, c.1960, 23 x 15 In., Pair .........*illus* | 4375 |
| **Plaque,** 4 Fishes, Multicolor, Pablo Picasso, 1947, 15 ¼ x 12 ¼ In. | 8750 |
| **Plate,** Abuja, Blue Bug, Glazed Stoneware, Incised, Ladi Kwali, 1960s, 2 x 10 ½ In. ....... | 540 |
| **Plate,** Bunch With Apple, White, Green, P. Picasso, Madoura, 1956 ......................... | 3375 |
| **Plate,** Cavalier On Horseback, Relief, Unglazed White, P. Picasso, Madoura, 17 In. | 5310 |
| **Plate,** Corrida, Bullfighting, Black, P. Picasso, 1953, 14 ½ In. | 8125 |
| **Plate,** Face No.125, Multicolor, P. Picasso, Madoura, 1962, 10 In. | 8125 |
| **Plate,** Faun's Head, White, P. Picasso, Madoura, 1955, 10 In. | 3250 |
| **Plate,** Picador, Black On White, Dotted Border, P. Picasso, Madoura, 1952, 8 In. | 1625 |
| **Plate,** Tauromachy Scene, Brown, P. Picasso, Madoura, 1959, 16 ½ In. | 9375 |
| **Plate,** Turquoise Glaze, Crystalline Center, Jade Snow Wong, c.1955, 10 In. ........*illus* | 584 |
| **Plate,** Vase With Bunch, Brown, Green, P. Picasso, Madoura, 1956, 9 ½ In. | 4062 |
| **Platter,** Fish, Glazed, Kenji Fujita, Incised Tackett, 1950s, 19 ½ x 13 ¼ In. .........*illus* | 1250 |
| **Platter,** Nature Morte, Partial Glaze, Pablo Picasso, 1953, 12 x 15 In. ..............*illus* | 6490 |
| **Platter,** Visage D'Une Etoile, Star Face, Picasso, Madoura, 1947, 12 x 14 In. | 5900 |
| **Pot,** Green Glaze, Flared, Cylindrical Top, Rolled Rim, P. Voulkos, 1950s, 14 x 14 In. ....... | 1188 |
| **Rattle,** Abstract Designs, Brown, Green, Cream Ground, Ribbed, T. Takezu, 22 In. ......... | 3172 |
| **Sculpture,** Figural, Abstract, Glazed, Marcello Fantoni, 1955, 25 ½ In. ...........*illus* | 2125 |
| **Sculpture,** Multicolor, Signed Hui, 22 x 13 In. | 2625 |
| **Sculpture,** Village Smithy, Signed, Viktor Schreckengost, 17 x 9 In. ..............*illus* | 11250 |
| **Shaving Mug,** Fish Sgrafitto, Glazed, Signed, James Seagreaves, 4 ½ In. | 35 |
| **Stein,** Abuja, Blue, Glazed Stoneware, Ladi Kwali, 1960s, 6 ½ x 5 ½ In., Pair | 270 |
| **Stein,** Abuja, Incised, Glaze Stoneware, Handle, Ladi Kwali, 1960s, 6 x 4 In., 4 Piece | 62 |
| **Tea Set,** Black, Squat, Teapot, Mugs, Tray, P. Saenger, c.1970, 9 x 9 In., 6 Piece | 46 |
| **Teapot,** Stylized Trees, Green, Black, Speckled, P. Voulkos, c.1958, 7 x 6 In. | 4880 |
| **Vase,** Alligatored Red Matte Glaze, Bulbous, Squat, Pinched Neck, Doyle Lane, 4 In. | 1750 |
| **Vase,** Ash Glaze, Wax Resist, Signed Shoji Hamada, 7 ¾ x 3 ¾ In. | 3250 |
| **Vase,** Ash Glazed Stoneware, Shoji Hamada, c.1965, 11 ½ x 6 ¼ In. | 3240 |
| **Vase,** Bottle, Horses, Manganese & Yellow, Cream Ground, G. Gambone, 12 In. | 531 |
| **Vase,** Bottle, Teardrops, Green, Beige, Speckled, Squat, H. McIntosh, 11 x 9 In. | 3750 |
| **Vase,** Curdled Mustard Glaze, Round, Small Opening, Doyle Lane, 3 In. | 1375 |
| **Vase,** Diane, Man, Spear, Multicolor, R.T. Lallemant, 1930s, 10 ¾ In. | 1500 |
| **Vase,** Feelie, Bright Blue & Green Matte Glaze, Bulbous, Rose Cabat, 3 ½ In. | 531 |
| **Vase,** Feelie, Green High Glaze, Crystalline Accents, Rose Cabat, 3 In. | 549 |
| **Vase,** Figures, Stoneware, Glazed, F.C. Ball, A. Bohrod, 22 x 10 In. ...............*illus* | 2500 |
| **Vase,** Geometric Design, Blue, Brown, Edgar Littlefield Logo, 1954, 13 ⅛ In. ........*illus* | 633 |
| **Vase,** Incised Vertical Lines, Blue Matte, Flared Foot, H. McIntosh, 5 x 6 In. | 732 |
| **Vase,** Little Master Cat, Seated, Signed, Louis Wain, 6 In. .......................*illus* | 2370 |
| **Vase,** Mr. Pointy Ears Cat, Seated, Stylized, Signed, Louis Wain, 5 In. ...........*illus* | 2074 |
| **Vase,** Smiling Face, Handle, Gambone, Donkey Cipher, 1960s, 23 x 22 In. .........*illus* | 10000 |
| **Vase,** Vertical Lines, Speckled Tan, Oval, Flared Rim, H. McIntosh, 6 x 3 In. | 563 |
| **Vase,** White Ground, Athletic Figures, Gold Rim, Footed, Gio Ponti, c.1930, 6 x 5 In., Pair ......... | 7500 |

**POWDER FLASKS AND POWDER HORNS** were made to hold the gunpowder used in antique firearms. The early examples were made of horn or wood; later ones were of copper or brass.

### POWDER FLASK

| | |
|---|---|
| **Brass,** Bald Eagle, Shield, Arrows, Olive Branch, Stars, Remington, 4 In. ................ | 1093 |
| **Copper,** Stags, 9 ½ In. | 132 |

**Pottery-Midcentury,** Pitcher, Sculpted Figures, Iridescent Glaze, Beatrice Wood, 9 In.
$2,250

Rago Arts & Auction Center

**Pottery-Midcentury,** Planter, Cylindrical, Green, Blue Glaze, David Cressey, c.1960, 23 x 15 In., Pair
$4,375

Los Angeles Modern Auctions (LAMA)

**Pottery-Midcentury,** Plate, Turquoise Glaze, Crystalline Center, Jade Snow Wong, c.1955, 10 In.
$584

Skinner Auctioneers & Appraisers

P

**Pottery-Midcentury,** Platter, Fish, Glazed, Kenji Fujita, Incised Tackett, 1950s, 19½ x 13¼ In. $1,250

Rago Arts & Auction Center

**Pottery-Midcentury,** Platter, Nature Morte, Partial Glaze, Pablo Picasso, 1953, 12 x 15 In. $6,490

Brunk Auctions

**Pottery-Midcentury,** Sculpture, Figural, Abstract, Glazed, Marcello Fantoni, 1955, 25½ In. $2,125

Rago Arts & Auction Center

| | |
|---|---:|
| **Double-Entwined Dolphin,** Bantram & Co., c.1850, 8 In. | 861 |
| **Engraved John Boyd,** c.1810, 12 In. | 1800 |
| **Measure,** Adjustable Measures, Spouted Cup, Wood-Handled, 5¼ In. | 60 |
| **Metal,** Thumb-Operated Opener, 9½ In. | 84 |
| **Silver Gilt,** Gazelle Coming Out, Sea Creature Head, 9¾ In. | 16063 |
| **Stamped Silver,** Trapezoid, Leaves, Cone Stopper, 15 x 4½ In. | 196 |
| **Wood,** Iron, Wolves, Flowers, Rosette, Musketeers, 1600s, 10½ x 8 In. | 1020 |
| **Wood,** Pierced Iron, Embossed, Leaves, Flowers, Cloth, Italy, c.1600 | 2550 |

## POWDER HORN

| | |
|---|---:|
| **Brass,** 1760 Boston Harbor Scene, c.1850, 8 In. | 180 |
| **Brass,** Birds, Animals, Flowers, Engraved, c.1910, 14 In. | 500 |
| **Brass,** Carved, Monogram TSR On Brass Spout, Animals, People, 1699, 7 In. | 960 |
| **Horn,** 3 Roses, Carved Inset Wood Cap, Fixed Rim, c.1800, 12 In. | 161 |
| **Horn,** Engraved Virginia Map, Native American, Soldier, c.1945, 12½ In. | 180 |
| **Horn,** Incised, Monograms, Name, Trees, Figure, French & Indian Wars, c.1780 | 2079 |
| **Horn,** Inscribed, Bird, Weapons, 1780, 10½ In. ......................................*illus* | 510 |
| **Whale's Teeth,** Engraved Masted Ships, Nautical Symbols, Chain, c.1762, 11⅞ In., c.1762 | 5280 |
| **Wood End,** Carved MP, c.1810, 12 In. | 37 |
| **Wood,** Carved, Applied Wood Cap, Threaded End, Inscribed, c.1815, 16 In. | 460 |

**PRATT** ware means two different things. It was an early Staffordshire pottery, cream-colored with colored decorations, made by Felix Pratt during the late eighteenth century. There was also Pratt ware made with transfer designs during the mid-nineteenth century in Fenton, England. Reproductions of the transfer-printed Pratt are being made.

**PRATT FENTON**

| | |
|---|---:|
| **Creamer,** Cameo, Lion & Boy, Lion & Dog, Fluted Panels, Basketweave, 19th Century, 4 In. | 145 |
| **Creamer,** Cow Shape, Sponged Painted, Yellow, Black, Green Base, c.1810, 6½ In. | 111 |
| **Figurine,** Baby, In Cradle, Green, Staffordshire, Pearlware, c.1800, 5 x 2 In. | 450 |
| **Figurine,** Horseman, Leaning On Stump, Hat, Tail Coat, c.1790, 4¼ In. | 445 |
| **Figurine,** Ophelia, Painted, May 26, 1810, 13 In. | 2006 |
| **Flask,** Cauliflower Shape, Leaves, 18th Century, 5 In. | 485 |
| **Jug,** Leaves, Dark Red Highlights, Enameled Flowers, Pearlware, c.1820, 5 In. | 295 |
| **Loving Cup,** Handles, Windmill, Valley, Horses, Pink, Transfer, c.1850, 4 In. | 650 |
| **Meat Jar,** Hunting Scene, Blue, Gold, c.1856, 4 In. | 50 |
| **Pitcher,** Greek Warriors, Horses, Chariots, Pearlware, Green, c.1860, 7 In. | 300 |
| **Plate,** Chinoiserie Scene, Cobalt Blue, Shaped Edge, 8 In. | 85 |
| **Plate,** Goats, Ruins, Pink Border, c.1860, 8½ In. | 48 |
| **Plate,** Herd Of Deer, River, c.1860, 7¼ In. | 135 |
| **Plate,** Skewbald Horse, Transferware, 19th Century, 7¼ In. | 100 |
| **Plate,** Village Wedding, Transferware, Pink, Ocher Border, 1800s, 7 In. | 75 |
| **Plate,** Waterfall, Plum & Gold Border, Transfer, 19th Century, 7¼ In. | 56 |
| **Potlid,** A Pair, Couple, Playing Cards, Fireplace, 1800s, 4 In. | 200 |
| **Potlid,** A. Fix, Men Playing Checkers, Woman, Child, Dog, c.1865, 4½ In. | 125 |
| **Potlid,** Bears, Outdoor School, Dunce Hat, 1800s, 3 In. | 135 |
| **Potlid,** French Street Scene, 4¾ In. | 110 |
| **Potlid,** Landscape, House, Man & Woman In Boat, Cows, 5¼ In. | 125 |
| **Potlid,** Late Duke Of Wellington, Portrait, 1870s, 6 In. | 100 |
| **Potlid,** Late Prince Consort, 19th Century, 4 In. | 150 |
| **Potlid,** Lobster Sauce, Cat, Lobster, 1840s, 3¾ In. | 135 |
| **Potlid,** River, Bridge, People, Dogs, 5¼ In. | 105 |
| **Potlid,** Uncle Tobey, Young Woman, Parson's Bench, c.1850, 4¼ In. | 110 |
| **Potlid,** Village Wedding, Musicians, Dancers, 6½ In. | 225 |
| **Sauceboat,** Fox Head Shape, Swan Handle, Pearlware, c.1790, 7 In. | 600 |
| **Tea Caddy,** Blue Macaroni Figures, Arched Rectangle, Pearlware, Staffordshire, c.1790, 6 In. | 420 |
| **Toby Jug,** Satyr, Pointed Nose, Beard, Rosy Cheeks, c.1790, 3½ In. | 1650 |
| **Watch Hutch,** Figural, Tall Case Clock, Children, Dixon, Austin & Co., c.1826, 11 In. | 2242 |

**PRESSED GLASS,** or pattern glass, was first made in the United States in the 1820s after the invention of glass pressing machines. Hundreds of patterns of pressed glass were made in complete table settings. Although the Boston and Sandwich Works was the most famous of the pressed glass factories, there were about sixteen other factories making pressed glass from 1830 to 1850, and still more from 1850 to 1900, when pressed glass reached its greatest popularity. It is now being widely reproduced. The pattern names used in this listing are based on the information in the book *Pressed Glass in America* by John and Elizabeth Welker. There may be pieces of pressed glass listed in this book in other categories, such as Lamp, Ruby Glass, Sandwich Glass, and Souvenir.

**101** pattern is listed here as One-Hundred-One.

P

| | |
|---|---:|
| **Albany,** Compote, Tarentum Glass Co., 8 x 6 In. | 55 |
| **Apollo,** Compote, Adams & Co., c.1875, 7 In. | 18 |
| **Banded Portland,** Pitcher, Water, Maiden's Blush, Purple, Clear, Gilt Virginia, c.1890, 7¾ In. | 150 |
| **Barberry,** Pitcher, Water, Bulbous, McKee & Brothers, c.1880, 8 In. | 38 |
| **Beatty Waffle,** Toothpick Holder, Opalescent, Beatty & Sons, c.1888 | 55 |
| **Beveled Diamond & Star** pattern is listed here as Albany. | |
| **Bird & Strawberry,** Cake Stand, Indiana Glass, c.1914, 9 x 3 In. | 95 |
| **Bluebird** pattern is listed here as Bird & Strawberry. | |
| **Bungalow,** Saltshaker | 34 |
| **Cabbage Leaf,** Plate, Riverside Glass, 1880s, 9½ In. | 210 |

**Candlewick** as a pressed glass pattern is properly named Banded Raindrop. There is also a pattern called Candlewick, which has been made by Imperial Glass Corporation since 1936. It is listed in this book in the Imperial Glass category.

| | |
|---|---:|
| **Candlewick,** Bowl, Green Satin, 11 In. | 41 |
| **Candlewick,** Punch Cup | 5 |
| **Cherry & Cable,** Butter, Red, 6 In. | 48 |
| **Church Windows** pattern is listed here as Columbia. | |
| **Clematis & Scroll,** Saltshaker | 32 |
| **Coin Spot** pattern is listed in this book in its own category. | |
| **Colonial,** Tumbler, Cobalt Blue, Hexagonal, c.1870, 3¾ x 3¼ In. | 431 |
| **Columbia,** Bowl, Purple, Ribbed, c.1875, 8 In. | 115 |
| **Columbia,** Compote, Teal, Fluted, Scalloped Rim, Figural Stem, c.1875, 7½ In. | 126 |
| **Compote,** Shell Shape Bowl, White Dolphin Standard, Dome Foot, c.1875, 7¾ x 10½ In. | 690 |
| **Cornucopia,** Candlestick, 3½ In., Pair | 30 |
| **Cosmos** pattern is listed in this book as its own category. | |
| **Crossbars,** Daisy & Button, Saltshaker, Amber | 45 |
| **Cupid & Venus,** Plate, Amber, c.1875, 10½ In. | 275 |
| **Dahlia,** Dish, Round, Handles, 9 In. | 28 |
| **Dahlia,** Dish, Round, Handles, Vaseline, 9 In. | 30 |
| **Dahlia,** Platter, Blue, Grape Cluster Handles, Oval, Flint Glass, 11 In. | 85 |
| **Daisy & Button,** Goblet, Amberina, Smith Glass | 35 |
| **Daisy & Button,** Goblet, Water, Green, Smith Glass, 6¾ In. | 21 |
| **Daisy & Button,** Top Hat, Green, Smith Glass, 3¼ In. | 7 |
| **Decanter,** 8-Flute, Amethyst, Prussian Shape, Applied Bar Lip, c.1870, 10½ In., 1 Qt. | 1035 |
| **Dewdrop In Points,** Plate, Open Handles, Peg Feet, 9 x 11 In. | 42 |
| **Diamond Prisms,** see also the related pattern Albany. | |
| **Diamond Quilted,** Pitcher, Cobalt Blue, Stiegel Type, Flared, Scrolled Handle, 4 In. | 92 |
| **Diamond Quilted,** Plate, Leaf Shape, Amber, 1880s, 10 x 12 In. | 65 |
| **Diamond Quilted,** Plate, Leaf Shape, Blue, 1880s, 10 x 12 In. | 62 |
| **Doric** pattern is listed here as Feather. | |
| **Dot Optic,** Pitcher, Mottled, Maroon & Opal, Crimped Rim, Reeded Handle, 9 In. | 55 |
| **Eureka,** Saltshaker, McKee | 32 |
| **Feather,** Plate, McKee, c.1890, 10 In. | 62 |
| **Feather,** Saltshaker, Cylindrical | 95 |
| **Fine Cut & Feather** pattern is listed here as Feather. | |
| **Finecut & Panel,** Plate, Blue, Bryce Brothers, c.1886, 7¼ In. | 62 |
| **First Love,** Relish, 3 Sections, 8 In. | 34 |
| **First Love,** Relish, 4 Sections, 10½ In. | 55 |
| **Floradora,** Salt & Pepper, Green, Gold Trim, 4 Squared Feet, Metal Cap, 3¾ In. | 115 |
| **Flower Band,** Salt & Pepper, Pink, Ribbed, 2¾ In. | 85 |
| **Forget-Me-Not,** Sugar Shaker, Mottled Butterscotch, Challinor, Taylor & Co., c.1900, 4 In. | 219 |
| **Frolicking Bears,** Tumbler, Clear | 475 |
| **Frosted** patterns may also be listed under the name of the main pattern. | |
| **Frosted Lion,** Platter, Gillinder, c.1877, 13 In. | 125 |
| **Georgian,** Sherbet, Ruby, 3 In. | 15 |
| **Hercules Pillar,** Eggcup, Double, Opalescent, 6 Panels, c.1870, 4½ x 2⅝ In. | 288 |
| **Hobnail** pattern is in this book as its own category. | |
| **Horizontal Ribs,** Creamer, Staffordshire Shape, C-Scrolls, Rope Border, 4-Footed, 4½ In. | 316 |
| **Ida** pattern is listed here as Sheraton. | |
| **Indian Tree,** Tray, c.1870, 9½ x 11¾ In. | 110 |
| **Indiana Swirl** pattern is listed here as Feather. | |
| **Inverted Thistle,** Egg Plate, Pink, 11½ In. | 38 |
| **Lacy Gothic Arch,** Sugar, Lid, Opalescent, Octagonal, Scalloped Foot, c.1850, 5 x 5 In. | 345 |
| **Lacy Heart & Scale,** Creamer, Opalescent, Medial Ring, Molded Handle, c.1850, 4½ In. | 345 |

**Pottery-Midcentury,** Sculpture, Village Smithy, Signed, Viktor Schreckengost, 17 x 9 In.
$11,250

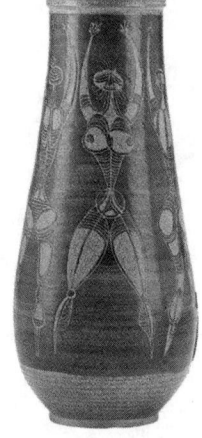

**Pottery-Midcentury,** Vase, Figures, Stoneware, Glazed, F.C. Ball, A. Bohrod, 22 x 10 In.
$2,500

**P**

**Pottery-Midcentury,** Vase, Geometric Design, Blue, Brown, Edgar Littlefield Logo, 1954, 13⅛ In.
$633

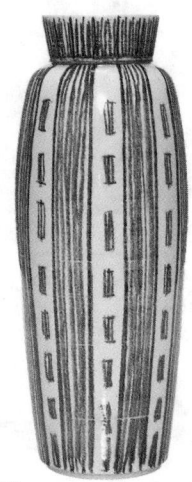

**Pottery-Midcentury,** Vase, Little Master Cat, Seated, Signed, Louis Wain, 6 In. $2,370

James D. Julia Auctioneers

**Pottery-Midcentury,** Vase, Mr. Pointy Ears Cat, Seated, Stylized, Signed, Louis Wain, 5 In. $2,074

James D. Julia Auctioneers

**Pottery-Midcentury,** Vase, Smiling Face, Handle, Gambone, Donkey Cipher, 1960s, 23 x 22 In. $10,000

Rago Arts & Auction Center

**Powder Horn,** Inscribed, Bird, Weapons, 1780, 10½ In. $510

Morphy Auctions

| | |
|---|---|
| **Late Thistle** pattern is listed here as Inverted Thistle. | |
| **Lincoln Drape,** Pitcher, Beaded, Rose Satin Glass, Crimped Rim, Reeded Camphor Handle, 13 In... | 173 |
| **Manhattan,** Plate, U.S. Glass, c.1902, 10 In. | 38 |
| **Marsh Pink,** Plate, c.1880, 10 x 10 In. | 55 |
| **Moon & Stars,** Bowl, Olive Green, 6 In. | 13 |
| **Moon & Stars,** Candlestick, Amberina, 4½ In. | 18 |
| **Moon & Stars,** Compote, Amber, 4 In. | 12 |
| **Moon & Stars,** Compote, Blue, 4 In. | 15 |
| **Moon & Stars,** Compote, Lid, Amber, 10 In. | 50 |
| **Moon & Stars,** Goblet, Water, Blue, 6 In. | 18 |
| **Moon & Stars,** Relish, 3 Sections, Amber, 8⅜ In. | 10 |
| **Moon & Stars,** Sherbet, Amber, 4½ In. | 12 |
| **Moon & Stars,** Sherbet, Amberina, 4⅛ In. | 15 |
| **Moon & Stars,** Sherbet, Green, 4½ In. | 18 |
| **Moon & Stars,** Sugar & Creamer, Amber | 23 |
| **Moon & Stars,** Sugar & Creamer, Green | 36 |
| **One-Hundred-One,** Plate, Give Us This Day, c.1885, 9½ In. | 68 |
| **One-O-One** pattern is listed here as One-Hundred-One. | |
| **One-Thousand Eye** pattern is listed here as Thousand Eye. | |
| **Overshot,** Pitcher, Lemonade, Glass Roping, Braided Handle, 13 x 7 In. | 58 |
| **Rosette,** Curtain Pin, Split Petal, Opalescent, Rope Edge, c.1840, 6 x 8 In., Pair | 58 |
| **Sawtooth,** Compote, Bryce Brothers, 6 x 9 In. | 125 |
| **Saxon,** Plate, Oval, Pineapple Handles, c.1875, 10 x 12 In. | 75 |
| **Sheraton,** Plate, Amber, Higbee, c.1885, 8 x 10 In. | 65 |
| **Star Of David,** Butter, Cover, 1960s, ¼ Lb. | 10 |
| **Stars & Stripes,** Toothpick Holder, McKee, c.1898. | 85 |
| **Stippled Cherry,** Plate, Our Daily Bread, 8 In. | 55 |
| **Teardrop & Thumbprint,** Butter, Cover | 12 |
| **Teardrop & Thumbprint,** Celery Vase, 10 In. | 21 |
| **Teardrop & Thumbprint,** Cocktail, 4⅝ In. | 6 |
| **Teardrop & Thumbprint,** Dish, Footed, Fan Edge, Sunburst Base, Round Foot, c.1850, 3¾ x 4 In. . | 46 |
| **Teardrop & Thumbprint,** Nut Dish, 7 In. | 7 |
| **Teardrop** pattern is listed here as Teardrop & Thumbprint. | |
| **Thousand Eye,** Plate, Adams, Amber, c.1870 | 68 |
| **Thousand Eye,** Plate, Adams, Blue, 10 x 10 In. | 65 |
| **Thousand Eye,** Plate, Amber, 8 x 8 In. | 55 |
| **Thousand Eye,** Plate, Apple Green, 7 x 7 In. | 65 |
| **Toltec,** Toothpick Holder, Footed, McKee, c.1900 | 25 |
| **Tree Of Life,** Salt & Pepper, Oval, Pink Slag | 75 |
| **Two Bands,** Tray, Handles, c.1880, 10½ In. | 58 |
| **Wildflower,** Tray, Adams, c.1870, 8½ x 11 In. | 55 |

**PRINT,** in this listing, means any of many printed images produced on paper by one of the more common methods, such as lithography. The prints listed here are of interest primarily to the antiques collector, not the fine arts collector. Many of these prints were originally part of books. Other prints will be found in the Advertising, Currier & Ives, Movie, and Poster categories.

| | |
|---|---|
| **Allison,** Kurz R., Battle Of Chancellorsville, Color Lithograph, Frame, 1889, 28 x 22 In. | 300 |

**Audubon** bird prints were originally issued as part of books printed from 1826 to 1854. They were issued in two sheet sizes, 26½ inches by 39½ inches and 11 inches by 7 inches. The height of a picture is listed before the width. The quadrupeds were issued in 28-by-22-inch prints. Later editions of the Audubon books were done in many sizes, and reprints of the books in the original sizes were also made. The words *After John James Audubon* appear on all of the prints, including the originals, because the pictures were made as copies of Audubon's original oil paintings. The bird pictures have been so popular they have been copied in myriad sizes using both old and new printing methods. This list includes originals and later copies because Audubon prints of all ages are sold in antiques shops.

*J.W.Audubon*

| | |
|---|---|
| **Audubon,** American Bittern, Havell, c.1832, 27¾ x 22¾ In. | 861 |
| **Audubon,** American Robin, Havell, 1834, 38 x 25 In. | 6765 |
| **Audubon,** Black-Billed Cuckoo, Engraved, Havell, Birds Of America, 25 x 38 In. | 1168 |
| **Audubon,** Black-Billed Cuckoo, Havell, Frame, c.1830, 27 x 19 In. | 3198 |
| **Audubon,** Boat-Tailed Grackle, Birds Of America, Havell, Frame, 25½ x 20¼ In. | 400 |
| **Audubon,** Bonapart's Flycatcher, Engraved, Hand Colored, Frame, 20⅜ x 12⅜ In. | 472 |
| **Audubon,** Brown Pelican, Leipzig Edition, Colortype, 26 x 38 In. | 1195 |
| **Audubon,** Cow Bunting, Havell, Frame, 22 x 15 In. | 246 |
| **Audubon,** Golden-Eye Duck, Engraving, R. Havell, 1838, 24 x 35 In. | 575 |

**P**

**Print,** Calder, Alexander, Multicolor Shapes, Lithograph, Signed, U.S.A., c.1940, 15 x 22 In. $1,840

Cottone Auctions

**Print,** Icart, Fruit, Woman, Lounging, Erotic Position, Frame, Signed, 1926, 15 x 20 ⅝ In. $590

Brunk Auctions

**Print,** Icart, Impudence, Woman, Dog Tugging On Her Wrap, Frame, Signed, 18 x 13 ½ In. $594

Rago Arts & Auction Center

**Print,** Icart, Joy Of Life, Seminude Woman, 2 Dogs, Stamped, Signed, 1929, 24 x 16 In. $1,125

Rago Arts & Auction Center

**Print,** Japanese, Hasui, Kawase, Evening Snow At Terashima, Signed, 1920, 15 x 10 ⅝ In. $8,610

Skinner Auctioneers & Appraisers

**Print,** Japanese, Hasui, Kawase, Lingering Snow At Hikone Castle, Signed, 1934, 15 ½ x 10 ⅛ In. $1,353

Skinner Auctioneers & Appraisers

**Print,** Japanese, Hasui, Kawase, Snow At Zojoji Temple, Shiba, 1925, 15 x 10 In. $5,228

Skinner Auctioneers & Appraisers

**Print,** Japanese, Kuniyoshi, Utagawa, Triptych, 3 Women, Frame, c.1850, 13 x 28 In., Pair $984

New Orleans Auction Galleries, Inc.

P

**Print,** Japanese, Munakata, Shiko, Owl On Tree Branch, Landscape Setting, Mat, 23 x 18 In.
$1,107

Garth's Auctioneers & Appraisers

**Print,** Japanese, Saito, Kiyoshi, Garden & Path, Frame, c.1955, 10 x 17 In.
$430

New Orleans Auction Galleries, Inc.

**Print,** Japanese, Toyokuni, Samurai Warriors, Frame, Triptych, c.1850, 13 x 28 In.
$240

DuMouchelles Art Gallery

**Print,** Woodblock, Achillea, Edna Boies Hopkins, Mat, Frame, c.1910, 10¾ x 7 In.
$8,750

Rago Arts & Auction Center

**Print,** Woodblock, Baumann, Gustave, Pines-Grand Canon, Color, Signed, 1921, 12 x 12 In.
$9,375

Rago Arts & Auction Center

**Print,** Woodblock, Esherick, W., Theodore Dreiser, Of A Great City, Signed, Frame, 1928, 10 x 6 In.
$3,375

Rago Arts & Auction Center

**Print,** Woodblock, Esherick, Wharton, Song Of The Broad Axe, Building, c.1924, 10½ x 9 In.
$2,432

Rago Arts & Auction Center

**Print,** Woodblock, Grand Canyon, Niagara Falls, Signed, Hiroshi Yoshida, 1925, 10¼ x 15½ In., Set Of 2
$5,313

Rago Arts & Auction Center

**Print,** Woodblock, Paule, Hans, The Oarsmen, Color, Monogram, Frame, 1932, 12½ x 20½ In.
$800

Skinner Auctioneers & Appraisers

**Print,** Woodblock, Rice, William, Bolinas Bay, Color, Signed, 6 x 8 In.
$2,000

Rago Arts & Auction Center

| | |
|---|---|
| **Audubon,** Great American Cock, Wild Turkey, Offset Lithograph, Frame, 39 x 25 In. | 276 |
| **Audubon,** Great Auk, Chromolithograph, Bien Edition, c.1860, 27 x 44 In. | 1125 |
| **Audubon,** Labrador Falcon, Havell, Frame, 37 ½ x 25 In. | 2583 |
| **Audubon,** Lincoln Finch, Birds Of America, Havell, 38 ¼ x 25 ½ In. | 615 |
| **Audubon,** Louisiana Heron, Colortype, Leipzig Edition, 25 x 38 In. | 1076 |
| **Audubon,** Louisiana Water Thrush, Aquatint, Engraving, Elephant Folio, 38 x 25 In. | 1315 |
| **Audubon,** Mallard Duck, Collotype, Leipzig Edition, Frame, 25 x 38 In. | 488 |
| **Audubon,** Musk Ox, J.T. Bowen, 24 x 19 ¼ In. | 738 |
| **Audubon,** Nuttall's Starling, Yellow-Headed Troopial, Bullock's Oriole, Aquatint, 39 x 26 In. | 777 |
| **Audubon,** Quadrupeds Of North America, Lithograph, Color, 155 Plates, 11 x 7 In. | 5500 |
| **Audubon,** Red-Tailed Squirrel, Color Lithograph, J.T. Bowen, 1844, Full Folio Sheet | 585 |
| **Audubon,** Swift Fox, Lithograph, 22 x 27 In. | 1673 |
| **Audubon,** Texan Lynx, Frame, J.T. Bowen, 24 x 19 In. | 461 |
| **Audubon,** Velvet Duck, Birds Of America, Engraved, 20 ¾ x 30 ³/₁₆ In. | 1652 |
| **Audubon,** White-Eyed Flycatcher, Aquatint, Engraving, Elephant Folio, 38 x 25 In. | 956 |
| **Audubon,** Wood Pewee, Engraved, Aquatint, R. Havell, Frame, 38 ¾ x 26 In. | 461 |
| **Binion,** Samuel Augustus, Ancient Egypt Of Mizrim, 72 Plates, Color, 1887, 26 x 19 In. | 1820 |
| **Calder,** Alexander, Multicolor Shapes, Lithograph, Signed, U.S.A., c.1940, 15 x 22 In. .........*illus* | 1840 |
| **Currier & Ives** prints are listed in the Currier & Ives category. | |
| **Farny,** Henri F., Indian Hunter, Lithograph, Shadow Box, Signed, Dated 1903, 7 x 5 In. | 1076 |
| **Gorman,** Bread Maker, Color Lithograph, Frame, 1988, 29 x 37 In. | 330 |
| **Hirschfield,** Al, Tootsie, Etching, 1984, 13 x 9 In. | 480 |

**Icart** prints were made by Louis Icart, who worked in Paris from 1907 as an employee of a postcard company. He then started printing magazines and fashion brochures. About 1910 he created a series of etchings of fashionably dressed women, and he continued to make similar etchings until he died in 1950. He is well known as a printmaker, painter, and illustrator. Original etchings are much more expensive than the later photographic copies.

| | |
|---|---|
| **Icart,** Carnival, Masked Women Figures, Color Etching, Aquatint, Signed, 19 ¼ x 23 In. | 400 |
| **Icart,** Cigarette Memories, Color Etching, Signed, 1931, 14 ¼ x 17 ¾ In. | 1080 |
| **Icart,** Fruit, Woman, Lounging, Erotic Position, Frame, Signed, 1926, 15 x 20 ⅝ In. .........*illus* | 590 |
| **Icart,** Impudence, Woman, Dog Tugging On Her Wrap, Frame, Signed, 18 x 13 ½ In. .........*illus* | 594 |
| **Icart,** Joy Of Life, Seminude Woman, 2 Dogs, Stamped, Signed, 1929, 24 x 16 In. ..............*illus* | 1125 |
| **Icart,** Les Hortensias, Etching, Aquatint, 1929, 16 x 21 In. | 660 |
| **Icart,** Lilies, Etching, On Paper, Signed, 1934, 28 ½ x 19 ½ In. | 1125 |
| **Icart,** Red Cage, Drypoint, Etching, Signed, Frame, 1928, 11 ⅜ x 9 In. | 431 |
| **Icart,** Snowstorm, Hand Colored, Etching, Frame. | 540 |
| **Icart,** Speed, Etching, On Paper, Signed, Frame, c.1933, 16 x 25 ¼ In. | 875 |
| **Icart,** Woman & Greyhounds, Aquatint, Engraving, Signed, 1925, 20 ¾ x 17 ¼ In. | 717 |

**Jacoulet** prints were designed by Paul Jacoulet (1902–1960), a Frenchman who spent most of his life in Japan. He was a master of Japanese woodblock print technique. Subjects included life in Japan, the South Seas, Korea, and China. His prints were sold by subscription and issued in series. Each series had a distinctive seal, such as a sparrow or butterfly. Most Jacoulet prints are approximately 15 x 10 inches.

| | |
|---|---|
| **Jacoulet,** Chinese Players, 2 Men, Rolling Dice, On Cardboard, c.1950, 12 x 15 In. | 420 |
| **Jacoulet,** Oyster Stew, 2 Figures, Seated, Drinking, Multicolor, France, c.1945, 15 x 12 In. | 210 |
| **Jacoulet,** Souvenirs D'Autrefois, Woodblock, Color, Signed, Seal, 1941, 18 ½ x 14 In. | 311 |
| **Jacoulet,** Vieillard Au Chapelet, Kawadzu, Woodcut, Stamped, 18 ½ x 14 In. | 360 |

**Japanese** woodblock prints are listed as follows: Print, Japanese, name of artist, title or description, type, and size. Dealers use the following terms: Tate-e is a vertical composition. Yoko-e is a horizontal composition. The words Aiban (13 by 9 inches), Chuban (10 by 7 ½ inches), Hosoban (13 by 6 inches), Koban (7 by 4 inches), Nagaban (20 by 9 inches), Oban (15 by 10 inches), Shikishiban (8 by 9 inches), and Tanzaku (15 by 5 inches) denote approximate size. Modern versions of some of these prints have been made. Other woodblock prints that are not Japanese are listed under Print, Woodblock.

| | |
|---|---|
| **Japanese,** 3 Geishas, Sitting At Table, Frame, 1700s, 6 ½ x 14 In. | 69 |
| **Japanese,** Anaki, Hoku, Black, Gray Abstracts, Frame, 18 x 12 In. | 263 |
| **Japanese,** Bijin, Holding Pipe, Embossed, Silver Pigment, Glossy, Frame, 1900s, 10 x 14 In. | 115 |
| **Japanese,** Cherry Blossoms By Gate, Signed, Mat, Frame, 15 ½ x 10 ½ In. | 138 |
| **Japanese,** Enkyo, Portrait Of Nakayama Tomisaburo, Mat, Frame, 1800s, 20 x 15 In. | 652 |
| **Japanese,** Hasui, Kawase, Evening Snow At Terashima, Signed, 1920, 15 x 10 ⅝ In. ..........*illus* | 8610 |
| **Japanese,** Hasui, Kawase, Kamino Hashi, Bridge Over Fukagawa, 9 x 14 In. | 2875 |
| **Japanese,** Hasui, Kawase, Kayagafuchi Nagato, Color, Signed, 1922, 9 x 12 In. | 4305 |

**Print,** Woodblock, Rice, William, Witch Tree, Handmade Paper, Frame, 8 ½ x 4 ¾ In.
$2,875

Rago Arts & Auction Center

**Print,** Wotherspoon, G., Gossip, House Of Art, 1925, 11 x 15 ½ In.
$90

Showtime Auction Services

P

**Purse,** Canvas, Leather Trim, Repeating Logo, Crossbody Strap, Gucci, 7 x 6 In.
$96

Garth's Auctioneers & Appraisers

**Purse,** Crystal, Green Cabochon, Frog Shape, Leather & Metal Frame, Judith Leiber, Box, 1900s, 5 In.
$2,006

Brunk Auctions

**Purse,** Leather, Tooled, Hand Laced, Lined, Shoulder Strap, Mexico, 1960s, 8 x 10 In.
$207

Allard Auctions

| | |
|---|---:|
| **Japanese,** Hasui, Kawase, Lingering Snow At Hikone Castle, Signed, 1934, 15 ½ x 10 ⅛ In. *illus* | 1353 |
| **Japanese,** Hasui, Kawase, Rapids Of Nakabusa River, Signed, 1926, 11 ¼ x 16 ½ In. | 3444 |
| **Japanese,** Hasui, Kawase, Road To Nikko, Color, Signed, 1930, 15 ½ x 10 In. | 1230 |
| **Japanese,** Hasui, Kawase, Snow At Hiei Shrine, 14 ¼ x 9 ½ In. | 780 |
| **Japanese,** Hasui, Kawase, Snow At Shibozojoji, 14 x 9 ½ In. | 3900 |
| **Japanese,** Hasui, Kawase, Snow At Zojoji Temple, Shiba, 1925, 15 x 10 In. *illus* | 5228 |
| **Japanese,** Hasui, Kawase, Zentsu Temple, 14 x 10 In. | 300 |
| **Japanese,** Heirinji, Temple Bell, Signed, Mat, Frame, 15 ½ x 10 ½ In. | 242 |
| **Japanese,** Hiroshige, Ando, Fireworks At Ryogoku, Color, c.1858, 20 x 16 In. | 6150 |
| **Japanese,** Hiroshige, Crane Flying Down To Pool, 13 ½ x 8 ½ In. | 593 |
| **Japanese,** Hiroshige, Ichiryusai, Daikokuya At Mukojima, Japan, c.1810, 9 x 14 In. | 29 |
| **Japanese,** Hiroshige, Utagawa, 53 Stations Of Tokaido Road, Kyoto, Oban, 10 x 15 In. | 250 |
| **Japanese,** Hiroshige, Utagawa, 53 Stations Of Tokaido Road, Miya, Oban, 10 x 15 In. | 75 |
| **Japanese,** Hiroshige, Utagawa, Plum Estate, Kameido, Color, Mat, Frame, 13 x 8 ½ In. | 702 |
| **Japanese,** Hiroshige, Woman Wanders With 3 Children In Snow, c.1820, 9 ¼ x 14 In. | 500 |
| **Japanese,** Hoichi, Joichi, Red Tree, Frame, 1973, 18 x 23 In. | 2640 |
| **Japanese,** Kason, Suzuki, Man & Child At Beach, Multicolor, c.1900, 8 ½ x 11 In. | 242 |
| **Japanese,** Kawase, Snow, Building, Inokashira, Frame, 1928, 20 x 14 In. | 2125 |
| **Japanese,** Kitaoka, Fumio, Autumn, Leaf, Green, Black, Brown, Frame, 1960, 17 x 11 In. | 146 |
| **Japanese,** Kiyochika, Kobayashi, Benten Shrine In Snow, Fukagawa, 14 x 9 In. | 492 |
| **Japanese,** Kuniyoshi, Utagawa, Triptych, 3 Women, Frame, c.1850, 13 x 28 In., Pair *illus* | 984 |
| **Japanese,** Munakata, Shiko, Owl On Tree Branch, Landscape Setting, Mat, 23 x 18 In. *illus* | 1107 |
| **Japanese,** Sadao, Beggar & Saints, Frame, 1965, 26 x 23 In. | 375 |
| **Japanese,** Saito, Kiyoshi, Garden & Path, Frame, c.1955, 10 x 17 In. *illus* | 430 |
| **Japanese,** Saito, Kiyoshi, Winter Village Scene, Color, Pencil Signed, Frame, 10 x 15 In. | 210 |
| **Japanese,** Shunga, Man & Woman Erotic Position, Hand Colored, Frame, 1700s, 6 ½ x 14 In. | 104 |
| **Japanese,** Temple Grounds In Winter, 14 x 9 ½ In. | 480 |
| **Japanese,** Toyokuni, Samurai Warriors, Frame, Triptych, c.1850, 13 x 28 In. *illus* | 240 |
| **Japanese,** Xuetao, Wang, Wisteria With Rooster & Hen, 72 ½ x 27 ½ In. | 738 |
| **Japanese,** Yoshida, Hiroshi, Daibutsu Temple Gate, Signed, Frame, 15 ¼ x 10 In. | 240 |
| **Japanese,** Yoshida, Hodaka, Diety Of Roads, Brown Abstract, Frame, 1961, 17 x 11 In. | 322 |
| **Japanese,** Yoshida, Toshi, Plum Tree & Blue Magpie, Color, Mat, Frame, 1951, 10 x 15 In. | 430 |
| **Japanese,** Yoshimi, Kidodoro, Wind, Red, Black, Abstract, Frame, 17 x 11 ½ In. | 146 |
| **Lichtenstein,** I Love Liberty, People For American Way, Offset Litho, 1982, 37 x 22 In. | 1135 |
| **Lithograph,** Paris Courses, Signed, Jules Cheret, Frame, 49 x 33 In. | 1353 |
| **MacPhearson,** Marian Francis Acker, Balcony, Old Mobile, Lithograph, 3 ½ x 2 ½ In. | 615 |
| **Mato-Tope,** Mandan Chief, Engraving, Aquatint, Travels North America, c.1840, 25 x 18 In. | 1076 |
| **Max,** Peter, Psychedelic Profile, Screen Print, Signed, Dated 71, 28 ¾ x 20 ¾ In. | 480 |
| **Moore,** Henry, Reclining Figures, Lithograph, 1973, 11 ½ x 8 ½ In. | 1080 |

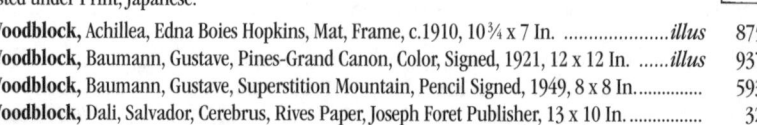

**Nutting** prints are popular with collectors. Wallace Nutting is known for his pictures, furniture, and books. Collectors call his pictures Nutting prints although they are actually hand-colored photographs issued from 1900 to 1941. There are over 10,000 different titles. Wallace Nutting furniture is listed in the Furniture category.

| | |
|---|---:|
| **Nutting,** Hollyhock Cottage, Frame, 7 ½ x 9 ½ In. | 23 |
| **Nutting,** Interior Scene, Fireplace, Braided Rugs, Chairs, Frame, 6 ½ x 9 In. | 26 |
| **Owen,** Charles, Essay, Natural History Of Serpents, 7 Engraved Plates, 1742, 10 x 8 In. | 813 |

**Parrish** prints are wanted by collectors. Maxfield Frederick Parrish was an illustrator who lived from 1870 to 1966. He is best known as a designer of magazine covers, posters, calendars, and advertisements. His prints have been copied in recent years. Some Maxfield Parrish items may be listed in Advertising.

| | |
|---|---:|
| **Parrish,** Daybreak, Lithograph, Frame, 1922, 10 ⅝ x 6 ⅝ In. | 32 |
| **Sinclair,** Isabella, Flowers Of Hawaiian Islands, 44 Chromolithographed Plates, 1885 | 3000 |

**Woodblock** prints that are not in the Japanese tradition are listed here. Most were made in England and the United States during the Arts and Crafts period. Japanese woodblock prints are listed under Print, Japanese.

| | |
|---|---:|
| **Woodblock,** Achillea, Edna Boies Hopkins, Mat, Frame, c.1910, 10 ¾ x 7 In. *illus* | 8750 |
| **Woodblock,** Baumann, Gustave, Pines-Grand Canon, Color, Signed, 1921, 12 x 12 In. *illus* | 9375 |
| **Woodblock,** Baumann, Gustave, Superstition Mountain, Pencil Signed, 1949, 8 x 8 In. | 5938 |
| **Woodblock,** Dali, Salvador, Cerebrus, Rives Paper, Joseph Foret Publisher, 13 x 10 In. | 322 |
| **Woodblock,** Esherick, W., Theodore Dreiser, Of A Great City, Signed, Frame, 1928, 10 x 6 In. *illus* | 3375 |
| **Woodblock,** Esherick, Wharton, Song Of The Broad Axe, Building, c.1924, 10 ½ x 9 In. *illus* | 2432 |

| | |
|---|---|
| Woodblock, Gearhart, Frances, Rincon, Pencil Signed, Frame, 10 x 9 In. | 2750 |
| Woodblock, Grand Canyon, Niagara Falls, Signed, Hiroshi Yoshida, 1925, 10¼ x 15½ In., Set Of 2 . *illus* | 5313 |
| Woodblock, Irvine, Sadie, Sailboats, Signed, Frame, 11 x 6¼ In. | 1625 |
| Woodblock, Paule, Hans, The Oarsmen, Color, Monogram, Frame, 1932, 12½ x 20½ In. ..*illus* | 800 |
| Woodblock, Rice, William, Bolinas Bay, Color, Signed, 6 x 8 In. .....................................*illus* | 2000 |
| Woodblock, Rice, William, Thaw, Pencil Signed, 8¾ x 12 In. | 3750 |
| Woodblock, Rice, William, Witch Tree, Handmade Paper, Frame, 8½ x 4¾ In. ...............*illus* | 2875 |
| Woodcut, Gearhart, F.H., Lonely Sierra, Multicolored, Frame, c.1950, 9 x 6½ In. | 2625 |
| Woodcut, Leschorn, Paul, Path In Snow, Germany, c.1945, 17 x 13¼ In. | 427 |
| Woodcut, Lum, Bertha, Wind & Rain, Color, Frame, 1917, 9½ x 15 In. | 1037 |
| Wotherspoon, G., Gossip, House Of Art, 1925, 11 x 15½ In. .................................*illus* | 90 |
| Yoshida, Kodomo, Portrait Of Boy, Toy Horse In Hand, c.1927, 22 x 17½ In. | 375 |

---

**PURINTON POTTERY COMPANY** was incorporated in Wellsville, Ohio, in 1936. The company moved to Shippenville, Pennsylvania, in 1941 and made a variety of hand-painted ceramic wares. By the 1950s Purinton was making dinnerware, souvenirs, cookie jars, and florist wares. The pottery closed in 1959.

*Purinton Pottery*

| | |
|---|---|
| Apple, Bowl, Vegetable, Oval, 8 In. | 18 |
| Apple, Cup & Saucer | 10 |
| Apple, Tumbler, 12 Oz., 4¾ In. | 19 |
| Fruit, Creamer, 1945, 4½ In. | 24 |
| Fruit, Creamer, 3 In. | 16 |
| Fruit, Jug, 4½ In. | 18 |
| Fruit, Sugar, Lid, Handles, 3⅛ In. | 28 |
| Heather Plaid, Cup & Saucer | 14 |
| Intaglio, Bowl, Dessert, Brown, 4 In. | 7 |
| Intaglio, Bowl, Vegetable, Oval, Brown, 7 In. | 20 |
| Intaglio, Chop Plate, Brown, 11 In. | 43 |
| Intaglio, Cup & Saucer, Brown. | 9 |
| Intaglio, Jug, Brown, 16 Oz., 4½ In. | 27 |
| Mountain Rose, Vase, Basket Shape, Double Spouted, Oval, 6 x 6 x 3 In. | 25 |
| Normandy Plaid, Bowl, Dessert, 4 In. | 9 |
| Normandy Plaid, Chop Plate, 11 In. | 48 |
| Normandy Plaid, Creamer, 8 Oz., 3 In. | 20 |
| Normandy Plaid, Cup & Saucer | 8 |
| Normandy Plaid, Oil & Vinegar, Square, 4¾ In. | 23 |
| Normandy Plaid, Plate, Salad, 6¾ In. | 9 |
| Shooting Star, Vase, 5 In. | 16 |

---

**PURSES** have been recognizable since the eighteenth century, when leather and needlework purses were preferred. Beaded purses became popular in the nineteenth century, went out of style, but are again in use. Mesh purses date from the 1880s and are still being made. How to carry a handkerchief and lipstick is a problem today for every woman, including the Queen of England.

| | |
|---|---|
| Alligator, Cognac, Envelope, Argentina | 120 |
| Alligator, Orange, Kelly Bag, Gold Plate Mounts, Shoulder Strap, Hermes, Stamped 1997 | 19120 |
| Alligator, Tote, Green, Zipper, Goldtone Metal, Double Handles, Prada, 8 x 12 In. | 834 |
| Beaded, Crystal, Satin, Multicolor, 007, Shoulder Strap, Tassels, Judith Leiber, 5 x 6 In. | 265 |
| Beaded, Flower Design, White Ground, Multicolor, Drawstring, Silk, 19th Century | 70 |
| Canvas, Brown Leather, Desk Agenda, Louis Vuitton, 6¾ x 9¼ In. | 155 |
| Canvas, Ebene Orav, PM Messenger, Shoulder, Goldtone Hardware, Louis Vuitton, 8 x 8 In. | 357 |
| Canvas, Envelope Clutch, Monogram, Suede Lined, Louis Vuitton, 13 In. | 360 |
| Canvas, Leather Trim, Repeating Logo, Crossbody Strap, Gucci, 7 x 6 In. ............................*illus* | 96 |
| Canvas, Leather, Brown, Mini Lin Mono, Goldtone Hardware, Louis Vuitton, 7 x 12 In. | 127 |
| Canvas, Leather, Duffel, Bandouliere 45, Monograms, Brass Trim, L. Vuitton, 10 x 18 In. | 1416 |
| Canvas, Leather, Hobo, Jackie, Silver Buckle, Shoulder Strap, Gucci, c.1980, 8 x 13 In. | 180 |
| Canvas, Leather, White Stripes, Flap Top, Cross Body, Fendi, 6¼ x 6¾ In. | 132 |
| Canvas, Mini Speedy, Brown, Monogram, Cross Body, Louis Vuitton, 4 x 6½ In. | 207 |
| Canvas, Monogram, Shoulder, Louis Vuitton, 14 x 19 In. | 450 |
| Canvas, Petit Point, Brown, Flowers, Envelope Shape, c.1940 | 120 |
| Canvas, Tote, Beige, Signature Embossed, Leather Trim, Louis Vuitton, 11½ x 14 In. | 449 |
| Canvas, Tote, Green, Black Skull Print, Goldtone Chain, Alexander McQueen, 16 x 16 In. | 259 |
| Canvas, Tote, Multicolor Graphics, Double Handles, Open Top, Pucci, 15½ x 9½ In. | 178 |
| Canvas, Zucca, Burgundy, Hobo, Asymmetrically Shaped, Zipper, Fendi, 13 x 15 In. | 35 |
| Coconut Shell, Brown Leather, Zipper, Beach Bar, Cross Body, April Comell, 5 x 5 In. | 35 |

**Purse**, Mesh, Silver, Enamel, Mandalian Mfg. Co., c.1920, 4½ In.
$84

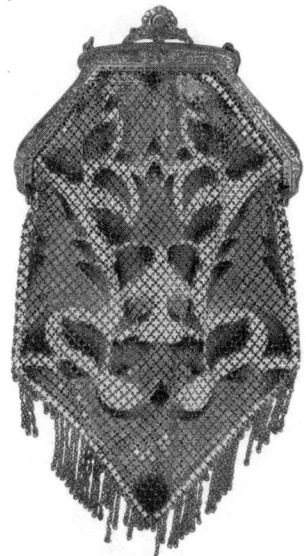

DuMouchelles Art Gallery

**Purse**, Mohair, Dog, Charly, Jointed Head, Embroidered, Ear Tag, Steiff, c.1935, 10 In.
$948

James D. Julia AuctioneersL

**Purse**, Silk, Beaded, Semiprecious Stones, Foldover, 5 x 9 In.
$799

New Orleans Auction Galleries, Inc.

**P**

### Necessaire

A necessaire is an expensive vanity case used for formal events. The case, usually silver and enamel, had compartments for powder, rouge, lipstick, and cigarettes. They were popular from 1915 into the 1930s.

PURuntitled# PURSE

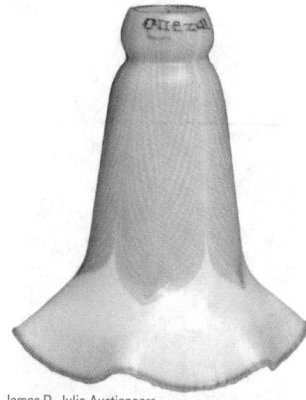

**Quezal,** Shade, Green Pulled Feathers, Lily, White, Gold Iridescent Trim, 4¾ In. **$592**

James D. Julia Auctioneers

**TIP**

*If you are having your antiques moved in a van to a new home, watch out for damage. Check the antiques as they are unloaded. Sweep the inside of the moving van and save any small pieces of veneer or wood that might have chipped off your furniture.*

**Quezal,** Vase, Gold Iridescent, Pink Highlights, White Swirled Threads, Marked, 9½ In. **$474**

James D. Julia Auctioneers

| | |
|---|---:|
| **Coin,** Victorian, Silver, Wood, Geometric Inlay, Red, Black, White, 1800s, 3¼ In. | 84 |
| **Crochet,** Knit, Satchel, Coin Purse Shape, Cotton, Brown Leather, Miu, 8 x 13 In. | 150 |
| **Crocodile,** Black, Foldover Flap, Gold Square Clasp, Strap Handle, Hermes, 1950s, 7 x 9 In. | 2714 |
| **Crocodile,** Brown, Shoulder, Foldover Flap, Buckle, Snap, Gucci, c.1970, 8½ x 11 In. | 1121 |
| **Crystal,** Green Cabochon, Frog Shape, Leather & Metal Frame, Judith Leiber, Box, 1900s, 5 In. *illus* | 2006 |
| **Enamel Flowers,** Silver Plated Frame, Yellow Silk Lining, Mandalian Mfg., c.1930, 4 x 9 In. | 127 |
| **Faux Alligator,** Box Style, Brown, Arched Handle, Twisted Plastic, 1940s, 7 x 3 x 4 In. | 38 |
| **Hemp,** Leather, Woven, Beige Double Handles, Zipper, Bottega Veneta, 11 In. | 86 |
| **Karung,** Leather, Cream, Goldtone Mount, Gem Clasp, Chain, Judith Leiber, 7½ x 9 In. | 155 |
| **Knit,** Beaded, Dog, Sitting, Grass, Sky, Loop Fringe, Drawstring, Germany, c.1900, 5 x 8 In. | 495 |
| **Lambskin Quilted,** Waist Belt Bag, Flap Top, Goldtone Hardware, Chanel, 5½ x 4½ In. | 380 |
| **Lambskin,** Black, Entwined Gold, Leather Straps, Chanel, 9 x 11½ In. | 826 |
| **Leather,** 2-Tone, Shoulder, Chanel, 9 In. | 540 |
| **Leather,** Beige, Flap Top, Shoulder Strap, Goldtone, Signature Horse Bit, Gucci, 8 x 12 In. | 270 |
| **Leather,** Black, Bucket Bag, Drawstring, Goldtone Hardware, Fendi, 9 x 9 In. | 351 |
| **Leather,** Black, Epi, Brea Handbag, Double Handles, Shoulder Strap, Louis Vuitton, 13 x 9 In. | 1955 |
| **Leather,** Black, Epi, Petit Noe, Drawstring, Goldtone Hardware, Louis Vuitton, 10 x 10 In. | 414 |
| **Leather,** Black, Epi, Zipper, Loop Handles, Louis Vuitton, 7½ x 10¾ In. | 289 |
| **Leather,** Black, Glossy, Cutout Handle, Salvatore Ferragamo, Italy, 9½ x 11 In. | 180 |
| **Leather,** Black, Goldtone Accents, Long Strap, Bottega Veneta, 10 x 10 In. | 84 |
| **Leather,** Black, Hobo, Half Ring Shell Handles, Chanel, 10 x 12 In. | 826 |
| **Leather,** Black, Mademoiselle, Flap Closure, Lock, Shoulder Bag, Chanel, 10¾ x 6½ In. | 932 |
| **Leather,** Black, Speedy Doctor Bag, Pocket, Double Handles, Zippers, Gucci, 6 x 10 In. | 357 |
| **Leather,** Black, Vert Fonce Gulliver, Birkin, Goldtone Hardware, Hermes, 12 x 8 In. | 9600 |
| **Leather,** Blue Vernis, Brea, Doctor's Bag Shape, Double Handles, Louis Vuitton, 13 x 10 In. | 1725 |
| **Leather,** Brown, Woven, Roll Bar Closure, Gold Metal, Judith Leiber, 10 In. | 431 |
| **Leather,** Faux Crocodile, Hobo, Shoulder, Chain Link & Leather Strap, Ferragamo, 8 x 10 In. | 207 |
| **Leather,** Gold, Soho, Shoulder Chain, Zipper, Tassel, Gucci, 7 x 11 In. | 130 |
| **Leather,** Intrecatto, Tote, White, Camel, Embroidered Handles, Bottega Veneta, 8 x 16 In. | 575 |
| **Leather,** Lamb, Black, Quilted, Goldtone Hardware, Shoulder, Chanel, c.1988, 5 x 7 In. | 1058 |
| **Leather,** Lamb, Black, Super Nova Warrior Sling, Metal Hardware, Burberry, 8 x 18 In. | 587 |
| **Leather,** Quilted, Shoulder Bag, Chanel, 7 x 10 In. | 450 |
| **Leather,** Quilted, Tan, Navy, Shoulder, Chanel, 8 In. | 600 |
| **Leather,** Rectangular, Central Compartment, 2 Handles, Abercrombie & Fitch, 11 In. | 313 |
| **Leather,** Shoulder, Navy, Chain & Leather Strap, Chanel, 8 In. | 1722 |
| **Leather,** Shoulder, Tan, Chanel, 12 In. | 923 |
| **Leather,** Tooled, Hand Laced, Lined, Shoulder Strap, Mexico, 1960s, 8 x 10 In. *illus* | 207 |
| **Leather,** Vernis, Bronze, Flap Top, Goldtone Hardware, Shoulder, Louis Vuitton, 9½ x 8 In. | 656 |
| **Lizard,** Black, Kelly, Gold Hardware, Hermes, 12½ In. | 5228 |
| **Lucite,** Amber, Flowers In Clear Loop Handle, Presto Lock Co., Rialto, 1950s, 4 x 7½ In. | 299 |
| **Mesh,** 18K Gold, Pierced Leaf Rondels, Diamonds, Rubies, Acorn Clasp, Edwardian, 6 In. | 9840 |
| **Mesh,** Cream, Goldtone Mount, Amber Lucite Handle, Whiting & Davis, 1950s, 5¾ x 9 In. | 84 |
| **Mesh,** Silver, Enamel, Mandalian Mfg. Co., c.1920, 4½ In. *illus* | 84 |
| **Minaudiere,** Beaded, Flowers & Leaves, Blue, Gray, Tan, Chatelaine Style, Judith Leiber, 5 In. | 590 |
| **Minaudiere,** Crystal, Coin Purse, Mirror, Comb, Faux Gem Clasp, Chain, J. Leiber, 3½ x 7 In. | 359 |
| **Minaudiere,** Multicolor Beads, 3 Books, Judith Leiber, 7 x 3¼ In. | 1845 |
| **Minaudiere,** Multicolor Beads, Penguin, Art Nouveau, Judith Leiber, 5½ x 3½ In. | 1968 |
| **Minaudiere,** Multicolor Beads, Stained Glass, Judith Leiber, 5½ x 2½ In. | 1353 |
| **Minaudiere,** Multi-Metallic, Faceted, Flush Clasp, Judith Leiber, 3½ x 4 In. | 1168 |
| **Minaudiere,** Panda, Multicolor Crystals, Goldtone Chain Strap, J. Leiber, 5 x 3½ In. | 978 |
| **Minaudiere,** Pineapple, Sequins, Beaded, Multicolor, Judith Leiber, 3½ In. | 1020 |
| **Mohair,** Dog, Charly, Jointed Head, Embroidered, Ear Tag, Steiff, c.1935, 10 In. *illus* | 948 |
| **Needlework,** Beadwork, Swans, Flowers, Silver Frame, Medallions, Beaded, Chain, 9 In. | 1064 |
| **Needlework,** Roses, Wavy Borders, Sampler Style, Silver Frame, Swan Chain Handles, 6 In. | 336 |
| **Needlework,** Urn, Flowers, 2 Pockets, Foldover, Va., c.1750, 5 x 5 In. | 316 |
| **Nylon,** Black, Waist Bag, Front Zipper, Interlocking CC Logo, Chanel, 8 x 16 In. | 121 |
| **Nylon,** Gold, Red, Black Print, Greek Key Zipper Pull, Backpack, Chain Straps, Versace, 9 In. | 329 |
| **Patent Leather,** Black, Clutch, Faux Onyx, Goldtone Chain, Judith Leiber, 7½ x 9 In. | 131 |
| **Pony Hair,** Deer Print, Faux Tortoise Shell, Chain Link Strap, 11 x 12 In. | 414 |
| **Purse,** Evening, Green Beaded, Goldtone Shoulder Strap, Judith Leiber, 3 In. | 390 |
| **Python Skin,** Yellow, Brown, Green, Burgundy, Clasp, Goldtone Frame, J. Leiber, 9 x 3 In. | 207 |
| **Rabbit Fur,** Black, Quilted, Goldtone Hardware, Metal & Leather Strap, Chanel, 8 x 11 In. | 920 |
| **Satin,** Black, Clutch, Intrecciato, Wristlet Strap, Fringe, Bottega Veneta, 3½ x 6½ In. | 380 |
| **Satin,** Black, Flap, Goldtone Metal CC, Braided Metal Chain Strap, Chanel, 6½ x 5 In. | 834 |
| **Satin,** Black, Quilted, Shoulder, Flap Top, Leather Trim, Chanel, c.1991, 6 x 8 In. | 932 |

| | |
|---|---|
| **Silk,** Beaded, Semiprecious Stones, Foldover, 5 x 9 In. .....................*illus* | 799 |
| **Silk,** Metallic Thread, Needlework, Flowers, Brown Ground, Flap, c.1740, 5 x 6 In...................... | 2640 |
| **Silver,** Enamel, Telescope & Beetle, Gold Dragon, Chain, Russia, 1908, 8½ In. | 984 |
| **Silver,** Mesh, Enameled, Art Deco, Clasp, Multicolor, Chain Handle, 1920, 5 In. | 390 |
| **Silver,** Oval, Hinged, Crosshatched Pattern, Beads, Mexico, c.1964, 1½ x 3⅝ x 3 In................. | 2375 |
| **Snakeskin,** Red, Triangular, Goldtone Chain, Salvatore Ferragamo, 3¼ x 4½ In. | 167 |
| **Snakeskin,** Shoulder, Python, Judith Leiber, 6 In. ................................................ | 553 |
| **Straw,** Cream, Leather, Black, Long Handles, Coach, 9½ x 9½ In. .............................. | 36 |
| **Swarovski Crystals,** Stepped Box Shape, Coral Clasp, Link Chain, Cover, Judith Leiber, 6 In...... | 750 |
| **Tapestry,** Vanity Set, Gold Plated, Petit Point, Wiener Wertarbeit, 8½ x 5¼ In. ........................... | 121 |
| **Velvet,** Seed Beads, Multicolor, c.1825, 7½ x 6½ In. .............................................. | 225 |
| **Velvet,** Watercolor, Ink, Fruit, Flowers, Ribbon Handle, Ruth Brown, c.1830, 9 x 9 In. ................. | 2280 |

---

**QUEZAL** glass was made from 1901 to 1924 at the Queens, New York, company started by **Quezal** Martin Bach. Other glassware by other firms, such as Loetz, Steuben, and Tiffany, resembles this gold-colored iridescent glass. Martin Bach died in 1921. His son-in-law, Conrad Vahlsing Jr., went to work at the Lustre Art Company about 1920. Bach's son, Martin Bach Jr., worked at the Durand Art Glass division of the Vineland Flint Glass Works after 1924.

| | |
|---|---|
| **Bowl,** Footed, Gold Iridescent Interior, Green Iridescent Exterior, Signed, 9¾ In. ........................ | 1422 |
| **Bowl,** Gold Iridescent, Straight-Sided, Flared Rim, Dome Foot, 6 In............................................ | 243 |
| **Compote,** White Iridescent, White Pulled Feather, Gold Inside, Ruffled, Blue Zipper Foot, 6 In. .. | 1896 |
| **Jar,** Orange Gold Iridescent, Oval, 3 Looped Feet, Dome Lid, Oval Finial, 12 In............................ | 1701 |
| **Lamp Base,** Gold Iridescent Wave, Cream Ground, Brass Foot, 2 Socket, 19 In. ........................ | 829 |
| **Lamp,** Hanging, Opal Glass Shade, Flower Shape, Gold Pulled Feather, 21 In., Pair .................... | 4740 |
| **Salt,** Gold Iridescent, Pink Highlights, Squat, Ribbed, 3 In., Pair............................................ | 244 |
| **Salt,** Gold Iridescent, Vertical Ribs, Squat, 2½ In............................................................. | 122 |
| **Shade,** Blue Pulled Feather, Tipped In Gold, Signed, 6 In., Pair............................................. | 460 |
| **Shade,** Cream, Blue Hooked Feather, Gold Iridescent Outlines, Squat, 5 In., Pair................... | 304 |
| **Shade,** Cream, Gold Iridescent Fishnet, Platinum Vertical Zipper, Helmet Shape, 10 In. ............. | 2133 |
| **Shade,** Flower Shape, Gold Iridescent, Ruby Overtones, 5 x 1¾ In. ....................................... | 75 |
| **Shade,** Gold Aurene, Pulled Feathers, Marked, 6 In., 2 Piece ............................................. | 338 |
| **Shade,** Gold Hooked Pulled Feather, Gold Interior, Signed, 5 In. ........................................ | 533 |
| **Shade,** Gold Iridescent, Double Hooked Feather, White Ground, 5¼ In. ................................ | 177 |
| **Shade,** Gold Iridescent, Green & Opal Pulled Feather, Helmet Shape, 10 In. ......................... | 1896 |
| **Shade,** Gold Iridescent, Pulled Feather, Cream Ground, Signed, 6½ In. ............................... | 355 |
| **Shade,** Gold Iridescent, Ribbed, Signed, 5¼ In. ............................................................ | 115 |
| **Shade,** Gold Iridescent, Snakeskin Design, Signed, 6 In. ................................................. | 288 |
| **Shade,** Gold Iridescent, Vertical Ribs, Bulbous, Flared Rim, 4½ In., 6 Piece ......................... | 948 |
| **Shade,** Green Iridescent, Gold Ribbons, Cream Ground, 5¼ In., 3 Piece............................... | 2073 |
| **Shade,** Green Pulled Feathers, Lily, White, Gold Iridescent Trim, 4¾ In. ...........................*illus* | 592 |
| **Shade,** Opal, Green Heart & Vine, Overall Gold Threading, Signed, 4½ In. ............................ | 173 |
| **Shade,** Orange Iridescent, Vertically Ribbed, Pulled Feather, Green Outline, 4¼ In. ................... | 414 |
| **Shade,** White Pulled Feather, Light Green Ground, Signed, 5 In............................................ | 1303 |
| **Shade,** White, Yellow Pulled Feather, Cylindrical, Swollen Base, 5 x 4 In., Pair....................... | 313 |
| **Tray,** Gold Iridescent, Optic Ribbed, c.1920, 6 In............................................................. | 92 |
| **Vase,** Blue Iridescent, Double Gourd Shape, Flared Rim, 8 In. ............................................ | 668 |
| **Vase,** Blue, Green Swirls, Cream Opaque Ground, 6½ In. ................................................. | 1440 |
| **Vase,** Bud, Cream, Green & Gold Pulled Feather, Stick Shape, Gold Saucer Foot, 4½ In. ............. | 356 |
| **Vase,** Cream Iridescent, Green & Gold Pulled Feather, Gold Iridescent Tendrils, 10 In................ | 3555 |
| **Vase,** Cream Opalescent, Green & Gold Pulled Feather, Flower Shape, Ribs, 7½ In.................... | 1304 |
| **Vase,** Cream, Green Pulled Feather, Gold Zipper, Flared, Ruffled, Dome Foot, 8½ In. .................. | 2370 |
| **Vase,** Gold Iridescent, Blue Coil, Applied Handles, Foot, Signed, c.1910, 12 In. ........................... | 2760 |
| **Vase,** Gold Iridescent, Cream Hooked Feather, Shouldered, 11 In. ...................................... | 2963 |
| **Vase,** Gold Iridescent, Lily, Elongated, Rolled Ruffled Rim, Bronze Foot, 20 In. ...................... | 668 |
| **Vase,** Gold Iridescent, Pink Highlights, White Swirled Threads, Marked, 9½ In. ................*illus* | 474 |
| **Vase,** Gold Iridescent, Silver Overlay, Art Nouveau, Pontil, Signed, 8½ In. .........................*illus* | 3910 |
| **Vase,** Gold, Platinum Iridescent, Coil Pattern, Blue, Green, Shouldered, Signed, 6½ In. .............. | 748 |
| **Vase,** Green To Gold Iridescent, Lily Pads, Oval, 6½ x 5 In.................................................. | 3775 |
| **Vase,** Green, Gold & Platinum Iridescent Feathering, Shaded, Oval, 5¼ In. ............................ | 3555 |
| **Vase,** Hooked Feathers, Yellow, Gold, Cream, Green, Iridescent, Signed, 12 In. ..................*illus* | 2963 |
| **Vase,** Jack-In-The-Pulpit, Gold Luster Oval Head, Green, Gold, White Pulled Feathers, 13 In....... | 11400 |
| **Vase,** Jack-In-The-Pulpit, Green, Pulled Feather, Gold Face, Ruffled, 11 In................................ | 5925 |
| **Vase,** King Tut, Cream, Blue & Gold Iridescent Design, Flared Rim & Foot, 12¾ In. ................... | 2074 |
| **Vase,** Opal, Gold Pulled Feathers, Green Feathers, Pontil, Signed, 9¼ In. .........................*illus* | 2185 |
| **Vase,** Opal, Green Pulled Feathers, Gold Tips, Flower Shape, Signed, 4½ In. ......................*illus* | 1840 |

**Quezal,** Vase, Gold Iridescent, Silver Overlay, Art Nouveau, Pontil, Signed, 8½ In.
$3,910

Early Auction Co.

---

**Quezal,** Vase, Hooked Feathers, Yellow, Gold, Cream, Green, Iridescent, Signed, 12 In.
$2,963

James D. Julia Auctioneers

Q

**Quezal,** Vase, Opal, Gold Pulled Feathers, Green Feathers, Pontil, Signed, 9¼ In.
$2,185

Early Auction Co.

**Quezal,** Vase, Opal, Green Pulled Feathers, Gold Tips, Flower Shape, Signed, 4 ½ In.
$1,840

Early Auction Co.

**Quilt,** Amish, Wool, Diamond In Square, Borders, Cotton Backing, Pa., c.1910, 74 x 75 In.
$500

Garth's Auctioneers & Appraisers

**Quilt,** Appliqued, Birds, Lattice, White, Yellow, Red, Green, Swag Borders, 1800s, 99 x 87 In.
$3,220

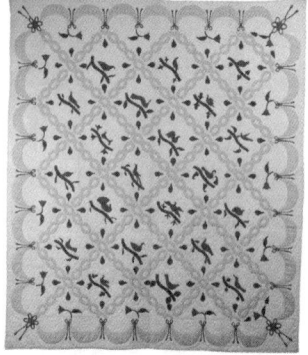

Cottone Auctions

**QUILTS** have been made since the seventeenth century. Early textiles were very precious and every scrap was saved to be reused. A quilt is a combination of fabrics joined to a filler and a backing by small stitched designs known as quilting. An appliqued quilt has pieces stitched to the top of a large piece of background fabric. A patchwork, or pieced, quilt is made of many small pieces stitched together. Embroidery can be added to either type.

| | |
|---|---:|
| **Amish,** Barn Raising, Concentric Diamonds, Multicolor, Signed QT, c.1900, 67 x 67 In. | 593 |
| **Amish,** Log Cabin, Orange, Green, Yellow, Hannah Stoltzfoos, 89 x 103 In. | 75 |
| **Amish,** Patchwork, 9-Patch, Red Center, Border, 71 x 84 In. | 406 |
| **Amish,** Patchwork, Bars, Aqua, Pink, Reversible, Ohio, c.1930, 72 x 84 In. | 246 |
| **Amish,** Patchwork, Bars, Red & Green, Brown Border, Black Trim, 15 ½ x 16 In. | 266 |
| **Amish,** Patchwork, Geometric, Olive, Blue, Red, Wool, Mounted, c.1900, 84 x 65 In. | 338 |
| **Amish,** Patchwork, Sunshine & Shadow, Flowers, Leaves, Green, Purple Border, 87 x 87 In. | 384 |
| **Amish,** Sunshine & Shadow, Feathers & Diamonds, Rayon, Cotton, c.1925, 87 x 89 In. | 246 |
| **Amish,** Sunshine & Shadow, Hannah Stoltzfoos, 106 x 106 In. | 100 |
| **Amish,** Trip Around The World, Blue, Red, Green, Black Border, Pa., c.1830, 72 x 75 In. | 900 |
| **Amish,** Whole Cloth, Violet, Leah Graber, Geneva, Indiana, c.1925, 72 x 88 In. | 400 |
| **Amish,** Wool, Diamond In Square, Borders, Cotton Backing, Pa., c.1910, 74 x 75 In. ........*illus* | 500 |
| **Appliqued,** 4 Eagle, Center Flower, Red, Cream, Yellow, Black Sawtooth Border, 1893, 87 In. | 338 |
| **Appliqued,** Album, 25 Blocks, Flowers, Red, Multicolor, Red Border, 1800s, 82 x 82 In. | 10665 |
| **Appliqued,** Birds, Lattice, White, Yellow, Red, Green, Swag Borders, 1800s, 99 x 87 In. .......*illus* | 3220 |
| **Appliqued,** Blue, Red Tulip, White Ground, c.1955, 79 x 58 In. | 60 |
| **Appliqued,** Coxcomb, Eagles, Flower Baskets, Green, Orange, Red, White, 1880, 76 x 78 In. | 923 |
| **Appliqued,** Democratic Rose, Red, Green, Orange, White, Flowering Vine Border, 94 x 94 In. | 1320 |
| **Appliqued,** Eagle Center, Flower, Vine Border, Green, Red, Yellow, White, c.1845, 91 x 76 In. | 277 |
| **Appliqued,** Four Tulips, Red, Green Birds, Grapes, Leaf Border, c.1875, 76 x 77 In. | 345 |
| **Appliqued,** Friendship Album, Red, White Sawtooth Border, Flowers, Blocks, 1853, 83 x 85 In. | 2760 |
| **Appliqued,** Grapevines, Red, Green, Yellow, 9 Blocks, Sarah Cobb, c.1850, 99 x 99 In. | 2880 |
| **Appliqued,** Rose Of Sharon, Pink, Green, White, Quilted Plume, Diamonds, Stars, 69 x 82 In. | 74 |
| **Appliqued,** Rose Of Sharon, Red, Green, Orange Ground, Green Border, 51 x 52 In. | 384 |
| **Appliqued,** Rose Of Sharon, Vines, Red, Green, Yellow, 1875, 78 x 79 In. | 900 |
| **Appliqued,** Snowflake, Red, White Ground, 20 Blocks, 83 x 99 In. | 295 |
| **Appliqued,** Star Of Bethlehem, Sawtooth Edge, Cotton, Chintz Sprigs, c.1850, 113 x 114 In. | 896 |
| **Appliqued,** Star Of Bethlehem, Tulip Vine, Birds, Flags, 32 Embroidered Stars, 114 x 118 In. | 11875 |
| **Appliqued,** Sunburst, Green, White, Orange, Swag Border, c.1855, 102 x 102 In. | 390 |
| **Appliqued,** Tulip & Vine, 4 Baskets, Heart Wreath, Red, Green, White, Border, 1876, 80 In. | 1800 |
| **Appliqued,** Tulips, Double Vine Border, Flower Basket Stitching, Kentucky, c.1853, 89 x 92 In. | 1200 |
| **Appliqued,** Tulips, Red, Green, Yellow, White, Wreath, Fan Stitching, 9 Blocks, 80 x 78 In. | 1920 |
| **Appliqued,** Whig Rose, Embroidery, Vines, Red, Green, Teal, 1860, 81 x 84 In. | 1020 |
| **Appliqued,** Wild Goose Chase, White, Green & Yellow Calico, Feather Stitching, 88 x 90 In. | 1046 |
| **Appliqued,** Wreath Of Roses, White Ground, Red, Green, Red Lattice, Border, 44 x 44 In. | 236 |
| **Appliqued,** Wreaths, Flowers, Red, Green, White Ground, 87 x 89 In. | 960 |
| **Crazy,** Silk, Velvet, Cotton, Taffeta, Multicolor, Greene County, Va., 1800s, 83 x 85 In. | 4956 |
| **Embroidered,** Pink, Sawtooth Edge, Green Border, Flowers, Wool, Cotton, c.1810, 83 x 91 In. | 923 |
| **Mennonite,** Appliqued, Leaf Medallion, Tulip Trees, Birds, Calico, 87 x 90 In. | 1353 |
| **Mennonite,** Patchwork, Blazing Stars, Red, Black, c.1900, 76 x 84 In. | 563 |
| **Mennonite,** Patchwork, Windmill, Red, Yellow, Green, Blue, Rope Stitching, c.1890, 90 x 88 In. | 3480 |
| **Patchwork,** 12 Feathered Stars, White, Green Calico, Meandering Feather Stitching, 88 x 70 In. | 308 |
| **Patchwork,** 16 Squares, Red & Green Flowers, Draped & Tassel Border, 92 x 92 In. ...........*illus* | 1896 |
| **Patchwork,** 4-Patch, Geometric, Multicolor, Floral Print Back, 81 x 82 In. | 71 |
| **Patchwork,** 9-Patch Alternating Geometrics, Gray, White, 70 x 88 In. | 106 |
| **Patchwork,** Appliqued, Red, Green, Lily, Bow Borders, 74 x 90 In. | 1200 |
| **Patchwork,** Blue Border, Striped Backing, Cotton, 88 x 100 In. | 480 |
| **Patchwork,** Brown, Green, Silk, 91 x 93 In. | 71 |
| **Patchwork,** Double Irish Chain, Red, Green, White, Bird On Branch, Stitching, 79 x 82 In. | 246 |
| **Patchwork,** Dresden Plate, Multicolor, c.1900, 87 x 87 In. | 212 |
| **Patchwork,** Eyes Of God, Ocean Waves, Brown, White, 76 x 66 In. | 308 |
| **Patchwork,** Feathered Star Variant, Cranberry, Green, Cream, Pa., c.1885, 71 x 93 In. | 120 |
| **Patchwork,** Flowers, Baskets, Birds, 4 Sections, 1880, 81 x 84 In. | 1560 |
| **Patchwork,** Flying Geese, Alternating Stripes, White, Green, Teacup Stitching, 94 x 98 In. | 277 |
| **Patchwork,** Friendship, Multicolor Chains, Pa., c.1890, 77 x 94 In. | 330 |
| **Patchwork,** Grandmother's Flower Garden, Multicolor Hexagon Patches, 73 x 94 In. | 118 |
| **Patchwork,** Grannie's Garden, Multicolor Flowers, 6-Sided Patches, 1930s, 82 x 60 In. | 59 |
| **Patchwork,** Honeybee Block, Blue On White, Crosshatching, Zigzag Border, 75 x 66 In. | 338 |
| **Patchwork,** Ocean Waves, Calico, Pink Seaweed Pattern, c.1885, 76 x 86 In. ....................*illus* | 593 |
| **Patchwork,** Ohio Star, Multicolor, Early 1900s, 66 x 68 In. | 154 |

Q

| | |
|---|---|
| **Patchwork,** Ohio Star, White Ground, Red Stars, Lattice, Zigzag Border, c.1875, 62 x 78 In. ...... | 711 |
| **Patchwork,** Pine Tree, Green, Red, Wreaths, Feathers, Cotton, c.1875, 79 x 81 In. ...................... | 690 |
| **Patchwork,** Red Sawtooth Diamond, Blue Ground, Pa., c.1890, 72 x 68 In. .............................. | 210 |
| **Patchwork,** Road To California, Red, Brown, White, Mustard, Cotton, 67 x 86 In. ............... | 180 |
| **Patchwork,** Star Variant Pattern, Cranberry, Cream, Green Ground, Pa., c.1895, 80 x 80 In....... | 150 |
| **Patchwork,** Star, 8-Pointed, White Ground, 9 Blocks, 74 x 74 In. ...................................... | 178 |
| **Patchwork,** Stars, Green, Lilac, White Ground, 78 x 80 In. ............................................. | 153 |
| **Patchwork,** Sunburst, 16 Blocks, Multicolor, Cotton, Wide Border, c.1900, 92 x 95 In. ............. | 984 |
| **Patchwork,** Texas Lone Star, Green, Brown, Yellow, 1970s, 100 x 114 In. ........................ | 100 |
| **Patchwork,** Triple Irish Chain, Red, White, Knotted, 1800s, 78 x 78 In. ............................ | 92 |
| **Patchwork,** Tumbling Blocks, Calico, Challis Backing, 80 x 82 In. ................................. | 660 |
| **Patchwork,** Tumbling Blocks, Multicolor, Red Border, c.1890, 87 x 78 In.......................... | 120 |

**QUIMPER** pottery has a long history. Tin-glazed, hand-painted pottery has been made in Quimper, France, since the late seventeenth century. The earliest firm was founded in 1708 by Pierre Bousquet. In 1782, Antoine de la Hubaudiere became the manager of the factory and the factory became known as the HB Factory (for Hubaudiere-Bousquet), de la Hubaudiere, or Grande Maison. Another firm, founded in 1772 by Francois Eloury, was known as Porquier. The third firm, founded by Guillaume Dumaine in 1778, was known as HR or Henriot Quimper. All three firms made similar pottery decorated with designs of Breton peasants and sea and flower motifs. The Eloury (Porquier) and Dumaine (Henriot) firms merged in 1913. Bousquet (HB) merged with the others in 1968. The group was sold to an American holding company in 1984. More changes followed, and in 2011 Jean-Pierre Le Goff became the owner and the name was changed to Henriot-Quimper.

*H.R. Quimper*

| | |
|---|---|
| **Bowl,** Fluted, Breton Child, Pipe, Scalloped, Blue Border, Marked, c.1895, 5 In. ............................ | 165 |
| **Bowl,** Handles, Bird, Footed, 1880s, 7 In. ............................................................. | 200 |
| **Bowl,** Yellow, Footed, Marked, c.1928, 10 x 3 In.......................................................... | 185 |
| **Centerpiece,** Faience, Griffin Handles, Scalloped Edge, Multicolor, Oval, Footed, 20 x 9 In. ........ | 575 |
| **Oyster Plate,** 6 Wells, Fish Shape, Flowers, c.1935, 10 x 8 ¼ In......................................... | 150 |
| **Oyster Plate,** 6 Wells, Flowers, Blue Border, c.1875, 9 In. ............................................ | 95 |
| **Plate,** Breton Woman, Yellow & Blue Border, 1880s, 8 ½ In.......................................... | 160 |

**RADIO** broadcast receiving sets were first sold in New York City in 1910. They were used to pick up the experimental broadcasts of the day. The first commercial radios were made by Westinghouse Company for listeners of the experimental shows on KDKA Pittsburgh in 1920. Collectors today are interested in all early radios, especially those made of Bakelite plastic or decorated with blue mirrors. Figural advertising radios and transistor radios are also collected.

| | |
|---|---|
| **Addison,** Model L2, Molded Plastic, Red & White, Tombstone Dial, AM, c.1940....................*illus* | 1920 |
| **Airline,** Electric Clock, Borg, Wood, 3 Dials, Metal Escutcheon, Floor Model, 47 x 29 In.............. | 120 |
| **Arvin,** Metal, Red, Gold Foil, AM, 1946, 5 x 6 ¼ x 4 In.................................................. | 180 |
| **Atwater Kent,** Model 55, Golden Voiced Table, Flip-Top Cabinet.......................................... | 60 |
| **Atwater Kent,** Model 60, Pooley Cabinet, Model 1700, 3 Dials, 50 x 31 In. ..........................*illus* | 120 |
| **Audiola,** Model 13-4T, Monarch, Art Deco, Cathedral, Leatherette Case, Table Model, 11 x 13 In. | 330 |
| **Beco Mfg.,** Best, 2 Knobs, Molded Leatherette Case, 7 x 10 In. ...................................... | 30 |
| **Bendix,** Catalin, 2 Knobs, AM, Slide Rule Dial, Horizontal Louvers Grill, Table Model................. | 570 |
| **Brunswick,** Shortwave, AM, 4 Pushbutton Dials, Magic Eye, Wood End Table ....................*illus* | 30 |
| **Cheney,** Clock, AM, 3 Dials, Metal Clock Face, Escutcheon, 12 x 19 In. ............................. | 60 |
| **Crosley,** Model D-25, Plastic, Alarm Clock, AM Tube, Table Model, 13 ¼ x 7 x 7 ½ In.................. | 48 |
| **Detrola,** Model 302, Cathedral-C, Wood, Triangular Shape, Upper Round Clock Face, c.1938..... | 316 |
| **Emerson,** Aristocrat, Catalin, Butterscotch, 2 Knobs, Dial On Right, Black Handle, Table Model | 240 |
| **Emerson,** Model EP375, Catalin, Yellow, Rectangular, AM, Tabletop, c.1941 ......................... | 720 |
| **Fada Model 700,** Cloud, Catalin, Brown, 2 Knobs, Handle, AM, Tabletop, 1946........................ | 2700 |
| **Fada,** Brown, Yellow Retractable Handle, Bakelite, 1930s-40s, 10 ½ In. .............................. | 555 |
| **Fada,** Bullet Streamliner, Model 115, Maroon Catalin Plastic, Handle, c.1941, 6 ½ In. .............. | 960 |
| **Fada,** Bullet Streamliner, Model 1000, Butterscotch Catalin Plastic, Handle, c.1946, 6 ½ x 10 In. | 660 |
| **Fada,** Bullet Streamliner, Model 1000, Dark Brown Catalin Plastic, Handle, c.1946, 6 ½ x 10 In. | 1320 |
| **Fada,** Catalin, Bullet, Model 100, Burgundy, Butterscotch, Bakelite, c.1940, 14 ½ In. ................. | 720 |
| **Fada,** Catalin, Orange, Bakelite, Art Deco, 10 ½ In. ................................................ | 300 |
| **Fada,** Model 115, Bullet, Catalin, Brown, Orange, Handle, AM, c.1941 ...........................*illus* | 570 |
| **Fada,** NA Series, AM, Wood, 3 Knobs, Vertical Column Speaker Grill, Table Model, 9 x 13 ½ In. *illus* | 30 |
| **Fada,** Temple, Catalin, 2 Knobs, AM, Table Model ................................................... | 270 |
| **Fish Radioette,** A.W.A., Amalgamated Wireless, Polished Radelec Cabinet.............................. | 720 |
| **Freshman Products,** Clock, Wood, Skyscraper Case, 3 Knobs, Metal Clock Face, 11 x 18 In....... | 300 |
| **Garod,** Commander, Catalin, AM, 2 Knobs, Handle, Slide Rule Dial, Red Grill, Table Model ........ | 450 |
| **General Electric,** Model J-82, Superheterodyne, Cathedral, 3 Dials, Table Model, Wood .....*illus* | 150 |
| **Grebe,** Wood, 3 Dials, Metal Escutcheon, Floor Model, 39 x 25 In........................................ | 120 |

**Quilt,** Patchwork, 16 Squares, Red & Green Flowers, Draped & Tassel Border, 92 x 92 In.
$1,896

James D. Julia Auctioneers

**Quilt,** Patchwork, Ocean Waves, Calico, Pink Seaweed Pattern, c.1885, 76 x 86 In.
$593

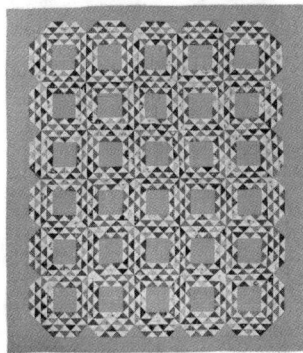

James D. Julia Auctioneers

**Radio,** Addison, Model L2, Molded Plastic, Red & White, Tombstone Dial, AM, c.1940
$1,920

Victorian Casino Antiques

**Early Transistor Radios**
The first American transistor radio was the Regency TR-1 made in 1954. The best color is red or black; the least expensive is ivory or gray. These early transistor radios sell for about $300 to $1,000.

R

**Radio,** Atwater Kent, Model 60, Pooley Cabinet, Model 1700, 3 Dials, 50 x 31 In.
$120

Morphy Auctions

**Radio,** Brunswick, Shortwave, AM, 4 Pushbutton Dials, Magic Eye, Wood End Table
$30

Morphy Auctions

**Radio,** Fada, Model 115, Bullet, Catalin, Brown, Orange, Handle, AM, c.1941
$570

Victorian Casino Antiques

| | |
|---|---|
| **Guild Radio & Television Co.,** Teakettle, Wood, Ceramic, Dial Under Lid, AM, 1957 .........*illus* | 150 |
| **Guild,** Novelty, AM, Wood, Ceramic, Teapot Shape, Brown, White, Handle..................................... | 150 |
| **Magic Eye,** Tube, Wood, Swings On Base, 3 Knobs, AM & Shortwave, 18½ x 16 In. .............*illus* | 900 |
| **Microphone Shape,** KWBE 1450, 1940s Model, Hard Rubber, Promotional, 13 In. ...........*illus* | 120 |
| **Microphone,** Argonne Crystal, Capsule Shape, Model AR-57, Base ......................................... | 330 |
| **Microphone,** Chromed, Short Desk Base, Spherical, Brown ..................................................... | 120 |
| **Microphone,** Electro-Voice, Cardax, Model 950, CBS, Aluminum, Plastic, Base .................*illus* | 450 |
| **Microphone,** Electro-Voice, Dynamic, Impedance, Hi-Z Model 638, Base........................... | 120 |
| **Microphone,** General Electric, Wood, Piano Key, Slide Rule Dials, Floor Model ...................... | 120 |
| **Microphone,** Selector Mfg. Corp., Long Cable, Model WS, Base........................................ | 120 |
| **Microphone,** Shure Brothers, Unidyne, Dynamic, Model 55S, Base.................................. | 480 |
| **Microphone,** Shure Brothers, Unidyne, Model 55S, Blue, Unidirectional Dynamic..................... | 390 |
| **Ozarka,** Model 90, 2 Speakers, Wood, 2 Dials, Metal Escutcheon, 39 x 48 In. ....................... | 300 |
| **Philco,** Model 46, Tombstone, Wood Case, AM, 1931.................................................*illus* | 120 |
| **Pla-Pal,** Wood, 2 Cabinets, Card Deck, Poker Chips, Decanters, Glasses, 9¾ x 14½ In........... | 430 |
| **RCA,** Catalin, 3 Knobs, AM, Paper Dial, Bowed Wood Grill, 4¾ x 6¾ In............................ | 330 |
| **RCA,** Model 66X8, Catalin, Brown, 3 Knobs, Slide Rule Dial, AM, Shortwave, 1946................ | 540 |
| **RCA,** Radiola, Loud Speaker, Black Horn ..................................................................... | 30 |
| **Silver-Marshal,** Console, Superheterodyne Wood, Center Dial, Floor Model, 32 x 18 x 52 In. ..... | 403 |
| **Silvertone,** Electric Clock, Hammond, Wood, Tall Case, 6 Knobs, 63 x 16 In........................ | 240 |
| **Silvertone,** Electric Clock, Tall Case, Wood, 4 Knobs, 61 x 14 In. ................................... | 540 |
| **Silvertone,** Model 13281-1, Metal, AM Tube, AC 100 60 Cycle, 6¼ x 4 x 5 In. ..................... | 58 |
| **Sparton,** Art Deco, Blue Mirror Reproduction, Round, Table Model, 14½ In. ........................ | 150 |
| **Sparton,** Console, Wood, Metal Escutcheon, Floor Model, 36 x 26 In.................................. | 210 |
| **Speaker,** Table, Wood, Turned Legs, Stretcher, Enclosed 7-In. Speaker, 30 x 32 In. ............... | 90 |
| **Tesla,** Talisman, Bakelite, Stamped, Czech Republic, 1950s, 6½ x 11¼ In. .;....................*illus* | 875 |
| **TSM,** Reproduction Art Deco, Model AR, Peach, Mirror, AM/FM, France, 10 x 14 In. ............... | 120 |
| **Walter Dorwin,** Teague Sparton, Glass, Metal, Wood, Blue, c.1936, 9 x 18 In. .............*illus* | 2250 |
| **Westinghouse,** Wood, Carved Grill, Mini Tombstone, 2 Knobs, 10 x 8½ In........................... | 90 |
| **Zenith,** Consol-Tone, Model S-17697, Plastic, AM Tube, AC 110 60 Cycle, Table Model, 14 x 6 In. | 48 |
| **Zenith,** Model 6D030WZ, Molded Plywood Case, Eames, c.1946, 7¾ x 13½ In. .............*illus* | 189 |

**RAILROAD** enthusiasts collect any train memorabilia. Everything is wanted, from oilcans to whole train cars. The Chessie system has a store that sells many reproductions of its old dinnerware and uniforms.

| | |
|---|---|
| **Chronometer,** Howard, Series 11, Sunken Seconds, Gold Filled Case, 2 In............................ | 277 |
| **Clock,** Station, Hanging, Copper, Enamel, Glass, 24 Hour Face, Behrens, AEG, 1910, 29 In. ......... | 2250 |
| **Cup & Saucer,** Greek Key Border, Flowers, Pullman Railroad .......................................... | 132 |
| **Lantern,** 3 Tiers, Black Metal, Brass Bezels, Fresnel Glass Lenses, Vented Top, Ring, 70 x 13 In... | 901 |
| **Lantern,** Central Railroad, Brass, Glass, Etched CRR, Metal Chain & Loop Handle, 15 In........... | 420 |
| **Lantern,** Dressel Lineman, 4-Way Blue & Red Lights, 16½ x 11 In...................................... | 210 |
| **Lantern,** Handlan, Lineman, 4-Way Blue, Orange & Green Lights, 14 x 11 In. ....................... | 330 |
| **Lantern,** Non-Sweating, 4-Way Orange & Blue Lights, Adlake, 15 x 9 In. .............................. | 330 |
| **Lantern,** Southern Railroad, Adlake Reliable, Sheet Iron, Adams & Westlake Co., c.1930, 16 In. | 81 |
| **Poster,** Pennsylvania Railroad, North South East West, Gouache, J. Collins, c.1950, 47 x 31 In... | 1250 |
| **Poster,** Pennsylvania Railroad, Visit Washington Symbol Of Democracy, J. Collins, c.1950, 46 x 29 In... | 1250 |
| **Sign,** Crossing X, Porcelain, Black & White, Reflective Buttons, 48 x 48 In. ......................... | 660 |
| **Sign,** Railway Agency Express, Diamond Shape, 49 x 49 In................................................ | 420 |
| **Sign,** Railway Express, Porcelain, Metal, Enamel, Tan, Red, Green, 2 Sections, 39 In. .................. | 369 |
| **Tray,** Pullman Railroad, White, Greek Key Border, Flowers, Oval, 10½ In............................... | 118 |

**RAZORS** were used in ancient Egypt and subsequently wherever shaving was in fashion. The metal razor used in America until about 1870 was made in Sheffield, England. After 1870, machine-made hollow-ground razors were made in Germany or America. Plastic or bone handles were popular. The razor was often sold in a set of seven, one for each day of the week. The set was often kept by the barber who shaved the well-to-do man each day in the shop.

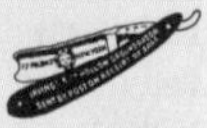

| | |
|---|---|
| **Bone Handle,** Pewter Inlay, Leather Case, W.M. Graves Sheffield, 2 Piece ..................................... | 180 |
| **Cast Aluminum,** Scenes Of Women, Looking Glass, Cattaraugus Cutlery Co............................... | 360 |
| **Double Bladed,** Naval, Straight, Bone Handle, Etched Blade .......................................... | 328 |
| **Gold Washed,** Roses, Thistles, Morocco Leather Case, Joseph Rodgers & Sons, 2 Piece ............... | 3300 |
| **Horn Handle,** Pearl Escutcheons, Twisted Edge, Morocco Leather Case, Wade & Butcher ......... | 210 |
| **Ivory Handle,** Inlaid Nickel Shields, Silk Lining Case, Houghton & Co., 2 Piece ...................... | 300 |
| **Ivory Handle,** Leather Case, Joseph Rodgers & Sons, c.1850 ............................................. | 210 |
| **Ivory Handle,** Straight, Inlaid Pique, Carved, Checkered, c.1825 ......................................... | 408 |

| | |
|---|---|
| **Pearl Pique Handle,** Silver Inlaid Pins, Morocco Leather Case, Joseph Rodgers & Sons | 420 |
| **Pressed Horn,** Hunters, Horses, Farm, Dogs, Wilson | 240 |
| **Pressed Horn,** Locomotive Scene, Locomotive Razor, Wilson, 1820s | 300 |
| **Shaving Kit,** Razor, Brush, Cup, Embossed, Velvet Box, 8 In. | 660 |
| **Sterling Over Celluloid,** Flowers, Pressed Cardboard Case, Superior & Warranted Razors | 510 |
| **Straight,** Pine, Hand Carved Handle, Paint, c.1900, 14 In. | 127 |
| **Straight,** Set, Elephant Ivory Handles, Engraved Shakespeare Bust, Box, c.1905, 7 Piece | 472 |

**REAMERS,** or juice squeezers, have been known since 1767, although most of those collected today date from the twentieth century. Figural reamers are among the most prized.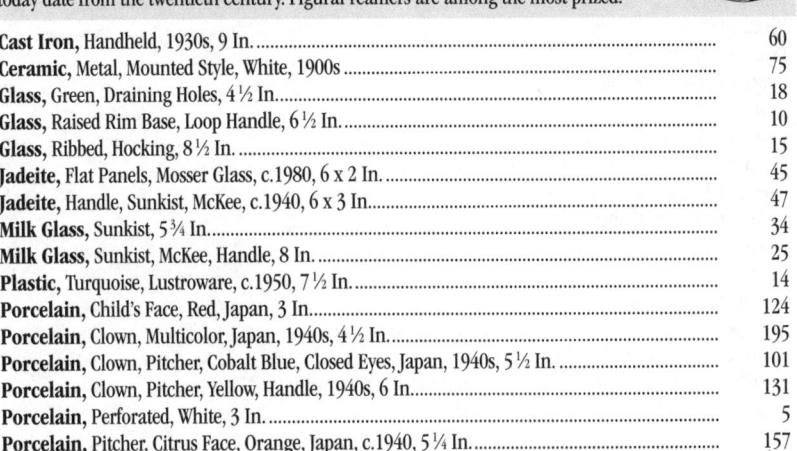

| | |
|---|---|
| **Cast Iron,** Handheld, 1930s, 9 In. | 60 |
| **Ceramic,** Metal, Mounted Style, White, 1900s | 75 |
| **Glass,** Green, Draining Holes, 4½ In. | 18 |
| **Glass,** Raised Rim Base, Loop Handle, 6½ In. | 10 |
| **Glass,** Ribbed, Hocking, 8½ In. | 15 |
| **Jadeite,** Flat Panels, Mosser Glass, c.1980, 6 x 2 In. | 45 |
| **Jadeite,** Handle, Sunkist, McKee, c.1940, 6 x 3 In. | 47 |
| **Milk Glass,** Sunkist, 5¾ In. | 34 |
| **Milk Glass,** Sunkist, McKee, Handle, 8 In. | 25 |
| **Plastic,** Turquoise, Lustroware, c.1950, 7½ In. | 14 |
| **Porcelain,** Child's Face, Red, Japan, 3 In. | 124 |
| **Porcelain,** Clown, Multicolor, Japan, 1940s, 4½ In. | 195 |
| **Porcelain,** Clown, Pitcher, Cobalt Blue, Closed Eyes, Japan, 1940s, 5½ In. | 101 |
| **Porcelain,** Clown, Pitcher, Yellow, Handle, 1940s, 6 In. | 131 |
| **Porcelain,** Perforated, White, 3 In. | 5 |
| **Porcelain,** Pitcher, Citrus Face, Orange, Japan, c.1940, 5¼ In. | 157 |
| **Porcelain,** Pitcher, Citrus Face, Yellow, Japan, 1940s, 5¼ In. | 148 |
| **Porcelain,** Pitcher, Duck, Blue, Red, Yellow, Japan, 2½ In. | 124 |

**RECORDS** have changed size and shape through the years. The cylinder-shaped phonograph record for use with the early Edison models was made about 1889. Disc records were first made by 1894, the double-sided disc by 1904. High-fidelity records were first issued in 1944, the first vinyl disc in 1946, the first stereo record in 1958. The 78 RPM became the standard in 1926 but was discontinued in 1957. In 1932, the first 33⅓ RPM was made but was not sold commercially until 1948. In 1949, the 45 RPM was introduced. Compact discs became available in the U.S. in 1982 and many companies began phasing out the production of phonograph records.

| | |
|---|---|
| **Alvin & The Chipmunks,** Christmas With The Chipmunks, Tree, 78 RPM, 1962 | 12 |
| **Beatles,** Get Back, Don't Let Me Down, Apple, 45 RPM, 1970s | 5 |
| **Elvis Presley,** Elvis' Christmas Album, RCA, 1970 | 45 |
| **Johnny Mathis,** Greatest Hits, Columbia 6-Eye Label, LP, 1958 | 30 |
| **Kenny Rogers,** Dolly Parton, I Will Always Love You, Islands In The Stream, 45 RPM, 1983 | 8 |
| **South Pacific,** Soundtrack, RCA Victor, 1958 | 23 |
| **Yankee Doodle Mickey,** Walt Disney, 78 RPM, c.1980 | 8 |

**RED WING POTTERY** of Red Wing, Minnesota, was a firm started in 1878. The company first made utilitarian pottery, including stoneware jugs and canning jars. In the 1920s art pottery was introduced. Many dinner sets and vases were made before the company closed in 1967. Rumrill pottery made by the Red Wing Pottery for George Rumrill is listed in its own category. For more prices, go to kovels.com.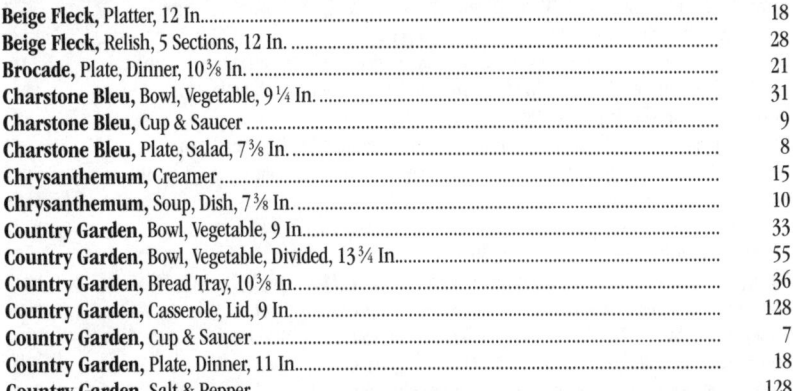

| | |
|---|---|
| **Beige Fleck,** Platter, 12 In. | 18 |
| **Beige Fleck,** Relish, 5 Sections, 12 In. | 28 |
| **Brocade,** Plate, Dinner, 10⅜ In. | 21 |
| **Charstone Bleu,** Bowl, Vegetable, 9¼ In. | 31 |
| **Charstone Bleu,** Cup & Saucer | 9 |
| **Charstone Bleu,** Plate, Salad, 7⅜ In. | 8 |
| **Chrysanthemum,** Creamer | 15 |
| **Chrysanthemum,** Soup, Dish, 7⅜ In. | 10 |
| **Country Garden,** Bowl, Vegetable, 9 In. | 33 |
| **Country Garden,** Bowl, Vegetable, Divided, 13¾ In. | 55 |
| **Country Garden,** Bread Tray, 10⅜ In. | 36 |
| **Country Garden,** Casserole, Lid, 9 In. | 128 |
| **Country Garden,** Cup & Saucer | 7 |
| **Country Garden,** Plate, Dinner, 11 In. | 18 |
| **Country Garden,** Salt & Pepper | 128 |

**Radio,** Fada, NA Series, AM, Wood, 3 Knobs, Vertical Column Speaker Grill, Table Model, 9 x 13½ In.
$30

Morphy Auctions

**Radio,** General Electric, Model J-82, Superheterodyne, Cathedral, 3 Dials, Table Model, Wood
$150

Morphy Auctions

## Clock Radios

There were clock radios in the 1950s. Peter Max added decoration to clock radios made by General Electric in the 1960s. A clock radio was cased with a tiny television set in the 1980s.

**Radio,** Guild Radio & Television Co., Teakettle, Wood, Ceramic, Dial Under Lid, AM, 1957
$150

Victorian Casino Antiques

**Radio,** Magic Eye, Tube, Wood, Swings On Base, 3 Knobs, AM & Shortwave, 18½ x 16 In.
$900

Victorian Casino Antiques

**Radio,** Microphone Shape, KWBE 1450, 1940s Model, Hard Rubber, Promotional, 13 In.
$120

Morphy Auctions

**Radio,** Microphone, Electro-Voice, Cardax, Model 950, CBS, Aluminum, Plastic, Base
$450

Morphy Auctions

| | |
|---|---:|
| **Crazy Rhythm,** Butter, Cover, ¼ Lb................................................. | 22 |
| **Crazy Rhythm,** Relish, 2 Sections, 13¼ In..................................... | 20 |
| **Driftwood,** Bread Tray, 10⅜ In...................................................... | 37 |
| **Driftwood,** Casserole, Lid, 1¾ Qt................................................... | 128 |
| **Driftwood,** Creamer, 5½ In............................................................. | 19 |
| **Driftwood,** Plate, Bread & Butter, 6½ In........................................ | 5 |
| **Fruit,** Celery Dish, 11⅜ In.............................................................. | 14 |
| **Fruit,** Creamer.................................................................................. | 20 |
| **Fruit,** Cup & Saucer......................................................................... | 8 |
| **Fruit,** Owl, Soup, Dish, 7½ In......................................................... | 8 |
| **Fruit,** Plate, Salad, 7½ In................................................................ | 7 |
| **Fruit,** Platter, Oval, 13 In............................................................... | 30 |
| **Granada,** Casserole, Lid, 2 Qt......................................................... | 36 |
| **Greenwichstone,** Creamer............................................................... | 12 |
| **Greenwichstone,** Cup & Saucer....................................................... | 6 |
| **Greenwichstone,** Plate, Bread & Butter, 6⅜ In.............................. | 9 |
| **Greenwichstone,** Plate, Dinner, 10¼ In.......................................... | 9 |
| **Greenwichstone,** Platter, Oval, 13 In.............................................. | 22 |
| **Hearthside,** Platter, Oval, 13 In...................................................... | 30 |
| **Lanterns,** Creamer, 3½ In............................................................... | 14 |
| **Lanterns,** Nappy, 8⅝ In................................................................... | 18 |
| **Lexington,** Plate, Bread & Butter, 6¼ In........................................ | 4 |
| **Lexington,** Platter, Oval, 13 In....................................................... | 30 |
| **Vase,** Bud, U Shape, Double, Woman, Between Holders, Impressed, 10¾ In. .......................*illus* | 316 |
| **Vase,** Nokomis Glaze, High Loop Handles, Stamped, 8½ In............ | 100 |

**REDWARE** is a hard, red stoneware that originated in the late 1600s and continues to be made. The term is also used to describe any common clay pottery that is reddish in color.

| | |
|---|---:|
| **Bank,** African American Face, Black, Red, Pink, White, Cold Painted, 1870, 3¾ In. ..................... | 316 |
| **Bank,** Cat, Seated, 19th Century ................................................... | 1725 |
| **Bank,** Coin Slot On Shoulder, Knob Finial, Rounded, Tapered, 1800s, 8 In............................... | 69 |
| **Bank,** Conestoga Wagon, Oval Base, 6 x 6 In................................ | 7590 |
| **Bank,** Crock, Bulbous, Incised Bird, Floral, Leaves, 3 Panels, Breininger, 13½ In.................... | 266 |
| **Bank,** Dog, On Tree Stump, 5 x 6 In.............................................. | 1725 |
| **Bank,** Green & Brown Glaze, Cream Ground, Shenandoah Valley, Va., 1800s, 4¼ In................. | 1440 |
| **Bank,** Owl, On Stump, 8 In............................................................. | 1725 |
| **Bank,** Rhinoceros, 7½ x 4½ In....................................................... | 805 |
| **Bank,** Still, Bird Shape, Yellow, Green, Manganese Mottled Glaze, 1998, 6¾ In. .................... | 130 |
| **Bean Pot,** Lid, Impressed John Bell Waynesboro, 1800s, 6¼ x 8 In. ................................... | 1920 |
| **Birdhouse,** Old White Paint, Cylindrical, Dome Top, Finial, Wooden Perch, c.1870, 7 In............ | 863 |
| **Bottle,** Squirrel Shape, Streaked, Mottled, R. Christ, N.C., Moravian, c.1810, 7⅜ In. ............. | 6325 |
| **Bowl,** Black Squiggle Rim, Signed Greg Shooner, 1999, 5 x 11 In. ................................... | 111 |
| **Bowl,** Cream, Brown, Green Slip Trailed Wavy Lines, I. Bell, c.1840, 2¾ x 10⅜ In. ............... | 4025 |
| **Bowl,** Green & Yellow Stripes, Manganese Ground, Wavy Rim, Flared, c.1810, 3 x 13 In. ........ | 17250 |
| **Bowl,** Green, White Slip Flowers, Continental, 2½ x 11½ In. ....... | 62 |
| **Bowl,** Milk, Rust Glaze, 6 Manganese Vertical Sponge Bands, Pa., 1800s, 3½ x 7 In. ............ | 130 |
| **Bowl,** Rounded Sides, Rim, Copper Slip, 1823, 10 x 2¼ In............. | 920 |
| **Bowl,** Slip Decorated Dots, Triple Wavy Lines, Shallow, Penn., c.1800, 11½ In. ................... | 394 |
| **Bowl,** Slip Trailed Interlaced Swirling Bands, Early 1800s, 12¼ In. ................................. | 840 |
| **Bowl,** Tapered, Rounded Rim, Wavy Stripes, c.1875, 14 x 3 In........ | 517 |
| **Bowl,** Trailing Yellow, Green, Black Slip, 5¼ x 13¼ In.................. | 180 |
| **Bowl,** Wavy Slip, Red, Cream, Brown, 3 Bead Rim., Hagerstown, Md., c.1800, 5 x 15 In. ......... | 978 |
| **Bowl,** Yellow & Brown Arches, Iron Oxide Ground, Flared, Shenandoah Valley, 4 x 12 In........... | 920 |
| **Bowl,** Yellow, Brown Stripe Slip, 1800s, 1⅜ x 4½ In.................... | 144 |
| **Bust,** Woman, Exposed Breasts, Downcast Eyes, White Paint, c.1875, 11½ x 10 In. ............... | 633 |
| **Charger,** Copper Slip Flying Bird, Inscription, Coggled Rim, Simon Singer, Pa., 12⅞ In. ........... | 8625 |
| **Charger,** Crosshatch Slip, Manganese, England, c.1790, 3 x 15 In. | 4888 |
| **Charger,** Dense Brown, Yellow Slip, Over Manganese Wash, c.1750, 2 x 13 In........................ | 4025 |
| **Charger,** Sgraffito, Horse & Rider, Greg Shooner, 1999, 13¾ In. ... | 320 |
| **Charger,** Slip Decoration, Bird On Branch, Inscribed Snipe, Matawan, N.J., 1800s, 11¼ In........ | 1722 |
| **Charger,** Slip Design, Cream, Green Zigzag Border, Bristol, Connecticut, c.1850, 13 In............ | 600 |
| **Charger,** Slip Swags, Zigzag Lines, Coggle Wheel Rim, 1800s, Pa., 12½ In........................... | 160 |
| **Charger,** Tree Of Life Yellow Slip, c.1825, 11½ In........................ | 1380 |
| **Charger,** Waves & Lines, Yellow & Green Slip, Coggled Rim, 12 In. | 5000 |

R

| | |
|---|---|
| Charger, Yellow Combed Slip, Over Manganese Wash, c.1765, 2 ½ x 13 In. | 4600 |
| Charger, Yellow Slip Crossed Lines, Green Splotches, 19th Century, 13 ¼ In. | 3120 |
| Charger, Yellow Slip Geometrics, c.1850, 11 ¾ In. | 900 |
| Charger, Yellow Slip Snake Lines, Pie Crimped Rim, Lead Glaze, c.1805, 3 x 14 In. | 546 |
| Charger, Yellow Slip Waves, Copper Splotches, Coggled Rim, c.1770, 2 ¾ x 14 In. | 374 |
| Charger, Yellow Slip, Copper Splotches, c.1765, 2 ¾ x 13 In. | 546 |
| Charger, Yellow Slip, Copper Splotches, Lead Glaze, c.1770, 2 ½ x 13 ½ In. | 546 |
| Charger, Yellow Slip, Copper Splotches, Pa., c.1770, 2 ½ x 13 ½ In. | 518 |
| Charger, Yellow Slip, Manganese Splotches, Pa., c.1765, 2 x 12 In. | 345 |
| Chest, Tortoiseshell Glaze, 6 Drawers, Scalloped Apron, c.1870, 10 x 12 In. | 240 |
| Churn, Stick, Yellow Curlicues, Jug Handles, 14 In. | 146 |
| Creamer, Green & Brown Glaze, Flattened Handle, 7 In. | 360 |
| Creamer, Green, Orange, Copper, Lead Glaze, Shenandoah Valley, c.1830, 4 ¾ x 3 ⅜ In. | 1380 |
| Creamer, Mottled Cream, Green, Brown, Flared, Handle, Strasburg, Va., c.1890, 6 ⅜ In. | 1093 |
| Crock, Bulbous, Molded Lip, Tooled Shoulder, Mottled Glaze, Penn., 1800s, 9 ½ In. | 106 |
| Crock, Cake, Cobalt Blue Flower, Leaf Swag, Handles, Baltimore, c.1870, 6 Gal., 13 x 15 In. | 546 |
| Crock, Lid, Mottled Manganese, Rope Twist Handles, J. Bell, c.1875, 7 x 6 In. | 1265 |
| Crock, Manganese Splash, Cylindrical, c.1850, 12 In. | 185 |
| Crock, Mottled Glaze, 11 In. | 180 |
| Crock, Mottled Glaze, Ringed Neck, 10 ¾ In. | 219 |
| Crock, Mottled Orange Glaze, Cylindrical, Raised Rim, Galena, Ill., 8 ¼ In. | 360 |
| Crock, Red, Green Splotches, Rolled Rim, 7 ½ In. | 120 |
| Crock, Yellow Scroll Band, Jug Handles, 7 ¾ x 9 ½ In. | 94 |
| Cup, Footed, Semi Oval, Tooled, Strap Handle, c.1875, 3 ½ In. | 259 |
| Cuspidor, Branches, Miniature, c.1875 | 1840 |
| Cuspidor, Manganese, Coggled Rim, Sawtooth Rim, Pa., c.1840, 5 x 8 ½ In. | 345 |
| Dish, Green, White, Black Blossoms, Vines Slip, c.1805, 9 ½ In. | 575 |
| Dish, Slip Decorated, 4 Rows Of 3 Undulating Flourishes, Coggled Rim, c.1850, 10 ¼ In. | 430 |
| Dish, Slip Decorated, Squiggle Flourish, S-Scrolls, Dots, Dashes, Coggled Rim, 11 ¼ In. | 540 |
| Dish, Yellow, Green Slip, Tulips, Double Bands, c.1830, 2 x 11 In. | 690 |
| Dish, Yellow, Green Stripe Slip, Swirled, Rounded Rim, Moravian, c.1780, 2 x 10 In. | 978 |
| Face Jug, Black Preacher, Clasped Hands, Red Accents, Alabama, c.1885, 17 In. | 52900 |
| Figurine, Bear, Holding Hollow Trunk, c.1860, 5 ⅜ In. | 9600 |
| Figurine, Bear, Seated, Beehive, Signed, Breininger, 1984, 5 ¼ In. | 295 |
| Figurine, Bear, Standing, By Tree, Molded Square Base, 1800s, 6 ¼ x 4 ½ In. | 1200 |
| Figurine, Bear, Walking, Head Down, Black, 10 ½ In. | 94 |
| Figurine, Cat, Seated, Manganese Glaze, John Bell, Pa., c.1870, 5 In. | 1495 |
| Figurine, Deer, Seated, Manganese Glaze, John Bell, Pa., c.1840, 2 x 2 In. | 1035 |
| Figurine, Deer, Standing, Gunmetal Black Glaze, 8 x 6 ½ In. | 6325 |
| Figurine, Dog, Begging, Basket In Mouth, Stump Base, 4 In. | 1265 |
| Figurine, Dog, Curly Tail, 9 x 9 In. | 2185 |
| Figurine, Dog, Spaniel, Cream Spots, 7 In., Pair | 4600 |
| Figurine, Dog, Spaniel, Incised Poodle, Apples In Basket, Pa., c.1870, 5 ½ x 6 In. | 6240 |
| Figurine, Dog, Spaniel, Mottled Manganese, Yellow Slip, Stamped John Bell, c.1860, 9 In. | 4888 |
| Figurine, Dog, Standing, Holding Jug, Brown, Orange, Pa., 5 ¾ In. | 16800 |
| Figurine, Dog, Standing, Over Child, 7 x 4 In. | 5980 |
| Figurine, Dog, Whippet, Lying, John Bell, Stamped, 7 x 10 In. | 14950 |
| Figurine, Dog, Whippet, Seated, Black Paint, Solomon Bell, Va., c.1840, 10 In. | 25300 |
| Figurine, Lamb, Reclining, Press Molded, Oval Base, Paint, c.1865, 9 x 10 In. | 184 |
| Figurine, Lamp, Reclining, White Paint, Shenandoah Valley, c.1890, 3 ½ x 12 In. | 3450 |
| Figurine, Lion, Standing, Oval Base, Pa., c.1850, 6 In. | 13200 |
| Figurine, Man, Hobo, Standing, Smoking, Hat, Arm Raised, 1800s, 22 ½ In. | 1093 |
| Figurine, Monkey, Holding Jug, Sitting On Reclining Dog, Pa., c.1850, 5 In. | 21600 |
| Figurine, Monkey, With Pipe, Riding Dog, Pa., c.1850, 6 In. | 10800 |
| Figurine, Rooster, Molded, Glazed, 3 ¾ In. | 201 |
| Figurine, Squirrel, Sitting, Holding Nut, Oval Base | 4830 |
| Flask, Donut, Signed, H.T. Kellogg, Ohio, c.1850, 8 In. | 300 |
| Flowerpot, 2 Slip Tulips, Rope Twist Handles, Square Rim, J. Bell, Pennsylvania, 11 In. | 900 |
| Flowerpot, Stand, Crimped Rim, Molded Band, Orange, Brown Glaze, Pa., c.1845, 8 x 10 In. | 540 |
| Jar, Apple Butter, Oval, Handle, D. Swope & Son, c.1860, 6 ⅞ In. | 431 |
| Jar, Cobalt Blue Tulip, Leaves, 3 Neck Rings, Handles, Md., c.1850, 3 Gal., 15 x 8 In. | 207 |
| Jar, Creamer, Cream, Brown, Green Splash Glaze, S. Bell & Son, Va., c.1890, 7 In. | 863 |
| Jar, Cylindrical, Squared Rim, Impressed, John Bell, Waynesboro, Pa., c.1850, 4 ¾ In. | 210 |
| Jar, Green & Brown Mottled Glaze, Cream Ground, Shenandoah Valley, Va., 1800s, 4 ¾ In. | 2160 |

**Radio,** Philco, Model 46, Tombstone, Wood Case, AM, 1931
$120

Victorian Casino Antiques

**Radio,** Tesla, Talisman, Bakelite, Stamped, Czech Republic, 1950s, 6 ½ x 11 ¼ In.
$875

Rago Arts & Auction Center

**Radio,** Walter Dorwin, Teague Sparton, Glass, Metal, Wood, Blue, c.1936, 9 x 18 In.
$2,250

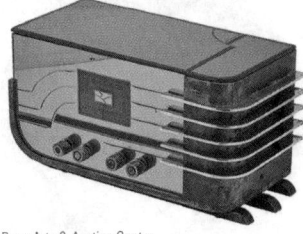

Rago Arts & Auction Center

**Radio,** Zenith, Model 6D030WZ, Molded Plywood Case, Eames, c.1946, 7 ¾ x 13 ½ In.
$189

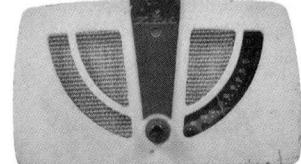

Conestoga Auction Co., Inc.

R

**Red Wing,** Vase, Bud, U Shape, Double, Woman, Between Holders, Impressed, 10¾ In.
$316

Humler & Nolan

---

**Redware,** Mold, Turks, Loop Handles, Glazed, 15½ In.
$24

Conestoga Auction Co., Inc.

---

**Rookwood,** Vase, Fish, Crabs, Gold Netting, Limoges Glaze, M.L. Nichols, 1883, 14 In.
$5,290

Humler & Nolan

---

**Rookwood,** Bookends, Elephant, Celadon Glaze, McDonald, 1918, 4½ In.
$390

Cowan's Auctions

| | |
|---|---:|
| **Jar,** Impressed W. McLeen, Glazed Interior, 19th Century, 6¾ In. | 63 |
| **Jar,** Incised Wave, Yellow Slip, Bulbous, 2 Strap Handles, c.1800, 7 x 8 In. | 488 |
| **Jar,** Lid, Green Glaze, Flecked, Oval, New England, c.1800, 6 In. | 8640 |
| **Jar,** Manganese Dropped Tulips, Stamped Upton M. Bell, Handles, c.1890, 4 Gal., 14 x 10 In. | 1380 |
| **Jar,** Manganese, Lead, 3 Incised Bands, Rounded Rim, Gal., c.1840, 10 x 5 In. | 288 |
| **Jar,** Mottled Glaze, Swollen Shape, Flared Rim, New England, 19th Century, 11 In. | 300 |
| **Jar,** Orange Yellow Ground, Brushed Manganese Mottled Glaze, c.1810, 10½ x 9½ In. | 1540 |
| **Jar,** Rolled Rim, Smith Womeldorf, 5¼ In. | 60 |
| **Jar,** Slip Trail, Yellow, Copper, Manganese, Green Bands, Oval, Strap Handles, c.1800, 8 x 6 In. | 403 |
| **Jar,** Storage, Manganese Glazed, Molded Lip, Oval, Turned Rings, 1800s, 8½ In. | 59 |
| **Jar,** Storage, Mottled Glaze, Splayed Rim, Oval Body, Applied Ear Handles, Pa., 1800s, 8½ In. | 118 |
| **Jar,** Tin Lid, Adam & Eve, Sgraffito, Greg Shooner, 12 In. | 1180 |
| **Jar,** Wave Band, Tapered Oval Shape, Mask Handles, Pa., c.1845, ½ Gal., 8 x 4 In. | 288 |
| **Jug,** Green, Orange Speckled Glaze, Loop Handles, 9 In. | 480 |
| **Jug,** Green, Orange, Manganese Sponging, Cylindrical, Footed, New Eng., c.1845, 9⅞ In. | 345 |
| **Jug,** Harvest, Sgraffito, Perched Bird, Floral Tree, 14 In. | 118 |
| **Jug,** Manganese Splotches, Oval, 8½ In. | 390 |
| **Jug,** Manganese, Lead Glaze, Double Ridge Strap Handle, New Eng., c.1820, Gal., 11 In. | 460 |
| **Jug,** Mottled Glaze, Bulbous, Tapered, Strap Handled, New Hampshire, 7½ In. | 300 |
| **Jug,** Mottled Orange, Brown, Green Glaze, Incised Neckband, 1800s, 6 In. | 960 |
| **Jug,** Olive Green Glaze, Peach Spots, Reeded Strap Handle, Flaring Lip, c.1800, 10½ In. | 652 |
| **Jug,** Oval, 5 Concentric Lines, Loop Handle, 13 In. | 360 |
| **Jug,** Oval, Stamped E.J. Miller, c.1870, 2 Gal., 14 In. | 104 |
| **Jug,** Sgraffito Eagle, Dotted Line Border, Coggled Rim, Bulbous, Flared, Glazed, 7½ In. | 554 |
| **Jug,** Splotchy Glaze, Oval, Applied Handle, 10½ In. | 300 |
| **Loaf Pan,** Blessed Are Poor In Spirit For Thars Is The Kingdom Of Heven, c.1850, 13 x 11 In. | 13800 |
| **Loaf Pan,** Coggled Rim, Looping & Wavy Lines, c.1840, 11¾ x 7⅞ In. | 431 |
| **Loaf Pan,** Trailing Slip Wavy Bands, Manganese Splotching, 1800s, 15 x 10½ In. | 510 |
| **Loaf Pan,** Yellow Slip, Coggled Rim, c.1810, 17 x 12 In. | 518 |
| **Loaf Pan,** Yellow Slip, Copper Splotches, c.1800, 2¾ x 11 In. | 431 |
| **Loaf Pan,** Yellow Slip, Oval, Pa., 1800s, 11 x 15¾ In. | 2160 |
| **Match Holder,** Slip Wash, Tan & Brown Glaze, Cylindrical, Flared Foot, 1⅝ In. | 288 |
| **Milk Pan,** Cobalt Blue Feathers, Tab Handles, Baltimore, c.1880, 2 Gal., 5 x 14 In. | 431 |
| **Milk Pan,** Impressed J.L. Blaney, 4½ x 18 In. | 1320 |
| **Mixing Bowl,** Manganese, Ribbed, Green Slip, Handles, Maryland, 4¾ x 13 In. | 840 |
| **Mold,** Food, Fish Shape, Glazed Interior, Scales, Fins, Trestle Legs, 1800s, 12 In. | 295 |
| **Mold,** Turks, Loop Handles, Glazed, 15½ In. ............................................*illus* | 24 |
| **Pie Plate,** Sgraffito Lady & Gentleman, Flowers, Inscription, 1805, 12 In. | 6250 |
| **Pie Plate,** Sgraffito, Tulips, Green, Yellow, Blue, Undulating Border, J. Neis, c.1820, 10 In. | 33750 |
| **Pie Plate,** Yellow Slip Decorated, Coggled Rim, Concentric Rings, Dots, c.1810, 9 In. | 584 |
| **Pie Plate,** Yellow Slip Squiggles, Pennsylvania, 1800s, 6⅜ In. | 123 |
| **Pipe Bowl,** Green & Yellow Marbleized Slip Decoration, 1800s, 3 In. | 2160 |
| **Pitcher,** Fish, Tail Looped To Touch Head, Red, Silver, Black Paint, c.1925, 7 In. | 115 |
| **Pitcher,** Green & Brown Splotching, Cream Ground, Shenandoah Valley, 1800s, 8½ In. | 600 |
| **Pitcher,** Green Glaze, Bulbous, Stahls Pottery, 1938, 6½ In. | 153 |
| **Pitcher,** Green, Brown, Red, Cream Splash Glaze, Flared, Richard Bell, Va., c.1890, 7 In. | 4888 |
| **Pitcher,** Lead Glaze, Manganese Splotch, Cylindrical, Round Hill Pottery, 7 In. | 2530 |
| **Pitcher,** Manganese Glaze, Squat, 3 Bead Rings, Strap Handle, c.1805, Gal., 9 In. | 374 |
| **Pitcher,** Manganese Streaks, Footed, Flared, 1800, 2 In. | 115 |
| **Pitcher,** Marbled Manganese Glaze, Oval, Flared Collar, Pa., c.1860, 3½ In. | 173 |
| **Pitcher,** Mottled Green, Brown, Cream, Shenandoah Valley, c.1860, 10 In. | 840 |
| **Pitcher,** Mottled Red, Green, Slip Wash, Incised Shoulder Ring, Strasburg, Va., c.1890, 8 x 4 In. | 805 |
| **Pitcher,** Slip Wash, Lead, Copper & Manganese Glaze, Spur Handle, Virginia, 11 In. | 8625 |
| **Planter,** Hanging, Bowl Shape, Crimped Rim Chain Holes, c.1875, 4 x 12 In. | 92 |
| **Plate,** 11 Yellow Slip Designs, Pa., c.1890, 9 In. | 863 |
| **Plate,** ABC, Coggled Rim, c.1840, 9 In. | 489 |
| **Plate,** Coggle Rim, Yellow Slip Wavy Line, Pa., 1800s, 11¾ In. | 413 |
| **Plate,** Coggle Rim, Yellow Slip, Wavy Line, Clef, Pa., 1800s, 10 In. | 708 |
| **Plate,** Manganese Splotching, Pennsylvania, 1800s, 9 In. | 62 |
| **Plate,** Rolled Rim, Wave Decoration, Copper Dotting, c.1830, 9 In. | 1380 |
| **Plate,** Scalloped Edge, Slip Decorated Center Star, Asterisks, Initials, Pa., 1800s, 6¾ In. | 960 |
| **Plate,** Sgraffito Stag, Red, Yellow, Green, Pa., c.1900, 9½ In. | 240 |
| **Plate,** Sgraffito, Center Star, Incised Swag Rim, Pennsylvania, c.1810, 7¼ In. | 720 |
| **Plate,** Sgraffito, Potted Tulip, Solomon Grimm, Berks County, Pa., c.1820, 9¾ In. | 21600 |
| **Plate,** Slip Trail Dot & Circle Decoration, Chester County, 1800s, 9 In. | 1680 |

R

| | |
|---|---|
| **Plate,** Wavy Yellow Slip, 4 Flowers, Coggled Rim, Pa., 10¾ In. | 690 |
| **Plate,** Wavy Yellow Slip, Coggled Rim, Pa., c.1845, 4 In. | 748 |
| **Plate,** Wavy Yellow Slip, Coggled Rim, Pa., c.1860, 4 In. | 1495 |
| **Plate,** Yellow Slip, Copper Splashes, Crisscrossed, c.1800, 1½ x 9 In. | 403 |
| **Plate,** Yellow Slip Lines, Waves, Coggled Rim, Lead Glaze, 1800s, 2 x 11 In. | 288 |
| **Plate,** Yellow Slip, Lines, Waves, Lead Glaze, c.1800, 1½ x 9 In. | 863 |
| **Plate,** Yellow Slip, Manganese Pea Pod Design, Lead Glaze, Pa., c.1820, 6 In. | 489 |
| **Platter,** Slip Swags, Zigzag Lines, Coggle Wheel Rim, 1800s, Pa., 10 x 13¼ In. | 354 |
| **Porringer,** Manganese Slashes, Ribbed Handles, New England, c.1820, 3¼ In. | 86 |
| **Porringer,** Slip Wash, Strap Handle, Stamped, Baecher, c.1870, 3 Gal., 4 x 4 In. | 403 |
| **Pot Saucer,** Manganese, Slip Wash, Baecher, c.1887, 1 x 5½ In. | 288 |
| **Rattle,** Bird Form, Incised Oval Base, Pennsylvania, 19th Century, 3 x 4 In. | 1500 |
| **Sauceboat,** Glazed, Heart Shape, 1800s, 2½ x 7½ In. | 944 |
| **Stew Pot,** No. 3, Rolled Rim, Footed, Stamped John Safford, Maine, c.1840, 6 x 4 In. | 1840 |
| **Strainer,** Slip Decorated, Round, Yellow, Brown Striped, 4 Wavy Lines, 1800s, 11¼ In. | 2214 |
| **Sugar,** Cover, Lead, Copper & Manganese Glaze, Oval, Footed, Ear Handles, 4½ In. | 1840 |
| **Sugar,** Lid, Bird Finial, Nest Shape Bowl, c.1870, 7½ In. | 259 |
| **Sugar,** Lid, Green, Orange, White Slip, Oval, Squat, Alamance County, N.C., c.1800, 10 In. | 35650 |
| **Sugar,** Lid, Green, Yellow, Black Mottled Glaze, Finial, Handle, Pa., c.1810, 4 In. | 154 |
| **Sugar,** Sponged Manganese, Flower Stamped Handles, Pedestal Base, 1800s, 4½ x 5½ In. | 259 |
| **Teapot,** Dome Lid, Coggled, Footed, Gooseneck Spout, 19th Century, 6½ In. | 776 |
| **Trivet,** Embossed Eagle Flower, John Bell Pottery, Pa., c.1850, 7¼ In. | 240 |
| **Trivet,** Flowers, Grapes, Mottled, Round, Stamped John Bell, Waynesboro, Pa., 8⅜ In. | 6990 |
| **Trivet,** Sponged Manganese, Serrated, Coggled Rim, Round, 8-Footed, John Bell, c.1850, 8 In. | 460 |
| **Tub,** Butter, Mottled Glaze, Diagonally Striped Band, Down-Turned Handles, J. Bell, 7 In. | 780 |
| **Umbrella Stand,** Tree Trunk Shape, Vine, Black, Yellow Paint, c.1910, 21 x 9 In. | 288 |
| **Urn,** 8 Spheres, Black, Handles, Crosswicks, N.J., Dated 1852, 13 In. | 780 |
| **Urn,** Applied Roses, Paint, Loop Handles, Mid-Atlantic, c.1876, 14 In. | 288 |
| **Urn,** Brushed Copper Double Swag, Flowers, Stamped S. Bell & Son, 13 x 9 In. | 2185 |
| **Urn,** Tea, Faux Bois, Brown, Applied Yellow Flowers, England, 1902, 17½ In. | 246 |
| **Vase,** Mottled Glaze, Double Handle, Bulbous, Flared Top, Jacob Medinger, 10¾ In. | 266 |
| **Vase,** Mottled Green, Orange, Tooled Rim, Loop Handles, c.1840, 9½ In. | 259 |
| **Vase,** Pedestal, Applied Whistle At Shoulder, 19th Century, 3½ In. | 546 |
| **Vase,** Shenandoah Valley Style, Glaze, Applied Bird, Flowers, Oval, Tall Collar, 8¼ In. | 35 |
| **Wall Pocket,** Manganese Splotch, Applied Bird & 3 Flowers, Arched Handle, 7 In. | 3335 |
| **Water Cooler,** Copper, Glazed, Slip Wash, Mask, Spigot, Twist Handles, Va., c.1880, 18 x 16 In. | 978 |
| **Whistle,** Stylized Bird Shape, Glazed, Pa., 2¼ x 5¼ In. | 720 |

**RIDGWAY** pottery has been made in the Staffordshire district in England since 1808 by a series of companies with the name Ridgway. Ridgway became part of Royal Doulton in the 1960s. The transfer-design dinner sets are the most widely known product. Other pieces of Ridgway may be listed under Flow Blue.

| | |
|---|---|
| **Chamber Pot,** Japanese Boys, Bow & Arrows, Palm Trees, Brown, c.1880, 10 x 5 In. | 125 |
| **Chop Plate,** Blue Willow, Village, Love Birds, c.1920, 12½ In. | 75 |
| **Jug,** Hunt Scene, Hound Handle, Relief, Scalloped Banner, Green, c.1835, 6⅜ In. | 495 |
| **Pitcher,** Jousting Knights, Pewter Hinged Lid, Footed, c.1840, 6¾ In. | 595 |
| **Pitcher,** Neoclassical Scenes, Raised Panels, Spout Rim, Lavender, Gilt, c.1840, 4½ In. | 395 |
| **Pitcher,** Stagecoach, Horse & Rider, Amber, 3¼ In. | 39 |
| **Plate,** Blue Pearlware Glaze, Boat On River, House, c.1840, 7½ In. | 65 |
| **Plate,** Botanicals, Hunter Green Scalloped Border, Gilt, 1840, 10 In. | 275 |
| **Plate,** Dinner, Roslyn, Multicolor Transfer Flowers, Leaves, 10¾ In., 12 Piece | 39 |
| **Plate,** Green Transferware, Ships, Working River, Grecian Scene, c.1830, 9¾ In. | 50 |
| **Platter,** View From Port Putnam, Hudson River, Purple Transferware, Staffordshire, 15 In. | 92 |
| **Platter,** Wadham College, Blue & White, Flower Border, 8-Sided, c.1835, 17 x 12 In. | 486 |
| **Washbowl & Pitcher,** Corinthian Pattern, c.1820, Child's | 120 |

**RIVIERA** dinnerware was made by the Homer Laughlin Co. of Newell, West Virginia, from 1938 to 1950. The pattern was similar in coloring and in mood to Fiesta and Harlequin. The Riviera plates and cup handles were square. For more prices, go to kovels.com.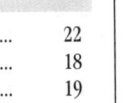

| | |
|---|---|
| **Ivory,** Creamer | 22 |
| **Red,** Baker, 6 x 9 In. | 18 |
| **Yellow,** Creamer | 19 |
| **Yellow,** Cup, Footed | 21 |
| **Yellow,** Pepper | 19 |

**Rookwood,** Fountain, Child & Dolphin, Faience, c.1910, 32¾ x 22 In.
$2,714

Brunk Auctions

**Rookwood,** Jug, Sparrow, Oriental Grasses, Gold Highlights, A. Valentien, 1884, 8 In.
$1,035

Humler & Nolan

**Rookwood,** Pencil Holder, Panels, Birds, Flowers, Geometrics, 6-Sided, Conant, 1900s, 5 In.
$210

Cowan's Auctions

R

**Rookwood,** Plaque, Scenic, River, Trees, Vellum Glaze, Marked, E.T. Hurley, 11 x 8 In.
$5,000

Rago Arts & Auction Center

---

**Rookwood,** Tray, Fish, Bird, Weeds, Blue, Martin Rettig, 1884, 5¾ In.
$431

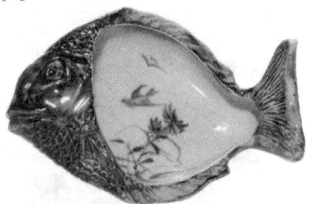

Humler & Nolan

---

**TIP**

*Mayonnaise can be used to remove old masking tape, stickers, or labels from glass or china.*

---

**Rookwood,** Vase, Flowers, Anniversary Glaze, Jens Jensen, 1931, 7 In.
$575

Humler & Nolan

---

**ROCKINGHAM,** in the United States, is a pottery with a brown glaze that resembles tortoiseshell. It was made from 1840 to 1900 by many American potteries. Mottled brown Rockingham wares were first made in England at the Rockingham factory. Other types of ceramics were also made by the English firm. Related pieces may be listed in the Bennington category.

| | |
|---|---:|
| **Crock,** Winged Feather, Cobalt Blue, 2 Incised Rings, Va., c.1855, 9 x 9 In., 2 Gal. | 431 |
| **Figurine,** Dog, Spaniel, Sitting, Brown Glaze, c.1875, 10¼ In. | 540 |
| **Pitcher,** Triple Tulip, Cobalt Blue, Va., c.1860, 10 x 4¾ In., Gal. | 431 |

---

**ROGERS**, *see John Rogers category.*

---

**ROOKWOOD** pottery was made in Cincinnati, Ohio, beginning in 1880. All of this art pottery is marked, most with the famous flame mark. The *R* is reversed and placed back to back with the letter *P*. Flames surround the letters. After 1900, a Roman numeral was added to the mark to indicate the year. The company went bankrupt in 1941. It was bought and sold several times after that. For several years various owners tried to revive the pottery, but by 1967 it was out of business. The name and some of the molds were bought by a collector in 1982. In 2005, a group of Cincinnati investors bought the company and 3,700 original molds, the name, and trademark. Martin and Marilyn Wade bought the company in 2011. Today they make new items and remake some old items, architectural tile, art pottery, and special commissions. Pieces are marked with the RP mark and a Roman numeral for the four-digit date.

| | |
|---|---:|
| **Ashtray,** Bat Shape, Orange Brown Matte Glaze, 1928, 2⅛ x 6⅛ In. | 863 |
| **Ashtray,** Rook Shape, Green Glaze, Impressed, 1914, 7 In. | 420 |
| **Bookends,** Buddha, Seated, Green, Blue Matte Glaze, William P. McDonald, 1930, 7 In. | 978 |
| **Bookends,** Cornucopia, Matte & Gloss Glaze, Logo, 1945, 5 In. | 805 |
| **Bookends,** Elephant, Celadon Glaze, McDonald, 1918, 4½ In. ............*illus* | 390 |
| **Bookends,** Fruit, Brown Over Tan Matte Glaze, Shirayamadani, 1937, 3 In. | 460 |
| **Bookends,** Horse Head, Ivory Matte Glaze, William McDonald, 1934, 6⅛ In. | 316 |
| **Bookends,** Lotus, Blue Matte Glaze, 1935, 3⅝ In. | 173 |
| **Bookends,** Owl, Standing On Book, Taupe Glaze, Impressed, 1941, 6 x 4 In. | 184 |
| **Bookends,** Pelican, Blue Matte Glaze, 1923, 7 In. | 2530 |
| **Bookends,** Puppy, Seated, Head Down, Tan Glaze, Louise Abel Mark, 1928, 5 In. | 161 |
| **Bookends,** Rook, Blue Over Blue Matte Glaze, Logo, 1927, 5⅜ In. | 518 |
| **Bookends,** Rook, Facing Left, Blue Glaze, 1921, 6 x 5 x 6 In. | 525 |
| **Bookends,** Rook, Ivory Glaze, William McDonald, 1943, 5½ In. | 240 |
| **Bookends,** Turkey, Coromandel Glaze, Arthur Conant, 1933, 5⅝ In. | 3680 |
| **Bowl,** Blue Glaze, Cascading Micro Crystalline Glaze, 1928, 3 x 5 In. | 115 |
| **Bowl,** Blue, Rooks, Animals, Flowers, Relief Design On Shoulder, c.1927, 8 x 3 In. | 121 |
| **Bowl,** Brown Matte Glaze, Round, Squat, 1921, 9½ In. | 150 |
| **Bowl,** Butterfat, Geometrics, 6-Pointed Star, Lorinda Epply, 1930, 2½ x 10½ In. | 403 |
| **Bowl,** Floral Ring On Shoulder, Matte Glaze, Charles Todd, 1913, 5⅛ x 7¼ In. | 518 |
| **Bowl,** Flowers, Yellow, Green, Brown, Flared Rim, S. Sax, 1927, 5½ x 7¾ In. | 2000 |
| **Bowl,** Leaping Rabbits At Rim, Green Over Rose Matte Glazes, 1920, 2⅜ x 5 In. | 173 |
| **Bowl,** Rooks In Flight Border, Green Matte Glaze, 1918, 3½ x 6¾ In. | 489 |
| **Bowl,** Roses, Yellow, Glaze, Edith Hoonan, 1905, 5½ In. | 173 |
| **Box,** Lid, Flowers, Blue & Brown, Green Ground, Lorinda Epply, 1926, 2¾ x 4 In. | 345 |
| **Candlestick,** Classical Columns, Green Over Blue Matte Glaze, 1920, 13 In., Pair | 230 |
| **Candlestick,** Columnar, Cherubs, Flower Garlands, Matte Glaze, 1922, 13 In., Pair | 230 |
| **Centerpiece,** Multicolor Flowers, Glossy Glaze, Green Matte Leaves, 1921, 11 In. | 1380 |
| **Cherub,** Wall Pocket, Orange, Green, Putto In Oval, 11¾ In. | 63 |
| **Ewer,** Blossoms, Ivory, Green, Stems, Yellow, Orange, Shirayamadani, c.1889, 23 In. | 938 |
| **Ewer,** Flower On Shoulders, Dark Brown, Ed Diers, c.1898, 6 In. | 180 |
| **Ewer,** Flowers, Dogwood, Standard Glaze, Wavy Rim, J. Zettel, 1893, 9 x 7 In. | 344 |
| **Ewer,** Mums, Gold, Glazed, Silver Overlay, William P. McDonald, 1892, 9 In. | 2070 |
| **Ewer,** Mums, Gold, Leaves, Orange, Brown, Silver Overlay, 1894, 10 In. | 3105 |
| **Fountain,** Child & Dolphin, Faience, c.1910, 32¾ x 22 In. .........*illus* | 2714 |
| **Humidor,** Lid, Standard Glaze, Pipes, Cigars, Grace Young, 1896, 7 In. | 390 |
| **Jar,** Lid, White, 1943, 3¾ In. | 173 |
| **Jardiniere,** Mountain, Forest, Gold, Orange, Beige, Bulbous, 1882, 11 x 12 In. | 1150 |
| **Jug,** Portrait, Buffalo Horn, Comanche, Sadie Markland, 1898, 6 In. | 3105 |
| **Jug,** Puzzle, Portrait, Black Man, Standard Glaze, Pierced Band, G. Young, 1897, 5 In. | 1375 |
| **Jug,** Sparrow, Oriental Grasses, Gold Highlights, A. Valentien, 1884, 8 In. .........*illus* | 1035 |
| **Lilacs,** Purple, Green & Lilac Ground, Iris Glaze, Albert Valentien, 1904, 11⅜ In. | 5175 |
| **Mug,** Corn & Wheat, Standard Glaze, 3 Handles, Mary Nourse, 1900, 5 x 6 In. | 250 |
| **Mug,** Flowers, Carved, Green Matte Glaze, John Wareham, 1901, 5 In. | 173 |

| | |
|---|---|
| **Mug**, Holly Leaves, Berries, Red, Green, Incised, Matte Glaze, 1907, 6 In. | 489 |
| **Paperweight**, Cardinal, Perched On Branch, HF, 1946, 7 1/8 In. | 242 |
| **Paperweight**, Cat, Seated, Green Matte Glaze, Louis Abel, 1941, 6 3/4 In. | 431 |
| **Paperweight**, Dog, Seated, Tan Glaze, 1946, 4 3/4 In. | 184 |
| **Paperweight**, Green Matte, 1920, 4 1/2 In. | 431 |
| **Paperweight**, Mandarin Duck, Ivory Matte Glaze, Arthur Conant, 1933, 2 3/8 In. | 184 |
| **Paperweight**, Rook, Advertising, Brown Matte Glaze, 4 In. | 1150 |
| **Pencil Holder**, Panels, Birds, Flowers, Geometrics, 6-Sided, Conant, 1900s, 5 In. ............*illus* | 210 |
| **Pipe Tamper**, Mummy In Sarcophagus Shape, E.T. Hurley, 2 5/8 In. | 403 |
| **Pitcher**, 2-Tone, Berries, Branch, Gloss Glaze, Fred Rothenbusch, c.1901, 4 1/4 In. | 180 |
| **Pitcher**, Fish, Sea Grass, Blue, Green Matte Glazes, Albert Pons, 1907, 4 1/4 In. | 863 |
| **Plaque**, Cherry Blossoms, Blue Glaze, Frame, E.T. Hurley, 1920, 11 x 16 In. | 2432 |
| **Plaque**, Chrysanthemums, Sea Green Glaze, A. Valentien, 1896, Frame, 9 x 13 In. | 7320 |
| **Plaque**, Portrait, Man, Standard Glaze, Frame, S. Laurence, 1898, 16 x 12 In. | 1875 |
| **Plaque**, River Scene, Vellum Glaze, Frame, L. Asbury, 1920, 10 x 13 In. | 4270 |
| **Plaque**, Scenic, River, Trees, Vellum Glaze, Marked, E.T. Hurley, 11 x 8 In. ...........*illus* | 5000 |
| **Plaque**, Trees, Dirt Road, Vellum Gaze, Frame, Lorinda Epply, c.1917, 9 1/4 x 5 In. | 2645 |
| **Plaque**, Vase, Trumpet Flowers, Orange, Standard Glaze, K. Shirayamadani, 1902, 12 x 7 In. | 1125 |
| **Plaque**, Winter Scene, Snowy Pine Trees, Vellum Glaze, Sallie Coyne, 1914, 11 x 8 1/2 In. | 6900 |
| **Plaque**, Woman, Standing, Iris Glaze, K. Shirayamadani, 1896, 12 x 9 In. | 3125 |
| **Plaque**, Woods, River, Vellum, Fred Rothenbusch, 1920, 12 x 9 In. | 3250 |
| **Teapot**, Art Nouveau, White, Blue Fluid Rim, Sara Sax, 1909, 6 1/4 In. | 1840 |
| **Tile**, 3 Seahorses, Green Matte Glaze, Square, Faience, Frame, 8 In. | 1586 |
| **Tile**, Birches, Scenic, Vellum, Lenore Asbury, Frame, c.1927, 11 1/2 x 9 3/8 In. | 3068 |
| **Tile**, Bounty Ships, Sea, Blue, Brown, Tan, Faience, 8 x 8 In. | 390 |
| **Tile**, Elephant, Molded, Brown Matte Glaze, 1919, 3 3/4 In. | 259 |
| **Tile**, Landscape, Trees, Lakes, Carved, Square, 12 In. | 1342 |
| **Tile**, Leaf, Molded, Green Leathery Matte Glaze, Faience, 6 x 6 In. | 374 |
| **Tile**, Scottish Rose, Earth Tones, Faience, Arts & Crafts Frame, 4 Tiles, 24 x 6 In. | 920 |
| **Tile**, Tea, Girl, Blond, Yellow Hat, Sitting In Garden, 1940, 5 1/4 In. | 230 |
| **Tile**, Urn & Grapes, Carved, Green & Blue Matte Glaze, Frame, 12 x 6 In. | 915 |
| **Tile**, Wisteria, Faience, Carved, 10 x 11 1/2 In. | 2760 |
| **Tray**, Fish, Bird, Weeds, Blue, Martin Rettig, 1884, 5 3/4 In. ............*illus* | 431 |
| **Trivet**, Blue Glossy Glaze, Scrolling Design, Logo, 1953, 5 3/4 In. | 92 |
| **Trivet**, Sea Gulls, White Ground, Turquoise Glaze Depicting Sky, Round, Stamped, 5 3/4 In. | 121 |
| **Vase**, 3 Peacock Feathers, Green, Plum, Blue, Oval, Sara Sax, 1916, 10 3/4 In. | 3125 |
| **Vase**, 5 Repeating Rook Panels, Puce Matte Glaze, 1921, 7 3/8 In. | 431 |
| **Vase**, Abstract, Blue, White, Brown, Black, Jens Jensen, 1943, 7 3/8 In. | 518 |
| **Vase**, Apple Blossoms, Iris Glaze, Marked Sallie E. Coyne, c.1910, 7 3/4 In. | 690 |
| **Vase**, Apple Blossoms, Iris Glaze, Sallie E. Coyne, 1906, 7 3/4 In. | 690 |
| **Vase**, Art Deco, Horses, Celadon Glossy Glaze, Wilhelmine Rehm, 1945, 4 1/2 In. | 115 |
| **Vase**, Art Deco, Matte Glaze, Slip Applied Shapes, Apricot Glaze, Wilhelmine Rehm, 7 1/2 In. | 575 |
| **Vase**, Arts & Crafts, Stylized, Green Ground, Blue, Matte Glaze, Squat, 1907, 4 In. | 345 |
| **Vase**, Asters, Standard Glaze, Cylindrical, K. Shirayamadani, 1902, 11 1/2 x 4 In. | 1875 |
| **Vase**, Bearded Iris, Iris Glaze, Cylindrical, Swollen, Lenore Asbury, 1906, 10 x 5 In. | 1586 |
| **Vase**, Beige Mottled Glaze, 3 Handles, Stamped, c.1921, 3 x 4 In. | 276 |
| **Vase**, Beige, Matte, Incised Flowers, Tapered, 1937, 8 In. | 127 |
| **Vase**, Bellflowers, Green, Aventurine, Lorinda Epply, 1920, 11 1/4 In. | 690 |
| **Vase**, Bengal Brown Glaze, Gray White Glaze Drip, Rust Ground, 1951, 14 In. | 230 |
| **Vase**, Blossoms, Rust, Cream, Blue Ground, Jens Jensen, 1934, 4 1/2 In. | 575 |
| **Vase**, Blossoms, White, Blue Ground, Cylindrical, Footed, Jens Jensen, 8 1/2 In. | 138 |
| **Vase**, Blue Over Tan Glaze, Crystalline, 1928, 3 In. | 259 |
| **Vase**, Bud, Autumn Leaves, Standard Glaze, Wide Squat Base, C. Schmidt, 6 In. | 546 |
| **Vase**, Cabbage Rose, Blue, Green, White Ground, Margaret McDonald, 1944, 5 1/2 In. | 288 |
| **Vase**, Carnation, Red, Brown, Standard Glaze, 1898, 20 In. | 1035 |
| **Vase**, Carnations, White, Vellum Glaze, Fred Rothenbusch, 1906, 8 In. | 1725 |
| **Vase**, Cherry Branch, Green To Ivory Ground, Vellum Glaze, Ed Diers, 1907, 9 In. | 690 |
| **Vase**, Clematis, Blue, Pink Ground, High Shouldered, C. Covalenco, 1925, 8 x 5 In. | 1063 |
| **Vase**, Clematis, Blue, Repeating Scroll, Arthur Conant, 1919, 7 In. | 2530 |
| **Vase**, Clover, Molded, Yellow Matte Glaze, Logo, 1929, 6 1/4 In. | 288 |
| **Vase**, Clover, Vellum Glaze, Tapered, Flared Rim, F. Rothenbusch, 1908, 8 3/4 In. | 750 |
| **Vase**, Cobalt Blue, White, Checkered Pattern, Sara Sax, 1923, 8 1/2 In. | 334 |
| **Vase**, Collie, Brown, Standard Glaze, E.T. Hurley, Logo, 1904, 9 3/4 In. | 677 |
| **Vase**, Cornucopia, Chartreuse Matte Glaze, 1936, 8 3/4 In., Pair | 288 |
| **Vase**, Crocus, Vellum Glaze, Oval, K. Shirayamadani, 1935, 6 x 4 In. | 1125 |

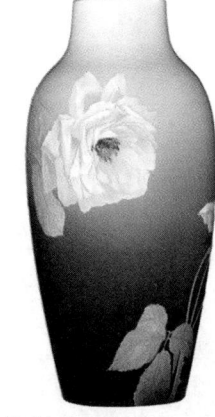

**Rookwood,** Vase, Roses, Iris Glaze, Albert Valentien, 1904, 12 1/2 x 6 In.
$2,375

Rago Arts & Auction Center

**Rookwood,** Vase, Sparrow, Oriental Grasses, Die Stamped Collar, Fired On Gold, 1885, 9 In.
$345

Humler & Nolan

**Rorstrand,** Vase, Blossoming Branches, Petal Rim, Marked, c.1900, 19 x 7 In.
$1,750

Rago Arts & Auction Center

R

**Rose Mandarin,** Jar, Lid, Historical Scenes, Flowers, Gilt, Porcelain, 1800s, 24 In.
$1,896

James D. Julia Auctioneers

**Rose Mandarin,** Platter, Scholars, Flower Border, Birds & Flowers, 1800s, 14½ In.
$593

James D. Julia Auctioneers

**Rose Mandarin,** Vase, Orange Leaves, Gilt Dragons, 1800s, 10 In.
$246

Skinner Auctioneers & Appraisers

| | |
|---|---|
| **Vase,** Cyclamen, Gold, Orange, Green, Vellum Glaze, Lorinda Epply, 1907, 7 In. | 288 |
| **Vase,** Daisies, Incised, Brown Matte Glaze, Rose Fechheimer, 1905, 10 In. | 546 |
| **Vase,** Daisies, Iris Glaze, Elongated Oval, Sara Sax, 1905, 10 x 5 In. | 1830 |
| **Vase,** Daisies, Leaf & Lattice, Glaze, Silver Overlay, Squat, W. McDonald, 9 In. | 2440 |
| **Vase,** Daisies, Red, Yellow, Green, Brown Matte Glaze, Rose Fechheimer, c.1905, 10 In. | 431 |
| **Vase,** Daylilies, Margaret McDonald, Logo, 1943, 8 In. | 1150 |
| **Vase,** Fawns, Blue, Flowers, Pink, Blue, Brown, Matte Glaze, Elizabeth Barrett, 1945, 8 In. | 3220 |
| **Vase,** Fish, Crabs, Gold Netting, Limoges Glaze, M.L. Nichols, 1883, 14 In. *illus* | 5290 |
| **Vase,** Fish, Dancing, Brown Matte Glaze, 1915, 8⅜ In. | 1725 |
| **Vase,** Fish, White, Red Mottled Ground, Jens Jensen, Logo, 1932, 5¾ In. | 1495 |
| **Vase,** Fish, Yellow Tint, Monogram, Lorinda Epply, 1931, 12 In. | 345 |
| **Vase,** Flower Band At Shoulder, Matte Glaze, Rose Ground, Charles Todd, 1919, 5¾ In. | 316 |
| **Vase,** Flower, Blue, Stick Neck, Jens Jensen, 1947, 10 x 4½ In. | 406 |
| **Vase,** Flower, Dogwood, Standard Glaze, Tapered, A.D. Sehon, 1902, 6 x 4 In. | 250 |
| **Vase,** Flower, Exotic, Standard Glaze, Kataro Shirayamadani, Logo, 1894, 12½ In. | 1150 |
| **Vase,** Flowers At Shoulder, Multicolor, Blue Ground, Charles Todd, 1921, 5¾ In. | 403 |
| **Vase,** Flowers, 5-Petal, Pastel, Flared Rim, Elizabeth Barrett, 1945, 5⅛ In. | 489 |
| **Vase,** Flowers, Anniversary Glaze, Jens Jensen, 1931, 7 In. *illus* | 575 |
| **Vase,** Flowers, At Shoulder, Blue, Green, Turquoise Matte Glaze, 1918, 4½ In. | 345 |
| **Vase,** Flowers, Blue Anniversary Glaze, Logo, Lorinda Epply, 1925, 13 In. | 2530 |
| **Vase,** Flowers, Blue Mottled Ground, Matte Glaze, Charles Todd, 1922, 5⅜ In. | 690 |
| **Vase,** Flowers, Blue, Embossed, 1927, 8 In. | 330 |
| **Vase,** Flowers, Blue, Embossed, Tapered, 1935, 6½ In. | 120 |
| **Vase,** Flowers, Blue, Green Ground, Neck Handles, W. Rehm, 1928, 10 x 7 In. | 875 |
| **Vase,** Flowers, Blue, Green Leaves, Mottled Brown Interior, Lorinda Epply, 1943, 6½ In. | 345 |
| **Vase,** Flowers, Blue, Green Leaves, Purple Ground, Elizabeth Lincoln, 1929, 13 In. | 1200 |
| **Vase,** Flowers, Blue, Purple, Pink, Brown Slip Monogram, Lorinda Epply, 1927, 6 In. | 460 |
| **Vase,** Flowers, Blue, Tapered, Bulbous, Lorinda Epply, 1932, 5 In. | 360 |
| **Vase,** Flowers, Blue, Turquoise, Bulbous, Tapered Base, 12½ In. | 184 |
| **Vase,** Flowers, Blue, Yellow, Red, Green Matte Glaze, Charles Todd, 1921, 7⅜ In. | 575 |
| **Vase,** Flowers, Carved, Blue, Red, Green, Puce Ground, Charles Todd, 1912, 10 In. | 805 |
| **Vase,** Flowers, Cascading, Vellum Glaze, Swollen Cylinder, L. Asbury, 1928, 8 In. | 976 |
| **Vase,** Flowers, Dogwood, Black Opal, Handles, Footed, H. Wilcox, 1927, 8 x 3 In. | 500 |
| **Vase,** Flowers, Dogwood, Sea Green Glaze, Squat, E.T. Hurley, 1900, 6 x 7 In. | 2684 |
| **Vase,** Flowers, Exotic, Jens Jensen, Logo, 1945, 5⅛ In. | 316 |
| **Vase,** Flowers, Gold Ground, Matte Glaze, Charles Klinger, 1925, 9 In. | 920 |
| **Vase,** Flowers, Green Matte, Rose Fechheimer, 1906, 8 In. | 253 |
| **Vase,** Flowers, Incised, Blue, Green Matte Glaze, Charles Todd, 1921, 7⅝ In. | 230 |
| **Vase,** Flowers, Incised, Maroon, Pink Matte Glaze, 1922, 7¾ In. | 345 |
| **Vase,** Flowers, Incised, Orange Ground, L. Abel, 1921, 9 x 3 In. | 438 |
| **Vase,** Flowers, Molded, Blue Matte Glaze, Logo, 1914, 11¾ In. | 690 |
| **Vase,** Flowers, Multicolor, Incised, Bulbous, Charles Todd, 1916, 4⅜ In. | 288 |
| **Vase,** Flowers, Mustard & Tan Gloss Glaze, Charles Todd, 1912, 9 In. | 230 |
| **Vase,** Flowers, Ombroso Glaze, William Hentschel, Logo, 1905, 18½ In. | 1840 |
| **Vase,** Flowers, Pink & White, Vellum Glaze, Lorinda Epply, 1907, 6 In. | 374 |
| **Vase,** Flowers, Pink To Tan Glaze, Tapered, Marked, 1930, 5 In. | 70 |
| **Vase,** Flowers, Pink, Brown Leaves, Elizabeth Barrett, 1945, 6¾ In. | 184 |
| **Vase,** Flowers, Pink, Purple, Wilhelmine Rehm, Logo, 1944, 4 In. | 230 |
| **Vase,** Flowers, Red, Lorinda Epply, 1943, 5¾ In. | 173 |
| **Vase,** Flowers, Standard Glaze, Yellow Ground, Matt Daly, 1887, 13½ In. | 127 |
| **Vase,** Flowers, Tan Shaded To Brown, Melon Ribbed, Tall Neck, Flared, 1895, 7 In. | 304 |
| **Vase,** Flowers, Turquoise Blue, Lorinda Epply, 1923, 10¾ In. | 1035 |
| **Vase,** Flowers, Vellum Glaze, Sara Sax, 1905, 7¾ In. | 805 |
| **Vase,** Flowers, Yellow Tint, Monogram, Lorinda Epply, Paper Label, 1923, 11 In. | 805 |
| **Vase,** Flowers, Yellow, Blue, Elizabeth Barrett, 1945, 6½ In. | 240 |
| **Vase,** Flowers, Yellow, Green, Blue Ground, Vellum, MM Initial, 1930, 8 In. | 1080 |
| **Vase,** Frans Hals Portrait, Standard Glaze, G. Young, 1902, 8¾ x 3½ In. | 594 |
| **Vase,** Futura, Butterscotch Brown, Tombstone Shape, Flared Base, 6 In. | 184 |
| **Vase,** Geometric Designs, Sea Green, 1939, 5½ In. | 94 |
| **Vase,** Geometric, Matte Glaze, Anna Marie Valentien, 1901, 3¾ In. | 489 |
| **Vase,** Glaze Effect, Green, Olive, Blue Drip, Flat Rim, 1932, 6¼ In. | 230 |
| **Vase,** Glaze Effect, Tan Base, Blue Drip Glaze, Bulbous, 1932, 3 In. | 184 |
| **Vase,** Glaze Effect, Yellow, Mauve Gloss Glaze, Bulbous, Footed, Logo, 1932, 4 In. | 58 |
| **Vase,** Goldenrod, Standard Glaze, Amelia Sprague, 1902, 10 In. | 1840 |
| **Vase,** Gothic Arch, Green Matte Glaze, 1922, 10¼ In. | 207 |

| | |
|---|---|
| **Vase,** Grapes, Purple, Matte Glaze, Sallie Coyne, 1925, 7 ⅝ In. | 518 |
| **Vase,** Grapes, Tapered, Base Handles, M. McDonald, 1929, 9 x 6 ½ In. | 813 |
| **Vase,** Grapes, Vines, Matte Glaze, Vera Tischler, 1920, 6 ¾ In. | 316 |
| **Vase,** Greek Key Design, Green Matte Glaze, Tooled, 1907, 10 ¼ In. | 431 |
| **Vase,** Green Over Pink Matte Glaze, Handles, 1931, 6 ½ In. | 138 |
| **Vase,** Green Over Rose Matte Glaze, Hand Tooled, Vellum, c.1909, 9 ¾ In. | 230 |
| **Vase,** Green, Blue Matte Glaze, C.S. Todd, 1913, 4 ½ In. | 184 |
| **Vase,** Green, Blue, Vellum, Charles Todd, 1919, 8 In. | 510 |
| **Vase,** Holly Sprig, Standard Glaze, Edith Felton, 7 x 4 In. | 242 |
| **Vase,** Holly, Standard Glaze, Squat, 2 Handles, W. Klemm, 2 ½ x 4 In. | 144 |
| **Vase,** Horses, Galloping, Cream, Rust, Anniversary Glaze, Jens Jensen, 1934, 5 In. | 1955 |
| **Vase,** Impressed Leaves, Blue, 1930, 4 ½ In. | 75 |
| **Vase,** Impressed Leaves, Green Matte Glaze, Tapered, 1930, 6 In. | 138 |
| **Vase,** Iris Glaze, Harriet Elizabeth Wilcox, Cincinnati, 1918, 6 ¼ In. | 540 |
| **Vase,** Iris Glaze, Logo, Sallie Coyne, 1907, 9 ½ In. | 2880 |
| **Vase,** Iris, Black Iris Glaze, Tapered, C. Schmidt, 1911, 8 x 4 ¼ In. | 6100 |
| **Vase,** Iris, Peach Flowers, Sara Sax, 1905, 7 In. | 1140 |
| **Vase,** Irises, Purple, Red, Blue, Rose, Mottled Ground, Elizabeth Lincoln, 1929, 17 In. | 3450 |
| **Vase,** Landscape, Green, Buttressed Cylinder, K. Shirayamadani, 1908, 11 x 5 In. | 1250 |
| **Vase,** Landscape, Vellum, Ed Diers, 1919, 12 ¼ In. | 863 |
| **Vase,** Laurel Leaves, Berries, Glaze, Matt Daly, 1900, 5 ⅜ In. | 6325 |
| **Vase,** Leaf & Berry, Lorinda Epply, 1943, Slip Monogram, 5 ½ In. | 288 |
| **Vase,** Leaf Band, Spiky, Blue, Mauve, Tan Matte Glaze, William Hentschel, 1914, 14 In. | 978 |
| **Vase,** Leaf Relief, Beige Matte Glaze, Insignia, c.1922, 6 x 3 ½ In. | 98 |
| **Vase,** Leaves, Berries On Shoulder, Blue Vellum Glaze, 1926, 4 ½ In. | 115 |
| **Vase,** Leaves, Berries, Red Ground, Matte Glaze, Olga Geneva Reed, 1906, 4 x 2 In. | 978 |
| **Vase,** Leaves, Brown, Blue, Slip Trail, Gold Matte Glazes, Elizabeth Barrett, 1928, 4 In. | 518 |
| **Vase,** Leaves, Geometric Shaped Sprays, Yellow Tint, Sara Sax, 1930, 6 In. | 2875 |
| **Vase,** Leaves, Green, Orange Ground, Standard Glaze, Matt Daly, 1899, 11 In. | 1093 |
| **Vase,** Leaves, Multicolor, Black Opal, Bulbous, Tapered Neck, Sara Sax, 1928, 11 ¾ In. | 4025 |
| **Vase,** Leaves, Tan Gloss, Bulbous, 1944, 6 ¾ In. | 86 |
| **Vase,** Lotus Blossom, Leaves, Incised, Mahogany Glaze, William McDonald, 1898, 8 In. | 10063 |
| **Vase,** Lotus Blossom, Pink & White Tulips, Vellum Glaze, Sallie Coyne, 1905, 10 ½ In. | 690 |
| **Vase,** Magnolia, Kataro Shirayamadani, 1946, 7 ½ In. | 805 |
| **Vase,** Mistletoe, Iris Glaze, Sara Sax, 1902, 7 ¼ In. | 1035 |
| **Vase,** Morning Glories, Matte Glaze, Sallie Coyne, 1926, 10 In. | 978 |
| **Vase,** Moth, White Iris Glaze, Elizabeth Lincoln, 1911, 6 ¼ In. | 863 |
| **Vase,** Mums, Gold, Brown, Mottled Ground, Standard Glaze, Albert Valentien, 1885, 13 In. | 633 |
| **Vase,** Narcissus, Vellum Glaze, Olga Geneva Reed, 1912, 6 In. | 489 |
| **Vase,** Narcissus, White, Double, Iris Glaze, Silver Overlay, 1905, 8 In. | 1725 |
| **Vase,** Nasturtium, Orange, Brown Ground, Elizabeth Wheldon Brail, 5 ½ In. | 246 |
| **Vase,** Oak Leaves, Acorns, Green Vellum, Lorinda Epply, 1911, 7 In. | 575 |
| **Vase,** Orange, Green Flowers, Yellow Ground, Flared, K. Jones, 1927, 11 x 7 In. | 813 |
| **Vase,** Parrots, Flowers, Multicolor, Rose Ground, E.T. Hurley, 1927, 14 ¼ In. | 1610 |
| **Vase,** Peace Lilies, Leaves, Glaze, Wilhelmine Rehm, 1944, 8 In. | 345 |
| **Vase,** Peacock Feather, Green, Purple, Vellum Glaze, Tapered, S. Sax, 1916, 11 In. | 6100 |
| **Vase,** Pillow, Pansy, Yellow, Silver Overlay, Gorham, Footed, O. Reed, 1891, 4 x 4 In. | 1500 |
| **Vase,** Poppies In Relief, Blue Matte Glaze, c.1917, 10 ½ In. | 253 |
| **Vase,** Poppies, Red, Iris Glaze, Rose Fechheimer, Logo, 1903, 5 ½ In. | 863 |
| **Vase,** Poppies, Red, Standard Glaze, Spiral Ribbed, Ruffled Rim, Shirayamadani, 1892, 8 In. | 805 |
| **Vase,** Poppy Relief, Brown Matte Glazes, Logo, 1910, 9 ¾ In. | 978 |
| **Vase,** Purple Matte Glaze, Blue Gloss Glaze Inside, Ribbed Body, 1916, 13 In. | 546 |
| **Vase,** River Landscape, Blue, Purple, Green, E. Hurley, 1916, 9 In. | 1150 |
| **Vase,** River Landscape, Green, Blue, Cylindrical, c.1917, 8 In. | 400 |
| **Vase,** Roses, Iris Glaze, Albert Valentien, 1904, 12 ½ x 6 In. ...........*illus* | 2375 |
| **Vase,** Roses, Molded, Purple Matte Glaze, Shirayamadani, 1914, 10 In. | 1093 |
| **Vase,** Roses, White, Incised, Logo, Elizabeth Barrett, 1945, 7 In. | 518 |
| **Vase,** Roses, Yellow, Standard Glaze, Lorinda Epply, 1906, 6 ¼ In. | 259 |
| **Vase,** Round, Painted Oak Leaves, Lenore Asbury, c.1920, 4 x 8 In. | 406 |
| **Vase,** Scroll, Panels, Yellow & Brown, Semigloss Glaze, Cylindrical, 1925, 9 In. | 800 |
| **Vase,** Seahorse, Bronze, Sea Green, Round, 1900, 5 x 5 ½ In. | 9375 |
| **Vase,** Seahorse, Paneled, Blue Glaze, 1929, 5 ¾ x 3 In. | 440 |
| **Vase,** Ship, Rough Seas, Vellum Glaze, Fred Rothernbusch, 1908, 10 ⅝ In. | 3450 |
| **Vase,** Ships, Carved, Green Matte Glaze, Cylindrical, W. Hentschel, 1911, 8 x 4 In. | 1500 |
| **Vase,** Sparrow, Oriental Grasses, Die Stamped Collar, Fired On Gold, 1885, 9 In. ...........*illus* | 345 |
| **Vase,** Stream, Landscape, Blue, Green Vellum Glaze, F. Rothenbusch, 1911, 15 In. | 1320 |

**Rose Medallion,** Basin, Figures, Birds, Butterflies, Flowers, 1800s, 15 ¾ x 4 ½ In. $486

James D. Julia Auctioneers

**Rosenthal,** Vase, Face, Signed, Jean Cocteau, 1952, c.1960, 8 ½ x 4 ¾ In. $338

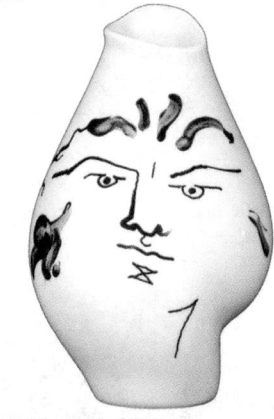

New Orleans Auction Galleries, Inc.

**Roseville,** Baneda, Vase, Footed, Green Glaze, Handles, Round, 9 ¾ x 9 In. $805

Humler & Nolan

R

**TIP**

*Bone china is a special type of porcelain that has bone ash added to the clay. This makes a stronger, whiter porcelain.*

**Roseville,** Baneda, Vase, Green,
2 Handles, Marked, 4 In.
**$403**

Humler & Nolan

**Roseville,** Blackberry, Vase, Oval Shape,
Loop Handles At Neck, 8¼ In.
**$288**

Humler & Nolan

**Roseville,** Bushberry, Vase, Blue, Round,
Twig Shape Handles, Leaves,
9 x 12¼ In.
**$316**

Humler & Nolan

| | | |
|---|---|---|
| **Vase,** Summer Landscape, Barn, Trees, Vellum Glaze, Fred Rothenbusch, 1930, 8 In. | | 805 |
| **Vase,** Swirl, Green Matte Glaze, Cylindrical, Signed DZ, 1904, 7½ In. | | 295 |
| **Vase,** Teasels, Green Ground, Iris Glaze, Albert Valentien, 1902, 14½ In. | | 7475 |
| **Vase,** Thistles, Vellum Glaze, Lenore Asbury, 1904, 5½ In. | | 575 |
| **Vase,** Thistles, White Iris Glaze, Carl Schmidt, Logo, 1909, 10¾ In. | | 2300 |
| **Vase,** Trees, Lake Shore, Vellum Glaze, Charles J. McLoughlin, 1914, 6⅜ In. | | 748 |
| **Vase,** Triangular Designs, Red, Blue Berries, Ivory Vellum Glaze, Todd, 1918, 3 In. | | 374 |
| **Vase,** Turquoise Glaze, Tapered, 1918, 15½ In., Pair | | 600 |
| **Vase,** Water Hyacinth, White, Iris Glaze, Pastel, John Dee Wareham, 1902, 12 In. | | 6325 |
| **Vase,** Water Lilies, Pink, Ivory Ground, E. Barrett, 1945, 12 x 4½ In. | | 750 |
| **Vase,** Wild Roses Band, Vellum Glaze, Fred Rothenbusch, 2½ x 5½ In. | | 316 |
| **Vase,** Wild Roses, Sea Green, Logo, Sallie Coyne, 1903, 6¾ In. | | 1035 |
| **Vase,** Wild Roses, Standard Glaze, High Shoulder, Tapered, C. Baker, 1893, 7 x 4½ In. | | 375 |
| **Vase,** Wisteria, Green Over Blue Matte Glaze, Charles Todd, 1913, 13⅝ In. | | 1265 |
| **Vase,** Wisteria, Purple Glaze, Tapered Cylinder, c.1941, 14 In. | | 540 |
| **Vase,** Wisteria, Vellum Glaze, E.T. Hurley, 1926, 14 In. | | 2300 |

**RORSTRAND** was established near Stockholm, Sweden, in 1726. By the nineteenth century Rorstrand was making English-style earthenware, bone china, porcelain, ironstone china, and majolica. The company is still working and is now owned by Fiskars Sweden. The three-crown mark has been used since 1884.

| | | |
|---|---|---|
| **Pitcher,** Gilt, Multicolor, Bulldog Mask, Strapwork, Leaves, Rope Twist Handle, 10 In. | | 246 |
| **Vase,** Blossoming Branches, Petal Rim, Marked, c.1900, 19 x 7 In. | *illus* | 1750 |
| **Vase,** Brown, Mottled Matte Glaze, Bottle Shape, C. Stalhane, 9 x 5 In. | | 406 |
| **Vase,** Brown, Mottled Matte Glaze, Swollen Cylinder Shape, G. Nylund, 7 x 3 In. | | 156 |
| **Vase,** Embossed Basket Weave, Brown Matte Glaze, Lug Handles, Nylund, 1900s, 22 x 12 In. | | 4375 |
| **Vase,** Igloo, Ribbed Neck, G. Nylund, 4½ x 10¼ In. | | 244 |
| **Vase,** Owls, Feathers, Footed, Alf Wallander, 11¾ In. | | 978 |
| **Vase,** Purple, Brown, G. Nylund, 6½ x 3 In. | | 122 |

**ROSALINE,** *see Steuben category.*

**ROSE BOWLS** were popular during the 1880s. Rose petals were kept in the open bowl to add fragrance to a room, a popular idea in a time of limited personal hygiene. The glass bowls were made with crimped tops, which kept the petals inside. Many types of Victorian art glass were made into rose bowls.

| | | |
|---|---|---|
| **Flowers,** Ferns, Cross Cuts, Ovals, Rogaska Crystal, 6¼ In. | | 50 |
| **Mother-Of-Pearl,** Diamond Quilt, Cranberry To Pink, Crimped Top, 5¼ In. | | 184 |
| **Porcelain,** Bird's Nest Mold, Robin, Leaves, Berries, Branch Base, Continental, c.1870, 7 In. | | 69 |
| **Purple Flower,** Enamel, Cameo, Gold Trim, France, 2⅛ In. | | 395 |

**ROSE CANTON** china is similar to Rose Mandarin and Rose Medallion, except that no people or birds are pictured in the decoration. It was made in China during the nineteenth and twentieth centuries in greens, pinks, and other colors.

| | | |
|---|---|---|
| **Bowl,** Flowers, Cream Ground, 5 x 12 In. | | 282 |
| **Charger,** Peonies, Butterflies, Yellow Border, Green Scrollwork, 15 In. | | 333 |
| **Dish,** Roses, Leaves, Pink, Green, 9½ In. | | 30 |
| **Planter,** Underliner, Flower Reserves, 13 x 19 In., Pair | | 237 |
| **Plate,** Peonies, Leaves, 20th Century, 10 In. | | 31 |
| **Platter,** Multicolor, 6 Reserves, 16 In. | | 210 |
| **Platter,** Peonies, Butterflies, Pink, Blue, Green, 18 In. | | 363 |
| **Soup,** Dish, Peonies, Butterflies, 8½ In., Pair | | 73 |
| **Tazza,** Birds, Butterfly, Flowers, Stylized Bats, 9½ In., Pair | | 484 |
| **Teapot,** Lid, Peonies, Leaves, Ball Finial, Round Foot, 8 In. | | 500 |
| **Vase,** Panels, Flowers, Leaves, White Ground, 8½ In. | | 12 |
| **Warming Dish,** Armorial Center, c.1850, 9⅝ In. | | 3120 |

**ROSE MANDARIN** china is similar to Rose Canton and Rose Medallion. If the panels in the design picture only people and not birds, it is Rose Mandarin.

| | | |
|---|---|---|
| **Bowl,** Junks, In Canal, c.1800, 4 x 9 In. | | 492 |
| **Jar,** Lid, Historical Scenes, Flowers, Gilt, Porcelain, 1800s, 24 In. | *illus* | 1896 |
| **Platter,** Scholars, Flower Border, Birds & Flowers, 1800s, 14½ In. | *illus* | 593 |
| **Punch Bowl,** Panels, Figures, Lancet Border, c.1775, 4 x 11 In. | | 1107 |

R

| | |
|---|---|
| **Vase,** Double Gourd, Chinese, c.1900, 9 ¼ x 4 ½ In., Pair ................................. | 960 |
| **Vase,** Orange Leaves, Gilt Dragons, 1800s, 10 In. .................................*illus* | 246 |

---

**ROSE MEDALLION** china was made in China during the nineteenth and twentieth centuries. It is a distinctive design with four or more panels of decoration around a central medallion that includes a bird or a peony. The panels show birds and people. The background is a design of tree peonies and leaves. Pieces are colored in greens, pinks, and other colors. It is similar to Rose Canton and Rose Mandarin.

| | |
|---|---|
| **Basin,** Figures, Birds, Butterflies, Flowers, 1800s, 15 ¾ x 4 ½ In. ...........................................*illus* | 486 |
| **Bowl,** Courtyard Scenes, c.1870, 5 x 16 In. ................................................ | 360 |
| **Bowl,** Flower Reserves, 6 ¼ x 15 ¾ In. ...................................................... | 840 |
| **Candlestick,** Courtyard Scenes, Bobeche, Spread Foot, 1800s, 11 ½ In., Pair ................................ | 369 |
| **Centerpiece,** White Ground, Tapered, 1800s, 5 ¾ x 14 ½ In. ......................... | 480 |
| **Charger,** Interior Scenes, 13 ¼ In. ........................................................... | 188 |
| **Fish Bowl,** Stand, Reserves, Court Scenes, Flowers, Buddha's Hand, c.1900, 21 x 14 In., Pair...... | 984 |
| **Plate,** Figures, Birds, Flowers, Scalloped, c.1890, 8 In. ................................. | 100 |
| **Punch Bowl,** Figures, Flowers, Fruit, 6 Panels, Gold Accented Rim, 6 x 14 In. ................. | 575 |
| **Punch Bowl,** Reserves, Figures, Flowers, Birds, Butterflies, c.1890, 7 x 16 In. ............... | 1845 |
| **Teapot,** Lid, Peonies, Birds, Leaves, Rope Handle, c.1850, 6 ½ In. ................ | 182 |
| **Teapot,** Lid, Peonies, Birds, Leaves, Rope Handles, 5 ½ In. ........................ | 91 |
| **Teapot,** Multicolor Enamel, Cord Wrapped Double Wire Handles, 1800s, 6 In. ................. | 59 |
| **Teapot,** Women At Table, Having Tea, Cylindrical, Tapered Top, 6 In. ................. | 420 |
| **Tray,** Birds, Flowers, Peaches, Leaves, Green Ground, 8 ½ x 7 In. ................. | 121 |
| **Tureen,** Lid, Cut Corners, Bamboo Handle, c.1875, 5 x 9 In. ........................ | 1045 |
| **Vase,** Birds, Butterflies, Flower Bands, Flared Base, 13 x 9 In. .................... | 545 |
| **Vase,** Downward Flaring Base, Round Center, Saucer Top, 12 ¾ In. ............... | 431 |
| **Vase,** Figures, Flowers, Hydra On Shoulders, Gilt, 1900s, 17 ½ x 8 In., Pair........ | 414 |
| **Vase,** Figures, Interior Scenes, c.1850, 10 In., Pair ................................... | 480 |
| **Vase,** Foo Dog, Gilded, Salamanders, Figures, Flowers, 1800s, 14 x 7 In., Pair.... | 1168 |
| **Vase,** Lid, Birds, Flowers, Court Scenes, Foo Dog Handles, Knop, 27 x 14 In., Pair ........ | 2091 |
| **Vase,** People, Flowers, Fruit, Baluster, Painted, Chinese, 1800s, 8 x 9 ¼ In. ............. | 474 |
| **Vase,** Reserves, Figures, Birds, Flowers, Shouldered, Chinese, 1800s, 25 x 8 In. ............. | 984 |
| **Vase,** Reserves, Flowers, Birds, Chinese, 18 ½ x 11 ¾ In. ......................... | 180 |
| **Vase,** Zun Shape, Chinese, c.1900, 14 x 8 ¾ In., Pair................................. | 1476 |

---

**ROSE O'NEILL,** *see Kewpie category.*

---

**ROSE TAPESTRY** porcelain was made by the Royal Bayreuth factory of Tettau, Germany, during the late nineteenth century. The surface of the porcelain was pressed against a coarse fabric while it was still damp, and the impressions remained on the finished porcelain. It looks and feels like a textured cloth. Very skillful reproductions are being made that even include a variation of the Royal Bayreuth mark, so be careful when buying.

| | |
|---|---|
| **Candleholder,** Handle, Royal Bayreuth, 4 In., Pair........................................ | 118 |

---

**ROSEMEADE POTTERY** of Wahpeton, North Dakota, worked from 1940 to 1961. The pottery was operated by Laura A. Taylor and her husband, R.I. Hughes. The company was also known as the Wahpeton Pottery Company. Art pottery and commercial wares were made.

| | |
|---|---|
| **Salt & Pepper,** Bulldog Head, Green, 2 ½ In. .............................................. | 90 |
| **Salt & Pepper,** Quail, Foil Label, c.1950.................................................... | 48 |

---

**ROSENTHAL** porcelain was made at the factory established in Selb, Bavaria, in 1880. The factory is still making fine-quality tablewares and figurines. A series of Christmas plates was made from 1910. Other limited edition plates have been made since 1971. In 1998 Rosenthal was acquired by the Waterford Wedgwood Group. Rosenthal was bought by Sambonet Paderno Industries, headquartered in Orfento, Novaro, Italy, in 2009. Rosenthal china is still being produced in Bavaria.

| | |
|---|---|
| **Bookends,** Marabou, Gray, Brown, Black, Hans Kuster, 7 In. ........................ | 180 |
| **Charger,** Le Roi Soleil, Red, Blue, Yellow, Versace, 20th Anniversary Plate, 12 In. .......... | 81 |
| **Figurine,** Bird, Black & Yellow Plumage, On Tree Stump, 7 ½ In. ................ | 95 |
| **Figurine,** Bird, Long Tail, Perched On Tree Stump With Berries, 10 In. ......... | 221 |
| **Figurine,** Bird, Perched On Tree Stump, Black & Yellow Plumage, 7 ½ In....... | 95 |
| **Figurine,** Bird, Tropical, Blue & Yellow Feathers, On White Leaf & Berry Branch, 9 In............. | 118 |
| **Figurine,** Girl With Roses, Blue, White Gown, A. Caasmann, 10 In............... | 180 |
| **Figurine,** Magic Of Love, A. Caasmann, 10 In. ......................................... | 240 |
| **Figurine,** Snake Charmer, Woman Blowing Horn, Coiled Snake, B. Boehs, 6 ⅝ In........ | 247 |

Roseville, Carnelian II, Vase, Tan, Gray, Drip Glaze, c.1926, 14 x 12 In.
$2,750

Rago Arts & Auction Center

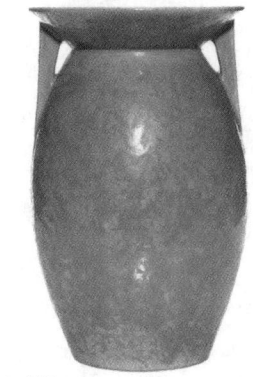

Roseville, Carnelian II, Vase, Turquoise, Gray, Square Handles, Flared Rim, 12 x 8 ½ In.
$374

Humler & Nolan

Roseville, Falline, Vase, Loop Handles, Saucer Foot, Flat Rim, Blue, Green, 6 ¼ In.
$546

Humler & Nolan

**TIP**
*Don't soak old ceramic pieces in water for a long time. Old repairs may be loosened.*

**Roseville,** Futura, Vase, Urn Shape, Emerald Green, Square Handles, Stepped Neck, 9 1/8 In.

**$633**

Humler & Nolan

**Roseville,** Juvenile, Dish, Feeding, Rabbit, Rolled Rim, 6 3/4 In.

**$47**

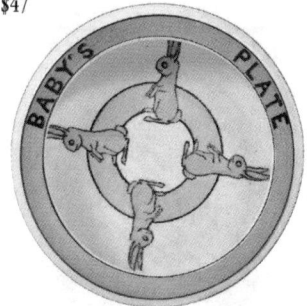

Conestoga Auction Co., Inc.

**Roseville,** Juvenile, Plate, Santa Claus, Rolled Rim, Green Bands, 7 3/4 In.

**$546**

Humler & Nolan

**TIP**

*It is said creativity comes from a messy, cluttered environment. It inspires ideas. Remember that the next time you rearrange your collectibles.*

| | |
|---|---|
| **Figurine,** Woodpecker, Perched On Decaying Tree Stump, 11 In. | 177 |
| **Group,** Faun With Nymphs, Walter Schott Design, c.1913, 11 x 9 In. | 1500 |
| **Plaque,** Depicting Mona Lisa, Porcelain, Germany, 1925-1941, 20 x 17 In. | 338 |
| **Plate,** Old Dutch, Cabernet Red, Pictorial Center, Gilt Stenciling, 10 In., 10 Piece | 529 |
| **Plate,** Service, Bavarian, Cobalt Blue Border, Raised Gilt Trim, 1922, 10 In., 10 Piece | 922 |
| **Plate,** White Roses, Blue Ground, Signed, c.1920, 8 In. | 150 |
| **Sugar & Creamer,** Violets, Gilt Handle & Trim, Bavaria, c.1915 | 185 |
| **Vase,** Face, Signed, Jean Cocteau, 1952, c.1960, 8 1/2 x 4 3/4 In. ...............*illus* | 338 |
| **Vase,** Trumpet, Pink, Silver Inlay, Round Base, 7 1/2 x 11 1/2 In. | 305 |

**ROSEVILLE POTTERY COMPANY** was organized in Roseville, Ohio, in 1890. Another plant was opened in Zanesville, Ohio, in 1898. Many types of pottery were made until 1954. Early wares include Sgraffito, Olympic, and Rozane. Later lines were often made with molded decorations, especially flowers and fruit. Most pieces are marked *Roseville*. Many reproductions made in China have been offered for sale the past few years.

*Roseville U.S.A.*

| | |
|---|---|
| **Artcraft,** Sand Jar, Mottle Blue Green, Footed, 12 In. | 69 |
| **Artcraft,** Vase, Mottled Orange, Green Interior, High Shouldered, 18 In. | 460 |
| **Artware,** Mug, Flowers, Berries, Brown Handles, 6 In. | 115 |
| **Artwood,** Vase, Open Green Block, Flowering Branch, 10 x 7 1/4 In. | 104 |
| **Ashtray & Matchbox,** Fatima Turkish Cigarettes, Cream, Yellow, 4 x 3 1/2 In. | 129 |
| **Aztec,** Pitcher, Squat, Arts & Crafts, Applied White Flower, 4 3/4 x 7 1/4 In. | 172 |
| **Aztec,** Vase, Blue, Matte Glaze, Squares, Cylindrical, Bulbous Base, 11 In. | 366 |
| **Aztec,** Vase, Triangle Shape, Peacock Feathers, Panels, 8 In. | 196 |
| **Azurean,** Mug, Blackberries, Paneled, Signed, Walter Myers, 5 5/8 In. | 230 |
| **Azurean,** Vase, Flowers, Blue, Tapered Bulbous, Small Mouth, 8 In. | 316 |
| **Bandeda,** Vase, Handles, Footed, 9 x 7 1/2 In. | 600 |
| **Baneda,** Bowl, Globular, Tab Handles, Footed, Green, 5 x 6 3/4 In. | 286 |
| **Baneda,** Jardiniere, Pedestal, Plum Red, Multicolor Flower Bands, Handles, 24 In. | 1265 |
| **Baneda,** Vase, Footed, Green Glaze, Handles, Round, 9 3/4 x 9 In. ...............*illus* | 805 |
| **Baneda,** Vase, Green, 2 Handles, Marked, 4 In. ...............*illus* | 403 |
| **Baneda,** Vase, Green, Embossed Leaves, Footed, High Handles, 7 In. | 420 |
| **Baneda,** Vase, Pink, Green, Orange Band, Neck Handles, 7 1/2 In. | 270 |
| **Baneda,** Vase, Pink, Handles, Footed, 6 In. | 173 |
| **Baneda,** Vase, Pink, Low Handles, Flared, 5 In. | 259 |
| **Blackberry,** Jardiniere, Orange, Green, Pedestal, Handles, 28 1/4 In. | 489 |
| **Blackberry,** Vase, Green, Brown, Globular, 6 In. | 250 |
| **Blackberry,** Vase, Green, Brown, Leaves, 2 Handles, 8 1/8 In. | 460 |
| **Blackberry,** Vase, Green, Brown, Squat, 2 Handles, 4 In. | 250 |
| **Blackberry,** Vase, Green, Yellow, Gold, Handles, 4 In. | 207 |
| **Blackberry,** Vase, Oval Shape, Loop Handles At Neck, 8 1/4 In. ...............*illus* | 288 |
| **Bleeding Heart,** Basket, Blue, Angular Rim, Flared Base, Loop Handle, 9 In. | 120 |
| **Bleeding Heart,** Jardiniere, Pedestal, Pink, 25 1/2 In. | 460 |
| **Bleeding Heart,** Vase, Blue, Shaped Rim, One Small, One Large Handle, 10 1/2 In. | 180 |
| **Bleeding Heart,** Vase, Rose, Peach, Flared Star Rim, 8 In. | 121 |
| **Bottle,** Monkey, Seated, Thinking, 4 3/4 In. | 115 |
| **Bushberry,** Vase, Blue, Round, Twig Shape Handles, Leaves, 9 x 12 1/4 In. ...............*illus* | 316 |
| **Carnelian I,** Vase, Blue Volcanic Glaze, Stepped Buttress Shape, 16 1/2 In. | 780 |
| **Carnelian II,** Vase, Gray, Pink, Handles, Bulbous, 10 In. | 94 |
| **Carnelian II,** Vase, Gray, Shaped Handles, Marked, 10 1/4 In. | 161 |
| **Carnelian II,** Vase, Green, Mottled, Drip Glaze, Angular Handles, c.1920, 9 x 9 In. | 600 |
| **Carnelian II,** Vase, Rocket Ship, Red Drip Glaze, 15 In. | 960 |
| **Carnelian II,** Vase, Tan, Gray, Drip Glaze, c.1926, 14 x 12 In. ...............*illus* | 2750 |
| **Carnelian II,** Vase, Turquoise, Gray, Square Handles, Flared Rim, 12 x 8 1/2 In. ...............*illus* | 374 |
| **Cherry Blossom,** Bowl, Rectangular, 3 x 10 3/4 In. | 189 |
| **Cherry Blossom,** Jardiniere, Pink Striped Base, 6 x 8 In. | 390 |
| **Cherry Blossom,** Pedestal, Blue, Pink, Ribbed, 18 1/2 In. | 184 |
| **Cherry Blossom,** Vase, Blue, Pink, Brown Striped Base, Small Handles, 6 In. | 270 |
| **Cherry Blossom,** Vase, Brown, Marked, 12 1/4 In. | 345 |
| **Cherry Blossom,** Vase, White Flowers, Stripes, Brown, High Handles, 7 1/4 In. | 173 |
| **Clemana,** Vase, White Flowers, Blue, Bulbous Base, 9 3/8 In. | 150 |
| **Clematis,** Basket, 10 In. | 47 |
| **Corinthian,** Jardiniere, Pedestal, 1923, 30 x 13 In. | 512 |
| **Corinthian,** Vase, Green, Yellow, Ribbed, Footed, 7 In. | 35 |
| **Cosmos,** Vase, Blue, Flared, Scalloped Rim, Loop Handles, 8 In. | 120 |
| **Creamware,** Humidor, Native American Indian, Lined Lid, Green, Orange, Red, 7 In. | 173 |

| | | |
|---|---|---:|
| **Creamware,** Persian, Jardiniere, Brown, Green Designs, 9 ½ In. | ...... | 253 |
| **Crystal Green,** Wall Shelf, 5 ¾ In. | ...... | 138 |
| **Crystallis,** Pitcher, High Handle, Mottled Orange, Mongol Mold, 7 ½ In. | ...... | 660 |
| **Dahlrose,** Vase, Pagoda Shape, Tapered, 6 In. | | 184 |
| **Della Robbia,** Bowl, Brown, White Flower, 6 ½ x 3 In. | | 2250 |
| **Della Robbia,** Mug, 1905, 6 x 5 In. | | 750 |
| **Della Robbia,** Teapot, Blue, Owl, 7 ½ x 7 In. | | 3172 |
| **Della Robbia,** Teapot, Green, 7 ½ x 6 ¼ In. | | 5490 |
| **Della Robbia,** Teapot, Hearts, Blue, Rozane, 9 x 5 ½ In. | | 1830 |
| **Donatello,** Hanging Basket, Frolicking Putti, Green Band, 10 ¼ In. | ...... | 52 |
| **Donatello,** Window Box, Frolicking Putti, Green Band, 16 x 6 ½ In. | | 81 |
| **Earlam,** Bowl, Brown, Flared, Handles, 10 x 4 In. | | 161 |
| **Egypto,** Jardiniere, Pedestal, Indented Bowl, Green Matte Glaze, c.1915, 31 x 23 In. | ...... | 3750 |
| **Egypto,** Vase, Green Matte Glaze, Embossed Iris, Overlapping Leaves, 14 In. | | 2160 |
| **Egypto,** Vase, Green, Rozane, 5 ½ x 11 ½ In. | | 518 |
| **Egypto,** Vase, Olive Green, Branch Shape Handles, Leaves, Fruit, 5 ⅛ x 7 ½ In. | ...... | 600 |
| **Falline,** Vase, Blue, Yellow Green Pea Pod Banded, Bulbous, Scrolled Handles, 7 ½ In. | ... | 510 to 720 |
| **Falline,** Vase, Brown, Green Leaves, Bulbous, Stepped Neck, Curled Handles, 8 In. | ...... | 360 |
| **Falline,** Vase, Loop Handles, Saucer Foot, Flat Rim, Blue, Green, 6 ¼ In. | ...*illus* | 546 |
| **Ferella,** Vase, Brown, Handles, 5 In. | | 259 |
| **Ferella,** Vase, Openwork Rim, Squat, Footed, 4 ¼ x 6 In. | | 288 |
| **Ferella,** Vase, Red, Stylized Flower Rim & Foot, Loop Handles, Footed, 6 ¼ In. | ...... | 320 to 420 |
| **Foxglove,** Jardiniere, Pedestal, Green, Pink Flowers, 30 ¾ In. | | 546 |
| **Foxglove,** Jardiniere, Pedestal, Handles, 24 ½ In. | | 288 |
| **Foxglove,** Vase, Cornucopia, Green, Pink, 6 In. | | 90 |
| **Freesia,** Vase, Yellow Flowers, Orange, Brown, Handles, 10 ¼ In. | | 40 |
| **Fuchsia,** Vase, Tan, Large Loop Handles, Footed, 12 In. | | 240 |
| **Futura,** Hanging Basket, Gray, Peach, 7 ½ In. | | 150 |
| **Futura,** Jardiniere, Pedestal, Pink Flowers, Gray, Angular, Handles, 28 In. | | 863 |
| **Futura,** Vase, Ball Shape, Stepped Neck, 8 In. | | 177 |
| **Futura,** Vase, Blue Box, Blue, Green, 3 ½ x 3 ⅝ In. | | 316 |
| **Futura,** Vase, Blue Christmas Tree, Stacked Graduated Cones, Multicolor, 10 In. | | 1020 |
| **Futura,** Vase, Chinese Pillow, Mauve, Green, Flowers, 9 ⅛ In. | | 1100 |
| **Futura,** Vase, Christmas Tree, Cones, Dark Orange, Geometric Shapes, 10 ¼ In. | | 195 |
| **Futura,** Vase, Graduated Spherical Neck, Green Bulbous Base, Zanesville, 1924, 8 x 5 In. | | 375 |
| **Futura,** Vase, Green Fan, Footed, 9 In. | | 2040 |
| **Futura,** Vase, Ostrich Egg, Green, Blue, Orange Matte Glaze, 7 x 7 ½ In. | | 316 |
| **Futura,** Vase, Ostrich Egg, Mottled Green To Orange, Square Foot, 7 ⅝ In. | | 316 |
| **Futura,** Vase, Ostrich Egg, Orange, Green Splatter, Footed, Square Base, 7 ½ In. | | 540 |
| **Futura,** Vase, Pleated Star, Black Paper Label, 8 In. | | 207 |
| **Futura,** Vase, The Bottle, Pink, Green, Black Label, .9 In. | | 360 |
| **Futura,** Vase, Triangle Shape, Blue, Geometric Shapes, 9 ⅛ In. | | 345 |
| **Futura,** Vase, Twist, Green, Yellow, Crystalline Glaze, 6 ½ In. | | 230 |
| **Futura,** Vase, Urn Shape, Emerald Green, Square Handles, Stepped Neck, 9 ⅛ In. | ...*illus* | 633 |
| **Futura,** Vase, V-Shape Pattern, Rose, Pink, Teal, 7 ⅛ In. | | 201 |
| **Futura,** Vase, V-Shape, Pink, Green Glaze, Footed, 7 In. | | 230 |
| **Hexagon,** Vase, Green, Square Lobed, 4 In. | | 138 |
| **Imperial II,** Vase, Blue & Yellow Glaze, Flared, Horizontal Ribs, 9 ½ In. | | 375 |
| **Imperial II,** Vase, Bulbous, Green Drip, Rose Ground, 9 In. | | 510 |
| **Imperial II,** Vase, Horizontal Ribs, Purple, Yellow, Flared, 6 In. | | 127 |
| **Imperial II,** Vase, Pink, Cream, Band At Rim, 8 ½ In. | | 575 |
| **Imperial II,** Vase, Runny Orange Drip, Blue Ground, Squat, 6 In. | | 540 |
| **Imperial II,** Wall Pocket, Verdigris Glaze Over Lavender, Tapered Shape, 6 ½ x 6 ½ In. | | 230 |
| **Jardiniere,** Scarabs, Green, 3 ¾ In. | | 373 |
| **Jonquil,** Jardiniere, White Flower, Textured Ground, 4 In. | | 83 |
| **Juvenile,** Creamer, Pig, Standing, Hat In Hand Band, 3 ½ In. | | 480 |
| **Juvenile,** Dish, Feeding, Rabbit, Rolled Rim, 6 ¾ In. | ...*illus* | 47 |
| **Juvenile,** Mug, Chick, Double Handle, 3 In. | | 59 |
| **Juvenile,** Plate, Santa Claus, Rolled Rim, Green Bands, 7 ¾ In. | ...*illus* | 546 |
| **Lombardy,** Hanging Basket, Round, Lobed, 7 ¾ In. | | 104 |
| **Luffa,** Vase, Green, Angular Handles, Gold Paper Label, 6 ½ In. | | 150 |
| **Luffa,** Vase, Green, Orange, Handles, 6 ¼ In. | | 150 |
| **Magnolia,** Vase, 2 Handles, 16 In. | ...*illus* | 90 |
| **Magnolia,** Vase, Brown, Green, Footed, Handles, c.1940, 15 In. | | 365 |
| **Matte Blue,** Jardiniere, Tan Geometric Neck Band, 6 In. | | 288 |
| **Matte Green,** Vase, Olive, Cylindrical, 1921, 6 ¾ In. | | 184 |

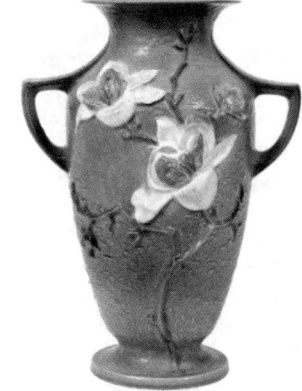

**Roseville,** Magnolia, Vase, 2 Handles, 16 In.
$90

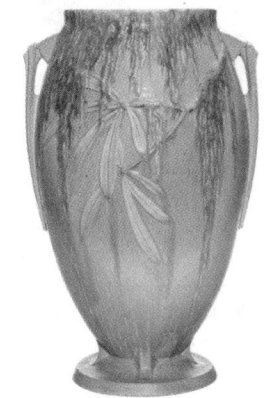

**Roseville,** Moss, Vase, Green, Beige, Shaped Handles, Bulbous, Tapered, Round Foot, 14 ½ In.
$345

**Roseville,** Peony, Vase, Yellow, Flowers, Shaped Handles, Flared Rim, 14 ¼ In.
$230

R

This is an edited listing of current prices. Visit Kovels.com to check thousands of prices from previous years and sign up for free information on trends, tips, reproductions, marks, and more.

**Roseville,** Pine Cone, Basket, Blue, Handle, Marked, 10 x 13 ½ In. $546

Humler & Nolan

**Roseville,** Pine Cone, Vase, Shaped Handles, Round Foot, Blue, Green, 10 ½ In. $489

Humler & Nolan

**Roseville,** Wisteria, Jardiniere, Pedestal, Brown, Green, Leaves, 28 In. $1,150

Humler & Nolan

| | |
|---|---:|
| **Monticello,** Vase, Blue, Brown Bands, Handles, 5 ¼ In. | 150 |
| **Monticello,** Vase, Orange, Green, White Runny Glaze, Handles, 8 ¼ In. | 230 |
| **Morning Glory,** Vase, Pink, Turquoise Vines, Angled Handles, 8 ⅜ In. | 253 |
| **Moss,** Vase, Green, Beige, Shaped Handles, Bulbous, Tapered, Round Foot, 14 ½ In. ......*illus* | 345 |
| **Mostique,** Jardiniere, Pedestal, Multicolor Flowers, Designs, Gray Ground, 28 In. | 173 |
| **Mostique,** Vase, Arts & Crafts, Taupe Ground, Spades, Green Interior, 8 In. | 47 |
| **Mostique,** Vase, Tan, Yellow, Red Geometrics, Cylindrical, 8 In. | 120 |
| **Mostique,** Vase, Tapered, Flared Rim, 10 x 6 In. | 108 |
| **Olympic,** Vase, Classical Figure, Playing Lute, Red, Flared Base, Rozane, 14 In. | 2400 |
| **Orion,** Vase, Rose Matte Glaze, Green Highlights, Handles, 6 ¼ In. | 115 |
| **Pauleo,** Vase, Flower Band, Tan, Luster Glaze, Bulbous, Elongated Neck, 13 x 9 In. | 750 |
| **Pauleo,** Vase, Grapes, Leaves, Vines, Cream & Gray Ground, 18 ¾ In. | 920 |
| **Peony,** Vase, Yellow, Flowers, Shaped Handles, Flared Rim, 14 ¼ In. ......*illus* | 230 |
| **Peony,** Wall Pocket, Brown, 8 ½ x 5 ½ In., Pair | 300 |
| **Persian,** Jardiniere, Creamware, Multicolor, Stylized Flowers, 9 x 6 ½ In. | 92 |
| **Pine Cone,** Basket, Blue, Handle, Marked, 10 x 13 ½ In. ......*illus* | 546 |
| **Pine Cone,** Pitcher, Brown Ground, Zanesville, Ohio, 1935, 10 x 8 In. | 281 |
| **Pine Cone,** Vase, 7 ⅜ In. | 142 |
| **Pine Cone,** Vase, Fan Shape, Green, Marked, 6 ⅝ In. | 173 |
| **Pine Cone,** Vase, Marked, 10 ¼ In. | 242 |
| **Pine Cone,** Vase, Shaped Handles, Round Foot, Blue, Green, 10 ½ In. ......*illus* | 489 |
| **Pine Cone,** Wall Bucket, Green, 3 Cups, Marked, 8 ¾ In. | 242 |
| **Poppy,** Centerpiece, Brown, 7 x 3 In. | 265 |
| **Poppy,** Ewer, Green Matte Glaze, Impressed Logo, 18 ½ In. | 288 |
| **Poppy,** Hanging Basket, Peach, Pink Flower, 9 In. | 92 |
| **Poppy,** Vase, Basket, Yellow Flower, Green Leaves, Gray Ground, 12 ⅜ In. | 345 |
| **Primrose,** Vase, White Flowers, Pink, Handles, 10 ½ In. | 173 |
| **Roma,** Urn, Pedestal, Pastel Flowers, Beige, Lobed, Lion's Head Ring Handles, Footed, 12 In. | 345 |
| **Rosecraft,** Vase, Hexagonal, Green & Orange Glaze, Marked, c.1925, 8 ¼ In. | 180 |
| **Rozane,** Pitcher, Roman Chariot, Horses, Della Robbia, c.1910, 8 x 10 In. | 2750 |
| **Rozane,** Tankard, Leaf & Berry, Signed CL Leiffler, 10 ½ In. | 127 |
| **Rozane,** Teapot, Della Robbia, Verse On Leaves, White, Blue, Arts & Crafts, 6 x 9 In. | 2928 |
| **Rozane,** Urn, Champagne Bucket, Flowers, Cream, Lug Handles, 10 ½ In. | 35 |
| **Rozane,** Vase, Della Robbia, Penguin Band, Green, Oval, Cinched Neck, 8 ½ In. | 3500 |
| **Rozane,** Vase, Flared Rim, Long Neck, Signed A.B., 7 ¼ In. | 98 |
| **Rozane,** Vase, Fujiyama, Flowers, Slip Trailing, Brown, Blue, Cream, Wafer Seal, 10 In. | 633 |
| **Rozane,** Vase, Mara, Iridescent, Purple, Mauve, 4 Handles, 6 In. | 575 |
| **Rozane,** Vase, Olympic, Persia, Ionia, Greek Key, Red, Black, Footed, c.1910, 14 x 7 In. | 3125 |
| **Rozane,** Vase, Pillow, Brown, Yellow, Man, Walking, Pond, Ruffled Rim, Handles, 12 x 9 In. | 414 |
| **Silhouette,** Vase, White, Reclining Nudes, Fan Shape, 7 ⅜ In. | 173 |
| **Snowberry,** Bookends, Open Book Shape, c.1947, 5 ½ x 4 ¾ In. | 145 |
| **Sunflower,** Basket, Hanging, Yellow Flowers, Green Leaves, 7 In. | 230 |
| **Sunflower,** Vase, Blue, Green, Yellow, Flowers, 2 Handles, 6 In. | 575 |
| **Sunflower,** Vase, Green, Orange, Cylindrical, Triangular Handles, 6 In. | 316 |
| **Sunflower,** Vase, Neck Handles, 1930, 9 x 7 In. | 625 |
| **Sunflower,** Vase, Orange, Yellow, Green, 2 Handles, 5 In. | 345 |
| **Sunflower,** Vase, Triangular Neck Handles, 6 ¼ In. | 450 |
| **Sunflower,** Wall Pocket, Green Yellow Flower, 7 ¼ In. | 374 |
| **Thornapple,** Basket, Blue, Green, Tapered, Footed, Handle, 10 ½ In. | 242 |
| **Thornapple,** Hanging Basket, Apple, Orange, Round, Lug Handles, 7 ¾ In. | 58 |
| **Thornapple,** Vase, Blue, Pink Flower Spray, Star Rim, Handles, Footed, 9 In. | 127 |
| **Thornapple,** Vase, On Stand, White Flower, Rose, Green, Tapered, 8 ⅜ In. | 138 |
| **Tourist,** Vase, Landscape, Multicolor, Car, Cream Ground, Flared, 12 In. | 2400 |
| **Tuscany,** Vase, Pink, Green Handles, 10 In. | 104 |
| **Velmoss,** Vase, Green, Striated, Leaves, 9 ⅞ In. | 690 |
| **Vista,** Wall Pocket, Blue, Green, Hanging Hole, 9 ⅝ In. | 518 |
| **Water Lily,** Vase, Angular Handles, 12 x 8 In. | 108 |
| **White Rose,** Wall Pocket, Pink, Green, Asymmetrical Handles, 9 In. | 242 |
| **Wincraft,** Vase, Panther, Blue Ground, Branch, Leaves, 10 ½ In. | 546 |
| **Windsor,** Vase, Blue, Green Leafy Vine Neck Border, High Handles, 10 ½ In. | 480 |
| **Windsor,** Vase, Blue, Handles, 5 ¼ In. | 259 |
| **Windsor,** Vase, Blue, Yellow Flowers, Cylindrical Handles, 9 In. | 540 |
| **Wisteria,** Jardiniere, Green Vine Leaves, Lavender Flowers, 4 ¼ In. | 130 |
| **Wisteria,** Jardiniere, Pedestal, Brown, Green, Leaves, 28 In. ......*illus* | 1150 |
| **Wisteria,** Vase, Blue Ground, Angled Handles, 10 In. | 1200 |

| | |
|---|---|
| **Wisteria,** Vase, Brown, Silver Triangle Label, 6½ In. | 230 |
| **Wisteria,** Vase, Small Handles, 5½ In. | 253 |
| **Woodland,** Vase, Red Flower, Tan Ground, 10¾ In. | 431 |
| **Woodland,** Yellow, Brown Flowers, Beige, Square, 5¼ In. | 150 |
| **Zephyr Lily,** Jardiniere, Pedestal, White Flowers, Orange, Green, Handles, 24½ In. | 345 |
| **Zephyr Lily,** Vase, Flared Rim, Handles, Footed, 8 In. | 45 |

**ROWLAND & MARSELLUS COMPANY** is part of a mark that appears on historical Staffordshire dating from the late nineteenth and early twentieth centuries. *Rowland & Marsellus* is the mark used by an American importing company in New York City. The company worked from 1893 to about 1937. Some of the pieces may have been made by the British Anchor Pottery Co. of Longton, England, for export to a New York firm. Many American views were made. Of special interest to collectors are the plates with rolled edges, usually blue and white.

| | |
|---|---|
| **Bowl,** Courtship Scene, Cobalt Blue, 7½ In. | 80 |
| **Plate,** Historical Boston, Faneuil Hall, Rolled Edge, 10 In. | 50 |
| **Plate,** Independence Hall, Flow Blue, Rolled Edge, 9¾ In. | 85 |
| **Plate,** Landing Of Hendrick Hudson, 10 In. | 125 |
| **Plate,** Penn's Treaty, Flow Blue, 10 In. | 75 |
| **Plate,** View Of Denver, Blue & White, 10 In. | 100 |

**ROY ROGERS** was born in 1911 in Cincinnati, Ohio. In the 1930s, he made a living as a singer; in 1935, his group started work at a Los Angeles radio station. He appeared in his first movie in 1937. From 1952 to 1957, he made 101 television shows. The other stars in the show were his wife, Dale Evans, his horse, Trigger, and his dog, Bullet. Roy Rogers memorabilia, including items from the Roy Rogers restaurants, are collected.

| | |
|---|---|
| **Alarm Clock,** Desert Scene, 40 Hour, E. Ingraham Co., 1951, 4 x 4½ In. | 338 |
| **Comic Book Corral,** Roy Riding Trigger, Lasso, Tin Lithograph, 12 x 9 x 8 In. | 175 |
| **Figure,** Roy Riding Trigger, Waving, Hartland Toys, 1950s, 8 In. | 165 |
| **Lantern,** Horseshoe Shape, 2 Handles, Box, 1950s, 8⅜ In. | 126 |
| **Mug,** Head, Hat, Scarf, Porcelain, 4 In. | 38 |
| **Paper Dolls,** Roy, Dale Evans, Trigger, 6 Pages Of Clothes, Whitman, 1950 | 145 |
| **Pin,** Dale's Brand, Red, Blue, Grape Nuts, Premium, 1953, ¾ In. | 14 |
| **Poster,** Roy Rogers Holding Bridle, Trigger, 1957, 67¼ x 24 In. | 208 |
| **Poster,** Sunset On The Desert, Gabby Hayes, Republic, 1942, 27 x 41 In. | 500 |
| **Record,** Happy Trail, Yellow Rose Of Texas, 78 RPM, 1952 | 45 |
| **Record,** Roy & Dale Evans, Happy Trails, RCA Victor Records, 78 RPM | 45 |
| **Ring,** Microscope, Trigger, Brass, Plastic, Quaker Oaks Premium, 1949 | 158 |
| **Rocking Horse,** Cottontail, Gabby Hayes, Red, 1950s, 10¼ x 20¼ In. | 115 |
| **Rocking Horse,** Platform Base, Red, White, Black, Wood, c.1950, 15 x 37 In. | 644 |
| **Salt & Pepper,** Boot Shape, Polished Metal, Box, Japan, 2 In. | 18 |
| **Sign,** Punch Out Card, Roy Rogers Cookies, Multicolor, 1950, 13 x 16¾ In. | 172 |
| **Stopwatch,** Chrome, Headshot, Rearing Trigger, 1959, 2 In. | 227 |
| **Store Display,** Post Raisin Bran, Roy Rogers Western Medals, 16½ x 23 In. | 506 |
| **Toy,** Horseshoe Set, Ohio Art Co., 1950s | 48 |
| **Toy,** Play Set, Rodeo Ranch, Box, Marx, 22 x 9 In. | 146 |
| **Watch,** Roy Riding Trigger, Leather, 1950s, 7⅝ In. | 35 |
| **Wristwatch,** Dale Evans, Queen Of The West, Horse, Leather Band, 3 x 8½ In. | 115 |
| **Wristwatch,** Rearing Trigger, Box, 1950s | 253 |

**ROYAL BAYREUTH** is the name of a factory that was founded in Tettau, Bavaria, in 1794. It has continued to modern times. The marks have changed through the years. A stylized crest, the name Royal Bayreuth, and the word *Bavaria* appear in slightly different forms from 1870 to about 1919. Later dishes may include the words *U.S. Zone* (1945–1949), the year of the issue, or the word *Germany* instead of *Bavaria*. Related pieces may be found listed in the Rose Tapestry, Sand Babies, Snow Babies, and Sunbonnet Babies categories.

| | |
|---|---|
| **Bowl,** Poppy, Red, Scalloped Rim, 4½ x 8½ In. | 127 |
| **Box,** Art Nouveau Woman Lid, Prone, 5 x 3¼ In. | 374 |
| **Candleholder,** Poppy, Handle, Blue Mark, 2¾ x 5 In. | 249 |
| **Candy Dish,** Clown, Red, White, Hands Up, 6¼ x 7 In. | 40 |
| **Chocolate Pot,** Poppy, Red, Green Leaves, 8 x 7 In. | 81 |
| **Creamer,** Art Nouveau Woman, Allover Swirl, 4 x 5¼ In. | 150 |
| **Creamer,** Black Devil, Orange Eyes, Interior, 4 x 5 In. | 661 |
| **Creamer,** Hat & Coat, Yellow, 6 x 5 In. | 127 |
| **Creamer,** Santa Claus, Brown, Seated, 4¼ x 4¾ In. | 891 |
| **Hatpin Holder,** Tray, Sheep Landscape, Green, Gilt, 6 x 3 In. | 350 |

**Royal Copenhagen,** Bottle, Silver Mounted, Flowering Vines, Marked, c.1920, 8½ In.
$923

Skinner Auctioneers & Appraisers

**Royal Copenhagen,** Figurine, Woman With Child, Holding Fan, Shaped Base, c.1926, 4½ x 5 In.
$1,599

New Orleans Auction Galleries, Inc.

**Royal Copenhagen,** Group, 2 Women & Man, Multicolor, Marked, 1900s
$3,321

R

Skinner Auctioneers & Appraisers

**Royal Copenhagen,** Plate, Christmas, 1909, Jul, Snow Covered Landscape, Starry Sky, 6 In.
$48

DuMouchelles Art Gallery

**Royal Copenhagen,** Vase, Marabou Stork, Green Stamp, c.1900, 14 x 6 In.
$2,625

Rago Arts & Auction Center

**Royal Doulton,** Figurine, Henry Irvine, Cardinal Wolsey, Standing, Red Robe & Cap, HN 344, c.1950, 13 In.
$738

Skinner Auctioneers & Appraisers

| | |
|---|---:|
| **Humidor,** Lobster, Red, Folded Shape, 8 x 5 In. | 150 |
| **Marmalade,** Pineapple, Orange, Tan, Green Leaves, 5 x 3 ½ In. | 288 |
| **Mug,** Clown, Red, Arms Around Cup, 4 ½ x 3 ¾ In. | 69 |
| **Nodder,** Crying Child, 5 x 2 ½ In. | 81 |
| **Pitcher,** Bell Ringer, Tricorn Hat, Yellow Bell, 7 ½ In. | 138 |
| **Pitcher,** Clown, Yellow, Green Buttons, 5 x 6 ½ In. | 92 |
| **Pitcher,** Dutch Women Working, Landscape Top Band, Corset Shape, 8 In. | 94 |
| **Pitcher,** Elk, Brown To Peach, 4 ¼ x 3 ¾ In. | 431 |
| **Pitcher,** Lamplighter, Green, 7 ¾ x 7 In. | 138 |
| **Pitcher,** Lemon, Yellow, Green, 6 ¾ x 8 In. | 173 |
| **Pitcher,** Maple Leaf, Orange, Green, 5 ½ x 8 ½ In. | 633 |
| **Pitcher,** Orange, Green, Leaves, 7 ¼ x 7 ¾ In. | 345 |
| **Pitcher,** Orchid, Rosy Cream, Red, 6 ½ x 7 ½ In. | 1725 |
| **Pitcher,** Perch, Pearly Underbelly, Green Gills, 7 ½ x 7 ½ In. | 805 |
| **Pitcher,** Poodle, Black, On Hind Legs, 5 ½ x 6 In. | 115 |
| **Pitcher,** Rooster, Red, Brown, Black, 7 ½ x 8 ½ In. | 1150 |
| **Pitcher,** Tomato, Red, Green Leaves, 6 ¼ x 8 ½ In. | 92 |
| **Pitcher,** Woman, Bonnet, Red Dress, 4 ½ x 4 ½ In. | 29 |
| **Plate,** Lemon Yellow Ground, Flowers, Gilt, Scalloped Edge, 11 In., 10 Piece | 219 |
| **Salt & Pepper,** Corn Ears, 4 ¼ In. | 546 |
| **Stringholder,** Wall, Rooster, 6 ¼ x 3 ¼ In. | 92 |
| **Vase,** Woman, Long Brown Hair, White Gown, 7 ½ x 6 ¾ In. | 805 |

**ROYAL BONN** is the nineteenth- and twentieth-century trade name used by Franz Anton Mehlem, who had a pottery in Bonn, Germany, from 1836 to 1931. Porcelain and earthenware were made. The factory was purchased by Villeroy & Boch in 1921 and closed in 1931. Many marks were used, most including the name Bonn, the initials FM, and a crown.

| | |
|---|---:|
| **Charger,** Blue Delft, White, Fruit Border, Landscape, Cows, 19 ¾ In. | 523 |
| **Clock,** Shelf, Ansonia Works, Le Handre, Pink Rose, Blue, Green, Cream, 15 x 13 In. | 826 |
| **Plaque,** Fruit, Painted, Leaf Shape, Wavy Rim, Signed W. Stanway, 1903, 4 x 24 In. | 518 |
| **Plaque,** Landscape, Cows, Blue, White, 14 x 13 In. | 123 |
| **Stein,** Stoneware, Painted, Marked, Pewter Lid, Inscription, ½ Liter. | 450 |
| **Urn,** Lid, Maiden, Flower Basket, Cobalt Blue Ground, Gold Trim, 17 x 9 In. | 544 |
| **Vase,** Art Nouveau, Blue Poppies, Signed, 5 ¾ In. | 219 |
| **Vase,** Dome Lid, Gilt Knops, Yellow Roses, Blue Ground, Mauney, c.1900, 51 In. | 2300 |
| **Vase,** White, Orange Castle, Village, Reticulated Applied Handles, 16 ½ In., Pair | 236 |
| **Vase,** Woman, Art Nouveau, Landscape, Green, Gold Trim, Sinewy, 2 Handles, 12 In. | 369 |
| **Vase,** Woman, Standing By Wall, Blue, Green Trim, Signed Heinen, 8 In. | 148 |

**ROYAL COPENHAGEN** porcelain and pottery have been made in Denmark since 1775. The Christmas plate series started in 1908. The figurines with pale blue and gray glazes have remained popular in this century and are still being made. Many other old and new style porcelains are made today.

| | |
|---|---:|
| **Basket,** Flora Danica, Apple Blossoms, Apples, Paint, 9 ½ In. | 1250 |
| **Berry Bowl,** Flora Danica, Blueberries, Pansies, Flared, Reticulated, 7 In. | 1098 |
| **Bottle,** Blue Daisy, Silver Lid, c.1915, 5 ½ In. | 615 |
| **Bottle,** Silver Mounted, Flowering Vines, Marked, c.1920, 8 ½ In. ................*illus* | 923 |
| **Bowl,** Flora Danica, Painted With A. Sauaveolons, c.1975, 9 ¾ In. | 1375 |
| **Chestnut Dish,** Silver Mounted, Leaves, c.1920, 8 ⅞ In. | 984 |
| **Figurine,** Boy With Umbrella, No. 3556, 7 In. | 140 |
| **Figurine,** Faun, With Bird, Christian Thomsen, 6 ¾ x 5 In. | 357 |
| **Figurine,** Fyen, Seated Girl, Ethnic Clothing, 4 In. | 240 |
| **Figurine,** Girl, Kneeling, Cradling Doll, 5 In. | 199 |
| **Figurine,** Iceland Falcon, 8 ¾ x 12 In. | 175 |
| **Figurine,** Polar Bear, Sitting, Head Up, Mouth Open, 12 ½ In. | 207 |
| **Figurine,** Woman With Child, Holding Fan, Shaped Base, c.1926, 4 ½ x 5 In. .........*illus* | 1599 |
| **Flask,** Rose, Butterfly, Silver Lid, c.1915, 7 ¾ In. | 923 |
| **Flask,** Silver Mounted, Orchid, Silver Lid, 6 ¾ In. | 461 |
| **Group,** 2 Women & Man, Multicolor, Marked, 1900s ..................*illus* | 3321 |
| **Group,** 3 Women Holding Flag, Headscarves, Kerchiefs, 12 ½ In. | 2583 |
| **Group,** Woman In Skirt, Sitting Man, 20th Century, 12 In. | 800 |
| **Lamp,** Faience, Elliptical Body, Multicolor, Geometric Detail, c.1960, 19 In. | 120 |
| **Perfume Bottle,** Silver Mounted, Grape Hyacinths, Leaves, c.1920, 8 ⅜ In. | 2460 |
| **Plate,** Christmas, 1909, Jul, Snow Covered Landscape, Starry Sky, 6 In. .........*illus* | 48 |
| **Plate,** Christmas, 1921, Market Place In Aabenraa, 7 In. | 175 |

| | | |
|---|---|---:|
| **Plate,** Christmas, 1956, Rosenburg Castle, Copenhagen, 7¼ In. | | 270 |
| **Plate,** Dessert, Flower Spray, Pierced Basketweave Rim, c.1900, 8 In., 12 Piece | | 381 |
| **Plate,** Flora Danica, Botanical Design, Reticulated & Gilt Border, 8 In., 8 Piece | | 345 |
| **Plate,** Flora Danica, Botanicals, Reticulated Band, 8¾ In., 10 Piece | | 6710 |
| **Plate,** Flora Danica, Pierced Gilt, Pink Border, Scalloped Rim, c.1970, 9 In., 12 Piece | | 4688 |
| **Plate,** Flora Danica, Sassafras, 9½ x 7¾ In. | | 540 |
| **Plate,** Lugomkloster Kirke, 1173-1973, Church, Meadow, Horses, 7 In. | | 15 |
| **Serving Dish,** Flora Danica, Round, Multicolor, Gilt, 8¼ In. | | 54 |
| **Teapot,** Lid, Blue Fluted, Plain, Blue & White, Flowers, 6 In. | | 36 |
| **Tray,** Ink, Coiled Snake, Toad Inkpot, Flowers, 10¾ In. | | 2460 |
| **Tureen,** Flora Danica, Lid, Flower Branch Handle, Stamped, 6½ In. | | 1000 |
| **Tureen,** Lid, Flora Danica, Botanicals, Pierced Gilt, Pink Border, 15½ In. | | 1875 |
| **Urn,** English Ivy On Trellis, Ricard Bocher, 3 Waves Mark, c.1913, 10¼ In. | | 863 |
| **Vase,** Chick, Silver Icicle Shoulder, Ring Foot, c.1915, 5¾ In. | | 1107 |
| **Vase,** Marabou Stork, Green Stamp, c.1900, 14 x 6 In. | *illus* | 2625 |
| **Vase,** Silver Mounted, 3 Ducks, Leaf, Thistle, Fitted Box, 7¼ In. | | 2091 |
| **Vase,** Silver Mounted, Bulbous Shape, Sailing Ships, c.1915, 8¼ In. | | 2952 |
| **Vase,** Silver Mounted, Bulbous Shape, Sailing Ships, c.1915, 12 In. | | 8610 |
| **Vase,** Silver Mounted, Daffodils, Leaves, Flowers, c.1910, 17 In. | | 10455 |
| **Vase,** Silver Mounted, Fish, Seaweed, Lily Pad Rim, c.1920, 5 In. | | 1169 |
| **Vase,** Silver Mounted, Flowers, Leaves, 7⅛ In. | | 800 |
| **Vase,** Silver Mounted, Nasturtiums, c.1915, 5⅛ In. | | 523 |
| **Vase,** Tulip, Silver Rim, Swirling Bands, Footed, c.1920, 5¼ In. | | 308 |
| **Vial,** Lid, Calla Lilies, Dragonflies, Silver Mounted, 4⅜ In. | | 1046 |

**ROYAL CROWN DERBY COMPANY, LTD.,** is a name used on porcelain beginning in 1890. There is a complex family tree that includes the Derby, Crown Derby, and Royal Crown Derby porcelains. The Royal Crown Derby mark includes the name and a crown. The words *Made in England* were used after 1921. The company became part of Allied English Potteries Group in 1964. It was bought in 2000 and is now privately owned.

| | | |
|---|---|---:|
| **Candlestick,** Imari, Tapering Stem, Canted Square Foot, Gilt, 10½ x 9 In., Pair | | 587 |
| **Ewer,** Cobalt Blue, Iron Red, White, Gilt, c.1897, 7½ In. | | 104 |
| **Lazy Susan,** Imari, Wavy Rim, Socle Foot, c.1890, 17 In. | | 466 |
| **Sauceboat,** Liner Plate, Imari, Oval, c.1980, 5¼ x 8¼ In. | | 127 |
| **Serving Dish,** Lid, Imari, Pedestal Base, Oval, c.1940, 12 x 8½ In. | | 150 |
| **Tureen,** Beaumont, Flowers, 4-Footed, 2 Scrolled Handles & Finial, 9 In. | | 295 |
| **Urn,** Lid, Painted, Squat, Reticulated Handles, Flowers, Geometrics, 11 x 13 In. | | 992 |

**ROYAL DOULTON** is the name used on Doulton and Company pottery made from 1902 to the present. Doulton and Company of England was founded in 1853. Pieces made before 1902 are listed in this book under Doulton. Royal Doulton collectors search for the out-of-production figurines, character jugs, vases, and series wares. Some vases and animal figurines were made with a special red glaze called flambe. Sung and Chang glazed pieces are rare. The multicolored glaze is very thick and looks as if it were dropped on the clay. In 2005 Royal Doulton was acquired by the Waterford Wedgwood Group, which was bought by KPS Capital Partners of New York in 2009 and became part of WWRD Holdings.

**Royal Doulton** character jugs depict the head and shoulders of the subject. They are made in four sizes: large, 5¼ to 7 inches; small, 3¼ to 4 inches; miniature, 2¼ to 2½ inches; and tiny, 1¼ inches. Toby jugs portray a seated, full figure.

| | | |
|---|---|---:|
| **Animal,** Cat, Persian, 5 x 5 In. | | 75 |
| **Animal,** Dog, Cocker Spaniel, Curled In Wicker Basket, 4 x 2¼ In. | | 125 |
| **Animal,** Dog, German Shepherd, Black & Tan, Seated, 3 In. | | 48 |
| **Animal,** Rabbit, Stretched Legs, Flambe, 5 1/4 In. | | 106 |
| **Animal,** Tiger, On Rock, 12 x 15 x 11 In. | | 325 |
| **Character Jug,** Bacchus, D 6505, 4 In. | | 39 |
| **Character Jug,** Fat Boy, D 6142, 1940s, 3½ In. | | 39 |
| **Character Jug,** Groucho Marx, D 6710, 7 In. | | 85 |
| **Character Jug,** Lumberjack, D 6613, 3½ In. | | 25 |
| **Character Jug,** Night Watchman, D 6569, 7 In. | | 175 |
| **Character Jug,** North American Indian, D 6611, 7¾ In. | | 100 |
| **Character Jug,** Old Salt, Mermaid Handle, D 6554, 4 In. | | 78 |
| **Character Jug,** Romeo, D 6670, 7½ In. | | 40 |
| **Character Jug,** Sairey Gamp, D 5528, 3¼ In. | | 44 |
| **Character Jug,** Sleuth, D 6635, 3¼ In. | | 75 |

Royal Doulton, Figurine, Picardy Peasant, HN 17, Phoebe Stabler, 9½ In. $2,583

Royal Doulton, Figurine, Wolf, HN 7, Blue Cloak, Charles Noke, c.1920, 5⅜ In. $6,150

R

Royal Doulton, Loving Cup, Lord Nelson, Rope Handles, Signed, Noke, H. Fenton, 1935, 10 In. $800

**Royal Doulton,** Match Holder, Man Seated By Barrel, Celadon Glaze, H. Simeon, c.1925, 4 In.

$523

Skinner Auctioneers & Appraisers

**Royal Doulton,** Toby Jug, George Robey, Hat Cover, Charles Noke, c.1925, 9¾ In.

$1,107

Skinner Auctioneers & Appraisers

**R**

**Royal Doulton,** Vase, Chang Ware, Flambe Glaze, Charles Noke, Harry Nixon, c.1925, 7 In.

$4,375

Rago Arts & Auction Center

| | |
|---|---|
| **Figurine,** Fox, Model 102, Flambe, Charles Noke, 9⅜ In. | 677 |
| **Figurine,** Gollywog, HN 2040, 1945, 5½ In. | 106 to 193 |
| **Figurine,** Henry Irvine, Cardinal Wolsey, Standing, Red Robe & Cap, HN 344, c.1950, 13 In. *illus* | 738 |
| **Figurine,** Jester, HN 2016, 10 In. | 207 |
| **Figurine,** Mr. Furrow, D 6701, 4 In. | 45 |
| **Figurine,** Persian Cat, White, Seated, DA 126 | 195 |
| **Figurine,** Picardy Peasant, HN 17, Phoebe Stabler, 9½ In. *illus* | 2583 |
| **Figurine,** Polar Bear, Cub, HN 4178, 9½ In. | 246 |
| **Figurine,** Rhinoceros, Model 615, 8½ x 17 In. | 531 |
| **Figurine,** Sea Harvest, HN 2257, 7½ In. | 35 |
| **Figurine,** Shepherd, HN 1975, 1945, 8¾ In. | 178 |
| **Figurine,** St. George, HN 2051, 8 In. | 172 |
| **Figurine,** Wolf, HN 7, Blue Cloak, Charles Noke, c.1920, 5⅜ In. *illus* | 6150 |
| **Figurine,** Yellow-Throated Warbler, HN 2546, 4⅜ In. | 18 |
| **Flask,** Kingsware, Standing Figure, Multicolor, Whip, 8¾ In. | 461 |
| **Loving Cup,** Lord Nelson, Rope Handles, Signed, Noke, H. Fenton, 1935, 10 In. *illus* | 800 |
| **Match Holder,** Man Seated By Barrel, Celadon Glaze, H. Simeon, c.1925, 4 In. *illus* | 523 |
| **Pitcher,** Stoneware, Oval Cartouches, Stags, Leaves, 19th Century, 14¾ In. | 1230 |
| **Plate,** Dinner, Raised Gilt, Marked Marshall Field, 1902-1922, 10¼ In., 12 Piece | 3936 |
| **Plate,** Dinner, White, Gold Scalloped Rim, Gold Garland, Medallion Edge, 10 In., 12 Piece | 500 |
| **Plate,** Jackdaw Of Rheims, c.1910, 10¾ In. | 100 |
| **Plate,** Matsumai Pattern, 10¼ In., 8 Piece | 813 |
| **Plate,** Swimming Trout Borders, Gilt Rim, 9 In., 12 Piece | 1250 |
| **Toby Jug,** Albert Sagger The Potter, D 6745, 4 In. | 150 |
| **Toby Jug,** Cap'n Cuttle, Seated, Hook Hand, D 6266, 20th Century, 4¼ In. | 55 |
| **Toby Jug,** Falstaff, Seated, Holding Beer Mugs, D 6063, 5 In. | 45 |
| **Toby Jug,** George Robey, Hat Cover, Charles Noke, c.1925, 9¾ In. *illus* | 1107 |
| **Toby Jug,** Major Green The Golfer, D 6740, 4 In. | 85 |
| **Toby Jug,** Sgt. Peeler, D 6720, 4 In. | 50 |
| **Toby Jug,** Town Crier, Holding Notes & Bell, D 6920, 5½ In. | 90 |
| **Vase,** 2 Panels, Horses, Leaves, 11¾ In. | 1476 |
| **Vase,** Blue, Brown, White, Geometric, E. Simmance, 1900, 11 x 6 In. | 768 |
| **Vase,** Blue, White Flowers, Beige Band, 6 x 10 In. | 122 |
| **Vase,** Bulls, Horned, Green Pasture, Sunset, Bushes, 6¼ In., Pair | 161 |
| **Vase,** Chang Ware, Blue, White, Bottle Shape, Charles Noke, 7 In. | 554 |
| **Vase,** Chang Ware, Flambe Glaze, Charles Noke, Harry Nixon, c.1925, 7 In. *illus* | 4375 |
| **Vase,** Chang Ware, Multicolor, Harry Nixon, Charles Noke, c.1920, 13½ In. *illus* | 4720 |
| **Vase,** Chang Ware, Red, White, Globe Shape, Charles Noke, Harry Nixon, 7⅜ In. | 1230 |
| **Vase,** Chang Ware, Thick Runny Glaze, Charles Noke, Fred Moore, 7⅛ In. *illus* | 7475 |
| **Vase,** Farm Animals, Stoneware, H. Barlow, 1872, 10 x 5½ In. | 1750 |
| **Vase,** Flambe Glaze, Bottle Shape, Impressed Marks, 6 In. | 265 |
| **Vase,** Flambe, Hunter, Rifle, Forest, Slope Shoulder, 13½ In., Pair | 293 |
| **Vase,** Flambe, Red, Landscape, House, 5 x 7 In. | 92 |
| **Vase,** Flambe, Red, Landscape, Trees, 5½ x 11 In. | 183 |
| **Vase,** Flambe, Sung, Peacock In Flight, Red Purple, Charles Noke, 6¼ In. *illus* | 1495 |
| **Vase,** Gray Crows, Branch, Moonlight, 1920s, 5¼ In. | 1968 |
| **Vase,** Plants, Art Nouveau, Stoneware, Mark V. Marshall, Lambeth, c.1903, 15 In. *illus* | 1107 |
| **Vase,** Stoneware, Beaded Blue Leaves, Flowers, 11½ In. | 923 |
| **Vase,** Stoneware, Central Band, Flowers, Leaves, Simeon, Early 1900s, 10 In. | 400 |
| **Vase,** Stoneware, Central Band, Pigs Grazing, Landscape, Barlow, 14⅛ In. | 2460 |
| **Vase,** Stoneware, Globular, Stylized Leaves, Mottled Blue, Simmance, 8 In., Pair | 584 |
| **Vase,** Stoneware, Leaves, Brown, Blue, 19th Century, 12 In., Pair | 1169 |
| **Vase,** Stoneware, Stylized Flowers, Leaves, Mottle Blue, Red, 8¾ In., Pair | 215 |
| **Vase,** Sung, Mottled Green, Blue Flambe Glaze, Squat, Lobed, C. Noke, 7 In. | 708 |
| **Vase,** Sung, Red, Green, Blue, Yellow Glazes, Charles Noke, Fred Moore, 7⅛ In. | 805 |
| **Vase,** Titanian, Bird In Orange Tree, Multicolor, 7½ In. | 633 |
| **Vase,** Titanian, Flying Crane, Pale Blue, Henri, 5⅞ In. | 615 |
| **Vase,** Titanian, Nomads, Landscape, Allen, 1920, 5¾ In. | 1968 |
| **Vase,** Titanian, Young Mavis, Bird, Flower, Branch, Blue, Allen, c.1920, 8½ In. | 1599 |

**ROYAL DUX** is the more common name for the Duxer Porzellanmanufaktur, which was founded by E. Eichler in Dux, Bohemia (now Duchov, Czech Republic), in 1860. By the turn of the twentieth century, the firm specialized in porcelain statuary and busts of Art Nouveau–style maidens, large porcelain figures, and ornate vases with three-dimensional figures climbing on the sides. The firm is still in business.

| | |
|---|---|
| **Figurine,** Cupid, Lute, 25 In. | 375 |

| | |
|---|---|
| **Figurine,** Madonna, Holding Infant, Halo, Starred Base, 5 In. | 39 |
| **Figurine,** Mahatma Gandhi, Seated, Crossed Legs, 10 In. | 219 |
| **Figurine,** Mother & Daughter, Dancing, Marked, 1896, 19 In. | 2160 |
| **Figurine,** Water Carrier, Turban, Ewer In Each Hand, Green, Brown, Pink, 25 In. | 423 |
| **Vase,** Art Nouveau, Vase, Reclining Woman, Handles, Oval, c.1915, 6 1/4 x 9 1/2 In. | 240 |
| **Vase,** Crane, Standing, Flowers, Leaves, 25 1/2 In., Pair | 120 |

**ROYAL FLEMISH** glass was made during the late 1880s in New Bedford, Massachusetts, by the Mt. Washington Glass Works. It is a colored satin glass decorated with dark colors and raised gold designs. The glass was patented in 1894. It was supposed to resemble stained glass windows.

| | |
|---|---|
| **Biscuit Jar,** Lid, Gold Grids, Multicolor Body, Coin, Rampant Lion, Handle, 8 In. ...............*illus* | 920 |
| **Bowl,** Shear Top, Enameled Pink & Blue Flowers, Satin Swirl, Mt. Washington, 2 x 3 1/2 In. | 489 |
| **Jar,** Lid, Coin Medallions, Gilt Webbing, Squat, Squared Handles, Flame Finial, 6 In. | 2070 |
| **Jar,** Lid, Raised Panels, 4 Romanesque Medallions, Handles, Mt. Washington, 7 In. | 3105 |
| **Jug,** Spiral Finial, Long Neck, Roped Handle, Coat Of Arms, Gilding, 18 In. | 6843 |
| **Vase,** Arabian Scene, Arab On Camel, Medallions, Pyramids, Gold Stars, 13 In. | 18368 |
| **Vase,** Flattened, Coins, Medallions, Gilt Grid, Trefoil Cup Mouth, 7 1/4 In. ...................*illus* | 2185 |
| **Vase,** Flowers, Gryphons' Heads, Frosted Ground, Bulbous Base, 12 x 7 In. | 1875 |

**ROYAL HAEGER**, *see Haeger category.*

**ROYAL HICKMAN** designed pottery, glass, silver, aluminum, furniture, lamps, and other items. From 1938 to 1944 and again from the 1950s to 1969, he worked for Haeger Potteries. Mr. Hickman operated his own pottery in Tampa, Florida, during the 1940s. He moved to California and worked for Vernon Potteries. During the last years of his life he lived in Guadalajara, Mexico, and continued designing for Royal Haeger. Pieces made in his pottery listed here are marked *Royal Hickman* or *Hickman*.

| | |
|---|---|
| **Bowl,** Centerpiece, Free-Form, Wave Crest, Brown, Cream, 11 x 8 In. | 75 |
| **Figurine,** Leopard, Plinth, c.1946, 11 In., Pair | 301 |
| **Vase,** Beehive, Purple Glaze, c.1938, 8 x 6 In. | 120 |
| **Vase,** Bow Foot, Blue Petty Glaze, c.1940, 11 In. | 60 |
| **Vase,** Bow Foot, Chartreuse, 11 In. | 40 |
| **Vase,** Gladiola, Chartreuse Drip Glaze, Pierced, c.1949, 11 x 14 In. | 155 |
| **Vase,** Gray, Greek Key, Marked, 1940s, 4 x 6 In. | 78 |
| **Vase,** Horn, Blue, 1940s, 7 1/4 In. | 20 |
| **Vase,** Oil Jar, Green Petty Crystal Glaze, Long Neck, 8 In. | 150 |
| **Vase,** Terraceware, Purple, 20 1/2 In. | 109 |

**ROYAL NYMPHENBURG** is the modern name for the Nymphenburg porcelain factory, which was established at Neudeck-ob-der-Au, Germany, in 1753 and moved to Nymphenburg in 1761. The company is still in existence. Marks include a checkered shield topped by a crown, a crowned *CT* with the year, and a contemporary shield mark on reproductions of eighteenth-century porcelain.

| | |
|---|---|
| **Candlestick,** Ram's Head, Acanthus Leaf, Gold, Black, 8 1/4 In., Pair | 725 |
| **Figurine,** Capitano, Man Holding Hat, Blanc De Chine, 7 1/2 In. | 281 |
| **Vase,** Bud, Baluster Shape, 4 Concave Recesses, Historical Busts, 9 In. | 625 |

**ROYAL RUDOLSTADT**, *see Rudolstadt category.*

**ROYAL VIENNA**, *see Beehive category.*

**ROYAL WORCESTER** is a name used by collectors. Worcester porcelains were made in Worcester, England, from about 1751. The firm went through many different periods and name changes. It became the Worcester Royal Porcelain Company, Ltd., in 1862. Today collectors call the porcelains made after 1862 "Royal Worcester." In 1976, the firm merged with W.T. Copeland to become Royal Worcester Spode. The company was bought by the Portmeirion Group in 2009. Some early products of the factory are listed under Worcester. Related pieces may be listed under Copeland, Copeland Spode, and Spode.

| | |
|---|---|
| **Basket,** Wild Flowers, Grass, Ivory Ground, Bent Handle, Oval Foot, c.1901, 5 In. | 205 |
| **Biscuit Stand,** 2 Children, Seated Under Trees, Porcelain, c.1890, 7 In., Pair | 875 |
| **Bowl,** Lotus Shape, Gilt Mounts, Marked, 7 x 11 1/2 In. | 531 |
| **Candlestick,** Ivory, Lion Masks, Leaves, Gilt, Claw Feet, c.1895, 16 In., Pair | 211 |
| **Castor,** Sugar, Boy, Girl, 1800s Attire, c.1910, 7 In., Pair | 875 |

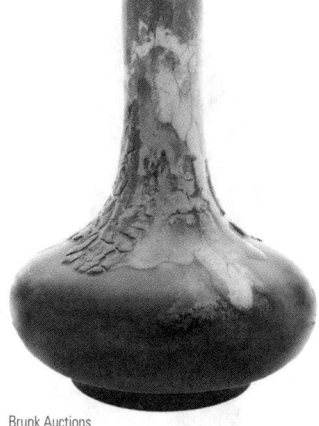

**Royal Doulton,** Vase, Chang Ware, Multicolor, Harry Nixon, Charles Noke, c.1920, 13 1/2 In.
$4,720

Brunk Auctions

**Royal Doulton,** Vase, Chang Ware, Thick Runny Glaze, Charles Noke, Fred Moore, 7 1/8 In.
$7,475

Humler & Nolan

**Royal Doulton,** Vase, Flambe, Sung, Peacock In Flight, Red Purple, Charles Noke, 6 1/4 In.
$1,495

Humler & Nolan

R

**Royal Doulton,** Vase, Plants, Art Nouveau, Stoneware, Mark V. Marshall, Lambeth, c.1903, 15 In.
$1,107

Skinner Auctioneers & Appraisers

**Royal Flemish,** Biscuit Jar, Lid, Gold Grids, Multicolor Body, Coin, Rampant Lion, Handle, 8 In.
$920

Early Auction Co.

**Royal Flemish,** Vase, Flattened, Coins, Medallions, Gilt Grid, Trefoil Cup Mouth, 7¼ In.
$2,185

Early Auction Co.

| | |
|---|---:|
| **Cup & Saucer,** Demitasse, Highland Cattle, Harry Stinton, 3¾ In. Diam. | 431 |
| **Ewer,** Grazing Sheep, Buff Ground, High Scroll Handle, Harry Davis, 13 In., Pair | 11070 |
| **Ewer,** Owl, On Branch, Blackbird, Dragon Handle, 11 In. | 649 |
| **Ewer,** Squat, Shaped Handle, White, Painted Gold Flowers, c.1886, 7½ In. | 180 |
| **Ewer,** White & Gold Decoration, Elongated Neck, Gilt Dragon Handle, 11 In. | 590 |
| **Figurine,** Hunter, Shirtless, Stick, Dead Rabbit, Pheasant, Majolica, 17⅞ In. | 1968 |
| **Goblet,** Pierced Lid, Pink, Red Flowers, Gilt, Raised Stem, 11 In. | 974 |
| **Jar,** Temple, Fruit, Natural Ground, Gilt Trim, Hexagonal, E. Townsend, 1939, 4 In. | 247 |
| **Jardiniere,** Water Lily, Cream, Gold, Water Lily Brass Base, 15 x 10½ In. | 472 |
| **Jug,** Salamander, Orange, Green, Angled Handle, Basketweave Ground, 6 In. | 207 |
| **Moon Flask,** Imari Palette, Stork In Flight, c.1890, 10 In. | 344 |
| **Planter,** Renaissance Style, Flowers, c.1910, 10 x 14 In. | 438 |
| **Plaque,** Children & Flowers, Pate-Sur-Pate, Salmon Ground, 8 x 18 In. | 1046 |
| **Plate,** Chinoiserie, Figures, Landscape, White Ground, c.1910, 12 Piece | 608 |
| **Plate,** Luncheon, Floral Bouquets, Green Rim, Square, c.1917, 8 In., 13 Piece | 240 |
| **Plate,** Vines, Flowers, Star Design, England, c.1915, 10¼ In., 11 Piece | 594 |
| **Potpourri Jar,** Lid, Cottage, Birds Panels, Reticulated, 6-Sided, 6 In. | 1770 |
| **Teapot,** Figural, Woman, Mustached Dandy On Reverse, Patience, Signed, c.1882, 6 In. ......*illus* | 9225 |
| **Urn,** Lid, Gold Enamel, Flowers, Yellow, Pink, Blue, Scroll Handles, 8 In. | 266 |
| **Vase,** Cattle, White, Oval, Gilt Handles, Footed, J. Stinton, 1920, 12 In. | 1906 |
| **Vase,** Flower Sprays, White Ground, Gilt, Flared, Handles, c.1889, 11½ In. | 281 |
| **Vase,** Gold, Pink, Blue Flowers, Reticulated, Pedestal Handles, 6 In. | 944 |
| **Vase,** Highland Cattle, Gilt Acanthus Leaf Handles, John Stinton, 10 In. | 253 |
| **Vase,** Lid, Grazing Sheep, Buff Ground, Footed, 2 Handles, H. Davis, 16 In. | 11685 |
| **Vase,** Lid, Musical Symbols, Angels, Pink, Flat, Flared, T. Bott, 1865, 14 In. | 4666 |
| **Vase,** Lid, Sheep, Misty Landscape, Painted, Harry Davis, 1909, 15¾ In. | 6355 |
| **Vase,** Nautilus Shell Shape, Parcel Gilt, Coral Branch Support, 9 x 5¼ In. | 253 |
| **Vase,** Peaches, Grapes, Berries, Brown Ground, Gilt, Baluster, Y.H. Price, 6 x 4 In. | 190 |

**ROYCROFT** products were made by the Roycrofter community of East Aurora, New York, in the late nineteenth and early twentieth centuries. The community was founded by Elbert Hubbard, famous philosopher, writer, and artist. The workshops owned by the community made furniture, metalware, leatherwork, embroidery, and jewelry. A printshop produced many signs, books, and the magazines that promoted the sayings of Elbert Hubbard. Furniture by the Roycroft community is listed in the Furniture category.

| | |
|---|---:|
| **Ashtray,** Copper, Hammered, Cylindrical Stem, Loop Handle, Match Holder, 29 In. | 295 |
| **Bookends,** Copper, Hammered, Agate, Orb & Cross Mark, c.1925, 4½ x 5½ In., Pair ......*illus* | 1000 |
| **Bowl,** Copper, Hammered, Modeled Ferns, Victor Toothaker, 7½ x 3 In. | 1830 |
| **Bowl,** Copper, Hammered, Round, Curved Sides, Small Pulled Feet, 13 In. | 708 |
| **Bowl,** Copper, Round, Flaring Rim, c.1910, 4½ x 12 In. | 246 |
| **Candelabrum,** 3-Light, Copper, Hammered, Twisted, Curled, 20 x 9¾ In. | 732 |
| **Candleholder,** Copper, Hammered, Dish Bobeche & Base, Flattened Handle, 3 x 4 In. | 488 |
| **Candlestick,** Copper, Hammered, 2 Legs, Square Base, 7 In. | 1220 |
| **Candlestick,** Copper, Silver, Secessionist, Dard Hunter, c.1905, 8 x 4¾ In. | 1750 |
| **Clock,** Wood, Arched, Leather Wrap, Tooled Flowers, Braided Edge, 4½ x 6 In. | 2125 |
| **Goodie Box,** Wood, Hammered Iron Handles, Orb Mark, 25 x 12 x 9 In. | 1375 |
| **Humidor,** Copper, Hammered, Footed, Handles, c.1915, 6 x 6 In. | 625 |
| **Inkwell,** Copper, Ceramic Insert, c.1925, 2 x 9 In. | 875 |
| **Inkwell,** Copper, Hammered, Tooled, Bell Form, Flared-Out Base, 3 x 5 In. | 188 |
| **Jardiniere,** Copper, Riveted Straps, Cylindrical, Bulbous, Flared Rim, 3-Footed, 11 In. | 4270 |
| **Lamp,** Copper Base, Hammered, Strapping, Ribbed Aurene Bell Shade, 15 x 11 In. | 6710 |
| **Lamp,** Copper Shade, Hammered, Strapwork, Mica Band, Column Support, 14 In. | 3068 |
| **Plate,** Trillium Designs, Copper, Hammered, Beaded, Tooled, 10 In. | 336 |
| **Vase,** Bud, Copper, Hammered, 3 Buttresses, Karl Kipp, 7 x 3 In. | 3965 |
| **Vase,** Bud, Copper, Silver Decoration, Cylindrical, Buttressed Feet, K. Kipp, 8 In. | 3540 |
| **Vase,** Copper, Beaker Shape, Round Foot, Pinched Rim, Hammered, 7½ In. | 288 |
| **Vase,** Copper, Brass Wash, Silver Decoration, Dard Hunter, c.1915, 6 x 3 In. ......*illus* | 500 |
| **Vase,** Copper, Hammered, Riveted Band, Bulbous, Marked, Orb & Cross, 15 x 7 In. | 3660 |
| **Vase,** Dogwood Pattern, Copper, Hammered, Brass, Cylindrical, c.1905, 7 x 2 In. | 1375 |
| **Vase,** Nickel Plate, Hammered, Band Of Squares, 5 x 3½ In. | 580 |
| **Wastebasket,** Oak, Slatted Sides, Square, Orb & Cross Mark, c.1910, 13 x 12 In. ......*illus* | 2000 |

**ROZANE,** *see Roseville category.*

**ROZENBURG** worked at The Hague, Holland, from 1890 to 1914. The most important pieces were earthenware made in the early twentieth century with pale-colored Art Nouveau designs.

| | |
|---|---|
| **Charger,** Yellow Dandelions, Blue Ribbon, Den Haag, c.1894, 17¾ In. | 403 |
| **Vase,** Flowers, Art Nouveau, Eggshell, Tapered, Narrow Neck, Bulbous, 9½ In. | 4370 |
| **Vase,** Multicolor Bird, Flowers, Glossy Glaze, Marked, Stork, Den Haag, 9⅜ In. | 230 |
| **Vase,** Stylized Flowers, Netherlands, c.1900, 10 x 6½ In. ........................*illus* | 625 |

**RRP,** or RRP Roseville, is the mark used by the firm of Robinson-Ransbottom. It is not a mark of the more famous Roseville Pottery. The Ransbottom brothers started a pottery in 1900 in Ironspot, Ohio. In 1920, they merged with the Robinson Clay Product Company of Akron, Ohio, to become Robinson-Ransbottom. The factory closed in 2005.

| | |
|---|---|
| **Bowl,** Brown Bands, Geometric Design, Marked, 14 x 7½ In. | 68 |
| **Cookie Jar,** Apples, Branch Handles, Round, Pedestal Foot, 8½ x 9 In. | 48 |
| **Cookie Jar,** Moon Girl, Closed Eyes, Blond, Marked, 1940s | 395 |
| **Crock,** Spongeware, Blue, Cream, 2¼ x 3¾ In. | 8 |
| **Cuspidor,** Dark Brown, Scalloped & Ribbed Rim, 4¾ x 8 In. | 37 |
| **Figurine,** Dog, Pug, Glass Eyes, Red, Black Trim, 13½ x 12 In. | 345 |
| **Jardiniere,** Sun & Moon, Brown, Blue, Green Glaze, 8 x 9¼ In. | 40 |
| **Mixing Bowl,** Yellowware, Geometric Design, Marked, 9 x 4¾ In. | 68 |
| **Pitcher,** Brown Drip Glaze, Marked, 7½ x 5½ In. | 23 |
| **Umbrella Stand,** 4 Panels, Poppies, Green Ground, 21½ x 10 In. | 225 |
| **Vase,** Mottled Green, Blue Over Purple, 9 In. | 230 |
| **Wall Pocket,** Birds, Flowers, Impressed, Conical, 8¼ In. | 29 |

**RS GERMANY** is part of the wording in marks used by the Tillowitz, Germany, factory of Reinhold Schlegelmilch from 1914 until about 1945. The porcelain was sold decorated and undecorated. The Schlegelmilch families made porcelains marked in many ways. See also ES Germany, RS Poland, RS Prussia, RS Silesia, RS Suhl, and RS Tillowitz.

| | |
|---|---|
| **Bowl,** Sheep Herder, Sheep, Cottage, Square, 8¼ In. | 89 |
| **Bowl,** Woman, Watering Flowers, Green, Iridescent Border, Steeple Mold, 11 In. | 826 |
| **Toothbrush Holder,** Cattails, Marked | 45 |
| **Toothbrush Holder,** Pink Roses, 3 Openings, Wall Mount, 3 x 3 In. | 175 |
| **Toothbrush Holder,** Roses, Dogwood, Leaves, Curved & Raised Edges, 4 x 4 In. | 75 |

**RS POLAND** (German) is a mark used by the Reinhold Schlegelmilch factory at Tillowitz from about 1946 to 1956. After 1956, the factory made porcelain marked *PT Poland*. This is one of many of the RS marks used. See also ES Germany, RS Germany, RS Prussia, RS Silesia, RS Suhl, and RS Tillowitz.

| | |
|---|---|
| **Biscuit Jar,** Flowers, Purple Ground, Finial, Lid, 7 x 7 In. | 325 |
| **Bowl,** White & Lavender Flowers, 3-Footed, 7 x 3 In. | 350 |
| **Centerpiece,** Rose Garlands, Footed, Gold Trim, Raised Dots | 675 |
| **Dish,** Mayonnaise, Hydrangea, Footed | 125 |
| **Dish,** Shell Shape, Reticulated, Pink & White Roses | 125 |
| **Plate,** White Flowers, Gold Rim, c.1935, 7½ In. | 37 |
| **Vase,** 2 Women, Working Yarn, Green Ground, Tapered, Prussia Mold, 6¼ In. | 767 |
| **Vase,** Bird Of Paradise Scene, Green Ground, Handles, 8 In. | 590 |
| **Vase,** Farm, Sheep, Herder, Handles, 9½ In. | 580 |
| **Vase,** Hummingbirds, Flowers, Pedestal, Handles, 9¼ In. | 1003 |
| **Vase,** White, Yellow Roses, Green Ground, Cylindrical, Prussia Mold, 3½ In. | 59 |
| **Vase,** Woodland Scene, Figures, Pheasants, Marked, 11 In. | 1295 |

**RS PRUSSIA** appears in several marks used on porcelain before 1917. Reinhold Schlegelmilch started his porcelain works in Suhl, Germany, in 1869. See also ES Germany, RS Germany, RS Poland, RS Silesia, RS Suhl, and RS Tillowitz.

| | |
|---|---|
| **Biscuit Jar,** Flowers, Scrolled Handles, 4-Footed, Wavy Rim, Lid, c.1900, 6¾ In. | 180 |
| **Biscuit Jar,** Lid, Snowball, Flowers, Leaves, White, Brown Ground, Gilt, 6½ In. | 118 |
| **Bowl,** Blackberry, Branch, Leaves, White, Green Border, Iris Mold, 10¼ In. | 59 |
| **Bowl,** Flowers, Snowball, Cream, Green Ground, Flower Border, 10½ In. | 207 |
| **Bowl,** Iris Mold, Wild Poppy Design, Multicolor, Gilt Trim, 10½ In. | 207 |
| **Bowl,** LeBrun Portrait, Green Ground, Purple Dome Border, Lily Mold, 9¼ In. | 295 |
| **Bowl,** Multicolor Fruit, Black Border, Gold Stencil Rim, 10¼ In. | 708 |
| **Bowl,** Pink Poppies, White, Green Ground, Iris Mold, 10½ In. | 118 |
| **Bowl,** Pink, White Flowers, Hidden Cottage Mold, 10 In. | 944 |

## The Monteith Bowl

Mr. Monteith was a Scotsman who wore a cloak with a scalloped hem. A large punch bowl with a similar scalloped edge is called a "Monteith bowl." It is usually at least 12 inches in diameter.

**Royal Worcester,** Teapot, Figural, Woman, Mustached Dandy On Reverse, Patience, Signed, c.1882, 6 In.
$9,225

Skinner Auctioneers & Appraisers

**Roycroft,** Bookends, Copper, Hammered, Agate, Orb & Cross Mark, c.1925, 4½ x 5½ In., Pair
$1,000

Rago Arts & Auction Center

**Roycroft,** Vase, Copper, Brass Wash, Silver Decoration, Dard Hunter, c.1915, 6 x 3 In.
$500

R

Rago Arts & Auction Center

**Roycroft,** Wastebasket, Oak, Slatted Sides, Square, Orb & Cross Mark, c.1910, 13 x 12 In.
$2,000

Rago Arts & Auction Center

**Rozenburg,** Vase, Stylized Flowers, Netherlands, c.1900, 10 x 6½ In.
$625

Rago Arts & Auction Center

**RS Prussia,** Pitcher, Water, Hydrangeas, Wreath, Star, Tankard, Molded Rim, Handle, c.1910, 12 In.
$207

Jeffrey S. Evans & Assoc.

| | |
|---|---|
| **Bowl,** Potacka Portrait, Gold Ground, Pink, Cream Border, Lily Mold, 10 In. | 767 |
| **Bowl,** Rose Basket Transfer, Red Star, 10½ In. | 47 |
| **Bowl,** Swan In Lake, Scalloped Edge, Red Star, 11 In. | 59 |
| **Bowl,** Winter Season, Blond Woman, Green, White, Lavender, Iris Mold, 10 In. | 767 |
| **Bowl,** Yellow, White Roses, Flower & Dotted Belt Rim, c.1910, 3 x 11 In. | 92 |
| **Cake Plate,** 12-Sided, 3 White Swans, Blue Lake, Birds, Cutout Handles, 10 In. | 295 |
| **Cake Plate,** Pink Flowers, Green, Cutout Handles, Hidden Image Mold, 11 In. | 177 |
| **Cake Plate,** Wildflowers, Cream, Cobalt Blue, Gold Trim, Cutout Handles, 10¼ In. | 266 |
| **Cake Plate,** Winter Season, Woman, Scalloped, Flower Mold, c.1900, 2 x 11 In. | 863 |
| **Celery Dish,** Roses, Lavender, Green, White, Satin Finish, Iris Mold, Cutout Handles, 12 In. | 59 |
| **Chocolate Pot,** Lid, Cream Ground, Red Roses, Fired Gold | 480 |
| **Chocolate Pot,** Lid, Roses, Pink, Yellow, Blue, Poppy Mold, Intertwined Handle, 9 In. | 531 |
| **Chocolate Service,** Pot, 6 Cups, Swans, Cream, Green, Blue Ground, Pot 10¼ In., 7 Piece | 413 |
| **Chocolate Set,** Pot, 6 Cups, Saucers, Roses, Green, Point & Clover Mold, Pot 10 In., 13 Piece | 885 |
| **Dresser Tray,** Spilled Flower Basket, White, Green Ground, Scalloped Rim, 11½ In. | 94 |
| **Pitcher,** Water, Hydrangeas, Wreath, Star, Tankard, Molded Rim, Handle, c.1910, 12 In. ....illus | 207 |
| **Pitcher,** Water, Pink Roses, Hydrangeas, Molded Rim & Handle, c.1910, 12 In. | 207 |
| **Plate,** 3 Scenes, Pheasant, Ducks, Farmyard, Cobalt Blue, Gilt Center Trim, 7 In. | 1298 |
| **Plate,** Flowers, Brown Scalloped Rim, Wreath Mark, 11¼ In. | 65 |
| **Plate,** Flowers, Pink, Wreath Mark, 10½ In. | 40 to 70 |
| **Plate,** Water Lilies, Icicle Mold, Green, Blue, 9¾ In. | 40 |
| **Plate,** Winter Season, Charmer, Woman, Red Cape, Gilt Edge, 8½ In. | 3250 |
| **Plate,** Woman, Portrait, Iridescent Green, Lily Border, Lily Mold, Germany, c.1900, 8 In. | 316 |
| **Relish,** Rose, Flower, White, Portrait Medallion, Cutout Handles, Gilt, 10 In. | 531 |
| **Tankard,** 6-Sided, Flowers, White, Pink Ground, Swag & Tassel Mold, Gilt, 10 In. | 235 |
| **Tankard,** Scattered Flowers, Scalloped Base, Gilt Trim, 11¼ In. | 295 |
| **Toothpick Holder,** Bust, Woman, Dark Hair, Lily Mold, Double Handles, Gilt, 2 In. | 2360 |
| **Vase,** 8-Sided, Roses, Pink, Satin Glaze, Trumpet Rim, Silver Plated Stand, 12 In. | 1180 |
| **Vase,** Painted, Cherubs, Multicolor, Shaped Handles, Finial, After Murillo, c.1900, 9 In. | 1320 |
| **Vase,** Swan, Evergreen Landscape, White Ground, Double Handles, Gilt, 8½ In. | 1003 |

**RS SILESIA** appears on porcelain made at the Reinhold Schlegelmilch factory in Tillowitz, Germany, from the 1920s to the 1940s. The Schlegelmilch families made porcelains marked in many ways. See also ES Germany, RS Germany, RS Poland, RS Prussia, RS Suhl, and RS Tillowitz.

| | |
|---|---|
| **Bowl,** Footed, Willow Tree, Medieval Building, 6¼ In. | 400 |
| **Dish,** Grapes, 6⅛ In. | 148 |

**RS SUHL** is a mark used by the Reinhold Schlegelmilch factory in Suhl, Germany, between 1900 and 1917. The Schlegelmilch families made porcelains in many places. See also ES Germany, RS Germany, RS Poland, RS Prussia, RS Silesia, and RS Tillowitz.

| | |
|---|---|
| **Bowl,** Sheep Herder, Village, Brown, 10 In. | 148 |
| **Fernery,** Pink, Yellow Roses, Gold Feet, Handles, Bands, Round, 4 x 5 In. | 142 |
| **Vase,** Cage Design, Blue Border, Gilt Trim, Handles, Gilt, Cylindrical, Prussia Mold, 10 In. | 472 |
| **Vase,** Medieval Castle, Pink & Yellow Roses, Shouldered, 4½ In. | 450 |
| **Vase,** Melon Eaters, Mountain Scene, Rolled Lip, 5 In. | 675 |

**RS TILLOWITZ** was marked on porcelain by the Reinhold Schlegelmilch factory at Tillowitz from the 1920s to the 1940s. Table services and ornamental pieces were made. See also ES Germany, RS Germany, RS Poland, RS Prussia, RS Silesia, and RS Suhl.

| | |
|---|---|
| **Celery Dish,** Black Swans, Heavy Gold Trim, Oval, Cutout Ends, 10½ In. | 295 |
| **Vase,** Chinese Pheasant, Brown, Gray Ground, Flared Cylinder, 8½ In. | 266 |
| **Vase,** Red-Breasted Pheasant, Brown, Gray Ground, Flared Cylinder, 8½ In. | 177 |
| **Vase,** Round, Flowers, Orange Ground, Footed, 5 In. | 35 |

**RUBINA** is a glassware that shades from red to clear. It was first made by George Duncan and Sons of Pittsburgh, Pennsylvania, in about 1885. This coloring was used on many types of glassware.

| | |
|---|---|
| **Pitcher,** Inverted Thumbprint, 8¾ In. | 89 |
| **Pitcher,** Water, Spot-Optic, Flowers, Multicolor, Triangular Crimped Rim, c.1900, 8 In. | 184 |

**RUBINA VERDE** is a Victorian glassware that was shaded from red to green. It was first made by Hobbs, Brockunier and Company of Wheeling, West Virginia, about 1890.

| | |
|---|---|
| **Pitcher,** Water, Coin Spot, Vaseline Handle, 8 In. | 288 |

R

| | |
|---|---|
| **Pitcher,** Water, Dew Drop, Hobnail No. 5, Square Rim, Hobbs, c.1890, 9 In. | 150 |
| **Pitcher,** Water, Hobnail, Vaseline Handle, 7 ½ In. | 374 |
| **Vase,** Jack-In-The-Pulpit, Applied Green Foot, c.1900, 12 In. | 161 |

**RUBY GLASS** is the dark red color of a ruby, the precious gemstone. It was a popular Victorian color that never went completely out of style. The glass was shaped by many different processes to make many different types of ruby glass. There was a revival of interest in the 1940s when modern-shaped ruby table glassware became fashionable. Sometimes the red color is added to clear glass by a process called flashing or staining. Flashed glass is clear glass dipped in a colored glass, then pressed or cut. Stained glass has color painted on a clear glass. Then it is refired so the stain fuses with the glass. Pieces of glass colored in this way are indicated by the word *stained* in the description. Related items may be found in other categories, such as Cranberry Glass, Pressed Glass, and Souvenir.

| | |
|---|---|
| **Compote,** White Design, Scalloped Rim, 8 ½ x 12 In. | 300 |
| **Vase,** Portrait, Young Bohemian Woman, 1875, 17 In. | 1960 |

**RUDOLSTADT** was a faience factory in the Thuringia region of Germany from 1720 to about 1791. In 1854, Ernst Bohne began working in the area. From about 1887 to 1918, the New York and Rudolstadt Pottery made decorated porcelain marked with the RW and crown familiar to collectors. This porcelain was imported by Lewis Straus and Sons of New York, which later became Nathan Straus and Sons. The word *Royal* was included in their import mark. Collectors often call it "Royal Rudolstadt." Most pieces found today were made in the late nineteenth or early twentieth century. Additional pieces may be listed in the Kewpie category.

| | |
|---|---|
| **Bust,** Woman, Hat, Ruffled Blouse, Necklace, Pink, Yellow, 6 ¼ In. | 525 |
| **Bust,** Woman, Ruffled Dress & Bonnet, Nouveau, 10 x 7 ½ In. | 775 |
| **Chocolate Pot,** Spray, Blue & Purple, Rococo Style Scrolls, Gilt Handle, Lid, 8 ¾ In. | 75 |
| **Console,** Poppies, Shell Shape, 11 ¾ x 10 ½ In. | 235 |
| **Group,** Boys, Around Fire, 6 In. | 155 |
| **Group,** Girls, In A Circle, Holding Hands, Blue Anchor Mark, E. Bohne Sohne, 6 In. | 177 |
| **Teapot,** Strawberry Shape, Strawberry Finial, Leaves, Flowers, c.1916, 6 ¼ In. | 58 |
| **Vase,** Beaded Ground, Pink Ribbon, Flowers & Scrolls, Scroll Handles, 8 In. | 125 |
| **Vase,** Bulbous, Stick Neck, Flared Rim, Pink Flowers, Gilt, c.1875, 6 In. | 75 |
| **Vase,** Faux Ivory, Cylindrical, Geisha, Fans, 8 In. | 225 |
| **Vase,** Women, Holding Instruments, Cobalt Blue, Gilt Handles, Ruffled Rim, 7 In. | 275 |

**RUGS** have been used in the American home since the seventeenth century. The oriental rug of that time was often used on a table, not on the floor. Rag rugs, hooked rugs, and braided rugs were made by housewives from scraps of material. American Indian rugs are listed in the Indian category.

| | |
|---|---|
| **Afshar,** 2 Medallions On Boteh, Geometrics, Ivory, Cobalt, Red Field, 5 Ft. x 6 Ft. 6 In. | 590 |
| **Afshar,** Diamond Medallions, Borders, Boteh Rows, Red Field, 5 Ft. x 6 Ft. 8 In. | 472 |
| **Anatolian,** Red & Ivory Crosses, Swastikas, Blue Field, Borders, 10 Ft. 9 In. x 5 Ft. 8 In. | 740 |
| **Angora,** Stylized Flowers, Cream Border, Red Ground, Turkey, 9 Ft. 8 In x 14 Ft. 5 In. | 2214 |
| **Aubusson,** Ivory Field, Red, Tan, Flower Medallion, Leaves, c.1890, 12 Ft. 4 In. x 9 Ft. 9 In. | 813 |
| **Bakhtiari,** Flower Medallion, Navy Ground, Canted Corners, c.1910, 4 Ft. 5 In. x 6 Ft. 8 In. | 3060 |
| **Bakhtiari,** Garden Panel, Octofoil Reserves, Flowers, Palmette Border, 14 Ft. 4 In. x 10 Ft. 10 In. | 2760 |
| **Bakhtiari,** Geometric Rows, Flower, Cross & Hook Border, Ivory Ground, 7 Ft. x 12 Ft. 8 In. | 944 |
| **Bakhtiari,** Tree, Exotic Birds, Blue, Green, Yellow, Red, Ivory Field, 4 Ft. x 5 Ft. 9 In. | 2832 |
| **Baluchi,** Geometric, Diamond Medallions, Red, Brown, Green, Saffron, 3 Ft. 7 In. x 6 Ft. 7 In. | 207 |
| **Bessarabian,** Navy Field, Red, Light Blue Roses, Geometric Border, 8 Ft. x 3 Ft. 6 In. | 540 |
| **Bidjar,** Blue, Cream Border, Persian, Late 20th Century, 11 Ft. 9 In. x 18 Ft. 2 In. | 923 |
| **Bidjar,** Flowers, Trelliswork, Ivory, Red, Pink, Blue Field, 9 x 11 Ft. | 1185 |
| **Bidjar,** Red, Blue, Green, Flowers, Diamonds, Borders, c.1910, 6 Ft. 7 In. x 4 Ft. 4 In. *illus* | 3852 |
| **Bokhara,** Gul Rows, Diamonds, Camel Field, Borders, c.1910, 4 Ft. 2 In. x 6 Ft. 7 In. | 177 |
| **Bokhara,** Hooks, Stars, 3 Repeating Rows Octagonal Shapes, c.1910, 8 Ft. 7 In. x 9 Ft. 9 In. | 354 |
| **Braided,** Multicolor, Oval, 20th Century, 12 Ft. x 9 Ft. 4 In. | 566 |
| **Caucasian,** Kazak, 3 Stepped Medallions, 3 Ft. 8 In. x 5 Ft. 11 In. *illus* | 649 |
| **Caucasian,** Kuba, Sejshore, Flowers, Leaves, Blue Ground, c.1890, 3 Ft. 1 In. x 4 Ft. | 3900 |
| **Chichi,** Blue Field, Stylized Palmettes, Borders, Multicolor, c.1890, 5 Ft. x 3 Ft. 11 In. | 523 |
| **Chinese,** Art Deco, Blue, Peonies, Shou Medallions, Wool, 11 Ft. 6 In. x 8 Ft. 9 In. | 1046 |
| **Chinese,** Camel Field, Ton-Sur-Ton Medallions, Blue Border, c.1925, 11 Ft. x 8 Ft. 6 In. | 875 |
| **Chinese,** Dueling Dragons, Blue Field, Ivory & Blue Stripe Border, c.1910, 3 Ft. x 5 Ft. | 413 |
| **Chinese,** Purple Flowers, Green Leaves, Yellow Ground, Wool, 4 Ft. 10 In. x 2 Ft. 6 In. | 531 |
| **Concentric Squares,** Brown, Gold, Orange, Black Border, Wool, 1950s, 9 Ft. 8 In. x 13 Ft. 4 In. | 1586 |
| **Felt,** Penny, 6-Sided, Multicolor, c.1885, 31 In. | 135 |

**Rug,** Bidjar, Red, Blue, Green, Flowers, Diamonds, Borders, c.1910,
6 Ft. 7 In. x 4 Ft. 4 In.
$3,852

Cottone Auctions

**Rug,** Caucasian, Kazak, 3 Stepped Medallions, 3 Ft. 8 In. x 5 Ft. 11 In.
$649

Brunk Auctions

**Rug,** Hand Woven, Wool, Geometric Shapes, Signed CC, 1960s,
4 Ft. 5 In. x 6 Ft. 9 In.
$1,875

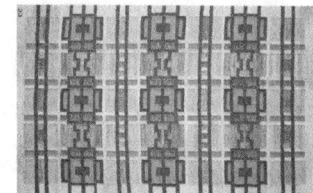

Rago Arts & Auction Center

R

**TIP**
*Keep weavings like rugs and tapestries away from air ducts, heaters, and sunlight.*

487

**Rug,** Hooked, Dogs, Black, White, Trees, Flowers, Mixed Fabric, Burlap, c.1930, 24 x 36 In.
$300

Garth's Auctioneers & Appraisers

**Rug,** Hooked, Horse & Buggy, Dog Chasing, Bird, Wood, Cotton, c.1910, 37 x 66 In.
$360

Garth's Auctioneers & Appraisers

**Rug,** Hooked, Matisse Style Design, Edward Fields, 1981, 82 x 104 In.
$472

Brunk Auctions

**Rug,** Hooked, Pictorial, Christmas Tree, Toys, Face Border, Stretcher, c.1930, 30 x 58 In.
$1,020

Garth's Auctioneers & Appraisers

**Rug,** Hooked, Smiling Cat, Red Pillow, Wool On Burlap, Mounted, c.1900, 20 x 38 In.
$390

Garth's Auctioneers & Appraisers

**Rug,** India, Hand Knotted, Wool, Overlapping Blocks, 8 x 11 Ft.
$4,063

Rago Arts & Auction Center

R

| | |
|---|---|
| **Feraghan,** Sarouk, Cobalt Blue Medallion & Pendants, Brick Red Field, 9 Ft. 11 In. x 13 Ft. | 2124 |
| **Gabbeh,** Checkerboard, Variegated Red, Pink, Brown, Wool, 3 Ft. x 5 Ft. 3 In. | 81 |
| **Gabbeh,** Variegated Red, Rust, Orange, Small Blue Animal, Wool, 4 Ft. 8 In. x 6 Ft. 7 In. | 207 |
| **Guatemalan,** Multicolor, Reds, Green, Woven, Wool, c.1950, 5 Ft. 3 In. x 4 Ft. | 115 |
| **Hamadan,** 17 Floral Medallions, Vines, Leaves, c.1950, Runner, 3 Ft. 6 In. x 16 Ft. 5 In. | 531 |
| **Hamadan,** 3 Medallions, Corner Work, Blue & Black Field, Multiple Borders, 3 x 9 Ft. | 590 |
| **Hamadan,** Flowers, Rust, Ivory, Yellow, Cobalt Blue Ground, Runner, 3 Ft. 4 In. x 12 Ft. | 531 |
| **Hamadan,** Medallion, Serrated Edges, Arrows, Cobalt Blue Ground, 4 Ft. 8 In. x 6 Ft. 6 In. | 295 |
| **Hamadan,** Variegated Red Ground, Medallion, Geometric Border, 5 Ft. 8 In. x 9 Ft. 9 In. | 427 |
| **Hand Woven,** Wool, Geometric Shapes, Signed CC, 1960s, 4 Ft. 5 In. x 6 Ft. 9 In. ...............*illus* | 1875 |
| **Hereke,** Hunting Scene, Elephant, Leopard, Ox Cart, Attendants, 4 Ft. 8 In. x 2 Ft. 7 In. | 2300 |
| **Heriz,** Arabesque Medallion, Red Field, Ivory Spandrels, Blue Border, 8 Ft. x 10 Ft. 10 In. | 1540 |
| **Heriz,** Blue Ground, Multicolor Borders, Ivory, Honey, Rust, Green, 8 Ft. 10 In. x 11 Ft. 10 In. | 259 |
| **Heriz,** Center Medallion, Cobalt Blue Border, Flowers, Leaves, Persia, c.1950, 8 Ft. x 11 Ft. | 1534 |
| **Heriz,** Center Medallion, Red Field, Ivory, Olive, Persia, 10 Ft. 4 In. x 12 Ft. 10 In. | 1003 |
| **Heriz,** Central Medallion, Navy, Gold, Rust Red, 8 Ft. x 11 Ft. 9 In. | 1888 |
| **Heriz,** Flower Border, Medallion, Palmettes, Red, Navy, Gold, 8 Ft. 11 In. x 5 Ft. 5 In. | 357 |
| **Heriz,** Ivory Field, Vines, Flowers, Medallion, Persia, c.1950, 8 Ft. 8 In. x 12 Ft. 4 In. | 708 |
| **Heriz,** Medallion, Corner Work, Brick Red Field, Geometric Border, 8 Ft. x 11 Ft. 5 In. | 885 |
| **Heriz,** Medallions, Flowers, Geometrics, Red Field, Trefoil Border, 3 Ft. 6 In. x 10 Ft. 7 In. | 1180 |
| **Heriz,** Multicolor Medallion, Ivory Spandrels, Blue Border, Persia, c.1945, 11 Ft. 11 In. x 8 Ft. | 2250 |
| **Heriz,** Red Center Panel, Ivory, Blue, Olive Highlights, Persia, c.1950, 8 Ft. 3 In. x 10 Ft. 1 In. | 649 |
| **Heriz,** Red Ground, Blue Zigzag, 4 Borders, Oriental, 9 x 12 Ft. | 2640 |
| **Heriz,** Red, Navy Blue, Ivory, Blues, Wool, Cotton, 9 Ft. 10 In. x 13 Ft. 9 In. | 805 |
| **Heriz,** Runner, Medallions, White Ground, Red, Blue, Pink, Wool, 6 Ft. 8 In. x 2 Ft. 3 ½ In. | 75 |
| **Hooked,** Animal Pairs, Boarding Noah's Ark, c.1950, 26 x 41 In. | 230 |
| **Hooked,** Bird, Tulip Branch Center Medallion, Flowers, Hearts, 28 x 45 In. | 177 |
| **Hooked,** Black Cat, Smiling, Striped Rug, Blue, Wool, Cotton, 22 x 33 In. | 780 |
| **Hooked,** Cat, Reclining, Multicolor, Wood Stretcher Frame, 26 x 35 In. | 59 |
| **Hooked,** Center Flower Spray, Undulating Border, Smyth Co., c.1920, 40 x 71 In. | 58 |
| **Hooked,** Center Lyres, White Field, Shell Border, c.1900, 29 x 58 In. | 360 |
| **Hooked,** Center Rose, 4 Radiating Petals, Buff Ground, Round, c.1910, 36 In. | 138 |
| **Hooked,** Diamond Pattern, Variegated, Multicolor, Early 1900s, 36 x 31 In. | 270 |
| **Hooked,** Dog, Resting On Bed Of Leaves, Flowers, Red Border, 53 x 101 In. | 1320 |
| **Hooked,** Dog, White, Black Spots, Demilune Shape, Pink Flower Border, 24 x 36 In. | 84 |
| **Hooked,** Dogs, Black, White, Trees, Flowers, Mixed Fabric, Burlap, c.1930, 24 x 36 In. .......*illus* | 300 |
| **Hooked,** Duck, Multicolored Checkered Ground, Stretcher Mount, 26 x 44 In. | 120 |
| **Hooked,** Embroidered, Houses, Deer, Man, Black Ground, New England, c.1910, 26 x 36 In. | 176 |
| **Hooked,** Flower Baskets, Multicolor, c.1940, 53 x 39 In. | 145 |
| **Hooked,** Flowers, Grapes, Vines, Strawberries, Rag, Yarn, Waldoboro Style, 31 x 54 In. | 1481 |
| **Hooked,** Flowers, On Branches, Black Ground, c.1900, 24 x 37 In. | 150 |
| **Hooked,** Geometric Wheel, Round, Braided Border, Wool On Burlap, c.1930, 36 In. | 316 |
| **Hooked,** Green, Gold Leaves, Maple, 70 x 77 In. | 826 |
| **Hooked,** Horse & Buggy, Dog Chasing, Bird, Wood, Cotton, c.1910, 37 x 66 In. ..................*illus* | 360 |
| **Hooked,** Horse, 4-Leaf Clover, Multicolor Stripe Border, Early 1900s, 19 x 36 In. | 431 |
| **Hooked,** Horse, Prancing, Striated Ground, Wool On Burlap, Virginia, c.1900, 40 x 42 In. | 3220 |
| **Hooked,** Horse, Running, Landscape, Multicolor, c.1915, 22 x 38 In. | 600 |
| **Hooked,** Houses, Ship, Scroll, Leaf Border, Orange, Red, Green, New England, 32 x 54 In. | 1800 |
| **Hooked,** Indian In Canoe, Hunting, 19 x 35 In. | 360 |
| **Hooked,** Landscape, Fruit, Flowers, After Currier & Ives Print, Wool, 36 x 48 In. | 480 |
| **Hooked,** Log Cabin, Geometric Shapes, c.1860, 36 x 71 In. | 840 |
| **Hooked,** Mat, Orange Tulips, Blue, Black, Sunburst, Leaves, 1920s, 19 x 19 In. | 176 |
| **Hooked,** Matisse Style Design, Edward Fields, 1981, 82 x 104 In. .........................*illus* | 472 |
| **Hooked,** Matisse Style, Yellow, Dark Red, Beige, Green, Edward Fields, 1981, 72 x 108 In. | 472 |
| **Hooked,** Moose, Landscape, Va., Verda H. Brenneman, c.1930, 27 x 44 In. | 288 |
| **Hooked,** New England Winter Scene, Church, Covered Bridge, Mountains, c.1910, 28 x 40 In. | 570 |
| **Hooked,** Octagon Medallion, Various Geometric Designs, Sawtooth Border, 1800s, 47 x 23 In. | 480 |
| **Hooked,** Parrots, Perched On Floral Branches, Multicolor, c.1910, 59 x 33 ½ In. | 98 |
| **Hooked,** Pictorial, Christmas Tree, Toys, Face Border, Stretcher, c.1930, 30 x 58 In. ..........*illus* | 1020 |
| **Hooked,** Pig, Red Back Marks, Black Border, Monogram, c.1950, 22 x 39 In. | 259 |
| **Hooked,** Pink Flowers, Gray Ground, Black Border, 38 ½ x 44 In. | 130 |
| **Hooked,** Potted Plant, Butterflies, Fleur-De-Lis, Red, c.1890, 26 x 39 In. | 259 |
| **Hooked,** Rooster, Standing, Red Ground, Scalloped Border, Cotton, c.1930, 24 x 36 In. | 575 |
| **Hooked,** Shirred, Urn, Flowers, Wool Strips, Yarn, Multicolored, Vt., c.1850, 30 x 42 In. | 3125 |
| **Hooked,** Smiling Cat, Red Pillow, Wool On Burlap, Mounted, c.1900, 20 x 38 In. ...............*illus* | 390 |
| **Hooked,** Spread Wing Eagle, Arrows, Shield, Stars, Welcome, Semicircular, c.1930 | 2850 |

**Rug,** Kazak, Eagle, Caucasian,
2 Sunburst Medallions, Red, Yellow, Blue,
c.1915, 7 Ft. 4 In. x 4 Ft. 3 In.
$900

Cowan's Auctions

**Rug,** Peking Chinese, Blue, Gray,
Flowers, Stark Carpets, 1976,
10 Ft. 2 In. x 13 Ft. 10 In.
$1,107

New Orleans Auction Galleries, Inc.

**Rug,** Persian, Red, Cream, Flowers,
Shiraz, 5 Ft. 4 In. x 8 Ft. 3 In.
$1,315

Neal Auction Co.

**Rug,** Pictorial, Eagle, Banner,
E Pluribus Unum, Sewn Yarn, S. Colburn,
Massachusetts, 1836, 33 x 69 In.
$8,610

Skinner Auctioneers & Appraisers

### TIP
*If you have Oriental or
Indian or other woven
rugs displayed on the
floor, put them on an all-
fabric padding. Do not
use rubber.*

**Rug,** Prayer, Silk, Brown, Beige, Orange,
Multiple Borders, Building, c.1900,
62 x 45 In.
$1,035

Cottone Auctions

**Rug,** Verner Panton, Wool, Black, Circles
Of Dots, Multicolor, Round, 5 Ft. 10 In.
$923

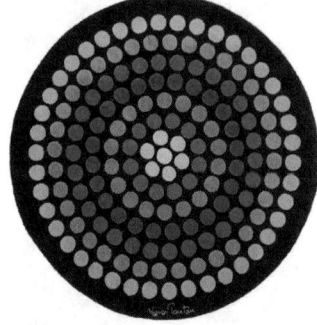

Skinner Auctioneers & Appraisers

| | |
|---|---|
| **Hooked,** Squirrel Playing With Ball, Multicolor, 1800s, 43 x 27 In. | 91 |
| **Hooked,** Stag, Geometric Corners, Multicolor, 1800s, 24 ½ x 31 ½ In. | 180 |
| **Hooked,** Stag, Trees, Flowers, Stripe Border, 1800s, 40 x 23 In. | 369 |
| **Hooked,** Strawberries, Red, Black, c.1925, 19 ½ x 28 ½ In. | 85 |
| **Hooked,** Swans, Swimming, Plants, Tree Landscape, 23 ½ x 43 ½ In. | 94 |
| **Hooked,** Terrier, Oval Reserve, Red Collar, Trees, Striated Border, Wool, c.1910, 32 x 55 In. | 575 |
| **Hooked,** Village, Victorian, Colonial Houses, Church, Signed B.E.M., 1900s, 18 x 44 In. | 356 |
| **Hooked,** Welcome, White Cat, Kitten, Flowers, Multicolor, Demilune Shape, 38 x 25 In. | 1778 |
| **India,** Hand Knotted, Wool, Overlapping Blocks, 8 x 11 Ft. ...........................*illus* | 4063 |
| **Isfahan,** Diamond Shape, Cream, Blue, Corner Guards, Wool, 9 Ft. 5 In. x 6 Ft. | 489 |
| **Jaipur,** Rust, Ivory, Honey, Salmon, Black, Wool, Fringe, 6 Ft. 2 In. x 4 Ft. 1 In. | 92 |
| **Kashan,** Cerulean Ground, Orange, Red, Blue, Medallion, c.1920, 4 Ft. 4 In. x 6 Ft. 8 In. | 3300 |
| **Kashan,** Medallion, Burgundy, Black, Tan, Green Wool, c.1950, 6 Ft. 10 In. x 4 Ft. 3 In. | 750 |
| **Kashan,** Prayer, Blue, Vase, Flowers, Guard Border, Persia, 4 Ft. 5 In. x 6 Ft. 9 In. | 1121 |
| **Kashan,** Red Ground, Blue Accented Medallion, Flowers, 3 Ft. 4 In. x 4 Ft. 8 In. | 244 |
| **Kashan,** Red, Blue, 3 Borders, Blue Ground, Red Center Diamond, 10 x 13 Ft. | 922 |
| **Kashan,** Tree Of Life, Birds Of Paradise, Multicolor, Wool, Silk, 3 Ft. 10 In. x 2 Ft. 10 In. | 265 |
| **Kasvin,** Geometric Medallion, Wreaths, Sprays, Pink, Beige, Ivory, Blue, 3 Ft. 6 In. x 5 Ft. | 533 |
| **Kazak,** Cinnamon Ground, Geometric Lozenges, Yellow, Red, 7 Ft. 3 In. x 4 Ft. 4 In. | 1037 |
| **Kazak,** Double Square Medallions, Pastels, Orange, Teal, Wool, 6 Ft. 6 In. x 4 Ft. 8 In. | 150 |
| **Kazak,** Eagle, Caucasian, 2 Sunburst Medallions, Red, Yellow, Blue, c.1915, 7 Ft. 4 In. x 4 Ft. 3 In. *illus* | 900 |
| **Kerman,** Diamonds, Scrolls, Tan, Burgundy, Wool, c.1945, 9 Ft. 3 In. x 5 Ft. 10 In. | 875 |
| **Kerman,** Hand Woven, Wool, Light Blue Field, Medallion Center, c.1960, 12 x 9 Ft. | 510 |
| **Kerman,** Medallion, Cream, Cartouche Blue Border, Iran, c.1950, 16 Ft. 6 In. x 11 Ft. 8 In. | 625 |
| **Kerman,** Multicolor Medallion, Flowers, Beige Gold Ground, Silk Wool, 1950s, 15 x 12 In. | 891 |
| **Kerman,** Prayer, Tree Of Life, Pairs Of Animals, Inscriptions, Silk, 2 Ft. 2 In. x 10 In. | 590 |
| **Kerman,** Red Ground, Medallion, Spandrels, Flower Borders, 10 Ft. 2 In. x 15 Ft. 8 In. | 615 |
| **Kerman,** Rose, Cream Borders, Blue Detail, Wool, Cotton, 24 Ft. 4 In. x 12 Ft. | 3778 |
| **Kerman,** Tree Of Life, Bird Border, Beige, Blue, Red, c.1900, 7 Ft. x 4 Ft. 8 In. | 1610 |
| **Kerman,** Vines, Flowers, Geometrics, Ivory Field, Red, Blue, Gold, Green, 13 Ft. 2 In. x 18 Ft. | 1298 |
| **Kuba,** Flower Vases, Multicolor, Caucasus, 1800s, 4 Ft. 8 In. x 3 Ft. 2 In. | 584 |
| **Kurdish,** Gold, Blue Boteh, Geometric Border, Wool, Runner, 3 Ft. 6 In. x 9 Ft. 9 In. | 1180 |
| **Mahal,** Leaves, Celadon, Tan, Brown, Ivory, Gray, Blue, Wool, Fringe, 8 Ft. 1 In. x 5 Ft. 2 In. | 150 |
| **Mahal,** Red, Gray, Black, Tan, Peach, Geometric, Medallion, Wool, 6 Ft. x 4 Ft. 3 In. | 184 |
| **Mahal,** Stylized Flowers, Ivory, Peach, Tan, Gray, Wool, Fringe, 10 Ft. 1 In. x 13 Ft. 10 In. | 253 |
| **Malayer,** Red Panel, Navy Medallion, Drops, Borders, 5 Ft. 7 In. x 11 Ft. 2 In. | 472 |
| **Marasali Shirvan,** Prayer, Flower, Ivory Field, Eagle Border, c.1900, 5 Ft. 6 In. x 3 Ft. | 1625 |
| **Needlepoint,** Flowers, Amber Field, Tile Pattern, Trefoil Border, c.1935, 9 Ft. 4 In. x 7 Ft. 7 In. | 4375 |
| **Needlepoint,** Taupe, Red, Blue Allover Flower Sprays, Saffron Field, 3 Ft. 11 In. x 2 Ft. 11 In. | 125 |
| **Oushak,** Angora, 3 Borders, Wide Blue Border, Stylized, Turkey, 10 x 13 Ft. 7 In. | 2706 |
| **Oushak,** Geometric, Leaf Medallion, Cream, Green, Iron Red, 6 Ft. 5 In. x 4 Ft. 5 In. | 426 |
| **Oushak,** Runner, Palmettos, Leaves, Amber Field, Flower Border, c.1900, 10 Ft. 8 In. x 21 In. | 563 |
| **Peking Chinese,** Blue, Gray, Flowers, Stark Carpets, 1976, 10 Ft. 2 In. x 13 Ft. 10 In. .........*illus* | 1107 |
| **Peking,** Flowers, Vines, Blue Ground, Red, Rust Detail, Chinese, 11 Ft. 7 In. x 9 Ft. 8 In. | 1750 |
| **Persian Tafresh,** Blue, Lobed Medallion, Red, Birds, Leaves, Spandrels, 5 Ft. x 6 Ft. 6 In. | 1003 |
| **Persian,** Center Flowers, Floral & Vine Border, 32 x 59 In. | 472 |
| **Persian,** Geometric, Flower Medallion, Brown, Blue Ground, 4 Ft. 6 In. x 6 Ft. 8 In. | 2390 |
| **Persian,** Lotus, Chrysanthemum, Leaves, Ivory, Red Border, c.1920, 10 Ft. 5 In. x 14 Ft. | 1422 |
| **Persian,** Red, Cream, Flowers, Shiraz, 5 Ft. 4 In. x 8 Ft. 3 In. ..........................................*illus* | 1315 |
| **Pictorial,** Eagle, Banner, E Pluribus Unum, Sewn Yarn, S. Colburn, Massachusetts, 1836, 33 x 69 In. *illus* | 8610 |
| **Prayer,** Silk, Brown, Beige, Orange, Multiple Borders, Building, c.1900, 62 x 45 In. ...........*illus* | 1035 |
| **Sarouk,** Blue Flowers, Vines, Palmette Border, Persia, c.1925, 15 Ft. 4 In. x 13 Ft. 5 In. | 625 |
| **Sarouk,** Flower Medallions, Blue Palmette Border, Persia, c.1925, 13 Ft. 6 In. x 9 Ft. 10 In. | 688 |
| **Sarouk,** Mat, Blue Border, Burgundy Ground, Wool, 4 Ft. 10 In. x 3 Ft. 2 In. | 200 |
| **Sarouk,** Pennant Medallion, Red Ground, Ivory Palmette, Iran, c.1950, 15 Ft. 2 In. x 8 Ft. 9 In. | 1750 |
| **Sarouk,** Red Ground, Blue Bouquets, Wool, Cotton, Fringe, 12 Ft. 10 In. x 10 Ft. 2 In. | 1121 |
| **Sarouk,** Urn & Flower, Red Ground, 5 Ft. 2 In. x 6 Ft. 2 In. | 708 |
| **Sarouk,** Urn & Flower, Red Ground, Persia, c.1950, 8 Ft. 11 In. x 12 Ft. 2 In. | 1652 |
| **Scandinavian,** Navy, Teal, Striped Bands, Wool, Handwoven, 7 Ft. 2 In. x 4 Ft. 10 In. | 625 |
| **Serafin,** Medallions, Olive, Navy, Serrated & Hooked, Red Field, 2 Ft. 10 In. x 6 Ft. | 649 |
| **Serapi,** Cream, Geometric Medallion, Salmon Border, Flowers, 6 Ft. 6 In. x 8 Ft. 10 In. | 3585 |
| **Serapi,** Red, Cream, Flower Medallion, Geometric, Vine Border, 18 Ft. 8 In. x 11 Ft. 7 In. | 10158 |
| **Serapi,** Tan, Gray, Honey, Celadon, Flowers, Geometric, Wool, 6 Ft. 1 In. x 8 Ft. 9 In. | 489 |
| **Shiraz,** Salmon, Gray, Off White, Yellow Geometric, Wool, 4 Ft. 6 In. x 7 Ft. 6 In. | 127 |
| **Shirvan,** Prayer, Serrated Edges, Blue Field, Flowers, Lattice, c.1900, 2 Ft. 9 In. x 4 Ft. 9 In. | 830 |

| | |
|---|---|
| **Soumak,** Blue Ground, Square Shapes, Cream Zag Border, 15 Ft. 8 In. x 9 Ft. 4 In. | 633 |
| **Soumak,** Medallion, Spandrels, Zoomorphic Animals, Multicolor, c.1890, 9 Ft. 5 In. x 7 Ft. | 1722 |
| **Sultanabad,** Teal, Green, Salmon Ground, Flowers, Salmon Border, Persia, 13 x 19 Ft. | 10980 |
| **Tabriz,** Arabesque Central Medallion, Flowers, Blue, Yellow, Ivory, Red, 8 Ft. 10 In. x 12 Ft. | 649 |
| **Tabriz,** Geometric Medallion, Red, Cream, Blue, Wool, Cotton, 11 Ft. 9 In. x 8 Ft. 1 In. | 834 |
| **Tabriz,** Leaf Patterns, Red, Yellow, Green, Navy, Brown, Wool, 9 Ft. 9 In. x 13 Ft. 1 In. | 874 |
| **Tabriz,** Medallion, Spandrels, Gray, Red, Blue, Palmetto Border, Iran, 12 Ft. 8 In. x 9 Ft. 10 In. | 4375 |
| **Tabriz,** Red Ground, Blue & White Medallion, Blue Border, Wool, 11 Ft. 3 In. x 8 Ft. 6 In. | 431 |
| **Turkoman,** Mat, Geometric Design, Borders, Brown, White, Red, Persia, 26 x 26 In. | 90 |
| **Verner Panton,** Wool, Black, Circles Of Dots, Multicolor, Round, 5 Ft 10 In. ...............*illus* | 923 |

**RUMRILL POTTERY** was designed by George Rumrill of Little Rock, Arkansas. From 1933 to 1938, it was produced by the Red Wing Pottery of Red Wing, Minnesota. In January 1938, production was transferred to the Shawnee Pottery in Zanesville, Ohio. It was moved again in December of 1938 to Florence Pottery Company in Mt. Gilead, Ohio, where Rumrill ware continued to be manufactured until the pottery burned in 1941. It was then produced by Gonder Ceramic Arts in South Zanesville until early 1943.

*RumRill*

| | |
|---|---|
| **Vase,** Cornucopia, White Matte Glaze, Marked, 7 ½ In., Pair | 60 |
| **Vase,** Dancing Nude, Green Glaze, Leaf Handles, 7 ½ In. | 395 |
| **Vase,** Flared Ruffled Rim, Green Matte Glaze, Ribbed Neck, Squat Bulbous, 7 In. | 48 |
| **Vase,** Leaf Design, Base, Green Matte Glaze, Scrolled Ringed Handles, 7 In. | 110 |
| **Vase,** Pink Matte Glaze, Tapered Neck, Flared Rim, Scroll Handle, 10 In. | 59 |

**RUSKIN** is a British art pottery of the twentieth century. The Ruskin Pottery was started by William Howson Taylor, and his name was used as the mark until about 1899. The factory, at West Smethwick, Birmingham, England, stopped making new pieces in 1933 but continued to glaze and sell the remaining wares until 1935. The art pottery is noted for its exceptional glazes.

*RUSKIN POTTERY WEST SMETHWICK*

| | |
|---|---|
| **Jar,** Lid, Luster Ware, Caramel Mottled Glaze, Gold, Blue, Green, Mauve, Red, 1923, 7 In. | 546 |
| **Vase,** Mauve Souffle Glaze, Flower Stem Silver Overlay, Flared, Impressed, 1905, 7 In. | 2400 |
| **Vase,** Mottled Turquoise & Green Glaze, Marked, 1918, 10 ½ In. | 1062 |

**RUSSEL WRIGHT** designed dinnerware in modern shapes for many companies. Iroquois China Company, Harker China Company, Steubenville Pottery, and Justin Tharaud and Sons made dishes marked *Russel Wright*. The Steubenville wares, first made in 1938, are the most common today. Wright was a designer of domestic and industrial wares, including furniture, aluminum, radios, interiors, and glassware. A new company, Bauer Pottery Company of Los Angeles, is making Russel Wright's American Modern dishes using molds made from original pieces. The pottery is made in Highland, California. Pieces are marked *Russel Wright by Bauer Pottery California USA*. Russel Wright Dinnerware and other original pieces by Wright are listed here. For more prices, go to kovels.com.

*Russel Wright MFG. BY STEUBENVILLE*

| | |
|---|---|
| **American Modern,** Cup & Saucer, Coral | 25 |
| **Doorstop,** Hokus, Stylized Elephant, Nickel Plate Brass, 1930s, 12 x 5 In. ...............*illus* | 5000 |
| **Iroquois Casual,** Casserole, Lid, Avocado, 3 x 10 In. | 35 |
| **Iroquois Casual,** Cup & Saucer, Yellow | 12 |
| **Iroquois Casual,** Platter, Green, 14 In. Diam. | 15 |
| **Iroquois Casual,** Sugar & Creamer, Blue, Stacking | 40 |
| **Vase,** Dark Mustard, Bulbous, c.1945, 5 ½ In. | 39 |

**SABINO** glass was made in the 1920s and 1930s in Paris, France. Founded by Marius-Ernest Sabino (1878–1961), the firm was noted for Art Deco lamps, vases, figurines, and animals in clear, colored, and opalescent glass. Production stopped during World War II but resumed in the 1960s with the manufacture of nude figurines and small opalescent glass animals. Pieces made in recent years are a slightly different color and can be recognized. Only vintage pieces are listed here.

*Sabino France*

| | |
|---|---|
| **Figurine,** Serenity, Nude, Opalescent, Inscribed Sabino Paris, c.1928, 8 ½ In. | 368 |
| **Lamp,** Electric, Molded Glass, Art Deco, Marked, 1900s, 10 x 10 In. | 923 |
| **Perfume Bottle,** Stopper, Molded, Opalescent, Nude Reliefs, Marked Sabino Paris, 6 In. | 357 |
| **Vase,** Birds, Globular, Opalescent, Art Deco, 9 ½ In. | 650 |
| **Vase,** Honey Bees, Honeycombs, Art Deco, Frosted Teal Green, 6 ¾ x 7 ½ In. ...............*illus* | 460 |

**SALOPIAN** ware was made by the Caughley factory of England during the eighteenth century. The early pieces were blue and white with some colored decorations. Another ware referred to as Salopian is a late nineteenth-century tableware decorated with color transfers.

**Salopian**

| | |
|---|---|
| **Cup & Saucer,** Cottage & Stag, Handleless, Soft Paste, 19th Century ...............*illus* | 189 |

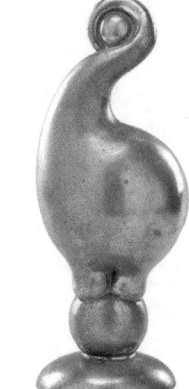

**Russel Wright,** Doorstop, Hokus, Stylized Elephant, Nickel Plate Brass, 1930s, 12 x 5 In.
$5,000

Rago Arts & Auction Center

**Sabino,** Vase, Honey Bees, Honeycombs, Art Deco, Frosted Teal Green, 6 ¾ x 7 ½ In.
$460

Humler & Nolan

> **TIP**
> *Cups are best stored by hanging them on cup hooks. Stacking cups inside each other can cause chipping.*

**S**

**Salopian,** Cup & Saucer, Cottage & Stag, Handleless, Soft Paste, 19th Century
$189

Conestoga Auction Co., Inc.

**Sampler,** Alphabet, Lucy A. Webb, 11th Year, Rockingham, Silk, Linen, 1808, 10 x 8 In.
$450

Garth's Auctioneers & Appraisers

**Samson,** Figurine, Monkey Sitting On Stump, Wooden Pedestal, Marked, c.1950, 28 x 14 In.
$1,168

New Orleans Auction Galleries, Inc.

**Sandwich Glass,** Cologne Bottle, Waisted Loop, Gilt, 6-Sided, Flower Stopper, 5 ¼ In.
$556

Norman C. Heckler & Company

| | |
|---|---:|
| **Cup & Saucer,** Stag, Multicolor, Flower & Leaf Border, Handless, 5 ½ In. | 236 |
| **Plate,** Toddy, Bird, Fruit, Flowers, Multicolor, Leaf Border, 6 ¼ In. | 59 |

**SALT AND PEPPER SHAKERS** in matched sets were first used in the nineteenth century. Collectors are primarily interested in figural examples made after World War I. Huggers are pairs of shakers that appear to embrace each other. Many salt and pepper shakers are listed in other categories and can be located through the index at the back of this book.

| | |
|---|---:|
| **Agway Gas Pump,** Gray, Red Logo, 2 ¾ In. | 1560 |
| **Agway Gas Pump,** Water Transfer, Paper Label, Purple, Blue, 2 ¾ In. | 330 |
| **Ball Point,** Yellow Plastic, Stanley, V.A. Kasin Molded Prods., 3 ⅛ In. | 14 |
| **Chevron Gas Pump,** Red, Blue, Transfer, Ink Stamp, 2 ¾ In., Pair | 1680 |
| **Clark Gas Pump,** White, Red, 2 ¾ In. | 960 |
| **Crystal,** Glandore Pattern, Waterford, Green Label, 2 ½ In. | 98 |
| **Dog & Cat,** Ken-L-Ration, Black Cat, Yellow Dog, F & F Mold & Dye Works, 1950 | 28 |
| **Forget-Me-Nots,** 4-Sided, Tapered, Multicolor, Bavaria, Joseph Kittler, 1900s, 3 In. | 35 |
| **Gas Pump Shape,** Midland, Plastic Decals, 2 ¾ In. | 90 |
| **Grapes,** Milk Glass, Paneled, Footed, Westmoreland, 4 ¾ In. | 22 |
| **Polka Dot,** Cranberry Opalescent, West Virginia Glass Co., c.1894, 3 x 3 ⅜ In. | 345 |
| **Rooster,** Hen, Puffed Chest, Cork Stopper, Japan, 1950s, 2 ¾ In. | 12 |
| **Spiral Shell,** Tray, Tan, Carlton Ware, 3 ¾ In., Tray 5 x 3 In. | 58 |
| **Tower Shape,** Bakelite, Green, Orange, Art Deco, 3 ½ In. | 125 |
| **Ultramarine,** Footed, Jenny Ware, 1930s, 4 ¼ x 2 ¼ In. | 80 |
| **Willie & Millie Penguins,** Kool Cigarette Mascots, Multicolor, Stopper, 3 ½ In. | 36 |

**SAMPLERS** were made in America from the early 1700s. The best examples were made from 1790 to 1840. Long, narrow samplers are usually older than square ones. Early samplers just had stitching or alphabets. The later examples had numerals, borders, and pictorial decorations. Those with mottoes are mid-Victorian. A revival of interest in the 1930s produced simpler samplers, usually with mottoes.

| | |
|---|---:|
| **Alphabet,** Ann Evelina Dray, Frame, June 1838, 12 x 14 In. | 135 |
| **Alphabet,** Basket, Fruit Tree, Strawberries, Aged 11, Silk, 1827, 13 ¾ x 12 In. | 1063 |
| **Alphabet,** Birds, Trees, Catherine Haines, Silk On Linen, Frame, 1825, 18 x 17 In. | 960 |
| **Alphabet,** Bluebirds, Baskets, Tree, Time Is Precious, 1823, 21 ½ x 17 ½ In. | 360 |
| **Alphabet,** Flower Border, Mahitable HC, Aged 13, Silk, Linen, Frame, 1823, 9 x 8 In. | 523 |
| **Alphabet,** Flowers, Birds, Lions, Mary Hayward, 1779, 15 x 11 In. | 450 |
| **Alphabet,** Flowers, Hearts, Birds, Silk On Linen, Mary Earnshaw, Frame, 1723, 15 x 8 In. | 240 |
| **Alphabet,** Flowers, Ribbon, Strawberry, Sawtooth Border, 1800, Silk, 20 ½ x 18 ¼ In. | 1080 |
| **Alphabet,** Geometric Border, Mary Roundle, 11 Years, Frame, 1809, 13 ½ x 9 ¾ In. | 118 |
| **Alphabet,** Hearts, Potted Flowers, Crowns, Silk, Gilt Frame, 1765, 11 x 9 In. | 420 |
| **Alphabet,** House, Birds, Berries, Basket, Forget-Me-Not, 1840, 16 ½ x 14 ½ In. | 330 |
| **Alphabet,** Lucy A. Webb, 11th Year, Rockingham, Silk, Linen, 1808, 10 x 8 In. ............*illus* | 450 |
| **Alphabet,** Marking, 1819, Medina, Ohio, 5 ½ x 9 ½ In. | 720 |
| **Alphabet,** Marking, Multicolor, Birds, c.1850, 16 x 19 In. | 188 |
| **Alphabet,** Numbers, Floral Urns, Mary Burton, Aged 9, Silk, Linen, Frame, 1827, 20 x 20 In. | 330 |
| **Alphabet,** Numbers, Houses, Fence, Trees, M.L. Savage, Silk On Linen, Va., 1830, 21 In. | 7475 |
| **Alphabet,** Numbers, Linen, Red Silk Needlework, Maria Davister Hodimont, 1892, 14 x 14 In. | 153 |
| **Alphabet,** Numbers, Margaret Wilson, Born October 22, Shenandoah County, 1783, 11 In. | 4600 |
| **Alphabet,** Peacocks, Flower Baskets, Isa Jessimank, Aged 9, 1834, 20 x 15 ¼ In. | 510 |
| **Alphabet,** Pictorial, Needlework, Trees, Building, Frame, 1845, 23 x 17 In. | 240 |
| **Alphabet,** Pink Band, Vines, Trees, Rebecca Marietta Butler, 1798, 11 ¾ x 10 ¼ In. | 6240 |
| **Alphabet,** School, Trees, Amanda Morris, 9th Year Of Her Age, 1818, Bucks County, 10 In. | 2125 |
| **Alphabet,** Trees, Birds, Silk, Linen, E. Dillir, Lancaster, Pa., 1821, 10 x 10 In. | 2400 |
| **Alphabet,** Verse, 1811, 7 ½ x 6 In. | 188 |
| **Alphabet,** Verse, 2-Story House, Butterflies, Flowers, Birds, Silk, 25 ½ x 23 ¾ In. | 510 |
| **Alphabet,** Verse, 2-Story House, Trees, Lawn, Block Corners, 15 ¼ x 17 ½ In. | 1063 |
| **Alphabet,** Verse, Flower Border, Lucy Ruggles, Aged 10, Mass., 1810, 16 ½ x 14 In. | 1968 |
| **Alphabet,** Verse, Flowers, Abigail Starr, 11th Year, October 17th 1799, Frame, 13 In. | 1875 |
| **Alphabet,** Verse, Flowers, Needlework, Maryann Johnson, 1820, 17 x 13 In. | 390 |
| **Alphabet,** Verse, Flowers, Numbers, Wrought By Deborah Tarr Aged 9, 1827, 10 x 8 In. | 1750 |
| **Alphabet,** Verse, Flowers, Red House, Birds, Alice Ann Grofs, Wool, 1846, 15 x 14 In. | 3456 |
| **Alphabet,** Verse, Flowers, Silk On Linen, Unity Lewis, 1789, Frame, Pa., 16 x 17 In. | 5520 |
| **Alphabet,** Verse, House, Flowers, Basket, Trees, Sarah Vaughn, Silk, 1783, 19 ½ x 16 In. | 480 |
| **Alphabet,** Verse, Mary Pratt, Silk, Linen, 1751, 17 x 8 In. | 540 |
| **Alphabet,** Verse, Owls, 1821, 15 ½ x 16 In. | 570 |
| **Alphabet,** Vine, Emaline White, 1825, 14 ¼ x 14 In. | 840 |

S

| | |
|---|---|
| **Birds,** Turkey, Anna Maria Brown, Silk On Linen, Frame, 1832, 12 x 12¾ In. | 325 |
| **Family Record,** Joseph Foster & Mary Foster, Flowers, Basket, 1820-31, 17 x 17 In. | 480 |
| **Friendship,** Flowers, Names, Silk, Satin, 16¼ x 15½ In. | 1200 |
| **Pictorial,** Adam & Eve, Mary Shields Aged 11, Taught By B. Walker, 1811, 18 x 12 In. | 1003 |
| **Pictorial,** Flowers, Sheep, House, Silk, Linen, Catherine Meyer, Springfield, Pa., 1820, 18 x 17 In. | 3360 |
| **Pictorial,** Fraternal Symbols, Silk On Linen, Mary Scott, Lurenckirk, 1835, 19 x 20 In. | 2400 |
| **Pictorial,** House, Trees, Flowers, Birds, Flower Border, Lucy White, 1792, 21 x 13 In. | 1680 |
| **Pictorial,** Needlework, Potted Flowers, Geometric Designs, Frame, 16 x 14 In. | 142 |
| **Verse,** Adam & Eve, House, Tree, Anne Large, Aged 5, c.1809, 10 x 15 In. | 975 |
| **Verse,** Adam & Eve, Man, Field, Sheep, Flower Border, 1836, 18 x 21 In. | 1250 |
| **Verse,** Bird, Flower, Martha Wyeth, Frame, England, 1830, 18 x 14 In. | 480 |
| **Verse,** Blackbirds, Fruit, Elizabeth Towt, Aged 8, Silk, 1802, 11½ x 11¼ In. | 390 |
| **Verse,** Flowers, Leaves, Animals, Geometric Border, Mary Ann Lines, 1804, 19 x 13 In. | 1400 |
| **Verse,** Flowers, Vines, Sprigs, Sarah Grafflin, Aged 10, 1807, 16 x 12 In. | 563 |
| **Verse,** Girl With Cat, Flowers, Dog, Elizabeth Drummond Taylor, Age 13, Frame, 24 x 24 In. | 2510 |
| **Verse,** Hearts, Baskets, Birds, Sheep, Elizabeth Lindy, 1802, 18 x 18 In. | 1750 |
| **Verse,** House, 4-Story, Brown, Trees, Stream, Janet Greenlie, Frame, 19 x 18 In. | 720 |
| **Verse,** House, Shepherd, Crowns, Cherubs, Butterflies, Birds, Silk, Linen, 1826, 28 x 27 In. | 1260 |
| **Verse,** Memorial, Tree, Urn, Mourning Woman, Abigail Leonard, c.1828, 17 x 20 In. | 1850 |
| **Verse,** Pictorial, Building, Fenced, Gate, Birds, Sarah Jane Carter, Frame, 1837, 19 x 18 In. | 2360 |
| **Verse,** Trees, Berry Vine Border, Family Record, Almira Stiles, Aged 12, 1827, 15 In. | 1250 |
| **Verse,** Trees, Flowers, Silk On Linen, Hetty Ann Kennedy, Pa., Frame, 1822, 20½ x 22 In. | 1680 |
| **Wreath,** Flowers, Anna Maria Grantwine, Seminary, August 10th, 1835, Frame, 12 x 18 In. | 960 |

**SAMSON** and Company, a French firm specializing in the reproduction of collectible wares of many countries and periods, was founded in Paris in the early nineteenth century. Chelsea, Meissen, Famille Verte, and Chinese Export porcelain are some of the wares that have been reproduced by the company. The firm used a variety of marks on the reproductions. It closed in 1969.

| | |
|---|---|
| **Bowl,** Navy, Orange, Gilt Bands, Landscape Rondels, Chinese, c.1885, 4 x 9¾ In. | 90 |
| **Figurine,** Monkey Sitting On Stump, Wooden Pedestal, Marked, c.1950, 28 x 14 In. ............*illus* | 1168 |
| **Mug,** Building Landscape Reserve, Flower, Insect Ground, Cylindrical, c.1890, 6 In. | 531 |
| **Tureen,** Lid, Multicolor Bouquets, Fluted, Lattice Borders, Mark, 1800s, 9 x 13 In. | 83 |

**SANDWICH GLASS** is any of the myriad types of glass made by the Boston & Sandwich Glass Company of Sandwich, Massachusetts, between 1825 and 1888. It is often very difficult to be sure whether a piece was really made at the Sandwich factory because so many types were made there and similar pieces were made at other glass factories. Additional pieces may be listed under Pressed Glass and in other related categories.

| | |
|---|---|
| **Candlestick,** Canary Yellow, Hexagonal Socket, 3-Step Standard, c.1840, 5 In., Pair | 720 |
| **Candlestick,** Dolphin, Canary Yellow, c.1865, 10¼ In., Pair | 840 |
| **Candlestick,** Dolphin, Starch Blue Over Clambroth, c.1860, 9¾ In., Pair | 900 |
| **Candlestick,** Hexagonal, Peacock Blue, Flared Base, c.1860, 7 x 4 In. | 1610 |
| **Candlestick,** Petal & Loop, Canary Yellow, c.1860, 6½ In., Pair | 180 |
| **Cologne Bottle,** Waisted Loop, Gilt, 6-Sided, Flower Stopper, 5¼ In. ............................*illus* | 556 |
| **Dish,** Hen On Nest, Clam Broth, Oval, 5½ x 7¾ In. | 176 |
| **Hat,** Diamond Quilted, 3-Piece Mold, Blown, 2⅜ In. ......................................*illus* | 153 |
| **Lamp,** Canary, Octagonal Font, Monument Base, Brass Collar, 10½ In., Pair | 380 |
| **Lamp,** Oil, Clear, Globular Font, Knop & Button Stem, Dish Base, 8 In. | 164 |
| **Lamp,** Opaque White, Cutout Emerald Green Geometrics, Woman's Bust Base, c.1850, 12 In. | 266 |
| **Vase,** Blue Crystal, Icicle Decoration, 7½ x 6 In. | 690 |
| **Vase,** Gothic Arch, 9½ In., Pair | 142 |
| **Vase,** Tulip, Cobalt Blue, Amethyst Tone, Ruffled Rim, Octagonal Foot, 9⅞ In. | 2925 |
| **Vase,** Tulip, Forest Green, Octagonal Bowl, Flared Rim, Base, Panels, c.1865, 10 x 5 In. | 2415 |
| **Vase,** Tulip, Peacock Blue, c.1850, 11 x 5½ In., Pair | 2375 |
| **Whimsy,** Hat, Flared Tricorn Brim, Pontil, 3½ In. | 644 |

**SARREGUEMINES** is the name of a French town that is used as part of a china mark. Utzschneider and Company, a porcelain factory, made ceramics in Sarreguemines, Lorraine, France, from about 1775. Transfer-printed wares and majolica were made in the nineteenth century. The nineteenth-century pieces, most often found today, usually have colorful transfer-printed decorations showing peasants in local costumes.

| | |
|---|---|
| **Bowl,** Cabbage Leaf Shape, Green Glaze, 8 x 8 x 2 In. | 140 |
| **Dish,** Fence, Flowers, Faience, 9½ In. ............................................................*illus* | 84 |
| **Jug,** Figural, Black Bill, 5½ In. | 295 |

**Sandwich Glass,** Hat, Diamond Quilted, 3-Piece Mold, Blown, 2⅜ In.
$153

Conestoga Auction Co., Inc.

**Sarreguemines,** Dish, Fence, Flowers, Faience, 9½ In.
$84

DuMouchelles Art Gallery

**TIP**

*When cleaning ceramics be sure to remove your rings so you don't scratch the dishes. Wear tight sleeves to avoid snagging any figurine's arms or legs. Hold pieces with both hands. Don't pick up teapots by the handles or spouts.*

**Sarreguemines,** Pitcher, Ram's Head, Turquoise Interior, Handle, Marked, c.1900, 9½ x 6¼ In.
$281

Rago Arts & Auction Center

**Sarreguemines,** Vase, Leaves, Reeds, Dark Blue Ground, Majolica, Marked, 16½ In.
$461

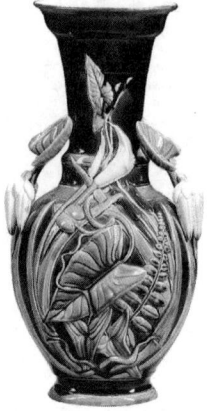

Skinner Auctioneers & Appraisers

**Satsuma,** Censer, Flowers, Brocade, Gilt, Square, Openwork Chrysanthemum On Cover, 6¼ In.
$800

Skinner Auctioneers & Appraisers

**Satsuma,** Urn, Gilt, Enamel, Palace, Figures, Flowers, Scallop Rim, Foo Dog Handles, Saucer Foot, c.1900, 42 In.
$1,003

Brunk Auctions

| | |
|---|---:|
| **Pitcher,** Figural, Scotsman, c.1875, 7¾ In. | 125 |
| **Pitcher,** Ram's Head, Turquoise Interior, Handle, Marked, c.1900, 9½ x 6¼ In. ...............*illus* | 281 |
| **Pitcher,** Tulips, Curling Leaves, Yellow, Green, Majolica, 7 In. | 295 |
| **Plate,** Asparagus, Green Glaze, 10 x 10 In. | 115 |
| **Plate,** Dessert, Flowers, Gilt Edge, c.1910, 7½ In., 8 Piece | 210 |
| **Plate,** Joan Of Arc, King, Half Moon Border, Flags, Shield, 8½ In. | 140 |
| **Plate,** Strawberries, Blossoms, Majolica, 8 In. | 128 |
| **Platter,** Majolica, Palissy Relief, Quail, Grain, Lily Pond, Twig Rim, 23 x 16 In. | 1438 |
| **Stein,** Stoneware, Blue, Green, Brown Salt Glaze, Pewter Lid, Incised, 1 Liter. | 300 |
| **Tile,** Art Nouveau, Stylized Flower, Stem, Leaf, Green, Pink, 6 x 6 In. | 149 |
| **Tray,** Handles, Villagers, Houses, Faience, 15 x 6 In. | 79 |
| **Tray,** Tomatoes, Basket Weave Border, Faience, 11 x 7 In. | 135 |
| **Vase,** Leaves, Reeds, Dark Blue Ground, Majolica, Marked, 16½ In. ...............*illus* | 461 |

**SASCHA BRASTOFF** made decorative accessories, ceramics, enamels on copper, and plastics of his own design. He headed a factory, Sascha Brastoff of California, Inc., in West Los Angeles, from 1953 until about 1973. He died in 1993. Pieces signed with the signature *Sascha Brastoff* were his work and are the most expensive. Other pieces marked *Sascha B.* or with a stamped mark were made by others in his company. Pieces made by Matt Adams after he left the factory are listed here with his name.

*Sascha Brastoff*

| | |
|---|---:|
| **Bowl,** Flowers, Free-Form, White Satin Finish, c.1950, 7 x 5 In. | 32 |
| **Bowl,** Flowers, Green Copper Enamel, Footed, 1970s, 3¼ x 8 In. | 28 |
| **Charger,** Birds, Gold Trim, Signed, 11¾ In. | 52 |
| **Dish,** Stylized Tulip, Black Ground, c.1950, 9¾ x 5½ In. | 64 |
| **Mug,** Gold Over Pink, Surf Ballet Pattern, Demitasse | 14 |
| **Pipe,** Rooftops, c.1955, 4¼ In. | 35 |
| **Planter,** Pagodas, Trees, 3-Footed, Marked, 1950s, 7½ x 5 In. | 75 |
| **Salt & Pepper,** Igloo, Mountains, Gray, White, 1940s | 42 |
| **Sculpture,** Face, Openwork, Marked, 7¾ x 4 In. | 450 |
| **Vase,** Cylindrical, Green, Brown, Pagoda, Lanterns, 1950s, 8 In. | 35 |
| **Vase,** Flowers, Leaves, Gold, Silver, 2⅝ x 2½ In. | 55 |
| **Vase,** Pagoda, Black, Green, Gold, Cylindrical, 1950s, 8 x 3 In. | 35 |

**SATIN GLASS** is a late nineteenth-century art glass. It has a dull finish that is caused by hydrofluoric acid vapor treatment. Satin glass was made in many colors and sometimes has applied decorations. Satin glass is also listed by factory name, such as Webb, or in the Mother-of-Pearl category in this book.

| | |
|---|---:|
| **Basket,** Pink, Swirl Pattern, Camphor Thorny Handle, Rigaree Footed, 11 In. | 144 |
| **Bowl,** Pink, Ruffled Rim, Silver Plated Caddy, 13 In. | 201 |
| **Bowl,** Rainbow Mother-Of-Pearl, Diamond Quilted, Yellow Rigaree Ruffles & Feet, 6 In. | 649 |
| **Epergne,** Drape, Pink, Ruffled Rim Trumpet, Bowl, Metal Standard, 14 In. | 259 |
| **Lemonade Set,** Pitcher, 6 Tumblers, White Shaded To Yellow, 9 In. | 120 |
| **Rose Bowl,** Blue, Yellow Striated Body, Rigaree Collar, Silver Aventurine, 3-Footed, 4¼ In. | 316 |
| **Vase,** Blue Flower, Branches, Amber, Gilt, Oval, Bohemia, c.1895, 7 In. | 1625 |
| **Vase,** Blue, Pink Interior, Egg Form, Flared Out Ruffled Rim, 3 Rigaree Feet, 4½ In. | 40 |
| **Vase,** Diamond-Quilted, Opaque Green, White, Pinched Neck, Eng., c.1910, 8 In. | 118 |
| **Vase,** Pink, Black & Gold Stemmed Flowers, Ruffled Rim, 6½ In. | 29 |
| **Vase,** Pink, Yellow Coralene, 8 In. | 201 |
| **Vase,** Rainbow Mother-Of-Pearl, Swirled Ribs, Bowling Pin Shape, 9¼ In. | 472 |
| **Vase,** Yellow, Gold Enamel Bird, Branch, Flower, Bowling Pin Shape, 9½ In. | 236 |

**SATSUMA** is a Japanese pottery with a distinctive creamy beige crackled glaze. Most of the pieces were decorated with blue, red, green, orange, or gold. Almost all Satsuma found today was made after 1860, especially during the Meiji Period, 1868–1912. During World War I, Americans could not buy undecorated European porcelains. Women who liked to make hand-painted porcelains at home began to decorate plain Satsuma. These pieces are known today as "American Satsuma."

| | |
|---|---:|
| **Bowl,** Chrysanthemum, Thousand Flowers, Lobed Sides, Scalloped Lip, Multicolor, 2 x 8 In. | 178 |
| **Bowl,** Gilt, Bird Finial, Double-Wall, Round Foot, 9½ x 7⅜ In. | 708 |
| **Bowl,** Scalloped Edge, Pond, Ducks, Figures, 3½ x 9½ In. | 246 |
| **Bowl,** Thousand Saints, Borders, Multicolor, Gilt Highlights, Fluted, Marked, 4¾ x 2 In. | 265 |
| **Buckle,** 7 Women, Blue Border, Gilt, 2 Silver Metal Plaque Mounts, c.1910, 2 x 3 In. | 270 |
| **Censer,** Flowers, Brocade, Gilt, Square, Openwork Chrysanthemum On Cover, 6¼ In. ........*illus* | 800 |
| **Censer,** Pierced Brass Lid, Flowers, Phoenix, Gosu Blue Accents, Wood Base, c.1900, 10 In. | 1320 |

| | |
|---|---|
| **Ginger Jar,** Stylized Flower Heads, White Ground, Shield Bands, Pierced Lid, 8 x 6 In. | 295 |
| **Jardiniere,** Pedestal, Birds, Flowers, Yellow, Black, Relief, 35 ½ In. | 246 |
| **Plaque,** Vignettes, Family Life, Round, 13 In. | 180 |
| **Plate,** Boat Scenes, 2 Rectangular, Cobalt Blue & Gilt Ground, Footed, 8 ⅜ In. | 1416 |
| **Plate,** Double Dragon, Stand, Multicolor, Gilt, Flared Border, Footed, Meizan Hododa, 8 In. | 334 |
| **Tray,** Oval, Figures, Dragons, c.1900, 12 x 14 ¾ In. | 270 |
| **Umbrella Stand,** Dragons, Horseback Rider, Servant, Flowers, Gilt, Cylindrical, c.1910, 25 In. | 120 |
| **Urn,** Gilt, Enamel, Palace, Figures, Flowers, Scallop Rim, Foo Dog Handles, Saucer Foot, c.1900, 42 In. *illus* | 1003 |
| **Urn,** Lid, Stand, Warrior Scenes, Gilt Scroll Ground, Monumental, 1900s, 10 In. | 1320 |
| **Urn,** Warriors, Applied Winged Dragons, Orange, Tan, Brown, c.1900, 10 ¾ In., Pair | 123 |
| **Vase,** Brown Amber Glaze, Baluster Shape, Flared Rim, Iridescent Glaze Ground, 13 x 9 In. | 345 |
| **Vase,** Cobalt Blue Ground, Scenic With Figures, Textile Design, Gilt, 2 ½ In. | 69 |
| **Vase,** Earthenware, Painted, Figures, Baluster Shape, Footed, c.1910, 15 In., Pair | 84 |
| **Vase,** Flowers, Enameled, Gold Ground, 3 Panels, Signed JHM, 1934, 9 ⅜ In. | 196 |
| **Vase,** Geisha, River, Bridge, Oval, Shouldered, c.1850, 10 In. | 175 |
| **Vase,** Gilt, Man, Woman, Ring Handles, c.1900, 18 In. | 123 |
| **Vase,** Gilt, Multicolored, Holy Men, Landscape, Dragon, Signed, 9 ½ In. | 120 |
| **Vase,** Gold, Landscape, 14 ½ In. | 493 |
| **Vase,** Holy Men Meditating, Geisha On Reverse, Samurai Panels, Gilt Handles, 7 In., Pair | 210 |
| **Vase,** Mallet Shape, Gilt, Flowers, Moriage, c.1900, 18 In., Pair | 610 |
| **Vase,** Panels, Figures, Landscape, Gilt Trim, c.1825, 12 ⅝ In. | 600 |
| **Vase,** Tall Neck, Decoration, 1900s, 24 ½ In. | 120 |
| **Vase,** Textile Designs, Gilt, Moriage, Scrolling Handles, Ruffled Lip, Cone Shape, 19 x 10 In. | 472 |
| **Vase,** Women, Landscape Ovals, Multicolor, Gilt, Tapered, 22 In. | 563 |

**SATURDAY EVENING GIRLS**, *see Paul Revere Pottery category.*

**SCALES** have been made to weigh everything from babies to gold. Collectors search for all types. Most popular are small gold dust scales and special grocery scales.

| | |
|---|---|
| **Balance,** Beam, Fairbanks, Weights, Maroon, Gold, Red Detail | 90 |
| **Balance,** Brass Tray, Red, Gray Pinstripe, 3 Lb. | 180 |
| **Balance,** Brass, 2 Trays, 2 Horn-Shape Supports, Black | 540 |
| **Balance,** Brass, Henry Troemner, Philadelphia, c.1850, 39 x 47 In. | 861 |
| **Balance,** Brass, Steel, Mahogany Case, Drawer, Adjustable Feet, Brass Weights, 15 In. | 500 |
| **Balance,** Brass, Tapering Shaft, Balance Arm, 3 Chains, 2 Pans, 13 x 9 ½ In. | 156 |
| **Balance,** Dayton, Fan Style, No. 121, Scoop, Mirror, Computing Scale Co., 1903-06, 2 Lb. | 259 |
| **Balance,** Farm, Walnut, Plumb Nob, Salesman's Sample, 11 x 5 In. | 4147 |
| **Balance,** Mahogany, Glass Door, Brass, Weights, Seederer-Kohlbusch, c.1920, 18 x 17 In. | 230 |
| **Balance,** Micrometer, Brass Base, Marble Ledge, Dodge Mfg. | 330 |
| **Balance,** Pewter, Scrolled Arm, Support, Link Chain, 19 x 14 In. | 84 |
| **Balance,** Spring, Frary's Improved, Metal, Embossed, 1800s, 9 In. | 15 |
| **Bathroom,** Sanisah, Porcelain Dial, Arrow Hand, Cast Iron, Germany, 22 x 33 In. | 120 |
| **Beam,** Black, Metal Tray, W.M. Scientific Co, Countertop | 84 |
| **Brass,** Balance, 2 Pans, Adjustable Stand, Degrave & Co., London, 27 x 21 In. | 59 |
| **Butcher Shop,** Brass, Balance Arm, Horned Steer's Head Finial, 2 Pans, France, 61 x 40 In. | 1180 |
| **Candy,** Dayton, Fan Style, Scoop, Red, Black Striping, Computing Scale Co., 1903-06 | 1020 |
| **Candy,** Dayton, Fan, Chrome Tray, Green, Gold Pinstripe, Computing Scale Co. | 780 |
| **Candy,** Dayton, No. 166, Fan, Brass Scoop, Petrol Blue, Brass, 1900-06, 18 x 14 In. | 840 to 1200 |
| **Candy,** Stimpson, Fan, Glass Tray, Nickel Trim, 30 Lb. Capacity, 30 x 27 In. | 1080 |
| **Candy,** Stimpson, Leander, No. 40, Red, White, 2-Tone, Brass Trim | 1080 |
| **Candy,** Toledo, Fan Shape, Model 405C, Brass Tray, Gold Pinstripes, 3 Lb. *illus* | 780 |
| **Candy,** Toledo, Model 405AR, Fan, Scoop, Red, Gold Pinstripe, Honest Weight No Springs | 600 |
| **Candy,** Toledo, Model 405AR, Green, Gold Pinstripe, Canada | 210 |
| **Candy,** White Porcelain, Black Trim, No. 4, National Store Specialty Co. | 69 |
| **Computing,** Dayton, No. 144, Barrel, Red, Brass, Front Indicator, Oval Glass Tray, 32 x 20 In. | 780 |
| **Computing,** Dayton, Wood, Metal, Countertop, 44 In. | 480 |
| **Computing,** Platform, c.1930, 19 x 23 In. | 360 |
| **Cup Weights,** Nesting, Brass, Handle, Germany, 5 ½ In. | 90 |
| **Kitchen,** Montgomery Ward, 9 x 6 ½ x 6 In. | 25 |
| **Kitchen,** White, Cattails Decal, Maid Of Honor, Up To 25 Lbs., 6 x 6 ⅝ In. | 32 |
| **Postage,** Silver, Spread Wing American Eagle, Gorham, 6 In. | 300 |
| **Postal,** Metal, Wood Base, Bun Feet, 4 Weights, England, c.1900, 6 ½ x 3 ½ In. | 230 |
| **Postal,** Verdigris, Pierced Leaf Sides, Green Glass, Beaded Edge, Apollo Studios, 3 x 2 x 3 In. | 213 |
| **Weighing,** Angldile, Style 303, GE, Open Face, Countertop, Tray, Honest Weight Sign, 1904 | 1800 |

**Scale,** Candy, Toledo, Fan Shape, Model 405C, Brass Tray, Gold Pinstripes, 3 Lb. $780

Morphy Auctions

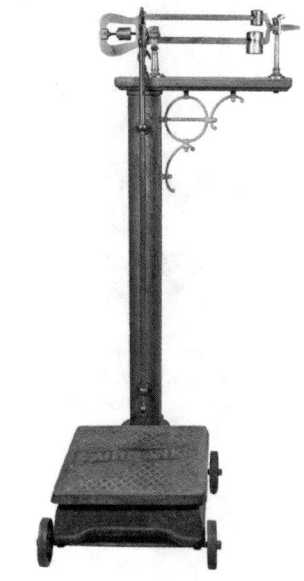

**Scale,** Weighing, Fairbanks, No. 11 ½, Wood, Brass, Metal, Floor Beam, Wheels, 58 In. $270

Morphy Auctions

**Schafer & Vater,** Black, Figurine, Suffragette, Bisque, 7 ½ In. $960

**Schafer & Vater,** Bottle, Skeleton, Spirits, Music Box, 11 ¾ In. $1,620

The Stein Auction Company

---

**Schafer & Vater,** Bottle, Uncle Sam, 5 ¾ In. $180

The Stein Auction Company

---

**Schafer & Vater,** Figurine, Peek-A-Boo Golfer, Bisque, Painted, Chloe Preston, c.1925, 4 In. $627

Theriault's

---

**Schafer & Vater,** Nodder, Bug On Nose, Porcelain, 4 In. $222

The Stein Auction Company

---

| | |
|---|---:|
| **Weighing,** Brass, Iron, Up To 24 Lbs., Chatillon, c.1800s | 18 |
| **Weighing,** Coin-Operated, Enameled, Watling Scale Co., 1900s, 47 In. | 90 |
| **Weighing,** Dayton, Red, Cast Iron, 15 In. | 960 |
| **Weighing,** Fairbanks, No. 11 ½, Wood, Brass, Metal, Floor Beam, Wheels, 58 In. ........*illus* | 270 |
| **Weighing,** Floor, Coin-Operated, 1 Cent, Fortune, Character Readings Your Future, Porcelain | 120 |
| **Weighing,** Floor, Coin-Operated, 1 Cent, Guess-Your-Weight, Blue, Mirror, Red Dial | 210 |
| **Weighing,** Floor, Coin-Operated, 1 Cent, Lollipop Shape, Did You Weigh Yourself Today | 480 |
| **Weighing,** Floor, Coin-Operated, Yellow, Lollipop Shape, Height Weight Chart, Porcelain | 900 |
| **Weighing,** Floor, Oak, Brass, 9 Weights, De Grace, Short, Fannier & Co., England, c.1900, 50 In. | 1625 |
| **Weighing,** Horoscope & Weight, 5 Cents, Watling, Stand, 63 x 16 x 24 In. | 213 |
| **Weighing,** Metal, Glass, No. 383 Toledo, c.1945, 30 In. | 115 |
| **Weighing,** Money Computing, Dayton, Oval Base, Maroon, Red, Brass Trim | 1200 |
| **Weighing,** Peerless, Coin-Operated, Tile Footrest, 66 In. | 510 |
| **Weighing,** Porcelain, 1 Cent, Mills, 60 In. | 180 |
| **Weighing,** Wallawalla Gum Co., Cast Iron, Embossed, 2 Lb., 12 ¾ In. | 480 |

---

**SCHAFER & VATER,** makers of small ceramic items, are best known for their amusing figurals. The factory was located in Volkstedt-Rudolstadt, Germany, from 1890 to 1962. Some pieces are marked with the crown and *R* mark, but many are unmarked.

| | |
|---|---:|
| **Black,** Figurine, Suffragette, Bisque, 7 ½ In. .......*illus* | 960 |
| **Bottle,** Baker, Blue, Life Saver On Apron, Music, Plays How Dry I Am, 11 ½ x 4 ¾ In. | 138 |
| **Bottle,** Skeleton, Spirits, Music Box, 11 ¾ In. .......*illus* | 1620 |
| **Bottle,** Uncle Sam, 5 ¾ In. .......*illus* | 180 |
| **Creamer,** Bear, Dressed, Green, Pink, Brown, 4 ½ In. | 69 |
| **Creamer,** Black Cat, Seated, Green Eyes, 4 ¾ x 4 ¾ In. | 288 |
| **Creamer,** Chinese Man, Holding Crying Baby, Yellow, White, Black, 5 ½ x 5 In. | 230 |
| **Creamer,** Cow, Blue, Dressed, 6 ½ x 6 In. | 52 |
| **Creamer,** Cow, Milkmaid, Chicken House Body, Blue, 5 ½ x 4 In. | 316 |
| **Creamer,** Cow, Tan, Dressed, 5 x 55 In. | 52 |
| **Creamer,** Gnome, Smiling, Red Clothes, 4 x 4 In. | 104 |
| **Creamer,** Goat, Seated, Red, White, Black, 5 ½ In. | 52 |
| **Creamer,** Indian, Crouching, Open Mouth, Hatchet, 5 x 5 In. | 259 |
| **Creamer,** Man, Monkey On Back, Green, Brown, 5 ½ x 5 In. | 92 |
| **Creamer,** Monk Pig, Gray, Pink, 4 ¾ x 2 ¾ In. | 69 |
| **Creamer,** Smiling Chinese Man, Seated, 5 x 5 In. | 138 |
| **Figurine,** Peek-A-Boo Golfer, Bisque, Painted, Chloe Preston, c.1925, 4 In. .......*illus* | 627 |
| **Incense Burner,** Indian, Seated, Tan, 3 ½ x 3 In. | 81 |
| **Nodder,** Bug On Nose, Porcelain, 4 In. .......*illus* | 222 |
| **Pin Holder,** Figural Head, Woman, Red Hair, Open Mouth, Marked, 4 ¼ In. .......*illus* | 138 |
| **Pitcher,** Chinese Man, Goose, 5 ¼ x 5 ¼ In. | 115 |
| **Pitcher,** Girl Holding Extended Creamer, White, Green, 5 ¼ x 5 ¼ In. | 58 |
| **Pitcher,** Man, Monkey On His Back, Blue, 5 ½ In. | 58 |
| **Pitcher,** Woman, Seated, Blue Skirt, 6 ¾ x 5 ¼ In. | 104 |
| **Tea Service,** Mad Hatter, Lids & Handles, Costumed Women, 6 ½-In. Teapot, 7 Piece | 1035 |

---

**SCHEIER POTTERY** was made by Edwin Scheier (1910–2008) and his wife, Mary (1908–2007). They met while they both worked for the WPA, and married in 1937. In 1939, they established their studio, Hillcrock Pottery, in Glade Spring, Virginia. From 1940 to 1968, Edwin taught at the University of New Hampshire and Mary was artist-in-residence. They moved to Oaxaca, Mexico, in 1968 to study the arts and crafts of the Zapotec Indians. When the Scheiers moved to Green Valley, Arizona, in 1978, Ed returned to pottery, making some of his biggest and best-known pieces.

*Scheier* (handwritten)

| | |
|---|---:|
| **Bowl,** Blue Semigloss Interior, Edwin & Mary Scheier, 1955, 2 x 8 In. | 369 |
| **Bowl,** Faces, Tan, 5 ¼ x 11 ¼ In. | 2500 |
| **Bowl,** Fish, Figures, Brown, 5 ¾ x 12 ¾ In. | 4062 |
| **Bowl,** Incised Stylized Fish & Figures, Blue, Gray, Flared, Signed, 7 In. | 813 |
| **Bowl,** Olive & Cream Mottled Glaze, Abstract Design, 8 x 7 In. | 1380 |
| **Bowl,** Red Clay, Mottled Glazes, Rust Rim, Edwin & Mary Scheier, 1955, 6 x 4 ¼ In. | 677 |
| **Bowl,** Sgraffito Decoration, Fish, Conjoined Twin, Blue Glaze, 8 In. | 748 |
| **Bowl,** Sgraffito Flowers, Blue Overglaze, Signed, 3 x 5 ¼ In. | 345 |
| **Bowl,** Sgraffito Shapes, Signed, 1950s, 3 ½ x 8 ½ In. | 1875 |
| **Bowl,** Sgraffito, Bands Of Vertical Lines, Signed, 1960s, 10 In. | 6875 |
| **Bowl,** Turquoise Glaze, Abstract Figures, Faces, Multicolor Mottled Inside, 5 x 6 In. | 1845 |
| **Mug,** Gray, Black Animals, Flowers, Cream Glaze, Banded Handle, c.1960, 5 In., 7 Piece | 200 |
| **Vase,** Coupe, Stylized Figures, Arched Hair, Incised, Glazed, Footed, Signed, 1960s, 9 ½ In. | 1500 |

S

**SCHNEIDER GLASSWORKS** was founded in 1917 at Epinay-sur-Seine, France, by Charles and Ernest Schneider. Art glass was made between 1917 and 1930. The company still produces clear crystal glass. See also the Le Verre Francais category.

| | |
|---|--:|
| **Ewer,** Art Deco, Orange Mottled, Amethyst Handle, Rippled Tail, Acid Signed, 6 In. | 431 |
| **Tazza,** Blue Shaded To Orange Mottled, Pink Wrap, Green, Flared Rim, c.1930, 11 ½ In. | 923 |
| **Tazza,** Pink Bowl, Shaded & Mottled, Black Paperweight Stem & Foot, Striations, 7 x 9 In. | 296 |
| **Vase,** Amethyst Mottled, Blown, Metal Frame, Marked, Ovington, France, 5 ½ In. *illus* | 575 |
| **Vase,** Art Deco, Cameo, Cobalt Blue Columbine, Netted Design Silhouette, 6 In. | 690 |
| **Vase,** Blue, Frosted, Lobed, Long Neck, 14 ½ In. | 369 |
| **Vase,** Escargots, Brown Lip, Neck, Snails Vines, Cameo, 9 ½ In. | 1777 |
| **Vase,** Mottled, Deep Purple To Pink, Yellow Orange Flecks, Long Tapered Neck, 13 In. | 288 |
| **Vase,** Orange, Plum To Mottled Yellow, Flowers, France, c.1925, 9 ¾ In. | 1380 |
| **Vase,** Red Mottled, Orange, Yellow, Flared Rim, Stamped, c.1910, 18 In. *illus* | 288 |

**SCIENTIFIC INSTRUMENTS** of all kinds are included in this category. Other categories such as Barometer, Binoculars, Dental, Medical, Nautical, and Thermometer may also price scientific apparatus.

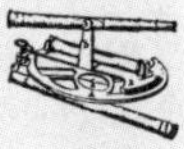

| | |
|---|--:|
| **Assayer's Kit,** Mahogany Case, August Lingke & Co., Germany, 12 In. | 2214 |
| **Bearing Scope,** Brass, Removable Eyepiece, Compass Dial, 9 In. | 90 |
| **Chronometer,** Mahogany Box, No. 739, Bliss & Creighton, N.Y., c.1860, 9 In. | 1725 |
| **Compass,** Beam, Brass, Mahogany, Adjustable Slides, 25 ½ In. | 344 |
| **Compass,** Brass, Surveyor's, H.M. Pool, 19th Century, 13 ¾ In. | 677 |
| **Compass,** Dial, 3 Swivel Arms, Mahogany Case, 18 ¼ x 6 ½ In. | 188 |
| **Compass,** Surveyor's, Brass, J. Pool, 19th Century, 14 ¾ In. | 861 |
| **Compass,** Surveyor's, Brass, Steel, Eagle, Heisely, 13 ½ In. | 1625 |
| **Compass,** Telltale, Brass, Dry Card, F.W. Lincoln Jr. & Co., Boston, 8 In. | 584 |
| **Compensator,** Brass, Silver Tone Face, Plastic Cover, Negretti & Sambra, 2 In. | 69 |
| **Dipleidoscope,** Brass, Bronze, Glass Prism, Scrolled Sides, 3 x 2 ¼ In. | 840 |
| **Drafting Set,** Brass, Steel, Folding Ruler, Velvet Lined Case, 8 x 2 In. | 330 |
| **Gyroscope,** Brass, Cylindrical Base, Mahogany Case, 4 ½ In. | 330 |
| **Gyroscope,** Iron S-Shape Armature, Gyroscopic Disc, 7 x 5 ½ In. | 480 |
| **Hourglass,** Pine Frame, 4 Spindles, 2-Part Glass Bulbs, Sand, 5 ⅜ In. *illus* | 738 |
| **Mapping Tool,** Brass, Adjustable Dials, Rectangular, 24 In. | 60 |
| **Microscope,** Brass, Dollond, London, c.1810, 12 In. | 360 |
| **Microscope,** Brass, Late 19th Century, Mahogany Case, 10 ¼ In. | 1250 |
| **Microscope,** Brass, Rich. Belle Of Aachen, Fruitwood Case, 14 x 8 In. | 330 |
| **Microscope,** Martin, Single Draw, Monocular Tube, 6 In. | 123 |
| **Octant,** Mahogany, Brass Index Arm, Bone Vernier, H. Rehme, c.1790, 17 In. | 1845 |
| **Optical Apparatus,** Electrical Eye Tester, Bausch & Lomb, 16 ½ In. | 210 |
| **Periscope,** Steel, Sliding Lens Hood, Tripod, Carl Zeiss, c.1960, 72 In. | 5500 |
| **Protractor,** Brass, 360-Degree, Folding Arm, W. & S. Jones, Case, c.1810, 6 In. | 406 |
| **Radius Gauge,** Brass, Tapers, Removable Arm, Elliot Bros., 19 In. | 120 |
| **Ruler,** Greek Gods, Embossed 22K Gold, Bone Edges & Markings, Case, 1851 | 2829 |
| **Sextant,** Eagle Finial, Wood Pulley, Composite, 24 In. | 300 |
| **Sextant,** Ebony, Brass, Mahogany Case, 19th Century, 11 In. | 450 |
| **Sextant,** Mounted, Tube Shaft, 19 ½ x 5 In. | 875 |
| **Solar System Model,** Trippensee Planetarium Co., 13 In. | 308 |
| **Spectroscope,** Brass, Cast Iron, 8 Prism, Rotates, Cast Iron Tripod, 17 In. | 1230 |
| **Spectroscope,** Horizontal Disc, John Browning, London, 1876, 11 ½ In. | 615 |
| **Spyglass,** Enamel, Collapsible, Flower Sprays, 3 ¼ x 1 ¾ In. | 149 |
| **Spyglass,** Single Draw, Blue, White, Diamond Pattern, 17 In. | 185 |
| **Steam Whistle,** Acorn Finial, Iron Lever, Buckeye Brass Works, Dayton, 12 In. | 230 |
| **Table With Arms & Microscope,** Mirror, Queen & Co., 4 ¾ x 3 ¾ In. | 120 |
| **Telescope,** Alvan Clark & Sons, Circular, Erector Prism | 1722 |
| **Telescope,** Bardou & Son, Rack & Pinion Focus, Oak Tripod, 39 In. | 615 |
| **Telescope,** Base, Spunpak QSX, Sky View Pro, Prion Optics, 46 In. | 180 |
| **Telescope,** Brass, Finderscope, Walnut Tripod, 19th Century, 54 In. | 2829 |
| **Telescope,** Brass, Leather, Wood, Single Draw, Sliding Cover, 1800s, 21 In. | 425 |
| **Telescope,** Brass, Marked Thos. Evans, London, 1900s, 29 x 18 ½ In. | 406 |
| **Telescope,** Brass, Repeating Circle, 19-In. Tube, 20 x 11 In. | 2625 |
| **Telescope,** Brass, Wood Stand, 74 x 54 In. | 2160 |
| **Telescope,** Broadhurst Clarkson & Co., Refracting, Brass, c.1980, 64 In. | 1169 |
| **Telescope,** Embossed Eagle, Collapsible, Leather Case, 16 In. | 250 |
| **Telescope,** J. Lizars, 3-In. Refractor, 35-In. Brass Main Tube, Box, 48 In. | 984 |

**Schafer & Vater,** Pin Holder, Figural Head, Woman, Red Hair, Open Mouth, Marked, 4 ¼ In.
$138

The Stein Auction Company

**Schneider,** Vase, Amethyst Mottled, Blown, Metal Frame, Marked, Ovington France, 5 ½ In.
$575

Early Auction Co.

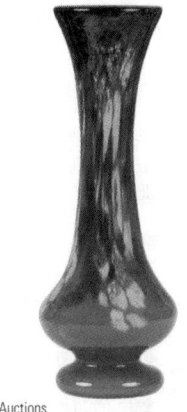

**Schneider,** Vase, Red Mottled, Orange, Yellow, Flared Rim, Stamped, c.1910, 18 In.
$288

Cottone Auctions

This is an edited listing of current prices. Visit **Kovels.com** to check thousands of prices from previous years and sign up for free information on trends, tips, reproductions, marks, and more.

**Scientific Instrument,** Hourglass, Pine Frame, 4 Spindles, 2-Part Glass Bulbs, Sand, 5⅜ In.
$738

Skinner Auctioneers & Appraisers

**Scientific Instrument,** Telescope, Ross, Brass, Collapsible, Engraved, England, 1800s, 40 In.
$2,460

Skinner Auctioneers & Appraisers

**Scientific Instrument,** Telescope, Thomas Jones, Brass, Adjustable, Engraved, London, c.1890, 17 In.
$5,400

Garth's Auctioneers & Appraisers

| | |
|---|---:|
| **Telescope,** J. Seal & Son, Day Or Night, Brass, 3 Draw, London, 35 x 3 In. | 472 |
| **Telescope,** James Short, Reflecting, Library, Box, 14 x 17¼ In. | 6765 |
| **Telescope,** Newtonian, Brass, 6½-In. Mirror, Tripod Base, 34½ In. | 1125 |
| **Telescope,** Refractor, Brass, Germany, 43½ In. | 2460 |
| **Telescope,** Ross, Brass, Collapsible, Engraved, England, 1800s, 40 In. ............*illus* | 2460 |
| **Telescope,** Stand, Leather Wrapped, 35-In. Telescope, 60 In. | 657 |
| **Telescope,** Thomas Jones, Brass, Adjustable, Engraved, London, c.1890, 17 In. .......*illus* | 5400 |
| **Telescope,** Wood Barrel, Polished Brass, Lerebour, Paris, 21 x 3 In. | 501 |
| **Transit,** Engineer's, Buff & Buff, 12-In. Scope, Bubble Level, 14 In. | 338 |
| **Transit,** Engineer's, W. & L.E. Gurley, 4 Quadrants, 19th Century, 10 In. | 738 |
| **Transit,** Surveyor's, Brass, Engraved Pewter Dial, John Heilig, 9 x 14½ In. | 3068 |
| **Transit,** Surveyor's, Frederick Fink, St. Louis, c.1914, 7 x 11 In. | 201 |
| **Transit,** Surveyor's, Keuffel & Esser, Copper, Brass, 9-In. Scope, Box, 14 In. | 403 |
| **Transit,** Surveyor's, W. & L.E. Gurley, Steel, Brass, c.1910, Case, 11 In. | 625 |

**SCRIMSHAW** is bone or ivory or whale's teeth carved by sailors and others for entertainment during the sailing-ship days. Some scrimshaw was carved as early as 1800. There are modern scrimshanders making pieces today on bone, ivory, or plastic. Other pieces may be found in the Ivory and Nautical categories. Collectors should be aware of the recent laws limiting the buying and selling of scrimshaw and elephant ivory.

| | |
|---|---:|
| **Riding Crop,** Narwhal Handle, Baleen Rod, 26 In. | 219 |
| **Rolling Pin,** Sailor's, Lignum Vitae, Walrus Ivory Handles, Knob Ends, 14 In. | 540 |
| **Swift,** Heart Design, Whale Bone, Rosewood, 27 In. | 5400 |
| **Walrus Tusk,** Tower, Hearts, Rosettes, Laurel Sprigs, 22¼ In. | 1230 |
| **Whale's Tooth,** Engraved, 3 Ships, American Flag, Banner, Fort, Cathedral, 7 In. | 660 |
| **Whale's Tooth,** Engraved, 5 Men In Farmyard, Shearing Boar, 7 In. | 720 |
| **Whale's Tooth,** Engraved, Eagle, Spread Wings, Patriotic Shield, Cannons, 5½ In. | 660 |
| **Whale's Tooth,** Engraved, Whaling Scene, Harpoon Boats, Whale, Geometrics, 7 In. | 2760 |
| **Whale's Tooth,** Engraved, Woman, 19th Century Dress, Wood Block Stand, 5¼ In. | 480 |
| **Whale's Tooth,** Inscribed Sloop Of War Wasp Engaged, H.M.S. Avon 1814, c.1850, 6 In. | 1920 |
| **Whale's Tooth,** Sailor, With Book, Seated On Cannon, 2 Ships, Palm Trees, 6¾ In. | 1353 |
| **Whale's Tooth,** Whaling Scenes, W.B., c.1850, 8½ In. | 2400 |

**SEG,** *see Paul Revere Pottery category.*

**SEVRES** porcelain has been made in Sevres, France, since 1769. Many copies of the famous ware have been made. The name originally referred to the works of the Royal Porcelain factory. The name now includes any of the wares made in the town of Sevres, France. The entwined lines with a center letter used as the mark is one of the most forged marks in antiques. Be very careful to identify Sevres by quality, not just by mark.

| | |
|---|---:|
| **Bottle,** Barber, Flowers, Blue, White, Scalloped Bulbous Base, Octagonal Finial, 8 In., Pair | 700 |
| **Bowl,** Art Deco, Gilt Bronze Rim, Flambe, Handles, Glazed Inside, Paul Milet, 7 x 2¾ In. | 161 |
| **Bowl,** Young Amorous Couple, Garden, Oak Leaf, Acorn, Gilt Metal, Mounted, 24 In. | 750 |
| **Box,** Egg Shape, Painted, Romantic Couple, Curving Legs, Gilt Metal Mounts, 7¾ x 11 In. | 178 |
| **Candelabrum,** 3-Light, Cartouches, Nymph, Cherub, Gilt, Blue Ground, 16¼ In. | 1599 |
| **Centerpiece,** Cherub Painted Bowl, Bronze Mounts, France, c.1890, 8 x 12 In. | 2500 |
| **Centerpiece,** Courting Scene, Bronze Dore Frame, Gilt Base, Handles, Oval, 4 x 13 In. | 2415 |
| **Cup & Saucer,** Bleu Celeste, Garden, Gilt, 3⅛ x 6 In. | 1200 |
| **Ewer,** Classical Courting Scene, White, Green, Gold, Pedestal, Scroll Handle, 11½ In. | 590 |
| **Figurine,** Imperial Prince, Dog, Parian, France, 19th Century, 16¼ In. | 1968 |
| **Garniture,** 6-Light Candelabrum, Gilt Metal, Clock, Putti, Fruit, Porcelain Panels, 19 In. | 4688 |
| **Jardiniere,** Gilt Ram's Head Masks, Tapered, 9½ In., Pair | 750 |
| **Jardiniere,** Turquoise Blue, 2 Putti Holding Helmet, C. Ficquenet, 27 In. | 369 |
| **Plaque,** Allegorical Fairy Scene, Painted, Round, Frame, c.1890, 14 In. | 416 |
| **Plaque,** Portrait, Woman, Pate-Sur-Pate, Taxile Doat, Frame, 1875, 10½ x 8 In. .........*illus* | 1250 |
| **Plate,** Dinner, Intertwined Monogram, Marked 1872, 9½ In., 12 Piece | 1045 |
| **Plate,** Portrait, Louise De Bourbon, Flowers, Gilt, Enamel, Cobalt Blue Border, 10 In. | 1750 |
| **Sculpture,** Mermaid, Jean-Baptiste Gauvenet, c.1940, 8¾ x 12 In. | 1375 |
| **Tea Set,** Traveling, Court Ladies, Cherubs, Blue Ground, Fitted Case, 10-In. Tray, 8 Piece | 5938 |
| **Urn,** Cobalt Blue, Gilt Bronze, Footed, Handles, 27 In. | 1875 |
| **Urn,** Courting Scene, Cobalt Blue, Metal Pierced Rim, Cherub Handles, Pedestal, 15 x 14 In. | 2478 |
| **Urn,** Cover, Spirals, White, Blue, Flowers, Cavetto Neck, Birds, Bronze Mount, 17 In., Pair | 3840 |
| **Urn,** Landscape, Lovers Painted Reserves, Tapered, Footed, France, c.1850, 26 In. | 813 |
| **Urn,** Mythological Panels, Pink Ground, Gilt, c.1850, 24 In. | 4063 |

S

| | | |
|---|---|---:|
| **Urn,** Portrait, Marie Antoinette, Louis XVI, Pierced Lid, Artichoke Finial, 25 In., Pair | *illus* | 1770 |
| **Vase,** Blue & Green Mottled Glaze, Paul Milet, 11 ¼ x 7 ¼ In. | | 239 |
| **Vase,** Blue, Green, Yellow Crystalline Glaze, Metal Mounts, Paul Milet, c.1920, 9 ⅜ In. | | 403 |
| **Vase,** Bud, Blue Drip, Brown, Sloped Shoulder, Signed, Taxile Doat, 1902, 6 ½ x 3 In. | | 2000 |
| **Vase,** Empire, Swan Head Handles, Bronze Socle, Crystal Base | | 492 |
| **Vase,** Pate-Sur-Pate Medallions, Taxile Doat, France, c.1890, 14 In., Pair | *illus* | 5625 |

**SEWER TILE** figures were made by workers at the sewer tile and pipe factories in the Ohio area during the late nineteenth and early twentieth centuries. Figurines, small vases, and cemetery vases were favored. Often the finished vase was a piece of the original pipe with added decorations and markings. All types of sewer tile work are now considered folk art by collectors.

| | | |
|---|---|---:|
| **Bank,** Log Cabin, Tooled Details, Indiana, Late 19th Century, 4 In. | | 210 |
| **Birdhouse,** Low Sloping Roof, c.1900, 8 In. | | 390 |
| **Bookends,** Native American, Headdress, Grand Ledge Sewer Pipe Co., c.1900, 6 In. | | 185 |
| **Bust,** Statue Of Liberty, 1918, 9 ¼ In. | | 4500 |
| **Chair,** Tree Branch Style, Arms, c.1950, 42 In. | *illus* | 900 |
| **Figure,** Dog, Poodle, Marked, Roy Blind, 1977, 15 In. | | 240 |
| **Figure,** Dog, Seated, Dimples, Ohio, c.1875, 9 ½ In. | *illus* | 2640 |
| **Figure,** Dog, Spaniel, Curly Coat, Seated, Gray Glaze, 10 ½ In. | | 360 |
| **Figure,** Dog, Spaniel, Flathead, Seated, 11 In. | | 450 |
| **Figure,** Dog, Spaniel, Seated, Incised Details, Ohio, 1931, 9 ½ In. | | 240 |
| **Figure,** Dog, Spaniel, Seated, Unglazed, Ohio, c.1875 | *illus* | 2760 |
| **Figure,** Frog, Inscribed, 1924, 4 ½ In. | | 630 |
| **Figure,** Lion, Reclining, Base, Stamped, c.1900, 11 ½ In. | | 300 |
| **Figure,** Lion, Reclining, Ohio, 6 ¾ x 10 ¼ In. | | 240 |
| **Figure,** Locomotive Engine, W. Smith, Uhrichsville, Ohio, 18 In. | | 450 |
| **Figure,** Napoleon, Full Body, Military Uniform, Crossed Arms, 1800s, 17 In. | | 295 |
| **Figure,** Pig, Seated, Brown Speckled Glaze, 10 ½ In. | | 570 |
| **Figure,** Pig, Standing, c.1900, 9 In. | | 2160 |
| **Figure,** Raven, Marked, c.1900, 9 In. | | 1680 |
| **Planter,** Flower Band Relief, Geometrics, End Of Day, Flower Frog Insert, Ohio, 11 In. | | 246 |
| **Planter,** Stamped Stylized Stars, Square, Arched Legs, c.1925, 11 x 9 x 9 In. | | 120 |
| **Planter,** Tree Trunk, Branches, 22 x 26 In. | | 120 |
| **Planter,** Tree Trunk, Branches, 25 x 32 In. | | 990 |
| **Plaque,** Relief Heron, Inscribed 1890 Maud Perdue, 6 ½ In. | | 344 |
| **Roof Vent,** Eagle, Spread Wings, Inscribed WS, c.1925, 23 ½ In. | *illus* | 390 |
| **Skull,** Incised EJE, c.1950, 5 ½ In. | | 630 |
| **Umbrella Stand,** Tree Trunk, Vining Leaves, Ohio, c.1900, 22 ½ In. | *illus* | 360 |
| **Urn,** Applied Lattice Band, Flared, Egg & Dart Rim, Pedestal Base, Dragon Handles, 25 In. | | 960 |
| **Urn,** Attached Lid, Eagle Finial, c.1900, 27 In. | | 960 |
| **Vase,** Spill, Central Hand Flaked By Seated Dogs, 7 In. | | 270 |

**SEWING** equipment of all types is collected, from sewing birds that held the cloth to tape measures, needle books, and old wooden spools. Sewing machines are included here. Needlework pictures are listed in the Picture category.

| | | |
|---|---|---:|
| **Bird,** Green Pincushion, Brass, Heart Handle, Watterman's, 1853, 5 In. | | 81 |
| **Board,** Pine, 3 Hearts, Corner Roses, Inlays, Paint, c.1820, 16 x 37 In. | | 58 |
| **Bodkin Case,** Rococo, Thimble, Enamel, White, Pink, Gilt, Staffordshire, 5 In. | | 489 |
| **Box,** Anglo-Colonial, Hardwood, Bone Inlays, Stepped Lid, Carved, 1800s, 5 x 13 In. | | 150 |
| **Box,** Black Lacquer, Figures, Flowers Gilt, Fitted Interior, Octagonal, Chinese, 6 x 14 In. | | 625 |
| **Box,** Embroidery, Wood, Faux Leather, Thread, Scissors, Accessories, c.1890, 12 x 8 In. | | 840 |
| **Box,** Exotic Wood, Marquetry, Inlaid Scissors, Thimble, Flowers, 14 x 8 In. | | 1568 |
| **Box,** Hinged Lid, Wood, Pincushion, 3 Drawers, Painted Figures, 6 ½ x 12 In. | | 150 |
| **Box,** Lid, Lacquer, Gilt, Brass, Fitted Interior, Bone Tools, Chinese Export, 15 x 11 In. | *illus* | 458 |
| **Box,** Lid, Mahogany, Inlaid Scissors, Heart Escutcheon, Compartments, 4 x 10 In. | | 240 |
| **Box,** Mixed Woods, Dovetail, Inlay, Spool Caddy, c.1850, 5 ½ x 13 In. | | 240 |
| **Box,** Needle, Grapevine, Silver Gilt, Lid, Hinged, 3 ⅛ In. | | 960 |
| **Box,** Painted, Mahogany, Parcel Gilt, Lift-Out Tray, Pincushion, Ball Feet, c.1835, 7 x 9 In. | | 923 |
| **Box,** Regency, Burl Walnut, Banded, Accessories, 5 ½ x 12 ¾ In. | | 90 |
| **Box,** Sailor's, Inlaid, Hinged Top, Interior Shelf, 1800s, 7 ¾ x 12 ½ In. | | 413 |
| **Box,** Tool, Gilt Bronze, Opaline, Oval, Gargoyle Handles, 4-Footed, France, c.1810, 7 In. | | 8960 |
| **Box,** Wood, Drawer, Thread Dispensers, 2-Tier, Pincushion Top, c.1865, 7 x 6 In. | | 115 |
| **Box,** Wood, Victorian House, Hinged Top, Pincushion, c.1890, 16 ½ x 20 ½ In. | *illus* | 3075 |
| **Cabinet,** Spool, see also the Advertising category under Cabinet, Spool. | | |

**Sevres,** Plaque, Portrait, Woman, Pate-Sur-Pate, Taxile Doat, Frame, 1875, 10 ½ x 8 In.
$1,250

Rago Arts & Auction Center

**Sevres,** Urn, Portrait, Marie Antoinette, Louis XVI, Pierced Lid, Artichoke Finial, 25 In., Pair
$1,770

Brunk Auctions

**Sevres,** Vase, Pate-Sur-Pate Medallions, Taxile Doat, France, c.1890, 14 In., Pair
$5,625

Rago Arts & Auction Center

**S**

**Sewer Tile,** Chair, Tree Branch Style, Arms, c.1950, 42 In.
$900

Garth's Auctioneers & Appraisers

**Sewer Tile,** Figure, Dog, Seated, Dimples, Ohio, c.1875, 9½ In.
$2,640

Garth's Auctioneers & Appraisers

**Sewer Tile,** Figure, Dog, Spaniel, Seated, Unglazed, Ohio, c.1875
$2,760

Garth's Auctioneers & Appraisers

| | |
|---|---|
| **Caddy,** Walnut, Tower Shape, Square Base, 3 Round Shelves, Turned Supports, 15 In. | 123 |
| **Case,** Scissors, 4 Romantic Scenes, Flowers, Gilt Trim, Hinged, Meissen, 5 In. | 1680 |
| **Case,** Screw Lid, Vegetable Ivory, Figures, Woman's Head Finial, 1800s, 2½ In. ...........*illus* | 106 |
| **Case,** Thimble, Castle, Village Scenes, Porcelain, Hinged, 4 In. | 1792 |
| **Case,** Tool, Swaddled Baby Shape, Porcelain, Flowers, Pink Ruffled Bonnet, c.1840, 5 In. | 672 |
| **Darner,** Mushroom Shape, Glass, Multicolor Stripes & Swags, c.1820, 6 In. | 448 |
| **Darning Ball,** Blue, Green, Maroon, Opal Cased, Blown, c.1850, 7½ In. | 81 |
| **Darning Ball,** Glass, Blue, White, Home, Landscape, Home Sweet Home On Handle, 7 x 3 In. | 316 |
| **Darning Ball,** Glass, Marbrie Loop, Amber, White, c.1870, 7½ x 3 In. | 184 |
| **Darning Ball,** Glass, Swirled Red, Yellow, White Canes, c.1970, 6¾ x 2⅝ In. | 345 |
| **Darning Egg,** Ceramic, Silver Handle. .........................*illus* | 85 |
| **Dress Form,** Child's Torso, Silk Cover, Turned & Painted Wood Stand, 28 In. | 510 |
| **Dress Form,** Half Scale, Cast Iron Base, Wolf Form Co., 28 In. | 399 |
| **Dress Form,** Muslin Covered, Cast Iron Base, Rollers, Marked J.R. Bauman, 1900s, 62 In. | 322 |
| **Etui,** Asparagus Spear Form, Porcelain, Painted Bug, Silver Hinged Cap, Germany, 1840, 5 In. | 448 |
| **Etui,** Enamel, Flowers, Scrolled Cartouche, Green Ground, Cylindrical, Hinged, 3¼ In. | 896 |
| **Hem Marker,** Sterling, Tiger Cat Finial, Revere Silversmiths, 6 In. | 130 |
| **Lacemaker's Lamp,** Blown Glass, Baluster, Spread Foot, Globular Top, c.1820, 7¼ In. | 210 |
| **Loom,** Walnut, Poplar, Table Top, Arch Crest, Pa., c.1845, 14 In. | 330 |
| **Necessaire,** Gilt Scrolls, 5 Scenes, Cylindrical, Hinged, Meissen, c.1840, 4 In. | 1008 |
| **Necessaire,** Grand Piano Form, Rosewood Veneer, Inlaid, Brass Appliques, Claw Feet, 12 In. | 17920 |
| **Needle Case,** Chinese Man Shape, Floral Tunic, Chinoiserie, Meissen, 2¼ In. | 2016 |
| **Needle Case,** Hinged Angled Lid, Tortoiseshell, Mother-Of-Pearl Inlay, Bone Rim, 2¼ In. | 280 |
| **Needle Case,** Lady's Leg Shape, Porcelain, Flowers, Lavender Heel, c.1780, 3¼ In. | 840 |
| **Needle Case,** Man, Woman, Figural, Silver, Traditional Costumes, France, c.1800, 2 In., Pair | 1008 |
| **Needle Case,** Straw Work, Wood, Multicolor, c.1820, 3⅜ In. | 175 |
| **Notions Holder,** Thread Spindles, Pincushion Lifts Off, Round, Plastic, 6 In. | 24 |
| **Pincushion Dolls** are listed in their own category. | |
| **Pincushion,** Bird, Amish Or Mennonite Style Fabric, Pennsylvania, 5½ In. ..............*illus* | 71 |
| **Pincushion,** Bird, Stitched, Stuffed, Va., c.1890, 3 x 5 In. | 207 |
| **Pincushion,** Brass, Gnome, On Snail, Under Textured Cotton Mound, c.1900, 6 x 4½ In. | 230 |
| **Pincushion,** Mahogany Inlay, Drawer, Greek Key Border, Clamp, 1800s, 6 In. | 418 |
| **Pincushion,** Metal, Flower Scrolls, Stamped WB Mfg. Co., 5½ In. | 125 |
| **Pincushion,** Porcelain, Girl Holding Basket, Thimble Cap, Germany, 4½ In. | 224 |
| **Pincushion,** Shoe Shape, Metal, Black, Heel, Upturned Toe, Purple Velvet Cushion, 6 In. | 504 |
| **Pincushion,** Turtle, Cast Metal, Pink Velvet, Rhinestone Eyes, 3½ x 2½ In. | 35 |
| **Pincushion,** Woven Basket, Ivory, Velvet, France, 2½ x 2½ In. | 75 |
| **Spool Cabinets** are listed here or in the Advertising category under Cabinet, Spool. | |
| **Spool Stand,** Treen, 4 Round Tiers, Spikes, Stepped Base, Red Paint, c.1850, 11 x 4 In. | 345 |
| **Swift,** Winder, Wood, Table Top, Set Screw, Clamp, Yarn Cup, 1800s, 21 In. | 35 |
| **Swift,** Wood, Folded, Turned, c.1860, 27 In. | 60 |
| **Tailor's Chalk,** 2 White, 1 Blue, 1 Red, Box, John Dritz & Sons, 1949 | 14 |
| **Tape Loom,** Pine, Forged Nail, Square Handle, Shenandoah Valley, c.1800, 15 x 9¼ In. | 374 |
| **Tape Loom,** Pine, Paint, Pa., c.1820, 12 x 17 In. | 540 |
| **Tape Measure,** Mammy, Painted, Metal, Crank Windup, 4 In. | 2400 |
| **Tape Measure,** Porcelain, Pierrot, Open Mouth, Germany, 1⅞ In. | 95 |
| **Thimble,** 14K Yellow Gold, Engraved, Bird, Pitted, Size 6, ¾ In. | 230 |
| **Thimble,** Beehive Design, Red Flower Band, Gold Trim, Meissen, 1 In. | 1344 |
| **Thimble,** Gold, Beehive Design, Floral Panels, Leather Case, England, c.1850, 1 In. | 616 |
| **Thimble,** Olive Wood, Flowers, Leaves, Paint, Italy, c.1970, 1 In. | 8 |
| **Thimble,** Scroll, Zigzag Design, 14K Gold, ¾ x ½ In. | 127 |
| **Thread Holder,** Wood, Barrel, Embroidered Band, Vines, Gold Edges, Pedestal Base, 4 In. | 392 |
| **Tracing Wheel,** Caramel Swirl Bakelite Handle, Box, c.1949 | 22 |
| **Trim,** Embroidered, Scalloped, Red, Lady Chic DeLuxe Trimming, c.1900, ⅜ In. x 3 Yards | 19 |
| **Winding Spool,** Clamp, Wood, Metal Screw, 19th Century, 7 In., Pair | 728 |
| **Work Bag,** Crewell, Vines, Birds, Butterflies, Wool, Linen, Jane Hoopes, 1768, 29 x 20 In. | 7500 |
| **Yarn Winder,** 4 Arms, 4 Sawtooth Holders, Crossed Base, Wood, 18 In. | 59 |
| **Yarn Winder,** Mixed Wood, Mortised Stretchers, Gray Paint, c.1850, 27 x 22 In. | 138 |

**SHAKER** items are characterized by simplicity, functionalism, and orderliness. There were many Shaker communities in America from the eighteenth century to the present day. The religious order made furniture, small wooden pieces, and packaged medicines, herbs, and jellies to sell to "outsiders." Other useful objects were made for use by members of the community. Shaker furniture is listed in this book in the Furniture category.

| | |
|---|---|
| **Apple Peeler,** Maple, Handle, Table Clamp, Swinging Arm, Peeler Blade, 14½ In. ............*illus* | 4130 |

**Sewer Tile,** Roof Vent, Eagle, Spread Wings, Inscribed WS, c.1925, 23 ½ In.
$390

**Sewer Tile,** Umbrella Stand, Tree Trunk, Vining Leaves, Ohio, c.1900, 22 ½ In.
$360

**Sewing,** Box, Lid, Lacquer, Gilt, Brass, Fitted Interior, Bone Tools, Chinese Export, 15 x 11 In.
$458

**Sewing,** Box, Wood, Victorian House, Hinged Top, Pincushion, c.1890, 16 ½ x 20 ½ In.
$3,075

**Sewing,** Case, Screw Lid, Vegetable Ivory, Figures, Woman's Head Finial, 1800s, 2 ½ In.
$106

**Sewing,** Darning Egg, Ceramic, Silver Handle
$85

**Sewing,** Pincushion, Bird, Amish Or Mennonite Style Fabric, Pennsylvania, 5 ½ In.
$71

**Shaker,** Apple Peeler, Maple, Handle, Table Clamp, Swinging Arm, Peeler Blade, 14 ½ In.
$4,130

**Shaker,** Basket, Berry, Picket Fence, Tulip Poplar, Wire, Tin Base, 2 Handles, Ky., 4 x 6 In.
$177

**Shaker,** Box, 3-Finger, Oval, Maple, Pine, Copper Tacks, c.1830, 2 x 4 In.
$2,124

**Shaker,** Box, 4-Finger, Pantry, Oval, Bentwood, Maple, Copper Tacks, 1800s, 11 ¼ In.
$615

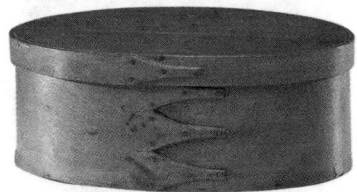

**Shaker,** Box, Wood, Pine, ¾ Hinged Lid, Breadboard Ends, Painted, c.1850, 22 x 27 In. $2,360

Willis Henry Auctions, Inc.

**Shaker,** Carrier, Kindling, Poplar, Dovetailed Sides, Hoop Handle, 15 ½ x 19 In. $4,130

Willis Henry Auctions, Inc.

**Shaker,** Doll, Bisque, Blond Wig, Wool Cloak, Beige Dress, Silk Ribbon, Germany, 12 ¾ In. $472

Willis Henry Auctions, Inc.

**Shaker,** Mixing Paddle, Pine, Carved, Cutout Handle, Rivets, Signed, New Lebanon, 40 ½ In. $885

Willis Henry Auctions, Inc.

**Shaker,** Model, Well, Pine, Walnut, Brass, Steel, Tin, Hinged Roof, Gears, 15 x 8 ⅜ In. $590

Willis Henry Auctions, Inc.

**Shaker,** Sconce, Candle, Tin, Forward Bent Top, 11 x 5 In., Pair $1,180

Willis Henry Auctions, Inc.

**Shaker,** Shovel, Garden, Maple, Steel, Carved Handle, Stamped, F.W. Evans, 38 ½ In. $10,030

Willis Henry Auctions, Inc.

**Shaker,** Sign, Shaker Cloaks, Emma J. Neale, Card Stock, Frame, 23 x 29 ½ In. $767

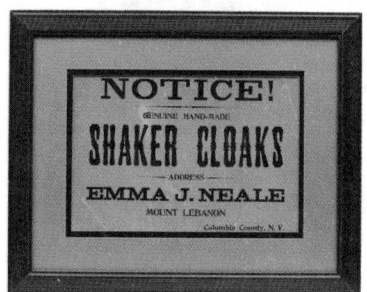

NOTICE!
GENUINE HAND-MADE
SHAKER CLOAKS
ADDRESS
EMMA J. NEALE
MOUNT LEBANON
Columbia County, N.Y.

Willis Henry Auctions, Inc.

**Shaker,** Tub, Pine, Ash, Canted Side, Green, Overlapped Bands, Tapered, Inset Bottom, c.1850 $533

James D. Julia Auctioneers

| | |
|---|---|
| **Basket,** Ash, Carved Handles, Round, Flared Sides, c.1830, 12 x 25 In. ........................ | 590 |
| **Basket,** Berry, Picket Fence, Tulip Poplar, Wire, Tin Base, 2 Handles, Ky., 4 x 6 In.............*illus* | 177 |
| **Basket,** Laundry, Maple, Hickory, Canted Spokes, 6-Spoke Bottom, 17 ½ In. Diam. ............ | 3186 |
| **Basket,** Sisters, Handles, Cloth Lined, Double Wrapped Rim, 4 x 13 In. ............................ | 1298 |
| **Basket,** Sisters, Work, Black Ash Split, Wrapped Rim, 23 x 16 In. .................................. | 1062 |
| **Basket,** Splint, Gathering, Fabric Lining, Handles, c.1890, 6 x 12 In. .............................. | 215 |
| **Blanket,** Cotton, Wool, Blue, White, Jacquard Woven, 86 x 78 In., Pair............................. | 1180 |
| **Bowl,** Red Painted Exterior, Orange Interior, 6 ¼ x 18 ½ In. ...................................... | 2950 |
| **Box,** 2-Finger, Lid, Oval, Green Over Red, 3 x 7 ½ In. ............................................... | 1320 |
| **Box,** 2-Finger, Oval, Maple, Pine, Red Paint, Copper Tacks, c.1830, 2 ½ x 6 In. .................. | 5192 |
| **Box,** 2-Finger, Oval, Maple, Pine, Yellow Paint, 8 Spools, c.1830, 1 ³⁄₁₆ x 3 ¼ In. ............... | 16520 |
| **Box,** 2-Finger, Oval, Maple, Pine, Yellow Stain, Copper Tacks, 7 x 9 In. ......................... | 708 |
| **Box,** 2-Finger, Oval, Maple, Pine, Yellow Stain, Copper Tacks, c.1830, 2 x 5 In. ................ | 3658 |
| **Box,** 2-Finger, Red, Oval, Lid, Inscribed Lebanon Springs 1839, 5 In. ............................ | 480 |
| **Box,** 3-Finger, Lid, Oval, Red Wash, 5 x 12 In. .................................................... | 840 |
| **Box,** 3-Finger, Oval, Maple, Pine, Copper Tacks, c.1830, 2 x 4 In. ........................*illus* | 2124 |
| **Box,** 3-Finger, Oval, Pine Top, Bent Maple Sides, Yellow, Copper Tacks, 3 x 8 x 12 In. ............. | 3900 |
| **Box,** 4-Finger, Lid, Oval, Copper Tacks, Painted Town Scene, 10 x 7 In. .......................... | 633 |
| **Box,** 4-Finger, Lid, Oval, Painted, Flowers, Leaves, 19th Century, 5 x 12 In......................... | 300 |
| **Box,** 4-Finger, Oval, Maple, Pine, Copper Tacks, c.1830, 4 x 10 In. ................................ | 1180 |
| **Box,** 4-Finger, Pantry, Oval, Bentwood, Maple, Copper Tacks, 1800s, 11 ¼ In. ...................*illus* | 615 |
| **Box,** 5-Finger, Oval, Maple & Pine, Blue, Copper Tacks, 4 x 11 In. ................................ | 4130 |
| **Box,** Dome Lid, Wire Hinges, Green Paint, 1800s, 3 ½ x 8 In. .................................... | 2091 |
| **Box,** Sisters, Maple, Pine, Signed Martha Perry, 3 ½ In. ......................................... | 1298 |
| **Box,** Split, 3-Finger, Maple, Pine, Yellow Paint, 8 ¾ In. ......................................... | 1239 |
| **Box,** Wood, Pine, ¾ Hinged Lid, Breadboard Ends, Painted, c.1850, 22 x 27 In. ...........*illus* | 2360 |
| **Box,** Writing, Hinged Lid, Beadboard Ends, Paint, New Lebanon, c.1830, 5 x 16 ⅝ In. ............ | 3198 |
| **Bucket,** Pine, Ash, Button Pins, Paint, Handle, c.1820, 18 ¾ x 13 In. ............................ | 1476 |
| **Bucket,** Pine, Blue, Brown, Diamond Shape Bail Plates, 2 Steel Binding Straps, 9 In. ............. | 531 |
| **Candlestick,** Tin, Cone Shape Snuff, Ring Finger Hold, Label, 4 ½ In. ............................ | 2478 |
| **Carrier,** 2-Finger, Pine, Maple, Oval, Handle, G. Roberts, Mt. Lebanon, c.1930, 7 ½ x 11 In. ........ | 738 |
| **Carrier,** Kindling, Poplar, Dovetailed Sides, Hoop Handle, 15 ½ x 19 In. ...................*illus* | 4130 |
| **Doll,** Bisque, Blond Wig, Wool Cloak, Beige Dress, Silk Ribbon, Germany, 12 ¾ In................*illus* | 472 |
| **Foot Warmer,** Maple, Wire Handle, 4 Rows Of Holes, Dovetailed, 7 x 12 In......................... | 1180 |
| **Kerchief,** Beige Silk, Tan, Blue, Stripe Border ................................................... | 1121 |
| **Mittens,** Uncut White Pile, Red Flower, Blue Wool Interior, 11 In. ................................ | 354 |
| **Mixing Paddle,** Pine, Carved, Cutout Handle, Rivets, Signed, New Lebanon, 40 ½ In. .........*illus* | 885 |
| **Model,** Well, Pine, Walnut, Brass, Steel, Tin, Hinged Roof, Gears, 15 x 8 ⅜ In. .............*illus* | 590 |
| **Sconce,** Candle, Tin, Forward Bent Top, 11 x 5 In., Pair............................*illus* | 1180 |
| **Seed Box,** Pine, Red Paint, Shakers Genuine Garden Seeds, 3 x 23 x 11 In. ..................... | 2124 |
| **Shovel,** Garden, Maple, Steel, Carved Handle, Stamped, F.W. Evans, 38 ½ In...............*illus* | 10030 |
| **Shovel,** Maple, Cutout Handle, Carved R.C.......................................................... | 4248 |
| **Sign,** Shaker Cloaks, Emma J. Neale, Card Stock, Frame, 23 x 29 ½ In.......................*illus* | 767 |
| **Sock Dryer,** Maple, Flat Panels, No. 11, 22 ¼ x 10 In., Pair ..................................... | 2583 |
| **Sock Stretcher,** Wood, 8 ¾ x 4 In. ................................................................ | 40 |
| **Spool Holder,** Sisters, Red, Green Interior, Turned Handle, 22 Spools, 2 In........................ | 9145 |
| **Tray,** Pine, Maple Sides, Yellow Stain, Oval, c.1800, 4 x 6 In. .................................. | 1968 |
| **Tub,** Pine, Ash, Canted Side, Green, Overlapped Bands, Tapered, Inset Bottom, c.1850.........*illus* | 533 |
| **Tub,** Pine, Forged Steel Bands, White Paint Interior, Shaped Handles, 5 ¼ x 11 In. ............... | 8260 |
| **Yarn Reel,** Maple, Red Stain, 4 Arms, Base, c.1840, 32 In. ...................................... | 472 |

**SHAVING MUGS** were popular from 1860 to 1900. Many types were made, including occupational mugs featuring pictures of men's jobs. There were scuttle mugs, silver-plated mugs, glass-lined mugs, and others.

| | |
|---|---|
| **Occupational,** Barber, Razor, Scissors, Weimar, Germany, c.1900, 3 ⅝ In. .................... | 161 |
| **Occupational,** Blacksmith, Shop Scene In Horseshoe, Gold Trim, C.S. Hain, 4 In........................ | 207 |
| **Occupational,** Bowling, John Monnet, 1913, 3 In. ...... ...................................... | 341 |
| **Occupational,** Butcher, J.P. Brenner, Cutting Meat, Limoges, Stamped, 3 ½ In.....................*illus* | 36 |
| **Occupational,** Captain, Chas Jarvis, 4 In. ...................................................... | 1790 |
| **Occupational,** Insurance Salesman, Charles W. Verney, Burning Building, 1800s, 4 In.............. | 3600 |
| **Pug Dogs,** Joseph William Parr, Tressemann & Vogt, Limoges, c.1900, 3 ½ In........................ | 1020 |
| **Sailor,** Tugboat, On Sea, T.J. O'Brien, 4 In. ................................................... | 1140 |
| **Wagon,** Horse Drawn, V.F. Hardwick, Gilt, Limoges, Stamped, 3 ½ In.....................*illus* | 210 |

**Shaving Mug,** Occupational, Butcher, J.P. Brenner, Cutting Meat, Limoges, Stamped, 3 ½ In.
$36

Morphy Auctions

**Shaving Mug,** Wagon, Horse Drawn, V.F. Hardwick, Gilt, Limoges, Stamped, 3 ½ In.
$210

Morphy Auctions

**Shearwater,** Cup & Saucer, Shoal Glaze, Monkey Handle, Anderson, c.1940, Saucer 5 ⅞ In.
$488

Neal Auction Co.

**Shearwater,** Figurine, Horse, Chesty, Blue Glaze, Marked, c.1970, 12 ½ In.
$2,390

Neal Auction Co.

S

**Shearwater,** Plate, 2 Pelicans, Walter Anderson, Impressed Mark, c.1945, 10 ½ In.
$3,075

Neal Auction Co.

---

**Shearwater,** Plate, Butterfly, Flower, Leaves, Walter Anderson, c.1950, 8 In.
$5,079

Neal Auction Co.

---

**Shearwater,** Plate, Duck, Waves, Multicolor, Applied Slip, Incised, W. Anderson, 1950s, 6 In.
$3,998

Neal Auction Co.

---

**TIP**

*Remove stains from dishes with hydrogen peroxide or bicarbonate of soda, not with bleach, which was the suggested way years ago. The bleach may damage the finish.*

---

**SHAWNEE POTTERY** was started in Zanesville, Ohio, in 1937. The company made vases, novelty ware, flowerpots, planters, lamps, and cookie jars. Three dinnerware lines were made: Corn, Lobster Ware, and Valencia (a solid color line). White Corn pattern utility pieces were made in 1945. Corn King was made from 1946 to 1954; Corn Queen, with darker green leaves and lighter colored corn, from 1954 to 1961. Shawnee produced pottery for George Rumrill during the late 1930s. The company closed in 1961.

Shawnee USA

| | |
|---|---:|
| **Ashtray,** Boomerang Shape, Splattered Pink & Gold, 13 In. | 45 |
| **Cookie Jar,** Lucky Elephant, Head, Gold Bow, 6 ¼ x 5 ½ In. | 49 |
| **Cookie Jar,** Muggsy, Dog, Blue Bow, 11 In. | 295 |
| **Planter,** Boy, With Fish, Tree Stump, 6 In. | 32 |
| **Planter,** Deer, Fawn, 5 ½ x 5 x 3 In. | 21 |
| **Planter,** Deer, Tree Stump, Yellow, Brown, 5 ¼ x 6 ½ x 7 In. | 44 |
| **Planter,** Elephant, 4 ½ x 3 ½ x 3 ¼ In. | 19 |
| **Planter,** Mallard, In Flight, 6 x 5 x 3 In. | 28 |
| **Planter,** Old Chinese Man, Umbrella, Basket, c.1945, 5 ¼ x 5 ¼ x 3 In. | 18 |
| **Planter,** Watering Can, Embossed Tulips, Basket Weave, 5 x 3 In. | 24 |
| **Salt & Pepper,** Chef, Ivory, Red, 3 ½ In. | 23 |
| **Salt & Pepper,** Fruit Bowl, 1940s, 3 ½ In. | 30 |
| **Salt & Pepper,** Muggsy, Gold, Blue Bow, 3 ¼ In. | 39 |
| **Salt & Pepper,** Smiley Pig, Green Collar, c.1945, 3 ¼ In. | 85 |
| **Vase,** Art Deco, Open Handles, Footed, Yellow, 8 In. | 32 |
| **Vase,** Ivory, Stippled, Bud, 10 ½ In. | 12 |
| **Vase,** Raised Daisies & Tulips, Swirling Leaves, Turquoise, 7 ½ x 3 In. | 36 |
| **Vase,** Tufted Buttons, Diamond Pattern, Green, Footed, 1950s, 8 ¾ In. | 40 |

**SHEARWATER POTTERY** is a family business started by Mr. and Mrs. G.W. Anderson Sr. and their three sons. The local Ocean Springs, Mississippi, clays were used to make the wares in the 1930s. The company was damaged by Hurricane Katrina in 2005 but was rebuilt and is still in business.

SHEARWATER

| | |
|---|---:|
| **Bookends,** Androcles & Lion, Yellow, Red, White Ground, c.1985, 6 ⅛ In. | 230 |
| **Bottle,** Wine, Plantation, Bronze Over Blue, Walter Anderson, Impressed Mark, 13 In. | 4063 |
| **Bowl,** Camellia Shape, Impressed Mark, Ocean Springs, Miss., 2 ¾ x 10 ¼ In. | 246 |
| **Bowl,** Camellia Shape, Seafoam Glaze, Peter Anderson, c.1947, 2 x 8 In. | 1793 |
| **Cup & Saucer,** Shoal Glaze, Monkey Handle, Anderson, c.1940, Saucer 5 ⅞ In. .................*illus* | 488 |
| **Figurine,** Baby Head, Glossy, Green, Brown Underglaze, 7 ½ In. | 230 |
| **Figurine,** Horse, Chesty, Blue Glaze, Marked, c.1970, 12 ½ In. ................*illus* | 2390 |
| **Figurine,** Horse, Grazing, Dapple Gray, Walter Anderson, c.1948, 4 ⅜ x 8 In. | 316 |
| **Figurine,** Rapunzel, Multicolor, Horse, Prince, Signed Shearwater, 10 ¼ In. | 185 |
| **Jug,** Fish, Cast, Seafoam, Gold Double Glaze, Walter Anderson, 4 ¼ In. | 478 |
| **Plate,** 2 Pelicans, Walter Anderson, Impressed Mark, c.1945, 10 ½ In. ................*illus* | 3075 |
| **Plate,** Butterfly, Flower, Leaves, Walter Anderson, c.1950, 8 In. ................*illus* | 5079 |
| **Plate,** Duck, Waves, Multicolor, Applied Slip, Incised, W. Anderson, 1950s, 6 In. ................*illus* | 3998 |
| **Vase,** Alkaline Blue, White, Sea Green, Peter Anderson, Marked, c.1935, 6 ½ In. ................*illus* | 717 |
| **Vase,** Bacchante, Blue Green Alkaline Glaze, Walter Inglis Anderson, 1930s, 9 ½ x 8 ½ In. | 23900 |
| **Vase,** Bird & Wave, Brown, Black, Tan, White, Peter & Walter Anderson, 12 x 4 ⅜ In. | 4674 |
| **Vase,** Blue Alkaline Glaze, Impressed Mark, 1930s, 6 ⅛ In. | 418 |
| **Vase,** Blue Rain Glaze, Marked, Jim Anderson, 1999, 9 In. | 427 |
| **Vase,** Bristol Glaze, Impressed Mark, 1950s, 8 In. | 732 |
| **Vase,** Cylindrical, Multicolor, Shapes, c.2002, 10 In. | 230 |
| **Vase,** Dancing Man, Blue Rain Glaze, Walter Anderson, 1945, 7 ¾ In. | 2390 |
| **Vase,** Floral Reticulated Rim, Border, Blue, Green Glaze, Peter Anderson, c.1946, 5 x 8 In. | 3286 |
| **Vase,** Geckos, Butterflies, Flowers, Multicolor, Patricia Anderson Findeisen, 6 In. ................*illus* | 460 |
| **Vase,** Multicolor, Woman, Red Flowers, Impressed Shearwater, 7 ⅞ In. | 748 |
| **Vase,** Sea, Earth & Sky, Cast, Turquoise & Green Glaze, Impressed Crescent Mark, 12 x 6 In. | 2460 |
| **Vase,** Turquoise & Brown Matte Glaze, Bulbous, Tapered, 6 x 4 In. | 244 |
| **Vase,** Woman, Checkered Table, High Glaze, J. McConnel, 9 x 4 In. | 6710 |

**SHEET MUSIC** from the past centuries is now collected. The favorites are examples with covers featuring artistic or historic pictures. Early sheet music covers were lithographed, but by the 1900s photographic reproductions were used. The early music was larger than more recent sheets, and you must watch out for examples that were trimmed to fit in a twentieth-century piano bench.

| | |
|---|---:|
| **Abby Road,** Beatles, 1969 | 20 |
| **Buttons & Bows,** The Paleface, Signed Bob Hope & Jane Russell, 1948, 9 x 12 In. | 115 |
| **Georgy Girl,** Lynn Redgrave, Springfield & Dale, 1966, 9 x 12. | 15 |

**S**

| | |
|---|---|
| **Hey Holy Mackerel,** I.C. Haag & John Frigo, 1969, 9 x 12 In. | 50 |
| **Lady In The Dark,** Famous Music Corporation, 1943, 12 x 9 In. | 7 |
| **Over The Waves,** Juventino Rosas, 1933 | 5 |
| **Peace At Last,** U.S. Grant, H.P. Danks, 1885, 10 x 13¾ In. | 50 |
| **Prisoner Of War Ballad,** George Russell, ST Gordon, 4 Pages, 1864, 10 x 13 In. | 45 |
| **Rhythm On The Range,** Bing Crosby, Shapiro, Bernstein & Co., 1936 | 36 |
| **Song Sung Blue,** Neil Diamond, 1972 | 7 |
| **That's My Boy,** Martin & Lewis, Edward B. Marks Music | 7 |
| **Wait Love Until The War Is Over,** Lithograph, Lee & Walker, 1864 | 115 |
| **Way Down South In Dixie,** E.L. Bolling, 1905, 10¾ x 13¾ In. | 30 |
| **Whatever You Got I Want,** Jackson 5, Motown Records, 1974, 11 x 8½ In. | 25 |

**SHEFFIELD** *items are listed in the Silver Plate and Silver-English categories.*

**SHELLEY** first appeared on English ceramics about 1912. The Foley China Works started in England in 1860. Joseph Ball Shelley joined the company in 1862 and became a partner in 1872. Percy Shelley joined the firm in 1881. The company went through a series of name changes and in 1910 the then Foley China Company became Shelley China. In 1929 it became Shelley Potteries. The company was acquired in 1966 by Allied English Potteries, then merged with the Doulton group in 1971. The name Shelley was put into use again in 1980. A trio is the name for a cup, saucer, and cake plate set.

| | |
|---|---|
| **Cheese Dish,** Dome Lid, Blue, Dainty, Handles, c.1960, 4 x 7 In. | 127 |
| **Coffeepot,** Chrysanthemum, Ripon, Blue Rim, 1950s, 9 In. | 72 |
| **Creamer,** Bridal Rose, Fluted, 2½ In. | 40 |
| **Creamer,** Cornflower, Scalloped Rim, 3½ In. | 68 |
| **Cup & Saucer,** Blossoms, Ludlow | 52 |
| **Cup & Saucer,** Blue Rose | 60 |
| **Cup & Saucer,** Daisy Chintz, Green | 48 |
| **Cup & Saucer,** Ludlow, Green, Gold | 98 |
| **Cup & Saucer,** Poppies | 50 |
| **Cup & Saucer,** Red Daisy | 53 |
| **Cup & Saucer,** Thistle, Dainty | 92 |
| **Eggcup,** Blue, Dainty, 3 In. | 49 |
| **Gravy Boat,** Bridal Rose, 8 In. | 75 |
| **Luncheon Trio,** Woodland, Plate, Cup, Saucer, Henley Shape | 95 |
| **Plate,** White, Yellow Pink Bubbles, Black Ground, Bubbles Pattern, c.1930, 6¾ In. | 69 |
| **Sugar & Creamer,** Daffodil Time, Corset Shape | 75 |
| **Teapot,** Blue Phlox, Regent Shape, c.1925, 5¾ In. | 104 |
| **Vase,** Butterfly, Iridescent, 6-Sided, Marked, 7 In. | 175 |

**SHIRLEY TEMPLE,** the famous movie star, was born in 1928. She made her first movie in 1932. She died in 2014. Thousands of items picturing Shirley have been and still are being made. Shirley Temple dolls were first made in 1934 by Ideal Toy Company. Millions of Shirley Temple cobalt blue glass dishes were made by Hazel Atlas Glass Company and U.S. Glass Company from 1934 to 1942. They were given away as premiums for Wheaties and Bisquick. A bowl, mug, and pitcher were made as a breakfast set. Some pieces were decorated with the picture of a very young Shirley, others used a picture of Shirley in her 1936 *Captain January* costume. Although collectors refer to a cobalt creamer, it is actually the 4½-inch-high milk pitcher from the breakfast set. Many of these items are being reproduced today.

| | |
|---|---|
| **4 Paper Dolls,** Outfits, Accessories, Saalfield Publishing Co., 1934, 8 In. | 75 |
| **Advertisement,** This Is My Cereal, Quaker Puffed Wheat, 1937, 10 x 14 In. | 15 |
| **Doll,** Blue & White Jumper, Wrist Tag, Ideal, Box, 1957, 12 In. | 365 |
| **Doll,** Composition, Sleep Eyes, Teeth, Blond Curls, Pink Pleated Dress, Ideal, 13 In. | 560 |
| **Doll,** Composition, Socket Head, Sleep Eyes, Mohair Wig, Ideal, Box, c.1935, 18 In. ...........*illus* | 1120 |
| **Doll,** Curled Wig, Pink Dress, Ideal, 35 In. | 240 |
| **Doll,** Vinyl Head, Ringlets, Blue & White Embroidered Dress, Ideal, Box, 1958, 15 In. .........*illus* | 513 |
| **Doll,** Vinyl Socket Head, Jointed, Saran Hair, Blue Flowers, Box, Ideal, 1958, 19 In. | 399 |
| **Doll,** Vinyl Socket Head, Jointed, Saran Hair, Captain January, Ideal, 1958, 12 In. | 285 |
| **Doll,** Vinyl Socket Head, Jointed, Saran Hair, Signature Pin, Ideal, 1958, 12 In. | 171 |
| **Doll,** Vinyl Socket Head, Jointed, Saran Hair, Sleep Eyes, Ideal, 1958, 17 In. | 228 |
| **Doll,** Vinyl Socket Head, Jointed, Saran Hair, Wrist Tag, Ideal, 1958, 15 In. | 456 |
| **Mirror,** Portrait, Celluloid, Fox Film Corp., 1935, 1¾ In. | 33 |
| **Pen & Pencil,** My Writing Set, Fountain Pen, Box | 275 |
| **Wig,** Mohair, Blond, Curls, 14 In. | 68 |

**Shearwater,** Vase, Alkaline Blue, White, Sea Green, Peter Anderson, Marked, c.1935, 6½ In.
$717

Neal Auction Co.

**Shearwater,** Vase, Geckos, Butterflies, Flowers, Multicolor, Patricia Anderson Findeisen, 6 In.
$460

Humler & Nolan

**Shirley Temple,** Doll, Composition, Socket Head, Sleep Eyes, Mohair Wig, Ideal, Box, c.1935, 18 In.
$1,120

Theriault's

S

**Shirley Temple,** Doll, Vinyl Head, Ringlets, Blue & White Embroidered Dress, Ideal, Box, 1958, 15 In.
$513

Theriault's

**Silver Deposit,** Jug, Art Nouveau Style, Green Glass, Engraved, Old Kentucky Home, 8 x 5 In.
$750

Rago Arts & Auction Center

**Silver Plate,** Ashtray, Man's Head, Holding Funnel, Marked, Prof. Phil Kittler, 3 ½ In.
$313

The Stein Auction Company

SILVER, *Sheffield, see Silver Plate; Silver-English categories.*

**SILVER DEPOSIT** glass was first made during the late nineteenth century. Solid sterling silver is applied to the glass by a chemical method so that a cutout design of silver metal appears against a clear or colored glass. It is sometimes called silver overlay.

| | |
|---|---:|
| **Bonbon,** Amber, 8-Sided, Handles, Art Nouveau, 6 x 5 x 2 In. | 65 |
| **Bonbon,** Poppies, 3-Footed, 6 x 2 In. | 120 |
| **Bottle,** Diamond Shapes, Angular Shape, Long Neck, Stopper, 7 ¼ In. | 60 |
| **Cake Plate,** Flowers, Bees, Scalloped Rim, 4 Raised Feet, 1930s, 11 ¾ In. | 105 |
| **Candlestick,** Black Glass, Art Deco, Leaf, c.1900, 9 In., Pair | 80 |
| **Decanter,** Brown Matte Glaze, Bulbous, Corn & Grape Overlay, 8 x 6 In. | 406 |
| **Dish,** Cranberry Glass, Gondola, Gondolier, Swirls, Curled Edge, 3 ½ In. | 85 |
| **Jug,** Art Nouveau Style, Green Glass, Engraved, Old Kentucky Home, 8 x 5 In. ........*illus* | 750 |
| **Perfume Bottle,** Etched, Flowers, Stopper, Bulbous, 4 ¾ In. | 1250 |
| **Pitcher,** Cranberry Glass, Flowers, Scrolling, Bulbous, c.1920, 8 ½ x 9 In. | 338 |
| **Pitcher,** Flowers, Footed, Pinched Spout, 6 In. | 125 |
| **Pitcher,** Green Glass, Flowers, Ribbed Base, c.1930, 8 ¾ x 9 In. | 550 |
| **Tray,** Amber, Urns, 4-Leaf Clovers, Center Handle, c.1900, 10 In. | 95 |
| **Vase,** Cobalt Blue Glass, Flowers, Leaves, Bulbous, 6 In. | 148 |

**SILVER FLATWARE** includes many of the current and out-of-production silver and silver-plated flatware patterns made in the past eighty years. Other silver is listed under Silver-American, Silver-English, etc. Most silver flatware sets that are missing a few pieces can be completed through the help of a silver matching service.

### SILVER FLATWARE PLATED

| | |
|---|---:|
| **Abington,** Fork, Oneida, 1910, 6 ⅞ In. | 6 |
| **Alhambra,** Tomato Server, Rogers, 7 ¼ In. | 28 |
| **American Landmarks,** Teaspoon, Reed & Barton, 5 ⅞ In. | 17 |
| **Aurora,** Ladle, Oneida, 1930, 6 ¾ In. | 13 |
| **Aurora,** Sugar Spoon, Oneida, 1930, 6 In. | 14 |
| **Aurora,** Teaspoon, Oneida, 1930, 6 In. | 7 |
| **Bancroft,** Fruit Spoon, Oneida, 1915, 5 ⅞ In. | 7 |
| **Bancroft,** Seafood Fork, Oneida, 1915, 6 ¼ In. | 8 |
| **Bennington,** Feeding Spoon, Oneida, 1959, 5 ½ In. | 5 |
| **Bennington,** Fork, Oneida, 1959, 7 ⅜ In. | 6 |
| **Bennington,** Iced Tea Spoon, Oneida, 1959, 7 ½ In. | 5 |
| **Bennington,** Meat Fork, Oneida, 1959, 8 ⅝ In. | 18 |
| **Bennington,** Teaspoon, Oneida, 1959, 6 In. | 6 |
| **Bouquet,** Cake Server, International Silver, c.1924, 10 ½ In. | 15 |
| **Cosmopolitan,** Cocktail Fork, Reed & Barton, 1968, 5 ¾ In. | 9 |
| **Cosmopolitan,** Fork, Reed & Barton, 7 ⅛ In. | 14 |
| **Cottage Rose,** Fork, Reed & Barton, 1985, 7 ⅜ In. | 11 |
| **Cottage Rose,** Ladle, Reed & Barton, 1985, 6 ½ In. | 6 |
| **Del Mar,** Dinner Fork, Rogers, 7 ½ In. | 10 |
| **Del Mar,** Salad Fork, Rogers, 6 ⅝ In. | 8 |
| **Del Mar,** Teaspoon, Rogers, 6 In. | 8 |
| **Denmark,** Ladle, Reed & Barton, 1963, 7 In. | 10 |
| **Denmark,** Salad Fork, Reed & Barton, 6 ¾ In. | 7 |
| **Denmark,** Sugar Spoon, Reed & Barton, 1963, 6 ⅛ In. | 5 |
| **Duchess,** Pickle Fork, Oneida Community, 6 ⅜ In. | 8 |
| **Enchanted Rose,** Meat Fork, Wm. Rogers & Son, 9 In. | 18 |
| **Enchanted Rose,** Serving Spoon, Wm. Rogers & Son, 11 In. | 22 |
| **Enchanted Rose,** Serving Spoon, Wm. Rogers & Son, 9 In. | 15 |
| **Enchanted Rose,** Teaspoon, Wm. Rogers & Son, 6 In. | 8 |
| **Epicure,** Iced Tea Spoon, Reed & Barton, 1970, 10 In. | 6 |
| **Epicure,** Meat Fork, Reed & Barton, 1970, 8 ¾ In. | 11 |
| **Epicure,** Serving Fork, Reed & Barton, 1970, 8 ⅝ In. | 3 |
| **Fantasy,** Cream Ladle, Oneida Community, 1941, 5 In. | 6 |
| **Floral,** Dinner Fork, Wallace, 7 ⅜ In. | 12 |
| **Floral,** Meat Fork, Wallace, 1902, 8 In. | 18 |
| **Floral,** Sugar Spoon, Wallace, 1902, 6 In. | 12 |
| **Floral,** Teaspoon, Wallace, 6 In. | 8 |
| **Fruit Set,** Reed & Vine Molded Hollow Handles, Walnut Case, 24 Piece | 420 |
| **Morning Rose,** Fork, Oneida, 1960, 7 ⅜ In. | 16 |
| **Morning Rose,** Salad Fork, Oneida, 1960, 6 ¾ In. | 12 |

S

| | |
|---|---|
| **Morning Rose,** Sugar Spoon, Oneida, 1960, 5 ¾ In. | 4 |
| **Norwood,** Butter Knife, William Brothers, 7 In. | 22 |
| **Old London,** Oyster Fork, Reed & Barton, 5 ¾ In. | 7 |
| **Old London,** Salad Fork, Reed & Barton, 6 ¼ In. | 12 |
| **Old London,** Teaspoon, Reed & Barton, 6 In. | 7 |
| **Plantation,** Dinner Fork, Rogers, 1948, 7 ⅝ In. | 10 |
| **Plantation,** Knife, Rogers, 1948, 9 ¼ In. | 12 |
| **Plantation,** Serving Spoon, Rogers, 8 ¼ In. | 18 |
| **Saybrooke,** Sugar Spoon, Universal Silver, 6 In. | 12 |

## SILVER FLATWARE STERLING

| | |
|---|---|
| **Acorn,** Cake Knife, Stainless Steel Blade, Georg Jensen, 10 ½ In. | 374 |
| **Acorn,** Salad Set, Georg Jensen, 7 ¾ In., 2 Piece | 368 |
| **Athene,** Utensils, Fillet Knife, Cheese Server, Bacon Fork, Amston | 115 |
| **Cambridge,** Ladle, Peach Shape Bowl, Curved Handle, Leaves, Gorham, 12 ¾ In. | 167 |
| **Chesterfield,** Demitasse Spoon, Gold Washed Bowl, Gorham, c.1906, Case, 6 Piece | 111 |
| **Dauphin,** Dessert Spoon, Gold Washed Bowl, B. Durgin, c.1900, 5 ¾ In., 6 Piece | 325 |
| **Etruscan,** Salad Set, Gold Washed, Lobed Bowl, Reticulated Fork, Gorham, 1913, 9 In. | 138 |
| **Francis I,** Butter Spreader, Gilt Blade, Reed & Barton, 1907, 5 ¾ In., 12 Piece | 1107 |
| **Honeysuckle,** Teaspoon, Whiting, c.1900, 6 In., 12 Piece | 180 |
| **Jacobean,** Soup Spoon, Reed & Barton, 7 In., 6 Piece | 150 |
| **King's Pattern,** Punch Ladle, Monogram, Marquand, 10 ½ In. | 478 |
| **Knife Set,** Luncheon, Grand Baroque, Stainless Steel Blade, Wallace, 9 In., 8 Piece | 184 |
| **Ladle,** Round Bowl, Curved Handle, Flowers, Reed & Barton, 10 ¼ x 4 In. | 132 |
| **Louis XIV,** Ladle, Gorham, 13 ½ In. | 295 |
| **Louis XV,** Serving Spoon, Oval Bowl, Scroll On Handle, Whiting Mfg., 1891, 9 In. | 282 |
| **Love Disarmed,** Meat Fork, Charles A. Bennett, Reed & Barton, 1899, 10 ½ In. | 399 |
| **Love Disarmed,** Serving Fork & Spoon, Art Nouveau Maiden, Reed & Barton, 10 In. | 237 |
| **Marie Antoinette,** Salad Servers, Fork & Spoon, Alvin, c.1910, 11 ¼ In. | 130 |
| **Morning Glory,** Pie Server, Engraved Blade, Gorham, 11 In. | 531 |
| **Mountain Rose,** Serving Set, David-Andersen, Norway, 9 In., 3 Piece | 826 |
| **New Queens,** Serving Set, Fork, Spoon, Gorham, Enamel, 8 ¾ x 2 ½ & 9 x 3 In. | 265 |
| **Old Master,** Serving Spoon, Spoon Rest, Harold E. Nock, Towle, 1942, 13 ½ In. | 240 |
| **Royal Danish,** Ladle, Oblong Bowl, Double Spout, International, 17 x 5 ½ In. | 575 |
| **Troubadour,** Dinner Knife, Concord Silversmith, 9 ¾ In., 12 Piece | 120 |
| **Versailles,** Fish Serving Set, Fork, Knife, Gorham, 10 ½ In. | 450 |
| **Versailles,** Pastry Fork, Gorham, 6 In., 8 Piece | 360 |
| **Vine,** Peapod, Pea Spoon, Tiffany & Co., c.1880, 9 In. | 720 |

**SILVER PLATE** is not solid silver. It is a ware made of a metal, such as nickel or copper, that is covered with a thin coating of silver. The letters *EPNS* are often found on American and English silver-plated wares. *Sheffield* is a term with two meanings. Sometimes it refers to sterling silver made in the town of Sheffield, England. Sometimes it refers to an old form of plated silver.

| | |
|---|---|
| **Ashtray,** Man's Head, Holding Funnel, Marked, Prof. Phil Kittler, 3 ½ In. ...............*illus* | 313 |
| **Biscuit Barrel,** Edwardian, Ringed Masque Handles, Dog Finial, c.1900, 8 x 8 In. | 522 |
| **Biscuit Barrel,** Lid, Chased Cherubs, Instruments, Footed, Elkington & Co., c.1900, 8 ½ In. | 1063 |
| **Biscuit Box,** Shell Shape, Folding, Israel Freeman & Son, 1928, 10 In. | 179 |
| **Bowl,** Flower Frog, Monogram, Reed & Barton, 4 ½ x 16 In. ...............*illus* | 132 |
| **Bowl,** Vegetable, Warming Stand, England, 8 x 13 ¾ In. | 120 |
| **Box,** Tantalus, Crystal, 2 Decanters, Wooden Insets, Betjemann, 12 ¾ x 12 In. | 369 |
| **Carving Set,** Steel, Antler Handles, Knife, Fork, Sharpening Steel, Sprock's, c.1900, 16 In. | 246 |
| **Carving Trolley,** Revolving Dome Lid, Louis XVI, Creme Peinte, Plate Stand, 43 In. | 1793 |
| **Centerpiece,** Central Tureen, Dolphin, Poseidon, Shell Shape Base, Mermaids | 3690 |
| **Centerpiece,** Edwardian, Tripod Standard, Round Base, Scroll Feet, Cut Glass Dish, 20 x 11 In. | 861 |
| **Centerpiece,** Maiden, Raised Arms, Shaped Oval Base, Leaves, 17 In. | 1500 |
| **Champagne Cooler,** Round, Offset Opening, Flutes Fit Around Equator, Footed, France | 210 |
| **Cocktail Shaker,** Bakelite, F. Arstrom, 1930, 3 ½ x 8 ½ In. | 976 |
| **Cocktail Shaker,** Bell Shape, Turned Wood Handle, Engraved C, 11 x 6 In. | 100 |
| **Cocktail Shaker,** Lighthouse, Hallmarks, 14 In. | 1016 |
| **Decanter,** Cut Glass Barrel, George V, Straps, Spigot, Bucket, 7 ½ x 9 ¼ In. | 264 |
| **Dish,** Entree Lid, Pierced Interior, Scroll Feet, Old Sheffield, c.1810, 9 x 14 In. ..............*illus* | 295 |
| **Dish,** Leaf Shape, Hammered, Rose Quartz Handle, 3-Footed, Sylvester, 15 In. | 120 |
| **Dresser Mirror,** Relief Fruit Rim, Oval, Hinged Leg, Marked, 14 x 10 ½ In. | 311 |
| **Entree Lid,** Shaped Dome, Scroll, Shell, Acanthus Border, Sheffield, c.1830, 16 x 8 ¼ In. | 531 |
| **Epergne,** Empire Style, 5 Clear Cut Glass Bowls, Scrolled Frame, Paw Feet, 1800s, 16 In. | 800 |
| **Epergne,** Georgian, 6 Arms, Crystal Bowls, Armorial Engraved, England, c.1900, 26 x 24 In. | 1375 |

**Silver Plate,** Bowl, Flower Frog, Monogram, Reed & Barton, 4 ½ x 16 In.
$132

Gray's Auctioneers LLC

**Silver Plate,** Dish, Entree Lid, Pierced Interior, Scroll Feet, Old Sheffield, c.1810, 9 x 14 In.
$295

Brunk Auctions

**Silver Plate,** Pitcher, Duck Shape, Brass Bill Shape Spout, Los Castillo, Mexico, c.1950, 10 ¾ In.
$1,121

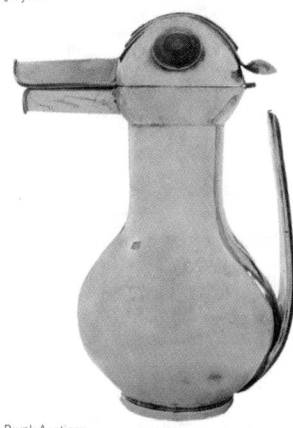

Brunk Auctions

**S**

**Silver Plate,** Pitcher, Stand, Tilting, 2 Cups, Meriden Brittania, Marked, c.1880, 12 ½ x 16 In.
$1,250

Heritage Auction Galleries

**Silver-American,** Basket, Pierced, Applied Rococo Trim, Swing Handle, Gorham, 1873, 17 x 16 In.
$3,125

Rago Arts & Auction Center

**Silver-American,** Basket, Sweetmeat, Swing Handle, Natchez, Marked, E. Profilet, Coin, 1823-68, 7 x 6 In.
$9,859

Neal Auction Co.

| | |
|---|---:|
| **Epergne,** Tree Shape Shaft, Putti, Flowers, Acanthus, Cut Glass Bowls, 25 ¼ In. | 2318 |
| **Fighting Cocks,** Realistically Modeled, 10 In., 2 Piece | 688 |
| **Food Trolley,** Figural Dome Lid, Fox, Branches, Towel Bar, Franco Lafinia, 36 x 44 In. | 7475 |
| **Frame,** Repousse, Fruit, Flowers, Leaves, Oval, 13 ¾ x 11 In. | 92 |
| **Hot Water Urn,** Georgian Neoclassical Style, Handles, Square Base, 21 In. | 236 |
| **Hot Water Urn,** Handles, Square Base, 4-Footed, Engraved, 19 ¾ In. | 244 |
| **Hot Water Urn,** Neo-Grec, Handles, Chased, Round Pedestal Base, 1800s, 19 In. | 179 |
| **Hot Water Urn,** Regency Style, Gadroon, Fluted Lid, Ball Feet, 17 ½ In. | 250 |
| **Hot Water Urn,** Ring Handles, Bacchus Mounts, Stepped Base, Sheffield, c.1850, 13 In. | 154 |
| **Ice Bucket,** Snail Shape, 9 ½ x 14 ¾ In. | 677 |
| **Jam Jar,** Victorian, Gilt, Fitted Liner, Acanthus Banding, Fenton, 5 ½ x 7 ¼ In. | 615 |
| **Jardiniere,** Belle Epoque, Shell & Scroll Rim, Scroll Feet, Christofle, 11 x 12 In. | 522 |
| **Ladle,** Reeded Shaft, Scalloped Bowl, Cut Glass Handle, Hobstar, Fan, J.D. Bergen, 15 In. | 403 |
| **Meat Dish,** Dome Lid, Lion Rampant Finial, Gadroon Border, 14 x 26 In. | 598 |
| **Pitcher,** Duck Shape, Brass Bill Shape Spout, Los Castillo, Mexico, c.1950, 10 ¾ In. ............*illus* | 1121 |
| **Pitcher,** Ram's Head Lid, Frosted Body, 7 ¼ In., Pair | 438 |
| **Pitcher,** Stand, Tilting, 2 Cups, Meriden Brittania, Marked, c.1880, 12 ½ x 16 In. ...........*illus* | 1250 |
| **Pitcher,** Tilting, Stand, Meriden Britannia, 1868 | 239 |
| **Plaque,** Collie, Relief Decoration, 19th Century, 9 ½ x 7 ½ In. | 86 |
| **Plate Set,** King Francis, Reed & Barton, c.1960, 12 In., 12 Piece | 2091 |
| **Plate,** Dublin Pattern, Ogee Rim, Worden-Munnis Co., 10 ½ In. | 250 |
| **Plate,** Service, Baroque Charger, Godinger Silver Arts Co., 11 ⅝ In., 16 Piece | 338 |
| **Plateau,** Mirrored, 3 Stage Heads, Oak Leaf & Acorn, Round, 14 x 22 In. | 587 |
| **Plateau,** Mirrored, Leaf Border, Ball Feet, Round, 1800s, 22 ½ In. | 657 |
| **Punch Bowl,** Laurel Swags, Acanthus & Dart Banding, c.1900, 6 ¾ x 11 ¼ In. | 369 |
| **Server,** Dome Top, Fluted Legs, Paw Feet, 2 Interior Trays, England, c.1900, 12 x 9 ½ In. | 59 |
| **Spoon,** Souvenir, see Souvenir category. | |
| **Tankard,** Coin Inset, Sheffield, 18th Century | 795 |
| **Tea & Coffee Set,** Hot Water Urn With Stand, Sugar & Creamer, Tray | 150 |
| **Tray,** Crest, 2 Handles, Elkington & Co., 29 ⅜ x 19 In. | 420 |
| **Tray,** Federal Style, Open Wirework, Oval, Ellis-Baker Mark, Birmingham, 25 x 15 In. | 944 |
| **Tray,** Figural, Bullfrogs Seated At Pond, Fish, Flute, 3 ¼ x 9 In. | 374 |
| **Tray,** Figural, Mermaid Climbing Onto Open Shell, Frog, 5 ¾ x 14 ½ In. | 288 |
| **Tray,** Geometric Etched Center, Raised Rim, Molded Fish Handles, Oval, 29 x 21 In. | 430 |
| **Tray,** Handles, Israel Freeman & Son, London, c.1930, 30 In. | 240 |
| **Tray,** Pierced Gallery, Handles, Footed, Engraved, Daniel & Arter, c.1910, 38 x 17 In., Pair | 615 |
| **Tray,** Reeded Rim, Handles, Footed, Engraved, Floral Band, Stag's Head, c.1880, 36 x 24 In. | 584 |
| **Tray,** Regency Style, Applied Flowers, Leaves, Pierced, Lion Masks, 29 ½ In. | 688 |
| **Tray,** Round, Etched Leaves, Mask Handles, c.1890, 38 x 23 In. | 313 |
| **Tray,** Shells & Scrolls, Shaped Handles, Cardeilhac, France, 33 x 21 In. | 649 |
| **Tray,** Truncated, Handles, Fan, Branches, Butterflies, Elkington & Co., c.1880, 27 x 17 In. | 406 |
| **Trophy Cup,** Engraved, Best Display S.C. Rhode Island Reds, 1914-15, 10 ½ x 9 ½ In. | 155 |
| **Tureen,** Lid, Flower Embossed Rim, Raised Paw Feet, Sheffield, c.1835, 13 x 15 In., Pair | 1200 |
| **Tureen,** Lid, Spanish Colonial Style, Spherical Shape, Repousse Fruit, 3 Claw Feet, 1 x 15 In. | 399 |
| **Tureen,** Sauce, Lid, Double Oval Shape, Paw Feet, Gadroon Rim, Handle, 5 ¾ x 9 In. | 246 |
| **Tureen,** Soup, Dome Lid, Shell, Leaf Gadroon, Armorial Engraved, Footed, 1800s, 13 In. | 420 |
| **Tureen,** William IV, Old Sheffield, Oval, Gadroon Rim, Acanthus Feet, 10 x 16 In. | 553 |
| **Urn,** Trumpet Shape, Reeded Band, Square Base, 4 Spherical Feet, 19 ¼ In. | 1168 |
| **Vase,** Glass, Cranberry To Clear, Holder, James Tufts, c.1890, 8 ½ In. | 246 |
| **Vase,** Moon, Christian Dior, 1970s, 11 x 11 ¾ In. | 978 |
| **Vase,** Trumpet, Wirework, Floral Swags, Emerald Green Liners, Royal Castle, 15 ¾ In., Pair | 1135 |
| **Wine Coaster,** Reticulated Lion Mask, England, c.1860, 5 x 7 ½ In., 4 Piece | 406 |
| **Wine Coaster,** Scroll & Shell Border, Wood Base, Sheffield, 1900s, 7 ¼ In., Pair | 248 |
| **Wine Cooler,** Acanthus Ruffle Upper Rim, 2 Handles, c.1850s, 12 ½ In., Pair | 1500 |
| **Wine Cooler,** Campana, Cast Grapes, Vines, Flared Ruffled Rim, Elkington, 11 In., Pair | 1476 |
| **Wine Cooler,** Georgian Style, Urn Shape, Gadroon Lip, Rampant Lion, 10 x 8 In., Pair | 460 |
| **Wine Trolley,** Cannon Shape, Movable Acanthus Decorated Wheels, Beaded, 12 ½ In., Pair | 956 |

---

**SILVER-AMERICAN.** American silver is listed here. Coin and sterling silver are included. Most of the sterling silver listed in this book is subdivided by country. There are also other pieces of silver and silver plate listed under special categories, such as Candelabrum, Napkin Ring, Silver Flatware, Silver Plate, Silver-Sterling, and Tiffany Silver. These prices are based on current silver values.

| | |
|---|---:|
| **Basket,** Bouquet, Handle, Flower Garlands, Gorham, 1920, 14 In. | 923 |
| **Basket,** Centerpiece, Woodside Sterling Co., c.1910, 15 x 12 In. | 480 |

**Silver-American,** Bowl, Repousse, Gilt Metal Flower Frog, Gorham, c.1907, 7 x 24 x 17 In.
$7,500

Heritage Auction Galleries

**Silver-American,** Canister, Lid, Malachite, Repousse, Hammered, Henry Petzal, c.1979, 8 In.
$9,375

Heritage Auction Galleries

**Silver-American,** Charger, Hammered, Flared Rim, Allan Adler, c.1950, 12 In., 12 Piece
$9,375

Heritage Auction Galleries

**Silver-American,** Coffeepot, Hinged, Butterfly Finial, Feather Shape Handle, Gorham, c.1850, 8 ¼ In.
$420

Cowan's Auctions

**Silver-American,** Cup, Agricultural Premium, Chased, Repousse, Handle, Engraved, Boston, 1850s, 4 In.
$308

Cowan's Auctions

**Silver-American,** Cup, Caudle, C-Scroll Handles, Marked, Gale & Hayden, 1849, 5 ⅝ In.
$406

Heritage Auction Galleries

**Silver-American,** Cup, South Central Agricultural Society, Handle, Marked E.J. Johnston, 1850, 3 In.
$3,884

Neal Auction Co.

**Silver-American,** Cup, Tapered, Molded Rim, Medallion, Strapwork, Engraved, E.A. Tyler, 3 In.
$956

Neal Auction Co.

**TIP**

*Very elaborate epergnes and candelabra can be protected with lacquer but do not use it on tableware. Be sure an expert applies the lacquer because tarnish will show in any place that has not been covered. The lacquer may have to be replaced about every ten years.*

S

**Silver-American,** Dish, Figural, Repousse Lion, Stippled, Gorham, 1883, 6 ⅞ In.
$938

Heritage Auction Galleries

**Silver-American,** Fish Slice, Hizen Pattern, Marked, Gorham, 1880, 11 ⅞ In.
$469

Heritage Auction Galleries

**Silver-American,** Goblet, Rococo Revival, Chased, Flowers, Marked, J. Rafel N.O., c.1858, 6 In.
$1,793

Neal Auction Co.

**Silver-American,** Grape Shears, Chased, Foxes, Vines, Gorham, c.1910, 6 ¾ In.
$406

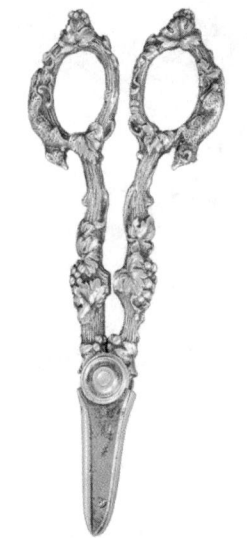

Heritage Auction Galleries

**Silver-American,** Julep Cup, Presentation Inscription, DDE, Mark J. Scearce, 1955, 3 ¾ In.
$330

Garth's Auctioneers & Appraisers

**Silver-American,** Kettle, Hot Water, Stand, Urn Shape, Monogram, Gorham, 10 In.
$850

James D. Julia Auctioneers

**TIP**

*Use tarnish-preventing strips or cloth to keep silver clean in a closed cupboard.*

**Silver-American,** Meat Tray, Plymouth, Reeded Rim, Tree & Well, Gorham, 23 x 17 In.
$1,793

Neal Auction Co.

**Silver-American,** Nut Dish, Chased Lines, Squirrel Finial, Footed, Gorham, c.1930, 5 ¾ In.
$938

Heritage Auction Galleries

**Silver-American,** Pitcher, Beaded, Scroll Handle, Engraved, Eoff & Shepherd, Coin, c.1850, 7 ½ In.
$360

DuMouchelles Art Gallery

Basket, Engine Turned, Cartouche, Round, Bail Handle, Coin, Gorham, c.1860, 7 x 4 In. ........... 413
Basket, Handle, Splay Foot, Towle, 8 In. ............................................. 189
Basket, Openwork, Handles, Underplate, Cylindrical, Webster Co., 4 In. ..................................... 210
Basket, Pierced, Applied Rococo Trim, Swing Handle, Gorham, 1873, 17 x 16 In. ...............*illus* 3125
Basket, Reticulated, Double Handle, Reed & Barton, 6 x 12½ In. ......................................... 270
Basket, Scrolling Handle, Engraved Urn & Scrolls, Pierced Work, International, 12 x 9 In........ 533
Basket, Sweetmeat, Swing Handle, Natchez, Marked, E. Profilet, Coin, 1823-68, 7 x 6 In. .....*illus* 9859
Basting Spoon, Down-Turned Fiddle, Engraved Crest, 1841, 12 In. ..................................... 418
Beaker, Marked, Wm. F. Baab, 6th Ave., Erstes Nationales Bundes Schiessen, 1895, 8 In. ..... 690
Berry Bowl, Relief Berries, Flowers, Round, Ball Feet, S. Kirk & Son, 5¾ In. ............................. 242
Bonbon, Flared-Out Undulating Rim, Leaves, Scrolls, Martele, Gorham, 1906, 7 In. .............. 2048
Bottle Tickets, Bourbon, Brandy, Gin, Rum, Scotch, Sherry, Cutout, Kalo, 3 In., 6 Piece ............ 1464
Bowl, Art Nouveau, Embossed Flowers, Alvin, 8¾ In. ........................................................... 106
Bowl, Art Nouveau, Flowers, Leaves, Pierced Border, Gorham Mfg., 18½ x 14½ In. ................ 1888
Bowl, Beaded Rim, Monogram, Flowers, Gorham, 1890, 8¼ In. ......................................... 554
Bowl, Chased Flowers, Monogram In Cartouche, Footed, Shreve, Crump & Low, 5 x 10 In......... 593
Bowl, Chased Rim, S. Kirk & Sons Inc., 11¼ In. ................................................................. 563
Bowl, Chased, Embossed, Leaf Scrolls, Cartouche, Low Foot, Davis & Galt, 9 In. ................. 461
Bowl, Circular, Flowers, Leaf Sprays, Black, Starr & Frost, 15 In. ........................................ 1500
Bowl, Claw Foot, Fluted Sides, Undulating Rim, Acanthus Leaves, Oval, Watson, 5 x 4 In. .......... 98
Bowl, Daisies, Monogram, Marked, Late 1800s, 13 In. Diam. ............................................... 813
Bowl, Decorated Rim, Strawberries, Grapes, Apples, Flowers, Leaves, Gorham, 10½ In. .............. 384
Bowl, Deep, Footed, Tapered, Turned-Out Rim, Paul Revere Reproduction, 4 x 8 In. .................... 196
Bowl, Engraved Thistle Stems, Arts & Crafts, Arthur Stone, 1906-37, 4 In. ......................... 4800
Bowl, Engraved, Pierced, Leaf, Scalloped Rim, Frank W. Smith Silver Co., c.1920, 15 x 12 In. ..... 1063
Bowl, Flower, Swag Around Rim, Short Foot, Durgin, 9 In. .................................................. 360
Bowl, Francis I, Ernest Meyers, 1907, 11½ In. ................................................................... 1045
Bowl, Francis I, Flowers, Flutes, Oval, Footed, Reed & Barton, 3 x 13 x 10 In. ....................... 531
Bowl, Furrowed Oval Sides, Scalloped Border, Animal Feet, Reed & Barton, 3¾ x 13 In. .......... 316
Bowl, Hammered, Applied Copper Berries On Branch, Birds, Butterflies, Gorham, 8 In. ............... 2500
Bowl, Hammered, Beaded Rim, Footed, Elongated Loop Handles, Marcus, 3 x 13 In. ............... 4956
Bowl, Hammered, Ivy, 2 Handles, Copper Ring Base, Gorham, 9¾ x 5 In. ............................ 8750
Bowl, Heavy Repousse Rim, Flowers, C-Scrolls, Lobed Sides, Oval, Whiting, 12 x 9 In. ............ 750
Bowl, Interlocking Lobes, Banded Rim & Foot, c.1973, 3 x 10 In. ........................................ 3500
Bowl, Ladle, Flared Rim, Tooled Bands, Round Foot, Pierced Terminal, Arthur Stone.................. 584
Bowl, Lid, Allover Repousse Flowers, Demilune Handle, Kirk, 5 x 10 In., Pair ......................... 3068
Bowl, Lid, Dominick & Haff, 11½ In., Pair ...................................................................... 1875
Bowl, Lobed Body, Scrolled & Shaped Rim, Whiting Co., c.1900, 9 In., Pair......................... 225
Bowl, Monogram, Engraved 1901, Scalloped Lobed Rim, Gorham, 14 x 18½ In. ................. 1035
Bowl, Overlapping Petals, Hammered, Undulating Rim, Peer Smed, 1933, 7 In. ..................... 2375
Bowl, Pedestal, Leaf Reticulated Waist, Durham, 5½ x 8¼ In. ........................................... 518
Bowl, Pedestal, Neoclassical, Whiting, 1914, 6 x 12 In. ...................................................... 891
Bowl, Pierced Flower Rim, Over Green, Etched Glass, Gorham, c.1898, 9½ In. ..................... 1375
Bowl, Pierced, Reticulated, Monogram, Graff, Washbourne & Dunn, c.1945, 2½ x 11 In. ........... 344
Bowl, Radiant Design, Flared Rim, Footed, Round, Wallace & Co., 10 In. ........................... 265
Bowl, Relief, Flowers, Leaves, Stems, 10¼ In. .................................................................. 2270
Bowl, Repousse Flowers & Scrolls, Round, T.B. Starr, 8½ In. ............................................. 1200
Bowl, Repousse Flowers, Flared Undulating Rim, S. Kirk, 1896-1924, 2 x 10 In. ..................... 236
Bowl, Repousse Flowers, Landscapes, Footed, S. Kirk & Sons, 3 x 7½ In. ........................ 584
Bowl, Repousse Flowers, Leaves, Footed, Stieff, 1927, 16½ In. ......................................... 3300
Bowl, Repousse Grapevines, Branch Rim, Footed, Black, Starr & Frost, 1900, 9 x 4 In................. 640
Bowl, Repousse, Gilt Metal Flower Frog, Gorham, c.1907, 7 x 24 x 17 In.............................*illus* 7500
Bowl, Reticulated, Grapevine Rim, 4-Footed, Bailey Banks & Biddle, 3¼ x 10 In........................ 600
Bowl, Revere, Flared, Footed, Stieff, 5 x 9 In. ................................................................. 295
Bowl, Ring Footed, Weidlich Sterling Silver Spoon, Ct., c.1935, 4 x 8 In............................... 250
Bowl, Roses, Hexagonal, Lobed, Undulating Rim, Whiting, 12 In. ........................................ 1285
Bowl, Rounded, Hammered, 4 Ball Feet, Whiting, 1916, 4 x 9 In. ...................................... 625
Bowl, Scalloped Rim, Reed & Barton, 7½ x 15 In. ............................................................ 5000
Bowl, Scalloped, Flower Border, Gorham, 1898, 11 x 3 In. ............................................... 360
Bowl, Squared Rim, Reeded Foot, Fisher, 10½ In. ............................................................ 277
Bowl, Squat, 4 Paw Feet, Leaf Relief, Monogram, Mark, Wm. B. Durgin Co., 2¾ x 6 In............. 368
Bowl, Squat, Footed, Gorham, c.1900, 2½ x 9 In. ............................................................. 270
Bowl, Swan Shape, Gorham, Early 20th Century, 8¼ In. ................................................... 738
Bowl, Trophy, 2 Handles, Harlem Yacht Club, Gorham, 1909, 14⅜ In. ................................. 584
Bowl, Trophy, Scroll, Leaves, Round Foot, Metcalf Co., 1906, 10½ In. ................................. 492

**Silver-American,** Pitcher, Water, Riverside Village Scene, Hausmann & Son, 1890, 9¾ In.
$1,164

New Orleans Auction Galleries, Inc.

**TIP**
*To clean crevices in old silver, use a cotton-tipped cuticle stick.*

**Silver-American,** Punch Bowl, Enamel Interior, 12 Cups, Towle, c.1955, 6⅝ x 12 In.
$3,000

Heritage Auction Galleries

**Silver-American,** Punch Ladle, Medallion, Bust, Mercury, Lobed Bowl, Gilt, Presentation, 1869, 15 In.
$777

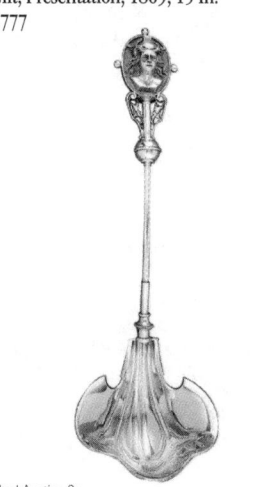

Neal Auction Co.

**Silver-American,** Soup Ladle, Hammered, Copper Crab, Bailey Banks & Biddle, c.1880, 12 In.
$938

Heritage Auction Galleries

---

**Silver-American,** Sugar & Creamer, Kem Weber, Silver Style Line, Friedman, c.1928, 4 ½ In. & 3 In.
$3,750

Los Angeles Modern Auctions (LAMA)

---

**Silver-American,** Sugar Urn, Oval, Monogram, Pedestal Foot, Finial, Walter Vogel, 10 In.
$805

Cottone Auctions

---

**Silver-American,** Tureen, Lid, Acanthus, Oval, Coin, Inscription, 1837, Jones, Low & Ball, 9 In.
$2,596

Brunk Auctions

| | |
|---|---|
| **Bowl,** Trophy, Sonderklasse, Marblehead, Arthur Stone, 8 In. | 1599 |
| **Bowl,** Turned-Out Rim, Stamped International, 10 x 3 In. | 414 |
| **Bowl,** Vegetable, Lid, Repousse Leaves & Flowers, Oval, S. Kirk, 7 x 10 In. | 1750 |
| **Box,** Etched Art Nouveau Flowers Overall, Hinged Lid, Reed & Barton, 4 In. | 861 |
| **Bread Tray,** Art Nouveau, George Shiebler Co., 14 In. | 330 |
| **Butter Chip,** Embossed Rim, Woodside Sterling, c.1910, 3 ½ In., 12 Piece | 276 |
| **Butter,** Cover, Flowers, Repousse, Cow Finial, Footed, Wm. Gale & Son, c.1853, 7 In. | 1250 |
| **Butter,** Cover, Repousse, Vines, Finial, Bull-Head Handles, Peter Krider, c.1855, 6 In. | 1875 |
| **Cake Basket,** Oval, Swing Handle, Pedestal Foot, 12 ½ x 13 ⅝ In. | 1553 |
| **Cake Basket,** Reticulated, Leaf Design Arched Handle, Simpson, Hall & Miller Co., 10 In. | 265 |
| **Cake Plate,** Arts & Crafts, Hammered, Leaf Banding, Round, Gorham, 11 ½ In. | 246 |
| **Calling Card Case,** Repousse, Engraved, Philadelphia Scenes, Leonard & Wilson, 3 ½ In. | 240 |
| **Candelabra** are listed in the Candelabrum category. | |
| **Candlesticks** are listed in their own category. | |
| **Canister,** Dome Lid, Spherical Finial, Bulbous, Hammered, c.1950, 5 In. | 812 |
| **Canister,** Lid, Malachite, Repousse, Hammered, Henry Petzal, c.1979, 8 In. ............*illus* | 9375 |
| **Card Tray,** Arts & Crafts, Relief Leaves, Vines, Mother-Of-Pearl, Kalo Shop, 1912, 4 x 8 In. | 4859 |
| **Castor,** Salt & Pepper, Orchid Pattern, International, 6 ¾ In., 4 Piece | 316 |
| **Centerpiece,** Inverted Undulating Rim, Garlands, International, 15 In. | 826 |
| **Centerpiece,** Oval, Lobster Handles, Pedestal Foot, J.E. Caldwell & Co., c.1890, 10 In. | 1188 |
| **Centerpiece,** Peacock, Gold Washed, Repousse Tail, Galt & Bro., 10 x 5 ⅜ In. | 265 |
| **Chalice,** 14K Gold Bowl, Leaf Tips, Hexagon Foot, Applied Cross, 9 ⅛ In. | 3198 |
| **Chalice,** Paneled, Repousse Flowers, Inscribed, 1865, 8 In. | 300 |
| **Charger,** Art Deco, Stylized Flowers, Gorham, c.1910, 11 ½ In., 12 Piece | 5228 |
| **Charger,** Flower Repousse Border, S. Kirk & Sons, c.1945, 11 In., 12 Piece | 9375 |
| **Charger,** Hammered, Flared Rim, Allan Adler, c.1950, 12 In., 12 Piece ............*illus* | 9375 |
| **Chatelaine,** Chain, Pincushion Ring, Shield Shape Hook, Triple Chain, 1700s, 2 ¾ In. | 1534 |
| **Chocolate Pot,** Repousse, Footed, S. Kirk & Son, c.1855, 10 ¼ In. | 1180 |
| **Cigar Holder,** Double, Gold Washed, Geometric Striped, Oval, Gorham, 5 x 1 In. | 92 |
| **Cigarette Box,** Monogram, Gorham, 1 ¾ x 5 In. | 120 |
| **Cigarette Case,** Flower Border, Cartouche, Chain, Blackinton & Co., c.1900, 3 ¾ In. | 187 |
| **Cigarette Case,** Indian Head, Headdress, Repousse, Unger Bros., c.1900, 2 ⅞ In. | 406 |
| **Cocktail Shaker,** Lid, Strainer, Shreve, Crump & Low, 7 ½ x 3 ½ In. | 541 |
| **Cocktail Shaker,** Manchester, Silver Co., 10 ¼ In. | 531 |
| **Cocktail Shaker,** Tapered, Half Dome Lid, Lip Shape Opening, Totten-Sommer, 7 x 3 In. | 234 |
| **Coffee Set,** Coffeepot, Sugar & Creamer, Monogram, Lenox, 8 ¼ In. | 200 |
| **Coffee Set,** Diamond Pattern, Black Plastic Handle, Reed & Barton, 12 x 8 In. | 863 |
| **Coffeepot,** Acanthus Leaves, Squat, Butterfly Finial, Charters, Cann & Dunn, 10 In. | 640 |
| **Coffeepot,** Champlain, Hand Chased, Flowers, Acanthus, Whiting, 11 In. | 678 |
| **Coffeepot,** Colonial Williamsburg, Lighthouse Shape, Ebonized Handle, Stieff, 12 x 8 In. | 861 |
| **Coffeepot,** Hammered, Cylindrical, 6 Lobes, Ebony Finial, Kalo Shop, 1916, 7 x 7 In. | 2928 |
| **Coffeepot,** Hinged, Butterfly Finial, Feather Shape Handle, Gorham, c.1850, 8 ¼ In. ............*illus* | 420 |
| **Coffeepot,** Rose Scroll Design, Gorham, c.1951, 10 In. | 342 |
| **Coffeepot,** Trophy, Scroll, Larchmont Yacht Club, Whiting, 9 In. | 492 |
| **Cold Meat Fork,** Imperial Chrysanthemum, Gorham, 8 In. | 86 |
| **Compote,** Flattened Rim, Round Base, Hirsch & Co., 6 In. | 82 |
| **Compote,** Flowers, Scrolls, Reticulated Edge, Domed Foot, T. Starr, 11 ⅝ In. | 923 |
| **Compote,** Gadroon Rim, Weighted Base, Marked, Fred Hirsch, 6 x 6 In., Pair | 81 |
| **Compote,** Grapevine Rim, Flowers, S. Kirk & Son Co., 1903-07, 5 In. | 984 |
| **Compote,** Pierced, Cone Shape Foot, Gorham, 1900, 6 In., Pair | 215 |
| **Compote,** Ribbed, Daisies, Leaves, Scalloping, Whiting, 4 x 10 ⅛ In. | 345 |
| **Compote,** Squat, Footed, Handles, Frank M. Whiting Co., 5 x 14 In. | 480 |
| **Compote,** Trophy, Carnations, Larchmont Yacht Club, Whiting, 1901, 4 ¾ In. | 615 |
| **Compote,** Trophy, Leaves, Larchmont Yacht Club, Whiting, 1899, 5 ¾ In. | 861 |
| **Corbeille,** Scroll, Shell, c.1925-32, 10 In. Diam. | 478 |
| **Creamer,** Beaded Rim, Square Base, Christian Wiltberger, Philadelphia, c.1795, 7 ½ In. | 1440 |
| **Creamer,** Classical, Vase Shape, Dolphin Shape Handle, Footed, E.A. Tyler, 5 ¾ In. | 836 |
| **Creamer,** Elongated Helmet Shape, Threaded Rim, Laurel Wreath, 14 x 6 ½ In. | 277 |
| **Creamer,** Lid, Clark, Rackett & Co., 1840-52, 7 ¼ In. | 3660 |
| **Creamer,** Lid, Repousse, Chased, Railroad, Landscape, Hyde & Goodrich, 8 ¼ In. | 861 |
| **Cup,** Aesthetic, Lily-Of-The-Valley Handle, Engraved, Jno. P. Madison, 1874, 3 ¼ In. | 310 |
| **Cup,** Agricultural Premium, Chased, Repousse, Handle, Engraved, Boston, 1850s, 4 In. ........*illus* | 308 |
| **Cup,** Caudle, C-Scroll Handles, Marked, Gale & Hayden, 1849, 5 ⅝ In. ............*illus* | 406 |
| **Cup,** Child, Rivet Applied Strapwork, Geometric, Hammered, C-Scroll Handle, c.1900, 2 In. | 375 |
| **Cup,** Medallions, Helmeted Figure, Strapwork, Shaped Handle, E.A. Tyler, 14 In. | 2629 |

| | |
|---|---|
| **Cup,** Presentation, Renaissance Style, Engraved Borders, Footed, c.1890, 3¾ In. | 478 |
| **Cup,** South Central Agricultural Society, Handle, Marked E.J. Johnston, 1850, 3 In. ...........*illus* | 3884 |
| **Cup,** Tapered, Molded Rim, Medallion, Strapwork, Engraved, E.A. Tyler, 3 In. ...........*illus* | 956 |
| **Cup,** Trophy Shape, Flowers, Howard & Co., Late 1800s, 15¼ x 14¼ In. | 3438 |
| **Cup,** Trophy, Shells, Leaves, Handles, Sharpie Club, 4 In. | 338 |
| **Decanter,** Trophy, Silver Overlay Bottle, Larchmont Yacht Club, 8½ In. | 338 |
| **Dish Set,** Plate, Bowl, Spoon, Inscribed, Child, 1918, 3 Piece | 960 |
| **Dish,** Arts & Crafts, Flower & Vine Handle, Signed, 6½ In. | 150 |
| **Dish,** Boat Shape, Men Handle, Shell Feet, Gorham, c.1873, 3 x 7 x 3 In. | 5937 |
| **Dish,** Entree, Lid, Tray, Chippendale, Gorham, 1947, 5 x 11 In. | 1080 |
| **Dish,** Entree, Lid, Whiting, 1919, 9½ In. | 300 |
| **Dish,** Entree, Trophy, Dome Lid, Nautilus, Black, Starr & Frost, 1923, 12 In. | 923 |
| **Dish,** Figural, Repousse Lion, Stippled, Gorham, 1883, 6⅞ In. ...........*illus* | 938 |
| **Dish,** Grape Leaf Shape, Spherical Feet, Mauser, c.1900, 3 x 8 x 7 In. | 937 |
| **Dish,** Inset Center, Line & Dart Band, Arthur Stone, c.1925, 8¼ In. | 312 |
| **Dish,** Leaf Shape, Repousse Strawberries, Flared Rim, 3 Ball Feet, George K. Webster, 11 x 9 In. . | 357 |
| **Dish,** Lobed Border, Undulating Rim, Stepped Round Foot, Gorham, 1930, 1¾ x 13 In. | 594 |
| **Dish,** Meat, Oval, Undulating Rim, Chased Flowers, Leaves, Martele, Gorham, 1917, 17 In. | 3250 |
| **Dish,** Narragansett Oyster Shell Shape, 2 Shell Feet, Gorham, 1886, 5 In. | 480 |
| **Dish,** Narragansett, Oyster Shell, Barnacles, Clamshell Foot, Gorham, 4¾ x 2½ In. | 1722 |
| **Dish,** Oblong, Leaves, Flower Heads, Pierced Edges, Gorham, 1909, 11⅝ In. | 338 |
| **Dish,** Oval, Scrollwork Border, 1907, 13¾ In. | 584 |
| **Dish,** Oyster Shape, Napkin Fold Handle, Monogram, Wood & Hughes, 6 In. | 338 |
| **Dish,** Redlich, J.E. Caldwell & Co., 5½ x 7½ In. | 369 |
| **Dish,** Repousse Flowers On Undulating Rim, Almond Form, Unger, c.1905, 14 x 10 In. | 259 |
| **Dish,** Round, Shaped, Lobed Cover, Removable Handle, Dominick & Haff, 9 In. | 480 |
| **Dish,** Square, Fluted Wide Rim, Marked, Reed & Barton, 8½ x 8½ In. | 173 |
| **Dresser Set,** Art Nouveau, Brush, Shoehorn, File, Alvin & Whiting, c.1912, 13-In. Mirror | 150 |
| **Dresser Set,** Rococo Leaves, Repousse, Clothing Brush, Hairbrush, Mirror, Gorham | 167 |
| **Egg Spoon,** Fiddle & Thread, Gilt Bowl, Monogram, Mobile, Ala., 5¼ In., 6 Piece | 806 |
| **Epergne,** 3 Crystal Bowl Inserts, Concave Base, 4 Paw Feet, 13¼ In. | 259 |
| **Ewer,** Flower, Leaf Repousse, Dragon's Head Top, S. Kirk & Sons, c.1900, 11½ In. | 2478 |
| **Ewer,** Glass Mounted In Silver, Grapevines, Clear To Cranberry, 13⅞ In. | 677 |
| **Ewer,** Stopper, Overlay, Footed, Monogram, 13 In. | 334 |
| **Fish Serving Set,** Hammered, Fork & Slice, Kalo Shop, 9 In. | 344 |
| **Fish Serving Set,** Relief Fish & Scroll Designs, Reticulated Blades, c.1860, 13½ & 10 In. | 391 |
| **Fish Slice,** Engraved Fish, Flowers, Fiddle Tipt Handle, Monogram, Knapp & Leslie, Ala., 12¼ In. | 826 |
| **Fish Slice,** Hizen Pattern, Marked, Gorham, 1880, 11⅞ In. ...........*illus* | 469 |
| **Fish Slice,** Upturned Fiddle Tip, Curved In, Pierced Scimitar Blade, 1855, 11½ In. | 359 |
| **Flask,** 19th Hole, Golfers, Kerr & Co., c.1920, ½ Pt., 6 x 4 In. | 246 |
| **Flask,** Cartouche Shape, Embossed Maidens, Hinged Cap, 1890, 6½ x 4 In. | 738 |
| **Flask,** Flowers, Repousse, Hinged, Gorham, c.1890 | 950 |
| **Flask,** Golfer, Knickers, Cap, Swinging Club, Wm. B. Kerr & Co., 7 x 5 In. | 826 |
| **Flask,** Hammered, Chased Lines, Monogram Plaque, Rounded Corners, Lebolt, 5 In. | 518 |
| **Flask,** Scottish Terriers, Hinged Lid, We're Both Scotch, 8 In. | 554 |
| **Flask,** Sterling Silver, Men Drinking Around Table, R. Wallace & Sons, c.1900, 5¼ In. | 469 |
| **Fork Set,** Cocktail, Leaf Etched, Bailey Banks & Biddle, 5½ In., 12 Piece | 109 |
| **Funnel,** Reed Rim Base, Strainer, Bread Rim, Marked SK, c.1846, 4¼ In. | 944 |
| **Goblet,** Monogram, Marked, Bentley Studios, Towle, 5¼ In., 6 Piece | 391 |
| **Goblet,** Rococo Revival, Chased, Flowers, Marked, J. Rafel N.O., c.1858, 6 In. ...........*illus* | 1793 |
| **Goblet,** Tapering Tulip Shape, Segmented Stem, c.1850, 8⅜ In. | 531 |
| **Goblet,** Trophy, Flowers, Wood & Hughes, 1884, 7 In. | 277 |
| **Goblet,** Water, Ogee Dome Trumpet Foot, Reeded Rim, Maryland, 6¾ In., 14 Piece | 2091 |
| **Grape Shears,** Chased, Foxes, Vines, Gorham, c.1910, 6¾ In. ...........*illus* | 406 |
| **Grape Shears,** Hammered, Applied Birds, Fish, Insects, Gorham, c.1880, 6 In. | 500 |
| **Gravy Boat,** Attached Underplate, Banded Border, C-Scroll Handle, c.1930, 5 In. | 500 |
| **Hair Comb,** Rounded Ends, 9 Tines, Monogram, W.H. Calhoun, Nashville, Tenn., 3½ x 3¾ In. . | 590 |
| **Jardiniere,** Swan Shape, Flower Frog, Repousse, Electroplated, Gorham, c.1920, 6 x 4 In., Pair. | 1750 |
| **Jigger,** Double, Cone On Cone Shape, Kalo, 4½ x 2 In. | 366 |
| **Julep Cup,** Adolphe Himmel, Hyde & Goodrich, New Orleans, c.1850, 3 x 2¾ In. | 777 |
| **Julep Cup,** Molded Rim, Reeded Base, Inscription, S. Kirk & Son, 3¾ In., 6 Piece | 2091 |
| **Julep Cup,** Presentation Inscription, DDE, Mark J. Scearce, 1955, 3¾ In. ...........*illus* | 330 |
| **Julep Cup,** Tapered, Molded Rim, Monogram, Preisner, c.1950, 4 In., 10 Piece | 2684 |
| **Kettle,** Hot Water, Stand, Urn Shape, Monogram, Gorham, 10 In. ...........*illus* | 850 |
| **Knife Set,** Fruit, Mother-Of-Pearl, Leaves, Scrolls, Box, c.1900, 7½ In., 12 Piece | 104 |
| **Ladle,** Asa Blansett, Southern Coin, c.1800, 13½ In. | 8850 |

**Silver-American,** Tureen, Lid, Claw Feet, Leaf Supports, Coin, W. Adams, c.1825, 11 x 16 In.
$11,850

James D. Julia Auctioneers

**Silver-American,** Vase, Bud, Neo-Grec, Arched Handles, Putti, Coin, Gorham, 1865, 9 x 4 In.
$615

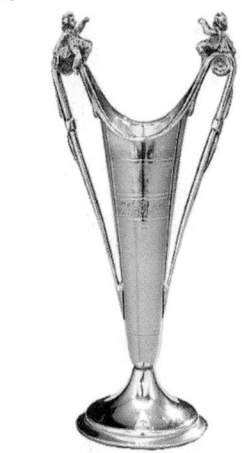

New Orleans Auction Galleries, Inc.

**Silver-American,** Vase, Trumpet, Art Nouveau, Relief, Shreve & Co., 1900s, 20½ In.
$4,248

Brunk Auctions

**Silver-Chinese,** Box, Lid, Enamel, Butterfly, Flowers, Marked, c.1910, 1 ¾ In.
$90

Cowan's Auctions

**Silver-Chinese,** Goblet, Repousse, Bamboo Stalks Support, Tien Shing, Chinese Export, 8 ⅜ In.
$246

Neal Auction Co.

---

### TIP
*Polish silver by rubbing it with a woolen blanket or piece of carpet.*

---

**Silver-Chinese,** Strainer, Tea, Stand, Inscribed Base, Early 20th Century, 2 x 3 ¾ In.
$413

Brunk Auctions

| | |
|---|---:|
| **Ladle,** Down Turned Tipt Back, Fiddle Handle, Marked, Penfield & Co., 14 ¼ In. | 1534 |
| **Ladle,** Fiddle Tipt Handle, Monogram, Natchez, Coit & Whittemore, c.1830, 13 In. | 2988 |
| **Ladle,** Helmet Handle Finial, Reeded Stem, G.B. Sharp, c.1865, 13 ¾ In. | 2700 |
| **Ladle,** John Brenise, York, Pennsylvania, c.1830, 13 ¾ In. | 660 |
| **Ladle,** Mid Rib Fiddle Pattern, Creole, Monogram, Pierre Lamothe, New Orleans, 12 ¾ In. | 2478 |
| **Ladle,** Portrait Medallion, Fluted Shell Bowl, Peter Krider, c.1885, 12 In. | 656 |
| **Ladle,** Serrated Rectangle, Eagles In Cartouches, Fiddle Handle, Natchez, 14 In. | 1434 |
| **Meat Platter,** Draining Reservoir, Lawrence B. Smith, 17 ⅞ In. | 677 |
| **Meat Tray,** Plymouth, Reeded Rim, Tree & Well, Gorham, 23 x 17 In. ............*illus* | 1793 |
| **Medal,** Dolphins, Corinthian Yacht Club, Reed & Barton, 1919, 3 ½ In. | 338 |
| **Napkin Rings** are listed in their own category. | |
| **Nut Dish,** Boat Shape, Reticulated, Marked Gorham, 4 x 2 ½ In., 12 Piece | 276 |
| **Nut Dish,** Chased Lines, Squirrel Finial, Footed, Gorham, c.1930, 5 ¾ In. ............*illus* | 938 |
| **Page Cutter,** Indian Head, Black, Starr & Frost, c.1900, 10 In. | 1937 |
| **Papboat,** Floral Repousse, Open Loop Handle, Bailey & Co., 6 ¾ In. | 266 |
| **Papboat,** Serrated Rectangle Bottom, Molded Rim, Scroll Handle, J. Ewan, 5 ¾ In. | 837 |
| **Paper Knife,** Knight's Helmet, Sword & Shield, Gorham, 4 ¾ In. | 244 |
| **Pill Box,** Lily Of The Valley Relief, Hinged Lid, Frank Whiting, 1888, 1 ¾ x 1 ¾ In. | 178 |
| **Pin Tray,** Hammered, Applied Blossoming Branch & Shell, Rectangular, Whiting, 5 In. | 500 |
| **Pitcher,** 8-Sided, Alternating Panels Of Engraved Floral Scrolls, W. Durgin, 7 In. | 688 |
| **Pitcher,** Baluster, Applied Monogram, Kalo Shop, Chicago, 6 ½ In. | 3050 |
| **Pitcher,** Beaded, Scroll Handle, Engraved, Eoff & Shepherd, Coin, c.1850, 7 ½ In. ......*illus* | 360 |
| **Pitcher,** Bulbous, Applied Scroll Handle, Durgin Silver Co., 8 In. | 384 |
| **Pitcher,** Chased Allover Scrolls, Leaves, Flowers, Whiting, 8 In. | 1230 |
| **Pitcher,** Chased Landscape, Branch & Vine Handle, C. Childs, c.1840, 9 In. | 1440 |
| **Pitcher,** C-Scroll Handle, Pinched Spout, Leaf Thumb Rest, Gorham, c.1870, 11 In. | 2000 |
| **Pitcher,** Egg & Dart, Beaded Borders, Scroll Handle, William Gale, c.1856, 11 ½ In. | 2032 |
| **Pitcher,** Federal, Triangular Spout, Scroll Handle, Saunders Pitman, c.1800, 9 In. | 4800 |
| **Pitcher,** Fluted Base, Bead & Dart Rim, Baluster, Spread Foot, Rogers & Wendt, 13 In. | 1845 |
| **Pitcher,** Hampton Court, Reed & Barton, 9 In. | 840 |
| **Pitcher,** Hexagonal, Flowers, Round Foot, J.C. Moore, 1840s, 9 ¼ In. | 1625 |
| **Pitcher,** Lobed Body, Applied Die Rolled Border, c.1810, 5 ⅝ In. | 598 |
| **Pitcher,** Paneled, Scrolled Handle, Dove, 12 ⅜ In. | 677 |
| **Pitcher,** Revere Pattern, Swollen, Hardy & Hayes Co., Pittsburgh, 1928, 8 In. | 649 |
| **Pitcher,** Scrolled Flowers, Conrad Bard, Philadelphia, c.1840, 11 ¾ In. | 1353 |
| **Pitcher,** Stylized Leaves & Beaded Accents, Chicago Silver Co., 10 In. | 1464 |
| **Pitcher,** Underplate, Relief Rose, Baltimore Silver, 9 ¾ In., 2 Piece | 2250 |
| **Pitcher,** Water, Angular Handle, Footed, Reed & Barton, 1947, 9 ½ In. | 600 |
| **Pitcher,** Water, Arc, Baluster, Molded Lip, Foot Trim, Scroll Handle, 9 ¾ In. | 1793 |
| **Pitcher,** Water, Arts & Crafts, Hammered, Whiting Mfg., c.1912, 9 In. | 861 |
| **Pitcher,** Water, Chased, Reeded, Helmet Shape, Gorham, Bailey Banks & Biddle, c.1914, 8 In. | 750 |
| **Pitcher,** Water, C-Scroll, Cartouche, Floral Repousse, Scroll Handle, 8 ¾ In. | 1722 |
| **Pitcher,** Water, Engraved, Monogram, 1860, 11 ¼ In. | 540 |
| **Pitcher,** Water, Flowers, Scrolls, Applied Masks, Footed, Theodore B. Starr, 9 ½ In. | 1625 |
| **Pitcher,** Water, Hammered, Flower Chased, Dominick & Haff, 8 ½ In. | 6875 |
| **Pitcher,** Water, Laurel Wreath, Scroll Handle, Durgin, Early 20th Century, 8 In. | 660 |
| **Pitcher,** Water, Monogram, Gorham, 4 ½ Pt., 8 In. | 644 |
| **Pitcher,** Water, Octagonal Urn Shape, Dome Foot, Wm. B. Durgin Co., 11 In. | 1000 |
| **Pitcher,** Water, Pear Shape, Arched, Flared Spout, C-Shape Handle, S. Cockrell, Miss., 9 In. | 2950 |
| **Pitcher,** Water, Repousse Flowers, Flared Spout, Oval Foot, Gorham, c.1949, 7 ½ In. | 690 |
| **Pitcher,** Water, Riverside Village Scene, Hausmann & Son, 1890, 9 ¾ In. ............*illus* | 1164 |
| **Pitcher,** Water, Scroll Handle, Ball Tompkins, Black, Coin, c.1845, 13 ½ x 8 ½ In. | 182 |
| **Plaque,** Mt. Rushmore, Signed, 5 x 8 In. | 450 |
| **Plate,** Bread & Butter, Art Deco, Shaped, Stylized Flowers, Gorham, 6 In., 9 Piece | 1680 |
| **Plate,** Bread & Butter, Flower Repousse Border, Kirk & Sons, c.1930, 6 ¼ In., 12 Piece | 1500 |
| **Plate,** Bread & Butter, Serpentine Rim, Wallace, 6 ⅜ In., 12 Piece | 1380 |
| **Plate,** Child's, Repousse Rim, Bear, Elk, Wolf, Kalo Shop, 8 In. | 793 |
| **Plate,** Dessert, Scrolled Border, Fruit Cavetto, Gorham Mfg. Co., c.1912, 9 In., 14 Piece | 4375 |
| **Plate,** Engraved Panels, Flower Swags, Bailey Banks & Biddle, c.1920, 11 In., 12 Piece | 10000 |
| **Plate,** Marie Antoinette, Embossed Border, Floral Swag, Footed, Gorham, c.1947, 10 In. | 184 |
| **Plate,** Service, Marie Antoinette, International Silver, Engraved, 10 ½ In., 6 Piece | 2640 |
| **Plate,** The Road, 24K Gold, Copper, Danbury Mint, Box, 8 In. | 173 |
| **Platter,** Engraved, Scalloped Oval Shape, Monogram, Gorham, 17 x 12 In. | 533 |
| **Platter,** Hanover, Monogram, Reed & Barton, c.1920, 18 x 13 In. | 738 |
| **Platter,** Meat, Maintenon Pattern, Laurel Border, Oval, Gorham Mfg., 1925, 18 ½ In. | 1188 |
| **Platter,** Meat, Shaped Oval, Gadroon Border, Gorham, c.1892, 24 In. | 2500 |

| | |
|---|---|
| **Platter,** Meat, Well & Tree, Footed, Chippendale, Frank Smith Silver Co., 18 In. | 720 |
| **Platter,** Oval, Whiting Mfg., c.1917, 14 In. | 420 |
| **Porringer,** Handle, Webster Co., 5 ½ In. | 60 |
| **Porringer,** Keyhole Handle, Boston, Nathan Hobbs, c.1800, 4 ½ In. | 960 |
| **Punch Bowl,** Athena Pattern, Art Nouveau, 2 Handles, 4 Pad Feet, Gorham, 7 x 14 In. | 1625 |
| **Punch Bowl,** Chased Scrolls, Garland, Flared, Simons Bros., Phila., c.1900, 16 In. | 4063 |
| **Punch Bowl,** Enamel Interior, 12 Cups, Towle, c.1955, 6 ⅝ x 12 In. ...........*illus* | 3000 |
| **Punch Bowl,** Repousse, Chased, S. Kirk & Son, 7 ¼ x 13 ¾ In. | 2360 |
| **Punch Ladle,** Back Tipped Fiddle Handle, c.1830, 13 In. | 161 |
| **Punch Ladle,** Beaded Handle, Coin, Va., 11 ½ In. | 316 |
| **Punch Ladle,** Coral, Matte Gilt Bowl, Bright Cut Rim, Knowles & Ladd, 11 In. | 399 |
| **Punch Ladle,** Medallion, Bust, Mercury, Lobed Bowl, Gilt, Presentation, 1869, 15 In. .........*illus* | 777 |
| **Punch Ladle,** Onslow Pattern, Scroll Handle, Oval, Monogram, Arthur Stone, 11 In. | 431 |
| **Salad Servers,** Hammered, Notched Ends, Saw Pierced Bowl, Kalo Shop, 9 In. | 344 |
| **Salad Servers,** Love Disarmed, Gilt Bowl, Tines, Reed & Barton, 1899, 10 ½ In. | 922 |
| **Salt & Pepper,** Baluster, Beaded Rim, Stepped Foot, F.W. Cooper, c.1865, 6 In. | 375 |
| **Salt Cellar,** Basketweave, Inverted Rim, Whiting Mfg., 1890, 3 ¼ x 1 ½ In., 8 Piece | 799 |
| **Salver,** Floral Repousse, Ball & Claw Feet, Jenkins & Jenkins, 1910, 11 In. | 590 |
| **Salver,** Repousse Border, Hairy Paw Feet, Round, S. Kirk & Son, 15 In. | 1888 |
| **Sauceboat,** Leaves, Scroll, Handles, Stepped Molded Foot, Star, 5 x 8 ⅞ In. | 1015 |
| **Server,** 2 Overlapping Leaf Plates, Twisted Handle, Reed & Barton, 1945, 6 ½ x 13 In. | 350 |
| **Server,** Croquette, Engraved, Iris Flowers, Carter Brothers, 9 x 3 In. | 293 |
| **Serving Dish,** Undulating Sides, Shield Shape, Leaf Medallion, Gorham, 12 ½ In. | 633 |
| **Serving Ladle,** Shell Bowl, Bellflower, Leaves, A.C. Benedict, 13 ¼ In. | 153 |
| **Serving Set,** Love Disarmed, Spoon, Fork, C.A. Bennet, 10 ¾ In., 2 Piece | 984 |
| **Serving Spoon & Fork,** Whiting Div. Of Gorham & Gorham, c.1900, 8 ½ In. | 330 |
| **Sherbet,** Colonial Pattern, Spread Foot, Stieff, 3 ¾ In., 12 Piece | 767 |
| **Sherbet,** Pedestal, Lobed Sides, Marked, Richard Dines Co., 3 ¼ In., 12 Piece | 1064 |
| **Shoehorn,** Roman Soldier Profile, Etruscan Pattern, George Shiebler, c.1880, 6 ¾ In. | 312 |
| **Skewer,** Tapered, Marked, Joseph Richardson, Loop Handle, 1700s, 12 ¼ In. | 531 |
| **Soup Ladle,** Double Struck Eagles, Fiddle Handle, 15 In. | 4270 |
| **Soup Ladle,** Hammered, Copper Crab, Bailey Banks & Biddle, c.1880, 12 In. ..........*illus* | 938 |
| **Soup Ladle,** Imperial Chrysanthemum, Gold Wash, Gorham, 12 ½ In. | 360 |
| **Soup Ladle,** King Edward, Gold Wash, Whiting, 1901, 12 ½ In. | 288 |
| **Spoon,** Ragout, Ursuline Convent, Fiddle Handle, Engraved, c.1830, 11 In. | 2135 |
| **Stamp Dispenser,** Round, Beaded, Ebony Flame Finial, Kalo Shop, 2 ½ x 2 In. | 366 |
| **Stoplight Jigger,** Mixing Spoon, Gorham, 2 ⅓ x 2 ¼ & 12 In., 2 Piece | 121 |
| **Strawberry Fork,** Old Orange Blossom, Monogram, Alvin, 4 ¾ In., 12 Piece | 338 |
| **Strawberry Pierced Pattern,** Kidney Shape Bowl, Twisted Vine Handle, 9 In. | 469 |
| **Sugar & Creamer,** Bulbous, Lobed, Hammered, Engraved, Wood & Hughes | 861 |
| **Sugar & Creamer,** Kem Weber, Silver Style Line, Friedman, c.1928, 4 ½ In. & 3 In. .........*illus* | 3750 |
| **Sugar & Creamer,** Lid, Repousse, Henegan, Bates Co., 1904, 4 ¾ In. | 826 |
| **Sugar & Creamer,** Louis XIV, Towle, 1924, 5 ¾ & 6 ½ In. | 676 |
| **Sugar & Creamer,** Oval Tray, Scroll Handles, Footed, Gorham, 1900s, 3 x 9 In. | 180 |
| **Sugar & Creamer,** Plymouth, Engraved, Gorham | 150 |
| **Sugar & Creamer,** Urn Shape, Thistle Die-Rolled Borders, John Ewan Mark, 1800s, 9 & 7 In. ... | 1121 |
| **Sugar Tongs,** Shaped Handle, Round Grip, Robert Titus, Knoxville, Tenn., c.1827, 6 In. | 531 |
| **Sugar Urn,** Lowry Wister Monogram, Wister Genealogy, Philadelphia, c.1790, 10 ½ In. | 1320 |
| **Sugar Urn,** Oval, Monogram, Pedestal Foot, Finial, Walter Vogel, 10 In. .........*illus* | 805 |
| **Sugar,** Castor, Baluster, Pierced Top, Turned Finial, Gorham, 9 In. | 293 |
| **Sugar,** Dome Lid, Berry Finial, Pear Shape, Footed, Benjamin Burt, 1790, 6 In. | 1020 |
| **Sugar,** Duster, Cabbage Leaf Sides, Chased Veins, Swirled Handles, T.B. Starr, 1883 | 2133 |
| **Sugar,** Lid, Pear Shape, Engraved, Scrolling Clover, Adolphe Himmel, c.1870, 6 ½ x 8 In. | 2091 |
| **Tablespoon,** Medallion, Gorham, Lion Marked, 1864, 8 ½ In., 4 Piece | 369 |
| **Tankard,** Tree Trunk Shape, Acorn, Branches, S. Kirk & Son, c.1880, 7 In. | 2125 |
| **Tazza,** Art Nouveau, Grape, Leaf, Stylized Lattice, Marcus & Co., 1890-1910, 4 x 8 In. | 354 |
| **Tazza,** Floral Repousse, Monogram, Stieff Mark, 1900s, 3 ½ x 7 ¼ In. | 1416 |
| **Tazza,** Louis XVI Style, Embossed Edge, Trumpeting Foot, Reed & Barton, 4 x 8 ¾ In., Pair | 369 |
| **Tazza,** Reticulated, Engraved, Reeded Stem, Cone Shape Base, Durgin, c.1927, 6 x 12 In., 4 Piece | 375 |
| **Tazza,** Round, Fruit Swags, Short Stem, Domed Foot, Gorham, 12 ¼ In., Pair | 3690 |
| **Tazza,** Round, Leaves, Urns, 10 ½ In. | 492 |
| **Tazza,** Shallow Bowl, Trumpet Base, Kalo Shops, 3 ½ x 7 In. | 366 |
| **Tea & Coffee Set,** Bakelite Insulators, Gorham, Durgin, Fairfax, 1927, 4 Piece | 1200 |
| **Tea & Coffee Set,** Dorian Pattern, Tapered, Vertical Bands, Art Deco, Watson, 5 Piece | 1599 |
| **Tea & Coffee Set,** Francis I, Gilt Interior, Reed & Barton, c.1952, 8 Piece | 1725 |
| **Tea & Coffee Set,** Minuet, Shield Form, International, 12-In. Coffeepot, 5 Piece | 1180 |

**Silver-Danish,** Compote, Flared Bowl, Leafy Open Column, Ring Foot, Georg Jensen, c.1930, 5 x 6 In.
$1,375

Rago Arts & Auction Center

---

**TIP**

*Silverware tarnished by eggs will come clean if rubbed with damp salt.*

---

**Silver-Danish,** Pitcher, Handle, Johan Rohde, Georg Jensen, Marked, 9 In.
$3,250

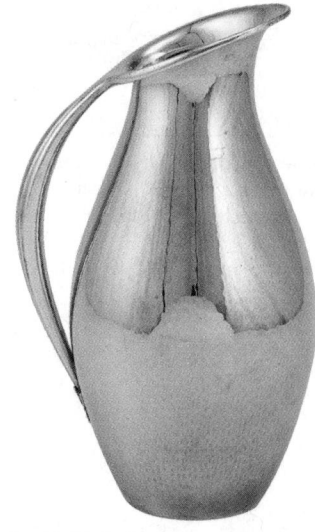

Rago Arts & Auction Center

---

**Silver-Danish,** Teapot, Stylized Flowers, Ebony Handle, Evald Nielsen, c.1929, 6 x 9 ½ In.
$5,312

Rago Arts & Auction Center

S

**Silver-English,** Mug, George III, Scroll Handle, William Shaw II, 1764, 4⅝ In. **$359**

Neal Auction Co.

**Silver-English,** Salver, Octagonal, Gadroon, Hamilton Coat Of Arms, Paul Storr, 1806, 8 In. **$3,625**

Rago Arts & Auction Center

**Silver-English,** Teapot, Curved Spout, Wood Handle, Peter, Ann, William Bateman, c.1800, 7 x 11 In. **$863**

Cottone Auctions

**S**

> **TIP**
> *You don't have to remove a monogram from a piece of silver. It is part of the history. Just say it belonged to an elderly relative.*

| | |
|---|---:|
| **Tea & Coffee Set,** Octagonal, Tapered, Reeded, Angular Handle, Newburyport, 3 Piece | 431 |
| **Tea & Coffee Set,** Plymouth, Shaped Handles, Gorham, 9-In. Coffeepot, 5 Piece | 1416 |
| **Tea & Coffee Set,** Repousse, Vase Shape, Footed, S. Kirk & Sons | 3884 |
| **Tea & Coffee Set,** Sugar & Creamer, Lid, Reed & Barton, 9¼ In. | 1046 |
| **Tea & Coffee Set,** Taper, Round Foot, Sugar & Creamer, Lid, Waste, 10 In., 5 | 1599 |
| **Tea & Coffee Set,** Teapot, Coffeepot, Sugar & Creamer, Scroll, Grapes, 4 Piece | 1912 |
| **Tea & Coffee Set,** Tray, Teapot, Coffeepot, Sugar, Monogram, Durgin, 4 Piece | 3600 |
| **Tea Canister,** Trophy, Flowers, Lid, Indian Harbor Yacht Club, 1892, 3¾ In. | 308 |
| **Tea Set,** Flower & Leaf Bands, Melon Form, Orb Finials, H. Thomas, Nashville, 3 Piece | 1500 |
| **Tea Set,** Long Neck Demitasse Teapot, Cream Jug, Sugar Bowl, 1800s, 3 Piece | 813 |
| **Tea Set,** Plymouth Pattern, Gorham, c.1955, 5 Piece | 2214 |
| **Tea Set,** Repousse, Grapevines, Cartouche, Oval, Footed, Stebbins & Co., N.Y., 3 Piece | 1185 |
| **Tea Set,** Round, Tapered, Bead Border, 1936, 9¼-In. Teapot, 4 Piece | 767 |
| **Tea Set,** Teapot, Sugar & Creamer, Bowl, Footed, Urn Shape, Greek Key, 4 Piece | 1098 |
| **Tea Set,** Teapot, Sugar & Creamer, Reeding, Scroll Handles, Gorham, 4 Piece | 533 |
| **Teapot,** Bulbous, Palmette Band, Stippled Ground, Wood Finial, Gorham, 1886, 9 In. | 500 |
| **Teapot,** Straight Spout, Shield Engraved, Eoff & Shepard, c.1850, 8¾ In. | 2500 |
| **Teaspoon,** Fiddle Handle, Marked L. Welch, c.1820, 5⅝ In. | 115 |
| **Teaspoon,** Fiddleback, Birds On Bowl, c.1800, 6 In., 6 Piece | 561 |
| **Teaspoon,** Mignonette, Lunt, 6 In., 8 Piece | 155 |
| **Teaspoon,** Shell Drop, Monogram, Samuel Drowne II, New Hampshire, c., 1800 | 450 |
| **Teaspoon,** Shell On Bowl, Lancaster, Marked C.H., c.1783, 6 Piece | 1180 |
| **Teaspoon,** Versailles, Monogram, Gorham, c.1910, 6 In., 12 Piece | 236 |
| **Tongs,** Asparagus, R. & W. Wilson, c.1850, 9½ In. | 531 |
| **Top,** Spinning, 6 Lobes, Stockbroker Tips, Sell High, Buy Low, Gorham, 2½ In. | 800 |
| **Tray,** Cartouche Form, Shaped Flower & Scroll Border, Gorham, 1907, 16 x 11 In. | 885 |
| **Tray,** Edwardian, Ribbons, Garlands, Rose Trellis Handles, Bailey Banks & Biddle, 14 In. | 750 |
| **Tray,** Hammered, Rectangular & Circular Openwork Border, Sturm, c.1920, 15 In. | 937 |
| **Tray,** Handles, Footed, Grape & Vase Border, Oval, Gorham, 16 In. | 84 |
| **Tray,** Handles, Grapevines, Animals, William Forbes, c.1825, 26 x 16 In. | 3500 |
| **Tray,** Leaf Border, Round, Reed & Barton, c.1950, 15 In. | 600 |
| **Tray,** Lobed Border, Repousse, Flowering Vines, Inset Corners, c.1905, 15 x 12 In. | 3125 |
| **Tray,** Neoclassical, Loop Handles, Swag Border, Monogram, Gorham, 30 x 19 In. | 3346 |
| **Tray,** Octagonal, Richard Dimes Co., 14 In. | 750 |
| **Tray,** Openwork, Swag & Bellflower, Graff, Washbourne & Dunn, 1900s, 10 In. | 531 |
| **Tray,** Oval, John Alden Pattern, Monogram, Watson, 16⅛ In. | 369 |
| **Tray,** Plymouth, Scalloped, Oval, Gorham, 1926, 16½ In. | 480 |
| **Tray,** Presentation, USS LST-470, Shreve & Co., 14¾ x 14¾ In. | 688 |
| **Tray,** Serpentine Rim, Scalloped, Hallmark, Graff, Washbourne & Dunn, c.1900s, 12 x 12 In. | 724 |
| **Tray,** Stepped Border, Banded Rim, Bun Feet, Newell Harding & Co., c.1850, 10 In. | 375 |
| **Tray,** Trophy, Reeded Rim, Larchmont Yacht Club, 1909, 12 In. | 215 |
| **Tray,** Undulating Furrowed Rim, Oval, Marked, Reed & Barton, 18½ x 13½ In. | 949 |
| **Tray,** USS Huntington, Handles, Hand Hammered, 11 In. | 150 |
| **Trophy,** Pitcher, Buildings, Ram's Head Handle, New York Yacht Club, S. Kirk, 1853, 16 In. | 2952 |
| **Tureen,** Lid, Acanthus, Oval, Coin, Inscription, 1837, Jones, Low & Ball, 9 In. ...*illus* | 2596 |
| **Tureen,** Lid, Claw Feet, Leaf Supports, Coin, W. Adams, c.1825, 11 x 16 In. ...*illus* | 11850 |
| **Tureen,** Lid, Oval, Masks, 1850-66, 10¾ In. | 1169 |
| **Tureen,** Lid, Scrolled Leaves, Shell Border, 4-Footed, Cooper & Fisher, c.1860, 10 x 17 x 9 In. | 5937 |
| **Tureen,** Lid, Swags, Stepped Foot, Handles, Finial, J & I Cox, c.1840, 13 x 15 x 12 In. | 3250 |
| **Tureen,** Oval Shape, Banding, 2 Handles, Strawberry Finial, Gorham, 11½ In. | 3936 |
| **Tureen,** Oval, Cast Handles, Paw Feet, Acanthus, Marked, Inscribed, 1837, 9½ In. | 2596 |
| **Vanity Set,** Brush, Beveled Glass Mirror, Repousse Flowers, Scrolls, Gorham, 10 & 8 In. | 104 |
| **Vase,** Bud, Neo-Grec, Arched Handles, Putti, Coin, Gorham, 1865, 9 x 4 In. ...*illus* | 615 |
| **Vase,** Inverted Tapering, Spreading Round Foot, Hammered, Lebolt & Co., c.1920, 15 In. | 937 |
| **Vase,** Key Fret Detail, Dominick & Haff, 13¾ In. | 541 |
| **Vase,** Openwork Floral & Scroll Top, Base, Apron, Trumpet Shape, Black, Starr & Frost, 10¼ In. | 354 |
| **Vase,** Shells, Flower, Trumpet Shape, Angled Handles, Cowell & Hubbard Co., 11 In. | 938 |
| **Vase,** Trophy, 2 Handles, New York Yacht Club, Black, Starr & Frost, 7½ In. | 923 |
| **Vase,** Trophy, 2 Handles, Pearl Harbor Yacht Club, Gorham, 10¼ In. | 400 |
| **Vase,** Trophy, Corinthian Yacht Club, Gorham, 13¼ In. | 923 |
| **Vase,** Trophy, Trumpet Shape, Ruby Glass, Dominick & Haff, 13½ In. | 523 |
| **Vase,** Trumpet Shape, Blue Glass Liner, Pierced, Roger Williams, c.1910, 9½ In., Pair | 246 |
| **Vase,** Trumpet Shape, Etched, Incised, Signed J.E. Caldwell, 12⅛ In. | 1375 |
| **Vase,** Trumpet Shape, Flared Reticulated Rim, Footed, Gorham, 1924, 9 x 5½ In., Pair | 437 |
| **Vase,** Trumpet, Art Nouveau, Relief, Shreve & Co., 1900s, 20½ In. ...*illus* | 4248 |
| **Vase,** Trumpet, Engraved Glass, Undulating Rim, Dominick & Haff, c.1910, 14 In., Pair | 240 |

| | |
|---|---|
| **Vase,** Trumpet, Satyr Masks, Oak Leaf Border, Monogram, Gorham, Florenz, 29 In. | 2832 |
| **Vase,** Urn, Trumpet, Handles, Reed & Barton, 20th Century, 18 x 6 x 5 In. | 720 |
| **Waiter,** Arts & Crafts, Hammered, Ball Feet, Monogram, Dominick & Haff, 1882, 10 In. | 1599 |
| **Waste Bowl,** Lobed, Floral Repousse, Scroll Feet, Engraved, Profilet, c.1850, 4½ x 6 In. | 5079 |
| **Wine Bucket,** Scrolling Floral Lip, c.1910, 10¾ In. | 2057 |
| **Wine Coaster,** Wedge Handle, Oval Turquoise Cabochon, F. Patania, c.1960, 6 In. | 437 |
| **Wine Cooler,** Cylindrical, Tapered, D-Shape Handles, c.1970, 10 x 9 x 8 In. | 4687 |

## SILVER-ARGENTINIAN

| | |
|---|---|
| **Parade Stirrups,** Plated, Flared, Oval Shape, Incised Flowers, c.1890, 8¼ x 6 In. | 492 |

## SILVER-AUSTRIAN

| | |
|---|---|
| **Box,** Enamel, Fish Scale Pattern, Cobalt Ground, Hinged Lid, 3⅝ In. | 738 |
| **Ewer,** Silver Neck, Cut Crystal Body, Trigger Handle, 13½ In., Pair | 1573 |
| **Hot Water Pot,** Lobed, Beaded, U-Shape Handle, Fluted Finial, Footed, c.1920, 18 In. | 1750 |
| **Tray,** Oval, Pierced Gallery, Urns, Vines, Rope Twist Handles, 3¾ x 26½ In. | 1800 |

## SILVER-AUSTRO-HUNGARIAN

| | |
|---|---|
| **Platter,** Fish, Oval, 28½ In. | 1125 |

## SILVER-BURMESE

| | |
|---|---|
| **Bowl,** Bulbous, Repousse, Figures, Battle, c.1950, 6 x 8½ In. | 1375 |

## SILVER-CANADIAN

| | |
|---|---|
| **Bowl,** Flowers, Leaves, Geometric & Leaf Border, Birks, 1940s, 8¼ In. | 106 |

## SILVER-CHINESE

| | |
|---|---|
| **Box,** Lid, Enamel, Butterfly, Flowers, Marked, c.1910, 1¾ In. ................*illus* | 90 |
| **Bucket,** Repousse Animals, Lobed, 2 Swing Handles, c.1870, 5¾ In. | 1080 |
| **Cigarette Case,** Bamboo Sprigs, Stippled Ground, Monogram P.K.S., 4¼ In. | 128 |
| **Cocktail Shaker,** Hammered, Dragons, 21 In. | 5748 |
| **Goblet,** Repousse, Bamboo Stalks Support, Tien Shing, Chinese Export, 8⅜ In. ......*illus* | 246 |
| **Scroll Weights,** Sterling, Immortals, Calligraphy, Monk's Journey, 9 x 1 In., Pair | 207 |
| **Strainer,** Tea, Stand, Inscribed Base, Early 20th Century, 2 x 3¾ In. ......*illus* | 413 |
| **Tea Set,** Birds, Prunus Branches, Faux Bamboo Kettle Stand, 4 Piece | 5843 |

## SILVER-CONTINENTAL

| | |
|---|---|
| **Bowl,** Chased Cupids, Medallions, Swags, Pierced Border, Scroll Handles, c.1910, 15½ In. | 2000 |
| **Canister,** Lid, Renaissance Battle Scene, Cylindrical, c.1890, 9¼ In. | 875 |
| **Centerpiece,** Scalloped, Leaf Capped, Oval, Lobed, Footed, Scroll Handles, 18 In. | 1188 |
| **Charger,** Reeded Rim, Engraved Crest, Round, Footed, c.1890, 12 In. | 560 |
| **Charger,** Repousse, Chased Hunter, Women Bathing, Grotesques Border, Oval, c.1890, 20 In. | 2375 |
| **Compote,** Reticulated, Putti, Leaves, 2 Eagle Heads, 12 In. | 80 |
| **Compote,** Scroll Handles, Swan Standard, Pierced Foot, Cut Glass Bowl, c.1905, 9 In., Pair | 1250 |
| **Cooler,** Round, Cast Lion Mask Ring Handles, Inset Coins, Repousse, c.1910, 10 x 13 In. | 10158 |
| **Cream Pot,** Allover Rococo Engraved, c.1820, 4¼ In. | 215 |
| **Creamer,** Engraved Scrolls, Lion's Paw Feet, 4½ In. | 83 |
| **Dish,** Triangular, Glass Mounted, 3 Agate Cabochons, 1⅝ x 6⅜ In. | 120 |
| **Ewer,** Basin, Filter, Istanbul, 2 Piece | 800 |
| **Salt,** Sleigh Shape, Cherub, Footed, Italy, c.1900, 3 In., Pair | 480 |
| **Server,** Flat, Engraved, Upturned Handle, Reticulated Blade, 11 x 12 In. | 209 |
| **Spice Box,** Fish Form, Articulated, Engraved Scales, Hinged Head, Red Stone Eye, 10 In. | 625 |
| **Tea & Coffee Set,** Coffeepot, Teapot, Sugar & Creamer, Swirl, 5 Piece | 1722 |
| **Tray,** Egg & Dart Band, Wreath Tied Handles, Monogram, Friedlander, c.1900, 26 In. | 1500 |
| **Tureen,** Dome Lid, 10 In. | 177 |
| **Vase,** Baroque Style, Lobed, Flared, Footed, 9¾ In. | 750 |

## SILVER-DANISH

| | |
|---|---|
| **Bowl,** Hammered, Repousse Iris Band, Ruffled Edge, A. Michelsen, 1914, 4 x 10 In. | 1500 |
| **Bowl,** Inverted Rim, Round Foot, Nut Spoon, Curved Terminus, Georg Jensen, 2¾ x 5 In. | 817 |
| **Bowl,** Lid, Ebony Finial, Beaded Edge, Georg Jensen, 1925-30, 9 In. | 1875 |
| **Bowl,** Round, Gadroon Rim, Georg Jensen, 8¾ In. | 1625 |
| **Box,** Lid, Hammered, Melon Ribs, Citron Feet, Amber Bud Finial, Georg Jensen, 5 x 4 In. | 21240 |
| **Coffee Set,** Blossom, Ivory Handles, 2 Trays, Georg Jensen, 1930s, 5 Piece | 15860 |
| **Coffee Set,** Coffeepot, Sugar & Creamer, Ebony Handles, E. Nielsen, 3 Piece | 4062 |
| **Compote,** Flared Bowl, Leafy Open Column, Ring Foot, Georg Jensen, c.1930, 5 x 6 In. ......*illus* | 1375 |
| **Compote,** Flared Cup, Openwork Stem, Banded Foot., J. Rohde, Georg Jensen, 5¼ In. | 625 |
| **Gravy Boat,** Schilling, Oval Foot, Curled Flattened Handle, Georg Jensen, c.1942, 5 In. | 2875 |
| **Humidor,** Georg Jensen, c.1920, 2½ x 8¾ In. | 8400 |
| **Pitcher,** Beaded Foot, Rim, Ebony Handle, Georg Jensen, c.1930, 10½ In. | 3125 |
| **Pitcher,** Handle, Johan Rohde, Georg Jensen, Marked, 9 In. ......*illus* | 3250 |

**Silver-English,** Teapot, Shield, Bellflower, Oval, Beaded, Pear Wood Handle, H. Bateman, 6 In.
$2,832

Brunk Auctions

**Silver-French,** Ewer, Louis XV Provencal, Rococo Cartouches, Swags, Hinged, Durand, 1773, 11 In.
$4,182

New Orleans Auction Galleries, Inc.

**Silver-Irish,** Goblet, George III, Repousse Acanthus, Gadroon Band On Foot, 6⅜ In., Pair
$2,952

New Orleans Auction Galleries, Inc.

This is an edited listing of current prices. Visit **Kovels.com** to check thousands of prices from previous years and sign up for free information on trends, tips, reproductions, marks, and more.

S

**Silver-Mexican,** Bowl, Flat Band Rim, Cabochon Amethysts, William Spratling, c.1944, 11¾ In.
**$3,250**

Heritage Auction Galleries

**Silver-Mexican,** Bowl, Fruit, Flared Rim, 3-Footed, William Spratling, Taxco, c.1943, 7⅝ In.
**$1,599**

New Orleans Auction Galleries, Inc.

> **TIP**
> *Toothpaste is not a good polish for silver. It works but it is abrasive.*

**Silver-Mexican,** Bowl, Repousse, Rope Rim, Handles, Jose Marmolejo, c.1958, 8 x 26 In.
**$1,188**

Heritage Auction Galleries

**Silver-Mexican,** Box, Hinged Lid, Raised Bands, Rectangular Amethyst, Sanborns, c.1940, 9 x 4 In.
**$1,375**

Heritage Auction Galleries

| | |
|---|---:|
| **Sauceboat,** Scrolled Blossom Handle, Footed, Georg Jensen, c.1970, 5 In. | 2250 |
| **Server,** Pastry, Blossom, Georg Jensen, c.1908, 9½ In. | 840 |
| **Spoon Set,** Enameled, Yellow, White, Turquoise, Red, Egon Lauridsen, 8 Piece | 210 |
| **Spoon,** Enamel Handles, Gold Washed, Meka, Lined Box, c.1950, 6 Piece | 60 |
| **Tazza,** Grape Pattern, Flared Rim, Grape Cluster Pendants, Swirl Stem, Georg Jensen, 11 In. | 4560 |
| **Tazza,** Grape Pattern, Round Foot, Pendant Bunches, 1925-32, 10½ In. | 6120 |
| **Tazza,** Hammered, Grape Clusters, Swirled Stem, Flared Foot, Georg Jensen, 10 In. | 6765 |
| **Tazza,** Rope Twist Stem, Grapes, c.1925, 7¼ In. | 2750 |
| **Tea & Coffee Set,** Beaded Neck Band, Berry Finial, Ebony Handle, Georg Jensen, 7 Piece | 13530 |
| **Tea & Coffee Set,** Cosmos, Bulbous, Paneled Base, Berry Handles, Georg Jensen, 6 Piece | 18880 |
| **Teapot,** Bulbous, Squat, Partially Black Handle, Georg Jensen, 8 In. | 2000 |
| **Teapot,** Stylized Flowers, Ebony Handle, Evald Nielsen, c.1929, 6 x 9½ In. ....................*illus* | 5312 |
| **Tray,** Flower Blossom, Rounded Corners, Single Band Border, Georg Jensen, 13 x 10 In. | 2750 |
| **Tray,** Handles, Modernist, Georg Jensen Silversmithy, Copenhagen, 14½ In. | 5250 |

## SILVER-DUTCH

| | |
|---|---:|
| **Basket,** Fruit, Pierced Oval, Engraved Scrolls, Loop Handles, c.1750, 14½ In. | 540 |
| **Castors,** Louis XV Style, Baluster Shape, Spiral Gadroons, Garlands, 1896, 7¾ In., Pair | 738 |
| **Coffeepot,** Scroll Handle, Footed, S. Gravenhage, c.1790, 13 x 7½ In. | 1416 |
| **Cup,** Marriage, Maid Shape, Arms Up, 9½ In. | 875 |
| **Pill Box,** Windmill Scene, Repousse, Hinged, Round, Marked, c.1935, 1¾ In. | 135 |
| **Trinket Box,** Repousse, Night Watch Relief, Paw Feet, 2 x 6 In. | 431 |

**SILVER-ENGLISH.** English sterling silver is marked with a series of four or five small hallmarks. The standing lion mark is the most commonly seen sterling quality mark. The other marks indicate the city of origin, the maker, and the year of manufacture. These dates can be verified in many good books on silver. These prices are based on current silver values.

| | |
|---|---:|
| **Asparagus Tongs,** Feather Edge Shell Pattern, Goldsmiths & Silversmiths Co., 1901, 3 In. | 95 |
| **Basket Dish,** Deep Relief, Reticulated, Leaves, Marked, Henry Matthews, 1896, 4¾ In. | 247 |
| **Basket,** Bail Handle, Oval, c.1939, 14⅝ In. | 1353 |
| **Basket,** Fruit, Relief Fruit, Flowers, Vines, Bail Handle, William Allen, 14 In. | 800 |
| **Basket,** George III, Bucket Shape, William Cripps, 1764, 4½ In. | 657 |
| **Beaker,** Flaring Rim, Relief, Radishes, Molded Foot, c.1774, 3⅝ In. | 615 |
| **Berry Spoon,** Victorian, Repousse, Gilt Bowl, Engraved Handle, 9 In., Pair | 180 |
| **Bowl,** Edwardian, Repousse, C-Scrolls, Flowers, Footed, c.1905, 5 x 7 In. | 330 |
| **Bowl,** George III, Round, Swirled Lobes, Flowers, Squat Foot, Scroll Handles, 10 In. | 861 |
| **Bowl,** George V, Footed, Lional Alfred Crichton, 1922, 2 x 10 In. | 732 |
| **Bowl,** Oval, Lobed Sides, Upright Handles, London, 1799, 13½ In. | 1534 |
| **Bowl,** Punch, Repousse, Rococo Scrolls, Floral Swags, Footed, 8½ x 14 In. | 127 |
| **Bowl,** Vegetable, Lid, George III, Gadroon Rim, Flower Loop Handle, c.1812, 11 In. | 1140 |
| **Box,** 4 Legs With Hooves, Laurel Garlands, Man, Ice Skates, 3⅛ x 2⅛ In. | 518 |
| **Box,** Art Nouveau, Woman's Profile, Scrolling, Oval, Hinged Lid, Walker & Hall, 4 x 2 In. | 180 |
| **Box,** Turquoise Cabochons, Round, Anchor, Lion, 1909, 4 In. | 1150 |
| **Brandy Warmer,** George II, Flared Body, Molded Foot, George Campar, 1752, 8½ In. | 625 |
| **Butter,** Dome Cover, Spiral Twist Rim, Yellow Bakelite Finial, Elkington, 6 In. | 460 |
| **Cake Basket,** George III, Oval, Beaded Spiral Gadroons, Reticulated Panels, Handles, 11 In. | 6457 |
| **Cake Basket,** George III, Pierced Leaves, Scrolls, Handle, Emick Romer, c.1763 | 2160 |
| **Candelabra** are listed in the Candelabrum category. | |
| **Candlesticks** are listed in their own category. | |
| **Card Tray,** Shell & Scroll Rim, Monogram, 3 Spade Shape Feet, c.1761, 6½ In. | 338 |
| **Castor,** Octagonal Design, Atkin Brothers, England, 1898, 6½ In. | 123 |
| **Chalice,** Presentation, Couples In Relief, Knights, Shields, 1901, 6⅝ In. | 403 |
| **Chalice,** Victorian, Berry, Vine Embossed, John S. Hunt, 1856, 7½ In. | 1125 |
| **Cigarette Box,** Rectangular, Bands Of Colored Gold, Applied Crest, 9 In. | 813 |
| **Cigarette Case,** Checkered, Engraved, Birmingham, S.B & S.L.D., c.1860, 3 x 2 In. | 380 |
| **Claret Jug,** Edwardian, Presentation, William Hutton & Sons, 1902, 11¼ In. | 492 |
| **Claret Jug,** Mounted Glass, Lion & Shield Finial, Cylindrical, Elkington & Co., c.1890, 11 In. | 875 |
| **Coaster,** Engraved Grapes, Leaves, Round, Wood, 1809, 2 x 5¾ In. | 750 |
| **Coffee Service,** Persian Style, Coffeepot, Cups, Box, Asprey, 1975, 13 In., 7 Piece | 2250 |
| **Coffeepot,** Flower, Hinged Lid, Wood Scroll Handle, c.1743, 8¼ In. | 984 |
| **Coffeepot,** George II, Chased Scrolls, Shells, Tapered, Ayme Videau, 1739, 8 In. | 1063 |
| **Coffeepot,** George II, Engraved Crest, Swan Head Spout Tip, Baluster Shape, c.1752, 10 In. | 1020 |
| **Coffeepot,** George II, Repousse, Leaves, Treen Handle, William Holmes, 1767, 12 In. | 1625 |
| **Coffeepot,** George III, Footed, Wood Handle, London, 1763, 10 In. | 1063 |
| **Coffeepot,** George III, Repousse, Armorial, Pear Shape, L.C. & G. Cowles, c.1770, 12 In. | 4560 |
| **Coffeepot,** Hinged Lid, Acorn Finial, Scrolled Spout, John Payne, 1767, 10½ In. | 813 |

| | |
|---|---|
| **Coffeepot,** Urn Shape Finial, Hinged Lid, Wood Handle, 1775, 12 ½ In............................................. | 677 |
| **Coffeepot,** Wood Scroll Handle, Chased Leaves, Stag, Laurel Leaf, 10 ¾ In.................................... | 1230 |
| **Compote,** Lobed Bowl, Scroll Handles, Footed, Docker & Burn, c.1927, 7 x 11 In. ...................... | 1440 |
| **Cup,** 2 Handles, Engraved, Boar's Head, c.1805, 6 ¾ In. ........................................................ | 330 |
| **Cup,** Lid, Chased Scrolls, Leafy Scroll Handles, Parker & Wakelin, 1763, 14 In............................ | 2700 |
| **Cup,** Lid, Nike Finial, Amazons, Battle, Greeks, Hallmark J. S. Hunt, 1849, 22 In. ...................... | 6765 |
| **Cup,** Trophy Shape, Leaves, Flowers, Handles, Grapevines, Gilt Interior, 11 In. ......................... | 625 |
| **Demitasse Spoon,** Art Deco, Enameled Handle, Barker Bros., Box, 4 ¼ In., 6 Piece..................... | 207 |
| **Fish Service,** For 12, Edward VII, Mother-Of-Pearl Handle, Sheffield, 1902, 24 Piece.................... | 300 |
| **Flask,** Cigar Holder Shape, 6 In. ........................................................................ | 420 |
| **Fork & Knife Set,** Ivory Handles, Thomas Willmore, Box, c.1904, 9 & 7 In., 12 Piece..................... | 196 |
| **Fork,** Spoon, Flared Fluted Handles, Hallmark, Gilt Tooled Box, Atkin Bros., 1906, 5 & 6 In. ...... | 92 |
| **Frame,** Scrolling Relief, Navy Velvet Backing, Carr, 1900s, 10 x 8 In. ................................. | 127 |
| **Fruit Strainer,** George III, Pierced Bowl, 2 Scroll Handles, c.1825, 9 In. ........................... | 288 |
| **Goblet,** Sterling, Etched Crest, Birmingham, c.1937, 10 x 5 In. ........................................ | 420 |
| **Grape Scissors,** Cast Grapevine Handles, 8 In. ........................................................ | 224 |
| **Hot Water Urn,** George III, Armorial, 2 Handles, Spigot, 1805, 22 ½ In............................... | 3585 |
| **Hot Water Urn,** George III, Engraved, Bead Border, Ball Feet, C-Handles, London, c.1782, 15 In. | 1440 |
| **Hot Water Urn,** George III, Leaf Banding, Arched Handles, Oval, 23 x 14 In. ......................... | 14760 |
| **Jar,** Hinged Lid, 4 Scrolled Feet, Henry Wigfull, 6 ¼ x 4 ½ In. ....................................... | 540 |
| **Ladle,** Fiddle Thread & Shell, Engraved, William Schofield, 13 In. .................................... | 492 |
| **Ladle,** Stag Crest, Crowned Leopard, King's Profile, Marked WE, WF, 12 ¾ In. ....................... | 185 |
| **Marrow Scoop,** Hester Bateman, 1790, 9 In. .......................................................... | 575 |
| **Muffineer,** Edwardian, Baluster Shape, Neoclassical, Swags, Leaves, 1905, 8 In. .................... | 219 |
| **Mug,** Baluster, Double Scroll Handle, Stag Hunt, George II, 4 ¾ x 3 ¾ In. ........................... | 1353 |
| **Mug,** George III, Double Scroll Handle, William Justis, c.1762, 3 In. ................................. | 420 |
| **Mug,** George III, Scroll Handle, William Shaw II, 1764, 4 ⅝ In.............................*illus* | 359 |
| **Napkin Rings** are listed in their own category. | |
| **Nutmeg Grater,** Barrel Shape, Hooped Sides, Thomas Meriton, 1797, 1 ½ In. ......................... | 510 |
| **Nutmeg Grater,** George III, Engraved, Hinge, Screen, W. Robertson, c.1790, 2 ½ In., Pair.......... | 1125 |
| **Nutmeg Grater,** George III, Reeded Hinged Lid, c.1803, 1 ⅛ In. ..................................... | 837 |
| **Pitcher,** Cream, Helmet Shape, Square Base, Beaded Trim, John Lambe, 1785, 6 In. ................ | 253 |
| **Pitcher,** Scroll Handle, Charles Wright, 1770, 7 ½ In. ................................................ | 1750 |
| **Plate,** George III, 5-Sided, Beaded Rim, William Southey, c.1814, 9 ½ In. ........................... | 330 |
| **Plate,** George III, Gadroon, Scalloped Rim, Motto, Crest, Paul Storr, c.1805, 11 In. ............... | 1140 |
| **Punch Bowl,** 8 Panels, Lionel A. Crichton, 1914-15, 5 In. ............................................ | 1560 |
| **Punch Bowl,** Openwork Shell, Scroll Border, Round, Sheffield, 1903, 6 ¾ x 10 ½ In. ................ | 1534 |
| **Roast Cover,** Lion Finial, Engraved Armorial, Robert Gerrard, 1827-28, 9 ½ In. ..................... | 4613 |
| **Salt,** Beaded Lip, 3 Legs, Leaves, Robert Harper, 1846, 1 ¼ x 2 In., Pair............................ | 150 |
| **Salver,** Beaded Rim, 3-Footed, Peter, Ann & William Bateman, c.1805, 10 In. ....................... | 369 |
| **Salver,** Circular, Reed & Ribbon Rim, 3-Footed, W. Burwash, 9 ⅝ In. ................................ | 1845 |
| **Salver,** Gadroon, Engraved Armorial Shield, Footed, Marked WB, c.1812, 10 In........................ | 1320 |
| **Salver,** George II, Engraved, Scalloped Shell, Edge, Footed, R. Abercromby, 1741, 10 In............ | 594 |
| **Salver,** George II, Sterling, Raised Serpentine Lobed Rim, 3 Shell Feet, Engraved, c.1759, 14 In. | 6765 |
| **Salver,** George III, Beaded, Shaped Round Rim, Footed, John Hutson, London, 1786, 13 In. ....... | 1500 |
| **Salver,** George III, Shells, Leaves, 3-Footed, 7 ¼ In. ................................................ | 369 |
| **Salver,** George III, Wavy, Bead Border, JW Monogram, 3 Ball Feet, E. Cooke, c.1770, 12 In. ......... | 4680 |
| **Salver,** Molded Piecrust Border, 3 Stepped Feet, Dennis Langton, c.1733, 7 In....................... | 369 |
| **Salver,** Octagonal, Gadroon, Hamilton Coat Of Arms, Paul Storr, 1806, 8 In. .......................*illus* | 3625 |
| **Salver,** Raised & Beaded Rim, Cradock & Reid Touchmark, 1815, 8 In........................... | 360 |
| **Salver,** Scroll Feet, Scalloped Edge, Engraved, Thomas Bradbury, 8 ½ In. ........................... | 652 |
| **Salver,** Shells, Flowers, Wreath, John Edmund Terry, London, 1930, 21 In. .......................... | 3125 |
| **Sauceboat,** Scalloped Rim, 3-Footed, 5 x 7 ¾ In., Pair................................................ | 2706 |
| **Serving Spoon,** Plaque, Roman Soldier's Bust, Gold Wash Bowl, 9 In. ................................ | 225 |
| **Spoon Set,** Floral Enameled Bowl, Turner & Simpson, 6 Piece ....................................... | 330 |
| **Spoon Set,** George III, Gold Washed, W. Eley & W. Fearn, c.1802, 5 ¼ In., 9 Piece.................. | 253 |
| **Spoon Set,** George William Adams, Encased, 1879, 5 Piece ......................................... | 185 |
| **Spoon,** George III, Armorial Engraved Handles, 9 In., 5 Piece ....................................... | 246 |
| **Spoon,** Rocco, Diana The Huntress, Pierced, Francis Higgins II, c.1846, 7 ½ x 2 ½ In. ............. | 276 |
| **Stand,** Teapot, Bellflower Band, Beaded Rim, Oval, 4-Footed, H. Bateman, 1782, 6 x 5 In............ | 531 |
| **Stuffing Spoon,** Stag Crest, Lion Pheasant, Eley & Fearn, 12 ¾ In. ................................. | 98 |
| **Sugar Basket,** Reeded Oval Foot, Chawner, c.1790, 6 ¼ x 6 ⅛ In. .................................. | 1045 |
| **Sugar Castor,** Pierced, Dolphin, Swan's Head Handle Ends, Scroll Supports, c.1840, 5 ½ In. ...... | 900 |
| **Sugar Castor,** Rococo, Shield Shape Reserve, Sheffield, c.1890, 8 ½ In. ............................ | 300 |
| **Sugar Castor,** Tower Shape, Sterling, Pierced Dome Lid, Monogram, 6 ½ In. ........................ | 127 |

**Silver-Mexican,** Pitcher, Water, Rosewood Handle, Openwork Foot, Codan, c.1950, 10 ¼ In.
**$844**

Heritage Auction Galleries

**TIP**
*Do not leave salt in a silver saltshaker or open salt. Salt corrodes silver.*

**Silver-Mexican,** Salt Shaker & Pepper Grinder, Chased, Janna Thomas De Velarde, c.1970, 6 In.
**$813**

Heritage Auction Galleries

**Silver-Mexican,** Tea & Coffee Set, Rosewood Handles, Codan, c.1950, 7 Piece
**$11,563**

Heritage Auction Galleries

519

**Silver-Mexican,** Vase Base, 6 Faces, Profiles Form Prongs, Emilia Castillo, Taxco, c.2000, 8 ½ In.
$750

Heritage Auction Galleries

---

**Silver-Russian,** Cup, Gilt, Enamel, Neoclassical Designs, Handle, Marked, c.1890, 1 ¾ In.
$300

Cowan's Auctions

---

**Silver-Russian,** Ewer, Applied Copper Decoration, Hinged Lid, Art Nouveau, 13 In.
$1,476

Skinner Auctioneers & Appraisers

| | |
|---|---:|
| **Sugar Tongs,** Egg Shape Terminal, 1803, 5 ½ In. | 403 |
| **Sugar,** Edwardian, Urn Shape, Gadroon, Footed, Sydney Bellamy Harman, 1910, 7 x 5 In. | 219 |
| **Tablespoon,** Hanoverian Pattern, Engraved Shell, c.1740, Pair | 240 |
| **Tablespoon,** Regency, Fiddle, Paul Storr, Stork Crest, 8 ⅝ In. | 799 |
| **Tankard,** George I, Repousse Flowers, C-Scrolls, Stippled, Dome Lid, 7 In. | 2048 |
| **Tankard,** George II, Baluster Body, Scroll Handle, Thomas Whipham, 1746, 7 ½ In. | 1298 |
| **Tankard,** George III, Dome Lid, Scroll Handle, Pierced Thumbpiece, Langlands, c.1715, 8 In. | 3480 |
| **Tankard,** George III, Repousse Flowers, Berries, London, c.1773, 5 In. | 480 |
| **Tea & Coffee Set,** Flowers, Leaves, Waste Bowl, Sugar & Creamer, c.1841, 5 Piece | 6150 |
| **Tea & Coffee Set,** Repousse, Basket Weave, Pear Shape, 9 ¾-In. Coffeepot, 5 Piece | 6150 |
| **Tea & Coffee Set,** Round Shape, Leaves, Medallions, Coffeepot, Pitcher, 2 Piece | 1062 |
| **Tea & Coffee Set,** Tapering Body, Circular Foot, Sugar & Creamer, Tray, c.1944 | 2214 |
| **Tea & Coffee Set,** Teapot, Coffeepot, Sugar & Creamer, Shell, Leaves, Snake, 4 Piece | 2760 |
| **Tea & Coffee Set,** Teapot, Coffeepot, Sugar, Adie Brothers, c.1930 | 750 |
| **Tea & Coffee Set,** Urn Shape, Kettle, Stand, Teapot, Coffeepot, Sugar, 4 Piece | 2706 |
| **Tea Box,** Art Nouveau Design, Birds, Vines, Flowers, Cylindrical, Tapered, 1901, 4 ½ In. | 351 |
| **Tea Service,** Chester, Teapot, Open Sugar, Creamer, Blankensee Mark, 1925, 5 ½ In. | 354 |
| **Tea Set,** Gadroon, Rounded Rectangle, Squat, Ball Feet, Sheffield, 1897, 3 Piece | 413 |
| **Teapot Stand,** George III, Oval, Footed, William Plummer, c.1782, 6 In. | 270 |
| **Teapot,** Acanthus Leaves, Wood Handle, Samuel Hennell, 1814, 5 ½ In. | 431 |
| **Teapot,** Bulbous, Reeded Band, Hinged Lid, Leaves, Acanthus, 9 ¼ x 12 In. | 2214 |
| **Teapot,** Curved Spout, Wood Handle, Peter, Ann, William Bateman, c.1800, 7 x 11 In. .......*illus* | 863 |
| **Teapot,** Flared Cylinder Shape, Scrolled Wood Handle, Joseph Collier, c.1724, 8 ¾ In. | 3120 |
| **Teapot,** George III, Duncan Urquhart & Naphtali Hart, London, c.1800, 6 x 11 In. | 660 |
| **Teapot,** George III, Fluted, Shields, Repousse Rim, Flowers, Sea Shells, 6 x 11 ½ In. | 518 |
| **Teapot,** George III, Oval, Etched Garland, Robert Makepeace, c.1778, 4 ¾ x 9 ½ In. | 600 |
| **Teapot,** Ivory Handle, Flower & Scroll Relief, Phoenix Spout, 6 ¼ In. | 1150 |
| **Teapot,** Shield, Bellflower, Oval, Beaded, Pear Wood Handle, H. Bateman, 6 In. ..............*illus* | 2832 |
| **Teaspoon,** George III, S. Royes, J. Dix, London, 12 Piece | 120 |
| **Toast Rack,** George III, 6-Slice, Bead & Reel Handles, John Emes, c.1805, 7 ½ In. | 480 |
| **Toast Rack,** George III, Gadroon Rim, Rocaille, Paw Feet, c.1810, 6 x 7 ½ In., Pair | 2214 |
| **Toast Rack,** Triangular Handle, William Hutton & Sons, 3 x 2 ½ In., Pair | 196 |
| **Tray,** Engraved, Pad Feet, Oval, Alexander Field, London, 1799, 6 ¾ x 5 In. | 649 |
| **Tray,** Engraved, Whippet, Ball & Claw, 4-Footed, 21 In. | 1003 |
| **Tray,** Gadroon Rim, Scrollwork Handles, Armorial, Unicorn, 30 In. | 3900 |
| **Tray,** George II, Shell Borders, Engraved, Panels, Swans, Ducks, 1754, 14 ½ In. | 1416 |
| **Tray,** George III, Engraved Fern Border, Oval, Reeded Rim, Handles, c.1797, 22 x 14 In. | 4674 |
| **Tray,** George V, Galleried, Oval, Cutout Handles, Birmingham, c.1912, 24 ½ In. | 3125 |
| **Tray,** Oval, Beaded Rim, Handles, Feet, Crouch & Hannam, c.1794, 21 ½ In. | 2829 |
| **Tray,** Pierced Gallery, Embossed Medallions, 8-Sided, Martin Hall & Co., c.1950, 25 In. | 625 |
| **Tray,** Square, Stepped Edge, 2 Handles, Thomas Bradbury & Sons, 26 In. | 2460 |
| **Tureen,** Lid, George III, Gadroon, Reeded, Crest, A. Folgelberg & S. Gilbert, c.1780, 12 In. | 6300 |
| **Waiter,** Circular, Shell & Scroll Rim, Center Arms, 3-Footed, c.1754, 7 In. | 864 |
| **Waiter,** George III, Beaded Rim, 3 Spade Feet, Engraved, Bellflower, Round, c.1787, 10 In. | 1476 |
| **Waste Bowl,** George III, 1786-87, 3 In. | 540 |

## SILVER-FRENCH

| | |
|---|---:|
| **Chocolate Pot & Beaker,** Treen Handle, Flared Cup, Hoof Feet, 2 Piece | 1020 |
| **Coffeepot,** Restauration, Oval, Waisted Collar, Horse Head Spout, Louis Filette, 13 x 9 In. | 1353 |
| **Creamer,** Lid, Rosewood Handle, Finial, Emile Puiforcat, c.1857, 6 ¾ In. | 478 |
| **Cruet Set,** Dolphins, Blue Glass, Garlands, Pierced Body, c.1781-83, 2 Piece | 563 |
| **Dresser Set,** 3 Brushes, Hand Mirror, Comb, 4 Boxes, Cartier, 1900s, 9 Piece | 750 |
| **Ewer,** Louis XV Provencal, Rococo Cartouches, Swags, Hinged, Durand, 1773, 11 In. ..........*illus* | 4182 |
| **Figurine,** Putto, Winged, Standing On Mound Base, Flowers, Marble Base, c.1897, 7 In. | 920 |
| **Placecard Holder,** 1900s, 1 ¼ In., 24 Piece | 1250 |
| **Plate,** Round, Stylized Leaf Edge, Marc-Augustin Lebrun, c.1838, 9 ½ In. | 180 |
| **Platter,** Oval, Reed & Ribbon Rim, Maison Odiot, Late 19th Century, 16 ¾ In. | 984 |
| **Salt,** Beaded, Putti, Garlands, Cobalt Blue Liner, Spoon, Paillard Freres, c.l880, 3 In., Pair | 210 |
| **Salt,** High Relief, Game Bird, Stem, Seated Hunter, Hound, 2 ⅝ x 5 ¼ In. | 60 |
| **Sauceboat,** Stand, Spiral Fluted Double Lip, Flower Scroll Handles, Boin-Taburet, c.1910, 11 In. | 1188 |
| **Server,** Lid, Cabbage Finial, Stand, Spiral Fluted, Pierced Flower Handles, c.1910, 13 In. | 2500 |
| **Sundial,** Pocket, 8-Sided, Hinged, Scrolling Leaves, Inset Compass, 3 In. | 4160 |
| **Tea & Coffee Set,** Angular, Glass Handle, J. Puiforcat, 1925, 5-In. Coffeepot, 4 Piece | 31250 |
| **Tea & Coffee Set,** Teapot, Coffeepot, Sugar & Creamer, Tray, 1925-50, 5 Piece | 2460 |
| **Trinket Box,** Oval, Hinged, Tooled Sides, Scroll Border, Watercolor In Lid, 6 ¾ x 5 ¼ In. | 495 |

| | |
|---|---|
| **Tureen,** Oval, Reeded Feet, Lid, Fruit Finial, Handles, 9¼ In. | 938 |
| **Wine Trolley,** Chariot Shape, Grapevines, Late 19th Century, 12¼ In. | 1353 |

## SILVER-GERMAN

| | |
|---|---|
| **Ashtray,** Hammered, Jakob Grimminger, c.1930, 8¼ In. | 437 |
| **Basket,** Pierced Swags, Griffins, Glass Insert, Creature Stem Supports, Roth, c.1900, 8 x 9 In. | 900 |
| **Bowl,** 4 Putti, Garlands, Oval Glass Bowl, 16¼ x 14 In. | 2091 |
| **Bowl,** Boat Shape, Swags, Ribbons, Cobalt Blue Glass Insert, 9½ x 6 In. | 265 |
| **Bowl,** Condiment, Goats Pulling Cart, Satyr Driver, Neresheimer & Sohne, c.1900, 9 x 5 In., Pair | 1200 |
| **Bowl,** Reticulated, Pierced, Oval, 8½ In. | 192 |
| **Bowl,** Square, Crescent, Crown, Fruit, Beaded Rim, 2¼ x 4¾ In., 6 Piece | 600 |
| **Bowl,** Sterling, Repousse Flowers, Glass Liner, Footed, Stamped, 11½ x 8 In. | 828 |
| **Box,** Guilloche Enamel Cover, Lavender, 2 Court Figures, Heart Vines, 8-Sided, 5 In. | 1536 |
| **Box,** Lid, Oval Shape, 4 Scrolled Feet, Leaf Handle, Hammered, 4 x 6 x 5 In. | 345 |
| **Box,** Relief Leaves, Pheasant Standing On Top, 5 x 3 In. | 437 |
| **Bread Basket,** Open Ivy Pattern, Ivory Handle, J. Hoffman, Wiener Werkstatte, 10 In. | 33750 |
| **Bread Plate,** Reeded Rim, 5⅞ In., 12 Piece | 600 |
| **Casket,** Ball Feet, Rectangular Shape, Swivel Handle, 6½ x 5 In. | 345 |
| **Centerpiece,** Oval, Lattice, Floral, Scroll Handles, Putti, Domed Foot, c.1890, 19 In. | 5000 |
| **Centerpiece,** Reticulated Scrolls, Children, Winged Putti Stem, Footed, c.1900, 9 In. | 510 |
| **Centerpiece,** Reticulated Urns, Scrolls, Tavern Scenes, G. Roth, Hanau, c.1900, 4 x 11 In. | 240 |
| **Centerpiece,** Scalloped Etched Glass Bowl, Scroll & Cherub Handles, 9 x 18 In. | 1560 |
| **Coffeepot,** Swags, Medallions, Ludwig Neresheimer & Co., c.1900, 11 x 6 In. | 237 |
| **Compote,** Reticulated Fruit, Footed, c.1890, 6 x 13 In. | 738 |
| **Decanter,** Holder, Grape, Grape Leaf, Nude Woman, Decanter, Stopper, 13¾ In. | 3704 |
| **Decanter,** Putto Finial, Engraved Shells, Flowers, Etched Liquor Bottle, c.1890, 11 In. | 420 |
| **Dish,** Lid, Dancers, Flowers, Scrollwork, Dolphin Finial, Dolphin Feet, 10¾ In. | 1353 |
| **Ewer,** Putto Handle, Flowers, Scroll Feet, 14½ x 6½ In., Pair | 3750 |
| **Figurine,** Fox, Sitting, Meresheimer Of Hanau, 12½ In. | 7500 |
| **Figurine,** Horse & Rider, Cabochon Jewels, Jouster, 1930, 12½ In. | 5937 |
| **Figurine,** Pheasants, Walking, 13 In., Pair | 3125 |
| **Flask,** Mushroom Stopper, Flowers, Scrolls, Serpentine Shape, Narrow Neck, 6 x 4 In. | 224 |
| **Fruit Service,** Flower, Leaf Border, Engraved, Germany, 6¼ In., 22 Piece | 207 |
| **Jar,** Ship Finial, Waves, Glass Body, Schleissner Sohne, Early 1900s, 6 In. | 738 |
| **Napkin Holder,** Basket, Roses, Repousse, Marked, 4½ x 3 x 1 In. | 150 |
| **Pitcher,** Cream, Figural Ornament, Women Under Urn, Applied Handle, 1828, 4¾ In. | 86 |
| **Pitcher,** Wood Panels, Tapered Cylinder, Hinged Lid, 1900s, 13½ In. | 1125 |
| **Plateau,** Embossed Rim, Mirror, Oval, 10¾ x 15¾ In. | 390 |
| **Salt & Pepper,** Figural, Reclining Foxes, Marked, 4½ x 1¼ In. | 414 |
| **Stamp,** Wax Seal, Art Nouveau, Marked, c.1900, 2¾ In. | 450 |
| **Sugar & Creamer,** Streamlined, Hammered, Rounded Square, Tapered Foot | 115 |
| **Tea & Coffee Set,** Coffeepot, Teapot, Sugar & Creamer, 4 Piece | 677 |
| **Tea & Coffee Set,** Coffeepot, Teapot, Sugar & Creamer, Tray, Roses, 5 Piece | 1997 |
| **Tea & Coffee Set,** Sugar & Creamer, Tray, Globe Shape, Spiral Fluting, 5 Piece | 2500 |
| **Tray,** Molded Rim, 17¼ In. | 720 |
| **Vase,** Hexagonal, Pierced, Flower Swags, 2 Scrolled Handles, 11¼ In. | 2250 |

## SILVER-GREEK

| | |
|---|---|
| **Cup,** Wine, Hammered, Incised Quarry Scene, Marked, 4¾ x 2 In. | 75 |

## SILVER-INDIAN

| | |
|---|---|
| **Bowl,** Colonial, Repousse Band Panels, Zodiac, Cylindrical, 1800s, 3½ x 4½ In. | 522 |
| **Hookah,** Bell Shape Base, Lotus Shape Bowl, Peacock Finial, Chimera, 19 In. | 1187 |
| **Tea Set,** Swami Style, Teapot, Sugar & Creamer, Elephant Handles, 3 Piece | 531 |

## SILVER-IRISH

| | |
|---|---|
| **Basket,** Ireland, George IV, 1822, 11 In. | 1920 |
| **Bowl,** George II, Gadroon Rim, James LeBas, 1818, 6¾ In. | 1063 |
| **Goblet,** George III, Repousse Acanthus, Gadroon Band On Foot, 6⅜ In., Pair ...............*illus* | 2952 |
| **Salver,** George IV, Scroll, Shell Rim, Chased Birds, 4 Paw Feet, James Le Bas, 1824, 22 In. | 4688 |
| **Serving Spoon,** Cutout Fish, Pierced Stars, Engraved Scrollwork, Dublin, 12¼ In. | 374 |
| **Tray,** 4 Portraits, Flowers, Leaves, Grapes, Beast, 4-Footed, c.1825, 26 In. | 8610 |
| **Wine Cooler,** 2 Ball Handles, Grapevine Register, Gadroon, c.1970, 7⅞ In. | 2091 |

## SILVER-ISRAELI

| | |
|---|---|
| **Kettle,** Stand, Rococo Style, Ebonized Wood, Paw Feet, 12¼ In. | 1952 |

## SILVER-ITALIAN

| | |
|---|---|
| **Basin,** Shell, Cockleshell Feet, 6¼ x 12½ In. | 360 |

**Silver-Sterling,** Bowl, Lobed, Reticulated Rim, Scrolling Flowers, Leaves, Shreve & Co., c.1900, 12 x 3 In.
$777

Neal Auction Co.

**Silver-Tibetan,** Ewer, Jade Plaques, Coral, Lapis, Turquoise Inlay, Bulbous, Loop Handle, 1800s, 17 In.
$5,036

James D. Julia Auctioneers

**Silver-Tibetan,** Ewer, Wine, Turquoise & Coral Cabochons, Dragon Handle, 1800s, 19 x 10 In.
$2,370

James D. Julia Auctioneers

S

**Sinclaire,** Candlestick, Sapphire Blue, Spiral Optic Ribbing, Drip Rim, Marked, 4 In., Pair
$230

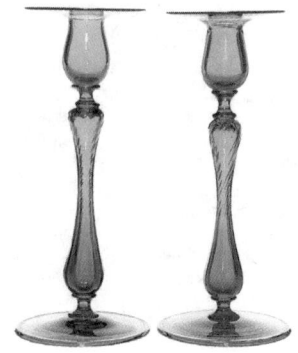

Humler & Nolan

**Sleepy Eye,** Mug, Blue, White, Indian Chief, Teepee, 7 ½ In.
$138

Humler & Nolan

**Sleepy Eye,** Sign, Old Sleepy Eye, Meritorious Flour, Indian Chief, Tin, c.1905, 24 x 20 In.
$10,800

Morphy Auctions

| | |
|---|---:|
| **Basket,** Flower, Swing Handle, Applied Flowers, 7 ¾ x 7 In. | 478 |
| **Box,** Lid, Walnut Form, Naturalistic Finish, Buccellati, 5 x 5 x 7 In. | 2560 |
| **Centerpiece,** Cabbage Form, Naturalistically Molded, Buccellati, 10 x 15 In. | 6080 |
| **Centerpiece,** Spiral Fluted, Round, 4 Scrolled Feet, Buccellati, 13 ½ In. | 2375 |
| **Coffeepot,** Undulating Fluted Body, Hammered, Mask Spout, S-Scroll Handle, c.1960, 10 In. | 2500 |
| **Figure,** Bull, Charging, Chased Fur, Buccellati, 7 x 14 In. | 10000 |
| **Jar,** Leaf & Stem Finial, Cap, Yellow Pear Shape Body, Buccellati, 5 ¼ In. | 2214 |
| **Jardiniere,** Hammered, Oval, Buccellati, 8 ½ x 18 In. | 9375 |
| **Pitcher,** Fluted, Scroll Handle, Domed Foot, Buccellati, 1845, 10 In. | 1845 |
| **Pitcher,** Water, Torchon Pattern, Twisted Baluster, 3 Scroll Feet, Buccellati, 12 In. | 2432 |
| **Salt & Pepper,** Poppy, Rocky Base, Pods Detach, Ilario Pradella, Buccellati, 7 ½ x 5 ¼ In. | 1599 |
| **Salt & Pepper,** Thistle Shape, Buccellati, 8 In. | 1092 |
| **Shaker,** Flower Form, 2 Removable Stems, Leaves, Buds, M. Buccellati, 7 In., Pair | 2006 |
| **Spoon Warmer,** Nautilus Shell Shape, 2 Whelk Shell Feet, Buccellati, 4 In., Pair | 3712 |
| **Tray,** Torchon Pattern, Shaped Oval, Reeded Edge, 4 Shell Tabs, Buccellati, 20 In. | 3712 |
| **Tureen,** Lid, Cabbage Shape, Buccellati, 13 In. | 3750 |
| **Vase,** Dimpled, Buccellati, 9 x 7 In. | 7500 |
| **Vase,** Flared, Cylindrical, Pierced, Lion Paw Feet, 1800s, 4 ½ x 4 In., Pair | 984 |

## SILVER-JAPANESE

| | |
|---|---:|
| **Cigar Box,** Chased Dragons, Stippled, Arthur Bond Yokohama, c.1900, 9 ¾ In. | 4375 |
| **Jewelry Box,** Sterling, Trefoil Handle, Wood Base, Engraved Flowers, 7 ½ x 12 In. | 3198 |
| **Placecard Holders,** Fishermen, Fish, Basket & Cage Carriers, Japan, 2 In., 10 Piece | 587 |
| **Tea Caddy,** Engraved Bamboo Shoots, Birds, Branches, Oval, 4 In. | 625 |
| **Teapot,** Art Deco, Oval, Footed, Swan Neck Spout, Fluted, Dome Lid, Miyata, 7 x 10 In. | 575 |
| **Tray,** Square, Daisies, Dragonflies, Whiting Mfg. Co., 1887, 8 ½ In. | 2750 |
| **Vase,** Enameled Blossom & Leaves, Long Neck, Flared, Rim, c.1910, 5 ¼ In., Pair | 2125 |

## SILVER-MEXICAN

| | |
|---|---:|
| **Bowl,** Applied Handles, Ball Decoration, Footed, 5 ¾ x 4 ¼ In. | 173 |
| **Bowl,** Conquistador Pattern, Footed, Scroll & Leaf Rim, 20th Century, 4 x 9 ⅝ In. | 413 |
| **Bowl,** Flat Band Rim, Cabochon Amethysts, William Spratling, c.1944, 11 ¾ In. ............*illus* | 3250 |
| **Bowl,** Fruit, Flared Rim, 3-Footed, William Spratling, Taxco, c.1943, 7 ⅝ In. .............*illus* | 1599 |
| **Bowl,** Liner Plate, Lobbed Shape, Pedestal, Hammered, Marked, Sanborns, 3 x 5 In., 5 In. | 184 |
| **Bowl,** Modernist, Organic Shape, 4 Cone Shape Legs, 14 x 8 In. | 472 |
| **Bowl,** Pedestal, 4 Dolphin Feet, Meandering Leaf Relief, Engraved, 4 x 5 ½ In. | 414 |
| **Bowl,** Quatrefoil Shape, Fluted Corners, Round Foot, 2 x 6 x 5 In., Pair | 1125 |
| **Bowl,** Repousse, Rope Rim, Handles, Jose Marmolejo, c.1958, 8 x 26 In. ............*illus* | 1188 |
| **Bowl,** Round, Lobed, Scroll Handles, Sanborns, 1900s, 4 ¾ x 12 ½ x 10 ½ In. | 1180 |
| **Bowl,** Spanish Colonial, Rococo Scroll Rim, Salvador De La Serna, 6 x 13 In. | 1107 |
| **Bowl,** Squat, Oval, Fish, Repousse, Hammered, Stepped Lid, 6 x 8 In. | 312 |
| **Box,** Hinged Lid, Raised Bands, Rectangular Amethyst, Sanborns, c.1940, 9 x 4 In. ...........*illus* | 1375 |
| **Centerpiece,** 2 Handles, c.1950, 5 ½ In. x 21 In. | 2460 |
| **Centerpiece,** Oval, Lobed, 2 Scrolled Handles, 4 Scrolled Feet, 19 ½ In. | 707 |
| **Cigarette Box,** 4 ⅜ x 3 ⅝ In. | 63 |
| **Cup,** Ducks, Cattle, Chicks, Birds At Play, Signed, Sanborns, 3 ¼ x 1 ½ In. | 121 |
| **Dish,** Shell Shape, Scrolled End, Footed Base, Marked, Sanborns, Mexico, 5 x 8 ½ In., Pair | 575 |
| **Pitcher,** Copper, Shaped Handle, Applied Leaf, Emilia Castillo, 14 In. | 450 |
| **Pitcher,** Water, Bulbous, Banded Handle With Thumb Tab, C. Flez, 8 In. | 225 |
| **Pitcher,** Water, Modernist, Juventino Lopez Reyes, c.1950, 12 In. | 984 |
| **Pitcher,** Water, Pear Shape, Integral Spout, Domed Foot, Salvador De La Serna, 11 x 5 In. | 584 |
| **Pitcher,** Water, Rosewood Handle, Openwork Foot, Codan, c.1950, 10 ¼ In. ...........*illus* | 844 |
| **Salad Server,** Inlay On Wood Handle, 12 ¼ In., Pair | 178 |
| **Salt & Pepper,** Twisted, Baluster, Antonia Pineda, c.1962, 3 In. | 531 |
| **Salt Shaker & Pepper Grinder,** Chased, Janna Thomas De Velarde, c.1970, 6 In. ...........*illus* | 813 |
| **Salt,** Tapering Round Bowl, Looped Openwork Base, c.1942, 1 x 3 In., 4 Piece | 625 |
| **Salver,** Shaped Banded Rim, Stepped Border, Scroll Feet, 12 In. | 812 |
| **Serving Spoon,** Fiddle Handle, Long Oval Bowl, Wm. Spratling, c.1967, 12 ¼ In. | 312 |
| **Serving Spoon,** William Spratling, Mexico, c.1940, 9 In. | 150 |
| **Tea & Coffee Set,** Kettle, Burner, Coffeepot, Teapot, Sugar & Creamer, 5 Piece | 2625 |
| **Tea & Coffee Set,** Lobed, Inverted Baluster, Scrolled Edge, Footed, 31-In. Tray, 7 Piece | 5904 |
| **Tea & Coffee Set,** Rosewood Handles, Codan, c.1950, 7 Piece ...........*illus* | 11563 |
| **Tea Set,** Repousse, Flowers, Melon Shape, 2 Teapots, Tongs, 24 ½-In. Tray, 7 Piece | 2370 |
| **Tray,** Applied Cast Leaf Relief Rim, Leaf Handles, 31 x 19 ½ In. | 1840 |
| **Tray,** Oval, Raised Edge, Marked CLS, 15 ½ x 9 ⅛ In. | 461 |
| **Tray,** Oval, Scrolled Handles, William Spratling, 13 ¼ In. | 3444 |
| **Tray,** Reeded, Gadroon Rim, Palmettes, Oval, Stamped, Sanborns, c.1910, 22 In. | 1476 |

| | |
|---|---|
| **Tray,** Repousse Lobes, Flower, Stippled Ground, Fan Feet, c.1900, 21 In. | 1875 |
| **Tureen,** Lid, Loop Handles, Sanborns, 14 ⅛ In. | 1599 |
| **Vase Base,** 6 Faces, Profiles Form Prongs, Emilia Castillo, Taxco, c.2000, 8 ½ In. .......*illus* | 750 |
| **Vase,** Elongated, Berry Clusters, Footed, c.1958, 10 ½ In. | 406 |

### SILVER-MIDDLE EASTERN

| | |
|---|---|
| **Ewer,** Pear Shape, Slender Spout, Curved Handle, Dome Lid, 1800s, 6 ½ x 4 ¼ In. | 138 |

### SILVER-NORWEGIAN

| | |
|---|---|
| **Desk Blotter,** Blue Enamel, Handle, Marius Hammer, Bergen, 4 x 2 ½ In. | 177 |
| **Fork Set,** Enamel Handle, Multicolor, David Andersen, 6 Piece | 540 |
| **Servers,** Stylized Leaf Handles, Engraved, Theo. Olsen, Norway, 7 ½ In., Pair | 213 |
| **Spoon Set,** Demitasse, Sterling, Blue Enamel Coat Of Arms Handles, Box, 4 In., 6 Piece | 75 |
| **Spoon Set,** Enamel Handle, Multicolor, 6 Piece | 120 |
| **Spoon Set,** Enamel Handle, Multicolor, David Andersen, 6 Piece | 330 |

### SILVER-PERSIAN

| | |
|---|---|
| **Box,** Arabesques, Gold Wash Interior, 5 ¾ x 5 ¾ In. | 322 |
| **Tea Set,** Teapot, Samovar, Bowl, Tray, Early 1900s, 12 In., 4 Piece | 1968 |

### SILVER-PERUVIAN

| | |
|---|---|
| **Candy Dish,** 3 Stylized Leaves, Rose Cluster, 9 ½ In. | 173 |
| **Goblet,** Inca Design, Repousse, Figural Stem, Stepped Foot, 6 ½ x 3 In. | 81 |
| **Tea & Coffee Set,** Creamer, Sugar, Waste Bowl, 7 ¾ & 7 ⅛ In. | 1265 |

### SILVER-PORTUGUESE

| | |
|---|---|
| **Bread Basket,** Pierced, Swing Handle, 4-Footed, 15 ½ x 15 ¼ In. | 813 |
| **Ewer,** High Relief Bunches Of Grapes, Vines, Leafy Handle, c.1928, 13 ½ In. | 938 |
| **Toothpick Holder,** Figural, Cupid, On Column, Leaf Relief, Paw Feet, 5 ¼ In. | 483 |

**SILVER-RUSSIAN.** Russian silver is marked with the Cyrillic, or Russian, alphabet. The numbers 84, 88, or 91 indicate the silver content. Russian silver may be higher or lower than sterling standard. Other marks indicate maker, assayer, or city of manufacture. Many pieces of silver made in Russia are decorated with enamel. These prices are based on current silver values. Faberge pieces are listed in their own category.

| | |
|---|---|
| **Basket,** Gold Wash Interior, Bail Handle, G.M. Okerblom, c.1848, 10 ¾ In. | 554 |
| **Beaker,** Thimble Tumblers, Sterling, Flared, Footed, Turned-Out Rim, Chased, c.1908, 3 Piece .. | 127 |
| **Bowl,** Gilt Wash Lobed Interior, Scalloped Rim, P. Syevrugeen, c.1885, 4 x 10 In. | 420 |
| **Bowl,** Shallow, Scalloped Apron, Knobbed Column, Cloisonne, Dome Base, 6 In. | 4687 |
| **Cigarette Box,** Embossed, Napoleon, Stallion, Bear, Cubs, 5 x 3 ½ In. | 863 |
| **Cigarette Case,** Buildings Scene, Moscow, c.1879, 3 ½ In. | 625 |
| **Cigarette Case,** Slavic Warrior, Gold Monogram, Gilt Interior, 5 ⅜ x 3 ½ In. | 1250 |
| **Creamer,** Classical Bands, Ebonized Handle, Gilt Interior, Lobed Base, Oval, 4 x 5 ½ In. | 359 |
| **Cup,** Gilt, Enamel, Neoclassical Designs, Handle, Marked, c.1890, 1 ¾ In. ...........*illus* | 300 |
| **Cup,** Presentation, Engraved, Knopped Stem, Stepped Base, Monogram, c.1878, 8 In. | 242 |
| **Ewer,** Applied Copper Decoration, Hinged Lid, Art Nouveau, 13 In. ...........*illus* | 1476 |
| **Kovsh,** Cloisonne, Enamel, Beaded Trim, Multicolor, c.1900, 2 x 5 ½ In. | 4600 |
| **Mug,** Podstakannik, Presentation, Applied Leaf Scrolling, Nicholas II, 5 x 3 ¼ In. | 522 |
| **Soup Spoon,** Enamel, Meandering Flower, Scrolling, Cloisonne, Twist Handle, 7 ½ In., 3 Piece . | 690 |
| **Spoon,** Enamel Cloisonne, Sterling, Almond Shape, Flowers, Leaves, 7 ¾ In. | 805 |
| **Tankard,** Repousse Diaper Pattern, Flower Heads, Putto Finial, Grachev Bros., 13 In. | 3998 |

### SILVER-SCANDINAVIAN

| | |
|---|---|
| **Tankard,** Cylindrical, Hinged, Wreath Border, Acorn Thumbpiece, 1700s, 4 In. | 1062 |

### SILVER-SCOTTISH

| | |
|---|---|
| **Creamer,** Hinged Lid, Ruby Glass Animal Eyes, Curved Tail Is Handle, c.1910, 6 ½ In. | 1062 |
| **Goblet,** Beaker Shape, Banded Pedestal Base, E Monogram, Wm. Marshall, 1805, 6 In., Pair. | 708 |

### SILVER-SIAMESE

| | |
|---|---|
| **Coaster Set,** Niello, Marked, 3 ¼ In., 8 Piece | 351 |

### SILVER-SPANISH

| | |
|---|---|
| **Bowl,** Hammered Over Mold, Ribbed, Heavy Scalloped Edge, 5 x 2 In., 9 Piece | 604 |

**SILVER-STERLING.** Sterling silver is made with 925 parts silver out of 1,000 parts of metal. The word *sterling* is a quality guarantee used in the United States after about 1860. The word was used much earlier in England and Ireland. Pieces listed here are not identified by country. These prices are based on current silver values. Other pieces of sterling quality silver are listed under Silver-American, Silver-English, etc.

| | |
|---|---|
| **Asparagus Server,** George IV, Bow Style, Fiddle Tongs, Leaf Pierced Blades, 10 In. | 738 |

**Snow Babies,** Figurine, Child, On Sled, Red Silk Ribbon, Germany, c.1910, 3 ¼ In., 2 Piece
$189

Conestoga Auction Co., Inc.

**Snuffbox,** Shell, Cowrie, Hinged Lid, Silver Mounted, c.1800, 3 In.
$240

DuMouchelles Art Gallery

**Snuffbox,** Tortoiseshell, Louis XV, Embossed Basket Weave, 20K Gold, Paris, c.1740, 2 ½ In.
$1,845

New Orleans Auction Galleries, Inc.

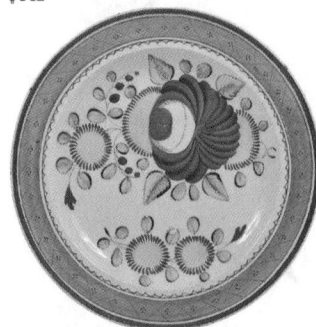

**Soft Paste,** Plate, Kings Rose, Solid Border, 9 ⅞ In.
$142

Conestoga Auction Co., Inc.

S

**Soft Paste,** Toddy Plate, King's Rose & Oyster Variant, 6¼ In.
$83

Conestoga Auction Co., Inc.

**Souvenir,** Button, Chiquita, Cuban Midget, Gown, Holding Fan, Pan-Am Expo, c.1901, 2⅛ In.
$325

Hake's Americana & Collectibles

**Spatterware,** Pitcher, Rainbow, Molded Handle, c.1835, 7 In.
$360

Garth's Auctioneers & Appraisers

**Spatterware,** Plate, Columbine, Stick Spatter, Flowers, Leaves, Daisy Border, 8⅝ In.
$118

Conestoga Auction Co., Inc.

| | |
|---|---:|
| **Basket,** Trumpet Vase, Swivel Handle, Weighted, 14 x 5 In. | 276 |
| **Bowl,** Embossed, Chased Flowers, Scrolling Leaves, Footed, 1896, 4½ x 7 In. | 478 |
| **Bowl,** Leaf Repousse, Pierced Rim, Oval, Marked, c.1893, 18 x 14½ In. | 2185 |
| **Bowl,** Lobed, Reticulated Rim, Scrolling Flowers, Leaves, Shreve & Co., c.1900, 12 x 3 In. ...*illus* | 777 |
| **Bowl,** Vegetable, Molded Banding, Steeply Dome Lid, Round, Monogram, 4 x 9½ In. | 430 |
| **Box,** Calling Card, Architectural, Cathedral, Scrolls, Shells, Flowers, 3½ x 2 In. | 138 |
| **Butter,** Cover, Repousse, Gold Flashed Liner, Monogram, c.1900, 3¼ x 7 In. | 767 |
| **Butter,** Cover, William IV, Tub Shape, Reeded Hoops, Incised Staves, Flower Finial, 3 x 6 In. | 610 |
| **Cake Plate,** Round, Pierced Floral Rim, Marked, 9½ In. | 178 |
| **Candelabra** are listed in the Candelabrum category. | |
| **Candlesticks** are listed in their own category. | |
| **Card Tray,** Leaf Relief Lip, Square, Engraved From Antionette Lord Whiton, 6½ x 6½ In. | 305 |
| **Carving Set,** Repousse, 8½-In. Bone Holder, 12¾-In. Knife, 10¾-In. Fork, 1800s | 144 |
| **Christening,** Cup, Gold Wash, Repousse, Cylindrical, C-Scroll Handle, c.1915, 3 x 4 In. | 161 |
| **Cigar Cutter,** Eagle Head, Boar's Head Tusk Handle, c.1900, 9 In. | 2625 |
| **Cigarette Case,** Engraved Vertical Line Bonds, Monogram, 3¼ x 3¼ In. | 81 |
| **Cigarette Case,** Scroll Work, Hinged, Push Button, 1900s, 4 x 3 In. | 350 |
| **Corncob Holders,** Corncob Husk Handle, Diamond Shape Prong, 3 x ½ In., 13 Piece | 282 |
| **Dish,** Art Deco, Flared Border, Stylized Bamboo Rim, Monogram, Oblong, 12 x 7 In. | 173 |
| **Dish,** Serpentine Rim, Footed, Square, Monogram, Hallmark, c.1942, 9 In. | 426 |
| **Figure,** Pheasant, Inset Glass Bead Eyes, Hinged Articulated Wings, 18½ In., Pair | 1170 |
| **Fish Serving Set,** Mother-Of-Pearl, Case, c.1890, 14 Piece | 540 |
| **Flask,** Repousse Flowers, Matte Ground, Gilt-Lined Shot Cup, Engraved, 1884, 5 x 2½ In. | 1845 |
| **Frame,** Repousse Putti, Flowers, Beaded, Easel Back, 9 x 7¼ In. | 293 |
| **Hip Flask,** Hinge Cap, Monogram Plaque, Texture Background, 7 In. | 71 |
| **Hot Water Jug,** Victorian, Teardrop Shape, Chased, Monogram, 1861, 11¼ In. | 308 |
| **Humidor,** Presentation, Facsimile Signatures, Monogram, c.1950, 8¾ x 5½ In. | 296 |
| **Ink Blotter Rocker,** Guilloche, Engraved, Blue, Enameled Pink Rose Garlands, 2 x 5 In. | 230 |
| **Letter Opener,** Indian Chief Head Handle, Bellflowers, 10¼ In. | 362 |
| **Napkin Rings** are listed in their own category. | |
| **Pillbox,** Guilloche Green Enamel, Flowers, Round, Hinged Lid, 1¾ In. | 190 |
| **Pillbox,** Woman Playing Lute, Blue Enamel, Scroll Border, 2 x 1½ In. | 104 |
| **Pitcher,** Milk, Furrowed Sided, Leaf Repousse, Leaf Feet, Applied Handle, 1916, 6 In. | 472 |
| **Pitcher,** Serpentine Lobed, Pear Shape, Conforming Foot, Scroll Handle, 10½ x 10 In. | 984 |
| **Pitcher,** Water, Art Deco, Incurved Neck, Stylized Band, Footed, Angular Handle, 8½ In. | 717 |
| **Pitcher,** Water, Bulbous, Rope Twist Handles, Borders, Footed, c.1860, 12 In. | 1003 |
| **Pitcher,** Water, Gadroon Shoulder, Curvilinear Handle, Monogram, 9¾ In. | 667 |
| **Punch Bowl,** Bulbous, Round, Repousse Flowers, Scroll Edge, 7 x 11 In. | 1599 |
| **Punch Ladle,** Flower Shape Cup, Mermaid Handle Terminal, c.1890, 16 In. | 1500 |
| **Salt & Pepper,** Bowl Shape, Rosewood Block Base, Spratling, c.1960, 1½ In. | 177 |
| **Salt & Pepper,** Cylindrical, Norbert Mfg. Co., 1¾ x 2 In. | 75 |
| **Salt & Pepper,** Urn Shape, Whiting, 6¼ In. | 87 |
| **Salt Cellar,** Figural, Dolphin, Sphere, Whelk Shell, Cobalt Blue Liner, 3 x 3 In., 12 Piece | 1845 |
| **Salt,** Pepper Shaker, Footed, 4 Piece | 150 |
| **Salt,** Spoon, Repousse, Oval, Cut Crystal Insert, Monogram, 3 x 2½ In., Pair | 201 |
| **Salver,** George III, Beaded Edge, Flat Rim, Engraved Crest, Footed, Round, 1783, 13 In. | 4780 |
| **Salver,** George III, Beaded, Serpentine Lobes, Round, Ball & Claw Feet, 15 In. | 5904 |
| **Salver,** George III, Serpentine Lobed, Round, Beaded Rim, Footed, c.1778, 13½ In. | 3690 |
| **Sauceboat,** Aesthetic, Tiffany's Union Square, J.C. Moore & Son, 5¾ In. | 1180 |
| **Serving Fork,** Acorn, 2 Tines, 8 In. | 180 |
| **Serving Tongs,** Lion Head, Grape Clusters, Lion Paw Feet Terminals, 6¾ In. | 295 |
| **Tea & Coffee Set,** Fluted, Maciel, Teapot, Coffeepot, Sugar, Creamer, Tray, c.1935, 29 In. | 3444 |
| **Tea & Coffee Set,** Sugar, Creamer, Hammered, Leaf, Bud, Ebonized Wood Handles, 9½ In. | 2629 |
| **Tea Set,** Coffeepot, Teapot, Sugar & Creamer, Tray, c.1920, 5 Piece | 1920 |
| **Tea Set,** Gilt, Solitaire, Crested, Scroll Supports, Fruit Finial, c.1873, 6 In., 3 Piece | 836 |
| **Tray,** Chippendale Style, Footed, Rounded Rectangular, Scroll Feet, 1900s, 14 In. | 1534 |
| **Trophy,** Bowl, Reticulated Rim, Grapevines, Footed, Corinthian Yacht Club, 1896, 11 In. | 1046 |
| **Trophy,** Butter, Cover, Larchmont Yacht Club, Dome Lid, Scrolled, Handles, 1902, 9 In. | 984 |
| **Trophy,** Cocktail Shaker, Larchmont Yacht Club, Insignia, 1893, 8 In. | 554 |
| **Trophy,** Coffeepot, Leaf Handle, Horsehead Spout, Larchmont Yacht Club, 1888, 10 In. | 1722 |
| **Trophy,** Crumb Brush, Figures, Scrolled Leaves, New Rochelle Yacht Club, c.1887, 14 In. | 185 |
| **Trophy,** Pitcher, Eagle Head Spout, Leafy Handle, Larchmont Yacht Club, c.1892, 10 In. | 2829 |
| **Trophy,** Tray, Art Nouveau, Newport Citizens Club, 1895, 18½ In. | 3690 |
| **Warming Pot,** Bulbous, Flaring Rim, Pronounced Spout, Handle, Turned Grip, 3 x 5 In. | 144 |

| | | |
|---|---|---|
| **Wine Coaster,** Magnum, Classical Relief Design, Putti, Lion, Leaf Border | | 777 |
| **Wine Coaster,** Pierced Scrollwork Sides, Wood Base, Scrolled Rim, c.1840, 3 x 5 In., Pair | | 1195 |

### SILVER-SWEDISH

| | |
|---|---|
| **Bowl,** Art Deco, Flared, Borgil, 1935, 10 ¼ In. | 450 |

### SILVER-TIBETAN

| | |
|---|---|
| **Container,** Lid, Repousse, Fluted Sides, c.1900, 4 ½ In. | 830 |
| **Ewer,** Repousse, Floral Patterns, c.1900, 9 ½ In. | 711 |
| **Ewer,** Jade Plaques, Coral, Lapis, Turquoise Inlay, Bulbous, Loop Handle, 1800s, 17 In. ....*illus* | 5036 |
| **Ewer,** Wine, Turquoise & Coral Cabochons, Dragon Handle, 1800s, 19 x 10 In. ....*illus* | 2370 |

### SILVER-VIETNAMESE

| | |
|---|---|
| **Tea Strainer,** Dragon Shape, Open Mouth, Stand, Bowl Swivels, Tail Handle, 5 ½ x 2 In. | 196 |

**SINCLAIRE** cut glass was made by H.P. Sinclaire and Company of Corning, New York, between 1904 and 1929. He cut glass made at other factories until 1920. Pieces were made of crystal as well as amber, blue, green, or ruby glass. Only a small percentage of Sinclaire glass is marked with the *S* in a wreath.

| | |
|---|---|
| **Bowl,** 3 Fruits, Rectangle, 3 ½ x 15 ½ In. | 848 |
| **Bread Plate,** 3 Fruits, Grapes, Pears, Apples, Shaped Oval, 14 x 10 In. | 275 |
| **Candlestick,** Sapphire Blue, Spiral Optic Ribbing, Drip Rim, Marked, 4 In., Pair ....*illus* | 230 |
| **Centerpiece,** Engraved Garland, Assyrian Border, Faceted Ring Stem, 6 x 12 In. | 650 |
| **Compote,** Intertwined Geometric Designs, Vines, Latticework, Marked, 10 In. | 345 |
| **Punch Bowl,** Vintage & Hobstar, Flared, Pedestal Stand, 13 x 14 In. | 1900 |
| **Salt Shaker,** Diamond Point Pattern, Tin Cap, Loop Handle, Signed | 68 |
| **Tray,** Assyrian Pattern, c.1909, 14 In. | 2700 |
| **Vase,** Bouquet, American Brilliant Cut, Signed, 3 ½ x 3 ½ In. | 135 |
| **Vase,** Trumpet, Roses, Daisies, Footed, Signed, 13 In. | 1400 |
| **Vase,** Tulip, Pedestal Shape, Signed, 13 ¾ In. | 254 |

**SLAG GLASS** resembles a marble cake. It can be streaked with different colors. There were many types made from about 1880. Caramel slag is the incorrect name for chocolate glass. Pink slag was an American product made by Harry Bastow and Thomas E.A. Dugan at Indiana, Pennsylvania, about 1900. Purple and blue slag were made in American and English factories in the 1880s. Red slag is a very late Victorian and twentieth-century glass. Other colors are known but are of less importance to the collector. New versions of chocolate glass and colored slag glass have been made.

| | |
|---|---|
| **Blue,** Powder Box, Figural, Scottie Dog, c.1940, 6 x ¾ In. | 245 |
| **Caramel Slag** is listed in the Imperial Glass category. | |
| **Green & White,** Compote, Swirl & Ball, c.1973, 4 ½ x 5 ⅛ In. | 30 |
| **Green,** Salt, Carved Flowers, 6-Sided, 1930s, 1 ½ In. | 18 |
| **Green,** Spooner, Lacy Edge | 250 |
| **Jade Green,** Dish, Fish Shape, 5 x 3 ½ In. | 28 |
| **Orange,** Compote, Star Shape, Retro, 12 x 4 In. | 33 |
| **Pink,** Tumbler, Inverted Fan & Feather, c.1880, 4 In. | 299 |
| **Purple & White,** Pitcher, Oval Panels, Windmill, House, Lake, c.1962, 6 ½ In. | 18 |
| **Red,** Ashtray, 6 In. | 10 |
| **Red,** Yellow & Orange, Pitcher, Scalloped Lip, 6 ¼ In. | 52 |
| **Yellow,** Ashtray, Dog, Laying On Rim, Art Deco, 5 x 5 ¼ In. | 41 |

**SLEEPY EYE** collectors look for anything bearing the image of the nineteenth-century Indian chief with the drooping eyelid. The Sleepy Eye Milling Co., Sleepy Eye, Minnesota, used his portrait in advertising from 1883 to 1921. It offered many premiums, including stoneware and pottery steins, crocks, bowls, mugs, and pitchers, all decorated with the famous profile of the Indian. The popular pottery was made by Weir Pottery Co. from c.1899-1905. Weir merged with six other potteries and became Western Stoneware in 1906. Western Stoneware Co. made blue and white Sleepy Eye from 1906 until 1937, long after the flour mill went out of business in 1921. Reproductions of the pitchers are being made today. The original pitchers came in only five sizes: 4 inches, 5 ¼ inches, 6 ½ inches, 8 inches, and 9 inches. The Sleepy Eye image was also used by companies unrelated to the flour mill.

| | | |
|---|---|---|
| **Letter Opener** | | 1000 |
| **Mug,** Blue, White, Indian Chief, Teepee, 7 ½ In. | *illus* | 138 |
| **Pitcher,** Blue, Teepees, Marked 30S, 6 ½ In. | | 245 |
| **Sign,** Old Sleepy Eye, Meritorious Flour, Indian Chief, Tin, c.1905, 24 x 20 In. | *illus* | 10800 |
| **Stein,** Indian, Profile, Indian Head On Handle, Embossed S, c.1903, 7 ¾ In. | | 560 |
| **Vase,** Cattail, Blue, Cylindrical, 8 ½ In. | | 344 |

**Spatterware,** Plate, Rabbits Playing, Field, Border, Blue & Red Leaves, 9 ¼ In., Pair
$325

Conestoga Auction Co., Inc.

**Spatterware,** Plate, Tulip, Blue & Red, Paneled, 8 ⅜ In.
$502

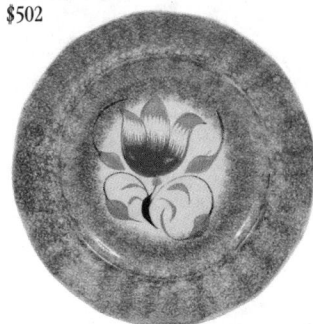

Conestoga Auction Co., Inc.

**Spinning Wheel,** Chestnut, Mixed Woods, Signed, S. Humes, Pennsylvania, 1811, 46 ½ In.
$212

Conestoga Auction Co., Inc.

### Sleepy Eye Repros

Original Sleepy Eye pitchers were made in five sizes. Each was made in one piece. Reproduction pitchers are two pieces, the body and an attached handle.

S

**Spode,** Platter, Hunting Campsite, Indian Sporting Series, Blue Transfer, c.1815, 14 x 18 In.
**$420**

DuMouchelles Art Gallery

---

**Sports,** Baseball, Badge, 1943, St. Louis, 2 Cardinals, Perched On Baseball Bat, Celluloid, 2 In.
**$1,123**

Hake's Americana & Collectibles

---

**Sports,** Baseball, Ball, Autographed, Babe Ruth, Additional Inscription, c.1946
**$4,500**

DuMouchelles Art Gallery

**S**

### Stitches Tell Baseball's Age

Baseball's National League used black and red stitches on baseballs until about 1934. American League balls had blue and red stitching.

---

**Vase,** Cylindrical, Indian Profile, Cattails, 1900s, 8 ½ x 4 In. .......... 175

---

**SLOT MACHINES** *are included in the Coin-Operated Machine category.*

---

**SMITH BROTHERS** glass was made after 1878. Alfred and Harry Smith had worked for the Mt. Washington Glass Company in New Bedford, Massachusetts, for seven years before going into their own shop. They made many pieces with enamel decoration.

*Smith Bros. Co.*

| | |
|---|---|
| **Biscuit Jar,** Leaves, Acorns, Cream Melon Ribbed, Silver Plated Lid, Bail, 7 In. | 177 |
| **Cologne Bottle,** Flowers, Cream, Yellow Ground, Melon Ribbed, Silver Flip Lid, 1894, 5 In. | 472 |
| **Sugar & Creamer,** Satin Glass, Shaded Opal To Blue, Gold Gingko, 3 ½ In. | 86 |
| **Sweetmeat,** Pink Flowers, Cream Ground, Melon Ribbed, Marked, 4 In. | 325 |
| **Vase,** Pink Roses, Cream, Green Ground, Melon Ribbed, Tapered, 8 ¼ In. | 413 |
| **Vase,** Purple, Blue Iris, Cream Ground, Ball Shape, Marked, 4 In. | 94 |

---

**SNOW BABIES,** made from bisque and spattered with glitter sand, were first manufactured in 1864 by Hertwig and Company of Thuringia. Other German and Japanese companies copied the Hertwig designs. Originally, Snow Babies were made of candy and used as Christmas decorations. There are also Snow Babies tablewares made by Royal Bayreuth. Copies of the small Snow Babies figurines are being made today and a line called "Snowbabies" was introduced by Department 56 in 1987. Don't confuse these with the original Snow Babies.

| | |
|---|---|
| **Figurine,** Boy, Arms Out, 3 In. | 43 |
| **Figurine,** Boy, Seated, Reaching Out Arms, c.1910, 1 ¾ x 2 In. | 75 |
| **Figurine,** Boy, Sitting On Red Sled, 1 ½ In. | 105 |
| **Figurine,** Child, On Sled, Red Silk Ribbon, Germany, c.1910, 3 ¼ In., 2 Piece ................*illus* | 189 |
| **Figurine,** Girl, On Sled, c.1900, 1 ¼ In. | 175 |
| **Figurine,** Girl, Riding Snow Bear, 2 ⅞ x 3 In. | 325 |
| **Figurine,** Girl, Santa, On Teeter-Totter, Feather Tree, 1910s, 3 In. | 275 |
| **Figurine,** Lamb, Bonzo, On Skis, c.1920, 2 In. | 195 |
| **Group,** Girl, Boy On Sled, 1920s, 2 In. | 89 |
| **Salt & Pepper,** Painted, 1 Blond, 1 Brunette, 4 In. | 53 |

---

**SNUFF BOTTLES** *are listed in the Bottle category.*

---

**SNUFFBOXES** held snuff. Taking snuff was popular long before cigarettes became available. The gentleman or lady would take a small pinch of the ground tobacco or snuff in the fingers, then sniff it and sneeze. Snuffboxes were made of many materials, including gold, silver, enameled metal, and wood. Most snuffboxes date from the late eighteenth or early nineteenth centuries.

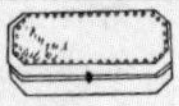

| | |
|---|---|
| **Brass,** Engraved Marriage Scene, 2 Hinged Lids, Oval, Dutch, 1700s, 3 x 4 In. | 805 |
| **Copper,** Embossed Man, Balance Scales, Oval, 1700s, 2 ⅞ x 3 ¾ In. | 259 |
| **Coquilla Wood,** Man, Tricorn Hat, Umbrella, Carved, Dutch, 3 ⅞ In. | 750 |
| **Enamel,** Chinoiserie Scenes, Gilt Metal Rims, Shell Shape, Hinged, England, 1847, 3 x 2 In. | 3450 |
| **Enamel,** Figural, Mouse, Sitting On Lid, Flowers, Under Base & Lid, 2 ¼ x 3 In. | 840 |
| **Hinged Lid,** Hobby Horse, Green, Men, Bicycles, 1 ¾ x 1 ¼ In. | 150 |
| **Horn,** Pressed, Queen Anne, Oval, Early 18th Century, 3 ¾ x 3 ⅛ In. | 360 |
| **Lacquer,** Hinged Lid, Valkhol Te Nymegen, Castle, Dutch, 1795, 5 In. | 84 |
| **Mother-Of-Pearl,** Gold Mounted, Glass, Jockey In Pursuit, 2 In. | 510 |
| **Mother-Of-Pearl,** Silver, Carved Figures, Pavilions, Mountain, Chinese, c.1850, 2 ½ In. | 600 |
| **Papier-Mache,** Horses, Riders, Spectators, 3 ½ x 2 ¼ In. | 330 |
| **Rose & Yellow Gold,** Engine Turned, Oval, Leaf Border, ¾ x 2 In. | 2500 |
| **Shell,** Cowrie, Hinged Lid, Silver Mounted, c.1800, 3 In. ..............*illus* | 240 |
| **Silver,** Hinged Dome Lid, Relief Musical Cherubs, Rococo Leaves, Shell, Round, 3 ½ In. | 270 |
| **Silver,** Hinged Lid, Engraved Flowers, Lattice, Latin Text, J. Shaw, 1809, 1 ¾ x 2 ⅞ In. | 230 |
| **Silver,** Hinged Lid, Relief Oriental Figures, Leeching, China Mark, c.1850, 2 ¾ x 1 ¾ In. | 874 |
| **Silver,** Leopard Head Shape, Hinged Jaw, Italy, 2 In. | 177 |
| **Silver,** Painted Porcelain Plaque Insert, Man, With Clay Pipe, c.1904, 1 ¼ x 2 ½ In. | 109 |
| **Silver,** Queen Anne, Oval, Bevel Edge, Lion, c.1710, ⅔ x 2 ⅞ In. | 450 |
| **Silver,** Repousse, Tavern Scene, Leaf Relief Sides, Mark, Scotland, 6 ½ x 4 ¾ In. | 529 |
| **Silver,** Sapphire, Hinged Lid, Simulated Amber, Rococo Scrolls, Applied Rim, c.1915, 3 x 2 In. | 984 |
| **Stone,** Mosaic Waterfall, Landscape, 14K Gold Trim, c.1900, 8 In. Diam. | 11244 |
| **Tortoiseshell,** Louis XV, Embossed Basket Weave, 20K Gold, Paris, c.1740, 2 ½ In. ..............*illus* | 1845 |

---

**SOAPSTONE** is a mineral that was used for foot warmers or griddles because of its heat-retaining properties. Soapstone was carved into figurines and bowls in many countries in the nineteenth and twentieth centuries. Most of the soapstone seen today is from China or Japan. It is still being carved in the old styles.

| | |
|---|---|
| **Boulder,** Carved, Elephants, Ocher To Gray, Carved Wood Base, Chinese, 1900s, 21 x 16 In......... | 590 |
| **Carving,** Fan, Archaic Style, Brownish Olive, Chinese, 1800s, 8 x 4½ In............................. | 119 |
| **Dish,** Lotus, Brown Mottled, Buds, Seed Pods, Chinese, 4 x 13 x 11 In............................. | 400 |
| **Figurine,** Arhat, Man Seated, Carved, Chinese, 4½ In................................................ | 115 |
| **Figurine,** Cockerel, Flowering Plum Branch, Yellow, Orange, Chinese, 1900s, 18 In................. | 246 |
| **Figurine,** Guanyin, Carved, Standing, Holding Lotus, Chinese, 14 In................................ | 450 |
| **Figurine,** Hawk, 2 Hatchlings, Northwest Coast, 18¾ x 13 x 6 In.................................. | 325 |
| **Figurine,** Inuit, Owl, Caravaggio, Signed, 12¾ In.................................................. | 1200 |
| **Figurine,** Quanyin, Green, Robed, Standing, Red Rock Base, Chinese, c.1950, 18½ In............... | 492 |
| **Group,** Boy, Standing On Basket, Offering Peach To Robed Man, Carved, Chinese, 10 In............ | 480 |
| **Group,** Rocky Landscape, Squirrels, Vines, Berries, Red, Brown, Wood Stand, 7¾ x 10 In. ......... | 900 |
| **Vase,** Flowering Bushes, Rocks, Birds, Chinese, 20th Century, 8⅜ x 6½ In........................ | 369 |
| **Wax Seal,** Foo Dog Finial, Tien Huang Shih, Chinese, c.1910, 2¼ In. .............................. | 7110 |
| **Wax Seal,** Inuit, 20th Century, 12 In................................................................ | 120 |

---

**SOFT PASTE** is a name for a type of pottery. Although it looks very much like porcelain, it is a chemically different material. Most of the soft-paste wares were made in the early nineteenth century. Other pieces may be listed under Gaudy Dutch or Leeds.

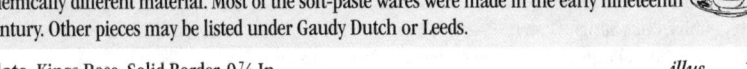

| | | |
|---|---|---|
| **Plate,** Kings Rose, Solid Border, 9⅞ In....................................................*illus* | 142 |
| **Toddy Plate,** King's Rose & Oyster Variant, 6¼ In.......................................*illus* | 83 |

---

**SOUVENIRS** of a trip—what could be more fun? Our ancestors enjoyed the same thing and souvenirs were made for almost every location. Most of the souvenir pottery and porcelain pieces of the nineteenth century were made in England or Germany, even if the picture showed a North American scene. In the twentieth century, the souvenir china business seems to have been dominated by the manufacturers in Japan, Taiwan, Hong Kong, England, and the United States. Another popular souvenir item is the souvenir spoon, made of sterling or silver plate. These are usually made in the country pictured on the spoon. Related pieces may be found in the Coronation and World's Fair categories.

| | | |
|---|---|---|
| **Bottle Stopper,** SS Orsiva, Orient Line Crest, Brass, Enamel, 1909, 4 In........................ | 59 |
| **Button,** Chiquita, Cuban Midget, Gown, Holding Fan, Pan-Am Expo, c.1901, 2⅛ In. ..........*illus* | 325 |
| **Button,** Yazoo Valley, Cotton Field, Black Workers, Cello, 1¼ In.................................. | 109 |
| **Medal,** Olympics, 1964, Tokyo, Silver, Runners, Torch, 2⅜ In. ................................... | 86 |
| **Plate,** Minnesota, Gopher State, Images, 22K Gold Trim, 7⅜ In.................................... | 15 |
| **Thimble,** Grand Canyon National Park, Incised, Juniper Wood, 1970s, 1¼ In..................... | 12 |
| **Thimble,** Lincoln Cathedral, Gold Trim, Cotswold China, 1 In. .................................... | 8 |

---

**SPANISH LACE** *is listed in the Opalescent category as Opaline Brocade.*

---

**SPATTER GLASS** is a multicolored glass made from many small pieces of different colored glass. It is sometimes called End-of-Day glass. It is still being made.

| | |
|---|---|
| **Biscuit Jar,** Multicolor, White Interior, Brass Fitting, Handle, c.1900, 7½ In................. | 92 |
| **Carafe,** Water, Opal & Cranberry Flakes, Multicolor Flowers, c.1900, 6¼ In. ................. | 196 |

---

**SPATTERWARE** and spongeware are terms that have changed in meaning in recent years, causing much confusion for collectors. Some say that *spatterware* is the term used by Americans, *sponged ware* or *spongeware* by the English. Spatterware is creamware or soft paste dinnerware decorated with colored spatter designs. The earliest pieces were made in the late eighteenth century, but most of the spatterware found today was made from about 1800 to 1850. Early spatterware was made in the Staffordshire district of England for sale in America. Collectors also use the word *spatterware* to refer to kitchen crockery with added spatter made in America during the late nineteenth and early twentieth centuries. Spongeware is very similar to spatterware in appearance. Designs were applied to ceramics by daubing the color on with a sponge or cloth. Many collectors do not differentiate between spongeware and spatterware and use the names interchangeably. Modern pottery is being made to resemble old spongeware, but careful examination will show it is new.

| | |
|---|---|
| **Creamer,** Blue, Rooster, 2-Sided, Yellow Body, Blue Wing, Red Tail, 3½ In................................... | 767 |
| **Creamer,** Peafowl, 4 In. ............................................................................ | 75 |
| **Cup & Saucer,** Blue Flower Pattern, Yellow, Handleless, c.1825 ................................ | 600 |
| **Cup & Saucer,** Blue, Demitasse, 2 x 4¼ In. ...................................................... | 12 |
| **Cup & Saucer,** Bull's-Eye, Rainbow, Red & Purple, Handleless ................................ | 210 |
| **Cup & Saucer,** Morning Glory, Yellow, Handleless, c.1825 ...................................... | 330 |
| **Cup & Saucer,** Rainbow, Red & Yellow Thistle, Handleless Cups, 6 Piece ..................... | 1320 |
| **Cup & Saucer,** Rainbow, Red, Green, Blue, Bull's-Eye Center, Handleless, 5¾ In. ..................... | 2596 |

**Sports,** Baseball, Catcher's Mask, Winchester
$1,900

**Sports,** Baseball, Nodder, Chief Wahoo, Cleveland Indians, Composition, Japan, c.1961, 4 In.
$221

**Sports,** Baseball, Pennant, 1971 World Series Champs, Pittsburgh Pirates, 29 x 12 In.
$47

S

# SPATTERWARE

**Sports,** Baseball, Ticket Stub, 1920 World Series, Cleveland Indians, Dunn Field, Game 3
$569

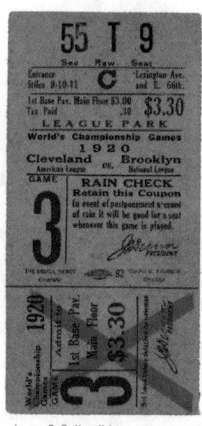

**Sports,** Baseball, Ticket, 1915 World Series, Game 1, Red Sox At Phillies, 1½ x 4¼ In.
$5,452

**Sports,** Football, Card, Rookie, Jimmy Brown, Fullback, Cleveland Browns, 1958, 2½ x 3½ In.
$253

| | |
|---|---:|
| **Cup & Saucer,** Rainbow, Red, Yellow, Thistle, Handleless, c.1825 | 330 |
| **Cup & Saucer,** Red & Blue, Central Bull's-Eye, Handleless, 5¾ In. | 24 |
| **Cup & Saucer,** Red & Green Rainbow, Handleless | 106 |
| **Cup & Saucer,** Red, Blue Tick, Child's, 4¼ In. | 142 |
| **Cup & Saucer,** Red, Green Rainbow, Center Bull's-Eye, Handless, 5¾ In. | 295 |
| **Cup & Saucer,** Thistle, Red & Yellow, Handleless | 540 |
| **Cup & Saucer,** Tulip, Red, Blue, 1800s | 332 |
| **Mixing Bowl,** Brown, Green, Early 20th Century, 5½ x 12½ In. | 221 |
| **Pitcher,** Molded Handle & Spout, Multicolor Stripes, c.1825, 7 In. | 1020 |
| **Pitcher,** Rainbow, Molded Handle, c.1835, 7 In. ...............................*illus* | 360 |
| **Pitcher,** Washbowl, Cobalt Blue, White Ground, Oval, Footed Base, Scroll Handle, c.1900, 11 In. | 58 |
| **Pitcher,** Water, Rainbow, Red, Blue, Green, Shaped Handle, 8¾ In. | 2360 |
| **Pitcher,** Yellow, Red Tulip, Green Leaves, Paneled, Tapered, Shaped Handle, 9¾ In. | 649 |
| **Plate,** Blue, Red Rose, Green Leaves, 9½ In. | 47 |
| **Plate,** China Fort, Blue, Red, Green Trees, 9⅝ In. | 212 |
| **Plate,** Columbine, Stick Spatter, Flowers, Leaves, Daisy Border, 8⅝ In. ..........*illus* | 118 |
| **Plate,** Dahlia, Blue, Scalloped Border, England, 8 In., 3 Piece | 960 |
| **Plate,** Dahlia, Blue, Sprigs, Flowers, Paneled, 9 In. | 323 |
| **Plate,** Pansy, Stick, Purple, Yellow Flower, Green, Red Bowtie Border, 2¾ In., 5 Piece | 266 |
| **Plate,** Peafowl, Red, Blue, Green, Blue Border, 7½ In. | 154 |
| **Plate,** Peafowl, Red, Blue, Yellow, 9⅜ In. | 295 |
| **Plate,** Rabbits Playing, Field, Border, Blue & Red Leaves, 9¼ In., Pair ...............*illus* | 325 |
| **Plate,** Rabbitware, Leaf Stick, Multicolor Flowers, Ironstone, 9¼ In. | 189 |
| **Plate,** Rabbitware, Virginia Rose, Multicolor, Ironstone, 9¼ In. | 177 |
| **Plate,** Rainbow, Purple & Black, 8¼ In. | 240 |
| **Plate,** Rainbow, Red, Blue, Green, Scalloped Edge, 9¼ In. | 236 |
| **Plate,** Schoolhouse, Blue, Green Tree, Red Border, c.1855, 8 In. | 960 |
| **Plate,** Schoolhouse, Red, 10⅜ In. | 960 |
| **Plate,** Toddy, China Rose, Red Rose, Blue Bed, Green Leaves, Paneled, Ironstone, 6⅜ In. | 266 |
| **Plate,** Tulip, Blue & Red, Paneled, 8⅜ In. ...............................*illus* | 502 |
| **Platter,** Blue & Purple, Nesting Ovals, Alternating Stripe Border, 8-Sided, 15¾ In. | 246 |
| **Platter,** Peafowl, Blue Center & Border, 8-Sided, England, 14 x 18 In. | 1200 |
| **Platter,** Peafowl, Octagonal Molded Edge, Red, c.1825, 10 x 13 In. | 420 |
| **Platter,** Stylized Cluster Of Rosebuds, Blue Border, 8-Sided, 12 x 15 In. | 840 |
| **Saucer,** Peafowl, Green Ground, 4¾ In. | 210 |
| **Sugar,** Lid, Blue, Rooster, c.1825, 5 In. | 308 |
| **Sugar,** Rainbow, Green, Blue, Paneled, Bulbous, Footed, Leaf Shape Handles, 6¾ In. | 590 |
| **Sugar,** Rainbow, Thistle, Red, Yellow, Paneled, Tapered, Footed, Shaped Open Handles, 8 In. | 5310 |
| **Sugar,** Rainbow, Tulip, Red, Purple, 4½ In. | 118 |
| **Tea Set,** Individual, Blue, Rooster, Handleless Cup, 3 Piece, 6 In. | 720 |

**SPELTER** is a synonym for a zinc alloy. Figurines, candlesticks, and other pieces were made of spelter and given a bronze or painted finish. The metal has been used since about the 1860s to make statues, tablewares, and lamps that resemble bronze. Spelter is soft and breaks easily. To test for spelter, scratch the base of the piece. Bronze is solid; spelter will show a silvery scratch.

| | |
|---|---:|
| **Bust,** Woman, Headdress, Coral, Gold, Beaded Jewelry, Paint, c.1900, 28½ In. | 720 |
| **Pocket Watch Holder,** Dog, Going Over Fence, Signed C. Valton, 8 In. | 185 |
| **Sculpture,** Arab Man, Pipe, Arab Woman, Thread Spool, Cold Paint, c.1905, 20¾ In., Pair | 2125 |
| **Sculpture,** Bedouin Prince, Horseback, Cold Paint, E. Guillemin, c.1895, 32 x 24 In. | 2000 |
| **Sculpture,** Cleopatra, Lamp, Wood Base, 20 In. | 106 |
| **Sculpture,** Fireman Charging, Signed X. Rapahanel, 20 In., Pair | 510 |
| **Sculpture,** Good Fairy, Patina, Round Base, Raleigh Jessie, Signed J.M.R., 11 In. | 62 |
| **Sculpture,** Horse, Saddled, Standing, 23¼ In. | 281 |

**SPINNING WHEELS** in the corner have been symbols of earlier times for the past 100 years. Although spinning wheels date back to medieval days, the ones found today are rarely more than 200 years old. Because the style of the spinning wheel changed very little, it is often impossible to place an exact date on a wheel.

| | |
|---|---:|
| **Castle,** Mixed Wood, Pa., 1800s, 55½ In. | 1180 |
| **Chestnut,** Mixed Woods, Signed, S. Humes, Pennsylvania, 1811, 46½ In. ............*illus* | 212 |
| **Flax,** Mixed Woods, Blue Paint, c.1810, 43½ In., Wheel 25 In. | 173 |
| **Mixed Woods,** Black Paint, 1800s, 46½ x 31 In. | 81 |
| **Mixed Woods,** Flax, 29 In. | 92 |
| **Wood,** White Paint, Gilt Accents, c.1850, 48 x 24 In. | 92 |

S

**SPODE** pottery, porcelain, and bone china were made by the Stoke-on-Trent factory of England founded by Josiah Spode about 1770. The firm became Copeland and Garrett from 1833 to 1847, then W.T. Copeland or W.T. Copeland and Sons until 1976. It then became Royal Worcester Spode Ltd. The company was bought by the Portmeirion Group in 2009. The word *Spode* appears on many pieces made by the factories. Most collectors include all the wares under the more familiar name of Spode. Porcelains are listed in this book by the name that appears on the piece. Related pieces may be listed under Copeland, Copeland Spode, and Royal Worcester.

| | |
|---|---|
| **Basket,** Under Tray Reticulated, Blue Flower Transfer, Gilt, c.1850, 8 ½ In. | 200 |
| **Cup,** Tulip Form, Single Flower, Green, Red, White, Octagonal Base, Handle, c.1820, 3 In., Pair.. | 554 |
| **Ginger Jar,** Lid, Flowers, Blue Ground, Gilt, Copeland, 12 x 8 ½ In. | 113 |
| **Plate,** Dinner, Stafford Flowers, 1900s, 11 In., 12 Piece | 1722 |
| **Platter,** Campsite, Figures, Dogs, Exotic Animal Border, Indian Sporting Series, 14 x 18 In. | 420 |
| **Platter,** Hunting Campsite, Indian Sporting Series, Blue Transfer, c.1815, 14 x 18 In. ..........*illus* | 420 |
| **Platter,** Imari, Frog Pattern, Blue, Red Transfer, Raised Wood Stand, c.1825, 16 ¾ In. | 780 |
| **Tureen,** Sauce, Lid, Blue, Flowers, Gilt, Lobed Sides, Leaf Relief, Handles, Footed, 5 x 8 In. | 98 |

**SPORTS** equipment, sporting goods, brochures, and related items are listed here. Items are listed by sport. Other categories of interest are Bicycle, Card, Fishing, Sword, Toy, and Trap.

| | |
|---|---|
| **Baseball,** Badge, 1943, St. Louis, 2 Cardinals, Perched On Baseball Bat, Celluloid, 2 In.......*illus* | 1123 |
| **Baseball,** Ball, Autographed, 26 Players, New York Yankees, 1970 | 813 |
| **Baseball,** Ball, Autographed, 28 Spring Training Players, Pittsburgh Pirates, 1947 | 1625 |
| **Baseball,** Ball, Autographed, 34 Players, New York Yankees, 1954 | 2125 |
| **Baseball,** Ball, Autographed, Babe Ruth, Additional Inscription, c.1946 .........................*illus* | 4500 |
| **Baseball,** Ball, Autographed, Cy Young, Milwaukee Braves, 1955 | 1375 |
| **Baseball,** Ball, Autographed, Reggie Jackson, 44, Mr. October, Selig | 74 |
| **Baseball,** Ball, Autographed, Ted Williams, Harridge, Vintage | 1033 |
| **Baseball,** Ball, Autographed, Walter Johnston, Signed On Sweet Spot | 2625 |
| **Baseball,** Ball, Autographed, Yankees, 1925-27, 16 Signatures, Fountain Pen | 6250 |
| **Baseball,** Baseball, Team Autographed, Detroit Tigers, 1948 | 210 |
| **Baseball,** Bat, Autographed, 60 Players, Cooperstown Hall Of Fame, 1989, 34 In. | 1063 |
| **Baseball,** Bat, Ross Young's Model, Wood, Marked Louisville Slugger, 34 In. | 4500 |
| **Baseball,** Button, Ribbon, All-Star Game, Washington, American League Roster, 1937, 2 In., Pair | 196 |
| **Baseball,** Catcher's Mask, Winchester.................................................................*illus* | 1900 |
| **Baseball,** Cuff Links, Red Sox, Socks, Baseball, Gold Tone, Reverse Painted, 1950s | 69 |
| **Baseball,** Jersey, Autographed, 23 Players, New York Mets World Series, 1986 | 750 |
| **Baseball,** Lithograph, On Paper, Double Play, Fletcher Martin, Frame, c.1950, 9 x 13 In. | 375 |
| **Baseball,** Nodder, Chief Wahoo, Cleveland Indians, Composition, Japan, c.1961, 4 In..........*illus* | 221 |
| **Baseball,** Pen & Pencil, Bat Shape, Faux Signature, Mize, DiMaggio, Hillerich, Bradsby, 1940s, 5 In. | 29 |
| **Baseball,** Pennant, 1971 World Series Champs, Pittsburgh Pirates, 29 x 12 In.....................*illus* | 47 |
| **Baseball,** Pennant, Dodger Stadium Grand Opening, Dodgers, Angels, 1962, 29 x 11 In. | 47 |
| **Baseball,** Photograph, 1922 Cleveland Indians, Panoramic, 8 ½ x 28 In. | 665 |
| **Baseball,** Press Pin, All-Star Game, St. Louis, Converted To Charm, Balfour, 1966 | 38 |
| **Baseball,** Program, Sluggers Of 1930, Louisville Slugger Ruth, Gehrig On Cover, 5 x 8 In. | 93 |
| **Baseball,** Ticket Stub, 1920 World Series, Cleveland Indians, Dunn Field, Game 3 ...............*illus* | 569 |
| **Baseball,** Ticket, 1915 World Series, Game 1, Red Sox At Phillies, 1 ½ x 4 ¼ In. ...................*illus* | 5452 |
| **Baseball,** Traffic Light, Round Lamp Cover, New York Yankees, Green Metal, 13 x 15 In. | 345 |
| **Baseball,** Uniform, Denver Bears, Strike Zone, Flannel, Western League Jersey, Pants, 1952 | 780 |
| **Basketball,** Gold Medal, Howard Cann, NYU, Helms Olympic Foundation | 213 |
| **Billiards,** Table, Oak, Ivory Inlay, Leather Pockets, Narragansett, Brunswick, 1898 | 2875 |
| **Boxing,** Clock, Shelf, Embossed Joe Louis World Champion, Electric, Marked Sessions, 12 In. .... | 300 |
| **Boxing,** Poster, Autographed, Muhammad Ali, Joe Frazier, L. Neiman, Frame, c.1975, 14 x 22 In. | 1250 |
| **Boxing,** Presentation Glove, Muhammad Ali Signed, To Bob Finkel, Oversize, 1975 | 1202 |
| **Canoeing,** Paddle, Figured Maple, 19th Century, 59 In. | 277 |
| **Canoeing,** Paddle, Figured Maple, Flared Knob End, 19th Century, 56 In. | 800 |
| **Canoeing,** Paddle, Punting, Wood, Iron End, 114 In. | 215 |
| **Exercise,** Club, Wood, Twisted Rope Carved, Turk's Head End, 20 In. | 150 |
| **Exercise,** Indian Club, Gold Medal, Spalding, Francais Expositionale 1900, Pair | 72 |
| **Exercise,** Indian Club, Wood, Red Paint, c.1900, 14 ½ In., Pair | 37 |
| **Football,** Award, Hertz, Reggie White, O.J. Simpson, Tennessee No. 1, c.1980, 16 x 20 In. | 225 |
| **Football,** Card, Rookie, Jimmy Brown, Fullback, Cleveland Browns, 1958, 2 ½ x 3 ½ In.......*illus* | 253 |
| **Football,** Game Ball, Reggie White, Green Bay Packers, Against Tampa Bay, 1994 | 944 |
| **Football,** Helmet, Bob Avellini, Chicago Bears, No. 7, Riddell Suspension, 1970s | 707 |
| **Football,** Helmut, Brett Favre Signature, Super Bowl XXXII, White, Logo | 481 |
| **Football,** Helmut, Vaughan Johnson, New Orleans Saints, Dome Patrol, 1986-1993 | 1143 |
| **Football,** Pennant, Wilberforce, Green, Yellow, Felt, c.1940, 31 ½ In. | 60 |

**Sports,** Skating, Roller Skates, 3 Wheels, Leather Straps, Shoelace, Metal Platform, 11 x 5 In.
$146

Copake Auction

**Sports,** Skating, Roller Skates, Metal, Leather, 2 Wheels, Kennedy Pat.'d May 5th 09, 11 ½ In.
$70

Copake Auction

**Sports,** Skating, Roller Skates, Wood, Metal, 4 Wheels, Leather Straps, 9 In.
$47

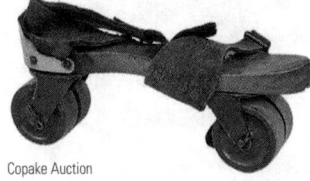

Copake Auction

**TIP**

*Avoid hanging your sports pennants in direct sunlight. They fade rapidly. Even indirect sunlight can fade the felt. Display pennants in frames with UV glass. Avoid thumbtacks, which leave rusty holes.*

S

**Staffordshire,** Bowl, Agateware, Blue, Rust, Brown, 1700s, 15 ½ In.
$2,360

Brunk Auctions

**Staffordshire,** Creamer, Hunt Scene, Blue Transfer, Silver, 4 In.
$354

Conestoga Auction Co., Inc.

**Staffordshire,** Cup & Saucer, Bee Skep Pattern, Purple Transfer, Handleless, Child's
$71

Conestoga Auction Co., Inc.

**Staffordshire,** Dish, Hen On Nest Lid, Painted, 9 x 6½ In.
$266

Conestoga Auction Co., Inc.

**Staffordshire,** Figurine, Ben Franklin, Blue & White, Titled Washington, 1800s, 16 In.
$1,552

Cottone Auctions

| | |
|---|---:|
| **Football,** Poster, Ballplayer, Jersey, Richmond College Emblem, c.1911, Frame, 22 x 14 In. | 184 |
| **Football,** Ticket Stub, Program, Super Bowl VII, Jan. 14, 1973 | 116 |
| **Golf,** Award, Gold Putter, Peter Oosterhuis, Schoeman Park Open, Ping Anser, 1971 | 498 |
| **Golf,** Marker, Zinc, Painted, Heart Shape, 1900s, 3 Piece | 545 |
| **Golf,** Wire Photograph, Henry Cotton, British Open Champion, 1934, 5 x 8 In. | 59 |
| **Hunting,** Duck Call, Raised Checkered Panels, c.1930, 4 In. | 3998 |
| **Hunting,** Duck Call, Raised Checkered Panels, Carved Bird-Like S, c.1920, 6⅜ In. | 1920 |
| **Hunting,** Duck Call, Raised Checkered Panels, Flying Duck, Marked, Crooks, c.1930, 6½ In. | 180 |
| **Hunting,** Duck Call, Raised Checkered Panels, Silver Stars, Marked, W.E. Boyd, 5½ In. | 3383 |
| **Hunting,** Trap Thrower, Spring Action, Green, 21 x 17 In. | 480 |
| **Lawn Tennis,** Poster, Turneir Heiligendammn, Woman Player, Hans Rudi Erdt, 1908, 38 x 27 In. | 4750 |
| **Polo,** Rack, Oak, 8 Top Bar Holes, Turned Supports, Continental, c.1860, 40 x 53 In., Pair | 480 |
| **Skating,** Ice Skates, Oak, Steel Curlicue Terminals, c.1870, 12½ In., Pair | 480 |
| **Skating,** Ice Skates, Tall, Wrought Iron, Leather, 34 In. | 263 |
| **Skating,** Roller Skates, 2 Wheels, Metal, Pat's Aug. 18, 1896, Buffalo Foot Cycle, 10 In. | 23 |
| **Skating,** Roller Skates, 3 Wheels, Leather Straps, Shoelace, Metal Platform, 11 x 5 In.........*illus* | 146 |
| **Skating,** Roller Skates, Metal, Leather, 2 Wheels, Kennedy Pat.'d May 5th 09, 11½ In. .........*illus* | 70 |
| **Skating,** Roller Skates, Wood, Metal, 4 Wheels, Leather Straps, 9 In. ......................*illus* | 47 |
| **Skating,** Roller Skates, Wood Body, Nickel Plated Heel, Cast Iron Wheel Holders, c.1890, 8½ In. | 47 |
| **Snowshoes,** Leather, Wood, A.G. Spalding, c.1910, 40 In., Pair. | 86 |
| **Snowshoes,** Wood, Leather, Marked U.S., C.A. Lund, Hastings, Minn., 1942, 56 In. | 34 |
| **Stationary Bicycle,** Gym-Cycle, Everlast Sporting Goods, c.1930s, 53 x 14 In. | 660 |
| **Tennis,** Poster, Davis Cup Wimbledon, Interzone Final, 1936, Walter Goetz, 9¾ x 12 In. | 1792 |
| **Tennis,** Poster, Dunlop Tennis, Boy, Armful Of Balls, Franz Jakob Hinklein, 1926, 36 x 24 In. | 1875 |
| **Tennis,** Poster, Health! Is Priceless, Man, Woman Playing Tennis, 1928, 27 x 22 In. | 1875 |
| **Tennis,** Poster, Nationale Lawn-Tennis Kampionenschppen, Orange, Blue, Kalff, 1922, 37 x 22 In. | 3750 |
| **Tennis,** Poster, Western Lawn Tennis Tournament, Kenwood Club, Penfield, 1896, 28 x 19 In. | 1000 |
| **Tennis,** Poster, What's Your Score, Man, Playing Tennis, Mather & Co., 1929, 44 x 36 In. | 2500 |
| **Tennis,** Sign, Dunlop Frank Sedgman, Man, Playing Tennis, Racket, Yellow, 1954, 30 x 40 In. | 1188 |
| **Tennis,** Sign, Tennis Platze, Woman, Yellow Tennis Attire, R. Matouschek, c.1927, 33 x 21 In. | 2125 |
| **Wrestling,** Boots, White Leather, Simple Ravishing, Rick Rude, Size 10½, 17 In. | 160 |

**STAFFORDSHIRE,** England, has been a district making pottery and porcelain since the 1700s. Hundreds of kilns are still working in the area. Thousands of types of pottery and porcelain have been made in the many factories that worked and still work in the area. Some of the most famous factories have been listed separately, such as Adams, Davenport, Ridgway, Rowland & Marsellus, Royal Doulton, Royal Worcester, Spode, Wedgwood, and others. Some Staffordshire pieces are listed under categories like Fairing, Flow Blue, Mulberry, Shaving Mug, etc.

| | |
|---|---:|
| **Basin,** Rebecca At The Well, Dark Blue Transfer, James & Ralph Clews, c.1820, 12¾ In. | 240 |
| **Bidet,** Castle, River, Flower Border, Transfer, Blue, 9 x 16 In. | 420 |
| **Bowl,** Agateware, Blue, Rust, Brown, 1700s, 15½ In. ......................................*illus* | 2360 |
| **Bowl,** Vegetable, Capitol Washington, Blue Transfer, Octagonal, T. Godwin, 9⅜ In., c.1844 | 300 |
| **Bowl,** Vegetable, Lid, Blue Transfer, Reclining Lion Finial, Sea Scene, 6¾ x 10¼ In. | 94 |
| **Bust,** George Washington, Marbleized Plinth Base, 8½ In. | 600 |
| **Card Tray,** Playing Card Center, Pierced Blue Ground, Scalloped Rim, c.1775, 3¾ In., Pair | 360 |
| **Casserole,** Hen On Nest Cover, Bisque, Colors, 7½ x 9 In. | 325 |
| **Charger,** Salt Glaze, Snakeskin Banding, Open Center, 1700s, 15 In. | 649 |
| **Creamer,** Baltimore Masonic Hall, Dark Blue, c.1820, 5½ In. | 3840 |
| **Creamer,** Hunt Scene, Blue Transfer, Silver, 4 In. ...................................*illus* | 354 |
| **Creamer,** Lamb, Flowers, 8½ x 4½ In. | 125 |
| **Creamer,** Lid, Cow, Milkmaid, Painted, c.1810, 5½ x 6¾ In. | 561 |
| **Cup & Saucer,** Bee Skep Pattern, Purple Transfer, Handleless, Child's ..................*illus* | 71 |
| **Cup & Saucer,** Children Playing, Dog, Leaf Border | 158 |
| **Cup & Saucer,** Peafowl, Blue, Yellow, Red, Branch, Green Leaves, Handleless, 5¾ In. | 266 |
| **Dish,** Entree, Lid, Black Finial, 3 Peasants, Landscape, Blue, White, Oval, c.1870, 6 x 13 In. | 400 |
| **Dish,** Hen On Nest Lid, Painted, 9 x 6½ In. ........................................*illus* | 266 |
| **Figurine,** Abraham Lincoln, On Horseback, Waistcoat, Cloak, Yellow Saddle, c.1870, 15 In. | 480 |
| **Figurine,** Ben Franklin, Blue & White, Titled Washington, 1800s, 16 In. .............*illus* | 1552 |
| **Figurine,** Ben Franklin, Labeled As General Washington, c.1820, 15 In. .............*illus* | 330 |
| **Figurine,** Benjamin Franklin, Holding Hat, Paper, Painted, 1800s, 14 In. | 900 |
| **Figurine,** Bird, Manganese, Yellow Spots, Painted, c.1800, 3⅞ In. | 345 |
| **Figurine,** Boy, Girl, Pink, Green, Bush, 11 In., 2 Piece | 180 |
| **Figurine,** Cow, Calf, Brown, White, 7 x 8 In. | 329 |
| **Figurine,** Dog, Bulldog, Holding Basket In Mouth, 2 Puppies, Blue Bow, 6 In., Pair | 266 |
| **Figurine,** Dog, Poodle, Curly, Sitting, White, c.1875, 3 In., Pair | 145 |
| **Figurine,** Dog, Spaniel, Black, White Spots, c.1850, 12½ In., Pair | 480 |

**Staffordshire,** Figurine, Ben Franklin, Labeled As General Washington, c.1820, 15 In. $330

DuMouchelles Art Gallery

**Staffordshire,** Group, Tam O'Shanter, Scooter Johnny, Seated, Barrel, c.1850, 9½ In. $240

DuMouchelles Art Gallery

**Staffordshire,** Group, Uncle Tom, Eva, Standing On His Knee, Flowered Vest, c.1850, 10 In. $480

DuMouchelles Art Gallery

**Staffordshire,** Inkwell, Figural, Dog, Whippet, Resting, Natural Colors, Cobalt Blue Base, 5¾ In. $59

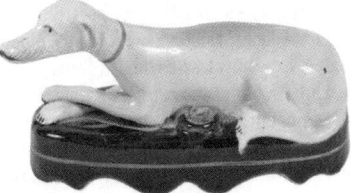

Conestoga Auction Co., Inc.

**Staffordshire,** Mug, A Present For A Good Boy, Archery Scene, Transfer, Child's, 2½ In. $295

Conestoga Auction Co., Inc.

**Staffordshire,** Pitcher, Figural, Bear, Chain, Dog Is Spout, Bears Grease, c.1825, 12 In. $61

James D. Julia Auctioneers

**Staffordshire,** Plate, Chief Justice Marshall, Paddleboat, Blue, Enoch Wood & Sons, c.1830, 10 In. $590

Conestoga Auction Co., Inc.

**Staffordshire,** Plate, Commodore MacDonnough's Victory, Blue Transfer, Wood, c.1820, 10½ In. $180

DuMouchelles Art Gallery

**Staffordshire,** Plate, Peace On Earth, Millennium, Brown Transfer, 7½ In. $83

Conestoga Auction Co., Inc.

S

**Staffordshire,** Plate, Soup, Residence Of The Late Richard Jordan, New Jersey, Red Transfer, 10¾ In.
**$212**

Conestoga Auction Co., Inc.

**Staffordshire,** Platter, View Of London, Thames River, T. & B. Godwin, 1800s, 17 In.
**$360**

DuMouchelles Art Gallery

**Staffordshire,** Stand, Pocket Watch, Figural, Man & Woman, Scottish Attire, Wreath, 1800s, 9 x 5 In.
**$72**

DuMouchelles Art Gallery

| | |
|---|---:|
| **Figurine,** Dog, Spaniel, Multicolor, Gilt, 12 x 11 In., Pair | 123 |
| **Figurine,** Dog, Spaniel, Spotted, Pink, White, 10½ x 14 In., Pair | 150 |
| **Figurine,** Duke Of Wellington, Seated, Book In Hand, 1800s, 12 In. | 190 |
| **Figurine,** George Washington, White Suit, Gilt Trim, 1800s, 15 In. | 2280 |
| **Figurine,** Girl, Blue Dress, Horse, Yellow Saddle, 12 In. | 60 |
| **Figurine,** Girl, In Dress, Dog, Mid 19th Century, 9 x 7½ In. | 300 |
| **Figurine,** Girl, Pointing Upward, Old Woman, Tree Trunk, 12 In. | 59 |
| **Figurine,** Lion, 10¾ In., Pair | 360 |
| **Figurine,** Musicians, Reclining, Man, Woman, Book, Mandolin, c.1860, 8 In., Pair | 150 |
| **Figurine,** Protestantism, Popery, Painted, Holding Bible, Scrolls, 1800s, 8¾ x 9 In. | 590 |
| **Figurine,** Robert Burns, Holding Book, Leaning On Tree, Painted, Gilt, 13 x 7 In. | 58 |
| **Figurine,** Shakespeare, Leaning In Stack Of Books, Pedestal, c.1770, 12 In. | 313 |
| **Figurine,** Sultan Abd-Ul-Medjid, Sultan Of Turkey, 1800s, 15 In. | 954 |
| **Figurine,** Uncle Tom & Eva, Uncle Tom's Cabin Characters, 7 In. | 215 |
| **Figurine,** Widow Of Zarephat, Holding Sticks, Boy, Standing, c.1815, 10 In. | 104 |
| **Game Pie Dish,** Hen On Nest Cover, Painted, c.1850, 9½ In. | 270 |
| **Group,** London 30 Miles, Man, Holding Hat, Woman Sitting By Mile Marker, c.1840, 11 In. | 81 |
| **Group,** Tam O'Shanter, Scooter Johnny, Seated, Barrel, c.1850, 9½ In. ......*illus* | 240 |
| **Group,** Uncle Tom, Eva, Standing On His Knee, Flowered Vest, c.1850, 10 In. ......*illus* | 480 |
| **Inkwell,** Figural, Dog, Whippet, Resting, Natural Colors, Cobalt Blue Base, 5¾ In. ......*illus* | 59 |
| **Jug,** Fruit Basket, Sparrow Beak, Wm. Greatbach, c.1770, 4½ In. | 288 |
| **Jug,** Green, Swirl Molded, Concentric Bands, c.1800, 4½ In. | 1265 |
| **Jug,** Milk, Footed, Lion, Paw Feet, c.1700s, 3½ In. | 1625 |
| **Jug,** Silver Resist Luster, Peacock, Robin, Greek Key Border, Brown, Tan, c.1820, 6½ In. | 300 |
| **Mug,** A Present For A Good Boy, Archery Scene, Transfer, Child's, 2½ In. ......*illus* | 295 |
| **Mug,** A Trifle For Thomas, Acorn Border, Red, Yellow Glaze, c.1820, 2¼ In. | 540 |
| **Mug,** Blue, Black & White Band, Molded Swag, Barrel Shape, c.1800, 3¾ In. | 431 |
| **Mug,** Christmas Musicians, Taking The Sharp Edge Of Text, Black Transfer, c.1815, 2½ In. | 1200 |
| **Mug,** Martha, Brown, Transfer Printed, 1810-20, 2⅜ In. | 660 |
| **Mug,** October, Mother, Child, Goat, Grapes, Brown Transfer, c.1815, 2⅜ In. | 570 |
| **Mug,** Samuel, Child, Kneeling, Stairs, Column, Black Transfer, c.1815, 2½ In. | 240 |
| **Pitcher & Bowl Set,** Asiatic Fountain, Red Transfer, 10 & 12¼ In. | 59 |
| **Pitcher & Bowl Set,** Bologna, Purple Transfer, Impressed Adams, 12½ x 9½ In. | 142 |
| **Pitcher,** Basin, Blue Transfer, Landscape, 1800s, Pitcher 8¾ In., Basin 4 x 12 In., 2 Piece | 180 |
| **Pitcher,** Basin, Calico, Blue Chintz, White Flowers, Blue Ground, 14¾ In. | 86 |
| **Pitcher,** Figural, Bear, Chain, Dog Is Spout, Bears Grease, c.1825, 12 In. ......*illus* | 61 |
| **Plate,** Arms Of The States, Rhode Island, Dark Blue, T. Mayer, c.1830, 8½ In. | 300 |
| **Plate,** Chief Justice Marshall, Paddleboat, Blue, Enoch Wood & Sons, c.1830, 10 In. ......*illus* | 590 |
| **Plate,** Commodore MacDonnough's Victory, Blue Transfer, Wood, c.1820, 10½ In. ......*illus* | 180 |
| **Plate,** Dinner, Brunswick Star, Brown Transfer, Scalloped Edge, 10¼ In. | 47 |
| **Plate,** Early Train In Landscape, Blue Transfer, Shell Border, E. Wood & Sons, c.1820, 10 In. | 660 |
| **Plate,** Fairmount Near Philadelphia, Blue, 10¼ In. | 85 |
| **Plate,** Historical Blue Transfer, Fall Of Montmorenci, Flowers, 9 In. | 354 |
| **Plate,** Park Theater New York, Blue Transfer, Acorn & Leaf Border, 10⅛ In. | 248 |
| **Plate,** Peace On Earth, Millennium, Brown Transfer, 7½ In. ......*illus* | 83 |
| **Plate,** Soup, Residence Of The Late Richard Jordan, New Jersey, Red Transfer, 10¾ In. ......*illus* | 212 |
| **Plate,** Soup, William Penn's Treaty, Blue Transfer, Geometric Border, Scalloped, 10½ In. | 94 |
| **Plate,** Toddy, Proverb, Mill, House, Gardening, Blue Transfer, Embossed, 4½ In. | 71 |
| **Plate,** Winter View Of Pittsfield, Mass., Blue Transfer, Scalloped Rim, Clews, c.1830, 8 In. | 180 |
| **Platter,** Alms House, New York, Historical, Blue, 19th Century, 13 x 17 In. | 570 |
| **Platter,** Blue, Grazing Deer, Blue, Round, Marked Adams, 15½ In. | 344 |
| **Platter,** Castle On Gold Coast Africa, Shell Border, Blue, Enoch Wood & Sons, 17 In. | 750 |
| **Platter,** Errand Boy, Dark Blue, James & Ralph Clews, c.1830, 19 In. | 720 |
| **Platter,** Knight Of The Wood Conquer'd, Blue, 1800s, 13¼ x 16½ In. | 360 |
| **Platter,** Oval, Painted Musician, Woman, Scalloped Rim, c.1765, 11½ In. | 660 |
| **Platter,** Texas Battle Scene In Cartouche, Blue Transfer, Oval, 17½ In. | 1200 |
| **Platter,** View Of London, Thames River, T. & B. Godwin, 1800s, 17 In. ......*illus* | 360 |
| **Platter,** View Of Newburgh, New York, Red Transfer, Oval, 19½ In. | 369 |
| **Platter,** Well & Tree, Upper Ferry Bridge Over River Schuylkill, Blue, 1800s, 15½ x 19 In. | 600 |
| **Saucer,** Woodlands Near Philadelphia, Blue Transfer, Stubbs, 3¼ In. | 177 |
| **Stand,** Pocket Watch, Figural, Man & Woman, Scottish Attire, Wreath, 1800s, 9 x 5 In. ......*illus* | 72 |
| **Teapot,** Lid, Salt Glaze Blue, Painted Rose, Green, Pink, Yellow, 3¾ In. | 600 |
| **Teapot,** Lid, Salt Glaze, Building, Fence, Vine, Red Crabstock Spout, Handle, c.1760, 4½ In. | 1062 |
| **Teapot,** Lid, Salt Glaze, Fruit, Vines, Scorn Knop, 3 Tall Supports, c.1740, 4¾ In. | 1062 |
| **Teapot,** Lid, Stand, Leaf Swags, Stems, 6½ x 8¼ In. | 264 |

| | |
|---|---:|
| **Teapot,** Mount Vernon, Seat Of Late Gen'l Washington, Dark Blue, c.1810, 6¾ In. | 720 |
| **Toby Jugs** are listed in their own category. | |
| **Tureen,** Bellville On Passaic River, Historical, Blue, 19th Century, 11 x 15 In. | 3120 |
| **Tureen,** Cover, Underplate, Ladle, Mosque Of Sultan Achmet, Blue Transfer, 14 In. ...........*illus* | 360 |
| **Vase,** Dome Lid, Applied Flowers, Handles, Lamp Mounted, c.1840, 18 x 35 In. | 316 |
| **Vase,** Spill, Dog, Spaniel, White, Tree Trunk, Flat Back, c.1900, 13 x 14 In., Pair | 300 |
| **Vase,** Spill, Hunter, Antelope, Cape, 17 In. | 180 |
| **Vase,** Spill, Man, White Horse, Grass, Bush, Red Saddle, 8 In. | 240 |
| **Vase,** Tree Shape, Base Swans, 1800s, 5¾ In., Pair | 106 |

**STAINLESS STEEL** became available to artists and manufacturers about 1920. They used it to make flatware, tableware, and many decorative items.

| | |
|---|---:|
| **Bookends,** Double Rolled Steel, Art Deco, Green Base, 10 x 6 In. | 75 |
| **Bowl,** Tab Handles, Gemco, 1950s, 4 x 2 In. | 10 |
| **Butter,** Cover, Glass Insert, 8 x 4 In. | 15 |
| **Casserole,** Wood Handles, Lid, Gense Of Sweden, 1950s, 9 x 7 In. | 45 |
| **Cocktail Shaker,** 2-Piece, Patented April 15, 1919, 9 In. | 10 |
| **Ice Bucket,** Bail Handle, Wood Finial, West Bend, 1950s, 4 Qt. | 35 |
| **Ice Cream Scoop,** Plastic Handle, Hamilton Beach, Thumb Lever, 8 In. | 35 |
| **Napkin Holder,** Crescent Moon Man Face, 1960s, 4 x 4 x 1¾ In. | 35 |
| **Sculpture,** Watermelon, C. Weed, c.1980, 16 x 29 In. | 938 |
| **Tea Set,** Michael Graves, Post Modern, Kettle, Sugar, Spoon, Creamer, Alessi, c.1985. | 150 |
| **Tray,** Atomic, Gense, Sweden, 10 x 4 In. | 24 |

**STANGL POTTERY** traces its history back to the Fulper Pottery of New Jersey. In 1910, Johann Martin Stangl started working at Fulper. He left to work at Haeger Pottery from 1915 to 1920. Stangl returned to Fulper Pottery in 1920, became president in 1926, and changed the company name to Stangl Pottery in 1929. Stangl acquired the firm in 1930. The pottery is known for dinnerware and a line of bird figurines. Martin Stangl died in 1972 and the pottery was sold to Frank Wheaton Jr. of Wheaton Industries. Production continued until 1978, when Pfaltzgraff Pottery purchased the right to the Stangl trademark and the remaining inventory was liquidated. A single bird figurine is identified by a number. Figurines made up of two birds are identified by a number followed by the letter *D* indicating Double.

| | |
|---|---:|
| **Amber Glo,** Cup | 6 |
| **Ashtray,** Quail, 11 In. | 25 |
| **Bird,** Blue Jays, Double, No. 3276D, 7¾ In. ...........................*illus* | 30 |
| **Bird,** Flycatcher, Scissortail No. 3757, Blue, Black, Yellow Crest, On Branch, 11 x 6½ In. | 230 |
| **Bird,** Multicolor, Open Wings, 1940s, 5¼ In. | 49 |
| **Bird,** Orioles, Double, No. 3402D, 6 In. | 69 |
| **Bird,** Parrots, Double, No. 35820, Painted, 7 In. | 53 |
| **Birds,** 5 Yellow Finches On Branch, 4 x 12¼ In. | 55 |
| **Bittersweet,** Cup & Saucer | 11 |
| **Blue Daisy,** Bowl, Fruit, 5⅝ In. | 15 |
| **Blue Daisy,** Gravy Boat | 52 |
| **Blue Daisy,** Plate, Dinner, 10 In. | 22 |
| **Blueberry,** Bowl, Vegetable, 10 In. | 55 |
| **Blueberry,** Plate, Salad, 8⅛ In. | 28 |
| **Blueberry,** Skillet, 8½ In. | 56 |
| **Caughley,** Plate, Salad, 7½ In. | 12 |
| **Chicory,** Plate, Dinner, 10⅛ In. | 28 |
| **Country Garden,** Bowl, Fruit, 5½ In. | 10 |
| **Country Garden,** Bowl, Fruit, Lug Handle, 6 In. | 21 |
| **Country Garden,** Creamer | 14 |
| **Country Garden,** Plate, Dinner, 10⅛ In. | 22 |
| **Country Garden,** Plate, Salad, 8½ In. | 21 |
| **Fruit & Flowers,** Relish, 11¼ In. | 32 |
| **Fruit & Flowers,** Saucer, 6¼ In. | 5 |
| **Fruit,** Bowl, Vegetable, 2-Sections, 10¾ In. | 48 |
| **Fruit,** Bowl, Vegetable, 9⅞ In. | 55 |
| **Fruit,** Bread Tray, 15 In. | 41 |
| **Fruit,** Creamer, 3⅛ In. | 17 |
| **Fruit,** Plate, Salad, 8⅛ In. | 15 |
| **Fruit,** Salt & Pepper | 28 |
| **Fruit,** Soup, Dish, Lug Handle, 6¼ In. | 35 |
| **Golden Blossom,** Plate, Bread & Butter, 6⅛ In. | 4 |

**Staffordshire,** Tureen, Cover, Underplate, Ladle, Mosque Of Sultan Achmet, Blue Transfer, 14 In. $360

DuMouchelles Art Gallery

**Stangl,** Bird, Blue Jays, Double, No. 3276D, 7¾ In. $30

Conestoga Auction Co., Inc.

**Stein,** Character, Jester, Pottery, Diesinger, 1 Liter
$840

Fox Auctions

**Stein,** Character, Uncle Sam, Porcelain, Schierholz, ½ Liter
$5,040

Fox Auctions

**Stein,** Character, Woman, Coffee, Kathreiner's Kneipp Malzkaffee, Porcelain, ½ Liter
$3,360

The Stein Auction Company

| | |
|---|---:|
| **Golden Grape,** Creamer, 3 In. | 12 |
| **Golden Harvest,** Plate, Dinner, 10⅛ In. | 18 |
| **Golden Harvest,** Plate, Salad, 8⅛ In. | 10 |
| **Hotpoint,** Relish, 2 Sections, 7¾ In. | 28 |
| **Magnolia,** Cup | 15 |
| **Orchard Song,** Plate, Bread & Butter, 6⅛ In. | 5 |
| **Terra Rose,** Pitcher, Basket Shape, Blue, Pink Braided Handle, 9½ x 12 In., Pair | 40 |
| **Thistle,** Saucer | 4 |
| **Toothbrush Holder,** Round Flat Rim, Blue Spatter, c.1970, 6 In. | 39 |
| **Windfall,** Bread Tray, 15¼ In. | 42 |
| **Windfall,** Plate, Bread & Butter, 6⅛ In. | 8 |
| **Windfall,** Plate, Dinner, 10 In. | 15 |
| **Windfall,** Saucer | 4 |

**STAR TREK AND STAR WARS** collectibles are included here. The original *Star Trek* television series ran from 1966 through 1969. The series spawned an animated TV series, three TV sequels, and a TV prequel. The first Star Trek movie was released in 1979 and eleven others followed, the most recent in 2013. The movie *Star Wars* opened in 1977. Sequels were released in 1980 and 1983; prequels in 1999, 2002, and 2005. *Star Wars: Episode VII* is scheduled to open in 2015, which will increase interest in Star Wars collectibles. The latest episode will include actors from the original cast. Other science fiction and fantasy collectibles can be found under Batman, Buck Rogers, Captain Marvel, Flash Gordon, Movie, Superman, and Toy.

### STAR TREK

| | |
|---|---:|
| **Action Figure,** Aliens Cheron, Plastic, Fabric Costume, Package, Mego, 1975, 8 In. | 363 |
| **Action Figure,** Aliens The Keeper, Plastic, Fabric Costume, Mego, Package, 1975, 8 In. | 348 |
| **Frisbee,** Spaceship, Flying U.S.S. Enterprise Label, Yellow Plastic, 1967, 8½ In. | 165 |
| **Ornament,** Klingon Bird Of Prey, Blinking Lights, Hallmark, Box, 1994 | 22 |
| **Star Trek Game,** Ideal, Board, Box, 1967 | 45 |
| **Toy,** Klingon Cruiser, Cast Iron, On Card, Dinky Toys, 1979 | 30 |
| **Toy,** USS Enterprise, Dinky Toys, Box, 9 x 3 x 5 In. | 190 |
| **View-Master,** 3 Disks, Omega Glory, 1968 | 12 |

### STAR WARS

| | |
|---|---:|
| **Action Figure,** Boba Fett, A Wookie Holiday, Box, 3¾ In. | 361 |
| **Action Figure,** Boba Fett, Unpainted, Star Wars Micro Collection, Kenner, c.1980, 5½ In. | 1645 |
| **Action Figure,** C-3PO, Blister Card, 20th Century Fox, 1977, 3¾ In. | 386 |
| **Action Playset,** Jabba The Hutt, Salacious Crumb, Prisoner Gates, Box, 8 x 13 In. | 126 |
| **Bank,** Mechanical, Qui-Gon Jinn, Interactive, Talking, Episode 1, Box, 1980 | 60 |
| **Cookie Jar,** R2-D2, C-3PO & Darth Vader, Porcelain, 6-Sided | 110 |
| **Figure,** Anakin Skywalker, Helmet, Flight Goggles, Crossed Arms, 72 In. | 780 |
| **Lunch Box,** Metal, Plastic Thermos, Empire Strikes Back, 1980 | 186 |
| **Pendant,** C-3PO, Jointed, Metal, 20th Century Fox, 1977, 2 In. | 22 |
| **Plate,** Princess Leia, Hamilton Collection, 1987, 8½ In. | 75 |
| **Plate,** R2-D2 & Wicket, Gold Trim, 1987, 8½ In. | 75 |
| **Poster,** Movie, Leia, Luke In White Attire, Paper, 1977, 27 x 41 In. | 370 |
| **Sign,** Twelve Action Figures, Graphics, Cardboard, General Mills Fun Group, 14 x 24 In. | 595 |
| **Toy,** Vehicle, Return Of The Jedi Imperial Shuttle, Box, Kenner, 1984, 17 x 20 In. | 346 |
| **Watch,** Digital, Quartz, LCD, On Card, 1984 | 30 |

**STEINS** have been used by beer and ale drinkers for over 500 years. They have been made of ivory, porcelain, stoneware, faience, silver, pewter, wood, or glass in sizes up to nine gallons. Although some were made by Mettlach, Meissen, Capo-di-Monte, and other famous factories, most were made by less important German potteries. The words *Geschutz* or *Musterschutz* on a stein are the German words for "patented" or "registered design," not company names. Steins are still being made in the old styles.

| | |
|---|---:|
| **Character,** Alpine Man, Porcelain, Lithophane, ½ Liter | 724 |
| **Character,** Bottle Shape, Devil Handle, Stoneware, Inlaid Lid, Marked LB & C, ½ Liter | 420 |
| **Character,** Cat With Hangover, Porcelain, Schierholz, ½ Liter | 420 |
| **Character,** Devil, Red, Porcelain, Inlaid Lid, E. Bohne & Sohne, ½ Liter | 750 |
| **Character,** Dog, Gentleman, Porcelain, Musterschutz, Schierholz, ½ Liter | 780 |
| **Character,** Fox, Feather In Hat, Porcelain, Musterschutz, Schierholz, ½ Liter | 660 |
| **Character,** Fox, Gentleman, Porcelain, Marked Musterschutz, By Schierholz, ½ Liter | 1284 |
| **Character,** Frauenkirche Tower, Porcelain, Josef Mayer, ½ Liter | 1110 |
| **Character,** Frauenkirche Tower, Stoneware, 1 Liter | 276 |

S

| | | |
|---|---|---|
| Character, Gnome, Pottery, Inlaid Lid, Diesinger, No. 694, ½ Liter | | 402 |
| Character, Happy Radish, Sad Radish, Porcelain, Musterschutz, Schierholz, ½ Liter, Pair | | 240 |
| Character, Jester, Pottery, Diesinger, 1 Liter | *illus* | 840 |
| Character, Little Red Riding Hood, Stoneware, By F. Ringer, ¼ Liter | | 660 |
| Character, Munich Child, Eckhardt & Engler Hohr-Grenze, Marked, Germany, 10½ In. | | 35 |
| Character, Munich Child, Pottery, Inlaid Lid, Marked, J. Reinemann, Munchen, ½ Liter | | 78 |
| Character, Mushroom Lady, Porcelain, Marked Musterschutz, By Schierholz, ½ Liter | | 7200 |
| Character, Sad Radish, Porcelain, Marked Musterschutz, 3 Liter | | 630 |
| Character, Skull On Book, Porcelain, E. Bohne & Sohne, ½ Liter | | 294 |
| Character, Umbrella Men, Porcelain, Lithophane, Pewter, ½ Liter | | 420 |
| Character, Uncle Sam, Porcelain, Schierholz, ½ Liter | *illus* | 5040 |
| Character, Woman, Coffee, Kathreiner's Kneipp Malzkaffee, Porcelain, ½ Liter | *illus* | 3360 |
| Character, Woman, Hat, Caroline, Porcelain, Musterschutz, ½ Liter | | 216 |
| Earthenware, Courting Couple, Castle, Pewter Lid, Branch Handle, Simon Peter Gerz, 21½ In. | | 94 |
| Elephant Leg, Tusk Handle, Brass Mounts, Semiprecious Stones, 1½ Liter | *illus* | 200 |
| Faience, Bird On Hill, Clouds, Pewter Lid & Footring, Bayreuther Walzenkrug, 9 In. | | 480 |
| Faience, Blue & Yellow Flowers, Baluster, Pewter Lid, Frankfurter, c.1785, 9½ In. | | 240 |
| Faience, Cupid, Engraved Pewter Lid, 1835, Carpenter Tools, North German Walzenkrug, 8 In. | | 360 |
| Faience, Deer With Antlers, Leaping, Pewter Lid, Schrattenhoffener Walzenkrug, 9 In. | | 360 |
| Faience, Erfurter Walzenkrug, Pewter Lid, Footring, c.1759, 8¼ In. | | 420 |
| Faience, Erfurter Walzenkrug, Seahorses, Fountain, Pewter Lid, Footring, c.1750, 11½ In. | | 240 |
| Faience, Figure, Bridge, Trees, Stylized Chinoiserie, Blue & White, Pewter Lid, 1722, 10 In. | | 420 |
| Faience, Gmundner Walzenkrug, Pewter Lid, c.1800, 8¼ In. | | 240 |
| Faience, Hanauer Walzenkrug, Pewter Lid, Footring, Late 1700s, 7¼ In. | | 240 |
| Faience, Stylized Flowers, Pewter Lid & Footring, Frankfurter, Walzenkrug, c.1780, 10 In. | | 288 |
| Faience, Stylized Fruit, Leaves, Pewter Lid, Bayreuther Walzenkrug, c.1770, 10 In. | | 450 |
| Faience, Stylized Man Walking, Waving, Trees, Pewter Lid, Bayreuther Walzenkrug, 9 In. | | 360 |
| Glass, Blown, Amber, Green Prunts, Rigaree, Glass Inlaid Lid, 3 Liter | | 420 |
| Glass, Blown, Engraved, Pewter Base & Lid, ½ Liter | | 219 |
| Glass, Blown, Red Flashed, Cut Design, Gilded, Inlaid Lid, Mid 1800s, ½ Liter, 6½ In. | | 312 |
| Glass, Clear, Etched, Gambrinus, Pewter Lid, 2½ Liter, 15 In. | | 96 |
| Glass, Clear, Fluted, Engraved Stag, Tapered, Footed, Pewter Inlaid Lid, ½ Liter | | 192 |
| Glass, Cut Diamond Band, Engraved, Cinched Waist, Pewter Sachsen Helmet Lid, ½ Liter | | 480 |
| Glass, Flowers, Scrolls, Art Nouveau Style, ½ Liter | *illus* | 120 |
| Glass, Man Holding Stein, Banner, Painted, Pewter Lid, ½ Liter | *illus* | 60 |
| Glass, Ruby Flashed, Engraved Stag, Leaves, Tapered, Inlaid Lid, Ducks, ¾ Liter | | 264 |
| Glass, Wedding, Enameled Pink Roses, Blue Banner, Spread Foot, Pewter Lid, 1856, 1 Liter | | 312 |
| Glass, White Over Clear, Cut Circles, Brass Relief Lid, Bohemia, c.1850, ½ Liter | *illus* | 570 |
| Ivory, Carved, Cherubs Drinking Wine, Figural Lid & Handle, 1 Liter | *illus* | 4800 |
| Metal, Gilt, Electrotyping, Relief, Marked Department Of Science & Art, Elkington, 2 Liter | | 1440 |
| Mettlach Steins are listed in the Mettlach category. | | |
| Military, Third Reich, 1 Btl., I.R. 61, Munchen, 1937, Stoneware, Pewter Lid, 1 Liter | *illus* | 540 |
| Military, Third Reich, Abt. Stab II, A.R., 53, 1936, Pottery, Pewter Lid, Name On Lid, ½ Liter | | 900 |
| Military, Third Reich, Artl. Regt. Nr. 45, Wetzlar, Pottery, Pewter, Helmet, Swastika, ½ Liter | | 462 |
| Military, Third Reich, Machine Gun Scene, Pottery, Pewter Lid, Eagle, Swastika, ½ Liter | | 450 |
| Military, Third Reich, Roster, Darmstadt, 9 Swastikas, Pottery, Metal Lid, c.1938, ½ Liter | | 900 |
| Military, Third Reich, Stalag VII A. Kriegsweihnacht, Stoneware, Metal Lid, 1940, ½ Liter | | 396 |
| Military, Third Reich, Unteroffiziers Korps. Der 13, Koln, Stoneware, Pewter, 1938, ½ Liter | | 900 |
| Military, Third Reich, Villingen Waldkaserne, Pottery, Pewter Lid, Helmet, 1935, ½ Liter | | 390 |
| Milk Glass, Colonial Man & Woman, Flowers, Multicolored, Pewter Lid, c.1780, 1 Liter | | 1920 |
| Occupational, Brenner, Liquor, Transfer, Enameled, Pewter Lid, Ludwig Baumann, ½ Liter | | 840 |
| Occupational, Brewer, Wood, Tapered, Horizontal Red Bands, Pewter Lid, c.1850, 8½ In. | | 276 |
| Occupational, Schreiner, Cabinet Maker, Enamel, Transfer, Pewter Lid, ½ Liter | | 252 |
| Occupational, Stadt Courier, City Postal Delivery, Enamel, Transfer, Pewter, c.1898, ½ Liter | | 360 |
| Occupational, Strassenwerk, Street Repair, Transfer, Enameled, Pewter Lid, Inscription, ½ Liter | | 540 |
| Porcelain, Family In Village Scene, Painted, Relief Silver Lid, 7 In. | | 1620 |
| Porcelain, King Ludwig, Military Uniform, Bavarian Lion Finial, 1 Liter | *illus* | 168 |
| Porcelain, Landscape, Rearing Horse, Multicolored, Pewter Lid, Delft, 8½ In. | | 360 |
| Porcelain, Men Drinking, Brass Lid, Marked, Beehive, Royal Vienna Type, 1 Liter | *illus* | 600 |
| Porcelain, Nude Woman, Trees, Painted, Gold Trim, Footed, Cherub Lid, Beehive, ½ Liter | | 1560 |
| Porcelain, Relief, Dancing Drinkers, Painted, Berry Finial, c.1885, ¾ Liter | | 420 |
| Porcelain, Rinaldo Und Armida, Painted, Gold Trim, Inlaid Lid, ½ Liter | | 2520 |
| Porcelain, Royal Vienna Style, Painted, Venus & Merkur, Beehive Mark, ½ Liter | | 420 |
| Pottery, Dwarfs, Flowers, Relief, Diesinger, No. 811, 2 Liter | *illus* | 390 |
| Pottery, Lawn Tennis Rackets, Relief, Stacked Tennis Ball Lid, 1 Liter | *illus* | 264 |

Stein, Elephant Leg, Tusk Handle, Brass Mounts, Semiprecious Stones, 1½ Liter
$200

Fox Auctions

Stein, Glass, Flowers, Scrolls, Art Nouveau Style, ½ Liter
$120

Fox Auctions

Stein, Glass, Man Holding Stein, Banner, Painted, Pewter Lid, ½ Liter
$60

The Stein Auction Company

S

535

**Stein,** Glass, White Over Clear, Cut Circles, Brass Relief Lid, Bohemia, c.1850, ½ Liter
$570

Fox Auctions

**Stein,** Porcelain, King Ludwig, Military Uniform, Bavarian Lion Finial, 1 Liter
$168

Fox Auctions

**Stein,** Pottery, Lawn Tennis Rackets, Relief, Stacked Tennis Ball Lid, 1 Liter
$264

Fox Auctions

**Stein,** Ivory, Carved, Cherubs Drinking Wine, Figural Lid & Handle, 1 Liter
$4,800

Fox Auctions

**Stein,** Porcelain, Men Drinking, Brass Lid, Marked, Beehive, Royal Vienna Type, 1 Liter
$600

The Stein Auction Company

**Stein,** Schmuckung Der Venus, Venus, Handmaids, Porcelain, Beehive Mark, 7 In., ½ Liter
$2,040

The Stein Auction Company

**Stein,** Military, Third Reich, 1 Btl., I.R. 61, Munchen, 1937, Stoneware, Pewter Lid, 1 Liter
$540

The Stein Auction Company

**Stein,** Pottery, Dwarfs, Flowers, Relief, Diesinger, No. 811, 2 Liter
$390

Fox Auctions

**Stein,** Stoneware, Royal Figure, Annaberg Factory, ¾ Liter
$5,760

Fox Auctions

| | |
|---|---|
| **Regimental,** 2 Comp., Eisenbahn Bat., Munchen, Winged Wheel Thumblift, ½ Liter................... | 491 |
| **Regimental,** 4 F. Batt. Wurzburg, 3 Vignettes, Soldiers, Cannons, Bullet Form, 10 In. .................. | 369 |
| **Regimental,** 5 Battr., Feld Artl. Regt. Nr. 26, Verden, Porcelain, Eagle Thumblift, ½ Liter............ | 420 |
| **Regimental,** 5 Comp., Fuss Art. Regt., Ingolstadt, Farming, Bavarian Thumblift, ½ Liter............ | 180 |
| **Regimental,** 6 Comp., Bayr. Inft. Regt. Nr. 21, Lion Thumblift, 1902, Lithophane, ½ Liter.......... | 2116 |
| **Regimental,** 9 Comp., Inft. Regt. Nr. 123, Ulm, Scenes, Floral Thumblift, c.1900, ½ Liter............ | 132 |
| **Regimental,** Roster, 2 Comp., Jager Bat. Nr. 8, Schlettstadt, 2 Scenes, Eagle, c.1905, ½ Liter ....... | 750 |
| **Regimental,** Roster, 10 Komp., Inft. Regt. Nr. 106, Leipzig, Scenes, Saxon Thumblift, ½ Liter ..... | 252 |
| **Regimental,** Roster, 2 Comp., Train Bat., Nr. 13, Ludwigsburg, Porcelain, ½ Liter, 11 ¾ In........... | 336 |
| **Regimental,** Roster, 5 Comp., Inft. Regt. Nr. 90, Wismar, 2 Scenes, Eagle Thumblift, ½ Liter......... | 540 |
| **Regimental,** Roster, 7 Komp., Inft. Regt. Nr. 94, Eisenach, 4 Scenes, Eagle, c.1910, ½ Liter ......... | 780 |
| **Regimental,** Roster, Eisenbahn Regt. Nr. 2, Berlin, 4 Scenes, Stoneware, Winged Wheel, ½ Liter | 516 |
| **Regimental,** Roster, Eisenbahn Regt. Nr. II, Berlin-Schoneberg, Scenes, ½ Liter ...................... | 990 |
| **Regimental,** Roster, Kgl. Sachs, Garde Reiter Rgt. 3, Scenes, Saxon Lift, 1913, ½ Liter................ | 1800 |
| **Regimental,** Soldier On Horseback, Cavalry, 1901, Alfonds Kreimer, 11 ¼ In............................... | 73 |
| **Schmuckung Der Venus,** Venus, Handmaids, Porcelain, Beehive Mark, 7 In., ½ Liter........*illus* | 2040 |
| **Serpentine,** Pewter Lid, Footring, Handle, Early 1700s, 7 In. ............................................... | 1080 |
| **Stoneware,** Art Nouveau, Blue & Gray Glaze, Pewter Lid, L. M. K. Capeller, ½ Liter ..................... | 630 |
| **Stoneware,** Art Nouveau, Blue Salt Glaze, Pewter Lid, Relief, Gerz, 2 Liter........................... | 252 |
| **Stoneware,** Brown, Fluted Swirls, Bulbous, Footed, Pewter Lid, Bunzlauer Melonkrug, 9 In....... | 144 |
| **Stoneware,** Creussen Style, Planets, Pewter Lid, Footring, Late 1900s, 1 Liter...................... | 348 |
| **Stoneware,** Impressed HB Kgl. Hof-Brauhaus, Munchen, Relief Pewter Lid, 1 Liter................ | 252 |
| **Stoneware,** Paul Revere, Horse, Silver Plated Pewter Lid, Whites, New York, 1 Liter.................... | 216 |
| **Stoneware,** Royal Figure, Annaberg Factory, ¾ Liter ...........................................*illus* | 5760 |
| **Stoneware,** Stylized Stag, Incised, Cobalt Blue, Gray, Pewter Lid, c.1780, 10 In. ..................... | 300 |
| **Stoneware,** Transfer, Enameled, HB, Kgl. Hofbrauhaus, Munchen, ½ Liter............................. | 192 |
| **Stoneware,** Transfer, Verse, Enameled, Pewter Lid, F. Ringer, ½ Liter.........................*illus* | 78 |
| **Stoneware,** Westerwalder Walzenkrug, 2-Headed Eagle, Salt Glaze, Pewter Lid, 1787, 9 In..*illus* | 581 |
| **Stoneware,** Westerwalder Walzenkrug, Incised, Applied Relief, Salt Glaze, Pewter Lid, 10 In. ..... | 192 |
| **Tankard,** Glass, Pewter Rim, Handle, Base, A. Knox, Liberty & Co., Tudric, c.1905, 7 ¼ In....*illus* | 2000 |

**STEREO CARDS** that were made for stereoscope viewers became popular after 1840. Two almost identical pictures were mounted on a stiff cardboard backing so that, when viewed through a stereoscope, a three-dimensional picture could be seen. Value is determined by maker and by subject. These cards were made in quantity through the 1930s.

| | |
|---|---|
| **2 Boys,** Dog In Wagon, Webster Albee, c.1890.......................................................... | 28 |
| **Couple Kissing,** On Porch, Stolen Sweets, Griffith & Griffith, No. 84 ............................. | 7 |
| **Girl,** Donkeys, Underwood & Underwood................................................................. | 12 |
| **Jackson Square,** New Orleans, Keystone.................................................................. | 22 |
| **Locomotive,** Railroad Yard, c.1880......................................................................... | 20 |
| **New York City,** Manhattan, Lower East Side, Docks, Steamships, c.1907 ..................... | 25 |
| **New York Railroad Bridge,** Centennial Views............................................................. | 24 |
| **Race Horse,** Hal Pointer, c.1890 ........................................................................... | 24 |
| **World's Fair,** St. Louis, Palace Of Mines From East Pavilion .......................................... | 15 |

**STEREOSCOPES** were used for viewing stereo cards. The hand viewer was invented by Oliver Wendell Holmes, although more complicated table models were used before his was produced in 1859. Do not confuse the stereoscope with the stereopticon, a magic lantern that used glass slides.

| | |
|---|---|
| **Aluminum,** Folding Handle, Cards, c.1900, 7 x 12 x 8 In................................................ | 95 |
| **Brewster Style,** Hand Held, Metal Barrels, Rosewood Veneer, c.1870, 7 x 4 x 6 In. ....................... | 250 |
| **Brewster,** Mahogany, 1850s, 7 ¾ x 3 ¾ x 6 ⅜ In.......................................................... | 1250 |
| **Monarch Co.,** Wood, Metal, Pat April 12, 1904, 12 ½ In.................................................. | 150 |
| **Perfecscope,** H.C. White, Wood, Metal, Engraved, Adjustable, c.1895, 12 x 5 In. ................... | 125 |
| **Underwood & Underwood,** Tilt Handle, Wood, White Metal, 1901, 12 x 5 In. ............................ | 105 |

**STERLING SILVER**, *see Silver-Sterling category.*

**STEUBEN** glass was made at the Steuben Glass Works of Corning, New York. The factory, founded by Frederick Carder and T.G. Hawkes, Sr., was purchased by the Corning Glass Company. Corning continued to make glass called Steuben. Many types of art glass were made at Steuben. Aurene is an iridescent glass. Schottenstein Stores Inc. bought 80 percent of the business in 2008. The factory closed in 2011 and no more of this quality glass will be made. Additional pieces may be found in the Cluthra and Perfume Bottle categories.

| | |
|---|---|
| **Ashtray,** Amber, Celeste Blue Handle.................................................................. | 201 |

**Stein,** Stoneware, Transfer, Verse, Enameled, Pewter Lid, F. Ringer, ½ Liter
$78

The Stein Auction Company

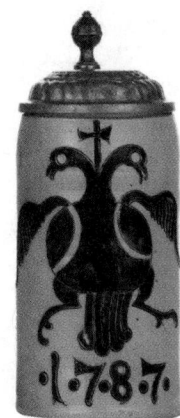

**Stein,** Stoneware, Westerwalder Walzenkrug, 2-Headed Eagle, Salt Glaze, Pewter Lid, 1787, 9 In.
$581

The Stein Auction Company

**Stein,** Tankard, Glass, Pewter Rim, Handle, Base, A. Knox, Liberty & Co., Tudric, c.1905, 7 ¼ In.
$2,000

Rago Arts & Auction Center

S

**Steuben,** Compote, Stretched Rim, Twisted Stem, Prunts, Gold, Aurene, 7 In. $920

Early Auction Co.

**Steuben,** Figurine, Eagle, 18K Gold, On Crystal Rock, Box, 7½ In. $8,888

James D. Julia Auctioneers

**Steuben,** Jar, Lid, Rosaline To Alabaster, Chinese Pattern, Acid Cut Back, 6¾ In. $1,035

Early Auction Co.

| | |
|---|---:|
| **Ashtray,** Green Jade, Alabaster, Leaf Handle | 201 |
| **Atomizer,** Gold, Triangular, Birds, Flowers, Acorn Finial, 10 In. | 173 |
| **Atomizer,** Tapered, Round Foot, Gilt Metal Cap, Aurene, Signed, Carder, 8 x 2 In. | 230 |
| **Basket,** Pomona, Green Lattice Basket, Flared Rim, Applied Handles, Prunts, 3¾ x 6¾ In. | 115 |
| **Basket,** Selenium Red, Pinched Waist, Ruffled Rim, Cabochons On Handle, 12 In. | 1208 |
| **Basket,** Verre De Soie, Flared Ruffled Rim, Applied Handle, Flower Button Ends, 15 In. | 296 |
| **Basket,** Verre De Soie, Pinched Waist, Ruffled Rim, Cabochon On Handle, 15 In. | 460 |
| **Bowl,** Amethyst, Engraved, Stylized Flowers & Stems, Stylized Wheel Centers, 10 In. | 415 |
| **Bowl,** Blue Aurene, 3-Footed, c.1920, 8¼ x 2¼ In. | 175 |
| **Bowl,** Blue Aurene, Marked, 6 In. | 215 |
| **Bowl,** Blue, Calcite, Aurene, 10 In. | 259 |
| **Bowl,** Calcite, Blue Aurene Interior, Flared, Stretched Rim, Rolled Foot, 10 In. | 365 |
| **Bowl,** Calcite, Gold Aurene Interior, Scalloped Stretch Border Rim, 3 x 9¾ In. | 259 |
| **Bowl,** Calyx, 5 x 10 In. | 240 |
| **Bowl,** Chinese Pattern, Blue Cut To Alabaster, Acid Cut Back, Signed Frederick Carder | 863 |
| **Bowl,** Cintra, Pink, Bulbous, Applied Black Wafer, Domed & Flared Foot, 6 In. | 356 |
| **Bowl,** Cyprian, Aquamarine Iridescent, Celeste Blue Rim, Rounded Sides, 5 x 10 In. | 365 |
| **Bowl,** Dolphin, Waves, Footed, Steuben, 11½ In. | 305 |
| **Bowl,** Gold, Aurene, Calcite, c.1915, 5 x 12½ In. | 688 |
| **Bowl,** Gold, Aurene, Calcite, Round, c.1910, 2¾ x 10 In. | 375 |
| **Bowl,** Gold, Curving Sides, Flat Rim, Aurene, 11¼ In. | 247 |
| **Bowl,** Gold, Green Hooked Coils, Inverted Folded Rim, Aurene, 3 In. | 1553 |
| **Bowl,** Gold, Rolled Rim, Aurene, Signed, 3 x 5¾ In. | 259 |
| **Bowl,** Green Jade, Ribbed, Elongated Oval, 6 x 12 In. | 690 |
| **Bowl,** Green Jade, Shaded, Flared, 12 In. | 533 |
| **Bowl,** Grotesque, 5 x 8 In. | 150 |
| **Bowl,** Holly, Acid Cut Back, 8¾ x 5 In. | 58 |
| **Bowl,** Ivrene, Grotesque, Free-Form, Folded, Ribbed, 7 In. | 123 |
| **Bowl,** Medallions, Branches, Plum Jade, Acid Cut Back, Rounded Form, 3 x 6 In. | 1150 |
| **Bowl,** Silverina Lattice, Amethyst, Flared, 5 x 10 In. | 474 |
| **Bowl,** Swirl, George Thompson, 1952, 13¼ In. | 420 |
| **Bowl,** Verre De Soie, Light Blue Jade, Threading, Side Prunts, Conical, Footed, 6½ In. | 546 |
| **Bowl,** Wisteria, Grotesque Form, Vertical Ribs, Ruffled Rim, Squared Feet, 4¾ x 8 In. | 486 |
| **Box,** Lid, French Blue, Swirled Optic Ribbing, Round, Threaded Ball Handle, 6 In. | 356 |
| **Candlestick,** Amber, Translucent, Tulip Shape, Thorns, Pomona Green Cups, 12½ In., Pair | 3220 |
| **Candlestick,** Amber, Twisted Stem, Applied Vertical Celeste Blue Rib, 9 In., Pair | 486 |
| **Candlestick,** Amethyst, Engraved Leaf & Vine, Baluster, Flattened Foot, 16 In., Pair | 1265 |
| **Candlestick,** Blue, Double Knop, Spread Foot, Aurene, 10 In., Pair | 1778 |
| **Candlestick,** Clear, 4½ In., Pair | 100 |
| **Candlestick,** Cobalt Blue, Inverted Saucer Foot, Cylindrical Stem, Flat Rim, 4 In. | 237 |
| **Candlestick,** Flemish Blue, Swirled Cups, Twisted Stem, Flattened Wafer & Foot, 6 In., Pair | 711 |
| **Candlestick,** Frederick Carder, 9 In., 4 Piece | 1020 |
| **Candlestick,** Pomona Green Ribbed, Amber Disc Foot, 12 In. | 115 |
| **Candlestick,** Verre De Soie, Diamond Pattern, Out Turned Rim, Footed, 4½ In., Pair | 575 |
| **Candlestick,** Verre De Soie, Lightly Iridized, Baluster, 2 Wafers, Rounded Foot, 8 In., Pair | 356 |
| **Centerpiece,** Alabaster, Flared-Out, Green Lip, 10 In. | 243 |
| **Centerpiece,** Amber, Optic Ribbed, Applied Green Glass Foot, 7 x 12 In. | 237 |
| **Champagne,** Strawberry Mansion, Spread Wing Eagle Crest, F. Carder, 1931, 4½ In. | 259 |
| **Chandelier,** Inverted Dome, Acid Cut, Flowers, Garlands, Ribbons, 4 Brackets, 31 In. | 1790 |
| **Charger,** Green, Engraved Border, Flowers, Leaves & Dots, 14 In. | 119 |
| **Charger,** Rosaline Cut To Alabaster, Acid Cut Back, 16 In. | 489 |
| **Cocktail,** Blue, Alabaster Stem, Base, Stevens & Carder, 6¼ In., 5 Piece | 253 |
| **Cocktail,** Lavender, Alabaster Stem, Base, Stevens & Carder, 6¼ In., 3 Piece | 150 |
| **Compote,** Blue Jade, Flared Out Form, Calcite Stem & Foot, 3 x 8 In. | 652 |
| **Compote,** Calcite, Gold, Aurene, c.1910, 7 x 9¾ In. | 360 |
| **Compote,** Gold, Ruffled Rim, Tall Twist Stem, Aurene, 6 x 6 In. | 460 |
| **Compote,** Lily, Crystal, Flashed Green Acid Cut Back Rim, 7¼ x 7 In. | 115 |
| **Compote,** Pomona, Amber Stem, Green Optic Ribbed Dish, Spread Foot, 6¼ In. | 115 |
| **Compote,** Purple, Ribbed, Inverted Saucer Foot, 6¾ In. | 370 |
| **Compote,** Stretched Rim, Twisted Stem, Prunts, Gold, Aurene, 7 In. ............*illus* | 920 |
| **Compote,** Verre De Soie, Footed, Latticework Lid, Stylized Leaf Finial, 9 In. | 748 |
| **Cordial,** Oriental Poppy, Opalescent Banding, Green Translucent Stem, Foot, Mark, 5½ In. | 575 |
| **Darning Ball,** Blue, Aurene, Open Pontil, c.1925, 7 x 2½ In. | 316 |
| **Darning Ball,** Flint White, Handle, Open Pontil, c.1930, 7 In. | 69 |
| **Darning Ball,** Gold, Open Pontil, Aurene, c.1925, 6½ x 2½ In. | 316 |

**Steuben,** Lamp, Blue, Over Alabaster, Corintha Pattern, Metal Finial, Aurene, c.1929, 29 ½ In. $1,150

Early Auction Co.

**Steuben,** Perfume Atomizer, Gold Cloth, Blue Aurene, Jeweled Finial, c.1925, 9 ½ In. $431

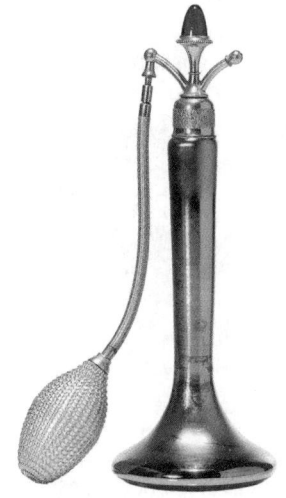

Cowan's Auctions

**Steuben,** Vase, 3 Tree Trunks, Blue, Purple Highlights, Spread Base, Aurene, 6 In. $948

James D. Julia Auctioneers

**Steuben,** Vase, Blue Jade, Optic Ribbed, Spreading Rim, Signed, F. Carder, 7 ½ In. $1,150

Early Auction Co.

**Steuben,** Vase, Blue, Applied Button Design, Aurene, Signed, c.1910, 10 x 7 In. $2,645

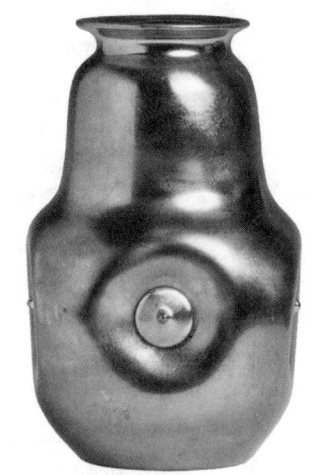

Cottone Auctions

**Steuben,** Vase, Blue, Green, Acid Cut Back, Aurene, Fleur-De-Lis Mark, 1900s, 12 x 5 ½ In. $2,250

Rago Arts & Auction Center

**Steuben,** Vase, Blue, Urn Shape, Scrolled Handles, Aurene, Marked, Paper Label, 11 ¾ In. $1,840

Early Auction Co.

**Steuben,** Vase, Bud, Tree Trunk, 3-Prong, Aurene, c.1914, 5 ¾ In. $523

Cowan's Auctions

**Steuben,** Vase, Calcite Body, Acid Carved Flowers, Green Highlights, Blue Aurene, 5 In. $5,036

James D. Julia Auctioneers

S

539

**Steuben,** Vase, Candlestick, Silver Leaf & Vine Design, Green, Aurene, Signed, 10 In.
$3,000

DuMouchelles Art Gallery

**Steuben,** Vase, Fan, Optic Rib, Celeste Blue, Amber Disc Foot & Stem, 8 ½ In.
$230

Early Auction Co.

**Steuben,** Vase, Jack-In-The-Pulpit, Gold, Blue, Purple, Pink, Aurene, Signed, 12 In.
$1,094

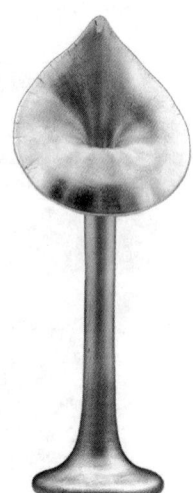

James D. Julia Auctioneers

**Steuben,** Vase, Nude, Etched, Stars, Sprigs, Walter Dorwin Teague, 1932, 11 ¾ x 4 ½ In.
$1,250

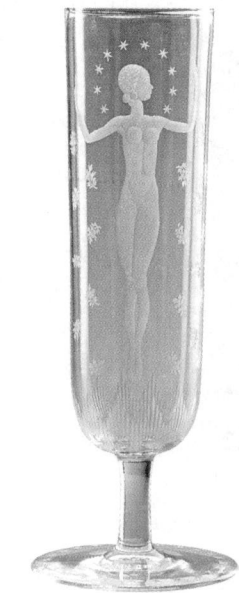

Rago Arts & Auction Center

**Steuben,** Vase, Tricornered, Opal & Green Pulled Feather, Aurene, 2 In.
$633

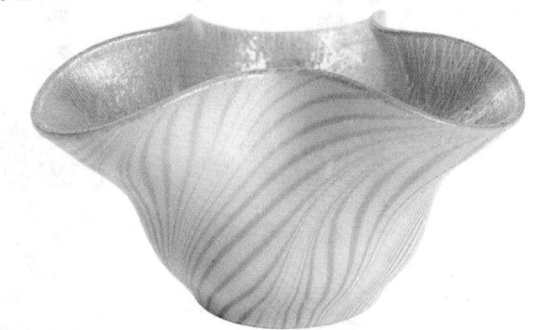

Early Auction Co.

**Steuben,** Vase, Verre De Soie, Pink Rim, Footed, Label, c.1915, 5 x 3 ¾ In.
$210

DuMouchelles Art Gallery

| | |
|---|---|
| **Darning Ball,** Gold, Pulled Feathers, Swollen Handle, Aurene, 6½ In. | 1007 |
| **Decanter,** 6400, Amethyst To Clear, Bird Of Paradise, 17 In. | 848 |
| **Dish,** Gold, Flared Bowl Base, Handle, Looped & Wrapped, Aurene, 6 x 5½ In. | 165 |
| **Figurine,** Eagle, 18K Gold, On Crystal Rock, Box, 7½ In. .....................*illus* | 8888 |
| **Figurine,** Eagle, Perched, Cut & Faceted Feathers, 8 In., Pair | 851 |
| **Figurine,** Elephant, Trumpeting, Clear, Etched Steuben, 8½ x 5½ In. | 311 |
| **Figurine,** Seahorse, Upright, Clear, Domed Base, 1900s, 10 In. | 189 |
| **Figurine,** Swan, Clear, Etched, Head Up, Down, 7 In., Pair | 234 |
| **Figurine,** Swiss Cheese Wedge, Bubbles, 18K Gold Mouse On Top, Fitted Box, 4 In. | 3125 |
| **Figurine,** Whale, Tail Up, Clear, 5 In. | 120 |
| **Fish,** Tropical, Clear, Signed, 10¾ In. | 200 |
| **Jar,** Lid, Rosaline To Alabaster, Chinese Pattern, Acid Cut Back, 6¾ In. ...............*illus* | 1035 |
| **Jardiniere,** Green Jade, Swirl Pattern, 6¼ x 8 In. | 150 |
| **Lamp Base,** Black, Turquoise Thread At Shoulder, 12 In. | 533 |
| **Lamp Base,** Green, White, Crackle Decoration, Rounded Shoulder, 11 In. | 1185 |
| **Lamp Base,** Selenium Red, Diagonal Ribs, Bulbous, Long Neck, Brass Base, 4-Footed, 24 In. | 851 |
| **Lamp,** Blue, Over Alabaster, Corintha Pattern, Metal Finial, Aurene, c.1929, 29½ In. ..........*illus* | 1150 |
| **Lamp,** Cobalt Blue On Flint, White Cased, Gold Leaf & Vine Shade, Harp Base, 57 In. | 5750 |
| **Lamp,** Green & Gold Pulled Feathers, Opaline Ground, Domed & Flared Shade, 17 In. | 8295 |
| **Lamp,** Green, Threaded Heart & Vine, Aurene, Brass Base, Leaves, Vines, 8 x 16 In. | 529 |
| **Lamp,** Hanging, Pink Aurene, Gold Iridescent Leaves & Vine, 4 Square Link Chains, 24 In. | 8888 |
| **Lamp,** Moss Agate, Blue & Yellow Mottled, Cobalt Blue Highlights, Mica, 33 In. | 3335 |
| **Lamp,** Moss Agate, Blue Mottled, Yellow, Cobalt Blue Highlights, Silver Mica, Metal, 33 In. | 2415 |
| **Lamp,** Yellow Jade, Acid Cut Back, Art Deco Flower, Leaf, Rectangular, 19 In. | 604 |
| **Nappy,** Gold, Trifold Rim, Applied Reeded Handle, Aurene, Signed, 2 In. | 259 |
| **Perfume Atomizer,** Gold Cloth, Blue Aurene, Jeweled Finial, c.1925, 9½ In. ...............*illus* | 431 |
| **Perfume Bottle,** Gold, Aurene, Footed, Teardrop Stopper, Signed, 1988, 8 In. | 575 |
| **Perfume Bottle,** Verre De Soie, Green Threads, Button Stopper, 3½ x 2¾ In., Pair | 316 |
| **Perfume Bottle,** Verre De Soie, Rose Du Berry Lip, Pear Shape Stopper, 9½ In. | 575 |
| **Plate,** Audubon, Engraved Pelican, 10 In. | 240 |
| **Plate,** Luncheon, Gold Ruby, Signed, Fleur-De-Lis Acid Mark, 8½ In. | 58 |
| **Puff Box,** Gold Ruby Lid, Squat Tapioca Base, Bubbles, 5¼ In. | 288 |
| **Rose Bowl,** Rosaline, White Blossom, Branch, Round, 6¾ x 8 In. | 531 |
| **Salt,** Verre De Soie, Ruffled Rim, c.1920, 1 x 3½ In. | 115 |
| **Scent Bottle,** Clear, Melon Ribbed, Silver Overlay, Flowers, Flame Stopper, 5½ In. | 356 |
| **Scent Bottle,** Oriental Poppy, Pink, Vertical Ribbons, 5 In. | 1777 |
| **Sculpture,** Cathedral, Prismatic Shape, Engraved, George Thompson, 1955, 1¼ x 3 In. | 4305 |
| **Sculpture,** Gilded Partridge Mounted, Crystal Pear, 6 In. | 5332 |
| **Sculpture,** Leopard In The Moonlight, Perched On Tree Branch, Stars, Box, 7½ x 8 In. | 4305 |
| **Sculpture,** Partridge In Pear Tree, Pear Shape, 18K Gold Inside, Atkins, 1968, 6 In. | 2006 |
| **Sculpture,** Thistle Rock, Carved, Jagged Rock, 7½ In. | 4740 |
| **Sculpture,** Under The Sea, Disc Shape, Fish, Coral, Weeds, Engraved, 6¾ x 7¾ In. | 3998 |
| **Shade,** Blue, Gold Heart & Vine, White Interior, Aurene, 4¾ In. | 1890 |
| **Shade,** Brown, Applied Intarsia Border, Flared, Aurene, Marked, 7½ In. | 1422 |
| **Shade,** Brown, Gold, Heart & Vine, Aurene, 4⅜ In. | 1777 |
| **Shade,** Brown, Heart & Vine, White Interior, Aurene, 4½ In. | 1718 |
| **Shade,** Calcite, White, Gold Leaves, Green, Gold Lined, Aurene, c.1920, 4 In., Pair | 344 |
| **Shade,** Gold Heart & Vine, Cream Ground, Gold Interior, Aurene, 4½ In. | 237 |
| **Shade,** Gold, Heart, Vine, Opal, Aurene Interior, 4½ In., 6 Piece | 923 |
| **Shade,** Gold, Pink Iridescence, Bell Shape, Aurene, 4½ In., 8 Piece | 1126 |
| **Shade,** Gold, Red Highlights, Aurene, Cylindrical, 6⅜ In., Pair | 237 |
| **Shade,** Gold, Ribbed, Flared Rims, Red, Aurene, 4¾ In., 4 Piece | 523 |
| **Shade,** Green, Gold, Pulled Feather, Aurene, Silver Fleur-De-Lis Mark, 5½ In. | 518 |
| **Shade,** Yellow & Gold Zipper, Pink Highlights, 5¼ In. | 237 |
| **Shaker,** Salt, Red, Gold Heart & Vines, Blue, Double Bulbous Shape, Aurene, 3⅛ In. | 719 |
| **Tazza,** Fluted Rim, Stretched Iridescence, Twisted Stem, Aurene, 6⅛ In. | 431 |
| **Tile,** Gazelle Leaping, 2 Pillars, Scrolling Leaves, Frosted, Square, 8½ In. | 889 |
| **Urn,** Golf, Magenta, Aurene, 6⅞ x 5½ In. | 488 |
| **Vase,** 3 Tree Trunks, Blue, Purple Highlights, Spread Base, Aurene, 6 In. .............*illus* | 948 |
| **Vase,** Acid Cut Back, Goblet Shape, Footed, Green Geometric Flowers, Textured Alabaster, 6 In. | 575 |
| **Vase,** Acid Cut, Stylized Flowers, Pink, Inverted Saucer Foot, 6 In. | 770 |
| **Vase,** Blue Jade, Optic Ribbed, Spreading Rim, Signed, F. Carder, 7½ In. ...............*illus* | 1150 |
| **Vase,** Blue To Platinum, Flared, Spread Foot, Aurene, 12 In. | 1519 |
| **Vase,** Blue Urn Shape, Aurene, c.1910, 2¾ In. | 460 |
| **Vase,** Blue, 3 Tree Trunks, Round Webbed Base, Aurene, 6 In. | 948 |
| **Vase,** Blue, Applied Button Design, Aurene, Signed, c.1910, 10 x 7 In. ...............*illus* | 2645 |

**Stevens & Williams,** Fairy Lamp, Satin, Peppermint Stripes, 6½ In.
$460

Early Auction Co.

**Stevens & Williams,** Inkwell, Glass, Green Cut To Clear, Sterling Silver Mounted, c.1898, 4 In.
$13,200

DuMouchelles Art Gallery

**Stevens & Williams,** Jug, Claret, Intaglio, Green To Pink, Overlay, Flowers, Stopper, c.1900, 11 In., Pair
$10,800

DuMouchelles Art Gallery

S

**Stevens & Williams,** Plate, Intaglio Cut Glass, Green, Pink Accents, Grapevines, c.1910, 8 In.
$1,080

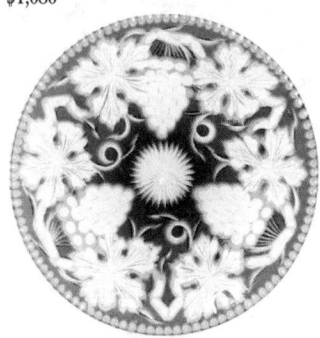

DuMouchelles Art Gallery

**Stevens & Williams,** Vase, Silveria, Green Threading, 2 Loop Handles, Signed, 4 ½ In.
$2,990

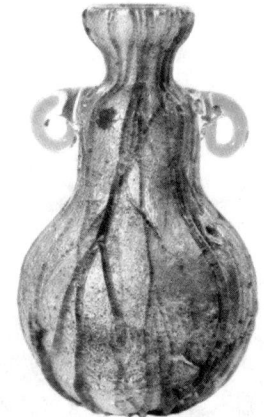

Early Auction Co.

**Stevens & Williams,** Vase, Stick, Blue To Rose, Green Trailing, Iridescent Finish, Signed, 10 ½ In.
$3,738

Early Auction Co.

| | |
|---|---|
| **Vase,** Blue, Aurene, Signed, c.1910, 1 ¼ x 2 In. | 240 |
| **Vase,** Blue, Green, Acid Cut Back, Aurene, Fleur-De-Lis Mark, 1900s, 12 x 5 ½ In. *illus* | 2250 |
| **Vase,** Blue, High Shouldered, Aurene, c.1910, 10 ½ In. | 780 |
| **Vase,** Blue, Inverted Saucer Foot, Swirled Ribbing, Aurene, 9 ¾ In. | 592 |
| **Vase,** Blue, Jug Shape, Handle, Bulbous, Cylindrical Neck, Aurene, 5 ½ x 3 ¼ In. | 403 |
| **Vase,** Blue, Opal Heart & Vine Band, Shouldered, Aurene, 6 ¼ In. | 2070 |
| **Vase,** Blue, Ribbed, Scalloped Flared Rim, Footed, Aurene, Signed, 5 ¾ In. | 316 |
| **Vase,** Blue, Shouldered, Tapered, Aurene, 1900s, 11 x 9 In. | 1408 |
| **Vase,** Blue, Twig Style, Ribbed Cylinder, Pinched Thorns, Aurene, 6 ¼ In. | 266 |
| **Vase,** Blue, Urn Shape, Scrolled Handles, Aurene, Marked, Paper Label, 11 ¾ In. *illus* | 1840 |
| **Vase,** Bubble, Clear, Round, c.1940, 4 ⅝ x 5 In. | 196 |
| **Vase,** Bud, Blue, Stick Shape, Disc Foot, Aurene Signed, 8 ½ In. | 173 |
| **Vase,** Bud, Calcite, Carved Garland, Black Foot, 5 ½ In. | 178 |
| **Vase,** Bud, Calcite, Flared, Narrow Neck, Ruffled Rim, Spread Foot, 4 In. | 304 |
| **Vase,** Bud, Ivrene, Trumpet Shape, Opalescent, Blown, 7 ⅜ In. | 106 |
| **Vase,** Bud, Tree Trunk, 3-Prong, Aurene, c.1914, 5 ¾ In. *illus* | 523 |
| **Vase,** Calcite Body, Acid Carved Flowers, Green Highlights, Blue Aurene, 5 In. *illus* | 5036 |
| **Vase,** Calcite, Gold Hooked Feathers, Squat, Aurene, 1 ¾ In. | 518 |
| **Vase,** Calcite, Gold Inside, Flared, Stretched Lip, Inverted Saucer Foot, Aurene, 6 In. | 119 |
| **Vase,** Calcite, Gold Inside, Pinched Waist, Undulating Edge, Onionskin Rim, Aurene, 5 In. | 173 |
| **Vase,** Calcite, Ruffle, Aurene, Gold, 8 ¾ In. | 154 |
| **Vase,** Candlestick, Silver Leaf & Vine Design, Green, Aurene, Signed, 10 In. *illus* | 3000 |
| **Vase,** Cased Amethyst Over Opalescent Lavender, Acid Cut, Lotus Design, 7 x 8 ½ In. | 1840 |
| **Vase,** Cintra, Pink, Mottled, Footed, 7 In. | 259 |
| **Vase,** Cobalt Blue, Vertical Ribs, Flared, Inverted Saucer Foot, 9 ¼ In. | 182 |
| **Vase,** Cornucopia, White, 6 In. | 62 |
| **Vase,** Crystal, Round Tapered Base, 7 ½ In. | 90 |
| **Vase,** Dark Blue Jade, Curvy Body, Sun Ray Ribbing, Undulating Edge, 6 x 5 ½ In. | 1035 |
| **Vase,** Dragon Pattern, Jade Green Cut To Alabaster, Double Acid Cut Back, 9 In. | 1265 |
| **Vase,** Dragon, Silver Iridescent, Yellow, c.1825, 12 In. | 2375 |
| **Vase,** Evelyn, Rosaline Cut To Alabaster, Signed, 7 ½ In. | 834 |
| **Vase,** Fan, Ivory, Ribbed, Pinched, Ruffled, Footed, 6 ¼ In. | 173 |
| **Vase,** Fan, Optic Rib, Celeste Blue, Amber Disc Foot & Stem, 8 ½ In. *illus* | 230 |
| **Vase,** Fan, Pomona, Green, Optic Ribbed Body, Alabaster Stem, Foot, 8 ¼ In. | 230 |
| **Vase,** Finger, Gold, Magenta, Ruffled Rim, Aurene, 8 ¼ In. | 288 |
| **Vase,** Fir, Cone, Alabaster, Jade, Acid Cut Back, Round, c.1915, 7 ½ In. | 1440 |
| **Vase,** Flowers, Acid Cut, Dark Cut To Light Amethyst, Baluster, F. Carder, 18 In. | 7110 |
| **Vase,** Flowers, Amethyst, Over Alabaster, Cutback, F. Carder, 1900s, 15 In. | 3125 |
| **Vase,** Glass, 4 Scrolled Feet, Flared Lip, Signed, 9 ½ In. | 270 |
| **Vase,** Gold, Green Lily Pads & Vines, White Millefiori, Swollen, Aurene, 4 ¾ In. | 2645 |
| **Vase,** Gold, Red Highlights, Aurene, 10 ½ In. | 829 |
| **Vase,** Green, Bubble Decoration, Threaded Near Mouth, 9 ¾ In. | 207 |
| **Vase,** Green, Gold, Pulled Feather, Aurene, 9 In. | 5925 |
| **Vase,** Green, Metal, Pinched Waist, Heart, Gold Vines, Aurene, Signed, 4 In. | 81 |
| **Vase,** Green, Platinum Threading, Aurene, 6 In. | 592 |
| **Vase,** Grotesque, Ruby, Handkerchief Rim, Ribbed, Acid Stamped, 6 ¼ In. | 184 |
| **Vase,** Intarsia, Clear, Amethyst Flowers & Winding Stems, 6-Sided Foot, Carder, 12 In. | 14550 |
| **Vase,** Intarsia, Clear, Blue Leaves & Vines, Flared, 6-Sided Foot, F. Carder, 7 In. | 11850 |
| **Vase,** Ivory, 2 Raised Pillars, Flared, Ruffled Edge, Black Inverted Saucer Foot, 8 ½ In. | 356 |
| **Vase,** Ivrene, Calla Lily, 3 Buds, Opalescent, Blown, Signed, 12 ½ In. | 649 |
| **Vase,** Jack-In-The-Pulpit, Blue, Aurene, Signed, c.1910, 6 ¼ In. | 1093 |
| **Vase,** Jack-In-The-Pulpit, Gold, Blue, Purple, Pink, Aurene, Signed, 12 In. *illus* | 1094 |
| **Vase,** Jade Green, Alabaster, Acid Cutback, Bird Of Paradise, 9 x 8 In. | 288 |
| **Vase,** Majestic Pattern, Acid Cut, Black Cut To Celeste Blue, Swollen, 6 ¾ In. | 593 |
| **Vase,** Matzu Trees, Stylized Clouds, Acid Cut, Green To Alabaster, Round, 7 In. | 474 |
| **Vase,** Millefiori, Gold, Heart, Vine, Flower, Inverted Saucer Foot, Aurene, 7 ¾ In. | 5925 |
| **Vase,** Nimbus, Clear, Slanted Lobes, 6 In. | 313 |
| **Vase,** Nude, Etched, Stars, Sprigs, Walter Dorwin Teague, 1932, 11 ¾ x 4 ½ In. *illus* | 1250 |
| **Vase,** Peacock Eye, Feathers, Opal, Green Eyes, Gold, Aurene, Signed, 10 ¼ In. | 3738 |
| **Vase,** Phoenix, 13 ½ x 8 In. | 780 |
| **Vase,** Rosaline Over Alabaster, Scrolls, Leaves, Cutback, c.1950, 8 In. | 1750 |
| **Vase,** Rose Quartz, Cutback Leaves, Flowers, 3 Frosted Loop Feet, 7 x 8 In. | 2950 |
| **Vase,** Ruffle, Gold, Aurene, Fleur-De-Lis Stamp, 9 ¼ In. | 369 |
| **Vase,** Silverina Lattice, French Blue, Cylindrical, Flared Rim, 8 In. | 365 |
| **Vase,** Stick, Gold, Aurene, c.1935, 8 In. | 196 |
| **Vase,** Stump, 3-Prong, Blue, Disc Foot, Aurene 6 In. | 805 |

| | |
|---|---|
| **Vase,** Translucent Amber, Rolled Rim, Urn Shape, Gold, Aurene, c.1920, 10 In. .......................... | 1250 |
| **Vase,** Translucent Amber, Urn Shape, Gold Aurene, c.1920, 12 ¼ In. ....................................... | 1250 |
| **Vase,** Tricornered, Opal & Green Pulled Feather, Aurene, 2 In................................*illus* | 633 |
| **Vase,** Trumpet, Florentia, 5 Green Leaves, Ruffled Rim, Disc Foot, 13 In........................ | 2300 |
| **Vase,** Verre De Soie Glass, Fluted Rim, Blue Threading, c.1915, 6 In. .......................... | 360 |
| **Vase,** Verre De Soie, Pink Rim, Footed, Label, c.1915, 5 x 3 ¾ In. ......................*illus* | 210 |
| **Vase,** Verre De Soie, Twisted Stem, Ribbed Opalescent Cup, Crimped Rim, Footed, 8 In. ......... | 201 |
| **Wine,** Calcite, Gold Aurene Inside & Rim, Spread Foot, 6 ⅝ In., 4 Piece ............................. | 296 |

**STEVENS & WILLIAMS** of Stourbridge, England, made many types of glass, including layered, etched, cameo, and art glass, between the 1830s and 1930s. Some pieces are signed *S & W.* Many pieces are decorated with flowers, leaves, and other designs based on nature.

| | |
|---|---|
| **Biscuit Jar,** Blue Body, Perched Bird, Tree Branch, 5 ½ In. ........................................ | 1265 |
| **Bowl,** Cranberry Cut To Amber, Stemmed Flowering Branch, Arrows, Grapes, 8 In. ................... | 3450 |
| **Decanter,** Globe Shape Stopper, Paneled, Intaglio Cut, 2 Colors, c.1910, 9 In. ................ | 4200 |
| **Decanter,** Green Intaglio Cut To Green, c.1910, 17 In. ................................ | 6600 |
| **Decanter,** Thistle, Green Glass Cut To Clear, c.1910, 8 In............................... | 960 |
| **Dish,** Sweetmeat, Opal Body, Pull Up Decoration, Red, Yellow, Embossed Lid, 4 ¼ In. ............... | 288 |
| **Ewer,** Green Glass Cut To Clear, Sterling Silver Handle, Spout, Lid, c.1897, 10 In........................ | 7800 |
| **Fairy Lamp,** Satin, Peppermint Stripes, 6 ½ In....................................*illus* | 460 |
| **Inkwell,** Glass, Green Cut To Clear, Sterling Silver Mounted, c.1898, 4 In. ...................*illus* | 13200 |
| **Jar,** Green Cut To Clear, Sterling Silver, Embossed Lid, c.1896, 4 In. ........................ | 1440 |
| **Jug,** Blossom Overlay, Pink Opalescent Ground, Amber Handle, Metal Spout, Lid, 9 In. .......... | 413 |
| **Jug,** Claret, Intaglio, Green To Pink, Overlay, Flowers, Stopper, c.1900, 11 In., Pair..............*illus* | 10800 |
| **Jug,** Whiskey, Rock Crystal, Engraved Tusks, Flowers, Scrolls, 8 ½ In., Pair. ................. | 1500 |
| **Northwood Pink,** Yellow, White, Pull Up Glass, Silver Lid, Bail, 6 ½ In. ...................... | 236 |
| **Pitcher,** Applied Branch, Flowers, Peachblow Body, Amber Glass Feet, Handle, Rim, 14 In. ........ | 177 |
| **Pitcher,** Pink Opalescent Glass, Applied, Red Apple, Amber Thorn Handle, Sway Back, 7 In. ....... | 472 |
| **Plate,** Intaglio Cut Glass, Green, Pink Accents, Grapevines, c.1910, 8 In............................*illus* | 1080 |
| **Rose Bowl,** Branch, Blossom, Matsu-No-Ke, Brown, Yellow, Blue, 3-Footed, 6 x 7 In. ............. | 472 |
| **Rose Bowl,** Crimson, Exaggerated Zigzag Decoration, Ruffled, 6 In. ........................ | 3450 |
| **Rose Bowl,** Peacock Eye, Cream, Cranberry, Blue, Ruffled, 3 Rigaree Feet, 5 In........................ | 2185 |
| **Rose Bowl,** Pink Cased, Diamond, 3 Opalescent Lizards, 4 ½ In........................... | 489 |
| **Scent Bottle,** Silveria, Tapered, Embossed Metal Flip Lid, Collar, Glass Stopper, 5 In................. | 3105 |
| **Tumbler,** Landscape, Pond, Swans, Birds, Green, To Clear, c.1910, 4 ¼ In. .................. | 443 |
| **Vase,** Amber, Optic Ribbed, Undulating Rim, 2 Shaped Blue Handles, 9 ¾ In. ................ | 86 |
| **Vase,** Apricot Satin, Swirled Lines, Bottle Shape, 9 In................................ | 236 |
| **Vase,** Cranberry, Applied Petals, Thorn Feet, Green Leaves, Flower Blossom, Shape, 3 ¾ In. ......... | 413 |
| **Vase,** Flowers, Stems, Leaves, Pale Blue Ground, Cameo, Signed, 7 In. ..................... | 1049 |
| **Vase,** Green, White Satin, Thorn Feet, Branch, Ruffled Rim, 3-Footed, 6 x 7 In. ................... | 89 |
| **Vase,** Herringbone, Mother-Of-Pearl, Red & White Vertical Stripe, 6 x 3 ¾ In. ................... | 2415 |
| **Vase,** Jack-In-The-Pulpit, Green, Pink, Optic Rib, Clear Vine Wrap, 11 In. ...................... | 173 |
| **Vase,** Matsu-No-Ke, Pink, Crystal Gingko, Bulbous, Raspberry Prunt, 5 In. ...................... | 259 |
| **Vase,** Mother-Of-Pearl, Amber, Red Pull-Up, Peacock Eye, Cylindrical, 6 ½ In. ................. | 2645 |
| **Vase,** Pink, Flowers, Leaves, Yellow Ground, Butterfly, Cameo, 3 ⅜ In........................... | 711 |
| **Vase,** Pink, Purple Diagonal Lines, Pompeiian Swirl, Genie Lamp Shape.7 ½ In................. | 1298 |
| **Vase,** Pink, White Overlay, Serpents, 2 Birds In Nest, Striped Handles, Footed, 8 In. ................ | 2950 |
| **Vase,** Pompeiian Swirl, Blue, Red & Purple Opalescent, Shouldered, 5 In.................... | 575 |
| **Vase,** Pompeiian Swirl, Oval, Crimped Rim, 5 In.................................. | 1150 |
| **Vase,** Pulled Blue, White, Vertical Rows, Bottle Shape, Northwood, 7 ½ In........................ | 1003 |
| **Vase,** Scallop Rim, Peachblow Glass, Clear Applied Branch Blossom, Footed, 9 In. ................ | 177 |
| **Vase,** Silver Foil, Blue, Green, Gold Highlights, Ribbed Melon Shape, c.1910, 7 In. .............. | 1500 |
| **Vase,** Silveria, Green Threading, 2 Loop Handles, Signed, 4 ½ In. .............................*illus* | 2990 |
| **Vase,** Stick, Blue To Rose, Green Trailing, Iridescent Finish, Signed, 10 ½ In. ...................*illus* | 3738 |

**STIEGEL TYPE** glass is listed here. It is almost impossible to be sure a piece was actually made by Stiegel, so the knowing collector refers to this glass as "Stiegel type." Henry William Stiegel, a colorful immigrant to the colonies, started his first factory in Pennsylvania in 1763. He remained in business until 1774. Glassware was made in a style popular in Europe at that time and was similar to the glass of many other makers. It was made of clear or colored glass and was decorated with enamel colors, mold blown designs, or etching.

| | |
|---|---|
| **Cologne Bottle,** Blown, Multicolor Flowers, Leaves, Pewter Collar, Screw Cap, 5 ⅝ In................. | 266 |
| **Creamer,** Cobalt Blue, Flint, Expanded Diamond, Footed, Comet Tail, Loop Handle, 4 In............ | 502 |
| **Tumbler,** Blown, Enameled, Bird, Flowers, 1800s, 4 In................................. | 295 |

**Stone,** Bowl, Turquoise, Cover, Bas Relief Carved, Chinese, 2 ¼ x 3 ⅜ In.
$35,670

**Stone,** Figure, Dignitary, Seated, Official Belt, Jadeite, Pale Green, c.1850, 9 ¼ x 4 In.
$356

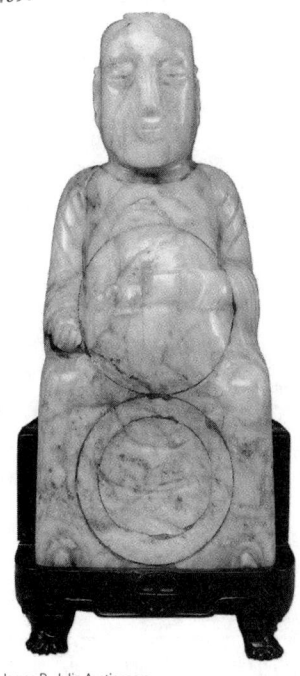

**Stone,** Figure, Rose Quartz, Water Buffalo, Reclining, Hardwood Stand, Chinese, c.1900, 10 In.
$1,112

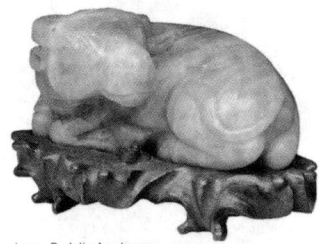

S

**Stone,** Seal, 2 Men, Calligraphy, Carved, Tan, Cream & Gray Inclusions, Chinese, 2 In.

$338

Skinner Auctioneers & Appraisers

**Stone,** Vase, Cover, Rose Quartz, Phoenixes, Flowers, Stand, Chinese, 1800s, 14 In.

$1,540

James D. Julia Auctioneers

**Stone,** Vase, Lapis Lazuli Carved, Foo Dog, Loose Ring Handles, 1900s, 5 x 6 In.

$1,000

Rago Arts & Auction Center

**STONE** includes those articles made of stones, coral, shells, and some other natural materials not listed elsewhere in this book. Micro mosaics (small decorative designs made by setting pieces of stone into a pattern), urns, vases, and other pieces made of natural stone are listed here. Stoneware is pottery and is listed in the Stoneware category. Alabaster, Jade, Malachite, Marble, and Soapstone are in their own categories.

| | |
|---|---:|
| **Bell Push,** Shaped Lapis Lazuli Body, Sterling Footed Base, Glass Button, 1½ x 1½ In. | 196 |
| **Bowl,** Turquoise, Cover, Bas Relief Carved, Chinese, 2¼ x 3⅜ In. ...............................*illus* | 35670 |
| **Buddha,** Hardstone, Serene Features, Burma, 1800s, 8¾ In. | 308 |
| **Buddha,** Pink Quartz, Seated, Round Green Marble Base, Bulb Inside, Electric, 3½ In. | 380 |
| **Bust,** Buddha, Hardstone, Zitan Base, 20th Century, 16 In. | 1152 |
| **Bust,** Woman, Curly Hair, Carved, Painted, New England, c.1840, 5 In. | 600 |
| **Figure,** Baptism, Man Pouring Water On Man's Head, Staff, P. Watts, c.1980, 11 x 6 In. | 120 |
| **Figure,** Beryl, Blue, Bamboo Section, Chinese, 1900s, 2¼ In. | 119 |
| **Figure,** Buddha, Sandstone, Lotus Position, Thailand, 1800s, 15½ x 10 x 7 In. | 281 |
| **Figure,** Dignitary, Seated, Official Belt, Jadeite, Pale Green, c.1850, 9¼ x 4 In. ..........*illus* | 356 |
| **Figure,** Elephant, Hardstone, Trunk Up, Carved, 1900s, 11 In. | 30 |
| **Figure,** Hardstone, Goddess Of Mercy, Guanyin, Holding Vase, Celadon, 1910, 12 In. | 369 |
| **Figure,** Ox, Lying Down, Hardstone, Carved, Applied Brown Patina, Wood Base, 7¾ x 18 In. | 253 |
| **Figure,** Rose Quartz, Guanyin, Holding Chrysanthemum, Carved, Wood Stand, 9 x 3 In., Pair | 184 |
| **Figure,** Rose Quartz, Water Buffalo, Reclining, Hardwood Stand, Chinese, c.1900, 10 In. .....*illus* | 1112 |
| **Figure,** Wild Boar, Base, Prato, Italy, 6 x 5 In. | 595 |
| **Fruit,** Cantaloupe, Traces Of Paint, 1890-1910, 7 In. | 240 |
| **Group,** Moorland Flight, Woman Holding Child In Arms, A. Sveubsson, 14¼ In. | 2176 |
| **Head,** Buddha, Borobudur Style, Indonesia, c.1910, 13 In. | 119 |
| **Head,** Buddha, Hair In Bun, Extended Ears, Carved, Gilt Trace, 8½ In. | 248 |
| **Inkstone,** Case, Carved, Green, 2 Phoenix-Head Wells, Shield Shape Well, 4 x 5¼ In. | 2390 |
| **Inkstone,** Tuan, Case, Carved Pinecone Section, Chinese, 1700s, 5½ x 4 In. | 10665 |
| **Keystone,** Limestone, Head In Rectangular Cavity, Tapered Frame, 1800s, 11½ x 10 In. | 2717 |
| **Medallion,** Depicting Diana, Carved Shell, Micro Mosaic Frame, c.1860, 5 x 4¼ In. | 920 |
| **Millstone,** Grinding Wheel, c.1800, 16 In. | 120 |
| **Millstone,** Sandstone, Red Hill Mill, Montgomery County, Pa., c.1790, 30 In. | 189 |
| **Obelisk,** Pietra Dura, Black Belgian Marble, Inlaid Flowers, Stones, Italy, 14 x 4 In., Pair | 2091 |
| **Picture,** Micro Mosaic, Rialto Bridge In Venice, Wood Frame, 4¼ x 6 In. | 288 |
| **Sages Climbing Mountain,** Attendant, Amber, Chinese, 7 x 5⅛ In. | 5412 |
| **Scroll Press,** Slate, Floral Relief Carving, Foo Dog Handle, Chinese, c.1900, 6 x 12 In. | 420 |
| **Seal,** 2 Men, Calligraphy, Carved, Tan, Cream & Gray Inclusions, Chinese, 2 In. ............*illus* | 338 |
| **Seal,** 6 Rotating Insets, Gilt Bronze Mount, Faceted Purple Handle, France, c.1890, 3¾ In. | 540 |
| **Seal,** Chicken Blood, Gray Ground, Red Reserves, Inscription, Box, Chinese, 1930s, 3 In. | 615 |
| **Seal,** Yellow, Old Man In Robes, Calligraphy Near Base, Chinese, 8 In. | 450 |
| **Sphere,** Agate, Polished, Caramel Color, Striated, Pedestal, 8 In. | 368 |
| **Tazza,** Blue John, English Neoclassical, Black Marble Base, 1800s, 5 x 5¼ In. | 1250 |
| **Tazza,** Blue John, Late Regency, Cylindrical Base, c.1825, 6½ x 4¾ In. | 8750 |
| **Vase,** Cover, Rose Quartz, Phoenixes, Flowers, Stand, Chinese, 1800s, 14 In. ...............*illus* | 1540 |
| **Vase,** Garniture, Seashell, Marble, Gilt Bronze, Vines, Leaves, Bird Finial, 8½ x 7 In., Pair | 922 |
| **Vase,** Lapis Lazuli Carved, Foo Dog, Loose Ring Handles, 1900s, 5 x 6 In. ...............*illus* | 1000 |
| **Vinaigrette,** Quartz, Gold Mounted, 2 Panels, Flower Rondel, Vinework, 1⅜ x 3 In. | 4500 |

**STONEWARE** is a coarse, glazed, and fired potter's ceramic that is used to make crocks, jugs, bowls, etc. It is often decorated with cobalt blue decorations. In the nineteenth and early twentieth centuries, potters often decorated crocks with blue numbers indicating the size of the container. A *2* meant 2 gallons. Stoneware is still being made. American stoneware is listed here.

| | |
|---|---:|
| **Bank,** Bulbous, Hand Molded Rooster Finial, Cobalt Blue Tulip, Vine, 10 In. | 59 |
| **Bank,** Cobalt Blue Flowers, Bell Shape Finial, Oval, R. Remmey, c.1870, 7¼ In. | 2300 |
| **Batter Jug,** Cobalt Blue Snowflake, Impressed F.H. Cowden, Harrisburg, 1800s, 8 In. | 420 |
| **Batter Pail,** Cobalt Blue Brushwork, Tube Spout, Bail Handle, T.G. Daub, c.1895, Gal. | 1495 |
| **Batter Pail,** Fan Shape Flowers, Cobalt Blue, Oval, Spout, c.1865, Gal. | 1150 |
| **Bottle,** Soda, J.A. Lagrange, Cobalt Blue Spout, Neck, c.1870, 9¾ In. | 115 |
| **Bottle,** Soda, J.E. Ferris, Cobalt Blue Spout, Shoulder, c.1870, 10 In. | 86 |
| **Bottle,** Soda, Laubenheimer & Kohl, Cobalt Blue Spout, Neck, c.1875, 10¼ In. | 57 |
| **Bottle,** Soda, P. Pfannebecker, Cobalt Blue Spout, Neck, c.1870, 9½ In. | 58 |
| **Bowl,** Cobalt Blue Stripes, Vines, Script, Lug Handles, Boughner, c.1855, 2 Gal., 8 x 11 In. | 2645 |
| **Bowl,** Peach Shape, Leaves, Exterior Inscription, Seal Signed, Chinese, 1800s, 6 x 9½ In. | 1007 |
| **Bowl,** Scalloped Rim, Red Glaze, Round Foot, Shoji Hamada, 4 x 7¼ In. | 984 |
| **Bowl,** Turquoise, Incised, Alev Ebuzziya Siesbye, c.1993, 5½ x 9½ In. ...............*illus* | 4500 |
| **Butter,** Cover, Cobalt Blue Feather, Flower, Hug Handles, 10 In. | 390 |
| **Charger,** Salt Glaze, Molded, Scalloped Rim, c.1800, 15 In. | 219 |

| | |
|---|---|
| **Chicken Waterer,** Blue Slip, Remmy, 9 In. | 5100 |
| **Chicken Waterer,** Dome Shape, Applied Trough & Handles, Button Finial, c.1850, 13 In. | 489 |
| **Churn,** Alkaline Glaze, Stand-Up Rim, Handle, Dasher, 19th Century, 17½ In. | 60 |
| **Churn,** Cobalt Blue Bird, Flower, White's, Utica, c.1880, 18 In. | 480 |
| **Churn,** Cobalt Blue Civil War Soldiers, Lug Handles, N.Y., c.1862, 5 Gal, 15½ In. | 402500 |
| **Churn,** Cobalt Blue Crested Bird, Flower, Lug Handles, White's, Utica, c.1800, 18 In. | 3360 |
| **Churn,** Cobalt Blue Flower, 3 Beaded Shoulder Rings, c.1880, 3 Gal., 15 x 8½ In. | 575 |
| **Churn,** Cobalt Blue Flower, Cowden & Wilcox, Pa., 3 Gal., 17 In. | 390 |
| **Churn,** Cobalt Blue Flower, Petals, Salt Glaze, Dish Rim, H. Smith & Co., 2 Gal. | 1840 |
| **Churn,** Cobalt Blue Horizontal Flower, Arch Handles, Baltimore, c.1875, 2 Gal., 13 x 7 In. | 196 |
| **Churn,** Cobalt Blue Leaves, 18 In. | 330 |
| **Churn,** Cobalt Blue Starburst Flower, Oval, Lug Handles, H.W. Whitman, c.1860, 5 Gal. | 2300 |
| **Churn,** Cobalt Blue, Bird, Salt Glaze, Dasher, S. Taft & Co., Keene, 3 Gal. | 1120 |
| **Churn,** Lid, Cobalt Blue Fantail Bird, Slip Trailed, Lug Handles, White's Utica, c.1870, 5 Gal. | 431 |
| **Churn,** Parrot, On Leaf, Cobalt Blue, Semi-Oval, Tooled Shoulder, Lug Handles, c.1880, 4 Gal. | 489 |
| **Churn,** Semi-Oval, Tooled Shoulder, Lug Handles, Wood Lid, Cornucopia, c.1880, 6 Gal. | 431 |
| **Churn,** Stencil, Hamilton & Jones, Greensboro, Pa., 5 Gal., 17¼ In. ........*illus* | 224 |
| **Churn,** Wood Lid, Cobalt Blue Bee Sting, 4, Applied Handles, Dasher, 14 In. ........*illus* | 240 |
| **Coffeepot,** Faust Blend, Relief Faust, Blanke's Drip, Blue, Cream, Whites, Utica, 9 In. | 420 |
| **Colander,** Basket Shape, Olive Green Glaze, 11½ In. | 266 |
| **Crock,** Albany Slip Glaze, N.Y., Impressed C. Colton & Co., No. 2, 5 x 6½ In. | 86 |
| **Crock,** Branch, Cobalt Blue Slip, Bird, Rowe Pottery Works, 1989, 11 In. | 12 |
| **Crock,** Butter, Cobalt Blue Flowers, Incised Lines, Flat Rim, 4 x 7 In. | 177 |
| **Crock,** Butter, Cobalt Blue Flowers, Richey & Hamilton, W. Va., c.1875, ½ Gal. | 230 |
| **Crock,** Cake, Cobalt Blue Dry Goods, Lug Handles, Hannibal, Ohio, c.1875, 2 Gal. | 1093 |
| **Crock,** Cake, Cobalt Blue Flower, Impressed T.G. Daub, Easton, Pa., 6 x 10¾ In. | 420 |
| **Crock,** Cake, Cobalt Blue Flowers, Tab Handles, B.C. Milburn, c.1856, ½ Gal., 5 x 7 In. | 863 |
| **Crock,** Cake, Cobalt Blue Slip Leaf, Applied Handles, Cowden & Wilcox, 5 x 10 In. | 189 |
| **Crock,** Cake, Lid, Blue Slip Flowers, Square Rim, Applied Handles, 1800s, 5½ x 9¼ In. | 295 |
| **Crock,** Cake, Lid, Cobalt Blue Flowers, Swags, Ribbed Lug Handles, c.1865, 11¾ x 7 In. | 978 |
| **Crock,** Cake, Swag, Cobalt Blue, Tooled Shoulder, Albany Slip Glaze, c.1875, Gal. | 230 |
| **Crock,** Cobalt Blue Apple, Tornado, Leaf, Lug Handles, Ohio, c.1875, 10 Gal. | 776 |
| **Crock,** Cobalt Blue Bird On Stump, Lug Handles, Cylindrical, E.R. Jones, 5 Gal., 13 In. | 2700 |
| **Crock,** Cobalt Blue Bird On Stylized Branch, 2 Blue Loop Handles, Germany, 20 In. | 150 |
| **Crock,** Cobalt Blue Bird, Branch, Arch Handles, Brady & Ryan, c.1890, 2 Gal., 11 x 11 In. | 374 |
| **Crock,** Cobalt Blue Bird, Branch, Cylindrical, N.Y., c.1850, 11 In. | 308 |
| **Crock,** Cobalt Blue Bird, Branch, Lug Handles, N.A. White & Sons, Utica, 10½ In. | 390 |
| **Crock,** Cobalt Blue Bird, Bush, Evan Jones, Pittston, Pa., 3 Gal., 11 In. | 2280 |
| **Crock,** Cobalt Blue Bird, F.B. Norton, Worcester, Ma., 3 Gal., 10 In. | 600 |
| **Crock,** Cobalt Blue Bird, Lug Handles, Impressed S.W. Schlock Crockery Store, 1800s, 12 In. | 450 |
| **Crock,** Cobalt Blue Bird, Lug Handles, White & Son, Utica, N.Y, 2 Gal., 11 In. | 570 |
| **Crock,** Cobalt Blue Bird, Twig, Lug Handles, J. Norton & Co., c.1860, 1½ x 7 In. | 390 |
| **Crock,** Cobalt Blue Chrysanthemum & Script, Cylindrical, Atwater, Ohio, 1879, 22 In. | 900 |
| **Crock,** Cobalt Blue Dashes, 2 Rows, Salt Glaze, Flattened Rim, J. Heatwole, c.1875, 4½ In. | 1955 |
| **Crock,** Cobalt Blue Decoration, P.H. Smith, c.1850, 12½ In. | 240 |
| **Crock,** Cobalt Blue Dove, Branch, Cylindrical, Square Rim, c.1890, 2 Gal., 11½ x 8 In. | 2415 |
| **Crock,** Cobalt Blue Eagle, Flowers, Stencil, Ear Handles, A. Conrad, Pa., 4 Gal., 15 In. | 984 |
| **Crock,** Cobalt Blue Eagle, Oval, Tapered, 2 Ear Handles, Rolled Rim, W.N. Craven, 17 In. | 2124 |
| **Crock,** Cobalt Blue Fish, Impressed 3, c.1850, 13 In. | 510 |
| **Crock,** Cobalt Blue Flower Basket, Lug Handles, J.A. & C.W. Underwood, c.1865, 6 Gal. | 403 |
| **Crock,** Cobalt Blue Flower Swag, Banded Rim, Tapered, 1800s, 8 In. | 160 |
| **Crock,** Cobalt Blue Flower, Leaf, Lug Handles, Solomon Bell, Va., c.1870, Gal., 7 x 9 In. | 230 |
| **Crock,** Cobalt Blue Flower, Slip Trailed, Lug Handles, J. Burger, c.1860, 3 Gal. | 1725 |
| **Crock,** Cobalt Blue Flowers, Brushed, Applied Handles, Tom Suttle, c.1850, 15½ In. ........*illus* | 4125 |
| **Crock,** Cobalt Blue Flowers, Glazed, Burger & Co., Rochester, 5 Gal., 13½ In. | 270 |
| **Crock,** Cobalt Blue Flowers, Higgins & Co., c.1850, 12½ In. | 360 |
| **Crock,** Cobalt Blue Flowers, Impressed J.M. Hickerson, Strasburg, Va., 10¾ In. | 120 |
| **Crock,** Cobalt Blue Flowers, Leaves, Impressed Circle, 1, Ear Handles, 10¼ In. | 236 |
| **Crock,** Cobalt Blue Flowers, Leaves, Molded Rim, Tapered, Applied Handles, 1800s, 9¾ In. | 295 |
| **Crock,** Cobalt Blue Flowers, Lug Handles, A.O. Whitmore, American, 12 In. | 94 |
| **Crock,** Cobalt Blue Flowers, Lug Handles, Cowden & Wilcox, Pa., Gal., 9¾ In. | 600 |
| **Crock,** Cobalt Blue Flowers, Lug Handles, D. Roberts & Co., Utica, c.1830, 5 Gal. | 403 |
| **Crock,** Cobalt Blue Flowers, Lug Handles, John Young & Co., Pa., 3 Gal., 13¼ In. | 570 |
| **Crock,** Cobalt Blue Flowers, Lug Handles, Pfaltzgraff, York, Pa., 4 Gal., 13 In. | 660 |
| **Crock,** Cobalt Blue Flowers, Lug Handles, Stamped F.T. Wright & Sons, 2 Gal., 9¼ In. | 130 |
| **Crock,** Cobalt Blue Flowers, Lug Handles, Wilson & Young, Harrisburg, c.1855, 10 In. | 960 |

**Stoneware,** Bowl, Turquoise, Incised, Alev Ebuzziya Siesbye, c.1993, 5½ x 9½ In.
$4,500

**Stoneware,** Churn, Stencil, Hamilton & Jones, Greensboro, Pa., 5 Gal., 17¼ In.
$224

**Stoneware,** Churn, Wood Lid, Cobalt Blue Bee Sting, 4, Applied Handles, Dasher, 14 In.
$240

S

**Stoneware,** Crock, Cobalt Blue Flowers, Brushed, Applied Handles, Tom Suttle, c.1850, 15 ½ In.
$4,125

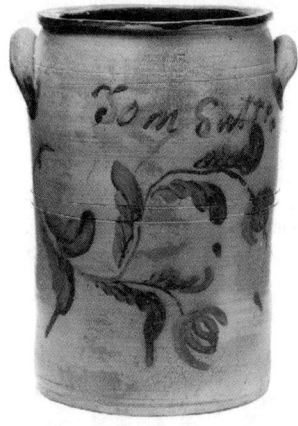

Garth's Auctioneers & Appraisers

**Stoneware,** Crock, Cobalt Blue, 4, Stenciled, McClellandtown Pa., Handles, c.1850, 14 ½ In.
$1,080

Garth's Auctioneers & Appraisers

**Stoneware,** Jug, Hunting Scene, Hunter On Horseback, Deer, Salt Glaze, Charles Graham, 7 ¼ In.
$633

Humler & Nolan

| | | |
|---|---|---:|
| **Crock,** Cobalt Blue House, Lug Handles, A.O. Whittemore, Havana, N.Y., 3 Gal., 11 In. | | 10880 |
| **Crock,** Cobalt Blue Leaves, Lug Handles, Lid, c.1865, 6 x 10 In. | | 175 |
| **Crock,** Cobalt Blue Pecking Chicken, Impressed Brady & Ryan Ellenville, N.Y., c.1890, 10 In. | | 510 |
| **Crock,** Cobalt Blue Script, Summit County, Ohio, Straight-Sided, Ear Handles, 11 In. | | 720 |
| **Crock,** Cobalt Blue Slip Flowers, Leaves, N.A. White & Son, 3 Gal., 10 In. | | 71 |
| **Crock,** Cobalt Blue Slip Trailed Flowers, Oval, Tab Handles, Baltimore, c.1820, 4 Gal. | | 489 |
| **Crock,** Cobalt Blue Stencil, 20, 2 Ear Handles, Donaghho Co., Parkersburg, W. Va., 25 In. | | 738 |
| **Crock,** Cobalt Blue Stenciled Designs, Flowers, Lug Handles, 6 Gal., 16 In. | | 570 |
| **Crock,** Cobalt Blue Stenciled Label, 2, G.A. & J.E. McCarthey, 11 ½ In. | | 780 |
| **Crock,** Cobalt Blue Stenciled, West Virginia Merchant, c.1885, Qt., 5 ½ x 6 In. | | 431 |
| **Crock,** Cobalt Blue Sunflower, Impressed N. Clark Jr., Athens, N.Y., 1800s, 11 ¼ In. | | 338 |
| **Crock,** Cobalt Blue Tree, Lug Handles, Impressed Haxton, Ottoman & Co., c.1870, 12 In. | | 19200 |
| **Crock,** Cobalt Blue Trumpet Flowers, Cylindrical, Incised Rings, 9 x 7 In. | | 863 |
| **Crock,** Cobalt Blue Tulips, A. Keister & Co., Arched Handles, Va., c.1840, 3 Gal., 13 In. | | 633 |
| **Crock,** Cobalt Blue Tulips, Lug Handles, Cylindrical, Cowden & Wilcox, Pa., Gal., 9 In. | | 480 |
| **Crock,** Cobalt Blue Tulips, Lug Handles, Impressed Somerfield Penn., 12 ½ In. | | 9900 |
| **Crock,** Cobalt Blue Tulips, Squared Rim, B.C. Milburn, Va., c.1850, Gal., 10 ½ In. | | 1840 |
| **Crock,** Cobalt Blue Vines, Incised Bands, Lug Handles, N. Cooper & Power, c.1860, 6 Gal. | | 2185 |
| **Crock,** Cobalt Blue, 4, Stenciled, McClellandtown Pa., Handles, c.1850, 14 ½ In. *illus* | | 1080 |
| **Crock,** Impressed Cowden & Son, Harrisburg, Pennsylvania, c.1900, 6 In. | | 62 |
| **Crock,** Impressed T.J. Shuttle, Cobalt Blue Tulip, Lug Handles, 17 ½ In. | | 1750 |
| **Crock,** Lid, Cobalt Blue Chicken Pecking Corn, Slip Trailed, Lug Handles, c.1885, 3 Gal. | | 230 |
| **Crock,** Lid, Cobalt Blue Incised Bands, Stencil, Barrel Shape, W.M. Rowe, 17 In. | | 415 |
| **Crock,** Lid, Cobalt Blue Peaches, Leaves, W.A. MacQuoid & Co., N.Y., c.1870, 3 Gal. | | 633 |
| **Crock,** Lid, Cobalt Blue, Bowers Three Thistles Snuff, Shouldered, 14 In. | | 720 |
| **Crock,** Lovebird, Cobalt Blue, Ear Handles, S. Hart Fulton, New York, 11 ½ In. | | 570 |
| **Crock,** Magnesium Brown, Stamped Paul Cushman, c.1810, 7 In. | | 584 |
| **Crock,** Rooster, Brushed Cobalt Blue, 2 Ear Handles, Oval, W.H. Farrar, 11 In. | | 2214 |
| **Crock,** Storage, Cobalt Blue 8, Stylized Loop, Cylindrical, Ear Handles, 18 x 11 ¾ In. | | 142 |
| **Crock,** Storage, Cobalt Blue Flowers, Leaves, Ear Handles, 3 Gal., 14 In. | | 236 |
| **Crock,** Tin Glaze, Brushed Manganese Swags, Lug Handles, Pennsylvania, 10 In. | | 90 |
| **Cuspidor,** Cobalt Blue Brushed Swags, R.J. Grier, Pa., c.1880, 4 ½ x 9 In. | | 518 |
| **Cuspidor,** Cobalt Blue Feathers, Drain Hole, Tapered, W.H. Lehew & Co., c.1865, 4 x 7 In. | | 690 |
| **Cuspidor,** Cobalt Blue Flowers, Footed, Concave Sides, Lug Handles, c.1875, 5 x 10 In. | | 1150 |
| **Doorstop,** Lamb, Resting, Bristol Slip Glaze, H.B. Pfaltzgraff, Pa., c.1925, 8 ¾ In. | | 201 |
| **Ewer,** Cobalt Blue Emblems, Gray Salt Glaze, 2 Intersecting Rings, Eagle Neck, 30 In. | | 177 |
| **Figurine,** Friar, Child, Manganese, Blue, Westerwald, c.1780, 10 ½ In. | | 154 |
| **Figurine,** Whippet, Reclining, Collar, Base, Painted, c.1875, 10 ¼ In. | | 287 |
| **Flask,** Cobalt Blue, Wreath, Square Spout, Flat Sides, Strap Handle, 1867, 10 In. | | 3335 |
| **Flask,** Ring, Brown Glaze, Snake Handle, Elliptical Base, c.1900, 13 ¼ In. | | 575 |
| **Flask,** Ring, Cobalt Blue Vines, Leaves, Buds, Applied Tapered Spout, c.1800, 10 In. | | 4600 |
| **Flowerpot,** Albany Slip, Tapered, Lugged Rim, Stamped, 1875, 10 ¾ In. | | 172 |
| **Flowerpot,** Cobalt Blue Leaves, Coved Rim, Attached Saucer, 19th Century, 7 x 9 In. | | 201 |
| **Ginger Jar,** Lid, Musicians, Flowers, Asia, 6 x 5 In. | | 32 |
| **Jar,** Brown, Albany Slip, Impressed Cushmans, 1811, 8 ½ In. | | 688 |
| **Jar,** Canning, Cobalt Blue Vine, Flowers, Gray, Bulbous, Squat, Handles, Coffman, 7 In. | | 4106 |
| **Jar,** Canning, Cobalt Blue Woman, Rifle, Flower, Bird, Tree, Morgantown, c.1870, 8 ¾ In. | | 7475 |
| **Jar,** Canning, Cylindrical, Stamped E.J. Miller, c.1865, ½ Gal., 8 x 2 In. | | 173 |
| **Jar,** Canning, Stamped, Cobalt Blue Plums, Rounded Rim, c.1840, 1 ½ Gal., 12 x 6 In. | | 748 |
| **Jar,** Celadon, Mottled, Alkaline Glaze, Turned Rim, Edgefield, c.1860, 10 ½ In. | | 236 |
| **Jar,** Cobalt Blue Bird On Stump, Leaves, Vines, Remmey, Philadelphia, c.1830, ½ Gal., 9 In. | | 2875 |
| **Jar,** Cobalt Blue Brushed Flowers, Lug Handles, Impressed E.L., c.1840, 3 ½ In. | | 1610 |
| **Jar,** Cobalt Blue Brushwork, Tooled Shoulder, Lug Handles, Greensboro, Pa., c.1875, 6 Gal. | | 374 |
| **Jar,** Cobalt Blue Chain Border, Flower, Leaf, Wavy Line, B.C. Milburn, c.1850, 4 Gal., 8 x 15 In. | | 3450 |
| **Jar,** Cobalt Blue Eagle, Shield, Salt Glaze, Swollen, Ear Handles, c.1825, 3 Gal., 12 In. | | 74750 |
| **Jar,** Cobalt Blue Feathers, Thin Rim, Cylindrical, Mid-Atlantic, c.1865, 8 x 6 In. | | 104 |
| **Jar,** Cobalt Blue Fish, Bands, Sponged Lug Handles, Uniontown, c.1870, 4 Gal. | | 2300 |
| **Jar,** Cobalt Blue Flower, Tapered, Arched Handles, James River, c.1825, 2 Gal., 13 x 7 In. | | 2070 |
| **Jar,** Cobalt Blue Flowers, B.C. Milburn, c.1840, 1 ½ Gal., 11 x 7 In. | | 460 |
| **Jar,** Cobalt Blue Flowers, Branches, Lug Handles, Va., c.1850, 11 x 7 In. | | 3450 |
| **Jar,** Cobalt Blue Flowers, Footed, Tall Collar, Oval, c.1865, ½ Gal. | | 288 |
| **Jar,** Cobalt Blue Flowers, Incised Bands, Tapered, Pocket Handles, Pa., c.1860, 4 Gal. | | 546 |
| **Jar,** Cobalt Blue Flowers, Rolled Handles, S. Frayser, c.1840, Gal., 9 x 5 In. | | 920 |
| **Jar,** Cobalt Blue Flowers, Swags, Ribbed Handles, Philadelphia, c.1860, Gal., 10 In. | | 259 |
| **Jar,** Cobalt Blue Inscribed, Bayless McCarthy & Co., Kentucky, 1800s, 8 In. | | 246 |
| **Jar,** Cobalt Blue Leaves, Lug Handles, Tapered, Rockingham Co., c.1860, 2 Gal., 12 x 8 In. | | 863 |

| | |
|---|---|
| **Jar**, Cobalt Blue Neck Band, Impressed John Bell, Waynesboro, Pa., 5¾ In. | 246 |
| **Jar**, Cobalt Blue Quatrefoil, Tapered, Tab Handles, James River, c.1845, 3 Gal., 13 x 7 In. | 8050 |
| **Jar**, Cobalt Blue Running Rabbit, Flared Rim, Lug Handles, Cylindrical, c.1870, Gal. | 1150 |
| **Jar**, Cobalt Blue Shield, Tree, Salt Glaze, Flared Rim, Tab Handles, Oval, 10 x 6 In. | 2300 |
| **Jar**, Cobalt Blue Stencil, Lipscomb & Somerville, Va., c.1880, 10 x 6 In. | 259 |
| **Jar**, Cobalt Blue Stripes, Stenciled WM. H. Overholt & Co., W. Va., c.1880, 10 x 6 In. | 403 |
| **Jar**, Cobalt Blue Sunflower, Leaves, B.C. Milburn, c.1845, 1 ½ Gal., 11 x 7⅜ In. | 431 |
| **Jar**, Cobalt Blue Tulip, Feathers, H.C. Smith, Tab Handles, Va., c.1845, Gal., 9 x 5 In. | 1150 |
| **Jar**, Cobalt Blue Tulip, Leaves, Colored Neck, B.C. Milburn, c.1860, ½ Gal., 8 x 6 In. | 2990 |
| **Jar**, Cobalt Blue Vines, Tooled Shoulder, Lug Handles, Pa., c.1870, 4 Gal. | 345 |
| **Jar**, Cobalt Blue Wreath, Albany Ware, Flared Rim, Incised Shoulder, Lug Handles, 16 In. | 307 |
| **Jar**, Cobalt Blue Y-Shape Flower, H.C. Smith, Irregular Rim, c.1845, Gal., 10 x 6 In. | 489 |
| **Jar**, Cobalt Blue, Stripes, J.A. Miller, Staple & Fancy Groceries, c.1870, Gal., 10 x 6 In. | 546 |
| **Jar**, Collared Neck, Squared Rim, Stamped S.C. Milburn, Gal., c.1870, 10 x 7 In. | 184 |
| **Jar**, Cream, Cobalt Blue Tulip, Flattened Rim, H.B. Pfaltzgraff, Pa., c.1875, ½ Gal. | 518 |
| **Jar**, Cylindrical, Stamped B.C. Milburn, c.1865, ½ Gal., 7¾ x 5 In. | 150 |
| **Jar**, Lid, Cobalt Blue Bird, Glazed, Ear Handles, Lamson & Swasey, Portland, Me., 14 In. | 240 |
| **Jar**, Lid, Cobalt Blue Bird, Lug Handles, West Troy Pottery, c.1875, 2 Gal. | 546 |
| **Jar**, Lid, Impressed Bands, Ribbed Strap Handles, Jeremiah Burpee, 10 ½ In. | 531 |
| **Jar**, Olive, Glazed Rim, Bulbous, Footed, France, 1800s Style, 24 x 16 In. | 1045 |
| **Jar**, Oyster, Red, Cylindrical, T. Commeraw, c.1820, 8 In. | 5175 |
| **Jardiniere**, Classical Figures, Flowers, Blue, Cream, Footed, Germany, 34 In. | 120 |
| **Jardiniere**, Tree Trunk Shape, 7 x 8¼ In. | 270 |
| **Jug**, Alkaline Glaze, Amber Olive Drips, Handle, Incised, c.1870, Georgia, 15 ½ In. | 1534 |
| **Jug**, Alkaline Glaze, Incised 3, Strap Handle, 15¼ In. | 531 |
| **Jug**, Batter, Cobalt Blue Dotted Squiggle, Brown Interior, New England, c.1850, 10 In. | 330 |
| **Jug**, Batter, Cobalt Blue Flowers, Banded, Bulbous, Virginia, c.1855, 11 In. | 900 |
| **Jug**, Batter, Cobalt Blue Flowers, Leaf Wreath, Wood Grip Handle, Evan R. Jones, 10 In. | 885 |
| **Jug**, Batter, Cobalt Blue Slip Flowers, Leaves, Cowden & Wilcox, Harrisburg, 9 ½ In. | 1121 |
| **Jug**, Beehive Shape, Lime Glaze, Brown Mottling, Washington Becham, 8 In. | 590 |
| **Jug**, Bellarmine, Applied Face, Applied Handle, Medallion, 11 In. | 1020 |
| **Jug**, Bellarmine, Applied Face, Beard, Applied Handle, Stamped Design, 17 In. | 1200 |
| **Jug**, Bellarmine, Applied Face, Beard, Impressed 2, Strap Handle, 1700s, 14 In. | 960 |
| **Jug**, Cobalt Blue 3 Branched Flowers, Applied Strap Handle, Oval, 13 In. | 130 |
| **Jug**, Cobalt Blue Bellflowers, Impressed 10, Applied Handles, 1840-60, 24 In. | 1800 |
| **Jug**, Cobalt Blue Bird & Flower, Sloped Shoulder, S. Hart, Fulton, 2 Gal., 13 In. | 960 |
| **Jug**, Cobalt Blue Bird On Blossoming Branch, Glazed, D. Melvin, 17 In. | 420 |
| **Jug**, Cobalt Blue Bird On Branch, Applied Strap Handle, Flattened Rim, 2 Gal., 13¾ In. | 266 |
| **Jug**, Cobalt Blue Bird On Stump, Slip, Squared Spout, Fort Edward Pottery, c.1859, 4 Gal. | 633 |
| **Jug**, Cobalt Blue Bird, Flower, Slip Trailed, W.H. Farrar, Geddes N.Y., c.1860, 3 Gal. | 805 |
| **Jug**, Cobalt Blue Bird, Flowers, Ribbed Handle, N.Y., c.1825, 2 Gal. | 575 |
| **Jug**, Cobalt Blue Bird, Gray Glaze, E.A. Buck & Co., Boston, 5 Gal. | 468 |
| **Jug**, Cobalt Blue Bird, Tapered Foot, Oval, H. & G. Nash, Utica, c.1830, 2 ½ Gal. | 1150 |
| **Jug**, Cobalt Blue Cornucopias, Beehive Shape, A. Conrad, West Virginia, c.1860, Gal., 12 In. | 518 |
| **Jug**, Cobalt Blue Daisy, Slip Trailed, Handle, Baltimore, c.1820, Gal., 11¾ In. | 1725 |
| **Jug**, Cobalt Blue Deer, Sloped, Giles & Co. Dealer In Variety Store, Cherry Valley, 16 In. | 15600 |
| **Jug**, Cobalt Blue Dot & Loop, 1800s, Miniature, 4 ½ In. | 1320 |
| **Jug**, Cobalt Blue Dotted Flower, Leaves, Impressed J.W. Greene & Brother, 3 Gal., 15 ½ In. | 420 |
| **Jug**, Cobalt Blue Double Flower, Moyer, Pa., Gal., 11 ½ In. | 450 |
| **Jug**, Cobalt Blue Dove Of Peace, H.B. Pfaltzgraff, Pa., c.1875, Gal. | 690 |
| **Jug**, Cobalt Blue Eagle, Inscribed Star Pottery, Pa., 1800s, 2 Gal., 13 ½ In. | 1020 |
| **Jug**, Cobalt Blue F.H. Cowden Harrisburg, Pa., c.1860, 10 ½ In. | 360 |
| **Jug**, Cobalt Blue Fish, Tooled Spout, J. Fenton, c.1800, Gal., 11¾ In. | 805 |
| **Jug**, Cobalt Blue Flower, Cowden & Wilcox, Harrisburg Pa., 10 ½ In. | 135 |
| **Jug**, Cobalt Blue Flower, Stamped H. Smith & Co., c.1830, 4 Gal., 18 In. | 12650 |
| **Jug**, Cobalt Blue Flowers, Applied Handle, Ringed Neck, Incised FW, 13 In. | 390 |
| **Jug**, Cobalt Blue Flowers, Squared Spout, Cowden & Wilcox, Pa., c.1865, Gal. | 201 |
| **Jug**, Cobalt Blue Flowers, Tapered Spout, Cowden & Wilcox, Pa., c.1865, 4 Gal. | 546 |
| **Jug**, Cobalt Blue Flowers, Vine, Stripes, Strap Handle, Pa., c.1860, 2 Gal., 14 In. | 690 |
| **Jug**, Cobalt Blue Grass, Tree, Sloped Shoulder, Squared Spout, c.1870, 3 Gal. | 517 |
| **Jug**, Cobalt Blue Heart, Applied Handle, Impressed, Burger, Rochester, 14 In. | 210 |
| **Jug**, Cobalt Blue Horse, Cantering, Oval, c.1840, 4 Gal., 17 In. | 6900 |
| **Jug**, Cobalt Blue Line, Ribbed Handle, Oval, Paul Cushman, N.Y., c.1810, 2 Gal. | 661 |
| **Jug**, Cobalt Blue Spotted Bird, Impressed Edmands & Co., N.Y., 1800s, 13 ½ In. | 420 |
| **Jug**, Cobalt Blue Stencil, Rose, Hamilton & Jones, Pa., 2 Gal., 15 In. | 403 |
| **Jug**, Cobalt Blue Triple Flower Bouquet, Salt Glaze, W.H. Farrar, 16 ½ In. | 461 |

**Stoneware**, Pepper Pot, Dome Top, Incised Scroll, F.H Cowden, Harrisburg, Pa., 1861, 3¾ In.
$47,200

Conestoga Auction Co., Inc.

**Stoneware**, Pitcher, Ale, Cobalt Blue, Flowers, Leaves, Wanner & Kline, Pa., c.1850, 11 In.
$2,074

James D. Julia Auctioneers

**Stoneware**, Planter, Peony, White, Green, Brown, Marked, Chinese, 7 ½ x 5 x 2 In.
$948

James D. Julia Auctioneers

S

## Stoneware Face Jugs

Face jugs are jugs with distorted faces, crooked teeth, and big eyes. Older face jugs, pieces with alkaline glaze, and jars with cobalt decorations—animals, plants, or people—sell for the highest prices.

---

**Stoneware,** Teapot, Cobalt Blue Sponged Glaze, 19th Century, 6 In.
$295

Conestoga Auction Co., Inc.

---

**Stoneware,** Teapot, Engraved Calligraphy, Yi Hsing, Signed, Gu Jingzhou, Chinese, c.1910, 7 In.
$3,555

James D. Julia Auctioneers

---

**Stoneware,** Teapot, Flowering Scrolls, Signed, Yi Hsing Ware, Chinese, c.1890, 3 x 3¼ In.
$119

James D. Julia Auctioneers

---

**Stoneware,** Vase, Incised Design, Salt Glazed, Shoji Hamada, Signed, Box, c.1938, 8 x 8½ In.
$3,000

Cowan's Auctions

| | |
|---|---|
| **Jug,** Cobalt Blue Tulip, Tooled Spout, Oval, Manhattan, c.1810, 3 Gal. | 863 |
| **Jug,** Cobalt Blue Tulips, Oval, H.B. Pfaltzgraff, Pa., c.1860, 3 Gal. | 345 |
| **Jug,** Cobalt Blue Tulips, Strap Handle, Ohio, c.1870, 3 Gal., 16 In. | 81 |
| **Jug,** Cobalt Blue Vine & Stripe, Tooled Spout, Oval, Pa., c.1870, 2 Gal. | 748 |
| **Jug,** Face, Amber, Smiling, Handle, 4-Sided, David & Flossie Meaders, Ga., 10¾ x 12 In. | 201 |
| **Jug,** Face, Brown Glaze, Strap Handle, Incised Eyes, Teeth, Bands, Leftwich, 1900s, 12 In. | 316 |
| **Jug,** Face, Cobalt Blue Eyes, Coleslaw Beard, Handle, Cylindrical, Va., c.1880, 8½ In. | 12650 |
| **Jug,** Face, Dark Alkaline, Nose Off Face, Inscribed Ouch, Handles, S. Abee, c.1995, 19½ In. | 173 |
| **Jug,** Face, Green Streaky Glaze, Large Ears, Eyes, L. Meaders, Cleveland, Ga., c.1980, 10 In. | 805 |
| **Jug,** Face, Inset Rock Eyes, Olive Green, Black, Georgia, c.1950, 9 In. | 1485 |
| **Jug,** Face, Matte Glaze, Inset Crooked Eyes, Signed Lanier Meaders, Ga., c.1960, 9 In. | 1380 |
| **Jug,** Face, Olive Green, Brown, Protruding Eyes, Nose, China Teeth, Reinhardt, c.1937, 8 In. | 2530 |
| **Jug,** Face, Runny Olive Green, Brown, Ceramic Eyes, Smirk, Signed Lanier Meaders, 9 In. | 1150 |
| **Jug,** Face, Stone Teeth, Painted Eyes, Olive Mottled Glaze, Handle, L. Meaders, 9 In. | 1140 |
| **Jug,** Flower Basket, Cobalt Blue, Tan Glaze, Tapered, F.B. Norton, Worcester, 4 Gal. | 761 |
| **Jug,** Flower, Cobalt Blue, Salt Glaze, Strap Handle, Oval, 3 Gal., 15¼ In. | 330 |
| **Jug,** Hot Water, Handle, Half Cylinder Shape, 10 In. | 30 |
| **Jug,** Hunting Scene, Hunter On Horseback, Deer, Salt Glaze, Charles Graham, 7¼ In. ... *illus* | 633 |
| **Jug,** Incised Horses, Flowers, Blue, Green, Gray, Germany, c.1820, 19 In. | 3750 |
| **Jug,** Incised Man, Smoking, Initials, Squat, Oval, G. Suttles, Texas, c.1900, 9 In. | 661 |
| **Jug,** Incised Wave Band, Stamped Miller & Woodward, Va., c.1885, 9 In. | 748 |
| **Jug,** Lid, Lead Glaze, Manganese Spatter, Oval, William Packer, 10 In. | 1800 |
| **Jug,** Sgraffito Flower Decoration, Swollen, Handle, 9½ In. | 270 |
| **Jug,** Wood Stopper, 2 Handles, Cylindrical, c.1875, 5 Gal. | 345 |
| **Milk Pan,** Cobalt Blue, Spout, Flared, Tapered, Handles, c.1875 | 173 |
| **Mortar & Pestle,** Albany Slip Glaze, W.J. & E.G. Schrop, Springfield, Ohio, 6¼ In. | 150 |
| **Mug,** Cobalt Blue Drape & Dot, Barrel Shape, Handle, 1890, Inscribed A.L.H., Ohio, 3 In. | 690 |
| **Mug,** Oak Tree, Leaves, Acorns, Molded, Naturalistic Glaze, Tapered, Twig Handle, 4 In. | 403 |
| **Pan,** Cobalt Blue Tulip, Squared Rim, Lug Handles, Tapered, G & A Black, c.1860 | 2990 |
| **Pepper Pot,** Dome Top, Incised Scroll, F.H. Cowden, Harrisburg, Pa., 1861, 3¾ In. ... *illus* | 47200 |
| **Pitcher,** Albany Slip Glaze, 12 Fluted Panels, Scrolls, John T. Winslow, Maine, c.1860, 9 In. | 210 |
| **Pitcher,** Ale, Cobalt Blue, Flowers, Leaves, Wanner & Kline, Pa., c.1850, 11 In. ... *illus* | 2074 |
| **Pitcher,** Cobalt Blue Accents, Incised Stylized Feathers, Strap Handle, Oval, 9 In. | 360 |
| **Pitcher,** Cobalt Blue Brushed Swags, Buds, Banding, J. Eberly & Bro., c.1885, Gal. | 3450 |
| **Pitcher,** Cobalt Blue Brushed Tulips, 2 Spouts, Flat Arched Top Handle, 14 In. | 180 |
| **Pitcher,** Cobalt Blue Clover, Flared Rim, Oval, c.1875, 3½ In. | 1840 |
| **Pitcher,** Cobalt Blue Dashes, Pinched Spout, Incised M.C.M., 1884, 4½ In. | 1080 |
| **Pitcher,** Cobalt Blue Feather, Low Belly, c.1880, Gal., 5 x 9 In. | 920 |
| **Pitcher,** Cobalt Blue Flower, Feathers, Waves, Incised Bands, Strap Handle, S. Bell, 12 In. | 6325 |
| **Pitcher,** Cobalt Blue Flower, Swag, Incised Neck, Strap Handle, c.1870, 2 Gal., 13 In. | 805 |
| **Pitcher,** Cobalt Blue Flowers, Incised T, 10 In. | 1560 |
| **Pitcher,** Cobalt Blue Flowers, Leaves, Clover Plant, Baltimore, c.1870, Gal. | 920 |
| **Pitcher,** Cobalt Blue Flowers, Leaves, Oval, Signed R.C.R., c.1870, ½ Gal. | 575 |
| **Pitcher,** Cobalt Blue Flowers, Swags, 9½ In. | 224 |
| **Pitcher,** Cobalt Blue Flowers, Tan Salt Glaze, Rockingham Co., Pt., 5½ In. | 2530 |
| **Pitcher,** Cobalt Blue Fruit, Vines, Oval, Incised, Rockingham County, Va., c.1866, Gal. | 978 |
| **Pitcher,** Cobalt Blue Hanging Flowers, Leaves, c.1850, 7 In. | 431 |
| **Pitcher,** Cobalt Blue Incised Bird, Squat, Flared Collar, Indiana, 1844, 6¾ In. | 6325 |
| **Pitcher,** Cobalt Blue Initials, Brushwork, Cylindrical, Pa., c.1890, 5 In. | 3220 |
| **Pitcher,** Cobalt Blue Lady Liberty, Flag, Spongeware, Bristol Slip Ground, c.1900, 10⅜ In. | 345 |
| **Pitcher,** Cobalt Blue Leaves, Grapes, Bulbous, Molded Rim, Strap Handle, 12½ In. | 189 |
| **Pitcher,** Cobalt Blue Leaves, Impressed 1, Strap Handle, c.1850, 10 In. | 450 |
| **Pitcher,** Cobalt Blue Leaves, Molded Figures, Seated Women, Incised, 1909, 12 In. | 120 |
| **Pitcher,** Cobalt Blue Slip, Flowers, Leaves, Rowe Pottery Works, 6¼ In. | 24 |
| **Pitcher,** Cobalt Blue Slip, Tulip & Leaves, Beaumont Pottery, 1983, 10¾ In. | 12 |
| **Pitcher,** Cobalt Blue Tulips, Applied Strap Handle, c.1850, 7 In. | 1020 |
| **Pitcher,** Cobalt Blue Vine, Flower, Slip Tailed, Flared Collar, New England, Gal. | 403 |
| **Pitcher,** Cobalt Blue Vines, Coggled Flower, Ribbed Rim, Thompson Pottery, Gal., 9⅜ In. | 2875 |
| **Pitcher,** Dogs Attacking Stag & Boar, Molded, Branch Handle, Solomon Bell, 7 In. | 1495 |
| **Pitcher,** Grapes, Leaves, Panels, Albany Slip Glaze, S. Risely, Conn., c.1845, 10 In. | 1020 |
| **Pitcher,** Lion, Standing, Blue Slip, R.H. Diebboll, 9 In. | 59 |
| **Pitcher,** Long Haired Man, Blue, Cream, Germany, c.1890, 11 In. | 90 |
| **Pitcher,** Slip Fuchsia, Tanware, Applied Strap Handle, New Geneva, 9 In. | 570 |
| **Pitcher,** Stag & Boar, Dark Brown Glaze, American Pottery, N.J., c.1850 | 270 |
| **Pitcher,** Tanware, 2 Blossoms, Brushwork, Flared Spout, c.1890, 6¾ In. | 374 |
| **Pitcher,** Tanware, Fuchsia Vines, Albany Slip Dashes, Stripes, Stepped Collar, c.1890, 7 In. | 978 |

**Pitcher,** Water, Cobalt Blue Flowers, Slip Design, Signed John Bell Waynesboro, Gal., 11 In. ....... 4800
**Planter,** Peony, White, Green, Brown, Marked, Chinese, 7 ½ x 5 x 2 In................................*illus* 948
**Porringer,** Salt Glaze, Flared Bowl, Strap Handle, Bead Foot, Virginia, 2 ½ x 5 In. .................... 115
**Pot,** Cobalt Blue Script, Elizabeth Heatwole, Squat, Neck Ring, Handles, Oval, 1851, 8 In. ........... 11500
**Pot,** Lid, Cobalt Blue Branch, Salt Glaze, Neck Ring, Handles, Oval, Rockingham Co., 7 In. ........ 9775
**Punch Bowl,** Cobalt Blue, Flower Rim, Footed, 1880s, 19 ½ In. ......................................... 360
**Sugar,** Cobalt Blue Flowers, Leaves, Lug Handles, Pa., 5 In. ............................................. 3000
**Teapot,** Cobalt Blue Sponged Glaze, 19th Century, 6 In. ..........................................*illus* 295
**Teapot,** Creamer, Embossed, Classical Figures, Acanthus Leaves, Enameled, c.1810, 5 ¾ In......... 236
**Teapot,** Engraved Calligraphy, Yi Hsing, Signed, Gu Jingzhou, Chinese, c.1910, 7 In............*illus* 3555
**Teapot,** Flowering Scrolls, Signed, Yi Hsing Ware, Chinese, c.1890, 3 x 3 ¼ In. ....................*illus* 119
**Tobacco Jar,** Manganese Glaze, Applied Branch, 3 Leaves, Stepped Shoulder, 7 x 4 In. ............ 6900
**Tureen,** Castle Scene, Stag Finial, Handles, Germany, 1800s, 15 In. ..................................... 300
**Umbrella Stand,** Cobalt Blue, Cattails, Insects, Pond Life, Utica, c.1910, 20 x 9 In. .................. 403
**Urn,** Eagle, Banner, Open Dolphin Handles, Unglazed, Molded John Bell, c.1876, 10 x 15 In. ...... 1265
**Vase,** Abstract Design, Green, Red, Blue, Black, Blob Foot, Oval, P. Voulkos, 14 In. .................. 3250
**Vase,** Bamboo Brush Strokes, Bottle Shape, Shoji Hamada, Japan, c.1960, 6 ½ In. ................... 813
**Vase,** Incised Design, Salt Glazed, Shoji Hamada, Signed, Box, c.1938, 8 x 8 ½ In. .............*illus* 3000
**Vase,** Incised, Glazed, Emile Lenoble, Choisy-Le-Roi, Marked, c.1930, 8 ½ x 9 In. .............*illus* 5312
**Water Cooler,** Blue Flower, Beehive Shape, Handles, J. Lew, c.1875, 10 Gal., 22 x 13 In. ............. 3738
**Water Cooler,** Blue Stag, Doe, Forest Design, Pinecone Wreath Design On Lid, 12 x 10 ¼ In....... 325
**Water Cooler,** Cobalt Blue Bird, Bands, Ottman Bro's, Fort Edward, N.Y., 15 x 14 In. ................ 593
**Water Cooler,** Cobalt Blue Flowers, Lug Handles, Cylindrical, 7 In. ..................................... 900
**Water Cooler,** Cobalt Blue Flowers, Lug Handles, Oval, Stamped Russell, c.1850, 5 Gal. ............ 805
**Water Cooler,** Cobalt Blue Flowers, Square, Lug Handles, H. Remmey, c.1835, 4 Gal., 18 In. ...... 1035
**Water Cooler,** Lid, Clover, Squat, Tapered, Bunghole, Applied Tab Handles, c.1870, 2 Gal. .......... 431
**Wine Cooler,** Admiral Nelson, Royal Navy Insignia, Davenport, c.1830, 10 In. ....................... 2813

---

**STORE** fixtures, cases, cutters, and other items that have no advertising as part of the decoration are listed here. Most items found in an old store are listed in the Advertising category in this book.

---

**Alarm,** Till, Tucker & Dorsey Mfg. Co., Drawer, Cast Bell, c.1890, 19 x 16 In................................. 150
**Bench,** Watchmaker's, Oak, Roll Top, 13 Drawers, J.H. Rosenberg, Chicago, 48 x 43 In. ........... 1046
**Bin,** Grain, Pine, Painted Blue, Cleated Ends, 4 Interior Sections, c.1810, 77 x 28 In. .................... 1845
**Cabinet,** Pine, Poplar, 7 Drawers, Carved Scrolls, Diamonds, Crosses, c.1890, 18 x 16 In. ............. 219
**Cabinet,** Spool, Walnut, 4 Drawers, Victorian, 10 ½ x 25 In. ............................................. 225
**Cabinet,** X-Ray Shoe Fitter, Wood, Metal, Shoe Flouroscope, c.1938. .................................. 330
**Case,** Display, Canes, Umbrellas, Oak, Slanted Hinged Lid, Stick & Ball Dividers, 48 In. .............. 708
**Case,** Display, Slant Front, Glass, Carved Wood Frame, 28 ½ In............................................ 570
**Cigar Cutter,** Figural, Waiter, Bronze, 7 ½ In. .......................................................... 330
**Cigarette Dispenser,** Elephant, Iron, 9 In. .............................................................. 60
**Coffee Grinders** are listed in the Coffee Mill category.
**Coin Counter,** Brandt, Automatic, Footed, 14 x 12 In.................................................*illus* 210
**Counter,** Oak, 28 Spool Drawers, Display Cases, J.D. Warren, 1910s, 85 x 30 In..................*illus* 1680
**Display Case,** Brass, Gilt, Beveled Glass, Trapezoid, Bracket Feet, Cherubs, 6 x 6 x 7 In. .............. 236
**Display,** Fly Swatters, Buy One For Every Room, Wood, Cardboard, c.1930, 25 x 21 In. ............... 345
**Display,** Ice Cream Cone, Glass, Metal, Round, 12 In. ................................................... 150
**Display,** Postcard, Ferris Wheel, Metal, Flowers, Rotates, Seats For Cards, 30 x 36 In. ................. 978
**Display,** Tobacco, Shelf, Pullout Tin Tray, Sliding Doors, Oak, Md., c.1890, 44 x 42 In. ............... 288
**Display,** Top Hat, Metal, Painted, Red, Black Band, Hudson's, Detroit, 10 ¼ x 14 ½ In. ............... 420
**Figure,** Lobster, Rolling Stand, Open Claw, Red, 63 In. .................................................. 660
**Head,** Mannequin, Gentleman, Handlebar Mustache, Beard, Plaster, Painted, Malley's, 14 In. ..... 308
**Ladder,** Oak, Galvanized Metal Rollers, c.1915, 10 In. .................................................... 115
**Mannequin,** Boy, Blond, Blue Eyes, Sailor Outfit, Fiberglass, 43 In...................................... 240
**Merchandise Grabber,** Clamp, Hook, Wood, Pressed Steel, c.1900, 50 In. ............................. 115
**Milliner's Figure,** Boy, Standing, Painted Face, Papier-Mache, Cast Iron Boots, 40 In................. 403
**Milliner's Figure,** Woman, Top Half, Jointed Arms, Wood, Carved, Painted, c.1840, 37 In. .......... 2415
**Shopping Cart,** 2 Tiers, Green Paint, Metal, Mack Store, Harrisonburg, Va., 1920, 37 x 24 In.. 259
**Showcase,** Nickel Plated Counter Top, Cathedral Arch, 40 x 32 x 16 ½ In. ............................ 510
**Showcase,** Ribbon Display, Glass, Interior Metal Racks, Wood Frame, 38 ½ In. ....................... 300
**Sign,** Antiques, Paint, Wood, 35 x 8 ¾ In.................................................................. 176
**Sign,** Apothecary, Mortar & Pestle, Zinc, Die Cut, Old Gold Paint, 31 In. ............................ 510
**Sign,** Cafe, 2-Sided, Yellow Paint, 1900s, 25 x 32 In. .................................................... 115
**Sign,** Car Park, Pointing Hand, Black, White Paint, Wood, 12 ½ x 10 ½ In.............................. 410
**Sign,** Chopsticks, Neon, Outdoor, 10 In. ................................................................. 780
**Sign,** Compass, Wood, c.1900, 51 ½ In. ................................................................... 450

**Stoneware,** Vase, Incised, Glazed, Emile Lenoble, Choisy-Le-Roi, Marked, c.1930, 8 ½ x 9 In.
**$5,312**

Rago Arts & Auction Center

**Store,** Coin Counter, Brandt, Automatic, Footed, 14 x 12 In.
**$210**

Showtime Auction Services

**Store,** Counter, Oak, 28 Spool Drawers, Display Cases, J.D. Warren, 1910s, 85 x 30 In.
**$1,680**

Morphy Auctions

**Store,** Sign, Optometrist, Glasses, Painted Eyes, Steel, Gilt, Light Bulbs, c.1910, 81 In.
**$7,380**

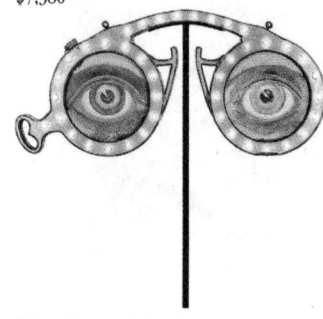

Skinner Auctioneers & Appraisers

S

**Store,** Sign, Pipe Fitter, Pipe & Turn Handle, Plugs, Wood, Gold Paint, c.1910, 21 In.
$540

Garth's Auctioneers & Appraisers

**Store,** Turk's Head, Man's Face, Carved, Display, Tobacco, Counter, c.1890, 20 x 17 In.
$1,845

Skinner Auctioneers & Appraisers

**Store,** Stove, Heating, Belleville Stove Co., Cast Iron, Chrome Trim, 1910s, 56 x 38 In.
$300

Morphy Auctions

| | |
|---|---:|
| **Sign,** Dentist, Up Stairs, Sheet Metal, Gold On Black, 52 x 5 In. | 390 |
| **Sign,** Do Not Ask For Credit, Pine, Black, Yellow Lettering, New England, 1800s, 7 x 18 In. | 1422 |
| **Sign,** Druggist, Pestle & Mortar, Carved, Painted, Gilded, 12 x 81 In. | 3000 |
| **Sign,** Figural, Eyeglasses, Painted Eyes, Metal, 33 In. | 702 |
| **Sign,** Fish Shape, Wood, Carved, Paper Label, 166 Piccadilly, 1800s, 9 x 42 In. | 1135 |
| **Sign,** Fountain Lunch, Neon, Red, Green, Glass Frame, 29 x 14 In. | 320 |
| **Sign,** Fresh N' Hot Popcorn, Mechanical, c.1960 | 1560 |
| **Sign,** Fresh Squeezed Orange Juice, Plastic, Light-Up, 18½ x 11¾ In. | 120 |
| **Sign,** Grubs, Wood, White, Black Lettering, Border, 18 x 10½ In. | 45 |
| **Sign,** Hand, Figural, Straight Fingers, Metal, Old Varnish, 1800s, 20 In. | 1800 |
| **Sign,** Hanger, Fish, Carved, Painted, Iron Hook, c.1920, 44 In. | 1320 |
| **Sign,** Horseshoe, Horse, Prancing, In Horseshoe Arch, 23 x 31 In. | 585 |
| **Sign,** Jeweler's, Watch, Wood Fob, Iron Ring, Painted Face, Gold Frame, c.1890, 21 x 15 In. | 1353 |
| **Sign,** Just Picked Strawberries, 3 Pine Boards, Bread Board Ends, 1900s, 12 x 38 In. | 711 |
| **Sign,** Lingerie, Metal, Arched, Blue Paint, 1930s, 36 x 10 In. | 556 |
| **Sign,** Mermaid, Bird, Sheet Iron, Shaped, Painted, Pulley Attached To Hands, c.1910, 26 In. | 1476 |
| **Sign,** Mortician, Wood, Painted, Turned Post, Ball Finial, Medial Ball, c.1890, 48 In. | 431 |
| **Sign,** Office, Pointing Finger, Pine, Black, Brown, Gilt, Silver Border, c.1850, 7½ x 29 In. | 770 |
| **Sign,** Optician, Eyeglass Shape, Blue Eyes, Cast Iron, 2-Sided, 5 x 18 In. | 978 |
| **Sign,** Optometrist, Glasses With Eyes, Wrought Iron, Multicolored Glass, c.1890, 14 x 25 In. | 492 |
| **Sign,** Optometrist, Glasses, Painted Eyes, Steel, Gilt, Light Bulbs, c.1910, 81 In. ...............*illus* | 7380 |
| **Sign,** Pipe Fitter, Pipe & Turn Handle, Plugs, Wood, Gold Paint, c.1910, 21 In. ...........*illus* | 540 |
| **Sign,** Please Do Not Annoy The Workers, Yellow Paint, Wood, c.1915, 13¾ x 24 In. | 920 |
| **Sign,** Rambler Tea Garden, Tourists Accommodated, Reverse Painted Glass, Frame, 45 x 24 In. | 644 |
| **Sign,** Refreshments, Neon, Outdoor, 72½ x 12 In. | 210 |
| **Sign,** Salmon, Carved, Painted, c.1900, 73 In. | 1599 |
| **Sign,** Scissors, Tailor's, Laminated Wood, Painted, Shaped Handles, Blades, 1900s, 62 In. | 415 |
| **Sign,** Shoe Repairing, Single Sided, Light-Up, Glass, Hanging, 4 x 26 In. | 210 |
| **Sign,** Sidewalk, Painted, Black Man, Indian Man, Cigars No. 1 Tobacco, Wood, Folding, 30 x 16 In. | 4305 |
| **Sign,** Smith's Skate Repair, Wood, Painted, Forged Iron Hooks, 10 x 24 In. | 83 |
| **Sign,** Sow, Pine, Painted, Mortised Legs, Attached Ears, Iron Tail, Glass Eyes, 22 x 49 In. | 2074 |
| **Sign,** Tack Shop, Horse's Head, Papier-Mache, Painted, c.1900, 25 In. | 480 |
| **Sign,** Tennis Racket, Blue, White Paint, 64¾ In. | 720 |
| **Sign,** Top Hat, Tole, Burgundy, Black Buckle Band, Stand, c.1880, 13 x 10 In. | 590 |
| **Sign,** Toy Manchester Terriers, Wood, Painted, Dog Cutout, 2-Sided, 21 x 16 In. | 322 |
| **Sign,** Upholstering, Wood, 2-Sided, Cut Corners, Black, Gold Letters, Hooks, 65 In. | 295 |
| **Sign,** Watch Repairing, Single Sided, Light-Up, Glass, Hanging, 4 x 26 In. | 150 |
| **Sign,** Welcome, Cowboy Boot Shape, Wood, 32 In. | 270 |
| **Table,** Chopping Block, Oak, Raised Legs, c.1950, 35 x 17 In. | 138 |
| **Tobacco Plug Cutter,** Jester Figure On Handle, Cast Iron, Brighton | 71 |
| **Turk's Head,** Man's Face, Carved, Display, Tobacco, Counter, c.1890, 20 x 17 In. ...........*illus* | 1845 |
| **Wig Stand,** Women's Bust, Elongated Neck, Composite, Painted, 1950s, 19 In., Pair | 826 |

**STOVES** have been used in America for heating since the eighteenth century and for cooking since the nineteenth century. Most types of wood, coal, gas, kerosene, and even some electric stoves are collected.

| | |
|---|---:|
| **Cook,** Independent Stove Co., Cast Iron, Chrome Trim, Burners, Oven, 32 x 52¾ In. | 900 |
| **Heating,** Belleville Stove Co., Cast Iron, Chrome Trim, 1910s, 56 x 38 In. ...........*illus* | 300 |
| **Heating,** Great Western, Cast Iron, Wood Burning, 4 Dogs, Scrollwork, c.1910, 59 x 25 In. | 660 |
| **Heating,** Hays & Co., 3 Hinged Lift-Off Doors, 4-Footed, Cast Iron, Pa., c.1820, 18 x 23 In. | 518 |
| **Heating,** Tiles, Iris, Leaves, Pink, Green, France, c.1875, 38 x 19½ In. | 2500 |
| **Heating,** Vina, No. 13, Iron, Nickel, Removable Top, Footed, Bridge Beach & Co., 47 In. | 540 |
| **Heating,** Wick, Kerosene, Blue, 16 x 24 In. | 30 |
| **Heating,** Woods-Evertz, Cast Iron, Wood Burning, Scrollwork, Chrome, 1903, 26 x 38½ In. | 450 |
| **Jewel Range Jr.,** Iron, Nickel, Detroit Stove Works, Salesman's Sample, 16 x 18 In. | 677 |
| **Majestic Jr.,** Cast Iron, Nickel & Black Finish, Salesman's Sample, 31 x 24 In. | 3600 |
| **Mascot Stove Mfg. Co.,** Enameled Mascot, Iron, Salesman's Sample, 16 x 18 In. | 360 |
| **Parlor,** Art Nouveau, Slate Top, Cast Iron Mounted Doors, Majolica, 30 x 19 x 17 In. ...........*illus* | 212 |
| **Parlor,** Manard, Black Cast Iron, Stove Pipe, 24 x 39 x 18 In. | 342 |
| **Parlor,** Steel, Enamel, Glass Panel, Salesman's Sample, 15 In. | 240 |
| **Pottery,** French Style, Tiered, Cream, Gold & Pink Accents, 72 x 25 In. | 960 |
| **Royal American,** Nickel, Iron, Bridgeford & Co. Louisville, Salesman's Sample, 14 x 12 In. | 360 |
| **Shaker,** Wood, Cast Iron, Canted Sides, Hinged Door, Long Front, Pipe, 21 x 31 In. ...........*illus* | 1239 |
| **Star Range,** Cast Iron, Nickel, Kenton, Salesman's Sample, 19 x 24 In. | 180 |
| **Steel,** Enameled, Nickeled, Cast Iron, Salesman's Sample, Qualified Range Co., 21 In. ...........*illus* | 7410 |

| | | |
|---|---|---|
| **Stove Plate,** Cast Iron, Log Cabin, Moose, 13½ x 27 In. | | 450 |
| **Stove Plate,** Double Canopy, Twisted Columns, Flowering Tulips, Iron, 22 x 24 In. | | 443 |
| **Stove Plate,** Pharisee & Publican, Cast Iron, Image, Text, 1742, 25 x 25 In. | | 295 |
| **Tappan Eclipse,** Cast Iron, Tin, Enameled Paint, Salesman's Sample, 17 x 16 In. | | 600 |
| **U.S. Gothic 16-18,** Nickel, Green Enameled Paint, Salesman's Sample, 17 x 17¾ In. | | 390 |

**SUMIDA** is a Japanese pottery that was made from about 1895 to 1941. Pieces are usually everyday objects—vases, jardinieres, bowls, teapots, and decorative tiles. Most pieces have a very heavy orange-red, blue, brown, black, green, purple, or off-white glaze, with raised three-dimensional figures as decorations. The unglazed part is painted red, green, black, or orange. Sumida is sometimes mistakenly called Sumida gawa, but true Sumida gawa is a softer pottery made in the early 1800s.

| | | |
|---|---|---|
| **Creamer,** Man, Hands Crossed, Animal Handle, Toby Style, c.1900, 4 x 4 In. | | 250 |
| **Humidor,** Man & Woman, Man Finial, Heart Shape, c.1910, 6 x 4 In. | | 125 |
| **Mug,** Monkeys, On Bridge, 5 x 3½ In. | | 94 |
| **Teapot,** Tiger, Leopard, Mountains, Black, Brown, Red Glaze, Bamboo Handle, 5 In. | | 599 |
| **Vase,** Flower Frog, Woman, Child, Fish, Monkey, 10 In. | | 350 |

**SUNBONNET BABIES** were introduced in 1900 in the book *The Sunbonnet Babies*. The stories were by Eulalie Osgood Grover, illustrated by Bertha Corbett. The children's faces were completely hidden by the sunbonnets. The children had been pictured in black and white before this time, but the color pictures in the book were immediately successful. The Royal Bayreuth China Company made a full line of children's dishes decorated with the Sunbonnet Babies. Some Sunbonnet Babies plates have been reproduced, but they are clearly marked.

| | | |
|---|---|---|
| **Bell,** 7 Days Of Week, Royal Bayreuth, 3¼ In., 7 Piece | | 225 |
| **Candleholder,** Fishing, Royal Bayreuth, Blue Mark, 5¼ In. | | 59 |
| **Chocolate Pot,** Ironing, Green Ground, Gilt, Royal Bayreuth, 8½ In. | | 177 |
| **Creamer,** Thursday, Scrubbing, Royal Bayreuth, 3¼ x 3¼ In. | | 145 |
| **Plate,** Friday, Sweeping, 1974, 7 In. | | 201 |
| **Plate,** Monday, Washing, 1974, 7 In. | | 159 |
| **Plate,** Saturday, Baking, 1974, 7 In. | | 199 |
| **Plate,** Sunday, Fishing, 1974, 7 In. | | 199 |
| **Plate,** Sunday, Fishing, Pewter Border, 11 In. | | 79 |
| **Plate,** Thursday, Scrubbing, c.1974, 7 In. | | 190 |
| **Plate,** Wednesday, Mending, 1974, 7 In. | | 212 |
| **Postcard,** Girl, Kneeling, Bull Dog, 1905 | | 15 |
| **Postcard,** Upset Girl, Sitting On Chair, 1920 | | 18 |
| **Tray,** Thursday, Scrubbing, Center Handle, 7 In. | | 225 |
| **Vase,** Sewing, Handle, Footed, 3¾ In. | | 125 |

**SUNDERLAND** luster is a name given to a special type of pink luster made by Leeds, Newcastle, and other English firms during the nineteenth century. The luster glaze is metallic and glossy and appears to have bubbles in it. Other pieces of luster are listed in the Luster category.

| | | |
|---|---|---|
| **Chamber Pot,** Pink Luster, Verse, Leaf Mounts, Strap Handles, c.1830, 11 x 5 In. | | 1340 |
| **Goblet,** Lid, Moonlight Luster, Footed, Button Knop Stems, 9½ In., Pair | | 561 |
| **Luster,** Pitcher, Embossed Multicolor Band, Bulbous, Snake Handle, 1800s | | 83 |
| **Mug,** Luster, Embossed Profile, Royal, Crown, Plumed Hat, 1700s, 4½ In. | | 826 |
| **Mug,** Pink Luster, Mariner's Compass, Reeded Strap Handle, 1800, 4¾ In. | | 275 |
| **Pitcher,** Pink Luster, Bridge, Verse, c.1850, 9 x 6½ In. | | 895 |
| **Pitcher,** Pink Luster, Maritime Scenes, Multicolor Transfer, 8 In. | | 384 |
| **Plate,** William Gladstone, Portrait, Transfer, Cobalt Border, 1880s, 8 x 8 In. | | 100 |

**SUPERMAN** was created by two seventeen-year-olds in 1938. The first issue of Action comics had the strip. Superman remains popular and became the hero of a radio show in 1940, cartoons in the 1940s, a television series, and several major movies.

| | | |
|---|---|---|
| **Badge,** Pin, Breaking Chains, Sunburst, Stars, Fo-Lee Gum, Brass Luster, 1⅝ In. | | 4807 |
| **Badge,** Superman Gum, Flying, Holding Flag, Colors, Die Cut, 1940s, 1½ In. | | 170 |
| **Bank,** Superman Breaking Chains, Yellow, Tin, Marked Dime Register Bank, c.1940, 2½ In. | | 108 |
| **Button,** Pin Back, White Ground, Lithograph, 1939, 1 In. | | 222 |
| **Card,** Saylor's Bread, Burning Wheat, Superman Throwing Building Into Harbor | *illus* | 153 |
| **Comic Book,** Action Comics, First Supergirl Appearance, No. 252, May 1959 | | 732 |
| **Comic Book,** DC Comics, July-August 1941, Leo Novak Art | | 350 |
| **Comic Book,** No. 22, 1943, 10½ x 7½ In. | | 80 |

**Stove,** Parlor, Art Nouveau, Slate Top, Cast Iron Mounted Doors, Majolica, 30 x 19 x 17 In.
$212

Conestoga Auction Co., Inc.

**Stove,** Shaker, Wood, Cast Iron, Canted Sides, Hinged Door, Long Front, Pipe, 21 x 31 In.
$1,239

Willis Henry Auctions, Inc.

**Stove,** Steel, Enameled, Nickeled, Cast Iron, Salesman's Sample, Qualified Range Co., 21 In.
$7,410

Theriault's

**S**

**Superman,** Card, Saylor's Bread, Burning Wheat, Superman Throwing Building Into Harbor
$153

Hake's Americana & Collectibles

**Superman,** Gum Card Wrapper, Superman, Waxed Paper, Join Club, Membership Application, 1940, 4 x 6 In.
$1,035

Hake's Americana & Collectibles

**Superman,** Sign, Superman Comes To Cleveland, Cardboard, Plain Dealer, 1940, 12 x 15 In.
$1,968

Hake's Americana & Collectibles

| | |
|---|---:|
| **Cutout Book,** 4 Superman Action Scenes, Saalfield Pub. Co., 1940, 10 ½ x 14 ½ In. | 3352 |
| **Doll,** Superman, Wood, Composition, Fabric, Jointed, Ideal, 1940, 13 In. | 974 |
| **Doll,** Wood, Composition, Jointed, Red, Blue, Ideal, 13 In. | 506 |
| **Figure,** Metal, Plastic Base, 1 Bent Leg, 1 Extended Arm, 1 ½ In. | 417 |
| **Figure,** Plaster, Hands On Hips, Strength, Courage, Justice, 1940s, 7 In. | 345 |
| **Figure,** Superman, Blue Suit, Pocket Super Hero, Original Package, Mego, 1979, 4 ¼ In. | 115 |
| **Figure,** Wood, Composition, Brown, Red, Wayne Boring, 1942, 5 ½ In. | 2142 |
| **Game,** Board, Superman Die Playing Pieces, Graphics, Box, Milton Bradley, 1940, 14 x 17 In. | 190 |
| **Gum Card Wrapper,** Superman, Waxed Paper, Join Club, Membership Application, 1940, 4 x 6 In. ... *illus* | 1035 |
| **Handkerchief,** Superman, Broken Chains, Multicolor, Navy, 1940s, 12 x 12 In. | 5705 |
| **Patch,** Supermen Of America Club, Superman Breaking Chains, Motto, Fabric, 2 x 2 ½ In. | 633 |
| **Pen & Pencil Set,** Yellow, Plastic, Superman, Cape, Clip, Gold Foil, 6 ⅛ x 2 ¼ In. | 4174 |
| **Phonograph,** Superman In Space, White Player, Handle, Box, 1978, 9 ¼ x 12 In. | 172 |
| **Poster,** Superman's Peril, Daybill, George Reeves, Laminated, Australia, 1954, 14 x 30 In. | 411 |
| **Ring,** Portrait, Brass Medallion, Action Comics, 1940 | 3450 |
| **Ring,** Secret Chamber, Adjustable, Ostby & Barton, Superman Defense Club, Brass | 2087 |
| **Ring,** Secret Chamber, Brass, Star, Planet, Milk Program Premium, 1941 | 4592 |
| **Ring,** Superman Smashing Anvil, Flasher, Multicolor, 1960s | 127 |
| **Shirt,** Red, Short Sleeve, Satin S Emblem, Body Gear, Parkley, 1960s, 14 x 25 In. | 100 |
| **Sign,** Superman Comes To Cleveland, Cardboard, Plain Dealer, 1940, 12 x 15 In. ... *illus* | 1968 |
| **Socks,** Superman Scenes, Sport-Wear Hosiery Mills, Inc., Box, 1949, 7 ¾ x 10 ¼ In. | 380 |
| **Sticker,** Macy's Department Store, Red, White, Blue, Gummed Back, 2 ¾ x 4 ⅜ In. | 345 |
| **Sticker,** Tune In KECA, Eat Town Talk Bread, Hands On Hips, 2 x 4 In. | 345 |
| **Toy,** Krypto-Raygun, Steel Film Viewer Gun, Filmstrips, Daisy, Box, c.1940, 8 x 10 In. | 462 |
| **Toy,** Superman, Rollover Tank, Tin Lithograph, Linemar, 4 In. | 150 |
| **Watch,** Stopwatch, Flying Superman, City Skyline, Metal Case, Bradley, 1959, 2 In. ... *illus* | 230 |

**SUSIE COOPER** began as a designer in 1925 working for the English firm A.E. Gray & Company. In 1932 she formed Susie Cooper Pottery, Ltd. In 1950 it became Susie Cooper China, Ltd., and the company made china and earthenware. In 1966 it was acquired by Josiah Wedgwood & Sons, Ltd. The name *Susie Cooper* appears with the company names on many pieces of ceramics.

| | |
|---|---:|
| **Cup & Saucer,** Pink & Blue Flowers, Gold Trim | 38 |
| **Cup & Saucer,** White Orchid, Gray, Gold Trim | 60 |
| **Mustard Jar,** Feather, Teal Blue, 3 ⅛ x 2 In. | 35 |
| **Pitcher,** Art Deco, Cubist Pattern, Multicolor, c.1930, 4 ¾ In. | 450 |
| **Pitcher,** Wedding Ring Pattern, Green, Taupe, Cream, c.1935, 3 ½ In. | 55 |

**SWANKYSWIGS** are small drinking glasses. In 1933, the Kraft Food Company began to market cheese spreads in these decorated, reusable glass tumblers. They were discontinued from 1941 to 1946, then made again from 1947 to 1958. Then plain glasses were used for most of the cheese, although a few special decorated Swankyswigs have been made since that time. For more prices, go to kovels.com.

| | |
|---|---:|
| **Blue Tulips,** Green Leaves, 2 ⅛ x 3 ⅜ In. | 6 |
| **Cornflower,** No. 2, Blue, 1947, 3 ½ In., Pair | 19 |
| **Red & White Stripe** | 12 |

**SWASTIKA KERAMOS** is a line of art pottery made from 1906 to 1908 by the Owen China Company of Minerva, Ohio. Many pieces were made with an iridescent glaze.

| | |
|---|---:|
| **Vase,** Coraline, White Beads, Green & Gold Squiggles, Signed, 5 ⅝ In. ... *illus* | 115 |
| **Vase,** Green Trailing Edge, Gold Ground, White Beading, 3 Handles, 7 ¼ In. | 230 |

**SWORDS** of all types that are of interest to collectors are listed here. The military dress sword with elaborate handle is probably the most wanted. A tsuba is a hand guard fitted to a Japanese sword between the handle and the blade. Be sure to display swords in a safe way, out of reach of children.

| | |
|---|---:|
| **Brass Hilt,** Eagle Head Pommel, Sea Serpent Terminals, Reeded Bone Grip, 30 ⅜ In. | 1250 |
| **Brass Hilt,** Hawk Head Pommel, Metal Scabbard, Recurve Blade, c.1880, 22 In. | 180 |
| **Cutlass,** Naval, Steel, Brass Hilt, Leather-Covered Wood Grip, Model 1860, c.1875, 32 In. | 615 |
| **Cutlass,** Navy, Brass Hilt, Fish Scale Pattern, c.1850, 26 In. | 840 |
| **Dagger,** Scabbard, Hanger, Officer, Nazi, Germany | 300 |
| **Dagger,** Scabbard, Portapee, Nazi Luftwaffe, Germany | 360 |
| **Imperial German,** Leather Scabbard, Black Snakeskin Grip, Brass Fittings, Blade, 32 In. | 236 |
| **Iron,** Pierced Basket, Hearts, Circles, Wood Grip, Engraved Pommel, c.1750, 38 In. | 2829 |
| **Naval,** Officer's, Lion's Head Pommel, Sharkskin Grips, Leather, Brass Scabbard, 1827, 3 ⅓ In. | 443 |

S

| | |
|---|---|
| **Openwork Metal,** Shagreen Handle, Tassel, Leather & Metal Scabbard, U.S. Navy, c.1850 | 125 |
| **Rapier,** Swept Hilt, Running Wolf Mark, Germany, c.1650, 46 In. | 2375 |
| **Saber,** Cavalry, Steel, Leather Grip Cover, Scabbard, Nathan Starr, c.1800, 37 In. | 338 |
| **Saber,** Dragoon, U.S. Model 1799, Buell & Greenleaf, Cartouche Marked, 29¼ In. | 5000 |
| **Tanto,** Engraved Silver Blade, Black Mottled, Red Lacquer Scabbard, 1800s, 17 In. | 350 |
| **Topographical Engineers,** Painted, c.1840, 34½ In. | 330 |
| **Yataghan,** Wood Grip, Brass D-Guard, 1800s, 22 In. | 104 |

**SYRACUSE** is a trademark used by the Onondaga Pottery of Syracuse, New York. The company was established in 1871. The name became the Syracuse China Company in 1966. Syracuse China closed in 2009. It was known for fine dinnerware and restaurant china.

SYRACUSE China

| | |
|---|---|
| **Accent,** Creamer | 10 |
| **Alpine,** Bowl, Cereal, 5½ In. | 31 |
| **Alpine,** Bowl, Fruit, 5 In. | 12 |
| **Alpine,** Bowl, Vegetable, Oval, 8¼ In. | 46 |
| **Alpine,** Coffeepot, Lid, 7¾ In. | 125 |
| **Alpine,** Creamer, 4 In. | 32 |
| **Alpine,** Cup & Saucer | 22 |
| **Alpine,** Gravy Boat, Underplate | 82 |
| **Alpine,** Plate, Bread & Butter, 6⅜ In. | 6 |
| **Alpine,** Plate, Dinner, 10⅝ In. | 28 |
| **Alpine,** Plate, Salad, 8⅛ In. | 8 |
| **Alpine,** Platter, 12½ In. | 68 |
| **Berkeley,** Bowl, Fruit, 4¼ In. | 8 |
| **Berkeley,** Cup & Saucer | 8 |
| **Berkeley,** Plate, Bread & Butter, 4 In. | 5 |
| **Berkeley,** Plate, Salad, 7¾ In. | 8 |
| **Corabel,** Bowl, Vegetable, Lid, 9 In. | 75 |
| **Corabel,** Cup & Saucer | 21 |
| **Corabel,** Plate, Bread & Butter, 6¼ In. | 5 |
| **Corabel,** Plate, Dinner, 9¾ In. | 21 |
| **Corabel,** Plate, Salad, 8 In. | 12 |
| **Coventry,** Bowl, Vegetable, 10⅜ In. | 35 |
| **Coventry,** Plate, Bread & Butter, 6¼ In. | 9 |
| **Coventry,** Plate, Dinner, 9¾ In. | 22 |
| **Coventry,** Plate, Salad, 8 In. | 15 |
| **Gardenia,** Cup & Saucer, Demitasse | 20 |
| **Gardenia,** Plate, Dinner, 10 In. | 24 |
| **Ivory,** Cup, Footed | 8 |
| **Lady Louise,** Bowl, Vegetable, Lid, Handles, 1949, 8 x 4 In. | 129 |
| **Madison,** Plate, Bread & Butter, 6¼ In. | 6 |
| **Madison,** Plate, Dinner, 10¾ In. | 12 |
| **Madison,** Saucer | 4 |
| **Marlene,** Bowl, Berry, 5¼ In. | 12 |
| **Marlene,** Cup & Saucer | 26 |
| **Marlene,** Plate, Bread & Butter, 6¼ In. | 10 |
| **Marlene,** Plate, Dinner, 9¾ In. | 26 |
| **Marlene,** Plate, Salad, 8 In. | 15 |
| **Milwaukee Railroad,** Traveler, Platter, c.1947, 6 x 8 In. | 80 |
| **Puritan,** Pitcher, 32 Oz. | 32 |
| **Rose Marie,** Bowl, Vegetable, Lid, Handles, 11 In. | 95 |
| **Selma,** Chop Plate, Round, 12 In. | 74 |
| **Sherwood,** Creamer | 18 |
| **Suzanne,** Bowl, Soup, 8 In. | 28 |
| **Suzanne,** Bowl, Vegetable, Oval, 10 In. | 45 |
| **Suzanne,** Bowl, Vegetable, Round, Footed, 9 In. | 75 |
| **Suzanne,** Creamer | 38 |
| **Suzanne,** Cup & Saucer, Footed | 30 |
| **Suzanne,** Gravy Boat, Underplate | 65 |
| **Suzanne,** Plate, Bread & Butter, 6⅜ In. | 12 |
| **Suzanne,** Plate, Dinner, 10½ In. | 35 |
| **Suzanne,** Platter, 12 In. | 30 |
| **Suzanne,** Platter, 14 In. | 48 |
| **Woodbine,** Cup & Saucer | 12 |
| **Woodbine,** Plate, Dinner, 10 In. | 12 |

**Superman,** Watch, Stopwatch, Flying Superman, City Skyline, Metal Case, Bradley, 1959, 2 In.
$230

Hake's Americana & Collectibles

**Swastika Keramos,** Vase, Coraline, White Beads, Green & Gold Squiggles, Signed, 5⅝ In.
$115

Humler & Nolan

**Tea Caddy,** Burl, Brass Paw Feet, Coffin Shape, Regency, 1800s, 29 x 16 In.
$615

Neal Auction Co.

S

**Tea Caddy,** Fruitwood, Pear Shape, Carved, Stem, Lock & Key, Tinned Paper Lining, 6 ½ In.
$1,659

**Tea Caddy,** Fruitwood, Pear Shape, Stem, Carved, Tinned Paper Lining, Lock & Key, 1800s, 6 ½ In.
$1,853

### Fake Tea Caddies

Eighteenth- and early-nineteenth-century tea caddies were sometimes made of wood. Some were shaped like apples or pears. These have been reproduced. The old ones may have cracks because wood shrinks with age. They should have a plug in the middle of the bottom and most have a lock.

**TAPESTRY,** *Porcelain, see Rose Tapestry category.*

**TEA CADDY** is the name for a small box made to hold tea leaves. In the eighteenth century, tea was very expensive and it was stored under lock and key. The first tea caddies were made with locks. By the nineteenth century, tea was more plentiful and the tea caddy was larger. Often there were two sections, one for green tea, one for black tea.

| | |
|---|---:|
| **Black Lacquer,** Gilt Figures, Landscape, Shaped, Wing Feet, 4 x 11 In. ....................... | 688 |
| **Burl Walnut,** Hinged Lid, 19th Century, 8 ½ x 5 In. ........................................... | 480 |
| **Burl,** Brass Paw Feet, Coffin Shape, Regency, 1800s, 29 x 16 In. .......................*illus* | 615 |
| **Chippendale,** Mahogany Veneer, Ogee Feet, Brass Bail Handle, 1700s, 6 x 9 In. ........... | 400 |
| **Fruitwood,** Apple Shape, George III, c.1800, 4 In. ............................................. | 1680 |
| **Fruitwood,** Apple Shape, George III, c.1820, 4 ¾ In. .......................................... | 1200 |
| **Fruitwood,** Apple Shape, Inlaid Shield Escutcheon, Hinged Lid, Foil Lining, 6 In. ......... | 295 |
| **Fruitwood,** Carved, Apple Shape, Stem, Locking Mechanism, Key, 4 ¾ In. ................... | 296 |
| **Fruitwood,** Figural, Apple, 5 In. ................................................................. | 840 |
| **Fruitwood,** Inlay, Flowers, Octagonal, c.1820, 4 ½ In. ....................................... | 720 |
| **Fruitwood,** Ivory Escutcheon, Pear Shape, Key, England, 8 ½ In. ........................... | 615 |
| **Fruitwood,** Pear Shape, Carved, Stem, Lock & Key, Tinned Paper Lining, 6 ½ In. ........*illus* | 1659 |
| **Fruitwood,** Pear Shape, Stem, Carved, Tinned Paper Lining, Lock & Key, 1800s, 6 ½ In. .....*illus* | 1853 |
| **Green & Yellow Dragons,** Black Ground, Chinese, 6-Footed, Hexagonal, 5 x 4 In. ......... | 125 |
| **Hunter,** Shooting, Dog, Papier-Mache, England, c.1850, 3 ¾ x 2 ¾ In. ..................... | 259 |
| **Inlay,** Banded Top, Herringbone, Satinwood Trim, 8-Sided, c.1790, 4 ½ x 6 In. .......*illus* | 1185 |
| **Lacquer,** Black, Gilt, Loop Handles, Garden Scenes, 8 x 13 ⅜ In. ........................... | 359 |
| **Lacquer,** Gilt Birds, Flowers, Butterflies, Insects, Engraved, Chinese, 8 x 13 x 10 In. .... | 531 |
| **Lacquer,** Tea Trade Scenes, Gilt, Red, Blue, Brass Bail Handles, China, 1840, 6 In. ....... | 660 |
| **Mahogany,** Brass Flower Heads, Scrolled Paper, Hexagonal, 5 x 7 In. ....................... | 660 |
| **Mahogany,** Brass Mounted, Handle, Bracket Feet, George II, 7 x 10 In. ..................... | 570 |
| **Mahogany,** Fitted Interior, Regency, Lion Mask, Loop Handles, c.1805, 6 ½ x 12 In. ...... | 180 |
| **Mahogany,** Flower, Scroll Inlay, England, 1800s, 6 x 9 In. ................................... | 300 |
| **Mahogany,** Fruitwood Inlay, George III, 5 x 7 ½ In. .......................................... | 313 |
| **Mahogany,** Handle, Bracket Feet, George II, 7 ¼ x 11 In. ................................... | 660 |
| **Mahogany,** Inlay, 1800-50, 6 ½ x 12 In. ....................................................... | 360 |
| **Mahogany,** Inlay, Fan Corners, Checker Banded Top, 4 ¾ x 6 ¾ In. ...................*illus* | 1185 |
| **Mahogany,** Oak, Divided Interior, Brass Handle, Key, George III, 5 ½ x 8 ¾ In. ........... | 360 |
| **Mahogany,** Shell Inlays, Hepplewhite, c.1800, 4 ½ x 4 ¾ In. ............................... | 390 |
| **Mother-Of-Pearl,** Bow Front, Horn Bun Feet, White Cartouche, 5 In. ...................... | 915 |
| **Mother-Of-Pearl,** Double, Shield, Escutcheon, 5 x 7 In. ..................................... | 2160 |
| **Mother-Of-Pearl,** Ebonized, Inlay, Leaves, Hinged, 4 ⅝ x 7 In. ............................ | 269 |
| **Papier-Mache,** Flowers, Gilt, Black Ground, Fitted Interior, 8 ½ x 15 In. .................. | 295 |
| **Penwork,** Neoclassical, Gilt Brass Handles, Paw Feet, c.1810, 5 x 11 In. ................... | 469 |
| **Pine,** Dovetailed, 2 Silver Trays, Red, Black, 19th Century, 12 x 14 ½ In. ................. | 344 |
| **Porcelain,** 3-Masted Ship, 2 Flags, Flowers, Arched Shoulder, 5 In. ........................ | 4375 |
| **Quillwork,** George III, 6-Sided, Flowers, Gilt Loop Handle, c.1800, 5 x 7 ½ In. .......*illus* | 431 |
| **Quillwork,** Swags, Medallion, Inlaid Trim, Lozenge Shape, c.1825, 5 x 8 In. ............... | 240 |
| **Rococo Style,** Hand Chased, Figures, Courting Scenes, Germany, 1800s, 4 ¼ In. .......... | 295 |
| **Rosewood,** Coffin Shape, Plaque Top, Inlaid Ivory Lock, Ball Feet, England, c.1820 ....... | 150 |
| **Rosewood,** Inlaid Geometrics, 3 Compartments, Wood Ring Handles, 6 x 12 In. .......*illus* | 492 |
| **Satinwood,** George III, Shell Inlay, Double Compartment, 5 x 7 In. ......................... | 369 |
| **Satinwood,** George III, Shell Inlay, Urn, Foil Lined, 4 ¾ x 4 ¼ In. ......................... | 299 |
| **Satinwood,** Striped, Seashell Inlay, Ebony Corner Trim, Mother-Of-Pearl, 1700s, 9 x 5 In. ...... | 1244 |
| **Silver,** Oval, Scrolling Acanthus Bands, Beaded Edge, Hinged Lid, London, 1893, 5 In. ..... | 767 |
| **Silver,** Repousse Japanesque Decoration, Crabs, Plants, Baluster, Gorham, 1897, 4 In. ..... | 1500 |
| **Silver,** Victorian, Etched Curvilinear Design, Birmingham, c.1899, 2 ½ x 4 In. ............. | 210 |
| **Tortoiseshell,** 2 Compartments, Mother-Of-Pearl Inlay, c.1885, 6 x 7 In. ............*illus* | 1968 |
| **Tortoiseshell,** Blond, Sheffield Silver Mounts, Regency, Coffin Shape, c.1810, 6 x 7 In. .... | 2271 |
| **Tortoiseshell,** Bowfront, Mother-Of-Pearl Inlay, Flowers, England, c.1835, 6 x 7 In. .....*illus* | 1168 |
| **Tortoiseshell,** Coffin Shape, 8-Sided, Cinched, 2 Compartments, England, 6 x 7 In. .....*illus* | 1440 |
| **Tortoiseshell,** Mother-Of-Pearl Inlay, George III, Gilt, Incised, c.1800, 7 x 9 ½ In. .....*illus* | 1553 |
| **Tortoiseshell,** Octagonal, Hinged Lid, 2 Compartments, Bun Feet, 5 ⅛ In. ................. | 1315 |
| **Walnut,** Brass Bound, English, Early 1800s, 4 ¾ x 6 In. ..................................... | 269 |
| **Walnut,** Brass Mounted, Pharaoh Mask, Divided Compartments, 7 x 10 In. ................. | 360 |
| **Wood,** Ormolu Mounts, Top Handle, c.1910, 5 ½ x 9 In. ..................................... | 154 |
| **Yew,** Canted Corners, Dome Lid, Ivory Finial, 6 x 7 ½ In. ................................... | 720 |

**Tea Caddy,** Inlay, Banded Top, Herringbone, Satinwood Trim, 8-Sided, c.1790, 4½ x 6 In.
$1,185

James D. Julia Auctioneers

**Tea Caddy,** Mahogany, Inlay, Fan Corners, Checker Banded Top, 4¾ x 6¾ In.
$1,185

James D. Julia Auctioneers

**Tea Caddy,** Quillwork, George III, 6-Sided, Flowers, Gilt Loop Handle, c.1800, 5 x 7½ In.
$431

Neal Auction Co.

**Tea Caddy,** Rosewood, Inlaid Geometrics, 3 Compartments, Wood Ring Handles, 6 x 12 In.
$492

New Orleans Auction Galleries, Inc.

**Tea Caddy,** Tortoiseshell, 2 Compartments, Mother-Of-Pearl Inlay, c.1885, 6 x 7 In.
$1,968

New Orleans Auction Galleries, Inc.

**Tea Caddy,** Tortoiseshell, Bowfront, Mother-Of-Pearl Inlay, Flowers, England, c.1835, 6 x 7 In.
$1,168

New Orleans Auction Galleries, Inc.

**Tea Caddy,** Tortoiseshell, Coffin Shape, 8-Sided, Cinched, 2 Compartments, England, 6 x 7 In.
$1,440

DuMouchelles Art Gallery

**Tea Caddy,** Tortoiseshell, Mother-Of-Pearl Inlay, George III, Gilt, Incised, c.1800, 7 x 9½ In.
$1,553

Neal Auction Co.

**Tea Leaf Ironstone,** Chamber Pot, Lid, Mellor & Taylor
$28

Strawser Auction Group

**Teco,** Vase, Green Glaze With Charcoaling, Buttressed Handles, c.1910, 9¼ x 8½ In.
$1,750

Rago Arts & Auction Center

**Teco,** Vase, Green Matte Glaze, 4 Buttresses, Charcoaling, Impressed Mark, 10¼ In.
$2,875

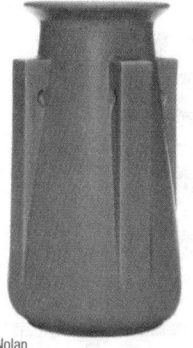

Humler & Nolan

**Teco,** Vase, Green Matte Glaze, Lobed, Footed, Stamped Mark, c.1910, 9 x 7 In.
$2,500

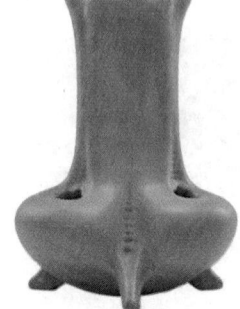

Rago Arts & Auction Centera

**TEA LEAF IRONSTONE** dishes are named for their decorations. There was a superstition that it was lucky if a whole tea leaf unfolded at the bottom of your cup. This idea was translated into the pattern of dishes known as "tea leaf." By 1850 at least twelve English factories were making this pattern, and by the 1870s it was a popular pattern in many countries. The tea leaf was always a luster glaze on early wares, although now some pieces are made with a brown tea leaf. There are many variations of tea leaf designs, such as Teaberry, Pepper Leaf, and Gold Leaf. The designs were used on many different white ironstone shapes, such as Bamboo, Lily of the Valley, Empress, and Cumbow.

| | |
|---|---:|
| **Basin,** Ewer, Cable, Anthony Shaw | 43 |
| **Bonbon,** Red Cliff, 4 x 4 In. | 15 |
| **Bowl,** Mush, Alfred Meakin, c.1880, 6 In. | 40 |
| **Bowl,** Vegetable, Anthony Shaw, 10 In. | 74 |
| **Bowl,** Vegetable, Empress, Oval, Adams, 9 In. | 24 |
| **Bowl,** Vegetable, Fluted Sides, Alfred Meakin, c.1897, 7½ x 7½ In. | 21 |
| **Bowl,** Vegetable, Grindley, 9 In. | 97 |
| **Bowl,** Vegetable, Lid, Footed, Grindley | 175 |
| **Bowl,** Vegetable, Lid, Wedgwood | 259 |
| **Bowl,** Vegetable, Wedgwood, 8 x 8 In. | 132 |
| **Cake Plate,** Brocade, Alfred Meakin, 9 In. | 102 |
| **Chamber Pot,** Lid, Mellor & Taylor | *illus* 28 |
| **Coffeepot,** Lid, Wedgwood, 7 Cup, 7 In. | 178 |
| **Compote,** Red Cliff, 8 x 8 x 4 In. | 55 |
| **Creamer,** Pankhurst Rosetta, 5 In. | 36 |
| **Cup & Saucer,** Empress, Adams | 9 |
| **Cup & Saucer,** Furnivals | 32 |
| **Cup & Saucer,** Red Cliff | 22 |
| **Cup & Saucer,** William Adams | 14 |
| **Gravy Boat,** Alfred Meakin | 89 |
| **Gravy Boat,** Copper Trim, Alfred Meakin | 90 |
| **Gravy Boat,** Furnivals | 109 |
| **Gravy Boat,** Grindley | 119 |
| **Gravy Boat,** Underplate, Wedgwood | 189 |
| **Mug,** Cable, Anthony Shaw | 47 |
| **Mug,** Scroll, Meakin | 50 |
| **Nappy,** Wedgwood, 4⅜ In. | 17 |
| **Pitcher,** Lily Of The Valley, Anthony Shaw, 7½ In. | 143 |
| **Pitcher,** Paneled, Ribbed Bottom, Footed, Red Cliff, 64 Oz., 8 x 8 In. | 125 |
| **Plate,** Bread & Butter, Mellor Taylor | 14 |
| **Plate,** Dinner, Anthony Shaw, 10 In. | 28 |
| **Plate,** Luncheon, Alfred Meakin, 8¾ In. | 15 |
| **Plate,** Salad, 7¾ In. | 12 |
| **Plate,** Salad, Alfred Meakin, 7¾ In. | 12 |
| **Plate,** Salad, Wedgwood, 7¾ In. | 12 |
| **Platter,** Alfred Meakin, 14 In. | 50 |
| **Platter,** Copper Luster Stripe Border, A.J. Wilkinson, c.1896, 10 x 14 In. | 30 |
| **Platter,** Copper Trim, Alfred Meakin, 14 In. | 50 |
| **Platter,** Empress, Oval, Adams, 13 In. | 114 |
| **Platter,** Furnivals, 13 In. | 67 |
| **Platter,** Mellor Taylor, 14 In. | 139 |
| **Platter,** Oval, Anthony Shaw, 16 In. | 199 |
| **Platter,** Wedgwood, 13 In. | 94 |
| **Relish,** Wedgwood, 7 In. | 35 |
| **Saucer,** Wedgwood, 6 In. | 10 |
| **Sugar,** Lid, Fish Hook Body, Alfred Meakin, 7 In. | 85 |
| **Teapot,** Lid, Fish Hook, Alfred Meakin, 9 In. | 61 |
| **Vase,** Fish Hook, Alfred Meakin, 5½ In. | 72 |

**TECO** is the mark used on the art pottery line made by the American Terra Cotta and Ceramic Company of Terra Cotta and Chicago, Illinois. The company was an offshoot of the firm founded by William D. Gates in 1881. The Teco line was first made in 1885 but was not sold commercially until 1902. It continued in production until 1922. Over 500 designs were made in a variety of colors, shapes, and glazes. The company closed in 1930.

| | |
|---|---:|
| **Bowl,** Blue Green Glaze, Buttressed, c.1910, 6 x 12 In. | 3500 |
| **Bowl,** Green Matte Glaze, Flared, 4 Square Feet, 2½ x 10½ In. | 2806 |
| **Chamberstick,** Green Matte Glaze, Tapered, Dish Base, Loop Handle, W.D. Gates, 6 In. | 732 |

| | |
|---|---|
| **Jardiniere**, Green Matte, 4-Footed, 10 x 7 In. | 3750 |
| **Jardiniere**, Green Matte, Globe Shape, Footed, 8 x 7 In. | 3660 |
| **Lamp**, Shade, Green Matte, Red & Green Glass, 12 x 5½ In. | 1342 |
| **Pitcher**, Tan Matte, 4 x 4 In. | 250 |
| **Shade**, Geometric Glass Panels, Green, Yellow, Stylized Leaves, Pyramid Form, 17 x 15 In. | 3172 |
| **Vase**, 4 Buttress Handles, Green, Stamped, c.1905, 7 x 4¼ In. | 2000 |
| **Vase**, Bud, Green Matte Glaze, Charcoaling, 3⅛ In. | 546 |
| **Vase**, Cattail Incised, Cylindrical, c.1910, 12 x 5 In. | 8125 |
| **Vase**, Green Glaze With Charcoaling, Buttressed Handles, c.1910, 9¼ x 8½ In. ............*illus* | 1750 |
| **Vase**, Green Matte Glaze, 4 Buttresses, Charcoaling, Impressed Mark, 10¼ In. ............*illus* | 2875 |
| **Vase**, Green Matte Glaze, Bulbous, Flared Square Mouth, W.B. Mundie, 11 In. | 5490 |
| **Vase**, Green Matte Glaze, Buttress Handles, Marked, 9½ In. | 1150 |
| **Vase**, Green Matte Glaze, Double Gourd, Handles, 11 x 13 In. | 9760 |
| **Vase**, Green Matte Glaze, Floor, 14 x 37 In. | 9760 |
| **Vase**, Green Matte Glaze, Hugh Garden, 20 x 9½ In. | 4575 |
| **Vase**, Green Matte Glaze, Lobed, Footed, Stamped Mark, c.1910, 9 x 7 In. ............*illus* | 2500 |
| **Vase**, Green Matte Glaze, Organic Decoration, Cylindrical, Square Base, Moreau, 17 x 7 In. ......... | 14640 |
| **Vase**, Green, 3 Raised Feet, 3 Handles, Terra-Cotta, c.1905, 3 x 5 In. | 406 |
| **Vase**, Green, Cylindrical, High Inset Handles, 11 In. | 480 |
| **Vase**, Green, Speckled Brown, Flattened Rim, 5¾ In. | 489 |
| **Vase**, Leaves In Recessed Panels, Green Matte Glaze, Square Base, Cinched, Neck, 12 In. | 9760 |
| **Vase**, Light Green, Shoulder Fold, 4½ In. | 316 |
| **Vase**, Tulips, Embossed, Green Matte Glaze, Melon Base, c.1910, 13½ x 5 In. ............*illus* | 25000 |
| **Vase**, Water Lilies, Reticulated Leaves, Green & Charcoal Matte Glaze, W.J. Dodd, 10 In. | 12200 |

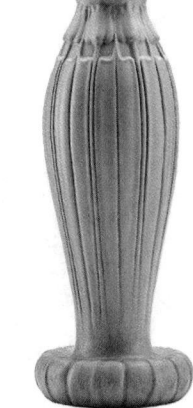

**Teco**, Vase, Tulips, Embossed, Green Matte Glaze, Melon Base, c.1910, 13½ x 5 In.
$25,000

Rago Arts & Auction Center

---

**TEDDY BEARS** were named for a president of the United States. The first teddy bear was a cuddly toy said to be inspired by a hunting trip made by Teddy Roosevelt in 1902. Morris and Rose Michtom started selling their stuffed bears as "teddy bears" and the name stayed. The Michtoms founded the Ideal Novelty and Toy Company. The German version of the teddy bear was made about the same time by the Steiff Company. There are many types of teddy bears and all are collected. The old ones are being reproduced. Other bears are listed in the Toy section.

| | |
|---|---|
| **Bing**, Mohair, Blond, Jointed, Shoebutton Eyes, Lace Collar, c.1910, 21 In. | 1519 |
| **Bing**, Mohair, Tan, Curly, Glass Pupil Eyes, Jointed, 1920s, 30 In. | 5332 |
| **Farnell**, 5 Ways Jointed, c.1930, 26 In. | 1659 |
| **Ideal**, Mohair, Yellow, Excelsior Stuffing, Jointed, Shoebutton Eyes, 19 In. | 4740 |
| **J.K. Farnell**, Mohair, Brown, Excelsior Stuffing, Jointed, Glass Eyes, 1920s, 27 In. | 2962 |
| **Mohair**, Golden, Sailor, Swivel Head, Jointed Limbs, Pointy Snout, Glass Eyes, c.1935, 27 In. | 168 |
| **Mohair**, Red, Electric Eye, Light-Up Bulb, Elongated Neck, Jointed, c.1930, 22 In. ............*illus* | 448 |
| **Sherlock**, Mohair, Blond, Straw Filled, Pointy Embroidered Nose, Jointed, c.1925, 30 In. | 224 |
| **Steiff**, Almond Buff, Ear Button, Leather Collar, Pull Toy, c.1920, 15 x 12 In. | 1777 |
| **Steiff**, Mohair, Apricot, Button Eyes, Shaved Muzzle, c.1907, 19 In. | 2607 |
| **Steiff**, Mohair, Blond, Jointed, Back Hump, Shoebutton Eyes, c.1905, 12 In. | 4147 |
| **Steiff**, Mohair, Blond, Jointed, Glass Eyes, Ear Button, 1920s, 18 In. | 4740 |
| **Steiff**, Mohair, Blond, Jointed, Shoebutton Eyes, Ear Tag, 1920s, 28 In. | 5332 |
| **Steiff**, Mohair, Golden, Rattle, Glass Pupil Eyes, Jointed, Ear Tag, 1920s, 5 In. | 1837 |
| **Steiff**, Mohair, Golden, Shoebutton Eyes, Leather Muzzle, 24 In. | 10030 |
| **Steiff**, Mohair, Yellow, Ear Tag, Jointed, 1940s, 14 In. | 1777 |
| **Steiff**, White, Brown Nose, 5 Ways Jointed, 10 In. | 1303 |
| **Steiff**, White, Brown Nose, 5 Ways Jointed, 1907, 15 In. | 2844 |
| **Steiff**, Wool, Yellow, Jointed, Glass Eyes, Ear Tag, c.1930, 18 In. | 1007 |
| **Sussenguth**, Peter, Plush, Straw, Swivel Head, Tongue, Eyes, Germany, 1925, 14 In. ............*illus* | 2240 |
| **Wool Plush**, Automobile, Open Mouth, Tongue, Swivel Head, Shoulder Joint, c.1935, 27 In. | 336 |

**Teddy Bear**, Mohair, Red, Electric Eye, Light-Up Bulb, Elongated Neck, Jointed, c.1930, 22 In.
$448

Theriault's

---

**TELEPHONES** are wanted by collectors if the phones are old enough or unusual enough. The first telephone may have been made in Havana, Cuba, in 1849, but it was not patented. The first publicly demonstrated phone was used in Frankfurt, Germany, in 1860. The phone made by Alexander Graham Bell was shown at the Centennial Exhibition in Philadelphia in 1876, but it was not until 1877 that the first private phones were installed. Collectors today want all types of old phones, phone parts, and advertising. Even recent figural phones are popular.

| | |
|---|---|
| **Automatic Electric Co.**, Strowger Desk, Sunburst Dial, 1903, 12 In. ............*illus* | 11400 |
| **Automatic Electric**, Pay, Wall Mount, Long Distance Telephone, 5, 10, 25, Cent, Keys | 360 |
| **Booth**, Edw. Melchior Co., Oak, Paneled, Quarter Sawn, 27¼ x 84 In. ............*illus* | 1938 |
| **Candlestick**, Brass, 5 Cent Local Calls, Pay Box, Key, 12¼ In. | 180 |
| **Chicago Phone Supply Co.**, Oak, Wall Mount, Ringer, Speaker, Headset, 12 x 33 In. .........*illus* | 180 |

**Teddy Bear**, Sussenguth, Peter, Plush, Straw, Swivel Head, Tongue, Eyes, Germany, 1925, 14 In.
$2,240

Theriault's

T

**Telephone,** Automatic Electric Co., Strowger Desk, Sunburst Dial, 1903, 12 In.
$11,400

**Telephone,** Booth, Edw. Melchior Co., Oak, Paneled, Quarter Sawn, 27 ¼ x 84 In.
$1,938

**Telephone,** Chicago Phone Supply Co., Oak, Wall Mount, Ringer, Speaker, Headset, 12 x 33 In.
$180

**Telephone,** Sign, Public Telephone, Porcelain, Flange, 2-Sided, 11 ¼ In. Diam.
$120

**Telephone,** Western Electric, Candlestick, Hammered Copper, Roycroft, 1915, 12 In.
$8,400

**Telephone,** Western Electric, Potbelly, Long Distance, No. 9, 1897, 12 ½ In.
$8,400

T

| | |
|---|---:|
| **Intercontinental,** Mandarin, Ivory, Brass, Rotary Dial, Black Lacquer, Dragons, 1966, 12 In..... | 144 |
| **Manhattan Electrical Supply,** Candlestick, Nickel, Square Plate, 1898, 12 ½ In. ....................... | 18000 |
| **Pay,** Coin-Operated, Gray Telephone, Black, 1900s, 18 In................................................ | 210 |
| **Pay,** Wall Mount, Receiver, Automatic, Old Chrome, Push Button, 5, 10, 15, Cent .................. | 300 |
| **Rotary,** Black Standard, Brown Receiver, 11 In........................................................... | 120 |
| **Rotary,** Explosion Proof, Round, Wood Base, Western Electric, 520 Type.............................. | 690 |
| **Sign,** Ameritech, Phone Handle, Bell, Metal, 2-Sided, 24 x 24 In...................................... | 60 |
| **Sign,** Bell Telephone, Payment Agency, Porcelain, Steel Hanger, 2-Sided, 24 x 30 In............... | 652 |
| **Sign,** Bell Telephone, Porcelain, Blue, White, Round, 7 In. ............................................ | 84 |
| **Sign,** Porcelain, Flange, Black, Gray, 18 x 18 In....................................................... | 150 |
| **Sign,** Public Telephone Bell System, DSP, 11 x 11 In................................................... | 180 |
| **Sign,** Public Telephone, Porcelain, Flange, 2-Sided, 11 ¼ In. Diam...........................*illus* | 120 |
| **Stromberg-Carlson,** Ringer Bells, Receiver, Crank, Mouthpiece, 10 x 54 In.......................... | 510 |
| **Telcer Telefonia,** Rotary, Polished Onyx Insets, 18K Gold Plated Brass, Bakelite, 11 x 8 In........ | 311 |
| **Western Electric,** Candlestick, Dial, Black ............................................................ | 90 |
| **Western Electric,** Candlestick, Hammered Copper, Roycroft, 1915, 12 In....................*illus* | 8400 |
| **Western Electric,** Candlestick, Potbelly, Brass, 1895, 12 In. ....................................... | 16800 |
| **Western Electric,** Candlestick, Potbelly, Brass, c.1898, 12 In. ..................................... | 9000 |
| **Western Electric,** Peg Dialer, 1904, 13 ½ In. ......................................................... | 12000 |
| **Western Electric,** Potbelly, Long Distance, No. 9, 1897, 12 ½ In...........................*illus* | 8400 |
| **Western Electric,** Wood, c.1891-1906, 9 x 9 In. ...................................................... | 120 |

---

**TELEVISION** sets are twentieth-century collectibles. Although the first television transmission took place in England in 1925, collectors find few sets that pre-date 1946. The first sets had only five channels, but by 1949 the additional UHF channels were included. The first color television set became available in 1951.

| | |
|---|---:|
| **JVC,** Video Sphere, Space Helmet Shape, Radio, Clock, Rabbit Ears, Remote, 1960s ..................... | 85 |
| **Philco,** Predicta, Stand, Shelf, Beige Metal.............................................................. | 450 |
| **Philco,** Predicta, Wood Case, Metal Legs...........................................................*illus* | 600 |

---

**TEPLITZ** refers to art pottery manufactured by a number of companies in the Teplitz-Turn area of Bohemia during the late nineteenth and early twentieth centuries. Two of these companies were the Alexandra Works founded by Ernst Wahliss, and the Amphora Porcelain Works, run by Riessner, Stellmacher, and Kessel.

| | |
|---|---:|
| **Bowl,** Art Nouveau, Nymph Kneeling, Lily Plant Shape Bowl, 19 ½ In............................... | 800 |
| **Bowl,** Flowers, Gold Paint, Nude Woman, Devil, Scalloped Rim, E. Wahliss, c.1910, 5 x 8 In........ | 196 |
| **Bust,** Woman, Banner Inscribed 1830, Cherub, Flowers, Ernst Wahliss, c.1900, 17 x 13 ¼ In....... | 1920 |
| **Tray,** Leaf, Pink, White, Maiden, Figural, Flowing Hair, Outstretched Arm Rim, Amphora, 8 In... | 237 |
| **Vase,** Art Nouveau, Applied Wisteria, Vine Handles, Swags, Flowers, Leaves, 20 ¼ In. ..................... | 173 |
| **Vase,** Autumn Leaves, Green Enamel Dots, Handles, 4 Spouts, Dachsel, 10 In. ............................. | 161 |
| **Vase,** Cobalt Blue Daisies, Gold Stems Handles, Textured Body, 6 In............................... | 316 |
| **Vase,** Cream, Orange Butterfly & Web, Jewels, Green Ground, Amphora, 11 In. ...................... | 2280 |
| **Vase,** Dandelions, Stippled Tan Ground, Tapered, 4 Buttressed Handles, Amphora, 11 In............ | 241 |
| **Vase,** Flower Band, Pink, Blue, Stippled Iridescence, Raised Gold Swirls, Amphora, 6 In. ............. | 711 |
| **Vase,** Gold Leaves, Blue & Gold Ground, Paul Dachsel, Impressed, Crown Mark, 12 In................ | 2990 |
| **Vase,** Gold Paste Butterfly, Pierced Rosebush Rim, Amphora, RStK, 7 In. ............................*illus* | 1003 |
| **Vase,** Gourd, Woman's Portrait, Flowers In Hair, Trees, Rust Neck, Raised Gold, 5 ½ In............. | 920 |
| **Vase,** Green Leaves, Pink Ground, 4 Bottom Handles, Amphora, 16 In. ............................... | 960 |
| **Vase,** Green, Chrysanthemum, Amphora, Ernst Wahliss, 15 x 7 In. ................................. | 427 |
| **Vase,** Green, Pink, 4 Gold Painted Handles, Oval, Amphora, 9 ½ In. ............................... | 780 |
| **Vase,** Jeweled, Globular, Amphora, 7 In................................................................ | 780 |
| **Vase,** Jeweled, Reticulated, Double Wall Interior, Gilded Rim, Amphora, Austria, 16 In. .......*illus* | 1792 |
| **Vase,** Klimt Style, Spiders, Webs, 9 Panels, Stylized Leaves, Reticulated, Enameled, 6 In. ............. | 2645 |
| **Vase,** Leaves, Cream, Brown, 4 Handles, Riessner, Stellmacher & Kessel, c.1900, 10 x 6 In. ......... | 2500 |
| **Vase,** Leaves, Gray, Orange, 4 Handles, Amphora, P. Dachsel, E. Wahliss, c.1911, 13 x 7 In. .......... | 3250 |
| **Vase,** Maiden, Riessner, Stellmacher & Kessel, Amphora, c.1900, 10 ¾ x 8 ¼ In. ..................*illus* | 3584 |
| **Vase,** Metallic Luster Flowers, Icicles, Golden Pierced Berry Handles, 12 In. ..................... | 460 |
| **Vase,** Portrait, Art Nouveau, Allegory Of Russia, Poppy Seed Pod Shape, Austria, 6 In. ................ | 1093 |
| **Vase,** Stylized Yellow Flowers, Dark Ground, Handle, Amphora, 8 ½ In. ........................... | 1080 |
| **Vase,** Wide Sloped Mouth Large Feathered Bird, Green, Amphora, 20 In. ............................ | 900 |
| **Vase,** Woman, Crown, Allegory Of Austria-Hungary, Tapered, N. Kannhauser, c.1900, 15 In........ | 7500 |
| **Vase,** Woman's Portrait, Enameled, Handles, Amphora, c.1900, 10 x 5 In............................ | 3840 |
| **Vase,** Woodbine, Glossy Glaze, Gold & Maroon Luster, Paul Dachsel, 11 ½ In. ............................. | 1380 |

**Television,** Philco, Predicta, Wood Case, Metal Legs
$600

Morphy Auctions

---

**Teplitz,** Vase, Gold Paste Butterfly, Pierced Rosebush Rim, Amphora, RStK, 7 In.
$1,003

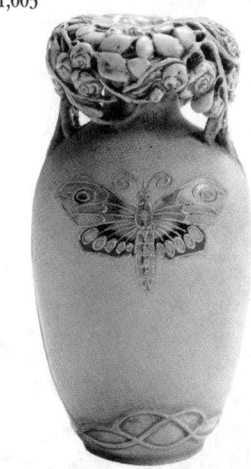

Brunk Auctions

---

**Teplitz,** Vase, Jeweled, Reticulated, Double Wall Interior, Gilded Rim, Amphora, Austria, 16 In.
$1,792

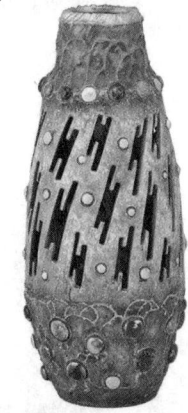

Rago Arts & Auction Center

This is an edited listing of current prices. Visit **Kovels.com** to check thousands of prices from previous years and sign up for free information on trends, tips, reproductions, marks, and more.

T

**Teplitz,** Vase, Maiden, Riessner, Stellmacher & Kessel, Amphora, c.1900, 10¾ x 8¼ In.
$3,584

Rago Arts & Auction Center

**Terra-Cotta,** Figurine, 2 Putti, Grapes, Apples, Basket, Bell Epoque, France, c.1885, 20 x 17 In.
$2,706

New Orleans Auction Galleries, Inc.

**Terra-Cotta,** Figurine, Creche, Painted, Wooden Hands, Silver Dagger, Clothing, Italy, c.1835, 16 In.
$984

New Orleans Auction Galleries, Inc.

**TERRA-COTTA** is a special type of pottery. It ranges from pale orange to dark reddish-brown in color. The color comes from the clay, which is fired but not always glazed in the finished piece.

| Item | Price |
|---|---|
| **Bowl,** Multicolor, Repeating Design, Cream, Black, Red Ground, Persia, 2½ x 8½ In. | 46 |
| **Bowl,** Yellow Glaze, Brown, Green Bands, c.1780, 12 x 4 In. | 489 |
| **Bust,** English Gentleman, W.J. Coffee, 1814, 9½ In. | 2400 |
| **Bust,** Woman, Blue Dress, Continental, c.1890, 18 In. | 90 |
| **Bust,** Woman, Egyptian Headdress, Fras, Painted, Austria, c.1910, 15¾ In. | 313 |
| **Bust,** Woman, Half Draped, Piled, Curled Hair, Raised Socle, 27 In. | 750 |
| **Figurine,** 2 Children, German Clothing, Hats, Marked J.M., 9629, 9¾ In. | 84 |
| **Figurine,** 2 Putti, Grapes, Apples, Basket, Bell Epoque, France, c.1885, 20 x 17 In. ...illus | 2706 |
| **Figurine,** Boy & Girl On Sled, Gnome Miners In Base, Lights With Lamp, Marked 847, 20 In. | 570 |
| **Figurine,** Cat, Seated On Pedestal, White Glaze, Articulated Fur, Yellow Eyes, Italy, 38 In. | 531 |
| **Figurine,** Children, Depicting Summer & Winter, Mounted As Lamps, 19 x 29 In., Pair | 369 |
| **Figurine,** Circus Women, Elie Nadelman, c.1931, 6 x 2½ In. | 6600 |
| **Figurine,** Creche, Painted, Wooden Hands, Silver Dagger, Clothing, Italy, c.1835, 16 In. ...illus | 984 |
| **Figurine,** Horse, Scratching Nose With Hind Hoof, Saddle, Chinese, c.1890, 14 x 15½ In. | 299 |
| **Figurine,** Nude Woman, Kneeling, Glazed, Waylande Gregory, c.1934, 18 x 11 In. ...illus | 9375 |
| **Figurine,** Owl On Books, Cicero & Tacitus, Eyes Light Up With Lamp, Marked, 16½ In. | 1080 |
| **Figurine,** Woman, Bathing, Rocky Base, Birds, Nest Overhead, France, 28¾ In. | 625 |
| **Humidor,** Figural, Turk's Head, Molded, Painted, Turban Lifts Off, c.1875, 11 In. | 184 |
| **Jardiniere,** Swags, Ram's Head Handles, Tapered, Italy, c.1920, 31 In. | 300 |
| **Plaque,** Italian Renaissance Style, Virgin Mother, Child, Flowers, Blue, Green, 31 x 24 In. | 2250 |
| **Platter,** Ivory, Pink, Scalloped Blue Border, Glazed, Charles Ardlett, 1986, 19 x 12 In. ...illus | 60 |
| **Sculpture,** Fruit Basket, c.1920, 18 x 19 In., Pair | 720 |
| **Teapot,** Square, Rounded Corners, Glazed Blue, Poems, Lotus, Bamboo, Chinese, 1800s, 8 In. | 119 |
| **Tile,** Architectural, Curvilinear, Chimera Relief, Scrolls, Burmese, 14 x 7½ In. | 230 |
| **Urn,** Lid, Leaves, Flowers, Cabochons, Metal Mounted, Finial, 20 In. | 300 |

**TEXTILES** listed here include many types of printed fabrics and table and household linens. Some other textiles will be found under Clothing, Coverlet, Rug, Quilt, etc.

| Item | Price |
|---|---|
| **Bag,** Drawstring, Beaded, Tassel, Shadow Box Frame, Signed, 1846, 8½ In. | 35 |
| **Banner,** Canvas, Chamber Of Horrors, Torture Devices, Fred Johnson, 8 x 8 Ft. | 4500 |
| **Banner,** Circus, Master Juggler, Alive, Juggling Objects On Stage, Canvas, 117 x 94 In. ...illus | 1180 |
| **Banner,** Eagle, Crossed Flags, Shield, E. Pluribus Unum, Glass Eye, Frame, 24 x 27 In. | 960 |
| **Banner,** Sideshow, Dwarf American Goat, Fred Johnson, 107 x 107 In. | 1940 |
| **Banner,** Sideshow, Half Boy, Fred Johnson, 92 x 116 In. | 2800 |
| **Banner,** Sideshow, Last Mile, Gallows, Garotte, Electric Chair, 4 Panels, 137 x 90 In. | 3776 |
| **Banner,** Sideshow, Monkey Speedway, Start, Sigler Studios, c.1950, 125 x 108 In. | 3360 |
| **Banner,** Sideshow, Woman Snake Handler, Fred Johnson, 83 x 83 In. | 3185 |
| **Bed Cover,** Crewelwork, Multicolor, Linen, 3-Part Backing, Middle Eastern, 62 x 81 In. | 522 |
| **Bed Cover,** Vase Of Flowers, Wool, Black Ground, 1826, 96 x 84 In. | 13800 |
| **Bed Rug,** Blue, Green, Salmon, Flowers, Wool, Joseph & Olive Abbott, 1775, 83 x 88 In. | 28290 |
| **Bedspread,** Green, Red Dots, Stars, Flowers, Block Printed, New Eng., c.1810, 83 x 76 In. | 660 |
| **Blanket,** Cotton, Woven, Stenciled, Flower Baskets, c.1775, 78 x 66 In. | 9480 |
| **Blanket,** Pelt, Skunk, 7 Ft. 10 In. x 8 Ft. 8 In. | 2520 |
| **Blanket,** Wool, Hudson's Bay Point, Stripes, England, 88 x 68 In. ...illus | 270 |
| **Drapery,** Coral, Silk, 5 Swags & Cascades, 10 Panels, 8 Tiebacks, 134 x 75 In., 23 Piece | 4674 |
| **Drapery,** Cream, Damask, Beaded Fringe, 6 Panels, 3 Cornices, 24 x 66 In., 9 Pieces | 1107 |
| **Drapery,** Damask, Gold, Patterned Organza, Serpentine Cornice Boards, 131 x 65 In., 6 Sets | 4674 |
| **Drapery,** Gold, Blue Fringe, 4 Swags, 8 Panels & Tiebacks, 128 x 72 In., 24 Piece | 5658 |
| **Drapery,** Lined Silk, Embroidery, Floral, Leaves, Orange Ground, 94 x 64 In., 4 Pair | 549 |
| **Embroidered,** Silk, Birds, Blossoms, Butterflies, Frame, Chinese, 17½ x 33½ In. | 69 |
| **Embroidered,** Silk, Crane, Peony Trees, Chinese, 56 x 63 In. | 600 |
| **Embroidered,** Silk, Flowers, Figures, Red Ground, Chinese, c.1900, 16 x 16 In. | 90 |
| **Embroidered,** Silk, Warriors, Figures In Garden, Frame, Chinese, c.1890, 27 x 15 In. | 474 |
| **Flag,** American, 13 Stars, 13 Stripes, Cowpens Pattern, Wool, Cotton, c.1900, 29 x 60 In. | 461 |
| **Flag,** American, 13 Stars, Betsy Ross, Rachel Albright, 10¾ x 19 In. | 2640 |
| **Flag,** American, 13 Stars, Centennial, Civil War Reunion Presentation, c.1876, 22 x 40 In. | 3220 |
| **Flag,** American, 13 Stars, Great Star Variation, 19¼ x 22¼ In. | 3600 |
| **Flag,** American, 13 Stars, Hickory Pole, Machine Stitched, c.1900, 25 x 33 In. | 259 |
| **Flag,** American, 13 Stars, Wool, Cotton, 46½ x 84 In. | 1875 |
| **Flag,** American, 33 Stars, 11 Stripes, Bunting, Cotton Stars & Hoist, Civil War, 104 In. ...illus | 1725 |
| **Flag,** American, 34 Stars, Civil War, 7 x 12 Ft. | 3300 |
| **Flag,** American, 34 Stars, Star Pattern, Cotton, Red, White, Blue, c.1861, 28 x 46 In. | 7380 |
| **Flag,** American, 36 Stars, Grand Luminary Pattern, Cotton, Wool | 3600 |

T

| | |
|---|---|
| **Flag,** American, 38 Stars, White Hoist, Grommets, Hemp Cord, c.1876, 12 x 20 Ft........................ | 1493 |
| **Flag,** Confederate, 7 Stars, Silk Ribbon, Embroidered, Fringe, Missouri, 1861, 5 ½ x 15 In........... | 14813 |
| **Flag,** Confederate, 11 Stars, c.1861, 12 ½ x 16 ½ In. | 7380 |
| **Flag,** Confederate, 11 Stars, Red, White, Blue, c.1861, 12 ½ x 16 ½ In. | 7380 |
| **Flag,** GAR, Membership Badge, 38 Stars, Silk, Framed, 1881-96, 15 x 23 In.....................*illus* | 1230 |
| **Furoshiki,** Wrapping Cloth, Cotton, Blue, Family Crest, Friends Of Winter, Japan, 46 x 44 In...... | 46 |
| **Handkerchief,** How To Speak French, Phrases, Translations, Cotton, 1950s, 13 x 13 In. ............. | 16 |
| **Hanging,** Goldwork, Peacock, Flowers, Cotton Back, Persia, 45 x 67 In......................... | 1845 |
| **Hanging,** Jute, Entwined Snakes, After Alexander Calder, Bon Art, 1975, 85 x 56 In. ................... | 8125 |
| **Hanging,** Maguey Fiber, Swirls, After Alexander Calder, Bon Art, 1975, 84 x 56 In. .................. | 8960 |
| **Hanging,** Wool Fiber, Shaped & Tucked On Frame, Multicolor, 31 x 64 In........................ | 1845 |
| **Panel,** Appliqued, Geese, Sheep, Stripes, Schoolhouse, Girl, Swing, Tree, 39 x 60 In................. | 600 |
| **Panel,** Embroidered, Allover Leaves, Red, Blue, Middle Eastern, 1875, 70 x 37 In. ..................... | 1875 |
| **Panel,** Embroidered, Tree, Crane, Pond, Black Ground, Japan, 50 x 19 In., Pair...................... | 140 |
| **Panel,** Embroidered, Velvet, Gold Thread, Flowers, Lattice Border, 4 Ft. 9 In. x 3 Ft. 4 In............ | 184 |
| **Panel,** Embroidered, Velvet, Urn, Bouquet, Birds, Claret Velvet Ground, c.1700, 32 x 69 In......... | 1875 |
| **Panel,** Embroidery, Leaf Urn Design, 46 x 46 In.................................... | 625 |
| **Panel,** Hindu God Brahma, 77 x 44 In........................................ | 72 |
| **Panel,** Linen, Embroidered, Nude Woman, Blond, Chaise, Cat, 1920s, 27 ½ x 54 In................. | 360 |
| **Panel,** Paisley, Red, Black Medallions, 123 x 60 In. .................................... | 300 |
| **Panel,** Silk Cigar Bands, Pieces, Fringe, Metal Frame, c.1860, 32 x 32 In. ..........................*illus* | 1416 |
| **Panel,** Silk Embroidered, Red, Gold Threads, Elephant, Howdah, Satin Stitch, Chinese, 30 x 26 In. . | 1673 |
| **Panel,** Silk, Embroidered, Center Cartouche, Linked Bats, Gold Thread, c.1910, 57 x 82 In......... | 2124 |
| **Panel,** Wool, Linen, Embroidered, Chain Stitch, Royal Procession, England, 16 x 109 In. ........... | 1599 |
| **Shade,** Window, Painted, Man, Top Hat, Paying 3 Workers, Carpenters, Builders, 59 x 55 In. ...... | 1375 |
| **Tablecloth,** Velvet, Green, Embroidered, 72 x 60 In................................... | 660 |
| **Tapestry,** 18th Century Music Room Scene, Belgium, Signed J. Stevaert, c.1900, 56 x 37 In. ....... | 450 |
| **Tapestry,** Aubusson Style, Flower Borders, Swags, France, c.1900, 114 x 49 In., Pair.................. | 2337 |
| **Tapestry,** Aubusson, Drapery Style, Flower Bouquets, Red Borders, 2 Ft. 10 In. x 20 Ft. ............ | 1080 |
| **Tapestry,** Aubusson, Game Park, Hunters, Prey, Forest, France, c.1860, 8 Ft. 6 In. x 10 Ft. ......... | 6875 |
| **Tapestry,** Aubusson, Shepherd, Bucolic Landscape, Floral Swag, Scrolls, c.1800, 91 x 47 In......... | 1250 |
| **Tapestry,** Center Panel, Oval Floral Cartouche, Floral Border, c.1900, 4 Ft. 6 In. x 5 Ft. 6 In....... | 590 |
| **Tapestry,** Coat Of Arms Crest, Cupids, Garlands Over River Landscape, 80 x 66 In..................... | 575 |
| **Tapestry,** Courting Scene, c.1850, 81 x 69 In. ....................................... | 1625 |
| **Tapestry,** Embroidered, Arts & Crafts, Flowers, Blue, Yellow, Cotton, 9 ½ x 25 In................. | 488 |
| **Tapestry,** Four Seasons, After Alphonse Mucha, Frame, 43 x 27 In., 4 Piece ....................... | 2400 |
| **Tapestry,** Lake Landscape, Church, Flower Border, Sage, Olive, Brussels, 1600s, 58 x 87 In. ....... | 3690 |
| **Tapestry,** L'Aube, Wool, Multicolor, Branches, Flower, Man Ray, 1960s, 43 ½ x 98 In................... | 3438 |
| **Tapestry,** Medieval Style, Nobility, Apple Orchard, Castle, Border, Multicolor, 61 x 42 In. ............ | 615 |
| **Tapestry,** Oil Paint, Landscape, Winter, Summer On Reverse, Fringe, c.1900, 41 x 31 In............ | 160 |
| **Tapestry,** Red, Gold, Samuel Rowe, Wool, Cotton, 46 ½ x 84 In. ...................... | 4575 |
| **Tapestry,** Trees, Birds, Beige Ground, Stylized, Wool, Scandinavia, 28 x 54 In........................ | 685 |
| **Tapestry,** Verdure, 2 Hunters, Dog, Wooded Landscape, 1700s, 24 x 80 In. .......................... | 1845 |
| **Tapestry,** Verdure, Landscape, Northern Europe, 1700s, 112 x 90 In................................. | 1440 |
| **Tapestry,** Verdure, Rape Of Europa, Green, Brown, Cream, Continental, 1700s, 112 x 155 In...... | 1320 |
| **Tapestry,** Woodland Scene, Trees, Animal, Birds, Silk Embroidery, 1800s, 171 x 91 In. ........... | 5625 |
| **Tapestry,** Wool, Birds, Landscape, Flowers, c.1900, 8 Ft. 10 In. x 4 Ft. 5 ½ In. .............. | 1875 |
| **Tapestry,** Wool, House, Figures, Animals, Multicolor, Poitr Grabowski, 60 x 41 ½ In. ................. | 984 |
| **Thangka,** Deities Border, Center Mandala, Oak Frame, Tibet, 22 x 16 ¼ In......................... | 119 |
| **Thangka,** Sambhava, Sakti, Palace Of Copper Mountain Paradise, Tibet, c.1910, 43 x 28 In....... | 625 |
| **Throw,** Sable, Chocolate Brown, Silk Velvet Lined, 72 x 48 In.................................. | 5166 |
| **Towel,** Sun, Blue, Hermes, Box, 55 x 70 In........................................ | 540 |
| **Towel,** Tambour, Knotted Fringe, Monogram, c.1800, 52 x 25 In. .............................. | 175 |
| **Trapunto,** Oni Eating Octopus, Gold Ground, Red Maker's Mark, Japan, c.1900, 33 x 27 In...... | 615 |
| **Tray,** Embroidered, Quail, Waves, Clouds, Chain Stitch, Mounted, Chinese, 1800s, 10 x 9 In.*illus* | 711 |
| **Upholstery,** Velvet, Black, Amber, Cream Faux Leopard Print, 7 Yd. ......................... | 42 |
| **Wall Hanging,** Embroidered, Arts & Crafts, Silk, Pink Flowers, Frame, 25 x 35 In..................... | 152 |

**THERMOMETER** is a name that comes from the Greek word for heat. The thermometer was invented in 1731 to measure the temperature of either water or air. All kinds of thermometers are collected, but those with advertising messages are the most popular.

| | |
|---|---|
| **7Up,** Fresh-Up, Ca Ravigote, Bottle, Tin, Red, White, Green ............................... | 150 |
| **Atlantic City,** Steel Pier, Fun For All, Steel, Wood Frame, c.1960, 41 In........................ | 531 |
| **Black Arrow Coal,** Blue, White, Porcelain, 38 In. ................................. | 360 |
| **Campbell's Soup Can,** Tomato, Porcelain, 7 ¼ x 12 ¼ In.......................*illus* | 19200 |

**Terra-Cotta,** Figurine, Nude Woman, Kneeling, Glazed, Waylande Gregory, c.1934, 18 x 11 In.
$9,375

Rago Arts & Auction Center

**Terra-Cotta,** Platter, Ivory, Pink, Scalloped Blue Border, Glazed, Charles Ardlett, 1986, 19 x 12 In.
$60

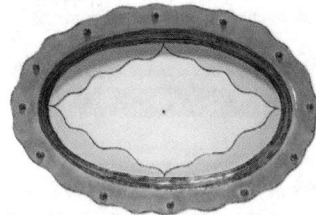

Cowan's Auctions

**Textile,** Banner, Circus, Master Juggler, Alive, Juggling Objects On Stage, Canvas, 117 x 94 In.
$1,180

Mosby Auctions

**Textile,** Blanket, Wool, Hudson's Bay Point, Stripes, England, 88 x 68 In.
$270

DuMouchelles Art Gallery

**Textile,** Flag, American, 33 Stars, 11 Stripes, Bunting, Cotton Stars & Hoist, Civil War, 104 In.
$1,725

James D. Julia Auctioneers

**Textile,** Flag, GAR, Membership Badge, 38 Stars, Silk, Framed, 1881-96, 15 x 23 In.
$1,230

Cowan's Auctions

**Textile,** Panel, Silk Cigar Bands, Pieces, Fringe, Metal Frame, c.1860, 32 x 32 In.
$1,416

Brunk Auctions

**Textile,** Tray, Embroidered, Quail, Waves, Clouds, Chain Stitch, Mounted, Chinese, 1800s, 10 x 9 In.
$711

James D. Julia Auctioneers

| | |
|---|---:|
| **Chew Wow Tobacco,** Red, Tin, c.1940, 38 In. | 1200 |
| **Columbia Records,** On Sale Here, Tin, Wood Frame, 61 x 18 In. | 1140 |
| **Cream Of Wheat,** Paint, Metal, 1970s, 48 In. | 48 |
| **Dr Pepper,** Bottle, Embossed Tin, 1930s, 17 ¼ In. | 1080 |
| **Drink Orange-Crush,** Feel Fresh, Bottle, Metal, 1943, 16 x 4 ½ In. | 588 |
| **Ex-Lax,** Blue, White, Porcelain, 38 ½ In. | 330 |
| **Ex-Lax,** Chocolate Laxative, Black, Yellow, Porcelain, 38 x 9 In. | 420 |
| **Ex-Lax,** The Chocolated Laxative, Millions Prefer Ex-Lax, 36 x 8 In. | 210 |
| **Figural,** Organ Grinder Playing Instrument, Monkey Holding Broom, Slate, 1800s, 7 x 6 In. | 311 |
| **Have Fun With NuGrape,** Delicious Anytime, Bottle, 12 In. Diam. | 180 |
| **Hills Bros. Coffee,** Man In White Cap, Porcelain, 21 ½ In. | 360 |
| **Hills Bros. Coffee,** Porcelain, Pat. March 16, 1915, Beach, Coshocton, O. *illus* | 1534 |
| **Hills Bros.,** Man Wearing Nightgown Drinking Coffee, 8 ¾ x 20 ¾ In. | 360 to 420 |
| **Ken-L Ration,** For Best Results, Tin, White, Blue, 26 x 7 In. | 390 |
| **Kirk's Jap Rose Soap,** Toilet, Bath, Shampoo, Blue, Yellow, Porcelain, 27 In. | 450 |
| **Mail Pouch Chewing Tobacco,** New Larger Size, Blue, Silver, Red, Tin, c.1950, 39 x 8 In. | 92 |
| **Mail Pouch Tobacco,** Navy Blue, Porcelain, 38 ½ In. | 240 |
| **Mail Pouch Tobacco,** Porcelain, Blue Ground, White, Yellow Lettering, 19 x 73 In. | 1368 |
| **Mail Pouch Tobacco,** Tin, Blue, 38 ½ In. | 180 |
| **Mail Pouch,** Tall Chew, Treat Yourself To The Best, c.1950, 8 x 39 In. | 210 to 240 |
| **Mail Pouch,** Treat Yourself To The Best, SSP, 12 x 2 ¾ In. | 90 |
| **McKeeson's Aspirin,** Best For Pain, Porcelain, Brown, c.1925, 27 x 7 In. | 480 |
| **Pepsi Please,** Yellow, 1965, 28 x 7 In. | 90 |
| **Polarine Red Crown Gasoline,** Porcelain, Wood Frame, 73 x 19 In. | 18000 |
| **Prestone Anti-Freeze,** Navy, Gray, Porcelain, 37 x 9 In. | 210 |
| **Pyro Anti-Freeze,** Yellow, Blue, Embossed, Tin, 32 x 18 In. | 540 |
| **Ramon's Pink Pills,** Doctor, Top Hat, Bag, Metal, 21 In. | 240 |
| **Red Seal Dry Batteries,** Red, Blue, Porcelain, 27 x 7 In. | 360 |
| **Red Seal Dry Battery,** Guarantee Protects You, Beach Co., c.1918, 7 x 27 In. | 420 |
| **Rose Quartz Tablet,** 14K Gold, Sapphires, Cartier, 7 In. *illus* | 26250 |
| **Royal Crown Cola,** Cream, Red, Tin, 26 x 10 In. | 240 |
| **Stephenson Union Suits,** 39 x 8 In. | 300 |
| **Tums,** Black, Red, Porcelain, Glass, 27 In. | 240 |
| **Wall,** Wood, Red, White, Taylor, 8 x 1 ¾ In. | 22 |
| **Ward's Vitovim Bread,** Blond Boy, Holding Bread, Porcelain, 21 x 9 In. | 1320 |
| **Whistle,** Any Time Any Weather Thirsty Just Whistle, Boy, Bottle, Chalkware, 12 In. | 300 |

**TIFFANY** is a name that appears on items made by Louis Comfort Tiffany, the American glass designer who worked from about 1879 to 1933. His work included iridescent glass, Art Nouveau styles of design, and original contemporary styles. He was also noted for stained glass windows, unusual lamps, bronze work, pottery, and silver. Tiffany & Company, often called "Tiffany," is also listed in this section. The company was started by Charles Lewis Tiffany and Teddy Young in 1837 in New York City. In 1853 the name was changed to Tiffany & Company. Louis Tiffany (1848–1933), Charles Tiffany's son, started his own business in 1879. It was named Louis Comfort Tiffany and Associated American Artists. In 1902 the name was changed to Tiffany Studios. Tiffany & Company is still working today and is best known for silver and fine jewelry. Louis worked for his father's company as a decorator in 1900 but at the same time was working for his Tiffany Studios. Other types of Tiffany are listed under Tiffany Glass, Tiffany Gold, Tiffany Pottery, or Tiffany Silver. The famous Tiffany lamps are listed in this section. Tiffany jewelry is listed in the Jewelry and Wristwatch categories. Some Tiffany Studio desk sets have matching clocks. They are listed here. Clocks made by Tiffany & Co. are listed in the Clock category. Reproductions of some types of Tiffany are being made.

*Louis C. Tiffany*

| | |
|---|---:|
| **Ashtray,** Bronze, Gold Dore, Ribbed Handles, Signed, 4 In. | 150 |
| **Blotter Ends,** Adam, Bronze, Cast, Swag & Ribbons, 13 x 2 ¼ In., Pair | 242 |
| **Blotter Ends,** Pine Needle, Gilt Bronze, c.1920, 19 In. | 180 |
| **Blotter,** Pine Needle, Bronze, Dark Patina, Green Slag Glass, Signed | 650 |
| **Bookends,** Art Deco, Bronze, Furnaces, Enameled Borders, Gold Patina, 5 x 5 In. *illus* | 2370 |
| **Bookends,** Bronze, Enamel, Gold Dore, Line & Scroll, Gold Plate, Signed, 5 x 6 In. | 3000 |
| **Bookends,** Buddha, Seated, Bronze, Low Relief, Arched Shape, 6 x 4 ½ In. | 489 |
| **Bookends,** George Washington Crest, Bronze, Stamped, Tiffany Studios, 5 x 3 ½ In., Pair | 510 |
| **Bookends,** Spanish Pattern, Bronze Dore, Stylized Bird In Arch, 1897, 5 ¾ x 4 In. | 2370 |
| **Bookends,** Trees, Branches, Scrolls, Gold Dore, Stamped, 5 x 6 In. | 3500 |
| **Bookends,** Venetian, Gilt Bronze, Stamped Tiffany Studios, 6 In., Pair | 1625 |
| **Bottle,** Gray, Green Pulled Feather, Yellow Dots, Pinched Sides, Silver Cap, 8 In. | 7500 |
| **Bowl,** Bronze Dore, Flared, Stylized Flowers On Rim, Pedestal Foot, 10 In. | 608 |
| **Bowl,** Geometric, Bronze Dore, Mother-Of-Pearl, Flared, Footed, 9 x 1 ½ In. | 230 |

T

| | |
|---|---|
| **Bowl,** Gold Iridescent, Ribbed, Scalloped Rim, Favrile, Signed, 7 In. .................*illus* | 690 |
| **Bowl,** Greek Key Rim, Enameled Lozenges, Gold Dore, Leaf Tip Border, c.1918, 2 x 8 In. ............. | 523 |
| **Bowl,** Lily Pad, Bronze, 2 Pads, 3 Pods, Brown Patina, Stamped, 4 ½ x 11 In. | 661 |
| **Bowl,** Lily Pad, Bronze, Brown Patina, Lily Pad Handles, Stamped, 4 ½ x 11 x 8 In. ...... | 489 |
| **Bowl,** Opalescent, Pastel Ribbons, Flared, Bronze Fleur-De-Lis Foot, 12 ½ In. ...... | 1185 |
| **Bowl,** Ribbed, Bronze Dore, Marked, c.1910, 2 x 8 In. ...... | 492 |
| **Bowl,** Spun Metal, Decorated Rim, c.1910, 9 In. ...... | 210 |
| **Box,** Bronze, Enamel, Gold Dore, Fleur-De-Lis, Multicolor, Signed, 6 x 5 x 2 In. ...... | 3000 |
| **Box,** Card, Pine Needle, Green Slag, Dark Patina, Hinged, Compartments, 3 x 4 x 2 In. ...... | 2500 |
| **Box,** Glove, Pine Needle, Bronze, Green Slag Glass, Bun Feet, 3 x 13 ¾ In. ...... | 575 |
| **Box,** Stamp, Bookmark Pattern, Gold Dore, Raised Leaves, Signed, 2 ½ x 2 x 1 ½ In. ...... | 950 |
| **Box,** Zodiac, Bronze, Dark Patina, Hinged, Cedar Lined, Signed, 6 ½ x 6 x 2 In. ...... | 3000 |
| **Calendar Frame,** Spanish Pattern, Daily, Gold Patina, Stamped, 6 x 5 In. .................*illus* | 1481 |
| **Candelabrum,** 3-Light, Bronze, Beaded Reticulated Cups, Green Glass Inserts, 14 In., Pair....... | 5925 |
| **Candelabrum,** 4-Light, Bronze, Bulbous Cups, Snuffer, Iridescent Cabochons, 15 In., Pair....... | 17775 |
| **Candelabrum,** 6-Light, Gold Dore, Urn Shape Cup, 3-Prong Arm, Center Stem, c.1910, 15 In.... | 1599 |
| **Candelabrum,** 7-Light, Bronze, Tapered Stem, Upturned Branches, Bulbous Cups, 14 In. ...... | 2500 |
| **Candelabrum,** 7-Light, Knop, Upturned Branches, Bulb Shape Sockets, Stamped, c.1920, 14 In. | 2125 |
| **Candle Lamp,** Blue Favrile, Pulled Feather, Electrified, Signed L.C.T., 1900s, 12 x 7 In. ...... | 1599 |
| **Candlestick,** Blue & Pink Enameled Rim, Bronze Dore, Blue Glass Stem, c.1920, 9 In., Pair ...... | 1968 |
| **Candlestick,** Bronze, Bamboo Stem, Flared Base, Stamped, 10 ½ In., Pair....... | 1680 |
| **Candlestick,** Bronze, Glass, Reticulated Pineapple Cup, Artichoke Stem, Saucer Foot, 15 In....... | 3402 |
| **Candlestick,** Bronze, Green Art Glass, c.1910, 13 In. ...... | 523 |
| **Candlestick,** Bronze, Green Glass, Pod Shape Cup, Round Base, 1900s, 17 ½ x 6 In., Pair....... | 540 |
| **Candlestick,** Bronze, Groundhog, Supporting Holder, Sitting On Book, J.L. Clark, 1903, 9 In....... | 4830 |
| **Candlestick,** Bronze, Teardrop Cutouts, Green Glass, Tripod Stand, Snuffer, 21 In....... | 5866 |
| **Candlestick,** Cobra, Lily Pad Foot, Candle Cup, Gold Dore Patina, Stamped, 8 In.........*illus* | 1778 |
| **Candlestick,** Gilt Bronze, Nude Woman, Holding Cup, 9 ¾ x 4 ½ In., Pair ...... | 8750 |
| **Candlestick,** Green Favrile Glass Insets, Bronze, Thin Knop Stem, 17 ¾ In. ...... | 875 |
| **Candlestick,** Groundhog On Book, Rowfant Club, Cleveland, J.L. Clark, 1903, 8 x 4 In.......*illus* | 8960 |
| **Candlestick,** Pastel, Sea Foam Green, Onionskin Stretch Border, Opalescent Snowflake, 4 In..... | 748 |
| **Candlestick,** Poppy, Bronze, Sage Glass Insert, Verdigris, Lily Pad Base, 17 x 6 In. ...... | 472 |
| **Candlestick,** Queen Anne's Lace, Bronze, Spread Base, Blown-Out Green Glass, 18 In. ...... | 1298 |
| **Centerpiece,** Glass, Bronze, Enamel, Favrile, Open Curve Design, Flared, 4 x 8 In. ...... | 2500 |
| **Chamberstick,** 2-Light, Bronze, Fleur-De-Lis Base, Snuffer, Signed, 8 ½ In. ...... | 5000 |
| **Charger,** Gilt Bronze, Round, Incised, Tiffany Studios, c.1915, 9 In. ...... | 1800 |
| **Clock,** Brass, Marble, Side Columns, Rectangular Base, 5 ½ x 9 In. ...... | 270 |
| **Clock,** Bronze Dore Movement, Pierced Case, Porcelain Over Copper Face, 14 x 8 In....... | 374 |
| **Clock,** Carriage, Gilt Bronze, Steel, Spiral Reeded, Scrollwork Beaver, Guy Lamaille, 6 x 4 In. ...... | 2952 |
| **Clock,** Crystal Palace Regulator, Bronze, Beveled Glass Sides, Doors, Swags, 14 x 8 In. ...... | 949 |
| **Clock,** Desk, Adam, Goldtone Face, Octagonal Case, Multicolor, Stamped, c.1910, 4 In....... | 923 |
| **Clock,** Travel, Grand Sonnerie, Sterling Silver Case, Porcelain Dial, Handle, c.1890, 3 ½ In. ....... | 2706 |
| **Clock,** Weather Station, Brass, Batons, Thermometer, Pedestal Base, Cut Corners, 4 In....... | 295 |
| **Compote,** Bronze Dore, Stylized Greek Key Band, Tapered Stem, Spread Foot, 4 x 6 ½ In............ | 266 |
| **Compote,** Bronze, Enamel, Flower Border, Geometric Border, Pedestal, Signed, 10 x 3 In............ | 1200 |
| **Compote,** Double Shaped Ribbed Body, Gold Iridescent, Scalloped Rim, Signed, 4 In. ...... | 750 |
| **Cribbage Pad,** Venetian, Bronze, Hinged, Wooden Back, 8 x 4 In.......................*illus* | 1422 |
| **Desk Blotter,** Grapevine, Etched Metal, Stamped Tiffany Studios, 4 Piece...... | 281 |
| **Desk Set,** Abalone Pattern, Bronze, 2 Inkwells, Blotter Ends, Box, 4 Piece...... | 889 |
| **Desk Set,** Abalone Pattern, Bronze, Octagonal Inkwell, Stamp Box, Paper Knife, 3 Piece........... | 1094 |
| **Desk Set,** Grapevine, Bronze, Caramel Slag, Inkwell, Letter Rack & Hook, 4 Piece ...... | 1215 |
| **Desk Set,** Pine Needle, Gilt Bronze, Glass, c.1920, 5 Piece...... | 1020 |
| **Desk Tray,** Bronze, Enameled, Blue, Green, Yellow, Stylized Leaf Corners, 5 In. ...... | 354 |
| **Frame,** Bronze, Easel, Ornate & Curve Border, Signed, 6 ¾ x 9 In. ...... | 3500 |
| **Frame,** Grapevine, Bronze, Beaded Rim, Oval Opening, Green Slag Glass, 10 x 8 In.................. | 2074 |
| **Frame,** Grapevine, Bronze, Caramel Slag Glass, Beaded Edges, 7 ¾ x 6 ½ In. ...... | 518 |
| **Frame,** Zodiac, Bronze, Easel, Patina, Signed, 7 x 8 In....... | 2400 |
| **Glass,** Jar, Gold Iridescent, Lid, Knob Handle, Sunburst, Signed, 4 x 7 ½ In. ...... | 2000 |
| **Glass,** Jar, Gold Iridescent, Silver Lid, Bail Handle, Signed, 3 ½ x 2 ¾ In. ...... | 2000 |
| **Inkwell & Pen Tray,** Zodiac, Bronze, Marked Tiffany Studios, 2 ½ In....... | 246 |
| **Inkwell,** American Indian, Bronze, Marked, 3 ¾ In. ...................*illus* | 277 |
| **Inkwell,** Bookmark Pattern, Bronze, Octagonal, Hinged, Signed, 4 ½ x 2 ½ In. ...... | 1200 |
| **Inkwell,** Bookmark Pattern, Gold Dore, Square, Diagonal Corners, Signed, 3 x 3 x 2 In. ...... | 750 |
| **Inkwell,** Geometric, Bronze, Hinged Lid, Acid Etched, Lime Green, 7 In. ...... | 5332 |
| **Inkwell,** Grapevine, Bronze, Green Slag Glass, 2 Clear Glass Inserts, 3 x 5 In. ...... | 4740 |

**Thermometer,** Campbell's Soup Can, Tomato, Porcelain, 7 ¼ x 12 ¼ In.
**$19,200**

**Thermometer,** Hills Bros. Coffee, Porcelain, Pat. March 16, 1915, Beach, Coshocton, O.
**$1,534**

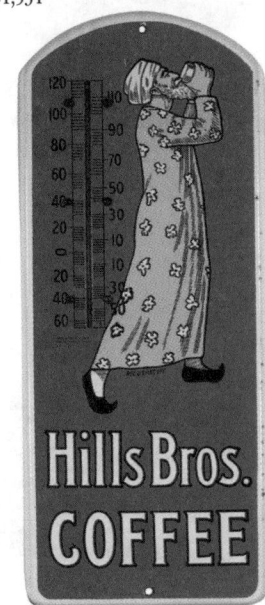

**Thermometer,** Rose Quartz Tablet, 14K Gold, Sapphires, Cartier, 7 In.
**$26,250**

**Tiffany,** Bookends, Art Deco, Bronze, Furnaces, Enameled Borders, Gold Patina, 5 x 5 In.
$2,370

James D. Julia Auctioneers

**Tiffany,** Bowl, Gold Iridescent, Ribbed, Scalloped Rim, Favrile, Signed, 7 In.
$690

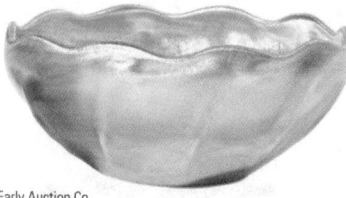

Early Auction Co.

**Tiffany,** Calendar Frame, Spanish Pattern, Daily, Gold Patina, Stamped, 6 x 5 In.
$1,481

James D. Julia Auctioneers

**Tiffany,** Candlestick, Cobra, Lily Pad Foot, Candle Cup, Gold Dore Patina, Stamped, 8 In.
$1,778

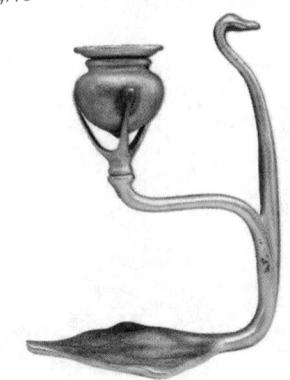

James D. Julia Auctioneers

**Tiffany,** Candlestick, Groundhog On Book, Rowfant Club, Cleveland, J.L. Clark, 1903, 8 x 4 In.
$8,960

Rago Arts & Auction Center

**Tiffany,** Cribbage Pad, Venetian, Bronze, Hinged, Wooden Back, 8 x 4 In.
$1,422

James D. Julia Auctioneers

**Tiffany,** Inkwell, American Indian, Bronze, Marked, 3 ¾ In.
$277

Cowan's Auctions

**Tiffany,** Lamp Socket, 6-Light Cluster, Bronze, Curved Arms, 4 x 8 In.
$296

James D. Julia Auctioneers

**Tiffany,** Lamp, Black-Eyed Susan, Bronze Mushroom Base, Signed, 23 x 16 In.
$34,500

Cottone Auctions

**Tiffany,** Lamp, Bronze, Gilt, Stamped, Tiffany Studios New York, 54 ½ In.
$3,304

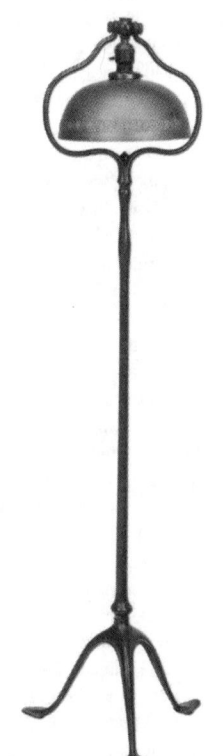

Brunk Auctions

T

| | | |
|---|---|---|
| **Inkwell**, Grapevine, Bronze, Slag Glass, 7 In. | | 246 |
| **Inkwell**, Heraldic, Canister, Green Enamel, Lid, Hinged, Shield, Hobnail, Signed, 3 In. | | 3500 |
| **Inkwell**, Pine Needle, Green Slag, Beaded, Ball Feet, 4 x 4 x 3 In. | | 950 |
| **Inkwell**, Zodiac, Bronze, Gold Dore, Crab Symbol, 2 ⅛ x 4 In. | | 374 |
| **Inkwell**, Zodiac, Gilt Bronze, Enamel, Stamped, 2 ½ In. | | 360 |
| **Jewelry Box**, Bronze, Raised Posts, Hinged, Ball Feet, Signed, 8 x 3 x 3 In. | | 4000 |
| **Lamp Socket**, 6-Light Cluster, Bronze, Curved Arms, 4 x 8 In. | *illus* | 296 |
| **Lamp**, 6-Light, Bronze, Gooseneck Arms, Artichoke Foot, Green Ribbed Lily Shades, 20 In. | | 11850 |
| **Lamp**, Acorn Shade, Mottled Green Leaded Glass, Bulbous Bronze Base, 14 In. | | 9440 |
| **Lamp**, Acorn, Leaded Glass, Green & Gold, Bronze Base, Signed, c.1910, 10 In. | | 3795 |
| **Lamp**, Aladdin, Gold Iridescent King Tut Pattern, Lion Feet, 54 ½ In. | | 10665 |
| **Lamp**, Arabian, Green, Cream, Gold Iridescent Zipper, Applied Gold Prunts, 14 In. | | 5333 |
| **Lamp**, Black-Eyed Susan, Bronze Mushroom Base, Signed, 23 x 16 In. | *illus* | 34500 |
| **Lamp**, Bronze, Gilt, Stamped, Tiffany Studios New York, 54 ½ In. | *illus* | 3304 |
| **Lamp**, Bronze, Lead Glass Acorn Style Shade, Tri-Petal Base, 56 x 10 In. | | 1495 |
| **Lamp**, Bronze, Lily Pad Base, 6-Sided Filigree Panel Shade, 18 ¾ x 21 In. | | 4945 |
| **Lamp**, Bronze, Ribbed, Spread Foot, Mottled Cream & Green Geometric Shade, 21 In. | | 14220 |
| **Lamp**, Bronze, Student, Iridescent Gold Shade, Blue Highlights, 26 In. | | 5925 |
| **Lamp**, Candlestick, Bronze Cobra, White, Green Pulled Feather, Flattened Base, 12 ½ In. | | 1481 |
| **Lamp**, Candlestick, Favrile Glass, Ruffled Shade, Twisted Base, Signed, 12 ½ In. | *illus* | 1003 |
| **Lamp**, Candlestick, Gold Iridescent, Honeycomb Fluted Shade, Favrile, 12 ½ In. | | 1298 |
| **Lamp**, Colonial, Leaded Geometric Shade, Bronze Base, 3-Light, Signed, 22 ½ In. | | 288 |
| **Lamp**, Counterbalance, Green Domed Shade, Signed LCT, 53 In. | | 7702 |
| **Lamp**, Desk, Adjustable, Gold Domed Shade, Diamond Quilted, 4-Footed, 20 ¾ In. | | 8295 |
| **Lamp**, Desk, Bronze, 3 Spider Arms, Round Onion Base, Domed Damascene Shade, 16 In. | | 948 |
| **Lamp**, Desk, Bronze, Forked Stem, Round Ribbed Base, Nautilus Shell Shade, 13 In. | | 7703 |
| **Lamp**, Desk, Bronze, Shaped Harp, Ribbed Base, Gold Iridescent Bell Shade, 13 In. | | 2370 |
| **Lamp**, Desk, Graduate Pattern, Acid Etched Shade Holder, Gold Shade, 18 In. | | 2964 |
| **Lamp**, Desk, Harp, Gilt Bronze, Amber Shade, Iridized, c.1920, 13 x 4 ½ In. | | 4688 |
| **Lamp**, Desk, Mottled Green Glass, Geometric Down Shape, Square Base, 17 ¾ In. | | 8887 |
| **Lamp**, Desk, Nautilus Shell, Abalone, Gilt Bronze, Marked, c.1910, 13 ½ In. | *illus* | 6600 |
| **Lamp**, Desk, Weight-Balance, Bronze, Shaped Arm, Green Shade, Twisted Prunts, 14 In. | | 6900 |
| **Lamp**, Dragonfly, Leaded Slag Glass, Bronze, Tiffany Studios, c.1920, 64 In. | *illus* | 68750 |
| **Lamp**, Electric, 3-Light, Bronze, Pulled Feather Tulip Shades, c.1910, 23 ½ In. | | 9600 |
| **Lamp**, Floor, Weight-Balance, Metal, Stamped Tiffany Studios, c.1900, 56 x 13 In. | | 1875 |
| **Lamp**, Gas, Ruffled Shade, Amber, Gold, 14 In. | | 938 |
| **Lamp**, Gold Iridescent Shade, Bronze, 5 Lily Pad Feet, Marked, 56 In. | | 5000 |
| **Lamp**, Green Damascene Shade, Purple Highlights, 5 Lily Pad Feet, 57 ½ In. | | 5925 |
| **Lamp**, Green Pulled Feather Shade, Bronze, Harp Base, 13 ½ In. | | 1896 |
| **Lamp**, Hanging, Gold Iridescent, Feather, Swirls, Ribbed, Bulbous, Favrile, 6 x 13 In. | | 2500 |
| **Lamp**, Hanging, Stalactite, Gold Iridescent, Ribbed, 3 Bronze Ball Chains, 26 In. | | 5333 |
| **Lamp**, Harp, Green Damascene Domed Shade, Favrile, Frame, c.1915, 55 x 9 In. | | 8750 |
| **Lamp**, Heat Cap, Bronze, Brown Patina, Acid Etched Flower & Cutouts, 4 In. | *illus* | 2074 |
| **Lamp**, Heat Cap, Bronze, Brown Patina, Ribbed, Acid Etched Vent Holes, 6 x 5 In. | *illus* | 1837 |
| **Lamp**, Iridescent Green Damascene Shade, Bronze, 5 Ball Feet, Signed LCT, 16 In. | | 6517 |
| **Lamp**, Leaded Glass, Acorn Band, Amber, Green Geometric Ground, Torpedo Base, 18 In. | | 5333 |
| **Lamp**, Leaded Glass, Greek Key Band, Mottled Amber & Green Tiles, Library Base, 23 In. | | 11543 |
| **Lamp**, Lily, 3-Light, Gold Dore, Gold Favrile Shades, c.1910, 12 ¾ In. | | 2214 |
| **Lamp**, Linenfold Shade, Bronze Trim & Dore Geometric Base, Marked, 23 In. | *illus* | 14500 |
| **Lamp**, Linenfold Shade, Tapered, Patinated Bronze Colonial Base, 1920s, 22 x 19 In. | | 17500 |
| **Lamp**, Mosque, Cream Iridescent, Blue & Gold Pulled Feather, 8-Sided Wood Base, 8 In. | | 4444 |
| **Lamp**, Oil, Gold Favrile, Twisted Stem Oil Font, Chimney, Ruffled Shade, 7 ¼ In. | *illus* | 1265 |
| **Lamp**, Papyrus, Bronze, Tapered, Stylized Egyptian Decor, Stepped Round Base, 24 In. | | 4500 |
| **Lamp**, Smoking Stand, Book Rack, Bronze, Mahogany, Glass Etruscan Shade, 1900s, 56 In. | *illus* | 5938 |
| **Lamp**, Student, 2-Light, Bronze, Arched Arms, Sawtooth Base, Gold Tulip Shades, 19 In. | | 7110 |
| **Lamp**, Turtleback Tile Band, Mottled Green Geometric Panels, Root Base, Arched Feet, 23 In. | | 18250 |
| **Lamp**, Tyler Scroll Shade, Green & Caramel Slag Glass, Bronze Pineapple Base, 24 In. | | 21250 |
| **Lamp**, Weight-Balance, Bronze, Ribbed, Lily Pad Feet, Green Damascene Shade, 53 In. | | 8888 |
| **Lamp**, Weight-Balance, Gilt Bronze, Leafy Column, Tapered White Shade, 55 ¼ In. | | 3068 |
| **Lamp**, Zodiac, Verdigris, Adjustable Bronze Shade, Shaped Harp, Footed Base, c.1910, 14 In. | | 1476 |
| **Letter Box**, Bronze, Agate Cabochons, Chased, Scrolling Fern, Openwork Lid, 6 x 9 In. | | 800 |
| **Letter Holder**, Pine Needle, Bronze, Green Slag Glass, 3 Tiers, 12 ⅝ x 3 ½ In. | | 863 |
| **Letter Rack**, Pine Needle, Bronze, Compartments, Green Slag, Signed, 10 x 6 x 2 In. | | 1500 |
| **Magnifying Glass**, Zodiac, Patinated Bronze Dore, Glass, Stamped, c.1910, 9 In. | | 215 |
| **Match Holder**, Pine Needle, Bronze, Green Slag Glass, 2 ¼ In. | | 345 |
| **Matchbox Stand**, Bronze, Gold Dore, Dish Base, Enamel Geometric Border, 3 ¾ In. | | 207 |

**Tiffany**, Lamp, Candlestick, Favrile Glass, Ruffled Shade, Twisted Base, Signed, 12 ½ In.
$1,003

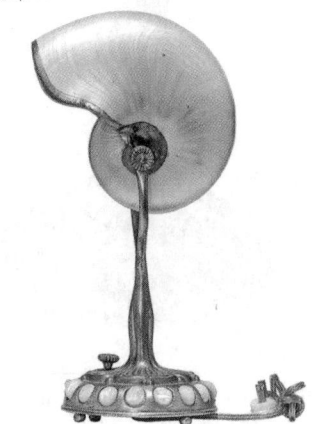

Brunk Auctions

**Tiffany**, Lamp, Desk, Nautilus Shell, Abalone, Gilt Bronze, Marked, c.1910, 13 ½ In.
$6,600

Cowan's Auctions

**Tiffany**, Lamp, Dragonfly, Leaded Slag Glass, Bronze, Tiffany Studios, c.1920, 64 In.
$68,750

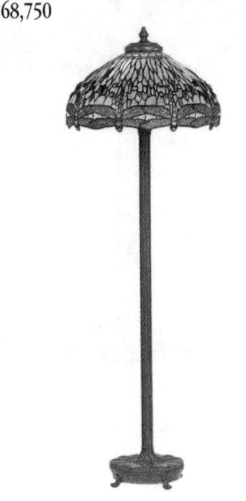

Rago Arts & Auction Center

565

**Tiffany,** Lamp, Heat Cap, Bronze, Brown Patina, Acid Etched Flower & Cutouts, 4 In.
$2,074

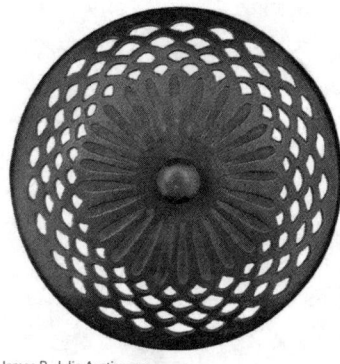

James D. Julia Auctioneers

**Tiffany,** Lamp, Heat Cap, Bronze, Brown Patina, Ribbed, Acid Etched Vent Holes, 6 x 5 In.
$1,837

James D. Julia Auctioneers

**Tiffany,** Lamp, Linenfold Shade, Bronze Trim & Dore Geometric Base, Marked, 23 In.
$14,500

James D. Julia Auctioneers

**Tiffany,** Lamp, Oil, Gold Favrile, Twisted Stem Oil Font, Chimney, Ruffled Shade, 7 ¼ In.
$1,265

Early Auction Co.

**Tiffany,** Lamp, Smoking Stand, Book Rack, Bronze, Mahogany, Glass Etruscan Shade, 1900s, 56 In.
$5,938

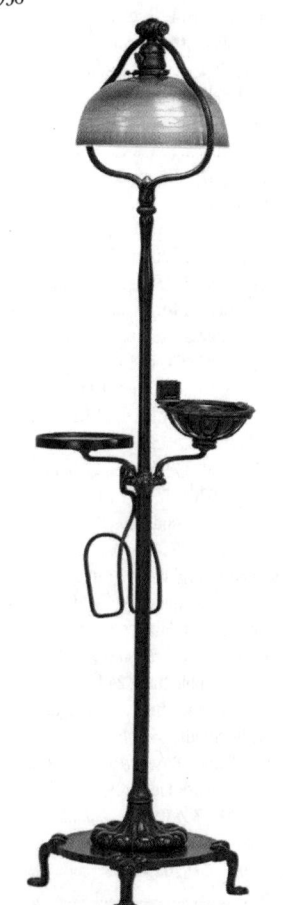

Rago Arts & Auction Center

**Tiffany,** Vase, Tulips, Favrile, Silvered Copper Clad, Signed, c.1910, 7 x 2 ½ In.
$4,063

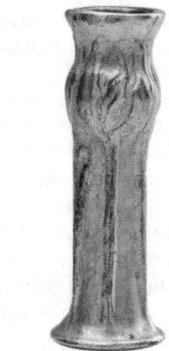

Rago Arts & Auction Center

**Tiffany Glass,** Bowl, Flower Frog, Lily Pads, Blue, Favrile, Marked, c.1910, 4 x 9 ¾ In.
$2,242

Brunk Auctions

**Tiffany Glass,** Shade, Lily, Green Pulled Feathers, Gold Iridescent Trim, Favrile, 4 ⅝ In.
$1,304

James D. Julia Auctioneers

**Tiffany Glass,** Vase, Amber, Maroon & Yellow Flowers, Green Vines, Cameo, Favrile, 11 In.
$13,035

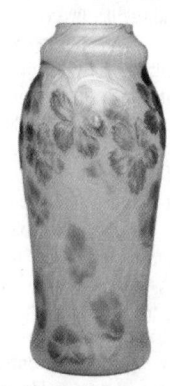

James D. Julia Auctioneers

T

| | |
|---|---|
| **Notepad,** Pine Needle, Bronze, Gold Patina, Caramel Slag Glass, 5 x 8 In. | 365 |
| **Paper Knife,** Zodiac, Bronze, Gold Dore, 10 In. | 365 |
| **Paper Rack,** Graduate, Bronze, Gilt, Marked Tiffany Studios, 7¼ In. | 369 |
| **Paper Rack,** Pine Needle, Gold, Tiffany Studios, 12 In. | 960 |
| **Paperweight,** Lion, Lying Down, Bronze, 2 x 2 x 5 In. | 580 |
| **Paperweight,** Pine Needle, Bronze, Glass, Curved Spine, 7½ x 3½ In. | 1500 |
| **Paperweight,** Turtleback, Green, Cream Swirls, Bronze Frame, 4-Footed, 5 x 6 In. | 2962 |
| **Pen Rest,** Trophy, Zodiac Pattern, New York Yacht Club, 1913, 6¼ In. | 923 |
| **Pen Tray,** Pine Needle, Bronze, Green Slag Glass, Bun Feet, 9⅝ x 2¾ In. | 316 |
| **Pen Wipe,** Bronze, Swirling Ribbons, Cartouche, Mosaic Favrile Glass, 1¼ x 3 In. | 5925 |
| **Penholder,** Spanish, Bronze, Gold Patina, 2 Swivel Bakelite Holders, 7 In. | 1778 |
| **Picture Frame,** Abalone Pattern, Art Nouveau, Oval Opening, 7¼ x 10¼ In. | 3705 |
| **Planter,** Pine Needle, Copper Lining, Tiffany Studios, 8 In. | 1020 |
| **Platter,** Dore Bronze Mottled, Round, Shallow, Wide Flat Border, Marked, 14 In. | 34 |
| **Postal Scale,** Bronze, Art Glass, Verdigris, Grapevine, Green Glass, 3¼ In. | 861 |
| **Scale,** Letter, Bookmark, Bronze, Gold Dore, Raised Leaves, Signed, 3 x 3 In. | 2500 |
| **Smoking Stand,** Poppy Buds, Leaves, Meandering Stem, Cast Iron, Bronze Ashtray, 28 In. | 4148 |
| **Standish,** Art Nouveau, Silvered Bronze, Round, Celtic Design, Tripod Base, 7½ x 6½ In. | 230 |
| **Tazza,** Gold Dore, Greek Key Rim, Leaf Tip Border, Round Foot, c.1918, 2½ x 7 In. | 523 |
| **Tea Screen,** Bronze, Glass, 3 Panels, Multicolor Swirls, Ball Feet, 12 x 21 In. | 4500 |
| **Thermometer,** Byzantine, Bronze, Gold Patina, Beaded, Coral Glass Inlay, 7¾ In. | 1600 |
| **Thermometer,** Venetian, Gold Dore, Raised, Sculptured Minks, Signed, 8 x 4 In. | 3000 |
| **Toiletry Set,** Man's, Silver, Glass, Comb, Brushes, Buttonhook, Mirror, Leather Case, 15 In. | 813 |
| **Tray,** Bronze, Gold Dore, Raised Edge, Signed, 9 In. Diam. | 250 |
| **Vase,** Bronze, Gold Favrile Body, Dore Base, Marked, c.1920, 14¾ In. | 923 |
| **Vase,** Bud, Gold Enameled Bronze, Favrile, c.1900, 13 x 4 In. | 1000 |
| **Vase,** Bud, Gold Favrile, Pairpoint Sheffield Holder, Signed, 8 In. | 483 |
| **Vase,** Gold Iridescent, Hooked Band At Shoulder, Cup Mouth, Favrile, 1965, 10 In. | 863 |
| **Vase,** Tulips, Favrile, Silvered Copper Clad, Signed, c.1910, 7 x 2½ In. ........*illus* | 4063 |

### TIFFANY GLASS

| | |
|---|---|
| **Bottle,** Turquoise, Cased White Inside, Bulbous, Tapered Neck, Ball Stopper, 7½ In. | 486 |
| **Bowl,** Engraved Leaves, Vine Encircling Rim, Gold, Magenta Highlight, 2¼ x 6⅜ In. | 546 |
| **Bowl,** Flower Frog, Lily Pads, Blue, Favrile, Marked, c.1910, 4 x 9¾ In. .........*illus* | 2242 |
| **Bowl,** Gold Iridescent, Flared, Green Rim, 3 Curled Reeded Feet, Favrile, 8 In. | 770 |
| **Bowl,** Gold Iridescent, Lobed, Paneled, Favrile, c.1920, 3 x 9¾ In. | 325 |
| **Bowl,** Gold Iridescent, Orange, Green Cross Band, Signed L.C. Tiffany, Favrile, 4 x 7 In. | 3540 |
| **Bowl,** Gold Iridescent, Translucent Amber, Lobed, Round, Signed, c.1920, 4 x 10 In. | 531 |
| **Bowl,** Gold Iridescent, Vertical Ribs On Sides, Undulating Rim, 9¼ In. | 152 |
| **Bowl,** Gold Iridescent, Wide Flaring Ruffled Rim, 4-Footed, Signed LCT, 7¾ In. | 494 |
| **Bowl,** Gold, Iridescent, Protrusion, Indentations, Amber Favrile, Signed L.C.T., 2 x 5 In. | 313 |
| **Bowl,** Green Heart & Trailing Vine, Squat, Gold Favrile, Signed L.C.T., 3½ In. | 690 |
| **Bowl,** Leaf & Vine Pattern, Iridescent Blue Ground, Round, 6½ In. | 1560 |
| **Bowl,** Ribbed, Flaring, Scalloped Rim, Gold Favrile, Signed, 2½ x 8½ In. | 288 |
| **Bowl,** Round, Shaped Rim, Body, Gold Favrile, Signed, c.1910, 2 x 6 In. | 330 |
| **Bowl,** Saucer, Water Lily, Millefiori, Gold Favrile, Inscribed L.C.T., 2 x 4 & 5¼ In. | 949 |
| **Bowl,** Wide Flaring Rim, Signed Tiffany Favrile, 12 In. | 440 |
| **Bowls,** Centerpiece, Candlesticks, Lavender, Opalescent Bands, Flared Out Rim, 3 Piece | 1540 |
| **Candlestick,** Gold Iridescent, Pedestal Form, Squat Knop, Flattened Rim, 5 In., Pair | 649 |
| **Candlestick,** Gold Iridescent, Ribbed, Domed Laurel Leaf Foot, Favrile, 11 In. | 2370 |
| **Candlestick,** Gold Iridescent, Short Stem, Flattened Rim, Spread Foot, 4 In., Pair | 711 |
| **Candlestick,** Gold Iridescent, Twist Stem, Signed L.C.T., Paper Label, 9 In. | 288 |
| **Candlestick,** White Ribbons, Blue Candle Cup, Signed LCT, 11¾ In. | 1066 |
| **Charger,** Daffodil Center, Yellow Iridescent, Favrile, c.1896, 10½ In. | 1063 |
| **Compote,** Amber, Opalescent Leaves, Pastel Favrile, Footed, Signed, 6 In. | 1150 |
| **Compote,** Gold Iridescent, Onionskin Finish, Blue, Magenta, Favrile, Signed, 6 x 2 In. | 546 |
| **Compote,** Soap Bubble Rainbow Iridescent, Scalloped Stretch Border, 4½ x 8½ In. | 431 |
| **Cup,** Gold Iridescent, Green Zigzag Line Band & Border, Gold Handle, Favrile, 3 In. | 365 |
| **Decanter,** Amber, Gold Iridescent Favrile, Signed L.C.T. c.1910, 12 In. | 750 |
| **Decanter,** Gold Iridescent, Bulbous, Pinched Sides, Elongated Neck, Favrile, 11 In. | 1003 |
| **Finger Bowl,** Gold Iridescent, Ribbed Sides, Scalloped Edges, 2¼ x 4½ In. | 150 |
| **Finger Bowl,** Underplate, Green Pastel, Amber, Onionskin Finish, Signed, 6 In. | 1150 |
| **Flower Bowl,** Gold Iridescent, Green Lily Pads, 2-Tier Flower Frog, 10 In. | 1035 |
| **Goblet,** Translucent Amber, Iridescent Gold, Knopped Stem, Signed, c.1904, 6 In., 4 Piece | 1375 |
| **Lamp,** Candlestick, Glass Base, Shade, Gold, Signed L.C.T., 18 In. | 3690 |
| **Medal,** Eagle, Liberty Bell, Victory 1918, Relief, Blue & Gold Iridescent, 2¾ In. | 415 |

**Tiffany Glass,** Vase, Crisscrossing Bands, Green, Gold Iridescence, Platinum, 6½ In.
**$9,480**

James D. Julia Auctioneers

**Tiffany Glass,** Vase, Lava, Gold Iridescent Drips, L.C. Tiffany-Favrile, Alaska-Yukon-X, 5 In.
**$14,220**

James D. Julia Auctioneers

**Tiffany Pottery,** Vase, Savoy Cabbage, Favrile, Incised Mark, LCT, 1900s, 9 x 8 In.
**$16,250**

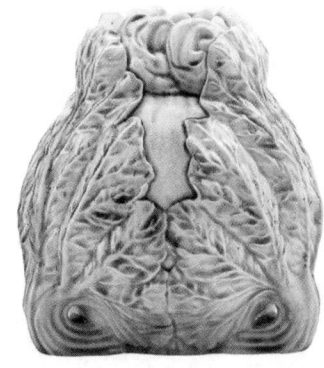

Rago Arts & Auction Center

T

**Tiffany Silver,** Asparagus Server, Regent Pattern, Pierced, Marked, 1884, 7 ½ In. $312

Heritage Auction Galleries

## Bad Company

Never put silverware and stainless-steel flatware in the dishwasher basket together. The stainless can damage the silver.

**Tiffany Silver,** Asparagus Server, Vine Pattern, Grapevines, Splayed Tines, 1872, 9 ½ In. $375

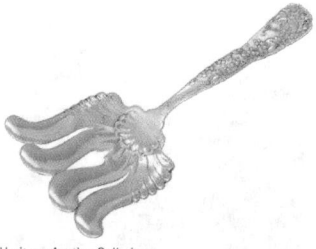

Heritage Auction Galleries

**Tiffany Silver,** Chip Server, Saratoga, Chrysanthemum Pattern, Marked, 1880, 8 ¾ In. $1,625

Heritage Auction Galleries

**Tiffany Silver,** Crumb Brush, Neoclassical, Inscription, New Rochelle Yacht Club, 1887, 14 In. $185

Skinner Auctioneers & Appraisers

| | |
|---|---:|
| **Panel,** Stained, St. Paul, Holding Sword, Memorial Verse, c.1900, 96 x 57 In. | 10000 |
| **Paperweight,** Turtleback, Gold Iridescent, Green Highlights, 5 ¾ x 4 ⅝ In. | 2962 |
| **Plate,** Pastel, Chartreuse Opalescent Fern Pattern, Favrile, c.1930, 9 In. | 460 |
| **Plate,** Pastel, Shell Pink Border, Scalloped Edge, Center Pinwheel, 11 In. | 259 |
| **Plate,** Pulled White Bands, Wisteria Pink Opalescent Edge, Inscribed, 8 ½ In. | 403 |
| **Prisms,** Iridescent, Favrile, c.1910, 6 x 1 In., 32 Piece | 2048 |
| **Rose Bowl,** Iridescent, Green Hearts, Vines, Gold Favrile, Oval, 4 In. | 1035 |
| **Salt,** Gold Iridescent, Ruffled Edge, Rainbow Highlights, Signed, 2 ½ In. | 200 |
| **Salt,** Master, Blue Iridescent, Compote Shape, Footed, 3 In. | 374 |
| **Scent Bottle,** Gold Iridescent, Green Heart & Vine, Pink Highlights, Stopper, 4 In. | 4148 |
| **Shade,** Cream, Red Fishnet, Faint Ribbing, Squat Base, Waisted Neck, 5 ⅜ In. | 1422 |
| **Shade,** Damascene, Green, Gold & Blue, Iridescent, Squat, 5 x 10 In. | 7320 |
| **Shade,** Diamond Quilted Body, Gold, Purple & Pink Highlights, 4 ⅝ In. | 948 |
| **Shade,** Gold Iridescent Shaded To Clambroth, Green Hooked Feather, Flared, 6 In. | 1422 |
| **Shade,** Green Pulled Feathers, Gold Pulled Feather Overlay, 5 ¼ In. | 1111 |
| **Shade,** Light Green Pulled Feather, Iridescent, Cream Ground, 4 ½ In. | 1296 |
| **Shade,** Lily, Green Pulled Feathers, Gold Iridescent Trim, Favrile, 4 ⅝ In. .......*illus* | 1304 |
| **Shade,** Opalescent Ribbons & Rim, Tulip Shape, 4 ⅝ In., Pair | 1823 |
| **Sherbet,** Underplate, Green, Opalescent Ribbons, Flared Rim, Iridescent Foot | 474 |
| **Tazza,** Gold Iridescent, Flared, Ribbed Support, Inverted Saucer Foot, Favrile, 3 x 6 In. | 178 |
| **Tile,** Turtleback, Blue & Gold Iridescent, 6 x 4 ½ In. | 610 |
| **Tile,** Turtleback, Favrile, Gold, 1900s, 5 ¾ x 4 ¼ In. | 719 |
| **Tile,** White Opalescent, Butterscotch Iridescent, Undulating Surface, 4 x 5 In. | 237 |
| **Toothpick Holder,** Gold Iridescent, Pinched Sides, Favrile, c.1920, 2 x 1 ⅜ In. | 259 |
| **Toothpick Holder,** Gold Iridescent, Spiral Threading, 3 In. | 189 |
| **Vase,** Amber, Gold Wave Pattern, Bulbous, Iridescent, Signed L.C.T., c.1920, 7 In. | 1063 |
| **Vase,** Amber, Maroon & Yellow Flowers, Green Vines, Cameo, Favrile, 11 In. ......*illus* | 13035 |
| **Vase,** Black, Applied Gold & Blue Tendrils, 9 ⅜ In. | 3555 |
| **Vase,** Blue Iridescent, Flower Form, Bulbous, Stretched & Riffled Rim, 4 x 5 In. | 1185 |
| **Vase,** Blue Iridescent, Flower Form, Vertical Ribs, Pedestal Foot, 12 ¾ In. | 1750 |
| **Vase,** Blue Iridescent, Green, White & Black Hearts & Vines, Onion Form, 9 In. | 3259 |
| **Vase,** Blue Iridescent, Light Blue & Gold Hearts & Vines, Swollen Shoulder, 6 In. | 2726 |
| **Vase,** Blue Iridescent, Outer Diatreta Latticework, Ruffled Edge, Favrile, 3 ¼ In. | 111 |
| **Vase,** Brown Iridescent, Yellow, Gold Pulled Design, Onion Base, Elongated Neck, 11 In. | 2963 |
| **Vase,** Bud, Flared Mouth, Amber, Feathered, Green, 4 In. | 2000 |
| **Vase,** Bud, Gold Iridescent, Pulled Green Leaf & Vine, Swollen Top, Favrile, 12 In. | 1875 |
| **Vase,** Bud, Iridescent Gold, Impressed Leaf, Flowers, Pink Highlights, 8 In. | 592 |
| **Vase,** Bulbous Shape, Green Leaves, Dark Blue Stems, Blue Iridescent, 2 ½ In. | 1722 |
| **Vase,** Bulbous, Stick Neck, Favrile, Paper Label, Signed, c.1910, 6 ½ In. | 2400 |
| **Vase,** Corona, Opal Glass, Green Pulled Feather Design, 5 ½ In. | 690 |
| **Vase,** Crisscrossing Bands, Green, Gold Iridescence, Platinum, 6 ½ In. ......*illus* | 9480 |
| **Vase,** Dark Green, Gold Pulled Feather, Squat, Pinched Neck, Signed, 3 x 3 In. | 438 |
| **Vase,** El Armana, Butterscotch Shaded To Brown, Platinum Lip, Bulbous, Squat, 8 In. | 2370 |
| **Vase,** Fan Shape, Amber, Lime Green, Peacock Feathers, 7 ¼ x 7 ¾ In. | 1750 |
| **Vase,** Flared Rim, Tapered, Ribbed Gold Iridescent Body, Favrile, Round Foot, 9 In. | 984 |
| **Vase,** Flower Shape, 5-Fold Flared Rim, Gold Iridescent, Pedestal, Signed, 4 In. | 1800 |
| **Vase,** Flower Shape, Bulbous Mouth, Round Foot, Iridescent, 7 ½ In. | 1875 |
| **Vase,** Frosted, Leaf, Lavender Vine, Flower, Carved, Signed L.C. Tiffany, Favrile, 13 In. | 12980 |
| **Vase,** Gold Favrile, Flared, Scalloped Rim, Footed, 4 ½ In. | 813 |
| **Vase,** Gold Favrile, Flower Shape, 1908, 10 x 5 In. | 1375 |
| **Vase,** Gold Iridescent, Green Heart & Vine, Favrile, c.1910, 8 ¾ In. | 1968 |
| **Vase,** Gold Iridescent, Green Leaves, Vines, Swollen Top, Favrile, 10 ¼ In. | 3911 |
| **Vase,** Gold Iridescent, Green Pulled Feather, Gold Hooked Border, Swollen, 7 In. | 2300 |
| **Vase,** Gold Iridescent, Leaves, Vines, Millefiori, Shouldered, 6 x 4 In. | 2760 |
| **Vase,** Gold Iridescent, Pinched Shoulders, Bulbous Rim, 6 ½ x 5 ½ In. | 1495 |
| **Vase,** Gold Iridescent, Platinum Highlights, Rolled Rim, Signed LCT, 6 In. | 494 |
| **Vase,** Gold Iridescent, Vertically Ribbed, Blue & Pink Highlights, Signed, 13 In. | 829 |
| **Vase,** Gold Iridescent, White Flowers, Red Centers, Stylized Leaves, Swollen, 6 In. | 7110 |
| **Vase,** Gold Swirl, Marked LCT, 10 ½ In. | 2280 |
| **Vase,** Gold, Green Heart & Vine, Favrile, Tulip Shape, Footed, Signed, 6 ¾ In. | 1495 |
| **Vase,** Gold, Green Heart & Vine, White Millefiori, Flowers, Favrile, 5 ⅞ In. | 1722 |
| **Vase,** Gold, Green Leaves, Vines, Long Neck, Bulbous Shape, 5 ¾ In. | 1230 |
| **Vase,** Gold, Jack-In-The-Pulpit, Elongated Twist Stem, Signed L.C.T., 14 In. | 2013 |
| **Vase,** Gold, Knopped Stem, Footed, Tulip Shape Bowl, Iridescent Favrile, Signed, 4 x 4 In. | 564 |
| **Vase,** Gold, Ribbed, Flower Shape, Domed Circular Foot, Signed, 11 ½ In. | 1250 |
| **Vase,** Gold, Trumpet, Footed, Ball Standard, Iridescent Favrile, Signed, 16 In. | 1840 |

T

| | |
|---|---:|
| **Vase,** Gold, Trumpet, Ribbed, Blue & Green Stretch Border, Footed, Favrile, 10 In. | 920 |
| **Vase,** Golden Red, Coiled Feathers At Shoulder, Pulled Feather From Base, 6 In. | 7475 |
| **Vase,** Green & Gold Iridescent, Pulled Design, Favrile, c.1905, 4 x 5 In. | 2875 |
| **Vase,** Green & Yellow Hooked Feather, Gold Iridescent Ground, Signed, 5 In. | 2074 |
| **Vase,** Green King Tut Pattern, Gold Iridescent Ground, Signed, 9¼ In. | 2779 |
| **Vase,** Green Translucent Body, Dimpled Sides, Iridescent Hooked Coil, 6 In. | 2300 |
| **Vase,** Green, Flared To Hexagonal Rim, Bronze Artichoke Shape Base, 16 In. | 1605 |
| **Vase,** Green, Iridescent Coiling, King Tut, Gold, Swollen, Square Mouth, 9 In. | 2645 |
| **Vase,** Heart & Vine, Favrile, c.1916, 2¾ x 3½ In. | 1265 |
| **Vase,** Indigo, Hooked Iridescent Band, Squat, Favrile, 4 In. | 1495 |
| **Vase,** Iridescent, Flared, Footed, 1918, 10 x 6 In. | 1000 |
| **Vase,** Iridescent, Opalescent Ribbons, Swirls, Bottle Form, Rolled Rim, 6½ In. | 1422 |
| **Vase,** Iridescent, Stylized Leaves, Yellow, Green, Vines, Brown, Maroon, Swollen, 6 In. | 7898 |
| **Vase,** Lava, Gold Iridescent Drips, L.C. Tiffany-Favrile, Alaska-Yukon-X, 5 In. .................*illus* | 14220 |
| **Vase,** Looped Organic Designs, Iridescent, Blue Ground, Signed L.C. Tiffany, 11 In. | 6000 |
| **Vase,** Millefiori, Green, Iridescent Heart & Vine, Shouldered, 6¼ In. | 3853 |
| **Vase,** Mottled Red, Silver, Flared Rim, High Shoulders, Paper Label, 8 In. | 9000 |
| **Vase,** Mottled Sea Foam, Blue Green, Signed, 6½ In. | 3900 |
| **Vase,** Paperweight, Tapered, White Narcissus, Pink Centers, Leaves, Signed, 8½ In. | 9200 |
| **Vase,** Pastel Green, Trumpet Shape, White Ribbons, Inverted Saucer Foot, 10 In. | 2014 |
| **Vase,** Peacock Feather, Blue & Platinum, Green, Swollen Top, Favrile, 8 In. | 7110 |
| **Vase,** Pinched Neck, Raised Twists, Gold Iridescent, Favrile, Signed, 6½ In. | 2500 |
| **Vase,** Pulled Feathers, Blue, Gold, Purple, Cream, Tapered, Favrile, c.1895, 5 In. | 1200 |
| **Vase,** Pulled Leaves, Opalescent, Flower Shape, Favrile, Signed L.C.T., c.1905, 14 In. | 3125 |
| **Vase,** Purple, Gold, Cream Swirling Strands On Shoulder, 9 In. | 7110 |
| **Vase,** Purple, Green, Reactive Glass, Vertical Ribs, Spread Base, 6½ In. | 4255 |
| **Vase,** Red Agata, Faceted Sides, Intaglio Carved Leaves, Signed, 5½ In. | 10497 |
| **Vase,** Red Agata, Flared Rim, Wide Shoulder, Taper, 3⅛ In. | 5843 |
| **Vase,** Ribbed Body, Mottled Gold, Opalescent Designs, Favrile, Footed, 9 In. | 4485 |
| **Vase,** Ribbed, Flared & Petal Neck, Rainbow Iridescent, Favrile, c.1910, 5¾ In. | 2200 |
| **Vase,** Shaped Rim, Ribbed Body, Favrile, Paper Label, c.1910, 9½ In. | 1046 |
| **Vase,** Stick, Cone Shape, Gold Iridescent, 5 Green Pulled Feathers, Favrile, 12 In. | 1150 |
| **Vase,** Stylized Flowers, Purple, Blue, Orange, Red Ground, Shouldered, 6 In. | 11875 |
| **Vase,** Tel El Amarna Banding, Gold, Bulbous, Smokestack Neck, Footed, 6 In. | 2875 |
| **Vase,** Tel El Amarna, Amber, Cobalt, Globular, Intarsia, Favrile, c.1910, 7½ In. | 2813 |
| **Vase,** Tel El Amarna, Blue, Intarsia Band At Neck, Iridescent, 4¾ In. | 4688 |
| **Vase,** Trumpet, Blue Iridescent, Favrile, c.1900, 8½ x 4¼ In. | 1722 |
| **Vase,** Trumpet, Blue Iridescent, Vertical Ribs, Flared, Footed, Favrile, 9¾ In. | 1185 |
| **Vase,** Tulip Shape, Gold Iridescent, Leaves, Vines, 12¼ In. | 3585 |
| **Vase,** Urn Shape, Red, Amber Zigzag At Shoulder, Favrile, 8 In. | 1188 |
| **Vase,** Urn Shape, Ribbed Scroll Handles, Amber, Gold, 6½ In. | 1625 |
| **Vase,** Urn Shape, Wheel Engraved, Flowers At Shoulder, Amber, 4¾ In. | 1188 |
| **Vase,** White Opalescent, Gold Pulled Feathers, Tapered, Favrile, 14¾ In. | 2074 |
| **Vase,** White Opalescent, Green Pulled Feather & Stem, Flower Form, Ruffled Rim, 13 In. | 2666 |
| **Vase,** White Opalescent, Green Pulled Leaves, Flower Shape, Inverted Foot, 11 In. | 5925 |
| **Wine,** Pastel, Aqua, Spoke Opal Blades, Reed Stems, 7½ In., Pair | 690 |

## TIFFANY GOLD

| | |
|---|---:|
| **Magnifying Glass,** Letter Opener, 18K, Reticulated Squirrel, Leaves, 6½ In., 2 Piece | 2252 |
| **Paper Knife,** 18K Gold, Pierced Squirrel & Oak Leaves, Dated 1916, 6½ In. | 2337 |

## TIFFANY POTTERY

| | |
|---|---:|
| **Vase,** Raised Flowers, Green Glaze, Oval, Inward Folded Rim, Incised LCT, 5½ In. | 2596 |
| **Vase,** Raised Squash Blossoms & Leaves, Cream Glaze, Green Accents, Oval, 8 In. | 4740 |
| **Vase,** Savoy Cabbage, Favrile, Incised Mark, LCT, 1900s, 9 x 8 In. ............................*illus* | 16250 |

## TIFFANY SILVER

| | |
|---|---:|
| **Asparagus Server,** Regent Pattern, Pierced, Marked, 1884, 7½ In. .........................*illus* | 312 |
| **Asparagus Server,** Vine Pattern, Grapevines, Splayed Tines, 1872, 9½ In. .................*illus* | 375 |
| **Basket,** Lobed Body, Bail Handle, Monogram, Leaf Tip, 6¾ In. | 738 |
| **Bowl,** Center, Cone Shape, Sine Wave Foot, c.1956, 3⅝ x 11 In. | 1062 |
| **Bowl,** Center, Gilt Brass Inset Frog, Overhanding Rim, Names, Dates, 12 In. | 800 |
| **Bowl,** Flared Rim, Footed, 1906, 4½ x 9 In. | 652 |
| **Bowl,** Flower Band At Rim, Fluted Body, 1884, 3¼ x 8¼ In. | 937 |
| **Bowl,** Flower Frog, Brass Reticulated, Etched, Repousse, Flared Rim, 4½ x 14 In. | 2963 |
| **Bowl,** Flower Shape, William Lusk, c.1960, 2 x 7 In. | 84 |
| **Bowl,** Fruit, Engraved Laurel Edge, Wavy Lobed, Round, 2½ x 11¾ In. | 553 |

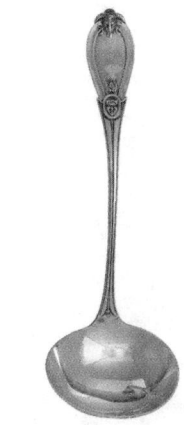

**Tiffany Silver,** Ladle, Grecian Pattern, c.1862, 12⅝ In.

$799

New Orleans Auction Galleries, Inc.

**Tiffany Silver,** Oyster Fork, Vine Pattern, Flowers, Marked, 1872, 6⅛ In., 11 Piece

$438

Heritage Auction Galleries

**Tiffany Silver,** Pitcher, Water, Catfish, Hammered, Applied Whiskers, Cattails, Handle, 8½ In.

$18,750

Rago Arts & Auction Center

T

**Tiffany Silver,** Tomato Server, Pointed Terminal, Beaded, Pierced, Scalloped, 1855, 10¾ In.
$375

Heritage Auction Galleries

**Tile,** Landscape, Glaze, Frame, Square, Henrietta Ord Jones, c.1930, 4 In.
$1,125

Rago Arts & Auction Center

**Tile,** Maiden, Daffodils, Frame, Johann Von Schwarz, Germany, c.1900, 10 x 5¾ In.
$625

Rago Arts & Auction Center

| | |
|---|---:|
| **Bowl,** Lid, Twist-Off Finial, Monogram, c.1910, 8 x 10¾ In. | 748 |
| **Bowl,** Salad, Tomato, Pumpkin, Vine, Spoon, Fork, c.1935, 10 In., 3 Piece | 2375 |
| **Bowl,** Trophy, Commodores Cup, 1934, 9⅛ In. | 1107 |
| **Bowl,** Trophy, Round Foot, New York Yacht Club, 1896, 8 In. | 461 |
| **Bowl,** Turned Out Rim, Repousse Blackberry Clusters, Scrolling, Monogram, 10 x 3 In. | 437 |
| **Bowl,** Vertical Ribs, Flared, 3 Ball Feet, 6 In., Pair | 425 |
| **Cake Stand,** Footed, Engraved Strapwork, Shell Border, Molded Shell Rim, 10½ In. | 720 |
| **Candlestick,** Cylindrical, Vertical Ribs, Inverted Saucer Foot, 1971, 5 In., Pair | 415 |
| **Card Holder,** Brushed Radiating Design, Foldover Clasp, 3¾ x 2¼ In. | 299 |
| **Charger,** Gadroon Corfer, Leaf Scrolls, 1907-38, 10¾ In., 12 Piece | 7500 |
| **Chip Server,** Saratoga, Chrysanthemum Pattern, Marked, 1880, 8¾ In. ...............*illus* | 1625 |
| **Chip Server,** Seahorse, Pierced Bowl, Scrolls, c.1880, 9 In. | 1062 |
| **Chop Plate,** Shaped Rim, 13 In. | 826 |
| **Cigar Cutter,** Altas, Blue Pouch, Marked, 1995, 2 x 1⅜ In. | 207 |
| **Cocktail Shaker,** Art Deco, Bulbous, Tapered, Incised Bands, Shot Cup, c.1918, 9 x 4 In. | 2706 |
| **Cocktail Shaker,** Reeded Waist, Pierced Strainer, Cylindrical, Tapered, Monogram, 9 In. | 1125 |
| **Coffeepot,** After Dinner, Tapered, Stippled Ground, Chased, Masques, Scrolls, 8 In. | 1464 |
| **Coffeepot,** Hinged Lid, Leaf Spout, Ebonized Finial, Monogram, 7½ In. | 461 |
| **Compact,** Pushbutton Closure, 2⅝ In. | 308 |
| **Corncob Holder,** Corn Husk Handles, 2¾ In., 12 Piece | 236 |
| **Crumb Brush,** Neoclassical, Inscription, New Rochelle Yacht Club, 1887, 14 In. ...............*illus* | 185 |
| **Crumb Tray,** 3-Sided Serpentine Border, Beaded Handle, Monogram, 13 x 3 In. | 288 |
| **Cup,** Cylindrical, Flared Braided Rim, Footed, 2¼ In., Pair | 89 |
| **Dish,** Lily Of The Valley, Shallow, Reticulated Relief Rim, Monogram, 8 In. | 644 |
| **Figurine,** Frog, Sterling, Cast, Stamped Tiffany & Co., 1996, 1¾ In., Pair | 644 |
| **Flask,** Art Nouveau, Hinged Top, Putti, Grapevines, c.1900, 5⅝ In. | 2337 |
| **Frame,** Scrolling Leaves, Splayed Paw Feet, A-Form Hinged Support, c.1883, 11 x 8 In. | 1250 |
| **Kettle,** Stand, Gooseneck Spout, Raised Ivy, Cartouche, Coin, 14¼ In. | 6457 |
| **Knife Set,** Audubon, Solid Handles, 8 In., 6 Piece | 1298 |
| **Knife,** Chrysanthemum, Marked, 1900s, 9⅛ In., 10 Piece | 813 |
| **Knife,** Fruit, Art Nouveau Style, Lap Over Edge, Charles Grosjean, c.1880, 7 In., 4 Piece | 242 |
| **Ladle,** Grecian Pattern, c.1862, 12⅝ In. .........................*illus* | 799 |
| **Ladle,** Persian Pattern, Monogram, c.1885, 12½ In. | 750 |
| **Ladle,** Tomatoes, Vines, Curved Tapered Handle, Heart Bowl, c.1880, 13 In. | 531 |
| **Ladle,** Vine Squash, Curved Handle, Relief Design, Monogram, c.1872, 7 x 2 In. | 207 |
| **Lettuce Fork,** Old Ivy, Flared, Rounded Handle, c.1900, 7 x 2¼ In., Pair | 184 |
| **Mustard Pot,** Lid, Ladle, Urn Shape, Leaf, Branch Engraved, Handles | 767 |
| **Oyster Fork,** Vine Pattern, Flowers, Marked, 1872, 6⅛ In., 11 Piece.................*illus* | 438 |
| **Pitcher,** Flower & Scroll Band, Oval, Squat, Leaf Tip Handle, 8¼ In. | 2214 |
| **Pitcher,** Hammered, Handle, 7½ In. | 1722 |
| **Pitcher,** Repousse, Flowers, Bulbous, Cylindrical Neck, Incised Leaf Handle, 7 In. | 2673 |
| **Pitcher,** Water, Catfish, Hammered, Applied Whiskers, Cattails, Handle, 8½ In. ...............*illus* | 18750 |
| **Pitcher,** Water, Repousse, Baluster, Water Lilies, Young & Ellis, c.1850, 10 In. | 2091 |
| **Plate,** Stepped Rim, Round, Mark, 11 In., 8 Piece | 3540 |
| **Platter,** Plain Molded Rim, Monogram, Round, c.1923, 12 In. | 676 |
| **Platter,** Scalloped Rim, 2 Handles, 26⅜ In. | 2583 |
| **Salad Set,** Pierced & Shaped Tines, Navette Bowl, Banded Orb, G. Sharp, 11 In., 2 Piece | 563 |
| **Salt Cellar Set,** Shell Shape, Ball Feet, Marked, Master, 6 Individual, 5 & 2¾ In. | 270 |
| **Sandwich Tray,** Pierced Flowers, Shell Shape, Scroll Handle, Bun Feet, 16 In., Pair | 4920 |
| **Spoon,** Demitasse, Persian, Edward C. Moore, 1872, 4⅛ In., 12 Piece | 276 |
| **Spoon,** Shoeshine Boy, Hobby Horse, Rifle, Lap Over Edge Pattern, 6¾ In. | 188 |
| **Sugar & Creamer,** Curved Handles, Footed, Monogram, c.1930, 4 In. | 180 |
| **Tazza,** Blackberry, 4⅞ In. | 2390 |
| **Tazza,** Round, Knopped Stem, Applied Border, Trumpet Foot, c.1915, 9 In., Pair | 1375 |
| **Tea & Coffee Set,** Leaf Bands, Sugar & Creamer, c.1886, 9½ In. | 3198 |
| **Tea Caddy,** Globe Shape, Cherubs, Flowers, Musical Instruments, 3 In. | 625 |
| **Tea Caddy,** Oval, Flowers On Vines, c.1870, 6¼ In. | 750 |
| **Teapot,** Greek Key, Stand, Burner, 11 In. | 800 |
| **Teaspoon,** Nursery Rhyme, Jack & Jill Handle, Impressed, 6½ In. | 115 |
| **Tomato Server,** Pointed Terminal, Beaded, Pierced, Scalloped, 1855, 10¾ In. ...............*illus* | 375 |
| **Tray,** Cake, Round, Rope Twist Border, Early 20th Century, 13½ In. | 832 |
| **Tray,** Chrysanthemum, Cast Border, Flowers, 28½ In. | 10455 |
| **Tray,** Flowers, Leaves, Pierced Rim, Shell & Acanthus Feet, 20 In. | 1210 |
| **Tray,** Octagonal, Integrated Handles, Inset Center, c.1907, 24 x 20 In. | 4687 |
| **Tray,** Oval, Engraved Field, Flower Swags, Applied Reeded Border, c.1902, 30 In. | 4688 |
| **Tray,** Oval, Shaped, Applied Border, 16 In. | 1375 |

**T**

| | |
|---|---:|
| **Tray,** Rectangular, Central Monogram, 18 In. | 1722 |
| **Tray,** Reticulated Gallery, 2 Handles, Engraved Leaves, Flowers, 20 ⅜ In. | 3198 |
| **Trophy,** Bamboo Arms, Pedestal, Larchmont Yacht Club, 1886, 13 In. | 4305 |
| **Trophy,** Flared, Repousse Band, 2 Tennis Racket Handles, 4 Ball Feet, 1883, 8 In. | 3250 |
| **Tureen,** Dome Lid, Loop Handle, Acanthus, Monogram, 4-Footed, 1870-75, 17 In. | 5535 |
| **Vase,** Japanesque, Embossed Trees, Figures, Tapered, Footed, c.1880, 8 x 4 In. | 2000 |
| **Vase,** Trumpet, 1910, 12 In. | 660 |
| **Vase,** Trumpet, Beveled, Flared Foot, Stamped, 11 ½ x 5 In. | 886 |
| **Vase,** Trumpet, Footed, 9 ½ In. | 390 |
| **Vase,** Trumpet, Molded Rim, Engraved, 1920, 19 ⅞ In. | 3198 |
| **Vase,** Trumpet, Ribbon Tied Swags, Cartouches, Monogram, 11 ½ In. | 923 |
| **Vase,** Trumpet, Sterling, Incised, Reeded, Engraved Palmette Band, c.1907, 12 x 5 In. | 1599 |

**TIFFIN** Glass Company of Tiffin, Ohio, was a subsidiary of the United States Glass Co. of Pittsburgh, Pennsylvania, in 1892. The U.S. Glass Co. went bankrupt in 1963, and the Tiffin plant employees purchased the building and the inventory. They continued running it from 1963 to 1966, when it was sold to Continental Can Company. In 1969, it was sold to Interpace, and in 1980, it was closed. The black satin glass, made from 1923 to 1926, and the stemware of the last twenty years are the best-known products.

| | |
|---|---:|
| **Allegro,** Cordial, 5 ¼ In. | 30 |
| **Allegro,** Plate, Luncheon, 8 ¼ In. | 28 |
| **Allegro,** Sherbet, 4 ⅞ In. | 10 |
| **Aster,** Sherbet, 4 ⅜ In. | 12 |
| **Aster,** Vase, Flared Rim, Footed, 10 ⅛ In. | 38 |
| **Atwater,** Goblet, Water, 7 ¾ In. | 43 |
| **Atwater,** Wine, Stem, 7 In. | 72 |
| **Beaumont,** Cocktail, Stem, 4 ¼ In. | 8 |
| **Beaumont,** Sherbet, 4 ½ In. | 7 |
| **Bridal Rose,** Tumbler, Iced Tea, 5 ¾ In. | 24 |
| **Bridal Rose,** Wine, 6 ¾ In. | 22 |
| **Cadena,** Cordial, Amber, 5 ⅜ In. | 70 |
| **Cadena,** Cup & Saucer, Amber. | 37 |
| **Cadena,** Plate, Bread & Butter, Amber, 6 ⅛ In. | 10 |
| **Cadena,** Tumbler, Footed, Amber, 2 Oz., 3 ⅜ In. | 32 |
| **Cadena,** Wine, Amber, 6 In. | 75 |
| **Cerice,** Champagne | 11 |
| **Cherokee Rose,** Bowl, Flared, Beaded Edging, 12 ¾ In. | 77 |
| **Cherokee Rose,** Relish, 3 Sections, Oval, Scalloped Beaded Edge, Handle, 12 ½ In. | 56 |
| **Cherokee Rose,** Vase, Bud, Tapered, 10 ½ In. | 65 |
| **Christina,** Juice, 4 ½ In. | 8 |
| **Christina,** Sherbet, 4 ⅛ In. | 13 |
| **Dish,** Ram's Head Shape, Translucent Green, Molded, Shallow Foot, 4 ½ x 5 In. | 184 |
| **Eternity,** Cocktail, Stem, 4 ½ In. | 28 |
| **Eternity,** Goblet, Water, 6 ⅜ In. | 30 |
| **Felicity,** Parfait, 6 ⅛ In. | 35 |
| **Florian,** Champagne, 5 ⅜ In. | 20 |
| **Florian,** Plate, Luncheon, 8 ⅛ In. | 19 |
| **Florian,** Tumbler, Iced Tea, 7 In. | 19 |
| **Forever Yours,** Juice, 5 In. | 27 |
| **Forever Yours,** Plate, Luncheon, 8 ⅛ In. | 20 |
| **Forever Yours,** Tumbler, Footed, 5 ½ In. | 8 |
| **Fuchsia,** Candlestick, 2-Light, Pair | 90 |
| **Fuchsia,** Centerpiece, 12 ½ In. | 57 |
| **Fuchsia,** Vase, Flared, Footed, Bud, c.1949, 6 ½ In. | 45 |
| **Harvest Gold,** Goblet, Water, 8 ⅛ In. | 79 |
| **King's Crown,** Bowl, Dessert, Ruby, 4 In. | 15 |
| **King's Crown,** Cocktail, 3 ¾ In. | 6 |
| **King's Crown,** Compote, 6 ⅛ x 5 ⅞ In. | 17 |
| **King's Crown,** Compote, Cranberry Flash, 5 ¼ In. | 28 |
| **King's Crown,** Goblet, Water, 5 ⅝ In. | 8 |
| **King's Crown,** Goblet, Water, Cranberry, 5 ⅝ In. | 17 |
| **King's Crown,** Plate, Salad, Cranberry Flash, 7 ½ In. | 22 |
| **King's Crown,** Sherbet, Cranberry Flash, 3 In. | 12 |
| **King's Crown,** Sherbet, Cranberry, 3 In. | 8 |
| **King's Crown,** Tumbler, Cranberry, 5 ⅝ In. | 15 |

**Tile,** New York City Scenes, Brooklyn Bridge, Cityscape, Frame, Harris Strong, 12 In., Pair
$288

Humler & Nolan

**Tile,** Nursery Rhyme, Gentleman, Gray Beard, Long Coat, Top Hat, Mosaic, Square, 6 In.
$175

Humler & Nolan

**Tinware,** Box, Little Piggy's, Hand, Pigs On Fingertips, Lid, 1879, 4 x 2 x 6 In.
$228

Showtime Auction Services

### Tinware

After 1850 canisters and spice boxes, cans that held tea, coffee, and spices, were japanned and stenciled with the name of the product. By 1880 names and designs were printed directly on metal cans and boxes.

T

**Tinware,** Sconce, 1-Light, Candle, Diamond Shape, Pinwheel Discs, c.1810, 12½ In., Pair
**$6,150**

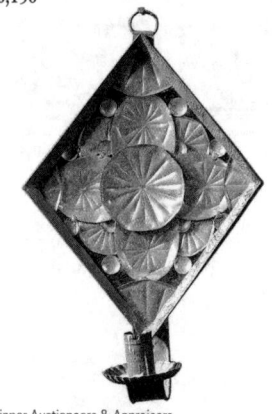

Skinner Auctioneers & Appraisers

**Tobacco Jar,** Hunter, Sitting On Stump, Figural, Terra-Cotta
**$288**

Fox Auctions

**Tobacco Jar,** Man Holding Stein, Terra-Cotta
**$480**

Fox Auctions

| | |
|---|---:|
| **King's Crown,** Wine, Cranberry, 4⅜ In. | 15 |
| **Leona Gold,** Goblet, Water, 6½ In. | 9 |
| **Leona Gold,** Sherbet, 4⅞ In. | 9 |
| **Madeira,** Goblet, Water, Apple Green, 5½ In. | 10 |
| **Madeira,** Goblet, Water, Citron, 5½ In. | 7 |
| **Madeira,** Goblet, Water, Cornsilk, 5½ In. | 10 |
| **Madeira,** Goblet, Water, Plum, 5½ In. | 15 |
| **Madeira,** Goblet, Water, Ruby, 5½ In. | 30 |
| **Madeira,** Sherbet, Apple Green, 3⅝ In. | 7 |
| **Madeira,** Sherbet, Citron, 3⅝ In. | 6 |
| **Madeira,** Sherbet, Cornsilk, 3⅝ In. | 8 |
| **Madeira,** Sherbet, Plum, 3⅝ In. | 10 |
| **Madeira,** Tumbler, Apple Green, 5⅝ In. | 15 |
| **Madeira,** Tumbler, Cornsilk, 5⅝ In. | 18 |
| **Madeira,** Tumbler, Iced Tea, Citron, 6½ In. | 9 |
| **Madeira,** Tumbler, Iced Tea, Cornsilk, 6½ In. | 13 |
| **Madeira,** Tumbler, Iced Tea, Plum, 6½ In. | 18 |
| **Madeira,** Tumbler, Old-Fashioned, Cornsilk, 4 In. | 16 |
| **Madeira,** Wine, Apple Green, 4⅜ In. | 8 |
| **Madeira,** Wine, Citron, 4⅜ In. | 5 |
| **Moon & Stars,** Punch Bowl | 75 |
| **Moon & Stars,** Punch Cup | 6 |
| **Mt. Vernon,** Cordial | 18 |
| **Mt. Vernon,** Tumbler, Iced Tea, 6 In. | 35 |
| **Nymph,** Plate, Dinner, Green, 10⅛ In. | 93 |
| **Nymph,** Wine, Green, 6 In. | 64 |
| **Octagon,** Plate, Salad, Pink, 8 In. | 18 |
| **Optic Blue,** Vase, Rectangular, 10½ In. | 41 |
| **Special Thistle,** Sherbet, 4⅛ In. | 12 |
| **Vintage Pink,** Wine, 6½ In. | 19 |
| **Williamsburg,** Sherbet, Cranberry Flash | 6 |
| **Wisteria,** Goblet, Footed, Pink, 5¾ In. | 32 |

**TILES** have been used in most countries of the world as a sturdy building material for floors, roofs, fireplace surrounds, and surface toppings. The cuerda seca (dry cord) technique of decoration uses a greasy pigment to separate different glaze colors during firing. In cuenca (raised line) decorated tiles, the design is impressed, leaving ridges that separate the glaze colors. Many of the American tiles are listed in this book under the factory name.

| | |
|---|---:|
| **Castle,** Trees, Yellow, Green, 6 In. | 115 |
| **Dog,** Dancing, Pink Ground, Marked Empire, 3 In. | 75 |
| **Duchess,** Green, Brown, Semimatte, Alice In Wonderland, Cuerda Seca, C. Pardee, 4½ In. | 492 |
| **Face,** King, Queen, Blue, Green, 12 Tiles, Wood Panel, Harris Strong, 48 x 16 In., Pair | 1150 |
| **Fireplace,** Goose Chasing Children, In Room, Cats, Multicolor, c.1859, 17 x 15 In. | 531 |
| **Flowers In A Pot,** Oak Frame, Claycraft, 14 x 14 In. | 240 |
| **Flying Gull,** Blue, Black, White, Red, Faience, Wide Wood Frame, 3 x 3 In. | 230 |
| **Girl,** Flouncy Dress, Birds On Hand, Multicolor, Frame, Marked AETCO, 12 x 15 In. | 161 |
| **Harbor Scene,** Walnut Frame, Harris Strong, 9½ x 40 In., 6 Tiles | 244 |
| **Horse,** Rider, Multicolor, Wood Frame, 5¾ x 10½ In. | 63 |
| **Horseback Rider,** Feeding Phoenix Bird, Multicolor, 12 x 8½ In. | 161 |
| **Jester Head,** Orange, Blue, Oak Frame, Moravian, Mercer, 5 x 6 In. | 63 |
| **Knight,** Yellow Outline, Plum Ground, 4½ In. | 8 |
| **Landscape,** Glaze, Frame, Square, Henrietta Ord Jones, c.1930, 4 In. ............*illus* | 1125 |
| **Leaves,** Cobalt Blue Star Shape, Black, White Ground, Persia, c.1800, 10 x 10 In. | 357 |
| **Maiden,** Daffodils, Frame, Johann Von Schwarz, Germany, c.1900, 10 x 5¾ In. ............*illus* | 625 |
| **Man,** Making Fire, Openwork, Green Black Glaze, Moravian, 6¾ In. | 17 |
| **Mosaic,** Diamond Shape Tiles, Green, Beige, Stylized Flowers, Syria, 16 x 16 In. | 69 |
| **Muresque,** Tree, Stream, Mill, Pastel, Oak Frame, 12⅜ x 4 In. | 288 |
| **New York City Scenes,** Brooklyn Bridge, Cityscape, Frame, Harris Strong, 12 In., Pair .......*illus* | 288 |
| **Nude Woman,** Impressed AETCO, Squeezebag Design, 9 x 9 In. | 330 |
| **Nursery Rhyme,** Gentleman, Gray Beard, Long Coat, Top Hat, Mosaic, Square, 6 In. ..........*illus* | 175 |
| **Palmetto,** Leaf Scroll, Blue, Turquoise, Green, Syria, 8¼ x 8¼ In. | 109 |
| **Roof,** Earthenware, Demon, Standing At Angle Sloped Roof, Glazed, Chinese, 13 x 12 In. | 708 |
| **Roof,** Figure, Official, Green, Brown, Amber Sancai Glaze, Ming, c.1600, 16½ In. | 369 |
| **Roof,** Foo Dogs, Green, Yellow Paint, 9½ x 13 In., Pair | 117 |
| **Ship,** Lighthouse, Multicolor Matte Glaze, Mueller, Oak Frame, 30 x 11 In., 10 Piece | 2875 |

| | | |
|---|---|---:|
| **Ship,** Wide Oak Frame, Marked Wheeling, 6 In. | | 63 |
| **Spider Web,** Black, Pink, Green, Oak Frame, Franklin, 8 ½ x 8 ½ In. | | 390 |
| **Squirrel,** Blue Translucent Gloss Glaze, Russell Crook, 3 ⅝ x 3 ⅝ In. | | 259 |
| **Stove Chimney,** Cartouche, Mask, Grotesques, Swags, Green Glaze, 11 x 11 In., Pair | | 495 |
| **Trees In Snow,** Green, White, Blue, Wooden Frame, National Tile Co., 13 In., 2 Tiles | | 671 |
| **Victorian Mansion,** Egyptian Blue Glaze, Katrich Studios, c.1995, 6 ½ In. | | 75 |
| **Viking Ship,** Sail Blowing, Marked Franklin, 9 In. | | 150 |
| **Wheeling Lighthouse,** Frame, Marked Wheeling, 6 In. | | 29 |
| **Woman In Garden,** Spraying Water, Oak Frame, Marked Mosaic, 6 In. | | 63 |
| **Woman,** Dog, Cupboard, Multicolor, Oak Frame, 5 ¾ In. | | 98 |

---

**TINWARE** containers for household use have been made in America since the seventeenth century. The first tin utensils were brought from Europe, but by 1798, tin plate was imported and local tinsmiths made the wares. Painted tin is called tole and is listed separately. Some tin kitchen items may be found listed under Kitchen. The lithographed tin containers used to hold food and tobacco are listed in the Advertising category under Tin.

| | | |
|---|---|---:|
| **Box,** Little Piggy's, Hand, Pigs On Fingertips, Lid, 1879, 4 x 2 x 6 In. | *illus* | 228 |
| **Coffeepot,** Punched Tulip & Swags, Angular Shape & Handle, Berks County, Pa., 12 In. | | 4500 |
| **Coffeepot,** Punched Tulips, Brass Finial, 1825-50, 11 ½ In. | | 780 |
| **Coffeepot,** Punched, Tapered, Angular Spout, Shaped Handle, 11 ½ In. | | 1208 |
| **Coffeepot,** Wrigglework, Eagle, Flag, Tulip, Serpent Handle, Pa., c.1810, 9 ¼ In. | | 1560 |
| **Coffeepot,** Wrigglework, Flower, Cone Shape, Gooseneck Spout, 1800s, 10 ½ In. | | 502 |
| **Cooling Rack,** Footed, c.1900, 12 ½ In. | | 65 |
| **Foot Warmer,** Hearts, Circles, Punched, Hinged, Bail Handle, 7 ¼ x 6 x 4 ¾ In. | | 46 |
| **Match Holder,** Tin, Black Paint, Curved Shell Pockets, Scalloped Rim, 5 x 4 ¼ In. | | 69 |
| **Mold,** Candle, 12 Tube, 1800s, 11 ¼ x 9 In. | | 135 |
| **Mold,** Candle, 18 Tube, Pine Frame, 1800s, 14 x 24 ¼ In. | | 600 |
| **Mold,** Candle, 36 Tube, Pine Frame, Tinned Iron Tubes, 11 ¼ x 14 x 11 ¼ In. | | 1080 |
| **Plate,** Woman, Long Brown Hair, Profile, Vienna Art, 10 In. | | 210 |
| **Sconce,** 1-Light, Candle, Diamond Shape, Pinwheel Discs, c.1810, 12 ½ In., Pair | *illus* | 6150 |
| **Urn,** Cone Shape Lid, Shield Shape Body, Ram's Head, Ring Handles, 1800s, 13 In., Pair | | 826 |

---

**TOBACCO CUTTERS** *may be listed in either the Advertising or Store categories.*

---

**TOBACCO JAR** collectors search for those made in odd shapes and colors. Because tobacco needs special conditions of humidity and air, it has been stored in special containers since the eighteenth century.

| | | |
|---|---|---:|
| **Bird Watcher,** Sitting, Binoculars, Bowler Hat, Jacket, Moustache | | 296 |
| **Black & White Songbird,** Log, Stump, Wood, Carved Drawer, Claw Feet, 14 ½ x 12 In. | | 2640 |
| **Elephant,** Seated, Dressed, Majolica, 8 In. | | 84 |
| **Faux Book Front,** Leather, Hinged, Square Feet, Humidor, 10 ¼ x 12 In. | | 375 |
| **Franz Josef,** Terra-Cotta, Marked, J.M., 11 In. | | 78 |
| **Frog,** Seated, Wearing Puce Jacket, Smoking Pipe, Continental, 1900s, 6 ½ In. | | 115 |
| **Fruits,** Mouse On Pillow Smoking A Pipe Finial, Lambeth, Doulton, 7 In. | | 984 |
| **Hunter,** Sitting On Stump, Figural, Terra-Cotta | *illus* | 288 |
| **Man Holding Stein,** Terra-Cotta | *illus* | 480 |
| **Owl,** Lid, Stoneware, Lambeth, Doulton, 7 ½ In. | | 738 |
| **Tobacco Products,** Caramel Glaze, Rookwood, 1884, 5 ½ In. | | 58 |

---

**TOBY JUG** is the name of a very special form of pitcher. It is shaped like the full figure of a man or woman. A pitcher that shows just the top half of a person is not correctly called a toby. More examples of toby jugs can be found under Royal Doulton and other factory names.

| | | |
|---|---|---:|
| **Hearty Good Fellow,** Painted, Staffordshire, c.1850, 12 In. | | 72 |
| **Jester,** Standing, Holding Staff, Royal Worcester, 7 ¼ In. | | 750 |
| **Man,** Seated, Drinking, Smoking, England, c.1790 | | 995 |
| **Man,** Seated, Holding Jug, Tricorn Hat, Open Mouth, Staffordshire, c.1800, 9 In. | | 845 |
| **Man,** Seated, Rockingham Glaze, Yellowware, 9 ½ In. | *illus* | 24 |
| **Man,** Standing, Holding Bottle & Mug, Somber Face, Doulton, 8 ½ In. | | 400 |
| **Man,** Standing, Holding Mug, Waistcoat, c.1825, 8 In. | | 1800 |
| **Mr. Punch,** Seated, Jester Costume, c.1850, 9 ¾ In. | | 475 |
| **Shorter & Son Guardsman,** Seated, Holding Mug, Staffordshire, 8 In. | | 48 |
| **Spud & Bulldog,** Standing, Flower In Mouth, Handing In Pocket, 1930s, 6 In. | | 24 |
| **Woman,** Pink Ruffled Dress, Ribbons, Curly Hair, 4 ¾ In. | | 45 |

**Toby Jug,** Man, Seated, Rockingham Glaze, Yellowware, 9 ½ In.
$24

Conestoga Auction Co., Inc.

**Tole,** Urn, Georgian, Chestnut, Grape Leaf Band, Lion Mask Handles, 13 x 7 In., Pair
$1,220

Neal Auction Co.

**Tole,** Wine Carriage, William IV, Cast Iron Wheels, Chinoiserie Painted, c.1835, 14 x 25 In.
$1,476

New Orleans Auction Galleries, Inc.

**Tom Mix,** Window Card, Tom Mix Circus, Will Positively Appear, Cardboard, 1937, 14 x 22 In.
$334

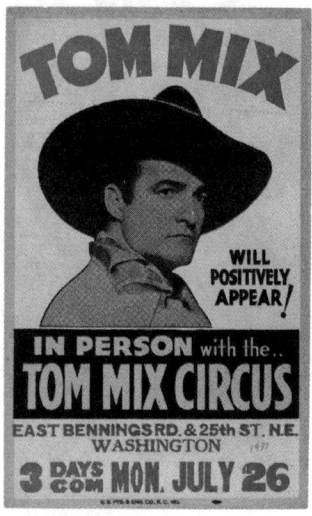

Hake's Americana & Collectibles

**Tool,** Cobbler's Bench, Mixed Woods, Painted, 2 Drawers, Tools, 1800s, 14 x 41 In.
$500

Garth's Auctioneers & Appraisers

**Tool,** Ladder, Pine, Reeded Steps, c.1900, 49½ x 32¼ x 14½ In.
$307

New Orleans Auction Galleries, Inc.

T

**TOLE** is painted tin. It is sometimes called japanned ware, pontypool, or toleware. Most nineteenth-century tole is painted with an orange-red or black background and multicolored decorations. Many recent versions of toleware are made and sold. Related items may be listed in the Tinware category.

| | |
|---|---|
| **Box,** Document, Black, Red Flowers, Gold Leaves, Hammered Handle, Dome, 7 x 9 In. | 210 |
| **Box,** Document, Flowers, Leaves, Wire Ring, Scrolled Hasp, Dome Lid, 5¼ x 9¼ In. | 384 |
| **Box,** Document, Green, Stenciled Flowers, Dome Lid, 6½ x 9½ In. | 246 |
| **Box,** Document, Painted Red, Hinge, Latch, Dome Lid, Pennsylvania, c.1810, 6¼ x 9½ In. | 160 |
| **Box,** Flower Garland, Bouquet, Orange Ground, Painted, 16 x 30 In. | 250 |
| **Box,** Lid, Stylized Urn, Motto, Peace & Plenty, Red, Gold, Black Ground, Oval, 6 In. | 123 |
| **Box,** Multicolor Paint, Handle, Dome Lid, 1800s, 5½ x 9 In. | 120 |
| **Box,** Tin, Japanned Black Finish, Loop Handle, Oval, 10 x 12¾ x 9 In. | 85 |
| **Bread Tray,** Asphaltum, Flowers, Fruit, Swags, Red, Green, Yellow, Phila., c.1845, 12 In. | 360 |
| **Bread Tray,** Red, Acorns, c.1835, 3 x 12½ In. | 360 |
| **Bread Tray,** Red, Fruit, Gold Border, Rectangular, 19th Century, 12 In. | 150 |
| **Canister,** Tea, Mother-Of-Pearl, Dome Lid, Cartouches, Landscapes, Buildings, 8 In., Pair | 2400 |
| **Coal Scuttle,** Black, Birds, Flowers, Egyptian Handles, Paw Feet, 1800s, 25 x 11 In. | 179 |
| **Coffeepot,** Multicolor Flowers, Black Ground, Gooseneck Spout, Pa., c.1810, 10 In. | 450 |
| **Coffeepot,** Red, Yellow Flowers, Lighthouse Shape, Gooseneck Spout, Domed Lid, 10 In. | 413 |
| **Coffeepot,** Red, Yellow, Cylindrical, Tapered, Gooseneck Spout, Dome Lid, 10½ In. | 295 |
| **Cooler,** Urn Shape, Painted, Ring Handles, Maltese Cross, Firefighter's Symbol, 33 x 13 In. | 738 |
| **Fire Starter,** Painted Red, Gold, Handle, Wood, 19th Century, 10¾ In. | 234 |
| **Hyacinth Bloom,** Pink, Fitted Into Cast Iron Pot, 16½ x 5 In. | 510 |
| **Jardiniere,** Green Ground, Yellow Band, Flowers, Ball Feet, 37 x 10 In. | 1554 |
| **Pail,** Lid, Roman Soldier, Woman, 2 Handles, 12 x 13 In. | 150 |
| **Plaque,** Eagle On Shield, Stars & Stripes, Tin, Paint, Wooden Support, c.1900, 40 x 48 In. | 3240 |
| **Spice Box,** Tin, Domed, 6 Compartments, Japanned, Hinged, 19th Century, 9 x 6 x 3 In. | 72 |
| **Tea Canister,** Chinoiserie Woman, Yellow Ground, Cylindrical, England, 1700s, 18 In. | 688 |
| **Tray,** Apple, Painted Flowers, Red Ground, Cut Out Handles, Oval, 3¾ x 13½ In. | 106 |
| **Tray,** Blackstone Footbridge, Walkers, Trees, Grassy Hills, 1800s, 28½ x 21 In. | 206 |
| **Tray,** Comb, Tin, Hanging, Blue, Red Paint, White Flowers, V-Shape, Back Panel, 8 x 7 In. | 246 |
| **Tray,** Fruit, Gold Trim, Scalloped, Signed, 17 x 14 In. | 36 |
| **Tray,** Lady Liberty, Patriotic Symbols, Patriot Portraits, Black Ground, c.1830, 24 In. | 5520 |
| **Tray,** Little Red Riding Hood, Wolf, Forest, Tin, Multicolor, 10 x 6½ In. | 90 |
| **Tray,** Mermaid, Sailor, Ships, Whales, Sea, Cutout Handles, M. Cahoon, c.1980, 15 x 20 In. | 2640 |
| **Tray,** Painted Bird, Flower, Gilt Border, Round, 11½ In., Pair | 300 |
| **Tray,** Seashell, Fruit, Striped Rim, Tin, Black, Yellow, Red, 2 Pierced Handles, 27½ In. | 1216 |
| **Tray,** Tin, Painted Red Leaves, Flowers, Oval, c.1840, 2 x 7 In. | 259 |
| **Tray,** Woman, Holding Hat, Flower, Cream, Black, Leaf Border, Red Ground, 1800s, 24 In. | 600 |
| **Urn,** Georgian, Chestnut, Grape Leaf Band, Lion Mask Handles, 13 x 7 In., Pair ...............*illus* | 1220 |
| **Urn,** Lid, Lion Masks, Ring, Pedestal Foot, 15½ In., Pair | 210 |
| **Urn,** On Pedestal, Lid, Bowed Panels, Painted Green, Black, Red, White, c.1810, 8 x 4 In. | 948 |
| **Urn,** Regency, White, Lion's Head Ring Handles, Acorn Knops, c.1810, 14 x 7 In., Pair | 1230 |
| **Urn,** Yellow, Painted Landscape, Leaf Band, Lion's Head Ring Handles, 13 In. | 2125 |
| **Wine Caddy,** Yellow, Bouquets, 2 Cylinders, Loop Handle, 15¾ x 13 In. | 120 |
| **Wine Carriage,** William IV, Cast Iron Wheels, Chinoiserie Painted, c.1835, 14 x 25 In. .......*illus* | 1476 |

**TOM MIX** was born in 1880 and died in 1940. He was the hero of over 100 silent movies from 1910 to 1929, and 25 sound films from 1929 to 1935. There was a Ralston Tom Mix radio show from 1933 to 1950, but the original Tom Mix was not in the show. Tom Mix comics were published from 1942 to 1953.

| | |
|---|---|
| **Badge,** Checkerboard Panel, Profile Portrait, Hat, Die Cut, 1938 | 506 |
| **Button,** Ralston Straight Shooter, Pistol, 1930s, 2 In. | 65 |
| **Button,** Spring Pin, Strap, Holster, Single Shot Cap Gun, 1935-38, 5½ In. | 382 |
| **Charm Bracelet,** Brass Links, 4 Charms, 6 Gun, Steerhead, Tony, 1936, 7 In. | 284 |
| **Charm,** Sterling Silver, Horseshoe Around Tom Mix Logo, 1 In. | 126 |
| **Paint Book,** 1935, 11 x 14 In. | 30 |
| **Patch,** Tom Mix Ralston Shooters, Red & White Checkered, 1933 | 49 |
| **Photograph,** Tom, Silent Film Stars, In Field, 1920s, 8 x 10 In. | 60 |
| **Poster,** Broncho Twister, Mix Fighting, Stiff Cardboard ½ Sheet, 1927, 22 x 28 In. | 253 |
| **Ring,** Marlin Guns, Black Target Design, Golden Luster | 143 |
| **Rocking Horse,** Profile On Rump, Red Saddle, 39½ x 24¼ In. | 139 |
| **Window Card,** Tom Mix Circus, Will Positively Appear, Cardboard, 1937, 14 x 22 In. .........*illus* | 334 |

## TOOLS

**TOOLS** of all sorts are listed here, but most are related to industry. Other tools may be found listed under Iron, Kitchen, Tinware, and Wooden.

| | |
|---|---:|
| **Ax Holder,** Conestoga Wagon, Fish Shape, Wrought Iron, c.1800 | 3840 |
| **Box,** Carpenter, Pine, Cutout Handle, Drawer, Green Paint, c.1885, 14 x 18 In. | 111 |
| **Box,** Wood, Leather Handle, Union Steel Chest Corporation, 20 x 8 x 13 In. | 118 |
| **Carrier,** Walnut, Carved, Open Compartment, c.1920, 11 x 31 ½ In. | 240 |
| **Chest,** Pine, Yellow Grain Painted, Pennsylvania, 19th Century, 11 ½ x 32 In. | 185 |
| **Chest,** Wood, Grain Painted, Dovetailed, Hinged Lid, Iron Lock, 1800s, 8 x 18 x 9 In. | 180 |
| **Clamp,** Iron, Gilt Tulip & Bird Terminals, Initials, Heart Shape Base Plate, c.1810, 9 In. | 4560 |
| **Cobbler's Bench,** Mixed Woods, Painted, 2 Drawers, Tools, 1800s, 14 x 41 In. ............*illus* | 500 |
| **Drying Rack,** Candle, 2 Rails, Pierced Board, 36 Holes, Carved Handle, 1800s, 17 x 11 In. | 1353 |
| **Drying Rack,** Federal, Turned Column, Tiers, Paint, Shenandoah Valley, c.1820, 40 x 24 In. | 546 |
| **Drying Rack,** Hanging, Walnut, Porcelain Tabs, Slated Base, c.1900, 30 x 19 In. | 104 |
| **Hair Dryer,** Stand, Wheels, Automatic Cycle, Acme Engineers, c.1950 | 210 |
| **Hat Block Form,** Wood, 1930s, 8 ½ x 5 ½ In. | 265 |
| **Hatchel,** Oak Frame, Iron Spikes, Canted Box Lid, Va., 1801, 5 x 4 In. | 184 |
| **Insect Sprayer,** Gilmore Oil Co., Lion Logo, Tin, Wood Handle Plunger, 13 In. | 1150 |
| **Jigsaw,** Boice, Iron, Red, Black Paint, Marked, Toledo Ohio, 1900s, 16 x 16 In. | 117 |
| **Key Grinder,** Wood Crank, Black Paint, Metal, c.1920, 12 x 7 In. | 70 |
| **Ladder,** Elephant, Camphor Wood, Leather Cover, Folding, Chinese, 1800s, 91 In. | 1541 |
| **Ladder,** Pine, Reeded Steps, c.1900, 49 ½ x 32 ¼ x 14 ½ In. .........................*illus* | 307 |
| **Level,** Engineer's, A. Meneely, Rack Focusing, Tripod, 10 ½ In. | 277 |
| **Level,** Red, Always On The Level, Farmers Union Oil Co., Printed Inch Marks, 12 In. | 24 |
| **Lock,** Combination, 4 Barrels, Rotating, Engraved Letters, Brass, c.1862, 1 ½ In. | 615 |
| **Mold,** Spoon, Brass, Pewter, 2 Sections, 7 ¾ In. | 201 |
| **Pitchfork,** Oak, 3 Tines, Pair | 1062 |
| **Plane,** Carpenter, Beechwood, Walnut Heart, Diamond Shape Inlay | 118 |
| **Plane,** Stanley No. 220, Type 1, Nickel Plated | 55 |
| **Plow,** Leroy Plow Co., Reversible, Spring, Nickel Plated Blade, Salesman's Sample, 10 In. | 2666 |
| **Pump,** Well, Wood, Iron, Painted, c.1895, 46 ½ In. | 270 |
| **Rule,** Lufkin, Folding, Lock Joints, White, Black & Red Lettering, 6 Ft. | 14 |
| **Scoop,** Cranberry, Handles, Pierced Opening, Stamped E. Atwood, c.1910, 18 In. | 200 |
| **Seed Stripper,** Pine, Metal Teeth, Blue Paint Traces, 1875-1900, 19 In. | 150 |
| **Shoe Lathe,** Cast Iron, Pine, Painted, Shoe Shape, Inscribed Bernier, 1800s, 28 In., 2 Piece | 180 |
| **Spoke Wrench,** High Wheel Ordinary, King Dick, Bull Dog Logo | 263 |
| **Steering Assembly,** Hip Wheel, Rudder, G. & E. Robinson, Salesman's Sample, c.1862, 8 x 12 In. | 3840 |
| **Surveyor's Box,** Tripod, Wood, c.1910 | 360 |
| **Threshing Machine,** Model, Wood, Metal, Crank, c.1910, 14 x 20 In. | 120 |
| **Wagon Box,** Wood, Conestoga, Wrought Iron Hardware, Backboard Mount, c.1820, 30 x 44 In. | 960 |
| **Wagon Jack,** Conestoga, Chestnut, Punched Design, Red Paint, Iron, c.1825, 28 x 7 In. | 288 |
| **Wagon Jack,** Conestoga, Wrought Iron, Marked GW 1838, 1925-50, 27 In. | 270 |
| **Wagon Jack,** Wood, Wrought Iron Bands, Lift & Handle, Pa., 1767, 20 x 7 In. | 480 |
| **Wheel Stop,** Conestoga Wagon, Iron, 17 In. | 189 |
| **Wheelbarrow,** Pine, Iron, Czechoslovakia, c.1850, 23 x 76 In. | 230 |
| **Workbench,** Hardwood, Dovetailed, 2 Vises, Hammacher Schlemmer & Co., c.1875, 32 x 83 In. ......*illus* | 1914 |

## TOOTHBRUSH HOLDERS

**TOOTHBRUSH HOLDERS** were part of every bowl and pitcher set in the late nineteenth century. Most were oblong covered dishes. About 1920, manufacturers started to make children's toothbrush holders shaped like animals or cartoon characters. A few modern toothbrush holders are still being made.

| | |
|---|---:|
| **Beaded,** Nickel Plated Brass, c.1899, 3 ½ x 2 In. | 18 |
| **Box,** Celluloid, Hinged, Geometric Designs, 1940s, 6 x 1 x 1 In. | 18 |
| **Boxer,** Gloves, Porcelain, Germany, 1920s, 5 x 3 x 2 In. | 149 |
| **Calf,** Brown, Leaning Forward, Gold Hooves, Paper Label, Japan, 5 x 5 In. | 32 |
| **Cat,** Art Deco, Stylized, Porcelain, White, Japan, 5 x 2 In. | 65 |
| **Chrome,** 2 Holes, Glass Tray, Riccardo Barthel, Italy | 45 |
| **Cylindrical,** Brown Transfer, Swans, Fence, Staffordshire, c.1875, 4 x 3 In. | 113 |
| **Dish,** Charlotte Pattern, Brown Transfer, Wall Mount, Crown Devon, c.1940, 6 x 4 In. | 55 |
| **Dutch Girl,** Chalkware, Wall Mount, 1960s, 6 ¾ x 4 In. | 55 |
| **Herons,** Water's Edge, Black Transfer, Ridgway, c.1877, 5 ¾ x 3 In. | 95 |
| **Little Bear,** Brown, Victoria Ceramics, 5 ¼ In. | 48 |
| **Mammy,** Hands On Hips, Pottery, c.1945, 5 In. | 59 |
| **Pirate,** Patch, Mustache, Curved Arms, Open Boots, Porcelain, 1940s, 5 In. | 135 |
| **Rabbit,** Red & Yellow, Brush Your Teeth, Chalkware, 7 In. | 55 |

**Tool,** Workbench, Hardwood, Dovetailed, 2 Vises, Hammacher Schlemmer & Co., c.1875, 32 x 83 In.
$1,914

James D. Julia Auctioneers

**Toy,** Amos 'n' Andy, Andy, Walker, Rolling Eyes, Tin Litho, Clockwork, Marx, c.1930, 11 ½ In.
$384

Bertoia Auctions

**Toy,** Baby In High Chair, Converts To Table, Tin Lithograph, Meier, Germany, 2 ¾ In.
$240

Bertoia Auctions

T

Toy, Bed, Doll's, Four-Poster, Curly Maple, Mattress, Pillow, Quilt, c.1810, 15 x 11 In. $448

Rago Arts & Auction Center

Toy, Bell Ringer, Camel, Tin, Painted, Wire Rocker Base, Althof Bergmann, 9 In. $3,000

Bertoia Auctions

Toy, Bell Ringer, Hunter, Rabbit Pops Out, Tree Trunk, Wheels, N.N. Hill Brass Co., c.1905, 6 In. $1,440

Bertoia Auctions

## Rules for Dating Most Toy Cars by the Wheels

Before World War II, toy car wheels were open-spoked metal wheels, solid metal disc wheels, solid metal disc wheels with embossed spokes, white rubber tires with metal rims, or solid white rubber tires mounted directly on the axles. The rule is that white rubber tires were used before World War II, black tires after. Since the 1960s, black plastic wheels have been used.

| | |
|---|---:|
| **Shell,** Gold Glitter Lucite, Cast Iron, Ball & Claw Feet, 3 x 4 In. | 65 |
| **Toothbrush Pattern,** Green, U.S. Glass, 3 Brush Feet, 4¾ In. | 65 |
| **Tulip,** Celluloid, 1930s, 6 In. | 70 |
| **Woman's Head,** Art Deco, Hat, Closed Eyes, Ceramic, 4 x 4 x 2 In. | 29 |

**TOOTHPICK HOLDERS** are sometimes called *toothpicks* by collectors. The variously shaped containers used to hold small wooden toothpicks are made of glass, china, or metal. Most of the toothpick holders are made of Victorian pressed glass. Additional items may be found in other categories, such as Bisque, Silver Plate, Slag Glass, etc.

| | |
|---|---:|
| **Beaded Ovals In Sand,** Green, Dugan | 195 |
| **Brown Glass,** Michigan, Boyd Glass, 2¾ In. | 22 |
| **Crystal,** Crosshatch Pattern, Sawtooth Cut Top, 2½ In. | 12 |
| **Double Dahlia,** Lens, Clear, Rose Stain | 75 |
| **Double Dahlia,** Lens, Green With Gold | 125 |
| **Elephant Toes,** Clear, Gold, US Glass | 35 |
| **Gaelic,** Clear, Enameled, Indiana Glass | 45 |
| **Jeweled Heart,** Victor, Apple Green Opalescent, Dugan Glass, c.1900, 2⅜ In. | 316 |
| **Lacy Medallion,** Green, Gold, Summit | 9 |
| **Tortoiseshell,** Folding Case, Tortoiseshell, c.1820, 1¾ In. | 100 |

**TORQUAY** is the name given to ceramics by several potteries working near Torquay, **TORQUAY** England, from 1870 until 1962. Until about 1900, the potteries used local red clay to make classical-style art pottery vases and figurines. Then they turned to making souvenir wares. Items were dipped in colored slip and decorated with painted slip and sgraffito designs. They often had mottoes or proverbs, and scenes of cottages, ships, birds, or flowers. The Scandy design was a symmetrical arrangement of brushstrokes and spots done in colored slips. Potteries included Watcombe Pottery (1870–1962), Torquay Terra-Cotta Company (1875–1905), Aller Vale (1881–1924), Torquay Pottery (1908–1940), and Longpark (1883–1957).

| | |
|---|---:|
| **Cheese Keeper,** Lid, Mouse Hole, Help Yourself To Cheese, Ship, 6 x 5 x 2 In. | 135 |
| **Eggcup,** Fresh Laid, Rooster, Attached Underplate | 85 |
| **Hatpin Holder,** I'll Take Care Of The Pins, Scandy, 5 In. | 135 |
| **Mustard Pot,** Lid, Hot & Strong, Scandy, 2 x 3 In. | 24 |
| **Pot,** Right Wrongs No Man, Fruit, Leaves, c.1905, 4 x 4½ In. | 38 |
| **Soup,** Dish, Slotted Lid, An Old Friend Is Better Than 2 New Ones, Cottages, Handle, c.1900 | 65 |
| **Tobacco Jar,** Tobacco Help Yersel, Ships, Lid, 5 x 3¼ In. | 130 |
| **Vase,** Black Bird, Tree Trunk, Cobalt Blue, Sponged, Flared, c.1920, 9½ In. | 75 |

**TORTOISESHELL** is the shell of the tortoise. It has been used as inlay and to make small decorative objects since the seventeenth century. Some species of tortoise are now on the endangered species list, and old or new objects made from these shells cannot be sold legally.

| | |
|---|---:|
| **Bodkin,** Silver Inlays, Flowers, Leaves, c.1800 | 235 |
| **Box,** Card, Gold Inlay, Silver, Mother-Of-Pearl, Oval Cartouche, c.1865, 4 x 2 In. | 984 |
| **Box,** Sterling, 4 Shaped Legs, Round, Deakin & Francis, 1918, 1¾ In. | 149 |
| **Card Case,** Cognac Flames, Velvet Lining, Cushion Shape, c.1850, 4 x 3 In. | 450 |
| **Comb,** Carved, Box Inscribed Mrs. Boles, Boston, c.1820, 7¾ In. | 1230 |
| **Comb,** Case, Bees, Rhinestones, Pearls, France, 4 x 1½ In. | 30 |
| **Dresser Box,** Hinged Lid, Medallion, Leaves, Silver Mount, Cloth Lining, 2 x 6 In. | 518 |
| **Dresser Box,** Lid, Silver Antelope, Antlers, Round, 19th Century, 2 x 3 In. | 201 |
| **Frame,** Silver Rim, Heart Shape, c.1876, 6 x 6 In. | 2865 |
| **Jewel Coffer,** Rococo Style, Bronze, Scrolled Corners, Bombe Shape Box, 9 x 7 In. | 3444 |
| **Letter Opener,** Pen, Knife, c.1885, 11¾ In. | 195 |
| **Paper Knife,** Rectangular, Rounded, Monogram, Mappin & Webb, Case, 17 In. | 460 |
| **Tea Caddy,** Double Well, Mother-Of-Pearl Inlay, Raised Ball Feet, 6 x 4 x 5 In. | 2956 |
| **Tray,** Rectangular, Dished Center, Victorian, 9 In. | 163 |

**TOY** collectors have special clubs, magazines, and shows. Toys are designed to entice children, and today they have attracted new interest among adults who are still children at heart. All types of toys are collected. Tin toys, iron toys, battery-operated toys, and many others are collected by specialists. Dolls, games, teddy bears, and bicycles are listed in their own categories. Other toys may be found under company or celebrity names.

| | |
|---|---:|
| **Acrobat,** Wood, Painted, Covered Box, Stepped Platform, 7 In. | 767 |
| **Acrobats,** Climb Up & Down Stairs, Painted, Wood, 1890, 7 In. | 840 |
| **Action Figure,** Alien, His Evil Brains Glow In The Dark, Kenner, Box, 1979, 18 In. | 957 |

T

**Toy,** Bell Ringer, Mr. Flip, Cast Iron, Nickel, Painted, Little Nemo Series, Watrous, 6½ In.
$960

**Toy,** Bell Ringer, Suffragette Pushing Hoop, Tin, Wheels, George Brown, 9½ In.
$6,000

**Toy,** Boob McNutt, Flat Hat, Tin Litho, Clockwork, Walker, Ferdinand Strauss, 8 In.
$295

**Toy,** Boat, Paddlewheel, 2 Stacks, Cabin, Flywheel, Tin Litho, Hess, Germany, 10 In.
$472

**Toy,** Box For Robot, Zoomer, Original $1.98 Price Tag, Japan, 8⅛ In.
$470

**Toy,** Box Lid, Dolly's Play House, McLoughlin Bros., c.1900, 24 x 15 In.
$171

**Toy,** Boy, Cross-Country Skis, Tin Lithograph, Levy, Germany, 3 In.
$240

**Toy,** Bus, Inter-State, Double-Decker, Rear Stairs, Tin Lithograph, Clockwork, Strauss, 10 In.
$177

Bertoia Auctions

---

**Toy,** Busy Bridge, 6 Autos, Tracks, 2 Terminals, Tin Litho, Clockwork, Marx, 24 In.
$354

Bertoia Auctions

---

> **TIP**
> To keep tin toys from rusting further, try this: Rinse the metal, scrub, dry, then coat with a thin layer of petroleum jelly.

---

**Toy,** Car, Charger, Custom, Hot Pink, Die Cast, Mattel, Hot Wheels, 1969, 5½ x 6 In.
$297

Hake's Americana & Collectibles

---

**Toy,** Car, Ford, Model T, Sedan, 2-Door, Spoke Wheels, Iron, Arcade, 1926, 6½ In.
$295

Bertoia Auctions

| | |
|---|---:|
| **Adam The Porter,** Pushing Handcar, Tin Lithograph, Painted, Clockwork, Lehmann, 8 In. | 1003 |
| **Airplane,** Air Mail, Green Paint, Kenton Toys, 6½ In. | 210 |
| **Airplane,** Ambulance, Sanitats-Korps, Red Crosses, 3½ In. | 826 |
| **Airplane,** Army Scout, Gray, Red Paint, Decals, Pressed Steel, Steelcraft, 23 In. | 210 |
| **Airplane,** Biplane, American Flyer, Green Paint, Tri-Motor, 23½ In. | 2700 |
| **Airplane,** Express, Tri-Motor, Tin, Green, Gold, Pop Windup, Japan, Prewar, 15-In. Wingspan | 649 |
| **Airplane,** Folker, Green, Nickel Wheels, Vindex, 1920s-30s, 8-In. Wingspan | 2844 |
| **Airplane,** Friendship Seaplane, Cast Iron, Yellow, Pull Toy, Hubley, 12-In. Wingspan | 3555 |
| **Airplane,** Little Jim, Orange, Body, Green Wings, Pressed Steel, Steelcraft, 22½ In. | 360 |
| **Airplane,** Lockheed Sirius, Cream Body, Red Paint, Pressed Steel, 1931, 21 In. | 1560 |
| **Airplane,** Lucky Boy, Red, Embossed, Dent Mfg., 1930s, 10-In. Wingspan | 770 |
| **Airplane,** Orange, Gray Wings, Cast Iron, Kilgore, 8-In. Wingspan | 3555 |
| **Airplane,** Pilot, Tin Lithograph, Clockwork, Fischer Bleriot, Germany, 11 In. | 1800 |
| **Airplane,** Pilots, Open Cockpit, America, Stars, Cast Iron, Pull Toy, Hubley, 17 In. | 2962 |
| **Airplane,** Pilotto, Lehmann, 4¾-In. Wingspan | 2015 |
| **Airplane,** Royal Dutch, Blue, Tin Lithograph, Friction, Marked Intercontinental, Box, 15 In. | 150 |
| **Airplane,** Sea Gull, Embossed, Passengers, Yellow, Blue, Pull Toy, Kilgore, 8 In. | 1185 |
| **Airplane,** Sir Mail, Red, Silver, Pressed Steel, Keystone, 23½ In. | 180 |
| **Airplane,** Skycruiser Aircraft, Silver, Red, Tin, Friction, Marx, 18 In. | 210 |
| **Airplane,** UX166, Embossed, Red Paint, Cast Iron, Kenton, 6 In. | 210 |
| **Alligator,** Manell, Platform, Paint, Cast Iron, Bell, c.1903, 9 In. | 1920 |
| **Ambulance,** Driver, Red, Silver Paint, Nickel Plated, 10 In. | 900 |
| **Amos 'N' Andy,** Andy, Walker, Rolling Eyes, Tin Litho, Clockwork, Marx, c.1930, 11½ In. *illus* | 384 |
| **Amos 'N' Andy,** Tin Litho, Rolling Eyes, Swinging Arms, Walker, Marx, 11 In., Pair | 944 |
| **Amusement Park Ride,** Gondolas, Riders, Paint, Cast Iron, Clockwork, Hubley, c.1900, 19 In. | 20400 |
| **Amusement Roundabout,** 5 Riders, Flag, Paint, Tin, 11 In. | 3300 |
| **Anxious Bride,** 3-Wheel Rad Cycle, Woman, Holding Hanky, Driver, Tin Litho, Lehmann, 9 In. | 2006 |
| **Armoire,** Doll's, Country French, Wood, Arched, Paneled Doors, Drawer, c.1860, 20 In. | 560 |
| **Baby Carriage,** Tin Baby, Quilted Blanket, Penny, Distler, 4½ In. | 134 |
| **Baby In High Chair,** Converts To Table, Tin Lithograph, Meier, Germany, 2¾ In. *illus* | 240 |
| **Baby Quieter,** Peg Leg Newspaper Reader, Child, Wheel, Paint, Cast Iron, Bell, J. & E. Stevens, 7½ In. | 3600 |
| **Baggage Porter,** Black, Man Carrying 2 Suitcases, Tin, Windup, Distler, 7¼ In. | 538 |
| **Barbie Car,** Jaguar XJS, Sparkly Pink, Marx, Box | 79 |
| **Barnacle Bill,** Waddler, Tin Lithograph, Windup, Chein, 6¼ In. | 150 |
| **Bavarian Dancers,** Tin Lithograph, Lever, Penny, Meier, 3½ In. | 1080 |
| **Bears** are also listed in the Teddy Bear category. | |
| **Bear,** Black Fur, Toothy Grin, Clockwork, Ives, Box, 1872, 9 In. | 525 |
| **Bear,** Dentist, Drilling, Crying Bear, Tin Litho, Cloth, Battery Operated, S&E, Box, 9½ In. | 502 |
| **Bear,** On Wheels, Ear Button, Ring Pull Growler, Leather Handle, 1956, 18 x 21 In. | 450 |
| **Bear,** On Wheels, Silk Plush, Cast Iron Wheels, Embroidered Nose, Felt Paws, c.1925, 12 In. | 224 |
| **Bed,** Doll's, Canopy, Tiger Maple, Carved, Slat Boards, 29 x 29 In. | 325 |
| **Bed,** Doll's, Cast Iron, Openwork Scrolls, 15¾ x 14½ In. | 60 |
| **Bed,** Doll's, Federal, Cherry, Arched Canopy, Roped Rails, Straw Stuffed Mattress, 17 In. | 300 |
| **Bed,** Doll's, Four-Poster, Curly Maple, Mattress, Pillow, Quilt, c.1810, 15 x 11 In. *illus* | 448 |
| **Bed,** Doll's, Four-Poster, Walnut, Shaped Head & Foot Boards, Turned Posts, Cup Finials, 25 In. | 185 |
| **Bell Ringer,** Camel, Tin, Painted, Wire Rocker Base, Althof Bergmann, 9 In. *illus* | 3000 |
| **Bell Ringer,** Eskimo, Polar Bear, Bells, Platform, White, Yellow Paint, Iron, Watrous, 10 In. | 960 |
| **Bell Ringer,** Hunter, Rabbit Pops Out, Tree Trunk, Wheels, N.N. Hill Brass Co., c.1905, 6 In.*illus* | 1440 |
| **Bell Ringer,** Jack & Jill, Platform, Paint, Cast Iron, 2 Bells, Watrous, 7 In. | 840 |
| **Bell Ringer,** Landing Of Columbus, Platform, Paint, Cast Iron, Bell, J. & E. Stevens, c.1910, 7 In. | 720 |
| **Bell Ringer,** Leapfrog, 2 Clowns, Wheels, Paint, Cast Iron, Bell, Ives, 8¾ In. | 16800 |
| **Bell Ringer,** Monkey, Jim-Along-Jose, Red Carriage, Paint, Cast Iron, Bell, Kyser & Rex, c.1881, 7 In. | 4500 |
| **Bell Ringer,** Monkey, Platform, Paint, Tin, Bell, Merriam, 6 In. | 900 |
| **Bell Ringer,** Mr. Flip, Cast Iron, Nickel, Painted, Little Nemo Series, Watrous, 6½ In. *illus* | 960 |
| **Bell Ringer,** Sailors, Open Bed Wagon, Silver, Blue, Iron, Pull Toy, Bells, Watrous, 9½ In. | 840 |
| **Bell Ringer,** Suffragette Pushing Hoop, Tin, Wheels, George Brown, 9½ In. *illus* | 6000 |
| **Ben Hur Horse,** Cart, Tin, Windup, Japan, 9 In. | 175 |
| **Bench,** Doll's, Sheraton, Tiger Maple, Shaped Crest, Plank Seat, Scrolled Arms, 17 x 27 In. | 780 |
| **Betty Cashier,** Plush Bear, Tin Lithograph, Battery, Linemar, Japan, 9 In. | 300 |
| **Bicycles** that are large enough to ride are listed in the Bicycle category. | |
| **Bicycle Riders,** Seated, Joined By 2 Wires, Cast Iron, Painted, Ideal, 5 In. | 3540 |
| **Black Washwoman,** Wood, Carved, Painted, Cotton Suds, Cigar Box, Pull String, c.1900, 9 In. | 1500 |
| **Black Woman,** Suffragette, Book, Podium, Tin, Wood, Clockwork, Ives, 11 In. | 11400 |
| **Blackie Drummer,** Bear In Suit, Red Wheels, Pull Toy, Fisher-Price, c.1939, 11 In. | 354 |
| **Blimp,** Akron, Metal, Silver Paint, 3 Wheels, Steelcraft, Murray Ohio, Cleveland, c.1933, 25 In. | 300 |
| **Blocks,** Alphabet, Pictorial, Wood, Paper Lithograph, Fisk & Little, Box, c.1885, 8 In. | 325 |

T

| | |
|---|---|
| **Blocks,** Animal Scenes, Lithograph, France, c.1870, 2 ¼ In., 48 Piece | 660 |
| **Boat,** 2 Sailors, Eagle Finial, Platform, Red, Green Paint, Cast Iron, Tin, Bell, Ives, 8 In. | 3600 |
| **Boat,** 8-Man Racing Scull, Iron, Red Wheels, Spokes, Yellow, c.1895, 18 ½ In. | 9000 |
| **Boat,** Destroyer, U.S. Navy, Gray Paint, Tin, Wood, Plastic, c.1950, 23 In. | 30 |
| **Boat,** Driver, Crank, Sea Hawk, Japan, 1950s, 11 In. | 120 |
| **Boat,** Jet Patrol, Tin Crank, Japan, 1950s, 10 In. | 145 |
| **Boat,** Motor, Driver, Green, Red Paint, Wood, Tin, Orkin Craft, 26 In. | 960 |
| **Boat,** New Mexico Dreadnought, Wood, Tin Hull, Clockwork, 25 In. | 1920 |
| **Boat,** Ocean Liner, Tin, Painted, Clockwork, Paper Labels, Arnold, Box, 13 In. | 767 |
| **Boat,** Paddlewheel, 2 Stacks, Cabin, Flywheel, Tin Litho, Hess, Germany, 10 In. ...............*illus* | 472 |
| **Boat,** R.M.S. Queen Mary, Red, Black, White Paint, Wood, Chad Valley, Box, 12 In. | 60 |
| **Boat,** Rowboat, 3 Oarsmen, Wood, Etienne Et Mandonnand, c.1922, 18 ½ In. | 472 |
| **Boat,** Sailboat, Exploding, Open Gun Ports, Heyde, Germany, 5 ¼ In. | 590 |
| **Boat,** Sailboat, Flywheel Power, Red, White, Green, Hess, 11 ¾ In. | 207 |
| **Boat,** Shore Patrol, 2 Guns, Battery Operated, Japan, 1950s, 9 In. | 120 |
| **Boat,** Steamship, 2 Masts, Clockwork, Fleischmann, c.1920, 13 In. | 1003 |
| **Boat,** Steamship, 3 Masts, 5 Sailors, Smoke, Flags, Heyde, 5 ½ In. | 325 |
| **Boob McNutt,** Flat Hat, Tin Litho, Clockwork, Walker, Ferdinand Strauss, 8 In. ...............*illus* | 295 |
| **Box For Robot,** Zoomer, Original $1.98 Price Tag, Japan, 8 ⅛ In. ...............*illus* | 470 |
| **Box Lid,** Dolly's Play House, McLoughlin Bros., c.1900, 24 x 15 In. ...............*illus* | 171 |
| **Boy Scouts,** 4 Bells, Platform, Paint, Cast Iron, Watrous, 13 In. | 660 |
| **Boy,** Cat, Bell, Platform, Brass, N.N. Hill Brass Co., c.1910, 5 ¾ In. | 4200 |
| **Boy,** Cross-Country Skis, Tin Lithograph, Levy, Germany, 3 In. ...............*illus* | 240 |
| **Boy,** Dog, Chasing Pigs, Platform, Paint, Cast Iron, c.1880, 9 ½ In. | 3600 |
| **Boy,** Feeding Chicken, Tin, Made In Japan, Toyodo & Co., 7 ¼ In. | 291 |
| **Boy,** Fishing, Bell, Paint, Cast Iron, N.M. Brass Co., 6 In. | 3000 |
| **Boy,** Fishing, Platform, Multicolor Paint, Cast Iron, Pull Toy, J. & E. Stevens, 8 In. | 6600 |
| **Boy,** Legs Up, Smiling, Sled, Wheels, Tin Lithograph, Penny, Meier, 3 ½ In. | 510 |
| **Boy,** On Sled, Wheels Under Runners, Embossed, Tin Lithograph, Penny, Meier, 3 In. | 325 |
| **Boy,** Whipping Donkey, Sleeping Dog, Moveable Arms, Brass, J. & E. Stevens, 9 In. | 780 |
| **Buckboard,** 2 White Goat Drawn, Woman Driver, Painted, Cast Iron, Harris, 13 In. | 3900 |
| **Bumper Car,** Pier 39, Red, No. 15, Soli S.R.L. Reggio E., Restored, 12 Volt Battery | 6325 |
| **Bus,** Century Of Progress, Tandem, Cast Iron, Blue, White, Rubber Tires, Arcade, 1933, 14 In. | 502 |
| **Bus,** Coast-To-Coast, No. 84, Gray Paint, Pressed Steel, Keystone, 31 ½ In. | 2160 |
| **Bus,** Cream, Green Paint, Cast Iron, Arcade, 14 In. | 210 |
| **Bus,** De-Luxe, Blue, Driver, Tin Litho, Curtain Window Graphic, Strauss, 13 ½ In. | 413 |
| **Bus,** Double-Decker, Bus To Joyville, 3 Passengers, Tin Lithograph, 8 In. | 1303 |
| **Bus,** Double-Decker, Driver, Window Passenger Graphics, Tin Litho, Penny, Meier, 3 In. | 2242 |
| **Bus,** Driver, Nickel Plated, Red, Decals, Rubber Tires, Cast Iron, Arcade, Box, 8 In. | 1298 |
| **Bus,** Green Paint, Pressed Steel, Buddy L, 28 ½ In. | 1599 |
| **Bus,** Inter-State, Double-Decker, Green, Lithograph, Clockwork, Strauss, 10 In. | 325 |
| **Bus,** Inter-State, Double-Decker, Rear Stairs, Tin Lithograph, Clockwork, Strauss, 10 In.......*illus* | 177 |
| **Bus,** Inter-State, Double-Decker, Tin Litho, Rooftop Seating, Strauss, 10 ½ In. | 413 to 741 |
| **Bus,** Metal, Friction, Peru, c.1940, 14 In. | 275 |
| **Bus,** Mobile Post Office, Japan, 1950s, 5 ½ In. | 75 |
| **Bus,** New York Sightseeing, 5 Katzenjammer Characters, Paint, Iron, c.1905, 10 In. | 5100 |
| **Bus,** Royal Blue Line Coast To Coast Service, Tin Lithograph, Chein, 18 In. | 364 |
| **Bus,** Safety Coach, 5-Seat Passenger, Green, En-Es, 1925, 29 In. | 600 |
| **Bus,** Schuco Piccolo, Metal, Painted Green, Clear Plastic Roof, Black Tires, 2 ¾ In. | 35 |
| **Bus,** Wisconsin Bus Lines, Black Painted Roof Ad, Green 2-Tone, Disc Wheels, Arcade, 8 In. | 826 |
| **Bus,** Yellow Paint, White Rubber Tires, Cast Iron, Kenton, c.1936, 7 In. | 1298 |
| **Busy Bridge,** 6 Autos, Tracks, 2 Terminals, Tin Litho, Clockwork, Marx, 24 In. ...............*illus* | 354 |
| **Busy Secretary,** Woman, Switchboard, Headphones, Tin, Battery, Linemar, Japan, Box, 7 In. | 330 |
| **Camel,** Bactrian, Mohair, Stuffed, Button Eyes, Cast Iron Base, Wheels, 15 x 11 In. | 708 |
| **Camel,** Bell, Rocking Base, Paint, Tin, Althof Bergmann, 9 In. | 3000 |
| **Camel,** Cotton, Rag Stuffed, Humps, Floppy Legs, Button Eyes, Bendable Knees, 1941, 12 In. | 168 |
| **Camel,** Plush, Head Down, Red Blanket, 4 Metal Wheels, Push Pull, Germany, 1800s, 16 In. | 492 |
| **Cap Gun,** Black, Box, Instructions, Last Minute Manufacturing, Canada, 5 ½ In. | 78 |
| **Cap Gun,** Buffalo Bill, Gold Metal, White Plastic Handle, On Card, Stevens, 9 ¼ In. | 90 |
| **Cap Gun,** Cast Iron, Chick In Egg, Ives, 1884, 5 ¾ In. | 1416 |
| **Car,** Alphonse & Gaston, Comic Characters, Bowing, Paint, Cast Iron, Kenton, c.1911, 8 In. | 4200 |
| **Car,** Andy Gump, 348 License Plate, Red Paint, Cast Iron, Arcade, 7 ½ In. | 480 |
| **Car,** Andy Gump, Man In Red Convertible, Cast Iron, Arcade, 7 In. | 450 |
| **Car,** Army Command, Plastic Windshield, Tin Lithograph, Marx, Box, 20 In. | 480 |
| **Car,** Buick, Sedan, Cast Iron, Green, Black Paint, Nickel-Plated Spoke Wheels, Arcade, 8 In. | 4425 |
| **Car,** Bump, Circus, Seated Clown, Roof Lifts, Tin Lithograph, Multicolor, 7 In. | 236 |

**Toy,** Car, Racing, Driver, Embossed, Iron, Rubber Tires, Nickel, Vindex, c.1929, 11 In.
$2,950

Bertoia Auctionsa

**Toy,** Car, Racing, Tin Lithograph, Clockwork, Mettoy, 1930s, 15 In.
$531

Bertoia Auctions

**Toy,** Car, Soapbox Derby, Cracker 7, Super Turbo, Metal Body, Wood Frame, 78 In.
$270

Morphy Auctions

**Toy,** Car, Station Wagon, Toytown Estate, Roof Rack, Wood Sides, Tin Litho, Wyandotte, 20 In.
$531

Bertoia Auctions

**Toy,** Car, Touring, Painted, Nickel Lamps, Rubber Tires, Clockwork, Bing, c.1904, 10¾ In.
$3,835

Bertoia Auctions

---

**Toy,** Carousel, Tin Lithograph, Windup, Germany, 7½ x 5½ In.
$863

Wm Morford Auctions

---

**Toy,** Cart, Horse Drawn, Whipping Horse, Cast Iron, J. & E. Stevens, Repainted, 8¾ In.
$180

Bertoia Auctions

| | |
|---|---:|
| **Car,** Cadillac, 1950 Model, Black, Battery Operated, Nickel Grill, Japan, Nomura, Box, 13 In. | 1298 |
| **Car,** Cadillac, 1959 Model, Sedan, 4 Door, Black, Bandai, Japan, 12 In. | 472 |
| **Car,** Champion, 3 Windows, Green, Blue Paint, Nickel Grill, 7½ In. | 1440 |
| **Car,** Charger, Custom, Hot Pink, Die Cast, Mattel, Hot Wheels, 1969, 5½ x 6 In. *illus* | 297 |
| **Car,** Chevrolet, Coupe, Cast Iron, Dark Gray, Andirons, Arcade, c.1925, 8 In. | 651 |
| **Car,** Chrysler, Airflow, Coupe, Iron, Black, Orange, Nickel, Rubber Tires, 1934, 6½ In. | 2360 |
| **Car,** Clown, Artie, Dog On Hood, Unique Art, Box, 7½ In. | 413 |
| **Car,** Convertible, Tin, Windup, US Zone Of Germany, Distler, 9¾ In. | 120 |
| **Car,** Coupe, Red, Black Chassis, Spoke Disc Wheels, Driver, Cast Iron, Kenton, 1926, 10 In. | 3540 |
| **Car,** Crazy, Tin, Marx, 8 In. | 213 |
| **Car,** Doodlebug, Light Blue, Tootsietoy, c.1936, 5 In. | 150 |
| **Car,** Edsel, Convertible, Cream, Green, New Edsel, Child Land, Haji, Japan, Box, 10¾ In. | 3300 |
| **Car,** Electric, Riding, Blue, Red Stripe, Tin Lithograph, Battery Operated, Marx, Box, 24 In. | 450 |
| **Car,** English Sedan, Wells-O-London, Extended Trunk, Tin Litho, Painted, Clockwork, 8 In. | 236 |
| **Car,** Fire Chief, Pressed Steel, Windup, Kingsbury, 10½ In. | 270 |
| **Car,** Fire Chief, Red, Gray, Pressed Steel, Windup, Marx, 1939, 14 In. | 510 |
| **Car,** Fire Chief, Siren, Red Paint, Tin, Windup, Marx, 14½ In. | 300 |
| **Car,** Fire Department, Tin, Friction, Lupor, USA, Box, 10½ In. | 145 |
| **Car,** Ford, 4 Door, Sedan, Cast Iron, Paint, Nickel Spoke Wheels, Driver, Arcade, 1920s, 5 In. | 148 |
| **Car,** Ford, Model A, Coupe, Rumble Seat, Iron, Green Paint, Rubber Tires, Arcade, 7 In. | 561 |
| **Car,** Ford, Model T, Coupe, Cast Iron, Black Paint, Spoke Wheels, Arcade, 6½ In. | 236 |
| **Car,** Ford, Model T, Sedan, 2-Door, Spoke Wheels, Iron, Arcade, 1926, 6½ In. *illus* | 295 |
| **Car,** Ford, Phaeton, White, Windup, 1910-15, 9 In. | 1422 |
| **Car,** Ford, Thunderbird, Dealer Promo Model, Unique In All The World, Plastic, 1964, 8 In. | 48 |
| **Car,** Ford, Tin, Friction, Japan, 1957, 11½ In. | 375 |
| **Car,** Funny Flivver, Driver, Dog On Running Boards, Tin Litho, Windup, Louis Marx, 7 In. | 325 |
| **Car,** Grand Sedan, Burgundy Red, Pressed Steel, Battery Headlights, Cor-Cor Toys, 1932, 20 In. | 510 |
| **Car,** Grand Sedan, Gray, Pressed Steel, Cor-Cor Toys, 1932, 20 In. | 570 |
| **Car,** Hand, Standing Driver, Windup, Tin Lithograph, Unique Art, 13¼ In. | 236 |
| **Car,** Hot Rod, Tin, Friction, Marx, Japan, 8 In. | 195 |
| **Car,** Kit, Orange, Black Paint, Pressed Steel, Original Plans, Structo, 15½ In. | 450 |
| **Car,** LaSalle, Sedan, Trailer, Pressed Steel, Green, Wyandotte, 1930s, 25½ In. | 518 |
| **Car,** Model T, Seated Woman Driver, Spoke Wheels, Clockwork, Bing, 1921, 6½ In. | 384 |
| **Car,** Motor Coach, Driver, Tin Litho, Red, Clockwork, Adjustable Tiller, Lehmann, 5 In. | 443 |
| **Car,** Nash, General Motors, Lights, Wipers, Japan, 1950s, 8 In. | 175 |
| **Car,** New Century Cycle, Driver, Passenger, Umbrella Roof, Tin, Windup, Lehmann, 5 In. | 390 |
| **Car,** Packard, Metal, Friction, Germany, 1950s, 10 In. | 175 |
| **Car,** Plastic, Shark, Battery Operated, Remco, USA, Box, 19 In. | 175 |
| **Car,** Police, Chevrolet, Impala, Driver, Japan, 1963, 14½ In. | 275 |
| **Car,** Police, Siren, Pressed Steel, Green Stenciling, Nickel Plated Grille, Marx, 14 In. | 266 |
| **Car,** Racing, Art Nouveau, Tin Plated, Open Wheel, Windup, Green, JEP, 1930s, 14 In. | 805 |
| **Car,** Racing, Benz, Yellow, Driver, Friction, S.H., Japan, Box, 11 In. | 360 |
| **Car,** Racing, Captain Campbell's Blue Bird, High Tail Fin, 19¾ In. | 2950 |
| **Car,** Racing, Champion, Red, Cast Iron, White Rubber Tires, Driver, 9 In. | 207 |
| **Car,** Racing, Champion's Racer, No. 98, Rubber Tires, Tin Litho, Friction, Y Co., 1950s, 18 In. | 1560 |
| **Car,** Racing, Driver, Embossed, Iron, Rubber Tires, Nickel, Vindex, c.1929, 11 In. *illus* | 2950 |
| **Car,** Racing, Driver, Flywheel, Avanti, Hess, Germany, 5 In. | 660 |
| **Car,** Racing, Driver, Tin, Windup, Penny, Fisher, 4½ In. | 450 |
| **Car,** Racing, Golden Arrow, Iron, 12 Piston Articulated, Driver, Hubley, 11 In. | 1298 |
| **Car,** Racing, Golden Arrow, Pressed Steel, Clockwork, Driver, Kingsbury, 20 In. | 1180 |
| **Car,** Racing, Gordon Bennet, Aerodynamic Bonnet, Balloon Wheels, Gunthermann, 9 In. | 9440 |
| **Car,** Racing, JEP, Tin, Clockwork, Rubber Tires, 13½ In. | 531 |
| **Car,** Racing, Long Nose, Seated Driver, Tail Fin, Hadson, Japan, 11½ In. | 295 to 354 |
| **Car,** Racing, No. 16, Motor Driven, Green, Driver, Jetex, England, Box, 6 In. | 173 |
| **Car,** Racing, Open Cockpit, Gas Powered Motor, Drive Line, Bunch, c.1935, 20 In. | 2160 |
| **Car,** Racing, Rubber Tires, Windup, Lupor, 10 In. | 205 |
| **Car,** Racing, Schuco Micro, Ferrari, Key, Red, Silver, Rubber Tires, Metal, Plastic, 4½ In. | 59 |
| **Car,** Racing, Spare Wheels On Side, Light Green, Penny Toy, Meier, 3½ In. | 708 |
| **Car,** Racing, Tin Lithograph, Clockwork, Mettoy, 1930s, 15 In. *illus* | 531 |
| **Car,** Racing, Tin Lithograph, Windup, Driver, Rocket Racer, Marx, 15¾ In. | 531 |
| **Car,** Roadster, Bugatti, Royal Esders, Silver, 4-Door, Open Touring Model, Dresden, 6 In. | 1534 |
| **Car,** Roadster, Stutz, Nickel Plated Parts, Yellow, Green, Kilgore, 10½ In. | 1777 |
| **Car,** Roadster, Stutz, Open, Iron, Blue, Orange Running Boards, Nickel Grill, Kilgore, 10 In. | 767 |
| **Car,** Sedan, Cast Iron, Driver, Disc Wheels, Spare Tire, Paint, Hubley, 6 In. | 885 |
| **Car,** Soapbox Derby, Cracker 7, Super Turbo, Metal Body, Wood Frame, 78 In. *illus* | 270 |
| **Car,** Sports, Convertible, Yellow Paint, Die Cast, Box, 7¼ In. | 215 |

**Toy,** Cat & Mouse, Nina, Attached Wire, Tin Litho, Lehmann, Germany, 11 In.
$1,298

Bertoia Auctions

**Toy,** Chicken Cracking Open Egg, Tin Lithograph, Lever In Base, Fischer, Germany, 3 In.
$840

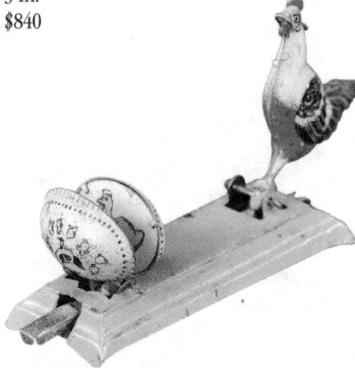

Bertoia Auctions

**Toy,** Clancy The Comical Cop, Built-In Key, Windup, Tin Litho, Walker, Marx, 10¾ In.
$558

Hake's Americana & Collectibles

**Toy,** Clown, Roly Poly, Punch Type, Musical, Glass Eyes, Cloth Collar, 12¾ In.
$179

Mosby Auctions

**Toy,** Dollhouse, 2 Story, Folding, Cardboard, Litho, McLoughlin Bros., c.1890, 16 In.
$560

Theriault's

**Toy,** Dollhouse, 2 Story, Wood, Paper, Painted, 1907, 4 Rooms, Staircase, 14 x 22 In.
$1,254

Theriault's

**Toy,** Driver Training Car, Learn To Drive, Tin Litho, Plastic Roof, Windup, Marx, Box, 6¾ In.
$159

Hake's Americana & Collectibles

**Toy,** Drum, Punched Tin, Spread Wing Eagle, American Flag, Wood Bands, 1800s, 6½ x 8 In.
$593

James D. Julia Auctioneers

**Toy,** Drummer Boy, Pushing Drum, Front Wheel, Tin Litho, Windup, Marx, c.1940, 8½ In.
$354

Bertoia Auctions

T

**Toy,** Flintstones, Wilma, On Tricycle, Tin, Celluloid, Clockwork, Marx, Box, 4 In.
$236

Bertoia Auctions

**Toy,** Frankenstein, Tin Litho, Vinyl, Remote Control, Battery Operated, Marx, 1963, 13 In.
$835

Hake's Americana & Collectibles

**Toy,** G.I. Joe, Adventurer, Camo Fatigues, Brown Life-Like Hair, Beard, Hasbro, Box, 1970, 12 In.
$127

Hake's Americana & Collectibles

**Toy,** Gas Pump, Yellow, Stamped Arcade Gas, Dial Meter, Cast Iron, Decal, Arcade, 6 In.
$472

Bertoia Auctions

**Toy,** Grasshopper, Green Paint, Rubber Tires, Cast Iron, Aluminum, Pull Toy, Hubley, 10 In.
$384

Bertoia Auctions

**Toy,** Great Garloo, Remote Control, Hard Plastic, Battery Operated, Marx, 1960s, 22 In.
$417

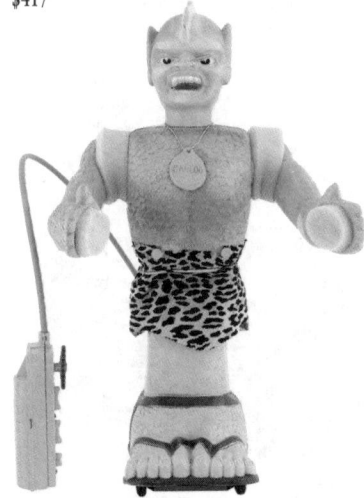

Hake's Americana & Collectibles

**Toy,** Horse & Wagon, Transfer, Cast Iron, Embossed, Painted, Dent, 17 In.
$720

Bertoia Auctions

**Toy,** Horse Stable, 2 Story, Stalls, Wood, Paper Litho, Gottschalk, Germany, 18 x 19 In.
$413

Bertoia Auctions

**Toy,** Horse, Rocking, Pine, Bench Seat, Green & White Paint, c.1890, 41 In.
$480

Garth's Auctioneers & Appraisers

**Toy,** Horse, Wheeled Platform, Dexter, Painted, Tan, Red, Black, G. Brown, 1880s, 9 In.
$648

Bertoia Auctions

| | |
|---|---|
| Car, Sportster, Metal, Friction, Marx, USA, 20 In. | 275 |
| Car, Station Wagon, Toytown Estate, Roof Rack, Wood Sides, Tin Litho, Wyandotte, 20 In....*illus* | 531 |
| Car, Thimble Drome Special, Red, Cox, 1950s, 9 In. | 145 |
| Car, Tin, Electric, Knapp, 12 In. | 4130 |
| Car, Tin, Windup, Driver, England, 9 In. | 195 |
| Car, Topsy-Turvy-Tom, Roll Over, Clown Driver, Tin Lithograph, Eberl, Box, 9¾ x 6 In. | 3920 |
| Car, Touring, Painted, Nickel Lamps, Rubber Tires, Clockwork, Bing, c.1904, 10¾ In..........*illus* | 3835 |
| Car, Toytown Delivery, Red, Yellow, Tin Lithograph, Wyandotte, 21 In. | 360 |
| Car, Tut-Tut, Driver, Tin Lithograph, Clockwork, Bellows, Lehmann, 7 In. | 590 |
| Car, Tut-Tut, Open, Portly Driver, Holding Horn, Tin Litho, Clockwork, Lehmann, 6¾ In. | 2950 |
| Car, Uncle Wiggly, Clockwork, Louis Marx, Box, 7¼ In. | 502 |
| Car, Uncle Wiggly, Clockwork, Marx, 7¼ In. | 472 |
| Car, Volkswagen, Convertible, Tin Litho, Plastic, Friction, Battery, Worldwide, 1950s, 10 In. | 288 |
| Car, Whoopee, Cowboy, Red, Clockwork, Marx, 8 In. | 118 |
| Carnival Ride, Rocket Ship, Tin, Chein, 9 In. | 240 |
| Carousel, Airplane, 6 Men, Flags, Paint, Tin, Clockwork, 16½ In. | 4500 |
| Carousel, Animals, Metal Crank, Wyandotte, c.1930, 6 In. | 175 |
| Carousel, Characters In Swings, Clockwork, Tin Lithograph, Germany, 10 x 7 In. | 184 |
| Carousel, Flying Airplanes, Steam Powered, Tin, Painted, Doll & Co., 10½ x 7 In. | 756 |
| Carousel, Horses, Swings, Open Chairs, Tin Litho Figures, Clockwork, Gunthermann, 12 In. | 944 |
| Carousel, Tin Lithograph, Windup, Germany, 7½ x 5½ In.............*illus* | 863 |
| Carriage, 2 Horses, Driver, Open Seats, Brake, Cast Iron, Yellow, Hubley, c.1900, 18 In. | 2124 |
| Carriage, Doll's, Adjustable Canopy, Wood Wheels, Red, Black, Yellow Paint, c.1890, 22 x 36 In. | 92 |
| Carriage, Doll's, Wicker, Iron, Painted Yellow, Scrolled Details, 30 x 24 x 13 In. | 57 |
| Carriage, Doll's, Wicker, Metal Frame, Wheels, 27 x 24 In. | 35 |
| Carriage, Doll's, Wood, Open Seats, Canopy Roof, Spoke Wheels, Blue Paint, 31 x 35 In. | 89 |
| Carriage, Driver, Passenger, Horse, Red, Blue, Yellow Paint, c.1890, 16 In. | 108 |
| Carriage, Phaeton, Driver, Woman, Open, Horse, White, Red, Black Paint, Iron, Kenton, 17 In. . | 1140 |
| Cart & Dog, Driver, Japanned, Cast Iron, Pull Toy, Ives, 8 In. | 5100 |
| Cart & Ox, Iron, Red Paint, Open Box Style, Seated Driver, Spoke Wheels, Hubley, 14 In. | 561 |
| Cart, 2 Oxen, Paint, Cast Iron, Welker Crosby, 10¾ In. | 600 |
| Cart, Amish, Horses, Tin, 19th Century, 12½ In. | 547 |
| Cart, Donkey Drawn, Black Driver, Paint, Cast Iron, 9 In. | 1140 |
| Cart, Dynamite Rail, Tin Lithograph, Windup, Marx, 7 In. | 180 |
| Cart, Hayrake, Horse, Driver, Paint, Cast Iron, Wilkins, 8½ In. | 6600 |
| Cart, Horse Drawn, Whipping Horse, Cast Iron, J. & E. Stevens, Repainted, 8¾ In. ...............*illus* | 180 |
| Cart, Horse Drawn, Woman Driver, Paint, Cast Iron, Shimer, 10½ In. | 246 |
| Cart, Horse Drawn, Woman Driver, Railed Seat, Nickel Plated Cast Iron, Shimer, 10 In. | 270 |
| Cart, Horse, Paint, Cast Iron, Ives, c.1893, 18 In. | 19200 |
| Cat & Mouse, Nina, Attached Wire, Tin Litho, Lehmann, Germany, 11 In.............................*illus* | 1298 |
| Cat, Felix, Chasing Mice, Tin Lithograph, Disc Wheeled Platform, Nifty, Pull Toy, 7¼ In. | 1003 |
| Cat, Felix, On Scooter, Tin Lithograph, Disc Wheels, Windup, Nifty, 7½ In. | 443 to 826 |
| Cat, Fluffy, Mohair, Red Stitched Claws, F Style Button, Steiff, 1926-43, 5 In. | 432 |
| Cat, Tabby, Woolen, Gray, Painted Stripes, Stitched Ear, Tail, Shoebutton Eyes, Steiff, 9 In. | 1568 |
| Cattle Hauler, Structo, 1956, 2 In. | 95 |
| Chair, Doll's, Wood, Faux Bamboo Spindle Back, Arms & Legs, France, c.1880, 11 In. | 504 |
| Chariot, 2 Horses, Uncle Sam, Paint, Red, Silver Paint, Cast Iron, Kenton, c.1911, 11½ In. | 2280 |
| Chariot, Rabbit Drawn, Rabbit Driver, Spoke Wheel, At Hitch, Paint, Cast Iron, Ideal, 9 In. | 2160 |
| Charleston Trio, Dancing Figure, Fiddler, Dog, Tin Litho, Clockwork, Louis Marx, 10 In. | 767 |
| Chest, Doll's, 3 Drawers, Leaf, Berry, Ribbed Feet, Brass Pulls, 12¼ x 8¼ In. | 296 |
| Chest, Doll's, Lift Top, Shaped Backsplash, Applied Leaf & Diamond, Drawers, 6 x 15 In. | 431 |
| Chicken Cracking Open Egg, Tin Lithograph, Lever In Base, Fischer, Germany, 3 In.........*illus* | 840 |
| Child In High Chair, Converts To Table & Chair, Tin, Penny, 4 In. | 101 |
| Chompy The Beetle, Red, Yellow, Orange, Tin Litho, Windup, Marx, Japan, Box, 1965, 6 In. | 180 |
| Clancy The Comical Cop, Built-In Key, Windup, Tin Litho, Walker, Marx, 10¾ In..............*illus* | 558 |
| Clown Face, Mechanical, White, Round, Tin Lithograph, Germany, c.1930, 3 In. | 1080 |
| Clown, Chasing Donkey, Platform, Tin Lithograph, Penny, Meier, 3¾ In. | 390 |
| Clown, Chasing Donkey, Tin, Shaped Green Base, Penny, Meier, 4 In. | 157 |
| Clown, Driving Car, Yellow Cone Hat, Tin Litho, Windup, Unique Art, Box, 10½ In. | 300 |
| Clown, In Donkey Cart, Holding Reins, Tin, Lehmann, 8 In. | 210 |
| Clown, Juggling Balls, Arm Motions, Tin, Painted, Clockwork, Germany, 9½ In. | 2124 |
| Clown, On Bicycle, Velocipede, Cloth, Tin, Clockwork, Stevens & Brown, c.1880s, 11 In. | 1800 |
| Clown, On Motorcycle, Acrobat, Tin, Windup, 5½ In. | 196 |
| Clown, Playing Harp, On Drum, Plink-Plunk Music, Lacy Clothes, Gunthermann, 8 In. | 2950 |
| Clown, Racing Horses, Tin Litho, Rubber Wheels, Push Pull, Wolverine, c.1930, 10 In. | 314 |
| Clown, Riding Pig, Tin, Painted, Gunthermann, Windup, 5½ In. | 493 to 652 |

Toy, Jack-In-The-Box, Happy Hooligan, Composition, Paper Litho, Wood, Germany, 3½ In.
$266

Toy, Li'l Abner Dogpatch Band, Tin Lithograph, Unique Art, c.1945, 10 x 8 In.
$210

Toy, Little Housekeeper, Young Girl, Rolling Pin, Paper Over Wood, Lever Turns, 12 In.
$266

T

**Toy,** Mary & Her Little Lamb, Celluloid, Tin Wheel Platform, Windup, Japan, Box, 6½ In. $295

Bertoia Auctions

**Toy,** Monkey Bass Player, Tin, Painted, Windup, Germany, 8¾ In. $336

Mosby Auctions

**Toy,** Mystery Ball, Fernand Martin, Spiral Action, Tin Lithograph, France, 14½ In. $649

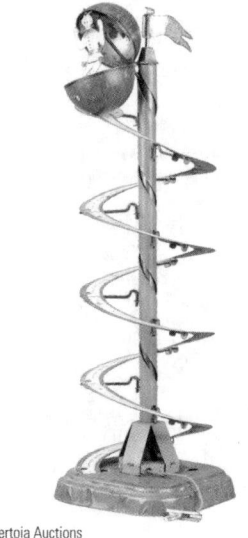

Bertoia Auctions

| | |
|---|---|
| **Clown,** Roller Skates, Hair, Japan, T.P.S., Box, 6¼ In. | 148 |
| **Clown,** Roly Poly, Punch Type, Musical, Glass Eyes, Cloth Collar, 12¾ In. ...........*illus* | 179 |
| **Clown,** Unicyclist, Tin, Windup, Japan, 5½ In. | 90 |
| **Clown,** Waddling, Composition Head, Paint, Cloth Outfit, Lead Shoes, Windup, Germany, 7 In... | 413 |
| **Clowns,** Barrel, Banjo, Tin, Clockwork, Plink-Plunk Music, Gunthermann, 9 In. | 2360 |
| **Coach,** Horse Drawn, Horse On Wheeled Platform, Tin, Painted, 7 In. | 236 |
| **Coast Defense,** Zeppelin Circles, Guns Raise & Lower, Hangar, Tin Litho, Marx, Box, 9 In. | 590 |
| **Cossack & Japanese Men,** Fighting, Gong Bell, Flags, Open Wagon, c.1902, 7 In. | 4800 |
| **Country House,** Trees, Fence, Composition Rooster, Chickens, Germany, 8 x 10 In. | 708 |
| **Cow Puncher Porky,** Plastic Hat, Lasso, Tin Lithograph, Windup, Marx, 12 In. | 300 |
| **Cow,** Wood, Jointed, Leather Horns, Ears & Collar, Brass Bell, Schoenhut, 9 In. | 354 |
| **Cowboy Rider,** Lasso, Gun, Windup, Louis Marx, Box, 6½ In. | 295 |
| **Cradle,** Doll's, Painted, Faux Graining, Shaped Sides, Cutout Ends, 1882, 6 x 15 In. | 123 |
| **Cradle,** Doll's, Pine, Heart Cutouts, c.1890, 9¾ x 19 In. | 30 |
| **Crane,** Wood, Painted, Marked STC, Seaver Toy Co., Burbank, Ca., c.1950, 19 x 16 In. | 30 |
| **Crocodile,** Walking, Jaw Opens, Tin, Windup, Distler, Germany, 8 In. | 224 |
| **Cupboard,** Doll's, Walnut, 2 Doors, Drawers, Shelves, Glass Doors, Acanthus, 19 x 21 In. | 474 |
| **Cupid,** Slipper Cart, Horse, Paint, Cast Iron, Kenton, 9½ In. | 300 |
| **Cyclist,** Metal, Windup, USA Unique Art, 1930s, 9 In. | 245 |
| **Dagwood Solo Flight,** Tin Lithograph, Mechanical, Windup, Marx, 5¾ x 8⅝ In. | 518 |
| **Dancer,** Twilby, Bell, Wheels, Tin Face, Paint, Cloth, Cast Iron, Ives, 8 In. | 9600 |
| **Dancers,** 2 Couples, Flags, Bell, Platform, Paint, Tin, Cast Iron, Althof Bergmann, 9 In. | 1560 |
| **Dancers,** Tango, Paint, Tin, Clockwork, Gunthermann, Germany, c.1900, 8 In. | 1440 |
| **Dandy Jim,** Clown Dancer, Dancing On Stage, Tin Litho, Clockwork, Unique Art, 1922, 10 In. ... | 708 |
| **Dapper Dan,** Admission 1 Cent, Black Dancer, Striped Pants, Green Jacket, Marx, 10¼ In. ........ | 924 |
| **Dapper Dan,** Jigger Dancing On Suitcase Stage, Tin Litho, Clockwork, Marx, Box, 10½ In. ........ | 1298 |
| **Dentist,** Plush Bear Dentist, Patient, Tin Lithograph, Battery, Rhi Brand, Japan, 7½ In. | 390 |
| **Derrick,** Red Boom, Black, Gray Base, Pressed Steel, Kiddies Toys, 22 In. | 450 |
| **Desk,** Doll's, Georgian, Kneehole, 7 Drawers, 1 Cabinet, 9 In. | 237 |
| **Diner,** Steaks, Chops, 2 Doors At Ends, Metal, Yellow, Red Trim, American Flyer, 12 In. | 78 |
| **Dinner Set,** Doll's, Soft Paste, Pink Flowers, Plates, Serving Ware, Napkins, Box, 35 Piece | 1064 |
| **Dirigible,** Model 651, Tin Lithograph, Lehmann, Windup, c.1907, 7½ In. | 225 |
| **Dog,** Bell, Green Platform, Bell, Brown, Red Paint, Tin, 9 In. | 480 |
| **Dog,** Bully, Horsehair Collar, Posable Ears, Embroidered Claws, Steiff, 1927-39, 5½ In. | 2964 |
| **Dog,** Cocker Spaniel, Open Mouth, Black, White Mohair, Red Collar, Ear Tag, Steiff, 27 In. | 590 |
| **Dog,** Fabric, Tan, Brown Spots, Wheels, Pull Toy, c.1905, 12¾ In. | 510 |
| **Dog,** German Shepherd, Brown, Tan, Mohair, Glass Eyes, 1923-28, 11 In. | 711 |
| **Dog,** Growler, Nodder, Rollers, Leash, Metal, Cloth, c.1960, 15 x 17 In. | 1250 |
| **Dog,** Trainer, Bell, Platform, Multicolor Paint, Tin, Althof Bergmann, 11½ In. | 4800 |
| **Dog,** Walking, Platform, Tin Lithograph, Penny, Meier, Germany, 3 In. | 540 |
| **Dolls** are listed in the Doll category. | |
| **Dollhouse Furniture,** Mule Chest, Walnut, Hinged Lid, False Upper, Dovetailed, Va., 1800s, 6 x 3 In. | 431 |
| **Dollhouse Furniture,** Bedroom Suite, Oak Stain, F.A.O. Schwarz Label, c.1885, 9 Piece | 1121 |
| **Dollhouse Furniture,** Bedroom Suite, Stained Wood, Gilt Transfers, Waltershausen, 7 Piece | 767 |
| **Dollhouse Furniture,** Etagere, Chandelier, Chair, Art Nouveau, Gilt Ormolu, Erhard & Sohne, 6 Piece | 1680 |
| **Dollhouse Furniture,** Parlor Suite, Victorian Style, Oval Backs, Stevens & Brown, 1890s, 5 Piece.. | 325 |
| **Dollhouse Furniture,** Sofa, Empire Style, Tin, Faux Wood Grain, Evans & Cartwright, 7 In. | 1652 |
| **Dollhouse Furniture,** Wash Stand, Tin, Painted, Pitcher, Basin, Evans & Cartwright, c.1850, 5 In. | 1298 |
| **Dollhouse,** 1 Story, Colonnade Porch, White, Blue, 2 Red Chimneys, 25½ x 26 In. | 450 |
| **Dollhouse,** 2 Rooms, Blue Roof, Wood, Painted, Paper Lithograph, Gottschalk, 15 x 7 In. | 708 |
| **Dollhouse,** 2 Story, 4 Room, Red Roof, Bay Window, Hinged Door, Gottschalk, 17 x 21 In. | 1007 |
| **Dollhouse,** 2 Story, Blue Roof, Elevator, Awnings, Porches, Gottschalk, 18 x 10 x 28 In. | 1033 |
| **Dollhouse,** 2 Story, Folding, Cardboard, Litho, McLoughlin Bros., c.1890, 16 In. ..............*illus* | 560 |
| **Dollhouse,** 2 Story, Wood, Paper, Painted, 1907, 4 Rooms, Staircase, 14 x 22 In..............*illus* | 1254 |
| **Dollhouse,** 3 Story, Victorian, Porch, Blue Roof, Gottschalk, Germany, c.1890, 17 x 9¾ In. | 461 |
| **Dollhouse,** 4 Rooms, English Manor, Faux Brick, Columns, Balustrade, c.1840, 42 x 35 In. | 3540 |
| **Dollhouse,** 4 Rooms, Victorian, Arched Door, Bay Windows, Widow's Walk, G.J. Lines, 31 In. | 5015 |
| **Dollhouse,** 4 Rooms, Wood, Tin, Bay Windows, Red Door, Furniture, Triang, 19 x 16 In. | 89 |
| **Dollhouse,** 4 Story, Wood, Lithograph Interiors, Cocoanut, Dunham, c.1905, 29 x 12 In. | 403 |
| **Dollhouse,** 6 Rooms, Wood, 10 Windows, Side Porch, Garage, Gottschalk, c.1930, 35 In. | 472 |
| **Dollhouse,** 8 Rooms, Colonial Revival, Wood, Board, Attic, Schoenhut, c.1927, 25 x 24 In. | 649 |
| **Dollhouse,** Bungalow, Porch, Cardboard Roof & Faux Stone, Schoenhut, 1920s, 15 In. | 590 |
| **Double Swing,** Man & Woman In Swing Gondola, Tin Lithograph, Meier, 3 In. | 236 |
| **Dresser,** Doll's, Oak, Mirror, Carved, Beaded, 4 Drawers, c.1900, 30 x 17 In. | 240 |
| **Driver Training Car,** Learn To Drive, Tin Litho, Plastic Roof, Windup, Marx, Box, 6¾ In...*illus* | 159 |
| **Drum,** Punched Tin, Spread Wing Eagle, American Flag, Wood Bands, 1800s, 6½ x 8 In. ...*illus* | 593 |

| | |
|---|---|
| **Drummer Boy,** Pushing Drum, Front Wheel, Tin Litho, Windup, Marx, c.1940, 8 ½ In.......*illus* | 354 |
| **Elephant & Wagon,** Cairo Express, Driver, Painted, Cast Iron, Kenton, 10 In............................. | 2700 |
| **Elephant,** Gray Paint, Wood, Wheeled Platform, Pull Toy, c.1920, 16 ½ x 18 In........................ | 90 |
| **Elephant,** Head Moves, Musical, Bell, Pull Toy, Fisher-Price, c.1948, 10 ¼ In. ....................... | 89 |
| **Elephant,** Mohair, Wheel Base, Pull Toy, Steiff, c.1950, 15 ½ In............................................ | 2640 |
| **Elephant,** On Wheels, Tan, Green, Red Paint, Cast Iron, Pull Toy, Kenton, 4 In......................... | 1320 |
| **Erector Set,** Gilbert, Rocket Launcher Set, Box, 1959 .......................................................... | 35 |
| **Fernand Martin Barrel Roller,** Man Walking, Rolling Barrels, Tin Lithograph, 7 ½ In............. | 1121 |
| **Ferris Wheel,** 3 Horses, Riders, Paint, Tin, Windup, Germany, 9 In. ...................................... | 1800 |
| **Ferris Wheel,** 4 Horses, Acrobat, Paint, Tin, Hull & Stafford, 1890s, 14 In. ........................... | 13200 |
| **Ferris Wheel,** 6 Carriage Seats, Windup, Tin, 15 In. ........................................................... | 829 |
| **Ferris Wheel,** 6 Rocket Cars, Tin, Windup, Blomer & Schuler, W. Germany, 11 In..................... | 90 |
| **Ferris Wheel,** Clown Face, 6 Gondolas, Chein, Box, 16 ½ In. ............................................... | 325 |
| **Ferris Wheel,** Crank Handle, Ticket Booth, Fenced Base, Multicolor Paint, Wood, 22 In............. | 30 |
| **Fire Bell,** Gong, Eagle, Paint, Cast Iron, c.1876, 8 In. ......................................................... | 2040 |
| **Fire Pumper,** 2 Horses, Cast Iron, Black & Yellow Paint, 14 In............................................. | 60 |
| **Fire Pumper,** Iron, Red, Nickel Boiler, Open Body, Rubber Tires, Hubley, 1930s, 13 In............. | 413 |
| **Fire Pumper,** Ladders, Red, Pressed Steel, Structo, 22 In..................................................... | 840 |
| **Fire Pumper,** Red, Pressed Steel, Buddy L, 23 ½ In............................................................. | 570 |
| **Fire Pumper,** Red, Silver Paint, Cast Iron, Hubley, 11 In. .................................................... | 210 |
| **Fire Station,** Wood, Cast Iron, Pumper Wagon, Driver, Horses, Clockwork, Ives, 1890s, 16 In. .... | 5700 |
| **Fire Steamer,** Tin Lithograph, Driver, Penny, Germany, 3 In.................................................. | 330 |
| **Fire Truck,** Aerial Ladder, Painted Red, Buddy L, c.1930, 39 In. ........................................... | 480 |
| **Fire Truck,** Driver, Tin Lithograph, Windup, Germany, 8 In. ................................................. | 84 |
| **Fire Truck,** Hose, Reel, 2 Firemen Pulled, Dog, Painted, Tin, George Brown, c.1870, 9 ½ In....... | 5700 |
| **Fire Truck,** Ladder, 3 Firemen, Ladder Extends, Schuco, Box, 18 In. ...................................... | 2124 |
| **Fire Truck,** Ladder, 6 Firemen, Tin Lithograph, Windup, Germany, c.1935, 13 In. .................... | 240 |
| **Fire Truck,** Ladder, L.A.F.D., Red Paint, Pressed Steel, Smith-Miller, 27 In............................. | 720 |
| **Fire Truck,** Ladder, Pressed Steel, Buddy L, 39 In. ............................................................ | 480 |
| **Fire Truck,** Painted Red, Cast Iron, White Rubber Wheels, 6 ½ In. ....................................... | 69 |
| **Fire Truck,** Water Tower, Pressed Steel, Sturditoy, 33 ½ In................................................... | 2040 |
| **Fire Truck,** Water Tower, Red, Pressed Steel, American LaFrance, Sturditoy, 34 In. ................... | 1200 |
| **Fire Wagon,** 2 Horses, 7 Firemen, Platform, Paint, Cast Iron, c.1895, 20 In............................. | 1320 |
| **Fire Wagon,** 2 Horses, Driver, Embossed Chemical, Paint, Cast Iron, Ives.c.1912, 22 In............. | 12000 |
| **Fire Wagon,** 3 Horses, Hose Reel, Driver, Red, Yellow Paint, Cast Iron, Kenton, 13 In............... | 450 |
| **Fire Wagon,** Hook & Ladder, 3 Horses, Cast Iron, Painted, Red, Gold Highlights, 19 In.............. | 35 |
| **Fire Wagon,** Hook & Ladder, Fireman, Embossed Eagle, Paint, Cast Iron, Hubley, 33 In............. | 1440 |
| **Fire Wagon,** Hook & Ladder, Horses, Articulating, Gong Bell, Hubley, c.1910, 24 In. ................ | 825 |
| **Fire Wagon,** Horse Drawn, Driver, Hose Reel, Cast Iron, 16 In. ............................................. | 390 |
| **Fire Wagon,** Horse Drawn, Driver, Hose, Reel, Paint, Cast Iron, Pratt & Letchworth, 14 In.......... | 900 |
| **Fire Wagon,** Ladder, 2 Firemen, Meier, 3 ½ In................................................................... | 531 |
| **Fire Wagon,** Ladder, 2 Horses, Drivers, Paint, Cast Iron, Ideal, 26 In. .................................... | 720 |
| **Fire Wagon,** Ladder, 3 Horses, 2 Ladders, Painted, Cast Iron, Kenton, 16 In............................ | 132 |
| **Fire Wagon,** Ladder, 3 Horses, Pressed Steel, Cast Iron, 2 Firemen, 3 Ladders, Wilkins, 27 In...... | 472 |
| **Fire Wagon,** Ladder, Clockwork, Germany, c.1930, 9 ½ In. .................................................. | 295 |
| **Fire Wagon,** Open Truck, 4 Firemen, Windup, Mettoy, England, Box, 14 ½ In. ......................... | 1770 |
| **Fire Wagon,** Patrol, Cast Iron, Gold Letters, 2 Galloping Horses, 7 Men, Hubley, 19 In............. | 944 |
| **Fire Wagon,** Pumper, 2 Horses, 2 Men, Bell, Cast Iron, Dent, 20 In....................................... | 330 |
| **Fire Wagon,** Pumper, 2 Horses, 2 Men, Cast Iron, Painted, Hubley, 20 In. ............................. | 303 |
| **Fire Wagon,** Pumper, 3 Horses, Painted Cast Iron, Kenton, 13 In. ........................................ | 154 |
| **Fire Wagon,** Pumper, Deluxe, Cast Iron, Red, Fireman, 2 Black Horses, Wilkins, 21 In.............. | 826 |
| **Fire Wagon,** Pumper, Horse Drawn, Cast Iron, Driver, Cast Iron, 21 In. ................................. | 540 |
| **Fire Wagon,** Pumper, Steam, Paint, Copper Finish, Cast Iron, Union, 1880s, 12 In. ................. | 2040 |
| **Fireman,** Climbing Ladder, Tin Lithograph, Windup, Louis Marx, 22-In. Ladder ...................... | 288 |
| **Flashlight Target Gun,** Astro Ray, Darts, Planets Target, Plastic, Ohio Art Co., Box, 1960s......... | 115 |
| **Flintstones,** Dino On Tricycle, Windup, Linemar, Box 4 In. .................................................. | 236 |
| **Flintstones,** Fred, Bedrock Band, Brass Drum Set, Cymbals, Box, 9 In. .................................. | 246 |
| **Flintstones,** Wilma, Celluloid, Tin, Windup, Marx, 3 ½ In. .................................................. | 120 |
| **Flintstones,** Wilma, On Tricycle, Tin, Celluloid, Clockwork, Marx, Box, 4 In.......................*illus* | 236 |
| **Flying Circus,** Elephant Base, Clown, Airplane, Tin Litho, Windup, Unique Art, 10 ½ In............ | 300 |
| **Football Player,** Running, Ball, Helmet, Celluloid, Windup, Marked Japan, c.1935, 8 In. ........... | 1920 |
| **Football Player,** Touchdown Pete, Ball In Hand, Tin Litho, Windup, Linemar, Box, 5 ¾ In........ | 443 |
| **Fort,** 3 Tiers, Revolving Platform, German, Marklin, 21 In. .................................................. | 5036 |
| **Foxy Grandpa Flip,** Cast Iron, Painted, Hat Flips Onto Head, Ives Blakeslee, 4 In..................... | 177 |
| **Frankenstein,** Mod Monster, Blushing, Tin Litho, Vinyl, Cloth, Battery, Japan, 1960s, 13 In........ | 180 |
| **Frankenstein,** Tin Litho, Vinyl, Remote Control, Battery Operated, Marx, 1963, 13 In. .......*illus* | 835 |

**Toy,** Panel Van, Yellow Cab, Orange, Black Roof, Spare Tire, Cast Iron, Arcade, 8 In.
$2,950

Bertoia Auctions

**Toy,** Pedal Car, Airplane, Air Knight, Red & White, 1930s
$2,750

Grogan & Company

**Toy,** Pedal Car, Buick, Luggage Rack, Tonneau Cover, Restored, Steelcraft, c.1930s, 48 In.
$4,480

Mosby Auctions

**Toy,** Pedal Car, Chrysler, Airflow, Pressed Steel, Blue, Bulb Horn, Starcraft, 1930s
$1,800

DuMouchelles Art Gallery

T

**TIP**

*Reproduction cast-iron toys and banks are heavier and thicker than the originals.*

**Toy,** Pedal Car, Fire Chief, Red Paint, Disc Wheels, Pressed Steel, Gendron, 1920s, 44 In.
$1,416

Bertoia Auctions

**Toy,** Pedal Car, Kidillac, No Top, Red & Black
$1,300

Grogan & Company

**Toy,** Pedal Car, Mogul, Pressed Steel, Spoke Wheels, American National, 1920s, 48 In.
$1,652

Bertoia Auctions

**Toy,** Pip-Squeak, Woman, Crouched Position, Papier-Mache, Germany, c.1890, 5 In.
$246

Garth's Auctioneers & Appraisers

| | |
|---|---|
| **Fuhrer Wagon,** Hitler Figure, Tin Lithograph, Clockwork, Tipp & Co., 9 In. | 632 |
| **G.I. Joe,** Adventurer, Camo Fatigues, Brown Life-Like Hair, Beard, Hasbro, Box, 1970, 12 In.*illus* | 127 |
| **G.I. Joe,** K-9 Pups, Soldier, Carrying Dog Plaques, Tin Litho, Windup, Unique Art, Box, 9 In. | 270 |
| **G.I. Joe,** Tin, Windup, Unique Art, Windup, 1950s, 9 In. | 295 |
| **Games** are listed in the Game category. | |
| **Garage,** Lift, Clockwork, 2 Cars, Box, Technofix, Germany, Box, 10 x 14 In. | 148 |
| **Gas Pump,** Yellow, Stamped Arcade Gas, Dial Meter, Cast Iron, Decal, Arcade, 6 In.*illus* | 472 |
| **Gentleman Rider,** Platform, Brown Horse, Green, Tin, Pull Toy, G. Brown, 1890s, 14 In. | 2040 |
| **Giraffe,** Studio, Steiff, 8 Ft. | 1541 |
| **Girl Jumping Rope,** Composition, Paint, Cloth Skirt, Blouse, Wire Swing, Clockwork, 11 In. | 266 |
| **Girl,** 2 Bears, Bell, Platform, Paint, Tin, Merriam, 1890s, 6½ In. | 1440 |
| **Girl,** Feeding Chicken, Pecking At Apron, Mechanical, Penny, Meier, 3¾ In. | 480 |
| **Girl,** Goat Pulling Cart, Bell Toy, Paint, Tin, Clockwork, Althof Bergmann, c.1875, 16 In. | 14400 |
| **Girl,** Riding Side Saddle, White Horse, Platform, Paint, Tin, G. Brown, 8 In. | 1200 |
| **Gnome,** On Egg, Hidden Bunny, Tin Lithograph, Lever, Penny, Meier, 3 In. | 1020 |
| **Gnomes,** Sawing Wood, Tin Lithograph, Fischer, 4 In. | 480 |
| **Goat & Boy,** Bell Toy, Platform, Paint, Tin, Althof Bergmann, 9 In. | 2400 |
| **Goat,** Platform, Cream, Red, Green Paint, Wood, Pull, Walter Gottshall, 1981, 7 x 9 In. | 108 |
| **Gong Bell,** Eagle, Platform, Paint, Cast Iron, Pull Toy, 5¾ In. | 1920 |
| **Graf Zeppelin Jr.,** Embossed, Silver Body, Metal Prop, Gondola, Clockwork, Strauss, Box, 9 In. | 296 |
| **Grandpa Bell,** Pulled By 2 Children On Bikes, Paint, Cast Iron, Watrous, Kenton, 6¼ In. | 1320 |
| **Granny Doodle,** Makes Sound When Pulled, Pull Toy, Fisher-Price, c.1933, 9½ In. | 354 |
| **Grasshopper,** Green Paint, Rubber Tires, Cast Iron, Aluminum, Pull Toy, Hubley, 10 In.*illus* | 384 |
| **Grasshopper,** Iron, Aluminum Legs, Green, Rubber Tires, Articulated, Pull, Hubley, 10 In. | 502 |
| **Great Garloo,** Remote Control, Hard Plastic, Battery Operated, Marx, 1960s, 22 In.*illus* | 417 |
| **Gun & Holster Set,** Wyatt Earp, Leather Belt, 2 Guns, 12 Bullets, Box, 1950s, 12 x 14 In. | 321 |
| **Gun & Holster Set,** Wyatt Earp, Leather Belt, 2 Guns, 1950s, 12 x 14 In. | 172 |
| **Gymnast,** Full Figure, Wire Bars, Celluloid, Painted, CK, Japan, Prewar, 9¼ In. | 295 |
| **Ham 'N Sam,** Minstrel Band, Piano Player, Dancer, Tin Litho, Windup, Linemar, 1950s, 5 x 7 In. | 1003 |
| **Hansom Cab,** Horse Drawn, Driver, Painted Cast Iron, Hubley, 9¼ In. | 137 |
| **Hansom Cab,** Horse, Wheeled, Paint, Glass, Tin, Cast Iron, Marklin, 28 In. | 13200 |
| **Harold Lloyd,** Walker, Funny Face, Windup, Marx, 11 In. | 290 |
| **Helicopter,** Hiller, Metal, Plastic, Blue, White, Tootsietoy, 3¾ In. | 180 |
| **Helicopter,** Sikorsky, Metal, Plastic Rotors, Red, White, Tootsietoy, 3 In. | 125 |
| **High Chair,** Converts To Table, Baby, Yellow, Penny Toy, Meier, Germany, 2¾ In. | 177 |
| **High Chair,** Doll's, Maple, Faux Bamboo Style, Woven Rush Seat, France, 18 In. | 280 |
| **Hobbyhorse,** Carved, Black, White, Red Paint, c.1905, 35 In. | 62 |
| **Hobbyhorse,** Carved, Red, White Paint, c.1905, 26 x 32 In. | 400 |
| **Hobbyhorse,** Mobo Bronco, It Steers!, Metal, Painted, D. Sebel & Co., England, 1940s | 106 |
| **Hobbyhorse,** Red, Green, White Paint, Wood, Metal Stirrups, c.1800, 43 x 35 In. | 556 |
| **Hobbyhorse,** Running, Dappled Gray, Glass Eyes, Hair Mane & Tail, Leather, Cloth, 36 In. | 1320 |
| **Hopewell Flyer Roundabout,** 2 Zeppelins, Tin Litho, Spins, Tripod Base, Hoproco, 14 x 15 In. | 1003 |
| **Horse & Carriage,** 1 Horse, Green Carriage, Fischer, Germany, Penny Toy, 4¾ In. | 826 |
| **Horse & Cart,** Coal, Red Paint, Japanned Finish, Cast Iron, Kyser & Rex, 10 In. | 420 |
| **Horse & Plow,** Driver, Paint, Cast Iron, Lever, Farm Series, Wilkins, 10½ In. | 5100 |
| **Horse & Rider,** Tin, Curved Rod, Embossed Wheels, Flange Base, Balance, 1880s, 14 In. | 8260 |
| **Horse & Wagon,** 2 Horses, Driver, Multicolor Paint, Cast Iron, Kenton, 15 In. | 120 |
| **Horse & Wagon,** City Sprinkler, Cast Iron, Painted, Hubley | 193 |
| **Horse & Wagon,** Coal, Black Horse, Driver, 1880s, 12½ In. | 950 |
| **Horse & Wagon,** Coal, Driver, Painted Cast Iron, Kenton, No. 143 | 66 |
| **Horse & Wagon,** Dairy, Tin Lithograph, Painted, 13 In. | 148 |
| **Horse & Wagon,** Dray, 2 Horses, Driver, Cast Iron, Painted, Kenton, 14½ In. | 44 |
| **Horse & Wagon,** Driver, Groceries & Provisions, Paint, Tin, George Brown, 1890s, 22 In. | 960 |
| **Horse & Wagon,** Driver, Horse, Red, Yellow Paint, Cast Iron, c.1900, 11 In. | 240 |
| **Horse & Wagon,** Driver, Open Bed, Transfer On Side, Painted, Cast Iron, 17 In. | 720 |
| **Horse & Wagon,** Ice, Horses, Driver, Cast Iron, Green, Gold Letters, Red Wheels, Hubley | 248 |
| **Horse & Wagon,** Sand & Gravel, 2 Horses, Driver, Cast Iron, Painted, Kenton, 9¾ In. | 55 |
| **Horse & Wagon,** Seated Driver, Green, Penny Toy, Fischer, 4¾ In. | 649 |
| **Horse & Wagon,** Stake, Driver, Painted Cast Iron, Kenton, Box, 11 In. | 110 |
| **Horse & Wagon,** Tetter, Driver, Paint, Cast Iron, Wilkens, 9 In. | 15600 |
| **Horse & Wagon,** Transfer, Cast Iron, Embossed, Painted, Dent, 17 In.*illus* | 720 |
| **Horse Stable,** 2 Story, Stalls, Wood, Paper Litho, Gottschalk, Germany, 18 x 19 In.*illus* | 413 |
| **Horse,** Composition, Platform, Wheels, Push Handle, 19 x 17 In. | 293 |
| **Horse,** Equestrian, Monkey, Small Horse, Bell, Platform, Paint, Tin, Pull Toy, c.1900, 11 In. | 5400 |
| **Horse,** Felt, Black, Leather Saddle, Reins, Pull Toy, c.1890, 29 x 32 In. | 270 |
| **Horse,** Gliding, Wood, Leather Ears & Saddle, Canvas Reins, 27 x 33 In. | 300 |

| | | |
|---|---|---|
| **Horse,** Gliding, Wood, Paint, Leather & Corduroy Saddle, Reins, 1800s, 32 x 38 In...... | | 523 |
| **Horse,** Jumping, Wood, Metal, Mojo, c.1950, 20½ In....... | | 24 |
| **Horse,** Pedal, Hide, Saddle, Head Turns, Wood Base, Wheels, Metal Stirrup Pedals, 40 In. | | 443 |
| **Horse,** Platform, Leather Saddle, Cloth Body, Pull, Germany, c.1900, 18 x 17½ In..... | | 369 |
| **Horse,** Platform, Wood, String Mane, Yarn Tail, Handle, Push, c.1930, 19 x 21 In....... | | 219 |
| **Horse,** Rocking, Art Moderne, 1940s ..... | | 30 |
| **Horse,** Rocking, Carved, Painted, Wood, c.1920, 29 x 54 In........ | | 69 |
| **Horse,** Rocking, Carved, Wing Pedestal, Painted Brown, Red Saddle, Victorian, 1800s ..... | | 173 |
| **Horse,** Rocking, Pine, Bench Seat, Green & White Paint, c.1890, 41 In. .................*illus* | | 480 |
| **Horse,** Rocking, Pine, Red & White Paint, Horsehair Mane & Tail, 59 In. ..... | | 120 |
| **Horse,** Rocking, Platform, Hair Mane, Saddle, Blanket, Iron Mounts, Paint, c.1910, 37 x 44 In.. | | 288 |
| **Horse,** Rocking, Swinging, Wood, Iron, Composition, Whitney Reed, c.1920, 46 In. ...... | | 590 |
| **Horse,** Rocking, Wood, Carved, White, Black, Green Paint, 1800s, 28 In. ..... | | 523 |
| **Horse,** Rocking, Wood, Dapple Gray, Galloping, Bow Runners, 54 x 32 In..... | | 1298 |
| **Horse,** Rocking, Wood, Gray, White, Red, Hair Tail, Leather Saddle, Bridle, 1800s, 25 x 32 In...... | | 480 |
| **Horse,** Rocking, Wood, Stylized, Racing Pose, Painted, c.1880, 42 In. ..... | | 616 |
| **Horse,** Running, Hollow Body, Iron, c.1950, 22 x 40 In..... | | 489 |
| **Horse,** Trotting, Tin, Wheeled Platform, George Brown, Pull Toy, 9 In. ..... | | 729 |
| **Horse,** Walking, 3-Wheel, Brown Paint, Cast Iron, Ives, c.1890, 7 In. ..... | | 3000 |
| **Horse,** Walking, Carved, Leather Reins, White, Gray Paint, Wheeled Platform, 27 x 24 In. ..... | | 480 |
| **Horse,** Wheeled Platform, Dexter, Painted, Tan, Red, Black, G. Brown, 1880s, 9 In. ..........*illus* | | 648 |
| **Horse,** White, In Blue Hoop, Paint, Tin, 7⅝ In..... | | 2700 |
| **Horse,** Wood, Carved, Fleece, Glass Eyes, Platform, Cast Wheels, Pull, Germany, 12 In..... | | 280 |
| **Horse,** Wood, White, Black Paint, Wheel Platform, Pull Toy, England, 13¼ In..... | | 210 |
| **Hot Air Balloon,** Tin Lithograph, String Slide, Penny, Meier, 4¼ In..... | | 1080 |
| **Housemaid,** Busy Lizzie, Sweeps, Tin Lithograph, Felt Sweeper, Clockwork, 7 In...... | | 443 |
| **Humphrey Mobile,** Outhouse On Wheels, Humphrey On Tricycle, Clockwork, Wyandotte, 8 In. | | 236 |
| **Humphrey Mobile,** Plastic Chimney, Tin Lithograph, Wyandotte, 7 In..... | | 180 |
| **Ice Cream Cart,** Driver, Tin, Friction, Japan, 1950s, 5½ In..... | | 345 |
| **Irish Mail,** 2 Riders, Tin Lithograph, Penny, Kellermann, 4¼ In..... | | 960 |
| **Jack-In-The-Box,** Black Child, Watermelon Base, Papier-Mache, Wood, 5 In..... | | 540 |
| **Jack-In-The-Box,** Clown, Composition, Wood Box, Kids Playing, c.1900, 4 x 4 In..... | | 180 |
| **Jack-In-The-Box,** Happy Hooligan, Composition, Paper Litho, Wood, Germany, 3½ In. ......*illus* | | 266 |
| **Jazzbo Jim & Fiddler,** Tin Lithograph, Clockwork, Unique Art, 10 In..... | | 384 |
| **Jazzbo Jim,** Dances On Roof, Tin Lithograph, Clockwork, Unique Art, 10 In................... | 384 to 590 | |
| **Jazzbo Jim,** Dances On Roof, Tin Lithograph, Windup, Strauss, 10 In. ..... | | 300 |
| **Jazzbo Jim,** Dances On Roof, Tin Lithograph, Windup, Strauss, Box, 10 In..... | | 354 |
| **Jeep,** Jumpin', 4 Yellow Helmeted Riders, Tin Lithograph, Windup, Marx, Box, 6 In...... | | 270 |
| **Jeep,** M.P., Friction, Bright Lithograph Japan, 1960s, 9½ In..... | | 75 |
| **Jeepster,** Convertible, Cast Aluminum, Al-Toy, 15½ In..... | | 780 |
| **Jockey,** On Goat, Tin Plate, Platform, Wheels, Painted, Pull Toy, 9 x 8½ In..... | | 850 |
| **Jockey,** Rocking Horse, Tin Lithograph, Penny, Meier, 3¾ In..... | | 1080 |
| **Jockeys,** Horses, Pole, Wire Spiral, Cast Iron, Gravity, c.1900, 14 In..... | | 600 |
| **Joe Penner & His Duck,** Tips Hat, Tin Lithograph, Clockwork, Louis Marx, 8½ In..... | | 531 |
| **Joy Rider,** Boy Driving Convertible, Back Trunk, Suitcase, Tin Lithograph, Marx, 8 In. ..... | | 150 |
| **Jumping Jack,** Frog Head, Wood, Carved, Composition, Suit, Articulated, Pull String, 11 In. ...... | | 649 |
| **Kaleidoscope,** Brass, Table Top, Round Wood Base, Inscribed Van Cort, c.1890, 14 In..... | | 554 |
| **Kangaroo,** Glass Eyes, Wood, Jointed, Balanced On Tail, Leather Ears, Schoenhut, 7 x 8 In. ...... | | 944 |
| **Leopard,** Walking, Platform, Tin Lithograph, Penny, Distler, 3¾ In. ..... | | 1440 |
| **Li'l Abner Dogpatch Band,** 4 Characters, Tin Litho, Painted, Unique Art, 1945, 8 x 9 In. ..... | | 767 |
| **Li'l Abner Dogpatch Band,** Tin Lithograph, Unique Art, c.1945, 10 x 8 In. ......................*illus* | | 210 |
| **Limousine,** Chauffeur, Moving Pistons, Tin Lithograph, Windup, Moko, 8½ In..... | | 1458 |
| **Limousine,** Chauffeur, Windup, William Rissman, Germany, Box, c.1920, 9½ In..... | | 3555 |
| **Limousine,** Luggage Rack, Red, Doors Open, Chauffer, Tin Tires, Carette, 9 In..... | | 1659 |
| **Limousine,** Rubber Tires, Luggage Rack, Clockwork, Blue Roof, Carette, 12 In..... | | 4252 |
| **Lincoln Tunnel,** Tin Lithograph, Clockwork, Unique Art, 24 In..... | | 325 |
| **Lincoln Tunnel,** Tunnels, 6 Vehicles, Policeman, Tin Litho, Windup, Unique Art, 24 In. ..... | | 210 |
| **Little Housekeeper,** Young Girl, Rolling Pin, Paper Over Wood, Lever Turns, 12 In. ..........*illus* | | 266 |
| **Log Cabin,** 2 Story, Pitched Roof, Chimney, Windows, D. Johnson, Maryland, 21 x 19 In..... | | 320 |
| **Log Wagon,** Plantation Worker Driver, Log, Cast Iron, Yellow Spoke Wheels, Kenton, 15 In. ...... | | 531 |
| **Maggie & Jiggs,** Bringing Up Father, Cigar, Rolling Pin, Books, Schoenhut, 7 To 9 In.................. | | 443 |
| **Maggie & Jiggs,** Fighting, 2 2-Wheel Carts, Lithograph, Fischer, 8 In. ..... | | 924 |
| **Main Street Bridge,** Buildings, Trolleys, Policeman, Tin Litho, Windup, Marx, Box, 24 In. ...... | | 300 |
| **Main Street Bridge,** Clockwork, Traffic Cop, Trestles, Tin Lithograph, Marx, Box, 24 In............ | | 207 |
| **Mama Katzenjammer,** Spanking, Paint, Cast Iron, Kenton, 4 In....... | | 185 |

**Toy,** Record Player, Rootie Kazootie Fono-Rootie, Symphonic Radio & Electronic, 1950s, 10 x 12 In.
**$285**

**Toy,** Ring, Crackle, Rice Krispies, Movable Face, Rubber, Kellogg's Premium, 1952, 3 In.
**$115**

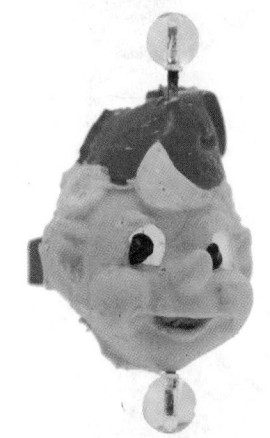

**Toy,** Robot, Mr. Machine, Plastic, Metal Bell, Arms Move, Sounds, Ideal, Box, 1960, 18 In.
**$260**

**Toy,** Roly Poly, Dutch Girl, Papier-Mache, Composition, Movable Head, Schoenhut, 14½ In.
$1,541

James D. Julia Auctioneers

**Toy,** Sand Loader, Pressed Steel, Upright Model, Chained Buckets, Keystone, 1920s, 18 In.
$1,481

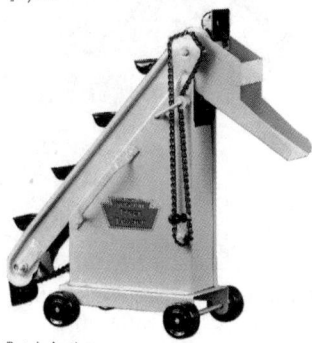

Bertoia Auctions

**Toy,** Scooter, Kick 'n Go, 3 Wheels, Hand Brake, Rubber Tires, Honda, c.1976, 33 x 34 In.
$90

Morphy Auctions

| | |
|---|---:|
| **Mammy's Boy,** Black Man Dancing, Face Moves, Tin, Windup, Marx, 11 x 5 In. | 426 |
| **Man With Duck,** Hat Falling Off, Tin Lithograph, Windup, Marx, 8 In. | 390 |
| **Man,** Playing Harpsichord, On Drum, Celluloid Head, Clockwork, Gunthermann, 12 In. | 1888 |
| **Marchers,** Rifles, Flags, Bell, Paint, Tin, Clockwork, A. Bergmann, c.1874, 9 In. | 18000 |
| **Marionettes,** 2 Minstrels, Sing A Good Old Ragtime Song, Lucite Case, Orlando, 25 x 22 In. | 177 |
| **Mary & Her Little Lamb,** Celluloid, Tin Wheel Platform, Windup, Japan, Box, 6½ In. ........*illus* | 295 |
| **Max & Moritz,** Pig, Wheel Barrow, Wood, Jointed, Cloth & Leather, Schoenhut, 8 In. | 708 |
| **May Queen,** Swan, Cart, Umbrella, Paint, Cast Iron, U.S. Hardware, 7 In. | 600 |
| **Merry-Go-Round,** 4 Horses, Calliope Decoration, Tin, Windup, Chein, 10 x 11 In. | 291 |
| **Merry-Go-Round,** 6 Bucket Carts, Tin Lithograph, Chain Driven, Lever, 16½ In. | 476 |
| **Merry-Go-Round,** Play Land, Tin Lithograph, Chein, 9½ x 11¼ In. | 246 |
| **Merry-Go-Round,** Ride-A-Rocket, Tin, Windup, Chein, 18 In. | 246 |
| **Merry-Go-Round,** Tin Lithograph, Chein & Co., 9¾ x 11⅛ In. | 472 |
| **Merrymakers Band,** Mice, Instruments, Conductor, Windup, Marx, Box, 9 x 8 In. | 885 to 1298 |
| **Military Figure On Horse,** Nazi Flag, Swastikas, Windup, B&S, 1930s-40s, 5¼ In. | 3555 |
| **Milton,** In Car, Red Plastic Hat, Tin Lithograph, Windup, Marx, 5½ In. | 180 |
| **Minstrel,** Mechanical, Tin Lithograph, Saalheimer & Strauss, c.1930, 7 In. | 780 |
| **Model Kit,** Car, Lincoln Convertible, Model 1574, Black, Red, White Top, 1941, 35 In. | 3198 |
| **Monkey Bass Player,** Tin, Painted, Windup, Germany, 8¾ In. ........*illus* | 336 |
| **Monkey,** Climbing On String, Tin Litho, Green Jacket, Red Hat, Box, Lehmann, 8 In. | 118 |
| **Monkey,** Climbing Pole, String, Tin Lithograph, Penny, Distler, Germany, 6¾ In. | 240 |
| **Monkey,** On Horse, Platform, Paint, Tin, George Brown, 9 In. | 3900 |
| **Monkey,** Playing Cymbal, Japan, 1950s | 50 |
| **Moon Patrol,** Remote Control, Battery Operated, Gakkaen, Japan, Box, 12 In. | 510 |
| **Mother Goose,** Walker, Cat Riding, Marx, Box, 8¾ In. | 649 |
| **Motorboat,** Pilot Waves, Paint, Cast Iron, Static, Hubley, c.1929, 9½ In. | 5400 |
| **Motorcycle,** Champion, Sidecar, Rider, Cast Iron, Blue, Red, Rubber Wheels, 4 In. | 94 |
| **Motorcycle,** Dismounting Policeman, Battery, Modern Toys, 11½ In. | 443 |
| **Motorcycle,** Driver, Tin Lithograph, Windup, Technofix, U.S. Zone, Germany, Box, 7 In. | 540 |
| **Motorcycle,** Harley-Davidson, Driver, Iron, Green Paint, Nickel Spoke Wheels, Hubley, 6 In. | 502 |
| **Motorcycle,** Hillclimber, No. 2, Cast Iron, Drier, Rubber Tires, Hubley, 1930s, 6½ In. | 360 |
| **Motorcycle,** Police Dept., Driver, 3 Wheels, Tin Crank, Japan, 1950s, 6½ In. | 295 |
| **Motorcycle,** Rookie Cop, Tin Lithograph, Red, Yellow, Windup, Marx, 5 x 8 x 2 In. | 517 |
| **Motorcycle,** Sidecar, Cast Iron, 2 Cylinder Engine, Driver, Hubley, 8½ In. | 443 |
| **Motorcycle,** Speed Boy Delivery, Electric Light, Stake-Sided Wagon, 10 In. | 295 |
| **Motorcycle,** Tricky Motorcycle, Policeman Driver, Tin, Louis Marx, Box, 4¼ In. | 140 |
| **Mr. Fox The Magician,** Disappearing Rabbit, Cape, Tin, Battery, Cragstan, Japan, Box, 10 In. | 570 |
| **Musical Figures,** Playing Drum, Trumpet, Violin, Horn, Crank. | 944 |
| **Musicians,** On Stage, Violinist, Bass Player, Harp Player, Plinking Sound, Einfalt, 9 In. | 1180 |
| **Mystery Ball,** Fernand Martin, Spiral Action, Tin Lithograph, France, 14½ In. ........*illus* | 649 |
| **New York Skyline,** Tin Lithograph, Windup, Marx, 10 In. | 300 |
| **Nite Coach,** Pickwick, Iron, Blue Body, Orange Side Stripe, Embossed, Kenton, 1930s, 7 In. | 1062 |
| **Oarsman,** Boat, Cloth Outfit, Paint, Tin, Clockwork, Ives, c.1870, 10¾ In. | 4500 |
| **Omnibus,** Horses, Driver, Paint, Tin, Althof Bergmann, 17 In. | 3300 |
| **Paddlewheel,** Adirondack, Iron, White, Red Trim, Yellow Deck, Articulated, Wilkins, 14 In. | 236 |
| **Paddy,** Riding Pig, Tin, Windup, Lehmann, 1920s, 5½ In. | 1777 |
| **Pail,** Shovel, Carousel Decoration, Animals, Band Organ, Blue Inside, Converse, 3 x 5 In. | 314 |
| **Pail,** Tin Lithograph, Atlantic City, Eagle Image, Red, Blue, White, 6½ x 6½ In. | 540 |
| **Panel Van,** Yellow Cab, Orange, Black Roof, Spare Tire, Cast Iron, Arcade, 8 In. ........*illus* | 2950 |
| **Parrot,** On Stand, Wings Flap, Tin, Painted, Lithographed Tail, Windup, Gunthermann, 11 In. | 504 |
| **Parrot,** Pretty Peggy, Eyes Light-Up, Wings Flap, Squawks, Tin, Battery, Rosko, Japan, Box, 13 In. | 210 |
| **Peacock,** Standing, Paint, Tin, Windup, Hans Ebrle, 9½ In. | 338 |
| **Peacock,** Walker, Fan Opens, Multicolored, Tin, Windup, Japan, 7¼ In. | 112 |
| **Peacock,** Walker, Tin Lithograph, Embossed Tail, Clockwork, Germany, Ebo, 9¼ In. | 354 |
| **Pedal Car,** Airplane, Air Knight, Red & White, 1930s ........*illus* | 2750 |
| **Pedal Car,** Airplane, Pursuit, Metal, Rubber, Signed, Viktor Schreckengost, Murray, 40 In. | 748 |
| **Pedal Car,** AMF Firefighter, Bell, Red, Black Paint, c.1965, 42 In. | 62 |
| **Pedal Car,** Buick, Luggage Rack, Tonneau Cover, Restored, Steelcraft, c.1930s, 48 In. ........*illus* | 4480 |
| **Pedal Car,** Bumblebee, Train Car, Headlight & Bell, 39 In. | 300 |
| **Pedal Car,** Chrysler, Airflow, Pressed Steel, Blue, Bulb Horn, Starcraft, 1930s ........*illus* | 1800 |
| **Pedal Car,** Corvette, 1956, Green, White, Pedal Classics, 1980s, 50 In. | 2700 |
| **Pedal Car,** Fire Chief, Red Paint, Disc Wheels, Pressed Steel, Gendron, 1920s, 44 In. ........*illus* | 1416 |
| **Pedal Car,** Ford Street Rod, Gas Power, Inflated Tires, Red, White, 1932, 50 In. | 5100 |
| **Pedal Car,** Instep, Red, Metal, 21 x 15 x 36 In. | 330 |
| **Pedal Car,** Kidillac, No Top, Red & Black ........*illus* | 1300 |
| **Pedal Car,** Mogul, Pressed Steel, Spoke Wheels, American National, 1920s, 48 In. ........*illus* | 1652 |

| | | |
|---|---|---|
| **Pedal Car,** Oakland, Running Board, Lithograph, Green, Yellow, Gendron, 1930s, 38 In. | | 3259 |
| **Pedal Car,** Open, Red, Spoke Wheels, Wood Frame, Brighton Manufacturer, 1907, 45 In. | | 1440 |
| **Pedal Car,** Racer, Indy No. 5 Pennzoil, Gas, Belt Driven, Radio Controlled, 1970s, 43 In. | | 2280 |
| **Pedal Car,** Roadster, Tandem, American National, c.1933, 61 ½ In. | | 7840 |
| **Pedal Car,** Sports Car, Convertible, English Style, Red, 1970s, 48 In. | | 960 |
| **Pedal Car,** Steel, Wood, Painted, Wire Spoke Wheels, Rubber Tires, c.1915, 40 In. | | 826 |
| **Pedal Car,** Tow, Red, Wood Frame, 1930s, 58 In. | | 1680 |
| **Pedal Car,** Tractor, Green, Yellow, John Deere, 1950s, | | 210 |
| **Pedal Car,** Whippet, Iron Steering Wheel, Spoke Wheels, American National, c.1925, 32 In. | | 94 |
| **Peter Rabbit Car,** Peter, Plastic Ears, Hat, Ducklings, Carrot, Tin Litho, Windup, Marx, 8 In. | | 210 |
| **Pip-Squeak,** Woman, Crouched Position, Papier-Mache, Germany, c.1890, 5 In. | *illus* | 246 |
| **Playland Merry-Go-Round,** Carousel Figures, Tin Litho, Bell Sound, Windup, Chein, 10 In. | | 443 |
| **Playset,** Battle Of The Blue & Gray, Series 3000, Marx, Box, 29 x 15 In. | | 358 |
| **Playset,** Big Top Circus, Marx, Box, 28 x 11 ½ In. | | 672 |
| **Playset,** Fort Apache Stockade, Fort, Marx, Box, 22 x 12 In. | | 67 |
| **Playset,** Robin Hood Castle, Marx, Box, 26 x 11 In. | | 101 |
| **Playset,** Toy Town Railroad, Cardboard, Tin Lithograph, Figures, Parker Bros., 31 In. | | 1062 |
| **Plink-Plunk Dog House,** Dog Moves In & Out, Tin, Painted, Faux Grain Roof, Crank, 5 In. | | 531 |
| **Police Motorcycle,** Siren On Side, Tin Lithograph, Clockwork, Marx, Box, 8 ¼ In. | | 472 |
| **Police Wagon,** Horses, 4 Seated Policemen, Paint, Nickeled Iron, Schimer, c.1890, 21 In. | | 16800 |
| **Policeman,** Riding 3 Wheeler, Bell On Handlebars, Paint, Tin, Clockwork, 10 In. | | 15600 |
| **Policeman,** Standing, Lights Change, Arm Moves, Flic 4520, Clockwork, Schuco, 5 In. | | 384 |
| **Pony Blimp,** Cast Iron, Silver, Kenton, c.1930, 5 ¾ In. | | 50 |
| **Porky Pig,** Tipping Top Hat, Umbrella, Mechanical, Tin Litho, Louis Marx, 1939, 8 ½ In. | | 360 |
| **Porter,** Red Cap, Carrying Suitcases, Tin Lithograph, Windup, Marx, 8 ½ In. | | 210 to 354 |
| **Puppet Set,** Punch & Judy, Composition, Wood, Gesso, Cloth, 14-16 In. Each, 9 Piece | | 2950 |
| **Puppet Set,** Punch & Judy, Stage, Tin Lithograph, Lever, Penny, Meier, 3 ⅝ In. | | 3000 |
| **Puppet Stage,** Punch & Judy, Papier-Mache, Crane-Operated Curtain, Wood Puppets, 58 In. | | 3245 |
| **Push Cart,** Spoke Wheels, Hand Enameled, Marklin, Germany, 12 ¾ In. | | 3245 |
| **Rabbit,** Brown Mohair, Egg Shape Head, Glass Eyes, Embroidered Nose, Mouth, 1930s, 11 In. | | 504 |
| **Rabbit,** Couching, Velvet, Stuffed, Shoebutton Eyes, Ribbon With Bell, c.1900, 7 In. | | 280 |
| **Rabbit,** Munches Cloth Lettuce Leaf, Rocks, White Fur, Pink Glass Eyes, Decamps, 9 In. | | 590 |
| **Rabbit,** Standing, Slide Action, Tin Lithograph, Penny, Fischer, 1 ⅞ In. | | 720 |
| **Race Track,** 2 Cars, 20 Volt Drive, Tin Track Sections, Marklin, Germany, 47 x 96 In. | | 6490 |
| **Racing Scull,** 8-Man, Movable Rowers, Wheels, Iron, U.S. Hardware Co., 19 In. | | 9000 |
| **Range Rider,** Rider Lasso, Tin Lithograph, Marx, Box, 11 In. | | 210 |
| **Rap & Tap Boxers,** Fighting In Raised Ring, Tin Litho, Windup, Unique Art, 6 ½ In. | | 210 |
| **Rastos & Mother,** Push Cart, Bell, Paint, Cast Iron, c.1902, 7 ½ In. | | 3900 |
| **Rattle,** Wood, Bell, Doepke, 1957, 8 In. | | 35 |
| **Record Player,** Rootie Kazootie Fono-Rootie, Symphonic Radio & Electronic, 1950s, 10 x 12 In. | *illus* | 285 |
| **Rickshaw,** Masuyama, Woman In Kimono, Windup, Lehmann, Box, 7 ¼ In. | | 3087 |
| **Ride-A-Rocket,** Spaceships, Children, Celluloid Propellers, Tin Litho, Windup, Chein, 18 In. | | 472 |
| **Ring,** Crackle, Rice Krispies, Movable Face, Rubber, Kellogg's Premium, 1952, 3 In. | *illus* | 115 |
| **Ring-A-Ling Circus,** Ringmaster, Animals, Round, Tin Lithograph, Windup, Marx, 8 In. | | 270 |
| **Ring-A-Ling Circus,** Tin Lithograph, Clockwork, Elephant, Clown, Louis Marx, 7 In. | | 531 |
| **Ringmaster,** Wood Body, Jointed, Bisque Head, Felt Suit, Black Hat, Staff, Schoenhut, 7 In. | | 472 |
| **Robot,** Back & Forth Direction, Yonezawa, Japan, Box, 11 In. | | 3300 |
| **Robot,** Moon Creature, Antennae, Yellow White Stripes, Windup, Tin, Marx, c.1968, 6 In. | | 185 |
| **Robot,** Moon, Explorer, Battery Operated, Alps, Box, 15 In. | | 4500 |
| **Robot,** Mr. Machine, Plastic, Metal Bell, Arms Move, Sounds, Ideal, Box, 1960, 18 In. | *illus* | 260 |
| **Robot,** Planet, Black, Helmet, Nickel Grille, Windup, Yoshida, Japan, Box, 9 In. | | 502 |
| **Robot,** Smoking Spaceman, Battery Operated, Linemar, Japan, Box, 12 In. | | 780 |
| **Robot,** Sparky, Silver, Windup, KO, Box, 7 ½ In. | | 354 |
| **Rocker,** Doll's, Mixed Woods, Turned Posts, Woven Back, Seat, Pa., c.1920, 5 ½ In. | | 58 |
| **Rocket Fighter,** Pilot, Tin Lithograph, Windup, Marx, 12 In. | | 270 |
| **Rocket Fighter,** Seated Pilot, Holding Gun, Tin Litho, Side Fins, Windup, Marx, Box, 12 In. | | 767 |
| **Rocket Police Patrol,** Pilot, Gun, Tin Lithograph, Windup, Marx, 12 In. | | 330 |
| **Rocket Racer,** Driver, Multicolor Body, Tin Lithograph, Windup, Marx, 16 ½ In. | | 360 |
| **Rocket,** Sparkler, Tin Lithograph, Windup, Marx, Box, 12 In. | | 1920 |
| **Roller Coaster,** Tin Lithograph, Chein, Box, 19 ½ In. | | 168 |
| **Rolling Gondolas,** Hoop Frame, Vis-A-Vis Seats, Tin Litho Figures, Windup, Germany, 9 In. | | 443 |
| **Rollo Chair,** Riding On Boardwalk, Rolling Wicker Chair, Tin Litho, Strauss, 7 In. | | 885 |
| **Roly Poly,** Dutch Girl, Papier-Mache, Composition, Movable Head, Schoenhut, 14 ½ In. | *illus* | 1541 |
| **Room Box,** Bathroom, Wood, Tin Roof, Window, Wall Paper, Electric Lights, 11 x 17 In. | | 708 |
| **Roosters,** Fighting, Banded Platform, Tin Lithograph, Clockwork, Einfalt, 10 In. | | 502 |
| **Rowers,** Rowboat, Bisque Head Figures, Cloth Outfit, Wood, Painted, Clockwork | | 3835 |

**Toy,** Sleigh, 2 Horses, Seated Woman Rider, Green, Gold Highlights, Cast Iron, Hubley, 14 In.
$325

Bertoia Auctions

**Toy,** Smitty Scooter, Boy Rider, 3 Wheels, Windup, Marx, 8 In.
$851

James D. Julia Auctioneers

**Toy,** Speed King, Soap Box Derby, Boy On Soap Box Racer, Tin Litho, Wyandotte, 6 ¼ In.
$384

Bertoia Auctions

**TIP**
*Don't let plastic toys or dishes touch each other. Different types of plastic may react to each other and be damaged.*

**Toy,** Stove, Great Majestic Junior, Steel, Iron, Tin, Accessories, Salesman's Sample, 34 In.
$4,320

Pook & Pook, Inc.

**Toy,** Stove, J.H. Potthoff, Scrolling, Footed, 1878, 19 x 13 ½ In.
$600

Showtime Auction Services

**Toy,** Stove, Karr Range Co., Iron, Tin, Blue Mottled Enamel, Nickel Trim, 21 x 13 In.
$1,020

Pook & Pook, Inc.

| | |
|---|---:|
| **Sailboat,** Man, Platform, Tin Lithograph, Penny, Meier, 3 In. | 480 |
| **Sammy Wong The Tea Totaler,** Cloth Sammy, Pouring Tea, Rosko, Japan, Box, 10 ½ In. | 330 |
| **Sand Boat,** Tin Lithograph, Pull, Chein Co., c.1935, 8 ½ x 4 x 3 In. | 60 |
| **Sand Loader,** Driver, Red Paint, Cast Iron, Arcade, 8 ½ In. | 1080 |
| **Sand Loader,** Pressed Steel, Upright Model, Chained Buckets, Keystone, 1920s, 18 In. ........*illus* | 1481 |
| **Sand,** Hod Carrier, Ladder, Chute, Worker, Tin, Chein, Box, 10 ½ In. | 291 |
| **Scooter,** Baby Silver Pigeon, Driver, Rider On Back, Tin, Friction, Marusan, 5 ¼ In. | 616 |
| **Scooter,** Heavy Steel, Platform, Rubber Tires, Auto Wheel Coaster Co., c.1925, 32 x 36 In. | 35 |
| **Scooter,** Henley Roll About, 4 Wheels, Flat Platform, 27 x 34 In. | 176 |
| **Scooter,** Kick 'n Go, 3 Wheels, Hand Brake, Rubber Tires, Honda, c.1976, 33 x 34 In.........*illus* | 90 |
| **Scooter,** Pump Action, Wood Slat, Painted Red, 3 Red Wheels, c.1900, 39 x 33 In. | 82 |
| **Scooter,** Vespa G.S., Tin, Friction, Japan, 1950s, 9 In. | 245 |
| **Seal,** Tin Lithograph, Painted, Windup, Lehmann, Germany, 7 In. | 295 |
| **Seal,** Tin, Jointed Flippers, Bell, Lithograph, Windup, Lehmann, Germany, 7 ½ In. | 120 |
| **Secretary,** Doll's, Louis XVI Style, Bronze, Curved Front, Painted Scenes, France, 11 In. | 4480 |
| **Sedan Chair,** 2 Mandarin Men Carrying, Tin Lithograph, Clockwork, Lehmann, 7 In. | 1416 |
| **Seesaw,** Boy, Girl, Platform, Paint, Tin Strap, Cast Iron, Watrous, 9 In. | 900 |
| **Service Station,** Fuel Pumps, Folding Ramp, Tin Lithograph, Marx, 10 x 12 ½ In. | 649 |
| **Sewing Machine,** Footed, Black Metal, Singer, 7 In. | 31 to 60 |
| **Sewing Machine,** Singer, Metal, Inscribed Plate, Box, Booklet, c.1955, 6 x 7 In. | 84 |
| **Shop,** Butcher, Wood, Painted, Paper Litho, Butcher, Scale, Meats, Gottschalk, 1910, 13 In. | 944 |
| **Shop,** General Store, Wood, Paint, Sewing Notions, Hats, Fabric, Germany, c.1910, 15 In. | 1534 |
| **Shop,** Grocery, Wood, Open Front, Counter, Figures, Merchandise, Erzgebirge, 9 x 10 In. | 2655 |
| **Shop,** Grocery, Wood, Paint, Wall Paper, Scale, Bottles, Crockery, Foods, Germany, c.1910, 23 In. | 944 |
| **Shop,** Grocery, Wood, Paper Litho, Canisters, Barrels, Scale, C. Hacker, Germany, 16 In. | 2242 |
| **Shop,** Pastry, Wood, Paint, Drawers, Glass Case, Composition Goods, Germany, c.1920, 23 In. | 1121 |
| **Shop,** Silversmith, Wood, 9-Pane Window, Lights, 22 Silver Items, Kupjack, 12 x 18 In. | 1770 |
| **Ski Ride,** Sloped Trail, Skiers, Tin Lithograph, Painted, Clockwork, 10 ½ x 10 In. | 531 |
| **Skipping Couple,** Boy & Girl Skipping Rope, Celluloid, Metal, Occupied Japan, Box, 4 ¾ In. | 112 |
| **Sky Rangers,** Plane, Zeppelin, Tower, Tin Litho, Windup, S-R8, Unique Art, Tower, 9 In. | 360 |
| **Sled,** Aluminum, Steel, Vinyl, Blue, White, Art Deco 18 x 54 In. | 7320 |
| **Sled,** Doll's, Wood, Red, Flowers, Steel Runners, Marked Marguerite, Christmas 1897, 15 In. | 649 |
| **Sled,** Double Ripper, Wheels, 4 Children Riders, Brass, N.N. Hill Brass Co., 8 ½ In. | 4500 |
| **Sled,** Horse Head, Painted Church Seat, Yellow, Blue, 1800s, 34 In. | 560 |
| **Sled,** King Of The Hill, Wood, Painted Red, Embossed Stenciling, 32 In. | 86 |
| **Sled,** Pine, Sunflower Painted, Iron Runners, 1800s, 15 In. | 840 |
| **Sled,** Steering Wheel, Wood, Metal Runners, Early 20th Century, 38 In. | 117 |
| **Sled,** Wood, Cast Iron Swan's Neck Ends, Red, Black Paint, 1800s, 37 In. | 160 |
| **Sled,** Wood, Paint, Orange Runners, Handle, 47 In. | 153 |
| **Sled,** Wood, Red, Black, Cushion, Push Handle, 32 x 54 In. | 84 |
| **Sled,** Wood, Red, Navy Banding, c.1890, Child's, 38 In. | 246 |
| **Sled,** Wood, Upturned Runners, Painted Flowers, Victorian, 37 ½ In. | 246 |
| **Sled,** Wood, Wood Carved Runners, Painted, Stylized Tree, Red Ground, 1800s, 11 x 31 In. | 330 |
| **Sleigh,** 2 Horses, Bell, Platform, Paint, Cast Iron, Fallows, c.1880, 11 In. | 3900 |
| **Sleigh,** 2 Horses, Seated Woman Rider, Green, Gold Highlights, Cast Iron, Hubley, 14 In. ....*illus* | 325 |
| **Sleigh,** Cutter, Woman Driver, Cloth Hat, Coat, Paint, Cast Iron, Ives, c.1893, 19 ½ In. | 234000 |
| **Sleigh,** Eskimo Driver, Dog Pulling, Plastic, Lithograph, Battery, T.M., Japan, Box, 16 In. | 450 |
| **Sleigh,** Push, Upholstery, Red, Green Paint, Bentwood, Iron Runners, c.1895, 34 x 49 In. | 127 |
| **Sleigh,** Woman Driver, Black Paint, Cast Iron, Arcade, 13 In. | 600 |
| **Smitty Scooter,** Boy Rider, 3 Wheels, Windup, Marx, 8 In. ........*illus* | 851 |
| **Smoking Grandpa,** Man In Rocker, Red Shoes, Pipe, Tin, Batteries, Marusan, Box, 8 In. | 123 |
| **Soldier,** Indian, Crawling, Tin, Windup, USA Ohio Art, 1950s, 8 ½ In. | 145 |
| **Soldier,** World War I British, Bisque, Painted, Clothing, Gear, 13-In. Box, 10 Piece | 885 |
| **Soldier,** Zouave, 3-Wheel Platform, Blue Jacket, Red Pants, Boots, Rifle, Clockwork, 8 In. | 502 |
| **Soldiers,** Wood, Multicolor, Drummer, Flag Bearer, Erzgebirge, Germany, 6 In., 12 Piece | 1770 |
| **Space Rocket,** Yellow, Orange, Friction, Automatic Toy Company, Box, 8 ¾ In. | 660 |
| **Speed Boat,** Tin, Crank, Japan, 1950s, 9 ½ In. | 95 |
| **Speed King,** Soap Box Derby, Boy On Soap Box Racer, Tin Litho, Wyandotte, 6 ¼ In.........*illus* | 384 |
| **Spic & Span Band,** 2 Minstrels, Playing Cymbals & Drums, Fiddle, Tin Litho, Louis Marx, 10 In. | 1652 |
| **Stable,** Pine, Painted, 3 Stalls, 2 Story Enclosure With Doors, c.1900, 21 x 26 In. | 394 |
| **Steam Shovel & Trailer,** Green, Orange, Structo, c.1949, 30 In. | 235 |
| **Steam Shovel,** Blue Paint, Structo, 25 ½ In. | 40 |
| **Steam Shovel,** Green, Black, Red, Pressed Steel, Sturditoy, 1926, 21 In. | 240 |
| **Steam Shovel,** Panama, Red, Yellow Paint, Cast Iron, Hubley, 9 In. | 270 |
| **Steam Shovel,** Rubber Wheels, Blue, Red, Yellow, Wyandotte, c.1950, 20 In. | 105 |
| **Steam Tractor,** Brass, Wilesco, 7 ¾ x 11 In. | 246 |

| | |
|---|---|
| **Steamroller,** Red Paint, Pressed Steel, Keystone, 20 In. | 270 |
| **Steamroller,** Ride 'Em, Keystone, Pressed Steel, Red, Black, Bell, c.1929, 20 x 12 In. | 230 |
| **Steer,** Pine, Painted, Leather Wrapped Horns, Platform Base, 4 Wheels, Push Pull, 14 x 20 In. | 720 |
| **Stork,** Standing, Push Slide, Tin Lithograph, Penny, Fischer, Germany, 1⅞ In. | 480 |
| **Stove,** Cast Iron, Nickel, Brass, Copper Cookware, 10½ x 23 In. | 210 |
| **Stove,** Cooking Accessories, Mercury, Cast Iron, Nickel, 11½ x 11¼ In. | 240 |
| **Stove,** Detroit Stove Works, Cast Iron, Nickel, Tin, Jewel Range Jr., 16 x 18¼ In. | 1353 |
| **Stove,** Dolly's Favorite, Cast Iron, 6 Burners, Scrolling Backsplash, Shelf, Favorite, 22 In. | 570 |
| **Stove,** Engman-Matthews, Range Eternal, Cast Iron, Nickel, Tin, 30 x 25 In. | 1140 |
| **Stove,** Globe Range, Copper Flashed, Tin, Cast Iron, 17 x 22 In. | 660 |
| **Stove,** Great Majestic Junior, Steel, Iron, Tin, Accessories, Salesman's Sample, 34 In. ...........*illus* | 4320 |
| **Stove,** Ideal, Cook, Cast Iron, 13 x 18 In. | 480 |
| **Stove,** J.H. Potthoff, Scrolling, Footed, 1878, 19 x 13½ In. ......................................*illus* | 600 |
| **Stove,** Karr Range Co., Iron, Tin, Blue Mottled Enamel, Nickel Trim, 21 x 13 In....................*illus* | 1020 |
| **Stove,** Kenton, Marvel Range, Cast Iron, Nickel, 15½ x 19½ In. | 308 |
| **Stove,** Kenton, Painted Cast Iron, Nickel Plated, Fully Opening Doors, 11 In. ......*illus* | 413 |
| **Stove,** Kenton, Royal, Silver Paint, Cast Iron, 11½ x 14 In. | 123 |
| **Stove,** Kenton, Triumph, Tin, Nickel, Cast Iron, 15½ x 15½ In. | 246 |
| **Stove,** Leader Washington, Cast Iron, Nickel, Enamel, 29 x 21 In. | 1800 |
| **Stove,** Lionel, Electric, c.1930, 33½ x 25 In. .........................................*illus* | 2400 |
| **Stove,** Parlor, Steel, Enamel, 15 In. | 240 |
| **Stove,** Plymouth Rock, Cast Iron, G.F. Filley, Patented 1858, 7 x 7 In. | 360 |
| **Stove,** Pot Belly, Gray Iron, Inscribed Spark, Early 20th Century, 13¾ In. | 541 |
| **Stove,** Queen Stove, Cast Iron, Nickel, 19 x 20 In. | 240 |
| **Stove,** St. Clair, Cast Iron, Nickel, Tin, Enameled Paint, 29½ x 16 In. | 1140 |
| **Stove,** St. Nicholas Revin, Cast Iron, Enamel, 10¼ x 12 In. | 120 |
| **Stove,** Stella, Black Paint, Cast Iron, M. Greenwood, Dec. 25, 1870, 7½ x 7 In. | 360 |
| **Stove,** Sterling, Cast Iron, Nickel, Ideal, 12¼ x 13½ In. | 185 |
| **Stove,** Tettenborn & Co., Iron, 4 Burners, 2 Doors, Embossed Leaves, Cincinnati, 14 x 18 In. | 270 |
| **Stove,** Uncle Sam, Black, Cast Iron, Abendroth, 13 x 24½ In. | 180 |
| **Stove,** Washington Leader, Cast Iron, Nickel, Enamel, 28½ x 20½ In.............................*illus* | 1800 |
| **Stove,** Wetter Manufacturing Co., Cast Iron, Nickel, 17½ x 17¾ In.........................*illus* | 1200 |
| **Streamline Railway Car,** Tin Lithograph, Wood Wheels, Wolverine Supply Co., 18 In. | 36 |
| **Street Sweeper,** Schuco Piccolo, Metal, Painted Silver, Yellow, Black Tires, 2¼ In. | 35 |
| **Stroller,** Taylor Tot, Custom, Reclining Seat Back, Oak Arm Rests, Fenders, Restored | 280 |
| **Suffragette In Hoop,** Holding American Flag, Tin, Clockwork, Geo. Brown, c.1880, 10 x 8 In. | 36000 |
| **Suffragette,** 2 Horses, Flag, Platform, c.1910, 8½ In. | 2040 |
| **Suffragette,** Pushing Hoop, Bell, Platform, Paint, Tin, Geo. Brown, c.1875, 9½ In. | 6000 |
| **Sulky,** Horse, Driver, Cast Iron, Pratt & Letchworth | 275 |
| **Sulky,** Horse, Driver, Cast Iron, Silver & Yellow Paint, Kenton, 8½ In. | 55 |
| **Sulky,** Iron, Red Cart, Jockey, Embossed Seating, Spoke Wheels, Gold Trim, Pratt & Letchworth, 8 In. | 236 |
| **Sulky,** Jockey, Paint, Cast Iron, Clockwork, Hubley, 8½ In. | 1080 |
| **Sunny Side Service Station,** Tin Lithograph, Marx, 13½ In. | 270 |
| **Surfer Girl,** On Board, Rides Waves, Cast Iron, 3 Wheels, Pull Toy, Hubley, 7½ In. .............*illus* | 12000 |
| **Suzy Bouncing Ball,** Girl, Ponytail, Plaid Skirt, Tin, Windup, Box, 6 In. | 78 |
| **Swan,** Platform, Tin Lithograph, Penny, Meier, Germany, 3 In. | 600 |
| **Swings,** Man, Woman, In Gondola, Tin Lithograph, Penny, Meier, Germany, 3½ In. | 180 |
| **Tank,** M4 Sherman Combat, US Army, Battery, Taiyo, Box, 12½ x 6 x 7 In. | 90 |
| **Tank,** Metal, Windup, Marx, USA, Box, 10 In. | 295 |
| **Tank,** Sparkling Space, Driver, Tin Lithograph, Windup, Marx, Box, 10 In. | 300 |
| **Tap-Tap Man,** Pushing Wheelbarrow, Spoke Wheels, Tin Litho, Clockwork, Lehmann, 6 In. | 266 |
| **Taxi,** Amos 'N' Andy Fresh Air Taxicab, Driver, Dog, Passenger, Paint, Cast Iron, Dent, 7 In. | 523 |
| **Taxi,** Amos 'N' Andy, Cpt. Correll & Gosden, Orange, 8 In. | 948 |
| **Taxi,** Amos 'N' Andy, Fresh Air, Tin Lithograph, Dog, Louis Marx, Box, 8 In. | 502 |
| **Taxi,** Celluloid Windows, Embossed Seats, Spare Tire, Citroen, France, 20½ In. .................*illus* | 885 |
| **Taxi,** Chauffeur, Doors Open, Orange, Ormolu, G&K, 7 In. | 888 |
| **Taxi,** Check-A-Cab, Green, Checker Stripe, Disc Wheels, Tin Litho, Clockwork, Strauss, 8 In. | 767 |
| **Taxi,** Check-A-Cab, Orange, Checker Stripe, Disc Wheels, Clockwork, Strauss, 8 In. | 443 |
| **Taxi,** Gundka, Luggage Rack, Driver, Orange, Black, Windup, 7 In. | 708 |
| **Taxi,** Yellow Cab, Decal, Driver, White Rubber Tires, Luggage Rack, Hubley, c.1940, 8 In. | 266 |
| **Taxi,** Yellow Cab, Driver, Orange, Black, Disc Wheels, Cast Iron, Arcade, 7¾ In. ..................*illus* | 443 |
| **Taxi,** Yellow Cab, Tin Litho, Orange, Black, Lettering On Doors, Spare Wheel, Strauss, 8 In. | 325 |
| **Tea Set,** Porcelain, Court Scenes, Blue Border, Leather & Silk Box, 5-In. Teapot, 8 Piece | 1120 |
| **Tea Set,** Strawberry Shape, Porcelain, Germany, Child's, 4¼-In. Teapot, 3 Piece | 12 |
| **Teddy Bears** are also listed in the Teddy Bear category. | |

**Toy,** Stove, Kenton, Painted Cast Iron, Nickel Plated, Fully Opening Doors, 11 In.
$413

Bertoia Auctions

**Toy,** Stove, Lionel, Electric, c.1930, 33½ x 25 In.
$2,400

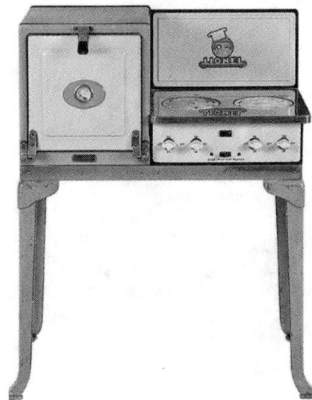

Pook & Pook, Inc.

**Toy,** Stove, Washington Leader, Cast Iron, Nickel, Enamel, 28½ x 20½ In.
$1,800

Pook & Pook, Inc.

T

**Toy,** Stove, Wetter Manufacturing Co., Cast Iron, Nickel, 17 ½ x 17 ¾ In.
$1,200

Pook & Pook, Inc.

**Toy,** Surfer Girl, On Board, Rides Waves, Cast Iron, 3 Wheels, Pull Toy, Hubley, 7 ½ In.
$12,000

Bertoia Auctions

**Toy,** Taxi, Celluloid Windows, Embossed Seats, Spare Tire, Citroen, France, 20 ½ In.
$885

Bertoia Auctions

**Toy,** Taxi, Yellow Cab, Driver, Orange, Black, Disc Wheels, Cast Iron, Arcade, 7 ¾ In.
$443

Bertoia Auctions

| | |
|---|---:|
| **Theater,** Myriopticon, Historical Panorama, Rebellion, Milton Bradley, 1860s, 8 In. ............*illus* | 3000 |
| **Theater,** Stage Dancers, Clock, Wood, Tin, Clockwork, c.1880, 10 x 6 In. ................................ | 3000 |
| **Thresher,** McCormick Deering, Cast Iron, Gray Painted, Red Highlights, Arcade, 12 In. .............. | 207 |
| **Tidy Tim,** Man Pushing Cart With Pail, Tin, Marx, 8 ½ In. ................................................ | 358 |
| **Tiger,** Walking, Platform, Tin Lithograph, Penny, 2 ¼ In. ................................................ | 1080 |
| **Toboggan,** Bentwood, Hardwood Ribs, Rawhide Laced, Painted Wreaths, c.1850, 77 In. ............ | 3425 |
| **Tom Corbett Space Cadet,** Blue, Yellow Lettering, Tin Lithograph, Windup, Marx, 12 In. ............ | 360 |
| **Toonerville Trolley,** Cast Iron, Conductor, Paint, Fontaine Fox, 5 ¾ In. ................................ | 330 |
| **Toonerville Trolley,** Cast Iron, Conductor, Paint, Fontaine Fox, Box, 5 ¾ In. ........................ | 413 |
| **Toonerville Trolley,** Clockwork, Fontaine Fox, c.1922, 7 In. ............................................ | 413 |
| **Toonerville Trolley,** Green, Red Paint, Cast Iron, Dent, 3 In. .......................................... | 180 |
| **Toy,** Sedan, Hillclimber, Green Paint, Pressed Steel, 11 ½ In. .......................................... | 215 |
| **Tractor,** Caterpillar, Cast Iron, Yellow, Silver Engine, Embossed, Driver, Arcade, 1930s, 8 In. ....... | 354 |
| **Tractor,** Crawler, Green, Yellow Pressed Steel, John Deere, Box, 8 In. ................................ | 450 |
| **Tractor,** Digger, Red, Black Cast Treads, Nickel Shovel, Cast Iron, Hubley, 6 In. .............*illus* | 236 |
| **Tractor,** Driver, Plow, Tin Lithograph, Windup, Woodhaven Metal Stamping Co., Box, 9 In. .......... | 150 |
| **Tractor,** Farmall, Cast Iron, Red, Driver, Drawbar, Rubber Tires, Decal, Arcade, 7 In. .............. | 502 |
| **Tractor,** Fordson, 1930s Model, Nickel Driver, Cast Iron, Painted, Arcade, 5 ¾ In. ...........*illus* | 177 |
| **Tractor,** John Deere, Cast Iron, Green, Seated Nickel Driver, Rubber Tires, Arcade, 7 In. ........... | 236 |
| **Tractor,** John Deere, Green, Yellow, Die Cast, Ertl, 1953, 8 x 5 In. .................................... | 58 |
| **Tractor,** Reversing, Tin Driver, Rubber Treads, Tin Lithograph, Windup, Marx, Box, 14 In. ......... | 390 |
| **Traffic Cop,** In Car, Beat It The Komikal Kop, Tin Lithograph, Windup, Marx, 8 In. .................. | 300 |
| **Traffic Light,** Steel, Yellow & Black, Tapered Base, Be Careful, Play Safe, 47 x 11 In. ............... | 146 |
| **Train & Trolley Set,** World's Fair Greyhound, Tin Lithograph, Cast Iron, Arcade, 6 ½ In. ........... | 330 |
| **Train Accessory,** Bing, Engine Shed, Paint, Tin, 8 ¾ x 14 ¼ In. ...................................... | 150 |
| **Train Accessory,** Bing, Station, Embossed Yellow & Red Brick, Arched Opening, 10 x 13 In. ....... | 649 |
| **Train Accessory,** Bing, Station, Tin, Multicolor Paint, 12 ¾ x 15 In. ................................ | 400 |
| **Train Accessory,** Carlisle & Finch, Switcher, Nickel Boiler & Cab, Paint, 10 ½ In. ................... | 1652 |
| **Train Accessory,** Carlisle & Finch, Truss Bridge, Cast Iron, Orange, c.1910, 22 In. ................. | 4720 |
| **Train Accessory,** Lionel, Signal Tower, Green, Yellow Orange Paint, 8 x 10 In. ....................... | 90 |
| **Train Accessory,** Marklin, Bridge, Suspension, 4 Towers, Steel Arches, c.1912, 30 In. .............. | 6490 |
| **Train Accessory,** Marklin, Bridge, Wood, 3 Sections, Arches, Faux Brick, 1 Gauge, 50 In. .......... | 354 |
| **Train Accessory,** Marklin, Crossing Platform, Guard House, Shed, Track Bumper, 14 In., Pair .. | 325 |
| **Train Accessory,** Marklin, Gantry Crane, 2 Cranks, Cabin Rotates, Lowers Weight, 16 In. ......... | 708 |
| **Train Accessory,** Marklin, Lamp, Arc, Cast Iron, Green, Maroon, Frosted Globe, Chain, 12 In. .... | 590 |
| **Train Accessory,** Marklin, Platform, Ribbed Canopy, 6 Posts, Bench, Green, Gold, 9 x 15 In. ...... | 649 |
| **Train Accessory,** Marklin, Station, Central, Canopied Platform, O Gauge, 10 x 9 In. ............... | 2360 |
| **Train Accessory,** Marklin, Station, Paint, Tin, 9 ½ x 16 In. .......................................... | 510 |
| **Train Accessory,** Marklin, Tunnel, Tower On Top, Electric Lamp, 1 & 2 Gauge, 18 x 13 In. ........ | 3540 |
| **Train Accessory,** Roundabout, Tin Litho, Hand Crank Moves Train On Track, Penny, 4 ½ In. .... | 561 |
| **Train Accessory,** Roundhouse, Tin, Standard Gauge, 15 x 24 In. ..................................... | 185 |
| **Train Accessory,** Shed, Freight, Sliding Doors, Pivoting Derrick, Wiring, 14 x 10 In. ............... | 472 |
| **Train Car,** Bassett, Locomotive, Brass Boiler, 9 ¾ In. ................................................ | 1652 |
| **Train Car,** Bassett, Locomotive, Lowke O Gauge, Tender, Black, Logo, 11 ¾ In. .................... | 472 |
| **Train Car,** Boxcar, Wood, Paint, Steel, c.1926, 11 ½ In. .............................................. | 2124 |
| **Train Car,** Buddy L, Boxcar, Pressed Steel, Red, Sliding Door, Decals, c.1928, 20 ½ In..........*illus* | 708 |
| **Train Car,** Buddy L, Coal, Stamped Sides, Decals, Pressed Steel, c.1927, 22 ½ In...................*illus* | 177 |
| **Train Car,** Buddy L, Railroad Pile Driver, Accessories, Red, Black Pressed Steel, 21 In............... | 420 |
| **Train Car,** Carlisle & Finch, Baggage, Tin Curved Roof, Cast Iron Wheels, c.1900, 12 In. ........... | 384 |
| **Train Car,** Carlisle & Finch, Locomotive, Mining, Hump Type, Pressed Steel, c.1912, 7 In. .......... | 944 |
| **Train Car,** Carlisle & Finch, Pullman, 5 Window, Brass, Sheet Metal, 6 Wheels, c.1905, 18 In. ..... | 7670 |
| **Train Car,** Hubley, Locomotive, 2-2-0, Headlamp, Cow Catcher, Clockwork, 7 ½ In. ............... | 266 |
| **Train Car,** Ives, Inboard Truck Live Stock Car, Tin Lithograph, 8 Wheels, c.1906, 9 In................ | 4720 |
| **Train Car,** Ives, Locomotive & Tender, Standard Gauge ............................................. | 1230 |
| **Train Car,** Ives, Locomotive, Dome & Spoke Wheels, Cast Iron, Clockwork, Pat. 1884, 7 In. ........ | 1652 |
| **Train Car,** Ives, Semaphore, Double Arm, Mechanical, Tin Litho, O Gauge, c.1905, 12 x 5 In. ..... | 3245 |
| **Train Car,** Lionel, Locomotive, Green Paint, Metal ................................................... | 180 |
| **Train Car,** Lionel, Locomotive, Green Paint, Williams Reproduction ............................... | 185 |
| **Train Car,** Lionel, Locomotive, Green, Brass Plates, Standard Gauge, 19 In. ...................... | 5310 |
| **Train Car,** Lionel, Log Dump, Planks, Restored, Prewar, 14 x 4 ½ In...............................*illus* | 30 |
| **Train Car,** Lionel, Observation, New York, Green, Apple Green Window Inserts, 21 In............... | 590 |
| **Train Car,** Lionel, Tender, NYC & HRRR, Black, Prewar, 11 x 3 ¾ In. ..............................*illus* | 150 |
| **Train Car,** Lionel, Trolley, Electric Rapid Transit, Blue, Yellow Paint ............................... | 4182 |
| **Train Car,** Little Wonder, Paper Over Wood, Revolving, Passengers, 20 In.........................*illus* | 590 |
| **Train Car,** Locomotive, Cast Iron Frame, Red, Paint, Voltamp Steeple, 10 In. ..................... | 1062 |
| **Train Car,** Marklin, Baggage, Tin Hoop Style, T-Strap, Red, Orange, Green, 2 Gauge, 14 In........ | 2491 |

| | |
|---|---|
| Train Car, Marklin, Caboose, PRR 90309, Tin, Sliding Roof, Bench, Stove, O Gauge, 5 In. | 767 |
| Train Car, Marklin, Locomotive, Tender, Black, 10¼ In. | 2360 |
| Train Car, Marklin, Locomotive, Tender, Green, Box, 8½ In. | 148 |
| Train Car, Marklin, Sleep Car, Grande Express, Tin, Iron, 8 Compartments, 1 Gauge, 21 In. | 502 |
| Train Car, Marklin, Snow Plow Car, Tin, St. E.V., Cast Iron Wheels, 1 Gauge, 8 In. | 561 |
| Train Car, Welker & Crosby, Locomotive, Steam, Cast Iron, Wood, Engineer, 1885, 13 In. | 1063 |
| Train Set, Ives, Pullman, Locomotive, Cars, O Gauge, 16-In. Locomotive, 5 Piece | 560 |
| Train Set, Kenton, Erie, Electroplated Cast Iron, Tender, 3 Passenger Coaches, 30½ In. | 885 |
| Train, Mountain Tunnel, Station, Mechanical, Tin Lithograph, Germany, 3¾ In. | 180 |
| Train, Rapid Transit, Tin, 3 Figures, Electric, Lionel, 10½ In. | 2006 |
| Train, Trolley, Cast Iron, Spring Axles, Paint, Electric, Voltamp United, c.1907, 10 In. | 3245 |
| Trolley, Fulton Ferry, 2 Horses, Paint, Tin, George Brown, c.1830, 24 In. | 3600 |
| Trolley, Horse Drawn, Wheels, Consolidated Street R.R. Side, Red, Brown, Iron, Harris, 14 In. | 480 |
| Trolley, Railway, Electric, Brass, Open Windows, Carlisle & Finch, c.1906, 8 In. | 885 |
| Truck, 7Up, Green, Red Logs, Box, 1960s, 10½ In. | 150 |
| Truck, American Railway Express, Iron, Green, Embossed, Yellow Trim, Kenton, 1930s, 7 In. | 531 |
| Truck, Anti-Aircraft Gun, Camouflaged, Windup, 8 Soldiers, Hausser, c.1920, 13½ In. | 1003 |
| Truck, Army Motor, Iron, Open Stake Body, Green, Embossed, Driver, Jones & Bixler, 15 In. | 500 |
| Truck, Army, Mack, Pressed Steel, Canvas Cargo Cover, U.S. Army, Smith-Miller, 20 In. | 270 |
| Truck, Army, Star, Metal, Marx, Box, 1950s, 21 In. | 195 |
| Truck, Baggage, Red, Pressed Steel, Rider, Buddy L, 1935, 26 In. | 900 |
| Truck, Baggage, Steel, Black Cab, Yellow Stake Body, Buddy L, 26 In. | 1976 |
| Truck, Bell Telephone, Green Paint, 12½ In. | 240 |
| Truck, Car Carrier, Cab, 3 Austin Cars, Iron, Plated Steel Wheels, A.C. Williams, 12 In. | 384 |
| Truck, Cattle Hauler, Structo, 1956, 22 In. | 95 |
| Truck, Cement Mixer, Jaeger, Cast Iron, Orange, Blue, Aluminum, Kenton, 6½ In. ........illus | 236 |
| Truck, Cement Mixer, Yellow Pressed Steel, Box, Model Toys Co., 15½ In. | 450 |
| Truck, Cement, Blue Diamond Service, White Blue, Smith-Miller, 20 In. | 840 |
| Truck, City Coal Co., Mack C Cab, Tin Litho, Blue, Green, Clockwork, Marx, 13½ In. | 649 |
| Truck, Coal, Hi Cab, Black, Red Chassis, Pressed Steel, Buddy L, 1930s, 25 In. | 5100 |
| Truck, Delivery, Express Line, Red, Green Paint, Pressed Steel, Buddy L, 25 In. | 523 |
| Truck, Delivery, Heinz, Pressed Steel, Battery Operated Headlights, Metalcraft, 12 In. | 83 |
| Truck, Delivery, Milk, Open Stake, License, Rubber Tires, Buddy L, Junior, 1930s, 24 In. ......illus | 2006 |
| Truck, Delivery, Wrigley's Spearmint Chewing Gum, Paint, Pressed Steel, Buddy L, 25 In. | 600 |
| Truck, Deluxe Hydraulic, Blue, Gray, Pressed Steel, Rider, Buddy L, 1948, 26 In. | 3000 |
| Truck, Dump, Hydraulic, Black Paint, Pressed Steel, Buddy L, 24 In. | 300 |
| Truck, Dump, Junior, Black Front, Red Body, Pressed Steel, Buddy L, c.1933, 24½ In. | 1440 |
| Truck, Dump, Mack, Hercules Dump, Pressed Steel, Open Cab, 1920s, Chein, 18 In. | 502 |
| Truck, Dump, Metallic Blue & Orange, Structo, 1957, 20 In. | 110 |
| Truck, Dump, Orange, Blue Paint, Cast Iron, Kilgore, 8½ In. | 308 |
| Truck, Dump, Orange, Red, Black Pressed Steel, Wood Wheels, Wyandotte, Box, 9½ In. | 270 |
| Truck, Dump, Red Diamond, Silver, Smith-Miller, 19 In. | 840 |
| Truck, Dump, Red, Yellow, Green, Pressed Steel, Turner, 1938, 28 In. | 210 |
| Truck, Dump, Ride On, Steel, Removable Seat, Gemstone Lights, Structo, 20 In. ...........illus | 120 |
| Truck, Dump, Side, Red, Orange, Pressed Steel, Electric Lights, Marx, 10½ In. | 330 |
| Truck, Dump, Wyandotte, USA, 1950s, 19½ In. | 175 |
| Truck, Emergency Auto Service, Pressed Steel, Banner Plastic Co., Box, 12 In. | 210 |
| Truck, First National Bank & Trust, Black, Metal, Smith-Miller, 16 In. | 300 |
| Truck, Flivver Dump, Black, Buddy L, 12 In. | 1185 |
| Truck, Flivver Huckster, Movable Tailgate, Cast Red Spokes, Buddy L, 14 In. | 3851 |
| Truck, Flivver Pick Up, Movable Tailgate, Cast Spoke Wheels, Buddy L, 12 In. | 494 |
| Truck, Ford, Pickup, Dark Blue, Tonka, 1956, 13 In. | 125 |
| Truck, Ford, Stake, Nickel Grill, Green, Arcade, 1935, 4½ In. | 385 |
| Truck, Hoist, Mack, Driver, Side Cranks, Swivel, Paint, Iron, Arcade, c.1932, 11 In. | 1416 to 2360 |
| Truck, Huckster, Green, Rubber Tires, Kingsbury, Windup, 1930, 14½ In. | 2370 |
| Truck, International, Pickup, Cast Aluminum, Yellow, Arcade, 9 In. | 290 |
| Truck, International, Stake, Cast Iron, Yellow Painted Cab, Coe, White Rubber Tires, 9½ In. | 708 |
| Truck, International, Stake, Open Body, Iron, Red, Decal, Rubber Tires, Arcade, 11½ In. | 266 |
| Truck, Ladder, Iron, Red, Gold Trim Embossed Fires Car, Lights, Nickel Drivers, Hubley, 16 In. | 1652 |
| Truck, Log, Wood Logs, Barrels, Yellow Cab, Pressed Steel, Smith-Miller, 14 In. | 120 |
| Truck, Long Haulage, Stake Side, Disc Wheels, Clockwork, Strauss, c.1940, 10½ In. | 325 |
| Truck, Mack Railway Express, Pressed Steel Steelcraft, c.1930, 12¾ x 24 In. | 489 |
| Truck, Mechanical Crane, Green, Yellow, Pressed Steel, Buddy L, 1952, 20 In. | 390 |
| Truck, Milk, Elsie's Dairy, Delivery, Elsie Driver, Bell, Wooden, Pull Toy, c.1948, 8¾ In. .......illus | 89 |
| Truck, Motor Express, Green, Red Cab, Die Cast, Hubley, Box, 18 In. | 180 |
| Truck, Moving, Allied Van Lines, Orange, Pressed Steel, Tonka, 23 In. | 150 |

**Toy,** Theater, Myriopticon, Historical Panorama, Rebellion, Milton Bradley, 1860s, 8 In.
$3,000

Cowan's Auctions

**Toy,** Tractor, Digger, Red, Black Cast Treads, Nickel Shovel, Cast Iron, Hubley, 6 In.
$236

Bertoia Auctions

**Toy,** Tractor, Fordson, 1930s Model, Nickel Driver, Cast Iron, Painted, Arcade, 5¾ In.
$177

Bertoia Auctions

**Tractor Toys**

The first tractor was built by J.I. Case in 1892, so no tractor toys were made before that date.

**Toy,** Train Car, Buddy L, Boxcar, Pressed Steel, Red, Sliding Door, Decals, c.1928, 20½ In.
$708

Bertoia Auctions

T

**Toy,** Train Car, Buddy L, Coal, Stamped Sides, Decals, Pressed Steel, c.1927, 22½ In.
$177

Bertoia Auctions

**Toy,** Train Car, Lionel, Log Dump, Planks, Restored, Prewar, 14 x 4½ In.
$30

Morphy Auctions

**Toy,** Train Car, Lionel, Tender, NYC & HRRR, Black, Prewar, 11 x 3¾ In.
$150

Morphy Auctions

**Toy,** Train Car, Little Wonder, Paper Over Wood, Revolving, Passengers, 20 In.
$590

Bertoia Auctions

**Toy,** Truck, Cement Mixer, Jaeger, Cast Iron, Orange, Blue, Aluminum, Kenton, 6½ In.
$236

Bertoia Auctions

**Toy,** Truck, Delivery, Milk, Open Stake, License, Rubber Tires, Buddy L, Junior, 1930s, 24 In.
$2,006

Bertoia Auctions

**Toy,** Truck, Dump, Ride On, Steel, Removable Seat, Gemstone Lights, Structo, 20 In.
$120

Morphy Auctions

**Toy,** Truck, Milk, Elsie's Dairy, Delivery, Elsie Driver, Bell, Wooden, Pull Toy, c.1948, 8¾ In.
$89

Bertoia Auctions

T

| | |
|---|---|
| **Truck,** Open Bed, White, Blue, Pressed Steel, Smith-Miller, 14 In. | 150 |
| **Truck,** Piccolo, Thermo, Metal, Painted Silver, Blue Cab, Door Opens, Schuco, 4 In. | 18 |
| **Truck,** Pyro Canteen, Plastic, Yellow, Blue, c.1950, 5 ½ In. | 125 |
| **Truck,** Pyro Express, Plastic, Blue, Red, c.1950, 5 ½ In. | 135 |
| **Truck,** Railway Express Agency, Van Body, Pressed Steel, Painted, Buddy L, 22 In. ...........*illus* | 944 |
| **Truck,** Robert's Circus, Pressed Steel, Van Body, Rear Doors, Box, 1940s, 22 In. ..............*illus* | 590 |
| **Truck,** Sand & Gravel, Black, Red, Still Wheel, Pressed Steel, No. 202, Buddy L, 1926, 26 In. | 3900 |
| **Truck,** Sand & Gravel, Marx, USA, 1950s, 14 In. | 175 |
| **Truck,** Sand & Stone, Pressed Steel, Yellow, Rubber Tires, Buddy L, Box, 14 In. | 561 |
| **Truck,** Sand Loader, Gray, Black, Pressed Steel, Buddy L, 1924, 21 x 18 In. | 510 |
| **Truck,** See's Candies, Tin, Friction, Japan, 1950s, 8 ½ In. | 75 |
| **Truck,** Semi-Trailer, International Harvester, Pressed Steel, Boxes, McCormick-Deering, 8 In. | 480 |
| **Truck,** Semi-Trailer, Maroon, Gray, Pressed Steel, Smith-Miller, 23 In. | 210 |
| **Truck,** Semi-Trailer, Ranger Motor Line, Tin Litho, Yellow, Red, Blue, Metal, Key, 6 In. | 24 |
| **Truck,** Semi-Trailer, Red, Pressed Steel, Rubber Wheels, Structo, Box, 18 In. | 240 |
| **Truck,** Semi-Trailer, White, Cargo Liner, All American Toy Co., 36 In. | 450 |
| **Truck,** Stake Bed, Nickel, Orange, Cast Iron, Hubley, 5 In. | 90 |
| **Truck,** Stake Body, Junior Series, Black, Yellow, Rubber Tires, Buddy L, c.1925, 17 In. | 2370 |
| **Truck,** Stake Rack, Yellow, Green, Wood Wheels, Restored, Wyandotte, 9 ½ In. .................*illus* | 60 |
| **Truck,** Stake, Mack, Cast Iron, Red Paint, Champion, 2 ½ In. | 94 |
| **Truck,** Tank Department, Green, Orange Paint, Pressed Steel, Keystone, 25 In. | 554 |
| **Truck,** Tanker, Die Cast, Aluminum Body, Rubber Tires, L Mack, 28 In. | 325 |
| **Truck,** Tanker, Gasoline, Iron, Green, Yellow Wheel Rims, Embossed Cans, Kenton, 10 In. | 1180 |
| **Truck,** Tanker, Shell Oil, 1996, 36 In. | 1175 |
| **Truck,** Tanker, Standard Oil, Orange, Green Paint, Tin Litho, Windup, Strauss, 11in. | 570 |
| **Truck,** Tanker, Tank Line, Painted, Black, Red, Buddy L, 26 In. | 540 |
| **Truck,** Tow, Black Open Cab, Boom, Steel, Buddy L, 27 In. | 1605 |
| **Truck,** Tow, Chain, Tow Hook, Red, Pressed Steel, Marx, 18 In. | 270 |
| **Truck,** Tow, Iron, Rear Compartment, Boom, Red, Silver, Yellow, Kenton, c.1927, 9 ½ In. | 1298 |
| **Truck,** Tow, Schuco Piccolo, Metal, Red, Green Hoist, Crank Works, Black Tires, 3 ¼ In. | 47 |
| **Truck,** Tow, White Paint, Pressed Steel, Smith-Miller, 16 ¼ In. | 431 |
| **Truck,** Transport, Army, Paint, Canvas, Steelcraft, 1920s, 23 In. | 350 |
| **Truck,** U.S. Mail Carrier, Porter, Luggage, Tin Lithograph, Windup, Unique Art, 13 In. | 96 |
| **Truck,** U.S. Treasury Bank, Pressed Steel, Aluminum, Smith-Miller, 14 In. | 210 |
| **Truck,** United Parcel Delivery, Brown, Pressed Steel, Pull Handle, Buddy L, c.1942, 25 In. | 1200 |
| **Truck,** Wild Animal Circus On Wheels, Cages, Red, Pressed Steel, Buddy L, Box, 26 In. | 330 |
| **Truck,** Wood, Wisa Gloria, Red, Yellow, Red Paint, c.1950, 23 In. | 25 |
| **Trunk,** Doll's, Dome Top, Paper Cover, Interior Tray, c.1890, 10 x 16 In. | 80 |
| **Turkey,** Tin Tail, Cloth Body, Windup, Alps, Box, 6 In. | 175 |
| **Turtle,** Native Rider, Mechanical, Orange, Red, Yellow, Blue, Windup, M. Chein & Co. | 234 |
| **Uncle Wiggily,** Muslin, Button Eyes, Painted Face, Georgene Novelties, c.1934, 19 In. | 112 |
| **Van,** Healthy Milk Truck, Sliding Door, Gong Bell, Box, 12 In. | 207 |
| **Velocipede,** Boy, Paint, Composition, Tin, Clockwork, Stevens & Brown, c.1880, 11 In. | 5100 |
| **Violin Player,** Le Gaye Violiniste, Composition, Cloth, Martin, 8 In. | 885 |
| **Wagon,** Artillery, Cannon, 2 Horses, Driver, Paint, Cast Iron, Ives, c.1890, 21 In. | 5400 |
| **Wagon,** Badger Coaster Jr., Handle, Red Paint, Wood, c.1900, 12 ½ x 28 In. | 104 |
| **Wagon,** Band, 4 White Horses, Paint, Cast Iron, Hubley, 28 In. | 3300 |
| **Wagon,** Circus, 3 Bandsmen, 2 Horses, Wood, Jointed, Instruments, Schoenhut, 21 In. | 708 |
| **Wagon,** Circus, Calliope, Open Body, Bells, Pipes, Cast Iron, Hubley, c.1920, 16 In. | 1320 |
| **Wagon,** Circus, Horse, Driver, Pacing Lion, Tin, Clockwork, George Brown, 13 In. | 27000 |
| **Wagon,** Circus, Revolving Monkey Cage, Driver, Horses, Paint, Iron, Hubley, 1920s, 16 In. | 114000 |
| **Wagon,** Circus, Royal Circus, Cast Iron, Brown Bear, Door Opens, Horses, Hubley, 12 In. | 266 |
| **Wagon,** Circus, Royal Circus, Driver, Brown Bear, Yellow Cage, Cast Iron, Hubley, 16 In. | 5700 |
| **Wagon,** Circus, Royal, Sliding Cage Door, Bears, Driver, 2 Horses, Cast Iron, Hubley, 16 In. | 590 |
| **Wagon,** Circus, Trapeze, Clown, 2 Horses, Paint, Cast Iron, Hubley, 16 In. | 1400 |
| **Wagon,** Dairy, Horse Drawn, Fairmount Farms, Driver, Bottles, Wood, Schoenhut, 25 In. | 1652 |
| **Wagon,** Driver, Yellow Green, Cast Iron, c.1900, 14 ½ In. | 210 |
| **Wagon,** Ice, Covered Style, White, Blue Roof, Embossed ICE, Spoke Wheels, Hubley, 15 In. | 413 |
| **Wagon,** Milk, Abbotts, Milk Crate, 6 Bottles, Schoenhut, 11 ¼ In. | 741 |
| **Wagon,** Milk, Horse Drawn, Borden's Milk & Cream, Tin Litho, Wood, Morrison Rich, 19 In. | 150 |
| **Wagon,** Milk, Horse Drawn, Driver, Cast Iron, Painted, Kenton, 13 In. | 99 |
| **Wagon,** Red, Black Paint, Wood, Pull Handle, c.1900, 22 x 40 In. | 164 |
| **Wagon,** Star Coaster, Wood, Spoke Wheels, Hand Brake, Hunt, Helm, Perris, c.1905, 41 In. | 224 |
| **Wagon,** Studebaker Junior, Raised Seat, Green, Orange, Black Paint, Pull Toy, 44 In. | 1920 |
| **Wagon,** Victory Flyer, Wood, Metal Wheels, Hand Wheels, c.1925, 41 In. | 78 |
| **Waltzing Couple,** Tin, Gunthermann, 7 ¾ In. | 700 |

**Toy,** Truck, Railway Express Agency, Van Body, Pressed Steel, Painted, Buddy L, 22 In.
$944

Bertoia Auctions

**Toy,** Truck, Robert's Circus, Pressed Steel, Van Body, Rear Doors, Box, 1940s, 22 In.
$590

Bertoia Auctions

**Toy,** Truck, Stake Rack, Yellow, Green, Wood Wheels, Restored, Wyandotte, 9 ½ In.
$60

Morphy Auctions

**Toy,** Washtub, 3 Little Pigs, Washboard, Tin Lithograph, Scenes, Ohio Art, c.1934, 6 ½ In.
$115

Hake's Americana & Collectibles

T

**Toy,** Woman, Pushing Fruit Cart, Composition, Painted, Embossed Cart, Clockwork, 6 In.
$325

Bertoia Auctions

**Toy,** Zeppelin, Hangar, Tin Litho, Push Lever, Hinged Door, Meier, Germany, c.1910, 4 In.
$631

Hake's Americana & Collectibles

**Tramp Art,** Box, Wood, Chip Carved, Stepped Pyramid Design, Hinged Lid, 4 x 10 In.
$20

Conestoga Auction Co., Inc.

**Tramp Art,** Cabinet, Hanging, Walnut, 12 Cubby Drawers, White Knobs, Pointed Crest, c.1890
$443

Conestoga Auction Co., Inc.

| | |
|---|---:|
| **Wash Stand,** Doll's, Wood, Soft Paste Pitcher, Wash Bowl, Kate Greenaway Style, 18 In. | 1008 |
| **Washer Woman,** Tub, Blue Platform, Bell, Paint, Wood, Cast Iron, Ives, 7½ In. | 6600 |
| **Washtub,** 3 Little Pigs, Washboard, Tin Lithograph, Scenes, Ohio Art, c.1934, 6½ In. .........*illus* | 115 |
| **Wee Washer,** Laundry Accessories, Washtub, Soaking Liner, Scrub Board, Quilt, c.1900, 16 In. | 168 |
| **Wheel Of Fortune,** Candy Drop, Green, Gold Paint, Tin Litho, Meier, Germany, Penny, 3 In. | 600 |
| **Wheelbarrow,** Rolls Racer Express-Barrow, Iron, Wood Wheel, Green, c.1920, 18 x 47 In. | 207 |
| **Whistling Spooky Kooky Tree,** Japan, Battery Operated, Marx, Box, c.1950, 14½ In. | 708 |
| **Whoopee Car,** Cowboy, Open Auto, Bucked Out Of Seat, Tin Litho, Clockwork, Marx, 8 In. | 325 |
| **Wild Boar,** Standing, Platform, Tin Lithograph, Penny, HMN, 2½ In. | 540 |
| **Woman,** In Shoe, Children, Horse, Paint, Tin, Cast Iron, Clockwork, Ives, 14½ In. | 6600 |
| **Woman,** In Velocipede Carriage, Bisque Head, Wicker, 3 Wheels, 9 In. | 3080 |
| **Woman,** Pushing Fruit Cart, Composition, Painted, Embossed Cart, Clockwork, 6 In. .......*illus* | 325 |
| **Woman,** With Pram, Penny, Meier, 3½ In. | 246 |
| **Yellow Kid,** Dangling Arms, String Joints, Clay, 1896, 5½ In. | 137 |
| **Zebra,** Unjointed, Painted Stripes, Metal Wheels, Steiff, 1910-19, 10½ In. | 988 |
| **Zeppelin,** Basket Gondola, Blue Side Propellers, Tin Litho, Meier, Germany, Penny, 3⅛ In. | 502 |
| **Zeppelin,** Green Enamel, 4 Additional Nickel Cabins, Kenton, 14 In. | 2725 |
| **Zeppelin,** Hangar, Tin Litho, Push Lever, Hinged Door, Meier, Germany, c.1910, 4 In. .........*illus* | 631 |
| **Zeppelin,** Rear Prop, Windup, Gondola, Battery Operated Light, Tipp & Co., 15 In. | 502 |
| **Zeppelin,** Solid Gondola, Tin Lithograph, Painted, Clockwork, Orobr, 8 In. | 944 |
| **Zick Zack,** 2 Wheels, 2 Men, Rolls Back & Forth, Tin Litho, Clockwork, Lehmann, 6 In. | 1003 |
| **Zig Zag,** Rocking Big Wheeled Car, 2 Figures, Tin Litho, Paint, Clockwork, Lehmann, 4 In. | 2006 |

**TRAMP ART** is a form of folk art made since the Civil War. It is usually made from chip-carved cigar boxes. Examples range from small boxes and picture frames to full-sized pieces of furniture.

| | |
|---|---:|
| **Box,** Coffin Top, Marquetry, Stars, Chevrons, Jackson Prison, 19th Century, 8 x 12 In. | 461 |
| **Box,** Sewing, Hinged Lid, Star, Pincushion, Cupids, Birds, Flowers, c.1902, 8 x 11 In. | 489 |
| **Box,** Storage, Wood, Chip Carved, Hinged Lid, 10 x 16¼ x 10¾ In. | 71 |
| **Box,** Wood, Chip Carved, Stepped Pyramid Design, Hinged Lid, 4 x 10 In. ..........*illus* | 20 |
| **Cabinet,** Hanging, Walnut, 12 Cubby Drawers, White Knobs, Pointed Crest, c.1890 .......*illus* | 443 |
| **Frame,** Carved, Stepped, Crosshatched, Tiered, Diamonds, Spiked Border, 30 x 27 In. | 1778 |
| **Frame,** Chip Carved, 6 Stepped Rows, Cross Corners, Square, c.1906, 35 In. | 1093 |
| **Frame,** Chip Carved, Flowers, 3 Sections, 12 x 16 In. | 118 |
| **Frame,** Pine, Mixed Woods, Chip Carved, Appliqued Geometrics, c.1900, 16 x 11 In. | 184 |
| **Frame,** Stepped, Crosshatched, Tiers, Carved, Notched, Spikes, c.1900, 30 x 27 In. .......*illus* | 1778 |
| **Mirror,** American Flags, Red Cross Merit Medallion, c.1960, 26 x 21 In. | 660 |
| **Plaque,** Geometric Stepped Designs, Peaked, Cloth Head, Antlers, c.1890, 16 x 19 In. | 554 |
| **Tray,** Pine, Oval, Brown, Crazed, Acorn, Leaf, Border, 13 In. | 35 |
| **Tray,** Rectangular, Dished Center, Victorian, 9 In. | 12 |
| **Wall Pocket,** Grid Design, Wood, Paint, Brown, Double, c.1910, 28 x 12 In. | 78 |

**TRAPS** for animals may be handmade. One of the most unusual is the mousetrap made so that when the mouse entered the trap, it was hit on the head with a mallet. Other traps were commercially manufactured and often are marked with the name of the manufacturer. Many traps were designed to be as humane as possible, and they would trap the live animal so it could be released in the woods.

| | |
|---|---:|
| **Animal,** Oneida, No. 4, Jump Trap, Steel | 50 |
| **Bear,** Wrought Iron, Anchor Chain, Hook, 1800s, 7½ x 32½ In. | 219 |
| **Fish,** Wire Mesh, Cylindrical, 36½ x 14 In. | 125 |
| **Minnow,** Woven, Demilune Opening, Willow, 29 In. | 59 |
| **Mouse,** McGill Metal Products, Alsteel, Serrated Top Jaw, c.1955, 2¾ x 1¾ In. | 28 |
| **Mouse,** Wood, 3 Holes, c.1875, 5½ x 2¾ In. | 30 |
| **Mouse,** Wood, End Spring, 1880s, 6½ x 5 In. | 100 |
| **Rat,** Wood, Rounded Front, Lovell Mfg., Paper Label, 1880s, 7 x 4 x 6 In. | 100 |
| **Snare,** Thompson Self-Locking, No. 00, Steel, c.1960, 30 In. | 22 |
| **Wolf,** Wrought Iron, Hand Forged, 1800s, 4½ x 25½ In. | 127 |

**TREEN,** *see Wooden category.*

**TRENCH ART** is a form of folk art made by soldiers. Metal casings from bullets and mortar shells were cut and decorated to form useful objects, such as vases.

| | |
|---|---:|
| **Artillery Shell Casing,** Brass, Incised Flowers, Cylindrical, 1900s, c.1917, 9 x 3½ In. | 90 |
| **Artillery Shell,** Hammered, Flower, 11 In. .........................*illus* | 114 |

| | |
|---|---|
| **Frame,** Heart, Scalloped, 5¼ x 5 In. | 145 |
| **Lamp,** Electric, Shade, 105 mm Shell, Marked, c.1945, 30 In., Pair | 23 |
| **Parlor Stove,** Mortar Shell, Copper, Brass Cylinder Shape, Animal Paw Feet, 9 In. | 104 |
| **Vase,** 105 mm Shell Casing, 1944, 14½ x 4 In., Pair ..................*illus* | 72 |
| **Vase,** Artillery Shell, Brass, Hammered, Boy, 14 In. | 192 |
| **Vase,** Artillery Shell, Brass, Hammered, Leaves, Acorns, 14 In. | 132 |
| **Vase,** Artillery Shell, Engraved, Verdun, Soldier, 13½ In. ..................*illus* | 336 |

---

**TRIVETS** are now used to hold hot dishes. Most trivets of the late nineteenth and early twentieth centuries were made to hold hot irons. Iron or brass reproductions are being made of many of the old styles.

| | |
|---|---|
| **Brass,** Forget-Me-Not, Ball Feet, 8½ x 4½ In. | 45 |
| **Cast Iron,** Enclosed Heart, Heart-Shape Finial, 3-Footed, Round, c.1829, 11 x 6 In. ......*illus* | 492 |
| **Cast Iron,** Griswold No. 299, 8¼ In. | 85 |
| **Cast Iron,** Iron Shape, Colt, 6 In. | 200 |
| **Cast Iron,** Maple Leaf, 4 Legs, Ober Mfg. Co., c.1930, 5¼ In. Diam. | 45 |
| **Cast Iron,** Triangular, Howell, 4 x 6 x 5 In. | 18 |
| **Ceramic Tile,** Fruit & Vegetable Figures, Multicolor, White Ground, 4¼ x 4¼ In. | 16 |
| **Earthenware,** Farm Scene, Transfer, Brown, Wire Rim, Minton's China Works, 6 x 6 In. | 195 |
| **Glass,** Sterling Overlay, Flowers, Scrolls, Monogram, Round, Marked, 1930s, 8 In. | 199 |
| **Glass,** Sterling Rim, Pressed Butterfly & Milkweed, c.1915, 6 In. | 45 |
| **Iron,** Brass, Georgian, Pierced Top, Reticulated Shelf, 12¾ x 12 In. ..................*illus* | 179 |
| **Iron,** Fender, Face Cutouts, Handle Marked, England, 6 x 12 x 18 In. | 245 |
| **Iron,** Heart In Heart Shape, 3-Footed, c.1800, 6¼ x 4⅝ In. | 584 |
| **Iron,** Heart Shape, 3 Penny Feet, Handle, c.1800, 10 x 5 x 4 In. | 123 |
| **Iron,** Round Head, Heart Cutouts, Handle, Pa., c.1850, 13 In. | 480 |
| **Majolica,** Wirework, Pink, Green, 8½ In. | 149 |
| **Pierced Heart,** Raised Penny Feet, Iron, c.1800, 5½ x 10 In. | 360 |
| **Porcelain Tile,** Art Nouveau, Pink Flowers, Gold Trim, Bavaria, 6 x 6 In. | 65 |
| **Porcelain,** Art Deco, Green, Blue, Yellow, Noritake, c.1925, 8 In. | 68 |
| **Porcelain,** Sprays, Pink Border, Painted, 6¼ In. | 25 |
| **Porcelain,** Windmill Scene, Blue & White, Tressemann & Voght, c.1898, 6¾ In. | 139 |
| **Silver Plate,** Flowers, Pierced Border, Oval, Wallace, Sticker, 1960s, 8 x 6 In. | 48 |
| **Wrought Iron,** 4 Hearts, c.1900, 7 x 7 In. | 25 |
| **Wrought Iron,** Hearth, Hearts, Curls, Hook Terminal, 3-Footed, c.1820, 3 x 19 In. | 805 |
| **Wrought Iron,** Triangle, Curved Handle, Heart Shape Terminal, Ogee Legs, 14 In. ......*illus* | 4920 |

---

**TRUNKS** of many types were made. The nineteenth-century sea chest was often handmade of unpainted wood. Brass-fitted camphorwood chests were brought back from the Orient. Leather-covered trunks were popular from the late eighteenth to mid-nineteenth centuries. By 1895, trunks were covered with canvas or decorated sheet metal. Embossed metal coverings were used from 1870 to 1910. By 1925, trunks were covered with vulcanized fiber or undecorated metal. Suitcases are listed here.

| | |
|---|---|
| **Campaign,** Painted, Metal Banded Corners, Hinged, Footed, 1900s, 36 x 19 In. | 70 |
| **Camphorwood,** Brass Fittings, Chinese, 19th Century, 20 x 41 x 22 In. | 1200 |
| **Camphorwood,** Iron Latch, Chinese, 18 x 37 x 20 In. | 70 |
| **Camphorwood,** Leather, Brass Tacks, Handles, Chinese, 10 x 25 In. | 120 |
| **Canvas & Wooden Latticework,** Lacquered Surface, 22 x 31 In. | 63 |
| **Dome Top,** Hinged, Geometric Nail Head Decoration, Leather, 42½ x 21 In. | 180 |
| **Dome Top,** Leather, Straps, Brass Studs, 19th Century, 24 x 36 In. ..................*illus* | 59 |
| **Dome Top,** Pine, Blue Paint, Yellow Border, Tulips, Ships, Man's Portrait, 1801, 13 x 30 In. | 472 |
| **Dome Top,** Pine, Iron Mounts, Carved Animals, Scrolls, Leaves, Flowers, c.1850, 22 x 34 In. | 1125 |
| **Dome Top,** Pine, Side Handles, Paint, New England, c.1810, 14 x 25 In. | 150 |
| **Dome Top,** Steamer, c.1900, 26 x 36 In. | 30 |
| **Dome Top,** Steamer, Fitted Interior, c.1850, 28 x 23 In. | 82 |
| **Dome Top,** Steamer, Wood Bands, Metal Lock, Clasps, 1800s, 28 x 18 In. | 47 |
| **Dome Top,** Walnut, Oak, Forged Hardware, 24 x 44 x 22 In. | 738 |
| **Dome Top,** Wood, Oak Staves, Storage Tray, 24½ x 36 In. | 127 |
| **Fitted Interior,** Painted Panels, Flower Basket, Georg Kirchner, 1845, 20 x 55 In. | 480 |
| **Goyard Style,** Leather, Green Print, 19 x 39 In. | 1375 |
| **Gucci,** Briefcase, Black Leather, Flap Top, Belt, Silvertone Hardware, c.1998, 13 x 17 In. | 242 |
| **Gucci,** Train Case, Brown Pigskin, Top Folds, Double Handles, 1970s, 18 x 10 In. | 518 |
| **Holdall,** Suitcase, Tan Leather, England, c.1950, 14 x 23 In. | 406 |
| **Immigrant's,** Dome Top, Ironwork, Painted Flowers, 1857, 22 x 43 x 20 In. | 400 |
| **Leather,** Black, Brass Trim, B.D.E. & Son, London, c.1885, 20 x 43 In. | 750 |

**Tramp Art,** Frame, Stepped, Crosshatched, Tiers, Carved, Notched, Spikes, c.1900, 30 x 27 In.
$1,778

James D. Julia Auctioneers

---

**Trench Art,** Artillery Shell, Hammered, Flower, 11 In.
$114

The Stein Auction Company

---

**Trench Art,** Vase, 105 mm Shell Casing, 1944, 14½ x 4 In., Pair
$72

Gray's Auctioneers LLC

T

**Trench Art,** Vase, Artillery Shell, Engraved, Verdun, Soldier, 13 ½ In.
**$336**

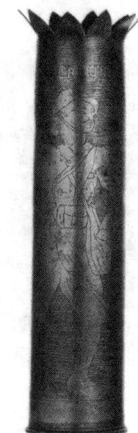

The Stein Auction Company

**Trivet,** Cast Iron, Enclosed Heart, Heart Shape Finial, 3-Footed, Round, c.1829, 11 x 6 In.
**$492**

Skinner Auctioneers & Appraisers

**Trivet,** Iron, Brass, Georgian, Pierced Top, Reticulated Shelf, 12 ¾ x 12 In.
**$179**

Neal Auction Co.

**Trivet,** Wrought Iron, Triangle, Curved Handle, Heart Shape Terminal, Ogee Legs, 14 In.
**$4,920**

Skinner Auctioneers & Appraisers

| | |
|---|---:|
| **Leather,** Red, Gilt Flowers, Wood Stand, Chinese, 18 x 33 In. | 625 |
| **Leather,** Tack Outlines, Side Handles, Wallpaper Interior, c.1850, 22 x 15 In. | 146 |
| **Louis Vuitton,** Brass Hardware, Leather Handles, 6 Drawers, 1930-40, 26 x 44 In. | 9150 |
| **Louis Vuitton,** Briefcase, Canvas, Monogram, 20 In. | 600 |
| **Louis Vuitton,** Cabin, Leather, Birch Slats, Wheels, Label, c.1920, 13 x 44 x 22 In. | 11950 |
| **Louis Vuitton,** Canvas, Stencil Painted, 19th Century, 22 ½ x 35 x 21 In. | 600 |
| **Louis Vuitton,** Fabric, Leather, Side Metal Handles, 13 x 43 In. | 4500 |
| **Louis Vuitton,** Garment Bag, Monogram Canvas, Leather Handle & Trim, Casters, 22 x 23 In. | 210 |
| **Louis Vuitton,** Keepall, Bandouliere 45, Monogrammed Canvas, Shoulder Strap, 10 x 18 In. | 466 |
| **Louis Vuitton,** Keepall, Monogram Canvas, 2 Leather Handles & Trim, 15 x 23 In. | 540 |
| **Louis Vuitton,** Lift Top, Checkerboard Design, Stencil, San Souci, Providence, RI, 35 x 20 In. | 5192 |
| **Louis Vuitton,** Logo Fabric, Embossed Leather Edges, 4 Trays, 20 x 24 x 15 In. | 9000 |
| **Louis Vuitton,** Sailor Bag, Monogram, Canvas, Marin, 26 x 14 In. | 1107 |
| **Louis Vuitton,** Specially Made For Encyclopedia Britannica, 10 ½ x 35 ½ In. | 3998 |
| **Louis Vuitton,** Steamer, Canvas Strap, Metal Bound, c.1910, 28 x 44 x 24 In. .....*illus* | 4674 |
| **Louis Vuitton,** Steamer, Damier Checkered Canvas, Black Metal Corners, 21 x 18 x 24 In. | 1534 |
| **Louis Vuitton,** Steamer, Fitted Interior, France, c.1910, 23 x 44 In. | 8960 |
| **Louis Vuitton,** Steamer, Fitted Interior, Tray, France, c.1910, 13 x 40 In. | 3500 |
| **Louis Vuitton,** Steamer, Metal Side Handles, c.1910, 22 x 40 x 22 In. .....*illus* | 8750 |
| **Louis Vuitton,** Steamer, Metal Side Handles, Monogram, c.1910, 20 ½ x 24 x 18 ½ In. | 7500 |
| **Louis Vuitton,** Steamer, Wood, Iron, Flat Top, Front Handle, 2 Trays, c.1885, 22 x 43 In. | 5400 |
| **Louis Vuitton,** Suitcase, Alzer 60, Monogrammed Canvas, 1980s, 16 x 24 In. | 1495 |
| **Louis Vuitton,** Suitcase, Brown Canvas, Monogram, Rolled Handle, Straps, 18 x 27 In. | 437 |
| **Louis Vuitton,** Suitcase, Canvas, Leather, Brass Corners, c.1940, 16 x 24 In. | 688 |
| **Louis Vuitton,** Suitcase, Canvas, Stencil, Brass, Leather, Interior Tray, 1800s, 21 x 32 In. | 1230 |
| **Louis Vuitton,** Suitcase, Leather, Brass, Cunard Stickers, 28 x 17 x 9 In. | 1380 |
| **Louis Vuitton,** Suitcase, Leather, Brass, Repeating Logo, 29 x 20 x 9 In. | 1265 |
| **Louis Vuitton,** Suitcase, Leather, Canvas, Monogram, Camalier & Buckley, 18 x 29 In. | 1200 |
| **Louis Vuitton,** Suitcase, Leather, Monogram, Square, Brass Lock, 19 x 19 x 9 In. | 704 |
| **Louis Vuitton,** Suitcase, Monogrammed Canvas, Leather, 1970s, 17 x 23 In. | 184 |
| **Louis Vuitton,** Suitcase, Sirus 45, Brown Canvas, Leather Trim, Monogram, 20 x 15 In. | 705 |
| **Louis Vuitton,** Suitcase, Soft Sided, Monogram Canvas, Beige Leather Trim, 20 x 27 In. | 600 |
| **Louis Vuitton,** Travel Bag, Keepall 50, Canvas, Monogram, Goldtone Hardware, 12 x 22 In. | 817 |
| **Louis Vuitton,** Vanity Case, Black Leather, Fitted Interior, Bottles, Brushes, 10 x 12 In. | 1250 |
| **Louis Vuitton,** Wardrobe, Canvas, Monogram, Banded, Interior Drawers, 22 x 45 In. | 9600 |
| **Louis Vuitton,** Wardrobe, Fabric, Leather, Side Handles, 22 x 44 In. | 9000 |
| **Louis Vuitton,** Wardrobe, Fitted Interior, Fabric, Leather Edges, 13 x 40 ½ In. | 7800 |
| **Louis Vuitton,** Wardrobe, Leather, Canvas, Monogram, J. Wanamaker, 44 x 26 In. | 11400 |
| **Malles Goyard,** Canvas, Lozine & Brass Hardware, Leather Handles, Monogram, 12 x 18 In. | 1476 |
| **Painted,** English Bulldog, Union Jack Flag, Hinged, Capt. A.W. Taylor, England, 1800s.....*illus* | 406 |
| **Pine,** Sprays, Red & Blue Ground, Continental, 19th Century, 22 x 48 x 26 In. | 400 |
| **Steamer,** Cunard Sticker, c.1905, 42 x 22 In. | 250 |
| **Steamer,** Metal Clasps, Black Straps, 25 x 38 In. | 123 |
| **Storage,** Nesting Set, Pigskin, Paint, Chinese Scene, 8 x 11 In. To 17 x 25 In., 5 Piece | 2520 |
| **Suitcase,** Alligator, Fabric Lined, Zipper, Brown, 18 ½ x 29 ½ In. | 413 |
| **Travel Box,** Campaign Style, Leather, 2 Drawers, Metal Corners, 12 ½ x 28 x 20 ½ In. | 344 |
| **Wood,** Finest Billiard Room, Man Playing Pool, Flynn's, c.1900, 19 x 25 In. .....*illus* | 240 |
| **Wood,** Leather, Building Interior, Painted, Brass Tacks, c.1825, 12 x 31 In. | 8750 |

**TUTHILL** Cut Glass Company of Middletown, New York, worked from 1902 to 1923. Of special interest are the finely cut pieces of stemware and tableware.

| | |
|---|---:|
| **Basket,** 4 Fruits, Intaglio, Grapes, Cherries, Pears, Apples, Tuthill, 17 In. | 700 |
| **Dish,** Athena Pattern, Round, American Brilliant, 6 In. | 295 |
| **Nappy,** Vintage Pattern, Engraved Grapes, Raised Rim, 5 ¾ x 4 ½ In. | 472 |
| **Tray,** Intaglio, Flowers, Chain Of Hobstar Border, Oval, 10 In. | 350 |
| **Tray,** Vintage Pattern, Grapes, Ivy, Signed, 1 ¾ x 12 In. | 2542 |
| **Vase,** Floral Cutting, Leaves, Honeycomb, Ruffled Sawtooth Rim, Notched Stem, 12 In. | 219 |

**TYPEWRITER** collectors divide typewriters into two main classifications: the index machine, which has a pointer and a dial for letter selection, and the keyboard machine, most commonly seen today. The first successful typewriter was made by Sholes and Glidden in 1874.

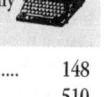

| | |
|---|---:|
| **Advertisement,** Framed, Oliver Bat Wing | 148 |
| **Blickensderfer,** No. 5, Ink From Roller, Wood Case, 13 In. | 510 |
| **Corona,** Folding, Case, 1917 | 80 |
| **L.C. Smith Corona,** No. 3, Case, 1917 | 34 |

| | | |
|---|---|---|
| **Oliver,** Printype, No. 9, Pat. Nov. 1912, 16 x 11 In. ............................*illus* | 300 |
| **Remington Rand Noiseless,** Model 7, Hard Case............................. | 85 |
| **Remington Standard,** No. 10, Cast Iron, Metal, c.1908 ....................... | 225 |
| **Remington,** Model 3, Portable, Green, c.1930, 12 x 9 ½ x 4 In............... | 425 |
| **Royal,** Model KMM, Pat. Magic Margin System, 1940s......................... | 130 |
| **Royal,** No. 10, Glass Side Keys, Manual............................................. | 100 |
| **Underwood,** No. 5, Black, Metal, 59 In. ........................................... | 59 |
| **Underwood,** No. 5, c.1916 ............................................................. | 75 |
| **Underwood,** Standard, No. 5, White Glass Keys, 1924 ..................... | 160 |
| **Williams,** No. 1 Straight, Grasshopper Mechanism, Oak Case, c.1893, 15 In. ..................*illus* | 1046 |

**TYPEWRITER RIBBON TINS** are now being collected. The lithographed tin containers have been used since the 1870s. Most popular with collectors are tins with pictorial graphics.

| | |
|---|---|
| **American Brand,** Blue, Silver, Hess-Hawkins Co., 2 x 2 In........................ | 26 |
| **Battleship,** Boat, Blue, Black, White, F.S. Webster, 2 x 2 In..................... | 23 |
| **Burroughs,** Silver, Orange, 2 ½ In........................................................ | 12 |
| **Caribonum,** Red, Beveled Edge Top, Rounded Corners, c.1901, 2 x 2 In..... | 29 |
| **Gibraltar,** Mountain, Sunset, Round, 2 ½ In............................................ | 45 |
| **Hercules,** Red, White, M.S. Apter Mfg. Co., 2 ½ x 2 ½ In......................... | 14 |
| **L.C. Smith & Corona,** Type Bar, Blue, 2 ½ x 2 ½ In................................. | 16 |
| **Miller Carnation,** White, Red, Black, 2 ½ In........................................... | 23 |
| **Old Town,** Blue, Orange, 2 x 2 In....................................................... | 12 |
| **Park Avenue,** Dark Blue, Silver, 2 ½ In................................................. | 15 |
| **Preferred,** Aristocrat, Crest, Blue, 2 ½ In.............................................. | 22 |
| **Remranco,** Woman, Yellow Dress, 1930s, 1 x 2 ½ In.............................. | 15 |
| **Royal-Nylon,** Art Deco, Black, c.1935, 2 ½ In....................................... | 18 |
| **Silver Medal,** Hand Holding Torch, Silver, Blue, 2 ½ In........................... | 21 |
| **Underwood Elliott Fisher Co.,** Orange, Silver, 2 ⅛ In............................. | 19 |
| **Vogue,** Roytype, Flowers, c.1935, 2 ½ In............................................. | 19 |

**UHL POTTERY** was made in Evansville, Indiana, in 1854. The pottery moved to Huntingburg, Indiana, in 1908. Stoneware and glazed pottery were made until the mid-1940s.

| | |
|---|---|
| **Bottle,** Figural, Elephant, Black, 3 In................................................... | 6 |
| **Crock,** 2 Handles, 3 Gal.................................................................... | 104 |
| **Jug,** Acorn Shape, Yellow, Footed,...................................................... | 6 |
| **Jug,** Glenmore Distilleries, Brown, White, Blue Writing, Handle, 6 ¼ In...... | 29 |
| **Pitcher,** Lid, Blue, Grapes, Lattice, 6 ½ In............................................ | 29 |
| **Planter,** Figural, Rabbit, Pink, 7 In..................................................... | 29 |
| **Salt & Pepper,** Pink, 3 In.................................................................. | 29 |
| **Shoes,** Baby, Red, 5 In..................................................................... | 6 |

**UMBRELLA** collectors like rain or shine. The first known umbrella was owned by King Louis XIII of France in 1637. The earliest umbrellas were sunshades, not designed to be used in the rain. The umbrella was embellished and redesigned many times. In 1852, the fluted steel rib style was developed and it has remained the most useful style.

| | |
|---|---|
| **Bamboo,** Paper, Painted Lanterns, 1940s, 27 ½ In................................. | 80 |
| **Engraved Flower Handle,** P.J. Cernus ................................................. | 94 |
| **Gold Embossed Handle,** Mother-Of-Pearl Inserts, Black Fabric.............. | 94 |
| **Gold Embossed Handle,** Thorn Design, Mother-Of-Pearl Panel ............. | 118 |
| **Gold Rolled Embossed Handle,** Shepherd's Crook, Black Fabric ........... | 59 |
| **Gold Rolled Handle,** Loop Shape, Black Fabric ................................... | 94 |
| **Hot Air Balloons,** Piero Fornasetti, 37 x 45 In........................*illus* | 488 |
| **Parasol Handle,** Silver, Abalone Inlay, Octagonal, Shells & Scrolls, Tiffany, 1800s, 6 x 1 ½ In.... | 132 |

**UNION PORCELAIN WORKS** was originally William Boch & Brothers, located in Greenpoint, New York. Thomas C. Smith bought the company in 1861 and renamed it Union Porcelain Works. The company went through a series of ownership changes and finally closed about 1922. The company made a fine quality white porcelain that was often decorated in clear, bright colors. Don't confuse this company with its competitor, Charles Cartlidge and Company, also in Greenpoint.

| | |
|---|---|
| **Oyster Plate,** 4 Wells, Albino, Gilt, Shell Shape, 8 x 6 In....................... | 250 |
| **Oyster Plate,** 4 Wells, Seaweed, Sea Life, Yellow, Shell Shape, 8 x 6 In...... | 795 |
| **Oyster Plate,** 5 Wells, Mussel, Crab, Snail, 1881, 8 x 6 In. ................... | 245 |
| **Oyster Plate,** 5 Wells, Whimsical Sea Creatures, Moss, 8 x 6 In............. | 375 |
| **Oyster Plate,** 6 Wells, Frog, Pink, Shell Shape, 10 x 7 ½ In.................. | 650 |

**Trunk,** Dome Top, Leather, Straps, Brass Studs, 19th Century, 24 x 36 In.
$59

Brunk Auctions

### TIP
*To remove the musty smell from an old trunk, put a bowl of freshly ground coffee inside.*

**Trunk,** Louis Vuitton, Steamer, Canvas Strap, Metal Bound, c.1910, 28 x 44 x 24 In.
$4,674

New Orleans Auction Galleries, Inc.

**Trunk,** Louis Vuitton, Steamer, Metal Side Handles, c.1910, 22 x 40 x 22 In.
$8,750

Rago Arts & Auction Center

**Trunk,** Painted, English Bulldog, Union Jack Flag, Hinged, Capt. A.W. Taylor, England, 1800s
$406

**U
V**

Garth's Auctioneers & Appraisers

**Trunk,** Wood, Finest Billiard Room, Man Playing Pool, Flynn's, c.1900, 19 x 25 In. $240

Garth's Auctioneers & Appraisers

**Typewriter,** Oliver, Printype, No. 9, Pat. Nov. 1912, 16 x 11 In. $300

Morphy Auctions

**Typewriter,** Williams, No. 1 Straight, Grasshopper Mechanism, Oak Case, c.1893, 15 In. $1,046

Skinner Auctioneers & Appraisers

**U**
**V**

**TIP**

*When you can't decide whether or not to buy a treasure at a show or flea market, remember the classic slogan, "Buy now or cry later."*

---

| | |
|---|---|
| **Oyster Plate,** 6 Wells, Pink, Round, 9¾ In. | 425 |
| **Oyster Plate,** 6 Wells, Sea Life, White, Gilt, 7½ x 10 In. | 495 |

**UNIVERSITY OF NORTH DAKOTA,** *see North Dakota School of Mines category.*

**VAL ST. LAMBERT** Cristalleries of Belgium was founded by Messieurs Kemlin and Lelievre in 1825. The company is still in operation. All types of table glassware and decorative glassware have been made. Pieces are often decorated with cut designs.

| | |
|---|---|
| **Compote,** Clear, Ribbon & Pillar Design, 7¾ x 10 In., Pair | 106 |
| **Vase,** Chalice Shape, Cranberry Cut To Clear, Grouse, Falcon, Footed, 11 x 7 In. | 150 |
| **Vase,** Flowers, Leaves, Textured Ground, Signed, 16½ In. *illus* | 9720 |
| **Wine Rinse,** Green Cut To Clear, 3 x 6 In. | 90 |

**VALLERYSTHAL GLASSWORKS** was founded in 1836 in Lorraine, France. In 1854, the firm became Klenglin et Cie. It made table and decorative glass, opaline, cameo, and art glass. A line of covered, pressed glass animal dishes was made in the nineteenth century. The firm is still working.

| | |
|---|---|
| **Candy Dish,** Pineapple Shape, Amber, Footed, c.1910, 7 In. | 18 |
| **Compote,** Amber, Plumes, c.1900, 6 In. | 130 |
| **Compote,** Dolphin Stem, Vaseline, c.1920, 8 In. | 850 |
| **Dish,** Robin, On Nest, White, Milk Glass, 4 x 4½ In. | 40 |
| **Figurine,** Elephant, Rider, Blue, Milk Glass, Marked, c.1900, 7 x 6 In. | 425 |
| **Ice Bucket,** Blue, Tab Handles, Opaline, Lid, 4⅞ In. | 245 |
| **Vase,** 3 Enameled Purple Cabochon Flowers, Olive Green Ground, 8¾ In. | 767 |
| **Vase,** Frosted Body, Shaded Amber To Rose, Acid Cut Flowers, Gold Enamel, 12 In. | 1150 |
| **Vase,** Stylized Allium, Pink & Frosted, Gold Trim, Squat Base, Stick Neck, 12 In. | 1481 |

**VAN BRIGGLE POTTERY** was started by Artus Van Briggle in Colorado Springs, Colorado, after 1901. Van Briggle had been a decorator at Rookwood Pottery of Cincinnati, Ohio. He died in 1904 and his wife took over managing the pottery. One of the employees, Kenneth Stevenson, took over the company in 1969. He died in 1990 and his wife and son ran the pottery. She died in 2010 and the company closed in 2012. The wares usually had modeled relief decorations and a soft, dull glaze.

| | |
|---|---|
| **Bookends,** Bear, Cliff, Mulberry, 4¼ In. | 403 |
| **Bowl,** Blue Matte Dragonfly, 3¼ x 8½ In. | 236 |
| **Bowl,** Molded Clover, Reddish Brown Over Green Matte Glaze, 1907, 5½ In. | 316 |
| **Plate,** Repeating Leaves, Green Matte Glaze, Incised, c.1910, 13 x 6 In. | 345 |
| **Tile,** Kingfisher On Branch, Purple, Brown, Turquoise Ground, Square, 6¼ In. | 793 |
| **Tile,** Water Lilies, Green, Blue, White, Frame, 6 x 6 In. | 2440 |
| **Vase,** Arrowroot Design, Feathery Green Glaze, c.1900, 6½ In. *illus* | 978 |
| **Vase,** Bird Design, Turquoise Blue Glaze, Baluster, 18 In. | 406 |
| **Vase,** Brown, Cylindrical, Marked Anna Van Briggle, 9 In. | 127 |
| **Vase,** Bud, Poppy, Green, 1905, 10¾ In. | 1093 |
| **Vase,** Calla Lily, Turquoise Glaze, Gourd Shape, Incised Colo., c.1950, 10 In. | 115 |
| **Vase,** Central Leaf Band, Marked, 9¼ In. | 344 |
| **Vase,** Flower Shape, Mulberry Glaze, Logo, Early 1900s, 4 In. | 288 |
| **Vase,** Gray, Rolled Rim, Squat, 1905, 3½ x 6½ In. | 390 |
| **Vase,** Green, Brown, Pinecones, Needles, Round, c.1935, 5 x 10 In. | 431 |
| **Vase,** Green, Flowers, 1904, 5⅝ In. | 690 |
| **Vase,** Incised Designs, Blue Green Glaze, Cinched Neck, 1903, 9 x 7 In. | 2375 |
| **Vase,** Incised Scroll Neck Band, High Shoulder, Colo., c.1906, 5 x 4 In. | 281 |
| **Vase,** Leaf Design, Mountain Craig Glaze, Tapered, Incised Colo., 5¼ In. | 250 |
| **Vase,** Leaves, Green Curdled Glaze Tapered Cylinder, 1914, 16 x 7 In. | 6875 |
| **Vase,** Leaves, Turquoise Blue Glaze, Tapered Cylinder, 17½ In. | 125 |
| **Vase,** Lorelei, Ming Turquoise, 11 In. | 207 |
| **Vase,** Lorelei, Turquoise, Woman, Flowing From Rim, Incised Colo., 11 In. | 259 |
| **Vase,** Mulberry Glaze, Leaves, 8⅛ In. | 403 |
| **Vase,** Pinecones, Needles, Green, Brown, Squat, c.1945, 5 x 10 In. | 431 |
| **Vase,** Poppy Pods, Ocher, Inverted Funnel Shape, c.1905, 9 x 7½ In. | 3000 |
| **Vase,** Poppy, Blue Green Glaze, Marked, 1902, 7¾ x 3½ In. *illus* | 15000 |
| **Vase,** Poppy, Maroon Matte Glaze, Cylindrical, Swollen Top, c.1903, 10½ x 7 In. | 6250 |
| **Vase,** Stylized Tulips, Turquoise Blue Glaze, Incised, 1920s, 9⅝ In. | 173 |
| **Vase,** Terra-Cotta, Unglazed, Carved Arrowhead Plant, Blossoms, Bulbous, 1907, 9 x 9 In. | 1625 |

**VASA MURRHINA** is the name of a glassware made by the Vasa Murrhina Art Glass Company of Sandwich, Massachusetts, about 1884. The glassware was transparent and was embedded with small pieces of colored glass and metallic flakes. The mica flakes were coated with silver, gold, copper, or nickel. Some of the pieces were cased. The same type of glass was made in England. Collectors often confuse Vasa Murrhina glass with aventurine, spatter, or spangle glass. There is uncertainty about what actually was made by the Vasa Murrhina factory. Related pieces may be listed under Spangle Glass.

| | |
|---|---:|
| Pitcher, Water, Clear, Mottled Pink, White, Silver Mica, 8 In. | 118 |
| Pitcher, Water, End Of Day Colors, Silver Mica, Ruffled Rim, Swirl Mold, 8 In. | 148 |
| Pitcher, Water, Lines, White Ground, Silver Mica, Clear Handle, Swirled Rib Mold, 8 In. | 59 |

**VASELINE GLASS** is a greenish-yellow glassware resembling petroleum jelly. Pressed glass of the 1870s was often made of vaseline-colored glass. Some vaseline glass is still being made in old and new styles. Additional pieces of vaseline glass may also be listed under Pressed Glass in this book.

| | |
|---|---:|
| Basket, Yellow, Green, Amber, Painted Flowers, Applied Handle, 3 Footed, c.1880, 4 x 6 In. | 115 |
| Berry Bowl, Wreath & Shell, Opalescent, 3-Footed, Model Flint Glass Co., c.1900, 4 x 9 In. | 46 |
| Bowl, Rose Sprig, Footed, Hexagonal Foot, Campbell, Jones, & Co., c.1886, 7 x 8 In. | 35 |
| Celery Dish, Inverted Thumbprint, Birds, Footed, c.1875, 6 x 15 In. | 345 |
| Cheese Dish, Lid, Inverted Thumbprint, King Glass, 6 ½ x 9 In. | 115 |
| Compote, Opalescent, Stemmed Tulips, Footed, Powell, 3 ½ In. | 115 |
| Dish, Swan Shape, Central Glass Co., c.1890, 3 ¾ x 9 In. | 219 |
| Epergne, 3 Jack-In-The-Pulpit Vases, Fenton Art Glass Co., c.1975, 13 x 12 In. | 196 |
| Epergne, Opalescent, 5 Vases, Scalloped, Flared Rim, Underplate, c.1890, 21 In. | 800 |
| Epergne, Opalescent, Ruffled Rim, Gold Paint, Metal Stand, 3 Tiers, c.1890, 27 x 22 In. | 219 |
| Epergne, Opalescent, Ruffled Rim, Trumpet Vase, Crooked Arms, Baskets, c.1890, 18 x 10 In. | 575 |
| Pitcher, Vertical Cabochon Designs, Tankard Shape, c.1890, 8 x 4 In. | 184 |
| Pitcher, Water, Cranberry To Green Hobnail, 7 ¾ In. | 148 |
| Pitcher, Water, Daisy & Fern, Flared Crimped Rim, Reeded Handle, L.W. Wright, 1900s, 9 In. | 150 |
| Pitcher, Water, Opalescent Hobnail, 7 ½ In. | 148 |
| Sleigh, Daisy & Button, c.1890, 7 x 10 In. | 161 |
| Spooner, Log Cabin Shape, Central Glass Co., c.1890, 4 ¾ x 3 In. | 431 |
| Tumbler, Opaline Brocade, Spanish Lace, Opalescent, Northwood, c.1899, 3 ½ In. | 173 |
| Tumbler, Ruby Stained Rim, Medial Band, Hobnail, c.1890, 3 ⅞ In. | 259 |
| Vase, 3-Printie Block, 8-Petal Rim, Tapered, Hexagonal Base, c.1860, 9 x 4 In. | 127 |
| Vase, Bud, Luxorette, Automobile Shape, c.1945, 7 In. | 58 |
| Vase, Corn Husk, Opalescence, Curved Handle, Dugan Glass, c.1900, 8 In., Pair | 161 |
| Vase, Daisy & Button, Umbrella Shape, Metal Handle, G. Duncan, 6 ½ In. | 518 |
| Vase, Opalescent, Fern Optic & Drape, Trumpet Shape, England, c.1890, 10 x 5 In. | 259 |
| Vase, Red, White, Blue Designs, Crimped Rim, Tapered, Czechoslovakia, c.1925, 8 In. | 184 |
| Vase, Trumpet Shape, Silvered, Fluted, Gilt Swan & Flower Base, 15 ¾ In., Pair | 1125 |
| Water Dispenser, 2 Parts, Radium Emanator Filter Co., c.1930, 22 x 10 In. | 374 |

**VENETIAN GLASS**, *see Glass-Venetian category.*

**VENINI GLASS**, *see Glass-Venetian category.*

**VERLYS** glass was made in Rouen, France, by the Societe Holophane Français, a company that started in 1920. It was made in Newark, Ohio, from 1935 to 1951. The art glass is either blown or molded. The American glass is signed with a diamond-point-scratched name, but the French pieces are marked with a molded signature. The designs resemble those used by Lalique.

| | |
|---|---:|
| Ashtray, Doves, Flowers, Frosted, Marked, 3 ½ x 4 ⅝ In. | 30 |
| Bowl, Dragonflies, Flowers, Frosted, 13 ¾ x 3 In. | 1258 |
| Bowl, Orchids, Marked, 14 In. | 175 |
| Bowl, Thistle, Marked, c.1955, 7 In. | 35 |
| Tray, Palms, 14 x 11 In. | 192 |

**VERNON KILNS** was the name used by Vernon Potteries, Ltd. The company, which started in 1931 in Vernon, California, made dinnerware and figurines until it went out of business in 1958. The molds were bought by Metlox, which continued to make some patterns. Collectors search for the brightly colored dinnerware and the pieces designed by Rockwell Kent, Walt Disney, and Don Blanding. For more prices, go to kovels.com.

| | |
|---|---:|
| Brown-Eyed Susan, Teapot, 6 ½ x 6 In. | 80 |
| Calico, Bowl, Lugged, Pink & Blue, 7 ½ In., 4 Piece | 75 |
| Figurine, Fantasia, Ostrich, Ballet Shoes, Ceramic, 1940, 6 In. | 377 |

**Umbrella,** Hot Air Balloons, Piero Fornasetti, 37 x 45 In. $488

Palm Beach Modern Auctions

**Val St.Lambert,** Vase, Flowers, Leaves, Textured Ground, Signed, 16 ½ In. $9,720

James D. Julia Auctioneers

**Van Briggle,** Vase, Arrowroot Design, Feathery Green Glaze, c.1900, 6 ½ In. $978

Humler & Nolan

U
V

This is an edited listing of current prices. Visit **Kovels.com** to check thousands of prices from previous years and sign up for free information on trends, tips, reproductions, marks, and more.

**Van Briggle,** Vase, Poppy, Blue Green Glaze, Marked, 1902, 7 ¾ x 3 ½ In.
$15,000

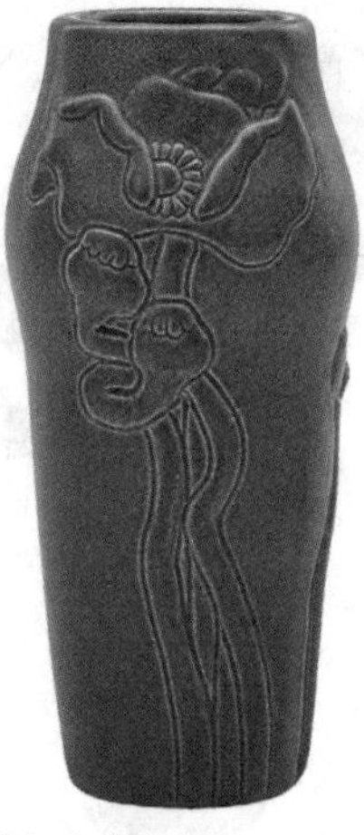

Rago Arts & Auction Center

**TIP**

*Be sure that any restorer, refinisher, or upholsterer working on your antique is insured.*

**Villeroy & Boch,** Beaker, Portrait, Wilhelm II, Blue, Dresden, ¼ Liter
$144

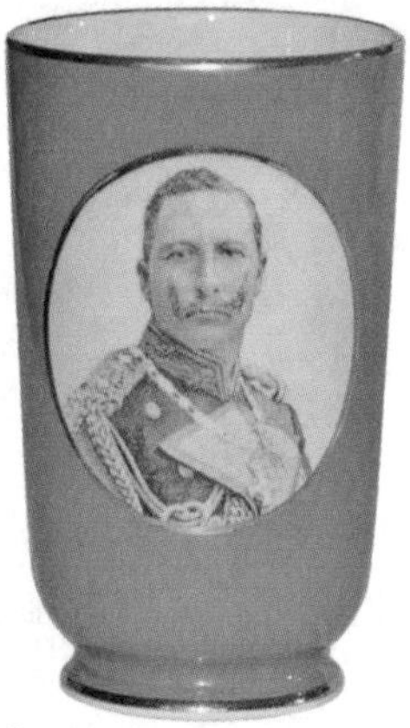

Fox Auctions

**Villeroy & Boch,** Paperweight, Dresden, Gnome, 3 x 5 ¾ In.
$96

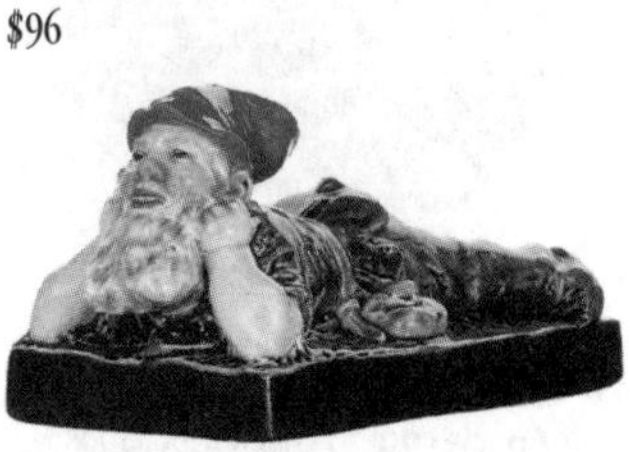

The Stein Auction Company

**Figurine,** Fantasia, Unicorn, Blue Flower, Ceramic, 1940, 4 ½ In. .... 411
**Gingham,** Carafe, Lid, Bulbous, 7 ½ In. .... 48
**Gingham,** Platter, 14 x 10 In. .... 30
**Harvest,** Chop Plate, 12 In. .... 30
**Hawaiian Flowers,** Plate, Dinner, c.1942, 10 ½ In. .... 90
**Hawaiian Flowers,** Salt & Pepper .... 85
**Hawaiian Flowers,** Sugar & Creamer .... 135
**Heavenly Days,** Coffeepot, Lid, 10 ¾ In. .... 55
**Homespun,** Salt & Pepper, Bulbous, 3 In. .... 18
**Organdie,** Chop Plate, 14 In. .... 28
**Organdie,** Eggcup, Double, 3 ½ In. .... 24
**Rosalie,** Coffeepot, Upside Down Handle, 8 ½ In. .... 62
**Tam O'Shanter,** Bowl, Vegetable, 8 ⅞ In. .... 37
**Tam O'Shanter,** Bowl, Vegetable, Divided, 11 ½ x 6 In. .... 18
**Tickled Pink,** Creamer .... 12
**Tickled Pink,** Cup, 2 ¾ x 4 ¾ In. .... 6
**Tickled Pink,** Plate, Dinner, 9 ⅞ In. .... 10
**Tickled Pink,** Soup, Dish, 8 In. .... 10

**VIENNA**, *see Beehive category.*

**VIENNA ART** plates are round metal serving trays produced at the turn of the century. The designs, copied from Royal Vienna porcelain plates, usually featured a portrait of a woman encircled by a wide, ornate border. Many were used as advertising or promotional items and were produced in Coshocton, Ohio, by J. F. Meeks Tuscarora Advertising Co. and H.D. Beach's Standard Advertising Co.

**Plate,** Cupid, Seated Woman, Banded Border, 10 In. .... 60
**Plate,** Flower Girl Jane, Blond, Roses, c.1909, 10 In. .... 85
**Plate,** Jamestown, Pocahontas, 1905, 10 In. .... 125
**Plate,** Louise, Long Hair, Flower, c.1907, 9 ⅝ In. .... 85
**Plate,** Phantasie, Hat, Holding Flower, c.1907, 10 ¼ In. .... 75
**Plate,** Sappho, Pink Gown, Holding Lyre, 8 ⅞ In. .... 65
**Plate,** Woman, Cupid, Bow & Arrows, Banded Border, 10 In. .... 55
**Plate,** Woman, Partially Nude, Long Hair, Blue & Gold Border, 1905, 10 In. .... 259

**VILLEROY & BOCH POTTERY** of Mettlach was founded in 1836. The firm made many types of wares, including the famous Mettlach steins. Collectors can be confused because although Villeroy & Boch made most of its pieces in the city of Mettlach, Germany, the company also had factories in other locations. The dating code impressed on the bottom of most pieces makes it possible to determine the age of the piece. Additional items, including steins and earthenware pieces marked with the famous castle mark or the word *Mettlach*, may be found in the Mettlach category.

**Beaker,** Portrait, Wilhelm II, Blue, Dresden, ¼ Liter .... *illus* 144
**Bowl,** Vegetable, Lid, Vieux Bruxelles, 3 Qt. .... 249
**Bowl,** Vegetable, Verona, 8 ⅜ In. .... 45
**Box,** Octagonal, King Of Hearts, Queen Of Spades, 4 x 2 In. .... 20
**Butter,** Cover, Vieux Bruxelles, ½ Lb. .... 99
**Chop Plate,** Verona, 12 ⅜ In. .... 55
**Chop Plate,** Vieux Bruxelles, 13 ¼ In. .... 79
**Coaster Set,** No. 1395, No. 1397, No. 1399, No. 1400, Children, 5 Piece .... 114
**Coffeepot,** Lid, Vieux Bruxelles, 6 Cup .... 99
**Cup & Saucer,** Vieux Bruxelles .... 28
**Gravy Boat,** Underplate, Vieux Bruxelles .... 79
**Paperweight,** Dresden, Gnome, 3 x 5 ¾ In. .... *illus* 96
**Platter,** Vieux Bruxelles, Oval, 14 ¼ In. .... 89
**Soup,** Dish, Ascoli, Rimmed, 8 ⅞ In. .... 15
**Tray,** Dresden, Shields, Broken Branches, 1888, Wood Frame, 15 x 23 In. .... *illus* 1680
**Vase,** Tulips, 2 Handles, Stamped, c.1904, 15 ½ x 7 ½ In. .... 1000

**VOLKSTEDT** was a soft-paste porcelain factory started in 1760 by Georg Heinrich Macheleid at Volkstedt, Thuringia. Volkstedt-Rudolstadt was a porcelain factory started at Volkstedt-Rudolstadt by Beyer and Bock in 1890. Most pieces seen in shops today are from the later factory.

**Group,** 2 Women Dancing, Stamped, c.1920, 12 ¾ x 7 In. .... 210
**Group,** 3 Ballerinas Dancing, Lace Dresses, Germany, 11 x 11 In. .... 1121
**Group,** 3 Women Having Tea, Man Attending, Painted, Lace, 5 x 7 ¼ In. .... 115
**Group,** Gentleman & Lady At Small Table, Man Offering Snuff, Crinoline, 9 x 11 In. .... 325

**Group,** Musical Family, 1700s Style, 7 Figures, Piano, Harp, 20 x 14 In. ...................................... 1150

---

**WADE** pottery is made by the Wade Group of Potteries started in 1810 near Burslem, England. Several potteries merged to become George Wade & Son, Ltd., early in the twentieth century, and other potteries have been added through the years. The best-known Wade pieces are the small figurines called Whimsies. They were first were made in 1954. Special Whimsies were given away with Red Rose Tea beginning in 1967. The Disney figures are listed in this book in the Disneyana category.

**WADE**
*figures*
c. 1936+

| | |
|---|---:|
| **Ashtray,** Fisherman, Fly Fishing, Crimped Edge, 4¾ In. ........................................ | 10 |
| **Ashtray,** Horse Drawn Coach, Passengers, Crimped Rim, 4¾ In. ........................ | 10 |
| **Bank,** Truck, Thornton's Chocolates, 1911, 4 x 8 x 3 In. ...................................... | 28 |
| **Bowl,** Flowers, Copper Luster, c.1925, 4 In. ........................................................ | 79 |
| **Cream & Sugar,** Bramble Pattern, c.1940 ............................................................ | 25 |
| **Creamer,** Peonies, c.1950, 3½ In. ........................................................................ | 35 |
| **Dish,** Figural, Pelican, Open Beak, White, Yellow, c.1945, 6 x 7½ In. ................ | 275 |
| **Figurine,** Baby Scruple, Green, 3 In. .............................................................*illus* | 496 |
| **Figurine,** Beaver, Holding Stump, 1½ In. ............................................................ | 6 |
| **Figurine,** Bison, Brown, Tan, 1½ In. .................................................................... | 5 |
| **Figurine,** Blynken, Marked, c.1950, 2½ In. ......................................................... | 90 |
| **Figurine,** Character, Red Jacket, Blue Pants, I'm A Wade Collector .................... | 98 |
| **Figurine,** Circus Lion, 1¾ In. .............................................................................. | 8 |
| **Figurine,** Doctor Foster, 1½ In. ........................................................................... | 5 |
| **Figurine,** Duck, Blue, Tan, 1½ In. ....................................................................... | 5 |
| **Figurine,** Hickory Dickory Dock, 1¾ In. ............................................................ | 6 |
| **Figurine,** Irish Setter, 2½ x 2½ In. ...................................................................... | 40 |
| **Figurine,** Jack & Jill, Carrying Buckets, 1970s, 3 In., 2 Piece ............................ | 48 |
| **Figurine,** Kangaroo, 1½ In. .................................................................................. | 9 |
| **Figurine,** Little Bo Peep, 1½ In. .......................................................................... | 5 |
| **Figurine,** Little Boy Blue, 1½ In. ......................................................................... | 5 |
| **Figurine,** Little Jack Horner, 1½ In. ................................................................... | 24 |
| **Figurine,** Old King Cole, 1½ In. ......................................................................... | 25 |
| **Figurine,** Orangutan, Hands Over Face, 1½ In. .................................................. | 10 |
| **Figurine,** Peregrine Falcon, 1¾ In. ..................................................................... | 7 |
| **Figurine,** Pied Piper, 1½ In. ................................................................................ | 19 |
| **Figurine,** Pied Piper, 1¾ In. ................................................................................ | 5 |
| **Figurine,** Poodle, White, 1½ In. .......................................................................... | 8 |
| **Figurine,** Queen Of Hearts, 1¾ In. ..................................................................... | 10 |
| **Figurine,** Wee Willie Winkle, 1½ In. ................................................................... | 5 |
| **Pipe Holder,** Spaniel, Green Base, 3 x 3 In. ........................................................ | 44 |
| **Planter,** Viking Ship, Brown Glaze, 7⅜ x 3½ In. ................................................ | 62 |
| **Salt & Pepper,** Branch, Leaf, Yellow, 2¾ In. ........................................................ | 30 |
| **Teapot,** Scottish Golfer, Tartan Cap, 1950s, 5 In. ................................................ | 45 |
| **Trinket Box,** Treasure Chest Shape, Brown, 1961, 1½ x 3⅝ In. ........................... | 18 |
| **Trinket Box,** Turtle Shape, Marked, 4 In. ............................................................ | 35 |
| **Vase,** Dogwood, Brown, Green, Bud, 3½ x 3½ In. ............................................... | 29 |

---

**WAHPETON POTTERY**, *see Rosemeade category.*

---

**WALL POCKETS** were popular in the 1930s. They were made by many American and European factories. Glass, pottery, porcelain, majolica, chalkware, and metal wall pockets can be found in many fanciful shapes.

| | |
|---|---:|
| **Flowers,** Butterfly, Cream Ground, Blue Lake Scene, Marked Luneville, France, 12½ In. ............. | 118 |
| **Majolica,** Leaves, Yellow Bird's Nest Pocket, Blackbird, c.1890, 11½ In. ............................ | 250 |
| **Pine,** Half Hull Pocket, Carved, Pierced, Stars, Heart, c.1865, 9½ x 20 In. .................................... | 1080 |

---

**WALLACE NUTTING** *photographs are listed under Print, Nutting. His reproduction furniture is listed under Furniture.*

---

**WALRATH** was a potter who worked in New York City; Rochester, New York; and at the Newcomb Pottery in New Orleans, Louisiana. Frederick Walrath died in 1920. Pieces listed here are from his Rochester period.

Walrath
Pottery

| | |
|---|---:|
| **Bowl,** Seated Nude Figure, Green Matte, Signed, 7 x 6 In. ..................................... | 207 |
| **Lamp,** Flower Shape, Green Glaze, Marked, c.1910, 12½ x 8 In. ..............*illus* | 5938 |
| **Vase,** Arrow Root Decoration, Green Matte Glaze, Rose Highlights, Reticulated, 8½ In. ............... | 978 |
| **Vase,** Arts & Crafts, Incised, Green Matte Glaze, Stylized Flowers, 8 In. .................. | 3105 |
| **Vase,** Calla Lilies, Cylindrical, c.1910, 7 x 3½ In. ................................................ | 5937 |

**Villeroy & Boch,** Tray, Dresden, Shields, Broken Branches, 1888, Wood Frame, 15 x 23 In.
$1,680

The Stein Auction Company

**Wade,** Figurine, Baby Scruple, Green, 3 In.
$496

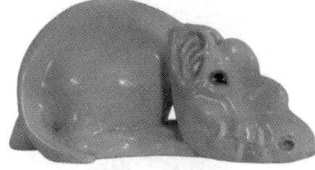

Potteries Specialist Auctions (PSA)

**Walrath,** Lamp, Flower Shape, Green Glaze, Marked, c.1910, 12½ x 8 In.
$5,938

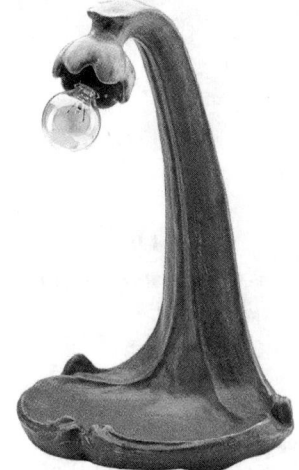

Rago Arts & Auction Center

W

**Watch,** E. Howard, Hunter Case, 14K Gold, Engraved, Crown Wind, c.1880, 1 ½ In.
$923

**Watch,** Gruen, Verithin Octagon, 14K Bicolor Gold, Parchment, 17 Jewel, Pocket
$390

### TIP
*Restoring and reusing old things is the purest form of recycling.*

**Weather Vane,** Codfish, Full Body, Copper, Gilt, Applied Sheet Iron Fins, c.1910, 30 In.
$3,998

**W**

---

**WALT DISNEY**, *see Disneyana category.*

---

**WALTER**, *see A. Walter category.*

---

**WARWICK** china was made in Wheeling, West Virginia, in a pottery working from 1887 to 1951. Many pieces were made with hand painted or decal decorations. The most familiar Warwick has a shaded brown background. The name *Warwick* is part of the mark and sometimes the mysterious word *IOGA* is also included.

| | |
|---|---:|
| **Chamber Pot,** Flowers, Buds, Leaves, Blue, Green, Finial, c.1890, 10 In. | 60 |
| **Compote,** Intertwined L & C, Restaurant Ware, 3 x 6 In. | 25 |
| **Mug,** Monks, Drinking, Reading, c.1925, 3 In., 4 Piece | 69 |
| **Plate,** Fish, Shells, Brown Band, Scalloped Edge, 8 ½ In. | 120 |
| **Plate,** Fort Harrison Hotel, Clearwater, Florida, Logo, c.1925, 8 In. | 48 |
| **Platter,** Trees & Golfer Border, Black, Broadmoor Golf Course, 1970s, 12 x 8 In. | 45 |
| **Vase,** Portrait, Handles, Footed, 10 In. | 375 |

**WATCH** pockets held the pocket watch that was important in Victorian times because it was not until World War I that the wristwatch was used. All types of watches are collected: silver, gold, or plated. Watches are listed here by company name or by style. Wristwatches are a separate category.

| | |
|---|---:|
| **Alfred Gerard,** 18K Gold, Porcelain Face, Sunken Sub Second Hand, c.1872 | 1064 |
| **Allport & Sons,** Uttoxeter, Sterling Case, Engraved, c.1851 | 180 |
| **Ancre Remontoir,** Demi-Hunting, Silver, 15 Jewel, Switzerland, c.1910 | 154 |
| **Bonnett,** Hunting Case, 14K Yellow Gold, Lever Set, White Enamel Dial, Swiss, c.1910 | 540 |
| **Borquin,** Hunting Case, 18K Gold, 2nd Hand Dial, Blue, White Enameled Leaves, Star, 1800s | 540 |
| **Bucherer,** Blue Guilloche Enamel, Roses, Ball Shape, Chain, Bar Pin, Sterling, ¾ x 30 In. | 259 |
| **Cartier,** Silver, Envelope Shape, Slides Open, Addressed, White Dial Inside, 1941, 1 ½ In. | 2125 |
| **Cavour,** Pendant, Silver Repousse, Open Face, Engraved, Painted Dial, c.1910 | 60 |
| **E. Howard,** Hunter Case, 14K Gold, Engraved, Crown Wind, c.1880, 1 ½ In. ...............*illus* | 923 |
| **Elgin,** 14K Gold, Porcelain Dial, Roman Numerals, Breguet Hands, JRD, Box Case | 1230 |
| **Elgin,** Hunting Case, 14K Gold, Stippled, Enamel Flowers, Diamond, Woman's, 1 ½ In. | 690 |
| **Elgin,** Open Face, 14K Yellow Gold, Silvertone Dial, 24 Jewel, Chain, 1 ¾ In. | 506 |
| **George Hooper,** Hunting Case, 18K Yellow Gold, White Porcelain Dial, 1800s | 1200 |
| **Golay-Lerescme & Fils,** 18K Yellow Gold, Open Face, Enamel Woman's Portrait, 1800s, 1 In. | 1035 |
| **Gruen,** Verithin Octagon, 14K Bicolor Gold, Parchment, 17 Jewel, Pocket................*illus* | 390 |
| **Hamilton,** 14K Yellow Gold Case, Open Face, Silvertone Dial, 1 ¾ In. | 472 |
| **Hampden,** New Railway, 23 Jewel, Double Roller, 5 ½ In. | 196 |
| **Harris & Shafer,** Silver, Goliath, Seconds Dial, Spade Hands, France, c.1910, Pocket | 338 |
| **Howard & Co.,** Opens To Reveal Key Winding, 1860, 2 ⅛ In., Pocket | 379 |
| **Howard,** Art Deco, 14K White Gold, Open Face, Engraved, Silvertone Dial, 2 In. | 644 |
| **Hunting Case,** 18K Gold, 5-Minute Repeat, Seconds Dial, Arabic Numerals, Tiffany & Co. | 4920 |
| **Hunting Case,** 18K Gold, Enamel Peacock, Roses, Stones, Arabic Numerals, Chain, Woman's | 369 |
| **Illinois Watch Co.,** Bunn Special, 1 ⅝ In. | 210 |
| **J. Roulet,** Hunting Case, 14K Gold, Engine Turned, Porcelain Dial, Seconds, Roman Numerals | 615 |
| **Jules Jurgensen,** 14K Gold, Sunk Seconds Dial, Repeating, Copenhagen, c.1890, Pocket | 3998 |
| **L. Raby,** Hunting Case, 18K Gold, Porcelain Dial, Moon Hands, Roman Numerals, Repeating | 1845 |
| **Lady Waltham,** 14K Gold, Monogram, Lapel, 1915, 1 In. | 81 |
| **Longines,** Hunting Case, Minute Repeat, 14K Gold, Porcelain Dial, Spade Hands, c.1900 | 4920 |
| **New England Co.,** Duplex Escapement, Glass Front & Back, Seconds Dial, 2 In. | 284 |
| **Open Face,** 18K Gold, Engine Turned, Champleve Dial, Quarter Repeat, Music | 4920 |
| **Open Face,** Gold, Ruby, Diamonds, Cream Color Dial, Arabic Numerals, Woman's, 1 In. | 472 |
| **Patek Philippe,** Open Face, 5-Minute Repeat, Porcelain Dial, Arabic Numerals, Box, Chain | 9225 |
| **Patek Philippe,** Silvertone Case, Gold Plated Fob, Engraved Patennaude Bros., 1 ¾ In. | 2760 |
| **Pendant,** 18K Yellow Gold Case, Branch Pin, Blue Enamel, Gilt, Le Monde, 1 ¾ x 1 In. | 357 |
| **Pendant,** Omega, 14K Hexagonal Case, Round Cut Diamonds, Goldtone Dial, Woman's, 1 In. | 460 |
| **Roulette,** Red, White, Black, France, Pocket, c.1890 | 100 |
| **Tiffany & Co.,** Sterling Silver, Repousse Carved | 338 |
| **Tiffany,** 18K Gold, Spade Hands, Sunk Seconds Dial, Open Face Case, Geneva, Pocket | 3690 |
| **Tiffany,** Chronograph, Sunk Seconds Dial, Moon Hands, Stem Wind, c.1900, Pocket | 5843 |
| **Waltham,** Hunting Case, Raised Flowers, 14K Gold, 15 Jewel, Signed Face, Woman's, 1 ¾ In. | 322 |

**WATCH FOBS** were worn on watch chains. They were popular during Victorian times and after. Many styles, especially advertising designs, are still made today.

| | |
|---|---:|
| **9K Rose Gold,** Woven Hair, Victorian, c.1875, 8 ¾ In. | 185 |
| **Binoculars,** Brass, Leather, Italy, 1900s, 3 ½ In. | 139 |

| | |
|---|---|
| **Buick Motor Cars,** Shield Shape, Inlaid Cloisonne Enamel, 1¾ x 1¼ In. | 218 |
| **Unger Brothers,** Art Nouveau, Figural, Silver, Woman, Profile, Long Hair, 6¼ In. | 826 |
| **Zeolene Motor Oil,** Car, Embossed, Metal, 1¾ x 1 In. | 207 |

**WATERFORD** type glass resembles the famous glass made from 1783 to 1851 in the Waterford Glass Works in Ireland. It is a clear glass that was often decorated by cutting. Modern glass is being made again in Waterford, Ireland, and is marketed under the name Waterford. Waterford merged with Wedgwood in 1986 to form the Waterford Wedgwood Group. Most Waterford Wedgwood assets were bought by KPS Capital Partners of New York in 2009 and became part of WWRD Holdings.

| | |
|---|---|
| **Bowl,** Liberty, Benjamin Franklin, 6 x 9¾ In. | 150 |
| **Bowl,** Metra, Crystal, Square, 4 x 10 In. | 84 |
| **Candleholder,** Crystal, Hurricane, Scalloped Rim, 12 In. | 150 |
| **Chess Set,** Velvet-Lined Case, King, 6⅛ In. | 1000 |
| **Sconce,** 2-Light, Clear Prisms, c.1890, 22 In., Pair | 313 |
| **Tumbler,** Old Fashioned, Lismore, Cut Crystal, 8 Piece | 450 |
| **Vase,** Cut Crystal, Globe Shape, 7½ In. | 60 |
| **Vase,** Maritana, Flared, Crystal, 14 x 9¼ In. | 270 |

**WATT** family members bought the Globe pottery of Crooksville, Ohio, in 1922. They made pottery mixing bowls and tableware of the type made by Globe. In 1935 they changed the production and made the pieces with the freehand decorations that are popular with collectors today. Apple, Starflower, Rooster, Tulip, and Autumn Foliage are the best-known patterns. Pansy, also called Rio Rose, was the earliest pattern. Apple, the most popular pattern, can be dated from the leaves. Originally, the apples had three leaves; after 1958 two leaves were used. The plant closed in 1965. For more prices, go to kovels.com.

| | |
|---|---|
| **Apple,** Ice Bucket, 3-Leaf, Lid, 7 x 8½ In. | 145 |
| **Apple,** Mixing Bowl, No. 7, 3-Leaf | 45 |
| **Apple,** Pie Plate, No. 33, 3-Leaf, 9½ In. | 15 |
| **Apple,** Pitcher, No. 15, 3-Leaf, 5½ In. | 29 |
| **Apple,** Pitcher, No. 16, 3-Leaf, 7 In. | 56 |
| **Apple,** Pitcher, No. 62, 3-Leaf, Long Lake Elev. & Lbr. Co., 4½ In. | 165 |
| **Apple,** Salt & Pepper, 3-Leaf, 4½ In. | 40 |
| **Autumn Foliage,** Bowl, No. 65, 6 Pt., 9 x 6 In. | 85 |
| **Autumn Foliage,** Creamer, No. 62, 4¼ In. | 190 |
| **Cherry,** Mixing Bowl, No. 4, 4 In. | 75 |
| **Moonflower,** Cup & Saucer | 125 |
| **Pansy,** Bowl, 5 In., 4 Piece | 65 |
| **Pansy,** Pitcher, No. 17, 8 In. | 128 |
| **Pansy,** Serving Bowl, 13 In. | 18 |
| **Pansy,** Serving Bowl, 14¾ In. | 100 |
| **Rio Rose,** see Pansy. | |
| **Rooster,** Mixing Bowl, No. 9, 9 In. | 20 |
| **Rooster,** Pitcher, No. 15, M.N. Kunkel, Kempton, Pa., 5½ In. | 115 |
| **Silhouette,** Casserole, No. 18, Lid, Tab Handles | 100 |
| **Starflower,** Pitcher, No. 16, 5-Petal, 6½ In. | 32 to 45 |
| **Starflower,** Pitcher, No. 17, 5-Petal, 8 In. | 85 to 100 |
| **Starflower,** Salt & Pepper, 4½ In. | 10 |
| **Tear Drop,** Bowl, No. 5, Rounded Sides, Ribbed, No. 5, 5¼ x 2½ In. | 35 |
| **Tear Drop,** Pitcher, No. 15, 5⅝ In. | 32 |
| **Tulip,** Bowl, Spaghetti, No. 39, 13 In. | 32 |
| **Tulip,** Pitcher, No. 15, 5 In. | 140 |

**WAVE CREST** glass is an opaque white glassware manufactured by the Pairpoint Manufacturing Company of New Bedford, Massachusetts, and some French factories. It was decorated by the C.F. Monroe Company of Meriden, Connecticut. The glass was painted in pastel colors and decorated with flowers. The name Wave Crest was used starting in 1892.

WAVE CREST WARE

| | |
|---|---|
| **Biscuit Jar,** Enameled Flowers, Swirl Mold, White, Lavender, Silver Plate Lid, Bail, 7½ In. | 177 |
| **Box,** Egg Crate Shape, Flower Sprays, Cream, Enameled Collars & Cuffs, 7½ x 5 In. | 944 |
| **Dresser Box,** Bishop's Hat, Iris, Brown & Yellow Ground, Footed, Nakara, 6 x 8 In. | 944 |
| **Dresser Box,** White Ground, Pink, Yellow Flowers, Round, Swirl Mold, 4 x 6½ In. | 148 |
| **Dresser Box,** Yellow Flowers, Shaded Brown, Lobed, Puffy, Metal Cherub Head Feet, 6 In. | 1180 |
| **Fernery,** Flowers, Pink, Green, 7½ In. | 55 |
| **Jewelry Box,** Cherub Playing Mandolin, Pink, White Flowers, Round, Nakara, 4 In. | 472 |
| **Jewelry Box,** Cobalt Blue, Pink Swags, Beaded, 6-Sided, Hinged, Kelva, 3½ In. | 295 |

## WAVE CREST

**Weather Vane,** Horse, Prancing, Enameled, Wrought Iron, William H. Diederich, 1930s, 40 x 49 In.
$59,375

Rago Arts & Auction Centera

**Weather Vane,** Locomobile, Flattened Full Body, Copper, E.G. Washburne Co., c.1910, 43 In.
$7,380

Skinner Auctioneers & Appraisers

**Weather Vane,** Pig, Sheet Iron, Painted, Applied Ears, Virginia, 23 x 47 In.
$4,248

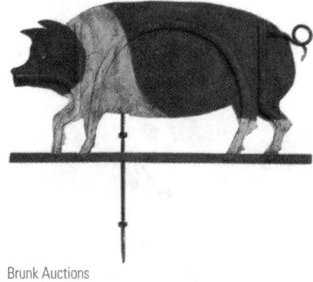

Brunk Auctions

**Weather Vane,** Rooster, Arrow, Full Body, Copper Gilt, U.S.A., c.1890, 26½ In.
$2,952

**W**

Skinner Auctioneers & Appraisers

# WAVE CREST

**Weather Vane,** Rooster, Copper, Molded, Hollow Arrow, Zinc, Gilt, Cushing, c.1890, 19 x 25 In. $2,074

James D. Julia Auctioneers

**Webb,** Coupe, Cameo, 3 Colors, Flowers, Leaves, Curling Handle, Signed, 9½ In. $2,875

Early Auction Co.

**Webb,** Finger Bowl, Alexandrite, Ruffled Rim, Underplate, Honeycomb Pattern, 5½ In. $805

Early Auction Co.

**Webb,** Perfume Bottle, Blue, Cameo Flower Cuttings, Laydown, 9½ In. $1,725

Early Auction Co.

| | |
|---|---|
| **Jewelry Box,** Hinged, Blue Flowers, Cherub, Yellow, White, Lobed, Square, 4 x 5 In. | 413 |
| **Powder Box,** Gray Blue, Flowers, White Enameling, Gilt Metal Mounts, Hinged Lid, 2 x 3 In. | 81 |
| **Sugar Shaker,** Erie Twist, Blue, Flower Panels, Silver Plate Lid, C.F. Monroe, c.1902, 3 In. | 173 |
| **Sugar Shaker,** No. 69, Opal, Flowers, Green, Silver Plate Lid, C.F. Monroe, c.1880, 5 In. | 80 |
| **Vase,** Opal Body, Purple Enamel, Chrysanthemum, Metal Frame, 4-Footed, 11 In. | 316 |

**WEAPONS** listed here include instruments of combat other than guns, knives, rifles, or swords and clothing worn in combat. Firearms made after 1900 are not listed in this book. Knives and Swords are listed in their own categories.

| | |
|---|---|
| **Artillery Grease Bucket,** Iron, Handle, Chain, Lid, c.1861, 9 In. | 369 |
| **Ax,** Iron Handle, Dagger Shaped Head, Leaves, Lions, Elephant, Persia, 24½ In. | 338 |
| **Ax,** Iron Handle, Spear Point, Crescent Shape Head, Persia, 26½ In. | 215 |
| **Cannon,** Brass, Cast Iron Carriage, 12 In. | 94 |
| **Cannon,** Ringed Muzzle, Brass Barrel, Wood Carriage, 8-Spoke Wheels, Model, 7 In. | 624 |
| **Club,** Akau-Ta, Lancet Shape Paddle, Center Rib, Tapering Haft, Tonga Islands, 1800s, 45 In. | 925 |
| **Halberd,** Curved Sides, Tapered Spike, Iron, 22 In. | 293 |
| **Man Catcher,** Rattan, Center Wood Barbed Spear, Jute, Papua New Guinea, 1800s, 74 In. | 2774 |
| **Mortar,** Bronze, U.S. Model 1838, Ames Coehorn Co., c.1865, 16½ In. | 19680 |
| **Shield,** Kalam Simbai, Highlands, Carved Pattern, Red, Black, Papua New Guinea, 49 x 28 In. | 979 |
| **Suit Of Armor,** Chased Silver Metal, Plumed Helmet, Acid Etched Relief, Spain, 1900s, 69 In. | 1581 |
| **Throwing Club,** Gourd Shape Head, Carved Grip, Indented Handle, Fiji Islands, 1800s, 16 In. | 1904 |
| **Torpedo Director,** Brass, Compass Settings, Japanese Characters, 1900-25, 11 x 11 In. | 215 |

**WEATHER VANES** were used in seventeenth-century Boston. The direction of the wind was an indication of coming weather, important to the seafaring and farming communities. By the mid-nineteenth century, commercial weather vanes were made of metal. Many were shaped like animals. Ethan Allen, Dexter, and St. Julian are famous horses that were depicted. Today's collectors often consider weather vanes to be examples of folk art, even though they may not have been handmade.

| | |
|---|---|
| **Airplane,** Wood, Tin, Primitive, c.1905, 22½ In. | 111 |
| **Angel Gabriel,** Blowing Trumpet, Sheet Iron, Paint, Stand, 48 In. | 540 |
| **Arrow,** Copper, Molded, Belted Ball, Sheet Copper Feather, c.1890, 18 x 37 In. | 677 |
| **Arrow,** Directional, Shaped Shaft, On Pole, Scroll Base, Iron, 41 In., Pair | 330 |
| **Arrow,** Gilt, Turned 3-Tier Giltwood Finial, 16 x 26 In. | 900 |
| **Arrow,** Molded Top Finial, Cast Iron, Sheet Copper Feathers, Verdigris, 19 x 36 In. | 1185 |
| **Banner,** Cutout, Copper, Zinc, Verdigris, c.1865, 34 In. | 2700 |
| **Banner,** Horse, Bull, Paint, Sheet Iron, 1800s, 21 x 36 In. | 1320 |
| **Banner,** Pierced 1869, Bullet Holes, Sheet Metal, Weathered, Sawtooth Edge, 36 In. | 720 |
| **Beaver,** Sheet Iron, Riveted, Red Paint, Steel Mounting Rod, 9 x 15 In. | 960 |
| **Bicycle,** Penny Farthing, Copper, Tubular, Wire, Sheet, Arrow Base, 1900s, 20 x 33 In. | 1185 |
| **Blacksmith,** Hammer, Mallet, Painted, 33½ In. | 720 |
| **Boat Paddle,** Wood, Black Paint, Architectural Ball On Top, 36 x 41 In. | 300 |
| **Bull,** Sheet Iron, 32 x 22½ In. | 351 |
| **Butterfly,** Sheet Copper, Spread Wings, J.W. Fiske, New York, 10½ x 23 In. | 3318 |
| **Coaching Horn,** Copper, Molded & Cast, Tilt, Verdigris, c.1890, 50 x 4½ In. | 1422 |
| **Cockerel,** Standing, Directional, Metal, Green, Red Patina, c.1950, 34 In. | 1080 |
| **Cockerel,** Swelled Body, Gold Paint, Verdigris, c.1845, 30½ In. | 1440 |
| **Codfish,** Full Body, Copper, Gilt, Applied Sheet Iron Fins, c.1910, 30 In. *illus* | 3998 |
| **Copper,** Sailboat, c.1935, 46 In. | 330 |
| **Cow,** Cast Aluminum, c.1900, 24 x 21 In. | 140 |
| **Cow,** Copper, Full Body, c.1950, 20 x 23 In. | 1320 |
| **Cow,** Iron, Full Body, Standing, Weathered, Zinc Horns, c.1900, 27 x 34 In. | 4888 |
| **Crow,** Iron, Perched On Directional Arrow, Black, Red Tip, c.1910, 28 x 31 In. | 863 |
| **Dog,** Running, Sheet Iron, 35 x 11 In. | 761 |
| **Dove,** White, Carved, Blue Paint, Tin, Wood, 1920, 10 x 15 In. | 1920 |
| **Eagle,** Ball, Cast Metal Directional, 24-In. Wing Span, 39½ In. | 384 |
| **Eagle,** Copper, Gold Paint, Iron Stand, c.1920, 21 x 15 In. | 1265 |
| **Eagle,** Copper, Raised Wings, Clutching Serpent, Verdigris, c.1880, 28 In. | 3738 |
| **Eagle,** Spread Wings, Copper, Gilt Paint, c.1890, 18 x 32 In. | 720 |
| **Eagle,** Spread Wings, On Ball, Directionals, Sheet Copper, Molded, Gilt, c.1890, 72 In. | 1230 |
| **Eagle,** Wings Up, Copper, Gilding, c.1880, 20 x 25 In. | 3960 |
| **Fire Engine,** Horse Drawn, Sheet Metal, c.1880, 33 In. | 780 |
| **Fish,** Copper, 15½ x 31½ In. | 1180 |
| **Fish,** Green, Rust, White, Tin, 34 In. | 540 |
| **Fish,** Iron, Weathered, Painted Eye, Mounting Rod, c.1900, 46 x 26 In. | 2300 |

W

| | |
|---|---|
| **Fish,** Sheet Iron, Rust, c.1910, 22 In. | 600 |
| **Fish,** Wood, Eyes, Mouth Gills Carved, 20 ½ In. | 600 |
| **Flag,** Sheet Iron, Painted Horse, Bull On Reverse, 19th Century, 21 x 36 In. | 1320 |
| **Fox,** Running, Copper, Hammered, Gilt, Mounted, 20 x 32 In. | 15600 |
| **Fox,** Running, Iron, Old Black Over Old Red Paint, Mounting Rod, 16 x 23 In. | 2760 |
| **Grasshopper,** Copper, Molded, Outstretched Tongue, Zinc Eyes, Verdigris, 26 x 34 In. | 3555 |
| **Horse,** Jumping, Jockey Rider, Molded Copper, Cast Zinc, Gilt, Cushing & Son, 28 x 31 In. | 5535 |
| **Horse,** Leaping, Copper Sheet, Molded, Gilt, Full Body, Verdigris, A.L. Jewell & Co., 58 In. | 24600 |
| **Horse,** Leaping, With Rider, Wearing Top Hat, Copper, Molded, Full Body, c.1890, 32 In. | 7995 |
| **Horse,** Prancing, Enameled, Wrought Iron, William H. Diederich, 1930s, 40 x 49 In. ..........*illus* | 59375 |
| **Horse,** Running, Cast Iron Head, Copper, Verdigris Patina, c.1890, 21 x 41 In. | 2880 |
| **Horse,** Running, Copper, Brass Head, Wood Stand, c.1900, 17 x 32 In. | 1265 |
| **Horse,** Running, Copper, Cast Zinc Head, c.1850, 27 ½ In. | 780 |
| **Horse,** Running, Copper, Gilt, 18 ½ In. | 2520 |
| **Horse,** Running, Copper, Verdigris Patina, Stand, 40 In. | 3600 |
| **Horse,** Running, Copper, Zinc Mounts, 16 x 38 In. | 1875 |
| **Horse,** Running, Molded Copper, Flattened Full Body, A.L. Jewell, c.1860, 21 x 32 In. | 4920 |
| **Horse,** Running, Zinc, Patinated, 24 In. | 1003 |
| **Horse,** Sulky, Driver, Copper, c.1895, 18 x 34 In. | 1500 |
| **Horse,** Trotting, Full Body, Sheet Iron, Gilt, Rochester Iron Works, c.1880, 26 x 37 In. | 11685 |
| **Horse,** Trotting, Sheet Iron, Cutout, Gray Paint, c.1925, 9 x 20 In. | 207 |
| **Horse,** Trotting, Woman Rider, Arrow Directional, Sheet Iron, Early 1900s, 19 x 31 In. | 390 |
| **Horses,** Mare, Foal, Standing, Directional, Green Paint, Sheet Iron, Va., 50 x 48 In. | 920 |
| **Lighthouse,** Copper, Zinc, Gilt, 27 ½ In. | 1560 |
| **Lion,** Wrought Iron, Scrolling, Flowers, Directional Arrow, 8 ½ In. | 960 |
| **Lobster,** Copper, Molded, Gilt, Full Body, Stand, c.1950, 15 x 32 In. | 14220 |
| **Locomobile,** Flattened Full Body, Copper, E.G. Washburne Co., c.1910, 43 In. .................*illus* | 7380 |
| **Locomotive,** Copper, Cast Bronze Wheels, Engine, Tender, Cowcatcher, 1900s, 12 x 31 In. | 4740 |
| **Native American,** On Knee, Holding Knife & Ax, Sheet Iron, Painted, Rod, 14 In. | 480 |
| **Owl On Broom,** Copper, Molded, Weathered Gilt, 22 x 42 In. | 6814 |
| **Owl,** Perched On Arrow, Gilt Copper, Molded, 23 x 29 In. | 12980 |
| **Peacock,** Sheet Iron, Wrought Iron Comb & Tail, Pennsylvania, 58 x 30 In. | 3300 |
| **Pen Mightier Than The Sword,** Quill Pen Breaking Sword, Copper, Zinc, c.1890, 40 x 36 In. | 47400 |
| **Pig,** Copper, Flattened, Hammered, Patinated, 19 x 43 In. | 3600 |
| **Pig,** Molded Copper, Flattened Full Body, Applied Sheet Copper, c.1900, 21 x 33 In. | 4920 |
| **Pig,** Sheet Iron, Painted, Applied Ears, Virginia, 23 x 47 In. ..................*illus* | 4248 |
| **Pig,** Tin, Milk Glass Insulator, 59 ¾ In. | 590 |
| **Roadster,** Silhouette, Woman Driving, Billowing Dust, Chicken In Front, Zinc, 29 In. | 2006 |
| **Rooster,** Arrow, Full Body, Copper Gilt, U.S.A., c.1890, 26 ½ In. ..................*illus* | 2952 |
| **Rooster,** Cast Iron, Yellow Paint, Cast Iron, Full Body, Pierced Tail, c.1890, 33 x 35 In. | 3444 |
| **Rooster,** Copper, Molded, Hollow Arrow, Zinc, Gilt, Cushing, c.1890, 19 x 25 In. .................*illus* | 2074 |
| **Rooster,** Sheet Iron, 36 x 27 In. | 1053 |
| **Rooster,** Silhouette, Sheet Iron, Red Paint, 18 x 17 In. | 510 |
| **Rooster,** Strutting, Sheet Iron, Cutout Tail, On Ball, Multicolor Paint, Virginia | 5750 |
| **Sailing Ship,** 3-Masted, Carved Wood Hull, Wire Rigging, Tin Sails, 1900s, 45 x 26 In. | 1896 |
| **School Of Fish,** 3 Graduated Fish, Cast Zinc, Copper, 44 In. | 3600 |
| **Scrolled Banner,** Copper, Verdigris, Zinc Arrow Tip, 16 x 29 In. | 1560 |
| **Ship's Captain,** Silhouette, Holds Telescope, Sheet Iron, Iron Straps, 54 In. | 5400 |
| **Stag,** Leaping, Copper, Molded, Cast Zinc, Gilt, Full Body, c.1890, 30 x 30 In. | 7380 |
| **Steer,** Copper, Brass Horns, Directional, c.1950, 29 x 62 In. | 3738 |
| **Steer,** Copper, Full Body, Standing, Cast Zinc Head, 22 x 33 In. | 5280 |
| **Trade Sign,** Blacksmith's Anvil, Hammer, Feathered Arrow, Copper, 1900s, 26 x 54 In. | 5628 |
| **Whale,** Copper, 2 Sections, Applied Fins, Verdigris, c.1900, 38 ½ In. | 1003 |
| **Whale,** Copper, Full Body, Applied Verdigris Patina, c.1950, 38 In. | 461 |
| **Winged Angel,** Trumpeting, Full Body, Molded Copper, Mounted, 1900s, 17 x 38 In. | 12443 |
| **Woman,** Sitting At Spinning Wheel, Directionals, Wrought Iron, Weathered, 44 x 30 In. | 375 |
| **Woman,** With Tennis Racket, Molded Copper, c.1910, 28 x 24 In. | 710 |

**WEBB** glass was made by Thomas Webb & Sons of Ambelcot, England. Many types of art and cameo glass were made by them during the Victorian era. Production ceased by 1991 and the factory was demolished in 1995. Webb Burmese and Webb Peachblow are special colored glasswares of the Victorian era. They are listed at the end of this section. Glassware that is not Burmese or Peachblow is included here.

*Webb*

| | |
|---|---|
| **Biscuit Jar,** Morning Glory, Cameo Glass, Opaque Cut To Citron, 5 In. | 460 |
| **Bowl,** Bronze, Green, Blue, Red, Gold Iridescence, Footed, 4 x 8 In. | 316 |
| **Bowl,** Queen's Burmese, Flowers, Buds, Scalloped Rim, 2 Clear Frosted Handles, 4 x 6 In. | 649 |

**Webb,** Vase, Blue, White Honeysuckle, Stems & Leaves, Cameo, Signed, 6 ½ In.
$830

James D. Julia Auctioneers

**Webb,** Vase, Prussian Blue, Stemmed Flowers, Arrowpoint Rim, Cameo, Signed, 6 ¼ In.
$3,163

Early Auction Co.

**Webb Burmese,** Vase, Cherry & Vines, Leaves, Crimped Rim, Squat, c.1890, 3 In.
$161

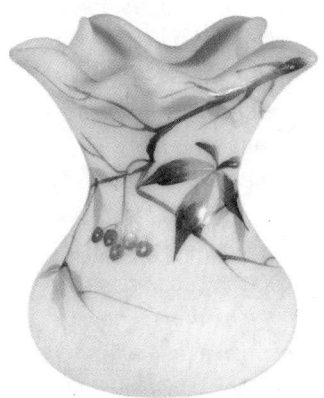

Jeffrey S. Evans & Assoc.

**W**

Wedgwood, Bowl, Fairyland Luster, Dragons, Mottled, Iridescent Blue, Stamped, c.1920, 10½ In.
$960

Cowan's Auctions

Wedgwood, Bowl, Fairyland Luster, Woodland Bridge, Picnic By River Interior, Fairies, 8 In.
$3,555

James D. Julia Auctioneers

Wedgwood, Dispenser, Lid, Spigot, Jockey, Racehorse, Marked, 1800s, 11¼ In.
$478

Neal Auction Co.

**TIP**

*Metal buttons made during World War II are often made of a nickel alloy that is silver and does not tarnish but is soft. Clean them by rubbing with a soft cloth. Examine any glass or plastic decorations like rhinestones. The glue shrinks eventually so the pieces may have to be re-glued.*

| | |
|---|---:|
| **Bowl,** Ruffled Rim, Berries, Branches, Flowers, Stems, Leaves, Green, Cameo, 2½ In. | 1244 |
| **Coupe,** Cameo, 3 Colors, Flowers, Leaves, Curling Handle, Signed, 9½ In. ............*illus* | 2875 |
| **Finger Bowl,** Alexandrite, Ruffled Rim, Underplate, Honeycomb Pattern, 5½ In. .........*illus* | 805 |
| **Goblet,** Alexandrite, Amber To Rose To Blue, Honeycomb, Spread Foot, 4½ In. | 575 |
| **Perfume Bottle,** Blue, Cameo Flower Cuttings, Laydown, 9½ In. ............*illus* | 1725 |
| **Perfume Bottle,** Blue, White Flowers, Silver Lid, Sampson & Mordan Co., 1887, 2¼ In. | 2125 |
| **Perfume Bottle,** Laydown, Butterfly, Citrine Ground, Silver Lid, Cameo, 4½ In. | 1481 |
| **Perfume Bottle,** Roses Yellow Ground, c.1890, 4 In. | 1500 |
| **Perfume Bottle,** White Cased Leaves & Stems, Translucent Blue, Cameo, Silver Cap, 3 In. | 1896 |
| **Perfume Bottle,** White Vine, Blue Ground, Laydown, Cameo, Gorham Silver Cap, 6½ In. | 2074 |
| **Perfume Burner,** Cameo, Ivory, Dogwood Blossom, Oval, Half Moon Mark, 4½ In. | 690 |
| **Pitcher,** Creamer, Alexandrite, Honeycomb, Shaded Amber Rose To Blue, 2½ In. | 661 |
| **Pitcher,** Flowers, Stems, Leaves, Yellow Ground, Cameo, 5 In. | 555 |
| **Plate,** Alexandrite, Moire, Ruffled Rim, 6 In. | 316 |
| **Rose Bowl,** Cased, Amber To Brown, Gold Flowers, Stand-Up Rim, 4 In. | 115 |
| **Rose Bowl,** Moire, Mother-Of-Pearl, 3 Thorny Feet, 5½ In. | 230 |
| **Scent Bottle,** Ivory, Cameo, Flask Shape, Cut Blossoms, Embossed Floral Lip, Stopper, 3 In. | 1495 |
| **Scent Bottle,** Laydown, Teardrop Shape, Red, Opal Flowers, Silver Collar, Presentation Box, 5 In. | 1495 |
| **Vase,** Alexandrite, Bulbous Smokestack Shape, Hexagonal Rim, 3¼ In. | 719 |
| **Vase,** Blue, White Honeysuckle, Stems & Leaves, Cameo, Signed, 6½ In. ............*illus* | 830 |
| **Vase,** Bud, Alexandrite, Amber To Blue To Fuchsia, Optic Rib, Flared Mushroom Rim, 3 In. | 575 |
| **Vase,** Damask Rose, Stems, Leaves, Buds, Carved Rim, Yellow Ground, Cameo, 8 In. | 1422 |
| **Vase,** Dragon, Stylized Clouds, Grasses, Rocks, Frosted, Round, Squat, Cameo, 7 x 8 In. | 1896 |
| **Vase,** Flower, Leaf, Vine, Pale Blue Ground, Cameo, Signed, 8¼ In. | 829 |
| **Vase,** Flowers, Stem, Leaves, Honeybees, Butterflies, Cameo, Signed, 9¼ In. | 2310 |
| **Vase,** Honeysuckle, Stems, Leaves, Red Ground Cameo, 6½ In. | 1836 |
| **Vase,** Ivory, Bottle Shape, Mythological Moorish Panels, Elephant Handles, Cameo, 7½ In. | 3565 |
| **Vase,** Ivory, Red Bird, Butterfly, Flowers, 6-Sided Rim, 4 In. | 531 |
| **Vase,** Leaves & Berries, Burmese, 6-Sided Rim, 3 x 3¾ In. | 354 |
| **Vase,** Prussian Blue, Stemmed Flowers, Arrowpoint Rim, Cameo, Signed, 6¼ In. ............*illus* | 3163 |
| **Vase,** Red Frosted, Stemmed Flowering Branch, Butterfly, Bulbous, Moorish Rim, Cameo, 8 In. | 1150 |
| **Vase,** Red Satin Glass, White Floral Cameo, Butterfly, Bulbous, Marked, c.1900, 4 In. | 492 |
| **Vase,** Red Satin, White Over Blue Oak Branch, Leaves, Seed Pods, Bulbous, Cameo, 8 In. | 9488 |
| **Vase,** Stick, Alexandrite, Honeycomb Pattern, Elongated Neck, Blue Undulating Rim, 13 In. | 2875 |
| **Vase,** White Cabbage Rose, Stems, Leaves, Bird, Yellow Ground, Cameo, Signed, 9½ In. | 2370 |
| **Vase,** White Flowers & Leaves, Red Ground, Bulbous, Flared Neck, Cameo, 4⅝ In. | 2252 |
| **Vase,** White Grapevines, Leaves, Frosted Red Ground, Cameo, Signed, 11 In. | 7121 |
| **Vase,** White Leaves, Flowers, Insect, Amber Ground, Cameo, Signed, 9 In. | 711 |
| **Vase,** White Morning Glory Flowers, Stick Neck, Cranberry, Carved, England, 3¾ In. | 944 |

**WEBB BURMESE** is a shaded Victorian glass made by Thomas Webb & Sons of Stourbridge, England, from 1886. Pieces are shades of pink to yellow.

| | |
|---|---:|
| **Epergne,** 3 Arms, Center Vase, Stand, Painted, Flowers, Buds, Leaves, Brass, 9½ In. | 2645 |
| **Fairy Lamp,** Red Berries, Green Leafy Branch, Clarke Clear Holder, 5½ In. | 633 |
| **Lamp,** Oil, Holly Leaves, Berries, Graduated Colors, 13½ x 4 In. | 3910 |
| **Vase,** Bottle, Yellow Shaded To Rose, Yellow, Green & Blue Leaves, Stems, 10 In. | 119 |
| **Vase,** Cherry & Vines, Leaves, Crimped Rim, Squat, c.1890, 3 In. ............*illus* | 161 |
| **Vase,** Hawthorn Pattern, Barrel Shape, 3½ In. | 173 |
| **Vase,** Melon Ribbed, Red Berries, Green Vines, 3½ In. | 259 |

**WEBB PEACHBLOW** is a shaded Victorian glass made by Thomas Webb & Sons of Stourbridge, England, from 1885.

| | |
|---|---:|
| **Biscuit Jar,** Rose Shaded, Gold Enamel Branch Flower, Silver Plate Lid, Bail, 7 In. | 236 |
| **Rose Bowl,** Amber Shaded To Rose, Cascading Gingko Branch, Oval, 5½ In. | 230 |
| **Vase,** Cascading Gold Ginko, Bulbous Smokestack Form, 6½ In. | 288 |
| **Vase,** Matsu-No-Ke, Gloss Glaze, Spiraling Branches, 14 In., Pair | 115 |

**WEDGWOOD,** one of the world's most successful potteries, was founded by Josiah Wedgwood, who was considered a cripple by his brother and was forbidden to work at the family business. The pottery was established in England in 1759. The company used a variety of marks, including Wedgwood, Wedgwood & Bentley, Wedgwood & Sons, and Wedgwood's Stone China. A large variety of wares has been made, including the well-known jasperware, basalt, creamware, and even a limited amount of porcelain. There are two kinds of jasperware. One is made from two colors of clay; the other is made from one color of clay with a color dip to create the contrast in design. In 1986 Wedgwood and Waterford Crystal merged to form the Waterford Wedgwood Group. Most Waterford

WEDGWOOD

Wedgwood assets were bought by KPS Capital Partners of New York in 2009 and became part of WWRD Holdings. Some manufacturing will be transferred to Germany, Indonesia, and Slovakia. Other Wedgwood pieces may be listed under Flow Blue, Majolica, Tea Leaf Ironstone, or in other porcelain categories.

| | |
|---|---:|
| **Biscuit Jar,** Green, White, Classical Scene, Silver Plated Lid, 6 In. | 177 |
| **Biscuit Jar,** Jasper Dip, Black, Yellow, Silver Plated Rim, c.1900, 5 ½ In. | 277 |
| **Biscuit Jar,** Lid, Jasper Dip, Crimson, Classical Figures, Acorns, c.1920, 4 ½ In. | 584 |
| **Bough Pot,** Lid, Queen's Ware, Purple Luster, Flowers, Stripes, 8 In. | 308 |
| **Bowl,** Black Basalt, Painted Flowers, Gold Trim, Marshall Field, 10 In. | 1476 |
| **Bowl,** Butterfly Luster, Mother-Of-Pearl, Mottled Orange Inside, 9 In. | 369 |
| **Bowl,** Chinese Ornaments Luster, Mottled Orange, Dragons, 9 In. | 923 |
| **Bowl,** Dragon Luster, Mottled Green & Yellow Ground, Gilt, 8 ¼ In. | 593 |
| **Bowl,** Fairyland Luster, Bridge, Trees, Buildings, Night Sky, Fitted Box, 9 In. | 3087 |
| **Bowl,** Fairyland Luster, Daventry, Hexagonal, Orange, Oriental Scene, 4 In. | 1150 |
| **Bowl,** Fairyland Luster, Dragons, Mottled, Iridescent Blue, Stamped, c.1920, 10 ½ In...........*illus* | 960 |
| **Bowl,** Fairyland Luster, Jumping Faun, Gilt Birds, Mottled Green Ground, 9 In. | 2844 |
| **Bowl,** Fairyland Luster, Leapfrogging Elves, Grassy, Midnight Luster, 3 x 5 In. | 3851 |
| **Bowl,** Fairyland Luster, Light Of Birds, Green Medallion, Gilt Rim, 8 ¾ In. | 4740 |
| **Bowl,** Fairyland Luster, Moorish, Smoke & Ribbons, 8-Sided, 8 ½ In. | 4860 |
| **Bowl,** Fairyland Luster, Nazami, King Watching Physicians Duel, Flared, Footed, 6 In. | 10665 |
| **Bowl,** Fairyland Luster, Octagonal, Leapfrogging Elves, Fairy In A Cage, 9 In. | 5843 |
| **Bowl,** Fairyland Luster, Pheasant, Peony, Leaves, 8 In. | 2370 |
| **Bowl,** Fairyland Luster, Willow, Coral, Bronze, Hanging Lantern Band, 8-Sided, 7 In. | 1046 |
| **Bowl,** Fairyland Luster, Woodland Bridge, Picnic By River Interior, Fairies, 8 In..................*illus* | 3555 |
| **Bowl,** Salad, Jasper Dip, Tricolor, Green, Lilac, Classical Figures, 6 In. | 400 |
| **Box,** Lid, Jasper Dip, Crimson, Classical Figures, Flowers, c.1920, 4 In. | 308 |
| **Cachepot,** Jasper Dip, Sage Green, White Relief, Lion Head, Figures, Swags, 7 x 8 In. | 266 |
| **Candlestick,** Blue Jasper Base, Classical Figures, Cut Glass Cup, Lustres, 10 In., Pair | 2304 |
| **Candlestick,** Jasper Dip, Blue, Columnar Shape, White, Leaves, 8 In., Pair | 923 |
| **Case,** Lid, Jasperware, Tricolor, Lilac Band, Leaves, Green, White, 8 In., Pair | 3075 |
| **Cassolette,** Lid, Black Basalt, Flower, 3-Footed, 11 In. | 800 |
| **Cheese Dish,** Lid, Jasper Dip, Lilac, White Classical Figures, Oak Leaves, 11 ¾ In. | 1046 |
| **Cup & Saucer,** Jasperware, Diceware, Green, Yellow, c.1900, 5 ¼ In. | 2214 |
| **Dinner Set,** Black Florentine, Service For 12, Dinner Plate, 10 ¾ In., 60 Piece | 1250 |
| **Dish,** Game Pie, Lid, Caneware, Molded Relief, Dead Game Birds, Oval, 10 ½ In. | 153 |
| **Dispenser,** Lid, Spigot, Jockey, Racehorse, Marked, 1800s, 11 ¼ In. ....................................*illus* | 478 |
| **Eggcup,** Lid, Dark Blue Ferrara Pattern, c.1832, 4 In. | 600 |
| **Ewer,** Black Basalt, Triton, Waves, Bacchus, Ram, Vines, 15 In., Pair | 3883 |
| **Figurine,** Sphinx, Black Basalt, Winged, Seated, Facing, Early 1800s, 9 In., Pair | 3585 |
| **Jar,** Lid, Hieroglyphs, Zodiac Symbols, Egyptian Designs, Beige, Blue, 10 ¼ In. | 6765 |
| **Jar,** Lid, Jasper Dip, Crimson, Classical Figures, Leaves, c.1920, 4 ⅜ In. | 738 |
| **Jug,** Caneware, Bacchanalian Boys, Feathered Crown, Faux Bamboo Neck & Handle, 7 In. | 2829 |
| **Jug,** Jasper Dip, Crimson, Classical Figures, Grapes, Grapevine, c.1920, 5 ⅜ In. | 984 |
| **Lamp,** Black Basalt, Aladdin Shape, Classical Maiden, 9 ¼ x 7 ¾ In., Pair | 1792 |
| **Pie Dish,** Lid, Caneware, Impressed Animals, Flowers, c.1850, 6 ½ x 11 In. | 180 |
| **Pitcher,** Jasperware, Sage Green, Neoclassical Figures, Trees, Swags, 6 In. | 75 |
| **Pitcher,** Jasperware, White, Lilac, Green, Trophies, Swags, Barrel Form, 5 ⅜ In..................*illus* | 400 |
| **Pitcher,** Lid, Black Basalt, Molded Leaves, Flowers, Marked, 1800s, 7 ⅝ In. ..........................*illus* | 1845 |
| **Pitcher,** Water, Lid, Black Basalt, Scrolled Leaf Handle, Flowers, 9 ⅝ In. | 1599 |
| **Plaque,** Black Basalt, Muse, Oval, 6 ⅞ x 4 ¾ In. | 660 |
| **Plaque,** Fairyland Luster, Elves In Pine Tree, c.1925, 7 ½ x 10 ½ In. .............................*illus* | 6765 |
| **Plaque,** Fairyland Luster, Enchanted Palace, Imps, Starry Sky, Frame, 13 x 9 In.................*illus* | 5333 |
| **Plaque,** Fairyland Luster, Picnic By A River, Rectangular, Cymbals, 4 ½ x 10 In. | 6150 |
| **Plaque,** Jasper Dip, Dark Blue, White Relief, Marriage Of Cupid & Psyche, 6 x 12 In. | 1169 |
| **Plaque,** Jasper Dip, Tricolor, Lilac, Dancing Hours, Navy, Green, 6 ⅜ x 19 In. | 5535 |
| **Plate,** Dessert, Columbia Pattern, 8 ¼ In., 16 Piece | 313 |
| **Plate,** Dinner, Columbia-Drakes Neck, Green Border, Medallion Center, 11 In., 12 Piece | 984 |
| **Plate,** Fairyland Luster, Bubbles II Pattern, 4 Brown Fairies, Green Wings, Water, 9 In. | 16590 |
| **Plate,** Fairyland Luster, Canoe Under Bridge, Bat, Goblins, Faces, 9 In. | 2990 |
| **Plate,** Fairyland Luster, Imps On Bridge, Canoe, Bat, Goblins, 9 In. | 2415 |
| **Plate,** Majolica, Green Basket Woven, Leaf Molded, c.1850, 8 In., 6 Piece | 104 |
| **Plate,** Patrician, Hunt Scenes, 10 ½ In., 10 Piece | 420 |
| **Plate,** Soup, Barley Pattern, Shell Rim, Sheaves, Berries, c.1950, 8 ³⁄₁₆ In., 6 Piece | 115 |
| **Plate,** U.S. Naval Academy Scene, Seal & Symbols On Border, Blue & White, 10 In. | 120 |
| **Plate,** Yale University, Blue Transfer, c.1945, 10 ½ In., 18 Piece | 1920 |
| **Potpourri,** Blue Jasper, Beaker Shape, Frog Insert, Mark, 6 ¾ In. | 63 |
| **Punch Bowl,** Fairyland Luster, Poplar Tree, Black Sky, Daylit Interior, 9 ½ In. | 4613 |

**Wedgwood,** Pitcher, Jasperware, White, Lilac, Green, Trophies, Swags, Barrel Form, 5 ⅜ In.
$400

Skinner Auctioneers & Appraisers

---

**Wedgwood,** Pitcher, Lid, Black Basalt, Molded Leaves, Flowers, Marked, 1800s, 7 ⅝ In.
$1,845

Skinner Auctioneers & Appraisers

---

**Wedgwood,** Plaque, Fairyland Luster, Elves In Pine Tree, c.1925, 7 ½ x 10 ½ In.
$6,765

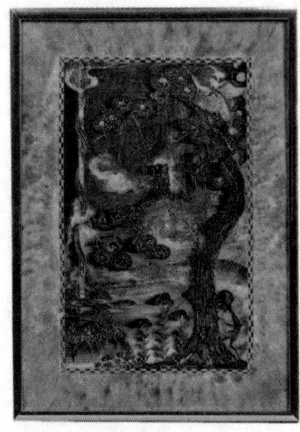

Skinner Auctioneers & Appraisers

**W**

**Wedgwood,** Plaque, Fairyland Luster, Enchanted Palace, Imps, Starry Sky, Frame, 13 x 9 In.

**$5,333**

James D. Julia Auctioneers

**Wedgwood,** Sugar, Lid, Flowers, Oriental Design, Red, Black, Gilt Edge, Marked, c.1950, 3¾ In.

**$60**

James D. Julia Auctioneers

**Wedgwood,** Urn, Lid, Jasperware, Gilt, Bronze, Oval Medallion, Swags, c.1898, 12 In., Pair

**$2,706**

New Orleans Auction Galleries, Inc.

| | |
|---|---:|
| **Punch Bowl,** Fairyland Luster, Swags, Lanterns, Yellow, Horses, Camels, 9 In. | 1845 |
| **Punch Bowl,** Fairyland Luster, Woodland Bridge, Trees, Bird Nest, Clouds, 11 In. | 5925 |
| **Sphinx,** Black Basalt, Hieroglyph Border, Late 20th Century, 8¾ In., Pair | 2091 |
| **Sugar,** Lid, Flowers, Oriental Design, Red, Black, Gilt Edge, Marked, c.1950, 3¾ In. ............*illus* | 60 |
| **Sugar,** Lid, Loop Handles, Squat, Red, White, Florets, Drapery Swags, 4½ In. | 1722 |
| **Tea Set,** Jasperware, Tricolor, Teapot, Sugar & Creamer, Leaves, c.1920, 3 Piece | 923 |
| **Teapot,** Black Basalt, Faux Bamboo, Inverted Baluster, Bail Handle, c.1875, 6¼ In. | 1046 |
| **Tray,** Fairyland Luster, Garden Of Paradise, Trees, Gondola, Blue, Green, 11 In. | 2962 |
| **Tray,** Fairyland Luster, Nizami, Seated Man, Tree, Flowers, Pavilion, Gold Band, 6 In. | 948 |
| **Urn,** Jasperware, Green, White Garlands, Leaves, Bacchus Heads, 10 In. | 316 |
| **Urn,** Lid, Gilt Mounts, Mask Handles, Marked, c.1850, 8 In. | 938 |
| **Urn,** Lid, Jasper, Lilac Medallions & Leaves, Green Festoons, White Figures, 8 In. | 800 |
| **Urn,** Lid, Jasperware, Gilt, Bronze, Oval Medallion, Swags, c.1898, 12 In., Pair..............*illus* | 2706 |
| **Vase,** Black Basalt, White, Portland, Gilt Metal Plinth, c.1860, 10 In. | 1188 |
| **Vase,** Black Jasper Dip, Portland, White Classical Figures, Column, 2 Handles, 10 In. | 2829 |
| **Vase,** Bowl Shape, Long Stem, White, Lilac, Green, Leaves, c.1920, 4¼ In. | 1845 |
| **Vase,** Bud, Jasper Dip, Classical Figures, c.1920, 5 In. | 492 |
| **Vase,** Fairyland Luster, Candlemas, Bronze Ground, Coral Accents, Spread Base, 10 In. | 5925 |
| **Vase,** Fairyland Luster, Daventry, Landscapes In Panels, Trumpet Form, 9¾ In.............*illus* | 3998 |
| **Vase,** Fairyland Luster, Ghostly Woods, Ghosts, Gnarled Tree, Signed, 13⅝ In. ..........*illus* | 44438 |
| **Vase,** Fairyland Luster, Imps On Bridge, Green, Blue, Mauve, Daisy Makeig-Jones, 9 In. | 6900 |
| **Vase,** Fairyland Luster, Imps On Bridge, Treehouse, Squat Base, Flared, 16 In. | 44438 |
| **Vase,** Fairyland Luster, Square, Flared Sides, Castle On A Road, c.1925, 7¾ In. | 2337 |
| **Vase,** Fairyland Luster, Sycamore Tree, 3 Panels, Feng Hwang, Ship & Tree, Bridge, 8 In. | 5925 |
| **Vase,** Fairyland Luster, Trumpet, Firbolgs, Imps, Fairies, 9½ In. | 1380 |
| **Vase,** Fish, Terra-Cotta, Enamel, Gold Trim, Christopher Dresser, c.1872, 6½ In.............*illus* | 23370 |
| **Vase,** Geisha, Garden, Gilt, Cobalt Blue Ground, Marked, 10¾ In. | 199 |
| **Vase,** Jasper Dip, Black, Bottle Shape, Foliage, Grapevines, c.1900, 7⅜ In. | 984 |
| **Vase,** Jasper Dip, Black, Classical Maidens, Zodiac Symbols, Swags, Lid, 12 In. ..........*illus* | 1722 |
| **Vase,** Jasper Dip, Black, Yellow, Blue Medallions, White Drapery, Lid, 8¼ In. ..........*illus* | 2829 |
| **Vase,** Jasper Dip, Blue, Flowers, Bottle Form, Branch Handles, 1800s, 10 In............*illus* | 4305 |
| **Vase,** Jasper Dip, Blue, White Classical Figures, Man, 10 In. | 1353 |
| **Vase,** Jasper Dip, Light Blue, Lovebird Finial, Arabesque Flowers, Shells, 7 In. | 431 |
| **Vase,** Jasper Dip, Portland, Crimson, Classical Figures, c.1920, 7 In. | 2214 |
| **Vase,** Jasperware, Black, Portland, Classical Figures, Late 1800s, 9¾ In. | 800 to 1968 |
| **Vase,** Jasperware, Tricolor, Lilac Columns, Medallions, Green, 7¼ In., Pair. | 1169 |
| **Vase,** Lid, Dragon Luster, Blue Ground, Gilt Trim, Oval, Knop Handles, 11 In., Pair. | 1059 |
| **Vase,** Lid, Fairyland Luster, Argus Pheasant, Pink & Red Flowers, Gold Trim, 10 In. | 7110 |
| **Vase,** Lid, Fairyland Luster, Candlemas, Woman's Head, Flowers, 9 In. | 6517 |
| **Vase,** Lid, Jasper Dip, Black, Yellow, Blue Medallion, Classical Figures, 8¼ In. | 2706 |
| **Vase,** Lid, Jasper Dip, Lilac, Lovebird Finial, Vertical Bands, Flowers, Shells, 6¾ In. | 1599 |
| **Vase,** Lid, Jasperware, Diceware, Scrolled Leaves, Molded Handles, Lilac, 6¾ In. | 3998 |
| **Vase,** Lid, Jasperware, Leaves, Handles, Lilac, Green, White, 8½ In. | 615 |
| **Vase,** Lid, Jasperware, Tricolor, Lilac, Green, 9 In. | 1230 |
| **Vase,** Ribbed, Yellow Matte Glaze, Keith Murray, Marked, c.1930, 7¼ In. | 316 |
| **Vase,** Rosso Antico, Applied Bats & Egyptian Decoration, 3 Hoof Feet, 9 In. ..........*illus* | 3998 |
| **Vase,** Spill, Jasper Dip, Tricolor, Bellflowers, Acanthus, 7¾ In., Pair. | 2460 |
| **Vestal Lamp,** Black Basalt, Fluted, Classical Woman On Lid, Pouring From Jug, 9 In. | 2829 |

**WELLER** pottery was first made in 1872 in Fultonham, Ohio. The firm moved to Zanesville, Ohio, in 1882. Artwares were introduced in 1893. Hundreds of lines of pottery were produced, including Louwelsa, Eocean, Dickens Ware, and Sicardo, before the pottery closed in 1948.

LOUWELSA WELLER

| | |
|---|---:|
| **Arcadia,** Vase, Light Blue, 7¾ In. | 35 |
| **Ardsley,** Bowl, Green Lines, Orange Tips, Flared, 12½ In. | 52 |
| **Art Deco,** Vase, White, Nude Woman, Fawn, Ivoris Glaze, Leaves, 8¼ In. | 1495 |
| **Athens,** Vase, Green Matte, Cream, 10 x 6½ In. | 196 |
| **Aurelian,** Jardiniere, Pedestal, Yellow Iris, 38 In. | 460 |
| **Aurelian,** Jug, Cherries, Swirled Black Ground, c.1900, 9 x 4¾ In. | 188 |
| **Aurelian,** Vase, Flowers, Black Ground, Bulbous, Signed AC, 6½ In. | 360 |
| **Baldin,** Vase, Red Apples, Green Leaves, Blue, 9¾ In. | 230 |
| **Bedford,** Jardiniere, Green, 4 Tapered Leaves, Tapered, c.1910, 10 In. | 840 |
| **Brighton,** Figurine, Dodo, White, Black Matte Glaze, 8½ x 4½ In. | 1668 |
| **Brighton,** Pheasant, Blue, Yellow, Black, 6½ In. | 345 |
| **Bronze Ware,** Vase, Purple, 17¾ In. | 242 |
| **Chase,** Jar, Lid, White, Cobalt Blue Ground, Man, Jumping Horse, Fence, 15 In. | 127 |

**W**

| | | |
|---|---|---|
| Chase, Vase, Tapered, Blue Matte Glaze, White Design, 7½ In. | | 70 |
| Coppertone, Basin, Turtle On Edge, Mottled Green, 17½ In. | | 900 |
| Coppertone, Flower Frog, Green Glaze, 5¼ In. | | 58 |
| Coppertone, Flower Frog, Green Glaze, Marked, 4½ In. | | 52 |
| Coppertone, Gnome, Seated, Blue Cap Feather, Tights, Orange Jacket, Round Base, 14 In. | | 960 |
| Coppertone, Sprinkler, Frog, Marked, 8 x 11 In. | | 575 |
| Coppertone, Sprinkler, Green, Tan, Marked, 8¼ x 7½ In. | | 1093 |
| Coppertone, Vase, Climbing Frogs, Inkstamp, 7 In. | | 546 |
| Cretone, Vase, Gazelle, Flowers, Mustard Yellow Ground, Hester Pillsbury, 8¼ x 6 In. | | 345 |
| Dickens Ware, Humidor, Turk Head, Turban, 7 In. | | 184 |
| Dickens Ware, Jug, Mt. Vernon Bridge Co., Mt. Vernon O., Brown, Blue, Peach, 6 x 5 In. | | 489 |
| Dickens Ware, Lamp Base, Stovepipe Neck, Yellow Irises, 17 In. | | 230 |
| Dickens Ware, Pitcher, Native American Chief, Wolfrobe, Signed G. Mull, 11⅜ In. | | 350 |
| Dickens Ware, Tobacco Jar, Captain, Incised, Blue, Brown, Cream, 7 x 6¼ In. | | 374 |
| Dickens Ware, Vase, Bleak House, Man, Top Hat, Holding Child's Hand, Rusty Glaze, 16 x 7 In. | | 374 |
| Dickens Ware, Vase, Classical Figure, Green Robe, Black Ground, Marked, 12¼ In. | | 460 |
| Dickens Ware, Vase, Fat Boy, Pickwick Papers, Mauve Ground, 7¾ In. | | 316 |
| Dickens Ware, Vase, Golfer, Cylindrical, Signed Edwin Pickens, 9⅜ In. | | 633 |
| Dickens Ware, Vase, Incised Coach, Horse, Sunset, Blue, Tapered, 11 In. | | 403 |
| Dickens Ware, Vase, Incised Scrolling, Maroon, Gold Ground, Cylindrical, 10½ In. | | 460 |
| Dickens Ware, Vase, Landscape, Stag, Twist Shape, Signed A. Daugherty, 11½ In. | | 431 |
| Dickens Ware, Vase, Mr. Micawber, From David Copperfield, Green, Cylindrical, 10 In. | | 345 |
| Dickens Ware, Vase, Old Toymaker, Toy Horse, Marked, 13½ In. | | 259 |
| Dickens Ware, Woman, Holding Bouquet, Brown Matte Glaze, 13½ x 4½ In. | | 288 |
| Dickens Ware, Woman, White Cap, Flowers, Handles, 5½ In. | | 115 |
| Eocean, Vase, Applied Frog, Snake, Ivory Ground, Ohio, 8 x 5 In. | | 438 |
| Eocean, Vase, Cylindrical, Green To Cream Ground, 6⅝ In. | | 138 |
| Eocean, Vase, Light Blue, Flowers, 6-Sided, Pink & Yellow Roses, 11¾ In. | | 115 |
| Eocean, Vase, Lilacs, Green Ground, Sarah McLaughlin, 16¼ In. | | 489 |
| Eocean, Vase, Pink Poppies, White Ground, 12⅝ In. | | 518 |
| Eocean, Vase, Purple, Flowers, 9¾ In. | | 219 |
| Eocean, Vase, Red Flowers, Gray Green Ground, Tapered, 3 In. | | 92 |
| Eocean, Vase, Rose, Horned Owl, On Branch, Full Moon, Elizabeth Blake, 10⅝ In. | | 1725 |
| Eocean, Vase, Yellow, Pink Roses, Blue Ground, 12½ In. | | 540 |
| Etna, Vase, Frog, Snake, Green, Cream, Tapered, Shouldered, Incised, 7¾ x 5 In. | | 431 |
| Figurine, Dog, Three Faces, Planter, White, Black, 6¾ In. | | 58 |
| Figurine, Pan, With Flute, Multicolor, Zanesville, c.1910, 16½ x 10 In. | | 2500 |
| Figurine, Parrot, Green, Red, Yellow & Blue Plumage, Black Matte Stand, 13 In. | | 649 |
| Figurine, Pop-Eye Dog, Black & Brown Patches, White Glaze, 4 In. | *illus* | 259 |
| Flemish, Vase, Blue Berries, Green, Cylindrical, 12 In. | | 104 |
| Fleron, Bowl, Purple, Wavy Rim, Low, 8 In. | | 46 |
| Flower Frog, Dish, Green, Applied Frog On Rim, Leaves, Marked Weller, 1920s, 10½ In. | | 338 |
| Forest, Basket, Hanging, Multicolor Landscape, Flared Shape, 8 In. | | 120 |
| Forest, Jardiniere, Brown, Green, Blue Trees, Wide Cylindrical Shape, 10 In. | | 330 |
| Forest, Jardiniere, Stand, Molded Landscape, Multicolor, 29 x 12 In. | | 615 |
| Fru Russet, Vase, 2 Handles, Acorn, Leaves, Green, 6½ In. | | 518 |
| Fru Russet, Vase, Cream To Purple, Thistles, Leaves, 2 Twist Open Handles, c.1905, 11 In. | | 3220 |
| Fru Russet, Vase, Green, Engraved Flowers, Squat, Handles, 3 x 5 In. | | 150 |
| Fru Russet, Vase, Lilies, Embossed, Greens, Rose Glaze, Impressed, 12⅝ In. | | 748 |
| Fru Russet, Vase, Thistle, Molded, Twist Handle, 11½ In. | *illus* | 4255 |
| Fru Russet, Vase, Thistles, Leaves, Cream To Purple, Twisted Open Handles, c.1920, 11 In. | | 3220 |
| Fruitone, Vase, Brown Glaze, Flared Green Rim, 7¼ In. | | 127 |
| Gardenware, Dog, Scottie, Seated, Black & White, 12½ In. | *illus* | 805 |
| Gardenware, Gnome, Seated, Ski-Jump Nose, Blue, Pants, Cap, Round Base, 15 x 10 In. | | 1610 |
| Gardenware, Gnomes, Toadstools, Green, Red, Cream, Incised, 16½ x 14 In. | | 6325 |
| Gardenware, Squirrel, Brown Glaze, 12 x 6⅓ In. | | 2900 |
| Gardenware, Squirrel, Brown, Tan, 13½ In. | | 1323 |
| Glendale, Vase, Brown Bird, Blue Sky, Green Plants, Incised, 7 In. | | 450 |
| Glendale, Vase, Double Bud, Bird, Nest, Eggs, 7 In. | | 270 |
| Hudson, Figurine, Bird On Pine Branch, White, Cylindrical, Marked, 8⅜ In. | | 322 |
| Hudson, Vase, 2 Birds On Branch, Blue Matte Glaze, Cylindrical, Tapered, 13 x 4½ In. | | 793 |
| Hudson, Vase, Asian Fishing Boat, Mountains, Shoreline, Handles, Signed, 9⅞ In. | *illus* | 2875 |
| Hudson, Vase, Blue & Yellow Irises, Celadon To Pink Ground, 14⅞ In. | | 373 |
| Hudson, Vase, Blue Flowers, Cream, Cylindrical, Marked, 7 In. | | 173 |
| Hudson, Vase, Blue Iris, Green Ground, S. McLaughlin, c.1930, 15 x 6 In. | | 688 |
| Hudson, Vase, Blue, Fades To Pink, Neck Handles, Sara Timberlake, 7¾ In. | | 230 |

**Wedgwood**, Vase, Fairyland Luster, Daventry, Landscapes In Panels, Trumpet Form, 9¾ In.
$3,998

Skinner Auctioneers & Appraisers

**Wedgwood**, Vase, Fairyland Luster, Ghostly Woods, Ghosts, Gnarled Tree, Signed, 13⅝ In.
$44,438

James D. Julia Auctioneers

**Wedgwood**, Vase, Fish, Terra-Cotta, Enamel, Gold Trim, Christopher Dresser, c.1872, 6½ In.
$23,370

Skinner Auctioneers & Appraisers

W

**Wedgwood,** Vase, Jasper Dip, Black, Classical Maidens, Zodiac Symbols, Swags, Lid, 12 In.
$1,722

Skinner Auctioneers & Appraisers

**Wedgwood,** Vase, Jasper Dip, Black, Yellow, Blue Medallions, White Drapery, Lid, 8¼ In.
$2,829

Skinner Auctioneers & Appraisers

**Wedgwood,** Vase, Jasper Dip, Blue, Flowers, Bottle Form, Branch Handles, 1800s, 10 In.
$4,305

Skinner Auctioneers & Appraisers

| | | |
|---|---|---:|
| **Hudson,** | Vase, Blue, Flowers, Leaves, Loop Handles, Sarah R. McLaughlin, 7 x 6½ In. | 316 |
| **Hudson,** | Vase, Blue, Pink Flowers, Green Leaves, Handles, McLaughlin, 10 In. | 510 |
| **Hudson,** | Vase, Bud, Cobalt Blue Ground, Flowers, Marked, 10¼ In. | 58 |
| **Hudson,** | Vase, Cosmos, White, Pink, Blue Ground, Handles, 7¾ In. | 242 |
| **Hudson,** | Vase, Daffodils, Cylindrical, Marked, 12 In. | 276 |
| **Hudson,** | Vase, Dogwood, Hexagonal Shape, White, Marked, 11¾ In. | 82 |
| **Hudson,** | Vase, Flowers, Blue, To Purple, Tapered, Signed M. Yinger, 9 In. | 322 |
| **Hudson,** | Vase, Glossy, White Ground, Zebra, Leaves, Flat Rim, 10⅜ In. | 1265 |
| **Hudson,** | Vase, Green, White Flowers, Cylindrical, Signed McLaughlin, 6⅞ In. | 334 |
| **Hudson,** | Vase, Hollyhocks, Pink, White, Green, Mae Timberlake, Signed, 11¾ In. | 575 |
| **Hudson,** | Vase, Light Blue, 6-Sided, Signed Hester Pillsbury, 11¾ In. | 173 |
| **Hudson,** | Vase, Light Purple, Orchids, Tapered, Marked, 11½ In. | 431 |
| **Hudson,** | Vase, Lilacs, Blue To Celadon Ground, Signed Hester Pillsbury, 13⅛ In. | 345 |
| **Hudson,** | Vase, Lily Of The Valley, Blue Vellum Glaze, Signed S. McLaughlin, 9 In. | 391 |
| **Hudson,** | Vase, Lily Of The Valley, Pastel, Glazed, Impressed, 5 In. | 98 |
| **Hudson,** | Vase, Pink Flowers, Gray, Ball Shape, Mae Timberlake, 3½ In. | 253 |
| **Hudson,** | Vase, Square Handles, Signed McLaughlin, 9⅜ In. | 207 |
| **Hudson,** | Vase, Suitor, Lute, Woman, Pale Purple, Yellow Figures, 10 In. | 891 |
| **Hudson,** | Vase, Tulip, Tapered Cylindrical, 11 In. | 173 |
| **Hudson,** | Vase, Wild Roses, Charles Chilcote, Ink Stamp, 6½ In. | 1725 |
| **Hudson,** | Vase, Wild Roses, Impressed, 4⅝ In. | 81 |
| **Hudson,** | Vase, Wisteria, Purple To Yellow, Cylindrical, Marked, 9¼ In. | 109 |
| **Hudson,** | Vase, Yellow & White Roses, Impressed Weller, 13 In. | 489 |
| **Hudson,** | Vase, Yellow Warbler, Leaves, Mountain Ash Berries, White Ground, 10¾ In. | 640 |
| **Hunter,** | Vase, Flying Duck, Choppy Water, Yellow Sky, 6⅞ In. | 218 |
| **Ivory,** | Jardiniere, Embossed Flowers, Basket, 11 x 9 In. | 127 |
| **Jap Birdimal,** | Vase, 7 Fish, Pink Ground, Impressed Name, 10¼ In. | 805 |
| **Jap Birdimal,** | Vase, Geisha, Butterflies, Orange Glaze, Squeezebag, 2 Handles, 10 x 8 In. | 1342 |
| **Jap Birdimal,** | Vase, Green, Black, Cranes, 3-Sided, 9¾ x 3¼ In. | 1208 |
| **Jap Birdimal,** | Vase, Red Ground, Geisha, Trees, Squeezebag, 10½ In. | 2040 |
| **Jap Birdimal,** | Vase, Red, Orange Blossom, Green Ground, High Handles, 9 In. | 720 |
| **Jap Birdimal,** | Vase, Snow Geese, Teal Gloss Glaze, Swirl Shape, Nub Handles, 4½ x 7 In. | 230 |
| **Jardiniere,** | Pedestal, Geese, Trees, Sgraffito & Squeezebag, F. Rhead, c.1905, 25 In. *illus* | 2625 |
| **Knifewood,** | Humidor, Lid, 3 English Pointer Dogs, Ducks, Reeds, Impressed, 6½ In. *illus* | 748 |
| **Knifewood,** | Vase, Goldfinches, Wisteria, Multicolor, Impressed, 5 In. | 431 |
| **Knifewood,** | Vase, Peacock, Tree, 11½ x 4½ In. | 719 |
| **L'Art Nouveau,** | Pitcher, Woman, Gown, Green, Pink, Frosted, 10½ In. | 316 |
| **Lasa,** | Vase, Gold, Palm Trees, Signed, Cylindrical, 8½ In. | 150 |
| **Lasa,** | Vase, Landscape, Hills, Trees, Multicolor, Iridescent, 8⅞ In. | 316 |
| **Lasa,** | Vase, Landscape, Palm Trees, Lake, Hills, Clouds, Castle, Multicolor, Iridescent, 12 In. | 460 |
| **Lasa,** | Vase, Palm Trees, Landscape, Yellow, Purple, Signed Weller Lasa, 12 In. | 258 |
| **Lasa,** | Vase, Palm Trees, Mountains, Red & Gold, Signed, 6¼ In. *illus* | 104 |
| **Lasa,** | Vase, Trees, Clouds, Hills, Signed, 4⅜ In. | 173 |
| **Lebanon,** | Vase, Animals, Man Working, Green, Brown, Lines, Scrolls, Impressed, 11 x 7 In. | 863 |
| **Louwelsa,** | Chamberstick, Rose, Dark Green, 5¼ In. | 184 |
| **Louwelsa,** | Tankard, Blackberries, Brown, Green, Leaves, Berries, 11¼ In. | 173 |
| **Louwelsa,** | Tankard, Corn, Red, Glossy, 11 In. | 115 |
| **Louwelsa,** | Vase, Blue, Flowers, Cylindrical, Marked, 12 In. | 720 |
| **Louwelsa,** | Vase, Daffodils, Brown, Orange, Glossy, Flat Rim, 17¾ In. | 632 |
| **Louwelsa,** | Vase, Flowers, Leaves, Blue, High Shoulder, 7 x 3½ In. | 288 |
| **Louwelsa,** | Vase, Irises, Gold, Yellow, Green Ground, Levi Burgess Initials, 12 In. | 138 |
| **Marengo,** | Vase, Red Ground, Silver Trees, Cream Under Layer, 8½ In. | 230 |
| **Marvo,** | Jardiniere, Pedestal, Green, 32½ In. | 460 |
| **Matte Ware,** | Green, Vase, Pinched Rim, Base Band, 6¼ In. | 230 |
| **Matte Ware,** | Green, Vase, Yellow Flowers, Etched, Cylindrical, Marked, 6¾ In. | 253 |
| **Matte Ware,** | Umbrella Stand, Green Matte Glaze, 10½ In. | 960 |
| **Matte Ware,** | Vase, Green, Horizontal Ribbed Neck, Tapered, 3½ In. | 104 |
| **Mermaid,** | Vase, Riding Seal, Seahorse, Applied Rope Handles, Signed, 7⅝ In. | 316 |
| **Muskota,** | Bowl, Butterflies, Bulbous Lobes, Squat, 6¼ x 6¼ In. | 1006 |
| **Muskota,** | Figurine, 2 Chicks, Grass, 5⅛ In. | 184 |
| **Muskota,** | Figurine, Elephant, Trunk Down, White, 7 x 10 In. | 661 |
| **Muskota,** | Flower Frog, Fisher Boy, 6¾ In. *illus* | 115 |
| **Muskota,** | Flower Frog, Nude, Swan, Marked, 6¾ In. | 207 |
| **Muskota,** | Flower Frog, Squirrel, Holding Nut, 3⅞ In. *illus* | 345 |
| **Rosemont,** | Vase, Cream Birds, Black Ground, Cylindrical, Marked, 10⅜ In. | 265 |
| **Sicardo,** | Vase, 6-Pointed Shape, Flowers, Multicolor, 4¾ In. | 747 |

**Wedgwood,** Vase, Rosso Antico, Applied Bats & Egyptian Decoration, 3 Hoof Feet, 9 In. $3,998

Skinner Auctioneers & Appraisers

**Weller,** Figurine, Pop-Eye Dog, Black & Brown Patches, White Glaze, 4 In. $259

Humler & Nolan

**Weller,** Fru Russet, Vase, Thistle, Molded, Twist Handle, 11 ½ In. $4,255

Humler & Nolan

**Weller,** Gardenware, Dog, Scottie, Seated, Black & White, 12 ½ In. $805

Humler & Nolan

**Weller,** Hudson, Vase, Asian Fishing Boat, Mountains, Shoreline, Handles, Signed, 9 ⅞ In. $2,875

Humler & Nolan

**Weller,** Jardiniere, Pedestal, Geese, Trees, Sgraffito & Squeezebag, F. Rhead, c.1905, 25 In. $2,625

Rago Arts & Auction Center

**Weller,** Knifewood, Humidor, Lid, 3 English Pointer Dogs, Ducks, Reeds, Impressed, 6 ½ In. $748

Humler & Nolan

**Weller,** Lasa, Vase, Palm Trees, Mountains, Red & Gold, Signed, 6 ¼ In. $104

Humler & Nolan

**Weller,** Muskota, Flower Frog, Fisher Boy, 6 ¾ In. $115

Humler & Nolan

W

**Weller,** Muskota, Flower Frog, Squirrel, Holding Nut, 3 ⅞ In.
$345

Humler & Nolan

---

**Weller,** Sicardo, Vase, Daisies, Panels, Signed, 4 ¼ In.
$518

Humler & Nolan

---

**Wheatley,** Tile, Fruit Basket, Flower Band, Matte Glaze, Round, 15 In.
$345

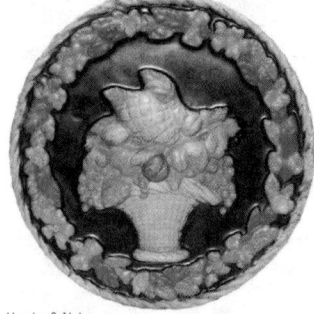

Humler & Nolan

---

### Buffalo Pottery Willow Pattern

The first Willow pattern dishes made in the United States were produced in 1905 at the Buffalo Pottery Company of Buffalo, New York. Earlier Willow was made in China and England. Some Willow was made with added touches of red.

---

| | |
|---|---:|
| **Sicardo,** Vase, Blue, Purple, Green, Cylindrical, Signed, 5 ½ In. | 345 |
| **Sicardo,** Vase, Blue, Red Metallic Glaze, Flared, 10 In. | 840 |
| **Sicardo,** Vase, Daisies, Panels, Signed, 4 ¼ In. ............*illus* | 518 |
| **Sicardo,** Vase, Iris, Etched, Burnished Gold, Signed John Lessell, 12 ½ In. | 242 |
| **Sicardo,** Vase, Ivy Leaf Cascade, Green Luster Glaze, Purple, Blue, Signed, 9 In. | 575 |
| **Sicardo,** Vase, Lobed, Blue, Red Metallic Glaze, Signed, 15 ½ In. | 3600 |
| **Sicardo,** Vase, Scenic, Flowers, Signed, 7 ⅜ In. | 1380 |
| **Sicardo,** Vase, Stylized Clover, Metallic Glaze, Undulating, Double Handles, 5 x 9 In. | 1098 |
| **Sicardo,** Vase, Stylized Flowers, Rim, Small Rim, Tapered, 8 ½ In. | 890 |
| **Sicardo,** Vase, Thistles, Metallic Glaze, Signed, 17 In. | 863 |
| **Sicardo,** Vase, Yellow, Red Flower Metallic Glaze, Signed, 15 In. | 1200 |
| **Silvertone,** Vase, Butterflies, Flowers, Wavy Rim, Handles, Tapered, 12 x 7 ½ In. | 316 |
| **Souevo,** Vase, Native American Symbols, 8 In. | 104 |
| **Stellar,** Vase, Inscribed, 6 x 6 In. | 374 |
| **Tutone,** Vase, Green Orange, Bottle Shape, Marked, 7 ¼ In. | 92 |
| **Umbrella Stand,** Cattail, Majolica, Green, Brown Glazes, Incised, 23 x 10 In. | 874 |
| **Vase,** Bird, Nest, Grass, Sky, 4 In. | 240 |
| **Vase,** Dark Blue, Cylinder Shape, Bird, Pine Branch, Impressed Weller, 13 In. | 575 |
| **Vase,** Nasturtium, Blue & Decorated, Band, Impressed, 9 ½ In. | 150 |
| **Vase,** Nude Woman, Crouched, Cliff, Seascape, Blue, Brown, Pink, Tapered, 9 x 7 In. | 4063 |
| **Vase,** Oxblood Drip Glaze, Handles, c.1930, 14 In. | 295 |
| **Vase,** Painted Iris, Cylindrical, Mae Timberlake, 9 ½ In. | 308 |
| **Vase,** Painted, Repeating Flowers, Matte Glaze, Impressed, 7 In. | 374 |
| **Vase,** Purple, Maroon Luster, Twist Design, Flared, 5 In. | 253 |
| **Vase,** Yellow, Flower Band, Squat, 6 ½ x 4 In. | 81 |
| **Woodcraft,** Fishbowl Holder, Kingfisher, Green, Brown, Impressed Weller, 13 ¼ In. | 348 |
| **Woodcraft,** Vase, Blossoms, Leaves, Tree Root Supports, 9 In. | 138 |
| **Woodcraft,** Vase, Bud, Wrapped Vines, Green, Flared, 8 ⅝ In. | 52 |
| **Woodcraft,** Vase, Tree Trunk, 9 ¼ In. | 47 |
| **Xenia,** Vase, Blue, Purple Matte Glaze, Stylized Flowers, Wide Base, 12 x 7 ½ In. | 633 |

---

**WESTMORELAND GLASS** was made by the Westmoreland Glass Company of Grapeville, Pennsylvania, from 1889 to 1984. The company made clear and colored glass of many varieties, such as milk glass, pressed glass, and slag glass.

| | |
|---|---:|
| **American Hobnail,** Compote, Blue Opalescent, Ruffled | 30 |
| **American Hobnail,** Dish, Mayonnaise, Blue Opalescent, Ruffled | 23 |
| **American Hobnail,** Puff Box, Blue Opalescent, Lid | 32 |
| **Ashburton,** Goblet, Water, 6 ¼ In. | 15 |
| **Ashburton,** Wine, 5 ¼ In. | 12 |
| **Atlanta,** Creamer, 3 ½ In. | 14 |
| **Atlanta,** Goblet, Water, 5 ⅜ In. | 24 |
| **Bramble,** Creamer, Milk Glass, 3 ½ In. | 6 |
| **Bramble,** Trinket Box, Milk Glass, 6 In. Diam. | 37 |
| **Daisy,** Trinket Box, Decal, Green, 4-Footed, 2 ¾ x 2 ¾ In. | 27 |
| **Della Robbia,** Creamer | 12 |
| **Della Robbia,** Punch Cup, Amber Flash, 4 Oz., 2 ½ In. | 15 |
| **Dolphin,** Centerpiece, Milk Glass, Handles, Footed, 16 In. | 143 |
| **Doric,** Compote, Moss Green, 6 ⅞ In. | 26 |
| **Doric,** Sweetmeat, Compote, Ruffled Rim, 5 x 5 In. | 35 |
| **English Hobnail,** Goblet, Water, 6 ⅛ | 10 |
| **English Hobnail,** Salt Dip, 3 In. | 12 |
| **English Hobnail,** Sherbet, 3 ½ In. | 5 |
| **Grape,** Cup & Saucer, Paneled, Milk Glass | 9 |
| **Lace,** Bowl, Fruit, 12 ½ x 10 ¼ In. | 35 |
| **Lattice Edge,** Banana Stand, Footed, 8 ⅜ In. | 26 |
| **Lattice Edge,** Bowl, Flowers | 28 |
| **Lily Of The Valley,** Vase, Milk Glass, Footed, 7 ⅛ In. | 17 |
| **Milk Glass,** Bowl, Beaded, 7 x 7 In. | 13 |
| **Old Quilt,** Iced Tea, Amethyst, 10 Oz., 5 ¼ In. | 18 |
| **Old Quilt,** Punch Cup, Milk Glass, 2 ⅜ In. | 11 |
| **Old Quilt,** Sugar & Creamer, Milk Glass | 35 |
| **Old Quilt,** Sweetmeat, Milk Glass, 4 ⅛ In. | 12 |
| **Old Quilt,** Tumbler, Milk Glass, 5 Oz. | 28 |
| **Paneled Grape,** Candleholder, Handle, Milk Glass | 18 |
| **Paneled Grape,** Creamer | 30 |
| **Paneled Grape,** Cup & Saucer, Milk Glass | 10 |

| | |
|---|---:|
| **Paneled Grape,** Goblet, Water, Blue, 5⅞ In. | 14 |
| **Paneled Grape,** Pitcher, Pt. | 21 |
| **Paneled Grape,** Puff Box, Blue, Beaded, 5⅜ x 5⅜ In. | 22 |
| **Paneled Grape,** Punch Bowl, Ruby, 9¾ In. | 119 |
| **Paneled Grape,** Punch Cup, Ruby, Footed, 2⅜ In. | 12 |
| **Paneled Grape,** Salt & Pepper | 25 |
| **Paneled Grape,** Sugar & Creamer | 28 |
| **Paneled Grape,** Vase, Flared, Milk Glass, 6 In. | 9 |
| **Paneled Grape,** Wine, 4 In. | 10 |
| **Pearly Dots,** Bowl, Marigold, Iridescent, 9¼ In. | 38 |
| **Princess Feather,** Cup & Saucer | 14 |
| **Princess Feather,** Dish, Jelly | 17 |
| **Princess Feather,** Goblet, Water, 5⅞ In. | 8 |
| **Princess Feather,** Plate, Bread & Butter, 6½ In. | 7 |
| **Princess Feather,** Sherbet, 4¾ In. | 6 |
| **Princess Feather,** Tumbler, Footed, 8 Oz., 5¼ In. | 6 |
| **Princess Feather,** Wine, 4⅜ In. | 7 |
| **Ring & Petal,** Candlestick, Pink, 3⅜ In. | 28 |
| **Roses & Bows,** Basket, Footed, 3 In. | 15 |
| **Roses & Bows,** Bell, 5¼ In. | 30 |
| **Roses & Bows,** Dish, Heart Shape, Milk Glass, 8 x 7 In. | 20 |
| **Roses & Bows,** Tray, Dresser, Handles, Oval, 13½ In. | 118 |
| **Sawtooth,** Compote, Milk Glass, 7⅛ In. | 30 |
| **Square S,** Plate, Dinner, 8 x 8 In. | 20 |
| **Swan,** Toothpick Holder, Black, 2⅜ In. | 23 |
| **Swan,** Toothpick Holder, Milk Glass, 2⅜ In. | 11 |
| **Swan,** Vase, Blue Opal | 35 |
| **Swirl & Ball,** Cruet, 5¼ In. | 35 |
| **Swirl & Ball,** Sugar & Creamer | 62 |
| **Thousand Eye,** Torte Plate, Ruby, 18 In. | 189 |

**WHEATLEY POTTERY** was established in 1880. Thomas J. Wheatley had worked in Cincinnati, Ohio, with the founders of the art pottery movement, including M. Louise McLaughlin of the Rookwood Pottery. Wheatley Pottery was purchased by the Cambridge Tile Manufacturing Company in 1927.

| | |
|---|---:|
| **Tile,** Fruit Basket, Flower Band, Matte Glaze, Round, 15 In. ........................*illus* | 345 |
| **Tile,** Viking Ship, Seahorse & Anchor Border, c.1928, 12¾ In. | 978 |
| **Vase,** Carved Organic Stylized Leaves, Cylindrical, Slightly Cinched Waist, 9 x 8 In. | 854 |
| **Vase,** Incised Geometrics, Green Matte Glaze, Bulbous, Pinched Neck, 6½ x 7 In. | 313 |
| **Vase,** Stylized Leaves, Incised Band, Black, c.1905, 11 x 8 In. | 750 |
| **Vase,** Stylized Leaves, Incised Band, Green, c.1905, 11 x 8 In. | 1188 |

**WILLETS MANUFACTURING COMPANY** of Trenton, New Jersey, began work in 1879. The company made belleek in the late 1880s and 1890s in shapes similar to those used by the Irish Belleek factory. It stopped working about 1912. A variety of marks were used, most including the name *Willets*.

| | |
|---|---:|
| **Mug,** Blackberries, Flowers, Leaves, Gold, Scrollwork, Belleek, 5¼ In. | 345 |
| **Salt,** Green Leaves & Flowers, Scalloped Ruffled Edge, 1¾ In. | 36 |
| **Vase,** Sailboats, Landscape, Belleek, c.1910, 15 In. | 660 |
| **Vase,** Wings, Flowers, Blue, Yellow, Belleek, c.1910, 12¼ In. | 549 |

**WILLOW** pattern has been made in England since 1780. The pattern has been copied by factories in many countries, including Germany, Japan, and the United States. It is still being made. Willow was named for a pattern that pictures a bridge, birds, willow trees, and a Chinese landscape. Most pieces are blue and white. Some made after 1900 are pink and white.

| | |
|---|---:|
| **Bowl,** Foot Ring, China, 19th Century, 8¼ In. | 65 |
| **Bowl,** Vegetable, 8 In. | 17 |
| **Candlestick,** Baluster, Scalloped Rim, Blue Danube, 6¼ In. | 24 |
| **Candlestick,** Square Base, Panels, Transfer, Deltonware, 12 In. | 79 |
| **Gravy Boat,** Scroll Handle, England | 25 |
| **Mug,** Wood & Sons, c.1950, 3¼ In. | 16 |
| **Plate,** Basket Weave Edge, Reticulated Rim, 1800s, 7¼ In. | 180 |
| **Platter,** Oval, Booths, 14 x 11 In. | 125 |
| **Platter,** Oval, Reticulated Rim, Pearlware, England, c.1810, 9 x 7 In. | 210 |

**Window,** Stained, Church, Arched, Crown, Anchor, Wood Frame, c.1906, 111 In., 2 Piece
$1,770

Brunk Auctions

**Window,** Stained, Musician, Blue Border, Red Corners, Signed, F. Ringer, 1900s, 8 x 13 In.
$450

The Stein Auction Company

**W**

**Wood Carving,** Boy, Articulated, Shoulders, Elbows, Hips, Knees, Painted, c.1825, 30½ In.
$4,920

Skinner Auctioneers & Appraisers

**Wood Carving,** Buddha Of Da Mo, Beast Biting Earring, Bamboo, Chinese, 1800s, 4 In.
$390

Garth's Auctioneers & Appraisers

**Wood Carving,** Bust, Marie Antoinette, Walnut, Wrapped In Cloak, 1800s, 32 x 20 In.
$1,168

New Orleans Auction Galleries, Inc.

| | |
|---|---:|
| **Platter,** Transferware, Staffordshire, c.1840, 19 x 15 In. | 395 |
| **Salt & Pepper,** Cylindrical, Cork, 3¾ In. | 24 |
| **Sugar & Creamer,** Old Willow English Ironstone, 1970s. | 65 |
| **Tureen,** Tab Handles, Lid, Old Willow Empire, England, 9 In. | 60 |

**WINDOW** glass that was stained and beveled was popular for houses during the late nineteenth and early twentieth centuries. The old windows became popular with collectors in the 1970s; today, old and new examples are seen.

| | |
|---|---:|
| **Leaded,** Art Nouveau, Tulips, Wooden Frame, 18 x 42½ In. | 150 |
| **Leaded,** Art Nouveau, Woman, Seminude, Green, Blue, 1900-25, 73 x 55½ In. | 1250 |
| **Leaded,** Center Medallion, Fruit Bowl, Green, Pink, Blue, Paneled Ground, 23 x 56 In. | 948 |
| **Leaded,** Grapes, Vines, Leaves, Sunset Sky, Clear Border, Frame, 44 x 43 In. | 711 |
| **Leaded,** Grapevine Pattern, Pine Frame, Arts & Crafts, 1900s, 18 x 38 In. | 2500 |
| **Leaded,** Peacock, Fountain, Flowers, Chipped Ice Ground, 50 x 43 In. | 5333 |
| **Leaded,** Plums, Green Leaves, Striated Gold Textured Ground, 48⅜ x 25¾ In. | 1476 to 1968 |
| **Leaded,** Stained, Geometric Design, Multicolor, Victorian, 44 x 24 In. | 210 |
| **Leaded,** Stained, Scrolls, Blue Border, Wood Frame, 48 x 41 In. | 188 |
| **Leaded,** Stained, Stylized Flowers, Painted Frame, 62 x 30 In. | 188 |
| **Leaded,** Transom, Multicolor, Banner Center, Wood Frame, c.1910, 37 x 60 In. | 178 |
| **Leaded,** Urn, Flowers, Blue Outer Border, Garland, 70½ x 46 In. | 625 |
| **Leaded,** Woman, Bench, Marble Patio, Reading, Purple Sky, Pink Flowers, 60 x 48 In. | 5628 |
| **Leaded,** Women, Harp, Flute, Blue Striated Sky, Frame, 38¾ x 39¼ In. | 948 |
| **Stained,** Arts & Crafts, Castle Scene, Multicolor, Yellow, Green Panes, c.1910, 23 x 42 In. | 270 |
| **Stained,** Caramel Slag Border, Blue Glass Web, Milk Glass Cabochons, Oval, 38 x 28 In. | 207 |
| **Stained,** Church, Arched, Crown, Anchor, Wood Frame, c.1906, 111 In., 2 Piece ...............*illus* | 1770 |
| **Stained,** Clear Paneled, Multicolor Border, Jewels, Frame, 47 x 44 In. | 115 |
| **Stained,** Enamel Sprite, Butterfly Net, Garlands, Ripple Glass, Jewels, 1885, 55 x 45 In., Pair ..... | 2460 |
| **Stained,** Mosaic, Geometric, Flowers, Frame, William McPherson, c.1860, 36 x 36 In. | 1968 |
| **Stained,** Musician, Blue Border, Red Corners, Signed, F. Ringer, 1900s, 8 x 13 In. ...............*illus* | 450 |
| **Stained,** Transom, Multicolor Geometric Flowers, Gold Border, 1900s, 56 x 31 In. | 92 |
| **Stained,** Transom, Red, Purple Shield & Spear, Caramel Slag Glass, Green Border, 71 x 17 In. | 242 |
| **Stained,** Victorian Style, Red, Blue, Green, Amber, Geometric, Wood Frame, 25 x 24 In., Pair ..... | 938 |
| **Zinc,** Slag Glass, Pink Rose, Leaves, Frame, 14 x 36 In. | 1125 |

**WOOD CARVINGS** and wooden pieces are listed separately in this book. There are also wooden pieces found in other categories, such as Folk Art, Kitchen, and Tool.

| | |
|---|---:|
| **Angel,** Walnut, Baroque, Holding Cornucopia, Flowers, 27¾ In., Pair | 1815 |
| **Barn Owl,** On Stump, Harold Gibbs, c.1960, 3 In. | 1080 |
| **Bear,** Painted Open Mouth, Glass Eyes, Black Forest, Walnut, Germany, c.1890, 33 x 57 In. | 79950 |
| **Bear,** Standing, Black Forest, Glass Eyes, c.1900, 15½ In. | 480 |
| **Bear,** Walnut, A. Crowe, Cherokee, Swain Co., N.C., 6 x 8 In. | 1652 |
| **Bird,** Green, Red Paint, Signed Joseph Moyer 1946, Pa., 3¼ In. | 2640 |
| **Black Bellied Plover,** On Driftwood, Painted, G. Boyd, c.1900, 4½ x 11 In. | 3840 |
| **Black Duck,** Paint, Stand, 3½ x 6 In. | 960 |
| **Blackamoor,** Holding Trays, Painted, Venice, c.1900, 43½ In. | 688 |
| **Blessed Virgin & Angels,** Multicolor, Continental, 1790-1810, 15 In. | 590 |
| **Boar,** Standing, Walnut, Black Forest, c.1910, 10 In. | 560 |
| **Boy,** Articulated, Shoulders, Elbows, Hips, Knees, Painted, c.1825, 30½ In. .........................*illus* | 4920 |
| **Bracket,** Winged Lion Shape, Shelf, 24 x 19 In. | 420 |
| **Buddha Of Da Mo,** Beast Biting Earring, Bamboo, Chinese, 1800s, 4 In. ...........................*illus* | 390 |
| **Buddha,** Headdress, Long Gown, Seated, Gilt Lacquered, Stand, Japan, c.1900, 14 In. | 944 |
| **Buddhist Monk,** Folded Hands, Multicolor, Chinese, 1800s, 30 x 13 In. | 2460 |
| **Bust,** Madonna, Eyes Cast Down, Gilt Garment, 21 x 16 In. | 1440 |
| **Bust,** Marie Antoinette, Walnut, Wrapped In Cloak, 1800s, 32 x 20 In. .........................*illus* | 1168 |
| **Bust,** Woman, Grapevines, Musical Scroll, 15¼ In. | 313 |
| **Candle Screen,** Burr Maple, Leaf Shape, Treen, Pennsylvania, c.1800, 16 In. | 594 |
| **Candlestick,** Black Forest, Stag, Tree, Late 19th Century, 10 x 7 In., Pair | 403 |
| **Child,** Robes, Arm Raised, Scrolled Base, Paint, Continental, 27 In. | 875 |
| **Clown,** Circus, Painted, Circus Tent Background, c.1920, 73 x 21 In. | 1680 |
| **Coat Hook,** Antlers, Black Forest, Cowled Gnome, Drinking Cup, 1800s, 15 In., Pair | 932 |
| **Cobra,** Loosely Coiled, 1900s, 28½ x 17 In. | 403 |
| **Compote,** Man, Raised Hand, Stepped Base, Italy, 23½ In. | 6765 |
| **Crane,** Painted, 1900s, 18¼ In. | 1121 |
| **Crucifix,** Body, Applied Gesso, Gilt, c.1880, 22 In. | 420 |
| **Crucifix,** Iron, Christ, Starburst, 18½ In. | 215 |

| | |
|---|---:|
| **Crucifix,** Multicolor, Guatemala, 17th Century, 24 In. | 141 |
| **Crucifix,** Walnut, Stepped Plinth, Germany, c.1920, 23 In. | 188 |
| **Cup & Saucer,** Poplar, Turned, Pussy Willow Rose Decal, Joseph Lehn, 1888, 3 ⅝ In. ....*illus* | 2360 |
| **Diorama,** Bar Room Scene, Painted, Figures, Tables, Bottles, Jailhouse Carver, 12 x 22 In. | 1770 |
| **Eagle,** Chesapeake Model, Painted, Artistic Carving Co., c.1950, 23 x 73 In. | 5040 |
| **Eagle,** Chip Carved, Talons, Holding Snake, Column, Painted, c.1930, 14 x 5 ½ In. | 2337 |
| **Eagle,** Folded Wings, Giltwood, 32 ¾ In. | 1250 |
| **Eagle,** Giltwood, 6 ½ x 14 ¾ In. | 780 |
| **Eagle,** On Sphere, Entwined Snake, Giltwood, 31 x 31 In. | 720 |
| **Eagle,** Spread Wings, Clasping American Shield, Marine Emblem, 1900s, 23 x 19 In. | 3450 |
| **Eagle,** Spread Wings, Giltwood, 11 x 35 In. | 1680 |
| **Eagle,** Spread Wings, Giltwood, Leaf Base Up, c.1945, 26 x 37 In. | 246 |
| **Eagle,** Spread Wings, Painted, Parcel Gilt, 24 x 37 In. | 1875 |
| **Eagle,** Spread Wings, Patriotic Shield, Banner, Block Base, c.1900, 24 In. .....*illus* | 960 |
| **Eagle,** Spread Wings, Signed N.R. Harris, 1900s, 24 x 63 In. | 768 |
| **Eagle,** Spread Wings, Stepped Base, Gilt, 19th Century, 18 x 24 In. | 480 |
| **Face,** C-Shape Profile, Long Nose, Eyes Hang From Rod, Modernist, c.1970, 23 x 10 In. | 805 |
| **Fishmonger,** Japan, c.1900, 28 In. | 180 |
| **Fish,** Arctic Char Salmon, Wood Backboard, Signed, Lawrence C. Irvine, 16 x 36 In. | 5925 |
| **Fish,** Atlantic Salmon, Male, Double Hook Fly, Lawrence C. Irvine, 33 ½ In. | 4444 |
| **Fish,** Hardwood, Ben Christian, Pitcairn Island, 11 ¾ In. | 420 |
| **Flag,** Red, White, Blue, Elongated, Applied Gesso Stars, George Stapf, c.1900, 36 In. | 2091 |
| **Foo Dogs,** Giltwood, Chinese, c.1845, 14 x 9 In., Pair | 1063 |
| **Fork,** Cannibal, Ceremonial, Crosshatched, Iron Stand, Fiji Islands, 1800s, 17 ½ In. | 3318 |
| **Girl,** Mallard Drakes, Painted, Signed Stan Sparre, 6 ½ In. | 266 |
| **Gnome,** Miner, On Rock, Black Forest, Switzerland, c.1900, 6 In. | 216 |
| **Great Horned Owl,** Glass Eyes, Painted, 19 ½ In. | 960 |
| **Guanyin,** Standing, Boxwood, Fly Whisk, Rosary, Rosewood Stand, Chinese, 16 In. .....*illus* | 1778 |
| **Haitian Man,** Articulated Arms, Metal Hat Visor, Japonai, 1888, 26 x 10 In. | 1076 |
| **Hand,** Painted Gray, 10 In. | 234 |
| **Hat Stand,** Zitan, Splayed Round Base, Globe Shape Bulb, Dragons, Chinese, 1800s, 11 In. | 1464 |
| **Horse,** Mahogany, Stallion, Standing, Rectangular Base, Charles Mankin, 24 In. | 720 |
| **Hourglass,** Green, Gold, Ring Handle, c.1920, 8 ¾ In. | 660 |
| **Hunter,** Hat, Mustache, Dog, White, Tan Paint, c.1920, 43 In. | 600 |
| **Indian,** Hand To Brow, Holding Drum, Painted, 25 In. | 120 |
| **Lion,** Yellow, Brown Paint, Signed Paul Tyson, 1979, 6 ½ x 13 In. | 1560 |
| **Madonna,** Giltwood, Arm Outstretched, c.1800, 17 In. | 510 |
| **Madonna,** Hands Out, Child, In Bed, Blue, White, Paint, Gilt, c.1700s, 18 In. | 1560 |
| **Madonna,** Standing On Clouds, c.1750, 19 ¾ In. | 500 |
| **Man,** Ancestral Figure, Yellow, Orange, Black, Papua New Guinea, 51 In. | 313 |
| **Man,** Articulated Arms, Hat, Blue Overalls, Round Platform Base, 1900s, 6 ¾ In. | 83 |
| **Man,** Black Mustache, Gray Suit, Painted, Stand, c.1910, 8 ½ In. | 150 |
| **Man,** Gray Suit Coat, Top Hat, Cane, Mustache, 24 ½ In. | 438 |
| **Man,** Li Tieguai, Daoist Immortal, Boxwood, 1800s, 12 ¼ In. .....*illus* | 923 |
| **Man,** Pine, Arms Raised, Orange, Brown Paint, Charlie Willeto, c.1955, 24 In. | 2400 |
| **Man,** Tuxedo, Black, White Paint, c.1895, 12 In. | 300 |
| **Mannequin,** Artist, Woman, Articulated Joints, 1900s, 35 In. | 900 |
| **Marionette,** Thai Man, Sword, Papier-Mache Head, Hinged Body, Painted, 29 In. | 708 |
| **Milliner's Form,** Woman's Head, Painted, Pole, Stand, France, c.1865, 9 ½ In. | 1320 |
| **Monkey,** Seated, Holding Ball, Black, Red, Yellow Paint, Leather Tail, 1800s, 16 In. | 2400 |
| **Mug,** Ducks, Flying, Cattails, Walnut, R. Lee, 5 ½ In. | 89 |
| **Napoleon,** Holding Telescope, Painted, Block Base, 44 In. | 3125 |
| **Panel,** Lacquered, Reticulated, Pheasants, Sparrows, Gilt, Chinese, 20 x 7 In., Pair | 190 |
| **Panel,** Pine, St. Matthew, Painted, Hanging Hook, c.1790, 30 x 25 In. | 210 |
| **Parrot,** Painted Green, Red, Orange, Turned Pedestal, Keith Collis, 8 ¼ In. | 165 |
| **Parrot,** Walnut, Perch, Turned Standard, c.1950, 32 ½ In. | 150 |
| **Partridge,** Wildlife, M. Van Houzen, 1979, 17 x 8 ¼ In. | 580 |
| **Pigeon,** Zitterhal, Painted, John Fliegerbauer, Pa., 10 ½ In. | 360 |
| **Plaque,** 8 Men, Grouped, Oak, c.1800, 10 x 16 In. | 2125 |
| **Plaque,** Bear Head, Black Forest, c.1950, 13 x 11 In. | 492 |
| **Plaque,** Crew Team Illustrious, 8 Passing The Line, Harvard Univ., 1901, 27 x 45 In. | 153 |
| **Plaque,** Deer Head, Walnut, Gilt Antlers, John Bellamy, c.1880, 17 x 15 In. | 4320 |
| **Plaque,** Eagle, Clutching Arrow, J. Bellamy, 8 x 23 In. | 4800 |
| **Plaque,** Eagle, Federal Style, Clutching Shield & Crossed Flags, 23 x 42 In. | 920 |
| **Plaque,** Eagle, Spread Wings, Shield, Banner, Live & Let Live, Painted, c.1910, 72 In. | 6900 |
| **Plaque,** Eagle, War & Peace, Red, White, Blue, John Bellamy, c.1900, 43 In., Pair | 126000 |

**Wood Carving,** Cup & Saucer, Poplar, Turned, Pussy Willow Rose Decal, Joseph Lehn, 1888, 3 ⅝ In.
**$2,360**

Conestoga Auction Co., Inc.

**Wood Carving,** Eagle, Spread Wings, Patriotic Shield, Banner, Block Base, c.1900, 24 In.
**$960**

Cowan's Auctions

**Wood Carving,** Guanyin, Standing, Boxwood, Fly Whisk, Rosary, Rosewood Stand, Chinese, 16 In.
**$1,778**

James D. Julia Auctioneers

W

**Wood Carving,** Man, Li Tieguai, Daoist Immortal, Boxwood, 1800s, 12¼ In.
**$923**

Skinner Auctioneers & Appraisers

---

**Wood Carving,** Rabbits & Baskets, 11 x 11 In.
**$192**

Fox Auctions

---

**Wood Carving,** Sculpture, Hand, Foot, Base, Gilt, Signed, Pedro Friedeberg, 5¾ In.
**$2,091**

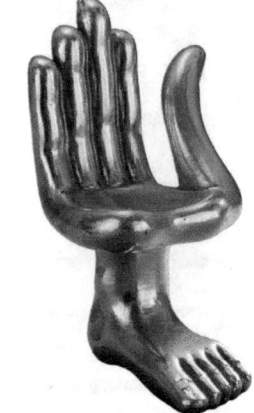

New Orleans Auction Galleries, Inc.

| | |
|---|---:|
| **Plaque,** Hanging Game, Game Bag, Deer, Partridge, Rifle, c.1880, 24 x 12 In. | 354 |
| **Plaque,** Lion, Reclining, Black Forest, Anri, Italy, 1950s, 24 x 22 In. | 630 |
| **Plaque,** Mahogany, Rape Of Europa, Signed Luigi Bonfanti Grignasco, 26 x 32 In. | 6000 |
| **Plaque,** Medallion, Cherubs Making Wine, 19th Century, 11 x 8 In. | 270 |
| **Plaque,** Raised Eagle, Gilt, Shield, Arrows, 45 In. | 840 |
| **Plaque,** Stag, Rocky Outcrop, Leather Backing, Black Forest Style, 11 x 9 In. | 86 |
| **Plaque,** Walnut, Angels, Medallion, Coat Of Arms, Gesso, Gilt, 1700s, 40 x 21 In. | 1481 |
| **Pope,** On Pedestal, White, Red, Brown Paint, c.1870, 59 x 36 In. | 3750 |
| **Putto,** Arm Raised, Gesso, Continental, c.1800, 33 In., Pair | 1476 |
| **Putto,** Holding Cornucopia, Giltwood, 32 In. | 2750 |
| **Rabbits & Baskets,** 11 x 11 In. _illus_ | 192 |
| **Reliquary,** Bust, Saint, Toga, Tassels, 17¾ x 8¼ In. | 300 |
| **Reliquary,** Pavilion, Christ, Continental, 1800s, 24 x 12½ In. | 480 |
| **Robin,** On Stand, Painted, Incised Wings, Tail, Wire Legs, Turned Base, 1800s, 8½ In. | 1353 |
| **Robin,** Painted, Signed On Base, Joseph Moyer, Berks County, Pa., 5½ In. | 1200 |
| **Rooster,** Balsa Wood, 20th Century, 7½ In. | 98 |
| **Rooster,** Gray, Red Paint, c.1850, 12 In. | 270 |
| **Rooster,** Painted, Bone Fins, Stand, 15½ In. | 300 |
| **Rooster,** Twisted Wire Legs, Nicodemus Demon Adams, Virginia, c.1910, 9¼ x 14 In. | 750 |
| **Ruby-Throated Hummingbird,** Wood Stand, Paint, Frank Finney, c.1976, 7¾ x 9½ In. | 1020 |
| **Santo,** 3 Magi, Horses, Red, Cream, Black, 19th Century, 7¾ x 12 In. | 645 |
| **Santo,** Angel, Gloria Patri, Multicolor, 1790-1810, 15 In. | 295 |
| **Santo,** Jesus Of Nazarene, Holding Cross, Multicolor, Colombia, 18th Century, 10⅝ In. | 129 |
| **Santo,** Lamp Base, Multicolor, 19¼ In. | 236 |
| **Santo,** Michael The Archangel, The Devil, Multicolor, 1790-1810, 16¼ In. | 767 |
| **Santo,** Painted, Multicolor, c.1815, 18 In. | 458 |
| **Santo,** St. Joseph, Wood, Multicolor, Guatemala, 17th Century, 14⅜ In. | 118 |
| **Santo,** Virgin Mary, Paint, 1800s, 10½ In. | 104 |
| **Santo,** Woman, Pivoting Upper, Cage Lower Body, Blue Paint, Portugal, 1700s, 62 x 18 In. | 1800 |
| **Sculpture,** Hand, Foot, Base, Gilt, Signed, Pedro Friedeberg, 5¾ In. _illus_ | 2091 |
| **Sculpture,** Kneeling Man, Robe, Cherry, Round Base, Signed, Sol Bauer, 1949, 15 In. _illus_ | 212 |
| **Shoes,** Flowers, Continental, 1890-1910, 11½ In. | 96 |
| **Shopping Bag,** Woven Handles, Livio De Marchi, Italy, 1990, 21¼ x 7¼ In. | 1843 |
| **Shovel,** Apple, Figured Maple, Wide Brim, Open Handle, 19th Century, 38 In. | 270 |
| **Simmons Bird,** Multicolor Paint, No. 1, Signed, Paul Tyson, Pottstown, Penn., 1979, 8 In. | 720 |
| **Snowy Owl,** Ocher Paint, Black Accents, Glass Eyes, F. Finney, Va., 26 In. | 2124 |
| **St. Ambrose,** Miter, Crozier, Bible, Reliquary In Base, 1800s, France, 41 In. | 805 |
| **St. Anthony,** Gesso, Multicolor, c.1910, 57 x 32 In. | 1353 |
| **St. Catherine Of Alexandra,** Painted, Continental, 1800s, 17 x 5½ In. | 676 |
| **St. Francis,** Standing, Flowing Robe, Painted, Continental, c.1800, 28 In. _illus_ | 1045 |
| **Staff,** Figural, Indonesia, 20th Century, 40 In. | 36 |
| **Statue Of Liberty,** Natural Finish, Early 20th Century, 38 In. _illus_ | 2520 |
| **Swan,** Black Paint, Curved Neck, Glass Eyes, c.1910, 21 x 29 In. | 2252 |
| **Temptress Of The King,** Bust, Headdress, Giltwood, Paint, A. Clark, c.1940, 19 x 12 In. | 21250 |
| **Totem Pole,** Eagle Top, Figures, Multicolor, William Kuhnley Sr., 82 x 64 In. | 2006 |
| **Towel Holder,** Figural, Woman In Medieval Dress, Holding Rod, Pine, Painted, 18 In. | 510 |
| **Vase,** Turned, Leopard Maple, Acer Rubrum, Signed, Ed Moulthrop, 7¾ x 6½ In. _illus_ | 4688 |
| **Wall Bracket,** Maiden, Hunter, Stag, Grouse, Black Forest, Swiss, 30 x 22 In. | 13750 |
| **Wall Hanging,** Giltwood, Putti, Scrolled Ground, Italy, 1900s, 11¼ x 17¾ In., Pair | 461 |
| **Waxwing,** Driftwood Base, Signed Lester Braddock | 180 |
| **Wayside Shrine,** St. Louis, Being Blessed, Mary, Jesus, Bas Relief, c.1750, 25 x 19 In. | 2160 |
| **Woman,** Depicting Summer, Pine, Floral Crown, Garland, Painted Gray, 1800s, 78 In. | 20910 |
| **Womb,** Egg, Stylized, Life, Bronze Base, R.G. Barger, 1973, 25¼ In. | 1750 |
| **Wrist Rest,** Bamboo, Engraved Buddhist Saint, Inscription, Chinese, 6½ In. | 830 |

---

**WOODEN** wares were used in all parts of the home. Wood was used for many containers and tools. Small wooden pieces are called _treenware_ in England, but the term _woodenware_ is more common in the United States. Additional pieces may be found in the Advertising, Kitchen, and Tool categories.

| | |
|---|---:|
| **Barrel,** Iron Bands, Blue Paint, 22 x 15 In. | 118 |
| **Barrel,** Oak, Lid, Cylindrical, Staved, 1800s, 30 In. | 60 |
| **Barrel,** Oak, Round Lid, Staved, c.1850, 29½ In. | 180 |
| **Berry Bucket,** 2 Iron Bands, Bail Handle, Green Paint, c.1865, 3½ x 4 In. | 575 |
| **Bin,** Rice, Square, Tapered, Nails, Center Handle, China, 19th Century, 9 x 14 In. | 58 |
| **Bookrack,** Gustav Stickley, Revolving, Branded Mark, c.1912, 10 x 12¾ In. _illus_ | 1216 |
| **Bowl,** Ash Burl, Turned, Flared, 19th Century, 10½ In. | 1320 |

W

| | |
|---|---|
| **Bowl**, Big Leaf, Maple Burl, Long Natural Handle, Signed B. Womack, 26 In. | 1000 |
| **Bowl**, Black Walnut, Turned, Bob Stockdale, c.1965, 3¾ x 17 In. | 1750 |
| **Bowl**, Burl, Banded Rim, New England, c.1810, 4½ x 14½ In. | 1440 |
| **Bowl**, Burl, Flared, 4 x 11¼ In. | 360 |
| **Bowl**, Burl, Flattened Bottom, Curved Sides, Concave Interior, c.1800, 5 x 17 In. | 593 |
| **Bowl**, Burl, Molded Rim, 9½ In. | 480 |
| **Bowl**, Burl, Patina, Flared, Inscribed, 1818, 7¼ In. | 570 |
| **Bowl**, Burl, Treen, Dark Brown, c.1810, 6 x 15 In. | 431 |
| **Bowl**, Burl, Turned, Footed, c.1810, 6¼ x 11¾ In. | 3198 |
| **Bowl**, Figured Tulipwood, Turned, Folded Rim, Signed, P. Moulthrop, 8 x 26 In. | 2500 |
| **Bowl**, Leopard Maple, Turned, Ring Foot, Ed Moulthrop, 5¾ x 13 In. | 2250 |
| **Bowl**, Maple, Tab Handles, New England, c.1810, 25 x 7 In. | 277 |
| **Bowl**, Nut, Cherry, Shaped & Flared-Out Rim, Wharton Esherick, 2 x 13 x 4 In. | 4063 |
| **Bowl**, Pine, Narrow Pedestal Base, Signed, Ron Kent, 1993, 7½ x 8 In. ...........*illus* | 2125 |
| **Bowl**, Raised Ends, Cutout Handles, c.1810, 16 x 13 In. ...........*illus* | 5333 |
| **Bowl**, Red Paint, Curved Handle, Scandinavia, c.1775, 16 x 18 In. | 840 |
| **Bowl**, Sweetgum, Tree Rings, Trunk Slice, Signed E. Moulthrop, 13¼ In. | 1250 |
| **Bowl**, Treen, Oval, c.1860, 7 x 19 In. | 288 |
| **Bowl**, Treen, Red & Black Paint, 19th Century, 4½ x 14½ In. | 150 |
| **Bowl**, Treen, Vinegar Sponging, Flared, 12½ In. | 185 |
| **Bowl**, Turned, Blue Paint, 1800s, 10¾ In. | 144 |
| **Bowl**, Turned, Protruding Rim, Painted Blue, 18½ In. | 1230 |
| **Bowl**, Walnut, Canted Sides, 1800s, 5 x 11 In. | 259 |
| **Bowl**, Wild Cherry, Varnished, Rounded, Squat Foot, Moulthrop, 7 x 14 In. | 3450 |
| **Box**, Donut, Lid, Wood, Stenciled, Round, Twisted Handle, Pennsylvania, 5 x 11 In. | 246 |
| **Box**, Wall, Queen Anne, Pine, Butt Joinery, Molded Base, Red Paint, c.1750, 9½ x 12 In. | 711 |
| **Brushpot**, Natural Root Section, Hollowed, Chinese, 1900s, 5½ x 5 In. | 119 |
| **Brushpot**, Scholar's, Burl, Patina, Chinese, 20th Century, 9½ In. | 240 |
| **Brushpot**, Straight-Sided, 3-Footed, Hexagonal, Chinese, 1900s, 5¼ x 5¾ In. | 237 |
| **Brushpot**, Zitan, Gilding, Round Reserves, Birds, Flowers, Chinese, 1800s, 7 x 5¾ In. | 584 |
| **Bucket**, Lid, Pine, Dark Paint, 1800s, 11½ In. | 148 |
| **Bucket**, Lid, Pine, Porcelain Knob, Painted Green, Tapered, Staved, 11 x 12½ In. | 369 |
| **Bucket**, Lid, Sugar, Tacked Bands, Bail Handle, Black Paint, c.1970, 9 x 9¾ In. | 150 |
| **Bucket**, Lid, Sugar, Treen, Staved, Bail Handle, Green Paint, c.1850, 10 x 9½ In. | 259 |
| **Bucket**, Lid, Treen, Metal Bands, Staved, Bail Handle, Red Paint, c.1900, 14 x 13 In. | 288 |
| **Bucket**, Peat, George III Style, Mahogany, Brass Bound, 15 In. | 188 |
| **Bucket**, Peat, Plank Sides, Wood Straps, Painted, Loop Handles, c.1875, 12¾ In. | 89 |
| **Bucket**, Piggin, Pine, Shaped Stave Handle, Pa., 1800s, 12 In. | 148 |
| **Bucket**, Sugar, 2 Finger Bands, Bentwood Handle, Blue Paint, 4¾ In. | 390 |
| **Bucket**, Sugar, Staved, Single Finger Bands, Bail Handle, Blue Paint, 7 x 7 In. | 1140 |
| **Bucket**, Sugar, Treen, Finger Hoops, Swing Bail, Gray Paint, c.1870, 10 x 10 In. | 92 |
| **Bucket**, Turned, Carved Ears, Bentwood Swing Handle, Blue Paint, c.1810, 6 x 5½ In. | 4148 |
| **Canister**, Blue & White Sponged Paint, Treen, New England, 1800s, 10¾ In. | 5040 |
| **Canister**, Lid, Treen, Yellow Poplar, Green Paint, 8½ x 7 In. | 615 |
| **Canister**, Lid, Treen, Yellow Poplar, Vinegar Graining, Tacks, Footed, 1847, 12 In. | 960 |
| **Carrier**, Dog, Dome Top, Spring-Loaded Food Chute, A. Backus Jr. & Sons, 36 x 41 In. ...........*illus* | 1007 |
| **Cask**, Oak Staves, 1780-1820, 9¼ x 8 In. | 338 |
| **Coffer**, Multicolor, Chinoiserie, Figural Landscape, Brass Handles, 14 x 19 In. | 1434 |
| **Compote**, Burl, Turned Foot, c.1900, 3 x 8 In. | 240 |
| **Compote**, Lid, Maple, Urn Shape, Stemmed Foot, c.1850, 5⅝ In. | 425 |
| **Compote**, Painted, Blue, Red, Gilt, White Base, Ring Turned Column, c.1810, 8 x 10 In. | 1007 |
| **Cup**, Saffron, Dome Lid, Poplar, Turned, Ball Finial, Salmon Ground, Flowers, Lehn, 5½ In. | 472 |
| **Cup**, Saffron, Lid, Painted, Strawberries, Signed John R. Dierwechter, 5½ In. | 35 |
| **Cup**, Saffron, Lid, Poplar, Turned, Painted Salmon, Strawberries, Footed, Lehn, 5 In. | 2124 |
| **Eggcup**, Turned, Painted, Salmon Ground, Multicolor Flowers, Leaves, Lehn, 3 In. | 236 |
| **Firkin**, Lid, Softwood, Aqua, Staved, Lap Joint, Bentwood Swing Handle, 10 x 10 In. | 236 |
| **Firkin**, Lid, Softwood, Green, Staved, Lap Joint, Bentwood Swing Handle, 9 x 9¾ In. | 354 |
| **Firkin**, Lid, Softwood, Sponge Painted, Staved, Bands, Bentwood Handle, 9¾ x 10¼ In. | 83 |
| **Firkin**, Lid, Softwood, Tongue & Groove Staves, Blue Paint, Penn., 10 x 10 In. ...........*illus* | 354 |
| **Firkin**, Lid., Pine, Gray Paint, Handle, 1800s, 12 In. | 234 |
| **Firkin**, Pine, Apple Green Paint, Pennsylvania, 19th Century, 13¾ In. | 357 |
| **Firkin**, Pine, Banded, Flat Lid, Green Paint, 1800s, 12 In. | 84 |
| **Firkin**, Pine, Black Paint, Handle, 1800s, 10 In. | 221 |
| **Firkin**, Pine, Brown Paint, Swing Handle, 1800s, 14½ In. | 123 |
| **Firkin**, Red Paint, Loop Handle, c.1840, 9½ x 10½ In. | 12 |
| **Firkin**, Softwood, Red Wash, Salmon Paint, Staved, Bands, Wire Handle, 6¾ x 6⅝ In. | 295 |

**Wood Carving**, Sculpture, Kneeling Man, Robe, Cherry, Round Base, Signed, Sol Bauer, 1949, 15 In.
**$212**

Rachel Davis Fine Arts

**Wood Carving**, St. Francis, Standing, Flowing Robe, Painted, Continental, c.1800, 28 In.
**$1,045**

New Orleans Auction Galleries, Inc.

**Wood Carving**, Statue Of Liberty, Natural Finish, Early 20th Century, 38 In.
**$2,520**

Garth's Auctioneers & Appraisers

# WOODEN

**Wood Carving,** Vase, Turned, Leopard Maple, Acer Rubrum, Signed, Ed Moulthrop, 7 ¾ x 6 ½ In.
$4,688

Rago Arts & Auction Center

**Wooden,** Bookrack, Gustav Stickley, Revolving, Branded Mark, c.1912, 10 x 12 ¾ In.
$1,216

Rago Arts & Auction Center

**Wooden,** Bowl, Pine, Narrow Pedestal Base, Signed, Ron Kent, 1993, 7 ½ x 8 In.
$2,125

Los Angeles Modern Auctions (LAMA)

**Wooden,** Bowl, Raised Ends, Cutout Handles, c.1810, 16 x 13 In.
$5,333

James D. Julia Auctioneers

| | |
|---|---:|
| **House Marker,** Pine, Painted, Green, Black, Ivory, Andreeas Henne Anno, 1816, 24 x 16 In. | 3840 |
| **Humidor,** Burl, Inlaid Banding, Cut Corners, Hinged Lid, Cedar Inside, 9 x 14 In. | 105 |
| **Ice Bucket,** Lid, Danish Modern, Teak, Handle, Liner, Sake Keg Shape, Denmark, 19 x 9 In. | 144 |
| **Ice Bucket,** Teak, Plastic Insert, Jens Quistgaard, Dansk, c.1960, 19 In. ..........*illus* | 120 |
| **Jar,** Lid, Peaseware, Round, Squat, Turned, Bail Handle, Finial, 9 In. | 523 |
| **Mangle Board,** Horse Handle, Carved Designs, Continental, 1800s, 28 ¾ In. | 270 |
| **Mangle Board,** Horse Handle, Carved, Multicolor Paint, Scandinavia, 1800s, 25 x 8 In. | 720 |
| **Mold,** Foundry, Pine, Painted, Inscribed F.X. Hooper Co., Glenarm, Md., 1800s, 43 x 34 In. | 86 |
| **Mortar & Pestle,** Lignum Vitae, 1800s, 9 In. | 180 |
| **Mortar & Pestle,** Walnut, Lignum Vitae, 1700s, 10 & 13 In. | 172 |
| **Palette,** Artist's, Curved, Thumb Hole, 28 x 17 ½ In. | 117 |
| **Pipe Holder,** Bamboo, Inlay, Mother-Of-Pearl, Brass, Garden, Men, Japan, 3 ⅛ In. | 84 |
| **Propeller,** Walnut, 72 ½ In. | 325 |
| **Salt,** Burl, Turned, Pedestal Base, Patina, c.1810, 3 ½ x 2 ¾ In. ..........*illus* | 711 |
| **Sculpture,** 1 Body, 2 Heads, c.1960, 18 In. | 120 |
| **Sculpture,** Abstract, Donn Enger, 12-In. Base, 23 In. | 450 |
| **Sign,** House Date Board, Yellow, Black Paint, Lancaster Co., 1837, 15 ¾ x 23 In. | 550 |
| **Sugar Bucket,** Lid, 3 Bands, Oak, Iron, Painted, J.J. Lehn, Lancaster County, Pa., 1885, 9 In. | 688 |
| **Tankard,** Burl, Bird's-Eye Maple, Turned, Lion Thumbpiece, Scandinavia, c.1800, 8 In. | 533 to 1680 |
| **Tankard,** Medieval Style, Carved, Scandinavia, c.1900, 9 In., Pair | 922 |
| **Torso,** Woman, c.1920, 24 ½ x 17 In. | 196 |
| **Tray,** Aluminum Rounded Corners, Reed Hall, Tea Rooms, 18 x 12 In. | 135 |
| **Tray,** Cutlery, Divided, Cutout Handle, Green Paint, Gold Flowers, c.1850, 5 x 13 In. | 207 |
| **Tray,** Cutlery, Mahogany, Rosewood, Carved, Cutout Handle, c.1840, 13 x 8 In. | 240 |
| **Tray,** Cutlery, Pine, Yellow Grained & Blue Paint, Henry Lapp, Pa., c.1900, 4 ½ x 12 In. | 600 |
| **Tray,** Cutlery, Tiger Maple, 2 Compartments, Cutout Divider Handle, c.1845, 6 x 14 In. | 489 |
| **Tray,** Cutlery, Walnut, Cutout Heart Shape Handle, Va., c.1920, 5 x 7 ¾ In. | 34 |
| **Tray,** George III, Mahogany, Fretwork, c.1800, 25 ½ x 5 In. | 120 |
| **Tray,** Knife, Walnut, Vine Inlays, Heart Cutout, Pa., c.1850, 5 ¾ x 12 In. | 840 |
| **Tray,** Mahogany, Satinwood, Oval, Handles, 24 In. | 75 |
| **Tray,** Mahogany, Scalloped Rim, Brass Bound, Oval, England, c.1820, 4 x 19 ¾ In. | 375 |
| **Trough,** Pine Planks, Drainage Hole, Sleigh Sides, Rustic Style, 6 x 46 x 21 In. | 86 |
| **Trough,** Pine, Carved, Inverted Trapezoid, Curved Legs, 19th Century, 31 x 66 x 25 In. | 288 |
| **Vase,** Ashleaf Maple, Turned, Glossy, Brown, Pink, Signed C. Moulthrop, 11 x 14 In. | 3200 |
| **Vase,** Ashleaf Maple, Turned, Spherical, Glossy, Signed C. Moulthrop, 11 ½ x 11 In. | 3200 |

**WORCESTER** porcelains were made in Worcester, England, from 1751. The firm went through many name changes and eventually, in 1862, became The Royal Worcester Porcelain Company Ltd. Collectors often refer to Dr. Wall, Barr, Flight, and other names that indicate time periods or artists at the factory. It became part of Royal Worcester Spode Ltd. in 1976. The company was bought by the Portmeirion Group in 2009. Related pieces may be found in the Royal Worcester category.

| | |
|---|---:|
| **Bowl,** Blue & White, 4 ¾ In. | 63 |
| **Castor Jar,** Pickle, Pinecone, 9 In. | 144 |
| **Cup & Saucer,** Camaieu Vert, Trailing Flowers, Green, Gold, Gilt, c.1765, 5 In. | 275 |
| **Cup & Saucer,** Camaieu, Puce, Flower Sprays, c.1770, 5 In. | 100 |
| **Cup & Saucer,** Rose, Yellow Red Flowers, Turquoise Rim, Fluted, c.1775, 3 x 6 In. | 660 |
| **Cup,** Queen Charlotte Pattern, Red, White Blue, Scroll, Flower Vertical Bands, c.1765, 2 ½ In. | 50 |
| **Dish,** Blue, White, Flowers, Shell Shape, 6 ½ In. | 625 |
| **Dish,** Pickle, Pickle Leaf Vine Pattern, Serrated Rim, Organic Shape, c.1765, 3 ½ In. | 138 |
| **Mustard Pot,** Lid, Fence Pattern, Flower Finial, 3 ¾ In. | 113 |
| **Plate,** Jabberwocky Pattern, Scalloped Rim, Chamberlain's Worcester, c.1835, 10 ½ In., 4 Piece. | 480 |
| **Platter,** Bengal Tiger, Armorials, Orange, Green, c.1790, 8 x 10 In., Pair | 1140 |
| **Rice Spoon,** Flower Sprays, Blue & White, Reticulated, c.1770, 5 ½ In. | 469 |
| **Saucer,** Marchioness Of Huntley, Green Band, Gilt Scrolls, Flowers, c.1770, 7 ½ In. | 35 |
| **Sugar,** Lid, Chinoiserie, Imari Colors, Gilt, Handles, Chamberlain's Worcester, 5 x 7 In. | 380 |
| **Sugar,** Lid, Three Flowers, Flower Finial, Blue, White, c.1775, 4 ½ In. | 281 |
| **Tankard,** Fisherman & Cormarant, Blue, White, c.1780, 5 ¾ In. | 281 |
| **Tea Bowl,** Chinoiserie Pattern, Figures, c.1765, 2 ⅞ In. | 175 |
| **Tea Bowl,** Saucer, Milkmaids Pattern, Black & White, c.1760, 4 ½ In. | 94 |
| **Teapot,** Dome Lid, Flower Knop, Chinese Family Scenes, Round Shape, c.1770, 6 ½ In. | 546 |
| **Teapot,** Dome Lid, Flower Knop, Flowers, Gilt Rims, c.1775, 6 In. | 207 |
| **Teapot,** Dome Lid, Onion Knop, Flowers, Gilt Lines, c.1770, 5 ½ In. | 345 |
| **Teapot,** Fence Pattern, Blue & White, Crescent Mark, 1700s, 6 x 7 In..........*illus* | 345 |
| **Teapot,** Flat Lid, Blue, Gilt Bands, Reeded Barrel Shape, c.1790, 5 ¾ In. | 518 |
| **Teapot,** Furrows, Rust Flowers, Vines, Blue Panels, Gilt, Chamberlain's Worcester, 10 x 7 In. | 368 |
| **Teapot,** Lid, Dalhousie, Scenic Ovals, Reeded, Barrel Shape, c.1780, 5 In. | 466 |

| | |
|---|---|
| **Teapot,** Stand, Imari Pattern, Flowers, Lobed, Hexagonal Stand, c.1770, 4 In. | 813 |
| **Tureen,** Sauce, Imari, Fan Pattern, Dr. Wall, c.1765, 4¾ x 6½ In. ............................*illus* | 657 |
| **Urn,** Lid, Irish Landscape Reserves, Hexagonal, Gilt Dolphin Handles, c.1850, 19 In., Pair | 1625 |
| **Vase,** Telephone Box Pattern, Knopped, Flared, c.1760, 7 In. | 281 |

**WORLD WAR** I and World War II souvenirs are collected today. Be careful not to store anything that includes live ammunition. Your local police will tell you how to dispose of the explosives. See also Sword and Trench Art.

## WORLD WAR I

| | |
|---|---|
| **Binoculars,** Brass, Naval, Marked, Mk.V Wide 60903 | 110 |
| **Bugle,** Trench, Wurlitzer, 8 In. | 30 |
| **Cap,** Black Patent Leather, Side Vents, Eagle, Jager Shako, Germany, c.1916, 6 In. | 288 |
| **Cup,** Pewter, Wilhelm II-Franz Joseph, Profile Plaques, Inscribed, c.1916, 4 x 2 In. | 180 |
| **Poster,** America Calls, Enlist In The Navy, Liberty, Sailor, J. Leyendecker, 1917, 41 x 28 In. | 2750 |
| **Poster,** Boys, Come Along You're Wanted, Yellow, Britain, 19¾ x 29 In. | 158 |
| **Poster,** Canadiens Francais, Venez Avec Nous Dans Le 150ieme Battaillon, 1915, 41 x 27 In. | 1125 |
| **Poster,** Daddy, What Did YOU Do In The Great War?, S. Lumley, 1915, 29 x 19 In. | 1875 |
| **Poster,** Destroy This Mad Brute, Enlist, Gorilla, Woman, H.R. Hopps, c.1917, 42 x 28 In. | 18750 |
| **Poster,** Empire Needs Men, Enlist Now, Lion, With Pride, A. Wardle, 30 x 20 In. | 1125 |
| **Poster,** Enlist, On Which Side Of The Window Are You, Soldiers, L. Brey, 1917, 39 x 26 In. | 1152 |
| **Poster,** Food Will Win The War, Yiddish, Statue Of Liberty, C. Chambers, 1918, 30 x 20 In. | 750 |
| **Poster,** Forward! Enlist Now, Lucy Kemp Walsh, Frame, 1915, 30 x 19 In. | 2000 |
| **Poster,** Gee!! I Wish I Were A Man, Girl, In Sailor Uniform, H.C. Christy, 1918, 40 x 26 In. | 6656 |
| **Poster,** Help Buy An Aeroplane, Army War Savings Assoc., Bert Thomas, 1918, 30 x 20 In. | 832 |
| **Poster,** I Want You For The Navy, Girl, In Navy Uniform, Frame, H.C. Christy, 40 x 26 In. | 5000 |
| **Poster,** I Want You For The U.S. Army, Uncle Sam Pointing, J.M. Flagg, 1917, 40 x 30 In. | 8125 |
| **Poster,** If You Want To Fight, Join The Marines, Woman, H. C. Christy, 1915, 37 x 27 In. | 7680 |
| **Poster,** It Takes A Man To Fill It, Sailor Uniform, C. S. Duncan, 1918, 42 x 28 In. | 3500 |
| **Poster,** It's Nice In Surf But What About Men In Trenches, D.H. Souter, 1917, 30 x 20 In. | 1500 |
| **Poster,** Join An Irish Regiment Today, Paper, 29½ x 19 In. | 2014 |
| **Poster,** Join The Air Service & Serve In France, Plane, J. Paul Verrees.1917, 37 x 25 In. | 1250 |
| **Poster,** Join The Army Air Service, Hawk & Eagle Fighting, C.L. Bull, c.1917, 27 x 20 In. | 3000 |
| **Poster,** Peace Loan, Ship Steaming Into Port, E.B. Studios, Sydney, 26 x 20 In. | 938 |
| **Poster,** Peace, Evening News, Angels, Heralding In Night Sky, 1919, 30 x 20 In. | 1125 |
| **Poster,** See Him Through, Burton Rice, National Catholic War Council, 1918, 30 x 20 In. | 46 |
| **Poster,** Shove Off, Join The Navy, Sailors On Elephant, J. Daugherty, c.1918, 41 x 27 In. | 813 |
| **Poster,** There Is Still A Place In The Line For You Will You Fill It?, 1915, 30 x 20 In. | 688 |
| **Poster,** Travel, Adventure, Join Marines, Hunter, Leopard, J.M. Flagg, c.1918, 40 x 30 In. | 4608 |
| **Poster,** U.S. Marine, Be A Sea Soldier, C. Underwood, c.1914, 38 x 28 In. | 1125 |
| **Poster,** U.S. Navy, Help Your Country, Battleship, H. Reuterdahl, Frame, c.1917, 39 x 26 In. | 2000 |
| **Poster,** Victory Liberty Loan, Woman, Flag, 26¾ x 40 In. | 230 |
| **Poster,** Wake Up America Day, Woman Paul Revere, Flag, J.M. Flagg, 1917, 41 x 27 In. | 8750 |
| **Poster,** Were You There Then?, Woman, Australian Flag, Harry Weston, c.1916, 36 x 23 In. | 1125 |
| **Poster,** Women Of Britain Say-GO, Women Watching Soldiers, E.V. Kealey, 1915, 29 x 19 In. | 1625 |

## WORLD WAR II

| | |
|---|---|
| **Badge,** Wound, Silver, Helmet, Crossed Swords, German | 129 |
| **Button,** Celluloid, Say It With Flyers, Airplane, Pinback, 1¼ In. | 45 |
| **Button,** V.E. Day Victory, Flags, Red, White, Blue, 1945, 1¼ In. | 35 |
| **Caricature,** Hirohito, Hitler, Mussolini, Board, 56 x 19 In. | 265 |
| **Carnival Game Target,** Anti-Hitler, Cast Iron Smiling Head, Composition Nose, 10 In. | 765 |
| **Compass,** Lensatic, Corps Of Engineers, Superior Magneto Corp. | 249 |
| **Dagger,** Nazi Hewer, Stamped Carl Eickhorn, 9¾-In. Blade. | 360 |
| **Flag,** Nazi, Swastika Cross, Red, White, Black, American Soldiers Signed, c.1943, 32 x 26 In. | 246 |
| **Game,** Arcade, Poison The Rat, Hitler, Steel Ball, Head Tilts, Groetchen, 1942, 24 In. | 9440 |
| **Helmet,** German, Metal, SS Decal, Leather Interior, 1943, 6½ x 9¼ In. | 237 |
| **Helmet,** Steel, Continental | 148 |
| **Mess Kit,** Tin, Latch Handle, Marked, U.S. E.A. Co., 1944, 16 x 6 x 2 In. | 37 |
| **Paper Doll,** War Girls, Sybil, Florence, Eleanor, Samuel Lowe, 12¾ x 8 In. | 90 |
| **Pin,** American Red Cross Volunteer, Cross, Red, Blue, 1940s, 1 In. | 22 |
| **Pin,** Quartermaster, Sterling, Eagle, Crossed Swords, 1940s, 1 x 1 In. | 19 |
| **Poster,** 7th War Loan, Now All Together, C.C. Beall, 1945, 28 x 11 In. | 150 |
| **Poster,** Books Are Weapons In The War Of Ideas, Books Cannot Be Killed, 1942, 28 x 20 In. | 1408 |
| **Poster,** Buy War Bonds, Uncle Sam, Stars, Stripes, 41 x 26½ In. | 592 |
| **Poster,** Free A Man To Fight, Woman Riveter, Leslie Ragan, 1943, 28 x 20 In. | 1125 |
| **Poster,** Give It Your Best, American Flag, Charles Coiner, 1942, 20 x 28 In. | 1216 |

**Wooden,** Carrier, Dog, Dome Top, Spring-Loaded Food Chute, A. Backus Jr. & Sons, 36 x 41 In.
$1,007

James D. Julia Auctioneers

**Wooden,** Firkin, Lid, Softwood, Tongue & Groove Staves, Blue Paint, Penn., 10 x 10 In.
$354

Conestoga Auction Co., Inc.

**Wooden,** Ice Bucket, Teak, Plastic Insert, Jens Quistgaard, Dansk, c.1960, 19 In.
$120

DuMouchelles Art Gallery

**W**

This is an edited listing of current prices. Visit **Kovels.com** to check thousands of prices from previous years and sign up for free information on trends, tips, reproductions, marks, and more.

**Wooden,** Salt, Burl, Turned, Pedestal Base, Patina, c.1810, 3 ½ x 2 ¾ In.
$711

James D. Julia Auctioneers

**Worcester,** Teapot, Fence Pattern, Blue & White, Crescent Mark, 1700s, 6 x 7 In.
$345

Cottone Auctions

**Worcester,** Tureen, Sauce, Imari, Fan Pattern, Dr. Wall, c.1765, 4 ¾ x 6 ½ In.
$657

Neal Auction Co.

**World's Fair,** Bank, 1893, Chicago, Half Globe, Image Of Columbus, Grover Cleveland, Palmer
$200

RSL Auction

| | |
|---|---|
| **Poster,** Jap, You're Next, Buy Extra Bonds, Uncle Sam, Ready To Fight, J.M. Flagg, 1945, 28 x 20 In. | 2048 |
| **Poster,** Keep Calm & Carry On, Crown, Red Ground, 1939, 30 x 20 In. | 17500 |
| **Poster,** Keep 'Em Coming, & Coming Right, Men, Torpedoes, W. Pursell, 1942, 40 x 29 In. | 2000 |
| **Poster,** Keep 'Em Rolling!, Planes, Mechanics, Flag Ground, Leo Lionni, 1941, 40 x 29 In. | 750 |
| **Poster,** Keep 'Em Shooting, U.S. Tank Rolling German Debris, Mead Schaeffer, 1943, 39 In. | 480 |
| **Poster,** Keep Us Flying, Buy War Bonds, African-American Airman, 1943, 28 x 20 In. | 1750 |
| **Poster,** Kinda Give It Your Personal Attention, More Production, Green, 40 x 27 In. | 23 |
| **Poster,** Let's Give Him Enough & On Time, Machine Gunner, N. Rockwell, 1943, 28 x 39 In. | 768 |
| **Poster,** Let's Go Forward Together, Winston Churchill, Blue, Black, White, 1940, 30 x 20 In. | 5500 |
| **Poster,** Never Was So Much Owed By So Many To So Few, London, c.1940, 30 x 20 In. | 4864 |
| **Poster,** Parade, Metropolitan Opera, Diorama Opera Scenes, David Hockney, 1982, 80 x 41 In. | 3125 |
| **Poster,** Remember December 7th, Issued In 1942, 24 x 30 In. | 450 |
| **Poster,** Together We Win, 3 Hands Shaking, Courtney Allen, 40 x 28 In. | 625 |
| **Poster,** Victory Is Sure But You Must Help Crush War Dogs, N. Chaubal, c.1941, 30 x 20 In. | 875 |
| **Poster,** Your Farm Can Help, Gov. Printing Office, Waving To Planes, 1941, 40 x 27 In. | 500 |
| **Training Center Camp Book,** Maxwell Field, Alabama, 1941, 9 x 6 In. | 42 |

**WORLD'S FAIR** souvenirs from all of the fairs are collected. The first fair was the Great Exhibition of 1851 in London. Some other important exhibitions and fairs include Philadelphia, 1876 (Centennial); Chicago, 1893 (World's Columbian); Buffalo, 1901 (Pan-American); St. Louis, 1904 (Louisiana Purchase); Portland, 1905 (Lewis & Clark Centennial Exposition); San Francisco, 1915 (Panama-Pacific); Philadelphia, 1926 (Sesquicentennial); Chicago, 1933 (Century of Progress); Cleveland, 1936 (Great Lakes); San Francisco, 1939 (Golden Gate International); New York, 1939 (World of Tomorrow); Seattle, 1962 (Century 21); New York, 1964; Montreal, 1967; Knoxville (Energy Turns the World) 1982; New Orleans, 1984; Tsukuba, Japan, 1985; Vancouver, Canada, 1986; Brisbane, Australia, 1988; Seville, Spain, 1992; Genoa, Italy, 1992; Seoul, South Korea, 1993; Lisbon, Portugal, 1998; Hanover, Germany, 2000; and Aichi, Japan, 2005. Memorabilia of fairs include directories, pictures, fabrics, ceramics, etc. Memorabilia from other similar celebrations may be listed in the Souvenir category.

| | |
|---|---|
| **Baby Dish,** 1939, New York, Trylon & Perisphere, 3 Sections, Cat, Bear, Blocks, 8 In. | 143 |
| **Bank,** 1893, Chicago, Building, Red, White, Gold Roof, 6 In. | 300 |
| **Bank,** 1893, Chicago, Half Globe, Image Of Columbus, Grover Cleveland, Palmer............*illus* | 19200 |
| **Bank,** Thermometer, 1939, New York, Sphere & Ball, Lithograph, 12 ¼ In. | 502 |
| **Bookends,** 1939, New York, Trylon & Perisphere, White, Marble, Italy, 4 ½ x 5 In. | 126 |
| **Bookmark,** 1876, Philadelphia, Centennial Exposition, George Washington Portrait, 8 In. | 240 |
| **Bottle,** 1939, New York, Milk Glass, Dawn Of A New Day, Anchor Hocking, 8 In. | 48 |
| **Chair,** 1939, New York, Trylon & Perisphere, Progressive Table Co., 36 In., Pair .......*illus* | 443 |
| **Clock,** 1939, New York, Electric, Trylon & Perisphere, Inlay, United Clock, 17 x 12 In. .......*illus* | 403 |
| **Creamer,** 1893, Chicago, Ribbed, Handle, Pastel Blue, Mt. Washington, 2 ½ In. ..........*illus* | 230 |
| **Directional Street Sign,** 1964, New York, Trapezoidal, Aluminum, 30 x 24 In. | 184 |
| **Dish,** 1939, New York, 3 Compartments, Flowers, White, 3 ¾ x 6 ½ In. | 115 |
| **Fan,** 1904, St. Louis, Gold Dust Twins, Cardboard, 15 x 12 In. | 150 |
| **Hatchet,** 1893, Chicago, Vaseline Glass, Embossed, Geo. Washington Bust, Libbey, 8 In. | 104 |
| **Pear,** 1893, Chicago, Blown Glass, White, Cranberry Shading, Peachblow, 5 In. ..........*illus* | 266 |
| **Pendant,** Expo '86, Vancouver, Canada, 10K Gold, 1986 | 60 |
| **Pocket Watch,** 1939, New York, Trylon & Perisphere, Case, Ingersoll | 506 |
| **Postcard,** 1893 Chicago, Puck, 3 x 5 In. | 90 |
| **Postcard,** 1904, St. Louis, Inside Inn, Color, Hold To Light, Mailed, 3 x 5 In. | 150 |
| **Postcard,** 1915, Panama-Pacific Expo, Kewpies Above Fair, Rose O'Neil Kever, 3 x 5 In. | 210 |
| **Poster,** 1933, Chicago, Century Of Progress, Hall Of Science, Blue, Red, Yellow, 42 x 28 In. | 1320 |
| **Poster,** 1933, Chicago, Century Of Progress, Triumphant Figure On Globe, 42 x 28 In. | 2040 |
| **Poster,** 1939, New York, World Of Tomorrow, Trylon & Perisphere, 30 x 20 In. ......*illus* | 1725 |
| **Radio,** 1939, New York, Victor RCA, Cabinet, Trylon & Perisphere, 7 x 9 ¼ In. | 632 |
| **Sign,** 1939, New York, N.B.C. Premium Crackers, Pride Assortment, 11 ½ x 17 In. | 115 |
| **Sign,** 1939, New York, Welcome, Bronze, Gold Highlights, Plaster, 25 x 17 In. ...........*illus* | 539 |
| **Sign,** 1982, Knoxville, Your Host, Holiday Inn, World's Fair, 32 x 14 In. | 60 |
| **Teapot,** 1939, New York, Blue, Gold, Trylon & Perisphere, Hall, 6 x 9 In. ...........*illus* | 316 |
| **Textile,** 1893, Chicago, George Washington, Building, New World, 24 x 34 In. ...........*illus* | 115 |
| **Tin,** 1915, San Francisco, Palace Of Fine Arts, Tin Lithograph, Gold Rim, 10 In. | 77 |
| **Toy,** 1933, Chicago, Century Of Progress, Truck, Steel, Wyandotte, 20 In. ...........*illus* | 300 |
| **Toy,** 1939, New York, Tractor Train, Trylon & Perisphere, Iron, Greyhound, 11 ½ In. | 278 |
| **Toy,** 1939, New York, Tram, Greyhound, Cast Iron, Tin Lithograph Arcade, 7 ½ In. | 236 |
| **Tray,** 1939, New York, Rio De Janeiro, Reverse Painted, Brazil, 13 x 21 In. ...........*illus* | 153 |
| **Typewriter,** 1939, New York, Hinged Case, Blue, Art Deco, Trylon & Perisphere | 345 |
| **Vase,** 1893, Chicago, Jack-In-The-Pulpit, Amberina, Fuchsia, Flowers, 7 In. | 243 |
| **Vase,** 1939, New York, Trylon & Perisphere, Lenox China, Pink, 5 ⅛ In. | 172 |
| **Water Cycle,** 1939, New York, Pontoon, 44 x 87 x 51 In. | 585 |

**World's Fair,** Chair, 1939, New York, Trylon & Perisphere, Progressive Table Co., 36 In., Pair
$443

Hake's Americana & Collectibles

**World's Fair,** Clock, 1939, New York, Electric, Trylon & Perisphere, Inlay, United Clock, 17 x 12 In.
$403

Hake's Americana & Collectibles

**World's Fair,** Creamer, 1893, Chicago, Ribbed, Handle, Pastel Blue, Mt. Washington, 2 ½ In.
$230

Early Auction Co.

**World's Fair,** Pear, 1893, Chicago, Blown Glass, White, Cranberry Shading, Peachblow, 5 In.
$266

Conestoga Auction Co., Inc.

**World's Fair,** Poster, 1939, New York, World Of Tomorrow, Trylon & Perisphere, 30 x 20 In.
$1,725

Hake's Americana & Collectibles

**World's Fair,** Sign, 1939, New York, Welcome, Bronze, Gold Highlights, Plaster, 25 x 17 In.
$539

Hake's Americana & Collectibles

**World's Fair,** Teapot, 1939, New York, Blue, Gold, Trylon & Perisphere, Hall, 6 x 9 In.
$316

Hake's Americana & Collectibles

**World's Fair,** Textile, 1893, Chicago, George Washington, Building, New World, 24 x 34 In.
$115

Hake's Americana & Collectibles

**World's Fair,** Toy, 1933, Chicago, Century Of Progress, Truck, Steel, Wyandotte, 20 In.
$300

Morphy Auctions

**World's Fair,** Tray, 1939, New York, Rio De Janeiro, Reverse Painted, Brazil, 13 x 21 In.
$153

Hake's Americana & Collectibles

**W**

WPA, Group, Pilgrim Family, Marked, Cleveland, O., Grace Luse, 10 In. $230

Humler & Nolan

**Wristwatch**, Benrus, 14K White Gold, Diamonds, 21 Jewel, Black Silk Band, Woman's $219

Garth's Auctioneers & Appraisers

---

**TIP**

*Don't stop your mail and newspapers when you go away if you can get a friend to pick them up. A stop-order may alert a burglar.*

---

**W**

---

**Water Set,** 1939, New York, Ceramic, 7-In. Pitcher, 4-In. Tumblers, Japan .......................... 313

**WPA** is the abbreviation for Works Progress Administration, a program created by executive order in 1935 to provide jobs for millions of unemployed Americans. Artists were hired to create murals, paintings, drawings, and sculptures for public buildings. Pieces are marked *WPA* and may have the artist's name on them.

| | |
|---|---:|
| **Group,** Pilgrim Family, Marked, Cleveland, O., Grace Luse, 10 In. .......................... *illus* | 230 |
| **Museum Diorama,** Cultivating Tobacco, Delaware, Label, 8 ½ x 13 In. ......................... | 130 |
| **Museum Diorama,** Grinding Corn, Hopi, Label, 8 ½ x 13 In. ...................................... | 443 |
| **Poster,** Lake Placid Bobsled Run, Red Sled, Blue White Ground, 1930s, 25 x 17 In. ......... | 840 to 1560 |

**WRISTWATCHES** came into use during World War I. Wristwatches are listed here by manufacturer or as advertising or character watches. Wristwatches may also be listed in other categories. Pocket watches are listed in the Watch category.

| | |
|---|---:|
| **Baume & Mercier,** 14K Yellow Gold, Tiffany & Co. Box, Woman's, 6 ½ In. ......................... | 600 |
| **Benrus,** 14K White Gold, Diamonds, 21 Jewel, Black Silk Band, Woman's ......................... | 219 |
| **Breitling,** Chrono Avenger M1, Model E73360 Titanium, Quartz, Water Resistant, 1 ¼ In. ......... | 1783 |
| **Breitling,** Chronograph Avenger, Titanium, Automatic, Model E13360, 2 In. ......................... | 1668 |
| **Breitling,** Chronomat, Stainless Steel Case, Bracelet, Blue Dial, Case, Box, 7 In. ......... | 1770 |
| **Breitling,** Cosmonaute Special Edition, Model A, Navitimer, Sapphire, Box, 1 ½ In. ......... | 3450 |
| **Brequet,** Sunk Seconds Dial, Manual Winding, Speidel Leather Band, 1 ⅓ In. ......... | 2091 |
| **Bulgari,** Diagono, 18K Yellow Gold, Automatic, Date, Sweep Second, Leather Band ......... | 4674 |
| **Bulova,** 14K White Gold Mesh Bracelet, Mother-Of-Pearl Dial, Woman's, 6 In. ......... | 322 |
| **Bulova,** Ultime, 14K Gold, Diamonds, Mesh Band, Quartz, Woman's, 6 In. .......................... *illus* | 360 |
| **Cartier,** 18K Yellow Gold, Round Case, Woman's, 7 In. .......................... | 1020 |
| **Cartier,** Baignoire, Textured Oval Dial, Pave Diamond Bezel, Black Cloth Band, Woman's ......... | 7995 |
| **Cartier,** Black Enamel, Gold Case, Square, Open Face, Persian Pattern, 1924, 1 ½ x 2 In. ......... | 7763 |
| **Cartier,** Gold Tonneau Case, Textured, White Dial, Leather Band, Signed, Woman's, ¾ In. ......... | 1323 |
| **Cartier,** Santos 100, Automatic, Stainless Steel, Pink Leather Band, Woman's, 1900s ......... | 1046 |
| **Cartier,** Sapphire Crown, Black Lizard Leather Band, 8 In. ......... | 480 |
| **Cartier,** Stainless Steel, White Dial, Roman Numerals, Panthere Links, Woman's ......... | 984 |
| **Cartier,** Tank Divan, Diamonds, 18K White Gold, Leather Band, Woman's .......................... *illus* | 5843 |
| **Cartier,** Tank Francaise, Stainless Steel, White Dial, Roman Numerals, Woman's ......... | 1476 |
| **Cartier,** Tank, 18K Gold Americaine XL, Mechanical Wind, Alligator Band, Box, 1 ½ In. ......... | 4485 |
| **Concord,** 14K Yellow Gold, 18K Band, For Cartier ......... | 960 |
| **Concord,** Bennington, 18K Gold, Quartz, Sapphire Stem, Alligator Band, 1 ½ In. ......... | 633 |
| **Concord,** Digital Display, Square, Rounded Corners, 18K Gold, Flexible Band, 1970s ......... | 2706 |
| **Concord,** Lapis Dial, Diamond Bezel, 18K Gold Flexible Link Band, Woman's ......... | 3321 |
| **Corum,** 1886 Gold Coin, 18 Jewel, Sapphire Stem, Mesh Band, Woman's, 6 ¾ In. ......... | 1955 |
| **Ebel,** 1911 Series, Diamonds, Sapphires, Stainless Steel Case, Blue Alligator Band, 1 In. ......... | 661 |
| **Ebel,** Diamonds, Stainless Steel Case, Sapphires, Mother-Of-Pearl Dial, 1911 Series, Woman's.... | 719 |
| **Elgin,** Art Deco Style, Platinum, Diamonds, Silvertone Dial, Cable Bracelet, Woman's, ½ In. ......... | 322 |
| **Elgin,** Deluxe, 10K Rose Gold Filled, 1900s, 1 ½ x 1 In. ......... | 98 |
| **Girard Perregaux,** Art Deco, 14K Rose Gold, 17 Jewel, Mesh Band, 1 x 2 In. ......... | 368 |
| **Gruen,** Yellow Gold Filled, Rectangular Face, Leather Strap, 1 ½ x 1 In. ......... | 360 |
| **Gucci,** 18K Gold, Blue Enamel Inlay, 17 Jewel, Buckle Closure, Woman's .......................... *illus* | 5000 |
| **Gucci,** Goldtone Case, Round, Black Roman Numerals, Leather Band, Woman's, 1 In. ......... | 92 |
| **Hamilton,** 14K White Gold, Diamonds, 22 Jewel, Woman's, 20th Century ......... | 431 |
| **Hamilton,** 14K Yellow Gold, Leather Band ......... | 240 |
| **Hamilton,** Art Deco, Platinum, Diamond, 19 Jewel, Silvertone Face, 1 ½ In. ......... | 1783 |
| **Hamilton,** Electric, Trapezoidal Face, 2-Tone Dial, Leather Band, 1950s .......................... *illus* | 923 |
| **Hamilton,** Platinum Case, Round Cut Diamonds, Gold Filled Bracelet, Woman's, ¾ In. ......... | 414 |
| **Hamilton,** Platinum, Diamonds, Model 911, 17 Jewel, Woman's, 20th Century ......... | 1140 |
| **Jaccard,** Platinum, Rhinestones, Cord Band, Woman's ......... | 390 |
| **LeCoultre,** Mystery, 14K Gold, Diamond, Cacheron Constainin, Lizard Band, 1 ¼ In. ......... | 1783 |
| **LeCoultre,** Polaris, Stainless Steel, Gridwork, Diver's Bezel, Alarm, Date, c.1968 ......... | 14760 |
| **Longines,** 14K Gold, Opal Mosaic Dial, Diamonds, Woman's, c.1965, 7 In. .......................... *illus* | 1375 |
| **Longines,** 14K Yellow Gold, Silvertone, Round Case, c.1960s, 1 ¼ In. ......... | 587 |
| **Longines,** Mystery, 14K White Gold, Diamonds, Round Case, Stretch Bracelet, 1 ¾ In. ......... | 661 |
| **Lucien Piccard,** 14K Gold, Automatic, Black Lizard Band ......... | 193 |
| **Lucien Piccard,** 14K Yellow Gold, Hexagonal Bezel, Goldtone Dial, Leather Band, 1 ½ In. ......... | 265 |
| **Lucien Piccard,** 18K Yellow Gold, Silvertone Satin Dial, Round Case, Signed, 1 ¼ In. ......... | 713 |
| **Movado,** 18K Yellow Gold, Square Case, Black Leather Strap, 1 In. ......... | 437 |
| **Movado,** Doctor's, 14K Yellow Gold, 15 Jewel, Leather Band, 1 In. ......... | 230 |
| **Movado,** Dress, Gold Mirrored Dish Face, Black Band, Woman's, 1 x 7 ½ In. ......... | 483 |

**Wristwatch,** Bulova, Ultime, 14K Gold, Diamonds, Mesh Band, Quartz, Woman's, 6 In.
$360

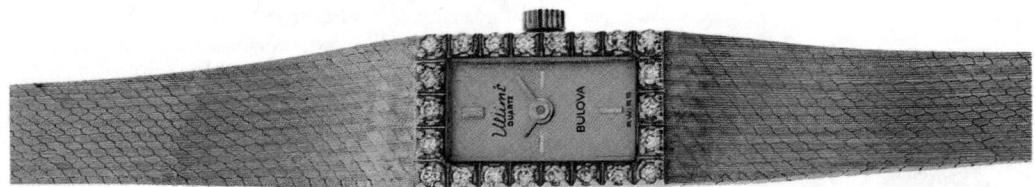

Cowan's Auctions

## Watches

Collectible watches range from expensive Cartier women's watches and Rolex watches that tell the time, day, date, month, and moon phase to inexpensive novelty and fashion watches, like Mickey Mouse watches, introduced in 1933, and Swatch watches, first sold in 1983.

**Wristwatch,** Cartier, Tank Divan, Diamonds, 18K White Gold, Leather Band, Woman's
$5,843

Skinner Auctioneers & Appraisers

**Wristwatch,** Gucci, 18K Gold, Blue Enamel Inlay, 17 Jewel, Buckle Closure, Woman's
$5,000

Rago Arts & Auction Center

**Wristwatch,** Hamilton, Electric, Trapezoidal Face, 2-Tone Dial, Leather Band, 1950s
$923

Cowan's Auctions

**Wristwatch,** Longines, 14K Gold, Opal Mosaic Dial, Diamonds, Woman's, c.1965, 7 In.
$1,375

Rago Arts & Auction Center

**Wristwatch,** Piaget, 18K Gold, Diamond Bezel, Flexible Band, Woman's, c.1980, 6 ½ In.
$2,500

Rago Arts & Auction Center

**Wristwatch,** Piaget, 18K Yellow Gold, Roman Numerals, Diamonds, Woven Band, Woman's
**$3,000**

DuMouchelles Art Gallery

**Wristwatch,** Piaget, Polo, 18K Gold, Quartz Movement, Woman's, 6½ In.
**$2,214**

Skinner Auctioneers & Appraisers

**Wristwatch,** Rolex, Oyster, Datejust, Stainless Steel, Diamonds, Quartz Movement, Woman's
**$4,375**

Garth's Auctioneers & Appraisers

| | |
|---|---:|
| **Omega,** 14K Yellow Gold, Diamond Shape Case, Leather Bracelet, Woman's | 414 |
| **Omega,** 18K Yellow Gold, Integral Mesh Bracelet, Round Case, Stamped, 1 x 7½ In. | 1323 |
| **Omega,** Chronometer, Black Pie Pan Dial, Leather Band, c.1960, 1¾ In. | 984 |
| **Omega,** Cosmic, Triple Date, Moonphase, Steel, 17 Jewel, Champagne Face, 1940s | 2990 |
| **Omega,** Seamaster, 18K Gold Bracelet, Textured Bezel, Silvertone Dial, Square Case, 1 In. | 1783 |
| **Omega,** Speedmaster, Chronometer, 3 Sunken Dials, Stainless Steel Band, 1⅔ In. | 1845 |
| **Patek Philippe,** 18K Rose Gold Face, Roman Numerals, Round, Geneva, 1940s | 4200 |
| **Patek Philippe,** Aquanaut, Stainless Steel Case, Deployment Buckle, 1999, 1¼ In. | 9200 |
| **Patek Philippe,** Golden Ellipse, Blue Dial, Baton Numerals, 18K Gold, Leather | 3075 |
| **Piaget,** 18K Gold, Diamond Bezel, Flexible Band, Woman's, c.1980, 6½ In. ............*illus* | 2500 |
| **Piaget,** 18K White Gold, Oval Dial, Diamond Surround, Mesh Band, Woman's | 3690 |
| **Piaget,** 18K Yellow Gold, Diamonds, Round Case, Integral Bracelet, Woman's, 6½ In. | 3738 |
| **Piaget,** 18K Yellow Gold, Roman Numerals, Diamonds, Woven Band, Woman's ............*illus* | 3000 |
| **Piaget,** Polo, 18K Gold, Quartz Movement, Woman's, 6½ In. ............*illus* | 2214 |
| **Rolex,** 14K Gold, Stainless Steel, Box, c.1992, Woman's, 6 In. | 1888 |
| **Rolex,** Aviator, Sky Rocket, Stainless Steel, Shockproof, Manual Wind, c.1936, 1¼ In. | 978 |
| **Rolex,** Date, Diamond Bezel, Stainless Steel, 14K Gold Jubilee Band | 3444 |
| **Rolex,** Datejust, 18K Yellow Gold, Diamonds, Presidential Style Bracelet, c.1974, Woman's | 8610 |
| **Rolex,** Datejust, Stainless Steel, Jubilee Bracelet, Silvertone, Deployment Buckle, 1¼ In. | 2875 |
| **Rolex,** Oyster Perpetual Datejust, 18K Gold, Stainless Steel, White Dial, Baton, Woman's | 2706 |
| **Rolex,** Oyster, Datejust, Stainless Steel, Diamonds, Quartz Movement, Woman's ............*illus* | 4375 |
| **Rolex,** Oyster, Perpetual Datejust, Model 16030, Stainless Steel, 1¾ In. | 3105 |
| **Rolex,** Oyster, Rolex, 14K Gold, Perpetual Date, Satin Gold Face, 26 Jewel, 1¼ In. | 3105 |
| **Rolex,** Oyster, Stainless Steel, Band, Manual Wind, 1950s, 1 In. | 633 |
| **Rolex,** Tudor, Art Deco, Model 7904, 17 Jewels, Brushed Copper Face, 1½ In. | 1323 |
| **Royce,** Diamond, Platinum, Woman's, 6 In. | 600 |
| **Tiffany & Co.,** 14K Yellow Gold, Leather Band, 1½ x 1⅜ In. | 1230 |
| **Tiffany & Co.,** Portfolio, Stainless Steel Case, Bracelet, White Dial, Case, Box, 1¼ In. | 161 |
| **Tiffany,** 18K Yellow Gold, Color Dial, Quartz, Oval, Leather Band, Woman's, 1¼ x 1 In. | 380 |
| **Universal Geneve,** 18K White Gold, Diamonds, 17 Jewels, Square Case, Woman's | 489 |
| **Vacheron & Constantin,** 18K Yellow Gold, Hang Tag, Guilloche Dial, Manual Wind | 2214 |
| **Vacheron & Constantin,** Platinum Case, 14K White Gold, Diamonds, Woman's, 7 In. | 4025 |
| **Van Cleef & Arpels,** 18K Gold, Diamonds, Rectangular, Flexible Band, Woman's, 6½ In. | 3600 |
| **Wakmann,** Chronograph, Triple Date, Stainless Steel, 17 Jewel, Red Seconds Hand ............*illus* | 800 |

**YELLOWWARE** is a heavy earthenware made of a yellowish clay. It varies in color from light yellow to orange-yellow. Many nineteenth- and twentieth-century kitchen bowls and jugs were made of yellowware. It was made in England and in the United States. Another form of pottery that is sometimes classed as yellowware is listed in this book in the Mocha category.

| | |
|---|---:|
| **Bank,** Log Cabin, 2 Chimneys, Barrel, Open Door Slot, Moriah Weir, 1858, 4½ x 4½ In. | 920 |
| **Bank,** Seated Spaniel, Manganese, Copper Designs, Oval Base, c.1870, 5 In. | 259 |
| **Chamber Pot,** Cobalt Blue Seaweed, Mocha, White Band, Ribbed Handle, c.1850, 6 x 9 In. | 58 |
| **Chamber Pot,** Seaweed, Blue, Mocha, White Band, 5½ In. ............*illus* | 153 |
| **Figurine,** Dog, Spaniel, Brown Mottled Glaze, Ohio, 19th Century, 11 In. | 210 |
| **Figurine,** Dog, Spaniel, Seated, Blue, Brown, c.1850, 7⅜ x 7⅝ In. | 600 |
| **Milk Pan,** Flared Sides, Ohio, 19th Century, 13¼ In. | 123 |
| **Mixing Bowl,** Nesting Set, Red, White Bands, 1800s, Largest 6 x 12½ In., 5 Piece | 111 |
| **Mixing Bowl,** White Band Below Rim, c.1904, 7¾ x 16 In. | 138 |
| **Mold,** Food, Lion, Reclining, Detailed, Oval, 1800s, 4½ x 8¾ In. | 106 |
| **Mold,** Food, Pineapple, 3 x 6½ In. | 200 |
| **Pitcher,** Green, Black, Brown Roses, R. Web & Co., Salineville, Ohio, c.1890, 10 In. | 575 |
| **Salt,** Master, Bulbous, 3 Blue Bands, Footed, 1800s, 2¼ x 3 In. | 266 |

**ZANESVILLE** Art Pottery was founded in 1900 by David Schmidt in Zanesville, Ohio. The firm made faience umbrella stands, jardinieres, and pedestals. The company closed in 1920 and Weller bought the factory. Many pieces are marked with just the words *La Moro.*   **LA MORO**

| | |
|---|---:|
| **Crock,** Liver Pudding, Z.P. Co., 9 x 5 In. | 135 |
| **Planter,** Duck, Satin Turquoise Glaze, 5½ x 3½ In. | 37 |
| **Urn,** Blue Glossy Glaze, Handles, 12 In. | 95 |
| **Vase,** Angular Panels, Flowers, Green Matte Glaze, 7¼ In. | 125 |
| **Vase,** Black Drip Glaze, Shouldered, 4 x 5 In. | 35 |
| **Vase,** Blue Glaze, Indented Lip, 7 In. | 125 |
| **Vase,** Engraved Ivy, Cylindrical, 9¼ In. | 127 |
| **Vase,** Flared Trumpet Shape, Green Matte Glaze, 6 In. | 115 |
| **Vase,** Green Matte Glaze, Rolled Lip, Shouldered, 11 In. | 225 |

W

| | |
|---|---|
| **Vase**, Molded Flower, Green Matte Glaze, Oval, 8¼ In............ | 94 |
| **Vase**, Turquoise Glossy Glaze, Ribbed, 4 x 5¼ In.............. | 29 |

**ZSOLNAY** pottery was made in Hungary after 1853 and was characterized by Persian, Art Nouveau, or Hungarian motifs. A series of new Zsolnay figurines with green-gold luster finish is available in many shops today. Early Zsolnay was not marked, but by 1878 the tower trademark was used.

| | |
|---|---|
| **Bowl**, 2 Parrots, Red Marbleized Eosin Glaze, c.1930, 6½ x 15 In. .... | 1625 |
| **Bowl**, 2 Red Parrots, Iridescent, Green Eosin Glaze, Hungary, c.1930, 6½ x 15 In. ....... | 1664 |
| **Bowl**, Flower Bud Shape, Iridescent Gold, 4⅛ In. ............ | 423 |
| **Bowl**, Horses, Riders, Green Eosin Glaze, 5 Churches Stamp, 4¼ x 8¼ In. ...... | 403 |
| **Box**, Lid, Stylized Flowers & Leaves, Dark Blue, Red, Stamped Pecs, Round, 3 In. ....... | 363 |
| **Charger**, Flowers, Leaves, Gilt, Pierced, Scalloped Edge, 14 In. .... | 565 |
| **Charger**, Flowers, Pink Yellow, Gilt, Pierced, Signed, 18½ In. .... | 654 |
| **Charger**, Flowers, Pink, Yellow, Reticulated Border, 15 In. ...... | 194 |
| **Figurine**, Falcon, Green Eosin, Signed, Hungary, 6½ In. .... | 61 |
| **Figurine**, Fox Terrier, Green Eosin, Signed, Hungary, 4 In. .... | 61 |
| **Figurine**, Frog, Green Eosin, Stylized, Hungary, 6½ In. .... | 121 |
| **Figurine**, Meditazione, Monk, Purple, Blue Eosin Glaze, 5 Churches Logo, 1933, 14½ In. ... | 863 |
| **Figurine**, Musician, Harp, Green Eosin, Stylized, 12¾ In. .... | 177 |
| **Figurine**, Nude Woman, Green Iridescent, c.1930, 10 In. .... | 210 |
| **Figurine**, Nun, Walking, Bundle Over Shoulder, Red Glossy Glaze, 14⅝ In. ....... | 847 |
| **Figurine**, Woman, Nude, Sitting, Green Eosin, 9½ In. .... | 177 |
| **Figurine**, Woman, Pitcher, Stick, Dog, Blue Headscarf, Blue Apron, 12½ x 5 In. .... | 130 |
| **Figurine**, Woman, Seated On Bundle Of Sticks, Marked Sinko, 10 x 10 In. ...... | 109 |
| **Jardiniere**, 2 Birds, In Field, Landscape, Orange, Green, Brown, Marked, 10½ x 14 In. ... | 8260 |
| **Jardiniere**, Gold, Iridescent, 8 Emus, Field, Trees, 10½ x 14 In. .... | 8260 |
| **Jug**, Birds, Flowers, Blue, Purple, Gold, Cream Ground, Handle, 10½ In. .... | 272 |
| **Jug**, Exotic Flowers, Birds, Butterflies, Insects, Ink Stamp Logo, 10½ In. .... | 259 |
| **Jug**, Multicolor Flowers, Applied Organic Designs, Handle, 7 In. .... | 210 |
| **Lamp**, Art Nouveau, Robed Woman, White Flowers, Gilt Leaves, 27 In. .... | 3600 |
| **Paperweight**, Blue Eosin, Skull On Bible, Rosary, 3 In. .... | 786 |
| **Pitcher**, 2 Woman Clinging To Rim, Green & Gold Iridescent, Pinched, 6½ In. ....... | 316 |
| **Pitcher**, Cream, 8 Cartouches, Central Band, Handle, Spigot, 10½ In. .... | 242 |
| **Pitcher**, Otter, White, Iridescent, Pecs, 5 Churches Mark, c.1900, 15½ In. .... | 2688 |
| **Plaque**, Nude Maidens, Satyr, Green, Orange, Eosin Glaze, L. Mack, c.1900, 13 In. .... | 2125 |
| **Plaque**, Nude Women, Satyr, Green Eosin, Yellow, Purple, Pecs, 5 Churches, c.1900, 13 In. .... | 2176 |
| **Plate**, Cobra, Coiled Body, Eosin Glaze, 5 Churches Seal, c.1900, 3 x 13 In. .... | 32500 |
| **Vase**, 2 Handles, Marbleized Eosin Glaze, Bulbous, Footed, 9 x 5 In. .... | 2250 |
| **Vase**, Art Nouveau Woman, Flowing Hair & Skirt Wraps Around, Waves, Iridescent, 9 In. ...... | 9480 |
| **Vase**, Art Nouveau, Stylized Leaf Stems, Green Eosin, 11 In. .... | 2541 |
| **Vase**, Blue Marbleized, Eosin Glaze, c.1900, 21 x 10 In., Pair ....... | 2375 |
| **Vase**, Copper Tone, 2 Twisted Ribbons, Handles, Flared Rim, Flower Bud Shape, 5 In. .... | 1722 |
| **Vase**, Floral Shape, Labrador Glaze, Pecs, 5 Churches Logo, 8⅝ In. .... | 374 |
| **Vase**, Flowering Branches, Cream Ground, Canteen Shape, 4-Footed, 19 In. .... | 598 |
| **Vase**, Gourd Gilt Rim, Multicolor Flowers, Gilt, J. Fischer, c.1900, 10½ In., Pair .... | 127 |
| **Vase**, Gourd, Red, Nude Maiden, Tip Toes, Logo, 8 In. .... | 920 |
| **Vase**, Green Iridescent, Ribbed, Wavy Ruffled Rim, 4½ In. .... | 50 |
| **Vase**, Green, Iridescent, Stamped, c.1918, 10 In. .... | 1353 |
| **Vase**, Iridescent, Green, Gold, Flowers, Marked, Hungary, c.1920, 9½ In. .... | 303 |
| **Vase**, Koi Fish, Teal, Flared Rim, Gilt, 10½ In. .... | 91 |
| **Vase**, Leaf Pattern, Raised, Eosin Glaze, c.1900, 7¾ x 4 In. .... | 4375 |
| **Vase**, Leaves, Vines, Eosin Glaze, 5 Churches Logo, 8¼ In. .... | 230 |
| **Vase**, Nabis Style, Garden Flowers, Foxglove, Leaves, Cherry Trees, 6 In. .... | 8338 |
| **Vase**, Nabis, Multicolor, Foxglove, Leaves, Cherry Trees, Pecs 5 Church Mark, 6 In. .... | 8482 |
| **Vase**, Nude Woman, Billowing Cloak, Eosin Glaze, Marked, c.1910, 9½ In. .... | 1353 |
| **Vase**, Orientalist, Peacock, Flowers, Brown Ground, 7¾ In. .... | 2420 |
| **Vase**, Peacock Feathers, Iridescent Eosin, White Ground, Marked Pecs, 3½ In. .... | 2541 |
| **Vase**, Relief Flowers, Reticulated, Multicolor, Marked, 1800s, 11 x 7⅝ x 7 In. .... | 610 |
| **Vase**, Relief, Flowers, Leaves, Reticulated, 2 Handles, 11 In. .... | 605 |
| **Vase**, Reticulated Rim, Melon Ribbed Body, Persian Floral, White Ground, Pecs, 9 In. .... | 184 |
| **Vase**, Reticulated, Latticed Vines, Lavender Orchids, Pink Flowers, Pecs, 10 In. .... | 518 |
| **Vase**, Rooster, Hen, Peonies, Leaves, Flow Blue Sides, Canteen Shape, Pecs, 12 x 9 In. .... | 460 |
| **Vase**, Roosters, Hen, Peonies, Cream Ground, Canteen Shape, 4-Footed, 12 In. .... | 484 |
| **Vase**, Teal, Handle, Oval & Cone Shape Cartouches, Finial, 18 x 11 In. .... | 121 |
| **Vase**, Wave, Green, Blue, Iridescent, Mermaid, Merman, Catfish, Ocean, 8½ x 10 In. .... | 2875 |

**Wristwatch**, Wakmann, Chronograph, Triple Date, Stainless Steel, 17 Jewel, Red Seconds Hand
**$800**

Cowan's Auctions

**Yellowware**, Chamber Pot, Seaweed, Blue, Mocha, White Band, 5½ In.
**$153**

Conestoga Auction Co., Inc.

### Magnify the Marks

I always wear a magnifying glass on a chain when "antiquing." Last month I went to help a friend empty her grandfather's house. One drawer was filled with "junk wristwatches." The first one I examined with the magnifier was marked "14K." I advised her to take the watches, her grandfather's jewelry, and old coins to a jeweler who buys jewelry and gold. The jeweler will tell her the meltdown value and the intrinsic value of the jewelry and coins. She can decide what to give to a thrift store, what to melt down or sell, and what to keep.

X
Y
Z

# INDEX

This index is computer-generated, making it as complete and accurate as possible. References in uppercase type are category listings. Those in lowercase letters refer to additional pages where pieces can be found. There is also an internal cross-referencing system used in the main part of the book, so if you look for a Kewpie doll in the Doll category, you will be told it is in its own category. There is additional information at the end of many paragraphs about where to find prices of pieces similar to yours.

## A

A. WALTER   1
ABC   1, 468
ABINGDON POTTERY   1
ADAMS   1–2, 272, 453–454, 519, 556
Admiral Dewey   163–164
ADVERTISING   2–23, 95, 113–114, 162, 181, 340, 378, 408, 471
AGATA   23, 569
Airplane   2, 31, 66, 112, 161, 192, 355, 578, 583, 588, 606, 621
AKRO AGATE   23–24, 362
ALABASTER   24, 119, 238, 538, 541–542
Album   45, 274, 462, 465
Almanac   328
ALUMINUM   24–25, 70, 99, 126, 211, 269, 274, 331, 335, 343–344, 366, 464, 537, 586–587, 590, 606, 620
AMBER GLASS   25, 37, 343, 409
AMBERINA   25
Ambrotype   420
AMERICAN ENCAUSTIC TILING CO.   26
AMETHYST GLASS   26
Amos 'N' Andy   578, 591
Amphora, see Teplitz
Andirons   71, 187–188
ANIMAL TROPHY   26–27
ANIMATION ART   27
ANNA POTTERY   27
Apothecary   10, 17, 60, 275, 371, 549
Apple Peeler   500; see Kitchen, Peeler, Apple
ARABIA   27
ARCHITECTURAL   27–29, 560
AREQUIPA POTTERY   30
ARITA   30
ART DECO   1, 16, 29–31, 66, 74, 79, 85, 103, 111–112, 114, 116, 123, 136, 138, 159, 176, 199, 203, 208, 218, 228, 230, 232–233, 238, 241, 245, 247–248, 275, 282, 287, 299, 332, 339, 341, 343, 348–349, 351–352, 354, 356, 365, 385, 394, 434, 447, 464, 471, 487, 497–498, 504, 506, 512, 514, 519, 522, 524–525, 533, 552, 562, 570, 575–576, 597, 599, 604, 610, 624, 626
Art Glass, see Glass-Art
ART NOUVEAU   24, 30, 53, 68, 73–74, 84, 89, 91, 93, 100–101, 116, 148, 199, 201–203, 208, 213, 215, 218, 223, 228–229, 231–233, 241, 247, 251, 256, 260, 263, 265, 274–275, 290, 306, 309, 317, 343, 349, 354, 360, 374–375, 377, 379, 385, 395, 403, 417–419, 422, 426, 444, 471, 479–480, 482–483, 485, 494, 506, 507, 511–513, 515–516, 518, 520–521, 524, 535, 537, 550, 559, 567, 570, 580, 597, 605, 612, 616, 627

## ARTS & CRAFTS

ARTS & CRAFTS   30, 43, 67, 71, 81, 84, 113–114, 116, 119, 139, 179, 187–189, 202–204, 206, 208, 212, 228–229, 231–233, 239–240, 242, 248, 251, 255, 265, 286, 317, 340, 343, 348, 350, 354, 385, 400, 403, 444, 471, 478, 511–514, 517, 561, 603, 616
Ashtray   2, 23, 25, 48, 51, 72, 87, 111, 125, 140, 159, 184, 193, 195, 247, 282, 284, 290, 300, 305, 338, 352, 374, 378, 399, 404, 422, 449, 470, 476, 484, 504, 507, 521, 525, 533, 537–538, 562, 601, 603
Atomizer   148, 266, 371, 417, 538, 541
Aunt Jemima   51, 137
Austria, see Royal Dux; Porcelain
AUTO   30–34, 85, 442, 557, 579, 593, 596
Automaton   2, 162
AUTUMN LEAF   34
Avon, see Bottle, Avon
AZALEA   34–35, 83

## B

Babe Ruth   335
BACCARAT   35
Backbar   29, 40, 56, 65
BADGE   35–36, 70, 81, 94, 157, 274, 357, 366, 429, 432–433, 529, 551, 561, 574, 621
Banana Boat   97, 137, 183–184
Banana Stand   614
BANK   27, 36–40, 43, 83, 103, 104, 159, 175, 297, 357, 402, 427, 433, 466, 499, 534, 544, 551, 593, 595, 603, 622, 626
Banner   2, 19, 93, 286, 354, 392, 429, 490, 535, 549, 559–560, 606–607
BARBER   40–41, 54, 129, 182, 498, 503
BAROMETER   41, 114, 390
Baseball, see Card, Baseball
BASKET   24, 41–43, 47–48, 71, 85–86, 92, 95, 113, 125, 138, 141, 144, 155, 159, 173–176, 178, 180–185, 189, 193, 198, 225, 272, 275, 277, 279, 281, 294–295, 297–298, 301, 309, 312, 328, 343, 351, 360, 363, 368, 370, 372–374, 377, 380, 393, 395, 400, 404, 409–410, 414, 418, 423, 425–426, 434, 436, 444, 459, 476–478, 480, 483, 486, 492, 494, 500, 503, 508, 511–512, 518–519, 521–524, 527, 529, 532, 538, 545, 548, 560, 569, 596–598, 601, 611, 615
BATCHELDER   43
Bathtub   27
BATMAN   43–44, 337
BATTERSEA   44
BAUER   44, 74
BAVARIA   44, 374
Beaded Bag, see Purse
BEATLES   45, 465, 504
Bed Warmer   71, 138
BEEHIVE   36–37, 45, 49, 87, 121, 307, 483, 500, 547, 549

ROCKINGHAM   47, 114, 470, 573

Rogers, see John Rogers

Rolling Pin   8, 334, 401, 498, 587

ROOKWOOD   470–474, 573

Rosaline, see Steuben

ROSE BOWL   25, 83, 96, 129, 143, 146, 148, 183–185, 274, 282, 292, 329, 356, 360, 370, 384–385, 413, 474, 494, 541, 543, 568, 608

ROSE CANTON   474

ROSE MANDARIN   474

ROSE MEDALLION   107, 250, 272, 366, 475

Rose O'Neill, see Kewpie

ROSE TAPESTRY   475

ROSEMEADE POTTERY   475

ROSENTHAL   269, 475–476

ROSEVILLE POTTERY   476–479

ROWLAND & MARSELLUS   479

ROY ROGERS   479

ROYAL BAYREUTH   475, 479–480, 551

ROYAL BONN   114, 480

ROYAL COPENHAGEN   480–481

ROYAL CROWN DERBY   481

ROYAL DOULTON   274, 481–482

ROYAL DUX   482–483

ROYAL FLEMISH   483

Royal Haeger, see Haeger

ROYAL HICKMAN   483

Royal Ivy, see Northwood, Royal Ivy

ROYAL NYMPHENBURG   483

Royal Oak, see Northwood, Royal Oak

Royal Rudolstadt, see Rudolstadt

Royal Vienna, see Beehive

ROYAL WORCESTER   483–484

ROYCROFT   210, 215, 242, 484

Rozane, see Roseville

ROZENBURG   485

RRP   485

RS GERMANY   485

RS POLAND   485

RS PRUSSIA   485–486

RS SILESIA   486

RS SUHL   486

RS TILLOWITZ   486

RUBINA   399, 486

RUBINA VERDE   486–487

RUBY GLASS   359, 487, 523

RUDOLSTADT   487

RUG   17, 26–27, 74, 160, 192, 301, 305, 351, 487–491

Ruler   497

RUMRILL POTTERY   491

RUSKIN   491

RUSSELL WRIGHT   491

## S

SABINO   347, 491

Sailor's Valentine   392

SALOPIAN   101, 491–492

SALT & PEPPER SHAKERS   34, 44, 89, 103, 146, 154–156, 184–185, 195–197, 282, 285, 288, 290, 294, 296, 328, 370, 374, 377–378, 382, 388, 397, 400, 404, 413, 453–454, 465, 475, 479–480, 492, 494, 504, 512, 515, 521–522, 524, 526, 533, 599, 602–603, 605, 615–616

Saltshaker   183, 285, 453

Samovar   523

SAMPLER   492–493

SAMSON   493

SANDWICH GLASS   143, 493

Santa Claus   39–40, 92, 108–109, 111, 128, 161, 176, 477, 479

SARREGUEMINES   493–494

SASCHA BRASTOFF   494

SATIN GLASS   72, 143, 348, 494, 526, 608

SATSUMA   494–495

Saturday Evening Girls, see Paul Revere Pottery

SCALE   127, 392, 495–496, 567

Scarf   71, 80, 109, 123, 179, 364, 385

SCHAFER & VATER   496

SCHEIER   496

SCHNEIDER   351, 497

SCIENTIFIC INSTRUMENTS   497–498

Scissors   160, 500, 519, 550

Scoop   8, 10, 212, 334, 519, 533, 575

Screen   29, 181, 188–189, 205, 240, 310, 383, 567, 616

SCRIMSHAW   498

SEG, see Paul Revere Pottery

SEVRES   435, 498–499

SEWER TILE   28, 50, 369, 499

SEWING   14, 17, 39, 42, 240, 259–260, 416, 499–500, 551, 590, 596

SHAKER   61, 120, 122, 202, 215, 219, 222, 225, 227, 230–231, 233, 236, 239–240, 242, 247–248, 260, 266, 330, 500–503

SHAVING MUG   451, 503

SHAWNEE POTTERY   504

SHEARWATER POTTERY   504

SHEET MUSIC   337, 432, 504–505

Sheffield, see Silver Plate; Silver-English

SHELLEY   505

SHIRLEY TEMPLE   383, 505

Shotgun   8, 17

Sideboard   242, 245

Sign   10, 13–14, 16–17, 19, 23, 29, 31, 32–34, 40–41, 43, 51, 66, 83, 127–128, 153, 186, 197, 392, 407, 416, 464, 479, 503, 530, 534, 549–550, 552, 559, 607, 620, 622

Silent Butler   8, 25

Silhouette   45, 275, 285, 375, 398, 423, 425, 478, 605, 607

SILVER DEPOSIT   506

SILVER FLATWARE   506–507

SILVER PLATE   66, 89–91, 100–101, 142, 146, 159, 186, 299, 309, 312, 327, 340, 354, 372, 389, 399, 402, 406, 507–508

SILVER-AMERICAN   508–517

SILVER-ARGENTINIAN   517

SILVER-AUSTRIAN   517

SILVER-AUSTRO-HUNGARIAN   517

SILVER-BURMESE   517

SILVER-CANADIAN   517

SILVER-CHINESE   517

SILVER-CONTINENTAL   517

SILVER-DANISH   517–518

SILVER-DUTCH   518

SILVER-ENGLISH   518–520

SILVER-FRENCH   520–521

SILVER-GERMAN   521

SILVER-GREEK   521

SILVER-INDIAN   521

SILVER-IRISH   521

SILVER-ISRAELI   521

SILVER-ITALIAN   521–522

SILVER-JAPANESE   522

SILVER-MEXICAN   522–523

SILVER-MIDDLE EASTERN   523

SILVER-NORWEGIAN   523

SILVER-PERSIAN   523

SILVER-PERUVIAN   523

SILVER-PORTUGUESE   523

SILVER-RUSSIAN   523

SILVER-SCANDINAVIAN   523

SILVER-SCOTTISH   523

SILVER-SIAMESE   523

SILVER-SPANISH   523

SILVER-STERLING   523–525

SILVER-SWEDISH   525

SILVER-TIBETAN   525

SILVER-VIETNAMESE   525

Silver, Sheffield, see Silver Plate; Silver-English

SINCLAIRE   525

Singing Bird   386

Skiing, see Sports

Slag, Caramel, see Imperial Glass

SLAG GLASS   71, 287–288, 343–344, 347, 350, 525, 565, 616

Sled   92, 526, 560, 579, 590, 624

SLEEPY EYE   16, 525–526

Sleigh   46, 81, 94, 99, 109, 144, 201, 245, 517, 590, 601

Slot Machine, see Coin-Operated Machine

SMITH BROTHERS   526

Smoking Set   71

Smoking Stand   30, 112, 565, 567

SNOW BABY   526

Snuff Bottle, see bottle, snuff

SNUFFBOX   44, 192, 432, 526

## PHOTO CREDITS

We have included the name of the auction house or photographer with each pictured object. This is a list of the addresses, websites, and phone numbers of those who have contributed photographs and information for this book. Every dealer or auction has to buy antiques to have items to sell. Call or email a dealer or auction house if you want to discuss buying or selling. If you need an appraisal or advice, remember that appraising is part of their business and fees may be charged.

**Ahlers & Ogletree Auction Gallery**
715 Miami Cir. NE, Ste. 210
Atlanta, GA 30324
aandoauctions.com
404-869-2478

**Aleph-Bet Books**
85 Old Mill River Rd.
Pound Ridge, NY 10576
alephbet.com
914-764-7410

**Allard Auctions**
P.O. Box 1030
St. Ignatius, MT 59865
allardauctions.com
406-745-0500

**American Bottle Auctions**
915 28th St.
Sacramento, CA 95816
americanbottle.com
800-806-7722

**Arus Auctions**
305 Lincoln St.
Marlboro, MA 01752
arusauctions.com
617-669-6170

**Bertoia Auctions**
2141 DeMarco Dr.
Vineland, NJ 08360
bertoiaauctions.com
856-692-1881

**Brunk Auctions**
P.O. Box 2135
Asheville, NC 28802
brunkauctions.com
828-254-6846

**Bowers & Merena Auctions**
1063 Mcgaw Ave., Ste. 250
Irvine, CA 92614-5506
bowersandmerena.com
949-253-0916

**Burchard's Galleries**
2528 30th Ave., No.
St. Petersburg, FL 33713
burchardgalleries.com
727-821-1167

**Clars Auction Gallery**
5644 Telegraph Ave.
Oakland, CA 94609
clars.com
510-428-0100

**Conestoga Auction Co.**
P.O. Box 1
Manheim, PA 17545
conestogaauction.com
717-898-7284

**Copake Auction**
266 Route 7A
Copake, NY 12516
copakeauction.com
518-329-1142

**Cottone Auctions**
120 Court St.
Geneseo, NY 14454
cottoneauctions.com
585-243-3100

**Cowan's Auctions**
6270 Este Ave.
Cincinnati, OH 45232
cowanauctions.com
513-871-1670

**Dallas Auction Gallery**
2235 Monitor St.
Dallas, TX 75207
dallasauctiongallery.com
214-653-3900

**Dirk Soulis Auctions**
P.O. Box 17
Lone Jack, MO 64070
dirksoulisauctions.com
816-697-3830

**DuMouchelles Art Gallery**
409 East Jefferson Ave.
Detroit, MI 48226
dumouchelles.com
313-963-6255

**Early Auction Co.**
123 Main St.
Milford, OH 45150
earlyauctionco.com
513-831-4833

**Eldred's Auctioneers**
P.O. Box 796
1483 Route 6A
East Dennis, MA 02641
eldreds.com
508-385-3116

**Fox Auctions**
P.O. Box 4069
Vallejo, CA 94590
foxauctionsonline.com
631-553-3841

**Garth's Auctioneers & Appraisers**
P.O. Box 369
Delaware, OH 43015
Garths.com
740-362-4771

**Glass Works Auctions**
P.O. Box 180
East Greenville, PA 18041
glswrk-auction.com
215-679-5849

Graceland Auctions
3734 Elvis Presley Blvd.
Memphis, TN 38116
graceland.com
901-332-3322

**Gray's Auctioneers**
10717 Detroit Ave.
Cleveland, OH 44102
graysauctioneers.com
216-458-7695

**Grogan & Co.**
20 Charles St.
Boston, MA 02114
groganco.com
617-720-2020

**Hake's Americana & Collectibles**
P.O. Box 12001
York, PA 17402
hakes.com
717-434-1600

**Heritage Auction Galleries**
3500 Maple Avenue, 17th Floor
Dallas, TX 75219-3941
ha.com
214-528-3500

**Humler & Nolan**
225 E. Sixth St., 4th Floor
Cincinnati, OH 45202
humlernolan.com
513-381-2041

**James D. Julia Auctioneers**
203 Skowhegan Rd.
Fairfield, Maine 04937
jamesdjulia.com
207-453-7125

**Jeffrey S. Evans & Associates**
2177 Green Valley Ln.
Mt. Crawford, VA 22841
jeffreysevans.com
540-434-3939

**Leonard Auction**
1765 Cortland Ct.
Addison, IL 60101
leonardauction.com
630-495-0229

**Los Angeles Modern Auctions (LAMA)**
16145 Hart St.
Van Nuys, CA 91406
lamodern.com
323-904-1950

**Merriman Auction**
2415 Shoaff Rd.
Huntertown, IN 46748
merrimanauctions.com
260-479-0399

**Morphy Auctions**
2000 North Reading Rd.
Denver, PA 17517
morphyauctions.com
717-335-3435

**Mosby & Co. Auctions**
5714 Industry Ln.
Frederick, MD 21704
mosbyauctions.net
240-629-8139

**Neal Auction Co.**
4038 Magazine St.
New Orleans, LA 70115
nealauction.com
800-467-5329

**New Orleans Auction Galleries**
801 Magazine St.
New Orleans, LA 70130
neworleansauction.com
800-501-0277

**Norman C. Heckler & Co.**
79 Bradford Corner Rd.
Woodstock Valley, CT 06282
hecklerauction.com
860-974-1634

**Old Barn Auction**
10040 State Route 224
Findlay, OH 45840
oldbarn.com
419-422-8531

**Palm Beach Modern Auctions**
417 Bunker Rd.
West Palm Beach, FL 33405
modernauctions.com
561-586-5500

**Pook & Pook, Inc. Auctioneers and Appraisers**
463 East Lancaster Ave.
Downingtown, PA 19335
pookandpook.com
610-269-4040

**Potter & Potter Auctions**
3759 N. Ravenswood Ave., #121
Chicago, IL 60613
potterauctions.com
773-472-1442

**Potteries Specialist Auctions**
271 Waterloo Road
Cobridge
Stoke on Trent Staffordshire ST6 3HR
United Kingdom
potteriesauctions.com
+44 (0)1782 286622

**Rachel Davis Fine Arts**
1301 West 79th St.
Cleveland, OH 44102
racheldavisfinearts.com
216-939-1190

**Rago Arts and Auction Center**
333 North Main St.
Lambertville, NJ 08530
ragoarts.com
609-397-9374

**Replacements Ltd.**
P.O. Box 26029
Greensboro, NC 27420-6029
replacements.com
800-737-5223

**RSL Auction**
P.O. Box 635
Oldwick, NJ 08858
rslauctions.com
908-823-4049

**Santa Margarita Auction Barn**
3850 El Camino Real
Atascadero, CA 93422
smab.com
805-466-7296

**Seeck Auctions**
P.O. Box 377
Mason City, IA 50402
seeckauction.com
641-424-1116

**Showtime Auction Services**
22619 Monterey Dr.
Woodhaven, MI 48183
showtimeauctions.com
951-453-2415

**Skinner Auctioneers & Appraisers**
274 Cedar Hill St.
Marlborough, MA 01752
skinnerinc.com
508-970-3000

**Strawser Auction Group**
200 N. Main St.
Wolcottville, IN 46795
strawserauctions.com
260-854-2859

**The Stein Auction Co.**
P.O. Box 136
Palatine, IL 60078
tsaco.com
847-991-5927

**Theriault's**
P.O. Box 151
Annapolis, MD 21404
theriaults.com
800-638-0422

**Treadway Toomey Galleries**
c/o Treadway Gallery
2029 Madison Rd.
Cincinnati, OH 45208
treadwaygallery.com
513-321-6742

**Victorian Casino Antiques**
4520 Arville St., #1
Las Vegas, NV 89103
vcaauction.com
702-382-2466

**Waterford's Art & Antiques**
147 Jackson Rd.
Berlin, NJ 08009
waterfordsauction.com
856-336-5551

**Willis Henry Auctions**
22 Main St.
Marshfield, MA 02050
willishenry.com
781-834-7774

**Wm Morford Auctions**
RD #2 Cobb Hill Rd.
Cazenovia, NY 13035
morfauction.com
315-662-7625

**Woody Auction**
P.O. Box 618
317 S. Forrest
Douglass, KS 67039
woodyauction.com
316-747-2694

**Worthridge Auctions**
568 Arbor Hill Rd.
Kernersville, NC 27284
worthridge.com
877-539-3952

**Wright**
1440 W. Hubbard St.
Chicago, IL 60642
wright20.com
312-563-0020